THE NORTON
INTRODUCTION TO
LITERATURE

Third Edition

W · W · NORTON & COMPANY · NEW YORK · LONDON

Carl E. Bain
Late of Emory University

Jerome Beaty
Emory University

J. Paul Hunter
The University of Rochester

THE NORTON
INTRODUCTION TO
LITERATURE

Third Edition

Library of Congress Cataloging in Publication Data
Bain, Carl E   comp.
The Norton introduction to literature.
Third Edition
Includes indexes.
1. Literature—Collections. I. Beaty, Jerome,
1924—   joint comp. II. Hunter, J. Paul, 1934—
joint comp. III. Title.
PN6014.B27 1981   808.8   80-24324

W. W. Norton & Company, Inc. 500 Fifth Avenue, New York, N.Y. 10110
W. W. Norton & Company Ltd. 25 New Street Square, London EC4A 3NT

4 5 6 7 8 9 0

ISBN 0-393-95146-4

In memory of Carl E. Bain
1930–1979

Contents

Foreword to the Third Edition   xxi
Acknowledgments   xxiii

FICTION

SPENCER HOLST • The Zebra Storyteller   3

A Preface to Fiction   4

ELEMENTS   7

1 PLOT   7

EDGAR ALLAN POE • The Cask of Amontillado   12
RICHARD CONNELL • The Most Dangerous Game   17
ERNEST HEMINGWAY • The Short Happy Life
   of Francis Macomber   32

2 FOCUS AND VOICE   55

AMBROSE BIERCE • An Occurrence at Owl Creek Bridge   59
SHIRLEY JACKSON • The Lottery   66
MORDECAI RICHLER • The Summer My Grandmother
   Was Supposed to Die   72

3 CHARACTERIZATION   83

SHERWOOD ANDERSON • The Egg   88
TONI CADE BAMBARA • My Man Bovanne   95
DORIS LESSING • Our Friend Judith   100

4 SYMBOLS   113

NATHANIEL HAWTHORNE • Young Goodman Brown   117
FLANNERY O'CONNOR • The Artificial Nigger   127

5 THEME   142

KATHERINE MANSFIELD • Her First Ball   146
ANTON CHEKHOV • The Lady with the Dog   151

vii

KINDS AND MODES   163

6   A KIND: INITIATION   163

   JAMES JOYCE • Araby   165
   ALICE MUNRO • Boys and Girls   169
   TILLIE OLSEN • O Yes   180
   WILLIAM FAULKNER • The Old People   191

7   A MODE: FANTASY   204

   ARTHUR C. CLARKE • Hide and Seek   207
   JORGE LUIS BORGES • The Garden of Forking Paths   215 ✓
   HAL BENNETT • Dotson Gerber Resurrected   223
   GABRIEL GARCIA MARQUEZ • A Very Old Man with
   Enormous Wings   234 ✓

CONTEXTS   239

8   THE AUTHOR'S WORK   239

   D. H. LAWRENCE • Odour of Chrysanthemums   244
   D. H. LAWRENCE • The Horse Dealer's Daughter   259 ✓
   D. H. LAWRENCE • The Rocking-Horse Winner   271 ✓
   D. H. LAWRENCE • Passages from Essays and Letters   282

9   TRADITION   288

   AUGUSTUS BALDWIN LONGSTREET • The Horse-Swap   290
   SAMUEL CLEMENS • The Celebrated Jumping Frog
   of Calaveras County   296 ✓
   WILLIAM FAULKNER • Spotted Horses   300 ✓

10   SETTING   314

   KATE CHOPIN • Beyond the Bayou   320
   F. SCOTT FITZGERALD • Babylon Revisited   320
   JAMES BALDWIN • Sonny's Blues   336

STORIES FOR FURTHER READING   359

   GEORGE WASHINGTON HARRIS • Mrs. Yardley's Quilting   359
   HERMAN MELVILLE • Bartleby, the Scrivener   365 ✓
   HENRY JAMES • The Tree of Knowledge   392
   JOSEPH CONRAD • The Secret Sharer   403
   SIR ARTHUR CONAN DOYLE • The Adventure of the Speckled
   Band   432 ✓
   FRANZ KAFKA • A Hunger Artist   451 ✓
   ISAAC BASHEVIS SINGER • Tanhum   457
   JOHN CHEEVER • The Country Husband   466
   ALBERT MURRAY • Train Whistle Guitar   484

GRACE PALEY • A Conversation with My Father   497
URSULA K. LE GUIN • The Ones Who Walk Away
from Omelas   501
WOODY ALLEN • The Kugelmass Episode   506
JOYCE CAROL OATES • The Lady with the Pet Dog   515

POETRY

A Preface to Poetry   531

ANONYMOUS • Western Wind   531
E. E. CUMMINGS • l(a   532
LOUIS MAC NEICE • Aubade   534

SUBJECT, THEME, AND TONE   537

1   EXPERIENCING POETRY   537

ELIZABETH BARRETT BROWNING • How Do I Love Thee?   538
JAROLD RAMSEY • The Tally Stick   538
EZRA POUND • The River-Merchant's Wife: A Letter   540
DIANE WAKOSKI • Uneasy Rider   542
TOM WAYMAN • Wayman in Love   543
JOHN CROWE RANSOM • Bells for John Whiteside's
Daughter   544
BEN JONSON • On My First Son   545
HOWARD NEMEROV • The Vacuum   546
LADY CATHERINE DYER • Epitaph On the Monument of
Sir William Dyer at Colmworth, 1641   548

A Gathering of Love Poems   548

ANONYMOUS • My Love in Her Attire   548
ROBERT HERRICK • Upon Julia's Clothes   549
THEODORE ROETHKE • I Knew a Woman   549
CHRISTINA ROSSETTI • Echo   550
AUDRE LORDE • Recreation   550
JOHN WILMOT, EARL OF ROCHESTER • Love
and Life   551
EDNA ST. VINCENT MILLAY • What Lips My Lips Have
Kissed   552
WILLIAM SHAKESPEARE • Let Me Not to the Marriage of
True Minds   552
WILLIAM CONGREVE • Song   553
ADRIENNE RICH • Two Songs   553

A Gathering of Poems about Death   554

A. E. HOUSMAN • To an Athlete Dying Young   554

WILLIAM WORDSWORTH • A Slumber Did My Spirit Seal   555
MARK TWAIN • Ode to Stephen Dowling Bots, Dec'd   555
DYLAN THOMAS • Do Not Go Gentle into That Good
   Night   556
EMILY DICKINSON • Because I Could Not Stop for Death   557
JOHN DONNE • Death Be Not Proud   558
SYLVIA PLATH • Lady Lazarus   558

2 EXPECTATION AND SURPRISE   561

MARGE PIERCY • Barbie Doll   561
W. D. SNODGRASS • Leaving the Motel   562
JONI MITCHELL • Woodstock   564
ETHERIDGE KNIGHT • Hard Rock Returns to Prison from the
   Hospital for the Criminal Insane   566
WILLIAM BLAKE • London   567
MAXINE KUMIN • Woodchucks   569
ADRIENNE RICH • Aunt Jennifer's Tigers   570

A Gathering of Poems about Animals   571

JOHN BUNYAN • Of the Boy and the Butterfly   573
EMILY DICKINSON • A Narrow Fellow in the Grass   573
KARL SHAPIRO • The Fly   574
OGDEN NASH • The Turtle   575
LEWIS CARROLL • How Doth the Little Crocodile   576
SUSAN MITCHELL • From the Journals of the Frog
   Prince   576
DELMORE SCHWARTZ • The Heavy Bear Who Goes
   with Me   577
JOHN STONE • Explaining About the Dachshund   578
JOHN MASEFIELD • The Lemmings   579

A Gathering of Poems on Family and Ancestry   580

RICHARD HUGO • What Thou Lovest Well, Remains
   American   580
JOHN STONE • Coming Home   580
DIANE WAKOSKI • The Photos   581
DOROTHY LIVESAY • Green Rain   583
ANN DEAGON • There Is No Balm in Birmingham   583
ETHERIDGE KNIGHT • The Idea of Ancestry   584
A. M. KLEIN • Heirloom   585

A Gathering of Poems on Poetry   586

A. E. HOUSMAN • Terence, This Is Stupid Stuff   586
MARIANNE MOORE • Poetry   587
NIKKI GIOVANNI • Poetry   589
EMILY DICKINSON • I Dwell in Possibility   590
ARCHIBALD MAC LEISH • Ars Poetica   590
ISHMAEL REED • beware: do not read this poem   591
WILLIAM SHAKESPEARE • Not Marble, Nor the Gilded
   Monuments   592

ARCHIBALD MAC LEISH • "Not Marble Nor the Gilded
  Monuments" 593
ROBINSON JEFFERS • To the Stone-Cutters 594

A Gathering of Poems of Satire and Protest 594

TOM WAYMAN • Picketing Supermarkets 594
DUDLEY RANDALL • Ballad of Birmingham 595
DENISE LEVERTOV • What Were They Like 596
DELAWARE INDIAN SONG • Who Are They? 597
ANONYMOUS • The Lady Fortune 597
ANONYMOUS • The Silver Swan 597
AUDRE LORDE • Outside 598
W. H. AUDEN • The Unknown Citizen 599
CLAUDE MCKAY • America 600
LANGSTON HUGHES • Harlem (A Dream Deferred) 600

CRAFT

601

3 SPEAKER

601

THOMAS HARDY • The Ruined Maid 601
X. J. KENNEDY • In a Prominent Bar in Secaucus
  One Day 602
ROBERT BROWNING • Soliloquy of the Spanish Cloister 604
DOROTHY PARKER • A Certain Lady 607
A. R. AMMONS • Needs 609
WILLIAM WORDSWORTH • She Dwelt Among the Untrodden
  Ways 610

JOHN BETJEMAN • In Westminster Abbey 612
HENRY REED • Lessons of the War: Judging Distances 613
AUDRE LORDE • Hanging Fire 614
HOWARD NEMEROV • Boom! 615
GEORGE HERBERT • The Collar 616
JOHN DONNE • Song ("Go, and catch a falling star") 617

4 SITUATION AND SETTING

618

JAMES DICKEY • Cherrylog Road 619
JOHN DONNE • The Flea 623
ROBERT FROST • U.S. 1946 King's X 624
SYLVIA PLATH • Point Shirley 626
MATTHEW ARNOLD • Dover Beach 628

ROBERT BROWNING • My Last Duchess 629
JOHN DONNE • A Valediction: Forbidding Mourning 631
JAROLD RAMSEY • Lupine Dew 632
GALWAY KINNELL • To Christ our Lord 632
ANNE SEXTON • The Truth the Dead Know 633
DONALD JUSTICE • Here in Katmandu 634

5 WORDS   635

RICHARD ARMOUR • Hiding Place 635
YVOR WINTERS • At the San Francisco Airport 636
WALTER DE LA MARE • Slim Cunning Hands 638
BEN JONSON • Still to Be Neat 639
ROBERT HERRICK • Delight in Disorder 640
THEODORE ROETHKE • My Papa's Waltz 642

GERARD MANLEY HOPKINS • Pied Beauty 643
EMILY DICKINSON • After Great Pain 644
WILLIAM CARLOS WILLIAMS • The Red Wheelbarrow 644
ANN DEAGON • Certified Copy 645
E. E. CUMMINGS • anyone lived in a pretty how town 645
JOHN MILTON • *from* Paradise Lost 646

6 FIGURATIVE LANGUAGE   649

Metaphor and Simile   649

WILLIAM SHAKESPEARE • That Time of Year 650
LINDA PASTAN • Marks 652
ROBERT BURNS • A Red, Red Rose 653

RANDALL JARRELL • The Death of the Ball Turret
   Gunner 655
JOHN DONNE • Batter My Heart 655
ANONYMOUS • The Twenty-Third Psalm 655
BOB DYLAN • Mr. Tambourine Man 656
PHILIP BOOTH • One Man's Wife 657

Symbol   657

SHARON OLDS • Leningrad Cemetery, Winter of 1941 658
JAMES DICKEY • The Leap 659
JOHN CLARE • Love's Emblem 663
WILLIAM BLAKE • The Sick Rose 664

WILLIAM HABINGTON • To Roses in the Bosom of
   Castara 665
ROBERT FROST • The Rose Family 666
DOROTHY PARKER • One Perfect Rose 666
DONALD JUSTICE • Southern Gothic 667
DUDLEY RANDALL • Roses and Revolutions 667
WILLIAM CARLOS WILLIAMS • Poem ("The rose
   fades") 668

7 STRUCTURE   668

ANONYMOUS • Frankie and Johnny 669
HOWARD NEMEROV • The Goose Fish 671
PHILIP LARKIN • Church Going 674
JAMES WRIGHT • Arrangements with Earth for Three Dead
   Friends 676

M. CARL HOLMAN • Three Brown Girls Singing 678

ANONYMOUS • Lord Randal 680
KARL SHAPIRO • Auto Wreck 681
LUCILLE CLIFTON • At Last We Killed the Roaches 682
ANONYMOUS • Sir Patrick Spens 682
EDMUND SPENSER • Happy Ye Leaves 683
PERCY BYSSHE SHELLEY • Ode to the West Wind 684
ROBERT FROST • Stopping by Woods on a Snowy
Evening 686

8 SOUND AND SIGHT   **687**

The Sounds of Poetry   687

HELEN CHASIN • The Word *Plum* 687
MONA VAN DUYN • What the Motorcycle Said 688
KENNETH FEARING • Dirge 690
ALEXANDER POPE • [Sound and Sense] 692
SAMUEL TAYLOR COLERIDGE • Metrical Feet 695
ARTHUR W. MONKS • Twilight's Last Gleaming 695
ANONYMOUS • Limericks 696
SIR JOHN SUCKLING • Song ("Why so pale and wan, fond
Lover?") 697
JOHN DRYDEN • To the Memory of Mr. Oldham 697

ALFRED, LORD TENNYSON • Break, Break, Break 699
DONALD JUSTICE • Counting the Mad 699
THOMAS NASHE • Spring, the Sweet Spring 700
GERARD MANLEY HOPKINS • Spring and Fall 700
WILLIAM SHAKESPEARE • Like as the Waves 701
STEPHEN SPENDER • The Express 701
MICHAEL HARPER • Dear John, Dear Coltrane 702
BOB KAUFMAN • Blues Note 703

The Way a Poem Looks   704

FRANKLIN P. ADAMS • Composed in the Composing
Room 705
E. E. CUMMINGS • portrait 705

GEORGE HERBERT • Easter Wings 707
ROBERT HERRICK • The Pillar of Fame 707
ANONYMOUS • Love Knot 708
EDWIN MORGAN • Message Clear 709
EDWIN MORGAN • The Computer's First Christmas Card 710
JOHN HOLLANDER • A State of Nature 711
ROBERT HOLLANDER • You Too? Me Too—Why Not?
Soda Pop 712

9 STANZAS AND VERSE FORMS   **713**

WILLIAM WORDSWORTH • Nuns Fret Not 717

HENRY CONSTABLE • My Lady's Presence Makes the Roses
   Red   718

WILLIAM WORDSWORTH • Scorn Not the Sonnet   720
JOHN KEATS • On the Sonnet   720
PERCY BYSSHE SHELLEY • Ozymandias   721
WILLIAM WORDSWORTH • London, 1802   722
JOHN MILTON • On the Late Massacre in Piedmont   722
GWENDOLYN BROOKS • First Fight. Then Fiddle.   723
JOHN KEATS • On First Looking into Chapman's Homer   723
GEORGE STARBUCK • On First Looking in on Blodgett's
   Keats's "Chapman's Homer" (*Sum.*1/2C.M9–11)   724
SIR PHILIP SIDNEY • When Nature Made Her Chief Work,
   Stella's Eyes   724
WILLIAM SHAKESPEARE • My Mistress' Eyes Are Nothing
   like the Sun   725
HELEN CHASIN • Joy Sonnet in a Random Universe   725

10 POETIC "KINDS"   726

CHRISTOPHER MARLOWE • The Passionate Shepherd to His
   Love   727

SAMUEL TAYLOR COLERIDGE • What Is an Epigram?   730
ANONYMOUS • [Epigrams]   730
WILLIAM WALSH • An Epigram   730
WILLIAM BLAKE • Her Whole Life Is an Epigram   730
BEN JONSON • Epitaph on Elizabeth, L.H.   731
MELEAGER • I'll Twine White Violets   731
MARTIAL • You've Told Me, Maro   731
MARTIAL • Tomorrow You Will Live   732
JOHN GAY • My Own Epitaph   732
J. V. CUNNINGHAM • Here Lies My Wife   732
SIR HENRY WOTTON • Upon the Death of Sir Albert
   Morton's Wife   732
WALTER SAVAGE LANDOR • Various the Roads of Life   733
SARAH CLEGHORN • Quatrain   733
THEODORE ROETHKE • Epigram: The Mistake   733
MATTHEW PRIOR • A True Maid   733
SIR JOHN HARINGTON • Epigram: Of Treason   734
HOWARD NEMEROV • Epigram: Political Reflexion   734
HENRY ALDRICH • Why I Drink   734
DAVID MCCORD • History of Education   734
RICHARD HARTER FOGLE • A Hawthorne Garland:
   Scarlet Letter   735
COUNTEE CULLEN • For a Lady I Know   735
X. J. KENNEDY • Epitaph for a Postal Clerk   735
DAVID MCCORD • Epitaph on a Waiter   735
DOROTHY PARKER • Comment   736
J. V. CUNNINGHAM • All in Due Time   736
FRANCES CORNFORD • Parting in Wartime   736
FRANCIS QUARLES • Be Sad, My Heart   736

CONTEXTS 737

11 THE AUTHOR'S WORK 737

HOWARD NEMEROV • A Way of Life 738
JOHN DONNE • The Sun Rising 740

JOHN KEATS
On the Grasshopper and the Cricket 742
from Endymion (Book I) 743
When I Have Fears 743
Bright Star 744
La Belle Dame sans Merci (original version) 744
Ode to a Nightingale 746
Ode on a Grecian Urn 748
Ode on Melancholy 749
To Autumn 750
from Letter to Benjamin Bailey, November 22, 1817 751
from Letter to George and Thomas Keats, December 21, 1817 752
Letter to John Hamilton Reynolds, February 19, 1818 753
from Letter to John Taylor, February 27, 1818 754
from the Preface to Endymion, dated April 10, 1818 755
from Letter to James Augustus Hessey, October 8, 1818 755
Chronology 756
ADRIENNE RICH
A Clock in the Square 757
At a Bach Concert 757
Storm Warnings 758
Snapshots of a Daughter-in-Law 758
Necessities of Life 762
Orion 764
Planetarium 765
Trying to Talk with a Man 766
Diving into the Wreck 767
Origins and History of Consciousness 770
from Talking with Adrienne Rich 771
from an Interview with Adrienne Rich 773
from When We Dead Awaken: Writing as Re-Vision 775
Chronology 776

12 HISTORICAL CONTEXTS 778

RAYMOND R. PATTERSON • You Are the Brave 779

The Need for Factual Information 783

AMIRI BARAKA (LEROI JONES) • In Memory of Radio 783
E. E. CUMMINGS • poem, or beauty hurts mr. vinal 784
EUGENE MCCARTHY • Kilroy 785
JAMES A. EMANUEL • Emmett Till 786

World War I   787

•• WILFRED OWEN • Dulce Et Decorum Est 787
ISAAC ROSENBERG • Break of Day in the Trenches   788
EZRA POUND • There Died a Myriad   788
EDGAR A. GUEST • The Things that Make a Soldier Great   789
SIEGFRIED SASSOON • Repression of War Experience   789
SIEGFRIED SASSOON • Base Details   790
RUPERT BROOKE • The Soldier   791
W. B. YEATS • On Being Asked for a War Poem   791

13   LITERARY TRADITION   791

The Carpe Diem *Motif*   794

ROBERT HERRICK • To the Virgins, to Make Much
   of Time   794
EDMUND WALLER • Song ("Go, lovely rose!")   794
RICHARD LOVELACE • To Amarantha, that She Would
   Dishevel Her Hair   795
BEN JONSON • Come, My Celia   796
DONALD J. LLOYD • Bridal Couch   796
ANDREW MARVELL • To His Coy Mistress   796
E. E. CUMMINGS • (ponder, darling, these busted
   statues   798

Replies to The Passionate Shepherd   799

SIR WALTER RALEGH • The Nymph's Reply to the
   Shepherd   799
C. DAY LEWIS • Song ("Come, live with me and be my
   love")   800
JOHN DONNE • The Bait   800
PETER DE VRIES • Bacchanal   801

Another Version   802

KENNETH KOCH • Variations on a Theme by William
   Carlos Williams   802
DESMOND SKIRROW • Ode on a Grecian Urn Summarized   802
ANTHONY HECHT • The Dover Bitch   803

14   FRAMES OF REFERENCE: CONTEXTS OF MYTH   803

Judaeo-Christian History and Myth   805

JOHN MILTON • [Before the Fall]   805
JOHN HOLLANDER • Adam's Task   807
LINDA PASTAN • A Symposium: Apples   807
VASSAR MILLER • Adam's Footprint   808
CHRISTINA ROSSETTI • Eve   809
ROB HOLLAND • Eve in Old Age   811
NANCY SULLIVAN • The Death of the First Man   812

Classical History and Myth 812

    ALFRED, LORD TENNYSON • Ulysses 812
    PETER VIERECK • Kilroy 814
    WALLACE STEVENS • The World as Meditation 816
    EDMUND SPENSER • Penelope for Her Ulysses' Sake 817

Non-Western History and Myth 817

    LANGSTON HUGHES • The Negro Speaks of Rivers 817
    GABRIEL OKARA • Piano and Drums 818
    MAYA ANGELOU • Africa 818
    BRUCE MCM. WRIGHT • The African Affair 819
    ISHMAEL REED • Sermonette 820

Private History and Myth 820

    W. B. YEATS
    Easter 1916 820
    The Second Coming 823
    Leda and the Swan 823
    Sailing to Byzantium 824
    Among School Children 825
    Byzantium 827
    The Circus Animals' Desertion 828

POEMS FOR FURTHER READING 830

    A. R. AMMONS • Cascadilla Falls 830
    MARGARET ATWOOD • Five Poems for Dolls 831
    W. H. AUDEN • In Memory of W. B. Yeats 832
    W. H. AUDEN • Musée des Beaux Arts 834
    JOHN BERRYMAN • 1 September 1939 835
    EARLE BIRNEY • From the Hazel Bough 835
    EARLE BIRNEY • Irapuato 836
    WILLIAM BLAKE • Ah Sunflower 837
    WILLIAM BLAKE • The Lamb 837
    WILLIAM BLAKE • The Tiger 838
    LOUISE BOGAN • The Dragonfly 838
    JULIAN BOND • The Bishop of Atlanta: Ray Charles 839
    JULIAN BOND • Rotation 839
    LEONARD COHEN • Suzanne Takes You Down 840
    SAMUEL TAYLOR COLERIDGE • Kubla Khan: or, a Vision in a Dream 841
    E. E. CUMMINGS • the season 'tis, my lovely lambs 842
    E. E. CUMMINGS • chanson innocente 844
    EMILY DICKINSON • The Brain Is Wider than the Sky 844
    EMILY DICKINSON • My Life Closed Twice 845
    EMILY DICKINSON • Wild Nights! Wild Nights! 845
    JOHN DONNE • The Good-Morrow 846
    JOHN DONNE • The Canonization 846

T. S. ELIOT • Journey of the Magi   848
T. S. ELIOT • The Love Song of J. Alfred Prufrock   849
LAWRENCE FERLINGHETTI • Christ Climbed Down   852
JULIA FIELDS • Madness One Monday Evening   854
ROBERT FROST • Range-Finding   855
THOMAS HARDY • The Darkling Thrush   855
THOMAS HARDY • During Wind and Rain   856
THOMAS HARDY • Hap   857
THOMAS HARDY • Channel Firing   857
ANTHONY HECHT • "It Out-Herods Herod. Pray You,
    Avoid It."   858
GERARD MANLEY HOPKINS • The Windhover   860
RICHARD HUGO • To Women   860
JOHN KEATS • The Eve of St. Agnes   861
D. H. LAWRENCE • Piano   871
D. H. LAWRENCE • Snake   871
ROBERT LOWELL • Skunk Hour   874
ELI MANDEL • Houdini   875
ANDREW MARVELL • The Garden   876
JAMES MERRILL • Watching the Dance   878
CZESLAW MILOSZ • A Poor Christian Looks at the
    Ghetto   878
HOWARD NEMEROV • Life Cycle of Common Man   879
SYLVIA PLATH • Black Rook in Rainy Weather   880
EZRA POUND • In a Station of the Metro   882
EZRA POUND • A Virginal   882
JOHN PRESS • Womanizers   882
DAVID RAY • A Piece of Shrapnel   883
EDWIN ARLINGTON ROBINSON • Mr. Flood's Party   883
EDWIN ARLINGTON ROBINSON • Richard Cory   885
EDWIN ARLINGTON ROBINSON • Uncle Ananias   885
THEODORE ROETHKE • The Dream   886
THEODORE ROETHKE • She   887
THEODORE ROETHKE • The Waking   887
ANNE SEXTON • The Kiss   888
WILLIAM SHAKESPEARE • Th'Expense of Spirit   889
WILLIAM SHAKESPEARE • Hark, Hark! the Lark   889
WILLIAM SHAKESPEARE • Spring   890
WILLIAM SHAKESPEARE • Winter   890
PERCY BYSSHE SHELLEY • England in 1819   891
STEPHEN SPENDER • An Elementary School Classroom in
    a Slum   891
STEPHEN SPENDER • Judas Iscariot   892
WALLACE STEVENS • Anecdote of the Jar   893
WALLACE STEVENS • The Idea of Order at Key West   894
WALLACE STEVENS • The Emperor of Ice-Cream   895
WALLACE STEVENS • Sunday Morning   896
JONATHAN SWIFT • On Stella's Birthday, 1719   899
DYLAN THOMAS • Fern Hill   899
DYLAN THOMAS • The Force that Through the Green Fuse
    Drives the Flower   901

DYLAN THOMAS • In My Craft or Sullen Art 901
WALT WHITMAN • When Lilacs Last in the Dooryard
   Bloomed 902
RICHARD WILBUR • The Beautiful Changes 908
RICHARD WILBUR • Love Calls Us to the Things of This
   World 909
WILLIAM CARLOS WILLIAMS • This Is Just to Say 910
WILLIAM WORDSWORTH • Lines Composed a Few Miles
   above Tintern Abbey on Revisiting the Banks of the
   Wye During a Tour, July 13, 1798 910
SIR THOMAS WYATT • They Flee from Me 913

A Glossary of Poetic Terms (915)

DRAMA

ELEMENTS 935

1 AUDIENCE, RITUAL, AND MYTH 935

ANONYMOUS • The Sacrifice of Isaac 938
HAROLD PINTER • The Dumb Waiter 950

2 DRAMATIC STRUCTURE AND THE STAGE 978

WILLIAM SHAKESPEARE • Hamlet (984)

READING AND PERFORMANCE 1077

3 PAGE, STAGE, AND SCREEN 1077

ARTHUR MILLER • Death of a Salesman 1083
HERMAN J. MANKIEWICZ AND ORSON WELLES • Citizen
   Kane 1156

CONTEXTS 1235

4 THE AUTHOR'S WORK 1235

TENNESSEE WILLIAMS • The Glass Menagerie (1238)
TENNESSEE WILLIAMS • The Long Goodbye 1297

5 TRAGEDY, COMEDY, AND THE MODERN DRAMA 1310

SOPHOCLES • Oedipus Tyrannus (1313)
OSCAR WILDE • The Importance of Being Earnest 1342

6 HISTORICAL SETTING   1391

    ANTON CHEKHOV • Three Sisters 1393

PLAYS FOR FURTHER READING   1443

    HENRIK IBSEN • Hedda Gabler 1443
    ED BULLINS • A Son, Come Home 1508

Index of Authors   1526
Index of Titles and First Lines   1533

FOREWORD TO THE THIRD EDITION

The Norton Introduction to Literature is both an anthology and a textbook—a "teaching anthology"—for the indispensable course in which college student and college teacher begin to read literature seriously together. In this, the Third Edition, we have pursued two central aims: we have freshened the *anthology* with new selections that, like those they join, are both enjoyable to read and profitable to learn about. And we have strengthened the *textbook* with a reorganization of chapters and new chapter introductions, so that students might hold, within a single volume, not merely literature worth studying but also assistance in developing the critical tools needed for that study.

In all our work on this edition we have been guided by teachers in other English departments and our own, and by students who addressed us simply as authors of the textbook they were using and by those who were able to approach us after class as their teachers: we feel confident that the result culls from the experience of many all the necessary ingredients for a solid introduction to the experience of literature.

We now offer 44 stories, 21 of which are new, nearly 350 poems, 95 of which are new, and 11 plays and a screenplay, 4 of which are new. Among the additions are both deservedly familiar stories and stories that we hope will provide instructor as well as student with the quickening thrill of discovery; we have added stories by Spencer Holst, Edgar Allan Poe, Ambrose Bierce, Mordecai Richler, Toni Cade Bambara, Doris Lessing, James Joyce, Alice Munro, Arthur C. Clarke, Jorge Luis Borges, Gabriel García Márquez, Augustus Baldwin Longstreet, Samuel Clemens, William Faulkner, Kate Chopin, F. Scott Fitzgerald, George Washington Harris, Grace Paley, Ursula K. LeGuin, Woody Allen, and Joyce Carol Oates.

The poetry section has been similarly infused with selections familiar and fresh, with newly included works by such poets as Jarold Ramsey, Lady Catherine Dyer, Audre Lorde, Dylan Thomas, Marge Piercy, Maxine Kumin, John Bunyan, Lewis Carroll, Richard Hugo, Nikki Giovanni, Emily Dickinson, Dudley Randall, Thomas Hardy, Dorothy Parker, William Wordsworth, Linda Pastan, Mona van Duyn, Margaret Atwood, Theodore Roethke, and Anne Sexton.

In drama, many instructors have requested the inclusion of *Hedda Gabler* and *Death of a Salesman,* and we are pleased to comply. (We now offer both *Death of a Salesman* and *The Glass Menagerie.*) We have also added a brilliant contemporary play by Harold Pinter, *The Dumb Waiter,* and the complete screenplay of the film *Citizen Kane.*

As before, however, *The Norton Introduction to Literature* is more than a grab-bag of good things to read. The works are not only selected but arranged in order to introduce a reader to the serious study of literature. Each genre—fiction, poetry, drama—is approached in three logical steps. Fiction, for example, is first analyzed by questions of craft, the so-called elements of fiction, such as plot, characterization, and theme. Then the student is shown how stories may be studied in groups, connected by subject matter, theme, or mode: initiation stories and fantasy stories are the examples. Finally, broader contexts are pointed up: an author's *oeuvre*, a particular literary tradition, and historical or cultural setting. (A fourth section of stories is left simply for further reading, for independent study, or as a reservoir of additional examples for the instructor who has a different plan of attack.) The first two sections within each genre are intended to support the close-reading and/or generic approach that has been familiar in literature classrooms for many years; the third section is intended to supplement and augment that approach, to suggest to teacher and student some ways of seeing a work of literature within its temporal and cultural frameworks. All in all, the book's arrangement is intended to facilitate a student's movement from narrower to broader questions, since it mirrors the way people read—wanting to learn more as they experience more.

In the Third Edition we have reshaped our own editorial helps, striving in these revisions for ever clearer explanation, ever more straightforward organization. Each chapter is now introduced by a discussion of basic concepts the student will need for classroom discussion or writing assignments. "Dramatic Structure and the Stage," for example, includes definitions and discussion of the terms used in analyzing the dramatic structure of a play and those used for the physical structure of a stage. Students, therefore, have this information available alongside the plays they are reading, and the instructor may spend valuable classroom time on the plays themselves. (Instructors who prefer their own definitions will find ours discrete from the literature and easy to use or ignore.) In preparing these pedagogical aids, we have restrained ourselves from overexplaining, or from dictating readers' responses in advance (some teachers and students will want to use the book, as indeed it can be used, as a quarry for their own discoveries).

We have retained certain editorial procedures that proved their usefulness in the First and Second Editions. First of all, the works are annotated, as is customary in Norton anthologies: beginning readers need help with references and allusions, and the fact that we supply that help frees the teacher for more important activities in the classroom. To offer the texts in the form most immediately available to their particular audience, we have normalized spelling according to modern American usage (but only in cases where the change does not alter semantic, phonological, or metric qualities). In order to avoid giving the impression that all literature was written at the same time, we have dated the selections: the date to the right is that of first book publication or performance (when preceded by a *p* it refers to periodical publication); a date to the left, when it occurs, is that of composition.

As in previous editions, Jerome Beaty has taken primary responsibility for the Fiction section, J. Paul Hunter for the Poetry, and Carl E. Bain for the Drama, the work on which he had all but completed before his untimely death. But we have collaborated on every aspect of the book from the beginning, learning from each other in ways that suggest that literature is still very much worth studying.

J.B., J.P.H.

ACKNOWLEDGMENTS

We would like to thank our teachers, for their example in the love of literature and in the art of sharing that love; our students, for their patience as we are learning from them to be better teachers of literature; our wives and children, for their understanding when the work of preparing this text made us seem less than perfectly loving husbands and fathers.

We would also like to thank our colleagues, many of whom have taught our book and evaluated our efforts, for their constant encouragement and enlightenment. Of our colleagues at Emory University, we would like especially to thank Michaelyn Burnette, Lore Metzger, Lee Pederson, Harry Rusche, Ronald Schuchard, Kristina Straub, Floyd C. Watkins, and Sally Wolff. And we thank also Paula R. Backscheider (University of Rochester); T. E. Blom (University of British Columbia); Patricia Brocker; Thomas R. Carper (University of Maine); Frank W. Childrey (Northwest Mississippi Junior College); Randy R. Conine (El Centro College); Michael P. Dean (University of Mississippi); Stephen F. Evans (University of Kansas); Norman Feltes (York University); Lila F. Fink (Pepperdine University); Frederick Goldberg (Clayton Junior College); Larry Gray (Southeastern Louisiana University); Alan Grob (Rice University); Christopher Hudgins (University of Nevada); Kristin Hunter (University of Pennsylvania); Lisa Hunter; Elizabeth Lunz; William Morgan (Illinois State University); Nils Peterson (San Jose State University); Ellanor Pruitt (Oxford College); Richard Quaintance (Douglass College); Joseph N. Riddell (University of California at Los Angeles); Ronald Schleifer (University of Oklahoma); John Shaw (Florida State University); John R. Shriver (Wayne State University); Irwin Simpkins (DeKalb College); Frederick Stocking (Williams College); Rae

Thompson (University of Guelph); Dennis Todd (Wayne State University); Richard Turner (Indiana University-Purdue University at Indianapolis); Patricia Vicari (Scarborough College of the University of Toronto); Melissa Walker (Mercer University); Arthur Williams (Oxford College); Dorothy A. Winsor (Wayne State University); and Curt R. Zimansky (University of Colorado).

On several occasions during the preparation of this work a retreat from everyday was needed. The Ossabaw Island Project provided it, and we wish to thank the Ossabaw Island Foundation and particularly Eleanor West for the provision and for the grace with which it was offered.

We would also like to thank our friends at W. W. Norton & Company, especially John Benedict, Karen Fischer, John W. N. Francis, Josepha Gutelius, Debbie Hunter, Fred McFarland, Diane O'Connor, Jennifer Sutherland, Roy Tedoff, and Barry Wade.

Our friend, colleague, and co-editor Carl E. Bain died just before completing work on this edition. Scott Wilson undertook the sad task of bringing the remaining materials to their present form, and we would like to express to him our deep appreciation. His work on *Death of a Salesman* and *Citizen Kane* in the spirit of Carl Bain's approach, we wish especially to acknowledge.

J.B., J.P.H.

FICTION

The Zebra Storyteller

Once upon a time there was a Siamese cat who pretended to be a lion and spoke inappropriate Zebraic.

That language is whinnied by the race of striped horses in Africa.

Here now: An innocent zebra is walking in a jungle and approaching from another direction is the little cat; they meet.

"Hello there!" says the Siamese cat in perfectly pronounced Zebraic. "It certainly is a pleasant day, isn't it? The sun is shining, the birds are singing, isn't the world a lovely place to live today!"

The zebra is so astonished at hearing a Siamese cat speaking like a zebra, why—he's just fit to be tied.

So the little cat quickly ties him up, kills him, and drags the better parts of the carcass back to his den.

The cat successfully hunted zebras many months in this manner, dining on filet mignon of zebra every night, and from the better hides he made bow neckties and wide belts after the fashion of the decadent princes of the Old Siamese court.

He began boasting to his friends he was a lion, and he gave them as proof the fact that he hunted zebras.

The delicate noses of the zebras told them there was really no lion in the neighborhood. The zebra deaths caused many to avoid the region. Superstitious, they decided the woods were haunted by the ghost of a lion.

One day the storyteller of the zebras was ambling, and through his mind ran plots for stories to amuse the other zebras, when suddenly his eyes brightened, and he said, "That's it! I'll tell a story about a Siamese cat who learns to speak our language! What an idea! That'll make 'em laugh!"

Just then the Siamese cat appeared before him, and said, "Hello there! Pleasant day today, isn't it!"

The zebra storyteller wasn't fit to be tied at hearing a cat speaking his language, because he'd been thinking about that very thing.

He took a good look at the cat, and he didn't know why, but there was something about his looks he didn't like, so he kicked him with a hoof and killed him.

That is the function of the storyteller.

1971

A PREFACE TO FICTION

The Zebra Storyteller seems to suggest that the purpose of stories is to prepare us for the unexpected. Though the storyteller thinks he is just spinning stories out of his own imagination, in order to amuse, his stories prove to be practical. When the extraordinary, the unheard-of occurs—like a Siamese cat speaking Zebraic—he is prepared because he has already imagined it, and he alone is able to protect his tribe against the unusual.

Other storytellers make the function of fiction less direct and less extraordinary. According to them, fiction prevents readers from projecting false hopes and fears (such as the zebras' superstitious belief that they are being preyed on by the ghost of a lion and so are helpless) and shows them what they can actually expect in their everyday lives, so that they can protect themselves. Hetty Sorrel, in George Eliot's novel *Adam Bede*, is being paid admiring attention by the young squire (who, by the way, eventually seduces her), and she dreams of marriage, elopement, and all sorts of vague pleasures. Her imagination has not been trained by narrative to project possible "stories": "Hetty had never read a novel," George Eliot tells us, "[so] how could she find a shape for her expectations?"

We are all storytellers, then, of one stripe or another. Whenever we plan the future or ponder a decision, we are telling stories, projecting expectations through narrative. Even scientists tell stories that begin with a fiction called a hypothesis ("What if . . .") and travel mentally through the unknown toward invention. Whenever we tell stories or read them, we are educating our imaginations, either extending our mental experience in the actual, as Hetty might have done by reading novels, or preparing ourselves for the extraordinary and unexpected, like the Zebra storyteller.

The actual and the extraordinary suggest what two different kinds of readers or a reader in two different moods looks for in fiction. Some readers like fiction, they say, because they enjoy reading about people like themselves, or about places, things, experiences, and ideas that are familiar and agreeable. Most of us initially prefer American literature and twentieth-century literature to literature remote in time or place. Indeed, stories must somehow be related to our own lives before we can find them intellectually or emotionally meaningful. Similarity of fictional characters, times, and places to those we know is only the most direct and obvious form of this relationship. No matter what our literary experience and taste, most of us relate in a special way to stories about people like us, experiences like our own, and especially to a story that mentions our home town or our neighborhood or the name of the street that we used to walk along on our way to school. (I got particular enjoyment, for example, in annotating the name of the station called out by the train conductor in *The Artificial Nigger*.) Whether we call this reading for identification or for relevance, no one would deny that one of the many things that fiction may be "for" is learning about ourselves and the world around us.

However, there are probably many readers—or all readers in certain moods—who would say that the last things they want in a story are people like themselves, experiences like those of their everyday lives, and places and times like here and now. They want to (or are accused of wanting to) escape. The desire to escape through literature, like the desire to identify, defines what is in fact one basic motive in reading fiction. If fiction must be relevant enough to relate meaningfully to us, it must also be "irrelevant," different, other, strange—as strange, perhaps, as a Siamese cat speaking Zebraic. That is, it must take us out of ourselves, out of the confining vision of our own eyes, conditioned by our own background and experience. It must show us that there are ways of looking at the world other than our own, other human and limited but also viable ways of looking at reality. So this collection includes a sprinkling of stories written in the last century, a few written in vastly different cultures, and a fair number written about worlds that have not existed or do not (yet) exist, as well as many stories about approximately our own time and place.

What a story shows us or teaches us many readers at first call a story's **message**—an objective, universal truth that they were unaware of before reading the story. We gradually become aware, however, that stories tell us not so much what life means as what it's like. They deal with perceptions rather than abstract or "objective" truths. These perceptions may be translated into messages, but we soon discover that the messages boil down to things like "There's good and bad in everybody," "Hurting people is wrong," and "Everything is not what it seems"—messages that Western Union, much less Western literature, might not find too urgent or startlingly illuminating. Indeed, it may not even be the truth of the perception embodied in a story (truth in the sense of our agreement or conversion) that is at the heart of the reading experience so much as the human or subjective truth: are we convinced that if we had those eyes rather than our own and were there rather than here, this is what we might see, or how we might see? Whenever we can say yes, we have expanded our consciousness: we have been able to escape or transcend the limitations of our own vision, our own past and conditions, and we are able to see, to a greater or lesser extent, a new world, or the world in a new way. Even more important, perhaps, is to recognize through apprehension of another's "distortion" of reality that objects do not in fact exist for us in themselves, as they are supposed to, but as they are perceived by us—a discovery that may awaken us to actively looking at things for ourselves rather than accepting them at conventional face value. For example, we "know" a table top is rectangular, but in a story we are told it is diamond-shaped. We understand that if we were to look at the table top from a certain angle it would look diamond-shaped. But doesn't that imply that the table top is rectangular only when we look from a certain angle? And are we looking at it from that angle? We look again, and we recognize that though we've always known it's a rectangle, we've never really *seen* it as one. The story has not only allowed us to see reality from another angle, but it has helped us to sharpen our own vision.

Stories, then, educate our perceptions—of others and of ourselves —as well as educating our expectations—of the ordinary and the extraordinary.

Elements

1 PLOT

If you have not yet read the very brief story that precedes the Preface, Spencer Holst's *The Zebra Storyteller,* you may want to glance at it now, for you can see in the arrangement of the action there the skeleton of the typical short story **plot** or **plot structure**. Plot simply means the arrangement of the action. The **action** refers to an imagined event or happening or to a series of such events. These events have a kind of imagined reality of their own, almost, we feel, separate from the words of the story and the plot or arrangement. The **arrangement,** on the other hand, suggests not a real or imagined world but manipulation by someone: the author. We shall refer to that imaginary world and the events in it as the story's **history,** and to all kinds of manipulation or arrangement, including plot, language, point of view, and many other fictional devices, as the **structure** of the story.

The action of a story usually involves **conflict** (a struggle between opposing forces), and it often falls into something like the same five parts that we find in a play (see p. 979). The conflict in this little tale is between the Siamese cat and the zebras, especially the zebra storyteller. The first part of the action, called the **exposition,** introduces characters, situation, and, usually, time and place. The exposition here is achieved in three sentences: the time is "once upon a," the place Africa, the characters a Siamese cat who speaks Zebraic and an innocent zebra, and the situation (which includes the cat's linguistic prowess) their meeting. From that point on we are in the second part of the plot, the **rising action:** events that complicate the situation and intensify or multiply the conflict or conflicts. The first conflict here is over in a hurry—the zebra who is "fit to be tied" is tied up and eaten. Complications build with the cat's continuing success in killing zebras, and the zebras' growing fears and consequent superstitious belief that the ghost of a lion haunts the region, preying on zebras. The **turning point** (or **climax**) of the action is the third part of the story, the appearance of the zebra storyteller. From this point on the complications that grew in the first part of the story are untangled—the zebra storyteller, for example, is not surprised when he meets a Siamese cat speaking Zebraic. This is the fourth part of the story, the **falling action.** The story ends at the fifth part, the **conclusion** or **catastrophe:** the point at which the situation that was destabilized at the beginning of the story (when the Zebraic-speaking cat appears) becomes stable once more: Africa is once again free of cats speaking the language of zebras.

Before the parts of the action can be arranged, of course, they must be selected. The opening passages of the first two stories in this chapter may show some of the things involved in selection.

7

"The thousand injuries of Fortunato I had borne as I best could, but when he ventured upon insult I vowed revenge." So begins Edgar Allan Poe's *The Cask of Amontillado*. What kinds of injuries? Were there actually that many? Were they real injuries or imaginary? What was the insult? Why was the insult worse than all the injuries? Poe could have invented answers for these questions, but he chose not to.

The first scene of Richard Connell's *The Most Dangerous Game* provides some information—the general location of the yacht, the superstition about the island, the fact that Rainsford is an expert hunter —but it is a rather full scene for one that, on first reading at least, seems to have no essential connection with the exciting events that follow. And Whitney, who appears to be a major character here, we see no more. Why does Connell include this scene and this character?

Authors leave out some things that seem to be important to the story and include some things that do not seem very important. Selection of events is a significant element of storytelling.

But what do we mean when we say an author selects events? Selects from where? It's not as if these events exist somewhere, as, say, historical events do. Like scientists with their hypotheses and philosophers with their premises, many of us who talk or write about fiction begin with a fiction: we speak as if the people and places exist and the events of a story take place in a world of the author's imagination, a world from which he or she chooses the story elements, a world we can understand and almost re-create, in terms of our own; a world I've already called the history behind the story, as opposed to the structure (which is anything that we can assume a storyteller has done to that imaginary world).

This chapter is concerned with one specific kind of structure, that which has to do with the selection, connection, and ordering of the events: the structure known as plot.

Once events have been selected, they must be connected. In the history, events take place in simple chronological sequence: "The king died and then the queen died," to use one critic's example. This sequential narrative of events, the critic says, is not a plot. But if we connect the events, if we structure the history—"The king died and then the queen died of grief"—then we have a plot.

Many of us are used to thinking of cause-and-effect as a natural part of an event, as somehow *in* the event, rather than as an interpretation of a relationship between two events. Often authors, bent on "telling the truth by lying" (as some have described the function of fiction) and getting us to accept the fiction as a kind of truth, try to exploit this misperception on our part. They try to hide their structuring of that history from us. Sometimes they will put the causes of events inside the fiction itself: Montresor's scheme of revenge against Fortunato in *The Cask of Amontillado* is not the author's plot, Poe seems to tell us, but Montresor's; it is he, not the author, who interprets Fortunato's insult as cause for revenge and generates the events that follow. Sometimes, when the characters do not make the connections, the author makes the reader do it. Hemingway is very reluctant to structure his stories by connecting events or other details. He just puts down one after another, as if they came into the story that way directly from the history. He uses few connectives, and most of these are "neutral," noninterpretive *ands*. In the eleventh paragraph of *The Short Happy Life of Francis Macomber*, for example, an *and* appears where many of us would expect (and perhaps silently insert) a *so*: Macomber is waiting for his wife to enter their tent: "She did not speak to him when she came in *and* he left the tent at once. . . ." Consider the *and* in this sentence: "He was dressed in the same sort of safari clothes that Wilson wore except that his were new, he was thirty-five years old, kept himself very fit, was good at court games, had a number of big-game fishing records, and had just shown himself, very publicly, to be a coward." Wouldn't *but* seem more natural here? And how about the odd selection and collection of details in this sentence? What relationship is there between Macomber's just having revealed his cowardice and his dress, age, physical condition, fishing ability? Why, without interpretation, reasons, connection, lay out these details in a sentence whose major purpose seems to be to tell us of the recent act of cowardice? Despite their innocent appearance, the selection and connection are not part of an unmediated factual report of the history: they are elements of a carefully contrived plot structure. Poe puts the causal connection on a character; Hemingway puts it on the reader. The hand of the author in the structuring is obscured, if not invisible.

In the history, events exist in chronological sequence, and they can be reported that way in the story: "The king died and then the queen died." But the story can be ordered differently without changing or concealing the order in the history. "The queen died after the king died" recounts the same history, but the sequence in the sentence is not the sequence of events in the history. The history has been structured. The reader of the first sentence focuses on the king first, the reader of the second sentence on the queen. The difference in emphasis can be significant.

In some stories, such as *The Most Dangerous Game*, the events of the history are not reordered in the telling but seem to come unstructured from the history: Rainsford speaks with Whitney aboard the yacht; Whitney goes below; Rainsford falls overboard. The events are presented one after another in the same sequence as in the history. The reader reads along finding out what happens next. In a good many stories, however, the sequence in the story is not the sequence in which the supposed events occurred. In a detective story, for example, the major action (the crime) has taken place before the story begins, and the forward action of the story is the detective's attempt to re-create the past and figure out what happened. The reader does not ask *What will happen?* but *What has happened?* In such stories it is obvious that the author is creating a plot, ordering the events in a sequence different from that of the history.

Though the sequence of events in the detective story is reordered in terms of the reader's knowledge of the events—we learn who done it in the past only long after the story begins—the past is not usually replayed. We do not see the crime reenacted before us (although the detective may describe the crime when he gives his solution). The story simply begins in the middle of the history—after the crime—and moves forward as the detective figures out what happened. In *The Short Happy Life of Francis Macomber*, however, there is a replay or **flashback.** As in a detective story, *Macomber* begins in the middle of the history. The history is made up essentially of two hunting episodes. The story begins not with the first but between the two. The first sentence of the story ends, "pretending that nothing had happened," clearly suggesting that, as in the detective story, something significant *had* happened. The reader asks what it was, with curiosity and interest aroused. There are some clues in the first few pages, but neither a detective nor the reader has to reconstruct the past episode from clues. That episode is brought forward into the fictional present and re-presented. About six pages into the story we are told, "It had started the night before," and the following paragraph begins a scene that took place before the first hunt (the lion hunt)—before the time of the opening of the story. Our curiosity is satisfied, but the events of the hunt are so exciting that we shift into suspense, wondering what will happen next.

One reason for structuring the history into plot is to engage, intensify, and keep the reader's attention, to make the reader read on. The story of a crime can be written chronologically, so that we know who done it from the beginning and are just reading on to discover if, when, how the criminal is caught; Dostoevsky tells the story of *Crime and Punishment* this way. Such stories are not, strictly speaking, detective stories. They play on suspense, but not quite so much on curiosity. It is the sheer power of curiosity that keeps us reading intensely when we know as little as Watson or Sherlock Holmes himself at the beginning. Nor is it only the detective story that plays upon our curiosity. We have already seen how the phrase "pretending that nothing had happened" at the end of the first sentence of *Macomber* sets us to wondering just what had happened; by the time we find out, six pages later, we are already deep into the characters and situation—we're hooked. Even titles, such as *The Artificial Nigger* and *A Very Old Man with Enormous Wings,* can make us pick up a story; after that, it's up to the story to keep us engaged.

As strong as, perhaps stronger than curiosity—the desire to know what is happening or has happened—is suspense, the expectation of and doubt about what is *going* to happen next, as in the lion hunt in *Macomber.* Some of the stories in this volume have titles which promise suspense: *The Most Dangerous Game, The Lottery, Hide and Seek.* The first of these may be the best in which to examine how plot can arouse, modify, and satisfy our expectations, in which to watch not only the story but our own minds as we read the story.

What *is* the most dangerous game? Russian roulette, perhaps? Within the first fifty words we run across such terms as *mystery, suggestive, curious dread, superstition,* and we may begin to think of the supernatural (but what kind of "game" does that suggest?). In the same passage is *Ship-Trap,* and another possible meaning for game, another direction for our anticipation, opens up: hunting and trapping game. This is reinforced in the next twenty-five lines by the talk of hunting. The game must be some exceedingly fierce animal. All sorts of expectations build: supernatural animals, monsters, prehistoric animals, cannibals, Satan himself—worse! By the time Whitney says good night and we come to the first break on the page, our expectations are at a pretty high pitch. There's a good deal of suspense, and our minds are actively scanning four, five, maybe six possibilities of what kinds of things might happen next.

Try reading another couple of pages—say, down to Rainsford's introducing himself ("I'm Sanger Rainsford of New York")—watching yourself anticipate and put together details or clues. What kind of reinforcement do those early references to mystery and superstition get from the unexpected, mirage-like appearance of a palatial château, a tall spiked iron gate, a gargoyle on the door knocker, and a gigantic man opening the door? Don't you find yourself trying to fit these things into a pattern? Sooner or later some possibilities are eliminated and one pattern dominates; the story may at some point simply tell you what possibility will be pursued. It is not too long before you learn for sure what the game is. But by that time there are new reasons for suspense—how will it come out? You get to another layer of suspense following Rainsford through a **serial ordeal,** a series of dangerous episodes.

Stories are not all fun and games, no matter how dangerous. Many of them seek to give you new insights into human perception, experience, meaning. They strive to tell truths—new, subjective truths, but truths—even though they "lie" about the actuality of the people and events represented. But first they have to get your attention, and one way is by arousing your curiosity and exciting your anticipation; that's what plot is primarily for. In order to keep you engaged and alert, a story must make you ask questions about what will happen or what will be revealed next. To fully respond to a story you must be alert to the signals and guess along with the author. For at least in one aspect, fiction is a guessing game. Like all guessing games, from quiz shows to philosophy, the plot game in fiction has certain guidelines. A good (well structured) plot will play fair with you, offering at appropriate points all the necessary indicators or clues to what will happen next, not just springing new and essential information on you at the last minute ("Meanwhile, unknown to our hero, the Marines were just on the other side of the hill . . ."). It is this playing fair that makes the ending of a well-structured story satisfying or, when you look back on it, inevitable. Most stories also offer a number of reasonable but false signals (red herrings) to get you off the scent, so that in a well-structured story the ending, though inevitable, is also surprising. And though there is usually an overarching action from beginning to end, in many stories there are layers of expectation or suspense, so that as soon as one question is answered another comes forth to replace it, keeping you in doubt and suspense as to the final outcome.

Unlike most guessing games, however, the reward is not for the right guess—anticipating the outcome before the final paragraph—but for the number of guesses, right *and* wrong, that you make, the number of signals you respond to. If you are misled by none of the false signals in the early pages of *The Most Dangerous Game,* you may be closer to being "right," but you've missed a good deal of both the experience and the implication of the story. How do you react, in *The Cask of Amontillado,* to Montresor's concern for Fortunato's coughing? What do you anticipate? What is it that you later discover? Alertness to signals, anticipating what is to come next, remembering what has been said and signaled earlier, are essential to fully appreciating and understanding stories. By the time you finish the Connell story, you should be able to figure out why he structured it so, why the first scene was there. You might have some idea—though not necessarily a firm and simple answer—as to why, in addition to arousing suspense, Hemingway wanted *The Short Happy Life of Francis Macomber* to begin in the middle of the history and later flash back to the beginning. You may know why insult is more important to Montresor than injury; you may even be able to suggest why Poe did not recount the thousand injuries or the fatal insult.

EDGAR ALLAN POE

The Cask of Amontillado

The thousand injuries of Fortunato I had borne as I best could, but when he ventured upon insult I vowed revenge. You, who so well know the nature of my soul, will not suppose, however, that I gave utterance to a threat. *At length* I would be avenged; this was a point definitely settled—but the very definitiveness with which it was resolved precluded the idea of risk. I must not only punish but punish with impunity. A wrong is unredressed when retribution overtakes its redresser. It is equally unredressed when the avenger fails to make himself felt as such to him who has done the wrong.

It must be understood that neither by word nor deed had I given Fortunato cause to doubt my good will. I continued, as was my wont, to smile in his face, and he did not perceive that my smile *now* was at the thought of his immolation.

He had a weak point—this Fortunato—although in other regards he was a man to be respected and even feared. He prided himself on his connoisseurship in wine. Few Italians have the true virtuoso spirit. For the most part their enthusiasm is adopted to suit the time and opportunity, to practice imposture upon the British and Austrian millionaires. In painting and gemmary, Fortunato, like his countrymen, was a quack, but in the matter of old wines he was sincere. In this respect I did not differ from him materially;—I was skilful in the Italian vintages myself, and bought largely whenever I could.

It was about dusk, one evening during the supreme madness of the carnival season, that I encountered my friend. He accosted me with excessive warmth, for he had been drinking much. The man wore motley. He had on a tight-fitting parti-striped dress, and his head was surmounted by the conical cap and bells. I was so pleased to see him that I thought I should never have done wringing his hand.

I said to him—"My dear Fortunato, you are luckily met. How remarkably well you are looking to-day. But I have received a pipe[1] of what passes for Amontillado, and I have my doubts."

"How?" said he. "Amontillado? A pipe? Impossible! And in the middle of the carnival!"

"I have my doubts," I replied; "and I was silly enough to pay the full Amontillado price without consulting you in the matter. You were not to be found, and I was fearful of losing a bargain."

"Amontillado!"

"I have my doubts."

"Amontillado!"

"And I must satisfy them."

"Amontillado!"

"As you are engaged, I am on my way to Luchresi. If any one has a critical turn, it is he. He will tell me——"

"Luchresi cannot tell Amontillado from Sherry."

"And yet some fools will have it that his taste is a match for your own."

"Come, let us go."

"Whither?"

"To your vaults."

"My friend, no; I will not impose upon your good nature. I perceive you have an engagement. Luchresi——"

"I have no engagement;—come."

"My friend, no. It is not the engagement, but the severe cold with which I perceive you are afflicted. The vaults are insufferably damp. They are encrusted with niter."

"Let us go, nevertheless. The cold is merely nothing. Amontillado! You have been imposed upon. And as for Luchresi, he cannot distinguish Sherry from Amontillado."

Thus speaking, Fortunato possessed himself of my arm; and putting on a mask of black silk and drawing a *roquelaire*[2] closely about my person, I suffered him to hurry me to my palazzo.

There were no attendants at home; they had absconded to make merry in honor of the time. I had told them that I should not return until the morning, and had given them explicit orders not to stir from the house. These orders were sufficient, I well knew, to insure their immediate disappearance, one and all, as soon as my back was turned.

I took from their sconces two flambeaux, and giving one to Fortunato, bowed him through several suites of rooms to the archway that led into the vaults. I passed down a long and winding staircase, requesting him to be cautious as he followed. We came at length to the foot of the descent, and stood together on the damp ground of the catacombs of the Montresors.

The gait of my friend was unsteady, and the bells upon his cap jingled as he strode.

"The pipe?" said he.

"It is farther on," said I; "but observe the white web-work which

---

1. A cask holding 126 gallons.
2. Roquelaure, man's heavy, knee-length

cloak, usually trimmed in fur and silk-lined, 18th century.

gleams from these cavern walls."

He turned towards me, and looked into my eyes with two filmy orbs that distilled the rheum of intoxication.

"Niter?" he asked, at length.

"Niter," I replied. "How long have you had that cough?"

"Ugh! ugh! ugh!—ugh! ugh! ugh!—ugh! ugh! ugh! ugh! ugh! ugh!—ugh! ugh! ugh!"

My poor friend found it impossible to reply for many minutes.

"It is nothing," he said, at last.

"Come," I said, with decision, "we will go back; your health is precious. You are rich, respected, admired, beloved; you are happy, as once I was. You are a man to be missed. For me it is no matter. We will go back; you will be ill, and I cannot be responsible. Besides, there is Luchresi———"

"Enough," he said; "the cough is a mere nothing; it will not kill me. I shall not die of a cough."

"True—true," I replied; "and, indeed, I had no intention of alarming you unnecessarily—but you should use all proper caution. A draft of this Medoc will defend us from the damps."

Here I knocked off the neck of a bottle which I drew from a long row of its fellows that lay upon the mold.

"Drink," I said, presenting him the wine.

He raised it to his lips with a leer. He paused and nodded to me familiarly, while his bells jingled.

"I drink," he said, "to the buried that repose around us."

"And I to your long life."

He again took my arm, and we proceeded.

"These vaults," he said, "are extensive."

"The Montresors," I replied, "were a great and numerous family."

"I forget your arms."

"A huge human foot d'or,[3] in a field azure; the foot crushes a serpent rampant whose fangs are imbedded in the heel."

"And the motto?"

"Nemo me impune lacessit."[4]

"Good!" he said.

The wine sparkled in his eyes and the bells jingled. My own fancy grew warm with the Medoc. We had passed through long walls of piled skeletons, with casks and puncheons intermingling, into the inmost recesses of the catacombs. I paused again, and this time I made bold to seize Fortunato by an arm above the elbow.

"The niter!" I said; "see, it increases. It hangs like moss upon the vaults. We are below the river's bed. The drops of moisture trickle among the bones. Come, we will go back ere it is too late. Your cough———"

"It is nothing," he said; "let us go on. But first, another draft of the Medoc."

I broke and reached him a flagon of De Grâve.[5] He emptied it at a breath. His eyes flashed with a fierce light. He laughed and threw the

---

3. Of gold.
4. No one provokes me with impunity.

5. Like Médoc, a French wine.

bottle upward with a gesticulation I did not understand.

I looked at him in surprise. He repeated the movement—a grotesque one.

"You do not comprehend?" he said.

"Not I," I replied.

"Then you are not of the brotherhood."

"How?"

"You are not of the masons."[6]

"Yes, yes," I said; "yes, yes."

"You? Impossible! A mason?"

"A mason," I replied.

"A sign," he said, "a sign."

"It is this," I answered, producing from beneath the folds of my *roquelaire* a trowel.

"You jest," he exclaimed, recoiling a few paces. "But let us proceed to the Amontillado."

"Be it so," I said, replacing the tool beneath the cloak and again offering him my arm. He leaned upon it heavily. We continued our route in search of the Amontillado. We passed through a range of low arches, descended, passed on, and descending again, arrived at a deep crypt, in which the foulness of the air caused our flambeaux rather to glow than flame.

At the most remote end of the crypt there appeared another less spacious. Its walls had been lined with human remains, piled to the vault overhead, in the fashion of the great catacombs of Paris. Three sides of this interior crypt were still ornamented in this manner. From the fourth the bones had been thrown down, and lay promiscuously upon the earth, forming at one point a mound of some size. Within the wall thus exposed by the displacing of the bones, we perceived a still interior crypt or recess, in depth about four feet, in width three, in height six or seven. It seemed to have been constructed for no especial use within itself, but formed merely the interval between two of the colossal supports of the roof of the catacombs, and was backed by one of their circumscribing walls of solid granite.

It was in vain that Fortunato, uplifting his dull torch, endeavored to pry into the depth of the recess. Its termination the feeble light did not enable us to see.

"Proceed," I said; "herein is the Amontillado. As for Luchresi——"

"He is an ignoramus," interrupted my friend, as he stepped unsteadily forward, while I followed immediately at his heels. In an instant he had reached the extremity of the niche, and finding his progress arrested by the rock, stood stupidly bewildered. A moment more and I had fettered him to the granite. In its surface were two iron staples, distant from each other about two feet, horizontally. From one of these depended a short chain, from the other a padlock. Throwing the links about his waist, it was but the work of a few seconds to secure it. He was too much astounded to resist. Withdrawing the key I stepped back from the recess.

---

6. Masons or Freemasons, an international secret society condemned by the Catholic church. Montresor means by mason one who builds with stone, brick, etc.

"Pass your hand," I said, "over the wall; you cannot help feeling the niter. Indeed it is *very* damp. Once more let me *implore* you to return. No? Then I must positively leave you. But I must first render you all the little attentions in my power."

"The Amontillado!" ejaculated my friend, not yet recovered from his astonishment.

"True," I replied; "the Amontillado."

As I said these words I busied myself among the pile of bones of which I have before spoken. Throwing them aside, I soon uncovered a quantity of building stone and mortar. With these materials and with the aid of my trowel, I began vigorously to wall up the entrance of the niche.

I had scarcely laid the first tier of the masonry when I discovered that the intoxication of Fortunato had in a great measure worn off. The earliest indication I had of this was a low moaning cry from the depth of the recess. It was *not* the cry of a drunken man. There was then a long and obstinate silence. I laid the second tier, and the third, and the fourth; and then I heard the furious vibrations of the chain. The noise lasted for several minutes, during which, that I might hearken to it with the more satisfaction, I ceased my labors and sat down upon the bones. When at last the clanking subsided, I resumed the trowel, and finished without interruption the fifth, the sixth, and the seventh tier. The wall was now nearly upon a level with my breast. I again paused, and holding the flambeaux over the mason-work, threw a few feeble rays upon the figure within.

A succession of loud and shrill screams, bursting suddenly from the throat of the chained form, seemed to thrust me violently back. For a brief moment I hesitated, I trembled. Unsheathing my rapier, I began to grope with it about the recess; but the thought of an instant reassured me. I placed my hand upon the solid fabric of the catacombs, and felt satisfied. I reapproached the wall. I replied to the yells of him who clamored. I reechoed, I aided, I surpassed them in volume and in strength. I did this, and the clamorer grew still.

It was now midnight, and my task was drawing to a close. I had completed the eighth, the ninth and the tenth tier. I had finished a portion of the last and the eleventh; there remained but a single stone to be fitted and plastered in. I struggled with its weight; I placed it partially in its destined position. But now there came from out the niche a low laugh that erected the hairs upon my head. It was succeeded by a sad voice, which I had difficulty in recognizing as that of the noble Fortunato. The voice said—

"Ha! ha! ha!—he! he! he!—a very good joke, indeed—an excellent jest. We will have many a rich laugh about it at the palazzo[7]—he! he! he!—over our wine—he! he! he!"

"The Amontillado!" I said.

"He! he! he!—he! he! he!—yes, the Amontillado. But is it not getting late? Will not they be awaiting us at the palazzo, the Lady Fortunato and the rest? Let us be gone."

"Yes," I said, "let us be gone."

7. Palace.

"*For the love of God, Montresor!*"

"Yes," I said, "for the love of God!"

But to these words I hearkened in vain for a reply. I grew impatient. I called aloud—

"Fortunato!"

No answer. I called again—

"Fortunato!"

No answer still. I thrust a torch through the remaining aperture and let it fall within. There came forth in return only a jingling of the bells. My heart grew sick; it was the dampness of the catacombs that made it so. I hastened to make an end of my labor. I forced the last stone into its position; I plastered it up. Against the new masonry I re-erected the old rampart of bones. For the half of a century no mortal has disturbed them. *In pace requiescat!*[8]

p. 1846

RICHARD CONNELL

The Most Dangerous Game

"Off there to the right—somewhere—is a large island," said Whitney. "It's rather a mystery—"

"What island is it?" Rainsford asked.

"The old charts call it 'Ship-Trap Island,'" Whitney replied. "A suggestive name, isn't it? Sailors have a curious dread of the place. I don't know why. Some superstition—"

"Can't see it," remarked Rainsford, trying to peer through the dank tropical night that was palpable as it pressed its thick warm blackness in upon the yacht.

"You've good eyes," said Whitney, with a laugh, "and I've seen you pick off a moose moving in the brown fall bush at four hundred yards, but even you can't see four miles or so through a moonless Caribbean night."

"Nor four yards," admitted Rainsford. "Ugh! It's like moist black velvet."

"It will be light in Rio," promised Whitney. "We should make it in a few days. I hope the jaguar guns have come from Purdey's. We should have some good hunting up the Amazon. Great sport, hunting."

"The best sport in the world," agreed Rainsford.

"For the hunter," amended Whitney. "Not for the jaguar."

"Don't talk rot, Whitney," said Rainsford. "You're a big-game hunter, not a philosopher. Who cares how a jaguar feels?"

"Perhaps the jaguar does," observed Whitney.

"Bah! They've no understanding."

"Even so, I rather think they understand one thing—fear. The fear of pain and the fear of death."

8. May he rest in peace.

"Nonsense," laughed Rainsford. "This hot weather is making you soft, Whitney. Be a realist. The world is made up of two classes—the hunters and the huntees. Luckily, you and I are hunters. Do you think we've passed that island yet?"

"I can't tell in the dark. I hope so."

"Why?" asked Rainsford.

"The place has a reputation—a bad one."

"Cannibals?" suggested Rainsford.

"Hardly. Even cannibals wouldn't live in such a God-forsaken place. But it's gotten into sailor lore, somehow. Didn't you notice that the crew's nerves seemed a bit jumpy today?"

"They were a bit strange, now you mention it. Even Captain Nielsen—"

"Yes, even that tough-minded old Swede, who'd go up to the devil himself and ask him for a light. Those fishy blue eyes held a look I never saw there before. All I could get out of him was: 'This place has an evil name among sea-faring men, sir.' Then he said to me, very gravely: 'Don't you feel anything?'—as if the air about us was actually poisonous. Now, you mustn't laugh when I tell you this—I did feel something like a sudden chill.

"There was no breeze. The sea was as flat as a plate-glass window. We were drawing near the island then. What I felt was a—a mental chill; a sort of sudden dread."

"Pure imagination," said Rainsford. "One superstitious sailor can taint the whole ship's company with his fear."

"Maybe. But sometimes I think sailors have an extra sense that tells them when they are in danger. Sometimes I think evil is a tangible thing—with wave lengths, just as sound and light have. An evil place can, so to speak, broadcast vibrations of evil. Anyhow, I'm glad we're getting out of this zone. Well, I think I'll turn in now, Rainsford."

"I'm not sleepy," said Rainsford. "I'm going to smoke another pipe up on the after deck."

"Good night, then, Rainsford. See you at breakfast."

"Right. Good night, Whitney."

There was no sound in the night as Rainsford sat there, but the muffled throb of the engine that drove the yacht swiftly through the darkness, and the swish and ripple of the wash of the propeller.

Rainsford, reclining in a steamer chair, indolently puffed on his favorite brier. The sensuous drowsiness of the night was on him. "It's so dark," he thought, "that I could sleep without closing my eyes; the night would be my eyelids—"

An abrupt sound startled him. Off to the right he heard it, and his ears, expert in such matters, could not be mistaken. Again he heard the sound, and again. Somewhere, off in the blackness, some one had fired a gun three times.

Rainsford sprang up and moved quickly to the rail, mystified. He strained his eyes in the direction from which the reports had come, but it was like trying to see through a blanket. He leaped upon the rail and balanced himself there, to get greater elevation; his pipe, striking a rope, was knocked from his mouth. He lunged for it; a short, hoarse cry came from his lips as he realized he had reached too far and had lost his balance. The cry was pinched off short as the blood-warm waters of the Caribbean Sea closed over his head.

He struggled up to the surface and tried to cry out, but the wash from the speeding yacht slapped him in the face and the salt water in his open mouth made him gag and strangle. Desperately he struck out with strong strokes after the receding lights of the yacht, but he stopped before he had swum fifty feet. A certain cool-headedness had come to him; it was not the first time he had been in a tight place. There was a chance that his cries could be heard by some one aboard the yacht, but that chance was slender, and grew more slender as the yacht raced on. He wrestled himself out of his clothes, and shouted with all his power. The lights of the yacht became faint and ever-vanishing fireflies; then they were blotted out entirely by the night.

Rainsford remembered the shots. They had come from the right, and doggedly he swam in that direction, swimming with slow, deliberate strokes, conserving his strength. For a seemingly endless time he fought the sea. He began to count his strokes; he could do possibly a hundred more and then—

Rainsford heard a sound. It came out of the darkness, a high scream-ing sound, the sound of an animal in an extremity of anguish and terror.

He did not recognize the animal that made the sound; he did not try to; with fresh vitality he swam toward the sound. He heard it again; then it was cut short by another noise, crisp, staccato.

"Pistol shot," muttered Rainsford, swimming on.

Ten minutes of determined effort brought another sound to his ears —the most welcome he had ever heard—the muttering and growling of the sea breaking on a rocky shore. He was almost on the rocks before he saw them; on a night less calm he would have been shattered against them. With his remaining strength he dragged himself from the swirling waters. Jagged crags appeared to jut into the opaqueness; he forced himself upward, hand over hand. Gasping, his hands raw, he reached a flat place at the top. Dense jungle came down to the very edge of the cliffs. What perils that tangle of trees and under-brush might hold for him did not concern Rainsford just then. All he knew was that he was safe from his enemy, the sea, and that utter weariness was on him. He flung himself down at the jungle edge and tumbled headlong into the deepest sleep of his life.

When he opened his eyes he knew from the position of the sun that it was late in the afternoon. Sleep had given him new vigor; a sharp hunger was picking at him. He looked about him, almost cheerfully.

"Where there are pistol shots, there are men. Where there are men, there is food," he thought. But what kind of men, he wondered, in so forbidding a place? An unbroken front of snarled and ragged jungle fringed the shore.

He saw no sign of a trail through the closely knit web of weeds and trees; it was easier to go along the shore, and Rainsford floundered along by the water. Not far from where he had landed, he stopped.

Some wounded thing, by the evidence a large animal, had thrashed about in the underbrush; the jungle weeds were crushed down and the moss was lacerated; one patch of weeds was stained crimson. A small, glittering object not far away caught Rainsford's eye and he picked it up. It was an empty cartridge.

"A twenty-two," he remarked. "That's odd. It must have been a fairly large animal too. The hunter had his nerve with him to tackle it with a light gun. It's clear that the brute put up a fight. I suppose the first three shots I heard was when the hunter flushed his quarry and wounded it. The last shot was when he trailed it here and finished it."

He examined the ground closely and found what he had hoped to find—the print of hunting boots. They pointed along the cliff in the direction he had been going. Eagerly he hurried along, now slipping on a rotten log or a loose stone, but making headway; night was beginning to settle down on the island.

Bleak darkness was blacking out the sea and jungle when Rainsford sighted the lights. He came upon them as he turned a crook in the coast line, and his first thought was that he had come upon a village, for there were many lights. But as he forged along he saw to his great astonishment that all the lights were in one enormous building—a lofty structure with pointed towers plunging upward into the gloom. His eyes made out the shadowy outlines of a palatial château; it was set on a high bluff, and on three sides of it cliffs dived down to where the sea licked greedy lips in the shadows.

"Mirage," thought Rainsford. But it was no mirage, he found, when he opened the tall spiked iron gate. The stone steps were real enough; the massive door with a leering gargoyle for a knocker was real enough; yet about it all hung an air of unreality.

He lifted the knocker, and it creaked up stiffly, as if it had never before been used. He let it fall, and it startled him with its booming loudness. He thought he heard steps within; the door remained closed. Again Rainsford lifted the heavy knocker, and let it fall. The door opened then, opened as suddenly as if it were on a spring, and Rainsford stood blinking in the river of glaring gold light that poured out. The first thing Rainsford's eyes discerned was the largest man Rainsford had ever seen—a gigantic creature, solidly made and black-bearded to the waist. In his hand the man held a long-barreled revolver, and he was pointing it straight at Rainsford's heart.

Out of the snarl of beard two small eyes regarded Rainsford.

"Don't be alarmed," said Rainsford, with a smile which he hoped was disarming. "I'm no robber. I fell off a yacht. My name is Sanger Rainsford of New York City."

The menacing look in the eyes did not change. The revolver pointed as rigidly as if the giant were a statue. He gave no sign that he understood Rainsford's words, or that he had even heard them. He was dressed in uniform, a black uniform trimmed with gray astrakhan.

"I'm Sanger Rainsford of New York," Rainsford began again. "I fell off a yacht. I am hungry."

The man's only answer was to raise with his thumb the hammer of his revolver. Then Rainsford saw the man's free hand go to his forehead in a military salute, and he saw him click his heels together and stand at attention. Another man was coming down the broad marble steps, an erect, slender man in evening clothes. He advanced to Rainsford and held out his hand.

In a cultivated voice marked by a slight accent that gave it added precision and deliberateness, he said: "It is a very great pleasure and honor to welcome Mr. Sanger Rainsford, the celebrated hunter, to my home."

Automatically Rainsford shook the man's hand.

"I've read your book about hunting snow leopards[1] in Tibet, you see," explained the man. "I am General Zaroff."

Rainsford's first impression was that the man was singularly handsome; his second was that there was an original, almost bizarre quality about the general's face. He was a tall man past middle age, for his hair was a vivid white; but his thick eyebrows and pointed military mustache were as black as the night from which Rainsford had come. His eyes, too, were black and very bright. He had high cheek bones, a sharp-cut nose, a spare, dark face, the face of a man used to giving orders, the face of an aristocrat. Turning to the giant in uniform, the general made a sign. The giant put away his pistol, saluted, withdrew.

"Ivan is an incredibly strong fellow," remarked the general, "but he has the misfortune to be deaf and dumb. A simple fellow, but, I'm afraid, like all his race, a bit of a savage."

"Is he Russian?"

"He is a Cossack,"[2] said the general, and his smile showed red lips and pointed teeth. "So am I."

"Come," he said, "we shouldn't be chatting here. We can talk later. Now you want clothes, food, rest. You shall have them. This is a most restful spot."

Ivan had reappeared, and the general spoke to him with lips that moved but gave forth no sound.

"Follow Ivan, if you please, Mr. Rainsford," said the general. "I was about to have my dinner when you came. I'll wait for you. You'll find that my clothes will fit you, I think."

It was to a huge, beam-ceilinged bedroom with a canopied bed big enough for six men that Rainsford followed the silent giant. Ivan laid out an evening suit, and Rainsford, as he put it on, noticed that it came from a London tailor who ordinarily cut and sewed for none below the rank of duke.

The dining room to which Ivan conducted him was in many ways remarkable. There was a medieval magnificence about it; it suggested a baronial hall of feudal times with its oaken panels, its high ceiling, its vast refectory table where twoscore men could sit down to eat. About the hall were the mounted heads of many animals—lions, tigers, elephants, moose, bears; larger or more perfect specimens Rainsford had never seen. At the great table the general was sitting, alone.

"You'll have a cocktail, Mr. Rainsford," he suggested. The cocktail was surpassingly good; and, Rainsford noted, the table appointments were of the finest—the linen, the crystal, the silver, the china.

They were eating *borsch*, the rich, red soup with whipped cream so dear to Russian palates. Half apologetically General Zaroff said: "We do our best to preserve the amenities of civilization here. Please forgive any lapses. We are well off the beaten track, you know. Do

---

1. The ounce, native to the Himalayas, and quite rare.

2. From the southern part of European Russia, the Cossacks were known as exceptionally fine horsemen and light cavalrymen and, under the Czars, were feared for their ruthless raids.

you think the champagne has suffered from its long ocean trip?"

"Not in the least," declared Rainsford. He was finding the general a most thoughtful and affable host, a true cosmopolite. But there was one small trait of the general's that made Rainsford uncomfortable. Whenever he looked up from his plate he found the general studying him, appraising him narrowly.

"Perhaps," said General Zaroff, "you were surprised that I recognized your name. You see, I read all books on hunting published in English, French, and Russian. I have but one passion in my life, Mr. Rainsford, and it is the hunt."

"You have some wonderful heads here," said Rainsford as he ate a particularly well cooked filet mignon. "That Cape buffalo[3] is the largest I ever saw."

"Oh, that fellow. Yes, he was a monster."

"Did he charge you?"

"Hurled me against a tree," said the general. "Fractured my skull. But I got the brute."

"I've always thought," said Rainsford, "that the Cape buffalo is the most dangerous of all big game."

For a moment the general did not reply; he was smiling his curious red-lipped smile. Then he said slowly: "No. You are wrong, sir. The Cape buffalo is not the most dangerous big game." He sipped his wine. "Here in my preserve on this island," he said in the same slow tone, "I hunt more dangerous game."

Rainsford expressed his surprise. "Is there big game on this island?"

The general nodded. "The biggest."

"Really?"

"Oh, it isn't here naturally, of course. I have to stock the island."

"What have you imported, general?" Rainsford asked. "Tigers?"

The general smiled. "No," he said. "Hunting tigers ceased to interest me some years ago. I exhausted their possibilities, you see. No thrill left in tigers, no real danger. I live for danger, Mr. Rainsford."

The general took from his pocket a gold cigarette case and offered his guest a long black cigarette with a silver tip; it was perfumed and gave off a smell like incense.

"We will have some capital hunting, you and I," said the general. "I shall be most glad to have your society."

"But what game—" began Rainsford.

"I'll tell you," said the general. "You will be amused, I know. I think I may say, in all modesty, that I have done a rare thing. I have invented a new sensation. May I pour you another glass of port, Mr. Rainsford?"

"Thank you, general."

The general filled both glasses, and said: "God makes some men poets. Some He makes kings, some beggars. Me He made a hunter. My hand was made for the trigger, my father said. He was a very rich man with a quarter of a million acres in the Crimea, and he was an ardent sportsman. When I was only five years old he gave me a little gun, specially made in Moscow for me, to shoot sparrows with. When I shot some of his prize turkeys with it, he did not punish me; he

---

3. Big, quick, intelligent, when separated from the herd ("rogue"), one of the most dangerous of African game animals.

complimented me on my marksmanship. I killed my first bear in the Caucasus when I was ten. My whole life has been one prolonged hunt. I went into the army—it was expected of noblemen's sons—and for a time commanded a division of Cossack cavalry, but my real interest was always the hunt. I have hunted every kind of game in every land. It would be impossible for me to tell you how many animals I have killed."

The general puffed at his cigarette.

"After the debacle in Russia[4] I left the country, for it was imprudent for an officer of the Czar to stay there. Many noble Russians lost everything. I, luckily, had invested heavily in American securities, so I shall never have to open a tea room in Monte Carlo or drive a taxi in Paris. Naturally, I continued to hunt—grizzlies in your Rockies, crocodiles in the Ganges, rhinoceroses in East Africa. It was in Africa that the Cape buffalo hit me and laid me up for six months. As soon as I recovered I started for the Amazon to hunt jaguars, for I had heard they were unusually cunning. They weren't." The Cossack sighed. "They were no match at all for a hunter with his wits about him, and a high-powered rifle. I was bitterly disappointed. I was lying in my tent with a splitting headache one night when a terrible thought pushed its way into my mind. Hunting was beginning to bore me! And hunting, remember, had been my life. I have heard that in America business men often go to pieces when they give up the business that has been their life."

"Yes, that's so," said Rainsford.

The general smiled. "I had no wish to go to pieces," he said. "I must do something. Now, mine is an analytical mind, Mr. Rainsford. Doubtless that is why I enjoy the problems of the chase."

"No doubt, General Zaroff."

"So," continued the general, "I asked myself why the hunt no longer fascinated me. You are much younger than I am, Mr. Rainsford, and have not hunted as much, but you perhaps can guess the answer."

"What was it?"

"Simply this: hunting had ceased to be what you call 'a sporting proposition.' It had become too easy. I always got my quarry. Always. There is no greater bore than perfection."

The general lit a fresh cigarette.

"No animal had a chance with me any more. That is no boast; it is a mathematical certainty. The animal had nothing but his legs and his instinct. Instinct is no match for reason. When I thought of this it was a tragic moment for me, I can tell you."

Rainsford leaned across the table, absorbed in what his host was saying.

"It came to me as an inspiration what I must do," the general went on.

"And that was?"

The general smiled the quiet smile of one who had faced an obstacle and surmounted it with success. "I had to invent a new animal to hunt," he said.

"A new animal? You're joking."

---

4. The Revolution of 1917 which overthrew the Czar and prepared the way for Communist rule.

"Not at all," said the general. "I never joke about hunting. I needed a new animal. I found one. So I bought this island, built this house, and here I do my hunting. The island is perfect for my purposes—there are jungles with a maze of trails in them, hills, swamps—"

"But the animal, General Zaroff?"

"Oh," said the general, "it supplies me with the most exciting hunting in the world. No other hunting compares with it for an instant. Every day I hunt, and I never grow bored now, for I have a quarry with which I can match my wits."

Rainsford's bewilderment showed in his face.

"I wanted the ideal animal to hunt," explained the general. "So I said: 'What are the attributes of an ideal quarry?' And the answer was, of course: 'It must have courage, cunning, and, above all, it must be able to reason.'"

"But no animal can reason," objected Rainsford.

"My dear fellow," said the general, "there is one that can."

"But you can't mean—" gasped Rainsford.

"And why not?"

"I can't believe you are serious, General Zaroff. This is a grisly joke."

"Why should I not be serious? I am speaking of hunting."

"Hunting? Good God, General Zaroff, what you speak of is murder."

The general laughed with entire good nature. He regarded Rainsford quizzically. "I refuse to believe that so modern and civilized a young man as you seem to be harbors romantic ideas about the value of human life. Surely your experiences in the war—"

"Did not make me condone cold-blooded murder," finished Rainsford stiffly.

Laughter shook the general. "How extraordinarily droll you are!" he said. "One does not expect nowadays to find a young man of the educated class, even in America, with such a naïve, and, if I may say so, mid-Victorian point of view. It's like finding a snuff-box in a limousine. Ah, well, doubtless you had Puritan ancestors. So many Americans appear to have had. I ll wager you'll forget your notions when you go hunting with me. You've a genuine new thrill in store for you, Mr. Rainsford."

"Thank you, I'm a hunter, not a murderer."

"Dear me," said the general, quite unruffled, "again that unpleasant word. But I think I can show you that your scruples are quite ill founded."

"Yes?"

"Life is for the strong, to be lived by the strong, and, if need be, taken by the strong. The weak of the world were put here to give the strong pleasure. I am strong. Why should I not use my gift? If I wish to hunt, why should I not? I hunt the scum of the earth—sailors from tramp ships—lascars, blacks, Chinese, whites, mongrels—a thoroughbred horse or hound is worth more than a score of them."

"But they are men," said Rainsford hotly.

"Precisely," said the general. "That is why I use them. It gives me pleasure. They can reason, after a fashion. So they are dangerous."

"But where do you get them?"

The general's left eyelid fluttered down in a wink. "This island is called Ship-Trap," he answered. "Sometimes an angry god of the high seas sends them to me. Sometimes, when Providence is not so kind, I help Providence a bit. Come to the window with me."

Rainsford went to the window and looked out toward the sea.

"Watch! Out there!" exclaimed the general, pointing into the night. Rainsford's eyes saw only blackness, and then, as the general pressed a button, far out to sea Rainsford saw the flash of lights.

The general chuckled. "They indicate a channel," he said, "where there's none: giant rocks with razor edges crouch like a sea monster with wide-open jaws. They can crush a ship as easily as I crush this nut." He dropped a walnut on the hardwood floor and brought his heel grinding down on it. "Oh, yes," he said, casually, as if in answer to a question, "I have electricity. We try to be civilized here."

"Civilized? And you shoot down men?"

A trace of anger was in the general's black eyes, but it was there for but a second, and he said, in his most pleasant manner: "Dear me, what a righteous young man you are! I assure you I do not do the thing you suggest. That would be barbarous. I treat these visitors with every consideration. They get plenty of good food and exercise. They get into splendid physical condition. You shall see for yourself tomorrow."

"What do you mean?"

"We'll visit my training school," smiled the general. "It's in the cellar. I have about a dozen pupils down there now. They're from the Spanish bark San Lucar that had the bad luck to go on the rocks out there. A very inferior lot, I regret to say. Poor specimens and more accustomed to the deck than to the jungle."

He raised his hand, and Ivan, who served as waiter, brought thick Turkish coffee. Rainsford, with an effort, held his tongue in check.

"It's a game, you see, pursued the general blandly. "I suggest to one of them that we go hunting. I give him a supply of food and an excellent hunting knife. I give him three hours' start. I am to follow, armed only with a pistol of the smallest caliber and range. If my quarry eludes me for three whole days, he wins the game. If I find him"—the general smiled—"he loses."

"Suppose he refuses to be hunted?"

"Oh," said the general, "I give him his option, of course. He need not play that game if he doesn't wish to. If he does not wish to hunt, I turn him over to Ivan. Ivan once had the honor of serving as official knouter[5] to the Great White Czar,[6] and he has his own ideas of sport. Invariably, Mr. Rainsford, invariably they choose the hunt."

"And if they win?"

The smile on the general's face widened. "To date I have not lost," he said.

Then he added, hastily: "I don't wish you to think me a braggart, Mr. Rainsford. Many of them afford only the most elementary sort of problem. Occasionally I strike a tartar. One almost did win. I eventually had to use the dogs."

"The dogs?"

---

5. In Czarist Russia the official flogger of criminals.
6. Probably Nicholas II (1868–1918) who was overthrown by the Revolution and executed; "White" designates those opposed to the Communists, or "Reds."

"This way, please. I'll show you."

The general steered Rainsford to a window. The lights from the windows sent a flickering illumination that made grotesque patterns on the courtyard below, and Rainsford could see moving about there a dozen or so huge black shapes; as they turned toward him, their eyes glittered greenly.

"A rather good lot, I think," observed the general. "They are let out at seven every night. If anyone should try to get into my house—or out of it—something extremely regrettable would occur to him." He hummed a snatch of song from the Folies Bergère.[7]

"And now," said the general, "I want to show you my new collection of heads. Will you come with me to the library?"

"I hope," said Rainsford, "that you will excuse me tonight, General Zaroff. I'm really not feeling at all well."

"Ah, indeed?" the general inquired solicitously. "Well, I suppose that's only natural, after your long swim. You need a good, restful night's sleep. Tomorrow you'll feel like a new man, I'll wager. Then we'll hunt, eh? I've one rather promising prospect—"

Rainsford was hurrying from the room.

"Sorry you can't go with me tonight," called the general. "I expect rather fair sport—a big, strong black. He looks resourceful—Well, good night, Mr. Rainsford; I hope you have a good night's rest."

The bed was good, and the pajamas of the softest silk, and he was tired in every fiber of his being, but nevertheless Rainsford could not quiet his brain with the opiate of sleep. He lay, eyes wide open. Once he thought he heard stealthy steps in the corridor outside his room. He sought to throw open the door; it would not open. He went to the window and looked out. His room was high up in one of the towers. The lights of the château were out now; and it was dark and silent, but there was a fragment of sallow moon, and by its wan light he could see, dimly, the courtyard; there, weaving in and out in the pattern of shadow, were black, noiseless forms; the hounds heard him at the window and looked up, expectantly, with their green eyes. Rainsford went back to bed and lay down. By many methods he tried to put himself to sleep. He had achieved a doze when, just as morning began to come, he heard, far off in the jungle, the faint report of a pistol.

General Zaroff did not appear until luncheon. He was dressed faultlessly in the tweeds of a country squire. He was solicitous about the state of Rainsford's health.

"As for me," sighed the general, "I do not feel so well. I am worried, Mr. Rainsford. Last night I detected traces of my old complaint."

To Rainsford's questioning glance the general said: "Ennui. Boredom."

Then, taking a second helping of *crêpes suzette,* the general explained: "The hunting was not good last night. The fellow lost his head. He made a straight trail that offered no problems at all. That's the trouble with these sailors; they have dull brains to begin with, and they do not know how to get about in the woods. They do excessively stupid and obvious things. It's most annoying. Will you have another

---

7. Paris theater and music hall which in 1918 reestablished itself as the scene for revues, spectaculars, etc.

glass of Chablis, Mr. Rainsford?"

"General," said Rainsford firmly, "I wish to leave this island at once."

The general raised his thickets of eyebrows; he seemed hurt. "But, my dear fellow," the general protested, "you've only just come. You've had no hunting—"

"I wish to go today," said Rainsford. He saw the dead black eyes of the general on him, studying him. General Zaroff's face suddenly brightened.

He filled Rainsford's glass with venerable Chablis from a dusty bottle.

"Tonight," said the general, "we will hunt—you and I."

Rainsford shook his head. "No, general," he said, "I will not hunt."

The general shrugged his shoulders and delicately ate a hothouse grape. "As you wish, my friend," he said. "The choice rests entirely with you. But may I not venture to suggest that you will find my idea of sport more diverting than Ivan's?"

He nodded toward the corner to where the giant stood, scowling, his thick arms crossed on his hogshead of a chest.

"You don't mean—" cried Rainsford.

"My dear fellow," said the general, "have I not told you I always mean what I say about hunting? This is really an inspiration. I drink to a foeman worthy of my steel—at last."

The general raised his glass, but Rainsford sat staring at him.

"You'll find this game worth playing," the general said enthusiastically. "Your brain against mine. Your woodcraft against mine. Your strength and stamina against mine. Outdoor chess! And the stake is not without value, eh?"

"And if I win—" began Rainsford huskily.

"I'll cheerfully acknowledge myself defeated if I do not find you by midnight of the third day," said General Zaroff. "My sloop will place you on the mainland near a town."

The general read what Rainsford was thinking.

"Oh, you can trust me," said the Cossack. "I will give you my word as a gentleman and a sportsman. Of course you, in turn, must agree to say nothing of your visit here."

"I'll agree to nothing of the kind," said Rainsford.

"Oh," said the general, "in that case—But why discuss that now? Three days hence we can discuss it over a bottle of Veuve Cliquot,[8] unless—"

The general sipped his wine.

Then a businesslike air animated him. "Ivan," he said to Rainsford, "will supply you with hunting clothes, food, a knife. I suggest you wear moccasins; they leave a poorer trail. I suggest too that you avoid the big swamp in the southeast corner of the island. We call it Death Swamp. There's quicksand there. One foolish fellow tried it. The deplorable part of it was that Lazarus followed him. You can imagine my feelings, Mr. Rainsford. I loved Lazarus; he was the finest hound in my pack. Well, I must beg you to excuse me now. I always take a siesta after lunch. You'll hardly have time for a nap, I fear. You'll want to start, no doubt. I shall not follow till dusk. Hunting at night is so

8. A fine champagne; Chablis, above, is a very dry white Burgundy table wine; Chambertin, later, is a highly esteemed red Burgundy wine.

much more exciting than by day, don't you think? Au revoir, Mr. Rainsford, au revoir."

General Zaroff, with a deep, courtly bow, strolled from the room.

From another door came Ivan. Under one arm he carried khaki hunting clothes, a haversack of food, a leather sheath containing a long-bladed hunting knife; his right hand rested on a cocked revolver thrust in the crimson sash about his waist. . . .

Rainsford had fought his way through the bush for two hours. "I must keep my nerve. I must keep my nerve," he said through tight teeth.

He had not been entirely clear-headed when the château gates snapped shut behind him. His whole idea at first was to put distance between himself and General Zaroff, and, to this end, he had plunged along, spurred on by the sharp rowels of something very like panic. Now he had got a grip on himself, had stopped, and was taking stock of himself and the situation.

He saw that straight flight was futile; inevitably it would bring him face to face with the sea. He was in a picture with a frame of water, and his operations, clearly, must take place within that frame.

"I'll give him a trail to follow," muttered Rainsford, and he struck off from the rude paths he had been following into the trackless wilderness. He executed a series of intricate loops; he doubled on his trail again and again, recalling all the lore of the fox hunt, and all the dodges of the fox. Night found him leg-weary, with hands and face lashed by the branches, on a thickly wooded ridge. He knew it would be insane to blunder on through the dark, even if he had the strength. His need for rest was imperative and he thought: "I have played the fox, now I must play the cat of the fable."[9] A big tree with a thick trunk and outspread branches was nearby, and, taking care to leave not the slightest mark, he climbed up into the crotch, and stretching out on one of the broad limbs, after a fashion, rested. Rest brought him new confidence and almost a feeling of security. Even so zealous a hunter as General Zaroff could not trace him there, he told himself; only the devil himself could follow that complicated trail through the jungle after dark. But, perhaps, the general was a devil—

An apprehensive night crawled slowly by like a wounded snake, and sleep did not visit Rainsford, although the silence of a dead world was on the jungle. Toward morning when a dingy gray was varnishing the sky, the cry of some startled bird focused Rainsford's attention in that direction. Something was coming through the bush, coming slowly, carefully, coming by the same winding way Rainsford had come. He flattened himself down on the limb, and through a screen of leaves almost as thick as tapestry, he watched. The thing that was approaching was a man.

It was General Zaroff. He made his way along with his eyes fixed in utmost concentration on the ground before him. He paused, almost beneath the tree, dropped to his knees and studied the ground. Rainsford's impulse was to hurl himself down like a panther, but he saw

---

9. The fox boasts of his many tricks to elude the hounds; the cat responds he knows only one—to climb the nearest tree—but that this is worth more than all the fox's tricks.

that the general's right hand held something metallic—a small automatic pistol.

The hunter shook his head several times, as if he were puzzled. Then he straightened up and took from his case one of his black cigarettes; its pungent incense-like smoke floated up to Rainsford's nostrils.

Rainsford held his breath. The general's eyes had left the ground and were traveling inch by inch up the tree. Rainsford froze there, every muscle tensed for a spring. But the sharp eyes of the hunter stopped before they reached the limb where Rainsford lay; a smile spread over his brown face. Very deliberately he blew a smoke ring into the air; then he turned his back on the tree and walked carelessly away, back along the trail he had come. The swish of the underbrush against his hunting boots grew fainter and fainter.

The pent-up air burst hotly from Rainsford's lungs. His first thought made him feel sick and numb. The general could follow a trail through the woods at night; he could follow an extremely difficult trail; he must have uncanny powers; only by the merest chance had the Cossack failed to see his quarry.

Rainsford's second thought was even more terrible. It sent a shudder of cold horror through his whole being. Why had the general smiled? Why had he turned back?

Rainsford did not want to believe what his reason told him was true, but the truth was as evident as the sun that had by now pushed through the morning mists. The general was playing with him! The general was saving him for another day's sport! The Cossack was the cat; he was the mouse.[1] Then it was that Rainsford knew the full meaning of terror.

"I will not lose my nerve. I will not."

He slid down from the tree, and struck off again into the woods. His face was set and he forced the machinery of his mind to function. Three hundred yards from his hiding place he stopped where a huge dead tree leaned precariously on a smaller, living one. Throwing off his sack of food, Rainsford took his knife from its sheath and began to work with all his energy.

The job was finished at last, and he threw himself down behind a fallen log a hundred feet away. He did not have to wait long. The cat was coming again to play with the mouse.

Following the trail with the sureness of a bloodhound, came General Zaroff. Nothing escaped those searching black eyes, no crushed blade of grass, no bent twig, no mark, no matter how faint, in the moss. So intent was the Cossack on his stalking that he was upon the thing Rainsford had made before he saw it. His foot touched the protruding bough that was the trigger. Even as he touched it, the general sensed his danger and leaped back with the agility of an ape. But he was not quite quick enough; the dead tree, delicately adjusted to rest on the cut living one, crashed down and struck the general a glacing blow on the shoulder as it fell; but for his alertness, he must have been smashed beneath it. He staggered, but he did not fall; nor did he drop his revolver. He stood there, rubbing his injured shoulder, and Rainsford,

---

1. A cat, sure of his prey, plays with a mouse before killing him.

with fear again gripping his heart, heard the general's mocking laugh ring through the jungle.

"Rainsford," called the general, "if you are within sound of my voice, as I suppose you are, let me congratulate you. Not many men know how to make a Malay man-catcher. Luckily, for me, I too have hunted in Malacca. You are proving interesting, Mr. Rainsford. I am going now to have my wound dressed; it's only a slight one. But I shall be back. I shall be back."

When the general, nursing his bruised shoulder, had gone, Rainsford took up his flight again. It was flight now, a desperate, hopeless flight, that carried him on for some hours. Dusk came, then darkness, and still he pressed on. The ground grew softer under his moccasins; the vegetation grew ranker, denser; insects bit him savagely. Then, as he stepped forward, his foot sank into the ooze. He tried to wrench it back, but the muck sucked viciously at his foot as if it were a giant leech. With a violent effort, he tore his foot loose. He knew where he was now. Death Swamp and its quicksand.

His hands were tight closed as if his nerve were something tangible that someone in the darkness was trying to tear from his grip. The softness of the earth had given him an idea. He stepped back from the quicksand a dozen feet or so and, like some huge prehistoric beaver, he began to dig.

Rainsford had dug himself in in France[2] when a second's delay meant death. That had been a placid pastime compared to his digging now. The pit grew deeper; when it was above his shoulders, he climbed out and from some hard saplings cut stakes and sharpened them to a fine point. These stakes he planted in the bottom of the pit with the points sticking up. With flying fingers he wove a rough carpet of weeds and branches and with it he covered the mouth of the pit. Then, wet with sweat and aching with tiredness, he crouched behind the stump of a lightning-charred tree.

He knew his pursuer was coming; he heard the padding sound of feet on the soft earth, and the night breeze brought him the perfume of the general's cigarette. It seemed to Rainsford that the general was coming with unusual swiftness; he was not feeling his way along, foot by foot. Rainsford, crouching there, could not see the general, nor could he see the pit. He lived a year in a minute. Then he felt an impulse to cry aloud with joy, for he heard the sharp crackle of the breaking branches as the cover of the pit gave way; he heard the sharp scream of pain as the pointed stakes found their mark. He leaped up from his place of concealment. Then he cowered back. Three feet from the pit a man was standing, with an electric torch in his hand.

"You've done well, Rainsford," the voice of the general called. "Your Burmese tiger pit has claimed one of my best dogs. Again you score. I think, Mr. Rainsford, I'll see what you can do against my whole pack. I'm going home for a rest now. Thank you for a most amusing evening."

At daybreak Rainsford, lying near the swamp, was awakened by a sound that made him know that he had new things to learn about

---

2. During World War I he had quickly dug a hole or trench to shelter himself from exploding shells, bullets, etc.

fear. It was a distant sound, faint and wavering, but he knew it. It was the baying of a pack of hounds.

Rainsford knew he could do one of two things. He could stay where he was and wait. That was suicide. He could flee. That was postponing the inevitable. For a moment he stood there, thinking. An idea that held a wild chance came to him, and, tightening his belt, he headed away from the swamp.

The baying of the hounds drew nearer, then still nearer, nearer, ever nearer. On a ridge Rainsford climbed a tree. Down a watercourse, not a quarter of a mile away, he could see the bush moving. Straining his eyes, he saw the lean figure of General Zaroff; just ahead of him Rainsford made out another figure whose wide shoulders surged through the tall jungle weeds; it was the giant Ivan, and he seemed pulled forward by some unseen force; Rainsford knew that Ivan must be holding the pack in leash.

They would be on him any minute now. His mind worked frantically. He thought of a native trick he had learned in Uganda. He slid down the tree. He caught hold of a springy young sapling and to it he fastened his hunting knife, with the blade pointing down the trail; with a bit of wild grapevine he tied back the sapling. Then he ran for his life. The hounds raised their voices as they hit the fresh scent. Rainsford knew now how an animal at bay feels.

He had to stop to get his breath. The baying of the hounds stopped abruptly, and Rainsford's heart stopped too. They must have reached the knife.

He shinned excitedly up a tree and looked back. His pursuers had stopped. But the hope that was in Rainsford's brain when he climbed died, for he saw in the shallow valley that General Zaroff was still on his feet. But Ivan was not. The knife, driven by the recoil of the springing tree, had not wholly failed.

Rainsford had hardly tumbled to the ground when the pack took up the cry again.

"Nerve, nerve, nerve!" he panted, as he dashed along. A blue gap showed between the trees dead ahead. Ever nearer drew the hounds. Rainsford forced himself on toward that gap. He reached it. It was the shore of the sea. Across a cove he could see the gloomy gray stone of the château. Twenty feet below him the sea rumbled and hissed. Rainsford hesitated. He heard the hounds. Then he leaped far out into the sea. . . .

When the general and his pack reached the place by the sea, the Cossack stopped. For some minutes he stood regarding the blue-green expanse of water. He shrugged his shoulders. Then he sat down, took a drink of brandy from a silver flask, lit a perfumed cigarette, and hummed a bit from "Madame Butterfly."

General Zaroff had an exceedingly good dinner in his great paneled dining hall that evening. With it he had a bottle of Pol Roger and half a bottle of Chambertin. Two slight annoyances kept him from perfect enjoyment. One was the thought that it would be difficult to replace Ivan; the other was that his quarry had escaped him; of course the American hadn't played the game—so thought the general as he tasted his after-dinner liqueur. In his library he read, to soothe himself, from the works of Marcus Aurelius.[3] At ten he went up to his bedroom. He was deliciously tired, he said to himself, as he locked himself in. There was a little moonlight, so, before turning on his light, he went to the window and looked down at the courtyard. He could see the great hounds, and he called: "Better luck another time," to them. Then he switched on the light.

A man, who had been hiding in the curtains of the bed, was standing there.

"Rainsford!" screamed the general. "How in God's name did you get here?"

"Swam," said Rainsford. "I found it quicker than walking through the jungle."

The general sucked in his breath and smiled. "I congratulate you," he said. "You have won the game."

Rainsford did not smile. "I am still a beast at bay," he said, in a low, hoarse voice. "Get ready, General Zaroff."

The general made one of his deepest bows. "I see," he said. "Splendid! One of us is to furnish a repast for the hounds. The other will sleep in this very excellent bed. On guard, Rainsford. . . ."

He had never slept in a better bed, Rainsford decided.

1924

ERNEST HEMINGWAY

The Short Happy Life of Francis Macomber

It was now lunch time and they were all sitting under the double green fly of the dining tent pretending that nothing had happened.

"Will you have lime juice or lemon squash?" Macomber asked.

"I'll have a gimlet,"[1] Robert Wilson told him.

"I'll have a gimlet too. I need something," Macomber's wife said.

"I suppose it's the thing to do," Macomber agreed. "Tell him to make three gimlets."

The mess boy had started them already, lifting the bottles out of the canvas cooling bags that sweated wet in the wind that blew through the trees that shaded the tents.

"What had I ought to give them?" Macomber asked.

"A quid[2] would be plenty," Wilson told him. "You don't want to spoil them."

"Will the headman distribute it?"

"Absolutely."

---

3. Roman Emperor (A.D. 161–180), Stoic philosopher, writer, and humanitarian, who, though good to the poor and opposed to the cruelty of gladiatorial shows, persecuted early Christians.

1. Drink of lime juice, gin, and soda or water.

2. Slang for a British pound.

Francis Macomber had, half an hour before, been carried to his tent from the edge of the camp in triumph on the arms and shoulders of the cook, the personal boys, the skinner and the porters. The gunbearers had taken no part in the demonstration. When the native boys put him down at the door of his tent, he had shaken all their hands, received their congratulations, and then gone into the tent and sat on the bed until his wife came in. She did not speak to him when she came in and he left the tent at once to wash his face and hands in the portable wash basin outside and go over to the dining tent to sit in a comfortable canvas chair in the breeze and the shade.

"You've got your lion," Robert Wilson said to him, "and a damned fine one too."

Mrs. Macomber looked at Wilson quickly. She was an extremely handsome and well-kept woman of the beauty and social position which had, five years before, commanded five thousand dollars as the price of endorsing, with photographs, a beauty product which she had never used. She had been married to Francis Macomber for eleven years.

"He is a good lion, isn't he?" Macomber said. His wife looked at him now. She looked at both these men as though she had never seen them before.

One, Wilson, the white hunter, she knew she had never truly seen before. He was about middle height with sandy hair, a stubby mustache, a very red face and extremely cold blue eyes with faint white wrinkles at the corners that grooved merrily when he smiled. He smiled at her now and she looked away from his face at the way his shoulders sloped in the loose tunic he wore with the four big cartridges held in loops where the left breast pocket should have been, at his big brown hands, his old slacks, his very dirty boots and back to his red face again. She noticed where the baked red of his face stopped in a white line that marked the circle left by his Stetson hat[3] that hung now from one of the pegs of the tent pole.

"Well, here's to the lion," Robert Wilson said. He smiled at her again and, not smiling, she looked curiously at her husband.

Francis Macomber was very tall, very well built if you did not mind that length of bone, dark, his hair cropped like an oarsman, rather thin-lipped, and was considered handsome. He was dressed in the same sort of safari clothes that Wilson wore except that his were new, he was thirty-five years old, kept himself very fit, was good at court games, had a number of big-game fishing records, and had just shown himself, very publicly, to be a coward.

"Here's to the lion," he said. "I can't ever thank you for what you did."

Margaret, his wife, looked away from him and back to Wilson.

"Let's not talk about the lion," she said.

Wilson looked over at her without smiling and now she smiled at him.

"It's been a very strange day," she said. "Hadn't you ought to

---

3. Cowboy-type hat.

put your hat on even under the canvas at noon? You told me that, you know."

"Might put it on," said Wilson.

"You know you have a very red face, Mr. Wilson," she told him and smiled again.

"Drink," said Wilson.

"I don't think so," she said. "Francis drinks a great deal, but his face is never red."

"It's red today," Macomber tried a joke.

"No," said Margaret. "It's mine that's red today. But Mr. Wilson's is always red."

"Must be racial," said Wilson. "I say, you wouldn't like to drop my beauty as a topic, would you?"

"I've just started on it."

"Let's chuck it," said Wilson.

"Conversation is going to be so difficult," Margaret said.

"Don't be silly, Margot," her husband said.

"No difficulty," Wilson said. "Got a damn fine lion."

Margot looked at them both and they both saw that she was going to cry. Wilson had seen it coming for a long time and he dreaded it. Macomber was past dreading it.

"I wish it hadn't happened. Oh, I wish it hadn't happened," she said and started for her tent. She made no noise of crying but they could see that her shoulders were shaking under the rose-colored, sun-proofed shirt she wore.

"Women upset," said Wilson to the tall man. "Amounts to nothing. Strain on the nerves and one thing'n another."

"No," said Macomber. "I suppose that I rate that for the rest of my life now."

"Nonsense. Let's have a spot of the giant killer," said Wilson. "Forget the whole thing. Nothing to it anyway."

"We might try," said Macomber. "I won't forget what you did for me though."

"Nothing," said Wilson. "All nonsense."

So they sat there in the shade where the camp was pitched under some wide-topped acacia trees with a boulder-strewn cliff behind them, and a stretch of grass that ran to the bank of a boulder-filled stream in front with forest beyond it, and drank their just-cool lime drinks and avoided one another's eyes while the boys set the table for lunch. Wilson could tell that the boys all knew about it now and when he saw Macomber's personal boy looking curiously at his master while he was putting dishes on the table he snapped at him in Swahili. The boy turned away with his face blank.

"What were you telling him?" Macomber asked.

"Nothing. Told him to look alive or I'd see he got about fifteen of the best."

"What's that? Lashes?"

"It's quite illegal," Wilson said. "You're supposed to fine them."

"Do you still have them whipped?"

"Oh, yes. They could raise a row if they chose to complain. But they don't. They prefer it to the fines."

"How strange!" said Macomber.

"Not strange, really," Wilson said. "Which would you rather do? Take a good birching or lose your pay?"

Then he felt embarrassed at asking it and before Macomber could answer he went on, "We all take a beating every day, you know, one way or another."

This was no better. "Good God," he thought. "I am a diplomat, aren't I?"

"Yes, we take a beating," said Macomber, still not looking at him. "I'm awfully sorry about that lion business. It doesn't have to go any further, does it? I mean no one will hear about it, will they?"

"You mean will I tell it at the Mathaiga Club?" Wilson looked at him now coldly. He had not expected this. So he's a bloody four-letter man as well as a bloody coward, he thought. I rather liked him too until today. But how is one to know about an American?

"No," said Wilson. "I'm a professional hunter. We never talk about our clients. You can be quite easy on that. It's supposed to be bad form to ask us not to talk though."

He had decided now that to break would be much easier. He would eat, then, by himself and could read a book with his meals. They would eat by themselves. He would see them through the safari on a very formal basis—what was it the French called it? Distinguished consideration[4]—and it would be a damn sight easier than having to go through this emotional trash. He'd insult him and make a good clean break. Then he could read a book with his meals and he'd still be drinking their whisky. That was the phrase for it when a safari went bad. You ran into another white hunter and you asked, "How is everything going?" and he answered, "Oh, I'm still drinking their whisky," and you knew everything had gone to pot.

"I'm sorry," Macomber said and looked at him with his American face that would stay adolescent until it became middle-aged, and Wilson noted his crew-cropped hair, fine eyes only faintly shifty, good nose, thin lips and handsome jaw. "I'm sorry I didn't realize that. There are lots of things I don't know."

So what could he do, Wilson thought. He was all ready to break it off quickly and neatly and here the beggar was apologizing after he had just insulted him. He made one more attempt. "Don't worry about me talking," he said. "I have a living to make. You know in Africa no woman ever misses her lion and no white man ever bolts."

"I bolted like a rabbit," Macomber said.

Now what in hell were you going to do about a man who talked like that, Wilson wondered.

Wilson looked at Macomber with his flat, blue, machine-gunner's eyes and the other smiled back at him. He had a pleasant smile if you did not notice how his eyes showed when he was hurt.

"Maybe I can fix it up on buffalo," he said. "We're after them next, aren't we?"

"In the morning if you like," Wilson told him. Perhaps he had been wrong. This was certainly the way to take it. You most cer-

4. Highest regard.

tainly could not tell a damned thing about an American. He was all for Macomber again. If you could forget the morning. But, of course, you couldn't. The morning had been about as bad as they come.

"Here comes the Memsahib," he said. She was walking over from her tent looking refreshed and cheerful and quite lovely. She had a very perfect oval face, so perfect that you expected her to be stupid. But she wasn't stupid, Wilson thought, no, not stupid.

"How is the beautiful red-faced Mr. Wilson? Are you feeling better, Francis, my pearl?"

"Oh, much," said Macomber.

"I've dropped the whole thing," she said, sitting down at the table. "What importance is there to whether Francis is any good at killing lions? That's not his trade. That's Mr. Wilson's trade. Mr. Wilson is really very impressive killing anything. You do kill anything, don't you?"

"Oh, anything," said Wilson. "Simply anything." They are, he thought, the hardest in the world; the hardest, the cruelest, the most predatory and the most attractive and their men have softened or gone to pieces nervously as they have hardened. Or is it that they pick men they can handle? They can't know that much at the age they marry, he thought. He was grateful that he had gone through his education on American women before now because this was a very attractive one.

"We're going after buff in the morning," he told her.

"I'm coming," she said.

"No, you're not."

"Oh, yes, I am. Mayn't I, Francis?"

"Why not stay in camp?"

"Not for anything," she said. "I wouldn't miss something like today for anything."

When she left, Wilson was thinking, when she went off to cry, she seemed a hell of a fine woman. She seemed to understand, to realize, to be hurt for him and for herself and to know how things really stood. She is away for twenty minutes and now she is back, simply enamelled in that American female cruelty. They are the damnedest women. Really the damnedest.

"We'll put on another show for you tomorrow," Francis Macomber said.

"You're not coming," Wilson said.

"You're very mistaken," she told him. "And I want *so* to see you perform again. You were lovely this morning. That is if blowing things' heads off is lovely."

"Here's the lunch," said Wilson. "You're very merry, aren't you?"

"Why not? I didn't come out here to be dull."

"Well, it hasn't been dull," Wilson said. He could see the boulders in the river and the high bank beyond with the trees and he remembered the morning.

"Oh, no," she said. "It's been charming. And tomorrow. You don't know how I look forward to tomorrow."

"That's eland he's offering you," Wilson said.

"They're the big cowy things that jump like hares, aren't they?"

"I suppose that describes them," Wilson said.

"It's very good meat," Macomber said.

"Didn't you shoot it, Francis?" she asked.

"Yes."

"They're not dangerous, are they?"

"Only if they fall on you," Wilson told her.

"I'm so glad."

"Why not let up on the bitchery just a little, Margot," Macomber said, cutting the eland steak and putting some mashed potato, gravy and carrot on the down-turned fork that tined through the piece of meat.

"I suppose I could," she said, "since you put it so prettily."

"Tonight we'll have champagne for the lion," Wilson said. "It's a bit too hot at noon."

"Oh, the lion," Margot said. "I'd forgotten the lion!"

So, Robert Wilson thought to himself, she *is* giving him a ride, isn't she? Or do you suppose that's her idea of putting up a good show? How should a woman act when she discovers her husband is a bloody coward? She's damn cruel but they're all cruel. They govern, of course, and to govern one has to be cruel sometimes. Still, I've seen enough of their damn terrorism.

"Have some more eland," he said to her politely.

That afternoon, late, Wilson and Macomber went out in the motor car with the native driver and the two gun-bearers. Mrs. Macomber stayed in the camp. It was too hot to go out, she said, and she was going with them in the early morning. As they drove off Wilson saw her standing under the big tree, looking pretty rather than beautiful in her faintly rosy khaki, her dark hair drawn back off her forehead and gathered in a knot low on her neck, her face as fresh, he thought, as though she were in England. She waved to them as the car went off through the swale of high grass and curved around through the trees into the small hills of orchard bush.

In the orchard bush they found a herd of impala,[5] and leaving the car they stalked one old ram with long, wide-spread horns and Macomber killed it with a very creditable shot that knocked the buck down at a good two hundred yards and sent the herd off bounding wildly and leaping over one another's backs in long, leg-drawn-up leaps as unbelievable and as floating as those one makes sometimes in dreams.

"That was a good shot," Wilson said. "They're a small target."

"Is it a worthwhile head?" Macomber asked.

"It's excellent," Wilson told him. "You shoot like that and you'll have no trouble."

"Do you think we'll find buffalo tomorrow?"

"There's a good chance of it. They feed out early in the morning and with luck we may catch them in the open."

"I'd like to clear away that lion business," Macomber said. "It's not very pleasant to have your wife see you do something like that."

5. Antelope of bush country of east and south Africa with lyre-shaped horns.

I should think it would be even more unpleasant to do it, Wilson thought, wife or no wife, or to talk about it having done it. But he said, "I wouldn't think about that any more. Anyone could be upset by his first lion. That's all over."

But that night after dinner and a whisky and soda by the fire before going to bed, as Francis Macomber lay on his cot with the mosquito bar over him and listened to the night noises, it was not all over. It was neither all over nor was it beginning. It was there exactly as it happened with some parts of it indelibly emphasized and he was miserably ashamed at it. But more than shame he felt cold, hollow fear in him. The fear was still there like a cold slimy hollow in all the emptiness where once his confidence had been and it made him feel sick. It was still there with him now.

It had started the night before when he had wakened and heard the lion roaring somewhere up along the river. It was a deep sound and at the end there were sort of coughing grunts that made him seem just outside the tent, and when Francis Macomber woke in the night to hear it he was afraid. He could hear his wife breathing quietly, asleep. There was no one to tell he was afraid, nor to be afraid with him, and, lying alone, he did not know the Somali proverb that says a brave man is always frightened three times by a lion; when he first sees his track, when he first hears him roar and when he first confronts him. Then while they were eating breakfast by lantern light out in the dining tent, before the sun was up, the lion roared again and Francis thought he was just at the edge of camp.

"Sounds like an old-timer," Robert Wilson said, looking up from his kippers and coffee. "Listen to him cough."

"Is he very close?"

"A mile or so up the stream."

"Will we see him?"

"We'll have a look."

"Does his roaring carry that far? It sounds as though he were right in camp."

"Carries a hell of a long way," said Robert Wilson. "It's strange the way it carries. Hope he's a shootable cat. The boys said there was a very big one about here."

"If I get a shot, where should I hit him," Macomber asked, "to stop him?"

"In the shoulders," Wilson said. "In the neck if you can make it. Shoot for bone. Break him down."

"I hope I can place it properly," Macomber said.

"You shoot very well," Wilson told him. "Take your time. Make sure of him. The first one in is the one that counts."

"What range will it be?"

"Can't tell. Lion has something to say about that. Won't shoot unless it's close enough so you can make sure."

"At under a hundred yards?" Macomber asked.

Wilson looked at him quickly.

"Hundred's about right. Might have to take him a bit under. Shouldn't chance a shot at much over that. A hundred's a decent range. You can hit him wherever you want at that. Here comes the Memsahib."

"Good morning," she said. "Are we going after that lion?"

"As soon as you deal with your breakfast," Wilson said. "How are you feeling?"

"Marvellous," she said. "I'm very excited."

"I'll just go and see that everything is ready," Wilson went off. As he left the lion roared again.

"Noisy beggar," Wilson said. "We'll put a stop to that."

"What's the matter, Francis?" his wife asked him.

"Nothing," Macomber said.

"Yes, there is," she said. "What are you upset about?"

"Nothing," he said.

"Tell me," she looked at him. "Don't you feel well?"

"It's that damned roaring," he said. "It's been going on all night, you know."

"Why didn't you wake me," she said. "I'd love to have heard it."

"I've got to kill the damned thing," Macomber said, miserably.

"Well, that's what you're out here for, isn't it?"

"Yes. But I'm nervous. Hearing the thing roar gets on my nerves."

"Well then, as Wilson said, kill him and stop his roaring."

"Yes, darling," said Francis Macomber. "It sounds easy, doesn't it?"

"You're not afraid, are you?"

"Of course not. But I'm nervous from hearing him roar all night."

"You'll kill him marvellously," she said. "I know you will. I'm awfully anxious to see it."

"Finish your breakfast and we'll be starting."

"It's not light yet," she said. "This is a ridiculous hour."

Just then the lion roared in a deep-chested moaning, suddenly guttural, ascending vibration that seemed to shake the air and ended in a sigh and a heavy, deep-chested grunt.

"He sounds almost here," Macomber's wife said.

"My God," said Macomber. "I hate that damned noise."

"It's very impressive."

"Impressive. It's frightful."

Robert Wilson came up then carrying his short, ugly, shockingly big-bored .505 Gibbs and grinning.

"Come on," he said. "Your gun-bearer has your Springfield and the big gun. Everything's in the car. Have you solids?"[6]

"Yes."

"I'm ready," Mrs. Macomber said.

"Must make him stop that racket," Wilson said. "You get in front. The Memsahib can sit back here with me."

They climbed into the motor car and, in the gray first daylight, moved off up the river through the trees. Macomber opened the breech of his rifle and saw he had metal-cased bullets, shut the bolt and put the rifle on safety. He saw his hand was trembling. He felt in his pocket for more cartridges and moved his fingers over the cartridges in the loops of his tunic front. He turned back to where

6. They are using jacketed bullets for quick, clean kill; the Springfield is a   thirty-caliber rifle as opposed to Wilson's fifty-caliber Gibbs.

Wilson sat in the rear seat of the doorless, box-bodied motor car beside his wife, them both grinning with excitement, and Wilson leaned forward and whispered,

"See the birds dropping. Means the old boy has left his kill."

On the far bank of the stream Macomber could see, above the trees, vultures circling and plummeting down.

"Chances are he'll come to drink along here," Wilson whispered. "Before he goes to lay up. Keep an eye out."

They were driving slowly along the high bank of the stream which here cut deeply to its boulder-filled bed, and they wound in and out through big trees as they drove. Macomber was watching the opposite bank when he felt Wilson take hold of his arm. The car stopped.

"There he is," he heard the whisper. "Ahead and to the right. Get out and take him. He's a marvellous lion."

Macomber saw the lion now. He was standing almost broadside, his great head up and turned toward them. The early morning breeze that blew toward them was just stirring his dark mane, and the lion looked huge, silhouetted on the rise of bank in the gray morning light, his shoulders heavy, his barrel of a body bulking smoothly.

"How far is he?" asked Macomber, raising his rifle.

"About seventy-five. Get out and take him."

"Why not shoot from where I am?"

"You don't shoot them from cars," he heard Wilson saying in his ear. "Get out. He's not going to stay there all day."

Macomber stepped out of the curved opening at the side of the front seat, onto the step and down onto the ground. The lion still stood looking majestically and coolly toward this object that his eyes only showed in silhouette, bulking like some super-rhino. There was no man smell carried toward him and he watched the object, moving his great head a little from side to side. Then watching the object, not afraid, but hesitating before going down the bank to drink with such a thing opposite him, he saw a man figure detach itself from it and he turned his heavy head and swung away toward the cover of the trees as he heard a cracking crash and felt the slam of a .30–06 220-grain solid bullet that bit his flank and ripped in sudden hot scalding nausea through his stomach. He trotted, heavy, big-footed, swinging wounded full-bellied, through the trees toward the tall grass and cover, and the crash came again to go past him ripping the air apart. Then it crashed again and he felt the blow as it hit his lower ribs and ripped on through, blood sudden hot and frothy in his mouth, and he galloped toward the high grass where he could crouch and not be seen and make them bring the crashing thing close enough so he could make a rush and get the man that held it.

Macomber had not thought how the lion felt as he got out of the car. He only knew his hands were shaking and as he walked away from the car it was almost impossible for him to make his legs move. They were stiff in the thighs, but he could feel the muscles fluttering. He raised the rifle, sighted on the junction of the lion's head and shoulders and pulled the trigger. Nothing happened though he pulled until he thought his finger would break. Then he knew he had the safety on and as he lowered the rifle to move the safety over he moved another frozen pace forward, and the lion seeing his silhouette now clear of the silhouette of the car, turned and started off at a trot, and, as Macomber fired, he heard a whunk that meant that the bullet was home; but the lion kept on going. Macomber shot again and everyone saw the bullet throw a spout of dirt beyond the trotting lion. He shot again, remembering to lower his aim, and they all heard the bullet hit, and the lion went into a gallop and was in the tall grass before he had the bolt pushed forward.

Macomber stood there feeling sick at his stomach, his hands that held the Springfield still cocked, shaking, and his wife and Robert Wilson were standing by him. Beside him too were the two gun-bearers chattering in Wakamba.[7]

"I hit him," Macomber said. "I hit him twice."

"You gut-shot him and you hit him somewhere forward," Wilson said without enthusiasm. The gun-bearers looked very grave. They were silent now.

"You may have killed him," Wilson went on. "We'll have to wait a while before we go in to find out."

"What do you mean?"

"Let him get sick before we follow him up."

"Oh," said Macomber.

"He's a hell of a fine lion," Wilson said cheerfully. "He's gotten into a bad place though."

"Why is it bad?"

"Can't see him until you're on him."

"Oh," said Macomber.

"Come on," said Wilson. "The Memsahib can stay here in the car. We'll go to have a look at the blood spoor."

"Stay here, Margot," Macomber said to his wife. His mouth was very dry and it was hard for him to talk.

"Why?" she asked.

"Wilson says to."

"We're going to have a look," Wilson said. "You stay here. You can see even better from here."

"All right."

Wilson spoke in Swahili to the driver. He nodded and said, "Yes, Bwana."

Then they went down the steep bank and across the stream, climbing over and around the boulders and up the other bank, pulling up by some projecting roots, and along it until they found where the lion had been trotting when Macomber first shot. There was dark blood on the short grass that the gun-bearers pointed out with grass stems, and that ran away behind the river bank trees.

"What do we do?" asked Macomber.

"Not much choice," said Wilson. "We can't bring the car over. Bank's too steep. We'll let him stiffen up a bit and then you and

7. A Bantu dialect spoken in Kenya.

I'll go in and have a look for him."

"Can't we set the grass on fire?" Macomber asked.

"Too green."

"Can't we send beaters?"

Wilson looked at him appraisingly. "Of course we can," he said. "But it's just a touch murderous. You see we know the lion's wounded. You can drive an unwounded lion—he'll move on ahead of a noise— but a wounded lion's going to charge. You can't see him until you're right on him. He'll make himself perfectly flat in cover you wouldn't think would hide a hare. You can't very well send boys in there to that sort of a show. Somebody bound to get mauled."

"What about the gun-bearers?"

"Oh, they'll go with us. It's their *shauri*.[8] You see, they signed on for it. They don't look too happy though, do they?"

"I don't want to go in there," said Macomber. It was out before he knew he'd said it.

"Neither do I," said Wilson very cheerily. "Really no choice though." Then, as an afterthought, he glanced at Macomber and saw suddenly how he was trembling and the pitiful look on his face.

"You don't have to go in, of course," he said. "That's what I'm hired for, you know. That's why I'm so expensive."

"You mean you'd go in by yourself? Why not leave him there?"

Robert Wilson, whose entire occupation had been with the lion and the problem he presented, and who had not been thinking about Macomber except to note that he was rather windy, suddenly felt as though he had opened the wrong door in a hotel and seen something shameful.

"What do you mean?"

"Why not just leave him?"

"You mean pretend to ourselves he hasn't been hit?"

"No. Just drop it."

"It isn't done."

"Why not?"

"For one thing, he's certain to be suffering. For another, some one else might run onto him."

"I see."

"But you don't have to have anything to do with it."

"I'd like to," Macomber said. "I'm just scared, you know."

"I'll go ahead when we go in," Wilson said, "with Kongoni tracking. You keep behind me and a little to one side. Chances are we'll hear him growl. If we see him we'll both shoot. Don't worry about anything. I'll keep you backed up. As a matter of fact, you know, perhaps you'd better not go. It might be much better. Why don't you go over and join the Memsahib while I just get it over with?"

"No, I want to go."

"All right," said Wilson. "But don't go in if you don't want to. This is my *shauri* now, you know."

"I want to go," said Macomber.

They sat under a tree and smoked.

8. Problem (a Swahili word).

"Want to go back and speak to the Memsahib while we're waiting?" Wilson asked.

"No."

"I'll just step back and tell her to be patient."

"Good," said Macomber. He sat there, sweating under his arms, his mouth dry, his stomach hollow feeling, wanting to find courage to tell Wilson to go on and finish off the lion without him. He could not know that Wilson was furious because he had not noticed the state he was in earlier and sent him back to his wife. While he sat there Wilson came up. "I have your big gun," he said. "Take it. We've given him time, I think. Come on."

Macomber took the big gun and Wilson said:

"Keep behind me and about five yards to the right and do exactly as I tell you." Then he spoke in Swahili to the two gun-bearers, who looked the picture of gloom.

"Let's go," he said.

"Could I have a drink of water?" Macomber asked. Wilson spoke to the older gun-bearer, who wore a canteen on his belt, and the man unbuckled it, unscrewed the top and handed it to Macomber, who took it noticing how heavy it seemed and how hairy and shoddy the felt covering was in his hand. He raised it to drink and looked ahead at the high grass with the flat-topped trees behind it. A breeze was blowing toward them and the grass rippled gently in the wind. He looked at the gun-bearer and he could see the gun-bearer was suffering too with fear.

Thirty-five yards into the grass the big lion lay flattened out along the ground. His ears were back and his only movement was a slight twitching up and down of his long, black-tufted tail. He had turned at bay as soon as he had reached this cover and he was sick with the wound through his full belly, and weakening with the wound through his lungs that brought a thin foamy red to his mouth each time he breathed. His flanks were wet and hot and flies were on the little openings the solid bullets had made in his tawny hide, and his big yellow eyes, narrowed with hate, looked straight ahead, only blinking when the pain came as he breathed, and his claws dug in the soft baked earth. All of him, pain, sickness, hatred and all of his remaining strength, was tightening into an absolute concentration for a rush. He could hear the men talking and he waited, gathering all of himself into this preparation for a charge as soon as the men would come into the grass. As he heard their voices his tail stiffened to twitch up and down, and, as they came into the edge of the grass, he made a coughing grunt and charged.

Kongoni, the old gun-bearer, in the lead watching the blood spoor, Wilson watching the grass for any movement, his big gun ready, the second gun-bearer looking ahead and listening, Macomber close to Wilson, his rifle cocked, they had just moved into the grass when Macomber heard the blood-choked coughing grunt, and saw the swishing rush in the grass. The next thing he knew he was running; running wildly, in panic in the open, running toward the stream.

He heard the *ca-ra-wong!* of Wilson's big rifle, and again in a second crashing *carawong!* and turning saw the lion, horrible-looking now, with half his head seeming to be gone, crawling toward Wilson in the edge of the tall grass while the red-faced man worked the bolt on the short ugly rifle and aimed carefully as another blasting *carawong!* came from the muzzle, and the crawling, heavy, yellow bulk of the lion stiffened and the huge, mutilated head slid forward and Macomber, standing by himself in the clearing where he had run, holding a loaded rifle, while two black men and a white man looked back at him in contempt, knew the lion was dead. He came toward Wilson, his tallness all seeming a naked reproach, and Wilson looked at him and said:

"Want to take pictures?"

"No," he said.

That was all any one had said until they reached the motor car. Then Wilson had said:

"Hell of a fine lion. Boys will skin him out. We might as well stay here in the shade."

Macomber's wife had not looked at him nor he at her and he had sat by her in the back seat with Wilson sitting in the front seat. Once he had reached over and taken his wife's hand without looking at her and she had removed her hand from his. Looking across the stream to where the gun-bearers were skinning out the lion he could see that she had been able to see the whole thing. While they sat there his wife had reached forward and put her hand on Wilson's shoulder. He turned and she had leaned forward over the low seat and kissed him on the mouth.

"Oh, I say," said Wilson, going redder than his natural baked color.

"Mr. Robert Wilson," she said. "The beautiful red-faced Mr. Robert Wilson."

Then she sat down beside Macomber again and looked away across the stream to where the lion lay, with uplifted, white-muscled, tendon-marked naked forearms, and white bloating belly, as the black men fleshed away the skin. Finally the gun-bearers brought the skin over, wet and heavy, and climbed in behind with it, rolling it up before they got in, and the motor car started. No one had said anything more until they were back in camp.

That was the story of the lion. Macomber did not know how the lion had felt before he started his rush, nor during it when the unbelievable smash of the .505 with a muzzle velocity of two tons had hit him in the mouth, nor what kept him coming after that, when the second ripping crash had smashed his hind quarters and he had come crawling on toward the crashing, blasting thing that had destroyed him. Wilson knew something about it and only expressed it by saying, "Damned fine lion," but Macomber did not know how Wilson felt about things either. He did not know how his wife felt except that she was through with him.

His wife had been through with him before but it never lasted. He was very wealthy, and would be much wealthier, and he knew she would not leave him ever now. That was one of the few things that he really knew. He knew about that, about motorcycles—that was earliest—about motor cars, about duck-shooting, about fishing, trout, salmon and big-sea, about sex in books, many books, too many books, about all court games, about dogs, not much about horses, about hanging on to his money, about most of the other things his world dealt in, and about his wife not leaving him. His wife had been a great beauty and she was still a great beauty in Africa, but she was not a great enough beauty any more at home to be able to leave him and better herself and she knew it and he knew it. She had missed the chance to leave him and he knew it. If he had been better with women she would probably have started to worry about him getting another new, beautiful wife; but she knew too much about him to worry about him either. Also, he had always had a great tolerance which seemed the nicest thing about him if it were not the most sinister.

All in all they were known as a comparatively happily married couple, one of those whose disruption is often rumored but never occurs, and as the society columnist put it, they were adding more than a spice of *adventure* to their much envied and ever-enduring *Romance* by a *Safari* in what was known as *Darkest Africa* until the Martin Johnsons lighted it on so many silver screens where they were pursuing *Old Simba* the lion, the buffalo, *Tembo* the elephant and as well collecting specimens for the Museum of Natural History.[9] This same columnist had reported them *on the verge* at least three times in the past and they had been. But they always made it up. They had a sound basis of union. Margot was too beautiful for Macomber to divorce her and Macomber had too much money for Margot ever to leave him.

It was now about three o'clock in the morning and Francis Macomber, who had been asleep a little while after he had stopped thinking about the lion, wakened and then slept again, woke suddenly, frightened in a dream of the bloody-headed lion standing over him, and listening while his heart pounded, he realized that his wife was not in the other cot in the tent. He lay awake with that knowledge for two hours.

At the end of that time his wife came into the tent, lifted her mosquito bar and crawled cozily into bed.

"Where have you been?" Macomber asked in the darkness.

"Hello," she said. "Are you awake?"

"Where have you been?"

"I just went out to get a breath of air."

"You did, like hell."

"What do you want me to say, darling?"

"Where have you been?"

"Out to get a breath of air."

"That's a new name for it. You *are* a bitch."

"Well, you're a coward."

"All right," he said. "What of it?"

"Nothing as far as I'm concerned. But please let's not talk, darling, because I'm very sleepy."

"You think that I'll take anything."

---

9. Martin and Osa Johnson from 1921 to 1936 made nature films in Africa.

"I know you will, sweet."

"Well, I won't."

"Please, darling, let's not talk. I'm so very sleepy."

"There wasn't going to be any of that. You promised there wouldn't be."

"Well, there is now," she said sweetly.

"You said if we made this trip that there would be none of that. You promised."

"Yes, darling. That's the way I meant it to be. But the trip was spoiled yesterday. We don't have to talk about it, do we?"

"You don't wait long when you have an advantage, do you?"

"Please let's not talk. I'm so sleepy, darling."

"I'm going to talk."

"Don't mind me then, because I'm going to sleep." And she did.

At breakfast they were all three at the table before daylight and Francis Macomber found that, of all the many men that he had hated, he hated Robert Wilson the most.

"Sleep well?" Wilson asked in his throaty voice, filling a pipe.

"Did you?"

"Topping," the white hunter told him.

You bastard, thought Macomber, you insolent bastard.

So she woke him when she came in, Wilson thought, looking at them both with his flat, cold eyes. Well, why doesn't he keep his wife where she belongs? What does he think I am, a bloody plaster saint? Let him keep her where she belongs. It's his own fault.

"Do you think we'll find buffalo?" Margot asked, pushing away a dish of apricots.

"Chance of it," Wilson said and smiled at her. "Why don't you stay in camp?"

"Not for anything," she told him.

"Why not order her to stay in camp?" Wilson said to Macomber.

"You order her," said Macomber coldly.

"Let's not have any ordering, nor," turning to Macomber, "any silliness, Francis," Margot said quite pleasantly.

"Are you ready to start?" Macomber asked.

"Any time," Wilson told him. "Do you want the Memsahib to go?"

"Does it make any difference whether I do or not?"

The hell with it, thought Robert Wilson. The utter complete hell with it. So this is what it's going to be like. Well, this is what it's going to be like, then.

"Makes no difference," he said.

"You're sure you wouldn't like to stay in camp with her yourself and let me go out and hunt the buffalo?" Macomber asked.

"Can't do that," said Wilson. "Wouldn't talk rot if I were you."

"I'm not talking rot. I'm disgusted."

"Bad word, disgusted."

"Francis, will you please try to speak sensibly?" his wife said.

"I speak too damned sensibly," Macomber said. "Did you ever eat such filthy food?"

"Something wrong with the food?" asked Wilson quietly.

"No more than with everything else."

"I'd pull yourself together, laddybuck," Wilson said very quietly. "There's a boy waits at table that understands a little English."

"The hell with him."

Wilson stood up and putting on his pipe strolled away, speaking a few words in Swahili to one of the gun-bearers who was standing waiting for him. Macomber and his wife sat on at the table. He was staring at his coffee cup.

"If you make a scene I'll leave you, darling," Margot said quietly.

"No, you won't."

"You can try it and see."

"You won't leave me."

"No," she said. "I won't leave you and you'll behave yourself."

"Behave myself? That's a way to talk. Behave myself."

"Yes. Behave yourself."

"Why don't *you* try behaving?"

"I've tried it so long. So very long."

"I hate that red-faced swine," Macomber said. "I loathe the sight of him."

"He's really *very* nice."

"Oh, *shut up*," Macomber almost shouted. Just then the car came up and stopped in front of the dining tent and the driver and the two gun-bearers got out. Wilson walked over and looked at the husband and wife sitting there at the table.

"Going shooting?" he asked.

"Yes," said Macomber, standing up. "Yes."

"Better bring a woolly. It will be cool in the car," Wilson said.

"I'll get my leather jacket," Margot said.

"The boy has it," Wilson told her. He climbed into the front with the driver and Francis Macomber and his wife sat, not speaking, in the back seat.

Hope the silly beggar doesn't take a notion to blow the back of my head off, Wilson thought to himself. Women *are* a nuisance on safari.

The car was grinding down to cross the river at a pebbly ford in the gray daylight and then climbed, angling up the steep bank, where Wilson had ordered a way shovelled out the day before so they could reach the parklike wooded rolling country on the far side.

It was a good morning, Wilson thought. There was a heavy dew and as the wheels went through the grass and low bushes he could smell the odor of the crushed fronds. It was an odor like verbena and he liked this early morning smell of the dew, the crushed bracken and the look of the tree trunks showing black through the early morning mist, as the car made its way through the untracked, parklike country. He had put the two in the back seat out of his mind now and was thinking about buffalo. The buffalo that he was after stayed in the daytime in a thick swamp where it was impossible to get a shot, but in the night they fed out into an open stretch of country and if he could come between them and their swamp with the car, Macomber would have a good chance at them in the open. He did not want to hunt buff with Macomber in thick cover. He did not want to hunt buff or anything else with Macomber at all, but he was a professional hunter and he had hunted with some rare ones in his time. If they got buff today there would only be rhino to come and the poor man would have gone through his dangerous game and things might pick up. He'd have nothing more to do with the woman and Macomber would get over that too. He must have gone through plenty of that before by the look of things. Poor beggar. He must have a way of getting over it. Well, it was the poor sod's[1] own bloody fault.

He, Robert Wilson, carried a double size cot on safari to accommodate any windfalls he might receive. He had hunted for a certain clientele, the international, fast, sporting set, where the women did not feel they were getting their money's worth unless they had shared that cot with the white hunter. He despised them when he was away from them although he liked some of them well enough at the time, but he made his living by them; and their standards were his standards as long as they were hiring him.

They were his standards in all except the shooting. He had his own standards about the killing and they could live up to them or get some one else to hunt them. He knew, too, that they all respected him for this. This Macomber was an odd one though. Damned if he wasn't. Now the wife. Well, the wife. Yes, the wife. Hm, the wife. Well he'd dropped all that. He looked around at them. Macomber sat grim and furious. Margot smiled at him. She looked younger today, more innocent and fresher and not so professionally beautiful. What's in her heart God knows, Wilson thought. She hadn't talked much last night. At that it was a pleasure to see her.

The motor car climbed up a slight rise and went on through the trees and then out into a grassy prairie-like opening and kept in the shelter of the trees along the edge, the driver going slowly and Wilson looking carefully out across the prairie and all along its far side. He stopped the car and studied the opening with his field glasses. Then he motioned to the driver to go on and the car moved slowly along, the driver avoiding wart-hog holes and driving around the mud castles ants had built. Then, looking across the opening, Wilson suddenly turned and said,

"By God, there they are!"

And looking where he pointed, while the car jumped forward and Wilson spoke in rapid Swahili to the driver, Macomber saw three huge, black animals looking almost cylindrical in their long heaviness, like big black tank cars, moving at a gallop across the far edge of the open prairie. They moved at a stiff-necked, stiff bodied gallop and he could see the upswept wide black horns on their heads as they galloped heads out; the heads not moving.

"They're three old bulls," Wilson said. "We'll cut them off before they get to the swamp."

The car was going a wild forty-five miles an hour across the open and as Macomber watched, the buffalo got bigger and bigger until he could see the gray, hairless, scabby look of one huge bull and how his neck was a part of his shoulders and the shiny black of his

---

1. Chap or fellow, now nonpejorative but originally "sodomite" (cp. "bugger").

horns as he galloped a little behind the others that were strung out
in that steady plunging gait; and then, the car swaying as though
it had just jumped a road, they drew up close and he could see
the plunging hugeness of the bull, and the dust in his sparsely haired
hide, the side boss of horn and his outstretched, wide-nostrilled
muzzle, and he was raising his rifle when Wilson shouted, "Not from
the car, you fool!" and he had no fear, only hatred of Wilson, while
the brakes clamped on and the car skidded, plowing sideways to
an almost stop and Wilson was out on one side and he on the other,
stumbling as his feet hit the still speeding-by of the earth, and then
he was shooting at the bull as he moved away, hearing the bullets
whunk into him, emptying his rifle at him as he moved steadily away,
finally remembering to get his shots forward into the shoulder, and
as he fumbled to re-load, he saw the bull was down. Down on his
knees, his big head tossing, and seeing the other two still galloping
he shot at the leader and hit him. He shot again and missed and
he heard the *carawonging* roar as Wilson shot and saw the leading
bull slide forward onto his nose.
"Get that other," Wilson said. "Now you're shooting!"
But the other bull was moving steadily at the same gallop and he
missed, throwing a spout of dirt, and Wilson missed and the dust
rose in a cloud and Wilson shouted, "Come on. He's too far!" and
grabbed his arm and they were in the car again, Macomber and
Wilson hanging on the sides and rocketing swayingly over the uneven ground, drawing up on the steady, plunging, heavy-necked,
straight-moving gallop of the bull.
They were behind him and Macomber was filling his rifle, dropping
shells onto the ground, jamming it, clearing the jam, then they were
almost up with the bull when Wilson yelled "Stop," and the car
skidded so that it almost swung over and Macomber fell forward
onto his feet, slammed his bolt forward and fired as far forward
as he could aim into the galloping, rounded black back, aimed and
shot again, then again, then again, and the bullets, all of them hitting,
had no effect on the buffalo that he could see. Then Wilson shot,
the roar deafening him, and he could see the bull stagger. Macomber
shot again, aiming carefully, and down he came, onto his knees.
"All right," Wilson said. "Nice work. That's the three."
Macomber felt a drunken elation.
"How many times did you shoot?" he asked.
"Just three," Wilson said. "You killed the first bull. The biggest one.
I helped you finish the other two. Afraid they might have got into
cover. You had them killed. I was just mopping up a little. You
shot damn well."
"Let's go to the car," said Macomber. "I want a drink."
"Got to finish off that buff first," Wilson told him. The buffalo was
on his knees and he jerked his head furiously and bellowed in pig-
eyed, roaring rage as they came toward him.
"Watch he doesn't get up," Wilson said. Then, "Get a little broadside and take him in the neck just behind the ear."
Macomber aimed carefully at the center of the huge, jerking, rage-
driven neck and shot. At the shot the head dropped forward.
"That does it," said Wilson. "Got the spine. They're a hell of a

looking thing, aren't they?"

"Let's get the drink," said Macomber. In his life he had never felt so good.

In the car Macomber's wife sat very white faced. "You were marvellous, darling," she said to Macomber. "What a ride."

"Was it rough?" Wilson asked.

"It was frightful. I've never been more frightened in my life."

"Let's all have a drink," Macomber said.

"By all means," said Wilson. "Give it to the Memsahib." She drank the neat whisky from the flask and shuddered a little when she swallowed. She handed the flask to Macomber who handed it to Wilson.

"It was frightfully exciting," she said. "It's given me a dreadful headache. I didn't know you were allowed to shoot them from cars though."

"No one shot from cars," said Wilson coldly.

"I mean chase them from cars."

"Wouldn't ordinarily," Wilson said. "Seemed sporting enough to me though while we were doing it. Taking more chance driving that way across the plain full of holes and one thing and another than hunting on foot. Buffalo could have charged us each time we shot if he liked. Gave him every chance. Wouldn't mention it to any one though. It's illegal if that's what you mean."

"It seemed very unfair to me," Margot said, "chasing those big helpless things in a motor car."

"Did it?" said Wilson.

"What would happen if they heard about it in Nairobi?"

"I'd lose my license for one thing. Other unpleasantnesses," Wilson said, taking a drink from the flask. "I'd be out of business."

"Really?"

"Yes, really."

"Well," said Macomber, and he smiled for the first time all day. "Now she has something on you."

"You have such a pretty way of putting things, Francis," Margot Macomber said. Wilson looked at them both. If a four-letter man marries a five-letter woman, he was thinking, what number of letters would their children be? What he said was, "We lost a gun-bearer. Did you notice it?"

"My God, no," Macomber said.

"Here he comes," Wilson said. "He's all right. He must have fallen off when we left the first bull."

Approaching them was the middle-aged gun-bearer, limping along in his knitted cap, khaki tunic, shorts and rubber sandals, gloomy-faced and disgusted looking. As he came up he called out to Wilson in Swahili and they all saw the change in the white hunter's face.

"What does he say?" asked Margot.

"He says the first bull got up and went into the bush," Wilson said with no expression in his voice.

"Oh," said Macomber blankly.

"Then it's going to be just like the lion," said Margot, full of anticipation.

"It's not going to be a damned bit like the lion," Wilson told her.

"Did you want another drink, Macomber?"

"Thanks, yes," Macomber said. He expected the feeling he had had about the lion to come back but it did not. For the first time in his life he really felt wholly without fear. Instead of fear he had a feeling of definite elation.

"We'll go and have a look at the second bull," Wilson said. "I'll tell the driver to put the car in the shade."

"What are you going to do?" asked Margaret Macomber.

"Take a look at the buff," Wilson said.

"I'll come."

"Come along."

The three of them walked over to where the second buffalo bulked blackly in the open, head forward on the grass, the massive horns swung wide.

"He's a very good head," Wilson said. "That's close to a fifty-inch spread."

Macomber was looking at him with delight.

"He's hateful looking," said Margot. "Can't we go into the shade?"

"Of course," Wilson said. "Look," he said to Macomber, and pointed. "See that patch of bush?"

"Yes."

"That's where the first bull went in. The gun-bearer said when he fell off the bull was down. He was watching us helling along and the other two buff galloping. When he looked up there was the bull up and looking at him. Gun-bearer ran like hell and the bull went off slowly into that bush."

"Can we go in after him now?" asked Macomber eagerly.

Wilson looked at him appraisingly. Damned if this isn't a strange one, he thought. Yesterday he's scared sick and today he's a ruddy[2] fire eater.

"No, we'll give him a while."

"Let's please go into the shade," Margot said. Her face was white and she looked ill.

They made their way to the car where it stood under a single, wide-spreading tree and all climbed in.

"Chances are he's dead in there," Wilson remarked. "After a little we'll have a look."

Macomber felt a wild unreasonable happiness that he had never known before.

"By God, that was a chase," he said. "I've never felt any such feeling. Wasn't it marvellous, Margot?"

"I hated it."

"Why?"

"I hated it," she said bitterly. "I loathed it."

"You know I don't think I'd ever be afraid of anything again," Macomber said to Wilson. "Something happened in me after we first saw the buff and started after him. Like a dam bursting. It was pure excitement."

"Cleans out your liver," said Wilson. "Damn funny things happen to people."

---

2. Euphemism for the stronger "bloody."

Macomber's face was shining. "You know something did happen to me," he said. "I feel absolutely different."

His wife said nothing and eyed him strangely. She was sitting far back in the seat and Macomber was sitting forward talking to Wilson who turned sideways talking over the back of the front seat.

"You know, I'd like to try another lion," Macomber said. "I'm really not afraid of them now. After all, what can they do to you?"

"That's it," said Wilson. "Worst one can do is kill you. How does it go? Shakespeare. Damned good. See if I can remember. Oh, damned good. Used to quote it to myself at one time. Let's see. 'By my troth, I care not; a man can die but once; we owe God a death and let it go which way it will he that dies this year is quit for the next.'[3] Damned fine, eh?"

He was very embarrassed, having brought out this thing he had lived by, but he had seen men come of age before and it always moved him. It was not a matter of their twenty-first birthday.

It had taken a strange chance of hunting, a sudden precipitation into action without opportunity for worrying beforehand, to bring this about with Macomber, but regardless of how it had happened it had most certainly happened. Look at the beggar now, Wilson thought. It's that some of them stay little boys so long, Wilson thought. Sometimes all their lives. Their figures stay boyish when they're fifty. The great American boy-men. Damned strange people. But he liked this Macomber now. Damned strange fellow. Probably meant the end of cuckoldry too. Well, that would be a damned good thing. Damned good thing. Beggar had probably been afraid all his life. Don't know what started it. But over now. Hadn't had time to be afraid with the buff. That and being angry too. Motor car too. Motor cars made it familiar. Be a damn fire eater now. He'd seen it in the war work the same way. More of a change than any loss of virginity. Fear gone like an operation. Something else grew in its place. Main thing a man had. Made him into a man. Women knew it too. No bloody fear.

From the far corner of the seat Margaret Macomber looked at the two of them. There was no change in Wilson. She saw Wilson as she had seen him the day before when she had first realized what his great talent was. But she saw the change in Francis Macomber now.

"Do you have that feeling of happiness about what's going to happen?" Macomber asked, still exploring his new wealth.

"You're not supposed to mention it," Wilson said, looking in the other's face. "Much more fashionable to say you're scared. Mind you, you'll be scared too, plenty of times."

"But you *have* a feeling of happiness about action to come?"

"Yes," said Wilson. "There's that. Doesn't do to talk too much about all this. Talk the whole thing away. No pleasure in anything if you mouth it up too much."

"You're both talking rot," said Margot. "Just because you've chased

---

3. Shakespeare, *Henry IV Part 2*, III, 2, 250–55. There are some differences in punctuation, and after "owe God a death," the following is omitted: "I'll ne'er bear a base mind. An't be my destiny, so; an't be not, so. No man's too good to serve's prince."

some helpless animals in a motor car you talk like heroes."

"Sorry," said Wilson. "I have been gassing too much." She's worried about it already, he thought.

"If you don't know what we're talking about why not keep out of it?" Macomber asked his wife.

"You've gotten awfully brave, awfully suddenly," his wife said contemptuously, but her contempt was not secure. She was very afraid of something.

Macomber laughed, a very natural hearty laugh. "You know I *have*," he said. "I really have."

"Isn't it sort of late?" Margot said bitterly. Because she had done the best she could for many years back and the way they were together now was no one person's fault.

"Not for me," said Macomber.

Margot said nothing but sat back in the corner of the seat.

"Do you think we've given him time enough?" Macomber asked Wilson cheerfully.

"We might have a look," Wilson said. "Have you any solids left?"

"The gun-bearer has some."

Wilson called in Swahili and the older gun-bearer, who was skinning out one of the heads, straightened up, pulled a box of solids out of his pocket and brought them over to Macomber, who filled his magazine and put the remaining shells in his pocket.

"You might as well shoot the Springfield," Wilson said. "You're used to it. We'll leave the Mannlicher in the car with the Memsahib. Your gun-bearer can carry your heavy gun. I've this damned cannon. Now let me tell you about them." He had saved this until the last because he did not want to worry Macomber. "When a buff comes he comes with his head high and thrust straight out. The boss of the horns covers any sort of a brain shot. The only shot is straight into the nose. The only other shot is into his chest or, if you're to one side, into the neck or the shoulders. After they've been hit once they take a hell of a lot of killing. Don't try anything fancy. Take the easiest shot there is. They've finished skinning out that head now. Should we get started."

He called to the gun-bearers, who came up wiping their hands, and the older one got into the back.

"I'll only take Kongoni," Wilson said. "The other can watch to keep the birds away."

As the car moved slowly across the open space toward the island of brushy trees that ran in a tongue of foliage along a dry water course that cut the open swale, Macomber felt his heart pounding and his mouth was dry again, but it was excitement, not fear.

"Here's where he went in," Wilson said. Then to the gun-bearer in Swahili, "Take the blood spoor."

The car was parallel to the patch of bush. Macomber, Wilson and the gun-bearer got down. Macomber, looking back, saw his wife, with the rifle by her side, looking at him. He waved to her and she did not wave back.

The brush was very thick ahead and the ground was dry. The middle-aged gun-bearer was sweating heavily and Wilson had his hat down over his eyes and his red neck showed just ahead of

Macomber. Suddenly the gun-bearer said something in Swahili to Wilson and ran forward.

"He's dead in there," Wilson said. "Good work," and he turned to grip Macomber's hand and as they shook hands, grinning at each other, the gun-bearer shouted wildly and they saw him coming out of the brush sideways, fast as a crab, and the bull coming, nose out, mouth tight closed, blood dripping, massive head straight out, coming in a charge, his little pig eyes bloodshot as he looked at them. Wilson, who was ahead was kneeling shooting, and Macomber, as he fired, unhearing his shot in the roaring of Wilson's gun, saw fragments like slate burst from the huge boss of the horns, and the head jerked, he shot again at the wide nostrils and saw the horns jolt again and fragments fly, and he did not see Wilson now and, aiming carefully, shot again with the buffalo's huge bulk almost on him and his rifle almost level with the on-coming head, nose out, and he could see the little wicked eyes and the head started to lower and he felt a sudden white-hot, blinding flash explode inside his head and that was all he ever felt.

Wilson had ducked to one side to get in a shoulder shot. Macomber had stood solid and shot for the nose, shooting a touch high each time and hitting the heavy horns, splintering and chipping them like hitting a slate roof, and Mrs. Macomber, in the car, had shot at the buffalo with the 6.5 Mannlicher as it seemed about to gore Macomber and had hit her husband about two inches up and a little to one side of the base of his skull.

Francis Macomber lay now, face down, not two yards from where the buffalo lay on his side and his wife knelt over him with Wilson beside her.

"I wouldn't turn him over," Wilson said.

The woman was crying hysterically.

"I'd get back in the car," Wilson said. "Where's the rifle?"

She shook her head, her face contorted. The gun-bearer picked up the rifle.

"Leave it as it is," said Wilson. Then, "Go get Abdulla so that he may witness the manner of the accident."

He knelt down, took a handkerchief from his pocket, and spread it over Francis Macomber's crew-cropped head where it lay. The blood sank into the dry, loose earth.

Wilson stood up and saw the buffalo on his side, his legs out, his thinly-haired belly crawling with ticks. "Hell of a good bull," his brain registered automatically. "A good fifty inches, or better. Better." He called to the driver and told him to spread a blanket over the body and stay by it. Then he walked over to the motor car where the woman sat crying in the corner.

"That was a pretty thing to do," he said in a toneless voice. "He *would* have left you too."

"Stop it," she said.

"Of course it's an accident," he said. "I know that."

"Stop it," she said.

"Don't worry," he said. "There will be a certain amount of unpleasantness but I will have some photographs taken that will be very useful at the inquest. There's the testimony of the gun-bearers and the driver too. You're perfectly all right."

"Stop it," she said.

"There's a hell of a lot to be done," he said. "And I'll have to send a truck off to the lake to wireless for a plane to take the three of us into Nairobi. Why didn't you poison him? That's what they do in England."

"Stop it. Stop it. Stop it," the woman cried.

Wilson looked at her with his flat blue eyes.

"I'm through now," he said. "I was a little angry. I'd begun to like your husband."

"Oh, please stop it," she said. "Please, please stop it."

"That's better," Wilson said. "Please is much better. Now I'll stop."

p. 1936

2   FOCUS AND VOICE

Who is telling us the story—whose words are we reading? Where does this person stand with relation to what is going on in the story? In narrative someone is always between us and the events—a viewer, a speaker, or both; narrative, unlike drama, is always mediated. The way a story is mediated—the way the distance and angle of perspective and the language mold the subject matter—is a key element in fictional structure.

This mediation, or structuring, is usually called **point of view,** a perfectly satisfactory term for the angle of vision, the point from which the people, events, and other details (the history) are viewed. But there are also the words of the story between us and the history, and the words are not always those of the person who is the viewing point. So we shall distinguish between the two, calling the viewing aspect the **focus** and the verbal aspect the **voice.**

Focus acts much as a movie camera does, choosing what we can look at and the angle at which we can view it, framing, proportioning, emphasizing, even distorting. Plot is a structure that places us in a time relationship to the history; focus places us in a spatial relationship.

There are several things to notice about focus at any given point in a story. Is it fixed or mobile; that is, does it stay at more or less the same angle to, and at the same distance from, the characters and action, or does it move around or in and out? In the first three and a half paragraphs of *An Occurrence at Owl Creek Bridge*, for example, we seem to be seeing through the lens of a camera that can swing left or right, up or down, but stays pretty much at the same angle and distance from the bridge. In *The Lottery* that seems true of the focus for the entire story (unless you feel the camera moves in a little closer toward the end). In *Owl Creek Bridge*, however, by the middle of the fourth paragraph we're inside the mind of the man who's about to be hanged: "The arrangement commended itself to his judgment. . . . He looked a moment. . . . A piece of dancing driftwood caught his attention. . . . How slowly it appeared to move!" From now on we are inside the condemned man's head. The focus is more limited in scope—for almost all of the rest of the story we can see and hear only what he sees and hears. But because the focus is internal as well as limited, we can also know what he thinks. This limited, internal focus, used here as well as in *The Most Dangerous Game,* is usually called the **centered** or **central consciousness.**

The centered consciousness has been a popular, perhaps *the* most popular focus in fiction of the past hundred years—through most of the history of the modern short story, in fact—and its tightly controlled range and concentration on a single individual seem particularly suited for the short form. During much of this period, fiction, both long and short, has been in one sense realistic—that is, treating the everyday and the natural. It has become increasingly clear, however, that to the individual, what is real is what is perceived (**psychological realism**). The centered consciousness, in which things, people, and events are perceived through the filter of the individual character's consciousness, has therefore been ideally appropriate. It is a comfortable focus for readers, too. On the one hand, they can identify with someone whose thoughts and perception they share, even if the character is fallible, like Rainsford in *The Most Dangerous Game* or Young Goodman Brown, or even reprehensible, like the womanizing Gurov at the beginning of Chekhov's *The Lady with the Dog.* On the other hand, readers are distanced enough from the focal character to escape. The third person keeps us "other"—we are outside a bit, even as we identify—and the camera eye can pull back, as it cannot do spatially from the first-person narrator.

First-person stories, like *The Summer My Grandmother Was Supposed to Die,* are always limited too, and almost all the time are internal as well (though Montresor, in *The Cask of Amontillado,* hides his plans from us), and though they cannot retract spatially from the narrator, they not only can be but almost always are withdrawn temporally. That is, the "I" telling the story is older than the "I" experiencing the events of the story. Indeed, it may be this temporal distancing in first-person narration that seems to give the centered-consciousness, third-person narration the edge in excitement and suspense; though both types of stories usually use the past tense, the first-person past seems less a narrative convention and more a real pastness than does the third-person past.

The psychological realism gained by having a limited narrator exacts a price from the reader. If you don't hold the author (or the story) responsible for the absolute truth, validity, accuracy, and opinions of the focal character—if he or she is just telling us what he or she thinks, feels, sees—we must accept the possibility that the character's vision may be unreliable. At a significant point in *Owl Creek Bridge,* for example, you will find that the camera pulls back from Peyton

Farquhar and we are made to recognize to what extent his consciousness is a reliable witness to what has been going on. The history here is only an occurrence; the limited focus structures the mere occurrence into a story.

There is no doubt about reliability at the end of *Owl Creek Bridge*, nor in a story like *The Tree of Knowledge* ("Stories for Further Reading"), but there may be considerable difference of opinion about whether the lawyer-narrator in *Bartleby, the Scrivener* (also in "Stories for Further Reading") is meant to be unreliable. (By the way, **unreliable narrator** is the term most often used to refer to this aspect of fiction, though neither Farquhar nor Peter Brench in *Tree of Knowledge* is in fact the narrator.) One of the great puzzles and glories of the limited focus is the need for readers to be actively engaged in weighing the evidence presented, involving them deeply in the story, even, you might say, in participating in the making of the story out of the history.

When the focus is limited, whether to a first-person narrator or to a centered consciousness, it is tied to that individual. When he or she leaves the room, the camera must go too, and if we are to know what happens in the room when the focal character is gone, some means of bringing the information to that character must be devised, such as a letter or a report by another character. The camera may pull back out of the character's mind or even, as in *Owl Creek Bridge*, above and away from the character, but it does not generally jump around. An **unlimited focus** permits such freedom. In *The Short Happy Life of Francis Macomber* we enter the minds of each of the main characters periodically throughout the story. We get inside Margot Macomber's consciousness on the first page as she looks at Wilson and knows she hasn't seen him before, and on another page Macomber and Robert Wilson "both saw that she was going to cry. Wilson had seen it coming for a long time and he dreaded it. Macomber was past dreading it." Throughout, the story seems free to dip inside one consciousness or another, and can move with any of the characters. This unlimited, internal/external focus is called **omniscient**. Though the camera eye in *The Lottery* seems unlimited in that it can focus on one character or another and to some degree move in or out, we are never allowed to get into any character's mind; the focus is consistently external. It is almost as if we were standing back from the crowd watching and listening, or in an audience watching a play. That's why this focus is sometimes called **dramatic**.

There are no laws governing focus in fiction, but there is a general feeling that once a focus is chosen that ought to be the law for that story. Do you feel manipulated when the focus, which has been on Rainsford for the entire length of *The Most Dangerous Game*, shifts, very near the end, from him to the general, apparently just to heighten our suspense? Do you feel betrayed by the fact that we are not allowed to enter Margot Macomber's mind at one crucial moment, even though the focus has shifted freely at less crucial times?

Focus and voice often coincide. There is no discrepancy that I can see (or hear) between the viewing and the telling in *The Cask of*

Amontillado, for example. But wouldn't that always be true in first-person narration, where the "I" who sees is the same person as the "I" who tells the story? Not necessarily. Look at *The Summer My Grandmother Was Supposed to Die.* The "I" telling the story is older than the "I" experiencing the events of the story. Notice how many phrases there are like "years later I was shown the telegram" and "In those days . . ." So, too, the language of the story is clearly not that of a young boy: "She arrived punctually at noon"; "I've been told that to study Talmud with him had been a rare pleasure"; "lots of slender volumes of sermons, chassidic tales, and rabbinical commentaries." Such expressions may deal with incidents and information within the boy's perception, but the language in which they are expressed is clearly beyond him.

The voice in *Owl Creek Bridge,* like the focus, at the beginning of the story is not centered in Peyton Farquhar, but even when the focus narrows on him the voice telling the story is not his; note, for example, "As these thoughts, *which have here to be set down in words,* were flashed into the doomed man's brain" (emphasis added). The discrepancy may prepare a careful reader for later developments in the story.

At times, too, the voice may help to define the narration more fully and more precisely than can the position of the focus alone. The dispassionate narrator of *The Lottery* seems to know all about the history of the lottery and about most of the townspeople's feelings about it, but only from reports of what they said or from general knowledge. It is as if that narrator is a member of the community, an onlooker or participant somewhere in the crowd, where the focus of narration seems located. But the language of the narration, though simple and direct, is not so provincial and colloquial as the language we hear about us in the dialogue. The voice seems that of an educated outsider, present today in the crowd perhaps, but coolly observing the villagers, almost as if they were specimens.

I have used the common term **narrator** in the usual way—to mean the person who tells the story. You will have noticed that often the narrator really is a person in the story, like Muttel, the narrator in *The Summer My Grandmother Was Supposed to Die.* But how about the narrator in *Owl Creek Bridge* or in *Macomber?* Who is it who sets down Farquhar's words and can say things like this: "Death is a dignitary who when he comes announced is to be received with formal manifestations of respect, even by those most familiar with him. In the code of military etiquette silence and fixity are forms of deference." Where is he or she standing? What kind of person is this narrator? It seems even more difficult to imagine or identify than the voice of *The Lottery.* In such cases we tend to identify the narrator with the author; we call the narrator of this story "Bierce," of *Macomber* "Hemingway." This is not necessarily wrong, but it can be misleading. We can dig up a few facts about the author's life and read them into the story, or, worse, read the character or detail of the story into the author's life. It is more prudent, therefore, especially on the basis of a single story, not to speak of the author but of the author's

persona, the voice or figure of the author who tells and structures the story, who may or may not resemble in nature or values the actual person of the author. Mary Ann Evans wrote novels under the name of George Eliot; the first-person narrator speaks of "himself." That male narrator may be a good example of the persona or representative that most authors construct to "write" their stories.

We say *write* the stories. The narrator of *Owl Creek Bridge* has to "set down in words" what Farquhar is thinking. But, just as poets write of singing their songs (poems), so we often speak of telling a story, and we speak of a narrator, which means a teller (and we say we speak when we are writing). There are stories, usually with first-person narrators, that make much of the convention of oral story-telling: *My Man Bovanne,* for example, or Faulkner's *Spotted Horses.* Often these stories not only have an "oral" taleteller but imply a certain audience. Sometimes, as in Mark Twain's *Celebrated Jumping Frog,* there is a narrator who tells the story within the story to some-one else who retells it or writes it down, and the nature and re-sponse of this auditor can be a significant part of the meaning and effect of the story.

To see how focus and voice structure history into story, you might want to try rewriting *The Lottery* with the same focus but with a dif-ferent voice (perhaps that of one of the villagers), or *Macomber* with any one character as the focus, or *The Summer My Grandmother Was Supposed to Die* with the focus and perhaps with the voice of Muttel's mother.

AMBROSE BIERCE

An Occurrence at Owl Creek Bridge

I

A man stood upon a railroad bridge in northern Alabama, looking down into the swift water twenty feet below. The man's hands were behind his back, the wrists bound with a cord. A rope closely encircled his neck. It was attached to a stout cross-timber above his head and the slack fell to the level of his knees. Some loose boards laid upon the sleepers[1] supporting the metals of the railway supplied a footing for him and his executioners—two private soldiers of the Federal army, directed by a sergeant who in civil life may have been a deputy sheriff. At a short remove upon the same temporary platform was an officer in the uniform of his rank, armed. He was a captain. A sentinel at each end of the bridge stood with his rifle in the position known as "support," that is to say, vertical in front of the left shoulder, the hammer resting on the forearm thrown straight across the chest—a for-

---

1. Crossties that support railroad track.

mal and unnatural position, enforcing an erect carriage of the body. It did not appear to be the duty of these two men to know what was occurring at the center of the bridge; they merely blockaded the two ends of the foot planking that traversed it.

Beyond one of the sentinels nobody was in sight; the railroad ran straight away into a forest for a hundred yards, then, curving, was lost to view. Doubtless there was an outpost farther along. The other bank of the stream was open ground—a gentle acclivity topped with a stockade of vertical tree trunks, loopholed for rifles, with a single embrasure through which protruded the muzzle of a brass cannon commanding the bridge. Midway of the slope between bridge and fort were the spectators—a single company of infantry in line, at "parade rest," the butts of the rifles on the ground, the barrels inclining slightly backward against the right shoulder, the hands crossed upon the stock. A lieutenant stood at the right of the line, the point of his sword upon the ground, his left hand resting upon his right. Excepting the group of four at the center of the bridge, not a man moved. The company faced the bridge, staring stonily, motionless. The sentinels, facing the banks of the stream, might have been statues to adorn the bridge. The captain stood with folded arms, silent, observing the work of his subordinates, but making no sign. Death is a dignitary who when he comes announced is to be received with formal manifestations of respect, even by those most familiar with him. In the code of military etiquette silence and fixity are forms of deference.

The man who was engaged in being hanged was apparently about thirty-five years of age. He was a civilian, if one might judge from his habit, which was that of a planter. His features were good—a straight nose, firm mouth, broad forehead, from which his long, dark hair was combed straight back, falling behind his ears to the collar of his well-fitting frock coat. He wore a mustache and pointed beard, but no whiskers; his eyes were large and dark gray, and had a kindly expression which one would hardly have expected in one whose neck was in the hemp. Evidently this was no vulgar assassin. The liberal military code makes provision for hanging many kinds of persons, and gentlemen are not excluded.

The preparations being complete, the two private soldiers stepped aside and each drew away the plank upon which he had been standing. The sergeant turned to the captain, saluted and placed himself immediately behind that officer, who in turn moved apart one pace. These movements left the condemned man and the sergeant standing on the two ends of the same plank, which spanned three of the crossties of the bridge. The end upon which the civilian stood almost, but not quite, reached a fourth. This plank had been held in place by the weight of the captain; it was now held by that of the sergeant. At a signal from the former the latter would step aside, the plank would tilt and the condemned man go down between two ties. The arrangement commended itself to his judgment as simple and effective. His face had not been covered nor his eyes bandaged. He looked a moment at his "unsteadfast footing," then let his gaze wander to the swirling water of the stream racing madly beneath his feet. A piece of dancing driftwood caught his attention and his eyes followed it down the current. How slowly it appeared to move! What a sluggish stream!

He closed his eyes in order to fix his last thoughts upon his wife and children. The water, touched to gold by the early sun, the brooding mists under the banks at some distance down the stream, the fort, the soldiers, the piece of drift—all had distracted him. And now he became conscious of a new disturbance. Striking through the thought of his dear ones was a sound which he could neither ignore nor understand, a sharp, distinct, metallic percussion like the stroke of a blacksmith's hammer upon the anvil; it had the same ringing quality. He wondered what it was, and whether immeasurably distant or near by—it seemed both. Its recurrence was regular, but as slow as the tolling of a death knell. He awaited each stroke with impatience and—he knew not why —apprehension. The intervals of silence grew progressively longer; the delays became maddening. With their greater infrequency the sounds increased in strength and sharpness. They hurt his ear like the thrust of a knife; he feared he would shriek. What he heard was the ticking of his watch.

He unclosed his eyes and saw again the water below him. "If I could free my hands," he thought, "I might throw off the noose and spring into the stream. By diving I could evade the bullets and, swimming vigorously, reach the bank, take to the woods and get away home. My home, thank God, is as yet outside their lines; my wife and little ones are still beyond the invader's farthest advance."

As these thoughts, which have here to be set down in words, were flashed into the doomed man's brain rather than evolved from it the captain nodded to the sergeant. The sergeant stepped aside.

II

Peyton Farquhar was a well-to-do planter, of an old and highly respected Alabama family. Being a slave owner and like other slave owners a politician he was naturally an original secessionist and ardently devoted to the Southern cause. Circumstances of an imperious nature, which it is unnecessary to relate here, had prevented him from taking service with the gallant army that had fought the disastrous campaigns ending with the fall of Corinth,[2] and he chafed under the inglorious restraint, longing for the release of his energies, the larger life of the soldier, the opportunity for distinction. That opportunity, he felt, would come, as it comes to all in war time. Meanwhile he did what he could. No service was too humble for him to perform in aid of the South, no adventure too perilous for him to undertake if consistent with the character of a civilian who was at heart a soldier, and who in good faith and without too much qualification assented to at least a part of the frankly villainous dictum that all is fair in love and war.

One evening while Farquhar and his wife were sitting on a rustic bench near the entrance to his grounds, a gray-clad soldier rode up to

2. Corinth, Mississippi, captured by General Grant in April 1862.

the gate and asked for a drink of water. Mrs. Farquhar was only too happy to serve him with her own white hands. While she was fetching the water her husband approached the dusty horseman and inquired eagerly for news from the front.

"The Yanks are repairing the railroads," said the man, "and are getting ready for another advance. They have reached the Owl Creek bridge, put it in order and built a stockade on the north bank. The commandant has issued an order, which is posted everywhere, declaring that any civilian caught interfering with the railroad, its bridges, tunnels or trains will be summarily hanged. I saw the order."

"How far is it to the Owl Creek bridge?" Farquhar asked.

"About thirty miles."

"Is there no force on this side the creek?"

"Only a picket post half a mile out, on the railroad, and a single sentinel at this end of the bridge."

"Suppose a man—a civilian and student of hanging—should elude the picket post and perhaps get the better of the sentinel," said Farquhar, smiling, "what could he accomplish?"

The soldier reflected. "I was there a month ago," he replied. "I observed that the flood of last winter had lodged a great quantity of driftwood against the wooden pier at this end of the bridge. It is now dry and would burn like tow."

The lady had now brought the water, which the soldier drank. He thanked her ceremoniously, bowed to her husband and rode away. An hour later, after nightfall, he repassed the plantation, going northward in the direction from which he had come. He was a Federal scout.

III

As Peyton Farquhar fell straight downward through the bridge he lost consciousness and was as one already dead. From this state he was awakened—ages later, it seemed to him—by the pain of a sharp pressure upon his throat, followed by a sense of suffocation. Keen, poignant agonies seemed to shoot from his neck downward through every fiber of his body and limbs. These pains appeared to flash along well-defined lines of ramification and to beat with an inconceivably rapid periodicity. They seemed like streams of pulsating fire heating him to an intolerable temperature. As to his head, he was conscious of nothing but a feeling of fulness—of congestion. These sensations were unaccompanied by thought. The intellectual part of his nature was already effaced; he had power only to feel, and feeling was torment. He was conscious of motion. Encompassed in a luminous cloud, of which he was now merely the fiery heart, without material substance, he swung through unthinkable arcs of oscillation, like a vast pendulum. Then all at once, with terrible suddenness, the light about him shot upward with the noise of a loud plash; a frightful roaring was in his ears, and all was cold and dark. The power of thought was restored; he knew that the rope had broken and he had fallen into the stream. There was no additional strangulation; the noose about his neck was already suffocating him and kept the water from his lungs.

To die of hanging at the bottom of a river!—the idea seemed to him ludicrous. He opened his eyes in the darkness and saw above him a gleam of light, but how distant, how inaccessible! He was still sinking, for the light became fainter and fainter until it was a mere glimmer. Then it began to grow and brighten, and he knew that he was rising toward the surface—knew it with reluctance, for he was now very comfortable. "To be hanged and drowned," he thought, "that is not so bad; but I do not wish to be shot. No; I will not be shot; that is not fair."

He was not conscious of an effort, but a sharp pain in his wrist appraised him that he was trying to free his hands. He gave the struggle his attention, as an idler might observe the feat of a juggler, without interest in the outcome. What splendid effort!—what magnificent, what superhuman strength! Ah, that was a fine endeavor! Bravo! The cord fell away; his arms parted and floated upward, the hands dimly seen on each side in the growing light. He watched them with a new interest as first one and then the other pounced upon the noose at his neck. They tore it away and thrust it fiercely aside, its undulations resembling those of a water snake. "Put it back, put it back!" He thought he shouted these words to his hands, for the undoing of the noose had been succeeded by the direct pang that he had yet experienced. His neck ached horribly; his brain was on fire; his heart, which had been fluttering faintly, gave a great leap, trying to force itself out at his mouth. His whole body was racked and wrenched with an insupportable anguish! But his disobedient hands gave no heed to the command. They beat the water vigorously with quick, downward strokes, forcing him to the surface. He felt his head emerge; his eyes were blinded by the sunlight; his chest expanded convulsively, and with a supreme and crowning agony his lungs engulfed a great draught of air, which instantly he expelled in a shriek!

He was now in full possession of his physical senses. They were, indeed, preternaturally keen and alert. Something in the awful disturbance of his organic system had so exalted and refined them that they made record of things never before perceived. He felt the ripples upon his face and heard their separate sounds as they struck. He looked at the forest on the bank of the stream, saw the individual trees, the leaves and the veining of each leaf—saw the very insects upon them: the locusts, the brilliant-bodied flies, the gray spiders stretching their webs from twig to twig. He noted the prismatic colors in all the dewdrops upon a million blades of grass. The humming of the gnats that danced above the eddies of the stream, the beating of the dragonflies' wings, the strokes of the waterspiders' legs, like oars which had lifted their boat—all these made audible music. A fish slid along beneath his eyes and he heard the rush of its body parting the water.

He had come to the surface facing down the stream; in a moment the visible world seemed to wheel slowly round, himself the pivotal point, and he saw the bridge, the fort, the soldiers upon the bridge, the captain, the sergeant, the two privates, his executioners. They were in silhouette against the blue sky. They shouted and gesticulated, pointing at him. The captain had drawn his pistol, but did not fire; the others were unarmed. Their movements were grotesque and horrible, their forms gigantic.

Suddenly he heard a sharp report and something struck the water smartly within a few inches of his head, spattering his face with spray. He heard a second report, and saw one of the sentinels with his rifle at his shoulder, a light cloud of blue smoke rising from the muzzle. The man in the water saw the eye of the man on the bridge gazing into his own through the sights of the rifle. He observed that it was a gray eye and remembered having read that gray eyes were keenest, and that all famous marksmen had them. Nevertheless, this one had missed.

A counter-swirl had caught Farquhar and turned him half round; he was again looking into the forest on the bank opposite the fort. The sound of a clear, high voice in a monotonous singsong now rang out behind him and came across the water with a distinctness that pierced and subdued all other sounds, even the beating of the ripples in his ears. Although no soldier, he had frequented camps enough to know the dread significance of that deliberate, drawling, aspirated chant; the lieutenant on shore was taking a part in the morning's work. How coldly and pitilessly—with what an even, calm intonation, presaging, and enforcing tranquility in the men—with what accurately measured intervals fell those cruel words:

"Attention, company! . . . Shoulder arms! . . . Ready! . . . Aim! . . . Fire!"

Farquhar dived—dived as deeply as he could. The water roared in his ears like the voice of Niagara, yet he heard the dulled thunder of the volley and, rising again toward the surface, met shining bits of metal, singularly flattened, oscillating slowly downward. Some of them touched him on the face and hands, then fell away, continuing their descent. One lodged between his collar and neck; it was uncomfortably warm and he snatched it out.

As he rose to the surface, gasping for breath, he saw that he had been a long time under water; he was perceptibly farther downstream —nearer to safety. The soldiers had almost finished reloading; the metal ramrods flashed all at once in the sunshine as they were drawn from the barrels, turned in the air, and thrust into their sockets. The two sentinels fired again, independently and ineffectually.

The hunted man saw all this over his shoulder; he was now swimming vigorously with the current. His brain was as energetic as his arms and legs; he thought with the rapidity of lightning.

"The officer," he reasoned, "will not make that martinet's error a second time. It is as easy to dodge a volley as a single shot. He has probably already given the command to fire at will. God help me, I cannot dodge them all!"

An appalling plash within two yards of him was followed by a loud, rushing sound, diminuendo, which seemed to travel back through the air to the fort and died in an explosion which stirred the very river to its deeps! A rising sheet of water curved over him, fell down upon him, blinded him, strangled him! The cannon had taken a hand in the game. As he shook his head free from the commotion of the smitten water he heard the deflected shot humming through the air ahead, and in an instant it was cracking and smashing the branches in the forest beyond.

"They will not do that again," he thought; "the next time they will use a charge of grape.[3] I must keep my eye upon the gun; the smoke will apprise me—the report arrives too late; it lags behind the missile. That is a good gun."

Suddenly he felt himself whirled round and round—spinning like a top. The water, the banks, the forests, the now distant bridge, fort and men—all were commingled and blurred. Objects were represented by their colors only; circular horizontal streaks of color—that was all he saw. He had been caught in a vortex and was being whirled on with a velocity of advance and gyration that made him giddy and sick. In a few moments he was flung upon the gravel at the foot of the left bank of the stream—the southern bank—and behind a projecting point which concealed him from his enemies. The sudden arrest of his motion, the abrasion of one of his hands on the gravel, restored him, and he wept with delight. He dug his fingers into the sand, threw it over himself in handfuls and audibly blessed it. It looked like diamonds, rubies, emeralds; he could think of nothing beautiful which it did not resemble. The trees upon the bank were giant garden plants; he noted a definite order in their arrangement, inhaled the fragrance of their blooms. A strange, roseate light shone through the spaces among their trunks and the wind made in their branches the music of aeolian harps. He had no wish to perfect his escape—was content to remain in that enchanting spot until retaken.

A whiz and rattle of grapeshot among the branches high above his head roused him from his dream. The baffled cannoneer had fired him a random farewell. He sprang to his feet, rushed up the sloping bank, and plunged into the forest.

All that day he traveled, laying his course by the rounding sun. The forest seemed interminable; nowhere did he discover a break in it, not even a woodman's road. He had not known that he lived in so wild a region. There was something uncanny in the revelation.

By nightfall he was fatigued, footsore, famishing. The thought of his wife and children urged him on. At last he found a road which led him in what he knew to be the right direction. It was as wide and straight as a city street, yet it seemed untraveled. No fields bordered it, no dwelling anywhere. Not so much as the barking of a dog suggested human habitation. The black bodies of the trees formed a straight wall on both sides, terminating on the horizon in a point, like a diagram in a lesson in perspective. Overhead, as he looked up through this rift in the wood, shone great golden stars looking unfamiliar and grouped in strange constellations. He was sure they were arranged in some order which had a secret and malign significance. The wood on either side was full of singular noises, among which—

---

3. Grapeshot, a cluster of small iron balls that scatter when fired from cannon.

once, twice, and again—he distinctly heard whispers in an unknown tongue.

His neck was in pain and lifting his hand to it he found it horribly swollen. He knew that it had a circle of black where the rope had bruised it. His eyes felt congested; he could no longer close them. His tongue was swollen with thirst; he relieved its fever by thrusting it forward from between his teeth into the cold air. How softly the turf had carpeted the untraveled avenue—he could no longer feel the roadway beneath his feet!

Doubtless, despite his suffering, he had fallen asleep while walking, for now he sees another scene—perhaps he has merely recovered from a delirium. He stands at the gate of his own home. All is as he left it, and all bright and beautiful in the morning sunshine. He must have traveled the entire night. As he pushes upon the gate and passes up the wide white walk, he sees a flutter of female garments; his wife, looking fresh and cool and sweet, steps down from the veranda to meet him. At the bottom of the steps she stands waiting, with a smile of ineffable joy, an attitude of matchless grace and dignity. Ah, how beautiful she is! He springs forward with extended arms. As he is about to clasp her he feels a stunning blow upon the back of the neck; a blinding white light blazes all about him with a sound like the shock of a cannon—then all is darkness and silence!

Peyton Farquhar was dead; his body, with a broken neck, swung gently from side to side beneath the timbers of the Owl Creek bridge.

1891

SHIRLEY JACKSON

The Lottery

The morning of June 27th was clear and sunny, with the fresh warmth of a full-summer day; the flowers were blossoming profusely and the grass was richly green. The people of the village began to gather in the square, between the post office and the bank, around ten o'clock; in some towns there were so many people that the lottery took two days and had to be started on June 26th, but in this village, where there were only about three hundred people, the whole lottery took less than two hours, so it could begin at ten o'clock in the morning and still be through in time to allow the villagers to get home for noon dinner.

The children assembled first, of course. School was recently over for the summer, and the feeling of liberty sat uneasily on most of them; they tended to gather together quietly for a while before they broke into boisterous play, and their talk was still of the classroom and the teacher, of books and reprimands. Bobby Martin had already stuffed his pockets full of stones, and the other boys soon followed his example, selecting the smoothest and roundest stones; Bobby and Harry Jones and Dickie Delacroix—the villagers pronounced this name "Dellacroy" —eventually made a great pile of stones in one corner of the square and guarded it against the raids of the other boys. The girls stood aside, talking among themselves, looking over their shoulders at the boys, and the very small children rolled in the dust or clung to the hands of their older brothers or sisters.

Soon the men began to gather, surveying their own children, speaking of planting and rain, tractors and taxes. They stood together, away from the pile of stones in the corner, and their jokes were quiet and they smiled rather than laughed. The women, wearing faded house dresses and sweaters, came shortly after their menfolk. They greeted one another and exchanged bits of gossip as they went to join their husbands. Soon the women, standing by their husbands, began to call to their children, and the chidren came reluctantly, having to be called four or five times. Bobby Martin ducked under his mother's grasping hand and ran, laughing, back to the pile of stones. His father spoke up sharply, and Bobby came quickly and took his place between his father and his oldest brother.

The lottery was conducted—as were the square dances, the teenage club, the Halloween program—by Mr. Summers, who had time and energy to devote to civic activities. He was a round-faced, jovial man and he ran the coal business, and people were sorry for him, because he had no children and his wife was a scold. When he arrived in the square, carrying the black wooden box, there was a murmur of conversation among the villagers, and he waved and called, "Little late today, folks." The postmaster, Mr. Graves, followed him, carrying a three-legged stool, and the stool was put in the center of the square and Mr. Summers set the black box down on it. The villagers kept their distance, leaving a space between themselves and the stool, and when Mr. Summers said, "Some of you fellows want to give me a hand?" there was a hesitation before two men, Mr. Martin and his oldest son, Baxter, came forward to hold the box steady on the stool while Mr. Summers stirred up the papers inside it.

The original paraphernalia for the lottery had been lost long ago, and the black box now resting on the stool had been put into use even before Old Man Warner, the oldest man in town, was born. Mr. Summers spoke frequently to the villagers about making a new box, but no one liked to upset even as much tradition as was represented by the black box. There was a story that the present box had been made with some pieces of the box that had preceded it, the one that had been constructed when the first people settled down to make a village here. Every year, after the lottery, Mr. Summers began talking again about a new box, but every year the subject was allowed to fade off without anything's being done. The black box grew shabbier each year; by now it was no longer completely black but splintered badly along one side to show the original wood color, and in some places faded or stained.

Mr. Martin and his oldest son, Baxter, held the black box securely on the stool until Mr. Summers had stirred the papers thoroughly with his hand. Because so much of the ritual had been forgotten or discarded, Mr. Summers had been successful in having slips of paper substituted for the chips of wood that had been used for generations. Chips of wood, Mr. Summers had argued, had been all very well when the village was tiny, but now that the population was more than three hundred and likely to keep on growing, it was necessary to use something that would fit more easily into the black box. The night before the lottery, Mr. Summers and Mr. Graves made up the slips of paper and put them in the box, and it was then taken to the safe of Mr. Summers' coal company and locked up until Mr. Summers was ready to take it to the square next morning. The rest of the year, the box was put away, sometimes one place, sometimes another; it had spent one year in Mr. Graves's barn and another year underfoot in the post office, and sometimes it was set on a shelf in the Martin grocery and left there.

There was a great deal of fussing to be done before Mr. Summers declared the lottery open. There were the lists to make up—of heads of families, heads of households in each family, members of each household in each family. There was the proper swearing-in of Mr. Summers by the postmaster, as the official of the lottery; at one time, some people remembered, there had been a recital of some sort, performed by the official of the lottery, a perfunctory, tuneless chant that had been rattled off duly each year; some people believed that the official of the lottery used to stand just so when he said or sang it, others believed that he was supposed to walk among the people, but years and years ago this part of the ritual had been allowed to lapse. There had been, also, a ritual salute, which the official of the lottery had had to use in addressing each person who came up to draw from the box, but this also had changed with time, until now it was felt necessary only for the official to speak to each person approaching. Mr. Summers was very good at all this; in his clean white shirt and blue jeans, with one hand resting carelessly on the black box, he seemed very proper and important as he talked interminably to Mr. Graves and the Martins.

Just as Mr. Summers finally left off talking and turned to the assembled villagers, Mrs. Hutchinson came hurriedly along the path to the square, her sweater thrown over her shoulders, and slid into place in the back of the crowd. "Clean forgot what day it was," she said to Mrs. Delacroix, who stood next to her, and they both laughed softly. "Thought my old man was out back stacking wood," Mrs. Hutchinson went on, "and then I looked out the window and the kids was gone, and then I remembered it was the twenty-seventh and came a-running." She dried her hands on her apron, and Mrs. Delacroix said, "You're in time, though. They're still talking away up there."

Mrs. Hutchinson craned her neck to see through the crowd and found her husband and children standing near the front. She tapped Mrs. Delacroix on the arm as a farewell and began to make her way through the crowd. The people separated good-humoredly to let her through; two or three people said, in voices just loud enough to be heard across the crowd, "Here comes your Missus, Hutchinson," and "Bill, she made it after all." Mrs. Hutchinson reached her husband, and Mr. Summers, who had been waiting, said cheerfully, "Thought we were going to have to get on without you, Tessie." Mrs. Hutchinson said, grinning, "Wouldn't have me leave m'dishes in the sink, now, would you, Joe?," and soft laughter ran through the crowd as the people stirred back into position after Mrs. Hutchinson's arrival.

"Well, now," Mr. Summers said soberly, "guess we better get started, get this over with, so's we can go back to work. Anybody ain't here?"

"Dunbar," several people said. "Dunbar, Dunbar."

Mr. Summers consulted his list. "Clyde Dunbar," he said. "That's right. He's broke his leg, hasn't he? Who's drawing for him?"

"Me, I guess," a woman said, and Mr. Summers turned to look at her. "Wife draws for her husband," Mr. Summers said. "Don't you have a grown boy to do it for you, Janey?" Although Mr. Summers and everyone else in the village knew the answer perfectly well, it was the business of the official of the lottery to ask such questions formally. Mr. Summers waited with an expression of polite interest while Mrs. Dunbar answered.

"Horace's not but sixteen yet," Mrs. Dunbar said regretfully. "Guess I gotta fill in for the old man this year."

"Right," Mr. Summers said. He made a note on the list he was holding. Then he asked, "Watson boy drawing this year?"

A tall boy in the crowd raised his hand. "Here," he said. "I'm drawing for m'mother and me." He blinked his eyes nervously and ducked his head as several voices in the crowd said things like "Good fellow, Jack," and "Glad to see your mother's got a man to do it."

"Well," Mr. Summers said, "guess that's everyone. Old Man Warner make it?"

"Here," a voice said, and Mr. Summers nodded.

A sudden hush fell on the crowd as Mr. Summers cleared his throat and looked at the list. "All ready?" he called. "Now, I'll read the names —heads of families first—and the men come up and take a paper out of the box. Keep the paper folded in your hand without looking at it until everyone has had a turn. Everything clear?"

The people had done it so many times that they only half listened to the directions; most of them were quiet, wetting their lips, not looking around. Then Mr. Summers raised one hand high and said, "Adams." A man disengaged himself from the crowd and came forward. "Hi, Steve," Mr. Summers said, and Mr. Adams said, "Hi, Joe." They grinned at one another humorlessly and nervously. Then Mr. Adams reached into the black box and took out a folded paper. He held it firmly by one corner as he turned and went hastily back to his place in the crowd, where he stood a little apart from his family, not looking down at his hand.

"Allen," Mr. Summers said. "Anderson. . . . Bentham."

"Seems like there's no time at all between lotteries any more," Mrs. Delacroix said to Mrs. Graves in the back row. "Seems like we got through with the last one only last week."

"Time sure goes fast," Mrs. Graves said.

"Clark. . . . Delacroix."

"There goes my old man," Mrs. Delacroix said. She held her breath while her husband went forward.

"Dunbar," Mr. Summers said, and Mrs. Dunbar went steadily to the box while one of the women said, "Go on, Janey," and another said, "There she goes."

"We're next," Mrs. Graves said. She watched while Mr. Graves came around from the side of the box, greeted Mr. Summers gravely, and selected a slip of paper from the box. By now, all through the crowd there were men holding the small folded papers in their large hands, turning them over and over nervously. Mrs. Dunbar and her two sons stood together, Mrs. Dunbar holding the slip of paper.

"Harburt. . . . Hutchinson."

"Get up there, Bill," Mrs. Hutchinson said, and the people near her laughed.

"Jones."

"They do say," Mr. Adams said to Old Man Warner, who stood next to him, "that over in the north village they're talking of giving up the lottery."

Old Man Warner snorted. "Pack of crazy fools," he said. "Listening to the young folks, nothing's good enough for *them*. Next thing you know, they'll be wanting to go back to living in caves, nobody work any more, live *that* way for a while. Used to be a saying about 'Lottery in June, corn be heavy soon.' First thing you know, we'd all be eating stewed chickweed and acorns. There's *always* been a lottery," he added petulantly. "Bad enough to see young Joe Summers up there joking with everybody."

"Some places have already quit lotteries," Mrs. Adams said.

"Nothing but trouble in *that*," Old Man Warner said stoutly. "Pack of young fools."

"Martin." And Bobby Martin watched his father go forward. "Overdyke. . . . Percy."

"I wish they'd hurry," Mrs. Dunbar said to her older son. "I wish they'd hurry."

"They're almost through," her son said.

"You get ready to run tell Dad," Mrs. Dunbar said.

Mr. Summers called his own name and then stepped forward precisely and selected a slip from the box. Then he called, "Warner."

"Seventy-seventh year I been in the lottery," Old Man Warner said as he went through the crowd. "Seventy-seventh time."

"Watson." The tall boy came awkwardly through the crowd. Someone said, "Don't be nervous, Jack," and Mr. Summers said, "Take your time, son."

"Zanini."

After that, there was a long pause, a breathless pause, until Mr. Summers, holding his slip of paper in the air, said, "All right, fellows." For a minute, no one moved, and then all the slips of paper were opened. Suddenly, all the women began to speak at once, saying, "Who is it?," "Who's got it?," "Is it the Dunbars?," "Is it the Watsons?" Then the voices began to say, "It's Hutchinson. It's Bill," "Bill Hutchinson's got it."

"Go tell your father," Mrs. Dunbar said to her older son.

People began to look around to see the Hutchinsons. Bill Hutchinson was standing quiet staring down at the paper in his hand. Suddenly, Tessie Hutchinson shouted to Mr. Summers, "You didn't give him time enough to take any paper he wanted. I saw you. It wasn't fair."

"Be a good sport, Tessie," Mrs. Delacroix called, and Mrs. Graves said, "All of us took the same chance."

"Shut up, Tessie," Bill Hutchinson said.

"Well, everyone," Mr. Summers said, "that was done pretty fast, and now we've got to be hurrying a little more to get done in time." He consulted his next list. "Bill," he said, "you draw for the Hutchinson family. You got any other households in the Hutchinsons?"

"There's Don and Eva," Mrs. Hutchinson yelled. "Make *them* take their chance!"

"Daughters draw with their husbands' families, Tessie," Mr. Summers said gently. "You know that as well as anyone else."

"It wasn't *fair*," Tessie said.

"I guess not, Joe," Bill Hutchinson said regretfully. "My daughter draws with her husband's family, that's only fair. And I've got no other family except the kids."

"Then, as far as drawing for families is concerned, it's you," Mr. Summers said in explanation, "and as far as drawing for households is concerned, that's you, too. Right?"

"Right," Bill Hutchinson said.

"How many kids, Bill?" Mr. Summers asked formally.

"Three," Bill Hutchinson said. "There's Bill, Jr., and Nancy, and little Dave. And Tessie and me."

"All right, then," Mr. Summers said. "Harry, you got their tickets back?"

Mr. Graves nodded and held up the slips of paper. "Put them in the box, then," Mr. Summers directed. "Take Bill's and put it in."

"I think we ought to start over," Mrs. Hutchinson said, as quietly as she could. "I tell you it wasn't *fair*. You didn't give him time enough to choose. *Every*body saw that."

Mr. Graves had selected the five slips and put them in the box, and he dropped all the papers but those onto the ground, where the breeze caught them and lifted them off.

"Listen, everybody," Mrs. Hutchinson was saying to the people around her.

"Ready, Bill?" Mr. Summers asked, and Bill Hutchinson, with one quick glance around at his wife and children, nodded.

"Remember," Mr. Summers said, "take the slips and keep them folded until each person has taken one. Harry, you help little Dave." Mr. Graves took the hand of the little boy, who came willingly with him up to the box. "Take a paper out of the box, Davy," Mr. Summers said. Davy put his hand into the box and laughed. "Take just *one* paper." Mr. Summers said. "Harry, you hold it for him." Mr. Graves took the child's hand and removed the folded paper from the tight fist and held it while little Dave stood next to him and looked up at him wonderingly.

"Nancy next," Mr. Summers said. Nancy was twelve, and her school friends breathed heavily as she went forward, switching her skirt, and took a slip daintily from the box. "Bill, Jr.," Mr. Summers said, and Billy, his face red and his feet over-large, nearly knocked the box over as he got a paper out. "Tessie," Mr. Summers said. She hesitated for a minute, looking around defiantly, and then set her lips and went up to the box. She snatched a paper out and held it behind her.

"Bill," Mr. Summers said, and Bill Hutchinson reached into the box and felt around, bringing his hand out at last with the slip of paper in it.

The crowd was quiet. A girl whispered, "I hope it's not Nancy," and the sound of the whisper reached the edges of the crowd.

"It's not the way it used to be," Old Man Warner said clearly. "People ain't the way they used to be."

"All right," Mr. Summers said. "Open the papers. Harry, you open little Dave's."

Mr. Graves opened the slip of paper and there was a general sigh through the crowd as he held it up and everyone could see that it was blank. Nancy and Bill, Jr., opened theirs at the same time, and both beamed and laughed, turning around to the crowd and holding their slips of paper above their heads.

"Tessie," Mr. Summers said. There was a pause, and then Mr. Summers looked at Bill Hutchinson, and Bill unfolded his paper and showed it. It was blank.

"It's Tessie," Mr. Summers said, and his voice was hushed. "Show us her paper, Bill."

Bill Hutchinson went over to his wife and forced the slip of paper out of her hand. It had a black spot on it, the black spot Mr. Summers had made the night before with the heavy pencil in the coal-company office. Bill Hutchinson held it up, and there was a stir in the crowd.

"All right, folks," Mr. Summers said. "Let's finish quickly."

Although the villagers had forgotten the ritual and lost the original black box, they still remembered to use stones. The pile of stones the boys had made earlier was ready; there were stones on the ground with the blowing scraps of paper that had come out of the box. Mrs. Delacroix selected a stone so large she had to pick it up with both hands and turned to Mrs. Dunbar. "Come on," she said. "Hurry up."

Mrs. Dunbar had small stones in both hands, and she said, gasping for breath, "I can't run at all. You'll have to go ahead and I'll catch up with you."

The children had stones already, and someone gave little Davy Hutchinson a few pebbles.

Tessie Hutchinson was in the center of a cleared space by now, and she held her hands out desperately as the villagers moved in on her. "It isn't fair," she said. A stone hit her on the side of the head.

Old Man Warner was saying, "Come on, come on, everyone." Steve Adams was in the front of the crowd of villagers, with Mrs. Graves beside him.

"It isn't fair, it isn't right," Mrs. Hutchinson screamed, and then they were upon her.

1948

MORDECAI RICHLER

The Summer My Grandmother Was Supposed to Die

Dr. Katzman discovered the gangrene on one of his monthly visits. "She won't last a month," he said.

He repeated that the second month, the third, and the fourth, and now she lay dying in the heat of the back bedroom.

"If only she'd die," my mother said. "Oh, God, why doesn't she die? God in heaven, what's she holding on for?"

The summer my grandmother was supposed to die we did not chip in with the Breenbaums to take a cottage in the Laurentians.[1] It wouldn't have been practical. The old lady couldn't be moved, the nurse came daily and the doctor twice a week, and so it seemed best to stay in the city and wait for her to die or, as my mother said, pass away. It was a hot summer, her bedroom was just behind the kitchen, and when we sat down to eat we could smell her. The dressings on my grandmother's left leg had to be changed several times a day and, according to Dr. Katzman, her condition was hopeless. "It's in the hands of the Almighty," he said.

"It won't be long now," my father said, "and she'll be better off, if you know what I mean."

"Please," my mother said.

A nurse came every day from the Royal Victorian Order.[2] She arrived punctually at noon and at five to twelve I'd join the rest of the boys under the outside staircase to look up her dress as she climbed to our second-story flat. Miss Monohan favored lacy pink panties and that was better than waiting under the stairs for Cousin Bessie, for instance. She wore enormous cotton bloomers, rain or shine.

I was sent out to play as often as possible, because my mother felt it was not good for me to see somebody dying. Usually I'd just roam the scorched streets shooting the breeze. There was Arty, Gas sometimes, Hershey, Stan, and me. We talked about everything from A to Z.

"Why is it," Arty wanted to know, "that Tarzan never shits?"

"Dick Tracy too."

"Or Wonder Woman."

"She's a dame."

"So?"

"Jees, wouldn't it be something if Superman crapped in the sky? He could just be flying over Waverly Street when, whamo, Mr. Rabinovitch catches it right in the kisser."

Mr. Rabinovitch was our Hebrew teacher.

"But there's Tarzan," Arty insisted, "in the jungle, week in and week out, and never once does he need to go to the toilet. It's not real, that's all."

Arty told me, "Before your grandma dies she's going to roll her eyes and gurgle. That's what they call the death-rattle."

"Aw, you know everything. Big shot."

"I *read* it, you jerk," Arty said, whacking me one, "in Perry Mason."

Home again I'd find my mother weeping.

"She's dying by inches," she said to my father one stifling night, "and none of them even come to see her. Oh, such children! They should only rot in hell."

"They're not behaving right. It's certainly not according to Hoyle," my father said.

"When I think of all the money and effort that went into making

1. Mountains in eastern Canada between Hudson Bay and the St. Lawrence River.   2. The Victorian Order of Nurses for Canada.

a rabbi out of Israel—the way Mother doted on him—and for what?
Oh, what's the world coming to? God."

"It's not right."

Dr. Kaztman was amazed. "I never believed she'd last this long.
Really, it must be will-power alone that keeps her going. And your
excellent care."

"I want her to die, Doctor. That's not my mother in the back room.
It's an animal. I want her to please please die."

"Hush. You don't mean it. You're tired." And Dr. Katzman gave my
father some pills for my mother to take. "A remarkable woman," he
said. "A born nurse."

At night in bed my brother Harvey and I used to talk about our
grandmother. "After she dies," I said, "her hair will go on growing
for another twenty-four hours."

"Sez who?"

"Arty. It's a scientific fact. Do you think Uncle Lou will come from
New York for the funeral?"

"Sure."

"Boy, that means another fiver for me. You too."

"You shouldn't say things like that, kiddo, or *her ghost will come
back to haunt you.*"

"Well," I said, "I'll be able to go to her funeral, anyway. I'm not
too young any more."

I was only six years old when my grandfather died, and I wasn't
allowed to go to his funeral.

I have only one memory of my grandfather. Once he called me into
his study, set me down on his lap, and made a drawing of a horse for
me. On the horse he drew a rider. While I watched and giggled he
gave the rider a beard and the round fur-trimmed cap of a rabbi.

My grandfather was a Zaddik,[3] one of the Righteous, and I've been
told that to study Talmud with him had been a rare pleasure. I wasn't
allowed to go to his funeral, but years after I was shown the telegram
of condolence that had come from Eire and Poland and Israel and
even Japan. My grandfather had written many books: a translation
of the Zohar[4] into modern Hebrew—some twenty years' work—and lots
of slender volumes of sermons, chassidic tales, and rabbinical commentaries. His books had been published in Warsaw and later in New
York. He had been famous.

"At the funeral," my mother told me, "they had to have six motorcycle policemen to control the crowds. It was such a heat that twelve
women fainted—and I'm *not* counting Mrs. Waxman from upstairs.
With her, you know, *anything* to fall into a man's arms. Even Pinsky's.
And did I tell you that there was even a French-Canadian priest
there?"

"No kidding?"

"The priest was a real big *knacker.*[5] A bishop maybe. He used to
study with the *zeyda.*[6] The *zeyda* was some personality, you know.

---

3. "Righteous man" in Hebrew.
4. "The Book of Splendor," the central
part of the Kabbalah, the esoteric teach-
ings of Judaism and the source of Jewish

mysticism.
5. Big shot.
6. Grandfather.

Spiritual and wordly-wise at the same time. Such personalities they don't make any more. Today, rabbis and peanuts are the same size."

But, according to my father, the *zeyda* (his father-in-law) hadn't been as famous as all that. "There are things I could say," he told me. "There was another side to him."

My grandfather had come from generations and generations of rabbis, his youngest son was a rabbi, but none of his grandchildren would be one. My brother Harvey was going to be a dentist and at the time, 1937, I was interested in flying and my cousin Jerry was already a communist. I once heard Jerry say, "Our grandpappy wasn't all he was cracked up to be." When the men at the kosher bakeries went out on strike he spoke up against them on the streets where they were picketing and in the *shule*.[7] It was of no consequence to him that they were grossly underpaid. His superstitious followers had to have bread. "Grandpappy," Jerry said, "was a prize reactionary."

A week after my grandfather died my grandmother suffered a stroke. Her right side was completely paralyzed. She couldn't speak. At first, it's true, my grandmother could say a few words and move her right hand enough to write her name in Hebrew. Her name was Malka. But her condition soon began to deteriorate.

My grandmother had six children and seven stepchildren, for my grandfather had been married before. His first wife had died in the old country. Two years later he had married my grandmother, the only daughter of the richest man in the village, and their marriage had been a singularly happy one. My grandmother had been a beautiful girl. She had also been a wise, resourceful, and patient wife. Qualities, I fear, indispensable to life with a Zaddik. For the synagogue had paid my grandfather no stipulated salary and much of the money he had picked up here and there he had habitually distributed among rabbinical students, needy immigrants, and widows. A vice, and such it was to his hard-pressed family, which made him as unreliable a provider as a drunkard. And indeed, to carry the analogy further, my grandmother had had to make many hurried trips to the pawnbroker with her jewelry. Not all of it had been redeemed, either. But her children had been looked after. The youngest, her favorite, was a rabbi in Boston, the eldest was the actor-manager of a Yiddish theater in New York, and another was a lawyer. One daughter lived in Toronto, two in Montreal. My mother was the youngest daughter, and when my grandmother had her stroke there was a family meeting and it was decided that my mother would take care of her. This was my father's fault. All the other husbands spoke up—they protested their wives had too much work, they could never manage it—but my father detested quarrels, and he was silent. So my grandmother came to stay with us.

Her bedroom, the back bedroom, had actually been promised to me for my seventh birthday. But all that was forgotten now, and I had to go on sharing a bedroom with my brother Harvey. So naturally I was resentful when each morning before I left for school my mother said, "Go in and kiss the *baba*[8] good-bye."

All the same I'd go into the bedroom and kiss my grandmother hastily. She'd say "Bouyo-bouyo," for that was the only sound she could make. And after school it was, "Go in and tell the *baba* you're home."

"I'm home, *baba*."

"Bouyo-bouyo."

During those first hopeful months—"Twenty years ago who would have thought there'd be a cure for diabetes?" my father asked; "where there's life there's hope, you know"—she'd smile at me and try to speak, her eyes charged with effort. And even later there were times when she pressed my head urgently to her bosom with her surprisingly strong left arm. But as her illness dragged on and on and she became a condition in the house, something beyond hope or reproach, like the leaky icebox, there was less recognition and more ritual in those kisses. I came to dread her room. A clutter of sticky medicine bottles and the cracked toilet chair beside the bed; glazed but imploring eyes and a feeble smile, the wet slap of her lips against my cheeks. I flinched from her touch. After two years of it I protested to my mother. "Look, what's the use of telling her I'm going or I'm here. She doesn't even recognize me any more."

"Don't be fresh. She's your grandmother."

My uncle who was in the theater in New York sent money regularly to help support my grandmother and, for the first few months, so did the other children. But once the initial and sustaining excitement had passed and it became likely that my grandmother might linger in her invalid condition for two or maybe even three more years, the checks began to drop off, and the children seldom came to our house any more. Anxious weekly visits—"and how is she today, poor lamb?"—quickly dwindled to a dutiful monthly looking in, then a semi-annual visit, and these always on the way to somewhere.

"The way they act," my father said, "you'd think that if they stayed long enough to take off their coats we'd make them take the *baba* home with them."

When the children did come to visit, my mother made it difficult for them.

"It's killing me," she said. "I have to lift her onto that chair three times a day maybe. Have you any idea how heavy she is? And what makes you think I always catch her in time? Sometimes I have to change her bed twice a day. That's a job I'd like to see your wife do," she said to my uncle, the rabbi.

"We could send her to the Old People's Home," the rabbi said.

"Now there's an idea," my father said.

But my mother began to sob. "Not as long as I'm alive," she said. And she gave my father a stony look. "Say something."

"It wouldn't be according to Hoyle."

"You want to be able to complain to everybody in town about all the other children," the rabbi said. "You've got a martyr complex."

"Everybody has a point of view, you know. You know what I mean?" my father said. "So what's the use of fighting?"

Meanwhile, Dr. Katzman came once a month to examine my grandmother. "It's remarkable, astonishing," he'd say each time. "She's as strong as a horse."

"Some life for a person," my father said. "She can't speak—she doesn't recognize anybody—what is there for her?"

The doctor was a cultivated man; he spoke often for women's clubs, sometimes on Yiddish literature and other times, his rubicund face hot with impatience, the voice taking on a doomsday tone, on the cancer threat.

"Who are we to judge?" he asked.

Every evening, during the first months of my grandmother's illness, my mother read her a story by Sholem Aleichem.[9] "Tonight she smiled," my mother would say. "She understood. I can tell." And my father, my brother, and I would not comment. Once a week my mother used to give the old lady a manicure. Sunny afternoons she'd lift her into a wheelchair and put her out in the sun. Somebody always had to stay in the house in case my grandmother called. Often, during the night, she would begin to wail unaccountably, and my mother would get up and rock the old lady in her arms for hours. But in the fourth year of my grandmother's illness the strain and fatigue began to tell on my mother. Besides looking after my grandmother—"and believe you me," the doctor assured her with a clap on the back, "it would be a full-time job for a professional nurse"—she had to keep house for a husband and two sons. She began to quarrel with my father and she became sharp with Harvey and me. My father started to spend his evenings playing pinochle at Tansky's Cigar & Soda. Weekends he took Harvey and me to visit his brothers and sisters. And everywhere he went people had little bits of advice for him.

"Sam, you might as well be a bachelor. You're just going to have to put your foot down for once."

"Yeah, in your face maybe."

My cousin Libby, who was at McGill,[1] said, "This could have a very damaging effect on the development of your boys. These are their formative years, Uncle Samuel, and the omnipresence of death in the house . . ."

"What you need," my father said, "is a boy friend. *And how.*"

At Tansky's Cigar & Soda it was, "Come clean, Sam. It's no hardship. If I know you, the old lady's got a big insurance policy and when the time comes . . ."

My mother lost lots of weight. After dinner she'd fall asleep in her chair in the middle of Lux Radio Theater.[2] One minute she'd be sewing a patch on my breeches or be making a list of girls to call for a bingo party (proceeds for the Talmud Torah),[3] and the next she'd be snoring. Then, one morning, she just couldn't get out of bed, and Dr. Katzman came round a week before his regular visit. "Well, well, this won't do, will it?" He sat in the kitchen with my father and the two men drank apricot brandy out of small glasses.

"Your wife is a remarkable woman," Dr. Katzman said.

9. "Peace be with you," pen name of Yiddish author and humorist Shalom Rabinovitz (1859–1916).
1. University in Montreal.
2. Radio weekly drama sponsored by Lux soap.
3. Orthodox Jewish school for boys.

"You don't say?"

"She's got a gallstone condition."

My father shrugged. "Have another one for the road," he said.

"Thank you, but I have several more calls to make." Dr. Katzman rose, sighing. "There she lies in that back room, poor old woman," he said, "hanging desperately onto life. There's food for thought there."

My grandmother's children met again, and the five of them sat around my mother's bed embarrassed, irritated, and quick to take insult. All except my uncle who was in the theater. He sucked a cigar and drank whisky. He teased my mother, the rabbi, and my aunts, and if not for him I think they would have been at each other's throats. It was decided, over my mother's protests, to send my grandmother to the Old People's Home on Esplanade Street. An ambulance came to take my grandmother away and Dr. Katzman said, "It's for the best." But my father had been in the back bedroom when the old lady had held on tenaciously to the bedpost, not wanting to be moved by the two men in white—"Easy does it, granny," the younger one had said—and afterwards he could not go in to see my mother. He went out for a walk.

"She looked at me with such a funny expression," he told my brother. "Is it my fault?"

My mother stayed in bed for another two weeks. My father cooked for us and we hired a woman to do the housework. My mother put on weight quickly, her cheeks regained their normal pinkish hue and, for the first time in months, she actually joked with Harvey and me. She became increasingly curious about our schools and whether or not we shined our shoes regularly. She began to cook again, special dishes for my father, and she resumed old friendships with women on the parochial school board. The change reflected on my father. Not only did his temper improve, but he stopped going to Tansky's every other night, and began to come home early from work. Life at home had never been so rich. But my grandmother's name was never mentioned. The back bedroom remained empty and I continued to share a room with Harvey. I couldn't see the point and so one evening I said, "Look, why don't I move into the back bedroom?"

My father glared at me across the table.

"But it's empty like."

My mother left the table. And the next afternoon she put on her best dress and coat and new spring hat.

"Where are you going?" my father asked.

"To see my mother."

"Don't go looking for trouble."

"It's been a month. Maybe they're not treating her right."

"They're experts."

"Did you think I was never going to visit her? I'm not inhuman, you know."

"All right, go," he said.

But after she'd gone my father went to the window and said, "Son-of-a-bitch."

Harvey and I sat outside on the steps watching the cars go by. My father sat on the balcony above, cracking peanuts. It was six o'clock, maybe later, when the ambulance turned the corner, slowed down, and parked right in front of the house.

"Son-of-a-bitch," my father said. "I knew it."

My mother got out first, her eyes red and swollen, and hurried up-stairs to make my grandmother's bed.

"I'm sorry, Sam, I had to do it."

"You'll get sick again, that's what."

"You think she doesn't recognize people. From the moment she saw me she cried and cried. Oh, it was terrible."

"They're experts there. They know how to handle her better than you do."

"Experts? Expert murderers you mean. She's got bedsores, Sam. Those dirty little Irish nurses they don't change her linen often enough, they hate her. She must have lost twenty pounds there."

"Another month and you'll be flat on your back again."

"Sam, what could I do? Please Sam."

"She'll outlive all of us. Even Muttel.[4] I'm going out for a walk."

She was back and I was to blame.

My father became a regular at Tansky's Cigar & Soda again and every morning I had to go in and kiss my grandmother. She began to look like a man. Little hairs had sprouted on her chin, she had a spiky gray mustache and, of course, she was practically bald. This near-baldness, I guess, sprang from the fact that she had been shaving her head ever since she had married my grandfather the rabbi.[5] My grandmother had four different wigs, but she had not worn one since the first year of her illness. She wore a little pink cap instead. And so, as before, she said, "bouyo-bouyo," to everything.

Once more uncles and aunts sent five-dollar bills, though erratically, to help pay for my grandmother's support. Elderly people, former followers of my grandfather, came to inquire after the old lady's health. They sat in the back bedroom with her for hours, leaning on their canes, talking to themselves, rocking, always rocking to and fro. "The Holy Shakers," my father called them, and Harvey and I avoided them, because they always wanted to pinch our cheeks, give us a dash of snuff and laugh when we sneezed, or offer us a sticky old candy from a little brown bag with innumerable creases in it. When the visit was done the old people would unfailingly sit in the kitchen with my mother for another hour, watching her make lock-shen[6] or bake bread. My mother always served them lemon tea and they would talk about my grandfather, recalling his books, his sayings, and his charitable deeds.

And so another two years passed, with no significant change in my grandmother's condition. But fatigue, bad temper, and even morbid-ity enveloped my mother again. She fought with her brothers and sisters and once, when I stepped into the living room, I found her sitting with her head in her hands, and she looked up at me with such anguish that I was frightened.

4. The narrator's Yiddish name; could be the equivalent of Mordecai.
5. Married Orthodox Jewish women customarily either shave their heads or cover their hair.
6. Noodles.

"What did I do now?" I asked.

"If, God forbid, I had a stroke, would you send me to the Old People's Home?"

"Don't be a joke. Of course not."

"I hope that never in my life do I have to count on my children for anything."

The summer my grandmother was supposed to die, the seventh year of her illness, my brother took a job as a shipper and he kept me awake at night with stories about the factory. "What we do, see, is clear out the middle of a huge pile of lengths of material. That makes for a kind of secret cave. A hideout. Well, then you coax one of the *shiksas*[7] inside and hi-diddle-diddle."

One night Harvey waited until I had fallen asleep and then he wrapped himself in a white sheet, crept up to my bed, and shouted, "Bouyo-bouyo."

I hit him. He shouted.

"Children. Children, please," my mother called. "I must get some rest."

As my grandmother's condition worsened—from day to day we didn't know when she'd die—I was often sent out to eat at my aunt's or at my other grandmother's house. I was hardly ever at home. On Saturday mornings I'd get together with the other guys and we'd walk all the way past the mountain to Eaton's, which was our favorite department store for riding up and down escalators and stealing.

In those days they let boys into the left-field bleachers free during the week and we spent many an afternoon at the ball park. The Montreal Royals, part of the Dodger farm system, was some ball club too. There was Jackie Robinson and Roy Campanella, Honest John Gabbard, Chuck Connors, and Kermit Kitman was our hero. It used to kill us to see that crafty little hebe[8] running around there with all those tall dumb *goyim*.[9] "Hey, Kitman," we'd yell. "Hey, hey, sho-head,[1] if your father knew you played ball on *shabus*—"[2] Kitman, unfortunately, was all field and no hit. He never made the majors. "There goes Kermit Kitman," we'd yell, after he'd gone down swinging again, "the first Jewish strike-out king of the International League." This we usually followed up by bellowing some choice imprecations in Yiddish.

It was after one of these games, on a Friday afternoon, that I came home to find a small crowd gathered in front of the house.

"That's the grandson."

"Poor kid."

Old people stood silent and expressionless across the street staring at our front door. A taxi pulled up and my aunt hurried out, hiding her face in her hands.

"After so many years," somebody said.

7. Gentile girls.
8. Hebrew, Jew.
9. Gentiles.
1. Possibly *shorn-head* (?), referring to

short hair or crew cut of athlete, in contrast to traditional long locks of Orthodox Jews (?).
2. Sabbath.

"And probably next year they'll discover a cure. Isn't that *always* the case?"

I took the stairs two at a time. The flat was full. Uncles and aunts from my father's side of the family, odd old people, Dr. Katzman, Harvey, neighbors, were all standing around and talking in hushed voices in the living room. I found my father in the kitchen, getting out the apricot brandy. "Your grandmother's dead," he said.

"She didn't suffer," somebody said. "She passed away in her sleep."

"A merciful death."

"Where's Maw?"

"In the bedroom with . . . you'd better not go in," my father said.

"I want to see her."

My mother's face was long with grief. She wore a black shawl, and glared down at a knot of handkerchief clutched in a fist that had been cracked by washing soda. "Don't come in here," she said.

Several bearded, round-shouldered men in black shiny coats stood round the bed. I couldn't see my grandmother.

"Your grandmother's dead."

"Daddy told me."

"Go and wash your face and comb your hair. You'll have to get your own supper."

"O.K."

"One minute. The *baba* left some jewelry. The ring is for Harvey's wife and the necklace is for yours."

"Who's getting married?"

"Better go and wash your face. And remember behind the ears, Muttel."

Telegrams were sent, long-distance calls were made, and all through the evening relatives and neighbors came and went like swarms of fish when crumbs have been dropped into the water.

"When my father died," my mother said, "they had to have *six* motorcycle policemen to control the crowds. Twelve people fainted, such a heat . . ."

The man from the funeral parlor came.

"There goes the only Jewish businessman in town," my Uncle Harry said, "who wishes all his customers were Germans."

"This is no time for jokes."

"Listen, life goes on."

My cousin Jerry had begun to use a cigarette holder. "Everyone's going to be sickeningly sentimental," he said. "Soon the religious mumbo-jumbo starts. I can hardly wait."

Tomorrow was the Sabbath and so, according to the law, my grandmother couldn't be buried until Sunday. She would have to lie on the floor all night. Two old grizzly women in white came to move and wash the body and a professional mourner arrived to sit up and pray for her.

"I don't trust his face," my mother said. "He'll fall asleep. You watch him, Sam."

"A fat lot of good prayers will do her now."

"Will you just watch him, please."

"I'll watch him, I'll watch him." My father was livid about my

Uncle Harry. "The way he's gone after that apricot brandy you'd think that guy never saw a bottle in his life before."

Harvey and I were sent to bed, but we couldn't sleep. My aunt was sobbing over the body in the living room—"That dirty hypocrite," my mother said—there was the old man praying, coughing, and spitting into his handkerchief each time he woke; and hushed voices and whimpering from the kitchen, where my father and mother sat. Harvey was in a good mood, he let me have a few puffs of his cigarette.

"Well, kiddo, this is our last night together. Tomorrow you can take over the back bedroom."

"*Are you crazy?*"

"You always wanted it for yourself."

"She died in there, but. You think I'm going to sleep in there?"

"Good night. Happy dreams, kiddo."

"Hey, let's talk some more."

Harvey told me a ghost story. "Did you know that when they hang a man," he said, "the last thing that happens is that he has an orgasm?"

"A what?"

"Forget it. I forgot you were still in kindergarten."

"I know plenty. Don't worry."

"At the funeral they're going to open her coffin to throw dirt in her face. It's supposed to be earth from Eretz.[3] They open it and you're going to have to look." Harvey stood up on his bed, holding his hands over his head like claws. He made a hideous face. "Bouyo-bouyo. Who's that sleeping in my bed? Woo-woo."

My uncle who was in the theater, the rabbi, and my aunt from Toronto, all came to Montreal for the funeral. Dr. Katzman came too.

"As long as she was alive," my mother said, "he couldn't even send five dollars a month. Some son! What a rabbi! I don't want him in my house, Sam. I can't bear the sight of him."

"You don't mean a word of that and you know it," Dr. Katzman said.

"Maybe you'd better give her a sedative," the rabbi said.

"Sam. Sam, will you say something, please."

My father stepped up to the rabbi, his face flushed. "I'll tell you this straight to your face, Israel," he said. "You've gone down in my estimation."

"Really," the rabbi said, smiling a little.

My father's face burned a deeper red. "Year by year," he said, "your stock has gone down with me."

And my mother began to weep bitterly, helplessly, without control. She was led unwillingly to bed. While my father tried his best to comfort her, as he said consoling things, Dr. Katzman plunged a needle into her arm. "There we are," he said.

I went to sit in the sun on the outside stairs with Arty. "I'm going to the funeral," I said.

"I couldn't go anyway."

Arty was descended from the tribe of high priests and so was not

3. Eretz Yisrael, the Land of Israel.

allowed to be in the presence of a dead body. I was descended from the Yisroelis.[4]

"The lowest of the low," Arty said.

"Aw."

My uncle, the rabbi, and Dr. Katzman stepped into the sun to light cigarettes.

"It's remarkable that she held out for so long," Dr. Katzman said.

"Remarkable?" my uncle said. "It's written that if a man has been married twice he will spend as much time with his first wife in heaven as he did on earth. My father, may he rest in peace, was married to his first wife for seven years and my mother, may she rest in peace, has managed to keep alive for seven years. Today in heaven she will be able to join my father, may he rest in peace."

Dr. Katzman shook his head, he pursed his lips. "It's amazing," he said. "The mysteries of the human heart. Astonishing."

My father hurried outside. "Dr. Katzman, please. It's my wife. Maybe the injection wasn't strong enough? She just doesn't stop crying. It's like a tap. Could you come please?"

"Excuse me," Dr. Katzman said to my uncle.

"Of course."

My uncle approached Arty and me.

"Well, boys," he said, "what would you like to be when you grow up?"

1961

3   CHARACTERIZATION

In a good many stories we read we know very little about the narrator, who is a disembodied offstage voice, without an identity or a personal history, without influence on the action, without qualities other than those that a voice and style may suggest. So it is in most of the earlier stories in this volume—*The Most Dangerous Game, Macomber, Owl Creek Bridge,* and especially *The Lottery.* Poe's narrator, however, not only tells us the story but acts out the action; without him we not only would not know the story, there just would not be any. Richler's narrator looks back into his past; he is there in the story, speaking, listening, reacting—so he is, then, a **character.** Hazel, in *My Man Bovanne,* is both character and narrator. In fiction a character is simply someone who acts, appears, or is referred to in a work, so that narrators may or may not be characters.

The whole cast of characters is called the **dramatis personae** (literally, characters or actors of the drama). Most discussions of char-

4. The lowest of the three categories into which the Jewish people are tradition-   ally divided.

acter, however, concentrate on the narrator or on the main characters. The most common term for the character with the leading male role is **hero**, the "good guy" who opposes the **villain**, or "bad guy." The leading female character is the **heroine**. Heroes are usually larger than life, stronger, better than most human beings, almost godlike (and there's even a brand of heroes nowadays so close to being godlike that they are called superheroes). In most modern fiction, however, the leading character is much more ordinary, more like the rest of us, as is the father in Sherwood Anderson's *The Egg* or the grandfather in *The Artificial Nigger*, a story in the next chapter, or almost anyone played by Dustin Hoffman. Such a character is called the **antihero**, not because he opposes the hero but because he is not like a hero in stature or perfection. An older and more neutral term than *hero* for the leading character, a term that does not imply either the presence or absence of outstanding virtue (and with the added advantage of referring equally to male and female), is **protagonist**, whose opponent is not the villain but the **antagonist**. You might get into long and pointless arguments by calling Hazel, Raskolnikov in *Crime and Punishment*, or Bonnie's Clyde or Clyde's Bonnie a hero or heroine, so it can be useful to have the more neutral term 'protagonist.'

Because we see more of the major characters over a longer period of time, we learn more about them, and we think of them as more complex and frequently therefore more "realistic" than the minor characters. They can grow and change, as Macomber does, as the father does in *The Egg*, and as Judith does in Doris Lessing's *Our Friend Judith*; by the end of these stories all these have acted in a way not predictable from what we learned earlier in the story about their character and their past actions. Characters who can thus "surprise convincingly," an influential critic says, are **round characters**. Major or minor characters who have only a single trait (or very few traits), and who remain consistent throughout the story, are called **flat characters**. Perhaps the most famous and beloved flat characters are those of Dickens, but Poe's characters are rather flat, and those in *The Lottery* seem so too.

I mention the characters of Dickens to bring out the point that flat characters, though less complex than round characters, are not necessarily inferior artistically. You may recall admirably presented flat characterizations in other media: Shakespeare's Falstaff, Charlie Chaplin's Little Tramp, Little Orphan Annie, the "Jack Benny" portrayed by Jack Benny, Archie Bunker.

Nor are all notable flat characters comic. Dickens's Fagin (in *Oliver Twist*) and Scrooge (in *A Christmas Carol*) are memorable, flat, and unfunny. Nor are flat characters necessarily uninteresting psychological types. Doesn't Iago (in *Othello*) fit the description of a flat character? How does his characterization differ from that of Montresor? Are both flat? equally flat? well presented? equally well presented?

Descriptive terms like *flat* and *round* have a disconcerting way of magically turning into value judgments, a transformation we must constantly discourage. Such terms also seem magically to turn into pigeonholes, so I said that Poe's characters were only "rather" flat, and said that those in *The Lottery* "seem" to be flat. Like *hero*, *round* and *flat* are useful but not wholly precise terms: they designate extremes or tendencies, matters of degree. Still, it will surely sharpen our perception and deepen our understanding of stories to try to define just how much we know about someone like Wilson in *Macomber*, or Hazel, the delightful narrator of *Bovanne*, to what degree they can be summed up in a phrase or sentence, to what degree they are flat, round, or lumpy.

Though most of Dickens's flat characters are highly individualized, not to say unique, some, like Fagin, the avaricious Jewish moneylender, are **stereotypes**. Stereotypes are characters based on conscious or unconscious cultural assumptions that sex, age, ethnic or national identification, occupation, marital status, and so on are predictably accompanied by certain character traits, actions, even values.

The stereotype may be very useful in creating a round character, one who can surprise convincingly: Macomber is a spoiled, rich American; Judith, according to a Canadian woman, "one of your typical English spinsters." Both Macomber and Judith, however, act in ways that deny the limitations of the stereotype, which is, after all, only a quick—and somewhat superficial—form of classification, and classification is a common first step in definitions. One of the chief ways we have of describing or defining is by placing the thing to be defined in a category and then distinguishing it from the other members of that category. A good deal of **characterization**—the art, craft, method of presentation or even creation of fictional personages—involves a similar process. Characters are almost inevitably identified by category— by sex, age, nationality, occupation, etc. We soon learn that the father in *The Egg* is a male middle-aged American Midwestern farmer, that the narrator of *My Man Bovanne* is a middle-aged urban black woman, and, as we have seen, that Judith is an English spinster.

Not all generalizations involve cultural stereotypes, of course. Some may involve generalized character traits that the story or narrator defines for us (and that we must accept unless events in the story prove otherwise). The father in *The Egg* is said to have been "intended by nature to be a cheerful, kindly man" with "no notion of trying to rise in the world." Bovanne is said to be "just a nice old gent from the block," the kind of man whose conversation is "Comfy and cheery."

You may have noticed something that may seem odd at first: putting a character in more than one general group makes that character more of an individual. The category *middle-aged* includes the father in *The Egg*, the narrator of *Bovanne*, and Judith. That the first is male separates him from the other two; that Judith is British distinguishes her from the other two; that the narrator of *Bovanne* is black separates her from both the father and Judith, though she is American like the first and a woman like the second. So Hazel is to some degree particularized by being identified as a member of three general categories. Similarly, there are more cheerful men and there are more kindly men than there are men who are both cheerful and kindly, and there are still fewer men who are cheerful, kindly, and without ambition.

Physical characteristics also serve as categories. Bovanne is blind. Before we are introduced to him, we are told that blind people hum, and that a blind man called Shakey Bee hums. Only then are we told that there is a blind man named Bovanne who also has the habit of humming. As physical characteristics are multiplied, as with other categories, the result is more and more particularizing or individualizing. That the father in *The Egg* at forty-five is bald and "a little fat" narrows the category of middle-aged male only slightly, but that Judith is beautiful though a fortyish English spinster considerably narrows that category, and detailed physical description makes it possible to visualize her rather fully, almost to recognize her as an individual:

> Judith is tall, small-breasted, slender. Her light brown hair is parted in the center and cut straight around her neck. A high straight forehead, straight nose, a full grave mouth are setting for her eyes, which are green, large and prominent. Her lids are very white, fringed with gold, and molded close over the eyeball. . . .

There are many other ways in which a character is characterized and individualized besides stereotyping and "de-stereotyping," and besides classifying and particularizing by physical description. In most cases we see what characters do and hear what they say; we sometimes learn what they think, and what other people think or say about them; we often know what kind of clothes they wear, what and how much they own, treasure, or covet; we may be told about their childhood, parents, or some part or parts of their past. We learn a bit about Hazel, the narrator of *Bovanne*, from her age, sex, ethnic identification. We learn a great deal more from the way she talks to her children and they to her, from the fact that men call her "long distance and in the middle of the night for a little Mama comfort," the fact that she carried her baby daughter strapped to her chest until the baby was nearly two years old, and from her short, low-cut dress. We even know what she is thinking. We are not privileged to know what the father in *The Egg* thinks from moment to moment, though we are told his general motives, and we do learn how he acts, what others think of him, and, finally, how he feels. And we know more of his earlier life than we know of Hazel's.

No matter how many methods of characterization are employed, however, at some point the particularization of the individual stops. Few characters are described down to the ridges of their fingerprints. No matter how individualized the character may be, he or she remains a member of a number of groups, and we make certain assumptions about the character based on our fixed or stereotyped notions of the groups. To destroy a stereotype, a story must introduce a stereotype to destroy. And somehow the de-stereotyped character, no matter how particularized, remains to some degree representative. If Judith turns out to be not as prudish and prissy as the stereotype of the English spinster has led us to believe, we may well conclude that the stereotype is false and Judith is more representative of the real English spinster than the stereotype is. Indeed, this tendency to generalize from the particulars of a story extends beyond cultural groups sometimes to human character at large: if Francis Macomber can change his ways after years of habitual conduct, then human character, the story might seem to say, is not permanently fixed at birth, in infancy, childhood, ever. If decent and ordinary people like those in *The Lottery* can cast destructive stones, human beings may not be entirely good by nature.

One of the reasons it is so difficult to discuss characters is precisely because the principles of definition and evaluation of fictional characters (not of their characterization) are the same as those we use for real people, an area of violent controversy and confusion. The very term *character* itself, when it refers not to a fictional personage but to a combination of qualities in a human being, is somewhat ambiguous. It usually has moral overtones, often favorable (a man of character); it is sometimes neutral but evaluative (character reference). Judgment about character (not characterization, remember) usually involves moral terms like *good* and *bad* or *strong* and *weak*. *Personality* usually implies that which distinguishes or individualizes a person, and the judgment called for is not so much moral as social —*pleasing* or *displeasing*. An older term, *nature* (it is his nature to be so or do such), usually implies something inherent or inborn, something fixed and thus predictable. The **existential character** implies the opposite; that is, whatever our past, our conditioning, our pattern of previous behavior, we can, by an act of will, change all that right this minute, as Macomber does.

Fictional characters thus frequently seem to be part of the history that lies behind the story or beyond the story as part of our own world, to exist in a reality that is detachable from the words and events of the story in which they appear. We feel we might recognize Tom Jones, Jane Eyre, or Sherlock Holmes on the street, and we might be able to anticipate what they might say or do in *our* world, outside the story. Fictional characters are neither real nor detachable, of course, and they exist only in the words of the works in which they are presented. We must not forget the distinction between the character and the method by which he or she is presented, the characterization; so we must be careful to distinguish the good character, meaning someone whom, if real, we would consider virtuous, and the good characterization, meaning a fictional person who, no matter what his or her morality or behavior, is well presented.

To recognize that characters are not finally detachable, that they have roles, functions, limitations, and their very existence in the context of other elements in the story, and not to confuse them with real people, character with characterization, is not to say that we may not learn about real people from characters in fiction or learn to understand fictional characters in part from what we know about real people. Indeed, it may be worth paying particular attention to how stories create the images of people and what those images assume about human character precisely because this process and these assumptions are so similar to the way we get to know and understand real people. We may be able to enrich both our reading and our lives

SHERWOOD ANDERSON

The Egg

My father was, I am sure, intended by nature to be a cheerful, kindly man. Until he was thirty-four years old he worked as a farmhand for a man named Thomas Butterworth whose place lay near the town of Bidwell, Ohio. He had then a horse of his own, and on Saturday evenings drove into town to spend a few hours in social intercourse with other farmhands. In town he drank several glasses of beer and stood about in Ben Head's saloon—crowded on Saturday evenings with visiting farmhands. Songs were sung and glasses thumped on the bar. At ten o'clock father drove home along a lonely country road, made his horse comfortable for the night, and himself went to bed, quite happy in his position in life. He had at that time no notion of trying to rise in the world.

It was in the spring of his thirty-fifth year that father married my mother, then a country schoolteacher, and in the following spring I came wriggling and crying into the world. Something happened to the two people. They became ambitious. The American passion for getting up in the world took possession of them.

It may have been that mother was responsible. Being a schoolteacher she had no doubt read books and magazines. She had, I presume, read of how Garfield,[1] Lincoln, and other Americans rose from poverty to fame and greatness, and as I lay beside her—in the days of her lying-in —she may have dreamed that I would some day rule men and cities. At any rate she induced father to give up his place as a farmhand, sell his horse, and embark on an independent enterprise of his own. She was a tall silent woman with a long nose and troubled gray eyes. For herself she wanted nothing. For father and myself she was incurably ambitious.

The first venture into which the two people went turned out badly. They rented ten acres of poor stony land on Grigg's Road, eight miles from Bidwell, and launched into chicken-raising. I grew into boyhood on the place and got my first impression of life there. From the beginning they were impressions of disaster, and if, in my turn, I am a gloomy man inclined to see the darker side of life, I attribute it to the fact that what should have been for me the happy joyous days of childhood were spent on a chicken farm.

One unversed in such matters can have no notion of the many and tragic things that can happen to a chicken. It is born out of an egg, lives for a few weeks as a tiny fluffy thing such as you will see pictured on Easter cards, then becomes hideously naked, eats quantities of corn and meal bought by the sweat of your father's brow, gets diseases called pip, cholera, and other names, stands looking with stupid eyes at the sun, becomes sick and dies. A few hens and now and then a rooster, intended to serve God's mysterious ends, struggle through to

---

1. James Abram Garfield (1831–1881), twentieth President of the United States, was born on a frontier farm in Ohio, spent his early years in poverty, worked as farmer, canal boatman, carpenter, sent himself through Williams College, to become teacher, principal, Congressman, President; like Lincoln, he was assassinated.

maturity. The hens lay eggs out of which come other chickens and the dreadful cycle is thus made complete. It is all unbelievably complex. Most philosophers must have been raised on chicken farms. One hopes for so much from a chicken and is so dreadfully disillusioned. Small chickens, just setting out on the journey of life, look so bright and alert and they are in fact so dreadfully stupid. They are so much like people they mix one up in one's judgments of life. If disease does not kill them, they wait until your expectations are thoroughly aroused and then walk under the wheels of a wagon—to go squashed and dead back to their maker. Vermin infest their youth, and fortunes must be spent for curative powders. In later life I have seen how a literature has been built up on the subject of fortunes to be made out of the raising of chickens. It is intended to be read by the gods who have just eaten of the tree of the knowledge of good and evil.[2] It is a hopeful literature and declares that much may be done by simple ambitious people who own a few hens. Do not be led astray by it. It was not written for you. Go hunt for gold on the frozen hills of Alaska, put your faith in the honesty of a politician, believe if you will that the world is daily growing better and that good will triumph over evil, but do not read and believe the literature that is written concerning the hen. It was not written for you.

I, however, digress. My tale does not primarily concern itself with the hen. If correctly told it will center on the egg. For ten years my father and mother struggled to make our chicken farm pay and then they gave up that struggle and began another. They moved into the town of Bidwell, Ohio, and embarked in the restaurant business. After ten years of worry with incubators that did not hatch, and with tiny— and in their own way lovely—balls of fluff that passed on into semi-naked pullethood and from that into dead henhood, we threw all aside and, packing our belongings on a wagon, drove down Grigg's Road toward Bidwell, a tiny caravan of hope looking for a new place from which to start on our upward journey through life.

We must have been a sad-looking lot, not, I fancy, unlike refugees fleeing from a battlefield. Mother and I walked in the road. The wagon that contained our goods had been borrowed for the day from Mr. Albert Griggs, a neighbor. Out of its sides stuck the legs of cheap chairs, and at the back of the pile of beds, tables, and boxes filled with kitchen utensils was a crate of live chickens, and on top of that the baby carriage in which I had been wheeled about in my infancy. Why we stuck to the baby carriage I don't know. It was unlikely other children would be born and the wheels were broken. People who have few possessions cling tightly to those they have. That is one of the facts that make life so discouraging.

Father rode on top of the wagon. He was then a bald-headed man of forty-five, a little fat, and from long association with mother and the chickens he had become habitually silent and discouraged. All during our ten years on the chicken farm he had worked as a laborer on

2. See *Genesis* 2:9 and 3, esp. 3:22–23: "And the Lord God said, Behold, the man is become as one of us, to know good and evil; and now, lest he put forth his hand, and take also of the tree of life, and eat, and live for ever: / Therefore the Lord God sent him forth from the Garden of Eden, to till the ground from whence he was taken."

neighboring farms and most of the money he had earned had been spent for remedies to cure chicken diseases, on Wilmer's White Wonder Cholera Cure or Professor Bidlow's Egg Producer or some other preparations that mother found advertised in the poultry papers. There were two little patches of hair on father's head just above his ear. I remember that as a child I used to sit looking at him when he had gone to sleep in a chair before the stove on Sunday afternoons in the winter. I had at that time already begun to read books and have notions of my own, and the bald path that led over the top of his head was, I fancied, something like a broad road, such a road as Caesar might have made on which to lead his legions out of Rome and into the wonders of an unknown world. The tufts of hair that grew above father's ears were, I thought, like forests. I fell into a half-sleeping, half-waking state and dreamed I was a tiny thing going along the road into a far beautiful place where there were no chicken farms and where life was a happy eggless affair.

One might write a book concerning our flight from the chicken farm into town. Mother and I walked the entire eight miles—she to be sure that nothing fell from the wagon and I to see the wonders of the world. On the seat of the wagon beside father was his greatest treasure. I will tell you of that.

On a chicken farm, where hundreds and even thousands of chickens come out of eggs, surprising things sometimes happen. Grotesques are born out of eggs as out of people. The accident does not often occur— perhaps once in a thousand births. A chicken is, you see, born that has four legs, two pairs of wings, two heads, or what not. The things do not live. They go quickly back to the hand of their maker that has for a moment trembled. The fact that the poor little things could not live was one of the tragedies of life to father. He had some sort of notion that if he could but bring into henhood or roosterhood a five-legged hen or a two-headed rooster his fortune would be made. He dreamed of taking the wonder about the county fairs and of growing rich by exhibiting it to other farmhands.

At any rate, he saved all the little monstrous things that had been born on our chicken farm. They were preserved in alcohol and put each in its own glass bottle. These he had carefully put into a box, and on our journey into town it was carried on the wagon seat beside him. He drove the horses with one hand and with the other clung to the box. When we got to our destination, the box was taken down at once and the bottles removed. All during our days as keepers of a restaurant in the town of Bidwell, Ohio, the grotesques in their little glass bottles sat on a shelf back of the counter. Mother sometimes protested, but father was a rock on the subject of his treasure. The grotesques were, he declared, valuable. People, he said, liked to look at strange and wonderful things.

Did I say that we embarked in the restaurant business in the town of Bidwell, Ohio? I exaggerated a little. The town itself lay at the foot of a low hill and on the shore of a small river. The railroad did not run through the town and the station was a mile away to the north at a place called Pickleville. There had been a cider mill and pickle factory at the station, but before the time of our coming they had both gone out of business. In the morning and in the evening busses came down to the station along a road called Turner's Pike from the hotel on the main street of Bidwell. Our going to the out-of-the-way place to embark in the restaurant business was mother's idea. She talked of it for a year and then one day went off and rented an empty store building opposite the railroad station. It was her idea that the restaurant would be profitable. Traveling men, she said, would be always waiting around to take trains out of town and town people would come to the station to await incoming trains. They would come to the restaurant to buy pieces of pie and drink coffee. Now that I am older I know that she had another motive in going. She was ambitious for me. She wanted me to rise in the world, to get into a town school and become a man of the towns.

At Pickleville father and mother worked hard, as they always had done. At first there was the necessity of putting our place into shape to be a restaurant. That took a month. Father built a shelf on which he put tins of vegetables. He painted a sign on which he put his name in large red letters. Below his name was the sharp command—"EAT HERE"—that was so seldom obeyed. A showcase was bought and filled with cigars and tobacco. Mother scrubbed the floor and the walls of the room. I went to school in the town and was glad to be away from the farm, from the presence of the discouraged, sad-looking chickens. Still I was not very joyous. In the evening I walked home from school along Turner's Pike and remembered the children I had seen playing in the town schoolyard. A troop of little girls had gone hopping about and singing. I tried that. Down along the frozen road I went hopping solemnly on one leg. "Hippity Hop To The Barber Shop,"[3] I sang shrilly. Then I stopped and looked doubtfully about. I was afraid of being seen in my gay mood. It must have seemed to me that I was doing a thing that should not be done by one who, like myself, had been raised on a chicken farm where death was a daily visitor.

Mother decided that our restaurant should remain open at night. At ten in the evening a passenger train went north past our door followed by a local freight. The freight crew had switching to do in Pickleville, and when the work was done they came to our restaurant for hot coffee and food. Sometimes one of them ordered a fried egg. In the morning at four they returned north-bound and again visited us. A little trade began to grow up. Mother slept at night and during the day tended the restaurant and fed our boarders while father slept. He slept in the same bed mother had occupied during the night and I went off to the town of Bidwell and to school. During the long nights, while mother and I slept, father cooked meats that were to go into sandwiches for the lunch baskets of our boarders. Then an idea in regard to getting up in the world came into his head. The American spirit took hold of him. He also became ambitious.

In the long nights when there was little to do, father had time to think. That was his undoing. He decided that he had in the past been an unsuccessful man because he had not been cheerful enough and that in the future he would adopt a cheerful outlook on life. In the early morning he came upstairs and got into bed with mother. She woke and the two talked. From my bed in the corner I listened.

---

3. Children's song and dance: "Hippety hop to the barber shop to buy a stick of candy./ One for you, and one for me, and one for Sister Annie."

It was father's idea that both he and mother should try to entertain the people who came to eat at our restaurant. I cannot now remember his words, but he gave the impression of one about to become in some obscure way a kind of public entertainer. When people, particularly young people from the town of Bidwell, came into our place, as on very rare occasions they did, bright entertaining conversation was to be made. From father's words I gathered that something of the jolly inn-keeper effect was to be sought. Mother must have been doubtful from the first, but she said nothing discouraging. It was father's notion that a passion for the company of himself and mother would spring up in the breasts of the younger people of the town of Bidwell. In the evening bright happy groups would come singing down Turner's Pike. They would troop shouting with joy and laughter into our place. There would be song and festivity. I do not mean to give the impression that father spoke so elaborately of the matter. He was, as I have said, an uncommunicative man. "They want some place to go. I tell you they want some place to go," he said over and over. That was as far as he got. My own imagination has filled in the blanks.

For two or three weeks this notion of father's invaded our house. We did not talk much, but in our daily lives tried earnestly to make smiles take the place of glum looks. Mother smiled at the boarders and I, catching the infection, smiled at our cat. Father became a little fever-ish in his anxiety to please. There was, no doubt, lurking somewhere in him, a touch of the spirit of the showman. He did not waste much of his ammunition on the railroad men he served at night, but seemed to be waiting for a young man or woman from Bidwell to come in to show what he could do. On the counter in the restaurant there was a wire basket kept always filled with eggs, and it must have been before his eyes when the idea of being entertaining was born in his brain. There was something pre-natal about the way eggs kept themselves connected with the development of his idea. At any rate, an egg ruined his new impulse in life. Late one night I was awakened by a roar of anger coming from father's throat. Both mother and I sat upright in our beds. With trembling hands she lighted a lamp that stood on a table by her head. Downstairs the front door of our restaurant went shut with a bang and in a few minutes father tramped up the stairs. He held an egg in his hand and his hand trembled as though he were having a chill. There was a half-insane light in his eyes. As he stood glaring at us I was sure he intended throwing the egg at either mother or me. Then he laid it gently on the table beside the lamp and dropped on his knees beside mother's bed. He began to cry like a boy, and I, carried away by his grief, cried with him. The two of us filled the little upstairs room with our wailing voices. It is ridiculous, but of the pic-ture we made I can remember only the fact that mother's hand con-tinually stroked the bald path that ran across the top of his head. I have forgotten what mother said to him and how she induced him to tell her of what had happened downstairs. His explanation also has gone out of my mind. I remember only my own grief and fright and the shiny path over father's head glowing in the lamplight as he knelt by the bed..

As to what happened downstairs. For some unexplainable reason I know the story as well as though I had been a witness to my father's discomfiture. One in time gets to know many unexplainable things. On that evening young Joe Kane, son of a merchant of Bidwell, came to Pickleville to meet his father, who was expected on the ten-o-clock evening train from the South. The train was three hours late and Joe came into our place to loaf about and to wait for its arrival. The local freight train came in and the freight crew were fed. Joe was left alone in the restaurant with father.

From the moment he came into our place the Bidwell young man must have been puzzled by my father's actions. It was his notion that father was angry at him for hanging around. He noticed that the restaurant-keeper was apparently disturbed by his presence and he thought of going out. However, it began to rain and he did not fancy the long walk to town and back. He bought a five-cent cigar and ordered a cup of coffee. He had a newspaper in his pocket and took it out and began to read. "I'm waiting for the evening train. It's late," he said apologetically.

For a long time father, whom Joe Kane had never seen before, remained silently gazing at his visitor. He was no doubt suffering from at attack of stage fright. As so often happens in life he had thought so much and so often of the situation that now confronted him that he was somewhat nervous in its presence.

For one thing, he did not know what to do with his hands. He thrust one of them nervously over the counter and shook hands with Joe Kane. "How-de-do," he said. Joe Kane put his newspaper down and stared at him. Father's eyes lighted on the basket of eggs that sat on the counter and he began to talk. "Well," he began hesitatingly, "well, you have heard of Christopher Columbus, eh?" He seemed to be angry. "That Christopher Columbus was a cheat," he declared emphatically. "He talked of making an egg stand on its end. He talked, he did, and then he went and broke the end of the egg."[4]

My father seemed to his visitor to be beside himself at the duplicity of Christopher Columbus. He muttered and swore. He declared it was wrong to teach children that Christopher Columbus was a great man when, after all, he cheated at the critical moment. He had declared he would make an egg stand on end and then, when his bluff had been called, he had done a trick. Still grumbling at Columbus, father took an egg from the basket on the counter and began to walk up and down. He rolled the egg between the palms of his hands. He smiled genially. He began to mumble words regarding the effect to be produced on an egg by the electricity that comes out of the human body. He declared that, without breaking its shell and by virtue of rolling it back and forth in his hands, he could stand the egg on its end. He explained that the warmth of his hands and the gentle rolling move-

4. Washington Irving, attributing it to the 16th-century Italian historian Benzoni, recounts, in *The Life and Voyages of Christopher Columbus,*
the well known anecdote of the egg. A shallow courtier . . . impatient of the honors paid to Columbus . . . abruptly asked him whether he thought that, in case he had not discovered the Indies, there were not other men in Spain who would have been capable of the enterprise? To this Columbus made no immediate reply, but, taking an egg, invited the company to make it stand on one end. Everyone attempted it, but in vain; whereupon he struck it upon the table so as to break the end, and left it standing on the broken part: illustrating in this simple manner that when he had once shown the way to the New World nothing was easier than to follow it.

ment he gave the egg created a new center of gravity, and Joe Kane was mildly interested. "I have handled thousands of eggs," father said. "No one knows more about eggs than I do."

He stood the egg on the counter and it fell on its side. He tried the trick again and again, each time rolling the egg between the palms of his hands and saying the words regarding the wonders of electricity and the laws of gravity. When after a half-hour's effort he did succeed in making the egg stand for a moment, he looked up to find that his visitor was no longer watching. By the time he had succeeded in calling Joe Kane's attention to the success of his effort, the egg had rolled over and lay on its side.

Afire with the showman's passion and at the same time a good deal disconcerted by the failure of his first effort, father now took the bottles containing the poultry monstrosities down from their place on the shelf and began to show them to his visitor. "How would you like to have seven legs and two heads like this fellow?" he asked, exhibiting the most remarkable of his treasures. A cheerful smile played over his face. He reached over the counter and tried to slap Joe Kane on the shoulder as he had seen men do in Ben Head's saloon when he was a young farmhand and drove to town on Saturday evenings. His visitor was made a little ill by the sight of the body of the terribly deformed bird floating in the alcohol in the bottle and got up to go. Coming from behind the counter, father took hold of the young man's arm and led him back to his seat. He grew a little angry and for a moment had to turn his face away and force himself to smile. Then he put the bottles back on the shelf. In an outburst of generosity he fairly compelled Joe Kane to have a fresh cup of coffee and another cigar at his expense. Then he took a pan and filling it with vinegar, taken from a jug that sat beneath the counter, he declared himself about to do a new trick. "I will heat this egg in this pan of vinegar," he said. "Then I will put it through the neck of a bottle without breaking the shell. When the egg is inside the bottle it will resume its normal shape and the shell will become hard again. Then I will give the bottle with the egg in it to you. You can take it about with you wherever you go. People will want to know how you got the egg in the bottle. Don't tell them. Keep them guessing. That is the way to have fun with this trick."

Father grinned and winked at his visitor. Joe Kane decided that the man who confronted him was mildly insane but harmless. He drank the cup of coffee that had been given him and began to read his paper again. When the egg had been heated in vinegar, father carried it on a spoon to the counter and going into a back room got an empty bottle. He was angry because his visitor did not watch him as he began to do his trick, but nevertheless went cheerfully to work. For a long time he struggled, trying to get the egg to go through the neck of the bottle. He put the pan of vinegar back on the stove, intending to reheat the egg, then picked it up and burned his fingers. After a second bath in the hot vinegar, the shell of the egg had been softened a little, but not enough for his purpose. He worked and worked and a spirit of desperate determination took possession of him. When he thought that at last the trick was about to be consummated, the delayed train came

in at the station and Joe Kane started to go nonchalantly out at the
door. Father made a last desperate effort to conquer the egg and make
it do the thing that would establish his reputation as one who knew
how to entertain guests who came into his restaurant. He worried the
egg. He attempted to be somewhat rough with it. He swore and the
sweat stood out on his forehead. The egg broke under his hand. When
the contents spurted over his clothes, Joe Kane, who had stopped at
the door, turned and laughed.

A roar of anger rose from my father's throat. He danced and shouted
a string of inarticulate words. Grabbing another egg from the basket
on the counter, he threw it, just missing the head of the young man as
he dodged through the door and escaped.

Father came upstairs to mother and me with an egg in his hand. I
do not know what he intended to do. I imagine he had some idea of
destroying it, of destroying all eggs, and that he intended to let
mother and me see him begin. When, however, he got into the presence
of mother, something happened to him. He laid the egg gently on the
table and dropped on his knees by the bed as I have already explained.
He later decided to close the restaurant for the night and to come up
stairs and get into bed. When he did so, he blew out the light and
after much muttered conversation both he and mother went to sleep.
I suppose I went to sleep also, but my sleep was troubled. I awoke at
dawn and for a long time looked at the egg that lay on the table. I
wondered why eggs had to be and why from the egg came the hen who
again laid the egg. The question got into my blood. It has stayed there,
I imagine, because I am the son of my father. At any rate, the problem
remains unsolved in my mind. And that, I conclude, is but another
evidence of the complete and final triumph of the egg—at least as far
as my family is concerned.

1920

TONI CADE BAMBARA

My Man Bovanne

Blind people got a hummin jones[1] if you notice. Which is understandable completely once you been around one and notice what no eyes
will force you into to see people, and you get past the first time,
which seems to come out of nowhere, and it's like you in church
again with fat-chest ladies and old gents gruntin a hum low in the
throat to whatever the preacher be saying. Shakey Bee bottom lip
all swole up with Sweet Peach[2] and me explainin how come the
sweet-potato bread was a dollar-quarter this time stead of dollar regular and he say uh hunh he understand, then he break into this
thizzin kind of hum which is quiet, but fiercesome just the same, if

---

1. A compelling need.   2. A brand of dipping snuff.

you ain't ready for it. Which I wasn't. But I got used to it and the onliest time I had to say somethin bout it was when he was playin checkers on the stoop one time and he commenst to hummin quite churchy seem to me. So I says, "Look here Shakey Bee, I can't beat you and Jesus too." He stop.

So that's how come I asked My Man Bovanne to dance. He ain't my man mind you, just a nice ole gent from the block that we all know cause he fixes things and the kids like him. Or used to fore Black Power got hold their minds and mess em around till they can't be civil to ole folks. So we at this benefit for my niece's cousin who's runnin for somethin with this Black party somethin or other behind her. And I press up close to dance with Bovanne who blind and I'm hummin and he hummin, chest to chest like talkin. Not jammin my breasts into the man. Wasn't bout tits. Was bout vibrations. And he dug it and asked me what color dress I had on and how my hair was fixed and how I was doin without a man, not nosy but nice-like, and who was at this affair and was the canapés dainty-stingy or healthy enough to get hold of proper. Comfy and cheery is what I'm tryin to get across. Touch talkin like the heel of the hand on the tambourine or on a drum.

But right away Joe Lee come up on us and frown for dancin so close to the man. My own son who knows what kind of warm I am about; and don't grown men all call me long distance and in the middle of the night for a little Mama comfort? But he frown. Which ain't right since Bovanne can't see and defend himself. Just a nice old man who fixes toasters and busted irons and bicycles and things and changes the lock on my door when my men friends get messy. Nice man. Which is not why they invited him. Grass roots you see. Me and Sister Taylor and the woman who does heads at Mamies and the man from the barber shop, we all there on account of we grass roots. And I ain't never been souther than Brooklyn Battery and no more country than the window box on my fire escape. And just yesterday my kids tellin me to take them countrified rags off my head and be cool. And now can't get Black enough to suit em. So everybody passin sayin My Man Bovanne. Big deal, keep steppin and don't even stop a minute to get the man a drink or one of them cute sandwiches or tell him what's goin on. And him standin there with a smile ready case someone do speak he want to be ready. So that's how come I pull him on the dance floor and we dance squeezin past the tables and chairs and all them coats and people standin round up in each other face talkin bout this and that but got no use for this blind man who mostly fixed skates and skooters for all these folks when they was just kids. So I'm pressed up close and we touch talkin with the hum. And here come my daughter cuttin her eye[3] at me like she do when she tell me about my "apolitical" self like I got hoof and mouf disease and there ain't no hope at all. And I don't pay her no mind and just look up in Bovanne shadow face and tell him his stomach like a drum and he laugh. Laugh real loud. And here come my youngest, Task, with a tap on my elbow like he the third grade

3. Giving a sharp look.

monitor and I'm cuttin up on the line to assembly.

"I was just talkin on the drums," I explained when they hauled me into the kitchen. I figured drums was my best defense. They can get ready for drums what with all this heritage business. And Bovanne stomach just like that drum Task give me when he come back from Africa. You just touch it and it hum thizzm, thizzm. So I stuck to the drum story. "Just drummin that's all."

"Mama, what are you talkin about?"

"She had too much to drink," say Elo to Task cause she don't hardly say nuthin to me direct no more since that ugly argument about my wigs.

"Look here Mama," say Task, the gentle one. "We just tryin to pull your coat. You were makin a spectacle of yourself out there dancing like that."

"Dancin like what?"

Task run a hand over his left ear like his father for the world and his father before that.

"Like a bitch in heat," say Elo.

"Well uhh, I was goin to say like one of them sex-starved ladies gettin on in years and not too discriminating. Know what I mean?"

I don't answer cause I'll cry. Terrible thing when your own children talk to you like that. Pullin me out the party and hustlin me into some stranger's kitchen in the back of a bar just like the damn police. And ain't like I'm old old. I can still wear me some sleeveless dresses without the meat hangin off my arm. And I keep up with some thangs through my kids. Who ain't kids no more. To hear them tell it. So I don't say nuthin.

"Dancin with that tom," say Elo to Joe Lee, who leanin on the folks' freezer. "His feet can smell a cracker a mile away and go into their shuffle number post haste. And them eyes. He could be a little considerate and put on some shades. Who wants to look into them blown-out fuses that—"

"Is this what they call the generation gap?" I say.

"Generation gap," spits Elo, like I suggested castor oil and fricassee possum in the milk-shakes or somethin. "That's a white concept for a white phenomenon. There's no generation gap among Black people. We are a col—"

"Yeh, well never mind," says Joe Lee. "The point is Mama . . . well, it's pride. You embarrass yourself and us too dancin like that."

"I wasn't shame." Then nobody say nuthin. Them standin there in they pretty clothes with drinks in they hands and gangin up on me, and me in the third-degree chair and nary a olive to my name. Felt just like the police got hold to me.

"First of all," Task say, holdin up his hand and tickin off the offenses, "the dress. Now that dress is too short, Mama, and too low-cut for a woman your age. And Tamu's going to make a speech tonight to kick off the campaign and will be introducin you and expecting you to organize the council of elders—"

"Me? Didn nobody ask me nuthin. You mean Nisi? She change her name?"

"Well, Norton was supposed to tell you about it. Nisi wants to

introduce you and then encourage the older folks to form a Council
of the Elders to act as an advisory—"

"And you going to be standing there with your boobs out and that
wig on your head and that hem up to your ass. And people'll say,
'Ain't that the horny bitch that was grindin with the blind dude?' "

"Elo, be cool a minute," say Task, gettin to the next finger. "And
then there's the drinkin. Mama, you know you can't drink cause next
thing you know you be laughin loud and carryin on," and he grab
another finger for the loudness. "And then there's the dancin. You
been tattooed on the man for four records straight and slow draggin
even on the fast numbers. How you think that look for a woman
your age?"

"What's my age?"

"What?"

"I'm axin you all a simple question. You keep talkin bout what's
proper for a woman my age. How old am I anyhow?" And Joe Lee
slams his eyes shut and squinches up his face to figure. And Task
run a hand over his ear and stare into his glass like the ice cubes
goin calculate for him. And Elo just starin at the top of my head
like she goin rip the wig off any minute now.

"Is your hair braided up under that thing? If so, why don't you
take it off? You always did do a neat cornroll."[4]

"Uh huh," cause I'm thinkin how she couldn't undo her hair fast
enough talking bout cornroll so countrified. None of which was the
subject. "How old, I say?"

"Sixtee-one or—"

"You a damn lie Joe Lee Peoples."

"And that's another thing," say Task on the fingers.

"You know what you all can kiss," I say, gettin up and brushin the
wrinkles out my lap.

"Oh, Mama," Elo say, puttin a hand on my shoulder like she hasn't
done since she left home and the hand landin light and not sure it
supposed to be there. Which hurt me to my heart. Cause this was
the child in our happiness fore Mr. Peoples die. And I carried that
child strapped to my chest till she was nearly two. We was close
is what I'm tryin to tell you. Cause it was more me in the child than
the others. And even after Task it was the girlchild I covered in the
night and wept over for no reason at all less it was she was a chub-
chub like me and not very pretty, but a warm child. And how did
things get to this, that she can't put a sure hand on me and say
Mama we love you and care about you and you entitled to enjoy yourself cause you a good woman?

"And then there's Reverend Trent," say Task, glancin from left to
right like they hatchin a plot and just now lettin me in on it. "You
were suppose to be talking with him tonight, Mama, about giving us
his basement for campaign headquarters and—"

"Didn nobody tell me nuthin. If grass roots mean you kept in the
dark I can't use it. I really can't. And Reven Trent a fool anyway the

---

4. Cornrow, a hairstyle in which all the hair is interwoven from the scalp into
small braids.

way he tore into the widow man up there on Edgecomb cause he wouldn't take in three of them foster children and the woman not even comfy in the ground yet and the man's mind messed up and—"

"Look here," say Task. "What we need is a family conference so we can get all this stuff cleared up and laid out on the table. In the meantime I think we better get back into the other room and tend to business. And in the meantime, Mama, see if you can't get to Reverend Trent and—"

"You want me to belly rub with the Reven, that it?"

"Oh damn," Elo say and go through the swingin door.

"We'll talk about all this at dinner. How's tomorrow night, Joe Lee?" While Joe Lee being self-important I'm wonderin who's doin the cookin and how come no body ax me if I'm free and do I get a corsage and things like that. Then Joe nod that it's O.K. and he go through the swingin door and just a little hubbub come through from the other room. Then Task smile his smile, lookin just like his daddy, and he leave. And it just me in this stranger's kitchen, which was a mess I wouldn't never let my kitchen look like. Poison you just to look at the pots. Then the door swing the other way and it's My Man Bovanne standin there sayin Miss Hazel but lookin at the deep fry and then at the steam table, and most surprised when I come up on him from the other direction and take him on out of there. Pass the folks pushin up towards the stage where Nisi and some other people settin and ready to talk, and folks gettin to the last of the sandwiches and the booze fore they settle down in one spot and listen serious. And I'm thinkin bout tellin Bovanne what a lovely long dress Nisi got on and the earrings and her hair piled up in a cone and the people bout to hear how we all gettin screwed and gotta form our own party and everybody there listenin and lookin. But instead I just haul the man on out of there, and Joe Lee and his wife look at me like I'm terrible, but they ain't said boo to the man yet. Cause he blind and old and don't nobody there need him since they grown up and don't need they skates fixed no more.

"Where we goin, Miss Hazel?" Him knowin all the time.

"First we gonna buy you some dark sunglasses. Then you comin with me to the supermarket so I can pick up tomorrow's dinner, which is goin to be a grand thing proper and you invited. Then we goin to my house."

"That be fine. I surely would like to rest my feet." Bein cute, but you got to let men play out they little show, blind or not. So he chat on bout how tired he is and how he appreciate me takin him in hand this way. And I'm thinkin I'll have him change the lock on my door first thing. Then I'll give the man a nice warm bath with jasmine leaves in the water and a little Epsom salt on the sponge to do his back. And then a good rubdown with rose water and olive oil. Then a cup of lemon tea with a taste in it. And a little talcum, some of that fancy stuff Nisi mother sent over last Christmas. And then a massage, a good face massage round the forehead which is the worryin part. Cause you gots to take care of the older folks. And let them know they still needed to run the mimeo machine and keep the spark plugs clean and fix the mailboxes for folks who might help us get the breakfast program goin, and the school for the little kids and the campaign and all. Cause old folks in the nation. That what Nisi was sayin and I mean to do my part.

"I imagine you are a very pretty woman, Miss Hazel."

"I surely am," I say just like the hussy my daughter always say I was.

1972

DORIS LESSING

Our Friend Judith

I stopped inviting Judith to meet people when a Canadian woman remarked, with the satisfied fervor of one who has at last pinned a label on a rare specimen: "She is, of course, one of your typical English spinsters."

This was a few weeks after an American sociologist, having elicited from Judith the facts that she was fortyish, unmarried, and living alone, had inquired of me: "I suppose she has given up?" "Given up what?" I asked; and the subsequent discussion was unrewarding.

Judith did not easily come to parties. She would come after pressure, not so much—one felt—to do one a favor, but in order to correct what she believed to be a defect in her character. "I really ought to enjoy meeting new people more than I do," she said once. We reverted to an earlier pattern of our friendship: odd evenings together, an occasional visit to the cinema, or she would telephone to say: "I'm on my way past you to the British Museum. Would you care for a cup of coffee with me? I have twenty minutes to spare."

It is characteristic of Judith that the word "spinster," used of her, provoked fascinated speculation about other people. There are my aunts, for instance: aged seventy-odd, both unmarried, one an ex-missionary from China, one a retired matron of a famous London hospital. These two old ladies live together under the shadow of the cathedral in a country town. They devote much time to the Church, to good causes, to letter writing with friends all over the world, to the grandchildren and the great-grandchildren of relatives. It would be a mistake, however, on entering a house in which nothing has been moved for fifty years, to diagnose a condition of fossilized late-Victorian integrity. They read every book reviewed in the *Observer* or the *Times*,[1] so that I recently got a letter from Aunt Rose inquiring whether I did not think that the author of *On the Road*[2] was not—perhaps?—exaggerating his difficulties. They know a good deal about music, and write letters of encouragement to young composers they

---

1. Prestigious London newspapers representing roughly the younger more liberal establishment and the Establishment proper.
2. Jack Kerouac (1922–69), leader of the beatniks, 1950s forerunners of the hippies. Kerouac heroes felt themselves completely cut off from and victimized by American society.

feel are being neglected—"You must understand that anything new and original takes time to be understood." Well-informed and critical Tories, they are as likely to dispatch telegrams of protest to the Home Secretary[3] as letters of support. These ladies, my aunts Emily and Rose, are surely what is meant by the phrase "English spinster." And yet, once the connection has been pointed out, there is no doubt that Judith and they are spiritual cousins, if not sisters. Therefore it follows that one's pitying admiration for women who have supported manless and uncomforted lives needs a certain modification?

One will, of course, never know; and I feel now that it is entirely my fault that I shall never know. I had been Judith's friend for upwards of five years before the incident occurred which I involuntarily thought of—stupidly enough—as the first time Judith's mask slipped.

A mutual friend, Betty, had been given a cast-off Dior[4] dress. She was too short for it. Also she said: "It's not a dress for a married woman with three children and a talent for cooking. I don't know why not, but it isn't." Judith was the right build. Therefore one evening the three of us met by appointment in Judith's bedroom, with the dress. Neither Betty nor I was surprised at the renewed discovery that Judith was beautiful. We had both often caught each other, and ourselves, in moments of envy when Judith's calm and severe face, her undemonstratively perfect body, succeeded in making everyone else in a room or a street look cheap.

Judith is tall, small-breasted, slender. Her light brown hair is parted in the center and cut straight around her neck. A high straight forehead, straight nose, a full grave mouth are setting for her eyes, which are green, large and prominent. Her lids are very white, fringed with gold, and molded close over the eyeball, so that in profile she has the look of a staring gilded mask. The dress was of dark green glistening stuff, cut straight, with a sort of loose tunic. It opened simply at the throat. In it Judith could of course evoke nothing but classical images. Diana, perhaps, back from the hunt, in a relaxed moment? A rather intellectual wood nymph who had opted for an afternoon in the British Museum Reading Room? Something like that. Neither Betty nor I said a word, since Judith was examining herself in a long mirror, and must know she looked magnificent.

Slowly she drew off the dress and laid it aside. Slowly she put on the old cord skirt and woolen blouse she had taken off. She must have surprised a resigned glance between us, for she then remarked, with the smallest of mocking smiles: "One surely ought to stay in character, wouldn't you say?" She added, reading the words out of some invisible book, written not by her, since it was a very vulgar book, but perhaps by one of us: "It does everything *for* me, I must admit."

"After seeing you in it," Betty cried out, defying her, "I can't bear for anyone else to have it. I shall simply put it away." Judith shrugged, rather irritated. In the shapeless skirt and blouse, and with-

---

3. Head of the British government department responsible for domestic matters.   4. Famous French designer of high fashions.

out makeup, she stood smiling at us, a woman at whom forty-nine out of fifty people would not look twice.

A second revelatory incident occurred soon after. Betty telephoned me to say that Judith had a kitten. Did I know that Judith adored cats? "No, but of course she would," I said.

Betty lived in the same street as Judith and saw more of her than I did. I was kept posted about the growth and habits of the cat and its effect on Judith's life. She remarked for instance that she felt it was good for her to have a tie and some responsibility. But no sooner was the cat out of kittenhood than all the neighbors complained. It was a tomcat, ungelded, and making every night hideous. Finally the landlord said that either the cat or Judith must go, unless she was prepared to have the cat "fixed."[5] Judith wore herself out trying to find some person, anywhere in Britain, who would be prepared to take the cat. This person would, however, have to sign a written statement not to have the cat "fixed." When Judith took the cat to the vet to be killed, Betty told me she cried for twenty-four hours.

"She didn't think of compromising? After all, perhaps the cat might have preferred to live, if given the choice?"

"Is it likely I'd have the nerve to say anything so sloppy to Judith? It's the nature of a male cat to rampage lustfully about, and therefore it would be morally wrong for Judith to have the cat fixed, simply to suit her own convenience."

"She said that?"

"She wouldn't have to *say* it, surely?"

A third incident was when she allowed a visiting young American, living in Paris, the friend of a friend and scarcely known to her, to use her flat while she visited her parents over Christmas. The young man and his friends lived it up for ten days of alcohol and sex and marijuana, and when Judith came back it took a week to get the place clean again and the furniture mended. She telephoned twice to Paris, the first time to say that he was a disgusting young thug and if he knew what was good for him he would keep out of her way in the future; the second time to apologize for losing her temper. "I had a choice either to let someone use my flat, or to leave it empty. But having chosen that you should have it, it was clearly an unwarrantable infringement of your liberty to make any conditions at all. I do most sincerely ask your pardon." The moral aspects of the matter having been made clear, she was irritated rather than not to receive letters of apology from him—fulsome, embarrassed, but above all, baffled.

It was the note of curiosity in the letters—he even suggested coming over to get to know her better—that irritated her most. "What do you suppose he means?" she said to me. "He lived in my flat for ten days. One would have thought that should be enough, wouldn't you?"

The facts about Judith, then, are all in the open, unconcealed, and plain to anyone who cares to study them; or, as it became plain she feels, to anyone with the intelligence to interpret them.

---

5. Gelded, castrated.

She has lived for the last twenty years in a small two-room flat high over a busy West London street. The flat is shabby and badly heated. The furniture is old, was never anything but ugly, is now frankly rickety and fraying. She has an income of two hundred pounds[6] a year from a dead uncle. She lives on this and what she earns from her poetry, and from lecturing on poetry to night classes and extramural university classes.

She does not smoke or drink, and eats very little, from preference, not self-discipline.

She studied poetry and biology at Oxford, with distinction.

She is a Castlewell. That is, she is a member of one of the academic upper-middle-class families, which have been producing for centuries a steady supply of brilliant but sound men and women who are the backbone of the arts and sciences in Britain. She is on cool good terms with her family, who respect her and leave her alone.

She goes on long walking tours, by herself, in such places as Exmoor[7] or West Scotland.

Every three or four years she publishes a volume of poems.

The walls of her flat are completely lined with books. They are scientific, classical and historical; there is a great deal of poetry and some drama. There is not one novel. When Judith says: "Of course I don't read novels," this does not mean that novels have no place, or a small place, in literature; or that people should not read novels; but that it must be obvious she can't be expected to read novels.

I had been visiting her flat for years before I noticed two long shelves of books, under a window, each shelf filled with the works of a single writer. The two writers are not, to put it at the mildest, the kind one would associate with Judith. They are mild, reminiscent, vague and whimsical. Typical English *belles-lettres,* in fact, and by definition abhorrent to her. Not one of the books in the two shelves has been read; some of the pages are still uncut. Yet each book is inscribed or dedicated to her: gratefully, admiringly, sentimentally and, more than once, amorously. In short, it is open to anyone who cares to examine these two shelves, and to work out dates, to conclude that Judith from the age of fifteen to twenty-five had been the beloved young companion of one elderly literary gentleman, and from twenty-five to thirty-five the inspiration of another.

During all that time she had produced her own poetry, and the sort of poetry, it is quite safe to deduce, not at all likely to be admired by her two admirers. Her poems are always cool and intellectual; that is their form, which is contradicted or supported by a gravely sensuous texture. They are poems to read often; one has to, to understand them.

I did not ask Judith a direct question about these two eminent but rather fusty lovers. Not because she would not have answered, or because she would have found the question impertinent, but because such questions are clearly unnecessary. Having those two shelves of books where they are, and books she could not conceivably care for,

6. About $500–$550 at the time of the story, but probably close to one-third or even one-half of a subsistence income.

7. Swampy or heathery wastelands in western Britain, from southwestern coast to north of England.

for their own sake, is publicly giving credit where credit is due. I can imagine her thinking the thing over, and deciding it was only fair, or perhaps honest, to place the books there; and this despite the fact that she would not care at all for the same attention to be paid to her. There is something almost contemptuous in it. For she certainly despises people who feel they need attention.

For instance, more than once a new emerging wave of "modern" young poets have discovered her as the only "modern" poet among their despised and well-credited elders. This is because, since she began writing at fifteen, her poems have been full of scientific, mechanical and chemical imagery. This is how she thinks, or feels.

More than once has a young poet hastened to her flat, to claim her as an ally, only to find her totally and by instinct unmoved by words like "modern," "new," "contemporary." He has been outraged and wounded by her principle, so deeply rooted as to be unconscious, and to need no expression but a contemptuous shrug of the shoulders, that publicly seeking or to want critical attention is despicable. It goes without saying that there is perhaps one critic in the world she has any time for. He has sulked off, leaving her on her shelf, which she takes it for granted is her proper place, to be read by an appreciative minority.

Meanwhile she gives her lectures, walks alone through London, writes her poems, and is seen sometimes at a concert or a play with a middle-aged professor of Greek, who has a wife and two children.

Betty and I had speculated about this professor, with such remarks as: Surely she must sometimes be lonely? Hasn't she ever wanted to marry? What about that awful moment when one comes in from somewhere at night to an empty flat?

It happened recently that Betty's husband was on a business trip, her children visiting, and she was unable to stand the empty house. She asked Judith for a refuge until her own home filled again.

Afterwards Betty rang me up to report: "Four of the five nights Professor Adams came in about ten or so."

"Was Judith embarrassed?"

"Would you expect her to be?"

"Well, if not embarrassed, at least conscious there was a situation?"

"No, not at all. But I must say I don't think he's good enough for her. He can't possibly understand her. He calls her Judy."

"Good God."

"Yes. But I was wondering. Suppose the other two called her Judy '—little Judy'—imagine it! Isn't it awful? But it does rather throw a light on Judith?"

"It's rather touching."

"I suppose it's touching. But *I* was embarrassed—oh, not because of the situation. Because of how she was, with him. 'Judy, is there another cup of tea in that pot?' And she, rather daughterly and demure, pouring him one."

"Three of the nights he went to her bedroom with her—very casual about it, because she was being. But he was not there in the mornings. So I asked her. You know how it is when you ask her a question. As if you've been having long conversations on that very subject

for years and years, and she is merely continuing where you left off
last. So when she says something surprising, one feels such a fool to
be surprised?"

"Yes. And then?"

"I asked her if she was sorry not to have children. She said yes,
but one couldn't have everything."

"One can't have everything, she said?"

"Quite clearly feeling she *has* nearly everything. She said she
thought it was a pity, because she would have brought up children
very well."

"When you come to think of it, she would, too."

"I asked about marriage, but she said on the whole the role of a
mistress suited her better."

"She used the word 'mistress'?"

"You must admit it's the accurate word."

"I suppose so."

"And then she said that while she liked intimacy and sex and
everything, she enjoyed waking up in the morning alone and *her
own person*."

"Yes, *of course*."

"Of course. But now she's bothered because the professor would
like to marry her. Or he feels he ought. At least, he's getting all guilty
and obsessive about it. She says she doesn't see the point of divorce,
and anyway, surely it would be very hard on his poor old wife after
all these years, particularly after bringing up two children so satisfactorily. She talks about his wife as if she's a kind of nice old
charwoman, and it wouldn't be *fair* to sack her, you know. Anyway.
What with one thing and another. Judith's going off to Italy soon in
order *to collect herself*."

"But how's she going to pay for it?"

"Luckily the Third Program's[8] commissioning her to do some arty
programs. They offered her a choice of The Cid—El Thid,[9] you know
—and the Borgias. Well, the Borghese, then. And Judith settled for
the Borgias."

"The Borgias," I said, "*Judith?*"

"Yes, quite. I said that too, in that tone of voice. She saw my
point. She says the epic is right up her street, whereas the Renaissance
has never been on her wave length. Obviously it couldn't be, all the
magnificence and cruelty and *dirt*. But of course chivalry and a high
moral code and all those idiotically noble goings-on are right on her
wave length."

"Is the money the same?"

"Yes. But is it likely Judith would let money decide? No, she said
that one should always choose something new, that isn't up one's
street. Well, because it's better for her character, and so on, to get
herself unsettled by the Renaissance. She didn't say *that*, of course."

"Of course not."

8. British Broadcasting Corporation public radio service (and now also television
channel) specializing in classical music,
literature and plays, lectures, etc.

9. Castilian, standard Spanish, pronunciation of El Cid, the title of an eleventh-
century soldier-hero and hero of many
works of literature.

Judith went to Florence; and for some months postcards informed us tersely of her doings. Then Betty decided she must go by herself for a holiday. She had been appalled by the discovery that if her husband was away for a night she couldn't sleep; and when he went to Australia for three weeks, she stopped living until he came back. She had discussed this with him, and he had agreed that if she really felt the situation to be serious, he would dispatch her by air, to Italy, in order to recover her self-respect. As she put it.

I got this letter from her: "It's no use, I'm coming home. I might have known. Better face it, once you're really married you're not fit for man nor beast. And if you remember what I used to be like! *Well!* I moped around Milan. I sunbathed in Venice, then I thought my tan was surely worth something, so I was on the point of starting an affair with another lonely soul, but I lost heart, and went to Florence to see Judith. She wasn't there. She'd gone to the Italian Riviera. I had nothing better to do, so I followed her. When I saw the place I wanted to laugh, it's so much not Judith, you know, all those palms and umbrellas and gaiety at all costs and ever such an ornamental blue sea. Judith is in an enormous stone room up on the hillside above the sea, with grape vines all over the place. You should see her, she's got beautiful. It seems for the last fifteen years she's been going to Soho[1] every Saturday morning to buy food at an Italian shop. I must have looked surprised, because she explained she liked Soho. I suppose because all that dreary vice and nudes and prostitutes and everything prove how right she is to be as she is? She told the people in the shop she was going to Italy, and the *signora*[2] said, what a coincidence, she was going back to Italy too, and she did hope an old friend like Miss Castlewell would visit her there. Judith said to me: 'I felt lacking, when she used the word friend. Our relations have always been formal. Can you understand it?' she said to me. 'For fifteen years,' I said to her. She said: 'I think I must feel it's a kind of imposition, don't you know, expecting people to feel friendship for one.' *Well.* I said: 'You ought to understand it, because you're like that yourself.' 'Am I?' she said. 'Well, think about it,' I said. But I could see she didn't want to think about it. Anyway, she's here, and I've spent a week with her. The widow Maria Rineiri inherited her mother's house, so she came home, from Soho. On the ground floor is a tatty little *rosticceria*[3] patronized by the neighbors. They are all working people. This isn't tourist country, up on the hill. The widow lives above the shop with her little boy, a nasty little brat of about ten. Say what you like, the English are the only people who know how to bring up children, I don't care if that's insular. Judith's room is at the back, with a balcony. Underneath her room is the barber's shop, and the barber is Luigi Rineiri, the widow's younger brother. Yes, I was keeping him until the last. He is about forty, tall dark handsome, a great *bull*, but rather a sweet fatherly bull. He has cut Judith's hair and made it lighter. Now it looks like a sort of gold helmet.

---

1. A section of London roughly equivalent to Greenwich Village in New York— foreign restaurants and groceries, haunt of writers, painters, etc.—but in recent years increasingly known for prostitutes and pornography.
2. Proprietress.
3. Grill.

Judith is all brown. The widow Rineiri has made her a white dress and a green dress. They fit, for a change. When Judith walks down the street to the lower town, all the Italian males take one look at the golden girl and melt in their own oil like ice cream. Judith takes all this in her stride. She sort of acknowledges the homage. Then she strolls into the sea and vanishes into the foam. She swims five miles every day. *Naturally.* I haven't asked Judith whether she has collected herself, because you can see she hasn't. The widow Rineiri is match-making. When I noticed this I wanted to laugh, but luckily I didn't because Judith asked me, really wanting to know: 'Can you see me married to an Italian barber?' (Not being snobbish, but stating the position, so to speak.) 'Well yes,' I said, 'you're the only woman I know who I can see married to an Italian barber.' Because it wouldn't matter who she married, she'd always be her *own person.* 'At any rate, for a time,' I said. At which she said, asperously:[4] 'You can use phrases like for a time in England but not in Italy.' Did you ever see England, at least London, as the home of license, liberty and free love? No, neither did I, but of course she's right. Married to Luigi it would be the family, the neighbors, the church and the *bambini.*[5] All the same she's thinking about it, believe it or not. Here she's quite different, all relaxed and free. She's melting in the attention she gets. The widow mothers her and makes her coffee all the time, and listens to a lot of good advice about how to bring up that nasty brat of hers. Unluckily she doesn't take it. Luigi is crazy for her. At mealtimes she goes to the *trattoria*[6] in the upper square and all the workmen treat her like a goddess. Well, a film star then. I said to her, you're mad to come home. For one thing her rent is ten bob[7] a week, and you eat *pasta* and drink red wine till you bust for about one and sixpence. No, she said, it would be nothing but self-indulgence to stay. Why? I said. She said, she's got nothing to stay for. (Ho ho.) And besides, she's done her research on the Borghese, though so far she can't see her way to an honest presentation of the facts. What made these people tick? she wants to know. And so she's only staying because of the cat. I forgot to mention the cat. This is a town of cats. The Italians here love their cats. I wanted to feed a stray cat at the table, but the waiter said no; and after lunch, all the waiters came with trays crammed with leftover food and stray cats came from everywhere to eat. And at dark when the tourists go in to feed and the beach is empty—you know how empty and forlorn a beach is at dusk?—well cats appear from everywhere. The beach seems to move, then you see it's cats. They go stalking along the thin inch of gray water at the edge of the sea, shaking their paws crossly at each step, snatching at the dead little fish, and throwing them with their mouths up onto the dry sand. Then they scamper after them. You've never seen such a snarling and fighting. At dawn when the fishing boats come in to the empty beach, the cats are there in dozens. The fishermen throw them bits of fish. The cats snarl and fight over it. Judith gets up early and

---

4. Sharply, harshly.
5. Children.
6. Restaurant.
7. Shillings. There are twenty shillings to the pound; *one and sixpence* below is one and a half shillings. Living in Italy at the time was very inexpensive by British standards.

goes down to watch. Sometimes Luigi goes too, being tolerant. Because what he really likes is to join the evening promenade with Judith on his arm around and around the square of the upper town. Showing her off. Can you *see* Judith? But she does it. Being tolerant. But she smiles and enjoys the attention she gets, there's no doubt of it.

"She has a cat in her room. It's a kitten really, but it's pregnant. Judith says she can't leave until the kittens are born. The cat is too young to have kittens. Imagine Judith. She sits on her bed in that great stone room, with her bare feet on the stone floor, and watches the cat, and tries to work out why a healthy uninhibited Italian cat always fed on the best from the *rosticceria* should be neurotic. Because it is. When it sees Judith watching it gets nervous and starts licking at the roots of its tail. But Judith goes on watching, and says about Italy that the reason why the English love the Italians is because the Italians make the English feel superior. They have no discipline. And that's a despicable reason for one nation to love another. Then she talks about Luigi and says he has no sense of guilt, but a sense of sin; whereas she has no sense of sin but she has guilt. I haven't asked her if this has been an insuperable barrier, because judging from how she looks, it hasn't. She says she would rather have a sense of sin, because sin can be attoned for, and if she understood sin, perhaps she would be more at home with the Renaissance. Luigi is very healthy, she says, and not neurotic. He is a Catholic of course. He doesn't mind that she's an atheist. His mother has explained to him that the English are all pagans, but good people at heart. I suppose he thinks a few smart sessions with the local priest would set Judith on the right path for good and all. Meanwhile the cat walks nervously around the room, stopping to lick, and when it can't stand Judith watching it another second, it rolls over on the floor, with its paws tucked up, and rolls up its eyes, and Judith scratches its lumpy pregnant stomach and tells it to relax. It makes *me* nervous to see her, it's not like her. I don't know why. Then Luigi shouts up from the barber's shop, then he comes up and stands at the door laughing, and Judith laughs, and the widow says: Children, enjoy yourselves. And off they go, walking down to the town eating ice cream. The cat follows them. It won't let Judith out of its sight, like a dog. When she swims miles out to sea, the cat hides under a beach hut until she comes back. Then she carries it back up the hill, because that nasty little boy chases it. *Well.* I'm coming home tomorrow thank God, to my dear old Billy, I was mad ever to leave him. There is something about Judith and Italy that has upset me, I don't know what. The point is, what on earth can Judith and Luigi *talk* about? Nothing. How can they? And of course it doesn't matter. So I turn out to be a prude as well. See you next week."

It was my turn for a dose of the sun, so I didn't see Betty. On my way back from Rome I stopped off in Judith's resort and walked up through narrow streets to the upper town, where, in the square with the vine-covered *trattoria* at the corner, was a house with ROSTICCERIA written in black paint on a cracked wooden board over a low door. There was a door curtain of red beads, and flies settled on the beads. I opened the beads with my hands and looked into a small dark room with a stone counter. Loops of salami hung from metal hooks. A glass bell covered some plates of cooked meats. There were flies on the salami and on the glass bell. A few tins on the wooden shelves, a couple of pale loaves, some wine casks and an open case of sticky pale green grapes covered with fruit flies seemed to be the only stock. A single wooden table with two chairs stood in a corner, and two workmen sat there, eating lumps of sausage and bread. Through another bead curtain at the back came a short, smoothly fat, slender-limbed woman with graying hair. I asked for Miss Castlewell, and her face changed. She said in an offended, offhand way: "Miss Castlewell left last week." She took a white cloth from under the counter, and flicked at the flies on the glass bell. "I'm a friend of hers," I said, and she said: "*Si*,"[8] and put her hands palm down on the counter and looked at me, expressionless. The workmen got up, gulped down the last of their wine, nodded and went. She *ciao*'d[9] them; and looked back at me. Then, since I didn't go, she called: "Luigi!" A shout came from the back room, there was a rattle of beads, and in came first a wiry sharp-faced boy, and then Luigi. He was tall, heavy-shouldered, and his black rough hair was like a cap, pulled low over his brows. He looked good-natured, but at the moment uneasy. His sister said something, and he stood beside her, an ally, and confirmed: "Miss Castlewell went away." I was on the point of giving up, when through the bead curtain that screened off a dazzling light eased a thin tabby cat. It was ugly and it walked uncomfortably, with its back quarters bunched up. The child suddenly let out a "Sssss" through his teeth, and the cat froze. Luigi said something sharp to the child, and something encouraging to the cat, which sat down, looked straight in front of it, then began frantically licking at its flanks. "Miss Castlewell was offended with us," said Mrs. Rineiri suddenly, and with dignity. "She left early one morning. We did not expect her to go." I said: "Perhaps she had to go home and finish some work."

Mrs. Rineiri shrugged, then sighed. Then she exchanged a hard look with her brother. Clearly the subject had been discussed, and closed forever.

"I've known Judith a long time," I said, trying to find the right note. "She's a remarkable woman. She's a poet." But there was no response to this at all. Meanwhile the child, with a fixed bared-teeth grin, was staring at the cat, narrowing his eyes. Suddenly he let out another "Ssssssss" and added a short high yelp. The cat shot backwards, hit the wall, tried desperately to claw its way up the wall, came to its senses and again sat down and began its urgent, undirected licking at its fur. This time Luigi cuffed the child, who yelped in earnest, and then ran out into the street past the cat. Now that the way was clear the cat shot across the floor, up onto the counter, and bounded past Luigi's shoulder and straight through the bead curtain into the barber's shop, where it landed with a thud.

"Judith was sorry when she left us," said Mrs. Rineiri uncertainly. "She was crying."

"I'm sure she was."

"And so," said Mrs. Rineiri, with finality, laying her hands down again, and looking past me at the bead curtain. That was the end. Luigi nodded brusquely at me, and went into the back. I said good-bye to Mrs. Rineiri and walked back to the lower town. In the square I saw the child, sitting on the running board of a lorry[1] parked outside the *trattoria*, drawing in the dust with his bare toes, and directing in front of him a blank, unhappy stare.

I had to go through Florence, so I went to the address Judith had been at. No, Miss Castlewell had not been back. Her papers and books were still here. Would I take them back with me to England? I made a great parcel and brought them back to England.

I telephoned Judith and she said she had already written for the papers to be sent, but it was kind of me to bring them. There had seemed to be no point, she said, in returning to Florence.

"Shall I bring them over?"

"I would be very grateful, of course."

Judith's flat was chilly, and she wore a bunchy sage-green woolen dress. Her hair was still a soft gold helmet, but she looked pale and rather pinched. She stood with her back to a single bar of electric fire—lit because I demanded it—with her legs apart and her arms folded. She contemplated me.

"I went to the Rineiris' house."

"Oh. Did you?"

"They seemed to miss you."

She said nothing.

"I saw the cat too."

"Oh. Oh, I suppose you and Betty discussed it?" This was with a small unfriendly smile.

"Well, Judith, you must see we were likely to?"

She gave this her consideration and said: "I don't understand why people discuss other people. Oh—I'm not criticizing you. But I don't see why you are so interested. I don't understand human behavior and I'm not particularly interested."

"I think you should write to the Rineiris."

"I wrote and thanked them, of course."

"I don't mean that."

"You and Betty have worked it out?"

"Yes, we talked about it. We thought we should talk to you, so you should write to the Rineiris."

"Why?"

"For one thing, they are both very fond of you."

"Fond," she said smiling.

"Judith, I've never in my life felt such an atmosphere of being let down."

Judith considered this. "When something happens that shows one there is really a complete gulf in understanding, what is there to say?"

"It could scarcely have been a complete gulf in understanding. I suppose you are going to say we are being interfering?"

---

1. Truck.

Judith showed distaste. "That is a very stupid word. And it's a stupid idea. No one can interfere with me if I don't let them. No, it's that I don't understand people. I don't understand why you or Betty should care. Or why the Rineiris should, for that matter," she added with the small tight smile.

"Judith!"

"If you've behaved stupidly, there's no point in going on. You put an end to it."

"What happened? Was it the cat?"

"Yes, I suppose so. But it's not important." She looked at me, saw my ironical face, and said: "The cat was too young to have kittens. That is all there was to it."

"Have it your way. But that is obviously not all there is to it."

"What upsets me is that I don't understand at all why I was so upset then."

"What happened? Or don't you want to talk about it?"

"I don't give a damn whether I talk about it or not. You really do say the most extraordinary things, you and Betty. If you want to know, I'll tell you. What does it matter?"

"I would like to know, of course."

"*Of course!*" she said. "In your place I wouldn't care. Well, I think the essence of the thing was that I must have had the wrong attitude to that cat. Cats are supposed to be independent. They are supposed to go off by themselves to have their kittens. This one didn't. It was climbing up on to my bed all one night and crying for attention. I don't like cats on my bed. In the morning I saw she was in pain. I stayed with her all that day. Then Luigi—he's the brother, you know."

"Yes."

"Did Betty mention him? Luigi came up to say it was time I went for a swim. He said the cat should look after itself. I blame myself very much. That's what happens when you submerge yourself in somebody else."

Her look at me was now defiant; and her body showed both defensiveness and aggression. "Yes. It's true. I've always been afraid of it. And in the last few weeks I've behaved badly. It's because I let it happen."

"Well, go on."

"I left the cat and swam. It was late, so it was only for a few minutes. When I came out of the sea the cat had followed me and had had a kitten on the beach. That little beast Michele—the son, you know?—well, he always teased the poor thing, and now he had frightened her off the kitten. It was dead, though. He held it up by the tail and waved it at me as I came out of the sea. I told him to bury it. He scooped two inches of sand away and pushed the kitten in—on the beach, where people are all day. So I buried it properly. He had run off. He was chasing the poor cat. She was terrified and running up the town. I ran too. I caught Michele and I was so angry I hit him. I don't believe in hitting children. I've been feeling beastly about it ever since."

"You were angry."

"It's no excuse. I would never have believed myself capable of hitting a child. I hit him very hard. He went off, crying. The poor cat had got under a big lorry parked in the square. Then she screamed. And then a most remarkable thing happened. She screamed just once, and all at once cats just materialized. One minute there was just one cat, lying under a lorry, and the next, dozens of cats. They sat in a big circle around the lorry, all quite still, and watched my poor cat."

"Rather moving," I said.

"Why?"

"There is no evidence one way or the other," I said in inverted commas, "that the cats were there out of concern for a friend in trouble."

"No," she said energetically. "There isn't. It might have been curiosity. Or anything. How do we know? However, I crawled under the lorry. There were two paws sticking out of the cat's back end. The kitten was the wrong way round. It was stuck. I held the cat down with one hand and I pulled the kitten out with the other." She held out her long white hands. They were still covered with fading scars and scratches. "She bit and yelled, but the kitten was alive. She left the kitten and crawled across the square into the house. Then all the cats got up and walked away. It was the most extraordinary thing I've ever seen. They vanished again. One minute they were all there, and then they had vanished. I went after the cat, with the kitten. Poor little thing, it was covered with dust—being wet, don't you know. The cat was on my bed. There was another kitten coming, but it got stuck too. So when she screamed and screamed I just pulled it out. The kittens began to suck. One kitten was very big. It was a nice fat black kitten. It must have hurt her. But she suddenly bit out—snapped, don't you know, like a reflex action, at the back of the kitten's head. It died, just like that. Extraordinary, isn't it?" she said, blinking hard, her lips quivering. "She was its mother, but she killed it. Then she ran off the bed and went downstairs into the shop under the counter. I called to Luigi. You know, he's Mrs. Rineiri's brother."

"Yes, I know."

"He said she was too young, and she was badly frightened and very hurt. He took the alive kitten to her but she got up and walked away. She didn't want it. Then Luigi told me not to look. But I followed him. He held the kitten by the tail and he banged it against the wall twice. Then he dropped it into the rubbish heap. He moved aside some rubbish with his toe, and put the kitten there and pushed rubbish over it. Then Luigi said the cat should be destroyed. He said she was badly hurt and it would always hurt her to have kittens."

"He hasn't destroyed her. She's still alive. But it looks to me as if he were right."

"Yes, I expect he was."

"What upset you—that he killed the kitten?"

"Oh no, I expect the cat would if he hadn't. But that isn't the point, is it?"

"What is the point?"

"I don't think I really know." She had been speaking breathlessly, and fast. Now she said slowly: "It's not a question of right or wrong,

is it? Why should it be? It's a question of what one is. That night
Luigi wanted to go promenading with me. For him, that was *that*.
Something had to be done, and he'd done it. But I felt ill. He was
very nice to me. He's a very good person," she said, defiantly.

"Yes, he looks it."

"That night I couldn't sleep. I was blaming myself. I should never
have left the cat to go swimming. Well, and then I decided to leave
the next day. And I did. And that's all. The whole thing was a mistake from start to finish."

"Going to Italy at all?"

"Oh, to go for a holiday would have been all right."

"You've done all that work for nothing? You mean you aren't going
to make use of all that research?"

"No. It was a mistake."

"Why don't you leave it a few weeks and see how things are then?"

"Why?"

"You might feel differently about it."

"What an extraordinary thing to say. Why should I? Oh, you mean,
time passing, healing wounds—that sort of thing? What an extraordinary idea. It's always seemed to me an extraordinary idea. No, right
from the beginning I've felt ill at ease with the whole business, not
myself at all."

"Rather irrationally, I should have said."

Judith considered this, very seriously. She frowned while she
thought it over. Then she said: "But if one cannot rely on what one
feels, what can one rely on?"

"On what one thinks, I should have expected you to say."

"Should you? Why? Really, you people are all very strange. I
don't understand you." She turned off the electric fire, and her face
closed up. She smiled, friendly and distant, and said: "I don't really
see any point at all in discussing it."

1963

4   SYMBOLS

One of the chief devices for bridging the gap between the writer's
and the reader's vision is the symbol. A symbol is commonly defined
as something that stands for something else, but that may need some
qualification. Though a member of a class may stand for or represent
the class, it is not really a symbol. Symbols are generally **figurative**;
that is, they explicitly or implicitly compare or merge two *unlike*
things. A senator may represent a state, but he is not a symbol of that
state, for the state is a governmental unit and the senator, as a
member of the government, *literally* represents the state. A flower,

on the other hand, though it may be a native of the state, may very well be a symbol of the state; it has little to do with governing the state, and so represents it only figuratively. When a figure is expressed as an explicit comparison, often signaled by *like* or *as*, it is called a **simile**: "eyes as blue as the sky"; "the baby brother I'd never known looked out from the depths of his private life, like an animal waiting to be coaxed into the light" (*Sonny's Blues*). An implicit comparison or identification of one thing with another unlike itself, without a verbal signal but just seeming to say "A *is* B," is called a **metaphor**: "The sea was a sheet of glass"; "the grass was a green carpet"; "there was a boiling wave of dogs about them" (*The Old People*). Sometimes all figures are loosely referred to as metaphors.

An **allegory** is like a metaphor in that one thing (usually nonrational, abstract, religious) is implicitly spoken of in terms of something that is concrete and usually sensuous (perceptible by the senses), but the comparison in allegory is extended to include a whole work or a large portion of a work. It is therefore usually part of a whole system of equivalencies. *The Pilgrim's Progress* is probably the most famous prose allegory in English: its central character is named Christian; he was born in the City of Destruction and sets out for the Celestial City, passes through the Slough of Despond and Vanity Fair, meets men named Pliable and Obstinate, and so on.

A symbol can be as brief and local as a metaphor or as extended as an allegory, and like an allegory usually speaks in concrete terms of the non- or super-rational, the abstract, that which is not immediately perceived by the senses. Though some allegories can be complex, with many layers or levels of equivalency, and some symbols can be very simple, with paraphrasable equivalencies, allegory usually refers to a one-to-one relationship (as the names from *The Pilgrim's Progress* imply), and literary symbols usually have highly complex or even inexpressible equivalencies. *The Lottery* may be considered a symbolic story, but precisely what it "stands for" is extremely difficult to express briefly and satisfactorily—New England Puritanism? man's cruelty to man? original sin? the dulling of human sensibility by ritualistic actions?

When an entire story, like *The Lottery,* is symbolic, it is sometimes called a **myth** or mythic. *Myth* originally meant a story of communal origin that provided an explanation or religious interpretation of man, nature, the universe, and the relation between them; from the vantage point of another culture or set of beliefs, the word usually implied that the story was false. We speak of classical myths, but Christians do not speak of Christian myth. We also apply the term *myth* now to stories by individuals, sophisticated authors, but often there is still the implication that the mythic story relates to a communal or group experience whereas a symbolic story may be more personal or private. It is hard to draw the line firmly: *The Lottery* and *The Old People* seem to have clearly national, American implications, while *The Rocking-Horse Winner* may be a private Lawrencian symbol or a myth of modern bourgeois society. A plot or character element that recurs in cultural or cross-cultural myths, such as episodes involving descent into the underworld (as in the sewer incident in *The Artificial*

Nigger?) or images of the devil (as in *Young Goodman Brown*), is now widely called an **archetype.**

There is another figure of speech, which seems to border on the one hand on representation and on the other on symbol—the **synecdoche,** a figure in which the part stands for the whole ("Jaws"). At the other boundary line of the symbol, totally nonrepresentational but not quite a symbol, is the **sign,** an arbitrary mark that is assigned a meaning (#, $, %, &, =, to use examples that are handy on the typewriter).

Is there no nonarbitrary reason why snakes are commonly symbolic of evil? Sure, some snakes are poisonous, but for some people so are bees, and a lot of snakes are not only harmless but actually helpful ecologically. (In Kipling's *The Jungle Book* the python Ka is frightening but on the side of Law and Order.) Through repeated use over the centuries, the snake has become a traditional symbol of Evil —not just danger, sneakiness, repulsiveness, but theological, absolute Evil. Had Macomber been startled by a snake during the lion hunt, we would not necessarily have said, "Aha—snake, symbol of Evil," though that potential meaning would have hovered around the incident, perhaps, and sent us looking backward and forward in the story for supporting evidence that this snake was indeed being used symbolically. (I can recall none.) However, when we discover that the stranger in *Young Goodman Brown* has a walking stick upon which is carved the image of a snake, we are much more likely to find it such a symbol because of other, related potential symbols or meanings in the context. The term *Goodman* in the title of the story sets up the distinct possibility that Brown (how common a name) stands for more than a "mere" individual young man. (That this expectation is aroused in part because most of us are ignorant of the fact that in colonial New England *Goodman* was used to mean husband does not cancel the fact that it does—and no doubt did—suggest more than the title.) Brown's bride is named Faith—a common name among the early Puritans, but, together with Goodman, suggesting symbolic possibilities. Then, just before the stranger with the walking stick appears, Brown says, "What if the devil himself should be at my very elbow!"

A single item, even something as traditionally fraught with meaning as a snake or a rose, becomes a symbol only when its potentially symbolic meaning is confirmed by something else in the story, just as a point needs a second point to define a line. Multiple symbols or potential symbols, or these plus other kinds of direct and indirect hints, such as Brown's mention of the devil, are among the ways in which details may be identified as symbols (for interpreting symbols is relatively easy once you know what is and what is probably not a symbol).

One form of what may be called an indirect hint is repetition. That an "old maid" like Judith should have a cat seems so ordinary it borders on the trite. When she chooses to have her male cat put to death rather than neutered, it makes us sit up and take notice, doesn't it? This choice may suggest something about the unconventional in her character, but we probably don't think of the cat in itself representing anything. What happens, though, when there appears another cat, a female this time, whose sex life calls forth strange behavior on Judith's part? And when the killing of a kitten interrupts Judith's affair with Luigi? It is difficult to say when or if the literal cats shade off into symbols, they remain so solidly cats, things, in the story. All we can say for sure is that cats become more important in reading and understanding this story than, say, the cask of Amontillado does in the Poe story. The cask remains a thing pure and simple. Repetition, then, calls attention to details and may alert us to potential symbolic overtones, but it does not necessarily turn a thing into a symbol; nor is it important, so long as we get the suggestions of significance, whether we agree entirely on what—or when—is a symbol.

Direct hints may take the form of explicit statements. (Authors are not so anxious to hide their meanings as some readers are prone to believe.) Sherwood Anderson calls his story *The Egg*, and chickens and eggs figure in most of the incidents. To make sure you know he's writing about more than chickens and eggs, he says things like: "A few hens and now and then a rooster, intended to serve God's mysterious ends, struggle through to maturity. . . . Most philosophers must have been raised on chicken farms." And in case that slips by you: "One hopes for so much from a chicken and is so dreadfully disillusioned. Small chickens, just setting out on the journey of life, look so bright and alert and they are in fact so dreadfully stupid. They are so much like people they mix one up in one's judgments of life."

We also may be alerted to the fact that something is standing for something else when the something does not seem to make literal sense in itself. It does not take us long to realize that *Young Goodman Brown* is not entirely as realistic a story as *Bovanne* or *Macomber*. When things do not seem explicable in terms of everyday reality, we often look beyond them for some meaning, as we do in *The Lottery*.

We must remember, however, that symbols do not exist solely for the transmission of a meaning we can paraphrase; they do not disappear from the story, our memory, or our response once their "meaning" has been sucked out of them, any more than Francis Macomber ceases to exist as an individual after we recognize his representative or universal nature. Faith's pink ribbons, eggs, Judith's cats are all objects in their stories, whatever meanings or suggestions of meanings they have given rise to.

As I've often implied and occasionally said, few symbols can be exhausted, translated into an abstract phrase or equivalent: the "something else" that the "something" stands for is ultimately allusive. When you get to the scene in *The Artificial Nigger* in which Nelson and his grandfather are brought back together by their puzzlement over the function of the statue of a little black jockey, a once-common and now unlamentably rare suburban lawn decoration, try to paraphrase exactly what the "artificial nigger" stands for. Or explain with certainty what Faith's pink ribbon symbolizes. It is not that the statue and the ribbon mean nothing but that they mean so many things that no one equivalence will do; even an abstract statement seems to reduce rather than fully explain the significance for the reader. Yes, the "artificial nigger" is a mystery that unites the boy and his grandfather in their ignorance, but is that the whole meaning of the story's description of the statue as "some monument to another's victory that brought them together in their common defeat"? Do any other incidents involving blacks in the story—on the train, on the city streets—relate to the statue? How does "artificial" fit in? And how about the tone? The phrase is offensive, isn't it, and suggests prejudice and ignorance. But the incident and their ignorance are a little funny, too, and pathetic. Are this incident and this symbol representative of or disruptive of the tone of the story as a whole? It seems to me the statue appropriately encapsulates the unsettling, frightening, and revealing experiences of grandfather and grandson in the city, but I'm not sure I could say everything I thought the "artificial nigger" means or all the feelings it generates. So, too, reading *Young Goodman Brown*, you might want to think about how many things Faith's pink ribbon suggests.

The unparaphrasable nature of these images is not vagueness but richness, not disorder but complexity.

NATHANIEL HAWTHORNE

Young Goodman Brown

Young Goodman Brown came forth, at sunset, into the street of Salem village,[1] but put his head back, after crossing the threshold, to exchange a parting kiss with his young wife. And Faith, as the wife was aptly named, thrust her own pretty head into the street, letting the wind play with the pink ribbons of her cap, while she called to Goodman Brown.

"Dearest heart," whispered she, softly and rather sadly, when her lips were close to his ear, "pr'y thee, put off your journey until sunrise, and sleep in your own bed tonight. A lone woman is troubled with such dreams and such thoughts, that she's afeard of herself, sometimes. Pray, tarry with me this night, dear husband, of all nights in the year!"

"My love and my Faith," replied young Goodman Brown, "of all nights in the year, this one night must I tarry away from thee. My journey, as thou callest it, forth and back again, must needs be done 'twixt now and sunrise. What, my sweet, pretty wife, dost thou doubt me already, and we but three months married!"

"Then, God bless you!" said Faith, with the pink ribbons, "and may you find all well, when you come back."

"Amen!" cried Goodman Brown. "Say thy prayers, dear Faith, and go to bed at dusk, and no harm will come to thee."

1. Salem, Massachusetts, Hawthorne's birthplace (1804) was the scene of the famous witch trials of 1692; *Goodman:* husband, master of household.

So they parted; and the young man pursued his way, until, being about to turn the corner by the meeting-house, he looked back, and saw the head of Faith still peeping after him, with a melancholy air, in spite of her pink ribbons.

"Poor little Faith!" thought he, for his heart smote him. "What a wretch am I, to leave her on such an errand! She talks of dreams, too. Methought, as she spoke, there was trouble in her face, as if a dream had warned her what work is to be done tonight. But, no, no! 'twould kill her to think it. Well; she's a blessed angel on earth; and after this one night, I'll cling to her skirts and follow her to Heaven."

With this excellent resolve for the future, Goodman Brown felt himself justfiied in making more haste on his present evil purpose. He had taken a dreary road, darkened by all the gloomiest trees of the forest, which barely stood aside to let the narrow path creep through, and closed immediately behind. It was all as lonely as could be; and there is this peculiarity in such a solitude, that the traveler knows not who may be concealed by the innumerable trunks and the thick boughs overhead; so that, with lonely footsteps, he may yet be passing through an unseen multitude.

"There may be a devilish Indian behind every tree," said Goodman Brown, to himself; and he glanced fearfully behind him, as he added, "What if the devil himself should be at my very elbow!"

His head being turned back, he passed a crook of the road, and looking forward again, beheld the figure of a man, in grave and decent attire, seated at the foot of an old tree. He arose, at Goodman Brown's approach, and walked onward, side by side with him.

"You are late, Goodman Brown," said he. "The clock of the Old South[2] was striking as I came through Boston; and that is full fifteen minutes agone."

"Faith kept me back awhile," replied the young man, with a tremor in his voice, caused by the sudden appearance of his companion, though not wholly unexpected.

It was now deep dusk in the forest, and deepest in that part of it where these two were journeying. As nearly as could be discerned, the second traveler was about fifty years old, apparently in the same rank of life as Goodman Brown, and bearing a considerable resemblance to him, though perhaps more in expression than features. Still, they might have been taken for father and son. And yet, though the elder person was as simply clad as the younger, and as simple in manner too, he had an indescribable air of one who knew the world, and would not have felt abashed at the governor's dinner table, or in King William's[3] court, were it possible that his affairs should call him thither. But the only thing about him, that could be fixed upon as remarkable, was his staff, which bore the likeness of a great black snake, so curiously wrought, that it might almost be seen to twist and wriggle itself, like a living serpent. This, of course, must have been an ocular deception, assisted by the uncertain light.

2. The Third Church of Boston, established in 1669 in opposition to the requirement of church membership for political rights and thus a landmark of religious freedom.

3. William III—William of Orange—1650-1702, ruled England from 1689 to 1702, until 1694 jointly with his wife, Mary II.

"Come, Goodman Brown!" cried his fellow-traveler, "this is a dull pace for the beginning of a journey. Take my staff, if you are so soon weary."

"Friend," said the other, exchanging his slow pace for a full stop, "having kept covenant by meeting thee here, it is my purpose now to return whence I came. I have scruples, touching the matter thou wot'st of."

"Sayest thou so?" replied he of the serpent, smiling apart. "Let us walk on, nevertheless, reasoning as we go, and if I convince thee not, thou shalt turn back. We are but a little way in the forest, yet."

"Too far, too far!" exclaimed the goodman, unconsciously resuming his walk. "My father never went into the woods on such an errand, nor his father before him. We have been a race of honest men and good Christians, since the days of the martyrs. And shall I be the first of the name of Brown, that ever took this path, and kept—"

"Such company, thou wouldst say," observed the elder person, interpreting his pause. "Well said, Goodman Brown! I have been as well acquainted with your family as with ever a one among the Puritans; and that's no trifle to say. I helped your grandfather, the constable, when he lashed the Quaker woman so smartly through the streets of Salem. And it was I that brought your father a pitch-pine knot, kindled at my own hearth, to set fire to an Indian village, in King Philip's war.[4] They were my good friends, both; and many a pleasant walk have we had along this path, and returned merrily after midnight. I would fain be friends with you, for their sake."

"If it be as thou sayest," replied Goodman Brown, "I marvel they never spoke of these matters. Or, verily, I marvel not, seeing that the least rumor of the sort would have driven them from New England. We are a people of prayer, and good works, to boot, and abide no such wickedness."

"Wickedness or not," said the traveler with the twisted staff, "I have a very general acquaintance here in New England. The deacons of many a church have drunk the communion wine with me; the selectmen, of divers towns, make me their chairman; and a majority of the Great and General Court are firm supporters of my interest. The governor and I, too—but these are state secrets."

"Can this be so!" cried Goodman Brown, with a stare of amazement at his undisturbed companion. "Howbeit, I have nothing to do with the governor and council; they have their own ways, and are no rule for a simple husbandman, like me. But, were I to go on with thee, how should I meet the eye of that good old man, our minister, at Salem village? Oh, his voice would make me tremble, both Sabbath-day and lecture-day!"[5]

Thus far, the elder traveler had listened with due gravity, but now burst into a fit of irrepressible mirth, shaking himself so violently, that his snake-like staff actually seemed to wriggle in sympathy.

"Ha! ha! ha!" shouted he, again and again; then composing him-

4. Metacom or Metacomet, chief of the Wampanoag Indians, known as King Philip, led a war against the New England colonists in 1675–76 which devastated many frontier communities.

5. The day—in the New England colonies usually a Thursday—appointed for a periodical lecture, the lecture being less formal than a sermon or delivered on a different occasion.

self, "Well, go on, Goodman Brown, go on; but pr'y thee, don't kill me with laughing!"

"Well, then, to end the matter at once," said Goodman Brown, considerably nettled, "there is my wife, Faith. It would break her dear little heart; and I'd rather break my own!"

"Nay, if that be the case," answered the other, "e'en[6] go thy ways, Goodman Brown. I would not, for twenty old women like the one hobbling before us, that Faith should come to any harm."

As he spoke, he pointed his staff at a female figure on the path, in whom Goodman Brown recognized a very pious and exemplary dame, who had taught him his catechism, in youth, and was still his moral and spiritual adviser, jointly with the minister and Deacon Gookin.

"A marvel, truly, that Goody[7] Cloyse should be so far in the wilderness, at nightfall!" said he. "But, with your leave, friend, I shall take a cut through the woods, until we have left this Christian woman behind. Being a stranger to you, she might ask whom I was consorting with, and whither I was going."

"Be it so," said his fellow-traveler. "Betake you to the woods, and let me keep the path."

Accordingly, the young man turned aside, but took care to watch his companion, who advanced softly along the road, until he had come within a staff's length of the old dame. She, meanwhile, was making the best of her way, with singular speed for so aged a woman, and mumbling some indistinct words, a prayer, doubtless, as she went. The traveler put forth his staff, and touched her withered neck with what seemed the serpent's tail.

"The devil!" screamed the pious old lady.

"Then Goody Cloyse knows her old friend?" observed the traveler, confronting her, and leaning on his writhing stick.

"Ah, forsooth, and is it your worship, indeed?" cried the good dame. "Yea, truly is it, and in the very image of my old gossip, Goodman Brown, the grandfather of the silly fellow that now is. But—would your worship believe it?—my broomstick hath strangely disappeared, stolen, as I suspect, by that unhanged witch, Goody Cory, and that, too, when I was all anointed with the juice of smallage and cinque-foil and wolf's-bane—"

"Mingled with fine wheat and the fat of a new-born babe," said the shape of old Goodman Brown.

"Ah, your worship knows the receipt," cried the old lady, cackling aloud. "So, as I was saying, being all ready for the meeting, and no horse to ride on, I made up my mind to foot it; for they tell me, there is a nice young man to be taken into communion tonight. But now your good worship will lend me your arm, and we shall be there in a twinkling."

"That can hardly be," answered her friend. "I may not spare you my arm, Goody Cloyse, but here is my staff, if you will."

So saying, he threw it down at her feet, where, perhaps, it assumed life, being one of the rods which its owner had formerly lent to the

6. Just.   7. Short for "goodwife" or housewife.

Egyptian Magi.[8] Of this fact, however, Goodman Brown could not take cognizance. He had cast up his eyes in astonishment, and looking down again, beheld neither Goody Cloyse nor the serpentine staff, but his fellow-traveler alone, who waited for him as calmly as if nothing had happened.

"That old woman taught me my catechism!" said the young man; and there was a world of meaning in this simple comment.

They continued to walk onward, while the elder traveler exhorted his companion to make good speed and persevere in the path, discoursing so aptly, that his arguments seemed rather to spring up in the bosom of his auditor, than to be suggested by himself. As they went, he plucked a branch of maple, to serve for a walking stick, and began to strip it of the twigs and little boughs, which were wet with evening dew. The moment his fingers touched them, they became strangely withered and dried up, as with a week's sunshine. Thus the pair proceeded, at a good free pace, until suddenly, in a gloomy hollow of the road, Goodman Brown sat himself down on the stump of a tree, and refused to go any farther.

"Friend," said he, stubbornly, "my mind is made up. Not another step will I budge on this errand. What if a wretched old woman do choose to go to the devil, when I thought she was going to Heaven! Is that any reason why I should quit my dear Faith, and go after her?"

"You will think better of this, by-and-by," said his acquaintance, composedly. "Sit here and rest yourself awhile; and when you feel like moving again, there is my staff to help you along."

Without more words, he threw his companion the maple stick, and was as speedily out of sight, as if he had vanished into the deepening gloom. The young man sat a few moments, by the roadside, applauding himself greatly, and thinking with how clear a conscience he should meet the minister, in his morning walk, nor shrink from the eye of good old Deacon Gookin. And what calm sleep would be his, that very night, which was to have been spent so wickedly, but purely and sweetly now, in the arms of Faith! Amidst these pleasant and praiseworthy meditations, Goodman Brown heard the tramp of horses along the road, and deemed it advisable to conceal himself within the verge of the forest, conscious of the guilty purpose that had brought him thither, though now so happily turned from it.

On came the hoof-tramps and the voices of the riders, two grave old voices, conversing soberly as they drew near. These mingled sounds appeared to pass along the road, within a few yards of the young man's hiding-place; but owing, doubtless, to the depth of the gloom, at that particular spot, neither the travelers nor their steeds were visible. Though their figures brushed the small boughs by the wayside, it could not be seen that they intercepted, even for a moment, the faint gleam from the strip of bright sky, athwart which they must have passed. Goodman Brown alternately crouched and stood on tiptoe, pulling aside the branches, and thrusting forth

8. *Exodus* 7:9–12. The Lord instructs Moses to have his prophet Aaron throw down his rod before the Pharaoh, whereupon it will be turned into a serpent, and by which miracle the Pharaoh will be persuaded to let the Jews go into the wilderness to sacrifice to God. The Pharaoh has his magicians (Magi) do likewise, "but Aaron's rod swallowed up their rods."

his head as far as he durst, without discerning so much as a shadow. It vexed him the more, because he could have sworn, were such a thing possible, that he recognized the voices of the minister and Deacon Gookin, jogging along quietly, as they were wont to do, when bound to some ordination or ecclesiastical council. While yet within hearing, one of the riders stopped to pluck a switch.

"Of the two, reverend Sir," said the voice like the deacon's, "I had rather miss an ordination-dinner than tonight's meeting. They tell me that some of our community are to be here from Falmouth[9] and beyond, and others from Connecticut and Rhode Island; besides several of the Indian powows, who, after their fashion, know almost as much deviltry as the best of us. Moreover, there is a goodly young woman to be taken into communion."

"Mighty well, Deacon Gookin!" replied the solemn old tones of the minister. "Spur up, or we shall be late. Nothing can be done, you know, until I get on the ground."

The hoofs clattered again, and the voices, talking so strangely in the empty air, passed on through the forest, where no church had ever been gathered, nor solitary Christian prayed. Whither, then, could these holy men be journeying, so deep into the heathen wilderness? Young Goodman Brown caught hold of a tree, for support, being ready to sink down on the ground, faint and overburdened with the heavy sickness of his heart. He looked up to the sky, doubting whether there really was a Heaven above him. Yet there was the blue arch, and the stars brightening in it.

"With Heaven above, and Faith below, I will yet stand firm against the devil!" cried Goodman Brown.

While he still gazed upward, into the deep arch of the firmament, and had lifted his hands to pray, a cloud, though no wind was stirring, hurried across the zenith, and hid the brightening stars. The blue sky was still visible, except directly overhead, where this black mass of cloud was sweeping swiftly northward. Aloft in the air, as if from the depths of the cloud, came a confused and doubtful sound of voices. Once, the listener fancied that he could distinguish the accents of townspeople of his own, men and women, both pious and ungodly, many of whom he had met at the communion-table, and had seen others rioting at the tavern. The next moment, so indistinct were the sounds, he doubted whether he had heard aught but the murmur of the old forest, whispering without a wind. Then came a stronger swell of those familiar tones, heard daily in the sunshine, at Salem village, but never, until now, from a cloud of night. There was one voice, of a young woman, uttering lamentations, yet with an uncertain sorrow, and entreating for some favor, which, perhaps, it would grieve her to obtain. And all the unseen multitude, both saints and sinners, seemed to encourage her onward.

"Faith!" shouted Goodman Brown, in a voice of agony and desperation; and the echoes of the forest mocked him, crying—"Faith! Faith!" as if bewildered wretches were seeking her, all through the wilderness.

9. A port in extreme southern Massachusetts; Salem is in northern Massachusetts.

The cry of grief, rage, and terror, was yet piercing the night, when the unhappy husband held his breath for a response. There was a scream, drowned immediately in a louder murmur of voices, fading into far-off laughter, as the dark cloud swept away, leaving the clear and silent sky above Goodman Brown. But something fluttered lightly down through the air, and caught on the branch of a tree. The young man seized it, and beheld a pink ribbon.

"My Faith is gone!" cried he, after one stupefied moment. "There is no good on earth; and sin is but a name. Come, devil! for to thee is this world given."

And maddened with despair, so that he laughed loud and long, did Goodman Brown grasp his staff and set forth again, at such a rate, that he seemed to fly along the forest path, rather than to walk or run. The road grew wilder and drearier, and more faintly traced, and vanished at length, leaving him in the heart of the dark wilderness, still rushing onward, with the instinct that guides mortal man to evil. The whole forest was peopled with frightful sounds; the creaking of the trees, the howling of wild beasts, and the yell of Indians; while, sometimes, the wind tolled like a distant church bell, and sometimes gave a broad roar around the traveler, as if all Nature were laughing him to scorn. But he was himself the chief horror of the scene, and shrank not from its other horrors.

"Ha! ha! ha!" roared Goodman Brown, when the wind laughed at him. "Let us hear which will laugh loudest! Think not to frighten me with your deviltry! Come witch, come wizard, come Indian powow, come devil himself! and here comes Goodman Brown. You may as well fear him as he fear you!"

In truth, all through the haunted forest, there could be nothing more frightful than the figure of Goodman Brown. On he flew, among the black pines, brandishing his staff with frenzied gestures, now giving vent to an inspiration of horrid blasphemy, and now shouting forth such laughter, as set all the echoes of the forest laughing like demons around him. The fiend in his own shape is less hideous, than when he rages in the breast of man. Thus sped the demoniac on his course, until, quivering among the trees, he saw a red light before him, as when the felled trunks and branches of a clearing have been set on fire, and throw up their lurid blaze against the sky, at the hour of midnight. He paused, in a lull of the tempest that had driven him onward, and heard the swell of what seemed a hymn, rolling solemnly from a distance, with the weight of many voices. He knew the tune; it was a familiar one in the choir of the village meeting-house. The verse died heavily away, and was lengthened by a chorus, not of human voices, but of all the sounds of the benighted wilderness, pealing in awful harmony together. Goodman Brown cried out; and his cry was lost to his own ear, by its unison with the cry of the desert.

In the interval of silence, he stole forward, until the light glared full upon his eyes. At one extremity of an open space, hemmed in by the dark wall of the forest, arose a rock, bearing some rude, natural resemblance either to an altar or a pulpit, and surrounded by four blazing pines, their tops aflame, their stems untouched, like candles at an evening meeting. The mass of foliage, that had overgrown the

summit of the rock, was all on fire, blazing high into the night, and
fitfully illuminating the whole field. Each pendent twig and leafy
festoon was in a blaze. As the red light arose and fell, a numerous congregation alternately shone forth, then disappeared in shadow, and
again grew, as it were, out of the darkness, peopling the heart of the
solitary woods at once.

"A grave and dark-clad company!" quoth Goodman Brown.

In truth, they were such. Among them, quivering to-and-fro, between gloom and splendor, appeared faces that would be seen, next
day, at the council-board of the province, and others which, Sabbath
after Sabbath, looked devoutly heavenward, and benignantly over
the crowded pews, from the holiest pulpits in the land. Some affirm,
that the lady of the governor was there. At least, there were high
dames well known to her, and wives of honored husbands, and
widows, a great multitude, and ancient maidens, all of excellent
repute, and fair young girls, who trembled, lest their mothers should
espy them. Either the sudden gleams of light, flashing over the obscure field, bedazzled Goodman Brown, or he recognized a score of
the church-members of Salem village, famous for their especial sanc-
tity. Good old Deacon Gookin had arrived, and waited at the skirts
of that venerable saint, his revered pastor. But, irreverently consorting with these grave, reputable, and pious people, these elders of
the church, these chaste dames and dewy virgins, there were men of
dissolute lives and women of spotted fame, wretches given over to
all mean and filthy vice, and suspected even of horrid crimes. It was
strange to see, that the good shrank not from the wicked, nor were
the sinners abashed by the saints. Scattered, also, among their pale-
faced enemies, were the Indian priests, or powows, who had often
scared their native forest with more hideous incantations than any
known to English witchcraft.

"But, where is Faith?" thought Goodman Brown; and, as hope
came into his heart, he trembled.

Another verse of the hymn arose, a slow and mournful strain,
such as the pious love, but joined to words which expressed all that
our nature can conceive of sin, and darkly hinted at far more. Unfathomable to mere mortals is the lore of fiends. Verse after verse
was sung, and still the chorus of the desert swelled between, like
the deepest tone of a mighty organ. And, with the final peal of that
dreadful anthem, there came a sound, as if the roaring wind, the
rushing streams, the howling beasts, and every other voice of the
unconverted wilderness, were mingling and according with the voice
of guilty man, in homage to the prince of all. The four blazing pines
threw up a loftier flame, and obscurely discovered shapes and visages
of horror on the smoke-wreaths, above the impious assembly. At
the same moment, the fire on the rock shot redly forth, and formed
a glowing arch above its base, where now appeared a figure. With
reverence be it spoken, the figure bore no slight similitude, both in
garb and manner, to some grave divine of the New England churches.

"Bring forth the converts!" cried a voice, that echoed through the
field and rolled into the forest.

At the word, Goodman Brown stepped forth from the shadow of
the trees, and approached the congregation, with whom he felt a

loathful brotherhood, by the sympathy of all that was wicked in his heart. He could have well nigh sworn, that the shape of his own dead father beckoned him to advance, looking downward from a smoke-wreath, while a woman, with dim features of despair, threw out her hand to warn him back. Was it his mother? But he had no power to retreat one step, nor to resist, even in thought, when the minister and good old Deacon Gookin seized his arms, and led him to the blazing rock. Thither came also the slender form of a veiled female, led between Goody Cloyse, that pious teacher of the catechism, and Martha Carrier, who had received the devil's promise to be queen of hell. A rampant hag was she! And there stood the proselytes, beneath the canopy of fire.

"Welcome, my children," said the dark figure, "to the communion of your race! Ye have found, thus young, your nature and your destiny. My children, look behind you!"

They turned; and flashing forth, as it were, in a sheet of flame, the fiend-worshippers were seen; the smile of welcome gleamed darkly on every visage.

"There," resumed the sable form, "are all whom ye have reverenced from youth. Ye deemed them holier than yourselves, and shrank from your own sin, contrasting it with their lives of righteousness, and prayerful aspirations heavenward. Yet, here are they all, in my worshipping assembly! This night it shall be granted you to know their secret deeds; how hoary-bearded elders of the church have whispered wanton words to the young maids of their households; how many a woman, eager for widow's weeds, has given her husband a drink at bedtime, and let him sleep his last sleep in her bosom; how beardless youths have made haste to inherit their fathers' wealth; and how fair damsels—blush not, sweet ones!—have dug little graves in the garden, and bidden me, the sole guest, to an infant's funeral. By the sympathy of your human hearts for sin, ye shall scent out all the places—whether in church, bedchamber, street, field, or forest—where crime has been committed, and shall exult to behold the whole earth one stain of guilt, one mighty bloodspot. Far more than this! It shall be yours to penetrate, in every bosom, the deep mystery of sin, the fountain of all wicked arts, and which inexhaustibly supplies more evil impulses than human power—than my power, at its utmost!—can make manifest in deeds. And now, my children, look upon each other."

They did so; and, by the blaze of the hell-kindled torches, the wretched man beheld his Faith, and the wife her husband, trembling before that unhallowed altar.

"Lo! there ye stand, my children," said the figure, in a deep and solemn tone, almost sad, with its despairing awfulness, as if his once angelic nature could yet mourn for our miserable race. "Depending upon one another's hearts, ye had still hoped, that virtue were not all a dream. Now are ye undeceived! Evil is the nature of mankind. Evil must be your only happiness. Welcome, again, my children, to the communion of your race!"

"Welcome!" repeated the fiend-worshippers, in one cry of despair and triumph.

And there they stood, the only pair, as it seemed, who were yet hesitating on the verge of wickedness, in this dark world. A basin was hollowed, naturally, in the rock. Did it contain water, reddened by the lurid light? or was it blood? or, perchance, a liquid flame? Herein did the Shape of Evil dip his hand, and prepare to lay the mark of baptism upon their foreheads, that they might be partakers of the mystery of sin, more conscious of the secret guilt of others, both in deed and thought, than they could now be of their own. The husband cast one look at his pale wife, and Faith at him. What polluted wretches would the next glance shew them to each other, shuddering alike at what they disclosed and what they saw!

"Faith! Faith!" cried the husband. "Look up to Heaven, and resist the Wicked One!"

Whether Faith obeyed, he knew not. Hardly had he spoken, when he found himself amid calm night and solitude, listening to a roar of the wind, which died heavily away through the forest. He staggered against the rock and felt it chill and damp, while a hanging twig, that had been on fire, besprinkled his cheek with the coldest dew.

The next morning, young Goodman Brown came slowly into the street of Salem village, staring around him like a bewildered man. The good old minister was taking a walk along the graveyard, to get an appetite for breakfast and meditate his sermon, and bestowed a blessing, as he passed, on Goodman Brown. He shrank from the venerable saint, as if to avoid an anathema. Old Deacon Gookin was at domestic worship, and the holy words of his prayer were heard though the open window. "What God doth the wizard pray to?" quoth Goodman Brown. Goody Cloyse, that excellent old Christian, stood in the early sunshine, at her own lattice, catechizing a little girl, who had brought her a pint of morning's milk. Goodman Brown snatched away the child, as from the grasp of the fiend himself. Turning the corner by the meeting-house, he spied the head of Faith, with the pink ribbons, gazing anxiously forth, and bursting into such joy at sight of him, that she skipped along the street, and almost kissed her husband before the whole village. But, Goodman Brown looked sternly and sadly into her face, and passed on without a greeting.

Had Goodman Brown fallen asleep in the forest, and only dreamed a wild dream of a witch-meeting?

Be it so, if you will. But, alas! it was a dream of evil omen for young Goodman Brown. A stern, a sad, a darkly meditative, a distrustful, if not a desperate man, did he become, from the night of that fearful dream. On the Sabbath day, when the congregation were singing a holy psalm, he could not listen, because an anthem of sin rushed loudly upon his ear, and drowned all the blessed strain. When the minister spoke from the pulpit, with power and fervid eloquence, and, with his hand on the open Bible, of the sacred truths of our religion, and of saint-like lives and triumphant deaths, and of future bliss or misery unutterable, then did Goodman Brown turn pale, dreading, lest the roof should thunder down upon the gray blasphemer and his hearers. Often, awakening suddenly at midnight, he shrank from the bosom of Faith, and at morning or eventide, when the family knelt down at prayer, he scowled, and muttered to himself, and gazed sternly at his wife, and turned away. And when he had lived long, and was borne to his grave, a hoary corpse, followed by Faith, an aged woman, and children and grandchildren, a goodly procession, besides neighbors, not a few, they carved no hopeful verse upon his tombstone; for his dying hour was gloom.

1846

FLANNERY O'CONNOR

The Artificial Nigger

Mr. Head awakened to discover that the room was full of moonlight. He sat up and stared at the floor boards—the color of silver—and then at the ticking on his pillow, which might have been brocade, and after a second, he saw half of the moon five feet away in his shaving mirror, paused as if it were waiting for his permission to enter. It rolled forward and cast a dignifying light on everything. The straight chair against the wall looked stiff and attentive as if it were awaiting an order and Mr. Head's trousers, hanging to the back of it, had an almost noble air, like the garment some great man had just flung to his servant; but the face on the moon was a grave one. It gazed across the room and out the window where it floated over the horse stall and appeared to contemplate itself with the look of a young man who sees his old age before him.

Mr. Head could have said to it that age was a choice blessing and that only with years does a man enter into that calm understanding of life that makes him a suitable guide for the young. This, at least, had been his own experience.

He sat up and grasped the iron posts at the foot of his bed and raised himself until he could see the face on the alarm clock which sat on an overturned bucket beside the chair. The hour was two in the morning. The alarm on the clock did not work but he was not dependent on any mechanical means to awaken him. Sixty years had not dulled his responses; his physical reactions, like his moral ones, were guided by his will and strong character, and these could be seen plainly in his features. He had a long tube-like face with a long rounded open jaw and a long depressed nose. His eyes were alert but quiet, and in the miraculous moonlight they had a look of composure and of ancient wisdom as if they belonged to one of the great guides of men. He might have been Vergil summoned in the middle of the night to go to Dante, or better, Raphael, awakened by a blast of God's light to fly to the side of Tobias.[1] The only dark spot in the room was Nelson's pallet, underneath the shadow of the window.

1. Vergil, Publius Vergilius Maro (70–19 B.C.), author of the *Aeneid*, in *The Divine Comedy* of Dante Alighieri (1265–1321), is summoned by Beatrice (*Inferno*, II, 49–70) to assist Dante and serves as his guide through Hell and Purgatory; the angel Raphael in the Book of Tobit in the *Apocrypha* serves as Tobias's instructor and companion in the overcoming of the demon Asmodeus.

Nelson was hunched over on his side, his knees under his chin and his heels under his bottom. His new suit and hat were in the boxes that they had been sent in and these were on the floor at the foot of the pallet where he could get his hands on them as soon as he woke up. The slop jar, out of the shadow and made snow-white in the moonlight, appeared to stand guard over him like a small personal angel. Mr. Head lay back down, feeling entirely confident that he could carry out the moral mission of the coming day. He meant to be up before Nelson and to have the breakfast cooking by the time he awakened. The boy was always irked when Mr. Head was the first up. They would have to leave the house at four to get to the railroad junction by five-thirty. The train was to stop for them at five forty-five and they had to be there on time for this train was stopping merely to accommodate them.

This would be the boy's first trip to the city though he claimed it would be his second because he had been born there. Mr. Head had tried to point out to him that when he was born he didn't have the intelligence to determine his whereabouts but this had made no impression on the child at all and he continued to insist that this was to be his second trip. It would be Mr. Head's third trip. Nelson had said, "I will've already been there twict and I ain't but ten."

Mr. Head had contradicted him.

"If you ain't been there in fifteen years, how you know you'll be able to find your way about?" Nelson had asked. "How you know it hasn't changed some?"

"Have you ever," Mr. Head had asked, "seen me lost?"

Nelson certainly had not but he was a child who was never satisfied until he had given an impudent answer and he replied, "It's nowhere around here to get lost at."

"The day is going to come," Mr. Head prophesied, "when you'll find you ain't as smart as you think you are." He had been thinking about this trip for several months but it was for the most part in moral terms that he conceived it. It was to be a lesson that the boy would never forget. He was to find out from it that he had no cause for pride merely because he had been born in a city. He was to find out that the city is not a great place. Mr. Head meant him to see everything there is to see in a city so that he would be content to stay at home for the rest of his life. He fell asleep thinking how the boy would at last find out that he was not as smart as he thought he was.

He was awakened at three-thirty by the smell of fatback frying and he leaped off his cot. The pallet was empty and the clothes boxes had been thrown open. He put on his trousers and ran into the other room. The boy had a corn pone on cooking and had fried the meat. He was sitting in the half-dark at the table, drinking cold coffee out of a can. He had on his new suit and his new gray hat pulled low over his eyes. It was too big for him but they had ordered it a size large because they expected his head to grow. He didn't say anything but his entire figure suggested satisfaction at having arisen before Mr. Head.

Mr. Head went to the stove and brought the meat to the table in the skillet. "It's no hurry," he said. "You'll get there soon enough and it's no guarantee you'll like it when you do neither," and he sat down across from the boy whose hat teetered back slowly to reveal a fiercely expressionless face, very much the same shape as the old man's. They were grandfather and grandson but they looked enough alike to be brothers and brothers not too far apart in age, for Mr. Head had a youthful expression by daylight, while the boy's look was ancient, as if he knew everything already and would be pleased to forget it.

Mr. Head had once had a wife and daughter and when the wife died, the daughter ran away and returned after an interval with Nelson. Then one morning, without getting out of bed, she died and left Mr. Head with sole care of the year-old child. He had made the mistake of telling Nelson that he had been born in Atlanta. If he hadn't told him that, Nelson couldn't have insisted that this was going to be his second trip.

"You may not like it a bit," Mr. Head continued. "It'll be full of niggers."

The boy made a face as if he could handle a nigger.

"All right," Mr. Head said. "You ain't ever seen a nigger."

"You wasn't up very early," Nelson said.

"You ain't ever seen a nigger," Mr. Head repeated. "There hasn't been a nigger in this county since we run that one out twelve years ago and that was before you were born." He looked at the boy as if he were daring him to say he had ever seen a Negro.

"How you know I never saw a nigger when I lived there before?" Nelson asked. "I probably saw a lot of niggers."

"If you seen one you didn't know what he was," Mr. Head said, completely exasperated. "A six-month-old child don't know a nigger from anybody else."

"I reckon I'll know a nigger if I see one," the boy said and got up and straightened his slick sharply creased gray hat and went outside to the privy.

They reached the junction some time before the train was due to arrive and stood about two feet from the first set of tracks. Mr. Head carried a paper sack with some biscuits and a can of sardines in it for their lunch. A coarse-looking orange-colored sun coming up behind the east range of mountains was making the sky a dull red behind them, but in front of them it was still gray and they faced a gray transparent moon, hardly stronger than a thumbprint and completely without light. A small tin switch box and a black fuel tank were all there was to mark the place as a junction; the tracks were double and did not converge again until they were hidden behind the bends at either end of the clearing. Trains passing appeared to emerge from a tunnel of trees and, hit for a second by the cold sky, vanish terrified into the woods again. Mr. Head had had to make special arrangements with the ticket agent to have this train stop and he was secretly afraid it would not, in which case, he knew Nelson would say, "I never thought no train was going to stop for you." Under the useless morning moon the tracks looked white and fragile. Both the old man and the child stared ahead as if they were awaiting an apparition.

Then suddenly, before Mr. Head could make up his mind to turn back, there was a deep warning bleat and the train appeared, gliding very slowly, almost silently around the bend of trees about two hundred yards down the track, with one yellow front light shining. Mr. Head was still not certain it would stop and he felt it would make an even bigger idiot of him if it went by slowly. But he and Nelson, however, were prepared to ignore the train if it passed them.

The engine charged by, filling their noses with the smell of hot metal and then the second coach came to a stop exactly where they were standing. A conductor with the face of an ancient bloated bulldog was on the step as if he expected them, though he did not look as if it mattered one way or the other to him if they got on or not. "To the right," he said.

Their entry took only a fraction of a second and the train was already speeding on as they entered the quiet car. Most of the travelers were still sleeping, some with their heads hanging off the chair arms, some stretched across two seats, and some sprawled out with their feet in the aisle. Mr. Head saw two unoccupied seats and pushed Nelson toward them. "Get in there by the winder," he said in his normal voice which was very loud at this hour of the morning. "Nobody cares if you set there because it's nobody in it. Sit right there."

"I heard you," the boy muttered. "It's no use in you yelling," and he sat down and turned his head to the glass. There he saw a pale ghost-like face scowling at him beneath the brim of a pale ghost-like hat. His grandfather, looking quickly too, saw a different ghost, pale but grinning, under a black hat.

Mr. Head sat down and settled himself and took out his ticket and started reading aloud everything that was printed on it. People began to stir. Several woke up and stared at him. "Take off your hat," he said to Nelson and took off his own and put it on his knee. He had a small amount of white hair that had turned tobacco-colored over the years and this lay flat across the back of his head. The front of his head was bald and creased. Nelson took off his hat and put it on his knee and they waited for the conductor to come ask for their tickets.

The man across the aisle from them was spread out over two seats, his feet propped on the window and his head jutting into the aisle. He had on a light blue suit and a yellow shirt unbuttoned at the neck. His eyes had just opened and Mr. Head was ready to introduce himself when the conductor came up from behind and growled, "Tickets."

When the conductor had gone, Mr. Head gave Nelson the return half of his ticket and said, "Now put that in your pocket and don't lose it or you'll have to stay in the city."

"Maybe I will," Nelson said as if this were a reasonable suggestion.

Mr. Head ignored him. "First time this boy has ever been on a train," he explained to the man across the aisle, who was sitting up now on the edge of his seat with both feet on the floor.

Nelson jerked his hat on again and turned angrily to the window.

"He's never seen anything before," Mr. Head continued. "Ignorant as the day he was born, but I mean for him to get his fill once and for all."

The boy leaned forward, across his grandfather and toward the stranger. "I was born in the city," he said. "I was born there. This is my second trip." He said it in a high positive voice but the man across the aisle didn't look as if he understood. There were heavy purple circles under his eyes.

Mr. Head reached across the aisle and tapped him on the arm. "The thing to do with a boy," he said sagely, "is to show him all it is to show. Don't hold nothing back."

"Yeah," the man said. He gazed down at his swollen feet and lifted the left one about ten inches from the floor. After a minute he put it down and lifted the other. All through the car people began to get up and move about and yawn and stretch. Separate voices could be heard here and there and then a general hum. Suddenly Mr. Head's serene expression changed. His mouth almost closed and a light, fierce and cautious both, came into his eyes. He was looking down the length of the car. Without turning, he caught Nelson by the arm and pulled him forward. "Look," he said.

A huge coffee-colored man was coming slowly forward. He had on a light suit and a yellow satin tie with a ruby pin in it. One of his hands rested on his stomach which rode majestically under his buttoned coat, and in the other he held the head of a black walking stick that he picked up and set down with a deliberate outward motion each time he took a step. He was proceeding very slowly, his large brown eyes gazing over the heads of the passengers. He had a small white mustache and white crinkly hair. Behind him there were two young women, both coffee-colored, one in a yellow dress and one in a green. Their progress was kept at the rate of his and they chatted in low throaty voices as they followed him.

Mr. Head's grip was tightening insistently on Nelson's arm. As the procession passed them, the light from a sapphire ring on the brown hand that picked up the cane reflected in Mr. Head's eye, but he did not look up nor did the tremendous man look at him. The group proceeded up the rest of the aisle and out of the car. Mr. Head's grip on Nelson's arm loosened. "What was that?" he asked.

"A man," the boy said and gave him an indignant look as if he were tired of having his intelligence insulted.

"What kind of a man?" Mr. Head persisted, his voice expressionless.

"A fat man," Nelson said. He was beginning to feel that he had better be cautious.

"You don't know what kind?" Mr. Head said in a final tone.

"An old man," the boy said and had a sudden foreboding that he was not going to enjoy the day.

"That was a nigger," Mr. Head said and sat back.

Nelson jumped up on the seat and stood looking backward to the end of the car but the Negro had gone.

"I'd of thought you'd know a nigger since you seen so many when you was in the city on your first visit," Mr. Head continued. "That's his first nigger," he said to the man across the aisle.

The boy slid down into the seat. "You said they were black," he said in an angry voice. "You never said they were tan. How do you expect me to know anything when you don't tell me right?"

"You're just ignorant is all," Mr. Head said and he got up and moved over in the vacant seat by the man across the aisle.

Nelson turned backward again and looked where the Negro had disappeared. He felt that the Negro had deliberately walked down the aisle in order to make a fool of him and he hated him with a fierce raw fresh hate; and also, he understood now why his grandfather disliked them. He looked toward the window and the face there seemed to suggest that he might be inadequate to the day's exactions. He wondered if he would even recognize the city when they came to it.

After he had told several stories, Mr. Head realized that the man he was talking to was asleep and he got up and suggested to Nelson that they walk over the train and see the parts of it. He particularly wanted the boy to see the toilet so they went first to the men's room and examined the plumbing. Mr. Head demonstrated the ice-water cooler as if he had invented it and showed Nelson the bowl with the single spigot where the travelers brushed their teeth. They went through several cars and came to the diner.

This was the most elegant car in the train. It was painted a rich egg-yellow and had a wine-colored carpet on the floor. There were wide windows over the tables and great spaces of the rolling view were caught in miniature in the sides of the coffee pots and in the glasses. Three very black Negroes in white suits and aprons were running up and down the aisle, swinging trays and bowing and bending over the travelers eating breakfast. One of them rushed up to Mr. Head and Nelson and said, holding up two fingers, "Space for two!" but Head replied in a loud voice, "We eaten before we left!"

The waiter wore large brown spectacles that increased the size of his eye whites. "Stan' aside then please," he said with an airy wave of the arm as if he were brushing aside flies.

Neither Nelson nor Mr. Head moved a fraction of an inch. "Look," Mr. Head said.

The near corner of the diner, containing two tables, was set off from the rest by a saffron-colored curtain. One table was set but empty but at the other, facing them, his back to the drape, sat the tremendous Negro. He was speaking in a soft voice to the two women while he buttered a muffin. He had a heavy sad face and his neck bulged over his white collar on either side. "They rope them off," Mr. Head explained. Then he said, "Let's go see the kitchen," and they walked the length of the diner but the black waiter was coming fast behind them.

"Passengers are not allowed in the kitchen!" he said in a haughty voice. "Passengers are NOT allowed in the kitchen!"

Mr. Head stopped where he was and turned. "And there's good reason for that," he shouted into the Negro's chest, "because the cockroaches would run the passengers out!"

All the travelers laughed and Mr. Head and Nelson walked out, grinning. Mr. Head was known at home for his quick wit and Nelson felt a sudden keen pride in him. He realized the old man would be his only support in the strange place they were approaching. He would be entirely alone in the world if he were ever lost from his grandfather. A terrible excitement shook him and he wanted to take hold of Mr. Head's coat and hold on like a child.

As they went back to their seats they could see through the passing windows that the countryside was becoming speckled with small houses and shacks and that a highway ran alongside the train. Cars sped by on it, very small and fast. Nelson felt that there was less breath in the air than there had been thirty minutes ago. The man across the aisle had left and there was no one near for Mr. Head to hold a conversation with so he looked out the window, through his own reflection, and read aloud the names of the buildings they were passing. "The Dixie Chemical Corp!" he announced. "Southern Maid Flour! Dixie Doors! Southern Belle Cotton Products! Patty's Peanut Butter! Southern Mammy Cane Syrup!"

"Hush up!" Nelson hissed.

All over the car people were beginning to get up and take their luggage off the overhead racks. Women were putting on their coats and hats. The conductor stuck his head in the car and snarled, "Firstop-ppppmry,"[2] and Nelson lunged out of his sitting position, trembling. Mr. Head pushed him down by the shoulder.

"Keep your seat," he said in dignified tones. "The first stop is on the edge of town. The second stop is at the main railroad station." He had come by this knowledge on his first trip when he had got off at the first stop and had had to pay a man fifteen cents to take him into the heart of town. Nelson sat back down, very pale. For the first time in his life, he understood that his grandfather was indispensable to him.

The train stopped and let off a few passengers and glided on as if it had never ceased moving. Outside, behind rows of brown rickety houses, a line of blue buildings stood up, and beyond them a pale rose-gray sky faded away to nothing. The train moved into the railroad yard. Looking down, Nelson saw lines and lines of silver tracks multiplying and criss-crossing. Then before he could start counting them, the face in the window stared out at him, gray but distinct, and he looked the other way. The train was in the station. Both he and Mr. Head jumped up and ran to the door. Neither noticed that they had left the paper sack with the lunch in it on the seat.

They walked stiffly through the small station and came out of a heavy door into the squall of traffic. Crowds were hurrying to work. Nelson didn't know where to look. Mr. Head leaned against the side of the building and glared in front of him.

Finally Nelson said, "Well, how do you see what all it is to see?"

Mr. Head didn't answer. Then as if the sight of people passing had given him the clue, he said, "You walk," and started off down the street. Nelson followed, steadying his hat. So many sights and sounds were flooding in on him that for the first block he hardly knew what he was seeing. At the second corner, Mr. Head turned and looked behind him at the station they had left, a putty-colored terminal with a concrete dome on top. He thought that if he could keep the dome always in sight, he would be able to get back in the afternoon to catch the train again.

As they walked along, Nelson began to distinguish details and take note of the store windows, jammed with every kind of equipment—hardware, drygoods, chicken feed, liquor. They passed one that Mr. Head called his particular attention to where you walked in and sat on a chair with your feet upon two rests and let a Negro polish your shoes. They walked slowly and stopped and stood at the entrances so he could see what went on in each place but they did not go into any of them. Mr. Head was determined not to go into any city store because

2. "First stop, Emory," station in suburban Atlanta.

on his first trip here, he had got lost in a large one and had found his way out only after many people had insulted him.

They came in the middle of the next block to a store that had a weighing machine in front of it and they both in turn stepped up on it and put in a penny and received a ticket. Mr. Head's ticket said, "You weigh 120 pounds. You are upright and brave and all your friends admire you." He put the ticket in his pocket, surprised that the machine should have got his character correct but his weight wrong, for he had weighed on a grain scale not long before and knew he weighed 110. Nelson's ticket said, "You weigh 98 pounds. You have a great destiny ahead of you but beware of dark women." Nelson did not know any women and he weighed only 68 pounds but Mr. Head pointed out that the machine had probably printed the number upsidedown, meaning the 9 for a 6.

They walked on and at the end of five blocks the dome of the terminal sank out of sight and Mr. Head turned to the left. Nelson could have stood in front of every store window for an hour if there had not been another more interesting one next to it. Suddenly he said, "I was born here!" Mr. Head turned and looked at him with horror. There was a sweaty brightness about his face. "This is where I come from!" he said.

Mr. Head was appalled. He saw the moment had come for drastic action. "Lemme show you one thing you ain't seen yet," he said and took him to the corner where there was a sewer entrance. "Squat down," he said, "and stick you head in there," and he held the back of the boy's coat while he got down and put his head in the sewer. He drew it back quickly, hearing a gurgling in the depths under the sidewalk. Then Mr. Head explained the sewer system, how the entire city was underlined with it, how it contained all the drainage and was full of rats and how a man could slide into it and be sucked along down endless pitchblack tunnels. At any minute any man in the city might be sucked into the sewer and never heard from again. He described it so well that Nelson was for some seconds shaken. He connected the sewer passages with the entrance to hell and understood for the first time how the world was put together in its lower parts. He drew away from the curb.

Then he said, "Yes, but you can stay away from the holes," and his face took on that stubborn look that was so exasperating to his grandfather. "This is where I come from!" he said.

Mr. Head was dismayed but he only muttered, "You'll get your fill," and they walked on. At the end of two more blocks he turned to the left, feeling that he was circling the dome; and he was correct for in a half-hour they passed in front of the railroad station again. At first Nelson did not notice that he was seeing the same stores twice but when they passed the one where you put your feet on the rests while the Negro polished your shoes, he perceived that they were walking in a circle.

"We done been here!" he shouted. "I don't believe you know where you're at!"

"The direction just slipped my mind for a minute," Mr. Head said and they turned down a different street. He still did not intend to let the dome get too far away and after two blocks in their new direction, he turned to the left. This street contained two- and three-story wooden dwellings. Anyone passing on the sidewalk could see into the rooms and Mr. Head, glancing through one window, saw a woman lying on an iron bed, looking out, with a sheet pulled over her. Her knowing expression shook him. A fierce-looking boy on a bicycle came driving down out of nowhere and he had to jump to the side to keep from being hit. "It's nothing to them if they knock you down," he said. "You better keep closer to me."

They walked on for some time on streets like this before he remembered to turn again. The houses they were passing now were all unpainted and the wood in them looked rotten; the street between was narrower. Nelson saw a colored man. Then another. Then another. "Niggers live in these houses," he observed.

"Well come on and we'll go somewhere else," Mr. Head said. "We didn't come to look at niggers," and they turned down another street but they continued to see Negroes everywhere. Nelson's skin began to prickle and they stepped along at a faster pace in order to leave the neighborhood as soon as possible. There were colored men in their undershirts standing in the doors and colored women rocking on the sagging porches. Colored children played in the gutters and stopped what they were doing to look at them. Before long they began to pass rows of stores with colored customers in them but they didn't pause at the entrances of these. Black eyes in black faces were watching them from every direction. "Yes," Mr. Head said, "this is where you were born—right here with all these niggers."

Nelson scowled. "I think you done got us lost," he said.

Mr. Head swung around sharply and looked for the dome. It was nowhere in sight. "I ain't got us lost either," he said. "You're just tired of walking."

"I ain't tired, I'm hungry," Nelson said. "Give me a biscuit."

They discovered then that they had lost the lunch.

"You were the one holding the sack," Nelson said. "I would have kepaholt of it."

"If you want to direct this trip, I'll go on by myself and leave you right here," Mr. Head said and was pleased to see the boy turn white. However, he realized they were lost and drifting farther every minute from the station. He was hungry himself and beginning to be thirsty and since they had been in the colored neighborhood, they had both begun to sweat. Nelson had on his shoes and he was unaccustomed to them. The concrete sidewalks were very hard. They both wanted to find a place to sit down but this was impossible and they kept on walking, the boy muttering under his breath, "First you lost the sack and then you lost the way," and Mr. Head growling from time to time, "Anybody wants to be from this nigger heaven can be from it!"

By now the sun was well forward in the sky. The odor of dinners cooking drifted out to them. The Negroes were all at their doors to see them pass. "Whyn't you ast one of these niggers the way?" Nelson said. "You got us lost."

"This is where you were born," Mr. Head said. "You can ast one yourself if you want to."

Nelson was afraid of the colored men and he didn't want to be laughed at by the colored children. Up ahead he saw a large colored woman leaning in a doorway that opened onto the sidewalk. Her hair stood straight out from her head for about four inches all around and she was resting on bare brown feet that turned pink at the sides. She had on a pink dress that showed her exact shape. As they came abreast of her, she lazily lifted one hand to her head and her fingers disappeared into her hair.

Nelson stopped. He felt his breath drawn up by the woman's dark eyes. "How do you get back to town?" he said in a voice that did not sound like his own.

After a minute she said, "You in town now," in a rich low tone that made Nelson feel as if a cool spray had been turned on him.

"How do you get back to the train?" he said in the same reed-like voice.

"You can catch you a car," she said.

He understood she was making fun of him but he was too paralyzed even to scowl. He stood drinking in every detail of her. His eyes traveled up from her great knees to her forehead and then made a triangular path from the glistening sweat on her neck down and across her tremendous bosom and over her bare arm back to where her fingers lay hidden in her hair. He suddenly wanted her to reach down and pick him up and draw him against her and then he wanted to feel her breath on his face. He wanted to look down and down into her eyes while she held him tighter and tighter. He had never had such a feeling before. He felt as if he were reeling down through a pitchblack tunnel.

"You can go a block down yonder and catch you a car take you to the railroad station, Sugarpie," she said.

Nelson would have collapsed at her feet if Mr. Head had not pulled him roughly away. "You act like you don't have any sense!" the old man growled.

They hurried down the street and Nelson did not look back at the woman. He pushed his hat sharply forward over his face which was already burning with shame. The sneering ghost he had seen in the train window and all the foreboding feelings he had on the way returned to him and he remembered that his ticket from the scale had said to beware of dark women and that his grandfather's had said he was upright and brave. He took hold of the old man's hand, a sign of dependence that he seldom showed.

They headed down the street toward the car tracks where a long yellow rattling trolley was coming. Mr. Head had never boarded a streetcar and he let that one pass. Nelson was silent. From time to time his mouth trembled slightly but his grandfather, occupied with his own problems, paid him no attention. They stood on the corner and neither looked at the Negroes who were passing, going about their business just as if they had been white, except that most of them stopped and eyed Mr. Head and Nelson. It occurred to Mr. Head that since the streetcar ran on tracks, they could simply follow the tracks. He gave Nelson a slight push and explained that they would follow the tracks on into the railroad station, walking, and they set off.

Presently to their great relief they began to see white people again and Nelson sat down on the sidewalk against the wall of a building. "I got to rest myself some," he said. "You lost the sack and the direction. You can just wait on me to rest myself."

"There's the tracks in front of us," Mr. Head said. "All we got to do is keep them in sight and you could have remembered the sack as good as me. This is where you were born. This is your old home town. This is your second trip. You ought to know how to do," and he squatted down and continued in this vein but the boy, easing his burning feet out of his shoes, did not answer.

"And standing there grinning like a chim-pan-zee while a nigger woman gives you directions. Great Gawd!" Mr. Head said.

"I never said I was nothing but born here," the boy said in a shaky voice. "I never said I would or wouldn't like it. I never said I wanted to come. I only said I was born here and I never had nothing to do with that. I want to go home. I never wanted to come in the first place. It was all your big idea. How you know you ain't following the tracks in the wrong direction?"

This last had occurred to Mr. Head too. "All these people are white," he said.

"We ain't passed here before," Nelson said. This was a neighborhood of brick buildings that might have been lived in or might not. A few empty automobiles were parked along the curb and there was an occasional passer-by. The heat of the pavement came up through Nelson's thin suit. His eyelids began to droop, and after a few minutes his head tilted forward. His shoulders twitched once or twice and then he fell over on his side and lay sprawled in an exhausted fit of sleep.

Mr. Head watched him silently. He was very tired himself but they could not both sleep at the same time and he could not have slept anyway because he did not know where he was. In a few minutes Nelson would wake up, refreshed by his sleep and very cocky, and would begin complaining that he had lost the sack and the way. You'd have a mighty sorry time if I wasn't here, Mr. Head thought; and then another idea occurred to him. He looked at the sprawled figure for several minutes; presently he stood up. He justified what he was going to do on the grounds that it is sometimes necessary to teach a child a lesson he won't forget, particularly when the child is always reasserting his position with some new impudence. He walked without a sound to the corner about twenty feet away and sat down on a covered garbage can in the alley where he could look out and watch Nelson wake up alone.

The boy was dozing fitfully, half conscious of vague noises and black forms moving up from some dark part of him into the light. His face worked in his sleep and he had pulled his knees up under his chin. The sun shed a dull dry light on the narrow street; everything looked like exactly what it was. After a while Mr. Head, hunched like an old monkey on the garbage can lid, decided that if Nelson didn't wake up soon, he would make a loud noise by bamming his foot against the can. He looked at his watch and discovered that it was two o'clock. Their train left at six and the possibility of missing it was too awful for him to think of. He kicked his foot backwards on the can and a hollow boom reverberated in the alley.

Nelson shot up onto his feet with a shout. He looked where his grandfather should have been and stared. He seemed to whirl several times and then, picking up his feet and throwing his head back, he dashed down the street like a wild maddened pony. Mr. Head jumped off the can and galloped after but the child was almost out of sight. He saw a streak of gray disappearing diagonally a block ahead. He ran as fast as he could, looking both ways down every intersection, but without sight of him again. Then as he passed the third intersection completely winded, he saw about half a block down the street a scene that stopped him altogether. He crouched behind a trash box to watch and get his bearings.

Nelson was sitting with both legs spread out and by his side lay an elderly woman, screaming. Groceries were scattered about the sidewalk. A crowd of women had already gathered to see justice done and Mr. Head distinctly heard the old woman on the pavement shout, "You've broken my ankle and your daddy'll pay for it! Every nickel! Police! Police!" Several of the women were plucking at Nelson's shoulder but the boy seemed too dazed to get up.

Something forced Mr. Head from behind the trash box and forward, but only at a creeping pace. He had never in his life been accosted by a policeman. The women were milling around Nelson as if they might suddenly all dive on him at once and tear him to pieces, and the old woman continued to scream that her ankle was broken and to call for an officer. Mr. Head came on so slowly that he could have been taking a backward step after each forward one, but when he was about ten feet away, Nelson saw him and sprang. The child caught him around the hips and clung panting against him.

The women all turned on Mr. Head. The injured one sat up and shouted, "You sir! You'll pay every penny of my doctor's bill that your boy has caused. He's a juve-nile delinquent! Where is an officer? Somebody take this man's name and address!"

Mr. Head was trying to detach Nelson's fingers from the flesh in the back of his legs. The old man's head had lowered itself into his collar like a turtle; his eyes were glazed with fear and caution.

"Your boy has broken my ankle!" the old woman shouted. "Police!"

Mr. Head sensed the approach of the policeman from behind. He stared straight ahead at the women who were massed in their fury like a solid wall to block his escape. "This is not my boy," he said. "I never seen him before."

He felt Nelson's fingers fall out of his flesh.

The women dropped back, staring at him with horror, as if they were so repulsed by a man who could deny his own image and likeness that they could not bear to lay hands on him. Mr. Head walked on, through a space they silently cleared, and left Nelson behind. Ahead of him he saw nothing but a hollow tunnel that had once been the street.

The boy remained standing where he was, his neck craned forward and his hands hanging by his sides. His hat was jammed on his head so that there were no longer any creases in it. The injured woman got up and shook her fist at him and the others gave him pitying looks, but he didn't notice any of them. There was no policeman in sight.

In a minute he began to move mechanically, making no effort to catch up with his grandfather but merely following at about twenty paces. They walked on for five blocks in this way. Mr. Head's shoulders were sagging and his neck hung forward at such an angle that it was not visible from behind. He was afraid to turn his head. Finally he cut a short hopeful glance over his shoulder. Twenty feet behind him, he saw two small eyes piercing into his back like pitchfork prongs.

The boy was not of a forgiving nature but this was the first time he had ever had anything to forgive. Mr. Head had never disgraced himself before. After two more blocks, he turned and called over his shoulder in a high desperately gay voice, "Let's us go get a Co' Cola somewheres!"

Nelson, with a dignity he had never shown before, turned and stood with his back to his grandfather.

Mr. Head began to feel the depth of his denial. His face as they walked on became all hollows and bare ridges. He saw nothing they were passing but he perceived that they had lost the car tracks. There was no dome to be seen anywhere and the afternoon was advancing. He knew that if dark overtook them in the city, they would be beaten and robbed. The speed of God's justice was only what he expected for himself, but he could not stand to think that his sins would be visited upon Nelson and that even now, he was leading the boy to his doom.

They continued to walk on block after block through an endless section of small brick houses until Mr. Head almost fell over a water spigot sticking up about six inches off the edge of a grass plot. He had not had a drink of water since early morning but he felt he did not deserve it now. Then he thought that Nelson would be thirsty and they would both drink and be brought together. He squatted down and put his mouth to the nozzle and turned a cold stream of water into his throat. Then he called out in the high desperate voice, "Come on and getcher some water!"

This time the child stared through him for nearly sixty seconds. Mr. Head got up and walked on as if he had drunk poison. Nelson, though he had not had water since some he had drunk out of a paper cup on the train, passed by the spigot, disdaining to drink where his grandfather had. When Mr. Head realized this, he lost all hope. His face in the waning afternoon light looked ravaged and abandoned. He could feel the boy's steady hate, traveling at an even pace behind him and he knew that (if by some miracle they escaped being murdered in the city) it would continue just that way for the rest of his life. He knew that now he was wandering into a black strange place where nothing was like it had even been before, a long old age without respect and an end that would be welcome because it would be the end.

As for Nelson, his mind had frozen around his grandfather's treachery as if he were trying to preserve it intact to present at the final judgment. He walked without looking to one side or the other, but every now and then his mouth would twitch and this was when he felt, from some remote place inside himself, a black mysterious form reach up as if it would melt his frozen vision in one hot grasp.

The sun dropped down behind a row of houses and hardly noticing, they passed into an elegant suburban section where mansions were set back from the road by lawns with birdbaths on them. Here everything was entirely deserted. For blocks they didn't pass even a dog. The big white houses were like partially submerged icebergs in the distance. There were no sidewalks, only drives and these wound around and around in endless ridiculous circles. Nelson made no move to come nearer to Mr. Head. The old man felt that if he saw a sewer entrance he would drop down into it and let himself be carried away; and he could imagine the boy standing by, watching with only a slight interest, while he disappeared.

A loud bark jarred him to attention and he looked up to see a fat man approaching with two bulldogs. He waved both arms like someone shipwrecked on a desert island. "I'm lost!" he called. "I'm lost and can't find my way and me and this boy have got to catch this train and I can't find the station. Oh Gawd I'm lost! Oh hep me Gawd I'm lost!"

The man, who was bald-headed and had on golf knickers, asked him what train he was trying to catch and Mr. Head began to get out his tickets, trembling so violently he could hardly hold them. Nelson had come up to within fifteen feet and stood watching.

"Well," the fat man said, giving him back the tickets, "you won't have time to get back to town to make this but you can catch it at the suburb stop. That's three blocks from here," and he began explaining how to get there.

Mr. Head stared as if he were slowly returning from the dead and when the man had finished and gone off with the dogs jumping at his heels, he turned to Nelson and said breathlessly, "We're going to get home!"

The child was standing about ten feet away, his face bloodless under the gray hat. His eyes were triumphantly cold. There was no light in them, no feeling, no interest. He was merely there, a small figure, waiting. Home was nothing to him.

Mr. Head turned slowly. He felt he knew now what time would be like without seasons and what heat would be like without light and what man would be like without salvation. He didn't care if he never made the train and if it had not been for what suddenly caught his attention, like a cry out of the gathering dusk, he might have forgotten there was a station to go to.

He had not walked five hundred yards down the road when he saw, within reach of him, the plaster figure of a Negro sitting bent over on a low yellow brick fence that curved around a wide lawn. The Negro was about Nelson's size and he was pitched forward at an unsteady angle because the putty that held him to the wall had cracked. One of his eyes was entirely white and he held a piece of brown watermelon.

Mr. Head stood looking at him silently until Nelson stopped at a little distance. Then as the two of them stood there, Mr. Head breathed, "An artificial nigger!"

It was not possible to tell if the artificial Negro were meant to be young or old; he looked too miserable to be either. He was meant to look happy because his mouth was stretched up at the corners but the chipped eye and the angle he was cocked at gave him a wild look of misery instead.

"An artificial nigger!" Nelson repeated in Mr. Head's exact tone.

The two of them stood there with their necks forward at almost the same angle and their shoulders curved in almost exactly the same way and their hands trembling identically in their pockets. Mr. Head looked like an ancient child and Nelson like a miniature old man. They stood gazing at the artificial Negro as if they were faced with some great mystery, some monument to another's victory that brought them together in their common defeat. They could both feel it dissolving their differences like an action of mercy. Mr. Head had never known before what mercy felt like because he had been too good to deserve any, but he felt he knew now. He looked at Nelson and understood that he must say something to the child to show that he was still wise and in the look the boy returned he saw a hungry need for that assurance. Nelson's eyes seemed to implore him to explain once and for all the mystery of existence.

Mr. Head opened his lips to make a lofty statement and heard himself say, "They ain't got enough real ones here. They got to have an artificial one."

After a second, the boy nodded with a strange shivering about his mouth, and said, "Let's go home before we get ourselves lost again."

Their train glided into the suburb stop just as they reached the station and they boarded it together, and ten minutes before it was due to arrive at the junction, they went to the door and stood ready to jump off if it did not stop; but it did, just as the moon, restored to its full splendor, sprang from a cloud and flooded the clearing with light. As they stepped off, the sage grass was shivering gently in shades of silver and the clinkers under their feet glittered with a fresh black light. The treetops, fencing the junction like the protecting walls of a garden, were darker than the sky which was hung with gigantic white clouds illuminated like lanterns.

Mr. Head stood very still and felt the action of mercy touch him again but this time he knew that there were no words in the world that could name it. He understood that it grew out of agony, which is not denied to any man and which is given in strange ways to children. He understood it was all a man could carry into death to give his Maker and he suddenly burned with shame that he had so little of it to take with him. He stood appalled, judging himself with the thoroughness of God, while the action of mercy covered his pride like a flame and consumed it. He had never thought himself a great sinner before but he saw now that his true depravity had been hidden from him lest it cause him despair. He realized that he was forgiven for sins from the beginning of time, when he had conceived in his own heart the sin of Adam, until the present, when he had denied poor Nelson. He saw that no sin was too monstrous for him to claim as his own, and since God loved in proportion as He forgave, he felt ready at that instant to enter Paradise.

Nelson, composing his expression under the shadow of his hat brim, watched him with a mixture of fatigue and suspicion, but as the train glided past them and disappeared like a frightened serpent into the woods, even his face lightened and he muttered, "I'm glad I've went once, but I'll never go back again!"

1955

5   THEME

If you ask what a story is "about," an author is likely to answer by telling you the **subject**. Indeed, many authors tell you the subject in their titles: *An Occurrence at Owl Creek Bridge, The Lottery, Our Friend Judith, Her First Ball*. Though a subject is always concrete, it may be stated at somewhat greater length than the few words of a title: "a man's thoughts as he faces execution for spying during the Civil War" (*Owl Creek Bridge*); "a young girl's excitement at her first grown-up dance and an incident that temporarily depresses her" (*Her First Ball*).

A friend might be more likely to tell you what a story is about by giving you a summary of the action: "This guy shoots a lion but is too chicken to go in and put it out of its misery, so his wife . . ." (We sometimes call this a **plot summary**, but you will notice that this summary is of the history—that's the way people usually tell us about a story—while the plot is an arrangement or structuring of that history; in *Macomber*, remember, the lion incident is not told to us first, though it did happen first.)

Your teacher may well tell you what a story is about by summarizing its **theme**. Some refer to the central idea, the thesis, or even the message of a story, and that is roughly what we mean by theme: a generalization or abstraction from the story.

The subject of *Young Goodman Brown* may be said to be a coven (witches' meeting), or, more fully, "a young colonial New England husband is driven mad by finding everyone he thought good and pure attending a witches' meeting." The theme may be "everyone partakes of evil," or, more succinctly, "the Fall." The theme of *The Artificial Nigger* similarly may be said to be redemption. There are, as you can see, degrees of generalization and abstraction; subject (a young man finds that everyone is evil) shades off into theme, which itself can be more or less general and abstract.

Discussions of literature in or out of class sometimes seem to suggest that stories exist for their themes, that we read only to get the "point" or message. But most themes, you must admit, are somewhat less than earth-shattering. That all men (and women) are evil may be debatable, but it certainly isn't news. That living beings, human and otherwise, should not be divided into exploiters (hunters) and exploited (hunted)—the apparent theme of *The Most Dangerous Game*—is, if acceptable, pretty obvious, something we don't need to read fifteen pages of fiction to find out. No wonder, then, that some of our more skeptical friends contend that stories are only elaborate ways of "saying something simple"; that literature is a game in which authors hide their meanings under shells of words.

Of course, reading fifteen pages of a story like *The Most Dangerous Game* can be fun. Could it be that we really read fiction for the fun, and all our talk about themes is just hiding from our puritan natures the fact that we are goofing off, pretending there's some high moral purpose in it all ("football builds character")?

I don't believe that articulating the theme of a story is either the purpose of, or the excuse for, reading fiction, or that authors hide their meanings like Easter eggs. In order to relate his or her unique vision of reality to an absent and unknown reader, a writer must find a way of communicating, some common ground on which he or she can meet the various unique individuals who will read the story. Common experiences, common assumptions, common language, and commonplaces offer such ground. Readers reach out from their own subjective worlds toward that new and different vision of the author with the help of the common elements (the general), and especially through the commonplaces of theme, bringing back the particulars and generalizations of the story to their own reading and living experience. The reader sees a spoiled Easterner on safari in Africa overcome his cowardice in an attempt to put a dangerous animal out of its misery. Generalizing, the reader may conclude that what the story says (its theme) is that life (or happy life) is more than survival, that honor is more important than existence, and that when one's values change one's behavior can be changed. Not planning to go on safari in the very near future, the reader may test out the experience of the story by translating it through its theme to his or her own experience: does this mean that I can change long-standing patterns of behavior that I know are wrong? Do I have any ideals I believe greater than life itself?

We should not confuse these questions with the story, but the significance of any story is modified to some extent by the reader's experience of books and life. (If this suggests that only a reader who had read and experienced everything and understood it all perfectly could read a story perfectly, it is not unintentional.) This does not imply that you are to reduce every story to the dimensions of what you already know and feel, but rather that you reach out to the story and bring it back to your own experience as an addition and modification. If you're going to make a story yours, and if you are going to make it more than a yarn about a guy who drinks a lot, has an unfaithful wife, and hunts lions and water buffalos, you will translate it somehow into terms that, while not necessarily psychological or moral precepts, alter or broaden to some degree your own vision of yourself, others, life in general.

When I discussed symbols, I said that even while a symbol suggests a meaning beyond the particulars of the fiction, it remains a detail in the fictional world—the snakelike staff of the stranger in *Young Goodman Brown* remains a staff, the "artificial nigger" remains a statue. Some critics would say that this is true also of theme and that theme is related to the history as integrally as symbolic meaning is to detail; that is, rather than *Young Goodman Brown* telling us something we did not know before, or making hard truths palatable, its theme and its history modify each other. The theme as I've stated it relates to spiritual evil, the kind of evil suggested by the snake and Satan figures. There are other things in the story that seem to suggest the theme has to do with moral evil (specifically, sexuality) in addition to or as part of spiritual evil: the fact that Brown is a newlywed, that Faith wears pink (coquettish?) ribbons, and that she, whom Brown thought so pure and innocent, shows up at the meeting of witches and sinners. So any paraphrase of the theme needs to take both kinds of evil into account, and perhaps even to indicate what the story implies about the relationship between sex and virtue. A statement that can do justice to all the complexity and all the particulars of the story is not likely to take the simple form of a message. Indeed, it is the complex particularity of literature, its ultimate irreducibility, that makes critics and teachers reject *message* (which suggests a simple packaged statement) as a suitable term even for the paraphrasable thematic content of a story.

Young Goodman Brown is an allegorical story whose details do function as symbols with paraphrasable meanings, yet even its theme refuses to be reduced to a simple statement. How much more resistant, then, are more realistic stories that are not allegorical and whose details do not function as allegorical symbols. *Her First Ball* is a short, rather simple story that seems to have a simple theme overtly enunciated by one of the characters: Leila's elderly partner suggests that her first ball is "only the beginning of her last ball." That youth and life itself are fleeting (scarcely a new truth, but one that we must be reminded of from time to time, no doubt) would seem to be the simple theme of this story. But the scene with the elderly partner is not the end of the story. Leila goes on to dance with a young partner, doesn't recognize her former partner, has fun, and seems to have completely forgotten the man's "message." What is the story "saying"? Is her forgetting "bad" or "sad," or "good"? Does the theme suggest the thoughtlessness of youth, the incommunicability of experience, trapping us in inescapable patterns, dooming us to repeat the experiences of our predecessors? Or is it better for Leila to live while she's young, to make the most of life, rather than dwelling on life's brevity? The specifics of the story modify and enrich all the generalizations we can abstract from it, while these themes and questions, if we recognize them, modify and enrich our reading, our experience of the story.

I realize I have been talking as if a theme or themes spring out at the reader, while to some of you my inference of themes may seem more like pulling rabbits out of hats. But if you have been watching carefully you will have caught my left hand prestidigitating. You will have noticed, for example, that I derived the theme of theological evil in *Young Goodman Brown* from the symbols (the snake-staff, Satan figure, names) and that physical details like pink ribbons and the narrative situation (the three-month marriage) which had sexual implications were tested against the theme to see if I would have to modify my paraphrase. In *Her First Ball* a character raises a general issue that is tested by subsequent events in the story and modified by them. In *The Most Dangerous Game* the opening conversation raises thematic issues (the morality of hunting) that are dramatically reinforced by the subsequent action of the story (Rainsford now the hunted rather than hunter). In *The Lady with the Dog* you will see Gurov conjecturing or generalizing to himself—once by the sea, for example, when the sea's indifference to life and death seems, paradoxically, to suggest that life or the life force goes on in a "never-ceasing movement toward perfection," and later when he concludes that everyone's life, like his own, really goes on in secret and "revolves around mystery." We must try somehow to bring these two overt generalizations into some kind of accord, some vision that includes them both. We must decide whether the events in the story confirm Gurov's view, whether we can trust him, or whether, like Leila's partner, he speaks seeming truth that needs serious modification.

There are, of course, other means by which details suggest generalizations or meaning or by which meaning may be abstracted from detail. You no doubt noticed in the first footnote to *The Artificial Nigger* there are two **allusions**, references outside the story (in this case to literature and the Bible, but allusions can encompass history or other areas common to the culture). They have to do with someone guiding someone else through a realm of spirits or the underworld. In the story, the grandfather sets out to guide Nelson through Atlanta, and at one point he has Nelson stick his head into a sewer, telling him that at any time "a man could slide into it and be sucked along down endless pitchblack tunnels." Nelson quite naturally "connected the sewer passages with the entrance to hell." The descent to hell is a common narrative pattern, a common element in crosscultural myths: an **archetype**. So allusion and archetype as well as symbols and plot, narrative voice, and character are elements that contribute to and must be accounted for in paraphrasing a theme. That is why theme is important, and why it comes last in a discussion of the elements of fiction.

But remember, the theme is an inadequate abstraction from the story; the story and its details do not disappear or lose significance once distilled into theme, nor could you reconstruct a story merely from its paraphrased theme. Indeed, theme and story, history and structure, do not so much interact, are not so much interrelated, as they are fused, inseparable.

How would you paraphrase the theme of *Lady with the Dog*? On the one hand, your definition of the theme will depend on what you think of Gurov and Anna: are they having a rather commonplace affair out of boredom and desperation and deceiving themselves into believing it's some sort of grand passion and ideal love, or is their vision of their relationship, no matter how difficult that relationship is, the true one? On the other hand, your view of their relationship depends on your apprehension and acceptance of the theme; your guess about their future and your evaluation of their love may well depend on whether you believe there is a benign force or current underneath the surface of life that moves irresistibly toward something we can call "the good." The story defines and evaluates the theme, the theme interprets the details and evaluates them. That's what I meant when I said that history and structure, story and theme interact.

A story is a compound of elements, not a mixture. In a sense, though they are useful, may be necessary, and seem reasonable or even obvious, the elements of fiction—plot, focus and voice, character, symbol, and theme, as well as others we have not talked about—do not really exist. They are convenient ways for us to extricate inextricable threads from the fabric of fiction. As the Old Master, Henry James, himself said a hundred years ago:

> A novel is a living thing, all one and continuous, like any other organism, and in proportion as it lives will it be found . . . that in each of its parts there is something of each of the other parts. The critic who over the close texture of a finished work shall pretend to trace a geography of items will mark some frontiers as artificial, I fear, as any that have been known to history. . . . What is character but the determination of incident? What is incident but the illustration of character?

KATHERINE MANSFIELD

Her First Ball

Exactly when the ball began Leila would have found it hard to say. Perhaps her first real partner was the cab. It did not matter that she shared the cab with the Sheridan girls and their brother. She sat back in her own little corner of it, and the bolster on which her hand rested felt like the sleeve of an unknown young man's dress suit; and away they bowled, past waltzing lampposts and houses and fences and trees.

"Have you really never been to a ball before, Leila? But, my child, how too weird—" cried the Sheridan girls.

"Our nearest neighbor was fifteen miles," said Leila softly, gently opening and shutting her fan.

Oh, dear, how hard it was to be indifferent like the others! She tried not to smile too much; she tried not to care. But every single thing was so new and exciting . . . Meg's tuberoses, Jose's long loop of amber, Laura's little dark head, pushing above her white fur like a flower through snow. She would remember for ever. It even gave her a pang to see her cousin Laurie throw away the wisps of tissue paper he pulled from the fastenings of his new gloves. She would like to have kept those wisps as a keepsake, as a remembrance. Laurie leaned forward and put his hand on Laura's knee.

"Look here, darling," he said. "The third and the ninth as usual. Twig?"

Oh, how marvellous to have a brother! In her excitement Leila felt that if there had been time, if it hadn't been impossible, she couldn't have helped crying because she was an only child, and no brother had ever said "Twig?" to her; no sister would ever say, as Meg said to Jose that moment, "I've never known your hair go up more successfully than it has tonight!"

But, of course, there was no time. They were at the drill hall already; there were cabs in front of them and cabs behind. The road was bright on either side with moving fan-like lights, and on the pavement gay couples seemed to float through the air; little satin shoes chased each other like birds.

"Hold on to me, Leila; you'll get lost," said Laura.

"Come on, girls, let's make a dash for it," said Laurie.

Leila put two fingers on Laura's pink velvet cloak, and they were somehow lifted past the big golden lantern, carried along the passage, and pushed into the little room marked "Ladies." Here the crowd was so great there was hardly space to take off their things; the noise was deafening. Two benches on either side were stacked high with wraps. Two old women in white aprons ran up and down tossing fresh armfuls. And everybody was pressing forward trying to get at the little dressing table and mirror at the far end.

A great quivering jet of gas lighted the ladies' room. It couldn't wait; it was dancing already. When the door opened again and there came a burst of tuning from the drill hall, it leaped almost to the ceiling.

Dark girls, fair girls were patting their hair, tying ribbons again, tucking handkerchiefs down the fronts of their bodices, smoothing marble-white gloves. And because they were all laughing it seemed to Leila that they were all lovely.

"Aren't there any invisible hairpins?" cried a voice. "How most extraordinary! I can't see a single invisible hairpin."

"Powder my back, there's a darling," cried some one else.

"But I must have a needle and cotton. I've torn simply miles and miles of the frill," wailed a third.

Then, "Pass them along, pass them along!" The straw basket of programs was tossed from arm to arm. Darling little pink-and-silver programs, with pink pencils and fluffy tassels. Leila's fingers shook as she took one out of the basket. She wanted to ask someone, "Am I meant to have one too?" but she had just time to read: "Waltz 3. *Two, Two in a Canoe.* Polka 4. *Making the Feathers Fly,*" when Meg cried, "Ready, Leila?" and they pressed their way through the crush in the passage towards the big double doors of the drill hall.

Dancing had not begun yet, but the band had stopped tuning, and the noise was so great it seemed that when it did begin to play it would never be heard. Leila, pressing close to Meg, looking over Meg's shoulder, felt that even the little quivering colored flags strung across the ceiling were talking. She quite forgot to be shy; she forgot how in the middle of dressing she had sat down on the bed with one shoe off and one shoe on and begged her mother to ring up her cousins and say she couldn't go after all. And the rush of longing she had had to be sitting on the veranda of their forsaken upcountry home, listening to the baby owls crying "More pork" in the moonlight, was changed to a rush of joy so sweet that it was hard to bear alone. She clutched her fan, and, gazing at the gleaming, golden floor, the azaleas, the lanterns, the stage at one end with its red carpet and gilt chairs and the band in a corner, she thought breathlessly, "How heavenly; how simply heavenly!"

All the girls stood grouped together at one side of the doors, the men at the other, and the chaperones in dark dresses, smiling rather foolishly, walked with little careful steps over the polished floor towards the stage.

"This is my little country cousin Leila. Be nice to her. Find her partners; she's under my wing," said Meg, going up to one girl after another.

Strange faces smiled at Leila—sweetly, vaguely. Strange voices answered, "Of course, my dear." But Leila felt the girls didn't really see her. They were looking towards the men. Why didn't the men begin? What were they waiting for? There they stood, smoothing their gloves, patting their glossy hair and smiling among themselves. Then, quite suddenly, as if they had only just made up their minds that that was what they had to do, the men came gliding over the parquet. There was a joyful flutter among the girls. A tall, fair man flew up to Meg, seized her program, scribbled something; Meg passed him on to Leila. "May I have the pleasure?" He ducked and smiled. There came a dark man wearing an eyeglass, then cousin Laurie with a friend, and Laura with a little freckled fellow whose tie was crooked. Then quite an old man—fat, with a big bald patch on his head—took her program and murmured, "Let me see, let me see!" And he was a long time comparing his program, which looked black with names, with hers. It seemed to give him so much trouble that Leila was ashamed. "Oh, please don't bother," she said eagerly. But instead of replying the fat man wrote something, glanced at her again. "Do I remember this bright little face?" he said softly. "Is it known to me of yore?" At that moment the band began playing; the fat man disappeared. He was tossed away on a great wave of music that came flying over the gleaming floor, breaking the groups up into couples, scattering them, sending them spinning. . . .

Leila had learned to dance at boarding school. Every Saturday afternoon the boarders were hurried off to a little corrugated iron mission hall where Miss Eccles (of London) held her "select" classes. But the difference between that dusty-smelling hall—with calico texts on the walls, the poor terrified little woman in a brown velvet toque with rabbit's ears thumping the cold piano, Miss Eccles poking the girls' feet with her long white wand—and this was so tremendous that Leila was sure if her partner didn't come and she had to listen to that marvelous music and to watch the others sliding, gliding over the golden floor, she would die at least, or faint, or lift her arms and fly out of one of those dark windows that showed the stars.

"Ours, I think—" Some one bowed, smiled, and offered her his arm; she hadn't to die after all. Some one's hand pressed her waist, and she floated away like a flower that is tossed into a pool.

"Quite a good floor, isn't it?" drawled a faint voice close to her ear.

"I think it's most beautifully slippery," said Leila.

"Pardon!" The faint voice sounded surprised. Leila said it again. And there was a tiny pause before the voice echoed, "Oh, quite!" and she was swung round again.

He steered so beautifully. That was the great difference between dancing with girls and men, Leila decided. Girls banged into each other, and stamped on each other's feet; the girl who was gentleman always clutched you so.

The azaleas were separate flowers no longer; they were pink and white flags streaming by.

"Were you at the Bells' last week," the voice came again. It sounded tired. Leila wondered whether she ought to ask him if he would like to stop.

"No, this is my first dance," said she.

Her partner gave a little gasping laugh. "Oh, I say," he protested.

"Yes, it is really the first dance I've ever been to." Leila was most fervent. It was such a relief to be able to tell somebody. "You see, I've lived in the country all my life up until now. . . ."

At that moment the music stopped, and they went to sit on two chairs against the wall. Leila tucked her pink satin feet under and fanned herself, while she blissfully watched the other couples passing and disappearing through the swing doors.

"Enjoying yourself, Leila?" asked Jose, nodding her golden head.

Laura passed and gave her the faintest little wink; it made Leila wonder for a moment whether she was quite grown up after all. Certainly her partner did not say very much. He coughed, tucked his handkerchief away, pulled down his waistcoat, took a minute thread off his sleeve. But it didn't matter. Almost immediately the band started, and her second partner seemed to spring from the ceiling.

"Floor's not bad," said the new voice. Did one always begin with the floor? And then, "Were you at the Neaves' on Tuesday?" And again Leila explained. Perhaps it was a little strange that her partners were not more interested. For it was thrilling. Her first ball! She was only at the beginning of everything. It seemed to her that she had never known what the night was like before. Up till now it had been dark, silent, beautiful very often—oh, yes—but mournful somehow. Solemn. And now it would never be like that again—it had opened dazzling bright.

"Care for an ice?" said her partner. And they went through the swing doors, down the passage, to the supper room. Her cheeks burned, she was fearfully thirsty. How sweet the ices looked on little glass plates, and how cold the frosted spoon was, iced too! And when they came back to the hall there was the fat man waiting for her by the door. It gave her quite a shock again to see how old he was; he ought to have been on the stage with the fathers and mothers. And when Leila compared him with her other partners he looked shabby. His waistcoat was creased, there was a button off his glove, his coat looked as if it was dusty with French chalk.

'Come along, little lady," said the fat man. He scarcely troubled to clasp her, and they moved away so gently, it was more like walking than dancing. But he said not a word about the floor. "Your first dance, isn't it?" he murmured.

"How *did* you know?"

"Ah," said the fat man, "that's what it is to be old!" He wheezed faintly as he steered her past an awkward couple. "You see, I've been doing this kind of thing for the last thirty years."

"Thirty years?" cried Leila. Twelve years before she was born!

"It hardly bears thinking about, does it?" said the fat man gloomily.

Leila looked at his bald head, and she felt quite sorry for him.

"I think it's marvelous to be still going on," she said kindly.

"Kind little lady," said the fat man, and he pressed her a little closer, and hummed a bar of the waltz. "Of course," he said, "you can't hope to last anything like as long as that. No-o," said the fat man, "long before that you'll be sitting up there on the stage, looking on, in your nice black velvet. And these pretty arms will have turned into little short fat ones, and you'll beat time with such a different kind of fan—a black bony one." The fat man seemed to shudder. "And you'll smile away like the poor old dears up there, and point to your daughter, and tell the elderly lady next to you how some dreadful man tried to kiss her at the club ball. And your heart will ache, ache"—the fat man squeezed her closer still, as if he really was sorry for that poor heart—"because no one wants to kiss you now. And you'll say how unpleasant these polished floors are to walk on, how dangerous they are. Eh, Mademoiselle Twinkletoes?" said the fat man softly.

Leila gave a light little laugh, but she did not feel like laughing. Was it—could it all be true? It sounded terribly true. Was this first ball only the beginning of her last ball after all? At that the music seemed to change; it sounded sad, sad it rose upon a great sigh. Oh, how quickly things changed! Why didn't happiness last for ever? For ever wasn't a bit too long.

"I want to stop," she said in a breathless voice. The fat man led her to the door.

"No," she said, "I won't go outside. I won't sit down. I'll just stand here, thank you." She leaned against the wall, tapping with her foot, pulling up her gloves and trying to smile. But deep inside her a little girl threw her pinafore over her head and sobbed. Why had he spoiled it all?

"I say, you know," said the fat man, "you mustn't take me seriously, little lady."

"As if I should!" said Leila, tossing her small dark head and sucking her underlip. . . .

Again the couples paraded. The swing doors opened and shut. Now new music was given out by the bandmaster. But Leila didn't want to dance any more. She wanted to be home, or sitting on the veranda listening to those baby owls. When she looked through the dark windows at the stars, they had long beams like wings. . . .

But presently a soft, melting, ravishing tune began, and a young man with curly hair bowed before her. She would have to dance, out of politeness, until she could find Meg. Very stiffly she walked into the middle; very haughtily she put her hand on his sleeve. But in one minute, in one turn, her feet glided, glided. The lights, the azaleas, the dresses, the pink faces, the velvet chairs, all became one beautiful flying wheel. And when her next partner bumped her into the fat man and he said, "Par*don*," she smiled at him more radiantly than ever. She didn't even recognize him again.

1922

ANTON CHEKHOV

The Lady with the Dog

1

People were telling one another that a newcomer had been seen on the promenade—a lady with a dog. Dmitri Dmitrich Gurov had been a fortnight in Yalta, and was accustomed to its ways, and he, too, had begun to take an interest in fresh arrivals. From his seat in Vernet's outdoor café, he caught sight of a young woman in a toque, passing along the promenade; she was fair and not very tall; after her trotted a white pomeranian.

Later he encountered her in the municipal park, and in the square, several times a day. She was always alone, wearing the same toque, and the pomeranian always trotted at her side. Nobody knew who she was, and people referred to her simply as "the lady with the dog."

"If she's here without her husband, and without any friends," thought Gurov, "it wouldn't be a bad idea to make her acquaintance."

He was not yet forty, but had a twelve-year-old daughter and two schoolboy sons. He had been talked into marrying in his second year at college, and his wife now looked nearly twice as old as he was. She was a tall, black-browed woman, erect, dignified, imposing, and, as she said of herself, a "thinker." She was a great reader, omitted the "hard sign"[1] at the end of words in her letters, and called her husband "Dimitri" instead of Dmitri; and though he secretly considered her shallow, narrow-minded, and dowdy, he stood in awe of her, and disliked being at home. It was long since he had first begun deceiving her and he was now constantly unfaithful to her, and this was no doubt why he spoke slightingly of women, to whom he referred as *the lower race*.

He considered that the ample lessons he had received from bitter experience entitled him to call them whatever he liked, but without this "lower race" he could not have existed a single day. He was bored and ill-at-ease in the company of men, with whom he was always cold and reserved, but felt quite at home among women, and knew exactly what to say to them, and how to behave; he could even be silent in their company without feeling the slightest awkwardness. There was an elusive charm in his appearance and disposition which attracted women and caught their sympathies. He knew this and was himself attracted to them by some invisible force.

Repeated and bitter experience had taught him that every fresh intimacy, while at first introducing such pleasant variety into everyday life, and offering itself as a charming, light adventure, inevitably developed, among decent people (especially in Moscow, where they are so irresolute and slow to move), into a problem of excessive complication leading to an intolerably irksome situation. But every time he encountered an attractive woman he forgot all about this experience, the

---

1. Conventional sign that was used following consonants; to omit it was then "progressive," and it has in fact been eliminated in the reformed alphabet adopted by the Soviet government.

desire for life surged up in him, and everything suddenly seemed simple and amusing.

One evening, then, while he was dining at the restaurant in the park, the lady in the toque came strolling up and took a seat at a neighboring table. Her expression, gait, dress, coiffure, all told him that she was from the upper classes, that she was married, that she was in Yalta for the first time, alone and bored. . . . The accounts of the laxity of morals among visitors to Yalta are greatly exaggerated, and he paid no heed to them, knowing that for the most part they were invented by people who would gladly have transgressed themselves, had they known how to set about it. But when the lady sat down at a neighboring table a few yards away from him, the stories of easy conquests, of excursions to the mountains, came back to him, and the seductive idea of a brisk transitory liaison, an affair with a woman whose very name he did not know, suddenly took possession of his mind.

He snapped his fingers at the pomeranian, and when it trotted up to him, shook his forefinger at it. The pomeranian growled. Gurov shook his finger again.

The lady glanced at him and instantly lowered her eyes.

"He doesn't bite," she said, and blushed.

"May I give him a bone?" he asked, and on her nod of consent added in friendly tones: "Have you been in Yalta long?"

"About five days."

"And I am dragging out my second week here."

Neither spoke for a few minutes.

"The days pass quickly, and yet one is so bored here," she said, not looking at him.

"It's the thing to say it's boring here. People never complain of boredom in God-forsaken holes like Belyev or Zhizdra, but when they get here it's: 'Oh, the dullness! Oh, the dust!' You'd think they'd come from Granada,[2] to say the least."

She laughed. Then they both went on eating in silence, like complete strangers. But after dinner they left the restaurant together, and embarked upon the light, jesting talk of people free and contented, for whom it is all the same where they go, or what they talk about. They strolled along, remarking on the strange light over the sea. The water was a warm, tender purple, the moonlight lay on its surface in a golden strip. They said how close it was, after the hot day. Gurov told her he was from Moscow, that he was really a philologist,[3] but worked in a bank; that he had at one time trained himself to sing in a private opera company, but had given up the idea; that he owned two houses in Moscow. . . . And from her he learned that she had grown up in Petersburg, but had got married in the town of S., where she had been living two years, that she would stay another month in Yalta, and that perhaps her husband, who also needed a rest, would join her. She was quite unable to explain whether her husband was a member of the gubernia[4] council, or on the board of the Zemstvo,[5] and was greatly

2. City in southern Spain, site of the Alhambra and once capital of the Moorish kingdom.
3. In the older sense, classical scholar.

4. Czarist province.
5. In Czarist Russia an elective provincial council responsible for local government.

amused at herself for this. Further, Gurov learned that her name was Anna Sergeyevna.

Back in his own room he thought about her, and felt sure he would meet her the next day. It was inevitable. As he went to bed he reminded himself that only a very short time ago she had been a schoolgirl, like his own daughter, learning her lessons; he remembered how much there was of shyness and constraint in her laughter, in her way of conversing with a stranger—it was probably the first time in her life that she found herself alone, and in a situation in which men could follow her and watch her, and speak to her, all the time with a secret aim she could not fail to divine. He recalled her slender, delicate neck, her fine gray eyes.

"And yet there's something pathetic about her," he thought to himself as he fell asleep.

2

A week had passed since the beginning of their acquaintance. It was a holiday. Indoors it was stuffy, but the dust rose in clouds out of doors, and people's hats blew off. It was a thirsty day and Gurov kept going to the outdoor café for fruit-drinks and ices to offer Anna Sergeyevna. The heat was overpowering.

In the evening, when the wind had dropped, they walked to the pier to see the steamer come in. There were a great many people strolling about the landing-place; some, bunches of flowers in their hands, were meeting friends. Two peculiarities of the smart Yalta crowd stood out distinctly—the elderly ladies all tried to dress very young, and there seemed to be an inordinate number of generals about.

Owing to the roughness of the sea the steamer arrived late, after the sun had gone down, and it had to maneuver for some time before it could get alongside the pier. Anna Sergeyevna scanned the steamer and passengers through her lorgnette, as if looking for someone she knew, and when she turned to Gurov her eyes were glistening. She talked a great deal, firing off abrupt questions and forgetting immediately what it was she had wanted to know. Then she lost her lorgnette in the crush.

The smart crowd began dispersing, features could no longer be made out, the wind had quite dropped, and Gurov and Anna Sergeyevna stood there as if waiting for someone else to come off the steamer. Anna Sergeyevna had fallen silent, every now and then smelling her flowers, but not looking at Gurov.

"It's turned out a fine evening," he said. "What shall we do? We might go for a drive."

She made no reply.

He looked steadily at her and suddenly took her in his arms and kissed her lips, and the fragrance and dampness of the flowers closed round him, but the next moment he looked behind him in alarm—had anyone seen them?

"Let's go to your room," he murmured.

And they walked off together, very quickly.

Her room was stuffy and smelled of some scent she had bought in the Japanese shop. Gurov looked at her, thinking to himself: "How full of strange encounters life is!" He could remember carefree, good-natured women who were exhilarated by love-making and grateful to him for the happiness he gave them, however short-lived; and there had been others—his wife among them—whose caresses were insincere, affected, hysterical, mixed up with a great deal of quite unnecessary talk, and whose expression seemed to say that all this was not just love-making or passion, but something much more significant; then there had been two or three beautiful, cold women, over whose features flitted a predatory expression, betraying a determination to wring from life more than it could give, women no longer in their first youth, capricious, irrational, despotic, brainless, and when Gurov had cooled to these, their beauty aroused in him nothing but repulsion, and the lace trimming on their underclothes reminded him of fish-scales.

But here the timidity and awkwardness of youth and inexperience were still apparent; and there was a feeling of embarrassment in the atmosphere, as if someone had just knocked at the door. Anna Sergeyevna, "the lady with the dog," seemed to regard the affair as something very special, very serious, as if she had become a fallen woman, an attitude he found odd and disconcerting. Her features lengthened and drooped, and her long hair hung mournfully on either side of her face. She assumed a pose of dismal meditation, like a repentant sinner in some classical painting.

"It isn't right," she said. "You will never respect me anymore."

On the table was a watermelon. Gurov cut himself a slice from it and began slowly eating it. At least half an hour passed in silence.

Anna Sergeyevna was very touching, revealing the purity of a decent, naïve woman who had seen very little of life. The solitary candle burning on the table scarcely lit up her face, but it was obvious that her heart was heavy.

"Why should I stop respecting you?" asked Gurov. "You don't know what you're saying."

"May God forgive me!" she exclaimed, and her eyes filled with tears. "It's terrible."

"No need to seek to justify yourself."

"How can I justify myself? I'm a wicked, fallen woman, I despise myself and have not the least thought of self-justification. It isn't my husband I have deceived, it's myself. And not only now, I have been deceiving myself for ever so long. My husband is no doubt an honest, worthy man, but he's a flunkey. I don't know what it is he does at his office, but I know he's a flunkey. I was only twenty when I married him, and I was devoured by curiosity, I wanted something higher. I told myself that there must be a different kind of life. I wanted to live, to live. . . . I was burning with curiosity . . . you'll never understand that, but I swear to God I could no longer control myself, nothing could hold me back, I told my husband I was ill, and I came here. . . . And I started going about like one possessed, like a madwoman . . . and now I have become an ordinary, worthless woman, and everyone has the right to despise me."

Gurov listened to her, bored to death. The naïve accents, the remorse, all was so unexpected, so out of place. But for the tears in her eyes, she might have been jesting or play-acting.

"I don't understand," he said gently. "What is it you want?"

She hid her face against his breast and pressed closer to him.

"Do believe me, I implore you to believe me," she said. "I love all that is honest and pure in life, vice is revolting to me, I don't know what I'm doing. The common people say they are snared by the devil. And now I can say that I have been snared by the devil, too."

"Come, come," he murmured.

He gazed into her fixed, terrified eyes, kissed her, and soothed her with gentle affectionate words, and gradually she calmed down and regained her cheerfulness. Soon they were laughing together again.

When, a little later, they went out, there was not a soul on the promenade, the town and its cypresses looked dead, but the sea was still roaring as it dashed against the beach. A solitary fishing-boat tossed on the waves, its lamp blinking sleepily.

They found a droshky[6] and drove to Oreanda.

"I discovered your name in the hall, just now," said Gurov, "written up on the board. Von Diederitz. Is your husband a German?"

"No. His grandfather was, I think, but he belongs to the Orthodox church himself."

When they got out of the droshky at Oreanda they sat down on a bench not far from the church, and looked down at the sea, without talking. Yalta could be dimly discerned through the morning mist, and white clouds rested motionless on the summits of the mountains. Not a leaf stirred, the grasshoppers chirruped, and the monotonous hollow roar of the sea came up to them, speaking of peace, of the eternal sleep lying in wait for us all. The sea had roared like this long before there was any Yalta or Oreanda, it was roaring now, and it would go on roaring, just as indifferently and hollowly, when we have passed away. And it may be that in this continuity, this utter indifference to life and death, lies the secret of our ultimate salvation, of the stream of life on our planet, and of its never-ceasing movement toward perfection.

Side by side with a young woman, who looked so exquisite in the early light, soothed and enchanted by the sight of all this magical beauty—sea, mountains, clouds and the vast expanse of the sky—Gurov told himself that, when you came to think of it, everything in the world is beautiful really, everything but our own thoughts and actions, when we lose sight of the higher aims of life, and of our dignity as human beings.

Someone approached them—a watchman, probably—looked at them and went away. And there was something mysterious and beautiful even in this. The steamer from Feodosia could be seen coming toward the pier, lit up by the dawn, its lamps out.

"There's dew on the grass," said Anna Sergeyevna, breaking the silence.

"Yes. Time to go home."

They went back to the town.

After this they met every day at noon on the promenade, lunching and dining together, going for walks, and admiring the sea. She complained of sleeplessness, of palpitations, asked the same questions over and over again, alternately surrendering to jealousy and the fear that he did not really respect her. And often, when there was nobody in sight in the square or the park, he would draw her to him and kiss her

---

6. Horse-drawn, four-wheeled open carriage.

passionately. The utter idleness, these kisses in broad daylight, accompanied by furtive glances and the fear of discovery, the heat, the smell of the sea, and the idle, smart, well-fed people continually crossing their field of vision, seemed to have given him a new lease on life. He told Anna Sergeyevna she was beautiful and seductive, made love to her with impetuous passion, and never left her side, while she was always pensive, always trying to force from him the admission that he did not respect her, that he did not love her a bit, and considered her just an ordinary woman. Almost every night they drove out of town, to Oreanda, the waterfall, or some other beauty spot. And these excursions were invariably a success, each contributing fresh impressions of majestic beauty.

All this time they kept expecting her husband to arrive. But a letter came in which he told his wife that he was having trouble with his eyes, and implored her to come home as soon as possible. Anna Sergeyevna made hasty preparations for leaving.

"It's a good thing I'm going," she said to Gurov. "It's the intervention of fate."

She left Yalta in a carriage, and he went with her as far as the railway station. The drive took nearly a whole day. When she got into the express train, after the second bell had been rung, she said:

"Let me have one more look at you. . . . One last look. That's right."

She did not weep, but was mournful, and seemed ill, the muscles of her cheeks twitching.

"I shall think of you . . . I shall think of you all the time," she said. "God bless you! Think kindly of me. We are parting for ever, it must be so, because we ought never to have met. Good-bye—God bless you."

The train steamed rapidly out of the station, its lights soon disappearing, and a minute later even the sound it made was silenced, as if everything were conspiring to bring this sweet oblivion, this madness, to an end as quickly as possible. And Gurov, standing alone on the platform and gazing into the dark distance, listened to the shrilling of the grasshoppers and the humming of the telegraph wires, with a feeling that he had only just waked up. And he told himself that this had been just one more of the many adventures in his life, and that it, too, was over, leaving nothing but a memory. . . . He was moved and sad, and felt a slight remorse. After all, this young woman whom he would never again see had not been really happy with him. He had been friendly and affectionate with her, but in his whole behavior, in the tones of his voice, in his very caresses, there had been a shade of irony, the insulting indulgence of the fortunate male, who was, moreover, almost twice her age. She had insisted in calling him good, remarkable, high-minded. Evidently he had appeared to her different from his real self, in a word he had involuntarily deceived her. . . .

There was an autumnal feeling in the air, and the evening was chilly.

"It's time for me to be going north, too," thought Gurov, as he walked away from the platform. "High time!"

3

When he got back to Moscow it was beginning to look like winter, the stoves were heated every day, and it was still dark when the children got up to go to school and drank their tea, so that the nurse had to light the lamp for a short time. Frost had set in. When the first snow falls, and one goes for one's first sleigh ride, it is pleasant to see the white ground, the white roofs; one breathes freely and lightly, and remembers the days of one's youth. The ancient lime-trees and birches, white with rime, have a good-natured look, they are closer to the heart than cypresses and palms, and beneath their branches one is no longer haunted by the memory of mountains and the sea.

Gurov had always lived in Moscow, and he returned to Moscow on a fine frosty day, and when he put on his fur-lined overcoat and thick gloves, and sauntered down Petrovka Street, and when, on Saturday evening, he heard the church bells ringing, his recent journey and the places he had visited lost their charm for him. He became gradually immersed in Moscow life, reading with avidity three newspapers a day, while declaring he never read Moscow newspapers on principle. Once more he was caught up in a whirl of restaurants, clubs, banquets, and celebrations, once more glowed with the flattering consciousness that well-known lawyers and actors came to his house, that he played cards in the Medical Club opposite a professor.

He had believed that in a month's time Anna Sergeyevna would be nothing but a vague memory, and that hereafter, with her wistful smile, she would only occasionally appear to him in dreams, like others before her. But the month was now well over and winter was in full swing, and all was as clear in his memory as if he had only parted with Anna Sergeyevna the day before. And his recollections grew ever more insistent. When the voices of his children at their lessons reached him in his study through the evening stillness, when he heard a song, or the sounds of a musical-box in a restaurant, when the wind howled in the chimney, it all came back to him: early morning on the pier, the misty mountains, the steamer from Feodosia, the kisses. He would pace up and down his room for a long time, smiling at his memories, and then memory turned into dreaming, and what had happened mingled in his imagination with what was going to happen. Anna Sergeyevna did not come to him in his dreams, she accompanied him everywhere, like his shadow, following him everywhere he went. When he closed his eyes, she seemed to stand before him in the flesh, still lovelier, younger, tenderer than she had really been, and looking back, he saw himself, too, as better than he had been in Yalta. In the evenings she looked out at him from the bookshelves, the fireplace, the corner; he could hear her breathing, the sweet rustle of her skirts. In the streets he followed women with his eyes, to see if there were any like her. . . .

He began to feel an overwhelming desire to share his memories with someone. But he could not speak of his love at home, and outside his home who was there for him to confide in? Not the tenants living in his house, and certainly not his colleagues at the bank. And what was there to tell? Was it love that he had felt? Had there been anything exquisite, poetic, anything instructive or even amusing about his relations with Anna Sergeyevna? He had to content himself with uttering vague generalizations about love and women, and nobody guessed what he meant, though his wife's dark eyebrows twitched as she said:

"The role of a coxcomb doesn't suit you a bit, Dimitri."

One evening, leaving the Medical Club with one of his card-partners, a government official, he could not refrain from remarking:

"If you only knew what a charming woman I met in Yalta!"

The official got into his sleigh, and just before driving off turned and called out:

"Dmitri Dmitrich!"

"Yes?"

"You were quite right, you know—the sturgeon was just a *leetle* off."

These words, in themselves so commonplace, for some reason infuriated Gurov, seemed to him humiliating, gross. What savage manners, what people! What wasted evenings, what tedious, empty days! Frantic card-playing, gluttony, drunkenness, perpetual talk always about the same thing. The greater part of one's time and energy went on business that was no use to anyone, and on discussing the same thing over and over again, and there was nothing to show for it all but a stunted, earth-bound existence and a round of trivialities, and there was nowhere to escape to, you might as well be in a madhouse or a convict settlement.

Gurov lay awake all night, raging, and went about the whole of the next day with a headache. He slept badly on the succeeding nights, too, sitting up in bed, thinking, or pacing the floor of his room. He was sick of his children, sick of the bank, felt not the slightest desire to go anywhere or talk about anything.

When the Christmas holidays came, he packed his things, telling his wife he had to go to Petersburg in the interests of a certain young man, and set off for the town of S. To what end? He hardly knew himself. He only knew that he must see Anna Sergeyevna, must speak to her, arrange a meeting, if possible.

He arrived at S. in the morning and engaged the best room in the hotel, which had a carpet of gray military frieze, and a dusty ink-pot on the table, surmounted by a headless rider, holding his hat in his raised hand. The hall porter told him what he wanted to know: von Diederitz had a house of his own in Staro-Goncharnaya Street. It wasn't far from the hotel, he lived on a grand scale, luxuriously, kept carriage-horses, the whole town knew him. The hall porter pronounced the name "Drideritz."

Gurov strolled over to Staro-Goncharnaya Street and discovered the house. In front of it was a long gray fence with inverted nails hammered into the tops of the palings.

"A fence like that is enough to make anyone want to run away," thought Gurov, looking at the windows of the house and the fence.

He reasoned that since it was a holiday, her husband would probably be at home. In any case it would be tactless to embarrass her by calling at the house. And a note might fall into the hands of the husband, and bring about catastrophe. The best thing would be to wait about on the chance of seeing her. And he walked up and down the street, hovering in the vicinity of the fence, watching for his chance. A beggar entered the gate, only to be attacked by dogs; then, an hour later, the faint, vague sounds of a piano reached his ears. That would be Anna Sergeyevna playing. Suddenly the front door opened and an old woman came out, followed by a familiar white pomeranian. Gurov tried to call to it, but his heart beat violently, and in his agitation he could not remember its name.

He walked on, hating the gray fence more and more, and now ready to tell himself irately that Anna Sergeyevna had forgotten him, had already, perhaps, found distraction in another—what could be more natural in a young woman who had to look at this accursed fence from morning to night? He went back to his hotel and sat on the sofa in his room for some time, not knowing what to do, then he ordered dinner, and after dinner, had a long sleep.

"What a foolish, restless business," he thought, waking up and looking toward the dark windowpanes. It was evening by now. "Well, I've had my sleep out. And what am I to do in the night?"

He sat up in bed, covered by the cheap gray quilt, which reminded him of a hospital blanket, and in his vexation he fell to taunting himself.

"You and your lady with a dog . . . there's adventure for you! See what you get for your pains."

On his arrival at the station that morning he had noticed a poster announcing in enormous letters the first performance at the local theater of *The Geisha*.[7] Remembering this, he got up and made for the theater.

"It's highly probable that she goes to first-nights," he told himself.

The theater was full. It was a typical provincial theater, with a mist collecting over the chandeliers, and the crowd in the gallery fidgeting noisily. In the first row of the stalls[8] the local dandies stood waiting for the curtain to go up, their hands clasped behind them. There, in the front seat of the Governor's box, sat the Governor's daughter, wearing a boa, the Governor himself hiding modestly behind the drapes, so that only his hands were visible. The curtain stirred, the orchestra took a long time tuning up their instruments. Gurov's eyes roamed eagerly over the audience as they filed in and occupied their seats.

Anna Sergeyevna came in, too. She seated herself in the third row of the stalls and when Gurov's glance fell on her, his heart seemed to stop, and he knew in a flash that the whole world contained no one nearer or dearer to him, no one more important to his happiness. This little woman, lost in the provincial crowd, in no way remarkable, holding a silly lorgnette in her hand, now filled his whole life, was his grief, his joy, all that he desired. Lulled by the sounds coming from the wretched orchestra, with its feeble, amateurish violinists, he thought how beautiful she was . . . thought and dreamed. . . .

Anna Sergeyevna was accompanied by a tall, round-shouldered young man with small whiskers, who nodded at every step before taking the seat beside her and seemed to be continually bowing to someone. This must be her husband, whom, in a fit of bitterness, at Yalta, she had called a "flunkey." And there really was something of the lackey's servility in his lanky figure, his side-whiskers, and the little bald spot on the top of his head. And he smiled sweetly, and the badge of some scientific society gleaming in his buttonhole was like the number on a footman's livery.

The husband went out to smoke in the first interval, and she was

<hr>

7. Operetta by Sidney Jones (1861–1946) which toured Eastern Europe in 1898–99.

8. Seats at the front of a theater, near the stage and separated from nearby seats by a railing.

left alone in her seat. Gurov, who had taken a seat in the stalls, went up to her and said in a trembling voice, with a forced smile: "How d'you do?"

She glanced up at him and turned pale, then looked at him again in alarm, unable to believe her eyes, squeezing her fan and lorgnette in one hand, evidently struggling to overcome a feeling of faintness. Neither of them said a word. She sat there, and he stood beside her, disconcerted by her embarrassment, and not daring to sit down. The violins and flutes sang out as they were tuned, and there was a tense sensation in the atmosphere, as if they were being watched from all the boxes. At last she got up and moved rapidly toward one of the exits. He followed her and they wandered aimlessly along corridors, up and down stairs; figures flashed by in the uniforms of legal officials, high-school teachers, and civil servants, all wearing badges; ladies' coats hanging on pegs, flashed by; there was a sharp draft, bringing with it an odor of cigarette stubs. And Gurov, whose heart was beating violently, thought:

"What on earth are all these people, this orchestra for? . . ."

The next minute he suddenly remembered how, after seeing Anna Sergeyevna off that evening at the station, he had told himself that all was over, and they would never meet again. And how far away the end seemed to be now!

She stopped on a dark narrow staircase over which was a notice bearing the inscription "To the upper circle."

"How you frightened me!" she said, breathing heavily, still pale and half-stunned. "Oh, how you frightened me! I'm almost dead! Why did you come? Oh, why?"

"But, Anna," he said, in low, hasty tones. "But, Anna. . . . Try to understand . . . do try. . . ."

She cast him a glance of fear, entreaty, love, and then gazed at him steadily, as if to fix his features firmly in her memory.

"I've been so unhappy," she continued, taking no notice of his words. "I could think of nothing but you the whole time, I lived on the thoughts of you. I tried to forget—why, oh, why did you come?"

On the landing above them were two schoolboys, smoking and looking down, but Gurov did not care, and, drawing Anna Sergeyevna toward him, began kissing her face, her lips, her hands.

"What are you doing, oh, what are you doing?" she said in horror, drawing back. "We have both gone mad. Go away this very night, this moment. . . . By all that is sacred, I implore you. . . . Somebody is coming."

Someone was ascending the stairs.

"You must go away," went on Anna Sergeyevna in a whisper. "D'you hear me, Dmitri Dmitrich? I'll come to you in Moscow. I have never been happy, I am unhappy now, and I shall never be happy—never! Do not make me suffer still more! I will come to you in Moscow, I swear it! And now we must part! My dear one, my kind one, my darling, we must part."

She pressed his hand and hurried down the stairs, looking back at him continually, and her eyes showed that she was in truth unhappy. Gurov stood where he was for a short time, listening, and when all was quiet went to look for his coat, and left the theater.

4

And Anna Sergeyevna began going to Moscow to see him. Every two or three months she left the town of S., telling her husband that she was going to consult a specialist on female diseases, and her husband believed her and did not believe her. In Moscow she always stayed at the "Slavyanski Bazaar," sending a man in a red cap to Gurov the moment she arrived. Gurov went to her, and no one in Moscow knew anything about it.

One winter morning he went to see her as usual (the messenger had been to him the evening before, but had not found him at home). His daughter was with him for her school was on the way, and he thought he might as well see her to it.

"It is three degrees above zero,"[9] said Gurov to his daughter, "and yet it is snowing. You see it is only above zero close to the ground, the temperature in the upper layers of the atmosphere is quite different."

"Why doesn't it ever thunder in winter, Papa?"

He explained this, too. As he was speaking, he kept reminding himself that he was going to a rendezvous and that not a living soul knew about it, or, probably, ever would. He led a double life—one in public, in the sight of all whom it concerned, full of conventional truth and conventional deception, exactly like the lives of his friends and acquaintances, and another which flowed in secret. And, owing to some strange, possibly quite accidental chain of circumstances, everything that was important, interesting, essential, everything about which he was sincere and never deceived himself, everything that composed the kernel of his life, went on in secret, while everything that was false in him, everything that composed the husk in which he hid himself and the truth which was in him—his work at the bank, discussions at the club, his "lower race," his attendance at anniversary celebrations with his wife—was on the surface. He began to judge others by himself, no longer believing what he saw, and always assuming that the real, the only interesting life of every individual goes on as under cover of night, secretly. Every individual existence revolves around mystery, and perhaps that is the chief reason that all cultivated individuals insisted so strongly on the respect due to personal secrets.

After leaving his daughter at the door of her school Gurov set off for the "Slavyanski Bazaar." Taking off his overcoat in the lobby, he went upstairs and knocked softly on the door. Anna Sergeyevna, wearing the gray dress he liked most, exhausted by her journey and by suspense, had been expecting him since the evening before. She was pale and looked at him without smiling, but was in his arms almost before he was fairly in the room. Their kiss was lingering, prolonged, as if they had not met for years.

"Well, how are you?" he asked. "Anything new?"

"Wait. I'll tell you in a minute. . . . I can't. . . ."

She could not speak, because she was crying. Turning away, she held her handkerchief to her eyes.

"I'll wait till she's had her cry out," he thought, and sank into a chair.

9. Probably Réaumur thermometer; about 39 degrees Fahrenheit.

He rang for tea, and a little later, while he was drinking it, she was still standing there, her face to the window. She wept from emotion, from her bitter consciousness of the sadness of their life; they could only see one another in secret, hiding from people, as if they were thieves. Was not their life a broken one?

"Don't cry," he said.

It was quite obvious to him that this love of theirs would not soon come to an end, and that no one could say when this end would be. Anna Sergeyevna loved him ever more fondly, worshipped him, and there would have been no point in telling her that one day it must end. Indeed, she would not have believed him.

He moved over and took her by the shoulders, intending to fondle her with light words, but suddenly he caught sight of himself in the looking-glass.

His hair was already beginning to turn gray. It struck him as strange that he should have aged so much in the last few years. The shoulders on which his hands lay were warm and quivering. He felt a pity for this life, still so warm and exquisite, but probably soon to fade and droop like his own. Why did she love him so? Women had always believed him different from what he really was, had loved in him not himself but the man their imagination pictured him, a man they had sought for eagerly all their lives. And afterwards when they discovered their mistake, they went on loving him just the same. And not one of them had ever been happy with him. Time had passed, he had met one woman after another, become intimate with each, parted with each, but had never loved. There had been all sorts of things between them, but never love.

And only now, when he was gray-haired, had he fallen in love properly, thoroughly, for the first time in his life.

He and Anna Sergeyevna loved one another as people who are very close and intimate, as husband and wife, as dear friends love one another. It seemed to them that fate had intended them for one another, and they could not understand why she should have a husband, and he a wife. They were like two migrating birds, the male and the female, who had been caught and put into separate cages. They forgave one another all that they were ashamed of in the past, in their present, and felt that this love of theirs had changed them both.

Formerly, in moments of melancholy, he had consoled himself by the first argument that came into his head, but now arguments were nothing to him, he felt profound pity, desired to be sincere, tender.

"Stop crying, my dearest," he said. "You've had your cry, now stop. . . . Now let us have a talk, let us try and think what we are to do."

Then they discussed their situation for a long time, trying to think how they could get rid of the necessity for hiding, deception, living in different towns, being so long without meeting. How were they to shake off these intolerable fetters?

"How? How?" he repeated, clutching his head. "How?"

And it seemed to them that they were within an inch of arriving at a decision, and that then a new, beautiful life would begin. And they both realized that the end was still far, far away, and that the hardest, the most complicated part was only just beginning.

1899

Kinds and Modes

6   A KIND: INITIATION

Themes are useful for grouping stories together for comparison, both to highlight similarities and to reveal differences in history and structure and so to discover the uniqueness of the work. Types of character—stereotypes—are useful for the same purpose: to show both the common qualities and the unique combination of qualities in a particular character in a story. Though all grouping or classification, used poorly, can blur distinctions and make all members of a group seem the same, when used well it does not blur but brings into focus the individuality of the individual thing or being.

Literary criticism lacks the specific and agreed-on system of classification of biology, so that its terms are not so fixed as *phylum, genus, species,* even in the editors' own usage. In general, we use the term **genre** for the largest commonly agreed-on categories: fiction, poetry, drama. When I'm trying to be consistent, I use the term **subgenre** for the divisions of fiction—novel, novella, short story, etc. A **kind** is a species or subcategory within a subgenre.

There is one kind of short story that is so common that there are those who maintain it is not a kind but is equivalent to the subgenre short story itself. That pervasive kind is the **initiation** story, in which a character—often but not always a child or young person—first learns a significant, even life-determining truth about the universe, about reality, about society, about people or a person, or about himself or herself. Such a subject tends to dictate the main outlines of the action of the story: it begins with the protagonist in a state of innocence or mistaken belief (exposition); it leads up to the moment of illumination or the discovery of the truth (rising action to climax or turning point), and ends usually with some indication of the result of that discovery (falling action to conclusion). This kind is particularly suitable to a short story because it lends itself to brief treatment: the illumination is more or less sudden—there is no need for lengthy development, for multiple scenes or settings, for much time to pass, for too many complications of action or a large cast of characters—yet it can encapsulate a whole life or important segment of a life and wide-ranging, significant themes.

If you've been reading this anthology from the beginning, you have already run into a number of initiation stories, and you may have some idea of what kinds of truths their protagonists discover. Young Goodman Brown discovered the universality of evil in human beings. Nelson Head (*The Artificial Nigger*) discovered the ubiquity of evil in the world outside his Edenic rural home, while his grandfather—not a young person, but described as having a youthful expression and looking more like Nelson's brother than his grandfather—learns of his own capacity for evil. Leila (*Her First Ball*) comes across the truth that youth is fleeting (you cannot say she really learns it, since by the end of that very short story she has forgotten it). We have also seen that one may retreat from the truth physically or psychologically, as do Brown and Nelson, or remain unchanged or revert to one's former state, as Leila does.

Since to the young all things seem possible—one can be a doctor, novelist, tennis star, saint, and swinger, serially or simultaneously—many of the truths learned in initiation stories have to do with limitation. The girl in *Boys and Girls* learns that she is "only a girl." Fortunately, growing up is not just loss, and there are positive or "happy" initiation stories. The boy in *The Old People* is initiated first into "manhood," and takes his place among "the hunters," and then into a more exclusive, privileged fraternity, that of the owners or, as Faulkner would no doubt prefer it, "custodians" of the land.

Sometimes the initiation takes place as an unscheduled event. At other times there is a scheduled event, a ritual or **rite of passage**, such as a formal entry into society (*Her First Ball*) or a baptism (*O Yes*), which is the occasion for the initiation into adulthood or into the group. What do we usually think of as the purpose of a debut? How does the society intend to induct its new member? As you read *Her First Ball*, think about these questions and watch how Leila's debut fulfills its ritual role, how it differs from it, and how it may induct Leila into society more truly than intended. So, too, in *O Yes* (originally called *The Baptism*), Parialee is intentionally and ritualistically inducted into her cultural role and is led by the larger (white) society into a predetermined role without ritual. And isn't Carol, who is only a spectator at the first baptism, baptized too in this second predetermined but unritualistic way? The ritual in *The Old People* is formal, communal, and ceremonial. The formalities of the rite in this story may bring to the surface elements in the pattern that lie beneath the surface in other stories.

By the time you finish this chapter you should have some idea of the variations possible within the initiation story, and as you go on to read such stories as *The Horse Dealer's Daughter*, *The Secret Sharer*, and *Tanhum* and think back over *The Egg* and *Macomber*, you should have a still better idea of the range of stories in this kind. Adults may be initiated as well as children and adolescents; the truths may be bitter or pleasing, cosmic, social, psychological; the initiates may change forever, retreat, shrug off what they have learned. By seeing all these stories as part of the large group of initiation stories you may the more readily notice the differences in the protagonists, in the learning experience, in the results of the initiation on the protagonists and whether they are permanent or temporary, life-denying or life-enhancing. You may, in other words, have gone a long way toward defining the unique vision of the story, its precise and individual illumination of reality. And that's the function of classification in the first place.

JAMES JOYCE

Araby

North Richmond Street, being blind,[1] was a quiet street except at the hour when the Christian Brothers'[2] School set the boys free. An uninhabited house of two stories stood at the blind end, detached from its neighbors in a square ground. The other houses of the street, conscious of decent lives within them, gazed at one another with brown imperturbable faces.

The former tenant of our house, a priest, had died in the back drawing room. Air, musty from having been long enclosed, hung in all the rooms, and the waste room behind the kitchen was littered with old useless papers. Among these I found a few paper-covered books, the pages of which were curled and damp: *The Abbot*, by Walter Scott, *The Devout Communicant* and *The Memoirs of Vidocq*.[3] I liked the last best because its leaves were yellow. The wild garden behind the house contained a central apple tree and a few straggling bushes under one of which I found the late tenant's rusty bicycle pump. He had been a very charitable priest; in his will he had left all his money to institutions and the furniture of his house to his sister.

When the short days of winter came dusk fell before we had well eaten our dinners. When we met in the street the houses had grown somber. The space of sky above us was the color of ever-changing violet and towards it the lamps of the street lifted their feeble lanterns. The cold air stung us and we played till our bodies glowed. Our shouts echoed in the silent street. The career of our play brought us through the dark muddy lanes behind the houses where we ran the gantlet of the rough tribes from the cottages, to the back doors of the dark dripping gardens where odors arose from the ashpits,[4] to the dark odorous stables where a coachman smoothed and combed the horse or shook music from the buckled harness. When we returned to the street light from the kitchen windows had filled the areas. If my uncle was seen turning the corner we hid in the shadow until we had seen him safely housed. Or if Mangan's sister came out on the doorstep to call her brother in to his tea we watched her from our shadow peer up and down the street. We waited to see whether she would remain or go in and, if she remained, we left our shadow and walked up to Mangan's steps resignedly. She was waiting for us, her figure defined by the light from the half-opened door. Her brother always teased her before he obeyed and I stood by the railings looking at her. Her dress swung as she moved her body and the soft rope of her hair tossed from side to side.

1. Dead-end street. The story takes place in Dublin.
2. Conservative Irish lay order.
3. The 1820 novel by Sir Walter Scott (1771–1834) is a romance about the Catholic Mary Queen of Scots (1542–87), who was beheaded; a Catholic religious tract: *The Devout Communicant: or Pious Meditations and Aspirations for the Three* *Days Before and Three Days After Receiving the Holy Eucharist* (1813); François Vidocq (1775–1857), a French criminal who became chief of detectives, who died poor and disgraced for his part in a crime that he solved, and who probably did not write the book called his memoirs.
4. Where fireplace ashes were dumped.

Every morning I lay on the floor in the front parlor watching her door. The blind was pulled down to within an inch of the sash so that I could not be seen. When she came out on the doorstep my heart leaped. I ran to the hall, seized my books and followed her. I kept her brown figure always in my eye and, when we came near the point at which our ways diverged, I quickened my pace and passed her. This happened morning after morning. I had never spoken to her, except for a few casual words, and yet her name was like a summons to all my foolish blood.

Her image accompanied me even in places the most hostile to romance. On Saturday evenings when my aunt went marketing I had to go to carry some of the parcels. We walked through the flaring streets, jostled by drunken men and bargaining women, amid the curses of laborers, the shrill litanies of shop-boys who stood on guard by the barrels of pigs' cheeks, the nasal chanting of street-singers, who sang a *come-all-you* about O'Donovan Rossa,[5] or a ballad about the troubles in our native land. These noises converged in a single sensation of life for me: I imagined that I bore my chalice safely through a throng of foes. Her name sprang to my lips at moments in strange prayers and praises which I myself did not understand. My eyes were often full of tears (I could not tell why) and at times a flood from my heart seemed to pour itself out into my bosom. I thought little of the future. I did not know whether I would ever speak to her or not or, if I spoke to her, how I could tell her of my confused adoration. But my body was like a harp and her words and gestures were like fingers running upon the wires.

One evening I went into the back drawing room in which the priest had died. It was a dark rainy evening and there was no sound in the house. Through one of the broken panes I heard the rain impinge upon the earth, the fine incessant needles of water playing in the sodden beds. Some distant lamp or lighted window gleamed below me. I was thankful that I could see so little. All my senses seemed to desire to veil themselves and, feeling that I was about to slip from them, I pressed the palms of my hands together until they trembled, murmuring: *O love! O love!* many times.

At last she spoke to me. When she addressed the first words to me I was so confused that I did not know what to answer. She asked me was I going to *Araby*.[6] I forget whether I answered yes or no. It would be a splendid bazaar, she said; she would love to go.

—And why can't you? I asked.

While she spoke she turned a silver bracelet round and round her wrist. She could not go, she said, because there would be a retreat that week in her convent. Her brother and two other boys were fighting for their caps and I was alone at the railings. She held one of the spikes, bowing her head towards me. The light from the lamp opposite our door caught the white curve of her neck, lit up her hair that rested there and, falling, lit up the hand upon the railing.

---

5. A song, of which there were many, which began "Come, all you Irishmen." Jeremiah ("Dynamite Rossa") O'Donovan (1831–1915) was a militant Irish nationalist who fought on despite terms in prison and banishment.

6. A bazaar billed as a "Grand Oriental Fête," Dublin, May 1894.

It fell over one side of her dress and caught the white border of a petticoat, just visible as she stood at ease.

—It's well for you, she said.

—If I go, I said, I will bring you something.

What innumerable follies laid waste my waking and sleeping thoughts after that evening! I wished to annihilate the tedious intervening days. I chafed against the work of school. At night in my bedroom and by day in the classroom her image came between me and the page I strove to read. The syllables of the word *Araby* were called to me through the silence in which my soul luxuriated and cast an Eastern enchantment over me. I asked for leave to go to the bazaar on Saturday night. My aunt was surprised and hoped it was not some Freemason[7] affair. I answered few questions in class. I watched my master's face pass from amiability to sternness; he hoped I was not beginning to idle. I could not call my wandering thoughts together. I had hardly any patience with the serious work of life which, now that it stood between me and my desire, seemed to me child's play, ugly monotonous child's play.

On Saturday morning I reminded my uncle that I wished to go to the bazaar in the evening. He was fussing at the hallstand, looking for the hat brush, and answered me curtly:

—Yes, boy, I know.

As he was in the hall I could not go into the front parlor and lie at the window. I left the house in bad humor and walked slowly towards the school. The air was pitilessly raw and already my heart misgave me.

When I came home to dinner my uncle had not yet been home. Still it was early. I sat staring at the clock for some time and, when its ticking began to irritate me, I left the room. I mounted the staircase and gained the upper part of the house. The high cold empty gloomy rooms liberated me and I went from room to room singing. From the front window I saw my companions playing below in the street. Their cries reached me weakened and indistinct and, leaning my forehead against the cool glass, I looked over at the dark house where she lived. I may have stood there for an hour, seeing nothing but the brown-clad figure cast by my imagination, touched discreetly by the lamplight at the curved neck, at the hand upon the railings and at the border below the dress.

When I came downstairs again I found Mrs. Mercer sitting at the fire. She was an old garrulous woman, a pawnbroker's widow, who collected used stamps for some pious purpose. I had to endure the gossip of the tea-table. The meal was prolonged beyond an hour and still my uncle did not come. Mrs. Mercer stood up to go: she was sorry she couldn't wait any longer, but it was after eight o'clock and she did not like to be out late, as the night air was bad for her. When she had gone I began to walk up and down the room, clenching my fists. My aunt said:

I'm afraid you may put off your bazaar for this night of Our Lord.

7. The Masons, or Freemasons, were considered enemies of the Catholics.

At nine o'clock I heard my uncle's latchkey in the hall door. I heard him talking to himself and heard the hall stand rocking when it had received the weight of his overcoat. I could interpret these signs. When he was midway through his dinner I asked him to give me the money to go to the bazaar. He had forgotten.

—The people are in bed and after their first sleep now, he said.

I did not smile. My aunt said to him energetically:

—Can't you give him the money and let him go? You've kept him late enough as it is.

My uncle said he was very sorry he had forgotten. He said he believed in the old saying: *All work and no play makes Jack a dull boy.* He asked me where I was going and, when I had told him a second time he asked me did I know *The Arab's Farewell to His Steed.*[8] When I left the kitchen he was about to recite the opening lines of the piece to my aunt.

I held a florin[9] tightly in my hand as I strode down Buckingham Street towards the station. The sight of the streets thronged with buyers and glaring with gas recalled to me the purpose of my journey. I took my seat in a third-class carriage of a deserted train. After an intolerable delay the train moved out of the station slowly. It crept onward among ruinous houses and over the twinkling river. At Westland Row Station a crowd of people pressed to the carriage doors; but the porters moved them back, saying that it was a special train for the bazaar. I remained alone in the bare carriage. In a few minutes the train drew up beside an improvised wooden platform. I passed out on to the road and saw by the lighted dial of a clock that it was ten minutes to ten. In front of me was a large building which displayed the magical name.

I could not find any sixpenny entrance and, fearing that the bazaar would be closed, I passed in quickly through a turnstile, handing a shilling to a weary-looking man. I found myself in a big hall girdled at half its height by a gallery. Nearly all the stalls were closed and the greater part of the hall was in darkness. I recognized a silence like that which pervades a church after a service. I walked into the center of the bazaar timidly. A few people were gathered about the stalls which were still open. Before a curtain, over which the words *Café Chantant*[1] were written in colored lamps, two men were counting money on a salver. I listened to the fall of the coins.

Remembering with difficulty why I had come, I went over to one of the stalls and examined porcelain vases and flowered tea-sets. At the door of the stall a young lady was talking and laughing with two young gentlemen. I remarked their English accents[2] and listened vaguely to their conversation.

—O, I never said such a thing!

—O, but you did!

—O, but I didn't!

—Didn't she say that?

---

8. Or *The Arab's Farewell to His Horse,* sentimental nineteenth-century poem by Caroline Norton. The speaker has sold the horse.

9. Two-shilling piece; thus four times the "sixpenny entrance" fee.

1. Café with music.

2. Remember, the story is set in Ireland.

—Yes. I heard her.

—O, there's a . . . fib!

Observing me the young lady came over and asked me did I wish to buy anything. The tone of her voice was not encouraging; she seemed to have spoken to me out of a sense of duty. I looked humbly at the great jars that stood like eastern guards at either side of the dark entrance to the stall and murmured:

—No, thank you.

The young lady changed the position of one of the vases and went back to the two young men. They began to talk of the same subject. Once or twice the young lady glanced at me over her shoulder.

I lingered before her stall, though I knew my stay was useless, to make my interest in her wares seem the more real. Then I turned away slowly and walked down the middle of the bazaar. I allowed the two pennies to fall against the sixpence in my pocket. I heard a voice call from one end of the gallery that the light was out. The upper part of the hall was now completely dark.

Gazing up into the darkness I saw myself as a creature driven and derided by vanity; and my eyes burned with anguish and anger.

1914

ALICE MUNRO

Boys and Girls

My father was a fox farmer. That is, he raised silver foxes, in pens; and in the fall and early winter, when their fur was prime, he killed them and skinned them and sold their pelts to the Hudson's Bay Company or the Montreal Fur Traders. These companies supplied us with heroic calendars to hang, one on each side of the kitchen door. Against a background of cold blue sky and black pine forests and treacherous northern rivers, plumed adventurers planted the flags of England or of France; magnificent savages bent their backs to the portage.

For several weeks before Christmas, my father worked after supper in the cellar of our house. The cellar was whitewashed, and lit by a hundred-watt bulb over the worktable. My brother Laird and I sat on the top step and watched. My father removed the pelt inside-out from the body of the fox, which looked surprisingly small, mean and rat-like, deprived of its arrogant weight of fur. The naked, slippery bodies were collected in a sack and buried at the dump. One time the hired man, Henry Bailey, had taken a swipe at me with this sack, saying, "Christmas present!" My mother thought that was not funny. In fact she disliked the whole pelting operation—that was what the killing, skinning, and preparation of the furs was called—and wished it did not have to take place in the house. There was the smell. After the pelt had been stretched inside-out on a long board my father scraped away delicately, removing the little clotted webs of blood vessels, the bubbles of fat; the smell of blood and animal fat, with the strong primitive odor of the fox itself, penetrated all parts of the house. I found it reassuringly seasonal, like the smell of oranges and pine needles.

Henry Bailey suffered from bronchial troubles. He would cough and cough until his narrow face turned scarlet, and his light blue, derisive eyes filled up with tears; then he took the lid off the stove, and, standing well back, shot out a great clot of phlegm—hsss—straight into the heart of the flames. We admired him for this performance and for his ability to make his stomach growl at will, and for his laughter, which was full of high whistlings and gurglings and involved the whole faulty machinery of his chest. It was sometimes hard to tell what he was laughing at, and always possible that it might be us.

After we had been sent to bed we could still smell fox and still hear Henry's laugh, but these things, reminders of the warm, safe, brightly lit downstairs world, seemed lost and diminished, floating on the stale cold air upstairs. We were afraid at night in the winter. We were not afraid of *outside* though this was the time of year when snowdrifts curled around our house like sleeping whales and the wind harassed us all night, coming up from the buried fields, the frozen swamp, with its old bugbear chorus of threats and misery. We were afraid of *inside,* the room where we slept. At this time the upstairs of our house was not finished. A brick chimney went up one wall. In the middle of the floor was a square hole, with a wooden railing around it; that was where the stairs came up. On the other side of the stairwell were the things that nobody had any use for any more—a soldiery roll of linoleum, standing on end, a wicker baby carriage, a fern basket, china jugs and basins with cracks in them, a picture of the Battle of Balaclava,[1] very sad to look at. I had told Laird, as soon as he was old enough to understand such things, that bats and skeletons lived over there; whenever a man escaped from the county jail, twenty miles away, I imagined that he had somehow let himself in the window and was hiding behind the linoleum. But we had rules to keep us safe. When the light was on, we were safe as long as we did not step off the square of worn carpet which defined our bedroom-space; when the light was off no place was safe but the beds themselves. I had to turn out the light kneeling on the end of my bed, and stretching as far as I could to reach the cord.

In the dark we lay on our beds, our narrow life rafts, and fixed our eyes on the faint light coming up the stairwell, and sang songs. Laird sang "Jingle Bells," which he would sing any time, whether it was Christmas or not, and I sang "Danny Boy." I loved the sound of my own voice, frail and supplicating, rising in the dark. We could make out the tall frosted shapes of the windows now, gloomy and white. When I came to the part, *When I am dead, as dead I well may be*—a fit of shivering caused not by the cold sheets but by pleasurable emotion almost silenced me. *You'll kneel and say, an Ave there above me*—What was an Ave? Every day I forgot to find out.

1. An indecisive Crimean War battle fought on October 25, 1854.

Laird went straight from singing to sleep. I could hear his long, satisfied, bubbly breaths. Now for the time that remained to me, the most perfectly private and perhaps the best time of the whole day, I arranged myself tightly under the covers and went on with one of the stories I was telling myself from night to night. These stories were about myself, when I had grown a little older; they took place in a world that was recognizably mine, yet one that presented opportunities for courage, boldness and self-sacrifice, as mine never did. I rescued people from a bombed building (it discouraged me that the real war had gone on so far away from Jubilee). I shot two rabid wolves who were menacing the schoolyard (the teachers cowered terrified at my back). I rode a fine horse spiritedly down the main street of Jubilee, acknowledging the townspeople's gratitude for some yet-to-be-worked-out piece of heroism (nobody ever rode a horse there, except King Billy in the Orangemen's Day[2] parade). There was always riding and shooting in these stories, though I had only been on a horse twice—bareback because we did not own a saddle— and the second time I had slid right around and dropped under the horse's feet; it had stepped placidly over me. I really was learning to shoot, but I could not hit anything yet, not even tin cans on fence posts.

Alive, the foxes inhabited a world my father made for them. It was surrounded by a high guard fence, like a medieval town, with a gate that was padlocked at night. Along the streets of this town were ranged large, sturdy pens. Each of them had a real door that a man could go through, a wooden ramp along the wire, for the foxes to run up and down on, and a kennel—something like a clothes chest with airholes—where they slept and stayed in winter and had their young. There were feeding and watering dishes attached to the wire in such a way that they could be emptied and cleaned from the outside. The dishes were made of old tin cans, and the ramps and kennels of odds and ends of old lumber. Everything was tidy and ingenious; my father was tirelessly inventive and his favorite book in the world was Robinson Crusoe.[3] He had fitted a tin drum on a wheelbarrow, for bringing water down to the pens. This was my job in summer, when the foxes had to have water twice a day. Between nine and ten o'clock in the morning, and again after supper, I filled the drum at the pump and trundled it down through the barnyard to the pens, where I parked it, and filled my watering can and went along the streets. Laird came too, with his little cream and green gardening can, filled too full and knocking against his legs and slopping water on his canvas shoes. I had the real watering can, my father's, though I could only carry it three-quarters full.

The foxes all had names, which were printed on a tin plate and hung beside their doors. They were not named when they were born,

2. The Orange Society is an Irish Protestant group named after William of Orange, who, as King William III of England, defeated the Catholic James II. The Society sponsors an annual procession on July 12 to commemorate the victory of William III at the Battle of the Boyne.

3. Novel (1719) by Daniel Defoe that is about a man shipwrecked on a desert island and that goes into great detail about his ingenious contraptions.

but when they survived the first year's pelting and were added to
the breeding stock. Those my father had named were called names
like Prince, Bob, Wally and Betty. Those I had named were called
Star or Turk, or Maureen or Diana. Laird named one Maud after
a hired girl we had when he was little, one Harold after a boy at
school, and one Mexico, he did not say why.

Naming them did not make pets out of them, or anything like it.
Nobody but my father ever went into the pens, and he had twice
had blood-poisoning from bites. When I was bringing them their
water they prowled up and down on the paths they had made inside
their pens, barking seldom—they saved that for nighttime, when they
might get up a chorus of community frenzy—but always watching me,
their eyes burning, clear gold, in their pointed, malevolent faces.
They were beautiful for their delicate legs and heavy, aristocratic
tails and the bright fur sprinkled on dark down their backs—which
gave them their name—but especially for their faces, drawn exquisitely sharp in pure hostility, and their golden eyes.

Besides carrying water I helped my father when he cut the long
grass, and the lamb's quarter and flowering money-musk, that grew
between the pens. He cut with the scythe and I raked into piles.
Then he took a pitchfork and threw fresh-cut grass all over the top
of the pens, to keep the foxes cooler and shade their coats, which
were browned by two much sun. My father did not talk to me
unless it was about the job we were doing. In this he was quite
different from my mother, who, if she was feeling cheerful, would
tell me all sorts of things—the name of a dog she had had when
she was a little girl, the names of boys she had gone out with later
on when she was grown up, and what certain dresses of hers had
looked like—she could not imagine now what had become of them.
Whatever thoughts and stories my father had were private, and I
was shy of him and would never ask him questions. Nevertheless I
worked willingly under his eyes, and with a feeling of pride. One
time a feed salesman came down into the pens to talk to him and
my father said, "Like to have you meet my new hired man." I turned
away and raked furiously, red in the face with pleasure.

"Could of fooled me," said the salesman. "I thought it was only a
girl."

After the grass was cut, it seemed suddenly much later in the year.
I walked on stubble in the earlier evening, aware of the reddening
skies, the entering silences, of fall. When I wheeled the tank out of
the gate and put the padlock on, it was almost dark. One night at
this time I saw my mother and father standing talking on the little
rise of ground we called the gangway, in front of the barn. My father
had just come from the meathouse; he had his stiff bloody apron on,
and a pail of cut-up meat in his hand.

It was an odd thing to see my mother down at the barn. She did
not often come out of the house unless it was to do something—hang
out the wash or dig potatoes in the garden. She looked out of place,
with her bare lumpy legs, not touched by the sun, her apron still on
and damp across the stomach from the supper dishes. Her hair was
tied up in a kerchief, wisps of it falling out. She would tie her hair

up like this in the morning, saying she did not have time to do it properly, and it would stay tied up all day. It was true, too; she really did not have time. These days our back porch was piled with baskets of peaches and grapes and pears, bought in town, and onions and tomatoes and cucumbers grown at home, all waiting to be made into jelly and jam and preserves, pickles and chili sauce. In the kitchen there was a fire in the stove all day, jars clinked in boiling water, sometimes a cheesecloth bag was strung on a pole between two chairs straining blue-black grape pulp for jelly. I was given jobs to do and I would sit at the table peeling peaches that had been soaked in the hot water, or cutting up onions, my eyes smarting and streaming. As soon as I was done I ran out of the house, trying to get out of earshot before my mother thought of what she wanted me to do next. I hated the hot dark kitchen in summer, the green blinds and the flypapers, the same old oilcloth table and wavy mirror and bumpy linoleum. My mother was too tired and preoccupied to talk to me, she had no heart to tell about the Normal School Graduation Dance; sweat trickled over her face and she was always counting under her breath, pointing at jars, dumping cups of sugar. It seemed to me that work in the house was endless, dreary and peculiarly depressing; work done out of doors, and in my father's service, was ritualistically important.

I wheeled the tank up to the barn, where it was kept, and I heard my mother saying, "Wait till Laird gets a little bigger, then you'll have a real help."

What my father said I did not hear. I was pleased by the way he stood listening, politely as he would to a salesman or a stranger, but with an air of wanting to get on with his real work. I felt my mother had no business down here and I wanted him to feel the same way. What did she mean about Laird? He was no help to anybody. Where was he now? Swinging himself sick on the swing, going around in circles, or trying to catch caterpillars. He never once stayed with me till I was finished.

"And then I can use her more in the house," I heard my mother say. She had a dead-quiet, regretful way of talking about me that always made me uneasy. "I just get my back turned and she runs off. It's not like I had a girl in the family at all."

I went and sat on a feed bag in the corner of the barn, not wanting to appear when this conversation was going on. My mother, I felt, was not to be trusted. She was kinder than my father and more easily fooled, but you could not depend on her, and the real reasons for the things she said and did were not to be known. She loved me, and she sat up late at night making a dress of the difficult style I wanted, for me to wear when school started, but she was also my enemy. She was always plotting. She was plotting now to get me to stay in the house more, although she knew I hated it (*because* she knew I hated it) and keep me from working for my father. It seemed to me she would do this simply out of perversity, and to try her power. It did not occur to me that she could be lonely, or jealous. No grown-up could be; they were too fortunate. I sat and kicked my heels monotonously against a feed bag, raising dust, and did not come out till she was gone.

At any rate, I did not expect my father to pay any attention to what she said. Who could imagine Laird doing my work—Laird remembering the padlock and cleaning out the watering dishes with a leaf on the end of a stick, or even wheeling the tank without it tumbling over? It showed how little my mother knew about the way things really were.

I have forgotten to say what the foxes were fed. My father's bloody apron reminded me. They were fed horsemeat. At this time most farmers still kept horses, and when a horse got too old to work, or broke a leg or got down and would not get up, as they sometimes did, the owner would call my father, and he and Henry went out to the farm in the truck. Usually they shot and butchered the horse there, paying the farmer from five to twelve dollars. If they had already too much meat on hand, they would bring the horse back alive, and keep it for a few days or weeks in our stable, until the meat was needed. After the war the farmers were buying tractors and gradually getting rid of horses altogether, so it sometimes happened that we got a good healthy horse, that there was just no use for any more. If this happened in the winter we might keep the horse in our stable till spring, for we had plenty of hay and if there was a lot of snow—and the plow did not always get our road cleared—it was convenient to be able to go to town with a horse and cutter.[4]

The winter I was eleven years old we had two horses in the stable. We did not know what names they had had before, so we called them Mack and Flora. Mack was an old black workhorse, sooty and indifferent. Flora was a sorrel mare, a driver. We took them both out in the cutter. Mack was slow and easy to handle. Flora was given to fits of violent alarm, veering at cars and even at other horses, but we loved her speed and high-stepping, her general air of gallantry and abandon. On Saturdays we went down to the stable and as soon as we opened the door on its cosy, animal-smelling darkness Flora threw up her head, rolled her eyes, whinnied despairingly and pulled herself through a crisis of nerves on the spot. It was not safe to go into her stall; she would kick.

This winter also I began to hear a great deal more on the theme my mother had sounded when she had been talking in front of the barn. I no longer felt safe. It seemed that in the minds of the people around me there was a steady undercurrent of thought, not to be deflected, on this one subject. The word *girl* had formerly seemed to me innocent and unburdened, like the word *child*; now it appeared that it was no such thing. A girl was not, as I had supposed, simply what I was; it was what I had to become. It was a definition, always touched with emphasis, with reproach and disappointment. Also it was a joke on me. Once Laird and I were fighting, and for the first time ever I had to use all my strength against him; even so, he caught and pinned my arm for a moment, really hurting me. Henry saw this, and laughed, saying, "Oh, that there Laird's gonna show you, one

4. A small, light, one-horse sleigh.

of these days!" Laird was getting a lot bigger. But I was getting bigger too.

My grandmother came to stay with us for a few weeks and I heard other things. "Girls don't slam doors like that." "Girls keep their knees together when they sit down." And worse still, when I asked some questions, "That's none of girls' business." I continued to slam the doors and sit as awkwardly as possible, thinking that by such measures I kept myself free.

When spring came, the horses were let out in the barnyard. Mack stood against the barn wall trying to scratch his neck and haunches, but Flora trotted up and down and reared at the fences, clattering her hooves against the rails. Snow drifts dwindled quickly, revealing the hard gray and brown earth, the familiar rise and fall of the ground, plain and bare after the fantastic landscape of winter. There was a great feeling of opening-out, of release. We just wore rubbers now, over our shoes; our feet felt ridiculously light. One Saturday we went out to the stable and found all the doors open, letting in the unaccustomed sunlight and fresh air. Henry was there, just idling around looking at his collection of calendars which were tacked up behind the stalls in a part of the stable my mother had probably never seen.

"Come to say goodbye to your old friend Mack?" Henry said. "Here, you give him a taste of oats." He poured some oats into Laird's cupped hands and Laird went to feed Mack. Mack's teeth were in bad shape. He ate very slowly, patiently shifting the oats around in his mouth, trying to find a stump of a molar to grind it on. "Poor old Mack," said Henry mournfully. "When a horse's teeth's gone, he's gone. That's about the way."

"Are you going to shoot him today?" I said. Mack and Flora had been in the stable so long I had almost forgotten they were going to be shot.

Henry didn't answer me. Instead he started to sing in a high, trembly, mocking-sorrowful voice, *Oh, there's no more work, for poor Uncle Ned, he's gone where the good darkies go.*[5] Mack's thick, black-ish tongue worked diligently at Laird's hand. I went out before the song was ended and sat down on the gangway.

I had never seen them shoot a horse, but I knew where it was done. Last summer Laird and I had come upon a horse's entrails before they were buried. We had thought it was a big black snake, coiled up in the sun. That was around in the field that ran up beside the barn. I thought that if we went inside the barn, and found a wide crack or a knothole to look through, we would be able to see them do it. It was not something I wanted to see; just the same, if a thing really happened, it was better to see it, and know.

My father came down from the house, carrying the gun.

"What are you doing here?" he said.

"Nothing."

"Go on up and play around the house."

5. Lines from the Stephen Foster song "Old Uncle Ned."

He sent Laird out of the stable. I said to Laird, "Do you want to see them shoot Mack?" and without waiting for an answer led him around to the front door of the barn, opened it carefully, and went in. "Be quiet or they'll hear us," I said. We could hear Henry and my father talking in the stable, then the heavy, shuffling steps of Mack being backed out of his stall.

In the loft it was cold and dark. Thin, crisscrossed beams of sunlight fell through the cracks. The hay was low. It was a rolling country, hills and hollows, slipping under our feet. About four feet up was a beam going around the walls. We piled hay up in one corner and I boosted Laird up and hoisted myself. The beam was not very wide; we crept along it with our hands flat on the barn walls. There were plenty of knotholes, and I found one that gave me the view I wanted—a corner of the barnyard, the gate, part of the field. Laird did not have a knothole and began to complain.

I showed him a widened crack between two boards. "Be quiet and wait. If they hear you you'll get us in trouble."

My father came in sight carrying the gun. Henry was leading Mack by the halter. He dropped it and took out his cigarette papers and tobacco; he rolled cigarettes for my father and himself. While this was going on Mack nosed around in the old, dead grass along the fence. Then my father opened the gate and they took Mack through. Henry led Mack way from the path to a patch of ground and they talked together, not loud enough for us to hear. Mack again began searching for a mouthful of fresh grass, which was not to be found. My father walked away in a straight line, and stopped short at a distance which seemed to suit him. Henry was walking away from Mack too, but sideways, still negligently holding on to the halter. My father raised the gun and Mack looked up as if he had noticed something and my father shot him.

Mack did not collapse at once but swayed, lurched sideways and fell, first on his side; then he rolled over on his back and, amazingly, kicked his legs for a few seconds in the air. At this Henry laughed, as if Mack had done a trick for him. Laird, who had drawn a long, groaning breath of surprise when the shot was fired, said out loud, "He's not dead." And it seemed to me it might be true. But his legs stopped, he rolled on his side again, his muscles quivered and sank. The two men walked over and looked at him in a businesslike way; they bent down and examined his forehead where the bullet had gone in, and now I saw his blood on the brown grass.

"Now they just skin him and cut him up," I said. "Let's go." My legs were a little shaky and I jumped gratefully down into the hay. "Now you've seen how they shoot a horse," I said in a congratulatory way, as if I had seen it many times before. "Let's see if any barn cat's had kittens in the hay." Laird jumped. He seemed young and obedient again. Suddenly I remembered how, when he was little, I had brought him into the barn and told him to climb the ladder to the top beam. That was in the spring, too, when the hay was low. I had done it out of a need for excitement, a desire for something to happen so that I could tell about it. He was wearing a little bulky brown and white checked coat, made down from one of mine. He went all the way up just as I told him, and sat down on the top beam with the hay far below him on one side, and the barn floor and some old machinery on the other. Then I ran screaming to my father, "Laird's up on the top beam!" My father came, my mother came, my father went up the ladder talking very quietly and brought Laird down under his arm, at which my mother leaned against the ladder and began to cry. They said to me, "Why weren't you watching him?" but nobody ever knew the truth. Laird did not know enough to tell. But whenever I saw the brown and white checked coat hanging in the closet, or at the bottom of the rag bag, which was where it ended up, I felt a weight in my stomach, the sadness of unexorcised guilt.

I looked at Laird, who did not even remember this, and I did not like the look on this thin, winter-pale face. His expression was not frightened or upset, but remote, concentrating. "Listen," I said, in an unusually bright and friendly voice, "you aren't going to tell, are you?"

"No," he said absently.

"Promise."

"Promise," he said. I grabbed the hand behind his back to make sure he was not crossing his fingers. Even so, he might have a nightmare; it might come out that way. I decided I had better work hard to get all thoughts of what he had seen out of his mind—which, it seemed to me, could not hold very many things at a time. I got some money I had saved and that afternoon we went into Jubilee and saw a show, with Judy Canova,[6] at which we both laughed a great deal. After that I thought it would be all right.

Two weeks later I knew they were going to shoot Flora. I knew from the night before, when I heard my mother ask if the hay was holding out all right, and my father said, "Well, after tomorrow there'll just be the cow, and we should be able to put her out to grass in another week." So I knew it was Flora's turn in the morning.

This time I didn't think of watching it. That was something to see just one time. I had not thought about it very often since, but sometimes when I was busy, working at school, or standing in front of the mirror combing my hair and wondering if I would be pretty when I grew up, the whole scene would flash into my mind: I would see the easy, practiced way my father raised the gun, and hear Henry laughing when Mack kicked his legs in the air. I did not have any great feeling of horror and opposition, such as a city child might have had; I was too used to seeing the death of animals as a necessity by which we lived. Yet I felt a little ashamed, and there was a new wariness, a sense of holding-off, in my attitude to my father and his work.

It was a fine day, and we were going around the yard picking up tree branches that had been torn off in winter storms. This was something we had been told to do, and also we wanted to use them to make a teepee. We heard Flora whinny, and then my father's voice and Henry's shouting, and we ran down to the barnyard to see what was going on.

6. American comedian best known for her yodeling in hillbilly movies of the 1940s.

The stable door was open. Henry had just brought Flora out, and she had broken away from him. She was running free in the barn-yard, from one end to the other. We climbed up on the fence. It was exciting to see her running, whinnying, going up on her hind legs, prancing and threatening like a horse in a Western movie, an unbroken ranch horse, though she was just an old driver, an old sorrel mare. My father and Henry ran after her and tried to grab the dangling halter. They tried to work her into a corner, and they had almost succeeded when she made a run between them, wild-eyed, and dis-appeared around the corner of the barn. We heard the rails clatter down as she got over the fence, and Henry yelled, "She's into the field now!"

That meant she was in the long L-shaped field that ran up by the house. If she got around the center, heading towards the lane, the gate was open; the truck had been driven into the field this morning. My father shouted to me, because I was on the other side of the fence, nearest the lane, "Go shut the gate!"

I could run very fast. I ran across the garden, past the tree where our swing was hung, and jumped across a ditch into the lane. There was the open gate. She had not got out, I could not see her up on the road; she must have run to the other end of the field. The gate was heavy. I lifted it out of the gravel and carried it across the roadway. I had it halfway across when she came in sight, galloping straight towards me. There was just time to get the chain on. Laird came scrambling through the ditch to help me.

Instead of shutting the gate, I opened it as wide as I could. I did not make any decision to do this, it was just what I did. Flora never slowed down; she galloped straight past me, and Laird jumped up and down, yelling, "Shut it, shut it!" even after it was too late. My father and Henry appeared in the field a moment too late to see what I had done. They only saw Flora heading for the township road. They would think I had not got there in time.

They did not waste any time asking about it. They went back to the barn and got the gun and the knives they used, and put these in the truck; then they turned the truck around and came bouncing up the field toward us. Laird called to them, "Let me go too, let me go too!" and Henry stopped the truck and they took him in. I shut the gate after they were all gone.

I supposed Laird would tell. I wondered what would happen to me. I had never disobeyed my father before, and I could not under-stand why I had done it. Flora would not really get away. They would catch up with her in the truck. Or if they did not catch her this morning somebody would see her and telephone us this afternoon or tomorrow. There was no wild country here for her to run to, only farms. What was more, my father had paid for her, we needed the meat to feed the foxes, we needed the foxes to make our living. All I had done was make more work for my father who worked hard enough already. And when my father found out about it he was not going to trust me any more; he would know that I was not entirely on his side. I was on Flora's side, and that made me no use to any-body, not even to her. Just the same, I did not regret it; when she came running at me and I held the gate open, that was the only thing I could do.

I went back to the house, and my mother said, "What's all the commotion?" I told her that Flora had kicked down the fence and got away. "Your poor father," she said, "now he'll have to go chasing over the countryside. Well, there isn't any use planning dinner before one." She put up the ironing board. I wanted to tell her, but thought better of it and went upstairs and sat on my bed.

Lately I had been trying to make my part of the room fancy, spreading the bed with old lace curtains, and fixing myself a dressing table with some leftovers of cretonne for a skirt. I planned to put up some kind of barricade between my bed and Laird's, to keep my section separate from his. In the sunlight, the lace curtains were just dusty rags. We did not sing at night any more. One night when I was singing Laird said, "You sound silly," and I went right on but the next night I did not start. There was not so much need to anyway, we were no longer afraid. We knew it was just old furniture over there, old jumble and confusion. We did not keep to the rules. I still stayed awake after Laird was asleep and told myself stories, but even in these stories something different was happening, mysterious alterations took place. A story might start off in the old way, with a spectacular danger, a fire or wild animals, and for a while I might rescue people; then things would change around, and instead, somebody would be rescuing me. It might be a boy from our class at school, or even Mr. Campbell, our teacher, who tickled girls under the arms. And at this point the story concerned itself at great length with what I looked like—how long my hair was, and what kind of dress I had on; by the time I had these details worked out the real excitement of the story was lost.

It was later than one o'clock when the truck came back. The tarpaulin was over the back, which meant there was meat in it. My mother had to heat dinner up all over again. Henry and my father had changed from their bloody overalls into ordinary working overalls in the barn, and they washed their arms and necks and faces at the sink, and splashed water on their hair and combed it. Laird lifted his arm to show off a streak of blood. "We shot old Flora," he said, "and cut her up in fifty pieces."

"Well I don't want to hear about it," my mother said. "And don't come to my table like that."

My father made him go and wash the blood off.

We sat down and my father said grace and Henry pasted his chewing gum on the end of his fork, the way he always did; when he took it off he would have us admire the pattern. We began to pass the bowls of steaming, overcooked vegetables. Laird looked across the table at me and said proudly, distinctly, "Anyway it was her fault Flora got away."

"What?" my father said.

"She could of shut the gate and she didn't. She just open' it up and Flora run out."

"Is that right?" my father said.

Everybody at the table was looking at me. I nodded, swallowing food with great difficulty. To my shame, tears flooded my eyes.

My father made a curt sound of disgust. "What did you do that for?"

I did not answer. I put down my fork and waited to be sent from the table, still not looking up.

But this did not happen. For some time nobody said anything, then Laird said matter-of-factly, "She's crying."

"Never mind," my father said. He spoke with resignation, even good humor, the words which absolved and dismissed me for good. "She's only a girl," he said.

I didn't protest that, even in my heart. Maybe it was true.

1968

TILLIE OLSEN

O Yes

For Margaret Heaton, who always taught.

1

They are the only white people there, sitting in the dimness of the Negro church that had once been a corner store, and all through the bubbling, swelling, seething of before the services, twelve-year-old Carol clenches tight her mother's hand, the other resting lightly on her friend, Parialee Phillips, for whose baptism she has come.

The white-gloved ushers hurry up and down the aisle, beckoning people to their seats. A jostle of people. To the chairs angled to the left for the youth choir, to the chairs angled to the right for the ladies' choir, even up to the platform, where behind the place for the dignitaries and the mixed choir, the new baptismal tank gleams—and as if pouring into it from the ceiling, the blue-painted River of Jordan, God standing in the waters, embracing a brown man in a leopard skin and pointing to the letters of gold:

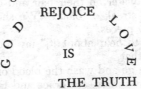

REJOICE

IS

G O D

L O V E

I AM THE WAY   THE TRUTH   THE LIFE

At the clear window, the crucified Christ embroidered on the starched white curtain leaps in the wind of the sudden singing. And the choirs march in. Robes of wine, of blue, of red.

"We stands and sings too," says Parialee's mother, Alva, to Helen; though already Parialee has pulled Carol up. Singing, little Lucinda Phillips fluffs out her many petticoats; singing, little Bubbie bounces up and down on his heels.

Any day now I'll reach that land of freedom,
                                            Yes, o yes

Any day now, know that promised land

The youth choir claps and taps to accent the swing of it. Beginning to tap, Carol stiffens. "Parry, look. Somebody from school."

"Once more once," says Parialee, in the new way she likes to talk now.

"Eddie Garlin's up there. He's in my math."

"Couple cats from Franklin Jr. chirps in the choir. No harm or alarm."

Anxiously Carol scans the faces to see who else she might know, who else might know her, but looks quickly down to Lucinda's wide skirts, for it seems Eddie looks back at her, sullen or troubled, though it is hard to tell, faced as she is into the window of curtained sunblaze.

> *I know my robe will fit me well*
> *I tried it on at the gates of hell*

If it were a record she would play it over and over, Carol thought, to untwine the intertwined voices, to search how the many rhythms rock apart and yet are one glad rhythm.

> *When I get to heaven gonna sing and shout*
> *Nobody be able to turn me out*

"That's Mr. Chairback Evans going to invocate," Lucinda leans across Parry to explain. "He don't invoke good like Momma."

"Shhhh."

"Momma's the only lady in the church that invocates. She made the prayer last week. (Last month, Lucy.) I made the children's 'nouncement last time. (That was way back Thanksgiving.) And Bubbie's 'nounced too. Lots of times."

"Lucy-inda. SIT!"

Bible study announcements and mixed-choir practice announcements and Teen Age Hearts meeting announcements.

If Eddie said something to her about being there, worried Carol, if he talked to her right in front of somebody at school.

Messengers of Faith announcements and Mamboettes announcement and Committee for the Musical Tea.

Parry's arm so warm. Not realizing, starting up the old game from grade school, drumming a rhythm on the other's arm to see if the song could be guessed. "Parry, guess."

But Parry is pondering the platform.

The baptismal tank? "Parry, are you scared . . . the baptizing?"

"This cat? No." Shaking her head so slow and scornful, the barrette in her hair, sun fired, strikes a long rail of light. And still ponders the platform.

New Strangers Baptist Church invites you and Canaan Fair Singers announcements and Battle of Song and Cosmopolites meet. "O Lord, I couldn't find no ease," a solo. The ladies' choir:

> *O what you say seekers, o what you say seekers,*
> *Will you never turn back no more?*

The mixed choir sings:

> *Ezekiel saw that wheel of time*
> *Every spoke was of humankind . . .*

And the slim worn man in the pin-stripe suit starts his sermon On the Nature of God. How God is long-suffering. Oh, how long he has suffered. Calling the roll of the mighty nations, that rose and fell and now are dust for grinding the face of man.

O voice of drowsiness and dream to which Carol does not need to listen. As long ago. Parry warm beside her too, as it used to be, there in the classroom at Mann Elementary, and the feel of drenched in sun and dimness and dream. Smell and sound of the chalk wearing itself away to nothing, rustle of books, drumming tattoo of fingers on her arm: *Guess*.

And as the preacher's voice spins happy and free, it is the used-to-be play-yard. Tag. Thump of the volley ball. Ecstasy of the jump rope. Parry, do pepper. Carol, do pepper. Parry's bettern Carol, Carol's bettern Parry. . . .

Did someone scream?

It seemed someone screamed—but all were sitting as before, though the sun no longer blared through the windows. She tried to see up where Eddie was, but the ushers were standing at the head of the aisle now, the ladies in white dresses like nurses or waitresses wear, the men holding their white-gloved hands up so one could see their palms.

"And God is Powerful," the preacher was chanting. "Nothing for him to scoop out the oceans and pat up the mountains. Nothing for him to scoop up the miry clay and create man. Man, I said, create Man."

The lady in front of her moaned "*O yes*" and others were moaning "*O yes.*"

"And when the earth mourned the Lord said, Weep not, for all will be returned to you, every dust, every atom. And the tired dust settles back, goes back. Until that Judgment Day. That great day."

"*O yes.*"

The ushers were giving out fans. Carol reached for one and Parry said: "What *you* need one for?" but she took it anyway.

"You think Satchmo can blow; you think Muggsy can blow; you think Dizzy can blow?"[1] He was straining to an imaginary trumpet now, his head far back and his voice coming out like a trumpet.

"Oh Parry, he's so good."

"Well. Jelly jelly."

"Nothing to Gabriel on that great getting-up morning. And the horn wakes up Adam, and Adam runs to wake up Eve, and Eve moans; Just one more minute, let me sleep, and Adam yells, Great Day, woman, don't you know it's the Great Day?"

"*Great Day, Great Day*," the mixed choir behind the preacher rejoices:

> *When our cares are past*
> *when we're home at last . . .*

"And Eve runs to wake up Cain." Running round the platform, stooping and shaking imaginary sleepers, "and Cain runs to wake up Abel." Looping, scalloping his voice—"Grea-aaa-aat Daaaay." All the choirs thundering:

---

1. Louis Armstrong (1900–1971); Francis ("Muggsy") Spanier (1906–1967); John ("Dizzy") Gillespie (b. 1917), all famous black jazz trumpeters.

> *Great Day*
> *When the battle's fought*
> *And the victory's won*

Exultant spirals of sound. And Carol caught into it (Eddie forgotten, the game forgotten) chanting with Lucy and Bubbie: "*Great Day*."

"Ohhhhhhhhhh," his voice like a trumpet again, "the re-unioning. Ohhhhhhhhh, the rejoicing. After the ages immemorial of longing."

Someone *was* screaming. And an awful thrumming sound with it, like feet and hands thrashing around, like a giant jumping of a rope.

"*Great Day*." And no one stirred or stared as the ushers brought a little woman out into the aisle, screaming and shaking, just a little shrunk-up woman, not much taller than Carol, the biggest thing about her her swollen hands and the cascades of tears wearing her face.

The shaking inside Carol too. Turning and trembling to ask: "What? . . . that lady?" But Parry still ponders the platform; little Lucy loops the chain of her bracelet round and round; and Bubbie sits placidly, dreamily. Alva Phillips is up fanning a lady in front of her; two lady ushers are fanning other people Carol cannot see. And her mother, her mother looks in a sleep.

Yes. He raised up the dead from the grave. He made old death behave.

Yes. Yes. From all over, hushed.   *O Yes*

He was your mother's rock. Your father's mighty tower. And he gave us a little baby. A little baby to love.

I am so glad

Yes, your friend, when you're friendless. Your father when you're fatherless. Way maker. Door opener.

Yes

When it seems you can't go on any longer, he's there. You can, he says, you can.

Yes

And that burden you been carrying—ohhhhh that burden—not for always will it be. No, not for always.

Stay with me, Lord

I will put my Word in you and it is power. I will put my Truth in you and it is power.

O Yes

Out of your suffering I will make you to stand as a stone. A tried stone. Hewn out of the mountains of ages eternal.

Yes

Ohhhhhhhhhhh. Out of the mire I will lift your feet. Your tired feet from so much wandering. From so much work and wear and hard times.

Yes

From so much journeying— and never the promised land. And I'll wash them in the well your tears made. And I'll shod them in the gospel of peace, and of feeling good. Ohhhhhhhhh.

O Yes.

Behind Carol, a trembling wavering scream. Then the thrashing. Up above, the singing:

They taken my blessed Jesus and flogged him to the woods

And they made him hew out his cross and they dragged him to
    Calvary
Shout brother, Shout shout shout. He never cried a word.

Powerful throbbing voices. Calling and answering to each other.

They taken my blessed Jesus and whipped him up the hill
With a knotty whip and a raggedy thorn he never cried a word
Shout, sister. Shout shout shout. He never cried a word.

Go tell the people the Saviour has risen
Has risen from the dead and will live forevermore
    And won't have to die no more.

                                                    Halleloo.
        Shout, brother, shout
        We won't have to die no more!

A single exultant lunge of shriek. Then the thrashing. All around a
clapping. Shouts with it. The piano whipping, whipping air to a froth.
Singing now.

        I once was lost who now am found
        Was blind who now can see

On Carol's fan, a little Jesus walked on wondrously blue waters to
where bearded disciples spread nets out of a fishing boat. If she
studied the fan—became it—it might make a wall around her. If she
could make what was happening (*what* was happening?) into a record
small and round to listen to far and far as if into a seashell—the stamp
and rills and spirals all tiny (but never any screaming).

        wade wade in the water

        Jordan's water is chilly and wild
        I've got to get home to the other side
        God's going to trouble the waters

Ladders of screamings. The music leaps and prowls. Drumming feet
of ushers running. And still little Lucy fluffs her skirts, loops the chain
on her bracelet; still Bubbie sits and rocks dreamily; and only eyes
turn for an instant to the aisle—as if nothing were happening. "Mother,
let's go home," Carol begs, but her mother holds her so tight. Alva
Phillips, strong Alva, rocking too and chanting, *O Yes.* No, do not
look.

        Wade,
        Sea of trouble all mingled with fire
        Come on my brethren it's time to go higher
        Wade wade

The voices in great humming waves, slow, slow (when did it become
the humming?), everyone swaying with it too, moving like in slow
waves and singing, and up where Eddie is, a new cry, wild and open,
"O help me, Jesus," and when Carol opens her eyes she closes them
again, quick, but still can see the new known face from school (not
Eddie), the thrashing, writhing body, struggling against the ushers

with the look of grave and loving support on their faces, and hear the torn, tearing cry: "Don't take me away, life everlasting, don't take me away."

And now the rhinestones in Parry's hair glitter wicked, the white hands of the ushers, fanning, foam in the air; the blue-painted waters of Jordan swell and thunder; Christ spirals on his cross in the window, and she is drowned under the sluice of the slow singing and the sway.

So high up and forgotten the waves and the world, so stirless the deep cool green and the wrecks of what had been. Here now Hostess Foods, where Alva Phillips works her nights—but different from that time Alva had taken them through before work, for it is all sunken under water, the creaking loading platform where they had left the night behind; the closet room where Alva's swaddles of sweaters, boots, and cap hung, the long hall lined with pickle barrels, the sharp freezer door swinging open.

Bubbles of breath that swell. A gulp of numbing air. She swims into the chill room where the huge wheels of cheese stand, and Alva swims too, deftly oiling each machine: slicers and wedgers and the convey, that at her touch start to roll and grind. The light of day blazes up and Alva is holding a cup, saying: Drink this, baby.

"DRINK IT." Her mother's voice and the numbing air demanding her to pay attention. Up through the waters and into the car.

"That's right, lambie, now lie back." Her mother's lap.

"Mother."

"Shhhhh. You almost fainted, lambie."

Alva's voice. "You gonna be all right, Carol . . . Lucy, I'm telling you for the last time, you and Buford get back into that church. Carol is *fine.*"

"Lucyinda, if I had all your petticoats I could float." Crying. "Why didn't you let me wear my full skirt with the petticoats, Mother."

"Shhhhh, lamb." Smoothing her cheek. "Just breathe, take long deep breaths."

". . . How you doing now, you little ol' consolation prize?" It is Parry, but she does not come in the car or reach to Carol through the open window: "No need to cuss and fuss. You going to be sharp as a tack, Jack."

Answering automatically: "And cool as a fool."

Quick, they look at each other.

"Parry, we have to go home now, don't we, Mother? I almost fainted, didn't I, Mother? . . . Parry, I'm sorry I got sick and have to miss your baptism."

"Don't feel sorry. I'll feel better you not there to watch. It was our mommas wanted you to be there, not me."

"Parry!" Three voices.

"Maybe I'll come over to play kickball after. If you feeling better. Maybe. Or bring the pogo." Old shared joys in her voice: "Or any little thing,"

In just a whisper: "Or any little thing. Parry. Good-bye, Parry."

And why does Alva have to talk now?

"You all right? You breathin' deep like your momma said? Was it too close 'n hot in there? Did something scare you, Carrie?"

Shaking her head to lie, "No."

"I blame myself for not paying attention. You not used to people letting go that way. Lucy and Bubbie, Parialee, they used to it. They been coming since they lap babies."

"Alva, that's all right. Alva, Mrs. Phillips."

"You *was* scared. Carol, it's something to study about. You'll feel better if you understand."

Trying not to listen.

"You not used to hearing what people keeps inside, Carol. You know how music can make you feel things? Glad or sad or like you can't sit still? That was religion music, Carol."

"I have to breathe deep, Mother said."

"Not everybody feels religion the same way. Some it's in their mouth, but some it's like a hope in their blood, their bones. And they singing songs every word that's real to them, Carol, every word out of they own life. And the preaching finding lodgment in their hearts."

The screaming was tuning up in her ears again, high above Alva's patient voice and the waves lapping and fretting.

"Maybe somebody's had a hard week, Carol, and they locked up with it. Maybe a lot of hard weeks bearing down."

"Mother, my head hurts."

"And they're home, Carol, church is home. Maybe the only place they can feel how they feel and maybe let it come out. So they can go on. And it's all right."

"Please, Alva. Mother, tell Alva my head hurts."

"Get Happy, we call it, and most it's good feeling, Carol, when you got all that locked up inside you."

"Tell her we have to go home. It's all right, Alva. Please, Mother. Say good-bye. Good-bye."

When I was carrying Parry and her father left me, and I fifteen years old, one thousand miles away from home, sin-sick and never really believing, as still I don't believe all, scorning, for what have it done to help, waiting there in the clinic and maybe sleeping, a voice called: Alva, Alva. So mournful and so sweet: Alva. Fear not, I have loved you from the foundation of the universe. And a little small child tugged on my dress. He was carrying a parade stick, on the end of it a star that outshined the sun. Follow me, he said. And the real sun went down and he hidden his stick. How dark it was, how dark. I could feel the darkness with my hands. And when I could see, I screamed. Dump trucks run, dumping bodies in hell, and a convey line run, never ceasing with souls, weary ones having to stamp and shove them along, and the air like fire. Oh I never want to hear such screaming. Then the little child jumped on a motorbike making a path no bigger than my little finger. But first he greased my feet with the hands of my momma when I was a knee baby. They shined like the sun was on them. Eyes he placed all around my head, and as I journeyed upward after him, it seemed I heard a mourning: "Mama Mama you must help carry the world." The rise and fall of nations I saw. And the voice called again Alva Alva, and I flew into a world of light, multitudes singing, Free, free, I am so glad.

2

Helen began to cry, telling her husband about it.

"You and Alva ought to have your heads examined, taking her there cold like that," Len said. "All right, wreck my best handkerchief. Anyway, now that she's had a bath, her Sunday dinner. . . ."

"And been fussed over," seventeen-year-old Jeannie put in.

"She seems good as new. Now *you* forget it, Helen."

"I can't. Something . . . deep happened. If only I or Alva had told her what it would be like. . . . But I didn't realize."

You don't realize a lot of things, Mother, Jeannie said, but not aloud.

"So Alva talked about it after instead of before. Maybe it meant more that way."

"Oh Len, she didn't listen."

"You don't know if she did or not. Or what there was in the experience for her. . . ."

Enough to pull that kid apart two ways even more, Jeannie said, but still not aloud.

"I was so glad she and Parry were going someplace together again. Now that'll be between them too. Len, they really need, miss each other. What happened in a few months? When I think of how close they were, the hours of makebelieve and dressup and playing ball and collecting. . . ."

"Grow up, Mother." Jeannie's voice was harsh. "Parialee's collecting something else now. Like her own crowd. Like jivetalk and rhythmandblues. Like teachers who treat her like a dummy and white kids who treat her like dirt; boys who think she's really something and chicks who. . . ."

"Jeannie, I know. It hurts."

"Well, maybe it hurts Parry too. Maybe. At least she's got a crowd. Just don't let it hurt Carol though, 'cause there's nothing she can do about it. That's all through, her and Parialee Phillips, put away with their paper dolls."

"No, Jeannie, no."

"It's like Ginger and me. Remember Ginger, my best friend in Horace Mann. But you hardly noticed when it happened to us, did you . . . because she was white? Yes, Ginger, who's got two kids now, who quit school year before last. Parry's never going to finish either. What's she got to do with Carrie any more? They're going different places. Different places, different crowds. And they're sorting. . . ."

"Now wait, Jeannie. Parry's just as bright, just as capable."

"They're in junior high, Mother. Don't you know about junior high? How they sort? And it's all where you're going. Yes and Parry's colored and Carrie's white. And you have to watch everything, what you wear and how you wear it and who you eat lunch with and how much homework you do and how you act to the teacher and what you laugh at. . . . And run with your crowd."

"It's that final?" asked Len. "Don't you think kids like Carol and Parry can show it doesn't *have* to be that way."

"They can't. They can't. They don't let you."

"No need to shout," he said mildly. "And who do you mean by 'they' and what do you mean by 'sorting'?"

How they sort. A foreboding of comprehension whirled within Helen. What was it Carol had told her of the Welcome Assembly the first day in junior high? The models showing How to Dress and How Not to Dress and half the girls in their loved new clothes watching their counterparts up on the stage—*their* straight skirt, their sweater, their earrings, lipstick, hairdo—"How Not to Dress," "a bad reputation for your school." It was nowhere in Carol's description, yet picturing it now, it seemed to Helen that a mute cry of violated dignity hung in the air. Later there had been a story of going to another Low 7 homeroom on an errand and seeing a teacher trying to wipe the forbidden lipstick off a girl who was fighting back and cursing. Helen could hear Carol's frightened, self-righteous tones: ". . . and I hope they expel her; she's the kind that gives Franklin Jr. a bad rep; she doesn't care about anything and always gets into fights." Yet there was nothing in these incidents to touch the heavy comprehension that waited. . . . Homework, the wonderings those times Jeannie and Carol needed help: "What if there's no one at home to give the help, and the teachers with their two hundred and forty kids a day can't or don't or the kids don't ask and they fall hopelessly behind, what then?"—but this too was unrelated. And what had it been that time about Parry? "Mother, Melanie and Sharon won't go if they know Parry's coming." Then of course you'll go with Parry, she's been your friend longer, she had answered, but where was it they were going and what had finally happened? Len, my head hurts, she felt like saying, in Carol's voice in the car, but Len's eyes were grave on Jeannie who was saying passionately:

"If you think it's so goddam important why do we have to live here where it's for real; why don't we move to Ivy like Betsy (yes, I know, money), where it's the deal to be buddies, in school anyway, three colored kids and their father's a doctor or judge or something big wheel and one always gets elected President or head song girl or something to prove oh how we're democratic. . . . What do you want of that poor kid anyway? Make up your mind. Stay friends with Parry —but be one of the kids. Sure. Be a brain—but not a square. Rise on up, college prep, but don't get separated. Yes, stay one of the kids, but. . . ."

"Jeannie. You're not talking about Carol at all, are you, Jeannie? Say it again. I wasn't listening. I was trying to think."

"She will not say it again," Len said firmly, "you look about ready to pull a Carol. One a day's our quota. And you, Jeannie, we'd better cool it. Too much to talk about for one session. . . . Here, come to the window and watch the Carol and Parry you're both so all worked up about."

In the wind and the shimmering sunset light, half the children of the block are playing down the street. Leaping, bouncing, hallooing, tugging the kites of spring. In the old synchronized understanding, Carol and Parry kick, catch, kick, catch. And now Parry jumps on her pogo stick (the last time), Carol shadowing her, and Bubbie, arching his body in a semicircle of joy, bounds after them, high, higher, higher.

And the months go by and supposedly it is forgotten, except for the now and then when, self-important, Carol will say: I really truly did nearly faint, didn't I, Mother, that time I went to church with Parry?

And now seldom Parry and Carol walk the hill together. Melanie's mother drives by to pick up Carol, and the several times Helen has suggested Parry, too, Carol is quick to explain: "She's already left" or "She isn't ready; she'll make us late."

And after school? Carol is off to club or skating or library or someone's house, and Parry can stay for kickball only on the rare afternoons when she does not have to hurry home where Lucy, Bubbie, and the cousins wait to be cared for, now Alva works the four to twelve-thirty shift.

No more the bending together over the homework. All semester the teachers have been different, and rarely Parry brings her books home, for where is there space or time and what is the sense? And the phone never rings with: what you going to wear tomorrow, are you bringing your lunch, or come on over, let's design some clothes for the Katy Keane comic-book contest. And Parry never drops by with Alva for Saturday snack to or from grocery shopping.

And the months go by and the sorting goes on and seemingly it is over until that morning when Helen must stay home from work, so swollen and feverish is Carol with mumps.

The afternoon before, Parry had come by, skimming up the stairs, spilling books and binders on the bed: Hey frail, lookahere and wail, your momma askin for homework, what she got against YOU? . . . looking quickly once then not looking again and talking fast. . . . Hey, you bloomed. You gonna be your own pumpkin, hallowe'en? Your momma know yet it's mu-umps? And lumps. Momma says: no distress, she'll be by tomorrow morning see do you need anything while your momma's to work. . . . (Singing: *whole lotta shakin goin on.*) All your 'signments is inside; Miss Rockface says the teachers to write 'em cause I mightn't get it right all right.

But did not tell: Does your mother work for Carol's mother? Oh, you're neighbors! Very well, I'll send along a monitor to open Carol's locker but you're only to take these things I'm writing down, nothing else. Now say after me: Miss Campbell is   trusting me to be   a good responsible girl. And go   right to Carol's house. After school. Not stop anywhere   on the way. Not lose anything. And only take. What's written on the list.

You really gonna mess with that book stuff? Sign on *mine* says do-not-open-until-eX-mas. . . . That Mrs. Fernandez doll she didn't send nothin, she was the only, says feel better and read a book to report if you feel like and I'm the most for takin care for you; she's my most, wish I could get her but she only teaches 'celerated. . . . Flicking the old read books on the shelf but not opening to mock-declaim as once she used to . . . Vicky, Eddie's g.f.[2] in Rockface office, she's on suspended for sure, yellin to Rockface: you bitchkitty don't you give me no more bad shit. That Vicky she can sure slinging-ring it. Staring out the window as if the tree not there in which they had hid out and rocked so often. . . . For sure. (*Keep mo-o-vin.*[3]) Got me a new pink top and lilac skirt. Look sharp with this purple?

2. Girl friend.
3. Words from "Whole Lotta Shakin' Goin' On" mentioned earlier in the passage and continued later; a famous Jerry Lee Lewis record of 1957.

Cinching in the wide belt as if delighted with what newly swelled above and swelled below. Wear it Saturday night to Sweet's, Sounds of Joy, Leroy and Ginny and me goin if Momma'll stay home. IF. (*Shake my baby shake.*) How come old folks still likes to party? Huh? Asking of Rembrandt's weary old face looking from the wall.[4] How come (softly) you long-gone you. Touching her face to his quickly, lightly. NEXT mumps is your buddybud Melanie's turn to tote your stuff. I'm gettin the hoovus groovus. Hey you so unneat, don't care what you bed with. Removing the books and binders, ranging them on the dresser one by one, marking lipstick faces— bemused or mocking or amazed—on each paper jacket. Better. Fluffing out smoothing the quilt with exaggerated energy. Any little thing I can get, cause I gotta blow. Tossing up and catching their year-ago, arm-in-arm graduation picture, replacing it deftly, upside down, into its mirror crevice. Joe. Bring you joy juice or fizz water or kickapoo? Adding a frown line to one bookface. Twanging the paper fishkite, the Japanese windbell overhead, setting the mobile they had once made of painted eggshells and decorated straws to twirling and rocking. And is gone.

She talked to the lipstick faces after, in her fever, tried to stand on her head to match the picture, twirled and twanged with the violent overhead.

Sleeping at last after the disordered night. Having surrounded herself with the furnishings of that world of childhood she no sooner learned to live in comfortably, then had to leave.

The dollhouse stands there to arrange and rearrange; the shell and picture card collections to re-sort and remember; the population of dolls given away to little sister, borrowed back, propped all round to dress and undress and caress.

She has thrown off her nightgown because of the fever, and her just budding breast is exposed where she reaches to hold the floppy plush dog that had been her childhood pillow.

Not for anything would her mother have disturbed her. Except that in the unaccustomedness of a morning at home, in the bruised restlessness after the sleepless night, Helen clicks on the radio—and the storm of singing whirls into the room:

> . . . *of trouble all mingled with fire*
> *Come on my brethren we've got to go higher*
> *Wade, wade. . . .*

And Carol runs down the stairs, shrieking and shrieking. "Turn it off, Mother, turn it off." Hurling herself at the dial and wrenching it so it comes off in her hand.

"Ohhhhh," choked and convulsive, while Helen tries to hold her, to quiet.

"Mother, why did they sing and scream like that?"

"At Parry's church?"

"Yes." Rocking and strangling the cries. "I hear it all the time." Clinging and beseeching. ". . . What was it, Mother? Why?"

---

4. Rembrandt van Rijn (1600–1669), the great Dutch painter, produced perhaps 100 self-portraits.

Emotion, Helen thought of explaining, *a characteristic of the religion of all oppressed peoples, yes your very own great-grandparents* —thought of saying. And discarded.

Aren't you now, haven't you had feelings in yourself so strong they had to come out some way? ("what howls restrained by decorum")— thought of saying. And discarded.

Repeat Alva: *hope . . . every word out of their own life. A place to let go. And church is home.* And discarded.

The special history of the Negro people—history?—just you try living what must be lived every day—thought of saying. And discarded.

And said nothing.

And said nothing.

And soothed and held.

"Mother, a lot of the teachers and kids don't like Parry when they don't even know what she's like. Just because. . ." Rocking again, convulsive and shamed. "And I'm not really her friend any more."

No news. Betrayal and shame. Who betrayed? Whose shame? Brought herself to say aloud: "But maybe friends again. As Alva and I are."

The sobbing a whisper. "That girl Vicky who got that way when I fainted, she's in school. She's the one keeps wearing the lipstick and they wipe it off and she's always in trouble and now maybe she's expelled. Mother."

"Yes, lambie."

"She acts so awful outside but I remember how she was in church and whenever I see her now I have to wonder. And hear . . . like I'm her, Mother, like I'm her." Clinging and trembling. "Oh why do I have to feel it happens to me too?

"Mother, I want to forget about it all, and not care,—like Melanie. Why can't I forget? *Oh why is it like it is and why do I have to care?*"

Caressing, quieting.

Thinking: *caring asks doing. It is a long baptism into the seas of humankind, my daughter. Better immersion than to live untouched. . . . Yet how will you sustain?*

Why is it like it is?

Sheltering her daughter close, mourning the illusion of the embrace.

And why do I have to care?

While in her, her own need leapt and plunged for the place of strength that was not—where one could scream or sorrow while all knew and accepted, and gloved and loving hands waited to support and understand.

1956

WILLIAM FAULKNER

The Old People

At first there was nothing. There was the faint, cold, steady rain, the gray and constant light of the late November dawn, with the voices of the hounds converging somewhere in it and toward them. Then Sam Fathers, standing just behind the boy as he had been standing when the boy shot his first running rabbit with his first gun and almost with the first load it ever carried, touched his shoulder and he began to shake, not with any cold. Then the buck was there. He did not come into sight; he was just there, looking not like a ghost but as if all of light were condensed in him and he were the source of it, not only moving in it but disseminating it, already running, seen first as you always see the deer, in that split second after he has already seen you, already slanting away in that first soaring bound, the antlers even in that dim light looking like a small rocking-chair balanced on his head.

"Now," Sam Fathers said, "shoot quick, and slow."

The boy did not remember that shot at all. He would live to be eighty, as his father and his father's twin brother and their father in his turn had lived to be, but he would never hear that shot nor remember even the shock of the gun-butt. He didn't even remember what he did with the gun afterward. He was running. Then he was standing over the buck where it lay on the wet earth still in the attitude of speed and not looking at all dead, standing over it shaking and jerking, with Sam Fathers beside him again, extending the knife. "Don't walk up to him in front," Sam said. "If he ain't dead, he will cut you all to pieces with his feet. Walk up to him from behind and take him by the horn first, so you can hold his head down until you can jump away. Then slip your other hand down and hook your fingers in his nostrils."

The boy did that—drew the head back and the throat taut and drew Sam Fathers' knife across the throat and Sam stooped and dipped his hands in the hot smoking blood and wiped them back and forth across the boy's face. Then Sam's horn rang in the wet gray woods and again and again; there was a boiling wave of dogs about them, with Tennie's Jim and Boon Hogganbeck whipping them back after each had had a taste of the blood, then the men, the true hunters—Walter Ewell whose rifle never missed, and Major de Spain and old General Compson and the boy's cousin, McCaslin Edmonds, grandson of his father's sister, sixteen years his senior and, since both he and McCaslin were only children and the boy's father had been nearing seventy when he was born, more his brother than his cousin and more his father than either —sitting their horses and looking down at them: at the old man of seventy who had been a Negro for two generations now but whose face and bearings were still those of the Chickasaw chief who had been his father; and the white boy of twelve with the prints of the bloody hands on his face, who had nothing to do now but stand straight and not let the trembling show.

"Did he do all right, Sam?" his cousin McCaslin said.

"He done all right," Sam Fathers said.

They were the white boy, marked forever, and the old dark man sired on both sides by savage kings, who had marked him, whose bloody hands had merely formally consecrated him to that which, under the man's tutelage, he had already accepted, humbly and joyfully, with abnegation and with pride too; the hands, the touch, the first worthy blood which he had been found at last worthy to draw, joining him and the man forever, so that the man would continue to live past the boy's seventy years and then eighty years, long after the man himself had entered the earth as chiefs and kings entered it;—the child, not yet a man, whose grandfather had lived in the same country and in almost the same manner as the boy himself would grow up to live, leaving his descendants in the land in his turn as his grandfather had done, and the old man past seventy whose grandfathers had owned the land long before the white men ever saw it and who had vanished from it now with all their kind, what of blood they left behind them running now in another race and for a while even in bondage and now drawing toward the end of its alien and irrevocable course, barren, since Sam Fathers had no children.

His father was Ikkemotubbe himself, who had named himself Doom. Sam told the boy about that—how Ikkemotubbe, old Issetibbeha's sister's son, had run away to New Orleans in his youth and returned seven years later with a French companion calling himself the Chevalier Soeur-Blonde de Vitry, who must have been the Ikkemotubbe of his family too and who was already addressing Ikkemotubbe as *Du Homme;*[1]—returned, came home again, with his foreign Aramis[2] and the quadroon slave woman who was to be Sam's mother, and a gold-laced hat and coat and a wicker wine-hamper containing a litter of month-old puppies and a gold snuff-box filled with a white powder resembling fine sugar. And how he was met at the River landing by three or four companions of his bachelor youth, and while the light of a smoking torch gleamed on the glittering braid of the hat and coat Doom squatted in the mud of the land and took one of the puppies from the hamper and put a pinch of the white powder on its tongue and the puppy died before the one who was holding it could cast it away. And how they returned to the Plantation where Issetibbeha, dead now, had been succeeded by his son, Doom's fat cousin Moketubbe, and the next day Moketubbe's eight-year-old son died suddenly and that afternoon, in the presence of Moketubbe and most of the others (the People, Sam Fathers called them) Doom produced another puppy from the wine-hamper and put a pinch of the white powder on its tongue and Moketubbe abdicated and Doom became in fact The Man which his French friend already called him. And how on the day after that, during the ceremony of accession, Doom pronounced a marriage between the pregnant quadroon and one of the slave men which he had just inherited (that was how Sam Fathers got his name, which in Chickasaw had been Had-Two-Fathers) and two years later sold the man and woman and the child who was his own son to his white neighbor, Carothers McCaslin.

That was seventy years ago. The Sam Fathers whom the boy knew was already sixty—a man not tall, squat rather, almost sedentary, flabby-looking though he actually was not, with hair like a horse's mane which even at seventy showed no trace of white and a face which

---

1. Mistaken or provincialized French for "The Man," with overtones of nobility. French nobility usually have, following their title, *de* or *d'* followed by a place name indicating their residence or seat— c.g., Duc d'Orléans. Even if "The Man," *l'homme,* were preceded by *de,* the proper form would be *de l'homme.*

2. One of Alexandre Dumas' three musketeers.

showed no age until he smiled, whose only visible trace of Negro blood was a slight dullness of the hair and the fingernails, and something else which you did notice about the eyes, which you noticed because it was not always there, only in repose and not always then—something not in their shape nor pigment but in their expression, and the boy's cousin McCaslin told him what that was: not the heritage of Ham, not the mark of servitude but of bondage; the knowledge that for a while that part of his blood had been the blood of slaves. "Like an old lion or a bear in a cage," McCaslin said. "He was born in the cage and has been in it all his life; he knows nothing else. Then he smells something. It might be anything, any breeze blowing past anything and then into his nostrils. But there for a second was the hot sand or the cane-brake that he never even saw himself, might not even know if he did see it and probably does know he couldn't hold his own with it if he got back to it. But that's not what he smells then. It was the cage he smelled. He hadn't smelled the cage until that minute. Then the hot sand or the brake blew into his nostrils and blew away, and all he could smell was the cage. That's what makes his eyes look like that."

"Then let him go!" the boy cried. "Let him go!"

His cousin laughed shortly. Then he stopped laughing, making the sound that is. It had never been laughing. "His cage ain't McCaslins'," he said. "He was a wild man. When he was born, all his blood on both sides, except the little white part, knew things that had been tamed out of our blood so long ago that we have not only forgotten them, we have to live together in herds to protect ourselves from our own sources. He was the direct son not only of a warrior but of a chief. Then he grew up and began to learn things, and all of a sudden one day he found out that he had been betrayed, the blood of the warriors and chiefs had been betrayed. Not by his father," he added quickly. "He probably never held it against old Doom for selling him and his mother into slavery, because he probably believed the damage was already done before then and it was the same warriors' and chiefs' blood in him and Doom both that was betrayed through the black blood which his mother gave him. Not betrayed by the black blood and not wilfully betrayed by his mother, but betrayed by her all the same, who had bequeathed him not only the blood of slaves but even a little of the very blood which had enslaved it; himself his own battleground, the scene of his own vanquishment and the mausoleum of his defeat. His cage aint us," McCaslin said. "Did you ever know anybody yet, even your father and Uncle Buddy, that ever told him to do or not do anything that he ever paid any attention to?"

That was true. The boy first remembered him as sitting in the door of the plantation blacksmith-shop, where he sharpened plow-points and mended tools and even did rough carpenter-work when he was not in the woods. And sometimes, even when the woods had not drawn him, even with the shop cluttered with work which the farm waited on, Sam would sit there, doing nothing at all for half a day or a whole one, and no man, neither the boy's father and twin uncle in their day nor his cousin McCaslin after he became practical though not yet titular master, ever to say to him, "I want this finished by sundown" or "why wasn't this done yesterday?" And once each year, in the late fall, in

November, the boy would watch the wagon, the hooped canvas top erected now, being loaded—the food, hams and sausage from the smokehouse, coffee and flour and molasses from the commissary, a whole beef killed just last night for the dogs until there would be meat in camp, the crate containing the dogs themselves, then the bedding, the guns, the horns and lanterns and axes, and his cousin McCaslin and Sam Fathers in their hunting clothes would mount to the seat and with Tennie's Jim sitting on the dog-crate they would drive away to Jefferson, to join Major de Spain and General Compson and Boon Hogganbeck and Walter Ewell and go on into the big bottom of the Tallahatchie where the deer and bear were, to be gone two weeks. But before the wagon was even loaded the boy would find that he could watch no longer. He would go away, running almost, to stand behind the corner where he could not see the wagon and nobody could see him, not crying, holding himself rigid except for trembling, whispering to himself: "Soon now. Soon now. Just three more years" (or two more or one more) "and I will be ten. Then Cass said I can go."

White man's work, when Sam did work. Because he did nothing else: farmed no allotted acres of his own, as the other ex-slaves of old Carothers McCaslin did, performed no field-work for daily wages as the younger and newer Negroes did—and the boy never knew just how that had been settled between Sam and old Carothers, or perhaps with old Carothers' twin sons after him. For, although Sam lived among the Negroes, in a cabin among the other cabins in the quarters, and consorted with Negroes (what of consorting with anyone Sam did after the boy got big enough to walk alone from the house to the blacksmith-shop and then to carry a gun) and dressed like them and talked like them and even went with them to the Negro church now and then, he was still the son of that Chickasaw chief and the Negroes knew it. And, it seemed to the boy, not only Negroes. Boon Hogganbeck's grandmother had been a Chickasaw woman too, and although the blood had run white since and Boon was a white man, it was not chief's blood. To the boy at least, the difference was apparent immediately you saw Boon and Sam together, and even Boon seemed to know it was there—even Boon, to whom in his tradition it had never occurred that anyone might be better born than himself. A man might be smarter, he admitted that, or richer (luckier, he called it) but not better born. Boon was a mastiff, absolutely faithful, dividing his fidelity equally between Major de Spain and the boy's cousin McCaslin, absolutely dependent for his very bread and dividing that impartially too between Major de Spain and McCaslin, hardy, generous, courageous enough, a slave to all the appetites and almost unratiocinative. In the boy's eyes at least it was Sam Fathers, the Negro, who bore himself not only toward his cousin McCaslin and Major de Spain but toward all white men, with gravity and dignity and without servility or recourse to that impenetrable wall of ready and easy mirth which Negroes sustain between themselves and white men, bearing himself toward his cousin McCaslin not only as one man to another but as an older man to a younger.

He taught the boy the woods, to hunt, when to shoot and when not to shoot, when to kill and when not to kill, and better, what to do with it afterward. Then he would talk to the boy, the two of them sitting beneath the close fierce stars on a summer hilltop while they waited for the hounds to bring the fox back within hearing, or beside a fire in the November or December woods while the dogs worked out a coon's trail along the creek, or fireless in the pitch dark and heavy dew of April mornings while they squatted beneath a turkey-roost. The boy would never question him; Sam did not react to questions. The boy would just wait and then listen and Sam would begin, talking about the old days and the People whom he had not had time ever to know and so could not remember (he did not remember ever having seen his father's face), and in place of whom the other race into which his blood had run supplied him with no substitute.

And as he talked about those old times and those dead and vanished men of another race from either that the boy knew, gradually to the boy those old times would cease to be old times and would become a part of the boy's present, not only as if they had happened yesterday but as if they were still happening, the men who walked through them actually walking in breath and air and casting an actual shadow on the earth they had not quitted. And more: as if some of them had not happened yet but would occur tomorrow, until at last it would seem to the boy that he himself had not come into existence yet, that none of his race nor the other subject race which his people had brought with them into the land had come here yet; that although it had been his grandfather's and then his father's and uncle's and was now his cousin's and someday would be his own land which he and Sam hunted over, their hold upon it actually was as trivial and without reality as the now faded and archaic script in the chancery book[3] in Jefferson which allocated it to them and that it was he, the boy, who was the guest here and Sam Fathers' voice the mouthpiece of the host.

Until three years ago there had been two of them, the other a full-blood Chickasaw, in a sense even more incredibly lost than Sam Fathers. He called himself Jobaker, as if it were one word. Nobody knew his history at all. He was a hermit, living in a foul little shack at the forks of the creek five miles from the plantation and about that far from any other habitation. He was a market hunter and fisherman and he consorted with nobody, black or white; no Negro would even cross his path and no man dared approach his hut except Sam. And perhaps once a month the boy would find them in Sam's shop—two old men squatting on their heels on the dirt floor, talking in a mixture of Negroid English and flat hill dialect and now and then a phrase of that old tongue which as time went on and the boy squatted there too listening, he began to learn. Then Jobaker died. That is, nobody had seen him in some time. Then one morning Sam was missing, nobody, not even the boy, knew when nor where, until that night when some Negroes hunting in the creek bottom saw the sudden burst of flame and approached. It was Jobaker's hut, but before they got anywhere near it, someone shot at them from the shadows beyond it. It was Sam who fired, but nobody ever found Jobaker's grave.

The next morning, sitting at breakfast with his cousin, the boy saw Sam pass the dining-room window and he remembered then that never in his life before had he seen Sam nearer the house than the blacksmith-

3. Public records or archives.

shop. He stopped eating even; he sat there and he and his cousin both heard the voices from beyond the pantry door, then the door opened and Sam entered, carrying his hat in his hand but without knocking as anyone else on the place except a house servant would have done, entered just far enough for the door to close behind him and stood looking at neither of them—the Indian face above the nigger clothes, looking at something over their heads or at something not even in the room.

"I want to go," he said. "I want to go to the Big Bottom to live."

"To live?" the boy's cousin said.

"At Major de Spain's and your camp, where you go to hunt," Sam said. "I could take care of it for you all while you aint there. I will build me a little house in the woods, if you rather I didn't stay in the big one."

"What about Isaac here?" his cousin said. "How will you get away from him? Are you going to take him with you?" But still Sam looked at neither of them, standing just inside the room with that face which showed nothing, which showed that he was an old man only when it smiled.

"I want to go," he said. "Let me go."

"Yes," the cousin said quietly. "Of course. I'll fix it with Major de Spain. You want to go soon?"

"I'm going now," Sam said. He went out. And that was all. The boy was nine then; it seemed perfectly natural that nobody, not even his cousin McCaslin, should argue with Sam. Also, since he was nine now, he could understand that Sam could leave him and their days and nights in the woods together without any wrench. He believed that he and Sam both knew that this was not only temporary but that the exigencies of his maturing, of that for which Sam had been training him all his life some day to dedicate himself, required it. They had settled that one night last summer while they listened to the hounds bringing a fox back up the creek valley; now the boy discerned in that very talk under the high, fierce August stars a presage, a warning, of this moment to-day. "I done taught you all there is of this settled country," Sam said. "You can hunt it good as I can now. You are ready for the Big Bottom now, for bear and deer. Hunter's meat," he said. "Next year you will be ten. You will write your age in two numbers and you will be ready to become a man. Your pa" (Sam always referred to the boy's cousin as his father, establishing even before the boy's orphanhood did that relation between them not of the ward to his guardian and kinsman and chief and head of his blood, but of the child to the man who sired his flesh and his thinking too.) "promised you can go with us then." So the boy could understand Sam's going. But he couldn't understand why now, in March, six months before the moon for hunting.

"If Jobaker's dead like they say," he said, "and Sam hasn't got any-body but us at all kin to him, why does he want to go to the Big Bottom now, when it will be six months before we get there?"

"Maybe that's what he wants," McCaslin said. "Maybe he wants to get away from you a little while."

But that was all right. McCaslin and other grown people often said things like that and he paid no attention to them, just as he paid no attention to Sam saying he wanted to go to the Big Bottom to live. After

all, he would have to live there for six months, because there would
be no use in going at all if he was going to turn right around and come
back. And, as Sam himself had told him, he already knew all about
hunting in this settled country that Sam or anybody else could teach
him. So it would be all right. Summer, then the bright days after the
first frost, then the cold and himself on the wagon with McCaslin this
time and the moment would come and he would draw the blood, the
big blood which would make him a man, a hunter, and Sam would
come back home with them and he too would have outgrown the
child's pursuit of rabbits and 'possums. Then he too would make one
before the winter fire, talking of the old hunts and the hunts to come as
hunters talked.

So Sam departed. He owned so little that he could carry it. He
walked. He would neither let McCaslin send him in the wagon, nor
take a mule to ride. No one saw him go even. He was just gone one
morning, the cabin which had never had very much in it, vacant and
empty, the shop in which there never had been very much done,
standing idle. Then November came at last, and now the boy made
one—himself and his cousin McCaslin and Tennie's Jim, and Major de
Spain and General Compson and Walter Ewell and Boon and old Uncle
Ash to do the cooking, waiting for them in Jefferson with the other
wagon, and the surrey in which he and McCaslin and General Compson
and Major de Spain would ride.

Sam was waiting at the camp to meet them. If he was glad to see
them, he did not show it. And if, when they broke camp two weeks
later to return home, he was sorry to see them go, he did not show that
either. Because he did not come back with them. It was only the boy
who returned, returning solitary and alone to the settled familiar land,
to follow for eleven months the childish business of rabbits and such
while he waited to go back, having brought with him, even from his
brief first sojourn, an unforgettable sense of the big woods—not a
quality dangerous or particularly inimical, but profound, sentient, gigantic and brooding, amid which he had been permitted to go to and
fro at will, unscathed, why he knew not, but dwarfed and, until he had
drawn honorably blood worthy of being drawn, alien.

Then November, and they would come back. Each morning Sam
would take the boy out to the stand allotted him. It would be one of
the poorer stands of course, since he was only ten and eleven and twelve
and he had never even seen a deer running yet. But they would stand
there, Sam a little behind him and without a gun himself, as he had
been standing when the boy shot the running rabbit when he was
eight years old. They would stand there in the November dawns, and
after a while they would hear the dogs. Sometimes the chase would
sweep up and past quite close, belling and invisible; once they heard
the two heavy reports of Boon Hogganbeck's old gun with which he
had never killed anything larger than a squirrel and that sitting, and
twice they heard the flat unreverberant clap of Walter Ewell's rifle,
following which you did not even wait to hear his horn.

"I'll never get a shot," the boy said. "I'll never kill one."

"Yes, you will," Sam said. "You wait. You'll be a hunter. You'll be a
man."

But Sam wouldn't come out. They would leave him there. He would come as far as the road where the surrey waited, to take the riding horses back, and that was all. The men would ride the horses and Uncle Ash and Tennie's Jim and the boy would follow in the wagon with Sam, with the camp equipment and the trophies, the meat, the heads, the antlers, the good ones, the wagon winding on among the tremendous gums and cypresses and oaks where no axe save that of the hunter had ever sounded between the impenetrable walls of cane and brier—the two changing yet constant walls just beyond which the wilderness whose mark he had brought away forever on his spirit even from that first two weeks seemed to lean, stooping a little, watching them and listening, not quite inimical because they were too small, even those such as Walter and Major de Spain and old General Compson who had killed many deer and bear, their sojourn too brief and too harmless to excite to that, but just brooding, secret, tremendous, almost inattentive.

Then they would emerge, they would be out of it, the line as sharp as the demarcation of a doored wall. Suddenly skeleton cotton- and corn-fields would flow away on either hand, gaunt and motionless beneath the gray rain; there would be a house, barns, fences, where the hand of man had clawed for an instant, holding, the wall of the wilderness behind them now, tremendous and still and seemingly impenetrable in the gray and fading light, the very tiny orifice through which they had emerged apparently swallowed up. The surrey would be waiting, his cousin McCaslin and Major de Spain and General Compson and Walter and Boon dismounted beside it. Then Sam would get down from the wagon and mount one of the horses and, with the others on a rope behind him, he would turn back. The boy would watch him for a while against that tall and secret wall, growing smaller and smaller against it, never looking back. Then he would enter it, returning to what the boy believed, and thought that his cousin McCaslin believed, was his loneliness and solitude.

2

So the instant came. He pulled trigger and Sam Fathers marked his face with the hot blood which he had spilled and he ceased to be a child and became a hunter and a man. It was the last day. They broke camp that afternoon and went out, his cousin and Major de Spain and General Compson and Boon on the horses. Walter Ewell and the Negroes in the wagon with him and Sam and his hide and antlers. There could have been (and were) other trophies in the wagon. But for him they did not exist, just as for all practical purposes he and Sam Fathers were still alone together as they had been that morning. The wagon wound and jolted between the slow and shifting yet constant walls from beyond and above which the wilderness watched them pass, less than inimical now and never to be inimical again since the buck still and forever leaped, the shaking gun-barrels coming constantly and forever steady at last, crashing, and still out of his instant of immortality the buck sprang, forever immortal;—the wagon jolting and bouncing on, the moment of the buck, the shot, Sam Fathers and himself and the blood with which Sam had marked him forever one with the wilderness which had accepted him since Sam said that he had done all right, when suddenly Sam reined back and stopped the wagon and they all heard the unmistakable and unforgettable sound of a deer breaking cover.

Then Boon shouted from beyond the bend of the trail and while they sat motionless in the halted wagon. Walter and the boy already reaching for their guns, Boon came galloping back, flogging his mule with his hat, his face wild and amazed as he shouted down at them. Then the other riders came around the bend, also spurring.

"Get the dogs!" Boon cried. "Get the dogs! If he had a nub on his head, he had fourteen points! Laying right there by the road in that pawpaw[4] thicket! If I'd a knowed he was there, I could have cut his throat with my pocket knife!"

"Maybe that's why he run," Walter said. "He saw you never had your gun." He was already out of the wagon with his rifle. Then the boy was out too with his gun, and the other riders came up and Boon got off his mule somehow and was scrabbling and clawing among the duffel[5] in the wagon, still shouting, "Get the dogs! Get the dogs!" And it seemed to the boy too that it would take them forever to decide what to do—the old men in whom the blood ran cold and slow, in whom during the intervening years between them and himself the blood had become a different and colder substance from that which ran in him and even in Boon and Walter.

"What about it, Sam?" Major de Spain said. "Could the dogs bring him back?"

"We wont need the dogs," Same said. "If he dont hear the dogs behind him, he will circle back in here about sundown to bed."

"All right," Major de Spain said. "You boys take the horses. We'll go on out to the road in the wagon and wait there." He and General Compson and McCaslin got into the wagon and Boon and Walter and Sam and the boy mounted the horses and turned back and out of the trail. Sam led them for an hour through the gray and unmarked afternoon whose light was little different from what it had been at dawn and which would become darkness without any graduation between. Then Sam stopped them.

"This is far enough," he said. "He'll be coming upwind, and he dont want to smell the mules." They tied the mounts in a thicket. Sam led them on foot now, unpathed through the markless afternoon, the boy pressing close behind him, the two others, or so it seemed to the boy, on his heels. But they were not. Twice Sam turned his head slightly and spoke back to him across his shoulder, still walking: "You got time. We'll get there fore he does."

So he tried to go slower. He tried deliberately to decelerate the dizzy rushing of time in which the buck which he had not even seen was moving, which it seemed to him must be carrying the buck farther and farther and more and more irretrievably away from them even though there were no dogs behind him now to make him run, even though, according to Sam, he must have completed his circle now and was heading back toward them. They went on; it could have been another hour or twice that or less than half, the boy could not have said. Then they were on a ridge. He had never been in here before and he

---

4. Papaw, tree of custard apple family.   5. Campers' personal gear.

could not see that it was a ridge. He just knew that the earth had risen slightly because the underbrush had thinned a little, the ground sloping invisibly away toward a dense wall of cane. Sam stopped. "This is it," he said. He spoke to Walter and Boon: "Follow this ridge and you will come to two crossings. You will see the tracks. If he crosses, it will be at one of these three."

Walter looked about for a moment. "I know it," he said. "I've even seen your deer. I was in here last Monday. He aint nothing but a yearling."

"A yearling?" Boon said. He was panting from the walking. His face still looked a little wild. "If the one I saw was any yearling, I'm still in kindergarden."

"Then I must have seen a rabbit," Walter said. "I always heard you quit school altogether two years before the first grade."

Boon glared at Walter. "If you dont want to shoot him, get out of the way," he said. "Set down somewhere. By God, I—"

"Aint nobody going to shoot him standing here," Sam said quietly.

"Sam's right," Walter said. He moved, slanting the worn, silver-colored barrel of his rifle downward to walk with it again. "A little more moving and a little more quiet too. Five miles is still Hoggan-beck range, even if he wasn't downwind." They went on. The boy could still hear Boon talking, though presently that ceased too. Then once more he and Sam stood motionless together against a tremendous pin oak in a little thicket, and again there was nothing. There was only the soaring and somber solitude in the dim light, there was the thin murmur of the faint cold rain which had not ceased all day. Then, as if it had waited for them to find their positions and become still, the wilderness breathed again. It seemed to lean inward above them, above himself and Sam and Walter and Boon in their separate lurking-places, tremendous, attentive, impartial and omniscient, the buck moving in it somewhere, not running yet since he had not been pursued, not frightened yet and never fearsome but just alert also as they were alert, perhaps already circling back, perhaps quite near, perhaps conscious also of the eye of the ancient immortal Umpire. Because he was just twelve then, and that morning something had happened to him: in less than a second he had ceased forever to be the child he was yesterday. Or perhaps that made no difference, perhaps even a city-bred man, let alone a child, could not have understood it; perhaps only a country-bred one could comprehend loving the life he spills. He began to shake again.

"I'm glad it's started now," he whispered. He did not move to speak; only his lips shaped the expiring words: "Then it will be gone when I raise the gun—"

Nor did Sam. "Hush," he said.

"Is he that near?" the boy whispered. "Do you think—"

"Hush," Sam said. So he hushed. But he could not stop the shaking. He did not try, because he knew it would go away when he needed the steadiness—had not Sam Fathers already consecrated and absolved him from weakness and regret too?—not from love and pity for all which lived and ran and then ceased to live in a second in the very midst of splendor and speed, but from weakness and regret. So they stood motionless, breathing deep and quiet and steady. If there had been any sun, it would be near to setting now; there was a condensing, a densifying, of what he had thought was the gray and unchanging light until he realized suddenly that it was his own breathing, his heart, his blood—something, all things, and that Sam Fathers had marked him indeed, not as a mere hunter, but with something Sam had had in his turn of his vanished and forgotten people. He stopped breathing then; there was only his heart, his blood, and in the following silence the wilderness ceased to breathe also, leaning, stooping overhead with its breath held, tremendous and impartial and waiting. Then the shaking stopped too, as he had known it would, and he drew back the two heavy hammers of the gun.

Then it had passed. It was over. The solitude did not breathe again yet; it had merely stopped watching him and was looking somewhere else, even turning its back on him, looking on away up the ridge at another point, and the boy knew as well as if he had seen him that the buck had come to the edge of the cane and had either seen or scented them and faded back into it. But the solitude did not breathe again. It should have suspired again then but it did not. It was still facing, watching, what it had been watching and it was not here, not where he and Sam stood; rigid, not breathing himself, he thought, cried *No! No!*, knowing already that it was too late, thinking with the old despair of two and three years ago: *I'll never get a shot.* Then he heard it—the flat single clap of Walter Ewell's rifle which never missed. Then the mellow sound of the horn came down the ridge and something went out of him and he knew then he had never expected to get the shot at all.

"I reckon that's it," he said. "Walter got him." He had raised the gun slightly without knowing it. He lowered it again and had lowered one of the hammers and was already moving out of the thicket when Sam spoke.

"Wait."

"Wait?" the boy cried. And he would remember that—how he turned upon Sam in the truculence of a boy's grief over the missed opportunity, the missed luck. "What for? Dont you hear that horn?"

And he would remember how Sam was standing. Sam had not moved. He was not tall, squat rather and broad, and the boy had been growing fast for the past year or so and there was not much difference between them in height, yet Sam was looking over the boy's head and up the ridge toward the sound of the horn and the boy knew that Sam did not even see him; that Sam knew he was still there beside him but he did not see the boy. Then the boy saw the buck. It was coming down the ridge, as if it were walking out of the very sound of the horn which related its death. It was not running, it was walking, tremendous, unhurried, slanting and tilting its head to pass the antlers through the undergrowth, and the boy standing with Sam beside him now instead of behind him as Sam always stood, and the gun still partly aimed and one of the hammers still cocked.

Then it saw them. And still it did not begin to run. It just stopped for an instant, taller than any man, looking at them; then its muscles suppled, gathered. It did not even alter its course, not fleeing, not

even running, just moving with that winged and effortless ease with
which deer move, passing within twenty feet of them, its head high
and the eye not proud and not haughty but just full and wild and unafraid, and Sam standing beside the boy now, his right arm raised at
full length, palm-outward, speaking in that tongue which the boy had
learned from listening to him and Jobaker in the blacksmith shop, while
up the ridge Walter Ewell's horn was still blowing them in to a dead
buck.

"Oleh, Chief," Sam said. "Grandfather."

When they reached Walter, he was standing with his back toward
them, quite still, bemused almost, looking down at his feet. He didn't
look up at all.

"Come here, Sam," he said quietly. When they reached him he
still did not look up, standing above a little spike buck which had still
been a fawn last spring. "He was so little I pretty near let him go,"
Walter said. "But just look at the track he was making. It's pretty near
big as a cow's. If there were any more tracks here beside the ones he
is laying in, I would swear there was another buck here that I never
even saw."

3

It was dark when they reached the road where the surrey waited. It
was turning cold, the rain had stopped, and the sky was beginning to
blow clear. His cousin and Major de Spain and General Compson had a
fire going. "Did you get him?" Major de Spain said.

"Got a good-sized swamp-rabbit with spike horns," Walter said.
He slid the little buck down from his mule. The boy's cousin McCaslin
looked at it.

"Nobody saw the big one?" he said.

"I dont even believe Boon saw it," Walter said. "He probably jumped
somebody's stray cow in that thicket." Boon started cursing, swearing
at Walter and at Sam for not getting the dogs in the first place and at
the buck and all.

"Never mind," Major de Spain said. "He'll be here for us next fall.
Let's get started home."

It was after midnight when they let Walter out at his gate two miles
from Jefferson and later still when they took General Compson to his
house and then returned to Major de Spain's, where he and McCaslin
would spend the rest of the night, since it was still seventeen miles
home. It was cold, the sky was clear now; there would be a heavy frost
by sunup and the ground was already frozen beneath the horses' feet
and the wheels and beneath their own feet as they crossed Major de
Spain's yard and entered the house, the warm dark house, feeling their
way up the dark stairs until Major de Spain found a candle and lit it,
and into the strange room and the big deep bed, the still cold sheets
until they began to warm to their bodies and at last the shaking stopped
and suddenly he was telling McCaslin about it while McCaslin listened,
quietly until he had finished. "You dont believe it," the boy said, "I
know you dont—"

"Why not?" McCaslin said. "Think of all that has happened here,
on this earth. All the blood hot and strong for living, pleasuring, that

has soaked back into it. For grieving and suffering too, of course, but still getting something out of it for all that, getting a lot out of it, because after all you dont have to continue to bear what you believe is suffering; you can always choose to stop that, put an end to that. And even suffering and grieving is better than nothing; there is only one thing worse than not being alive, and that's shame. But you cant be alive forever, and you always wear out life long before you have exhausted the possibilities of living. And all that must be somewhere; all that could not have been invented and created just to be thrown away. And the earth is shallow; there is not a great deal of it before you come to the rock. And the earth dont want to just keep things, hoard them; it wants to use them again. Look at the seed, the acorns, at what happens even to carrion when you try to bury it: it refuses too, seethes and struggles too until it reaches light and air again, hunting the sun still. And they—" the boy saw his hand in silhouette for a moment against the window beyond which, accustomed to the darkness now, he could see sky where the scoured and icy stars glittered "—they dont want it, need it. Besides, what would it want, itself, knocking around out there, when it never had enough time about the earth as it was, when there is plenty of room about the earth, plenty of places still unchanged from what they were when the blood used and pleasured in them while it was still blood?"

"But we want them," the boy said. "We want them too. There is plenty of room for us and them too."

"That's right," McCaslin said. "Suppose they dont have substance, cant cast a shadow—"

"But I saw it!" the boy cried. "I saw him!"

"Steady," McCaslin said. For an instant his hand touched the boy's flank beneath the covers. "Steady. I know you did. So did I. Sam took me in there once after I killed my first deer."

1942

7   A MODE: FANTASY

There is a looser and wider-ranging system of literary classification than genres and kinds, one that looks at works (or even parts of works) not as organisms but in terms of **modes,** ways of perceiving or presenting experience. If we call the conventional literary genres poetry, drama, fiction, we call the conventional modes the **poetic** (or **lyric**), the **dramatic,** and the **narrative.** A work that is classified in the subgenre short story, within the genre fiction, may have passages in the poetic mode—passages marked by heightened and highly figurative language, intensification of rhythms and emotions, often focusing on the ideal or spiritual. The final paragraphs of The Artificial Nigger, Gurov standing by the sea or contemplating the nails in the gray fence around Anna's home in *Lady with the Dog*, the boy wandering through the Dublin streets full of frustration and shame in *Araby* are examples of poetic passages. Some portion of a story, even a whole story, may be in the dramatic mode, like a play with unmediated or unnarrated dialogue or action. In *The Most Dangerous Game*, General Zaroff and Rainsford's conversation at their first dinner seems like a scene from a play; it could be transferred to the stage almost without change. *The Lottery*, made up of dialogue and seemingly objective descriptions of action, comes about as close as a short story can to being fully dramatic, short of being reduced to pure dialogue.

Befitting the looseness of the term, modes do not descend in an orderly way through subheadings, as do genres through subgenres and kinds. **Fantasy**, for example, a literary mode involving the consciously unreal—places, societies, or beings that never existed, do not exist, or do not yet exist, or with qualities that are beyond or counter to the ordinary or commonsensical—can be found in fiction, poetry, or drama.

Fantastic fiction sometimes signals its fictionality immediately or very soon: "Once upon a time . . ."; "The story begins about a million kilometers sunward of Mars, . . ." At other times, it goes to some lengths to establish its "reality": many eighteenth-century novels about medieval castles and ghosts (Gothic novels) pretend to be editions of some monk's dusty manuscript, for example. Still other stories, such as *Dotson Gerber* and *A Very Old Man with Enormous Wings*, simply treat the incredible—a buried corpse growing, a man with wings—as perfectly natural, if not perfectly common.

Much fantasy has as its aim to stretch or expand our consciousness, our perception and conception of reality, sometimes even questioning our beliefs about the nature of reality. Some stories seek to open us up to possibilities by disorienting us, alternating or mixing the realistic, the fictional, the fantastic in dizzying patterns. *The Garden of Forking Paths* begins realistically, with documentation and an essay-like manner that makes it seem not like a story at all. Then the confession begins, and we recognize that we are in the midst of a common fictional kind, the spy story or thriller. The shift does not bother us too much —it's like the dusty-manuscript device, and the fictional kind we've entered on is so familiar that we're reasonably comfortable. Suddenly the spy story shifts once again, toward fantasy and, just as we're getting used to fantasy, to mysterious Chinese gardens and riddles. The fantasy is used to question whether it is the fantastic that is incredible, or whether our assumption that time is uniform and absolute is merely arbitrary and too restrictive—itself a fantasy. Given eternity, we must admit that everything that might possibly happen *will* happen. So when we make a choice, the choice we did not make but might have made will yet be made; its potential must be realized; it must exist somewhere in the vastness of eternity in a world of events parallel to our own. No wonder, then, when we return to the world of the spy story, which, though fictional, operates within the same notions of uniform, absolute time, it seems credible that the writer of the confession is not concerned with whether he lives or dies, realities that are now "unreal, insignificant."

I don't think what I have told you about *Forking Paths* will destroy your interest in the story—indeed, everyone can probably do with a little help in reading this fascinating story for the first time. Its questioning of our assumptions about reality is not too different from what's going on in modern thought. It is precisely because history, psychology, science, philosophy—almost all the intellectual disciplines—have in recent years most urgently called into question our long-standing assumptions about reality that fantasy seems so congenial a mode for us today.

From the middle of the nineteenth century to the middle of ours, the rise of the novel and the rise of realism were assumed to be the same thing, and we looked back on literary history as progress toward the literal, the factual, the ordinary (just as some art historians saw the Renaissance and what followed as demonstrating progress in man's ability to represent things "as they really are"). Long narratives that dwelled on the extraordinary, unusual, bizarre, or supernatural were called **romances,** as opposed to the more realistic **novel.**

The early modern short story leaned more heavily toward romance. Poe was perhaps our most widely respected writer, and you can see that *The Cask of Amontillado* is not exactly a story of everyday life. Late in the century, with de Maupassant in France and Chekhov in Russia (see *The Lady with the Dog*), the realistic short story seemed to have caught up with the novel.

But already in the nineteenth century "common sense" notions of realism were beginning to give way before the discovery of worlds beyond our unaided senses, observable through microscope and telescope. Darwin, with his notion that species themselves were not fixed but moving and changing in time, made the solid earth under our feet a little less solid. With the rise of psychology, which too was meant to capture more realms for consciousness and science, we became more and more aware that there were realities only dreamed of in our philosophies. When physics, the most advanced and scientific of the sciences, began to tell us that all our knowledge is, if not subjective, at least limited to what the human brain and its instruments can perceive, and is altered by our perception, we were not so sure anymore that reality was what existed "out there" or that we were contained between our hat and boots.

Perhaps the unsettling "retrogression" of science toward subjectivity has spurred on our most recent spate of the unreal or superreal; perhaps it was the nightmare of a human reality that could create a barbaric holocaust at Dachau or a scientific one at Hiroshima that made *rationality* and *science* and *realism* less automatically terms of positive value. Even the positive side of scientific achievement—space travel, walking on the moon, television and laser beams—destroyed our sense of a real and stable world and opened up other possibilities.

A generation or two ago, *Rosemary's Baby* or *The Exorcist* could have had only one ending—a rational explanation for the appearance of the supernatural. Few viewers or readers then would take seriously a work that was not embedded in a world of more or less everyday reality. The supernatural or fantastic in such a world had to be explained away as a dream, hallucination, or other psychological aberration, or as a hoax of some sort, set up to take in the foolish or credulous. Similarly, we would have had to explain away stories like *The Lottery* and García Márquez's *Very Old Man* by treating them as allegories. Now we can accept them as symbolic, as experiences that cannot be explained away or reduced to everyday terms, but exist on their own terms, explaining in fantasy more than we might in our discursive prose, our scientific formulas, graphs, and charts.

Not all fantasies seek to undermine conventional assumptions about reality or even to set up alternative, symbolic ways of comprehending reality. *Dotson Gerber* seems to use a fantastic event as a comic catalyst to clarify certain destructive tendencies in contemporary society, though it may imply that our actuality is itself a kind of fantasy land. The fantasy land of science fiction is usually the future—not so much never-never as never-yet land—which does not necessarily undermine or question conventional reality but projects potential consequences of present knowledge. There are those who maintain that for this very reason it is a mistake to call sci fi fantasy. Fantasy, they say, involves the incredible or impossible. Science fiction, while it may take place in the future or outside earthly reality, is neither incredible nor impossible but wholly logical, often based on real scientific principles. Others say that's exactly why it's fantasy: historical reality is never predictable, and certainly not by that fantasy called logic.

Science-fiction people are passionate, dedicated, and argumentative, so if it's risky to suggest that science fiction is in the mode of fantasy, it's even riskier to try to define science fiction as a kind, even though everyone will grant that generic definitions are at best only loose approximations. Approximately, science fiction is a narrative about events outside the bounds of Earth history in which science or advanced technology is often centrally important. The term *Earth history* allows for both space travel (to imaginary life on real or imaginary planets) in the present and time travel to prehistory. Science and technology in the stories can be important as a means of transhistorical travel, or in the operation of that imaginary world, or simply, as in *Hide and Seek*, in their preponderant role in the working out of the details of the plot. I'm sure this loose baggy monster of a definition leaves something out or includes too much, but at least it separates *Hide and Seek* from the other three fantasy stories here, and from *The Lottery* and *The Rocking-Horse Winner*, and, in "Stories for Further Reading," from *The Kugelmass Episode* and *A Hunger Artist*. (What would you say about *The Ones Who Walk Away from Omelas?*)

ARTHUR C. CLARKE

Hide and Seek

We were walking back through the woods when Kingman saw the gray squirrel. Our bag was a small but varied one—three grouse, four rabbits (one, I am sorry to say, an infant in arms) and a couple of pigeons. And contrary to certain dark forecasts, both the dogs were still alive.

The squirrel saw us at the same moment. It knew that it was marked for immediate execution as a result of the damage it had done to the trees on the estate, and perhaps it had lost close relatives to Kingman's gun. In three leaps it had reached the base of the nearest tree, and vanished behind it in a flicker of gray. We saw its face once more, appearing for a moment round the edge of its shield a dozen feet from the ground; but though we waited, with guns leveled hopefully at various branches, we never saw it again.

Kingman was very thoughtful as we walked back across the lawn to the magnificent old house. He said nothing as we handed our victims to the cook—who received them without much enthusiasm—and only emerged from his reverie when we were sitting in the smoking room and he remembered his duties as a host.

"That tree-rat," he said suddenly (he always called them "tree-rats," on the grounds that people were too sentimental to shoot the dear little squirrels), "it reminded me of a very peculiar experience that happened shortly before I retired. Very shortly indeed, in fact."

"I thought it would," said Carson dryly. I gave him a glare: he'd been in the Navy and had heard Kingman's stories before, but they were still new to me.

"Of course," Kingman remarked, slightly nettled, "if you'd rather I didn't . . ."

"Do go on," I said hastily. "You've made me curious. What connection there can possibly be between a gray squirrel and the Second Jovian War I can't imagine."

Kingman seemed mollified.

"I think I'd better change some names," he said thoughtfully, "but I won't alter the places. The story begins about a million kilometers sunward of Mars. . . ."

K.15 was a military intelligence operative. It gave him considerable pain when unimaginative people called him a spy, but at the moment he had much more substantial grounds for complaint. For some days now a fast enemy cruiser had been coming up astern, and though it was flattering to have the undivided attention of such a fine ship and so many highly trained men, it was an honor that K.15 would willingly have forgone.

What made the situation doubly annoying was the fact that his friends would be meeting him off Mars in about twelve hours, aboard a ship quite capable of dealing with a mere cruiser—from which you will gather that K.15 was a person of some importance. Unfortunately, the most optimistic calculation showed that the pursuers would be within accurate gun range in six hours. In some six hours five minutes, therefore, K.15 was likely to occupy an extensive and still expanding volume of space.

There might just be time for him to land on Mars, but that would be one of the worst things he could do. It would certainly annoy the aggressively neutral Martians, and the political complications would be frightful. Moreover, if his friends *had* to come down to the planet to rescue him, it would cost them more than ten kilometers a second in fuel—most of their operational reserve.

He had only one advantage, and that a very dubious one. The commander of the cruiser might guess that he was heading for a rendezvous, but he would not know how close it was or how large was the ship that was coming to meet him. If he could keep alive for only twelve hours, he would be safe. The "if" was a somewhat considerable one.

K.15 looked moodily at his charts, wondering if it was worthwhile to burn the rest of his fuel in a final dash. But a dash to where? He would be completely helpless then, and the pursuing ship might still have enough in her tanks to catch him as he flashed outward into the empty darkness, beyond all hope of rescue—passing his friends as they came sunward at a relative speed so great that they could do nothing to save him.

With some people, the shorter the expectation of life, the more sluggish are the mental processes. They seem hypnotized by the approach of death, so resigned to their fate that they do nothing to avoid it. K.15, on the other hand, found that his mind worked better in such a desperate emergency. It began to work now as it had seldom done before.

Commander Smith—the name will do as well as any other—of the cruiser *Doradus* was not unduly surprised when K.15 began to decelerate. He had half expected the spy to land on Mars, on the principle that internment was better than annihilation, but when the plotting room brought the news that the little scout ship was heading for Phobos, he felt completely baffled. The inner moon was nothing but a jumble of rock some twenty kilometers across, and not even the economical Martians had ever found any use for it. K.15 must be pretty desperate if he thought it was going to be of any greater value to him.

The tiny scout had almost come to rest when the radar operator lost it against the mass of Phobos. During the braking maneuver, K.15 had squandered most of his lead and the *Doradus* was now only minutes away—though she was now beginning to decelerate lest she overrun him. The cruiser was scarcely three thousand kilometers from Phobos when she came to a complete halt: of K.15's ship, there was still no sign. It should be easily visible in the telescopes, but it was probably on the far side of the little moon.

It reappeared only a few minutes later, traveling under full thrust on a course directly away from the sun. It was accelerating at almost five gravities—and it had broken its radio silence. An automatic recorder was broadcasting over and over again this interesting message:

"I have landed on Phobos and am being attacked by a Z-class cruiser. Think I can hold out until you come, but hurry."

The message wasn't even in code, and it left Commander Smith a sorely puzzled man. The assumption that K.15 was still aboard the ship and that the whole thing was a ruse was just a little too naïve. But it might be a double bluff: the message had obviously been left in plain language so that he would receive it and be duly confused. He could afford neither the time nor the fuel to chase the scout if K.15

really had landed. It was clear that reinforcements were on the way, and the sooner he left the vicinity the better. The phrase "Think I can hold out until you come" might be a piece of sheer impertinence, or it might mean that help was very near indeed.

Then K.15's ship stopped blasting. It had obviously exhausted its fuel, and was doing a little better than six kilometers a second away from the sun. K.15 *must* have landed, for his ship was now speeding helplessly out of the solar system. Commander Smith didn't like the message it was broadcasting, and guessed that it was running into the track of an approaching warship at some indefinite distance, but there was nothing to be done about that. The *Doradus* began to move toward Phobos, anxious to waste no time.

On the face of it, Commander Smith seemed the master of the situation. His ship was armed with a dozen heavy guided missiles and two turrets of electromagnetic guns. Against him was one man in a space suit, trapped on a moon only twenty kilometers across. It was not until Commander Smith had his first good look at Phobos, from a distance of less than a hundred kilometers, that he began to realize that, after all, K.15 might have a few cards up his sleeve.

To say that Phobos has a diameter of twenty kilometers, as the astronomy books invariably do, is highly misleading. The word "diameter" implies a degree of symmetry which Phobos most certainly lacks. Like those other lumps of cosmic slag, the asteroids, it is a shapeless mass of rock floating in space with, of course, no hint of an atmosphere and not much more gravity. It turns on its axis once every seven hours thirty-nine minutes, thus keeping the same face always to Mars—which is so close that appreciably less than half the planet is visible, the poles being below the curve of the horizon. Beyond this, there is very little more to be said about Phobos.

K.15 had no time to enjoy the beauty of the crescent world filling the sky above him. He had thrown all the equipment he could carry out of the air lock, set the controls, and jumped. As the little ship went flaming out toward the stars he watched it go with feelings he did not care to analyze. He had burned his boats with a vengeance, and he could only hope that the oncoming battleship would intercept the radio message as the empty vessel went racing by into nothingness. There was also a faint possibility that the enemy cruiser might go in pursuit, but that was rather too much to hope for.

He turned to examine his new home. The only light was the ocher radiance of Mars, since the sun was below the horizon, but that was quite sufficient for his purpose and he could see very well. He stood in the center of an irregular plain about two kilometers across, surrounded by low hills over which he could leap rather easily if he wished. There was a story he remembered reading long ago about a man who had accidentally jumped off Phobos: that wasn't quite possible—though it was on Deimos—because the escape velocity was still about ten meters a second. But unless he was careful, he might easily find himself at such a height that it would take hours to fall back to the surface—and that would be fatal. For K.15's plan was a simple one: he must remain as close to the surface of Phobos as possible—

and diametrically opposite the cruiser. The *Doradus* could then fire
all her armament against the twenty kilometers of rock, and he
wouldn't even feel the concussion. There were only two serious dangers, and one of these did not worry him greatly.

To the layman, knowing nothing of the finer details of astro-
nautics, the plan would have seemed quite suicidal. The *Doradus* was
armed with the latest in ultrascientific weapons: moreover, the twenty
kilometers which separated her from her prey represented less than a
second's flight at maximum speed. But Commander Smith knew better,
and was already feeling rather unhappy. He realized, only too well,
that of all the machines of transport man has ever invented, a cruiser
of space is far and away the least maneuverable. It was a simple fact
that K.15 could make half a dozen circuits of his little world while her
commander was persuading the *Doradus* to make even one.

There is no need to go into technical details, but those who are still
unconvinced might like to consider these elementary facts. A rocket-
driven spaceship can, obviously, only accelerate along its major axis
—that is, "forward." Any deviation from a straight course demands a
physical turning of the ship, so that the motors can blast in another
direction. Everyone knows that this is done by internal gyros or tan-
gential steering jets, but very few people know just how long this simple maneuver takes. The average cruiser, fully fueled, has a mass of
two or three thousand tons, which does not make for rapid footwork.
But things are even worse than this, for it isn't the mass, but the moment of inertia that matters here—and since a cruiser is a long, thin
object, its moment of inertia is slightly colossal. The sad fact remains
(though it is seldom mentioned by astronautical engineers) that it
takes a good ten minutes to rotate a spaceship through one hundred
and eighty degrees, with gyros of any reasonable size. Control jets
aren't much quicker, and in any case their use is restricted because the
rotation they produce is permanent and they are liable to leave the
ship spinning like a slow-motion pinwheel, to the annoyance of all
inside.

In the ordinary way, these disadvantages are not very grave. One
has millions of kilometers and hundreds of hours in which to deal with
such minor matters as a change in the ship's orientation. It is definitely
against the rules to move in ten-kilometer-radius circles, and the commander of the *Doradus* felt distinctly aggrieved. K.15 wasn't playing
fair.

At the same moment that resourceful individual was taking stock
of the situation, which might very well have been worse. He had
reached the hills in three jumps and felt less naked than he had out in
the open plain. The food and equipment he had taken from the ship
he had hidden where he hoped he could find it again, but since his
suit could keep him alive for over a day that was the least of his worries. The small packet that was the cause of all the trouble was still
with him, in one of those numerous hiding places a well-designed
space suit affords.

There was an exhilarating loneliness about his mountain eyrie, even
though he was not quite as lonely as he would have wished. Forever
fixed in his sky, Mars was waning almost visibly as Phobos swept above

the night side of the planet. He could just make out the lights of some of the Martian cities, gleaming pinpoints marking the junctions of the invisible canals. All else was stars and silence and a line of jagged peaks so close it seemed he could almost touch them. Of the *Doradus* there was still no sign. She was presumably carrying out a careful telescopic examination of the sunlighted side of Phobos.

Mars was a very useful clock: when it was half full the sun would rise and, very probably, so would the *Doradus*. But she might approach from some quite unexpected quarter: she might even—and this was the one real danger—she might even have landed a search party.

This was the first possiblity that had occurred to Commander Smith when he saw just what he was up against. Then he realized that the surface area of Phobos was over a thousand square kilometers and that he could not spare more than ten men from his crew to make a search of that jumbled wilderness. Also, K.15 would certainly be armed.

Considering the weapons which the *Doradus* carried, this last objection might seem singularly pointless. It was very far from being so. In the ordinary course of business, sidearms and other portable weapons are as much use to a space cruiser as are cutlasses and crossbows. The *Doradus* happened, quite by chance—and against regulations at that—to carry one automatic pistol and a hundred rounds of ammunition. Any search party would therefore consist of a group of unarmed men looking for a well-concealed and very desperate individual who could pick them off at his leisure. K.15 was breaking the rules again.

The terminator of Mars was now a perfectly straight line, and at almost the same moment the sun came up, not so much like thunder as like a salvo of atomic bombs. K.15 adjusted the filters of his visor and decided to move. It was safer to stay out of the sunlight, not only because here he was less likely to be detected in the shadow but also because his eyes would be much more sensitive there. He had only a pair of binoculars to help him, whereas the *Doradus* would carry an electronic telescope of twenty-centimeter aperture at least.

It would be best, K.15 decided, to locate the cruiser if he could. It might be a rash thing to do, but he would feel much happier when he knew exactly where she was and could watch her movements. He could then keep just below the horizon, and the glare of the rockets would give him ample warning of any impending move. Cautiously launching himself along an almost horizontal trajectory, he began the circumnavigation of his world.

The narrowing crescent of Mars sank below the horizon until only one vast horn reared itself enigmatically against the stars. K.15 began to feel worried: there was still no sign of the *Doradus*. But this was hardly surprising, for she was painted black as night and might be a good hundred kilometers away in space. He stopped, wondering if he had done the right thing after all. Then he noticed that something quite large was eclipsing the stars almost vertically overhead, and was moving swiftly even as he watched. His heart stopped for a moment: then he was himself again, analyzing the situation and trying to discover how he had made so disastrous a mistake.

It was some time before he realized that the black shadow slipping across the sky was not the cruiser at all, but something almost equally deadly. It was far smaller, and far nearer, than he had at first thought. The *Doradus* had sent her television-homing guided missiles to look for him.

This was the second danger he had feared, and there was nothing he could do about it except to remain as inconspicuous as possible. *Doradus* now had many eyes searching for him, but these auxiliaries had very severe limitations. They had been built to look for sunlit spaceships against a background of stars, not to search for a man hiding in a dark jungle of rock. The definition of their television systems was low, and they could only see in the forward direction.

There were rather more men on the chessboard now, and the game was a little deadlier, but his was still the advantage.

The torpedo vanished into the night sky. As it was traveling on a nearly straight source in this low-gravitational field, it would soon be leaving Phobos behind, and K.15 waited for what he knew must happen. A few minutes later, he saw a brief stabbing of rocket exhausts and guessed that the projectile was swinging slowly back on its course. At almost the same moment he saw another flare far away in the opposite quarter of the sky, and wondered just how many of these infernal machines were in action. From what he knew of Z-class cruisers—which was a good deal more than he should—there were four missile-control channels, and they were probably all in use.

He was suddenly struck by an idea so brilliant that he was quite sure it couldn't possibly work. The radio on his suit was a tunable one, covering an unusually wide band, and somewhere not far away the *Doradus* was pumping out power on everything from a thousand megacycles upward. He switched on the receiver and began to explore.

It came in quickly—the raucous whine of a pulse transmitter not far away. He was probably only picking up a subharmonic, but that was quite good enough. It D/F'ed[1] sharply, and for the first time K.15 allowed himself to make long-range plans about the future. The *Doradus* had betrayed herself: as long as she operated her missiles, he would know exactly where she was.

He moved cautiously forward toward the transmitter. To his surprise the signal faded, then increased sharply again. This puzzled him until he realized that he must be moving through a diffraction zone. Its width might have told him something useful if he had been a good-enough physicist, but he couldn't imagine what.

The *Doradus* was hanging about five kilometers above the surface, in full sunlight. Her "nonreflecting" paint was overdue for renewal, and K.15 could see her clearly. Since he was still in darkness, and the shadow line was moving away from him, he decided that he was as safe here as anywhere. He settled down comfortably so that he could just see the cruiser and waited, feeling fairly certain than none of the guided projectiles would come so near the ship. By now, he calculated, the commander of the *Doradus* must be getting pretty mad. He was perfectly correct.

---

1. Detected or found the direction (thus D/F, direction finder) of the transmitter.

After an hour, the cruiser began to heave herself round with all the grace of a bogged hippopotamus. K.15 guessed what was happening. Commander Smith was going to have to look at the antipodes, and was preparing for the perilous fifty-kilometer journey. He watched very carefully to see the orientation the ship was adopting, and when she came to rest again was relieved to see that she was almost broadside to him. Then, with a series of jerks that could not have been very enjoyable aboard, the cruiser began to move down to the horizon. K.15 followed her at a comfortable walking pace—if one could use the phrase—reflecting that this was a feat very few people had ever performed. He was particularly careful not to overtake her on one of his kilometer-long glides, and kept a close watch for any missiles that might be coming up astern.

It took the *Doradus* nearly an hour to cover the fifty kilometers. This, as K.15 amused himself by calculating, represented considerably less than a thousandth of her normal speed. Once she found herself going off into space at a tangent, and rather than waste time turning end over end again fired off a salvo of shells to reduce speed. But she made it at last, and K.15 settled down for another vigil, wedged between two rocks where he could just see the cruiser and he was quite sure she couldn't see him. It occurred to him that by this time Commander Smith might have grave doubts as to whether he really was on Phobos at all, and he felt like firing off a signal flare to reassure him. However, he resisted the temptation.

There would be little point in describing the events of the next ten hours, since they differed in no important detail from those that had gone before. The *Doradus* made three other moves, and K.15 stalked her with the care of a big-game hunter following the spoor of some elephantine beast. Once, when she would have led him out into full sunlight, he let her fall below the horizon until he could only just pick up her signals. But most of the time he kept her just visible, usually low down behind some convenient hill.

Once a torpedo exploded some kilometers away, and K.15 guessed that some exasperated operator had seen a shadow he didn't like— or else that a technician had forgotten to switch off a proximity fuse. Otherwise nothing happened to enliven the proceedings: in fact, the whole affair was becoming rather boring. He almost welcomed the sight of an occasional guided missile drifting inquisitively overhead, for he did not believe that they could see him if he remained motionless and in reasonable cover. If he could have stayed on the part of Phobos exactly opposite the cruiser he would have been safe even from these, he realized, since the ship would have no control there in the moon's radio-shadow.[2] But he could think of no reliable way in which he could be sure of staying in the safety zone if the cruiser moved again.

The end came very abruptly. There was a sudden blast of steering jets, and the cruiser's main drive burst forth in all its power and splendor. In seconds the *Doradus* was shrinking sunward, free at last,

---

2. Since radio waves move in a straight line, so long as K.15 keeps the moon Phobos between himself and the *Doradus,* the ship cannot successfully fire radioguided missiles at him.

thankful to leave, even in defeat, this miserable lump of rock that had so annoyingly balked her of her legitimate prey. K.15 knew what had happened, and a great sense of peace and relaxation swept over him. In the radar room of the cruiser, someone had seen an echo of disconcerting amplitude approaching with altogether excessive speed. K.15 now had only to switch on his suit beacon and to wait. He could even afford the luxury of a cigarette.

"Quite an interesting story," I said, "and I see now how it ties up with that squirrel. But it does raise one or two queries in my mind."

"Indeed?" said Rupert Kingman politely.

I always like to get to the bottom of things, and I knew that my host had played a part in the Jovian War about which he very seldom spoke. I decided to risk a long shot in the dark.

"May I ask how you happen to know so much about this unorthodox military engagement? It isn't possible, is it, that *you* were K.15?"

There was an odd sort of strangling noise from Carson. Then Kingman said, quite calmly: "No, I wasn't."

He got to his feet and went off toward the gun room.

"If you'll excuse me a moment, I'm going to have another shot at that tree-rat. Maybe I'll get him this time." Then he was gone.

Carson looked at me as if to say: "This is another house you'll never be invited to again." When our host was out of earshot he remarked in a coldly cynical voice:

"You've done it. What did you have to say that for?"

"Well, it seemed a safe guess. How else could he have known all that?"

"As a matter of fact, I believe he met K.15 after the War: they must have had an interesting conversation together. But I thought you knew that Rupert was retired from the service with only the rank of lieutenant commander. The Court of Inquiry could never see his point of view. After all, it just wasn't reasonable that the commander of the fastest ship in the Fleet couldn't catch a man in a space suit."

p. 1949

JORGE LUIS BORGES

The Garden of Forking Paths*

On page 22 of Liddell Hart's *History of World War I* you will read that an attack against the Serre-Montauban[1] line by thirteen British

*Translated by Donald A. Yates.

1. Liddell Hart's work is entitled *The Real War, 1914–1918* (1930) and *A History of the World War, 1914–1918* in the enlarged English-language edition (1934). The events of July 1916 do not appear on page 22 in the first and are unlikely to appear so early in any edition. A line between Serre and Montauban forms a defensive position about a hundred miles north-northeast of Paris, north of the Somme River. There is a dizzying mixture of factual references and fiction in this story, the most unlikely often being the factual.

divisions (supported by 1,400 artillery pieces), planned for the 24th of July, 1916, had to be postponed until the morning of the 29th. The torrential rains, Captain Liddell Hart comments, caused this delay, an insignificant one, to be sure.

The following statement, dictated, reread and signed by Dr. Yu Tsun, former professor of English at the *Hochschule* at Tsingtao,[2] throws an unsuspected light over the whole affair. The first two pages of the document are missing.

". . . and I hung up the receiver. Immediately afterwards, I recognized the voice that had answered in German. It was that of Captain Richard Madden. Madden's presence in Viktor Runeberg's apartment meant the end of our anxieties and—but this seemed, *or should have seemed*, very secondary to me—also the end of our lives. It meant that Runeberg had been arrested or murdered.[3] Before the sun set on that day, I would encounter the same fate. Madden was implacable. Or rather, he was obliged to be so. An Irishman at the service of England, a man accused of laxity and perhaps of treason, how could he fail to seize and be thankful for such a miraculous opportunity: the discovery, capture, maybe even the death of two agents of the German Reich? I went up to my room; absurdly I locked the door and threw myself on my back on the narrow iron cot. Through the window I saw the familiar roofs and the cloud-shaded six o'clock sun. It seemed incredible to me that that day without premonitions or symbols should be the one of my inexorable death. In spite of my dead father, in spite of having been a child in a symmetrical garden of Hai Feng,[4] was I—now—going to die? Then I reflected that everything happens to a man precisely, precisely *now*. Centuries of centuries and only in the present do things happen; countless men in the air, on the face of the earth and the sea, and all that really is happening is happening to me . . . . The almost intolerable recollection of Madden's horselike face banished these wanderings. In the midst of my hatred and terror (it means nothing to me now to speak of terror, now that I have mocked Richard Madden, now that my throat yearns for the noose) it occurred to me that that tumultuous and doubtless happy warrior did not suspect that I possessed the Secret. The name of the exact location of the new British artillery park on the River Ancre.[5] A bird streaked across the gray sky and blindly I translated it into an airplane and that airplane into many (against the French sky) annihilating the artillery station with vertical bombs. If only my mouth, before a bullet shattered it, could cry out that secret name so it could be heard in Germany . . . My human voice was very weak. How might I make it carry to the ear of the Chief? To the ear of that sick and hateful man who knew nothing of Runeberg and me save that we were in Staffordshire[6] and who was wait-

2. The high school in what was the capital of the German colonial enclave until the First World War.

3. An hypothesis both hateful and odd. The Prussian spy Hans Rabener, alias Viktor Runeberg, attacked with drawn automatic the bearer of the warrant for his arrest, Captain Richard Madden. The latter, in self-defense, inflicted the wound which brought about Runeberg's death.

(Borges's note.)

4. Chinese gardens usually aim for the appearance of nature, so a symmetrical garden would be unusual. Hai Feng seems fictional, as many names here are, but Hai-fang is Chinese for the Vietnamese city of Haiphong and is near the Yunnan province mentioned later.

5. River in northeastern France.

6. County in English midlands.

ing in vain for our report in his arid office in Berlin, endlessly examining newspapers . . . I said out loud: *I must flee.* I sat up noiselessly, in a useless perfection of silence, as if Madden were already lying in wait for me. Something—perhaps the mere vain ostentation of proving my resources were nil—made me look through my pockets. I found what I knew I would find. The American watch, the nickel chain and the square coin, the key ring with the incriminating useless keys to Runeberg's apartment, the notebook, a letter which I resolved to destroy immediately (and which I did not destroy), a crown, two shillings and a few pence,[7] the red-and-blue pencil, the handkerchief, the revolver with one bullet. Absurdly, I took it in my hand and weighed it in order to inspire courage within myself. Vaguely I thought that a pistol report can be heard at a great distance. In ten minutes my plan was perfected. The telephone book listed the name of the only person capable of transmitting the message; he lived in a suburb of Fenton, less than a half hour's train ride away.

I am a cowardly man. I say it now, now that I have carried to its end a plan whose perilous nature no one can deny. I know its execution was terrible. I didn't do it for Germany, no. I care nothing for a barbarous country which imposed upon me the abjection of being a spy. Besides, I know of a man from England—a modest man—who for me is no less great than Goethe. I talked with him for scarcely an hour, but during that hour he was Goethe . . . I did it because I sensed that the Chief somehow feared people of my race—for the innumerable ancestors who merge within me. I wanted to prove to him that a yellow man could save his armies. Besides, I had to flee from Captain Madden. His hands and his voice could call at my door at any moment. I dressed silently, bade farewell to myself in the mirror, went downstairs, scrutinized the peaceful street and went out. The station was not far from my home, but I judged it wise to take a cab. I argued that in this way I ran less risk of being recognized; the fact is that in the deserted street I felt myself visible and vulnerable, infinitely so. I remember that I told the cab driver to stop a short distance before the main entrance. I got out with voluntary, almost painful slowness; I was going to the village of Ashgrove but I bought a ticket for a more distant station. The train left within a very few minutes, at eight-fifty. I hurried; the next one would leave at nine-thirty. There was hardly a soul on the platform. I went through the coaches; I remember a few farmers, a woman dressed in mourning, a young boy who was reading with fervor the *Annals* of Tacitus,[8] a wounded and happy soldier. The coaches jerked forward at last. A man whom I recognized ran in vain to the end of the platform. It was Captain Richard Madden. Shattered, trembling, I shrank into the far corner of the seat, away from the dreaded window.

From this broken state I passed into an almost abject felicity. I told myself that the duel had already begun and that I had won the first encounter by frustrating, even if for forty minutes, even if by a

---

7. Though the two dollars' worth of coins would be worth quite a bit more at present, it still is not much for a middle-class person to be carrying.

8. The Annals of Cornelius Tacitus (55?–

117?) treat the history of Rome from the death of Augustus in 14 to the end of Nero's reign in 68, and the military events of the period.

stroke of fate, the attack of my adversary. I argued that this slightest of victories foreshadowed a total victory. I argued (no less fallaciously) that my cowardly felicity proved that I was a man capable of carrying out the adventure successfully. From this weakness I took strength that did not abandon me. I foresee that man will resign himself each day to more atrocious undertakings; soon there will be no one but warriors and brigands; I give them this counsel: *The author of an atrocious undertaking ought to imagine that he has already accomplished it, ought to impose upon himself a future as irrevocable as the past.* Thus I proceeded as my eyes of a man already dead registered the elapsing of that day, which was perhaps the last, and the diffusion of the night. The train ran gently along, amid ash trees. It stopped, almost in the middle of the fields. No one announced the name of the station. "Ashgrove?" I asked a few lads on the platform. "Ashgrove," they replied. I got off.

A lamp enlightened the platform but the faces of the boys were in shadow. One questioned me, "Are you going to Dr. Stephen Albert's house?" Without waiting for my answer, another said, "The house is a long way from here, but you won't get lost if you take this road to the left and at every crossroads turn again to your left." I tossed them a coin (my last), descended a few stone steps and started down the solitary road. It went downhill, slowly. It was of elemental earth; overhead the branches were tangled; the low, full moon seemed to accompany me.

For an instant, I thought that Richard Madden in some way had penetrated my desperate plan. Very quickly, I understood that that was impossible. The instructions to turn always to the left reminded me that such was the common procedure for discovering the central point of certain labyrinths. I have some understanding of labyrinths: not for nothing am I the great grandson of that Ts'ui Pên who was governor of Yunnan[9] and who renounced worldly power in order to write a novel that might be even more populous than the *Hung Lu Meng*[1] and to construct a labyrinth in which all men would become lost. Thirteen years he dedicated to these heterogeneous tasks, but the hand of a stranger murdered him—and his novel was incoherent and no one found the labyrinth. Beneath English trees I meditated on that lost maze: I imagined it inviolate and perfect at the secret crest of a mountain; I imagined it erased by rice fields or beneath the water; I imagined it infinite, no longer composed of octagonal kiosks and returning paths, but of rivers and provinces and kingdoms . . . I thought of a labyrinth of labyrinths, of one sinuous spreading labyrinth that would encompass the past and the future and in some way involve the stars. Absorbed in these illusory images, I forgot my destiny of one pursued. I felt myself to be, for an unknown period of time, an abstract perceiver of the world. The vague, living countryside, the moon, the remains of the day worked on me, as well as the slope of the road, which eliminated any possibility of weariness. The

9. Southwesternmost of China's eighteen traditional provinces; beautiful but sparsely populated, damp and malarial (the name means "Cloudy South"); not an ideal diplomatic assignment.

1. *Dream of the Red Chamber*, long, semiautobiographical novel by Ts'ao Chan (1715–1763) about the decay of a wealthy noble family.

afternoon was intimate, infinite. The road descended and forked among the now confused meadows. A high-pitched, almost syllabic music approached and receded in the shifting of the wind, dimmed by leaves and distance. I thought that a man can be an enemy of other men, of the moments of other men, but not of a country: not of fireflies, words, gardens, streams of water, sunsets. Thus I arrived before a tall, rusty gate. Between the iron bars I made out a poplar grove and a pavilion. I understood suddenly two things, the first trivial, the second almost unbelievable: the music came from the pavilion, and the music was Chinese. For precisely that reason I had openly accepted it without paying it any heed. I do not remember whether there was a bell or whether I knocked with my hand. The sparkling of the music continued.

From the rear of the house within a lantern approached: a lantern that the trees sometimes striped and sometimes eclipsed, a paper lantern that had the form of a drum and the color of the moon. A tall man bore it. I didn't see his face for the light blinded me. He opened the door and said slowly, in my own language: "I see that the pious Hsi P'êng persists in correcting my solitude. You no doubt wish to see the garden?"

I recognized the name of one of our consuls and I replied, disconcerted, "The garden?"

"The garden of forking paths."

Something stirred in my memory and I uttered with incomprehensible certainty, "The garden of my ancestor Ts'ui Pên."

"Your ancestor? Your illustrious ancestor? Come in."

The damp path zigzagged like those of my childhood. We came to a library of Eastern and Western books. I recognized bound in a yellow silk several volumes of the Lost Encyclopedia, edited by the Third Emperor of the Luminous Dynasty[2] but never printed. The record on the phonograph revolved next to a bronze phoenix. I also recall a *famille rose*[3] vase and another, many centuries older, of that shade of blue which our craftsmen copied from the potters of Persia . . .

Stephen Albert observed me with a smile. He was, as I have said, very tall, sharp-featured, with gray eyes and a gray beard. He told me that he had been a missionary in Tientsin "before aspiring to become a Sinologist."

We sat down—I on a long, low divan, he with his back to the window and a tall circular clock. I calculated that my pursuer, Richard Madden, could not arrive for at least an hour. My irrevocable determination could wait.

"An astounding fate, that of Ts'ui Pên," Stephen Albert said. "Governor of his native province, learned in astronomy, in astrology and in the tireless interpretation of the canonical books,[4] chess player, famous poet and calligrapher—he abandoned all this in order to com-

2. The "Luminous" Dynasty is the Ming; its third emperor, Yung-lo, reigned 1402–1424. He commissioned a compilation of all significant work done on Chinese history, government, philosophy, geography, etc., which, though incomplete, ran to over 11,000 of the small Chinese volumes—too long to be printed.

3. "Rose family" Chinese porcelain, characterized by rose glaze over the decoration.

4. The Confucian classics which officials had to know thoroughly and apply to contemporary social and political issues.

pose a book and a maze. He renounced the pleasures of both tyranny and justice, of his populous couch, of his banquets and even of erudition—all to close himself up for thirteen years in the Pavilion of the Limpid Solitude.[5] When he died, his heirs found nothing save chaotic manuscripts. His family, as you may be aware, wished to condemn them to the fire, but his executor—a Taoist or Buddhist monk—insisted on their publication."

"We descendants of Ts'ui Pên," I replied, "continue to curse that monk. Their publication was senseless. The book is an indeterminate heap of contradictory drafts. I examined it once: in the third chapter the hero dies, in the fourth he is alive. As for the other undertaking of Ts'ui Pên, his labyrinth . . ."

"Here is Ts'ui Pên's labyrinth," he said, indicating a tall lacquered desk.

"An ivory labyrinth!" I exclaimed. "A minimum labyrinth."

"A labyrinth of symbols," he corrected. "An invisible labyrinth of time. To me, a barbarous Englishman, has been entrusted the revelation of this diaphanous mystery. After more than a hundred years, the details are irretrievable; but it is not hard to conjecture what happened. Ts'ui Pên must have said once: *I am withdrawing to write a book*. And another time: *I am withdrawing to construct a labyrinth*. Everyone imagined two works; to no one did it occur that the book and the maze were one and the same thing. The Pavilion of the Limpid Solitude stood in the center of a garden that was perhaps intricate; that circumstance could have suggested to the heirs a physical labyrinth. Ts'ui Pên died; no one in the vast territories that were his came upon the labyrinth; the confusion of the novel suggested to me that *it* was the maze. Two circumstances gave me the correct solution of the problem. One: the curious legend that Ts'ui Pên had planned to create a labyrinth which would be strictly infinite. The other: a fragment of a letter I discovered."

Albert rose. He turned his back on me for a moment; he opened a drawer of the black and gold desk. He faced me and in his hands he held a sheet of paper that had once been crimson, but was now pink and tenuous and cross-sectioned. The fame of Ts'ui Pên as a calligrapher had been justly won. I read, uncomprehendingly and with fervor, these words written with a minute brush by a man of my blood: *I leave to the various futures (not to all) my garden of forking paths*. Wordlessly, I returned the sheet. Albert continued:

"Before unearthing this letter, I had questioned myself about the ways in which a book can be infinite. I could think of nothing other than a cyclic volume, a circular one. A book whose last page was identical with the first, a book which had the possibility of continuing indefinitely. I remembered too that night which is at the middle of the Thousand and One Nights when Scheherazade (through a magical oversight of the copyist) begins to relate word for word the story of the Thousand and One Nights, establishing the risk of coming once again to the night when she must repeat it, and thus on to infinity. I imagined as well a Platonic, hereditary work, transmitted

---

5. The names of both Ts'ui Pên and the Pavilion seem fictitious.

from father to son, in which each new individual adds a chapter or corrects with pious care the pages of his elders. These conjectures diverted me; but none seemed to correspond, not even remotely, to the contradictory chapters of Ts'ui Pên. In the midst of this perplexity, I received from Oxford the manuscript you have examined. I lingered, naturally, on the sentence: *I leave to the various futures (not to all) my garden of forking paths.* Almost instantly, I understood: 'the garden of forking paths' was the chaotic novel; the phrase 'the various futures (not to all)' suggested to me the forking in time, not in space. A broad rereading of the work confirmed the theory. In all fictional works, each time a man is confronted with several alternatives, he chooses one and eliminates the others; in the fiction of Ts'ui Pên, he chooses—simultaneously—all of them. *He creates*, in this way, diverse futures, diverse times which themselves also proliferate and fork. Here, then, is the explanation of the novel's contradictions. Fang, let us say, has a secret; a stranger calls at his door; Fang resolves to kill him. Naturally, there are several possible outcomes: Fang can kill the intruder, the intruder can kill Fang, they both can escape, they both can die, and so forth. In the work of Ts'ui Pên, all possible outcomes occur; each one is the point of departure for other forkings. Sometimes, the paths of this labyrinth converge: for example, you arrive at this house, but in one of the possible pasts you are my enemy, in another, my friend. If you will resign yourself to my incurable pronunciation, we shall read a few pages."

His face, within the vivid circle of the lamplight, was unquestionably that of an old man, but with something unalterable about it, even immortal. He read with slow precision two versions of the same epic chapter. In the first, an army marches to a battle across a lonely mountain; the horror of the rocks and shadows makes the men undervalue their lives and they gain an easy victory. In the second, the same army traverses a palace where a great festival is taking place; the resplendent battle seems to them a continuation of the celebration and they win the victory. I listened with proper veneration to these ancient narratives, perhaps less admirable in themselves than the fact that they had been created by my blood and were being restored to me by a man of a remote empire, in the course of a desperate adventure, on a Western isle. I remember the last words, repeated in each version like a secret commandment: *Thus fought the heroes, tranquil their admirable hearts, violent their swords, resigned to kill and to die.*

From that moment on, I felt about me and within my dark body an invisible, intangible swarming. Not the swarming of the divergent, parallel and finally coalescent armies, but a more inaccessible, more intimate agitation that they in some manner prefigured. Stephen Albert continued:

"I don't believe that your illustrious ancestor played idly with these variations. I don't consider it credible that he would sacrifice thirteen years to the infinite execution of a rhetorical experiment. In your country, the novel is a subsidiary form of literature; in Ts'ui Pên's time it was a despicable form. Ts'ui Pên was a brilliant novelist, but he was also a man of letters who doubtless did not consider himself a mere novelist. The testimony of his contemporaries proclaims—and his life fully confirms—his metaphysical and mystical interests. Philosophic controversy usurps a good part of the novel. I know that of all problems, none disturbed him so greatly nor worked upon him so much as the abysmal problem of time. Now then, the latter is the only problem that does not figure in the pages of the *Garden*. He does not even use the word that signifies *time*. How do you explain this voluntary omission?"

I proposed several solutions—all unsatisfactory. We discussed them. Finally, Stephen Albert said to me:

"In a riddle whose answer is chess, what is the only prohibited word?"

I thought a moment and replied, "The word *chess*."

"Precisely," said Albert. "*The Garden of Forking Paths* is an enormous riddle, or parable, whose theme is time; this recondite cause prohibits its mention. To omit a word always, to resort to inept metaphors and obvious periphrases, is perhaps the most emphatic way of stressing it. That is the tortuous method preferred, in each of the meanderings of his indefatigable novel, by the oblique Ts'ui Pên. I have compared hundreds of manuscripts, I have corrected the errors that the negligence of the copyists has introduced, I have guessed the plan of this chaos, I have re-established—I believe I have re-established—the primordial organization, I have translated the entire work: it is clear to me that not once does he employ the word 'time.' The explanation is obvious: *The Garden of Forking Paths* is an incomplete, but not false, image of the universe as Ts'ui Pên conceived it. In contrast to Newton and Schopenhauer, your ancestor did not believe in a uniform, absolute time. He believed in an infinite series of times, in a growing, dizzying net of divergent, convergent and parallel times. This network of times which approached one another, forked, broke off, or were unaware of one another for centuries, embraces *all* possibilities of time. We do not exist in the majority of these times; in some you exist, and not I; in others I, and not you; in others, both of us. In the present one, which a favorable fate has granted me, you have arrived at my house; in another, while crossing the garden, you found me dead; in still another, I utter these same words, but I am a mistake, a ghost."

"In every one," I pronounced, not without a tremble to my voice, "I am grateful to you and revere you for your re-creation of the garden of Ts'ui Pên."

"Not in all," he murmured with a smile. "Time forks perpetually toward innumerable futures. In one of them I am your enemy."

Once again I felt the swarming sensation of which I have spoken. It seemed to me that the humid garden that surrounded the house was infinitely saturated with invisible persons. Those persons were Albert and I, secret, busy and multiform in other dimensions of time. I raised my eyes and the tenuous nightmare dissolved. In the yellow and black garden there was only one man; but this man was as strong as a statue . . . this man was approaching along the path and he was Captain Richard Madden.

"The future already exists," I replied, "but I am your friend. Could I see the letter again?"

Albert rose. Standing tall, he opened the drawer of the tall desk; for the moment his back was to me. I had readied the revolver. I fired with extreme caution. Albert fell uncomplainingly, immediately. I swear his death was instantaneous—a lightning stroke.

The rest is unreal, insignificant. Madden broke in, arrested me. I have been condemned to the gallows. I have won out abominably; I have communicated to Berlin the secret name of the city they must attack. They bombed it yesterday; I read it in the same papers that offered to England the mystery of the learned Sinologist Stephen Albert, who was murdered by a stranger, one Yu Tsun. The Chief had deciphered this mystery. He knew my problem was to indicate (through the uproar of the war) the city called Albert[6] and that I had found no other means to do so than to kill a man of that name. He does not know (no one can know) my innumerable contrition and weariness.

For Victoria Ocampo   p. 1958

HAL BENNETT

Dotson Gerber Resurrected

We saw the head of Mr. Dotson Gerber break ground at approximately nine o'clock on a bright Saturday morning in March out near our collard patch, where Poppa had started to dig a well and then filled it in. Of course, none of us knew then that the shock of red hair and part of a head sprouting from the abandoned well belonged to Mr. Dotson Gerber, who'd been missing from his farm since early last fall. We were black folk, and the fact that a white man like Mr. Dotson Gerber was missing from his home was of small importance to us. Unless that white man suddenly started growing from the ground near our collard patch like Mr. Dotson Gerber was doing now for Momma, my sister Millicent and me. We'd come running because of a commotion the chickens had made, thinking that a lynx or a weasel might have got after them. And found Mr. Dotson Gerber's head instead.

"Good Jesus," Millicent said, "I do think I'm going to faint." Millicent had been prone to fainting ever since she'd seen two black men kissing behind some boxes in the factory where she worked. Now she was getting ready to faint again. But Momma snatched her roughly by the apron.

"Girl, you *always* fainting, you don't hardly give other people a chance." And Momma fainted dead away, which left Millicent conscious for the time being and looking very desperate. But she didn't faint and I was glad of that, because I certainly didn't want to be

6. City on the Paris side (southwest) of the River Ancre.

alone with Mr. Dotson Gerber sprouting from the ground. A dozen or so chickens were still raising a ruckus about the unexpected appearance of a white man's head where they were accustomed to picking for grain. Screeching at the top of her voice, Millicent shooed the chickens away while I tugged Momma into the shade and propped her against the barn. Then we went back to looking at Mr. Dotson Gerber.

I have mentioned the well that Poppa started to dig because it was apparent that Mr. Dotson Gerber had been planted standing up in that hole. Which, of course, explained why his head was growing out first. Although, as I have said, neither Millicent nor I knew then that what we were looking at belonged to Mr. Dotson Gerber. It took Poppa to tell us that.

He came riding on Miss Tricia from the stable, where he'd been saddling her. "Why you children making all that noise out there?" he called from the road. When we didn't answer, he yanked the reins and rode Miss Tricia toward us. "Millicent, was that you I heard hollering? What you all doing out here?" Poppa asked again.

"There's a white man growing from the ground," I said.

Poppa nearly fell off Miss Tricia. "A *what?*"

"A white man. He's growing from that hole where you started to dig the well."

"I *know* I'm going to faint now," Millicent said. And she wrapped her hands around her throat as though to choke herself into unconsciousness. But Poppa and I both ignored her and she was too curious to faint right then. So she stopped choking herself and watched Poppa jump down from Miss Tricia to inspect the head. He walked all around it, poking it from time to time with his shoe.

"That'd be Mr. Dotson Gerber," he finally pronounced.

By this time, Momma had revived and was watching Poppa with the rest of us. "Poppa, how you know that's Mr. Dotson Gerber? Why, he could be any old white man! There's hardly enough of him above ground for anybody to recognize."

"I know it's Mr. Dotson Gerber because I planted him there," Poppa said. He told us how Mr. Gerber had come out to the farm last fall to inspect the well that he was digging, which had been part of Mr. Gerber's job here in Alcanthia County.[1] "He kept calling me Uncle," Poppa said, with some bitterness. "I told him respectfully that my name is Walter Beaufort, or that he could even call me *Mr.* Beaufort, if he'd a mind to. After all, things have changed so much nowadays, I told him I certainly wouldn't think any less of him if he called me Mr. Beaufort. I told him that black people don't appreciate white folks' calling us Uncle any longer. But he just kept on calling me that, so I hit him on the head with my shovel." We all looked at Mr. Dotson Gerber's head; and it was true that there was a wide gash in his skull that could only have been caused by a shovel. "I didn't intend to kill him," Poppa said. "I just wanted to teach him some respect. After all, things *have* changed. But when I found out he was dead, I stood him up in that hole I was digging and covered him up. I never expected to see him growing out of the ground this way."

1. Both this and Burnside mentioned below seem to be fictional; Dillwyn, mentioned later, is a very small town in Buckingham County, Virginia.

"Well, that's not the problem now," Millicent said. "The problem now is, what are we going to do with him?"

Momma moved a step closer to Mr. Gerber and cautiously poked him with her toe. "If it weren't for that red hair," she said, "somebody might mistake him for a cabbage."

"He don't look like no cabbage to me," Millicent said. It was clear that she was annoyed because Momma had fainted before she'd had a chance to.

"I didn't say he looked like a cabbage," Momma said. "I said somebody might mistake him for a cabbage."

"He too red to be a cabbage," Millicent said stubbornly. "Anyway, we still ought to do something about him. It just don't look right, a white man growing like this on a colored person's farm. Suppose some white people see it?"

The 9:10 Greyhound to Richmond went by then. Momma and Poppa shaded their eyes to watch it speed down the far road; but Millicent and I were of today's generation and we hardly looked. Although there had been a time when the passing of the Richmond bus was the most exciting event of everybody's day in Burnside. But the years in between had brought many changes. There was electricity now, and television and telephones. Several factories and supermarkets had opened up on the highway, so that farming became far less profitable than working in the factories and spending weekly wages in the glittering markets, where everything that had formerly come from soil was sold now in tin cans and plastic wrappers. Because nobody in Burnside farmed anymore. Like almost everyone else, Momma and Poppa and Millicent all worked in the factories. And Momma bought at the supermarkets, like everyone else. The land around us, given over to weeds, was overgrown now like a graveyard in those first green days of spring.

Momma and Poppa watched the bus until it disappeared. "That Greyhound, she sure do go," Momma said. "It's Saturday now and I bet she's crowded with nigger men going to Richmond for them white hussies on Clay Street."

Millicent grunted. "Let them help themselves," she said bitterly. "After what I seen, a nigger man don't mean a thing to me no more."

"You're right there, sugar," Momma agreed. "A nigger man, he ain't worth a damn."

Millicent curled her lip and she and Momma looked at Poppa and me as though there were something dirty and pathetic about being a black man. I had seen this expression on their faces before—a wan kind of pity mixed with distaste and the sad realization that being a black man is next to being nothing at all. And the black woman is always telling the black man that with her eyes and lips and hips, telling him by the way she moves beside him on the road and underneath him in the bed. *Nigger, oh, I love you, but I know you ain't never going to be as good as a white man.* That's the way Momma and Millicent looked at Poppa and me while they cut us dead right there on the spot. They almost fell over each other, talking about how low and no-good nigger men are. And they weren't just joking; they really meant it. I saw it in their faces and it hurt me to my heart. I just didn't know what to do. I reached out and caught Poppa's arm, that's how hurt I was. He seemed to understand, because he wrapped his arm around me and I could feel some of his strength draining into me. So Momma and Millicent stood there ridiculing us on one side of Mr. Dotson Gerber's head, and Poppa and I stood there on the other.

Then, when Momma and Millicent were all through with their tirade, Poppa said very quietly, "I'm riding in to Dillwyn now. I'm going to turn myself over to the sheriff for killing Mr. Gerber here."

There was a kind of joy in Poppa's voice that I suppose no black woman can ever understand, and Momma and Millicent looked at Poppa as though he had suddenly lost his mind. But I was sixteen years old, which is old enough to be a man if you're black, and I understood why Poppa was so happy about killing that white man. Until now, he'd always had to bury his rich, black male rage in the far corner of some infertile field, lest it do harm to him and to the rest of us as well. But by telling that he'd killed that white man, he would undo all the indignities he had ever suffered in the name of love.

Now Momma looked afraid. "Turn yourself in to the sheriff? What you talking about, Walter Beaufort? What kind of foolishness you talking?" She tried humor to change Poppa's somber mood, laughing in a big hullabaloo. "I bet you been hitting the plum wine again," she said joyously.

But Poppa shook his head. "You always accuse me of that when you want to make light of what I'm saying. But I haven't been near that plum wine, not today. And what I'm saying is plain enough. I've killed a white man and I want somebody to know it."

"*We* know it," Momma said. "Ain't that good enough?"

"I want them to know it," Poppa said. "I want them to know he's dead and I want them to know why he's dead."

"Because he didn't call you Mister?" Momma said. There wasn't a white man in Alcanthia County who didn't call her Auntie, and she started to rage scornfully at the idea of Poppa's rebelling at being called Uncle. "Now, I could see it if you said you were going to hide out for a while, killing that white man and all that—"

But Poppa stopped her with an angry jerk of his hand. "It's not that way at all, Hattie. I don't aim to hide no more. I been hiding too long already—if you understand what I mean. The time's come for me to stop hiding. I'm going to Dillwyn and tell the sheriff what I've done."

Momma jumped straight up in the air. "Walter Beaufort, you gone *crazy* or something? No, I don't understand what you mean. Why didn't you tell the sheriff last year? Why you got to tell him now? Nobody even knows you killed Mr. Gerber. And to give yourself up now, that don't make no sense at all."

"Some things don't never make no sense," Poppa said. He cocked his eye at me. "You coming with me to the sheriff, boy? Somebody's got to ride Miss Tricia back here to home."

I got up onto Miss Tricia with him and we rode off to find the sheriff.

"I think I'm going to faint," I heard Millicent say behind me. But when I looked around, she was still standing there with her mouth hanging open.

As Poppa and I went up the road, Momma's voice followed us like an angry wind. "You see what I mean about *niggers,* Millicent?" Moaning sadly, half happy and afraid at the same time, a kind of turbulent satisfaction marred her voice as she shrieked at Millicent. "You see what I mean about *niggers,* child?"

"That black bitch," Poppa muttered. I don't know whether he knew I heard him or not. He kicked Miss Tricia viciously in the ribs and the mule leaped into a surprised gallop, heading to Dillwyn for Poppa to give himself up to the sheriff. After the way Momma and Millicent had carried on, I didn't see what else he could do.

Even here in Burnside, we had heard that black is beautiful. But I don't think that many of us believed it, because black is ugly and desperate and degraded wherever the white man is sitting on your neck. Still, Millicent and I had worn Afros for a while to show our black pride; but they were too hard to keep clean here in the country, there is so much dust and dirt blowing about. And our kind of hair picks up everything that goes by. Besides, the white people who owned the factories took Afro hairdos as a sign of militancy and threatened to fire everybody who wore one. So everybody went back to getting their hair cut short or straightening it like before.

I was thinking about that as I rode with Poppa to the sheriff's office. I thought about Millicent, too, and the black men she'd seen kissing in the factory. She never would tell who they were, and sometimes I wondered whether it might not have been just a story that she made up to justify her saying that all black men are sissies. At any rate, she complained quite openly that no black man had made love to her since last Halloween, which was almost five months ago, and this probably explained why she was so jumpy and threatening to faint all the time.

As for me, I thought I knew why no black men were interested in Millicent. For one thing, they could go to Richmond and Charlottesville and get white women, now that they had money to spend on the whores there. Also, the black men I'd talked to told me that they didn't find black women so desirable anymore, the way they were dressing and acting and perfuming themselves like white women on television, now that they had money to do so.

So the black men went to Richmond and paid white women, because their own women were trying to act white. And the black women were turning their backs on their own men, because—if Millicent was any example—they thought that black men were sissies. It was all very confusing.

I was old enough to have had myself a woman or two by then. But I was very hung up on Mrs. Palmer and her five daughters; I hope you know what I mean. There was a time when black people said that doing something like that to yourself would make you crazy. Now they said that it would make you turn white. Which was sufficient reason for some black boys to stop. But not me. I actually did it more. But all that happened was that sometimes I felt dizzy and depressed.

Sometimes I felt weak. But I never did turn white.

Sheriff Dave Young's office was closed when we got to Dillwyn. Some white men sitting around told us that the sheriff was away to a Christian conference. "He's a deacon in the white Baptist church, you know. He'll be away for the rest of the week." There were some hounds lying around, sleeping in the dust, and one or two of them opened a drowsy eye and looked at Poppa and me without curiosity. The white men looked at us as though we were two hounds who had by some miracle managed to get up onto a mule. That's the way white men are in the South. As for Poppa and me, we looked right through those white men, which is really a very good way of rebelling by pretending that you're looking at nothing. There are other sly ways that we Southern black people have of rebelling—like grinning, or licking our tongue out behind the white man's back, spitting in his water when he's not looking, imitating his way of talking—which is why so many Northern black people think that Southern black people are such natural clowns, when what we're really doing is rebelling. Not as dramatic as a Molotov cocktail or a pipe bomb, but it certainly is satisfying, and a whole lot safer, too. Furthermore, it must be said that we do not hate whites here as black people apparently do in the North. Although we nearly always view them with pity and suspicion, for *they* think that we hate them, as they might well do if the tables were reversed.

"Uncle, is there any particular reason why you want to see the sheriff?"

"No, sir, no, sir, none at all," Poppa said. He thanked them the way he was supposed to, grinning a little, and rode away.

"Where we going now, Poppa? Back to home?"

He shook his head. "We going to Mr. Dotson Gerber's house up the street yonder. I expect his wife is home. I expect she'd like to know what happened to her husband."

When we got to Mrs. Dotson Gerber's, there was a decrepit old white lady sitting in a rocking chair on her porch and waving a small Confederate flag over the banister, like a child does at a parade. She was the mother of Mr. Dotson Gerber's wife. And while colored people said quite openly that the old lady was touched in the head, white people claimed that she had arthritis; and they said that she waved the Confederate flag to exercise her arm, as though to conceal from black people the fact that any white had ever lost his mind.

She waved the flag and rocked every once in a while, pushing at the banister with spidery legs that ended in two fluffy slippers that had once been white. Her pale-blue eyes were as sharp as a hawk's behind her wire-rimmed glasses; but it was hard to tell whether she was looking into the past or the future, waving and rocking, smiling from time to time.

Poppa got down from Miss Tricia and walked over to the fence. "Good morning, ma'am," he said respectfully. It was dangerous not to be respectful, just in case the old white woman wasn't crazy and really did have arthritis in her arm. She could raise a ruckus for Poppa's disrespecting her that could cause him to wind up on the end of a rope. "I came to see Mrs. Dotson Gerber, ma'am," Poppa said politely, while the old lady rocked and waved the flag outrageously. She might have been saluting Lee's army marching proudly on its way to Appomattox, which was only a few miles away. Her eyes grew large and happy. But she didn't pay any attention at all to Poppa, even when he asked a second and a third time for Mrs. Dotson Gerber. She had arthritis, all right, that old woman. She had arthritis in the brain, that's where she had it.

Just then, Mrs. Dotson Gerber came to the screen door. Drying her hands on a pink apron, she inspected Poppa for a minute, as though trying to figure out whether he was safe or not. "Is that you, Uncle Walter?" She squinted through the screen. "Did you want to talk to me?"

"Yes, ma'am, Mrs. Gerber. I did come to talk to you. I got something to tell you."

"I certainly don't see why you came to my front door," Mrs. Gerber said peevishly, coming out onto the porch. "I *never* receive colored people at my front door, and I'm sure you know that, Uncle Walter. Besides, it bothers my mother's arthritis, people talking all around her." She inspected the crazy old woman, who was waving the Confederate flag and rocking vigorously.

"Well, ma'am . . . I'm sorry I came to your front door. I certainly do know better than that. But I've come to tell you about your husband."

Mrs. Gerber seemed to stop breathing. "My husband?" She dashed from the porch and stood at the fence near Poppa. "You know where my husband is?"

"Yes, ma'am. He's out in my collard patch—where my collard patch used to be."

"What's he doing out there?"

Poppa looked embarrassed. "He came to inspect the well I was digging. We got in an argument and I hit him with my shovel."

Mrs. Gerber turned very white, indeed. "You killed him?"

"I'm afraid so, ma'am. I buried him there in the well."

Mrs. Gerber tapped her bottom teeth with her forefinger. She was a sort of pretty white woman and certainly a lot younger than Mr. Dotson Gerber had been. Behind her on the porch, the crazy old woman rocked on, waving the flag at Southern armies that only she could see. "Momma's arthritis isn't too good today," Mrs. Gerber said absently, patting her hair. After a while, she said, "So Dotson is dead. All of us wondered what happened when he didn't come home last year. Knowing him, I was almost certain that he'd gone and got himself killed." But she didn't seem too upset. "Actually, Uncle Walter, you've done me a big favor. Dotson used to treat my poor mother something terrible, laughing at her arthritis all the time." She patted her hair again, although every strand seemed to be perfectly in place. "I suppose you know that I'm to get married again this summer to a very respectable man here in Alcanthia?"

"No, ma'am, I didn't know that."

"Well, I'm surprised," Mrs. Gerber said. "I thought that colored people knew everything. Anyway, he's a very respectable man. Very decent and very intelligent, too, I need not say. We both figured that Dotson was dead after all these months. That's why we decided to get married." She looked at Poppa almost gently. "But I never supposed you'd be the one to kill him, Uncle Walter. Why, you've even been here and done a little work for Dotson and me around the house."

"Yes, ma'am."

"He really must've provoked you, Uncle Walter. What did he do?"

"He kept calling me Uncle. I asked him not to, but he kept on."

"Yes, that sounds like Dotson. He could be mean that way. I suppose you want me to stop calling you Uncle, too?"

"I'd appreciate it if you would, ma'am. I mean, it's an actual fact that I'm not your uncle, so I'd appreciate your not calling me that."

Now Mrs. Gerber nibbled on her thumb. Her mother rocked on and on, waving the flag. "All right, I'll stop calling you Uncle," Mrs. Gerber said, "if you promise not to tell anybody about my husband being buried out there in your collard patch. After all, I'm planning on being married to a very decent man. It would be a big embarrassment to me—and to him, too—if anybody found out about Dotson being buried in a collard patch. As much as he hates collard greens." It was clear from the tone of her voice that the disgrace lay not in Mr. Dotson Gerber's being dead but in his being buried in our collard patch.

"There ain't no collards there now," Poppa said, trying to placate Mrs. Gerber some. "Why, we haven't done any farming for years."

"But collards *were* there," Mrs. Gerber said, almost stomping her foot. "And Dotson couldn't stand collards. I just hope you won't tell anybody else about this, Uncle Walter. I don't know what my fiancé would say if he knew about this. Considering that he's willing to marry me and to put up with Momma's arthritis in the bargain, I certainly wouldn't want him to know about Dotson. Why, I don't know what he'd do if he ever found out about Dotson. You haven't told anybody else, have you?"

"I went to tell the sheriff, but he's out of town until next week."

"You went to tell the sheriff?" She seemed absolutely horrified. "Mr. Beaufort, I know I have no right asking you to think about me and my feelings in all this. But you ought to at least think about your own family. You know what they'll do to you if they find out about this?"

"I know," Poppa said.

"And you don't care?"

"I certainly do care. I don't want to die. I want to live. But I've killed me a white man. That's not something that somebody like me does every day. I think I want folks to know about it."

"But why now?" she cried. "Why didn't you say something before? Before I went out and got myself engaged?"

"It didn't seem important before. Besides, Mr. Gerber was still in the ground then. He ain't in the ground anymore, not exactly."

From time to time, white people had gone past and looked at Poppa and Mrs. Gerber as they talked. "I think you all ought to go around to the back door," Mrs. Gerber said. "My husband-to-be certainly wouldn't like it known that I stood on my own front porch and carried on a conversation with colored people . . ." She turned very red then and took a step or two away, as though she was afraid that Poppa might hit her with a shovel. But Poppa started laughing very gently, the way a man does when he weighs the value of things and finds out that what is important to other people seems absurd to him. And he looked at Mrs. Gerber with a kind of amused pity darkening his eyes, as though he realized now that no white person could ever understand why he wanted him to know about Mr. Dotson Gerber.

"We're going on home," Poppa said. "And don't you worry none about Mr. Gerber, ma'am. We'll take care of him. Your husband-to-be won't ever find out."

"What do you intend to do?" Mrs. Gerber wanted to know.

Poppa's face lit up with a great big grin. Not the kind of tame, painful grin that a black man puts on when he's rebelling. But a large, beautiful grin that showed all of his teeth and gums. "I'm going to plant collard greens around him," Poppa said.

Mrs. Gerber wrinkled her nose in distaste. "Dotson certainly wouldn't like that, if he knew. And you mean *over* him, don't you?"

Now Poppa and I both laughed. We hadn't told her that Mr. Gerber was growing straight up from the ground. And she wouldn't have believed us if we had told her. That's how white people are. "Good-bye, ma'am," Poppa said to Mrs. Gerber. She nodded and went into her house. On the porch, her mother waved the Confederate flag triumphantly. The rocker squeaked like the tread of strident ghosts. We climbed up onto Miss Tricia and rode home.

And we were nearly halfway there before I finally figured out why that old crazy white woman was on Mrs. Gerber's porch. They kept her there instead of buying a doorbell and using electricity. That way, when people talked to her, Mrs. Gerber heard them and came outside to see who it was. Smart. Sometimes I had to give it to white people. They were very smart indeed.

Momma and Millicent were waiting for us when we got home. "Did you tell the sheriff?" Momma said. She looked haggard and very unhappy.

"The sheriff wasn't there," Poppa said. "He won't be home until next week." With Momma and Millicent following us, he rode Miss Tricia out to the collard patch and gave me the reins. "Take her to the stable, boy." But I watched while he knelt and worked the dirt into a mound around Mr. Gerber's head. "There, that ought to do it," Poppa said. "Tomorrow, I'm going to plant me some collard greens here." He stood up happily and wiped his hands on the seat of his overalls.

Momma's mouth dropped open. She ran to Mr. Dotson Gerber's head and tried to stomp it back into the ground. But Poppa stopped her firmly. "You've gone stark crazy!" Momma cried.

Poppa slapped her right in the mouth. She spun around like a top. He slapped her again and sent her spinning the other way. "I don't want no more trouble out of you," Poppa said.

Momma melted against him like warm cheese. "All right, sugar. You won't have no more trouble out of me, sugar."

I rode Miss Tricia down to the stable. Millicent had enough sense to keep her mouth shut for a change, and Momma and Poppa went on up to the house with their arms wrapped around each other. I hadn't seen them together like that for years.

And that is how Poppa started farming again. Helped on by sun and spring rain, Mr. Dotson Gerber and the collards grew rapidly together. It would not be an exaggeration to say that Mr. Gerber's body growing there seemed to fertilize the whole field. Although in no time at all, he was taller than the collards and still growing. Most of his chest and arms was out of the ground by the end of March. And by the middle of April, he had cleared the ground down to his ankles. With his tattered clothes and wild red hair, his large blue eyes wide and staring, he seemed more some kind of monster than a resurrected man. The sun and wind had burned his skin nearly as black as ours. And while there was small chance of anybody seeing him—people in Burnside didn't visit anymore, now that most of them worked in the factories—Poppa still thought it might be a good idea to cover Mr. Gerber up. "You'd better put a sack over his head and some gloves on his hands," he said. Later on, Poppa put a coat and some sunglasses on Mr. Gerber, along with an old straw hat. He propped a stick behind Mr. Gerber and passed another one through the sleeves of Mr. Gerber's coat for him to rest his arms on. He really looked like a scarecrow then, and we stopped worrying about people finding out about him. In truth, however, it must be said that Mr. Gerber made a very poor scarecrow, indeed, because the birds hardly paid any attention to him. It was fortunate for us that birds don't especially like collard greens.

Poppa worked a few hours in the collard patch every night after he came home from the factory. Momma helped him sometimes. Sometimes Millicent and I helped him, too. Then one day, Poppa quit his job at the factory and hitched Miss Tricia to the plow. "You farming again?" Momma asked him. She had been very tame with Poppa since he'd slapped her.

"I'm farming again," Poppa said.

Momma just nodded. "That's very nice, sugar. That's really very nice."

In no time at all, Poppa had planted all the old crops that used to grow on our farm—all kinds of vegetables, wheat, corn. He went to Dillwyn and bought a couple of pigs and a cow. All the neighbors knew what he was doing. But they kept on working at the factories and spending their money at the supermarkets. Until one day, a neighbor woman showed up to buy some collard greens. Poppa sold her a large basketful for a dollar. "I'm just sick to death of store-bought food," she said.

"I know what you mean," Poppa said. "You come back, you hear?" In a little while, other people came to buy tomatoes, string beans, white potatoes, golden corn from the tall green stalks.

Summer droned on. Poppa worked his crops. Word reached us

that Mrs. Dotson Gerber had married her decent white man. After school had let out, I had begun to help Poppa full time. Momma finally quit her job at the factory and helped, too. But mostly, she took care of selling and managing the money that we were making. As for Millicent, I spied her one day making love down in the pea patch. And that black man she was with, he certainly was no sissy. That was all Millicent needed and all a black man needed, too—someplace green and growing to make love in. I never heard Millicent talk about fainting after that, although she did talk about getting married.

Around the end of summer, Sheriff Dave Young came to our farm. "Some of the fellows said you were looking for me," he told Poppa. "But I figured it wasn't really too important, since you never came back."

"It wasn't important, Sheriff."

He bought a watermelon that Poppa let him have very cheap. "You got a good business going here," Sheriff Young said. "Some of the white farmers been talking about doing the same thing."

"It'd be good if they did," Poppa said. The sheriff put his watermelon into his car and drove away.

When fall came and the leaves turned red and gold and brown, Mr. Dotson Gerber turned like all the other growing things and shriveled away to nothing. Poppa seemed very satisfied then, looking over his fields. And I knew how he must have felt, standing there looking at Mr. Dotson Gerber and all the other dead things that would live again next spring.

The Greyhound to Richmond went by and Poppa shielded his eyes to watch. I think that I understood everything about him then and it hurt me so much that I deliberately turned my back. The lesson of that summer seemed a particularly bitter one, because we had done everything and we had done nothing. Mr. Doston Gerber would certainly be growing in my father's fields every spring forever. And my father, my poor father would always watch and admire the Greyhound to Richmond. The same way that in the deepest and sincerest and blackest part of himself he would always hate himself and believe that God is the greatest white man of all.

"That Greyhound, she sure do run," Poppa said. He sounded very satisfied, indeed. God knew he'd killed a white man. With God knowing, that was knowledge enough. But I was thinking about how it feels to be black and forever afraid. And about the white man, god*damn* him, how he causes everything. Even when He is God. Even when he is dead.

p. 1970

GABRIEL GARCÍA MÁRQUEZ

A Very Old Man with Enormous Wings*

A TALE FOR CHILDREN

On the third day of rain they had killed so many crabs inside the house that Pelayo had to cross his drenched courtyard and throw them into the sea, because the newborn child had a temperature all night and they thought it was due to the stench. The world had been sad since Tuesday. Sea and sky were a single ash-gray thing and the sands of the beach, which on March nights glimmered like powdered light, had become a stew of mud and rotten shellfish. The light was so weak at noon that when Pelayo was coming back to the house after throwing away the crabs, it was hard for him to see what it was that was moving and groaning in the rear of the courtyard. He had to go very close to see that it was an old man, a very old man, lying face down in the mud, who, in spite of his tremendous efforts, couldn't get up, impeded by his enormous wings.

Frightened by that nightmare, Pelayo ran to get Elisenda, his wife, who was putting compresses on the sick child, and he took her to the rear of the courtyard. They both looked at the fallen body with mute stupor. He was dressed like a ragpicker. There were only a few faded hairs left on his bald skull and very few teeth in his mouth, and his pitiful condition of a drenched great-grandfather had taken away any sense of grandeur he might have had. His huge buzzard wings, dirty and half-plucked, were forever entangled in the mud. They looked at him so long and so closely that Pelayo and Elisenda very soon overcame their surprise and in the end found him familiar. Then they dared speak to him, and he answered in an incomprehensible dialect with a strong sailor's voice. That was how they skipped over the inconvenience of the wings and quite intelligently concluded that he was a lonely castaway from some foreign ship wrecked by the storm. And yet, they called in a neighbor woman who knew everything about life and death to see him, and all she needed was one look to show them their mistake.

"He's an angel," she told them. "He must have been coming for the child, but the poor fellow is so old that the rain knocked him down."

On the following day everyone knew that a flesh-and-blood angel was held captive in Pelayo's house. Against the judgment of the wise neighbor woman, for whom angels in those times were the fugitive survivors of a celestial conspiracy, they did not have the heart to club him to death. Pelayo watched over him all afternoon from the kitchen, armed with his bailiff's club, and before going to bed he dragged him out of the mud and locked him up with the hens in the wire chicken coop. In the middle of the night, when the rain stopped, Pelayo and Elisenda were still killing crabs. A short time afterward the child woke up without a fever and with a desire to eat. Then they

* Translated by Gregory Rabassa.

felt magnanimous and decided to put the angel on a raft with fresh water and provisions for three days and leave him to his fate on the high seas. But when they went out into the courtyard with the first light of dawn, they found the whole neighborhood in front of the chicken coop having fun with the angel, without the slightest reverence, tossing him things to eat through the openings in the wire as if he weren't a supernatural creature but a circus animal.

Father Gonzaga arrived before seven o'clock, alarmed at the strange news. By that time onlookers less frivolous than those at dawn had already arrived and they were making all kinds of conjectures concerning the captive's future. The simplest among them thought that he should be named mayor of the world. Others of sterner mind felt that he should be promoted to the rank of five-star general in order to win all wars. Some visionaries hoped that he could be put to stud in order to implant on earth a race of winged wise men who could take charge of the universe. But Father Gonzaga, before becoming a priest, had been a robust woodcutter. Standing by the wire, he reviewed his catechism in an instant and asked them to open the door so that he could take a close look at that pitiful man who looked more like a huge decrepit hen among the fascinated chickens. He was lying in a corner drying his open wings in the sunlight among the fruit peels and breakfast leftovers that the early risers had thrown him. Alien to the impertinences of the world, he only lifted his antiquarian eyes and murmured something in his dialect when Father Gonzaga went into the chicken coop and said good morning to him in Latin. The parish priest had his first suspicion of an imposter when he saw that he did not understand the language of God or know how to greet His ministers. Then he noticed that seen close up he was much too human: he had an unbearable smell of the outdoors, the back side of his wings was strewn with parasites and his main feathers had been mistreated by terrestrial winds, and nothing about him measured up to the proud dignity of angels. Then he came out of the chicken coop and in a brief sermon warned the curious against the risks of being ingenuous. He reminded them that the devil had the bad habit of making use of carnival tricks in order to confuse the unwary. He argued that if wings were not the essential element in determining the difference between a hawk and an airplane, they were even less so in the recognition of angels. Nevertheless, he promised to write a letter to his bishop so that the latter would write to his primate so that the latter would write to the Supreme Pontiff in order to get the final verdict from the highest courts.

His prudence fell on sterile hearts. The news of the captive angel spread with such rapidity that after a few hours the courtyard had the bustle of a marketplace and they had to call in troops with fixed bayonets to disperse the mob that was about to knock the house down. Elisenda, her spine all twisted from sweeping up so much marketplace trash, then got the idea of fencing in the yard and charging five cents admission to see the angel.

The curious came from far away. A traveling carnival arrived with a flying acrobat who buzzed over the crowd several times, but no one paid any attention to him because his wings were not those of an

angel but, rather, those of a sidereal bat. The most unfortunate invalids on earth came in search of health: a poor woman who since
childhood had been counting her heartbeats and had run out of numbers; a Portuguese man who couldn't sleep because the noise of the
stars disturbed him; a sleepwalker who got up at night to undo the
things he had done while awake; and many others with less serious
ailments. In the midst of that shipwreck disorder that made the
earth tremble, Pelayo and Elisenda were happy with fatigue, for in
less than a week they had crammed their rooms with money and the
line of pilgrims waiting their turn to enter still reached beyond the
horizon.

The angel was the only one who took no part in his own act. He
spent his time trying to get comfortable in his borrowed nest, be-
fuddled by the hellish heat of the oil lamps and sacramental candles
that had been placed along the wire. At first they tried to make him
eat some mothballs, which, according to the wisdom of the wise
neighbor woman, were the food prescribed for angels. But he turned
them down, just as he turned down the papal lunches[1] that the peni-
tents brought him, and they never found out whether it was because
he was an angel or because he was an old man that in the end he
ate nothing but eggplant mush. His only supernatural virtue seemed
to be patience. Especially during the first days, when the hens pecked
at him, searching for the stellar parasites that proliferated in his
wings, and the cripples pulled out feathers to touch their defective
parts with, and even the most merciful threw stones at him, trying to
get him to rise so they could see him standing. The only time they
succeeded in arousing him was when they burned his side with an
iron for branding steers, for he had been motionless for so many hours
that they thought he was dead. He awoke with a start, ranting in his
hermetic language and with tears in his eyes, and he flapped his wings
a couple of times, which brought on a whirlwind of chicken dung and
lunar dust and a gale of panic that did not seem to be of this world.
Although many thought that his reaction had been one not of rage
but of pain, from then on they were careful not to annoy him, because
the majority understood that his passivity was not that of a hero
taking his ease but that of a cataclysm in repose.

Father Gonzaga held back the crowd's frivolity with formulas of
maidservant inspiration while awaiting the arrival of a final judgment on the nature of the captive. But the mail from Rome showed no
sense of urgency. They spent their time finding out if the prisoner had
a navel, if his dialect had any connection with Aramaic, how many
times he could fit on the head of a pin, or whether he wasn't just a
Norwegian with wings. Those meager letters might have come and
gone until the end of time if a providential event had not put an end
to the priest's tribulations.

It so happened that during those days, among so many other
carnival attractions, there arrived in town the traveling show of the
woman who had been changed into a spider for having disobeyed
her parents. The admission to see her was not only less than the ad-

---

1. Choice, extremely expensive meals.

mission to see the angel, but people were permitted to ask her all manner of questions about her absurd state and to examine her up and down so that no one would ever doubt the truth of her horror. She was a frightful tarantula the size of a ram and with the head of a sad maiden. What was most heart-rending, however, was not her outlandish shape but the sincere affliction with which she recounted the details of her misfortune. While still practically a child she had sneaked out of her parents' house to go to a dance, and while she was coming back through the woods after having danced all night without permission, a fearful thunderclap rent the sky in two and through the crack came the lightning bolt of brimstone that changed her into a spider. Her only nourishment came from the meatballs that charitable souls chose to toss into her mouth. A spectacle like that, full of so much human truth and with such a fearful lesson, was bound to defeat without even trying that of a haughty angel who scarcely deigned to look at mortals. Besides, the few miracles attributed to the angel showed a certain mental disorder, like the blind man who didn't recover his sight but grew three new teeth, or the paralytic who didn't get to walk but almost won the lottery, and the leper whose sores sprouted sunflowers. Those consolation miracles, which were more like mocking fun, had already ruined the angel's reputation when the woman who had been changed into a spider finally crushed him completely. That was how Father Gonzaga was cured forever of his insomnia and Pelayo's courtyard went back to being as empty as during the time it had rained for three days and crabs walked through the bedrooms.

The owners of the house had no reason to lament. With the money they saved they built a two-story mansion with balconies and gardens and high netting so that crabs wouldn't get in during the winter, and with iron bars on the windows so that angels wouldn't get in. Pelayo also set up a rabbit warren close to town and gave up his job as bailiff for good, and Elisenda bought some satin pumps with high heels and many dresses of iridescent silk, the kind worn on Sunday by the most desirable women in those times. The chicken coop was the only thing that didn't receive any attention. If they washed it down with creolin[2] and burned tears of myrrh inside it every so often, it was not in homage to the angel but to drive away the dungheap stench that still hung everywhere like a ghost and was turning the new house into an old one. At first, when the child learned to walk, they were careful that he not get too close to the chicken coop. But then they began to lose their fears and got used to the smell, and before the child got his second teeth he'd gone inside the chicken coop to play, where the wires were falling apart. The angel was no less standoffish with him than with other mortals, but he tolerated the most ingenious infamies with the patience of a dog who had no illusions. They both came down with chicken pox at the same time. The doctor who took care of the child couldn't resist the temptation to listen to the angel's heart, and he found so much whistling in the heart and so many sounds in his kidneys that it seemed impossible for him to be alive.

2. A disinfectant.

What surprised him most, however, was the logic of his wings. They seemed so natural on that completely human organism that he couldn't understand why other men didn't have them too.

When the child began school it had been some time since the sun and rain had caused the collapse of the chicken coop. The angel went dragging himself about here and there like a stray dying man. They would drive him out of the bedroom with a broom and a moment later find him in the kitchen. He seemed to be in so many places at the same time that they grew to think that he'd been duplicated, that he was reproducing himself all through the house, and the exasperated and unhinged Elisenda shouted that it was awful living in that hell full of angels. He could scarcely eat and his antiquarian eyes had also become so foggy that he went about bumping into posts. All he had left were the bare cannulae of his last feathers. Pelayo threw a blanket over him and extended him the charity of letting him sleep in the shed, and only then did they notice that he had a temperature at night, and was delirious with the tongue twisters of an old Norwegian. That was one of the few times they became alarmed, for they thought he was going to die and not even the wise neighbor woman had been able to tell them what to do with dead angels.

And yet he not only survived his worst winter, but seemed improved with the first sunny days. He remained motionless for several days in the farthest corner of the courtyard, where no one would see him, and at the beginning of December some large, stiff feathers began to grow on his wings, the feathers of a scarecrow, which looked more like another misfortune of decrepitude. But he must have known the reason for those changes, for he was quite careful that no one should notice them, that no one should hear the sea chanteys that he sometimes sang under the stars. One morning Elisenda was cutting some bunches of onions for lunch when a wind that seemed to come from the high seas blew into the kitchen. Then she went to the window and caught the angel in his first attempts at flight. They were so clumsy that his fingernails opened a furrow in the vegetable patch and he was on the point of knocking the shed down with the ungainly flapping that slipped on the light and couldn't get a grip on the air. But he did manage to gain altitude. Elisenda let out a sigh of relief, for herself and for him, when she saw him pass over the last houses, holding himself up in some way with the risky flapping of a senile vulture. She kept watching him even when she was through cutting the onions and she kept on watching until it was no longer possible for her to see him, because then he was no longer an annoyance in her life but an imaginary dot on the horizon of the sea.

1972

Contexts

8 THE AUTHOR'S WORK

Stories do not exist by themselves. Each is, first of all, part of the author's entire body of work—the **canon**—which, taken together, forms something like a huge single entity, a "superwork."

Even if it were desirable to read a story as a thing in itself, separate from everything else we had ever read or seen and from everything else the author had written, it is in practice impossible. We can *first* look into Chapman's Homer or Faulkner's fiction only once. After we read a second and then a third story by an author, we recognize the voice and have a sense of familiarity, as we would with a growing acquaintance. The author's voice and vision soon create in us certain expectations—of action, structure, characterization, world view, language. We come to expect short sentences from Hemingway, long ones from Faulkner, a certain amount of violence from both; we are not surprised if a Hemingway story is set in Michigan or Montmartre or on Mount Kilimanjaro, but we are surprised if a Faulkner story takes place outside Mississippi (his portion of which, we soon learn, Faulkner calls Yoknapatawpha). We inevitably bring to our interpretations of Mrs. Macomber's actions what we have learned about Hemingway's view of women from his other writings.

When we find an author's vision attractive or challenging, we naturally want to find out more about it, reading not only the literary works in the canon but the author's nonfictional prose—essays, letters, anything we can find that promises a fuller or clearer view of that unique way of looking at the world. Such knowledge is helpful—within limits. It was D. H. Lawrence, whose stories and statements we are about to read, who warned us to trust the tale and not the teller. A statement of beliefs or of intentions is not necessarily the same as what a given work may show or achieve—otherwise we'd all be saints and masters. It works the other way, too: often writers embody in their art what they cannot articulate, what indeed may not be expressible, in discursive prose.

The three short stories and brief selections from Lawrence's letters and criticism in this chapter are meant to make you feel more at home (and interested) in Lawrence's world and to raise questions about the relationship of the individual work to an author's work as a whole. Of course, short stories and a few pages of nonfiction alone cannot adequately represent the career of a writer who was a novelist, poet, critic, and essayist as well as short story writer, nor can three stories represent the richness and variety of the fifty or more that he published. However, as each story comes from a different decade, they do represent somewhat the continuities and changes within the

239

three decades of his career. Two of the stories, *Odour of Chrysanthe-mums* and *The Horse Dealer's Daughter*, are characteristically set in the coal-mining region of his native English Midlands, the scene of many of his novels, including three of the most famous, which also span his career—*Sons and Lovers* (1913), *The Rainbow* (1915), and *Lady Chatterley's Lover* (1928). The emphasis on the Midlands setting may be justified in terms of the canon, but can be misleading; there is no way in so few selections to represent both the emphasis on the Midlands and the scope of Lawrence's settings—his stories take place all over Western Europe, in the Americas, and in Australia. The London setting of *The Rocking-Horse Winner* only faintly indicates Lawrence's growing cosmopolitanism socially as well as geographi-cally. It also suggests, though superficially, his developing interest in the superreal and the mythic, concerns most fully developed in *The Plumed Serpent* (1926) and *The Man Who Died* (1929), and his movement in content and style away from nineteenth-century notions of realism.

It may be useful to see the first story here (one of Lawrence's very first stories) through the eyes of its first "professional" reader as he remembers the experience. Not long before World War I, a young woman sent to Ford Madox Ford, then editor of *The English Review*, three poems and a short story written by a schoolmaster friend of hers, the then unknown D. H. Lawrence. Ford read the story first and, he recalls, knew immediately that he had a genius on his hands, "a big one." The very title, *Odour of Chrysanthemums*, Ford noted, "makes an impact on the mind," indicates that the writer is observant (not many people realize that chrysanthemums have an odor), and sets the dark autumnal tone of the story. From the very first sentence, Ford goes on to say,

> . . . you know that this fellow with the power of observation is going to write whatever he writes about from the inside. The "Number 4" shows that. He will be the sort of fellow who knows that for the sort of people who work about engines, engines have a sort of individuality. He had to give the engine the personality of a num-ber. . . . "With seven full wagons". . . . The "seven" is good. The ordinary careless writer would say "some small wagons." This man knows what he wants. He sees the scene of his story exactly. He has an authoritative mind.
>
> "It appeared round the corner with loud threats of speed." . . . Good writing; slightly, but not *too* arresting. . . . "But the colt that it startled from among the gorse . . . out-distanced it at a canter." Good again. This fellow does not "state." He doesn't say: "It was coming slowly," or—what would have been a little better—"at seven miles an hour." Because even "seven miles an hour" means nothing definite for the untrained mind. It might mean something for a trainer or pedestrian racers. The imaginative writer writes for all humanity; he does not limit his desired readers to specialists. . . . But anyone knows that an engine that makes a great deal of noise and yet cannot over-take a colt at a canter must be a ludicrously ineffective machine. We know then that this fellow knows his job.

"The gorse still flickered indistinctly in the raw afternoon. . . ." Good too, distinctly good. This is the just-sufficient observation of Nature that gives you, in a single phrase, landscape, time of day, weather, season. It is a raw afternoon in autumn in a rather accented countryside. The engine would not come round a bend if there were not some obstacle to a straight course—a watercourse, a chain of hills. Hills, probably, because gorse grows on dry, broken-up waste country. They won't also be mountains or anything spectacular or the writer would have mentioned them. It is, then, just "country."

Your mind does all this for you without any ratiocination on your part. You are not, I mean, purposedly sleuthing. The engine and the trucks are there, with the white smoke blowing away over hummocks of gorse. Yet there has been practically none of the tiresome thing called descriptive nature, of which the English writer is as a rule so lugubriously lavish. . . . And then the woman comes in, carrying her basket. That indicates her status in life. She does not belong to the comfortable classes. Nor, since the engine is small, with trucks on a dud line, will the story be one of the Kipling-engineering type, with gleaming rails and gadgets, and the smell of oil warmed by the bearings and all the other tiresomenesses.

You are, then, for as long as the story lasts, to be in one of those untidy, unfinished landscapes where locomotives wander innocuously amongst women with baskets. That is to say, you are going to learn how what we used to call "the other half"—though we might as well have said other ninety-nine hundredths—lives. And if you are an editor and that is what you are after, you know that you have got what you want and you can pitch the story straight away into your wicker basket with the few accepted manuscripts and go onto some other occupation. . . . Because this man knows. He knows how to open a story with a sentence of the right cadence for holding the attention. He knows how to construct a paragraph. He knows the life he is writing about in a landscape just sufficiently constructed with a casual word here and there. You can trust him for the rest. . . .
—from "Before the Wars," *Selected Memories, The Bodley Head Ford Madox Ford* (London, 1962), I, 322–323

You will find the same precision of detail, suggesting the author's "inside view," his mastery of his material, in *The Horse Dealer's Daughter* —in paragraph six, for example, or the later description of the cemetery and the pond. You will find it even in that strange and strangely different story *The Rocking-Horse Winner*, in the first description of Paul's riding the horse, for example; in the description of the horse's "lowered face" ("Its red mouth was slightly open, its big eye was wide and glassy-bright") and in the precise accounting of the races, the odds, the money.

Ford read *Odour of Chrysanthemums* outside the context available to us. He did not know anything of the author and had read nothing else by him. Ford was an excellent editor (as well as writer) and to his credit spotted Lawrence's genius, a genius quite different from his own. Lawrence's mastery of detail made Ford trust him, but what he trusted him for seems to have been knowledge of the "other ninety-nine hundredths" of the population, the working class. An English writer of genius with knowledge of the working class was no doubt rare and notable in those pre-war days, and Lawrence's early works are full of details of the lives of miners and their families. But Lawrence, we now know, considered not class but the man–woman relationship the "great relationship of humanity," all others being subsidiary. Because we know that, know of Lawrence's notoriety for describing sexual relations, know his later works in which sexual relations are the major or basic concern—and perhaps because of the emphasis on sex in our own time—in reading *Odour of Chrysanthemums* we focus our attention not on the working-class mores but on the strange relationship between the Bateses. We ponder over Elizabeth's recognition that she not only had never really known her husband as himself despite their marital intimacy, but that by thinking of him only as her husband she had denied his individual selfhood and his otherness. The class element is still in the story, but the context of Lawrence's other works and utterances highlights this other human relationship.

What is implied about "real" or "true" love in the criticism of Elizabeth Bates's possessive love? There is nothing in that story that would specifically suggest the terrible risk of loving or the inexplicable descent of love on the soul beyond all reason and intent, or love as transfiguration and new birth, the kind of love we see in *The Horse Dealer's Daughter*. We cannot legitimately go back and put that kind of love in the earlier story, and yet, knowing Lawrence's later work, we can see its potential definition lying there, can see in what Elizabeth Bates's love was not the shadowy suggestion of what love must be. At least love as defined in *The Horse Dealer's Daughter* is not inconsistent with what real love might be in *Chrysanthemums*. Similarly, the notion of an emotional knowledge deeper than reason, language, and appearance that we see in Fergusson's loving Mabel, the horse dealer's daughter—

> With an inward groan he gave way, and let his heart yield towards her. A sudden gentle smile came on his face. And her eyes, which never left his face, slowly, slowly filled with tears. He watched the strange water rise in her eyes, like some slow fountain coming up. And his heart seemed to burn and melt away in his breast.

—prepares us for the same kind of deep emotional knowledge in the mother of Paul, the rocking-horse rider—

> . . . when her children were present, she always felt the center of her heart go hard. This troubled her, and in her manner she was all the more gentle and anxious for her children, as if she loved them very much. Only she herself knew that at the center of her heart was a hard little place that could not feel love, no, not for anybody. Everybody else said of her: "She is such a good mother. She adores her children." Only she herself, and her children themselves, knew it was not so.

—only in her case the knowledge is of lack of love.

The central, sometimes obsessive concerns and assumptions that permeate an author's work not only relate the individual stories to each other, mutually illuminating and enriching them, but they also serve as the author's trademark. It is not difficult to recognize or even parody a story by Lawrence.

Embodying these larger concerns and underlying such larger structures as plot, focus, and voice are the basic characteristics of the author's language, such as **diction** (choice of words and their use), sentence structure, **rhetorical tropes** (figures of thought and speech), imagery and **rhythm**—in other words, the author's style.

Perhaps because of the uniqueness of style, the vocabulary for discussing stylistic elements is not very precise or accessible. We can broadly characterize diction as **formal** (*The Cask of Amontillado*) or **informal** (most of the stories in this collection), and within the broad term *informal* identify a level of language that approximates the speech of ordinary people and call it colloquial (*My Man Bovanne*). But to characterize precisely an author's diction so that it adequately describes his or her work and marks it off from the works of contemporaries is a very difficult task indeed. We can note Hemingway's short sentences and Faulkner's long sentences, but it is hard to get much definition in the stylistic fingerprint of an author merely by measuring the lengths of sentences or tabulating connectives (though these qualities no doubt do subliminally contribute to the effect of the works on readers and do help them identify an author's work).

Diction and sentence structure contribute to the tone of a work, or the implied attitude or stance of the author toward the characters and events, an aspect somewhat analogous to tone of voice. When what is being said and the tone are consistent, it is difficult to separate one from the other; when there seems to be a discrepancy, we have some words that are useful to describe the difference. If the language seems exaggerated, we call it **overstatement**. The narrator of *Spotted Horses* is very fond of overstatement: "Flem Snopes had filled that whole country full of spotted horses," he says, and one "flew right over my team, big as a billboard and flying through the air like a hawk." When Wilson, in *Macomber*, admits that if the authorities discovered they had hunted from cars he would lose his license and there might be "Other unpleasantnesses," he is indulging in a bit of obvious **understatement**. When a word or expression says virtually the opposite of its literal meaning, we have an example of **verbal irony**. Yellow Blossom, in *The Horse-Swap*, has been bragging that he is "a *leetle* of the best man at a horse-swap" that anyone has seen, but when his own words are thrown back at him mockingly later, their meaning is so different that the difference is painful to him. There are also nonverbal forms of irony, the most common of which is **dramatic irony**, in which a character holds a position or has an expectation that is reversed or fulfilled in an unexpected way. Knowing her husband's habit of drinking himself into unconsciousness, Elizabeth Bates expects him to be brought home like a log. How is her expectation fulfilled? She had also said bitterly, "But he needn't come rolling in here in his pit-dirt, for *I* won't wash him," and yet she does. Why is her determination altered? As you read through, or look back over this story, watch for other reversed or unexpectedly fulfilled expectations.

Another and highly emphasized element of style is **imagery.** In its broadest sense imagery includes any sensory detail or evocation in a work. Note how much more imagery in that sense we find in *The Old People* than in, say, *The Lottery.* Imagery in this broad sense, however, is so prevalent in literature that it would take exhaustive statistics to differentiate styles by counting the number of sensory elements per hundred or thousand words, categorizing the images as primarily visual, tactile, etc. In a more restricted sense imagery refers to figurative language (see Chapter 4 on symbols), particularly that which defines an abstraction or any emotional or psychological state with a sensory comparison. The opening paragraph of *Odour of Chrysanthemums* illustrates the broader definition of imagery, and this passage from later in the same story may represent the figurative sense: "Life with its smoky burning gone from him, had left him apart. . . . In her womb was ice of fear. . . ."

We might say that if an author's vision gives us his or her profile, the style gives us a fingerprint—though the fingerprint is unique and definitive, it is also harder to come by than a glimpse of a profile. Ultimately, however, vision and style are less distinguishable from each other than the profile-fingerprint image suggests. For vision and style, just like history and structure, do more than interact: they are inextricably fused or compounded. Let us look back at the Ford passage. He says this of "the gorse, which still flickered indistinctly in the raw afternoon" (though he misquotes it slightly and rather loosely calls it a phrase):

> . . . Good too, distinctly good. This is the just-sufficient observation
> of Nature that gives you, in a single phrase, landscape, time of day,
> weather, season.

Is this vision or style? The observation of Nature is clearly vision, but expressing that vision economically, tautly, is style. The two merge.

Whatever else this passage is, it is vintage, typical Lawrence. Perhaps it would take more than just these ten words, but surely in a paragraph or two we know we're in the fictional world that he perceived and that he embodied in his stories, novels, poems in a language of his own created out of that language we share.

D. H. LAWRENCE

Odour of Chrysanthemums

1

The small locomotive engine, Number 4, came clanking, stumbling down from Selston with seven full wagons. It appeared round the corner with loud threats of speed, but the colt that it startled from among the gorse, which still flickered indistinctly in the raw afternoon, out-distanced it at a canter. A woman, walking up the railway line to Underwood, drew back into the hedge, held her basket aside, and watched the footplate of the engine advancing. The trucks thumped heavily past, one by one, with slow inevitable movement, as she stood insignificantly trapped between the jolting black wagons and the hedge; then they curved away towards the coppice where the withered oak leaves dropped noiselessly, while the birds, pulling at the scarlet hips beside the track, made off into the dusk that had already crept into the spinney. In the open, the smoke from the engine sank and cleaved to the rough grass. The fields were dreary and forsaken, and in the marshy strip that led to the whimsey, a reedy pit-pond, the fowls had already abandoned their run among the alders, to roost in the tarred fowl-house. The pit-bank loomed up beyond the pond, flames like red sores licking its ashy sides, in the afternoon's stagnant light. Just beyond rose the tapering chimneys and the clumsy black headstocks of Brinsley Colliery. The two wheels were spinning fast up against the sky, and the winding engine rapped out its little spasms. The miners were being turned up.

The engine whistled as it came into the wide bay of railway lines[1] beside the colliery, where rows of trucks stood in harbor.

Miners, single, trailing and in groups, passed like shadows diverging home. At the edge of the ribbed level of sidings squat a low cottage, three steps down from the cinder track. A large bony vine clutched at the house, as if to claw down the tiled roof. Round the bricked yard grew a few wintry primroses. Beyond, the long garden sloped down to a bush-covered brook course. There were some twiggy apple trees, winter-crack trees, and ragged cabbages. Beside the path hung dishevelled pink chrysanthemums, like pink cloths hung on bushes. A woman came stooping out of the felt-covered fowl-house, half-way down the garden. She closed and padlocked the door, then drew herself erect, having brushed some bits from her white apron.

She was a tall woman of imperious mien, handsome, with definite black eyebrows. Her smooth black hair was parted exactly. For a few moments she stood steadily watching the miners as they passed along the railway: then she turned towards the brook course. Her face was calm and set, her mouth was closed with disillusionment. After a moment she called:

"John!" There was no answer. She waited, and then said distinctly: "Where are you?"

"Here!" replied a child's sulky voice from among the bushes. The woman looked piercingly through the dusk.

"Are you at that brook?" she asked sternly.

For answer the child showed himself before the raspberry-canes that rose like whips. He was a small, sturdy boy of five. He stood quite still, defiantly.

"Oh!" said the mother, conciliated. "I thought you were down at that wet brook—and you remember what I told you——"

The boy did not move or answer.

"Come, come on in," she said more gently, "it's getting dark. There's your grandfather's engine coming down the line!"

---

1. Flat, level area of railroad tracks, probably bending away.

The lad advanced slowly, with resentful, taciturn movement. He was dressed in trousers and waistcoat of cloth that was too thick and hard for the size of the garments. They were evidently cut down from a man's clothes.

As they went slowly towards the house he tore at the ragged wisps of chrysanthemums and dropped the petals in handfuls along the path. "Don't do that—it does look nasty," said his mother. He refrained, and she, suddenly pitiful, broke off a twig with three or four wan flowers and held them against her face. When mother and son reached the yard her hand hesitated, and instead of laying the flower aside, she pushed it in her apron-band. The mother and son stood at the foot of the three steps looking across the bay of lines at the passing home of the miners. The trundle of the small train was imminent. Suddenly the engine loomed past the house and came to a stop opposite the gate.

The engine-driver, a short man with round gray beard, leaned out of the cab high above the woman.

"Have you got a cup of tea?" he said in a cheery, hearty fashion.

It was her father. She went in, saying she would mash.[2] Directly, she returned.

"I didn't come to see you on Sunday," began the little gray-bearded man.

"I didn't expect you," said his daughter.

The engine-driver winced; then, reassuming his cheery, airy manner, he said:

"Oh, have you heard then? Well, and what do you think——?"

"I think it is soon enough," she replied.

At her brief censure the little man made an impatient gesture, and said coaxingly, yet with dangerous coldness:

"Well, what's a man to do? It's no sort of life for a man of my years, to sit at my own hearth like a stranger. And if I'm going to marry again it may as well be soon as late—what does it matter to anybody?"

The woman did not reply, but turned and went into the house. The man in the engine-cab stood assertive, till she returned with a cup of tea and a piece of bread and butter on a plate. She went up the steps and stood near the footplace of the hissing engine.

"You needn't 'a' brought me bread an' butter," said her father. "But a cup of tea"—he sipped appreciatively—"it's very nice." He sipped for a moment or two, then: "I hear as Walter's got another bout on," he said.

"When hasn't he?" said the woman bitterly.

"I heerd tell of him in the 'Lord Nelson'[3] braggin' as he was going to spend that b—— afore he went: half a sovereign[4] that was."

"When?" asked the woman.

"A' Sat'day night—I know that's true."

"Very likely," she laughed bitterly. "He gives me twenty-three shillings."

"Aye, it's a nice thing, when a man can do nothing with his money but make a beast of himself!" said the gray-whiskered man. The woman

2. Prepare (tea).
3. A public house, pub.
4. A sovereign is an English pound, then

worth $4.86+; there are 20 shillings (see below) to the pound.

turned her head away. Her father swallowed the last of his tea and handed her the cup.

"Aye," he sighed, wiping his mouth. "It's a settler, it is——"

He put his hand on the lever. The little engine strained and groaned, and the train rumbled towards the crossing. The woman again looked across the metals. Darkness was settling over the spaces of the railway and trucks; the miners, in gray somber group, were still passing home. The winding engine pulsed hurriedly, with brief pauses. Elizabeth Bates looked at the dreary flow of men, then she went indoors. Her husband did not come.

The kitchen was small and full of firelight; red coals piled glowing up the chimney mouth. All the life of the room seemed in the white, warm hearth and the steel fender reflecting the red fire. The cloth was laid for tea; cups glinted in the shadows. At the back, where the lowest stairs protruded into the room, the boy sat struggling with a knife and a piece of white wood. He was almost hidden in the shadow. It was half-past four. They had but to await the father's coming to begin tea. As the mother watched her son's sullen little struggle with the wood, she saw herself in his silence and pertinacity; she saw the father in her child's indifference to all but himself. She seemed to be occupied by her husband. He had probably gone past his home, slunk past his own door, to drink before he came in, while his dinner spoiled and wasted in waiting. She glanced at the clock, then took the potatoes to strain them in the yard. The garden and fields beyond the brook were closed in uncertain darkness. When she rose with the saucepan, leaving the drain steaming into the night behind her, she saw the yellow lamps were lit along the high road that went up the hill away beyond the space of the railway lines and the field.

Then again she watched the men trooping home, fewer now and fewer.

Indoors the fire was sinking and the room was dark red. The woman put her saucepan on the hob, and set a batter-pudding near the mouth of the oven. Then she stood unmoving. Directly, gratefully, came quick young steps to the door. Someone hung on the latch a moment, then a little girl entered and began pulling off her outdoor things, dragging a mass of curls, just ripening from gold to brown, over her eyes with her hat.

Her mother chid her for coming late from school, and said she would have to keep her at home the dark winter days.

"Why, mother, it's hardly a bit dark yet. The lamp's not lighted, and my father's not home."

"No, he isn't. But it's a quarter to five! Did you see anything of him?"

The child became serious. She looked at her mother with large wistful blue eyes.

"No, mother, I've never seen him. Why? Has he come up an' gone past, to Old Brinsley? He hasn't, mother, 'cos I never saw him."

"He'd watch that," said the mother bitterly, "he'd take care as you didn't see him. But you may depend upon it, he's seated in the 'Prince o' Wales.' He wouldn't be this late."

The girl looked at her mother piteously.

"Let's have our teas, mother, should we?" said she.

The mother called John to table. She opened the door once more and looked out across the darkness of the lines. All was deserted: she could not hear the winding engines.

"Perhaps," she said to herself, "he's stopped to get some ripping[5] done."

They sat down to tea. John, at the end of the table near the door, was almost lost in the darkness. Their faces were hidden from each other. The girl crouched against the fender slowly moving a thick piece of bread before the fire. The lad, his face a dusky mark on the shadow, sat watching her who was transfigured in the red glow.

"I do think it's beautiful to look in the fire," said the child.

"Do you?" said her mother. "Why?"

"It's so red, and full of little caves—and it feels so nice, and you can fair smell it."

"It'll want mending directly," replied her mother, "and then if your father comes he'll carry on and say there never is a fire when a man comes home sweating from the pit. A public house is always warm enough."

There was silence till the boy said complainingly: "Make haste, our Annie."

"Well, I am doing! I can't make the fire do it no faster, can I?"

"She keeps wafflin'[6] it about so's to make 'er slow," grumbled the boy.

"Don't have such an evil imagination, child," replied the mother.

Soon the room was busy in the darkness with the crisp sound of crunching. The mother ate very little. She drank her tea determinedly, and sat thinking. When she rose her anger was evident in the stern unbending of her head. She looked at the pudding in the fender, and broke out:

"It is a scandalous thing as a man can't even come home to his dinner! If it's crozzled[7] up to a cinder I don't see why I should care. Past his very door he goes to get to a public house, and here I sit with his dinner waiting for him——"

She went out. As she dropped piece after piece of coal on the red fire, the shadows fell on the walls, till the room was almost in total darkness.

"I canna see," grumbled the invisible John. In spite of herself, the mother laughed.

"You know the way to your mouth," she said. She set the dustpan outside the door. When she came again like a shadow on the hearth, the lad repeated, complaining sulkily:

"I canna see."

"Good gracious!" cried the mother irritably, "you're as bad as your father if it's a bit dusk!"

Nevertheless, she took a paper spill from a sheaf on the mantelpiece and proceeded to light the lamp that hung from the ceiling in the middle of the room. As she reached up, her figure displayed itself just rounding with maternity.

"Oh, mother——!" exclaimed the girl.

"What?" said the woman, suspended in the act of putting the lamp-

---

5. Coal-mining term for taking down the roof of an underground road in order to make it higher.

6. Waving.

7. Shriveled.

glass over the flame. The copper reflector shone handsomely on her, as she stood with uplifted arm, turning to face her daughter.

"You've got a flower in your apron!" said the child, in a little rapture at this unusual event.

"Goodness me!" exclaimed the woman, relieved. "One would think the house was afire." She replaced the glass and waited a moment before turning up the wick. A pale shadow was seen floating vaguely on the floor.

"Let me smell!" said the child, still rapturously, coming forward and putting her face to her mother's waist.

"Go along, silly!" said the mother, turning up the lamp. The light revealed their suspense so that the woman felt it almost unbearable. Annie was still bending at her waist. Irritably, the mother took the flowers out from her apron-band.

"Oh, mother—don't take them out!" Annie cried, catching her hand and trying to replace the sprig.

"Such nonsense!" said the mother, turning away. The child put the pale chrysanthemums to her lips, murmuring:

"Don't they smell beautiful!"

Her mother gave a short laugh.

"No," she said, "not to me. It was chrysanthemums when I married him, and chrysanthemums when you were born, and the first time they ever brought him home drunk, he'd got brown chrysanthemums in his buttonhole."

She looked at the children. Their eyes and their parted lips were wondering. The mother sat rocking in silence for some time. Then she looked at the clock.

"Twenty minutes to six!" In a tone of fine bitter carelessness she continued: "Eh, he'll not come now till they bring him. There he'll stick! But he needn't come rolling in here in his pit-dirt, for *I* won't wash him. He can lie on the floor—Eh, what a fool I've been, what a fool! And this is what I came here for, to this dirty hole, rats and all, for him to slink past his very door. Twice last week—he's begun now——"

She silenced herself, and rose to clear the table.

While for an hour or more the children played, subduedly intent, fertile of imagination, united in fear of the mother's wrath, and in dread of their father's homecoming, Mrs. Bates sat in her rocking-chair making a "singlet" of thick cream-colored flannel, which gave a dull wounded sound as she tore off the gray edge. She worked at her sewing with energy, listening to the children, and her anger wearied itself, lay down to rest, opening its eyes from time to time and steadily watching, its ears raised to listen. Sometimes even her anger quailed and shrank, and the mother suspended her sewing, tracing the footsteps that thudded along the sleepers outside; she would lift her head sharply to bid the children "hush," but she recovered herself in time, and the footsteps went past the gate, and the children were not flung out of their play-world.

But at last Annie sighed, and gave in. She glanced at her wagon of slippers, and loathed the game. She turned plaintively to her mother.

"Mother!"—but she was inarticulate.

John crept out like a frog from under the sofa. His mother glanced up.

"Yes," she said, "just look at those shirtsleeves!"

The boy held them out to survey them, saying nothing. Then somebody called in a hoarse voice away down the line, and suspense bristled in the room, till two people had gone by outside, talking.

"It is time for bed," said the mother.

"My father hasn't come," wailed Annie plaintively. But her mother was primed with courage.

"Never mind. They'll bring him when he does come—like a log." She meant there would be no scene. "And he may sleep on the floor till he wakes himself. I know he'll not go to work tomorrow after this!"

The children had their hands and faces wiped with a flannel.[8] They were very quiet. When they had put on their nightdresses, they said their prayers, the boy mumbling. The mother looked down at them, at the brown silken bush of intertwining curls in the nape of the girl's neck, at the little black head of the lad, and her heart burst with anger at their father, who caused all three such distress. The children hid their faces in her skirts for comfort.

When Mrs. Bates came down, the room was strangely empty, with a tension of expectancy. She took up her sewing and stitched for some time without raising her head. Meantime her anger was tinged with fear.

2

The clock struck eight and she rose suddenly, dropping her sewing on her chair. She went to the stair-foot door, opened it, listening. Then she went out, locking the door behind her.

Something scuffled in the yard, and she started, though she knew it was only the rats with which the place was overrun. The night was very dark. In the great bay of railway lines, bulked with trucks, there was no trace of light, only away back she could see a few yellow lamps at the pit-top, and the red smear of the burning pit-bank on the night. She hurried along the edge of the track, then, crossing the converging lines, came to the stile by the white gates, whence she emerged on the road. Then the fear which had led her shrank. People were walking up to New Brinsley; she saw the lights in the houses; twenty yards farther on were the broad windows of the 'Prince of Wales,' very warm and bright, and the loud voices of men could be heard distinctly. What a fool she had been to imagine that anything had happened to him! He was merely drinking over there at the 'Prince of Wales.' She faltered. She had never yet been to fetch him, and she never would go. So she continued her walk toward the long straggling line of houses, standing back on the highway. She entered a passage between the dwellings.

"Mr. Rigley?—Yes! Did you want him? No, he's not in at this minute."

The raw-boned woman leaned forward from her dark scullery and peered at the other, upon whom fell a dim light through the blind of the kitchen window.

"Is it Mrs. Bates?" she asked in a tone tinged with respect.

"Yes. I wondered if your Master was at home. Mine hasn't come yet."

"'Asn't 'e! Oh, Jack's been 'ome an' 'ad 'is dinner an' gone out. 'E's just gone for 'alf an hour afore bed-time. Did you call at the 'Prince of Wales'?"

8. Washrag.

"No——"

"No, you didn't like——! It's not very nice." The other woman was indulgent. There was an awkward pause. "Jack never said nothink about—about your Master," she said.

"No!—I expect he's stuck in there!"

Elizabeth Bates said this bitterly, and with recklessness. She knew that the woman across the yard was standing at her door listening, but she did not care. As she turned:

"Stop a minute! I'll just go an' ask Jack if 'e knows anythink," said Mrs. Rigley.

"Oh no—I wouldn't like to put——!"

"Yes, I will, if you'll just step inside an' see as th' childer doesn't come downstairs and set theirselves afire."

Elizabeth Bates, murmuring a remonstrance, stepped inside. The other woman apologized for the state of the room.

The kitchen needed apology. There were little frocks and trousers and childish undergarments on the squab[9] and on the floor, and a litter of playthings everywhere. On the black American cloth[1] of the table were pieces of bread and cake, crusts, slops, and a teapot with cold tea.

"Eh, ours is just as bad," said Elizabeth Bates, looking at the woman, not at the house. Mrs. Rigley put a shawl over her head and hurried out, saying:

"I shanna be a minute."

The other sat, noting with faint disapproval the general untidiness of the room. Then she fell to counting the shoes of various sizes scattered over the floor. There were twelve. She sighed and said to herself: "No wonder!"—glancing at the litter. There came the scratching of two pairs of feet on the yard, and the Rigleys entered. Elizabeth Bates rose. Rigley was a big man, with very large bones. His head looked particularly bony. Across his temple was a blue scar, caused by a wound got in the pit, a wound in which the coal-dust remained blue like tattooing.

"'Asna 'e come whoam yit?" asked the man, without any form of greeting, but with deference and sympathy. "I couldna say wheer he is—'e's non ower theer!"—he jerked his head to signify the 'Prince of Wales.'

" 'E's 'appen[2] gone up to th' 'Yew,' " said Mrs. Rigley.

There was another pause. Rigley had evidently something to get off his mind:

"Ah left 'im finishin' a stint," he began. "Loose-all[3] 'ad bin gone about ten minutes when we com'n away, an' I shouted: 'Are ter comin', Walt?' an' 'e said: 'Go on, Ah shanna be but a'ef a minnit,' so we com'n ter th' bottom, me an' Bowers, thinkin' as 'e wor just behint, an' 'ud come up i' th' next bantle[4]——"

He stood perplexed, as if answering a charge of deserting his mate. Elizabeth Bates, now again certain of disaster, hastened to reassure him:

"I expect 'e's gone up to th' 'Yew Tree,' as you say. It's not the first time. I've fretted myself into a fever before now. He'll come home when they carry him."

9. Sofa.
1. Enameled oilcloth.
2. Perhaps.
3. Signal to quit work and come to the surface.
4. An open seat or car of the lift or elevator that takes the miners to the surface.

"Ay, isn't it too bad!" deplored the other woman.

"I'll just step up to Dick's an' see if 'e *is* theer," offered the man, afraid of appearing alarmed, afraid of taking liberties.

"Oh, I wouldn't think of bothering you that far," said Elizabeth Bates, with emphasis, but he knew she was glad of his offer.

As they stumbled up the entry, Elizabeth Bates heard Rigley's wife run across the yard and open her neighbor's door. At this, suddenly all the blood in her body seemed to switch away from her heart.

"Mind!"[5] warned Rigley. "Ah've said many a time as Ah'd fill up them ruts in this entry, sumb'dy 'll be breakin' their legs yit."

She recovered herself and walked quickly along with the miner.

"I don't like leaving the children in bed, and nobody in the house," she said.

"No, you dunna!" he replied courteously. They were soon at the gate of the cottage.

"Well, I shanna be many minnits. Dunna you be frettin' now, 'e'll be all right," said the butty.[6]

"Thank you very much, Mr. Rigley," she replied.

"You're welcome!" he stammered, moving away. "I shanna be many minnits."

The house was quiet. Elizabeth Bates took off her hat and shawl, and rolled back the rug. When she had finished, she sat down. It was a few minutes past nine. She was startled by the rapid chuff of the winding engine at the pit, and the sharp whirr of the brakes on the rope as it descended. Again she felt the painful sweep of her blood, and she put her hand to her side, saying aloud: "Good gracious!—it's only the nine o'clock deputy going down," rebuking herself.

She sat still, listening. Half an hour of this, and she was wearied out.

"What am I working myself up like this for?" she said pitiably to herself, "I s'll only be doing myself some damage."

She took out her sewing again.

At a quarter to ten there were footsteps. One person! She watched for the door to open. It was an elderly woman, in a black bonnet and a black woollen shawl—his mother. She was about sixty years old, pale, with blue eyes, and her face all wrinkled and lamentable. She shut the door and turned to her daughter-in-law peevishly.

"Eh, Lizzie, whatever shall we do, whatever shall we do!" she cried.

Elizabeth drew back a little, sharply.

"What is it, mother?" she said.

The elder woman seated herself on the sofa.

"I don't know, child, I can't tell you!"—she shook her head slowly. Elizabeth sat watching her, anxious and vexed.

"I don't know," replied the grandmother, sighing very deeply. "There's no end to my troubles, there isn't. The things I've gone through, I'm sure it's enough——!" She wept without wiping her eyes, the tears running.

"But, mother," interrupted Elizabeth, "what do you mean? What is it?"

The grandmother slowly wiped her eyes. The fountains of her tears

---

5. Watch out.   6. Buddy, fellow worker.

were stopped by Elizabeth's directness. She wiped her eyes slowly.

"Poor child! Eh, you poor thing!" she moaned. "I don't know what we're going to do, I don't—and you as you are—it's a thing, it is indeed!"

Elizabeth waited.

"Is he dead?" she asked, and at the words her heart swung violently, though she felt a slight flush of shame at the ultimate extravagance of the question. Her words sufficiently frightened the old lady, almost brought her to herself.

"Don't say so, Elizabeth! We'll hope it's not as bad as that; no, may the Lord spare us that, Elizabeth. Jack Rigley came just as I was sittin' down to a glass afore going to bed, an' 'e said: ' 'Appen you'll go down th' line, Mrs. Bates. Walt's had an accident. 'Appen you'll go an' sit wi' 'er till we can get him home.' I hadn't time to ask him a word afore he was gone. An' I put my bonnet on an' come straight down, Lizzie. I thought to myself: 'Eh, that poor blessed child, if anybody should come an' tell her of a sudden, there's no knowin' what'll 'appen to 'er.' You mustn't let it upset you, Lizzie—or you know what to expect. How long is it, six months—or is it five, Lizzie? Ay!"—the old woman shook her head—"time slips on, it slips on! Ay!"

Elizabeth's thoughts were busy elsewhere. If he was killed—would she be able to manage on the little pension and what she could earn? —she counted up rapidly. If he was hurt—they wouldn't take him to the hospital—how tiresome he would be to nurse!—but perhaps she'd be able to get him away from the drink and his hateful ways. She would—while he was ill. The tears offered to come to her eyes at the picture. But what sentimental luxury was this she was beginning? She turned to consider the children. At any rate she was absolutely necessary for them. They were her business.

"Ay!" repeated the old woman, "it seems but a week or two since he brought me his first wages. Ay—he was a good lad, Elizabeth, he was, in his way. I don't know why he got to be such a trouble, I don't. He was a happy lad at home, only full of spirits. But there's no mistake he's been a handful of trouble, he has! I hope the Lord'll spare him to mend his ways. I hope so, I hope so. You've had a sight o' trouble with him, Elizabeth, you have indeed. But he was a jolly enough lad wi' me, he was, I can assure you. I don't know how it is. . . ."

The old woman continued to muse aloud, a monotonous irritating sound, while Elizabeth thought concentratedly, startled once, when she heard the winding-engine chuff quickly, and the brakes skirr with a shriek. Then she heard the engine more slowly, and the brakes made no sound. The old woman did not notice. Elizabeth waited in suspense. The mother-in-law talked, with lapses into silence.

"But he wasn't your son, Lizzie, an' it makes a difference. Whatever he was, I remember him when he was little, an' I learned to understand him and to make allowances. You've got to make allowances for them——"

It was half-past ten, and the old woman was saying: "But it's trouble from beginning to end; you're never too old for trouble, never too old for that——" when the gate banged back, and there were heavy feet on the steps.

"I'll go, Lizzie, let me go," cried the old woman, rising. But Elizabeth was at the door. It was a man in pit-clothes.

"They're bringin' 'im, Missis," he said. Elizabeth's heart halted a moment. Then it surged on again, almost suffocating her.

"Is he—is it bad?" she asked.

The man turned away, looking at the darkness:

"The doctor says 'e'd been dead hours. 'E saw 'im i' th' lamp-cabin."

The old woman, who stood just behind Elizabeth, dropped into a chair, and folded her hands, crying: "Oh, my boy, my boy!"

"Hush!" said Elizabeth, with a sharp twitch of a frown. "Be still, mother, don't waken th' children: I wouldn't have them down for anything!"

The old woman moaned softly, rocking herself. The man was drawing away. Elizabeth took a step forward.

"How was it?" she asked.

"Well, I couldn't say for sure," the man replied, very ill at ease. " 'E wor finishin' a stint an' th' butties 'ad gone, an' a lot o' stuff come down atop 'n 'im.'

"And crushed him?" cried the widow, with a shudder.

"No," said the man, "it fell at th' back of 'im. 'E wor under th' face, an' it niver touched 'im. It shut 'im in. It seems 'e wor smothered."

Elizabeth shrank back. She heard the old woman behind her cry:

"What?—what did 'e say it was?"

The man replied, more loudly: " 'E wor smothered!"

Then the old woman wailed aloud, and this relieved Elizabeth.

"Oh, mother," she said, putting her hand on the old woman, "don't waken th' children, don't waken th' children."

She wept a little, unknowing, while the old mother rocked herself and moaned. Elizabeth remembered that they were bringing him home, and she must be ready. "They'll lay him in the parlor," she said to herself, standing a moment pale and perplexed.

Then she lighted a candle and went into the tiny room. The air was cold and damp, but she could not make a fire, there was no fireplace. She set down the candle and looked round. The candlelight glittered on the luster-glasses[7] on the two vases that held some of the pink chrysanthemums, and on the dark mahogany. There was a cold, deathly smell of chrysanthemums in the room. Elizabeth stood looking at the flowers. She turned away, and calculated whether there would be room to lay him on the floor, between the couch and the chiffonier. She pushed the chairs aside. There would be room to lay him down and to step round him. Then she fetched the old red tablecloth, and another old cloth, spreading them down to save her bit of carpet. She shivered on leaving the parlor; so, from the dresser drawer she took a clean shirt and put it at the fire to air. All the time her mother-in-law was rocking herself in the chair and moaning.

"You'll have to move from there, mother," said Elizabeth. "They'll be bringing him in. Come in the rocker."

The old mother rose mechanically, and seated herself by the fire, continuing to lament. Elizabeth went into the pantry for another

7. **Glass pendants around the edge of an ornamental vase.**

candle, and there, in the little pent-house[8] under the naked tiles, she heard them coming. She stood still in the pantry doorway, listening. She heard them pass the end of the house, and come awkwardly down the three steps, a jumble of shuffling footsteps and muttering voices. The old woman was silent. The men were in the yard.

Then Elizabeth heard Matthews, the manager of the pit, say: "You go in first, Jim. Mind!"

The door came open, and the two women saw a collier backing into the room, holding one end of a stretcher, on which they could see the nailed pit-boots of the dead man. The two carriers halted, the man at the head stooping to the lintel of the door.

"Wheer will you have him?" asked the manager, a short, white-bearded man.

Elizabeth roused herself and came from the pantry carrying the unlighted candle.

"In the parlor," she said.

"In there, Jim!" pointed the manager, and the carriers backed round into the tiny room. The coat with which they had covered the body fell off as they awkwardly turned through the two doorways, and the women saw their man, naked to the waist, lying stripped for work. The old woman began to moan in a low voice of horror.

"Lay th' stretcher at th' side," snapped the manager, "an' put 'im on th' cloths. Mind now, mind! Look you now——!"

One of the men had knocked off a vase of chrysanthemums. He stared awkwardly, then they set down the stretcher. Elizabeth did not look at her husband. As soon as she could get in the room, she went and picked up the broken vase and the flowers.

"Wait a minute!" she said.

The three men waited in silence while she mopped up the water with a duster.

"Eh, what a job, what a job, to be sure!" the manager was saying, rubbing his brow with trouble and perplexity. "Never knew such a thing in my life, never! He'd no business to ha' been left. I never knew such a thing in my life! Fell over him clean as a whistle, an' shut him in. Not four foot of space, there wasn't—yet it scarce bruised him."

He looked down at the dead man, lying prone, half naked, all grimed with cold-dust.

"'Sphyxiated,' the doctor said. It *is* the most terrible job I've ever known. Seems as if it was done o' purpose. Clean over him, an' shut 'im in, like a mouse-trap"—he made a sharp, descending gesture with his hand.

The colliers standing by jerked aside their heads in hopeless comment.

The horror of the thing bristled upon them all.

Then they heard the girl's voice upstairs calling shrilly: "Mother, mother—who is it? Mother, who is it?"

Elizabeth hurried to the foot of the stairs and opened the door:

"Go to sleep!" she commanded sharply. "What are you shouting about? Go to sleep at once—there's nothing——"

8. Structure, usually with a sloping roof, attached to house.

Then she began to mount the stairs. They could hear her on the boards, and on the plaster floor of the little bedroom. They could hear her distinctly:

"What's the mater now?—what's the matter with you, silly thing?" —her voice was much agitated, with an unreal gentleness.

"I thought it was some men come," said the plaintive voice of the child. "Has he come?"

"Yes, they've brought him. There's nothing to make a fuss about. Go to sleep now, like a good child."

They could hear her voice in the bedroom, they waited whilst she covered the children under the bedclothes.

"Is he drunk?" asked the girl, timidly, faintly.

"No! No—he's not! He—he's asleep."

"Is he asleep downstairs?"

"Yes—and don't make a noise."

There was silence for a moment, then the men heard the frightened child again:

"What's that noise?"

"It's nothing, I tell you, what are you bothering for?"

The noise was the grandmother moaning. She was oblivious of everything, sitting on her chair rocking and moaning. The manager put his hand on her arm and bade her "Sh—sh!!"

The old woman opened her eyes and looked at him. She was shocked by this interruption, and seemed to wonder.

"What time is it?" the plaintive thin voice of the child, sinking back unhappily into sleep, asked this last question.

"Ten o'clock," answered the mother more softly. Then she must have bent down and kissed the children.

Matthews beckoned to the men to come away. They put on their caps and took up the stretcher. Stepping over the body, they tiptoed out of the house. None of them spoke till they were far from the wakeful children.

When Elizabeth came down she found her mother alone on the parlor floor, leaning over the dead man, the tears dropping on him.

"We must lay him out," the wife said. She put on the kettle, then returning knelt at the feet, and began to unfasten the knotted leather laces. The room was clammy and dim with only one candle, so that she had to bend her face almost to the floor. At last she got off the heavy boots and put them away.

"You must help me now," she whispered to the old woman. Together they stripped the man.

When they arose, saw him lying in the naïve dignity of death, the women stood arrested in fear and respect. For a few moments they remained still, looking down, the old mother whimpering. Elizabeth felt countermanded. She saw him, how utterly inviolable he lay in himself. She had nothing to do with him. She could not accept it. Stooping, she laid her hand on him, in claim. He was still warm, for the mine was hot where he had died. His mother had his face between her hands, and was murmuring incoherently. The old tears fell in succession as drops from wet leaves; the mother was not weeping, merely her tears flowed. Elizabeth embraced the body of her husband, with cheek and lips. She seemed to be listening, inquiring, trying to get some connection. But she could not. She was driven away. He was impregnable.

She rose, went into the kitchen, where she poured warm water into a bowl, brought soap and flannel and a soft towel.

"I must wash him," she said.

Then the old mother rose stiffly, and watched Elizabeth as she carefully washed his face, carefully brushing the big blond moustache from his mouth with the flannel. She was afraid with a bottomless fear, so she ministered to him. The old woman, jealous, said:

"Let me wipe him!"—and she kneeled on the other side drying slowly as Elizabeth washed, her big black bonnet sometimes brushing the dark head of her daughter-in-law. They worked thus in silence for a long time. They never forgot it was death, and the touch of the man's dead body gave them strange emotions, different in each of the women; a great dread possessed them both, the mother felt the lie was given to her womb, she was denied; the wife felt the utter isolation of the human soul, the child within her was a weight apart from her.

At last it was finished. He was a man of handsome body, and his face showed no traces of drink. He was blond, full-fleshed, with fine limbs. But he was dead.

"Bless him," whispered his mother, looking always at his face, and speaking out of sheer terror. "Dear lad—bless him!" She spoke in a faint, sibilant ecstasy of fear and mother love.

Elizabeth sank down again to the floor, and put her face against his neck, and trembled and shuddered. But she had to draw away again. He was dead, and her living flesh had no place against his. A great dread and weariness held her: she was so unavailing. Her life was gone like this.

"White as milk he is, clear as a twelve-month baby, bless him, the darling!" the old mother murmured to herself. "Not a mark on him, clear and clean and white, beautiful as ever a child was made," she murmured with pride. Elizabeth kept her face hidden.

"He went peaceful, Lizzie—peaceful as sleep. Isn't he beautiful, the lamb? Ay—he must ha' made his peace, Lizzie. 'Appen he made it all right, Lizzie, shut in there. He'd have time. He wouldn't look like this if he hadn't made his peace. The lamb, the dear lamb. Eh, but he had a hearty laugh. I loved to hear it. He had the heartiest laugh, Lizzie, as a lad——"

Elizabeth looked up. The man's mouth was fallen back, slightly open under the cover of the moustache. The eyes, half shut, did not show glazed in the obscurity. Life with its smoky burning gone from him, had left him apart and utterly alien to her. And she knew what a stranger he was to her. In her womb was ice of fear, because of this separate stranger with whom she had been living as one flesh. Was this what it all meant—utter, intact separateness, obscured by heat of living? In dread she turned her face away. The fact was too deadly. There had been nothing between them, and yet they had come to-gether, exchanging their nakedness repeatedly. Each time he had taken her, they had been two isolated beings, far apart as now. He was no more responsible than she. The child was like ice in her womb. For as she looked at the dead man, her mind, cold and detached, said clearly: "Who am I? What have I been doing? I have been fighting a husband who did not exist. *He* existed all the time. What wrong have I done? What was that I have been living with? There lies the reality, this man." And her soul died in her for fear: she knew she had never seen him, he had never seen her, they had met in the dark and had fought in the dark, not knowing whom they met nor whom they fought. And now she saw, and turned silent in seeing. For she had been wrong. She had said he was something he was not; she had felt familiar with him. Whereas he was apart all the while, living as she never lived, feeling as she never felt.

In fear and shame she looked at his naked body, that she had known falsely. And he was the father of her children. Her soul was torn from her body and stood apart. She looked at his naked body and was ashamed, as if she had denied it. After all, it was itself. It seemed awful to her. She looked at his face, and she turned her own face to the wall. For his look was other than hers, his way was not her way. She had denied him what he was—she saw it now. She had refused him as himself. And this had been her life, and his life. She was grateful to death, which restored the truth. And she knew she was not dead.

And all the while her heart was bursting with grief and pity for him. What had he suffered? What stretch of horror for this helpless man! She was rigid with agony. She had not been able to help him. He had been cruelly injured, this naked man, this other being, and she could make no reparation. There were the children—but the children belonged to life. This dead man had nothing to do with them. He and she were only channels through which life had flowed to issue in the children. She was a mother—but how awful she knew it now to have been a wife. And he, dead now, how awful he must have felt it to be a husband. She felt that in the next world he would be a stranger to her. If they met there, in the beyond, they would only be ashamed of what had been before. The children had come, for some mysterious reason, out of both of them. But the children did not unite them. Now he was dead, she knew how eternally he was apart from her, how eternally he had nothing more to do with her. She saw this episode of her life closed. They had denied each other in life. Now he had withdrawn. An anguish came over her. It was finished then: it had become hopeless' between them long before he died. Yet he had been her husband. But how little!

"Have you got his shirt, 'Lizabeth?"

Elizabeth turned without answering, though she strove to weep and behave as her mother-in-law expected. But she could not, she was silenced. She went into the kitchen and returned with the garment.

"It is aired," she said, grasping the cotton shirt here and there to try. She was almost ashamed to handle him; what right had she or anyone to lay hands on him; but her touch was humble on his body. It was hard work to clothe him. He was so heavy and inert. A terrible dread gripped her all the while: that he could be so heavy and utterly inert, unresponsive, apart. The horror of the distance between them was almost too much for her—it was so infinite a gap she must look across.

At last it was finished. They covered him with a sheet and left him lying, with his face bound. And she fastened the door of the little parlor, lest the children should see what was lying there. Then, with peace sunk heavy on her heart, she went about making tidy the kitchen. She knew she submitted to life, which was her immediate master. But from death, her ultimate master, she winced with fear and shame.

1914

D. H. LAWRENCE

The Horse Dealer's Daughter

"Well, Mabel, and what are you going to do with yourself?" asked Joe, with foolish flippancy. He felt quite safe himself. Without listening for an answer, he turned aside, worked a grain of tobacco to the tip of his tongue, and spat it out. He did not care about anything, since he felt safe himself.

The three brothers and the sister sat round the desolate breakfast table, attempting some sort of desultory consultation. The morning's post had given the final tap to the family fortunes, and all was over. The dreary dining room itself, with its heavy mahogany furniture, looked as if it were waiting to be done away with.

But the consultation amounted to nothing. There was a strange air of ineffectuality about the three men, as they sprawled at table, smoking and reflecting vaguely on their own condition. The girl was alone, a rather short, sullen-looking young woman of twenty-seven. She did not share the same life as her brothers. She would have been good-looking, save for the impassive fixity of her face, "bull dog," as her brothers called it.

There was a confused tramping of horses' feet outside. The three men all sprawled round in their chairs to watch. Beyond the dark holly bushes that separated the strip of lawn from the highroad, they could see a cavalcade of shire horses swinging out of their own yard, being taken for exercise. This was the last time. These were the last horses that would go through their hands. The young men watched with critical, callous look. They were all frightened at the collapse of their lives, and the sense of disaster in which they were involved left them no inner freedom.

Yet they were three fine, well-set fellows enough. Joe, the eldest, was a man of thirty-three, broad and handsome in a hot, flushed way. His face was red, he twisted his black mustache over a thick finger, his eyes were shallow and restless. He had a sensual way of uncovering his teeth when he laughed, and his bearing was stupid. Now he watched the horses with a glazed look of helplessness in his eyes, a certain stupor of downfall.

The great draft-horses swung past. They were tied head to tail, four of them, and they heaved along to where a lane branched off from the highroad, planting their great hoofs floutingly in the fine black mud, swinging their great rounded haunches sumptuously, and trotting a few sudden steps as they were led into the lane, round the corner. Every movement showed a massive, slumbrous strength, and a stupidity which held them in subjection. The groom at the head looked back, jerking the leading rope. And the cavalcade moved out of sight up the lane, the tail of the last horse, bobbed up tight and stiff, held out taut from the swinging great haunches as they rocked behind the hedges in a motion-like sleep.

Joe watched with glazed hopeless eyes. The horses were almost like his own body to him. He felt he was done for now. Luckily he was engaged to a woman as old as himself, and therefore her father, who was steward of a neighboring estate, would provide him with a job. He would marry and go into harness. His life was over, he would be a subject animal now.

He turned uneasily aside, the retreating steps of the horses echoing in his ears. Then, with foolish restlessness, he reached for the scraps of bacon-rind from the plates, and making a faint whistling sound, flung them to the terrier that lay against the fender.[1] He watched the dog swallow them, and waited till the creature looked into his eyes. Then a faint grin came on his face, and in a high, foolish voice he said:

"You won't get much more bacon, shall you, you little b——?"

The dog faintly and dismally wagged its tail, then lowered its haunches, circled round, and lay down again.

There was another helpless silence at the table. Joe sprawled uneasily in his seat, not willing to go till the family conclave was dissolved. Fred Henry, the second brother, was erect, clean-limbed, alert. He had watched the passing of the horses with more sang-froid. If he was an animal, like Joe, he was an animal which controls, not one which is controlled. He was master of any horse, and he carried himself with a well-tempered air of mastery. But he was not master of the situations of life. He pushed his coarse brown mustache upwards, off his lip, and glanced irritably at his sister, who sat impassive and inscrutable.

"You'll go and stop with Lucy for a bit, shan't you?" he asked. The girl did not answer.

"I don't see what else you can do," persisted Fred Henry.

"Go as a skivvy,"[2] Joe interpolated laconically.

The girl did not move a muscle.

"If I was her, I should go in for training for a nurse," said Malcolm, the youngest of them all. He was the baby of the family, a young man of twenty-two, with a fresh, jaunty *museau*.[3]

But Mabel did not take any notice of him. They had talked at her and round her for so many years, that she hardly heard them at all.

The marble clock on the mantelpiece softly chimed the half-hour, the dog rose uneasily from the hearthrug and looked at the party

---

1. Fire-screen or -guard.
2. Servant.
3. Face, "mug" (slightly derogatory).

at the breakfast table. But still they sat on in ineffectual conclave.

"Oh, all right," said Joe suddenly, apropos of nothing. "I'll get a move on."

He pushed back his chair, straddled his knees with a downward jerk, to get them free, in horsey fashion, and went to the fire. Still he did not go out of the room; he was curious to know what the others would do or say. He began to charge his pipe, looking down at the dog and saying, in a high, affected voice:

"Going wi' me? Going wi' me are ter? Tha'rt goin' further than tha counts on just now, dost hear?"

The dog faintly wagged its tail, the man stuck out his jaw and covered his pipe with his hands, and puffed intently, losing himself in the tobacco, looking down all the while at the dog with an absent brown eye. The dog looked up at him in mournful distrust. Joe stood with his knees stuck out, in real horsey fashion.

"Have you had a letter from Lucy?" Fred Henry asked of his sister.

"Last week," came the neutral reply.

"And what does she say?"

There was no answer.

"Does she *ask* you to go and stop there?" persisted Fred Henry.

"She says I can if I like."

"Well, then, you'd better. Tell her you'll come on Monday."

This was received in silence.

"That's what you'll do then, is it?" said Fred Henry, in some exasperation.

But she made no answer. There was a silence of futility and irritation in the room. Malcolm grinned fatuously.

"You'll have to make up your mind between now and next Wednesday," said Joe loudly, "or else find yourself lodgings on the curbstone."

The face of the young woman darkened, but she sat on immutable.

"Here's Jack Fergusson!" exclaimed Malcolm, who was looking aimlessly out of the window.

"Where?" exclaimed Joe, loudly.

"Just gone past."

"Coming in?"

Malcolm craned his neck to see the gate.

"Yes," he said.

There was a silence. Mabel sat on like one condemned, at the head of the table. Then a whistle was heard from the kitchen. The dog got up and barked sharply. Joe opened the door and shouted: "Come on."

After a moment a young man entered. He was muffled up in overcoat and a purple woolen scarf, and his tweed cap, which he did not remove, was pulled down on his head. He was of medium height, his face was rather long and pale, his eyes looked tired.

"Hello, Jack! Well, Jack!" exclaimed Malcolm and Joe. Fred Henry merely said, "Jack."

"What's doing?" asked the newcomer, evidently addressing Fred Henry.

"Same. We've got to be out by Wednesday. Got a cold?"

"I have—got it bad, too."

"Why don't you stop in?"[4]

"*Me* stop in? When I can't stand on my legs, perhaps I shall have a chance." The young man spoke huskily. He had a slight Scotch accent.

"It's a knockout, isn't it," said Joe, boisterously, "if a doctor goes round croaking with a cold. Looks bad for the patients, doesn't it?"

The young doctor looked at him slowly.

"Anything the matter with *you*, then?" he asked sarcastically.

"Not as I know of. Damn your eyes, I hope not. Why?"

"I thought you were very concerned about the patients, wondered if you might be one yourself."

"Damn it, no, I've never been patient to no flaming[5] doctor, and hope I never shall be," returned Joe.

At this point Mabel rose from the table, and they all seemed to become aware of her existence. She began putting the dishes together. The young doctor looked at her, but did not address her. He had not greeted her. She went out of the room with the tray, her face impassive and unchanged.

"When are you off then, all of you?" asked the doctor.

"I'm catching the eleven-forty," replied Malcolm. "Are you goin' down wi' th' trap, Joe?"

"Yes, I've told you I'm going down wi' th' trap, haven't I?"

"We'd better be getting her in then. So long, Jack, if I don't see you before I go," said Malcolm, shaking hands.

He went out, followed by Joe, who seemed to have his tail between his legs.

"Well, this is the devil's own," exclaimed the doctor, when he was left alone with Fred Henry. "Going before Wednesday, are you?"

"That's the orders," replied the other.

"Where, to Northampton?"[6]

"That's it."

"The devil!" exclaimed Fergusson, with quiet chagrin.

And there was silence between the two.

"All settled up, are you?" asked Fergusson.

"About."

There was another pause.

"Well, I shall miss yer, Freddy, boy," said the young doctor.

"And I shall miss thee, Jack," returned the other.

"Miss you like hell," mused the doctor.

Fred Henry turned aside. There was nothing to say. Mabel came in again, to finish clearing the table.

"What are *you* going to do, then, Miss Pervin?" asked Fergusson. "Going to your sister's, are you?"

Mabel looked at him with her steady, dangerous eyes, that always made him uncomfortable, unsettling his superficial ease.

"No," she said.

"Well, what in the name of fortune *are* you going to do? Say

4. Stay home.
5. Euphemism for "bloody," roughly equivalent to "darned."
6. Town about 65 miles north and slightly west of London.

what you mean to do," cried Fred Henry, with futile intensity.

But she only averted her head, and continued her work. She folded the white tablecloth, and put on the chenille cloth.

"The sulkiest bitch that ever trod!" muttered her brother.

But she finished her task with perfectly impassive face, the young doctor watching her interestedly all the while. Then she went out.

Fred Henry stared after her, clenching his lips, his blue eyes fixing in sharp antagonism, as he made a grimace of sour exasperation.

"You could bray[7] her into bits, and that's all you'd get out of her," he said, in a small, narrowed tone.

The doctor smiled faintly.

"What's she *going* to do, then?" he asked.

"Strike me if *I* know!" returned the other.

There was a pause. Then the doctor stirred.

"I'll be seeing you tonight, shall I?" he said to his friend.

"Ay—where's it to be? Are we going over to Jessdale?"[8]

"I don't know. I've got such a cold on me. I'll come round to the Moon and Stars, anyway."

"Let Lizzie and May miss their night for once, eh?"

"That's it—if I feel as I do now."

"All's one——"

The two young men went through the passage and down to the back door together. The house was large, but it was servantless now, and desolate. At the back was a small bricked house-yard, and beyond that a big square, graveled fine and red, and having stables on two sides. Sloping, dank, winter-dark fields stretched away on the open sides.

But the stables were empty. Joseph Pervin, the father of the family, had been a man of no education, who had become a fairly large horse dealer. The stables had been full of horses, there was a great turmoil and come-and-go of horses and of dealers and grooms. Then the kitchen was full of servants. But of late things had declined. The old man had married a second time, to retrieve his fortunes. Now he was dead and everything was gone to the dogs, there was nothing but debt and threatening.

For months, Mabel had been servantless in the big house, keeping the home together in penury for her ineffectual brothers. She had kept house for ten years. But previously it was with unstinted means. Then, however brutal and coarse everything was, the sense of money had kept her proud, confident. The men might be foul-mouthed, the women in the kitchen might have bad reputations, her brothers might have illegitimate children. But so long as there was money, the girl felt herself established, and brutally proud, reserved.

No company came to the house, save dealers and coarse men. Mabel had no associates of her own sex, after her sister went away. But she did not mind. She went regularly to church, she attended to her father. And she lived in the memory of her mother, who had died when she was fourteen, and whom she had loved. She had

7. Crush.   8. Apparently a fictional name.

loved her father, too, in a different way, depending upon him, and feeling secure in him, until at the age of fifty-four he married again. And then she had set hard against him. Now he had died and left them all hopelessly in debt.

She had suffered badly during the period of poverty. Nothing, however, could shake the curious sullen, animal pride that dominated each member of the family. Now, for Mabel, the end had come. Still she would not cast about her. She would follow her own way just the same. She would always hold the keys of her own situation. Mindless and persistent, she endured from day to day. Why should she think? Why should she answer anybody? It was enough that this was the end, and there was no way out. She need not pass any more darkly along the main street of the small town, avoiding every eye. She need not demean herself any more, going into the shops and buying the cheapest food. This was at an end. She thought of nobody, not even of herself. Mindless and persistent, she seemed in a sort of ecstasy to be coming nearer to her fulfilment, her own glorification, approaching her dead mother, who was glorified.

In the afternoon she took a little bag, with shears and sponge and a small scrubbing brush, and went out. It was a gray, wintry day, with saddened, dark green fields and an atmosphere blackened by the smoke of foundries not far off. She went quickly, darkly along the causeway, heeding nobody, through the town to the churchyard.

There she always felt secure, as if no one could see her, although as a matter of fact she was exposed to the stare of every one who passed along under the churchyard wall. Nevertheless, once under the shadow of the great looming church, among the graves, she felt immune from the world, reserved within the thick churchyard wall as in another country.

Carefully she clipped the grass from the grave, and arranged the pinky white, small chrysanthemums in the tin cross. When this was done, she took an empty jar from a neighboring grave, brought water, and carefully, most scrupulously sponged the marble head-stone and the coping-stone.[9]

It gave her sincere satisfaction to do this. She felt in immediate contact with the world of her mother. She took minute pains, went through the park in a state bordering on pure happiness, as if in performing this task she came into a subtle, intimate connection with her mother. For the life she followed here in the world was far less real than the world of death she inherited from her mother.

The doctor's house was just by the church. Fergusson, being a mere hired assistant, was slave to the countryside. As he hurried now to attend to the outpatients in the surgery, glancing across the graveyard with his quick eye, he saw the girl at her task at the grave. She seemed so intent and remote, it was like looking into another world. Some mystical element was touched in him. He slowed down as he walked, watching her as if spellbound.

She lifted her eyes, feeling him looking. Their eyes met. And each looked again at once, each feeling, in some way, found out by

9. Copestone, stone on top layer.

the other. He lifted his cap and passed on down the road. There remained distinct in his consciousness, like a vision, the memory of her face, lifted from the tombstone in the churchyard, and looking at him with slow, large, portentous eyes. It *was* portentous, her face. It seemed to mesmerize him. There was a heavy power in her eyes which laid hold of his whole being, as if he had drunk some powerful drug. He had been feeling weak and done before. Now the life came back into him, he felt delivered from his own fretted, daily self.

He finished his duties at the surgery as quickly as might be, hastily filling up the bottles of the waiting people with cheap drugs. Then, in perpetual haste, he set off again to visit several cases in another part of his round, before teatime. At all times he preferred to walk if he could, but particularly when he was not well. He fancied the motion restored him.

The afternoon was falling. It was gray, deadened, and wintry, with a slow, moist, heavy coldness sinking in and deadening all the faculties. But why should he think or notice? He hastily climbed the hill and turned across the dark green fields, following the black cinder-track. In the distance, across a shallow dip in the country, the small town was clustered like smouldering ash, a tower, a spire, a heap of low, raw, extinct houses. And on the nearest fringe of the town, sloping into the dip, was Oldmeadow, the Pervins' house. He could see the stables and the outbuildings distinctly, as they lay towards him on the slope. Well, he would not go there many more times! Another resource would be lost to him, another place gone: the only company he cared for in the alien, ugly little town he was losing. Nothing but work, drudgery, constant hastening from dwelling to dwelling among the colliers and the ironworkers. It wore him out, but at the same time he had a craving for it. It was a stimulant to him to be in the homes of the working people, moving as it were through the innermost body of their life. His nerves were excited and gratified. He could come so near, into the very lives of the rough, inarticulate, powerfully emotional men and women. He grumbled, he said he hated the hellish hole. But as a matter of fact it excited him, the contact with the rough, strongly-feeling people was a stimulant applied direct to his nerves.

Below Oldmeadow, in the green, shallow, soddened hollow of fields, lay a square, deep pond. Roving across the landscape, the doctor's quick eye detected a figure in black passing through the gate of the field, down towards the pond. He looked again. It would be Mabel Pervin. His mind suddenly became alive and attentive.

Why was she going down there? He pulled up on the path on the slope above, and stood staring. He could just make sure of the small black figure moving in the hollow of the failing day. He seemed to see her in the midst of such obscurity, that he was like a clairvoyant, seeing rather with the mind's eye than with ordinary sight. Yet he could see her positively enough, whilst he kept his eye attentive. He felt, if he looked away from her, in the thick, ugly, falling dusk, he would lose her altogether.

He followed her minutely as she moved, direct and intent, like something transmitted rather than stirring in voluntary activity, straight down the field towards the pond. There she stood on the bank for a moment. She never raised her head. Then she waded slowly into the water.

He stood motionless as the small black figure walked slowly and deliberately towards the center of the pond, very slowly, gradually moving deeper into the motionless water, and still moving forward as the water got up to her breast. Then he could see her no more in the dusk of the dead afternoon.

"There!" he exclaimed. "Would you believe it?"

And he hastened straight down, running over the wet, soddened fields, pushing through the hedges, down into the depression of callous wintry obscurity. It took him several minutes to come to the pond. He stood on the bank, breathing heavily. He could see nothing. His eyes seemed to penetrate the dead water. Yes, perhaps that was the dark shadow of her black clothing beneath the surface of the water.

He slowly ventured into the pond. The bottom was deep, soft clay, he sank in, and the water clasped dead cold round his legs. As he stirred he could smell the cold, rotten clay that fouled up into the water. It was objectionable in his lungs. Still, repelled and yet not heeding, he moved deeper into the pond. The cold water rose over his thighs, over his loins, upon his abdomen. The lower part of his body was all sunk in the hideous cold element. And the bottom was so deeply soft and uncertain, he was afraid of pitching with his mouth underneath. He could not swim, and was afraid.

He couched a little, spreading his hands under the water and moving them round, trying to feel for her. The dead cold pond swayed upon his chest. He moved again, a little deeper, and again, with his hands underneath, he felt all around under the water. And he touched her clothing. But it evaded his fingers. He made a desperate effort to grasp it.

And so doing he lost his balance and went under, horribly, suffocating in the foul earthy water, struggling madly for a few moments. At last, after what seemed an eternity, he got his footing, rose again into the air and looked around. He gasped, and knew he was in the world. Then he looked at the water. She had risen near him. He grasped her clothing, and drawing her nearer, turned to take his way to land again.

He went very slowly, carefully, absorbed in the slow progress. He rose higher, climbing out of the pond. The water was now only about his legs; he was thankful, full of relief to be out of the clutches of the pond. He lifted her and staggered on to the bank, out of the horror of wet, gray clay.

He laid her down on the bank. She was quite unconscious and running with water. He made the water come from her mouth, he worked to restore her. He did not have to work very long before he could feel the breathing begin again in her; she was breathing naturally. He worked a little longer. He could feel her live beneath his hands; she was coming back. He wiped her face, wrapped her in his overcoat, looked round into the dim, dark gray world, then lifted her and staggered down the bank and across the fields.

It seemed an unthinkably long way, and his burden so heavy he felt he would never get to the house. But at last he was in the stable-yard, and then in the house-yard. He opened the door and went into the house. In the kitchen he laid her down on the hearthrug, and called. The house was empty. But the fire was burning in the grate.

Then again he kneeled to attend to her. She was breathing regularly, her eyes were wide open and as if conscious, but there seemed something missing in her look. She was conscious in herself, but unconscious of her surroundings.

He ran upstairs, took blankets from a bed, and put them before the fire to warm. Then he removed her saturated, earthy-smelling clothing, rubbed her dry with a towel, and wrapped her naked in the blankets. Then he went into the diningroom, to look for spirits. There was a little whisky. He drank a gulp himself, and put some into her mouth.

The effect was instantaneous. She looked full into his face, as if she had been seeing him for some time, and yet had only just become conscious of him.

"Dr. Fergusson?" she said.

"What?" he answered.

He was divesting himself of his coat, intending to find some dry clothing upstairs. He could not bear the smell of the dead, clayey water, and he was mortally afraid for his own health.

"What did I do?" she asked.

"Walked into the pond," he replied. He had begun to shudder like one sick, and could hardly attend to her. Her eyes remained full on him, he seemed to be going dark in his mind, looking back at her helplessly. The shuddering became quieter in him, his life came back in him, dark and unknowing, but strong again.

"Was I out of my mind?" she asked, while her eyes were fixed on him all the time.

"Maybe, for the moment," he replied. He felt quiet, because his strength had come back. The strange fretful strain had left him.

"Am I out of my mind now?" she asked.

"Are you?" he reflected a moment. "No," he answered truthfully, "I don't see that you are." He turned his face aside. He was afraid now, because he felt dazed, and felt dimly that her power was stronger than his, in this issue. And she continued to look at him fixedly all the time. "Can you tell me where I shall find some dry things to put on?" he asked.

"Did you dive into the pond for me?" she asked.

"No," he answered. "I walked in. But I went in overhead as well."

There was silence for a moment. He hesitated. He very much wanted to go upstairs to get into dry clothing. But there was another desire in him. And she seemed to hold him. His will seemed to have gone to sleep, and left him, standing there slack before her. But he felt warm inside himself. He did not shudder at all, though his clothes were sodden on him.

"Why did you?" she asked.

"Because I didn't want you to do such a foolish thing," he said.

"It wasn't foolish," she said, still gazing at him as she lay on the floor, with a sofa cushion under her head. "It was the right thing to do. _I_ knew best, then."

"I'll go and shift [1] these wet things," he said. But still he had not the power to move out of her presence, until she sent him. It was as if she had the life of his body in her hands, and he could not extricate himself. Or perhaps he did not want to.

. Suddenly she sat up. Then she became aware of her own immediate condition. She felt the blankets about her, she knew her own limbs. For a moment it seemed as if her reason were going. She looked round, with wild eye, as if seeking something. He stood still with fear. She saw her clothing lying scattered.

"Who undressed me?" she asked, her eyes resting full and inevitable on his face.

"I did," he replied, "to bring you round."

For some moments she sat and gazed at him awfully, her lips parted.

"Do you love me, then?" she asked.

He only stood and stared at her, fascinated. His soul seemed to melt.

She shuffled forward on her knees, and put her arms round him, round his legs, as he stood there, pressing her breasts against his knees and thighs, clutching him with strange, convulsive certainty, pressing his thighs against her, drawing him to her face, her throat, as she looked up at him with flaring, humble eyes of transfiguration, triumphant in first possession.

"You love me," she murmured, in strange transport, yearning and triumphant and confident. "You love me. I know you love me, I know."

And she was passionately kissing his knees, through the wet clothing, passionately and indiscriminately kissing his knees, his legs, as if unaware of everything.

He looked down at the tangled wet hair, the wild, bare, animal shoulders. He was amazed, bewildered, and afraid. He had never thought of loving her. He had never wanted to love her. When he rescued her and restored her, he was a doctor, and she was a patient. He had had no single personal thought of her. Nay, this introduction of the personal element was very distasteful to him, a violation of his professional honor. It was horrible to have her there embracing his knees. It was horrible. He revolted from it, violently. And yet— and yet—he had not the power to break away.

She looked at him again, with the same supplication of powerful love, and that same transcendent, frightening light of triumph. In view of the delicate flame which seemed to come from her face like a light, he was powerless. And yet he had never intended to love her. He had never intended. And something stubborn in him could not give way.

"You love me," she repeated, in a murmur of deep, rhapsodic assurance. "You love me."

Her hands were drawing him, drawing him down to her. He was

1. Change.

afraid, even a little horrified. For he had, really, no intention of loving her. Yet her hands were drawing him towards her. He put out his hand quickly to steady himself, and grasped her bare shoulder. A flame seemed to burn the hand that grasped her soft shoulder. He had no intention of loving her: his whole will was against his yielding. It was horrible. And yet wonderful was the touch of her shoulders, beautiful the shining of her face. Was she perhaps mad? He had a horror of yielding to her. Yet something in him ached also.

He had been staring away at the door, away from her. But his hand remained on her shoulder. She had gone suddenly very still. He looked down at her. Her eyes were now wide with fear, with doubt, the light was dying from her face, a shadow of terrible grayness was returning. He could not bear the touch of her eyes' question upon him, and the look of death behind the question.

With an inward groan he gave way, and let his heart yield towards her. A sudden gentle smile came on his face. And her eyes, which never left his face, slowly, slowly filled with tears. He watched the strange water rise in her eyes, like some slow fountain coming up. And his heart seemed to burn and melt away in his breast.

He could not bear to look at her any more. He dropped on his knees and caught her head with his arms and pressed her face against his throat. She was very still. His heart, which seemed to have broken, was burning with a kind of agony in his breast. And he felt her slow, hot tears wetting his throat. But he could not move.

He felt the hot tears wet his neck and the hollows of his neck, and he remained motionless, suspended through one of man's eternities. Only now it had become indispensable to him to have her face pressed close to him; he could never let her go again. He could never let her head go away from the close clutch of his arm. He wanted to remain like that for ever, with his heart hurting him in a pain that was also life to him. Without knowing, he was looking down on her damp, soft brown hair.

Then, as it were suddenly, he smelt the horrid stagnant smell of that water. And at the same moment she drew away from him and looked at him. Her eyes were wistful and unfathomable. He was afraid of them, and he fell to kissing her, not knowing what he was doing. He wanted her eyes not to have that terrible, wistful, unfathomable look.

When she turned her face to him again, a faint delicate flush was glowing, and there was again dawning that terrible shining of joy in her eyes, which really terrified him, and yet which he now wanted to see, because he feared the look of doubt still more.

"You love me?" she said, rather faltering.

"Yes." The word cost him a painful effort. Not because it wasn't true. But because it was too newly true, the *saying* seemed to tear open again his newly-torn heart. And he hardly wanted it to be true, even now.

She lifted her face to him, and he bent forward and kissed her on the mouth, gently, with the one kiss that is an eternal pledge. And as he kissed her his heart strained again in his breast. He never intended to love her. But now it was over. He had crossed over the gulf to her, and all that he had left behind had shriveled and become void.

After the kiss, her eyes again slowly filled with tears. She sat still, away from him, with her face drooped aside, and her hands folded in her lap. The tears fell very slowly. There was complete silence. He too sat there motionless and silent on the hearthrug. The strange pain of his heart that was broken seemed to consume him. That he should love her? That this was love! That he should be ripped open in this way! Him, a doctor! How they would all jeer if they knew! It was agony to him to think they might know.

In the curious naked pain of the thought he looked again to her. She was sitting there drooped into a muse. He saw a tear fall, and his heart flared hot. He saw for the first time that one of her shoulders was quite uncovered, one arm bare, he could see one of her small breasts; dimly, because it had become almost dark in the room.

"Why are you crying?" he asked, in an altered voice.

She looked up at him, and behind her tears the consciousness of her situation for the first time brought a dark look of shame to her eyes.

"I'm not crying, really," she said, watching him half frightened.

He reached his hand, and softly closed it on her bare arm.

"I love you! I love you!" he said in a soft, low vibrating voice, unlike himself.

She shrank, and dropped her head. The soft, penetrating grip of his hand on her arm distressed her. She looked up at him.

"I want to go," she said. "I want to go and get you some dry things."

"Why?" he said. "I'm all right."

"But I want to go," she said. "And I want you to change your things."

He released her arm, and she wrapped herself in the blanket, looking at him rather frightened. And still she did not rise.

"Kiss me," she said wistfully.

He kissed her, but briefly, half in anger.

Then, after a second, she rose nervously, all mixed up in the blanket. He watched her in her confusion, as she tried to extricate herself and wrap herself up so that she could walk. He watched her relentlessly, as she knew. And as she went, the blanket trailing, and as he saw a glimpse of her feet and her white leg, he tried to remember her as she was when he had wrapped her in the blanket. But then he didn't want to remember, because she had been nothing to him then, and his nature revolted from remembering her as she was when she was nothing to him.

A tumbling, muffled noise from within the dark house startled him. Then he heard her voice—"There are clothes." He rose and went to the foot of the stairs, and gathered up the garments she had thrown down. Then he came back to the fire, to rub himself down and dress. He grinned at his own appearance when he had finished.

The fire was sinking, so he put on coal. The house was now quite dark, save for the light of a street-lamp that shone in faintly from beyond the holly trees. He lit the gas with matches he found on the mantelpiece. Then he emptied the pockets of his own clothes, and threw all his wet things in a heap into the scullery. After which he gathered up her sodden clothes, gently, and put them in a separate heap on the copper-top[2] in the scullery.

It was six o'clock on the clock. His own watch had stopped. He ought to go back to the surgery. He waited, and still she did not come down. So he went to the foot of the stairs and called:

"I shall have to go."

Almost immediately he heard her coming down. She had on her best dress of black voile, and her hair was tidy, but still damp. She looked at him—and in spite of herself, smiled.

"I don't like you in those clothes," she said.

"Do I look a sight?" he answered.

They were shy of one another.

"I'll make you some tea," she said.

"No, I must go."

"Must you?" And she looked at him again with the wide, strained, doubtful eyes. And again, from the pain of his breast, he knew how he loved her. He went and bent to kiss her, gently, passionately, with his heart's painful kiss.

"And my hair smells so horrible," she murmured in distraction. "And I'm so awful, I'm so awful! Oh, no, I'm too awful." And she broke into bitter, heartbroken sobbing. "You can't want to love me, I'm horrible."

"Don't be silly, don't be silly," he said, trying to comfort her, kissing her, holding her in his arms. "I want you, I want to marry you, we're going to be married, quickly, quickly—tomorrow if I can."

But she only sobbed terribly, and cried:

"I feel awful. I feel awful. I feel I'm horrible to you."

"No, I want you, I want you," was all he answered, blindly, with that terrible intonation which frightened her almost more than her horror lest he should *not* want her.

1922

D. H. LAWRENCE

The Rocking-Horse Winner

There was a woman who was beautiful, who started with all the advantages, yet she had no luck. She married for love, and the love turned to dust. She had bonny children, yet she felt they had been thrust upon her, and she could not love them. They looked at her coldly, as if they were finding fault with her. And hurriedly she felt she must cover up some fault in herself. Yet what it was that she must cover up she never knew. Nevertheless, when her children were present, she always felt the center of her heart go hard. This troubled her, and in her manner she was all the more gentle and anxious for her

2. Top of a washtub or cooking vessel, now usually made of iron.

children, as if she loved them very much. Only she herself knew that
at the center of her heart was a hard little place that could not feel
love, no, not for anybody. Everybody else said of her: "She is such a
good mother. She adores her children." Only she herself, and her children
themselves, knew it was not so. They read it in each other's eyes.

There were a boy and two little girls. They lived in a pleasant
house, with a garden, and they had discreet servants, and felt themselves
superior to anyone in the neighborhood.

Although they lived in style, they felt always an anxiety in the house.
There was never enough money. The mother had a small income, and
the father had a small income, but not nearly enough for the social
position which they had to keep up. The father went into town to
some office. But though he had good prospects, these prospects never
materialized. There was always the grinding sense of the shortage of
money, though the style was always kept up.

At last the mother said: "I will see if *I* can't make something." But
she did not know where to begin. She racked her brains, and tried this
thing and the other, but could not find anything successful. The failure
made deep lines come into her face. Her children were growing up,
they would have to go to school. There must be more money, there
must be more money. The father, who was always very handsome and
expensive in his tastes, seemed as if he never *would* be able to do anything
worth doing. And the mother, who had a great belief in herself,
did not succeed any better, and her tastes were just as expensive.

And so the house came to be haunted by the unspoken phrase: *There
must be more money! There must be more money!* The children could
hear it all the time, though nobody said it aloud. They heard it at
Christmas, when the expensive and splendid toys filled the nursery.
Behind the shining modern rocking-horse, behind the smart doll's
house, a voice would start whispering: "There *must* be more money!
There *must* be more money!" And the children would stop playing, to
listen for a moment. They would look into each other's eyes, to see if
they had all heard. And each one saw in the eyes of the other two that
they too had heard. "There *must* be more money! There *must* be more
money!"

It came whispering from the springs of the still-swaying rocking-horse,
and even the horse, bending his wooden, champing head, heard
it. The big doll, sitting so pink and smirking in her new pram,[1] could
hear it quite plainly, and seemed to be smirking all the more self-consciously
because of it. The foolish puppy, too, that took the place
of the teddy bear, he was looking so extraordinarily foolish for no
other reason but that he heard the secret whisper all over the house:
"There *must* be more money!"

Yet nobody ever said it aloud. The whisper was everywhere, and
therefore no one spoke it. Just as no one ever says: "We are breathing!"
in spite of the fact that breath is coming and going all the time.

"Mother," said the boy Paul one day, "why don't we keep a car of
our own? Why do we always use uncle's, or else a taxi?"

"Because we're the poor members of the family," said the mother.

---

1. Baby carriage.

"But why *are* we, mother?"

"Well—I suppose," she said slowly and bitterly, "it's because your father has no luck."

The boy was silent for some time.

"Is luck money, mother?" he asked, rather timidly.

"No, Paul. Not quite. It's what causes you to have money."

"Oh!" said Paul vaguely. "I thought when Uncle Oscar said *filthy lucker,* it meant money."

"*Filthy lucre* does mean money," said the mother. "But it's lucre, not luck."

"Oh!" said the boy. "Then what *is* luck, mother?"

"It's what causes you to have money. If you're lucky you have money. That's why it's better to be born lucky than rich. If you're rich, you may lose your money. But if you're lucky, you will always get more money."

"Oh! Will you? And is father not lucky?"

"Very unlucky, I should say," she said bitterly.

The boy watched her with unsure eyes.

"Why?" he asked.

"I don't know. Nobody ever knows why one person is lucky and another unlucky."

"Don't they? Nobody at all? Does *nobody* know?"

"Perhaps God. But He never tells."

"He ought to, then. And aren't you lucky either, mother?"

"I can't be, if I married an unlucky husband."

"But by yourself, aren't you?"

"I used to think I was, before I married. Now I think I am very unlucky indeed."

"Why?"

"Well—never mind! Perhaps I'm not really," she said.

The child looked at her to see if she meant it. But he saw, by the lines of her mouth, that she was only trying to hide something from him.

"Well, anyhow," he said stoutly, "I'm a lucky person."

"Why?" said his mother, with a sudden laugh.

He stared at her. He didn't even know why he had said it.

"God told me," he asserted, brazening it out.

"I hope He did, dear!" she said, again with a laugh, but rather bitter.

"He did, mother!"

"Excellent!" said the mother, using one of her husband's exclamations.

The boy saw she did not believe him; or rather, that she paid no attention to his assertion. This angered him somewhat, and made him want to compel her attention.

He went off by himself, vaguely, in a childish way, seeking for the clue to "luck." Absorbed, taking no heed of other people, he went about with a sort of stealth, seeking inwardly for luck. He wanted luck, he wanted it, he wanted it. When the two girls were playing dolls in the nursery, he would sit on his big rocking-horse, charging madly into space, with a frenzy that made the little girls peer at him uneasily.

Wildly the horse careered, the waving dark hair of the boy tossed, his eyes had a strange glare in them. The little girls dared not speak to him.

When he had ridden to the end of his mad little journey, he climbed down and stood in front of his rocking-horse, staring fixedly into its lowered face. Its red mouth was slightly open, its big eye was wide and glassy-bright.

"Now!" he would silently command the snorting steed. "Now, take me to where there is luck! Now take me!"

And he would slash the horse on the neck with the little whip he had asked Uncle Oscar for. He *knew* the horse could take him to where there was luck, if only he forced it. So he would mount again and start on his furious ride, hoping at last to get there. He knew he could get there.

"You'll break your horse, Paul!" said the nurse.

"He's always riding like that! I wish he'd leave off!" said his elder sister Joan.

But he only glared down on them in silence. Nurse gave him up. She could make nothing of him. Anyhow, he was growing beyond her.

One day his mother and his Uncle Oscar came in when he was on one of his furious rides. He did not speak to them.

"Hallo, you young jockey! Riding a winner?" said his uncle.

"Aren't you growing too big for a rocking-horse? You're not a very little boy any longer, you know," said his mother.

But Paul only gave a blue glare from his big, rather close-set eyes. He would speak to nobody when he was in full tilt. His mother watched him with an anxious expression on her face.

At last he suddenly stopped forcing his horse into the mechanical gallop and slid down.

"Well, I got there!" he announced fiercely, his blue eyes still flaring, and his sturdy long legs straddling apart.

"Where did you get to?" asked his mother.

"Where I wanted to go," he flared back at her.

"That's right, son!" said Uncle Oscar. "Don't you stop till you get there. What's the horse's name?"

"He doesn't have a name," said the boy.

"Gets on without all right?" asked the uncle.

"Well, he has different names. He was called Sansovino last week."

"Sansovino, eh? Won the Ascot. How did you know this name?"

"He always talks about horse-races with Bassett," said Joan.

The uncle was delighted to find that his small nephew was posted with all the racing news. Bassett, the young gardener, who had been wounded in the left foot in the war[2] and had got his present job through Oscar Cresswell, whose batman he had been, was a perfect blade[3] of the "turf." He lived in the racing events, and the small boy lived with him.

Oscar Cresswell got it all from Bassett.

"Master Paul comes and asks me, so I can't do more than tell him, sir," said Bassett, his face terribly serious, as if he were speaking of religious matters.

2. World War I, 1914–1918.   3. Dashing young man.

"And does he ever put anything on a horse he fancies?"

"Well—I don't want to give him away—he's a young sport, a fine sport, sir. Would you mind asking him himself? He sort of takes a pleasure in it, and perhaps he'd feel I was giving him away, sir, if you don't mind."

Bassett was serious as a church.

The uncle went back to his nephew and took him off for a ride in the car.

"Say, Paul, old man, do you ever put anything on a horse?" the uncle asked.

The boy watched the handsome man closely.

"Why, do you think I ougntn't to?" he parried.

"Not a bit of it! I thought perhaps you might give me a tip for the Lincoln."[4]

The car sped on into the country, going down to Uncle Oscar's place in Hampshire.

"Honor bright?" said the nephew.

"Honor bright, son!" said the uncle.

"Well, then, Daffodil."

"Daffodil! I doubt it, sonny. What about Mirza?"

"I only know the winner," said the boy. "That's Daffodil."

"Daffodil, eh?"

There was a pause. Daffodil was an obscure horse comparatively.

"Uncle!"

"Yes, son?"

"You won't let it go any further, will you? I promised Bassett."

"Bassett be damned, old man! What's he got to do with it?"

"We're partners. We've been partners from the first. Uncle, he lent me my first five shillings,[5] which I lost. I promised him, honor bright, it was only between me and him; only you gave me that ten-shilling note I started winning with, so I thought you were lucky. You won't let it go any further, will you?"

The boy gazed at his uncle from those big, hot, blue eyes, set rather close together. The uncle stirred and laughed uneasily.

"Right you are, son! I'll keep your tip private. Daffodil, eh? How much are you putting on him?"

"All except twenty pounds," said the boy. "I keep that in reserve."

The uncle thought it a good joke.

"You keep twenty pounds in reserve, do you, you young romancer? What are you betting, then?"

"I'm betting three hundred," said the boy gravely. "But it's between you and me, Uncle Oscar! Honor bright?"

The uncle burst into a roar of laughter.

"It's between you and me all right, you young Nat Gould,"[6] he said, laughing. "But where's your three hundred?"

4. Lincolnshire Handicap race then run at Lincoln Downs. Other races mentioned in the story include the St. Leger Stakes (the Leger) run at Doncaster; the Grand National Steeplechase run at Aintree, the most famous steeplechase in the world; the famous Derby, a mile-and-a-half race for three-year-olds run at Epsom Downs, and the Ascot (above) run at the course of that name in Berkshire.

5. Then just over a dollar. The English pound after World War I fluctuated considerably but was generally less than the $4.86 of the pre-War period and more than $1. There are 20 shillings to the pound.

6. Nathaniel Gould (1857–1919) novelist and journalist whose writings in both genres concerned horse-racing.

"Bassett keeps it for me. We're partners."

"You are, are you! And what is Bassett putting on Daffodil?"

"He won't go quite as high as I do, I expect. Perhaps he'll go a hundred and fifty."

"What, pennies?" laughed the uncle.

"Pounds," said the child, with a surprised look at his uncle. "Bassett keeps a bigger reserve than I do."

Between wonder and amusement Uncle Oscar was silent. He pursued the matter no further, but he determined to take his nephew with him to the Lincoln races.

"Now, son," he said, "I'm putting twenty on Mirza, and I'll put five on for you on any horse you fancy. What's your pick?"

"Daffodil, uncle."

"No, not the fiver on Daffodil!"

"I should if it was my own fiver," said the child.

"Good! Good! Right you are! A fiver for me and a fiver for you on Daffodil."

The child had never been to a race-meeting before, and his eyes were blue fire. He pursed his mouth tight and watched. A Frenchman just in front had put his money on Lancelot. Wild with excitement, he flayed his arms up and down, yelling *Lancelot! Lancelot!* in his French accent.

Daffodil came in first, Lancelot second, Mirza third. The child, flushed and with eyes blazing, was curiously serene. His uncle brought him four five-pound notes, four to one.

"What am I to do with these?" he cried, waving them before the boy's eyes.

"I suppose we'll talk to Bassett," said the boy. "I expect I have fifteen hundred now; and twenty in reserve; and this twenty."

His uncle studied him for some moments.

"Look here, son!" he said. "You're not serious about Bassett and that fifteen hundred, are you?"

"Yes, I am. But it's between you and me, uncle. Honor bright?"

"Honor bright all right, son! But I must talk to Bassett."

"If you'd like to be a partner, uncle, with Bassett and me, we could all be partners. Only, you'd have to promise, honor bright, uncle, not to let it go beyond us three. Bassett and I are lucky, and you must be lucky, because it was your ten shillings I started winning with. . . ."

Uncle Oscar took both Bassett and Paul into Richmond Park for an afternoon, and there they talked.

"It's like this, you see, sir," Bassett said. "Master Paul would get me talking about racing events, spinning yarns, you know, sir. And he was always keen on knowing if I'd made or if I'd lost. It's about a year since, now, that I put five shillings on Blush of Dawn for him: and we lost. Then the luck turned, with that ten shillings, he had from you: that we put on Singhalese. And since that time, it's been pretty steady, all things considering. What do you say, Master Paul?"

"We're all right when we're sure," said Paul. "It's when we're not quite sure that we go down."

"Oh, but we're careful then," said Bassett.

"But when are you *sure*?" smiled Uncle Oscar.

"It's Master Paul, sir," said Bassett in a secret, religious voice. "It's as if he had it from heaven. Like Daffodil, now, for the Lincoln. That was as sure as eggs."

"Did you put anything on Daffodil?" asked Oscar Cresswell.

"Yes, sir. I made my bit."

"And my nephew?"

Bassett was obstinately silent, looking at Paul.

"I made twelve hundred, didn't I, Bassett? I told uncle I was putting three hundred on Daffodil."

"That's right," said Bassett, nodding.

"But where's the money?" asked the uncle.

"I keep it safe locked up, sir. Master Paul he can have it any minute he likes to ask for it."

"What, fifteen hundred pounds?"

"And twenty! And *forty*, that is, with the twenty he made on the course."

"It's amazing!" said the uncle.

"If Master Paul offers you to be partners, sir, I would, if I were you: if you'll excuse me," said Bassett.

Oscar Cresswell thought about it.

"I'll see the money," he said.

They drove home again, and, sure enough, Bassett came round to the garden-house with fifteen hundred pounds in notes. The twenty pounds reserve was left with Joe Glee, in the Turf Commission deposit.

"You see, it's all right, uncle, when I'm *sure*! Then we go strong, for all we're worth. Don't we, Bassett?"

"We do that, Master Paul."

"And when are you sure?" said the uncle, laughing.

"Oh, well, sometimes I'm *absolutely* sure, like about Daffodil," said the boy; "and sometimes I have an idea; and sometimes I haven't even an idea, have I, Bassett? Then we're careful, because we mostly go down."

"You do, do you! And when you're sure, like about Daffodil, what makes you sure, sonny?"

"Oh, well, I don't know," said the boy uneasily. "I'm sure, you know, uncle; that's all."

"It's as if he had it from heaven, sir," Bassett reiterated.

"I should say so!" said the uncle.

But he became a partner. And when the Leger was coming on, Paul was "sure" about Lively Spark, which was a quite inconsiderable horse. The boy insisted on putting a thousand on the horse, Bassett went for five hundred, and Oscar Cresswell two hundred. Lively Spark came in first, and the betting had been ten to one against him. Paul had made ten thousand.

"You see," he said, "I was absolutely sure of him."

Even Oscar Cresswell had cleared two thousand.

"Look here, son," he said, "this sort of thing makes me nervous."

"It needn't, uncle! Perhaps I shan't be sure again for a long time."

"But what are you going to do with your money?" asked the uncle.

"Of course," said the boy, "I started it for mother. She said she had no luck, because father is unlucky, so I thought if *I* was lucky, it might stop whispering."

"What might stop whispering?"

"Our house. I *hate* our house for whispering."

"What does it whisper?"

"Why—why"—the boy fidgeted—"why, I don't know. But it's always short of money, you know, uncle."

"I know it, son, I know it."

"You know people send mother writs, don't you, uncle?"

"I'm afraid I do," said the uncle.

"And then the house whispers, like people laughing at you behind your back. It's awful, that is! I thought if I was lucky—"

"You might stop it," added the uncle.

The boy watched him with big blue eyes, that had an uncanny cold fire in them, and he said never a word.

"Well, then!" said the uncle. "What are we doing?"

"I shouldn't like mother to know I was lucky," said the boy.

"Why not, son?"

"She'd stop me."

"I don't think she would."

"Oh!"—and the boy writhed in an odd way—"I *don't* want her to know, uncle."

"All right, son! We'll manage it without her knowing."

They managed it very easily. Paul, at the other's suggestion, handed over five thousand pounds to his uncle, who deposited it with the family lawyer, who was then to inform Paul's mother that a relative had put five thousand pounds into his hands, which sum was to be paid out a thousand pounds at a time, on the mother's birthday, for the next five years.

"So she'll have a birthday present of a thousand pounds for five successive years," said Uncle Oscar. "I hope it won't make it all the harder for her later."

Paul's mother had her birthday in November. The house had been "whispering" worse than ever lately, and, even in spite of his luck, Paul could not bear up against it. He was very anxious to see the effect of the birthday letter, telling his mother about the thousand pounds.

When there were no visitors, Paul now took his meals with his parents, as he was beyond the nursery control. His mother went into town nearly every day. She had discovered that she had an odd knack of sketching furs and dress materials, so she worked secretly in the studio of a friend who was the chief "artist" for the leading drapers. She drew the figures of ladies in furs and ladies in silk and sequins for the newspaper advertisements. This young woman artist earned several thousand pounds a year, but Paul's mother only made several hundreds, and she was again dissatisfied. She so wanted to be first in something, and she did not succeed, even in making sketches for drapery advertisements.

She was down to breakfast on the morning of her birthday. Paul watched her face as she read her letters. He knew the lawyer's letter. As his mother read it, her face hardened and became more expressionless. Then a cold, determined look came on her mouth. She hid the letter under the pile of others, and said not a word about it.

"Didn't you have anything nice in the post for your birthday, mother?" said Paul.

"Quite moderately nice," she said, her voice cold and absent.

She went away to town without saying more.

But in the afternoon Uncle Oscar appeared. He said Paul's mother had had a long interview with the lawyer, asking if the whole five thousand could not be advanced at once, as she was in debt.

"What do you think, uncle?" said the boy.

"I leave it to you, son."

"Oh, let her have it, then! We can get some more with the other," said the boy.

"A bird in the hand is worth two in the bush, laddie!" said Uncle Oscar.

"But I'm sure to *know* for the Grand National; or the Lincolnshire; or else the Derby. I'm sure to know for one of them," said Paul.

So Uncle Oscar signed the agreement, and Paul's mother touched the whole five thousand. Then something very curious happened. The voices in the house suddenly went mad, like a chorus of frogs on a spring evening. There were certain new furnishings, and Paul had a tutor. He was *really* going to Eton, his father's school, in the following autumn. There were flowers in the winter, and a blossoming of the luxury Paul's mother had been used to. And yet the voices in the house, behind the sprays of mimosa and almond-blossom, and from under the piles of iridescent cushions, simply trilled and screamed in a sort of ecstasy: "There *must* be more money! Oh-h-h; there *must* be more money. Oh, now, now-w! Now-w-w—there *must* be more money! —more than ever! More than ever!"

It frightened Paul terribly. He studied away at his Latin and Greek with his tutor. But his intense hours were spent with Bassett. The Grand National had gone by: he had not "known," and had lost a hundred pounds. Summer was at hand. He was in agony for the Lincoln. But even for the Lincoln he didn't "know," and he lost fifty pounds. He became wild-eyed and strange, as if something were going to explode in him.

"Let it alone, son! Don't you bother about it!" urged Uncle Oscar. But it was as if the boy couldn't really hear what his uncle was saying.

"I've got to know for the Derby! I've got to know for the Derby!" the child reiterated, his big blue eyes blazing with a sort of madness.

His mother noticed how overwrought he was.

"You'd better go to the seaside. Wouldn't you like to go now to the seaside, instead of waiting? I think you'd better," she said, looking down at him anxiously, her heart curiously heavy because of him.

But the child lifted his uncanny blue eyes.

"I couldn't possibly go before the Derby, mother!" he said. "I couldn't possibly!"

"Why not?" she said, her voice becoming heavy when she was opposed. "Why not? You can still go from the seaside to see the Derby with your Uncle Oscar, if that's what you wish. No need for you to wait here. Besides, I think you care too much about these races. It's a bad sign. My family has been a gambling family, and you won't know till you grow up how much damage it has done. But it has done damage. I shall have to send Bassett away, and ask Uncle Oscar not to talk racing to you, unless you promise to be reasonable about it: go away to the seaside and forget it. You're all nerves!"

"I'll do what you like, mother, so long as you don't send me away till after the Derby," the boy said.

"Send you away from where? Just from this house?"

"Yes," he said, gazing at her.

"Why, you curious child, what makes you care about this house so much, suddenly? I never knew you loved it."

He gazed at her without speaking. He had a secret within a secret, something he had not divulged, even to Bassett or to his Uncle Oscar.

But his mother, after standing undecided and a little bit sullen for some moments, said:

"Very well, then! Don't go to the seaside till after the Derby, if you don't wish it. But promise me you won't let your nerves go to pieces. Promise you won't think so much about horse-racing and *events*, as you call them!"

"Oh, no," said the boy casually. "I won't think much about them, mother. You needn't worry. I wouldn't worry, mother, if I were you."

"If you were me and I were you," said his mother, "I wonder what we *should* do!"

"But you know you needn't worry, mother, don't you?" the boy repeated.

"I should be awfully glad to know it," she said wearily.

"Oh, well, you *can*, you know. I mean, you *ought* to know you needn't worry," he insisted.

"Ought I? Then I'll see about it," she said.

Paul's secret of secrets was his wooden horse, that which had no name. Since he was emancipated from a nurse and a nursery-governess, he had had his rocking-horse removed to his own bedroom at the top of the house.

"Surely you're too big for a rocking-horse!" his mother had remonstrated.

"Well, you see, mother, till I can have a *real* horse, I like to have *some* sort of animal about," had been his quaint answer.

"Do you feel he keeps you company?" she laughed.

"Oh, yes! He's very good, he always keeps me company, when I'm there," said Paul.

So the horse, rather shabby, stood in an arrested prance in the boy's bedroom.

The Derby was drawing near, and the boy grew more and more tense. He hardly heard what was spoken to him, he was very frail, and his eyes were really uncanny. His mother had sudden strange seizures of uneasiness about him. Sometimes, for half an hour, she would feel a sudden anxiety about him that was almost anguish. She wanted to rush to him at once, and know he was safe.

Two nights before the Derby, she was at a big party in town, when one of her rushes of anxiety about her boy, her first-born, gripped her heart till she could hardly speak. She fought with the feeling, might and main, for she believed in common sense. But it was too strong. She had to leave the dance and go downstairs to telephone to the country. The children's nursery-governess was terribly surprised and startled at being rung up in the night.

"Are the children all right, Miss Wilmot?"

"Oh, yes, they are quite all right."

"Master Paul? Is he all right?"

"He went to bed as right as a trivet. Shall I run up and look at him?"

"No," said Paul's mother reluctantly. "No! Don't trouble. It's all right. Don't sit up. We shall be home fairly soon." She did not want her son's privacy intruded upon.

"Very good," said the governess.

It was about one o'clock when Paul's mother and father drove up to their house. All was still. Paul's mother went to her room and slipped off her white fur cloak. She had told her maid not to wait up for her. She heard her husband downstairs, mixing a whisky and soda.

And then, because of the strange anxiety at her heart, she stole upstairs to her son's room. Noiselessly she went along the upper corridor. Was there a faint noise? What was it?

She stood, with arrested muscles, outside his door, listening. There was a strange, heavy, and yet not loud noise. Her heart stood still. It was a soundless noise, yet rushing and powerful. Something huge, in violent, hushed motion. What was it? What in God's name was it? She ought to know. She felt that she knew the noise. She knew what it was.

Yet she could not place it. She couldn't say what it was. And on and on it went, like a madness.

Softly, frozen with anxiety and fear, she turned the door-handle.

The room was dark. Yet in the space near the window, she heard and saw something plunging to and fro. She gazed in fear and amazement.

Then suddenly she switched on the light, and saw her son, in his green pajamas, madly surging on the rocking-horse. The blaze of light suddenly lit him up, as he urged the wooden horse, and lit her up, as she stood, blonde, in her dress of pale green and crystal, in the doorway.

"Paul!" she cried. "Whatever are you doing?"

"It's Malabar!" he screamed, in a powerful, strange voice. "It's Malabar!"

His eyes blazed at her for one strange and senseless second, as he ceased urging his wooden horse. Then he fell with a crash to the ground, and she, all her tormented motherhood flooding upon her, rushed to gather him up.

But he was unconscious, and unconscious he remained, with some brain-fever. He talked and tossed, and his mother sat stonily by his side.

"Malabar! It's Malabar! Bassett, Bassett, I *know*! It's Malabar!"

So the child cried, trying to get up and urge the rocking-horse that gave him his inspiration.

"What does he mean by Malabar?" asked the heart-frozen mother.

"I don't know," said the father stonily.

"What does he mean by Malabar?" she asked her brother Oscar.

"It's one of the horses running for the Derby," was the answer.

And, in spite of himself, Oscar Cresswell spoke to Bassett, and himself put a thousand on Malabar: at fourteen to one.

The third day of the illness was critical: they were waiting for a change. The boy, with his rather long, curly hair, was tossing ceaselessly on the pillow. He neither slept nor regained consciousness, and his eyes were like blue stones. His mother sat, feeling her heart had gone, turned actually into a stone.

In the evening, Oscar Cresswell did not come, but Bassett sent a message, saying could he come up for one moment, just one moment? Paul's mother was very angry at the intrusion, but on second thought she agreed. The boy was the same. Perhaps Bassett might bring him to consciousness.

The gardener, a shortish fellow with a little brown moustache and sharp little brown eyes, tiptoed into the room, touched his imaginary cap to Paul's mother, and stole to the bedside, staring with glittering, smallish eyes, at the tossing, dying child.

"Master Paul!" he whispered. "Master Paul! Malabar came in first all right, a clean win. I did as you told me. You've made over seventy thousand pounds, you have; you've got over eighty thousand. Malabar came in all right, Master Paul."

"Malabar! Malabar! Did I say Malabar, mother? Did I say Malabar? Do you think I'm lucky, mother? I knew Malabar, didn't I? Over eighty thousand pounds! I call that lucky, don't you, mother? Over eighty thousand pounds! I knew, didn't I know I knew? Malabar came in all right. If I ride my horse till I'm sure, then I tell you, Bassett, you can go as high as you like. Did you go for all you were worth, Bassett?"

"I went a thousand on it, Master Paul."

"I never told you, mother, that if I can ride my horse, and *get there*, then I'm absolutely sure—oh, absolutely! Mother, did I ever tell you? I *am* lucky!"

"No, you never did," said the mother.

But the boy died in the night.

And even as he lay dead, his mother heard her brother's voice saying to her: "My God, Hester, you're eighty-odd thousand to the good, and a poor devil of a son to the bad. But, poor devil, poor devil, he's best gone out of a life where he rides his rocking-horse to find a winner."

1932

D. H. LAWRENCE

Passages from Essays and Letters

from "Nottingham and the Mining Countryside"

I was born . . . in Eastwood, a mining village of some three thousand souls, about eight miles from Nottingham. . . . It is hilly country. . . . To me it seemed, and still seems, an extremely beautiful countryside, just between the red sandstone and the oak-trees of Nottingham, and the cold limestone, the ash-trees, the stone fences of Derbyshire. To me, as a child and a young man, it was still the old England of the forest and agricultural past; there were no motor-cars, the mines were, in a sense, an accident in the landscape, and Robin Hood and his merry men were not very far away.

. . . The people lived almost entirely by instinct, men of my father's age could not really read. And the pit did not mechanize men. . . . My father loved the pit. He was hurt badly, more than once, but he would never stay away. He loved the contact, the intimacy, as men in the war loved the intense male comradeship of the dark days.

Now the colliers had also an instinct for beauty. The colliers' wives had not. The colliers were deeply alive, instinctively. But they had no daytime ambition, and no daytime intellect. They avoided, really, the rational aspect of life. . . . They didn't even care very profoundly about wages. It was the women, naturally, who nagged on this score. . . . The collier went to the pub and drank in order to continue the intimacy with his mates.

. . . Life for him did not consist of facts, but in a flow. Very often he loved his garden. And very often he had a genuine love of the beauty of flowers. . . .

. . . Most women love flowers as possessions, and as trimmings. They can't look at a flower, and wonder a moment, and pass on. If they see a flower that arrests their attention, they must at once pick it, pluck it. Possession! A possession! Something added on to *me!*

from "Love"

. . . the love between a man and a woman . . . is dual. It is the melting into pure communion, and it is the friction of sheer sensuality, both. In pure communion I become whole in love. And in pure, fierce passion of sensuality, I am burned into essentiality. I am driven from the matrix unto sheer separate distinction. I become my single self, inviolable and unique, as the gems were perhaps once driven into themselves out of the confusion of earths. . . .

from "Women Are So Cocksure"

. . . [My mother] was convinced . . . that a man ought not to drink beer. This conviction developed from the fact, naturally, that my father drank beer. He sometimes drank too much. He sometimes boozed away the money necessary for the young family. When my father came in tipsy, she saw scarlet.

from "Art and Morality"

Apples are always apples! says Vox Populi, Vox Dei.[1]

Sometimes they're sin, sometimes they're a knock on the head, sometimes they're a bellyache, sometimes they're part of a pie, sometimes they're sauce for a goose.

1. The voice of the people [is] the voice of God.

What art has got to do, and will go on doing, is to reveal things in their different relationships. That is to say, you've got to see in the apples the bellyache, Sir Isaac's knock on the cranium, the vast, moist wall through which the insect bores to lay her eggs in the middle, and the untasted, unknown quality which Eve saw hanging on a tree.

from "Morality and the Novel"

The business of art is to reveal the relation between man and his circumambient universe, at the living moment. As mankind is always struggling in the toils of old relationships, art is always ahead of the "times," which themselves are always far in the rear of the living moment.

When Van Gogh paints sunflowers, he reveals, or achieves, the vivid relation between himself, as man, and the sunflowers, as sunflower, at that quick moment of time. His painting does not represent the sunflower itself. We shall never know what the sunflower itself is. And the camera will *visualize* the sunflower far more perfectly than van Gogh can.

The vision on the canvas is a third thing, utterly intangible and inexplicable, the offspring of the sunflower itself and van Gogh himself. . . .

. . . The novel is the highest example of subtle interrelatedness that man has discovered. Everything is true in its own time, place, and circumstance, and untrue outside of its own place, time, circumstance. If you try to nail anything down, in the novel, either it kills the novel, or the novel gets up and walks away with the nail.

. . . Love is a great emotion. But if you set out to write a novel, and you yourself are in the throes of the great predilection for love, love as the supreme, the only emotion worth living for, then you will write an immoral novel.

Because *no* emotion is supreme, or exclusively worth living for. *All* emotions go to the achieving of a living relationship between a human being and the other human being or creature or thing he becomes purely related to. All emotions, including love and hate, and rage and tenderness, go to the adjusting of the oscillating, unestablished balance between two people who amount to anything.

A new relation, a new relatedness hurts somewhat in the attaining; and will always hurt. So life will always hurt. . . .

Each time we strive to a new relation, with anyone or anything, it is bound to hurt somewhat. Because it means the struggle with and the displacing of old connections, and this is never pleasant. And, moreover, between living things at least, an adjustment means also a fight, for each party, inevitably, must "seek its own" in the other, and be denied. When, in the two parties, each of them seeks his own, her own, absolutely, then it is a fight to the death. And this is true of the thing called "passion."

The great relationship for humanity will always be the relation between man and woman. The relation between man and man, woman and woman, parent and child, will always be subsidiary.

And the relation between man and woman will change forever, and will forever be the new central clue to human life. It is the *relation itself* which is the quick and the central clue to life, not the man, nor the woman, nor the children that result from the relationship, as a contingency.

from "Why the Novel Matters"

We have curious ideas of ourselves. We think of ourselves as a body with a spirit in it, or a body with a soul in it, or a body with a mind in it. . . .

It is a funny sort of superstition. Why should I look at my hand, as it so cleverly writes these words, and decide that it is a mere nothing compared to the mind that directs it? Why should I imagine that there is a *me* which is more *me* than my hand is? Since my hand is absolutely alive, me alive.

And that's what you learn, when you're a novelist. And that's what you are liable *not* to know, if you're a parson, or a philosopher, or a scientist, or a stupid person.

Now I absolutely flatly deny that I am a soul, or a body, or a mind, or an intelligence, or a brain, or a nervous system, or a bunch of glands, or any of the rest of these bits of me. The whole is greater than the part. And therefore, I, who am man alive, am greater than my soul, or spirit, or body, or mind, or consciousness, or anything else that is merely a part of me. I am man a man, and alive. I am man alive, and as long as I can, I intend to go on being man alive.

For this reason I am a novelist. And being a novelist, I consider myself superior to the saint, the scientist, the philosopher, and the poet, who are all great masters of different bits of man alive, but never get the whole thing.

We should ask for no absolutes, or absolute. . . . There is no absolute good, there is nothing absolutely right. All things flow and change, and even change is not absolute. . . .

. . . If the one I love remains unchanged and unchanging, I shall cease to love her. It is only because she changes and startles me into change and defies my inertia, and is herself staggered in her inertia by my changing, that I can continue to love her. If she stayed put, I might as well love the pepper-pot.

In life, there is right and wrong, good and bad, all the time. But what is right in one case is wrong in another. And in the novel you see one man becoming a corpse, because of his so-called goodness, another going dead because of his so-called wickedness. Right and wrong is an instinct: but an instinct of the whole consciousness in a man, bodily, mental, spiritual at once. And only in the novel are *all* things given full play, or at least, they may be given full play, when we realize that life itself, and not inert safety, is the reason for living. For out of the full play of all things emerges the only thing that is anything, the wholeness of a man, the wholeness of a woman, man alive, and live woman.

from Autobiographical Sketch

They ask me; "Did you find it very hard to get on and to become a success?" And I have to admit that if I can be said to have got on, and if I can be called a success, then I *did not* find it hard.

I never starved in a garret, nor waited in anguish for the post to bring me an answer from editor or publisher, nor did I struggle in sweat and blood to bring forth mighty works, nor did I ever wake up and find myself famous.

. . . My father was a collier, and only a collier, nothing praiseworthy about him. He wasn't even respectable, in so far as he got drunk rather frequently, never went near a chapel, and was usually rather rude to his little immediate bosses at the pit.

My mother was, I suppose, superior. She came from town, and belonged really to the lower bourgeoisie. She spoke King's English, without an accent, and never in her life could even imitate a sentence of the dialect which my father spoke, and which we children spoke out of doors.

I have *wanted* to feel truly friendly with some, at least of my fellow-men. Yet I have never quite succeeded. Whether I got on *in* the world is a question; but I certainly don't get on very well *with* the world. And whether I am a worldly success or not I really don't know. But I feel, somehow, not much of a human success.

By which I mean that I don't feel there is any very cordial of fundamental contact between me and society, or me and other people. There is a breach. And my contact is with something that is nonhuman, nonvocal.

[Why?] The answer, as far as I can see, has something to do with class. Class makes a gulf, across which all the best human flow is lost. It is not exactly the triumph of the middle classes that has made the deadness, but the triumph of the middle-class *thing*.

As a man from the working class, I feel that the middle class cut off some of my vital vibration when I am with them. I admit them charming and educated and good people often enough. *But they just stop some part of me from working.* . . .

Then why don't I live with my working people? Because their vibration is limited in another direction. They are narrow, but still fairly deep and passionate, whereas the middle class is broad and shallow and passionless.

I cannot make the transfer from my own class into the middle class. I cannot, not for anything in the world, forfeit my passional consciousness and my old blood-affinity with my fellow-men and the animals and the land, for that other thin, spurious mental conceit which is all that is left of the mental consciousness once it has made itself exclusive.

from the Letters

TO A. W. MCLEOD, 26 APRIL 1913

I am so sure that only through a readjustment between men and women, and a making free and healthy of this sex, will she [England] get out of her present atrophy. Oh, Lord, and if I don't "subdue my art to a metaphysic," as somebody very beautifully said of Hardy, I do write because I want folk—English folk—to alter, and have more sense.

TO A. W. MCLEOD, 2 JUNE 1914

I think the only re-sourcing of art, revivifying it, is to make it more the joint work of man and woman. I think *the* one thing to do, is for men to have courage to draw nearer to women, expose themselves to them, and be altered by them; and for women to accept and admit men. That is the start—by bringing themselves together, men and women—revealing themselves to each other, gaining great blind knowledge and suffering and joy, which it will take a big further lapse of civilization to exploit and work out. Because the source of all life and knowledge is in man and woman, and the source of all living is in the interchange and the meeting and mingling of these two: man-life and woman-life, man-knowledge and woman-knowledge, man-being and woman-being.

TO J. B. PINKER, 16 DECEMBER 1915

. . . Tell Arnold Bennett [2] that all rules of construction hold good only for novels which are copies of other novels. A book which is not a copy of other books has its own construction and what he calls faults, he being an old imitator, I call characteristics.

TO ROLF GARDINER, 9 AUGUST 1924

What we need is to smash a few big holes in European suburbanity, let in a little real fresh air.

TO LADY OTTOLINE MORRELL, 5 FEBRUARY 1929

. . . Don't you think it's nonsense when Murry says that my world is not the ordinary man's world and that I am a sort of animal with a sixth sense. Seems to me more likely he's a sort of animal with only four senses—the real sense of touch missing. They all seem determined to make a freak of me—to save their own short-failings, and make them "normal."

2. An early twentieth-century novelist (1867–1931) whose major works—*The Old Wives' Tale* (1908) and *The Clayhanger Trilogy* (1910–15)—treat the middle classes in the pottery country of the English Midlands in a naturalistic manner (usually criticizing the money-grubbing, social-climbing selfishness of the society). In his later years he more or less turned into a hack, though a clever one, and it is to Bennett as a very popular, successful hack that Lawrence is referring.

9   TRADITION

What is a short story? a novel? When we sit down to read a short story, what do we expect? Our expectations, our very notion of what a short story or novel is, have been formed by other short stories and novels we have read or heard about. This body of work—all the stories, novels, even poems and plays—that the author and informed reader are in general familiar with is the literary tradition. Within the literary tradition are less all-inclusive traditions: there is the Western literary tradition, and the tradition of American literature, and the Puritan tradition, and so on. Within a **literary tradition** certain signals or **conventions** are developed with which readers become familiar, and which tell them, for example, whether to expect high adventure or everyday events, even whether there is likely to be a happy ending, an unhappy one, or not much of an ending at all.

Conventions are something like a second layer of language, an aid and structure for communicating meaning. We know from the conventions of punctuation—arbitrary signs such as ?, !, . —how to read certain sentences. We know from the conventions of English word order who did what to whom in the sentence "The girl hit the boy." We know that when type is set in blocks we are reading prose; when it is set in uneven lines beginning with capital letters, we are reading poetry. So we know what kind of story to expect when it begins, "Once upon a time . . ."

Of course, writers don't know exactly who *you* are. They must make certain assumptions and by some of their signals and devices try to make you the kind of reader they want. Sometimes, especially in the case of foreign or older literature, we are not the reader the author had in mind at all, and it is thus up to us either to resign ourselves to missing a good deal of what's going on, or to try to learn enough to become at least a reasonably informed reader.

The writer, then, expects the reader to share a common literary tradition in a general way, to understand most of the signals that further relate the individual work to a body of works, and thus to raise expectations that he can either fulfill or transform. We all know that if a television show is a series, both the young cop and his older partner will more than likely survive (and catch the bad guys), but if it's not a series and the older cop is near retirement, a widower living alone, and very kindly but a little lost, we fully expect him to fall heroically before the final commercial. Sometimes a writer will expect you to know a specific work and keep it in mind while you are reading the new work. A **parody**, or an imitation that makes fun of another work, like *Samurai Night Fever* or Fielding's *Shamela*, which parodies Richardson's *Pamela*, clearly assumes you remember the work being parodied.

As readers, the literary tradition is important to us primarily so that we can get the full enjoyment, the full experience, from reading the work. We want to be familiar with the Gothic tradition—with castles and ghosts—and its science-fiction aspect—the mad scientist, weird experiments—so that when, in *The Most Dangerous Game*, Rainsford comes upon the château in the middle of the jungle and Ivan answers the door, we can have the thrill of expectation—even though it's a false expectation, for it's not being right but being aware that's the important thing. If we know the tradition of the serial ordeal, in which the hero must accomplish three tasks or solve three problems, Rainsford's tricks of survival may build our expectations more intensely.

For writers the tradition is a necessary tool in defining their fictional world, both for themselves and for readers. Most want to write because there is some truth, some vision of reality they want to present that no one has quite got right. They want to tell it like it is, but in order to do so they have to work on what you already know. So they use the most appropriate portion of the tradition to "place" their work or frame it, and then they play off the tradition, or work against it, or define their world and its operations in terms of it, so that you can see the difference and significance more immediately and clearly. The narrator of *Catcher in the Rye*, for example, wants to deny the influence of his home and early years on his current "mad" behavior, so he says he will not tell *his* story the way Dickens told David Copperfield's: "If you really want to hear about it, the first thing you'll probably want to know is where I was born, and what my lousy childhood was like, and how my parents were occupied and all before they had me, and all that David Copperfield kind of crap, but I don't feel like going into it, if you want to know the truth. . . ."

The three stories in this chapter are in the tradition of what has been called "Southwest humor" (*Southwest* meaning the southern frontier wherever it happened to be; in Longstreet's day, then, no farther west than Georgia).

All these stories involve the trickster. The trickster—practical joker, shady trader, underhanded opponent; sometimes heroic, sometimes a rogue, at times a villain, respected or contemptible—appears in European, African, and other folk literature as well as in the American. In the American, as in other traditions, the trickster may be a braggart, like Yellow Blossom in the Longstreet story (and like Odysseus); sometimes more sly, like Longstreet's old man or Faulkner's Flem Snopes; sometimes downright sneaky, like the stranger in Samuel Clemens's story. Very often in the American tradition, as perhaps one might expect, the trick involves trading, as in Longstreet and Faulkner, or other forms of gain such as betting, as in Clemens.

The trickster is usually a local and his victim usually an outsider or stranger, often one who is himself trying to trick and who thus deserves to be bested. Often the stories are anti-urban or anti-intellectual, with the "folk" getting the better of his more sophisticated rival. For some reason, in the American stories within this tradition there is almost always a narrator between us and the trickster. Perhaps it is to insulate us morally from the trickster: the narrator, like the reader, is removed from the action and uninvolved, neither profiting nor losing by the tricks, and so disclaiming responsibility, as it were, for the morality of the action. Perhaps it is to make the tale, often a rather outlandish one, more credible: the narrator, someone like us, is merely reporting what he heard or testifying to the veracity of the story, no matter how strange it seems. Perhaps it is to make the story respectable or comprehensible, for the folk characters speak local dialect and the narrator usually speaks standard American.

Though the humor in these stories is based on verbal exaggeration (**hyperbole** or overstatement) and on physical, knockabout, pratfall, vaudeville-type comic action (**slapstick**), the folk characters, folk humor, dialect, and regional description and mores (**local color**) connect this tradition with the movement toward increased realism in nineteenth-century fiction. Historically the tradition is centered in the generation immediately preceding the Civil War, when American literature was first separating itself from its English predecessors and seeking local roots. (See Hennig Cohen and William B. Dillingham's Introduction to *Humor of the Old Southwest.*) It must have struck a taproot, for after the Civil War we find Clemens and a number of his contemporaries, and in our own century William Faulkner as well as many others (*Dotson Gerber* has many elements of the tradition), writing stories recognizably related to these.

It is more than likely that the later writers had read Longstreet; Faulkner had certainly read Longstreet and Clemens. However, we are not here primarily concerned with **influence**—the direct effect of one writer on another—or with **allusion**—reference within a work to another specific work, such as the early reference to Dante's epic in *The Artificial Nigger,* or Woody Allen's hilarious use of *Madame Bovary* in *The Kugelmass Episode.* What we are focusing on here is the later authors' reliance on reader familiarity not with any specific work but with a sufficient number of stories within the tradition to arouse certain expectations of plot and character, and in some cases voice, language, even setting.

The author can thus assume that the tradition itself, rather than any specific work or works within the tradition, is common knowledge. Clemens can write a story within the tradition that is at the same time a spoof of the tradition. The jumping frog contest is more ridiculous than a horse race or swap, and the trick is a rather blatant and flimsy one. You might think this is just Clemens writing a poor or strained example of the trickster-tricked story, but notice that Simon Wheeler tells story after story about Jim Smiley, and the narrator himself, a stand-in for the reader, recognizes the triteness of the trickster device and flees rather than listen to another such story, about "a yaller one-eyed cow that didn't have no tail." Faulkner shows how a master can revive and transform the tradition. *Spotted Horses* retains the trickster and the trick, the broad verbal humor and the slapstick, but he reveals within the jokes the trickster's essential cruelty and exploitation, and without sentimentality he creates out of comedy almost unbearable pathos.

AUGUSTUS BALDWIN LONGSTREET

The Horse-Swap

During the session of the Supreme Court, in the village of ―― about three weeks ago, when a number of people were collected in the principal street of the village, I observed a young man riding up and down the street, as I supposed, in a violent passion. He galloped this way, then that, and then the other; spurred his horse to one group of citizens, then to another, then dashed off at half speed, as if fleeing from danger; and, suddenly checking his horse, returned first in a pace, then in a trot, and then in a canter. While he was performing these various evolutions, he cursed, swore, whooped, screamed, and tossed himself in every attitude which man could assume on horseback. In short, he *cavorted* most magnanimously (a term which, in our tongue, expresses all that I have described, and a little more), and seemed to be setting all creation at defiance. As I like to see all that is passing, I determined to take a position a little nearer to him, and to ascertain, if possible, what it was that affected him so sensibly. Accordingly, I approached a crowd before which he had stopped for a moment, and examined it with the strictest scrutiny. But I could see nothing in it that seemed to have anything to do with the cavorter. Every man appeared to be in good humor, and all minding their own business. Not one so much as noticed the principal figure. Still he went on. After a semicolon pause, which my appearance seemed to produce (for he eyed me closely as I approached), he fetched a whoop, and swore that "he could out-swap any live man, woman, or child that ever walked these hills, or that ever straddled horseflesh since the days of old daddy Adam. Stranger," said he to me, "did you ever see the *Yellow* Blossom from Jasper?"

"No," said I, "but I have often heard of him."

"I'm the boy," continued he; "perhaps a *leetle*, jist a *leetle*, of the best man at a horse-swap that ever trod shoe-leather."

I began to feel my situation a little awkward, when I was relieved by a man somewhat advanced in years, who stepped up and began to survey the "*Yellow Blossom's*" horse with much apparent interest. This drew the rider's attention, and he turned the conversation from me to the stranger.

"Well, my old coon," said he, "do you want to swap *hosses?*"

"Why, I don't know," replied the stranger; "I believe I've got a beast I'd trade with you for that one, if you like him."

"Well, fetch up your nag, my old cock; you're jist the lark[1] I wanted to get hold of. I am perhaps a *leetle*, jist a *leetle*, of the best man at a horse-swap that ever stole *cracklins* out of his mammy's fat gourd. Where's your *hoss?*"

"I'll bring him presently; but I want to examine your horse a little."

"Oh! look at him," said the Blossom, alighting and hitting him a cut; "look at him. He's the best piece of *hoss*flesh in the thirteen united univarsal worlds. There's no sort o' mistake in little Bullet. He can pick up miles on his feet, and fling 'em behind him as fast as the next man's *hoss*, I don't care where he comes from. And he can keep at it as long as the sun can shine without resting."

During this harangue, little Bullet looked as if he understood it all, believed it, and was ready at any moment to verify it. He was a horse of goodly countenance, rather expressive of vigilance than fire; though

1. Game or trick.

an unnatural appearance of fierceness was thrown into it by the loss of his ears, which had been cropped pretty close to his head. Nature had done but little for Bullet's head and neck; but he managed, in a great measure, to hide their defects by bowing perpetually. He had obviously suffered severely for corn; but if his ribs and hip bones had not disclosed the fact, *he* never would have done it; for he was in all respects as cheerful and happy as if he commanded all the corn-cribs and fodder-stacks in Georgia. His height was about twelve hands; but as his shape partook somewhat of that of the giraffe, his haunches stood much lower. They were short, strait, peaked, and concave. Bullet's tail, however, made amends for all his defects. All that the artist could do to beautify it had been done; and all that horse could do to compliment the artist, Bullet did. His tail was nicked in superior style, and exhibited the line of beauty in so many directions, that it could not fail to hit the most fastidious taste in some of them. From the root it dropped into a graceful festoon; then rose in a handsome curve; then resumed its first direction; and then mounted suddenly upward like a cypress knee to a perpendicular of about two and a half inches. The whole had a careless and bewitching inclination to the right. Bullet obviously knew where his beauty lay, and took all occasions to display it to the best advantage. If a stick cracked, or if anyone moved suddenly about him, or coughed, or hawked, or spoke a little louder than common, up went Bullet's tail like lightning; and if the *going up* did not please, the *coming down* must of necessity, for it was as different from the other movement as was its direction. The first was a bold and rapid flight upward, usually to an angle of forty-five degrees. In this position he kept his interesting appendage until he satisfied himself that nothing in particular was to be done; when he commenced dropping it by half inches, in second beats, then in triple time, then faster and shorter, and faster and shorter still, until it finally died away imperceptibly into its natural position. If I might compare sights to sounds, I should say its *settling* was more like the note of a locust than anything else in nature.

Either from native sprightliness of disposition, from uncontrollable activity, or from an unconquerable habit of removing flies by the stamping of the feet, Bullet never stood still; but always kept up a gentle fly-scaring movement of his limbs, which was peculiarly interesting.

"I tell you, man," proceeded the Yellow Blossom, "he's the best live hoss that ever trod the grit of Georgia. Bob Smart knows the hoss. Come here, Bob, and mount this hoss, and show Bullet's motions." Here Bullet bristled up, and looked as if he had been hunting for Bob all day long, and had just found him. Bob sprang on his back. "Boo-oo-oo!" said Bob, with a fluttering noise of the lips; and away went Bullet, as if in a quarter race,[2] with all his beauties spread in handsome style.

"Now fetch him back," said Blossom. Bullet turned and came in pretty much as he went out.

"Now trot him by." Bullet reduced his tail to "*customary*"; sidled to

2. Quarter-mile race.

the right and left airily, and exhibited at least three varieties of trot in the short space of fifty yards.

"Make him pace!"[3] Bob commenced twitching the bridle and kicking at the same time. These inconsistent movements obviously (and most naturally) disconcerted Bullet; for it was impossible for him to learn, from them, whether he was to proceed or stand still. He started to trot, and was told that wouldn't do. He attempted a canter, and was checked again. He stopped, and was urged to go on. Bullet now rushed into the wide field of experiment, and struck out a gait of his own, that completely turned the tables upon his rider, and certainly deserved a patent. It seemed to have derived its elements from the jig, the minuet, and the cotillion. If it was not a pace, it certainly had *pace* in it, and no man would venture to call it anything else; so it passed off to the satisfaction of the owner.

"Walk him!" Bullet was now at home again; and he walked as if money was staked on him.

The stranger, whose name, I afterward learned, was Peter Ketch, having examined Bullet to his heart's content, ordered his son Neddy to go and bring up Kit. Neddy soon appeared upon Kit; a well-formed sorrel of the middle size, and in good order. His *tout ensemble*[4] threw Bullet entirely in the shade, though a glance was sufficient to satisfy anyone that Bullet had the decided advantage of him in point of intellect.

"Why, man," said Blossom, "do you bring such a hoss as that to trade for Bullet? Oh, I see you're no notion of trading."

"Ride him off, Neddy!" said Peter. Kit put off at a handsome lope.

"Trot him back!" Kit came in at a long, sweeping trot, and stopped suddenly at the crowd.

"Well," said Blossom, "let me look at him; maybe he'll do to plow."

"Examine him!" said Peter, taking hold of the bridle close to the mouth; "he's nothing but a tacky. He an't as *pretty* a horse as Bullet, I know; but he'll do. Start 'em together for a hundred and fifty *mile*; and if Kit an't twenty *mile* ahead of him at the coming out, any man may take Kit for nothing. But he's a monstrous mean horse, gentlemen; any man may see that. He's the scariest horse, too, you ever saw. He won't do to hunt on, no how. Stranger, will you let Neddy have your rifle to shoot off him? Lay the rifle between his ears, Neddy, and shoot at the blaze in that stump. Tell me when his head is high enough."

Ned fired, and hit the blaze; and Kit did not move a hair's breadth.

"Neddy, take a couple of sticks, and beat on that hogshead at Kit's tail."

Ned made a tremendous rattling, at which Bullet took fright, broke his bridle, and dashed off in grand style; and would have stopped all farther negotiations by going home in disgust, had not a traveler arrested him and brought him back; but Kit did not move.

"I tell you, gentlemen," continued Peter, "he's the scariest horse you ever saw. He ain't as gentle as Bullet, but he won't do any harm if you watch him. Shall I put him in a cart, gig, or wagon for you,

3. Display his abilities; a pace is a fast gait.   4. All-together.

stranger? He'll cut the same capers there he does here. He's a monstrous mean horse."

During all this time Blossom was examining him with the nicest scrutiny. Having examined his frame and limbs, he now looked at his eyes.

"He's got a curious look out of his eyes," said Blossom.

"Oh yes, sir," said Peter, "just as blind as a bat. Blind horses always have clear eyes. Make a motion at his eyes, if you please, sir."

Blossom did so, and Kit threw up his head rather as if something pricked him under the chin than as if fearing a blow. Blossom repeated the experiment, and Kit jerked back in considerable astonishment.

"Stone blind, you see, gentlemen," proceeded Peter; "but he's just as good to travel of a dark night as if he had eyes."

"Blame my buttons," said Blossom, "if I like them eyes."

"No," said Peter, "nor I neither. I'd rather have 'em made of diamonds; but they'll do, if they don't show as much white as Bullet's."

"Well," said Blossom, "make a pass at me."[5]

"No," said Peter; "you made the banter,[6] now make your pass."

"Well, I'm never afraid to price my hosses. You must give me twenty-five dollars boot."[7]

"Oh, certainly; say fifty, and my saddle and bridle in. Here, Neddy, my son, take away daddy's horse."

"Well," said Blossom, "I've made my pass, now you make yours."

"I'm for short talk in a horse-swap, and therefore always tell a gentleman at once what I mean to do. You must give me ten dollars."

Blossom swore absolutely, roundly, and profanely, that he never would give boot.

"Well," said Peter, "I didn't care about trading; but you cut such high shines[8] that I thought I'd like to back you out, and I've done it. Gentlemen, you see I've brought him to a hack."[9]

"Come, old man," said Blossom, "I've been joking with you. I begin to think you do want to trade; therefore, give me five dollars and take Bullet. I'd rather lose ten dollars any time than not make a trade, though I hate to fling away a good hoss."

"Well," said Peter, "I'll be as clever as you are. Just put the five dollars on Bullet's back, and hand him over; it's a trade."

Blossom swore again, as roundly as before, that he would not give boot; and, said he, "Bullet wouldn't hold five dollars on his back, no how. But as, I bantered you, if you say an even swap, here's at you."

"I told you," said Peter, "I'd be as clever as you; therefore, here goes two dollars more, just for trade sake. Give me three dollars, and it's a bargain."

Blossom repeated his former assertion; and here the parties stood for a long time, and the bystanders (for many were now collected) began to taunt both parties. After some time, however, it was pretty unanimously decided that the old man had backed Blossom out.

At length Blossom swore he "never would be backed out for three

5. Make me an offer.
6. Challenge.
7. To boot (in addition).

8. Such a big show.
9. Horse in bad physical condition.

dollars after bantering a man"; and, accordingly, they closed the trade.

"Now," said Blossom, as he handed Peter the three dollars, "I'm a man that, when he makes a bad trade, makes the most of it until he can make a better. I'm for no rues and after-claps."[1]

"That's just my way," said Peter; "I never goes to law to mend my bargains."

"Ah, you're the kind of boy I love to trade with. Here's your hoss, old man. Take the saddle and bridle off him, and I'll strip yours; but lift up the blanket easy from Bullet's back, for he's a mighty tender-backed hoss."

The old man removed the saddle, but the blanket stuck fast. He attempted to raise it, and Bullet bowed himself, switched his tail, danced a little, and gave signs of biting.

"Don't hurt him, old man," said Blossom, archly; "take it off easy. I am, perhaps, a leetle of the best man at a horse-swap that ever catched a coon."

Peter continued to pull at the blanket more and more roughly, and Bullet became more and more *cavortish*; insomuch that, when the blanket came off, he had reached the *kicking* point in good earnest.

The removal of the blanket disclosed a sore on Bullet's backbone that seemed to have defied all medical skill. It measured six full inches in length and four in breadth, and had as many features as Bullet had motions. My heart sickened at the sight; and I felt that the brute who had been riding him in that situation deserved the halter.

The prevailing feeling, however, was that of mirth. The laugh became loud and general at the old man's expense, and rustic witticisms were liberally bestowed upon him and his late purchase. These Blossom continued to provoke by various remarks. He asked the old man "if he thought Bullet would let five dollars lie on his back." He declared most seriously that he had owned that horse three months, and had never discovered before that he had a sore back, "or he never should have thought of trading him," etc., etc.

The old man bore it all with the most philosophic composure. He evinced no astonishment at his late discovery, and made no replies. But his son Neddy had not disciplined his feelings quite so well. His eyes opened wider and wider from the first to the last pull of the blanket; and, when the whole sore burst upon his view, astonishment and fright seemed to contend for the mastery of his countenance. As the blanket disappeared, he stuck his hands in his breeches pockets, heaved a deep sigh, and lapsed into a profound reverie, from which he was only roused by the cuts at his father. He bore them as long as he could; and, when he could contain himself no longer, he began, with a certain wildness of expression which gave a peculiar interest to what he uttered: "His back's mighty bad off; but dod drot[2] my soul if he's put it to daddy as bad as he thinks he has, for old Kit's both blind and *deef*, I'll be dod drot if he eint."

"The devil he is," said Blossom.

"Yes, dod drot my soul if he *eint*. You wulk him, and see if he *eint*. His eyes don't look like it; but he'd *jist as leve go agin* the house with

---

1. Regrets or unexpected consequences.　　2. God rot, an expletive.

you, or in a ditch, as any how. Now you go try him." The laugh was now turned on Blossom; and many rushed to test the fidelity of the little boy's report. A few experiments established its truth beyond controversy.

"Neddy," said the old man, "you oughtn't to try and make people discontented with their things. Stranger, don't mind what the little boy says. If you can only get Kit rid of them little failings, you'll find him all sorts of a horse. You are a *leetle* the best man at a horse-swap that ever I got hold of; but don't fool away Kit. Come, Neddy, my son, let's be moving; the stranger seems to be getting snappish."

1835

SAMUEL CLEMENS (MARK TWAIN)

The Celebrated Jumping Frog of Calaveras County

In compliance with the request of a friend of mine, who wrote me from the East, I called on good-natured, garrulous old Simon Wheeler, and inquired about my friend's friend, Leonidas W. Smiley, as requested to do, and I hereunto append the result. I have a lurking suspicion that *Leonidas* W. Smiley is a myth; that my friend never knew such a personage; and that he only conjectured that if I asked old Wheeler about him, it would remind him of his infamous *Jim* Smiley, and he would go to work and bore me to death with some exasperating reminiscence of him as long and as tedious as it should be useless to me. If that was the design, it succeeded.

I found Simon Wheeler dozing comfortably by the barroom stove of the dilapidated tavern in the decayed mining camp of Angel's, and I noticed that he was fat and bald-headed, and had an expression of winning gentleness and simplicity upon his tranquil countenance. He roused up, and gave me good day. I told him that a friend of mine had commissioned me to make some inquiries about a cherished companion of his boyhood named *Leonidas* W. Smiley—*Rev. Leonidas* W. Smiley, a young minister of the Gospel, who he had heard was at one time a resident of Angel's Camp. I added that if Mr. Wheeler could tell me anything about this Rev. Leonidas W. Smiley, I would feel under many obligations to him.

Simon Wheeler backed me into a corner and blockaded me there with his chair, and then sat down and reeled off the monotonous narrative which follows this paragraph. He never smiled, he never frowned, he never changed his voice from the gentle-flowing key to which he tuned his initial sentence, he never betrayed the slightest suspicion of enthusiasm; but all through the interminable narrative there ran a vein of impressive earnestness and sincerity, which showed me plainly that, so far from his imagining that there was anything ridiculous or funny about his story, he regarded it as a really important matter, and admired its two heroes as men of transcendent genius in *finesse*. I let him go on in his own way, and never interrupted him once.

"Rev. Leonidas W. H'm, Reverend Le—well, there was a feller here once by the name of *Jim* Smiley, in the winter of '49—or maybe it was the spring of '50—I don't recollect exactly, somehow, though what makes me think it was one or the other is because I remember the big flume[1] warn't finished when he first came to the camp; but anyway, he was the curiousest man about always betting on anything that turned up you ever see, if he could get anybody to bet on the other side; and if he couldn't he'd change sides. Any way that suited the other man would suit *him*—any way just so's he got a bet, *he* was satisfied. But still he was lucky, uncommon lucky; he most always come out winner. He was always ready and laying for a chance; there couldn't be no solit'ry thing mentioned but that feller'd offer to bet on it, and take ary side you please, as I was just telling you. If there was a horse-race, you'd find him flush or you'd find him busted at the end of it; if there was a dog-fight, he'd bet on it; if there was a cat-fight, he'd bet on it; if there was a chicken-fight, he'd bet on it; why, if there was two birds setting on a fence, he would bet you which one would fly first; or if there was a camp-meeting, he would be there reg'lar to bet on Parson Walker, which he judged to be the best exhorter about here, and so he was too, and a good man. If he even see a straddle-bug[2] start to go anywheres, he would bet you how long it would take him to get to—to wherever he was going to, and if you took him up, he would foller that straddle-bug to Mexico but what he would find out where he was bound for and how long he was on the road. Lots of the boys here has seen that Smiley, and can tell you about him. Why, it never made no difference to *him* —he'd bet on *any* thing—the dangdest feller. Parson Walker's wife laid very sick once, for a good while, and it seemed as if they warn't going to save her; but one morning he come in, and Smiley up and asked him how she was, and he said she was considerable better— thank the Lord for his inf'nite mercy—and coming on so smart that with the blessing of Prov'dence she'd get well yet; and Smiley, before he thought, says, 'Well, I'll resk two-and-a-half she don't anyway.'

"Thish-yer Smiley had a mare—the boys called her the fifteen-minute nag, but that was only in fun, you know, because of course she was faster than that—and he used to win money on that horse, for all she was so slow and always had the asthma, or the distemper, or the consumption, or something of that kind. They used to give her two or three hundred yards' start, and then pass her under way; but always at the fag end of the race she'd get excited and desperate like, and come cavoting and straddling up, and scattering her legs around limber, sometimes in the air, and sometimes out to one side among the fences, and kicking up m-o-r-e dust and raising m-o-r-e racket with her coughing and sneezing and blowing her nose—and *always* fetch up at the stand just about a neck ahead, as near as you could ciphor it down.

---

1. Artificial chute or trough for carry-ing water to gold diggings.　　2. Long-legged beetle.

"And he had a little small bull-pup, that to look at him you'd think he warn't worth a cent but to set around and look ornery and lay for a chance to steal something. But as soon as money was up on him he was a different dog; his under-jaw'd begin to stick out like the fo'castle of a steamboat, and his teeth would uncover and shine like the furnaces. And a dog might tackle him and bully-rag him, and bite him, and throw him over his shoulder two or three times, and Andrew Jackson[3]—which was the name of the pup—Andrew Jackson would never let on but what *he* was satisfied, and hadn't expected nothing else—and the bets being doubled and doubled on the other side all the time, till the money was all up; and then all of a sudden he would grab that other dog jest by the j'int of his hind leg and freeze to it—not chaw, you understand, but only just grip and hang on till they throwed up the sponge, if it was a year. Smiley always come out winner on that pup, till he harnessed a dog once that didn't have no hind legs, because they'd been sawed off in a circular saw, and when the thing had gone along far enough, and the money was all up, and he come to make a snatch for his pet holt, he see in a minute how he'd been imposed on, and how the other dog had him in the door, so to speak, and he 'peared surprised, and then he looked sorter discouraged-like, and didn't try no more to win the fight, and so he got shucked out bad. He give Smiley a look, as much as to say his heart was broke, and it was *his* fault, for putting up a dog that hadn't no hind legs for him to take holt of, which was his main dependence in a fight, and then he limped off a piece and laid down and died. It was a good pup, was that Andrew Jackson, and would have made a name for hisself if he'd lived, for the stuff was in him and he had genius—I know it, because he hadn't no opportunities to speak of, and it don't stand to reason that a dog could make such a fight as he could under them circumstances if he hadn't no talent. It always makes me feel sorry when I think of that last fight of his'n, and the way it turned out.

"Well, thish-yer Smiley had rat-tarriers, and chicken cocks, and tom-cats and all them kind of things, till you couldn't rest, and you couldn't fetch nothing for him to bet on but he'd match you. He ketched a frog one day, and took him home, and said he cal'lated to educate him; and so he never done nothing for three months but set in his back yard and learn that frog to jump. And you bet you he *did* learn him, too. He'd give him a little punch behind, and the next minute you'd see that frog whirling in the air like a doughnut—see him turn one summerset, or maybe a couple, if he got a good start, and come down flat-footed and all right, like a cat. He got him up so in the matter of ketching flies, and kep' him in practice so constant, that he'd nail a fly every time as fur as he could see him. Smiley said all a frog wanted was education, and he could do 'most anything—and I believe him. Why, I've seen him set Dan'l Webster[4] down here

---

3. President of the United States, 1829–1837; called Old Hickory because he was so tough and determined.
4. Famous congressman, senator, orator (1782–1852) whose independence—sup-porting Jackson on Union, running against him as a Whig, not resigning from Tyler's cabinet when other Whigs did—made him seem to some a great "jumper."

on this floor—Dan'l Webster was the name of the frog—and sing out, 'Flies, Dan'l, flies!' and quicker'n you could wink he'd spring straight up and snake a fly off'n the counter there, and flop down on the floor ag'in as solid as a gob of mud, and fall to scratching the side of his head with his hind foot as indifferent as if he hadn't no idea he'd been doin' any more'n any frog might do. You never see a frog so modest and straightfor'ard as he was, for all he was so gifted. And when it come to fair and square jumping on a dead level, he could get over more ground at one straddle than any animal of his breed you ever see. Jumping on a dead level was his strong suit, you understand; and when it come to that, Smiley would ante up money on him as long as he had a red.[5] Smiley was monstrous proud of his frog, and well he might be, for fellers that had traveled and been everywheres, all said he laid over any frog that ever *they* see.

"Well, Smiley kep' the beast in a little lattice box, and he used to fetch him downtown sometimes and lay for a bet. One day a feller— a stranger in the camp, he was—come acrost him with his box, and says:

" 'What might it be that you've got in the box?'

"And Smiley says, sorter indifferent-like, 'It might be a parrot, or it might be a canary, maybe, but it ain't—it's only just a frog.'

"And the feller took it, and looked at it careful, and turned it round this way and that, and says, 'H'm—so 'tis. Well, what's *he* good for?'

" 'Well,' Smiley says, easy and careless, 'he's good enough for *one* thing, I should judge—he can outjump any frog in Calaveras County.'

"The feller took the box again, and took another long, particular look, and give it back to Smiley, and says, very deliberate, 'Well,' he says, 'I don't see no p'ints about that frog that's any better'n any other frog.'

" 'Maybe you don't,' Smiley says. 'Maybe you understand frogs and maybe you don't understand 'em; maybe you've had experience, and maybe you ain't only a amature, as it were. Anyways, I've got *my* opinion, and I'll resk forty dollars that he can outjump any frog in Calaveras County.'

"And the feller studied a minute, and then says, kinder sadlike, 'Well, I'm only a stranger here, and I ain't got no frog; but if I had a frog, I'd bet you.'

"And then Smiley says, 'That's all right—that's all right—if you'll hold my box a minute, I'll go and get you a frog.' And so the feller took the box, and put up his forty dollars along with Smiley's, and set down to wait.

"So he set there a good while thinking and thinking to himself, and then he got the frog out and prized his mouth open and took a tea-spoon and filled him full of quail-shot—filled him pretty near up to his chin—and set him on the floor. Smiley he went to the swamp and slopped around in the mud for a long time, and finally he ketched a frog, and fetched him in, and give him to this feller, and says:

" 'Now, if you're ready, set him alongside of Dan'l, with his fore paws just even with Dan'l's, and I'll give the word.' Then he says,

5. A single (red) penny.

'One—two—three—*git!*' and him and the feller touched up the frogs from behind, and the new frog hopped off lively, but Dan'l give a heave, and hysted up his shoulders—so—like a Frenchman, but it warn't no use—he couldn't budge; he was planted as solid as a church, and he couldn't no more stir than if he was anchored out. Smiley was a good deal surprised, and he was disgusted too, but he didn't have no idea what the matter was, of course.

"The feller took the money and started away; and when he was going out at the door, he sorter jerked his thumb over his shoulder —so—at Dan'l, and says again, very deliberate, 'Well,' he says, 'I don't see no p'ints about that frog that's any better'n any other frog.'

"Smiley he stood scratching his head and looking down at Dan'l a long time, and at last he says, 'I do wonder what in the nation that frog throw'd off for—I wonder if there ain't something the matter with him—he 'pears to look mighty baggy, somehow.' And he ketched Dan'l by the nape of the neck, and hefted him, and says, 'Why blame my cats if he don't weigh five pound!' " and turned him upside down and he belched out a double handful of shot. And then he see how it was, and he was the maddest man—he set the frog down and took out after that feller, but he never ketched him. And—"

[Here Simon Wheeler heard his name called from the front yard, and got up to see what was wanted.] And turning to me as he moved away, he said: "Just set where you are, stranger, and rest easy—I ain't going to be gone a second."

But, by your leave, I did not think that a continuation of the history of the enterprising vagabond *Jim* Smiley would be likely to afford me much information concerning the Rev. *Leonidas* W. Smiley, and so I started away.

At the door I met the sociable Wheeler returning, and he button-holed me and recommended:

"Well, thish-yer Smiley had a yaller one-eyed cow that didn't have no tail, only just a short stump like a bannanner, and—"

However, lacking both time and inclination, I did not wait to hear about the afflicted cow, but took my leave.

1867

WILLIAM FAULKNER

Spotted Horses

Yes, sir. Flem Snopes has filled that whole country full of spotted horses. You can hear folks running them all day and all night, whooping and hollering, and the horses running back and forth across them little wooden bridges ever now and then kind of like thunder. Here I was this morning pretty near halfway to town, with the team ambling along and me setting in the buckboard about half asleep, when all of a sudden something come swurging[1] up outen the bushes and jumped the road clean, without touching hoof to it. It flew right over my team, big as a billboard and flying through the air like a hawk. It taken me thirty minutes to stop my team and untangle the harness and the buckboard and hitch them up again.

That Flem Snopes. I be dog if he ain't a case, now. One morning about ten years ago, the boys was just getting settled down on Varner's porch for a little talk and tobacco, when here come Flem out from behind the counter, with his coat off and his hair all parted like he might have been clerking for Varner for ten years already. Folks all knowed him; it was a big family of them about five miles down the bottom. That year, at least. Share-cropping. They never stayed on any place over a year. Then they would move on to another place, with the chap or maybe the twins of that year's litter. It was a regular nest of them. But Flem. The rest of them stayed tenant farmers, moving ever year, but here come Flem one day, walking out from behind Jody Varner's counter like he owned it. And he wasn't there but a year or two before folks knowed that, if him and Jody was both still in that store in ten years more, it would be Jody clerking for Flem Snopes. Why, that fellow could make a nickel where it wasn't but four cents to begin with. He skun[2] me in two trades, myself, and the fellow that can do that, I just hope he'll get rich before I do; that's all.

All right. So here Flem was, clerking at Varner's, making a nickel here and there and not telling nobody about it. No, sir. Folks never knowed when Flem got the better of somebody lessen the fellow he beat told it. He'd just set there in the store-chair, chewing his tobacco and keeping his own business to hisself, until about a week later we'd find out it was somebody else's business he was keeping to hisself—provided the fellow he trimmed was mad enough to tell it. That's Flem.

We give him ten years to own everthing Jody Varner had. But he never waited no ten years. I reckon you-all know that gal of Uncle Billy Varner's, the youngest one; Eula. Jody's sister. Ever Sunday ever yellow-wheeled buggy and curried riding horse in that country would be hitched to Bill Varner's fence, and the young bucks setting on the porch, swarming around Eula like bees around a honey pot. One of these here kind of big, soft-looking gals that could giggle richer than plowed newground. Wouldn't none of them leave before the others, and so they would set there on the porch until time to go home, with some of them with nine and ten miles to ride and then get up tomorrow and go back to the field. So they would all leave together and they would ride in a clump down to the creek ford and hitch them curried horses and yellow-wheeled buggies and get out and fight one another. Then they would get in the buggies again and go on home.

Well, one day about a year ago, one of them yellow-wheeled buggies and one of them curried saddle-horses quit this country. We heard they was heading for Texas. The next day Uncle Billy and

1. Surging.
2. Skinned, cheated.

Eula and Flem come in to town in Uncle Bill's surrey, and when they come back, Flem and Eula was married. And on the next day we heard that two more of them yellow-wheeled buggies had left the country. They mought have gone to Texas, too. It's a big place.

Anyway, about a month after the wedding, Flem and Eula went to Texas, too. They was gone pretty near a year. Then one day last month, Eula come back, with a baby. We figgered up, and we decided that it was as well-growed a three-months-old baby as we ever see. It can already pull up on a chair. I reckon Texas makes big men quick, being a big place. Anyway, if it keeps on like it started, it'll be chewing tobacco and voting time it's eight years old.

And so last Friday here come Flem himself. He was on a wagon with another fellow. The other fellow had one of these two-gallon hats and a ivory-handled pistol and a box of gingersnaps sticking out of his hind pocket, and tied to the tailgate of the wagon was about two dozen of them Texas ponies, hitched to one another with barbed wire. They was colored like parrots and they was quiet as doves, and ere a one of them would kill you quick as a rattlesnake. Nere a one of them had two eyes the same color, and nere a one of them had ever see a bridle, I reckon; and when that Texas man got down offen the wagon and walked up to them to show how gentle they was, one of them cut his vest clean offen him, same as with a razor.

Flem had done already disappeared; he had went on to see his wife, I reckon, and to see if that ere baby had done gone on to the field to help Uncle Billy plow, maybe. It was the Texas man that taken the horses on to Mrs. Littlejohn's lot. He had a litttle trouble at first, when they come to the gate, because they hadn't never see a fence before, and when he finally got them in and taken a pair of wire cutters and unhitched them and got them into the barn and poured some shell corn into the trough, they durn nigh tore down the barn. I reckon they thought that shell corn was bugs, maybe. So he left them in the lot and he announced that the auction would begin at sunup tomorrow.

That night we was setting on Mrs. Littlejohn's porch. You-all mind the moon was nigh full that night, and we could watch them spotted varmints swirling along the fence and back and forth across the lot same as minnows in a pond. And then now and then they would all kind of huddle up against the barn and rest themselves by biting and kicking one another. We would hear a squeal, and then a set of hoofs would go Bam! against the barn, like a pistol. It sounded just like a fellow with a pistol, in a nest of cattymounts,[3] taking his time.

II

It wasn't ere[4] a man knowed yet if Flem owned them things or not. They just knowed one thing: that they wasn't never going to know for sho if Flem did or not, or if maybe he didn't just get on that wagon at the edge of town, for the ride or not. Even Eck Snopes didn't know, Flem's own cousin. But wasn't nobody surprised at that. We knowed that Flem would skin Eck quick as he would ere a one of us.

---

3. Panthers.   4. There was not one.

They was there by sunup next morning, some of them come twelve and sixteen miles, with seed-money tied up in tobacco sacks in their overalls, standing along the fence, when the Texas man come out of Mrs. Littlejohn's after breakfast and clumb onto the gate post with that ere white pistol butt sticking outen his hind pocket. He taken a new box of gingersnaps outen his pocket and bit the end offen it like a cigar and spit out the paper, and said the auction was open. And still they was coming up in wagons and a horse-and-mule-back and hitching the teams across the road and coming to the fence. Flem wasn't nowhere in sight.

But he couldn't get them started. He begun to work on Eck, because Eck holp him last night to get them into the barn and feed them that shell corn. Eck got out jist in time. He come outen that barn like a chip of the crest of a busted dam of water, and clumb into the wagon just in time.

He was working on Eck when Henry Armstid come up in his wagon. Eck was saying he was skeered to bid on one of them, because he might get it, and the Texas man says, "Them ponies? Them little horses?" He clumb down offen the gate post and went toward the horses. They broke and run, and him following them, kind of chirping to them, with his hand out like he was fixing to catch a fly, until he got three or four of them cornered. Then he jumped into them, and then we couldn't see nothing for a while because of the dust. It was a big cloud of it, and them blare-eyed, spotted things swoaring outen it twenty foot to a jump, in forty directions without counting up. Then the dust settled and there they was, that Texas man and the horse. He had its head twisted clean around like a owl's head. Its legs was braced and it was trembling like a new bride and groaning like a saw mill, and him holding its head wrung clean around on its neck so it was snuffing sky. "Look it over," he says, with his heels dug too and that white pistol sticking outen his pocket and his neck swole up like a spreading adder's until you could just tell what he was saying, cussing the horse and talking to us all at once: "Look him over, the fiddle-headed son of fourteen fathers. Try him, buy him; you will get the best—" Then it was all dust again, and we couldn't see nothing but spotted hide and mane, and that ere Texas man's boot-heels like a couple of walnuts on two strings, and after a while that two-gallon hat come sailing out like a fat old hen crossing a fence.

When the dust settled again, he was just getting outen the far fence corner, brushing himself off. He come and got his hat and brushed it off and come and clumb onto the gate post again. He was breathing hard. He taken the gingersnap box outen his pocket and et one, breathing hard. The hammer-head horse was still running round and round the lot like a merry-go-round at a fair. That was when Henry Armstid come shoving up to the gate in them patched overalls and one of them dangle-armed shirts of hisn. Hadn't nobody noticed him until then. We was all watching the Texas man and the horses. Even Mrs. Littlejohn; she had done come out and built a fire under the washpot in her back yard, and she would stand at the fence a while and then go back into the house and come out again with a armful of wash and stand at the fence again. Well, here come Henry shoving up, and then we see Mrs. Armstid right behind him, in that ere faded wrapper and sunbonnet and them tennis shoes. "Git on back to that wagon," Henry says.

"Henry," she says.

"Here, boys," the Texas man says; "make room for missus to git up and see. Come on, Henry," he says; "here's your chance to buy that saddle-horse missus has been wanting. What about ten dollars, Henry?"

"Henry," Mrs. Armstid says. She put her hand on Henry's arm. Henry knocked her hand down.

"Git on back to that wagon, like I told you," he says.

Mrs. Armstid never moved. She stood behind Henry, with her hands rolled into her dress, not looking at nothing. "He hain't no more despair[5] than to buy one of them things," she says. "And us not five dollars ahead of the porehouse, he hain't no more despair." It was the truth, too. They ain't never made more than a bare living offen that place of theirs, and them with four chaps and the very clothes they wears she earns by weaving by the firelight at night while Henry's asleep.

"Shut your mouth and git on back to that wagon," Henry says. "Do you want I taken a wagon stake to you here in the big road?"

Well, that Texas man taken one look at her. Then he begun on Eck again, like Henry wasn't even there. But Eck was skeered. "I can git me a snapping turtle or a water moccasin for nothing. I ain't going to buy none."

So the Texas man said he would give Eck a horse. "To start the auction, and because you holp me last night. If you'll start the bidding on the next horse," he says, "I'll give you that fiddle-head horse."

I wish you could have seen them, standing there with their seed-money in their pockets, watching that Texas man give Eck Snopes a live horse, all fixed to call him a fool if he taken it or not. Finally Eck says he'll take it. "Only I just starts the bidding," he says. "I don't have to buy the next one lessen I ain't overtopped." The Texas man said all right, and Eck bid a dollar on the next one, with Henry Armstid standing there with his mouth already open, watching Eck and the Texas man like a mad dog or something. "A dollar," Eck says.

The Texas man looked at Eck. His mouth was already open too, like he had started to say something and what he was going to say had up and died on him. "A dollar?" he says. "One dollar? You mean, *one* dollar, Eck?"

"Durn it," Eck says; "two dollars, then."

Well, sir, I wish you could a seen that Texas man. He taken out that gingersnap box and held it up and looked into it, careful, like it might have been a diamond ring in it, or a spider. Then he throwed it away and wiped his face with a bandanna. "Well," he says. "Well. Two dollars. Two dollars. Is your pulse all right, Eck?" he says. "Do you have ager-sweats[6] at night, maybe?" he says. "Well," he says, "I got to take it. But are you boys going to stand there and see Eck

5. To spare.   6. Cold sweats, as in malaria.

get two horses at a dollar a head?"

That done it. I be dog if he wasn't nigh as smart as Flem Snopes. He hadn't no more than got the words outen his mouth before here was Henry Armstid, waving his hand. "Three dollars," Henry says. Mrs. Armstid tried to hold him again. He knocked her hand off, shoving up to the gate post.

"Mister," Mrs. Armstid says, "we got chaps in the house and not corn to feed the stock. We got five dollars I earned my chaps a-weaving after dark, and him snoring in the bed. And he hain't no more despair."

"Henry bids three dollars," the Texas man says. "Raise him a dollar, Eck, and the horse is yours."

"Henry," Mrs. Armstid says.

"Raise him, Eck," the Texas man says.

"Four dollars," Eck says.

"Five dollars," Henry says, shaking his fist. He shoved up right under the gate post. Mrs. Armstid was looking at the Texas man too.

"Mister," she says, "if you take that five dollars I earned my chaps a-weaving for one of them things, it'll be a curse onto you and yourn during all the time of man."

But it wasn't no stopping Henry. He had shoved up, waving his fist at the Texas man. He opened it; the money was in nickels and quarters, and one dollar bill that looked like a cow's cud. "Five dollars," he says. "And the man that raises it'll have to beat my head off, or I'll beat hisn."

"All right," the Texas man says. "Five dollars is bid. But don't you shake your hand at me."

III

It taken till nigh sundown before the last one was sold. He got them hotted up once and the bidding got up to seven dollars and a quarter, but most of them went around three or four dollars, him setting on the gate post and picking the horses out one at a time by mouthword, and Mrs. Littlejohn pumping up and down at the tub and stopping and coming to the fence for a while and going back to the tub again. She had done got done too, and the wash was hung on the line in the back yard, and we could smell supper cooking. Finally they was all sold; he swapped the last two and the wagon for a buckboard.

We was all kind of tired, but Henry Armstid looked more like a mad dog than ever. When he bought, Mrs. Armstid had went back to the wagon, setting in it behind them two rabbit-sized, bone-pore mules, and the wagon itself looking like it would fall all to pieces soon as the mules moved. Henry hadn't even waited to pull it outen the road; it was still in the middle of the road and her setting in it, not looking at nothing, ever since this morning.

Henry was right up against the gate. He went up to the Texas man. "I bought a horse and I paid cash," Henry says. "And yet you expect me to stand around here until they are all sold before I can get my horse. I'm going to take my horse outen that lot."

The Texas man looked at Henry. He talked like he might have

been asking for a cup of coffee at the table. "Take your horse," he says.

Then Henry quit looking at the Texas man. He begun to swallow, holding onto the gate. "Ain't you going to help me?" he says.

"It ain't my horse," the Texas man says.

Henry never looked at the Texas man again, he never looked at nobody. "Who'll help me catch my horse?" he says. Never nobody said nothing. "Bring the plowline," Henry says. Mrs. Armstid got outen the wagon and brought the plowline. The Texas man got down offen the post. The woman made to pass him, carrying the rope.

"Don't you go in there, missus," the Texas man says.

Henry opened the gate. He didn't look back. "Come on here," he says.

"Don't you go in there, missus," the Texas man says.

Mrs. Armstid wasn't looking at nobody, neither, with her hands across her middle, holding the rope. "I reckon I better," she says. Her and Henry went into the lot. The horses broke and run. Henry and Mrs. Armstid followed.

"Get him into the corner," Henry says. They got Henry's horse cornered finally, and Henry taken the rope, but Mrs. Armstid let the horse get out. They hemmed it up again, but Mrs. Armstid let it get out again, and Henry turned and hit her with the rope. "Why didn't you head him back?" Henry says. He hit her again. "Why didn't you?" It was about that time I looked around and see Flem Snopes standing there.

It was the Texas man that done something. He moved fast for a big man. He caught the rope before Henry could hit the third time, and Henry whirled and made like he would jump at the Texas man. But he never jumped. The Texas man went and taken Henry's arm and led him outen the lot. Mrs. Armstid come behind them and the Texas man taken some money outen his pocket and he give it into Mrs. Armstid's hand. "Get him into the wagon and take him on home," the Texas man says, like he might have been telling them he enjoyed his supper.

Then here come Flem. "What's that for, Buck?" Flem says.

"Thinks he bought one of them ponies," the Texas man says. "Get him on away, missus."

But Henry wouldn't go. "Give him back that money," he says. "I bought that horse and I aim to have him if I have to shoot him."

And there was Flem, standing there with his hands in his pockets, chewing, like he had just happened to be passing.

"You take your money and I take my horse," Henry says. "Give it back to him," he says to Mrs. Armstid.

"You don't own no horse of mine," the Texas man says. "Get him on home, missus."

Then Henry seen Flem. "You got something to do with these horses," he says. "I bought one. Here's the money for it." He taken the bill outen Mrs. Armstid's hand. He offered it to Flem. "I bought one. Ask him. Here. Here's the money," he says, giving the bill to Flem.

When Flem taken the money, the Texas man dropped the rope he had snatched outen Henry's hand. He had done sent Eck Snopes's boy up to the store for another box of gingersnaps, and he taken the box of gingersnaps, and he taken the box outen his pocket and looked into it. It was empty and he dropped it on the ground. "Mr. Snopes will have your money for you tomorrow," he says to Mrs. Armstid. "You can get it from him tomorrow. He don't own no horse. You get him into the wagon and get him on home." Mrs. Armstid went back to the wagon and got in. "Where's that ere buckboard I bought?" the Texas man says. It was after sundown then. And then Mrs. Littlejohn come out on the porch and rung the supper bell.

IV

I come on in and et supper. Mrs. Littlejohn would bring in a pan of bread or something, then she would go out to the porch a minute and come back and tell us. The Texas man had hitched his team to the buckboard he had swapped them last two horses for, and him and Flem had gone, and then she told that the rest of them that never had ropes had went back to the store with I. O. Snopes to get some ropes, and wasn't nobody at the gate but Henry Armstid, and Mrs. Armstid setting in the wagon in the road, and Eck Snopes and that boy of hisn. "I don't care how many of them fool men gets killed by them things," Mrs. Littlejohn says, "but I ain't going to let Eck Snopes take that boy into that lot again." So she went down to the gate, but she come back without the boy or Eck neither.

"It ain't no need to worry about that boy," I says. "He's charmed." He was right behind Eck last night when Eck went to help feed them. The whole drove of them jumped clean over that boy's head and never touched him. It was Eck that touched him. Eck snatched him into the wagon and taken a rope and frailed the tar outen him.

So I had done et and went to my room and was undressing, long as I had a long trip to make next day; I was trying to sell a machine to Mrs. Bundren up past Whiteleaf; when Henry Armstid opened that gate and went in by hisself. They couldn't make him wait for the balance of them to get back with their ropes. Eck Snopes said he tried to make Henry wait, but Henry wouldn't do it. Eck said Henry walked right up to them and that when they broke, they run clean over Henry like a hay-mow breaking down. Eck said he snatched that boy of hisn out of the way just in time and that them things went through that gate like a creek flood and into the wagons and teams hitched side the road, busting wagon tongues and snapping harness like it was fishing line, with Mrs. Armstid still setting in their wagon in the middle of it like something carved outen wood. Then they scattered, wild horses and tame mules with pieces of harness and single trees dangling offen them, both ways up and down the road.

"There goes ourn, paw!" Eck says his boy said. "There it goes, into Mrs. Littlejohn's house." Eck says it run right up the steps and into the house like a boarder late for supper. I reckon so. Anyway, I was in my room, in my underclothes, with one sock on and one sock in my hand, loaning out the window when the commotion busted out, when I heard something run into the melodeon in the hall; it sounded like a railroad engine. Then the door to my room come sailing in like when you throw a tin bucket top into the wind and I looked over my shoulder and see something that looked like a fourteen-foot pinwheel a-blaring its eyes at me. It had to blare them fast, because I was already done jumped out the window.

I reckon it was anxious, too. I reckon it hadn't never seen barbed wire or shell corn before, but I know it hadn't never seen underclothes before, or maybe it was a sewing-machine agent it hadn't never seen. Anyway, it swirled and turned to run back up the hall and outen the house, when it met Eck Snopes and that boy just coming in, carrying a rope. It swirled again and run down the hall and out the back door just in time to meet Mrs. Littlejohn. She had just gathered up the clothes she had washed, and she was coming onto the back porch with a armful of washing in one hand and a scrubbing board in the other, when the horse skidded up to her, trying to stop and swirl again. It never taken Mrs. Littlejohn no time a-tall.

"Git outen here, you son," she says. She hit it across the face with the scrubbing board; that ere scrubbing board split as neat as ere a axe could have done it, and when the horse swirled to run back up the hall, she hit it again with what was left of the scrubbing board, not on the head this time. "And stay out," she says.

Eck and that boy was halfway down the hall by this time. I reckon that horse looked like a pinwheel to Eck too. "Git to hell outen here, Ad!" Eck says. Only there wasn't time. Eck dropped flat on his face, but the boy never moved. The boy was about a yard tall maybe, in overhalls just like Eck's; that horse swoared over his head without touching a hair. I saw that, because I was just coming back up the front steps, still carrying that ere sock and still in my underclothes, when the horse come onto the porch again. It taken one look at me and swirled again and run to the end of the porch and jumped the banisters and the lot fence like a hen-hawk and lit in the lot running and went out the gate again and jumped eight or ten upside-down wagons and went on down the road. It was a full moon then. Mrs. Armstid was still setting in the wagon like she had done been carved outen wood and left there and forgot.

That horse. It ain't never missed a lick. It was going about forty miles a hour when it come to the bridge over the creek. It would have had a clear road, but it so happened that Vernon Tull was already using the bridge when it got there. He was coming back from town; he hadn't heard about the auction; him and his wife and three daughters and Mrs. Tull's aunt, all setting in chairs in the wagon bed, and all asleep, including the mules. They waked up when the horse hit the bridge one time, but Tull said the first he knew was when the mules tried to turn the wagon around in the middle of the bridge and he seen that spotted varmint run right twixt the mules and run up the wagon tongue like a squirrel. He said he just had time to hit it across the face with his whip-stock, because about that time the mules turned the wagon around on that ere one-way bridge and that horse clumb across one of the mules and jumped down onto the bridge again and went on, with Vernon standing up in the wagon and kicking at it.

Tull said the mules turned in the harness and clumb back into the wagon too, with Tull trying to beat them out again, with the reins wrapped around his wrist. After that he says all he seen was over-turned chairs and womenfolks' legs and white drawers shining in the moonlight, and his mules and that spotted horse going on up the road like a ghost.

The mules jerked Tull outen the wagon and drug him a spell on the bridge before the reins broke. They thought at first that he was dead, and while they was kneeling around him, picking the bridge splinters outen him, here come Eck and that boy, still carrying the rope. They was running and breathing a little hard. "Where'd he go?" Eck says.

V

I went back and got my pants and shirt and shoes on just in time to go and help get Henry Armstid outen the trash in the lot. I be dog[7] if he didn't look like he was dead, with his head hanging back and his teeth showing in the moonlight, and a little rim of white under his eyelids. We could still hear them horses, here and there; hadn't none of them got more than four–five miles away yet, not knowing the country, I reckon. So we could hear them and folks yelling now and then: "Whooey. Head him!"

We toted Henry into Mrs. Littlejohn's. She was in the hall; she hadn't put down the armful of clothes. She taken one look at us, and she laid down the busted scrubbing board and taken up the lamp and opened a empty door. "Bring him in here," she says.

We toted him in and laid him on the bed. Mrs. Littlejohn set the lamp on the dresser, still carrying the clothes. "I'll declare, you men," she says. Our shadows was way up the wall, tiptoeing too; we could hear ourselves breathing. "Better get his wife," Mrs. Littlejohn says. She went out, carrying the clothes.

"I reckon we had," Quick says. "Go get her, somebody."

"Whyn't you go?" Winterbottom says.

"Let Ernest git her," Durley says. "He lives neighbors with them."

Ernest went to fetch her. I be dog if Henry didn't look like he was dead. Mrs. Littlejohn come back, with a kettle and some towels. She went to work on Henry, and then Mrs. Armstid and Ernest come in. Mrs. Armstid come to the foot of the bed and stood there, with her hands rolled into her apron, watching what Mrs. Littlejohn was doing, I reckon.

"You men get outen the way," Mrs. Littlejohn says. "Git outside," she says. "See if you can't find something else to play with that will kill some more of you."

"Is he dead?" Winterbottom says.

"It ain't your fault if he ain't," Mrs. Littlejohn says. "Go tell Will Varner to come up here. I reckon a man ain't so different from a mule, come long come short. Except maybe a mule's got more sense."

We went to get Uncle Billy. It was a full moon. We could hear them, now and then, four mile away: "Whooey. Head him." The country was full of them, one on ever wooden bridge in the land, running across it like thunder: "Whooey. There he goes. Head him."

7. Darned.

We hadn't got far before Henry begun to scream. I reckon Mrs. Littlejohn's water had brung him to; anyway, he wasn't dead. We went on to Uncle Billy's. The house was dark. We called to him, and after a while the window opened and Uncle Billy put his head out, peart as a peckerwood,[8] listening. "Are they still trying to catch them durn rabbits?" he says.

He come down, with his britches on over his nightshirt and his suspenders dangling, carrying his horse-doctoring grip. "Yes, sir," he says, cocking his head like a woodpecker; "they're still a-trying."

We could hear Henry before we reached Mrs. Littlejohn's. He was going Ah-Ah-Ah. We stopped in the yard. Uncle Billy went on in. We could hear Henry. We stood in the yard, hearing them on the bridges, this-a-way and that: "Whooey. Whooey."

"Eck Snopes ought to caught hisn," Ernest says.

"Looks like he ought," Winterbottom said.

Henry was going Ah-Ah-Ah steady in the house; then he begun to scream. "Uncle Billy's started," Quick says. We looked into the hall. We could see the light where the door was. Then Mrs. Littlejohn come out.

"Will needs some help," she says. "You, Ernest. You'll do." Ernest went into the house.

"Hear them?" Quick said. "That one was on Four Mile bridge." We could hear them; it sounded like thunder a long way off; it didn't last long:

"Whooey."

We could hear Henry: "Ah-Ah-Ah-Ah-Ah."

"They are both started now," Winterbottom says. "Ernest too."

That was early in the night. Which was a good thing, because it taken a long night for folks to chase them things right and for Henry to lay there and holler, being as Uncle Billy never had none of this here chloryfoam to set Henry's leg with. So it was considerate in Flem to get them started early. And what do you reckon Flem's com-ment was?

That's right. Nothing. Because he wasn't there. Hadn't nobody see him since that Texas man left.

VI

That was Saturday night. I reckon Mrs. Armstid got home about daylight, to see about the chaps. I don't know where they thought her and Henry was. But lucky the oldest one was a gal, about twelve, big enough to take care of the little ones. Which she did for the next two days. Mrs. Armstid would nurse Henry all night and work in the kitchen for hern and Henry's keep, and in the afternoon she would drive home (it was about four miles) to see to the chaps. She would cook up a pot of victuals and leave it on the stove, and the gal would bar the house and keep the little ones quiet. I would hear Mrs. Littlejohn and Mrs. Armstid talking in the kitchen. "How are the chaps making out?" Mrs. Littlejohn says.

"All right," Mrs. Armstid says.

8. Woodpecker.

"Don't they git skeered at night?" Mrs. Littlejohn says.

"Ina May bars the door when I leave," Mrs. Armstid says. "She's got the axe in bed with her. I reckon she can make out."

I reckon they did. And I reckon Mrs. Armstid was waiting for Flem to come back to town; hadn't nobody seen him until this morning; to get her money the Texas man said Flem was keeping for her. Sho. I reckon she was.

Anyway, I heard Mrs. Armstid and Mrs. Littlejohn talking in the kitchen this morning while I was eating breakfast. Mrs. Littlejohn had just told Mrs. Armstid that Flem was in town. "You can ask him for that five dollars," Mrs. Littlejohn says.

"You reckon he'll give it to me?" Mrs. Armstid says.

Mrs. Littlejohn was washing dishes, washing them like a man, like they was made out of iron. "No," she says. "But asking him won't do no hurt. It might shame him. I don't reckon it will, but it might."

"If he wouldn't give it back, it ain't no use to ask," Mrs. Armstid says.

"Suit yourself," Mrs. Littlejohn says. "It's your money."

I could hear the dishes.

"Do you reckon he might give it back to me?" Mrs. Armstid says. "That Texas man said he would. He said I could get it from Mr. Snopes later."

"Then go and ask him for it," Mrs. Littlejohn says.

I could hear the dishes.

"He won't give it back to me," Mrs. Armstid says.

"All right," Mrs. Littlejohn says. "Don't ask him for it, then."

I could hear the dishes; Mrs. Armstid was helping. "You don't reckon he would, do you?" she says. Mrs. Littlejohn never said nothing. It sounded like she was throwing the dishes at one another. "Maybe I better go and talk to Henry about it," Mrs. Armstid says.

"I would," Mrs. Littlejohn says. I be dog if it didn't sound like she had two plates in her hands, beating them together. "Then Henry can buy another five-dollar horse with it. Maybe he'll buy one next time that will out and out kill him. If I thought that, I'd give you back the money, myself."

"I reckon I better talk to him first," Mrs. Armstid said. Then it sounded like Mrs. Littlejohn taken up all the dishes and throwed them at the cookstove, and I come away.

That was this morning. I had been up to Bundren's and back, and I thought that things would have kind of settled down. So after breakfast, I went up to the store. And there was Flem, setting in the store chair and whittling, like he might not have ever moved since he come to clerk for Jody Varner. I. O. was leaning in the door, in his shirt sleeves and with his hair parted too, same as Flem was before he turned the clerking job over to I. O. It's a funny thing about them Snopes: they all looks alike, yet there ain't ere a two of them that claims brothers. They're always just cousins, like Flem and Eck and Flem and I. O. Eck was there too, squatting against the wall, him and that boy, eating cheese and crackers outen a sack; they told me that Eck hadn't been home a-tall. And that Lon Quick hadn't got back to town, even. He followed his horse clean down to Samson's

Bridge, with a wagon and a camp outfit. Eck finally caught one of hisn. It run into a blind lane at Freeman's and Eck and the boy taken and tied their rope across the end of the lane, about three foot high. The horse come to the end of the lane and whirled and run back without ever stopping. Eck says it never seen the rope a-tall. He says it looked just like one of these here Christmas pinwheels. "Didn't it try to run again?" I says.

"No," Eck says, eating a bit of cheese offen his knife blade. "Just kicked some."

"Kicked some?" I says.

"It broke its neck," Eck says.

Well, they was squatting there, about six of them, talking, talking at Flem; never nobody knowed yet if Flem had ere a interest in them horses or not. So finally I come right out and asked him. "Flem's done skun all of us so much," I says, "that we're proud of him. Come on, Flem," I says, "how much did you and that Texas man make offen them horses? You can tell us. Ain't nobody here but Eck that bought one of them; the others ain't got back to town yet, and Eck's your own cousin; he'll be proud to hear, too. How much did you-all make?"

They was all whittling, not looking at Flem, making like they was studying. But you could a heard a pin drop. And I. O. He had been rubbing his back up and down on the door, but he stopped now, watching Flem like a pointing dog. Flem finished cutting the sliver offen his stick. He spit across the porch, into the road. " 'Twarn't none of my horses," he says.

I. O. cackled, like a hen, slapping his legs with both hands. "You boys might just as well quit trying to get ahead of Flem," he said.

Well, about that time I see Mrs. Armstid come outen Mrs. Little-john's gate, coming up the road. I never said nothing. I says, "Well, if a man can't take care of himself in a trade, he can't blame the man that trims him."

Flem never said nothing, trimming at the stick. He hadn't seen Mrs. Armstid. "Yes, sir," I says. "A fellow like Henry Armstid ain't got nobody but hisself to blame."

"Course he ain't," I. O. says. He ain't seen her, neither. "Henry Armstid's a born fool. Always is been. If Flem hadn't a got his money, somebody else would."

We looked at Flem. He never moved. Mrs. Armstid come on up the road.

"That's right," I says. "But, come to think of it, Henry never bought no horse." We looked at Flem; you could a heard a match drop. "That Texas man told her to get that five dollars back from Flem next day. I reckon Flem's done already taken that money to Mrs. Little-john's and give it to Mrs. Armstid."

We watched Flem. I. O. quit rubbing his back against the door again. After a while Flem raised his head and spit across the porch, into the dust. I. O. cackled, just like a hen. "Ain't he a beating fellow, now?" I. O. says.

Mrs. Armstid was getting closer, so I kept on talking, watching to see if Flem would look up and see her. But he never looked up. I went on talking about Tull, about how he was going to sue Flem, and Flem setting there, whittling his stick, not saying nothing clse after he said they wasn't none of his horses.

Then I. O. happened to look around. He seen Mrs. Armstid. "Psssst!" he says. Flem looked up. "Here she comes!" I. O. says. "Go out the back. I'll tell her you done went in to town today."

But Flem never moved. He just set there, whittling, and we watched Mrs. Armstid come up onto the porch, in that ere faded sunbonnet and wrapper and them tennis shoes that made a kind of hissing noise on the porch. She come onto the porch and stopped, her hands rolled into her dress in front, not looking at nothing.

"He said Saturday," she says, "that he wouldn't sell Henry no horse. He said I could get the money from you."

Flem looked up. The knife never stopped. It went on trimming off a sliver same as if he was watching it. "He taken that money off with him when he left," Flem says.

Mrs. Armstid never looked at nothing. We never looked at her, neither, except the boy of Eck's. He had a half-et cracker in his hand, watching her, chewing.

"He said Henry hadn't bought no horse," Mrs. Armstid says. "He said for me to get the money from you today."

"I reckon he forgot about it," Flem said. "He taken that money off with him Saturday." He whittled again. I. O. kept on rubbing his back, slow. He licked his lips. After a while the woman looked up the road, where it went on up the hill, toward the graveyard. She looked up that way for a while, with that boy of Eck's watching her and I. O. rubbing his back slow against the door. Then she turned back toward the steps.

"I reckon it's time to get dinner started," she says.

"How's Henry this morning, Mrs. Armstid?" Winterbottom says.

She looked at Winterbottom; she almost stopped. "He's resting, I thank you kindly," she says.

Flem got up, outen the chair, putting his knife away. He spit across the porch. "Wait a minute, Mrs. Armstid," he says. She stopped again. She didn't look at him. Flem went on into the store, with I. O. done quit rubbing his back now, with his head craned after Flem, and Mrs. Armstid standing there with her hands rolled into her dress, not looking at nothing. A wagon come up the road and passes; it was Freeman, on the way to town. Then Flem come out again, with I. O. still watching him. Flem had one of these little striped sacks of Jody Varner's candy; I bet he still owes Jody that nickel, too. He put the sack into Mrs. Armstid's hand, like he would have put it into a hollow stump. He spit again across the porch. "A little sweetening for the chaps," he says.

"You're right kind," Mrs. Armstid says. She held the sack of candy in her hand, not looking at nothing. Eck's boy was watching the sack, the half-et cracker in his hand; he wasn't chewing now. He watched Mrs. Armstid roll the sack into her apron. "I reckon I better get on back and help with dinner," she says. She turned and went back across the porch. Flem set down in the chair again and opened his knife. He spit across the porch again, past Mrs. Armstid where she hadn't went down the steps yet. Then she went on, in that ere sun-bonnet and wrapper all the same color, back down the road toward Mrs. Littlejohn's. You couldn't see her dress move, like a natural woman walking. She looked like a old snag still standing up and moving along on a high water. We watched her turn in at Mrs. Littlejohn's and go outen sight. Flem was whittling. I. O. begun to rub his back on the door. Then he begun to cackle, just like a durn hen.

"You boys might just as well quit trying," I. O. says. "You can't git ahead of Flem. You can't touch him. Ain't he a sight, now?"

I be dog if he ain't. If I had brung a herd of wild cattymounts into town and sold them to my neighbors and kinfolks, they would have lynched me. Yes, sir.

p. 1931

10   SETTING

All stories, like all individuals, are obviously part of their time, place, and culture, and are conditioned by them. The more we understand of the historical and cultural context, the more we may come to understand about a story (or about a person). The close relationship between historical, geographical, and cultural context—or setting—on the one hand, and people and events on the other, offers the author a means of reinforcing and communicating his or her vision and the reader therefore a means of understanding more fully the details of the story.

Setting is an important aspect even of the very first story in this collection. Montresor's character and plot can be called Machiavellian (characterized by subtle or unscrupulous cunning; after the Italian Renaissance politician and writer Niccolò Machiavelli, 1469–1527); no wonder Poe's story is set in Renaissance Italy. The Puritan Goodman Brown lives in the reign of King William (1689–1702) in Salem, Massachusetts, where in 1692 the famous witch trials were held—what better place for a story whose subject is a witches' meeting and whose theme is man's natural depravity? Not all of us who live in Atlanta will admit that it is a fit place for a fictional journey through Hell (as in *The Artificial Nigger*), or that rural Georgia (the scene of the novel *Deliverance*) is a fit image for the Garden of Eden, but the traditional image of rural innocence and virtue and urban sinfulness is long established and widely known in our culture, and even those of us who do not accept its validity understand its import. An *English* spinster seems (or seemed) much more prudish and virginal than just any old spinster, Italian lovers seem more sensual than Anglo-Saxon ones, and *Our Friend Judith* takes advantage of that cultural convention. Though few of us know Yalta, Chekhov has little trouble making us understand the contrast of that semitropical resort on the sea, whose very fruit, the melon, is sensuous, and the frozen world of Moscow, of everyday routine and emotions, of fish that's not quite fresh. And in Conrad's *Heart of Darkness,* which many of you may have read, the journey to the interior of the Dark Continent and the journey into the dark interior recesses of the human heart are parallel.

I've mentioned a number of other stories here toward the end of our discussions to emphasize what I hope you long ago understood: almost any story can be put in almost any chapter in this book; almost every aspect of fiction can be seen in almost any story. The stories here illustrate how geographical, historical, and cultural contexts may inform a work, but they are not exclusively local-color, historical, or sociological stories.

Beyond the Bayou, like *Heart of Darkness,* makes parallel or analogous psychic areas and geographical ones. La Folle, frightened "out of her senses" during the Civil War, deadens large areas of her emotional life and restricts herself to a narrow corner of her small world. Another trauma opens her to life, and she crosses into the territory "beyond the bayou." Besides this central analogy, the cultural context—the complex racial mix of Louisiana, which made race relations even in the time of slavery and Reconstruction unique, and even the physical nature of the bayou country—subtly modifies and defines the characters and their actions. While we can learn a good deal about that context from the story, we can also learn a good deal about the story from increased awareness of and knowledge of the context.

Charlie, in *Babylon Revisited,* so reflects his historical and cultural context that it is difficult to say whether he is a symbol or a product of his time and nation and social set; is he merely representative, or does the story imply that one's life is virtually determined by and therefore a reflection of its context? During the prosperous, dissolute Roaring Twenties, Charlie was prosperous and dissolute; an American in Paris, he roared with the loudest. Now, in the depressed thirties, he, like the times, has sobered up. Many of the geographical and historical details in these two stories need footnotes in order for us more fully to understand the relation between the individuals and their background and even the authors and their assumptions (since the first story was written nearly a hundred years ago and the second almost fifty). Now, however, even white readers may understand more of what it means to be a black living in Harlem in the mid-twentieth century than such readers would have a hundred years ago or will a hundred years from now. There is some question whether a white reader ever can understand a story like *Sonny's Blues* as well as a black reader can, whether it is ever possible to make the imaginative leap across ethnic, cultural, or historical dividing lines with complete success. Surely detailed knowledge and a sympathetic imagination sensitized by literature may at least help us approach such understanding, and understanding other subjective visions of the world is, after all, what literature is all about.

KATE CHOPIN

Beyond the Bayou

The bayou curved like a crescent around the point of land on which La Folle's cabin stood. Between the stream and the hut lay a big abandoned field, where cattle were pastured when the bayou supplied them with water enough. Through the woods that spread back into unknown regions the woman had drawn an imaginary line, and past this circle she never stepped. This was the form of her only mania.

She was now a large, gaunt black woman, past thirty-five. Her real name was Jacqueline, but everyone on the plantation called her La Folle,[1] because in childhood she had been frightened literally "out of her senses," and had never wholly regained them.

It was when there had been skirmishing and sharpshooting all day in the woods. Evening was near when P'tit Maître,[2] black with powder and crimson with blood, had staggered into the cabin of Jacqueline's mother, his pursuers close at his heels. The sight had stunned her childish reason.

She dwelt alone in her solitary cabin, for the rest of the quarters had long since been removed beyond her sight and knowledge. She had more physical strength than most men, and made her patch of cotton and corn and tobacco like the best of them. But of the world beyond the bayou she had long known nothing, save what her morbid fancy conceived.

People at Bellissime had grown used to her and her way, and they thought nothing of it. Even when "Old Mis' " died, they did not wonder that La Folle had not crossed the bayou, but had stood upon her side of it, wailing and lamenting.

P'tit Maître was now the owner of Bellissime. He was a middle-aged man, with a family of beautiful daughters about him, and a little son whom La Folle loved as if he had been her own. She called him Chéri,[3] and so did every one else because she did.

None of the girls had ever been to her what Chéri was. They had each and all loved to be with her, and to listen to her wondrous stories of things that always happened "yonda, beyon' de bayou."

But none of them had stroked her black hand quite as Chéri did, nor rested their heads against her knee so confidingly, nor fallen asleep in her arms as he used to do. For Chéri hardly did such things

1. The crazy woman.
2. Little Master.

3. Darling.

now, since he had become the proud possessor of a gun, and had had his black curls cut off.

That summer—the summer Chéri gave La Folle two black curls tied with a knot of red ribbon—the water ran so low in the bayou that even the little children at Bellissime were able to cross it on foot, and the cattle were sent to pasture down by the river. La Folle was sorry whan they were gone, for she loved these dumb companions well, and liked to feel that they were there, and to hear them browsing by night up to her own enclosure.

It was Saturday afternoon, when the fields were deserted. The men had flocked to a neighboring village to do their week's trading, and the women were occupied with household affairs—La Folle as well as the others. It was then she mended and washed her handful of clothes, scoured her house, and did her baking.

In this last employment she never forgot Chéri. Today she had fashioned croquignoles[4] of the most fantastic and alluring shapes for him. So when she saw the boy come trudging across the old field with his gleaming little new rifle on his shoulder, she called out gaily to him, "Chéri! Chéri!"

But Chéri did not need the summons, for he was coming straight to her. His pockets all bulged out with almonds and raisins and an orange that he had secured for her from the very fine dinner which had been given that day up at his father's house.

He was a sunny-faced youngster of ten. When he had emptied his pockets, La Folle patted his round red cheek, wiped his soiled hands on her apron, and smoothed his hair. Then she watched him as, with his cakes in his hand, he crossed her strip of cotton back of the cabin, and disappeared into the wood.

He had boasted of the things he was going to do with his gun out there.

"You think they got plenty deer in the wood, La Folle?" he had inquired, with the calculating air of an experienced hunter.

"*Non, non!*" the woman laughed. "Don't you look fo' no deer, Chéri. Dat 's too big. But you bring La Folle one good fat squirrel fo' her dinner to-morrow, an' she goin' be satisfi'."

"One squirrel ain't a bit. I'll bring you mo' 'an onc, La Folle," he had boasted pompously as he went away.

When the woman, an hour later, heard the report of the boy's rifle close to the wood's edge, she would have thought nothing of it if a sharp cry of distress had not followed the sound.

She withdrew her arms from the tub of suds in which they had been plunged, dried them upon her apron, and as quickly as her trembling limbs would bear her, hurried to the spot whence the ominous report had come.

It was as she feared. There she found Chéri stretched upon the ground, with his rifle beside him. He moaned piteously:

"I'm dead, La Folle! I'm dead! I'm gone!"

"*Non, non!*" she exclaimed resolutely, as she knelt beside him. "Put you' arm 'roun' La Folle's nake, Chéri. Dat's nuttin'; dat goin' be

4. Biscuits.

nuttin'." She lifted him in her powerful arms.

Chéri had carried his gun muzzle-downward. He had stumbled, he did not know how. He only knew that he had a ball lodged somewhere in his leg, and he thought that his end was at hand. Now, with his head upon the woman's shoulder, he moaned and wept with pain and fright.

"Oh, La Folle! La Folle! it hurt so bad! I can' stan' it, La Folle!"

"Don't cry, *mon bébé*,[5] *mon bébé, mon Chéri!*" the woman spoke soothingly as she covered the ground with long strides. "La Folle goin' mine you; Doctor Bonfils goin' come make *mon Chéri* well agin."

She had reached the abandoned field. As she crossed it with her precious burden, she looked constantly and restlessly from side to side. A terrible fear was upon her—the fear of the world beyond the bayou, the morbid and insane dread she had been under since childhood.

When she was at the bayou's edge she stood there, and shouted for help as if a life depended upon it:

"Oh, P'tit Maître! P'tit Maître! *Venez donc! Au secours! Au secours!*"[6]

No voice responded. Chéri's hot tears were scalding her neck. She called for each and every one upon the place, and still no answer came.

She shouted, she wailed; but whether her voice remained unheard or unheeded, no reply came to her frenzied cries. And all the while Chéri moaned and wept and entreated to be taken home to his mother.

La Folle gave a last despairing look around her. Extreme terror was upon her. She clasped the child close against her breast, where he could feel her heart beat like a muffled hammer. Then shutting her eyes, she ran suddenly down the shallow bank of the bayou, and never stopped till she had climbed the opposite shore.

She stood there quivering an instant as she opened her eyes. Then she plunged into the footpath through the trees.

She spoke no more to Chéri, but muttered constantly, "*Bon Dieu, ayez pitié La Folle! Bon Dieu, ayez pitié moi!*"[7]

Instinct seemed to guide her. When the pathway spread clear and smooth enough before her, she again closed her eyes tightly against the sight of that unknown and terrifying world.

A child, playing in some weeds, caught sight of her as she neared the quarters. The little one uttered a cry of dismay.

"La Folle!" she screamed, in her piercing treble. "La Folle done cross de bayer!"

Quickly the cry passed down the line of cabins.

"Yonda, La Folle done cross de bayou!"

Children, old men, old women, young ones with infants in their arms, flocked to doors and windows to see this awe-inspiring spectacle. Most of them shuddered with superstitious dread of what it might portend. "She totin' Chéri!" some of them shouted.

Some of the more daring gathered about her, and followed at her heels, only to fall back with new terror when she turned her distorted

5. My baby.
6. Come here! Help! Help!

7. Good Lord, have pity on La Folle! Good Lord, have pity on me!

face upon them. Her eyes were bloodshot and the saliva had gathered in a white foam on her black lips.

Some one had run ahead of her to where P'tit Maître sat with his family and guests upon the gallery.

"P'tit Maître! La Folle done cross de bayou! Look her! Look her yonda totin' Chéri!" This startling intimation was the first which they had of the woman's approach.

She was now near at hand. She walked with long strides. Her eyes were fixed desperately before her, and she breathed heavily, as a tired ox.

At the foot of the stairway, which she could not have mounted, she laid the boy in his father's arms. Then the world that had looked red to La Folle suddenly turned black—like that day she had seen powder and blood.

She reeled for an instant. Before a sustaining arm could reach her, she fell heavily to the ground.

When La Folle regained consciousness, she was at home again, in her own cabin and upon her own bed. The moon rays, streaming in through the open door and windows, gave what light was needed to the old black mammy who stood at the table concocting a tisane of fragrant herbs. It was very late.

Others who had come, and found that the stupor clung to her, had gone again. P'tit Maître had been there, and with him Doctor Bonfils, who said that La Folle might die.

But death had passed her by. The voice was very clear and steady with which she spoke to Tante[8] Lizette, brewing her tisane there in a corner.

"Ef you will give me one good drink tisane, Tante Lizette, I b'lieve I'm goin' sleep, me."

And she did sleep; so soundly, so healthfully, that old Lizette without compunction stole softly away to creep back through the moonlit fields to her own cabin in the new quarters.

The first touch of the cool gray morning awoke La Folle. She arose, calmly, as if no tempest had shaken and threatened her existence but yesterday.

She donned her new blue cottonade[9] and white apron, for she remembered that this was Sunday. When she had made for herself a cup of strong black coffee, and drunk it with relish, she quitted the cabin and walked across the old familiar field to the bayou's edge again.

She did not stop there as she had always done before, but crossed with a long, steady stride as if she had done this all her life.

When she had made her way through the brush and scrub cottonwood-trees that lined the opposite bank, she found herself upon the border of a field where the white, bursting cotton, with the dew upon it, gleamed for acres and acres like frosted silver in the early dawn.

La Folle drew a long, deep breath as she gazed across the country. She walked slowly and uncertainly, like one who hardly knows how, looking about her as she went.

8. Aunt.   9. Cotton fabric made to resemble wool.

The cabins, that yesterday had sent a clamor of voices to pursue her, were quiet now. No one was yet astir at Bellissime. Only the birds that darted here and there from hedges were awake, and singing their matins.

When La Folle came to the broad stretch of velvety lawn that surrounded the house, she moved slowly and with delight over the springy turf, that was delicious beneath her tread.

She stopped to find whence came those perfumes that were assailing her senses with memories from a time far gone.

There they were, stealing up to her from the thousand blue violets that peeped out from green, luxuriant beds. There they were, showering down from the big waxen bells of the magnolias far above her head, and from the jessamine clumps around her.

There were roses, too, without number. To right and left palms spread in broad and graceful curves. It all looked like enchantment beneath the sparkling sheen of dew.

When La Folle had slowly and cautiously mounted the many steps that led up to the veranda, she turned to look back at the perilous ascent she had made. Then she caught sight of the river, bending like a silver bow at the foot of Bellissime. Exultation possessed her soul.

La Folle rapped softly upon a door near at hand. Chéri's mother soon cautiously opened it. Quickly and cleverly she dissembled the astonishment she felt at seeing La Folle.

"Ah, La Folle? Is it you, so early?"

"*Oui*,[1] madame. I come ax how my po' li'le Chéri to, 's mo'nin'."

"He is feeling easier, thank you, La Folle. Dr. Bonfils says it will be nothing serious. He's sleeping now. Will you come back when he awakes?"

"*Non*, madame. I'm goin' wait yair tell Chéri wake up." La Folle seated herself upon the topmost step of the veranda.

A look of wonder and deep content crept into her face as she watched for the first time the sun rise upon the new, the beautiful world beyond the bayou.

1894

F. SCOTT FITZGERALD

Babylon Revisited

"And where's Mr. Campbell?" Charlie asked.

"Gone to Switzerland. Mr. Campbell's a pretty sick man, Mr. Wales."

"I'm sorry to hear that. And George Hardt?" Charlie inquired.

"Back in America, gone to work."

"And where is the Snow Bird?"

---

1. Yes.

"He was in here last week. Anyway, his friend, Mr. Schaeffer, is in Paris."

Two familiar names from the long list of a year and a half ago. Charlie scribbled an address in his notebook and tore out the page.

"If you see Mr. Schaeffer, give him this," he said. "It's my brother-in-law's address. I haven't settled on a hotel yet."

He was not really disappointed to find Paris was so empty. But the stillness in the Ritz bar was strange and portentous. It was not an American bar any more—he felt polite in it, and not as if he owned it. It had gone back into France. He felt the stillness from the moment he got out of the taxi and saw the doorman, usually in a frenzy of activity at this hour, gossiping with a *chasseur*[1] by the servants' entrance.

Passing through the corridor, he heard only a single, bored voice in the once-clamorous women's room. When he turned into the bar he traveled the twenty feet of green carpet with his eyes fixed straight ahead by old habit; and then, with his foot firmly on the rail, he turned and surveyed the room, encountering only a single pair of eyes that fluttered up from a newspaper in the corner. Charlie asked for the head barman, Paul, who in the latter days of the bull market[2] had come to work in his own custom-built car—disembarking, however, with due nicety at the nearest corner. But Paul was at his country house today and Alix giving him information.

"No, no more," Charlie said, "I'm going slow these days."

Alix congratulated him: "You were going pretty strong a couple of years ago."

"I'll stick to it all right," Charlie assured him. "I've stuck to it for over a year and a half now."

"How do you find conditions in America?"

"I haven't been to America for months. I'm in business in Prague, representing a couple of concerns there. They don't know about me down there."

Alix smiled.

"Remember the night of George Hardt's bachelor dinner here?" said Charlie. "By the way, what's become of Claude Fessenden?"

Alix lowered his voice confidentially: "He's in Paris, but he doesn't come here any more. Paul doesn't allow it. He ran up a bill of thirty thousand francs,[3] charging all his drinks and his lunches, and usually his dinner, for more than a year. And when Paul finally told him he had to pay, he gave him a bad check."

Alix shook his head sadly.

"I don't understand it, such a dandy fellow. Now he's all bloated up—" He made a plump apple of his hands.

Charlie watched a group of strident queens installing themselves in a corner.

"Nothing affects them," he thought. "Stocks rise and fall, people loaf or work, but they go on forever." The place oppressed him. He called for the dice and shook with Alix for the drink.

1. Hotel errand boy.
2. Rising stock market. The crash came in October 1929, beginning the Depression.
3. About $7,500. Below, 4 Swiss francs equals 18¢.

"Here for long, Mr. Wales?"

"I'm here for four or five days to see my little girl."

"Oh-h! You have a little girl?"

Outside, the fire-red, gas-blue, ghost-green signs shone smokily through the tranquil rain. It was late afternoon and the streets were in movement; the bistros gleamed. At the corner of the Boulevard des Capucines he took a taxi. The Place de la Concorde moved by in pink majesty; they crossed the logical Seine, and Charlie felt the sudden provincial quality of the Left Bank.[4]

Charlie directed his taxi to the Avenue de l'Opéra, which was out of his way. But he wanted to see the blue hour spread over the magnificent façade, and imagine that the cab horns, playing endlessly the first few bars of *Le Plus que Lent*,[5] were the trumpets of the Second Empire.[6] They were closing the iron grill in front of Brentano's Bookstore, and people were already at dinner behind the trim little bourgeois hedge of Duval's. He had never eaten at a really cheap restaurant in Paris. Five-course dinner, four francs fifty, eighteen cents, wine included. For some odd reason he wished that he had.

As they rolled on to the Left Bank and he felt its sudden provincialism, he thought, "I spoiled this city for myself. I didn't realize it, but the days came along one after another, and then two years were gone, and everything was gone, and I was gone."

He was thirty-five, and good to look at. The Irish mobility of his face was sobered by a deep wrinkle between his eyes. As he rang his brother-in-law's bell in the Rue Palatine, the wrinkle deepened till it pulled down his brows; he felt a cramping sensation in his belly. From behind the maid who opened the door darted a lovely little girl of nine who shrieked "Daddy!" and flew up, struggling like a fish, into his arms. She pulled his head around by one ear and set her cheek against his.

"My old pie," he said.

"Oh, daddy, daddy, daddy, daddy, dads, dads, dads!"

She drew him into the salon, where the family waited, a boy and a girl his daughter's age, his sister-in-law and her husband. He greeted Marion with his voice pitched carefully to avoid either feigned enthusiasm or dislike, but her response was more frankly tepid, though she minimized her expression of unalterable distrust by directing her regard toward his child. The two men clasped hands in a friendly way and Lincoln Peters rested his for a moment on Charlie's shoulder.

The room was warm and comfortably American. The three children moved intimately about, playing through the yellow oblongs that led to other rooms; the cheer of six o'clock spoke in the eager smacks of the fire and the sounds of French activity in the kitchen. But Charlie did not relax; his heart sat up rigidly in his body and he drew confidence from his daughter, who from time to time came close to him, holding in her arms the doll he had brought.

"Really extremely well," he declared in answer to Lincoln's question.

---

4. South of the Seine River; site of the student quarter and Bohemian section of Paris.
5. "More than Slow," a Debussy piano piece.
6. Reign of Louis Napoleon, 1852–1870; glamorous "good old days."

"There's a lot of business there that isn't moving at all, but we're doing even better than ever. In fact, damn well. I'm bringing my sister over from America next month to keep house for me. My income last year was bigger than it was when I had money. You see, the Czechs——"

His boasting was for a specific purpose; but after a moment, seeing a faint restiveness in Lincoln's eye, he changed the subject:

"Those are fine children of yours, well brought up, good manners."

"We think Honoria's a great little girl too."

Marion Peters came back from the kitchen. She was a tall woman with worried eyes, who had once possessed a fresh American loveliness. Charlie had never been sensitive to it and was always surprised when people spoke of how pretty she had been. From the first there had been an instinctive antipathy between them.

"Well, how do you find Honoria?" she asked.

"Wonderful. I was astonished how much she's grown in ten months. All the children are looking well."

"We haven't had a doctor for a year. How do you like being back in Paris?"

"It seems very funny to see so few Americans around."

"I'm delighted," Marion said vehemently. "Now at least you can go into a store without their assuming you're a millionaire. We've suffered like everybody, but on the whole it's a good deal pleasanter."

"But it was nice while it lasted," Charlie said. "We were a sort of royalty, almost infallible, with a sort of magic around us. In the bar this afternoon"—he stumbled, seeing his mistake—"there wasn't a man I knew."

She looked at him keenly. "I should think you'd have had enough of bars."

"I only stayed a minute. I take one drink every afternoon, and no more."

"Don't you want a cocktail before dinner?" Lincoln asked.

"I take only one drink every afternoon, and I've had that."

"I hope you keep to it," said Marion.

Her dislike was evident in the coldness with which she spoke, but Charlie only smiled; he had larger plans. Her very aggressiveness gave him an advantage, and he knew enough to wait. He wanted them to initiate the discussion of what they knew had brought him to Paris.

At dinner he couldn't decide whether Honoria was most like him or her mother. Fortunate if she didn't combine the traits of both that had brought them to disaster. A great wave of protectiveness went over him. He thought he knew what to do for her. He believed in character; he wanted to jump back a whole generation and trust in character again as the eternally valuable element. Everything else wore out.

He left soon after dinner, but not to go home. He was curious to see Paris by night with clearer and more judicious eyes than those of other days. He bought a *strapontin*[7] for the Casino and watched Josephine Baker go through her chocolate arabesques.

7. Cheap seat in the aisle. Josephine Baker (1906–1975) was a celebrated black singer of the blues in Paris in the 1920s.

After an hour he left and strolled toward Montmartre, up the Rue Pigalle into the Place Blanche. The rain had stopped and there were a few people in evening clothes disembarking from taxis in front of cabarets, and *cocottes*[8] prowling singly or in pairs, and many Negroes. He passed a lighted door from which issued music, and stopped with the sense of familiarity; it was Bricktop's, where he had parted with so many hours and so much money. A few doors farther on he found another ancient rendezvous and incautiously put his head inside. Immediately an eager orchestra burst into sound, a pair of professional dancers leaped to their feet and a maître d'hôtel swooped toward him, crying, "Crowd just arriving, sir!" But he withdrew quickly.

"You have to be damn drunk," he thought.

Zelli's was closed, the bleak and sinister cheap hotels surrounding it were dark; up in the Rue Blanche there was more light and a local, colloquial French crowd. The Poet's Cave had disappeared, but the two great mouths of the Café of Heaven and the Café of Hell still yawned—even devoured, as he watched, the meager contents of a tourist bus—a German, a Japanese, and an American couple who glanced at him with frightened eyes.

So much for the effort and ingenuity of Montmartre. All the catering to vice and waste was on an utterly childish scale, and he suddenly realized the meaning of the word "dissipate"—to dissipate into thin air; to make nothing out of something. In the little hours of the night every move from place to place was an enormous human jump, an increase of paying for the privilege of slower and slower motion.

He remembered thousand-franc notes given to an orchestra for playing a single number, hundred-franc notes tossed to a doorman for calling a cab.

But it hadn't been given for nothing.

It had been given, even the most wildly squandered sum, as an offering to destiny that he might not remember the things most worth remembering, the things that now he would always remember—his child taken from his control, his wife escaped to a grave in Vermont.

In the glare of a *brasserie*[9] a woman spoke to him. He bought her some eggs and coffee, and then, eluding her encouraging stare, gave her a twenty-franc note and took a taxi to his hotel.

II

He woke upon a fine fall day—football weather. The depression of yesterday was gone and he liked the people on the streets. At noon he sat opposite Honoria at Le Grand Vatel, the only restaurant he could think of not reminiscent of champagne dinners and long luncheons that began at two and ended in a blurred and vague twilight.

"Now, how about vegetables? Oughtn't you to have some vegetables?"

"Well, yes."

"Here's *épinards* and *chou-fleur* and carrots and *haricots*."[1]

"I'd like *chou-fleur*."

"Wouldn't you like to have two vegetables?"

8. Prostitutes.
9. Small restaurant and bar.

1. Spinach, cauliflower, and beans.

"I usually only have one at lunch."

The waiter was pretending to be inordinately fond of children. *"Qu'elle est mignonne la petite! Elle parle exactement comme une française."*[2]

"How about dessert? Shall we wait and see?"

The waiter disappeared. Honoria looked at her father expectantly.

"What are we going to do?"

"First, we're going to that toy store in the Rue Saint-Honoré and buy you anything you like. And then we're going to the vaudeville at the Empire."

She hesitated. "I like it about the vaudeville, but not the toy store."

"Why not?"

"Well, you brought me this doll." She had it with her. "And I've got lots of things. And we're not rich any more, are we?"

"We never were. But today you are to have anything you want."

"All right," she agreed resignedly.

When there had been her mother and a French nurse he had been inclined to be strict; now he extended himself, reached out for a new tolerance; he must be both parents to her and not shut any of her out of communication.

"I want to get to know you," he said gravely. "First let me introduce myself. My name is Charles J. Wales, of Prague."

"Oh, daddy!" her voice cracked with laughter.

"And who are you, please?" he persisted, and she accepted a role immediately: "Honoria Wales, Rue Palatine, Paris."

"Married or single?"

"No, not married. Single."

He indicated the doll. "But I see you have a child, madame."

Unwilling to disinherit it, she took it to her heart and thought quickly: "Yes, I've been married, but I'm not married now. My husband is dead."

He went on quickly, "And the child's name?"

"Simone. That's after my best friend at school."

"I'm very pleased that you're doing so well at school."

"I'm third this month," she boasted. "Elsie"—that was her cousin—"is only about eighteenth, and Richard is about at the bottom."

"You like Richard and Elsie, don't you?"

"Oh, yes. I like Richard quite well and I like her all right."

Cautiously and casually he asked: "And Aunt Marion and Uncle Lincoln—which do you like best?"

"Oh, Uncle Lincoln, I guess."

He was increasingly aware of her presence. As they came in, a murmur of ". . . adorable" followed them, and now the people at the next table bent all their silences upon her, staring as if she were something no more conscious than a flower.

"Why don't I live with you?" she asked suddenly. "Because mamma's dead?"

"You must stay here and learn more French. It would have been hard for daddy to take care of you so well."

---

2. "What a cute little girl! She talks just like a French girl."

"I don't really need much taking care of any more. I do everything for myself."

Going out of the restaurant, a man and a woman unexpectedly hailed him.

"Well, the old Wales!"

"Hello there, Lorraine. . . . Dunc."

Sudden ghosts out of the past: Duncan Schaeffer, a friend from college. Lorraine Quarrles, a lovely, pale blonde of thirty; one of a crowd who had helped them make months into days in the lavish times of three years ago.

"My husband couldn't come this year," she said, in answer to his question. "We're poor as hell. So he gave me two hundred a month and told me I could do my worst on that. . . . This your little girl?"

"What about coming back and sitting down?" Duncan asked.

"Can't do it." He was glad for an excuse. As always, he felt Lorraine's passionate, provocative attraction, but his own rhythm was different now.

"Well, how about dinner?" she asked.

"I'm not free. Give me your address and let me call you."

"Charlie, I believe you're sober," she said judicially. "I honestly believe he's sober, Dunc. Pinch him and see if he's sober."

Charlie indicated Honoria with his head. They both laughed.

"What's your address?" said Duncan skeptically.

He hesitated, unwilling to give the name of his hotel.

"I'm not settled yet. I'd better call you. We're going to see the vaudeville at the Empire."

"There! That's what I want to do," Lorraine said. "I want to see some clowns and acrobats and jugglers. That's just what we'll do, Dunc."

"We've got to do an errand first," said Charlie. "Perhaps we'll see you there."

"All right, you snob. . . . Good-by, beautiful little girl."

"Good-by."

Honoria bobbed politely.

Somehow, an unwelcome encounter. They liked him because he was functioning, because he was serious; they wanted to see him, because he was stronger than they were now, because they wanted to draw a certain sustenance from his strength.

At the Empire, Honoria proudly refused to sit upon her father's folded coat. She was already an individual with a code of her own, and Charlie was more and more absorbed by the desire of putting a little of himself into her before she crystallized utterly. It was hopeless to try to know her in so short a time.

Between the acts they came upon Duncan and Lorraine in the lobby where the band was playing.

"Have a drink?"

"All right, but not up at the bar. We'll take a table."

"The perfect father."

Listening abstractedly to Lorraine, Charlie watched Honoria's eyes leave their table, and he followed them wistfully about the room, wondering what they saw. He met her glance and she smiled.

"I liked that lemonade," she said.

What had she said? What had he expected? Going home in a taxi afterward, he pulled her over until her head rested against his chest.

"Darling, do you ever think about your mother?"

"Yes, sometimes," she answered vaguely.

"I don't want you to forget her. Have you got a picture of her?"

"Yes, I think so. Anyhow, Aunt Marion has. Why don't you want me to forget her?"

"She loved you very much."

"I loved her too."

They were silent for a moment.

"Daddy, I want to come and live with you," she said suddenly.

His heart leaped; he had wanted it to come like this.

"Aren't you perfectly happy?"

"Yes, but I love you better than anybody. And you love me better than anybody, don't you, now that mummy's dead?"

"Of course I do. But you won't always like me best, honey. You'll grow up and meet somebody your own age and go marry him and forget you ever had a daddy."

"Yes, that's true," she agreed tranquilly.

He didn't go in. He was coming back at nine o'clock and he wanted to keep himself fresh and new for the thing he must say then.

"When you're safe inside, just show yourself in that window."

"All right. Good-by, dads, dads, dads, dads."

He waited in the dark street until she appeared, all warm and glowing, in the window above and kissed her fingers out into the night.

III

They were waiting. Marion sat behind the coffee service in a dignified black dinner dress that just faintly suggested mourning. Lincoln was walking up and down with the animation of one who had already been talking. They were as anxious as he was to get into the question. He opened it almost immediately:

"I suppose you know what I want to see you about—why I really came to Paris."

Marion played with the black stars on her necklace and frowned.

"I'm awfully anxious to have a home," he continued. "And I'm awfully anxious to have Honoria in it. I appreciate your taking in Honoria for her mother's sake, but things have changed now"—he hesitated and then continued more forcibly—"changed radically with me, and I want to ask you to reconsider the matter. It would be silly for me to deny that about three years ago I was acting badly——"

Marion looked up at him with hard eyes.

"—but all that's over. As I told you, I haven't had more than a drink a day for over a year, and I take that drink deliberately, so that the idea of alcohol won't get too big in my imagination. You see the idea?"

"No," said Marion succinctly.

"It's a sort of stunt I set myself. It keeps the matter in proportion."

"I get you," said Lincoln. "You don't want to admit it's got any attraction for you."

"Something like that. Sometimes I forget and don't take it. But I try to take it. Anyhow, I couldn't afford to drink in my position. The people I represent are more than satisfied with what I've done, and I'm bringing my sister over from Burlington to keep house for me, and I want awfully to have Honoria too. You know that even when her mother and I weren't getting along well we never let anything that happened touch Honoria. I know she's fond of me and I know I'm able to take care of her and—well, there you are. How do you feel about it?"

He knew that now he would have to take a beating. It would last an hour or two hours, and it would be difficult, but if he modulated his inevitable resentment to the chastened attitude of the reformed sinner, he might win his point in the end.

Keep your temper, he told himself. You don't want to be justified. You want Honoria.

Lincoln spoke first: "We've been talking it over ever since we got your letter last month. We're happy to have Honoria here. She's a dear little thing, and we're glad to be able to help her, but of course that isn't the question——"

Marion interrupted suddenly. "How long are you going to stay sober, Charlie?" she asked.

"Permanently, I hope."

"How can anybody count on that?"

"You know I never did drink heavily until I gave up business and came over here with nothing to do. Then Helen and I began to run around with——"

"Please leave Helen out of it. I can't bear to hear you talk about her like that."

He stared at her grimly; he had never been certain how fond of each other the sisters were in life.

"My drinking only lasted about a year and a half—from the time we came over until I—collapsed."

"It was time enough."

"It was time enough," he agreed.

"My duty is entirely to Helen," she said. "I try to think what she would have wanted me to do. Frankly, from the night you did that terrible thing you haven't really existed for me. I can't help that. She was my sister."

"Yes."

"When she was dying she asked me to look out for Honoria. If you hadn't been in a sanitarium then, it might have helped matters."

He had no answer.

"I'll never in my life be able to forget the morning when Helen knocked at my door, soaked to the skin and shivering, and said you'd locked her out."

Charlie gripped the sides of the chair. This was more difficult than he expected; he wanted to launch out into a long expostulation and explanation, but he only said: "The night I locked her out—" and she interrupted, "I don't feel up to going over that again."

After a moment's silence Lincoln said: "We're getting off the subject. You want Marion to set aside her legal guardianship and give you Honoria. I think the main point for her is whether she has confidence in you or not."

"I don't blame Marion," Charlie said slowly, "but I think she can have entire confidence in me. I had a good record up to three years ago. Of course, it's within human possibilities I might go wrong any time. But if we wait much longer I'll lose Honoria's childhood and my chance for a home." He shook his head. "I'll simply lose her, don't you see?"

"Yes, I see," said Lincoln.

"Why didn't you think of all this before?" Marion asked.

"I suppose I did, from time to time, but Helen and I were getting along badly. When I consented to the guardianship, I was flat on my back in a sanitarium and the market had cleaned me out. I knew I'd acted badly, and I thought if it would bring any peace to Helen, I'd agree to anything. But now it's different. I'm functioning, I'm behaving damn well, so far as——"

"Please don't swear at me," Marion said.

He looked at her, startled. With each remark the force of her dislike became more and more apparent. She had built up all her fear of life into one wall and faced it toward him. This trivial reproof was possibly the result of some trouble with the cook several hours before. Charlie became increasingly alarmed at leaving Honoria in this atmosphere of hostility against himself; sooner or later it would come out, in a word here, a shake of the head there, and some of that distrust would be irrevocably implanted in Honoria. But he pulled his temper down out of his face and shut it up inside him; he had won a point, for Lincoln realized the absurdity of Marion's remark and asked her lightly since when she had objected to the word "damn."

"Another thing," Charlie said: "I'm able to give her certain advantages now. I'm going to take a French governess to Prague with me. I've got a lease on a new apartment——"

He stopped, realizing that he was blundering. They couldn't be expected to accept with equanimity the fact that his income was again twice as large as their own.

"I suppose you can give her more luxuries than we can," said Marion. "When you were throwing away money we were living along watching every ten francs. . . . I suppose you'll start doing it again."

"Oh, no," he said. "I've learned. I worked hard for ten years, you know—until I got lucky in the market, like so many people. Terribly lucky. It won't happen again."

There was a long silence. All of them felt their nerves straining, and for the first time in a year Charlie wanted a drink. He was sure now that Lincoln Peters wanted him to have his child.

Marion shuddered suddenly; part of her saw that Charlie's feet were planted on the earth now, and her own maternal feeling recognized the naturalness of his desire; but she had lived for a long time with a prejudice—a prejudice founded on a curious disbelief in her sister's happiness, which, in the shock of one terrible night, had turned to hatred for him. It had all happened at a point in her life where the discouragement of ill health and adverse circumstances made it necessary for her to believe in tangible villainy and a tangible villain.

"I can't help what I think!" she cried out suddenly. "How much you were responsible for Helen's death, I don't know. It's something you'll have to square with your own conscience."

An electric current of agony surged through him; for a moment he was almost on his feet, an unuttered sound echoing in his throat. He hung on to himself for a moment, another moment.

"Hold on there," said Lincoln uncomfortably. "I never thought you were responsible for that."

"Helen died of heart trouble," Charlie said dully.

"Yes, heart trouble." Marion spoke as if the phrase had another meaning for her.

Then, in the flatness that followed her outburst, she saw him plainly and she knew he had somehow arrived at control over the situation. Glancing at her husband, she found no help from him, and as abruptly as if it were a matter of no importance, she threw up the sponge.

"Do what you like!" she cried, springing up from her chair. "She's your child. I'm not the person to stand in your way. I think if it were my child I'd rather see her—" She managed to check herself. "You two decide it. I can't stand this. I'm sick. I'm going to bed."

She hurried from the room; after a moment Lincoln said:

"This has been a hard day for her. You know how strongly she feels—" His voice was almost apologetic: "When a woman gets an idea in her head."

"Of course."

"It's going to be all right. I think she sees now that you—can provide for the child, and so we can't very well stand in your way or Honoria's way."

"Thank you, Lincoln."

"I'd better go along and see how she is."

"I'm going."

He was still trembling when he reached the street, but a walk down the Rue Bonaparte to the *quais*[3] set him up, and as he crossed the Seine, fresh and new by the *quai* lamps, he felt exultant. But back in his room he couldn't sleep. The image of Helen haunted him. Helen whom he had loved so until they had senselessly begun to abuse each other's love, tear it into shreds. On that terrible February night that Marion remembered so vividly, a slow quarrel had gone on for hours. There was a scene at the Florida, and then he attempted to take her home, and then she kissed young Webb at a table; after that there was what she had hysterically said. When he arrived home alone he turned the key in the lock in wild anger. How could he know she would arrive an hour later alone, that there would be a snow storm in which she wandered about in slippers, too confused to find a taxi? Then the aftermath, her escaping pneumonia by a miracle, and all the attendant horror. They were "reconciled," but that was the beginning of the end, and Marion, who had seen with her own eyes and who imagined it to be one of many scenes from her sister's martyrdom, never forgot.

Going over it again brought Helen nearer, and in the white, soft

3. Paved walks along the Seine River.

light that steals upon half sleep near morning he found himself talking to her again. She said that he was perfectly right about Honoria and that she wanted Honoria to be with him. She said she was glad he was being good and doing better. She said a lot of other things—very friendly things—but she was in a swing in a white dress, and swinging faster and faster all the time, so that at the end he could not hear clearly all that she said.

IV

He woke up feeling happy. The door of the world was open again. He made plans, vistas, futures for Honoria and himself, but suddenly he grew sad, remembering all the plans he and Helen had made. She had not planned to die. The present was the thing—work to do and someone to love. But not to love too much, for he knew the injury that a father can do to a daughter or a mother to a son by attaching them too closely: afterward, out in the world, the child would seek in the marriage partner the same blind tenderness and, failing probably to find it, turn against love and life.

It was another bright, crisp day. He called Lincoln Peters at the bank where he worked and asked if he could count on taking Honoria when he left for Prague. Lincoln agreed that there was no reason for delay. One thing—the legal guardianship. Marion wanted to retain that a while longer. She was upset by the whole matter, and it would oil things if she felt that the situation was still in her control for another year. Charlie agreed, wanting only the tangible, visible child.

Then the question of a governess. Charles sat in a gloomy agency and talked to a cross Béarnaise and to a buxom Breton peasant,[4] neither of whom he could have endured. There were others whom he would see tomorrow.

He lunched with Lincoln Peters at Griffons, trying to keep down his exultation.

"There's nothing quite like your own child," Lincoln said. "But you understand how Marion feels too."

"She's forgotten how hard I worked for seven years there," Charlie said. "She just remembers one night."

"There's another thing." Lincoln hesitated. "While you and Helen were tearing around Europe throwing money away, we were just getting along. I didn't touch any of the prosperity because I never got ahead enough to carry anything but my insurance. I think Marion felt there was some kind of injustice in it—you not even working toward the end, and getting richer and richer."

"It went just as quick as it came," said Charlie.

"Yes, a lot of it stayed in the hands of *chasseurs* and saxophone players and maitres d'hôtel—well, the big party's over now. I just said that to explain Marion's feeling about those crazy years. If you drop in about six o'clock tonight before Marion's too tired, we'll settle the details on the spot."

Back at his hotel, Charlie found a *pneumatique*[5] that had been re

---

4. Woman from Béarn, a region of south-western France; peasant from Brittany.

5. Express message sent through Paris-wide system of air tubes.

directed from the Ritz bar, where Charlie had left his address for the purpose of finding a certain man.

DEAR CHARLIE: You were so strange when we saw you the other day that I wondered if I did something to offend you. If so, I'm not conscious of it. In fact, I have thought about you too much for the last year, and it's always been in the back of my mind that I might see you if I came over here. We *did* have such good times that crazy spring, like the night you and I stole the butcher's tricycle, and the time we tried to call on the president and you had the old derby rim and the wire cane. Everybody seems so old lately, but I don't feel old a bit. Couldn't we get together some time today for old time's sake? I've got a vile hangover for the moment, but will be feeling better this afternoon and will look for you about five in the sweatshop at the Ritz.

Always devotedly,
Lorraine

His first feeling was one of awe that he had actually, in his mature years, stolen a tricycle and pedaled Lorraine all over the Étoile between the small hours and dawn. In retrospect it was a nightmare. Locking out Helen didn't fit in with any other act of his life, but the tricycle incident did—it was one of many. How many weeks or months of dissipation to arrive at that condition of utter irresponsibility?

He tried to picture how Lorraine had appeared to him then—very attractive; Helen was unhappy about it, though she said nothing. Yesterday, in the restaurant, Lorraine had seemed trite, blurred, worn away. He emphatically did not want to see her, and he was glad Alix had not given away his hotel address. It was a relief to think, instead, of Honoria, to think of Sundays spent with her and of saying good morning to her and of knowing she was there in his house at night, drawing her breath in the darkness.

At five he took a taxi and bought presents for all the Peterses—a piquant cloth doll, a box of Roman soldiers, flowers for Marion, big linen handkerchiefs for Lincoln.

He saw, when he arrived in the apartment, that Marion had accepted the inevitable. She greeted him now as though he were a recalcitrant member of the family, rather than a menacing outsider. Honoria had been told she was going; Charlie was glad to see that her tact made her conceal her excessive happiness. Only on his lap did she whisper her delight and the question "When?" before she slipped away with the other children.

He and Marion were alone for a minute in the room, and on an impulse he spoke out boldly:

"Family quarrels are bitter things. They don't go according to any rules. They're not like aches or wounds; they're more like splits in the skin that won't heal because there's not enough material. I wish you and I could be on better terms."

"Some things are hard to forget," she answered. "It's a question of confidence." There was no answer to this and presently she asked, "When do you propose to take her?"

"As soon as I can get a governess. I hoped the day after tomorrow."

"That's impossible. I've got to get her things in shape. Not before Saturday."

He yielded. Coming back into the room, Lincoln offered him a drink.

"I'll take my daily whisky," he said.

It was warm here, it was a home, people together by a fire. The children felt very safe and important; the mother and father were serious, watchful. They had things to do for the children more important than his visit here. A spoonful of medicine was, after all, more important than the strained relations between Marion and himself. They were not dull people, but they were very much in the grip of life and circumstances. He wondered if he couldn't do something to get Lincoln out of his rut at the bank.

A long peal at the doorbell; the *bonne à tout faire*[6] passed through and went down the corridor. The door opened upon another long ring, and then voices, and the three in the salon looked up expectantly; Richard moved to bring the corridor within his range of vision, and Marion rose. Then the maid came back along the corridor, closely followed by the voices, which developed under the light into Duncan Schaeffer and Lorraine Quarrles.

They were gay, they were hilarious, they were roaring with laughter. For a moment Charlie was astounded; unable to understand how they ferreted out the Peterses' address.

"Ah-h-h!" Duncan wagged his finger roguishly at Charlie. "Ah-h-h!"

They both slid down another cascade of laughter. Anxious and at a loss, Charlie shook hands with them quickly and presented them to Lincoln and Marion. Marion nodded, scarcely speaking. She had drawn back a step toward the fire; her little girl stood beside her, and Marion put an arm about her shoulder.

With growing annoyance at the intrusion, Charlie waited for them to explain themselves. After some concentration Duncan said:

"We came to invite you out to dinner. Lorraine and I insist that all this shishi,[7] cagy business 'bout your address got to stop."

Charlie came closer to them, as if to force them backward down the corridor.

"Sorry, but I can't. Tell me where you'll be and I'll phone you in half an hour."

This made no impression. Lorraine sat down suddenly on the side of a chair, and focusing her eyes on Richard, cried, "Oh, what a nice little boy! Come here, little boy." Richard glanced at his mother, but did not move. With a perceptible shrug of her shoulders, Lorraine turned back to Charlie:

"Come and dine. Sure your cousins won' mine. See you so sel'om. Or solemn."

"I can't," said Charlie sharply. "You two have dinner and I'll phone you."

Her voice became suddenly unpleasant. "All right, we'll go. But I remember once when you hammered on my door at four A.M. I was enough of a good sport to give you a drink. Come on, Dunc."

6. Maid of all work.　　　　7. Chichi, showy.

Still in slow motion, with blurred, angry faces, with uncertain feet, they retired along the corridor.

"Good night," Charlie said.

"Good night!" responded Lorraine emphatically.

When he went back into the salon Marion had not moved, only now her son was standing in the circle of her other arm. Lincoln was still swinging Honoria back and forth like a pendulum from side to side.

"What an outrage!" Charlie broke out. "What an absolute outrage!"

Neither of them answered. Charlie dropped into an armchair, picked up his drink, set it down again and said:

"People I haven't seen for two years having the colossal nerve——"

He broke off. Marion had made the sound "Oh!" in one swift, furious breath, turned her body from him with a jerk and left the room.

Lincoln set down Honoria carefully.

"You children go in and start your soup," he said, and when they obeyed, he said to Charlie:

"Marion's not well and she can't stand shocks. That kind of people make her really physically sick."

"I didn't tell them to come here. They wormed your name out of somebody. They deliberately——"

"Well, it's too bad. It doesn't help matters. Excuse me a minute."

Left alone, Charlie sat tense in his chair, In the next room he could hear the children eating, talking in monosyllables, already oblivious to the scene between their elders. He heard a murmur of conversation from a farther room and then the ticking bell of a telephone receiver picked up, and in a panic he moved to the other side of the room and out of earshot.

In a minute Lincoln came back. "Look here, Charlie. I think we'd better call off dinner for tonight. Marion's in bad shape."

"Is she angry with me?"

"Sort of," he said, almost roughly. "She's not strong and——"

"You mean she's changed her mind about Honoria?"

"She's pretty bitter right now. I don't know. You phone me at the bank tomorrow."

"I wish you'd explain to her I never dreamed these people would come here. I'm just as sore as you are."

"I couldn't explain anything to her now."

Charlie got up. He took his coat and hat and started down the corridor. Then he opened the door of the dining room and said in a strange voice, "Good night, children."

Honoria rose and ran around the table to hug him.

"Good night, sweetheart," he said vaguely, and then trying to make his voice more tender, trying to conciliate something, "Good night, dear children."

V

Charlie went directly to the Ritz bar with the furious idea of finding Lorraine and Duncan, but they were not there, and he realized that in any case there was nothing he could do. He had not touched his drink at the Peters, and now he ordered a whisky-and-soda. Paul came over to say hello.

"It's a great change," he said sadly. "We do about half the business we did. So many fellows I hear about back in the States lost everything, maybe not in the first crash, but then in the second. Your friend George Hardt lost every cent, I hear. Are you back in the States?"

"No, I'm in business in Prague."

"I heard that you lost a lot in the crash."

"I did," and he added grimly, "but I lost everything I wanted in the boom."

"Selling short."[8]

"Something like that."

Again the memory of those days swept over him like a nightmare —the people they had met traveling; then people who couldn't add a row of figures or speak a coherent sentence. The little man Helen had consented to dance with at the ship's party, who had insulted her ten feet from the table; the women and girls carried screaming with drink or drugs out of public places——

The men who locked their wives out in the snow, because the snow of twenty-nine wasn't real snow. If you didn't want it to be snow, you just paid some money.

He went to the phone and called the Peterses' apartment; Lincoln answered.

"I called up because this thing is on my mind. Has Marion said anything definite?"

"Marion's sick," Lincoln answered shortly. "I know this thing isn't altogether your fault, but I can't have her go to pieces about it. I'm afraid we'll have to let it slide for six months; I can't take the chance of working her up to this state again."

"I see."

"I'm sorry, Charlie."

He went back to his table. His whisky glass was empty, but he shook his head when Alix looked at it questioningly. There wasn't much he could do now except send Honoria some things; he would send her a lot of things tomorrow. He thought rather angrily that this was just money—he had given so many people money. . . .

"No, no more," he said to another waiter. "What do I owe you?"

He would come back some day; they couldn't make him pay forever. But he wanted his child, and nothing was much good now, beside that fact. He wasn't young any more, with a lot of nice thoughts and dreams to have by himself. He was absolutely sure Helen wouldn't have wanted him to be so alone.

1931

---

8. Selling at too low a price.

JAMES BALDWIN

Sonny's Blues

I read about it in the paper, in the subway, on my way to work. I read it, and I couldn't believe it, and I read it again. Then perhaps I just stared at it, at the newsprint spelling out his name, spelling out the story. I stared at it in the swinging lights of the subway car, and in the faces and bodies of the people, and in my own face, trapped in the darkness which roared outside.

It was not to be believed and I kept telling myself that, as I walked from the subway station to the high school. And at the same time I couldn't doubt it. I was scared, scared for Sonny. He became real to me again. A great block of ice got settled in my belly and kept melting there slowly all day long, while I taught my classes algebra. It was a special kind of ice. It kept melting, sending trickles of ice water all up and down my veins, but it never got less. Sometimes it hardened and seemed to expand until I felt my guts were going to come spilling out or that I was going to choke or scream. This would always be at a moment when I was remembering some specific thing Sonny had once said or done.

When he was about as old as the boys in my classes his face had been bright and open, there was a lot of copper in it; and he'd had wonderfully direct brown eyes, and great gentleness and privacy. I wondered what he looked like now. He had been picked up, the evening before, in a raid on an apartment downtown, for peddling and using heroin.

I couldn't believe it: but what I mean by that is that I couldn't find any room for it anywhere inside me. I had kept it outside me for a long time. I hadn't wanted to know. I had had suspicions, but I didn't name them, I kept putting them away. I told myself that Sonny was wild, but he wasn't crazy. And he'd always been a good boy, he hadn't ever turned hard or evil or disrespectful, the way kids can, so quick, so quick, especially in Harlem. I didn't want to believe that I'd ever see my brother going down, coming to nothing, all that light in his face gone out, in the condition I'd already seen so many others. Yet it had happened and here I was, talking about algebra to a lot of boys who might, every one of them for all I knew, be popping off needles every time they went to the head.[1] Maybe it did more for them than algebra could.

I was sure that the first time Sonny had ever had horse,[2] he couldn't have been much older than these boys were now. These boys, now, were living as we'd been living then, they were growing up with a rush and their heads bumped abruptly against the low ceiling of their actual possibilities. They were filled with rage. All they really knew were two darknesses, the darkness of their lives, which was now closing in on them, and the darkness of the movies, which had blinded them to that other darkness, and in which they now, vindictively, dreamed, at once more together than they were at any other time, and more alone.

When the last bell rang, the last class ended, I let out my breath. It seemed I'd been holding it for all that time. My clothes were wet—I may have looked as though I'd been sitting in a steam bath, all dressed

---

1. Lavatory.   2. Heroin.

up, all afternoon. I sat alone in the classroom a long time. I listened to the boys outside, downstairs, shouting and cursing and laughing. Their laughter struck me for perhaps the first time. It was not the joyous laughter which—God knows why—one associates with children. It was mocking and insular, its intent was to denigrate. It was disenchanted, and in this, also, lay the authority of their curses. Perhaps I was listening to them because I was thinking about my brother and in them I heard my brother. And myself.

One boy was whistling a tune, at once very complicated and very simple, it seemed to be pouring out of him as though he were a bird, and it sounded very cool and moving through all that harsh, bright air, only just holding its own through all those other sounds.

I stood up and walked over to the window and looked down into the courtyard. It was the beginning of the spring and the sap was rising in the boys. A teacher passed through them every now and again, quickly, as though he or she couldn't wait to get out of that courtyard, to get those boys out of their sight and off their minds. I started collecting my stuff. I thought I'd better get home and talk to Isabel.

The courtyard was almost deserted by the time I got downstairs. I saw this boy standing in the shadow of a doorway, looking just like Sonny. I almost called his name. Then I saw that it wasn't Sonny, but somebody we used to know, a boy from around our block. He'd been Sonny's friend. He'd never been mine, having been too young for me, and, anyway, I'd never liked him. And now, even though he was a grown-up man, he still hung around that block, still spent hours on the street corners, was always high and raggy. I used to run into him from time to time and he'd often work around to asking me for a quarter or fifty cents. He always had some real good excuse, too, and I always gave it to him, I don't know why.

But now, abruptly, I hated him. I couldn't stand the way he looked at me, partly like a dog, partly like a cunning child. I wanted to ask him what the hell he was doing in the school courtyard.

He sort of shuffled over to me, and he said, "I see you got the papers. So you already know about it."

"You mean about Sonny? Yes, I already know about it. How come they didn't get you?"

He grinned. It made him repulsive and it also brought to mind what he'd looked like as a kid. "I wasn't there. I stay away from them people."

"Good for you." I offered him a cigarette and I watched him through the smoke. "You come all the way down here just to tell me about Sonny?"

"That's right." He was sort of shaking his head and his eyes looked strange, as though they were about to cross. The bright sun deadened his damp dark brown skin and it made his eyes look yellow and showed up the dirt in his kinked hair. He smelled funky.[3] I moved a little away from him and I said, "Well, thanks. But I already know about it and I got to get home."

"I'll walk you a little ways," he said. We started walking. There were a couple of kids still loitering in the courtyard and one of them said goodnight to me and looked strangely at the boy beside me.

3. Obnoxious.

"What're you going to do?" he asked me. "I mean, about Sonny?"

"Look. I haven't seen Sonny for over a year, I'm not sure I'm going to do anything. Anyway, what the hell *can* I do?"

"That's right," he said quickly, "ain't nothing you can do. Can't much help old Sonny no more, I guess."

It was what I was thinking and so it seemed to me he had no right to say it.

"I'm surprised at Sonny, though," he went on—he had a funny way of talking, he looked straight ahead as though he were talking to himself—"I thought Sonny was a smart boy, I thought he was too smart to get hung."

"I guess he thought so too," I said sharply, "and that's how he got hung. And how about you? You're pretty goddamn smart, I bet."

Then he looked directly at me, just for a minute. "I ain't smart," he said. "If I was smart, I'd have reached for a pistol a long time ago."

"Look. Don't tell *me* your sad story, if it was up to me, I'd give you one." Then I felt guilty—guilty, probably, for never having supposed that the poor bastard *had* a story of his own, much less a sad one, and I asked, quickly, "What's going to happen to him now?"

He didn't answer this. He was off by himself some place.

"Funny thing," he said, and from his tone we might have been discussing the quickest way to get to Brooklyn, "when I saw the papers this morning, the first thing I asked myself was if I had anything to do with it. I felt sort of responsible."

I began to listen more carefully. The subway station was on the corner, just before us, and I stopped. He stopped, too. We were in front of a bar and he ducked slightly, peering in, but whoever he was looking for didn't seem to be there. The juke box was blasting away with something black and bouncy and I half watched the barmaid as she danced her way from the juke box to her place behind the bar. And I watched her face as she laughingly responded to something someone said to her, still keeping time to the music. When she smiled one saw the little girl, one sensed the doomed, still-struggling woman beneath the battered face of the semi-whore.

"I never *give* Sonny nothing," the boy said finally, "but a long time ago I come to school high and Sonny asked me how it felt." He paused, I couldn't bear to watch him, I watched the barmaid, and I listened to the music which seemed to be causing the pavement to shake. "I told him it felt great." The music stopped, the barmaid paused and watched the juke box until the music began again. "It did."

All this was carrying me some place I didn't want to go. I certainly didn't want to know how it felt. It filled everything, the people, the houses, the music, the dark, quicksilver barmaid, with menace; and this menace was their reality.

"What's going to happen to him now?" I asked again.

"They'll send him away some place and they'll try to cure him." He shook his head. "Maybe he'll even think he's kicked the habit. Then they'll let him loose"—he gestured, throwing his cigarette into the gutter. "That's all."

"What do you mean, that's *all?*"

But I knew what he meant.

"I *mean,* that's *all.*" He turned his head and looked at me, pulling down the corners of his mouth. "Don't you know what I mean?" he asked, softly.

"How the hell *would* I know what you mean?" I almost whispered it, I don't know why.

"That's right," he said to the air, "how would *he* know what I mean?" He turned toward me again, patient and calm, and yet I somehow felt him shaking, shaking as though he were going to fall apart. I felt that ice in my guts again, the dread I'd felt all afternoon; and again I watched the barmaid, moving about the bar, washing glasses, and singing. "Listen. They'll let him out and then it'll just start all over again. That's what I mean."

"You mean—they'll let him out. And then he'll just start working his way back in again. You mean he'll never kick the habit. Is that what you mean?"

"That's right," he said, cheerfully. "*You* see what I mean."

"Tell me," I said at last, "why does he want to die? He must want to die, he's killing himself, why does he want to die?"

He looked at me in surprise. He licked his lips. "He don't want to die. He wants to live. Don't nobody want to die, ever."

Then I wanted to ask him—too many things. He could not have answered, or if he had, I could not have borne the answers. I started walking. "Well, I guess it's none of my business."

"It's going to be rough on old Sonny," he said. We reached the subway station. "This is your station?" he asked. I nodded. I took one step down. "Damn!" he said, suddenly. I looked up at him. He grinned again. "Damn it if I didn't leave all my money home. You ain't got a dollar on you, have you? Just for a couple of days, is all."

All at once something inside gave and threatened to come pouring out of me. I didn't hate him any more. I felt that in another moment I'd start crying like a child.

"Sure," I said. "Don't sweat." I looked in my wallet and didn't have a dollar, I only had a five. "Here," I said. "That hold you?"

He didn't look at it—he didn't want to look at it. A terrible, closed look came over his face, as though he were keeping the number on the bill a secret from him and me. "Thanks," he said, and now he was dying to see me go. "Don't worry about Sonny. Maybe I'll write him or something."

"Sure," I said. "You do that. So long."

"Be seeing you," he said. I went on down the steps.

And I didn't write Sonny or send him anything for a long time. When I finally did, it was just after my little girl died, he wrote me back a letter which made me feel like a bastard.

Here's what he said:

Dear brother,

You don't know how much I needed to hear from you. I wanted to write you many a time but I dug how much I must have hurt you and so I didn't write. But now I feel like a man who's been trying to climb up out of some deep, real deep and funky hole and just saw the sun up there, outside. I got to get outside.

I can't tell you much about how I got here. I mean I don't know how to tell you. I guess I was afraid of something or I was trying to escape from something and you know I have never been very strong in the head (smile). I'm glad Mama and Daddy are dead and can't see what's happened to their son and I swear if I'd known what I was doing I would never have hurt you so, you and a lot of other fine people who were nice to me and who believed in me.

I don't want you to think it had anything to do with me being a musician. It's more than that. Or maybe less than that. I can't get anything straight in my head down here and I try not to think about what's going to happen to me when I get outside again. Sometime I think I'm going to flip and *never* get outside and sometime I think I'll come straight back. I tell you one thing, though, I'd rather blow my brains out than go through this again. But that's what they all say, so they tell me. If I tell you when I'm coming to New York and if you could meet me, I sure would appreciate it. Give my love to Isabel and the kids and I was sure sorry to hear about little Gracie. I wish I could be like Mama and say the Lord's will be done, but I don't know it seems to me that trouble is the one thing that never does get stopped and I don't know what good it does to blame it on the Lord. But maybe it does some good if you believe it.

Your brother,
Sonny

Then I kept in constant touch with him and I sent him whatever I could and I went to meet him when he came back to New York. When I saw him many things I thought I had forgotten came flooding back to me. This was because I had begun, finally, to wonder about Sonny, about the life that Sonny lived inside. This life, whatever it was, had made him older and thinner and it had deepened the distant stillness in which he had always moved. He looked very unlike my baby brother. Yet, when he smiled, when we shook hands, the baby brother I'd never known looked out from the depths of his private life, like an animal waiting to be coaxed into the light.

"How you been keeping?" he asked me.

"All right. And you?"

"Just fine." He was smiling all over his face. "It's good to see you again."

"It's good to see you."

The seven years' difference in our ages lay between us like a chasm: I wondered if these years would ever operate between us as a bridge. I was remembering, and it made it hard to catch my breath, that I had been there when he was born; and I had heard the first words he had ever spoken. When he started to walk, he walked from our mother straight to me. I caught him just before he fell when he took the first steps he ever took in this world.

"How's Isabel?"

"Just fine. She's dying to see you."

"And the boys?"

"They're fine, too. They're anxious to see their uncle."

"Oh, come on. You know they don't remember me."

"Are you kidding? Of course they remember you."

He grinned again. We got into a taxi. We had a lot to say to each other, far too much to know how to begin.

As the taxi began to move, I asked, "You still want to go to India?"
He laughed. "You still remember that. Hell, no. This place is Indian
enough for me."

"It used to belong to them," I said.

And he laughed again. "They damn sure knew what they were
doing when they got rid of it."

Years ago, when he was around fourteen, he'd been all hipped on
the idea of going to India. He read books about people sitting on rocks,
naked, in all kinds of weather, but mostly bad, naturally, and walking
barefoot through hot coals and arriving at wisdom. I used to say that
it sounded to me as though they were getting away from wisdom as
fast as they could. I think he sort of looked down on me for that.

"Do you mind," he asked, "if we have the driver drive alongside the
park? On the west side—I haven't seen the city in so long."

"Of course not," I said. I was afraid that I might sound as though I
were humoring him, but I hoped he wouldn't take it that way.

So we drove along, between the green of the park and the stony,
lifeless elegance of hotels and apartment buildings, toward the vivid,
killing streets of our childhood. These streets hadn't changed, though
housing projects jutted up out of them now like rocks in the middle of
a boiling sea. Most of the houses in which we had grown up had
vanished, as had the stores from which we had stolen, the basements
in which we had first tried sex, the rooftops from which we had hurled
tin cans and bricks. But houses exactly like the houses of our past yet
dominated the landscape, boys exactly like the boys we once had been
found themselves smothering in these houses, came down into the
streets for light and air and found themselves encircled by disaster.
Some escaped the trap, most didn't. Those who got out always left
something of themselves behind, as some animals amputate a leg and
leave it in the trap. It might be said, perhaps, that I had escaped, after
all, I was a school teacher; or that Sonny had, he hadn't lived in
Harlem for years. Yet, as the cab moved uptown through streets
which seemed, with a rush, to darken with dark people, and as I
covertly studied Sonny's face, it came to me that what we both were
seeking through our separate cab windows was that part of ourselves
which had been left behind. It's always at the hour of trouble and
confrontation that the missing member aches.

We hit 110th Street and started rolling up Lenox Avenue. And I'd
known this avenue all my life, but it seemed to me again, as it had
seemed on the day I'd first heard about Sonny's trouble, filled with a
hidden menace which was its very breath of life.

"We almost there," said Sonny.

"Almost." We were both too nervous to say anything more.

We live in a housing project. It hasn't been up long. A few days after
it was up it seemed uninhabitably new, now, of course, it's already
rundown. It looks like a parody of the good, clean, faceless life—God
knows the people who live in it do their best to make it a parody. The
beat-looking grass lying around isn't enough to make their lives green,
the hedges will never hold out the streets, and they know it. The big
windows fool no one, they aren't big enough to make space out of no
space. They don't bother with the windows, they watch the TV screen

instead. The playground is most popular with the children who don't play at jacks, or skip rope, or roller skate, or swing, and they can be found in it after dark. We moved in partly because it's not too far from where I teach, and partly for the kids; but it's really just like the houses in which Sonny and I grew up. The same things happen, they'll have the same things to remember. The moment Sonny and I started into the house I had the feeling that I was simply bringing him back into the danger he had almost died trying to escape.

Sonny has never been talkative. So I don't know why I was sure he'd be dying to talk to me when supper was over the first night. Everything went fine, the oldest boy remembered him, and the youngest boy liked him, and Sonny had remembered to bring something for each of them; and Isabel, who is really much nicer than I am, more open and giving, had gone to a lot of trouble about dinner and was genuinely glad to see him. And she's always been able to tease Sonny in a way that I haven't. It was nice to see her face so vivid again and to hear her laugh and watch her make Sonny laugh. She wasn't, or, anyway, she didn't seem to be, at all uneasy or embarrassed. She chatted as though there were no subject which had to be avoided and she got Sonny past his first, faint stiffness. And thank God she was there, for I was filled with that icy dread again. Everything I did seemed awkward to me, and everything I said sounded freighted with hidden meaning. I was trying to remember everything I'd heard about dope addiction and I couldn't help watching Sonny for signs. I wasn't doing it out of malice. I was trying to find out something about my brother. I was dying to hear him tell me he was safe.

"Safe!" my father grunted, whenever Mama suggested trying to move to a neighborhood which might be safer for children. "Safe, hell! Ain't no place safe for kids, nor nobody."

He always went on like this, but he wasn't, ever, really as bad as he sounded, not even on weekends, when he got drunk. As a matter of fact, he was always on the lookout for "something a little better," but he died before he found it. He died suddenly, during a drunken weekend in the middle of the war, when Sonny was fifteen. He and Sonny hadn't ever got on too well. And this was partly because Sonny was the apple of his father's eye. It was because he loved Sonny so much and was frightened for him, that he was always fighting with him. It doesn't do any good to fight with Sonny. Sonny just moves back, inside himself, where he can't be reached. But the principal reason that they never hit it off is that they were so much alike. Daddy was big and rough and loud-talking, just the opposite of Sonny, but they both had—that same privacy.

Mama tried to tell me something about this, just after Daddy died. I was home on leave from the army.

This was the last time I ever saw my mother alive. Just the same, this picture gets all mixed up in my mind with pictures I had of her when she was younger. The way I always see her is the way she used to be on a Sunday afternoon, say, when the old folks were talking after the big Sunday dinner. I always see her wearing pale blue. She'd be sitting on the sofa. And my father would be sitting in the easy chair, not far

from her. And the living room would be full of church folks and relatives. There they sit, in chairs all around the living room, and the
night is creeping up outside, but nobody knows it yet. You can see the
darkness growing against the windowpanes and you hear the street
noises every now and again, or maybe the jangling beat of a tambourine from one of the churches close by, but it's real quiet in the
room. For a moment nobody's talking, but every face looks darkening,
like the sky outside. And my mother rocks a little from the waist, and
my father's eyes are closed. Everyone is looking at something a child
can't see. For a minute they've forgotten the children. Maybe a kid is
lying on the rug, half asleep. Maybe somebody's got a kid in his lap and
is absent-mindedly stroking the kid's head. Maybe there's a kid, quiet
and big-eyed, curled up in a big chair in the corner. The silence, the
darkness coming, and the darkness in the faces frighten the child
obscurely. He hopes that the hand which strokes his forehead will never
stop—will never die. He hopes that there will never come a time when
the old folks won't be sitting around the living room, talking about
where they've come from, and what they've seen, and what's happened
to them and their kinfolk.

But something deep and watchful in the child knows that this is
bound to end, is already ending. In a moment someone will get up and
turn on the light. Then the old folks will remember the children and
they won't talk any more that day. And when light fills the room, the
child is filled with darkness. He knows that every time this happens
he's moved just a little closer to that darkness outside. The darkness
outside is what the old folks have been talking about. It's what they've
come from. It's what they endure. The child knows that they won't talk
any more because if he knows too much about what's happened to
them, he'll know too much too soon, about what's going to happen to
him.

The last time I talked to my mother, I remember I was restless. I
wanted to get out and see Isabel. We weren't married then and we had
a lot to straighten out between us.

There Mama sat, in black, by the window. She was humming an old
church song, *Lord, you brought me from a long ways off*. Sonny was out
somewhere. Mama kept watching the streets.

"I don't know," she said, "if I'll ever see you again, after you go off
from here. But I hope you'll remember the things I tried to teach you."

"Don't talk like that," I said, and smiled. "You'll be here a long time
yet."

She smiled, too, but she said nothing. She was quiet for a long time.
And I said, "Mama, don't you worry about nothing. I'll be writing all
the time, and you be getting the checks. . . ."

"I want to talk to you about your brother," she said, suddenly. "If
anything happens to me he ain't going to have nobody to look out for
him."

"Mama," I said, "ain't nothing going to happen to you *or* Sonny.
Sonny's all right. He's a good boy and he's got good sense."

"It ain't a question of his being a good boy," Mama said, "nor of his
having good sense. It ain't only the bad ones, nor yet the dumb ones
that gets sucked under." She stopped, looking at me. "Your Daddy

once had a brother," she said, and she smiled in a way that made me
feel she was in pain. "You didn't never know that, did you?"

"No," I said, "I never knew that," and I watched her face.

"Oh, yes," she said, "your Daddy had a brother." She looked out of
the window again. "I know you never saw your Daddy cry. But *I* did
—many a time, through all these years."

I asked her, "What happened to his brother? How come nobody's
ever talked about him?"

This was the first time I ever saw my mother look old.

"His brother got killed," she said, "when he was just a little younger
than you are now. I knew him. He was a fine boy. He was maybe a little
full of the devil, but he didn't mean nobody no harm."

Then she stopped and the room was silent, exactly as it had sometimes been on those Sunday afternoons. Mama kept looking out into the
streets.

"He used to have a job in the mill," she said, "and, like all young
folks, he just liked to perform on Saturday nights. Saturday nights, him
and your father would drift around to different place, go to dances and
things like that, or just sit around with people they knew, and your
father's brother would sing, he had a fine voice, and play along with
himself on his guitar. Well, this particular Saturday night, him and
your father was coming home from some place, and they were both
a little drunk and there was a moon that night, it was bright like day.
Your father's brother was feeling kind of good, and he was whistling
to himself, and he had his guitar slung over his shoulder. They was
coming down a hill and beneath them was a road that turned off from
the highway. Well, your father's brother, being always kind of frisky,
decided to run down this hill, and he did, with that guitar banging and
clanging behind him, and he ran across the road, and he was making
water behind a tree. And your father was sort of amused at him and
he was still coming down the hill, kind of slow. Then he heard a car
motor and that same minute his brother stepped from behind the tree,
into the road, in the moonlight. And he started to cross the road. And
your father started to run down the hill, he says he don't know why.
This car was full of white men. They was all drunk, and when they
seen your father's brother they let out a great whoop and holler and
they aimed the car straight at him. They was having fun, they just
wanted to scare him, the way they do sometimes, you know. But they
was drunk. And I guess the boy, being drunk, too, and scared, kind of
lost his head. By the time he jumped it was too late. Your father says
he heard his brother scream when the car rolled over him, and he heard
the wood of that guitar when it give, and he heard them strings go
flying, and he heard them white men shouting, and the car kept on
a-going and it ain't stopped till this day. And, time your father got
down the hill, his brother weren't nothing but blood and pulp."

Tears were gleaming on my mother's face. There wasn't anything I
could say.

"He never mentioned it," she said, "because I never let him mention it before you children. Your Daddy was like a crazy man that
night and for many a night thereafter. He says he never in his life
seen anything as dark as that road after the lights of that car had gone

away. Weren't nothing, weren't nobody on that road, just your Daddy
and his brother and that busted guitar. Oh, yes. Your Daddy never did
really get right again. Till the day he died he weren't sure but that
every white man he saw was the man that killed his brother."

She stopped and took out her handkerchief and dried her eyes and
looked at me.

"I ain't telling you all this," she said, "to make you scared or bitter or
to make you hate nobody. I'm telling you this because you got a
brother. And the world ain't changed."

I guess I didn't want to believe this. I guess she saw this in my
face. She turned away from me, toward the window again, searching
those streets.

"But I praise my Redeemer," she said at last, "that He called your
Daddy home before me. I ain't saying it to throw no flowers at myself,
but, I declare, it keeps me from feeling too cast down to know I
helped your father get safely through this world. Your father always
acted like he was the roughest, strongest man on earth. And everybody took him to be like that. But if he hadn't had *me* there—to see
his tears!"

She was crying again. Still, I couldn't move. I said, "Lord, Lord,
Mama, I didn't know it was like that."

"Oh, honey," she said, "there's a lot that you don't know. But you
are going to find out." She stood up from the window and came over
to me. "You got to hold on to your brother," she said, "and don't let
him fall, no matter what it looks like is happening to him and no matter
how evil you gets with him. You going to be evil with him many a time.
But don't you forget what I told you, you hear?"

"I won't forget," I said. "Don't you worry, I won't forget. I won't let
nothing happen to Sonny."

My mother smiled as though she were amused at something she saw
in my face. Then, "You may not be able to stop nothing from happening. But you got to let him know you's *there*."

Two days later I was married, and then I was gone. And I had a
lot of things on my mind and I pretty well forgot my promise to Mama
until I got shipped home on a special furlough for her funeral.

And, after the funeral, with just Sonny and me alone in the empty
kitchen, I tried to find out something about him.

"What do you want to do?" I asked him.

"I'm going to be a musician," he said.

For he had graduated, in the time I had been away, from dancing
to the juke box to finding out who was playing what, and what they
were doing with it, and he had bought himself a set of drums.

"You mean, you want to be a drummer?" I somehow had the feeling
that being a drummer might be all right for other people but not for
my brother Sonny.

"I don't think," he said, looking at me very gravely, "that I'll ever
be a good drummer. But I think I can play a piano."

I frowned. I'd never played the role of the older brother quite so
seriously before, had scarcely ever, in fact, *asked* Sonny a damn thing.
I sensed myself in the presence of something I didn't really know how

to handle, didn't understand. So I made my frown a little deeper as I asked: "What kind of musician do you want to be?"

He grinned. "How many kinds do you think there are?"

"Be *serious*," I said.

He laughed, throwing his head back, and then looked at me. "I *am* serious."

"Well, then, for Christ's sake, stop kidding around and answer a serious question. I mean, do you want to be a concert pianist, you want to play classical music and all that, or—or what?" Long before I finished he was laughing again. "For Christ's *sake*, Sonny!"

He sobered, but with difficulty. "I'm sorry. But you sound so— *scared!*" and he was off again.

"Well, you may think it's funny now, baby, but it's not going to be so funny when you have to make your living at it, let me tell you *that.*" I was furious because I knew he was laughing at me and I didn't know why.

"No," he said, very sober now, and afraid, perhaps, that he'd hurt me, "I don't want to be a classical pianist. That isn't what interests me. I mean"—he paused, looking hard at me, as though his eyes would help me to understand, and then gestured helplessly, as though perhaps his hand would help—"I mean, I'll have a lot of studying to do, and I'll have to study *everything*, but, I mean, I want to play *with*—jazz musicians." He stopped. "I want to play jazz," he said.

Well, the word had never before sounded as heavy, as real, as it sounded that afternoon in Sonny's mouth. I just looked at him and I was probably frowning a real frown by this time. I simply couldn't see why on earth he'd want to spend his time hanging around nightclubs, clowning around on bandstands, while people pushed each other around a dance floor. It seemed—beneath him, somehow. I had never thought about it before, had never been forced to, but I suppose I had always put jazz musicians in a class with what Daddy called "good-time people."

"Are you *serious?*"

"Hell, *yes*, I'm serious."

He looked more helpless than ever, and annoyed, and deeply hurt.

I suggested, helpfully: "You mean—like Louis Armstrong?"

His face closed as though I'd struck him. "No. I'm not talking about none of that old-time, down home crap."

"Well, look, Sonny, I'm sorry, don't get mad. I just don't altogether get it, that's all. Name somebody—you know, a jazz musician you admire."

"Bird."

"Who?"

"Bird! Charlie Parker![4] Don't they teach you nothing in the goddamn army?"

I lit a cigarette. I was surprised and then a little amused to discover that I was trembling. "I've been out of touch," I said. "You'll have to be patient with me. Now. Who's this Parker character?"

---

4. Charlie ("Bird") Parker (1920–1955), for whom Birdland in New York was named, perhaps the greatest saxophonist and innovator of jazz; cofounder, with Dizzy Gillespie, of the new jazz, once called "bebop"; narcotics addict.

"He's just one of the greatest jazz musicians alive," said Sonny, sullenly, his hands in his pockets, his back to me. "Maybe *the* greatest," he added, bitterly, "that's probably why *you* never heard of him."

"All right," I said, "I'm ignorant. I'm sorry. I'll go out and buy all the cat's records right away, all right?"

"It don't," said Sonny, with dignity, "make any difference to me. I don't care what you listen to. Don't do me no favors."

I was beginning to realize that I'd never seen him so upset before. With another part of my mind I was thinking that this would probably turn out to be one of those things kids go through and that I shouldn't make it seem important by pushing it too hard. Still, I didn't think it would do any harm to ask: "Doesn't all this take a lot of time? Can you make a living at it?"

He turned back to me and half leaned, half sat, on the kitchen table. "Everything takes time," he said, "and—well, yes, sure, I can make a living at it. But what I don't seem to be able to make you understand is that it's the only thing I want to do."

"Well, Sonny," I said, gently, "you know people can't always do exactly what they *want* to do—"

"*No,* I don't know that," said Sonny, surprising me. "I think people *ought* to do what they want to do, what else are they alive for?"

"You getting to be a big boy," I said desperately, "it's time you started thinking about your future."

"I'm thinking about my future," said Sonny, grimly. "I think about it all the time."

I gave up. I decided, if he didn't change his mind, that we could always talk about it later. "In the meantime," I said, "you got to finish school." We had already decided that he'd have to move in with Isabel and her folks. I knew this wasn't the ideal arrangement because Isabel's folks are inclined to be dicty[5] and they hadn't especially wanted Isabel to marry me. But I didn't know what else to do. "And we have to get you fixed up at Isabel's."

There was a long silence. He moved from the kitchen table to the window. "That's a terrible idea. You know it yourself."

"Do you have a *better* idea?"

He just walked up and down the kitchen for a minute. He was as tall as I was. He had started to shave. I suddenly had the feeling that I didn't know him at all.

He stopped at the kitchen table and picked up my cigarettes. Looking at me with a kind of mocking, amused defiance, he put one between his lips. "You mind?"

"You smoking already?"

He lit the cigarette and nodded, watching me through the smoke. "I just wanted to see if I'd have the courage to smoke in front of you." He grinned and blew a great cloud of smoke to the ceiling. "It was easy." He looked at my face. "Come on, now. I bet you was smoking at my age, tell the truth."

I didn't say anything but the truth was on my face, and he laughed. But now there was something very strained in his laugh. "Sure. And

5. Snobbish, bossy.

I bet that ain't all you was doing."

He was frightening me a little. "Cut the crap," I said. "We already decided that you was going to go and live at Isabel's. Now what's got into you all of a sudden?"

"*You* decided it," he pointed out. "*I* didn't decide nothing." He stopped in front of me, leaning against the stove, arms loosely folded. "Look, brother. I don't want to stay in Harlem no more, I really don't." He was very earnest. He looked at me, then over toward the kitchen window. There was something in his eyes I'd never seen before, some thoughtfulness, some worry all his own. He rubbed the muscle of one arm. "It's time I was getting out of here."

"Where do you want to *go*, Sonny?"

"I want to join the army. Or the navy, I don't care. If I say I'm old enough, they'll believe me."

Then I got mad. It was because I was so scared. "You must be crazy. You goddamn fool, what the hell do you want to go and join the *army* for?"

"I just told you. To get out of Harlem."

"Sonny, you haven't even finished *school*. And if you really want to be a musician, how do you expect to study if you're in the *army*?"

He looked at me, trapped, and in anguish. "There's ways. I might be able to work out some kind of deal. Anyway, I'll have the G.I. Bill when I come out."

"*If* you come out." We stared at each other. "Sonny, please. Be reasonable. I know the setup is far from perfect. But we got to do the best we can."

"I ain't learning nothing in school," he said. "Even when I go." He turned away from me and opened the window and threw his cigarette out into the narrow alley. I watched his back. "At least, I ain't learning nothing you'd want me to learn." He slammed the window so hard I thought the glass would fly out, and turned back to me. "And I'm sick of the stink of these garbage cans!"

"Sonny," I said, "I know how you feel. But if you don't finish school now, you're going to be sorry later that you didn't." I grabbed him by the shoulders. "And you only got another year. It ain't so bad. And I'll come back and I swear I'll help you do *whatever* you want to do. Just try to put up with it till I come back. Will you please do that? For me?"

He didn't answer and he wouldn't look at me.

"Sonny. You hear me?"

He pulled away. "I hear you. But you never hear anything *I* say."

I didn't know what to say to that. He looked out of the window and then back at me. "OK," he said, and sighed. "I'll try."

Then I said, trying to cheer him up a little, "They got a piano at Isabel's. You can practice on it."

And as a matter of fact, it did cheer him up for a minute. "That's right," he said to himself. "I forgot that." His face relaxed a little. But the worry, the thoughtfulness, played on it still, the way shadows play on a face which is staring into the fire.

But I thought I'd never hear the end of that piano. At first, Isabel would write me, saying how nice it was that Sonny was so serious about his music and how, as soon as he came in from school, or wherever he had been when he was supposed to be at school, he went straight to that piano and stayed there until suppertime. And, after supper, he went back to that piano and stayed there until everybody went to bed. He was at the piano all day Saturday and all day Sunday. Then he bought a record player and started playing records. He'd play one record over and over again, all day long sometimes, and he'd improvise along with it on the piano. Or he'd play one section of the record, one chord, one change, one progression, then he'd do it on the piano. Then back to the record. Then back to the piano.

Well, I really don't know how they stood it. Isabel finally confessed that it wasn't like living with a person at all, it was like living with sound. And the sound didn't make any sense to her, didn't make any sense to any of them—naturally. They began, in a way, to be afflicted by this presence that was living in their home. It was as though Sonny were some sort of god, or monster. He moved in an atmosphere which wasn't like theirs at all. They fed him and he ate, he washed himself, he walked in and out of their door; he certainly wasn't nasty or unpleasant or rude, Sonny isn't any of those things; but it was as though he were all wrapped up in some cloud, some fire, some vision all his own; and there wasn't any way to reach him.

At the same time, he wasn't really a man yet, he was still a child, and they had to watch out for him in all kinds of ways. They certainly couldn't throw him out. Neither did they dare to make a great scene about that piano because even they dimly sensed, as I sensed, from so many thousands of miles away, that Sonny was at that piano playing for his life.

But he hadn't been going to school. One day a letter came from the school board and Isabel's mother got it—there had, apparently, been other letters but Sonny had torn them up. This day, when Sonny came in, Isabel's mother showed him the letter and asked where he'd been spending his time. And she finally got it out of him that he'd been down in Greenwich Village, with musicians and other characters, in a white girl's apartment. And this scared her and she started to scream at him and what came up, once she began—though she denies it to this day—was what sacrifices they were making to give Sonny a decent home and how little he appreciated it.

Sonny didn't play the piano that day. By evening, Isabel's mother had calmed down but then there was the old man to deal with, and Isabel herself. Isabel says she did her best to be calm but she broke down and started crying. She says she just watched Sonny's face. She could tell, by watching him, what was happening with him. And what was happening was that they penetrated his cloud, they had reached him. Even if their fingers had been a thousand times more gentle than human fingers ever are, he could hardly help feeling that they had stripped him naked and were spitting on that nakedness. For he also had to see that his presence, that music, which was life or death to him, had been torture for them and that they had endured it, not at all for his sake, but only for mine. And Sonny couldn't take that. He can take it a little better today than he could then but he's still not very good at it and, frankly, I don't know anybody who is.

The silence of the next few days must have been louder than the sound of all the music ever played since time began. One morning, before she went to work, Isabel was in his room for something and she suddenly realized that all of his records were gone. And she knew for certain that he was gone. And he was. He went as far as the navy would carry him. He finally sent me a postcard from some place in Greece and that was the first I knew that Sonny was still alive. I didn't see him any more until we were both back in New York and the war had long been over.

He was a man by then, of course, but I wasn't willing to see it. He came by the house from time to time, but we fought almost every time we met. I didn't like the way he carried himself, loose and dreamlike all the time, and I didn't like his friends, and his music seemed to be merely an excuse for the life he led. It sounded just that weird and disordered.

Then we had a fight, a pretty awful fight, and I didn't see him for months. By and by I looked him up, where he was living, in a furnished room in the Village, and I tried to make it up. But there were lots of other people in the room and Sonny just lay on his bed, and he wouldn't come downstairs with me, and he treated these other people as though they were his family and I weren't. So I got mad and then he got mad, and then I told him that he might just as well be dead as live the way he was living. Then he stood up and he told me not to worry about him any more in life, that he *was* dead as far as I was concerned. Then he pushed me to the door and the other people looked on as though nothing were happening, and he slammed the door behind me. I stood in the hallway, staring at the door. I heard somebody laugh in the room and then the tears came to my eyes. I started down the steps, whistling to keep from crying, I kept whistling to myself, *You going to need me, baby, one of these cold, rainy days.*

I read about Sonny's trouble in the spring. Little Grace died in the fall. She was a beautiful little girl. But she only lived a little over two years. She died of polio and she suffered. She had a slight fever for a couple of days, but it didn't seem like anything and we just kept her in bed. And we would certainly have called the doctor, but the fever dropped, she seemed to be all right. So we thought it had just been a cold. Then, one day, she was up, playing, Isabel was in the kitchen fixing lunch for the two boys when they'd come in from school, and she heard Grace fall down in the living room. When you have a lot of children you don't always start running when one of them falls, unless they start screaming or something. And, this time, Gracie was quiet. Yet, Isabel says that when she heard that *thump* and then that silence, something happened in her to make her afraid. And she ran to the living room and there was little Grace on the floor, all twisted up, and the reason she hadn't screamed was that she couldn't get her breath. And when she did scream, it was the worst sound, Isabel says, that she'd ever heard in all her life, and she still hears it sometimes in her dreams. Isabel will sometimes wake me up with a low, moaning, strangled sound and I have to be quick to awaken her and hold her to me and where Isabel is weeping against me seems a mortal wound.

I think I may have written Sonny the very day that little Grace was buried. I was sitting in the living room in the dark, by myself, and I suddenly thought of Sonny. My trouble made his real.

One Saturday afternoon, when Sonny had been living with us, or anyway, been in our house, for nearly two weeks, I found myself wandering aimlessly about the living room, drinking from a can of beer, and trying to work up courage to search Sonny's room. He was out, he was usually out whenever I was home, and Isabel had taken the children to see their grandparents. Suddenly I was standing still in front of the living room window, watching Seventh Avenue. The idea of searching Sonny's room made me still. I scarcely dared to admit to myself what I'd be searching for. I didn't know what I'd do if I found it. Or if I didn't.

On the sidewalk across from me, near the entrance to a barbecue joint, some people were holding an old-fashioned revival meeting. The barbecue cook, wearing a dirty white apron, his conked[6] hair reddish and metallic in the pale sun, and a cigarette between his lips, stood in the doorway, watching them. Kids and older people paused in their errands and stood there, along with some older men and a couple of very tough-looking women who watched everything that happened on the avenue, as though they owned it, or were maybe owned by it. Well, they were watching this, too. The revival was being carried on by three sisters in black, and a brother. All they had were their voices and their Bibles and a tambourine. The brother was testifying[7] and while he testified two of the sisters stood together, seeming to say, amen, and the third sister walked around with the tambourine outstretched and a couple of people dropped coins into it. Then the brother's testimony ended and the sister who had been taking up the collection dumped the coins into her palm and transferred them to the pocket of her long black robe. Then she raised both hands, striking the tambourine against the air, and then against one hand, and she started to sing. And the two other sisters and the brother joined in.

It was strange, suddenly, to watch, though I had been seeing these meetings all my life. So, of course, had everybody else down there. Yet, they paused and watched and listened and I stood still at the window. "*'Tis the old ship of Zion*," they sang, and the sister with the tambourine kept a steady, jangling beat, "*it has rescued many a thousand!*" Not a soul under the sound of their voices was hearing this song for the first time, not one of them had been rescued. Nor had they seen much in the way of rescue work being done around them. Neither did they especially believe in the holiness of the three sisters and the brother, they knew too much about them, knew where they lived, and how. The woman with the tambourine, whose voice dominated the air, whose face was bright with joy, was divided by very little from the woman who stood watching her, a cigarette between her heavy, chapped lips, her hair a cuckoo's nest, her face scarred and swollen from many beatings, and her black eyes glittering like coal. Perhaps they both knew this, which was why, when, as rarely, they addressed each other, they addressed each other as Sister. As the singing filled the air the watching, listening faces underwent a change, the eyes focusing on something within; the music seemed to soothe a poison out of them;

---

6. Processed: straightened and greased.   7. Publicly professing belief.

and time seemed, nearly, to fall away from the sullen, belligerent, battered faces, as though they were fleeing back to their first condition, while dreaming of their last. The barbecue cook half shook his head and smiled, and dropped his cigarette and disappeared into his joint. A man fumbled in his pockets for change and stood holding it in his hand impatiently, as though he had just remembered a pressing appointment further up the avenue. He looked furious. Then I saw Sonny, standing on the edge of the crowd. He was carrying a wide, flat notebook with a green cover, and it made him look, from where I was standing, almost like a schoolboy. The coppery sun brought out the copper in his skin, he was very faintly smiling, standing very still. Then the singing stopped, the tambourine turned into a collection plate again. The furious man dropped in his coins and vanished, so did a couple of the women, and Sonny dropped some change in the plate, looking directly at the woman with a little smile. He started across the avenue, toward the house. He has a slow, loping walk, something like the way Harlem hipsters walk, only he's imposed on this his own half-beat. I had never really noticed it before.

I stayed at the window, both relieved and apprehensive. As Sonny disappeared from my sight, they began singing again. And they were still singing when his key turned in the lock.

"Hey," he said.

"Hey, yourself. You want some beer?"

"No. Well, maybe." But he came up to the window and stood beside me, looking out. "What a warm voice," he said.

They were singing *If I could only hear my mother pray again!*

"Yes," I said, "and she can sure beat that tambourine."

"But what a terrible song," he said, and laughed. He dropped his notebook on the sofa and disappeared into the kitchen. "Where's Isabel and the kids?"

"I think they went to see their grandparents. You hungry?"

"No." He came back into the living room with his can of beer. "You want to come some place with me tonight?"

I sensed, I don't know how, that I couldn't possibly say no. "Sure. Where?"

He sat down on the sofa and picked up his notebook and started leafing through it. "I'm going to sit in with some fellows in a joint in the Village."

"You mean, you're going to play, tonight?"

"That's right." He took a swallow of his beer and moved back to the window. He gave me a sidelong look. "If you can stand it."

"I'll try," I said.

He smiled to himself and we both watched as the meeting across the way broke up. The three sisters and the brother, heads bowed, were singing *God be with you till we meet again*. The faces around them were very quiet. Then the song ended. The small crowd dispersed. We watched the three women and the lone man walk slowly up the avenue.

"When she was singing before," said Sonny, abruptly, "her voice reminded me for a minute of what heroin feels like sometimes—when it's in your veins. It makes you feel sort of warm and cool at the same time. And distant. And—and sure." He sipped his beer, very deliberately not looking at me. I watched his face. "It makes you feel—in control. Sometimes you've got to have that feeling."

"Do you?" I sat down slowly in the easy chair.

"Sometimes." He went to the sofa and picked up his notebook again. "Some people do."

"In order," I asked, "to play?" And my voice was very ugly, full of contempt and anger.

"Well"—he looked at me with great, troubled eyes, as though, in fact, he hoped his eyes would tell me things he could never otherwise say—"they *think* so. And *if* they think so—!"

"And what do *you* think?" I asked.

He sat on the sofa and put his can of beer on the floor. "I don't know," he said, and I couldn't be sure if he were answering my question or pursuing his thoughts. His face didn't tell me. "It's not so much to *play*. It's to *stand* it, to be able to make it at all. On any level." He frowned and smiled: "In order to keep from shaking to pieces."

"But these friends of yours," I said, "they seem to shake themselves to pieces pretty goddamn fast."

"Maybe." He played with the notebook. And something told me that I should curb my tongue, that Sonny was doing his best to talk, that I should listen. "But of course you only know the ones that've gone to pieces. Some don't—or at least they haven't *yet* and that's just about all *any* of us can say." He paused. "And then there are some who just live, really, in hell, and they know it and they see what's happening and they go right on. I don't know." He sighed, dropped the notebook, folded his arms. "Some guys, you can tell from the way they play, they on something *all* the time. And you can see that, well, it makes something real for them. But of course," he picked up his beer from the floor and sipped it and put the can down again, "they *want* to, too, you've got to see that. Even some of them that say they don't—*some*, not all."

"And what about you?" I asked—I couldn't help it. "What about you? Do *you* want to?"

He stood up and walked to the window and I remained silent for a long time. Then he sighed. "Me," he said. Then: "While I was downstairs before, on my way here, listening to that woman sing, it struck me all of a sudden how much suffering she must have had to go through—to sing like that. It's *repulsive* to think you have to suffer that much."

I said: "But there's no way not to suffer—is there, Sonny?"

"I believe not," he said and smiled, "but that's never stopped anyone from trying." He looked at me. "Has it?" I realized, with this mocking look, that there stood between us, forever, beyond the power of time or forgiveness, the fact that I had held silence—so long!—when he had needed human speech to help him. He turned back to the window. "No, there's no way not to suffer. But you try all kinds of ways to keep from drowning in it, to keep on top of it, and to make it seem—well, like *you*. Like you did something, all right, and now you're suffering for it. You know?" I said nothing. "Well you know," he said, impatiently, "why *do* people suffer? Maybe it's better to do something to give it a reason, *any* reason."

"But we just agreed," I said, "that there's no way not to suffer. Isn't it better, then, just to—take it?"

"But nobody just takes it," Sonny cried, "that's what I'm telling you! *Everybody* tries not to. You're just hung up on the *way* some people try—it's not *your* way!"

The hair on my face began to itch, my face felt wet. "That's not true," I said, "that's not true. I don't give a damn what other people do, I don't even care how they suffer. I just care how *you* suffer." And he looked at me. "Please believe me," I said, "I don't want to see you—die—trying not to suffer."

"I won't," he said flatly, "die trying not to suffer. At least, not any faster than anybody else."

"But there's no need," I said, trying to laugh, "is there? in killing yourself."

I wanted to say more, but I couldn't. I wanted to talk about will power and how life could be—well, beautiful. I wanted to say that it was all within; but was it? or, rather, wasn't that exactly the trouble? And I wanted to promise that I would never fail him again. But it would all have sounded—empty words and lies.

So I made the promise to myself and prayed that I would keep it.

"It's terrible sometimes, inside," he said, "that's what's the trouble. You walk these streets, black and funky and cold, and there's not really a living ass to talk to, and there's nothing shaking, and there's no way of getting it out—that storm inside. You can't talk it and you can't make love with it, and when you finally try to get with it and play it, you realize *nobody's* listening. So *you've* got to listen. You got to find a way to listen."

And then he walked away from the window and sat on the sofa again, as though all the wind had suddenly been knocked out of him. "Sometimes you'll do *anything* to play, even cut your mother's throat." He laughed and looked at me. "Or your brother's." Then he sobered. "Or your own." Then: "Don't worry. I'm all right now and I think I'll *be* all right. But I can't forget—where I've been. I don't mean just the physical place I've been, I mean where I've *been*. And *what* I've been."

"What have you been, Sonny?" I asked.

He smiled—but sat sideways on the sofa, his elbow resting on the back, his fingers playing with his mouth and chin, not looking at me. "I've been something I didn't recognize, didn't know I could be. Didn't know anybody could be." He stopped, looking inward, looking helplessly young, looking old. "I'm not talking about it now because I feel *guilty* or anything like that—maybe it would be better if I did, I don't know. Anyway, I can't really talk about it. Not to you, not to anybody," and now he turned and faced me. "Sometimes, you know, and it was actually when I was most *out* of the world, I felt that I was in it, that I was *with* it, really, and I could play or I didn't really have to *play*, it just came out of me, it was there. And I don't know how I played, thinking about it now, but I know I did awful things, those times, sometimes, to people. Or it wasn't that I *did* anything to them—it was that they weren't real." He picked up the beer can; it was empty; he rolled it between his palms: "And other times—well, I needed a fix, I needed to find a place to lean, I needed to clear a space to *listen*—and I couldn't find it, and I—went crazy, I did terrible things to *me*, I was terrible *for* me." He began pressing the beer can between his hands, I watched the metal begin to give. It glittered, as he played with it like a knife, and I was afraid he would cut himself, but I said nothing. "Oh well. I can never tell you. I was all by myself at the bottom of something, stinking and sweating and crying and shaking, and I smelled it, you know? *my* stink, and I thought I'd die if I couldn't get away from it and yet, all the same, I knew that everything I was doing was just locking me in with it. And I didn't know," he paused, still flattening the beer can, "I didn't know, I still *don't* know, something kept telling me that maybe it was good to smell your own stink, but I didn't think that *that* was what I'd been trying to do—and—who can stand it?" and he abruptly dropped the ruined beer can, looking at me with a small, still smile, and then rose, walking to the window as though it were the lodestone rock. I watched his face, he watched the avenue. "I couldn't tell you when Mama died—but the reason I wanted to leave Harlem so bad was to get away from drugs. And then, when I ran away, that's what I was running from—really. When I came back, nothing had changed, *I* hadn't changed, I was just—older." And he stopped, drumming with his fingers on the windowpane. The sun had vanished, soon darkness would fall. I watched his face. "It can come again," he said, almost as though speaking to himself. Then he turned to me. "It can come again," he repeated. "I just want you to know that."

"All right," I said, at last. "So it can come again. All right."

He smiled, but the smile was sorrowful. "I had to try to tell you," he said.

"Yes," I said. "I understand that."

"You're my brother," he said, looking straight at me, and not smiling at all.

"Yes," I repeated, "yes. I understand that."

He turned back to the window, looking out. "All that hatred down there," he said, "all that hatred and misery and love. It's a wonder it doesn't blow the avenue apart."

We went to the only nightclub on a short, dark street, downtown. We squeezed through the narrow, chattering, jampacked bar to the entrance of the big room, where the bandstand was. And we stood there for a moment, for the lights were very dim in this room and we couldn't see. Then, "Hello, boy," said a voice and an enormous black man, much older than Sonny or myself, erupted out of all that atmospheric lighting and put an arm around Sonny's shoulder. "I been sitting right here," he said, "waiting for you."

He had a big voice, too, and heads in the darkness turned toward us.

Sonny grinned and pulled a little away, and said, "Creole, this is my brother. I told you about him."

Creole shook my hand. "I'm glad to meet you, son," he said, and it was clear that he was glad to meet me *there*, for Sonny's sake. And he smiled, "You got a real musician in *your* family," and he took his arm from Sonny's shoulder and slapped him, lightly, affectionately, with the back of his hand.

"Well. Now I've heard it all," said a voice behind us. This was another musician, and a friend of Sonny's, a coal-black, cheerful-looking man, built close to the ground. He immediately began confiding to me, at the top of his lungs, the most terrible things about Sonny, his teeth gleaming like a lighthouse and his laugh coming up out of him like the beginning of an earthquake. And it turned out that everyone at the bar knew Sonny, or almost everyone; some were musicians, working there, or nearby, or not working, some were simply hangers-on, and some were there to hear Sonny play. I was introduced to all of them and they were all very polite to me. Yet, it was clear that, for them, I was only Sonny's brother. Here, I was in Sonny's world. Or, rather: his kingdom. Here, it was not even a question that his veins bore royal blood.

They were going to play soon and Creole installed me, by myself, at a table in a dark corner. Then I watched them, Creole, and the little black man, and Sonny, and the others, while they horsed around, standing just below the bandstand. The light from the bandstand spilled just a little short of them and, watching them laughing and gesturing and moving about, I had the feeling that they, nevertheless, were being most careful not to step into that circle of light too suddenly: that if they moved into the light too suddenly, without thinking, they would perish in flame. Then, while I watched, one of them, the small black man, moved into the light and crossed the bandstand and started fooling around with his drums. Then—being funny and being, also, extremely ceremonious—Creole took Sonny by the arm and led him to the piano. A woman's voice called Sonny's name and a few hands started clapping. And Sonny, also being funny and being ceremonious, and so touched, I think, that he could have cried, but neither hiding it nor showing it, riding it like a man, grinned, and put both hands to his heart and bowed from the waist.

Creole then went to the bass fiddle and a lean, very bright-skinned brown man jumped up on the bandstand and picked up his horn. So there they were, and the atmosphere on the bandstand and in the room began to change and tighten. Someone stepped up to the microphone and announced them. Then there were all kinds of murmurs. Some people at the bar shushed others. The waitress ran around, frantically getting in the last orders, guys and chicks got closer to each other, and the lights on the bandstand, on the quartet, turned to a kind of indigo. Then they all looked different there. Creole looked about him for the last time, as though he were making certain that all his chickens were in the coop, and then he—jumped and struck the fiddle. And there they were.

All I know about music is that not many people ever really hear it. And even then, on the rare occasions when something opens within, and the music enters, what we mainly hear, or hear corroborated, are personal, private, vanishing evocations. But the man who creates the music is hearing something else, is dealing with the roar rising from the void and imposing order on it as it hits the air. What is evoked in him, then, is of another order, more terrible because it has no words, and triumphant, too, for that same reason. And his triumph, when he triumphs, is ours. I just watched Sonny's face. His face was troubled, he was working hard, but he wasn't with it. And I had the feeling that, in a way, everyone on the bandstand was waiting for him, both waiting for him and pushing him along. But as I began to watch Creole, I realized that it was Creole who held them all back. He had them on a short rein. Up there, keeping the beat with his whole body, wailing on the fiddle, with his eyes half closed, he was listening to everything, but he was listening to Sonny. He was having a dialogue with Sonny. He wanted Sonny to leave the shoreline and strike out for the deep water. He was Sonny's witness that deep water and drowning were not the same thing—he had been there, and he knew. And he wanted Sonny to know. He was waiting for Sonny to do the things on the keys which would let Creole know that Sonny was in the water.

And, while Creole listened, Sonny moved, deep within, exactly like someone in torment. I had never before thought of how awful the relationship must be between the musician and his instrument. He has to fill it, this instrument, with the breath of life, his own. He has to make it do what he wants it to do. And a piano is just a piano. It's made out of so much wood and wires and little hammers and big ones, and ivory. While there's only so much you can do with it, the only way to find this out is to try; to try and make it do everything.

And Sonny hadn't been near a piano for over a year. And he wasn't on much better terms with his life, not the life that stretched before him now. He and the piano stammered, started one way, got scared, stopped; started another way, panicked, marked time, started again; then seemed to have found a direction, panicked again, got stuck. And the face I saw on Sonny I'd never seen before. Everything had been burned out of it, and, at the same time, things usually hidden were being burned in, by the fire and fury of the battle which was occurring in him up there.

Yet, watching Creole's face as they neared the end of the first set, I had the feeling that something had happened, something I hadn't heard. Then they finished, there was scattered applause, and then, without an instant's warning, Creole started into something else, it was almost sardonic, it was *Am I Blue*.[8] And, as though he commanded, Sonny began to play. Something began to happen. And Creole let out the reins. The dry, low, black man said something awful on the drums, Creole answered, and the drums talked back. Then the horn insisted, sweet and high, slightly detached perhaps, and Creole listened, commenting now and then, dry, and driving, beautiful and calm and old. Then they all came together again, and Sonny was part of the family again. I could tell this from his face. He seemed to have found, right there beneath his fingers, a damn brand-new piano. It seemed that he couldn't get over it. Then, for a while, just being happy with Sonny, they seemed to be agreeing with him that brand-new pianos certainly were a gas.

Then Creole stepped forward to remind them that what they were playing was the blues. He hit something in all of them, he hit something in me, myself, and the music tightened and deepened, apprehension began to beat the air. Creole began to tell us what the blues were all about. They were not about anything very new. He and his boys up

8. By Grant Clark and Harry Akst, sung by Ethel Waters in 1929 film, "On with the Show," brilliantly recorded by Billy Holiday, and a favorite blues piece.

there were keeping it new, at the risk of ruin, destruction, madness, and death, in order to find new ways to make us listen. For, while the tale of how we suffer, and how we are delighted, and how we may triumph is never new, it always must be heard. There isn't any other tale to tell, it's the only light we've got in all this darkness.

And this tale, according to that face, that body, those strong hands on those strings, has another aspect in every country, and a new depth in every generation. Listen, Creole seemed to be saying, listen. Now these are Sonny's blues. He made the little black man on the drums know it, and the bright, brown man on the horn. Creole wasn't trying any longer to get Sonny in the water. He was wishing him Godspeed. Then he stepped back, very slowly, filling the air with the immense suggestion that Sonny speak for himself.

Then they all gathered around Sonny and Sonny played. Every now and again one of them seemed to say, amen. Sonny's fingers filled the air with life, his life. But that life contained so many others. And Sonny went all the way back, he really began with the spare, flat statement of the opening phrase of the song. Then he began to make it his. It was very beautiful because it wasn't hurried and it was no longer a lament. I seemed to hear with what burning he had made it his, with what burning we had yet to make it ours, how we could cease lamenting. Freedom lurked around us and I understood, at last, that he could help us to be free if we would listen, that he would never be free until we did. Yet, there was no battle in his face now, I heard what he had gone through, and would continue to go through until he came to rest in earth. He had made it his: that long line, of which we knew only Mama and Daddy. And he was giving it back, as everything must be given back, so that, passing through death, it can live forever. I saw my mother's face again, and felt, for the first time, how the stones of the road she had walked on must have bruised her feet. I saw the moonlit road where my father's brother died. And it brought something else back to me, and carried me past it, I saw my little girl again and felt Isabel's tears again, and I felt my own tears begin to rise. And I was yet aware that this was only a moment, that the world waited outside, as hungry as a tiger, and that trouble stretched above us, longer than the sky.

Then it was over. Creole and Sonny let out their breath, both soaking wet, and grinning. There was a lot of applause and some of it was real. In the dark, the girl came by and I asked her to take drinks to the bandstand. There was a long pause, while they talked up there in the indigo light and after awhile I saw the girl put a Scotch and milk on top of the piano for Sonny. He didn't seem to notice it, but just before they started playing again, he sipped from it and looked toward me, and nodded. Then he put it back on top of the piano. For me, then, as they began to play again, it glowed and shook above my brother's head like the very cup of trembling.[9]

1965

9. See *Isaiah* 51:17, 22–23: "Awake, awake, stand up, O Jerusalem, which hast drunk at the hand of the Lord the cup of his fury; thou hast drunken the dregs of the cup of trembling, and wrung them out. . . . Behold, I have taken out of thine hand the cup of trembling, even the dregs of the cup of my fury; thou shalt no more drink it again: But I will put it into the hands of them that afflict thee; . . . ."

Stories for Further Reading

GEORGE WASHINGTON HARRIS

Mrs. Yardley's Quilting

"Thar's one durn'd nasty muddy job, an' I is jis' glad enuf tu take a ho'n[1] ur two, on the straingth ove hit."

"What have you been doing, Sut?"

"Helpin tu salt ole Missis Yardley down."

"What do you mean by that?"

"Fixin her fur rotten cumfurtably, kiverin her up wif sile, tu keep the buzzards from cheatin the wurms."

"Oh, you have been helping to bury a woman."

"That's hit, by golly! Now why the devil can't I 'splain myself like yu? I ladles out my words at random, like a calf kickin at yaller-jackids; yu jis' rolls em out tu the pint, likc a feller a-layin bricks—every one fits. How is it that bricks fits so clost enyhow? Rocks won't ni du hit."

"Becaze they'se all ove a size," ventured a man with a wen over his eye.

"The devil yu say, hon'ey-head![2] haint rcapin-mersheens ove a size? I'd likc tu see two ove em fit clost. Yu wait ontil yu sprouts tuther ho'n, afore yu venters tu 'splain mix'd questions. George did yu know ole Missis Yardley?"

"No."

"Well, she wer a curious 'oman in her way, an' she wore shiney specks. Now jis' listen: Whenever yu see a ole 'oman ahine a par ove *shiney* specks, yu keep yer eye skinn'd; they am dang'rus in the ex-treme. Thar is jis' no knowin' what they ken du. I hed one a-stradil ove me onsl, fur kissin her gal. She went fur my har, an' she went fur my skin, ontil I tho't she ment tu kill me, an' wud a-dun hit, ef my hollerin hadent fotch ole Dave Jordan, a *bacheler*, tu my aid. He, like a durn'd fool, cotch her by the laig, an' drug her back'ards ofen me. She jis' kivered him, an' I run, by golly! The nex time I seed him he wer bald headed, an' his face looked like he'd been a-fitin wildcats.

"Ole Missis Yardley wer a great noticer ove littil things, that nobody else ever seed. She'd say right in the middil ove sumbody's serious talk: 'Law sakes! thar goes that yaller slut ove a hen, a-flingin straws over her shoulder; she's arter settin now, an' haint laid but seven aigs. I'll disapint *her*, see ef I don't; I'll put a punkin in her nes', an' a feather in her nose. An' bless my soul! jis' look at that cow wif the wilted ho'n, a-flingin up dirt an' a-smellin the place whar hit cum frum, wif

1. "Horn": a drink.
2. "Horny-head" (because of a wen, or tumor); thus his reference to sporting
another horn and becoming wise (like the devil?).

the rale ginuine still-wurim twis'[3] in her tail, too; what upon the face
ove the yeath kin she be arter now, the ole fool? watch her, Sally.
An' sakes alive jis' look at that ole sow; she's a-gwine in a fas' trot,
wif her empty bag a-floppin agin her sides. Thar, she hes stop't,
an's a-listenin! massy on us! what a long yearnis grunt she gin; hit
cum frum way back ove her kidneys. Thar she goes agin; she's arter no
good, sich kerryin on means no good.'

"An' so she wud gabble, no odds who wer a-listenin. She looked
like she mout been made at fust 'bout four foot long, an' the common
thickness ove wimen when they's at tharsefs,[4] an' then had her har
tied tu a stump, a par ove steers hitched to her heels, an' then straiched
out a-mos' two foot more—mos' ove the straichin cumin outen her
laigs an' naik. Her stockins, a-hangin on the clothesline tu dry, looked
like a par ove sabre scabbards, an' her naik looked like a dry beef
shank smoked, an' mout been ni ontu es tough. I never felt hit mysef,
I didn't, I jis' jedges by looks. Her darter Sal wer bilt at fust 'bout
the laingth ove her mam, but wer never straiched eny by a par ove
steers an' she wer fat enuf tu kill; she wer taller lyin down than she
wer a-standin up. Hit wer her who gin me the 'hump shoulder.' Jis'
look at me; haint I'se got a tech ove the dromedary back thar bad?
haint I humpy? Well, a-stoopin tu kiss that squatty lard-stan[5] ove a
gal is what dun hit tu me. She wer the fairest-lookin gal I ever seed.
She allers wore thick woolin stockins 'bout six inches too long fur her
laig; they rolled down over her garters, lookin like a par ove life-
presarvers up thar. I tell yu she wer a tarin gal enyhow. Luved kissin,
wrastlin, an' biled cabbige, an' hated tite clothes, hot weather, an
suckit-riders.[6] B'leved strong in married folk's ways, cradles, an' the
remishun ove sins, an' didn't b'leve in corsets, fleas, peaners, nur the
fashun plates."

"What caused the death of Mrs. Yardley, Sut?"

"Nuffin, only her heart stop't beatin 'bout losin a nine dimunt quilt.[7]
True, she got a skeer'd hoss tu run over her, but she'd a-got over that
ef a quilt hadn't been mix'd up in the catastrophy. Yu see quilts wer
wun ove her speshul gifts; she run strong on the bed-kiver question.
Irish chain, star ove Texas, sun-flower, nine-dimunt, saw teeth,
checker board, an' shell quilts; blue, an' white, an' yaller an' black
coverlids, an' callickercumfurts[8] reigned triumphan' 'bout her hous'.
They wer packed in drawers, layin in shelfs full, wer hung four dubbil
on lines in the lof, packed in chists, piled on cheers, an' wer everywhar,
even ontu the beds, an' wer changed every bed-makin. She told everybody she cud git tu listen tu hit that she ment tu give every durn'd
one ove them tu Sal when she got married. Oh, lordy! what es fat a
gal es Sal Yardley cud ever du wif half ove em, an' sleepin wif a hus-
bun at that, is more nor I ever cud see through. Jis' think ove her
onder twenty layer ove quilts in July, an' yu in thar too. Gewhillikins!
George, look how I is sweatin' now, an' this is December. I'd 'bout es
lief be shet up in a steam biler wif a three-hundred-pound bag ove

<hr>

3. Still-worm is a spiralling tube in
whiskey stills.
4. Full-grown (and not pregnant).
5. Tub or crock of lard.
6. Circuit riders: preachers.

7. Nine-diamond, pattern of quilt;
others, like "Irish chain," "star over
Texas," are named below.
8. Coverlets (bedspreads) and calico
comforters or quilted bedcoverings.

lard, es tu make a bisiness ove sleepin wif that gal—'twould kill a glass-blower.

"Well, tu cum tu the serious part ove this conversashun, that is how the old quilt morsheen an' coverlid-loom cum tu stop opera-shuns on this yeath. She hed narrated hit thru the neighborhood that nex Saterday she'd gin a quiltin[9]—three quilts an' one cumfurt tu tie. 'Goblers,[1] fiddils, gals, an' whisky,' wer the words she sent tu the men-folk, an' more tetchin ur wakenin words never drap't ofen an 'oman's tongue. She sed tu the gals, 'Sweet toddy, huggin, dancin, an' huggers in 'bundance.' Them words struck the gals rite in the pit ove the stumick, an' spread a ticklin sensashun bof ways, ontil they scratched thar heads wif one han, an' thar heels wif tuther.

"Everybody, he an' she, what wer baptized b'levers in the righ-teousnes ove quiltins wer thar, an' hit jis' so happen'd that everybody in them parts, frum fifteen summers tu fifty winters, were unannamus b'levers. Strange, warn't hit? Hit wer the bigges' quiltin ever Missis Yardley hilt, an' she hed hilt hundreds; everybody wer thar, 'scept the constibil an' suckit-rider, two dam easily-spared pussons; the numbers ni ontu even too; jis' a few more boys nur gals; that made hit more exhitin, fur hit gin the gals a chance tu kick an' squeal a littil, wifout runnin eny risk ove not gittin kissed at all, an' hit gin reasonabil grouns fur a few scrimmages amung the he's. Now es kissin an' fitin am the pepper an' salt ove all soshul getherins, so hit were more espishully wif this ove ours. Es I swung my eyes over the crowd, George, I thought quiltins, managed in a morril an' sensibil way, truly am good things—good fur free drinkin, good fur free eatin, good fur free huggin, good fur free dancin, good fur free fitin, an' goodest ove all fur poperlatin a country fas'.

"Thar am a fur-seein wisdum in quiltins, ef they hes proper trim-mins: 'vittils, fiddils, an' sperrits in 'bundence.' One holesum quiltin am wuf three old pray'r meetins on the poperlashun pint, purtickerly ef hits hilt in the dark ove the moon, an' runs intu the night a few hours, an' April ur May am the time chosen. The moon don't suit quiltins whar everybody is well acquainted an' already fur along in courtin. She dus help pow'ful tu begin a courtin match onder, but when hit draws ni ontu a head, nobody wants a moon but the ole mammys.

"The mornin cum, still, saft, sunshiney; cocks crowin, hens singih, birds chirpin, tuckeys gobblin—jis' the day tu sun quilts, kick, kiss, squeal, an' make love.

"All the plow-lines an' clotheslines wer straiched tu every post an' tree. Quilts purvailed. Durn my gizzard ef two acres round that ar house warn't jis' one solid quilt, all out a-sunnin, an' tu be seed. They dazzled the eyes, skeered the hosses, gin wimen the heart-burn, an' perdominated.

"To'ards sundown the he's begun tu drap in. Yearnis' needil-drivin cummenced tu lose groun; threads broke ofen, thimbils got los', an' quilts needed anuther roll. Gigglin, winkin, whisperin, smoofin ove har, an' gals a-ticklin one anuther, wer a-gainin every inch ove groun what the needils los'. Did yu ever notis, George, at all soshul getherins, when the he's begin tu gather, that the young she's begin tu tickil one anuther an' the ole maids swell thar tails, roach[2] up thar backs, an' sharpen thar nails ontu the bed-posts an' door jams, an' spit an' groan sorter like cats a-courtin? Dus hit mean *rale* rath, ur is hit a dare tu the he's, sorter kivered up wif the outside signs ove danger? I honestly b'leve that the young shes' ticklin means, 'Cum an' take this job ofen our hans.' But that swellin I jis' don't onderstan; dus yu? Hit looks skeery, an' I never tetch one ove em when they am in the swellin way. I may be mistaken'd 'bout the ticklin bisiness too; hit may be dun like a feller chaws poplar bark when he haint got eny terbacker, a-sorter better nur nun make-shif. I dus know one thing tu a certainty: that is, when the he's take hold the ticklin quits, an' ef yu gits one ove the ole maids out tu hersef, then she subsides an' is the smoofes, sleekes, saft thing yu ever seed, an' dam ef yu can't hear her purr, jis' es plain!

"But then, George, gals an' ole maids haint the things tu fool time away on. Hits widders, by golly, what am the rale sensibil, steady-goin, never-skeerin, never-kickin, willin, sperrited, smoof pacers. They cum clost up tu the hoss-block,[3] standin still wif thar purty silky years playin, an' the naik-veins a-throbbin, an' waits fur the word, which ove course yu gives, arter yu finds yer feet well in the stirrup, an' away they moves like a cradil on cushioned rockers, ur a spring buggy runnin in damp san'. A tetch ove the bridil, an' they knows yu want em tu turn, an' they dus hit es willin es ef the idear wer thar own. I be dod rabbited[4] ef a man can't 'propriate happiness by the skinful ef he is in contack wif sumbody's widder, an' is smart. Gin me a willin widder, the yeath over: what they don't know, haint worth larnin. They hes all been tu Jamakey an' larnt how sugar's made, an' knows how tu sweeten wif hit; an' by golly, they is always ready tu use hit. All yu hes tu du is tu find the spoon, an' then drink cumfort till yer blind. Nex tu good sperrits an' my laigs, I likes a twenty-five-year-ole widder, wif roun ankils, an' bright eyes, honestly an' squarly lookin intu yurn, an' sayin es plainly es a partrige sez 'Bob White,' 'Don't be afraid ove me; I hes been thar; yu know hit ef yu hes eny sense, an' thar's no use in eny humbug, old feller—cum ahead!"

"Ef yu onderstans widder nater, they ken save yu a power ove troubil, onsartinty, an' time, an ef you is interprisin yu gits mons'rous well paid fur hit. The very soun ove thar littil shoe-heels speak full trainin, an' hes a knowin click as they tap the floor; an' the rustil ove thar dress sez, 'I dar yu tu ax me.'

"When yu hes made up yer mind tu court one, jis' go at hit like hit wer a job ove rail-maulin. Ware yer workin close, use yer common, every-day moshuns an' words, an' abuv all, fling away yer cinamint ile[5] vial an' burn all yer love songs. No use in tryin tu fool em, fur they sees plum thru yu, a durn'd sight plainer than they dus thru thar veils. No use in a pasted[6] shut; she's been thar. No use in bor-rowin a cavortin fat hoss; she's been thar. No use in har-dye; she's been thar. No use in cloves, tu kill whisky breff; she's been thar. No

---

2. Arch.
3. A platform used to mount or dis-mount a horse or to get into or out of a vehicle.
4. God-confounded.
5. Cinnamon oil perfume.
6. Starched.

use in buyin clost curtains fur yer bed, fur she has been thar. Widders am a speshul means, George, fur ripenin green men, killin off weak ones, an makin 'ternally happy the soun ones.

"Woll, es I sed afore, I flew the track an' got ontu the widders. The fellers begun tu ride up an' walk up, sorter slow, like they warn't in a hurry, the durn'd 'saitful[7] raskils, hitchin thar critters tu enything they cud find. One red-comb'd, long-spurr'd, dominecker[8] feller, frum town, in a red an' white grid-iron jackid an' patent leather gaiters,[9] hitched his hoss, a wild, skeery, wall-eyed devil, inside the yard palins, tu a cherry tree lim'. Thinks I, that hoss hes a skeer intu him big enuf tu run intu town, an' perhaps beyant hit, ef I kin only tetch hit off; so I sot intu thinkin.

"One aind ove a long clothesline, wif nine dimunt quilts ontu hit, wer tied tu the same cherry tree that the hoss wer. I tuck my knife and socked hit thru every quilt, 'bout the middil, an' jis' below the rope, an' tied them thar wif bark, so they cudent slip. Then I went tu the back aind, an' ontied hit frum the pos', knottin in a hoe-handil, by the middil, tu keep the quilts frum slippin off ef my bark strings failed, an' laid hit on the groun. Then I went tu the tuther aind: thar wer 'bout ten foot tu spar, a-lyin on the groun arter tyin tu the tree. I tuck hit atwix Wall-eye's hine laigs, an' tied hit fas' tu bof stirrups, an' then cut the cherry tree lim' betwix his bridil an' the tree, almos' off. Now, mine yu thar wer two ur three uther ropes full ove quilts atween me an' the hous', so I wer purty well hid frum thar. I jis' tore off a palin frum the fence, an' tuck hit in bof hans, an' arter raisin hit 'way up yander, I fotch hit down, es hard es I cud, flatsided to'ards the groun, an' hit acksidentally happen'd tu hit Wall-eye, 'bout nine inches ahead ove the root ove his tail. Hit landed so hard that hit made my hans tingle, an' then busted intu splinters. The first thing I did, wer tu feel ove mysef, on the same spot whar hit hed hit the hoss. I cudent help duin hit tu save my life, an' I swar I felt sum ove Wall-eye's sensashun, jis' es plain. The fust thing he did, wer tu tare down the lim' wif a twenty-foot jump, his head to'ards the hous'. Thinks I, now yu hev dun hit, yu durn'd wall-eyed fool! tarin down that lim' wer the beginin ove all the troubil, an' the hoss did hit hissef; my conshuns felt clar es a mountin spring, an' I wer in a frame ove mine tu obsarve things es they happen'd, an' they soon begun tu happen purty clost arter one anuther rite then, an' thar, an' tharabouts, clean ontu town, thru hit, an' still wer a-happenin, in the woods beyant thar ni ontu eleven mile frum ole man Yardley's gate, an' four beyant town.

"The fust line ove quilts he tried tu jump, but broke hit down; the nex one he ran onder; the rope cotch ontu the ho'n ove the saddil, broke at bof ainds, an' went along wif the hoss, the cherry tree lim' an' the fust line ove quilts, what I hed proverdensally tied fas' tu the rope. That's what I calls foresight, George. Right furnint[1] the frunt door he cum in contack wif ole Missis Yardley hersef, an' anuther ole 'oman; they wer a-holdin a nine-dimunt quilt spread out,

7. Deceitful.
8. Dominiques: yellow-legged chickens with gray-barred plumage.
9. High-topped shoes.
1. In front of.

a-'zaminin hit an' a-praisin hits perfeckshuns. The durn'd onmanerly, wall-eyed fool run plum over Missis Yardley frum ahine, stompt one hine foot through the quilt takin hit along, a-kickin ontil he made hits corners snap like a whip. The gals screamed, the men hollered wo! an' the ole 'oman wer toted intu the hous' limber es a wet string, an' every word she sed wer, 'Oh, my preshus nine-dimunt quilt!'

"Wall-eye busted thru the palins, an' Dominicker seed 'im, made a mortal rush fur his bitts, wer too late fur them, but in good time fur the strings ove flyin quilts, got tangled amung em, an' the gridiron jackid patren wer los' tu my sight amung star an' Irish chain quilts; he went frum that quiltin at the rate ove thuty miles tu the hour. Nuffin lef on the lot ove the hole consarn, but a nine biler[2] hat, a par ove gloves, an' the jack ove hearts.

"What a onmanerly, suddin way ove leavin places sum folks hev got, enyhow.

"Thinks I, well, that fool hoss, tarin down that cherry tree lim', hes dun sum good, enyhow; hit hes put the ole 'oman outen the way fur the balance ove the quiltin, an' tuck Dominicker outen the way an' outen danger, fur that gridiron jackid wud a-bred a scab on his nose afore midnite; hit wer morrily boun tu du hit.

"Two months arterwards, I tracked the route that hoss tuck in his kalamatus skeer, by quilt rags, tufts ove cotton, bunches ove har, (human an' hoss), an' scraps ove a gridiron jackid stickin ontu the bushes, an' plum at the aind ove hit, whar all signs gin out, I foun a piece ove watch chain an' a hosses head. The places what know'd Dominicker, know'd 'im no more.[3]

"Well, arter they'd tuck the ole 'oman up stairs an' camfired her tu sleep, things begun tu work agin. The widders broke the ice, an' arter a littil gigilin, goblin, an' gabblin, the kissin begun. *Smack!*—'Thar, now,' a widder sed that. *Pop!*—'Oh, don't!' *Pfip!*—'Oh, yu quit!' *Plosh!*—'Go *way* yu awkerd critter, yu kissed me in the eye!' anuther widder sed that. *Bop!*—'Now yu ar satisfied, I recon, big mouf!' *Vip!*—'That haint fair!' *Spat!*—'Oh, lordy! May, cum pull Bill away; he's a-tanglin my har.' *Thut!*—'I jis' d-a-r-e yu tu du that agin!'" a widder sed that, too. Hit sounded all 'roun that room like poppin co'n in a hot skillet, an' wer pow'ful sujestif.

"Hit kep on ontil I be durn'd ef *my* bristils didn't begin tu rise, an' sumthin like a cold buckshot wud run down the marrow in my backbone 'bout every ten secons, an' then run up agin, tolerabil hot. I kep a swallerin wif nuthin tu swaller, an' my face felt swell'd: an' yet I wer fear'd tu make a bulge. Thinks I, I'll ketch one out tu hersef torreckly, an' then I guess we'll rastil. Purty soon Sal Yardley started fur the smoke 'ous, so I jis' gin my head a few short shakes, let down one ove my wings a-trailin, an' sirkiled roun her wif a side twis' in my naik, steppin sidewise, an' a-fetchin up my hinmos' foot wif a sorter jerkin slide at every step. Sez I, 'Too coo-took a-too.' She onderstood hit, an stopt, sorter spreadin her shoulders. An' jis' es I hed pouch'd out my mouf, an' wer a-reachin forrid wif hit, fur the article hitself, sunthin interfared wif me, hit did. George, wer yu ever ontu yer hans

---

2. Unidentified.
3. Job 7: 9–10 ". . . he that goeth down to the grave shall come up no more.

He shall return no more to his house, neither shall his place know him any more."

an' knees, an' let a hell-tarin big, mad ram, wif a ten-yard run, but[4] yu yearnis'ly, jis' onst, right squar ontu the pint ove yer backbone?"

"No, you fool, why do you ask?"

"Kaze I wanted tu know ef yu cud hev a realizin' noshun ove my shock. Hits scarcely worth while tu try tu make yu onderstan the case by words only, onless yu hev been tetched in that way. Gr-eat golly! the fust thing I felt, I tuck hit tu be a back-ackshun yeathquake; an' the fust thing I seed wer my chaw'r terbacker a-flyin' over Sal's head like a skeer'd bat. My mouf wer pouch'd out, ready fur the article hitsef, yu know, an' hit went outen the roun hole like the wad outen a pop-gun—thug! an' the fust thing I know'd, I wer a flyin over Sal's head too, an' a-gainin on the chaw'r terbacker fast. I wer straitened out strait, toes hinemos', middil finger-nails foremos', an' the fust thing I hearn wer, 'Yu dam Shanghi!'[5] Great Jerus-a-lam! I lit ontu my all fours jis' in time tu but the yard gate ofen hits hinges, an' skeer loose sum more hosses—kep on in a four-footed gallop, clean acrost the lane afore I cud straiten up, an' yere I cotch up wif my chaw'r terbacker, stickin flat agin a fence-rail. I hed got so good a start that I thot hit a pity tu spile hit, so I jis' jump'd the fence an' tuck thru the orchurd. I tell yu I dusted those yere close, fur I tho't hit wer arter me.

"Arter runnin a spell, I ventered tu feel roun back thar, fur sum signs ove what hed happened tu me. George, arter two pow'ful hard tugs, I pull'd out the vamp an' sole ove one ove ole man Yardley's big brogans, what he hed los' amung my coattails. Dre'ful! dre'ful! Arter I got hit away frum thar, my flesh went fas' asleep, frum abuv my kidneys tu my knees; about now, fur the fust time, the idear struck me, what hit wer that hed interfar'd wif me, an' los' me the kiss. Hit wer ole Yardley hed kicked me. I walked fur a month like I wer straddlin a thorn hedge. Sich a shock, at sich a time, an' on sich a place—jis' think ove hit! hit am tremenjus, haint hit? The place feels num, right now."

"Well, Sut, how did the quilting come out?"

"How the hell du yu 'speck me tu know? I warn't thar eny more."

1867

HERMAN MELVILLE

Bartleby, the Scrivener

A STORY OF WALL STREET

I am a rather elderly man. The nature of my avocations for the last thirty years has brought me into more than ordinary contact with what would seem an interesting and somewhat singular set of men, of whom as yet nothing that I know of has ever been written: I mean the law-copyists or scriveners. I have known very many of them, professionally and privately, and if I pleased, could relate divers histories, at which

---

4. Butt.   5. Chicken with long feathered legs.

good-natured gentlemen might smile, and sentimental souls might weep. But I waive the biographies of all other scriveners for a few passages in the life of Bartleby, who was a scrivener the strangest I ever saw or heard of. While of other law-copyists I might write the complete life, of Bartleby nothing of that sort can be done. I believe that no materials exist for a full and satisfactory biography of this man. It is an irreparable loss to literature. Bartleby was one of those beings of whom nothing is ascertainable, except from the original sources, and in his case those are very small. What my own astonished eyes saw of Bartleby, *that* is all I know of him, except, indeed, one vague report which will appear in the sequel.

Ere introducing the scrivener, as he first appeared to me, it is fit I make some mention of myself, my *employées*, my business, my chambers, and general surroundings; because some such description is indispensable to an adequate understanding of the chief character about to be presented.

Imprimis:[1] I am a man who, from his youth upwards, has been filled with a profound conviction that the easiest way of life is the best. Hence, though I belong to a profession proverbially energetic and nervous, even to turbulence, at times, yet nothing of that sort have I ever suffered to invade my peace. I am one of those unambitious lawyers who never addresses a jury, or in any way draws down public applause; but in the cool tranquillity of a snug retreat, do a snug business among rich men's bonds and mortgages and title-deeds. All who know me, consider me an eminently *safe* man. The late John Jacob Astor,[2] a personage little given to poetic enthusiasm, had no hesitation in pronouncing my first grand point to be prudence; my next, method. I do not speak it in vanity, but simply record the fact, that I was not unemployed in my profession by the late John Jacob Astor; a name which, I admit, I love to repeat, for it hath a rounded and orbicular sound to it, and rings like unto bullion. I will freely add that I was not insensible to the late John Jacob Astor's good opinion.

Some time prior to the period at which this little history begins, my avocations had been largely increased. The good old office, now extinct in the State of New York, of a Master in Chancery,[3] had been conferred upon me. It was not a very arduous office, but very pleasantly remunerative. I seldom lose my temper; much more seldom indulge in dangerous indignation at wrongs and outrages; but I must be permitted to be rash here and declare, that I consider the sudden and violent abrogation of the office of Master in Chancery, by the new Constitution, as a—premature act; inasmuch as I had counted upon a life-lease of the profits, whereas I only received those of a few short years. But this is by the way.

My chambers were up stairs at No. —— Wall Street. At one end they looked upon the white wall of the interior of a spacious skylight shaft, penetrating the building from top to bottom. This view might have been considered rather tame than otherwise, deficient in what landscape painters call "life." But if so, the view from the other end of my chambers offered, at least, a contrast, if nothing more. In that direction

1. In the first place.
2. New York fur merchant and land owner (1763–1848) who died the richest man in the United States.

3. A court of chancery can temper the law, applying "dictates of conscience" or "the principles of natural justice"; the office of Master was abolished in 1847.

my windows commanded an unobstructed view of a lofty brick wall, black by age and everlasting shade; which wall required no spyglass to bring out its lurking beauties, but for the benefit of all near-sighted spectators, was pushed up to within ten feet of my window panes. Owing to the great height of the surrounding buildings, and my chambers being on the second floor, the interval between this wall and mine not a little resembled a huge square cistern.

At the period just preceding the advent of Bartleby, I had two persons as copyists in my employment, and a promising lad as an office-boy. First, Turkey; second, Nippers; third, Ginger Nut. These may seem names the like of which are not usually found in the Directory.[4] In truth they were nicknames, mutually conferred upon each other by my three clerks, and were deemed expressive of their respective persons or characters. Turkey was a short, pursy[5] Englishman of about my own age, that is, somewhere not far from sixty. In the morning, one might say, his face was of a fine florid hue, but after twelve o'clock, meridian —his dinner hour—it blazed like a grate full of Christmas coals; and continued blazing—but, as it were, with a gradual wane—till 6 o'clock, P.M. or thereabouts, after which I saw no more of the proprietor of the face, which gaining its meridian with the sun, seemed to set with it, to rise, culminate, and decline the following day, with the like regularity and undiminished glory. There are many singular coincidences I have known in the course of my life, not the least among which was the fact, that exactly when Turkey displayed his fullest beams from his red and radiant countenance, just then, too, at that critical moment, began the daily period when I considered his business capacities as seriously disturbed for the remainder of the twenty-four hours. Not that he was absolutely idle, or averse to business then; far from it. The difficulty was, he was apt to be altogether too energetic. There was a strange, inflamed, flurried, flighty recklessness of activity about him. He would be incautious in dipping his pen into his inkstand. All his blots upon my documents were dropped there after twelve o'clock, meridian. Indeed, not only would he be reckless and sadly given to making blots in the afternoon, but some days he went further, and was rather noisy. At such times, too, his face flamed with augmented blazonry, as if cannel coal had been heaped on anthracite.[6] He made an unpleasant racket with his chair; spilled his sand-box; in mending his pens, impatiently split them all to pieces, and threw them on the floor in a sudden passion; stood up and leaned over his table, boxing his papers about in a most indecorous manner, very sad to behold in an elderly man like him. Nevertheless, as he was in many ways a most valuable person to me, and all the time before twelve o'clock, meridian, was the quickest, steadiest creature too, accomplishing a great deal of work in a style not easy to be matched—for these reasons, I was willing to overlook his eccentricities, though indeed, occasionally, I remonstrated with him. I did this very gently, however, because, though the civilest, nay, the blandest and most reverential of men in the morning, yet in the afternoon he was disposed, upon provocation, to be slightly rash with his tongue, in fact, insolent. Now, valuing his morning services as I did, and resolved not to lose them; yet, at the same time made un-

4. Post Office Directory.
5. Fat, shortwinded.

6. A fast, bright-burning coal heaped on slow-burning, barely glowing coal.

comfortable by his inflamed ways after twelve o'clock; and being a man of peace, unwilling by my admonitions to call forth unseemly retorts from him; I took upon me, one Saturday noon (he was always worse on Saturdays), to hint to him, very kindly, that perhaps now that he was growing old, it might be well to abridge his labors; in short, he need not come to my chambers after twelve o'clock, but, dinner over, had best go home to his lodgings and rest himself till tea-time. But no; he insisted upon his afternoon devotions. His countenance became intolerably fervid, as he oratorically assured me—gesticulating with a long ruler at the other end of the room—that if his services in the morning were useful, how indispensable, then, in the afternoon?

"With submission, sir," said Turkey on this occasion, "I consider myself your right-hand man. In the morning I but marshal and deploy my columns; but in the afternoon I put myself at their head, and gallantly charge the foe, thus!"—and he made a violent thrust with the ruler.

"But the blots, Turkey," intimated I.

"True,—but, with submission, sir, behold these hairs! I am getting old. Surely, sir, a blot or two of a warm afternoon is not to be severely urged against gray hairs. Old age—even if it blot the page—is honorable. With submission, sir, we *both* are getting old."

This appeal to my fellow-feeling was hardly to be resisted. At all events, I saw that go he would not. So I made up my mind to let him stay, resolving, nevertheless, to see to it, that during the afternoon he had to do with my less important papers.

Nippers, the second on my list, was a whiskered, sallow, and, upon the whole, rather piratical-looking young man of about five and twenty. I always deemed him the victim of two evil powers—ambition and indigestion. The ambition was evinced by a certain impatience of the duties of a mere copyist, an unwarrantable usurpation of strictly professional affairs, such as the original drawing up of legal documents. The indigestion seemed betokened in an occasional nervous testiness and grinning irritability, causing the teeth to audibly grind together over mistakes committed in copying; unnecessary maledictions, hissed, rather than spoken, in the heat of business; and especially by a continual discontent with the height of the table where he worked. Though of a very ingenious mechanical turn. Nippers could never get this table to suit him. He put chips under it, blocks of various sorts, bits of pasteboard, and at last went so far as to attempt an exquisite adjustment by final pieces of folded blotting-paper. But no invention would answer. If, for the sake of easing his back, he brought the table lid at a sharp angle well up towards his chin, and wrote there like a man using the steep roof of a Dutch house for his desk:—then he declared that it stopped the circulation in his arms. If now he lowered the table to his waistbands, and stooped over it in writing, then there was a sore aching in his back. In short, the truth of the matter was, Nippers knew not what he wanted. Or, if he wanted any thing, it was to be rid of a scrivener's table altogether. Among the manifestations of his diseased ambition was a fondness he had for receiving visits from certain ambiguous-looking fellows in seedy coats, whom he called his clients. Indeed I was aware that not only was he, at times, considerable of a ward-politician, but he occasionally did a little business at the

Justices' courts, and was not unknown on the steps of the Tombs.[7] I have good reason to believe, however, that one individual who called upon him at my chambers, and who, with a grand air, he insisted was his client, was no other than a dun,[8] and the alleged title-deed, a bill. But with all his failings, and the annoyances he caused me, Nippers, like his compatriot Turkey, was a very useful man to me; wrote a neat, swift hand; and, when he chose, was not deficient in a gentlemanly sort of deportment. Added to this, he always dressed in a gentlemanly sort of way: and so, incidentally, reflected credit upon my chambers. Whereas with respect to Turkey, I had much ado to keep him from being a reproach to me. His clothes were apt to look oily and smell of eating-houses. He wore his pantaloons very loose and baggy in summer. His coats were execrable; his hat not to be handled. But while the hat was a thing of indifference to me, inasmuch as his natural civility and deference, as a dependent Englishman, always led him to doff it the moment he entered the room, yet his coat was another matter. Concerning his coats, I reasoned with him; but with no effect. The truth was, I suppose, that a man with so small an income, could not afford to sport such a lustrous face and a lustrous coat at one and the same time. As Nippers once observed, Turkey's money went chiefly for red ink. One winter day I presented Turkey with a highly-respectable looking coat of my own, a padded gray coat, of a most comfortable warmth, and which buttoned straight up from the knee to the neck. I thought Turkey would appreciate the favor, and abate his rashness and obstreperousness of afternoons. But no. I verily believe that buttoning himself up in so downy and blanket-like a coat had a pernicious effect upon him; upon the same principle that too much oats are bad for horses. In fact, precisely as a rash, restive horse is said to feel his oats, so Turkey felt his coat. It made him insolent. He was a man whom prosperity harmed.

Though concerning the self-indulgent habits of Turkey I had my own private surmises, yet touching Nippers I was well persuaded that whatever might be his faults in other respects, he was, at least, a temperate young man. But indeed, nature herself seemed to have been his vintner,[9] and at his birth charged him so thoroughly with an irritable, brandy-like disposition, that all subsequent potations were needless. When I consider how, amid the stillness of my chambers, Nippers would sometimes impatiently rise from his seat, and stooping over his table, spread his arms wide apart, seize the whole desk, and move it, and jerk it, with a grim, grinding motion on the floor, as if the table were a perverse voluntary agent, intent on thwarting and vexing him; I plainly perceive that for Nippers, brandy and water were altogether superfluous.

It was fortunate for me that, owing to its peculiar cause—indigestion—the irritability and consequent nervousness of Nippers, were mainly observable in the morning, while in the afternoon he was comparatively mild. So that Turkey's paroxysms only coming on about twelve o'clock, I never had to do with their eccentricities at one time. Their fits relieved each other like guards. When Nippers' was on,

7. **Prison in New York City.**
8. Bill collector.

9. Wine-seller.

Turkey's was off; and *vice versa*. This was a good natural arrangement under the circumstances.

Ginger Nut, the third on my list, was a lad some twelve years old. His father was a carman,[1] ambitious of seeing his son on the bench instead of a cart, before he died. So he sent him to my office as student at law, errand boy, and cleaner and sweeper, at the rate of one dollar a week. He had a little desk to himself, but he did not use it much. Upon inspection, the drawer exhibited a great array of the shells of various sorts of nuts. Indeed, to this quick-witted youth the whole noble science of the law was contained in a nutshell. Not the least among the employments of Ginger Nut, as well as one which he discharged with the most alacrity, was his duty as cake and apple purveyor for Turkey and Nippers. Copying law papers being proverbially a dry, husky sort of business, my two scriveners were fain to moisten their mouths very often with Spitzenbergs[2] to be had at the numerous stalls nigh the Custom House and Post Office. Also, they sent Ginger Nut very frequently for that peculiar cake—small, flat, round, and very spicy—after which he had been named by them. Of a cold morning when business was but dull, Turkey would gobble up scores of these cakes, as if they were mere wafers—indeed they sell them at the rate of six or eight for a penny—the scrape of his pen blending with the crunching of the crisp particles in his mouth. Of all the fiery afternoon blunders and flurried rashnesses of Turkey, was his once moistening a ginger-cake between his lips, and clapping it on to a mortgage for a seal. I came within an ace of dismissing him then. But he mollified me by making an oriental bow, and saying—"With submission, sir, it was generous of me to find you in[3] stationery on my own account."

Now my original business—that of a conveyancer and title hunter,[4] and drawer-up of recondite documents of all sorts—was considerably increased by receiving the master's office. There was now great work for scriveners. Not only must I push the clerks already with me, but I must have additional help. In answer to my advertisement, a motionless young man one morning stood upon my office threshold, the door being open, for it was summer. I can see that figure now—pallidly neat, pitiably respectable, incurably forlorn! It was Bartleby.

After a few words touching his qualifications, I engaged him, glad to have among my corps of copyists a man of so singularly sedate an aspect, which I thought might operate beneficially upon the flighty temper of Turkey, and the fiery one of Nippers.

I should have stated before that ground glass folding-doors divided my premises into two parts, one of which was occupied by my scriveners, the other by myself. According to my humor I threw open these doors, or closed them. I resolved to assign Bartleby a corner by the folding-doors, but on my side of them, so as to have this quiet man within easy call, in case any trifling thing was to be done. I placed his desk close up to a small side-window in that part of the room, a window which originally had afforded a lateral view of certain grimy backyards and bricks, but which, owing to subsequent erections, commanded at present no view at all, though it gave some light. Within

1. Driver of wagon or cart that hauls goods.
2. Red-and-yellow American apple.
3. Supply you with.

4. Lawyer who draws up deeds for transferring property, and one who searches out legal control of title deeds.

three feet of the panes was a wall, and the light came down from far above, between two lofty buildings, as from a very small opening in a dome. Still further to a satisfactory arrangement, I procured a high green folding screen, which might entirely isolate Bartleby from my sight, though not remove him from my voice. And thus, in a manner, privacy and society were conjoined.

At first Bartleby did an extraordinary quantity of writing. As if long famishing for something to copy, he seemed to gorge himself on my documents. There was no pause for digestion. He ran a day and night line, copying by sunlight and by candlelight. I should have been quite delighted with his application, had he been cheerfully industrious. But he wrote on silently, palely, mechanically.

It is, of course, an indispensable part of a scrivener's business to verify the accuracy of his copy, word by word. Where there are two or more scriveners in an office, they assist each other in this examination, one reading from the copy, the other holding the original. It is a very dull, wearisome, and lethargic affair. I can readily imagine that to some sanguine temperaments it would be altogether intolerable. For example, I cannot credit that the mettlesome poet Byron would have contentedly sat down with Bartleby to examine a law document of, say, five hundred pages, closely written in a crimpy hand.

Now and then, in the haste of business, it had been my habit to assist in comparing some brief document myself, calling Turkey or Nippers for this purpose. One object I had in placing Bartleby so handy to me behind the screen, was to avail myself of his services on such trivial occasions. It was on the third day, I think, of his being with me, and before any necessity had arisen for having his own writing examined, that, being much hurried to complete a small affair I had in hand, I abruptly called to Bartleby. In my haste and natural expectancy of instant compliance, I sat with my head bent over the original on my desk, and my right hand sideways, and somewhat nervously extended with the copy, so that immediately upon emerging from his retreat, Bartleby might snatch it and proceed to business without the least delay.

In this very attitude did I sit when I called to him, rapidly stating what it was I wanted him to do—namely, to examine a small paper with me. Imagine my surprise, nay, my consternation, when without moving from his privacy, Bartleby, in a singularly mild, firm voice, replied, "I would prefer not to."

I sat awhile in perfect silence, rallying my stunned faculties. Immediately it occurred to me that my ears had deceived me, or Bartleby had entirely misunderstood my meaning. I repeated my request in the clearest tone I could assume. But in quite as clear a one came the previous reply, "I would prefer not to."

"Prefer not to," echoed I, rising in high excitement, and crossing the room with a stride. "What do you mean? Are you moon-struck?[5] I want you to help me compare this sheet here—take it," and I thrust it towards him.

"I would prefer not to," said he.

I looked at him steadfastly. His face was leanly composed; his gray

5. Crazy.

eye dimly calm. Not a wrinkle of agitation rippled him. Had there been the least uneasiness, anger, impatience or impertinence in his manner; in other words, had there been anything ordinarily human about him, doubtless I should have violently dismissed him from the premises. But as it was, I should have as soon thought of turning my pale plaster-of-paris bust of Cicero[6] out-of-doors. I stood gazing at him awhile, as he went on with his own writing, and then reseated myself at my desk. This is very strange, thought I. What had one best do? But my business hurried me. I concluded to forget the matter for the present, reserving it for my future leisure. So calling Nippers from the other room, the paper was speedily examined.

A few days after this, Bartleby concluded four lengthy documents, being quadruplicates of a week's testimony taken before me in my High Court of Chancery. It became necessary to examine them. It was an important suit, and great accuracy was imperative. Having all things arranged I called Turkey, Nippers and Ginger Nut from the next room, meaning to place the four copies in the hands of my four clerks, while I should read from the original. Accordingly Turkey, Nippers and Ginger Nut had taken their seats in a row, each with his document in hand, when I called to Bartleby to join this interesting group.

"Bartleby! quick, I am waiting."

I heard a slow scrape of his chair legs on the uncarpeted floor, and soon he appeared standing at the entrance of his hermitage.

"What is wanted?" said he mildly.

"The copies, the copies," said I hurriedly. "We are going to examine them. There"—and I held towards him the fourth quadruplicate.

"I would prefer not to," he said, and gently disappeared behind the screen.

For a few moments I was turned into a pillar of salt,[7] standing at the head of my seated column of clerks. Recovering myself, I advanced towards the screen, and demanded the reason for such extraordinary conduct.

"*Why* do you refuse?"

"I would prefer not to."

With any other man I should have flown outright into a dreadful passion, scorned all further words, and thrust him ignominiously from my presence. But there was something about Bartleby that not only strangely disarmed me, but in a wonderful manner touched and disconcerted me. I began to reason with him.

"These are your own copies we are about to examine. It is labor saving to you, because one examination will answer for your four papers. It is common usage. Every copyist is bound to help examine his copy. Is it not so? Will you not speak? Answer!"

"I prefer not to," he replied in a flute-like tone. It seemed to me that while I had been addressing him, he carefully revolved every statement that I made; fully comprehended the meaning; could not gainsay the irresistible conclusion; but, at the same time, some paramount consideration prevailed with him to reply as he did.

"You are decided, then, not to comply with my request—a request

---

6. Marcus Tullius Cicero (106–43 B.C.), pro-republican Roman statesman, barrister, writer, who ranks with Demosthenes and Burke as orator.

7. Struck dumb; in *Genesis* 19:26, Lot's wife defies God's command and "looked back from behind him, and she became a pillar of salt."

made according to common usage and common sense?"

He briefly gave me to understand that on that point my judgment was sound. Yes: his decision was irreversible.

It is not seldom the case that when a man is browbeaten in some unprecedented and violently unreasonable way, he begins to stagger in his own plainest faith. He begins, as it were, vaguely to surmise that, wonderful as it may be, all the justice and all the reason is on the other side. Accordingly, if any disinterested persons are present, he turns to them for some reinforcement for his own faltering mind.

"Turkey," said I, "what do you think of this? Am I not right?"

"With submission, sir," said Turkey, with his blandest tone, "I think that you are."

"Nippers," said I, "what do *you* think of it?"

"I think I should kick him out of the office."

(The reader of nice perceptions will here perceive that, it being morning, Turkey's answer is couched in polite and tranquil terms, but Nippers replies in ill-tempered ones. Or, to repeat a previous sentence, Nippers's ugly mood was on duty, and Turkey's off.)

"Ginger Nut," said I, willing to enlist the smallest suffrage[8] in my behalf, "what do *you* think of it?"

"I think, sir, he's a little *luny*," replied Ginger Nut, with a grin.

"You hear what they say," said I, turning towards the screen, "come forth and do your duty."

But he vouchsafed no reply. I pondered a moment in sore perplexity. But once more business hurried me. I determined again to postpone the consideration of this dilemma to my future leisure. With a little trouble we made out to examine the papers without Bartleby, though at every page or two, Turkey deferentially dropped his opinion that this proceeding was quite out of the common; while Nippers, twitching in his chair with a dyspeptic nervousness, ground out between his set teeth occasional hissing maledictions against the stubborn oaf behind the screen. And for his (Nippers's) part, this was the first and the last time he would do another man's business without pay.

Meanwhile Bartleby sat in his hermitage, oblivious to everything but his own peculiar business there.

Some days passed, the scrivener being employed upon another lengthy work. His late remarkable conduct led me to regard his ways narrowly. I observed that he never went to dinner; indeed that he never went anywhere. As yet I had never of my personal knowledge known him to be outside of my office. He was a perpetual sentry in the corner. At about eleven o'clock though, in the morning, I noticed that Ginger Nut would advance toward the opening in Bartleby's screen, as if silently beckoned thither by a gesture invisible to me where I sat. The boy would then leave the office jingling a few pence, and reappear with a handful of ginger-nuts which he delivered in the hermitage, receiving two of the cakes for his trouble.

He lives, then, on ginger-nuts, thought I; never eats a dinner, properly speaking; he must be a vegetarian then; but no; he never eats even vegetables, he eats nothing but ginger-nuts. My mind then ran on in roveries concerning the probable effects upon the human constitution of living entirely on ginger-nuts. Ginger-nuts are so called because they

8. Favorable vote.

contain ginger as one of their peculiar constituents, and the final flavoring one. Now what was ginger? A hot, spicy thing. Was Bartleby hot and spicy? Not at all. Ginger, then, had no effect upon Bartleby. Probably he preferred it should have none.

Nothing so aggravates an earnest person as a passive resistance. If the individual so resisted be of a not inhumane temper, and the resisting one perfectly harmless in his passivity; then, in the better moods of the former, he will endeavor charitably to construe to his imagination what proves impossible to be solved by his judgment. Even so, for the most part, I regarded Bartleby and his ways. Poor fellow! thought I, he means no mischief; it is plain he intends no insolence; his aspect sufficiently evinces that his eccentricities are involuntary. He is useful to me. I can get along with him. If I turn him away, the chances are he will fall in with some less indulgent employer, and then he will be rudely treated, and perhaps driven forth miserably to starve. Yes. Here I can cheaply purchase a delicious self-approval. To befriend Bartleby; to humor him in his strange wilfulness, will cost me little or nothing, while I lay up in my soul what will eventually prove a sweet morsel for my conscience. But this mood was not invariable with me. The passiveness of Bartley sometimes irritated me. I felt strangely goaded on to encounter him in new opposition, to elicit some angry spark from him answerable to my own. But indeed I might as well have essayed to strike fire with my knuckles against a bit of Windsor soap.[9] But one afternoon the evil impulse in me mastered me, and the following little scene ensued:

"Bartleby," said I, "when those papers are all copied, I will compare them with you."

"I would prefer not to."

"How? Surely you do not mean to persist in that mulish vagary?"

No answer.

I threw open the folding-doors near by, and turning upon Turkey and Nippers, exclaimed in an excited manner—

"He says, a second time, he won't examine his papers. What do you think of it, Turkey?"

It was afternoon, be it remembered. Turkey sat glowing like a brass boiler, his bald head steaming, his hands reeling among his blotted papers.

"Think of it?" roared Turkey; "I think I'll just step behind his screen, and black his eyes for him!"

So saying, Turkey rose to his feet and threw his arms into a puglistic position. He was hurrying away to make good his promise, when I detained him, alarmed at the effect of incautiously rousing Turkey's combativeness after dinner.

"Sit down, Turkey," said I, "and hear what Nippers has to say. What do you think of it, Nippers? Would I not be justified in immediately dismissing Bartleby?"

"Excuse me, that is for you to decide, sir. I think his conduct quite unusual, and indeed unjust, as regards Turkey and myself. But it may only be a passing whim."

"Ah," exclaimed I, "you have strangely changed your mind then—you speak very gently of him now."

9. Scented soap, usually brown.

"All beer," cried Turkey; "gentleness is effects of beer—Nippers and I dined together today. You see how gentle *I* am, sir. Shall I go and black his eyes?"

"You refer to Bartleby, I suppose. No, not today, Turkey," I replied; "pray, put up your fists."

I closed the doors, and again advanced towards Bartleby. I felt additional incentives tempting me to my fate. I burned to be rebelled against again. I remembered that Bartleby never left the office.

"Bartleby," said I, "Ginger Nut is away; just step round to the Post Office, won't you? (it was but a three minutes' walk,) and see if there is anything for me."

"I would prefer not to."

"You *will* not?"

"I *prefer* not."

I staggered to my desk, and sat there in a deep study. My blind inveteracy returned. Was there any other thing in which I could procure myself to be ignominiously repulsed by this lean, penniless wight?— my hired clerk? What added thing is there, perfectly reasonable, that he will be sure to refuse to do?

"Bartleby!"

No answer.

"Bartleby," in a louder tone.

No answer.

"Bartleby," I roared.

Like a very ghost, agreeably to the laws of magical invocation, at the third summons, he appeared at the entrance of his hermitage.

"Go to the next room, and tell Nippers to come to me."

"I prefer not to," he respectfully and slowly said, and mildly disappeared.

"Very good, Bartleby," said I, in a quiet sort of serenely severe self-possessed tone, intimating the unalterable purpose of some terrible retribution very close at hand. At the moment I half intended something of the kind. But upon the whole, as it was drawing towards my dinner-hour, I thought it best to put on my hat and walk home for the day, suffering much from perplexity and distress of mind.

Shall I acknowledge it? The conclusion of this whole business was, that it soon became a fixed fact of my chambers, that a pale young scrivener, by the name of Bartleby, had a desk there; that he copied for me at the usual rate of four cents a folio (one hundred words); but he was permanently exempt from examining the work done by him, that duty being transferred to Turkey and Nippers, one of compliment doubtless to their superior acuteness; moreover, said Bartleby was never on any account to be dispatched on the most trivial errand of any sort; and that even if entreated to take upon him such a matter, it was generally understood that he would prefer not to—in other words, that he would refuse point-blank.

As days passed on, I became considerably reconciled to Bartleby. His steadiness, his freedom from all dissipation, his incessant industry (except when he chose to throw himself into a standing revery behind his screen), his great stillness, his unalterableness of demeanor under all circumstances, made him a valuable acquisition. One prime thing was this,—*he was always there;*—first in the morning, continually through the day, and the last at night. I had a singular confidence in his honesty. I felt my most precious papers perfectly safe in his hands. Sometimes to be sure I could not, for the very soul of me, avoid falling into sudden spasmodic passions with him. For it was exceeding difficult to bear in mind all the time those strange peculiarities, privileges, and unheard of exemptions, forming the tacit stipulations on Bartleby's part under which he remained in my office. Now and then, in the eagerness of dispatching pressing business, I would inadvertently summon Bartleby, in a short, rapid tone, to put his finger, say, on the incipient tie of a bit of red tape with which I was about compressing some papers. Of course, from behind the screen the usual answer, "I prefer not to," was sure to come; and then, how could a human creature with the common infirmities of our nature, refrain from bitterly exclaiming upon such perverseness—such unreasonableness? However, every added repulse of this sort which I received only tended to lessen the probability of my repeating the inadvertence.

Here it must be said, that according to the custom of most legal gentlemen occupying chambers in densely-populated law buildings, there were several keys to my door. One was kept by a woman residing in the attic, which person weekly scrubbed and daily swept and dusted my apartments. Another was kept by Turkey for convenience sake. The third I sometimes carried in my own pocket. The fourth I knew not who had.

Now, one Sunday morning I happened to go to Trinity Church, to hear a celebrated preacher, and finding myself rather early on the ground, I thought I would walk round to my chambers for a while. Luckily I had my key with me; but upon applying it to the lock, I found it resisted by something inserted from the inside. Quite surprised, I called out; when to my consternation a key was turned from within; and thrusting his lean visage at me, and holding the door ajar, the apparition of Bartleby appeared, in his shirt sleeves, and otherwise in a strangely tattered dishabille, saying quietly that he was sorry, but he was deeply engaged just then, and—preferred not admitting me at present. In a brief word or two, he moreover added, that perhaps I had better walk round the block two or three times, and by that time he would probably have concluded his affairs.

Now, the utterly unsurmised appearance of Bartleby, tenanting my law-chambers of a Sunday morning, with his cadaverously gentlemanly *nonchalance*, yet withal firm and self-possessed, had such a strange effect upon me, that incontinently I slunk away from my own door, and did as desired. But not without sundry twinges of impotent rebellion against the mild effrontery of this unaccountable scrivener. Indeed, it was his wonderful mildness, chiefly, which not only disarmed me, but unmanned me, as it were. For I consider that one, for the time, is sort of unmanned when he tranquilly permits his hired clerk to dictate to him, and order him away from his own premises. Furthermore, I was full of uneasiness as to what Bartleby could possibly be doing in my office in his shirt sleeves, and in an otherwise dismantled condition of a Sunday morning. Was anything amiss going on? Nay, that was out of the question. It was not to be thought of for a moment that Bartleby was an immoral person. But what could he be doing there?—

copying? Nay again, whatever might be his eccentricities, Bartleby was an eminently decorous person. He would be the last man to sit down to his desk in any state approaching to nudity. Besides, it was Sunday; and there was something about Bartleby that forbade the supposition that he would by any secular occupation violate the proprieties of the day.

Nevertheless, my mind was not pacified; and full of a restless curiosity, at last I returned to the door. Without hindrance I inserted my key, opened it, and entered. Bartleby was not to be seen. I looked round anxiously, peeped behind his screen; but it was very plain that he was gone. Upon more closely examining the place, I surmised that for an indefinite period Bartleby must have ate, dressed, and slept in my office, and that too without plate, mirror, or bed. The cushioned seat of a ricketty old sofa in one corner bore the faint impress of a lean, reclining form. Rolled away under his desk, I found a blanket under the empty grate, a blacking box[1] and brush; on a chair, a tin basin, with soap and a ragged towel; in a newspaper a few crumbs of ginger-nuts and a morsel of cheese. Yes, thought I, it is evident enough that Bartleby has been making his home here, keeping bachelor's hall all by himself. Immediately then the thought came sweeping across me, What miserable friendlessness and loneliness are here revealed! His poverty is great; but his solitude, how horrible! Think of it. Of a Sunday, Wall Street is deserted as Petra;[2] and every night of every day it is an emptiness. This building too, which of weekdays hums with industry and life, at nightfall echoes with sheer vacancy, and all through Sunday is forlorn. And here Bartleby makes his home; sole spectator of a solitude which he has seen all populous—a sort of innocent and transformed Marius brooding among the ruins of Carthage![3]

For the first time in my life a feeling of overpowering stinging melancholy seized me. Before, I had never experienced aught but a not-unpleasing sadness. The bond of a common humanity now drew me irresistibly to gloom. A fraternal melancholy! For both I and Bartleby were sons of Adam. I remembered the bright silks and sparkling faces I had seen that day, in gala trim, swan-like sailing down the Mississippi of Broadway; and I contrasted them with the pallid copyist, and thought to myself, Ah, happiness courts the light, so we deem the world is gay; but misery hides aloof, so we deem that misery there is none. These sad fancyings—chimeras, doubtless, of a sick and silly brain—led on to other and more special thoughts, concerning the eccentricities of Bartleby. Presentiments of strange discoveries hovered round me. The scrivener's pale form appeared to me laid out, among uncaring strangers, in its shivering winding sheet.

Suddenly I was attracted by Bartleby's closed desk, the key in open sight left in the lock.

1. Box of black shoe polish.
2. Once a flourishing Middle Eastern trade center, long in ruins.
3. Gaius (or Caius) Marius (157–86 B.C.), Roman consul and general, expelled from Rome in 88 B.C. by Sulla; when an officer of Sextilius, the governor, forbade him to land in Africa, Marius replied, "Go tell him that you have seen Caius Marius sitting in exile among the ruins of Carthage," applying the example of the fortune of that city to the change of his own condition. The image was so common that a few years after "Bartleby," Dickens apologizes for using it: ". . . like that lumbering Marius among the ruins of Carthage, who has sat heavy on a thousand millions of similes . . ." ("The Calais Night-Mail," in *The Uncommercial Traveller*).

I mean no mischief, seek the gratification of no heartless curiosity, thought I; besides, the desk is mine, and its contents too, so I will make bold to look within. Everything was methodically arranged, the papers smoothly placed. The pigeonholes were deep, and removing the files of documents, I groped into their recesses. Presently I felt something there, and dragged it out. It was an old bandanna handkerchief, heavy and knotted. I opened it, and saw it was a savings' bank.

I now recalled all the quiet mysteries which I had noted in the man. I remembered that he never spoke but to answer; that though at intervals he had considerable time to himself, yet I had never seen him reading—no, not even a newspaper; that for long periods he would stand looking out, at his pale window behind the screen, upon the dead brick wall; I was quite sure he never visited any refectory or eating house; while his pale face clearly indicated that he never drank beer like Turkey, or tea and coffee even, like other men; that he never went anywhere in particular that I could learn; never went out for a walk, unless indeed that was the case at present; that he had declined telling who he was, or whence he came, or whether he had any relatives in the world; that though so thin and pale, he never complained of ill health. And more than all, I remembered a certain unconscious air of pallid—how shall I call it?—of pallid haughtiness, say, or rather an austere reserve about him, which had positively awed me into my tame compliance with his eccentricities, when I had feared to ask him to do the slightest incidental thing for me, even though I might know, from his long-continued motionlessness, that behind his screen he must be standing in one of those dead-wall reveries of his.

Revolving all these things, and coupling them with the recently discovered fact that he made my office his constant abiding place and home, and not forgetful of his morbid moodiness; revolving all these things, a prudential feeling began to steal over me. My first emotions had been those of pure melancholy and sincerest pity; but just in proportion as the forlornness of Bartleby grew and grew to my imagination, did that same melancholy merge into fear, that pity into repulsion. So true it is, and so terrible too, that up to a certain point the thought or sight of misery enlists our best affections; but, in certain special cases, beyond that point it does not. They err who would assert that invariably this is owing to the inherent selfishness of the human heart. It rather proceeds from a certain hopelessness of remedying excessive and organic ill. To a sensitive being, pity is not seldom pain. And when at last it is perceived that such pity cannot lead to effectual succor, common sense bids the soul be rid of it. What I saw that morning persuaded me that the scrivener was the victim of innate and incurable disorder. I might give alms to his body; but his body did not pain him; it was his soul that suffered, and his soul I could not reach.

I did not accomplish the purpose of going to Trinity Church that morning. Somehow, the things I had seen disqualified me for the time from churchgoing. I walked homeward, thinking what I would do with Bartleby. Finally, I resolved upon this;—I would put certain calm questions to him the next morning, touching his history, &c., and if he declined to answer them openly and unreservedly (and I supposed he would prefer not), then to give him a twenty-dollar bill over and above whatever I might owe him, and tell him his services were no longer required; but that if in any other way I could assist him, I would be happy to do so, especially if he desired to return to his native place, wherever that might be, I would willingly help to defray the expenses. Moreover, if, after reaching home, he found himself at any time in want of aid, a letter from him would be sure of a reply.

The next morning came.

"Bartleby," said I, gently calling to him behind his screen.

No reply.

"Bartleby," said I, in a still gentler tone, "come here; I am not going to ask you to do anything you would prefer not to do—I simply wish to speak to you."

Upon this he noiselessly slid into view.

"Will you tell me, Bartleby, where you were born?"

"I would prefer not to."

"Will you tell me *anything* about yourself?"

"I would prefer not to."

"But what reasonable objection can you have to speak to me? I feel friendly towards you."

He did not look at me while I spoke, but kept his glance fixed upon my bust of Cicero, which as I then sat, was directly behind me, some six inches above my head.

"What is your answer, Bartleby?" said I, after waiting a considerable time for a reply, during which his countenance remained immovable, only there was the faintest conceivable tremor of the white attenuated mouth.

"At present I prefer to give no answer," he said, and retired into his hermitage.

It was rather weak in me I confess, but his manner on this occasion nettled me. Not only did there seem to lurk in it a certain calm disdain, but his perverseness seemed ungrateful, considering the undeniable good usage and indulgence he had received from me.

Again I sat ruminating what I should do. Mortified as I was at his behavior, and resolved as I had been to dismiss him when I entered my office, nevertheless I strangely felt something superstitious knocking at my heart, and forbidding me to carry out my purpose, and denouncing me for a villain if I dared to breathe one bitter word against this forlornest of mankind. At last, familiarly drawing my chair behind his screen, I sat down and said: "Bartleby, never mind then about revealing your history; but let me entreat you, as a friend, to comply as far as may be with the usages of this office. Say now you will help to examine papers tomorrow or next day: in short, say now that in a day or two you will begin to be a little reasonable:—say so, Bartleby."

"At present I would prefer not to be a little reasonable," was his mildly cadaverous reply.

Just then the folding-doors opened, and Nippers approached. He seemed suffering from an unusually bad night's rest, induced by severer indigestion than common. He overheard those final words of Bartleby.

"*Prefer not*, eh?" gritted Nippers—"I'd *prefer* him, if I were you, sir," addressing me—"I'd *prefer* him; I'd give him preferences, the stubborn mule! What is it, sir, pray, that he *prefers* not to do now?"

Bartleby moved not a limb.

"Mr. Nippers," said I, "I'd prefer that you would withdraw for the present."

Somehow, of late I had got into the way of involuntarily using this word "prefer" upon all sorts of not exactly suitable occasions. And I trembled to think that my contact with the scrivener had already and seriously affected me in a mental way. And what further and deeper aberration might it not yet produce? This apprehension had not been without efficacy in determining me to summary means.

As Nippers, looking very sour and sulky, was departing, Turkey blandly and deferentially approached.

"With submission, sir," said he, "yesterday I was thinking about Bartleby here, and I think that if he would but prefer to take a quart of good ale every day, it would do much towards mending him and enabling him to assist in examining his papers."

"So you have got the word too," said I, slightly excited.

"With submission, what word, sir?" asked Turkey, respectfully crowding himself into the contracted space behind the screen, and by so doing making me jostle the scrivener. "What word, sir?"

"I would prefer to be left alone here," said Bartleby, as if offended at being mobbed in his privacy.

"*That's* the word, Turkey," said I—"*that's* it."

"Oh, *prefer?* oh yes—queer word. I never use it myself. But, sir, as I was saying, if he would but prefer—"

"Turkey," interrupted I, "you will please withdraw."

"Oh certainly, sir, if you prefer that I should."

As he opened the folding-door to retire, Nippers at his desk caught a glimpse of me, and asked whether I would prefer to have a certain paper copied on blue paper or white. He did not in the least roguishly accent the word *prefer*. It was plain that it involuntarily rolled from his tongue. I thought to myself, surely I must get rid of a demented man, who already has in some degree turned the tongues, if not the heads of myself and clerks. But I thought it prudent not to break the dis-mission at once.

The next day I noticed that Bartleby did nothing but stand at his window in his dead-wall revery. Upon asking him why he did not write, he said that he had decided upon doing no more writing.

"Why, how now? what next?" exclaimed I, "do no more writing?"

"No more."

"And what is the reason?"

"Do you not see the reason for yourself," he indifferently replied.

I looked steadfastly at him, and perceived that his eyes looked dull and glazed. Instantly it occurred to me, that his unexampled diligence in copying by his dim window for the first few weeks of his stay with me might have temporarily impaired his vision.

I was touched. I said something in condolence with him. I hinted that of course he did wisely in abstaining from writing for a while; and urged him to embrace that opportunity of taking wholesome exercise in the open air. This, however, he did not do. A few days after this, my other clerks being absent, and being in a great hurry to dispatch certain letters by the mail, I thought that, having nothing else earthly to do,

Bartleby would surely be less inflexible than usual, and carry these letters to the post office. But he blankly declined. So, much to my inconvenience, I went myself.

Still added days went by. Whether Bartleby's eyes improved or not, I could not say. To all appearance, I thought they did. But when I asked him if they did, he vouchsafed no answer. At all events, he would do no copying. At last, in reply to my urgings, he informed me that he had permanently given up copying.

"What!" exclaimed I; "suppose your eyes should get entirely well—better than ever before—would you not copy then?"

"I have given up copying," he answered, and slid aside.

He remained, as ever, a fixture in my chamber. Nay—if that were possible—he became still more of a fixture than before. What was to be done? He would do nothing in the office: why should he stay there? In plain fact, he had now become a millstone[4] to me, not only useless as a necklace, but afflictive to bear. Yet I was sorry for him. I speak less than truth when I say that, on his own account, he occasioned me uneasiness. If he would but have named a single relative or friend, I would instantly have written, and urged their taking the poor fellow away to some convenient retreat. But he seemed alone, absolutely alone in the universe. A bit of wreck in the mid-Atlantic. At length, necessities connected with my business tyrannized over all other considerations. Decently as I could, I told Bartleby that in six days' time he must unconditionally leave the office. I warned him to take measures, in the interval, for procuring some other abode. I offered to assist him in this endeavor, if he himself would but take the first step towards a removal. "And when you finally quit me, Bartleby," added I, "I shall see that you go not away entirely unprovided. Six days from this hour, remember."

At the expiration of that period, I peeped behind the screen, and lo! Bartleby was there.

I buttoned up my coat, balanced myself; advanced slowly towards him, touched his shoulder, and said, "The time has come; you must quit this place; I am sorry for you; here is money; but you must go."

"I would prefer not," he replied, with his back still towards me.

"You *must*."

He remained silent.

Now I had an unbounded confidence in this man's common honesty. He had frequently restored to me sixpences and shillings[5] carelessly dropped upon the floor, for I am apt to be very reckless in such shirt-button affairs. The proceeding then which followed will not be deemed extraordinary.

"Bartleby," said I, "I owe you twelve dollars on account; here are thirty-two; the odd twenty are yours.—Will you take it?" and I handed the bills towards him.

But he made no motion.

"I will leave them here then," putting them under a weight on the table. Then taking my hat and cane and going to the door I tranquilly

---

4. Heavy stone for grinding grain. See *Matthew* 18:6: "But whoso shall offend one of these little ones which believe in me, it were better for him that a millstone were hanged about his neck, and that he were drowned in the depth of the sea."

5. Coins now worth six cents and 12 cents but once worth twice that.

turned and added—"After you have removed your things from these offices, Bartleby, you will of course lock the door—since everyone is now gone for the day but you—and if you please, slip your key underneath the mat, so that I may have it in the morning. I shall not see you again; so good-bye to you. If hereafter in your new place of abode I can be of any service to you, do not fail to advise me by letter. Goodbye, Bartleby, and fare you well."

But he answered not a word; like the last column of some ruined temple, he remained standing mute and solitary in the middle of the otherwise deserted room.

As I walked home in a pensive mood, my vanity got the better of my pity. I could not but highly plume myself on my masterly management in getting rid of Bartleby. Masterly I call it, and such it must appear to any dispassionate thinker. The beauty of my procedure seemed to consist in its perfect quietness. There was no vulgar bullying, no bravado of any sort, no choleric hectoring, and striding to and fro across the apartment, jerking out vehement commands for Bartleby to bundle himself off with his beggarly traps.[6] Nothing of the kind. Without loudly bidding Bartleby depart—as an inferior genius might have done—I *assumed* the ground that depart he must; and upon that assumption built all I had to say. The more I thought over my procedure, the more I was charmed with it. Nevertheless, next morning, upon awakening, I had my doubts,—I had somehow slept off the fumes of vanity. One of the coolest and wisest hours a man has is just after he awakes in the morning. My procedure seemed as sagacious as ever,—but only in theory. How it would prove in practice—there was the rub. It was truly a beautiful thought to have assumed Bartleby's departure; but, after all, that assumption was simply my own, and none of Bartleby's. The great point was, not whether I had assumed that he would quit me, but whether he would prefer so to do. He was more a man of preferences than assumptions.

After breakfast, I walked downtown, arguing the probabilities *pro* and *con*. One moment I thought it would prove a miserable failure, and Bartleby would be found all alive at my office as usual; the next moment it seemed certain that I should see his chair empty. And so I kept veering about. At the corner of Broadway and Canal Street, I saw quite an excited group of people standing in earnest conversation.

"I'll take odds he doesn't," said a voice as I passed.

"Doesn't go?—done!" said I, "put up your money."

I was instinctively putting my hand in my pocket to produce my own, when I remembered that this was an election day. The words I had overheard bore no reference to Bartleby, but to the success or nonsuccess of some candidate for the mayoralty. In my intent frame of mind, I had, as it were, imagined that all Broadway shared in my excitement, and were debating the same question with me. I passed on, very thankful that the uproar of the street screened my momentary absent-mindedness.

As I had intended, I was earlier than usual at my office door. I stood listening for a moment. All was still. He must be gone. I tried the knob. The door was locked. Yes, my procedure had worked to a charm; he

6. Personal belongings, luggage.

indeed must be vanished. Yet a certain melancholy mixed with this: I was almost sorry for my brilliant success. I was fumbling under the door mat for the key, which Bartleby was to have left there for me, when accidentally my knee knocked against a panel, producing a summoning sound, and in response a voice came to me from within—"Not yet; I am occupied."

It was Bartleby.

I was thunderstruck. For an instant I stood like the man who, pipe in mouth, was killed one cloudless afternoon long ago in Virginia, by summer lightning; at his own warm open window he was killed, and remained leaning out there upon the dreamy afternoon, till some one touched him, when he fell.

"Not gone!" I murmured at last. But again obeying that wondrous ascendancy which the inscrutable scrivener had over me, and from which ascendancy, for all my chafing, I could not completely escape, I slowly went downstairs and out into the street, and while walking round the block, considered what I should next do in this unheard-of perplexity. Turn the man out by an actual thrusting I could not; to drive him away by calling him hard names would not do; calling in the police was an unpleasant idea; and yet, permit him to enjoy his cadaverous triumph over me,—this too I could not think of. What was to be done? or, if nothing could be done, was there anything further that I could *assume* in the matter? Yes, as before I had prospectively assumed that Bartleby would depart, so now I might retrospectively assume that departed he was. In the legitimate carrying out of this assumption, I might enter my office in a great hurry, and pretending not to see Bartleby at all, walk straight against him as if he were air. Such a proceeding would in a singular degree have the appearance of a home-thrust.[7] It was hardly possible that Bartleby could withstand such an application of the doctrine of assumptions. But upon second thoughts the success of the plan seemed rather dubious. I resolved to argue the matter over with him again.

"Bartleby," said I, entering the office, with a quietly severe expression, "I am seriously displeased. I am pained, Bartleby. I had thought better of you. I had imagined you of such a gentlemanly organization, that in any delicate dilemma a slight hint would suffice—in short, an assumption. But it appears I am deceived. Why," I added, unaffectedly starting, "you have not even touched that money yet," pointing to it, just where I had left it the evening previous.

He answered nothing.

"Will you, or will you not, quit me?" I now demanded in a sudden passion, advancing close to him.

"I would prefer *not* to quit you," he replied, gently emphasizing the *not*.

"What earthly right have you to stay here? Do you pay any rent? Do you pay my taxes? Or is this property yours?"

He answered nothing.

"Are you ready to go on and write now? Are your eyes recovered? Could you copy a small paper for me this morning? or help examine a few lines? or step round to the post office? In a word, will you do any-

7. Thrust that reaches its mark.

thing at all, to give a coloring to your refusal to depart the premises?"
He silently retired into his hermitage.

I was now in such a state of nervous resentment that I thought it
but prudent to check myself at present from further demonstrations.
Bartleby and I were alone. I remembered the tragedy of the unfortunate Adams and the still more unfortunate Colt in the solitary office
of the latter; and how poor Colt, being dreadfully incensed by Adams,
and imprudently permitting himself to get wildly excited, was at
unawares hurried into his fatal act—an act which certainly no man
could possibly deplore more than the actor himself. Often it had occurred to me in my ponderings upon the subject, that had that alter-
cation taken place in the public street, or at a private residence, it
would not have terminated as it did. It was the circumstance of being
alone in a solitary office, up stairs, of a building entirely unhallowed by
humanizing domestic associations—an uncarpeted office, doubtless, of
a dusty, haggard sort of appearance;—this it must have been, which
greatly helped to enhance the irritable desperation of the hapless Colt.[8]

But when this old Adam[9] of resentment rose in me and tempted me
concerning Bartleby, I grappled him and threw him. How? Why, simply
by recalling the divine injunction: "A new commandment[1] give I unto
you, that ye love one another." Yes, this it was that saved me. Aside
from higher considerations, charity often operates as a vastly wise and
prudent principle—a great safeguard to its possessor. Men have committed murder for jealousy's sake, and anger's sake, and hatred's sake,
and selfishness' sake, and spiritual pride's sake; but no man that ever I
heard of, ever committed a diabolical murder for sweet charity's sake.
Mere self-interest, then, if no better motive can be enlisted, should,
especially with high-tempered men, prompt all beings to charity and
philanthropy. At any rate, upon the occasion in question, I strove to
drown my exasperated feelings towards the scrivener by benevolently
construing his conduct. Poor fellow, poor fellow! thought I, he don't
mean anything; and besides, he has seen hard times, and ought to be
indulged.

I endeavored also immediately to occupy myself, and at the same
time to comfort my despondency. I tried to fancy that in the course of
the morning, at such time as might prove agreeable to him, Bartleby,
of his own free accord, would emerge from his hermitage, and take up
some decided line of march in the direction of the door. But no. Half-
past twelve o'clock came; Turkey began to glow in the face, overturn
his inkstand, and become generally obstreperous; Nippers abated down
into quietude and courtesy; Ginger Nut munched his noon apple; and
Bartleby remained standing at his window in one of his profoundest
dead-wall reveries. Will it be credited? Ought I to acknowledge it? That
afternoon I left the office without saying one further word to him.

Some days now passed, during which, at leisure intervals I looked a

---

8. In 1841, John C. Colt, brother of
the famous gunmaker, unintentionally killed
Samuel Adams, a printer, when he hit him
on the head during a fight.

9. Sinful element in human nature; see,
e.g., "Invocation of Blessing on the Child,"
in the *Book of Common Prayer*: "Grant that

the old Adam in this child may be so
buried, that the new man may be raised
up in him." Christ is sometimes called the
"new Adam."

1. In *John* 13:34, where, however, the
phrasing is "I give unto . . ."

little into "Edwards on the Will," and "Priestley on Necessity."[2] Under the circumstances, those books induced a salutary feeling. Gradually I slid into the persuasion that these troubles of mine touching the scrivener, had been all predestinated from eternity, and Bartleby was billeted upon me for some mysterious purpose of an all-wise Providence, which it was not for a mere mortal like me to fathom. Yes, Bartleby, stay there behind your screen, thought I; I shall persecute you no more; you are harmless and noiseless as any of these old chairs; in short, I never feel so private as when I know you are here. At least I see it, I feel it; I penetrate to the predestinated purpose of my life. I am content. Others may have loftier parts to enact; but my mission in this world, Bartleby, is to furnish you with office-room for such period as you may see fit to remain.

I believe that this wise and blessed frame of mind would have continued with me, had it not been for the unsolicited and uncharitable remarks obtruded upon me by my professional friends who visited the rooms. But thus it often is, that the constant friction of illiberal minds wears out at last the best resolves of the more generous. Though to be sure, when I reflected upon it, it was not strange that people entering my office should be struck by the peculiar aspect of the unaccountable Bartleby, and so be tempted to throw out some sinister observations concerning him. Sometimes an attorney having business with me, and calling at my office, and finding no one but the scrivener there, would undertake to obtain some sort of precise information from him touching my whereabouts; but without heeding his idle talk, Bartleby would remain standing immovable in the middle of the room. So after contemplating him in that position for a time, the attorney would depart, no wiser than he came.

Also, when a Reference[3] was going on, and the room full of lawyers and witnesses and business was driving fast; some deeply occupied legal gentleman present, seeing Bartleby wholly unemployed, would request him to run round to his (the legal gentleman's) office and fetch some papers for him. Thereupon, Bartleby would tranquilly decline, and yet remain idle as before. Then the lawyer would give a great stare, and turn to me. And what could I say? At last I was made aware that all through the circle of my professional acquaintance, a whisper of wonder was running round, having reference to the strange creature I kept at my office. This worried me very much. And as the idea came upon me of his possibly turning out a long-lived man, and keep occupying my chambers, and denying my authority; and perplexing my visitors; and scandalizing my professional reputation; and casting a general gloom over the premises; keeping soul and body together to the last upon his savings (for doubtless he spent but half a dime a day), and in the end perhaps outlive me, and claim possession of my office by right of his perpetual occupancy: as all these dark anticipations crowded

2. Jonathan Edwards (1703–1758), New England Calvinist theologian and revivalist, in *The Freedom of the Will* (1754), argued that man is not in fact free, for though he chooses according to the way he sees things, that way is predetermined (by biography, environment, and character), and he acts out of personality rather than by will. Joseph Priestley (1733–1804), Dissenting preacher, scientist, grammarian, and philosopher, in *The Doctrine of Philosophical Necessity* (1777), argued that free will is theologically objectionable, metaphysically incomprehensible, and morally undesirable.

3. Consultation or committee meeting.

upon me more and more, and my friends continually intruded their relentless remarks upon the apparition in my room; a great change was wrought in me. I resolved to gather all my faculties together, and forever rid me of this intolerable incubus.

Ere revolving any complicated project, however, adapted to this end, I first simply suggested to Bartleby the propriety of his permanent departure. In a calm and serious tone, I commended the idea to his careful and mature consideration. But having taken three days to meditate upon it, he apprised me that his original determination remained the same; in short, that he still preferred to abide with me.

What shall I do? I now said to myself, buttoning up my coat to the last button. What shall I do? what ought I to do? what does conscience say I *should* do with this man, or rather ghost. Rid myself of him, I must; go, he shall. But how? You will not thrust him, the poor, pale, passive mortal,—you will not thrust such a helpless creature out of your door? you will not dishonor yourself by such cruelty? No, I will not, I cannot do that. Rather would I let him live and die here, and then mason up his remains in the wall. What then will you do? For all your coaxing, he will not budge. Bribes he leaves under your own paperweight on your table; in short, it is quite plain that he prefers to cling to you.

Then something severe, something unusual must be done. What! surely you will not have him collared by a constable, and commit his innocent pallor to the common jail? And upon what ground could you procure such a thing to be done?—a vagrant, is he? What! he a vagrant, a wanderer, who refuses to budge? It is because he will *not* be a vagrant, then, that you seek to count him *as* a vagrant. That is too absurd. No visible means of support: there I have him. Wrong again: for indubitably he *does* support himself, and that is the only unanswerable proof that any man can show of his possessing the means so to do. No more then. Since he will not quit me, I must quit him. I will change my offices; I will move elsewhere; and give him fair notice, that if I find him on my new premises I will then proceed against him as a common trespasser.

Acting accordingly, next day I thus addressed him: "I find these chambers too far from the City Hall; the air is unwholesome. In a word, I propose to remove my offices next week, and shall no longer require your services. I tell you this now, in order that you may seek another place."

He made no reply, and nothing more was said.

On the appointed day I engaged carts and men, proceeded to my chambers, and having but little furniture, everything was removed in a few hours. Throughout, the scrivener remained standing behind the screen, which I directed to be removed the last thing. It was withdrawn; and being folded up like a huge folio, left him the motionless occupant of a naked room. I stood in the entry watching him a moment, while something from within me upbraided me.

I re-entered, with my hand in my pocket—and—and my heart in my mouth.

"Good-bye, Bartleby; I am going—good-bye, and God some way bless you; and take that," slipping something in his hand. But it dropped upon the floor, and then,—strange to say—I tore myself from him whom I had so longed to be rid of.

Established in my new quarters, for a day or two I kept the door locked, and started at every footfall in the passages. When I returned to my rooms after any little absence, I would pause at the threshold for an instant, and attentively listen, ere applying my key. But these fears were needless. Bartleby never came nigh me.

I thought all was going well, when a perturbed-looking stranger visited me, inquiring whether I was the person who had recently occupied rooms at No. — Wall Street.

Full of forebodings, I replied that I was.

"Then sir," said the stranger, who proved a lawyer, "you are responsible for the man you left there. He refuses to do any copying; he refuses to do anything; he says he prefers not to; and he refuses to quit the premises."

"I am very sorry, sir," said I, with assumed tranquillity, but an inward tremor, "but, really, the man you allude to is nothing to me—he is no relation or apprentice of mine, that you should hold me responsible for him."

"In mercy's name, who is he?"

"I certainly cannot inform you. I know nothing about him. Formerly I employed him as a copyist; but he has done nothing for me now for some time past."

"I shall settle him then,—good morning, sir."

Several days passed, and I heard nothing more; and though I often felt a charitable prompting to call at the place and see poor Bartleby, yet a certain squeamishness of I know not what withheld me.

All is over with him, by this time, thought I at last, when through another week no further intelligence reached me. But coming to my room the day after, I found several persons waiting at my door in a high state of nervous excitement.

"That's the man—here he comes," cried the foremost one, whom I recognized as the lawyer who had previously called upon me alone.

"You must take him away, sir, at once," cried a portly person among them, advancing upon me, and whom I knew to be the landlord of No. — Wall Street. "These gentlemen, my tenants, cannot stand it any longer; Mr. B——" pointing to the lawyer, "has turned him out of his room, and he now persists in haunting the building generally, sitting upon the banisters of the stairs by day, and sleeping in the entry by night. Everybody is concerned; clients are leaving the offices; some fears are entertained of a mob; something you must do, and that without delay."

Aghast at this torrent, I fell back before it, and would fain have locked myself in my new quarters. In vain I persisted that Bartleby was nothing to me—no more than to anyone else. In vain:—I was the last person known to have anything to do with him, and they held me to the terrible account. Fearful then of being exposed in the papers (as one person present obscurely threatened) I considered the matter, and at length said, that if the lawyer would give me a confidential interview with the scrivener, in his (the lawyer's) own room, I would that afternoon strive my best to rid them of the nuisance they complained of.

Going upstairs to my old haunt, there was Bartleby silently sitting upon the banister at the landing.

"What are you doing here, Bartleby?" said I.

"Sitting upon the banister," he mildly replied.

I motioned him into the lawyer's room, who then left us.

"Bartleby," said I, "are you aware that you are the cause of great tribulation to me, by persisting in occupying the entry after being dismissed from the office?"

No answer.

"Now one of two things must take place. Either you must do something, or something must be done to you. Now what sort of business would you like to engage in? Would you like to re-engage in copying for someone?"

"No; I would prefer not to make any change."

"Would you like a clerkship in a drygoods store?"

"There is too much confinement about that. No, I would not like a clerkship; but I am not particular."

"Too much confinement," I cried, "why you keep yourself confined all the time!"

"I would prefer not to take a clerkship," he rejoined, as if to settle that little item at once.

"How would a bartender's business suit you? There is no trying of the eyesight in that."

"I would not like it at all; though, as I said before, I am not particular."

His unwonted wordiness inspirited me. I returned to the charge.

"Well then, would you like to travel through the country collecting bills for the merchants? That would improve your health."

"No, I would prefer to be doing something else."

"How then would going as a companion to Europe, to entertain some young gentleman with your conversation,—how would that suit you?"

"Not at all. It does not strike me that there is anything definite about that. I like to be stationary. But I am not particular."

"Stationary you shall be then," I cried, now losing all patience, and for the first time in all my exasperating connection with him fairly flying into a passion. "If you do not go away from these premises before night, I shall feel bound—indeed I *am* bound—to—to—to quit the premises myself!" I rather absurdly concluded, knowing not with what possible threat to try to frighten his immobility into compliance. Despairing of all further efforts, I was precipitately leaving him, when a final thought occurred to me—one which had not been wholly unindulged before.

"Bartleby," said I, in the kindest tone I could assume under such exciting circumstances, "will you go home with me now—not to my office, but my dwelling—and remain there till we can conclude upon some convenient arrangement for you at our leisure? Come, let us start now, right away."

"No: at present I would prefer not to make any change at all."

I answered nothing; but effectually dodging everyone by the suddenness and rapidity of my flight, rushed from the building, ran up Wall Street toward Broadway, and jumping into the first omnibus was soon removed from pursuit. As soon as tranquillity returned I distinctly perceived that I had now done all that I possibly could, both in respect to the demands of the landlord and his tenants, and with regard to my own desire and sense of duty, to benefit Bartleby, and shield him from rude persecution. I now strove to be entirely carefree and quiescent; and my conscience justified me in the attempt; though indeed it was not so successful as I could have wished. So fearful was I of being again hunted out by the incensed landlord and his exasperated tenants, that, surrendering my business to Nippers, for a few days I drove about the upper part of the town and through the suburbs, in my rockaway; crossed over to Jersey City and Hoboken, and paid fugitive visits to Manhattanville and Astoria. In fact I almost lived in my rockaway for the time.

When again I entered my office, lo, a note from the landlord lay upon the desk. I opened it with trembling hands. It informed me that the writer had sent to the police, and had Bartleby removed to the Tombs as a vagrant. Moreover, since I knew more about him than anyone else, he wished me to appear at that place, and make a suitable statement of the facts. These tidings had a conflicting effect upon me. At first I was indignant; but at last almost approved. The landlord's energetic, summary disposition had led him to adopt a procedure which I do not think I would have decided upon myself; and yet as a last resort, under such peculiar circumstances, it seemed the only plan.

As I afterwards learned, the poor scrivener, when told that he must be conducted to the Tombs, offered not the slightest obstacle, but in his pale unmoving way, silently acquiesced.

Some of the compassionate and curious bystanders joined the party; and headed by one of the constables arm in arm with Bartleby, the silent procession filed its way through all the noise, and heat, and joy of the roaring thoroughfares at noon.

The same day I received the note I went to the Tombs, or to speak more properly, the Halls of Justice. Seeking the right officer, I stated the purpose of my call, and was informed that the individual I described was indeed within. I then assured the functionary that Bartleby was a perfectly honest man, and greatly to be compassionated, however unaccountably eccentric. I narrated all I knew, and closed by suggesting the idea of letting him remain in as indulgent confinement as possible till something less harsh might be done—though indeed I hardly knew what. At all events, if nothing else could be decided upon, the alms-house must receive him. I then begged to have an interview.

Being under no disgraceful charge, and quite serene and harmless in all his ways, they had permitted him freely to wander about the prison, and especially in the inclosed grass-platted yards thereof. And so I found him there, standing all alone in the quietest of the yards, his face towards a high wall, while all around, from the narrow slits of the jail windows, I thought I saw peering out upon him the eyes of murderers and thieves.

"Bartleby!"

"I know you," he said, without looking round,—"and I want nothing to say to you."

"It was not I that brought you here, Bartleby," said I, keenly pained at his implied suspicion. "And to you, this should not be so vile a place. Nothing reproachful attaches to you by being here. And see, it is not so sad a place as one might think. Look, there is the sky, and here is the grass."

"I know where I am," he replied, but would say nothing more, and so I left him.

As I entered the corridor again, a broad meat-like man, in an apron, accosted me, and jerking his thumb over his shoulder said—"Is that your friend?"

"Yes."

"Does he want to starve? If he does, let him live on the prison fare, that's all."

"Who are you?" asked I, not knowing what to make of such an un-officially-speaking person in such a place.

"I am the grub-man. Such gentlemen as have friends here, hire me to provide them with something good to eat."

"Is this so?" said I, turning to the turnkey.

He said it was.

"Well then," said I, slipping some silver into the grub-man's hands (for so they called him). "I want you to give particular attention to my friend there; let him have the best dinner you can get. And you must be as polite to him as possible."

"Introduce me, will you?" said the grub-man, looking at me with an expression which seemed to say he was all impatience for an opportunity to give a specimen of his breeding.

Thinking it would prove of benefit to the scrivener, I acquiesced; and asking the grub-man his name, went up with him to Bartleby.

"Bartleby, this is Mr. Cutlets; you will find him very useful to you."

"Your sarvant, sir, your sarvant," said the grub-man, making a low salutation behind his apron. "Hope you find it pleasant here, sir;—spacious grounds—cool apartments, sir—hope you'll stay with us some time—try to make it agreeable. May Mrs. Cutlets and I have the pleasure of your company to dinner, sir, in Mrs. Cutlets' private room?"

"I prefer not to dine today," said Bartleby, turning away. "It would disagree with me; I am unused to dinners." So saying he slowly moved to the other side of the inclosure, and took up a position fronting the dead-wall.

"How's this?" said the grub-man, addressing me with a stare of astonishment. "He's odd, ain't he?"

"I think he is a little deranged," said I, sadly.

"Deranged? deranged is it? Well now, upon my word, I thought that friend of yourn was a gentleman forger; they are always pale and genteel-like, them forgers. I can't help pity 'em—can't help it, sir. Did you know Monroe Edwards?" he added touchingly, and paused. Then, laying his hand pityingly on my shoulder, sighed, "he died of consumption at Sing Sing. So you weren't acquainted with Monroe?"

"No, I was never socially acquainted with any forgers. But I cannot stop longer. Look to my friend yonder. You will not lose by it. I will see you again."

Some few days after this, I again obtained admission to the Tombs, and went through the corridors in quest of Bartleby; but without finding him.

"I saw him coming from his cell not long ago," said a turnkey, "may be he's gone to loiter in the yards."

So I went in that direction.

"Are you looking for the silent man?" said another turnkey passing me. "Yonder he lies—sleeping in the yard there. 'Tis not twenty minutes since I saw him lie down."

The yard was entirely quiet. It was not accessible to the common prisoners. The surrounding walls, of amazing thickness, kept off all sounds behind them. The Egyptian character of the masonry weighed upon me with its gloom. But a soft imprisoned turf grew under foot. The heart of the eternal pyramids, it seemed, wherein, by some strange magic, through the clefts, grass seed, dropped by birds, had sprung.

Strangely huddled at the base of the wall, his knees drawn up, and lying on his side, his head touching the cold stones, I saw the wasted Bartleby. But nothing stirred. I paused; then went close up to him; stooped over, and saw that his dim eyes were open; otherwise he seemed profoundly sleeping. Something prompted me to touch him. I felt his hand, when a tingling shiver ran up my arm and down my spine to my feet.

The round face of the grub-man peered upon me now. "His dinner is ready. Won't he dine today, either? Or does he live without dining?"

"Lives without dining," said I, and closed the eyes.

"Eh!—He's asleep, ain't he?"

"With kings and counsellors,"[4] murmured I.

There would seem little need for proceeding further in this history. Imagination will readily supply the meager recital of poor Bartleby's interment. But ere parting with the reader, let me say, that if this little narrative has sufficiently interested him, to awaken curiosity as to who Bartleby was, and what manner of life he led prior to the present narrator's making his acquaintance, I can only reply, that in such curiosity I fully share, but am wholly unable to gratify it. Yet here I hardly know whether I should divulge one little item of rumor, which came to my ear a few months after the scrivener's decease. Upon what basis it rested, I could never ascertain; and hence, how true it is I cannot now tell. But inasmuch as this vague report has not been without a certain strange suggestive interest to me, however sad, it may prove the same with some others; and so I will briefly mention it. The report was this: that Bartleby had been a subordinate clerk in the Dead Letter Office at Washington, from which he had been suddenly removed by a change in the administration. When I think over this rumor, I cannot adequately express the emotions which seize me. Dead letters! does it not sound like dead men? Conceive a man by nature and misfortune prone to a pallid hopelessness, can any business seem more fitted to heighten it than that of continually handling these dead letters, and assorting them for the flames? For by the cartload they are annually

---

4. I.e., dead. See *Job* 3:13–14; ". . . then had I been at rest, With kings and counsellors of the earth, which built desolate places for themselves."

burned. Sometimes from out the folded paper the pale clerk takes a ring:—the finger it was meant for, perhaps, molders in the grave; a banknote sent in swiftest charity:—he whom it would relieve, nor eats nor hungers any more; pardon for those who died despairing; hope for those who died unhoping; good tidings for those who died stifled by unrelieved calamities. On errands of life, these letters speed to death.

Ah Bartleby! Ah humanity!

p. 1853

HENRY JAMES

The Tree of Knowledge

1

It was one of the secret opinions, such as we all have, of Peter Brench that his main success in life would have consisted in his never having committed himself about the work, as it was called, of his friend Morgan Mallow. This was a subject on which it was, to the best of his belief, impossible with veracity to quote him, and it was nowhere on record that he had, in the connection, on any occasion and in any embarrassment, either lied or spoken the truth. Such a triumph had its honor even for a man of other triumphs—a man who had reached fifty, who had escaped marriage, who had lived within his means, who had been in love with Mrs. Mallow for years without breathing it, and who, last not least, had judged himself once for all. He had so judged himself in fact that he felt an extreme and general humility to be his proper portion; yet there was nothing that made him think so well of his parts as the course he had steered so often through the shallows just mentioned. It became thus a real wonder that the friends in whom he had most confidence were just those with whom he had most reserves. He couldn't tell Mrs. Mallow—or at least he supposed, excellent man, he couldn't—that she was the one beautiful reason he had never married; any more than he could tell her husband that the sight of the multiplied marbles in that gentleman's studio was an affliction of which even time had never blunted the edge. His victory, however, as I have intimated, in regard to these productions, was not simply in his not having let it out that he deplored them; it was, remarkably, in his not having kept it in by anything else.

The whole situation, among these good people, was verily a marvel, and there was probably not such another for a long way from the spot that engages us—the point at which the soft declivity of Hampstead began at that time to confess in broken accents to Saint John's Wood.[1] He despised Mallow's status and adored Mallow's wife, and yet was distinctly fond of Mallow, to whom, in turn, he was equally

1. Sections of northwest London.

dear. Mrs. Mallow rejoiced in the statues—though she preferred, when pressed, the busts; and if she was visibly attached to Peter Brench it was because of his affection for Morgan. Each loved the other more-over for the love borne in each case to Lancelot, whom the Mallows respectively cherished as their only child and whom the friend of their fireside identified as the third—but decidedly the handsomest—of his godsons. Already in the old years it had come to that—that no one, for such a relation, could possibly have occurred to any of them, even to the baby itself, but Peter. There was luckily a certain independence, of the pecuniary sort, all round: the Master could never otherwise have spent his solemn *Wanderjahre*[2] in Florence and Rome, and con-tinued by the Thames as well as by the Arno and the Tiber to add unpurchased group to group and model, for what was too apt to prove in the event mere love, fancy-heads of celebrities either too busy or too buried—too much of the age or too little of it—to sit. Neither could Peter, lounging in almost daily, have found time to keep the whole complicated tradition so alive by his presence. He was massive but mild, the depositary of these mysteries—large and loose and ruddy and curly, with deep tones, deep eyes, deep pockets, to say nothing of the habit of long pipes, soft hats and brownish grayish weather-faded clothes, apparently always the same.

He had "written," it was known, but had never spoken, never spoken in particular of that; and he had the air (since, as was believed, he continued to write) of keeping it up in order to have something more —as if he hadn't at the worst enough—to be silent about. Whatever his air, at any rate, Peter's occasional unmentioned prose and verse were quite truly the result of an impulse to maintain the purity of his taste by establishing still more firmly the right relation of fame to feebleness. The little green door of his domain was in a garden wall on which the discolored stucco made patches, and in the small detached villa be-hind it everything was old, the furniture, the servants, the books, the prints, the immemorial habits and the new improvements. The Mal-lows, at Carrara Lodge, were within ten minutes, and the studio there was on their little land, to which they had added, in their happy faith, for building it. This was the good fortune, if it was not the ill, of her having brought him in marriage a portion that put them in a manner at their ease and enabled them thus, on their side, to keep it up. And they did keep it up—they always had—the infatuated sculptor and his wife, for whom nature had refined on the impossible by relieving them of the sense of the difficult. Morgan had at all events everything of the sculptor but the spirit of Phidias—the brown velvet, the becoming *beretto*,[3] the "plastic" presence, the fine fingers, the beautiful accent in Italian and the old Italian factotum. He seemed to make up for every-thing when he addressed Egidio with the "tu"[4] and waved him to turn one of the rotary pedestals of which the place was full. They were tremendous Italians at Carrara Lodge, and the secret of the part played by this fact in Peter's life was in a large degree that it gave

---

2. A journeyman's year of travel before settling to work; also the title of the second volume (1821–29) of the famous novel *Wilhelm Meister* by Johann Wolf-gang von Goethe (1749–1832).

3. Cap with tassel, usually *berretto*.

4. The familiar form of the second-person pronoun, literally "thou," but roughly equivalent to first-naming some-one in English.

him, sturdy Briton as he was, just the amount of "going abroad" he could bear. The Mallows were all his Italy, but it was in a measure for Italy he liked them. His one worry was that Lance—to which they had shortened his godson—was, in spite of a public school,[5] perhaps a shade too Italian. Morgan meanwhile looked like somebody's flattering idea of somebody's own person as expressed in the great room provided at the Uffizzi Museum[6] for the general illustration of that idea by eminent hands. The Master's sole regret that he hadn't been born rather to the brush than to the chisel sprang from his wish that he might have contributed to that collection.

It appeared with time at any rate to be to the brush that Lance had been born; for Mrs. Mallow, one day when the boy was turning twenty, broke it to their friend, who shared, to the last delicate morsel, their problems and pains, that it seemed as if nothing would really do but that he should embrace the career. It had been impossible longer to remain blind to the fact that he was gaining no glory at Cambridge, where Brench's own college had for a year tempered its tone to him as for Brench's own sake. Therefore why renew the vain form of preparing him for the impossible? The impossible—it had become clear—was that he should be anything but an artist.

"Oh dear, dear!" said poor Peter.

"Don't you believe in it?" asked Mrs. Mallow, who still, at more than forty, had her violet velvet eyes, her creamy satin skin and her silken chestnut hair.

"Believe in what?"

"Why in Lance's passion."

"I don't know what you mean by 'believing in it.' I've never been unaware, certainly, of his disposition, from his earliest time, to daub and draw; but I confess I've hoped it would burn out."

"But why should it," she sweetly smiled, "with his wonderful heredity? Passion is passion—though of course indeed *you,* dear Peter, know nothing of that. Has the Master's ever burned out?"

Peter looked off a little and, in his familiar formless way, kept up for a moment a sound between a smothered whistle and a subdued hum. "Do you think he's going to be another Master?"

She seemed scarce prepared to go that length, yet she had on the whole a marvelous trust. "I know what you mean by that. Will it be a career to incur the jealousies and provoke the machinations that have been at times almost too much for his father? Well—say it may be, since nothing but claptrap, in these dreadful days, *can,* it would seem, make its way, and since, with the curse of refinement and distinction, one may easily find one's self begging one's bread. Put it at the worst —say he *has* the misfortune to wing his flight further than the vulgar taste of his stupid countrymen can follow. Think, all the same, of the happiness—the same the Master has had. He'll *know.*"

Peter looked rueful. "Ah but *what* will he know?"

"Quiet joy!" cried Mrs. Mallow, quite impatient and turning away.

---

5. English boarding-school, usually for the well-to-do.
6. Art Museum in Florence with world's finest collection of Italian Renaissance painting, the reference here being to artists' self-portraits.

2

He had of course before long to meet the boy himself on it and to hear that practically everything was settled. Lance was not to go up again,[7] but to go instead to Paris where, since the die was cast, he would find the best advantages. Peter had always felt he must be taken as he was, but had never perhaps found him so much of that pattern as on this occasion. "You chuck Cambridge then altogether? Doesn't that seem rather a pity?"

Lance would have been like his father, to his friend's sense, had he had less humor, and like his mother had he had more beauty. Yet it was a good middle way for Peter that, in the modern manner, he was, to the eye, rather the young stockbroker than the young artist. The youth reasoned that it was a question of time—there was such a mill to go through, such an awful lot to learn. He had talked with fellows and had judged. "One has got, today," he said, "don't you see? to know."

His interlocutor, at this, gave a groan. "Oh hang it, *don't* know!"

Lance wondered. " 'Don't'? Then what's the use—?"

"The use of what?"

"Why of anything. Don't you think I've talent?"

Peter smoked away for a little in silence; then went on; "It isn't knowledge, it's ignorance that—as we've been beautifully told—is bliss."

"Don't you think I've talent," Lance repeated.

Peter, with his trick of queer kind demonstrations, passed his arm round his godson and held him a moment. "How do I know?"

"Oh," said the boy, "if it's your own ignorance you're defending?—"

Again, for a pause, on the sofa, his godfather smoked. "It isn't. I've the misfortune to be omniscient."

"Oh well," Lance laughed again, "if you know *too* much—!"

"That's what I do, and it's why I'm so wretched."

Lance's gaiety grew. "Wretched? Come, I say!"

"But I forgot," his companion went on—"you're not to know about that. It would indeed for you too make the too much. Only I'll tell you what I'll do." And Peter got up from the sofa. "If you'll go up again I'll pay your way at Cambridge."

Lance stared, a little rueful in spite of being still more amused. "Oh Peter! You disapprove so of Paris?"

"Well, I'm afraid of it."

"Ah I see!"

"No, you don't see—yet. But you will—that is you would. And you mustn't."

The young man thought more gravely. "But one's innocence, already—!"

"Is considerably damaged? Ah that won't matter," Peter persisted—"we'll patch it up here."

"Here? Then you want me to stay at home?"

Peter almost confessed to it. "Well, we're so right—we four together—just as we are. We're so safe. Come, don't spoil it."

7. Not to return to the university.

The boy, who had turned to gravity, turned from this, on the real pressure in his friend's tone, to consternation. "Then what's a fellow to be?"

"My particular care. Come, old man"—and Peter now fairly pleaded—"*I'll* look out for you."

Lance, who had remained on the sofa with his legs out and his hands in his pockets, watched him with eyes that showed suspicion. Then he got up. "You think there's something the matter with me—that I can't make a success."

"Well, what do you call a success?"

Lance thought again. "Why the best sort, I suppose, is to please one's self. Isn't that the sort that, in spite of cabals and things, is—in his own peculiar line—the Master's?"

There were so much too many things in this question to be answered at once that they practically checked the discussion, which became particularly difficult in the light of such renewed proof that, though the young man's innocence might, in the course of his studies, as he contended, somewhat have shrunken, the finer essence of it still remained. That was indeed exactly what Peter had assumed and what above all he desired; yet perversely enough it gave him a chill. The boy believed in the cabals and things, believed in the peculiar line, believed, to be brief, in the Master. What happened a month or two later wasn't that he went up again at the expense of his godfather, but that a fortnight after he had got settled in Paris this personage sent him fifty pounds.

He had meanwhile at home, this personage, made up his mind to the worst; and what that might be had never yet grown quite so vivid to him as when, on his presenting himself one Sunday night, as he never failed to do, for supper, the mistress of Carrara Lodge met him with an appeal as to—of all things in the world—the wealth of the Canadians. She was earnest, she was even excited. "Are many of them *really* rich?"

He had to confess he knew nothing about them, but he often thought afterwards of that evening. The room in which they sat was adorned with sundry specimens of the Master's genius, which had the merit of being, as Mrs. Mallow herself frequently suggested, of an unusually convenient size. They were indeed of dimensions not customary in the products of the chisel, and they had the singularity that, if the objects and features intended to be small looked too large, the objects and features intended to be large looked too small. The Master's idea, either in respect to this matter or to any other, had in almost any case, even after years, remained undiscoverable to Peter Brench. The creations that so failed to reveal it stood about on pedestals and brackets, on tables and shelves, a little staring white population, heroic, idyllic, allegoric, mythic, symbolic, in which "scale" had so strayed and lost itself that the public square and the chimney piece seemed to have changed places, the monumental being all diminutive and the diminutive all monumental; branches at any rate, markedly, of a family in which stature was rather oddly irrespective of function, age, and sex. They formed, like the Mallows themselves, poor Brench's own family—having at least to such a degree the note of familiarity.

The occasion was one of those he had long ago learned to know and to name—short flickers of the faint flame, soft gusts of a kinder air. Twice a year regularly the Master believed in his fortune, in addition to believing all the year round in his genius. This time it was to be made by a bereaved couple from Toronto, who had given him the handsomest order for a tomb to three lost children, each of whom they desired to see, in the composition, emblematically and character- istically represented.

Such was naturally the moral of Mrs. Mallow's question: if their wealth was to be assumed, it was clear, from the nature of their ad- miration, as well as from mysterious hints thrown out (they were a little odd!) as to other possibilities for the same mortuary sort, that their further patronage might be; and not less evident that should the Master become at all known in those climes nothing would be more inevitable than a run of Canadian custom. Peter had been present before at runs of custom, colonial and domestic—present at each of those of which the aggregation had left so few gaps in the marble company round him; but it was his habit never at these junctures to prick the bubble in advance. The fond illusion, while it lasted, eased the wound of elections never won, the long ache of medals and diplomas carried off, on every chance, by everyone but the Master; it moreover lighted the lamp that would glimmer through the next eclipse. They lived, however, after all—as it was always beautiful to see—at a height scarce susceptible of ups and downs. They strained a point at times charmingly, strained it to admit that the public was here and there not too bad to buy; but they would have been no- where without their attitude that the Master was always too good to sell. They were at all events deliciously formed, Peter often said to himself, for their fate; the Master had a vanity, his wife had a loyalty, of which success, depriving these things of innocence, would have diminished the merit and the grace. Anyone could be charming under a charm, and as he looked about him at a world of prosperity more void of proportion even than the Master's museum he wondered if he knew another pair that so completely escaped vulgarity.

"What a pity Lance isn't with us to rejoice!" Mrs. Mallow on this oc- casion sighed at supper.

"We'll drink to the health of the absent," her husband replied, filling his friend's glass and his own and giving a drop to their companion; "but we must hope he's preparing himself for a happiness much less like this of ours this evening—excusable as I grant it to be!—than like the comfort we have always (whatever has happened or has not hap- pened) been able to trust ourselves to enjoy. The comfort," the Master explained, leaning back in the pleasant lamplight and firelight, holding up his glass and looking round at his marble family, quartered more or less, a monstrous brood, in every room—"the comfort of art in itself!"

Peter looked a little shyly at his wine. "Well—I don't care what you may call it when a fellow doesn't—but Lance must learn to *sell*, you know. I drink to his acquisition of the secret of a base popularity!"

"Oh yes, *he* must sell," the boy's mother, who was still more, how- ever, this seemed to give out, the Master's wife, rather artlessly allowed.

"Ah," the sculptor after a moment confidently pronounced, "Lance *will*. Don't be afraid. He'll have learned."

"Which is exactly what Peter," Mrs. Mallow gaily returned—"why in the world were you so perverse, Peter?—wouldn't when he told him hear of."

Peter, when this lady looked at him with accusatory affection—a grace on her part not infrequent—could never find a word; but the Master, who was always all amenity and tact, helped him out now as he had often helped him before. "That's his old idea, you know—on which we've so often differed: his theory that the artist should be all impulse and instinct. *I* go in of course for a certain amount of school. Not too much—but a due proportion. There's where his protest came in," he continued to explain to his wife, "as against what *might*, don't you see? be in question for Lance."

"Ah well"—and Mrs. Mallow turned the violet eyes across the table at the subject of this discourse—"he's sure to have meant of course nothing but good. Only that wouldn't have prevented him, if Lance *had* taken his advice, from being in effect horribly cruel."

They had a sociable way of talking of him to his face as if he had been in the clay or—at most—in the plaster, and the Master was unfailingly generous. He might have been waving Egidio to make him revolve. "Ah but poor Peter wasn't so wrong as to what it may after all come to that he *will* learn."

"Oh but nothing artistically bad," she urged—still, for poor Peter, arch and dewy.

"Why just the little French tricks," said the Master: on which their friend had to pretend to admit, when pressed by Mrs. Mallow, that these aestheic vices had been the objects of his dread.

3

"I know now," Lance said to him the next year, "why you were so much against it." He had come back supposedly for a mere interval and was looking about him at Carrara Lodge, where indeed he had already on two or three occasions since his expatriation briefly reappeared. This had the air of a longer holiday. "Something rather awful has happened to me. It *isn't* so very good to know."

"I'm bound to say high spirits don't show in your face," Peter was rather ruefully forced to confess. "Still, are you very sure you do know?"

"Well, I at least know about as much as I can bear." These remarks were exchanged in Peter's den, and the young man, smoking cigarettes, stood before the fire with his back against the mantel. Something of his bloom seemed really to have left him.

Poor Peter wondered. "You're clear then as to what in particular I wanted you not to go for?"

"In particular?" Lance thought. "It seems to me that in particular there can have been only one thing."

They stood for a little sounding each other. "Are you quite sure?"

"Quite sure I'm a beastly duffer? Quite—by this time."

"Oh!"—and Peter turned away as if almost with relief.

"It's *that* that isn't pleasant to find out."

"Oh I don't care for 'that,'" said Peter, presently coming round again. "I mean I personally don't."

"Yet I hope you can understand a little that I myself should!"

"Well, what do you mean by it?" Peter skeptically asked.

And on this Lance had to explain—how the upshot of his studies in Paris had inexorably proved a mere deep doubt of his means. These studies had so waked him up that a new light was in his eyes; but what the new light did was really to show him too much. "Do you know what's the matter with me? I'm too horribly intelligent. Paris was really the last place for me. I've learned what I can't do."

Poor Peter stared—it was a staggerer; but even after they had had, on the subject, a longish talk in which the boy brought out to the full the hard truth of his lesson, his friend betrayed less pleasure than usually breaks into a face to the happy tune of "I told you so!" Poor Peter himself made now indeed so little a point of having told him so that Lance broke ground in a different place a day or two after. "What was it then that—before I went—you were afraid I should find out?" This, however, Peter refused to tell him—on the ground that if he hadn't yet guessed perhaps he never would, and that in any case nothing at all for either of them was to be gained by giving the thing a name. Lance eyed him on this an instant with the bold curiosity of youth—with the air indeed of having in his mind two or three names, of which one or other would be right. Peter nevertheless, turning his back again, offered no encouragement, and when they parted afresh it was with some show of impatience on the side of the boy. Accordingly on their next encounter Peter saw at a glance that he had now, in the interval, divined and that, to sound his note, he was only waiting till they should find themselves alone. This he had soon arranged and he then broken straight out. "Do you know your conundrum has been keeping me awake? But in the watches of the night the answer came over me—so that, upon my honor, I quite laughed out. Had you been supposing I had to go to Paris to learn *that*?" Even now, to see him still so sublimely on his guard, Peter's young friend had to laugh afresh. "You won't give a sign till you're sure? Beautiful old Peter!" But Lance at last produced it. "Why, hang it, the truth about the Master."

It made between them for some minutes a lively passage, full of wonder for each at the wonder of the other. "Then how long have you understood—"

"The true value of his work? I understood it," Lance recalled, "as soon as I began to understand anything. But I didn't begin fully to do that, I admit, till I got *là-bas*."[8]

"Dear, dear!"—Peter gasped with retrospective dread.

"But for what have you taken me? I'm a hopeless muff[9]—that I *had* to have rubbed in. But I'm not such a muff as the Master!" Lance declared.

"Then why did you never tell me—?"

"That I hadn't, after all"—the boy took him up—"remained such an idiot? Just because I never dreamed *you* knew. But I beg your pardon.

8. Over there (that is, Paris).   a duffer.
9. Someone without skill or aptitude,

I only wanted to spare you. And what I don't now understand is how the deuce then for so long you've managed to keep bottled."

Peter produced his explanation, but only after some delay and with a gravity not void of embarrassment. "It was for your mother."

"Oh!" said Lance.

"And that's the great thing now—since the murder *is* out. I want a promise from you. I mean"—and Peter almost feverishly followed it up —"a vow from you, solemn and such as you owe me here on the spot, that you'll sacrifice anything rather than let her ever guess—"

"That *I've* guessed?"—Lance took it in. "I see." He evidently after a moment had taken in much. "But what is it you've in mind that I may have a chance to sacrifice?"

"Oh one has always something."

Lance looked at him hard. "Do you mean that *you've* had—?" The look he received back, however, so put the question by that he found soon enough another. "Are you really sure my mother doesn't know?"

Peter, after renewed reflection, was really sure. "If she does she's too wonderful."

"But aren't we all too wonderful?"

"Yes," Peter granted—"but in different ways. The thing's so desperately important because your father's little public consists only, as you know then," Peter developed—"well, of how many?"

"First of all," the Master's son risked, "of himself. And last of all too. I don't quite see of whom else."

Peter had an approach to impatience. "Of your mother, I say— *always.*"

Lance cast it all up. "You absolutely feel that?"

"Absolutely."

"Well then with yourself that makes three."

"Oh *me!*"—and Peter, with a wag of his kind old head, modestly excused himself. "The number's at any rate small enough for any individual dropping out to be too dreadfully missed. Therefore, to put it in a nutshell, take care, my boy—that's all—that *you're* not!"

"I've got to keep on humbugging?" Lance wailed.

"It's just to warn you of the danger of your failing of that that I've seized this opportunity."

"And what do you regard in particular," the young man asked, "as the danger?"

"Why this certainty: that the moment your mother, who feels so strongly, should suspect your secret—well," said Peter desperately, "the fat would be on the fire."

Lance for a moment seemed to stare at the blaze. "She'd throw me over?"

"She'd throw *him* over."

"And come round to us?"

Peter, before he answered, turned away. "Come round to *you.*" But he had said enough to indicate—and, as he evidently trusted, to avert —the horrid contingency.

4

Within six months again, none the less, his fear was on more occasions than one all before him. Lance had returned to Paris for another trial; then had reappeared at home and had had, with his father, for the first time in his life, one of the scenes that strike sparks. He described it with much expression to Peter, touching whom (since they had never done so before) it was the sign of a new reserve on the part of the pair at Carrara Lodge that they at present failed, on a matter of intimate interest, to open themselves—if not in joy then in sorrow—to their good friend. This produced perhaps practically between the parties a shade of alienation and a slight intermission of commerce—marked mainly indeed by the fact that to talk at his ease with his old playmate Lance had in general to come to see him. The closest if not quite the gayest relation they had yet known together was thus ushered in. The difficulty for poor Lance was a tension at home—begotten by the fact that his father wished him to be at least the sort of success he himself had been. He hadn't "chucked" Paris—though nothing appeared more vivid to him than that Paris had chucked him: he would go back again because of the fascination in trying, in seeing, in sounding the depths—in learning one's lesson, briefly, even if the lesson were simply that of one's impotence in the presence of one's larger vision. But what did the Master, all aloft in his senseless fluency, know of impotence, and what vision—to be called such—had he in all his blind life ever had? Lance, heated and indignant, frankly appealed to his godparent on this score.

His father, it appeared, had come down on him for having, after so long, nothing to show, and hoped that on his next return this deficiency would be repaired. *The* thing, the Master complacently set forth, was for any artist, however inferior to himself—at least to "do" something. "What can you do? That's all I ask!" *He* had certainly done enough, and there was no mistake about what he had to show. Lance had tears in his eyes when it came thus to letting his old friend know how great the strain might be on the "sacrifice" asked of him. It wasn't so easy to continue humbugging—as from son to parent—after feeling one's self despised for not groveling in mediocrity. Yet a noble duplicity was what, as they intimately faced the situation, Peter went on requiring; and it was still for a time what his young friend, bitter and sore, managed loyally to comfort him with. Fifty pounds more than once again, it was true, rewarded both in London and in Paris the young friend's loyalty; none the less sensibly, doubtless, at the moment, that the money was a direct advance on a decent sum for which Peter had long since privately prearranged an ultimate function. Whether by these arts or others, at all events, Lance's just resentment was kept for a season—but only for a season—at bay. The day arrived when he warned his companion that he could hold out—or hold in—no longer. Carrara Lodge had had to listen to another lecture delivered from a great height—an infliction really heavier at last than, without striking back or in some way letting the Master have the truth, flesh and blood could bear.

"And what I don't see is," Lance observed with a certain irritated eye for what was after all, if it came to that, owing to himself too; "what I don't see is, upon my honor, how *you*, as things are going, can keep the game up."

"Oh the game for me is only to hold my tongue," said placid Peter. "And I have my reason."

"Still my mother?"

Peter showed a queer face as he had often shown it before—that is by turning it straight away. "What will you have? I haven't ceased to like her."

"She's beautiful—she's a dear of course," Lance allowed; "but what is she to you, after all, and what is it to you that, as to anything whatever, she should or she shouldn't?"

Peter, who had turned red, hung fire a little. "Well—it's all simply what I make of it."

There was now, however, in his young friend a strange, an adopted insistence. "What are you after all to *her?*"

"Oh nothing. But that's another matter."

"She cares only for my father," said Lance the Parisian.

"Naturally—and that's just why."

"Why you've wished to spare her?"

"Because she cares so tremendously much."

Lance took a turn about the room, but with his eyes still on his host. "How awfully—always—you must have liked her!"

"Awfully. Always," said Peter Brench.

The young man continued for a moment to muse—then stopped again in front of him. "Do you know how much she cares?" Their eyes met on it, but Peter, as if his own found something new in Lance's, appeared to hesitate, for the first time in an age, to say he did know. "*I've* only just found out," said Lance. "She came to my room last night, after being present, in silence and only with her eyes on me, at what I had had to take from him: she came—and she was with me an extraordinary hour."

He had paused again and they had again for a while sounded each other. Then something—and it made him suddenly turn pale—came to Peter. "She *does* know?"

"She does know. She let it all out to me—so as to demand of me no more than 'that,' as she said, of which she herself had been capable. She has always, always known," said Lance without pity.

Peter was silent a long time; during which his companion might have heard him gently breathe, and on touching him might have felt within him the vibration of a long low sound suppressed. By the time he spoke at last he had taken everything in. "Then I do see how tremendously much."

"Isn't it wonderful?" Lance asked.

"Wonderful," Peter mused.

"So that if your original effort to keep me from Paris was to keep me from knowledge—!" Lance exclaimed as if with a sufficient indication of this futility.

It might have been at the futility Peter appeared for a little to gaze. "I think it must have been—without my quite at the time knowing it—to keep *me!*" he replied at last as he turned away.

1900

JOSEPH CONRAD

The Secret Sharer

1

On my right hand there were lines of fishing-stakes resembling a mysterious system of half-submerged bamboo fences, incomprehensible in its division of the domain of tropical fishes, and crazy[1] of aspect as if abandoned for ever by some nomad tribe of fishermen now gone to the other end of the ocean; for there was no sign of human habitation as far as the eye could reach. To the left a group of barren islets, suggesting ruins of stone walls, towers, and blockhouses, had its foundations set in a blue sea that itself looked solid, so still and stable did it lie below my feet; even the track of light from the westering sun shone smoothly, without that animated glitter which tells of an imperceptible ripple. And when I turned my head to take a parting glance at the tug which had just left us anchored outside the bar, I saw the straight line of the flat shore joined to the stable sea, edge to edge, with a perfect and unmarked closeness, in one leveled floor half brown, half blue under the enormous dome of the sky. Corresponding in their insignificance to the islets of the sea, two small clumps of trees, one on each side of the only fault in the impeccable joint, marked the mouth of the river Meinam[2] we had just left on the first preparatory stage of our homeward journey; and, far back on the inland level, a larger and loftier mass, the grove surrounding the great Paknam pagoda, was the only thing on which the eye could rest from the vain task of exploring the monotonous sweep of the horizon. Here and there gleams as of a few scattered pieces of silver marked the windings of the great river; and on the nearest of them, just within the bar, the tug steaming right into the land became lost to my sight, hull and funnel and masts, as though the impassive earth had swallowed her up without an effort, without a tremor. My eye followed the light cloud of her smoke, now here, now there, above the plain, according to the devious curves of the stream, but always fainter and farther away, till I lost it at last behind the mitre-shaped hill of the great pagoda. And then I was left alone with my ship, anchored at the head of the Gulf of Siam.

She floated at the starting-point of a long journey, very still in an immense stillness, the shadows of her spars flung far to the eastward by the setting sun. At that moment I was alone on her decks. There was not a sound in her—and around us nothing moved, nothing lived, not a canoe on the water, not a bird in the air, not a cloud in the sky. In this breathless pause at the threshold of a long passage we

1. Irregular, rickety.
2. The Menan (Chao Phraya) runs through Bangkok into the Gulf of Siam. The Paknam Pagoda (Wat Prachadi Klang-nam) is behind the Fort of Paknam at the mouth of the river. H. Warrington Smyth, in *Five Years in Siam* (1898), describes Bangkok as "a land of myths and terror," and says that when he first crossed the bar of the river his heart sank at the sight: "All around an expanse of dirty mud-brown water . . . stuck here and there with fishing stakes, which gave to the whole scene a disorderly, ragged sort of look. . . ."

seemed to be measuring our fitness for a long and arduous enterprise, the appointed task of both our existences to be carried out, far from all human eyes, with only sky and sea for spectators and for judges.

There must have been some glare in the air to interfere with one's sight, because it was only just before the sun left us that my roaming eyes made out beyond the highest ridge of the principal islet of the group something which did away with the solemnity of perfect solitude. The tide of darkness flowed on swiftly; and with tropical suddenness a swarm of stars came out above the shadowy earth, while I lingered yet, my hand resting lightly on my ship's rail as if on the shoulder of a trusted friend. But, with all that multitude of celestial bodies staring down at one, the comfort of quiet communion with her was gone for good. And there were also disturbing sounds by this time—voices, footsteps forward; the steward flitted along the main deck, a busily ministering spirit; a hand-bell tinkled urgently under the poop deck. . . .

I found my two officers waiting for me near the supper table, in the lighted cuddy. We sat down at once, and as I helped the chief mate, I said:

"Are you aware that there is a ship anchored inside the islands? I saw her mast-heads above the ridge as the sun went down."

He raised sharply his simple face, overcharged by a terrible growth of whisker, and emitted his usual ejaculations, "Bless my soul, sir! You don't say so!"

My second mate was a round-cheeked, silent young man, grave beyond his years, I thought; but as our eyes happened to meet I detected a slight quiver on his lips. I looked down at once. It was not my part to encourage sneering on board my ship. It must be said, too, that I knew very little of my officers. In consequence of certain events of no particular significance, except to myself, I had been appointed to the command only a fortnight before. Neither did I know much of the hands forward. All these people had been together for eighteen months or so, and my position was that of the only stranger on board. I mention this because it has some bearing on what is to follow. But what I felt most was my being a stranger to the ship; and if all the truth must be told, I was somewhat of a stranger to myself. The youngest man on board (barring the second mate), and untried as yet by a position of the fullest responsibility, I was willing to take the adequacy of the others for granted. They had simply to be equal to their tasks; but I wondered how far I should turn out faithful to that ideal conception of one's own personality every man sets up for himself secretly.

Meantime the chief mate, with an almost visible effect of collaboration on the part of his round eyes and frightful whiskers, was trying to evolve a theory of the anchored ship. His dominant trait was to take all things into earnest consideration. He was of a painstaking turn of mind. As he used to say, he "liked to account to himself" for practically everything that came in his way, down to a miserable scorpion he had found in his cabin a week before. The why and the wherefore of that scorpion—how it got on board and came to select his room rather than the pantry (which was a dark place and more what a scorpion would be partial to), and how on earth it managed to drown itself in the inkwell of his writing-desk—had exercised him infinitely. The ship within the islands was much more easily accounted for; and just as we were about to rise from table he made his pronouncement. She was, he doubted not, a ship from home lately arrived. Probably she drew too much water to cross the bar except at the top of spring tides. Therefore she went into that natural harbor to wait for a few days in preference to remaining in an open roadstead.

"That's so," confirmed the second mate suddenly, in his slightly hoarse voice. "She draws over twenty feet. She's the Liverpool ship *Sephora*[3] with a cargo of coal. Hundred and twenty-three days from Cardiff."

We looked at him in surprise.

"The tugboat skipper told me when he come on board for your letters, sir," explained the young man. "He expects to take her up the river the day after tomorrow."

After thus overwhelming us with the extent of his information he slipped out of the cabin. The mate observed regretfully that he "could not account for that young fellow's whims." What prevented him telling us all about it at once, he wanted to know.

I detained him as he was making a move. For the last two days the crew had had plenty of hard work, and the night before they had very little sleep. I felt painfully that I—a stranger—was doing something unusual when I directed him to let all hands turn in without setting an anchor-watch.[4] I proposed to keep on deck myself till one o'clock or thereabouts. I would get the second mate to relieve me at that hour.

"He will turn out the cook and the steward at four," I concluded, "and then give you a call. Of course at the slightest sign of any sort of wind we'll have the hands up and make a start at once."

He concealed his astonishment. "Very well, sir." Outside the cuddy he put his head in the second mate's door to inform him of my unheard-of caprice to take a five hours' anchor-watch on myself. I heard the other raise his voice incredulously—"What? The captain himself?" Then a few more murmurs, a door closed, then another. A few moments later I went on deck.

My strangeness, which had made me sleepless, had prompted that unconventional arrangement, as if I had expected in those solitary hours of the night to get on terms with the ship of which I knew nothing, manned by men of whom I knew very little more. Fast alongside a wharf, littered like any ship in port with a tangle of unrelated things, invaded by unrelated shore people, I had hardly seen her yet properly. Now, as she lay cleared for sea, the stretch of her main deck seemed to me very fine under the stars. Very fine, very roomy for her size, and very inviting. I descended the poop and paced the waist, my mind picturing to myself the coming passage through the Malay Archipelago, down the Indian Ocean, and up the Atlantic. All its phases were familiar enough to me, every characteris-

---

3. See *Leviticus* 23:15–16, for the system of counting days for offerings; *sephor*, to count, refers to a forty-day period during which no marriages can take place.

4. A detachment of seamen kept on deck while the ship lies at anchor.

tic, all the alternatives which were likely to face me on the high seas—everything! . . . except the novel responsibility of command. But I took heart from the reasonable thought that the ship was like other ships, the men like other men, and that the sea was not likely to keep any special surprises expressly for my discomfiture.

Arrived at that comforting conclusion, I bethought myself of a cigar and went below to get it. All was still down there. Everybody at the after end of the ship was sleeping profoundly. I came out again on the quarter-deck, agreeably at ease in my sleeping suit on that warm, breathless night, barefooted, a glowing cigar in my teeth, and, going forward, I was met by the profound silence of the fore end of the ship. Only as I passed the door of the forecastle I heard a deep, quiet, trustful sigh of some sleeper inside. And suddenly I rejoiced in the great security of the sea as compared with the unrest of the land, in my choice of that untempted life presenting no disquieting problems, invested with an elementary moral beauty by the absolute straightforwardness of its appeal and by the singleness of its purpose.

The riding-light [5] in the fore-rigging burned with a clear, untroubled, as if symbolic, flame, confident and bright in the mysterious shades of the night. Passing on my way aft along the other side of the ship, I observed that the rope side-ladder, put over, no doubt, for the master of the tug when he came to fetch away our letters, had not been hauled in as it should have been. I became annoyed at this, for exactitude in small matters is the very soul of discipline. Then I reflected that I had myself peremptorily dismissed my officers from duty, and by my own act had prevented the anchor-watch being formally set and things properly attended to. I asked myself whether it was wise ever to interfere with the established routine of duties even from the kindest of motives. My action might have made me appear eccentric. Goodness only knew how that absurdly whiskered mate would "account" for my conduct, and what the whole ship thought of that informality of their new captain. I was vexed with myself.

Not from compunction certainly, but, as it were mechanically, I proceeded to get the ladder in myself. Now a side-ladder of that sort is a light affair and comes in easily, yet my vigorous tug, which should have brought it flying on board, merely recoiled upon my body in a totally unexpected jerk. What the devil! . . . I was so astounded by the immovableness of that ladder that I remained stock-still, trying to account for it to myself like that imbecile mate of mine. In the end, of course, I put my head over the rail.

The side of the ship made an opaque belt of shadow on the darkling glassy shimmer of the sea. But I saw at once something elongated and pale floating very close to the ladder. Before I could form a guess a faint flash of phosphorescent light, which seemed to issue suddenly from the naked body of a man, flickered in the sleeping water with the elusive, silent play of summer lightning in a night sky. With a gasp I saw revealed to my stare a pair of feet, the long legs, a broad livid back immersed right up to the neck in a greenish cadaverous glow. One hand, awash, clutched the bottom rung of the ladder. He

---

5. Special light displayed by ship while ("riding") at anchor.

was complete but for the head. A headless corpse! The cigar dropped out of my gaping mouth with a tiny plop and a short hiss quite audible in the absolute stillness of all things under heaven. At that I suppose he raised up his face, a dimly pale oval in the shadow of the ship's side. But even then I could only barely make out down there the shape of his black-haired head. However, it was enough for the horrid, frost-bound sensation which had gripped me about the chest to pass off. The moment of vain exclamations was past too. I only climbed on the spare spar and leaned over the rail as far as I could, to bring my eyes nearer to that mystery floating alongside.

As he hung by the ladder, like a resting swimmer, the sea-lightning played about his limbs at every stir; and he appeared in it ghastly, silvery, fish-like. He remained as mute as a fish, too. He made no motion to get out of the water, either. It was inconceivable that he should not attempt to come on board, and strangely troubling to suspect that perhaps he did not want to. And my first words were prompted by just that troubled incertitude.

"What's the matter?" I asked in my ordinary tone, speaking down to the face upturned exactly under mine.

"Cramp," it answered, no louder. Then slightly anxious, "I say, no need to call any one."

"I was not going to," I said.

"Are you alone on deck?"

"Yes."

I had somehow the impression that he was on the point of letting go the ladder to swim away beyond my ken—mysterious as he came. But, for the moment, this being appearing as if he had risen from the bottom of the sea (it was certainly the nearest land to the ship) wanted only to know the time. I told him. And he, down there, tentatively:

"I suppose your captain's turned in?"

"I am sure he isn't," I said.

He seemed to struggle with himself, for I heard something like the low, bitter murmur of doubt. "What's the good?" His next words came out with a hesitating effort.

"Look here, my man. Could you call him out quietly?"

I thought the time had come to declare myself.

"*I* am the captain."

I heard a "By Jove!" whispered at the level of the water. The phosphorescence flashed in the swirl of the water all about his limbs, his other hand seized the ladder.

"My name's Leggatt."

The voice was calm and resolute. A good voice. The self-possession of that man had somehow induced a corresponding state in myself. It was very quietly that I remarked:

"You must be a good swimmer."

"Yes. I've been in the water practically since nine o'clock. The question for me now is whether I am to let go this ladder and go on swimming till I sink from exhaustion or—to come on board here."

I felt this was no mere formula of desperate speech, but a real alternative in the view of a strong soul. I should have gathered from this that he was young; indeed, it is only the young who are ever confronted by such clear issues. But at the time it was pure intuition on my part. A mysterious communication was established already between us two—in the face of that silent, darkened tropical sea. I was young, too; young enough to make no comment. The man in the water began suddenly to climb up the ladder, and I hastened away from the rail to fetch some clothes.

Before entering the cabin I stood still, listening in the lobby at the foot of the stairs. A faint snore came through the closed door of the chief mate's room. The second mate's door was on the hook, but the darkness in there was absolutely soundless. He, too, was young and could sleep like a stone. Remained the steward, but he was not likely to wake up before he was called. I got a sleeping suit out of my room, and, coming back on deck, saw the naked man from the sea sitting on the main-hatch, glimmering white in the darkness, his elbows on his knees and his head in his hands. In a moment he had concealed his damp body in a sleeping suit of the same gray-stripe pattern as the one I was wearing, and followed me like my double on the poop. Together we moved right aft, barefooted, silent.

"What is it?" I asked in a deadened voice, taking the lighted lamp out of the binnacle, and raising it to his face.

"An ugly business."

He had rather regular features; a good mouth; light eyes under somewhat heavy, dark eyebrows; a smooth, square forehead; no growth on his cheeks; a small, brown mustache, and a well-shaped, round chin. His expression was concentrated, meditative, under the inspecting light of the lamp I held up to his face; such as a man thinking hard in solitude might wear. My sleeping suit was just right for his size. A well-knit young fellow of twenty-five at most. He caught his lower lip with the edge of white, even teeth.

"Yes," I said, replacing the lamp in the binnacle. The warm, heavy tropical night closed upon his head again.

"There's a ship over there," he murmured.

"Yes, I know. The *Sephora*. Did you know of us?"

"Hadn't the slightest idea. I am the mate of her—" He paused and corrected himself. "I should say I *was*."

"Aha! Something wrong?"

"Yes. Very wrong indeed. I've killed a man."

"What do you mean? Just now?"

"No, on the passage. Weeks ago. Thirty-nine south. When I say a man—"

"Fit of temper," I suggested confidently.

The shadowy, dark head, like mine, seemed to nod imperceptibly above the ghostly gray of my sleeping suit. It was, in the night, as though I had been faced by my own reflection in the depths of a sombre and immense mirror.

"A pretty thing to have to own up to for a Conway boy," [6] murmured my double distinctly.

"You're a Conway boy?"

6. The wooden battleship Conway, which was used to train young officers for the Royal Navy and merchant service. She ran aground in the Menai Straits (Wales) in 1953 and burned in 1956.

"I am," he said, as if startled. Then, slowly . . . "Perhaps you too . . ."

It was so; but being a couple of years older I had left before he joined. After a quick interchange of dates a silence fell; and I thought suddenly of my absurd mate with his terrific whiskers and the "Bless my soul—you don't say so" type of intellect. My double gave me an inkling of his thoughts by saying:

"My father's a parson in Norfolk. Do you see me before a judge and jury on that charge? For myself I can't see the necessity. There are fellows that an angel from heaven—And I am not that. He was one of those creatures that are just simmering all the time with a silly sort of wickedness. Miserable devils that have no business to live at all. He wouldn't do his duty and wouldn't let anybody else do theirs. But what's the good of talking! You know well enough the sort of ill-conditioned snarling cur . . ."

He appealed to me as if our experiences had been as identical as our clothes. And I knew well enough the pestiferous danger of such a character where there are no means of legal repression. And I knew well enough also that my double there was no homicidal ruffian. I did not think of asking him for details, and he told me the story roughly in brusque, disconnected sentences. I needed no more. I saw it all going on as though I were myself inside that other sleeping suit.

"It happened while we were setting a reefed foresail, at dusk. Reefed foresail! You understand the sort of weather. The only sail we had left to keep the ship running; so you may guess what it had been like for days. Anxious sort of job, that. He gave me some of his cursed insolence at the sheet.[7] I tell you I was overdone with this terrific weather that seemed to have no end to it. Terrific, I tell you—and a deep ship. I believe the fellow himself was half crazed with funk. It was no time for gentlemanly reproof, so I turned round and felled him like an ox. He up and at me. We closed just as an awful sea made for the ship. All hands saw it coming and took to the rigging, but I had him by the throat, and went on shaking him like a rat, the men above us yelling. 'Look out! Look out!' Then a crash as if the sky had fallen on my head. They say that for over ten minutes hardly anything was to be seen of the ship—just the three masts and a bit of the forecastle head and of the poop all awash driving along in a smother of foam. It was a miracle that they found us, jammed together behind the forebits. It's clear that I meant business, because I was holding him by the throat still when they picked us up. He was black in the face. It was too much for them. It seems they rushed us aft together, gripped as we were, screaming 'Murder!' like a lot of lunatics, and broke into the cuddy. And the ship running for her life, touch and go all the time, any minute her last in a sea fit to turn your hair gray only a-looking at it. I understand that the skipper, too, started raving like the rest of them. The man had been deprived of sleep for more than a week, and to have this sprung on him at the height of a furious gale nearly drove him out of his mind. I wonder they didn't fling me overboard after getting the carcass of their precious shipmate out of my fingers. They had

---

7. Rope or chain attached to lower corner of sail used for shortening or slackening it.

rather a job to separate us, I've been told. A sufficiently fierce story to make an old judge and a respectable jury sit up a bit. The first thing I heard when I came to myself was the maddening howling of that endless gale, and on that the voice of the old man. He was hanging on to my bunk, staring into my face out of his sou'wester.

" 'Mr. Leggatt, you have killed a man. You can act no longer as chief mate of this ship.' "

His care to subdue his voice made it sound monotonous. He rested a hand on the end of the skylight to steady himself with, and all that time did not stir a limb, so far as I could see. "Nice little tale for a quiet tea party," he concluded in the same tone.

One of my hands, too, rested on the end of the skylight; neither did I stir a limb, so far as I knew. We stood less than a foot from each other. It occurred to me that if old "Bless my soul—you don't say so" were to put his head up the companion and catch sight of us, he would think he was seeing double, or imagine himself come upon a scene of weird witchcraft: the strange captain having a quiet confabulation by the wheel with his own gray ghost. I became very much concerned to prevent anything of the sort. I heard the other's soothing undertone:

"My father's a parson in Norfolk," it said. Evidently he had forgotten he had told me this important fact before. Truly a nice little tale.

"You had better slip down into my stateroom now," I said, moving off stealthily. My double followed my movements; our bare feet made no sound; I let him in, closed the door with care, and, after giving a call to the second mate, returned on deck for my relief.

"Not much sign of any wind yet," I remarked when he approached.

"No, sir. Not much," he assented sleepily in his hoarse voice, with just enough deference, no more, and barely suppressing a yawn.

"Well, that's all you have to look out for. You have got your orders."

"Yes, sir."

I paced a turn or two on the poop and saw him take up his position face forward with his elbow in the ratlines of the mizzen-rigging before I went below. The mate's faint snoring was still going on peacefully. The cuddy lamp was burning over the table on which stood a vase with flowers, a polite attention from the ship's provision merchant —the last flowers we should see for the next three months at the very least. Two bunches of bananas hung from the beam symmetrically, one on each side of the rudder-casing. Everything was as before in the ship—except that two of her captain's sleeping suits were simultaneously in use, one motionless in the cuddy, the other keeping very still in the captain's stateroom.

It must be explained here that my cabin had the form of the capital letter L, the door being within the angle and opening into the short part of the letter. A couch was to the left, the bedplace to the right; my writing-desk and the chronometers' table faced the door. But any one opening it, unless he stepped right inside, had no view of what I call the long (or vertical) part of the letter. It contained some lockers surmounted by a bookcase; and a few clothes, a thick jacket or two, caps, oilskin coat, and such-like, hung on hooks. There was at the bottom of that part a door opening into my bathroom, which could be entered also directly from the saloon. But that way was never used.

The mysterious arrival had discovered the advantage of this particular shape. Entering my room, lighted strongly by a big bulkhead lamp swung on gimbals above my writing-desk, I did not see him anywhere till he stepped out quietly from behind the coats hung in the recessed part.

"I heard somebody moving about, and went in there at once," he whispered.

I, too, spoke under my breath.

"Nobody is likely to come in here without knocking and getting permission."

He nodded. His face was thin and the sunburn faded, as though he had been ill. And no wonder. He had been, I heard presently, kept under arrest in his cabin for nearly nine weeks. But there was nothing sickly in his eyes or in his expression. He was not a bit like me, really; yet, as we stood leaning over my bedplace, whispering side by side, with our dark heads together and our backs to the door, anybody bold enough to open it stealthily would have been treated to the uncanny sight of a double captain busy talking in whispers with his other self.

"But all this doesn't tell me how you came to hang on to our side-ladder," I inquired, in the hardly audible murmurs we used, after he had told me something more of the proceedings on board the *Sephora* once the bad weather was over.

"When we sighted Java Head[8] I had had time to think all those matters out several times over. I had six weeks of doing nothing else, and with only an hour or so every evening for a tramp on the quarterdeck."

He whispered, his arms folded on the side of my bedplace, staring through the open port. And I could imagine perfectly the manner of this thinking out—a stubborn if not a steadfast operation; something of which I should have been perfectly incapable.

"I reckoned it would be dark before we closed with the land," he continued, so low that I had to strain my hearing, near as we were to each other, shoulder touching shoulder almost. "So I asked to speak to the old man. He always seemed very sick when he came to see me—as if he could not look me in the face. You know, that foresail saved the ship. She was too deep to have run long under bare poles. And it was I that managed to set it for him. Anyway, he came. When I had him in my cabin—he stood by the door looking at me as if I had the halter round my neck already I asked him right away to leave my cabin door unlocked at night while the ship was going through Sunda Straits. There would be the Java coast within two or three miles, off Anjer Point. I wanted nothing more. I've had a prize for swimming my second year in the Conway."

"I can believe it," I breathed out.

"God only knows why they locked me in every night. To see some of their faces you'd have thought they were afraid I'd go about at

8. A famous landmark for clipper ships engaged in the China trade on the western end of Java, the southern entrance to the Sunda Straits mentioned below; the Leggatt incident thus took place some 1,500 miles south of the present scene.

night strangling people. Am I a murdering brute? Do I look it? By Jove! if I had been he wouldn't have trusted himself like that into my room. You'll say I might have chucked him aside and bolted out, there and then—it was dark already. Well, no. And for the same reason I wouldn't think of trying to smash the door. There would have been a rush to stop me at the noise, and I did not mean to get into a confounded scrimmage. Somebody else might have got killed—for I would not have broken out only to get chucked back, and I did not want any more of that work. He refused, looking more sick than ever. He was afraid of the men, and also of that old second mate of his who had been sailing with him for years—a gray-headed old humbug; and his steward, too, had been with him devil knows how long—seventeen years or more—a dogmatic sort of loafer who hated me like poison, just because I was the chief mate. No chief mate ever made more than one voyage in the *Sephora,* you know. Those two old chaps ran the ship. Devil only knows what the skipper wasn't afraid of (all his nerve went to pieces altogether in that hellish spell of bad weather we had)—of what the law would do to him—of his wife, perhaps. Oh yes! she's on board. Though I don't think she would have meddled. She would have been only too glad to have me out of the ship in any way. The 'brand of Cain' business, don't you see? That's all right. I was ready enough to go off wandering on the face of the earth—and that was price enough to pay for an Abel[9] of that sort. Anyhow, he wouldn't listen to me. 'This thing must take its course. I represent the law here.' He was shaking like a leaf. 'So you won't?' 'No!' 'Then I hope you will be able to sleep on that," I said, and turned my back on him. 'I wonder that *you* can,' cries he, and locks the door.

"Well, after that, I couldn't. Not very well. That was three weeks ago. We have had a slow passage through the Java Sea; drifted about Carimata[1] for ten days. When we anchored here they thought, I suppose, it was all right. The nearest land (and that's five miles) is the ship's destination; the consul would soon set about catching me; and there would have been no object in bolting to these islets there. I don't suppose there's a drop of water on them. I don't know how it was, but tonight that steward, after bringing me my supper, went out to let me eat it, and left the door unlocked. And I ate it—all there was, too. After I had finished I strolled out on the quarter-deck. I don't know that I meant to do anything. A breath of fresh air was all I wanted, I believe. Then a sudden temptation came over me. I kicked off my slippers and was in the water before I had made up my mind fairly. Somebody heard the splash and they raised an awful hullabaloo. 'He's gone! Lower the boats! He's committed suicide! No, he's swimming.' Certainly I was swimming. It's not easy for a swimmer like me to commit suicide by drowning. I landed on the nearest islet before the boat left the ship's side. I heard them pulling

---

9. In *Genesis* (4:14-15) Cain says to the Lord, "Behold, though hast driven me out this day from the face of the earth; and from thy face shall I be hid; and I shall be a fugitive and a vagabond in the earth; and it shall come to pass, that every one that findeth me shall slay me. And the Lord said unto him, Therefore whosoever slayeth Cain, vengeance shall be taken on him sevenfold. And the Lord set a mark upon Cain, lest any finding him should kill him."

1. The Karimata Islands in the straits between Borneo and Sumatra, some three hundred miles northeast of the Sunda Straits.

about in the dark, hailing, and so on, but after a bit they gave up. Everything quieted down and the anchorage became as still as death. I sat down on a stone and began to think. I felt certain they would start searching for me at daylight. There was no place to hide on those stony things—and if there had been, what would have been the good? But now I was clear of that ship, I was not going back. So after a while I took off all my clothes, tied them up in a bundle with a stone inside, and dropped them in the deep water on the outer side of that islet. That was suicide enough for me. Let them think what they liked, but I didn't mean to drown myself. I meant to swim till I sank—but that's not the same thing. I struck out for another of these little islands, and it was from that one that I first saw your riding-light. Something to swim for. I went on easily, and on the way I came upon a flat rock a foot or two above water. In the day-time, I dare say, you might make it out with a glass from your poop. I scrambled up on it and rested myself for a bit. Then I made another start. That last spell must have been over a mile."

His whisper was getting fainter and fainter, and all the time he stared straight out through the porthole, in which there was not even a star to be seen. I had not interrupted him. There was something that made comment impossible, in his narrative, or perhaps in himself; a sort of feeling, a quality, which I can't find a name for. And when he ceased, all I found was a futile whisper, "So you swam for our light?"

"Yes—straight for it. It was something to swim for. I couldn't see any stars low down because the coast was in the way, and I couldn't see the land, either. The water was like glass. One might have been swimming in a confounded thousand feet deep cistern with no place for scrambling out anywhere; but what I didn't like was the notion of swimming round and round like a crazed bullock before I gave out; and as I didn't mean to go back . . . No. Do you see me being hauled back, stark naked, off one of these little islands by the scruff of the neck and fighting like a wild beast? Somebody would have got killed for certain, and I did not want any of that. So I went on. Then your ladder—"

"Why didn't you hail the ship?" I asked, a little louder.

He touched my shoulder lightly. Lazy footsteps came right over our heads and stopped. The second mate had crossed from the other side of the poop and might have been hanging over the rail, for all we knew.

"He couldn't hear us talking—could he?" My double breathed into my very ear anxiously.

His anxiety was an answer, a sufficient answer, to the question I had put to him. An answer containing all the difficulty of that situation. I closed the porthole quietly, to make sure. A louder word might have been overheard.

"Who's that?" he whispered then.

"My second mate. But I don't know much more of the fellow than you do."

And I told him a little about myself. I had been appointed to take charge while I least expected anything of the sort, not quite a fort-night ago. I didn't know either the ship or the people. Hadn't had the time in port to look about me or size anybody up. And as to the crew, all they knew was that I was appointed to take the ship home. For the rest, I was almost as much of a stranger on board as himself, I said. And at the moment I felt it most acutely. I felt that it would take very little to make me a suspect person in the eyes of the ship's company.

He had turned about meantime; and we, the two strangers in the ship, faced each other in identical attitudes.

"Your ladder—" he murmured, after a silence. "Who'd have thought of finding a ladder hanging over at night in a ship anchored out here! I felt just then a very unpleasant faintness. After the life I've been leading for nine weeks, anybody would have got out of condition. I wasn't capable of swimming round as far as your rudder-chains. And, lo and behold! there was a ladder to get hold of. After I gripped it I said to myself, 'What's the good?' When I saw a man's head looking over I thought I would swim away presently and leave him shouting—in whatever language it was. I didn't mind being looked at. I—I liked it. And then you speaking to me so quietly—as if you had expected me—made me hold on a little longer. It had been a confounded lonely time—I don't mean while swimming. I was glad to talk a little to somebody that didn't belong to the *Sephora*. As to asking for the captain, that was a mere impulse. It could have been no use, with all the ship knowing about me and the other people pretty certain to be round here in the morning. I don't know—I wanted to be seen, to talk with somebody, before I went on. I don't know what I would have said. . . . 'Fine night, isn't it?' or something of the sort."

"Do you think they will be round here presently?" I asked, with some incredulity.

"Quite likely," he said faintly.

He looked extremely haggard all of a sudden. His head rolled on his shoulders.

"H'm. We shall see then. Meantime get into that bed," I whispered. "Want help? There."

It was a rather high bedplace with a set of drawers underneath. This amazing swimmer really needed the lift I gave him by seizing his leg. He tumbled in, rolled over on his back, and flung one arm across his eyes. And then, with his face nearly hidden, he must have looked exactly as I used to look in that bed. I gazed upon my other self for a while before drawing across carefully the two green serge curtains which ran on a brass rod. I thought for a moment of pinning them together for greater safety, but I sat down on the couch, and once there I felt unwilling to rise and hunt for a pin. I would do it in a moment. I was extremely tired, in a peculiarly intimate way, by the strain of stealthiness, by the effort of whispering, and the general secrecy of this excitement. It was three o'clock by now, and I had been on my feet since nine, but I was not sleepy; I could not have gone to sleep. I sat there, fagged out, looking at the curtains, trying to clear my mind of the confused sensation of being in two places at once, and greatly bothered by an exasperating knocking in my head. It was a relief to discover suddenly that it was not in my head at all, but on the outside of the door. Before I could collect myself, the words "Come in" were out of my mouth, and the steward entered with a tray, bringing in my morning coffee. I had slept, after all, and I was so frightened that I shouted, "This way! I am here, steward," as though he had been miles away. He put down the tray on the table next the couch and only then said, very quietly, "I can see you are here, sir." I felt him give me a keen look, but I dared not meet his eyes just then. He must have wondered why I had drawn the curtains of my bed before going to sleep on the couch. He went out, hooking the door open as usual.

I heard the crew washing decks above me. I knew I would have been told at once if there had been any wind. Calm, I thought, and I was doubly vexed. Indeed, I felt dual more than ever. The steward reappeared suddenly in the doorway. I jumped up from the couch so quickly that he gave a start.

"What do you want here?"

"Close your port, sir—they are washing decks."

"It is closed," I said, reddening.

"Very well, sir." But he did not move from the doorway and returned my stare in an extraordinary, equivocal manner for a time. Then his eyes wavered, all his expression changed, and in a voice unusually gentle, almost coaxingly.

"May I come in to take the empty cup away, sir?"

"Of course!" I turned my back on him while he popped in and out. Then I unhooked and closed the door and even pushed the bolt. This sort of thing could not go on very long. The cabin was as hot as an oven, too. I took a peep at my double, and discovered that he had not moved; his arm was still over his eyes; but his chest heaved, his hair was wet, his chin glistened with perspiration. I reached over him and opened the port.

"I must show myself on deck," I reflected.

Of course, theoretically, I could do what I liked, with no one to say nay to me within the whole circle of the horizon; but to lock my cabin door and take the key away I did not dare. Directly I put my head out of the companion I saw the group of my two officers, the second mate barefooted, the chief mate in long india-rubber boots, near the break of the poop, and the steward half-way down the poop ladder talking to them eagerly. He happened to catch sight of me and dived, the second ran down on the main deck shouting some order or other, and the chief mate came to meet me, touching his cap.

There was a sort of curiosity in his eye that I did not like. I don't know whether the steward had told them that I was "queer" only, or downright drunk, but I know the man meant to have a good look at me. I watched him coming with a smile which, as he got into point-blank range, took effect and froze his very whiskers. I did not give him time to open his lips.

"Square the yards by lifts and braces before the hands go to breakfast."

It was the first particular order I had given on board that ship; and I stayed on deck to see it executed too. I had felt the need of asserting myself without loss of time. That sneering young cub got taken down a peg or two on that occasion, and I also seized the opportunity of having a good look at the face of every foremast man as they filed past me to go to the after braces. At breakfast time, eating nothing myself, I presided with such frigid dignity that the two mates were only too glad to escape from the cabin as soon as decency permitted; and all the time the dual working of my mind distracted me almost to the point of insanity. I was constantly watching myself, my secret self, as dependent on my actions as my own personality, sleeping in that bed, behind that door which faced me as I sat at the head of the table. It was very much like being mad, only it was worse, because one was aware of it.

I had to shake him for a solid minute, but when at last he opened his eyes it was in the full possession of his senses, with an inquiring look.

"All's well so far," I whispered. "Now you must vanish into the bathroom."

He did so, as noiseless as a ghost, and I then rang for the steward, and facing him boldly, directed him to tidy up my stateroom while I was having my bath—"and be quick about it." As my tone admitted of no excuses, he said, "Yes, sir," and ran off to fetch his dustpan and brushes. I took a bath and did most of my dressing, splashing, and whistling softly for the steward's edification, while the secret sharer of my life stood drawn bolt upright in that little space, his face looking very sunken in daylight, his eyelids lowered under the stern, dark line of his eyebrows drawn together by a slight frown.

When I left him there to go back to my room the steward was finishing dusting. I sent for the mate and engaged him in some insignificant conversation. It was, as it were, trifling with the terrific character of his whiskers; but my object was to give him an opportunity for a good look at my cabin. And then I could at last shut, with a clear conscience, the door of my stateroom and get my double back into the recessed part. There was nothing else for it. He had to sit still on a small folding stool, half smothered by the heavy coats hanging there. We listened to the steward going into the bathroom out of the saloon, filling the water-bottles there, scrubbing the bath, setting things to rights, whisk, bang, clatter—out again into the saloon —turn the key—click. Such was my scheme for keeping my second self invisible. Nothing better could be contrived under the circumstances. And there we sat: I at my writing-desk ready to appear busy with some papers, he behind me, out of sight of the door. It would not have been prudent to talk in daytime; and I could not have stood the excitement of that queer sense of whispering to myself. Now and then, glancing over my shoulder, I saw him far back there, sitting rigidly on the low stool, his bare feet close together, his arms folded, his head hanging on his breast—and perfectly still. Anybody would have taken him for me.

I was fascinated by it myself. Every moment I had to glance over my shoulder. I was looking at him when a voice outside the door said:

"Beg pardon, sir."

"Well!" . . . I kept my eyes on him, and so when the voice outside the door announced, "There's a ship's boat coming our way, sir," I saw him give a start—the first movement he had made for hours. But he did not raise his bowed head.

"All right. Get the ladder over."

I hesitated. Should I whisper something to him? But what? His immobility seemed to have been never disturbed. What could I tell him he did not know already? . . . Finally I went on deck.

2

The skipper of the *Sephora* had a thin, red whisker all round his face, and the sort of complexion that goes with hair of that color; also the particular, rather smeary shade of blue in the eyes. He was not exactly a showy figure; his shoulders were high, his stature but middling—one leg slightly more bandy than the other. He shook hands, looking vaguely around. A spiritless tenacity was his main characteristic, I judged. I behaved with a politeness which seemed to disconcert him. Perhaps he was shy. He mumbled to me as if he were ashamed of what he was saying; gave his name (it was something like Archbold—but at this distance of years I hardly am sure), his ship's name, and a few other particulars of that sort, in the manner of a criminal making a reluctant and doleful confession. He had had terrible weather on the passage out—terrible—terrible—wife aboard, too.

By this time we were seated in the cabin and the steward brought in a tray with a bottle and glasses. "Thanks! No." Never took liquor. Would have some water, though. He drank two tumblerfuls. Terrible thirsty work. Ever since daylight had been exploring the islands round his ship.

"What was that for—fun?" I asked with an appearance of polite interest.

"No!" He sighed. "Painful duty."

As he persisted in his mumbling and I wanted my double to hear every word, I hit upon the notion of informing him that I regretted to say I was hard of hearing.

"Such a young man too!" he nodded, keeping his smeary, blue, unintelligent eyes fastened upon me. "What was the cause of it—some disease?" he inquired, without the least sympathy and as if he thought that, if so, I'd got no more than I deserved.

"Yes; disease," I admitted in a cheerful tone which seemed to shock him. But my point was gained, because he had to raise his voice to give me his tale. It is not worth while to record that version. It was just over two months since all this had happened, and he had thought so much about it that he seemed completely muddled as to its bearings, but still immensely impressed.

"What would you think of such a thing happening on board your own ship? I've had the *Sephora* for these fifteen years. I am a well-known shipmaster."

He was densely distressed—and perhaps I should have sympathized with him if I had been able to detach my mental vision from the unsuspected sharer of my cabin as though he were my second self. There he was on the other side of the bulkhead, four or five feet from us, no more, as we sat in the saloon. I looked politely at Captain Archbold (if that was his name), but it was the other I saw, in a gray sleeping suit, seated on a low stool, his bare feet close together, his arms folded, and every word said between us falling into the ears of his dark head bowed on his chest.

"I have been at sea now, man and boy, for seven and thirty years, and I've never heard of such a thing happening in an English ship. And that it should be my ship. Wife on board, too."

I was hardly listening to him.

"Don't you think," I said, "that the heavy sea which, you told me, came aboard just then might have killed the man? I have seen the sheer weight of a sea kill a man very neatly, by simply breaking his neck."

"Good God!" he uttered impressively, fixing his smeary blue eyes on me. "The sea! No man killed by the sea ever looked like that." He seemed positively scandalized at my suggestion. And as I gazed at him, certainly not prepared for anything original on his part, he advanced his head close to mine and thrust his tongue out at me so suddenly that I couldn't help starting back.

After scoring over my calmness in this graphic way he nodded wisely. If I had seen the sight, he assured me, I would never forget it as long as I lived. The weather was too bad to give the corpse a proper sea burial. So next day at dawn they took it up on the poop, covering its face with a bit of bunting; he read a short prayer, and then, just as it was, in its oilskins and long boots, they launched it amongst those mountainous seas that seemed ready every moment to swallow up the ship herself and the terrified lives on board of her.

"That reefed foresail saved you," I threw in.

"Under God—it did," he exclaimed fervently. "It was by a special mercy, I firmly believe, that it stood some of those hurricane squalls."

"It was the setting of that sail which—" I began.

"God's own hand in it," he interrupted me. "Nothing less could have done it. I don't mind telling you that I hardly dared give the order. It seemed impossible that we could touch anything without losing it, and then our last hope would have been gone."

The terror of that gale was on him yet. I let him go on for a bit, then said casually—as if returning to a minor subject:

"You were very anxious to give up your mate to the shore people, I believe?"

He was. To the law. His obscure tenacity on that point had in it something incomprehensible and a little awful; something, as it were, mystical, quite apart from his anxiety that he should not be suspected of "countenancing any doings of that sort." Seven and thirty virtuous years at sea, of which over twenty of immaculate command, and the last fifteen in the *Sephora*, seemed to have laid him under some pitiless obligation.

"And you know," he went on, groping shamefacedly amongst his feelings, "I did not engage that young fellow. His people had some interest with my owners. I was in a way forced to take him on. He looked very smart, very gentlemanly, and all that. But do you know—

I never liked him, somehow. I am a plain man. You see, he wasn't exactly the sort for the chief mate of a ship like the *Sephora*."

I had become so connected in thoughts and impressions with the secret sharer of my cabin that I felt as if I, personally, were being given to understand that I, too, was not the sort that would have done for the chief mate of a ship like the *Sephora*. I had no doubt of it in my mind.

"Not at all the style of man. You understand," he insisted superfluously, looking hard at me.

I smiled urbanely. He seemed at a loss for a while.

"I suppose I must report a suicide."

"Beg pardon?"

"Sui-cide! That's what I'll have to write to my owners directly I get in."

"Unless you manage to recover him before tomorrow," I assented dispassionately. . . . "I mean, alive."

He mumbled something which I really did not catch, and I turned my ear to him in a puzzled manner. He fairly bawled:

"The land—I say, the mainland is at least seven miles off my anchorage."

"About that."

My lack of excitement, of curiosity, of surprise, of any sort of pronounced interest, began to arouse his distrust. But except for the felicitous pretense of deafness I had not tried to pretend anything. I had felt utterly incapable of playing the part of ignorance properly, and therefore was afraid to try. It is also certain that he had brought some ready-made suspicions with him, and that he viewed my politeness as a strange and unnatural phenomenon. And yet how else could I have received him? Not heartily! That was impossible for psychological reasons, which I need not state here. My only object was to keep off his inquiries. Surlily? Yes, but surliness might have provoked a point-blank question. From its novelty to him and from its nature, punctilious courtesy was the manner best calculated to restrain the man. But there was the danger of his breaking through my defense bluntly. I could not, I think, have met him by a direct lie, also for psychological (not moral) reasons. If he had only known how afraid I was of his putting my feeling of identity with the other to the test! But, strangely enough (I thought of it only afterward), I believe that he was not a little disconcerted by the reverse side of that weird situation, by something in me that reminded him of the man he was seeking—suggested a mysterious similitude to the young fellow he had distrusted and disliked from the first.

However that might have been, the silence was not very prolonged. He took another oblique step.

"I reckon I had no more than a two-mile pull to your ship. Not a bit more."

"And quite enough, too, in this awful heat," I said.

Another pause full of mistrust followed. Necessity, they say, is mother of invention, but fear, too, is not barren of ingenious suggestions. And I was afraid he would ask me point-blank for news of my other self.

"Nice little saloon, isn't it?" I remarked, as if noticing for the first time the way his eyes roamed from one closed door to the other. "And very well fitted out, too. Here, for instance," I continued, reaching over the back of my seat negligently and flinging the door open, "is my bathroom."

He made an eager movement, but hardly gave it a glance. I got up, shut the door of the bathroom, and invited him to have a look round, as if I were very proud of my accommodation. He had to rise and be shown round, but he went through the business without any raptures whatever.

"And now we'll have a look at my stateroom," I declared, in a voice as loud as I dared to make it, crossing the cabin to the starboard side with purposely heavy steps.

He followed me in and gazed around. My intelligent double had vanished. I played my part.

"Very convenient—isn't it?"

"Very nice. Very comf . . ." He didn't finish, and went out brusquely as if to escape from some unrighteous wiles of mine. But it was not to be. I had been too frightened not to feel vengeful; I felt I had him on the run, and I meant to keep him on the run. My polite insistence must have had something menacing in it, because he gave in suddenly. And I did not let him off a single item: mates' rooms, pantry, storerooms, the very sail-locker, which was also under the poop—he had to look into them all. When at last I showed him out on the quarter-deck he drew a long, spiritless sigh, and mumbled dismally that he must really be going back to his ship now. I desired my mate, who had joined us, to see to the captain's boat.

The man of whiskers gave a blast on the whistle which he used to wear hanging round his neck, and yelled, "*Sephora's* away!" My double down there in my cabin must have heard, and certainly could not feel more relieved than I. Four fellows came running out from somewhere forward and went over the side, while my own men, appearing on deck too, lined the rail. I escorted my visitor to the gangway ceremoniously, and nearly overdid it. He was a tenacious beast. On the very ladder he lingered, and in that unique, guiltily conscientious manner of sticking to the point:

"I say . . . you . . . you don't think that—"

I covered his voice loudly.

"Certainly not. . . . I am delighted. Goodbye."

I had an idea of what he meant to say, and just saved myself by the privilege of defective hearing. He was too shaken generally to insist, but my mate, close witness of that parting, looked mystified and his face took on a thoughtful cast. As I did not want to appear as if I wished to avoid all communication with my officers, he had the opportunity to address me.

"Seems a very nice man. His boat's crew told our chaps a very extraordinary story, if what I am told by the steward is true. I suppose you had it from the captain, sir?"

"Yes. I had a story from the captain."

"A very horrible affair—isn't it, sir?"

"It is."

"Beats all these tales we hear about murders in Yankee ships."

"I don't think it beats them. I don't think it resembles them in the least."

"Bless my soul—you don't say so! But of course I've no acquaintance whatever with American ships, not I, so I couldn't go against your knowledge. It's horrible enough for me. . . . But the queerest part is that those fellows seemed to have some idea the man was hidden aboard here. They had really. Did you ever hear of such a thing?"

"Preposterous—isn't it?"

We were walking to and fro athwart the quarter-deck. No one of the crew forward could be seen (the day was Sunday), and the mate pursued:

"There was some little dispute about it. Our chaps took offense. 'As if we would harbor a thing like that,' they said. 'Wouldn't you like to look for him in our coal-hole?' Quite a tiff. But they made it up in the end. I suppose he did drown himself. Don't you, sir?"

"I don't suppose anything."

"You have no doubt in the matter, sir?"

"None whatever."

I left him suddenly. I felt I was producing a bad impression, but with my double down there it was most trying to be on deck. And it was almost as trying to be below. Altogether a nerve-trying situation. But on the whole I felt less torn in two when I was with him. There was no one in the whole ship whom I dared take into my confidence. Since the hands had got to know his story, it would have been impossible to pass him off for any one else, and an accidental discovery was to be dreaded now more than ever. . . .

The steward being engaged in laying the table for dinner, we could talk only with our eyes when I first went down. Later in the afternoon we had a cautious try at whispering. The Sunday quietness of the ship was against us; the stillness of air and water around her was against us; the elements, the men were against us—everything was against us in our secret partnership; time itself—for this could not go on for ever. The very trust in Providence was, I supposed, denied to his guilt. Shall I confess that this thought cast me down very much? And as to the chapter of accidents which counts for so much in the book of success, I could only hope that it was closed. For what favorable accident could be expected?

"Did you hear everything?" were my first words as soon as we took up our position side by side, leaning over my bedplace.

He had. And the proof of it was his earnest whisper, "The man told you he hardly dared to give the order."

I understood the reference to be to that saving foresail.

"Yes. He was afraid of it being lost in the setting."

"I assure you he never gave the order. He may think he did, but he never gave it. He stood there with me on the break of the poop after the maintopsail blew away, and whimpered about our last hope —positively whimpered about it and nothing else—and the night coming on! To hear one's skipper go on like that in such weather was enough to drive any fellow out of his mind. It worked me up into a sort of desperation. I just took it into my own hands and. went away from him, boiling, and—But what's the use telling you? *You* know! . . . Do you think that if I had not been pretty fierce with them I should have got the men to do anything? Not it! The boss'en² perhaps? Perhaps! It wasn't a heavy sea—it was a sea gone mad! I suppose the end of the world will be something like that; and a man may have the heart to see it coming once and be done with it—but to have to face it day after day . . . I don't blame anybody. I was precious little better than the rest. Only—I was an officer of that old coal-wagon, anyhow. . . ."

"I quite understand," I conveyed that sincere assurance into his ear. He was out of breath with whispering; I could hear him pant slightly. It was all very simple. The same strung-up force which had given twenty-four men a chance, at least, for their lives had, in a sort of recoil, crushed an unworthy mutinous existence.

But I had no leisure to weigh the merits of the matter—footsteps in the saloon, a heavy knock. "There's enough wind to get under way with, sir." Here was the call of a new claim upon my thoughts and even upon my feelings.

"Turn the hands up," I cried through the door. "I'll be on deck directly."

I was going out to make the acquaintance of my ship. Before I left the cabin our eyes met—the eyes of the only two strangers on board. I pointed to the recessed part where the little camp-stool awaited him and laid my finger on my lips. He made a gesture—somewhat vague—a little mysterious, accompanied by a faint smile, as if of regret.

This is not the place to enlarge upon the sensations of a man who feels for the first time a ship move under his feet to his own independent word. In my case they were not unalloyed. I was not wholly alone with my command; for there was that stranger in my cabin. Or, rather, I was not completely and wholly with her. Part of me was absent. That mental feeling of being in two places at once affected me physically as if the mood of secrecy had penetrated my very soul. Before an hour had elapsed since the ship had begun to move, having occasion to ask the mate (he stood by my side) to take a compass bearing of the Pagoda, I caught myself reaching up to his ear in whispers. I say I caught myself, but enough had escaped to startle the man. I can't describe it otherwise than by saying that he shied. A grave, preoccupied manner, as though he were in possession of some perplexing intelligence, did not leave him henceforth. A little later I moved away from the rail to look at the compass with such a stealthy gait that the helmsman noticed it—and I could not help noticing the unusual roundness of his eyes. These are trifling instances, though it's to no commander's advantage to be suspected of ludicrous eccentricities. But I was also more seriously affected. There are to a seaman certain words, gestures, that should in given conditions come as naturally, as instinctively, as the winking of a menaced eye. A certain order should spring on to his lips without thinking; a certain sign

2. *Bosun* or *boatswain*, petty officer in charge of deck crew and of rigging.

should get itself made, so to speak, without reflection. But all unconscious alertness had abandoned me. I had to make an effort of will to
recall myself back (from the cabin) to the conditions of the moment.
I felt that I was appearing an irresolute commander to those people
who were watching me more or less critically.

And, besides, there were the scares. On the second day out, for
instance, coming off the deck in the afternoon (I had straw slippers
on my bare feet) I stopped at the open pantry door and spoke to the
steward. He was doing something there with his back to me. At the
sound of my voice he nearly jumped out of his skin, as the saying is,
and incidentally broke a cup.

"What on earth's the matter with you?" I asked, astonished.

He was extremely confused. "Beg your pardon, sir. I made sure
you were in your cabin."

"You see I wasn't."

"No, sir. I could have sworn I had heard you moving in there
not a moment ago. It's most extraordinary . . . very sorry, sir."

I passed on with an inward shudder. I was so identified with my
secret double that I did not even mention the fact in those scanty,
fearful whispers we exchanged. I suppose he had made some slight
noise of some kind or other. It would have been miraculous if he
hadn't at one time or another. And yet, haggard as he appeared,
he looked always perfectly self-controled, more than calm—almost
invulnerable. On my suggestion he remained almost entirely in the
bathroom, which, upon the whole, was the safest place. There could
be really no shadow of an excuse for any one ever wanting to go in
there, once the steward had done with it. It was a very tiny place.
Sometimes he reclined on the floor, his legs bent, his head sustained
on one elbow. At others I would find him on the camp-stool, sitting
in his gray sleeping suit and with his cropped dark hair like a patient,
unmoved convict. At night I would smuggle him into my bedplace,
and we would whisper together, with the regular footfalls of the
officer of the watch passing and repassing over our heads. It was an
infinitely miserable time. It was lucky that some tins of fine preserves were stowed in a locker in my stateroom; hard bread I could
always get hold of; and so he lived on stewed chicken, pâté de foie
gras, asparagus, cooked oysters, sardines—on all sorts of abominable
sham-delicacies out of tins. My early morning coffee he always drank;
and it was all I dared do for him in that respect.

Every day there was the horrible maneuvering to go through so
that my room and then the bathroom should be done in the usual
way. I came to hate the sight of the steward, to abhor the voice of
that harmless man. I felt that it was he who would bring on the
disaster of discovery. It hung like a sword over our heads.

The fourth day out, I think (we were then working down the east
side of the Gulf of Siam, tack for tack,[3] in light winds and smooth
water)—the fourth day, I say, of this miserable juggling with the
unavoidable, as we sat at our evening meal, that man, whose slightest

3. By a series of shiftings back and forth of sails.

movement I dreaded, after putting down the dishes ran up on deck busily. This could not be dangerous. Presently he came down again; and then it appeared that he had remembered a coat of mine which I had thrown over a rail to dry after having been wetted in a shower which had passed over the ship in the afternoon. Sitting stolidly at the head of the table I became terrified at the sight of the garment on his arm. Of course he made for my door. There was no time to lose.

"Steward!" I thundered. My nerves were so shaken that I could not govern my voice and conceal my agitation. This was the sort of thing that made my terrifically whiskered mate tap his forehead with his forefinger. I had detected him using that gesture while talking on deck with a confidential air to the carpenter. It was too far to hear a word, but I had no doubt that this pantomime could only refer to the strange new captain.

"Yes, sir," the pale-faced steward turned resignedly to me. It was this maddening course of being shouted at, checked without rhyme or reason, arbitrarily chased out of my cabin, suddenly called into it, sent flying out of his pantry on incomprehensible errands, that accounted for the growing wretchedness of his expression.

"Where are you going with that coat?"

"To your room, sir."

"Is there another shower coming?"

"I'm sure I don't know, sir. Shall I go up again and see, sir?"

"No! never mind."

My object was attained, as of course my other self in there would have heard everything that passed. During this interlude my two officers never raised their eyes off their respective plates; but the lip of that confounded cub, the second mate, quivered visibly.

I expected the steward to hook my coat on and come out at once. He was very slow about it; but I dominated my nervousness sufficiently not to shout after him. Suddenly I became aware (it could be heard plainly enough) that the fellow for some reason or other was opening the door of the bathroom. It was the end. The place was literally not big enough to swing a cat in. My voice died in my throat and I went stony all over. I expected to hear a yell of surprise and terror, and made a movement, but had not the strength to get on my legs. Everything remained still. Had my second self taken the poor wretch by the throat? I don't know what I could have done next moment if I had not seen the steward come out of my room, close the door, and then stand quietly by the sideboard.

"Saved," I thought. "But, no! Lost! Gone! He was gone!"

I laid my knife and fork down and leaned back in my chair. My head swam. After a while, when sufficiently recovered to speak in a steady voice, I instructed my mate to put the ship round at eight o'clock himself.

"I won't come on deck," I went on. "I think I'll turn in, and unless the wind shifts I don't want to be disturbed before midnight. I feel a bit seedy."

"You did look middling bad a little while ago," the chief mate remarked without showing any great concern.

They both went out, and I stared at the steward clearing the table. There was nothing to be read on that wretched man's face. But why did he avoid my eyes? I asked myself. Then I thought I should like to hear the sound of his voice.

"Steward!"

"Sir!" Startled as usual.

"Where did you hang up that coat?"

"In the bathroom, sir." The usual anxious tone. "It's not quite dry yet, sir."

For some time longer I sat in the cuddy. Had my double vanished as he had come? But of his coming there was an explanation, whereas his disappearance would be inexplicable. . . . I went slowly into my dark room, shut the door, lighted the lamp, and for a time dared not turn round. When at last I did I saw him standing bolt upright in the narrow recessed part. It would not be true to say I had a shock, but an irresistible doubt of his bodily existence flitted through my mind. Can it be, I asked myself, that he is not visible to other eyes than mine? It was like being haunted. Motionless, with a grave face, he raised his hands slightly at me in a gesture which meant clearly, "Heavens! what a narrow escape!" Narrow indeed. I think I had come creeping quietly as near insanity as any man who his not actually gone over the border. That gesture restrained me, so to speak.

The mate with the terrific whiskers was now putting the ship on the other tack. In the moment of profound silence which follows upon the hands going to their stations I heard on the poop his raised voice: "Hard alee!"[4] and the distant shout of the order repeated on the main deck. The sails, in that light breeze, made but a faint fluttering noise. It ceased. The ship was coming round slowly; I held my breath in the renewed stillness of expectation; one wouldn't have thought that there was a single living soul on her decks. A sudden brisk shout, "Mainsail haul!" broke the spell, and in the noisy cries and rush overhead of the men running away with the main brace we two, down in my cabin, came together in our usual position by the bedplace.

He did not wait for my question. "I heard him fumbling here and just managed to squat myself down in the bath," he whispered to me. "The fellow only opened the door and put his arm in to hang the coat up. All the same. . . ."

"I never thought of that," I whispered back, even more appalled than before at the closeness of the shave, and marveling at that something unyielding in his character which was carrying him through so finely. There was no agitation in his whisper. Whoever was being driven distracted, it was not he. He was sane. And the proof of his sanity was continued when he took up the whispering again.

"It would never do for me to come to life again."

It was something that a ghost might have said. But what he was alluding to was his old captain's reluctant admission of the theory of suicide. It would obviously serve his turn—if I had understood at all the view which seemed to govern the unalterable purpose of his action.

"You must maroon me as soon as ever you can get amongst these islands off the Cambodje[5] shore," he went on.

4. Put the helm all the way over to the side away from the wind.

5. Cambodian.

"Maroon you! We are not living in a boy's adventure tale," I protested. His scornful whispering took me up.

"We aren't indeed! There's nothing of a boy's tale in this. But there's nothing else for it. I want no more. You don't suppose I am afraid of what can be done to me? Prison or gallows or whatever they may please. But you don't see me coming back to explain such things to an old fellow in a wig and twelve respectable tradesmen, do you? What can they know whether I am guilty or not—or of *what* I am guilty, either? That's my affair. What does the Bible say? 'Driven off the face of the earth.'⁶ Very well. I am off the face of the earth now. As I came at night so I shall go."

"Impossible!" I murmured. "You can't."

"Can't? . . . Not naked like a soul on the Day of Judgment. I shall freeze on to this sleeping suit. The Last Day is not yet—and . . . you have understood thoroughly. Didn't you?"

I felt suddenly ashamed of myself. I may say truly that I understood—and my hesitation in letting that man swim away from my ship's side had been a mere sham sentiment, a sort of cowardice.

"It can't be done now till next night," I breathed out. "The ship is on the offshore tack and the wind may fail us."

"As long as I know that you understand," he whispered. "But of course you do. It's a great satisfaction to have got somebody to understand. You seem to have been there on purpose." And in the same whisper, as if we two whenever we talked had to say things to each other which were not fit for the world to hear, he added, "It's very wonderful."

We remained side by side talking in our secret way—but sometimes silent or just exchanging a whispered word or two at long intervals. And as usual he stared through the port. A breath of wind came now and again into our faces. The ship might have been moored in dock, so gently and on an even keel she slipped through the water, that did not murmur even at our passage, shadowy and silent like a phantom sea.

At midnight I went on deck, and to my mate's great surprise put the ship round on the other tack. His terrible whiskers flitted round me in silent criticism. I certainly should not have done it if it had been only a question of getting out of that sleepy gulf as quickly as possible. I believe he told the second mate, who relieved him, that it was a great want of judgment. The other only yawned. That intolerable cub shuffled about so sleepily and lolled against the rails in such a slack, improper fashion that I came down on him sharply.

"Aren't you properly awake yet?"

"Yes, sir! I am awake."

"Well, then, be good enough to hold yourself as if you were. And keep a look out. If there's any current we'll be closing with some islands long before daylight."

The east side of the gulf is fringed with islands, some solitary, others in groups. On the blue background of the high coast they seem to float on silvery patches of calm water, arid and gray, or dark green and rounded like clumps of evergreen bushes, with the larger

6. See note 9 above.

ones, a mile or two long, showing the outlines of ridges, ribs of gray
rock under the dank mantle of matted leafage. Unknown to trade, to
travel, almost to geography, the manner of life they harbor is an unsolved secret. There must be villages—settlements of fishermen at least
—on the largest of them, and some communication with the world is
probably kept up by native craft. But all that forenoon, as we headed
for them, fanned along by the faintest of breezes, I saw no sign of
man or canoe in the field of the telescope I kept on pointing at the
scattered group.

At noon I gave no orders for a change of course, and the mate's
whiskers became much concerned and seemed to be offering themselves unduly to my notice. At last I said:

"I am going to stand right in. Quite in—as far as I can take her."

The stare of extreme surprise imparted an air of ferocity also to
his eyes, and he looked truly terrific for a moment.

"We're not doing well in the middle of the gulf," I continued
casually. "I am going to look for the land breezes tonight."

"Bless my soul! Do you mean, sir, in the dark amongst the lot
of all them islands and reefs and shoals?"

"Well, if there are any regular land breezes at all on this coast
one must get close inshore to find them—mustn't one?"

"Bless my soul!" he exclaimed again under his breath. All that
afternoon he wore a dreamy, comtemplative appearance which in
him was a mark of perplexity. After dinner I went into my stateroom as if I meant to take some rest. There we two bent our dark
heads over a half-unrolled chart lying on my bed.

"There," I said. "It's got to be Koh-ring.[7] I've been looking at it
ever since sunrise. It has got two hills and a low point. It must be
inhabited. And on the coast opposite there is what looks like the
mouth of a biggish river—with some town, no doubt, not far up. It's
the best chance for you that I can see."

"Anything. Koh-ring let it be."

He looked thoughtfully at the chart as if surveying chances and
distances from a lofty height—and following with his eyes his own
figure wandering on the blank land of Cochin-China, and then passing off that piece of paper clean out of sight into uncharted regions.
And it was as if the ship had two captains to plan her course for her.
I had been so worried and restless running up and down that I had
not had the patience to dress that day. I had remained in my sleeping
suit, with straw slippers and a soft floppy hat. The closeness of the
heat in the gulf had been most oppressive, and the crew were used
to see me wandering in that airy attire.

"She will clear the south point as she heads now," I whispered
into his ear. "Goodness only knows when, though—but certainly after
dark. I'll edge her in to half a mile, as far as I may be able to judge
in the dark . . ."

"Be careful," he murmured warningly—and I realized suddenly that
all my future, the only future for which I was fit, would perhaps go
irretrievably to pieces in any mishap to my first command.

7. *Koh* or *Ko* means *island;* there are a large number of islands with that prefix at
the head of the Gulf of Siam, but not, apparently, a Koh-ring.

I could not stop a moment longer in the room. I motioned him to get out of sight and made my way on the poop. That unplayful cub had the watch. I walked up and down for a while thinking things out, then beckoned him over."

"Send a couple of hands to open the two quarter-deck ports," I said mildly.

He actually had the impudence, or else so forgot himself in his wonder at such an incomprehensible order, as to repeat:

"Open the quarter-deck ports! What for, sir?"

"The only reason you need concern yourself about is because I tell you to do so. Have them opened wide and fastened properly."

He reddened and went off, but I believe made some jeering remark to the carpenter as to the sensible practice of ventilating a ship's quarter-deck. I know he popped into the mate's cabin to impart the fact to him, because the whiskers came on deck, as it were by chance, and stole glances at me from below—for signs of lunacy or drunkenness, I suppose.

A little before supper, feeling more restless than ever, I rejoined, for a moment, my second self. And to find him sitting so quietly was surprising, like something against nature, inhuman.

I developed my plan in a hurried whisper.

"I shall stand in as close as I dare and then put her round. I shall presently find means to smuggle you out of here into the sail-locker, which communicates with the lobby. But there is an opening, a sort of square for hauling the sails out, which gives straight on the quarter-deck and which is never closed in fine weather, so as to give air to the sails. When the ship's way is deadened in stays[8] and all the hands are aft at the main braces you shall have a clear road to slip out and get overboard through the open quarter-deck port. I've had them both fastened up. Use a rope's end to lower yourself into the water so as to avoid a splash—you know. It could be heard and cause some beastly complication."

He kept silent for a while, then whispered, "I understand."

"I won't be there to see you go," I began with an effort. "The rest . . . I only hope I have understood too."

"You have. From first to last"—and for the first time there seemed to be a faltering, something strained in his whisper. He caught hold of my arm, but the ringing of the supper bell made me start. He didn't, though; he only released his grip.

After supper I didn't come below again till well past eight o'clock. The faint, steady breeze was loaded with dew; and the wet, darkened sails held all there was of propelling power in it. The night, clear and starry, sparkled darkly, and the opaque, lightless patches shifting slowly amongst the low stars were the drifting islets. On the port bow there was a big one more distant and shadowily imposing by the great space of sky it eclipsed.

On opening the door I had a back view of my very own self looking at a chart. He had come out of the recess and was standing near the table.

8. When the ship's forward motion is slowed or stopped while its head is being turned toward the wind for the purpose of shifting the sail.

"Quite dark enough," I whispered.

He stepped back and leaned against my bed with a level, quiet glance. I sat on the couch. We had nothing to say to each other. Over our heads the officer of the watch moved here and there. Then I heard him move quickly. I knew what that meant. He was making for the companion; and presently his voice was outside my door.

"We are drawing in pretty fast, sir. Land looks rather close."

"Very well," I answered. "I am coming on deck directly."

I waited till he was gone out of the cuddy, then rose. My double moved too. The time had come to exchange our last whispers, for neither of us was ever to hear each other's natural voice.

"Look here!" I opened a drawer and took out three sovereigns. "Take this, anyhow. I've got six and I'd give you the lot, only I must keep a little money to buy some fruit and vegetables for the crew from native boats as we go through Sunda Straits."

He shook his head.

"Take it," I urged him, whispering desperately. "No one can tell what . . ."

He smiled and slapped meaningly the only pocket of the sleeping jacket. It was not safe, certainly. But I produced a large old silk handkerchief of mine, and tying the three pieces of gold in a corner, pressed it on him. He was touched, I suppose, because he took it at last and tied it quickly round his waist under the jacket, on his bare skin.

Our eyes met; several seconds elapsed, till, our glances still mingled, I extended my hand and turned the lamp out. Then I passed through the cuddy, leaving the door of my room wide open. . . . "Steward!"

He was still lingering in the pantry in the greatness of his zeal, giving a rub-up to a plated cruet stand the last thing before going to bed. Being carful not to wake up the mate, whose room was opposite, I spoke in an undertone.

He looked round anxiously. "Sir!"

"Can you get me a little hot water from the galley?"

"I am afraid, sir, the galley fire's been out for some time now."

"Go and see."

He fled up the stairs.

"Now," I whispered loudly into the saloon—too loudly, perhaps, but I was afraid I couldn't make a sound. He was by my side in an instant—the double captain slipped past the stairs—through a tiny dark passage . . . a sliding door. We were in the sail-locker, scrambling on our knees over the sails. A sudden thought struck me. I saw myself wandering barefooted, bareheaded, the sun beating on my dark poll. I snatched off my floppy hat and tried hurriedly in the dark to ram it on my other self. He dodged and fended off silently. I wonder what he thought had come to me before he understood and suddenly desisted. Our hands met gropingly, lingered united in a steady, motionless clasp for a second. . . . No word was breathed by either of us when they separated.

I was standing quietly by the pantry door when the steward returned.

"Sorry, sir. Kettle barely warm. Shall I light the spirit-lamp?"

"Never mind."

I came out on deck slowly. It was now a matter of conscience to shave the land as close as possible—for now he must go overboard whenever the ship was put in stays. Must! There could be no going back for him. After a moment I walked over to leeward and my heart flew into my mouth at the nearness of the land on the bow. Under any other circumstances I would not have held on a minute longer. The second mate had followed me anxiously.

I looked on till I felt I could command my voice.

"She will weather," I said then in a quiet tone.

"Are you going to try that, sir?" he stammered out incredulously.

I took no notice of him and raised my tone just enough to be heard by the helmsman.

"Keep her good full."[9]

"Good full, sir."

The wind fanned my cheek, the sails slept, the world was silent. The strain of watching the dark loom of the land grow bigger and denser was too much for me. I had to shut my eyes—because the ship must go closer. She must! The stillness was intolerable. Were we standing still?

When I opened my eyes the second view started my heart with a thump. The black southern hill of Koh-ring seemed to hang right over the ship like a towering fragment of the everlasting night. On that enormous mass of blackness there was not a gleam to be seen, not a sound to be heard. It was gliding irresistibly towards us and yet seemed already within reach of the hand. I saw the vague figures of the watch grouped in the waist, gazing in awed silence.

"Are you going on, sir?" inquired an unsteady voice at my elbow.

I ignored it. I had to go on.

"Keep her full. Don't check her way. That won't do now," I said warningly.

"I can't see the sails very well," the helmsman answered me, in strange, quavering tones.

Was she close enough? Already she was, I won't say in the shadow of the land, but in the very blackness of it, already swallowed up as it were, gone too close to be recalled, gone from me altogether.

"Give the mate a call," I said to the young man who stood at my elbow as still as death. "And turn all hands up."

My tone had a borrowed loudness reverberated from the height of the land. Several voices cried out together, "We are all on deck, sir."

Then stillness again, with the great shadow gliding closer, towering higher, without a light, without a sound. Such a hush had fallen on the ship that she might have been a bark of the dead floating in slowly under the very gate of Erebus.

"My God! Where are we?"

It was the mate moaning at my elbow. He was thunderstruck, and as it were deprived of the moral support of his whiskers. He clapped his hands and absolutely cried out, "Lost!"

"Be quiet," I said sternly.

9. Keep the ship's sails filled with wind.

He lowered his tone, but I saw the shadowy gesture of his despair. "What are we doing here?"

"Looking for the land wind."

He made as if to tear his hair, and addressed me recklessly.

"She will never get out. You have done it, sir. I knew it'd end in something like this. She will never weather, and you are too close now to stay. She'll drift ashore before she's round. O my God!"

I caught his arm as he was raising it to batter his poor devoted head, and shook it violently.

"She's ashore already," he wailed, trying to tear himself away.

"Is she? . . . Keep good full there!"

"Good full, sir," cried the helmsman in a frightened, thin, childlike voice.

I hadn't let go the mate's arm and went on shaking it. "Ready about,[1] do you hear? You go forward"—shake—"and stop there"—shake—"and hold your noise"—shake—"and see these head-sheets properly overhauled"—shake, shake—shake.

And all the time I dared not look towards the land lest my heart should fail me. I released my grip at last and he ran forward as if fleeing for dear life.

I wondered what my double there in the sail-locker thought of this commotion. He was able to hear everything—and perhaps he was able to understand why, on my conscience, it had to be thus close—no less. My first order "Hard alee!" re-echoed ominously under the towering shadow of Koh-ring as if I had shouted in a mountain gorge. And then I watched the land intently. In that smooth water and light wind it was impossible to feel the ship coming-to.[2] No! I could not feel her. And my second self was making now ready to slip out and lower himself overboard. Perhaps he was gone already . . . ?

The great black mass brooding over our very mast-heads began to pivot away from the ship's side silently. And now I forgot the secret stranger ready to depart, and remembered only that I was a total stranger to the ship. I did not know her. Would she do it? How was she to be handled?

I swung the mainyard and waited helplessly. She was perhaps stopped, and her very fate hung in the balance, with the black mass of Koh-ring like the gate of the everlasting night towering over her taffrail. What would she do now? Had she way on her yet? I stepped to the side swiftly, and on the shadowy water I could see nothing except a faint phosphorescent flash revealing the glassy smoothness of the sleeping surface. It was impossible to tell—and I had not learned yet the feel of my ship. Was she moving? What I needed was something easily seen, a piece of paper, which I could throw overboard and watch. I had nothing on me. To run down for it I didn't dare. There was no time. All at once my strained, yearning stare distinguished a white object floating within a yard of the ship's side—white, on the black water. A phosphorescent flash passed under it.

1. Be ready to shift the sails (tack). The head-sheets, below, are the lines attached to the sails of the forward mast, and to overhaul is to slacken a rope by pulling it in the opposite direction to that used in hoisting a sail and thus loosening the blocks.
2. Coming to a standstill.

What was that thing? . . . I recognized my own floppy hat. It must have fallen off his head . . . and he didn't bother. Now I had what I wanted—the saving mark for my eyes. But I hardly thought of my other self, now gone from the ship, to be hidden for ever from all friendly faces, to be a fugitive and a vagabond on the earth, with no brand of the curse on his sane forehead to stay a slaying hand . . . too proud to explain.

And I watched the hat—the expression of my sudden pity for his mere flesh. It had been meant to save his homeless head from the dangers of the sun. And now—behold—it was saving the ship, by serving me for a mark to help out the ignorance of my strangeness. Ha! It was drifting forward, warning me just in time that the ship had gathered sternway.

"Shift the helm," I said in a low voice to the seaman standing still like a statue.

The man's eyes glistened wildly in the binnacle light as he jumped round to the other side and spun round the wheel.

I walked to the break of the poop. On the overshadowed deck all hands stood by the forebraces waiting for my order. The stars ahead seemed to be gliding from right to left. And all was so still in the world that I heard the quiet remark, "She's round," passed in a tone of intense relief between two seamen.

"Let go and haul."

The foreyards ran round with a great noise, amidst cheery cries. And now the frightful whiskers made themselves heard giving various orders. Already the ship was drawing ahead. And I was alone with her. Nothing! no one in the world should stand now between us, throwing a shadow on the way of silent knowledge and mute affection; the perfect communion of a seaman with his first command.

Walking to the taffrail, I was in time to make out, on the very edge of a darkness thrown by a towering black mass like the very gateway of Erebus—yes, I was in time to catch an evanescent glimpse of my white hat left behind to mark the spot where the secret sharer of my cabin and of my thoughts, as though he were my second self, had lowered himself into the water to take his punishment: a free man, a proud swimmer striking out for a new destiny.

1912

SIR ARTHUR CONAN DOYLE

The Adventure of the Speckled Band

In glancing over my notes of the seventy odd cases in which I have during the last eight years studied the methods of my friend Sherlock Holmes, I find many tragic, some comic, a large number merely strange, but none commonplace; for, working as he did rather for the love of his art than for the acquirement of wealth, he refused to associate himself with any investigation which did not tend towards the unusual, and even the fantastic. Of all these varied cases, however, I cannot recall any which presented more singular features than that which was associated with the well-known Surrey[1] family of the Roylotts of Stoke Moran. The events in question occurred in the early days of my association with Holmes, when we were sharing rooms as bachelors, in Baker Street.[2] It is possible that I might have placed them upon record before, but a promise of secrecy was made at the time, from which I have only been freed during the last month by the untimely death of the lady to whom the pledge was given. It is perhaps as well that the facts should now come to light, for I have reasons to know there are widespread rumors as to the death of Dr. Grimesby Roylott which tend to make the matter even more terrible than the truth.

It was early in April, in the year '83, that I woke one morning to find Sherlock Holmes standing, fully dressed, by the side of my bed. He was a late riser as a rule, and, as the clock on the mantelpiece showed me that it was only a quarter past seven, I blinked up at him in some surprise, and perhaps just a little resentment, for I was myself regular in my habits.

"Very sorry to knock you up,[3] Watson," said he, "but it's the common lot this morning. Mrs. Hudson has been knocked up, she retorted upon me, and I on you."

"What is it, then? A fire?"

"No, a client. It seems that a young lady has arrived in a considerable state of excitement, who insists upon seeing me. She is waiting now in the sitting room. Now, when young ladies wander about the metropolis at this hour of the morning, and knock sleepy people up out of their beds, I presume that it is something very pressing which they have to communicate. Should it prove to be an interesting case, you would, I am sure, wish to follow it from the outset. I thought at any rate that I should call you, and give you the chance."

"My dear fellow, I would not miss it for anything."

I had no keener pleasure than in following Holmes in his professional investigations, and in admiring the rapid deductions, as swift as intuitions, and yet always founded on a logical basis, with which he unraveled the problems which were submitted to him. I rapidly threw on my clothes, and was ready in a few minutes to accompany my friend down to the sitting room. A lady dressed in black and heavily veiled, who had been sitting in the window, rose as we entered.

"Good morning, madam," said Holmes cheerily. "My name is Sherlock Holmes. This is my intimate friend and associate, Dr. Watson, before whom you can speak as freely as before myself. Ha, I am glad to see that Mrs. Hudson has had the good sense to light the fire. Pray draw up to it, and I shall order you a cup of hot coffee, for I observe that you are shivering."

"It is not cold which makes me shiver," said the woman in a low

1. A county just south of London, one of the "Home Counties" around London—Berkshire, Hampshire, and Middlesex, mentioned later are also Home Counties. Stoke Moran is apparently fictional, though there is a Stoke D'Abernon three miles from the west Surrey town of Leatherhead, mentioned below, which is some 18 miles from London.
2. Near Regent's Park in north central London, a street that Holmes made famous.
3. Wake you up.

voice, changing her seat as requested.

"What then?"

"It is fear, Mr. Holmes. It is terror." She raised her veil as she spoke, and we could see that she was indeed in a pitiable state of agitation, her face all drawn and gray, with restless, frightened eyes, like those of some hunted animal. Her features and figure were those of a woman of thirty, but her hair was shot with premature gray, and her expression was weary and haggard. Sherlock Holmes ran her over with one of his quick, all-comprehensive glances.

"You must not fear," said he soothingly, bending forward and patting her forearm. "We shall soon set matters right, I have no doubt. You have come in by train this morning, I see."

"You know me, then?"

"No, but I observe the second half of a return ticket in the palm of your left glove. You must have started early, and yet you had a good drive in a dog cart, along heavy roads, before you reached the station."

The lady gave a violent start, and stared in bewilderment at my companion.

"There is no mystery, my dear madam," said he, smiling. "The left arm of your jacket is spattered with mud in no less than seven places. The marks are perfectly fresh. There is no vehicle save a dog cart which throws up mud in that way, and then only when you sit on the left-hand side of the driver."[4]

"Whatever your reasons may be, you are perfectly correct," said she. "I started from home before six, reached Leatherhead at twenty past, and came in by the first train to Waterloo.[5] Sir, I can stand this strain no longer, I shall go mad if it continues. I have no one to turn to—none, save only one, who cares for me, and he, poor fellow, can be of little aid. I have heard of you, Mr. Holmes; I have heard of you from Mrs. Farintosh, whom you helped in the hour of her sore need. It was from her that I had your address. Oh, sir, do you not think you could help me too, and at least throw a little light through the dense darkness which surrounds me? At present it is out of my power to reward you for your services, but in a month or two I shall be married, with the control of my own income, and then at least you shall not find me ungrateful."

Holmes turned to his desk, and unlocking it, drew out a small case-book which he consulted.

"Farintosh," said he. "Ah, yes, I recall the case; it was concerned with an opal tiara. I think it was before your time, Watson. I can only say, madam, that I shall be happy to devote the same care to your case as I did to that of your friend. As to reward, my profession is its reward; but you are at liberty to defray whatever expenses I may be put to, at the time which suits you best. And now I beg that you will lay before us everything that may help us in forming an opinion upon the matter."

"Alas!" replied our visitor. "The very horror of my situation lies in

4. In Britain the driver sits on the right; a lady would normally sit behind the driver, perhaps in the middle of the seat. The seats of the two benches of the dogcart are, however, back to back, and since even class distinction would not insist that the lady sit facing the rear, she perforce would sit on the left.

5. A main London railway station serving south and west of the metropolis.

the fact that my fears are so vague, and my suspicions depend so entirely upon small points, which might seem trivial to another, that even he to whom of all others I have a right to look for help and advice looks upon all that I tell him about it as the fancies of a nervous woman. He does not say so, but I can read it from his soothing answers and averted eyes. But I have heard, Mr. Holmes, that you can see deeply into the manifold wickedness of the human heart. You may advise me how to walk amid the dangers which encompass me."

"I am all attention, madam."

"My name is Helen Stoner, and I am living with my stepfather, who is the last survivor of one of the oldest Saxon families in England, the Roylotts of Stoke Moran, on the Western border of Surrey."

Holmes nodded his head. "The name is familiar to me," said he.

"The family was at one time among the richest in England, and the estate extended over the borders into Berkshire in the north, and Hampshire in the west. In the last century, however, four successive heirs were of a dissolute and wasteful disposition, and the family ruin was eventually completed by a gambler, in the days of the Regency.[6] Nothing was left save a few acres of ground and the two-hundred-year-old house, which is itself crushed under a heavy mortgage. The last squire dragged out his existence there, living the horrible life of an aristocratic pauper; but his only son, my stepfather, seeing that he must adapt himself to the new conditions, obtained an advance from a relative, which enabled him to take a medical degree, and went out to Calcutta, where, by his professional skill and his force of character, he established a large practice. In a fit of anger, however, caused by some robberies which had been perpetrated in the house, he beat his native butler to death, and narrowly escaped a capital sentence. As it was, he suffered a long term of imprisonment, and afterwards returned to England a morose and disappointed man.

"When Dr. Roylott was in India he married my mother, Mrs. Stoner, the young widow of Major-General Stoner, of the Bengal Artillery. My sister Julia and I were twins, and we were only two years old at the time of my mother's remarriage. She had a considerable sum of money, not less than a thousand a year,[7] and this she bequeathed to Dr. Roylott entirely whilst we resided with him, with a provision that a certain annual sum should be allowed to each of us in the event of our marriage. Shortly after our return to England my mother died—she was killed eight years ago in a railway accident near Crewe. Dr. Roylott then abandoned his attempts to establish himself in practice in London, and took us to live with him in the ancestral house at Stoke Moran. The money which my mother had left was enough for all our wants, and there seemed no obstacle to our happiness.

6. In 1811–20, the Prince of Wales, later George IV, served as Prince Regent in place of George III, who had been declared insane. The period was noted for the dandyism and dissoluteness of the court and London society.

7. Though only $5,000, its purchasing power may better be gauged by the fact that as late as 1905, according to Baedecker's famous guide of London, if a visitor "lives in a first-class hotel, dines at the table-d'hôte, drinks wine, frequents the theater and other places of amusement, and drives about in cabs . . . he must be prepared to spend 30–40 shillings a day"—that is, as much as *two* pounds a day!

"But a terrible change came over our stepfather about this time. Instead of making friends and exchanging visits with our neighbors, who had at first been overjoyed to see a Roylott of Stoke Moran back in the old family seat, he shut himself up in his house, and seldom came out save to indulge in ferocious quarrels with whoever might cross his path. Violence of temper approaching to mania has been hereditary in the men of the family, and in my stepfather's case it had, I believe, been intensified by his long residence in the tropics. A series of disgraceful brawls took place, two of which ended in the police court, until at last he became the terror of the village, and the folks would fly at his approach, for he is a man of immense strength, and absolutely uncontrollable in his anger.

"Last week he hurled the local blacksmith over a parapet into a stream and it was only by paying over all the money that I could gather together that I was able to avert another public exposure. He had no friends at all save the wandering gypsies, and he would give these vagabonds leave to encamp upon the few acres of bramble-covered land which represent the family estate, and would accept in return the hospitality of their tents, wandering away with them sometimes for weeks on end. He has a passion also for Indian animals, which are sent over to him by a correspondent, and he has at this moment a cheetah and a baboon, which wander freely over his grounds, and are feared by the villagers almost as much as their master.

"You can imagine from what I say that my poor sister Julia and I had no great pleasure in our lives. No servant would stay with us, and for a long time we did all the work of the house. She was but thirty at the time of her death, and yet her hair had already begun to whiten, even as mine has."

"Your sister is dead, then?"

"She died just two years ago, and it is of her death that I wish to speak to you. You can understand that, living the life which I have described, we were little likely to see anyone of our own age and position. We had, however, an aunt, my mother's maiden sister, Miss Honoria Westphail, who lives near Harrow, and we were occasionally allowed to pay short visits at this lady's house. Julie went there at Christmas two years ago, and met there a half-pay[8] Major of Marines, to whom she became engaged. My stepfather learned of the engagement when my sister returned, and offered no objection to the marriage; but within a fortnight of the day which had been fixed for the wedding, the terrible event occurred which has deprived me of my only companion."

Sherlock Holmes had been leaning back in his chair with his eyes closed, and his head sunk in a cushion, but he half opened his lids now, and glanced across at his visitor.

"Pray be precise as to details," said he.

"It is easy for me to be so, for every event of that dreadul time is seared into my memory. The manor house is, as I have already said, very old, and only one wing is now inhabited. The bedrooms in this wing are on the ground floor, the sitting rooms being in the

---

8. Reduced pay for service officer when he is on inactive duty.

central block of the buildings. Of these bedrooms the first is Dr. Roylott's, the second my sister's, and the third my own. There is no communication between them, but they all open out into the same corridor. Do I make myself plain?"

"Perfectly so."

"The windows of the three rooms open out upon the lawn. That fatal night Dr. Roylott had gone to his room early, though we knew that he had not retired to rest, for my sister was troubled by the smell of the strong Indian cigars which it was his custom to smoke. She left her room, therefore, and came into mine, where she sat for some time, chatting about her approaching wedding. At eleven o'clock she rose to leave me, but she paused at the door and looked back.

"'Tell me, Helen,' said she, 'have you ever heard anyone whistle in the dead of the night?'

"'Never,' said I.

"'I suppose that you could not possibly whistle yourself in your sleep?'

"'Certainly not. But why?'

"'Because during the last few nights I have always, about three in the morning, heard a low clear whistle. I am a light sleeper, and it has awakened me. I cannot tell where it came from—perhaps from the next room, perhaps from the lawn. I thought that I would just ask you whether you had heard it.'

"'No, I have not. It must be those wretched gypsies in the plantation.'

"'Very likely. And yet if it were on the lawn I wonder that you did not hear it also.'

"'Ah, but I sleep more heavily than you.'

"'Well, it is of no great consequence, at any rate,' she smiled back at me, closed my door, and a few moments later I heard her key turn in the lock."

"Indeed," said Holmes. "Was it your custom always to lock yourselves in at night?"

"Always."

"And why?"

"I think that I mentioned to you that the Doctor kept a cheetah and a baboon. We had no feeling of security unless our doors were locked."

"Quite so. Pray proceed with your statement."

"I could not sleep that night. A vague feeling of impending misfortune impressed me. My sister and I, you will recollect, were twins, and you know how subtle are the links which bind two souls which are so closely allied. It was a wild night. The wind was howling outside, and the rain was beating and splashing against the windows. Suddenly, amidst all the hubbub of the gale, there burst forth the wild scream of a terrified woman. I knew that it was my sister's voice. I sprang from my bed, wrapped a shawl round me, and rushed into the corridor. As I opened my door I seemed to hear a low whistle, such as my sister described, and a few moments later a clanging sound, as if a mass of metal had fallen. As I ran down the passage my sister's door was unlocked, and revolved slowly upon its hinges. I stared at it horror-stricken, not knowing what was about to issue from it. By the light of the corridor lamp I saw my sister appear at the opening, her face blanched with terror, her hands groping for help, her whole figure swaying to and fro like that of a drunkard. I ran to her and threw my arms round her, but at that moment her knees seemed to give way and she fell to the ground. She writhed as one who is in terrible pain, and her limbs were dreadfully convulsed. At first I thought that she had not recognized me, but as I bent over her she suddenly shrieked out in a voice which I shall never forget, 'Oh, my God! Helen! It was the band! The speckled band!' There was something else which she would fain have said, and she stabbed with her finger into the air in the direction of the Doctor's room, but a fresh convulsion seized her and choked her words. I rushed out, calling loudly for my stepfather, and I met him hastening from his room in his dressing gown. When he reached my sister's side she was unconscious, and though he poured brandy down her throat, and sent for medical aid from the village, all efforts were in vain, for she slowly sank and died without having recovered her consciousness. Such was the dreadful end of my beloved sister."

"One moment," said Holmes: "are you sure about this whistle and metallic sound? Could you swear to it?"

"That was what the county coroner asked me at the inquiry. It is my strong impression that I heard it, and yet among the crash of the gale, and the creaking of an old house, I may possibly have been deceived."

"Was your sister dressed?"

"No, she was in her nightdress. In her right hand was found the charred stump of a match, and in her left a matchbox."

"Showing that she had struck a light and looked about her when the alarm took place. That is important. And what conclusions did the coroner come to?"

"He investigated the case with great care, for Dr. Roylott's conduct had long been notorious in the county, but he was unable to find any satisfactory cause of death. My evidence showed that the door had been fastened upon the inner side, and the windows were blocked by old-fashioned shutters with broad iron bars, which were secured every night. The walls were carefully sounded, and were shown to be quite solid all round, and the flooring was also thoroughly examined, with the same result. The chimney is wide, but is barred up by four large staples. It is certain, therefore, that my sister was quite alone when she met her end. Besides, there were no marks of any violence upon her."

"How about poison?"

"The doctors examined her for it, but without success."

"What do you think that this unfortunate lady died of, then?"

"It is my belief that she died of pure fear and nervous shock, though what it was which frightened her I cannot imagine."

"Were there gypsies in the plantation at the time?"

"Yes, there are nearly always some there."

"Ah, and what did you gather from this allusion to a band—a speckled band?"

"Sometimes I have thought that it was merely the wild talk of delirium, sometimes that it may have referred to some band of people, perhaps to these very gypsies in the plantation. I do not know whether the spotted handkerchiefs which so many of them wear over their heads might have suggested the strange adjective which she used."

Holmes shook his head like a man who is far from being satisfied. "These are very deep waters," said he; "pray go on with your narrative."

"Two years have passed since then, and my life has been until lately lonelier than ever. A month ago, however, a dear friend, whom I have known for many years, has done me the honor to ask my hand in marriage. His name is Armitage—Percy Armitage—the second son of Mr. Armitage, of Crane Water, near Reading.[9] My stepfather has offered no opposition to the match, and we are to be married in the course of the spring. Two days ago some repairs were started in the west wing of the building, and my bedroom wall has been pierced, so that I have had to move into the chamber in which my sister died, and to sleep in the very bed in which she slept. Imagine, then, my thrill of terror when last night, as I lay awake, thinking over her terrible fate, I suddenly heard in the silence of the night the low whistle which had been the herald of her own death. I sprang up and lit the lamp, but nothing was to be seen in the room. I was too shaken to go to bed again, however, so I dressed, and as soon as it was daylight I slipped down, got a dog cart at the Crown Inn, which is opposite, and drove to Leatherhead, from whence I have come on this morning, with the one object of seeing you and asking your advice."

"You have done wisely," said my friend. "But have you told me all?"

"Yes, all."

"Miss Stoner, you have not. You are screening your stepfather."

"Why, what do you mean?"

For answer Holmes pushed back the frill of black lace which fringed the hand that lay upon our visitor's knee. Five little livid spots, the marks of four fingers and a thumb, were printed upon the white wrist.

"You have been cruelly used," said Holmes.

The lady colored deeply, and covered over her injured wrist. "He is a hard man," she said, "and perhaps he hardly knows his own strength."

There was a long silence, during which Holmes leaned his chin upon his hands and stared into the crackling fire.

"This is very deep business," he said at last. "There are a thousand details which I should desire to know before I decide upon our course of action. Yet we have not a moment to lose. If we were to come to Stoke Moran today, would it be possible for us to see over these rooms without the knowledge of your stepfather?"

"As it happens, he spoke of coming into town today upon some most important business. It is probable that he will be away all day, and that there would be nothing to disturb you. We have a house-

9. Berkshire town about 35 miles from London.

keeper now, but she is old and foolish, and I could easily get her out of the way."

"Excellent. You are not averse to this trip, Watson?"

"By no means."

"Then we shall both come. What are you going to do yourself?"

"I have one or two things which I would wish to do now that I am in town. But I shall return by the twelve o'clock train, so as to be there in time for your coming."

"And you may expect us early in the afternoon. I have myself some small business matters to attend to. Will you not wait and breakfast?"

"No, I must go. My heart is lightened already since I have confided my trouble to you. I shall look forward to seeing you again this afternoon." She dropped her thick black veil over her face, and glided from the room.

"And what do you think of it all, Watson?" asked Sherlock Holmes, leaning back in his chair.

"It seems to me to be a most dark and sinister business."

"Dark enough and sinister enough."

"Yet if the lady is correct in saying that the flooring and walls are sound, and that the door, window, and chimney are impassable, then her sister must have been undoubtedly alone when she met her mysterious end."

"What becomes, then, of these nocturnal whistles, and what of the very peculiar words of the dying woman?"

"I cannot think."

"When you combine the ideas of whistles at night, the presence of a band of gypsies who are on intimate terms with this old doctor, the fact that we have every reason to believe that the doctor has an interest in preventing his stepdaughter's marriage, the dying allusion to a band, and finally, the fact that Miss Helen Stoner heard a metallic clang, which might have been caused by one of those metal bars which secured the shutters falling back into their place, I think there is good ground to think that the mystery may be cleared along those lines."

"But what, then, did the gypsies do?"

"I cannot imagine."

"I see many objections to any such a theory."

"And so do I. It is precisely for that reason that we are going to Stoke Moran this day. I want to see whether the objections are fatal, or if they may be explained away. But what, in the name of the devil!"

The ejaculation had been drawn from my companion by the fact that our door had been suddenly dashed open, and that a huge man framed himself in the aperture. His costume was a peculiar mixture of the professional and of the agricultural, having a black top hat, a long frock coat, and a pair of high gaiters, with a hunting-crop swinging in his hand. So tall was he that his hat actually brushed the crossbar of the doorway, and his breadth seemed to span it across from side to side. A large face, seared with a thousand wrinkles, burned yellow with the sun, and marked with every evil passion, was turned from one to the other of us, while his deep-set, bile-shot eyes, and the high thin fleshless nose, gave him somewhat the resemblance to a fierce old bird of prey.

"Which of you is Holmes?" asked this apparition.

"My name, sir, but you have the advantage of me," said my companion quietly.

"I am Dr. Grimesby Roylott, of Stoke Moran."

"Indeed, Doctor," said Holmes blandly. "Pray take a seat."

"I will do nothing of the kind. My stepdaughter has been here. I have traced her. What has she been saying to you?"

"It is a little cold for the time of the year," said Holmes.

"What has she been saying to you?" screamed the old man furiously.

"But I have heard that the crocuses promise well," continued my companion imperturbably.

"Ha! You put me off, do you?" said our new visitor, taking a step forward, and shaking his hunting-crop. "I know you, you scoundrel! I have heard of you before. You are Holmes the meddler."

My friend smiled.

"Holmes the busybody!"

His smile broadened.

"Holmes the Scotland Yard jack-in-office." [1]

Holmes chuckled heartily. "Your conversation is most entertaining," said he. "When you go out close the door, for there is a decided draught."

"I will go when I have had my say. Don't you dare to meddle with my affairs. I know that Miss Stoner has been here—I traced her! I am a dangerous man to fall foul of! See here." He stepped swiftly forward, seized the poker, and bent it into a curve with his huge brown hands.

"See that you keep yourself out of my grip," he snarled, and hurling the twisted poker into the fireplace, he strode out of the room.

"He seems a very amiable person," said Holmes, laughing. "I am not quite so bulky, but if he had remained I might have shown him that my grip was not much more feeble than his own." As he spoke he picked up the steel poker, and with a sudden effort straightened it out again.

"Fancy his having the insolence to confound me with the official detective force! This incident gives zest to our investigation, however, and I only trust that our little friend will not suffer from her imprudence in allowing this brute to trace her. And now, Watson, we shall order breakfast, and afterwards I shall walk down to Doctors' Commons,[2] where I hope to get some data which may help us in this matter."

It was nearly one o'clock when Sherlock Holmes returned from his excursion. He held in his hand a sheet of blue paper, scrawled over with notes and figures.

"I have seen the will of the deceased wife," said he. "To determine its exact meaning I have been obliged to work out the present prices of the investments with which it is concerned. The total income, which at the time of the wife's death was little short of £1,100, is now

---

1. Self-important petty official.   marriage licenses, registration of wills, etc.
2. Office which had jurisdiction over

through the fall in agricultural prices not more than £750. Each daughter can claim an income of £250, in case of marriage. It is evident, therefore, that if both girls had married, this beauty would have had a mere pittance, while even one of them would cripple him to a serious extent. My morning's work has not been wasted, since it has proved that he has the very strongest motives for standing in the way of anything of the sort. And now, Watson, this is too serious for dawdling, especially as the old man is aware that we are interesting ourselves in his affairs, so if you are ready we shall call a cab and drive to Waterloo. I should be very much obliged if you would slip your revolver into your pocket. An Eley's No. 2 is an excellent argument with gentlemen who can twist steel pokers into knots. That and a toothbrush are, I think, all that we need."

At Waterloo we were fortunate in catching a train for Leatherhead, where we hired a trap at the station inn, and drove for four or five miles through the lovely Surrey lanes. It was a perfect day, with a bright sun and a few fleecy clouds in the heavens. The trees and wayside hedges were just throwing out their first green shoots, and the air was full of the pleasant smell of the moist earth. To me at least there was a strange contrast between the sweet promise of the spring and this sinister quest upon which we were engaged. My companion sat in front of the trap, his arms folded, his hat pulled down over his eyes, and his chin sunk upon his breast, buried in the deepest thought. Suddenly, however, he started, tapped me on the shoulder, and pointed over the meadows.

"Look there!" said he.

A heavily timbered park stretched up in a gentle slope, thickening into a grove at the highest point. From amidst the branches there jutted out the gray gables and high rooftree of a very old mansion.

"Stoke Moran?" said he.

"Yes, sir, that be the house of Dr. Grimesby Roylott," remarked the driver.

"There is some building going on there," said Holmes: "that is where we are going."

"There's the village," said the driver, pointing to a cluster of roofs some distance to the left; "but if you want to get to the house, you'll find it shorter to go over this stile, and so by the footpath over the fields. There it is, where the lady is walking."

"And the lady, I fancy, is Miss Stoner," observed Holmes, shading his eyes. "Yes, I think we had better do as you suggest."

We got off, paid our fare, and the trap rattled back on its way to Leatherhead.

"I thought it as well," said Holmes, as we climbed the stile, "that this fellow should think we had come here as architects, or on some definite business. It may stop his gossip. Good afternoon, Miss Stoner. You see that we have been as good as our word."

Our client of the morning had hurried forward to meet us with a face which spoke her joy. "I have been waiting so eagerly for you," she cried, shaking hands with us warmly. "All has turned out splendidly. Dr. Roylott has gone to town, and it is unlikely that he will be back before evening."

"We have had the pleasure of making the Doctor's acquaintance," said Holmes, and in a few words he sketched out what had occurred. Miss Stoner turned white to the lips as she listened.

"Good heavens!" she cried, "he has followed me, then."

"So it appears."

"He is so cunning that I never know when I am safe from him. What will he say when he returns?"

"He must guard himself, for he may find that there is someone more cunning than himself upon his track. You must lock yourself from him tonight. If he is violent, we shall take you away to your aunt's at Harrow. Now, we must make the best use of our time, so kindly take us at once to the rooms which we are to examine."

The building was of gray, lichen-blotched stone, with a high central portion, and two curving wings, like the claws of a crab, thrown out on each side. In one of these wings the windows were broken, and blocked with wooden boards, while the roof was partly caved in, a picture of ruin. The central portion was in little better repair, but the right-hand block was comparatively modern, and the blinds in the windows, with the blue smoke curling up from the chimneys, showed that this was where the family resided. Some scaffolding had been erected against the end wall, and the stonework had been broken into, but there were no signs of any workmen at the moment of our visit. Holmes walked slowly up and down the ill-trimmed lawn, and examined with deep attention the outsides of the windows.

"This, I take it, belongs to the room in which you used to sleep, the center one to your sister's, and the one next to the main building to Dr. Roylott's chamber?"

"Exactly so. But I am now sleeping in the middle one."

"Pending the alterations, as I understand. By the way, there does not seem to be any very pressing need for repairs at that end wall."

"There were none. I believe that it was an excuse to move me from my room."

"Ah! that is suggestive. Now, on the other side of this narrow wing runs the corridor from which these three rooms open. There are windows in it, of course?"

"Yes, but very small ones. Too narrow for anyone to pass through."

"As you both locked your doors at night, your rooms were unapproachable from that side. Now, would you have the kindness to go into your room, and to bar your shutters."

Miss Stoner did so, and Holmes, after a careful examination through the open window, endeavored in every way to force the shutter open, but without success. There was no slit through which a knife could be passed to raise the bar. Then with his lens he tested the hinges, but they were of solid iron, built firmly into the massive masonry. "Hum!" said he, scratching his chin in some perplexity, "my theory certainly presents some difficulties. No one could pass these shutters if they were bolted. Well, we shall see if the inside throws any light upon the matter."

A small side door led into the whitewashed corridor from which the three bedrooms opened. Holmes refused to examine the third chamber, so we passed at once to the second, that in which Miss

Stoner was now sleeping, and in which her sister had met her fate. It was a homely little room, with a low ceiling and a gaping fireplace, after the fashion of old country houses. A brown chest of drawers stood in one corner, a narrow white-counterpaned bed in another, and a dressing table on the left-hand side of the window. These articles, with two small wickerwork chairs, made up all the furniture in the room, save for a square of Wilton carpet in the center. The boards round and the paneling of the walls were brown, worm-eaten oak, so old and discolored that it may have dated from the original building of the house. Holmes drew one of the chairs into a corner and sat silent, while his eyes traveled round and round and up and down, taking in every detail of the apartment.

"Where does that bell communicate with?" he asked at last, pointing to a thick bell-rope which hung down beside the bed, the tassel actually lying upon the pillow.

"It goes to the housekeeper's room."

"It looks newer than the other things?"

"Yes, it was only put there a couple of years ago."

"Your sister asked for it, I suppose?"

"No, I never heard of her using it. We used always to get what we wanted for ourselves."

"Indeed, it seemed unnecessary to put so nice a bell-pull there. You will excuse me for a few minutes while I satisfy myself as to this floor." He threw himself down upon his face with his lens in his hand, and crawled swiftly backwards and forwards, examining minutely the cracks between the boards. Then he did the same with the woodwork with which the chamber was paneled. Finally he walked over to the bed and spent some time in staring at it, and in running his eye up and down the wall. Finally he took the bell-rope in his hand and gave it a brisk tug.

"Why, it's a dummy," said he.

"Won't it ring?"

"No, it is not even attached to a wire. This is very interesting. You can see now that it is fastened to a hook just above where the little opening of the ventilator is."

"How very absurd! I never noticed that before."

"Very strange!" muttered Holmes, pulling at the rope. "There are one or two very singular points about this room. For example, what a fool a builder must be to open a ventilator in another room, when, with the same trouble, he might have communicated with the outside air!"

"That is also quite modern," said the lady.

"Done about the same time as the bell-rope?" remarked Holmes.

"Yes, there were several little changes carried out about that time."

"They seem to have been of a most interesting character—dummy bell-ropes, and ventilators which do not ventilate. With your permission, Miss Stoner, we shall now carry our researches into the inner apartment."

Dr. Grimesby Roylott's chamber was larger than that of his step-daughter, but was as plainly furnished. A camp bed, a small wooden shelf full of books, mostly of a technical character, an armchair beside the bed, a plain wooden chair against the wall, a round table, and a large iron safe were the principal things which met the eye. Holmes walked slowly round and examined each and all of them with the keenest interest.

"What's in here?" he asked, tapping the safe.

"My stepfather's business papers."

"Oh! You have seen inside then?"

"Only once, some years ago. I remember that it was full of papers."

"There isn't a cat in it, for example?"

"No. What a strange idea!"

"Well, look at this!" He took up a small saucer of milk which stood on the top of it.

"No; we don't keep a cat. But there is a cheetah and a baboon."

"Ah, yes, of course! Well, a cheetah is just a big cat, and yet a saucer of milk does not go very far in satisfying its wants, I daresay. There is one point which I should wish to determine." He squatted down in front of the wooden chair, and examined the seat of it with the greatest attention.

"Thank you. That is quite settled," said he, rising and putting his lens in his pocket. "Hullo! here is something interesting!"

The object which had caught his eye was a small dog lash hung on one corner of the bed. The lash, however, was curled upon itself, and tied so as to make a loop of whipcord.

"What do you make of that, Watson?"

"It's a common enough lash. But I don't know why it should be tied."

"That is not quite so common, is it? Ah, me! it's a wicked world, and when a clever man turns his brain to crime it is the worst of all. I think that I have seen enough now, Miss Stoner, and, with your permission, we shall walk out upon the lawn."

I had never seen my friend's face so grim, or his brow so dark, as it was when we turned from the scene of his investigation. We had walked several times up and down the lawn, neither Miss Stoner nor myself liking to break in upon his thoughts before he roused himself from his reverie.

"It is very essential, Miss Stoner," said he, "that you should absolutely follow my advice in every respect."

"I shall most certainly do so."

"The matter is too serious for any hesitation. Your life may depend upon your compliance."

"I assure you that I am in your hands."

"In the first place, both my friend and I must spend the night in your room."

Both Miss Stoner and I gazed at him in astonishment.

"Yes, it must be so. Let me explain. I believe that that is the village inn over there?"

"Yes, that is the 'Crown.'"

"Very good. Your windows would be visible from there?"

"Certainly."

"You must confine yourself to your room, on pretense of a headache, when your stepfather comes back. Then when you hear him retire for the night, you must open the shutters of your window, undo the hasp, put your lamp there as a signal to us, and then withdraw with everything which you are likely to want into the room which you used to occupy. I have no doubt that, in spite of the repairs, you could manage there for one night."

"Oh, yes, easily."

"The rest you will leave in our hands."

"But what will you do?"

"We shall spend the night in your room, and we shall investigate the cause of this noise which has disturbed you."

"I believe, Mr. Holmes, that you have already made up your mind," said Miss Stoner, laying her hand upon my companion's sleeve.

"Perhaps I have."

"Then for pity's sake tell me what was the cause of my sister's death."

"I should prefer to have clearer proofs before I speak."

"You can at least tell me whether my own thought is correct, and if she died from some sudden fright."

"No, I do not think so. I think that there was probably some more tangible cause. And now, Miss Stoner, we must leave you, for if Dr. Roylott returned and saw us, our journey would be in vain. Goodbye, and be brave, for if you will do what I have told you, you may rest assured that we shall soon drive away the dangers that threaten you."

Sherlock Holmes and I had no difficulty in engaging a bedroom and sitting room at the Crown Inn. They were on the upper floor, and from our window we could command a view of the avenue gate, and of the inhabited wing of Stoke Moran Manor House. At dusk we saw Dr. Grimesby Roylott drive past, his huge form looming up beside the little figure of the lad who drove him. The boy had some slight difficulty in undoing the heavy iron gates, and we heard the hoarse roar of the Doctor's voice, and saw the fury with which he shook his clenched fists at him. The trap drove on, and a few minutes later we saw a sudden light spring up among the trees as the lamp was lit in one of the sitting rooms.

"Do you know, Watson," said Holmes, as we sat together in the gathering darkness, "I have really some scruples as to taking you tonight. There is a distinct element of danger."

"Can I be of assistance?"

"Your presence might be invaluable."

"Then I shall certainly come."

"It is very kind of you."

"You speak of danger. You have evidently seen more in these rooms than was visible to me."

"No, but I fancy that I may have deduced a little more. I imagine that you saw all that I did."

"I saw nothing remarkable save the bell-rope, and what purpose that could answer I confess is more than I can imagine."

"You saw the ventilator, too?"

"Yes, but I do not think that it is such a very unusual thing to have a small opening between two rooms. It was so small a rat could hardly pass through."

"I knew that we should find a ventilator before ever we came to Stoke Moran."

"My dear Holmes!"

"Oh, yes, I did. You remember in her statement she said that her sister could smell Dr. Roylott's cigar. Now, of course that suggests at once that there must be a communication between the two rooms. It could only be a small one, or it would have been remarked upon at the coroner's inquiry. I deduced a ventilator."

"But what harm can there be in that?"

"Well, there is at least a curious coincidence of dates. A ventilator is made, a cord is hung, and a lady who sleeps in the bed dies. Does not that strike you?"

"I cannot as yet see any connection."

"Did you observe anything very peculiar about that bed?"

"No."

"It was clamped to the floor. Did you ever see a bed fastened like that before?"

"I cannot say that I have."

"The lady could not move her bed. It must always be in the same relative position to the ventilator and to the rope—for so we may call it, since it was clearly never meant for a bell-pull."

"Holmes," I cried, "I seem to see dimly what you are hitting at. We are only just in time to prevent some subtle and horrible crime."

"Subtle enough and horrible enough. When a doctor does go wrong he is the first of criminals. He has nerve and he has knowledge. Palmer and Pritchard[3] were among the heads of their profession. This man strikes even deeper, but, I think, Watson, that we shall be able to strike deeper still. But we shall have horrors enough before the night is over: for goodness' sake let us have a quiet pipe, and turn our minds for a few hours to something more cheerful."

About nine o'clock the light among the trees was extinguished, and all was dark in the direction of the Manor House. Two hours passed slowly away, and then, suddenly, just at the stroke of eleven, a single bright light shone out right in front of us.

"That is our signal," said Holmes, springing to his feet; "it comes from the middle window."

As we passed out he exchanged a few words with the landlord, explaining that we were going on a late visit to an acquaintance, and that it was possible that we might spend the night there. A moment later we were out on the dark road, a chill wind blowing in our faces, and one yellow light twinkling in front of us through the gloom to guide us on our somber errand.

There was little difficulty in entering the grounds, for unrepaired breaches gaped in the old park wall. Making our way among the trees, we reached the lawn, crossed it, and were about to enter through the window, when out from a clump of laurel bushes there darted what seemed to be a hideous and distorted child, who threw

3. William Palmer was executed in 1856 for poisoning a friend, Edward William   Pritchard in 1865 for poisoning his wife and her mother. Both were physicians.

itself on the grass with writhing limbs, and then ran swiftly across the lawn into the darkness.

"My God!" I whispered, "did you see it?"

Holmes was for the moment as startled as I. His hand closed like a vise upon my wrist in his agitation. Then he broke into a low laugh, and put his lips to my ear.

"It is a nice household," he murmured, "that is the baboon."

I had forgotten the strange pets which the doctor affected. There was a cheetah, too; perhaps we might find it upon our shoulders at any moment. I confess that I felt easier in my mind when, after following Holmes's example and slipping off my shoes, I found myself inside the bedroom. My companion noiselessly closed the shutters, moved the lamp onto the table, and cast his eyes round the room. All was as we had seen it in the daytime. Then creeping up to me and making a trumpet of his hand, he whispered into my ear again so gently that it was all that I could do to distinguish the words:

"The least sound would be fatal to our plans."

I nodded to show that I had heard.

"We must sit without a light. He would see it through the ventilator."

I nodded again.

"Do not go to sleep; your very life may depend upon it. Have your pistol ready in case we should need it. I will sit on the side of the bed, and you in that chair."

I took out my revolver and laid it on the corner of the table.

Holmes had brought up a long thin cane, and this he placed upon the bed beside him. By it he laid the box of matches and the stump of a candle. Then he turned down the lamp and we were left in darkness.

How shall I ever forget that dreadful vigil? I could not hear a sound, not even the drawing of a breath, and yet I knew that my companion sat open-eyed, within a few feet of me, in the same state of nervous tension in which I was myself. The shutters cut off the least ray of light, and we waited in absolute darkness. From outside came the occasional cry of a night-bird, and once at our very window a long drawn, cat-like whine, which told us that the cheetah was indeed at liberty. Far away we could hear the deep tones of the parish clock, which boomed out every quarter of an hour. How long they seemed, those quarters! Twelve o'clock, and one, and two, and three, and still we sat waiting silently for whatever might befall.

Suddenly there was the momentary gleam of a light up in the direction of the ventilator, which vanished immediately, but was succeeded by a strong smell of burning oil and heated metal. Someone in the next room had lit a dark lantern. I heard a gentle sound of movement, and then all was silent once more, though the smell grew stronger. For half an hour I sat with straining ears. Then suddenly another sound became audible—a very gentle, soothing sound, like that of a small jet of steam escaping continually from a kettle. The instant, that we heard it, Holmes sprang from the bed, struck a match, and lashed furiously with his cane at the bell-pull.

"You see it, Watson?" he yelled. "You see it?"

But I saw nothing. At the moment when Holmes struck the light I heard a low, clear whistle, but the sudden glare flashing into my weary eyes made it impossible for me to tell what it was at which my friend lashed so savagely. I could, however, see that his face was deadly pale, and filled with horror and loathing.

He had ceased to strike, and was gazing up at the ventilator, when suddenly there broke from the silence of the night the most horrible cry to which I have ever listened. It swelled up louder and louder, a hoarse yell of pain and fear and anger all mingled in the one dreadful shriek. They say that away down in the village, and even in the distant parsonage, that cry raised the sleepers from their beds. It struck cold to our hearts, and I stood gazing at Holmes, and he at me, until the last echoes of it had died away into the silence from which it rose.

"What can it mean?" I gasped.

"It means that it is all over," Holmes answered. "And perhaps, after all, it is for the best. Take your pistol, and we shall enter Dr. Roylott's room."

With a grave face he lit the lamp, and led the way down the corridor. Twice he struck at the chamber door without any reply from within. Then he turned the handle and entered, I at his heels, with the cocked pistol in my hand.

It was a singular sight which met our eyes. On the table stood a dark lantern with the shutter half open, throwing a brilliant beam of light upon the iron safe, the door of which was ajar. Beside this table, on the wooden chair, sat Dr. Grimesby Roylott, clad in a long gray dressing gown, his bare ankles protruding beneath, and his feet thrust into red heelless Turkish slippers.[4] Across his lap lay the short stock with the long lash which we had noticed during the day. His chin was cocked upwards, and his eyes were fixed in a dreadful rigid stare at the corner of the ceiling. Round his brow he had a peculiar yellow band, with brownish speckles, which seemed to be bound tight round his head. As we entered he made neither sound nor motion.

"The band! the speckled band!" whispered Holmes.

I took a step forward: in an instant his strange headgear began to move, and there reared itself from among his hair the squat diamond-shaped head and puffed neck of a loathsome serpent.

"It is a swamp adder!"[5] cried Holmes—"the deadliest snake in India. He has died within ten seconds of being bitten. Violence does, in truth, recoil upon the violent, and the schemer falls into the pit which he digs for another.[6] Let us thrust this creature back into its den, and we can then remove Miss Stoner to some place of shelter, and let the county police know what has happened."

As he spoke he drew the dog whip swiftly from the dead man's lap, and throwing the noose round the reptile's neck, he drew it from its horrid perch, and, carrying it at arm's length, threw it into the iron safe, which he closed upon it.

4. Flat slipper of fabric or leather with elongated pointed toe.
5. There is no known snake of this name. The description most nearly fits, it is agreed, a cobra called the *Naja naja.*
6. *Ecclesiastes* 1:2—"He that diggeth a pit shall fall into it; and whoso breaketh a hedge, a serpent shall bite him."

Such are the true facts of the death of Dr. Grimesby Roylott, of Stoke Moran. It is not necessary that I should prolong a narrative which has already run to too great a length, by telling how we broke the sad news to the terrified girl, how we conveyed her by the morning train to the care of her good aunt at Harrow, of how the slow process of official inquiry came to the conclusion that the Doctor met his fate while indiscreetly playing with a dangerous pet. The little which I had yet to learn of the case was told me by Sherlock Holmes as we traveled back next day.

"I had," said he, "come to an entirely erroneous conclusion, which shows, my dear Watson, how dangerous it always is to reason from insufficient data. The presence of the gypsies, and the use of the word "band," which was used by the poor girl, no doubt, to explain the appearance which she had caught a horrid glimpse of by the light of her match, were sufficient to put me upon an entirely wrong scent. I can only claim the merit that I instantly reconsidered my position when, however, it became clear to me that whatever danger threatened an occupant of the room could not come either from the window or the door. My attention was speedily drawn, as I have already remarked to you, to this ventilator, and to the bell-rope which hung down to the bed. The discovery that this was a dummy, and that the bed was clamped to the floor, instantly gave rise to the suspicion that the rope was there as a bridge for something passing through the hole, and coming to the bed. The idea of a snake instantly occurred to me, and when I coupled it with my knowledge that the Doctor was furnished with a supply of creatures from India, I felt that I was probably on the right track. The idea of using a form of poison which could not possibly be discovered by any chemical test was just such a one as would occur to a clever and ruthless man who had had an Eastern training. The rapidity with which such a poison would take effect would also, from his point of view, be an advantage. It would be a sharp-eyed coroner indeed who could distinguish the two little dark punctures which would show where the poison fangs had done their work. Then I thought of the whistle. Of course, he must recall the snake before the morning light revealed it to the victim. He had trained it, probably by the use of the milk which we saw, to return to him when summoned. He would put it through the ventilator at the hour that he thought best, with the certainty that it would crawl down the rope, and land on the bed. It might or might not bite the occupant, perhaps she might escape every night for a week, but sooner or later she must fall a victim.

"I had come to these conclusions before ever I had entered his room. An inspection of his chair showed me that he had been in the habit of standing on it, which, of course, would be necessary in order that he should reach the ventilator. The sight of the safe, the saucer of milk, and the loop of whipcord were enough to finally dispel any doubts which may have remained. The metallic clang heard by Miss Stoner was obviously caused by her father hastily closing the door of his safe upon its terrible occupant. Having once made up my mind, you know the steps which I took in order to put the matter to the proof. I heard the creature hiss, as I have no doubt that you did also, and I instantly lit the light and attacked it."

"With the result of driving it through the ventilator."

"And also with the result of causing it to turn upon its master at the other side. Some of the blows of my cane came home, and roused its snakish temper, so that it flew upon the first person it saw. In this way I am no doubt indirectly responsible for Dr. Grimesby Roylott's death, and I cannot say that it is likely to weigh very heavily upon my conscience."

1892

FRANZ KAFKA

A Hunger Artist *

During these last decades the interest in professional fasting has markedly diminished. It used to pay very well to stage such great performances under one's own management, but today that is quite impossible. We live in a different world now. At one time the whole town took a lively interest in the hunger artist; from day to day of his fast the excitement mounted; everybody wanted to see him at least once a day; there were people who bought season tickets for the last few days and sat from morning till night in front of his small barred cage; even in the nighttime there were visiting hours, when the whole effect was heightened by torch flares; on fine days the cage was set out in the open air, and then it was the children's special treat to see the hunger artist; for their elders he was often just a joke that happened to be in fashion, but the children stood open-mouthed, holding each other's hands for greater security, marveling at him as he sat there pallid in black tights, with his ribs sticking out so prominently, not even on a seat but down among straw on the ground, sometimes giving a courteous nod, answering questions with a constrained smile, or perhaps stretching an arm through the bars so that one might feel how thin it was, and then again withdrawing deep into himself, paying no attention to anyone or anything, not even to the all-important striking of the clock that was the only piece of furniture in his cage, but merely staring into vacancy with half-shut eyes, now and then taking a sip from a tiny glass of water to moisten his lips.

Besides casual onlookers there were also relays of permanent watchers selected by the public, usually butchers, strangely enough, and it was their task to watch the hunger artist day and night, three of them at a time, in case he should have some secret recourse to nourishment. This was nothing but a formality, instituted to reassure the masses, for the initiates knew well enough that during his fast the artist would never in any circumstances, not even under forcible com-

* Translated by Willa and Edwin Muir.

pulsion, swallow the smallest morsel of food; the honor of his profession forbade it. Not every watcher, of course, was capable of understanding this, there were often groups of night watchers who were very lax in carrying out their duties and deliberately huddled together in a retired corner to play cards with great absorption, obviously intending to give the hunger artist the chance of a little refreshment, which they supposed he could draw from some private hoard. Nothing annoyed the artist more than such watchers; they made him miserable; they made his fast seem unendurable; sometimes he mastered his feebleness sufficiently to sing during their watch for as long as he could keep going, to show them how unjust their suspicions were. But that was of little use; they only wondered at his cleverness in being able to fill his mouth even while singing. Much more to his taste were the watchers who sat close up to the bars, who were not content with the dim night lighting of the hall but focused him in the full glare of the electric pocket torch given them by the impresario. The harsh light did not trouble him at all. In any case he could never sleep properly, and he could always drowse a little, whatever the light, at any hour, even when the hall was thronged with noisy onlookers. He was quite happy at the prospect of spending a sleepless night with such watchers; he was ready to exchange jokes with them, to tell them stories out of his nomadic life, anything at all to keep them awake and demonstrate to them again that he had no eatables in his cage and that he was fasting as not one of them could fast. But his happiest moment was when the morning came and an enormous breakfast was brought them, at his expense, on which they flung themselves with the keen appetite of healthy men after a weary night of wakefulness. Of course there were people who argued that this breakfast was an unfair attempt to bribe the watchers, but that was going rather too far, and when they were invited to take on a night's vigil without a breakfast, merely for the sake of the cause, they made themselves scarce, although they stuck stubbornly to their suspicions.

Such suspicions, anyhow, were a necessary accompaniment to the profession of fasting. No one could possibly watch the hunger artist continuously, day and night, and so no one could produce first-hand evidence that the fast had really been rigorous and continuous; only the artist himself could know that; he was therefore bound to be the sole completely satisfied spectator of his own fast. Yet for other reasons he was never satisfied; it was not perhaps mere fasting that had brought him to such skeleton thinness that many people had regretfully to keep away from his exhibitions, because the sight of him was too much for them, perhaps it was dissatisfaction with himself that had worn him down. For he alone knew, what no other initiate knew, how easy it was to fast. It was the easiest thing in the world. He made no secret of this, yet people did not believe him; at the best they set him down as modest; most of them, however, thought he was out for publicity or else was some kind of cheat who found it easy to fast because he had discovered a way of making it easy, and then had the impudence to admit the fact, more or less. He had to put up with all that, and in the course of time had got used to it, but his inner dis-

satisfaction always rankled, and never yet, after any term of fasting—
this must be granted to his credit—had he left the cage of his own free
will. The longest period of fasting was fixed by his impresario at forty
days, beyond that term he was not allowed to go, not even in great
cities, and there was good reason for it, too. Experience had proved
that for about forty days the interest of the public could be stimulated
by a steadily increasing pressure of advertisement, but after that the
town began to lose interest, sympathetic support began notably to fall
off; there were of course local variations as between one town and another or one country and another, but as a general rule forty days
marked the limit. So on the fortieth day the flower-bedecked cage was
opened, enthusiastic spectators filled the hall, a military band played,
two doctors entered the cage to measure the results of the fast,
which were announced through a megaphone, and finally two young
ladies appeared, blissful at having been selected for the honor, to help
the hunger artist down the few steps leading to a small table on which
was spread a carefully chosen invalid repast. And at this very moment the artist always turned stubborn. True, he would entrust his
bony arms to the outstretched helping hands of the ladies bending
over him, but stand up he would not. Why stop fasting at this particular moment, after forty days of it? He had held out for a long time, an
illimitably long time; why stop now, when he was in his best fasting
form, or rather, not yet quite in his best fasting form? Why should he
be cheated of the fame he would get for fasting longer, for being not
only the record hunger artist of all time, which presumably he was
already, but for beating his own record by a performance beyond human imagination, since he felt that there were no limits to his capacity
for fasting? His public pretended to admire him so much, why
should it have so little patience with him; if he could endure fasting
longer, why shouldn't the public endure it? Besides, he was tired, he
was comfortable sitting in the straw, and now he was supposed to lift
himself to his full height and go down to a meal the very thought of
which gave him a nausea that only the presence of the ladies kept
him from betraying, and even that with an effort. And he looked up
into the eyes of the ladies who were apparently so friendly and in
reality so cruel, and shook his head, which felt too heavy on its
strengthless neck. But then there happened yet again what always
happened. The impresario came forward, without a word—for the
band made speech impossible—lifted his arms in the air above the artist, as if inviting Heaven to look down upon its creature here in the
straw, this suffering martyr, which indeed he was, although in quite
another sense; grasped him round the emaciated waist, with exaggerated caution, so that the frail condition he was in might be appreciated; and committed him to the care of the blenching ladies, not
without secretly giving him a shaking so that his legs and body tot-
tered and swayed. The artist now submitted completely; his head
lolled on his breast as if it had landed there by chance; his body was
hollowed out; his legs in a spasm of self-preservation clung close to
each other at the knees, yet scraped on the ground as if it were not
really solid ground, as if they were only trying to find solid ground;
and the whole weight of his body, a featherweight after all, relapsed

onto one of the ladies, who, looking round for help and panting a little —this post of honor was not at all what she had expected it to be— first stretched her neck as far as she could to keep her face at least free from contact with the artist, then finding this impossible, and her more fortunate companion not coming to her aid but merely holding extended on her own trembling hand the little bunch of knucklebones that was the artist's, to the great delight of the spectators burst into tears and had to be replaced by an attendant who had long been stationed in readiness. Then came the food, a little of which the impresario managed to get between the artist's lips, while he sat in a kind of half-fainting trance, to the accompaniment of cheerful patter designed to distract the public's attention from the artist's condition; after that, a toast was drunk to the public, supposedly prompted by a whisper from the artist in the impresario's ear; the band confirmed it with a mighty flourish, the spectators melted away, and no one had any cause to be dissatisfied with the proceedings, no one except the hunger artist himself, he only, as always.

So he lived for many years, with small regular intervals of recuperation, in visible glory, honored by the world, yet in spite of that troubled in spirit, and all the more troubled because no one would take his trouble seriously. What comfort could he possibly need? What more could he possibly wish for? And if some good-natured person, feeling sorry for him, tried to console him by pointing out that his melancholy was probably caused by fasting, it could happen, especially when he had been fasting for some time, that he reacted with an outburst of fury and to the general alarm began to shake the bars of his cage like a wild animal. Yet the impresario had a way of punishing these outbreaks which he rather enjoyed putting into operation. He would apologize publicly for the artist's behavior, which was only to be excused, he admitted, because of the irritability caused by fasting; a condition hardly to be understood by well-fed people; then by natural transition he went on to mention the artist's equally incomprehensible boast that he could fast for much longer than he was doing; he praised the high ambition, the good will, the great self-denial undoubtedly implicit in such a statement; and then quite simply countered it by bringing out photographs, which were also on sale to the public, showing the artist on the fortieth day of a fast lying in bed almost dead from exhaustion. This perversion of the truth, familiar to the artist though it was, always unnerved him afresh and proved too much for him. What was a consequence of the premature ending of his fast was here presented as the cause of it! To fight against this lack of understanding, against a whole world of non-understanding, was impossible. Time and again in good faith he stood by the bars listening to the impresario, but as soon as the photographs appeared he always let go and sank with a groan back on to his straw, and the reassured public could once more come close and gaze at him.

A few years later when the witnesses of such scenes called them to mind, they often failed to understand themselves at all. For meanwhile the aforementioned change in public interest had set in; it seemed to happen almost overnight; there may have been profound causes for it, but who was going to bother about that; at any rate the pampered hunger artist suddenly found himself deserted one fine day by the amusement seekers, who went streaming past him to other more favored attractions. For the last time the impresario hurried him over half Europe to discover whether the old interest might still survive here and there; all in vain; everywhere, as if by secret agreement, a positive revulsion from professional fasting was in evidence. Of course it could not really have sprung up so suddenly as all that, and many premonitory symptoms which had not been sufficiently remarked or suppressed during the rush and glitter of success now came retrospectively to mind, but it was now too late to take any countermeasures. Fasting would surely come into fashion again at some future date, yet that was no comfort for those living in the present. What, then, was the hunger artist to do? He had been applauded by thousands in his time and could hardly come down to showing himself in a street booth at village fairs, and as for adopting another profession, he was not only too old for that but too fanatically devoted to fasting. So he took leave of the impresario, his partner in an unparalleled career, and hired himself to a large circus; in order to spare his own feelings he avoided reading the conditions of his contract.

A large circus with its enormous traffic in replacing and recruiting men, animals and apparatus can always find a use for people at any time, even for a hunger artist, provided of course that he does not ask too much, and in this particular case anyhow it was not only the artist who was taken on but his famous and long-known name as well; indeed considering the peculiar nature of his performance, which was not impared by advancing age, it could not be objected that here was an artist past his prime, no longer at the height of his professional skill, seeking a refuge in some quiet corner of a circus; on the contrary, the hunger artist averred that he could fast as well as ever, which was entirely credible; he even alleged that if he were allowed to fast as he liked, and this was at once promised him without more ado, he could astound the world by establishing a record never yet achieved, a statement which certainly provoked a smile among the other professionals, since it left out of account the change in public opinion, which the hunger artist in his zeal conveniently forgot.

He had not, however, actually lost his sense of the real situation and took it as a matter of course that he and his cage should be stationed, not in the middle of the ring as a main attraction, but outside, near the animal cages, on a site that was after all easily accessible. Large and gaily painted placards made a frame for the cage and announced what was to be seen inside it. When the public came thronging out in the intervals to see the animals, they could hardly avoid passing the hunger artist's cage and stopping there for a moment; perhaps they might even have stayed longer had not those pressing behind them in the narrow gangway, who did not understand why they should be held up on their way towards the excitements of the menagerie, made it impossible for anyone to stand gazing quietly for any length of time. And that was the reason why the hunger artist, who had of course been looking forward to these visiting hours as the main achievement of his life, began instead to shrink from them. At first he could hardly wait for the intervals; it was exhilarating to watch the crowds come streaming his way, until only too soon—not even the most obstinate self-deception, clung to almost consciously, could hold out against the fact

—the conviction was borne in upon him that these people, most of them, to judge from their actions, again and again, without exception, were all on their way to the menagerie. And the first sight of them from the distance remained the best. For when they reached his cage he was at once deafened by the storm of shouting and abuse that arose from the two contending factions, which renewed themselves continuously, of those who wanted to stop and stare at him—he soon began to dislike them more than the others—not out of real interest but only out of obstinate self-assertiveness, and those who wanted to go straight on to the animals. When the first great rush was past, the stragglers came along, and these, whom nothing could have prevented from stopping to look at him as long as they had breath, raced past with long strides, hardly even glancing at him, in their haste to get to the menagerie in time. And all too rarely did it happen that he had a stroke of luck, when some father of a family fetched up before him with his children, pointed a finger at the hunger artist and explained at length what the phenomenon meant, telling stories of earlier years when he himself had watched similar but much more thrilling performances, and the children, still rather uncomprehending, since neither inside nor outside school had they been sufficiently prepared for this lesson—what did they care about fasting?—yet showed by the brightness of their intent eyes that new and better times might be coming. Perhaps, said the hunger artist to himself many a time, things would be a little better if his cage were set not quite so near the menagerie. That made it too easy for people to make their choice, to say nothing of what he suffered from the stench of the menagerie, the animals' restlessness by night, the carrying past of raw lumps of flesh for the beasts of prey, the roaring at feeding times, which depressed him continually. But he did not dare to lodge a complaint with the management; after all, he had the animals to thank for the troops of people who passed his cage, among whom there might always be one here and there to take an interest in him, and who could tell where they might seclude him if he called attention to his existence and thereby to the fact that, strictly speaking, he was only an impediment on the way to the menagerie.

A small impediment, to be sure, one that grew steadily less. People grew familiar with the strange idea that they could be expected, in times like these, to take an interest in a hunger artist, and with this familiarity the verdict went out against him He might fast as much as he could, and he did so; but nothing could save him now, people passed him by. Just try to explain to anyone the art of fasting! Anyone who has no feeling for it cannot be made to understand it. The fine placards grew dirty and illegible, they were torn down; the little notice board telling the number of fast days achieved, which at first was changed carefully every day, had long stayed at the same figure, for after the first few weeks even this small task seemed pointless to the staff; and so the artist simply fasted on and on, as he had once dreamed of doing, and it was no trouble to him, just as he had always foretold, but no one counted the days, no one, not even the artist himself, knew what records he was already breaking, and his heart grew heavy. And when once in a time some leisurely passer-by stopped, made merry over the old figure on the board and spoke of swindling, that was in its way the stupidest lie ever invented by indifference and inborn malice, since it was not the hunger artist who was cheating; he was working honestly, but the world was cheating him of his reward.

Many more days went by, however, and that too came to an end. An overseer's eye fell on the cage one day and he asked the attendants why this perfectly good cage should be left standing there unused with dirty straw inside it; nobody knew, until one man, helped out by the notice board, remembered about the hunger artist. They poked into the straw with sticks and found him in it. "Are you still fasting?" asked the overseer. "When on earth do you mean to stop?" "Forgive me, everybody," whispered the hunger artist; only the overseer, who had his ear to the bars, understood him. "Of course," said the overseer, and tapped his forehead with a finger to let the attendants know what state the man was in, "we forgive you." "I always wanted you to admire my fasting," said the hunger artist. "We do admire it," said the overseer, affably. "But you shouldn't admire it," said the hunger artist. "Well, then we don't admire it," said the overseer, "but why shouldn't we admire it?" "Because I have to fast, I can't help it," said the hunger artist. "What a fellow you are," said the overseer, "and why can't you help it?" "Because," said the hunger artist, lifting his head a little and speaking, with his lips pursed, as if for a kiss, right into the overseer's ear, so that no syllable might be lost, "because I couldn't find the food I liked. If I had found it, believe me, I should have made no fuss and stuffed myself like you or anyone else." These were his last words, but in his dimming eyes remained the firm though no longer proud persuasion that he was still continuing to fast.

"Well, clear this out now!" said the overseer, and they buried the hunger artist, straw and all. Into the cage they put a young panther. Even the most insensitive felt it refreshing to see this wild creature leaping around the cage that had so long been dreary. The panther was all right. The food he liked was brought him without hesitation by the attendants; he seemed not even to miss his freedom; his noble body, furnished almost to the bursting point with all that it needed, seemed to carry freedom around with it too; somewhere in his jaws it seemed to lurk; and the joy of life streamed with such ardent passion from his throat that for the onlookers it was not easy to stand the shock of it. But they braced themselves, crowded round the cage, and did not want ever to move away.

1924

ISAAC BASHEVIS SINGER

Tanhum

Tanhum Makover buttoned his gaberdine and twisted his earlocks into curls. He wiped his feet on the straw mat before the door, as

he had been told to. His prospective father-in-law, Reb Bendit Waldman, often reminded him that one could study the Torah and serve
the Almighty and still not behave like an idle dreamer. Reb Bendit
Waldman offered himself as an example. He was everything at once—
a scholar, a fervent Chassid of the Sadgora rabbi [1] as well as a successful lumber merchant, a chess player, and the proprietor of a
water mill. There was time for everything if one wasn't lazy, Reb
Bendit said—even to teach yourself Russian and Polish and glance
into a newspaper. How his prospective father-in-law managed all this
was beyond Tanhum. Reb Bendit never seemed to hurry. He had a
friendly word for everyone, even an errand boy or servant girl. Women
burdened down by a heavy spirit came to him for advice. Nor did he
neglect to visit the sick or—God forbid—to escort a corpse. Tanhum
often resolved to be like his prospective father-in-law, but he simply
couldn't manage it. He would grow absorbed in some sacred book
and before he knew it half the day had gone by. He tried to maintain a proper appearance, but a button would loosen and dangle by
a thread until it dropped off and got lost. His boots were always
muddied, his shirt collars frayed. As often as he knotted the band
of his breeches it always came untied again. He resolved to commit
two pages of the Gemara [2] to memory each day so that in three and
a half years he might finish with the Talmud, but he couldn't manage
even this. He would become preoccupied with some Talmudic controversy and linger over it for weeks on end. The questions and doubts
wouldn't let him rest. Certainly there was mercy in Heaven, but
why did little children or even dumb animals have to suffer? Why did
man have to end up dying, and a steer under the slaughterer's knife?
Why had the miracles ceased and God's chosen people been forced
to suffer exile for two thousand years? Tanhum probed in the Chassidic lore, the cabala[3] volumes, the ancient philosophy books. The
questions they raised in his mind plagued him like flies. There were
mornings when Tanhum awoke with a weight in his limbs, a pain
in his temples, and no urge at all to study, pray, or even perform
his ablutions. Today was one of those days. He opened the Gemara
and sat there for two hours without turning a page. At prayer, he
couldn't seem to grasp the meaning of the words. While reciting the
eighteen benedictions,[4] he transposed the blessings. And it just so
happened that today he was invited for lunch at his prospective
father-in-law's.

Reb Bendit Waldman's house was constructed in such a way
that one had to pass through the kitchen to get to the dining room.
The kitchen was aswarm with women—Tanhum's prospective mother-
in-law, her daughters-in-law, her daughters, including Tanhum's
bride-to-be, Mira Fridl. Even before entering the house he heard the
racket and commotion inside. The women of the house were all noisy

---

1. A member of the Jewish mystic order
that orginated in Poland in the eighteenth
century, stressing the pure heart and devotion but not asceticism and, in Poland,
learning. Sadgora, a small town in Buko-
vina (now U.S.S.R.), whose Jewish residents in the nineteenth century were
mostly Chassidim.
2. The supplementary second part of

the Talmud, commentary on the first part
(Mishnah), together making up the Jewish
civil and religious law.
3. Mystical interpretation of Scriptures.
4. The principal Jewish prayer, which
includes blessings of praise, prayer re-
quests (for understanding, redemption,
etc.), and thanksgiving.

and inclined to laughter, and often there were neighbors present. The cooking, baking, knitting, and needlepoint went on with a vengeance, and games of checkers, knucklebones, hide-and-seek, and wolf-and-goat[5] were played. On Chanukkah they rendered chicken fat; after Sukkoth they made coleslaw and pickled cucumbers; in the summers they put up jam. A fire was always kept going in the stove and under a tripod. The kitchen smelled of chicken soup, braised meat, cinnamon, and saffron. Cakes and cookies were baked for the Sabbath and holidays, to go with the roast geese, chickens, and ducks. One day they prepared for a circumcision and another day for the ceremony of redeeming the firstborn son;[6] now one of the family was becoming engaged, and now they all trouped off to a wedding. Tailors fitted coats, cobblers measured feet for shoes. At Reb Bendit Waldman's there was ample occasion to have a drink of cherry or sweet brandy and to nibble at an almond cookie, a babka,[7] or a honey cake. If a guest from another town came to visit, half the town sent over a kugel.[8] Reb Bendit made fun of the women of the house and their exaggerated sense of hospitality, but apparently he, too, enjoyed having his house full of people. Each time he went to Warsaw or Krakow he brought back all kinds of trinkets for the women—embroidered headkerchiefs, rings, shawls, and pins— and for the boys, pocketknives, pens, gold embossed skullcaps, and ornate phylactery bags. Apart from the usual wedding gifts—a set of the Talmud, a gold watch, a wine goblet, a spice box, a prayer shawl with silver brocade—Tanhum had already received all kinds of other presents. It wasn't mere talk when Tanhum's former fellow-students at the Brisk Yeshiva[9] said that he had fallen into a gravy pot. His bride-to-be, Mira Fridl, was considered a beauty, but Tanhum had not yet had a good look at her. How could he? During the signing of the marriage contract the women's parlor was jammed, and in the kitchen Mira Fridl was always surrounded by her sisters and sisters-in-law.

The moment Tanhum crossed the threshhold he lowered his eyes. True, everyone had his destined mate; forty days before he, Tanhum, had been born it had already been decided that Mira Fridl would become his spouse.[1] Still, he fretted that he wasn't a suitable enough son-in-law for Reb Bendit Waldman. All the members of the family were jolly, while he was reticent. He wasn't good at business or quick of tongue, not playful, not good at games, unable to perform stunts or do swimming tricks in the river. At twelve he already had to take free board at the homes of strangers in the towns where he was sent to study at the various yeshivas. His father died when Tanhum was still a child. His mother had remarried. Tanhum's stepfather was a poor peddler and had six children from a previous marriage. From childhood on, Tanhum went around in rags and was

5. Unidentified: there are, however, a Russian children's game and a chess game called wolf-and-sheep.

6. Every firstborn of the womb, man or animal, belongs to the Lord; clean animals must be sacrificed and humans redeemed, usually by the payment of money or its equivalent to the rabbi thirty days after the birth of the firstborn son. See

Exodus 13:11–16, *Leviticus* 27:26.

7. A cake marblized with soft chocolate.

8. Pudding of noodles or potatoes.

9. The seminary of Brest-Litovsk, Lithuania.

1. Not a contractual arrangement; legend has it that a child's mate is determined in heaven forty days before he or she is born.

neglected. He constantly berated himself for not praying fervently enough or devoting himself sufficiently to Jewishness, and he warred eternally with evil thoughts.

This day, the tumult in the kitchen was louder than ever. Someone had apparently just told a joke or performed some antic, for the women laughed and clapped their hands. Usually when Tanhum came in, a respectful path was cleared for him, but now he had to push his way through the throng. Who knows, maybe they were making fun of him? The back of his neck felt hot and damp. He must be late, for Reb Bendit was already seated at the table, with his sons and sons-in-law, waiting for him to appear. Reb Bendit, in a flowered robe, his silver-white beard combed into two points and a silk skullcap down over his forehead, lolled grandly in his armchair at the head of the table. The men had apparently had a drink, for a carafe and glasses stood on the table, along with wafers to crunch on. The company was in a joking mood. Reb Bendit's eldest son, Leibush Meir, a big, fleshy fellow with a huge potbelly and a round reddish beard circling his fat face, shook with laughter. Yoshe, a son-in-law—short and round as a barrel and with liquid black eyes and thick lips—giggled into a handkerchief. Another son-in-law, Shlomele, the wag, jokester, and mimic, impudently imitated someone's gestures.

Reb Bendit asked Tanhum amiably, "You have a gold watch. Why aren't you on time?"

"It stopped running."

"You probably didn't wind it."

"He needs an alarm clock," Schlomele jested.

"Well, go wash your hands," and Reb Bendit pointed to the washstand.

While washing his hands Tanhum wet his sleeves. There was a towel hanging on the rack, but he stood helplessly dripping water on the floor. He often tripped, caught his clothing, and bumped into things, and he constantly had to be told where to go and what to do. There was a mirror in the dining room and Tanhum caught a glimpse of himself—a stooped figure with sunken cheeks, dark eyes below dishevelled brows, a tiny beard on the tip of the chin, a pale nose, and a pointed Adam's apple. It took him a few seconds to realize that he was looking at his reflection. At the table, Reb Bendit praised the dish of groats and asked the woman who had prepared it what ingredients she had used. Leibush Meir demanded a second helping as usual. Shlomele complained that he had found only one mushroom in his portion. After the soup, the conversation turned serious. Reb Bendit had bought a tract of forest in partnership with a Zamosc merchant, Reb Nathan Vengrover. The two partners had fallen out, and Reb Nathan had summoned Reb Bendit to the rabbi's the following Saturday night for a hearing. Reb Bendit complained to the company at lunch that his partner was totally lacking in common sense, a dolt, a ninny, a dunderhead. The sons and sons-in-law agreed that he was a jackass. Tanhum sat in terror. This was evil talk, slander, and who knows what else! According to the Gemara, one lost the world to come for speaking so disrespectfully of another man. Had they forgotten this or did they only pretend to forget? Tanhum wanted to warn them that they were violating the law: Thou shalt not go up and down as a talebearer among thy people. According to the Gemara, he should have stuffed up his ears with the lobes so as not to hear, but he couldn't embarrass his prospective father-in-law this way. He sank even lower in his chair. Two women now brought in the main course—a platter of beef cutlets and a tray of roast chicken floating in sauce. Tanhum grimaced. How could one eat such a repast on a weekday? Didn't they remember the destruction of the Temple?[2]

"Tanhum, are you eating or sleeping?"

It was his intended, Mira Fridl, speaking. Tanhum came to with a start. He saw her now for the first time—of medium build, fair, with golden hair and blue eyes, wearing a red dress. She smiled at him mischievously and even winked.

"Which would you prefer—beef or chicken?"

Tanhum wanted to answer, but the words stuck in his throat. For some time already, he had felt an aversion to meat. No doubt everything here was strictly kosher, but it seemed to him that the meat smelled of blood and that he could hear the bellowing of the cow writhing beneath the slaughterer's knife.

Reb Bendit said, "Give him some of each."

Mira Fridl served a cutlet and then, with her serving spoon poised over the platter of chicken, asked, "Which would you like—the breast or a leg?"

Again Tanhum was unable to answer. Instead, Shlomele the wag said with a leer, "He lusts for both."

As Mira Fridl bent over Tanhum to put a chicken leg on his plate, her bosom touched his shoulder. She added potatoes and carrots and Tanhum shrank away from her. He heard Shlomele snicker, and he was overcome with shame. I don't belong among them, he thought. They're making a fool of me. . . . He had an urge to stand up and flee.

"Eat, Tanhum, don't dillydally," Reb Bendit said. "One must have strength for the Torah."

Tanhum put his fork into the sauce and dug out a sliver of meat, doused it in horseradish, and sprinkled it with salt to blot out the taste. He ate a slice of bread. He was intimidated by Mira Fridl. What would they talk about after the wedding? She was a rich man's daughter, accustomed to a life of luxury. Her mother had told him that a goldsmith from Lublin had fashioned jewelry for Mira Fridl. All kinds of fur coats, jackets, and capes were being sewn for her, and she would be provided with furniture, rugs, and porcelain. How could he, Tanhum, exercise control over such a pampered creature? And why would she want him for a husband? Her father had undoubtedly coerced her into it. He wanted a Talmudist for a son-in-law. Tanhum envisioned himself standing under the wedding canopy with Mira Fridl, eating the golden soup,[3] dancing the wedding dance,

---

2. 2 *Chronicles* 36:19. Because of the wickedness of Israel and its kings, the Lord allows the Chaldeans to kill young men in Solomon's temple, burn it down, and break down the walls of Jerusalem.

3. The Jewish wedding ceremony takes place under a canopy (*chuppah*). The bride and groom fast until after the ceremony, then immediately go into a separate room to eat, sometimes a more or less ceremonial food—here, apparently, chicken soup.

and then being led off to the marriage chamber. He felt a sense of panic. None of this seemed fitting for his oppressed spirit. He began to sway and to beg the Almighty to guard him from temptations, impure thoughts, Satan's net. *Father in Heaven, save me!*

Leibush Meir burst into laughter. "What are you swaying for? It's a chicken leg, not Rashi's commentary."[4]

Reb Nathan was expected to bring his arbitrator, Reb Feivel, to the hearing. Reb Bendit Waldman also had his own arbitrator, Reb Fishel, but nevertheless he invited Tanhum to attend the proceedings too. He said that it would do Tanhum good to learn something about practical matters. If he turned to the rabbinate, he would have to know a little about business. It was entirely feasible that that stubborn villain, Reb Nathan, wouldn't agree to a compromise and would insist on the strict letter of the law, and Reb Bendit asked Tanhum therefore to take down the books and go over the sections that dealt with the codes governing business partnerships. Tanhum agreed reluctantly. The entire Torah was holy, of course, but Tanhum wasn't drawn to those laws dealing with money, manipulation, interests, and swindle. In former years when he studied these subjects in the Gemara, it hadn't occurred to him that there really were Jews who reneged on written agreements, stole, swore falsely, and cheated. The idea of meeting in the flesh a person who would deny a debt, violate a trust, and grow rich from deception was too painful to contemplate. Tanhum wanted to tell Reb Bendit that he had no intention of becoming a rabbi, and that it would be hard for him now to lay aside the treatise in which he was absorbed and turn to matters that were alien to him. But how could he refuse Reb Bendit, who had raised him out of poverty, and given him his daughter for a bride, and provided him with overcoats, underwear, a sheepskin coat, a residence, holy books, a prayer shawl with silver brocade, and a thirteen-pointed fur hat besides? This would have enraged his future mother-in-law and turned Mira Fridl against him. It would have incited a feud and provoked evil gossip. It would have led to who knows what quarrels.

During the next few days, Tanhum didn't have enough time to get deeply into "The Breastplate of Judgment"[5] and its many commentaries. He quickly scanned the text of Rabbi Caro and the annotations of Rabbi Moshe Isserles. He hummed and bit his lips. Obviously even in the old days there had been no lack of frauds and of rascals. Was it any wonder? Even the generation that received the Torah had its Korah, its Dathan, its Abiram.[6] Still, how could theft be reconciled with faith? How could one whose soul had stood on Mount Sinai defile it with crime?

4. Solomon Yitzhaki Rashi (1040–1105), French rabbinical scholar, whose commentary on the whole Talmud helped to establish the text, and whose commentary on the Pentateuch has served as the basis for most later scholarship.

5. The Talmud. Joseph Caro (1488–1575) author of a commentary and its abridgement, *Shulhan Arukh* ("The Pre-

pared Table," 1564–65), which, with Moses Isserles' (c.1525–72) critical strictures, *Ha Mappah* ("The Tablecloth") are still considered authoritative by Orthodox Jews.

6. Leaders of the revolt against Moses in the desert who were destroyed by fire and earthquake. *Numbers* 16 and 26:9–11.

The Din Torah, the hearing, began on Saturday evening, and it looked as though it would last a whole week. The rabbi, Reb Efraim Engel, a patriarch of seventy and author of a book of legal opinions, told his wife to send all those who came seeking advice about other matters to the assistant rabbi. He bolted the door of his study and ordered his beadle to let only the participants enter. On the table stood the candles that had ushered out the Sabbath. The room smelled of wine, wax, and the spice box. From the way the family had decribed Reb Nathan Vengrover as a tough man and a speculator, Tanhum expected him to be tall, dark, and with the wild gaze of a gypsy, but in came a thin, stooped little man with a sparse beard the color of pepper, with a milky-white cataract in his left eye, and wearing a faded gaberdine, a sheepskin hat, and coarse boots. Pouches of bluish flesh dangled beneath his eyes and he had warts on his nose. Being the plaintiff, he was the first to speak. He immediately began to shout in a hoarse voice, and he kept on shouting and grunting throughout the proceedings.

Reb Bendit smoked an aromatic blend of tobacco in a pipe with an amber cover; Reb Nathan rolled cigarettes of cheap, stinking tobacco. Reb Bendit spoke deliberately and graced his words with proverbs and quotations from the saints; Reb Nathan slammed the table with his fist, yanked hairs from his beard, and called Reb Bendit a thief. He wouldn't even let his own arbitrator, Reb Feivel—who was the size of a cheder boy,[7] with eyes green as gooseberries and a red beard that fell to his loins—get a word in edgewise. Reb Bendit recalled the details of the agreement from memory, but Reb Nathan consulted whole stackfuls of papers that were filled with row upon row of a clumsy scribble and stained with erasures and blots. He didn't sit in the chair provided for him but paced to and fro, coughed, and spat into a handkerchief. Reb Bendit was sent all kinds of refreshments and drinks from home, but Reb Nathan didn't even go near the tea that the rabbi's wife brought in. From day to day his face grew more drawn, and was gray as dust and wasted as if from consumption. From nervous tension, he chewed his fingernails and tore his own notes into tiny shreds.

For the first two days, Tanhum was completely bewildered by what went on. The rabbi again and again implored Reb Nathan to speak to the point, not to mix up dates or inject matters that had no bearing on the subject. But it all came gushing out of Reb Nathan like water fom a pump. Gradually Tanhum came to understand that his prospective father-in-law was being accused of holding back profits and falsifying accounts. Reb Nathan Vengrover maintained that Reb Bendit had bribed Prince Sapieha's steward to chop down more acres of timber than had been stipulated in the contract. Nor would Reb Bendit allow Reb Nathan and his associate near the Squire, or to get in contact with the merchants who purchased the timber, which was tied in rafts and floated down the Vistula to Danzig. Reb Bendit had allegedly announced one price to Reb Nathan, when he had in fact got a higher one from the merchants. Reb

7. Schoolboy.

Bendit had claimed to have paid the brokers, loggers, and sawyers more than he actually did. He employed every trick and device to oust Reb Nathan from the partnership and to seize all the profits for himself. Reb Nathan pointed out that Reb Bendit had already twice gone bankrupt and subsequently settled for a third of his debts.

Reb Bendit had kept silent most of the time, awaiting his turn to speak, but finally he lost his patience. "Savage!" he shouted. "Hothead! Lunatic!"

"Usurer! Swindler! Robber!" Reb Nathan responded.

On the third day, Reb Bendit calmly began to refute Reb Nathan's charges. He proved that Reb Nathan contradicted himself, exaggerated, and didn't know a pine from an oak. How could he be allowed near the Squire when his Polish was so broken? How could he lay claim to half the income when he, Reb Bendit, had to lay out hush money to the gentry, stave off unfavorable decrees, shower assessors and marshals with gifts out of his own pocket? The more glibly Reb Bendit spoke, the more apparent it became to Tanhum that his prospective father-in-law had broken his agreement and had indeed sought to rob Reb Nathan of the profits and even part of his original investment. But how could this be, Tanhum wondered. How could Reb Bendit, a man in his sixties, a scholar, and a Chassid, commit such iniquities? What was his justification? He knew all the laws. He knew that no repentance could excuse the sin of robbery and theft unless one paid back every penny. The Day of Atonement[8] didn't forgive such transgressions. Could a man who believed in the Creator, in reward and punishment and in immortality of the soul, risk the world to come for the sake of a few thousand gulden?[9] Or was Reb Bendit a secret heretic?

In the closing days, Reb Bendit, his arbitrator, Reb Fishel, and Tanhum didn't go home for dinner—the maid brought them meat and soup. But Tanhum didn't touch the food. There was a gnawing in his stomach. His tongue was dry. He had a bad taste in his mouth, and he felt like vomiting. Although he fasted, his belly was bloated. A lump formed in his throat that he could neither swallow nor disgorge. He didn't weep but his eyes kept tearing over, and he saw everything as if through a mist. Tanhum reminded himself that only that past Sukkoth, when Reb Bendit had gone to the Sadgora rabbi, he had brought the rabbi an ivory ethrog box that was decorated with silver and embossed in gold. Inside, couched in flax, lay an ethrog[10] from Corfu that was pocked and budding. The Chassidim knew that besides contributing generously to the community, of which he was an elder, Reb Bendit also gave the rabbi a tithe. But what was the sense of robbing one person to give to another? Did he do all this to be praised in the Sadgora study houses and be seated at the rabbi's table? Had the greed for money and honors so blinded him that he didn't know the wrongs he committed? Yes, so it seemed, for during evening prayers Reb Bendit piously washed

---

8. Yom Kippur, last of the ten days of Pentitence, upon which, by fasting and prayer one may be released from sins or promises made to God, but vows to other men, community, court, or political regime are not annulled.

9. Gold or silver coin of Austria and Germany in wide use through eastern Europe.
10. Citron fruit which, with palm branch (lulab) was used to celebrate—and still symbolizes—the festival of Sukkoth.

his fingers in the basin, girdled his loins with a sash, stationed himself to pray at the eastern wall, swayed, bowed, beat his breast, and sighed. From time to time he stretched his hands up to Heaven. Several times during the arbitration he had invoked God's name.

Thursday night, when it came time to pass judgment, Reb Nathan Vengrover demanded a clear-cut decision: "No compromises! If the law says that what my partner did was right, then I don't demand even a groschen." [1]

"According to law, Reb Bendit has to take an oath," Reb Nathan's arbitrator Reb Feivel, asserted.

"I wouldn't swear even for a sackful of gold," Reb Bendit countered.

"In that case, pay up!"

"Not on your life!"

Both arbitrators, Reb Feivel and Reb Fishel, began to dispute the law. The rabbi drew "The Breastplate of Judgment" down from the bookcase.

Reb Bendit cast a glance at Tanhum. "Tanhum, why don't you speak up?"

Tanhum wanted to say that to appropriate another's possession was as serious an offense as swearing falsely. He also wanted to ask, "Why did you do it?" But he merely mumbled, "Since Father-in-Law signed an agreement, he must honor it."

"So you, too, turn on me, eh?"

"God forbid, but—"

" 'Art thou for us or for our adversaries?' " Reb Bendit quoted from the Book of Joshua,[2] in a dry voice.

"We don't live forever," Tanhum said haltingly.

"You go home!" Reb Bendit ordered.

Tanhum left the rabbi's study and went straight to his room at the inn. He didn't recite the Shema,[3] or undress, but sat on the edge of his cot the whole night. When the light began to break, he packed his Sabbath gaberdine, a few shirts, socks, and books in a straw basket, and walked down Synagogue Street to the bridge that led out of town. Months went by without any news of him. They even dredged the river for his body. Reb Bendit Waldman and Reb Nathan Vengrover reached an agreement. The rabbi and the arbitrators wouldn't permit it to come to oath-taking. Mira Fridl became engaged to a youth from Lublin, the son of a sugar manufacturer. Tanhum had left all his presents behind at the inn, and the bridegroom from Lublin inherited them. One winter day, a shipping agent brought news of Tanhum: he had gone back to the Brisk Yeshiva, from which Reb Bendit originally brought him to his town. Tanhum had become a recluse. He ate no meat, drank no wine, put pebbles inside his shoes, and slept on a bench behind the stove at the study house. When a new match was proposed to him in Brisk, he responded, "My soul yearns for the Torah."

1975

1. I.e., not even a thin dime.
2. *Joshua* 5:13. Before Jericho, Joshua sees a man with drawn sword and asks him this question; the answer: "captain of the host of the Lord."

3. *Shema Yisrael,* "Hear O Israel," the Jewish confession of faith, proclaiming the unity of God, recited morning and evening and on certain special occasions.

JOHN CHEEVER

The Country Husband

To begin at the beginning, the airplane from Minneapolis in which Francis Weed was traveling East ran into heavy weather. The sky had been a hazy blue, with the clouds below the plane lying so close together that nothing could be seen of the earth. Then mist began to form outside the windows, and they flew into a white cloud of such density that it reflected the exhaust fires. The color of the cloud darkened to gray, and the plane began to rock. Francis had been in heavy weather before, but he had never been shaken up so much. The man in the seat beside him pulled a flask out of his pocket and took a drink. Francis smiled at his neighbor, but the man looked away; he wasn't sharing his painkiller with anyone. The plane had begun to drop and flounder wildly. A child was crying. The air in the cabin was overheated and stale, and Francis' left foot went to sleep. He read a little from a paper book that he had bought at the airport, but the violence of the storm divided his attention. It was black outside the ports. The exhaust fires blazed and shed sparks in the dark, and, inside, the shaded lights, the stuffiness, and the window curtains gave the cabin an atmosphere of intense and misplaced domesticity. Then the lights flickered and went out. "You know what I've always wanted to do?" the man beside Francis said suddenly. "I've always wanted to buy a farm in New Hampshire and raise beef cattle." The stewardess announced that they were going to make an emergency landing. All but the child saw in their minds the spreading wings of the Angel of Death. The pilot could be heard singing faintly, "I've got sixpence, jolly, jolly sixpence. I've got sixpence to last me all my life . . ."[1] There was no other sound.

The loud groaning of the hydraulic valves swallowed up the pilot's song, and there was a shrieking high in the air, like automobile brakes, and the plane hit flat on its belly in a cornfield and shook them so violently that an old man up forward howled, "Me kidneys! Me kidneys!" The stewardess flung open the door, and someone opened an emergency door at the back, letting in the sweet noise of their continuing mortality—the idle splash and smell of a heavy rain. Anxious for their lives, they filed out of the doors and scattered over the cornfield in all directions, praying that the thread would hold. It did. Nothing happened. When it was clear that the plane would not burn or explode, the crew and the stewardess gathered the passengers together and led them to the shelter of a barn. They were not far from Philadelphia, and in a little while a string of taxis took them into the city. "It's just like the Marne,"[2] someone said, but there was surprisingly little relaxation of that suspiciousness with which many Americans regard their fellow-travelers.

In Philadelphia, Francis Weed got a train to New York. At the end of that journey, he crossed the city and caught, just as it was about to pull out, the commuting train that he took five nights a week to his

1. Song popular with Allied troops in World War II.
2. On September 8, 1914, over 1000 Paris taxicabs were requisitioned to move troops to the Marne River to halt the encircling Germans in what turned out to be the first German defeat of World War I.

home in Shady Hill.

He sat with Trace Bearden. "You know, I was in that plane that just crashed outside Philadelphia," he said. "We came down in a field . . ." He had traveled faster than the newspapers or the train, and the weather in New York was sunny and mild. It was a day in late September, as fragrant and shapely as an apple. Trace listened to the story, but how could he get excited? Francis had no powers that would let him re-create a brush with death—particularly in the atmosphere of a commuting train, journeying through a sunny countryside where already, in the slum gardens, there were signs of harvest. Trace picked up his newspaper, and Francis was left alone with his thoughts. He said good night to Trace on the platform at Shady Hill and drove in his secondhand Volkswagen up to the Blenhollow neighborhood, where he lived.

The Weeds' Dutch Colonial house was larger than it appeared to be from the driveway. The living room was spacious and divided like Gaul into three parts.[3] Around an ell to the left as one entered from the vestibule was the long table, laid for six, with candles and a bowl of fruit in the center. The sounds and smells that came from the open kitchen door were appetizing, for Julia Weed was a good cook. The largest part of the living room centered around a fireplace. On the right were some bookshelves and a piano. The room was polished and tranquil, and from the windows that opened to the west there was some late-summer sunlight, brilliant and as clear as water. Nothing here was neglected; nothing had not been burnished. It was not the kind of household where, after prying open a stuck cigarette box, you would find an old shirt button and a tarnished nickel. The hearth was swept, the roses on the piano were reflected in the polish of the broad top, and there was an album of Schubert waltzes on the rack. Louisa Weed, a pretty girl of nine, was looking out the western windows. Her younger brother Henry was standing beside her. Her still younger brother, Toby, was studying the figures of some tonsured monks drinking beer on the polished brass of the wood box. Francis, taking off his hat and putting down his paper, was not consciously pleased with the scene; he was not that reflective. It was his element, his creation, and he returned to it with that sense of lightness and strength with which any creature returns to its home. "Hi, everybody," he said. "The plane from Minneapolis . . ."

Nine times out of ten, Francis would be greeted with affection, but tonight the children are absorbed in their own antagonisms. Francis has not finished his sentence about the plane crash before Henry plants a kick in Louisa's behind. Louisa swings around, saying, "*Damn* you!" Francis makes the mistake of scolding Louisa for bad language before he punishes Henry. Now Louisa turns on her father and accuses him of favoritism. Henry is always right; she is persecuted and lonely; her lot is hopeless. Francis turns to his son, but the boy has justification for the kick —she hit him first; she hit him on the ear, which is dangerous. Louisa agrees with this passionately. She hit him on the ear, and she *meant* to hit him on the ear, because he messed up her china collection. Henry says that this is a lie. Little Toby turns away from the

3. Ancient France (Gaul) is so described by Julius Caesar in *The Gallic War*.

wood box to throw in some evidence for Louisa. Henry claps his hand over little Toby's mouth. Francis separates the two boys but accidentally pushes Toby into the wood box. Toby begins to cry. Louisa is already crying. Just then, Julia Weed comes into that part of the room where the table is laid. She is a pretty, intelligent woman, and the white in her hair is premature. She does not seem to notice the fracas. "Hello, darling," she says serenely to Francis. "Wash your hands, everyone. Dinner is ready." She strikes a match and lights the six candles in this vale of tears.[4]

This simple announcement, like the war cries of the Scottish chieftains, only refreshes the ferocity of the combatants. Louisa gives Henry a blow on the shoulder. Henry, although he seldom cries, has pitched nine innings and is tired. He bursts into tears. Little Toby discovers a splinter in his hand and begins to howl. Francis says loudly that he has been in a plane crash and that he is tired. Julia appears again, from the kitchen, and, still ignoring the chaos, asks Francis to go upstairs and tell Helen that everything is ready. Francis is happy to go; it is like getting back to headquarters company.[5] He is planning to tell his oldest daughter about the airplane crash, but Helen is lying on her bed reading a *True Romance* magazine, and the first thing Francis does is to take the magazine from her hand and remind Helen that he has forbidden her to buy it. She did not buy it, Helen replies. It was given to her by her best friend, Bessie Black. Everybody reads *True Romance*. Bessie Black's father reads *True Romance*. There isn't a girl in Helen's class who doesn't read *True Romance*. Francis expresses his detestation of the magazine and then tells her that dinner is ready—although from the sounds downstairs it doesn't seem so. Helen follows him down the stairs. Julia has seated herself in the candlelight and spread a napkin over her lap. Neither Louisa nor Henry has come to the table. Little Toby is still howling, lying face down on the floor. Francis speaks to him gently: "Daddy was in a plane crash this afternoon, Toby. Don't you want to hear about it?" Toby goes on crying. "If you don't come to the table now, Toby," Francis says, "I'll have to send you to bed without any supper." The little boy rises, gives him a cutting look, flies up the stairs to his bedroom, and slams the door. "Oh dear," Julia says, and starts to go after him. Francis says that she will spoil him. Julia says that Toby is ten pounds underweight and has to be encouraged to eat. Winter is coming, and he will spend the cold months in bed unless he has his dinner. Julia goes upstairs. Francis sits down at the table with Helen. Helen is suffering from the dismal feeling of having read too intently on a fine day, and she gives her father and the room a jaded look. She doesn't understand about the plane crash, because there wasn't a drop of rain in Shady Hill.

Julia returns with Toby, and they all sit down and are served. "Do I have to look at that big, fat slob?" Henry says, of Louisa. Everybody but Toby enters into this skirmish, and it rages up and down the table for five minutes. Toward the end, Henry puts his napkin over his head and, trying to eat that way, spills spinach all over his shirt. Francis asks Julia if the children couldn't have their dinner earlier.

---

4. Common figurative reference to earthly life (vale is valley), though here the tears are literal.

5. That is, like escaping from combat to relative safety behind the lines.

Julia's guns are loaded for this. She can't cook two dinners and lay two tables. She paints with lightning strokes that panorama of drudgery in which her youth, her beauty, and her wit have been lost. Francis says that he must be understood; he was nearly killed in an airplane crash, and he doesn't like to come home every night to a battlefield. Now Julia is deeply committed. Her voice trembles. He doesn't come home every night to a battlefield. The accusation is stupid and mean. Everything was tranquil until he arrived. She stops speaking, puts down her knife and fork, and looks into her plate as if it is a gulf. She begins to cry. "Poor Mummy!" Toby says, and when Julia gets up from the table, drying her tears with a napkin, Toby goes to her side. "Poor Mummy," he says. "Poor Mummy!" And they climb the stairs together. The other children drift away from the battlefield, and Francis goes into the back garden for a cigarette and some air.

It was a pleasant garden, with walks and flower beds and places to sit. The sunset had nearly burned out, but there was still plenty of light. Put into a thoughtful mood by the crash and the battle, Francis listened to the evening sounds of Shady Hill. "Varmints! Rascals!" old Mr. Nixon shouted to the squirrels in his bird-feeding station. "Avaunt and quit my sight!" A door slammed. Someone was playing tennis on the Babcocks' court; someone was cutting grass. Then Donald Goslin, who lived at the corner, began to play the "Moonlight Sonata."[6] He did this nearly every night. He threw the tempo out the window and played it *rubato*[7] from beginning to end, like an outpouring of tearful petulance, lonesomeness, and self-pity—of everything it was Beethoven's greatness not to know. The music rang up and down the street beneath the trees like an appeal for love, for tenderness, aimed at some lonely housemaid—some fresh-faced, homesick girl from Galway, looking at old snapshots in her third-floor room. "Here, Jupiter, here, Jupiter," Francis called to the Mercers' retriever. Jupiter crashed through the tomato vines with the remains of a felt hat in his mouth.

Jupiter was an anomaly. His retrieving instincts and his high spirits were out of place in Shady Hill. He was as black as coal, with a long, alert, intelligent, rakehell face. His eyes gleamed with mischief, and he held his head high. It was the fierce, heavily collared dog's head that appears in heraldry, in tapestry, and that used to appear on umbrella handles and walking sticks. Jupiter went where he pleased, ransacking wastebaskets, clotheslines, garbage pails, and shoe-bags. He broke up garden parties and tennis matches, and got mixed up in the processional at Christ Church on Sunday, barking at the men in red dresses.[8] He crashed through old Mr. Nixon's rose garden two or three times a day, cutting a wide swath through the Condesa de Sastagos,[9] and as soon as Donald Goslin lighted his barbecue fire on Thursday nights, Jupiter would get the scent. Nothing the Goslins did could drive him away. Sticks and stones and rude commands only moved him to the edge of the terrace, where he remained, with his gallant and heraldic muzzle, waiting for Donald Goslin to turn his back and reach for the

---

6. Common title of Beethoven's *Sonata Quasi una Fantasia* (1802), one of the most famous, frequently played, and sentimentalized piano compositions.
7. With intentional deviations from strict tempo.
8. Probably the choir.
9. Rather uncommon yellow and red roses difficult to grow.

salt. Then he would spring onto the terrace, lift the steak lightly off the fire, and run away with the Goslins' dinner. Jupiter's days were numbered. The Wrightsons' German gardener or the Farquarsons' cook would soon poison him. Even old Mr. Nixon might put some arsenic in the garbage that Jupiter loved. "Here, Jupiter, Jupiter!" Francis called, but the dog pranced off, shaking the hat in his white teeth. Looking in at the windows of his house, Francis saw that Julia had come down and was blowing out the candles.

Julia and Francis Weed went out a great deal. Julia was well liked and gregarious, and her love of parties sprang from a most natural dread of chaos and loneliness. She went through her morning mail with real anxiety, looking for invitations, and she usually found some, but she was insatiable, and if she had gone out seven nights a week, it would not have cured her of a reflective look—the look of someone who hears distant music—for she would always suppose that there was a more brilliant party somewhere else. Francis limited her to two weeknight parties, putting a flexible interpretation on Friday, and rode through the weekend like a dory in a gale. The day after the airplane crash, the Weeds were to have dinner with the Farquarsons.

Francis got home late from town, and Julia got the sitter while he dressed, and then hurried him out of the house. The party was small and pleasant, and Francis settled down to enjoy himself. A new maid passed the drinks. Her hair was dark, and her face was round and pale and seemed familiar to Francis. He had not developed his memory as a sentimental faculty. Wood smoke, lilac, and other such perfumes did not stir him, and his memory was something like his appendix—a vestigial repository. It was not his limitation at all to be unable to escape the past; it was perhaps his limitation that he had escaped it so successfully. He might have seen the maid at other parties, he might have seen her taking a walk on Sunday afternoons, but in either case he would not be searching his memory now. Her face was, in a wonderful way, a moon face—Norman or Irish—but it was not beautiful enough to account for his feeling that he had seen her before, in circumstances that he ought to be able to remember. He asked Nellie Farquarson who she was. Nellie said that the maid had come through an agency, and that her home was Trénon, in Nor nandy—a small place with a church and a restaurant that Nellie had once visited. While Nellie talked on about her travels abroad, Francis realized where he had seen the woman before. It had been at the end of the war. He had left a replacement depot with some other men and taken a three-day pass in Trénon. On their second day, they had walked out to a crossroads to see the public chastisement of a young woman who had lived with the German commandant during the Occupation.

It was a cool morning in the fall. The sky was overcast, and poured down onto the dirt crossroads a very discouraging light. They were on high land and could see how like one another the shapes of the clouds and the hills were as they stretched off toward the sea. The prisoner arrived sitting on a three-legged stool in a farm cart. She stood by the cart while the mayor read the accusation and the sentence. Her head was bent and her face was set in that empty half smile behind which the whipped soul is suspended. When the mayor was finished, she undid her hair and let it fall across her back. A little man with a gray mustache cut off her hair with shears and dropped it on the ground. Then, with a bowl of soapy water and a straight razor, he shaved her skull clean. A woman approached and began to undo the fastenings of her clothes, but the prisoner pushed her aside and undressed herself. When she pulled her chemise over her head and threw it on the ground, she was naked. The women jeered; the men were still. There was no change in the falseness or the plaintiveness of the prisoner's smile. The cold wind made her white skin rough and hardened the nipples of her breasts. The jeering ended gradually, put down by the recognition of their common humanity. One woman spat on her, but some inviolable grandeur in her nakedness lasted through the ordeal. When the crowd was quiet, she turned—she had begun to cry—and, with nothing on but a pair of worn black shoes and stockings, walked down the dirt road alone away from the village. The round white face had aged a little, but there was no question but that the maid who passed his cocktails and later served Francis his dinner was the woman who had been punished at the crossroads.

The war seemed now so distant and that world where the cost of partisanship had been death or torture so long ago. Francis had lost track of the men who had been with him in Vésey. He could not count on Julia's discretion. He could not tell anyone. And if he had told the story now, at the dinner table, it would have been a social as well as a human error. The people in the Farquarsons' living room seemed united in their tacit claim that there had been no past, no war—that there was no danger or trouble in the world. In the recorded history of human arrangements, this extraordinary meeting would have fallen into place, but the atmosphere of Shady Hill made the memory unseemly and impolite. The prisoner withdrew after passing the coffee, but the encounter left Francis feeling languid; it had opened his memory and his senses, and left them dilated. He and Julia drove home when the party ended, and Julia went into the house. Francis stayed in the car to take the sitter home.

Expecting to see Mrs. Henlein, the old lady who usually stayed with the children, he was surprised when a young girl opened the door and came out onto the lighted stoop. She stayed in the light to count her textbooks. She was frowning and beautiful. Now, the world is full of beautiful young girls, but Francis saw here the difference between beauty and perfection. All those endearing flaws, moles, birthmarks, and healed wounds were missing, and he experienced in his consciousness that moment when music breaks glass, and felt a pang of recognition as strange, deep, and wonderful as anything in his life. It hung from her frown, from an impalpable darkness in her face—a look that impressed him as a direct appeal for love. When she had counted her books, she came down the steps and opened the car door. In the light, he saw that her cheeks were wet. She got in and shut the door.

"You're new," Francis said.

"Yes. Mrs. Henlein is sick. I'm Anne Murchison."

"Did the children give you any trouble?"

"Oh, no, no." She turned and smiled at him unhappily in the dim dashboard light. Her light hair caught on the collar of her jacket, and she shook her head to set it loose.

"You've been crying."

"Yes."

"I hope it was nothing that happened in our house."

"No, no, it was nothing that happened in your house." Her voice was bleak. "It's no secret. Everybody in the village knows. Daddy's an alcoholic, and he just called me from some saloon and gave me a piece of his mind. He thinks I'm immoral. He called just before Mrs. Weed came back."

"I'm sorry."

"Oh, *Lord!*" She gasped and began to cry. She turned toward Francis, and he took her in his arms and let her cry on his shoulder. She shook in his embrace, and this movement accentuated his sense of the fineness of her flesh and bone. The layers of their clothing felt thin, and when her shuddering began to diminish, it was so much like a paroxysm of love that Francis lost his head and pulled her roughly against him. She drew away. "I live on Belleview Avenue," she said. "You go down Lansing Street to the railroad bridge."

"All right." He started the car.

"You turn left at that traffic light. . . . Now you turn right here and go straight on toward the tracks."

The road Francis took brought him out of his own neighborhood, across the tracks, and toward the river, to a street where the near-poor lived, in houses whose peaked gables and trimmings of wooden lace conveyed the purest feelings of pride and romance, although the houses themselves could not have offered much privacy or comfort, they were all so small. The street was dark, and, stirred by the grace and beauty of the troubled girl, he seemed, in turning in to it, to have come into the deepest part of some submerged memory. In the distance, he saw a porch light burning. It was the only one, and she said that the house with the light was where she lived. When he stopped the car, he could see beyond the porch light into a dimly lighted hallway with an old-fashioned clothes tree. "Well, here we are," he said, conscious that a young man would have said something different.

She did not move her hands from the books, where they were folded, and she turned and faced him. There were tears of lust in his eyes. Determinedly—not sadly—he opened the door on his side and walked around to open hers. He took her free hand, letting his fingers in between hers, climbed at her side the two concrete steps, and went up a narrow walk through a front garden where dahlias, marigolds, and roses—things that had withstood the light frosts—still bloomed, and made a bittersweet smell in the night air. At the steps, she freed her hand and then turned and kissed him swiftly. Then she crossed the porch and shut the door. The porch light went out, then the light in the hall. A second later, a light went on upstairs at the side of the house, shining into a tree that was still covered with leaves. It took her only a few minutes to undress and get into bed, and then the house was dark.

Julia was asleep when Francis got home. He opened a second window and got into bed to shut his eyes on that night, but as soon as they were shut—as soon as he had dropped off to sleep—the girl entered his mind, moving with perfect freedom through its shut doors and

filling chamber after chamber with her light, her perfume, and the
music of her voice. He was crossing the Atlantic with her on the old
Mauretania[1] and, later, living with her in Paris. When he woke from
his dream, he got up and smoked a cigarette at the open window.
Getting back into bed, he cast around in his mind for something he
desired to do that would injure no one, and he thought of skiing. Up
through the dimness in his mind rose the image of a mountain deep in
snow. It was late in the day. Wherever his eyes looked, he saw broad
and heartening things. Over his shoulder, there was a snow-filled valley,
rising into wooded hills where the trees dimmed the whiteness like a
sparse coat of hair. The cold deadened all sound but the loud, iron
clanking of the lift machinery. The light on the trails was blue, and it
was harder than it had been a minute or two earlier to pick the turns,
harder to judge—now that the snow was all deep blue—the crust, the
ice, the bare spots, and the deep piles of dry powder. Down the mountain he swung, matching his speed against the contours of a slope that
had been formed in the first ice age, seeking with ardor some simplicity
of feeling and circumstance. Night fell then, and he drank a Martini
with some old friend in a dirty country bar.

In the morning, Francis' snow-covered mountain was gone, and he
was left with his vivid memories of Paris and the *Mauretania*. He had
been bitten gravely. He washed his body, shaved his jaws, drank his
coffee, and missed the seven-thirty-one. The train pulled out just as he
brought his car to the station, and the longing he felt for the coaches
as they drew stubbornly away from him reminded him of the humors
of love. He waited for the eight-two, on what was now an empty platform. It was a clear morning; the morning seemed thrown like a gleaming bridge of light over his mixed affairs. His spirits were feverish and
high. The image of the girl seemed to put him into a relationship to the
world that was mysterious and enthralling. Cars were beginning to
fill up the parking lot, and he noticed that those that had driven down
from the high land above Shady Hill were white with hoarfrost. This
first clear sign of autumn thrilled him. An express train—a night train
from Buffalo or Albany—came down the tracks between the platforms,
and he saw that the roofs of the foremost cars were covered with a
skin of ice. Struck by the miraculous physicalness of everything, he
smiled at the passengers in the dining car, who could be seen eating
eggs and wiping their mouths with napkins as they traveled. The
sleeping-car compartments, with their soiled bed linen, trailed through
the fresh morning like a string of rooming-house windows. Then he
saw an extraordinary thing; at one of the bedroom windows sat an un-
clothed woman of exceptional beauty, combining her golden hair. She
passed like an apparition through Shady Hill, combing and combing
her hair, and Francis followed her with his eyes until she was out of
sight. Then old Mrs. Wrightson joined him on the platform and began
to talk.

"Well, I guess you must be surprised to see me here the third morning in a row," she said, "but because of my window curtains I'm
becoming a regular commuter. The curtains I bought on Monday I

1. The original *Mauretania* (1907–1935), sister ship of the *Lusitania*, which was sunk by the Germans in 1915, was the most famous transatlantic liner of its day and held speed records for more than 20 years.

returned on Tuesday, and the curtains I bought Tuesday I'm returning today. On Monday, I got exactly what I wanted—it's a wool tapestry with roses and birds—but when I got them home, I found they were the wrong length. Well, I exchanged them yesterday, and when I got them home, I found they were still the wrong length. Now I'm praying to high Heaven that the decorator will have them in the right length, because you know my house, you *know* my living-room windows, and you can imagine what a problem they present. I don't know what to do with them."

"I know what to do with them," Francis said.

"What?"

"Paint them black on the inside, and shut up."

There was a gasp from Mrs. Wrightson, and Francis looked down at her to be sure that she knew he meant to be rude. She turned and walked away from him, so damaged in spirit that she limped. A wonderful feeling enveloped him, as if light were being shaken about him, and he thought again of Venus combing and combing her hair as she drifted through the Bronx. The realization of how many years had passed since he had enjoyed being deliberately impolite sobered him. Among his friends and neighbors, there were brilliant and gifted people—he saw that—but many of them, also, were bores and fools, and he had made the mistake of listening to them all with equal attention. He had confused a lack of discrimination with Christian love, and the confusion seemed general and destructive. He was grateful to the girl for this bracing sensation of independence. Birds were singing—cardinals and the last of the robins. The sky shone like enamel. Even the smell of ink from his morning paper honed his appetite for life, and the world that was spread out around him was plainly a paradise.

If Francis had believed in some hierarchy of love—in spirits armed with hunting bows, in the capriciousness of Venus and Eros[2]—or even in magical potions, philters, and stews, in scapulae and quarters of the moon,[3] it might have explained his susceptibility and his feverish high spirits. The autumnal loves of middle age are well publicized, and he guessed that he was face to face with one of these, but there was not a trace of autumn in what he felt. He wanted to sport in the green woods, scratch where he itched, and drink from the same cup.

His secretary, Miss Rainey, was late that morning—she went to a psychiatrist three mornings a week—and when she came in, Francis wondered what advice a psychiatrist would have for him. But the girl promised to bring back into his life something like the sound of music. The realization that this music might lead him straight to a trial for statutory rape[4] at the county courthouse collapsed his happiness. The photograph of his four children laughing into the camera on the beach at Gay Head reproached him. On the letterhead of his firm there was a drawing of the Laocoön[5] and the figure of the priest and his sons in

2. The Roman name for the goddess of love (Greek Aphrodite) and the Greek name for her son (Roman Cupid).

3. Love-inducing and predictive magic; *scapulae* are shoulderblades or bones of the back.

4. Criminal charge involving sexual relations with someone below the legal age of consent.

5. Famous Greek statue, described here, now in the Vatican museum; the "meaning" for Weed seems to reside in the physical struggle, not in the legend (in which the priest and his sons were punished for warning the Trojans about the wooden horse).

the coils of the snake appeared to him to have the deepest meaning.

He had lunch with Pinky Trabert. At a conversational level, the mores of his friends were robust and elastic, but he knew that the moral card house would come down on them all—on Julia and the children as well—if he got caught taking advantage of a babysitter. Looking back over the recent history of Shady Hill for some precedent, he found there was none. There was no turpitude; there had not been a divorce since he lived there; there had not even been a breath of scandal. Things seemed arranged with more propriety even than in the Kingdom of Heaven. After leaving Pinky, Francis went to a jeweler's and bought the girl a bracelet. How happy this clandestine purchase made him, how stuffy and comical the jeweler's clerks seemed, how sweet the women who passed at his back smelled! On Fifth Avenue, passing Atlas with his shoulders bent under the weight of the world,[6] Francis thought of the strenuousness of containing his physicalness within the patterns he had chosen.

He did not know when he would see the girl next. He had the bracelet in his inside pocket when he got home. Opening the door of his house, he found her in the hall. Her back was to him, and she turned when she heard the door close. Her smile was open and loving. Her perfection stunned him like a fine day—a day after a thunderstorm. He seized her and covered her lips with his, and she struggled but she did not have to struggle for long, because just then little Gertrude Flannery appeared from somewhere and said, "Oh, Mr. Weed . . ."

Gertrude was a stray. She had been born with a taste for exploration, and she did not have it in her to center her life with her affectionate parents. People who did not know the Flannerys concluded from Gertrude's behavior that she was the child of a bitterly divided family, where drunken quarrels were the rule. This was not true. The fact that little Gertrude's clothing was ragged and thin was her own triumph over her mother's struggle to dress her warmly and neatly. Garrulous, skinny, and unwashed, she drifted from house to house around the Blenhollow neighborhood, forming and breaking alliances based on an attachment to babies, animals, children her own age, adolescents, and sometimes adults. Opening your front door in the morning, you would find Gertrude sitting on your stoop. Going into the bathroom to shave, you would find Gertrude using the toilet. Looking into your son's crib, you would find it empty, and, looking further, you would find that Gertrude had pushed him in his baby carriage into the next village. She was helpful, pervasive, honest, hungry, and loyal. She never went home of her own choice. When the time to go arrived, she was indifferent to all its signs: "Go home, Gertrude," people could be heard saying in one house or another, night after night. "Go home, Gertrude. It's time for you to go home now, Gertrude." "You had better go home and get your supper, Gertrude." "I told you to go home twenty minutes ago, Gertrude." "Your mother will be worrying about you, Gertrude." "Go home, Gertude, go home."

There are times when the lines around the human eye seem like shelves of eroded stone and when the staring eye itself strikes us with

6. In Greek legend the Titan Atlas supported the heavens on his shoulders but has come to be depicted as bearing the globe; the statue is at Rockefeller Center.

such a wilderness of animal feeling that we are at a loss. The look Francis gave the little girl was ugly and queer, and it frightened her. He reached into his pocket—his hands were shaking—and took out a quarter. "Go home, Gertrude, go home, and don't tell anyone, Gertrude. Don't—" He choked and ran into the living room as Julia called down to him from upstairs to hurry and dress.

The thought that he would drive Anne Murchison home later that night ran like a golden thread through the events of the party that Francis and Julia went to, and he laughed uproariously at dull jokes, dried a tear when Mabel Mercer told him about the death of her kitten, and stretched, yawned, sighed, and grunted like any other man with a rendezvous at the back of his mind. The bracelet was in his pocket. As he sat talking, the smell of grass was in his nose, and he was wondering where he would park the car. Nobody lived in the old Parker mansion, and the driveway was used as a lovers' lane. Townsend Street was a dead end, and he could park there, beyond the last house. The old lane that used to connect Elm Street to the riverbanks was overgrown, but he had walked there with his children, and he could drive his car deep enough into the brushwoods to be concealed.

The Weeds were the last to leave the party, and their host and hostess spoke of their own married happiness while they all four stood in the hallway saying good night. "She's my girl," their host said, squeezing his wife. "She's my blue sky. After sixteen years, I still bite her shoulders. She makes me feel like Hannibal crossing the Alps."[7]

The Weeds drove home in silence. Francis brought the car up the driveway and sat still, with the motor running. "You can put the car in the garage," Julia said as she got out. "I told the Murchison girl she could leave at eleven. Someone drove her home." She shut the door, and Francis sat in the dark. He would be spared nothing then, it seemed, that a fool was not spared: ravening lewdness, jealousy, this hurt to his feelings that put tears in his eyes, even scorn—for he could see clearly the image he now presented, his arms spread over the steering wheel and his head buried in them for love.

Francis had been a dedicated Boy Scout when he was young, and, remembering the precepts of his youth, he left his office early the next afternoon and played some round-robin squash, but, with his body toned up by exercise and a shower, he realized that he might better have stayed at his desk. It was a frosty night when he got home. The air smelled sharply of change. When he stepped into the house, he sensed an unusual stir. The children were in their best clothes, and when Julia came down, she was wearing a lavender dress and her diamond sunburst. She explained the stir: Mr. Hubber was coming at seven to take their photograph for the Christmas card. She had put out Francis' blue suit and a tie with some color in it, because the picture was going to be in color this year. Julia was lighthearted at the thought of being photographed for Christmas. It was the kind of ceremony she enjoyed.

Francis went upstairs to change his clothes. He was tired from the

---

7. The Carthaginian general (274–183 B.C.) attacked the Romans from the rear by crossing the Alps, considered impregnable, with the use of elephants.

day's work and tired with longing, and sitting on the edge of the bed had the effect of deepening his weariness. He thought of Anne Murchison, and the physical need to express himself, instead of being restrained by the pink lamps on Julia's dressing table, engulfed him. He went to Julia's desk, took a piece of writing paper, and began to write on it. "Dear Anne, I love you, I love you, I love you . . ." No one would see the letter, and he used no restraint. He used phrases like "heavenly bliss," and "love nest." He salivated, sighed, and trembled. When Julia called him to come down, the abyss between his fantasy and the practical world opened so wide that he felt it affect the muscles of his heart.

Julia and the children were on the stoop, and the photographer and his assistant had set up a double battery of floodlights to show the family and the architectural beauty of the entrance to their house. People who had come home on a late train slowed their cars to see the Weeds being photographed for their Christmas card. A few waved and called to the family. It took half an hour of smiling and wetting their lips before Mr. Hubber was satisfied. The heat of the lights made an unfresh smell in the frosty air, and when they were turned off, they lingered on the retina of Francis' eyes.

Later that night, while Francis and Julia were drinking their coffee in the living room, the doorbell rang. Julia answered the door and let in Clayton Thomas. He had come to pay her for some theater tickets that she had given his mother some time ago, and that Helen Thomas had scrupulously insisted on paying for, though Julia had asked her not to. Julia invited him in to have a cup of coffee. "I won't have any coffee," Clayton said, "but I will come in for a minute." He followed her into the living room, said good evening to Francis, and sat awkwardly in a chair.

Clayton's father had been killed in the war, and the young man's fatherlessness surrounded him like an element. This may have been conspicuous in Shady Hill because the Thomases were the only family that lacked a piece; all the other marriages were intact and productive. Clayton was in his second or third year of college, and he and his mother lived alone in a large house, which she hoped to sell. Clayton had once made some trouble. Years ago, he had stolen some money and run away; he had got to California before they caught up with him. He was tall and homely, wore horn-rimmed glasses, and spoke in a deep voice.

"When do you go back to college, Clayton?" Francis asked.

"I'm not going back," Clayton said. "Mother doesn't have the money, and there's no sense in all this pretense. I'm going to get a job, and if we sell the house, we'll take an apartment in New York."

"Won't you miss Shady Hill?" Julia asked.

"No," Clayton said. "I don't like it."

"Why not?" Francis asked.

"Well, there's a lot here I don't approve of," Clayton said gravely. "Things like the club dances. Last Saturday night, I looked in toward the end and saw Mr. Granner trying to put Mrs. Minot into the trophy case. They were both drunk. I disapprove of so much drinking."

"It was Saturday night," Francis said.

"And all the dovecotes are phony," Clayton said. "And the way people clutter up their lives. I've thought about it a lot, and what seems to me to be really wrong with Shady Hill is that it doesn't have any future. So much energy is spent in perpetuating the place—in keeping out undesirables, and so forth—that the only idea of the future anyone has is just more and more commuting trains and more parties. I don't think that's healthy. I think people ought to be able to dream big dreams about the future. I think people ought to be able to dream great dreams."

"It's too bad you couldn't continue with college," Julia said.

"I wanted to go to divinity school," Clayton said.

"What's your church?" Francis asked.

"Unitarian, Theosophist, Transcendentalist, Humanist,"[8] Clayton said.

"Wasn't Emerson a transcendentalist?" Julia asked.

"I mean the English transcendentalists," Clayton said. "All the American transcendentalists were goops."

"What kind of a job do you expect to get?" Francis asked.

"Well, I'd like to work for a publisher," Clayton said, "but everyone tells me there's nothing doing. But it's the kind of thing I'm interested in. I'm writing a long verse play about good and evil. Uncle Charlie might get me into a bank, and that would be good for me. I need the discipline. I have a long way to go in forming my character. I have some terrible habits. I talk too much. I think I ought to take vows of silence. I ought to try not to speak for a week, and discipline myself. I've thought of making a retreat at one of the Episcopalian monasteries, but I don't like the Trinitarianism."

"Do you have any girl friends?" Francis asked.

"I'm engaged to be married," Clayton said. "Of course, I'm not old enough or rich enough to have my engagement observed or respected or anything, but I bought a simulated emerald for Anne Murchison with the money I made cutting lawns this summer. We're going to be married as soon as she finishes school."

Francis recoiled at the mention of the girl's name. Then a dingy light seemed to emanate from his spirit, showing everything—Julia, the boy, the chairs—in their true colorlessness. It was like a bitter turn of the weather.

"We're going to have a large family," Clayton said. "Her father's a terrible rummy, and I've had my hard times, and we want to have lots of children. Oh, she's wonderful, Mr. and Mrs. Weed, and we have so much in common. We like all the same things. We sent out the same Christmas card last year without planning it, and we both have an allergy to tomatoes, and our eyebrows grow together in the middle. Well, good night."

Julia went to the door with him. When she returned, Francis said that Clayton was lazy, irresponsible, affected, and smelly. Julia said that Francis seemed to be getting intolerant; the Thomas boy was young and should be given a chance. Julia had noticed other cases where Francis had been short-tempered. "Mrs. Wrightson has asked

---

8. All are deviations from orthodox Christianity and tend to be more man-than God-oriented, though their differences hardly seem reconcilable; the American Transcendentalists (see below) tended to change the emphasis from the study of thought rather than of sense objects among the English Transcendentalists to belief in "intuition."

everyone in Shady Hill to her anniversary party but us," she said.

"I'm sorry, Julia."

"Do you know why they didn't ask us?"

"Why?"

"Because you insulted Mrs. Wrightson."

"Then you know about it?"

"June Masterson told me. She was standing behind you."

Julia walked in front of the sofa with a small step that expressed, Francis knew, a feeling of anger.

"I did insult Mrs. Wrightson, Julia, and I meant to. I've never liked her parties, and I'm glad she's dropped us."

"What about Helen?"

"How does Helen come into this?"

"Mrs. Wrightson's the one who decides who goes to the assemblies."

"You mean she can keep Helen from going to the dances?"

"Yes."

"I hadn't thought of that."

"Oh, I knew you hadn't thought of it," Julia cried, thrusting hilt-deep into this chink of his armor. "And it makes me furious to see this kind of stupid thoughtlessness wreck everyone's happiness."

"I don't think I've wrecked anyone's happiness."

"Mrs. Wrightson runs Shady Hill and has run it for the last forty years. I don't know what makes you think that in a community like this you can indulge every impulse you have to be insulting, vulgar, and offensive."

"I have very good manners," Francis said, trying to give the evening a turn toward the light.

"Damn you, Francis Weed!" Julia cried, and the spit of her words struck him in the face. "I've worked hard for the social position we enjoy in this place, and I won't stand by and see you wreck it. You must have understood when you settled here that you couldn't expect to live like a bear in a cave."

"I've got to express my likes and dislikes."

"You can conceal your dislikes. You don't have to meet everything head-on, like a child. Unless you're anxious to be a social leper. It's no accident that we get asked out a great deal. It's no accident that Helen has so many friends. How would you like to spend your Saturday nights at the movies? How would you like to spend your Sundays raking up dead leaves? How would you like it if your daughter spent the assembly nights sitting at her window, listening to the music from the club? How would you like it—" He did something then that was, after all, not so unaccountable, since her words seemed to raise up between them a wall so deadening that he gagged: He struck her full in the face. She staggered and then, a moment later, seemed composed. She went up the stairs to their room. She didn't slam the door. When Francis followed, a few minutes later, he found her packing a suitcase.

"Julia, I'm very sorry."

"It doesn't matter," she said. She was crying.

"Where do you think you're going?"

"I don't know. I just looked at a timetable. There's an eleven-sixteen into New York. I'll take that."

"You can't go, Julia."

"I can't stay. I know that."

"I'm sorry about Mrs. Wrightson, Julia, and I'm—"

"It doesn't matter about Mrs. Wrightson. That isn't the trouble."

"What is the trouble?"

"You don't love me."

"I do love you, Julia."

"No, you don't."

"Julia, I do love you, and I would like to be as we were—sweet and bawdy and dark—but now there are so many people."

"You hate me."

"I don't hate you, Julia."

"You have no idea of how much you hate me. I think it's subconscious. You don't realize the cruel things you've done."

"What cruel things, Julia?"

"The cruel acts your subconscious drives you to in order to express your hatred of me."

"What, Julia?"

"I've never complained."

"Tell me."

"You don't know what you're doing."

"Tell me."

"Your clothes."

"What do you mean?"

"I mean the way you leave your dirty clothes around in order to express your subconscious hatred of me."

"I don't understand."

"I mean your dirty socks and your dirty pajamas and your dirty underwear and your dirty shirts!" She rose from kneeling by the suitcase and faced him, her eyes blazing and her voice ringing with emotion. "I'm talking about the fact that you've never learned to hang up anything. You just leave your clothes all over the floor where they drop, in order to humiliate me. You do it on purpose!" She fell on the bed, sobbing.

"Julia, darling!" he said, but when she felt his hand on her shoulder she got up.

"Leave me alone," she said. "I have to go." She brushed past him to the closet and came back with a dress. "I'm not taking any of the things you've given me," she said. "I'm leaving my pearls and the fur jacket."

"Oh, Julia!" Her figure, so helpless in its self-deceptions, bent over the suitcase made him nearly sick with pity. She did not understand how desolate her life would be without him. She didn't understand the hours that working women have to keep. She didn't understand that most of her friendships existed within the framework of their marriage, and that without this she would find herself alone. She didn't understand about travel, about hotels, about money. "Julia, I can't let you go! What you don't understand, Julia, is that you've come to be dependent on me."

She tossed her head back and covered her face with her hands. "Did you say that *I* was dependent on *you*?" she asked. "Is that what you said? And who is it that tells you what time to get up in the morning and when to go to bed at night? Who is it that prepares your meals and picks up your dirty clothes and invites your friends to dinner? If it weren't for me, your neckties would be greasy and your clothing would be full of moth holes. You were alone when I met you, Francis Weed, and you'll be alone when I leave. When Mother asked you for a list to send out invitations to our wedding, how many names did you have to give her? Fourteen!"

"Cleveland wasn't my home, Julia."

"And how many of your friends came to the church? Two!"

"Cleveland wasn't my home, Julia."

"Since I'm not taking the fur jacket," she said quietly, "you'd better put it back into storage. There's an insurance policy on the pearls that comes due in January. The name of the laundry and the maid's telephone number—all those things are in my desk. I hope you won't drink too much, Francis. I hope that nothing bad will happen to you. If you do get into serious trouble, you can call me."

"Oh, my darling, I can't let you go!" Francis said. "I can't let you go, Julia!" He took her in his arms.

"I guess I'd better stay and take care of you for a little while longer," she said.

Riding to work in the morning, Francis saw the girl walk down the aisle of the coach. He was surprised; he hadn't realized that the school she went to was in the city, but she was carrying books, she seemed to be going to school. His surprise delayed his reaction, but then he got up clumsily and stepped into the aisle. Several people had come between them, but he could see her ahead of him, waiting for someone to open the car door, and then, as the train swerved, putting out her hand to support herself as she crossed the platform into the next car. He followed her through that car and halfway through another before calling her name—"Anne! Anne!"—but she didn't turn. He followed her into still another car, and she sat down in an aisle seat. Coming up to her, all his feelings warm and bent in her direction, he put his hand on the back of her seat—even this touch warmed him—and, leaning down to speak to her, he saw that it was not Anne. It was an older woman wearing glasses. He went on deliberately into another car, his face red with embarrassment and the much deeper feeling of having his good sense challenged; for if he couldn't tell one person from another, what evidence was there that his life with Julia and the children had as much reality as his dreams of iniquity in Paris or the litter, the grass smell, and the cave-shaped trees in Lovers' Lane.

Late that afternoon, Julia called to remind Francis that they were going out for dinner. A few minutes later, Trace Bearden called. "Look, fellar," Trace said. "I'm calling for Mrs. Thomas. You know? Clayton, that boy of hers, doesn't seem able to get a job, and I wondered if you could help. If you'd call Charlie Bell—I know he's indebted to you— and say a good word for the kid, I think Charlie would—"

"Trace, I hate to say this," Francis said, "but I don't feel that I can do anything for that boy. The kid's worthless. I know it's a harsh thing to say, but it's a fact. Any kindness done for him would backfire in everybody's face. He's just a worthless kid, Trace, and there's nothing to be done about it. Even if we got him a job, he wouldn't be able to keep it for a week. I know that to be a fact. It's an awful thing, Trace, and I know it is, but instead of recommending that kid, I'd feel obliged to warn people against him—people who knew his father and would naturally want to step in and do something. I'd feel obliged to warn them. He's a thief . . ."

The moment this conversation was finished. Miss Rainey came in and stood by his desk. "I'm not going to be able to work for you any more, Mr. Weed," she said. "I can stay until the seventeenth if you need me, but I've been offered a whirlwind of a job, and I'd like to leave as soon as possible."

She went out, leaving him to face alone the wickedness of what he had done to the Thomas boy. His children in their photograph laughed and laughed, glazed with all the bright colors of summer, and he remembered that they had met a bagpiper on the beach that day and he had paid the piper a dollar to play them a battle song of the Black Watch.[9] The girl would be at the house when he got home. He would spend another evening among his kind neighbors, picking and choosing dead-end streets, cart tracks, and the driveways of abandoned houses. There was nothing to mitigate his feeling—nothing that laughter or a game of softball with the children would change—and, thinking back over the plane crash, the Farquarsons' new maid, and Anne Murchison's difficulties with her drunken father, he wondered how he could have avoided arriving at just where he was. He was in trouble. He had been lost once in his life, coming back from a trout stream in the north woods, and he had now the same bleak realization that no amount of cheerfulness or hopefulness or valor or perseverance could help him find, in the gathering dark, the path that he'd lost. He smelled the forest. The feeling of bleakness was intolerable, and he saw clearly that he had reached the point where he would have to make a choice.

He could go to a psychiatrist, like Miss Rainey; he could go to church and confess his lusts; he could go to a Danish massage parlor[1] in the West Seventies that had been recommended by a salesman; he could rape the girl or trust that he would somehow be prevented from doing this; or he could get drunk. It was his life, his boat, and, like every other man, he was made to be the father of thousands, and what harm could there be in a tryst that would make them both feel more kindly toward the world? This was the wrong train of thought, and he came back to the first, the psychiatrist. He had the telephone number of Miss Rainey's doctor, and he called and asked for an immediate appointment. He was insistent with the doctor's secretary—it was his manner in business—and when she said that the doctor's schedule was full for the next few weeks, Francis demanded an appointment that day and was told to come at five.

The psychiatrist's office was in a building that was used mostly by doctors and dentists, and the hallways were filled with the candy smell of mouthwash and memories of pain. Francis' character had been formed upon a series of private resolves—resolves about cleanliness, about going off the high diving board or repeating any other feat that

9. Originally a British Highland regiment that became a line regiment and distinguished itself in battle, including World War II battles.

1. Sometimes "fronts" for houses of prostitution.

The Country Husband 483

challenged his courage, about punctuality, honesty, and virtue. To
abdicate the perfect loneliness in which he had made his most vital decisions shattered his concept of character and left him now in a condition that felt like shock. He was stupefied. The scene for his *miserere
mei Deus*[2] was, like the waiting room of so many doctors' offices, a
crude token gesture toward the sweets of domestic bliss: a place arranged with antiques, coffee tables, potted plants, and etchings of
snow-covered bridges and geese in flight, although there were no
children, no marriage bed, no stove, even, in this travesty of a house,
where no one had ever spent the night and where the curtained windows looked straight onto a dark air shaft. Francis gave his name and
address to a secretary and then saw, at the side of the room, a policeman moving toward him. "Hold it, hold it," the policeman said. "Don't
move. Keep your hands where they are."

"I think it's all right, officer," the secretary began. "I think it will
be—"

"Let's make sure," the policeman said, and he began to slap Francis'
clothes, looking for what—pistols, knives, an icepick? Finding nothing,
he went off, and the secretary began a nervous apology: "When you
called on the telephone, Mr. Weed, you seemed very excited, and one
of the doctor's patients has been threatening his life, and we have to be
careful. If you want to go in now?" Francis pushed open a door connected to an electrical chime, and in the doctor's lair sat down heavily,
blew his nose into a handkerchief, searched in his pockets for cigarettes,
for matches, for something, and said hoarsely, with tears in his eyes,
"I'm in love, Dr. Herzog."

It is a week or ten days later in Shady Hill. The seven-fourteen has
come and gone, and here and there dinner is finished and the dishes
are in the dish-washing machine. The village hangs, morally and economically, from a thread; but it hangs by its thread in the evening light.
Donald Goslin has begun to worry the "Moonlight Sonata" again. *Mar-
cato ma sempre pianissimo!*[3] He seems to be wringing out a wet bath
towel, but the housemaid does not heed him. She is writing a letter to
Arthur Godfrey.[4] In the cellar of his house, Francis Weed is building
a coffee table. Dr. Herzog recommended woodwork as a therapy, and
Francis finds some true consolation in the simple arithmetic involved
and in the holy smell of new wood. Francis is happy. Upstairs, little
Toby is crying, because he is tired. He puts off his cowboy hat, gloves,
and fringed jacket, unbuckles the belt studded with gold and rubies,
the silver bullets and holsters, slips off his suspenders, his checked
shirt, and Levis, and sits on the edge of his bed to pull off his high
boots. Leaving this equipment in a heap, he goes to the closet and takes
his space suit off a nail. It is a struggle for him to get into the long
tights, but he succeeds. He loops the magic cape over his shoulders and,
climbing onto the footboard of his bed, he spreads his arms and flies
the short distance to the floor, landing with a thump that is audible to
everyone in the house but himself.

"Go home, Gertrude, go home," Mrs. Masterson says. "I told you to

<hr />

2. "Have mercy upon me, O God"; first
words of 51st Psalm.
3. Stressed but still very softly.

4. At the time of the story, host of a
daytime radio program especially popular
with housewives.

go home an hour ago, Gertrude. It's way past your suppertime, and your mother will be worried. Go home!" A door on the Babcocks' terrace flies open, and out comes Mrs. Babcock without any clothes on, pursued by her naked husband. (Their children are away at boarding school, and their terrace is screened by a hedge.) Over the terrace they go and in at the kitchen door, as passionate and handsome a nymph and satyr[5] as you will find on any wall in Venice. Cutting the last of the roses in her garden, Julia hears old Mr. Nixon shouting at the squirrels in his bird-feeding station. "Rapscallions! Varmints! Avaunt and quit my sight!" A miserable cat wanders into the garden, sunk in spiritual and physical discomfort. Tied to its head is a small straw hat—a doll's hat—and it is securely buttoned into a doll's dress, from the skirts of which protrudes its long, hairy tail. As it walks, it shakes its feet, as if it had fallen into water.

"Here, pussy, pussy, pussy!" Julia calls.

"Here, pussy, here, poor pussy!" But the cat gives her a skeptical look and stumbles away in its skirts. The last to come is Jupiter. He prances through the tomato vines, holding in his generous mouth the remains of an evening slipper. Then it is dark; it is a night where kings in golden suits ride elephants over the mountains.

1958

ALBERT MURRAY

Train Whistle Guitar

Lil' Buddy's color was that sky blue in which hens cackled; it was that smoke blue in which dogs barked and mosquito hawks lit on barbed-wire fences. It was the color above meadows. It was my color too because it was a boy's color. It was whistling blue and hunting blue, and it went with baseball, and that was old Lil' Buddy again, and that blue beyond outfields was exactly what we were singing about when we used to sing that old one about it ain't gonna rain no more no more.[1]

Steel blue was a man's color. That was the clean, oil-smelling color of rifle barrels and railroad iron. That was the color that went with Luzana Cholly, and he had a steel-blue 32–20 on a 44 frame.[2] His complexion was not steel blue but leather brown like dark rawhide, but steel blue was the color that went with what he was. His hands were just like rawhide, and when he was not dressed up he smelled like green oak steam. He had on slick starched blue denim overalls then, and when he was dressed up he wore a black broadcloth box-back coat with hickory-striped peg-top pants, and he smelled like the barber shop and new money.

Luzana Cholly was there in that time and place as far back as I can remember, even before Lil' Buddy was. Because I can remember

---

5. Minor nature goddesses and mythical woodland gods half man, half goat; the terms are often used to refer to beautiful young girls and to lecherous men.
1. Dance song with both mountaineer and Negro versions that moved west from Kentucky and other Southern states and

dates at least from the 1870s: "It ain't gonna rain, it ain't gonna snow,/It ain't gonna rain no mo';/Come on ev'rybody now,/Ain't gonna rain no mo'."
2. A smaller caliber barrel (32–20) on a larger mounting, more common in 1920s.

when I didn't know Lil' Buddy at all. I can remember when that house they moved to was built (Lil' Buddy's papa and mama were still living together when they came to Gasoline Point from Choctaw County, which was near the Mississippi line), and I can also remember when that street (which was called Chattanooga Lookout Street) was pushed all the way through to the AT&N[3] cut. That was before I had ever even heard of Lil' Buddy, and my buddy then was old Willie Marlowe. Lil' Buddy didn't come until after Willie Marlowe had gone to Detroit, Michigan, and that was not until after Mister One-Arm Will had been dead and buried for about nine months.

I can remember him there in that wee time when I couldn't even follow the stories I knew later they were telling about him, when it was only just grown folks talking, and all I could make of it was *Luzana, they are talking something about old Luzana again, and I didn't know what, to say nothing of where Louisiana was.* But old Luze was there even then and I could see him very clearly when they said his name because I had already seen him coming up that road that came by that house with the chinaberry yard, coming from around the bend and down in the railroad bottom; and I had already heard whatever that was he was picking on his guitar and heard that holler too. That was always far away and long coming. It started low like it was going to be a song, and then it jumped all the way to the very top of his voice and broke off, and then it started again, and this time was already at the top, and then it gave some quick jerking squalls and died away in the woods, the water, and the darkness (you always heard it at night), and Mama always said he was whooping and hollering like somebody back in the rosin-woods country, and Papa said it was one of them old Luzana swamp hollers. I myself always thought it was like a train, like a bad train saying look out this is me, and here I come, and I'm coming through.

That was even before I was big enough to climb the chinaberry tree. That was when they used to talk about the war and the Kaiser,[4] and I can remember that there was a war book with Germans in it, and I used to see sure-enough soldiers marching in the Mardi Gras parades. Soldier Boy Crawford was still wearing his Army coat then, and he was the one who used to tell about how Luze used to play his guitar in France, telling about how they would be going through some French town like the ones called Nancy and Saint Die and old Luze would drop out of the company and go and play around in the underground wine shops until he got as much cognac and as many French Frogs[5] as he wanted and then he would turn up in the company again and Capt'n would put him out by himself on the worst outpost he could find in No Man's Land and old Luze would stay out there sometimes for three or four days and nights knocking off patrol after patrol, and one time in another place, which was the Hindenburg Line,[6] old Luze was out there again and there were a few shots late in the afternoon and then it was all quiet until about three o'clock the next morning and then all hell broke loose, and the Capt'n thought that a whole German battalion was about to move in, and he sent five patrols out to find out

3. Alabama, Tennessee, and Northern Railroad.
4. Wilhelm II (1859–1941), ruler of Germany during World War I, 1914–1918.
5. Derogatory term for French.
6. Strong defense line established by the Germans in 1916 and the scene of heavy fighting, especially in 1917.

what was happening, but when they got there all they found was old Luze all dug in and bristling with enough ammunition to blow up kingdom come; he had crawled around all during the afternoon collecting hand grenades and a mortar and two machine guns and even a light two-wheel cannon, and when they asked him what was going on he told them that he had fallen off to sleep and when he woke up he didn't know whether or not any Germans had snuck up so he thought he'd better lay himself down a little light barrage. The next morning they found out that old Luze had wiped out a whole German platoon but when the Capt'n sent for him to tell him he was going to give him a medal, old Luze had cut out and was off somewhere picking the guitar and drinking cognac and chasing the mademoiselles again. He went through the whole war like that and he came out of the Army without a single scratch, didn't even get flat feet.

I heard a lot of stories about the war and I used to draw pictures of them fighting with bayonets in the Argonne Forest,[7] and Soldier Boy Crawford used to look at them and shake his head and give me a nickel and say that some day I was going to be a soldier too.

I used to draw automobiles too, especially the Hudson Super-Six, like old Long George Nisby had; he said it would do sixty on a straightaway, and he had a heavy blasting cut-out on it that jarred the ground. Old Man Perc Stranahan had a Studebaker but he was a white man and he didn't have a cut-out, and he drove as slow as a hearse. Old Gander said Old Man Perc always drove like he was trying to sneak up on something but he never was going to catch it like that. The cars I didn't like then were the flat-engine Buick and the old humpbacked Hupmobile. I liked the Maxwell and the Willys Knight and the Pierce Arrow.

I was playing train then too, and the trains were there before the automobiles were (there were many more horses and buggies in that part of town than there were automobiles then). I couldn't sit up in my nest in the chinaberry tree and see the trains yet, because I could not climb it yet, but I saw them when Papa used to take me to the L&N[8] bottom to see them come by and I knew them all, and the Pan American was the fastest and Number Four was the fastest that ran in the daytime. Old Luzana could tell you all about the Southern Pacific and the Santa Fe, but that was later. But I already knew something about the Southern Pacific because Cousin Roberta had already gone all the way to Los Angeles, California, on the Sunset Limited.

I used to be in bed and hear the night trains coming by. The Crescent came by at nine-thirty and if you woke up way in the middle of the night you could hear Number Two. I was in my warm bed in that house, and I could hear the whistle coming even before it got to Chickasabogue Bridge and it had a bayou sound then, and then I could hear the engine batting it hell-for-leather on down the line bound for Mobile and New Orleans, and the next time the whistle came it was for Three Mile Creek. It was getting on into the beel[9] then. I played train by myself in the daytime then, looking out the window

7. Forest in northeast France near Belgian border where Allies, including Americans, launched an offensive, September—

November 1918.
8. Louisville and Nashville Railroad.
9. *Beal*, mouth of creek or valley.

along the side of the house like an engineer looking down along the drivers.

I used to hear old Stagolee playing the piano over in Hot Water Shorty's jook[1] at night too, even then, especially on Saturday night. They rocked all night long, and I was lying in my warm quilted bed by the window. Uncle Jimmy's bed was by the window on the other side of the fireplace. When it was cold, you could wake up way in the night and still see the red embers in the ashes, and hear the wind whining outside, and sometimes you could hear the boat whistles too, and I could lie listening from where I was and tell you when it was a launch pulling a log raft or a tugboat pulling a barge or a riverboat like the *Nettie Queen*, and sometimes it was a big ship like the *Luchenback* called the Looking Back, which was all the way down at the city wharf at the foot of Government Street.

I knew a lot about the big ships because Uncle Jimmy worked on the wharf. That was before the state docks were built and the big Gulf-going and ocean-going ships didn't come on past Mobile then unless they were going up to Chickasaw to be overhauled, but I had already seen them and had been on ships from England and France and Holland and naturally there were always ships from the Caribbean and South America because that was where the fruit boats came from.

All I could do was see old Luzana Cholly and hear him coming. I didn't really know him then, but I knew that he was always blue steel and that he was always going and coming and that he had the best walk in the world, because I had learned how to do that walk and was already doing the stew out of it[2] long before Lil' Buddy ever saw it. They were calling me Mister Man, and that was when somebody started calling me The Little Blister, because they said I was calling myself blister trying to say Mister. Aun Tee called me My Mister and Mama called me My Little Man, but she had to drop the little part off when Lil' Buddy came, and that was how everybody started calling me The Man, although I was still nothing but a boy, and I said to myself old Luzana is the man, old Luzana is the one I want to be like.

Then I was getting to be big enough to go everywhere by myself and I was going to school. That was when I knew about Dunkin's Hill and going up through Egerton Lane. That was the short way to school, because that was the way the bell sound came. Buddy Babe and Sister Babe and old double-jointed, ox-jawed Jack Johnson all went that way too, but when it rained you couldn't get across the bottom, and that was when everybody went the Shelton way, going through behind Stranahan's store and Good Hope Baptist to the old car line and then along that red clay road by the Hillside store.

Then Lil' Buddy was there and it was sky blue and we were blue hunters and every day was for whistling and going somewhere to do something you had to be rawhide to do, and some day we were going to live in times and places that were blue steel too. We found out a lot about old Luzana then, and then we not only knew him we knew how to talk to him.

The best time (except when he was just sitting somewhere strumming on his guitar) was when he was on his way to the Gambling

1. Roadhouse, juke-joint.   2. Doing it expertly.

Woods. (So far as anybody knew, gambling and guitar picking and grabbing freight trains were the only steady jobs he ever had or ever would have, except during the time he was in the Army and the times he was in jail—and he not only had been in jail, he had been in the penitentiary!) We were his good luck when he was headed for a skin game, and we always used to catch him late Saturday afternoon right out there where Gins Alley came into the oil-tank road, because he would be coming from Miss Pauline's cookshop then. The Gambling Woods trail started right out across from Sargin' Jeff's. Sometimes old Luze would have the guitar slung across his back even then, and naturally he had his famous 32-20 in the holster under his right arm.

"Say now hey Mister Luzana," I would holler at him.

"Mister Luzana Cholly one-time," Lil' Buddy always said, and he said that was what old Luze's swamp holler said too.

"Mister Luzana Cholly all night long," I would say then.

"Nobody else!" he would holler back at us then, "nobody else but."

"The one and only Mister Luzana Cholly from Booze Ana Bolly come Solly go Molly hit 'em with the fun folly."

"Talk to me, little ziggy,[3] talk to me."

"Got the world in a jug," I might say then.

"And the stopper in your hand,"[4] old Lil' Buddy would say.

"You tell 'em, little crust busters, 'cause I ain't got the heart."

"He's a man among men."

"And Lord God among women!"

"Well tell the dy ya,"[5] old Luze would say then, standing wide-legged, laughing, holding a wad of Brown's Mule chewing tobacco in with his tongue at the same time. Then he would skeet[6] a stream of amber juice to one side like a batter does when he steps up to the plate and then he would wipe the back of his leathery hand across his mouth and squint his eyes.

"Tell the dy-damn-ya!"

"Cain't tell no more," Lil' Buddy would say then, and old Luze would frown and wink at me.

"How come, little sooner,[7] how goddam come?"

"'Cause money talks."

"Well shut my mouth and call me suitcase."

"Ain't nobody can do that."

"I knowed you could tell 'em little ziggabo, I knowed good and damn well you could tell 'em."

"But we ain't gonna tell 'em no more."

"We sure ain't."

"Talk ain't no good if you ain't got nothing to back it up with."

Old Luze would laugh again and we would stand waiting and then he would run his hands deep down into his pockets and come out with two quarters between his fingers. He would throw them into the air and catch them again, one in each hand, and then he would cross his hands and flip one to me and one to Lil' Buddy.

"Now talk," he would say then. "Now talk, but don't say too much

---

3. Prison slang variant of "jig," "jiga-boo," derogatory name for a black.
4. The two lines of dialogue are a common blues line.
5. Possibly Gullah phrase with variants used in songs, e.g., "Kushie Dye-yo."
6. Squirt.
7. Mongrel or bastard.

and don't talk too loud, and handle your money like the white folks does."

We were going to be like him even before we were going to be like cowboys. And we knew that blue steel was also root hog or die poor,[8] which was what we were going to have to do whether we liked it or not. Lil' Buddy said it was not just how rough-and-ready old hard-cutting Luze was and how nobody, black or white, was going to do him any dirt and get away with it, and all that. It was that too, but it was also something else. It was also the way he could do whatever he was doing and make it look so easy that he didn't even seem to have to think about it, and once he did it, that seemed to be just about the only real way to do it.

Old Luze did everything his own way just like old Satch[9] played baseball his way. But we knew that we wanted to be like him for more reasons than that too. Somehow or other just as he always seemed to be thirty-five years old and blue steel because he had already been so many places and done so many things you'd never heard of before, he also always seemed to be absolutely alone and not needing anybody else, self-sufficient, independent, dead sure, and at the same time so unconcerned.

Mama said he was don't-carified, and that was it too (if you know the full meaning of the Negro meaning of that expression). He was living in blue steel and his way was don't-carified, because he was blue steel too. Lil' Buddy said hellfied, and he didn't mean hell-defying either, you couldn't say he was hell-defying all the time, and you couldn't say he went for bad either, not even when he was doing that holler he was so notorious for. That *was* hell-defying in a way, but it was really I don't give a damn if I *am* hell-defying, and he was not going for bad because he didn't need to, since everybody, black and white, who knew anything about him at all already knew that when he made a promise it meant if it's the last thing I do, if it's the last thing I do on this earth—and they knew that could mean I'll kill you and pay for you as much as it meant anything else. Because the idea of going to jail didn't scare him at all, and the idea of getting shot at didn't seem to scare him either. *Because all he ever said about that was if they shoot at me they sure better not miss me, they sure better get me the first time.*

He was a Negro who was an out and out Nigger in the very best meaning of the word as Negroes use it among themselves (who are the only ones who can), and nobody in that time and that place seemed to know what to make of him. White folks said he was crazy, but what they really meant or should have meant was that he was confusing to them, because if they knew him well enough to say he was crazy they also had to know enough about him to know that he wasn't even foolhardy, not even careless, not even what they wanted to mean by biggity. The funny thing, as I remember it now, was how their confusion made them respect him in spite of themselves. Some-how or other it was as if they respected him precisely because he didn't

8. Work hard or die poor.
9. Satchell Paige, famed, almost legen-dary Negro league baseball player who was already in his forties when the major leagues admitted Negroes.

care anything about them one way or the other. They certainly respected the fact that he wasn't going to take any foolishness off of them.

Negroes said he was crazy too, but they meant their own meaning. They did not know what to make of him, but when they said he was crazy they almost did, because when they said it they really meant something else. They were not talking so much about what he did, but how he was doing it. They were talking about something like poetic madness, and that was the way they had of saying that he was doing something unheard of, doing the hell out of it, and getting away with whatever it was. You could tell that was what they meant by the very way they said it, by the sound of it, and by the way they were shaking their heads and laughing when they said it.

The way he always operated as a lone wolf and the unconcerned-, not the Negro-ness as such, were the main things then. (Naturally Lil' Buddy and I knew about Negroes and white folks, and we knew that there was something generally wrong with white folks, but it didn't seem so very important then. We knew that if you hit a white boy he would turn red and call you nigger that did not sound like the Nigger the Negroes said and he would run and get as many other white boys as he could and come back at you, and we knew that a full-grown white had to get somebody to back him up too, but we didn't really think about it much, because there were so many other things we were doing then.)

Nobody ever said anything about old Luzana's papa and mama, and when you suddenly wondered about them you realized that he didn't seem to have or need any family at all, it really was as if he had come full-grown out of the swamp somewhere. And he didn't seem to need a wife either. But that was because he was not going to settle down yet. Because he had lived with more women from time to time and place to place than the average man could even shake a stick at.

We knew somehow or other that the Negro-ness had something to do with the way we felt about him too, but except for cowboys and the New York Yankees and one or two other things, almost everything was Negro then; that is, everything that mattered was. So the Negro part was only natural, although I can see something special about it too now.

When you boil it all down, I guess the main thing was how when you no more than just said his name, *Louisiana Charlie, old Luzana Cholly, old Luze,* that was enough to make you know not only him and how he looked and talked and walked that sporty limp walk, but his whole way of being, and how you knew right off the bat that he all alone and unconcerned in his sharp-edged and rough-backed steel had made it what it was himself.

That was what old Lil' Buddy and I were going to do too, make a name for ourselves. Because we knew even then (and I already knew it before he came) that doing that was exactly what made you the kind of man we wanted to be. Mama said I was her little man, and Aun Tee always called me her little mister, but I wasn't anybody's man and mister yet and I knew it, and when I heard the sound of the name that Mama taught me how to write I always felt funny, and I always jumped even when I didn't move. That was in school, and I wanted to hide, and I always said *they are looking for me, they are trying to see who I am*, and I had to answer because it would be the teacher calling the roll, and I said Present, and it sounded like somebody else.

And when I found out what I found out about me and Aun Tee and knew that she was my flesh and blood mama, I also found out that I didn't know my real name at all, because I didn't know who my true father was. So I said *My name is Reynard the Fox*, and Lil' Buddy said *My name is Jack the Rabbit and my home is in the briar patch*.[1] That was old Luzana too, and when you heard that holler coming suddenly out of nowhere just as old Luze himself always seemed to come, it was just like it was coming from the briar patch.

So when Mama said what she said about me and Aun Tee at that wake that time and I heard it and had to believe it, I wished that old Luzana had been my real papa, but I didn't tell anybody that, not even Lil' Buddy although Lil' Buddy was almost in the same fix because he didn't have a mama any more and he didn't really love his papa because it was his papa that ran his mama away.

But we were buddies and we both did old Luzana's famous walk and we were going to be like him, and the big thing that you had to do to really get like him was to grab yourself a fast armful of fast freight train and get long gone from here. That was the real way to learn about the world, and we wanted to learn everything about it that we could. That was when we started practicing on the switch engine. That was down in the oilyards. You had to be slick to do even that because naturally your folks didn't want you doing stuff like that, because there was old Peg Leg Nat. Old Peg Leg butt-headed Nat could hop a freight almost as good as old Luzana could. He called himself mister-some-big-shit-on-a-stick. He spent most of his time fishing and sometimes he would come around pushing a wheelbarrow selling fresh fish, shrimps, and crabs, but every now and then he would strike out for somewhere on a freight just like old Luze did. Mama used to try to scare us with old Nat, telling us that a peg leg was just what messing around with freight trains would get you, and for a while she did scare us, but not for long, because then we found out that it never would have happened to old Nat if he hadn't been drunk and showing off. And anybody could see that getting his leg cut off hadn't stopped old Nat himself anyway since he could still beat any two-legged man we knew doing it except old Luze himself. Naturally we had to think about it, and naturally it did slow us up for a while, but it didn't really stop us. Because there was still old Luze, and that was who we were anyway, not old Peg Leg Nat.

Then that time when I found out all about me and Aun Tee, I was going to run away, and Lil' Buddy was ready too. Then old Lil' Buddy found out that old Luze was getting ready to get moving again and we were all set and just waiting and then it was the day itself.

I will always remember that one.

I had on my brogan shoes and I had on my corduroy pants under my overalls with my jumper tucked in. I had on my blue baseball cap

1. Reynard and Jack are traditional names for the fox and rabbit: the briar patch episode appears in the Uncle Remus story, by Joel Chandler Harris (1848–1908) in which the shrewd Br'er Rabbit, caught by Br'er Fox, pleads not to be thrown into the briar patch; so of course the fox throws him in and the rabbit escapes crying, "Bred en bawn in a briarpatch, Br'er Fox, bred en bawn in a brier-patch."

too and my rawhide wristband and I had my pitching glove folded in
my hip pocket. Lil' Buddy had on just about the same thing except that
he was carrying his first-base pad instead of his catcher's mitt. We had
our other things and something to eat rolled up in our blanket rolls so
that we could sling them over our shoulders and have our arms free.

Lil' Buddy had gotten his papa's pearl-handled .38 Smith & Wesson,
and we both had good jackknives. We had some hooks and twine to fish
with too, just in case, and of course we had our trusty old slingshots for
birds.

It was May and school was not out yet, and so not only were we
running away, we were playing hooky too. It was hot, and with that
many clothes on we were sweating, but you had to have them, and that
was the best way to carry them.

There was a thin breeze that came across the railroad from the river,
the marsh, and Pole Cat Bay, but the sun was hot and bright, and you
could see the rails downright shimmering under the high and wide
open sky. We had always said that we were going to wait until school
was out, but this was our chance now, and we didn't care about school
much any more anyhow. This was going to be school now anyway,
except it was going to be much better.

We were waiting in the thicket under the hill. That was between
where the Dodge mill road came down and where the oil spur started,
and from where we were, we could see up and down the clearing as
far as we needed to, to the south all the way across Three Mile Creek
bridge to the roundhouse, and where Mobile was, and to the north all
the way up past that mill to the Chickasabogue Bridge. We knew just
about from where old Luzana was going to come running, because we
had been watching him do it for a long time now. We had that part
down pat.

I don't know how long we had been waiting because we didn't have
a watch but it had been a long time, and there was nothing to do but
wait then.

"I wish it would hurry up and come on," Lil' Buddy said.

"Me too," I said.

"Got to get to splitting."

We were squatting on the blanket rolls, and Lil' Buddy was smoking
another Lucky Strike, smoking the way we both used to smoke them
in those old days, letting it hang dangling in the corner of your mouth,
and tilting your head to one side with one eye squinted up like a
gambler.

"Goddam it, watch me nail that sapsucker," he said.

"Man, you watch me."

You could smell the May woods there then, the dogwood, the honeysuckle, and the warm smell of the undergrowth; and you could hear
the birds too, the jays, the thrushes, and even a woodpecker somewhere on a dead tree. I felt how moist and cool the soft dark ground
was there in the shade, and you could smell that smell too, and smell
the river and the marsh too.

Lil' Buddy finished the cigarette and flipped it out into the sunshine, and then sat with his back against a sapling and sucked his

teeth. I looked out across the railroad to where the gulls were circling over the marsh and the river.

"Goddam it, when I come back here to this burg, I'm goddam man and a half," Lil' Buddy said all of a sudden.

"And don't care who knows it," I said.

"Boy, Chicago."

"Man, Detroit."

"Man, Philadelphia."

"Man, New York."

"Boy, I kinda wish old Gander was going too."

"I kinda wish so too."

"Old cat-eyed Gander."

"Old big-toed Gander."

"Old Gander is all right."

"Man, who you telling."

"That son of a bitch know his natural stuff."

"That bastard can steal lightning if he have to."

"Boy, how about that time."

"Man, hell yeah."

"Boy, but old Luze though."

"That Luze takes the cake for everything."

"Hot damn, boy we going!"

"It won't be long now."

"Boy, Los Angeles."

"Boy, St. Louis."

"Man, you know we going."

"Boy, you just watch me swing the sapsucker."

"Boy, snag it."

"Goddam."

"I'm going to natural-born kick that son of a bitch."

"Kick the living guts out of it."

"Boy and when we get back!" I said that and I could see it, coming back on the Pan American I would be carrying two suitcases and have a money belt and an underarm holster, and I would be dressed fit to kill.

"How long you think it will take us to get fixed to come back?" I said.

"Man, I don't know and don't care."

"You coming back when old Luze come back?"

"I don't know."

I didn't say anything else then. Because I was trying to think about how it was really going to be then. Because what I had been thinking about before was how I wanted it to be. I didn't say anything because I was thinking about myself then, thinking: *I always said I was going but I don't really know whether I want to go or not now. I want to go and I don't want to go.* I tried to see what was really going to happen and I couldn't, and I tried to forget it and think about something else, but I couldn't do that either.

I looked over at Lil' Buddy again. Who was lying back against the tree with his hands behind his head and his eyes closed. Whose legs were crossed, and who was resting easy like a ballplayer rests before time for the game to start. I wondered what he was really thinking. Did he really mean it when he said he did not know and didn't care? You couldn't tell what he was thinking, but you could tell that he wasn't going to back out now, no matter how he was feeling about it.

So I said to myself goddam it if Lil' Buddy can make it I can too, and I had more reason to be going away than he did anyway. *I had forgotten about that. I had forgotten all about it. And then I knew that I still loved Papa and they had always loved me and they had always known about me and Aun Tee.*

But I couldn't back out then, because what I had found out wasn't the real reason for going anyway. Old Luze was really the reason, old Luze and blue steel, old Luze and rawhide, old Luze and ever-stretching India Rubber.

"Hey Lebud."

"Hey."

"Going to the big league."

"You said it."

"Skipping city."

"You tell 'em."

"Getting further."

"Ain't no lie."

"Long gone."

"No crap."

That was when Lil' Buddy said my home is in the briar patch. My name is Jack the Rabbit and my natural home is in the briar patch. And I said it too, and I said that was where I was bred and born.

"Goddam it to hell," Lil' Buddy said then, "why don't it come on?"

"Son of a bitch," I said.

Then I was leaning back against my tree looking out across the sandy clearing at the sky and there were clean white pieces of clouds that looked like balled-up sheets in a washtub, and the sky was blue like rinse water with bluing in it, and I was thinking about Mama again, and hoping that it was all a dream.

But then the train was really coming and it wasn't a dream at all, and Lil' Buddy jumped up.

"Come on."

"I'm here."

The engine went by, and we were running across the clearing. My ears were ringing and I was sweating, and my collar was hot and my pants felt as if the seat had been ripped away. There was nothing but the noise and we were running into it, and then we were climbing up the hill and running along the slag and cinders. We were trotting along in reach of it then. We remembered to let an empty boxcar go by, and when the next gondola came, Lil' Buddy grabbed the front end and I got the back. I hit the hotbox with my right foot and stepped onto the step and pulled up. The wind was in my ears then, but I knew about that from practicing. I climbed on up the ladder and got down on the inside, and there was Lil' Buddy coming back toward me.

"Man, what did I tell you!"

"Did you see me lam into that sucker?"

"Boy, we low more nailed it."

"I bet old Luze will be kicking it any minute now."

"Cool hanging it."

"Boy, yair," I said, but I was thinking I hope old Luze didn't change his mind. I hope we don't miss him. I hope we don't have to start out all by ourselves.

"Going boy."

"Yeah."

"Going,
don't know where I'm going
but I'm going
Say now I'm going
don't know when I'm going
but I'm going."

We crawled up into the left front corner out of the wind, and there was nothing to do but wait then. We knew that she was going to have to pull into the hole for Number Four when she got twelve miles out, and that was when we were going to get to the open boxcar.

We got the cigarettes out and lit up, and there was nothing but the rumbling noise that the wide-open car made then, and the faraway sound of the engine and the low-rolling smoke coming back. That was just sitting there, and after we got a little more used to the vibration, nothing at all was happening except being there. You couldn't even see the scenery going by.

It was just being there and being in that time, and you never really remember anything about things like that except the sameness and the way you felt, and all I can remember now about that part is this nothingness of doing nothing and the feeling not of going but of being taken.

All I could see after we went through the bridge was the sky and the bare floor and the sides of the gondola, and all I can remember about myself is how I wished that something would happen, because I definitely did not want to be going then, and I was lost even though I knew good and well that I was not even twelve miles from home yet. Because although we certainly had been many times farther away and stayed longer, this already seemed to be farther and longer than all the other times put together.

Then we could tell that it was beginning to slow down, and we stood up and started getting ready. And then it was stopping and we were ready, and we climbed over and got down and started running for it. That was still in the bayou country and beyond the train smell there was the sour-sweet smell of the swamp. We were running on hard pounded slag then, and with the train quiet and waiting for Number Four, you could hear the double running of our feet echoing through the cypresses and the marshland.

The wide roadbed was almost half as high as the telegraph wires, and along the low right-of-way where the black creosote poles went along, you could see the blue and white lilies floating on the slimy green water. We came hustling hot to get to where we knew the empty car was, and then there we were.

And there old Luzana himself was.

He stood looking down at us from the door with an unlighted cigarette in his hand. We stopped dead in our tracks. I knew exactly what

was going to happen then. It was suddenly so quiet that you could
hear your heart pounding inside your head, and I was so embarrassed
I didn't know what to do and I thought *now he's going to call us a
name. Now he's never going to have anything to do with us anymore.*

We were just standing there waiting and he just let us stand there
and feel like two puppies with their tails tucked between their legs,
and then he started talking.

"It ain't like that. It ain't like that. It just ain't like that, it just ain't."

And he was shaking his head not only as if we couldn't understand
him but also as if we couldn't even hear him.

"It ain't. Oh, but it ain't."

We didn't move. Lil' Buddy didn't even dig his toe into the ground.

"So this is what y'all up to. Don't say a word, not a word. Don't
open your mouth."

I could have sunk right on down into the ground.

"What the hell y'all think y'all doing? Tell me that. Tell me. Don't
say a word. Don't say a goddam mumbling word to me."

We weren't even about to say anything.

"I got a good mind to whale the sawdust out of you both. That's just
what I oughta do."

But he didn't move. He just stood looking down.

"Well, I'll be a son of a bitch."

That was all he had said then, and then he jumped down, walked us
back to where the switch frog was, and then there was nothing but
just shamefaced waiting. Then Number Four came by and then finally
we heard the next freight coming south and when it got there and
slowed down for the switch he was standing waiting for a gondola and
when it came he picked me up and put me on and then he picked Lil'
Buddy up and put him on and then he caught the next car and came
to where we were.

So we came slowpoking it right on back and got back in Gasoline
Point before the whistles even started blowing for one o'clock. Imagine
that. All of that had happened and it wasn't really afternoon yet. I
could hardly believe it.

We came on until the train all but stopped for Three Mile Creek
bridge and then he hopped down and took us off. He led us down the
hill and went to a place the hobos used under the bridge. He sat down
and lit another cigarette and flipped the match into the water and
watched it float away and then he was looking at us and then he
motioned for us to sit down too.

That was when he really told us what hitting the road was, and
what blue steel was. He was talking evenly then, not scolding, just
telling us man to boys, saying he was talking for our own good because
doing what we were trying to do was more than a notion. He was
talking quietly and evenly but you still couldn't face him, I know I
couldn't and Lil' Buddy naturally couldn't because he never looked
anybody straight in the eye anyway.

We were back and sitting under Three Mile Creek bridge and he
was not really angry and then we were all eating our something-to-eat
and then we could talk too, but we didn't have much to say that day.

He was doing the talking and all we wanted to do was ask questions and listen.

That was when he told us all about the chain gang and the penitentiary and the white folks, and you could see everything he said and you were there too, but you were not really in it this time because it was happening to him, not you, and it was him and you were not him, you were you. You could be rawhide and you could be blue steel but you couldn't really be Luzana Cholly, because he himself was not going to let you.

Then he was talking about going to school and learning to use your head like the smart white folks. You had to be a rawhide but you had to be patent leather too, then you would really be nimble, then you would really be not only a man but a big man. He said we had a lot of spunk and that was good but it wasn't good enough, it wasn't nearly enough.

And then he was talking about Negroes and white folks again, and he said the young generation of Negroes were supposed to be like Negroes and be like white folks too and still be Negroes. He sat looking out across the water then, and then we heard another freight coming and he got up and got ready and he said we could watch him but we'd better not try to follow him.

Then we were back up on the hill again and the train was coming and he stood looking at us with the guitar slung over his shoulder and then he put his hands on our shoulders and looked straight at us, and we had to look at him then, and we knew that we were not to be ashamed in front of him any more.

"Make old Luze proud of you," he said then, *and he was almost pleading. "Make old Luze glad to take his hat off to you some of these days. You going further than old Luze ever even dreamed of. Old Luze ain't been nowhere. Old Luze don't know from nothing."*

And then the train was there and we watched him snag it and then he was waving good-bye.

p. 1953

GRACE PALEY

A Conversation with My Father

My father is eighty-six years old and in bed. His heart, that bloody motor, is equally old and will not do certain jobs any more. It still floods his head with brainy light. But it won't let his legs carry the weight of his body around the house. Despite my metaphors, this muscle failure is not due to his old heart, he says, but to a potassium shortage. Sitting on one pillow, leaning on three, he offers last-minute advice and makes a request.

"I would like you to write a simple story just once more," he says, "the kind de Maupassant wrote, or Chekhov,[1] the kind you used to write. Just recognizable people and then write down what happened to them next."

I say, "Yes, why not? That's possible." I want to please him, though I don't remember writing that way. I *would* like to try to tell such a story, if he means the kind that begins: "There was a woman . . ." followed by plot, the absolute line between two points which I've always despised. Not for literary reasons, but because it takes all hope away. Everyone, real or invented, deserves the open destiny of life.

Finally I thought of a story that had been happening for a couple of years right across the street. I wrote it down, then read it aloud. "Pa," I said, "how about this? Do you mean something like this?"

Once in my time there was a woman and she had a son. They lived nicely, in a small apartment in Manhattan. This boy at about fifteen became a junkie, which is not unusual in our neighborhood. In order to maintain her close friendship with him, she became a junkie too. She said it was part of the youth culture, with which she felt very much at home. After a while, for a number of reasons, the boy gave it all up and left the city and his mother in disgust. Hopeless and alone, she grieved. We all visit her.

"O.K., Pa, that's it," I said, "an unadorned and miserable tale."

"But that's not what I mean," my father said. "You misunderstood me on purpose. You know there's a lot more to it. You know that. You left everything out. Turgenev[2] wouldn't do that. Chekhov wouldn't do that. There are in fact Russian writers you never heard of, you don't have an inkling of, as good as anyone, who can write a plain ordinary story, who would not leave out what you have left out. I object not to facts but to people sitting in trees talking senselessly, voices from who knows where . . ."

"Forget that one, Pa, what have I left out now? In this one?"

"Her looks, for instance."

"Oh. Quite handsome, I think. Yes."

"Her hair?"

"Dark, with heavy braids, as though she were a girl or a foreigner."

"What were her parents like, her stock? That she became such a person. It's interesting, you know."

"From out of town. Professional people. The first to be divorced in their county. How's that? Enough?" I asked.

"With you, it's all a joke," he said. "What about the boy's father? Why didn't you mention him? Who was he? Or was the boy born out of wedlock?"

"Yes," I said. "He was born out of wedlock."

"For Godsakes, doesn't anyone in your stories get married? Doesn't anyone have the time to run down to City Hall before they jump into bed?"

---

1. Guy de Maupassant (1850–93) wrote heavily plotted, ironic stories, Chekhov realistic stories that often had no resolution (see *Lady with the Dog*) and sometimes with little plot.

2. Ivan Sergevich Turgenev (1818–1883) wrote stories and novels deeply embedded in the culture of his time; his best-known novel, *Fathers and Sons*, deals with the conflict between generations.

"No," I said. "In real life, yes. But in my stories, no."

"Why do you answer me like that?"

"Oh, Pa, this is a simple story about a smart woman who came to N.Y.C. full of interest love trust excitement very up to date, and about her son, what a hard time she had in this world. Married or not, it's of small consequence."

"It is of great consequence," he said.

"O.K.," I said.

"O.K. O.K. yourself," he said, "but listen. I believe you that she's good-looking, but I don't think she was so smart."

"That's true," I said. "Actually that's the trouble with stories. People start out fantastic. You think they're extraordinary, but it turns out as the work goes along, they're just average with a good education. Sometimes the other way around, the person's a kind of dumb inno-cent, but he outwits you and you can't even think of an ending good enough."

"What do you do then?" he asked. He had been a doctor for a couple of decades and then an artist for a couple of decades and he's still interested in details, craft, technique.

"Well, you just have to let the story lie around till some agreement can be reached between you and the stubborn hero."

"Aren't you talking silly, now?" he asked. "Start again," he said. "It so happens I'm not going out this evening. Tell the story again. See what you can do this time."

"O.K.," I said. "But it's not a five-minute job." Second attempt:

Once, across the street from us, there was a fine handsome woman, our neighbor. She had a son whom she loved because she'd known him since birth (in helpless chubby infancy, and in the wrestling, hugging ages, seven to ten, as well as earlier and later). This boy, when he fell into the fist of adolescence, became a junkie. He was not a hopeless one. He was in fact hopeful, an ideologue and successful converter. With his busy brilliance, he wrote persuasive articles for his high-school news-paper. Seeking a wider audience, using important connections, he drummed into Lower Manhattan newsstand distribution a periodical called *Oh! Golden Horse!*

In order to keep him from feeling guilty (because guilt is the stony heart of nine tenths of all clinically diagnosed cancers in America today, she said), and because she had always believed in giving bad habits room at home where one could keep an eye on them, she too became a junkie. Her kitchen was famous for a while—a center for intellectual addicts who knew what they were doing. A few felt artistic like Coleridge and others were scientific and revolutionary like Leary.[3] Although she was often high herself, certain good mothering reflexes remained, and she saw to it that there was lots of orange juice around and honey and milk and vitamin pills. However, she never cooked anything but chili, and that no more than once a week. She explained, when we talked to her, seriously, with neighborly concern, that it was

3. Samuel Taylor Coleridge (1772–1834), English Romantic poet, says he wrote his allegedly unfinished poem *Kubla Khan* in an opium dream. Timothy Leary (b. 1920), American psychologist who promoted the use of psychedelic drugs.

her part in the youth culture and she would rather be with the young, it was an honor, than with her own generation.

One week, while nodding through an Antonioni[4] film, this boy was severely jabbed by the elbow of a stern and proselytizing girl, sitting beside him. She offered immediate apricots and nuts for his sugar level, spoke to him sharply, and took him home.

She had heard of him and his work and she herself published, edited, and wrote a competitive journal called *Man Does Live By Bread Alone*. In the organic heat of her continuous presence he could not help but become interested once more in his muscles, his arteries, and nerve connections. In fact he began to love them, treasure them, praise them with funny little songs in *Man does Live* . . .

> *the fingers of my flesh transcend*
> *my transcendental soul*
> *the tightness in my shoulders end*
> *my teeth have made me whole*

To the mouth of his head (that glory of will and determination) he brought hard apples, nuts, wheat germ, and soybean oil. He said to his old friends, From now on, I guess I'll keep my wits about me. I'm going on the natch. He said he was about to begin a spiritual deep-breathing journey. How about you too, Mom? he asked kindly.

His conversion was so radiant, splendid, that neighborhood kids his age began to say that he had never been a real addict at all, only a journalist along for the smell of the story. The mother tried several times to give up what had become without her son and his friends a lonely habit. This effort only brought it to supportable levels. The boy and his girl took their electronic mimeograph and moved to the bushy edge of another borough. They were very strict. They said they would not see her again until she had been off drugs for sixty days.

At home alone in the evening, weeping, the mother read and reread the seven issues of *Oh! Golden Horse!* They seemed to her as truthful as ever. We often crossed the street to visit and console. But if we mentioned any of our children who were at college or in the hospital or dropouts at home, she would cry out, My baby! My baby! and burst into terrible, face-scarring, time-consuming tears. The End.

First my father was silent, then he said, "Number One: You have a nice sense of humor. Number Two: I see you can't tell a plain story. So don't waste time." Then he said sadly, "Number Three: I suppose that means she was alone, she was left like that, his mother. Alone. Probably sick?"

I said, "Yes."

"Poor woman. Poor girl, to be born in a time of fools, to live among fools. The end. The end. You were right to put that down. The end."

I didn't want to argue, but I had to say, "Well, it is not necessarily the end, Pa."

---

4. Michelangelo Antonioni (b. 1912), Italian director (*Blow-Up, Zabriskie Point*), whose neo-realist, often slow-moving films investigate society.

"Yes," he said, "what a tragedy. The end of a person."

"No, Pa," I begged him. "It doesn't have to be. She's only about forty. She could be a hundred different things in this world as time goes on. A teacher or a social worker. An ex-junkie! Sometimes it's better than having a master's in education."

"Jokes," he said. "As a writer that's your main trouble. You don't want to recognize it. Tragedy! Plain tragedy! Historical tragedy! No hope. The end."

"Oh, Pa," I said. "She could change."

"In your own life, too, you have to look it in the face." He took a couple of nitroglycerin.[5] "Turn to five," he said, pointing to the dial on the oxygen tank. He inserted the tubes into his nostrils and breathed deep. He closed his eyes and said, "No."

I had promised the family to always let him have the last word when arguing, but in this case I had a different responsibility. That woman lives across the street. She's my knowledge and my invention. I'm sorry for her. I'm not going to leave her there in that house crying. (Actually neither would Life, which unlike me has no pity.)

Therefore: She did change. Of course her son never came home again. But right now, she's the receptionist in a storefront community clinic in the East Village. Most of the customers are young people, some old friends. The head doctor has said to her, "If we only had three people in this clinic with your experiences . . ."

"The doctor said that?" My father took the oxygen tubes out of his nostrils and said, "Jokes. Jokes again."

"No, Pa, it could really happen that way, it's a funny world nowadays."

"No," he said. "Truth first. She will slide back. A person must have character. She does not."

"No, Pa," I said. "That's it. She's got a job. Forget it. She's in that storefront working."

"How long will it be?" he asked. "Tragedy! You too. When will you look it in the face?"

1974

URSULA K. LE GUIN

The Ones Who Walk Away from Omelas[1]

With a clamor of bells that set the swallows soaring, the Festival of Summer came to the city Omelas, bright-towered by the sea. The rigging of the boats in harbor sparkled with flags. In the streets between houses with red roofs and painted walls, between old moss-grown

---

5. Medicine for certain heart conditions.
1. The author says the name comes from "a road sign: Salem (Oregon) backwards. . . . Salem equals schelomo equals salaam equals Peace. Melas. O melas. Omelas. Homme hélas." The last phrase equals "Man, alas."

gardens and under avenues of trees, past great parks and public buildings, processions moved. Some were decorous: old people in long stiff
robes of mauve and gray, grave master workmen, quiet, merry women
carrying their babies and chatting as they walked. In other streets the
music beat faster, a shimmering of gong and tambourine, and the
people went dancing, the procession was a dance. Children dodged
in and out, their high calls rising like the swallows' crossing flights over
the music and the singing. All the processions wound towards the north
side of the city, where on the great water-meadow called the Green
Fields boys and girls, naked in the bright air, with mud-stained feet
and ankles and long, lithe arms, exercised their restive horses before
the race. The horses wore no gear at all but a halter without bit. Their
manes were braided with streamers of silver, gold, and green. They
flared their nostrils and pranced and boasted to one another; they
were vastly excited, the horse being the only animal who has adopted
our ceremonies as his own. Far off to the north and west the mountains
stood up half encircling Omelas on her bay. The air of morning was
so clear that the snow still crowning the Eighteen Peaks burned with
white-gold fire across the miles of sunlit air, under the dark blue of the
sky. There was just enough wind to make the banners that marked the
racecourse snap and flutter now and then. In the silence of the broad
green meadows one could hear the music winding through the city
streets, farther and nearer and ever approaching, a cheerful faint
sweetness of the air that from time to time trembled and gathered together and broke out into the great joyous clanging of the bells.

Joyous! How is one to tell about joy? How describe the citizens of
Omelas?

They were not simple folk, you see, though they were happy. But
we do not say the words of cheer much any more. All smiles have become archaic. Given a description such as this one tends to make certain assumptions. Given a description such as this one tends to look
next for the King, mounted on a splendid stallion and surrounded
by his noble knights, or perhaps in a golden litter borne by great-
muscled slaves. But there was no king. They did not use swords, or
keep slaves. They were not barbarians, I do not know the rules and
laws of their society, but I suspect that they were singularly few. As
they did without monarchy and slavery, so they also got on without
the stock exchange, the advertisement, the secret police, and the
bomb. Yet I repeat that these were not simple folk, not dulcet shepherds, noble savages, bland utopians. They were not less complex than
us. The trouble is that we have a bad habit, encouraged by pedants
and sophisticates, of considering happiness as something rather stupid.
Only pain is intellectual, only evil interesting. This is the treason of
the artist: a refusal to admit the banality of evil and the terrible boredom of pain. If you can't lick 'em, join 'em. If it hurts, repeat it. But
to praise despair is to condemn delight, to embrace violence is to
lose hold of everything else. We have almost lost hold; we can no
longer describe a happy man, nor make any celebration of joy. How
can I tell you about the people of Omelas? They were not naïve and
happy children—though their children were, in fact, happy. They
were mature, intelligent, passionate adults whose lives were not

wretched. O miracle! but I wish I could describe it better. I wish I could convince you. Omelas sounds in my words like a city in a fairy tale, long ago and far away, once upon a time. Perhaps it would be best if you imagined it as your own fancy bids, assuming it will rise to the occasion, for certainly I cannot suit you all. For instance, how about technology? I think that there would be no cars or helicopters in and above the streets; this follows from the fact that the people of Omelas are happy people. Happiness is based on a just discrimination of what is necessary, what is neither necessary nor destructive, and what is destructive. In the middle category, however—that of the unnecessary but undestructive, that of comfort, luxury, exuberance, etc. —they could perfectly well have central heating, subway trains, washing machines, and all kinds of marvelous devices not yet invented here, floating light-sources, fuelless power, a cure for the common cold. Or they could have none of that: it doesn't matter. As you like it. I incline to think that people from towns up and down the coast have been coming in to Omelas during the last days before the Festival on very fast little trains and double-decked trams, and that the train station of Omelas is actually the handsomest building in town, though plainer than the magnificent Farmers' Market. But even granted trains, I fear that Omelas so far strikes some of you as goody-goody. Smiles, bells, parades, horses, bleh. If so, please add an orgy. If an orgy would help, don't hesitate. Let us not, however, have temples from which issue beautiful nude priests and priestesses already half in ecstasy and ready to copulate with any man or woman, lover or stranger, who desires union with the deep godhead of the blood, although that was my first idea. But really it would be better not to have any temples in Omelas—at least, not manned temples. Religion yes, clergy no. Surely the beautiful nudes can just wander about, offering themselves like divine soufflés to the hunger of the needy and the rapture of the flesh. Let them join the processions. Let tambourines be struck above the copulations, and the glory of desire be proclaimed upon the gongs, and (a not unimportant point) let the off- spring of these delightful rituals be beloved and looked after by all. One thing I know there is none of in Omelas is guilt. But what else should there be? I thought at first there were no drugs, but that is puritanical. For those who like it, the faint insistent sweetness of *drooz* may perfume the ways of the city, *drooz* which first brings a great lightness and brilliance to the mind and limbs, and then after some hours a dreamy languor, and wonderful visions at last of the very arcana and inmost secrets of the Universe, as well as exciting the pleasure of sex beyond all belief; and it is not habit-forming. For more modest tastes I think there ought to be beer. What else, what else belongs in the joyous city? The sense of victory, surely, the cele- bration of courage. But as we did without clergy, let us do without soldiers. The joy built upon successful slaughter is not the right kind of joy; it will not do; it is fearful and it is trivial. A boundless and generous contentment, a magnanimous triumph felt not against some outer enemy but in communion with the finest and fairest in the souls of all men everywhere and the splendor of the world's summer: this is what swells the hearts of the people of Omelas, and the victory they celebrate is that of life. I really don't think many of them need to take *drooz*.

Most of the processions have reached the Green Fields by now. A marvelous smell of cooking goes forth from the red and blue tents of the provisioners. The faces of small children are amiably sticky; in the benign gray beard of a man a couple of crumbs of rich pastry are entangled. The youths and girls have mounted their horses and are beginning to group around the starting line of the course. An old woman, small, fat, and laughing, is passing out flowers from a basket, and tall young men wear her flowers in their shining hair. A child of nine or ten sits at the edge of the crowd, alone, playing on a wooden flute. People pause to listen, and they smile, but they do not speak to him, for he never ceases playing and never sees them, his dark eyes wholly rapt in the sweet, thin magic of the tune.

He finishes, and slowly lowers his hands holding the wooden flute.

As if that little private silence were the signal, all at once a trumpet sounds from the pavilion near the starting line: imperious, melancholy, piercing. The horses rear on their slender legs, and some of them neigh in answer. Sober-faced, the young riders stroke the horses' necks and soothe them, whispering, "Quiet, quiet, there my beauty, my hope. . . ." They begin to form in rank along the starting line. The crowds along the racecourse are like a field of grass and flowers in the wind. The Festival of Summer has begun.

Do you believe? Do you accept the festival, the city, the joy? No? Then let me describe one more thing.

In a basement under one of the beautiful public buildings of Omelas, or perhaps in the cellar of one of its spacious private homes, there is a room. It has one locked door, and no window. A little light seeps in dustily between cracks in the boards, secondhand from a cobwebbed window somewhere across the cellar. In one corner of the little room a couple of mops, with stiff, clotted, foul-smelling heads, stand near a rusty bucket. The floor is dirt, a little damp to the touch, as cellar dirt usually is. The room is about three paces long and two wide: a mere broom closet or disused tool room. In the room a child is sitting. It could be a boy or a girl. It looks about six, but actually is nearly ten. It is feeble-minded. Perhaps it was born defective, or perhaps it has become imbecile through fear, malnutrition, and neglect. It picks its nose and occasionally fumbles vaguely with its toes or genitals, as it sits hunched in the corner farthest from the bucket and the two mops. It is afraid of the mops. It finds them horrible. It shuts its eyes, but it knows the mops are still standing there; and the door is locked; and nobody will come. The door is always locked; and nobody ever comes, except that sometimes—the child has no understanding of time or interval—sometimes the door rattles terribly and opens, and a person, or several people, are there. One of them may come in and kick the child to make it stand up. The others never come close, but peer in at it with frightened, disgusted eyes. The food bowl and the water jug are hastily filled, the door is locked, the eyes disappear. The people at the door never say anything, but the child, who has not always lived in the tool room, and can remember sunlight and its mother's voice, sometimes speaks. "I will be good," it says. "Please let

me out. I will be good!" They never answer. The child used to scream
for help at night, and cry a good deal, but now it only makes a kind
of whining, "eh-haa, eh-haa," and it speaks less and less often. It is
so thin there are no calves to its legs; its belly protrudes; it lives on a
half-bowl of corn meal and grease a day. It is naked. Its buttocks and
thighs are a mass of festered sores, as it sits in its own excrement
continually.

They all know it is there, all the people of Omelas. Some of them
have come to see it, others are content merely to know it is there.
They all know that it has to be there. Some of them understand why,
and some do not, but they all understand that their happiness, the
beauty of their city, the tenderness of their friendships, the health of
their children, the wisdom of their scholars, the skill of their makers,
even the abundance of their harvest and the kindly weathers of
their skies, depend wholly on this child's abominable misery.

This is usually explained to children when they are between eight
and twelve, whenever they seem capable of understanding; and most
of those who come to see the child are young people, though often
enough an adult comes, or comes back, to see the child. No matter how
well the matter has been explained to them, these young spectators
are always shocked and sickened at the sight. They feel disgust, which
they had thought themselves superior to. They feel anger, outrage, impotence, despite all the explanations. They would like to do something
for the child. But there is nothing they can do. If the child were
brought up into the sunlight out of that vile place, if it were cleaned
and fed and comforted, that would be a good thing, indeed; but if it
were done, in that day and hour all the prosperity and beauty and
delight of Omelas would wither and be destroyed. Those are the terms.
To exchange all the goodness and grace of every life in Omelas for
that single, small improvement: to throw away the happiness of thousands for the chance of the happiness of one: that would be to let
guilt within the walls indeed.

The terms are strict and absolute; there may not even be a kind
word spoken to the child.

Often the young people go home in tears, or in a tearless rage,
when they have seen the child and faced this terrible paradox. They
may brood over it for weeks or years. But as time goes on they begin
to realize that even if the child could be released, it would not get
much good of its freedom: a little vague pleasure of warmth and
food, no doubt, but little more. It is too degraded and imbecile to
know any real joy. It has been afraid too long ever to be free of fear.
Its habits are too uncouth for it to respond to humane treatment. Indeed, after so long it would probably be wretched without walls about
it to protect it, and darkness for its eyes, and its own excrement to
sit in. Their tears at the bitter injustice dry when they begin to perceive the terrible justice of reality, and to accept it. Yet it is their
tears and anger, the trying of their generosity and the acceptance of
their helplessness, which are perhaps the true source of the splendor
of their lives. Theirs is no vapid, irresponsible happiness. They know
that they, like the child, are not free. They know compassion. It is the
existence of the child, and their knowledge of its existence, that makes

possible the nobility of their architecture, the poignancy of their music, the profundity of their science. It is because of the child that they are so gentle with children. They know that if the wretched one were not there sniveling in the dark, the other one, the flute-player, could make no joyful music as the young riders line up in their beauty for the race in the sunlight of the first morning of summer.

Now do you believe in them? Are they not more credible? But there is one more thing to tell, and this is quite incredible.

At times one of the adolescent girls or boys who go to see the child does not go home to weep or rage, does not, in fact, go home at all. Sometimes also a man or woman much older falls silent for a day or two, and then leaves home. These people go out into the street, and walk down the street alone. They keep walking, and walk straight out of the city of Omelas, through the beautiful gates. They keep walking across the farmlands of Omelas. Each one goes alone, youth or girl, man or woman. Night falls; the traveler must pass down village streets, between the houses with yellow-lit windows, and on out into the darkness of the fields. Each alone, they go west or north, towards the mountains. They go on. They leave Omelas, they walk ahead into the darkness, and they do not come back. The place they go towards is a place even less imaginable to most of us than the city of happiness. I cannot describe it at all. It is possible that it does not exist. But they seem to know where they are going, the ones who walk away from Omelas.

1975

WOODY ALLEN

The Kugelmass Episode

Kugelmass, a professor of humanities at City College, was unhappily married for the second time. Daphne Kugelmass was an oaf. He also had two dull sons by his first wife, Flo, and was up to his neck in alimony and child support.

"Did I know it would turn out so badly?" Kugelmass whined to his analyst one day. "Daphne had promise. Who suspected she'd let herself go and swell up like a beach ball? Plus she had a few bucks, which is not in itself a healthy reason to marry a person, but it doesn't hurt, with the kind of operating nut[1] I have. You see my point?"

Kugelmass was bald and as hairy as a bear, but he had soul.

"I need to meet a new woman," he went on. "I need to have an affair. I may not look the part, but I'm a man who needs romance. I need softness, I need flirtation. I'm not getting younger, so before it's too late I want to make love in Venice, trade quips at '21,'[2] and exchange coy glances over red wine and candlelight. You see what I'm saying?"

---

1. Budget, expenses.   2. Celebrity nightclub and restaurant.

Dr. Mandel shifted in his chair and said, "An affair will solve nothing. You're so unrealistic. Your problems run much deeper."

"And also this affair must be discreet," Kugelmass continued. "I can't afford a second divorce. Daphne would really sock it to me."

"Mr. Kugelmass—"

"But it can't be anyone at City College, because Daphne also works there. Not that anyone on the faculty at C.C.N.Y. is any great shakes, but some of those coeds . . ."

"Mr. Kugelmass—"

"Help me. I had a dream last night. I was skipping through a meadow holding a picnic basket and the basket was marked 'Options.' And then I saw there was a hole in the basket."

"Mr. Kugelmass, the worst thing you could do is act out. You must simply express your feelings here, and together we'll analyze them. You have been in treatment long enough to know there is no overnight cure. After all, I'm an analyst, not a magician."

"Then perhaps what I need is a magician," Kugelmass said, rising from his chair. And with that he terminated his therapy.

A couple of weeks later, while Kugelmass and Daphne were moping around in their apartment one night like two pieces of old furniture, the phone rang.

"I'll get it," Kugelmass said. "Hello."

"Kugelmass?" a voice said. "Kugelmass, this is Persky."

"Who?"

"Persky. Or should I say The Great Persky?"

"Pardon me?"

"I hear you're looking all over town for a magician to bring a little exotica into your life? Yes or no?"

"Sh-h-h," Kugelmass whispered. "Don't hang up. Where are you calling from, Persky?"

Early the following afternoon, Kugelmass climbed three flights of stairs in a broken-down apartment house in the Bushwick section of Brooklyn. Peering through the darkness of the hall, he found the door he was looking for and pressed the bell. I'm going to regret this, he thought to himself.

Seconds later, he was greeted by a short, thin, waxy-looking man.

"*You're* Persky the Great?" Kugelmass said.

"The Great Persky. You want a tea?"

"No, I want romance. I want music. I want love and beauty."

"But not tea, eh? Amazing. O.K., sit down."

Persky went to the back room, and Kugelmass heard the sounds of boxes and furniture being moved around. Persky reappeared, pushing before him a large object on squeaky roller-skate wheels. He removed some old silk handkerchiefs that were lying on its top and blew away a bit of dust. It was a cheap-looking Chinese cabinet, badly lacquered.

"Persky," Kugelmass said, "what's your scam?"[3]

"Pay attention," Persky said. "This is some beautiful effect. I developed it for a Knights of Pythias[4] date last year, but the booking fell through. Get into the cabinet."

---

3. Scheme, confidence trick.   4. Secret fraternal society.

"Why, so you can stick it full of swords or something?"

"You see any swords?"

Kugelmass made a face and, grunting, climbed into the cabinet. He couldn't help noticing a couple of ugly rhinestones glued onto the raw plywood just in front of his face. "If this is a joke," he said.

"Some joke. Now, here's the point. If I throw any novel into this cabinet with you, shut the doors, and tap it three times, you will find yourself projected into that book."

Kugelmass made a grimace of disbelief.

"It's the emess,"[5] Persky said. "My hand to God. Not just a novel, either. A short story, a play, a poem. You can meet any of the women created by the world's best writers. Whoever you dreamed of. You could carry on all you like with a real winner. Then when you've had enough you give a yell, and I'll see you're back here in a split second."

"Persky, are you some kind of outpatient?"

"I'm telling you it's on the level," Persky said.

Kugelmass remained skeptical. "What are you telling me—that this cheesy homemade box can take me on a ride like you're describing?"

"For a double sawbuck."[6]

Kugelmass reached for his wallet. "I'll believe this when I see it," he said.

Persky tucked the bills in his pants pocket and turned toward his bookcase. "So who do you want to meet? Sister Carrie? Hester Prynne? Ophelia? Maybe someone by Saul Bellow? Hey, what about Temple Drake?[7] Although for a man your age she'd be a workout."

"French. I want to have an affair with a French lover."

"Nana?"[8]

"I don't want to have to pay for it."

"What about Natasha in 'War and Peace'?"[9]

"I said French. I know! What about Emma Bovary? That sounds to me perfect."

"You got it, Kugelmass. Give me a holler when you've had enough." Persky tossed in a paperback copy of Flaubert's novel.

"You sure this is safe?" Kugelmass asked as Persky began shutting the cabinet doors.

"Safe. Is anything safe in this crazy world?" Persky rapped three times on the cabinet and then flung open the doors.

Kugelmass was gone. At the same moment, he appeared in the bedroom of Charles and Emma Bovary's house at Yonville.[1] Before him was a beautiful woman, standing alone with her back turned to him as she folded some linen. I can't believe this, thought Kugelmass, staring at the doctor's ravishing wife. This is uncanny. I'm here. It's her.

Emma turned in surprise. "Goodness, you startled me," she said.

---

5. Truth.

6. Twenty dollars.

7. Respectively, the fallen heroine of Theodore Dreiser's *Sister Carrie* (1900); the adulterous heroine of Nathaniel Hawthorne's *The Scarlet Letter* (1850); Hamlet's fiancée, who drowns herself; Bellow's heroines are intensely neurotic, sexual, and vindictive; the victim of a bizarre rape in Faulkner's *Sanctuary* (1931), who is also the heroine of his *Requiem for a Nun* (1950).

8. Prostitute-heroine of Émile Zola's *Nana* (1880).

9. Saucy heroine of the novel (1865–1869) by Tolstoy.

1. Town in Normandy, France, where much of Flaubert's novel *Madame Bovary* (1857) is set.

"Who are you?" She spoke in the same fine English translation as the paperback.

It's simply devastating, he thought. Then, realizing that it was he whom she had addressed, he said, "Excuse me. I'm Sidney Kugelmass. I'm from City College. A professor of humanities. C.C.N.Y.? Uptown. I—oh, boy!"

Emma Bovary smiled flirtatiously and said, "Would you like a drink? A glass of wine, perhaps?"

She is beautiful, Kugelmass thought. What a contrast with the troglodyte who shared his bed! He felt a sudden impulse to take this vision into his arms and tell her she was the kind of woman he had dreamed of all his life.

"Yes, some wine," he said hoarsely. "White. No, red. No, white. Make it white."

"Charles is out for the day," Emma said, her voice full of playful implication.

After the wine, they went for a stroll in the lovely French countryside. "I've always dreamed that some mysterious stranger would appear and rescue me from the monotony of this crass rural existence," Emma said, clasping his hand. They passed a small church. "I love what you have on," she murmured. "I've never seen anything like it around here. It's so . . . so modern."

"It's called a leisure suit," he said romantically. "It was marked down." Suddenly he kissed her. For the next hour they reclined under a tree and whispered together and told each other deeply meaningful things with their eyes. Then Kugelmass sat up. He had just remembered he had to meet Daphne at Bloomingdale's.[2] "I must go," he told her. "But don't worry, I'll be back."

"I hope so," Emma said.

He embraced her passionately, and the two walked back to the house. He held Emma's face cupped in his palms, kissed her again, and yelled, "O.K., Persky! I got to be at Bloomingdale's by three-thirty."

There was an audible pop, and Kugelmass was back in Brooklyn.

"So? Did I lie?" Persky asked triumphantly.

"Look, Persky, I'm right now late to meet the ball and chain at Lexington Avenue, but when can I go again? Tomorrow?"

"My pleasure. Just bring a twenty. And don't mention this to anybody."

"Yeah. I'm going to call Rupert Murdoch."[3]

Kugelmass hailed a cab and sped off to the city. His heart danced on point. I am in love, he thought, I am the possessor of a wonderful secret. What he didn't realize was that at this very moment students in various classrooms across the country were saying to their teachers, "Who is this character on page 100? A bald Jew is kissing Madame Bovary?" A teacher in Sioux Falls, South Dakota, sighed and thought, Jesus, these kids, with their pot and acid. What goes through their minds!

---

2. Chic New York department store.
3. Australian newspaper baron, who, in addition to several British papers, owns the New York *Post*, the *Village Voice*, and *New York* magazine.

Daphne Kugelmass was in the bathroom-accessories department at Bloomingdale's when Kugelmass arrived breathlessly. "Where've you been?" she snapped. "It's four-thirty."

"I got held up in traffic," Kugelmass said.

Kugelmass visited Persky the next day, and in a few minutes was again passed magically to Yonville. Emma couldn't hide her excitement at seeing him. The two spent hours together, laughing and talking about their different backgrounds. Before Kugelmass left, they made love. "My God, I'm doing it with Madame Bovary!" Kugelmass whispered to himself. "Me, who failed freshman English."

As the months passed, Kugelmass saw Persky many times and developed a close and passionate relationship with Emma Bovary. "Make sure and always get me into the book before page 120," Kugelmass said to the magician one day. "I always have to meet her before she hooks up with this Rodolphe character."[4]

"Why?" Persky asked. "You can't beat his time?"

"Beat his time. He's landed gentry. Those guys have nothing better to do than flirt and ride horses. To me, he's one of those faces you see in the pages of *Women's Wear Daily*. With the Helmut Berger[5] hairdo. But to her he's hot stuff."

"And her husband suspects nothing?"

"He's out of his depth. He's a lackluster little paramedic who's thrown in his lot with a jitterbug. He's ready to go to sleep by ten, and she's putting on her dancing shoes. Oh, well . . . See you later."

And once again Kugelmass entered the cabinet and passed instantly to the Bovary estate at Yonville. "How you doing, cupcake?" he said to Emma.

"Oh, Kugelmass," Emma sighed. "What I have to put up with. Last night at dinner, Mr. Personality dropped off to sleep in the middle of the dessert course. I'm pouring my heart out about Maxim's[6] and the ballet, and out of the blue I hear snoring."

"It's O.K., darling. I'm here now," Kugelmass said, embracing her. I've earned this, he thought, smelling Emma's French perfume and burying his nose in her hair. I've suffered enough. I've paid enough analysts. I've searched till I'm weary. She's young and nubile, and I'm here a few pages after Léon and just before Rodolphe. By showing up during the correct chapters, I've got the situation knocked.

Emma, to be sure, was just as happy as Kugelmass. She had been starved for excitement, and his tales of Broadway night life, of fast cars and Hollywood and TV stars, enthralled the young French beauty.

"Tell me again about O.J. Simpson,"[7] she implored that evening, as she and Kugelmass strolled past Abbé Bournisien's church.

"What can I say? The man is great. He sets all kinds of rushing records. Such moves. They can't touch him."

4. The provincial aristocratic womanizer who seduces Emma, after she has a first romantic, idealistic flirtation with the mooning young Léon (who is mentioned below). The Abbé Bournisien and Binet, mentioned later, are minor characters in the novel.

5. Gossipy New York fashion newspaper; handsome German actor (b. 1942) who often plays decadent characters (*The Damned, Portrait of Dorian Gray*).

6. Fashionable Paris restaurant.

7. Famous football running back, recently retired, though he's still seen running through airports in TV commercials.

"And the Academy Awards?" Emma said wistfully. "I'd give anything to win one."

"First you've got to be nominated."

"I know. You explained it. But I'm convinced I can act. Of course, I'd want to take a class or two. With Strasberg[8] maybe. Then, if I had the right agent—"

"We'll see, we'll see. I'll speak to Persky."

That night, safely returned to Persky's flat, Kugelmass brought up the idea of having Emma visit him in the big city.

"Let me think about it," Persky said. "Maybe I could work it. Stranger things have happened." Of course, neither of them could think of one.

"Where the hell do you go all the time?" Daphne Kugelmass barked at her husband as he returned home late that evening. "You got a chippie stashed somewhere?"

"Yeah, sure, I'm just the type," Kugelmass said wearily. "I was with Leonard Popkin. We were discussing Socialist agriculture in Poland. You know Popkin. He's a freak on the subject."

"Well, you've been very odd lately," Daphne said. "Distant. Just don't forget about my father's birthday. On Saturday?"

"Oh, sure, sure," Kugelmass said, heading for the bathroom.

"My whole family will be there. We can see the twins. And Cousin Hamish. You should be more polite to Cousin Hamish—he likes you."

"Right, the twins," Kugelmass said, closing the bathroom door and shutting out the sound of his wife's voice. He leaned against it and took a deep breath. In a few hours, he told himself, he would be back in Yonville again, back with his beloved. And this time, if all went well, he would bring Emma back with him.

At three-fifteen the following afternoon, Persky worked his wizardry again. Kugelmass appeared before Emma, smiling and eager. The two spent a few hours at Yonville with Binet and then remounted the Bovary carriage. Following Persky's instructions, they held each other tightly, closed their eyes, and counted to ten. When they opened them, the carriage was just drawing up at the side door of the Plaza Hotel, where Kugelmass had optimistically reserved a suite earlier in the day.

"I love it! It's everything I dreamed it would be," Emma said as she swirled joyously around the bedroom, surveying the city from their window. "There's F.A.O. Schwarz.[9] And there's Central Park, and the Sherry[1] is which one? Oh, there—I see. It's too divine."

On the bed there were boxes from Halston and Saint Laurent.[2] Emma unwrapped a package and held up a pair of black velvet pants against her perfect body.

"The slacks suit is by Ralph Lauren," Kugelmass said. "You'll look like a million bucks in it. Come on, sugar, give us a kiss."

---

8. Lee Strasberg's acting school taught the natural acting style known as "The Method" to such stars as Marlon Brando.
9. Well-known toy store.
1. Sherry-Netherland Hotel, also in Central Park area.
2. Famous and expensive fashion designers and couturiers, as is Ralph Lauren, below.

"I've never been so happy!" Emma squealed as she stood before the mirror. "Let's go out on the town. I want to see 'Chorus Line' and the Guggenheim and this Jack Nicholson[3] character you always talk about. Are any of his flicks showing?"

"I cannot get my mind around this," a Stanford professor said. "First a strange character named Kugelmass, and now she's gone from the book. Well, I guess the mark of a classic is that you can reread it a thousand times and always find something new."

The lovers passed a blissful weekend. Kugelmass had told Daphne he would be away at a symposium in Boston and would return Monday. Savoring each moment, he and Emma went to the movies, had dinner in Chinatown, passed two hours at a discothèque, and went to bed with a TV movie. They slept till noon on Sunday, visited SoHo, and ogled celebrities at Elaine's.[4] They had caviar and champagne in their suite on Sunday night and talked until dawn. That morning, in the cab taking them to Persky's apartment, Kugelmass thought, It was hectic, but worth it. I can't bring her here too often, but now and then it will be a charming contrast with Yonville.

At Persky's, Emma climbed into the cabinet, arranged her new boxes of clothes neatly around her, and kissed Kugelmass fondly. "My place next time," she said with a wink. Persky rapped three times on the cabinet. Nothing happened.

"Hmm," Persky said, scratching his head. He rapped again, but still no magic. "Something must be wrong," he mumbled.

"Persky, you're joking!" Kugelmass cried. "How can it not work?"

"Relax, relax. Are you still in the box, Emma?"

"Yes."

Persky rapped again—harder this time.

"I'm still here, Persky."

"I know, darling. Sit tight."

"Persky, we *have* to get her back," Kugelmass whispered. "I'm a married man, and I have a class in three hours. I'm not prepared for anything more than a cautious affair at this point."

"I can't understand it," Persky muttered. "It's such a reliable little trick."

But he could do nothing. "It's going to take a little while," he said to Kugelmass. "I'm going to have to strip it down. I'll call you later."

Kugelmass bundled Emma into a cab and took her back to the Plaza. He barely made it to his class on time. He was on the phone all day, to Persky and to his mistress. The magician told him it might be several days before he got to the bottom of the trouble.

"How was the symposium?" Daphne asked him that night.

"Fine, fine," he said, lighting the filter end of a cigarette.

"What's wrong? You're as tense as a cat."

"Me? Ha, that's a laugh. I'm as calm as a summer night. I'm

---

3. A Broadway musical; the Solomon R. Guggenheim Museum; Nicholson starred in the films *Easy Rider, One Flew Over the Cuckoo's Nest, Five Easy Pieces.*

4. SoHo is the new center of the contemporary art scene south of Greenwich Village. Elaine's restaurant is frequented by publishing and newspaper notables.

just going to take a walk." He eased out the door, hailed a cab, and flew to the Plaza.

"This is no good," Emma said. "Charles will miss me."

"Bear with me, sugar," Kugelmass said. He was pale and sweaty. He kissed her again, raced to the elevators, yelled at Persky over a pay phone in the Plaza lobby, and just made it home before midnight.

"According to Popkin, barley prices in Kraków have not been this stable since 1971," he said to Daphne, and smiled wanly as he climbed into bed.

The whole week went by like that. On Friday night, Kugelmass told Daphne there was another symposium he had to catch, this one in Syracuse. He hurried back to the Plaza, but the second weekend there was nothing like the first. "Get me back into the novel or marry me," Emma told Kugelmass. "Meanwhile, I want to get a job or go to class, because watching TV all day is the pits."

"Fine. We can use the money," Kugelmass said. "You consume twice your weight in room service."

"I met an Off Broadway producer in Central Park yesterday, and he said I might be right for a project he's doing," Emma said.

"Who is this clown?" Kugelmass asked.

"He's not a clown. He's sensitive and kind and cute. His name's Jeff Something-or-Other, and he's up for a Tony."[5]

Later that afternoon, Kugelmass showed up at Persky's drunk.

"Relax," Persky told him. "You'll get a coronary."

"Relax. The man says relax. I've got a fictional character stashed in a hotel room, and I think my wife is having me tailed by a private shamus."[6]

"O.K., O.K. We know there's a problem." Persky crawled under the cabinet and started banging on something with a large wrench.

"I'm like a wild animal," Kugelmass went on. "I'm sneaking around town, and Emma and I have had it up to here with each other. Not to mention a hotel tab that reads like the defense budget."

"So what should I do? This is the world of magic," Persky said. "It's all nuance."

"Nuance, my foot. I'm pouring Dom Pérignon and black eggs[7] into this little mouse, plus her wardrobe, plus she's enrolled at the Neighborhood Playhouse[8] and suddenly needs professional photos. Also, Persky, Professor Fivish Kopkind, who teaches Comp Lit and who has always been jealous of me, has identified me as the sporadically appearing character in the Flaubert book. He's threatened to go to Daphne. I see ruin and alimony jail. For adultery with Madame Bovary, my wife will reduce me to beggary."

"What do you want me to say? I'm working on it night and day. As far as your personal anxiety goes, that I can't help you with. I'm a magician, not an analyst."

5. Broadway Drama Critics' Award comparable to Oscar.
6. Detective.
7. An especially fine champagne and caviar.
8. Founded in 1915 to bring drama to the lower East Side of New York City, its productions tended to have social implications or to be experimental. The theater closed in 1927, but its production company continues to perform.

By Sunday afternoon, Emma had locked herself in the bathroom and refused to respond to Kugelmass's entreaties. Kugelmass stared out the window at the Wollman Rink[9] and contemplated suicide. Too bad this is a low floor, he thought, or I'd do it right now. Maybe if I ran away to Europe and started life over . . . Maybe I could sell the *International Herald Tribune*, like those young girls used to.[1]

The phone rang. Kugelmass lifted it to his ear mechanically.

"Bring her over," Persky said. "I think I got the bugs out of it."

Kugelmass's heart leaped. "You're serious?" he said. "You got it licked?"

"It was something in the transmission. Go figure."

"Persky, you're a genius. We'll be there in a minute. Less than a minute."

Again the lovers hurried to the magician's apartment, and again Emma Bovary climbed into the cabinet with her boxes. This time there was no kiss. Persky shut the doors, took a deep breath, and tapped the box three times. There was the reassuring popping noise, and when Persky peered inside, the box was empty. Madame Bovary was back in her novel. Kugelmass heaved a great sigh of relief and pumped the magician's hand.

"It's over," he said. "I learned my lesson. I'll never cheat again, I swear it." He pumped Persky's hand again and made a mental note to send him a necktie.

Three weeks later, at the end of a beautiful spring afternoon, Persky answered his doorbell. It was Kugelmass, with a sheepish expression on his face.

"O.K., Kugelmass," the magician said. "Where to this time?"

"It's just this once," Kugelmass said. "The weather is so lovely, and I'm not getting any younger. Listen, you've read 'Portnoy's Complaint'? Remember The Monkey?"[2]

"The price is now twenty-five dollars, because the cost of living is up, but I'll start you off with one freebie, due to all the trouble I caused you."

"You're good people," Kugelmass said, combing his few remaining hairs as he climbed into the cabinet again. "This'll work all right?"

"I hope. But I haven't tried it much since all that unpleasantness."

"Sex and romance," Kugelmass said from inside the box. "What we go through for a pretty face."

Persky tossed in a copy of "Portnoy's Complaint" and rapped three times on the box. This time, instead of a popping noise there was a dull explosion, followed by a series of crackling noises and a shower of sparks. Persky leaped back, was seized by a heart attack, and dropped dead. The cabinet burst into flames, and eventually the entire house burned down.

Kugelmass, unaware of this catastrophe, had his own problems. He had not been thrust into "Portnoy's Complaint," or into any other

9. Skating rink in Central Park.
1. This was what some American dropouts of the 1950s did; Jean Seberg portrayed one in the 1959 film *Breathless*.

2. The leading character in Philip Roth's 1969 novel, The Monkey is less romantic than Flaubert's Emma Bovary and sexually carefree and . . . experimental.

novel, for that matter. He had been projected into an old textbook, "Remedial Spanish," and was running for his life over a barren, rocky terrain as the word *"tener"* ("to have")—a large and hairy irregular verb—raced after him on its spindly legs.

p. 1977

JOYCE CAROL OATES

The Lady with the Pet Dog

1

Strangers parted as if to make way for him.

There he stood. He was there in the aisle, a few yards away, watching her.

She leaned forward at once in her seat, her hand jerked up to her face as if to ward off a blow—but then the crowd in the aisle hid him, he was gone. She pressed both hands against her cheeks. He was not there, she had imagined him.

"My God," she whispered.

She was alone. Her husband had gone out to the foyer to make a telephone call; it was intermission at the concert, a Thursday evening.

Now she saw him again, clearly. He was standing there. He was staring at her. Her blood rocked in her body, draining out of her head . . . she was going to faint. . . . They stared at each other. They gave no sign of recognition. Only when he took a step forward did she shake her head *no—no—keep away*. It was not possible.

When her husband returned, she was staring at the place in the aisle where her lover had been standing. Her husband leaned forward to interrupt that stare.

"What's wrong?" he said. "Are you sick?"

Panic rose in her in long shuddering waves. She tried to get to her feet, panicked at the thought of fainting here, and her husband took hold of her. She stood like an aged woman, clutching the seat before her.

At home he helped her up the stairs and she lay down. Her head was like a large piece of crockery that had to be held still, it was so heavy. She was still panicked. She felt it in the shallows of her face, behind her knees, in the pit of her stomach. It sickened her, it made her think of mucus, of something thick and gray congested inside her, stuck to her, that was herself and yet not herself—a poison.

She lay with her knees drawn up toward her chest, her eyes hotly open, while her husband spoke to her. She imagined that other man saying, *Why did you run away from me?* Her husband was saying other words. She tried to listen to them. He was going to call the doctor, he said, and she tried to sit up. "No, I'm all right now," she said quickly. The panic was like lead inside her, so thickly congested.

How slow love was to drain out of her, how fluid and sticky it was inside her head!

Her husband believed her. No doctor. No threat. Grateful, she drew her husband down to her. They embraced, not comfortably. For years now they had not been comfortable together, in their intimacy and at a distance, and now they struggled gently as if the paces of this dance were too rigorous for them. It was something they might have known once, but had now outgrown. The panic in her thickened at this double betrayal: she drew her husband to her, she caressed him wildly, she shut her eyes to think about that other man.

A crowd of men and women parting, unexpectedly, and there he stood—there he stood—she kept seeing him, and yet her vision blotched at the memory. It had been finished between them, six months before, but he had come out here . . . and she had escaped him, now she was lying in her husband's arms, in his embrace, her face pressed against his. It was a kind of sleep, this love-making. She felt herself falling asleep, her body falling from her. Her eyes shut.

"I love you," her husband said fiercely, angrily.

She shut her eyes and thought of that other man, as if betraying him would give her life a center.

"Did I hurt you? Are you—?" her husband whispered.

Always this hot flashing of shame between them, the shame of her husband's near failure, the clumsiness of his love—

"You didn't hurt me," she said.

2

They had said good-by six months before. He drove her from Nantucket, where they had met, to Albany, New York, where she visited her sister. The hours of intimacy in the car had sealed something between them, a vow of silence and impersonality: she recalled the movement of the highways, the passing of other cars, the natural rhythms of the day hypnotizing her toward sleep while he drove. She trusted him, she could sleep in his presence. Yet she could not really fall asleep in spite of her exhaustion, and she kept jerking awake, frightened, to discover that nothing had changed—still the stranger who was driving her to Albany, still the highway, the sky, the antiseptic odor of the rented car, the sense of a rhythm behind the rhythm of the air that might unleash itself at any second. Everywhere on this highway, at this moment, there were men and women driving together, bonded together—what did that mean, to be together? What did it mean to enter into a bond with another person?

No, she did not really trust him; she did not really trust men. He would glance at her with his small cautious smile and she felt a declaration of shame between them.

Shame.

In her head she rehearsed conversations. She said bitterly, "You'll be relieved when we get to Albany. Relieved to get rid of me." They had spent so many days talking, confessing too much, driven to a pitch of childish excitement, laughing together on the beach, breaking into that pose of laughter that seems to eradicate the soul, so many days of this that the silence of the trip was like the silence of a hospital—all these surface noises, these rattles and hums, but an interior silence, a befuddlement. She said to him in her imagination, "One of us should die." Then she leaned over to touch him. She caressed the back of his neck. She said, aloud, "Would you like me to drive for a while?"

They stopped at a picnic area where other cars were stopped—couples, families—and walked together, smiling at their good luck. He put his arm around her shoulders and she sensed how they were in a posture together, a man and a woman forming a posture, a figure, that someone might sketch and show to them. She said slowly, "I don't want to go back. . . ."

Silence. She looked up at him. His face was heavy with her words, as if she had pulled at his skin with her fingers. Children ran nearby and distracted him—yes, he was a father too, his children ran like that, they tugged at his skin with their light, busy fingers.

"Are you so unhappy?" he said.

"I'm not unhappy, back there. I'm nothing. There's nothing to me," she said.

They stared at each other. The sensation between them was intense, exhausting. She thought that this man was her savior, that he had come to her at a time in her life when her life demanded completion, an end, a permanent fixing of all that was troubled and shifting and deadly. And yet it was absurd to think this. No person could save another. So she drew back from him and released him.

A few hours later they stopped at a gas station in a small city. She went to the women's rest room, having to ask the attendant for a key, and when she came back her eye jumped nervously onto the rented car—why? did she think he might have driven off without her?—onto the man, her friend, standing in conversation with the young attendant. Her friend was as old as her husband, over forty, with lanky, sloping shoulders, a full body, his hair thick, a dark, burnished brown, a festive color that made her eye twitch a little—and his hands were always moving, always those rapid conversational circles, going nowhere, gestures that were at once a little aggressive and apologetic.

She put her hand on his arm, a claim. He turned to her and smiled and she felt that she loved him, that everything in her life had forced her to this moment and that she had no choice about it.

They sat in the car for two hours, in Albany, in the parking lot of a Howard Johnson's restaurant, talking, trying to figure out their past. There was no future. They concentrated on the past, the several days behind them, lit up with a hot, dazzling August sun, like explosions that already belonged to other people, to strangers. Her face was faintly reflected in the green-tinted curve of the windshield, but she could not have recognized that face. She began to cry; she told herself: *I am not here, this will pass, this is nothing.* Still, she could not stop crying. The muscles of her face were springy, like a child's, unpredictable muscles. He stroked her arms, her shoulders, trying to comfort her. "This is so hard . . . this is impossible . . ." he said. She felt panic for the world outside this car, all that was not herself and this man, and at the same time she understood that she was free of him, as people are free of other people, she would leave him soon, safely, and within a few days he would have fallen into the past, the impersonal past. . . .

"I'm so ashamed of myself!" she said finally.

She returned to her husband and saw that another woman, a shadow-woman, had taken her place—noiseless and convincing, like a dancer performing certain difficult steps. Her husband folded her in his arms and talked to her of his own loneliness, his worries about his business, his health, his mother, kept tranquilized and mute in a nursing home, and her spirit detached itself from her and drifted about the rooms of the large house she lived in with her husband, a shadow-woman delicate and imprecise. There was no boundary to her, no edge. Alone, she took hot baths and sat exhausted in the steaming water, wondering at her perpetual exhaustion. All that winter she noticed the limp, languid weight of her arms, her veins bulging slightly with the pressure of her extreme weariness. *This is fate,* she thought, to be here and not there, to be one person and not another, a certain man's wife and not the wife of another man. The long, slow pain of this certainty rose in her, but it never became clear, it was baffling and imprecise. She could not be serious about it; she kept congratulating herself on her own good luck, to have escaped so easily, to have freed herself. So much love had gone into the first several years of her marriage that there wasn't much left, now, for another man. . . . She was certain of that. But the bath water made her dizzy, all that perpetual heat, and one day in January she drew a razor blade lightly across the inside of her arm, near the elbow, to see what would happen.

Afterward she wrapped a small towel around it, to stop the bleeding. The towel soaked through. She wrapped a bath towel around that and walked through the empty rooms of her home, lightheaded, hardly aware of the stubborn seeping of blood. There was no boundary to her in this house, no precise limit. She could flow out like her own blood and come to no end.

She sat for a while on a blue love seat, her mind empty. Her husband telephoned her when he would be staying late at the plant. He talked to her always about his plans, his problems, his business friends, his future. It was obvious that he had a future. As he spoke she nodded to encourage him, and her heartbeat quickened with the memory of her own, personal shame, the shame of this man's particular, private wife. One evening at dinner he leaned forward and put his head in his arms and fell asleep, like a child. She sat at the table with him for a while, watching him. His hair had gone gray, almost white, at the temples—no one would guess that he was so quick, so careful a man, still fairly young about the eyes. She put her hand on his head, lightly, as if to prove to herself that he was real. He slept, exhausted.

One evening they went to a concert and she looked up to see her lover there, in the crowded aisle, in this city, watching her. He was standing there, with his overcoat on, watching her. She went cold. That morning the telephone had rung while her husband was still home, and she had heard him answer it, heard him hang up—it must have been a wrong number—and when the telephone rang again, at 9:30, she had been afraid to answer it. She had left home to be out of the range of that ringing, but now, in this public place, in this busy auditorium, she found herself staring at that man, unable to make any sign to him, any gesture of recognition. . . .

He would have come to her but she shook her head. *No. Stay away.*

Her husband helped her out of the row of seats, saying, "Excuse us, please. Excuse us," so that strangers got to their feet, quickly, alarmed, to let them pass. Was that woman about to faint? What was wrong?

At home she felt the blood drain slowly back into her head. Her husband embraced her hips, pressing his face against her, in that silence that belonged to the earliest days of their marriage. She thought, *He will drive it out of me.* He made love to her and she was back in the auditorium again, sitting alone, now that the concert was over. The stage was empty; the heavy velvet curtains had not been drawn; the musicians' chairs were empty, everything was silent and expectant; in the aisle her lover stood and smiled at her—Her husband was impatient. He was apart from her, working on her, operating on her; and then, stricken, he whispered, "Did I hurt you?"

The telephone rang the next morning. Dully, sluggishly, she answered it. She recognized his voice at once—that "Anna?" with its lifting of the second syllable, questioning and apologetic and making its claim—"Yes, what do you want?" she said.

"Just to see you. Please—"

"I can't."

"Anna, I'm sorry, I didn't mean to upset you—"

"I can't see you."

"Just for a few minutes—I have to talk to you—"

"But why, why now? Why now?" she said.

She heard her voice rising, but she could not stop it. He began to talk again, drowning her out. She remembered his rapid conversation. She remembered his gestures, the witty energetic circling of his hands.

"Please don't hang up!" he cried.

"I can't—I don't want to go through it again—"

"I'm not going to hurt you. Just tell me how you are."

"Everything is the same."

"Everything is the same with me."

She looked up at the ceiling, shyly. "Your wife? Your children?"

"The same."

"Your son?"

"He's fine—"

"I'm glad to hear that. I—"

"Is it still the same with you, your marriage? Tell me what you feel. What are you thinking?"

"I don't know. . . ."

She remembered his intense, eager words, the movement of his hands, that impatient precise fixing of the air by his hands, the jabbing of his fingers.

"Do you love me?" he said.

"No," she said.

She could not answer.

"I'll come over to see you," he said.

What will come next, what will happen?

Flesh hardening on his body, aging. Shrinking. He will grow old, but not soft like her husband. They are two different types: he is nervous, lean, energetic, wise. She will grow thinner, as the tension radiates out from her backbone, wearing down her flesh. Her collar-bones will jut out of her skin. Her husband, caressing her in their bed, will discover that she is another woman—she is not there with him—instead she is rising in an elevator in a downtown hotel, carrying a book as a prop, or walking quickly away from that hotel, her head bent and filled with secrets. Love, what to do with it? . . . Useless as moths' wings, as moths fluttering. . . . She feels the flutterings of silky, crazy wings in her chest.

He flew out to visit her every several weeks, staying at a different hotel each time. He telephoned her, and she drove down to park in an underground garage at the very center of the city.

She lay in his arms while her husband talked to her, miles away, one body fading into another. He will grow old, his body will change, she thought, pressing her cheek against the back of one of these men. If it was her lover, they were in a hotel room: always the propped-up little booklet describing the hotel's many services, with color photo-graphs of its cocktail lounge and dining room and coffee shop. Grow old, leave me, die, go back to your neurotic wife and your sad, ordi-nary children, she thought, but still her eyes closed gratefully against his skin and she felt how complete their silence was, how they had come to rest in each other.

"Tell me about your life here. The people who love you," he said, as he always did.

One afternoon they lay together for four hours. It was her birthday and she was intoxicated with her good fortune, this prize of the after-noon, this man in her arms! She was a little giddy, she talked too much. She told him about her parents, about her husband. . . . "They were all people I believed in, but it turned out wrong. Now, I believe in you. . . ." He laughed as if shocked by her words. She did not understand. Then she understood. "But I believe truly in you. I can't think of myself without you," she said. . . . He spoke of his wife, her ambitions, her intelligence, her use of the children against him, her use of his younger son's blindness, all of his words gentle and hypnotic and convincing in the late afternoon peace of this ho-tel room . . . and she felt the terror of laughter, threatening laughter. Their words, like their bodies, were aging.

She dressed quickly in the bathroom, drawing her long hair up around the back of her head, fixing it as always, anxious that every-thing be the same. Her face was slightly raw, from his face. The rubbing of his skin. Her eyes were too bright, wearily bright. Her hair was blond but not so blond as it had been that summer in the white Nantucket air.

She ran water and splashed it on her face. She blinked at the water. Blind. Drowning. She thought with satisfaction that soon, soon, he would be back home, in that house on Long Island she had never seen, with that woman she had never seen, sitting on the edge of another bed, putting on his shoes. She wanted nothing except to be free of him. Why not be free? *Oh*, she thought suddenly, *I will follow you back and kill you. You and her and the little boy. What is there to stop me?*

She left him. Everyone on the street pitied her, that look of absolute zero.

3

A man and a child, approaching her. The sharp acrid smell of fish. The crashing of waves. Anna pretended not to notice the father with his son—there was something strange about them. That frank, silent intimacy, too gentle, the man's bare feet in the water and the boy a few feet away, leaning away from his father. He was about nine years old and still his father held his hand.

A small yipping dog, a golden dog, bounded near them.

Anna turned shyly back to her reading; she did not want to have to speak to these neighbors. She saw the man's shadow falling over her legs, then over the pages of her book, and she had the idea that he wanted to see what she was reading. The dog nuzzled her; the man called him away.

She watched them walk down the beach. She was relieved that the man had not spoken to her.

She saw them in town later that day, the two of them brown-haired and patient, now wearing sandals, walking with that same look of care. The man's white shorts were soiled and a little baggy. His pullover shirt was a faded green. His face was broad, the cheekbones wide, spaced widely apart, the eyes stark in their sockets, as if they fastened onto objects for no reason, ponderous and edgy. The little boy's face was pale and sharp; his lips were perpetually parted.

Anna realized that the child was blind.

The next morning, early, she caught sight of them again. For some reason she went to the back door of her cottage. She faced the sea breeze eagerly. Her heart hammered. . . . She had been here, in her family's old house, for three days, alone, bitterly satisfied at being alone, and now it was a puzzle to her how her soul strained to fly outward, to meet with another person. She watched the man with his son, his cautious, rather stooped shoulders above the child's small shoulders.

The man was carrying something, it looked like a notebook. He sat on the sand, not far from Anna's spot of the day before, and the dog rushed up to them. The child approached the edge of the ocean, timidly. He moved in short jerky steps, his legs stiff. The dog ran around him. Anna heard the child crying out a word that sounded like "Ty"—it must have been the dog's name—and then the man joined in, his voice heavy and firm.

"Ty—"

Anna tied her hair back with a yellow scarf and went down to the beach.

The man glanced around at her. He smiled. She stared past him at the waves. To talk to him or not to talk—she had the freedom of that choice. For a moment she felt that she had made a mistake, that the child and the dog would not protect her, that behind the man's ordinary, friendly face there was a certain arrogant maleness—then she relented, she smiled shyly.

"A nice house you've got there," the man said.

She nodded her thanks.

The man pushed his sunglasses up on his forehead. Yes, she recognized the eyes of the day before—intelligent and nervous, the sockets pale, untanned.

"Is that your telephone ringing?" he said.

She did not bother to listen. "It's a wrong number," she said.

Her husband calling: she had left home for a few days, to be alone.

But the man, settling himself on the sand, seemed to misinterpret this. He smiled in surprise, one corner of his mouth higher than the other. He said nothing. Anna wondered: *What is he thinking?* The dog was leaping about her, panting against her legs, and she laughed in embarrassment. She bent to pet it, grateful for its busyness. "Don't let him jump up on you," the man said. "He's a nuisance."

The dog was a small golden retriever, a young dog. The blind child, standing now in the water, turned to call the dog to him. His voice was shrill and impatient.

"Our house is the third one down—the white one," the man said.

She turned, startled. "Oh, did you buy it from Dr. Patrick? Did he die?"

"Yes, finally. . . ."

Her eyes wandered nervously over the child and the dog. She felt the nervous beat of her heart out to the very tips of her fingers, the fleshy tips of her fingers: little hearts were there, pulsing. *What is he thinking?* The man had opened his notebook. He had a piece of charcoal and he began to sketch something.

Anna looked down at him. She saw the top of his head, his thick brown hair, the freckles on his shoulders, the quick, deft movement of his hand. Upside down, Anna herself being drawn. She smiled in surprise.

"Let me draw you. Sit down," he said.

She knelt awkwardly a few yards away. He turned the page of the sketch pad. The dog ran to her and she sat, straightening out her skirt beneath her, flinching from the dog's tongue. "Ty!" cried the child. Anna sat, and slowly the pleasure of the moment began to glow in her; her skin flushed with gratitude.

She sat there for nearly an hour. The man did not talk much. Back and forth the dog bounded, shaking itself. The child came to sit near them, in silence. Anna felt that she was drifting into a kind of trance while the man sketched her, half a dozen rapid sketches, the surface of her face given up to him. "Where are you from?" the man asked.

"Ohio. My husband lives in Ohio."

She wore no wedding band.

"Your wife—" Anna began.

"Yes?"

"Is she here?"

"Not right now."

She was silent, ashamed. She had asked an improper question. But the man did not seem to notice. He continued drawing her, bent over the sketch pad. When Anna said she had to go, he showed her the drawings—one after another of her, Anna, recognizably Anna, a woman in her early thirties, her hair smooth and flat across the top of her head, tied behind by a scarf. "Take the one you like best," he said, and she picked one of her with the dog in her lap, sitting very straight, her brows and eyes clearly defined, her lips girlishly pursed, the dog and her dress suggested by a few quick irregular lines.

"Lady with pet dog," the man said.

She spent the rest of that day reading, nearer her cottage. It was not really a cottage—it was a two-story house, large and ungainly and weathered. It was mixed up in her mind with her family, her own childhood, and she glanced up from her book, perplexed, as if waiting for one of her parents or her sister to come up to her. Then she thought of that man, the man with the blind child, the man with the dog, and she could not concentrate on her reading. Someone—probably her father—had marked a passage that must be important, but she kept reading and rereading it: *We try to discover in things, endeared to us on that account, the spiritual glamour which we ourselves have cast upon them; we are disillusioned, and learn that they are in themselves barren and devoid of the charm that they owed, in our minds, to the association of certain ideas. . . .*

She thought again of the man on the beach. She lay the book aside and thought of him: his eyes, his aloneness, his drawings of her.

They began seeing each other after that. He came to her front door in the evening, without the child; he drove her into town for dinner. She was shy and extremely pleased. The darkness of the expensive restaurant released her; she heard herself chatter; she leaned forward and seemed to be offering her face up to him, listening to him. He talked about his work on a Long Island newspaper and she seemed to be listening to him, as she stared at his face, arranging her own face into the expression she had seen in that charcoal drawing. Did he see her like that, then?—girlish and withdrawn and patrician? She felt the weight of his interest in her, a force that fell upon her like a blow. A repeated blow. Of course he was married, he had children—of course she was married, permanently married. This flight from her husband was not important. She had left him before, to be alone, it was not important. Everything in her was slender and delicate and not important.

They walked for hours after dinner, looking at the other strollers, the weekend visitors, the tourists, the couples like themselves. Surely they were mistaken for a couple, a married couple. *This is the hour in which everything is decided*, Anna thought. They had both had several drinks and they talked a great deal. Anna found herself saying too much, stopping and starting giddily. She put her hand to her forehead, feeling faint.

"It's from the sun—you've had too much sun—" he said.

At the door to her cottage, on the front porch, she heard herself asking him if he would like to come in. She allowed him to lead her inside, to close the door. *This is not important,* she thought clearly, *he doesn't mean it, he doesn't love me, nothing will come of it.* She was frightened, yet it seemed to her necessary to give in; she had to leave Nantucket with that act completed, an act of adultery, an accomplishment she would take back to Ohio and to her marriage.

Later, incredibly, she heard herself asking: "Do you . . . do you love me?"

"You're so beautiful!" he said, amazed.

She felt this beauty, shy and glowing and centered in her eyes. He stared at her. In this large, drafty house, alone together, they were like accomplices, conspirators. She could not think: how old was she? which year was this? They had done something unforgivable together, and the knowledge of it was tugging at their faces. A cloud seemed to pass over her. She felt herself smiling shrilly.

Afterward, a peculiar raspiness, a dryness of breath. He was silent. She felt a strange, idle fear, a sense of the danger outside this room and this old, comfortable bed—a danger that would not recognize her as the lady in that drawing, the lady with the pet dog. There was nothing to say to this man, this stranger. She felt the beauty draining out of her face, her eyes fading.

"I've got to be alone," she told him.

He left, and she understood that she would not see him again. She stood by the window of the room, watching the ocean. A sense of shame overpowered her: it was smeared everywhere on her body, the smell of it, the richness of it. She tried to recall him, and his face was confused in her memory: she would have to shout to him across a jumbled space, she would have to wave her arms wildly. *You love me! You must love me!* But she knew he did not love her, and she did not love him; he was a man who drew everything up into himself, like all men, walking away, free to walk away, free to have his own thoughts, free to envision her body, all the secrets of her body. . . . And she lay down again in the bed, feeling how heavy this body had become, her insides heavy with shame, the very backs of her eyelids coated with shame.

"This is the end of one part of my life," she thought.

But in the morning the telephone rang. She answered it. It was her lover: they talked brightly and happily. She could hear the eagerness in his voice, the love in his voice, that same still, sad amazement—she understood how simple life was, there were no problems.

They spent most of their time on the beach, with the child and the dog. He joked and was serious at the same time. He said, once, "You have defined my soul for me," and she laughed to hide her alarm. In a few days it was time for her to leave. He got a sitter for the boy and took the ferry with her to the mainland, then rented a car to drive her up to Albany. She kept thinking: *Now something will happen. It will come to an end.* But most of the drive was silent and hypnotic. She wanted him to joke with her, to say again that she had defined his soul for him, but he drove fast, he was serious, she distrusted the hawkish look of his profile—she did not know him at all. At a gas station she splashed her face with cold water. Alone in the grubby little rest room, shaky and very much alone. In such places are women totally alone with their bodies. The body grows heavier, more evil, in such silence. . . . On the beach everything had been noisy with sunlight and gulls and waves; here, as if run to earth, everything was cramped and silent and dead.

She went outside, squinting. There he was, talking with the station attendant. She could not think as she returned to him whether she wanted to live or not.

She stayed in Albany for a few days, then flew home to her husband. He met her at the airport, near the luggage counter, where her three pieces of pale-brown luggage were brought to him on a conveyor belt, to be claimed by him. He kissed her on the cheek. They shook hands, a little embarrassed. She had come home again.

"How will I live out the rest of my life?" she wondered.

In January her lover spied on her: she glanced up and saw him, in a public place, in the DeRoy Symphony Hall. She was paralyzed with fear. She nearly fainted. In this faint she felt her husband's body, loving her, working its love upon her, and she shut her eyes harder to keep out the certainty of his love—sometimes he failed at loving her, sometimes he succeeded, it had nothing to do with her or her pity or her ten years of love for him, it had nothing to do with a woman at all. It was a private act accomplished by a man, a husband or a lover, in communion with his own soul, his manhood.

Her husband was forty-two years old now, growing slowly into middle age, getting heavier, softer. Her lover was about the same age, narrower in the shoulders, with a full, solid chest, yet lean, nervous. She thought, in her paralysis, of men and how they love freely and eagerly so long as their bodies are capable of love, love for a woman; and then, as love fades in their bodies, it fades from their souls and they become immune and immortal and ready to die.

Her husband was a little rough with her, as if impatient with himself. "I love you," he said fiercely, angrily. And then, ashamed, he said, "Did I hurt you? . . ."

"You didn't hurt me," she said.

Her voice was too shrill for their embrace.

While he was in the bathroom she went to her closet and took out that drawing of the summer before. There she was, on the beach at Nantucket, a lady with a pet dog, her eyes large and defined, the dog in her lap hardly more than a few snarls, a few coarse soft lines of charcoal . . . her dress smeared, her arms oddly limp . . . her hands not well drawn at all. . . . She tried to think: did she love the man who had drawn this? did he love her? The fever in her husband's body had touched her and driven her temperature up, and now she stared at the drawing with a kind of lust, fearful of seeing an ugly soul in that woman's face, fearful of seeing the face suddenly through her lover's eyes. She breathed quickly and harshly, staring at the drawing.

And so, the next day, she went to him at his hotel. She wept, pressing against him, demanding of him. "What do you want? Why are you here? Why don't you let me alone?" He told her that he wanted nothing. He expected nothing. He would not cause trouble.

"I want to talk about last August," he said.

"Don't—" she said.

She was hypnotized by his gesturing hands, his nervousness, his obvious agitation. He kept saying, "I understand. I'm making no claims upon you."

They became lovers again.

He called room service for something to drink and they sat side by side on his bed, looking through a copy of *The New Yorker,* laughing at the cartoons. It was so peaceful in this room, so complete. They were on a holiday. It was a secret holiday. Four-thirty in the afternoon, on a Friday, an ordinary Friday: a secret holiday.

"I won't bother you again," he said.

He flew back to see her again in March, and in late April. He telephoned her from his hotel—a different hotel each time—and she came down to him at once. She rose to him in various elevators, she knocked on the doors of various rooms, she stepped into his embrace, breathless and guilty and already angry with him, pleading with him. One morning in May, when he telephoned, she pressed her forehead against the doorframe and could not speak. He kept saying, "What's wrong? Can't you talk? Aren't you alone?" She felt that she was going insane. Her head would burst. Why, why did he love her, why did he pursue her? Why did he want her to die?

She went to him in the hotel room. A familiar room: had they been here before? "Everything is repeating itself. Everything is stuck," she said. He framed her face in his hands and said that she looked thinner—was she sick?—what was wrong? She shook herself free. He, her lover, looked about the same. There was a small, angry pimple on his neck. He stared at her, eagerly and suspiciously. Did she bring bad news?

"So you love me? You love me?" she asked.

"Why are you so angry?"

"I want to be free of you. The two of us free of each other."

"That isn't true—you don't want that—"

He embraced her. She was wild with that old, familiar passion for him, her body clinging to his, her arms not strong enough to hold him. Ah, what despair!—what bitter hatred she felt!—she needed this man for her salvation, he was all she had to live for, and yet she could not believe in him. He embraced her thighs, her hips, kissing her, pressing his warm face against her, and yet she could not believe in him, not really. She needed him in order to live, but he was not worth her love, he was not worth her dying. . . . She promised herself this: when she got back home, when she was alone, she would draw the razor more deeply across her arm.

The telephone rang and he answered it: a wrong number.

"Jesus," he said.

They lay together, still. She imagined their posture like this, the two of them one figure, one substance; and outside this room and this bed there was a universe of disjointed, separate things, blank things, that had nothing to do with them. She would not be Anna out there, the lady in the drawing. He would not be her lover.

"I love you so much . . ." she whispered.

"Please don't cry! We have only a few hours, please. . . ."

It was absurd, their clinging together like this. She saw them as a single figure in a drawing, their arms and legs entwined, their heads pressing mutely together. Helpless substance, so heavy and warm and doomed. It was absurd that any human being should be so important

to another human being. She wanted to laugh: a laugh might free
them both.

She could not laugh.

Sometime later he said, as if they had been arguing, "Look. It's
you. You're the one who doesn't want to get married. You lie to me—"

"Lie to you?"

"You love me but you won't marry me, because you want something left over—Something not finished—All your life you can attribute your misery to me, to our not being married—you are using
me—"

"Stop it! You'll make me hate you!" she cried.

"You can say to yourself that you're miserable because of *me*. We
will never be married, you will never be happy, neither one of us
will ever be happy—"

"I don't want to hear this!" she said.

She pressed her hands flatly against her face.

She went to the bathroom to get dressed. She washed her face and
part of her body, quickly. The fever was in her, in the pit of her
belly. She would rush home and strike a razor across the inside of
her arm and free that pressure, that fever.

The impatient bulging of the veins: an ordeal over.

The demand of the telephone's ringing: that ordeal over.

The nuisance of getting the car and driving home in all that five
o'clock traffic: an ordeal too much for a woman.

The movement of this stranger's body in hers: over, finished.

Now, dressed, a little calmer, they held hands and talked. They had
to talk swiftly, to get all their news in: he did not trust the people
who worked for him, he had faith in no one, his wife had moved to a
textbook publishing company and was doing well, she had inherited
a Ben Shahn[1] painting from her father and wanted to "touch it up
a little"—she was crazy!—his blind son was at another school, doing
fairly well, in fact his children were all doing fairly well in spite of
the stupid mistake of their parents' marriage—and what about her?
What about her life? She told him in a rush the one thing he wanted
to hear: that she lived with her husband lovelessly, the two of them
polite strangers, sharing a bed, lying side by side in the night in that
bed, bodies out of which souls had fled. There was no longer even
any shame between them.

"And what about me? Do you feel shame with me still?" he asked.

She did not answer. She moved away from him and prepared to
leave.

Then, a minute later, she happened to catch sight of his reflection
in the bureau mirror—he was glancing down at himself, checking
himself mechanically, impersonally, preparing also to leave. He too
would leave this room: he too was headed somewhere else.

She stared at him. It seemed to her that in this instant he was
breaking from her, the image of her lover fell free of her, breaking
from her . . . and she realized that he existed in a dimension quite

1. Famous American painter (1898–1969) who specialized in scenes of social protest.

apart from her, a mysterious being. And suddenly, joyfully, she felt a miraculous calm. This man was her husband, truly—they were truly married, here in this room—they had been married haphazardly and accidentally for a long time. In another part of the city she had another husband, a "husband," but she had not betrayed that man, not really. This man, whom she loved above any other person in the world, above even her own self-pitying sorrow and her own life, was her truest lover, her destiny. And she did not hate him, she did not hate herself any longer; she did not wish to die; she was flooded with a strange certainty, a sense of gratitude, of pure selfless energy. It was obvious to her that she had, all along, been behaving correctly; out of instinct.

What triumph, to love like this in any room, anywhere, risking even the craziest of accidents!

"Why are you so happy? What's wrong?" he asked, startled. He stared at her. She felt the abrupt concentration in him, the focusing of his vision on her, almost a bitterness in his face, as if he feared her. What, was it beginning all over again? Their love beginning again, in spite of them? "How can you look so happy?" he asked. "We don't have any right to it. Is it because . . . ?"

"Yes," she said.

1972

POETRY

A PREFACE TO POETRY

ANONYMOUS

Western Wind

Western wind, when wilt thou blow,
  The small rain down can rain?
Christ, if my love were in my arms
  And I in my bed again!

ca. 1300   15th century

This poem is clearly not a story, although perhaps it could be part of
one: the beginning, the middle, or the end. (Perhaps the hero is saying these words on the eve of a battle—the beginning; perhaps the
heroine, banished for conduct unbecoming a heroine, is dying in the
wilderness—the end). But we are not told what happened—how the
lovers became separated, when, why, what happened meanwhile.
What we have is only the expression of the emotion itself: in the last
two short lines, nostalgia, outrage, lust, a sense of loss. The emotion is
directly, concisely, profanely expressed, and the narrative questions are
all left unanswered. Longer poems—and some short ones—sometimes
set the stage as carefully as a story does and fill out the plot, characters, and so on; often, however, we are alone out there with somebody
else's feelings.

Sound scary? Perhaps that's why people who enjoy stories and plays
often find it hard to "relate" to poetry; for one thing, it is hard to
"escape" into a poem—we haven't the chance that a story or play offers
to live with the characters for a while and share another existence.
Most poems move more quickly than stories—a moment and they are
over. A poem uses fewer words, so poets pack more into each word.

The following poem looks very different from *Western Wind*, by
once again somebody (the poet? someone he has overheard? someone
he has imagined being?) who is feeling lonely.

e. e. cummings

l(a

l(a

le
af
fa

ll   5

s)
one
l

iness

1958

Poetry usually looks different on the page from prose, but this poem really looks odd. The poet has tried to show, by imitation and analogy, a leaf falling, as we read. Visually, even the word "loneliness" is fragmented by the falling of the solitary leaf, and the poet even uses a typewriter pun in the second-to-last line to repeat the emphasis on "one." Not many poems use visual effects so heavily, and here the story element is almost nonexistent. But once again we are alone confronting a particular expression of feeling.

Which of these two is a typical poem? Neither, really, although both are well within what we might expect of poems to be read in a course in literature. It's hard to say what a typical poem is. Poetry has many subjects, many themes, many tones, and it uses a great variety of devices and strategies to affect us in a great variety of ways. Here are some things that all poems are often said to do:

—Rhyme.
—Have a regular rhythm.
—Describe something beautiful.
—State a universal truth.
—Elevate our thoughts.
—Make us feel better.
—Teach us something.
—Give us a broader perspective on ourselves and our world.
—Give us aesthetic pleasure.

Some poems do quite a few of these things, and most of them are decent enough things to do, but if we think of poems *having* to do these things we are in trouble. It's a bad list: forget it. Poems do share some common concerns: a sense of wordplay, a sharp consciousness of some particular feeling or emotion, tremendous concision of expression, whether the poem is long or short, the conscious use of sound effects, a constant concern with telling us what it is like to be in a particular situation, or feel a particular way. But even these persistent habits of poetry might be dangerous to codify as musts. Poems go better if you scrap preconceived notions about *all* poetry and are prepared to respond instead to the varieties of possibility that individual poems provide. Every poem is, like every person, individual, different, unique—not just a representative of a group.

Still, knowing how to read one poem can help you with other poems, and you can accumulate some skills that will help with difficulties that are likely to recur. This book is arranged to make it easier to develop such skills and to transfer them from one poem to another. Basically, we move from simpler problems in the early chapters to more complex ones, and from fairly accessible poems to more difficult ones. Groups of poems are arranged at the end of each chapter so as to facilitate comparison. A lot of the ability to read poetry well develops from a sense of knowing what to expect, and the groupings are there to help you develop that sense.

The first two chapters suggest some of the appeals and uses of poems, and the groupings of poems at the end of these chapters are by subjects—love, death, family, and so on—so that the many themes and tones of poems can readily be seen and distinguished from one another. The eight chapters in the second section are devoted to problems of craft. The craft of the poet has a lot to do with the skills needed by a reader of poetry, and in this section you will find introductory discussions of standard problems—speaker, situation and setting, figurative language, structure, stanza forms, and so on. The chapters in the third section raise "contextual" questions about poetry. Obviously, poems don't exist in a vacuum; like any other art objects or cultural phenomena they are part of the time and place from which they spring, and the groupings in this section illustrate a poem's connection to some larger cultural and historical forces. An anthology at the end includes some poems for further reading, and "A Glossary of Poetic Terms" (pp. 915–932) provides a review of the central points discussed in the individual chapters, a more detailed consideration of some technical points (directions on how to do metrical scansion, for example), and a ready reference guide to terminology.

Usually a reader can experience a poem in a satisfactory way without a lot of special knowledge, but additional knowledge and developed skill can heighten the experience of almost any poem. Poems do not "hide" their meanings, and good poets usually communicate rather quickly in some basic way. Rereadings, reconsiderations, and the application of additional knowledge allow us to hear resonances built into the poem, qualities that make it enjoyable to experience again and again. The route to meaning is often clear on first reading a poem, but the full possibilities of experience may require more time, energy, and knowledge of the right questions to ask.

This poem, for example, is fairly accessible, but far more pointed and complex if one brings a little knowledge to it:

LOUIS MACNEICE

Aubade

Having bitten on life like a sharp apple
Or, playing it like a fish, been happy,

Having felt with fingers that the sky is blue,
What have we after that to look forward to?

Not the twilight of the gods but a precise dawn   5
Of sallow and grey bricks, and newsboys crying war.

1935

Here is an expression of how the best of human desires for beauty is often frustrated by reality: instead of an eternal skyblueness and divine twilight, we discover a dull, gray reality of buildings and news of human conflict. The expression of the contrast is sharp, and there seems to be a hint of a specific reference. We can pin the situation down a bit if we know that the poem was written by an English poet in the mid-1930s, when fears of Hitler and of an imminent world war were rampant and likely to depress even the most determined of optimists and lovers. (Poems in this book are always dated at the end so it is easy to find out approximately when the poem was written.) The poem hints at a more specific situation, too; the "we" in line 4 suggests that whoever is talking is speaking for two, and the images of pleasure in the early lines imply a close and pleasant relationship that might well represent a love affair. Actually, this short poem gives us quite a bit of information—but indirectly. The title of the poem is *Aubade,* and the title tells us something about the tale. An aubade is a kind of poem (defined, along with other poetic kinds in "A Glossary of Poetic Terms," §10, p. 928) which features a particular setting and situation: it is a dawn song, involving lovers who regret the coming of the dawn after a night of love. We still are not told much about the narrative situation—only enough to let us share the sense of frustration and loss of awakening to a very grim world that seems light-years removed from moments ago.

The more you know, the better a reader of poems you are likely to be; the more practice you have had in reading other poems, the more likely you are to be able to experience a poem new to you. But knowing facts is not by itself enough; willingness to discover something new is a crucial quality of mind for reading poems well, and being willing to let the poem itself dictate which questions to ask is important to locating the right facts and discovering the right way of putting them together. Most readers can find out what they need to know for most poems if they figure out what questions to ask.

Poetry reading has many hazards, and almost as many of them result from overeagerness as from apathy; many people who read poetry enthusiastically do not read it well, just as many poems that mean well do not mean much. The questions you ask of poetry should channel your enthusiasm and direct it toward meaningful experience, but they should not destroy it. Some people are rather protective about poetry, and think it shouldn't be analyzed lest it shrivel or collapse. But such an attitude toward the "poor little poem" is finally rather patronizing; good poems are hardy, and they won't disintegrate when confronted with difficult questions. The techniques of analysis mean to make you both tougher-minded (less subject to gimmicks and quackery) and more sensitive (to the nuances and depths of good poems), and they also aim to allow the poem to open itself to you.

No one can give you a method that will offer you total experience of all poems. But because many characteristics of an individual poem are characteristics that one poem shares with other poems, there are guidelines which can prompt you to ask the right questions. The chapters that follow will help you in detail with a variety of problems, but meanwhile here is a checklist of some things to remember:

1. *Identify the poem's situation.* What is said is often conditioned by where it is said and by whom. Identifying the speaker and his or her place in the situation puts what he or she says in perspective.

2. *Read the syntax literally.* What the words say literally in normal sentences is only a starting point, but it is the place to start. Not all poems use normal prose syntax, but most of them do, and you can save yourself embarrassment by paraphrasing accurately (that is, rephrasing what the poem literally says, in plain prose) and not simply free-associating from an isolated word or phrase.

3. *Articulate for yourself what the title, subject, and situation make you expect.* Poets often use false leads and try to surprise you by doing shocking things, but defining expectation lets you be conscious of where you are when you begin.

4. *Be willing to be surprised.* Things often happen in poems that turn them around. A poem may seem to suggest one thing at first, then persuade you to its opposite, or at least to a significant qualification or variation.

5. *Find out what is implied by the traditions behind the poem.* Verse forms, poetic kinds, and metrical patterns all have a frame of reference, traditions of the way they are usually used and for what. For example, the anapest is usually used for comic poems, and if a poet uses it "straight" he is aware of his "departure" and is probably making a point by doing it.

6. *Remember that poems exist in time, and times change.* Not only the meanings of words, but whole ways of looking at the universe and man's role vary in different ages. Consciousness of time works two ways: your knowledge of history provides a context for reading the poem, and the poem's *use* of a word or idea may modify your notion of a particular age.

7. *Bother the reference librarian.* Look up anything you don't understand: an unfamiliar word (or an ordinary word used in an unfamiliar way), a place, a person, a myth, an idea—anything the poem uses. When you can't find what you need or don't know where to look, ask for help.

8. *Take a poem on its own terms.* Adjust to the poem; don't make

the poem adjust to you. Be prepared to hear things you do not want to hear. Not all poems are about your ideas, nor will they always present emotions you want to feel. But be tolerant and listen to the poem's ideas, not only to your desire to revise them for yourself.

9. *Argue*. Discussion usually results in clarification and keeps you from being too dependent on personal biases and preoccupations which sometimes mislead even the best readers. Talking a poem over with someone else (especially someone very different) can expand the limits of a too narrow perspective.

10. *Assume there is a reason for everything*. Poets do make mistakes, but in poems that show some degree of verbal control it is usually safest to assume that the poet chose each word carefully; if the choice seems peculiar to us, it is usually *we* who are missing something. Craftsmanship obliges us to try to account for the specific choices and only settle for conclusions of ineptitude if no hypothetical explanation will make sense.

What *is* poetry? Let your definition be cumulative as you read the poems in this book. No dictionary definition will cover all that you find, and it is better to discover for yourself poetry's many ingredients, its many effects, its many ways of acting. What can it do for you? Wait and see. Begin to add up its effects after you have read carefully —after you have studied and reread—a hundred or so poems; that will be a beginning, and you will be able to add to that total as long as you continue to read new poems or reread old ones.

Subject, Theme, and Tone

1   EXPERIENCING POETRY

People seldom feel neutral about poetry. Those who love it sometimes give the impression that it is an adequate substitute for food, shelter, and love. It isn't. It won't feed you or do your work for you or help you defeat your enemies, and, however satisfying words can be, they are never an equivalent for life itself and its human experiences. Those who dislike poetry on principle sometimes claim, on the other hand, that poetry is only words and good for nothing. That's not true either. It is easy to become frustrated by words—in poetry or in life—but when words represent, express, and recreate genuine human feelings, as they often do in poetry, they can be crucially important. Poetry is, in fact, more than just words. It is an *experience* of words, and those who know how to read poetry can easily extend their experience of life, their sense of what other people are like, and especially their awareness of personal feelings.

Feelings. One reason why poetry can be so important is that it is so intimately concerned with feelings. Poetry is often full of ideas, too, and sometimes poems can be powerful experiences of the mind, but most poems are primarily about how people feel rather than how people think. Poems provide, in fact, a language for feeling, and one of poetry's most insistent virtues involves its attempt to express the inexpressible. How can anyone, for example, put into words what it means to be in love? or what it feels like to lose to death someone one cares about? Poetry tries, and it often captures exactly the shade of emotion that feels just right to the reader. No one poem can be said to express all the things that love or death feels like, or means, but one of the joys of experiencing poetry occurs when we read a poem and want to say, "Yes, that is just what it is like; I know exactly what that line means but I've never been able to express it so well." Poetry can be the mouthpiece of our feelings even when our minds are speechless with grief or joy.

Here are two poems that talk about the sincerity and depth of love between two people. Each is written as if it were spoken or read by one person to his or her lover, and each is definite and powerful about the intensity and quality of love; but the poems work in quite different ways—the first one asserting the strength and depth of love, the second implying intense feeling by reminiscing about events in the relationship between the two people.

ELIZABETH BARRETT BROWNING

How Do I Love Thee?

How do I love thee? Let me count the ways.
I love thee to the depth and breadth and height
My soul can reach, when feeling out of sight
For the ends of Being and ideal Grace.
I love thee to the level of every day's   5
Most quiet need, by sun and candlelight.
I love thee freely, as men strive for Right;
I love thee purely, as they turn from Praise;
I love thee with the passion put to use
In my old griefs, and with my childhood's faith.   10
I love thee with a love I seemed to lose
With my lost saints—I love thee with the breath,
Smiles, tears of all my life!—and, if God choose,
I shall but love thee better after death.

1850

JAROLD RAMSEY

The Tally Stick

Here from the start, from our first of days, look:
I have carved our lives in secret on this stick
of mountain mahogany the length of your arms
outstretched, the wood clear red, so hard and rare.
It is time to touch and handle what we know we share.   5

Near the butt, this intricate notch where the grains
converge and join: it is our wedding.
I can read it through with a thumb and tell you now
who danced, who made up the songs, who meant us joy.
These little arrowheads along the grain,   10
they are the births of our children. See,
they make a kind of design with these heavy crosses,
the deaths of our parents, the loss of friends.

Over it all as it goes, of course, I
have chiseled Events, History—random   15
hashmarks cut against the swirling grain.
See, here is the Year the World Went Wrong,
we thought, and here the days the Great Men fell.
The lengthening runes of our lives run through it all.

See, our tally stick is whittled nearly end to end;   20
delicate as scrimshaw, it would not bear you up.

Regrets have polished it, hand over hand.
Yet let us take it up, and as our fingers
like children leading on a trail cry back
our unforgotten wonders, sign after sign,   25
we will talk softly as of ordinary matters,
and in one another's blameless eyes go blind.

p. 1977

The first poem is direct, but fairly abstract. It lists several ways in which the poet feels love and connects them to some noble ideas of higher obligations—to justice (line 7), for example, and to spiritual aspiration (lines 2–4). It suggests a wide range of things that love can mean and notices a variety of emotions. It is an ardent statement of feeling and asserts a permanence that will extend even beyond death. It contains admirable thoughts and memorable phrases that many lovers would like to hear said to themselves. What it does not do is say very much about what the relationship between the two lovers is like on an everyday basis, what experiences they have had together, what distinguishes their relationship from that of other devoted or ideal lovers. Its appeal is to our general sense of what love is like and how intense feelings can be; it does not offer everyday details. Love may differ from person to person and even from moment to moment, and so can poems about love.

The Tally Stick is much more concrete. The whole poem concentrates on a single object that, like the poem above, "counts" or "tallies" the ways in which this couple love one another. The stick stands for their love and becomes a kind of physical reminder of it: its natural features—the notches and arrowheads and cross marks (lines 6, 10, and 12) along with the marks carved on it (lines 15–16, 20–21)—indicate events in the story of the relationship. (We could say that the stick *symbolizes* their love; later on, we will look at a number of terms like this that can be used to make it easier to talk about some aspects of poems, but for now it is enough to notice that the stick serves the lovers as a reminder of some specific details of their love.) It is a special kind of reminder to them because its language is "secret" (line 2), something they can share privately (except that we as readers of the poem are sort of looking over their shoulders, not intruding but sharing their secret). The poet interprets the particular features of the stick as standing for particular events—their wedding and the births of their children, for example—and carves marks into it as reminders of other events (lines 15ff.). The stick itself becomes a very personal object, and in the last stanza of the poem it is as if we watch the lovers touching the stick together and reminiscing over it, gradually dissolving into their emotions and each other as they recall the "unforgotten wonders" (line 25) of their lives together.

Both poems are powerful statements of feelings, each in its own way. Some readers will prefer one and some the other. Personal preference does not mean that objective standards for poetry cannot be found (some poems are better than others, and later we will look in detail at features which help us to evaluate poems), but we need have no preconceived standard that all poetry must be one thing or another or work in one particular way. Some good poems are quite abstract, others quite specific. Any poem that helps us to articulate and clarify human feelings and ideas has a legitimate claim on us as readers. We tend to like poems (or people) for what they do, what they are, and what they represent to us.

Both *How Do I Love Thee* and *The Tally Stick* are written as if they were addressed to the partner in the love relationship, and both talk directly about the intensity of the love. The next poem we will look at talks only indirectly about the quality and intensity of love. It is written as if it were a letter from a woman to her husband who has gone on a long journey on business, and it clearly expresses how much she misses him, but indirectly suggests how much she cares about him.

EZRA POUND

The River-Merchant's Wife: A Letter

(*after Rihaku*[1])

While my hair was still cut straight across my forehead
I played about the front gate, pulling flowers.
You came by on bamboo stilts, playing horse,
You walked about my seat, playing with blue plums.
And we went on living in the village of Chokan: 5
Two small people, without dislike or suspicion.

At fourteen I married My Lord you.
I never laughed, being bashful.
Lowering my head, I looked at the wall.
Called to, a thousand times, I never looked back.   10

At fifteen I stopped scowling,
I desired my dust to be mingled with yours
For ever and for ever and for ever.
Why should I climb the look out?

At sixteen you departed,   15
You went into far Ku-to-yen, by the river of swirling eddies,
And you have been gone five months.
The monkeys make sorrowful noise overhead.

You dragged your feet when you went out.
By the gate now, the moss is grown, the different mosses,   20

1. The Japanese name for Li Po, an 8th-century Chinese poet. Pound's poem is a loose paraphrase of Li Po's.

Too deep to clear them away!
The leaves fall early this autumn, in wind.
The paired butterflies are already yellow with August
Over the grass in the West garden;
They hurt me. I grow older.   25
If you are coming down through the narrows of the river Kiang,
Please let me know beforehand,
And I will come out to meet you
    As far as Cho-fu-Sa.

1915

The "letter" tells us only a few facts about the nameless merchant's wife: that she is about sixteen and a half years old, that she married at fourteen and fell in love with her husband a year later, that she is now very lonely. And about their relationship we know only that they were childhood playmates in a small Chinese village, that their marriage originally was not a matter of personal choice, and that the husband unwillingly went away on a long journey five months ago. But the words tell us a great deal about how the young wife feels, and the simplicity of her language suggests her sincere and deep longing. The daily noises she hears seem "sorrowful" (line 18), and she worries about the dangers of the far-away place where her husband is, thinking of it in terms of its perilous "river of swirling eddies" (line 16). She thinks of how moss has grown up over the unused gate, and more time seems to her to have passed than actually has (lines 22–25). She remembers nostalgically their innocent childhood, when they played together without deeper love or commitment (lines 1–6), and contrasts that with her later satisfaction in their love (lines 11–14) and with her present anxiety, loneliness, and desire. We do not need to know the details of the geography of the river Kiang or how far Cho-fu-Sa is to sense that her wish to see him is very strong, that her desire is powerful enough to make her venture beyond the ordinary geographical bounds of her existence so that their reunion will come sooner. The closest she comes to a direct statement about her love is her statement that she desired that her dust be mingled with his "For ever and for ever and for ever" (lines 12–13). But her single-minded vision of the world, her perception of even the beauty of nature as only a record of her husband's absence and the passage of time, and her plain, apparently uncalculated language about her rejection of other suitors and her shutting out of the rest of the world all show her to be committed, desirous, nearly desperate for his presence. In a different sense, she has also counted the ways that she loves her man.

Here is another poem that similarly expresses a woman's intense desire for her lover, but here the expression is much more openly physical and sexual.

DIANE WAKOSKI

Uneasy Rider[2]

Falling in love with a mustache
is like saying
you can fall in love with
the way a man polishes his shoes
      which,
      of course,   5
      is one of the things that turns on
      my tuned-up engine

      those trim buckled boots

      (I feel like an advertisement   10
        for men's fashions
        when I think of your ankles)

Yeats was hung up with a girl's beautiful face[3]

and I find myself

a bad moralist,   15

a failing aesthetician,

a sad poet,

wanting to touch your arms and feel the muscles
that make a man's body have so much substance,
that makes a woman   20
lean and yearn in that direction
that makes her melt/ she is a rainy day
in your presence
the pool of wax under a burning candle
the foam from a waterfall   25

You are more beautiful than any Harley-Davidson
She is the rain,
waits in it for you,
finds blood spotting her legs
from the long ride.   30

                                           1971

---

2. From Wakoski's volume, *The Motor-cycle Betrayal Poems. Easy Rider* was one of the most popular motorcycle films of the late 1960s and early '70s.

3. See, for example, Yeats's "Among School Children," p. 825.

Physical details of the man's body and his clothing are plentiful here, and the woman is very direct about their effects—emotional and physical—upon her as she talks about what "turns on" her "tuned-up engine" (lines 7–8), and how his muscles make her "lean and yearn" and her body "melt" (lines 18–22). So vivid and intense are the various pictures of melting ("a rainy day," "a pool of wax," and "foam from a waterfall") that the poem pulls its focus back a bit from the couple near the end and talks of them as "a man" and "a woman": the woman who is speaking the poem adopts the third-person "she" to distance herself (and us) from the fire and energy of passion.

Poems can, of course, be about the meaning of a relationship or about disappointment just as easily as about sex or emotional fulfillment, and poets are often very good at suggesting the contradictions and uncertainties that tend to affect most relationships. Like other people, poets often find love and its complications quaint or downright funny, too, mainly because it involves human beings who, however serious their intentions and concerns, are often inept, uncertain, and self-contradictory—in short, human. Showing us ourselves as others see us is one of the more useful tasks that poems perform, but the poems that result can be just as entertaining and pleasurable as they are educational. Here is a poem which imagines a very strange scene, a kind of fantasy of what happens when we *think* too much about the implications of sex or love, and it is likely to leave us laughing, whether or not we take it seriously as a statement of human anxiety and of the tendency to intellectualize too much.

TOM WAYMAN

Wayman in Love

At last Wayman gets the girl into bed.
He is locked in one of those embraces
so passionate his left arm is asleep
when suddenly he is bumped in the back.
"Excuse me," a voice mutters, thick with German.   5
Wayman and the girl sit up astounded
as a furry gentleman in boots and a frock coat
climbs in under the covers.

"My name is Doktor Marx," the intruder announces
settling his neck comfortably on the pillow.   10
"I'm here to consider for you the cost of a kiss."
He pulls out a notepad. "Let's see now,
we have the price of the mattress, this room must be rented,
your time off work, groceries for two,
medical fees in case of accidents . . ."   15

"Look," Wayman says,
"couldn't we do this later?"
The philosopher sighs, and continues: "You are affected too,
    Miss.
If you are not working, you are going to resent   20
your dependent position. This will influence
I assure you, your most intimate moments . . ."

"Doctor, please," Wayman says. "All we want
is to be left alone."
But another beard, more nattily dressed,   25
is also getting into the bed.
There is a shifting and heaving of bodies
as everyone wriggles out room for themselves.
"I want you to meet a friend from Vienna,"
Marx says. "This is Doktor Freud."   30

The newcomer straightens his glasses,
peers at Wayman and the girl.
"I can see," he begins,
"that you two have problems . . ."

                              1973

    Another traditional subject of poetry is death, and on this subject, too, poets often describe frequent, recurrent human emotions in a variety of ways. In the following poem, the emphasis is on the shock and dismay we feel in perceiving the stillness of death in contrast to the energy and vitality of life. Here the dead person is a child, and the poet struggles with a sense of disbelief that someone so much alive could now be motionless.

JOHN CROWE RANSOM

Bells for John Whiteside's Daughter

There was such speed in her little body,
And such lightness in her footfall,
It is no wonder her brown study[4]
Astonishes us all.

Her wars were bruited in our high window.   5
We looked among orchard trees and beyond
Where she took arms against her shadow,
Or harried unto the pond

---

4. Stillness, as if in meditation or deep thought.

The lazy geese, like a snow cloud
Dripping their snow on the green grass,   10
Tricking and stopping, sleepy and proud,
Who cried in goose, Alas,

For the tireless heart within the little
Lady with rod that made them rise
From their noon apple-dreams and scuttle   15
Goose-fashion under the skies!

But now go the bells, and we are ready,
In one house we are sternly stopped
To say we are vexed at her brown study,
Lying so primly propped.   20

1924

After an opening stanza that introduces the basic contrast between
activity and stillness and between life and death, the center of the
poem concentrates on one vivid scene in the dead girl's life, a moment
when she played Mother Goose to her world and created a colorful,
energetic, and noisy dramatic scene. The three middle stanzas are
filled with a sense of energy and timelessness, and their main effect is
to recall the child at the peak of her vitality and activity, an emphasis
that heightens even more the stillness and quiet of the "brown study"
of the first and last stanzas. The final picture of the girl "Lying so
primly propped" seems grossly inappropriate for someone so restless
and active and thoroughly alive. The poet finds hard to bear the restraint of being "sternly stopped" to pay memorial homage and tries
to keep control by understating ("vexed," line 19) the deep feelings
about how all has gone wrong. We do not know much about the girl
except for her playful energy; we don't even know how she died. For
the purposes of the poem, those facts are not relevant. What we do
know is that her restless body is now at rest, and the stillness is eerie,
incomprehensible, unbelievable. The important thing to this poem is
the sense of inappropriateness and finality that death visits upon those
who seem to be its least likely targets.

The following poem is more openly about a personal reaction to the
death of a child. Here, a father struggles to understand and control his
grief.

BEN JONSON

On My First Son

Farewell, thou child of my right hand,[5] and joy;
My sin was too much hope of thee, loved boy:

5. A literal translation of the son's name, Benjamin.

Seven years thou'wert lent to me, and I thee pay,
Exacted by thy fate, on the just[6] day.
O could I lose all father now! for why   5
Will man lament the state he should envý,
To have so soon 'scaped world's and flesh's rage,
And, if no other misery, yet age?
Rest in soft peace, and asked, say, "Here doth lie
Ben Jonson his[7] best piece of poetry."   10
For whose sake henceforth all his vows be such
As what he loves may never like too much.

1616

The poem's attempts to rationalize the death are quite conventional, and although the father tries to be comforted by pious thoughts, his feelings keep showing through. The poem's beginning—with its formal "farewell" and the rather distant-sounding address to the dead boy ("child of my right hand")—cannot be sustained for long: both of the first two lines end with bursts of emotion. It is as if the father is trying to explain the death to himself and to keep his emotions under control, but cannot quite manage it. Even the punctuation suggests the way his feelings compete with conventional attempts to put the death into some sort of perspective that will soften the grief, and the comma near the end of each of the first two lines marks a pause that cannot quite hold back the overflowing emotion. But finally the only "idea" that the poem supports is that the father wishes he did not feel so intensely; in the fifth line he fairly blurts that he wishes he could lose his fatherly emotions, and in the final lines he resolves never again to "like" so much that he can be this deeply hurt. Philosophy and religion offer their useful counsels in this poem, but they prove far less powerful than feeling; and rather than drawing some kind of moral about what death means, the poem presents the actuality of feeling as inevitable and nearly all-consuming.

The poem that follows similarly tries to suppress the rawness of feelings about the death of a loved one, but here the survivor is haunted by memories of his wife when he sees a physical object—a vacuum cleaner—that was important in her life.

HOWARD NEMEROV

The Vacuum

The house is so quiet now
The vacuum cleaner sulks in the corner closet,

---

6. Exact; the son died on his seventh birthday, in 1603.

7. Ben Jonson's (a common Renaissance form of the possessive).

Its bag limp as a stopped lung, its mouth
Grinning into the floor, maybe at my
Slovenly life, my dog-dead youth   5

I've lived this way long enough,
But when my old woman died her soul
Went into that vacuum cleaner, and I can't bear
To see the bag swell like a belly, eating the dust
And the woolen mice, and begin to howl   10

Because there is old filth everywhere
She used to crawl, in the corner and under the stair.
I know now how life is cheap as dirt,
And still the hungry, angry heart
Hangs on and howls, biting at air.   15

1955

The poem is about a vacuum in the husband's life, but the title refers most obviously to the vacuum cleaner that, like the tally stick we looked at earlier, seems to stand for many of the things that were once important in their life together. The cleaner is a reminder of the dead wife ("my old woman," line 7) because of her devotion to cleanliness, but to the surviving husband buried in the filth of his life it seems as if the machine has become almost human, a kind of ghost of her: it "sulks" (line 2), it has lungs and a mouth (line 3), and it seems to grin, making fun of what has become of him. He "can't bear" (line 8) to see it in action because it then seems too much alive, too much a reminder of her life. The poem records his paralysis, his inability to do more than discover that life is "cheap as dirt" without her ordering and cleansing presence for him. At the end it is *his* angry heart that acts like the haunting machine, howling and biting at air as if he has merged with her spirit and the physical object that memorializes her. This poem, like *Bells for John Whiteside's Daughter,* puts a strong emphasis on the stillness of death and the way it makes things seem to stop; it captures in words the hurt, the anger, the inability to understand, the vacuum that remains when a loved one dies and leaves a vacant space. But here we do not see the body or hear a direct good-bye to the dead person; rather we encounter the feeling that lingers and won't go away, recalled through memory by an especially significant object, a mere thing but one that has been personalized to the point of becoming nearly human in itself. (The event described here is, by the way, fictional; the poet's wife did not in fact die. Like a dramatist or writer of fiction, the poet may simply *imagine* an event in order to analyze and articulate how such an event might feel in certain circumstances.)

The following poem, written three centuries earlier about an actual death, expresses a sense of love and loss much more directly. Here, the grieving widow addresses her beloved and expresses her desire to join him in death. Her terms are openly sexual, uniting a concern with love and death.

LADY CATHERINE DYER

Epitaph On the Monument of Sir William Dyer at Colmworth, 1641

My dearest dust, could not thy hasty day
Afford thy drowsy patience leave to stay
One hour longer: so that we might either
Sit up, or gone to bed together?
But since thy finished labor hath possessed   5
Thy weary limbs with early rest,
Enjoy it sweetly: and thy widow bride
Shall soon repose her by thy slumbering side.
Whose business, now, is only to prepare
My nightly dress, and call to prayer: 10
Mine eyes wax heavy and the day grows old,
The dew falls thick, my blood grows cold.
Draw, draw the closéd curtains: and make room:
My dear, my dearest dust; I come, I come.

1641

There is much more going on in the poems that we have glanced at than we have taken time to consider, but even the quickest look at these poems suggests something of the range of feelings that poems can offer—the depth of feeling, the clarity, the experience that may be articulately and precisely shared. Later we will look more carefully at *how* these things happen.

A Gathering of Love Poems

ANONYMOUS

My Love in Her Attire

My love in her attire doth show her wit,[1]
It doth so well become her:
For every season she hath dressings fit,
For winter, spring, and summer.
No beauty she doth miss,   5
When all her robes are on;

1. Cleverness.

But Beauty's self she is,
When all her robes are gone.

1602

ROBERT HERRICK

Upon Julia's Clothes

Whenas in silks my Julia goes
Then, then, methinks, how sweetly flows
That liquefaction of her clothes.

Next, when I cast mine eyes, and see
That brave[2] vibration, each way free,   5
O, how that glittering taketh me!

1648

THEODORE ROETHKE

I Knew a Woman

I knew a woman, lovely in her bones,
When small birds sighed, she would sigh back at them;
Ah, when she moved, she moved more ways than one:
The shapes a bright container can contain!
Of her choice virtues only gods should speak,   5
Or English poets who grew up on Greek
(I'd have them sing in chorus, cheek to cheek).

How well her wishes went! She stroked my chin,
She taught me Turn, and Counter-turn, and Stand;[3]
She taught me Touch, that undulant white skin;   10
I nibbled meekly from her proffered hand;
She was the sickle; I, poor I, the rake,
Coming behind her for her pretty sake
(But what prodigious mowing we did make).

Love likes a gander, and adores a goose: 15
Her full lips pursed, the errant note to seize;
She played it quick, she played it light and loose;
My eyes, they dazzled at her flowing knees;
Her several parts could keep a pure repose,
Or one hip quiver with a mobile nose   20
(She moved in circles, and those circles moved).

2. Handsome, showy.   Pindaric ode.
3. Literary terms for the parts of a

Let seed be grass, and grass turn into hay:
I'm martyr to a motion not my own;
What's freedom for? To know eternity.
I swear she cast a shadow white as stone.   25
But who would count eternity in days?
These old bones live to learn her wanton ways:
(I measure time by how a body sways).

                                                    1958

CHRISTINA ROSSETTI

Echo

Come to me in the silence of the night;
    Come in the speaking silence of a dream;
Come with soft rounded cheeks and eyes as bright
    As sunlight on a stream;
        Come back in tears,   5
O memory, hope, love of finished years.

O dream how sweet, too sweet, too bitter sweet,
    Whose wakening should have been in Paradise,
Where souls brimful of love abide and meet;
    Where thirsting longing eyes   10
        Watch the slow door
That opening, letting in, lets out no more.

Yet come to me in dreams, that I may live
    My very life again though cold in death:
Come back to me in dreams, that I may give   15
    Pulse for pulse, breath for breath:
        Speak low, lean low,
As long ago, my love, how long ago.

                                                    1862

AUDRE LORDE

Recreation

Coming together
it is easier to work
after our bodies
meet
paper and pen   5

neither care nor profit
whether we write or not
but as your body moves
under my hands
charged and waiting   10
we cut the leash
you create me against your thighs
hilly with images
moving through our word countries
my body   15
writes into your flesh
the poem
you make of me.

Touching you I catch midnight
as moon fires set in my throat   20
I love you flesh into blossom
I made you
and take you made
into me.

                                                    1978

JOHN WILMOT, EARL OF ROCHESTER

Love and Life

All my past life is mine no more;
    The flying hours are gone,
Like transitory dreams given o'er
Whose images are kept in store
    By memory alone.   5

Whatever is to come is not:
    How can it then be mine?
The present moment's all my lot,
And that, as fast as it is got,
    Phyllis, is wholly thine.   10

Then talk not of inconstancy,
    False hearts, and broken vows;
If I, by miracle, can be
This livelong minute true to thee,
    'Tis all that heaven allows.   15

                                                    1677

EDNA ST. VINCENT MILLAY

What Lips My Lips Have Kissed

What lips my lips have kissed, and where, and why,
I have forgotten, and what arms have lain
Under my head till morning; but the rain
Is full of ghosts tonight, that tap and sigh
Upon the glass and listen for reply,   5
And in my heart there stirs a quiet pain
For unremembered lads that not again
Will turn to me at midnight with a cry.
Nor knows what birds have vanished one by one,   10
Thus in the winter stands the lonely tree,
Yet knows its boughs more silent than before:
I cannot say what loves have come and gone;
I only know that summer sang in me
A little while, that in me sings no more.

1923

WILLIAM SHAKESPEARE

Let Me Not to the Marriage of True Minds

Let me not to the marriage of true minds
Admit impediments.[4] Love is not love
Which alters when it alteration finds,
Or bends with the remover to remove:
Oh, no! it is an ever-fixéd mark,   5
That looks on tempests and is never shaken;
It is the star to every wandering bark,
Whose worth's unknown, although his height be taken.[5]
Love's not Time's fool, though rosy lips and cheeks
Within his bending sickle's compass come;   10
Love alters not with his brief hours and weeks,
But bears it out even to the edge of doom.[6]
If this be error and upon me proved,
I never writ, nor no man ever loved.

1609

4. The Marriage Service contained this address to the observers: "If any of you know cause or just impediments why these persons should not be joined together . . . ."

5. I.e., measuring the altitude of stars (for purposes of navigation) is not a measurement of value.
6. End of the world.

WILLIAM CONGREVE

Song

> Pious Selinda goes to prayers,
>   If I but ask the favor;[7]
> And yet the tender fool's in tears,
>   When she believes I'll leave her.
>
> Would I were free from this restraint,   5
>   Or else had hopes to win her;
> Would she could make of me a saint,
>   Or I of her a sinner.

ca. 1690

ADRIENNE RICH

Two Songs

1.

Sex, as they harshly call it,
I fell into this morning
at ten o'clock, a drizzling hour
of traffic and wet newspapers.
I thought of him who yesterday   5
clearly didn't
turn me to a hot field
ready for plowing,
and longing for that young man
piercéd me to the roots   10
bathing every vein, etc.[8]
All day he appears to me
touchingly desirable,
a prize one could wreck one's peace for.
I'd call it love if love   15
didn't take so many years
but lust too is a jewel
a sweet flower and what
pure happiness to know
all our high-toned questions   20
breed in a lively animal.

2.

That "old last act"!
And yet sometimes

7. Sexual favor.
8. See the opening lines of the Prologue to Chaucer's *Canterbury Tales.*

all seems post coitum triste[9]
and I a mere bystander.   25
Somebody else is going off,
getting shot to the moon.
Or, a moon-race!
my opposite number lands
Split seconds after   30
I make it—
we lie fainting together
at a crater-edge
heavy as mercury in our moonsuits
till he speaks—   35
in a different language
yet one I've picked up
through cultural exchanges . . .
we murmur the first moonwords:
Spasibo. Thanks. O.K.   40

                                                       1964

A Gathering of Poems about Death

A. E. HOUSMAN

To an Athlete Dying Young

The time you won your town the race
We chaired[1] you through the marketplace;
Man and boy stood cheering by,
And home we brought you shoulder-high.

Today, the road all runners come,   5
Shoulder-high we bring you home,
And set you at your threshold down,
Townsman of a stiller town.

Smart lad, to slip betimes away
From fields where glory does not stay,   10
And early though the laurel[2] grows
It withers quicker than the rose.

Eyes the shady night has shut
Cannot see the record cut,

---

9. Sadness after sexual union.   2. Wreath of honor.
1. Carried aloft in triumph.

And silence sounds no worse than cheers   15
After earth has stopped the ears: BURIED

Now you will not swell the rout
Of lads that wore their honors out,
Runners whom renown outran
And the name died before the man.   20

So set, before its echoes fade,
The fleet foot on the sill of shade,
And hold to the low lintel[3] up
The still-defended challenge-cup.

And round that early-laureled head   25
Will flock to gaze the strengthless dead,
And find unwithered on its curls
The garland[4] briefer than a girl's.

ATHLETIC CLAIM MORE FLEETING THAN A GIRLS BEATY

1896

WILLIAM WORDSWORTH

A Slumber Did My Spirit Seal

A slumber did my spirit seal; A BELOVED
   I had no human fears:
She seemed a thing that could not feel
   The touch of earthly years.

MY SPIRIT

NEVER AGE

No motion has she now, no force: DEAD
   She neither hears nor sees;
Rolled round in earth's diurnal[5] course,
   With rocks, and stones, and trees.

1800

UNTOUCHED BY EARTHLY FEARS   ROCKS, STONES NOT PRETTY BUT ARE NATURE

MARK TWAIN

Ode to Stephen Dowling Bots, Dec'd [6]

And did young Stephen sicken,
   And did young Stephen die?

---

3. Upper part of a door frame.
4. Wreath of flowers.
5. Daily.
6. The ode is supposedly written by Emmeline Grangerford, the 13-year-old daughter of one of the feuding families in *Huckleberry Finn.* Huck says, "She could write about anything you choose [sic] to give her to write about just so it was sadful. Every time a man died, or a woman died, or a child died, she would be on hand with her 'tribute' before he was cold."

And did the sad hearts thicken,
    And did the mourners cry?

No; such was not the fate of   5
    Young Stephen Dowling Bots;
Though sad hearts round him thickened,
    'Twas not from sickness' shots.

No whooping-cough did rack his frame,
    Nor measles drear with spots;   10
Not these impaired the sacred name
    Of Stephen Dowling Bots.

Despised love struck not with woe
    That head of curly knots,
Nor stomach troubles laid him low,   15
    Young Stephen Dowling Bots.

O no. Then list with tearful eye,
    Whilst I his fate do tell.
His soul did from this cold world fly,
    By falling down a well.   20

They got him out and emptied him;
    Alas it was too late;
His spirit was gone for to sport aloft
    In the realms of the good and great.

                                                          1884

DYLAN THOMAS

Do Not Go Gentle into That Good Night[7]

Do not go gentle into that good night,
Old age should burn and rave at close of day;
Rage, rage against the dying of the light.

Though wise men at their end know dark is right,
Because their words had forked no lightning they   5
Do not go gentle into that good night.

Good men, the last wave by, crying how bright
Their frail deeds might have danced in a green bay,
Rage, rage against the dying of the light.

Wild men who caught and sang the sun in flight,   10
And learn, too late, they grieved it on its way,
Do not go gentle into that good night.

---

7. Written during the final illness of the poet's father.

Grave men, near death, who see with blinding sight
Blind eyes could blaze like meteors and be gay,
Rage, rage against the dying of the light.   15

And you, my father, there on the sad height,
Curse, bless, me now with your fierce tears, I pray.
Do not go gentle into that good night.
Rage, rage against the dying of the light.

1952

EMILY DICKINSON

Because I Could Not Stop for Death

Because I could not stop for Death—
He kindly stopped for me—
The Carriage held but just Ourselves—
And Immortality.

We slowly drove—He knew no haste   5
And I had put away
My labor and my leisure too,
For His Civility—

We passed the School, where Children strove
At Recess—in the Ring—   10
We passed the Fields of Gazing Grain—
We passed the Setting Sun—

Or rather—He passed Us—
The Dews drew quivering and chill—
For only Gossamer,[8] my Gown—   15
My Tippet[9]—only Tulle[1]—

We paused before a House that seemed
A Swelling of the Ground—
The Roof was scarcely visible—
The Cornice—in the Ground—   20

Since then—'tis Centuries—and yet
Feels shorter than the Day
I first surmised the Horses' Heads
Were toward Eternity—

ca. 1863

8. A soft sheer fabric.   1. A fine net fabric.
9. Scarf.

JOHN DONNE

Death Be Not Proud

Death be not proud, though some have callèd thee
Mighty and dreadful, for thou art not so;
For those whom thou think'st thou dost overthrow
Die not, poor Death, nor yet canst thou kill me.
From rest and sleep, which but thy pictures[2] be,   5
Much pleasure; then from thee much more must flow,
And soonest[3] our best men with thee do go,
Rest of their bones, and soul's delivery.[4]
Thou art slave to Fate, Chance, kings, and desperate men,
And dost with Poison, War, and Sickness dwell;   10
And poppy or charms can make us sleep as well,
And better than thy stroke; why swell'st[5] thou then?
One short sleep past, we wake eternally
And death shall be no more; Death, thou shalt die.

                                                            1633

SYLVIA PLATH

Lady Lazarus[6]

I have done it again.
One year in every ten
I manage it——

A sort of walking miracle, my skin
Bright as a Nazi lampshade,   5
My right foot

A paperweight,
My face a featureless, fine
Jew linen.

Peel off the napkin   10
O my enemy.
Do I terrify?——

The nose, the eye pits, the full set of teeth?
The sour breath
Will vanish in a day.   15

---

2. Likenesses.
3. Most willingly.
4. Deliverance.
5. Puff with pride.

6. According to *John* 11, Jesus raised Lazarus, the brother of Mary and Martha, from the dead.

Soon, soon the flesh
The grave cave ate will be
At home on me

And I a smiling woman.
I am only thirty.   20
And like the cat I have nine times to die.

This is Number Three.
What a trash
To annihilate each decade.

What a million filaments.   25
The peanut-crunching crowd
Shoves in to see

Them unwrap me hand and foot——
The big strip tease.
Gentlemen, ladies   30

These are my hands
My knees.
I may be skin and bone,

Nevertheless, I am the same, identical woman.
The first time it happened I was ten.   35
It was an accident.

The second time I meant
To last it out and not come back at all.
I rocked shut

As a seashell.   40
They had to call and call
And pick the worms off me like sticky pearls.

Dying
Is an art, like everything else.
I do it exceptionally well.   45

I do it so it feels like hell.
I do it so it feels real.
I guess you could say I've a call.

It's easy enough to do it in a cell.
It's easy enough to do it and stay put.   50
It's the theatrical

Comeback in broad day
To the same place, the same face, the same brute
Amused shout:

"A miracle!"   55
That knocks me out.
There is a charge

For the eyeing of my scars, there is a charge
For the hearing of my heart——
It really goes.   60

And there is a charge, a very large charge
For a word or a touch
Or a bit of blood

Or a piece of my hair or my clothes.
So, so, Herr Doktor.   65
So, Herr Enemy.

I am your opus,
I am your valuable,
The pure gold baby

That melts to a shriek.   70
I turn and burn.
Do not think I underestimate your great concern.

Ash, ash—
You poke and stir.
Flesh, bone, there is nothing there——   75

A cake of soap,
A wedding ring,
A gold filling.

Herr God, Herr Lucifer
Beware   80
Beware.

Out of the ash
I rise with my red hair
And I eat men like air.

                                                             1965

2 EXPECTATION AND SURPRISE

Poetry is full of surprises. Poems express anger or outrage just as effectively as love or sadness, and good poems can be written about going to a rock concert or having lunch or cutting the lawn, as well as about making love or gazing at a cloudless sky or smelling flowers. Even poems on "predictable" subjects can surprise us with unpredicted attitudes, unusual events, or a sudden twist. Knowing that a poem is about some particular subject—love, for example, or death—may give us a general idea of what to expect, but it never tells us altogether what we will find in a particular poem. Experiencing a poem fully means being open to the poem and its surprises, being willing to let the poem guide us to its own attitudes, feelings, and ideas. The following two poems—one about death and one about love —are rather different from those we looked at in Chapter 1.

MARGE PIERCY

Barbie Doll

This girlchild was born as usual
and presented dolls that did pee-pee
and miniature GE stoves and irons
and wee lipsticks the color of cherry candy.
Then in the magic of puberty, a classmate said: 5
You have a great big nose and fat legs.

She was healthy, tested intelligent,
possessed strong arms and back,
abundant sexual drive and manual dexterity.
She went to and fro apologizing.   10
Everyone saw a fat nose on thick legs.

She was advised to play coy,
exhorted to come on hearty,
exercise, diet, smile and wheedle.
Her good nature wore out   15
like a fan belt.
So she cut off her nose and her legs
and offered them up.

In the casket displayed on satin she lay
with the undertaker's cosmetics painted on,   20
a turned-up putty nose,
dressed in a pink and white nightie.
Doesn't she look pretty? everyone said.
Consummation at last.
To every woman a happy ending.   25

1973

W. D. SNODGRASS

Leaving the Motel

Outside, the last kids holler
Near the pool: they'll stay the night.
Pick up the towels; fold your collar
Out of sight.

Check: is the second bed   5
Unrumpled, as agreed?
Landlords have to think ahead
In case of need,

Too. Keep things straight: don't take
The matches, the wrong keyrings—   10
We've nowhere we could keep a keepsake—
Ashtrays, combs, things

That sooner or later others
Would accidentally find.
Check: take nothing of one another's   15
And leave behind

Your license number only,
Which they won't care to trace;
We've paid. Still, should such things get lonely,
Leave in their vase   20

An aspirin to preserve
Our lilacs, the wayside flowers
We've gathered and must leave to serve
A few more hours;

That's all. We can't tell when   25
We'll come back, can't press claims;
We would no doubt have other rooms then,
Or other names.

1968

The first poem has the strong note of sadness that characterizes
many death poems, but its emphasis is not on the response to the
girl's death but on the disappointments in her life. The only "scene"
in the poem (lines 19–23) portrays the unnamed girl at rest in her
casket, and as in *Bells for John Whiteside's Daughter*, her stillness contrasts with a restlessness in life, but the effect is very different. Here
the still body in the casket contrasts not with vitality but with frustra-

tion and anxiety: her life since puberty (lines 5–6) had been full of apologies and attempts to change her physical appearance and emotional makeup. The rest she achieves in death is not, however, a triumph, despite what people say (line 23). Although the poem's last two words are "happy ending" this girl without a name has died in embarrassment and without fulfillment, and the final lines are **ironic**, meaning the opposite of what they say. The cheerful comments at the end lack force and truth because of what we already know; we understand them as ironic because they emphasize how unhappy the girl was and how false her cosmeticized corpse is to the sad truth of her life.

The poem's concern is to suggest the falsity and destructiveness of those standards of beauty which have led to the tragedy of the girl's life. In an important sense, the poem is not really *about* death at all in spite of the fact that the girl's death and her repaired corpse are central to it. As the title suggests, the poem dramatizes how standardized, commercialized notions of femininity and prettiness can be painful and destructive to those whose bodies do not precisely fit the conformist models, and the poem attacks vigorously those conventional standards and the widespread, unthinking acceptance of them.

Leaving the Motel similarly goes in quite a different direction from many poems on the subject of love. Instead of expressing assurance about how love lasts and endures, or about the sincerity and depth of affection, this poem dramatizes a brief sexual encounter. But it does not emphasize sexuality or eroticism in the meeting of the nameless lovers (we see them only as they prepare to leave), nor does it suggest why or how they have found each other, or what either of them is like as a person. Its emphasis is on how careful they must be not to get caught, how exact and calculating they must be in their planning, how finite and limited their encounter must be, how sealed off this encounter is from the rest of their lives. The poem stresses the tiny details the lovers must think of, the agreements they must observe, and the ritual checklist of their duties ("Check . . . Keep things straight . . . Check . . ." lines 5, 9, 15). Affection and sentiment have their small place in the poem (notice the care for the flowers, lines 19–24, and the thought of "pressing claims," line 26), but the emphasis is on temporariness, uncertainty, and limits. The poem is about an illicit, perhaps adulterous sexual encounter, but there is no sex in the poem, only a kind of archeological record of lust.

Labeling a poem as a "love poem" or a "death poem" is primarily a matter of convenience, a grouping based on the **subject matter** in a poem or the event or **topic** it chooses to engage. But as the poems we have been looking at suggest, poems that may be loosely called love poems or death poems may differ widely from one another, express totally different attitudes or ideas, and concentrate on very different aspects of the subject. The main advantages of grouping poems in this way for study is that a reader can become conscious of individual differences: a reading of two poems side by side may suggest how each is distinctive in what it has to say and how it says it.

What a poem has to say is often called its **theme**, the kind of statement it makes about its subject. We could say, for example, that the theme of *Leaving the Motel* is that illicit love is secretive, careful, transitory, and short on emotion and sentiment, or that secret sexual encounters tend to be brief, calculated, and characterized by restrained and insecure feelings. The theme of a poem usually may be expressed in several different ways, and poems often have more than one theme. *Barbie Doll* suggests that commercialized standards destroy human values; that rigid and idealized notions of normalty cripple people who are different; that false standards of appearance and behavior can destroy human beings and lead to personal tragedy; that people are easily and tragically led to accept evaluations thrust upon them by others; that American consumers tend to be conformists, easily influenced in their outlook by advertising and by commercial products; that children who do not conform to middle-class standards and notions don't have a chance. Each of these statements could be demonstrated to be said or implied in the poem and rather central to it. But none of these statements individually nor all of them together would be an adequate substitute for the poem itself. To state the theme in such a brief and abstract way—while it may be helpful in clarifiying what the poem does and does not say—never does justice to the experience of the poem, the way it works on us as readers. Poems affect us in all sorts of ways—emotional and psychological as well as rational—and often a poem's dramatization of a story, an event, or a moment bypasses our rational responses and affects us far more deeply than a clear and logical argument would.

Poems, then, may differ widely from one another even when they share a common subject. And the subjects of poetry also vary widely. It isn't true that there are certain "poetic" subjects and that there are others which aren't appropriate to poetry. Any human activity, any thought or feeling can be the subject of poetry. Poetry often deals with beauty and the softer, more attractive human emotions, but it can deal with ugliness and less attractive human conduct as well, for poetry seeks to mirror human beings and human events, showing us ourselves not only as we'd like to be but as we are. Good poetry gets written about all kinds of topics, in all kinds of forms. This poem, for example, celebrates a famous rock concert.

JONI MITCHELL

Woodstock[1]

I came upon a child of God
He was walking along the road
And I asked him, where are you going
And this he told me

---

1. Written after the rock festival there in 1969, celebrating not only the festival but what came to be called the "Woodstock Nation."

I'm going on down to Yasgur's farm   5
I'm going to join in a rock'n'roll band
I'm going to camp out on the land
And try an' get my soul free
    We are stardust
    We are golden   10
    And we've got to get ourselves
    Back to the garden

Then can I walk beside you
I have come here to lose the smog
And I feel to be a cog in something turning   15
Well maybe it is just the time of year
Or maybe it's the time of man
I don't know who I am
But life is for learning
    We are stardust   20
    We are golden
    And we've got to get ourselves
    Back to the garden

By the time we got to Woodstock
We were half a million strong   25
And everywhere there was song and celebration
And I dreamed I saw the bombers
Riding shotgun in the sky
And they were turning into butterflies
Above our nation   30
    We are stardust
    We are golden
    And we've got to get ourselves
    Back to the garden

1969

This particular poem is also a song. (The lyrics to some songs "work" as poems; others don't because they aren't sufficiently verbal or because their particular effects depend too much on the music that goes with the words.) The account it gives of Woodstock may now seem rather dated in its optimism about transforming, through love and togetherness, the machines of war (lines 27–30), but its ideals of simplicity and peace are stated powerfully. The recurrent idea of returning somehow to an original ideal of innocence (the Garden of Eden) suggests the high aspirations ("stardust") and urgency ("got to") of the sixties' sense of things gone wrong. The mental pictures portray rural simplicity, freedom, the power of united efforts, and the joys of music as an alternative to urban crowding and pollution (line 14), political conflict (lines 27–28), and confusion over personal identity (lines 18–19). The poem's theme—that human beings can, through love and working together, recreate a perfect age of innocence and peace—represents human aspirations at a very high level and does so persuasively and highmindedly, despite the particular details of time and place that anchor the poem to a particular moment in history and a specific experience.

Much less flattering to human nature is this poem about a prison inmate.

ETHERIDGE KNIGHT

Hard Rock Returns to Prison from the Hospital for the Criminal Insane

Hard Rock was "known not to take no shit
From nobody," and he had the scars to prove it:
Split purple lips, lumped ears, welts above
His yellow eyes, and one long scar that cut
Across his temple and plowed through a thick   5
Canopy of kinky hair.

The WORD was that Hard Rock wasn't a mean nigger
Anymore, that the doctors had bored a hole in his head,
Cut out part of his brain, and shot electricity
Through the rest. When they brought Hard Rock back,   10
Handcuffed and chained, he was turned loose,
Like a freshly gelded stallion, to try his new status.
And we all waited and watched, like indians at a corral,
To see if the WORD was true.

As we waited we wrapped ourselves in the cloak   15
Of his exploits: "Man, the last time, it took eight
Screws[2] to put him in the Hole." "Yeah, remember when he
Smacked the captain with his dinner tray?" "He set
The record for time in the Hole—67 straight days!"
"Ol Hard Rock! man, that's one crazy nigger."   20
And then the jewel of a myth that Hard Rock had once bit
A screw on the thumb and poisoned him with syphilitic spit.

The testing came, to see if Hard Rock was really tame.
A hillbilly called him a black son of a bitch
And didn't lose his teeth, a screw who knew Hard Rock   25
From before shook him down and barked in his face.
And Hard Rock did *nothing*. Just grinned and looked silly,
His eyes empty like knot holes in a fence.

---

2. Guards. "Hole": solitary confinement.

And even after we discovered that it took Hard Rock
Exactly 3 minutes to tell you his first name,   30
We told ourselves that he had just wised up,
Was being cool; but we could not fool ourselves for long,
And we turned away, our eyes on the ground. Crushed.
He had been our Destroyer, the doer of things
We dreamed of doing but could not bring ourselves to do,   35
The fears of years, like a biting whip,
Had cut grooves too deeply across our backs.

                                                                                    1968

The picture of Hard Rock as a kind of hero to other prison in-
mates is established early in the poem through a retelling of the
legends circulated about him; the straightforward chronology of the
poem sets up the mystery of how he will react after his "treatment"
in the hospital. The poem identifies with those who wait; they are
hopeful that Hard Rock's spirit has not been broken by surgery or shock
treatments, and the lines crawl almost to a stop with disappointment
in stanza four. The "nothing" (line 27) of Hard Rock's response to
teasing and taunting and the emptiness of his eyes ("like knot holes
in a fence," line 28) reduce the heroic hopes and illusions to despair.
The final stanza recounts the observers' attempts to reinterpret, to hang
onto hope that their symbol of heroism could stand up against the
best efforts to tame him, but the spirit has gone out of the hero-
worshipers too, and the poem records them as beaten, conformed,
deprived of their spirit as Hard Rock has been of his. The poem
records the despair of the hopeless and it protests against the exercise
of power that can curb even as rebellious a figure as Hard Rock.

The following poem is equally full of anger and disappointment,
but it uses a kind of playfulness with words to make the seriousness of
the situation seem all the more relentless.

◊ WILLIAM BLAKE

London

I wander through each chartered street,
Near where the chartered Thames does flow,
And mark in every face I meet
Marks of weakness, marks of woe.

In every cry of every man,   5
In every Infant's cry of fear,
In every voice, in every ban,
The mind-forged manacles I hear.

How the Chimney-sweeper's cry
Every black'ning Church appalls;   10
And the hapless Soldier's sigh
Runs in blood down Palace walls.

But most through midnight streets I hear
How the youthful Harlot's curse
Blasts the new-born Infant's tear,   15
And blights with plagues the Marriage hearse.

                                                    1794

The poem gives a strong sense of how London feels to this particular observer; it is cluttered, constricting, oppressive. The wordplay here articulates and connects the strong emotions he associates with London experiences. The repeated words—"every," for example, or "cry"—intensify the sense of total despair in the city and weld connections between things not necessarily related—the cries of street vendors, for example, the cries for help. The word "chartered" implies strong feelings too, and the word gives a particularly rigid sense of streets. Instead of seeming alive with people or bustling with movement, they are rigidly, coldly determined, controlled, cramped. And the same word is used for the river, as if it too were planned, programed, laid out by an oppressor. In fact, the course of the Thames had been altered (slightly) by the government before Blake's time, but most important is the word's emotional force, the sense it projects of constriction and artificiality: the person speaking experiences London as if human artifice had totally altered nature. According to the poem, people are victimized too, "marked" by their confrontations with urbanness and the power of institutions: the "soldier's sigh" that "runs in blood down Palace walls" vividly suggests, through a metaphor that visually dramatizes the speaker's feelings, both the powerlessness of the individual and the callousness of power. The "description" of the city has clearly become, by now, a subjective, highly emotional, and vivid expression of how the speaker feels about London and what it represents to him.

One more thing about *London:* at first it looks like an account of a personal experience, as if the speaker is describing and interpreting as he goes along: "I wander through each chartered street." But soon it is clear that he is describing many wanderings, putting together impressions from many walks, recreating a generalized or typical walk— which shows him "every" person in the streets, allows him to generalize about the churches being "appalled" (literally, made white) by the cry of the representative Chimney-sweeper, presents his conclusions about soldiers, prostitutes, and infants. What we are given is not a personal record of an event, but a re-presentation of it, as it seems in the mind in retrospect—not a story, not a narrative or chronological account of events, but a dramatization of self that compresses many experiences into one.

The **tone** of *London* is somber in spite of the poet's playfulness with words. Wordplay may be witty and funny if it calls attention to its own cleverness, but here it involves the discovery of unsuspected (but meaningful) connections between things. The term **tone** is used to describe the attitude the poem takes toward its subject and theme. If the theme of a poem is *what* the poem says, the tone involves *how* one says it. The "how" involves feelings, attitudes that are expressed by how one says the words. The tone of *London* is sad, despairing, and angry; reading *London* aloud, one would try to show in one's voice the strong feelings that the poem expresses, just as one would try to reproduce tenderness and caring in reading aloud *The Tally Stick* or *How Do I Love Thee*.

Subject, theme, and tone. Each of these categories gives us a way to begin considering poems and showing how one poem differs from another. Comparing poems on the same subject, or with a similar theme or tone, can lead to a clearer understanding of each individual poem and can refine our responses to the subtleties of individual differences. The title of a poem (*Leaving the Motel*, for example) or the way the poem first introduces its subject often can give us a sense of what to expect, but we need to be open to surprise too. No two poems are going to be exactly alike in their effect on us; the variety of possible poems multiplies when you think of all the possible themes and tones that can be explored within any single subject. Varieties of feeling often coincide with varieties of thinking, and readers open to the pleasures of the unexpected may find themselves learning, growing, becoming more sensitive to ideas and human issues as well as more articulate about feelings and thoughts they already have.

The following two poems might be said to be about animals, although both of them place their final emphasis on what human beings are like: the animal in each case is only the means to the end of exploring human nature. The poems share a common assumption that animals reflect human habits and conduct and may reveal much about ourselves, and in each case the woman central to the poem is revealed to be surprisingly unlike the way she thinks of herself. But the poems are very different from one another. As you read them, see if you can think of appropriate words to describe the main character and to indicate the right tone of voice to use in reading each poem.

MAXINE KUMIN

Woodchucks

Gassing the woodchucks didn't turn out right.
The knockout bomb from the Feed and Grain Exchange
was featured as merciful, quick at the bone
and the case we had against them was airtight,
both exits shochorned shut with puddingstone,[3]   5
but they had a sub-sub-basement out of range.

3. A mixture of cement, pebbles, and gravel: a conglomerate.

Next morning they turned up again, no worse
for the cyanide than we for our cigarettes
and state-store Scotch, all of us up to scratch.
They brought down the marigolds as a matter of course   10
and then took over the vegetable patch
nipping the broccoli shoots, beheading the carrots.

The food from our mouths, I said, righteously thrilling
to the feel of the .22, the bullets' neat noses.
I, a lapsed pacifist fallen from grace   15
puffed with Darwinian pieties for killing,
now drew a bead on the littlest woodchuck's face.
He died down in the everbearing roses.

Ten minutes later I dropped the mother. She
flipflopped in the air and fell, her needle teeth   20
still hooked in a leaf of early Swiss chard.
Another baby next. O one-two-three
the murderer inside me rose up hard,
the hawkeye killer came on stage forthwith.

There's one chuck left. Old wily fellow, he keeps   25
me cocked and ready day after day after day.
All night I hunt his humped-up form. I dream
I sight along the barrel in my sleep.
If only they'd all consented to die unseen
gassed underground the quiet Nazi way.   30

                                                           1972

ADRIENNE RICH

Aunt Jennifer's Tigers

Aunt Jennifer's tigers prance across a screen,
Bright topaz denizens of a world of green.
They do not fear the men beneath the tree;
They pace in sleek chivalric certainty.

Aunt Jennifer's fingers fluttering through her wool   5
Find even the ivory needle hard to pull.
The massive weight of Uncle's wedding band
Sits heavily upon Aunt Jennifer's hand.

When Aunt is dead, her terrified hands will lie
Still ringed with ordeals she was mastered by.   10
The tigers in the panel that she made
Will go on prancing, proud and unafraid.

                                                           1951

How would your tone of voice change if you read *Woodchucks* aloud from beginning to end? What tone would you use to read the ending? How does the hunter feel about her increasing attraction to violence? Why does the poem begin by calling the gassing of the woodchucks "merciful" and end by describing it as "the quiet Nazi way"? What names does the hunter call herself? How does the name-calling affect your feelings about her? Exactly when does the hunter begin to *enjoy* the feel of the gun and the idea of killing? How does the poet make that clear?

Why are tigers a particularly appropriate contrast to the quiet and subdued manner of Aunt Jennifer? What words used to describe the tigers seem particularly significant? In what ways is the tiger an opposite of Aunt Jennifer? In what ways does it externalize her secrets? Why are Aunt Jennifer's hands described as "terrified"? What clues does the poem give about why Aunt Jennifer is so afraid? How does the poem make you feel about Aunt Jennifer? about her tigers? about her life? How would you describe the tone of the poem? How does the poet feel about Aunt Jennifer?

Twenty years after writing *Aunt Jennifer's Tigers*, Adrienne Rich said this about the poem:

> In writing this poem, composed and apparently cool as it is, I thought
> I was creating a portrait of an imaginary woman. But this woman
> suffers from the opposition of her imagination, worked out in tapestry,
> and her life style, "ringed with ordeals she was mastered by." It was
> important to me that Aunt Jennifer was a person as distinct from
> myself as possible—distanced by the formalism of the poem, by its
> objective, observant tone—even by putting the woman in a different
> generation. In those years formalism was part of the strategy—like
> asbestos gloves, it allowed me to handle materials I couldn't pick up
> bare-handed.[4]

Not often do we have such an explicit comment on a poem by its author, and we don't actually have to have it to understand and experience the force of the poem (although such a statement may clarify why the author chose particular modes of presentation and how the poem fits into the author's own patterns of thinking and growing). Most poems contain within them what we need to know in order to tap the human and artistic resources they offer us. Still, it is nice to have comments like this one, and later on (in Chapter 11) we will look at some of the advantages of knowing specific things about an author and other poems that he or she has written. (There, too, you will find a gathering of poems by Adrienne Rich.) In the chapters between now and then we will look at various technical aspects of poetry, considering how poems are put together and what sorts of things we need to know in order to read well, that is, how to experience sensitively and fully other poems you may want to read later. Not all poems are as accessible as those we've looked at so far, and even the

---

4. In *When We Dead Awaken: Writing as Re-Vision*, a talk given in December, 1971, at the Women's Forum of the Modern Language Association.

ones that are accessible usually yield themselves to us more readily and more completely if we approach them systematically by developing specific reading habits and skills—just as someone learning to play tennis systematically learns the rules, the techniques, the things to watch out for that are distinctive to the pleasures and hazards of that skill or craft. In the next eight chapters, we will consider the various aspects of language that come together in a poem, and we will methodically ask some questions that will help you to know how to approach a poem. It helps if you know what to expect, and the chapters that follow will help you to an understanding of the things that poets can do—and thus to what poems can do for you.

But knowing what to expect isn't everything, and I have one bit of advice to offer every prospective reader of poetry before going any further: Be open. Be open to new experience, be open to new feelings, be open to new ideas. No reader of poetry is perfect, and in learning what you learn in the next few chapters you will not become invincible and superior to all mistakes. It is important that you stay open to new information and new experiences—forever. Every poem in the world is a potential new experience, and no matter how sophisticated you become, you can still be surprised (and delighted) by new poems— and by rereading old ones. Good poems bear many, many rereadings, and often one discovers something new with every new reading. Learning about the standard devices and techniques of poetry can help you know what to expect, but it need not make you feel either overconfident or jaded; in fact, knowledge of poetry—like real knowledge of almost anything—will convince you that you do not know everything, or indeed as much as you want to know. No reader is a worse reader than a dogmatic or closed-minded one. This course will not teach you everything.

And it is especially important that you be open now. The information that follows will help give you a sense of what to expect, but will also count on your being open to surprises. Poetry is not Everything; there are many worthwhile things in the world besides poetry, but poetry considers most of these things and offers several perspectives on them. If you are open to poetry, you are open to much that the world can offer you. Be willing to let poems surprise you when you come to them; let them come on their own terms, let them be themselves. At the end of this chapter are four groups of poems on popular subjects of poetry. You can probably read most of them with interest and pleasure now. But you may want to come back to them later, too, when you have worked your way through some of the problems we will consider together in the chapters that follow, where you will become more familiar with what meeting a poem on its own terms can mean.

A Gathering of Poems about Animals

JOHN BUNYAN

Of the Boy and Butterfly

Behold, how eager this our little boy
Is for a butterfly, as if all joy,
All profits, honors, yea, and lasting pleasures,
Were wrapped up in her, or the richest treasures
Found in her would be bundled up together,   5
When all her all is lighter than a feather.

He halloos, runs, and cries out, "Here, boys, here!"
Nor doth he brambles or the nettles fear:
He stumbles at the molehills, up he gets,
And runs again, as one bereft of wits;   10
And all his labor and his large outcry
Is only for a silly butterfly.

Comparison

This little boy an emblem[1] is of those
Whose hearts are wholly at the world's dispose.
The butterfly doth represent to me   15
The world's best things at best but fading be.
All are but painted nothings and false joys,
Like this poor butterfly to these our boys.

His running through nettles, thorns, and briers,
To gratify his boyish fond desires,   20
His tumbling over molehills to attain
His end, namely, his butterfly to gain,
Doth plainly show what hazards some men run
To get what will be lost as soon as won.

1686

EMILY DICKINSON

A Narrow Fellow in the Grass

A narrow Fellow in the Grass
Occasionally rides—
You may have met Him—did you not
His notice sudden is—

1. Symbol.

The Grass divides as with a Comb—   5
A spotted shaft is seen—
And then it closes at your feet
And opens further on—

He likes a Boggy Acre
A Floor too cool for Corn—   10
Yet when a Boy, and Barefoot—
I more than once at Noon

Have passed, I thought, a Whip lash
Unbraiding in the Sun
When stooping to secure it   15
It wrinkled, and was gone—

Several of Nature's People
I know, and they know me—
I feel for them a transport
Of cordiality—   20

But never met this Fellow
Attended, or alone
Without a tighter breathing
And Zero at the Bone—

                                                    1866

KARL SHAPIRO

The Fly

O hideous little bat, the size of snot,
With polyhedral eye and shabby clothes,
To populate the stinking cat you walk
The promontory of the dead man's nose,
Climb with the fine leg of a Duncan-Phyfe[2]   5
    The smoking mountains of my food
        And in a comic mood
    In mid-air take to bed a wife.

Riding and riding with your filth of hair
On gluey foot or wing, forever coy,   10
Hot from the compost and green sweet decay,
Sounding your buzzer like an urchin toy—
You dot all whiteness with diminutive stool,
    In the tight belly of the dead
        Burrow with hungry head   15
    And inlay maggots like a jewel.

2. Furniture of the 19th-century Amer-   times featured delicate, sharply angled
ican cabinetmaker Duncan Phyfe some-   legs.

At your approach the great horse stomps and paws
Bringing the hurricane of his heavy tail;
Shod in disease you dare to kiss my hand
Which sweeps against you like an angry flail;   20
Still you return, return, trusting your wing
   To draw you from the hunter's reach
     That learns to kill to teach
   Disorder to the tinier thing.

My peace is your disaster. For your death   25
Children like spiders cup their pretty hands
And wives resort to chemistry of war.
In fens of sticky paper and quicksands
You glue yourself to death. Where you are stuck
   You struggle hideously and beg,   30
     You amputate your leg
   Imbedded in the amber muck.

But I, a man, must swat you with my hate,
Slap you across the air and crush your flight,
Must mangle with my shoe and smear your blood,   35
Expose your little guts pasty and white,
Knock your head sidewise like a drunkard's hat,
   Pin your wings under like a crow's,
     Tear off your flimsy clothes
   And beat you as one beats a rat.   40

Then like Gargantua[3] I stride among
The corpses strewn like raisins in the dust,
The broken bodies of the narrow dead
That catch the throat with fingers of disgust.
I sweep. One gyrates like a top and falls   45
   And stunned, stone blind, and deaf
     Buzzes its frightful F
   And dies between three cannibals.

1942

OGDEN NASH

The Turtle

   The turtle lives 'twixt plated decks
   Which practically conceal its sex.
   I think it clever of the turtle
   In such a fix to be so fertile.

1940

3. Legendary medieval giant.

LEWIS CARROLL

How Doth the Little Crocodile

How doth the little crocodile
　　Improve his shining tail,
And pour the waters of the Nile
　　On every golden scale!

How cheerfully he seems to grin　　　　　　　　5
　　How neatly spreads his claws,
And welcomes little fishes in,
　　With gently smiling jaws!

1865

SUSAN MITCHELL

From the Journals of the Frog Prince[4]

In March I dreamed of mud,
sheets of mud over the ballroom chairs and table,
rainbow slicks of mud under the throne.
In April I saw mud of clouds and mud of sun.
Now in May I find excuses to linger in the kitchen　　　5
for wafts of silt and ale,
cinnamon and river bottom,
tender scallion and sour underlog.

At night I cannot sleep.
I am listening for the dribble of mud　　　　　　　　10
climbing the stairs to our bedroom
as if a child in a wet bathing suit ran
up them in the dark.

Last night I said, "Face it, you're bored.
How many times can you live over　　　　　　　　15
with the same excitement
that moment when the princess leans
into the well, her face a petal
falling to the surface of the water
as you rise like a bubble to her lips,　　　　　　　　20
the golden ball bursting from your mouth?"
Remember how she hurled you against the wall,
your body cracking open,
skin shriveling to the bone,

4. According to a popular fairy tale, a
frog is transformed into a prince when a
girl for whom he performs a favor kisses
him and allows him to sleep in her bed.

the green pod of your heart splitting in two,   25
and her face imprinted with every moment
of your transformation?

I no longer tremble.

Night after night I lie beside her.
"Why is your forehead so cool and damp?" she asks.   30
Her breasts are soft and dry as flour.
The hand that brushes my head is feverish.
At her touch I long for wet leaves,
the slap of water against rocks.

"What are you thinking of?" she asks.   35
How can I tell her
I am thinking of the green skin
shoved like wet pants behind the Directoire desk?
Or tell her I am mortgaged to the hilt
of my sword, to the leek-green tip of my soul?   40
Someday I will drag her by her hair
to the river—and what? Drown her?
Show her the green flame of my self rising at her feet?
But there's no more violence in her
than in a fence or a gate.   45

"What are you thinking of?" she whispers.
I am staring into the garden.
I am watching the moon
wind its trail of golden slime around the oak,
over the stone basin of the fountain.   50
How can I tell her
I am thinking that transformations are not forever?

                                                             p. 1978

DELMORE SCHWARTZ

The Heavy Bear Who Goes with Me

"the withness of the body"[5]

The heavy bear who goes with me,
A manifold honey to smear his face,
Clumsy and lumbering here and there,
The central ton of every place,
The hungry beating brutish one   5
In love with candy, anger, and sleep,

---

5. Early editions attributed the epigraph to Alfred North Whitehead, the philosopher.

Crazy factotum, dishevelling all,
Climbs the building, kicks the football,
Boxes his brother in the hate-ridden city.

Breathing at my side, that heavy animal,   10
That heavy bear who sleeps with me,
Howls in his sleep for a world of sugar,
A sweetness intimate as the water's clasp,
Howls in his sleep because the tight-rope
Trembles and shows the darkness beneath.   15
—The strutting show-off is terrified,
Dressed in his dress-suit, bulging his pants,
Trembles to think that his quivering meat
Must finally wince to nothing at all.

That inescapable animal walks with me,   20
Has followed me since the black womb held,
Moves where I move, distorting my gesture,
A caricature, a swollen shadow,
A stupid clown of the spirit's motive,
Perplexes and affronts with his own darkness,   25
The secret life of belly and bone,
Opaque, too near, my private, yet unknown,
Stretches to embrace the very dear
With whom I would walk without him near,
Touches her grossly, although a word   30
Would bare my heart and make me clear,
Stumbles, flounders, and strives to be fed
Dragging me with him in his mouthing care,
Amid the hundred million of his kind,
The scrimmage of appetite everywhere.   35

1938

JOHN STONE

Explaining About the Dachshund

There's no badger in this sandbox.
There wasn't one here when I nailed it
four feet square and hauled
the sand ten miles.

There's not one in it now   5
despite this nosing
nosing around these tunnels
we dug by hand.

It's genes that have caught up with him,

an instinct for fur some ancestor   10
had to leave behind,
tremble-jawed but safe,
in other ground.

It's a grandfather's failure

makes him want to kill   15
something he hasn't seen
but can't forget

that comes back with him now to the house,
part of his cells, and sleeps beside him
in the red-eyed dark of my kitchen,   20

mixed in with the other smells.

1972

JOHN MASEFIELD

The Lemmings[6]

Once in a hundred years the Lemmings come
Westward, in search of food, over the snow,
Westward until the salt sea drowns them dumb,
Westward, till all are drowned, those Lemmings go.
Once, it is thought, there was a westward land   5
(Now drowned) where there was food for those starved things,
And memory of the place has burnt its brand
In the little brains of all the Lemming Kings.
Perhaps, long since, there was a land beyond
Westward from death, some city, some calm place,   10
Where one could taste God's quiet and be fond
With the little beauty of a human face;
But now the land is drowned. Yet still we press
Westward, in search, to death, to nothingness.

1920

6. Rodents noted for their periodic migrations caused by sharp population increases.

A Gathering of Poems on Family and Ancestry

RICHARD HUGO

What Thou Lovest Well, Remains American

You remember the name was Jensen. She seemed old
always alone inside, face pasted gray to the window,
and mail never came. Two blocks down, the Grubskis
went insane. George played rotten trombone
Easter when they flew the flag. Wild roses   5
remind you the roads were gravel and vacant lots
the rule. Poverty was real, wallet and spirit,
and each day slow as church. You remember threadbare
church groups on the corner, howling their faith
at stars, and the violent Holy Rollers[1]   10
renting the barn for their annual violent sing
and the barn burned down when you came back from war.
Knowing the people you knew then are dead,
you try to believe these roads paved are improved,
the neighbors, moved in while you were away, good-looking,   15
their dogs well fed. You still have need
to remember lots empty and fern.
Lawns well trimmed remind you of the train
your wife took one day forever, some far empty town,
the odd name you never recall. The time: 6:23.   20
The day: October 9. The year remains a blur.
You blame this neighborhood for your failure.
In some vague way, the Grubskis degraded you
beyond repair. And you know you must play again
and again Mrs. Jensen pale at her window, must hear   25
the foul music over the good slide of traffic.
You loved them well and they remain, still with nothing
to do, no money and no will. Loved them, and the gray
that was their disease you carry for extra food
in case you're stranded in some odd empty town   30
and need hungry lovers for friends, and need feel
you are welcome in the secret club they have formed.

                                                                    1975

JOHN STONE

Coming Home

About two thousand miles
into my life

1. Slang for emotional evangelical Christians.

the family bounced south
    west   east
in an old Oldsmobile.   5

    Two brothers tumbled
      on the back seat
  watching the world blur
upside down right side up
      through windows   10
    time fogged in
slowly from the corners.

      Nights
    cars came at us
      wall-eyed   15
   their lights sliding
  over the ceiling
  like night fighters

    while in the front
  they talked parental low   20
    in a drone
  we didn't hear .
tossing through Arkansas
  toward Mississippi.

When our eyes grew red   25
  and blood bulged
in our heads from laughing
    we slept
    he on the seat
  and I bent over   30
the humped transmission

  close to the only motor
    in the world.

                1972

DIANE WAKOSKI

The Photos

My sister in her well-tailored silk blouse hands me
the photo of my father
in naval uniform and white hat.
I say, "Oh, this is the one which Mama used to have on her
  dresser."

My sister controls her face and furtively looks at my mother,   5
a sad rag bag of a woman, lumpy and sagging everywhere,

like a mattress at the Salvation Army, though with no holes or
     tears,
and says, "No."

I look again,
and see that my father is wearing a wedding ring,   10
which he never did
when he lived with my mother. And that there is a legend on it,
"To my dearest wife,
          Love
          Chief"   15
And I realize the photo must have belonged to his second wife,
whom he left our mother to marry.

My mother says, with her face as still as the whole unpopulated
     part of the
state of North Dakota,
"May I see it too?"   20
She looks at it.

I look at my tailored sister
and my own blue-jeaned self. Have we wanted to hurt our
     mother,
sharing these pictures on this, one of the few days I ever visit or
spend with family? For her face is curiously haunted,   25
not now with her usual viperish bitterness,
but with something so deep it could not be spoken.

I turn away and say I must go on, as I have a dinner
     engagement with friends.
But I drive all the way to Pasadena from Whittier,
thinking of my mother's face; how I could never love her;   30
     how my father
could not love her either. Yet knowing I have inherited
the rag-bag body,
stony face with bulldog jaws.

I drive, thinking of that face.
Jeffers' California Medea[2] who inspired me to poetry.   35
I killed my children,
but there as I am changing lanes on the freeway, necessarily
     glancing in the
rearview mirror, I see the face,
not even a ghost, but always with me, like a photo in a   40
     beloved's wallet.

How I hate my destiny.

                                                          1978

2. Robinson Jeffers (1887–1962), Ameri-   *Solstice*, 1935. According to Greek leg-
can poet who migrated to California from   end, Medea was a sorceress who killed her
the East, retold the Medea story in   children.

DOROTHY LIVESAY

Green Rain

I remember long veils of green rain
Feathered like the shawl of my grandmother—
Green from the half-green of the spring trees
Waving in the valley.

I remember the road   5
Like the one which leads to my grandmother's house,
A warm house, with green carpets,
Geraniums, a trilling canary
And shining horse-hair chairs;
And the silence, full of the rain's falling   10
Was like my grandmother's parlor
Alive with herself and her voice, rising and falling—
Rain and wind intermingled.

I remember on that day
I was thinking only of my love   15
And of my love's house.
But now I remember the day
As I remember my grandmother.
I remember the rain as the feathery fringe of her shawl.

p. 1929

ANN DEAGON

There Is No Balm in Birmingham

Among the agents used by counterfeiters
to age their stock are: glycerine,
whale oil, rose water. I know this art.
To make their tender legal, to pass current,
my petaled, my limpid aunts   5
distilled in the coiled copper of their afternoons
animal, vegetable, mineral
into a balmy essence that preserved
their beauty moist.
            Leathered as I am,   10
Aunties, sisters, I smear my page
with crafty balsam, beauteous conceit,
hide to the last, last line the truth that's not
beauty but bone, bone, bone, bone.

1978

ETHERIDGE KNIGHT

The Idea of Ancestry

I

Taped to the wall of my cell[3] are 47 pictures: 47 black
faces: my father, mother, grandmothers (1 dead), grand
fathers (both dead), brothers, sisters, uncles, aunts,
cousins (1st & 2nd), nieces, and nephews. They stare
across the space at my sprawling on my bunk. I know
their dark eyes, they know mine. I know their style,   ·   5
they know mine. I am all of them, they are all of me;
they are farmers, I am a thief, I am me, they are thee.

I have at one time or another been in love with my mother,
1 grandmother, 2 sisters, 2 aunts (1 went to the asylum),   10
and 5 cousins. I am now in love with a 7 yr old niece
(she sends me letters written in large block print, and
her picture is the only one that smiles at me).

I have the same name as 1 grandfather, 3 cousins, 3 nephews,
and 1 uncle. The uncle disappeared when he was 15, just took   15
off and caught a freight (they say). He's discussed each year
when the family has a reunion, he causes uneasiness in
the clan, he is an empty space. My father's mother, who is 93
and who keeps the Family Bible with everybody's birth dates
(and death dates) in it, always mentions him. There is no   20
place in her Bible for "whereabouts unknown."

II

Each Fall the graves of my grandfathers call me, the brown
hills and red gullies of mississippi send out their electric
messages, galvanizing my genes. Last yr/like a salmon quitting
the cold ocean—leaping and bucking up his birthstream/I   25
hitchhiked my way from L.A. with 16 caps[4] in my pocket and a
monkey on my back, and I almost kicked it with the kinfolks.
I walked barefooted in my grandmother's backyard/I smelled
    the old
land and the woods/I sipped cornwhiskey from fruit jars with the
    men/
I flirted with the women/I had a ball till the caps ran out   30
and my habit came down. That night I looked at my grand-
    mother
and split/my guts were screaming for junk/but I was almost
contented/I had almost caught up with me.
    The next day in Memphis I cracked a croaker's crib[5]/for a fix.

---

3. This poem is from Knight's volume, *Poems from Prison*; Knight began to write poetry while serving a sentence for armed robbery in the Ohio State Penitentiary.

4. Doses of heroin (?); "monkey on my back": drug habit.
5. Burglarized a doctor's house (or a drugstore).

This yr there is a gray stone wall damming my stream, and when   35
the falling leaves stir my genes, I pace my cell or flop on my
    bunk
and stare at 47 black faces across the space. I am all of them,
they are all of me, I am me, they are thee, and I have no sons
to float in the space between.

1968

A. M. KLEIN

Heirloom

My father bequeathed me no wide estates;
No keys and ledgers were my heritage;
Only some holy books with *yahrzeit*[6] dates
Writ mournfully upon a blank front page—

Books of the Baal Shem Tov,[7] and of his wonders;   5
Pamphlets upon the devil and his crew;
Prayers against road demons, witches, thunders;
And sundry other tomes for a good Jew.

Beautiful: though no pictures on them, save
The scorpion crawling on a printed track;   10
The Virgin floating on a scriptural wave,
Square letters twinkling in the Zodiac.

The snuff left on this page, now brown and old,
The tallow stains of midnight liturgy—
These are my coat of arms, and these unfold   15
My noble lineage, my proud ancestry!

And my tears, too, have stained this heirloomed ground,
When reading in these treatises some weird
Miracle, I turned a leaf and found
A white hair fallen from my father's beard.   20

1940

---

6. Anniversary of the death of a parent or near relative.
7. A title given to someone who possesses the secret knowledge of Jewish holy men and who therefore could work miracles.

A Gathering of Poems on Poetry

A. E. HOUSMAN

Terence, This Is Stupid Stuff

"Terence,[1] this is stupid stuff:
You eat your victuals fast enough;
There can't be much amiss, 'tis clear,
To see the rate you drink your beer.
But oh, good Lord, the verse you make,   5
It gives a chap the belly-ache.
The cow, the old cow, she is dead;
It sleeps well, the horned head:
We poor lads, 'tis our turn now
To hear such tunes as killed the cow.   10
Pretty friendship 'tis to rhyme
Your friends to death before their time
Moping melancholy mad:
Come, pipe a tune to dance to, lad."

    Why, if 'tis dancing you would be,   15
There's brisker pipes than poetry.
Say, for what were hop-yards meant,
Or why was Burton built on Trent?[2]
Oh many a peer of England brews
Livelier liquor than the Muse,   20
And malt does more than Milton can
To justify God's ways to man.[3]
Ale, man, ale's the stuff to drink
For fellows whom it hurts to think:
Look into the pewter pot   25
To see the world as the world's not.
And faith, 'tis pleasant till 'tis past:
The mischief is that 'twill not last.
Oh I have been to Ludlow fair[4]
And left my necktie God knows where,   30
And carried half-way home, or near,
Pints and quarts of Ludlow beer:
Then the world seemed none so bad,
And I myself a sterling lad;
And down in lovely muck I've lain,   35
Happy till I woke again.
Then I saw the morning sky:
Heigho, the tale was all a lie;

---

1. Housman originally titled the volume in which this poem appeared "The Poems of Terence Hearsay."
2. Burton was famous for its ales, originally brewed from special springs there.
3. Milton said his purpose in *Paradise Lost* was to "justify the ways of God to men."
4. Ludlow was a market town in Shropshire, and its town fair would be a social high point for a youth growing up in the county.

The world, it was the old world yet,
I was I, my things were wet,   40
And nothing now remained to do
But begin the game anew.

Therefore, since the world has still
Much good, but much less good than ill,
And while the sun and moon endure   45
Luck's a chance, but trouble's sure,
I'd face it as a wise man would,
And train for ill and not for good.
'Tis true, the stuff I bring for sale
Is not so brisk a brew as ale: 50
Out of a stem that scored the hand
I wrung it in a weary land.
But take it: if the smack is sour,
The better for the embittered hour;
It should do good to heart and head   55
When your soul is in my soul's stead;
And I will friend you, if I may,
In the dark and cloudy day.

There was a king reigned in the East:
There, when kings will sit to feast,   60
They get their fill before they think
With poisoned meat and poisoned drink.
He gathered all that springs to birth
From the many-venomed earth;
First a little, thence to more,   65
He sampled all her killing store;
And easy, smiling, seasoned sound,
Sate the king when healths went round.
They put arsenic in his meat
And stared aghast to watch him eat;   70
They poured strychnine in his cup
And shook to see him drink it up:
They shook, they stared as white's their shirt:
Them it was their poison hurt.
—I tell the tale that I heard told.   75
Mithridates,[5] he died old.

1896

MARIANNE MOORE

Poetry

I, too, dislike it: there are things that are important beyond all this
   fiddle.

5. The king of Pontus, he was said to have developed a tolerance of poison by taking
gradually increasing quantities.

Reading it, however, with a perfect contempt for it, one discovers in
it after all, a place for the genuine.
    Hands that can grasp, eyes
       that can dilate, hair that can rise   5
         if it must, these things are important not because a

high-sounding interpretation can be put upon them but because they
      are
useful. When they become so derivative as to become unintelligible,
the same thing may be said for all of us, that we
    do not admire what   10
      we cannot understand: the bat
        holding on upside down or in quest of something to

eat, elephants pushing, a wild horse taking a roll, a tireless wolf under
a tree, the immovable critic twitching his skin like a horse that feels
    a flea, the base-
      ball fan, the statistician—   15
        nor is it valid
          to discriminate against "business documents and

school-books"[6]; all these phenomena are important. One must make a
      distinction
however: when dragged into prominence by half poets, the result is
    not poetry,
nor till the poets among us can be   20
    "literalists of
      the imagination"[7]—above
        insolence and triviality and can present

for inspection, "imaginary gardens with real toads in them," shall we
      have
it. In the meantime, if you demand on the one hand,   25
    the raw material of poetry in
      all its rawness and
        that which is on the other hand
          genuine, you are interested in poetry.

                                              1921

---

6. *"Diary of Tolstoy*, p. 84: 'Where the boundary between prose and poetry lies, I shall never be able to understand. The question is raised in manuals of style, yet the answer to it lies beyond me. Poetry is verse; prose is not verse. Or else poetry is everything with the exception of business documents and school books.' " (Moore's note)

7. " 'Literalists of the imagination.' Yeats, *Ideas of Good and Evil* (A. H. Bullen, 1903), p. 182. 'The limitation of his view was from the very intensity of his vision; he was a too literal realist of imagination, as others are of nature; and because he believed that the figures seen by the mind's eye, when exalted by inspiration, were "eternal existences," symbols of divine essences, he hated every grace of style that might obscure their lineaments.' " (Moore's note)

NIKKI GIOVANNI

Poetry

poetry is motion graceful
as a fawn
gentle as a teardrop
strong like the eye
finding peace in a crowded room   5

we poets tend to think
our words are golden
though emotion speaks too
loudly to be defined
by silence   10

sometimes after midnight or just before
the dawn
we sit typewriter in hand
pulling loneliness around us
forgetting our lovers or children   15
who are sleeping
ignoring the weary wariness
of our own logic
to compose a poem
    no one understands it   20
it never says "love me" for poets are
beyond love
it never says "accept me" for poems seek not
acceptance but controversy
it only says "i am" and therefore   25
i concede that you are too

a poem is pure energy
horizontally contained
between the mind
of the poet and the ear of the reader   30
if it does not sing discard the ear
for poetry is song
if it does not delight discard
the heart for poetry is joy
if it does not inform then close   35
off the brain for it is dead
if it cannot heed the insistent message
that life is precious

which is all we poets
wrapped in our loneliness   40
are trying to say

1975

EMILY DICKINSON

I Dwell in Possibility

I dwell in Possibility—
A fairer House than Prose—
More numerous of Windows—
Superior—for Doors—

Of Chambers as the Cedars—   5
Impregnable of Eye—
And for an Everlasting Roof
The Gambrels[8] of the Sky—

Of Visitors—the fairest—
For Occupation—This—   10
The spreading wide my narrow Hands
To gather Paradise—

ca. 1862

ARCHIBALD MACLEISH

Ars Poetica[9]

A poem should be palpable and mute
As a globed fruit,

Dumb
As old medallions to the thumb,

Silent as the sleeve-worn stone   5
Of casement ledges where the moss has grown—

A poem should be wordless
As the flight of birds.

A poem should be motionless in time
As the moon climbs,   10

Leaving, as the moon releases
Twig by twig the night-entangled trees,

Leaving, as the moon behind the winter leaves,
Memory by memory the mind—

---

8. **Roofs with double slopes.**
9. "The Art of Poetry," title of a poetical treatise by the Roman poet Horace (65–8 B.C.).

A poem should be motionless in time   15
As the moon climbs.

A poem should be equal to:
Not true.

For all the history of grief
An empty doorway and a maple leaf.   20

For love
The leaning grasses and two lights above the sea—

A poem should not mean
But be.

1926

ISHMAEL REED

beware : do not read this poem

tonite ,   thriller was
abt an ol woman , so vain she
surrounded herself w/
      many mirrors

it got so bad that finally she   5
locked herself indoors & her
whole life became the
      mirrors

one day the villagers broke
into her house ,   but she was too   10
swift for them .   she disappeared
      into a mirror

each tenant who bought the house   •
after that ,   lost a loved one to
      the ol woman in the mirror :   15
      first a little girl
      then a young woman
      then the young woman/s husband

the hunger of this poem is legendary
it has taken in many victims   20
back off from this poem
it has drawn in yr feet
back off from this poem
it has drawn in yr legs

back off from this poem   25
it is a greedy mirror
you are into this poem   .   from
      the waist down
nobody can hear you can they   ?
this poem has had you up to here   30
      belch
this poem aint got no manners
you cant call out frm this poem
relax now & go w/ this poem   35
move & roll on to this poem
do not resist this poem
this poem has yr eyes
this poem has his head
this poem has his arms
this poem has his fingers   40
this poem has his fingertips
this poem is the reader & the
reader this poem

statistic   :   the us bureau of missing persons reports
                   that in 1968 over 100,000 people disappeared
                   leaving no solid clues
                             nor trace   only
         a space   in the lives of their friends

                                                      1970

WILLIAM SHAKESPEARE

Not Marble, Nor the Gilded Monuments

Not marble, nor the gilded monuments
Of princes, shall outlive this powerful rhyme;
But you shall shine more bright in these conténts
Than unswept stone, besmeared with sluttish time.
When wasteful war shall statues overturn,   5
And broils root out the work of masonry,
Nor Mars his[1] sword nor war's quick fire shall burn
The living record of your memory.
'Gainst death and all-oblivious enmity
Shall you pace forth; your praise shall still find room   10
Even in the eyes of all posterity
That wear this world out to the ending doom.[2]
So, till the judgment that yourself arise,
You live in this, and dwell in lovers' eyes.

                                                      1609

1. Mars's (a common Renaissance form
of the possessive). "Nor . . . nor": neither
. . . nor.
2. Judgment Day.

ARCHIBALD MACLEISH

"Not Marble Nor the Gilded Monuments"

for Adele

The praisers of women in their proud and beautiful poems,
Naming the grave mouth and the hair and the eyes,
Boasted those they loved should be forever remembered:
These were lies.

The words sound but the face in the Istrian sun is forgotten.   5
The poet speaks but to her dead ears no more.
The sleek throat is gone—and the breast that was troubled to listen:
Shadow from door.

Therefore I will not praise your knees nor your fine walking
Telling you men shall remember your name as long   10
As lips move or breath is spent or the iron of English
Rings from a tongue.

I shall say you were young, and your arms straight, and your mouth
    scarlet:
I shall say you will die and none will remember you:
Your arms change, and none remember the swish of your garments,   15
Nor the click of your shoe.

Not with my hand's strength, not with difficult labor
Springing the obstinate words to the bones of your breast
And the stubborn line to your young stride and the breath to your
    breathing
And the beat to your haste   20
Shall I prevail on the hearts of unborn men to remember.

(What is a dead girl but a shadowy ghost
Or a dead man's voice but a distant and vain affirmation
Like dream words most)

Therefore I will not speak of the undying glory of women.   25
I will say you were young and straight and your skin fair
And you stood in the door and the sun was a shadow of leaves on your
    shoulders
And a leaf on your hair—

I will not speak of the famous beauty of dead women:
I will say the shape of a leaf lay once on your hair.   30
Till the world ends and the eyes are out and the mouths broken
Look! It is there!

1930

ROBINSON JEFFERS

To the Stone-Cutters

Stone-cutters fighting time with marble, you foredefeated
Challengers of oblivion
Eat cynical earnings, knowing rock splits, records fall down,
The square-limbed Roman letters
Scale in the thaws, wear in the rain. The poet as well   5
Builds his monument mockingly;
For the man will be blotted out, the blithe earth die, the brave sun
Die blind and blacken to the heart:
Yet stones have stood for a thousand years, and pained thoughts found
The honey of peace in old poems.   10

                                                          1924

A Gathering of Poems of Satire and Protest

TOM WAYMAN

Picketing Supermarkets

Because all this food is grown in the store
do not take the leaflet.
Cabbages, broccoli and tomatoes
are raised at night in the aisles.
Milk is brewed in the rear storage areas.   5
Beef produced in vats in the basement.
Do not take the leaflet.
Peanut butter and soft drinks
are made fresh each morning by store employees.
Our oranges and grapes   10
are so fine and round
that when held up to the lights they cast no shadow.
Do not take the leaflet.

And should you take one
do not believe it.   15
This chain of stores has no connection
with anyone growing food someplace else.
How could we have an effect on local farmers?
Do not believe it.

The sound here is Muzak, for your enjoyment.   20
It is not the sound of children crying.

There *is* a lady offering samples
to mark Canada Cheese Month.
There is no dark-skinned man with black hair beside her
wanting to show you the inside of a coffin.   25
You would not have to look if there was.
And there are no Nicaraguan heroes
in any way connected with the bananas.

Pay no attention to these people.
The manager is a citizen.   30
All this food is grown in the store.

                                                              1973

DUDLEY RANDALL

Ballad of Birmingham

(On the bombing of a church in Birmingham, Alabama, 1963)

"Mother dear, may I go downtown
Instead of out to play,
And march the streets of Birmingham
In a Freedom March today?"

"No, baby, no, you may not go,   5
For the dogs are fierce and wild,
And clubs and hoses, guns and jails
Aren't good for a little child."

"But, mother, I won't be alone.
Other children will go with me,   10
And march the streets of Birmingham
To make our country free."

"No, baby, no, you may not go,
For I fear those guns will fire.
But you may go to church instead   15
And sing in the children's choir."

She has combed and brushed her night-dark hair,
And bathed rose petal sweet,
And drawn white gloves on her small brown hands,
And white shoes on her feet.   20

The mother smiled to know her child
Was in the sacred place,
But that smile was the last smile
To come upon her face.

For when she heard the explosion,   25
Her eyes grew wet and wild.
She raced through the streets of Birmingham
Calling for her child.

She clawed through bits of glass and brick,
Then lifted out a shoe.   30
"Oh, here's the shoe my baby wore,
But, baby, where are you?"

                                                                            1969

DENISE LEVERTOV

What Were They Like?

1) Did the people of Viet Nam
   use lanterns of stone?
2) Did they hold ceremonies
   to reverence the opening of buds?
3) Were they inclined to rippling laughter?   5
4) Did they use bone and ivory,
   jade and silver, for ornament?
5) Had they an epic poem?
6) Did they distinguish between speech and singing?

1) Sir, their light hearts turned to stone.   10
   It is not remembered whether in gardens
   stone lanterns illumined pleasant ways.
2) Perhaps they gathered once to delight in blossom,
   but after the children were killed
   there were no more buds.   15
3) Sir, laughter is bitter to the burned mouth.
4) A dream ago, perhaps. Ornament is for joy.
   All the bones were charred.
5) It is not remembered. Remember,
   most were peasants; their life   20
   was in rice and bamboo.
   When peaceful clouds were reflected in the paddies
   and the water buffalo stepped surely along terraces,
   maybe fathers told their sons old tales.
   When bombs smashed the mirrors   25
   there was time only to scream.
6) There is an echo yet, it is said,
   of their speech which was like a song.
   It is reported their singing resembled
   the flight of moths in moonlight.   30
   Who can say? It is silent now.

                                                                            1966

DELAWARE INDIAN SONG

Who Are They?[1]

A great land and a wide land was the east land,
A land without snakes, a rich land, a pleasant land.
Great Fighter was chief, toward the north.
At the Straight river, River-Loving was chief.
Becoming-Fat was chief at Sassafras land . . .   5

Affable was chief, and made peace with all,
All were friends, all were united under this great chief.
Great-Beaver was chief, remaining in Sassafras land.
White-Body was chief on the seashore.
Peace-Maker was chief, friendly to all.   10
He-Makes-Mistakes was chief, hurriedly coming . . .

Coming-as-a-Friend was chief; he went to the Great Lakes,
Visiting all his children, all his friends.
Cranberry-Eater was chief, friend of the Ottawas.
North-Walker was chief; he made festivals.   15
Slow-Gatherer was chief at the shore . . .

White-Crab was chief; a friend of the shore.
Watcher was chief; he looked toward the sea.
At this time, from north and south, the whites came.
They are peaceful; they have great things; who are they?   20

> translated, 1885

ANONYMOUS

The Lady Fortune

The lady Fortune is bothe freend and fo.
Of poure she maketh riche, of riche poure also;
She turneth wo[2] al into wele,[3] and wele al into wo.
Ne truste no man to this wele, the wheel it turneth so.

ca. 1325

ANONYMOUS

The Silver Swan

The silver swan, who living had no note,
When death approached, unlocked her silent throat;

---

1. Translated by D. G. Brinton.   3. Weal: well-being, prosperity.
2. Woe.

Leaning her breast against the reedy shore,
Thus sung her first and last, and sung no more:
"Farewell, all joys; Oh death, come close mine eyes;   5
More geese than swans now live, more fools than wise."

1612

AUDRE LORDE

Outside

In the center of a harsh and spectrumed city
all things natural are strange.
I grew up in a genuine confusion
between grass and weeds and flowers
and what colored meant   5
except for clothes you couldn't bleach
and nobody called me nigger
until I was thirteen.
Nobody lynched my momma
but what she'd never been   10
had bleached her face of everything
but very private furies
and made the other children
call me yellow snot at school.

And how many times have I called myself back   15
through my bones confusion
black
like marrow meaning meat
and how many times have you cut me
and run in the streets   20
my own blood
who do you think me to be
that you are terrified of becoming
or what do you see in my face
you have not already discarded   25
in your own mirror
what face do you see in my eyes
that you will someday
come to
acknowledge your own?   30
Who shall I curse that I grew up
believing in my mother's face
or that I lived in fear of potent darkness
wearing my father's shape
they have both marked me   35
with their blind and terrible love
and I am lustful now for my own name.

Between the canyons of their mighty silences

mother bright and father brown
I seek my own shapes now   40
for they never spoke of me
except as theirs
and the pieces I stumble and fall over
I still record as proof
that I am beautiful   45
twice
blessed with the images
of who they were
and who I thought them once to be
of what I move   50
toward and through
and what I need
to leave behind me
most of all   55
I am blessed within my selves
who are come to make our shattered faces
whole.

1978

W. H. AUDEN

The Unknown Citizen

(To JS/07/M/378
This Marble Monument
Is Erected by the State)[4]

He was found by the Bureau of Statistics to be
One against whom there was no official complaint,
And all the reports on his conduct agree
That, in the modern sense of an old-fashioned word, he was a saint,
For in everything he did he served the Greater Community.   5
Except for the War till the day he retired
He worked in a factory and never got fired,
But satisfied his employers, Fudge Motors Inc.
Yet he wasn't a scab or odd in his views,
For his Union reports that he paid his dues,   10
(Our report on his Union shows it was sound)
And our Social Psychology workers found
That he was popular with his mates and liked a drink.
The Press are convinced that he bought a paper every day
And that his reactions to advertisements were normal in every way. 15
Policies taken out in his name prove that he was fully insured,
And his Health-card shows he was once in hospital but left it cured.
Both Producers Research and High-Grade Living declare
He was fully sensible to the advantages of the Installment Plan
And had everything necessary to the Modern Man,   20
A phonograph, a radio, a car and a frigidaire.
Our researchers into Public Opinion are content

---

4. The title and subtitle parallel the inscription on the Tomb of the Unknown Soldier.

That he held the proper opinions for the time of year;
When there was peace, he was for peace; when there was war, he
    went.
He was married and added five children to the population,   25
Which our Eugenist says was the right number for a parent of his
    generation,
And our teachers report that he never interfered with their education.
Was he free? Was he happy? The question is absurd:
Had anything been wrong, we should certainly have heard.

                                                        1940

CLAUDE MC KAY

America

Although she feeds me bread of bitterness,
And sinks into my throat her tiger's tooth,
Stealing my breath of life, I will confess
I love this cultured hell that tests my youth!
Her vigor flows like tides into my blood,   5
Giving me strength erect against her hate.
Her bigness sweeps my being like a flood.
Yet as a rebel fronts a king in state,
I stand within her walls with not a shred
Of terror, malice, not a word of jeer.   10
Darkly I gaze into the days ahead,
And see her might and granite wonders there,
Beneath the touch of Time's unerring hand,
Like priceless treasures sinking in the sand.

                                                        1922

LANGSTON HUGHES

Harlem (A Dream Deferred)

What happens to a dream deferred?

    Does it dry up
    like a raisin in the sun?
    Or fester like a sore—
    And then run?   5
    Does it stink like rotten meat?
    Or crust and sugar over—
    like a syrupy sweet?

    Maybe it just sags
    like a heavy load.   10

    Or does it explode?

                                                        1951

Craft

3   SPEAKER

Poems are personal. The thoughts and feelings they express belong to a specific person, and however "universal" or general their sentiments seem to be, poems come to us as the expression of a human voice—an individual voice. That voice is often the voice of the poet. But not always. Poets sometimes create a "character" just as writers of fiction or drama do—people who speak for them only indirectly. A character may, in fact, be very different from the poet, just as a character in a play or story is different from the author, and that person, the **speaker** of the poem, may express ideas or feelings very different from the poet's own. In the following poem, *two* individual voices in fact speak, and it is clear that, rather than himself speaking directly to us, the poet has chosen to create two speakers, each of whom has a distinctive voice.

THOMAS HARDY

The Ruined Maid

"O 'Melia,[1] my dear, this does everything crown!
Who could have supposed I should meet you in Town?
And whence such fair garments, such prosperi-ty?"—
"O didn't you know I'd been ruined?" said she.

—"You left us in tatters, without shoes or socks,   5
Tired of digging potatoes, and spudding up docks;[2]
And now you've gay bracelets and bright feathers three!"—
"Yes: that's how we dress when we're ruined," said she.

—"At home in the barton[3] you said 'thee' and 'thou,'
And 'thik oon,' and 'theäs oon,' and 't'other'; but now   10
Your talking quite fits 'ee for high compa-ny!"—
"Some polish is gained with one's ruin," said she.

—"Your hands were like paws then, your face blue and bleak
But now I'm bewitched by your delicate cheek,
And your little gloves fit as on any la-dy!"—   15
"We never do work when we're ruined," said she.

1. Short for Amelia.   3. Farmyard.
2. Spading up weeds.

—"You used to call home-life a hag-ridden dream,
And you'd sigh, and you'd sock;[4] but at present you seem
To know not of megrims[5] or melancho-ly!"—
"True. One's pretty lively when ruined," said she.   20

—"I wish I had feathers, a fine sweeping gown,
And a delicate face, and could strut about Town!"—
"My dear—a raw country girl, such as you be,
Cannot quite expect that. You ain't ruined," said she.
1866

The first voice, that of the sister who has stayed home, is designated typographically (that is, by the way the poem is printed):
there are dashes at the beginning and end of each of her speeches.
The second sister regularly gets the last line in each stanza (and in
the last stanza, two lines), so it is easy to tell who is talking at every
point. Also, the two speakers are just as clearly distinguished by what
they say, how they say it, and what sort of person each proves to be.
The nameless stay-at-home shows little knowledge of the world, and
everything surprises her: seeing her sister at all, but especially seeing
her well clothed, cheerful, and polished; and as the poem develops
she shows increasing envy of her more worldly sister. She is the "raw
country girl" (line 23) that her sister says she is, and she still speaks
the country dialect ("fits 'ee," line 11, for example) that she notices
her sister has lost (lines 9–11). The "ruined" sister ('Melia), on the
other hand, says little except to keep repeating the refrain about
having been ruined, but even the slight variations she plays on that
theme suggest her sophistication and amusement at her countrified
sister, although she still uses a rural "ain't" at the end. We are not
told the full story of their lives (was the ruined sister thrown out?
did she run away from home?), but we know enough (that they've
been separated for some time, that the stay-at-home did not know
where her sister had gone) to allow the dialogue to articulate the
contrast between them. The style of speech of each speaker then does
the rest.

It is equally clear that there is a speaker (or, in this case, actually
a singer) in stanzas two through nine of this poem:

X. J. KENNEDY

In a Prominent Bar in Secaucus One Day

*To the tune of "The Old Orange Flute" or
the tune of "Sweet Betsy from Pike"*

In a prominent bar in Secaucus[6] one day

4. Deliver angry blows.
5. Migraine headaches.
6. A small, smoggy town on the Hacken-

sack River in New Jersey, a few miles
west of Manhattan.

Rose a lady in skunk with a topheavy sway,
Raised a knobby red finger—all turned from their beer—
While with eyes bright as snowcrust she sang high and clear:

"Now who of you'd think from an eyeload of me   5
That I once was a lady as proud as could be?
Oh I'd never sit down by a tumbledown drunk
If it wasn't, my dears, for the high cost of junk.

"All the gents used to swear that the white of my calf
Beat the down of a swan by a length and a half.   10
In the kerchief of linen I caught to my nose
Ah, there never fell snot, but a little gold rose.

"I had seven gold teeth and a toothpick of gold,
My Virginia cheroot was a leaf of it rolled
And I'd light it each time with a thousand in cash—   15
Why the bums used to fight if I flicked them an ash.

"Once the toast of the Biltmore,⁷ the belle of the Taft,
I would drink bottle beer at the Drake, never draft,
And dine at the Astor on Salisbury steak
With a clean tablecloth for each bite I did take.   20

"In a car like the Roxy⁸ I'd roll to the track,
A steel-guitar trio, a bar in the back,
And the wheels made no noise, they turned over so fast,
Still it took you ten minutes to see me go past.

"When the horses bowed down to me that I might choose,   25
I bet on them all, for I hated to lose.
Now I'm saddled each night for my butter and eggs
And the broken threads race down the backs of my legs.

"Let you hold in mind, girls, that your beauty must pass
Like a lovely white clover that rusts with its grass.   30
Keep your bottoms off barstools and marry you young
Or be left—an old barrel with many a bung.

"For when time takes you out for a spin in his car
You'll be hard-pressed to stop him from going too far
And be left by the roadside, for all your good deeds,   35
Two toadstools for tits and a face full of weeds."

All the house raised a cheer, but the man at the bar
Made a phonecall and up pulled a red patrol car
And she blew us a kiss as they copped her away
From that prominent bar in Secaucus, N.J.   40

1961

---

7. Like the Taft, Drake, and Astor, a
once fashionable New York hotel.
8. A luxurious old New York theater
and movie house, the site of many "World
Premieres" in the heyday of Hollywood.

Again, we learn about the character primarily through her own words, although we don't have to believe everything she tells us about her past. From her introduction in the first stanza we get some general notion of her appearance and condition, but it is she who tells us that she is a junkie (line 8), a prostitute (line 27), and that her face and figure are pretty well shot (lines 32, 36). That information could make her a sad case, and the poem might lament her state or allow her to lament it, but instead the poem presents her cheerfully. She is anxious to give advice and sound moralistic (line 31, for example), but she's also enormously cheerful about herself, and her spirit repeatedly bursts through her song. Her performance gives her a lot of pleasure as she exaggerates outrageously about her former luxury and prominence, and even her departure in a patrol car she chooses to treat as a grand exit, throwing a kiss to her audience. The comedy is bittersweet, perhaps, but she is allowed to present herself, through her own words and attitudes, as a likable character. The glorious fiction of her life, narrated with energy and polish in the manner of a practiced and accomplished liar, betrays some rather naive notions of good taste and luxurious living (lines 18–26). But this "lady in skunk" has a picturesque and engaging style, a refreshing sense of humor about herself, and (like the cheap fur she wears) her experiences in what she considers high life satisfy her sense of style and drama. The self-portrait accumulates, almost completely through how she talks about herself, and the poet develops our attitude toward her by allowing her to recount her story herself, in her own words—or rather in words chosen for her by the author.

It is, of course, equally possible to create a speaker who makes us dislike himself or herself, also because of what the poet makes him or her say, as the following poem does. Here the speaker, as the title implies, is a monk, but he shows himself to be most unmonklike: mean, self-righteous, and despicable.

ROBERT BROWNING

Soliloquy of the Spanish Cloister[9]

Gr-r-r—there go, my heart's abhorrence!
    Water your damned flower-pots, do!
If hate killed men, Brother Lawrence,
    God's blood, would not mine kill you!
What? your myrtle-bush wants trimming?   5
    Oh, that rose has prior claims—
Needs its leaden vase filled brimming?
    Hell dry you up with its flames!

9. Monastery.

At the meal we sit together:
   Salve tibi![1] I must hear   10
Wise talk of the kind of weather,
   Sort of season, time of year:
Not a plenteous cork-crop: scarcely
   Dare we hope oak-galls,[2] *I doubt:*
What's the Latin name for "parsley"?   15
   What's the Greek name for Swine's Snout?

Whew! We'll have our platter burnished,
   Laid with care on our own shelf!
With a fire-new spoon we're furnished,
   And a goblet for ourself,   20
Rinsed like something sacrificial
   Ere 'tis fit to touch our chaps[3]—
Marked with L. for our initial!
   (He-he! There his lily snaps!)

Saint, forsooth! While brown Dolores   25
   Squats outside the Convent bank
With Sanchicha, telling stories,
   Steeping tresses in the tank,
Blue-black, lustrous, thick like horsehairs,
   —Can't I see his dead eye glow,   30
Bright as 'twere a Barbary corsair's?[4]
   (That is, if he'd let it show!)

When he finishes refection,[5]
   Knife and fork he never lays
Cross-wise, to my recollection,   35
   As do I, in Jesu's praise.
I the Trinity illustrate,
   Drinking watered orange-pulp—
In three sips the Arian[6] frustrate;
   While he drains his at one gulp.   40

Oh, those melons? If he's able
   We're to have a feast! so nice!
One goes to the Abbot's table,
   All of us get each a slice.
How go on your flowers? None double?   45
   Not one fruit-sort can you spy?
Strange!—And I, too, at such trouble,
   Keep them close-nipped on the sly!

There's a great text in Galatians,[7]

1. Hail to thee. Italics usually indicate the words of Brother Lawrence.
2. Abnormal growth on oak trees, used for tanning.
3. Jaws.
4. African pirate's.
5. A meal.
6. A heretical sect which denied the Trinity.
7. "Cursed is every one that continueth not in all things which are written in the book of law to do them," *Galatians* 3:10. *Galatians* 5:15–23 provides a long list of possible offenses, but they do not add up to 29.

Once you trip on it, entails   50
Twenty-nine distinct damnations,
    One sure, if another fails:
If I trip him just a-dying,
    Sure of heaven as sure can be,
Spin him round and send him flying   55
    Off to hell, a Manichee?[8]

Or, my scrofulous French novel
    On gray paper with blunt type!
Simply glance at it, you grovel
    Hand and foot in Belial's gripe:[9]   60
If I double down its pages
    At the woeful sixteenth print,
When he gathers his greengages,
    Ope a sieve and slip it in't?

Or, there's Satan!—one might venture   65
    Pledge one's soul to him, yet leave
Such a flaw in the indenture
    As he'd miss till, past retrieve,
Blasted lay that rose-acacia
    We're so proud of! *Hy, Zy, Hine* . . .[1]   70
'St, there's Vespers! *Plena gratiâ*
    Ave, Virgo.[2] Gr-r-r—you swine!

                                                                   1842

Not many poems begin with a growl, and in this one it turns out to
be fair warning that we are about to get to know a real beast, even
though he is in the clothing of a religious man. In line 1, he has
already shown himself to hold a most uncharitable attitude toward
his fellow monk, Brother Lawrence, and by line 4 he has uttered
two profanities and admitted his intense feelings of hatred and
vengefulness. His ranting and roaring is full of exclamation points
(four in the first stanza), and he reveals his own personality and
character when he imagines curses and unflattering nicknames for
Brother Lawrence or plots malicious jokes on him. By the end, we
have accumulated no knowledge of Brother Lawrence that makes
him seem a fit target for such rage (except that he is pious, dutiful,
and pleasant—perhaps enough to make this sort of speaker despise
him), but we have discovered the speaker to be lecherous (stanza 4),
full of false piety (stanza 5), malicious in trivial matters (stanza 6),
ready to use his theological learning to sponsor damnation rather
than salvation (stanza 7), a closet reader and viewer of pornography

8. A heretic. According to the Mani-
chean heresy, the world was divided into
the forces of good and evil, equally powerful.
9. In the clutches of Satan.

1. Possibly the beginning of an incantation or curse.
2. The opening words of the *Ave Maria*,
here reversed: "Full of grace, Hail, Virgin."

within the monastery (stanza 8)—even willing to risk his own soul in order to torment Brother Lawrence (last stanza). The speaker is made to characterize himself; the details accrue and accumulate into a fairly full portrait, and here we do not have even an opening and closing "objective" description (as in *In a Prominent Bar*) or another speaker (as in *The Ruined Maid*) to give us perspective. Except for the moments when the speaker mimics or parodies Brother Lawrence (usually in italic type), we have only the speaker's own words and thoughts. But that is enough; the poet has controlled them so carefully that we clearly know what he thinks of the speaker he has created— that he is a mean-spirited, vengeful hypocrite, a thoroughly disreputable and unlikable character. The whole poem has been about him and his attitudes; the point of the poem has been to characterize the speaker and develop in us a dislike of him and what he stands for—total hypocrisy. In reading a poem like this aloud, we would want our voice to suggest all the unlikable features of a hypocrite. We would also need to suggest, through the tone of voice we used, the author's contemptuous mocking of the rage and hypocrisy, and we would want, like an actor, to create strong disapproval in the hearer. The poem's words (the ones the author has given to the speaker) clearly imply those attitudes, and we would want our voice to express them. Usually there is much more to a poem than the identification and characterization of the speaker, but in many cases it is necessary to identify the speaker and determine his or her character before we can appreciate what else goes on in the poem. And sometimes, as here, in looking for the speaker of the poem, we come near to the center of the poem itself.

The speaker in the following poem is, from the first, clearly much more likable, but we do not get a very full sense of her until the poem is well along. As you read, try to imitate the tone of voice you think this kind of person would use. Exactly when do you begin to feel that you know what she is like?

DOROTHY PARKER

A Certain Lady

Oh, I can smile for you, and tilt my head,
  And drink your rushing words with eager lips,
And paint my mouth for you a fragrant red,
  And trace your brows with tutored finger-tips.
When you rehearse your list of loves to me,   5
  Oh, I can laugh and marvel, rapturous-eyed.
And you laugh back, nor can you ever see
  The thousand little deaths my heart has died.
And you believe, so well I know my part,
  That I am gay as morning, light as snow,   10

And all the straining things within my heart
　　You'll never know.

Oh, I can laugh and listen, when we meet,
　　And you bring tales of fresh adventurings—
Of ladies delicately indiscreet,   15
　　Of lingering hands, and gently whispered things.
And you are pleased with me, and strive anew
　　To sing me sagas of your late delights.
Thus do you want me—marveling, gay, and true—
　　Nor do you see my staring eyes of nights.   20
And when, in search of novelty, you stray,
　　Oh, I can kiss you blithely as you go . . .
And what goes on, my love, while you're away,
　　You'll never know.

1937

To whom does the speaker seem to be talking? What sort of person is he? How do you feel about him? Which habits and attitudes of his do you like least? How soon can you tell that the speaker is not altogether happy about his conversation and conduct? In what tone of voice would you read the first 22 lines aloud? What attitude would you try to express toward the person spoken to? What tone would you use for the last two lines? How would you describe the speaker's personality? What aspects of her behavior are most crucial to the poem's effect?

It is easy to assume that the speaker in a poem is an extension of the poet. Is the speaker in this poem Dorothy Parker?—Maybe. A lot of Parker's poems present a similar world-weary posture and a kind of cynicism about romantic love (look, for example, at *Comment*, p. 736). But the poem is hardly an example of self-revelation, a giving away of personal secrets. If it were, it would be silly, not to say risky, to address her lover in a way that gives damaging facts about a pose she has been so careful to set up. We may be *tempted* to think of the speaker as Dorothy Parker, but it is best to resist the temptation and think of the character as an imagined person. Besides, the poem is called *A Certain Lady*, as if it were a speaking portrait of someone. Is the speaker based on any real person at all? Probably not; we are given no reason to think that the speaker is anyone in particular or that the poet has done anything but create a fictional character and situation. In any case, the poem's effect does not depend on our thinking that the speaker is someone specific and historical; it depends on our surprise at her honesty and openness in giving away a secret, something more likely in a fictional speaker than in real life. In poetry we can be overhearers of a conversation; in real life such a role could be dangerous to hearer as well as speaker—and seldom in real life do we get so quick and pointed a characterization as this poem develops in just a few well-organized and well-calculated lines.

In poems like *The Ruined Maid, In a Prominent Bar*, and *Soliloquy*, we are in no danger of mistaking the speaker for the poet, once we have recognized that poets may create speakers who participate in specific situations much as in fiction or drama. When there is a pointed discrepancy between the speaker and what we know of the poet—when the speaker is a woman, for example, and the poet is a man—we know we have a created speaker to contend with and that the point (or at least *one* point) in the poem is to observe the characterization carefully. In *A Certain Lady* we may be less sure, and in other poems the discrepancy between speaker and poet may be even more uncertain. What are we to make, for example, of the speaker in *Woodchucks* in the previous chapter (p. 569)? Is that speaker the real Maxine Kumin? At best (without knowing something quite specific about the author) we can only say "maybe" to that question. What we can be sure of is the sort of person the speaker is portrayed to be—someone (man? or woman?) surprised to discover feelings and attitudes that contradict values apparently held confidently. And that is exactly what we need to know for the poem to have its effect.

A similar kind of self-mocking of the speaker is present in the following poem, but here the mockery is put to less revelatory, more comic ends.

A. R. AMMONS

Needs

I want something suited to my special needs
I want chrome hubcaps, pin-on attachments
and year round use year after year
I want a workhorse with smooth uniform cut,
dozer blade and snow blade & deluxe steering   5
wheel
I want something to mow, throw snow, tow
and sow with
I want precision reel blades
I want a console styled dashboard   10
I want an easy spintype recoil starter
I want combination bevel and spur gears, 14
gauge stamped steel housing and
washable foam element air cleaner
I want a pivoting front axle and extrawide   15
turf tires
I want an inch of foam rubber inside a vinyl
covering
and especially if it's not too much, if I
can deserve it, even if I can't pay for it   20
I want to mow while riding.

1970

The poet here may be teasing himself about his desire for comfort and ease—and showing how readily advertisements and catalog descriptions manipulate us. But the speaker doesn't have to be the author for the teasing to work. In fact, the effect is to tease those attitudes no matter who holds them by teasing a speaker who illustrates the attitudes. It doesn't matter to the poem whether the speaker is the poet himself or some totally invented character. If the speaker is a version of the poet himself—perhaps a *side* of his personality that he is exploring—the portrait is still fictional in an important sense. The poem presents not a whole human being (*no* poem could do that) but only a version of him—a mood perhaps, an aspect, an attitude, a part of that person. Here, the poet presents someone with an obsession, in this case a small and not very damaging one, and allows him to spurt phrases as if he were reciting from an ad. Here the "portrait" is made more comic by a clear sense the poem projects that what we have is only a part of the person, an interest grown too intense, gone askew, gotten out of proportion, something that happens to most of us from time to time. The speaker may be a side of the poet, or maybe not. All we know about the speaker is that he has a one-track mind, that he is obsessed by his own luxurious comfort. He may not even be a "he": there is nothing in the poem that makes us certain that the speaker is male. It is customary to think of the speaker in a poem written by a man as "he" and in a poem written by a woman as "she" (as in Maxine Kumin's *Woodchucks*) unless the poem presents contrary evidence, but it is merely a convenience, a habit, nothing more.

Even when poets present themselves as if they were speaking directly to us in their own voices, their poems present only a partial portrait, something considerably less than the full personality of the poet. Even when there is not an obviously created character—someone with distinct characteristics which are different from those of the poet—strategies of characterization are used to present the person speaking in one way and not another. Even in a poem like the following one, it is still a good idea to talk of the speaker instead of the poet, although here it is probable that the poet is writing about a personal, actual experience.

WILLIAM WORDSWORTH

She Dwelt Among the Untrodden Ways

> She dwelt among the untrodden ways
>   Beside the springs of Dove,[3]
> A Maid whom there were none to praise
>   And very few to love:

3. A small stream in the Lake District in northern England, near where Wordsworth lived in Dove Cottage at Grasmere.

A violet by a mossy stone
   Half hidden from the eye!
—Fair as a star, when only one 5
   Is shining in the sky.

She lived unknown, and few could know
   When Lucy ceased to be; 10
But she is in her grave, and, oh,
   The difference to me!

1800

It is hard to say whether this poem is more about Lucy or about how the speaker feels about her death. Her simple life, far removed from fame and known only to a few, is said nevertheless to have been beautiful. We know little else about her beyond her name and where she lived, in a beautiful but then isolated section of northern England. We don't know if she was young or old, only that the speaker thinks of her as "fair" and compares her to a "violet by a mossy stone." What we do know is that the speaker feels her loss deeply, so deeply that he is almost inarticulate with grief, lapsing into simple exclamation ("oh," line 11) and unable to articulate the "difference" that her death makes.

Did Lucy actually live? Was she a friend of the poet? We don't know; the poem doesn't tell us, and even biographers of Wordsworth are unsure. What we do know is that Wordsworth was able to represent grief over the death very powerfully. Whether the speaker is the historical Wordsworth or not, that speaker is a major focus of the poem, and it is his feelings which the poem isolates and expresses. We need to recognize some characteristics of the speaker and be sensitive to his feelings for the poem to work. We may be tempted to identify the speaker with the poet—it seems to be a natural tendency for most readers to make that assumption unless there is overwhelming evidence to the contrary in the poem—but it is still best to think of the voice we hear in the poem as that of the speaker. We don't need to give him a name, but we do need to understand his values as the poem expresses them and to recognize his deep feelings.

The poems we have looked at in this chapter—and the group that follows at the end of the chapter—all suggest the value of beginning the reading of any poem with a simple question: Who is speaking and what do we know about him or her? Putting together the evidence that the poem presents in answer to this question can often take us a long way into the poem. For some poems, this question won't help a great deal because the speaking voice is too indistinct or the character behind the poem too scantily presented, but in many cases asking this question will lead you toward the central experience the poem offers.

JOHN BETJEMAN

In Westminster Abbey[4]

Let me take this other glove off
  As the *vox humana*[5] swells,
And the beauteous fields of Eden
  Bask beneath the Abbey bells.
Here, where England's statesmen lie,   5
Listen to a lady's cry.

Gracious Lord, oh bomb the Germans.
  Spare their women for Thy Sake,
And if that is not too easy
  We will pardon Thy Mistake.   10
But, gracious Lord, whate'er shall be,
Don't let anyone bomb me.

Keep our Empire undismembered
  Guide our Forces by Thy Hand,
Gallant blacks from far Jamaica,   15
  Honduras and Togoland;
Protect them Lord in all their fights,
And, even more, protect the whites.

Think of what our Nation stands for,
  Books from Boots[6] and country lanes,   20
Free speech, free passes, class distinction,
  Democracy and proper drains.
Lord, put beneath Thy special care
One-eighty-nine Cadogan Square.[7]

Although dear Lord I am a sinner,   25
  I have done no major crime;
Now I'll come to Evening Service
  Whensoever I have the time.
So, Lord, reserve for me a crown,
And do not let my shares go down.   30

I will labor for Thy Kingdom,
  Help our lads to win the war,
Send white feathers to the cowards[8]
  Join the Women's Army Corps,[9]
Then wash the Steps around Thy Throne   35
In the Eternal Safety Zone.

---

4. The famous Gothic church in London in which English monarchs are crowned and famous Englishmen are buried (see lines 5, 39–40).
5. Organ tones which resemble the human voice.
6. A chain of London pharmacies.
7. Presumably where the speaker lives, in a fairly fashionable area.

8. White feathers were sometimes given, or sent, to men not in uniform, to suggest that they were cowards and should join the armed forces.
9. The speaker uses the old World War I name (Women's Army Auxiliary Corps) of the Auxiliary Territorial Service, an organization which performed domestic (and some foreign) defense duties.

Now I feel a little better,
    What a treat to hear Thy Word
Where the bones of leading statesmen,
    Have so often been interred.
And now, dear Lord, I cannot wait
Because I have a luncheon date.

1940

HENRY REED

Lessons of the War

Judging Distances

Not only far away, but the way that you say it
Is very important. Perhaps you may never get
The knack of judging a distance, but at least you know
How to report on a landscape: the central sector,
The right of arc and that, which we had last Tuesday,
    And at least you know

That maps are of time, not place, so far as the army
Happens to be concerned—the reason being,
Is one which need not delay us. Again, you know
There are three kinds of tree, three only, the fir and the poplar,
And those which have bushy tops to; and lastly
    That things only seem to be things.

A barn is not called a barn, to put it more plainly,
Or a field in the distance, where sheep may be safely grazing.
You must never be over-sure. You must say, when reporting:
At five o'clock in the central sector is a dozen
Of what appear to be animals; whatever you do,
    Don't call the bleeders *sheep*.

I am sure that's quite clear; and suppose, for the sake of example,
The one at the end, asleep, endeavors to tell us
What he sees over there to the west, and how far away,
After first having come to attention. There to the west,
On the fields of summer the sun and the shadows bestow
    Vestments of purple and gold.

The still white dwellings are like a mirage in the heat,
And under the swaying elms a man and a woman
Lie gently together. Which is, perhaps, only to say
That there is a row of houses to the left of arc,
And that under some poplars a pair of what appear to be humans
    Appear to be loving.

Well that, for an answer, is what we might rightly call

Moderately satisfactory only, the reason being,
Is that two things have been omitted, and those are important.
The human beings, now: in what direction are they,
And how far away, would you say? And do not forget   35
    There may be dead ground in between.

There may be dead ground in between; and I may not have got
The knack of judging a distance; I will only venture
A guess that perhaps between me and the apparent lovers,
(Who, incidentally, appear by now to have finished,)   40
At seven o'clock from the houses, is roughly a distance
    Of about one year and a half.

                                         1946

AUDRE LORDE

Hanging Fire

        I am fourteen
        and my skin has betrayed me
        the boy I cannot live without
        still sucks his thumb
        in secret   5
        how come my knees are
        always so ashy
        what if I die
        before morning
        and momma's in the bedroom   10
        with the door closed.

        I have to learn how to dance
        in time for the next party
        my room is too small for me
        suppose I die before graduation   15
        they will sing sad melodies
        but finally
        tell the truth about me
        There is nothing I want to do
        and too much   20
        that has to be done
        and momma's in the bedroom
        with the door closed.

        Nobody even stops to think
        about my side of it   25
        I should have been on Math Team
        my marks were better than his
        why do I have to be

the one
wearing braces   30
I have nothing to wear tomorrow
will I live long enough
to grow up
and momma's in the bedroom
with the door closed.   35

1978

HOWARD NEMEROV

Boom!

Sees Boom in Religion, Too

Atlantic City, June 23, 1957 (AP).—President Eisenhower's pastor said
tonight that Americans are living in a period of "unprecedented religious
activity" caused partially by paid vacations, the eight-hour day and modern
conveniences.
   "These fruits of material progress," said the Rev. Edward L. R. Elson
of the National Presbyterian Church, Washington, "have provided the
leisure, the energy, and the means for a level of human and spiritual
values never before reached."

Here at the Vespasian-Carlton,[1] it's just one
religious activity after another; the sky
is constantly being crossed by cruciform[2]
airplanes, in which nobody disbelieves
for a second and the tide, the tide   5
of spiritual progress and prosperity
miraculously keeps rising, to a level
never before attained. The churches are full,
the beaches are full, and the filling-stations
are full, God's great ocean is full   10
of paid vacationers praying an eight-hour day
to the human and spiritual values, the fruits,
the leisure, the energy, and the means, Lord,
the means for the level, the unprecedented level,
and the modern conveniences, which also are full.   15
Never before, O Lord, have the prayers and praises
from belfry and phonebooth, from ballpark and barbecue
the sacrifices, so endlessly ascended.

It was not thus when Job in Palestine
sat in the dust and cried, cried bitterly;[3]   20
when Damien kissed the lepers on their wounds

---

1. Vespasian was emperor of Rome 70–79, shortly after the reign of Nero. In French, *vespasienne* means public toilet.
2. Cross-shaped.
3. According to the *Book of Job*, he was afflicted with the loss of prosperity, children, and health as a test of his faith. His name means, in Hebrew, "he cries"; see especially *Job* 2:7–13.

it was not thus;[4] it was not thus
when Francis worked a fourteen-hour day
strictly for the birds;[5] when Dante took
a week's vacation without pay and it rained   25
part of the time,[6] O Lord, it was not thus.

But now the gears mesh and the tires burn
and the ice chatters in the shaker and the priest
in the pulpit and Thy Name, O Lord,
is kept before the public, while the fruits   30
ripen and religion booms and the level rises
and every modern convenience runneth over,
that it may never be with us as it hath been
with Athens and Karnak and Nagasaki,[7]
nor Thy sun for one instant refrain from shining   35
on the rainbow Buick by the breezeway
or the Chris Craft with the uplift life raft;
that we may continue to be the just folks we are,
plain people with ordinary superliners and
disposable diaperliners, people of the stop'n'shop   40
'n'pray as you go, of hotel, motel, boatel,
the humble pilgrims of no deposit no return
and please adjust thy clothing, who will give to Thee,
if Thee will keep us going, our annual
Miss Universe, for Thy Name's Sake, Amen.   45

1960

GEORGE HERBERT

The Collar

I struck the board[8] and cried, "No more;
          I will abroad!
What? shall I ever sigh and pine?
My lines[9] and life are free, free as the road,
Loose as the wind, as large as store.[1]   5
          Shall I be still in suit?[2]
Have I no harvest but a thorn
To let me blood, and not restore
What I have lost with cordial[3] fruit?

---

4. "Father Damien" (Joseph Damien de
Veuster, 1840–1889), a Roman Catholic
missionary from Belgium, was known for
his work among lepers in Hawaii; he ultimately contracted leprosy himself and died
there.
5. St. Francis of Assisi, 13th-century
founder of the Franciscan order, was noted
for his love of all living things, and one of
the most famous stories about him tells of
his preaching to the birds. "Strictly for the
birds": a mid-20th-century expression for
worthless or unfashionable activity.
6. Dante's journey through Hell, Purga-

tory, and Paradise (in *The Divine Comedy*)
takes a week, beginning on Good Friday,
1300. It rains in the third chasm of Hell.
7. Athens, the cultural center of ancient
civilization; Karnak, a village on the Nile,
built on the site of ancient Thebes; Nagasaki, a large Japanese port city, virtually
destroyed by a U.S. atomic bomb in 1945.
8. Table.
9. Lot.
1. A storehouse; i.e., in abundance.
2. In service to another.
3. Reviving, restorative.

Sure there was wine 10
Before my sighs did dry it; there was corn
Before my tears did drown it.
Is the year only lost to me?
Have I no bays[4] to crown it,
No flowers, no garlands gay? All blasted? 15
All wasted?
Not so, my heart; but there is fruit,
And thou hast hands.
Recover all thy sigh-blown age
On double pleasures: leave thy cold dispute 20
Of what is fit, and not. Forsake thy cage,
Thy rope of sands,[5]
Which petty thoughts have made, and made to thee
Good cable, to enforce and draw,
And be thy law, 25
While thou didst wink[6] and wouldst not see.
Away! take heed;
I will abroad.
Call in thy death's-head[7] there; tie up thy fears.
He that forbears 30
To suit and serve his need,
Deserves his load."
But as I raved and grew more fierce and wild
At every word,
Methought I heard one calling, *Child!* 35
And I replied, *My Lord.*

1633

JOHN DONNE

Song

Go, and catch a falling star,
Get with child a mandrake root,[8]
Tell me, where all past years are,
Or who cleft the devil's foot,
Teach me to hear mermaids singing 5
Or to keep off envy's stinging,
And find
What wind
Serves to advance an honest mind.

If thou beest born to strange sights,[9] 10
Things invisible to see,

---

4. Wreaths of triumph.
5. Moral restrictions.
6. I.e., close your eyes to the weaknesses of such restrictions.
7. *Memento mori*, a skull intended to

remind men of their mortality
8. The forked mandrake root is said to be shaped like the lower half of a human torso.
9. I.e., if you have supernatural powers.

Ride ten thousand days and nights,
  Till age snow white hairs on thee;
Thou, when thou return'st, wilt tell me
All strange wonders that befell thee,   15
      And swear,
      No where
Lives a woman true, and fair.

If thou find'st one, let me know:
  Such a pilgrimage were sweet.   20
Yet do not, I would not go,
  Though at next door we might meet:
Though she were true when you met her,
And last till you write your letter,
      Yet she   25
      Will be
False, ere I come, to two, or three.

                                                    1633

4   SITUATION AND SETTING

Questions about speaker ("Who?" questions) in a poem almost always lead to questions of "Where?" "When?" and "Why?" Identifying the speaker usually is, in fact, part of a larger process of defining the entire imagined **situation** in a poem: What is happening? Where is it happening? Who is the speaker speaking to? Who else is present? Why is this event occurring? In order to understand the dialogue in *The Ruined Maid*, for example, we need to become aware that the sisters are meeting again after a period of absence and that they are meeting in a town large enough to seem substantially different in setting from the rural area in which they grew up together. And we infer (from the opening lines) that the meeting is accidental, and that no other family members are present for the conversation. The poem's whole "story" depends upon the fact of their situation: after leading separate lives for some time they have some catching up to do. We don't know what specific town is involved, or what year, season, or time of day because those details are not important to the poem's effect. But crucial to the poem are the where and when questions that define the situation and relationship of the two speakers, and the answer to the why question—that the meeting is by chance—is important too. In another poem we looked at in the previous chapter, *A Certain Lady*, the specific moment and place are not important, but we do need to notice that the "lady" is talking to (or having an imaginary conversation with) her man and that they are talking about a relationship of some duration.

Sometimes a *specific* time and place (**setting**) may be important.

The "lady in skunk" sings her life story "in a prominent bar in Secaucus, N.J.," a smelly and unfashionable town, but on no particular occasion ("One Day"). In *Soliloquy of the Spanish Cloister,* the setting (a monastery) adds to the irony because of the gross inappropriateness of such sentiments and attitudes in such a supposedly holy place, and the setting of *In Westminster Abbey* similarly helps us to judge the speaker's ideas, attitudes, and self-conception.

The title of the following poem suggests that place may be important, and it is, although you may be surprised to discover exactly what exists at this address and what uses the speaker makes of it.

JAMES DICKEY

Cherrylog Road

Off Highway 106[1]
At Cherrylog Road I entered
The '34 Ford without wheels,
Smothered in kudzu,[2]
With a seat pulled out to run   5
Corn whiskey down from the hills,

And then from the other side
Crept into an Essex
With a rumble seat of red leather
And then out again, aboard   10
A blue Chevrolet, releasing
The rust from its other color,

Reared up on three building blocks.
None had the same body heat;
I changed with them inward, toward   15
The weedy heart of the junkyard,
For I knew that Doris Holbrook
Would escape from her father at noon

And would come from the farm
To seek parts owned by the sun   20
Among the abandoned chassis,
Sitting in each in turn
As I did, leaning forward
As in a wild stock-car race

In the parking lot of the dead,   25
Time after time, I climbed in

1. The poem is set in the mountains of North Georgia.
2. A rapidly growing vine, introduced from Japan to combat erosion but now covering whole fields and groves of trees.

And out the other side, like
An envoy or movie star
Met at the station by crickets.
A radiator cap raised its head,   30

Become a real toad or a kingsnake
As I neared the hub of the yard,
Passing through many states,
Many lives, to reach
Some grandmother's long Pierce-Arrow   35
Sending platters of blindness forth

From its nickel hubcaps
And spilling its tender upholstery
On sleepy roaches,
The glass panel in between   40
Lady and colored driver
Not all the way broken out,

The back-seat phone
Still on its hook.
I got in as though to exclaim,   45
"Let us go to the orphan asylum,
John; I have some old toys
For children who say their prayers."

I popped with sweat as I thought
I heard Doris Holbrook scrape   50
Like a mouse in the southern-state sun
That was eating the paint in blisters
From a hundred car tops and hoods.
She was tapping like code,

Loosening the screws,   55
Carrying off headlights,
Sparkplugs, bumpers,
Cracked mirrors and gear-knobs,
Getting ready, already,
To go back with something to show   60

Other than her lips' new trembling
I would hold to me soon, soon,
Where I sat in the ripped back seat
Talking over the interphone,
Praying for Doris Holbrook   65
To come from her father's farm

And to get back there
With no trace of me on her face
To be seen by her red-haired father
Who would change, in the squalling barn,   70

Her back's pale skin with a strop,
Then lay for me

In a bootlegger's roasting car
With a string-triggered 12-gauge shotgun
To blast the breath from the air.   75
Not cut by the jagged windshields,
Through the acres of wrecks she came
With a wrench in her hand,

Through dust where the blacksnake dies
Of boredom, and the beetle knows   80
The compost has no more life.
Someone outside would have seen
The oldest car's door inexplicably
Close from within:

I held her and held her and held her,   85
Convoyed at terrific speed
By the stalled, dreaming traffic around us,
So the blacksnake, stiff
With inaction, curved back
Into life, and hunted the mouse   90

With deadly overexcitement,
The beetles reclaimed their field
As we clung, glued together,
With the hooks of the seat springs
Working through to catch us red-handed   95
Amidst the gray breathless batting

That burst from the seat at our backs.
We left by separate doors
Into the changed, other bodies
Of cars, she down Cherrylog Road   100
And I to my motorcycle
Parked like the soul of the junkyard

Restored, a bicycle fleshed
With power, and tore off
Up Highway 106, continually   105
Drunk on the wind in my mouth,
Wringing the handlebar for speed,
Wild to be wreckage forever.

                                                            1964

The *exact* location of the junkyard is not important (there is no
Highway 106 near the real Cherrylog Road in North Georgia), but
we do need to know that the setting is rural, that the time is summer

and that the summer is hot, and that moonshine whiskey is native to the area. Following the story is no problem once we have sorted out these few facts, and we are prepared to meet the cast of characters: Doris Holbrook, her red-haired father, and the speaker. About each we learn just enough to appreciate the sense of vitality, adventure, and power that constitute the major effects of the poem.

The situation of love-making in another setting than the junkyard would not produce the same effects, and the exotic sense of a forbidden meeting in this unlikely place helps to recreate the speaker's sense of the episode. For him, it is memorable (notice all the tiny details he remembers), powerful (notice his reaction when he gets back on his motorcycle), dreamlike (notice the sense of time standing still, especially in lines 85–89), and important (notice how the speaker perceives his environment as changed by their love-making, lines 88–91 and 98–100). The wealth of details about setting also helps us to raise other, related questions. Why does the speaker fantasize about being shot by the father (lines 72–75)? Why, in a poem so full of details, do we find out so little about what Doris Holbrook looks like? What gives us the sense that this incident is a composite of episodes, an event that was repeated many times? What gives us the impression that the events occurred long ago? What makes the speaker feel so powerful at the end? What does he mean when he talks of himself as being "wild to be wreckage forever"? All of the poem's attention to the speaker's reactions, reflections, and memories is intricately tied up with the particulars of setting. Making love in a junkyard is crucial to the speaker's sense of both power and wreckage, and Doris is merely a matter of excitement, adventure, and pretty skin, appreciated because she makes the world seem different and because she is willing to take risks and to suffer for meeting him like this. The more we probe the poem with questions about situation, the more likely we are to catch the poem's full effect.

Cherrylog Road is a fairly easy poem to read, but its effect is more complex than its simple story line suggests. The next poem we will look at is, at first glance, much more difficult to follow. Part of the difficulty is that the poem is from an earlier age, and its language is a little different, and part is because the action in the poem is so closely connected to what is being said. But its opening lines— addressed to someone who is resisting the speaker's suggestions— disclose the situation, and gradually we can figure out the scene: a man is trying to convince a woman that they should make love. When a flea happens by, the speaker uses it for an unlikely example as part of his argument. And once we recognize the situation, we can readily follow (and be amused by) the speaker's witty and intricate argument.

JOHN DONNE

The Flea

Mark but this flea, and mark in this[3]
How little that which thou deny'st me is;
It sucked me first, and now sucks thee,
And in this flea our two bloods mingled be;
Thou know'st that this cannot be said   5
A sin, nor shame, nor loss of maidenhead,
   Yet this enjoys before it woo,
   And pampered[4] swells with one blood made of two,
   And this, alas, is more than we would do.[5]

Oh stay, three lives in one flea spare,   10
Where we almost, yea more than, married are.
This flea is you and I, and this
Our marriage bed, and marriage temple is;
Though parents grudge, and you, we're met
And cloistered in these living walls of jet.   15
   Though use[6] make you apt to kill me,
   Let not to that, self-murder added be,
   And sacrilege, three sins in killing three.

Cruel and sudden, hast thou since
Purpled thy nail in blood of innocence?   20
Wherein could this flea guilty be,
Except in that drop which it sucked from thee?
Yet thou triumph'st, and say'st that thou
Find'st not thyself, nor me, the weaker now;
   'Tis true; then learn how false, fears be;   25
   Just so much honor, when thou yield'st to me,
   Will waste, as this flea's death took life from thee.

1633

The scene in *The Flea* develops almost as in a play. Action even
occurs right along with the words. Between stanzas 1 and 2, the
woman makes a move to kill the flea (as stanza 2 opens, the speaker
is trying to stop her), and between stanzas 2 and 3 the woman
has squished the flea with her fingernail. Once we try to make sense
of what the speaker says, the action is just as clear from the words
as if we had stage directions in the margin. All of the speaker's
verbal cleverness and all of his specious arguments follow from the
situation, and in this poem (as in *Soliloquy of the Spanish Cloister*

3. Medieval preachers and rhetoricians
asked their hearers to "mark" (look at) an
object which illustrated a moral or philosophical lesson they wished to emphasize.
4. Fed luxuriously.

5. According to contemporary medical
theory, conception involved the literal
mingling of the lovers' blood.
6. Habit.

or *In Westminster Abbey*) we watch as if we were observing a scene on the stage. The speaker is, in effect, giving a dramatic monologue for our benefit. (You may have noticed that in seduction poems, the seducer usually does all the talking and the seducer seldom gets a chance to speak; for some amusing inversions (reversals) of this pattern, and some witty variations on it, see the group of poems on pp. 799–801).

Neither time nor place is important to *The Flea*, except in the sense that the speaker and his friend have to be assumed to be in the same place and have the leisure for some playfulness. The situation could occur in any place where a man, a woman, and a flea could be together. Indoors, outdoors, morning, evening, city, country, it is all one; the situation could occur in cottage or palace, on a boat or in a bedroom. We do know, from the date of publication of the poem (1633), that the poet was writing about people of more than three centuries ago, but the conduct he describes might equally happen in later ages just as well. Only the habits of language (and perhaps the speaker's religious attitudes) date the poem; the situation could equally be set in any age or place.

Some poems, are, however, specifically **referential** about time or place; that is, they refer to a certain actual place and time. The following poem depends upon historical information (it also assumes that we know the terminology of children's games); if you don't know the history of atomic warfare, you may want to read the footnote before you read the poem.

ROBERT FROST

U. S. 1946 King's X[7]

Having invented a new Holocaust,
And been the first with it to win a war,
How they make haste to cry with fingers crossed,
King's X—no fairs to use it any more!

p. 1946

Our knowledge of the relevant historical facts does not necessarily mean that we will agree with the poet's criticism of U. S. policy at

---

7. Shortly after exploding the two atomic bombs that ended World War II, the United States proposed to share nuclear information with other countries in exchange for an agreement that the information would be used only for peaceful purposes. In children's games, time out is sometimes signaled by crossing fingers and saying "King's X."

the end of World War II, but we certainly can't understand or appreciate the poem's equation of nuclear policy with a child's fear of consequence unless we do know the facts. Often it is hard to place ourselves fully enough in another time or place to imagine sympathetically what a particular historical moment would have been like, and even the best poetic efforts do not necessarily transport us there. But poets sometimes record a particular moment or event in order to commemorate it or comment upon it. A poem written about a specific occasion is usually called an **occasional poem,** and such a poem is **referential;** that is, it refers to a specific historical moment or event. For such poems we need, at the least, specific historical information—plus a willingness on our part as readers to be transported imaginatively to that particular time, sometimes (as in *U. S. 1946 King's X*) by mentioning explicitly a particular time, sometimes by recreating that moment in a dramatic situation. The poems about World War I on pp. 787–791 suggest something of the range of problems involved in reading consciously historical and referential poetry.

Time or place may, of course, be used much less specifically and still be important to a poem, and the most common uses of setting involve drawing upon common notions of a particular time or place. Setting a poem in a garden, for example, or writing about apples almost inevitably reminds us of the Garden of Eden because it is part of our common heritage of belief or knowledge. Even people who don't read at all or who lack Judaeo-Christian religious commitments are likely to know about Eden, and a poet writing in our culture can count on that. In Joni Mitchell's *Woodstock* (p. 564), for example (as we noticed in Chapter 2) the idea of the innocence in Woodstock is drawn into the poem by an allusion to Eden; the final refrain in each stanza of the poem insists that "we've got to get ourselves / Back to the garden." An **allusion** is a reference to something outside the poem that carries a history of meaning and strong emotional associations. For example, gardens may carry suggestions of innocence and order, or temptation and the fall, or both, depending on how the poem handles the allusion. Well-known places from history or myth may be popularly associated with particular ideas or values or ways of life.

The place involved in a poem is its **spatial setting,** and the time is its **temporal setting.** The temporal setting may involve a specific date or an era, a season of the year or a time of day. We tend, for example, to think of spring as a time of discovery and growth, and poems set in spring are likely to draw upon that association; morning usually suggests discovery as well—beginnings, vitality, the world fresh and new—even to those of us who in reality take our waking slow. Temporal or spatial setting are often used to influence our expectation of theme and tone in a specific way, although the poet may then go on to surprise us by making something very different of our expectation. Setting is often an important factor in creating the mood in poems just as in stories, plays, or films. Often the details of setting have a lot to do with the way we ultimately respond to the poem's subject or theme, as in this poem:

SYLVIA PLATH

Point Shirley

From Water-Tower Hill to the brick prison
The shingle booms, bickering under
The sea's collapse.
Snowcakes break and welter. This year
The gritted wave leaps   5
The seawall and drops onto a bier
Of quahog chips,[8]
Leaving a salty mash of ice to whiten

In my grandmother's sand yard. She is dead,
Whose laundry snapped and froze here, who   10
Kept house against
What the sluttish, rutted sea could do.
Squall waves once danced
Ship timbers in through the cellar window;
A thresh-tailed, lanced   15
Shark littered in the geranium bed—

Such collusion of mulish elements
She wore her broom straws to the nub.
Twenty years out
Of her hand; the house still hugs in each drab   20
Stucco socket
The purple egg-stones: from Great Head's knob
To the filled-in Gut
The sea in its cold gizzard ground those rounds.

Nobody wintering now behind   25
The planked-up windows where she set
Her wheat loaves
And apple cakes to cool. What is it
Survives, grieves
So, over this battered, obstinate spit   30
Of gravel? The waves'
Spewed relics clicker masses in the wind,

Gray waves the stub-necked eiders ride.
A labor of love, and that labor lost.
Steadily the sea   35
Eats at Point Shirley. She died blessed,
And I come by
Bones, bones only, pawed and tossed,
A dog-faced sea.
The sun sinks under Boston, bloody red.   40

8. Chips from quahog clam shells, common on the New England coast.

I would get from these dry-papped stones
The milk your love instilled in them.
The black ducks dive.
And though your graciousness might stream,
And I contrive,   45
Grandmother, stones are nothing of home
To that spumiest dove.
Against both bar and tower the black sea runs.

                                                        1960

One does not have to know the New England coast by personal
experience to have it vividly recalled by Plath's poem. A reader who
knows that coast or another like it may have an advantage in being
able to respond more quickly to the poem's precision of description,
but the poem does not depend on such knowledge from outside the
poem. The precise location of Point Shirley, near Boston, is not especially important, but visualization of the setting is. Crucial to the poem's
tone and mood is the sense of the sea as aggressor, a force powerful
enough to change the contours of the coast and invade the privacy of
yards and homes. The energy, relentlessness, and impersonality of the
sea met their match, though a temporary one, in the speaker's grandmother who "Kept house against / What the sluttish, rutted sea could
do" (lines 11–12). The grandmother *belonged* in this setting, and it
seemed hers, but twenty years of her absence (since her death) now
begin to show. Still, the marks of her obstinacy and love are there,
although ultimately doomed by the sea's more enduring power.

Details—and how they are amassed—are important here rather than
historic particulars of time and place. The grays and whites and drab
colors of the sea and its leavings provide both a visual sense of the
scene and the mood for the poem. The stubbornness which the
speaker admired in the grandmother comes to seem a part of that
tenacious grayness. Nothing happens rapidly here; things wear down.
Even the "bloody red" (line 40) of the sun's setting—an ominous sign
that adds a vivid fright to the dullness rather than brightening it—
makes promises that seem slow and long-term. The toughness of the
boarded-up house is a monument to the grandmother's loving care
and becomes a way for the speaker to touch her human spirit, but
the poem's final emphasis is on the relentless black sea which continues
to run against the landmarks and fortresses that had been identified
with the setting in the very first line.

Questions about situation and setting begin as simple questions of
identification but often become more complex when we sort out all
the implications. Often it takes only a moment to determine a poem's
situation, but it may take much longer to discover all of the things
that time and place imply, for their meanings may depend upon
visual details, or upon actual historical occurrences, or upon habitual
ways of thinking about certain times and places—or all three at once.

As you read the following poem, notice how the setting—another shore—prepares us for the speaker's moods and ideas, and then watch how the movement of his mind is affected by what he sees.

MATTHEW ARNOLD

Dover Beach[9]

The sea is calm tonight.
The tide is full, the moon lies fair
Upon the straits; on the French coast the light
Gleams and is gone; the cliffs of England stand,
Glimmering and vast, out in the tranquil bay.   5
Come to the window, sweet is the night-air!
Only, from the long line of spray
Where the sea meets the moon-blanched land,
Listen! you hear the grating roar
Of pebbles which the waves draw back, and fling,   10
At their return, up the high strand,
Begin, and cease, and then again begin,
With tremulous cadence slow, and bring
The eternal note of sadness in.

Sophocles long ago   15
Heard it on the Aegean, and it brought
Into his mind the turbid ebb and flow
Of human misery;[1] we
Find also in the sound a thought,
Hearing it by this distant northern sea.   20

The Sea of Faith
Was once, too, at the full, and round earth's shore
Lay like the folds of a bright girdle furled.
But now I only hear
Its melancholy, long, withdrawing roar,   25
Retreating, to the breath
Of the night-wind, down the vast edges drear
And naked shingles[2] of the world.

Ah, love, let us be true
To one another! for the world, which seems   30
To lie before us like a land of dreams,
So various, so beautiful, so new,

---

9. At the narrowest point on the English Channel. The lights on the French coast (lines 3–4) would be about 20 miles away.
1. In *Antigone*, lines 583–91, the chorus

compares the fate of the house of Oedipus to the waves of the sea.
2. Pebble-strewn beaches.

Hath really neither joy, nor love, nor light,
Nor certitude, nor peace, nor help for pain;
And we are here as on a darkling plain   35
Swept with confused alarms of struggle and flight,
Where ignorant armies clash by night.

ca. 1851

Exactly what is the dramatic situation in *Dover Beach*? How soon
are you aware that someone is being spoken to? How much are we
told about the person spoken to? How would you describe the speaker's mood? What does the speaker's mood have to do with time and
place? Do any details of present place and time help to account for
his tendency to talk repeatedly of the past and the future? How
important is it to the poem's total effect that the beach here involves
an international border? What particulars of the Dover Beach seem
especially important to the poem's themes? to its emotional effects?

Not all poems have an identifiable situation or setting, just as not
all poems have a speaker that is distinct from the author. Poems that
simply present a series of thoughts and feelings directly, in a con-
templative, meditative, or reflective way, may not set up any kind of
action, plot, or situation at all, preferring to speak directly without the
intermediary of a dramatic device. But most poems depend crucially
upon a sense of place, a sense of time, and an understanding of human
interaction in scenes that resemble the strategies of drama or film.
And questions about these matters will often lead you to define not
only the "facts" but also the feelings central to a poem's design upon us.

ROBERT BROWNING

My Last Duchess

Ferrara[3]

That's my last Duchess painted on the wall,
Looking as if she were alive. I call
That piece a wonder, now: Frà Pandolf's hands[4]
Worked busily a day, and there she stands.
Will't please you sit and look at her? I said   5
"Frà Pandolf" by design, for never read
Strangers like you that pictured countenance,

3. Alfonso II, Duke of Ferrara in Italy
in the mid-16th century, is the presumed
speaker of the poem, which is loosely based
on historical events. The Duke's first wife
—whom he had married when she was 14
—died under suspicious circumstances at
17, and he then negotiated through an
agent (to whom the poem is spoken) for
the hand of the niece of the Count of
Tyrol in Austria.
    4. Frà Pandolf is, like Claus (line 56),
fictitious.

The depth and passion of its earnest glance,
But to myself they turned (since none puts by
The curtain I have drawn for you, but I)   10
And seemed as they would ask me, if they durst,
How such a glance came there; so, not the first
Are you to turn and ask thus. Sir, 'twas not
Her husband's presence only, called that spot
Of joy into the Duchess' cheek: perhaps   15
Frà Pandolf chanced to say "Her mantle laps
Over my lady's wrist too much," or "Paint
Must never hope to reproduce the faint
Half-flush that dies along her throat": such stuff
Was courtesy, she thought, and cause enough   20
For calling up that spot of joy. She had
A heart—how shall I say?—too soon made glad,
Too easily impressed; she liked whate'er
She looked on, and her looks went everywhere.
Sir, 'twas all one! My favor at her breast,   25
The dropping of the daylight in the West,
The bough of cherries some officious fool
Broke in the orchard for her, the white mule
She rode with round the terrace—all and each
Would draw from her alike the approving speech,   30
Or blush, at least. She thanked men,—good! but thanked
Somehow—I know not how—as if she ranked
My gift of a nine-hundred-years-old name
With anybody's gift. Who'd stoop to blame
This sort of trifling? Even had you skill   35
In speech—which I have not—to make your will
Quite clear to such an one, and say, "Just this
Or that in you disgusts me; here you miss,
Or there exceed the mark"—and if she let
Herself be lessoned so, nor plainly set   40
Her wits to yours, forsooth, and made excuse,
—E'en then would be some stooping; and I choose
Never to stoop. Oh sir, she smiled, no doubt,
Whene'er I passed her; but who passed without
Much the same smile? This grew; I gave commands;   45
Then all smiles stopped together. There she stands
As if alive. Will't please you rise? We'll meet
The company below, then. I repeat,
The Count your master's known munificence
Is ample warrant that no just pretense   50
Of mine for dowry will be disallowed;
Though his fair daughter's self, as I avowed
At starting, is my object. Nay, we'll go
Together down, sir. Notice Neptune, though,
Taming a sea-horse, thought a rarity,   55
Which Claus of Innsbruck cast in bronze for me!

1842

JOHN DONNE

A Valediction: Forbidding Mourning

As virtuous men pass mildly away,
  And whisper to their souls to go,
Whilst some of their sad friends do say,
  "The breath goes now," and some say, "No,"

So let us melt, and make no noise,   5
  No tear floods, nor sigh-tempests move;
'Twere profanation of our joys
  To tell the laity our love.

Moving of the earth[5] brings harms and fears,
  Men reckon what it did and meant;   10
But trepidation of the spheres,[6]
  Though greater far, is innocent.

Dull sublunary[7] lovers' love
  (Whose soul is sense) cannot admit
Absence, because it doth remove   15
  Those things which elemented[8] it.

But we, by a love so much refined
  That our selves know not what it is,
Inter-assured of the mind,
  Care less, eyes, lips, and hands to miss.   20

Our two souls therefore, which are one,
  Though I must go, endure not yet
A breach, but an expansion,
  Like gold to airy thinness beat.

If they be two, they are two so   25
  As stiff twin compasses are two:
Thy soul, the fixed foot, makes no show
  To move, but doth, if the other do;

And though it in the center sit,
  Yet when the other far doth roam,   30
It leans, and hearkens after it,
  And grows erect, as that comes home.

---

5. Earthquakes.
6. The Renaissance hypothesis that the celestial spheres trembled and thus caused unexpected variations in their orbits. Such movements are "innocent" because earthlings do not observe or fret about them.
7. Below the moon; i.e., changeable.

According to the traditional cosmology which Donne invokes here, the moon was considered the dividing line between the immutable celestial world and the earthly mortal one.
8. Comprised.

Such wilt thou be to me, who must,
    Like the other foot, obliquely run;
Thy firmness makes my circle[9] just,   35
    And makes me end where I begun.

1611(?)

JAROLD RAMSEY

Lupine Dew[1]

For Sophia

That summer, you were game for anything.
Someday, stepping out of the rectilinear shade
of a building, bearing your own share of Atlas's burden,[2]
the stone cocoon of the world,
may you remember how we left the others   5
swigging canteen water under a juniper
to close the gate at the head of Garrett Canyon.[3]
Hot, too hot for purposes—
we played we were deer, breaking from willow to willow
shade and dazzle and dappled shade again,   10
until we sprawled in a bower.
There you drank the gems of dew on a purple lupine,
leaves and flower, and I told you
"Those who drink the lupine dew at noon
turn into many things, child, in the sun."   15
"Well then," you said, "I'll be a butterfly."
And when in a moment a lusty Monarch
veered at us through the boughs
you cried, "So long, Dad, I'm off and away!"
And you were a butterfly, remember,   20
oh remember, all that day.

p. 1979

GALWAY KINNELL

To Christ our Lord

The legs of the elk punctured the snow's crust
And wolves floated lightfooted on the land

---

9. A traditional symbol of perfection.
1. The lupine plant is a member of the genus *lupinus*, literally meaning wolflike; the plant was so named because of the ancient belief that it destroyed the soil. There are many other legends about the power of the plant.
2. In Greek mythology, Atlas was condemned to uphold the heavens on his shoulders.
3. In the state of Oregon.

Hunting Christmas elk living and frozen;
Inside snow melted in a basin, and a woman basted
A bird spread over coals by its wings and head.   5

Snow had sealed the windows; candles lit
The Christmas meal. The Christmas grace chilled
The cooked bird, being long-winded and the room cold.
During the words a boy thought, it is fitting
To eat this creature killed on the wing?   10

He had killed it himself, climbing out
Alone on snowshoes in the Christmas dawn,
The fallen snow swirling and the snowfall gone,
Heard its throat scream as the rifle shouted,
Watched it drop, and fished from the snow the dead.   15

He had not wanted to shoot. The sound
Of wings beating into the hushed air
Had stirred his love, and his fingers
Froze in his gloves, and he wondered,
Famishing, could he fire? Then he fired.   20

Now the grace praised his wicked act. At its end
The bird on the plate
Stared at his stricken appetite.
There had been nothing to do but surrender,
To kill and to eat; he ate as he had killed, with wonder.   25

At night on snowshoes on the drifting field
He wondered again, for whom had love stirred?
The stars glittered on the snow and nothing answered.
Then the Swan spread her wings, cross of the cold north,
The pattern and mirror of the acts of earth.   30

1960

ANNE SEXTON

The Truth the Dead Know

*for my mother, born March 1902, died March 1959
and my father, born February 1900, died June 1959*

Gone, I say and walk from church,
refusing the stiff procession to the grave,
letting the dead ride alone in the hearse.
It is June. I am tired of being brave.

We drive to the Cape.[4] I cultivate   5

4. Cape Cod, in Massachusetts.

myself where the sun gutters from the sky,
where the sea swings in like an iron gate
and we touch. In another country people die.

My darling, the wind falls in like stones
from the whitehearted water and when we touch   10
we enter touch entirely. No one's alone.
Men kill for this, or for as much.

And what of the dead? They lie without shoes
in their stone boats. They are more like stone
than the sea would be if it stopped. They refuse   15
to be blessed, throat, eye and knucklebone.

                                                        1962

DONALD JUSTICE

Here in Katmandu[5]

We have climbed the mountain,
There's nothing more to do.
It is terrible to come down
To the valley
Where, amidst many flowers,   5
One thinks of snow,

As, formerly, amidst snow,
Climbing the mountain,
One thought of flowers,
Tremulous, ruddy with dew,   10
In the valley.
One caught their scent coming down.

It is difficult to adjust, once down,
To the absence of snow.
Clear days, from the valley,   15
One looks up at the mountain.
What else is there to do?
Prayerwheels, flowers!

Let the flowers
Fade, the prayerwheels run down.   20
What have these to do
With us who have stood atop the snow
Atop the mountain,
Flags seen from the valley?

It might be possible to live in the valley,   25
To bury oneself among flowers,

5. The capital city of Nepal, about 100 miles west of Mt. Everest.

If one could forget the mountain,
How, setting out before dawn,
Blinded with snow,
One knew what to do.   30

Meanwhile it is not easy here in Katmandu,
Especially when to the valley
That wind which means snow
Elsewhere, but here means flowers,
Comes down,   35
As soon it must, from the mountain.

                                                              1960

5   WORDS

Fiction and drama depend upon language just as poetry does, but in
a poem almost everything comes down to words. In stories and plays,
we are likely to keep our attention primarily on narrative and plot—
what is happening in front of us or in the action as we imagine it in
our minds—and although words are crucial to how we imagine the
characters and how we respond to what happens to them, we are
less likely to pause over any one word as we may need to in a poem.
Besides, poems often are short and use only a few words, so a lot depends on every single one. Poetry sometimes feels like prose that is
distilled: only the most essential words are there, just barely
enough so that we communicate in the most basic way, using the most
elemental signs of meaning and feeling—and each one chosen for
exactly the right shade of meaning. But elemental does not necessarily
mean simple, and these signs may be very rich in their meanings and
complex in their effects.

Let's look first at two poems, each of which depends heavily upon a
single key word.

RICHARD ARMOUR

Hiding Place

A speaker at a meeting of the New York State Frozen Food Locker Association
declared that the best hiding place in event of an atomic explosion is a frozen-
food locker, where "radiation will not penetrate."[1]   NEWS ITEM.

    Move over, ham
    And quartered cow,
    My Geiger[2] says
    The time is now.

1. Before home freezers became popular,   2. Geiger counter: used to detect radia-
many Americans rented lockers in specially   tion.
equipped commercial buildings.

                    Yes, now I lay me   5
                    Down to sleep,
                  And if I die,
                    At least I'll keep.

                                                                    1954

YVOR WINTERS

At the San Francisco Airport

              To my daughter, 1954

This is the terminal: the light
Gives perfect vision, false and hard;
The metal glitters, deep and bright.
Great planes are waiting in the yard—
They are already in the night.   5

And you are here beside me, small,
Contained and fragile, and intent
On things that I but half recall—
Yet going whither you are bent.
I am the past, and that is all.   10

But you and I in part are one:
The frightened brain, the nervous will,
The knowledge of what must be done,
The passion to acquire the skill
To face that which you dare not shun.   15

The rain of matter upon sense
Destroys me momently. The score:
There comes what will come. The expense
Is what one thought, and something more—
One's being and intelligence.   20

This is the terminal, the break.
Beyond this point, on lines of air,
You take the way that you must take;
And I remain in light and stare—
In light, and nothing else, awake.   25

1954

In *Hiding Place*, almost all the poem's comedy depends on the final
word, "keep." In the child's prayer which the poem echoes, to "pray
the Lord my soul to keep" does not exactly involve cold storage, and
so the poem depends upon an outrageous double meaning. The key
word is chosen because it can mean more than one thing; in this case,
the importance of the word involves its **ambiguity** (an ability to mean

more than one thing) rather than its **precision** (exactness).

In the second poem, the several possible meanings of a single word are probed more soberly and thoughtfully. What does it *mean* to be in a place called a "terminal"? the poem asks. As the parting of father and daughter is explored, carefully, the place of parting and the means of transportation begin to take on meanings larger than their simple referential ones. The poem is full of contrasts—young and old, light and dark, past and present, security and adventure—as the parting of generations is pondered. The father ("I am the past," line 10) remains in the light, among known objects and experience familiar to his many years; the daughter is about to depart into the night, the unknown, the uncertain future. But they both share a sense of the necessity of the parting, of the need for the daughter to mature, gain knowledge, acquire experience. Is she going off to school? to college? to her first job? The specifics are not given, but her plane ride clearly means a new departure and a clean break with childhood, dependency, the past.

So much depends upon the meanings of "terminal." It is the airport building, of course, but it also implies a boundary, an extremity, an end, something that is limited, a place where a connection is broken. The clear, crisp meanings of other words are important too. The words "break," "point," "lines," "way," and "remain" all express literally and sharply what the event means. The final stanza of the poem is full of words that state flatly and **denote** exactly, as if the speaker has recovered completely from the momentary confusion of stanza 4, when "being and intelligence" are lost in the emotion of the parting itself. The crisp articulation of the last stanza puts an almost total emphasis on the precise meaning of each word, its **denotation**, what it precisely denotes or refers to. The words "break," "point," "way," and "remain" are almost completely unemotional and colorless; they do not make value judgments or offer personal views, but rather define and describe. It is as if the speaker is trying to disengage himself from the emotion of the situation and just give the facts.

Words, however, are more than hard blocks of meaning on whose sense everyone agrees. They also have a more personal side, and they carry emotional force and shades of suggestion. The words we use indicate not only what we mean but how we feel about it, and we choose words that we hope will carry a persuasive emotional engagement with others, in conversation and daily usage as well as in poems. A person who holds office is, quite literally (and unemotionally), an "officeholder," a word that clearly denotes what he or she does. But if we want to convince someone that an officeholder is wise, trustworthy, and deserving of political support we may call that person a "political leader" or perhaps a "statesman"; whereas if we want to promote distrust or contempt of officeholders we might call them "politicians" or "bureaucrats" or "political hacks." These latter words have clear **connotations**—suggestions of emotional coloration that imply our attitude and invite a similar one on the part of our hearers. What words **connote** can be just as important to a poem as what they denote, although some poems depend primarily on denotation and some more on connotation.

At the San Francisco Airport seems to depend primarily on denotation; the speaker tries to *specify* the meanings and implications of the parting with his daughter, and his tendency to split categories neatly for the two of them at first contributes to the sense of clarity and certainty which the speaker wants to project. He is the past (line 10) and what remains (line 24); he has age and experience, his life is the known quantity, he stands in the light. She, on the other hand, is committed to the adventure of going into the night; she seems small, fragile, and her identity exists in the uncertain future. Yet the connotations of some words carry strong emotional force as well as clear definition: that the daughter seems "small" and "fragile" to the speaker suggests his fear for her, something quite different from her sense of adventure. The neat, clean categories keep breaking down, and the speaker's feelings keep showing through. In stanza 1, the speaker tells us that the light in the terminal gives "perfect vision" but he also notices, indirectly, its artificial quality: it is "false" and "hard," suggesting the limits of the rationalism he tries to maintain. That artificial light shines over most of the poem and honors the speaker's effort, but the whole poem represents his struggle, and in stanza 4 the signals of disturbance are very strong as, despite an insistence on a vocabulary of calculation, his rational facade collapses completely. If we have observed his verbal strategies carefully, we should not be surprised to find him at the end just *staring* in the artificial light, merely awake, although the poem has shown him to be unconsciously awake to much more than he will candidly admit.

At the San Francisco Airport is an unusually intricate and complicated poem, and it offers us, if we are willing to examine very precisely its carefully crafted fabric, an unusually rich insight into how complex a thing it is to be human and have human feelings and foibles when we think we must be rational machines. Connotations often work more simply. The following poem, for example, even though it describes the mixed feelings one person has about another, depends heavily on the common connotations of fairly common words.

WALTER DE LA MARE

Slim Cunning Hands

Slim cunning hands at rest, and cozening eyes—
Under this stone one loved too wildly lies;
How false she was, no granite could declare;
    Nor all earth's flowers, how fair.

1950

What the speaker in *Slim Cunning Hands* remembers about the dead woman—her hands, her eyes—tells part of the story; her physical presence was clearly important to him, and the poem's other nouns—

stone, granite, flowers—all remind us of her death and its finality. All these words denote objects having to do with rituals that memorialize a departed life. Granite and stone connote finality as well, and flowers connote fragility and suggest the shortness of life (which is why they have become the symbolic language of funerals). The way the speaker talks about the woman expresses, in just a few words, how complexly he feels about his love for her. She was loved, he says, too "wildly"—by him perhaps, and by others. The excitement she offered is suggested by the word, and also the lack of control. The words "cunning" and "cozening" help us interpret both her wildness and falsity; they suggest her calculation, cleverness, and untrustworthiness as well as her skill, persuasiveness, and ability to place. And the word "fair," a simple yet very inclusive word, suggests how totally attractive the speaker finds her: her beauty is just as incapable of being expressed by flowers as her fickleness is of being expressed in something as permanent as stone. Simple words here tell us perhaps all we need to know of a long story.

Words like "fair" and "cozening" are clearly loaded: they have strong, clear connotations and tell us what to think, what evaluation to make. The connotations may also suggest or imply the basis for the evaluation. In the two poems that follow we can readily see why the specific words are chosen because, although both poems express a preference for the same sort of feminine appearance, the grounds of appeal are vastly different.

BEN JONSON

Still to Be Neat[3]

Still[4] to be neat, still to be dressed,
As you were going to a feast;
Still to be powdered, still perfumed;
Lady, it is to be presumed,
Though art's hid causes are not found,   5
All is not sweet, all is not sound.

Give me a look, give me a face
That makes simplicity a grace;
Robes loosely flowing, hair as free;
Such sweet neglect more taketh me   10
Than all th' adulteries of art.
They strike mine eyes, but not my heart.

1609

---

3. A song from Jonson's play, *The Silent Woman.*   4. Continually.

ROBERT HERRICK

Delight in Disorder

A sweet disorder in the dress
Kindles in clothes a wantonness.
A lawn[5] about the shoulders thrown
Into a fine distractiön;
An erring lace, which here and there   5
Enthralls the crimson stomacher,[6]
A cuff neglectful, and thereby
Ribbands[7] to flow confusedly;
A winning wave, deserving note,
In the tempestuous petticoat;   10
A careless shoestring, in whose tie
I see a wild civility;
Do more bewitch me than when art
Is too precise[8] in every part.

1648

The poem *Still to Be Neat* begins by describing a woman who looks too neat and orderly; she seems too perfect to be believed, the speaker says, and he has to assume that there is a reason for such overly fastidious grooming, that she is covering up something. He worries that something is wrong underneath—that not all is "sweet" and "sound." "Sweet" could mean several possible things, and its meaning becomes clearer when it is repeated in the next stanza in a more specific context. But "sound" begins to suggest the speaker's moral earnestness: it is a strong word, implying a suspicion that something is deeply wrong.

When "sweet" is repeated in line 10, it has taken on specific attributes from what the speaker has said about things he likes in a less calculated physical appearance. Now it appears to mean easy, attractive, unpremeditated. And when the speaker springs "adulteries" on us in the next line as a description of the woman's cosmeticizing, it is clear what he fears—that the appearance of the too neat, too made-up woman covers serious flaws, things which try to make her appear someone she is not. "Adulteries" suggests the addition of something foreign, something unlike her own nature, and it is a strong, disapproving word. The "soundness" he had worried about involves her integrity; his objection is certainly moral, probably sexual. He wants his women simple and chaste; he wants them to be just what they seem to be.

The speaker in *Delight in Disorder* wants his women easy and sim-

---

5. Scarf of fine linen.
6. Ornamental covering for the breasts.
7. Ribbons.

8. In the 16th and 17th centuries Puritans were often called Precisians because of their fastidiousness.

ple too, but for different reasons. He finds disorder "sweet" too (line 1), and seems almost to be answering the first speaker, providing a different rationale for artless appearance. His grounds of preference are clear early: his support of "wantonness" (line 2) is close to the opposite in its moral suppositions of the first speaker's disapproval of "adulteries." This speaker wants a careless look because he thinks it's sexy, and many of the words he chooses suggest sensuality and availability: "distraction" (line 4), "erring" (line 5), "tempestuous" (line 10), "wild" (line 12). The speakers in the two poems read informality of dress very differently and have very different expectations of the person who dresses in a particular way. We find out quite a lot about each speaker. Their common subject allows us to see clearly how different they both are, and how what one sees is in the eye of the beholder, how values and assumptions are built into the words one chooses even for description. Jonson has created a speaker who wants an informally clad woman who has a natural grace and ease of manner because she is confident of herself, dependable, and chaste. Herrick has created a speaker who finds informality of dress fetching and sexy and indicative of sensuality and availability.

It would be hard to exaggerate how important words are to poems. Poets who know their craft pick each word with care, so that each word will express exactly what needs to be expressed and suggest every emotional shade that the poem is calculated to evoke in us. Often individual words qualify and amplify one another—suggestions clarify other suggestions, and meanings grow upon meanings—and thus the way the words are put together can be important too. Notice, for example, that in *Slim Cunning Hands* the final emphasis is on how *fair* the speaker's woman was; that is his last word, the thing he can't forget in spite of his distrust of her, and that is where the poem chooses to leave the emphasis, on that one word which, even though it doesn't justify everything else, qualifies all the disappointment and hurt.

That word does not stand all by itself, however, any more than any other word in a poem can be considered all alone. Every word exists within larger units of meaning—sentences, patterns of comparisons and contrasts, the whole poem—and where the word is and how it is used often are very important. The final word or words may be especially emphatic (as in *Slim Cunning Hands*), and words that are repeated take on a special intensity, as "terminal" does in *At the San Francisco Airport* or as "chartered" and "cry" do in *London,* a poem we looked at in Chapter 2. Certain words often stand out, because they are used in an unusual way (like "chartered" in *London* or "adulteries" in *Still To Be Neat*) or because they are given an artificial prominence, through unusual sentence structure, for example, or because the title calls special attention to them. In the following poem, notice how the title calls upon us to wonder, from the beginning, how playful and how patterned the boy's bedtime romp with his father is. As you read it, try to be conscious of the emotional effects created by the choice of words that seem to be key ones. Which words establish the bond between the two males?

THEODORE ROETHKE

My Papa's Waltz

The whiskey on your breath
Could make a small boy dizzy;
But I hung on like death:
Such waltzing was not easy.

We romped until the pans   5
Slid from the kitchen shelf;
My mother's countenance
Could not unfrown itself.

The hand that held my wrist
Was battered on one knuckle;   10
At every step you missed
My right ear scraped a buckle.

You beat time on my head
With a palm caked hard by dirt,
Then waltzed me off to bed   15
Still clinging to your shirt.

1948

Exactly what is the situation in *My Papa's Waltz*? What are the economic circumstances in the family? How can you tell? What indications are there of the family's social class? of the father's line of work? How would you characterize the speaker? How does the poem indicate his pleasure in the bedtime ritual? Which words suggest the boy's excitement? Which suggest his anxiety? How can you tell how the speaker feels about his father? What clues are there about what the mother is like? How can you tell that the experience is remembered at some years' distance? What clues are there in the word choice that an adult is remembering a childhood experience? In what sense is the poem a tribute to memories of the father? How would you describe the poem's tone?

The subtlety and force of word choice is sometimes very much affected by **word order**, the way the sentences are put together. Sometimes poems are driven to unusual word order because of the demands of rhyme and meter, but ordinarily poets use word order very much as prose writers do, to create a particular emphasis. When an unusual word order is used, you can be pretty sure that something worth noticing is going on. Notice, for example, the odd constructions in the second and third stanzas of *My Papa's Waltz*. In the third stanza, the way the speaker talks about the abrasion of buckle on ear is very unusual. He does not say that the buckle scraped his ear, but rather puts it the other way round—a big difference in the kind of effect created, for it avoids placing blame and refuses to specify any unpleasant effect. Had he said that the buckle scraped his ear—the normal way of putting it—we would have to worry about the fragile ear. The syntax (sentence structure) of the poem channels our feeling and helps to control what we think of the waltz.

The most curious part of the poem is the second stanza, for it is there that the silent mother appears, and the syntax there is peculiar in two places. In lines 5–6, the connection between the romping and the pans falling is stated oddly: "We romped *until* the pans / Slid from the kitchen shelf." The speaker does not say that they knocked down the pans or imply that there was awkwardness, but he does suggest energetic activity and duration. He implies intensity, almost design—as though the romping were not complete until the pans fell. And the sentence about the mother—odd but effective—makes her position clear. She is a silent bystander in this male ritual, and her frown seems molded on her face. It is not as if she is frightened or angry but as if she too is performing a ritual, holding a frown on her face as if it is part of her role in the ritual, as well as perhaps a facet of her stern character. The syntax implies that she *has to* maintain the frown, and the falling of the pans almost seems to be for her benefit. She disapproves, but she is still their audience.

Word order is not always as complicated or crucial as it is in *My Papa's Waltz*, but poets often manipulate the ordinary prose order of a sentence to make a specific point or create a specific emphasis or effect. In the passage below (pp. 646–649) from *Paradise Lost*, for example, notice how the syntax first sets a formal tone for the passage, then calls attention to the complexities of theology which it expresses, and (in lines 44ff.) imitates, by holding back key elements of the grammar, the fall that is being described. The poems that follow suggest some of the ways in which poets use words and word order to create for us the various experiences they want us to have of their words.

GERARD MANLEY HOPKINS

Pied Beauty[9]

Glory be to God for dappled things—
  For skies of couple-color as a brinded[1] cow;
    For rose-moles all in stipple[2] upon trout that swim;
Fresh-firecoal chestnut-falls;[3] finches' wings;
    Landscape plotted and pieced—fold, fallow, and plow;   5
      And all trades, their gear and tackle and trim.

9. Particolored beauty: having patches or sections of more than one color.
1. Streaked or spotted.
2. Rose-colored dots or flecks.
3. Fallen chestnuts as red as burning coals.

All things counter, original, spare, strange;
   Whatever is fickle, freckled (who knows how?)
    With swift, slow; sweet, sour; adazzle, dim;
He fathers-forth whose beauty is past change: 10
          Praise him.

1877

EMILY DICKINSON

After Great Pain

After great pain, a formal feeling comes—
The Nerves sit ceremonious, like Tombs—
The stiff Heart questions was it He, that bore,
And Yesterday, or Centuries before?

The Feet, mechanical, go round—   5
Of Ground, or Air, or Ought—
A Wooden way
Regardless grown,
A Quartz contentment, like a stone—

This is the Hour of Lead—   10
Remembered, if outlived,
As Freezing Persons recollect the Snow—
First—Chill—then Stupor—then the letting go—

ca. 1862

WILLIAM CARLOS WILLIAMS

The Red Wheelbarrow

so much depends
upon

a red wheel
barrow

glazed with rain   5
water

beside the white
chickens.

1923

ANN DEAGON

Certified Copy

I have xeroxed my navel
bare-bellied in the public library
borne on the hymeneal cries
of hysteric librarians, inserted a coin
prone on the glass slab steeled myself against   5
the green light's insolent stroke
and viewed emerging
instantaneously, parthenogenously from the slit
this reproduction of my reproduction
this evidence of my most human birth.   10

Archives forget, Bibles[4] prevaricate
aged witnesses from age grow witless—
only the skin remembers, swirling to clench
the archetypal wound: the center holds.[5]

1978

e. e. cummings

anyone lived in a pretty how town

anyone lived in a pretty how town
(with up so floating many bells down)
spring summer autumn winter
he sang his didn't he danced his did.

Women and men (both little and small)   5
cared for anyone not at all
they sowed their isn't they reaped their same
sun moon stars rain

children guessed (but only a few
and down they forgot as up they grew   10
autumn winter spring summer)
that noone loved him more by more

when by now and tree by leaf
she laughed his joy she cried his grief
bird by snow and stir by still   15
anyone's any was all to her

---

4. Genealogies in family Bibles.   823), line 3.
5. See Yeats's *The Second Coming*, (p.

someones married their everyones
laughed their cryings and did their dance
(sleep wake hope and then) they
said their nevers they slept their dream   20

stairs rain sun moon
(and only the snow can begin to explain
how children are apt to forget to remember
with up so floating many bells down)

one day anyone died i guess   25
(and noone stooped to kiss his face)
busy folk buried them side by side
little by little and was by was

all by all and deep by deep
and more by more they dream their sleep   30
noone and anyone earth by april
wish by spirit and if by yes.

Women and men (both dong and ding)
summer autumn winter spring
reaped their sowing and went their came   35
sun moon stars rain

                                                            1940

JOHN MILTON

from Paradise Lost[6]

I

Of man's first disobedience, and the fruit[7]
Of that forbidden tree whose mortal taste
Brought death into the world, and all our woe,
With loss of Eden, till one greater Man
Restore us, and regain the blissful seat,   5
Sing, Heav'nly Muse,[8] that, on the secret top
Of Oreb, or Sinai, didst inspire
That shepherd who first taught the chosen seed

6. The opening lines of Books I and II
and a short passage from Book III. The first
passage states the poem's subject, and the
second describes Satan's beginning address
to the council of fallen angels meeting to
discuss strategy; in the third, God is looking down from Heaven at his new human
creation and watching Satan approach the
Earth.
7. The apple, but also the consequences.
8. Addressing one of the muses and asking for aid is a convention for the opening
lines of an epic; Milton complicates the
standard procedure here by describing
sources and circumstances of Judeo-Chris-
tian revelation rather than specifically invoking one of the nine classical muses.
Sinai is the spur of Mount Oreb, where
Moses ("That shepherd," line 8, who was
traditionally regarded as author of the first
five books of the Bible) received the Law;
Sion hill and Siloa (lines 10–11), near
Jerusalem, correspond to the traditional
mountain (Helicon) and springs of classical
tradition. Later, in Book VII, Milton calls
upon Urania, the muse of astronomy, but
he does not mention by name the muse
of epic poetry, Calliope.

In the beginning how the Heav'ns and Earth
Rose out of Chaos: or, if Sion hill   10
Delight thee more, and Siloa's brook that flowed
Fast[9] by the oracle of God, I thence
Invoke thy aid to my adventurous song,
That with no middle flight intends to soar
Above th' Aonian mount,[1] while it pursues   15
Things unattempted yet in prose or rhyme.
And chiefly thou, O Spirit,[2] that dost prefer
Before all temples th' upright heart and pure,
Instruct me, for thou know'st; thou from the first
Wast present, and, with mighty wings outspread,   20
Dovelike sat'st brooding on the vast abyss,
And mad'st it pregnant: what in me is dark
Illumine; what is low, raise and support;
That, to the height of this great argument,[3]
I may assert Eternal Providence,   25
And justify the ways of God to men.
   Say first (for Heav'n hides nothing from thy view,
Nor the deep tract of Hell), say first what cause
Moved our grand parents, in that happy state,
Favored of Heav'n so highly, to fall off   30
From their Creator, and transgress his will
For[4] one restraint, lords of the world besides?
Who first seduced them to that foul revolt?
Th' infernal serpent; he it was, whose guile,
Stirred up with envy and revenge, deceived   35
The mother of mankind, what time[5] his pride
Had cast him out from Heav'n, with all his host
Of rebel angels, by whose aid, aspiring
To set himself in glory above his peers,
He trusted to have equaled the Most High,   40
If he opposed; and with ambitious aim
Against the throne and monarchy of God,
Raised impious war in Heav'n and battle proud,
With vain attempt. Him the Almighty Power
Hurled headlong flaming from th' ethereal sky,   45
With hideous ruin and combustion down
To bottomless perdition, there to dwell
In adamantine chains and penal fire,
Who durst defy th' Omnipotent to arms.[6]

* * *

---

9. Close.
1. Mt. Helicon, home of the classical muses.
2. The divine voice that inspired the Hebrew prophets. *Genesis* 1:2 says that "the Spirit of God moved upon the face of the waters" as part of the process of the original creation; Milton follows tradition in making the inspirational and communicative function of God present in creation itself. The passage echoes and merges many Biblical references to divine creation and revelation.
3. Subject.
4. Because of. "besides": in all other respects.
5. When.
6. After invoking the muse and giving a brief summary of the poem's subject, an epic regularly begins in *medias res* (in the midst of things).

II

High on a throne of royal state, which far
Outshone the wealth of Ormus and of Ind,[7]
Or where the gorgeous East with richest hand
Show'rs on her kings barbaric pearl and gold,
Satan exalted sat, by merit raised   5
To that bad eminence; and, from despair
Thus high uplifted beyond hope, aspires
Beyond thus high, insatiate to pursue
Vain war with Heav'n, and by success[8] untaught,
His proud imaginations thus displayed: 10
"Powers and Dominions, Deities of Heav'n,
For since no deep within her gulf can hold
Immortal vigor, though oppressed and fall'n,
I give not Heav'n for lost. From this descent
Celestial virtues rising will appear   15
More glorious and more dread than from no fall,
And trust themselves to fear no second fate.
Me though just right and the fixed laws of Heav'n
Did first create your leader, next, free choice,
With what besides, in council or in fight,   20
Hath been achieved of merit, yet this loss,
Thus far at least recovered, hath much more
Established in a safe unenvied throne
Yielded with full consent. The happier state
In Heav'n, which follows dignity, might draw   25
Envy from each inferior; but who here
Will envy whom the highest place exposes
Foremost to stand against the Thunderer's aim
Your bulwark, and condemns to greatest share
Of endless pain? Where there is then no good   30
For which to strive, no strife can grow up there
From faction; for none sure will claim in hell
Precédence, none, whose portion is so small
Of present pain, that with ambitious mind
Will covet more. With this advantage then   35
To union, and firm faith, and firm accord,
More than can be in Heav'n, we now return
To claim our just inheritance of old,
Surer to prosper than prosperity
Could have assured us; and by what best way,   40
Whether of open war or covert guile,
We now debate; who can advise, may speak."

                    ❖   ❖   ❖

III

                    ❖   ❖   ❖

Now had th' Almighty Father from above,   56
From the pure empyrean where he sits

---

7. Hormuz, an island in the Persian   8. Outcome, either good or bad.
Gulf, famous for pearls, and India.

High throned above all height, bent down his eye,
His own works and their works at once to view:
About him all the sanctities of Heav'n[9]   60
Stood thick as stars, and from his sight received
Beatitude past utterance; on his right
The radiant image of his glory sat,
His only Son. On earth he first beheld
Our two first parents, yet the only two   65
Of mankind, in the happy garden placed,
Reaping immortal fruits of joy and love,
Uninterrupted joy, unrivaled love,
In blissful solitude. He then surveyed
Hell and the gulf between, and Satan there   70
Coasting the wall of Heav'n on this side Night
In the dun air sublime,[1] and ready now
To stoop[2] with wearied wings and willing feet
On the bare outside of this world, that seemed
Firm land embosomed without firmament,   75
Uncertain which, in ocean or in air.

1667

6   FIGURATIVE LANGUAGE

Metaphor and Simile

The language of poetry is almost always picturesque. Rather than depending primarily on abstract ideas and elaborate reasoning, poems depend mainly upon the creation of pictures in our minds, helping us to see things fresh and new, or to feel them suggestively through our other physical senses, such as hearing or the sense of touch. Poetry is most often vital in the sense that it helps us form, in our minds, visual impressions. We "see" a corpse at a funeral, a child chasing geese in the garden, or two lovers sitting together on the bank of a stream, so that our response begins from a vivid impression of exactly what is happening. Some people think that those arts and media which challenge the imagination of a reader or hearer—radio drama, for example, or poetry—allow us to respond more fully than arts (such as film or theater) that actually show things more fully to our physical senses. Certainly they leave more to our imagination, to our mind's eye.

But being visual does not just mean describing, telling us facts,

---

9. The hierarchies of angels.   2. Swoop down, like a bird of prey.
1. Aloft in the twilight atmosphere.

indicating shapes, colors, and specific details. Often the vividness of
the picture in our minds depends upon comparisons. What we are
trying to imagine is pictured in terms of something else familiar to us,
and we are asked to think of one thing as if it were something else.
Many such comparisons, or **figures of speech**, in which something is
pictured or imaged or figured forth in terms of something already
familiar to us, are taken for granted in daily life. Things we can't
see or which aren't familiar to us are pictured as things we can;
for example, God is said to be like a father, Italy is said to be shaped
like a boot. Poems use figurative language much of the time. A
speaker may tell us that his ladylove is like a red rose, or that the
way to imagine how it feels to be spiritually secure is to think of
the way a shepherd takes care of his sheep. The pictorialness of our
imagination may *clarify* things for us—scenes, states of mind, ideas—
but at the same time it stimulates us to think of how those pictures
make us *feel*. Pictures, even when they are mental pictures or imagined
visions, may be both denotative and connotative, just as individual
words are: they may clarify and make precise, and they may channel
our feelings. In this chapter, we will look at some of the ways that
poets create pictures in our minds—images that help us think clearly
about what they are saying and feel clearly the emotions they want
us to feel. Most poetry depends, at least in part, on the pictorial
quality of words and upon the notion that something becomes clearer
when we compare it with something else that is more familiar. In the
poem that follows, the poet helps us to visualize the old age and
approaching death of the speaker by making comparisons with familiar things—the coming of winter, the approach of sunset, and the
dying embers of a fire.

◊ WILLIAM SHAKESPEARE

That Time of Year

That time of year thou mayst in me behold
When yellow leaves, or none, or few, do hang
Upon those boughs which shake against the cold,
Bare ruined choirs, where late the sweet birds sang.
In me thou see'st the twilight of such day   5
As after sunset fadeth in the west;
Which by and by[1] black night doth take away,
Death's second self,[2] that seals up all in rest.
In me thou see'st the glowing of such fire,
That on the ashes of his youth doth lie,   10
As the deathbed whereon it must expire,
Consumed with that which it was nourished by.
This thou perceiv'st, which makes thy love more strong,
To love that well which thou must leave ere long.

1609

1. Shortly.   2. Sleep.

The first four lines of *That Time of Year* make the comparison to seasonal change; but notice that the poet does not have the speaker say directly that his physical condition and age make him resemble autumn. He draws the comparison without stating directly that it is a comparison: you can see, he says, my own state in the coming of winter in late autumn when the leaves are almost all off the trees. The speaker portrays himself *indirectly* by talking about the passing of the year. The poem uses **metaphor**; that is, one thing is pictured *as if* it were something else. *That Time of Year* goes on to another metaphor in lines 5–8 and still another in lines 9–12, and each of the metaphors contributes to our understanding of the speaker's sense of his old age and approaching death. Even more important, however, is the way the metaphors give us feelings, an emotional sense of the speaker's age and of his own attitude toward aging. Through the metaphors we come to understand, appreciate, and to some extent share the increasing sense of anxiety and urgency that the poem expresses. Our emotional sense of the poem is largely influenced by the way each metaphor is developed and by the way each metaphor leads, with its own kind of internal logic, to another.

The images of late autumn in the first four lines all suggest loneliness, loss, and nostalgia for earlier times. As in the rest of the poem, our eyes are imagined to be the main vehicle for noticing the speaker's age and condition; the phrase "thou mayst in me behold" (line 1) introduces what we are asked to see, and in both lines 5 and 9 we are similarly told "In me thou see'st. . . ." The picture of the trees shedding their leaves suggests that autumn is nearly over, and we can imagine trees either with yellow leaves, or without leaves, or with just a trace of foliage remaining—the latter perhaps most feelingly suggesting the bleakness and loneliness that characterize the change of seasons, the ending of the life cycle. But other senses are invoked too. The boughs shaking against the cold represent an appeal to our tactile sense, and the next line appeals to our sense of hearing, although only as a reminder that the birds no longer sing. (Notice how exact the visual representation is of the bare, or nearly bare, limbs, even as the cold and the lack of birds are noted; birds lined up like a choir on risers would have made a striking visual image on the barren limbs one above the other, but now there is only the *reminder* of what used to be. The present is quiet, bleak, trembly, and lonely.)

The next four lines are slightly different in tone, and the color changes. From a black-and-white landscape with a few yellow leaves, we come upon a rich and almost warm reminder of a faded sunset. But a somber note does enter the poem in these lines through another figure of speech, **personification**, which involves treating an abstraction, such as death or justice or beauty, as if it were a person. The poem is talking about the coming of night and of sleep, and Sleep is personified and identified as the "second self" of Death (that is, as a kind of reflection of death). The main emphasis is on how night and sleep close in on our sense of twilight, and only secondarily does a reminder of death enter the poem. But it does enter.

The third metaphor—that of the dying embers of a fire—begins in line 9 and continues to color and warm the bleak cold that the poem began with, but it also sharpens the reminder of death. The three main metaphors in the poem work in a way to make our sense of old age and approaching death more friendly, but also more immediate: moving from barren trees, to fading twilight, to dying embers suggests a sensuous increase of color and warmth, but also an increasing urgency. The first metaphor involves a whole season, or at least a segment of one, a matter of days or possibly weeks; the second involves the passing of a single day, reducing the time scale to a matter of minutes, and the third draws our attention to that split second when a glowing ember fades into a simple ash. The final part of the fire metaphor introduces the most explicit sense of death so far, as the metaphor of embers shifts into a direct reminder of death. Embers which had been a metaphor of the speaker's aging body now themselves become, metaphorically, a deathbed; the vitality that nourishes youth is used up just as a log in a fire is. The urgency of the reminder of coming death has now peaked. It is friendlier but now seems immediate and inevitable, a natural part of the life process, and the final two lines then make an explicit plea to make good and intense use of the remaining moments of human relationship.

That Time of Year represents an unusually intricate use of images to organize a poem and focus its emotional impact. Not all poems are so skillfully made, and not all depend on such a full and varied use of metaphor. But most poems use metaphors for at least part of their effect, and often a poem is based on a single metaphor which is fully developed as the major way of making the poem's statement and impact, as in this poem about the role of a mother and wife.

LINDA PASTAN

Marks

My husband gives me an A
for last night's supper,
an incomplete for my ironing,
a B plus in bed.
My son says I am average,   5
an average mother, but if
I put my mind to it
I could improve.
My daughter believes
in Pass/Fail and tells me   10
I pass. Wait 'til they learn
I'm dropping out.

1978

The speaker in *Marks* is obviously not thrilled with the idea of continually being judged, and the metaphor of marks (or grades) as a way of talking about her performance of roles in the family suggests her irritation. The list of the roles implies the many things expected of her, and the three different systems of marking (letter grades, categories to be checked off on a chart, and pass/fail) detail the difficulties of multiple standards. The poem retains the language of schooldays all the way to the end ("learn," line 11; "dropping out," line 12), and the major effect of the poem depends on the irony of the speaker's agreeing to surrender to the metaphor the family has thrust upon her; if she is to be judged as if she were a student, she retains the right to drop out. Ironically, she joins the system (adopts the metaphor for herself) in order to defeat it.

The difficulty of conveying what some experiences are like and how we feel about them sometimes leads poets to startling comparisons and figures of speech that may at first seem far-fetched but which, in one way or another, do in fact suggest the quality of the experience or the feelings associated with it. Sometimes a series of metaphors is used, as if no one kind of visualization will serve, but several together may suggest the full complexity of the experience or cumulatively define the feeling precisely. Metaphors open up virtually endless possibilities of comparison, giving words a chance to be more than words, offering our mind's eye a challenge to keep up with the fertile and articulate imagination of writers who make it their business to see things that ordinary people miss, noticing the most surprising likenesses.

Sometimes, in poetry as in prose, comparisons are made explicitly, as in the following poem.

ROBERT BURNS

A Red, Red Rose

> O, my luve's like a red, red rose
> That's newly sprung in June.
> O, my luve is like the melodie
> That's sweetly played in tune.
>
> As fair art thou, my bonnie lass,   5
> So deep in luve am I;
> And I will luve thee still, my dear,
> Till a' the seas gang[3] dry.
>
> Till a' the seas gang dry, my dear,
> And the rocks melt wi' the sun;   10
> And I will luve thee still, my dear,
> While the sands o' life shall run.
>
> And fare thee weel, my only luve,

---

3. Go.

And fare thee weel a while!
And I will come again, my luve,   15
Though it were ten thousand mile.

1796

The first four lines make two explicit comparisons: the speaker says that his love is "like a rose" and "like a melodie." Such *explicit* comparison is called a **simile,** and usually (as here) the comparison involves the words "like" or "as." Similes work much as do metaphors, except that they usually are used more passingly, more incidentally; they make a quick comparison and usually do not elaborate, whereas metaphors often extend over a long section of a poem (in which case they are called **extended metaphors**) or even over the whole poem as in Marks (in which case they are called **controlling metaphors**).

The two similes in *A Red, Red Rose* assume that we already have a favorable opinion of roses and of melodies. Here the poet does not develop the comparison or even remind us of attractive details about roses or tunes. He pays the quick compliment and moves on. Similes sometimes develop more elaborate comparisons than this and occasionally even control long sections of a poem (in which case they are called **analogies**), but usually a simile is briefer and relies more fully on something we already know. The speaker in *My Papa's Waltz* says that he hung on "like death"; he doesn't have to explain or elaborate the comparison: we know the anxiety he refers to.

Like metaphors, similes may imply both meaning and feeling; they may both explain something and invoke feelings about it. All figurative language involves an attempt to clarify something *and* to help readers feel a certain way about it. Saying that one's love is like a rose implies a delicate and fragile beauty and invites our senses into play so that we can share sensuously a response to fragrant appeal and soft touch, just as the shivering boughs and dying embers in Shakespeare's poem explain separation and loss at the same time that they allow us to share the cold sense of loneliness and the warmth of old friendship. The poems that follow suggest some other varieties of figures of speech in poems. But you will also find metaphors and similes elsewhere, in fact nearly everywhere. Once you are alerted to look for them you will find figures in poem after poem; they are among the most common devices through which poets share their vision with us.

RANDALL JARRELL

The Death of the Ball Turret Gunner[4]

From my mother's sleep I fell into the State,
And I hunched in its belly till my wet fur froze.
Six miles from earth, loosed from its dream of life,
I woke to black flak and the nightmare fighters.
When I died they washed me out of the turret with a hose.   5

1945

JOHN DONNE

Batter My Heart

Batter my heart, three-personed God; for You
As yet but knock, breathe, shine, and seek to mend;
That I may rise and stand, o'erthrow me, and bend
Your force, to break, blow, burn, and make me new.
I, like an usurped town, to another due,   5
Labor to admit You, but Oh, to no end!
Reason, Your viceroy[5] in me, me should defend,
But is captived, and proves weak or untrue.
Yet dearly I love You, and would be loved fain.[6]
But am betrothed unto Your enemy: 10
Divorce me, untie, or break that knot again,
Take me to You, imprison me, for I,
Except You enthrall me, never shall be free,
Nor ever chaste, except You ravish me.

1633

ANONYMOUS
(Traditionally attributed to King David)

The Twenty-Third Psalm

The Lord is my shepherd; I shall not want.

He maketh me to lie down in green pastures: he leadeth me beside
the still waters.

4. "A ball turret was a plexiglass sphere set into the belly of a B-17 or B-24 and inhabited by two .50 caliber machine-guns and one man, a short, small man. When this gunner tracked with his machine-guns a fighter attacking his bomber from below, he revolved with the turret; hunched upside-down in his little sphere, he looked like the foetus in the womb. The fighters which attacked him were armed with cannon firing explosive shells. The hose was a steam hose." (Jarrell's note)

5. One who rules as the representative of a higher power.

6. Gladly.

He restoreth my soul: he leadeth me in the paths of righteousness
        for his name's sake.
Yea, though I walk through the valley of the shadow of death,
        I will fear no evil: for thou art with me;
        thy rod and thy staff they comfort me.
Thou preparest a table before me in the presence of mine enemies:
        thou anointest my head with oil; my cup runneth over.
Surely goodness and mercy shall follow me all the days of my life:
        and I will dwell in the house of the Lord for ever.

BOB DYLAN

Mister Tambourine Man

Chorus

Hey, Mister Tambourine Man, play a song for me,
I'm not sleepy and there ain't no place I'm going to.
Hey, Mister Tambourine Man, play a song for me,
In the jingle, jangle morning I'll come followin' you.

I

Though I know that evenin's empire has returned into sand   5
Vanished from my hand,
Left me blindly here to stand
But still no sleepin'.
My weariness amazes me,
I'm branded on my feet,   10
I have no one to meet,
And the ancient empty street's
Too dead for dreamin'.
Chorus

II

Take me on a trip upon your magic swirlin' ship,
My senses have been stripped,   15
My hands can't feel to grip,
My toes too numb to step,
Wait only for my boot heels to be wanderin'.
I'm ready to go anywhere,
I'm ready for to fade   20
Into my own parade.
Cast your dancin' spell my way,
I promise to go under it.
Chorus

III

Though you might hear laughin', spinnin', swingin' madly through the
    sun,
It's not aimed at anyone,   25
It's just escapin' on the run,

And but for the sky there are no fences facin'.
And if you hear vague traces
Of skippin' reels of rhyme
To your tambourine in time,   30
It's just a ragged clown behind,
I wouldn't pay it any mind,
It's just a shadow
You're seein' that he's chasin'.
Chorus

                                    IV
Take me disappearin' through the smoke rings of my mind   35
Down the foggy ruins of time,
Far past the frozen leaves,
The haunted, frightened trees
Out to the windy beach
Far from the twisted reach of crazy sorrow.   40
Yes, to dance beneath the diamond sky
With one hand wavin' free,
Silhouetted by the sea,
Circled by the circus sands,
With memory and fate   45
Driven deep beneath the waves.
Let me forget about today until tomorrow.
Chorus

                                                          1964

PHILIP BOOTH

One Man's Wife

        Not that he promised not to windowshop,
        or refuse free samples; but he gave up
        exploring warehouse bargains, and forgot
        the trial offers he used to mail away for.

        After, that is, she laid on the counter what   5
        she'd long kept hidden under the penny-candy,
        and demonstrated (one up-country Sunday)
        the total inventory of one wife's general store.

                                                          1966

Symbol

One can get into a good argument with a literary critic, a philosopher,
or just about anybody else simply by mentioning the word symbol.
A symbol is many things to many people, and often it means no

more than that the person using the term is dealing with something he doesn't know how to describe or think about precisely. The term is difficult to be precise about, but it can be used quite sensibly. A **symbol** is, put simply, something which stands for something else. The everyday world is full of common examples; a flag, a logo, a trademark, or a skull and crossbones all suggest things beyond themselves, and everyone is likely to understand what their display is meant to signify, whether or not the viewer shares a commitment to what the object represents. In common usage a prison is a symbol of confinement, constriction, and loss of freedom, and in specialized traditional usage a cross may symbolize oppression, cruelty, suffering, death, resurrection, triumph, or the intersection of two separate things, traditions, or ideas (as in crossroads and crosscurrents, for example). The specific symbolic significance is controlled by the context; a reader may often decide by looking at contiguous details in the poem and by examining the poem's attitude toward a particular tradition or body of beliefs; a star means one kind of thing to a Jewish poet and something else to a Christian poet, still something else to a Nazi or to someone whose religion is surfing. In a very literal sense, words themselves are all symbols (they stand for an object, action, or quality, not just for letters or sounds), but symbols in poetry are said to be those words and groups of words which have a range of reference beyond their literal denotation.

Poems sometimes create a symbol out of a thing, action, or event which has no previously agreed upon symbolic significance. In the following poem, for example, a random gesture is given symbolic significance.

SHARON OLDS

Leningrad Cemetery, Winter of 1941[1]

That winter, the dead could not be buried.
The ground was frozen, the gravediggers weak from hunger,
the coffin wood used for fuel. So they were covered with
    something
and taken on a child's sled to the cemetery
in the sub-zero air. They lay on the soil,   5
some of them wrapped in dark cloth
bound with rope like the tree's ball of roots
when it waits to be planted; others wound in sheets,
their pale, gauze, tapered shapes
stiff as cocoons that will split down the center   10
when the new life inside is prepared;
but most lay like corpses, their coverings
coming undone, naked calves
hard as corded wood spilling

1. The 900-day siege of Leningrad during World War II began in September 1941.

from under a cloak, a hand reaching out   15
with no sign of peace, wanting to come back
even to the bread made of glue and sawdust,
even to the icy winter, and the siege.

p. 1979

All of the corpses—frozen, neglected, beginning to be in disarray—
vividly stamp upon our minds a sense of the horrors of war, and the
detailed picture of the random, uncounted clutter of bodies is likely
to stick in our minds long after we have finished reading the poem.
Several of the details are striking, and the poem's language heightens
our sense of them. The corpses wound in sheets, for example, are
described in "their pale, gauze, tapered shapes," and they are compared to cocoons that one day will split and emit new life; and the
limbs that dangle loose when the coverings come undone are said
to be "hard as corded wood spilling." But clearly the most memorable
sight is the hand dangling from one corpse that is coming unwrapped,
for the poet invests that hand with special significance, giving its
gesture *meaning*. The hand is described as "reaching out . . . wanting
to come back": it is as if the dead can still gesture even if they cannot speak, and the gesture seems to signify the desire of the dead
to come back at any price. They would be glad to be alive, even
under the grim conditions that attend the living in Leningrad during
this grim war. Suddenly the grimness which we—living—have been
witnessing pales by comparison with what the dead have lost simply
by being dead. The hand has been made to **symbolize** the desire
of the dead to return, to be alive, to be still among us, anywhere.
The hand reaches out in the poem as a gesture that means; the poet
has made it a symbol of desire.

The whole array of dead bodies in the poem might be said to be
symbolic as well. As a group, they stand for the human waste that
the war has produced, and their dramatic visual presence on the
scene provides the poem with a dramatic visualization of how war
and its requirements have no time for decency, not even the decency
of burial. The bodies are a symbol in the sense that they stand for
what the poem as a whole asserts.

This next poem also arises out of a historical moment, but this time
the event is a personal one which the poet gives a significance by the
interpretation he puts upon it.

JAMES DICKEY

The Leap

The only thing I have of Jane MacNaughton
Is one instant of a dancing-class dance.

She was the fastest runner in the seventh grade,
My scrapbook says, even when boys were beginning
To be as big as the girls,   5
But I do not have her running in my mind,
Though Frances Lane is there, Agnes Fraser,
Fat Betty Lou Black in the boys-against-girls
Relays we ran at recess: she must have run

Like the other girls, with her skirts tucked up   10
So they would be like bloomers,
But I cannot tell; that part of her is gone.
What I do have is when she came,
With the hem of her skirt where it should be
For a young lady, into the annual dance   15
Of the dancing class we all hated, and with a light
Grave leap, jumped up and touched the end
Of one of the paper-ring decorations

To see if she could reach it. She could,
And reached me now as well, hanging in my mind   20
From a brown chain of brittle paper, thin
And muscular, wide-mouthed, eager to prove
Whatever it proves when you leap
In a new dress, a new womanhood, among the boys
Whom you easily left in the dust   25
Of the passionless playground. If I said I saw
In the paper where Jane MacNaughton Hill,

Mother of four, leapt to her death from a window
Of a downtown hotel, and that her body crushed-in
The top of a parked taxi, and that I held   30
Without trembling a picture of her lying cradled
In that papery steel as though lying in the grass,
One shoe idly off, arms folded across her breast,
I would not believe myself. I would say
The convenient thing, that it was a bad dream   35
Of maturity, to see that eternal process

Most obsessively wrong with the world
Come out of her light, earth-spurning feet
Grown heavy: would say that in the dusty heels
Of the playground some boy who did not depend   40
On speed of foot, caught and betrayed her.
Jane, stay where you are in my first mind:
It was odd in that school, at that dance.
I and the other slow-footed yokels sat in corners
Cutting rings out of drawing paper   45

Before you leapt in your new dress
And touched the end of something I began,
Above the couples struggling on the floor,

New men and women clutching at each other
And prancing foolishly as bears: hold on   50
To that ring I made for you, Jane—
My feet are nailed to the ground
By dust I swallowed thirty years ago—
While I examine my hands.

1967

Memory is crucial to *The Leap*. The fact that Jane MacNaughton's graceful leap in dancing class has stuck in the speaker's mind for all these years means that this leap was important to him, meant something to him, stood for something in his mind. For the speaker, the leap is an "instant" and the "only thing" he has of Jane. Its grace and ease are what he remembers, and he struggles at several points to articulate its meaning (lines 15–26, 44–50), but even without articulation or explanation it is there in his head as a visual memory, a symbol for him of something beyond himself, something he cannot do, something he wanted to be. What that leap had stood for, or symbolized, was boldness, confidence, accomplishment, maturity, the ability to go beyond her fellow students in dancing class—the transcending of childhood by someone beginning to be a woman. Her feet now seem "earth-spurning" (line 38) in that original leap, and they separate her from everyone else. Jane MacNaughton was beyond the speaker's abilities and any attempt he could make to articulate his hopes, but not beyond his dreams. And even before articulation, she symbolized that dream.

The leap to her death seems cruelly ironic in the context of her earlier leap. In memory she is suspended in air, as if there were no gravity, no coming back to earth, as if life could exist as dream. And so the photograph, recreated in precise detail, is a cruel dashing of the speaker's dream—a detailed record of the ending of a leap, a denial of the suspension in which his memory had held her. His dream is grounded; her mortality is insistent. But what the speaker wants to hang on to (line 42) is still that symbolic moment which, although now confronted in more mature implications, will never be altogether replaced or surrendered.

The leap is ultimately symbolic in the *poem*, too, not just in the speaker's mind. In the poem (and for us as readers) the symbolism of the leap is double: the first leap is aspiration, and the second is frustration of high hopes; the two are complementary, one unable to be imagined without the other. The poem is horrifying in some ways, a dramatic reminder that human beings don't ultimately transcend their mortality, their limits, no matter how heroic or unencumbered by gravity they may seem to an observer. But it is not altogether sad and despairing either, partly because it notices and affirms the validity of the original leap and partly because another symbol is created and elaborated in the poem. That symbol is the paper chain.

The chain connects Jane to the speaker both literally and figuratively. It is, in part, *his* paper chain which she had leaped to touch in dancing class (lines 18–19), and he thinks of her first leap as "touch[ing] the end of something I began" (line 47). He and the other "slow footed," earthbound "yokels" (line 44) were the makers of the chain, and thus they are connected to her original leap, just as a photograph glimpsed in a paper connects the speaker to her second leap. The paper in the chain is "brittle" (line 21), and its creators seem dull artisans compared to the artistic performer that Jane was. They are heavy and left in the dust (lines 25, 52–53), and she is "light" (line 16) and able to transcend them but even in transcendence touching their lives and what they are able to do. And so the paper chain becomes the poem's symbol of linkage, connecting lower accomplishment to higher possibility, the artisan to the artist, material substance to the act of imagination. And the speaker at the end examines the hands that made the chain because those hands certify his connection to her and the imaginative leap she had made for him. The chain thus symbolizes not only the lower capabilities of those who cannot leap like the budding Jane could, but (later) the connection with her leap as both transcendence and mortality. Like the leap itself, the chain has been elevated to special meaning, given symbolic significance, by the poet's treatment of it. A leap and a chain have no necessary significance in themselves to most of us—at least no significance that we have all agreed upon together.

But some objects and acts do have such significance. Over the years some things have acquired an agreed-upon significance, an accepted value in our minds. They already stand for something before the poet cites them; they are **traditional symbols.** Their uses in poetry have to do with the fact that poets can count on a recognition of their traditional suggestions and meanings outside the poem, and the poem does not have to propose or argue a particular symbolic value. Birds, for example, traditionally symbolize flight, freedom from confinement, detachment from earthbound limits, the ability to soar beyond rationality and transcend mortal limits. Traditionally, birds have also been linked with imagination, especially poetic imagination, and poets often identify with them as ideal singers of songs, as in Keats's *Ode to a Nightingale* (p. 746). One of the most traditional symbols is that of the rose. It may be a simple and fairly plentiful flower in its season, but it has been allowed to stand for particular qualities for so long that to name it raises predictable expectations. Its beauty, delicacy, fragility, shortness of life, and depth of color have made it a symbol of the transitoriness of beauty, and countless poets have counted on its accepted symbolism—sometimes to compliment a friend (as Burns does in *A Red, Red Rose*) or sometimes to make a point about the nature of symbolism. The following poem draws on, in a quite traditional way, the traditional meanings.

JOHN CLARE

Love's Emblem

Go, rose, my Chloe's[2] bosom grace:
    How happy should I prove,
Could I supply that envied place
    With never-fading love.

Accept, dear maid, now summer glows,   5
    This pure, unsullied gem,
Love's emblem in a full-blown rose,
    Just broken from the stem.

Accept it as a favorite flower
    For thy soft breast to wear;   10
'Twill blossom there its transient hour,
    A favorite of the fair.

Upon thy cheek its blossom glows,
    As from a mirror clear,
Making thyself a living rose,   15
    In blossom all the year.

It is a sweet and favorite flower
    To grace a maiden's brow,
Emblem of love without its power—
    A sweeter rose art thou.   20

The rose, like hues of insect wing,
    May perish in an hour;
'Tis but at best a fading thing,
    But thou'rt a living flower.

The roses steeped in morning dews   25
    Would every eye enthrall,
But woman, she alone subdues;
    Her beauty conquers all.

1873

The speaker in *Love's Emblem* sends the rose to Chloe to decorate
her bosom (lines 1, 10) and reflect the blush of her cheek and brow
(lines 13, 18), and he goes on to mention some of the standard meanings: the rose is pure (line 6), transitory (line 11), fragrant, beautiful, and always appreciated (line 17). The poet need not elaborate
or argue these things; he can assume the reader's acquiescence. To

2. A standard "poetic" name for a woman in traditional love poetry.

say that the rose is an emblem of love is to say that it traditionally symbolizes love, and the speaker expects Chloe to accept his gift readily; she will understand it as a compliment, a pledge, and a bond. She will understand, too, that her admirer is being conventional and complimentary in going on to call her (and women in general) a rose (line 20), except that her qualities are said to be more lasting than those of a momentary flower.

Several of the poems at the end of this chapter explore the traditional meanings of the rose as symbol, sometimes playing with the meanings and modifying them, sometimes consciously trying to create new and untraditional meanings (as in *Roses and Revolutions*), sometimes calling attention to the deterioration of nature as well as to the tradition (*Southern Gothic*), or suggesting the primacy of symbol over physical artifact (*Poem*: "The rose fades").

Sometimes symbols—traditional or not—become so insistent in the world of a poem that the larger referential world is left almost totally behind. In such cases the symbol is everything, and the poem does not just *use* symbols but becomes a **symbolic poem.**

Here is an example of such a poem:

WILLIAM BLAKE

The Sick Rose[3]

O rose, thou art sick.
The invisible worm
That flies in the night
In the howling storm

Has found out thy bed   5
Of crimson joy,
And his dark secret love
Does thy life destroy.

1794

The poem does not seem to be about a rose, but about what the rose represents—not in this case something altogether understandable through the traditional meanings of rose.

We know that the rose is usually associated with beauty and love, often with sex; and here several key terms have sexual connotations: "bed," "worm," and "crimson joy." The violation of the rose by the

3. In Renaissance emblem books, the scarab beetle, worm, and rose are closely associated: The beetle feeds on dung, and the smell of the rose is fatal to it.

worm is the poem's main concern; the violation seems to have involved secrecy, deceit, and "dark" motives, and the result is sickness rather than the joy of love. The poem is sad; it involves a sense of hurt and tragedy, nearly of despair. The poem cries out against the misuse of the rose, against its desecration, implying that instead of a healthy joy in sensuality and sexuality, in this case, there has been destruction and hurt because of misunderstanding and repression and lack of sensitivity.

But to say so much about this poem I have had to extrapolate from other poems by this poet, and have introduced information from outside the poem. Fully symbolic poems often require that, and thus they ask us to go beyond the normal procedures of reading which we have discussed here. As presented in this poem, the rose is not part of the normal world that we ordinarily see, and it is symbolic in a special sense. The poet does not simply take an object from that everyday world and give it special significance, making it a symbol in the same sense that the leap is a symbol, or the corpse's hand. Here the rose seems to belong to its own world, a world made entirely inside the poem. The rose is not referential. The whole poem is symbolic; it is not paraphrasable; it lives in its own world. But what is the rose here a symbol of? In general terms, we can say from what the poem tells us; but we may not be as confident as we can be in the more nearly everyday world of *The Leap* or *Leningrad Cemetery, Winter of 1941*, poems that contain actions we recognize from the world of probabilities in which we live. In *The Sick Rose*, it seems inappropriate to ask the standard questions: What rose? Where? Which worm? What are the particulars here? In the world of this poem worms can fly and may be invisible. We are altogether in a world of meanings.

Negotiation of meanings in symbolic poems can be very difficult indeed; the skill of reading symbolic poems is an advanced skill that depends on special knowledge of authors and of the traditions they work from, and these skills need to be developed carefully and cautiously under the tutelage of a skilled teacher. You will find in this book some examples of symbolic poems (*Sailing to Byzantium,* for example), but the symbols you will usually find in poems are referential, and these meanings are readily discoverable from the careful study of the poems themselves, as in poems like *The Leap* and *Love's Emblem.*

―――――――

WILLIAM HABINGTON

To Roses in the Bosom of Castara

Ye blushing virgins happy are
In the chaste nunn'ry of her breasts,

For he'd profane so chaste a fair,[4]
Whoe'er should call them Cupid's nests.

Transplanted thus, how bright ye grow,   5
How rich a perfume do ye yield.
In some close garden, cowslips so
Are sweeter than i' th' open field.

In those white cloisters live secure
From the rude blasts of wanton breath,   10
Each hour more innocent and pure,
Till you shall wither into death.

Then that which living gave you room,
Your glorious sepulcher shall be;
There wants[5] no marble for a tomb,   15
Whose breast hath marble been to me.

                                        1634

ROBERT FROST

The Rose Family[6]

The rose is a rose,
And was always a rose.
But the theory now goes
That the apple's a rose,
And the pear is, and so's
The plum, I suppose.
The dear only knows
What will next prove a rose.
You, of course, are a rose—
But were always a rose.   10

                                        1928

DOROTHY PARKER

One Perfect Rose

A single flow'r he sent me, since we met.
    All tenderly his messenger he chose;
Deep-hearted, pure, with scented dew still wet—
    One perfect rose.

4. Beautiful woman.
5. Lacks.

6. A response to Gertrude Stein's famous
line, "A rose is a rose is a rose."

I knew the language of the floweret;   5
   "My fragile leaves," it said, "his heart enclose."
Love long has taken for his amulet
   One perfect rose.

Why is it no one ever sent me yet
   One perfect limousine, do you suppose?   10
Ah no, it's always just my luck to get
   One perfect rose.

                                                    1937

DONALD JUSTICE

Southern Gothic

(*for W.E.B. & P.R.*)

Something of how the homing bee at dusk
Seems to inquire, perplexed, how there can be
No flowers here, not even withered stalks of flowers,
Conjures a garden where no garden is
And trellises too frail almost to bear   5
The memory of a rose, much less a rose.
Great oaks, more monumentally great oaks now
Than ever when the living rose was new,
Cast shade that is the more completely shade
Upon a house of broken windows merely   10
And empty nests up under broken eaves.
No damask any more prevents the moon,
But it unravels, peeling from a wall,
Red roses within roses within roses.

                                                 1960

DUDLEY RANDALL

Roses and Revolutions

Musing on roses and revolutions,
I saw night close down on the earth like a great dark wing,
and the lighted cities were like tapers in the night,
and I heard the lamentations of a million hearts
regretting life and crying for the grave,   5
and I saw the Negro lying in the swamp with his face blown off,
and in northern cities with his manhood maligned and felt the
   writhing
of his viscera like that of the hare hunted down or the bear at bay,

and I saw men working and taking no joy in their work
and embracing the hard-eyed whore with joyless excitement   10
and lying with wives and virgins in impotence.

And as I groped in darkness
and felt the pain of millions,
gradually, like day driving night across the continent,
I saw dawn upon them like the sun a vision   15
of a time when all men walk proudly through the earth
and the bombs and missiles lie at the bottom of the ocean
like the bones of dinosaurs buried under the shale of eras,
and men strive with each other not for power or the accumulation
    of paper
but in joy create for others the house, the poem, the game of   20
    athletic beauty.

Then washed in the brightness of this vision,
I saw how in its radiance would grow and be nourished and
    suddenly
burst into terrible and splendid bloom
the blood-red flower of revolution.

                                                    1968

WILLIAM CARLOS WILLIAMS

Poem

The rose fades
and is renewed again
by its seed, naturally
but where

save in the poem   5
shall it go
to suffer no diminution
of its splendor

                                                    1962

7   STRUCTURE

"Proper words in proper places": that is the way one great writer of
English prose (Jonathan Swift) described good writing. Finding appropriate words is not the easiest of tasks for a poet, and in the last
two chapters we have looked at some of the implications for readers

of the choices a poet makes. But a poet's decision about where to put those words is also difficult, for individual words, metaphors, and symbols not only exist as part of a phrase or sentence or rhythmic pattern but also as part of the larger whole of the poem itself. How is the whole poem to be organized? What will come first and what last? How is some sort of structure to be created? How are words, sentences, images, ideas, feelings to be put together into something that holds together, seems complete, and will have a certain effect upon us as readers?

Looking at these questions from the point of view of the maker of the poem (What shall I plan? Where shall I begin?) can have the advantage of helping us as readers to notice the effect of structural decisions. In a sense, every single poem is different from every other, and therefore independent, individual decisions must be made about how to organize. But there are also patterns of organization that poems fall into, sometimes because of the subject matter, sometimes because of the effect intended, sometimes for other reasons. Often poets consciously decide on a particular organizational strategy, sometimes they may reach instinctively for one or happen into a structure that suits the needs of the moment, one onto which a creator can hang the words one by one.

When there is a story to be told, the organization of a poem may be fairly simple, as in this popular ballad:

ANONYMOUS

Frankie and Johnny

Frankie and Johnny were lovers,
    Lordy, how they could love,
Swore to be true to each other,
    True as the stars up above,
        He was her man, but he done her wrong.   5

Frankie went down to the corner,
    To buy her a bucket of beer,
Frankie says "Mister Bartender,
    Has my lovin' Johnny been here?
        He is my man, but he's doing me wrong."   10

"I don't want to cause you no trouble
    Don't want to tell you no lie,
I saw your Johnny half-an-hour ago
    Making love to Nelly Bly.
        He is your man, but he's doing you wrong."   15

Frankie went down to the hotel
    Looked over the transom so high,
There she saw her lovin' Johnny

Making love to Nelly Bly.
      He was her man; he was doing her wrong.   20

Frankie threw back her kimono,
    Pulled out her big forty-four;
Rooty-toot-toot: three times she shot
    Right through that hotel door,
      She shot her man, who was doing her wrong.   25

"Roll me over gently,
    Roll me over slow,
Roll me over on my right side,
    'Cause these bullets hurt me so,
      I was your man, but I done you wrong."   30

Bring all your rubber-tired hearses
    Bring all your rubber-tired hacks,
They're carrying poor Johnny to the burying ground
    And they ain't gonna bring him back,
      He was her man, but he done her wrong.   35

Frankie says to the sheriff,
    "What are they going to do?"
The sheriff he said to Frankie,
    "It's the 'lectric chair for you.
      He was your man, and he done you wrong."   40

"Put me in that dungeon,
    Put me in that cell,
Put me where the northeast wind
    Blows from the southeast corner of hell,
      I shot my man, 'cause he done me wrong."   45

                 (19th century)

When a strict narrative pattern organizes a poem, events follow upon one another in a generally chronological order, but even then a lot of artistic decisions need to be made just as in a short story or novel. Does one begin at the beginning, or begin in the middle at an exciting point, and then circle back and explain earlier events? How much detail should be given? How much description of setting is necessary and where should one stop or slow the narrative to insert it? How much explanation of motives is needed and when should it be provided? Should some details be held back for greater suspense? Should there be subplots or digressions? Is an interpretation or reflection desirable, at the end or at some earlier point?

Even in a poem with as straightforward a **narrative structure** as that of *Frankie and Johnny*, pure chronology is not the only consideration in finding places for the words. The first stanza of the poem provides an overview, some background, and even a hint of the catastrophe ("he done her wrong"). Stanzas 2 and 3 move the story along swiftly, but not by the most economical narrative means possible; instead, the poem adds some color and flavor by including the dialogue between Frankie and the bartender. Except for the repeated refrain (which keeps the whole story continuously in view), the next three stanzas are straightforward, and efficient, up through the shooting and Johnny's confession of infidelity. The final three stanzas also proceed chronologically—through the funeral, the conversation between Frankie and the sheriff, and Frankie's final reflections. The poem does not ever violate chronology, strictly speaking, but one can readily imagine quite a different emphasis from the very same facts told in much the same order. Chronology has guided the construction of the poem, but the final effects depend just as much upon the decision of which details to include, on the decision to include so much dialogue, on the decision to follow Frankie's progress through the events rather than Johnny's, and on the decision to include a summary refrain in each stanza.

Purely narrative poems can often be very long, much longer than can be included in a book like this, and often there are many features that are not, strictly speaking, closely connected to the narrative or linked to a strict chronology. Very often a poem moves on from a narrative of an event to some sort of commentary or reflection upon it, as in *Auto Wreck* (at the end of this chapter) or *When Lilacs Last in the Dooryard Bloomed* (p. 902). Reflection can be included along the way or may be implicit in the way the story is narrated, as in *Woodchucks* (p. 569) where our major attention is more on the narrator and her responses than on the events in the story as such.

Just as they sometimes take on a structure rather like that of a story, poems sometimes borrow the structures of plays. The following poem has a **dramatic structure**; it consists of a series of scenes, each of which is presented vividly and in detail:

HOWARD NEMEROV

The Goose Fish

On the long shore, lit by the moon
To show them properly alone,
Two lovers suddenly embraced
So that their shadows were as one.
The ordinary night was graced   5
For them by the swift tide of blood
That silently they took at flood,
And for a little time they prized
   Themselves emparadised.

Then, as if shaken by stage fright   10

Beneath the hard moon's bony light,
They stood together on the sand
Embarrassed in each other's sight
But still conspiring hand in hand,
Until they saw, there underfoot,   15
As though the world had found them out,
The goose fish turning up, though dead,
    His hugely grinning head.

There in the china light he lay,
Most ancient and corrupt and gray   20
They hesitated at his smile,
Wondering what it seemed to say
To lovers who a little while
Before had thought to understand,
By violence upon the sand,   25
The only way that could be known
    To make a world their own.

It was a wide and moony grin
Together peaceful and obscene;
They knew not what he would express,   30
So finished a comedian
He might mean failure or success,
But took it for an emblem of
Their sudden, new and guilty love
To be observed by, when they kissed,   35
    That rigid optimist.

So he became their patriarch,
Dreadfully mild in the half-dark.
His throat that the sand seemed to choke,
His picket teeth, these left their mark   40
But never did explain the joke
That so amused him, lying there
While the moon went down to disappear
Along the still and tilted track
    That bears the zodiac.   45

                           1955

The first stanza sets the scene—a sandy shore in moonlight—and presents, in fact, the major action of the poem. The rest of the poem dramatizes the lovers' reactions: their initial embarrassment and feelings of guilt (stanza 2), their attempt to interpret the goose fish's smile (stanza 3), their decision to make him, whatever his meaning, the "emblem" of their love (stanza 4), and their acceptance of the fish's ambiguity and of their own relationship (stanza 5). The five stanzas do not exactly present five different scenes, but they do present separate dramatic moments, even if only a few minutes apart. Almost like a play of five very short acts, the poem traces the drama of the lovers' discovery of themselves, of their coming to terms with the meaning of their action. As in many plays, the central event (their love-making) is not the central focus of the drama, although the drama is based upon that event and could not take place without it. Here, that event is depicted only briefly but very vividly through figurative language: "they took at flood" the "swift tide of blood," and the immediate effect is to make them briefly feel "emparadised." But the poem concentrates on their later reactions, not on the act of love itself.

Their sudden discovery of the fish is a rude shock and injects a grotesque, almost macabre note into the poem. From a vision of paradise, the poem seems for a moment to turn toward a gothic horror story when the lovers discover that they have, after all, been seen—and by such a ghoulish spectator. The last three stanzas gradually recreate the intruder in their minds, as they are forced to admit that their act of love does not exist in isolation as they had at first hoped, and they begin to see it as part of a continuum, as part of their relationship to the larger world, even (at the end) putting it into the context of the rotating world and its seasons as the moon disappears into its zodiac. In retrospect, we can see that even at the moment of passion they were in touch with larger processes controlled by the presiding mood (the "swift tide of blood"), but neither the lovers nor we had understood their act as such then, and the poem is about their gradual recognition.

Stages of feeling and knowing rather than specific visual scenes are responsible for the poem's progress, and its dramatic structure depends upon internal perceptions and internal states of mind rather than dialogue and events. Visualization and images help to organize the poem too. Notice in particular how the two most striking visual features of the poem—the fish and the moon—are presented stanza by stanza. In stanza 1, the fish is not yet noticed, and the moon exists plain; it is only mentioned, not described, and its light serves as a stage spotlight to assure not center-stage attention, but rather total privacy: it is a kind of lookout for the lovers. The stage imagery, barely suggested by the light in stanza 1, is articulated in stanza 2, and there the moon is said to be "hard" and its light "bony"; its features have characteristics that seem more appropriate to the fish which has now become visible. In stanza 3, the moon's light has come to seem fragile ("china") as it is said to expose the fish directly; the role of the moon as lookout and protector seems abandoned, or at least endangered. No moon appears in stanza 4, but the fish's grin is described as "wide and moony," almost as if the two onlookers, one earthly and dead, the other heavenly and eternal, had become merged in the poem, as they nearly had been by the imagery in stanza 2. And by stanza 5, the fish has become a friend—by now he is a comedian, optimist, emblem, and a patriarch of their love—and his new position in collaboration with the lovers is presided over by the moon going about its eternal business. The moon has provided the stage light for the poem and the means by which not only the fish but the meaning of the lovers' act has been discovered. The moon has also helped to organize the poem, partly as a dramatic accessory, partly as imagery.

The following poem is also dramatic, but it seems to represent a composite of several similar experiences rather than a single event—a fairly common pattern in dramatic poems:

PHILIP LARKIN

Church Going

Once I am sure there's nothing going on
I step inside, letting the door thud shut.
Another church: matting, seats, and stone,
And little books; sprawlings of flowers, cut
For Sunday, brownish now; some brass and stuff   5
Up at the holy end; the small neat organ;
And a tense, musty, unignorable silence,
Brewed God knows how long. Hatless, I take off
My cycle-clips in awkward reverence,

Move forward, run my hand around the font.[1]   10
From where I stand, the roof looks almost new—
Cleaned, or restored? Someone would know: I don't.
Mounting the lectern, I peruse a few
Hectoring[2] large-scale verses, and pronounce
"Here endeth" much more loudly than I'd meant.   15
The echoes snigger briefly. Back at the door
I sign the book, donate an Irish sixpence,
Reflect the place was not worth stopping for.

Yet stop I did: in fact I often do,
And always end much at a loss like this,   20
Wondering what to look for; wondering, too,
When churches fall completely out of use
What we shall turn them into, if we shall keep
A few cathedrals chronically on show,
Their parchment, plate and pyx[3] in locked cases,   25
And let the rest rent-free to rain and sheep.
Shall we avoid them as unlucky places?

Or, after dark, will dubious women come
To make their children touch a particular stone;
Pick simples[4] for a cancer; or on some   30
Advised night see walking a dead one?

1. A bowl for baptismal water, mounted on a stone pedestal.
2. Intimidating.
3. A container for the Eucharist.
4. Medicinal herbs.

Power of some sort or other will go on
In games, in riddles, seemingly at random;
But superstition, like belief, must die,
And what remains when disbelief has gone?   35
Grass, weedy pavement, brambles, buttress, sky,

A shape less recognizable each week,
A purpose more obscure. I wonder who
Will be the last, the very last, to seek
This place for what it was; one of the crew   40
That tap and jot and know what rood-lofts[5] were?
Some ruin-bibber,[6] randy for antique,
Or Christmas-addict, counting on a whiff
Of gown-and-bands and organ-pipes and myrrh?
Or will he be my representative,   45

Bored, uninformed, knowing the ghostly silt
Dispersed, yet tending to this cross of ground
Through suburb scrub because it held unspilt
So long and equably what since is found
Only in separation—marriage, and birth,   50
And death, and thoughts of these—for whom was built
This special shell? For, though I've no idea
What this accoutered frowsty barn is worth,
It pleases me to stand in silence here;

A serious house on serious earth it is,   55
In whose blent air all our compulsions meet,
Are recognized, and robed as destinies.
And that much never can be obsolete,
Since someone will forever be surprising
A hunger in himself to be more serious,   60
And gravitating with it to this ground,
Which, he once heard, was proper to grow wise in,
If only that so many dead lie round.

1955

Ultimately, the poem's emphasis is upon what it means to visit churches, what sort of phenomenon church buildings represent, and what one is to make of the fact that "church going" (in the usual sense of the word) has declined so much. The poem uses a *different* sort of church-going (visitation by tourists) to consider larger philosophical questions about the relationship of religion to culture and history. The poem is, finally, a rather philosophical one about the directions of English culture, and through an enumeration of religious

5. Galleries atop the screens (on which crosses are mounted) which divide the naves or main bodies of churches from the choirs or chancels.
6. Literally, ruin-drinker: someone extremely attracted to antiquarian objects.

objects and rituals it reviews the history of how we got to our present historical circumstance. It tells a kind of story first, through one lengthy dramatized scene, in order to comment later on what the place and the experience may mean, and the larger conclusion derives from the particulars of what the speaker does and touches. The action is really over by the end of stanza 2, and that action, we are told, stands for many such visits to similar churches; after that, all is reflection and discussion, five stanzas' worth.

Church Going is a curious, funny poem in many ways. It goes to a lot of trouble to characterize its speaker, who seems a rather odd choice as a commentator on the state of religion. His informal attire (he takes off his cycle-clips at the end of stanza 1) and his not exactly worshipful behavior do not at first make us expect him to be a serious philosopher about what all this means. He is not disrespectful or sacrilegious, and before the end of stanza 1 he has tried to describe the "awkward reverence" he feels, but his overly somber imitation of part of the service stamps him as playful and as a tourist here, not someone who regularly drops in for prayer or meditation in the usual sense. And yet those early details do give him credentials, in a way; he clearly knows the names of religious objects and has some of the history of churches in his grasp. Clearly he does this sort of church-going often ("Yet stop I did; in fact I often do," line 19) because he wonders seriously what it all means—now—in comparison to what it meant to religious worshipers in times past. Ultimately, he takes the church itself seriously and its cultural meaning and function just as seriously (lines 55ff.), understanding its important place in the history of his culture. In this poem, the drama is, relatively speaking, brief, but it gives a context for the more digressive and rambling free-floating reflections that grow out of the dramatic experience.

Poems often have **discursive structures** too; that is, they are sometimes organized like a treatise, an argument, or an essay. "First," they say, "and second . . . and third. . . ." This sort of 1–2–3 structure takes a variety of forms depending on what one is enumerating or arguing. Here, for example, is a poem that is about three people who have died. The poem honors all three, but makes clear and sharp distinctions between them. As you read the poem, try to articulate just what sort of person each of the three is represented to be.

JAMES WRIGHT

Arrangements with Earth for Three Dead Friends

Sweet earth, he ran and changed his shoes to go
Outside with other children through the fields.
He panted up the hills and swung from trees
Wild as a beast but for the human laughter
That tumbled like a cider down his cheeks.   5
Sweet earth, the summer has been gone for weeks,
And weary fish already sleeping under water

Below the banks where early acorns freeze.
Receive his flesh and keep it cured of colds.
Button his coat and scarf his throat from snow.   10

And now, bright earth, this other is out of place
In what, awake, we speak about as tombs.
He sang in houses when the birds were still
And friends of his were huddled round till dawn
After the many nights to hear him sing.   15
Bright earth, his friends remember how he sang
Voices of night away when wind was one.
Lonely the neighborhood beneath your hill
Where he is waved away through silent rooms.
Listen for music, earth, and human ways.   20

Dark earth, there is another gone away,
But she was not inclined to beg of you
Relief from water falling or the storm.
She was aware of scavengers in holes
Of stone, she knew the loosened stones that fell   25
Indifferently as pebbles plunging down a well
And broke for the sake of nothing human souls.
Earth, hide your face from her where dark is warm.
She does not beg for anything, who knew
The change of tone, the human hope gone gray.   30

1957

Why, in stanza 1, is the earth represented as a parent? What does addressing the earth here as "sweet" seem to mean? How does the address to earth as "bright" fit the dead person described in stanza 2? In what different senses is the person described in stanza 3 "dark"? Why is the earth asked to give attention secretly to this person? Exactly what kind of person was she? How does the poem make you feel about her? Is there any cumulative point in describing three such different people in the same poem? What is accomplished by having the poem's three stanzas addressed to various aspects of earth? Similar discursive structures help to organize poems such as Shelley's *Ode to the West Wind* (p. 684), where the wind is shown driving a leaf in Part I, a cloud in Part II, a wave in Part III, and then, after a summary and statement of the speaker's ambitious hope in Part IV, is asked to make the speaker a lyre in Part V; or Spenser's *Happy Ye Leaves* (p. 683), in which the speaker addresses in the first four lines the leaves of the book his love is holding, in the next four the lines of the poem she is reading, and in the next four the rhymes in that poem.

Different kinds of structures are sometimes combined for special effects:

M. CARL HOLMAN

Three Brown Girls Singing

In the ribs of an ugly school building
Three rapt faces
Fuse one pure sound in a shaft of April light:
Three girls, choir robes over their arms, in a stairwell singing
Compose the irrelevancies of a halting typewriter,   5
Chalk dust and orange peel,
A French class drilling,
Into a shimmering column of flawed perfection;
Lasting as long
As their fresh, self-wondering voices climb to security;   10
Outlasting
The childbed death of one,
The alto's divorce,
The disease-raddled face of the third
Whose honey brown skin   15
Glows now in a nimbus[7] of dust motes,
But will be as estranged
As that faceless and voiceless typist
Who, unknown and unknowing, enters the limpid column,
Joins chalk, French verbs, the acrid perfume of oranges,   20
To mark the periphery
Of what shall be saved from calendars and decay.

p. 1963

The poem begins like a narrative and fades into a single dramatic scene. But the scene itself receives little attention. We are told of the "pure sound" created by the music, but instead of detailing the sound or providing metaphoric equivalents so that we almost hear it, or dramatizing its effect on someone, the poem enumerates all the things that it "composes," that is, brings together as one. The various sounds, sights, and smells from the school building—the typewriter, the peeling of an orange, writing on a chalkboard—seem harmonized by their music, and so do the lives of the three singers, whose brief and turbulent histories are also enumerated. The poem brings together different organizational patterns much as the music is said to "compose" (or harmonize) the disparate, miscellaneous, and fragmented sounds, smells, sights, and histories of those who create it and those within the range of its notes.

Poems may borrow their organizational strategies from many places, imitating chronological, visual, or discursive shapes in reality or in other works of art. Sometimes poems strive to be almost purely descriptive of someone or something (using **descriptive structures**), in which case organizational decisions have to be made much as a

7. Halo.

painter or photographer would make them, deciding first how the whole scene should look, then putting the parts into proper place for the whole. But there are differences demanded by the poetic medium: a poem has to present the details sequentially, not all at once as an actual picture more or less can, so the poet must decide where the description starts (at the left? center? top?) and what sort of movement to use (linear across the scene? clockwise?). But if having words instead of paint or film has some disadvantages, it also has particular assets: figurative language can be a part of description, or an adjunct to it. A poet can insert a comparison at any point without necessarily disturbing the unity of what he or she describes—as long as the reader's main attention stays riveted on the tenor rather than the vehicle. A poem like Stevens's *Anecdote of the Jar* (p. 893) suggests some other complex things that a descriptive poem can do just *because* it has words to use to offer perspective on an object or scene.

Some poems use **imitative structures**, mirroring as exactly as possible the structure of something that already exists as an object and can be seen (another poem perhaps, as in Koch's *Variations on a Theme by William Carlos Williams*, p. 802) or a standard visual or vocal format, by asking and answering questions, as Levertov's *What Were They Like* (p. 596) does. Or a poem may use **reflective** (or **meditative**) **structures**, pondering a subject, theme, or event, and letting the mind play with it, skipping (sometimes illogically but still usefully) from one sound to another, or to related thoughts or objects as the mind receives them.

Patterns, forms, structures, models, paradigms—all these terms help to suggest ways that we organize experience every day on the basis of analogy, putting things into an order on the basis of some other order we already know about. And they help with organizing words, with putting together verbal structures into some kind of whole. But the whole process is hardly mechanical. We might try to draw diagrams and charts of the organizations of poems, but they wouldn't be very helpful, not nearly so accurate as a set of plans for a building or even a sketch of a painting might be. Words reflect and reverberate; they are always growing and expanding; they won't stay put in a single frame. Their shades of meaning, connotations, implications, and their participation in larger syntaxes and pictures mean that they modify structures even as they fill them out. No one has ever discovered how to talk precisely about the larger organizations of words, and yet we need some sense of how attempts are made to put words into orders that are, to some extent, controlled by larger principles. And so we use terms such as narrative and imitative structures as imprecise but suggestive indicators.

The paradigms (or models) for organizing poems are, finally, not all that different from those of prose. It may be easier to organize something short rather than something long, but the question of intensity becomes comparatively more important in shorter works. Basically, the problem of how to organize one's material is, for the writer, first of all a matter of deciding what kind of thing one wants to create, of having its purposes and effects clearly in mind, a matter we will look at from a different perspective in Chapter 10. That means that every poem will differ somewhat from every other, but it also means that patterns of purpose—narrative, dramatic, discursive, descriptive, imitative, or reflective—may help writers organize and formulate their ideas. A consciousness of purpose and effect can help the reader see *how* a poem proceeds toward its goal. Seeing how a poem is organized is, in turn, often a good way of seeing where it is going and what its real concerns and purposes may be. Often a poem's organization helps to make clear the particular effects that the poet wishes to generate. In a good poem, means and end are closely related, and a reader who is a good observer of one will be able to discover the other.

ANONYMOUS

Lord Randal

"O where hae ye been, Lord Randal, my son?
O where hae ye been, my handsome young man?"
"I hae been to the wild wood; mother, make my bed soon,
For I'm weary wi' hunting, and fain wald[8] lie down."

"Where gat ye your dinner, Lord Randal, my son?   5
Where gat ye your dinner, my handsome young man?"
"I dined wi' my true-love; mother, make my bed soon,
For I'm weary wi' hunting, and fain wald lie down."

"What gat ye to your dinner, Lord Randal, my son?
What gat ye to your dinner, my handsome young man?"   10
"I gat eels boiled in broo; mother, make my bed soon,
For I'm weary wi' hunting, and fain wald lie down."

"What became of your bloodhounds, Lord Randal, my son?
What became of your bloodhounds, my handsome young man?"
"O they swelled and they died; mother, make my bed soon,   15
For I'm weary wi' hunting, and fain wald lie down."

"O I fear ye are poisoned, Lord Randal, my son!
O I fear ye are poisoned, my handsome young man!"
"O yes! I am poisoned; mother, make my bed soon,
For I'm sick at the heart, and I fain wald lie down."   20

                                        (date of composition uncertain)

---

8. Would like to.

KARL SHAPIRO

Auto Wreck

Its quick soft silver bell beating, beating,
And down the dark one ruby flare
Pulsing out red light like an artery,
The ambulance at top speed floating down
Past beacons and illuminated clocks   5
Wings in a heavy curve, dips down,
And brakes speed, entering the crowd.
The doors leap open, emptying light;
Stretchers are laid out, the mangled lifted
And stowed into the little hospital.   10
Then the bell, breaking the hush, tolls once,
And the ambulance with its terrible cargo
Rocking, slightly rocking, moves away,
As the doors, an afterthought, are closed.

We are deranged, walking among the cops   15
Who sweep glass and are large and composed.
One is still making notes under the light.
One with a bucket douches ponds of blood
Into the street and gutter.
One hangs lanterns on the wrecks that cling,   20
Empty husks of locusts, to iron poles.

Our throats were tight as tourniquets,
Our feet were bound with splints, but now,
Like convalescents intimate and gauche,
We speak through sickly smiles and warn   25
With the stubborn saw of common sense,
The grim joke and the banal resolution.
The traffic moves around with care,
But we remain, touching a wound
That opens to our richest horror.   30
Already old, the question Who shall die?
Becomes unspoken Who is innocent?

For death in war is done by hands;
Suicide has cause and stillbirth, logic;
And cancer, simple as a flower, blooms.   35
But this invites the occult mind,
Cancels our physics with a sneer,
And spatters all we knew of denouement
Across the expedient and wicked stones.

1942

LUCILLE CLIFTON

At Last We Killed the Roaches

at last we killed the roaches.
mama and me. she sprayed,
i swept the ceiling and they fell
dying onto our shoulders, in our hair
covering us with red. the tribe was broken,   5
the cooking pots were ours again
and we were glad, such cleanliness was grace
when i was twelve. only for a few nights,
and then not much, my dreams were blood
my hands were blades and it was murder murder   10
all over the place.

1974

ANONYMOUS

Sir Patrick Spens

The king sits in Dumferling toune,[9]
    Drinking the blude-reid[1] wine:
"O whar will I get guid sailor,
    To sail this ship of mine?"

Up and spake an eldern knicht,   5
    Sat at the king's richt knee:
"Sir Patrick Spens is the best sailor
    That sails upon the sea."

The king has written a braid[2] letter
    And signed it wi' his hand,   10
And sent it to Sir Patrick Spens,
    Was walking on the sand.

The first line that Sir Patrick read,
    A loud lauch[3] lauched he;
The next line that Sir Patrick read,   15
    The tear blinded his ee.[4]

"O wha is this has done this deed,
    This il deed done to me,
To send me out this time o' the year,
    To sail upon the sea?   20

9. Town.   3. Laugh.
1. Blood-red.   4. Eye.
2. Broad: explicit.

"Make haste, make haste, my merry men all,
   Our guid ship sails the morn."
"O say na sae,[5] my master dear,
   For I fear a deadly storm.

"Late, late yestre'en I saw the new moon 25
   Wi' the auld moon in her arm,
And I fear, I fear, my dear mastér,
   That we will come to harm."

O our Scots nobles were richt laith[6]
   To weet their cork-heeled shoon,[7] 30
But lang owre a'[8] the play were played
   Their hats they swam aboon.[9]

O lang, lang, may their ladies sit,
   Wi' their fans into their hand,
Or ere they see Sir Patrick Spens 35
   Come sailing to the land.

O lang, lang, may the ladies stand
   Wi' their gold kems[1] in their hair,
Waiting for their ain[2] dear lords,
   For they'll see them na mair. 40

Half o'er, half o'er to Aberdour
   It's fifty fadom deep,
And there lies guid Sir Patrick Spens
   Wi' the Scots lords at his feet.

                      (probably 13th century)

EDMUND SPENSER

Happy Ye Leaves

Happy ye leaves[3] whenas those lily hands,
Which hold my life in their dead-doing[4] might,
Shall handle you and hold in love's soft bands,
Like captives trembling at the victor's sight.
And happy lines on which, with starry light, 5
Those lamping eyes will deign sometimes to look,
And read the sorrows of my dying sprite,[5]

---

5. Not so.
6. Right loath: very reluctant.
7. To wet their cork-heeled shoes. Cork was expensive, and therefore such shoes were a mark of wealth and status.
8. Before all.
9. Their hats swam above them.

1. Combs.
2. Own.
3. Of the book of poems celebrating the woman these "lines" (line 5) go on to describe.
4. Death-dealing.
5. Spirit.

Written with tears in heart's close[6] bleeding book.
And happy rhymes bathed in the sacred brook
Of Helicon,[7] whence she derivéd is;   10
When ye behold that angel's blessed look,
My soul's long-lackéd food, my heaven's bliss.
Leaves, lines and rhymes, seek her to please alone,
Whom if ye please, I care for other none!

1595

PERCY BYSSHE SHELLEY

Ode to the West Wind

I

O wild West Wind, thou breath of Autumn's being,
Thou, from whose unseen presence the leaves dead
Are driven, like ghosts from an enchanter fleeing,

Yellow, and black, and pale, and hectic red,
Pestilence-stricken multitudes: O thou,   5
Who chariotest to their dark wintry bed

The wingéd seeds, where they lie cold and low,
Each like a corpse within its grave, until
Thine azure sister of the Spring shall blow

Her clarion[8] o'er the dreaming earth, and fill   10
(Driving sweet buds like flocks to feed in air)
With living hues and odors plain and hill:

Wild Spirit, which art moving everywhere;
Destroyer and preserver; hear, oh, hear!

II

Thou on whose stream, mid the steep sky's commotion,   15
Loose clouds like earth's decaying leaves are shed,
Shook from the tangled boughs of Heaven and Ocean,

Angels[9] of rain and lightning: there are spread
On the blue surface of thine aëry surge,
Like the bright hair uplifted from the head   20

Of some fierce Maenad,[1] even from the dim verge
Of the horizon to the zenith's height,
The locks of the approaching storm. Thou dirge

---

6. Secretly.
7. A mountain sacred to the muses. Classical writers described a fountain or spring on the mountain as a source of poetic inspiration; medieval writers often called the spring itself Helicon.

8. Trumpet-call.
9. Messengers.
1. A frenzied female votary of Dionysus, the Greek god of vegetation and fertility who was supposed to die in the fall and rise again each spring.

Of the dying year, to which this closing night
Will be the dome of a vast sepulcher,   25
Vaulted with all thy congregated might

Of vapors, from whose solid atmosphere
Black rain, and fire, and hail will burst: oh, hear!

III
Thou who didst waken from his summer dreams
The blue Mediterranean, where he lay,   30
Lulled by the coil of his crystálline streams,

Beside a pumice isle in Baiae's bay,[2]
And saw in sleep old palaces and towers
Quivering within the wave's intenser day,

All overgrown with azure moss and flowers   35
So sweet, the sense faints picturing them! Thou
For whose path the Atlantic's level powers

Cleave themselves into chasms, while far below
The sea-blooms and the oozy woods which wear
The sapless foliage of the ocean, know   40

Thy voice, and suddenly grow gray with fear,
And tremble and despoil themselves:[3] oh, hear!

IV
If I were a dead leaf thou mightest bear;
If I were a swift cloud to fly with thee;
A wave to pant beneath thy power, and share   45

The impulse of thy strength, only less free
Than thou, O uncontrollable! If even
I were as in my boyhood, and could be

The comrade by thy wanderings over Heaven,
As then, when to outstrip thy skyey speed   50
Scarce seemed a vision; I would ne'er have striven

As thus with thee in prayer in my sore need.
Oh, lift me as a wave, a leaf, a cloud!
I fall upon the thorns of life! I bleed!

A heavy weight of hours has chained and bowed   55
One too like thee: tameless, and swift, and proud.

V
Make me thy lyre,[4] even as the forest is:

2. Where Roman emperors had erected villas, west of Naples. "pumice": made of porous lava turned to stone.
3. "The vegetation at the bottom of the sea . . . sympathizes with that of the land in the change of seasons." (Shelley's note)
4. Aeolian lyre, a wind harp.

What if my leaves are falling like its own!
The tumult of thy mighty harmonies

Will take from both a deep, autumnal tone,   60
Sweet though in sadness. Be thou, Spirit fierce,
My spirit! Be thou me, impetuous one!

Drive my dead thoughts over the universe
Like withered leaves to quicken a new birth!
And, by the incantation of this verse,   65

Scatter, as from an unextinguished hearth
Ashes and sparks, my words among mankind!
Be through my lips to unawakened earth

The trumpet of a prophecy! O Wind,
If Winter comes, can Spring be far behind?   70

                                                          1820

ROBERT FROST

Stopping by Woods on a Snowy Evening

Whose woods these are I think I know.
His house is in the village, though;
He will not see me stopping here
To watch his woods fill up with snow.

My little horse must think it queer   5
To stop without a farmhouse near
Between the woods and frozen lake
The darkest evening of the year.

He gives his harness bells a shake
To ask if there is some mistake.   10
The only other sound's the sweep
Of easy wind and downy flake.

The woods are lovely, dark, and deep,
But I have promises to keep,
And miles to go before I sleep,   15
And miles to go before I sleep.

                                                          1923

8   SOUND AND SIGHT

The Sounds of Poetry

A lot of what happens in a poem happens in your mind's eye, but some of it happens in your voice. Poems are full of sounds and silences as well as words and sentences that are meaningful. Besides choosing words for their meanings, poets sometimes choose words because they involve certain sounds, and use sound effects to create a mood or establish a tone, just as films do. Sometimes the sounds of words are crucial to what is happening in the text of the poem.

The following poem explores the sounds of a particular word, tries them on, and analyzes them in relation to the word itself.

HELEN CHASIN

The Word *Plum*

The word *plum* is delicious

pout and push, luxury of
self-love, and savoring murmur

full in the mouth and falling
like fruit   5

taut skin
pierced, bitten, provoked into
juice, and tart flesh

question
and reply, lip and tongue   10
of pleasure.

1968

The poem savors the sounds of the word as well as the taste and feel of the fruit itself. It is almost as if the poem is tasting the sounds and rolling them carefully on the tongue. The second and third lines even replicate the "p," "l," "uh," and "m" sounds of the word while at the same time imitating the squishy sounds of eating the fruit. Words like "delicious" and "luxury" sound juicy, and other words imitate sounds of satisfaction and pleasure—"murmur," for example. Even the process of eating is in part recreated aurally. The tight, clipped sounds of "taut skin / pierced" suggest the sharp breaking of the skin and solid flesh, and as the tartness is described, the words ("provoked," "question") force the mouth to pucker as it would if it were savoring a tart fruit. The poet is having fun here recreating the various sense appeals of a plum, teasing the sounds and meanings out of available words. The words must mean something appropriate and describe something accurately first of all, of course, but when they can also imitate the sounds and feel of the process, they can do double duty. Not all poems manipulate sound as consciously or as fully as *The Word Plum,* but many poems at least contain passages in which the sounds of life are reproduced by the human voice reading the poem. To get the full effect of this poem—and of many others— reading aloud is essential; that way, one can pay attention to the vocal rhythms and can articulate the sounds as the poem calls for them to be reproduced by the human voice.

Almost always a poem's effect will be helped by reading it aloud, using your voice to pronounce the words so that the poem becomes a spoken communication. Historically, poetry began as an oral phenomenon, and often poems that seem very difficult when looked at silently come alive when they are turned into sound. Early bards chanted their verses, and the music of poetry—its cadences and rhythms—developed from this kind of performance. Often in primitive poetry (and sometimes in later ages) poetry performances have been accompanied by some kind of musical instrument. The rhythms of any poem become clearer when you say or hear them.

Poetry is, almost always, a vocal art, dependent on the human voice to become its full self (for some exceptions look at the shaped verse at the end of this chapter). In a sense, it begins to exist as a real phenomenon when a reader reads and actualizes it. Poems don't really achieve their full meaning when they merely exist on a page; a poem on a page is more a set of stage directions for a poem than a poem itself. Sometimes, in fact, it is hard to experience the poem at all unless you hear it. A good poetry reading might easily convince you of the importance of a good voice sensitive to the poem's requirements, but you can also persuade yourself by reading poems aloud in the privacy of your own room. An audience is even better, however, because then there is someone to share the pleasure in the sounds themselves and consider what they imply.

MONA VAN DUYN

What the Motorcycle Said

Br-r-r-am-m-m, rackety-am-m, OM, *Am:*
All—r-r-room, r-r-ram, ala-bas-ter—
Am, the world's my oyster.

I hate plastic, wear it black and slick,

hate hardhats, wear one on my head,   5
that's what the motorcycle said.

Passed phonies in Fords, knocked down billboards, landed
on the other side of The Gap, and Whee,
bypassed history.

When I was born (The Past), baby knew best.   10
They shook when I bawled, took Freud's path,
threw away their wrath.

R-r-rackety-am-m, *Am*. War, rhyme,
soap, meat, marriage, the Phantom Jet
are shit, and like that.   15

Hate pompousness, punishment, patience, am into Love,
hate middle-class moneymakers, live on Dad,
that's what the motorcycle said.

Br-r-r-am-m-m. It's Nowsville, man. Passed Oldies, Uglies,
Straighties, Honkies. I'll never be   20
mean, tired or unsexy.

Passed cigarette suckers, souses, mother-fuckers,
losers, went back to Nature and found
how to get VD, stoned.

Passed a cow, too fast to hear her moo, "*I* rolled   25
our leaves of grass into one ball.
I am the grassy All."

Br-r-r-am-m-m, rackety-am-m, OM, *Am*:
All—gr-r-rin, oooohgah, gl-l-utton—
Am, the world's my smilebutton.   30

                                                                                             1973

Saying this poem as if you were a motorcycle with the power of
speech (sort of) is part of the poem's fun, and the rich, loud sounds
of a motorcycle revving up concentrate and intensify the effect and
enrich the pleasure. It's a shame not to hear a poem like this aloud;
a lot of it is missed if you don't try to imitate the sounds or if you
don't try to pick up the motor's rhythms in the poem. A performance here is clearly worth it: a human being as motorcycle,
motorcycle as human being.

And it's a good poem, too, that does something interesting, important, and maybe a bit subversive. The speaking motorcycle seems
to take on the values of some of its riders, the noisy and obtrusive
ones that readers are most likely to associate with motorcycles in
their minds. The riders made fun of here are themselves sort of mind-

less and mechanical; they are the sort who have cult feelings about their group, who travel in packs, and who live no life beyond their machines. The speaking motorcycle, like such riders, grooves on power and speed, lives for the moment, and has little respect for people, the past, for institutions, or for anything beyond its own small world. It is self-centered, modish, ignorant, and inarticulate; but proud, mighty proud, and feels important in its own sounds. That's what the motorcycle says.

The following poem uses sound effects efficiently, too.

KENNETH FEARING

Dirge

1-2-3 was the number he played but today the number came 3-2-1;
Bought his Carbide at 30, and it went to 29; had the favorite at Bowie
    but the track was slow—

O executive type, would you like to drive a floating-power, knee-action,
    silk-upholstered six? Wed a Hollywood star? Shoot the course in
    58? Draw to the ace, king, jack?
O fellow with a will who won't take no, watch out for three cigarettes
    on the same, single match; O democratic voter born in August
    under Mars, beware of liquidated rails—

Denouement to denouement, he took a personal pride in the certain,
    certain way he lived his own, private life,   5
But nevertheless, they shut off his gas; nevertheless, the bank foreclosed;
    nevertheless, the landlord called; nevertheless, the radio broke,

And twelve o'clock arrived just once too often,
Just the same he wore one gray tweed suit, bought one straw hat, drank
    one straight Scotch, walked one short step, took one long look,
    drew one deep breath,
Just one too many,

And wow he died as wow he lived,   10
Going whop to the office and blooie home to sleep and biff got married
    and bam had children and oof got fired,
Zowie did he live and zowie did he die,

With who the hell are you at the corner of his casket, and where the
    hell're we going on the right-hand silver knob, and who the hell
    cares walking second from the end with an American Beauty
    wreath from why the hell not,

Very much missed by the circulation staff of the New York Evening
    Post; deeply, deeply mourned by the B.M.T.[1]

1. A New York subway line.

Wham, Mr. Roosevelt; pow, Sears Roebuck; awk, big dipper; bop,
summer rain;   15
Bong, Mr., bong, Mr., bong, Mr., bong.

1935

As the title implies, this poem is a kind of musical lament, in this
case for a certain sort of businessman who took a lot of chances and
saw his investments and life go down the drain in the depression of
the early thirties. Reading this poem aloud is a big help partly because it contains expressive words which echo the action, words like
"oof" and "blooie" (which primarily carry their meaning in their sounds,
for they have no literal or referential meaning). Reading aloud also
helps us notice that the poem employs rhythms much as a song would
and that it frequently shifts its pace and mood. Notice how carefully
the first two lines are balanced, and then how quickly the rhythm
shifts as the "executive type" begins to be addressed directly in line
3. (Line 2 is long and dribbles over in the narrow pages of a book
like this; a lot of the lines here are especially long, and the irregu-
larity of the line lengths is one aspect of the special sound effects
the poem creates.) In the direct address, the poem first picks up a
series of advertising features which it recites in rapid-fire order rather
like the advertising phrases in *Needs* in Chapter 3. In stanza 3 here,
the rhythm shifts again, but the poem gives us helpful clues about
how to read. Line 5 sounds like prose and is long, drawn out, and
rather dull (rather like its subject), but line 6 sets up a regular
(and monotonous) rhythm with its repeated "nevertheless" which
punctuates the rhythm like a drumbeat: "But nevertheless *tuh-tuh-
tuh-tuh-tuh*; nevertheless *tuh-tuh-tuh-tuh*; nevertheless *tuh-tuh-tuh-
tuh*; nevertheless *tuh-tuh-tuh-tuh-tuh*." In the next stanza, the repetitive phrasing comes again, this time guided by the word "one" in
cooperation with other words of one syllable: "wore *one* gray tweed
suit, bought *one* straw hat, *tuh* one *tuh-tuh*; *tuh* one *tuh-tuh*; *tuh*
one *tuh-tuh*; *tuh* one *tuh-tuh*." And then a new rhythm and a new
technique in stanza 5 as the language of comic books is imitated
to describe in violent, exaggerated terms the routine of his life. You
have to say words like "whop" and "zowie" aloud and in the rhythm
of the whole sentence to get the full effect of how boring his life is,
no matter how he tries to jazz it up with exciting words. And so it
goes—repeated words, shifting rhythms, emphasis on routine and aver-
ageness—until the final bell ("Bong . . . bong . . . bong . . . bong")
tolls rhythmically for the dead man in the final clanging line.

Sometimes sounds in poems just provide special effects, rather like
a musical score behind a film, setting mood and getting us into an
appropriate frame of mind. But often sound and meaning go hand in
hand, and the poet finds words that in their sounds echo the action.
A word which captures or approximates the sound of what it describes, such as "splash" or "squish" or "murmur" is called an **onomatopoeic** word, and the device itself is called **onomatopoeia**. And similar things can be done poetically with pacing and rhythm, sounds and

pauses. The punctuation, the length of vowels, and the combination of consonant sounds help to control the way we read so that we imitate what is being described. The poems at the end of this discussion (pp. 699–703) suggest several ways that such imitations of pace and pause may occur: by echoing the lapping of waves on a shore, for example (*Like as the Waves*), or mimicking the sounds of a train on a variable terrain (*The Express*), or reproducing the rhythms of a musical style (*Dear John, Dear Coltrane*).

Here is a classic passage in which a skillful poet talks about the virtues of making the sound echo the sense—and shows at the same time how to do it:

ALEXANDER POPE

[Sound and Sense] [2]

But most by numbers[3] judge a poet's song,   337
And smooth or rough, with them, is right or wrong;
In the bright muse though thousand charms conspire,[4]
Her voice is all these tuneful fools admire,   340
Who haunt Parnassus[5] but to please their ear,
Not mend their minds; as some to church repair,
Not for the doctrine, but the music there.
These, equal syllables[6] alone require,
Though oft the ear the open vowels tire,   345
While expletives[7] their feeble aid do join,
And ten low words oft creep in one dull line,
While they ring round the same unvaried chimes,
With sure returns of still expected rhymes.
Where'e'er you find "the cooling western breeze,"   350
In the next line, it "whispers through the trees";
If crystal streams "with pleasing murmurs creep,"
The reader's threatened (not in vain) with "sleep."
Then, at the last and only couplet fraught
With some unmeaning thing they call a thought,   355
A needless Alexandrine[8] ends the song,
That, like a wounded snake, drags its slow length along.
Leave such to tune their own dull rhymes, and know
What's roundly smooth, or languishingly slow;
And praise the easy vigor of a line,   360
Where Denham's strength and Waller's[9] sweetness join.

2. From *An Essay on Criticism*, Pope's poem on the art of poetry and the problems of literary criticism. The passage excerpted here follows a discussion of several common weaknesses of critics: failure to regard an author's intention, for example, or over-emphasis on clever metaphors and ornate style.
3. Meter, rhythm, sound.
4. Unite.
5. A mountain in Greece, traditionally associated with the muses and considered the seat of poetry and music.
6. Regular accents.
7. Filler words, such as "do."
8. A six-foot line, sometimes used in pentameter poems to vary the pace mechanically. Line 357 is an alexandrine.
9. Sir John Denham and Edmund Waller, 17th-century poets credited with perfecting the heroic couplet.

True ease in writing comes from art, not chance,
As those move easiest who have learned to dance.
'Tis not enough no harshness gives offense,
The sound must seem an echo to the sense: 365
Soft is the strain when Zephyr[1] gently blows,
And the smooth stream in smoother numbers flows;
But when loud surges lash the sounding shore,
The hoarse, rough verse should like the torrent roar.
When Ajax[2] strives, some rock's vast weight to throw,   370
The line too labors, and the words move slow;
Not so, when swift Camilla[3] scours the plain,
Flies o'er th' unbending corn, and skims along the main.
Hear how Timotheus'[4] varied lays surprise,
And bid alternate passions fall and rise!   375
While, at each change, the son of Libyan Jove[5]
Now burns with glory, and then melts with love;
Now his fierce eyes with sparkling fury glow,
Now sighs steal out, and tears begin to flow:
Persians and Greeks like turns of nature[6] found,   380
And the world's victor stood subdued by sound!
The pow'r of music all our hearts allow,
And what Timotheus was, is DRYDEN now.

                                                          1711

A lot of things go on here simultaneously. The poem uses a number of
echoic or onomatopoeic words, and pleasant and unpleasant consonant sounds are used in some lines to underline a particular point or
add some mood music. When the poet talks about a particular weakness in poetry, he illustrates it at the same time—by using open vowels
(line 345), expletives (line 346), monosyllabic words (line 347),
predictable rhymes (lines 350–353), or long, slow lines (line 357).
And the good qualities of poetry he talks about and illustrates as well
(line 360, for example). But the main effects of the passage come
from an interaction of several strategies at once. The effects are fairly
simple and easy to spot, but their causes involve a lot of poetic ingenuity. In line 340, for example, a careful cacophonous effect is
achieved by the repetition of the $\overline{oo}$ vowel sound and the repetition
of the L consonant sound together with the interruption (twice) of
the rough F sound in the middle; no one wants to be caught admiring that music when the poet gets through with us, but the careful harmony of the preceding sounds has set us up beautifully. And
in lines 347, 357, and 359, the pace of the lines is carefully con-

---

1. The west wind.
2. A Greek hero of the Trojan War,
noted for his strength.
3. A woman warrior in *The Aeneid*.
4. The court-musician of Alexander the
Great, celebrated in a famous poem by
Dryden (see line 383) for the power of
his music over Alexander's emotions.

5. In Greek tradition, the chief god of
any people was often given the name Zeus
(Jove), and the chief god of Libya (the
Greek name for all of Africa) was called
Zeus Ammon. Alexander visited his oracle
and was proclaimed son of the god.
6. Similar alternations of emotion.

trolled by consonant sounds as well as by the use of long vowels. Line 347 moves incredibly slowly and seems much longer than it is because almost all the one-syllable words end in a consonant which refuses to blend with the beginning of the next word, making the words hard to say without distinct, awkward pauses between them. And in lines 357 and 359, long vowels such as those in "wounded," "snake," "slow," "along," "roundly," and "smooth" help to slow down the pace, and the same trick of juxtaposing awkward, unpronounceable consonants is also employed. The commas also provide nearly a full stop in the midst of each line to slow us down still more. Similarly, the harsh lashing of the shore in lines 368–69 is partly accomplished by onomatopoeia, partly by a shift in the pattern of stress which creates irregular waves in line 368, and partly by the dominance of rough consonants in line 369. (In Pope's time, the English *r* was still trilled gruffly so that it could be made to sound extremely rough and harsh.) Almost every line in this passage could serve as a demonstration of how to make sound echo sense.

As the passage from Pope and the poem *Dirge* suggest, sound is most effectively manipulated in poetry when the rhythm of the voice is carefully controlled so that not only are the proper sounds heard, but they are heard at precisely the right moment. Pace and rhythm are nearly as important to a good poem as they are to a good piece of music. The human voice naturally develops certain rhythms in speech; some syllables and some words receive more stress than others, and a careful poet controls the flow of stresses to that, in many poems, a certain basic rhythm develops almost like a quiet percussion instrument in the background. The most common rhythm in English is the regular alternation of unstressed and stressed syllables, as in the passage from Pope. There, most lines have five sets of unstressed/stressed syllables, although plenty of lines have slight variations so that there is little danger (if you read sensitively) of falling into too expected a rhythm, a dull sing-song. The unstressed/stressed pattern (in that order) is called **iambic** rhythm. Other fairly common rhythms are the **trochaic** (a stressed syllable followed by an unstressed one), the **anapestic** (two unstressed syllables followed by a stressed one), and **dactylic** (a stressed syllable followed by two unstressed ones). Each unit of measurement is called a **foot**. In "A Glossary of Poetic Terms," pp. 915–932, you will find definitions as well for some less frequently used rhythms, a list of terms used to describe lengths of lines, and some directions on how to **scan** (that is, analyze the rhythmic pattern of) metered verse.

Here is a poem which names and illustrates many of the meters. If you read it aloud and chart the unstressed (∪) and stressed (—) syllables you should have a chart similar to that done by the poet himself in the text.

SAMUEL TAYLOR COLERIDGE

Metrical Feet

Lesson for a Boy

Trŏchĕe trı̆ps frŏm lŏng tŏ shŏrt;[7]
From long to long in solemn sort
Slōw Spōndēe stālks; strŏng fōōt! yet ill able
Ēvĕr tŏ cōme ŭp wı̆th Dāctўl trı̆sŷllăblĕ.
Iămbı̆cs mārch frŏm short tŏ long—   5
Wı̆th ă lēap ănd ă bōūnd thĕ swı̆ft Ānăpĕsts thrōng;
One syllable long, with one short at each side,
Ămphı̆brăchŷs hāstes wı̆th ă stātelŷ stride—
Fı̆rst ănd lāst bēı̆ng lōng, mı̆ddlĕ shŏrt, Ămphı̆mācer
Strı̆kes hı̆s thūndĕrı̆ng hōōfs lı̆ke ă prōūd hı̆gh-brĕd Rācer.   10
If Derwent[8] be innocent, steady, and wise,
And delight in the things of earth, water, and skies;
Tender warmth at his heart, with these meters to show it,
With sound sense in his brains, may make Derwent a poet—
May crown him with fame, and must win him the love   15
Of his father on earth and his Father above.
       My dear, dear child!
Could you stand upon Skiddaw,[9] you would not from its whole ridge
See a man who so loves you as your fond s. t. coleridge.
1806

    The following poem exemplifies **dactylic** rhythm, and the limericks that follow are written in **anapestic** meter.

ARTHUR W. MONKS

Twilight's Last Gleaming

        Higgledy-piggledy
        President Jefferson
        Gave up the ghost on the
        Fourth of July.

        So did John Adams, which   5
        Shows that such patriots
        Propagandistically
        Knew how to die.

                       1967

7. The long and short marks over syllables are Coleridge's; the kinds of metrical feet named and exemplified here are defined in the glossary, p. 924.
8. Written originally for Coleridge's son Hartley, the poem was later adapted for his younger son, Derwent.
9. A mountain in the lake country of northern England (where Coleridge lived in his early years), near the town of Derwent.

ANONYMOUS

Limericks

There once was a spinster of Ealing,
Endowed with such delicate feeling,
    That she thought an armchair
    Should not have its legs bare—
So she kept her eyes trained on the ceiling.

* *

I sat next to the Duchess at tea.
It was just as I thought it would be:
    Her rumblings abdominal
    Were simply phenomenal
And everyone thought it was me.

* *

A charming young woman named Pat
Would invite one to do this and that.
    When speaking of this
    She meant more than a kiss
So imagine her meaning of that.

* *

A trendy young girl from St. Paul
Wore a newspaper dress to a ball,
    But the dress caught on fire
    And burned her entire
Front page, sporting section, and all.

* *

A swimmer whose clothing was strewed
By breezes that left her quite nude,
    Saw a man come along,
    And unless I am wrong
You expected this line to be lewd.

* *

A staid schizophrenic named Struther,
When told of the death of his brother,
    Said: "Yes, I am sad;
    It makes me feel bad,
But then, I still have each other."

* *

There once was a pious young priest
Who lived almost wholly on yeast.
    He said, "It's so plain
    We must all rise again
That I'd like to get started at least."

* *

God's plan had a hopeful beginning,
But man spoiled his chances by sinning.
    We trust that the story
    Will end in God's glory,
But right now the other side's winning.

This poem is composed in the more common **trochaic** meter.

SIR JOHN SUCKLING

Song

Why so pale and wan, fond Lover?
    Prithee why so pale?
Will, when looking well can't move her,
    Looking ill prevail?
    Prithee why so pale?   5

Why so dull and mute, young Sinner?
    Prithee why so mute?
Will, when speaking well can't win her,
    Saying nothing do 't?
    Prithee why so mute?   10

Quit, quit, for shame, this will not move,
    This cannot take her;
If of her self she will not love,
    Nothing can make her,
    The Devil take her.   15

                            1646

The basic meter in the following poem is the most common one in English, **iambic:**

JOHN DRYDEN

To the Memory of Mr. Oldham[1]

Farewell, too little, and too lately known,
Whom I began to think and call my own;

---

1. John Oldham (1653–83), who like Dryden (see lines 3–6) wrote satiric poetry.

For sure our souls were near allied, and thine
Cast in the same poetic mold with mine.
One common note on either lyre did strike,　　　　　5
And knaves and fools we both abhorred alike.
To the same goal did both our studies drive;
The last set out the soonest did arrive.
Thus Nisus fell upon the slippery place,
While his young friend performed and won the race.[2]　　　10
O early ripe! to thy abundant store
What could advancing age have added more?
It might (what nature never gives the young)
Have taught the numbers[3] of thy native tongue.
But satire needs not those, and wit will shine　　　　15
Through the harsh cadence of a rugged line.[4]
A noble error, and but seldom made,
When poets are by too much force betrayed.
Thy generous fruits, though gathered ere their prime,
Still showed a quickness; and maturing time　　　　20
But mellows what we write to the dull sweets of rhyme.
Once more, hail and farewell; farewell, thou young,
But ah too short, Marcellus[5] of our tongue;
Thy brows with ivy, and with laurels bound;
But fate and gloomy night encompass thee around.　　　25

1684

Once you have figured out the basic rhythm of a poem, you can often find some interesting things by looking carefully at the departures from the pattern. Departures from the basic iambic meter of *To the Memory of Mr. Oldham*, for example, suggest some of the imaginative things that poets can do within the apparently very restrictive requirements of traditional meter. Try marking the stressed and unstressed syllables in *To the Memory of Mr. Oldham* and then look carefully at each of the places which vary from the basic iambic pattern. Which of these variations call special attention to a particular sound or action being talked about in the poem? Which ones specifically mimic or echo the sense? Which variations seem to exist primarily for emphasis? Which ones seem primarily intended to mark structural breaks in the poem?

───────

2. In Vergil's *Aeneid* (Book V), Nisus (who is leading the race) falls and then trips the second runner so that his friend Euryalus can win.
3. Rhythms.

4. In Dryden's time, R's were pronounced with a harsh, trilling sound.
5. The nephew of the Roman emperor Augustus; he died at 20, and Vergil celebrated him in *The Aeneid*, Book VI.

ALFRED, LORD TENNYSON

Break, Break, Break

Break, break, break,
  On thy cold gray stones, O Sea!
And I would that my tongue could utter
  The thoughts that arise in me.

O well for the fisherman's boy,   5
  That he shouts with his sister at play!
O well for the sailor lad,
  That he sings in his boat on the bay!
And the stately ships go on
  To their haven under the hill;   10
But O for the touch of a vanished hand,
  And the sound of a voice that is still!

Break, break, break,
  At the foot of thy crags, O Sea!
But the tender grace of a day that is dead   15
  Will never come back to me.

ca. 1834

DONALD JUSTICE

Counting the Mad

This one was put in a jacket,
This one was sent home,
This one was given bread and meat
But would eat none,
And this one cried No No No No   5
All day long.

This one looked at the window
As though it were a wall,
This one saw things that were not there,
This one things that were,   10
And this one cried No No No No
All day long.

This one thought himself a bird,
This one a dog,
And this one thought himself a man,   15
An ordinary man,
And cried and cried No No No No
All day long.

1960

THOMAS NASHE

Spring, the Sweet Spring

Spring, the sweet spring, is the year's pleasant king,
Then blooms each thing, then maids dance in a ring,
Cold doth not sting, the pretty birds do sing:
    Cuckoo, jug-jug, pu-we, to-witta-woo![6]

The palm and may make country houses gay,   5
Lambs frisk and play, the shepherds pipe all day,
And we hear aye birds tune this merry lay:
    Cuckoo, jug-jug, pu-we, to-witta-woo!

The fields breathe sweet, the daisies kiss our feet,
Young lovers meet, old wives a-sunning sit,   10
In every street these tunes our ears do greet:
    Cuckoo, jug-jug, pu-we, to-witta-woo!
      Spring, the sweet spring!

                           1592

GERARD MANLEY HOPKINS

Spring and Fall:

To a Young Child

Márgarét áre you gríeving
Over Goldengrove unleaving?
Leáves, líke the things of man, you
With your fresh thoughts care for, can you?
Áh! ás the heart grows older   5
It will come to such sights colder
By and by, nor spare a sigh
Though worlds of wanwood[7] leafmeal lie;
And yet you wíll weep and know why.
Now no matter, child, the name: 10
Sórrow's spríngs áre the same.
Nor mouth had, no nor mind, expressed
What heart heard of, ghost[8] guessed:
It ís the blight man was born for,
It is Margaret you mourn for.   15

1880

---

6. The calls of the cuckoo, nightingale, lapwing, and owl, respectively.
7. Pale, gloomy woods. "leafmeal": broken up, leaf by leaf (analogous to "piecemeal").
8. Soul.

WILLIAM SHAKESPEARE

Like as the Waves

Like as the waves make towards the pebbled shore,
So do our minutes hasten to their end,
Each changing place with that which goes before,
In sequent[9] toil all forwards do contend.[1]
Nativity,[2] once in the main[3] of light,   5
Crawls to maturity, wherewith being crowned,
Crooked[4] eclipses 'gainst his glory fight,
And Time that gave doth now his gift confound.[5]
Time doth transfix[6] the flourish set on youth
And delves the parallels[7] in beauty's brow,   10
Feeds on the rarities of nature's truth,
And nothing stands but for his scythe to mow.
    And yet to times in hope[8] my verse shall stand,
    Praising thy worth, despite his cruel hand.

1609

STEPHEN SPENDER

The Express

After the first powerful, plain manifesto
The black statement of pistons, without more fuss
But gliding like a queen, she leaves the station.
Without bowing and with restrained unconcern
She passes the houses which humbly crowd outside,   5
The gasworks, and at last the heavy page
Of death, printed by gravestones in the cemetery.
Beyond the town, there lies the open country
Where, gathering speed, she acquires mystery,
The luminous self-possession of ships on ocean.   10
It is now she begins to sing—at first quite low
Then loud, and at last with a jazzy madness—
The song of her whistle screaming at curves,
Of deafening tunnels, brakes, innumerable bolts.
And always light, aerial, underneath,   15
Retreats the elate meter of her wheels.
Steaming through metal landscape on her lines,
She plunges new eras of white happiness,

9. Successive.
1. Struggle.
2. New-born life.
3. High seas.
4. Perverse.

5. Bring to nothing.
6. Pierce.
7. Lines, wrinkles.
8. In the future.

Where speed throws up strange shapes, broad curves
And parallels clean like trajectories from guns.   20
At last, further than Edinburgh or Rome,
Beyond the crest of the world, she reaches night
Where only a low stream-line brightness
Of phosphorus on the tossing hills is light.
Ah, like a comet through flame, she moves entranced,   25
Wrapt in her music no bird song, no, nor bough
Breaking with honey buds, shall ever equal.

                                                                   1933

MICHAEL HARPER

Dear John, Dear Coltrane

                          a love supreme, a love supreme[9]
                          a love supreme, a love supreme

Sex fingers toes
in the marketplace
near your father's church
in Hamlet, North Carolina—[1]
witness to this love   5
in this calm fallow
of these minds,
there is no substitute for pain:
genitals gone or going,
seed burned out,   10
you tuck the roots in the earth,
turn back, and move
by river through the swamps,
singing: *a love supreme, a love supreme;*
what does it all mean?   15
Loss, so great each black
woman expects your failure
in mute change, the seed gone.
You plod up into the electric city—
your song now crystal and   20
the blues. You pick up the horn
with some will and blow
into the freezing night:
a love supreme, a love supreme—

Dawn comes and you cook   25
up the thick sin 'tween

9. Coltrane's record of "A Love Supreme," released in 1965, represents his moment of greatest public acclaim. The record was named Record of the Year and Coltrane was named jazz musician of the year in the *Downbeat* poll.

1. Coltrane's birthplace. His family shared a house with Coltrane's grandfather, who was the minister of St. Stephen's AME Zion Church there.

impotence and death, fuel
the tenor sax cannibal
heart, genitals and sweat
that makes you clean—   30
a love supreme, a love supreme—

Why you so black?
cause I am
why you so funky?
cause I am   35
why you so black?
cause I am
why you so sweet?
cause I am
why you so black?   40
cause I am
a love supreme, a love supreme:

So sick
you couldn't play *Naima*,[2]
so flat we ached   45
for song you'd concealed
with your own blood,
your diseased liver gave
out its purity,
the inflated heart   50
pumps out, the tenor kiss,
tenor love:
a love supreme, a love supreme—
a love supreme, a love supreme—

                                                            1970

BOB KAUFMAN

Blues Note

Ray Charles is the black wind of Kilimanjaro,[3]
Screaming up-and-down blues,
Moaning happy on all the elevators of my time.

Smiling into the camera, with an African symphony
Hidden in his throat, and (*I Got a Woman*)[4] wails, too.   5

He burst from Bessie's crushed black skull

---

2. Another standard Coltrane song, recorded in 1966 at the Village Vanguard.
3. The highest mountain in Africa, where the high winds are legendary.

4. One of Ray Charles's most famous hit recordings, the phrase "'way cross town" (line 14) is also from this song.

One cold night outside of Nashville,[5] shouting,
And grows bluer from memory, glowing bluer, still.

At certain times you can see the moon
Balanced on his head.   10

From his mouth he hurls chunks of raw soul.
He separated the sea of polluted sounds
And led the blues into the Promised Land.[6]

Ray Charles is a dangerous man ('way cross town),
And I love him.   15

(for Ray Charles's birthday N.Y.C./1961)

The Way a Poem Looks

The way a poem looks is not nearly so important as the way it
sounds—usually. But there are exceptions. A few poems are written
to be seen rather than heard or read aloud, and their appearance
on the page is crucial to their effect. The poem *l(a*, for example
(discussed in the Preface, p. 532), tries to visualize typographically
what the poet asks you to see in your mind's eye. Occasionally, too,
poems are composed in a specific shape so that the poem looks like
a physical object. At the end of this chapter, several poems—some
old, some new—illustrate some of the ways in which visual effects may
be created. Even though poetry has traditionally been thought of as
oral—words to be said, sung, or performed rather than looked at—the
idea that poems can also be related to painting and the visual arts
is also an old one. Theodoric in ancient Greece is credited with in-
venting **technopaegnia**—that is, constructing poems with visual appeal.
Once, the shaping of words to resemble an object was thought to have
mystical power, and especially in the Renaissance there was an active
interest in **emblem poetry** (or **carmen figuratum**) such as that exemplified in *Easter Wings* (p. 707) or *The Pillar of Fame* (p. 707).
But more recent attempts at **shaped verse** (the general term that may
be applied to any poem that uses visual appeal dramatically) are
usually playful exercises (such as Robert Hollander's *You Too? Me
Too—Why Not? Soda Pop*, which is shaped like a Coke bottle),
attempting to supplement (or replace) verbal meanings with devices
from painting and sculpture.

'Reading a poem like *Easter Wings* aloud wouldn't make much
sense. Our eyes are everything for a poem like that. A more frequent

5. Bessie Smith (1898?–1937), American blues singer, died near Nashville when
a segregated hospital refused to treat her
after an accident.
6. According to *Exodus* 14, Moses

caused the Red Sea waters to part so that
the Israelites could cross and escape from
the Egyptians who were pursuing them;
he then led his people to the Promised
Land, Canaan.

poetic device is to ask us to use our eyes as a guide to sound. The following poem depends upon recognition of some standard typographical symbols and knowledge of their names. We have to say those names to read the poem:

FRANKLIN P. ADAMS

Composed in the Composing Room

At stated .ic times
I love to sit and — off rhymes
Till ,tose at last I fall
Exclaiming "I don't ∧ all."

Though I'm an * objection   5
By running this in this here §
This ☞ of the Fleeting Hour,
This lofty -ician Tower—

A ¶er's hope dispels   10
All fear of deadly ‖.
You think these [] are a pipe?
Well, not on your †eotype.

                                                        1914

We create the right term here when we verbalize, putting the visual signs together with the words or letters printed in the poem, for example making the word "periodic" out of ".ic" or "high Phoenician" out of "-ician." This, too, involves an extreme instance and involves a game more than any serious emotional effect. More often poets give us—by the visual placement of sounds—a guide to reading, inviting us to regulate the pace of our reading, notice pauses or silences, pay attention both to the syntax of the poem and to the rhetoric of the voice, thus providing us a set of stage directions for reading.

c. e. cummings

portrait

Buffalo Bill's
defunct
            who used to
            ride a watersmooth-silver

                              stallion   5
and break onetwothreefourfive pigeonsjustlikethat
                                        Jesus
he was a handsome man
                        and what i want to know is
how do you like your blueeyed boy   10
Mister Death

                                        1923

The unusual spacing of words here, with some run together and others widely separated, provides a guide to reading, regulating both speed and sense, so that the poem can capture aloud some of the excitement and wonder of a boy's enthusiasm for a theatrical act as spectacular as that of Buffalo Bill. A good reader-aloud, with only this typographical guidance, can capture some of the wide-eyed boy's responses, remembered now in retrospect long after Buffalo Bill's act is out of business and the man himself is dead.

In prose, syntax and punctuation are the main guides to the voice of a reader, providing indicators of emphasis, pace, and speed, and in poetry they are also more conventional and more common guides than extreme forms of unusual typography as in *portrait*. Reading a poem sensitively is in some ways a lot like reading a piece of prose sensitively: one has to pay close attention to the way the sentences are put together and how they are punctuated. A good reader makes use of appropriate pauses as well as thundering emphasis; silence as well as sound is part of any poem, and reading punctuation is as important as knowing how to say the words.

Beyond punctuation, the placement and spacing of lines on the page may be helpful to a reader even when that placement is not as radical as in *portrait*. The fact that poetry looks different from prose is not an accident; decisions to make lines one length instead of another have as much to do with vocal breaks and phrasing as they have to do with functions of syntax or meaning. In a good poem, there are no accidents, not even in the way the poem meets the eye, for as readers our eyes are the most direct route to our voices; they are our scanner and director, our prompter and guide.

GEORGE HERBERT

Easter Wings

Lord, who createdst man in wealth and store,[1]
Though foolishly he lost the same,
Decaying more and more,
Till he became
Most poor:
With thee
O let me rise
As larks,[2] harmoniously,
And sing this day thy victories:
Then shall the fall further the flight in me.

My tender age in sorrow did begin;
And still with sicknesses and shame
Thou didst so punish sin,
That I became
Most thin.
With thee
Let me combine,
And feel this day thy victory;
For, if I imp[3] my wing on thine,
Affliction shall advance the flight in me.

1633

ROBERT HERRICK

The Pillar of Fame

Fame's pillar here, at last, we set,
Out-during *Marble, Brass,* or *Jet*,[4]
Charmed and enchanted so,
As to withstand the blow
Of   overthrow:
Nor shall the seas,
Or   OUTRAGES
Of storms o'erbear
What we up-rear,
Tho Kingdoms fall,
This   pillar   never   shall
Decline or waste at all;
But stand for ever by his own
Firm and well fixed foundation.

1648

1. In plenty.
2. Which herald the morning.
3. Engraft. In falconry, to engraft feathers in a damaged wing, so as to re-

store the powers of flight (OED).
4. Black lignite or black marble. "Out-during", out-lasting.

ANONYMOUS

Love Knot

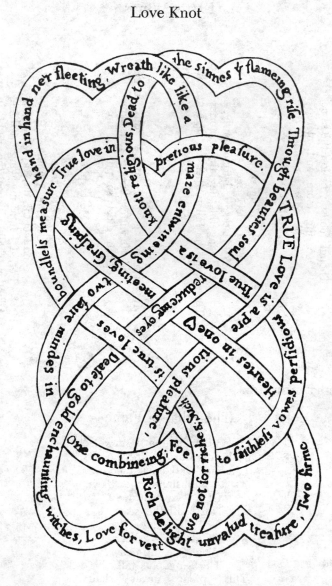

1640

EDWIN MORGAN

Message Clear

```
            am          i
                                if
        i am                he
            he r     o
            h    ur t                        5
            the re          and
            he    re     and
            he re
        a            n    d
            th  e    r         e               10
        i am  r                ife
                     i n
                  s     ion and
        i                d   i e
            am  e re   ct                      15
            am  e re   ction
                        o         f
            the               life
                     o         f
            m e         n                      20
                 sur e
            the          d   i e
        i      s
                  s  e t  and
        i am the  sur     d                    25
            a   t  res  t
                        o      life
        i am her            e
        i a         ct
        i     r   u     n                      30
        i  m e e    f
        i         t      i e
        i      s    t  and
        i am th     o     th
        i am   r      a                        35
        i am the  su    n
        i am the  s    on
        i am the  e  rect on     e if
        i am    re        n    t
        i am      s    a      fe               40
        i am      s  e  n    t
        i   he e          d
        i   t e s   t
        i      re      a d
        a   th re      a d                     45
        a     s    t on      e
        a   t  re      a d
        a   th r     on         e
        i      resurrect
                        a      life            50
        i am         i n      life
        i am    resurrection
        i am the resurrection and
        i am
        i am the resurrection and the life[b]   55
```

EDWIN MORGAN

The Computer's First Christmas Card

```
        jollymerry
        hollyberry
        jollyberry
        merryholly
        happyjolly                    5
        jollyjelly
        jellybelly
        bellymerry
        hollyheppy
        jollyMolly                    10
        marryJerry
        merryHarry
        hoppyBarry
        heppyJarry
        boppyheppy                    15
        berryjorry
        jorryjolly
        moppyjelly
        Mollymerry
        Jerryjolly                    20
        bellyboppy
        jorryhoppy
        hollymoppy
        Barrymerry
        Jarryhappy                    25
        happyboppy
        boppyjolly
        jollymerry
        merrymerry
        merrymerry                    30
        merryChris
        ammerryasa
        Chrismerry
        aSMERRYCHR
        YSANTHEMUM                    35
```

1968

JOHN HOLLANDER

A State of Nature

                                        Some broken
                                      Iroquois adze
                                     pounded southward
                                    and resembled this
                                   outline once But now
                                  boundaries foul-lines
                                 and even sea-coasts are
                                naturally involved with
                               mappers and followers of
                              borders So that we who grew
                             up here might think That steak is
                      shaped too much like New York to be real And like
            the shattered flinty implement whose ghost lives
            inside our sense of what this rough chunk should
            by right of history recall the language spoken by
            its shapers now inhabits only streams and lakes and
            hills The natural names are only a chattering and mean
only the land they label How shall we live in a forest of
                                        such murmurs with
                                         no ideas but in
                                        forms a state
                                          whose name
                                            passes
                                              for
                                            a city
                                            1969

ROBERT HOLLANDER

You Too? Me Too—Why Not?
Soda Pop

                    I am
                    look
                    ing at
                    the Co
                    caCola
                    bottle
                    which is
                    green wi
                    th ridges
                    just like
                c   c   c
                o   o   o
                l   l   l
                u   u   u
                m   m   m
                n   n   n
                s   s   s
            and on itself it says

                COCA-COLA
                reg.u.s.pat.off.

exactly like an art pop
statue of that kind of
bottle but not so green
that the juice inside
gives other than the co
lor it has when I pour
it out in a clear glass
glass on this table top
(It's making me thirsty
all this winking and
beading of Hippocrene
please let me pause
drinking the fluid in)
ah! it is enticing how
each color is the same
brown in green bottle
brown in uplifted glass
making each utensil on
the table laid a brown
fork in a brown shade
making me long to watch
them harvesting the crop
which makes the deep-aged
rich brown wine of America
that is to say which makes
soda   pop   p. 1968

9   STANZAS AND VERSE FORMS

Most poems of more than a few lines are divided into **stanzas,** groups of lines divided from other groups by white space on the page. Putting some space between the groupings of lines has the effect of sectioning off the poem, giving its physical appearance a series of divisions that often mark breaks in thought in the poem, or changes of scenery or imagery, or other shifts in the direction of the poem. In *The Flea* (p. 623), for example, the stanza divisions mark distinctive stages in the action; between the first and second stanzas, the speaker stops his companion from killing the flea, and between the second and third stanzas, the companion follows through on her intention and kills the flea. And in *The Goose Fish* (p. 671), the stanzas mark stages in the self-perception of the lovers; each of the stanzas is a more or less distinct scene, and the stanzas unfold almost like a series of slides. Not all stanzas are quite so neatly patterned, but any poem divided into stanzas calls attention on the page to the fact of the divisions and invites some sort of response to what appear to be gaps or silences that may be structural indicators.

Historically, stanzas have most often been organized internally by patterns of rhyme, and thus stanza divisions have been a visual indicator of patterns in sound. In most traditional stanza forms, the pattern of rhyme is repeated in stanza after stanza throughout the poem, and the voice and ear become familiar with the pattern so that, in a sense, we come to depend on it. We can thus "hear" variations, just as we do in music. In a poem of more than a few stanzas, the accumulation of pattern may even mean that our ear comes to expect repetition and finds a kind of comfort in its increasing familiarity. The rhyme thus becomes an organizational device in the poem, and ordinarily the metrical patterns stay constant from stanza to stanza. In Shelley's *Ode to the West Wind*, for example, the first and third lines in each stanza rhyme, and the middle line then rhymes with the first and third lines of the next stanza. (In indicating rhyme, a different letter of the alphabet is conventionally used to represent each sound; in the following example, if we begin with "being" as *a* and "dead" as *b*, then "fleeing" is also *a*, and "red" and "bed" are *b*.)

O wild West Wind, thou breath of Autumn's being,   a
Thou, from whose unseen presence the leaves dead   b
Are driven, like ghosts from an enchanter fleeing,   a

Yellow, and black, and pale, and hectic red,   b
Pestilence-stricken multitudes: O thou,   c
Who chariotest to their dark wintry bed   b

The wingéd seeds, where they lie cold and low,   c
Each like a corpse within its grave, until   d
Thine azure sister of the Spring shall blow   c

In this stanza form, known as **terza rima,** the stanzas are thus linked to each other by a common sound: one rhyme sound from each stanza is picked up in the next stanza, and so on to the end of the group of stanzas. This stanza form is the one used by Dante in *The Divine Comedy*; its use is not all that common in English because it is a rhyme-rich stanza form—that is, it requires many, many rhymes, and English is, relatively speaking, a rhyme-poor language (that is, not so rich in rhyme possibilities as are languages such as Italian or French). One reason for this is that English words derive from so many different language families that we have fewer similar word endings than languages that have remained more "pure," more dependent for vocabulary on roots and patterns in their own language system.

Shortly, we will look at some other stanza forms, but first a brief Defense of Rhyme, or at least an explanation of its uses. Contemporary poets seldom use it, finding it neither necessary nor appealing, but until the last half century or so rhyme was central to most poems. Historically, there are good reasons for rhyme. Why have most recent poets avoided rhyme as vigorously as older poets pursued it? There is no single easy answer, but one can suggest why poetry traditionally found rhyme attractive and notice that some of those needs no longer exist. Because poetry was originally an oral art (and its texts not always written down) various kinds of **memory devices** (sometimes called **mnemonic devices**) were built into poems to help reciters remember them. Rhyme was one such device, and most people still find it easier to memorize poetry that rhymes. The simple pleasure of hearing the repetition of familiar sounds may also help to account for the traditional popularity of rhyme, and perhaps plain habit (for both poets and hearers) had a lot to do with why rhyme flourished for so many centuries as a standard expectation. No doubt, too, rhyme helped to give poetry a special quality that distinguished it from prose, a significant advantage in ages that worried about decorum and propriety and that were anxious to preserve a strong sense of poetic tradition. Some ages have been very concerned that poetry should not in any way be mistaken for prose or made to serve prosaic functions, and the literary critics and theorists in those ages made extraordinary efforts to emphasize the distinctions between poetry, which was thought to be artistically superior, and prose, which was thought to be primarily utilitarian. A pride in elitism and a fear that an expanded reading public could ultimately mean a dilution of the possibilities of traditional art forms have been powerful cultural forces in Western civilization, and if such forces were not themselves responsible for creating rhyme in poetry, they did help to preserve a sense of its necessity.

But there are at least two other reasons for rhyme. One is complex and hard to state justly without long explanations. It involves traditional ideas of the symmetrical relationship of different aspects of the world and ideas about the function of poetry to reflect the universe as human learning understood it. Most poets in earlier centuries assumed that rhyme was proper to verse, perhaps even essential. They would have felt themselves eccentric to compose poems any other way. Some poets did experiment—very successfully—with **blank verse** (that is, verse which did not rhyme but which nevertheless had strict metrical requirements), but the cultural pressure was almost constantly for rhyme. Why? Custom or habit may account for part of the assumption that rhyme was necessary, but probably not all of it. Rather, the poets' sense that poetry was an imitation of larger relationships in the universe made it seem natural to use rhyme to recreate a sense of harmony, correspondence, symmetry, and order. The sounds of poetry were thus faint reminders of the harmonious cosmos, of the music of the spheres that animated the planets, the processes of nature, the interrelationship of all created things and beings. Probably poets never said to themselves, "I shall now tunefully emulate the harmony of God's carefully ordered universe," but the tendency to use rhyme and other repetitions or re-echoings of sound (such as **alliteration** or **assonance**, defined in "A Glossary of Poetic Terms" §8) nevertheless stems ultimately from basic assumptions about how the universe worked. In a modern world increasingly perceived as fragmented, rambling, and unrelated, there is of course a much lessened tendency to testify to a sense of harmony and symmetry. It would be too easy and too mechanical to think that rhyme in a poem specifically means that the poet has a firm sense of cosmic order, and that an unrhymed poem testifies to chaos, but cultural assumptions do affect the expectations of both poets and readers, and cultural tendencies create a kind of pressure upon the individual creator. In the third section, from Chapter 11 on, we will be looking at several similar effects upon individual poems of historical and cultural contexts.

One other reason for using rhyme is that it provides a kind of discipline for the poet, a way of harnessing poetic talents and keeping a rein on the imagination, so that the results are ordered, controlled, put into some kind of meaningful and recognizable form. Robert Frost used to be fond of saying that writing poems without rhyme was like playing tennis without a net. Writing good poetry does require a lot of discipline, and Frost speaks for many (perhaps most) traditional poets in suggesting that rhyme can be a major source of that discipline. But it is not the only possible source, and more recent poets have usually felt they would rather play by new rules or invent their own as they go along, and have therefore sought their sources of discipline elsewhere, preferring the more spare tones that unrhymed poetry provides. It is not that contemporary poets cannot think of rhyme words or that they do not care about the sounds of their poetry; rather, recent poets have consciously decided not to work with rhyme and to use instead other aural devices and other strategies for organizing stanzas, just as they have chosen to work with experimental and variable rhythms instead of writing primarily in the traditional English meters. Some few modern poets, though, have protested the abandonment of rhyme and have continued to write rhymed verse successfully in a more or less traditional way.

The amount and density of rhyme varies widely in stanza and verse forms, some requiring elaborate and intricate patterns of rhyme, oth-

ers more casual or spare sound repetitions. The **Spenserian stanza,**
for example, is even more rhyme rich than terza rima, using only
three rhyme sounds in nine rhymed lines.

Her falt'ring hand upon the balustrade,	a
Old Angela was feeling for the stair,	b
When Madeline, St. Agnes' charméd maid,	a
Rose, like a missioned spirit, unaware:	b
With silver taper's light, and pious care,	b
She turned, and down the agéd gossip led	c
To a safe level matting. Now prepare,	b
Young Porphyro, for gazing on that bed;	c
She comes, she comes again, like ring dove frayed and fled.	c

On the other hand, the **ballad stanza** has only one rhyme in four
lines; lines 1 and 3 in each stanza do not rhyme at all.

The king sits in Dumferling toune,	a
Drinking the blude-reid wine:	b
"O whar will I get guid sailor,	c
To sail this ship of mine?"	b

Most stanzas have a metrical pattern as well as a rhyme scheme.
Terza rima, for example, involves five-beat lines (iambic pentameter),
and most of the Spenserian stanza (the first 8 lines) is also in iambic
pentameter, but the ninth line in each stanza has one extra foot (it
is iambic hexameter). The ballad stanza, also iambic as are most
English stanza and verse forms, alternates three-beat and four-beat
lines; lines 1 and 3 are unrhymed iambic tetrameter, and lines 2
and 4 are rhymed iambic trimeter.

Several stanza forms are exemplified in this book, most of them
based on rhyme schemes, but some (such as blank verse or syllabic
verse) are based entirely on meter or other measures of sound, or
on some more elaborate scheme such as the measured repetition of
words, as in the **sestina,** or the repetition of whole lines, as in the
villanelle. You can probably deduce the principles involved in each of
the following stanza or verse forms by looking carefully at a poem
which uses it; if you have trouble, look at the definitions in "A
Glossary of Poetic Terms," §9.

To His Coy Mistress	tetrameter couplet	p. 796
There Once Was a Spinster of Ealing	limerick	p. 696
Twilight's Last Gleaming	double dactyl	p. 695
Dirge	free verse	p. 690
from *Paradise Lost*	blank verse	p. 646
Fern Hill	syllabic verse	p. 899
Here in Katmandu	sestina	p. 634
Do Not Go Gentle	villanelle	p. 556

What are stanza forms good for? What use is it to recognize them? Why do poets bother? Matters discussed in this chapter so far have suggested two reasons: 1. Breaks between stanzas provide convenient pauses for reader and writer, something roughly equivalent to paragraphs in prose. The eye thus picks up the places where some kind of pause or break occurs. 2. Poets sometimes use stanza forms, as they do rhyme itself, as a discipline: writing in a certain kind of stanza form imposes a shape on their act of imagination. To suggest some other uses, we will look in more detail at one particular verse form, the **sonnet**. A sonnet has only a single stanza and offers several related possibilities for its rhyme scheme, but it is always fourteen lines long and usually written in iambic pentameter. The sonnet has remained a popular verse form in English for more than four centuries, and even in an age that largely rejects rhyme it continues to attract a variety of poets, including (curiously) radical and even revolutionary poets who find its firm structure very useful. Its uses, although quite varied, can be illustrated fairly precisely.

As a verse form, the sonnet is contained, compact, demanding; whatever it does, it must do concisely and quickly. To be effective, it must take advantage of the possibilities inherent in its shortness and its relative rigidity. It is best suited to intensity of feeling and concentration of expression. Not too surprisingly, one subject it frequently discusses is confinement itself.

₰ WILLIAM WORDSWORTH

Nuns Fret Not

Nuns fret not at their convent's narrow room;
And hermits are contented with their cells;
And students with their pensive citadels;
Maids at the wheel, the weaver at his loom,
Sit blithe and happy; bees that soar for bloom,   5
High as the highest Peak of Furness-fells,[1]
Will murmur by the hour in foxglove bells:[2]
In truth the prison, unto which we doom
Ourselves, no prison is: and hence for me,
In sundry moods, 'twas pastime to be bound   10

1. Mountains in England's Lake District, where Wordsworth lived.   2. Flowers from which digitalis (a heart medicine) began to be made in 1799.

Within the sonnet's scanty plot of ground;
Pleased if some souls (for such there needs must be)
Who have felt the weight of too much liberty,
Should find brief solace there, as I have found.

1807

Most sonnets are structured according to one of two principles of division. On one principle, the sonnet divides into three units of four lines each and a final unit of two lines. On the other, the fundamental break is between the first eight lines (called an octave) and the last six (called a sestet). The 4-4-4-2 sonnet is usually called the **English** or **Shakespearean sonnet,** and ordinarily its rhyme scheme reflects the structure: the scheme of *abab cdcd efef gg* is the classic one, but many variations from that pattern still reflect the basic 4-4-4-2 division. The 8-6 sonnet is usually called the **Italian** or **Petrarchan sonnet** (the Italian poet Petrarch was an early master of this structure), and its "typical" rhyme scheme is *abbaabba cdecde,* although it too produces many variations that still reflect the basic division into two parts.

The two kinds of sonnet structures are useful for two different sorts of argument. The 4-4-4-2 structure works very well for constructing a poem that wants to make a three-step argument (with a quick summary at the end), or for setting up brief, cumulative images. *That Time of Year* (p. 650), for example, uses the 4-4-4-2 structure to mark the progressive steps toward death and the parting of friends by using three distinct images, then summarizing. Shakespeare's *Let Me Not to the Marriage of True Minds* (p. 552) and Spenser's *Happy Ye Leaves* (p. 683) work very similarly, following the kind of organization that in Chapter 7 I called the 1-2-3 structure—and doing it compactly and economically.

Here, on the other hand is a poem which uses the 8-6 pattern:

HENRY CONSTABLE

My Lady's Presence Makes the Roses Red

My lady's presence makes the roses red
Because to see her lips they blush for shame.
The lily's leaves, for envy, pale became,
And her white hands in them this envy bred.
The marigold the leaves abroad doth spread   5
Because the sun's and her power is the same.
The violet of purple color came,
Dyed in the blood she made my heart to shed.
In brief, all flowers from her their virtue take;
From her sweet breath their sweet smells do proceed;   10

The living heat which her eyebeams doth make
Warmeth the ground and quickeneth the seed.
The rain wherewith she watereth the flowers
Falls from mine eyes, which she dissolves in showers.

1594

Here, the first eight lines argue that the lady's presence is responsible for the color of all of nature's flowers, and the final six lines
summarize and extend that argument to smells and heat—and finally
to the rain that the lady draws from the speaker's eyes. That kind of
two-part structure, in which the octave states a proposition or generalization and the sestet provides a particularization or application of
it, has a variety of uses. The final lines may, for example, reverse
the first eight and achieve a paradox or irony in the poem, or the
poem may *nearly* balance two comparable arguments. Basically, the
8-6 structure lends itself to poems with two points to make, or to those
which wish to make one fairly brief point and illustrate it.

Sometimes the neat and precise structure I have described is altered—either slightly, as in *Nuns Fret Not* above (where the 8-6
structure is more of an 8½-5½ structure) or more radically as particular needs or effects may demand. And the two basic structures
certainly do not define all the structural possibilities within a fourteen-
line poem, even if they do suggest the most traditional ways of taking
advantage of the sonnet's compact and well-kept container. Radical
departures like the *Joy Sonnet in a Random Universe* (p. 725), for
example, toy with the rigidity and use it lightheartedly to mock the
form.

The sonnets here by Sidney, Shakespeare, and Constable survive
from a golden age of sonnet writing in the late 16th century, an age
that set the pattern for expectations of form, subject matter, and tone.
The sonnet came to England from Italy via France, and imitations of
Petrarch's famous sonnet sequence to Laura became the rage. Thousands upon thousands of sonnets were written in those years, often in
sequences of a hundred or more sonnets each; the sequences explored the many moods of love and usually had a light thread of narrative that purported to recount a love affair between the poet and a
mistress who was almost always golden-haired, beautiful, disdainful,
and inaccessible. Her beauty was described in a series of exaggerated
comparisons: her eyes were like the sun (*When Nature Made Her
Chief Work, Stella's Eyes*), her teeth like pearls, her cheeks like
roses, her skin like ivory, and so on, but the adherence to these
conventions was always playful, and it became a game of wit to play
variations upon expectations (*My Lady's Presence Makes the Roses Red*
and *My Mistress' Eyes Are Nothing Like the Sun*). Almost always
teasing and witty (*What, Have I Thus Betrayed My Liberty*), these
poems were probably not as true to life as they pretended, but they
provided historically an expectation of what sonnets were to be.

Many modern sonnets continue to be about love or private life, and
many continue to use a personal, apparently open and sincere tone.

But poets often find the sonnet's compact form and rigid demands
equally useful for many varieties of subject, theme, and tone. Besides
love, sonnets often treat other subjects: politics, philosophy, discovery
of a new world. And tones vary widely too, from the anger and remorse of *Th' Expense of Spirit* (p. 889) and righteous outrage of
On the Late Massacre in Piedmont (p. 722) to the tender awe of
How Do I Love Thee (p. 538). Many poets seem to take the kind
of comfort Wordsworth describes in the careful limits of the form,
finding in its two basic variations (the English sonnet such as *My
Mistress' Eyes* and the Italian sonnet such as *On First Looking*) a
sufficiency of convenient ways to organize their materials into coherent
structures.

WILLIAM WORDSWORTH

Scorn Not the Sonnet

Scorn not the Sonnet; Critic, you have frowned,
Mindless of its just honors; with this key
Shakespeare unlocked his heart; the melody
Of this small lute gave ease to Petrarch's[3] wound;
A thousand times this pipe did Tasso sound;   5
With it Camoëns soothed an exile's grief;
The Sonnet glittered a gay myrtle leaf
Amid the cypress with which Dante crowned
His visionary brow: a glow-worm lamp,
It cheered mild Spenser, called from Faeryland   10
To struggle through dark ways; and when a damp
Fell round the path of Milton, in his hand
The Thing became a trumpet; whence he blew
Soul-animating strains—alas, too few!

1827

JOHN KEATS

On the Sonnet

If by dull rhymes our English must be chained,
And like Andromeda,[4] the sonnet sweet

---

3. Petrarch (1304–1374), Italian poet,
was the model for English Renaissance
sonneteers. The other poets named by
Wordsworth—the Italians Tasso and Dante,
the Portuguese Camoëns, and the English
Shakespeare, Spenser, and Milton—also
wrote sonnets extensively.
4. Who, according to Greek myth, was
chained to a rock so that she would be
devoured by a sea monster. She was rescued by Perseus, who married her. When
she died she was placed among the stars.

Fettered, in spite of painéd loveliness,
Let us find, if we must be constrained,
Sandals more interwoven and complete   5
To fit the naked foot of Poesy: [5]
Let us inspect the lyre, and weigh the stress
Of every chord, [6] and see what may be gained
By ear industrious, and attention meet;
Misers of sound and syllable, no less   10
Than Midas [7] of his coinage, let us be
Jealous [8] of dead leaves in the bay-wreath crown; [9]
So, if we may not let the Muse be free,
She will be bound with garlands of her own.

1819

PERCY BYSSHE SHELLEY

Ozymandias [1]

I met a traveler from an antique land
Who said: Two vast and trunkless legs of stone
Stand in the desert. . . . Near them, on the sand,
Half sunk, a shattered visage lies, whose frown,
And wrinkled lip, and sneer of cold command,   5
Tell that its sculptor well those passions read
Which yet survive, stamped on these lifeless things,
The hand that mocked them, and the heart that fed:
And on the pedestal these words appear:
"My name is Ozymandias, King of Kings: 10
Look on my works, ye Mighty, and despair!"
Nothing beside remains. Round the decay
Of that colossal wreck, boundless and bare
The lone and level sands stretch far away.

1818

5. In a letter which contained this sonnet, Keats expressed impatience with the traditional Petrarchan and Shakespearean sonnet forms: "I have been endeavoring to discover a better sonnet stanza than we have."
6. Lyre-string.
7. The legendary king of Phrygia who asked, and got, the power to turn all he touched to gold.
8. Suspiciously watchful.
9. The bay tree was sacred to Apollo, god of poetry, and bay wreaths came to symbolize true poetic achievement. The withering of the bay tree is sometimes considered an omen of death.
1. The Greek name for Rameses II, 13th-century B.C. pharaoh of Egypt. According to a first century B.C. Greek historian, Diodorus Siculus, the largest statue in Egypt was inscribed: "I am Ozymandias, king of kings; if anyone wishes to know what I am and where I lie, let him surpass me in some of my exploits."

◦ WILLIAM WORDSWORTH

London, 1802

Milton! thou should'st be living at this hour:
England hath need of thee: she is a fen[2]
Of stagnant waters: altar, sword, and pen,
Fireside, the heroic wealth of hall and bower,
Have forfeited their ancient English dower[3]   5
Of inward happiness. We are selfish men;
Oh! raise us up, return to us again;
And give us manners, virtue, freedom, power.
Thy soul was like a star, and dwelt apart:
Thou hadst a voice whose sound was like the sea: 10
Pure as the naked heavens, majestic, free,
So didst thou travel on life's common way,
In cheerful godliness; and yet thy heart
The lowliest duties on herself did lay.

1802

◦ JOHN MILTON

On the Late Massacre in Piedmont[4]

Avenge, O Lord, thy slaughtered saints, whose bones
Lie scattered on the Alpine mountains cold;
Ev'n them who kept thy truth so pure of old,
When all our fathers worshiped stocks and stones,
Forget not: in thy book record their groans   5
Who were thy sheep, and in their ancient fold
Slain by the bloody Piedmontese, that rolled
Mother with infant down the rocks. Their moans
The vales redoubled to the hills, and they
To Heav'n. Their martyred blood and ashes sow   10
O'er all th' Italian fields, where still doth sway
The triple Tyrant:[5] that from these may grow
A hundredfold who, having learnt thy way,
Early may fly the Babylonian woe.[6]

1655

---

2. Marsh.
3. Inheritance.
4. On Easter Sunday, 1655, the Duke of Savoy's forces massacred 1700 members of the Waldensian sect in the Piedmont in northwestern Italy. The sect, founded in 1170, existed at first within the Roman Catholic Church, but its vigorous condemnation of church rites and policies (especially of the use of icons—see line 4)

led to a total break. Until the year of the massacre the group had been allowed freedom of worship.
5. The Pope's tiara has three crowns.
6. Protestants in Milton's day associated Catholicism with Babylonian decadence, called the church "the whore of Babylon," and read the prophecy of *Revelation* 17 and 18 as an allegory of its coming destruction.

GWENDOLYN BROOKS

First Fight. Then Fiddle.

First fight. Then fiddle. Ply the slipping string
With feathery sorcery; muzzle the note
With hurting love; the music that they wrote
Bewitch, bewilder. Qualify to sing
Threadwise. Devise no salt, no hempen thing   5
For the dear instrument to bear. Devote
The bow to silks and honey. Be remote
A while from malice and from murdering.
But first to arms, to armor. Carry hate
In front of you and harmony behind.   10
Be deaf to music and to beauty blind.
Win war. Rise bloody, maybe not too late
For having first to civilize a space
Wherein to play your violin with grace.

                                                       1949

JOHN KEATS

On First Looking into Chapman's Homer [7]

Much have I traveled in the realms of gold,
And many goodly states and kingdoms seen;
Round many western islands have I been
Which bards in fealty [8] to Apollo hold.
Oft of one wide expanse had I been told   5
That deep-browed Homer ruled as his demesne; [9]
Yet did I never breathe its pure serene [1]
Till I heard Chapman speak out loud and bold:
Then felt I like some watcher of the skies
When a new planet swims into his ken; [2]   10
Or like stout Cortez [3] when with eagle eyes
He stared at the Pacific—and all his men
Looked at each other with a wild surmise—
Silent, upon a peak in Darien.

                                                       1816

7. Chapman's were among the most famous Renaissance translations; his *Iliad* was completed in 1611, *The Odyssey* in 1616. Keats wrote the sonnet after being led to Chapman by his former teacher and reading *The Iliad* all night long.
8. Literally, the loyalty owed by a vas- sal to his feudal lord. Apollo was the Greek and Roman god of poetry and music.
9. Estate, feudal possession.
1. Atmosphere.
2. Range of vision.
3. Actually, Balboa; he first viewed the Pacific from Darien, in Panama.

GEORGE STARBUCK

On First Looking in on Blodgett's Keats's "Chapman's Homer" (Sum. ½C. M9–11)

Mellifluous as bees, these brittle men
droning of Honeyed Homer give me hives.
I scratch, yawn like a bear, my arm arrives
at yours—oh, Honey, and we're back again,
me the Balboa, you the Darien,   5
lording the loud Pacific sands, our lives
as hazarded as when a petrel dives
to yank the dull sea's coverlet, or when,
breaking from me across the sand that's rink
and record of our weekend boning up   10
on *The Romantic Agony*,[4] you sink
John Keats a good surf-fisher's cast out—plump
in the sun's wake—and the parched pages drink
that great whales' blanket party hump and hump.

                                                                 1960

SIR PHILIP SIDNEY

When Nature Made Her Chief Work, Stella's Eyes[5]

When Nature made her chief work, Stella's eyes,[6]
In color black[7] why wrapped she beams so bright?
Would she in beamy black, like painter wise,
Frame daintiest luster mixed of shades and light?
Or did she else that sober hue devise,   5
In object best to knit and strength our sight,
Lest if no veil those brave gleams did disguise,
They sunlike should more dazzle than delight?
Or would she her miraculous power show,
That, whereas black seems Beauty's contrary,   10
She even in black doth make all beauties flow?
Both so and thus: she, minding[8] Love should be
Placed ever there, gave him this mourning weed
To honor all their deaths who for her bleed.

1582

---

4. The title, conveniently enough, of a scholarly book about several writers, including Keats.
5. From Sidney's sonnet sequence, *Astrophel and Stella*, usually credited with having started the vogue of sonnet sequences in Elizabethan England.
6. Following Petrarch's lead, Sidney and other English sonneteers developed a series of exaggerated conventions to describe the physical features of the women they celebrated. The excessive brightness of the eyes—almost always compared favorably with the sun's brightness—was an expected feature.
7. Black was frequently used in the Renaissance to mean absence of light, and ugly or foul (see line 10).
8. Remembering that.

°WILLIAM SHAKESPEARE

My Mistress' Eyes Are Nothing like the Sun[9]

My mistress' eyes are nothing like the sun;
Coral is far more red than her lips' red;
If snow be white, why then her breasts are dun;[1]
If hairs be wires, black wires grow on her head.[2]
I have seen roses damasked[3] red and white,   5
But no such roses see I in her cheeks;
And in some perfumes is there more delight
Than in the breath that from my mistress reeks.
I love to hear her speak, yet well I know
That music hath a far more pleasing sound;   10
I grant I never saw a goddess go;[4]
My mistress, when she walks, treads on the ground.
And yet, by heaven, I think my love as rare
As any she belied with false compare.

1609

HELEN CHASIN

Joy Sonnet in a Random Universe

Sometimes I'm happy: la la la la la la la
la la la la la la la la la la la la la la la la la la
la la la la. Tum tum ti tum. La la la la la la
la la la la la la la la la la la la la la la la la la.
Hey nonny nonny. La la la la la la la la la   5
la la la la la la la la la la la. Vo do di o do.
Poo poo pi doo. La la la la la la la la la la
la la la la la la la la la la la la la la la la la la
la la. Whack a doo. La la la la la la la. Sh-
boom, sh-boom. La la la la la la la la la la   10
la la la la la la la la la la la la la la la la la la
la la. Dum di dum. La la la la la la la la la
la la la la la la la la la la. Tra la la. Tra la la
la la la la la la la la la la. Yeah yeah yeah.

1968

9. See Sidney's "When Nature Made
Her Chief Work, Stella's Eyes," and notes.
1. Mouse-colored.
2. Women in traditional sonnets have
hair of gold. Many poets who use the
Petrarchan conventions also wrote poems
which teased or deflated the conventions.
3. Variegated.
4. Walk.

10   POETIC "KINDS"

There are all sorts of poems. By now you have experienced poems on a variety of subjects and with a variation of tones, philosophical poems, political poems, witty poems, poems that tell stories, poems that recall events of long ago, poems of praise and of protest and attack, poems that concern abstractions and poems tied to a specific moment or occasion, poems that rhyme and poems that don't, short poems, long poems. And there are, of course, other sorts of poems which we haven't looked at. Some poems, for example, are thousands of lines long and differ rather substantially from the poems that can be included in a textbook like this. Poems may be classified in a variety of ways, by subject, topic, or theme; by their length, appearance, and formal features; by the way they are organized; by the level of language they use; by the poet's intention and what kinds of effects the poem tries to generate. Thinking about poems categorically can be useful in analytical ways because it enables us to put poems side by side for comparison and contrast, and in a sense almost any sort of sensible classification can help a reader experience a poem more precisely and fully. But, traditionally, there have been some more or less standard ways of classifying poems, ways that involve a combination of factors—subject matter, tone, style, intention, and effect. Knowledge of these classifications can help readers know what to expect. Poets, in fact, often consciously write a certain "kind" of poem and let us know what to expect, and when they do the poet and reader have entered into a kind of contract to think about a particular subject in a particular way. A poem that calls itself an "elegy," for example, gives us fair warning of what to expect: its label tells that it will be a serious poem memorializing the death of someone, and we may reasonably expect that its tone will be sad or angry about the death, and reflective about the meaning and direction of the dead person's life, and perhaps ruminative about the implications of the death itself.

Classification may be, of course, simply an intellectual exercise. Recognizing a poem that is an elegy, for example, or a satire, may be very much like the satisfaction involved in recognizing a scarlet tanager, a weeping willow tree, a Doric column, a French phrase, or a 1967 Ford Thunderbird. Just *knowing* what others don't know gives us a sense of importance, accomplishment, and power. But there are also *uses* for classification: we can experience a poem more fully if we understand early on exactly what kind of poem we are dealing with. A fuller response is possible because the poet has consciously chosen to play by certain defined rules, and the **conventions** he or she employs indicate that certain standard ways of saying things are being employed so as to achieve certain expected effects. The **tradition** that is involved in a particular poetic kind is thus employed by the poet and its effects are involved in us. For example, much of the humor and fun in the following poem is premised on the assumption that readers will know that they are reading a pastoral poem and will respond accordingly:

CHRISTOPHER MARLOWE

The Passionate Shepherd to His Love

Come live with me and be my love,
And we will all the pleasures prove[1]
That valleys, groves, hills, and fields,
Woods, or steepy mountain yields.

And we will sit upon the rocks,   5
Seeing the shepherds feed their flocks,
By shallow rivers to whose falls
Melodious birds sing madrigals.

And I will make thee beds of roses
And a thousand fragrant posies,   10
A cap of flowers, and a kirtle[2]
Embroidered all with leaves of myrtle;

A gown made of the finest wool
Which from our pretty lambs we pull;
Fair lined slippers for the cold,   15
With buckles of the purest gold;

A belt of straw and ivy buds,
With coral clasps and amber studs:
And if these pleasures may thee move,
Come live with me, and be my love.   20

The shepherd swains[3] shall dance and sing
For thy delight each May morning:
If these delights thy mind may move,
Then live with me and be my love.

1600

A naive reader might easily protest that a plea such as this one is unrealistic and fanciful and thus feel unsure of the poem's tone. What could such a reader think of a speaker who constructed his argument in such a dreamlike way? But the traditions behind the poem and the conventions of the poetic kind make its intention and effects quite clear. *The Passionate Shepherd* is a pastoral poem, a poetic kind that concerns itself with the simple life of country folk and describes that life in stylized, idealized terms. The people in a pastoral poem are usually (as here) shepherds, although they may be fishermen or other rustics who lead an outdoor life and are involved in tending basic human needs in a simplified society; the world of the poem is one

1. Try.
2. Gown.
3. Youths.

of simplicity, beauty, music, and love. The world always seems time-less in pastoral; people are eternally young, and the season is always spring, usually May. Nature seems endlessly green and the future entirely golden. Difficulty, frustration, disappointment, and obligation do not belong in this world at all; it is blissfully free of problems. Shepherds sing instead of tending sheep here, and they make love and play music instead of having to watch out for wolves in the night. If only the shepherd boy and shepherd girl can agree with each other to make love joyously and passionately, they will live happily ever after. The language of pastoral is informal and fairly simple, although always a bit more sophisticated than that of real shepherds with real problems and real sheep.

Unrealistic? Of course. No real shepherd gets to spend even a single whole day like that, and certainly the world of simple country folk has to cope with the ferocities of nature, human falsehood and knav-ery, disease, bad weather, old age, moments that are not all green and gold. And probably no poet ever thought that shepherds really live that way, but it is an attractive fantasy, and poets who write pastoral simply choose one formulaic way to isolate a series of ideal-ized moments. Fantasies can be personal and private, of course, but there is also a certain pleasure in shared public fantasies, and one central moment is that moment in a love relationship when two people are contemplating the joys of ecstatic love.

Pastoral poems are not written by shepherds. No doubt shepherds have fantasies too, but theirs probably involve ways of life far removed from sheepfolds and nights outdoors. Pastoral poems are usually written, as here, by city poets who are consciously indulging their "isn't it pretty to think so" thoughts. Pastoral poems involve an urban fantasy of rural bliss. It can be lovely to contemplate a world in which the birds sing only for our delight and other shepherds take care of the sheep, a world in which there is no work that does not turn into magic and in which the lambs bring themselves to us so that we can transform their wool instantly into a beautiful gown. It is also fun to "answer" such a vision. A group of poems on pp. 799–801 provide re-sponses to Marlowe's poem and thus offer a kind of critique of the pastoral vision. But in a sense none is necessary; the pastoral poet builds an awareness of artificiality into the whole idea of the poem. It is conceived in full consciousness that its fantasy avoids implication, and in filtering that implication carefully out of the poem, poets implicitly provide their own criticism of the fantasy world. Satire is, in a sense, the other side of the pastoral world—a city poet who fantasizes about being a shepherd usually knows all about dirt and grime and human failure and urban corruption—and satire and pas-toral are often seen as complementary poetic kinds.

Several other poetic kinds are exemplified in this book; and each has its own characteristics and conventions that have become estab-lished by tradition, repetition, and habit.

epic	*Paradise Lost* (excerpt)	p. 646
pastoral	*The Passionate Shepherd to His Love*	p. 727
elegy	*On My First Son*	p. 545

lyric	*The Lamb*	p. 837
ballad	*Sir Patrick Spens*	p. 682
satire	*The Love Song of J. Alfred Prufrock*	p. 849
protest poem	*Hard Rock Returns . . .*	p. 566
aubade	*The Sun Rising*	p. 740
confessional poem	*Skunk Hour*	p. 874
meditation	*Song* ("Go, lovely rose")	p. 794
dramatic monologue	*My Last Duchess*	p. 629
soliloquy	*Soliloquy of the Spanish Cloister*	p. 604

You will find definitions and brief descriptions of these poetic kinds in §10 of "A Glossary of Poetic Terms," p. 928. Each of these established kinds is worthy of detailed discussion and study, and your teacher may want to examine in depth how the conventions of several different kinds work. But rather than go through kind after kind with you, I have chosen to include quite a few poems that typify one particular kind, the epigram, so that you can examine one kind in some depth.

The poems at the end of this chapter are all epigrams, and together they add up almost to a definition of a poetic kind that has been in existence for centuries and that is still very popular. Some of these poems try definition directly (*What Is an Epigram?* or [*Epigrams*]); others, such as *Epitaph on Elizabeth, L. H.*, indirectly say what an epigram is for and how it works. Not all epigrams are so self-conscious, though, and they treat many subjects: politics (*Epigram: Of Treason*), love (*I'll Twine White Violets*), philosophies of life (*My Own Epitaph* and *Comment*), drinking (*Why I Drink*), social class (*For a Lady I Know*).

Like most poetic kinds, the epigram has a history that shaped its form and content. Originally, an **epigram** was an inscription upon some object such as a monument, triumphal arch, tombstone, or gate; hence it prized brevity and conciseness because they were absolutely necessary. But over a period of time, the term "epigram" came to mean a short poem that tried to attract attention in the same way that an inscription attracts the eyes of passersby.

As the poems here suggest, epigrams have been popular over a long period of time. The modern tradition of epigrams has two more or less separate ancient sources, one in Greece, one in Rome. In classical Greece, epigrams were composed over a period of 2,000 years; the earliest surviving ones date from the 8th century B.C. Apparently there were several anthologies of epigrams in early times, and fragments of these anthologies were later preserved, especially in large collections like the so-called *Greek Anthology*, which dates from the 10th century A.D. Largely short inscriptions, these epigrams also included some love poems (including many on homosexual love), comments on life and morality, riddles, etc. The father of the Roman tradition is generally agreed to be Martial (Marcus Valerius Martialis, A.D. 40–104 [?]), whose epigrams are witty and satirical. Modern epigrams have more frequently followed Martial's lead, but occasionally the distinctive influence of the older Greek tradition can be seen in the sadder poignancy of such poems as *Parting in Wartime*.

Knowing what to do with a poem often is aided by knowing what it is, or what it means to be. Many modern poems are not consciously conceived in terms of a traditional kind, and not all older poems are either, but a knowledge of kind can often provide one more way of deciding what to look for in a poem, helping one to find the right questions to ask.

_____

* short, witty, satiric poem [usually] *(handwritten annotation)*

SAMUEL TAYLOR COLERIDGE

What Is an Epigram?

> What is an epigram? a dwarfish whole,
> Its body brevity, and wit its soul.

p. 1802

ANONYMOUS translation of a Latin distich

[Epigrams]

> Three things must epigrams, like bees, have all,
> A sting, and honey, and a body small.

WILLIAM WALSH

An Epigram

> An epigram should be—if right—
> Short, simple, pointed, keen, and bright,
>   A lively little thing!
> Like wasp, with taper body—bound
> By lines—not many, neat and round,   5
>   All ending in a sting.

ca. 1690

WILLIAM BLAKE

Her Whole Life Is an Epigram

> Her whole life is an epigram: smack, smooth & neatly penned,
> Platted quite neat to catch applause, with a sliding noose at the end.

ca. 1793–1811

BEN JONSON

Epitaph on Elizabeth, L. H.

Wouldst thou hear what man can say
In a little? Reader, stay.
Underneath this stone doth lie
As much beauty as could die;
Which in life did harbor give   5
To more virtue than doth live.
If at all she had a fault,
Leave it buried in this vault.
One name was Elizabeth;
Th' other, let it sleep with death: 10
Fitter, where it died, to tell,
Than that it lived at all. Farewell.

                           1616

MELEAGER (from the *Greek Anthology*)

I'll Twine White Violets[4]

I'll twine white violets and the myrtle green;
Narcissus will I twine and lilies sheen;
I'll twine sweet crocus and the hyacinth blue;
And last I twine the rose, love's token true:
That all may form a wreath of beauty, meet[5]
To deck my Heliodora's tresses sweet.

ca. 90 B.C.

MARTIAL

You've Told Me, Maro[6]

You've told me, Maro, whilst you live
You'd not a single penny give,
But that whene'er you chanced to die,
You'd leave a handsome legacy;
You must be mad beyond redress,   5
If my next wish you cannot guess.

ca. 100

---

4. Translated from the Greek by Goldwin Smith.
5. Appropriate.
6. Translated from the Latin by F. Lewis.

MARTIAL

Tomorrow You Will Live[7]

Tomorrow you will live, you always cry;
In what fair country does this morrow lie,
That 'tis so mighty long ere it arrive?
Beyond the Indies does this morrow live?
'Tis so far-fetched, this morrow, that I fear   5
'Twill be both very old and very dear.
"Tomorrow I will live," the fool does say;
Today itself's too late—the wise lived yesterday.

ca. 85–90

JOHN GAY

My Own Epitaph

Life is a jest; and all things show it.
I thought so once; but now I know it.

1720

J. V. CUNNINGHAM

Here Lies My Wife

Here lies my wife. Eternal peace
Be to us both with her decease.

1959

SIR HENRY WOTTON

Upon the Death of Sir Albert Morton's Wife

He first deceased; she for a little tried
To live without him, liked it not, and died.

1651

---

7. Translated from the Latin by Abraham Cowley.

WALTER SAVAGE LANDOR

Various the Roads of Life

Various the roads of life; in one
All terminate, one lonely way.
We go; and "Is he gone?"
Is all our best friends say.

1846

SARAH CLEGHORN

Quatrain

The golf links lie so near the mill
That almost every day
The laboring children can look out
And see the men at play.

1936

THEODORE ROETHKE

Epigram: The Mistake

He left his pants upon a chair:
She was a widow, so she said:
But he was apprehended, bare,
By one who rose up from the dead.

p. 1957

MATTHEW PRIOR

A True Maid

No, no; for my virginity,
When I lose that, says Rose, I'll die:
Behind the elms, last night, cried Dick,
Rose, were you not extremely sick?

1718

SIR JOHN HARINGTON

Epigram: Of Treason

Treason doth never prosper, what's the reason?
For if it prosper, none dare call it treason.

1615

HOWARD NEMEROV

Epigram: Political Reflexion

loquitur[8] the sparrow in the zoo.

No bars are set too close, no mesh too fine
To keep me from the eagle and the lion,
Whom keepers feed that I may freely dine.
This goes to show that if you have the wit
To be small, common, cute, and live on shit,   5
Though the cage fret kings, you may make free with it.

1958

HENRY ALDRICH

Why I Drink

If on my theme I rightly think,
There are five reasons why I drink—
Good wine, a friend, because I'm dry,
Or lest I should be by and by,
Or any other reason why.

ca. 1690

DAVID MC CORD

History of Education

The decent docent doesn't doze:
He teaches standing on his toes.
His student dassn't[9] doze—and does,
And that's what teaching is and was.

1945

8. I.e., the sparrow is the speaker.   9. Dares not.

RICHARD HARTER FOGLE

A Hawthorne Garland

Scarlet Letter

Wrote the clergy: "Our Dear Madame Prynne:
We keep mighty close watch upon sin:
   And we think we had better
   Proclaim by this Letter
Our sense of how Active you've been."

1979

COUNTEE CULLEN

For a Lady I Know

She even thinks that up in heaven
Her class lies late and snores,
While poor black cherubs rise at seven
To do celestial chores.

1925

X. J. KENNEDY

Epitaph for a Postal Clerk

Here lies wrapped up tight in sod
Henry Harkins c/o God.
On the day of Resurrection
May be opened for inspection.

1961

DAVID MC CORD

Epitaph on a Waiter

By and by
God caught his eye.

1935

• DOROTHY PARKER

Comment

Oh, life is a glorious cycle of song,
A medley of extemporanea;
And love is a thing that can never go wrong;
And I am Marie of Rumania.

1926

J. V. CUNNINGHAM

All in Due Time

All in due time: love will emerge from hate,
And the due deference of truth from lies.
If not quite all things come to those who wait
They will not need them: in due time one dies.

1950

FRANCES CORNFORD

Parting in Wartime

How long ago Hector[1] took off his plume,
Not wanting that his little son should cry,
Then kissed his sad Andromache good-bye—
And now we three in Euston[2] waiting-room.

1948

FRANCIS QUARLES

Be Sad, My Heart

Be sad, my heart, deep dangers wait thy mirth:
Thy soul's waylaid by sea, by hell, by earth:
Hell has her hounds; earth, snares; the sea, a shelf;
But, most of all, my heart, beware thyself.

1635

1. The noblest chieftain in ancient Troy.   2. A London railway station.

Contexts

11   THE AUTHOR'S WORK

Poems are not all written in the same style, as if they were produced by a corporation or put together in a committee. Just as every human individual is unique and has a distinct personality, every poet leaves a distinctive stamp on his or her work. Even though all poets share the same material (language) and usually have some common notions of their craft, they put the unique resources of their individual minds and consciousnesses into what they create. A poet may use the tradition extensively and share the crafts that others have developed without surrendering his or her own individuality, just as the integrity and uniqueness of an individual is not compromised by characteristics the individual may share with others—political affiliations, religious beliefs, tastes in clothes and music. Sometimes the uniqueness is hard to define—what exactly is it that defines the unique personality of an individual?—but it is always there, and the recognition of the distinctive quality is a large part of what we depend upon in our relationship with other people. And so with poets: most poets don't make a conscious effort to put an individual stamp on their work; they don't have to. The stamp is there, just in the way they choose subjects, words, configurations. Every individual's consciousness is unique, and that consciousness uniquely marks what it records, imagines, and decides to print.

Experienced readers can often identify a poem as the distinctive work of an individual poet even though they may never have seen the poem before. That may surprise you, but it is a lot like identifying a particular singer or group after hearing only a few phrases of a new song. Such an ability depends upon experience—a lot of reading of that author, or a lot of listening to music—but any reasonably sensitive reader can learn to do it with great accuracy. Developing such an ability, however, is not really an end in itself; rather, it is a by-product of learning to notice the particular, distinctive qualities in the workmanship of any poet. Once you've read several poems by a particular poet, you will usually begin to notice some features that the poems have in common, and gradually you may come to think of those features as characteristic. The poem that follows was written by Howard Nemerov, whose work you have read in some earlier chapters. Before you read it, you may want to look back at some of his poems printed earlier in this book and remind yourself of what those poems were like (*The Vacuum*, p. 546; *Boom!*, p. 615; *The Goose Fish*, p. 671; *Epigram: Political Reflexion*, p. 734). Another poem by Nemerov (*Life Cycle of the Common Man*, p. 879) appears in the anthology at the back.

HOWARD NEMEROV

A Way of Life

It's been going on a long time.
For instance, these two guys, not saying much, who slog
Through sun and sand, fleeing the scene of their crime,
Till one turns, without a word, and smacks
His buddy flat with the flat of an axe,   5
Which cuts down on the dialogue
Some, but is viewed rather as normal than sad
By me, as I wait for the next ad.

It seems to me it's been quite a while
Since the last vision of blonde loveliness   10
Vanished, her shampoo and shower and general style
Replaced by this lean young lunk-
head parading along with a gun in his back to confess
How yestereve, being drunk
And in a state of existential despair,   15
He beat up his grandma and pawned her invalid chair.

But here at last is a pale beauty
Smoking a filter beside a mountain stream,
Brief interlude, before the conflict of love and duty
Gets moving again, as sheriff and posse expound,   20
Between jail and saloon, the American Dream
Where Justice, after considerable horsing around,
Turns out to be Mercy; when the villain is knocked off,
A kindly uncle offers syrup for my cough.

And now these clean-cut athletic types   25
In global hats are having a nervous debate
As they stand between their individual rocket ships
Which have landed, appropriately, on some rocks
Somewhere in Space, in an atmosphere of hate
Where one tells the other to pull up his socks   30
And get going, he doesn't say where; they fade,
And an angel food cake flutters in the void.

I used to leave now and again;
No more. A lot of violence in American life
These days, mobsters and cops all over the scene.   35
But there's a lot of love, too, mixed with the strife,
And kitchen-kindness, like a bedtime story
With rich food and a more kissable depilatory.
Still, I keep my weapons handy, sitting here
Smoking and shaving and drinking the dry beer.

1967

What does this poem have in common with Nemerov's other poems? The concern with contemporary life, the tendency to concentrate on modern conveniences and luxuries, and the interest in isolating and defining aspects of the distinctively modern sensibility are all characteristic of Nemerov, and so is the tendency to create a short drama, with a speaker who is not altogether admirable. Several of Nemerov's other poems also share an attitude that seems deeply imbedded in this poem, a kind of anti-romanticism that emerges when someone tries to sound or feel *too* proud or cheerful and is shown, by events in the poem, to be part of a grimmer reality instead. The concentration upon one or more physical objects is also characteristic, and often (as in *The Vacuum*) the main object is a mechanical one that symbolizes modernity and our modern dependency on things rather than our concern with human relationships. Americanness is made emphatic here too, as if the poem were concerned to help us define our culture and its habits and values. The mood of loneliness is also characteristic, and so is the poem's witty conversational style. The verbal wit here, although not as prominent as the puns and double-entendres of *Boom!* and *Life Cycle*, is characteristically informal. Often it seems to derive from the language of commercials and street speech, and the undercutting of this language by the poet—having a paranoid and simple-minded speaker talk about a gangster in "a state of existential despair"—is similar to the strategy of *Boom!* or *The Vacuum*. The regular stanzas, rhymed but not in a traditional or regular way and with a number of near-rhymes, are also typical. Nemerov's thematic interests and ideas, his verbal style, and his cast of mind are all plainly visible in *A Way of Life*.

Noticing common features does not mean that every poem by a particular author will be predictable and contain all these features. Most poets like to experiment with new subjects, tones, forms, and various kinds of poetic strategies and devices. But the way of approach—the distinct stamp imposed by a unique consciousness—is likely to be visible anyway. The work of any writer will have certain *tendencies* that are identifiable, although not every single tendency will show up in any one poem.

Of what practical use is it to notice the distinctive voice and mind of a particular poet? One use (not the most important one for the casual reader, but one that nonetheless gives pleasure) is the pleasant surprise that occurs when you recognize something familiar. Reading a new poem by a poet with whom you are already familiar is a bit like meeting an old friend whose face or conversation reminds you of experiences you have had together. Poetic friendships can be treasures just as personal friendships are, even though they are necessarily more distant and somewhat more abstract. Just as novelty—meeting something or someone altogether new to you—is one kind of pleasure, so revisiting or recalling the familiar is another, its equal and opposite. Just *knowing* and *recognizing* often feel good—in and for themselves.

But there are other reasons, also, to look at the various works of a single writer. Just as you learn from watching other people—seeing how they react and respond to people and events, observing how they cope with their lives—you also learn from watching poets at work, seeing how they learn and develop, how they change their minds about things, how they discover the reach and limits of their minds and talents, how they find their distinctive voices and come to terms with their own identities. Watching someone at work over a period of years (as you can Adrienne Rich in the selection at the end of this chapter) is a little like watching an autobiography unfold, except that the individual poems continue to exist separately and for themselves as well as provide a record of a distinctive but gradually changing and evolving consciousness.

A third reason to study in some detail the work of a single individual is a very practical one: the more you know about the poet, the better a reader you are likely to be of any individual poem by that poet. It is not so much that the external facts of a writer's life find their way into whatever he or she writes—a poem or essay, as well as a letter or an autobiography—but that a reader gets used to habits and manners, of knowing what to expect. Coming to a new poem by a poet you already know is not completely an experience fresh and new. You adjust faster, know better what to look for, have some specific expectations (although they may be unconscious and unarticulated) of what the poem will be like. The more poems you read by any author, the better a reader you are likely to be of any one poem.

Before you read the following poem by John Donne, look at the poems by him that appear elsewhere in this book: *Death Be Not Proud* (p. 558), *Song* (p. 617), *The Flea* (p. 623), *A Valediction: Forbidding Mourning* (p. 631), *Batter My Heart* (p. 655), and *The Canonization* (p. 846). What features in these poems seem most striking and distinctive to you as you review them as a group?

JOHN DONNE

The Sun Rising

Busy old fool, unruly sun,
    Why dost thou thus,
Through windows, and through curtains, call on us?
Must to thy motions lovers' seasons run?
    Saucy pedantic wretch, go chide   5
    Late schoolboys, and sour prentices,[1]
Go tell court-huntsmen that the king will ride,
    Call country ants[2] to harvest offices;
Love, all alike, no season knows, nor clime,
Nor hours, days, months, which are the rags of time.   10

---

1. Apprentices.   2. Farmworkers.

Thy beams, so reverend and strong
Why shouldst thou think?
I could eclipse and cloud them with a wink,
But that I would not lose her sight so long:
    If her eyes have not blinded thine,   15
Look, and tomorrow late, tell me
Whether both the Indias[3] of spice and mine
Be where thou left'st them, or lie here with me.
Ask for those kings whom thou saw'st yesterday,
And thou shalt hear, all here in one bed lay.   20

She is all states, and all princes I,
    Nothing else is.
Princes do but play us; compared to this,
All honor's mimic,[4] all wealth alchemy.[5]
    Thou, sun, art half as happy as we,   25
    In that the world's contracted thus;
Thine age asks[6] ease, and since thy duties be
To warm the world, that's done in warming us.
Shine here to us, and thou art every where;
This bed thy center[7] is, these walls thy sphere.   30

1633

Was *The Sun Rising* somewhat easier to read than the first Donne poem you read this term? What kind of expectations did you have of the poem, knowing it was by the same author as other poems you had read? How conscious were you of those expectations? Did those expectations enable you to ask more intelligent questions of the poem as you read it? How conscious were you, as you read, of the subject matter of other Donne poems? of their themes? tone? style? form? sound effects? of other poetic devices? Did you consciously expect a speaker and a dramatic situation? How quickly did you decide what the situation was? How quickly did you identify the setting? Did you find that you had certain expectations of the speaker once you had sensed the poem's subject and situation? In retrospect, how similar to other Donne poems does this one seem? In what specific ways?

The skills involved here are progressive: they don't come all at once like a flash of lightning. Rather, they develop over time, as do most of the more sophisticated reading skills we will be considering in the final chapters of this book, and they develop in conjunction with skills you have already worked on in the previous chapters. Don't worry if you still have difficulty with a new Donne poem. You are in good company: Donne isn't easy. But the more you read, the better you will get. Reading ten or a dozen poems by a single author

3. The East and West Indies, commercial sources of spices and gold.
4. Hypocritical.
5. Imposture, like the "scientific" procedures for turning base metals into gold.
6. Requires.
7. Of orbit.

is better than reading three or four, not only because your generalizations and the expectations they create will be more reliable but also because you will feel increasingly comfortable. Spending some hours in the library reading several new poems by a poet you like and admire can be a very satisfying experience: work with any author long enough, and you will begin to feel positively at home. But even then, a good poet will still surprise you in every new poem, at least to some extent. Being reliable and distinctive is not the same as being totally predictable.

The two groups of poems that follow indicate both the distinctiveness of an individual poet's voice and the variety that often exists within that distinctiveness. The poems by John Keats suggest the pervasive sensuous and sensual quality of his work, his fascination with medieval times and gothic states of mind, his attraction both to nature and to highly ornate artifices, his distinctive patterns of phrasing and use of poetic devices, and the recurrent contrasts in his work between an external world of "objective" reality and internal states of "subjective" consciousness. Prose selections from a preface and from several of Keats's personal letters underscore some of his most persistent poetic and personal concerns. The poems are arranged chronologically, and a chronology of his life suggests the potential relevance of biographical information.

Adrienne Rich's distinctive poetic voice also emerges from the representative selection here, but the corpus of her work also illustrates change and development. Rich herself describes these changes in the prose selections and in notes appended to *Snapshots of a Daughter-in-Law, Orion,* and *Planetarium.* You may also want to look back at what Rich has said about *Aunt Jennifer's Tigers* (p. 570).

JOHN KEATS

On the Grasshopper and the Cricket

The poetry of earth is never dead:
When all the birds are faint with the hot sun,
And hide in cooling trees, a voice will run
From hedge to hedge about the new-mown mead;
That is the grasshopper's—he takes the lead   5
In summer luxury—he has never done
With his delights; for when tired out with fun
He rests at ease beneath some pleasant weed.
The poetry of earth is ceasing never:
On a lone winter evening, when the frost   10
Has wrought a silence, from the stove there shrills
The cricket's song, in warmth increasing ever,
And seems to one in drowsiness half lost,
The grasshopper's among some grassy hills.

December 30, 1816

from Endymion (Book I)[8]

A thing of beauty is a joy for ever:
Its loveliness increases; it will never
Pass into nothingness; but still will keep
A bower quiet for us, and a sleep
Full of sweet dreams, and health, and quiet breathing.   5
Therefore, on every morrow, are we wreathing
A flowery band to bind us to the earth,
Spite of despondence, of the inhuman dearth
Of noble natures, of the gloomy days,
Of all the unhealthy and o'er-darkened ways   10
Made for our searching: yes, in spite of all,
Some shape of beauty moves away the pall
From our dark spirits. Such the sun, the moon,
Trees old, and young sprouting a shady boon
For simple sheep; and such are daffodils   15
With the green world they live in; and clear rills
That for themselves a cooling covert make
'Gainst the hot season; the mid forest brake,[9]
Rich with a sprinkling of fair musk-rose blooms:
And such too is the grandeur of the dooms[1]   20
We have imagined for the mighty dead;
All lovely tales that we have heard or read:
An endless fountain of immortal drink,
Pouring unto us from the heaven's brink.
　　Nor do we merely feel these essences   25
For one short hour; no, even as the trees
That whisper round a temple become soon
Dear as the temple's self, so does the moon,
The passion poesy, glories infinite,
Haunt us till they become a cheering light   30
Unto our souls, and bound to us so fast,
That, whether there be shine, or gloom o'ercast,
They always must be with us, or we die.

1817

When I Have Fears

When I have fears that I may cease to be
Before my pen has gleaned my teeming brain,
Before high-pilèd books, in charact'ry,
Hold like rich garners the full-ripened grain;
When I behold, upon the night's starred face,   5
Huge cloudy symbols of a high romance,
And think that I may never live to trace

8. Keats's long poem about the myth of
a mortal (Endymion) loved by the goddess
of the moon.

9. Thicket.
1. Judgments.

Their shadows, with the magic hand of chance;
And when I feel, fair creature of an hour!
That I shall never look upon thee more,   10
Never have relish in the faery power
Of unreflecting love!—then on the shore
Of the wide world I stand alone, and think
Till Love and Fame to nothingness do sink.

1818

Bright Star

Bright star! would I were steadfast as thou art—
    Not in lone splendor hung aloft the night
And watching, with eternal lids apart,
    Like nature's patient, sleepless Eremite,[2]
The moving waters at their priestlike task   5
    Of pure ablution round earth's human shores,
Or gazing on the new soft fallen mask
    Of snow upon the mountains and the moors—
No—yet still steadfast, still unchangeable,
    Pillowed upon my fair love's ripening breast,   10
To feel for ever its soft fall and swell,
    Awake for ever in a sweet unrest,
Still, still to hear her tender-taken breath,
And so live ever—or else swoon to death.

1819

La Belle Dame sans Merci[3]

A Ballad
(original version)

O what can ail thee, knight-at-arms,
    Alone and palely loitering?
The sedge has withered from the lake,
    And no birds sing.

O what can ail thee, knight-at-arms,   5
    So haggard and so woe-begone?
The squirrel's granary is full,
    And the harvest's done.

---

2. Religious hermit.
3. "The beautiful lady without pity." The title (but not the subject matter) de- rives from a medieval poem by Alain Chartier.

I see a lily on thy brow,
    With anguish moist and fever dew,   10
And on thy cheeks a fading rose
    Fast withereth too.

I met a lady in the meads,[4]
    Full beautiful—a faery's child,
Her hair was long, her foot was light,   15
    And her eyes were wild.

I made a garland for her head,
    And bracelets too, and fragrant zone;[5]
She looked at me as she did love,
    And made sweet moan.   20

I set her on my pacing steed,
    And nothing else saw all day long,
For sidelong would she bend, and sing
    A faery's song.

She found me roots of relish sweet,   25
    And honey wild, and manna dew,
And sure in language strange she said,
    "I love thee true."

She took me to her elfin grot,
    And there she wept, and sighed full sore,   30
And there I shut her wild wild eyes
    With kisses four.

And there she lulléd me asleep,
    And there I dreamed—Ah! woe betide!
The latest[6] dream I ever dreamed   35
    On the cold hill side.

I saw pale kings and princes too,
    Pale warriors, death-pale were they all;
They cried—"La Belle Dame sans Merci
    Hath thee in thrall!"   40

I saw their starved lips in the gloam,
    With horrid warning gapéd wide,
And I awoke and found me here,
    On the cold hill's side.

And this is why I sojourn here,   45
    Alone and palely loitering,
Though the sedge has withered from the lake,
    And no birds sing.

April, 1819

4. Meadows.
5. Girdle.

6. Last.

Ode to a Nightingale

I

My heart aches, and a drowsy numbness pains
  My sense, as though of hemlock[7] I had drunk,
Or emptied some dull opiate to the drains
  One minute past, and Lethe-wards[8] had sunk:
'Tis not through envy of thy happy lot,   5
    But being too happy in thine happiness,
      That thou, light-wingéd Dryad[9] of the trees,
        In some melodious plot
  Of beechen green, and shadows numberless,
    Singest of summer in full-throated ease.   10

II

O, for a draught of vintage! that hath been
  Cooled a long age in the deep-delvéd earth,
Tasting of Flora[1] and the country green,
  Dance, and Provençal song,[2] and sunburnt mirth!
O for a beaker full of the warm South,   15
  Full of the true, the blushful Hippocrene,[3]
    With beaded bubbles winking at the brim,
      And purple-stainéd mouth;
  That I might drink, and leave the world unseen,
    And with thee fade away into the forest dim: 20

III

Fade far away, dissolve, and quite forget
  What thou among the leaves hast never known,
The weariness, the fever, and the fret
  Here, where men sit and hear each other groan;
Where palsy shakes a few, sad, last gray hairs,   25
    Where youth grows pale, and specter-thin, and dies;
      Where but to think is to be full of sorrow
        And leaden-eyed despairs,
  Where Beauty cannot keep her lustrous eyes,
    Or new Love pine at them beyond tomorrow.   30

IV

Away! away! for I will fly to thee,
  Not charioted by Bacchus and his pards,[4]
But on the viewless wings of Poesy,
  Though the dull brain perplexes and retards:
Already with thee! tender is the night,   35
    And haply the Queen-Moon is on her throne,
      Clustered around by all her starry Fays;[5]

7. A poisonous drug.
8. Toward the river of forgetfulness (Lethe) in Hades.
9. Wood nymph.
1. Roman goddess of flowers.
2. The medieval troubadors of Provence (in southern France) were famous for their love songs.

3. The fountain of the Muses on Mt. Helicon, whose waters bring poetic inspiration.
4. The Roman god of wine was sometimes portrayed in a chariot drawn by leopards. "viewless": invisible.
5. Fairies.

But here there is no light,
　　Save what from heaven is with the breezes blown
　　　Through verdurous glooms and winding mossy ways.   40

V

I cannot see what flowers are at my feet,
　　Nor what soft incense hangs upon the boughs,
But, in embalméd[6] darkness, guess each sweet
　　Wherewith the seasonable month endows
The grass, the thicket, and the fruit-tree wild;   45
　　White hawthorn, and the pastoral eglantine;[7]
　　　Fast fading violets covered up in leaves;
　　　　And mid-May's eldest child,
　　The coming musk-rose, full of dewy wine,
　　　The murmurous haunt of flies on summer eves.   50

VI

Darkling[8] I listen; and, for many a time
　　I have been half in love with easeful Death,
Called him soft names in many a muséd rhyme,
　　To take into the air my quiet breath;
Now more than ever seems it rich to die,   55
　　To cease upon the midnight with no pain,
　　　While thou art pouring forth thy soul abroad
　　　　In such an ecstasy!
　　Still wouldst thou sing, and I have ears in vain—
　　　To thy high requiem become a sod.   60

VII

Thou wast not born for death, immortal Bird!
　　No hungry generations tread thee down;
The voice I hear this passing night was heard
　　In ancient days by emperor and clown:
Perhaps the selfsame song that found a path   65
　　Through the sad heart of Ruth,[9] when, sick for home,
　　　She stood in tears amid the alien corn;
　　　　The same that ofttimes hath
　　Charmed magic casements, opening on the foam
　　　Of perilous seas, in faery lands forlorn.   70

VIII

Forlorn! the very word is like a bell
　　To toll me back from thee to my sole self!
Adieu! the fancy cannot cheat so well
　　As she is famed to do, deceiving elf.
Adieu! adieu! thy plaintive anthem fades   75
　　Past the near meadows, over the still stream,

---

6. Fragrant, aromatic.
7. Sweetbriar or honeysuckle.
8. In the dark.
9. A virtuous Moabite widow who, ac-

cording to the Old Testament *Book of Ruth*, found a husband while gleaning in the wheat fields of Judah.

Up the hillside; and now 'tis buried deep
    In the next valley-glades:
Was it a vision, or a waking dream?
    Fled is that music:—Do I wake or sleep?   80

May, 1819

Ode on a Grecian Urn

I

Thou still unravished bride of quietness,
    Thou foster-child of silence and slow time,
Sylvan[1] historian, who canst thus express
    A flowery tale more sweetly than our rhyme:
What leaf-fringed legend haunts about thy shape   5
    Of deities or mortals, or of both,
        In Tempe or the dales of Arcady?[2]
What men or gods are these? What maidens loath?
    What mad pursuit? What struggle to escape?
        What pipes and timbrels? What wild ecstasy?   10

II

Heard melodies are sweet, but those unheard
    Are sweeter; therefore, ye soft pipes, play on;
Not to the sensual[3] ear, but, more endeared,
    Pipe to the spirit ditties of no tone:
Fair youth, beneath the trees, thou canst not leave   15
    Thy song, nor ever can those trees be bare;
        Bold Lover, never, never canst thou kiss,
Though winning near the goal—yet, do not grieve;
    She cannot fade, though thou hast not thy bliss,
        For ever wilt thou love, and she be fair!   20

III

Ah, happy, happy boughs! that cannot shed
    Your leaves, nor ever bid the Spring adieu;
And, happy melodist, unwearièd,
    For ever piping songs for ever new;
More happy love! more happy, happy love!   25
    For ever warm and still to be enjoyed,
        For ever panting, and for ever young;
All breathing human passion far above,
    That leaves a heart high-sorrowful and cloyed,
        A burning forehead, and a parching tongue.   30

1. Rustic. The urn depicts a woodland scene.
    2. Arcadia. Tempe is a beautiful valley near Mt. Olympus in Greece, and the valley ("dales") of Arcadia a picturesque section of the Peloponnesus; both came to be associated with the pastoral ideal.
    3. Of the senses, as distinguished from the "ear" of the spirit or imagination.

IV

Who are these coming to the sacrifice?
  To what green altar, O mysterious priest,
Lead'st thou that heifer lowing at the skies,
    And all her silken flanks with garlands dressed?
What little town by river or sea shore,   35
  Or mountain-built with peaceful citadel,
    Is emptied of this folk, this pious morn?
And, little town, thy streets for evermore
  Will silent be; and not a soul to tell
    Why thou art desolate, can e'er return.   40

V

O Attic[4] shape! Fair attitude! with brede[5]
  Of marble men and maidens overwrought,
With forest branches and the trodden weed;
  Thou, silent form, dost tease us out of thought
As doth eternity: Cold Pastoral!   45
  When old age shall this generation waste,
    Thou shalt remain, in midst of other woe
Than ours, a friend to man, to whom thou say'st,
  Beauty is truth, truth beauty[6]—that is all
    Ye know on earth, and all ye need to know.   50

May, 1819

Ode on Melancholy

I

No, no, go not to Lethe,[7] neither twist
  Wolfsbane, tight-rooted, for its poisonous wine;[8]
Nor suffer thy pale forehead to be kissed
  By nightshade, ruby grape of Proserpine;
Make not your rosary of yew-berries,[9]   5
  Nor let the beetle, nor the death-moth be
    Your mournful Psyche,[1] nor the downy owl
A partner in your sorrow's mysteries;
  For shade to shade will come too drowsily,
    And drown the wakeful anguish of the soul.   10

4. Attica was the district of ancient Greece surrounding Athens.
5. Woven pattern. "overwrought": ornamented all over.
6. In some texts of the poem "Beauty is truth, truth beauty" is in quotation marks and in some texts it is not, leading to critical disagreements about whether the last line and a half are also inscribed on the urn or spoken by the poet.
7. The river of forgetfulness in Hades.

8. Like nightshade (line 4), wolfsbane is a poisonous plant. "Proserpine": Queen of Hades.
9. Which often grow in cemeteries and which are traditionally associated with death.
1. *Psyche* means both "soul" and "breath," and sometimes it was anciently represented by a moth leaving the mouth at death. Owls and beetles were also traditionally associated with darkness and death.

II

But when the melancholy fit shall fall
   Sudden from heaven like a weeping cloud,
That fosters the droop-headed flowers all,
   And hides the green hill in an April shroud;
Then glut thy sorrow on a morning rose,   15
   Or on the rainbow of the salt sand-wave,
      Or on the wealth of globéd peonies;
Or if thy mistress some rich anger shows,
   Emprison her soft hand, and let her rave,
      And feed deep, deep upon her peerless eyes.   20

III

She[2] dwells with Beauty—Beauty that must die;
   And Joy, whose hand is ever at his lips
Bidding adieu; and aching Pleasure nigh,
   Turning to poison while the bee-mouth sips:
Ay, in the very temple of Delight   25
   Veiled Melancholy has her sov'reign shrine,
      Though seen of none save him whose strenuous tongue
Can burst Joy's grape against his palate fine;[3]
   His soul shall taste the sadness of her might,
      And be among her cloudy trophies hung.[4]   30

May, 1819

To Autumn

I

Season of mists and mellow fruitfulness,
   Close bosom-friend of the maturing sun;
Conspiring with him how to load and bless
   With fruit the vines that round the thatch-eves run;
To bend with apples the mossed cottage-trees,   5
   And fill all fruit with ripeness to the core;
      To swell the gourd, and plump the hazel shells
With a sweet kernel; to set budding more,
   And still more, later flowers for the bees,
      Until they think warm days will never cease,   10
      For Summer has o'er-brimmed their clammy cells.

II

Who hath not seen thee oft amid thy store?
   Sometimes whoever seeks abroad may find
Thee sitting careless on a granary floor,
   Thy hair soft-lifted by the winnowing wind;[5]   15

---

2. The goddess Melancholy, whose chief place of worship ("shrine") is described in lines 25–26.
3. Sensitive, discriminating.

4. The ancient Greeks and Romans hung trophies in their gods' temples.
5. Which sifts the grain from the chaff.

Or on a half-reaped furrow sound asleep,
   Drowsed with the fume of poppies, while thy hook[6]
   Spares the next swath and all its twinéd flowers:
And sometimes like a gleaner thou dost keep
   Steady thy laden head across a brook,   20
   Or by a cider-press, with patient look,
   Thou watchest the last oozings hours by hours.

                          III
Where are the songs of Spring? Ay, where are they?
   Think not of them, thou hast thy music too—
While barréd clouds bloom the soft-dying day,   25
   And touch the stubble-plains with rosy hue;
Then in a wailful choir the small gnats mourn
   Among the river sallows,[7] borne aloft
   Or sinking as the light wind lives or dies;
And full-grown lambs loud bleat from hilly bourn;[8]   30
   Hedge-crickets sing; and now with treble soft
   The red-breast whistles from a garden-croft;[9]
   And gathering swallows twitter in the skies.
September 19, 1819

---

from Letter to Benjamin Bailey, November 22, 1817[1]

° ° ° I am certain of nothing but of the holiness of the Heart's affections and the truth of Imagination—What the imagination seizes as Beauty must be truth—whether it existed before or not—for I have the same Idea of all our Passions as of Love they are all in their sublime, creative of essential Beauty ° ° ° The Imagination may be compared to Adam's dream[2]—he awoke and found it truth. I am the more zealous in this affair, because I have never yet been able to perceive how any thing can be known for truth by consequitive reasoning—and yet it must be—Can it be that even the greatest Philosopher ever ~~when~~ arrived at his goal without putting aside numerous objections—However it may be, O for a Life of Sensations rather than of Thoughts! It is "a Vision in the form of Youth" a Shadow of reality to come—and this consideration has further conv[i]nced me for it has come as auxiliary to another favorite Speculation of mine, that we shall enjoy ourselves here after by having what we called happiness on Earth repeated in a finer tone and so repeated—And yet such a fate can only befall those who delight in sensation rather than hunger as you do after Truth—Adam's dream will do here and seems to be a conviction that Imagination and its empyreal reflection is the same as human Life and its spiritual repetition. But as I was saying—the simple imaginative Mind may have its rewards in the repeti[ti]on of its own silent Working coming continually on the spirit with a fine suddenness—to compare

6. Scythe or sickle.
7. Willows.
8. Domain.
9. An enclosed garden near a house.

1. Keats's private letters, often carelessly written, are reprinted uncorrected.
2. In *Paradise Lost*, VIII, 460–90.

great things with small—have you never by being surprised with an old Melody—in a delicious place—by a delicious voice, fe[l]t over again your very speculations and surmises at the time it first operated on your soul—do you not remember forming to yourself the singer's face more beautiful that [*for* than] it was possible and yet with the elevation of the Moment you did not think so—even then you were mounted on the Wings of Imagination so high—that the Prototype must be here after—that delicious face you will see—What a time! I am continually running away from the subject—sure this cannot be exactly the case with a complex Mind—one that is imaginative and at the same time careful of its fruits—who would exist partly on sensation partly on thought—to whom it is necessary that years should bring the philosophic Mind—such an one I consider your's and therefore it is necessary to your eternal Happiness that you not only ~~have~~ drink this old Wine of Heaven which I shall call the redigestion of our most ethereal Musings on Earth; but also increase in knowledge and know all things. ° ° °

from Letter to George and Thomas Keats, December 21, 1817

° ° ° I spent Friday evening with Wells[3] & went the next morning to see *Death on the Pale horse.*[4] It is a wonderful picture, when West's age is considered; But there is nothing to be intense upon; no women one feels mad to kiss, no face swelling into reality. the excellence of every Art is its intensity, capable of making all disagreeables evaporate, from their being in close relationship with Beauty & Truth—Examine King Lear & you will find this examplified throughout; but in this picture we have unpleasantness without any momentous depth of speculation excited, in which to bury its repulsiveness—The picture is larger than Christ rejected—I dined with Haydon the sunday after you left, & had a very pleasant day, I dined too (for I have been out too much lately) with Horace Smith & met his two Brothers with Hill & Kingston & one Du Bois,[5] they only served to convince me, how superior humour is to wit in respect to enjoyment—These men say things which make one start, without making one feel, they are all alike; their manners are alike; they all know fashionables; they have a mannerism in their very eating & drinking, in their mere handling a Decanter—They talked of Kean[6] & his low company—Would I were with that company instead of yours said I to myself! I know such like acquaintance will never do for me & yet I am going to Reynolds, on wednesday—Brown & Dilke walked with me & back from the Christmas pantomime. I had not a dispute but a disquisition with Dilke, on various subjects; several things dovetailed in my mind, & at once it

---

3. Charles Wells (1800–1879), an author.
4. By Benjamin West (1738–1820), American painter and president of the Royal Academy; "Christ Rejected" (mentioned below) is also by West.

5. Thomas Hill (1760–1840), a book collector, and Edward duBois (1774–1850), a journalist.
6. Edmund Kean, a famous Shakespearean actor.

struck me, what quality went to form a Man of Achievement especially
in Literature & which Shakespeare posessed so enormously—I mean
Negative Capability, that is when man is capable of being in uncertainties, Mysteries, doubts, without any irritable reaching after fact &
reason—Coleridge, for instance, would let go by a fine isolated veri-
similitude caught from the Penetralium of mystery, from being incapable of remaining content with half knowledge. This pursued
through Volumes would perhaps take us no further than this, that with
a great poet the sense of Beauty overcomes every other consideration,
or rather obliterates all consideration.

Letter to John Hamilton Reynolds,
February 19, 1818

I have an idea that a Man might pass a very pleasant life in this
manner—let him on any certain day read a certain Page of full Poesy
or distilled Prose and let him wander with it, and muse upon it, and
reflect from it, and bring home to it, and prophesy upon it, and dream
upon it—untill it becomes stale—but when will it do so? Never—
When Man has arrived at a certain ripeness in intellect any one grand
and spiritual passage serves him as a starting post towards all "the two-
and-thirty Pallaces"[7] How happy is such a "voyage of conception,"
what delicious diligent Indolence! A doze upon a Sofa does not hinder
it, and a nap upon Clover engenders ethereal finger-pointings—the
prattle of a child gives it wings, and the converse of middle age a
strength to beat them—a strain of musick conducts to "an odd angle of
the Isle",[8] and when the leaves whisper it puts a "girdle round the
earth",[9] Nor will this sparing touch of noble Books be any irreverance
to their Writers—for perhaps the honors paid by Man to Man are trifles
in comparison to the Benefit done by great Works to the "Spirit and
pulse of good" by their mere passive existence. Memory should not be
called knowledge—Many have original minds who do not think it—
they are led away by Custom—Now it appears to me that almost any
Man may like the Spider spin from his own inwards his own airy
Citadel—the points of leaves and twigs on which the Spider begins
her work are few and she fills the Air with a beautiful circuiting: man
should be content with as few points to tip with the fine Webb of his
Soul and weave a tapestry empyrean—full of Symbols for his spiritual
eye, of softness for his spiritual touch, of space for his wandering of
distinctness for his Luxury— But the Minds of Mortals are so different
and bent on such diverse Journeys that it may at first appear impossible
for any common taste and fellowship to exist ~~bettween~~ between two
or three under these suppositions—It is however quite the contrary—
Minds would leave each other in contrary directions, traverse each
other in Numberless points, and all [*for* at] last greet each other at the
Journeys end—An old Man and a child would talk together and the old

---

7. "Places of delight" in Buddhism.
8. *The Tempest*, Act I, sc. ii, 223.

9. The phrase is from *Midsummer Night's Dream*, Act II, sc. i, 175.

Man be led on his Path, and the child left thinking—Man should not dispute or assert but whisper results to his neighbor, and thus by every germ of Spirit sucking the Sap from mould ethereal every human might become great, and Humanity instead of being a wide heath of Furse[1] and Briars with here and there a remote Oak or Pine, would become a grand democracy of Forest Trees. It has been an old Comparison for our urging on—the Bee hive—however it seems to me that we should rather be the flower than the Bee—for it is a false notion that more is gained by receiving than giving—no, the receiver and the giver are equal in their benefits—The f[l]ower I doubt not receives a fair guerdon from the Bee—its leaves blush deeper in the next spring—and who shall say between Man and Woman which is the most delighted? Now it is more noble to sit like Jove that [*for* than] to fly like Mercury—let us not therefore go hurrying about and collecting honey bee like, buzzing here and there impatiently from a knowledge of what is to be arrived at; but let us open our leaves like a flower and be passive and receptive—budding patiently under the eye of Apollo and taking hints from every noble insect that favors us with a visit—sap will be given us for Meat and dew for drink—I was led into these thoughts, my dear Reynolds, by the beauty of the morning operating on a sense of Idleness—I have not read any Books—the Morning said I was right —I had no Idea but of the Morning, and the Thrush said I was right— seeming to say—

> O thou whose face hath felt the Winter's wind,
> Whose eye has seen the snow-clouds hung in mist,
> And the black elm tops 'mong the freezing stars,
> To thee the spring will be a harvest-time.
> O thou, whose only book has been the light
> Of supreme darkness which thou feddest on
> Night after night when Phœbus was away,
> To thee the spring shall be a triple morn.
> O fret not after knowledge—I have none,
> And yet my song comes native with the warmth.
> O fret not after knowledge—I have none,
> And yet the Evening listens. He who saddens
> At thought of idleness cannot be idle,
> And he's awake who thinks himself asleep.

Now I am sensible all this is a mere sophistication, however it may neighbor to any truths, to excuse my own indolence—so I will not deceive myself that Man should be equal with jove—but think himself very well off as a sort of scullion-Mercury, or even a humble Bee—It is not [*for* no] matter whether I am right or wrong either one way or another, if there is sufficient to lift a little time from your Shoulders.

from Letter to John Taylor, February 27, 1818

° ° ° It is a sorry thing for me that any one should have to overcome Prejudices in reading my Verses—that affects me more than any hyper-

---

1. *The Tempest*, Act I, sc. i, 68–69.

criticism on any particular Passage. In *Endymion* I have most likely but moved into the Go-cart from the leading strings. In Poetry I have a few Axioms, and you will see how far I am from their Centre. 1ˢᵗ I think Poetry should surprise by a fine excess and not by Singularity—it should strike the Reader as a wording of his own highest thoughts, and appear almost a Remembrance—2ⁿᵈ Its touches of Beauty should never be half way therby making the reader breathless instead of content: the rise, the progress, the setting of imagery should like the Sun come natural natural too him—shine over him and set soberly although in magnificence leaving him in the Luxury of twilight—but it is easier to think what Poetry should be than to write it—and this leads me on to another axiom. That if Poetry comes not as naturally as the Leaves to a tree it had better not come at all. However it may be with me I cannot help looking into new countries with "O for a Muse of fire to ascend!"[2]—If Endymion serves me as a Pioneer perhaps I ought to be content. I have great reason to be content, for thank God I can read and perhaps understand Shakspeare to his depths, and I have I am sure many friends, who, if I fail, will attribute any change in my Life and Temper to Humbleness rather than to Pride—to a cowering under the Wings of great Poets rather than to a Bitterness that I am not appreciated. I am anxious to get Endymion printed that I may forget it and proceed. ° ° °

from the Preface to *Endymion,* dated April 10, 1818

The imagination of a boy is healthy, and the mature imagination of a man is healthy; but there is a space of life between, in which the soul is in a ferment, the character undecided, the way of life uncertain, the ambition thick-sighted: thence proceeds mawkishness, and all the thousand bitters which those men I speak of must necessarily taste in going over the following pages.

I hope I have not in too late a day touched the beautiful mythology of Greece, and dulled its brightness: for I wish to try once more, before I bid it farewell.

from Letter to James Augustus Hessey, October 8, 1818

° ° ° Praise or blame has but a momentary effect on the man whose love of beauty in the abstract makes him a severe critic on his own Works. My own domestic criticism has given me pain without comparison beyond what Blackwood or the ~~Edinburgh~~ Quarterly[3] could possibly inflict. and also when I feel I am right, no external praise can give me such a glow as my own solitary reperception & ratification of what is fine. J. S.[4] is perfectly right in regard to the slip-shod Endymion. That it is so is no fault of mine.—No!—though it may sound a little paradoxical. It is as good as I had power to make it—by myself—Had I been nervous about its being a perfect piece, & with that view asked advice, & trembled over every page, it would not have been written;

---

2. Shakespeare, *Henry V*, Prologue, 1.
3. *Endymion* was violently attacked by reviewers in *Blackwood's Edinburgh Maga-*

zine and *The Quarterly Review.*
4. Whose letter to the *Morning Chronicle* defended Keats.

for it is not in my nature to fumble—I will write independantly.—I have written independently *without Judgment.*—I may write independently & *with judgment* hereafter.—The Genius of Poetry must work out its own salvation in a man: It cannot be matured by law & precept, but by sensation & watchfulness in itself—That which is creative must create itself—In Endymion, I leaped headlong into the Sea, and thereby have become better acquainted with the Soundings, the quicksands & the rocks, than if I had ~~stayed~~ stayed upon the green shore, and piped a silly pipe, and took tea & comfortable advice.—I was never afraid of failure; for I would sooner fail than not be among the greatest—But I am nigh getting into a rant. * * *

Chronology

1795   John Keats born October 31 at Finsbury, just north of London, the eldest child of Thomas and Frances Jennings Keats. Thomas Keats was head ostler at a livery stable.

1797–1803   Birth of three younger brothers and sisters: George in 1797, Thomas in 1799, Frances Mary (Fanny) in 1803.

1803   With George, begins school in Enfield.

1804   Father killed by a fall from his horse, April 15. On June 27 his mother remarries, and the children go to live with their maternal grandparents at Enfield. The grandfather dies a year later, and the children move with their grandmother to Lower Edmonton.

1809   Begins a literary friendship with Charles Cowden Clarke, the son of the headmaster at the Enfield school, and develops a strong interest in reading.

1810   Mother dies of tuberculosis, after a long illness.

1811   Leaves school to become apprenticed to an apothecary-surgeon in Edmonton; completes a prose translation of the *Aeneid,* begun at school.

1814   Earliest known attempts at writing verse. In December his grandmother dies, and the family home is broken up.

1815   In October moves to next stage of his medical training at Guy's Hospital, south of the Thames in London.

1816   On May 5 his first published poem, *O Solitude,* appears in Leigh Hunt's *Examiner.* In October writes *On First Looking into Chapman's Homer,* published in December. Meets Hunt, Benjamin Haydon, John Hamilton Reynolds, and Shelley. By the spring of 1817, gives up the idea of medical practice.

1817   In March, moves with brothers to Hampstead, sees the Elgin Marbles with Haydon, and publishes his first collection of *Poems.* Composes *Endymion* between April and November. Reads Milton, Shakespeare, Coleridge and rereads Wordsworth during the year.

1818   *Endymion* published in April, unfavorably reviewed in September, defended by Reynolds in October. During the summer goes on walking tour of the lake country and Scotland, but returns to London in mid-August with a sore throat and severe chills. His brother Tom also seriously ill by late summer, dying on December 1. In

September, Keats first meets Fanny Brawne (18 years old), with whom he arrives at an "understanding" by Christmas.

1819   Writes *The Eve of St. Agnes* in January, revises it in September. Fanny Brawne and her mother move into the other half of the double house in which Keats lives in April. During April and May writes *La Belle Dame sans Merci* and all the major odes except *To Autumn*, written in September. Rental arrangements force separation from Fanny Brawne during the summer (Keats on Isle of Wight from June to August), and in the fall he tries to break his dependence on her, but they become engaged by Christmas. Earlier in December suffers a recurrence of his sore throat.

1820   In February has a severe hemorrhage and in June an attack of blood-spitting. In July his doctor orders him to Italy for the winter; he sails in September and finally arrives in Rome on November 15. In July a volume of poems published, *Lamia, Isabella, The Eve of St. Agnes and Other Poems*. Fanny Brawne nurses him through the late summer.

1821   Dies at 11 P.M., February 23. Buried in the English Cemetery at Rome.

———

ADRIENNE RICH

A Clock in the Square

This handless clock stares blindly from its tower,
Refusing to acknowledge any hour.
But what can one clock do to stop the game
When others go on striking just the same?
Whatever mite of truth the gesture held,   5
Time may be silenced but will not be stilled,
Nor we absolved by any one's withdrawing
From all the restless ways we must be going
And all the rings in which we're spun and swirled,
Whether around a clockface or a world.   10

1951

At a Bach Concert

Coming by evening through the wintry city
We said that art is out of love with life.
Here we approach a love that is not pity.

This antique discipline, tenderly severe,
Renews belief in love yet masters feeling,   5
Asking of us a grace in what we bear.

Form is the ultimate gift that love can offer—
The vital union of necessity
With all that we desire, all that we suffer.

A too-compassionate art is half an art.   10
Only such proud restraining purity
Restores the else-betrayed, too-human heart.

1951

Storm Warnings

The glass has been falling all the afternoon,
And knowing better than the instrument
What winds are walking overhead, what zone
Of gray unrest is moving across the land,
I leave the book upon a pillowed chair   5
And walk from window to closed window, watching
Boughs strain against the sky

And think again, as often when the air
Moves inward toward a silent core of waiting,
How with a single purpose time has traveled   10
By secret currents of the undiscerned
Into this polar realm. Weather abroad
And weather in the heart alike come on
Regardless of prediction.

Between foreseeing and averting change   15
Lies all the mastery of elements
Which clocks and weatherglasses cannot alter.
Time in the hand is not control of time,
Nor shattered fragments of an instrument
A proof against the wind; the wind will rise,   20
We can only close the shutters.

I draw the curtains as the sky goes black
And set a match to candles sheathed in glass
Against the keyhole draught, the insistent whine
Of weather through the unsealed aperture.   25
This is our sole defense against the season;
These are the things that we have learned to do
Who live in troubled regions.

1951

Snapshots of a Daughter-in-Law

1

You, once a belle in Shreveport,
with henna-colored hair, skin like a peachbud,

still have your dresses copied from that time,
and play a Chopin prelude
called by Cortot: *"Delicious recollections*   5
float like perfume through the memory."

Your mind now, mouldering like wedding-cake,
heavy with useless experience, rich
with suspicion, rumor, fantasy,
crumbling to pieces under the knife-edge   10
of mere fact. In the prime of your life.

Nervy, glowering, your daughter
wipes the teaspoons, grows another way.

2

Banging the coffee-pot into the sink
she hears the angels chiding, and looks out   15
past the raked gardens to the sloppy sky.
Only a week since They said: *Have no patience.*

The next time it was: *Be insatiable.*
Then: *Save yourself; others you cannot save.*[5]
Sometimes she's let the tapstream scald her arm,   20
a match burn to her thumbnail,

or held her hand above the kettle's snout
right in the woolly steam. They are probably angels,
since nothing hurts her any more, except
each morning's grit blowing into her eyes.   25

3

A thinking woman sleeps with monsters.
The beak that grips her, she becomes. And Nature,
that sprung-lidded, still commodious
steamer-trunk of *tempora* and *mores*[6]
gets stuffed with it all: the mildewed orange-flowers,   30
the female pills, the terrible breasts
of Boadicea[7] beneath flat foxes' heads and orchids.

Two handsome women, gripped in argument,
each proud, acute, subtle, I hear scream
across the cut glass and majolica   35
like Furies[8] cornered from their prey:
The argument *ad feminam*,[9] all the old knives

<hr/>

5. According to *Matthew* 27:42, the chief priests, scribes, and elders mocked the crucified Jesus by saying, "He saved others; himself he cannot save."
6. Times and customs.
7. Queen of the ancient Britons. When her husband died, the Romans seized the territory he ruled and scourged Boadicea; she then led a heroic but ultimately un-

successful revolt.
8. In Roman mythology, the three sisters were the avenging spirits of retributive justice.
9. Argument to the woman. The *argumentum ad hominem* (literally, argument to the man) is (in logic) an argument aimed at a person's individual prejudices or special interests.

that have rusted in my back, I drive in yours,
ma semblable, ma soeur![1]

4

Knowing themselves too well in one another: 40
their gifts no pure fruition, but a thorn,
the prick filed sharp against a hint of scorn . . .
Reading while waiting
for the iron to heat,
writing, *My Life had stood—a Loaded Gun—*[2]   45
in that Amherst pantry while the jellies boil and scum,
or, more often,
iron-eyed and beaked and purposed as a bird,
dusting everything on the whatnot every day of life.

5

Dulce ridens, dulce loquens,[3]   50
she shaves her legs until they gleam
like petrified mammoth-tusk.

6

When to her lute Corinna sings[4]
neither words nor music are her own;
only the long hair dipping   55
over her check, only the song
of silk against her knees
and these
adjusted in reflections of an eye.

Poised, trembling and unsatisfied, before   60
an unlocked door, that cage of cages,
tell us, you bird, you tragical machine—
is this *fertilisante douleur?*[5] Pinned down
by love, for you the only natural action,
are you edged more keen   65
to prise the secrets of the vault? has Nature shown
her household books to you, daughter-in-law,
that her sons never saw?

7

"To have in this uncertain world some stay
which cannot be undermined, is   70
of the utmost consequence."[6]

---

1. "My mirror-image (or 'double'), my sister." Baudelaire, in the prefatory poem to *Les Fleurs du Mal*, addresses (and attacks) his "hypocrite reader" as "mon semblable, mon frère" (my double, my brother).
2. " 'My Life had stood—a Loaded Gun' [Poem No. 754], Emily Dickinson, *Complete Poems*, ed. T. H. Johnson, 1960, p. 369." (Rich's note)
3. "Sweet (or winsome) laughter, sweet chatter." The phrase (slightly modified here) concludes Horace's *Ode*, 1, 22, describing the appeal of a mistress.
4. The opening line of a famous Elizabethan lyric (by Thomas Campion) in which Corinna's music is said to control totally the poet's happiness or despair.
5. Enriching pain.
6. " '. . . is of the utmost consequence,' from Mary Wollstonecraft, *Thoughts on the Education of Daughters*, London, 1787." (Rich's note)

Thus wrote
a woman, partly brave and partly good,
who fought with what she partly understood.
Few men about her would or could do more,
hence she was labeled harpy, shrew and whore.   75

8

"You all die at fifteen," said Diderot,[7]
and turn part legend, part convention.
Still, eyes inaccurately dream
behind closed windows blankening with steam.
Deliciously, all that we might have been,   80
all that we were—fire, tears,
wit, taste, martyred ambition—
stirs like the memory of refused adultery
the drained and flagging bosom of our middle years.

9

Not that it is done well, but   85
that it is done at all?[8] Yes, think
of the odds! or shrug them off forever.
This luxury of the precocious child,
Time's precious chronic invalid,—
would we, darlings, resign it if we could?   90
Our blight has been our sinecure:
mere talent was enough for us—
glitter in fragments and rough drafts.

Sigh no more, ladies.
                Time is male
and in his cups drinks to the fair.   95
Bemused by gallantry, we hear
our mediocrities over-praised,
indolence read as abnegation,
slattern thought styled intuition,
every lapse forgiven, our crime   100
only to cast too bold a shadow
or smash the mould straight off.

For that, solitary confinement,
tear gas, attrition shelling.
Few applicants for that honor.

10

                Well,   105
she's long about her coming, who must be

---

7. "'Vous mourez toutes à quinze ans,'
from the *Lettres à Sophie Volland*, quoted
by Simone de Beauvoir in *Le Deuxième
Sexe*, vol. II, pp. 123–4." (Rich's note)
Editor of the *Encyclopédie* (the central
document of the French Enlightenment),
Diderot became disillusioned with the traditional education of women and undertook an experimental education for his
own daughter.

8. Samuel Johnson's comment on women
preachers: "Sir, a woman's preaching is
like a dog's walking on his hinder legs. It
is not done well, but you are surprised to
find it done at all." (Boswell's *Life of
Johnson*, ed. Birbeck-Hill, I, 463)

more merciless to herself than history.[9]
Her mind full to the wind, I see her plunge
breasted and glancing through the currents,
taking the light upon her   110
at least as beautiful as any boy
or helicopter,
              poised, still coming,
her fine blades making the air wince

but her cargo
no promise then: 115
delivered
palpable
ours.

1958–60

[*In* When We Dead Awaken, *Rich described her consciousness during the time she was writing this poem:* "Over two years I wrote a 10-part poem called 'Snapshots of A Daughter-in-Law,' in a longer, looser mode than I've ever trusted myself with before. It was an extraordinary relief to write that poem. It strikes me now as too literary, too dependent on allusion; I hadn't found the courage yet to do without authorities, or even to use the pronoun 'I'—the woman in the poem is always 'she.' One section of it, #2, concerns a woman who thinks she is going mad; she is haunted by voices telling her to resist and rebel, voices which she can hear but not obey."]

Necessities of Life

Piece by piece I seem
to re-enter the world: I first began

a small, fixed dot, still see
that old myself, a dark-blue thumbtack

pushed into the scene,   5
a hard little head protruding

from the pointillist's[1] buzz and bloom.
After a time the dot

begins to ooze. Certain heats
melt it.
              Now I was hurriedly   10
blurring into ranges

9. "Cf. *Le Deuxième Sexe*, vol. II, p. 574: '. . . elle arrive du fond des ages, de Thèbes, de Minos, de Chichen Itza; et elle est aussi le totem planté au coeur de la brousse africaine; c'est un helicoptère et c'est un oiseau; et voilà la plus grande merveille: sous ses cheveux peints le bruisse- ment des feuillages devient une pensée et des paroles s'échappent de ses seins.' " (Rich's note)

1. Post-impressionist painters (Seurat, for example) who fused small dots of paint with brush strokes.

of burnt red, burning green,
whole biographies swam up and
swallowed me like Jonah.

Jonah! I was Wittgenstein,[2]   15
Mary Wollstonecraft, the soul

of Louis Jouvet, dead
in a blown-up photograph.

Till, wolfed almost to shreds,
I learned to make myself   20

unappetizing. Scaly as a dry bulb
thrown into a cellar

I used myself, let nothing use me.
Like being on a private dole,

sometimes more like kneading bricks in Egypt.[3]   25
What life was there, was mine,

now and again to lay
one hand on a warm brick

and touch the sun's ghost
with economical joy,   30

now and again to name
over the bare necessities.

So much for those days. Soon
practice may make me middling-perfect, I'll

dare inhabit the world   35
trenchant in motion as an eel, solid

as a cabbage-head. I have invitations:
a curl of mist steams upward

from a field, visible as my breath,
houses along a road stand waiting   40

like old women knitting, breathless
to tell their tales.

1962

2. Ludwig Wittgenstein (1889–1951),
Austrian born philosopher. His early thought
heavily influenced logical positivism, and
his later work expressed such strong skepticism about the reliability of language that
he ultimately resigned his chair of philosophy lest his ideas be misunderstood or
misinterpreted. Mary Wollstonecraft, an
early feminist, wrote *Vindication of the
Rights of Women* (1792). Louis Jouvet
(1887–1951), innovative French actor and
producer.
3. According to *Exodus* 5, one of the
most oppressive tasks imposed on the Israelites during their Egyptian bondage was
the making of bricks.

Orion

Far back when I went zig-zagging
through tamarack pastures
you were my genius, you
my cast-iron Viking, my helmed
lion-heart king in prison.   5
Years later now you're young

my fierce half-brother, staring
down from that simplified west
your breast open, your belt dragged down
by an oldfashioned thing, a sword   10
the last bravado you won't give over
though it weighs you down as you stride

and the stars in it are dim
and maybe have stopped burning.
But you burn, and I know it;   15
as I throw back my head to take you in
an old transfusion happens again:
divine astronomy is nothing to it.

Indoors I bruise and blunder,
break faith, leave ill enough   20
alone, a dead child born in the dark.
Night cracks up over the chimney,
pieces of time, frozen geodes
come showering down in the grate.

A man reaches behind my eyes   25
and finds them empty
a woman's head turns away
from my head in the mirror
children are dying my death
and eating crumbs of my life.   30

Pity is not your forte.
Calmly you ache up there
pinned aloft in your crow's nest,
my speechless pirate!
You take it all for granted   35
and when I look you back

it's with a starlike eye
shooting its cold and egotistical spear
where it can do least damage.
Breathe deep! No hurt, no pardon   40
out here in the cold with you
you with your back to the wall.

1965

[*In* When We Dead Awaken, *Rich described* Orion *as* "a poem of re-construction with a part of myself I had felt I was losing—the active principle, the energetic imagination, the 'half-brother' whom I projected, as I had for many years, into the constellation Orion. It's no accident that the words 'cold and egotistical' appear in this poem, and are applied to myself. The choice still seemed to be between 'love'—womanly, maternal love, altruistic love—a love defined and ruled by the weight of an entire culture—and egotism—a force directed by men into creation, achievement, ambition, often at the expense of others, but justifiably so. For weren't they men, and wasn't that their destiny as womanly love was ours? I know now that the alternatives are false ones—that the word 'love' is itself in need of re-vision."]

Planetarium

(*Thinking of Caroline Herschel, 1750–1848, astronomer, sister of William; and others*)

A woman in the shape of a monster
a monster in the shape of a woman
the skies are full of them

a woman   "in the snow
among the Clocks and instruments   5
or measuring the ground with poles"

in her 98 years to discover
8 comets

she whom the moon ruled
like us   10
levitating into the night sky
riding the polished lenses

Galaxies of women, there
doing penance for impetuousness
ribs chilled   15
in those spaces   of the mind

An eye,
          "virile, precise and absolutely certain"
          from the mad webs of Uranisborg

                    encountering the NOVA

every impulse of light exploding   20
from the core
as life flies out of us

Tycho[4] whispering at last
"Let me not seem to have lived in vain"

What we see, we see   25
and seeing is changing

the light that shrivels a mountain
and leaves a man alive

Heartbeat of the pulsar
heart sweating through my body   30

The radio impulse
pouring in from Taurus
        I am bombarded yet   I stand

I have been standing all my life in the
direct path of a battery of signals   35
the most accurately transmitted most
untranslatable language in the universe
I am a galactic cloud so deep   so invo-
luted that a light wave could take 15
years to travel through me   And has   40
taken   I am an instrument in the shape
of a woman trying to translate pulsations
into images   for the relief of the body
and the reconstruction of the mind.
1968

[*Rich described this poem, in* When We Dead Awaken, *as a* "companion poem to 'Orion,' " *above:* "at last the woman in the poem and
the woman writing the poem become the same person. . . . It was written after a visit to a real planetarium, where I read an account of the
work of Caroline Herschel, the astronomer, who worked with her
brother William, but whose name remained obscure, as his did not."]

Trying to Talk with a Man

Perhaps my life is nothing but an image of this kind; perhaps I am doomed to retrace my
steps under the illusion that I am exploring, doomed to try and learn what I should
simply recognize, learning a mere fraction of what I have forgotten.
                                              —Andre Breton, *Nadja*[5]

Out in this desert we are testing bombs,

that's why we came here.

4. Tycho Brahe (1546–1601), Danish
astronomer whose cosmology tried to fuse
the Ptolemaic and Copernican systems. He
discovered and described ("*De Nova Stella*,
1573) a new star in what had previously
been considered a fixed star-system. Uran-
iborg (line 19) was Tycho's famous and
elaborate palace-laboratory-observatory.
    5. Breton (1896–1968), a French poet
and critic, was one of the founders of both
Dadaism and Surrealism. His novel *Nadja*
was published in 1928.

Sometimes I feel an underground river
forcing its way between deformed cliffs
an acute angle of understanding   5
moving itself like a locus of the sun
into this condemned scenery.

What we've had to give up to get here—
Whole LP collections, films we starred in
playing in the neighborhoods, bakery windows   10
full of dry, chocolate-filled Jewish cookies,
the language of love-letters, of suicide notes,
afternoons on the riverbank
pretending to be children

Coming out to this desert   15
we meant to change the face of
driving among dull green succulents
walking at noon in the ghost-town
surrounded by a silence

that sounds like the silence of the place   20
except that it came with us
and is familiar
and everything we were saying until now
was an effort to blot it out
Coming out here we are up against it   25

Out here I feel more helpless
with you than without you.
You mention the danger
and list the equipment
we talk of people caring for each other   30
in emergencies—laceration, thirst—
but you look at me like an emergency

Your dry heat feels like power
your eyes are stars of a different magnitude
they reflect lights that spell out EXIT   35
when you get up and pace the floor

talking of the danger
as if it were not ourselves
as if we were testing anything else.

1971

Diving into the Wreck

First having read the book of myths,
and loaded the camera,
and checked the edge of the knife-blade,
I put on

the body-armor of black rubber   5
the absurd flippers
the grave and awkward mask.
I am having to do this
not like Cousteau with his
assiduous team   10
aboard the sun-flooded schooner
but here alone.

There is a ladder.
The ladder is always there
hanging innocently   15
close to the side of the schooner.
We know what it is for,
we who have used it.
Otherwise
it's a piece of maritime floss   20
some sundry equipment.

I go down.
Rung after rung and still
the oxygen immerses me
the blue light   25
the clear atoms
of our human air.
I go down.
My flippers cripple me,
I crawl like an insect down the ladder   30
and there is no one
to tell me when the ocean
will begin.

First the air is blue and then
it is bluer and then green and then   35
black I am blacking out and yet
my mask is powerful
it pumps my blood with power
the sea is another story
the sea is not a question of power   40
I have to learn alone
to turn my body without force
in the deep element.

And now: it is easy to forget
what I came for   45
among so many who have always
lived here
swaying their crenellated fans
between the reefs
and besides   50
you breathe differently down here.

I came to explore the wreck.
The words are purposes.
The words are maps.
I came to see the damage that was done   55
and the treasures that prevail.
I stroke the beam of my lamp
slowly along the flank
of something more permanent
than fish or weed   60

the thing I came for:
the wreck and not the story of the wreck
the thing itself and not the myth
the drowned face always staring
toward the sun   65
the evidence of damage
worn by salt and sway into this threadbare beauty
the ribs of the disaster
curving their assertion
among the tentative haunters.   70

This is the place.
And I am here, the mermaid whose dark hair
streams black, the merman in his armored body
We circle silently
about the wreck   75
we dive into the hold.
I am she: I am he

whose drowned face sleeps with open eyes
whose breasts still bear the stress
whose silver, copper, vermeil cargo lies   80
obscurely inside barrels
half-wedged and left to rot
we are the half-destroyed instruments
that once held to a course
the water-eaten log   85
the fouled compass

We are, I am, you are
by cowardice or courage
the one who find our way
back to this scene   90
carrying a knife, a camera
a book of myths
in which
our names do not appear.

1972

Origins and History of Consciousness

I

Night-life. Letters, journals, bourbon
sloshed in the glass. Poems crucified on the wall,
dissected, their bird-wings severed
like trophies. No one lives in this room
without living through some kind of crisis.   5

No one lives in this room
without confronting the whiteness of the wall
behind the poems, planks of books,
photographs of dead heroines.
Without contemplating last and late   10
the true nature of poetry. The drive
to connect. The dream of a common language.

Thinking of lovers, their blind faith, their
experienced crucifixions,
my envy is not simple. I have dreamed of going to bed   15
as walking into clear water ringed by a snowy wood
white as cold sheets, thinking, *I'll freeze in there.*
My bare feet are numbed already by the snow
but the water
is mild, I sink and float   20
like a warm amphibious animal
that has broken the net, has run
through fields of snow leaving no print;
this water washes off the scent—
You are clear now   25
of the hunter, the trapper
the wardens of the mind—

yet the warm animal dreams on
of another animal
swimming under the snow-flecked surface of the pool,   30
and wakes, and sleeps again.

No one sleeps in this room without
the dream of a common language.

II

It was simple to meet you, simple to take your eyes
into mine, saying: these are eyes I have known   35
from the first. . . . It was simple to touch you
against the hacked background, the grain of what we
had been, the choices, years. . . . It was even simple
to take each other's lives in our hands, as bodies.

What is not simple: to wake from drowning   40

from where the ocean beat inside us like an afterbirth
into this common, acute particularity
these two selves who walked half a lifetime untouching—
to wake to something deceptively simple: a glass
sweated with dew, a ring of the telephone, a scream   45
of someone beaten up far down in the street
causing each of us to listen to her own inward scream

knowing the mind of the mugger and the mugged
as any woman must who stands to survive this city,
this century, this life . . .   50

each of us having loved the flesh in its clenched or loosened
    beauty
better than trees or music (yet loving those too
as if they were flesh—and they are—but the flesh
of beings unfathomed as yet in our roughly literal life).

III

It's simple to wake from sleep with a stranger,   55
dress, go out, drink coffee,
enter a life again. It isn't simple
to wake from sleep into the neighborhood
of one neither strange nor familiar
whom we have chosen to trust. Trusting, untrusting,   60
we lowered ourselves into this, let ourselves
downward hand over hand as on a rope that quivered
over the unsearched. . . . We did this. Conceived
of each other, conceived each other in a darkness
which I remember as drenched in light.   65
                                        I want to call this, life.

But I can't call it life until we start to move
beyond this secret circle of fire
where our bodies are giant shadows flung on a wall
where the night becomes our inner darkness, and sleeps   70
like a dumb beast, head on her paws, in the corner.

1972–1974   1978

from Talking with Adrienne Rich[6]

* * * I think of myself as using poetry as a chief means of self-exploration—one of several means, of which maybe another would be dreams, really thinking about, paying attention to dreams, but the poem, like the dream, does this through images and it is in the images of my poems that I feel I am finding out more about my own expe-

6. A transcript of a conversation re-   *Ohio Review*, Fall, 1971.
corded March 9, 1971, and printed in *The*

rience, my sense of things. But I don't think of myself as having a position or a self-description which I'm then going to present in the poem.

* * *

When I started writing poetry I was tremendously conscious of, and very much in need of, a formal structure that could be obtained from outside, into which I could pour whatever I had, whatever I thought I had to express. But I think that was a part of a whole thing that I see, now as a teacher, very much with young writers, of using language more as a kind of façade than as either self-revelation or as a probe into one's own consciousness. I think I would attribute a lot of the change in my poetry simply to the fact of growing older, undergoing certain kinds of experiences, realizing that formal metrics were not going to suffice me in dealing with those experiences, realizing that experience itself is much more fragmentary, much more sort of battering, much ruder than these structures would allow, and it had to find its own form.

* * *

I have a very strong sense about the existence of poetry in daily life and poetry being part of the world as it is, and that the attempt to reduce poetry to what is indited on a page just limits you terribly. . . . The poem is the poetry of things lodged in the innate shape of the experience. My saying "The moment of change is the only poem" is the kind of extreme statement you feel the need to make at certain times if only to force someone to say, "But I always thought a poem is something written on a piece of paper," you know, and to say: "But look, how did those words get on that piece of paper." There had to be a mind; there had to be an experience; the mind had to go through certain shocks, certain stresses, certain strains, and if you're going to carry the poem back to its real beginnings it's that moment of change. I feel that we are always writing.

* * *

When I was in my twenties * * * I was going through a very sort of female thing—of trying to distinguish between the ego that is capable of writing poems, and then this other kind of being that you're asked to be if you're a woman, who is, in a sense, denying that ego. I had great feelings of split about that for many years actually, and there are a lot of poems I couldn't write even, because I didn't want to confess to having that much aggression, that much ego, that much sense of myself. I had always thought of my first book as being a book of very well-tooled poems of a sort of very bright student, which I was at that time, but poems in which the unconscious things never got to the surface. But there's a poem in that book about a woman who sews a tapestry and the tapestry has figures of tigers on it. But the woman is represented as being completely—her hand is burdened by the weight of the wedding band, and she's meek, and she's fearful, and the only way in which she can express any other side of her nature is in embroidering these tigers. Well, I thought of that as almost a formal exercise, but when I go back and look at that poem I really think it's saying something about what I was going through. And now that's lessened a great deal for all sorts of reasons—that split.

from An Interview with Adrienne Rich[7]

I would have said ten or fifteen years ago that I would not even want to identify myself as a woman poet. That term *has* been used pejoratively; I just don't think it can be at this point. You know, for a woman the act of creation is prototypically to produce children, while the act of creating with language—I'm not saying that women writers haven't been accepted; certainly, more have been accepted than women lawyers or doctors. Still, a woman writer feels, she is going against the grain—or there has been this sense until very recently (if there isn't still). Okay, it's all right to be a young thing and write verse. But a friend of mine was telling me about meeting a noted poet at a cocktail party. She'd sent him a manuscript for a contest he was judging. She went up to him and asked him about it, and he looked at her and said, "Young girls *are* poems; they shouldn't write them." This attitude toward women poets manifests itself so strongly that you are made to feel you are becoming the thing you are not.

* * *

If a man is writing, he's gone through all the nonsense and said "Okay, I am a poet and I'm still a man. They don't cancel each other out or, if they do, then I'll opt to be a poet." He's not writing for a hostile sex, a breed of critics who by virtue of their sex are going to look at his language and pass judgment on it. That does happen to a woman. I don't know why the woman poet has been slower than the woman novelist in taking risks though I'm very grateful that this is no longer so. I feel that I dare to think further than I would have dared to think ten years ago—and *that* certainly is going to affect my writing. And I now dare to entertain thoughts and speculations that then would have seemed unthinkable.

* * *

Many of the male writers whom I very much admire—Galway Kinnell, James Wright, W. S. Merwin—are writing poetry of such great desolation. They come from different backgrounds, write in different ways, and yet all seem to write out of a sense of doom, as if we were fated to carry on these terribly flawed relationships. I think it's expressive of a feeling that "we, the masters, have created a world that's impossible to live in and that probably may not be livable in, in a very literal sense. What we thought, what we'd been given to think is our privilege, our right, and our sexual prerogative has led to this, to our doom." I guess a lot of women—if not a lot of women poets—are feeling that there has to be some other way, that human life is messed up but that it doesn't have to be *this* desolate.

* * *

7. By David Kalstone, in *The Saturday Review*, April 22, 1972.

Today, much poetry by women is charged with anger and uses voices of rage and anger that I don't think were ever used in poetry before. In poets like Sylvia Plath and Diane Wakoski, say, those voices are so convincing that it is impossible to describe them by using those favorite adjectives of phallic criticism—shrill and hysterical. Well, Sylvia Plath is dead. I always maintained from the first time I read her last poems that her suicide was not necessary, that she could have gone on and written poems that would have given us even more insight into the states of anger and willfulness, even of self-destructiveness, that women experience. She didn't need literally to destroy herself in order to reflect and express those things. Diane Wakoski is a young woman. She's changing a lot and will continue to change. What I admire in her, besides her energy and dynamism and quite a beautiful gift for snatching the image that she wants out of the air, is her honesty. No woman has written before about her face and said she hated it, that it had served her ill, that she wished she could throw acid in it. That's very shocking. But I think all women, even the most beautiful women, at times have felt that in a kind of self-hatred. Because the *face* is supposed to be the *woman.*

* * *

A lot of poetry is becoming more oral. Certainly, it's true of women and black poets. Reading black poetry on the printed page gives no sense of the poem, if you're going to look at that poetry the way you look at poems by Richard Wilbur. Yet you can hear these poets read and realize it's the oldest kind of poetry.

* * *

I think the energy of language comes somewhat from the pressure and need and unbearableness of what's being done to you. It's not the same energy you find in the blues. The blues are a grief language, a lost language, and a cry of pain, usually in a woman's voice, which is interesting. For a long time you sing the blues, and then you begin to say, "I'm tired of singing the blues. I want something else." And that's what you're hearing now. There seems to be a connection between an oppressed condition and having access to certain kinds of energy, vitality, and subjectivity. For women as well as blacks. Though I don't feel there is a necessary cause-and-effect relationship; what seems to happen is that being on top, being in a powerful position leads to a divorce between one's unruly, chaotic, revolutionary sensitivity and one's reason, sense of order and of maintaining a hold. And, therefore, you have at the bottom of the pile, so to speak, a kind of churning energy that gets lost up there among the administrators.

* * *

I don't know how or whether poetry changes anything. But neither do I know how or whether bombing or even community organizing changes anything when we are pitted against a massive patriarchal system armed with supertechnology. I believe in subjectivity—that a lot of male Left leaders have turned into Omnipotent Administrators, because their "masculinity" forced them to deny their subjectivity. I believe in dreams and visions and "the madness of art." And at moments I can conceive of a women's movement that will show the way to humanizing technology and fusing dreams and skills and visions and reason to begin the healing of the human race. But I don't want women to take over the world and run it the way men have, or to take on—yet again!—the burden of carrying the subjectivity of the race. Women are a vanguard now, and I believe will increasingly become so, because we have—Western women, Third World women, all women—known and felt the pain of the human condition most consistently. But in the end it can't be women alone.

from When We Dead Awaken: Writing as Re-Vision

Most, if not all, human lives are full of fantasy—passive daydreaming which need not be acted on. But to write poetry or fiction, or even to think well, is not to fantasize or to put fantasies on paper. For a poem to coalesce, for a character or an action to take shape, there has to be an imaginative transformation of reality which is in no way passive. And a certain freedom of the mind is needed—freedom to press on, to enter the currents of your thought like a glider pilot, knowing that your motion can be sustained, that the buoyancy of your attention will not be suddenly snatched away. Moreover, if the imagination is to transcend and transform experience it has to question, to challenge, to conceive of alternatives, perhaps to the very life you are living at that moment. You have to be free to play around with the notion that day might be night, love might be hate, nothing can be too sacred for the imagination to turn into its opposite or to call experimentally by another name. For writing is re-naming.

Now, to be maternally with small children all day in the old way, to be with a man in the old way of marriage, requires a holding back, a putting aside of that imaginative activity, and seems to demand instead a kind of conservatism. I want to make it clear that I am *not* saying that in order to write well, or think well, it is necessary to become unavailable to others, or to become a devouring ego. This has been the myth of the masculine artist and thinker; and, I repeat, I do not accept it. But to be a female human being trying to fulfill traditional female functions in a traditional way *is* in direct conflict with the subversive function of the imagination. The word "traditional" is important here. There must be ways, and we will be finding out more and more about them, in which the energy of creation and the energy of relation can be united. But in those earlier years I always felt the conflict as a failure of love in myself. I had thought I was choosing a full life: the life available to most men, in which sexuality, work and parenthood could co-exist. But I felt, at 29, guilt toward the people closest to me, and guilty toward my own being.

I wanted, then, more than anything, the one thing of which there was never enough: time to think, time to write. The '50s and early '60s were years of rapid revelations: the sit-ins and marches in the South, the Bay of Pigs, the early antiwar movement, raised large questions—questions for which the masculine world of the academy around me seemed to have expert and fluent answers. But I needed desperately to think for myself—about pacifism and dissent and violence, about poetry and society, and about my own relationship to all these things. For about ten years I was reading in fierce snatches, scribbling in notebooks, writing poetry in fragments; I was looking desperately for clues,`because if there were no clues then I thought I might be insane. I wrote in a notebook about this time:

> Paralyzed by the sense that there exists a mesh of relationships —e.g. between my anger at the children, my sensual life, pacifism, sex (I mean sex in its broadest significance, not merely sexual desire)—an interconnectedness which, if I could see it. make it valid, would give me back myself, make it possible to function lucidly and passionately. Yet I grope in and out among these dark webs.

I think I began at this point to feel that politics was not something "out there" but something "in here" and of the essence of my condition.

In the late '50s I was able to write, for the first time, directly about experiencing myself as a woman. The poem was jotted in fragments during children's naps, brief hours in a library, or at 3 A.M. after rising with a wakeful child. I despaired of doing any continuous work at this time. Yet I began to feel that my fragments and scraps had a common consciousness and a common theme, one which I would have been very unwilling to put on paper at an earlier time because I had been taught that poetry should be "universal," which meant, of course, nonfemale. Until then I had tried very much *not* to identify myself as a female poet.

Chronology

1929   Born in Baltimore, Maryland, May 16. Began writing poetry as a child under the encouragement and supervision of her father, Dr. Arnold Rich, from whose "very Victorian, pre-Raphaelite" library, Rich later recalled, she read Tennyson, Keats, Arnold, Blake, Rossetti, Swinburne, Carlyle, and Pater.

1951   A.B., Radcliffe College. Phi Beta Kappa. *A Change of World* chosen by W. H. Auden for the Yale Younger Poets Award and published.

1952–53   Guggenheim Fellowship; travel in Europe and England. Marriage to Alfred H. Conrad, an economist who taught at Harvard. Residence in Cambridge, Massachusetts, 1953–66.

1955   Birth of David Conrad. Publication of *The Diamond Cutters and Other Poems,* which won the Ridgely Torrence Memorial Award of the Poetry Society of America.

1957   Birth of Paul Conrad.

1959   Birth of Jacob Conrad.

1960   National Institute of Arts and Letters Award for poetry. Phi Beta Kappa poet at William and Mary College.

1961–62   Guggenheim Fellowship; residence with family in the Netherlands.

1962   Bollingen Foundation grant for translation of Dutch poetry.

1962–63   Amy Lowell Travelling Fellowship.
1963   *Snapshots of a Daughter-in-Law* published. Bess Hokin
Prize of *Poetry* magazine.
1965   Phi Beta Kappa poet at Swarthmore College.
1966   *Necessities of Life* published, nominated for the National
Book Award. Phi Beta Kappa poet at Harvard College.
Move to New York City, where Alfred Conrad taught at
City College of New York. Residence there from 1966
on. Increasingly active politically in protests against the
Indochina war.
1966–68   Lecturer at Swarthmore College.
1967–69   Adjunct Professor of Writing in the Graduate School of
the Arts, Columbia University.
1967   *Selected Poems* published in Britain. Litt.D., Wheaton
College.
1968   Eunice Tietjens Memorial Prize of *Poetry* magazine. Began
teaching in the SEEK and Open Admissions Programs at
City College of New York.
1969   *Leaflets* published.
1970   Death of Alfred Conrad.
1971   *The Will to Change* published. Shelley Memorial Award
of the Poetry Society of America. Increasingly identifies
with the women's movement as a radical feminist.
1972–73   Fanny Hurst Visiting Professor of Creative Literature at
Brandeis University.
1973   *Diving into the Wreck* published.
1973–74   Ingram Merrill Foundation research grant; began work
on a book on the history and myths of motherhood.
1974   National Book Award for *Diving into the Wreck*. Rich
rejected the award as an individual, but accepted it, in a
statement written with Audre Lorde and Alice Walker,
two other nominees, in the name of all women:

> "We . . . together accept this award in the name of all the
> women whose voices have gone and still go unheard in a
> patriarchal world, and in the name of those who, like us, have
> been tolerated as token women in this culture, often at great cost
> and in great pain. . . . We symbolically join here in refusing the
> terms of patriarchal competition and declaring that we will share
> this prize among us, to be used as best we can for women. . . .
> We dedicate this occasion to the struggle for self-determination
> of all women, of every color, identification or derived class . . .
> the women who will not understand yet; the silent women whose
> voices have been denied us, the articulate women who have given
> us strength to do our work."

Professor of English, City College of New York
1975   *Poems: Selected and New* published.
1976   Professor of English at Douglass College.
Of Woman Born: Motherhood as Experience and Institution
published.
Twenty-one Love Poems published.

1978   *The Dream of a Common Language: Poems 1974–1977*
         published.
1979   *On Lies, Secrets, and Silence: Selected Prose 1966–1978*
         published. Leaves Douglass College and New York City;
         moves to a small town in western Massachusetts with "the
         woman who shares my life."

12   HISTORICAL CONTEXTS

The more you know, the better a reader of poetry you are capable
of being. Poems often draw upon a large fund of human knowledge,
and sometimes they require a great deal from the reader. The earlier
chapters in this book suggest some of the skills one needs to develop
in order to cope with the demands they make. In these final chapters
we will look at the knowledge poets often expect. Very little that you
know will ultimately go to waste in your reading of poetry. The best
potential reader of a poem is someone who has already developed
reading skills to perfection, read everything, thought deeply about
all sorts of things, and who is wise beyond belief—but that is the
ideal reader we all strive to be, not the one any of us is, and no
poet expects any reader to be all those things. Still, the point is to
try. By knowing that these things are important to the reading of
poetry, we won't discount too easily what we need, and so we will
keep trying to do better, trying to bring more to the poem. The chapters that follow suggest some of the ways that poetry draws specifically upon the traditional fund of human knowledge, how it uses
the history of literature, science, philosophy, religion—the "wisdom of
the ages" that traditional humanistic education has long relied upon
as the cornerstone of its existence. This chapter considers some of the
historical particulars, matters that relate specifically to the moment
in time when a particular poem was written, for every poem is, in
the beginning, a timely act of creation.

Things that happen every day frequently find their way into poetry
in an easy and yet often forceful manner. Making love in a junkyard,
as in *Cherrylog Road,* is one kind of example; a reader doesn't need
to know what particular junkyard was involved—or imaginatively involved—in order to understand the poem, but a reader does need
to know what an auto junkyard was like in the middle of the 20th
century, with more or less whole car bodies being scattered in various
states of disarray over a large plot of ground. But what if, over the
next generation or two, another way is developed to dispose of old
cars? What if the metal is all melted down, or the junk is orbited
into space? If something like that happens, readers then will need
a footnote explaining what junkyards were like. The history of junk-
yards will not be lost—there will be pictures, films, records, and some-

one will write definitive books about the forms and functions of junk-yards, probably even including the fact that lovers occasionally visited them—but the public memory of junkyards will soon disappear. No social customs, no things that are made, no institutions or sites last forever.

Readers may still be able to experience *Cherrylog Road* when that happens, but they will need some help, and they may think its par-ticulars a little quaint, much as we regard literature that involves horses and buggies—or even making love in the back seat of a parked car—as quaint now. Institutions change, habits change, times change, particulars change, even when people's wants, needs, and foibles pretty much go on in the same way. Footnotes never provide a precise or adequate substitute for the ease and pleasure that come from already knowing, but they can help us understand and pave the way for feeling and experience. A kind of imaginative historical sympathy can be simulated and in fact created, for poems from earlier times that refer to specific contemporary details (and that have now become to us, in our own time, *historical* details) often describe human nature and human experiences very much as we still know and experience them. Today's poem may need tomorrow's footnote, but the poem need not be tomorrow's puzzle or only a curiosity or fossil.

The following poem, not many years old, already requires some explanation, not only because the factual details of its occasion may not be known to every reader, but also because the whole spirit of the poem may be difficult to appreciate unless one knows its circumstances.

RAYMOND R. PATTERSON

You Are the Brave

You are the brave who do not break
In the grip of the mob when the blow comes straight
To the shattered bone; when the sockets shriek;
When your arms lie twisted under your back.

Good men holding their courage slack   5
In their frightened pockets see how weak
The work that is done; and feel the weight
Of your blood on the ground for their spirits' sake;

And build their anger, stone on stone;
Each silently, but not alone.   10

1962

I can remember teaching this poem in class during the Viet Nam War and finding that a lot of students were hostile to it because they assumed it to be a poem in praise of patriotism and war. Sometimes the difficulty about factual information is that one doesn't know that one *needs* specific information. In a poem like *You Are the Brave,* it is fairly easy to assume (incorrectly, but understandably) that the conflict involved is a war and that the speaker addresses, and honors, a group of soldiers. Actually, there are clues in the poem that this conflict is, if as bitter as war, one in which mob violence (line 2) and enforced restraint (line 4) are involved. The date of the poem is a clue too—1962, when the American civil rights struggle was at its height. Once that "fact" is noticed, the whole historical context of the poem, if not its *immediate* occasion in terms of one specific civil rights march in one place on one day, becomes clear. In fact, since the poem doesn't mention a particular time and place, we may assume that the poem is not about the particulars of one specific incident, but instead gathers the kind of details that characterized many moments of the early sixties. The poem's details (generalized details about mob resentments and brutalities in a situation of passive resistance), its metaphors in the second and third stanzas, and its dignified tone of praise for "the brave" all make sense readily when the right information is available. The poem does not mention specific time and place because its concern is not confined to one event, but its location in time is important to finding what it refers to. Poems may be referential to one single event or moment (as in Berryman's *1 September 1939,* p. 835) or to some larger situation that may span weeks, months, or even years. The amount of particularity in the poem will tell you.

How do you know what you need to know? The easiest clue is your own puzzlement. When it seems that something is happening in a poem that you don't recognize—and yet the poem makes no apparent effort in itself to clarify it—you have a clue that readers at the time the poem was written must have recognized something which is not now such common knowledge. Once you know you don't know, it's only work to find out: most college libraries contain far more information than you will ever need, and the trick is to learn to search efficiently; that's why I have left a group of poems unannotated at the end of this chapter. An hour or two in the library will turn up most of the facts you will need for those poems, but of course your ability to find the information efficiently will depend upon how well you know the kinds of reference materials available to you. Practice helps. Knowledge accumulates. Most poems printed in textbooks like this one will be annotated for you with minimal facts, but often you may need additional information to interpret the poem's full meaning and resonance. An editor, trying to decide on the needs of a variety of readers, may not always have decided to write the footnote you yourself may need, so there may be digging to be done in the library for any poem you read, certainly for those you may come upon in magazines and books of poetry without footnotes. Few poets like to footnote their own work (they'd rather let you struggle a little to appreciate them), and besides, many things that now need footnotes didn't when they were first written, as in *You Are the Brave.*

To get at appropriate factual and historical information, it is important to learn to ask three kinds of questions. One kind is obvious: it is the "Do I understand the reference to . . . ?" kind of question. When events, places, or people unfamiliar to you come up, you will need to find out what or who they are. The second kind of question is more difficult: How do you know, in a poem like *You Are the Brave*, that you need to know more? When there are no specific references to look up, no people or events to identify, how do you know that there is a specific context? To get at this sort of question, you have to trust two people: the poet, and yourself. Learning to trust yourself, your own responses, is the more difficult—you can just decide to trust the poet. Usually, good poets know what they are doing. If they do, they will not want to puzzle you more than necessary, so that you can safely assume that something which is not self-explanatory will merit close attention and possibly some digging in the library. (Poets do make mistakes and miscalculations about their readers, but it is safest to assume they know what they are doing and why they are doing it.) When a poem contains things that are not in themselves clear (such as "the grip of the mob" or the "arms . . . twisted under your back" in *You Are the Brave*) those things provide a strong clue that you need more information. And that is why you need to trust yourself: you need to be confident that when something doesn't click, when the information given you does not seem enough, that you trust your puzzlement and try to find the missing facts that will allow the poem to make sense. But how? Often the date of the poem is a help, as in *You Are the Brave*. Sometimes the title gives a clue or a point of departure. Sometimes you can discover, by reading about the author, some of the things he or she was interested in or concerned about. There is no single all-purpose way to discover what to look for, but that kind of research—looking for clues, adding up the evidence—can be interesting in itself and very rewarding when it is successful.

The third question is why? For every factual reference, one needs to ask why. Why does the poem refer to this particular person instead of some other? What function does the reference perform? Why, for example, does *In Memory of Radio* make such a big deal of its references to Lamont Cranston? What does that reference have to do with the whole poem? Why is Goody Knight mentioned in the poem? What particular aspect of Goodwin Knight's political career makes him useful to the poet in this poem?

Beyond the levels of simply understanding that a particular poem is about a particular event or place or movement is the matter of developing a full sense of historical context, a sense of the larger significance and resonance of the historical occurrence referred to. Often a poem expects you to bring some sense of that significance; equally often it wants to continue your education, telling you more, wanting you to understand and appreciate on a feeling level some further things about this occurrence. A second group of poems at the end of this chapter has as its point of reference World War I. These poems offer a variety of emphases and perspectives, and they isolate quite different facts about the war. What we need to bring to our reading varies from poem to poem. *Dulce et Decorum Est*, for example, needs our knowledge that poison gas was used in the war; the green tint through which the speaker sees the world in lines 13–14, comes from green-lensed glass in the goggles of the gas mask he has just put on. But some broader matters are important as well. Harder to specify but probably even more important is the climate of opinion that surrounded World War I. To idealists, it was "the war to end all wars," and many participants—as well as politicians and propagandists—felt holy about it, regarding the threat of Germany's expansionist policy as the potential destruction of Western civilization.

Here is some other background information you may find useful. The Allied Powers (France, Great Britain, and Russia, later joined by Japan, Italy, and the United States) early in the war were very much weaker militarily than the combined force of the Central Powers (Germany, Austria-Hungary, and Turkey). Battles were fought on both Eastern and Western fronts; the Western battles in Flanders were especially brutal, and a long stalemate developed there in 1917, with huge casualties. On the sea, too, casualties ran high; the development of submarine warfare made transportation of ammunition and supplies very difficult, and German U-boats often attacked ships even from neutral nations. The United States joined the allied forces after one of the most celebrated incidents, the sinking of the *Lusitania*. Air power became militarily important for the first time, too; by 1915 fighter aircraft were equipped with machine guns, and there was some strategic bombing as early as the autumn of 1914.

Not everyone, however, was convinced of the dire danger to Western civilization and enthusiastic about the war effort. Great Britain entered the war reluctantly; after the British insisted that Germany respect the neutrality of Belgium, Germany ignored the British request and continued to occupy Belgium as part of its assault on France. The United States was even more reluctant to enter the war and stayed out until 1917. In both countries there were—although nearly forgotten now—strong peace movements; in Great Britain there were more than 16,000 conscientious objectors to the war, and their feelings were, for the most part, honored, despite incredible shortages of military manpower: by early 1918 Britain had raised the age of compulsory military service to 51. One of the poets represented here (Siegfried Sassoon) was a strong force in the peace movement; he had enlisted in the British military service early in the war and was twice wounded; later in the war, after winning the Military Cross and while still an officer in the army, Sassoon publicly affirmed his pacifism.

Because of its late entrance into the war, U. S. casualties were, relatively speaking, light; more Americans died in the flu epidemic of 1919 than had been killed in the war. But Britain was hit much harder. Fighting close to home soil for nearly five years—much of the time in savage combat in the Flanders mud, but also contributing forces and equipment to other fronts—Great Britain counted more than a million war dead. But even these figures do not begin to suggest the human loss. Nearly a whole generation of British youth was lost in the war, including many of its brightest and most promising potential leaders, and ultimately Britain suffered a loss of leadership in many fields, a loss that was not entirely felt until later years. Besides, Britain's international power and prestige were severely damaged; the British empire had rested on Britain's sea power and isolation, and at the war's end Britain faced a staggering war debt and a severe shrinkage of foreign markets, in addition to major shifts in the international power balance and shocking human losses.

No doubt you will read the poems more intelligently, and more feelingly, if you know quite a bit about World War I, and the same is true of poems about any historical occurrence or of poems that refer specifically or generally to things that happen or situations that exist in a temporal context. But it is also true that your sense of these events will grow as a result of reading sensitively and thoughtfully the poems themselves. Facts are no substitute for skills. Once you have read individually the poems in this section, try taking a breather, and then at one sitting read them all again. Reading poetry can be a form of gaining knowledge as well as an aesthetic experience. One doesn't go to poetry to seek information as such, but poems often give us more than we came for. The ways to wisdom are paved with facts, and although poetry is not primarily a data-conscious art, it often requires us to be aware, sometimes in detail, of its referents in the real world.

The Need for Factual Information

AMIRI BARAKA (LE ROI JONES)

In Memory of Radio

Who has ever stopped to think of the divinity of Lamont Cranston?
(Only Jack Kerouac, that I know of: & me.
The rest of you probably had on WCBS and Kate Smith,
Or something equally unattractive.)

What can I say?   5
It is better to have loved and lost
Than to put linoleum in your living rooms?

Am I a sage or something?
Mandrake's hypnotic gesture of the week?
(Remember, I do not have the healing powers of Oral Roberts . . .   10
I cannot, like F. J. Sheen, tell you how to get saved & rich!
I cannot even order you to gaschamber satori like Hitler or Goody Knight
& Love is an evil word.
Turn it backwards/see, what I mean?
An evol word, & besides   15
Who understands it?
I certainly wouldn't like to go out on that kind of limb.

Saturday mornings we listened to *Red Lantern* & his undersea folk.
At 11, *Let's Pretend*/& we did/& I, the poet, still do, Thank God!

What was it he used to say (after the transformation, when he was safe   20
& invisible & the unbelievers couldn't throw stones?) "Heh, heh, heh,
Who knows what evil lurks in the hearts of men? The Shadow knows."

O, yes he does
O, yes he does.
An evil word it is,   25
This Love.

                                                                     1961

e. e. cummings

poem, or beauty hurts mr. vinal

        take it from me kiddo
        believe me
        my country, 'tis of

        you, land of the Cluett
        Shirt Boston Garter and Spearmint   5
        Girl With The Wrigley Eyes(of you
        land of the Arrow Ide
        and Earl &
        Wilson
        Collars) of you i   10
        sing:land of Abraham Lincoln and Lydia E. Pinkham,
        land above all of Just Add Hot Water And Serve—
        from every B. V. D.

        let freedom ring

        amen. i do however protest, anent the un   15
        -spontaneous and otherwise scented merde which
        greets one (Everywhere Why) as divine poesy per
        that and this radically defunct periodical. i would
        suggest that certain ideas gestures
        rhymes, like Gillette Razor Blades   20
        having been used and reused
        to the mystical moment of dullness emphatically are
        Not To Be Resharpened. (Case in point

        if we are to believe these gently O sweetly
        melancholy trillers amid the thrillers   25
        these crepuscular violinists among my and your
        skyscrapers—Helen & Cleopatra were Just Too Lovely,
        The Snail's On The Thorn enter Morn and God's
        In His andsoforth

do you get me?)according   30
to such supposedly indigenous
throstles Art is O World O Life
a formula:example, Turn Your Shirttails Into
Drawers and If It Isn't An Eastman It Isn't A
Kodak therefore my friends let   35
us now sing each and all fortissimo A-
mer
i

ca, I
love,   40
You. And there're a
hun-dred-mil-lion-oth-ers, like
all of you successfully if
delicately gelded(or spaded)
gentlemen(and ladies)—pretty   45

littleliverpill-
hearted-Nujolneeding-There's-A-Reason
americans(who tensetendoned and with
upward vacant eyes, painfully
perpetually crouched, quivering, upon the   50
sternly allotted sandpile
—how silently
emit a tiny violetflavoured nuisance:Odor?

ono.
comes out like a ribbon lies flat on the brush   55

1926

EUGENE MCCARTHY

Kilroy

Kilroy is gone,
the word is out,
absent without leave
from Vietnam.

Kilroy   5
who wrote his name
in every can
from Poland to Japan
and places in between
like Sheboygan and Racine   10
is gone
absent without leave
from Vietnam.

Kilroy
who kept the dice   15
and stole the ice
out of the BOQ
Kilroy
whose name was good
on every IOU   20
in World War II
and even in Korea
is gone
absent without leave
from Vietnam.   25

Kilroy
the unknown soldier
who was the first to land
the last to leave,
with his own hand   30
has taken his good name
from all the walls
and toilet stalls.
Kilroy
whose name around the world   35
was like the flag unfurled
has run it down
and left Saigon
and the Mekong
without a hero or a song   40
and gone
absent without leave
from Vietnam.

                                                                    1968

JAMES A. EMANUEL

Emmett Till

I hear a whistling
Through the water.
Little Emmett
Won't be still.
He keeps floating   5
Round the darkness,
Edging through
The silent chill.
Tell me, please,
That bedtime story   10
Of the fairy

River Boy
Who swims forever,
Deep in treasures,
Necklaced in   15
A coral toy.

                                                             1968

World War I

•

WILFRED OWEN

Dulce Et Decorum Est[1]

Bent double, like old beggars under sacks,
Knock-kneed, coughing like hags, we cursed through sludge,
Till on the haunting flares we turned our backs
And towards our distant rest began to trudge.
Men marched asleep. Many had lost their boots   5
But limped on, blood-shod. All went lame; all blind;
Drunk with fatigue; deaf even to the hoots
Of disappointed shells that dropped behind.

Gas! Gas! Quick, boys!—An ecstasy of fumbling,
Fitting the clumsy helmets just in time;   10
But someone still was yelling out and stumbling
And floundering like a man in fire or lime.—
Dim, through the misty panes and thick green light
As under a green sea, I saw him drowning.

In all my dreams, before my helpless sight,   15
He plunges at me, guttering, choking, drowning.

If in some smothering dreams you too could pace
Behind the wagon that we flung him in,
And watch the white eyes writhing in his face,
His hanging face, like a devil's sick of sin;   20
If you could hear, at every jolt, the blood
Come gargling from the froth-corrupted lungs,
Obscene as cancer, bitter as the cud
Of vile, incurable sores on innocent tongues,—
My friend, you would not tell with such high zest   25
To children ardent for some desperate glory,
The old Lie: Dulce et decorum est
Pro patria mori.

1917

1. Part of a phrase from Horace, quoted in full in the last lines: "It is sweet and proper to die for one's country."

ISAAC ROSENBERG

Break of Day in the Trenches

The darkness crumbles away—
It is the same old druid[2] Time as ever.
Only a live thing leaps my hand—
A queer sardonic rat—
As I pull the parapet's poppy[3]   5
To stick behind my ear.
Droll rat, they would shoot you if they knew
Your cosmopolitan sympathies.
Now you have touched this English hand
You will do the same to a German—   10
Soon, no doubt, if it be your pleasure
To cross the sleeping green between.
It seems you inwardly grin as you pass
Strong eyes, fine limbs, haughty athletes
Less chanced than you for life,   15
Bonds to the whims of murder,
Sprawled in the bowels of the earth,
The torn fields of France.
What do you see in our eyes
At the shrieking iron and flame   20
Hurled through still heavens?
What quaver—what heart aghast?
Poppies whose roots are in man's veins
Drop, and are ever dropping;
But mine in my ear is safe,   25
Just a little white with the dust.

c. 1917

EZRA POUND

There Died a Myriad[4]

There died a myriad,
And of the best, among them,
For an old bitch gone in the teeth,
For a botched civilization,

Charm, smiling at the good mouth,   5
Quick eyes gone under earth's lid,

For two gross of broken statues,
For a few thousand battered books.

1920

2. Magician or priest.
3. Flower growing on the earthwork
built to shield soldiers from enemy fire.
The poppy became a standard symbol for
the war dead because a large burial field
in Flanders was covered with poppies.
4. Section V of "E. P. Ode pour L'Élec-
tion de Son Sépulcre."

EDGAR A. GUEST

The Things that Make a Soldier Great

The things that make a soldier great and send him out to die,
To face the flaming cannon's mouth, nor ever question why,
Are lilacs by a little porch, the row of tulips red,
The peonies and pansies, too, the old petunia bed,
The grass plot where his children play, the roses on the wall: 5
'Tis these that make a soldier great. He's fighting for them all.

'Tis not the pomp and pride of kings that make a soldier brave;
'Tis not allegiance to the flag that over him may wave;
For soldiers never fight so well on land or on the foam
As when behind the cause they see the little place called home.   10
Endanger but that humble street whereon his children run—
You make a soldier of the man who never bore a gun.

What is it through the battle smoke the valiant soldier sees?
The little garden far away, the budding apple trees,
The little patch of ground back there, the children at their play,   15
Perhaps a tiny mound behind the simple church of gray.
The golden thread of courage isn't linked to castle dome
But to the spot, where'er it be—the humble spot called home.

And now the lilacs bud again and all is lovely there,
And homesick soldiers far away know spring is in the air;   20
The tulips come to bloom again, the grass once more is green,
And every man can see the spot where all his joys have been.
He sees his children smile at him, he hears the bugle call,
And only death can stop him now—he's fighting for them all.

          1918

SIEGFRIED SASSOON

Repression of War Experience

Now light the candles; one; two; there's a moth;
What silly beggars they are to blunder in
And scorch their wings with glory, liquid flame—
No, no, not that,—it's bad to think of war,
When thoughts you've gagged all day come back to scare you;   5
And it's been proved that soldiers don't go mad
Unless they lose control of ugly thoughts
That drive them out to jabber among the trees.

Now light your pipe; look, what a steady hand,
Draw a deep breath; stop thinking; count fifteen,   10
And you're as right as rain. . . .
          Why won't it rain? . . .

I wish there'd be a thunderstorm to-night,
With bucketsful of water to sluice the dark,
And make the roses hang their dripping heads.   15
Books; what a jolly company they are,
Standing so quiet and patient on their shelves,
Dressed in dim brown, and black, and white, and green,
And every kind of color. Which will you read?
Come on; O *do* read something; they're so wise.   20
I tell you all the wisdom of the world
Is waiting for you on those shelves; and yet
You sit and gnaw your nails, and let your pipe out,
And listen to the silence: on the ceiling
There's one big, dizzy moth that bumps and flutters;   25
And in the breathless air outside the house
The garden waits for something that delays.
There must be crowds of ghosts among the trees,—
Not people killed in battle—they're in France—
But horrible shapes in shrouds—old men who died   30
Slow, natural deaths—old men with ugly souls,
Who wore their bodies out with nasty sins.

You're quiet and peaceful, summering safe at home;
You'd never think there was a bloody war on! . . .
O yes, you would . . . why, you can hear the guns.   35
Hark! Thud, thud, thud—quite soft . . . they never cease—
Those whispering guns—O Christ, I want to go out
And screech at them to stop—I'm going crazy;
I'm going stark, staring mad because of the guns.

                                                      1918

SIEGFRIED SASSOON

Base Details

If I were fierce, and bald, and short of breath,
   I'd live with scarlet Majors at the Base,
And speed glum heroes up the line to death.
   You'd see me with my puffy petulant face,
Guzzling and gulping in the best hotel,   5
   Reading the Roll of Honor.[5] "Poor young chap,"
I'd say—"I used to know his father well;
   Yes, we've lost heavily in this last scrap."
And when the war is done and youth stone dead,
I'd toddle safely home and die—in bed.   10

                                                      1918

_____

5. List of dead.

RUPERT BROOKE

The Soldier

If I should die, think only this of me:
   That there's some corner of a foreign field
That is forever England. There shall be
   In that rich earth a richer dust concealed;
A dust whom England bore, shaped, made aware,   5
   Gave, once, her flowers to love, her ways to roam,
A body of England's, breathing English air,
   Washed by the rivers, blest by suns of home.

And think, this heart, all evil shed away,
   A pulse in the eternal mind, no less   10
Gives somewhere back the thoughts by England given;
Her sights and sounds; dreams happy as her day;
   And laughter, learnt of friends; and gentleness,
   In hearts at peace, under an English heaven.

1915

W. B. YEATS

On Being Asked for a War Poem

I think it better that in times like these
A poet's mouth be silent, for in truth
We have no gift to set a statesman right;
He has had enough of meddling who can please
A young girl in the indolence of her youth,   5
Or an old man upon a winter's night.

p. 1915

13   LITERARY TRADITION

The more poetry you read, the better a reader of poetry you are
likely to be. This is not just because your skills will improve and
develop, but also because you will come to know more about the
poetic tradition and can thus understand more fully how poets draw
upon each other. Poets are conscious of each other, and often they
refer to each other's work or use it as a starting point for their own
work in ways that may not be immediately obvious to an outsider.
Sometimes a quiet (or even noisy) competitiveness is at the bottom

of their concern with what other poems have done or can do; at other times, playfulness and a sense of humor about poetic possibilities take over, and the competitiveness dwindles to fun and poetic games. And often they want to tap the rich mine of artistic expression just to share in the bounty of our heritage. In any case, a poet's consciousness of what others have done leads to a sense of tradition that is often hard to articulate but nevertheless is very important to the effects of poetry —and this sense of tradition is something of a problem for a relatively new reader of poetry. How can I possibly read this poem intelligently, sometimes we are likely to ask in exasperation, until I've read all the other poems ever written? It's a real problem. Poets don't actually expect that all of their readers have Ph.D.s in literature, but sometimes it *seems* as if they do. For some poems—T. S. Eliot's *Love Song of J. Alfred Prufrock* (p. 849) is one example—it does help if one has read practically everything imaginable.

Why are poets so dependent on each other? What is the point of their continuous consciousness of what has already been done by others? Why do they repeatedly allude to and echo other poems? Why is a sense of tradition so important to them?

A sense of common task, a kind of communality of purpose, accounts for some traditional poetic practice, and the desire of individual poets to achieve a place in the English and American poetic tradition accounts for some more. Many poets show an anxiety to be counted among those who achieve, through their writing, a place in history, and a way of establishing that place is to define for oneself the relationship between one's own work and that of others whose place is already secure. There is, for many poets, a sense of a serious and abiding cultural tradition which they wish to share and pass on; but also important is a shared sense of playfulness, a kind of poetic gamesmanship. Making words dance on the page or in our heads provides in itself a satisfaction and delight for many writers; pride in craft that is rather like the pride of a painter or potter or tennis player. Often poets set themselves a particular task to see what they can do. One way of doing that is to introduce a standard traditional **motif** (a recurrent device, formula, or situation which deliberately connects a poem with common patterns of existing thought), and then to play variations on it much as a musician might do. Another way is to provide an alternative answer to a question that has repeatedly been asked and answered in a traditional way. Poetic playfulness by no means excludes serious intention—the poems in this chapter often make important statements about their subject, however humorous they may be in their method. Some teasing of the tradition and of other poets is pure fun, a kind of kidding among good friends; some is rather more harsh and represents an attempt to see the world very differently—to define and articulate a very different view.

The English poetic tradition is a rich and varied heritage, and individual poets draw upon it in countless ways. You have probably noticed, in the poems you have read so far, a number of allusions, glances at the tradition or at individual expressions of it, and the more poems you read the better equipped you will be to notice more. The more you read, the more you will yourself become a comfortable member of the audience poets write for. Poets do expect a lot—not

always but often enough to make a new reader feel nervous and sometimes inadequate. The other side of that discomfort comes when you
begin to notice things that other readers don't. *After* you've read
Yeats's *Second Coming* (p. 823), for example, you might want to
reread Deagon's *Certified Copy* (p. 646): the comedy of the Deagon
poem is funnier in the context of a knowledge of Yeats's serious worry
and serious statement. The poetic tradition is a vast and various mine;
poets find in it raw materials to make many fine things.

The three groups of poems in this chapter illustrate some of the
ways that the tradition energizes individual poets and suggests some
of the things poets like to do with their heritage. The first group consists of poems that share a common subject (love), theme (time is
short), and urgency of tone (let's not wait; let's make love now).
And most of them seem rather self-conscious—as if each poet is aware
of a common tradition and is trying to do something a little bit
different. However "sincere" these poems are as seduction poems (many
of them do present a convincing sense of love and desire), their sense
of play is equally important in its variation upon the standard *carpe
diem* (seize the day: live for the moment) motif. The motif is an old
one, dating back at least to classical Roman times; several of the
poems (*Come, My Celia; Bridal Couch; To the Virgins, to Make
Much of Time*) allude specifically to the following lines of a poem by
Catullus, which is one of the fountains of the tradition:

> Let us live, my Lesbia, and love
> And not care about the gossip of old men.
> The sun that sets may rise again,
> But when our light has once set
> Our night will be unbroken.

The second group consists of poems that pick on (playfully) one
poem which we looked at in Chapter 10, *The Passionate Shepherd
to His Love* (p. 727). In effect, all these poems provide "answers" to
that poem. It is as if "his love" were telling the shepherd what is the
matter with his argument, and the poets are answering Marlowe, too.
These poets know full well what Marlowe was doing in the fantasy
of his original poem, and they clearly have a lot of fun telling him
how people in various circumstances might feel about his fantasy. There
is, repeatedly, a lot of joy in their "realistic" deflation of his magic,
and not much hostility.

The third group similarly pokes fun at other famous poems, providing another version of what might have happened in each. Koch's
Variations on a Theme by William Carlos Williams is the only **parody**
in the group (that is, it pretends to write in the style of the original
poem, but comically exaggerates that style). The other two poems use
very different styles to alter, totally, the poetic intention of the original. *Ode on a Grecian Urn Summarized* teases Keats as well as the
whole notion of poetic summaries; the effects of the summary are not
very much like those of the Keats poem. *The Dover Bitch*, on the
other hand, is as its subtitle suggests much more than just a different
perspective on the situation portrayed in *Dover Beach*; it uses the
tradition to criticize art *and* life.

The Carpe Diem *Motif*

ROBERT HERRICK

To the Virgins, to Make Much of Time

Gather ye rosebuds while ye may,
  Old time is still a-flying;
And this same flower that smiles today
  Tomorow will be dying.

The glorious lamp of heaven, the sun,   5
  The higher he's a-getting,
The sooner will his race be run,
  And nearer he's to setting.

That age is best which is the first,
  When youth and blood are warmer;   10
But being spent, the worse, and worst
  Times still succeed the former.

Then be not coy, but use your time,
  And, while ye may, go marry;
For, having lost but once your prime,   15
  You may forever tarry.

                                                    1648

EDMUND WALLER

Song

Go, lovely rose!
Tell her that wastes her time and me
  That now she knows,
When I resemble[1] her to thee,
How sweet and fair she seems to be.   5

  Tell her that's young,
And shuns to have her graces spied,
  That hadst thou sprung
In deserts, where no men abide,
Thou must have uncommended died.   10

  Small is the worth
Of beauty from the light retired;

---

1. Compare.

> Bid her come forth,
> Suffer herself to be desired,
> And not blush so to be admired.   15
>
> Then die! that she
> The common fate of all things rare
>   May read in thee;
> How small a part of time they share
> That are so wondrous sweet and fair!   20

1645

RICHARD LOVELACE

To Amarantha, that She Would Dishevel Her Hair

> Amarantha sweet and fair,
> Ah, braid no more that shining hair!
>   As my curious hand or eye
> Hovering round thee, let it fly.
>
> Let it fly as unconfined   5
> As its calm ravisher, the wind,
>   Who hath left his darling, th' East,
> To wanton o'er that spicy nest.
>
> Every tress must be confessed
> But neatly tangled at the best,   10
>   Like a clue² of golden thread,
> Most excellently raveléd.
>
> Do not then wind up that light
> In ribands, and o'ercloud in night;
>   Like the sun in's early ray,   15
> But shake your head and scatter day.
>
> See, 'tis broke! Within this grove,
> The bower and the walks of love,
>   Weary lie we down and rest
> And fan each other's panting breast.   20
>
> Here we'll strip and cool our fire
> In cream below, in milk-baths higher;
>   And when all wells are drawn dry,
> I'll drink a tear out of thine eye.
>
> Which our very joys shall leave,   25

2. Ball.

That sorrows thus we can deceive;
Or our very sorrows weep,
That joys so ripe so little keep.

1649

BEN JONSON

Come, My Celia[3]

Come, my Celia, let us prove,[4]
While we can, the sports of love;
Time will not be ours forever:
He at length our good will sever.
Spend not, then, his gifts in vain;   5
Suns that set may rise again,
But if once we lose this light,
'Tis with us perpetual night.
Why should we defer our joys?
Fame and rumor are but toys.   10
Cannot we delude the eyes
Of a few poor household spies?
Or his easier ears beguile,
Thus removéd by our wile?
'Tis no sin love's fruits to steal,   15
But the sweet thefts to reveal;
To be taken, to be seen,
These have crimes accounted been.

1606

DONALD J. LLOYD

Bridal Couch

Follows this a narrower bed,
Wood at feet, wood at head;
Follows this a sounder sleep,
Somewhat longer and too deep.

All too meanly and too soon   5
Waxes once and wanes our moon;
All too swiftly for each one
Falls to dark our winter sun.

---

3. A song from *Volpone,* sung by the play's villain and would-be seducer. Part of the poem paraphrases Catullus, V.
4. Try.

Let us here then wrestle death,
Intermingled limb and breath,   10
Conscious both that we beget
End of rest, endless fret,

And come at last to permanence,
Tired dancers from a dance,
Yawning, and content to fall   15
Into any bed at all.

                                                        1956

ANDREW MARVELL

To His Coy Mistress

Had we but world enough, and time,
This coyness,[5] lady, were no crime.
We would sit down, and think which way
To walk, and pass our long love's day.
Thou by the Indian Ganges' side   5
Shouldst rubies[6] find: I by the tide
Of Humber[7] would complain. I would
Love you ten years before the Flood,
And you should if you please refuse
Till the conversion of the Jews.[8]   10
My vegetable love[9] should grow
Vaster than empires, and more slow;
An hundred years should go to praise
Thine eyes, and on thy forehead gaze;
Two hundred to adore each breast,   15
But thirty thousand to the rest.
An age at least to every part,
And the last age should show your heart.
For, lady, you deserve this state;[1]
Nor would I love at lower rate.   20
    But at my back I always hear
Time's wingèd chariot hurrying near;
And yonder all before us lie
Deserts of vast eternity.
Thy beauty shall no more be found,   25

5. Hesitancy, modesty (not necessarily suggesting calculation).
6. Talismans which are supposed to preserve virginity.
7. A small river which flows through Marvell's home town, Hull. "complain": write love complaints, conventional songs lamenting the cruelty of love.
8. Which, according to popular Christian belief, will occur just before the end of the world.
9. Which is capable only of passive growth, not of consciousness. The "Vegetable Soul" is lower than the other two divisions of the Soul, "Animal" and "Rational."
1. Dignity.

Nor, in thy marble vault, shall sound
My echoing song; then worms shall try
That long preserved virginity,
And your quaint honor turn to dust,
And into ashes all my lust: 30
The grave's a fine and private place,
But none, I think, do there embrace.
    Now therefore, while the youthful hue
Sits on thy skin like morning dew,[2]
And while thy willing soul transpires[3]   35
At every pore with instant fires,
Now let us sport us while we may,
And now, like am'rous birds of prey,
Rather at once our time devour
Than languish in his slow-chapped[4] pow'r.   40
Let us roll all our strength and all
Our sweetness up into one ball,
And tear our pleasures with rough strife
Thorough[5] the iron gates of life.
Thus, though we cannot make our sun   45
Stand still,[6] yet we will make him run.[7]

                                  1681

e. e. cummings

(ponder,darling,these busted statues

   (ponder,darling,these busted statues
of yon motheaten forum be aware
notice what hath remained
—the stone cringes
clinging to the stone,how obsolete   5

lips utter their extant smile . . . .
remark

a few deleted of texture
or meaning monuments and dolls

resist Them Greediest Paws of careful   10
time[8] all of which is extremely
unimportant)whereas Life

   matters if or

---

2. The text reads "glew." "Lew" (warmth) has also been suggested as an emendation.
3. Breathes forth.
4. Slow-jawed. Chronos (Time), ruler of the world in early Greek myth, devoured all of his children except Zeus, who was hidden. Later, Zeus seized power (see line 46 and note).
5. Through.
6. To lengthen his night of love with Alcmene, Zeus made the sun stand still.
7. Each sex act was believed to shorten life by one day.
8. See "To His Coy Mistress," above, especially lines 39–40.

when the your- and my-   15
idle vertical worthless
self unite in a peculiarly
momentary

partnership(to instigate
constructive
                    Horizontal   20
business . . . . even so,let us make haste
—consider well this ruined aqueduct

lady,
which used to lead something into somewhere)

                                                                    1926

Replies to the Passionate Shepherd

SIR WALTER RALEGH

The Nymph's Reply to the Shepherd

If all the world and love were young,
And truth in every shepherd's tongue,
These pretty pleasures might me move
To live with thee and be thy love.

Time drives the flocks from field to fold,   5
When rivers rage, and rocks grow cold,
And Philomel[1] becometh dumb;
The rest complain of cares to come.

The flowers do fade, and wanton fields
To wayward winter reckoning yields: 10
A honey tongue, a heart of gall,
Is fancy's spring, but sorrow's fall.

Thy gowns, thy shoes, they beds of roses,
Thy cap, thy kirtle, and thy posies
Soon break, soon wither, soon forgotten;   15
In folly ripe, in reason rotten.

Thy belt of straw and ivy buds,
Thy coral clasps and amber studs,
All these in me no means can move
To come to thee and be thy love.   20

---

1. The nightingale.

But could youth last, and love still breed,
Had joys no date,[2] nor age no need,
Then these delights my mind might move
To live with thee and be thy love.

                                                    1600

C. DAY LEWIS

Song

Come, live with me and be my love,
And we will all the pleasures prove
Of peace and plenty, bed and board,
That chance employment may afford.

I'll handle dainties on the docks   5
And thou shalt read of summer frocks:
At evening by the sour canals
We'll hope to hear some madrigals.

Care on thy maiden brow shall put
A wreath of wrinkles, and thy foot   10
Be shod with pain: not silken dress
But toil shall tire thy loveliness.

Hunger shall make thy modest zone
And cheat fond death of all but bone—
If these delights thy mind may move,   15
Then live with me and be my love.

                                                    1935

JOHN DONNE

The Bait

Come live with me, and be my love,
And we will some new pleasures prove,
Of golden sands, and crystal brooks:
With silken lines, and silver hooks.

There will the river whispering run   5
Warmed by thy eyes, more than the sun.
And there th' enamored fish will stay,
Begging themselves they may betray.

2. End.

When thou wilt swim in that live bath,
Each fish, which every channel hath,　　　　　　10
Will amorously to thee swim,
Gladder to catch thee, than thou him.

If thou to be so seen be'st loath
By sun, or moon, thou dark'nest both,
And if myself have leave to see,　　　　　　15
I need not their light, having thee.

Let others freeze with angling reeds,[3]
And cut their legs with shells and weeds,
Or treacherously poor fish beset
With strangling snare, or windowy net.　　　　　　20

Let coarse bold hands, from slimy nest
The bedded fish in banks out-wrest;
Or curious traitors, sleave-silk[4] flies,
Bewitch poor fishes' wand'ring eyes.

For thee, thou need'st no such deceit,　　　　　　25
For thou thyself art thine own bait;
That fish that is not catched thereby,
Alas, is wiser far than I.

1612

PETER DE VRIES

Bacchanal[5]

"Come live with me and be my love,"
　　He said, in substance. "There's no vine
We will not pluck the clusters of,
　　Or grape we will not turn to wine."

It's autumn of their second year.　　　　　　5
　　Now he, in seasonal pursuit,
With rich and modulated cheer,
　　Brings home the festive purple fruit;

And she, by passion once demented
　　—That woman out of Botticelli[6]—　　　　　　10
She brews and bottles, unfermented,
　　The stupid and abiding jelly.

1959

---

3. Rods.
4. Untwisted silk.
5. A drunken or riotous celebration.
6. Italian painter (1445–1510) of the Florentine school, famous for his sensuous paintings of Venus and the Virgin Mary.

Another Version

KENNETH KOCH

Variations on a Theme by
William Carlos Williams[1]

1

I chopped down the house that you had been saving to live in next
   summer.
I am sorry, but it was morning, and I had nothing to do
and its wooden beams were so inviting.

2

We laughed at the hollyhocks together
and then I sprayed them with lye.   5
Forgive me. I simply do not know what I am doing.

3

I gave away the money that you had been saving to live on for the
   next ten years.
The man who asked for it was shabby
and the firm March wind on the porch was so juicy and cold.

4

Last evening we went dancing and I broke your leg.   10
Forgive me. I was clumsy, and
I wanted you here in the wards, where I am the doctor!

1962

DESMOND SKIRROW

Ode on a Grecian Urn Summarized[2]

Gods chase
Round vase.
What say?
What play?
Don't know.
Nice, though.

p. 1960

---

1. See William Carlos Williams's *This
Is Just to Say*, p. 910. Williams was a
physician as well as poet (see line 12).

2. See Keats's *Ode on a Grecian Urn*
(p. 748).

ANTHONY HECHT

The Dover Bitch

A Criticism of Life

for Andrews Wanning

So there stood Matthew Arnold and this girl[3]
With the cliffs of England crumbling away behind them,
And he said to her, "Try to be true to me,
And I'll do the same for you, for things are bad
All over, etc., etc."   5
Well now, I knew this girl. It's true she had read
Sophocles in a fairly good translation
And caught that bitter allusion to the sea,[4]
But all the time he was talking she had in mind
The notion of what his whiskers would feel like   10
On the back of her neck. She told me later on
That after a while she got to looking out
At the lights across the channel, and really felt sad,
Thinking of all the wine and enormous beds
And blandishments in French and the perfumes.   15
And then she got really angry. To have been brought
All the way down from London, and then be addressed
As a sort of mournful cosmic last resort
Is really tough on a girl, and she was pretty.
Anyway, she watched him pace the room   20
And finger his watch-chain and seem to sweat a bit,
And then she said one or two unprintable things.
But you mustn't judge her by that. What I mean to say is,
She's really all right. I still see her once in a while
And she always treats me right. We have a drink   25
And I give her a good time, and perhaps it's a year
Before I see her again, but there she is,
Running to fat, but dependable as they come.
And sometimes I bring her a bottle of *Nuit d'Amour*.

1968

14   FRAMES OF REFERENCE: CONTEXTS OF MYTH

Whether or not we are a part of *all* that we have met, we take some
of our identity from the cultures into which we were born and the
traditions that lie behind them. Being so thoroughly culture-bound

3. See Arnold's poem *Dover Beach*, p. 628.   4. In *Antigone*, lines 583–91. See *Dover Beach*, lines 9–18.

doesn't please everybody, and rebels often use a lot of energy kicking against the values and assumptions built into the people and institutions with whom they have grown up. But even in rebelling, we are stuck with the terms, values, and assumptions we rebel against. No matter how "individual" we succeed in being, we are still a part of something larger, something that has been here longer than we have and that has managed to clarify and articulate its values over generations and centuries.

Every culture develops stories to explain itself. These stories try to explain to us who we are and why we are the way we are. Taken together, they constitute what is often called a **myth**. Calling it a myth does not mean that it is false. In fact, it means nearly the opposite, for a culture takes its myths seriously as explanations of why things are the way they are, why the history of the culture has gone in a particular way. Myth, in the sense in which it is used here, involves the explanations that are more or less universally shared within a particular culture; it is a frame of reference that people within the culture understand and share. A sharing of this frame of reference does not mean that all people within a culture are carbon copies of each other or that popular stereotypes represent reality accurately, nor does it mean that every individual in the culture *knows* the perceived history and can articulate its events, ideas, and values. But it does mean that a shared history and a shared set of symbols lie behind any particular culture and that the culture is to some extent aware of its distinctiveness from other cultures.

A **culture,** in the sense in which it is used here, may be of many sizes and shapes. Often we think of a nation as a culture (and so speak of American culture, American history, the myth of America, the American dream, the American frame of reference), and it is equally useful to make smaller and larger divisions—as long as there is some commonality of history and some cohesiveness of purpose within the group. One can speak of Southern culture, for example, or of urban culture, or of the drug culture, or the rock music culture, or of a culture associated with a particular political belief, economic class, or social group. Most of us belong, willingly or not, to a number of such cultures at one time, and to some extent our identity and destiny are linked with the distinctive features of those cultures and with the ways the culture perceives its identity, values, and history. Some of these cultures we choose to join; some are thrust upon us by birth and circumstances. It is these larger and more persistent kinds of cultures that are illustrated in the frames of reference sampled in this chapter.

Poets, aware of their heritage, often like to probe its history and beliefs and plumb its depths, just as they like to articulate and play variations on the poetic tradition they feel a part of. For poetry written in the English language over the last 400 years or so, both the Judaeo-Christian frame of reference and the classical frame of reference (involving the civilizations of ancient Greece and Rome) have been quite important. Western culture, a broad culture that includes many nations and many sorts of religious and social groups, is largely defined within these two frames of reference—or it has been until quite recently. As religious belief has eroded over the past two or three centuries, and as classical civilization has been less emphasized and less studied, poets have felt increasingly less comfortable in assuming that their audiences share a knowledge of their systems, but they have often continued to use them to isolate and articulate human traits that have cultural continuity and importance. The poems in this chapter exemplify various kinds of attempts to define and investigate cultural contexts and what they continue to mean.

The question of shared values and a common heritage is prominent in all the poems in this chapter. Because communication necessarily involves some kind of common ground, poets in homogeneous cultures have had a relatively easier time of it than poets in very diverse cultures, and modern poets often lament the lack of a received tradition that they can count on. Still, they have to work with what is available, and the poems in the first two subgroups here draw upon two traditional sources of history and myth—the Judaeo-Christian and classical frames of reference. The third subgroup introduces elements from some non-Western frames of reference. The final subgroup represents one modern poet's individual solution to the problem of decaying certitudes in communication; W. B. Yeats's own mythology is highly individual and even eccentric but it amalgamates elements from traditional classical and Judaeo-Christian frames of reference as well as adding novelties of its own.

Judaeo-Christian History and Myth

JOHN MILTON

[Before the Fall]¹

She as a veil down to the slender waist   304
Her unadorned golden tresses wore
Disheveled, but in wanton² ringlets waved
As the vine curls her tendrils, which implied
Subjection,³ but required with gentle sway,
And by her yielded, by him best received,
Yielded with coy⁴ submission, modest pride,   310
And sweet reluctant amorous delay.
Nor those mysterious parts were then concealed,
Then was not guilty shame, dishonest shame
Of nature's works, honor dishonorable,
Sin-bred, how have ye troubled all mankind   315

1. From *Paradise Lost,* Book IV. For the Biblical description of Eden, see *Genesis* 2.8–25.
2. Luxuriant.
3. The idea derives from *Genesis* 3:16 and *I Corinthians* 11:9–10.
4. Shy.

With shows instead, mere shows of seeming pure,
And banished from man's life his happiest life,
Simplicity and spotless innocence.
So passed they naked on, nor shunned the sight
Of God or angel, for they thought no ill.   320
So hand in hand they passed, the loveliest pair
That ever since in love's embraces met,
Adam the goodliest man of men since born
His sons, the fairest of her daughters Eve.
Under a tuft of shade that on a green   325
Stood whispering soft, by a fresh fountain side
They sat them down, and after no more toil
Of their sweet gardening labor than sufficed
To recommend cool zephyr, and made ease
More easy, wholesome thirst and appetite   330
More grateful, to their supper fruits they fell,
Nectarine[5] fruits which the compliant boughs
Yielded them, sidelong as they sat recline
On the soft downy bank damasked[6] with flowers:
The savory pulp they chew, and in the rind   335
Still as they thirsted scoop the brimming stream;
Nor gentle purpose,[7] nor endearing smiles
Wanted,[8] nor youthful dalliance as beseems
Fair couple, linked in happy nuptial league,
Alone as they. About them frisking played   340
All beasts of the earth, since wild, and of all chase[9]
In wood or wilderness, forest or den;
Sporting the lion ramped, and in his paw
Dandled the kid; bears, tigers, ounces,[1] pards,
Gamboled before them, the unwieldy elephant   345
To make them mirth used all his might, and wreathed
His lithe proboscis; close the serpent sly
Insinuating, wove with Gordian[2] twine
His braided train, and of his fatal guile
Gave proof unheeded; others on the grass   350
Couched, and now filled with pasture gazing sat,
Or bedward ruminating: for the sun
Declined was hasting now with prone career
To the Ocean Isles,[3] and in the ascending scale
Of heaven the stars that usher evening rose.   355

1667

---

5. Sweet as nectar, the traditional drink
of the gods.
6. Variegated.
7. Conversation. "Nor . . . nor": neither
. . . nor (a common 17th-century construction).
8. Were lacking.

9. Tracts of land.
1. Lynxes. "pards": leopards.
2. Like the Gordian knot, a legendary
intricate knot, finally cut by Alexander the
Great.
3. The Azores; i.e., westward.

JOHN HOLLANDER

Adam's Task

"And Adam gave names to all cattle, and to the fowl of the air, and to every beast of the field . . ."—*Gen.* 2:20

Thou, paw-paw-paw; thou, glurd; thou, spotted
   Glurd; thou, whitestap, lurching through
The high-grown brush; thou, pliant-footed,
   Implex; thou, awagabu.

Every burrower, each flier   5
   Came for the name he had to give:
Gay, first work, ever to be prior,
   Not yet sunk to primitive.

Thou, verdle; thou, McFleery's pomma;
   Thou; thou; thou—three types of grawl;   10
Thou, flisket; thou, kabasch; thou, comma-
   Eared mashawk; thou, all; thou, all.

Were, in a fire of becoming,
   Laboring to be burned away,
Then work, half-measuring, half-humming,   15
   Would be as serious as play.

Thou, pambler; thou, rivarn; thou, greater
   Wherret, and thou, lesser one;
Thou, sproal; thou, zant; thou, lily-eater.
   Naming's over. Day is done.   20

1971

LINDA PASTAN

A Symposium: Apples

Eve: Remember a season
of apples, the orchard
full of them, my apron
full of them. One day
we wandered from tree   5
to tree, sharing a basket
feeling the weight of apples
increase between us.
And how your muscles ripened
with all that lifting.   10
I felt them round and hard

under my teeth; white
and sweet the flesh
of men and apples.

Gabriel:[4] Nameless in Eden,   15
the apple itself
was innocent—an ordinary
lunchpail fruit.
Still it reddened
for the way it was used.   20
Afterward the apple
chose for itself
names untrusting
on the tongue: stayman,
gravenstein,   25
northern spy.

The Serpent: Ordinary, innocent
yes. But deep
in each center of whiteness
one dark star . . .   30

Adam: In the icebox
an apple
will keep
for weeks.
Then its skin   35
wrinkles up
like the skin of the old man
I have become,
from a single
bite.   40

1975

VASSAR MILLER

Adam's Footprint

Once as a child I loved to hop
On round plump bugs and make them stop
Before they crossed a certain crack.
My bantam brawn could turn them back,
My crooked step wrenched straight to kill   5
Live pods that then screwed tight and still.

Small sinner, stripping boughs of pears,
Shinnied past sweet and wholesome airs,

4. Traditionally, a messenger of God;   chief of the angelic guards in Paradise.
in *Paradise Lost,* Milton makes Gabriel the

How could a tree be so unclean?
Nobody knows but Augustine.[5]   10
He nuzzled pears for dam-sin's dugs[6]—
And I scrunched roly-poly bugs.

No wolf's imprint or tiger's trace
Does Christ hunt down to catch with grace
In nets of love the devious preys   15
Whose feet go softly all their days:
The foot of Adam leaves the mark
Of some child scrabbling in the dark.

                                                              1956

CHRISTINA ROSSETTI

Eve

"While I sit at the door,
Sick to gaze within,
Mine eye weepeth sore
For sorrow and sin:
As a tree my sin stands   5
To darken all lands;
Death is the fruit it bore.

"How have Eden bowers grown
Without Adam to bend them!
How have Eden flowers blown,   10
Squandering their sweet breath,
Without me to tend them!
The Tree of Life was ours,
Tree twelvefold fruited,[7]
Most lofty tree that flowers,   15
Most deeply rooted:
I chose the Tree of Death.[8]

"Hadst thou but said me nay,
    Adam, my brother,
I might have pined away—   20
    I, but none other:
God might have let thee stay
Safe in our garden,

5. In his *Confessions*, Book II, St. Augustine agonizes over his theft, from a nearby tree, of pears he did not really want and meditates on the human tendency to want what is forbidden.
6. I.e., as if they were the breasts of mother-sin (with, of course, more than one pun on "dam").
7. The tree of life is so described in Revelation 22:2, 14, but the account there is of the New Jerusalem, not of Eden.
8. The *Genesis* account distinguishes between the tree of life and the tree of the knowledge of good and evil; the latter is forbidden, and eating of it brings labor, sickness, and death into the world. See *Genesis* 2:9, 3:1–24.

By putting me away
Beyond all pardon.   25

"I, Eve, sad mother
Of all who must live,
I, not another,
Plucked bitterest fruit to give
My friend, husband, lover.   30
O wanton eyes run over!
Who but I should grieve?—
Cain hath slain his brother:[9]
Of all who must die mother,
Miserable Eve!"   35

Thus she sat weeping,
Thus Eve our mother,
Where one lay sleeping
Slain by his brother.
Greatest and least   40
Each piteous beast
To hear her voice
Forgot his joys
And set aside his feast.

The mouse paused in his walk   45
And dropped his wheaten stalk:
Grave cattle wagged their heads
In rumination;
The eagle gave a cry
From his cloud station: 50
Larks on thyme beds
Forbore to mount or sing;
Bees drooped upon the wing;
The raven perched on high
Forgot his ration;   55
The conies[1] in their rock,
A feeble nation,
Quaked sympathetical;
The mocking-bird left off to mock;
Huge camels knelt as if   60
In deprecation;
The kind hart's tears were falling;
Chattered the wistful stork;
Dove-voices with a dying fall
Cooed desolation   65
Answering grief by grief.

9. Abel (see *Genesis* 4:1–15).
1. A common term for rabbits, but here
probably the small pachyderms mentioned
in *Proverbs* 30:26.

Only the serpent in the dust,
Wriggling and crawling,
Grinned an evil grin, and thrust
His tongue out with its fork.   70

1865

ROB HOLLAND

Eve in Old Age

Over her shoulder, the window framed the stars.
The planets gathered—still, always for her,
Called out of the dark like thoughts. Venus a green
Firefly. The erratic pulse, Mars.
Inside the thoughts themselves gathered, the stir   5
Of a few leaves, the light fretful, serene.

The unicorn was not at her elbow now.
The pomegranate, split in the sudden cold,
Spilled its red chambers like a heart.[2]
She remembered it only so, and how   10
It was ever other she could not have told.
She was an old woman. This was God's part.

Her sons, once, had filled her like a snail,
Curled within her, beating like rain
Against a window. She remembered watching each   15
Drive into himself the hooked nail.
And the nameless daughters, who first had lain
With them. They watched the days pass without speech.

Adam, too, was silent. She could not forget
His calm weight beside her, as if nothing but light   20
Burned on the retina of God's eye.
There was a fine line where their bodies had met,
Crossed and yet never crossed. The white
Moon cut like a scythe across the sky.

She dreamed at last of the green skin of the snake,   25
In each scale the star, the tree, windless,
And her own face, scratched there like a mark.
The snow began to fall, flake by flake
Gathering the world around her. Transparent, endless,
The dark passed through her into the dark.

1977

2. In Christian iconography (most notably in the Flemish tapestry "The Unicorn in Captivity" in the Cloisters in New
York), a unicorn and pomegranate tree
are associated with the *hortus conclusus*
(enclosed garden) tradition. The unicorn
is a traditional symbol of Christ.

NANCY SULLIVAN

The Death of the First Man

What was it?
How could they know what it was?
It had never happened before.
No one had ever gone out.
Whatever it was was happening.   5
Something was over.
Curled in a loose shape
the first dead man
drained out of himself
while the others shifted   10
the dead weight
(because it was dead);
they tried to make him get up.
They kicked and prodded.
Where had he gone?   15
Dead we now call that place
where he stayed in a heap
for maybe a week
until the stink told them
something was wrong.   20
Someone thought to bury him.
How could they know
from the animals that fell to their clubs
that they too could go down?
The first grave   25
mounded up over his weight.

What was it,
this going out?
That was what no one knew
even as it happened.   30
Even as it happens.

1975

Classical History and Myth

ALFRED, LORD TENNYSON

Ulysses[1]

It little profits that an idle king,
By this still hearth, among these barren crags,

1. After the end of the Trojan War, Ulysses (or Odysseus), King of Ithaca and one of the Greek heroes of the war, returned to his island home (line 34). Homer's account of the situation is in the *Odyssey*, Book XI, but Dante's account of Ulysses in *The Inferno*, XXVI, is the more immediate background of the poem.

Matched with an agéd wife,[2] I mete and dole
Unequal laws unto a savage race,
That hoard, and sleep, and feed, and know not me.   5
    I cannot rest from travel; I will drink
Life to the lees.[3] All times I have enjoyed
Greatly, have suffered greatly, both with those
That loved me, and alone; on shore, and when
Through scudding drifts the rainy Hyades[4]   10
Vexed the dim sea. I am become a name;
For always roaming with a hungry heart
Much have I seen and known—cities of men
And manners, climates, councils, governments,
Myself not least, but honored of them all—   15
And drunk delight of battle with my peers,
Far on the ringing plains of windy Troy.
I am a part of all that I have met;
Yet all experience is an arch wherethrough
Gleams that untraveled world, whose margin fades   20
For ever and for ever when I move.
How dull it is to pause, to make an end,
To rust unburnished, not to shine in use!
As though to breathe were life. Life piled on life
Were all too little, and of one to me   25
Little remains; but every hour is saved
From that eternal silence, something more,
A bringer of new things; and vile it were
For some three suns to store and hoard myself,
And this gray spirit yearning in desire   30
To follow knowledge like a sinking star,
Beyond the utmost bound of human thought.

    This is my son, mine own Telemachus,
To whom I leave the scepter and the isle—
Well-loved of me, discerning to fulfill   35
This labor by slow prudence to make mild
A rugged people, and through soft degrees
Subdue them to the useful and the good.
Most blameless is he, centered in the sphere
Of common duties, decent not to fail   40
In offices of tenderness, and pay
Meet adoration to my household gods,
When I am gone. He works his work, I mine.

    There lies the port; the vessel puffs her sail:
There gloom the dark, broad seas. My mariners,   45
Souls that have toiled, and wrought, and thought with me—
That ever with a frolic welcome took
The thunder and the sunshine, and opposed
Free hearts, free foreheads—you and I are old;

2. Penelope.
3. All the way down to the bottom of
the cup.

4. A group of stars which were supposed to predict rain when they rose at the
same time as the sun.

Old age hath yet his honor and his toil.   50
Death closes all; but something ere the end,
Some work of noble note, may yet be done,
Not unbecoming men that strove with Gods.
The lights begin to twinkle from the rocks;
The long day wanes; the slow moon climbs; the deep   55
Moans round with many voices. Come, my friends.
'Tis not too late to seek a newer world.
Push off, and sitting well in order smite
The sounding furrows; for my purpose holds
To sail beyond the sunset, and the baths   60
Of all the western stars, until I die.
It may be that the gulfs will wash us down;[5]
It may be we shall touch the Happy Isles,[6]
And see the great Achilles, whom we knew.
Though much is taken, much abides; and though   65
We are not now that strength which in old days
Moved earth and heaven, that which we are, we are:
One equal temper of heroic hearts,
Made weak by time and fate, but strong in will
To strive, to seek, to find, and not to yield.   70

1833

PETER VIERECK

Kilroy[7]

Also Ulysses once—that other war.[8]
          (Is it because we find his scrawl
          Today on every privy door
          That we forget his ancient role?)
Also was there—he did it for the wages—   5
When a Cathay-drunk Genoese set sail.[9]
Whenever "longen folk to goon on pilgrimages,"[1]
Kilroy is there;
          he tells *The Miller's Tale.*

At times he seems a paranoiac king   10
Who stamps his crest on walls and says "My Own!"
But in the end he fades like a lost tune,
Tossed here and there, whom all the breezes sing.

5. Beyond the Gulf of Gibraltar was supposed to be a chasm that led to Hades.
6. Elysium, the Islands of the Blessed, where heroes like Achilles (line 64) abide after death.
7. A fictitious character in World War II who symbolized American daring and ingenuity; the phrase "Kilroy was here" was carved and scribbled everywhere, all over the world.
8. The Trojan War, in which Ulysses became a hero and a mythic symbol of the bold voyager who thrived on action and adventure.
9. When Columbus set sail from Genoa, he intended to find a new trade route to China (Cathay).
1. An early line in the "General Prologue" to Chaucer's *Canterbury Tales*, explaining the rationale for the journey on which the *Tales* are built. "The Miller's Tale" (line 9) is the bawdiest of the tales, and one of the most spirited.

"Kilroy was here"; these words sound wanly gay,
    Haughty yet tired with long marching.   15
He is Orestes[2]—guilty of what crime?—
    For whom the Furies still are searching;
    When they arrive, they find their prey
(Leaving his name to mock them) went away.
Sometimes he does not flee from them in time: 20
"Kilroy was—"
        (*with his blood a dying man*
        Wrote half the phrase out in Bataan.[3])

Kilroy, beware. "HOME" is the final trap
That lurks for you in many a wily shape: 25
In pipe-and-slippers plus a Loyal Hound
    Or fooling around, just fooling around.
Kind to the old (their warm Penelope[4])
But fierce to boys,
        thus "home" becomes that sea,   30
Horribly disguised, where you were always drowned—
    (How could suburban Crete[5] condone
The yarns you would have V-mailed[6] from the sun?)—
And folksy fishes sip Icarian tea.[7]

One stab of hopeless wings imprinted your   35
    Exultant Kilroy-signature
Upon sheer sky for all the world to stare:
    "I was there! I was there! I was there!"

God is like Kilroy. He, too, sees it all;
That's how He knows of every sparrow's fall;[8]   40
That's why we prayed each time the tightropes cracked
On which our loveliest clowns contrived their act.
The G. I. Faustus[9] who was
        everywhere
Strolled home again. "What was it like outside?"   45
Asked Can't, with his good neighbors Ought and But
And pale Perhaps and grave-eyed Better Not;
For "Kilroy" means: the world is very wide.
    He was there, he was there, he was there!

And in the suburbs Can't sat down and cried.   50
        1948

2. The son of Agamemnon and Clytemnestra in Greek myth. After his mother killed his father, he avenged the death by killing her, and the Furies (line 17) pursued him from country to country.
3. The site, in the Philippine Islands, of two major battle campaigns in World War II.
4. Wife of Ulysses.
5. According to Pindar, the Cretans were incredible liars.
6. V-Mail was an overseas military mail system used in World War II. Letters were microfilmed, for compact transportation, and then re-enlarged before delivery.

7. Icarus, the son of Daedalus, flew with his father from Crete (line 32), but he strayed too near the sun, the wax which attached his wings melted, and he fell into the sea, which then became known as the Icarian Sea. "Icarian" once meant venturesome.
8. According to *Matthew* 10:29, even a sparrow "shall not fall on the ground" without God's knowledge of it.
9. The 16th-century astrologer and magician who became a symbol of man's desire to know everything regardless of the cost.

WALLACE STEVENS

The World as Meditation

J'ai passé trop de temps à travailler mon violon, à voyager. Mais l'exercice essentiel du compositeur—la méditation—rien ne l'a jamais suspendu en moi . . . Je vis un rêve permanent, qui ne s'arrête ni nuit ni jour.

GEORGES ENESCO[1]

Is it Ulysses that approaches from the east,[2]
The interminable adventurer? The trees are mended.
That winter is washed away. Someone is moving

On the horizon and lifting himself up above it.
A form of fire approaches the cretonnes of Penelope,   5
Whose mere savage presence awakens the world in which she dwells.

She has composed, so long, a self with which to welcome him,
Companion to his self for her, which she imagined,
Two in a deep-founded sheltering, friend and dear friend.

The trees had been mended, as an essential exercise   10
In an inhuman meditation, larger than her own.
No winds like dogs watched over her at night.

She wanted nothing he could not bring her by coming alone.
She wanted no fetchings. His arms would be her necklace
And her belt, the final fortune of their desire.   15

But was it Ulysses? Or was it only the warmth of the sun
On her pillow? The thought kept beating in her like her heart.
The two kept beating together. It was only day.

It was Ulysses and it was not. Yet they had met,
Friend and dear friend and a planet's encouragement.   20
The barbarous strength within her would never fail.

She would talk a little to herself as she combed her hair,
Repeating his name with its patient syllables,
Never forgetting him that kept coming constantly so near.

1954

---

1. Rumanian violinist, conductor, and composer (1881–1955): "I have spent too much time working at my violin and traveling. But the essential exercise of the composer—meditation—nothing has ever kept me from that—I live a permanent dream which does not stop, night or day."

2. During Ulysses' absence to fight the Trojan War, Penelope remained at home for twenty years, besieged by suitors.

EDMUND SPENSER

Penelope, for Her Ulysses' Sake

Penelope,[3] for her Ulysses' sake,
Devised a web her wooers to deceive;
In which the work that she all day did make,
The same at night she did again unreave:
Such subtle craft my damsel[4] doth conceive,   5
Th' importune suit of my desire to shun:
For all that I in many days do weave,
In one short hour I find by her undone.
So, when I think to end that I begun,
I must begin and never bring to end: 10
For with one look she spills[5] that long I spun;
And with one word my whole year's work doth rend.
Such labor like the spider's web I find,
Whose fruitless work is broken with least wind.

1595

Non-Western History and Myth

LANGSTON HUGHES

The Negro Speaks of Rivers

I've known rivers:
I've known rivers ancient as the world and older than the flow of human
    blood in human veins.

My soul has grown deep like the rivers.

I bathed in the Euphrates when dawns were young.
I built my hut near the Congo and it lulled me to sleep.   5
I looked upon the Nile and raised the pyramids above it.
I heard the singing of the Mississippi when Abe Lincoln went down
    to New Orleans, and I've seen its muddy bosom turn all golden in
    the sunset.

I've known rivers:
Ancient, dusky rivers.

My soul has grown deep like the rivers.   10

1926

3. Famous for her long-suffering faithfulness to her husband, Ulysses, during the Trojan War. She ingeniously devised a series of tricks to deceive the men who pursued her during Ulysses' 20-year absence. The "never-ending, still beginning" web was a shroud she was weaving for her father-in-law; she promised her suitors she would make a choice when she finished, but each night she unraveled what she had done during the day. See Homer's *Odyssey*, II, XIX, and XXIV.
4. Spenser's sonnet is part of a sequence recounting a courtship.
5. Destroys.

GABRIEL OKARA

Piano and Drums

When at break of day at a riverside
I hear jungle drums telegraphing
the mystic rhythm, urgent, raw
like bleeding flesh, speaking of
primal youth and the beginning,   5
I see the panther ready to pounce,
the leopard snarling about to leap
and the hunters crouch with spears poised;

And my blood ripples, turns torrent,
topples the years and at once I'm   10
in my mother's lap a suckling;
at once I'm walking simple
paths with no innovations,
rugged, fashioned with the naked
warmth of hurrying feet and groping hearts   15
in green leaves and wild flowers pulsing.

Then I hear a wailing piano
solo speaking of complex ways
in tear-furrowed concerto;
of far-away lands   20
and new horizons with
coaxing diminuendo, counterpoint,
crescendo. But lost in the labyrinth
of its complexities, it ends in the middle
of a phrase at a daggerpoint.   25

And I lost in the morning mist
of an age at a riverside keep
wandering in the mystic rhythm
of jungle drums and the concerto.

                                                                   1963

MAYA ANGELOU

Africa

Thus she had lain
sugar cane sweet
deserts her hair
golden her feet
mountains her breasts   5
two Niles her tears

Thus she has lain
Black through the years.

Over the white seas
rime white and cold   10
brigands ungentled
icicle bold
took her young daughters
sold her strong sons
churched her with Jesus   15
bled her with guns.
Thus she has lain.

Now she is rising
remember her pain
remember the losses   20
her screams loud and vain
remember her riches
her history slain
now she is striding
although she had lain.   25

1975

BRUCE MCM. WRIGHT

The African Affair

Black is what the prisons are,
The stagnant vortex of the hours
Swept into totality,
Creeping in the perjured heart,
Bitter in the vulgar rhyme,   5
Bitter on the walls;

Black is where the devils dance
With time within
The creviced wall. Time pirouettes
A crippled orbit in a trance,   10
And crawls below, beneath the flesh
Where darkness flows;

Black is where the deserts burn,
The Niger and Sasandra flow,
From where the Middle Passage went   15
Within the Continent of Night
From Cameroons to Carisbrooke
And places conscience cannot go;

Black is where thatched temples burn

Incense to carved ebon-wood;   20
Where traders shaped my father's pain,
His person and his place,
Among dead statues in a frieze,
In the spectrum of his race.

1963

ISHMAEL REED

Sermonette

a poet was busted by a topless judge
his friends went to morristwn nj & put
black powder on his honah's doorstep
black powder into his honah's car
black powder on his honah's briefs   5
tiny dolls into his honah's mind

by nightfall his honah could a go go no mo
his dog went crazy & ran into a crocodile
his widow fell from a wall &
hanged herself   10
his daughter was run over by a black man
cming home for the wakes the two boys
skidded into mourning
all the next of kin's teeth fell out

gimmie dat ol time   15
                    religion
it's good enough
        for me!

1972

Private History and Myth

WILLIAM BUTLER YEATS

Easter 1916[1]

I have met them at close of day
Coming with vivid faces

1. The famous Easter uprising began on Easter Monday when an Irish republic was proclaimed by nationalist leaders, but English military forces responded quickly; by April 29, some 300 people were dead and the Nationalists surrendered. Early in May, 15 leaders (including the four mentioned in lines 75–76) were executed, and more than 2,000 were held prisoners.

From counter or desk among gray
Eighteenth-century houses.
I have passed with a nod of the head   5
Or polite meaningless words,
Or have lingered awhile and said
Polite meaningless words,
And thought before I had done
Of a mocking tale or a gibe   10
To please a companion
Around the fire at the club,
Being certain that they and I
But lived where motley[2] is worn:
All changed, changed utterly: 15
A terrible beauty is born.

That woman's[3] days were spent
In ignorant good-will,
Her nights in argument
Until her voice grew shrill.   20
What voice more sweet than hers
When, young and beautiful,
She rode to harriers?[4]
This man[5] had kept a school
And rode our wingéd horse;[6]   25
This other[7] his helper and friend
Was coming into his force;
He might have won fame in the end,
So sensitive his nature seemed,
So daring and sweet his thought.   30
This other man[8] I had dreamed
A drunken, vainglorious lout.
He had done most bitter wrong
To some who are near my heart,
Yet I number him in the song;   35
He, too, has resigned his part
In the casual comedy;
He, too, has been changed in his turn,
Transformed utterly:
A terrible beauty is born.   40

2. The particolored clothing of a professional fool or jester, at court or in a play.
3. Countess Constance Georgina Markiewicz, a beautiful and well-born young woman from County Sligo who became a vigorous and bitter nationalist. At first condemned to death, she later had her sentence commuted to life imprisonment, and she gained amnesty in 1917.
4. Hounds.
5. Patrick Pearse, who led the assault on the Dublin Post Office from which the proclamation of a republic was issued. A schoolmaster by profession, he had vigorously supported the restoration of the Gaelic language in Ireland and was an active political writer and poet.
6. Pegasus, the traditional symbol of poetic inspiration.
7. Thomas MacDonagh, also a writer and teacher.
8. Major John MacBride, who had married Yeats's beloved Maud Gonne in 1903 but separated from her two years later.

Hearts with one purpose alone
Through summer and winter seem
Enchanted to a stone
To trouble the living stream.
The horse that comes from the road,   45
The rider, the birds that range
From cloud to tumbling cloud,
Minute by minute they change;
A shadow of cloud on the stream
Changes minute by minute;   50
A horse-hoof slides on the brim,
And a horse plashes within it;
The long-legged moor-hens dive,
And hens to moor-cocks call;
Minute by minute they live: 55
The stone's in the midst of all.

Too long a sacrifice
Can make a stone of the heart.
O when may it suffice?
That is Heaven's part, our part   60
To murmur name upon name,
As a mother names her child
When sleep at last has come
On limbs that had run wild.
What is it but nightfall?   65
No, no, not night but death;
Was it needless death after all?
For England may keep faith[9]
For all that is done and said.
We know their dream; enough
To know they dreamed and are dead;   70
And what if excess of love
Bewildered them till they died?
I write it out in a verse—
MacDonagh and MacBride   75
And Connolly[1] and Pearse
Now and in time to be,
Wherever green is worn,
Are changed, changed utterly:
A terrible beauty is born.   80

1916

---

9. Before the uprising the English had
promised eventual home rule to Ireland.

1. James Connolly, the leader of the
Easter uprising.

The Second Coming[2]

Turning and turning in the widening gyre[3]
The falcon cannot hear the falconer;
Things fall apart; the center cannot hold;
Mere anarchy is loosed upon the world,
The blood-dimmed tide is loosed, and everywhere   5
The ceremony of innocence is drowned;
The best lack all conviction, while the worst
Are full of passionate intensity.

Surely some revelation is at hand;
Surely the Second Coming is at hand.   10
The Second Coming! Hardly are those words out
When a vast image out of *Spiritus Mundi*[4]
Troubles my sight: somewhere in sands of the desert
A shape with lion body and the head of a man,
A gaze blank and pitiless as the sun,   15
Is moving its slow thighs, while all about it
Reel shadows of the indignant desert birds.[5]
The darkness drops again; but now I know
That twenty centuries of stony sleep
Were vexed to nightmare by a rocking cradle,   20
And what rough beast, its hour come round at last,
Slouches towards Bethlehem to be born?

p. 1920

Leda and the Swan[6]

A sudden blow: the great wings beating still
Above the staggering girl, her thighs caressed
By the dark webs, her nape caught in his bill,
He holds her helpless breast upon his breast.

2. The Second Coming of Christ, according to *Matthew* 24:29–44, will come after a time of "tribulation." Disillusioned by Ireland's continued civil strife, Yeats saw his time as the end of another historical cycle. In *A Vision* (1937) Yeats describes his view of history as dependent on cycles of about 2000 years: the birth of Christ had ended the cycle of Greco-Roman civilization, and now the Christian cycle seemed near an end, to be followed by an antithetical cycle, ominous in its portents.
3. Literally, the widening spiral of a falcon's flight. "Gyre" is Yeats's term for a cycle of history, which he diagrammed in terms of a series of interpenetrating cones.
4. Or *Anima Mundi*, the spirit or soul of the world, a consciousness in which the individual participates. Yeats considered this universal consciousness or memory a fund from which poets drew their images and symbols. In *Per Amica Silentia Lunae* he wrote: "Before the mind's eye, whether in sleep or waking, came images that one was to discover presently in some book one

had never read, and after looking in vain for explanation . . . , I came to believe in a great memory passing on from generation to generation."
5. Yeats later writes of the "brazen winged beast . . . described in my poem *The Second Coming*" as "associated with laughing, ecstatic destruction." "Our civilization was about to reverse itself, or some new civilization about to be born from all that our age had rejected . . . ; because we had worshipped a single god it would worship many."
6. According to Greek myth, Zeus took the form of a swan to seduce Leda, who became the mother of Helen of Troy and also of Clytemnestra, Agamemnon's wife and murderer. Helen's abduction from her husband, Menelaus, brother of Agamemnon, began the Trojan War (line 10) Yeats described the visit of Zeus to Leda as an annunciation like that to Mary (see *Luke* 1:26–38): "I imagine the annunciation that founded Greece as made to Leda. . . ." (*A Vision*).

How can those terrified vague fingers push   5
The feathered glory from her loosening thighs?
And how can body, laid in that white rush,
But feel the strange heart beating where it lies?

A shudder in the loins engenders there
The broken wall, the burning roof and tower   10
And Agamemnon dead.
                          Being so caught up,
So mastered by the brute blood of the air,
Did she put on his knowledge with his power
Before the indifferent beak could let her drop?

1923

Sailing to Byzantium[7]

I

That[8] is no country for old men. The young
In one another's arms, birds in the trees
—Those dying generations—at their song,
The salmon-falls, the mackerel-crowded seas
Fish, flesh, or fowl, commend all summer long   5
Whatever is begotten, born, and dies.
Caught in that sensual music all neglect
Monuments of unaging intellect.

II

An aged man is but a paltry thing,
A tattered coat upon a stick, unless   10
Soul clap its hands and sing, and louder sing
For every tatter in its mortal dress,
Nor is there singing school but studying
Monuments of its own magnificence;
And therefore I have sailed the seas and come   15
To the holy city of Byzantium.

7. The ancient name of Istanbul, the capital and holy city of Eastern Christendom from the late fourth century until 1453. It was famous for its stylized and formal mosaics, its symbolic, nonnaturalistic art, and its highly developed intellectual life. Yeats repeatedly uses it to symbolize a world of artifice and timelessness, free from the decay and death of the natural and sensual world. In *A Vision*, Yeats wrote: "I think if I could be given a month of Antiquity and leave to spend it where I chose, I would spend it in Byzantium a little before Justinian opened St. Sophia and closed the Academy of Plato [about 535 A.D.]. I think I could find in some little wineshop some philosophical worker in mosaic who could answer all my questions, the supernatural descending nearer to him than to Plotinus even, for the pride of his delicate skill would make what was an instrument of power to princes and clerics, a murderous madness in the mob, show as a lovely flexible presence like that of a perfect human body. I think that in early Byzantium, maybe never before or since in recorded history, religious, aesthetic and practical life were one, that architect and artificers . . . spoke to the multitude and the few alike. The painter, the mosaic worker, the worker in gold and silver, the illuminator of sacred books, were almost impersonal, almost perhaps without the consciousness of individual design, absorbed in their subject-matter and that the vision of the whole people. They could . . . weave all into a vast design, the work of many that seemed the work of one, that made building, picture, metal-work or rail and lamp, seem but a single image. . . ."

8. Ireland, as an instance of the natural, temporal world.

III

O sages standing in God's holy fire
As in the gold mosaic of a wall,
Come from the holy fire, perne in a gyre,[9]
And be the singing masters of my soul.   20
Consume my heart away; sick with desire
And fastened to a dying animal
It knows not what it is; and gather me
Into the artifice of eternity.

IV

Once out of nature I shall never take   25
My bodily form from any natural thing,
But such a form as Grecian goldsmiths make
Of hammered gold and gold enameling
To keep a drowsy Emperor awake;[1]
Or set upon a golden bough[2] to sing   30
To lords and ladies of Byzantium
Of what is past, or passing, or to come.

1927

Among School Children

I

I walk through the long schoolroom questioning;
A kind old nun in a white hood replies;
The children learn to cipher and to sing,
To study reading-books and history,
To cut and sew, be neat in everything   5
In the best modern way—the children's eyes
In momentary wonder stare upon
A sixty-year-old smiling public man.[3]

II

I dream of a Ledaean body,[4] bent
Above a sinking fire, a tale that she   10
Told of a harsh reproof, or trivial event
That changed some childish day to tragedy—
Told, and it seemed that our two natures blent
Into a sphere from youthful sympathy,

9. I.e., whirl in a coiling motion, so that his soul may merge with its motion as the timeless world invades the cycles of history and nature. The gyre in "The Second Coming" moves in the opposite direction, up and out centripetally, so that "things fall apart." "Perne" is Yeats's coinage (from the noun "pirn"): to spin around in the kind of spiral pattern that thread makes as it comes off a bobbin or spool.

1. "I have read somewhere that in the Emperor's palace at Byzantium was a tree made of gold and silver, and artificial birds that sang." (Yeats's note)

2. In Book VI of *The Aeneid*, the sybil tells Aeneas that he must pluck a golden bough from a nearby tree in order to descend to Hades. There is only one such branch there, and when it is plucked an identical one takes its place.

3. At 60 (in 1925) Yeats had been a senator of the Irish Free State.

4. Like that of Helen of Troy, daughter of Leda. The memory dream is of Maud Gonne (see also lines 29–30), with whom Yeats had long been hopelessly in love.

Or else, to alter Plato's parable,   15
Into the yolk and white of the one shell.[5]

III

And thinking of that fit of grief or rage
I look upon one child or t'other there
And wonder if she stood so at that age—
For even daughters of the swan can share   20
Something of every paddler's heritage—
And had that color upon cheek or hair,
And thereupon my heart is driven wild:
She stands before me as a living child.

IV

Her present image floats into the mind—   25
Did Quattrocento finger[6] fashion it
Hollow of cheek as though it drank the wind
And took a mess of shadows for its meat?
And I though never of Ledaean kind
Had pretty plumage once—enough of that,   30
Better to smile on all that smile, and show
There is a comfortable kind of old scarecrow.

V

What youthful mother, a shape upon her lap
Honey of generation[7] had betrayed,
And that must sleep, shriek, struggle to escape   35
As recollection or the drug decide,
Would think her son, did she but see that shape
With sixty or more winters on its head,
A compensation for the pang of his birth,
Or the uncertainty of his setting forth?   40

VI

Plato thought nature but a spume that plays
Upon a ghostly paradigm of things;[8]
Solider Aristotle played the taws

5. In Plato's *Symposium*, the origin of human love is explained by parable: Human beings were once spheres, but Zeus was fearful of their power and cut them in half; now each half longs to be reunited with its missing half. Helen and Pollux were hatched from one of two eggs born to Leda after her union with Zeus in the form of a swan; the other contained Castor and Clytemnestra. According to Yeats in *A Vision*, "from one of [Leda's] eggs came Love and from the other War."

6. Fifteenth-century artists, who fall within the 15th Phase of the Christian cycle. Yeats especially admired Botticelli, and in *A Vision* praises his "deliberate strangeness everywhere [which] gives one an emotion of mystery which is new to painting." Botticelli is grouped with those who make "intellect and emotion, *primary* curiosity and the *antithetical* dream . . . for the moment one."

7. "I have taken the 'honey of generation' from Porphyry's essay on 'The Cave of the Nymphs' [*Odyssey*, Book XIII], but find no warrant in Porphyry for considering it the 'drug' that destroys the 'recollection' of prenatal freedom. He blamed a cup of oblivion given in the zodiacal sign of Cancer." (Yeats's note) Porphyry, a third-century Greek scholar and neoplatonic philosopher, says "honey of generation" means the "pleasure arising from copulation" which draws souls "downward" to generation.

8. Plato considered the world of nature an imperfect and illusory copy of the ideal world.

Upon the bottom of a king of kings;[9]
World-famous golden-thighed Pythagoras[1]   45
Fingered upon a fiddle-stick or strings
What a star sang and careless Muses heard:
Old clothes upon old sticks to scare a bird.

VII

Both nuns and mothers worship images,
But those the candles light are not as those   50
That animate a mother's reveries,
But keep a marble or a bronze repose.
And yet they too break hearts—O Presences
That passion, piety or affection knows,
And that all heavenly glory symbolize—   55
O self-born mockers of man's enterprise;

VIII

Labor is blossoming or dancing where
The body is not bruised to pleasure soul,
Nor beauty born out of its own despair,
Nor blear-eyed wisdom out of midnight oil.   60
O chestnut-tree, great-rooted blossomer,
Are you the leaf, the blossom or the bole?[2]
O body swayed to music, O brightening glance,
How can we know the dancer from the dance?

1927

Byzantium[3]

The unpurged images of day recede;
The Emperor's drunken soldiery are abed;
Night resonance recedes, night-walkers' song
After great cathedral gong;
A starlit or a moonlit dome[4] disdains   5
All that man is,
All mere complexities,
The fury and the mire of human veins.

Before me floats an image, man or shade,
Shade more than man, more image than a shade;   10

9. Aristotle, the teacher of Alexander the Great, disciplined him with a strap ("taw," line 43). His philosophy, insisting on the interdependence of form and matter, took the world of nature far more seriously than did Plato's.
1. Sixth-century B.C. Greek mathematician and philosopher, whose elaborate philosophical system included the doctrine of the harmony of the spheres. He was highly revered, and one legend describes his godlike golden thighs.
2. Trunk.
3. In his diary for April 30, 1930, Yeats sketched the following "Subject for a Poem": "Describe Byzantium as it is in the system towards the end of the first Christian millennium. A walking mummy. Flames at the street corners where the soul is purified, birds of hammered gold singing in the golden trees, in the harbor [dolphins], offering their backs to the wailing dead that they may carry them to paradise."
4. In *A Vision*, Yeats described the 28 phases of the moon in psychological terms related to his system. In Phase 1, only stars are visible ("starlit") and "body is completely absorbed in its supernatural environment." In its opposite, Phase 15, when the moon is full ("moonlit"), the mind is "completely absorbed in being."

For Hades' bobbin bound in mummy-cloth
May unwind the winding path;[5]
A mouth that has no moisture and no breath
Breathless mouths may summon;
I hail the superhuman;   15
I call it death-in-life and life-in-death.

Miracle, bird or golden handiwork,
More miracle than bird or handiwork,
Planted on the star-lit golden bough,
Can like the cocks of Hades crow,[6]   20
Or, by the moon embittered, scorn aloud
In glory of changeless metal
Common bird or petal
And all complexities of mire or blood.

At midnight on the Emperor's pavement flit   25
Flames that no fagot[7] feeds, nor steel has lit,
Nor storm disturbs, flames begotten of flame,
Where blood-begotten spirits come
And all complexities of fury leave,
Dying into a dance,   30
An agony of trance,
An agony of flame that cannot singe a sleeve.

Astraddle on the dolphin's mire and blood,[8]
Spirit after spirit! The smithies break the flood,
The golden smithies of the Emperor!   35
Marbles of the dancing floor
Break bitter furies of complexity,
Those images that yet
Fresh images beget,
That dolphin-torn, that gong-tormented sea.   40

1932

The Circus Animals' Desertion[9]

I

I sought a theme and sought for it in vain,
I sought it daily for six weeks or so.
Maybe at last, being but a broken man,

5. A volume in which "Byzantium" appeared, *The Winding Stair and Other Poems*, contains many similar images; of this volume Yeats wrote: "In this book and elsewhere I have used towers, and one tower in particular, as symbols and have compared their winding stairs to the philosophical gyres, but it is hardly necessary to interpret what comes from the main track of thought and expression. Shelley uses towers constantly as symbols, and there are gyres in Swedenborg, and in Thomas Aquinas and certain classical authors."

6. As the bird of dawn, the cock had from antiquity been a symbol of rebirth and resurrection.

7. Bundle of sticks.

8. In ancient art, dolphins symbolize the soul moving from one state to another, and sometimes they provide a vehicle for the dead. Palaemon, for example, in Greek tradition is often mounted on a dolphin.

9. The "animals" are early themes and images in Yeats's poetry, and he here reviews some of them.

I must be satisfied with my heart, although
Winter and summer till old age began   5
My circus animals were all on show,
Those stilted boys, that burnished chariot,
Lion and woman and the Lord knows what.

II

What can I but enumerate old themes?
First that sea-rider Oisin[1] led by the nose   10
Through three enchanted islands, allegorical dreams,
Vain gaiety, vain battle, vain repose,
Themes of the embittered heart, or so it seems,
That might adorn old songs or courtly shows;
But what cared I that set him on to ride,   15
I, starved for the bosom of his faery bride?

And then a counter-truth filled out its play,
The Countess Cathleen[2] was the name I gave it;
She, pity-crazed, had given her soul away,
But masterful Heaven had intervened to save it.   20
I thought my dear[3] must her own soul destroy,
So did fanaticism and hate enslave it,
And this brought forth a dream and soon enough
This dream itself had all my thought and love.

And when the Fool and Blind Man stole the bread   25
Cuchulain fought the ungovernable sea;[4]
Heart-mysteries there, and yet when all is said
It was the dream itself enchanted me:
Character isolated by a deed
To engross the present and dominate memory.   30
Players and painted stage took all my love,
And not those things that they were emblems of.

III

Those masterful images because complete
Grew in pure mind, but out of what began?
A mound of refuse or the sweepings of a street,   35
Old kettles, old bottles, and a broken can,
Old iron, old bones, old rags, that raving slut
Who keeps the till. Now that my ladder's gone,
I must lie down where all the ladders start,
In the foul rag-and-bone shop of the heart.   40

1939

---

1. The subject of an 1889 long poem. Oisin was a legendary figure, beguiled to faery land for 150 years, who returned to find his friends dead in his native Ireland.
2. An 1892 play, in which the countess sells her soul to the devil to get food for hungry people but nevertheless gains Heaven.
3. Maud Gonne.
4. In a 1904 play, *On Baile's Strand*.

Poems for Further Reading

A. R. AMMONS

Cascadilla Falls

I went down by Cascadilla
Falls this
evening, the
stream below the falls,
and picked up a   5
handsized stone
kidney-shaped, testicular, and

thought all its motions into it,
the 800 mph earth spin,
the 190-million-mile yearly   10
displacement around the sun,
the overriding
grand
haul

of the galaxy with the 30,000   15
mph of where
the sun's going:
thought all the interweaving
motions
into myself: dropped   20

the stone to dead rest:
the stream from other motions
broke
rushing over it:
shelterless,   25
I turned

to the sky and stood still:
oh
I do
not know where I am going   30
that I can live my life
by this single creek.

1970

MARGARET ATWOOD

Five Poems for Dolls

I

Behind glass in Mexico
this clay doll draws
its lips back in a snarl;
despite its beautiful dusty shawl,
it wishes to be dangerous.   5

II

See how the dolls resent us,
with their bulging foreheads
and minimal chins, their flat bodies
never allowed to bulb and swell,
their faces of little thugs.   10

This is not a smile,
this glossy mouth, two stunted teeth;
the dolls gaze at us
with the filmed eyes of killers.

III

There have always been dolls   15
as long as there have been people.
In the trash heaps and abandoned temples
the dolls pile up;
the sea is filling with them.

What causes them?   20
Or are they gods, causeless,
something to talk to
when you have to talk
something to throw against the wall?

A doll is a witness   25
who cannot die,
with a doll you are never alone.

On the long journey under the earth,
in the boat with two prows,
there were always dolls.   30

IV

Or did we make them
because we needed to love someone
and could not love each other?

It was love, after all,
that rubbed the skins from their gray cheeks,   35

crippled their fingers,
snarled their hair, brown or dull gold.
Hate would merely have smashed them.

You change, but the doll
I made of you lives on,   40
a white body leaning
in a sunlit window, the features
wearing away with time,
frozen in the gaunt pose
of a single day,   45
holding in its plaster hand
your doll of me.

                        V

Or: all dolls come
from the land of the unborn,
the almost-born; each   50
doll is a future
dead at the roots,
a voice heard only
on breathless nights,
a desolate white memento.   55

Or: these are the lost children,
those who have died or thickened
to full growth and gone away.

The dolls are their souls or cast skins
which line the shelves of our bedrooms   60
and museums, disguised as outmoded toys,
images of our sorrow,
shedding around themselves
five inches of limbo.

                                                    1978

W. H. AUDEN

In Memory of W. B. Yeats

(d. January, 1939)

                        I

He disappeared in the dead of winter:
The brooks were frozen, the airports almost deserted,
And snow disfigured the public statues;
The mercury sank in the mouth of the dying day.
What instruments we have agree   5
The day of his death was a dark cold day.

Far from his illness
The wolves ran on through the evergreen forests,
The peasant river was untempted by the fashionable quays;
By mourning tongues   10
The death of the poet was kept from his poems.

But for him it was his last afternoon as himself,
An afternoon of nurses and rumors;
The provinces of his body revolted,
The squares of his mind were empty,   15
Silence invaded the suburbs,
The current of his feeling failed; he became his admirers.

Now he is scattered among a hundred cities
And wholly given over to unfamiliar affections,
To find his happiness in another kind of wood   20
And be punished under a foreign code of conscience.
The words of a dead man
Are modified in the guts of the living.

But in the importance and noise of tomorrow
When the brokers are roaring like beasts on the floor of the Bourse,[1]   25
And the poor have the sufferings to which they are fairly accustomed,
And each in the cell of himself is almost convinced of his freedom,
A few thousand will think of this day
As one thinks of a day when one did something slightly unusual.
What instruments we have agree   30
The day of his death was a dark cold day.

II

You were silly like us; your gift survived it all:
The parish of rich women, physical decay,
Yourself. Mad Ireland hurt you into poetry.
Now Ireland has her madness and her weather still,   35
For poetry makes nothing happen: it survives
In the valley of its making where executives
Would never want to tamper, flows on south
From ranches of isolation and the busy griefs,
Raw towns that we believe and die in; it survives,   40
A way of happening, a mouth.

III

Earth, receive an honored guest:
William Yeats is laid to rest.
Let the Irish vessel lie
Emptied of its poetry.   45

In the nightmare of the dark
All the dogs of Europe bark,

---

1. The Paris stock exchange.

And the living nations wait,
Each sequestered in its hate;

Intellectual disgrace   50
Stares from every human face,
And the seas of pity lie
Locked and frozen in each eye.

Follow, poet, follow right
To the bottom of the night,   55
With your unconstraining voice
Still persuade us to rejoice;

With the farming of a verse
Make a vineyard of the curse,
Sing of human unsuccess   60
In a rapture of distress;

In the deserts of the heart
Let the healing fountain start,
In the prison of his days
Teach the free man how to praise.   65

1939

W. H. AUDEN

Musée des Beaux Arts[2]

About suffering they were never wrong,
The Old Masters: how well they understood
Its human position; how it takes place
While someone else is eating or opening a window or just walking dully
    along;
How, when the aged are reverently, passionately waiting   5
For the miraculous birth, there always must be
Children who did not specially want it to happen, skating
On a pond at the edge of the wood:
They never forgot
That even the dreadful martyrdom must run its course   10
Anyhow in a corner, some untidy spot
Where the dogs go on with their doggy life and the torturer's horse
Scratches its innocent behind on a tree.

In Brueghel's *Icarus*,[3] for instance: how everything turns away

2. The Museum of the Fine Arts, in Brussels.
3. "Landscape with the Fall of Icarus," by Pieter Brueghel the elder, located in the Brussels Museum. According to Greek myth, Daedalus and his son Icarus escaped from imprisonment by using home-made wings of wax; but Icarus flew too near the sun, the wax melted, and he fell into the sea and drowned. In the Brueghel painting the central figure is a peasant plowing, and several other figures are more immediately noticeable than Icarus who, disappearing into the sea, is easy to miss in the lower right-hand corner. Equally ignored by the figures is a dead body in the woods.

Quite leisurely from the disaster; the plowman may   15
Have heard the splash, the forsaken cry,
But for him it was not an important failure; the sun shone
As it had to on the white legs disappearing into the green
Water; and the expensive delicate ship that must have seen
Something amazing, a boy falling out of the sky,   20
Had somewhere to get to and sailed calmly on.
1938

JOHN BERRYMAN

1 September 1939 [4]

The first, scattering rain on the Polish cities.
That afternoon a man squat' on the shore
Tearing a square of shining cellophane.
Some easily, some in evident torment tore,
Some for a time resisted, and then burst.   5
All this depended on fidelity . . .
One was blown out and borne off by the waters,
The man was tortured by the sound of rain.

Children were sent from London in the morning
But not the sound of children reached his ear.   10
He found a mangled feather by the lake,
Lost in the destructive sand this year
Like feathery independence, hope. His shadow
Lay on the sand before him, under the lake
As under the ruined library our learning.   15
The children play in the waves until they break.

The Bear crept under the Eagle's wing and lay
Snarling; the other animals showed fear,
Europe darkened its cities. The man wept,
Considering the light which had been there,   20
The feathered gull against the twilight flying.
As the little waves ate away the shore
The cellophane, dismembered, blew away.
The animals ran, the Eagle soared and dropt.

1939

EARLE BIRNEY

From the Hazel Bough

I met a lady
on a lazy street

4. The first day of World War II.

   hazel eyes
    and little plush feet

   her legs swam by   5
    like lovely trout
   eyes were trees
    where boys leant out

   hands in the dark and
    a river side   10
   round breasts rising
    with the fingers' tide

   she was plump as a finch
    and live as a salmon
   gay as silk and   15
    proud as a Brahmin[5]

   we winked when we met
    and laughed when we parted
   never took time
    to be brokenhearted   20

   but no man sees
    where the trout lie now
   or what leans out
    from the hazel bough

1945–47

EARLE BIRNEY

Irapuato[6]

For reasons any
      brigadier
          could tell
this is a favorite nook for
         massacre   5

Toltex by Mixtex Mixtex by Aztex
Aztex by Spanishtex Spanishtex by
Mexitex by Mexitex by Mexitex by Texaco

So any farmer can see how the strawberries
are the biggest and reddest   10
   in the whole damn continent

---

5. A member of a socially elite class.
6. A city in central Mexico, northwest of Mexico City.

but why

     when arranged under

          the market flies

do they look like small clotting hearts?   15

                         1962

WILLIAM BLAKE

Ah Sunflower

Ah Sunflower! weary of time,
Who countest the steps of the Sun,
Seeking after that sweet golden clime
Where the traveler's journey is done,

Where the Youth pined away with desire,   5
And the pale Virgin shrouded in snow,
Arise from their graves and aspire,
Where my Sunflower wishes to go.

                         1794

WILLIAM BLAKE

The Lamb

Little Lamb, who made thee?
  Dost thou know who made thee?
Gave thee life, and bid thee feed
By the stream and o'er the mead;
Gave thee clothing of delight,   5
Softest clothing woolly bright;
Gave thee such a tender voice,
Making all the vales rejoice?
  Little Lamb, who made thee?
  Dost thou know who made thee?   10

Little Lamb, I'll tell thee!
Little Lamb, I'll tell thee:
He is callèd by thy name,
For he calls himself a Lamb,
He is meek and he is mild;   15
He became a little child.
I a child and thou a lamb,
We are callèd by his name.
  Little Lamb, God bless thee!
  Little Lamb, God bless thee!   20

                         1789

WILLIAM BLAKE

The Tiger

Tiger, Tiger, burning bright
In the forests of the night,
What immortal hand or eye
Could frame thy fearful symmetry?

In what distant deeps or skies   5
Burnt the fire of thine eyes?
On what wings dare he aspire?
What the hand dare seize the fire?

And what shoulder and what art,
Could twist the sinews of thy heart?   10
And when thy heart began to beat,
What dread hand, and what dread feet?

What the hammer? What the chain?
In what furnace was thy brain?
What the anvil? What dread grasp   15
Dare its deadly terrors clasp?

When the stars threw down their spears
And watered heaven with their tears,
Did he smile his work to see?
Did he who made the Lamb make thee?   20

Tiger, Tiger, burning bright
In the forests of the night,
What immortal hand or eye
Dare frame thy fearful symmetry?

1794

LOUISE BOGAN

The Dragonfly

You are made of almost nothing
But of enough
To be great eyes
And diaphanous double vans;[7]
To be ceaseless movement,   5
Unending hunger
Grappling love.

---

7. Delicate and translucent double wings.

Link between water and air,
Earth repels you.
Light touches you only to shift into iridescence   10
Upon your body and wings.

Twice-born, predator,
You split into the heat.
Swift beyond calculation or capture
You dart into the shadow   15
Which consumes you.

You rocket into the day.
But at last, when the wind flattens the grasses,
For you, the design and purpose stop.
And you fall   20
With the other husks of summer.

1968

JULIAN BOND

The Bishop of Atlanta: Ray Charles

The Bishop seduces the world with his voice
Sweat strangles mute eyes
As insinuations gush out through a hydrant of sorrow
Dreams, a world never seen
Molded on Africa's anvil, tempered down home   5
Documented in cries and wails
Screaming to be ignored, crooning to be heard
Throbbing from the gutter
On Saturday night
Silver offering only   10
The Right Reverend's back in town
Don't it make you feel all right?

p. 1963

JULIAN BOND

Rotation

Like plump green floor plans
the pool tables squat
Among fawning mahogany Buddhas with felt heads.
Like clubwomen blessed with adultery
The balls dart to kiss   5

and tumble erring members into silent oblivion.
Right-angled over the verdant barbered turf
Sharks point long fingers at the multi-colored worlds
and play at percussion
Sounding cheap plastic clicks   10
in an 8-ball universe built for ivory.

p. 1964

LEONARD COHEN

Suzanne Takes You Down

Suzanne takes you down
to her place near the river,
you can hear the boats go by
you can stay the night beside her.
And you know that she's half crazy   5
but that's why you want to be there
and she feeds you tea and oranges
that come all the way from China.
Just when you mean to tell her
that you have no gifts to give her,   10
she gets you on her wave-length
and she lets the river answer
that you've always been her lover.
    And you want to travel with her,
    you want to travel blind   15
    and you know that she can trust you
    because you've touched her perfect body
    with your mind.

Jesus was a sailor
when he walked upon the water[8]   20
and he spent a long time watching
from a lonely wooden tower
and when he knew for certain
only drowning men could see him
he said All men will be sailors then   25
until the sea shall free them,
but he himself was broken
long before the sky would open,
forsaken, almost human,
he sank beneath your wisdom like a stone.   30
    And you want to travel with him,
    you want to travel blind
    and you think maybe you'll trust him
    because he touched your perfect body
    with his mind.   35

8. According to *Matthew* 14:22–26 and   water in order to join his disciples in a
Mark 6:45–52, Jesus walked upon the   ship at sea.

Suzanne takes your hand
and she leads you to the river,
she is wearing rags and feathers
from Salvation Army counters.
The sun pours down like honey   40
on our lady of the harbor
as she shows you where to look
among the garbage and the flowers,
there are heroes in the seaweed
there are children in the morning,   45
they are leaning out for love
they will lean that way forever
while Suzanne she holds the mirror.
    And you want to travel with her
    and you want to travel blind   50
    and you're sure that she can find you
    because she's touched her perfect body
    with her mind.

1968

SAMUEL TAYLOR COLERIDGE

Kubla Khan: or, a Vision in a Dream[9]

In Xanadu did Kubla Khan
    A stately pleasure-dome decree:
Where Alph, the sacred river, ran
Through caverns measureless to man
    Down to a sunless sea.   5
So twice five miles of fertile ground
With walls and towers were girdled round:
And here were gardens bright with sinuous rills
Where blossomed many an incense-bearing tree;
And here were forests ancient as the hills,   10
Enfolding sunny spots of greenery.
But oh! that deep romantic chasm which slanted
Down the green hill athwart a cedarn cover![1]
A savage place! as holy and enchanted
As e'er beneath a waning moon was haunted   15
By woman wailing for her demon-lover![2]
And from this chasm, with ceaseless turmoil seething,
As if this earth in fast thick pants were breathing,
A mighty fountain momently was forced,
Amid whose swift half-intermitted burst   20
Huge fragments vaulted like rebounding hail,
Or chaffy grain beneath the thresher's flail:

9. Coleridge said he wrote this fragment immediately after waking from an opium dream and that after he was interrupted by a caller he was unable to finish the poem.
1. From side to side of a cover of cedar trees.
2. In a famous and often imitated German ballad, the lady Lenore is carried off on horseback by the specter of her lover and married to him at his grave.

And 'mid these dancing rocks at once and ever
It flung up momently the sacred river.
Five miles meandering with a mazy motion   25
Through wood and dale the sacred river ran,
Then reached the caverns measureless to man,
And sank in tumult to a lifeless ocean:
And 'mid this tumult Kubla heard from far
Ancestral voices prophesying war!   30

    The shadow of the dome of pleasure
    Floated midway on the waves;
    Where was heard the mingled measure
    From the fountain and the caves.
It was a miracle of rare device,   35
A sunny pleasure-dome with caves of ice!
    A damsel with a dulcimer[3]
    In a vision once I saw:
    It was an Abyssinian maid,
    And on her dulcimer she played,   40
    Singing of Mount Abora.
    Could I revive within me
    Her symphony and song,
    To such a deep delight 'twould win me,
That with music loud and long,   45
I would build that dome in air,
That sunny dome! those caves of ice!
And all who heard should see them there,
And all should cry, Beware! Beware!
His flashing eyes, his floating hair!   50
Weave a circle round him thrice,
And close your eyes with holy dread,
For he on honey-dew hath fed,
And drunk the milk of Paradise.

1798

e. e. cummings

the season 'tis, my lovely lambs

the season 'tis, my lovely lambs,

of Sumner Volstead Christ and Co.[4]
the epoch of Mann's righteousness
the age of dollars and no sense.

---

3. A stringed instrument, prototype of the piano.
4. The Volstead Act (1919) gave the federal government power to enforce Prohibition. "Sumner": possibly Charles Sumner, a late 19th-century U. S. senator who was considered the leading representative of the Puritan spirit in American politics, but more probably William Sumner, a late 19th and early 20th-century laissez-faire theorist who opposed laws regulating monopolies. The Mann Act (1910) made taking a woman across a state line "for immoral purposes" a federal offense.

Which being quite beyond dispute   5

as prove from Troy (N. Y.) to Cairo
(Egypt) the luminous dithyrambs[5]
of large immaculate unmute
antibolshevistic gents
(each manufacturing word by word   10
his own unrivalled brand of pyro
-technic blurb anent[6] the (hic)
hero dead that gladly (sic)
in far lands perished of unheard
of maladies including flu)   15

my little darlings, let us now
passionately remember how—
braving the worst, of peril heedless,
each braver than the other, each
(a typewriter within his reach)   20
upon his fearless derrière
sturdily seated—Colonel Needless
To Name and General You know who
a string of pretty medals drew

(while messrs jack james john and jim   25
in token of their country's love
received my dears the order of
The Artificial Arm and Limb)

—or, since bloodshed and kindred questions
inhibit unprepared digestions,   30
come: let us mildly contemplate
beginning with his wellfilled pants
earth's biggest grafter, nothing less;
the Honorable Mr. (guess)
who, breathing on the ear of fate,   35
landed a seat in the legislat-
ure whereas tommy so and so
(an erring child of circumstance
whom the bulls[7] nabbed at 33rd)

pulled six months for selling snow[8]   40
                                                                       1926

5. Vehement expressions on neon signs.
6. In reference to (a somewhat affected term common in early businessese). "Hic" (line 12), Latin for "here," and "sic" (line 13), Latin for "thus," sometimes appear in similar incongruent contexts, ostensibly as shortcuts to saying "here is an example" or "it is correct as it stands," but often to show off. There are, of course, also puns on both terms.
7. Police.
8. Cocaine, but also a reminder of the Season.

e. e. cummings

chanson innocente

in Just-
spring   when the world is mud-
luscious the little
lame balloonman

whistles   far   and wee   5

and eddieandbill come
running from marbles and
piracies and it's
spring

when the world is puddle-wonderful   10

the queer
old balloonman whistles
far   and   wee
and bettyandisbel come dancing

from hop-scotch and jump-rope and   15

it's
spring
and
   the

      goat-footed   20

balloonMan   whistles
far
and
wee[9]

1923

EMILY DICKINSON

The Brain Is Wider than the Sky

The Brain—is wider than the Sky—
For—put them side by side—
The one the other will contain
With ease—and You—beside—

---

9. Pan, whose Greek name means "everything," is traditionally represented with
a syrinx (or the pipes of Pan). The upper
half of his body is human, the lower half
goat, and as the father of Silenus he is
associated with the spring rites of Dionysus.

The Brain is deeper than the sea—   5
For—hold them—Blue to Blue—
The one the other will absorb—
As Sponges—Buckets—do—

The Brain is just the weight of God—
For—Heft them—Pound for Pound—   10
And they will differ—if they do—
As Syllable from Sound—

ca. 1862

EMILY DICKINSON

My Life Closed Twice

My life closed twice before its close—
It yet remains to see
If Immortality unveil
A third event to me

So huge, so hopeless to conceive   5
As these that twice befell.
Parting is all we know of heaven,
And all we need of hell.

1896

EMILY DICKINSON

Wild Nights! Wild Nights!

Wild Nights—Wild Nights!
Were I with thee
Wild Nights should be
Our luxury!

Futile—the Winds—   5
To a Heart in port—
Done with the Compass—
Done with the Chart!

Rowing in Eden—
Ah, the Sea!   10
Might I but moor—Tonight—
In Thee!

ca. 1861

JOHN DONNE

The Good-Morrow

I wonder, by my troth, what thou and I
    Did, till we loved? were we not weaned till then?
But sucked on country pleasures, childishly?
    Or snorted[1] we in the Seven Sleepers' den?[2]
'Twas so; but[3] this, all pleasures fancies be.   5
If ever any beauty[4] I did see,
Which I desired, and got,[5] 'twas but a dream of thee.

And now good-morrow to our waking souls,
    Which watch not one another out of fear;
For love, all love of other sights controls,   10
    And makes one little room an everywhere.
Let sea-discoverers to new worlds have gone,
Let maps to other,[6] worlds on worlds have shown,
Let us possess one world, each hath one, and is one.

My face in thine eye, thine in mine appears,[7]   15
    And true plain hearts do in the faces rest;
Where can we find two better hemispheres,
    Without sharp north, without declining west?
Whatever dies was not mixed equally,[8]
If our two loves be one, or, thou and I   20
Love so alike that none do slacken, none can die.

                          1633

JOHN DONNE

The Canonization

For God's sake hold your tongue and let me love!
    Or chide my palsy or my gout,
My five gray hairs or ruined fortune flout;
With wealth your state, your mind with arts improve,
    Take you a course, get you a place,   5
    Observe his Honor or his Grace,
Or the king's real or his stampéd face[9]
    Contemplate; what you will, approve,
        So you will let me love.

1. Snored.
2. According to tradition, seven Christian youths escaped Roman persecution by sleeping in a cave for 187 years.
3. Except for.
4. Beautiful woman.
5. Sexually possessed.

6. Other people.
7. I.e., each is reflected in the other's eyes.
8. Perfectly mixed elements, according to scholastic philosophy, were stable and immortal.
9. On coins.

Alas, alas, who's injured by my love?   10
  What merchant's ships have my sighs drowned?
Who says my tears have overflowed his ground?
  When did my colds a forward spring remove?
    When did the heats which my veins fill
    Add one man to the plaguy bill?[1]   15
Soldiers find wars, and lawyers find out still
  Litigious men which quarrels move,
    Though she and I do love.

Call us what you will, we are made such by love.
  Call her one, me another fly,   20
We're tapers[2] too, and at our own cost die;
  And we in us find th' eagle and the dove.[3]
    The phoenix riddle[4] hath more wit[5]
    By us; we two, being one, are it.
So to one neutral thing both sexes fit,   25
  We die and rise the same, and prove
    Mysterious by this love.

We can die by it, if not live by love;
  And if unfit for tombs and hearse
Our legend be, it will be fit for verse;   30
And if no piece of chronicle we prove,[6]
  We'll build in sonnets[7] pretty rooms
  (As well a well-wrought urn becomes[8]
The greatest ashes, as half-acre tombs),
  And by these hymns all shall approve   35
    Us canonized for love.

And thus invoke us: "You whom reverent love
  Made one another's hermitage,
You to whom love was peace, that now is rage,
Who did the whole world's soul extract, and drove[9]   40
  Into the glasses of your eyes
  (So made such mirrors and such spies
That they did all to you epitomize)
  Countries, towns, courts; beg from above
    A pattern of your love!"   45

1633

---

1. List of plague victims.
2. Which consume themselves. To "die" is Renaissance slang for consummating the sexual act, which was popularly believed to shorten life by one day. "fly": a traditional symbol of transitory life.
3. Traditional symbols of strength and purity.
4. According to tradition, only one phoenix existed at a time, dying in a funeral pyre of its own making and being reborn from its own ashes. The bird's existence was thus a riddle akin to a religious mystery (line 27), and a symbol sometimes fused with Christian representations of immortality.
5. Meaning.
6. I.e., if we don't turn out to be an authenticated piece of historical narrative.
7. Love poems. In Italian, *stanza* means rooms.
8. Befits.
9. Compressed.

T. S. ELIOT

Journey of the Magi[1]

"A cold coming we had of it,
Just the worst time of the year
For a journey, and such a long journey:
The ways deep and the weather sharp,
The very dead of winter."[2]   5
And the camels galled, sore-footed, refractory,
Lying down in the melting snow.
There were times we regretted
The summer palaces on slopes, the terraces,
And the silken girls bringing sherbet.   10
Then the camel men cursing and grumbling
And running away, and wanting their liquor and women,
And the night-fires going out, and the lack of shelters,
And the cities hostile and the towns unfriendly
And the villages dirty and charging high prices: 15
A hard time we had of it.
At the end we preferred to travel all night,
Sleeping in snatches,
With the voices singing in our ears, saying
That this was all folly.   20

Then at dawn we came down to a temperate valley,
Wet, below the snow line, smelling of vegetation;
With a running stream and a water-mill beating the darkness,
And three trees on the low sky,[3]
And an old white horse galloped away in the meadow.   25
Then we came to a tavern with vine-leaves over the lintel,
Six hands at an open door dicing for pieces of silver,
And feet kicking the empty wine-skins.
But there was no information, and so we continued
And arrived at evening, not a moment too soon   30
Finding the place; it was (you may say) satisfactory.

All this was a long time ago, I remember,
And I would do it again, but set down
This set down
This: were we led all that way for   35
Birth or Death? There was a Birth, certainly,
We had evidence and no doubt. I had seen birth and death,
But had thought they were different; this Birth was
Hard and bitter agony for us, like Death, our death.
We returned to our places, these Kingdoms,[4]   40

1. The wise men who followed the star of Bethlehem. See *Matthew* 2:1–12.
2. An adaptation of a passage from a 1622 sermon by Lancelot Andrewes.
3. Suggestive of the three crosses of the Crucifixion (*Luke* 23:32–33). The Magi see several objects which suggest later events in Christ's life: pieces of silver (see *Matthew* 26:14–16), the dicing (see *Matthew* 27:35), the white horse (see *Revelation* 6:2 and 19:11–16), and the empty wine-skins (see *Matthew* 9:14–17, possibly relevant also to lines 41–42).
4. The Bible only identifies the wise men as "from the East," and subsequent tradition has made them kings. In Persia, Magi were members of an ancient priestly caste.

But no longer at ease here, in the old dispensation,
With an alien people clutching their gods.
I should be glad of another death.

1927

T. S. ELIOT

The Love Song of J. Alfred Prufrock

> *S'io credesse che mia risposta fosse*
> *A persona che mai tornasse al mondo,*
> *Questa fiamma staria senza piu scosse.*
> *Ma perciocche giammai di questo fondo*
> *Non torno vivo alcun, s'i'odo il vero,*
> *Senza tema d'infamia ti rispondo.*[5]

Let us go then, you and I,
When the evening is spread out against the sky
Like a patient etherized upon a table;
Let us go, through certain half-deserted streets,
The muttering retreats   5
Of restless nights in one-night cheap hotels
And sawdust restaurants with oyster-shells:
Streets that follow like a tedious argument
Of insidious intent
To lead you to an overwhelming question . . .   10
Oh, do not ask, "What is it?"
Let us go and make our visit.

In the room the women come and go
Talking of Michelangelo.

The yellow fog that rubs its back upon the window-panes,   15
The yellow smoke that rubs its muzzle on the window-panes
Licked its tongue into the corners of the evening,
Lingered upon the pools that stand in drains,
Let fall upon its back the soot that falls from chimneys,
Slipped by the terrace, made a sudden leap,   20
And seeing that it was a soft October night,
Curled once about the house, and fell asleep.

And indeed there will be time[6]
For the yellow smoke that slides along the street,

---

5. Dante's *Inferno*, XXVII, 61–66. In the Eighth Chasm, Dante and Vergil meet Count Guido de Montefeltrano, one of the False Counselors. The spirits there are in the form of flames, and Guido speaks from the trembling tip of the flame, responding to Dante's request that he tell his life story: "If I thought that my answer were to someone who would ever go back to earth, this flame would be still, without any more movement. But because no one has ever gone back alive from this chasm (if what I hear is true) I answer you without fear of infamy."

6. See *Ecclesiastes* 3:1ff.: "To everything there is a season, and a time to every purpose under the heaven; A time to be born, and a time to die; a time to plant, and a time to pluck up that which is planted; A time to kill, and a time to heal. . . ." Also see Marvell's "To His Coy Mistress": "Had we but world enough and time. . . ."

Rubbing its back upon the window-panes;   25
There will be time, there will be time
To prepare a face to meet the faces that you meet;
There will be time to murder and create,
And time for all the works and days[7] of hands
That lift and drop a question on your plate;   30
Time for you and time for me,
And time yet for a hundred indecisions,
And for a hundred visions and revisions,
Before the taking of a toast and tea.

　　In the room the women come and go   35
Talking of Michelangelo.

　　And indeed there will be time
To wonder, "Do I dare?" and, "Do I dare?"
Time to turn back and descend the stair,
With a bald spot in the middle of my hair—   40
(They will say: "How his hair is growing thin!")
My morning coat, my collar mounting firmly to the chin,
My necktie rich and modest, but asserted by a simple pin—
(They will say: "But how his arms and legs are thin!")
Do I dare   45
Disturb the universe?

In a minute there is time
For decisions and revisions which a minute will reverse.

　　For I have known them all already, known them all:—
Have known the evenings, mornings, afternoons,   50
I have measured out my life with coffee spoons;
I know the voices dying with a dying fall
Beneath the music from a farther room.
　　So how should I presume?

　　And I have known the eyes already, known them all—   55
The eyes that fix you in a formulated phrase,
And when I am formulated, sprawling on a pin,
When I am pinned and wriggling on the wall,
Then how should I begin
To spit out all the butt-ends of my days and ways?   60
　　And how should I presume?

　　And I have known the arms already, known them all—
Arms that are braceleted and white and bare
(But in the lamplight, downed with light brown hair!)
Is it perfume from a dress   65
That makes me so digress?
Arms that lie along a table, or wrap about a shawl.

---

7. Hesiod's ancient Greek didactic poem   detail how to conduct one's life.
Works and Days prescribed in practical

And should I then presume?
And how should I begin?

. . . . .

Shall I say, I have gone at dusk through narrow streets   70
And watched the smoke that rises from the pipes
Of lonely men in shirt-sleeves, leaning out of windows? . . .

    I should have been a pair of ragged claws
Scuttling across the floors of silent seas.

. . . . .

And the afternoon, the evening, sleeps so peacefully!   75
Smoothed by long fingers,
Asleep . . . tired . . . or it malingers,
Stretched on the floor, here beside you and me.
Should I, after tea and cakes and ices,
Have the strength to force the moment to its crisis?   80
But though I have wept and fasted, wept and prayed,
Though I have seen my head (grown slightly bald) brought in upon
    a platter,[8]
I am no prophet—and here's no great matter;
I have seen the moment of my greatness flicker,
And I have seen the eternal Footman hold my coat, and snicker,   85
And in short, I was afraid.

    And would it have been worth it, after all,
After the cups, the marmalade, the tea,
Among the porcelain, among some talk of you and me,
Would it have been worth while,   90
To have bitten off the matter with a smile,
To have squeezed the universe into a ball[9]
To roll it toward some overwhelming question,
To say: "I am Lazarus,[1] come from the dead,
Come back to tell you all, I shall tell you all"—   95
If one, settling a pillow by her head,
    Should say:"That is not what I meant at all.
    That is not it, at all."

    And would it have been worth it, after all,
Would it have been worth while,   100
After the sunsets and the dooryards and the sprinkled streets,
After the novels, after the teacups, after the skirts that trail along the
    floor—
And this, and so much more?—
It is impossible to say just what I mean!
But as if a magic lantern[2] threw the nerves in patterns on a screen: 105
Would it have been worth while

---

8 See *Matthew* 14.1–12 and *Mark*
6:17–29: John the Baptist was decapitated,
upon Salome's request and at Herod's command, and his head delivered on a platter.
9. See Marvell's "To His Coy Mistress,"
lines 41–42: "Let us roll all our strength
and all / our sweetness up into one
ball. . . ."

1. One Lazarus was raised from the
dead by Jesus (see *John* 1:1 to 2:2), and
another (in the parable of the rich man
Dives) is discussed in terms of returning
from the dead to warn the living (*Luke*
16:19–31).
2. A nonelectric projector used as early
as the 17th century.

If one, settling a pillow or throwing off a shawl,
And turning toward the window, should say:
   "That is not it at all,
   That is not what I meant, at all."   110

   . . . . . .

No! I am not Prince Hamlet, nor was meant to be;
Am an attendant lord,[3] one that will do
To swell a progress,[4] start a scene or two,
Advise the prince; no doubt, an easy tool,
Deferential, glad to be of use,   115
Politic, cautious, and meticulous;
Full of high sentence, but a bit obtuse;
At times, indeed, almost ridiculous—
Almost, at times, the Fool.

   I grow old . . . I grow old . . .   120
I shall wear the bottoms of my trousers rolled.

   Shall I part my hair behind? Do I dare to eat a peach?
I shall wear white flannel trousers, and walk upon the beach.
I have heard the mermaids singing, each to each.

   I do not think that they will sing to me.   125

   I have seen them riding seaward on the waves
Combing the white hair of the waves blown back
When the wind blows the water white and black.

   We have lingered in the chambers of the sea
By sea-girls wreathed with seaweed red and brown   130
Till human voices wake us, and we drown.

                              1917

LAWRENCE FERLINGHETTI

Christ Climbed Down

     Christ climbed down
     from His bare Tree[5]
     this year
     and ran away to where
     there were no rootless Christmas trees   5
     hung with candycanes and breakable stars

     Christ climbed down
     from His bare Tree

---

3. Like Polonius in *Hamlet*, who is full of maxims ("high sentence," line 117).   4. Procession of state.
5. The cross on which he was crucified.

this year
and ran away to where
there were no gilded Christmas trees
and no tinsel Christmas trees
and no tinfoil Christmas trees
and no pink plastic Christmas trees
and no gold Christmas trees
and no black Christmas trees
and no powderblue Christmas trees
hung with electric candles
and encircled by tin electric trains
and clever cornball relatives

Christ climbed down
from His bare Tree
this year
and ran away to where
no intrepid Bible salesmen
covered the territory
in two-tone cadillacs
and where no Sears Roebuck creches[6]
complete with plastic babe in manger
arrived by parcel post
the babe by special delivery
and where no televised Wise Men
praised the Lord Calvert Whiskey

Christ climbed down
from His bare Tree
this year
and ran away to where
no fat handshaking stranger
in a red flannel suit
and a fake white beard
went around passing himself off
as some sort of North Pole saint
crossing the desert to Bethlehem
Pennsylvania
in a Volkswagen sled
drawn by rollicking Adirondack reindeer
with German names
and bearing sacks of Humble Gifts
from Saks Fifth Avenue[7]
for everybody's imagined Christ child

Christ climbed down
from His bare Tree
this year
and ran away to where

10

15

20

25

30

35

40

45

50

---

6. Representations of the nativity scene.
7. A fashionable store in New York City.

no Bing Crosby[8] carollers   55
groaned of a tight Christmas
and where no Radio City angels
iceskated wingless[9]
thru a winter wonderland
into a jinglebell heaven   60
daily at 8:30
with Midnight Mass matinees

Christ climbed down
from His bare Tree
this year   65
and softly stole away into
some anonymous Mary's womb again
where in the darkest night
of everybody's anonymous soul
He awaits again   70
an unimaginable
and impossibly
Immaculate Reconception
the very craziest
of Second Comings   75

1958

JULIA FIELDS

Madness One Monday Evening

Late that mad Monday evening
I made mermaids come from the sea
As the block sky sat
Upon the waves
And night came   5
Creeping up to me

    (I tell you I made mermaids
    Come from the sea)

The green waves lulled and rolled
As I sat by the locust tree   10
And the bright glare of the neon world
Sent gas-words bursting free—
Their spewed splendor fell on the billows
And gaudy it grew to me
As I sat up upon the shore   15
And made mermaids come from the sea.

1964

8. Popular midcentury singer whose record of "White Christmas" was a best-seller.
Crosby was nicknamed "the Groaner"
(line 56).
9. An outdoor ice-skating rink is located
in Rockefeller Center, near Radio City
Music Hall. Midnight mass has traditionally been televised from St. Patrick's
Cathedral nearby.

ROBERT FROST

Range-Finding

The battle rent a cobweb diamond-strung
And cut a flower beside a groundbird's nest
Before it stained a single human breast.
The stricken flower bent double and so hung.
And still the bird revisited her young.   5
A butterfly its fall had dispossessed,
A moment sought in air his flower of rest,
Then lightly stooped to it and fluttering clung.
On the bare upland pasture there had spread
O'ernight 'twixt mullein[1] stalks a wheel of thread   10
And straining cables wet with silver dew.
A sudden passing bullet shook it dry.
The indwelling spider ran to greet the fly,
But finding nothing, sullenly withdrew.

1916

THOMAS HARDY

The Darkling Thrush

I leant upon a coppice gate
    When Frost was specter gray,
And Winter's dregs made desolate
    The weakening eye of day.
The tangled bine-stems scored the sky   5
    Like strings of broken lyres,
And all mankind that haunted nigh
    Had sought their household fires.

The land's sharp features seemed to be
    The Century's corpse outleant,   10
His crypt the cloudy canopy,
    The wind his death-lament.
The ancient pulse of germ and birth
    Was shrunken hard and dry,
And every spirit upon earth   15
    Seemed fervorless as I.

At once a voice arose among
    The bleak twigs overhead
In a full-hearted evensong
    Of joy illimited;   20
An aged thrush, frail, gaunt, and small,
    In blast-beruffled plume,

---

1. Weed.

Had chosen thus to fling his soul
  Upon the growing gloom.

So little cause for carolings   25
  Of such ecstatic sound
Was written on terrestrial things
  Afar or nigh around,
That I could think there trembled through
  His happy good-night air   30
Some blessed Hope, whereof he knew
  And I was unaware.

December 31, 1900

THOMAS HARDY

During Wind and Rain

They sing their dearest songs—
  He, she, all of them—yea,
Treble and tenor and bass,
  And one to play;
With the candles mooning each face. . . .   5
  Ah, no; the years O!
How the sick leaves reel down in throngs!

They clear the creeping moss—
  Elders and juniors—aye,
Making the pathway neat   10
  And the garden gay;
And they build a shady seat. . . .
  Ah, no; the years, the years;
See, the white stormbirds wing across!

They are blithely breakfasting all—   15
  Men and maidens—yea,
Under the summer tree,
  With a glimpse of the bay,
While pet fowl come to the knee. . . .
  Ah, no; the years O!   20
And the rotten rose is ripped from the wall.

They change to a high new house,
  He, she, all of them—aye,
Clocks and carpets, and chairs
  On the lawn all day,   25
And brightest things that are theirs. . . .
  Ah, no; the years, the years;
Down their carved names the rain drop ploughs.

1917

THOMAS HARDY

Hap[2]

If but some vengeful god would call to me
From up the sky, and laugh: "Thou suffering thing,
Know that thy sorrow is my ecstasy,
That thy love's loss is my hate's profiting!"

Then would I bear it, clench myself, and die,   5
Steeled by the sense of ire unmerited;
Half-eased in that a Powerfuller than I
Had willed and meted me the tears I shed.

But not so. How arrives it[3] joy lies slain,
And why unblooms the best hope ever sown?   10
—Crass Casualty[4] obstructs the sun and rain,
And dicing Time for gladness casts a moan. . . .
These purblind Doomsters[5] had as readily strown
Blisses about my pilgrimage as pain.

1866

THOMAS HARDY

Channel Firing[6]

That night your great guns, unawares,
Shook all our coffins as we lay,
And broke the chancel window squares,[7]
We thought it was the Judgment-day[8]

And sat upright. While drearisome   5
Arose the howl of wakened hounds:
The mouse let fall the altar-crumb,[9]
The worms drew back into the mounds,

The glebe cow[1] drooled. Till God called, "No;
It's gunnery practice out at sea   10
Just as before you went below;
The world is as it used to be:

"All nations striving strong to make
Red war yet redder. Mad as hatters

---

2. Chance.
3. How does it happen that.
4. Chance.
5. Those who decide one's fate.
6. Naval practice on the English Channel preceded the outbreak of World War I in the summer of 1914.

7. The windows near the altar in a church.
8. When, according to tradition, the dead will be awakened.
9. Breadcrumbs from the sacrament.
1. Parish cow pastured on the meadow next to the churchyard.

They do no more for Christés sake   15
Than you who are helpless in such matters.

"That this is not the judgment-hour
For some of them's a blessed thing,
For if it were they'd have to scour
Hell's floor for so much threatening . . .   20

"Ha, ha. It will be warmer when
I blow the trumpet (if indeed
I ever do; for you are men,
And rest eternal sorely need)."

So down we lay again. "I wonder,   25
Will the world ever saner be,"
Said one, "than when He sent us under
In our indifferent century!"

And many a skeleton shook his head.
"Instead of preaching forty year,"   30
My neighbor Parson Thirdly said,
"I wish I had stuck to pipes and beer."

Again the guns disturbed the hour,
Roaring their readiness to avenge.
As far inland as Stourton Tower,   35
And Camelot, and starlit Stonehenge.[2]

April, 1914

ANTHONY HECHT

"It Out-Herods Herod. Pray You, Avoid It."[3]

Tonight my children hunch
Toward their Western, and are glad
As, with a Sunday punch,
The Good casts out the Bad.

And in their fairy tales   5
The warty giant and witch

2. Stourton Tower, built in the 18th century to commemorate King Alfred's ninth-century victory over the Danes, in Stourhead Park, Wiltshire. Camelot is the legendary site of King Arthur's court, said to have been in Cornwall or Somerset. Stonehenge, a circular formation of upright stones dating from about 1800 B.C., is on Salisbury Plain, Wiltshire; it is thought to have been a ceremonial site for political and religious occasions or an early scientific experiment in astronomy.

3. *Hamlet*, Act III, sc. ii. Hamlet's advice to the actors about to perform "The Mousetrap" includes a caution against overacting and excessive displays of passion. In medieval mystery plays, the character of Herod was portrayed as wild and bombastic, and the actor who played the part was sometimes allowed to improvise extravagant and spectacular behavior.

Get sealed in doorless jails
And the match-girl strikes it rich.

I've made myself a drink.
The giant and witch are set   10
To bust out of the clink
When my children have gone to bed.

All frequencies are loud
With signals of despair;
In flash and morse they crowd   15
The rondure of the air.

For the wicked have grown strong,
Their numbers mock at death,
Their cow brings forth its young,
Their bull engendereth.   20

Their very fund of strength,
Satan, bestrides the globe;
He stalks its breadth and length
And finds out even Job.[4]

Yet by quite other laws   25
My children make their case;
Half God, half Santa Claus,
But with my voice and face,

A hero comes to save
The poorman, beggarman, thief,   30
And make the world behave
And put an end to grief.

And that their sleep be sound
I say this childermas[5]
Who could not, at one time,   35
Have saved them from the gas.

1968

4. According to the *Book of Job* 1·7–12, Satan has been "going to and fro in the earth, and . . . walking up and down in it" before finding Job, a man of singular righteousness, to torment and tempt. 5. The festival of the Holy Innocents (Childermas) commemorates Herod's slaughter of the children; see *Matthew* 2:16.

GERARD MANLEY HOPKINS

The Windhover[6]

To Christ Our Lord

I caught this morning morning's minion,[7] king-
      dom of daylight's dauphin,[8] dapple-dawn-drawn Falcon, in his
         riding
    Of the rolling level underneath him steady air, and striding
High there, how he rung upon the rein of a wimpling[9] wing
In his ecstasy! then off, off forth on swing,   5
      As a skate's heel sweeps smooth on a bow-bend: the hurl and
         gliding
    Rebuffed the big wind. My heart in hiding
Stirred for a bird,—the achieve of, the mastery of the thing!

Brute beauty and valor and act, oh, air, pride, plume, here
      Buckle![1] AND the fire that breaks from thee then, a billion   10
Times told lovelier, more dangerous, O my chevalier![2]

      No wonder of it: sheér plód makes plow down sillion[3]
Shine, and blue-bleak embers, ah my dear,
    Fall, gall themselves, and gash gold-vermilion.
1877

RICHARD HUGO

To Women

    You start it all. You are lovely.
    We look at you and we flow.
    So a line begins, on the page, on air,
    in the all of self. We have misused you,
    invested you with primal sin. You bleed   5
    for our regret we are not more.
    The dragon wins. We come home and sob
    and you hold us and say we are brave
    and in the future will do better.
    So far, so good.   10

    Now some of you want out and I don't
    blame you, not a tiny bit. You've caught on.
    You have the right to veer off flaming

---

6. A small hawk, the kestrel, which habitually hovers in the air, headed into the wind.
7. Favorite, beloved.
8. Heir to regal splendor.
9. Rippling.
1. Several meanings may apply: to join closely, to prepare for battle, to grapple with, to collapse.
2. Horseman, knight.
3. The narrow strip of land between furrows in an open field divided for separate cultivation.

in a new direction, mud flat and diamond mine,
clavicord and dead drum. Whatever.   15
Please know our need remains the same.
It's a new game every time, one on one.

In me today is less rage than ever, less hurt.
When I imagine some good woman young
I no longer imagine her cringing   20
in cornstalks, cruel father four rows away
beating corn leaves aside with a club.
That is release you never expected
from a past you never knew you had.
My horse is not sure he can make it   25
to the next star. You are free.

                                                              1980

JOHN KEATS

The Eve of St. Agnes[4]

I

St. Agnes' Eve—Ah, bitter chill it was!
The owl, for all his feathers, was a-cold;
The hare limped trembling through the frozen grass,
And silent was the flock in woolly fold:
Numb were the Beadsman's[5] fingers, while he told   5
His rosary, and while his frosted breath,
Like pious incense from a censer old,
Seemed taking flight for heaven, without a death,
Past the sweet Virgin's picture, while his prayer he saith.

II

His prayer he saith, this patient, holy man;   10
Then takes his lamp, and riseth from his knees,
And back returneth, meager, barefoot, wan,
Along the chapel aisle by slow degrees:
The sculptured dead, on each side, seem to freeze,
Emprisoned in black, purgatorial rails: 15
Knights, ladies, praying in dumb orat'ries,[6]
He passeth by; and his weak spirit fails
To think[7] how they may ache in icy hoods and mails.

III

Northward he turneth through a little door,
And scarce three steps, ere Music's golden tongue   20

---

4. Martyred early in the fourth century at the age of 13, St. Agnes became the patron saint of virgins. According to popular belief, if a virgin performed the proper ritual on St. Agnes' Eve (January 20), she would dream of her future husband.

5. Someone paid to pray for the soul of another. "told": counted his beads.
6. Silent chapels inside the larger chapel.
7. When he thinks. "mails": suits of armor.

Flattered[8] to tears this aged man and poor;
But no—already had his deathbell rung:
The joys of all his life were said and sung:
His was harsh penance on St. Agnes' Eve:
Another way he went, and soon among   25
Rough ashes sat he for his soul's reprieve,
And all night kept awake, for sinners' sake to grieve.

IV

That ancient Beadsman heard the prelude soft;
And so it chanced, for many a door was wide,
From hurry to and fro. Soon, up aloft,   30
The silver, snarling trumpets 'gan to chide:
The level chambers, ready with their pride,[9]
Were glowing to receive a thousand guests:
The carvéd angels, ever eager-eyed,
Stared, where upon their heads the cornice rests,   35
With hair blown back, and wings put cross-wise on their breasts.

V

At length burst in the argent revelry,[1]
With plume, tiara, and all rich array,
Numerous as shadows haunting fairily
The brain, new stuffed, in youth, with triumphs gay   40
Of old romance. These let us wish away,
And turn, sole-thoughted, to one Lady there,
Whose heart had brooded, all that wintry day,
On love, and winged St. Agnes' saintly care,
As she had heard old dames full many times declare.   45

VI

They told her how, upon St. Agnes' Eve,
Young virgins might have visions of delight,
And soft adorings from their loves receive
Upon the honeyed middle of the night,
If ceremonies due they did aright;   50
As, supperless to bed they must retire,
And couch supine their beauties, lily white;
Nor look behind, nor sideways, but require
Of Heaven with upward eyes for all that they desire.

VII

Full of this whim was thoughtful Madeline: 55
The music, yearning like a God in pain,
She scarcely heard: her maiden eyes divine,
Fixed on the floor, saw many a sweeping train
Pass by—she heeded not at all: in vain
Came many a tiptoe, amorous cavalier,   60
And back retired; not cooled by high disdain,

8. Coaxed, beguiled.   1. Silver-clad revelers.
9. Splendor.

But she saw not: her heart was otherwhere:
She sighed for Agnes' dreams, the sweetest of the year.

VIII

She danced along with vague, regardless eyes,
Anxious her lips, her breathing quick and short: 65
The hallowed hour was near at hand: she sighs
Amid the timbrels,[2] and the thronged resort
Of whisperers in anger, or in sport;
'Mid looks of love, defiance, hate, and scorn,
Hoodwinked with faery fancy; all amort,[3]   70
Save to St. Agnes and her lambs unshorn,[4]
And all the bliss to be before tomorrow morn.

IX

So, purposing each moment to retire,
She lingered still. Meantime, across the moors,
Had come young Porphyro, with heart on fire   75
For Madeline. Beside the portal doors,
Buttressed[5] from moonlight, stands he, and implores
All saints to give him sight of Madeline,
But for one moment in the tedious hours,
That he might gaze and worship all unseen;   80
Perchance speak, kneel, touch, kiss—in sooth such things have been.

X

He ventures in: let no buzzed whisper tell:
All eyes be muffled, or a hundred swords
Will storm his heart, Love's fev'rous citadel:
For him, those chambers held barbarian hordes,   85
Hyena foemen, and hot-blooded lords,
Whose very dogs would execrations howl
Against his lineage:[6] not one breast affords
Him any mercy, in that mansion foul,
Save one old beldame,[7] weak in body and in soul.   90

XI

Ah, happy chance! the aged creature came,
Shuffling along with ivory-headed wand,[8]
To where he stood, hid from the torch's flame,
Behind a broad hall-pillar, far beyond
The sound of merriment and chorus bland:[9]   95
He startled her; but soon she knew his face,
And grasped his fingers in her palsied hand,
Saying, "Mercy, Porphyro! hie thee from this place;
They are all here tonight, the whole blood-thirsty race!

2. Small hand drums or tambourines.
3. Deadened: oblivious.
4. At the feast of St. Agnes the next day, lamb's wool was traditionally offered; later, nuns wove it into cloth (lines 115–17).
5. Shaded by the wall supports.
6. Because of the feud between his family and Madeline's.
7. Old, usually ugly, woman.
8. Walking stick, cane.
9. Soothing.

XII

Get hence! get hence! there's dwarfish Hildebrand;   100
He had a fever late, and in the fit
He curséd thee and thine, both house and land:
Then there's that old Lord Maurice, not a whit
More tame for his gray hairs—Alas me! flit!
Flit like a ghost away."—"Ah, Gossip[1] dear,   105
We're safe enough; here in this arm-chair sit,
And tell me how"—"Good Saints! not here, not here;
Follow me, child, or else these stones will be thy bier."

XIII

He followed through a lowly archéd way,
Brushing the cobwebs with his lofty plume,   110
And as she muttered "Well-a—well-a-day!"
He found him in a little moonlight room,
Pale, latticed, chill, and silent as a tomb.
"Now tell me where is Madeline," said he,
"O tell me, Angela, by the holy loom   115
Which none but secret sisterhood may see,
When they St. Agnes' wool are weaving piously."

XIV

"St. Agnes! Ah! it is St. Agnes' Eve—
Yet men will murder upon holy days:
Thou must hold water in a witch's sieve,   120
And be liege-lord of all the Elves and Fays,
To venture so:[2] it fills me with amaze
To see thee, Porphyro!—St. Agnes' Eve!
God's help! my lady fair the conjuror plays[3]
This very night: good angels her deceive!   125
But let me laugh awhile, I've mickle[4] time to grieve."

XV

Feebly she laugheth in the languid moon,
While Porphyro upon her face doth look,
Like puzzled urchin on an aged crone
Who keepeth closed a wond'rous riddle-book,   130
As spectacled she sits in chimney nook.
But soon his eyes grew brilliant, when she told
His lady's purpose; and he scarce could brook[5]
Tears, at the thought of those enchantments cold
And Madeline asleep in lap of legends old.   135

1. Old friend.
2. I.e., Porphyro would need to be a
magician to take such chances.
3. In trying to evoke the image of her
lover.
4. Plenty of.
5. Hold back.

XVI

Sudden a thought came like a full-blown rose,
Flushing his brow, and in his painéd heart
Made purple riot: then doth he propose
A stratagem, that makes the beldame start:
"A cruel man and impious thou art: 140
Sweet lady, let her pray, and sleep, and dream
Alone with her good angels, far apart
From wicked men like thee. Go, go!—I deem
Thou canst not surely be the same that thou didst seem."

XVII

"I will not harm her, by all saints I swear,"   145
Quoth Porphyro: "O may I ne'er find grace
When my weak voice shall whisper its last prayer,
If one of her soft ringlets I displace,
Or look with ruffian passion in her face:
Good Angela, believe me by these tears;   150
Or I will, even in a moment's space,
Awake, with horrid shout, my foemen's ears,
And beard[6] them, though they be more fanged than wolves and bears."

XVIII

"Ah! why wilt thou affright a feeble soul?
A poor, weak, palsy-stricken, churchyard thing,   155
Whose passing-bell[7] may ere the midnight toll;
Whose prayers for thee, each morn and evening,
Were never missed."—Thus plaining,[8] doth she bring
A gentler speech from burning Porphyro;
So woeful, and of such deep sorrowing,   160
That Angela gives promise she will do
Whatever he shall wish, betide her weal or woe.[9]

XIX

Which was, to lead him, in close secrecy,
Even to Madeline's chamber, and there hide
Him in a closet, of such privacy   165
That he might see her beauty unespied,
And win perhaps that night a peerless bride,
While legioned fairies paced the coverlet,
And pale enchantment held her sleepy-eyed.
Never on such a night have lovers met,   170
Since Merlin paid his Demon all the monstrous debt.[1]

---

6. Defy, affront.
7. Bell that rings for death.
8. Complaining.
9. Whatever happens to her, good or bad.

1. Merlin was a powerful magician in the Arthurian legends; the incident referred to here has not been identified.

XX

"It shall be as thou wishest," said the Dame:
"All cates[2] and dainties shall be storéd there
Quickly on this feast-night: by the tambour frame[3]
Her own lute thou wilt see: no time to spare,   175
For I am slow and feeble, and scarce dare
On such a catering trust my dizzy head.
Wait here, my child, with patience; kneel in prayer
The while: Ah! thou must needs the lady wed,
Or may I never leave my grave among the dead."   180

XXI

So saying, she hobbled off with busy fear.
The lover's endless minutes slowly passed;
The dame returned, and whispered in his ear
To follow her; with agéd eyes aghast
From fright of dim espial. Safe at last,   185
Through many a dusky gallery, they gain
The maiden's chamber, silken, hushed, and chaste;
Where Porphyro took covert, pleased amain.[4]
His poor guide hurried back with agues in her brain.

XXII

Her falt'ring hand upon the balustrade,   190
Old Angela was feeling for the stair,
When Madeline, St. Agnes' charméd maid,
Rose, like a missioned spirit,[5] unaware:
With silver taper's light, and pious care,
She turned, and down the agéd gossip led   195
To a safe level matting. Now prepare,
Young Porphyro, for gazing on that bed;
She comes, she comes again, like ring dove frayed[6] and fled.

XXIII

Out went the taper as she hurried in;
Its little smoke, in pallid moonshine, died: 200
She closed the door, she panted, all akin
To spirits of the air, and visions wide:
No uttered syllable, or, woe betide!
But to her heart, her heart was voluble,
Paining with eloquence her balmy side;   205
As though a tongueless nightingale should swell
Her throat in vain, and die, heart-stifled, in her dell.

XXIV

A casement[7] high and triple-arched there was,
All garlanded with carven imag'ries
Of fruits, and flowers, and bunches of knot-grass,   210

2. Delicacies.
3. Embroidery frame.
4. Greatly.
5. Angel on a mission.

6. Frightened.
7. Window, in which are stained-glass representations of many kinds, including a royal coat of arms (line 216).

And diamonded with panes of quaint device,
Innumerable of stains and splendid dyes,
As are the tiger moth's deep-damasked wings;
And in the midst, 'mong thousand heraldries,
And twilight saints, and dim emblazonings,   215
A shielded scutcheon blushed with blood of queens and kings.

XXV

Full on this casement shone the wintry moon,
And threw warm gules[8] on Madeline's fair breast,
As down she knelt for heaven's grace and boon;[9]
Rose-bloom fell on her hands, together pressed,   220
And on her silver cross soft amethyst,
And on her hair a glory,[1] like a saint:
She seemed a splendid angel, newly dressed,
Save wings, for heaven—Porphyro grew faint:
She knelt, so pure a thing, so free from mortal taint.   225

XXVI

Anon his heart revives: her vespers done,
Of all its wreathéd pearls her hair she frees;
Unclasps her warméd jewels one by one;
Loosens her fragrant bodice; by degrees
Her rich attire creeps rustling to her knees: 230
Half-hidden, like a mermaid in sea-weed,
Pensive awhile she dreams awake, and sees,
In fancy, fair St. Agnes in her bed,
But dares not look behind, or all the charm is fled.

XXVII

Soon, trembling in her soft and chilly nest,   235
In sort of wakeful swoon, perplexed she lay,
Until the poppied warmth of sleep oppressed
Her soothéd limbs, and soul fatigued away;
Flown, like a thought, until the morrow-day;
Blissfully havened both from joy and pain;   240
Clasped like a missal where swart Paynims[2] pray;
Blinded alike from sunshine and from rain,
As though a rose should shut, and be a bud again.

XXVIII

Stol'n to this paradise, and so entranced,
Porphyro gazed upon her empty dress,   245
And listened to her breathing, if it chanced
To wake into a slumberous tenderness;
Which when he heard, that minute did he bless,
And breathed himself: then from the closet crept,
Noiseless as fear in a wide wilderness,   250

8. Heraldic red.   1. Halo.
9. Gift, blessing.   2. Pagans.

And over the hushed carpet, silent, stepped,
And 'tween the curtains peeped, where, lo!—how fast she slept.

XXIX

Then by the bedside, where the faded moon
Made a dim, silver twilight, soft he set
A table, and, half anguished, threw thereon   255
A cloth of woven crimson, gold, and jet—
O for some drowsy Morphean amulet![3]
The boisterous, midnight, festive clarion,[4]
The kettledrum, and far-heard clarinet,
Affray his ears, though but in dying tone—   260
The hall door shuts again, and all the noise is gone.

XXX

And still she slept an azure-lidded sleep,
In blanchéd linen, smooth, and lavendered,
While he from forth the closet brought a heap
Of candied apple, quince, and plum, and gourd;   265
With jellies soother than the creamy curd,
And lucent syrups, tinct with cinnamon;
Manna[5] and dates, in argosy[6] transferred
From Fez; and spicéd dainties, every one,
From silken Samarcand to cedared Lebanon.   270

XXXI

These delicates he heaped with glowing hand
On golden dishes and in baskets bright
Of wreathéd silver: sumptuous they stand
In the retired quiet of the night,
Filling the chilly room with perfume light.   275
"And now, my love, my seraph[7] fair, awake!
Thou art my heaven, and I thine eremite:
Open thine eyes, for meek St. Agnes' sake,
Or I shall drowse beside thee, so my soul doth ache."

XXXII

Thus whispering, his warm, unnervéd arm   280
Sank in her pillow. Shaded was her dream
By the dusk curtains:—'twas a midnight charm
Impossible to melt as icéd stream:
The lustrous salvers in the moonlight gleam;
Broad golden fringe upon the carpet lies: 285
It seemed he never, never could redeem
From such a steadfast spell his lady's eyes;
So mused awhile, entoiled[8] in wooféd fantasies.

---

3. A charm of Morpheus, god of sleep.
4. Trumpet.
5. Sweet gum.
6. Merchant ships. Fez, Samarcand, and Lebanon are in Morocco, central Asia, and the Levant, respectively.
7. The highest order of angel. "eremite": devotee.
8. Entangled. "wooféd": woven.

XXXIII

Awakening up, he took her hollow lute—
Tumultuous—and, in chords that tenderest be,   290
He played an ancient ditty, long since mute,
In Provence called, "La belle dame sans merci": [9]
Close to her ear touching the melody—
Wherewith disturbed, she uttered a soft moan:
He ceased—she panted quick—and suddenly   295
Her blue affrayéd eyes wide open shone:
Upon his knees he sank, pale as smooth-sculptured stone.

XXXIV

Her eyes were open, but she still beheld,
Now wide awake, the vision of her sleep:
There was a painful change, that nigh expelled   300
The blisses of her dream so pure and deep,
At which fair Madeline began to weep,
And moan forth witless words with many a sigh;
While still her gaze on Porphyro would keep;
Who knelt, with joinéd hands and piteous eye,   305
Fearing to move or speak, she looked so dreamingly.

XXXV

"Ah, Porphyro!" said she, "but even now
Thy voice was at sweet tremble in mine ear,
Made tunable with every sweetest vow;
And those sad eyes were spiritual and clear: 310
How changed thou art! how pallid, chill, and drear!
Give me that voice again, my Porphyro,
Those looks immortal, those complainings dear!
Oh leave me not in this eternal woe,
For if thou diest, my Love, I know not where to go."   315

XXXVI

Beyond a mortal man impassioned far
At these voluptuous accents, he arose,
Ethereal, flushed, and like a throbbing star
Seen mid the sapphire heaven's deep repose
Into her dream he melted, as the rose   320
Blendeth its odor with the violet—
Solution sweet: meantime the frost-wind blows
Like Love's alarum pattering the sharp sleet
Against the windowpanes; St. Agnes' moon hath set.

XXXVII

'Tis dark: quick pattereth the flaw-blown[1] sleet: 325
"This is no dream, my bride, my Madeline!"
'Tis dark: the icéd gusts still rave and beat:
"No dream, alas! alas! and woe is mine!

---

9. "The beautiful lady without pity,"
the kind of love song played or sung in
medieval Provence.
1. Gust-blown.

Porphyro will leave me here to fade and pine.
Cruel! what traitor could thee hither bring?   330
I curse not, for my heart is lost in thine,
Though thou forsakest a deceivéd thing—
A dove forlorn and lost with sick unprunéd wing."

XXXVIII

"My Madeline! sweet dreamer! lovely bride!
Say, may I be for aye[2] thy vassal blest?   335
Thy beauty's shield, heart-shaped and vermeil[3] dyed?
Ah, silver shrine, here will I take my rest
After so many hours of toil and quest,
A famished pilgrim—saved by miracle.
Though I have found, I will not rob thy nest   340
Saving of thy sweet self; if thou think'st well
To trust, fair Madeline, to no rude infidel.

XXXIX

"Hark! 'tis an elfin-storm from faery land,
Of haggard[4] seeming, but a boon indeed:
Arise—arise! the morning is at hand—   345
The bloated wassailers[5] will never heed—
Let us away, my love, with happy speed;
There are no ears to hear, or eyes to see—
Drowned all in Rhenish and the sleepy mead:[6]
Awake! arise! my love, and fearless be,   350
For o'er the southern moors I have a home for thee."

XL

She hurried at his words, beset with fears,
For there were sleeping dragons all around,
At glaring watch, perhaps, with ready spears—
Down the wide stairs a darkling way they found.   355
In all the house was heard no human sound.
A chain-drooped lamp was flickering by each door;
The arras,[7] rich with horseman, hawk, and hound,
Fluttered in the besieging wind's uproar;
And the long carpets rose along the gusty floor.   360

XLI

They glide, like phantoms, into the wide hall;
Like phantoms, to the iron porch, they glide;
Where lay the Porter, in uneasy sprawl,
With a huge empty flagon by his side:
The wakeful bloodhound rose, and shook his hide,   365
But his sagacious eye an inmate[8] owns:
By one, and one, the bolts full easy slide—

2. Forever.
3. Vermilion: bright red.
4. Wild.
5. Drunken revelers.
6. Liquor made from honey. "Rhenish":
rhine wine.
7. Tapestry.
8. Member of the household. "owns": recognizes.

The chains lie silent on the footworn stones—
The key turns, and the door upon its hinges groans.

XLII

And they are gone: ay, ages long ago   370
These lovers fled away into the storm.
That night the Baron dreamt of many a woe,
And all his warrior-guests, with shade and form,
Of witch, and demon, and large coffin-worm,
Were long be-nightmared. Angela the old   375
Died palsy-twitched, with meager face deform;
The Beadsman, after thousand aves[9] told,
For aye unsought for slept among his ashes cold.

1819

D. H. LAWRENCE

Piano

Softly, in the dusk, a woman is singing to me;
Taking me back down the vista of years, till I see
A child sitting under the piano, in the boom of the tingling strings
And pressing the small, poised feet of a mother who smiles as she sings.

In spite of myself, the insidious mastery of song   5
Betrays me back, till the heart of me weeps to belong
To the old Sunday evenings at home, with winter outside
And hymns in the cozy parlor, the tinkling piano our guide.

So now it is vain for the singer to burst into clamor
With the great black piano appassionato. The glamour   10
Of childish days is upon me, my manhood is cast
Down in the flood of remembrance, I weep like a child for the past.

1918

D. H. LAWRENCE

Snake

A snake came to my water-trough
On a hot, hot day, and I in pajamas for the heat,
To drink there.

In the deep, strange-scented shade of the great dark carob-tree

9. Ave Maria's: Hail Mary's.

I came down the steps with my pitcher   5
And must wait, must stand and wait, for there he was at the trough
   before me.

He reached down from a fissure in the earth-wall in the gloom
And trailed his yellow-brown slackness soft-bellied down, over the
   edge of the stone trough
And rested his throat upon the stone bottom,
And where the water had dripped from the tap, in a small clearness,   10
He sipped with his straight mouth,
Softly drank through his straight gums, into his slack long body,
Silently.

Someone was before me at my water-trough,
And I, like a second comer, waiting.   15

He lifted his head from his drinking, as cattle do,
And looked at me vaguely, as drinking cattle do,
And flickered his two-forked tongue from his lips, and mused a
   moment,
And stooped and drank a little more,
Being earth-brown, earth-golden from the burning bowels of the
   earth
On the day of Sicilian July, with Etna[1] smoking.   20

The voice of my education said to me
He must be killed,
For in Sicily the black, black snakes are innocent, the gold are
   venomous.

And voices in me said, If you were a man   25
You would take a stick and break him now, and finish him off.

But must I confess how I liked him,
How glad I was he had come like a guest in quiet, to drink at my
   water-trough

And depart peaceful, pacified, and thankless,
Into the burning bowels of this earth?   30

Was it cowardice, that I dared not kill him?
Was it perversity, that I longed to talk to him?

Was it humility, to feel so honored?
I felt so honored.

And yet those voices: 35
If you were not afraid, you would kill him!

And truly I was afraid, I was most afraid,
But even so, honored still more

1. Mount Etna, the tallest active volcano in Europe. Lawrence wrote the poem in
Taormina, a town overlooking the Ionian Sea, not far from Etna.

That he should seek my hospitality
From out the dark door of the secret earth.   40

He drank enough
And lifted his head, dreamily, as one who has drunken,
And flickered his tongue like a forked night on the air, so black,
Seeming to lick his lips,
And looked around like a god, unseeing, into the air,   45
And slowly turned his head,
And slowly, very slowly, as if thrice adream,
Proceeded to draw his slow length curving round
And climb again the broken bank of my wall-face.

And as he put his head into that dreadful hole,   50
And as he slowly drew up, snake-easing his shoulders, and
   entered farther,
A sort of horror, a sort of protest against his withdrawing into that
   horrid black hole,
Deliberately going into the blackness, and slowly drawing himself
   after,
Overcame me now his back was turned.

I looked round, I put down my pitcher,   55
I picked up a clumsy log
And threw it at the water-trough with a clatter.

I think it did not hit him,
But suddenly that part of him that was left behind convulsed in
   undignified haste
Writhed like lightning, and was gone   60
Into the black hole, the earth-lipped fissure in the wall-front,
At which, in the intense still noon, I stared with fascination.

And immediately I regretted it.
I thought how paltry, how vulgar, what a mean act!
I despised myself and the voices of my accursed human education.   65
And I thought of the albatross[2]
And I wished he would come back, my snake.

For he seemed to me again like a king,
Like a king in exile, uncrowned in the underworld,
Now due to be crowned again.   70

And so, I missed my chance with one of the lords
Of life.
And I have something to expiate;
A pettiness.
Taormina, 1923

2. In Coleridge's poem *The Rime of the Ancient Mariner*, the mariner brings bad luck to his ship by gratuitously killing an albatross, and his shipmates hang the dead bird around his neck. As he comes to accept his kinship with the natural world, his act is expiated, and the bird finally falls to the ground when the mariner blesses a watersnake.

ROBERT LOWELL

Skunk Hour

(For Elizabeth Bishop)

Nautilus Island's hermit
heiress still lives through winter in her Spartan cottage;
her sheep still graze above the sea.
Her son's a bishop. Her farmer
is first selectman[3] in our village,   5
she's in her dotage.

Thirsting for
the hierarchic privacy
of Queen Victoria's century,
she buys up all   10
the eyesores facing her shore,
and lets them fall.

The season's ill—
we've lost our summer millionaire,
who seemed to leap from an L. L. Bean[4]   15
catalogue. His nine-knot yawl
was auctioned off to lobstermen.
A red fox stain covers Blue Hill.

And now our fairy
decorator brightens his shop for fall,   20
his fishnet's filled with orange cork,
orange, his cobbler's bench and awl,
there is no money in his work,
he'd rather marry.

One dark night,   25
my Tudor Ford climbed the hill's skull,
I watched for love-cars. Lights turned down,
they lay together, hull to hull,
where the graveyard shelves on the town. . . .
My mind's not right.   30

A car radio bleats,
"Love, O careless Love. . . ."[5] I hear
my ill-spirit sob in each blood cell,
as if my hand were at its throat. . . .
I myself am hell;   35
nobody's here—

only skunks, that search
in the moonlight for a bite to eat.

3. An elected New England town official.   5. A popular song.
4. Famous old Maine sporting goods firm.

They march on their soles up Main Street:
white stripes, moonstruck eyes' red fire   40
under the chalk-dry and spar spire
of the Trinitarian Church.

I stand on top
of our back steps and breathe the rich air—
a mother skunk with her column of kittens swills the garbage pail.   45
She jabs her wedge head in a cup
of sour cream, drops her ostrich tail,
and will not scare.

1959

ELI MANDEL

Houdini[6]

I suspect he knew that trunks are metaphors,
could distinguish between the finest rhythms
unrolled on rope or singing in a chain
and knew the metrics of the deepest pools

I think of him listening to the words   5
spoken by manacles, cells, handcuffs,
chests, hampers, roll-top desks, vaults,
especially the deep words spoken by coffins

escape, escape: quaint Harry in his suit
his chains, his desk, attached to all attachments   10
how he'd sweat in that precise struggle
with those binding words, wrapped around him
like that mannered style, his formal suit

and spoken when? by whom? What think first said
"there's no way out"?; so that he'd free himself,   15
leap, squirm, no matter how, to chain himself again,
once more jump out of the deep alive
with all his chains singing around his feet
like the bound crowds who sigh, who sigh.

1967

---

6. Harry Houdini (1874–1926), American magician and escape-artist; he was
especially famous for spectacular "challenge" acts in which he allowed members
of his audience to tie him up, handcuff
him, and lock him in boxes, trunks,
coffins, etc., and for an act in which he
escaped from a Water Torture Cell while
submerged upside down.

ANDREW MARVELL

The Garden

How vainly men themselves amaze[7]
To win the palm, the oak, or bays,[8]
And their incessant labors see
Crowned from some single herb, or tree,
Whose short and narrow-vergéd[9] shade   5
Does prudently their toils upbraid;
While all flowers and all trees do close[1]
To weave the garlands of repose!

Fair Quiet, have I found thee here,
And Innocence, thy sister dear?   10
Mistaken long, I sought you then
In busy companies of men.
Your sacred plants,[2] if here below,
Only among the plants will grow;
Society is all but rude[3]   15
To[4] this delicious solitude.

No white nor red was ever seen
So am'rous as this lovely green.
Fond lovers, cruel as their flame,
Cut in these trees their mistress' name: 20
Little, alas, they know, or heed
How far these beauties hers exceed!
Fair trees, wheresoe'er your barks I wound,
No name shall but your own be found.

When we have run our passion's heat,   25
Love hither makes his best retreat.
The gods, that mortal beauty chase,
Still in a tree did end their race:
Apollo hunted Daphne so,
Only that she might laurel grow;   30
And Pan did after Syrinx speed,
Not as a nymph, but for a reed.[5]

What wondrous life is this I lead!
Ripe apples drop about my head;
The luscious clusters of the vine   35
Upon my mouth do crush their wine;
The nectarine and curious[6] peach
Into my hands themselves do reach;

---

7. Become frenzied.
8. Awards for athletic, civic, and literary achievements.
9. Narrowly cropped.
1. Unite.
2. Cuttings.
3. Barbarous.

4. Compared to.
5. In Ovid's *Metamorphoses,* Daphne, pursued by Apollo, is turned into a laurel, and Syrinx, pursued by Pan, into a reed which Pan makes into a flute.
6. Exquisite.

Stumbling on melons, as I pass,
Insnared with flowers, I fall on grass.   40

    Meanwhile the mind, from pleasure less,
Withdraws into its happiness;[7]
The mind, that ocean where each kind
Does straight its own resemblance find;[8]
Yet it creates, transcending these,   45
Far other worlds and other seas,
Annihilating[9] all that's made
To a green thought in a green shade.

    Here at the fountain's sliding foot,
Or at some fruit tree's mossy root,   50
Casting the body's vest[1] aside,
My soul into the boughs does glide:
There, like a bird, it sits and sings,
Then whets[2] and combs its silver wings,
And, till prepared for longer flight,   55
Waves in its plumes the various[3] light.

    Such was that happy garden-state,
While man there walked without a mate:
After a place so pure, and sweet,
What other help could yet be meet![4]   60
But 'twas beyond a mortal's share
To wander solitary there:
Two paradises 'twere in one
To live in paradise alone.

    How well the skillful gardener drew   65
Of flowers and herbs this dial[5] new,
Where, from above, the milder sun
Does through a fragrant zodiac run;
And as it works, th' industrious bee
Computes its time as well as we!   70
How could such sweet and wholesome hours
Be reckoned but with herbs and flowers?

1681

---

7. I.e., the mind withdraws from lesser
sense pleasure into contemplation.
8. All land creatures were supposed to
have corresponding sea-creatures.
9. Reducing to nothing by comparison.
1. Vestment, clothing; the flesh is being
considered as simply clothing for the soul.
2. Preens.
3. Many-colored.
4. Appropriate.
5. A garden planted in the shape of a
sundial, complete with zodiac.

JAMES MERRILL

Watching the Dance

1. BALANCHINE'S[6]

> Poor savage, doubting that a river flows
> But for the myriad eddies made
> By unseen powers twirling on their toes,
>
> Here in this darkness it would seem
> You had already died, and were afraid.   5
> Be still. Observe the powers. Infer the stream.

2. DISCOTHÈQUE.

> Having survived entirely your own youth,
> Last of your generation, purple gloom
> Investing you, sit, Jonah,[7] beyond speech,
>
> And let towards the brute volume VOOM whale mouth   10
> VAM pounding viscera VAM VOOM
> A teenage plankton luminously twitch.

1967

CZESLAW MILOSZ

A Poor Christian Looks at the Ghetto[8]

Bees build around red liver,
Ants build around black bone.
It has begun: the tearing, the trampling on silks,
It has begun: the breaking of glass, wood, copper, nickel, silver, foam
Of gypsum, iron sheets, violin strings, trumpets, leaves, balls, crystals.   5
Poof! Phosphorescent fire from yellow walls
Engulfs animal and human hair.

Bees build around the honeycomb of lungs,
Ants build around white bone.
Torn is paper, rubber, linen, leather, flax,   10
Fiber, fabrics, cellulose, snakeskin, wire.

---

6. George Balanchine, Russian-born (1894) ballet choreographer and teacher.
7. According to *Jonah* 4, Jonah sat in gloom near Nineveh after its residents re-pented and God decided to spare the city from destruction.
8. Translated from the Polish by the author.

The roof and the wall collapse in flame and heat seizes the foundations.
Now there is only the earth, sandy, trodden down,
With one leafless tree.

Slowly, boring a tunnel, a guardian mole makes his way,   15
With a small red lamp fastened to his forehead.
He touches burned bodies, counts them, pushes on,
He distinguishes human ashes by their luminous vapor,
The ashes of each man by a different part of the spectrum.
Bees build around a red trace.   20
Ants build around the place left by my body.

I am afraid, so afraid of the guardian mole.
He has swollen eyelids, like a Patriarch
Who has sat much in the light of candles
Reading the great book of the species.   25
What will I tell him, I, a Jew of the New Testament,
Waiting two thousand years for the second coming of Jesus?
My broken body will deliver me to his sight
And he will count me among the helpers of death:
The uncircumcised.   30

         1943

HOWARD NEMEROV

Life Cycle of Common Man

Roughly figured, this man of moderate habits,
This average consumer of the middle class,
Consumed in the course of his average life span
Just under half a million cigarettes,
Four thousand fifths of gin and about   5
A quarter as much vermouth; he drank
Maybe a hundred thousand cups of coffee,
And counting his parents' share it cost
Something like half a million dollars
To put him through life. How many beasts   10
Died to provide him with meat, belt and shoes
Cannot be certainly said.
              But anyhow,
It is in this way that a man travels through time,
Leaving behind him a lengthening trail   15
Of empty bottles and bones, of broken shoes,
Frayed collars and worn out or outgrown
Diapers and dinnerjackets, silk ties and slickers.

Given the energy and security thus achieved,
He did . . . ? What? The usual things, of course,   20
The eating, dreaming, drinking and begetting,
And he worked for the money which was to pay
For the eating, et cetera, which were necessary
If he were to go on working for the money, et cetera,
But chiefly he talked. As the bottles and bones   25
Accumulated behind him, the words proceeded
Steadily from the front of his face as he
Advanced into the silence and made it verbal.
Who can tally the tale of his words? A lifetime
Would barely suffice for their repetition;   30
If you merely printed all his commas the result
Would be a very large volume, and the number of times
He said "thank you" or "very little sugar, please,"
Would stagger the imagination. There were also
Witticisms, platitudes, and statements beginning   35
"It seems to me" or "As I always say."

Consider the courage in all that, and behold the man
Walking into deep silence, with the ectoplastic
Cartoon's balloon of speech proceeding
Steadily out of the front of his face, the words   40
Borne along on the breath which is his spirit
Telling the numberless tale of his untold Word[6]
Which makes the world his apple, and forces him to eat.

1960

SYLVIA PLATH

Black Rook in Rainy Weather

On the stiff twig up there
Hunches a wet black rook
Arranging and rearranging its feathers in the rain.
I do not expect miracle
Or an accident   5

---

6. *Logos,* the principle of creation and order.

To set the sight on fire
In my eye, nor seek
Any more in the desultory weather some design,
But let spotted leaves fall as they fall,
Without ceremony, or portent   10

Although, I admit, I desire,
Occasionally, some backtalk
From the mute sky, I can't honestly complain:
A certain minor light may still
Leap incandescent   15

Out of kitchen table or chair
As if a celestial burning took
Possession of the most obtuse objects now and then—
Thus hallowing an interval
Otherwise inconsequent   20

By bestowing largesse, honor,
One might say love. At any rate, I now walk
Wary (for it could happen
Even in this dull, ruinous landscape); skeptical,
Yet politic; ignorant   25

Of whatever angel may choose to flare
Suddenly at my elbow. I only know that a rook
Ordering its black feathers can so shine
As to seize my senses, haul
My eyelids up, and grant   30

A brief respite from fear
Of total neutrality. With luck,
Trekking stubborn through this season
Of fatigue, I shall
Patch together a content   35

Of sorts. Miracles occur,
If you care to call those spasmodic
Tricks of radiance miracles. The wait's begun again,
The long wait for the angel,
For that rare, random descent.[7]   40

1960

---

7. According to *Acts* 2, the Holy Ghost at Pentecost descended like a dove upon Christ's disciples.

EZRA POUND

In a Station of the Metro[8]

The apparition of these faces in the crowd;
Petals on a wet, black bough.

p. 1913

EZRA POUND

A Virginal

No, no! Go from me. I have left her lately.
I will not spoil my sheath with lesser brightness,
For my surrounding air hath a new lightness;
Slight are her arms, yet they have bound me straitly
And left me cloaked as with a gauze of æther;   5
As with sweet leaves; as with a subtle clearness.
Oh, I have picked up magic in her nearness
To sheathe me half in half the things that sheathe her.
No, no! Go from me, I have still the flavor,
Soft as spring wind that's come from birchen bowers.   10
Green come the shoots, aye April in the branches,
As winter's wound with her sleight hand she staunches,
Hath of the trees a likeness of the savor:
As white their bark, so white this lady's hours.

1912

JOHN PRESS

Womanizers

Adulterers and customers of whores
And cunning takers of virginities
Caper from bed to bed, but not because
The flesh is pricked to infidelities.

The body is content with homely fare;   5
It is the avid, curious mind that craves
New pungent sauce and strips the larder bare,
The palate and not hunger that enslaves.

1959

8. The Paris subway.

DAVID RAY

A Piece of Shrapnel

The Rock That Doesn't Break, she calls
it that, picks it up in a field of clover,
brushes off the mud, asks me what it is
but who am I to explain war to a five-
year-old, who myself see something which   5
even to touch is dangerous, it is so sharp
and unshiny. I can feel it wanting
to hurt, to whizz through the air, land
in a tangle, be sold and resold. I can feel
how restless it is, not having found after   10
all this search a grave, where it can rest
and not be picked up, once more estranged,
searching again through hands and delicate
faces. It is like a small, tired heart
begging not to be stolen still again from   15
this grave, which is in a field of clover.

1974

EDWIN ARLINGTON ROBINSON

Mr. Flood's Party

Old Eben Flood, climbing alone one night
Over the hill between the town below
And the forsaken upland hermitage
That held as much as he should ever know
On earth again of home, paused warily.   5
The road was his and not a native near;
And Eben, having leisure, said aloud,
For no man else in Tilbury Town to hear:

"Well, Mr. Flood, we have the harvest moon
Again, and we may not have many more;   10
The bird is on the wing, the poet says,[9]
And you and I have said it here before.
Drink to the bird." He raised up to the light
The jug that he had gone so far to fill,
And answered huskily: "Well, Mr. Flood,   15
Since you propose it, I believe I will."

---

9. Edward Fitzgerald, in "The Rubáiyat of Omar Khayyám," so describes the "Bird
of Time."

Alone, as if enduring to the end
A valiant armor of scarred hopes outworn,
He stood there in the middle of the road
Like Roland's ghost winding a silent horn.[1]   20
Below him, in the town among the trees,
Where friends of other days had honored him,
A phantom salutation of the dead
Rang thinly till old Eben's eyes were dim.

Then, as a mother lays her sleeping child   25
Down tenderly, fearing it may awake,
He set the jug down slowly at his feet
With trembling care, knowing that most things break;
And only when assured that on firm earth
It stood, as the uncertain lives of men   30
Assuredly did not, he paced away,
And with his hand extended paused again:

"Well, Mr. Flood, we have not met like this
In a long time; and many a change has come
To both of us, I fear, since last it was   35
We had a drop together. Welcome home!"
Convivially returning with himself,
Again he raised the jug up to the light;
And with an acquiescent quaver said:
"Well, Mr. Flood, if you insist, I might.   40

"Only a very little, Mr. Flood—
For auld lang syne. No more, sir; that will do."
So, for the time, apparently it did,
And Eben evidently thought so too;
For soon amid the silver loneliness   45
Of night he lifted up his voice and sang,
Secure, with only two moons listening,
Until the whole harmonious landscape rang—

"For auld lang syne." The weary throat gave out,
The last word wavered, and the song was done.   50
He raised again the jug regretfully
And shook his head, and was again alone.
There was not much that was ahead of him,
And there was nothing in the town below—
Where strangers would have shut the many doors   55
That many friends had opened long ago.

1921

1. In French legend Roland's powerful ivory horn was used to warn his allies of impending attack.

EDWIN ARLINGTON ROBINSON

Richard Cory

Whenever Richard Cory went down town,
We people on the pavement looked at him:
He was a gentleman from sole to crown,
Clean favored, and imperially slim.

And he was always quietly arrayed,   5
And he was always human when he talked;
But still he fluttered pulses when he said,
"Good-morning," and he glittered when he walked.

And he was rich—yes, richer than a king—
And admirably schooled in every grace: 10
In fine, we thought that he was everything
To make us wish that we were in his place.

So on we worked, and waited for the light,
And went without the meat, and cursed the bread;
And Richard Cory, one calm summer night,   15
Went home and put a bullet through his head.

1897

EDWIN ARLINGTON ROBINSON

Uncle Ananias[2]

His words were magic and his heart was true,
    And everywhere he wandered he was blessed.
Out of all ancient men my childhood knew
    I choose him and I mark him for the best.
Of all authoritative liars, too,   5
    I crown him loveliest.

How fondly I remember the delight
    That always glorified him in the spring;
The joyous courage and the benedight[3]
    Profusion of his faith in everything!   10
He was a good old man, and it was right
    That he should have his fling.

And often, underneath the apple-trees,
    When we surprised him in the summer time,

2. The Biblical character Ananias was   5:1–10.
famous because he lied to God. See *Acts*   3. Blessed.

With what superb magnificence and ease   15
   He sinned enough to make the day sublime!
And if he liked us there about his knees,
   Truly it was no crime.

All summer long we loved him for the same
   Perennial inspiration of his lies;   20
And when the russet wealth of autumn came,
   There flew but fairer visions to our eyes—
Multiple, tropical, winged with a feathery flame,
   Like birds of paradise.

So to the sheltered end of many a year   25
   He charmed the seasons out with pageantry
Wearing upon his forehead, with no fear,
   The laurel of approved iniquity.
And every child who knew him, far or near,
   Did love him faithfully.   30

                                      1910

THEODORE ROETHKE

The Dream

1

I met her as a blossom on a stem
Before she ever breathed, and in that dream
The mind remembers from a deeper sleep:
Eye learned from eye, cold lip from sensual lip.
My dream divided on a point of fire;   5
Light hardened on the water where we were;
A bird sang low; the moonlight sifted in;
The water rippled, and she rippled on.

2

She came toward me in the flowing air,
A shape of change, encircled by its fire.   10
I watched her there, between me and the moon;
The bushes and the stones danced on and on;
I touched her shadow when the light delayed;
I turned my face away, and yet she stayed.
A bird sang from the center of a tree;   15
She loved the wind because the wind loved me.

3

Love is not love until love's vulnerable.
She slowed to sigh, in that long interval.
A small bird flew in circles where we stood;
The deer came down, out of the dappled wood.   20

All who remember, doubt. Who calls that strange?
I tossed a stone, and listened to its plunge.
She knew the grammar of least motion, she
Lent me one virtue, and I live thereby.

4

She held her body steady in the wind;   25
Our shadows met, and slowly swung around;
She turned the field into a glittering sea;
I played in flame and water like a boy
And I swayed out beyond the white seafoam;
Like a wet log, I sang within a flame.   30
In that last while, eternity's confine,
I came to love, I came into my own.

1958

THEODORE ROETHKE

She

I think the dead are tender. Shall we kiss?—
My lady laughs, delighting in what is.
If she but sighs, a bird puts out its tongue.
She makes space lonely with a lovely song.
She lilts a low soft language, and I hear   5
Down long sea-chambers of the inner ear.

We sing together; we sing mouth to mouth.
The garden is a river flowing south.
She cries out loud the soul's own secret joy;
She dances, and the ground bears her away.   10
She knows the speech of light, and makes it plain
A lively thing can come to life again.

I feel her presence in the common day,
In that slow dark that widens every eye.
She moves as water moves, and comes to me,   15
Stayed by what was, and pulled by what would be.

1956

THEODORE ROETHKE

The Waking

I wake to sleep, and take my waking slow.
I feel my fate in what I cannot fear.

I learn by going where I have to go.

We think by feeling. What is there to know?
I hear my being dance from ear to ear.   5
I wake to sleep, and take my waking slow.

Of those so close beside me, which are you?
God bless the Ground! I shall walk softly there,
And learn by going where I have to go.

Light takes the Tree; but who can tell us how?   10
The lowly worm climbs up a winding stair;
I wake to sleep, and take my waking slow.

Great Nature has another thing to do
To you and me; so take the lively air,
And, lovely, learn by going where to go.   15

This shaking keeps me steady. I should know.
What falls away is always. And is near.
I wake to sleep, and take my waking slow.
I learn by going where I have to go.

1953

ANNE SEXTON

The Kiss

My mouth blooms like a cut.
I've been wronged all year, tedious
nights, nothing but rough elbows in them
and delicate boxes of Kleenex calling *crybaby
crybaby, you fool!*   5

Before today my body was useless.
Now it's tearing at its square corners.
It's tearing old Mary's garments off, knot by knot
and see—Now it's shot full of these electric bolts.
Zing! A resurrection!   10

Once it was a boat, quite wooden
and with no business, no salt water under it
and in need of some paint. It was no more
than a group of boards. But you hoisted her, rigged her.
She's been elected.   15

My nerves are turned on. I hear them like
musical instruments. Where there was silence

the drums, the strings are incurably playing. You did this.
Pure genius at work. Darling, the composer has stepped
into fire.   20

1969

WILLIAM SHAKESPEARE

Th' Expense of Spirit

Th' expense[4] of spirit in a waste[5] of shame
Is lust in action; and, till action, lust
Is perjured, murderous, bloody, full of blame,
Savage, extreme, rude, cruel, not to trust;
Enjoyed no sooner but despiséd straight: 5
Past reason hunted; and no sooner had,
Past reason hated, as a swallowed bait,
On purpose laid to make the taker mad:
Mad in pursuit, and in possession so;
Had, having, and in quest to have, extreme;   10
A bliss in proof;[6] and proved, a very woe;
Before, a joy proposed; behind, a dream.
All this the world well knows; yet none knows well
To shun the heaven that leads men to this hell.

1609

WILLIAM SHAKESPEARE

Hark, Hark! the Lark[7]

Hark, hark! the lark at heaven's gate sings,
   And Phoebus[8] 'gins arise,
His steeds to water at those springs
   On chaliced[9] flowers that lies;
And winking Mary-buds[1] begin   5
   To ope their golden eyes:
With every thing that pretty is,
   My lady sweet, arise!
   Arise, arise!

ca. 1610

---

4. Expending.
5. Using up; also, desert.
6. In the act.
7. From *Cymbeline*, Act II, sc. iii.
8. Apollo, the sun god.
9. Cup-shaped.
1. Buds of marigolds.

WILLIAM SHAKESPEARE

Spring[2]

When daisies pied and violets blue
　　And ladysmocks all silver-white
And cuckoobuds of yellow hue
　　Do paint the meadows with delight,
The cuckoo then, on every tree,　　　　　　　　　5
Mocks married men;[3] for thus sings he,
　　　　　　Cuckoo;
Cuckoo, cuckoo: Oh word of fear,
Unpleasing to a married ear!

When shepherds pipe on oaten straws,　　　　　10
　　And merry larks are plowmen's clocks,
When turtles tread,[4] and rooks, and daws,
　　And maidens bleach their summer smocks,
The cuckoo then, on every tree,
Mocks married men; for thus sings he,　　　　　15
　　　　　　Cuckoo;
Cuckoo, cuckoo: Oh word of fear,
Unpleasing to a married ear!

ca. 1595

WILLIAM SHAKESPEARE

Winter

When icicles hang by the wall
　　And Dick the shepherd blows[5] his nail,
And Tom bears logs into the hall,
　　And milk comes frozen home in pail.
When blood is nipped and ways be foul,　　　　5
Then nightly sings the staring owl,
　　　　　　Tu-who;
Tu-whit, tu-who: a merry note,
While greasy Joan doth keel[6] the pot.

When all aloud the wind doth blow,　　　　　　10
　　And coughing drowns the parson's saw,[7]
And birds sit brooding in the snow,
　　And Marian's nose looks red and raw,
When roasted crabs[8] hiss in the bowl,

---

2. Like "Winter" (below), a song from *Love's Labors Lost*, Act V, sc. ii.
3. By the resemblance of its call to the word "cuckold."
4. Copulate. "turtles": turtledoves.
5. Breathes on for warmth. "nail":
fingernail; i.e., hands.
6. Cool: stir to keep it from boiling over.
7. Maxim, proverb.
8. Crabapples.

Then nightly sings the staring owl,
   Tu-who,
Tu-whit, tu-who: a merry note
While greasy Joan doth keel the pot.

ca. 1595

PERCY BYSSHE SHELLEY

England in 1819

An old, mad, blind, despised, and dying king[9]—
Princes, the dregs of their dull race, who flow
Through public scorn—mud from a muddy spring;
Rulers who neither see, nor feel, nor know,
But leechlike to their fainting country cling,
Till they drop, blind in blood, without a blow;
A people starved and stabbed in the untilled field—
An army, which liberticide and prey
Makes as a two-edged sword to all who wield;
Golden and sanguine[1] laws which tempt and slay;
Religion Christless, Godless—a book sealed;
A Senate—Time's worst statute[2] unrepealed—
Are graves, from which a glorious Phantom[3] may
Burst, to illumine our tempestuous day.

1819

STEPHEN SPENDER

An Elementary School Classroom in a Slum

Far far from gusty waves these children's faces.
Like rootless weeds, the hair torn round their pallor.
The tall girl with her weighed-down head. The paper-
seeming boy, with rat's eyes. The stunted, unlucky heir
Of twisted bones, reciting a father's gnarled disease,
His lesson from his desk. At back of the dim class
One unnoted, sweet and young. His eyes live in a dream
Of squirrel's game, in tree room, other than this.
On sour cream walls, donations. Shakespeare's head,
Cloudless at dawn, civilized dome riding all cities.
Belled, flowery, Tyrolese valley.[4] Open-handed map

9. George III, senile for many years, had ruled England since 1760. He died the year after the poem was written.
1. Motivated by greed, resulting in bloodshed.
2. A law discriminating against Catholics.
3. Revolution.
4. A rich and beautiful section of Austria with many scenes like those in typical paintings of hamlets and picturesque countrysides.

Awarding the world its world. And yet, for these
Children, these windows, not this world, are world,
Where all their future's painted with a fog,
A narrow street sealed in with a lead sky,   15
Far far from rivers, capes, and stars of words.

Surely, Shakespeare is wicked, the map a bad example
With ships and sun and love tempting them to steal—
For lives that slyly turn in their cramped holes
From fog to endless night? On their slag heap, these children   20
Wear skins peeped through by bones and spectacles of steel
With mended glass, like bottle bits on stones.
All of their time and space are foggy slum.
So blot their maps with slums as big as doom.

Unless, governor, teacher, inspector, visitor,   25
This map becomes their window and these windows
That shut upon their lives like catacombs,
Break O break open till they break the town
And show the children to green fields, and make their world
Run azure on gold sands, and let their tongues   30
Run naked into books, the white and green leaves open
History theirs whose language is the sun.

                                                                                    1939

STEPHEN SPENDER

Judas Iscariot[5]

The eyes of twenty centuries
Pursue me along corridors to where
I am painted at their ends on many walls.
    Ever-revolving future recognize
This red hair and red beard, where I am seated   5
Within the dark cave of the feast of light.
    Out of my heart-shaped shadow I stretch my hand
Across the white table into the dish
But not to dip the bread. It is as though
The cloth on each side of one dove-bright face   10
Spread dazzling wings on which the apostles ride
Uplifting them into the vision
Where their eyes watch themselves enthroned.
    My russet hand across the dish
Plucks enviously against one feather   15
    —But still the rushing wings spurn me below!

5. According to New Testament accounts, Judas, one of the twelve disciples,
betrayed Jesus to his enemies for 30 pieces
of silver. The betrayal occurred shortly
after the Last Supper; Judas indicated to
his confederates who Jesus was by kissing
him.

Saint Sebastian[6] of wickedness
I stand: all eyes legitimate arrows piercing through
The darkness of my wickedness. They recognize
My halo hammered from thirty silver pieces   20
And the hemp rope around my neck
Soft as that Spirit's hanging arms
When on my cheek he answered with the kiss
Which cuts for ever—
      My strange stigmata,   25
All love and hate, all fire and ice!

But who betrayed whom? O you,
Whose light gaze forms the azure corridor
Through which those other pouring eyes
Arrow into me—answer! Who   30
Betrayed whom? Who read
In his mind's light from the first day
That the kingdom of heaven on earth must always
Reiterate the garden of Eden,
And each day's revolution be betrayed   35
Within man's heart, each day?
      Who wrapped
The whispering serpent round the tree
And hung between the leaves the glittering purse
And trapped the fangs with God-appointed poison?   40
Who knew
I must betray the truth, and made the lie
Betray its truth in me?

Those hypocrite eyes which aimed at you
Now aim at me. And yet, beyond their world   45
Each turning on his pole of truth, your pole
Invisible light, and mine
Becoming what man is. We stare
Across two thousand years, and heaven, and hell,
Into each other's gaze.   50

           1949

WALLACE STEVENS

Anecdote of the Jar

I placed a jar in Tennessee,
And round it was, upon a hill.
It made the slovenly wilderness
Surround that hill.

---

6. Early Christian martyr who was a favorite subject of Renaissance painters. According to legend, St. Sebastian was sentenced to be shot with arrows, but his many wounds were miraculously healed.

The wilderness rose up to it,   5
And sprawled around, no longer wild.
The jar was round upon the ground
And tall and of a port in air.

It took dominion everywhere.
The jar was gray and bare.   10
It did not give of bird or bush,
Like nothing else in Tennessee.

                                                                 1923

WALLACE STEVENS

The Idea of Order at Key West

She sang beyond the genius of the sea.
The water never formed to mind or voice,
Like a body wholly body, fluttering
Its empty sleeves; and yet its mimic motion
Made constant cry, caused constantly a cry,   5
That was not ours although we understood,
Inhuman, of the veritable ocean.

The sea was not a mask. No more was she.
The song and water were not medleyed sound
Even if what she sang was what she heard,   10
Since what she sang was uttered word by word.
It may be that in all her phrases stirred
The grinding water and the gasping wind;
But it was she and not the sea we heard.

For she was the maker of the song she sang.   15
The ever-hooded, tragic-gestured sea
Was merely a place by which she walked to sing.
Whose spirit is this? we said, because we knew
It was the spirit that we sought and knew
That we should ask this often as she sang.   20

If it was only the dark voice of the sea
That rose, or even colored by many waves;
If it was only the outer voice of sky
And cloud, of the sunken coral water-walled,
However clear, it would have been deep air,   25
The heaving speech of air, a summer sound
Repeated in a summer without end
And sound alone. But it was more than that,
More even than her voice, and ours, among
The meaningless plungings of water and the wind,   30

Theatrical distances, bronze shadows heaped
On high horizons, mountainous atmospheres
Of sky and sea.
    It was her voice that made
The sky acutest at its vanishing.
She measured to the hour its solitude.   35
She was the single artificer of the world
In which she sang. And when she sang, the sea,
Whatever self it had, became the self
That was her song, for she was the maker. Then we,
As we beheld her striding there alone,   40
Knew that there never was a world for her
Except the one she sang and, singing, made.

Ramon Fernandez,[7] tell me, if you know,
Why, when the singing ended and we turned
Toward the town, tell why the glassy lights,   45
The lights in the fishing boats at anchor there,
As the night descended, tilting in the air,
Mastered the night and portioned out the sea,
Fixing emblazoned zones and fiery poles,
Arranging, deepening, enchanting night.   50

Oh! Blessed rage for order, pale Ramon,
The maker's rage to order words of the sea,
Words of the fragrant portals, dimly-starred,
And of ourselves and of our origins,
In ghostlier demarcations, keener sounds.   55

              1935

WALLACE STEVENS

The Emperor of Ice-Cream

Call the roller of big cigars,
The muscular one, and bid him whip
In kitchen cups concupiscent curds.[8]
Let the wenches dawdle in such dress
As they are used to wear, and let the boys   5

7. French classicist and critic, 1894–1944, who emphasized the ordering role of a writer's consciousness upon the materials he used. Stevens denied that he had Fernandez in mind, saying that he combined a Spanish first name and surname at random: "I knew of Ramon Fernandez, the critic, and had read some of his criticisms, but I did not have him in mind." (*Letters* [New York: Knopf, 1960], p. 798) Later, Stevens wrote to another correspondent that he did not have the critic "consciously" in mind. (*Letters*, p. 823)

8. "The words 'concupiscent curds' have no genealogy; they are merely expressive: at least, I hope they are expressive. They express the concupiscence of life, but, by contrast with the things in relation in the poem, they express or accentuate life's destitution, and it is this that gives them something more than a cheap lustre" Wallace Stevens, *Letters* (New York: Knopf, 1960), p. 500.

Bring flowers in last month's newspapers.
Let be be finale of seem.[9]
The only emperor is the emperor of ice-cream.

Take from the dresser of deal,
Lacking the three glass knobs, that sheet   10
On which she embroidered fantails [1] once
And spread it so as to cover her face.
If her horny feet protrude, they come
To show how cold she is, and dumb.
Let the lamp affix its beam.   15
The only emperor is the emperor of ice-cream.

1923

WALLACE STEVENS

Sunday Morning

I

Complacencies of the peignoir, and late
Coffee and oranges in a sunny chair,
And the green freedom of a cockatoo
Upon a rug mingle to dissipate
The holy hush of ancient sacrifice.   5
She dreams a little, and she feels the dark
Encroachment of that old catastrophe,[2]
As a calm darkens among water-lights.
The pungent oranges and bright, green wings
Seem things in some procession of the dead,   10
Winding across wide water, without sound.
The day is like wide water, without sound,
Stilled for the passing of her dreaming feet
Over the seas, to silent Palestine,
Dominion of the blood and sepulchre.   15

II

Why should she give her bounty to the dead?
What is divinity if it can come
Only in silent shadows and in dreams?
Shall she not find in comforts of the sun,
In pungent fruit and bright, green wings, or else   20
In any balm or beauty of the earth,
Things to be cherished like the thought of heaven?
Divinity must live within herself:

9. ". . . the true sense of Let be be the finale of seem is let being become the conclusion or denouement of appearing to be: in short, ice cream is an absolute good. The poem is obviously not about ice cream, but about being as distinguished from seeming to be." *Letters,* p. 341.
1. Fantail pigeons.
2. The Crucifixion.

Passions of rain, or moods in falling snow;
Grievings in loneliness, or unsubdued   25
Elations when the forest blooms; gusty
Emotions on wet roads on autumn nights;
All pleasures and all pains, remembering
The bough of summer and the winter branch.
These are the measures destined for her soul.   30

III

Jove[3] in the clouds had his inhuman birth.
No mother suckled him, no sweet land gave
Large-mannered motions to his mythy mind
He moved among us, as a muttering king,
Magnificent, would move among his hinds,[4]   35
Until our blood, commingling, virginal,
With heaven, brought such requital to desire
The very hinds discerned it, in a star.[5]
Shall our blood fail? Or shall it come to be
The blood of paradise? And shall the earth   40
Seem all of paradise that we shall know?
The sky will be much friendlier then than now,
A part of labor and a part of pain,
And next in glory to enduring love,
Not this dividing and indifferent blue.   45

IV

She says, "I am content when wakened birds,
Before they fly, test the reality
Of misty fields, by their sweet questionings;
But when the birds are gone, and their warm fields
Return no more, where, then, is paradise?"   50
There is not any haunt of prophecy,
Nor any old chimera of the grave,
Neither the golden underground, nor isle
Melodious, where spirits gat[6] them home,
Nor visionary south, nor cloudy palm   55
Remote on heaven's hill, that has endured
As April's green endures, or will endure
Like her remembrance of awakened birds,
Or her desire for June and evening, tipped
By the consummation of the swallow's wings.   60

V

She says, "But in contentment I still feel
The need of some imperishable bliss."
Death is the mother of beauty; hence from her,
Alone, shall come fulfillment to our dreams
And our desires. Although she strews the leaves   65
Of sure obliteration on our paths,

---

3. Jupiter, the chief Roman god.   5. The star of Bethlehem.
4. Lowliest rural subjects.   6. Got.

The path sick sorrow took, the many paths
Where triumph rang its brassy phrase, or love
Whispered a little out of tenderness,
She makes the willow shiver in the sun   70
For maidens who were wont to sit and gaze
Upon the grass, relinquished to their feet.
She causes boys to pile new plums and pears
On disregarded plate.[7] The maidens taste
And stray impassioned in the littering leaves.   75

VI

Is there no change of death in paradise?
Does ripe fruit never fall? Or do the boughs
Hang always heavy in that perfect sky,
Unchanging, yet so like our perishing earth,
With rivers like our own that seek for seas   80
They never find, the same receding shores
That never touch with inarticulate pang?
Why set the pear upon those river-banks
Or spice the shores with odors of the plum?
Alas, that they should wear our colors there,   85
The silken weavings of our afternoons,
And pick the strings of our insipid lutes!
Death is the mother of beauty, mystical,
Within whose burning bosom we devise
Our earthly mothers waiting, sleeplessly.   90

VII

Supple and turbulent, a ring of men
Shall chant in orgy[8] on a summer morn
Their boisterous devotion to the sun,
Not as a god, but as a god might be,
Naked among them, like a savage source.   95
Their chant shall be a chant of paradise,
Out of their blood, returning to the sky;
And in their chant shall enter, voice by voice,
The windy lake wherein their lord delights,
The trees, like serafin,[9] and echoing hills,   100
That choir among themselves long afterward.
They shall know well the heavenly fellowship
Of men that perish and of summer morn.
And whence they came and whither they shall go
The dew upon their feet shall manifest.   105

VIII

She hears, upon that water without sound,
A voice that cries, "The tomb in Palestine

7. "Plate is used in the sense of so-called family plate. Disregarded refers to the disuse into which things fall that have been possessed for a long time. I mean, therefore, that death releases and renews. What the old have come to disregard, the young inherit and make use of" (*Letters of Wallace Stevens* [1966], pp. 183–184).
8. Ceremonial revelry.
9. Seraphim, the highest of the nine orders of angels.

Is not the porch of spirits lingering.
It is the grave of Jesus, where he lay."
We live in an old chaos of the sun,   110
Or old dependency of day and night,
Or island solitude, unsponsored, free,
Of that wide water, inescapable.
Deer walk upon our mountains, and the quail
Whistle about us their spontaneous cries;   115
Sweet berries ripen in the wilderness;
And, in the isolation of the sky,
At evening, casual flocks of pigeons make
Ambiguous undulations as they sink,
Downward to darkness, on extended wings.   120

1915

JONATHAN SWIFT

On Stella's Birthday, 1719

Stella this day is thirty-four,[1]
(We shan't dispute a year or more)
However Stella, be not troubled,
Although thy size and years are doubled,
Since first I saw thee at sixteen   5
The brightest virgin on the green,
So little is thy form declined
Made up so largely in thy mind.
Oh, would it please the gods to split
Thy beauty, size, and years, and wit,   10
No age could furnish out a pair
Of nymphs so graceful, wise and fair
With half the luster of your eyes,
With half your wit, your years and size:
And then before it grew too late,   15
How should I beg of gentle Fate,
(That either nymph might have her swain,[2])
To split my worship too in twain.

1719

DYLAN THOMAS

Fern Hill

Now as I was young and easy under the apple boughs
About the lilting house and happy as the grass was green,

1. Stella is Swift's pet name for Hester   was actually 38.
Johnson, a close friend for many years. She   2. Servant, admirer, lover.

The night above the dingle starry,
    Time let me hail and climb
    Golden in the heydays of his eyes,
And honored among wagons I was prince of the apple towns
And once below a time I lordly had the trees and leaves
      Trail with daisies and barley
    Down the rivers of the windfall light.

And as I was green and carefree, famous among the barns
About the happy yard and singing as the farm was home,
    In the sun that is young once only,
      Time let me play and be
    Golden in the mercy of his means,
And green and golden I was huntsman and herdsman, the calves
Sang to my horn, the foxes on the hills barked clear and cold,
      And the sabbath rang slowly
    In the pebbles of the holy streams.

All the sun long it was running, it was lovely, the hay
Fields high as the house, the tunes from the chimneys, it was air
    And playing, lovely and watery
      And fire green as grass.
    And nightly under the simple stars
As I rode to sleep the owls were bearing the farm away,
All the moon long I heard, blessed among stables, the nightjars[3]
    Flying with the ricks,[4] and the horses
      Flashing into the dark.

And then to awake, and the farm, like a wanderer white
With the dew, come back, the cock on his shoulder: it was all
    Shining, it was Adam and maiden,
      The sky gathered again
    And the sun grew round that very day.
So it must have been after the birth of the simple light
In the first, spinning place, the spellbound horses walking warm
    Out of the whinnying green stable
      On to the fields of praise.

And honored among foxes and pheasants by the gay house
Under the new made clouds and happy as the heart was long,
    In the sun born over and over,
      I ran my heedless ways,
    My wishes raced through the house-high hay
And nothing I cared, at my sky-blue trades, that time allows
In all his tuneful turning so few and such morning songs
    Before the children green and golden
      Follow him out of grace,

Nothing I cared, in the lamb white days, that time would take me
Up to the swallow-thronged loft by the shadow of my hand,

---

3. Birds.   4. Haystacks.

In the moon that is always rising,
    Nor that riding to sleep
I should hear him fly with the high fields   50
And wake to the farm forever fled from the childless land.
Oh as I was young and easy in the mercy of his means,
    Time held me green and dying
Though I sang in my chains like the sea.

                        1946

DYLAN THOMAS

The Force that Through the Green Fuse
Drives the Flower

The force that through the green fuse drives the flower
Drives my green age; that blasts the roots of trees
Is my destroyer.
And I am dumb to tell the crooked rose
My youth is bent by the same wintry fever.   5

The force that drives the water through the rocks
Drives my red blood; that dries the mouthing streams
Turns mine to wax.
And I am dumb to mouth unto my veins
How at the mountain spring the same mouth sucks.   10

The hand that whirls the water in the pool
Stirs the quicksand; that ropes the blowing wind
Hauls my shroud sail.
And I am dumb to tell the hanging man
How of my clay is made the hangman's lime.   15

The lips of time leech to the fountain head;
Love drips and gathers, but the fallen blood
Shall calm her sores.
And I am dumb to tell a weather's wind
How time has ticked a heaven round the stars.   20

And I am dumb to tell the lover's tomb
How at my sheet goes the same crooked worm.

                        1934

DYLAN THOMAS

In My Craft or Sullen Art

In my craft or sullen art
Exercised in the still night

When only the moon rages
And the lovers lie abed
With all their griefs in their arms,   5
I labor by singing light
Not for ambition or bread
Or the strut and trade of charms
On the ivory stages
But for the common wages   10
Of their most secret heart.

Not for the proud man apart
From the raging moon I write
On these spindrift⁵ pages
Nor for the towering dead   15
With their nightingales and psalms
But for the lovers, their arms
Round the griefs of the ages,
Who pay no praise or wages
Nor heed my craft or art.   20

1946

WALT WHITMAN

When Lilacs Last in the Dooryard Bloomed⁶

1

When lilacs last in the dooryard bloomed,
And the great star early drooped in the western sky in the night,
I mourned, and yet shall mourn with ever-returning spring.

Ever-returning spring, trinity sure to me you bring,
Lilac blooming perennial and drooping star in the west,   5
And thought of him I love.

2

O powerful western fallen star!
O shades of night—O moody, tearful night!
O great star disappeared—O the black murk that hides the star!
O cruel hands that hold me powerless—O helpless soul of me!   10
O harsh surrounding cloud that will not free my soul.

3

In the dooryard fronting an old farm-house near the white-washed
    palings,
Stands the lilac-bush tall-growing with heart-shaped leaves of rich
    green,
With many a pointed blossom rising delicate, with the perfume strong
    I love,

5. Literally, wind-driven sea spray.   assassination of Abraham Lincoln.
6. The "occasion" of the poem is the

With every leaf a miracle—and from this bush in the dooryard,   15
With delicate-colored blossoms and heart-shaped leaves of rich green,
A sprig with its flower I break.

4

In the swamp in secluded recesses,
A shy and hidden bird is warbling a song.

Solitary the thrush,   20
The hermit withdrawn to himself, avoiding the settlements,
Sings by himself a song.

Song of the bleeding throat,
Death's outlet song of life (for well dear brother I know,
If thou wast not granted to sing thou would'st surely die).   25

5

Over the breast of the spring, the land, amid cities,
Amid lanes and through old woods, where lately the violets peeped
    from the ground, spotting the gray debris,
Amid the grass in the fields each side of the lanes, passing the endless
    grass,
Passing the yellow-speared wheat, every grain from its shroud in the
    dark-brown fields uprisen,
Passing the apple-tree blows of white and pink in the orchards,   30
Carrying a corpse to where it shall rest in the grave,
Night and day journeys a coffin.

6

Coffin that passes through lanes and streets,[7]
Through day and night with the great cloud darkening the land,
With the pomp of the inlooped flags with the cities draped in black,   35
With the show of the States themselves as of crepe-veiled women
    standing,
With processions long and winding and the flambeaus of the night,
With the countless torches lit, with the silent sea of faces and the un-
    bared heads,
With the waiting depot, the arriving coffin, and the somber faces,
With dirges through the night, with the thousand voices rising strong
    and solemn,   40
With all the mournful voices of the dirges poured around the coffin,
The dim-lit churches and the shuddering organs—where amid these
    you journey,
With the tolling tolling bells' perpetual clang,
Here, coffin that slowly passes,
I give you my sprig of lilac.   45

7

(Nor for you, for one alone,
Blossoms and branches green to coffins all I bring,
For fresh as the morning, thus would I chant a song for you O sane
    and sacred death.

---

7. The funeral cortege stopped at many towns between Washington and Springfield, Illinois, where Lincoln was buried.

All over bouquets of roses,
O death, I cover you over with roses and early lilies,   50
But mostly and now the lilac that blooms the first,
Copious I break, I break the sprigs from the bushes,
With loaded arms I come, pouring for you,
For you and the coffins all of you O death.)

8

O western orb sailing the heaven,   55
Now I know what you must have meant as a month since I walked,
As I walked in silence the transparent shadowy night,
As I saw you had something to tell as you bent to me night after night,
As you drooped from the sky low down as if to my side (while the
        other stars all looked on),
As we wandered together the solemn night (for something I know
        not what kept me from sleep),   60
As the night advanced, and I saw on the rim of the west how full you
        were of woe,
As I stood on the rising ground in the breeze in the cool transparent
        night,
As I watched where you passed and was lost in the netherward black
        of the night,
As my soul in its trouble dissatisfied sank, as where you sad orb,
Concluded, dropped in the night, and was gone.   65

9

Sing on there in the swamp,
O singer bashful and tender, I hear your notes, I hear your call,
I hear, I come presently, I understand you,
But a moment I linger, for the lustrous star has detained me,
The star my departing comrade holds and detains me.   70

10

O how shall I warble myself for the dead one there I loved?
And how shall I deck my song for the large sweet soul that has gone?
And what shall my perfume be for the grave of him I love?
Sea-winds blown from east and west,
Blown from the Eastern sea and blown from the Western sea, till there
        on the prairies meeting,   75
These and with these and the breath of my chant,
I'll perfume the grave of him I love.

11

O what shall I hang on the chamber walls?
And what shall the pictures be that I hang on the walls,
To adorn the burial-house of him I love?   80

Pictures of growing spring and farms and homes,
With the Fourth-month eve at sundown, and the gray smoke lucid and
        bright,
With floods of the yellow gold of the gorgeous, indolent, sinking sun,
        burning, expanding the air,

With the fresh sweet herbage under foot, and the pale green leaves of
    the trees prolific,
In the distance the flowing glaze, the breast of the river, with a wind-
    dapple here and there,   85
With ranging hills on the banks, with many a line against the sky, and
    shadows,
And the city at hand with dwellings so dense, and stacks of chimneys,
And all the scenes of life and the workshops, and the workmen home-
    ward returning.

12

Lo, body and soul—this land,
My own Manhattan with spires, and the sparkling and hurrying tides,
    and the ships,   90
The varied and ample land, the South and the North in the light,
    Ohio's shores and flashing Missouri,
And ever the far-spreading prairies covered with grass and corn.

Lo, the most excellent sun so calm and haughty,
The violet and purple morn with just-felt breezes,
The gentle soft-born measureless light,   95
The miracle spreading bathing all, the fulfilled noon,
The coming eve delicious, the welcome night and the stars,
Over my cities shining all, enveloping man and land.

13

Sing on, sing on you gray-brown bird,
Sing from the swamps, the recesses, pour your chant from the bushes, 100
Limitless out of the dusk, out of the cedars and pines.

Sing on dearest brother, warble your reedy song,
Loud human song, with voice of uttermost woe.
O liquid and free and tender!
O wild and loose to my soul—O wondrous singer!   105
You only I hear—yet the star holds me (but will soon depart),
Yet the lilac with mastering odor holds me.

14

Now while I sat in the day and looked forth,
In the close of the day with its light and the fields of spring, and the
    farmers preparing their crops,
In the large unconscious scenery of my land with its lakes and forests, 110
In the heavenly aerial beauty, (after the perturbed winds and the
    storms),
Under the arching heavens of the afternoon swift passing, and the
    voices of children and women.
The many-moving sea-tides, and I saw the ships how they sailed,
And the summer approaching with richness, and the fields all busy
    with labor,
And the infinite separate houses, how they all went on, each with its
    meals and minutia of daily usages,   115
And the streets how their throbbings throbbed, and the cities pent—lo,
    then and there,

Falling upon them all and among them all, enveloping me with the rest,
Appeared the cloud, appeared the long black trail,
And I knew death, its thought, and the sacred knowledge of death.

Then with the knowledge of death as walking one side of me,   120
And the thought of death close-walking the other side of me,
And I in the middle as with companions, and as holding the hands of
    companions,
I fled forth to the hiding receiving night that talks not,
Down to the shores of the water, the path by the swamp in the dim-
    ness,
To the solemn shadowy cedars and ghostly pines so still.   125

And the singer so shy to the rest received me,
The gray-brown bird I know received us comrades three,
And he sang the carol of death, and a verse for him I love.

From deep secluded recesses,
From the fragrant cedars and the ghostly pines so still,   130
Came the carol of the bird.

And the charm of the carol rapt me,
As I held as if by their hands my comrades in the night,
And the voice of my spirit tallied the song of the bird.

Come lovely and soothing death,   135
Undulate round the world, serenely arriving, arriving,
In the day, in the night, to all, to each,
Sooner or later delicate death.

Praised be the fathomless universe,
For life and joy, and for objects and knowledge curious,   140
And for love, sweet love—but praise! praise! praise!
For the sure-enwinding arms of cool-enfolding death.

Dark mother always gliding near with soft feet,
Have none chanted for thee a chant of fullest welcome?
Then I chant it for thee, I glorify thee above all,   145
I bring thee a song that when thou must indeed come, come unfalter-
*   ingly.*

Approach strong deliveress,
When it is so, when thou hast taken them I joyously sing the dead,
Lost in the loving floating ocean of thee,
Laved in the flood of thy bliss O death.   150

From me to thee glad serenades,
Dances for thee I propose saluting thee, adornments and feastings for
*   thee,*
And the sights of the open landscape and the high-spread sky are
*   fitting,*
And life and the fields, and the huge and thoughtful night.

The night in silence under many a star,   155
The ocean shore and the husky whispering wave whose voice I know,
And the soul turning to thee O vast and well-veiled death,
And the body gratefully nestling close to thee.

Over the tree-tops I float thee a song,
Over the rising and sinking waves, over the myriad fields and the
  prairies wide,   160
Over the dense-packed cities all and the teeming wharves and ways,
I float this carol with joy, with joy to thee O death.

15

To the tally of my soul,
Loud and strong kept up the gray-brown bird,
With pure deliberate notes spreading filling the night.   165

Loud in the pines and cedars dim,
Clear in the freshness moist and the swamp-perfume,
And I with my comrades there in the night.

While my sight that was bound in my eyes unclosed,
As to long panoramas of visions.   170

And I saw askant[8] the armies,
I saw as in noiseless dreams hundreds of battle-flags,
Borne through the smoke of the battles and pierced with missiles I saw
  them,
And carried hither and yon through the smoke, and torn and bloody,
And at last but a few shreds left on the staffs (and all in silence),   175
And the staffs all splintered and broken.

I saw battle-corpses, myriads of them,
And the white skeletons of young men, I saw them,
I saw the debris and debris of all the slain soldiers of the war,
But I saw they were not as was thought,   180
They themselves were fully at rest, they suffered not,
The living remained and suffered, the mother suffered,
And the wife and the child and the musing comrade suffered,
And the armies that remained suffered.

16

Passing the visions, passing the night,   185
Passing, unloosing the hold of my comrades' hands,
Passing the song of the hermit bird and the tallying song of my soul,
Victorious song, death's outlet song, yet varying ever-altering song,
As low and wailing, yet clear the notes, rising and falling, flooding the
  night,
Sadly sinking and fainting, as warning and warning, and yet again
  bursting with joy,   190
Covering the earth and filling the spread of the heaven,

8. Askance: sideways.

As that powerful psalm in the night I heard from recesses,
Passing, I leave thee lilac with heart-shaped leaves,
I leave thee there in the door-yard, blooming, returning with spring.

I cease from my song for thee,   195
From my gaze on thee in the west, fronting the west, communing with
    thee,
O comrade lustrous with silver face in the night.

Yet each to keep and all, retrievements out of the night,
The song, the wondrous chant of the gray-brown bird,
And the tallying chant, the echo aroused in my soul,   200
With the lustrous and drooping star with the countenance full of woe,
With the holders holding my hand nearing the call of the bird,
Comrades mine and I in the midst, and their memory ever to keep, for
    the dead I loved so well,
For the sweetest, wisest soul of all my days and lands—and this for his
    dear sake,
Lilac and star and bird twined with the chant of my soul,   205
There in the fragrant pines and the cedars dusk and dim.
1865–66

RICHARD WILBUR

The Beautiful Changes

One wading a Fall meadow finds on all sides
The Queen Anne's Lace[9] lying like lilies
On water; it glides
So from the walker, it turns
Dry grass to a lake, as the slightest shade of you   5
Valleys my mind in fabulous blue Lucernes.[1]

The beautiful changes as a forest is changed
By a chameleon's tuning his skin to it;
As a mantis, arranged
On a green leaf, grows
Into it, makes the leaf leafier, and proves   10
Any greenness is deeper than anyone knows.

Your hands hold roses always in a way that says
They are not only yours; the beautiful changes
In such kind ways,
Wishing ever to sunder   15
Things and things' selves for a second finding, to lose
For a moment all that it touches back to wonder.

1947

9. A delicate-looking plant, with finely divided leaves and flat clusters of small white flowers, sometimes called "wild carrot."
1. Alfalfa, a plant resembling clover, with small purple flowers. Lake Lucerne is famed for deep blue color and its picturesque Swiss setting amid limestone mountains.

RICHARD WILBUR

Love Calls Us to the Things of This World[2]

The eyes open to a cry of pulleys,[3]
And spirited from sleep, the astounded soul
Hangs for a moment bodiless and simple
As false dawn.
                Outside the open window   5
The morning air is all awash with angels.

    Some are in bed-sheets, some are in blouses,
Some are in smocks: but truly there they are.
Now they are rising together in calm swells
Of halcyon[4] feeling, filling whatever they wear   10
With the deep joy of their impersonal breathing;
    Now they are flying in place,[5] conveying
The terrible speed of their omnipresence, moving
And staying like white water; and now of a sudden
They swoon down into so rapt a quiet   15
That nobody seems to be there.
                   The soul shrinks

    From all that it is about to remember,
From the punctual rape of every blesséd day,
And cries,   20
        "Oh, let there be nothing on earth but laundry,
Nothing but rosy hands in the rising steam
And clear dances done in the sight of heaven."

    Yet, as the sun acknowledges
With a warm look the world's hunks and colors,   25
The soul descends once more in bitter love
To accept the waking body, saying now
In a changed voice as the man yawns and rises,

    "Bring them down from their ruddy gallows;
Let there be clean linen for the backs of thieves;   30
Let lovers go fresh and sweet to be undone,
And the heaviest nuns walk in a pure floating
Of dark habits,
              keeping their difficult balance."

                                      1956

2. A phrase from St. Augustine's *Commentary on the Psalms.*
3. Laundry pulleys, designed so that clothes can be hung on the line inside and then sent outdoors to dry.
4. Serene.
5. Like planes in a formation.

WILLIAM CARLOS WILLIAMS

This Is Just to Say

I have eaten
the plums
that were in
the icebox

and which   5
you were probably
saving
for breakfast

Forgive me
they were delicious   10
so sweet
and so cold

1934

WILLIAM WORDSWORTH

Lines Composed a Few Miles above Tintern Abbey on Revisiting the Banks of the Wye During a Tour, July 13, 1798[6]

Five years have passed; five summers, with the length
Of five long winters! and again I hear
These waters, rolling from their mountain-springs
With a soft inland murmur. Once again
Do I behold these steep and lofty cliffs,   5
That on a wild secluded scene impress
Thoughts of more deep seclusion; and connect
The landscape with the quiet of the sky.
The day is come when I again repose
Here, under this dark sycamore, and view   10
These plots of cottage-ground, these orchard tufts,
Which at this season, with their unripe fruits,
Are clad in one green hue, and lose themselves
'Mid groves and copses.[7] Once again I see
These hedge-rows, hardly hedge-rows, little lines   15
Of sportive wood run wild: these pastoral farms,
Green to the very door; and wreaths of smoke
Sent up, in silence, from among the trees!
With some uncertain notice, as might seem
Of vagrant dwellers in the houseless woods,   20
Or of some hermit's cave, where by his fire

6. Wordsworth had first visited the Wye valley and the ruins of the medieval abbey there in 1793, while on a solitary walking tour. He was 23 then, 28 when he wrote this poem.
7. Thickets.

The hermit sits alone.
               These beauteous forms,
Through a long absence, have not been to me
As is a landscape to a blind man's eye;
But oft, in lonely rooms, and 'mid the din   25
Of towns and cities, I have owed to them,
In hours of weariness, sensations sweet,
Felt in the blood, and felt along the heart;
And passing even into my purer mind,
With tranquil restoration—feelings too   30
Of unremembered pleasure: such, perhaps,
As have no slight or trivial influence
On that best portion of a good man's life,
His little, nameless, unremembered acts
Of kindness and of love. Nor less, I trust,   35
To them I may have owed another gift,
Of aspect more sublime; that blessèd mood,
In which the burthen[8] of the mystery,
In which the heavy and the weary weight
Of all this unintelligible world,   40
Is lightened—that serene and blessèd mood,
In which the affections gently lead us on—
Until, the breath of this corporeal frame
And even the motion of our human blood
Almost suspended, we are laid asleep   45
In body, and become a living soul;
While with an eye made quiet by the power
Of harmony, and the deep power of joy,
We see into the life of things.
                  If this
Be but a vain belief, yet, oh! how oft—   50
In darkness and amid the many shapes
Of joyless daylight; when the fretful stir
Unprofitable, and the fever of the world,
Have hung upon the beatings of my heart—
How oft, in spirit, have I turned to thee,   55
O sylvan Wye! thou wanderer through the woods,
How often has my spirit turned to thee!

    And now, with gleams of half-extinguished thought,
With many recognitions dim and faint,
And somewhat of a sad perplexity,   60
The picture of the mind revives again;
While here I stand, not only with the sense
Of present pleasure, but with pleasing thoughts
That in this moment there is life and food
For future years. And so I dare to hope,   65
Though changed, no doubt, from what I was when first
I came among these hills; when like a roe
I bounded o'er the mountains, by the sides
Of the deep rivers, and the lonely streams,

8. Burden.

Wherever nature led: more like a man   70
Flying from something that he dreads than one
Who sought the thing he loved. For nature then
(The coarser[9] pleasures of my boyish days,
And their glad animal movements all gone by)
To me was all in all—I cannot paint   75
What then I was. The sounding cataract
Haunted me like a passion; the tall rock,
The mountain, and the deep and gloomy wood,
Their colors and their forms, were then to me
An appetite; a feeling and a love,   80
That had no need of a remoter charm,
By thought supplied, nor any interest
Unborrowed from the eye. That time is past,
And all its aching joys are now no more,
And all its dizzy raptures. Not for this   85
Faint I,[1] nor mourn nor murmur; other gifts
Have followed; for such loss, I would believe,
Abundant recompense. For I have learned
To look on nature, not as in the hour
Of thoughtless youth; but hearing oftentimes   90
The still, sad music of humanity,
Nor harsh nor grating, though of ample power
To chasten and subdue. And I have felt
A presence that disturbs me with the joy
Of elevated thoughts; a sense sublime   95
Of something far more deeply interfused,
Whose dwelling is the light of setting suns,
And the round ocean and the living air,
And the blue sky, and in the mind of man:
A motion and a spirit, that impels   100
All thinking things, all objects of all thought,
And rolls through all things. Therefore am I still
A lover of the meadows and the woods
And mountains; and of all that we behold
From this green earth; of all the mighty world   105
Of eye, and ear—both what they half create,
And what perceive; well pleased to recognize
In nature and the language of the sense
The anchor of my purest thoughts, the nurse,
The guide, the guardian of my heart, and soul   110
Of all my moral being.
                              Nor perchance,
If I were not thus taught, should I the more
Suffer my genial spirits[2] to decay:
For thou art with me here upon the banks
Of this fair river; thou my dearest Friend,[3]   115
My dear, dear Friend; and in thy voice I catch
The language of my former heart, and read

---

9. Physical.
1. Am I discouraged.
2. Natural disposition; i.e., the spirits
that are part of his individual genius.
3. His sister Dorothy.

My former pleasures in the shooting lights
Of thy wild eyes. Oh! yet a little while
May I behold in thee what I was once, 120
My dear, dear Sister! and this prayer I make,
Knowing that Nature never did betray
The heart that loved her; 'tis her privilege,
Through all the years of this our life, to lead
From joy to joy: for she can so inform 125
The mind that is within us, so impress
With quietness and beauty, and so feed
With lofty thoughts, that neither evil tongues,
Rash judgments, nor the sneers of selfish men,
Nor greetings where no kindness is, nor all 130
The dreary intercourse of daily life,
Shall e'er prevail against us, or disturb
Our cheerful faith that all which we behold
Is full of blessings. Therefore let the moon
Shine on thee in thy solitary walk; 135
And let the misty mountain-winds be free
To blow against thee: and, in after years,
When these wild ecstasies shall be matured
Into a sober pleasure; when thy mind
Shall be a mansion for all lovely forms, 140
Thy memory be as a dwelling-place
For all sweet sounds and harmonies; oh! then,
If solitude, or fear, or pain, or grief,
Should be thy portion, with what healing thoughts
Of tender joy wilt thou remember me, 145
And these my exhortations! Nor, perchance—
If I should be where I no more can hear
Thy voice, nor catch from thy wild eyes these gleams
Of past existence—wilt thou then forget
That on the banks of this delightful stream 150
We stood together; and that I, so long
A worshiper of Nature, hither came
Unwearied in that service; rather say
With warmer love—oh! with far deeper zeal
Of holier love. Nor wilt thou then forget, 155
That after many wanderings, many years
Of absence, these steep woods and lofty cliffs,
And this green pastoral landscape, were to me
More dear, both for themselves and for thy sake!

1798

SIR THOMAS WYATT

They Flee from Me

They flee from me, that sometime did me seek,
With naked foot stalking in my chamber.
I have seen them, gentle, tame, and meek,

That now are wild, and do not remember
That sometime they put themselves in danger   5
To take bread at my hand; and now they range,
Busily seeking with a continual change.

Thankéd be Fortune it hath been otherwise,
Twenty times better; but once in special,
In thin array, after a pleasant guise,   10
When her loose gown from her shoulders did fall,
And she me caught in her arms long and small.[4]
And therewith all sweetly did me kiss
And softly said, "Dear heart, how like you this?"

It was no dream, I lay broad waking.   15
But all is turned, thorough[5] my gentleness,
Into a strange fashion of forsaking;
And I have leave to go, of her goodness,
And she also to use newfangleness.[6]
But since that I so kindely[7] am servéd,   20
I fain[8] would know what she hath deservéd.

1557

---

4. Slender.   7. In a way natural to women.
5. Through.   8. Eagerly.
6. Fondness for novelty.

A GLOSSARY OF POETIC TERMS

1. SUBJECT, THEME, AND MEANING

Most readers would agree with Archibald MacLeish that "a poem should not mean but be," but discovering what a poem "is" often involves identifying what it contains. Poets often used to provide an **argument** for their poems, a prose summary of what "happens"; now they seldom provide such a convenience, but to begin interpretation and experience of a poem readers often find it useful to **paraphrase**, put into prose exactly what the poem says, line by line, in words that are different but as nearly equivalent as possible.

The **subject,** or **topic,** of a poem is its general or specific area of concern, usually something categorical such as death (or the death of a particular person), war (or a specific war, or specific battle), love, or the simple life. Most poems make **statements** about a subject and define the degree and kind of their interest in it; a poem about war, for example, may ultimately be more concerned to say something about the nature of man or about honor or about peace than about war itself. Subjects offer a great variety of **themes:** that death is a release from pain, or a gateway to immortality, that war is senseless, or brutal, or a necessary evil, or a heroic quest for justice. A poem's theme is the statement it makes about its subject; summarizing a paraphrase in one or two sentences often yields the theme.

An **explication,** or **exegesis,** explains how all of the elements in an individual poem or passage work; in explication, a critic analyzes the various component parts in order to interpret the poem's statement. Explication takes a step beyond paraphrase in attempting to discover a poem's meaning. The terms **message** and **moral,** once used to summarize the poem's meaning, are now usually considered misleading because they tend to oversimplify and confuse statement with meaning. Similarly objectionable to many is the term **hidden meaning,** which implies that a poem is a puzzle or that the author is deliberately obscuring his or her point. **Meaning** is the poem's combination of themes and statements about a subject or series of subjects *and* the emotions that it artfully evokes toward them by means of poetic devices and strategies. But meaning—however well defined and articulated—is never the precise equivalent of the poem itself.

2. ATTITUDE, TONE, AND AUDIENCE

It is not only what is said that determines a poem's meaning and effect but how it is said and to whom. The term **tone** represents an attempt to be precise about the author's attitude toward what his or her poem literally says. Descriptions of tone try to characterize the way the words of the poem are (or should be) spoken when one sensitively reads the poem aloud. Tone literally tries to describe the vocal sounds which a poem seems to demand, and one may speak of the tone of an individual word or phrase, of a longer passsage, or of a whole poem. Words such as "ironic," "comic," "playful," "sincere," and "straightforward" may sometimes accurately describe tone, as may more particular adjectives such as "angry," "boastful," "taunting," "apologetic," "plaintive," or "bemused."

It is often useful, too, to know about the imagined **audience** of a poem, for much of what poets do involves an attempt to move and influence their hearers. Because poems are meant to be read and experienced by someone besides the poet, they are more than simple records of an event, or idea, or state of mind. Poets fictionalize or imagine circumstances and reflections, and they usually try to communicate by evoking in the reader a particular attitude or emotion.

The means by which poems generate an effect are usually called **poetic** (or **artistic**) **devices** or **strategies**. Almost everything in a poem is in some sense (but not a bad sense) a device: the choice of one word rather than another one, the use of metaphor, of certain sounds and rhythms, of allusions, conventions, forms—all contribute to a total effect. The **rhetoric** of a poem is the sum of the persuasive devices used to affect readers, with or without their consent.

Many of the most important **rhetorical devices** (or **rhetorical figures**) date from classical antiquity, and some of these are so common in ordinary life that we scarcely recognize them as devices, even in a poem. **Comparison** and **contrast** may clarify the identity and properties of a person, place, or thing, but persuasive values may also be built in, depending on what is being compared with what. Acceptance by **association** is as common as guilt by association; naming admired names may lull a reader into easy submission or be part of a complex web of interrelationships in which an author places his or her values among things certain to be admired, or expected to be admired among readers of a certain kind. An **allusion** is a reference to something outside the poem (in history, perhaps, or in another poem) which has built-in emotional associations. **Example** is simply the giving of a specific instance to back up a generalization, and many whole poems are built upon the principle, directly or indirectly.

Several classic figures of speech, though not restricted to poetry, are often found in poems. **Hyperbole** (or extravagant **exaggeration**) may be serious or comic or both at the same time, pushing something so far toward absurdity that its ordinary manifestation may seem normal and acceptable. **Meiosis** (or **understatement**) consciously underrates something or portrays it as lesser than it is usually thought to be; its psychology is to bring the reader instinctively to the defense of the thing being undervalued. It is closely related to **irony** (§3), especially in one of its forms, **litotes**, which affirms something by denying its opposite, as in colloquial expressions such as "He's no Einstein." **Periphrasis** (or **circumlocution**) is deliberate avoidance of the obvious, writing which circles its subject and refuses to take the simplest route toward clear meaning. **Synecdoche** is using a part of something to signify the whole (as in "hired hands" for "workmen"), and **metonymy** is naming something associated with what is being talked about rather than the thing itself, as in the use of "crown" for "king." **Hyperbaton** is the rearrangement of sentence elements for special effects; Milton, in *Paradise Lost*, for example, often uses extreme instances of the figure, as in the sentence beginning in line 44 of Book I (p. 647). **Prolepsis** is the **foreshadowing** of a future event as if it were already influencing the present, as in Eliot's *Journey of the Magi* (p. 848) when the wise men on their way to Bethlehem see objects suggestive of the Crucifixion.

These terms merely describe and categorize standard ways in which words may affect pyschological processes. Many kinds of attempts to persuade—sermons, political speeches, TV commercials, informal conversations—use some version of such devices, although often in more simple and less subtle ways than good poetry. Identifying the devices is only a way of discovering what a poem advocates, how it tries to develop emotional energy, and whether its methods are effective. Being able to identify the devices is useful but only as a means to a more important end.

Poems which openly and directly advocate a particular ideology, argue for a specific cause, or try to teach us something are called **didactic** poems. Critics sometimes distinguish between didactic poems and **mimetic** (or **imaginative**) poems, which are more concerned to present than to persuade. But the distinction is one of degree, for most poems mean at the very least to make their attitudes, their vision, their presentation of reality plausible and attractive. The term **propaganda** is almost always used pejoratively, to suggest that a writer's main aim is to arouse readers toward immediate action in a specific situation; poems so specifically and narrowly directed are usually assumed to be ephemeral, although good "occasional poems" (§11) and "satires" (§10) often transcend their occasions.

3. SPEAKER

It has become traditional to distinguish between the person who wrote the poem and the person who speaks in a poem, for an author often deliberately chooses to speak through a character quite different from his or her real self. Poets thus sometimes create a fictional person as a **speaker**, just as playwrights create a character who is then obliged to say things in a way appropriate to the character as created. In many poems the speaker is very like the author, or very like what the author wishes to think he or she is like. Between the speaker who is a fully distinct character and the author speaking honestly and directly are many degrees of detachment.

The term **persona** is often used synonymously with speaker, especially in satire, where the author usually speaks in a voice very like his own except that he often pretends to be more innocent, more earnest, and more pure than he knows himself to be. Such a **pose** (or **posture**, or **mask**) is not really dishonest any more than the creation of a character in a play or story is dishonest; it is part of the author's strategy of making a point effectively and persuasively.

When the author's attitude is different from that of the speaker the poem is said to be ironic, although the term **irony** also means several other things. Irony is not only saying one thing and meaning its opposite; it is also any manner of being oblique rather than straightforward and often involves **exaggeration** or **understatement**. A whole poem may be said to be ironic (or to have **structural irony**) when its total effect is to reverse the attitude presented by the speaker, but poems which are not wholly ironic may use ironic words and phrases (**verbal irony**) to generate a more complex statement or attitude.

When irony is stark, simple, snide, exactly inverted—that is, when what is said is exactly the opposite of what is meant—it is called **sarcasm.** The term "irony," qualified in various ways, may indicate almost any kind of discrepancy between what is apparent in a literary work and what someone else knows to be so. **Dramatic irony** (which may be used in a poem as well as in a play) occurs when the speaker is unaware of something about himself or his situation but the reader is not.

4. SITUATION AND SETTING

A poem's relationship to time and space is sometimes very simple and sometimes very complicated. Some poems have a **setting** specified as clearly as do stories and plays, and in many cases the effect of a poem may depend heavily upon our recognizing the setting. In *Channel Firing* (p. 857), for example, the setting has to be a graveyard in England just before Britain's entry into World War I for the poem to make any sense. But the poem does not immediately tell us where and when the action is taking place; in *Channel Firing* the facts accumulate: first a dead body awakens and sits up, wondering what the noise is about. A little later we find out that gunnery practice in the English channel is the cause of the commotion, and finally we are given information (about the echoes moving inland) that indicates which side of the channel we are concerned with.

Poems which celebrate a certain occasion (see **occasional poem,** §11) often depend upon a reader's knowledge of the event and its cultural context. Poems about specific events or circumstances may be said to be **referential** in their use of setting, and they generally require us to recognize not only historical facts but the cultural interpretation placed upon the facts at the time. If a poem requires a particular location, there is usually information in the poem that leads to such specificity. When no such information exists in the poem, it is safe to assume that you don't need it to understand the poem's use of setting. Even a general setting may, however, recall other settings in literature, art, history, or myth. Such **allusive settings** (for a definition of **allusion,** see §2) are very common; garden settings, for example, almost inevitably call up memories of the Garden of Eden and its features and events—innocence, perfection, temptation, or the fall. Closely related to allusive settings are **symbolic settings,** which depend upon the psychological association of a particular quality with a particular place.

Temporal settings (that is, settings in time) may be symbolic or allusive or both at the same time. *Sunday Morning* (p. 896) depends upon both the traditional sense of sabbath and the modern custom of using Sunday mornings for luxurious leisure. Temporal settings may also be historically specific, or depend instead upon time of day or season of the year. The temporal setting often helps to set a particular mood in the poem or anchors the poem in a particular psychological reality.

The **situation** may need to be identified even in poems that do not have a specific setting. In *The Flea* (p. 623), for example, a male speaker is delivering a monologue to a woman, but we don't know where or when; the significant thing is that the man is arguing for making love, and the woman is reluctant. In some poems, too, the situation is a remembered one from the distance of later years; such a device is called **retrospection**. *Cherrylog Road* (p. 619), for example, although detailed in its presentation of setting and situation, makes it clear that the speaker is recalling events from many years before.

5. LANGUAGE AND POETRY

Words are the bricks and mortar of poetry, and whatever design the poet has in mind has to be carried out through the words available in the language. Word choice (**diction**) in poems is usually calculated carefully; often words are chosen because of their **precision** or their **ambiguity**, the multiple possibilities of suggestivity which can complicate reader responses. Where words are placed is important, too; like prose, poetry usually follows the normal **syntax** (word order) of the language in which it is written, but sometimes words are moved around for special effects in sound, emphasis, or meaning.

Most nouns, verbs, adjectives, and adverbs not only **denote** a thing, action, or attribute, but also **connote** feelings and associations suggested by it. A horse is literally a four-legged, whinnying, rideable, workable animal, but the word "horse" connotes to most people strength, vitality, vigor. To be even more emphatic about its vigor and strength and to imply wildness as well, one might call it a steed or stallion. Not all words have clear, universally accepted connotations built into them, and writers often use the more elaborate devices of metaphor and symbolism (§6) to build a specific set of associations and values into the words and combinations of words that they use.

Imagery is used by different critics to mean three related but distinct things: 1. the mental pictures suggested by the verbal descriptions in a poem; 2. the visual descriptions in the poem itself; or 3. the figurative language (including metaphors, similes, and analogies) in the poem. In all three uses, imagery is technically a visual term, though other sense impressions are sometimes included under its large umbrella; imagery which mingles different sense impressions (sound or touch, for exmple, with sight) is said to be **synesthetic imagery**.

The first definition of imagery is the least precise one, for it tries to describe the effect of the poem on the reader; because each reader's response is likely to be a little different from every other reader's, critics usually find it safer and more precise to articulate the poem's efforts to create the effect; the second and third definitions of imagery are attempts to describe these efforts, the *means* of bringing about a certain effect. The third definition is the most common one, and it has the advantage of greater precision in describing different indirect ways that a poem may use to translate words into less abstract sense experience. Critics who use the term "imagery" in this third way may refer to nonfigurative description simply as description and to the presumed effect on the reader of both description and imagery as **visual impressions** or **sense impressions**. Imagery is the collective term for a group of individual images. One may speak of an **image cluster** (a group of similar images concentrated in a short passage), of a **controlling image** (when a single image seems to dominate a passage or even a whole poem, making other images subservient to it), or of an **image pattern** (when one or more images recur in a passage or poem). Sometimes it is convenient to speak of **kinds of imagery** ("animal imagery" or "architectural imagery") as well as to define individual images in greater detail. When imagery is defined in the third way, it is **figurative language**, which is defined in §6.

6. FIGURATIVE LANGUAGE

Figurative language (that is, language that uses figures of speech) includes the use of simile, metaphor, analogy, and personification. A **simile** is a direct, explicit comparison of one thing to another and usually uses "like" or "as" in drawing the connection. A simile may **extend** throughout a poem and be elaborated (it is then called an **analogy**) or be used to make a brief comparison in only one specified sense.

A **metaphor** pretends that one thing is something else, thus making an implicit comparison between the things. Even more than similes, metaphors are often **extended** because, in describing a thing in terms of something else, a metaphor often implies a detailed and complex resemblance between the two, one which may not be obvious at first glance. When a metaphor compares things which seem radically unlike, but which can be developed into a striking parallel, it is called a **conceit**; the "metaphysical poets" of the 17th century specialized in finding surprising likenesses in things usually considered unlike, and their poems often elaborate a single **metaphysical conceit**. The terms **tenor** and **vehicle** are often used to distinguish the primary object of attention from the thing being used to clarify that object. In Shakespeare's *That Time of Year* (p. 650) the primary object of attention (**tenor**) is the aging speaker, and late autumn is the **vehicle** which in the first few lines clarifies his aging. Metaphors are often said to be **extended metaphors** or **controlling metaphors** (in the same sense I have described above for images) when they dominate or organize a passage or poem.

A **mixed metaphor** is one in which terms from one metaphor are incorporated into another one, usually by mistake. A **dead metaphor** is one that has passed into such common usage as to have obscured its origins: we speak of a "leg" of a chair or the "heart" of the problem without remembering that the terms are metaphors implying a comparison to living bodies. When language, metaphorical or not, becomes unnecessarily specialized and self-consciously unavailable to an outsider, it is **jargon**. When such language is used mindlessly, it is called **cant**. When it is slangy and lives the short life of fashion among a select in-group, it is called **argot**. A **cliché** is any expression or idea which, through repeated use, has become commonplace, tiresome, and trite.

Personification (or **prosopopeia**) is the strategy of giving human qualities to abstract concepts or inanimate things: Beauty, Honor, Cruelty, Death, flowers, and various aspects of the natural landscape have been personified in various ages, but the strategy has been largely out of favor except for specialized and comic uses in the 20th century. Closely related is the strategy of ascribing to nature emotions which reflect human happenings (the **pathetic fallacy**), as in *The Darkling Thrush* (p. 855).

A **symbol** is something which stands for something else. In a very literal sense, words themselves are all symbols (they stand for an object, action, or quality, not just for letters or sounds), but symbols in poetry are said to be those words and groups of words which have a range of reference beyond their literal denotation. When a poem pervasively uses symbols as a major strategy and when the poem is more committed to the things which the symbols represent than to everyday reality, it is called a **symbolic poem** and is said to use **symbolism**. Poems, like everyday conversation, may use symbols occasionally and casually without being called symbolic.

In **allegory**, the action of the poem consistently and systematically describes another order of things beyond the obvious one. Spenser's *The Faerie Queene* is allegorical on several levels at the same time; the narrative action makes literal sense as a story, but the characters and actions also stand for political happenings, religious events, and moral values. *The Faerie Queene* is thus said to be a political, religious, and moral allegory.

Poets sometimes develop a highly specialized and personal set of **private symbols**—words, objects, and phrases which take on specific meanings as a result of repeated use by the poet in poem after poem. At the opposite extreme from private symbols are those which are universally shared within a defined culture. The framework of such shared symbols is called a **myth,** and the myth may include characters, events, and recurrent patterns of experience which the culture recognizes as, on some deep level, true. Poets sometimes too use particulars of a myth no longer literally or generally accepted; the wide recognition of standard myths allows writers to employ examples either in or out of their full mythic context. In recent years, critics have been heavily influenced by **myth criticism,** which usually signifies an attempt to discover **archetypes,** patterns of experience and action which are similar in different nations and cultures. In this sense, myth is not restricted to a single system, but rather attempts to transcend the particulars of time and place and locate fundamental recurrent patterns in human nature and human history.

7. FORM AND STRUCTURE

The form of a poem has to do with its appearance, just as does the form of a building, and one can describe that form in many different ways, just as a description of the form of a building depends upon the angle of vision (from the ground or from the air), the distance of the viewer, and to what other buildings the building is being compared. The simplest sense of poetic form involves the literal appearance on the page, the poem's shape seen physically, conceived literally. On the page most traditional poems look regular—that is, they are either divided into regular "stanzas" (§9) or they flow continually down the page in lines of more or less equal length. Modern poems tend to be less regular and thus to look more scattered and fragmented on the page, reflecting a general modern attitude that poetic meaning accumulates in a less regular and less programmed way. Occasionally the words are even shaped like a particular object, as in Renaissance **emblem poetry** (or **carmen figuratum** or **shaped verse**) or recent **concrete poetry.**

More enduring, more significant, and more complex senses of form involve less easily seeable ways of classifying external characteristics. Poetry is itself a sort of **formal** classification as distinguished from drama or fiction, and one can also distinguish between kinds of poetry (elegy, for example, or epigram) on the basis of subject matter, tone; conventions, etc. (see §10). Stanza varieties and rhythmic patterns (see §9 and §8) are also formal matters, for each involves external patterns which may be described relative to other poems.

As in a building, **structure** supports form and makes it possible. The order and arrangement of all of a poem's constituent parts—words, images, figures of speech, ideas, everything—involve structure, and the ways of discussing the relationship between parts vary from matters of word arrangement (grammar, syntax) to the development and presentation of ideas. Structure enables the form; the planning and craft of poetry are all, finally, structural matters.

The distinction I have made between form and structure corresponds to distinctions that some critics make between **external** and **internal form** (or external and internal structure). Another frequent distinction is that between **organic** structure or form and **architechtonic** structure or form (those who make this distinction do not necessarily use the terms "form" and "structure" as they have been explained above). Things organic are said to take their shape from natural forces, like living organisms, and things architechtonic to have shape artificially imposed upon them from without; a strong bias is usually implied toward the former, for the distinction implies the livingness, wholeness, and uniqueness of an individual poem.

Some works are shaped by other works which they **imitate** or **parody**; *The Dover Bitch* (p. 803), for example, is a response to *Dover Beach* (p. 628). An **imitation** which makes fun of another work is a **burlesque** or **parody** of it, exaggerating its distinctive features and holding them up to ridicule; it is a parody if its attitude is one of gentle teasing, a burlesque if it is harsh and vicious: Imitation may also be a kind of flattery, honoring the methods, values, and meanings of another work and expropriating them into the new one. Many great poems have their basis in imitation and a good imitation is never a simple copy; it often derives major effects from its similarities to and differences from the original.

Questions of form and structure are related to questions about the integrity and autonomy of individual poems. For many years, critics were reluctant to deal with **parts** of a poem, insisting that as self-existent **wholes** poems deserved to be dealt with **holistically**, as creations having their own laws. More recently, criticism has dealt more directly with parts of poems, admitting that they too have organizational principles and facing squarely the difficulty that knowing whether a poem is whole or not is, even for the author, very nearly a mystical matter. Besides, an individual poem is often part of a larger **sequence** or **cycle**—that is, a group of poems which have significant features in common: they may be about a similar subject, tell a story progressively, or be calculated to produce a particular effect. Almost all poets themselves arrange the poems in their individual volumes, and it is often useful and revealing to read individual poems in the context of these volumes.

8. PROSODY

Prosody is the study of sound and rhythm in poetry. It is not a very exact science, but properly used it can be an aid to reading and *hearing* poems more fully.

The **rhythm** of a passage—in prose or poetry—is the pattern of sound pulsations in the voice as one reads it. Almost all spoken language has some kind of rhythm, however irregular, and simply listening to a human voice reciting, reading, or talking informally reveals recurrent systems of **stress** or **accent**. Stress is a relative matter (and this fact is a major difficulty for prosodic analysis), but in listening to the human voice we can always hear that some words and syllables are **stressed** (accented), and that others are, relatively, **unstressed** (unaccented). When the stress recurs at quite regular intervals—that is, when the rhythm has a pattern—the result is **meter.** The systematic analysis of patterns of stress, syllable by syllable, sound unit by sound unit, is called **scansion;** a reader who can **scan** a poem will discern the poem's basic rhythmic pattern (meter) and may then notice variations in the pattern or departures from it.

In the sentence,

Throw the ball to me

stresses "naturally" fall on "throw," "ball," and "me," but another context of meaning might considerably alter the stress pattern:

I said, throw the ball to me, not over my head.

Stress here would likely fall on "to," and there might be some other "unusual" stresses, provided by the demands of meaning in particular instances or by particular speakers. When a sentence or phrase appears in a certain rhythmic context (in, for example, a poem written in a certain meter), the sound context also affects it, tending to bend it (or "wrench" it) toward the basic pattern in the surrounding passage. There are, then, three factors which determine stress: (1.) the "natural" stress or stresses of each word; (2.) meaning and emphasis in a sentence or phrase; and (3.) the patterns of stress in the surrounding context.

Meter is measured in feet; a **foot** normally consists of a stressed syllable and one or more unstressed syllables. In the following line, in which stressed syllables have marked "–" and unstressed syllables "∪," the division into five feet is indicated by a **virgule,** or **slash mark** (/):

∪ – / ∪ – / ∪ – / ∪ – / ∪ –
A lit/tle lear/ning is/a dang/'rous thing

Each of its feet is an *iambic* foot—that is, it has an unstressed syllable followed by a stressed one. Iambic meter is the most common one in English poetry, but three other meters are of some importance:

Trochaic (a stressed syllable followed by an unstressed one):

$$\text{Tell mé}/ \text{ nót ín}/ \text{ móurn fúl}/ \text{ núm bèrs}$$

Anapestic (two unstressed syllables followed by a stressed one):

$$\text{'Twas the níght}/ \text{ be fóre Chríst}/ \text{ mas and áll}/ \text{ through the hóuse}$$

Dactylic (a stressed syllable followed by two unstressed ones):

$$\text{Híg gle dy}/ \text{ píg gle dy}/ \text{ Ál fred Lórd}/ \text{ Tén ny sòn.}$$

Most English poems use one of these meters as their basic meter, but not with absolute regularity. An iambic poem will often contain trochaic feet (for emphasis, perhaps, or just for change), and some variation is almost a requirement if a poem is not to lull the ear into total dull deafness. Besides the standard meters, there are special feet used for variations.

Here is a table of the basic metrical feet and the most frequent variations:

ADJECTIVE FORM OF THE NAME	NOUN FORM	PATTERN
iambic	*iamb* (or *iambus*)	⌣ —
trochaic	*trochee*	— ⌣
anapestic	*anapest*	⌣ ⌣ —
dactylic	*dactyl*	— ⌣ ⌣
spondaic	*spondee*	— —
pyrrhic	*pyrrhic*	⌣ ⌣
amphibrachic	*amphibrach* (or *amphibrachys* or *rocking foot*)	⌣ — ⌣
amphimacric	*amphimacer* (or *amphimac* or *cretic*)	— ⌣ —

Coleridge's *Metrical Feet* (p. 695) exemplifies most of them.

The most common line length in English poetry is pentameter, five feet. Here is a table of all the common line lengths:

monometer	one foot
dimeter	two feet
trimeter	three feet
tetrameter	four feet
pentameter	five feet
hexameter	six feet
heptameter	seven feet
octameter	eight feet

Iambic and anapestic meters are sometimes called **rising rhythms** (or **rising meters**) because their basic movement is from unstressed to stressed syllables; and trochaic and dactylic meters are called **falling rhythms** (or **falling meters**). When a foot lacks a syllable it is called **catalectic;** the first foot of anapestic lines is often catalectic, and the final foot of most trochaic lines is catalectic because lines that end with an unstressed syllable are usually thought to "sound funny"; such lines usually occur only in comic poetry. Lines that rhyme by using an unstressed final syllable are said to have **feminine rhyme.** Certain meters are also said to incline toward comic effects; anapestic rhythm tends to produce comic effects, although it can be used to produce more serious tones. Iambic tetrameter also seems more liable than most meters to comic effects, though it also has been used for great varieties of tone. The number and length of pauses in a line affect the speed with which the line is read and, indirectly, the tone in any meter, for a slow-paced line seems less emphatic in its rhythm than a rapid-paced one. Almost all lines contain one or more natural pauses, some very short and some fairly long; any significant pause within a line is called a **caesura,** and in scansion it is indicated by a double virgule (//).

The distinction between stressed and unstressed is not a very precise one, for many degrees of stress are possible, and even an untrained ear can usually hear great variety of stress in the reading of a single line from a single poem. Division into feet is sometimes arbitrary, for there is often more than one way to count the number of feet, even assuming that the stresses are all accurately marked. Students often get bogged down in the technicalities of such matters and lose sight of the point of metrical analysis—which is to *hear* poems more accurately and notice those surprising places when the poem departs from its basic pattern.

Not all English poetry uses meter in the traditional senses I have described. Much modern poetry is in **free verse,** which avoids regularized meter and has no significant recurrent stress rhythms, although it may use other repetitive patterns—of words, phrases, structures—as Whitman often does. (**Free verse** should not be confused with **blank verse,** which is unrhymed but is by definition written in iambic pentameter.) Many modern poems that may appear unpatterned are, however, very tightly controlled metrically; the absence of rhyme does not mean the absence of metrical pattern, and many untraditional-looking modern poems use traditional meter in traditional ways. Many poems, old as well as new, experiment with meter too, trying odd combinations within the definitions I have given or using different principles altogether. The **sprung rhythm** used by Gerard Manley Hopkins avoids the usual distinctions about kinds of feet and only counts the numbers of stressed syllables; each foot begins with a stressed syllable, but any number of unstressed syllables may follow before the next foot begins, so that traditional scansion would make the pattern seem unpatterned. **Quantitative verse,** imitating the metrical principles used by Latin and Greek poets, has been attempted in almost every age, but seldom with success. Unlike stress meters of any kind, quantitative verse determines pattern by the duration of sounds and sets up various meters in combinations of long and short syllables. Some modern experimenters have fused quantitative and stress patterns, and still others have tried patterns based on the number of sounds (see the discussion of syllabic verse in §9), on the kind of sounds used rather than either duration or stress, or on attempts at precise distinctions in the *amount* of stress in stressed syllables.

Until recently **rhyme** has been nearly as important as meter to most poetry. Rhyme is based on the duplication of the vowel sound and all sounds after the vowel in the relevant words. Most rhyme is **end-rhyme** (that is, the near-duplication of sounds takes place at the ends of the lines), but other patterns are possible. **Internal rhyme** involves rhyming sounds within the same line; in **beginning rhyme**, the first word or syllable rhymes in two or more lines. Not-quite rhyme is often used to vary strict rhyme schemes; the most common form is **slant rhyme** (or **half rhyme**) in which the relevant words have similar but not exactly rhyming sounds because either the vowel or consonant varies slightly (as in backs/box, bent/want, or web/step). **Visual** (or **eye**) **rhyme** uses words with identical endings but different pronunciations (bread/bead), and **rime riche** uses words that sound exactly the same but have different spellings and meanings (knight/night; lead/led; him/hymn). In poetry of earlier ages, one needs to watch, too, for **historical rhyme**—rhyme that was perfect when the poem was written but, because of historical changes in pronunciation, is no longer so; tea/day and join/divine were once good rhymes in the easiest and simplest sense.

Sound effects not involving rhyme continue to be important to poetry, and many of them are (like rhyme and meter) based on the ordering principle of repetition. **Alliteration** is the repetition of sounds in nearby words; usually alliteration involves the initial consonant sounds of words (and sometimes internal consonants in stressed syllables). **Assonance** is a repetition of vowel sounds in a line or series of lines; assonance often affects pace (by unbalancing short and long vowel patterns) and the way words included in the pattern tend to seem underscored. **Consonance** involves a repeated sequence of consonants but with varied vowels (as in stop/step, rope/reap, or hip/hop).

Onomatopoeia is the attempt to imitate or echo sounds being described. Some words are in themselves **onomatopoeic** (buzz, fizz, murmur), and others suggest action or qualities related to their literal meaning (slippery, lull). Passages may use rhythms and vocal sounds for onomatopoeic purposes; the famous "Sound and Sense" passage by Pope (p. 692) exemplifies many of the possibilities of sound to produce imitative, hormonious, or cacophonous effects.

9. STANZA AND VERSE FORMS

Most poems of more than a few lines are divided into stanzas, groups of lines with a specific cogency of their own and usually set off from one another by a space. Traditionally, stanzas are linked by a common **rhyme scheme** (pattern of rhyme words) or by a common pattern of rhythms; modern poems which are divided into stanzas often, however, lack such patterns. Stanza lengths vary considerably, and so do the patterns and complexity of rhyme. Poets often invent distinctive patterns of their own—sometimes for novelty, sometimes to generate a particular effect—but over the years some stanza patterns have proved quite durable.

The **ballad stanza** is one of the oldest; it consists of four lines, the second and fourth of which are iambic trimeter and rhyme with each other. The first and third lines, in iambic tetrameter, do not rhyme. **Terza rima** is the three-line stanza in which Dante wrote *The Divine Comedy;* each iambic pentameter stanza (*aba*) interlocks with the next (*bcb, cdc, ded,* etc.). Among longer stanza forms are **ottava rima,** an Italian form adapted to English as eight lines of iambic pentameter rhyming *abababcc,* and the **Spenserian stanza,** the nine-line form Spenser invented for his *Faerie Queene*—eight lines of iambic pentameter and a ninth line of iambic hexameter, called an **alexandrine,** rhymed *ababbcbcc.* Stanzas with no official names are simply designated by the number of lines; a three-line stanza is called a **tristich, triplet,** or **tercet** (the latter is also a term for part of the sonnet—see the discussion below); a four-line stanza is a **quatrain;** a five-line stanza is a **quintain** or **quintet;** a six-line stanza is a **sextain** or **sixain.**

Many modern poems, rather than using traditional stanzas, are divided spatially according to breaks in syntax, meaning, or tone, and the individual characteristics of a particular poem may dictate such breaks. Some modern experiments have also produced patterns as demanding in their own way as rhyme-based stanzas. **Syllabic verse,** for example, requires that the number of syllables in each line of the first stanza be duplicated in each subsequent stanza; stanzas (and lines within them) may thus be of any length, but the poet commits himself or herself to a pattern in the first stanza and thereafter sticks to it.

The **couplet** is a rather special case among stanza forms. It consists of two lines (of any specifiable length or rhythm) which rhyme with one another, and seldom is one couplet divided by space from another one. Larger divisions within couplet verse are usually indicated (as in blank verse) by indentation, and the units are called **verse paragraphs,** which may or may not be separated by space. The **heroic couplet,** rhyming lines of iambic pentameter, has been the most popular and durable of couplet forms; it dominated English poetry during much of the 17th and 18th centuries and has been used successfully by many earlier and later poets. When the syntax of one couplet carries over into the next couplet, the couplets are said to be **open** or **enjambed; enjambment** is the continuation of syntax beyond the borders of a single couplet. **Closed** (or **end-stopped**) **couplets** are—as far as the technicalities of syntax are concerned— complete in themselves. Couplets written in iambic tetrameter tend to be used for comic effect because of the emphatic regularity of the rhythms and the abrupt underscoring of the rhyme.

Several **fixed poetic forms** (which contain a certain number of stanzas organized in a determined way) have been popular, from time to time, with English poets. Most of them were introduced by French troubadours in Provence, some of them as early as the 12th century. The **villanelle,** for example, contains five three-line stanzas and a final four-line stanza; only two rhyme sounds are permitted in the entire poem, and the first and third lines of the first stanza are repeated, alternately, as the third line of subsequent stanzas until the last. In the last stanza, the repeating lines become the final two lines of the poem. The **sestina** contains six six-line stanzas and a final three-line stanza, all unrhymed; but the final word in each line of the first stanza then becomes the final word in other stanzas (but in a different specified pattern); the final stanza uses these words again in a specified way, one in each half line. Some poets have even written **double** and **triple sestinas,** in which the demands increase geometrically. Repetition (probably originally for mnemonic purposes) is a major feature in fixed poetic forms.

10. GENRES AND KINDS

Here the term **genre** is used to indicate the traditional classroom distinction between fiction, poetry, and drama. Other less inclusive terms may then be used for subdividing genres and for different ways of classifying literary works according to characteristics they have in common.

A **mode** is, literally, a way of doing something; as a literary term it may most usefully be employed to indicate basic literary patterns of organizing experience. The **narrative mode** tells a story and organizes experience along a time continuum. The **dramatic mode** presents a change, usually an abrupt one, and organizes experience emotionally according to the rise and fall of someone's fortunes. The **lyric mode** reflects upon an experience or an idea and organizes experience irrespective of time and space, although it may describe a particular time or specific place. These traditional modes represent basic ways of viewing experience and have been around for a very long time. They obviously influenced the development of genres, which represent a somewhat artificial stiffening or rigidification of the narrative, dramatic, and lyric modes.

One may also think of modes in terms of the conclusions they draw about experience or the dominant emotions they arouse in their presentations of experience. **Tragedy,** or the **tragic mode,** describes someone's downfall, usually in stately language. **Comedy,** or the **comic mode,** describes in more common language someone's triumph or the successful emergence of some order which encompasses and mutes all disorderly forces. **Romance,** or the **romantic mode,** describes the ideal, or what ought to be, often in terms of nostalgia or fantasy or longing. **Satire,** or the **satiric mode,** attacks the way things are and usually distributes the blame. In *The Anatomy of Criticism,* Northrop Frye argues that these modes correspond to the **myths** of the four seasons (comedy–spring; romance–summer; tragedy–autumn; satire–winter) and thus considers them universal ways of organizing experience.

Poetry considered as a genre may also be subdivided into **kinds** (or **types,** or **subgenres**). The **epic,** or **heroic poetry,** has been traditionally regarded as the highest in a hierarchy of kinds because it describes the great deeds of mighty heroes and heroines, usually in founding a nation or developing a distinctive culture, and uses elevated language and a grand, high style. **Pastoral poetry** describes the simple life of country folk, usually shepherds who live a timeless, painless (and sheepless) life in a world that is full of beauty, music, and love, and that remains forever green. The pastoral poem is also sometimes called an **eclogue,** a **bucolic,** or an **idyll.** The **elegy** was, in classical times, a poem on any subject written in "elegiac" meter, but since the

Renaissance the term has usually indicated a formal lament for the death of a particular person; a **dirge**, or **threnody**, is similar but less formal and is supposed to be sung. A dirge or elegy supposed to be sung by one person is called a **monody**. An **epigram** was originally any poem carved in stone (on tombstones, buildings, gates, etc.), but in modern usage it denotes a very short, usually witty verse with a quick turn at the end; it is often, but not always, comic. The **epitaph** is a variety of epigram in which the poem is to be carved on someone's tombstone, but many epitaphs are comic, written about people not yet dead, and of course not really intended for engraving. A **lyric** is a short poem in which a speaker expresses intense personal emotion rather than describing a narrative or dramatic situation; sometimes the term is used even more broadly for *any* short poem. Originally the term "lyric" designated poems meant to be sung to the accompaniment of the lyre, and the names of several other kinds also specify their original connection with music. Many **songs** (whose words are usually called lyrics) are poems which have been set to music. A **ballad** is a narrative poem which is, or originally was, meant to be sung. Characterized by much repetition and often by a repeated **refrain** (recurrent phrase or series of phrases), ballads were originally a folk creation, transmitted orally from person to person and age to age. Once **folk ballads** began to be written down (in the 18th century), **literary ballads** in imitation of folk ballads began to be created by individual authors. A **hymn** is a song of praise, usually in praise of God but sometimes of abstract qualities. A **chanson** (which in French simply means "song") was originally a song written in **couplets** (§9), but the term now describes any simple song. An **aubade** is a morning song in which the coming of dawn is either celebrated or denounced as a nuisance. An **aube** is a more rigidly defined morning poem; the speaker of an aube is the woman in a love triangle, and she expresses regret that dawn is coming so that she and her lover must part. In a **complaint** a lover bemoans his sad condition as a result of neglect by his mistress. In a **palinode**, an author recants his previous attitude toward something, often apologizing for his earlier poetry, which he now claims to have been trivial. The **confessional poem** is a relatively new (or at least only recently defined) kind in which the speaker describes his confused chaotic state, which becomes a metaphor for the state of the world around him. A **meditation** is a contemplation of some physical object as a way of reflecting upon some larger truth, often (but not necessarily) a spiritual one.

Many of the kinds (confessional, complaint, aube, and many others) are traditionally **monologues** (one clearly distinguishable speaker does all the speaking). Monologues are sometimes called **interior monologues** (as in fiction) if the speaker seems to be thinking thoughts rather than speaking to someone. A monologue set in a specific situation and spoken to someone is called **dramatic monologue**; if the character is alone and speaking only to him- or herself, it is called **soliloquy**. **Light verse** encompasses many poems in many kinds; it is not necessarily trivial, but its speaker takes or affects a whimsical, twitting attitude toward his or her subject. Light verse that deals with the manners and mores of polite society is called **vers de société**. And some terms which properly describe a kind also properly describe some other sort of grouping. If **satire**, for example, is in one sense a mode, it is also a kind, for there is **formal verse satire** that attacks a specific vice in the manner of a verse essay. And the term "satire" also describes an attitude toward experience and a tone; as the opposite of **panegyric** (poetry praising something) satire attacks something, usually by analyzing, specifying, and naming names. **Satire** that is mild, civilized, and gentle is called **Horatian satire** (named after the Roman poet Horace); vicious, violent, loud satire is **Juvenalian satire** (named after Juvenal), or **invective**; a satire that attacks a specific person is a **lampoon**.

11. WIDER CONTEXTS

In a sense, every poem creates a world all its own, but every poem also reflects aspects of a larger world from which it derives. Often it is important—and sometimes it is crucial—for a reader to recognize **context**, the circumstances that surrounded the making of the poem. The most obvious and compelling contexts are in poems that refer explicitly to some historical event or situation. A poem written about a specific event or occasion is called an **occasional** poem; the occasion may be a well known public one or a private one. All matters of time and circumstance that might affect either the conception or execution are part of the poem's **historical** or **cultural context**. It is not always easy to determine exactly which factors are relevant to a poem and which are not; deciding just what information is necessary and how to use it once acquired is one of the most delicate tasks in good interpretation.

Literary historians often designate **periods** in which cultural and aesthetic assumptions are more or less shared, speaking, for example, of the Elizabethan period (literally, 1558–1603, the reign of Queen Elizabeth in England) or the Romantic period (approximately 1790–1830) to describe certain common tendencies in a given historical era. The ideas and assumptions built into poems often reflect trends of thinking in a particular historical period. Poets sometimes consciously evoke their sense of shared ideas by using a **motif** (plural, **motifs** or **motives**): a recurrent device, formula or situation which deliberately connects a poem with common patterns of existing thought. One common motif is that of **carpe diem**. The phrase literally means "seize the day," and *carpe diem* poems invariably remind us of the shortness of life and beauty and the necessity to take advantage of the present. Such recurring situations as temptations in the garden, flights into the country, and journeys into experience are also motifs.

Poets often consciously evoke, too, a particular frame of reference or system of belief as a way of anchoring their own vision in a common pattern of experience that is understandable to an audience. In English poetry, the Judaeo-Christian and classical frames of reference are the most common, and the events and symbols of Biblical and classical history and myth are often prominent. Poets have, however, increasingly worried, especially since the 18th century, about the deterioration of a common heritage that was once based in Judaeo-Christian or classical terms, and the use of other, non-Western myths has become increasingly popular. Some poets have also developed private symbolic systems, sometimes extended into full-blown myths as in the poetry of Yeats. Most authors do not, of course, develop a complex private system of their own, but all authors have individual traits which are a product of their individual consciousness. Reading a group of poems by an author usually clarifies every individual poem, for the reader can develop a sense of the poet's distinctive style, strategies, and ideas. The total work of an author is called a **canon**; one may speak of the Milton canon or the Eliot canon. But even a sampling of a poet's work often leads a reader to expect certain procedures and attitudes, enabling a more exact and intense response. In its broadest sense, the **authorial context** may include biographical detail, psychological analysis, and specific facts about the conditions under which a poem was created, as well as dominant characteristics or tendencies in poems by a certain author.

What kind of contextual knowledge and how much of it a poem requires varies, of course, from poem to poem; many poems are readily accessible without deliberate pursuit of historical, intellectual, or authorial background, but the range and intensity of experience available through a poem is almost always enhanced by more knowledge.

12. TRADITION AND CONVENTION

In its most inclusive sense, **tradition** is the influence—deliberate or not—of any previous event, technique, or consciousness upon subsequent ways of thought and action. Poetic tradition may involve an influence in ideas, or style, or both. Poets may deliberately seek to follow, refine, or respond to previous thinkers and poets, or they may find themselves conditioned by the past in ways over which they have no control.

Poetry, perhaps more than drama or fiction, is subject to the characteristic habits and limitations of a particular language, and it is common practice to speak of the **English tradition** (or the **English poetic tradition,** or simply the **tradition**) meaning all of the recurrent tendencies over the years, including many which oppose, modify, or contradict other tendencies. The poetry of Pound or cummings, for example, is as surely a part of the tradition as that of Milton or Tennyson, for the tradition is not something which once and for all defines itself but rather consists of continuity marked by continual modification. Participation in the tradition is not always easy to recognize or predict, for some of the English tradition's brightest lights (Shakespeare, Swift, Shelley, and Eliot are examples) at first seemed to their contemporaries most untraditional—in the sense of the tradition then understood. Tradition continually redefines itself to comprehend rebellious sons and daughters born into its line and intent on the old rituals of father-killing and mansion-burning. Sometimes the tradition is defined as if it were already complete, but it is more useful to consider it a living, changing thing which will, by definition, ultimately render any definition incomplete. Much (perhaps most) of what seems new and innovative does not, of course, last long enough in the public memory or evoke a substantial enough response in its audience to become part of the tradition. Contemporary with Shakespeare, for example, were many poets whose innovations did not "catch on" or whose distinctive appeal did not prove to be permanent; it is so in every age, and the process of developing a tradition is a perpetual matter of experimenting and sorting.

Within a language tradition are **national** and **regional traditions** as well; one may speak, for example, of a Canadian tradition, an Irish tradition, or a New England tradition. Such divisions have partly to do with local variations in linguistic usage, but they also relate to ideological concerns, cultural assumptions, and social, political, and economic movements. The same sort of division may be broadened, reaching beyond language barriers to comprehend the **European tradition** or the **Western tradition.** The latter term is often used nearly synonymously with the English tradition; such usage is not entirely precise, but many of the most characteristic features of English poetry do have origins or counterparts in ancient Greece or Rome or in more recent Continental cultures, especially those of France, Italy, and Germany.

Besides definitions based on linguistic, national, and cultural boundaries, there are other, more narrow senses of tradition in common use. Tradition may describe the history and accumulated characteristics of a literary kind or a stanza form (one might speak of the epic tradition, the sonnet tradition, the couplet tradition, or the tradition of free verse, §9 and 10), the recurrent appearances of a motif or theme (the *carpe diem* tradition, §11), the characteristics of a thought or value pattern (the Puritan tradition or the metaphysical tradition), or characteristics associated with a particular time or age (the Elizabethan tradition).

A **convention** is any characteristic which over a period of time has come to be expected in poetry or in a poem of a certain sort. There are conventions of subject matter and conventional ways of using the standard poetic devices, but conventions are especially associated with the older poetic kinds (§10). Following the standard conventions is usually less significant than not following them; when a poem ignores or contradicts a convention, a reader can be pretty sure that the convention is missing or altered for a specific reason. Conventions at their best are shortcuts in communication; they tell a reader what to look for and establish a beginning rapport between poet and reader; what happens as the expectations are satisfied or surprised is then up to the poet. Most conventions originated in the doctrine of **decorum,** which insists on appropriateness in all things: every poetic kind, for example, was assumed to require a certain level of language and persons and incidents of a specific level of dignity. Most conventions begin in necessity, flourish when they are recognizable to a large number of readers, and linger on simply as decoration, a memory of past needs. When specific conventions totally lose their use and force, they become merely ornamental, and sometimes seem amusing or absurd. This is why mechanical repetition of what is expected is often said to be "conventional" (or "merely conventional") in a negative sense. Sensible use of conventions involves taking advantage of the technical solutions and shortcuts they provide, but it involves too the personalized touch of an individual poet. No great poet leaves a convention exactly as he or she found it. In the hands of a shrewd craftsman, tradition and convention may be innovative and exciting; in the hands of a mindless ape of the past, they are nearly always dull and deadly.

DRAMA

Elements

1   AUDIENCE, RITUAL, AND MYTH

A play is different from other forms of literature because it is written
to be performed, to be acted out on a stage before an **audience,** a
group of people gathered at a specific time and place to share the
common experience of the theater. Many people watch and enjoy
even a film in privacy, but to watch a play by oneself is a highly unusual experience. Drama is meant to be public—a form of collective
behavior that persists in many forms in society. We go to football
games or rock concerts as our primitive ancestors went to rain dances
and fertility rites, to share an experience with others of similar attitudes and interests. Fifteen thousand people do not gather at a rock
concert with any real hope of personal contact with the performers.
They do not really go to hear the music, for there are too many people, creating too much extraneous noise. The live performance can
hardly equal one achieved by the sophisticated techniques of the re-
cording studio, but it *is* live and it is shared with thousands of
other people. The individual feels the spirit and enthusiasm that make
collective experience meaningful.

Whatever the nature of the performance, the individuals who make
up the audience have made separate but common decisions to attend
Hair or *Carmen* or *Annie.* They gather at the specified time and place,
and in a sense they assume new identities as members of the group,
partly expressed in their clothes—people dress one way for a football
game and another for the opera—but also in such obvious ways as
their new identities as seat numbers (Section 4, Row AA, Seat 103).
These group identities strongly influence behavior, as anyone who has
laughed at the wrong time in the theater or cheered for the visiting
team while sitting among the home fans can testify. The group
identity can become so strong that members of the group behave in
ways they would not as individuals; cheering loudly, booing, and crying "Encore!" are simple examples. At its worst, the group can become
a mob.

There are as many different audiences in the contemporary theater
as there are kinds of performances. On the one hand, there are people
who go to be entertained or to be seen at the latest hit. On the other
hand, there are audiences that are interested in the theater, the presentation of classic plays by Shakespeare or Molière, the innovative use of
stage space by such directors as Jerzy Grotowski, or the pioneering
ideas about the use of actors and settings of Bertolt Brecht. The
theater offers a wide variety of experience. There are theaters for
blacks and for homosexuals, cabaret and dinner theaters that offer food
and drink as an added attraction, outdoor historical dramas for tourists, and plays written especially for children.

What is said and done in a play must also be acceptable to the audience as a group and must engage the attention of the audience. In recent years, for example, we have seen a number of plays dealing with aging. Arthur Kopit's *Wings* deals with the recovery of a stroke victim, an aging aviatrix. Such plays have more obvious relevance to a society like ours, in which the average age is rising, than to one in which it is falling; a play like *Wings* assumes an audience whose members are interested in a stroke because of either their own situation or that of aging relatives. Plays that aim primarily to entertain may avoid such an issue as aging in favor of examining the prevailing attitudes of the society toward the difference between marrying and living together. What is relevant will vary with the historical situation. Most of Shakespeare's great tragedies, for example, deal with succession to a throne or other positions of power. They were written when Elizabeth I was an aging queen, too old to produce a legitimate heir even if she had chosen to marry. For two centuries England had suffered war and destruction over issues of succession; not surprisingly, Shakespeare's audience was interested in the problems of transfer of power. In America we have developed a relatively orderly way of transferring power; in other countries the transfer is less easy. Still, a play like *Hamlet* has relevance for us, not only because it explores that issue, but also because it explores issues of continuing interest and relevance: how does a young man who expects to inherit his father's business deal with the intervention of his mother's second husband between him and his rightful inheritance? How does he deal with his sexual attraction to his mother? How does he balance his attraction for a suitable young woman like Ophelia against his political ambitions? Such issues are relevant in every age, and give a play like *Hamlet* its lasting appeal.

The audience also determines what can be seen onstage. In *Oedipus Tyrannus*, for example, Jocasta hangs herself offstage and Oedipus puts out his eyes offstage because the audience did not like to see violence onstage. Shakespeare's audience, on the other hand, seems to have loved onstage violence, if we are to believe the evidence of the last scene of *Hamlet* or the scene in Thomas Kyd's popular *Spanish Tragedy* in which the central character, Hieronimo, bites off his tongue and spits out the piece he has bitten off. In our own day we are witnessing the breakdown of audience taboos against nudity and sexual activity on stage, in films, and in television.

Whatever the audience, however, group behavior involves rituals, elements of repetition in which the repetition is at least as important as what is done. The seventh-inning stretch, half-time activities, and intermissions may have real functions, but they are also rituals. Why, for example, is the national anthem played or sung at the beginning of sporting events but not before performances of plays? Theater audiences are surely not less patriotic than those at sporting events; they merely have different expectations about what is to be done. The elements of repetition in a ritual provide comforting transitions between the ways things have been done in the past and the ways they will be done in the future. They are the unvarying elements of collective activity, which endure though the time, place, and persons change. No two performances of a play can be exactly the same, but exact repetition is the implied goal of the rehearsals that precede the performances. Several modern playwrights make this explicit, as when the maid Sabrina in Wilder's *The Skin of Our Teeth* tells the audience to go home though the actors must remain and perform the play over and over again.

The ritual elements of many communal activities are based on mythical patterns. The struggle between the home team and the visiting team in many sports, for example, almost becomes the mythical struggle between good and evil. Certain teams customarily wear white uniforms at home and gray or colored uniforms on the road to clarify their identities as "good guys" at home and "bad guys" away. Myth originally meant a story of communal origin that provided an explanation or religious interpretation of man, nature, the universe, and the relations among them. Myth-making is a basic human activity and a communal one.

The first myths were specifically religious, but the basic narrative sequence of a myth retains an appeal even when the religious significance is no longer present. The stories of David slaying Goliath with a slingshot and of Hercules strangling two serpents with his bare hands in his crib are examples of a mythical narrative element in which the hero as a child performs prodigious or unusual feats. Centuries later the same kind of event recurs in the story of George Washington and the famous cherry tree, a political myth. A similar kind of repetition of narrative elements can be seen in the first two plays of this collection, *The Sacrifice of Isaac* and *The Dumb Waiter*. Two males journey to a distant place where one of them is to kill the other. In the medieval play, this is explained as God's testing of Abraham's faith. When Abraham's faith proves strong, God rewards him by providing a ram as substitute for his son. In the Pinter play there are no such certainties about the identity of the authority, its purposes, or even the outcome. We can make guesses about why Gus is to be killed—he has begun to question the organization and its purposes after their last job—but we cannot know. We are not even sure when Ben first knew what his mission was to be. Did he stop the car during the night to relieve his bladder or to receive his orders? One play deals with an age of simple faith, the other with the uncertainties of an absurd world, but both use the same myth.

ANONYMOUS

The Sacrifice of Isaac *

CHARACTERS

GOD   ISAAC, *his son*
AN ANGEL   A DOCTOR, *a learned man*
ABRAHAM, the patriarch

A field, near ABRAHAM'*s tent.*

ABRAHAM   Father of heaven omnipotent,
    With all my heart to thee I call.
Thou hast given me both land and rent;
And my livelihood thou hast me sent.
    I thank thee highly evermore of all.   5

First of the earth thou madest Adam
    And Eve also to be his wife;
All others creatures of them two came.
And now thou hast grant to me, Abraham,
    Here in this land to lead my life.   10

In my age thou hast granted me this,
    That this young child with me shall wone.[1]
I love no thing so much, y-wis,[2]
Except thine own self, dear Father of bliss,
    As Isaac here, my own sweet son.   15

I have diverse children mo,[3]
    The which I love not half so well;
This fair child he cheers me so
In every place where that I go
    That no dis-ease here may I feel.   20

And therefore, Father of heaven, I thee pray
    For his health and also for his grace.
Now, Lord, keep him both night and day,
That never disease nor no fray [4]
    Come to my child in no place.   25

Now come, Isaac, my own sweet child
    Go we home and take our rest.

---

* Often (and perhaps more accurately) called "The Brome *Sacrifice of Isaac*" (Brome was the name of the 19th-century owner of the manuscript in which the play appears). The events of the play are based on *Genesis* 22.
1. Dwell.
2. Certainly.
3. More.
4. Fright.

ISAAC   Abraham, mine own father so mild,
     To follow you I am full prest,[5]
       Both early and late.   30
ABRAHAM   Come on, sweet child. I love thee best
     Of all the children that ever I begat.

    Heaven.

GOD   Mine Angel, fast hie thee thy way
     And unto middle-earth[6] anon thou go;
   Abram's heart now will I assay,   35
     Whether that he be steadfast or no.

Say I commanded him for to take
     Isaac, his young son, that he loves so well,
And with his blood sacrifice he make
     If any of my friendship he will feel.   40

Show him the way unto the hill
     Where that his sacrifice shall be.
I shall assay now his good will,
     Whether he loveth better his child or me.
     All men shall take example by him   45
My commandments how they shall keep.

    The field, near ABRAHAM'S *tent.*

ABRAHAM   Now, Father of heaven, that formed all things,
     My prayers I make to thee again,
For this day my tender offering[7]
     Here must I give to thee certain.   50
Ah! Lord God, almighty king,
     What manner beast will make thee most fain?
If I had thereof very[8] knowing,
     It should be done with all my main[9]
       Full soon anon.   55
To do thy pleasing on an hill,
Verily it is my will,
       Dear Father, God in Trinity.

ANGEL   Abraham! Abraham! will thou rest!
     Our Lord commandeth thee for to take   60
Isaac, thy young son that thou lovest best,
     And with his blood sacrifice that thou make.
Into the Land of Vision[1] thou go,
     And offer thy child unto thy Lord;

---

5. Ready (Fr. *prêt*).
6. The earth.
7. Periodic sacrifice.
8. True.
9. Strength.

1. A translation of the phrase *in terram visionis* in *Genesis* 22:2 of the Vulgate, the standard Latin Bible of the Middle Ages. Other versions, including the Authorized or King James Version, read "the land of Moriah."

I shall thee lead and show also.   65
    Unto God's hest,[2] Abraham, accord.

And follow me upon this green.
ABRAHAM Welcome to me be my Lord's sond,[3]
    And his hest I will not withstand.
    Yet Isaac, my young son in land,   70
A full dear child to me hath been.

I had liefer,[4] if God had been pleased,
    For to have forborne all the good that I have
Than Isaac my son should have been dis-eased,
    So God in heaven my soul might save!   75

I loved never thing so much in earth.
    And now I must the child go kill.
Ah! Lord God! My conscience is strongly stirred!
And yet, my dear Lord, I am sore a-feared
    To grudge anything against your will.   80

I love my child as my life;
    But yet I love my God much more.
For though my heart would make any strife,
Yet will I not spare for child nor wife,
    But do after my Lord's lore.[5]   85

Though I love my son never so well,
    Yet smite off his head soon I shall.
Ah! Father of heaven, to thee I kneel;
An hard death my son shall feel
    For to honor thee, Lord, withall.   90

ANGEL Abraham! Abraham! This is well said!
    And all these commandments look that thou keep.
But in thy heart be nothing dismayed.
ABRAHAM Nay, nay, forsooth[6] I hold me well appayed[7]
    To please my God to the best that I have.   95

For though my heart be heavily set
    To see the blood of mine own dear son,
Yet for all this I will not let,[8]
But Isaac, my son, I will go fetch,
    And come as fast as ever we can.   100

    Another part of the field.

Now, Isaac, my own son dear,
    Where art thou, child? Speak to me.
ISAAC My father, sweet father, I am here,
    And make my prayers to the Trinity.

---

2. Command.   6. In truth.
3. Messenger.   7. Pleased.
4. Rather.   8. Refrain.
5. Teaching.

ABRAHAM   Rise up, my child, and fast come hither,   105
  My gentle bairn[9] that art so wise,
For we two, child, must go together
  And unto my Lord make sacrifice.

ISAAC   I am full ready, my father, lo!
  Even at your hands I stand right here;   110
And whatsoever ye bid me do,
  It shall be done with glad cheer,
    Full well and fine.
ABRAHAM   Ah! Isaac, my own son so dear,
  God's blessing I give thee and mine.   115

Hold this faggot upon thy back,
  And here myself fire shall bring.
ISAAC   Father, all this here will I pack;
  I am full fain to do your bidding.
ABRAHAM [*aside*]   Ah! Lord of heaven my hands I wring,   120
  This child's words all to-wound[1] my heart.

Now, Isaac, son, go we our way
  Unto yon mount, with all our main.[2]
ISAAC   Go we, my dear father, as fast as I may;
  To follow you I am full fain,   125
    Although I be slender.[3]
ABRAHAM [*aside*]   Ah! Lord, my heart breaketh in twain,
  This child's words they be so tender.

   ABRAHAM *and* ISAAC *arrive at the mountain.*

Ah! Isaac, son, anon lay it down;
  No longer upon thy back it hold.   130
For I must make ready bon[4]
  To honor my Lord God as I should.

ISAAC   Lo, my dear father, where it is!
  To cheer you alway I draw me near.
But, father, I marvel sore of this,   135
  Why that ye make this heavy cheer.[5]

And also, father, evermore dread I;
  Where is your quick[6] beast that ye should kill?
Both fire and wood we have ready,
  But quick beast have none on this hill.   140
A quick beast, I wot[7] well, must be dead
  Your sacrifice for to make.
ABRAHAM   Dread thee nought, my child, I thee rede,[8]
Our Lord will send me unto this stead[9]

---

9. Child.
1. Wound severely.
2. Strength.
3. Weak.
4. Quite ready.

5. Countenance.
6. Live.
7. Know.
8. Counsel.
9. Place.

Some manner of beast for to take,   145
    Through his sweet sond.[1]
ISAAC   Yea, father, but my heart beginneth to quake
    To see that sharp sword in your hand.

Why bear ye your sword drawn so?
    Of your countenance I have much wonder.   150
ABRAHAM [*aside*]   Ah! Father of heaven, so I am woe!
    This child here breaketh my heart asunder.

ISAAC   Tell me, dear father, ere that ye cease,
    Bear ye your sword drawn for me?
ABRAHAM   Ah! Isaac, sweet son, peace! peace!   155
    For, y-wis, thou break my heart in three.

ISAAC   Now, truly, somewhat, father, ye think
    That ye mourn thus more and more.
ABRAHAM [*aside*]   Ah! Lord of heaven, thy grace let sink,[2]
    For my heart was never half so sore.   160

ISAAC   I pray you, father, that ye will let me it wit[3]
    Whether shall I have any harm or no.
ABRAHAM   Y-wis, sweet son, I may not tell thee yet;
    My heart is now so full of woe.

ISAAC   Dear father, I pray you, hideth it not from me,   165
    But some of your thought that ye tell me.
ABRAHAM   Ah! Isaac, Isaac I must kill thee!
ISAAC   Kill me, father? Alas, what have I done?

If I have trespassed against you aught,
    With a yard[4] ye may make me full mild;   170
And with your sharp sword kill me nought,
    For, y-wis, father, I am but a child.

ABRAHAM   I am full sorry, son, thy blood for to spill
    But truly, my child, I may not choose.
ISAAC   Now I would to God my mother were here on his hill!   175
    She would kneel for me on both her knees
        To save my life.
And sithen[5] that my mother is not here,
I pray you, father, change your cheer,
        And kill me not with your knife.   180

ABRAHAM   Forsooth, son, but if[6] I thee kill,
    I should grieve God right sore, I dread.
It is his commandment, and also his will,
    That I should do this same deed.

He commanded me, son, for certain,   185
    To make my sacrifice with thy blood.
ISAAC   And is it God's will that I should be slain?

---

1. Messenger.
2. Descend.
3. Know.

4. Rod.
5. Since.
6. Unless.

ABRAHAM   Aye, truly, Isaac, my son so good;
    And therefore my hands I wring.
ISAAC   Now, father, against my Lord's will   190
 I will never grudge, loud nor still.[7]
    He might have sent me a better destiny
    If it had have been his pleasure.

ABRAHAM   Forsooth, son, but if I did this deed,
    Grievously displeased our Lord will be.   195
ISAAC   Nay, nay, father, God forbid
    That ever you should grieve him for me.

Ye have other children, one or two,
    The which ye should love well by kind.[8]
I pray you, father, make ye no woe;   200
For be I once dead, and from you go,
    I shall be soon out of your mind.

Therefore do our Lord's bidding,
    And when I am dead, then pray for me.
But, good father, tell ye my mother nothing;   205
Say that I am in another country dwelling.
ABRAHAM   Ah! Isaac, Isaac, blessed might thou be!

My heart beginneth strongly to rise,
    To see the blood of thy blessed body.
ISAAC   Father, since it may be no other wise.   210
    Let it pass over as well as I.

But, father, ere I go unto my death,
    I pray you bless me with your hand.
ABRAHAM   Now, Isaac, with all my breath
    My blessing I give thee upon this land,   215
    And God's also thereto, y-wis.
    Isaac, Isaac, son, up thou stand,
    Thy fair sweet mouth that I may kiss.

ISAAC   Now farewell, my own father so fine;
    And greet well my mother in earth.   220
But I pray you, father, to hide my eyen,[9]
    That I see not the stroke of your sharp sword,
    That my flesh shall defile.
ABRAHAM   Son, thy words make me weep full sore;
Now, my dear son Isaac, speak no more.   225
ISAAC   Ah! my own dear father, wherefore?
    We shall speak together here but a while.
And sithen[1] that I must needs be dead,
    Yet, my dear father, to you I pray,
Smite but few strokes at my head,   230
    And make an end as soon as ye may,
    And tarry not too long.

7. In any way.   9. Eyes.
8. Natural affection.   1. Since.

ABRAHAM   Thy meek words, child, make me affray;[2]
      So "Well-a-way!"[3] may be my song,

Except all-only God's will.   235
    Ah! Isaac, my own sweet child,
Yet kiss me again upon this hill!
    In all this world is none so mild.

ISAAC   Now truly, father, all this tarrying
    It doth my heart but harm;   240
I pray you, father, make an ending.
ABRAHAM   Come up, sweet son, into my arm.

I must bind thy hands too,
    Although thou be never so mild.
ISAAC   Ah! mercy, father! Why should ye do so?   245
ABRAHAM   That thou shouldst not let[4] me, my child.

ISAAC   Nay, y-wis, father, I will not let you.
    Do on, for me, your will;
And on the purpose that ye have set you,
    For God's love keep it forth[5] still.   250

I am full sorry this day to die,
    But yet I keep[6] not my God to grieve.
Do on your list[7] for me hardly;
    My fair sweet father, I give you leave.

But, father, I pray you evermore,   255
    Tell ye my mother no deal;
If she wost[8] it, she would weep full sore,
    For y-wis, father, she loveth me full well.
        God's blessing might she have!

Now farewell, my mother so sweet!   260
We two be like no more to meet,
ABRAHAM   Ah! Isaac, Isaac! son, thou makest me to grate[9]
    And with thy words thou distemperest me.

ISAAC   Y-wis, sweet father, I am sorry to grieve you.
    I cry you mercy of that I have done.   265
And of all trespass that ever I did move[1] you.
    Now, dear father, forgive me that I have done,
    God of heaven be with me!

ABRAHAM   Ah! dear child, leave off thy moans;
In all thy life thou grieved me never once.   270
Now blessed be thou, body and bones,
    That ever thou were bred and born!

2. Dread.   7. Pleasure, will.
3. Alas.   8. Knew.
4. Hinder.   9. Gnash my teeth.
5. Pursue it.   1. Perform against.
6. Wish.

Thou hast been to me child full good.
    But, y-wis, child, though I mourn never so fast
    Yet must I needs here at the last   275
In this place shed all thy blood.

Therefore, my dear son, here shall thou lie.
    Unto my work I must me stead.[2]
Y-wis, I had as lief[3] myself to die,
    If God will be pleased with my deed,   280
        And mine own body for to offer
ISAAC   Ah! mercy, father. Mourn ye no more!
Your weeping maketh my heart sore,
        As my own death that I shall suffer.

Your kerchief, father, about my eyen[4] ye wind.   285
ABRAHAM   So I shall, my sweetest child in earth.
ISAAC   Now yet, good father, have this in mind
    And smite me not often with your sharp sword,
        But hastily that it be sped.
ABRAHAM   Now farewell, my child, so full of grace.   290
ISAAC   Ah! father, father. Turn downward my face,
        For of your sharp sword I am ever a-dread.

ABRAHAM [*aside*]   To do this deed I am full sorry,
    But, Lord, thine hest[5] I will not withstand.
ISAAC   Ah! Father of heaven, to thee I cry;   295
    Lord, receive me into thy hand.

ABRAHAM [*aside*]   Lo! now is the time come, certain,
    That my sword in his neck shall bite.
Ah! Lord, my heart raiseth there-again;[6]
    I may not findeth it in my heart to smite;   300
        My heart will not know thereto.
Yet fain I would work my Lord's will,
But this young innocent lieth so still,
I may not findeth it in my heart him to kill.
        Oh, Father of heaven, what shall I do?   305

ISAAC   Ah! mercy, father. Why tarry ye so,
    And let me lay thus long on this heath?
Now I would to God the stroke were do!
Father, I pray you heartily, short me out of my woe,
    And let me not look thus after my death.   310

ABRAHAM   Now, heart, why wouldest not thou break in three?
    Yet shall thou not make me to my God unmild.
I will no longer let[7] for thee,
For that my God a-grieved would be.
    Now hold[8] the stroke, my own dear child.   315

---

2. Steady myself.   6. Rises in protest against the act.
3. Gladly.   7. Refrain.
4. Eyes.   8. Receive.
5. Command.

ANGEL *appears.*

ANGEL   I am an angel, thou mayest see blithe,[9]
    That from heaven to thee is sent.
Our Lord thank thee an hundred sithe[1]
    For the keeping of his commandment.

He knowest thy will and also thy heart,   320
    That thou dreadest him above all thing;
And some of thy heaviness for to depart[2]
    A fair ram yonder I gan bring;[3]

He standeth tied, lo! among the briars.
    Now, Abraham, amend thy mood,   325
For Isaac, thy young son that here is,
    This day shall not shed his blood.

Go, make thy sacrifice with yon ram.
Now farewell, blessed Abraham,
    For unto Heaven I now go home;   330
    The way is full gain[4] that I must go.
      Take up thy son so free.[5]   *Exit.*

ABRAHAM   Ah! Lord, I thank thee of thy great grace,
Now am I yethed[6] in diverse wise.
Arise up, Isaac, my dear son, arise;   335
    Arise up, sweet child, and come to me.

ISAAC   Ah! mercy, father. Why smite ye nought?
    Ah! smite on, father, once with your knife.
ABRAHAM   Peace, my sweet son, and take no thought,
    For our Lord of heaven hath grant thy life   340
      By his angel now.

That thou shalt not die this day, son, truly.
ISAAC   Ah, father, full glad then were I,
    Y-wis, father, I say, y-wis,
If this tale were true.   345
ABRAHAM   An hundred times, my son fair of hue,
    For joy thy mouth now will I kiss.

ISAAC   Ah! my dear father Abraham,
    Will not God be wroth that we do thus?
ABRAHAM   No, no, hardly, my sweet son,   350
For yon same ram he hath us sent
    Hither down to us.

Yon beast shall die here in thy stead,
    In the worship of our Lord alone.
Go, fetch him hither, my child, indeed.   355

---

9. At once.   4. Straight.
1. Times.   5. Noble.
2. Remove.   6. Comforted.
3. Have brought.

ISAAC   Father, I will go hent[7] him by the head,
    And bring yon beast with me anon.

Ah! sheep, sheep, blessed might thou be,
    That ever thou were sent down hither!
Thou shall this day die for me   360
In the worship of the Holy Trinity.
    Now come fast and go we together
      To my Father of heaven.
Though thou be never so gentle and good,
Yet had I liefer[8] thou sheddest thy blood,   365
      Y-wis, sheep, than I.

Lo! father, I have brought here full smart[9]
    This gentle sheep, and him to you I give.
But, Lord God, I thank thee with all my heart,
    For I am glad that I shall live,   370
      And kiss once my dear mother.
ABRAHAM   Now be right merry, my sweet child,
    For this quick[1] beast, that is so mild,
      Here I shall present before all other.
ISAAC   And I will fast begin to blow;   375
    This fire shall burn a full good speed.
But, father, will I stoop down low,
Ye will not kill me with your sword, I trow?[2]
ABRAHAM   No, hardly, sweet son, have no dread;
      My mourning is past.   380
ISAAC   Aye! but I would that sword were in a gled,[3]
      For, y-wis, father, it makes me full ill aghast.

ABRAHAM   Now, Lord God of heaven in Trinity,
    Almighty God omnipotent,
My offering I make in worship of thee,   385
    And with this quick beast I thee present.
    Lord, receive thou mine intent,
      As thou art God and ground of our grace.

      GOD *appears above.*

GOD   Abraham, Abraham, well might thou speed,
    And Isaac, thy young son thee by!   390
Truly, Abraham, for this deed
I shall multiply your bothers[4] seed
    As thick as stars be in the sky,
      Both more and less;
And as thick as gravel in the sea,   395
So thick multiplied your seed shall be.
      This grant I you for your goodness.

---

7. Seize.   2. Trust.
8. Rather.   3. Fire.
9. Quickly.   4. Both your.
1. Live.

Of you shall come fruit great won,[5]
    And ever be in bliss without end,
For ye dread me as God alone   400
And keep my commandments everyone;
    My blessing I give, wheresoever ye wend.[6]

ABRAHAM   Lo! Isaac, my son, how think ye
    By this work that we have wrought?
Full glad and blithe we may be,   405
    Against the will of God we grudged nought,
        Upon this fair heath.
ISAAC   Ah! father, I thank our Lord every deal,[7]
    That my wit served me so well
        For to dread God more than my death.   410

ABRAHAM   Why, dearworthy[8] son, were thou adread?[9]
    Hardly, my child, tell me thy lore.[1]
ISAAC   Aye! by my faith, father, now have I read,
    I was never so afraid before
        As I have been at yon hill.   415
But, by my faith, father, I swear,
I will nevermore come there
        But it be against my will.

ABRAHAM   Aye! come on with me, my own sweet son,
    And homeward fast now let us gone.   420
ISAAC   By my faith, father, thereto I grant;
    I had never so good will to go home,
        And to speak with my dear mother.
ABRAHAM   Ah! Lord of heaven, I thank thee,
    For now may I lead home with me   425
    Isaac, my young son so free,
        The gentlest child above all other.

    Now go we forth, my blessed son.
ISAAC   I grant, father, and let us gone;
    For, by my troth, were I at home,   430
    I would never go out under that form;
        This may I well avow.
        I pray God give us grace evermore,
        And all those we be holding to.[2]

    DOCTOR *comes forward and addresses the audience.*

DOCTOR   Lo! sovereigns and sires, now have we showed   435
    This solemn story to great and small.
It is good learning to learned and lewd,[3]
    And the wisest of us all,
        Withouten any barring

---

5. In great number.
6. Go.
7. In every way.
8. Beloved.

9. Afraid.
1. Knowledge.
2. To whom we are related.
3. Ignorant.

For this story shows you here   440
How we should keep to our power[4]
    God's commandment without grudging.

Trow ye,[5] sirs, and God sent an angel
    And commanded you your child to slain,
By my troth, is there any of you   445
    That either would grudge or strive thereagainst?

How think ye now, sirs, thereby?
    I trow there be three or four or more,
And these women that weep so sorrowfully
    Then that their children die them from,   450
        As nature will and kind;
It is but folly, I may well avow,
To grudge against God or to grieve you,
For ye shall never see them mischieved,[6] well I know,
    By land nor water, have this in mind.   455
And grudge not against our Lord God
    In wealth or woe, whether[7] that he you send,
Though ye be never so hard bestead;
    For when he will, he may it amend,

His commandments truly if ye keep with good heart,   460
    As this story hath now showed you before,
And faithfully serve him while ye be quart,[8]
    That ye may please God both even and morn.
    Now Jesu, that weareth the crown of thorn,
        Bring us all to heaven's bliss.   465

Finis.[9]

Ms. 1470–1480

---

4. As best we can.   7. Whichever.
5. Trust.   8. In good health.
6. In distress.   9. The end.

HAROLD PINTER

The Dumb Waiter

CHARACTERS

BEN   GUS

SCENE: *A basement room. Two beds, flat against the back wall. A serving hatch, closed, between the beds. A door to the kitchen and lavatory, left. A door to a passage, right.*

BEN *is lying on a bed, left, reading a paper.* GUS *is sitting on a bed, right, tying his shoelaces, with difficulty. Both are dressed in shirts, trousers and braces.[1]*
Silence.
GUS *ties his laces, rises, yawns and begins to walk slowly to the door, left. He stops, looks down, and shakes his foot.*
BEN *lowers his paper and watches him.* GUS *kneels and unties his shoelace and slowly takes off the shoe. He looks inside it and brings out a flattened matchbox. He shakes it and examines it. Their eyes meet.* BEN *rattles his paper and reads.* GUS *puts the matchbox in his pocket and bends down to put on his shoe. He ties his lace, with difficulty.* BEN *lowers his paper and watches him.* GUS *walks to the door, left, stops, and shakes the other foot. He kneels, unties his shoelace, and slowly takes off the shoe. He looks inside it and brings out a flattened cigarette packet. He shakes it and examines it. Their eyes meet.* BEN *rattles his paper and reads.* GUS *puts the packet in his pocket, bends down, puts on his shoe and ties the lace.*
He wanders off, left.
BEN *slams the paper down on the bed and glares after him. He picks up the paper and lies on his back, reading.*
Silence.
A lavatory chain is pulled twice off left, but the lavatory does not flush.
Silence.
GUS *re-enters, left, and halts at the door, scratching his head.*
BEN *slams down the paper.*

BEN   Kaw!

> *He picks up the paper.*

What about this? Listen to this!

> *He refers to the paper.*

1. Suspenders.

A man of eighty-seven wanted to cross the road. But there was a lot of traffic, see? He couldn't see how he was going to squeeze through. So he crawled under a lorry.[2]

GUS   He what?

BEN   He crawled under a lorry. A stationary lorry.

GUS   No?

BEN   The lorry started and ran over him.

GUS   Go on!

BEN   That's what it says here.

GUS   Get away.

BEN   It's enough to make you want to puke, isn't it?

GUS   Who advised him to do a thing like that?

BEN   A man of eighty-seven crawling under a lorry!

GUS   It's unbelievable.

BEN   It's down here in black and white.

GUS   Incredible.

>   *Silence.*
>
>   GUS *shakes his head and exits.* BEN *lies back and reads. The lavatory chain is pulled once off left, but the lavatory does not flush.* BEN *whistles at an item in the paper.* GUS *re-enters.*

I want to ask you something.

BEN   What are you doing out there?

GUS   Well, I was just—

BEN   What about the tea?

GUS   I'm just going to make it.

BEN   Well, go on, make it.

GUS   Yes, I will. [*He sits in a chair. Ruminatively.*] He's laid on some very nice crockery this time, I'll say that. It's sort of striped. There's a white stripe.

>   *Ben reads.*

It's very nice. I'll say that.

>   *Ben turns the page.*

You know, sort of round the cup. Round the rim. All the rest of it's black, you see. Then the saucer's black, except for right in the middle, where the cup goes, where it's white.

>   *Ben reads.*

Then the plates are the same, you see. Only they've got a black stripe—the plates right across the middle. Yes, I'm quite taken with the crockery.

BEN   [*still reading*]   What do you want plates for? You're not going to eat.

GUS   I've brought a few biscuits.

2. Truck.

BEN   Well, you'd better eat them quick.

GUS   I always bring a few biscuits. Or a pie. You know I can't drink tea without anything to eat.

BEN   Well, make the tea then, will you? Time's getting on.

> GUS *brings out the flattened cigarette packet and examines it.*

GUS   You got any cigarettes? I think I've run out.

> *He throws the packet high up and leans forward to catch it.*

I hope it won't be a long job, this one.

> *Aiming carefully, he flips the packet under his bed.*

Oh, I wanted to ask you something.

BEN   [*slamming his paper down*]   Kaw!

GUS   What's that?

BEN   A child of eight killed a cat!

GUS   Get away.

BEN   It's a fact. What about that, eh? A child of eight killing a cat!

GUS   How did he do it?

BEN   It was a girl.

GUS   How did she do it?

BEN   She—

> *He picks up the paper and studies it.*

It doesn't say.

GUS   Why not?

BEN   Wait a minute. It just says—Her brother, aged eleven, viewed the incident from the toolshed.

GUS   Go on!

BEN   That's bloody ridiculous.

> *Pause.*

GUS   I bet he did it.

BEN   Who?

GUS   The brother.

BEN   I think you're right.

> *Pause.*

[*Slamming down the paper.*] What about that, eh? A kid of eleven killing a cat and blaming it on his little sister of eight! It's enough to—

> *He breaks off in disgust and seizes the paper.* GUS *rises.*

GUS   What time is he getting in touch?

BEN *reads.*

What time is he getting in touch?
BEN   What's the matter with you? It could be any time. Any time.
GUS [*moves to the foot of* BEN's *bed*]   Well, I was going to ask you something.
BEN   What?
GUS   Have you noticed the time that tank takes to fill?
BEN   What tank?
GUS   In the lavatory.
BEN   No. Does it?
GUS   Terrible.
BEN   Well, what about it?
GUS   What do you think's the matter with it?
BEN   Nothing.
GUS   Nothing?
BEN   It's got a deficient ballcock, that's all.
GUS   A deficient what?
BEN   Ballcock.
GUS   No? Really?
BEN   That's what I should say.
GUS   Go on! That didn't occur to me.

GUS *wanders to his bed and presses the mattress.*

I didn't have a very restful sleep today, did you? It's not much of a bed. I could have done with another blanket too. [*He catches sight of a picture on the wall.*] Hello, what's this? [*Peering at it.*] "The First Eleven." Cricketers.[3] You seen this, Ben?
BEN [*reading*]   What?
GUS   The first eleven.
BEN   What?
GUS   There's a photo here of the first eleven.
BEN   What first eleven?
GUS [*studying the photo*]   It doesn't say.
BEN   What about the tea?
GUS   They all look a bit old to me.

GUS *wanders downstage, looks out front, then all about the room.*

I wouldn't like to live in this dump. I wouldn't mind if you had a window, you could see what it looked like outside.
BEN   What do you want a window for?
GUS   Well, I like to have a bit of a view, Ben. It whiles away the time.

He *walks about the room.*

I mean, you come into a place when it's still dark, you come into

---

3. A cricket team is routinely called an *eleven.*

a room you've never seen before, you sleep all day, you do your job, and then you go away in the night again.

> *Pause.*

I like to get a look at the scenery. You never get the chance in this job.

BEN　You get your holidays, don't you?

GUS　Only a fortnight.

BEN　[*lowering the paper*] You kill me. Anyone would think you're working every day. How often do we do a job? Once a week? What are you complaining about?

GUS　Yes, but we've got to be on tap though, haven't we? You can't move out of the house in case a call comes.

BEN　You know what your trouble is?

GUS　What?

BEN　You haven't got any interests.

GUS　I've got interests.

BEN　What? Tell me one of your interests.

> *Pause.*

GUS　I've got interests.

BEN　Look at me. What have I got?

GUS　I don't know. What?

BEN　I've got my woodwork. I've got my model boats. Have you ever seen me idle? I'm never idle. I know how to occupy my time, to its best advantage. Then when a call comes, I'm ready.

GUS　Don't you ever get a bit fed up?

BEN　Fed up? What with?

> *Silence.* BEN *reads.* GUS *feels in the pocket of his jacket, which hangs on the bed.*

GUS　You got any cigarettes? I've run out.

> *The lavatory flushes off left.*

There she goes.

> GUS *sits on his bed.*

No, I mean, I say the crockery's good. It is. It's very nice. But that's about all I can say for this place. It's worse than the last one. Remember that last place we were in? Last time, where was it? At least there was a wireless[4] there. No, honest. He doesn't seem to bother much about our comfort these days.

BEN　When are you going to stop jabbering?

GUS　You'd get rheumatism in a place like this, if you stay long.

BEN　We're not staying long. Make the tea, will you? We'll be on the job in a minute.

4. Radio.

GUS *picks up a small bag by his bed and brings out a packet of tea. He examines it and looks up.*

GUS   Eh, I've been meaning to ask you.

BEN   What the hell is it now?

GUS   Why did you stop the car this morning, in the middle of that road?

BEN   [*lowering the paper*]   I thought you were asleep.

GUS   I was, but I woke up when you stopped. You did stop, didn't you?

Pause.

In the middle of that road. It was still dark, don't you remember? I looked out. It was all misty. I thought perhaps you wanted to kip,[5] but you were sitting up dead straight, like you were waiting for something.

BEN   I wasn't waiting for anything.

GUS   I must have fallen asleep again. What was all that about then? Why did you stop?

BEN   [*picking up the paper*]   We were too early.

GUS   Early? [*He rises.*] What do you mean? We got the call, didn't we, saying we were to start right away. We did. We shoved out on the dot. So how could we be too early?

BEN   [*quietly*]   Who took the call, me or you?

GUS   You.

BEN   We were too early.

GUS   Too early for what?

Pause.

You mean someone had to get out before we got in?

He examines the bedclothes.

I thought these sheets didn't look too bright. I thought they ponged[6] a bit. I was too tired to notice when I got in this morning. Eh, that's taking a bit of a liberty, isn't it? I don't want to share my bed sheets. I told you things were going down the drain. I mean, we've always had clean sheets laid on up till now. I've noticed it.

BEN   How do you know those sheets weren't clean?

GUS   What do you mean?

BEN   How do you know they weren't clean? You've spent the whole day in them, haven't you?

GUS   What, you mean it might be my pong? [*He sniffs sheets.*] Yes. [*He sits slowly on bed.*] It could be my pong, I suppose. It's difficult to tell. I don't really know what I pong like, that's the trouble.

BEN   [*referring to the paper*]   Kaw!

GUS   Eh, Ben.

BEN   Kaw!

GUS   Ben.

5. Take a nap.   6. Smelled.

BEN   What?
GUS   What town are we in? I've forgotten.
BEN   I've told you. Birmingham.
GUS   Go on!

> *He looks with interest about the room.*

That's in the Midlands. The second biggest city in Great Britain. I'd never have guessed.

> *He snaps his fingers.*

Eh, it's Friday today, isn't it? It'll be Saturday tomorrow.
BEN   What about it?
GUS   [*excited*]   We could go and watch the Villa.[7]
BEN   They're playing away.
GUS   No, are they? Caarr! What a pity.
BEN   Anyway, there's no time. We've got to get straight back.
GUS   Well, we have done in the past, haven't we? Stayed over and watched a game, haven't we? For a bit of relaxation.
BEN   Things have tightened up, mate. They've tightened up.

> GUS *chuckles to himself.*

GUS   I saw the Villa get beat in a cup-tie once. Who was it against now? White shirts. It was one-all at half-time. I'll never forget it. Their opponents won by a penalty. Talk about drama. Yes, it was a disputed penalty. Disputed. They got beat two-one, anyway, because of it. You were there yourself.
BEN   Not me.
GUS   Yes, you were there. Don't you remember that disputed penalty?
BEN   No.
GUS   He went down just inside the area. Then they said he was just acting. I didn't think the other bloke touched him myself. But the referee had the ball on the spot.[8]
BEN   Didn't touch him! What are you talking about? He laid him out flat!
GUS   Not the Villa. The Villa don't play that sort of game.
BEN   Get out of it.

> *Pause.*

GUS   Eh, that must have been here, in Birmingham.
BEN   What must?
GUS   The Villa. That must have been here.
BEN   They were playing away.
GUS   Because you know who the other team was? It was the Spurs.

---

7. A soccer club.
8. On the penalty spot. Gus is describing a soccer match won on a penalty kick. When a defender fouls an attacker in the penalty area, a 44 × 18–yard rectangle outside the goal, the attacking team is awarded a penalty kick from a spot twelve yards from the goal mouth. Only the goalkeeper can attempt to block this shot, which is virtually unstoppable if well placed.

It was Tottenham Hotspur.

BEN   Well, what about it?

GUS   We've never done a job in Tottenham.

BEN   How do you know?

GUS   I'd remember Tottenham.

BEN turns on his bed to look at him.

BEN   Don't make me laugh, will you?

BEN turns back and reads. GUS yawns and speaks through his yawn.

GUS   When's he going to get in touch?

Pause.

Yes, I'd like to see another football match. I've always been an ardent football fan. Here, what about coming to see the Spurs tomorrow?

BEN   [*tonelessly*]   They're playing away.

GUS   Who are?

BEN   The Spurs.

GUS   Then they might be playing here.

BEN   Don't be silly.

GUS   If they're playing away they might be playing here. They might be playing the Villa.

BEN   [*tonelessly*]   But the Villa are playing away.

Pause. An envelope slides under the door, right. GUS sees it. He stands, looking at it.

GUS   Ben.

BEN   Away. They're all playing away.

GUS   Ben, look here.

BEN   What?

GUS   Look.

BEN turns his head and sees the envelope. He stands.

BEN   What's that?

GUS   I don't know.

BEN   Where did it come from?

GUS   Under the door.

BEN   Well, what is it?

GUS   I don't know.

They stare at it.

BEN   Pick it up.

GUS   What do you mean?

BEN   Pick it up!

> GUS *slowly moves towards it, bends and picks it up.*

What is it?
GUS   An envelope.
BEN   Is there anything on it?
GUS   No.
BEN   Is it sealed?
GUS   Yes.
BEN   Open it.
GUS   What?
BEN   Open it!

> GUS *opens it and looks inside.*

What's in it?

> GUS *empties twelve matches into his hand.*

GUS   Matches.
BEN   Matches?
GUS   Yes.
BEN   Show it to me.

> GUS *passes the envelope.* BEN *examines it.*

Nothing on it. Not a word.
GUS   That's funny, isn't it?
BEN   It came under the door?
GUS   Must have done.
BEN   Well, go on.
GUS   Go on where?
BEN   Open the door and see if you can catch anyone outside.
GUS   Who, me?
BEN   Go on!

> GUS *stares at him, puts the matches in his pocket, goes to his bed and brings a revolver from under the pillow. He goes to the door, opens it, looks out and shuts it.*

GUS   No one.

> *He replaces the revolver.*

BEN   What did you see?
GUS   Nothing.
BEN   They must have been pretty quick.

> GUS *takes the matches from his pocket and looks at them.*

GUS   Well, they'll come in handy.

BEN   Yes.

GUS   Won't they?

BEN   Yes, you're always running out, aren't you?

GUS   All the time.

BEN   Well, they'll come in handy then.

GUS   Yes.

BEN   Won't they?

GUS   Yes, I could do with them. I could do with them too.

BEN   You could, eh?

GUS   Yes.

BEN   Why?

GUS   We haven't got any.

BEN   Well, you've got some now, haven't you?

GUS   I can light the kettle now.

BEN   Yes, you're always cadging⁹ matches. How many have you got there?

GUS   About a dozen.

BEN   Well, don't lose them. Red too. You don't even need a box.

GUS *probes his ear with a match.*

[*Slapping his hand.*] Don't waste them! Go on, go and light it.

GUS   Eh?

BEN   Go and light it.

GUS   Light what?

BEN   The kettle.

GUS   You mean the gas.

BEN   Who does?

GUS   You do.

BEN [*his eyes narrowing*]   What do you mean, I mean the gas?

GUS   Well, that's what you mean, don't you? The gas.

BEN [*powerfully*]   If I say go and light the kettle I mean go and light the kettle.

GUS   How can you light a kettle?

BEN   It's a figure of speech! Light the kettle. It's a figure of speech!

GUS   I've never heard it.

BEN   Light the kettle! It's common usage!

GUS   I think you've got it wrong.

BEN [*menacing*]   What do you mean?

GUS   They say put on the kettle.

BEN [*taut*]   Who says?

They stare at each other, breathing hard.

[*Deliberately.*] I have never in all my life heard anyone say put on the kettle.

GUS   I bet my mother used to say it.

BEN   Your mother? When did you last see your mother?

GUS   I don't know, about—

9. Begging for.

BEN   Well, what are you talking about your mother for?

They stare.

Gus, I'm not trying to be unreasonable. I'm just trying to point out something to you.

GUS   Yes, but—

BEN   Who's the senior partner here, me or you?

GUS   You.

BEN   I'm only looking after your interests, Gus. You've got to learn mate.

GUS   Yes, but I've never heard—

BEN   [*vehemently*] Nobody says light the gas! What does the gas light?

GUS   What does the gas—?

BEN   [*grabbing him with two hands by the throat, at arm's length*] THE KETTLE, YOU FOOL!

GUS *takes the hands from his throat.*

GUS   All right, all right.

Pause.

BEN   Well, what are you waiting for?

GUS   I want to see if they light.

BEN   What?

GUS   The matches.

He takes out the flattened box and tries to strike.

No.

He throws the box under the bed.
  BEN *stares at him.*
  GUS *raises his foot.*

Shall I try it on here?

BEN *stares.* GUS *strikes a match on his shoe. It lights.*

Here we are.

BEN   [*wearily*] Put on the bloody kettle, for Christ's sake.

BEN *goes to his bed, but, realizing what he has said, stops and half turns. They look at each other.* GUS *slowly exits, left.* BEN *slams his paper down on the bed and sits on it, head in hands.*

GUS   [*entering*] It's going.

BEN   What?

GUS   The stove.

GUS *goes to his bed and sits.*

I wonder who it'll be tonight.

> *Silence.*

Eh, I've been wanting to ask you something.
BEN [*putting his legs on the bed*]   Oh, for Christ's sake.
GUS   No. I was going to ask you something.

> *He rises and sits on* BEN's *bed.*

BEN   What are you sitting on my bed for?

> GUS *sits.*

What's the matter with you? You're always asking me questions. What's the matter with you?
GUS   Nothing.
BEN   You never used to ask me so many damn questions. What's come over you?
GUS   No, I was just wondering.
BEN   Stop wondering. You've got a job to do. Why don't you just do it and shut up?
GUS   That's what I was wondering about.
BEN   What?
GUS   The job.
BEN   What job?
GUS [*tentatively*]   I thought perhaps you might know something.

> BEN *looks at him.*

I thought perhaps you—I mean—have you got any idea—who it's going to be tonight?
BEN   Who what's going to be?

> *They look at each other.*

GUS [*at length*]   Who it's going to be.

> *Silence.*

BEN   Are you feeling all right?
GUS   Sure.
BEN   Go and make the tea.
GUS   Yes, sure.

> GUS *exits, left,* BEN *looks after him. He then takes his revolver from under the pillow and checks it for ammunition.* GUS *re-enters.*

The gas has gone out.

BEN   Well, what about it?

GUS   There's a meter.

BEN   I haven't got any money.

GUS   Nor have I.

BEN   You'll have to wait.

GUS   What for?

BEN   For Wilson.

GUS   He might not come. He might just send a message. He doesn't always come.

BEN   Well, you'll have to do without it, won't you?

GUS   Blimey.

BEN   You'll have a cup of tea afterwards. What's the matter with you?

GUS   I like to have one before.

> BEN *holds the revolver up to the light and polishes it.*

BEN   You'd better get ready anyway.

GUS   Well, I don't know, that's a bit much, you know, for my money.

> *He picks up a packet of tea from the bed and throws it into the bag.*

I hope he's got a shilling, anyway, if he comes. He's entitled to have. After all, it's his place, he could have seen there was enough gas for a cup of tea.

BEN   What do you mean, it's his place?

GUS   Well, isn't it?

BEN   He's probably only rented it. It doesn't have to be his place.

GUS   I know it's his place. I bet the whole house is. He's not even laying on any gas now either.

> GUS *sits on his bed.*

It's his place all right. Look at all the other places. You go to this address, there's a key there, there's a teapot, there's never a soul in sight—[*He pauses.*] Eh, nobody ever hears a thing, have you ever thought of that? We never get any complaints, do we, too much noise or anything like that? You never see a soul, do you—except the bloke who comes. You ever notice that? I wonder if the walls are soundproof. [*He touches the wall above his bed.*] Can't tell. All you do is wait, eh? Half the time he doesn't even bother to put in an appearance, Wilson.

BEN   Why should he? He's a busy man.

GUS   [*thoughtfully*]   I find him hard to talk to, Wilson. Do you know that, Ben?

BEN   Scrub round it,[1] will you?

> *Pause.*

GUS   There are a number of things I want to ask him. But I can never get round to it, when I see him.

1. Forget it.

Pause.

I've been thinking about the last one.

BEN   What last one?

GUS   That girl.

BEN *grabs the paper, which he reads.*

[*Rising, looking down at* BEN.] How many times have you read that paper?

BEN *slams the paper down and rises.*

BEN [*angrily*]   What do you mean?

GUS   I was just wondering how many times you'd—

BEN   What are you doing, criticizing me?

GUS   No, I was just—

BEN   You'll get a swipe round your earhole if you don't watch your step.

GUS   Now look here, Ben—

BEN   I'm not looking anywhere! [*He addresses the room.*] How many times have I—! A bloody liberty!

GUS   I didn't mean that.

BEN   You just get on with it, mate. Get on with it, that's all.

BEN *gets back on the bed.*

GUS   I was just thinking about that girl, that's all.

GUS *sits on his bed.*

She wasn't much to look at, I know, but still. It was a mess though, wasn't it? What a mess. Honest, I can't remember a mess like that one. They don't seem to hold together like men, women. A looser texture, like. Didn't she spread, eh? She didn't half spread. Kaw! But I've been meaning to ask you.

BEN *sits up and clenches his eyes.*

Who clears up after we've gone? I'm curious about that. Who does the clearing up? Maybe they just leave them there, eh? What do you think? How many jobs have we done? Blimey, I can't count them. What if they never clear anything up after we've gone.

BEN [*pityingly*]   You mutt. Do you think we're the only branch of this organization? Have a bit of common. They got departments for everything.

GUS   What, cleaners and all?

BEN   You birk![2]

GUS   No, it was that girl made me start to think—

There is a loud clatter and racket in the bulge of wall between

2. Idiot.

the beds, of something descending. They grab their revolvers, jump up and face the wall. The noise comes to a stop. Silence. They look at each other. BEN *gestures sharply towards the wall.* GUS *approaches the wall slowly. He bangs it with his revolver. It is hollow.* BEN *moves to the head of his bed, his revolver cocked.* GUS *puts his revolver on his bed and pats along the bottom of the center panel. He finds a rim. He lifts the panel. Disclosed is a serving-hatch, a "dumb waiter." A wide box is held by pulleys.* GUS *peers into the box. He brings out a piece of paper.*

BEN   What is it?

GUS   You have a look at it.

BEN   Read it.

GUS   [*reading*]   Two braised steak and chips. Two sago puddings. Two teas without sugar.

BEN   Let me see that. [*He takes the paper.*]

GUS   [*to himself*]   Two teas without sugar.

BEN   Mmnn.

GUS   What do you think of that?

BEN   Well—

The box goes up. BEN *levels his revolver.*

GUS   Give us a chance! They're in a hurry, aren't they?

BEN *rereads the note.* GUS *looks over his shoulder.*

That's a bit—that's a bit funny, isn't it?

BEN   [*quickly*]   No. It's not funny. It probably used to be a café here, that's all. Upstairs. These places change hands very quickly.

GUS   A café?

BEN   Yes.

GUS   What, you mean this was the kitchen, down here?

BEN   Yes, they change hands overnight, these places. Go into liquidation. The people who run it, you know, they don't find it a going concern, they move out.

GUS   You mean the people who ran this place didn't find it a going concern and moved out?

BEN   Sure.

GUS   WELL, WHO'S GOT IT NOW?

Silence.

BEN   What do you mean, who's got it now?

GUS   Who's got it now? If they moved out, who moved in?

BEN   Well, that all depends—

The box descends with a clatter and bang. BEN *levels his revolver.* GUS *goes to the box and brings out a piece of paper.*

GUS   [*reading*]   Soup of the day. Liver and onions. Jam tart.

A pause. GUS *looks at* BEN. BEN *takes the note and reads it. He walks slowly to the hatch.* GUS *follows.* BEN *looks into the hatch but not up it.* GUS *puts his hand on* BEN's *shoulder.* BEN *throws it off.* GUS *puts his finger to his mouth. He leans on the hatch and swiftly looks up it.* BEN *flings him away in alarm.* BEN *looks at the note. He throws his revolver on the bed and speaks with decision.*

BEN We'd better send something up.
GUS Eh?
BEN We'd better send something up.
GUS Oh! Yes. Yes. Maybe you're right.

They are both relieved at the decision.

BEN [*purposefully*] Quick! What have you got in that bag?
GUS Not much.

GUS *goes to the hatch and shouts up it.*

Wait a minute!
BEN Don't do that!

GUS *examines the contents of the bag and brings them out, one by one.*

GUS Biscuits. A bar of chocolate. Half a pint of milk.
BEN That all?
GUS Packet of tea.
BEN Good.
GUS We can't send the tea. That's all the tea we've got.
BEN Well, there's no gas. You can't do anything with it, can you?
GUS Maybe they can send us down a bob.[3]
BEN What else is there?
GUS [*reaching into bag*] One Eccles cake.[4]
BEN One Eccles cake?
GUS Yes.
BEN You never told me you had an Eccles cake.
GUS Didn't I?
BEN Why only one? Didn't you bring one for me?
GUS I didn't think you'd be keen.
BEN Well, you can't send up one Eccles cake, anyway.
GUS Why not?
BEN All right.

GUS *goes towards the door, left, and stops.*

Do you mean I can keep the Eccles cake then?
BEN Keep it?

3. A shilling.
4. A cake made of sugared light pastry and currants.

GUS   Well, they don't know we've got it, do they?
BEN   That's not the point.
GUS   Can't I keep it?
BEN   No, you can't. Get the plate.

> GUS *exits, left.* BEN *looks in the bag. He brings out a packet of crisps.*[5] *Enter* GUS *with a plate.*

[*Accusingly, holding up the crisps.*] Where did these come from?

GUS   What?
BEN   Where did these crisps come from?
GUS   Where did you find them?
BEN   [*hitting him on the shoulder*] You're playing a dirty game, my lad!
GUS   I only eat those with beer!
BEN   Well, where were you going to get the beer?
GUS   I was saving them till I did.
BEN   I'll remember this. Put everything on the plate.

> *They pile everything onto the plate. The box goes up without the plate.*

Wait a minute!

> *They stand.*

GUS   It's gone up.
BEN   It's all your stupid fault, playing about!
GUS   What do we do now?
BEN   We'll have to wait till it comes down.

> BEN *puts the plate on the bed, puts on his shoulder holster, and starts to put on his tie.*

You'd better get ready.

> GUS *goes to his bed, puts on his tie, and starts to fix his holster.*

GUS   Hey, Ben.
BEN   What?
GUS   What's going on here?

> *Pause.*

BEN   What do you mean?
GUS   How can this be a café?
BEN   It used to be a café.
GUS   Have you seen the gas stove?
BEN   What about it?

5. Potato chips.

GUS   It's only got three rings.

BEN   So what?

GUS   Well, you couldn't cook much on three rings, not for a busy place like this.

BEN   [*irritably*]   That's why the service is slow!

BEN *puts on his waistcoat.*

GUS   Yes, but what happens when we're not here? What do they do then? All these menus coming down and nothing going up. It might have been going on like this for years.

BEN *brushes his jacket.*

What happens when we go?

BEN *puts on his jacket.*

They can't do much business.

The box descends. They turn about. GUS *goes to the hatch and brings out a note.*

GUS   [*reading*]   Macaroni Pastitsio. Ormitha Macarounada.

BEN   What was that?

GUS   Macaroni Pastitsio. Ormitha Macarounada.

BEN   Greek dishes.

GUS   No.

BEN   That's right.

GUS   That's pretty high class.

BEN   Quick before it goes up.

GUS *puts the plate in the box.*

GUS   [*calling up the hatch*]   Three McVitie and Price! One Lyons Red Label! One Smith's Crisps! One Eccles cake! One Fruit and Nut!

BEN   Cadbury's.

GUS   [*up the hatch*]   Cadbury's!

BEN   [*handing the milk*]   One bottle of milk.

GUS   [*up the hatch*]   One bottle of milk! Half a pint! [*He looks at the label.*] Express Dairy! [*He puts the bottle in the box.*]

The box goes up.

Just did it.

BEN   You shouldn't shout like that.

GUS   Why not?

BEN   It isn't done.

BEN *goes to his bed.*

Well, that should be all right, for the time being.

GUS   You think so, eh?

BEN   Get dressed, will you? It'll be any minute now.

> GUS *puts on his waistcoat.* BEN *lies down and looks up at the ceiling.*

GUS   This is some place. No tea and no biscuits.

BEN   Eating makes you lazy, mate. You're getting lazy, you know that? You don't want to get slack on your job.

GUS   Who me?

BEN   Slack, mate, slack.

GUS   Who me? Slack?

BEN   Have you checked your gun? You haven't even checked your gun. It looks disgraceful, anyway. Why don't you ever polish it?

> GUS *rubs his revolver on the sheet.* BEN *takes out a pocket mirror and straightens his tie.*

GUS   I wonder where the cook is. They must have had a few, to cope with that. Maybe they had a few more gas stoves. Eh! Maybe there's another kitchen along the passage.

BEN   Of course there is! Do you know what it takes to make an Ormitha Macarounada?

GUS   No, what?

BEN   An Ormitha—! Buck your ideas up,[6] will you?

GUS   Takes a few cooks, eh?

> GUS *puts his revolver in its holster.*

The sooner we're out of this place the better.

> *He puts on his jacket.*

Why doesn't he get in touch? I feel like I've been here years. [*He takes his revolver out of its holster to check the ammunition.*] We've never let him down though, have we? We've never let him down. I was thinking only the other day, Ben. We're reliable, aren't we?

> *He puts his revolver back in its holster.*

Still, I'll be glad when it's over tonight.

> *He brushes his jacket.*

I hope the bloke's not going to get excited tonight, or anything. I'm feeling a bit off. I've got a splitting headache.

> *Silence.*
> *The box descends.* BEN *jumps up.*
> GUS *collects the note.*

6. Keep your ideas to yourself; *buck* is slang for *chatter.*

[*Reading.*] One Bamboo Shoots, Water Chestnuts and Chicken. One Char Siu and Beansprouts.

BEN   Beansprouts?
GUS   Yes.
BEN   Blimey.
GUS   I wouldn't know where to begin.

> *He looks back at the box. The packet of tea is inside it. He picks it up.*

They've sent back the tea.
BEN   [*anxious*]   What'd they do that for?
GUS   Maybe it isn't tea-time.

> *The box goes up. Silence.*

BEN   [*throwing the tea on the bed, and speaking urgently*]   Look here. We'd better tell them.
GUS   Tell them what?
BEN   That we can't do it, we haven't got it.
GUS   All right then.
BEN   Lend us your pencil. We'll write a note.

> GUS, *turning for a pencil, suddenly discovers the speaking-tube, which hangs on the right wall of the hatch facing his bed.*

GUS   What's this?
BEN   What?
GUS   This
BEN   [*examining it*]   It's a speaking-tube.
GUS   How long has that been there?
BEN   Just the job. We should have used it before, instead of shouting up there.
GUS   Funny I never noticed it before.
BEN   Well, come on.
GUS   What do you do?
BEN   See that? That's a whistle.
GUS   What, this?
BEN   Yes, take it out. Pull it out.

> GUS *does so.*

That's it.
GUS   What do we do now?
BEN   Blow into it.
GUS   Blow?
BEN   It whistles up there if you blow. Then they know you want to speak. Blow.

> GUS *blows. Silence.*

GUS   [*tube at mouth*]   I can't hear a thing.

BEN   Now you speak! Speak into it!

> GUS *looks at* BEN, *then speaks into the tube.*

GUS   The larder's bare!
BEN   Give me that!

> *He grabs the tube and puts it to his mouth.*

[*speaking with great deference.*] Good evening. I'm sorry to— bother you, but we just thought we'd better let you know that we haven't got anything left. We sent up all we had. There's no more food down here.

> *He brings the tube slowly to his ear.*

What?

> *To mouth.*

What?

> *To ear. He listens. To mouth.*

No, all we had we sent up.

> *To ear. He listens. To mouth.*

Oh, I'm very sorry to hear that.

> *To ear. He listens. To* GUS.

The Eccles cake was stale.

> *He listens. To* GUS.

The chocolate was melted.

> *He listens. To* GUS.

The milk was sour.
GUS   What about the crisps?
BEN   [*listening*]   The biscuits were moldy.

> *He glares at* GUS. *Tube to mouth.*

Well, we're very sorry about that.

> *Tube to ear.*

What?

    To mouth.

What?

    To ear.

Yes. Yes.

    To mouth.

Yes certainly. Certainly. Right away.

    To ear. The voice has ceased. He hangs up the tube.

    [*Excitedly.*] Did you hear that?
GUS   What?
BEN   You know what he said? Light the kettle! Not put on the ket-
tle! Not light the gas! But light the kettle!
GUS   How can we light the kettle?
BEN   What do you mean?
GUS   There's no gas.
BEN   [*clapping hand to head*]   Now what do we do?
GUS   What did he want us to light the kettle for?
BEN   For tea. He wanted a cup of tea.
GUS   *He* wanted a cup of tea! What about me? I've been wanting a
cup of tea all night!
BEN   [*despairingly*]   What do we do now?
GUS   What are we supposed to drink?

    BEN *sits on his bed, staring.*

What about us?

    BEN *sits.*

I'm thirsty too. I'm starving. And he wants a cup of tea. That beats
the band, that does.

    BEN *lets his head sink onto his chest.*

I could do with a bit of sustenance myself. What about you? You
look as if you could do with something too.

    GUS *sits on his bed.*

We send him up all we've got and he's not satisfied. No, honest,
it's enough to make the cat laugh. Why did you send him up all
that stuff? [*Thoughtfully.*] Why did I send it up?

    Pause.

Who knows what he's got upstairs? He's probably got a salad bowl. They must have something up there. They won't get much from down here. You notice they didn't ask for any salads? They've probably got a salad bowl up there. Cold meat, radishes, cucumbers. Watercress. Roll mops.

Pause.

Hardboiled eggs.

Pause.

The lot. They've probably got a crate of beer too. Probably eating my crisps with a pint of beer now. Didn't have anything to say about those crisps, did he? They do all right, don't worry about that. You don't think they're just going to sit there and wait for stuff to come up from down here, do you? That'll get them nowhere.

Pause.

They do all right.

Pause.

And he wants a cup of tea.

Pause.

That's past a joke, in my opinion.

He looks over at BEN, *rises, and goes to him.*

What's the matter with you? You don't look too bright, I feel like an Alka-Seltzer myself.

BEN *sits up.*

BEN [*in a low voice*]   Time's getting on.
GUS   I know. I don't like doing a job on an empty stomach.
BEN [*wearily*]   Be quiet a minute. Let me give you your instructions.
GUS   What for? We always do it the same way, don't we?
BEN   Let me give you your instructions.

GUS *sighs and sits next to* BEN *on the bed. The instructions are stated and repeated automatically.*

When we get the call, you go over and stand behind the door.
GUS   Stand behind the door.
BEN   If there's a knock on the door you don't answer it.
GUS   If there's a knock on the door I don't answer it.
BEN   But there won't be a knock on the door.

GUS   So I won't answer it.

BEN   When the bloke comes in—

GUS   When the bloke comes in—

BEN   Shut the door behind him.

GUS   Shut the door behind him.

BEN   Without divulging your presence.

GUS   Without divulging my presence.

BEN   He'll see me and come towards me.

GUS   He'll see you and come towards you.

BEN   He won't see you.

GUS   [*absently*]   Eh?

BEN   He won't see you.

GUS   He won't see me.

BEN   But he'll see me.

GUS   He'll see you.

BEN   He won't know you're there.

GUS   He won't know you're there.

BEN   He won't know *you're* there.

GUS   He won't know I'm there.

BEN   I take out my gun.

GUS   You take out your gun.

BEN   He stops in his tracks.

GUS   He stops in his tracks.

BEN   If he turns round—

GUS   If he turns round—

BEN   You're there.

GUS   I'm here.

BEN *frowns and presses his forehead.*

You've missed something out.

BEN   I know. What?

GUS   I haven't taken my gun out, according to you.

BEN   You take your gun out—

GUS   After I've closed the door.

BEN   After you've closed the door.

GUS   You've never missed that out before, you know that?

BEN   When he sees you behind him—

GUS   Me behind him—

BEN   And me in front of him—

GUS   And you in front of him—

BEN   He'll feel uncertain—

GUS   Uneasy.

BEN   He won't know what to do.

GUS   So what will he do?

BEN   He'll look at me and he'll look at you.

GUS   We won't say a word.

BEN   We'll look at him.

GUS   He won't say a word.

BEN   He'll look at us.

GUS   And we'll look at him.

BEN   Nobody says a word.

> *Pause.*

GUS   What do we do if it's a girl?
BEN   We do the same.
GUS   .Exactly the same?
BEN   Exactly.

> *Pause.*

GUS   We don't do anything different?
BEN   We do exactly the same.
GUS   Oh.

GUS *rises, and shivers.*

Excuse me.

> *He exits through the door on the left.* BEN *remains sitting on the bed, still. The lavatory chain is pulled once off left, but the lavatory does not flush.*
> *Silence.* GUS *re-enters and stops inside the door, deep in thought. He looks at* BEN, *then walks slowly across to his own bed. He is troubled. He stands, thinking. He turns and looks at* BEN. *He moves a few paces towards him.*

[*Slowly in a low, tense voice.*] Why did he send us matches if he knew there was no gas?

> *Silence.* BEN *stares in front of him.* GUS *crosses to the left side of* BEN, *to the foot of his bed, to get to his other ear.*

Why did he send us matches if he knew there was no gas?

> BEN *looks up.*

Why did he do that?
BEN   Who?
GUS   Who sent us those matches?
BEN   What are you talking about?

> GUS *stares down at him.*

GUS [*thickly*]   Who is it upstairs?
BEN [*nervously*]   What's one thing to do with another?
GUS   Who is it, though?
BEN   What's one thing to do with another?

> BEN *fumbles for his paper on the bed.*

GUS   I asked you a question.

BEN   Enough!

GUS [*with growing agitation*] I asked you before. Who moved in? I asked you. You said the people who had it before moved out. Well, who moved in?

BEN [*hunched*]   Shut up.

GUS   I told you, didn't I?

BEN [*standing*]   Shut up!

GUS [*feverishly*] I told you before who owned this place, didn't I? I told you.

> BEN *hits him viciously on the shoulder.*

I told you who ran this place, didn't I?

> BEN *hits him viciously on the shoulder.*

[*Violently.*] Well, what's he playing all these games for? That's what I want to know. What's he doing it for?

BEN   What games?

GUS [*passionately, advancing*]   What's he doing it for? We've been through our tests, haven't we? We got right through our tests, years ago, didn't we? We took them together, don't you remember, didn't we? We've proved ourselves before now, haven't we? We've always done our job. What's he doing all this for? What's the idea? What's he playing these games for?

> *The box in the shaft comes down behind them. The noise is this time accompanied by a shrill whistle, as it falls.* GUS *rushes to the hatch and seizes the note.*

[*Reading.*] Scampi!

> *He crumples the note, picks up the tube, takes out the whistle, blows and speaks.*

WE'VE GOT NOTHING LEFT! NOTHING! DO YOU UNDERSTAND?

> BEN *seizes the tube and flings* GUS *away. He follows* GUS *and slaps him hard, backhanded, across the chest.*

BEN   Stop it! You maniac!

GUS   But you heard!

BEN [*savagely*]   That's enough! I'm warning you!

> *Silence.*
> BEN *hangs the tube. He goes to his bed and lies down. He picks up his paper and reads.*
> *Silence.*
> *The box goes up.*
> *They turn quickly, their eyes meet.* BEN *turns to his paper.*
> *Slowly* GUS *goes back to his bed, and sits.*
> *Silence.*

The hatch falls back into place.
They turn quickly, their eyes meet. BEN *turns back to his paper.*
Silence.
Ben throws his paper down.

BEN   Kaw!

He picks up the paper and looks at it.

Listen to this!

Pause.

What about that, eh?

Pause.

Kaw!

Pause.

Have you ever heard such a thing?
GUS [*dully*]   Go on!
BEN   It's true.
GUS   Get away.
BEN   It's down here in black and white.
GUS [*very low*]   Is that a fact?
BEN   Can you imagine it.
GUS   It's unbelievable.
BEN   It's enough to make you want to puke, isn't it?
GUS [*almost inaudible*]   Incredible.

Ben shakes his head. He puts the paper down and rises. He fixes the revolver in his holster.
    GUS *stands up. He goes towards the door on the left.*

BEN   Where are you going?
GUS   I'm going to have a glass of water.

He exits. BEN *brushes dust off his clothes and shoes. The whistle in the speaking-tube blows. He goes to it, takes the whistle out and puts the tube to his ear. He listens. He puts it to his mouth.*

BEN   Yes.

To ear. He listens. To mouth.

Straight away. Right.

> *To ear. He listens. To mouth.*

Sure we're ready.

> *To ear. He listens. To mouth.*

Understood. Repeat. He has arrived and will be coming in straight away. The normal method to be employed. Understood.

> *To ear. He listens. To mouth.*

Sure we're ready.

> *To ear. He listens. To mouth.*

Right.

> *He hangs the tube up.*

Gus!

> *He takes out a comb and combs his hair, adjusts his jacket to diminish the bulge of the revolver. The lavatory flushes off left.* BEN *goes quickly to the door, left.*

Gus!

> *The door right opens sharply.* BEN *turns, his revolver leveled at the door.*
> GUS *stumbles in.*
> *He is stripped of his jacket, waistcoat, tie, holster, and revolver.*
> *He stops, body stooping, his arms at his sides.*
> *He raises his head and looks at* BEN.
> *A long silence.*
> *They stare at each other.*

CURTAIN

1959

2 DRAMATIC STRUCTURE AND THE STAGE

The theater has emerged twice in Western culture, each time in connection with the religious rituals of a relatively sophisticated society. In Athens the festivals of Dionysus gave birth to the classical drama; in the later Middle Ages the services of the Christian church produced the drama from which all later Western plays are derived. Neither of these was a primitive society. In terms of what had preceded, they were urbanized and self-aware. The religious rites of both involved, among other things, a baptismal rite signifying that the person baptized had become new. The rite of rebirth implied a complete reversal in the life of the worshipper. As Saint Paul put it, "Therefore if any man be in Christ, he is a new creature; old things are passed away; behold, all things are become new." This feature of both religions is important for understanding the nature of drama.

When such a rebirth or change occurs in literature, it is called a **peripety**, a sudden change, brought about by some action or revelation, and a reversal in the direction of a situation. The old situation has passed away; everything has been made new. The first play of modern time will show how this works. It is called the *Quem quaeritis* trope, *Quem quaeritis* from its opening words in the original Latin, trope because it was a passage inserted in the liturgy. It was a dramatization performed by priests of one event of the biblical story of Easter. It survives in several forms, including the minimal one used here. The scene is the tomb of Jesus on Easter morning as three women, who have come to embalm the body, approach the tomb. They find the stone that had sealed the tomb rolled away and an angel present.

ANGEL   Whom do you seek in this sepulchre, Christians?
WOMEN   Jesus of Nazareth, who was crucified, heavenly one.
ANGEL   He is not here; he is risen as he foretold. Go, announce that he is risen from the grave.

The single dramatic event of this play, the angel's announcement of the resurrection, reverses the emotional tone of the situation and the direction of the action. Sorrow is replaced by elation, and embalming gives way to announcement.

Conflict is often defined as the basic element of drama, but conflict without peripety, or at least the possibility of peripety, is not truly dramatic. A struggle whose outcome is never in doubt may have other kinds of interest, but it makes for a dull play or a dull football game in dramatic terms. If, however, the opposing forces are matched so that neither can control the situation for any considerable period, or if the weaker antagonist can mount a credible threat against the stronger, or if the apparently weaker can overcome the stronger, then there is drama. In *Hamlet*, for example, the effectiveness of the struggle between Hamlet and Claudius depends on their being evenly matched. Claudius has possession of the throne and the Queen, but Hamlet has his relation to the late king and his popularity with the people to balance his opponent's strengths. Early in the play Claudius has the upper hand, but he realizes that he has underestimated Hamlet and he overreacts. Until he stops the play-within-the-play, the king seems firmly in command; the expectable outcome of his action seems to favor him. The play, however, does not end with Claudius's triumph.

The king's outburst in *Hamlet* is an example of a specific kind of peripety called a **climax**, the dramatic event about which the typical structure of a play is built. The typical dramatic structure of a play generally falls into five parts, which may or may not coincide with the division into acts and scenes. The first of these, the **exposition**, presents the situation as it exists at the opening of the play, introducing the characters and defining the relationships among them. In *The Sacrifice of Isaac* the exposition is presented concisely in Abraham's opening prayer; by contrast, some of the exposition is given immediately at the opening of *Hedda Gabler*, but certain parts of the material are presented at later points in the play. The second part of a play, the **rising action**, consists of a series of events that complicate the original situation and create conflicts among the characters. During the rising action, the flow of the action is in a single direction, but at some crucial moment an event occurs that changes the direction of the action. This is the third part of the play, the **climax**, or **turning point**. The fourth part of a play is the **falling action**, the changes that characterize the unwinding or unknotting of the complications. Generally the falling action requires less time than the rising action. The final part of the play is its **conclusion** or **catastrophe**. The conclusion reestablishes a stable situation to end the drama.

Although this structure does not work the same way in every play, we might find it helpful to see how it works in *Hamlet*. The exposition sets forth the established situation at the beginning of the play. In *Hamlet*, we need to know about the death of the old king, the accession of Claudius rather than young Hamlet, the marriage of Claudius and Gertrude, Hamlet's return from Wittenberg, and the threat of invasion from Fortinbras. Shakespeare uses two devices to present this information: the recent return of Horatio from Wittenberg (and his need to be brought up to date) and Claudius's speech at the beginning of Act 1, Scene 2. In these and other ways we learn where things stand. At the same time we are witnessing the beginning of the rising action, the introduction of new elements that are to affect the action of the play: the appearance of the ghost, Claudius's refusal to allow Hamlet to return to Wittenberg, Hamlet's growing involvement with Ophelia, the return of Rosencrantz and Guildenstern, and so forth. These and other complications affect the action without changing its basic direction. They also set up events that are to happen later in the play, e.g., Laertes's departure for Paris sets up his return in Act 4. The climax, or turning point, occurs when the King loses control of himself at the play. He loses his advantage over Hamlet, who is more or less in control of the situation. During the falling action the various strands of the plot begin to work themselves out. What happens to Ophelia? What is the result of Rosencrantz and Guildenstern's return? When such questions have been settled, we move to the conclusion of the play, the reestablishment of a new stable situation. In *Hamlet* the conclusion takes place in the final scene, where order is finally restored by the promise of Fortinbras as king.

Beside these structural divisions, most plays have formal divisions, such as **acts** and **scenes.** In the Greek theater scenes were separated by choral odes. In many French plays, a new scene begins with any significant entrance or exit. Many "classic" plays have five acts, because the poet Horace suggested that number, but modern plays tend to have two or three acts. Formal divisions are the result of the conventions of the periods and the content of the individual play, and may vary from the one-act (one-scene) play to such multi-act plays as O'Neill's *Mourning Becomes Electra.*

In performance a play takes place on a **stage** or acting area, whose design and significance vary in different times and places. In the Greek theater, the audience was seated on a raised semicircle of seats (**amphitheater**) halfway around a circular area (**orchestra**) used primarily for dancing by the chorus. At the back of orchestra was the **skene** or stage house, which represented the palace or temple before which the action took place. Shakespeare's stage, in contrast, basically involved a rectangular area built up within a generally round enclosure, so that the audience was on three sides of the principal acting area. However, there were subsidiary acting areas on either side as well as a recessed area at the back of the stage, which could represent Gertrude's chamber in *Hamlet* or the cave in *The Tempest,* and an upper acting area, which could serve as Juliet's balcony.

Modern stages are of three types. The **proscenium** stage evolved during the nineteenth century and is still the most common. For such a stage, the proscenium or proscenium arch is an architectural element that separates the auditorium from the stage and makes the action seem more real because the audience is viewing it through an invisible fourth wall. The proscenium stage lends itself to the use of a curtain, which can be lowered and raised or closed and parted between acts or scenes. Sometimes a part of the acting area is on the auditorium side of the proscenium. Such an area is an **apron** or forestage. In an **arena stage,** however, the audience is seated around the acting area. Entrances and exits are made through the auditorium, and restrictions on the sets are required to insure visibility. The third type of modern stage is the **thrust stage,** in which the audience is seated around three-fourths of the major acting area. All of the action may take place on this projecting area, or some may occur in the extended area of the fourth side.

At any given time and place the idea of what a stage is like is generally shared by audience and stage personnel, and most authors work with this conventional or generally understood notion of the kind of stage involved when they write a play. Of course, authors will sometimes innovate and work out new ways of using the stage, as Arthur Miller did when he devised ways of using flashbacks in *Death of a Salesman.* But even then he was working with the general understanding of the nature of one stage. Even greater differences are involved when we examine plays of different periods that have radically different conventions, such as those between Shakespeare's stage and Sophocles's.

One such convention involves the notion of place. The audience knows that the stage is a stage, but they accept it for something, a public square or a room in a castle or an empty road. In *The Dumb Waiter* we accept the stage as a room in the basement of a building somewhere in England. There must be two doors, one leading to the outside and one leading to the kitchen and bathroom. There must also be some way of representing a dumb waiter and a speaking-tube, and there must be two beds. The play is written for a proscenium stage. If the play is to work, the designer must make the audience aware of the objects, doors, beds, etc., required by the action. By contrast, *The Sacrifice of Isaac* was written to be performed outdoors on a wagon, probably with an elevated area to represent heaven and some indication that one part of the stage represents a field near Abraham's tent and another the place of sacrifice. There are no doors leading to specific places, and only a few objects are required. We do not know exactly how these were represented, but the representation was surely satisfactory to the audience.

The convention of place also involves how place is changed. In *The Sacrifice of Isaac* this was apparently accomplished by moving from one part of the wagon to another. In *The Dumb Waiter* such a change would involve, if it had been required, lowering a curtain or darkening the stage while the sets and props were changed to produce the new place. In Greek drama, generally there was no change of place and the action was set up to involve only one place. If the presence of Tiresias was required, someone would be sent to bring him.

In *Hamlet* all the conventions are quite different. In Shakespeare's theater the acting area does not represent a specific place, but assumes a temporary identity from the characters who inhabit it, their costumes, and their speeches. At the opening of the play we know we are at a sentry station because a man dressed as a soldier challenges two others. By line 15 we know that we are in Denmark because the actors profess to be "liegemen to the Dane." At the end of the scene the actors leave the stage and in a sense take the sentry station with them. Shortly a group of people dressed in court costumes and a man and a woman wearing crowns appear. The audience knows that the acting area has now become a "chamber of state." As the play progresses, we learn more about the characters and the action, and identification of place becomes easier. Although the conventions differ, there is always some tacit agreement between playwright and actors on the one hand and the audience on the other about how place is represented as well.

A similar set of conventions governs the treatment of time on stage. Only in special cases as in a modern one-act play like *The Dumb Waiter* do the elapsed time of the performance and the time covered by the action of the play coincide. The choral odes in *Oedipus Tyrannus* are an example of one convention for representing the passage of time. The elapsed time between scenes may be that necessary to send for the shepherd from Mount Cithaeron and allow for his return or the much shorter time needed for Oedipus to enter his palace, discover Jocasta's suicide, blind himself, and return. The time covered by the ode is shorter or longer as necessary, without real reference to the length of the ode. The total elapsed time of the action in a Greek tragedy, however, was almost universally limited to twenty-four hours or so. In the Elizabethan theater the break between scenes covered whatever time was necessary without a formal device like the choral odes. Sometimes the time was short as the break between Hamlet's departure to see his mother at the end of Act 3, Scene 2, and the opening of the King's prayer at the beginning of the next scene; at other times the elapsed time between might be as long as that between Scenes 4 and 5 of Act 4, in which the news of Polonius's death reached Paris and Laertes returned to Denmark and there rallied his friends. By contrast with the Greek drama, however, the total elapsed time might be years as in *The Winter's Tale*, where the action begins before Perdita's birth and ends after her marriage. In *Hamlet* we cannot tell exactly what the time span is, but in a time of relatively primitive transportation Laertes goes to Paris, remains there for a time, and returns to Denmark; Fortinbras goes from Norway to Poland, fights a war, and returns to Denmark; and news of the deaths of Rosencrantz and Guildenstern, who left England between Acts 3 and 4, is brought back.

In these plays, and in *The Sacrifice of Isaac*, there seems to be little concern with exact time relations. It does not matter whether the journey of Abraham and Isaac consumes three hours, three days, or three months. In more recent plays, however, the audience generally expects to know more about the amount of time involved. When everyone wears a wristwatch, we are perhaps more conscious of time.

A third area of convention in the presentation of plays is the relation between actors and characters. Sophocles wrote *Oedipus Tyrannus* for the festival of Dionysus and was assigned three men to play all the parts. We assume that the most talented of the three played Oedipus, the second most talented Creon and Messenger 2, and the third all the other parts. Sophocles had to write scenes so that there were no more than three speaking parts in each, and allow sufficient time for the performers to change the masks and costumes that told the audience whether the character was an old man or a young woman, a king or a shepherd. The author of *The Sacrifice of Isaac* was writing a play to be performed once a year by a group of tradesmen, who were largely amateurs. We do not know much about how parts were assigned, but unless human nature has changed drastically, we may assume that certain parts seemed more desirable than others, that some actors developed specialties playing angels or children, and that there were cast changes from time to time. Shakespeare also wrote for an all-male cast, but his performers are professional actors. The company included some young boys (presumably from about eleven to fifteen) to play the women's parts, but parts for the boys had to be written to allow for easy replacement as voices cracked with the onset of puberty. Because Shakespeare was a member of the company for which he wrote, he knew the special strengths and weaknesses of his colleagues, and seems to have written certain parts for special talents—Polonius for a specialist in sententious old men, Osric for one in effeminate young men.

After a period in the nineteenth century and early twentieth century when stock companies played many plays and had performers who specialized in such "lines" as leading men and women, juveniles of both sexes, heavies or villains, and character actors, our theater has evolved into one where performers are cast to conform as closely as possible in appearance and age to the characters they are to represent. Film has been an important influence here. In *The Dumb Waiter*, for example, we would expect to see two relatively mature males, who can convince us by their appearance that they could earn a living as professional assassins. We would expect that they be relatively robust, that they have no unusual features, and that Ben is somewhat older than Gus. Thus, at various times the theater has different conventions, but conventions there always are.

WILLIAM SHAKESPEARE

Hamlet

CHARACTERS

CLAUDIUS, *King of Denmark*
HAMLET, *son of the former and nephew to the present King*
POLONIUS, *Lord Chamberlain*
HORATIO, *friend of Hamlet*
LAERTES, *son of Polonius*
VOLTEMAND ⎫
CORNELIUS ⎪
ROSENCRANTZ ⎬ *courtiers*
GUILDENSTERN ⎪
OSRIC ⎪
A GENTLEMAN ⎭
A PRIEST

MARCELLUS ⎫ *officers*
BERNARDO ⎭
FRANCISCO, *a soldier*
REYNALDO, *servant to Polonius*
PLAYERS
TWO CLOWNS, *gravediggers*
FORTINBRAS, *Prince of Norway*
A NORWEGIAN CAPTAIN
ENGLISH AMBASSADORS
GERTRUDE, *Queen of Denmark, and mother of Hamlet*
OPHELIA, *daughter of Polonius*
GHOST OF HAMLET'S FATHER

LORDS, LADIES, OFFICERS, SOLDIERS, SAILORS, MESSENGERS, *and* ATTENDANTS

SCENE: *The action takes place in or near the royal castle of Denmark at Elsinore.*

Act 1

SCENE 1: *A guard station atop the castle. Enter* BERNARDO *and* FRANCISCO, *two sentinels.*

BERNARDO Who's there?
FRANCISCO Nay, answer me. Stand and unfold yourself.
BERNARDO Long live the king!
FRANCISCO Bernardo?
BERNARDO He.
FRANCISCO You come most carefully upon your hour.   5
BERNARDO 'Tis now struck twelve. Get thee to bed, Francisco.
FRANCISCO For this relief much thanks. 'Tis bitter cold,
And I am sick at heart.
BERNARDO Have you had quiet guard?
FRANCISCO   Not a mouse stirring.   10
BERNARDO Well, good night.
If you do meet Horatio and Marcellus,
The rivals[1] of my watch, bid them make haste.

Enter HORATIO *and* MARCELLUS.

FRANCISCO I think I hear them. Stand, ho! Who is there?
HORATIO Friends to this ground.

1. companions

MARCELLUS   And liegemen to the Dane.[2]   15
FRANCISCO   Give you good night.
MARCELLUS   O, farewell, honest soldier!
   Who hath relieved you?
FRANCISCO   Bernardo hath my place.
   Give you good night.   *Exit* FRANCISCO.
MARCELLUS   Holla, Bernardo!
BERNARDO   Say—
   What, is Horatio there?
HORATIO   A piece of him.
BERNARDO   Welcome, Horatio. Welcome, good Marcellus.   20
HORATIO   What, has this thing appeared again tonight?
BERNARDO   I have seen nothing.
MARCELLUS   Horatio says 'tis but our fantasy,
   And will not let belief take hold of him
   Touching this dreaded sight twice seen of us.   25
   Therefore I have entreated him along
   With us to watch the minutes of this night,
   That if again this apparition come,
   He may approve[3] our eyes and speak to it.
HORATIO   Tush, tush, 'twill not appear.
BERNARDO   Sit down awhile,   30
   And let us once again assail your ears,
   That are so fortified against our story,
   What we have two nights seen.
HORATIO   Well, sit we down,
   And let us hear Bernardo speak of this.
BERNARDO   Last night of all,   35
   When yond same star that's westward from the pole[4]
   Had made his course t' illume that part of heaven
   Where now it burns, Marcellus and myself,
   The bell then beating one—

      Enter GHOST.

MARCELLUS   Peace, break thee off. Look where it comes again.   40
BERNARDO   In the same figure like the king that's dead.
MARCELLUS   Thou art a scholar; speak to it, Horatio.
BERNARDO   Looks 'a[5] not like the king? Mark it, Horatio.
HORATIO   Most like. It harrows me with fear and wonder.
BERNARDO   It would be spoke to.
MARCELLUS   Speak to it, Horatio.   45
HORATIO   What art thou that usurp'st this time of night
   Together with that fair and warlike form
   In which the majesty of buried Denmark
   Did sometimes march? By heaven I charge thee, speak.
MARCELLUS   It is offended.
BERNARDO   See, it stalks away.   50

---

2. The "Dane" is the King of Denmark,   3. confirm the testimony of
who is also called "Denmark," as in line 48   4. polestar
of this scene. In line 61 the same figure is   5. he
used for the King of Norway.

HORATIO   Stay. Speak, speak. I charge thee, speak.   *Exit* GHOST.
MARCELLUS   'Tis gone and will not answer.
BERNARDO   How now, Horatio! You tremble and look pale.
  Is not this something more than fantasy?
  What think you on't?   55
HORATIO   Before my God, I might not this believe
  Without the sensible[6] and true avouch
  Of mine own eyes.
MARCELLUS   Is it not like the king?
HORATIO   As thou art to thyself.
  Such was the very armor he had on   60
  When he the ambitious Norway combated.
  So frowned he once when, in an angry parle,[7]
  He smote the sledded Polacks on the ice.
  'Tis strange.
MARCELLUS   Thus twice before, and jump[8] at this dead hour,   65
  With martial stalk hath he gone by our watch.
HORATIO   In what particular thought to work I know not,
  But in the gross and scope of mine opinion,
  This bodes some strange eruption to our state.
MARCELLUS   Good now, sit down, and tell me he that knows,   70
  Why this same strict and most observant watch
  So nightly toils the subject[9] of the land,
  And why such daily cast of brazen cannon
  And foreign mart for implements of war;
  Why such impress of shipwrights, whose sore task   75
  Does not divide the Sunday from the week.
  What might be toward that this sweaty haste
  Doth make the night joint-laborer with the day?
  Who is't that can inform me?
HORATIO   That can I.
  At least, the whisper goes so. Our last king,   80
  Whose image even but now appeared to us,
  Was as you know by Fortinbras of Norway,
  Thereto pricked on by a most emulate pride,
  Dared to the combat; in which our valiant Hamlet
  (For so this side of our known world esteemed him)   85
  Did slay this Fortinbras; who by a sealed compact
  Well ratified by law and heraldry,
  Did forfeit, with his life, all those his lands
  Which he stood seized of,[1] to the conqueror;
  Against the which a moiety competent[2]   90
  Was gagéd[3] by our king; which had returned
  To the inheritance of Fortinbras,
  Had he been vanquisher; as, by the same covenant
  And carriage of the article designed,
  His fell to Hamlet. Now, sir, young Fortinbras,   95

6. of the senses   1. possessed
7. parley   2. portion of similar value
8. precisely   3. pledged
9. people

Of unimprovéd mettle hot and full,
Hath in the skirts of Norway here and there
Sharked up a list of lawless resolutes
For food and diet to some enterprise
That hath a stomach in't; which is no other,   100
As it doth well appear unto our state,
But to recover of us by strong hand
And terms compulsatory, those foresaid lands
So by his father lost; and this, I take it,
Is the main motive of our preparations,   105
The source of this our watch, and the chief head
Of this post-haste and romage[4] in the land.
BERNARDO   I think it be no other but e'en so.
Well may it sort[5] that this portentous figure
Comes arméd through our watch so like the king   110
That was and is the question of these wars.
HORATIO   A mote[6] it is to trouble the mind's eye.
In the most high and palmy state of Rome,
A little ere the mightiest Julius fell,
The graves stood tenantless, and the sheeted dead   115
Did squeak and gibber in the Roman streets;
As stars with trains of fire, and dews of blood,
Disasters in the sun; and the moist star,
Upon whose influence Neptune's empire stands,[7]
Was sick almost to doomsday with eclipse.   120
And even the like precurse[8] of feared events,
As harbingers preceding still the fates
And prologue to the omen coming on,
Have heaven and earth together demonstrated
Unto our climatures[9] and countrymen.   125

    Enter GHOST.

But soft, behold, lo where it comes again!
I'll cross it[1] though it blast me.—Stay, illusion.

                        It spreads [*its*] *arms.*

If thou hast any sound or use of voice,
Speak to me.
If there be any good thing to be done,   130
That may to thee do ease, and grace to me,
Speak to me.
If thou art privy to thy country's fate,
Which happily foreknowing may avoid,
O, speak!   135
Or if thou hast uphoarded in thy life

4. stir
5. chance
6. speck of dust
7. Neptune was the Roman sea god; the "moist star" is the moon.
8. precursor
9. regions
1. Horatio means either that he will move across the Ghost's path in order to stop him or that he will make the sign of the cross to gain power over him. The stage direction which follows is somewhat ambiguous. "It" seems to refer to the Ghost, but the movement would be appropriate to Horatio.

Extorted treasure in the womb of earth,
For which, they say, you spirits oft walk in death,

The cock crows.

Speak of it. Stay, and speak. Stop it, Marcellus.
MARCELLUS   Shall I strike at it with my partisan[2]?   140
HORATIO   Do, if it will not stand.
BERNARDO   'Tis here.
HORATIO   'Tis here.
MARCELLUS   'Tis gone.   *Exit* GHOST.
    We do it wrong, being so majestical,
    To offer it the show of violence;
    For it is as the air, invulnerable,   145
    And our vain blows malicious mockery.
BERNARDO   It was about to speak when the cock crew.
HORATIO   And then it started like a guilty thing
    Upon a fearful summons. I have heard
    The cock, that is the trumpet to the morn,   150
    Doth with his lofty and shrill-sounding throat
    Awake the god of day, and at his warning,
    Whether in sea or fire, in earth or air,
    Th' extravagant and erring[3] spirit hies
    To his confine; and of the truth herein   155
    This present object made probation.[4]
MARCELLUS   It faded on the crowing of the cock.
    Some say that ever 'gainst that season comes
    Wherein our Savior's birth is celebrated,
    This bird of dawning singeth all night long,   160
    And then, they say, no spirit dare stir abroad,
    The nights are wholesome, then no planets strike,
    No fairy takes,[5] nor witch hath power to charm,
    So hallowed and so gracious is that time.
HORATIO   So have I heard and do in part believe it.   165
    But look, the morn in russet mantle clad
    Walks o'er the dew of yon high eastward hill.
    Break we our watch up, and by my advice
    Let us impart what we have seen tonight
    Unto young Hamlet, for upon my life   170
    This spirit, dumb to us, will speak to him.
    Do you consent we shall acquaint him with it,
    As needful in our loves, fitting our duty?
MARCELLUS   Let's do't, I pray, and I this morning know
    Where we shall find him most convenient.   *Exeunt.* 175

SCENE 2: *A chamber of state. Enter* KING CLAUDIUS, QUEEN GER-
TRUDE, HAMLET, POLONIUS, LAERTES, OPHELIA, VOLTEMAND, COR-
NELIUS *and other members of the court.*

---

2. halberd   4. proof
3. wandering out of bounds   5. enchants

KING   Though yet of Hamlet our dear brother's death
   The memory be green, and that it us befitted
   To bear our hearts in grief, and our whole kingdom
   To be contracted in one brow of woe,
   Yet so far hath discretion fought with nature   5
   That we with wisest sorrow think on him,
   Together with remembrance of ourselves.
   Therefore our sometime sister, now our queen,
   Th' imperial jointress[6] to this warlike state,
   Have we, as 'twere with a defeated joy,   10
   With an auspicious and a dropping eye,
   With mirth in funeral, and with dirge in marriage,
   In equal scale weighing delight and dole,
   Taken to wife; nor have we herein barred
   Your better wisdoms, which have freely gone   15
   With this affair along. For all, our thanks.
   Now follows that you know young Fortinbras,
   Holding a weak supposal of our worth,
   Or thinking by our late dear brother's death
   Our state to be disjoint and out of frame,   20
   Colleaguéd with this dream of his advantage,
   He hath not failed to pester us with message
   Importing the surrender of those lands
   Lost by his father, with all bands of law,
   To our most valiant brother. So much for him.   25
   Now for ourself, and for this time of meeting,
   Thus much the business is: we have here writ
   To Norway, uncle of young Fortinbras—
   Who, impotent and bedrid, scarcely hears
   Of this his nephew's purpose—to suppress   30
   His further gait[7] herein, in that the levies,
   The lists, and full proportions are all made
   Out of his subject; and we here dispatch
   You, good Cornelius, and you, Voltemand,
   For bearers of this greeting to old Norway,   35
   Giving to you no further personal power
   To business with the king, more than the scope
   Of these dilated[8] articles allow.
   Farewell, and let your haste commend your duty.

CORNELIUS ⎫
VOLTEMAND ⎭ In that, and all things will we show our duty.   40

KING   We doubt it nothing, heartily farewell.

                     Exeunt VOLTEMAND *and* CORNELIUS.

   And now, Laertes, what's the news with you?
   You told us of some suit. What is't, Laertes?
   You cannot speak of reason to the Dane
   And lose your voice. What wouldst thou beg, Laertes,   45

---

6. A "jointress" is a widow who holds a
jointure or life interest in the estate of her
deceased husband.

7. progress
8. fully expressed

That shall not be my offer, not thy asking?
The head is not more native to the heart,
The hand more instrumental[9] to the mouth,
Than is the throne of Denmark to thy father.
What wouldst thou have, Laertes?

LAERTES   My dread lord,   50
Your leave and favor to return to France,
From whence, though willingly, I came to Denmark
To show my duty in your coronation,
Yet now I must confess, that duty done,
My thoughts and wishes bend again toward France,   55
And bow them to your gracious leave and pardon.

KING   Have you your father's leave? What says Polonius?

POLONIUS   He hath, my lord, wrung from me my slow leave
By laborsome petition, and at last
Upon his will I sealed my hard consent.   60
I do beseech you give him leave to go.

KING   Take thy fair hour, Laertes. Time be thine,
And thy best graces spend it at thy will.
But now, my cousin[1] Hamlet, and my son—

HAMLET [*aside*]   A little more than kin, and less than kind.   65

KING   How is it that the clouds still hang on you?

HAMLET   Not so, my lord. I am too much in the sun.

QUEEN   Good Hamlet, cast thy nighted color off,
And let thine eye look like a friend on Denmark.
Do not for ever with thy vailéd lids[2]   70
Seek for thy noble father in the dust.
Thou know'st 'tis common—all that lives must die,
Passing through nature to eternity.

HAMLET   Ay, madam, it is common.

QUEEN   If it be,
Why seems it so particular with thee?   75

HAMLET   Seems, madam? Nay, it is. I know not "seems."
'Tis not alone my inky cloak, good mother,
Nor customary suits of solemn black,
Nor windy suspiration of forced breath,
No, nor the fruitful river in the eye,   80
Nor the dejected havior[3] of the visage,
Together with all forms, moods, shapes of grief,
That can denote me truly. These indeed seem,
For they are actions that a man might play,
But I have that within which passes show—   85
These but the trappings and the suits of woe.

KING   'Tis sweet and commendable in your nature, Hamlet,
To give these mourning duties to your father,
But you must know your father lost a father,
That father lost, lost his, and the survivor bound   90
In filial obligation for some term

9. serviceable   2. lowered eyes
1. "Cousin" is used here as a general   3. appearance
term of kinship.

To do obsequious[4] sorrow. But to persever
In obstinate condolement is a course
Of impious stubbornness. 'Tis unmanly grief.
It shows a will most incorrect to[5] heaven,   95
A heart unfortified, a mind impatient,
An understanding simple and unschooled.
For what we know must be, and is as common
As any the most vulgar thing to sense,
Why should we in our peevish opposition   100
Take it to heart? Fie, 'tis a fault to heaven,
A fault against the dead, a fault to nature,
To reason most absurd, whose common theme
Is death of fathers, and who still hath cried,
From the first corse[6] till he that died today,   105
"This must be so." We pray you throw to earth
This unprevailing woe, and think of us
As of a father, for let the world take note
You are the most immediate[7] to our throne,
And with no less nobility of love   110
Than that which dearest father bears his son
Do I impart toward you. For your intent
In going back to school in Wittenberg,
It is most retrograde[8] to our desire,
And we beseech you, bend you to remain   115
Here in the cheer and comfort of our eye,
Our chiefest courtier, cousin, and our son.

QUEEN   Let not thy mother lose her prayers, Hamlet.
I pray thee stay with us, go not to Wittenberg.

HAMLET   I shall in all my best obey you, madam.   120

KING   Why, 'tis a loving and a fair reply.
Be as ourself in Denmark. Madam, come.
This gentle and unforced accord of Hamlet
Sits smiling to my heart, in grace whereof,
No jocund health that Denmark drinks today   125
But the great cannon to the clouds shall tell,
And the king's rouse[9] the heaven shall bruit[1] again,
Respeaking earthly thunder. Come away.

Flourish. Exeunt all but HAMLET.

HAMLET   O, that this too too solid flesh would melt,
Thaw, and resolve itself into a dew,   130
Or that the Everlasting had not fixed
His canon[2] 'gainst self-slaughter. O God, God,
How weary, stale, flat, and unprofitable
Seem to me all the uses of this world!
Fie on't, ah, fie, 'tis an unweeded garden   135
That grows to seed. Things rank and gross in nature

---

4. suited for funeral obsequies
5. uncorrected toward
6. corpse
7. next in line
8. contrary
9. carousal
1. echo
2. law

Possess it merely.[3] That it should come to this,
But two months dead, nay, not so much, not two.
So excellent a king, that was to this
Hyperion to a satyr,[4] so loving to my mother,   140
That he might not beteem[5] the winds of heaven
Visit her face too roughly. Heaven and earth,
Must I remember? Why, she would hang on him
As if increase of appetite had grown
By what it fed on, and yet, within a month—   145
Let me not think on't. Frailty, thy name is woman—
A little month, or ere those shoes were old
With which she followed my poor father's body
Like Niobe,[6] all tears, why she, even she— .
O God, a beast that wants discourse of reason   150
Would have mourned longer—married with my uncle,
My father's brother, but no more like my father
Than I to Hercules.[7] Within a month,
Ere yet the salt of most unrighteous tears
Had left the flushing in her gallèd eyes,   155
She married. O, most wicked speed, to post
With such dexterity to incestuous sheets!
It is not, nor it cannot come to good.
But break my heart, for I must hold my tongue.

Enter HORATIO, MARCELLUS, *and* BERNARDO.

HORATIO   Hail to your lordship!
HAMLET   I am glad to see you well.   160
Horatio—or I do forget myself.
HORATIO   The same, my lord, and your poor servant ever.
HAMLET   Sir, my good friend, I'll change[8] that name with you.
And what make you from Wittenberg, Horatio?
Marcellus?   165
MARCELLUS   My good lord!
HAMLET   I am very glad to see you. [*To* BERNARDO.] Good even, sir.—
But what, in faith, make you from Wittenberg?
HORATIO   A truant disposition, good my lord.
HAMLET   I would not hear your enemy say so,   170
Nor shall you do my ear that violence
To make it truster of your own report
Against yourself. I know you are no truant.
But what is your affair in Elsinore?
We'll teach you to drink deep ere you depart.   175
HORATIO   My lord, I came to see your father's funeral.
HAMLET   I prithee do not mock me, fellow-student,
I think it was to see my mother's wedding.

---

3. entirely
4. Hyperion, a sun god, stands here for beauty in contrast to the monstrous satyr, a lecherous creature, half man and half goat.
5. permit
6. In Greek mythology Niobe was turned to stone after a tremendous fit of weeping over the death of her fourteen children, a misfortune brought about by her boasting over her fertility.
7. The demigod Hercules was noted for his strength and the series of spectacular labors which it allowed him to accomplish.
8. exchange

HORATIO   Indeed, my lord, it followed hard upon.
HAMLET   Thrift, thrift, Horatio. The funeral-baked meats   180
Did coldly furnish forth the marriage tables.
Would I had met my dearest[9] foe in heaven
Or ever I had seen that day, Horatio!
My father—methinks I see my father.
HORATIO   Where, my lord?
HAMLET   In my mind's eye, Horatio.   185
HORATIO   I saw him once, 'a was a goodly king.
HAMLET   'A was a man, take him for all in all,
I shall not look upon his like again.
HORATIO   My lord, I think I saw him yesternight.
HAMLET   Saw who?   190
HORATIO   My lord, the king your father.
HAMLET   The king my father?
HORATIO   Season[1] your admiration[2] for a while
With an attent[3] ear till I may deliver[4]
Upon the witness of these gentlemen
This marvel to you.
HAMLET   For God's love, let me hear!   195
HORATIO   Two nights together had these gentlemen,
Marcellus and Bernardo, on their watch
In the dead waste and middle of the night
Been thus encountered. A figure like your father,
Armed at point exactly,[5] cap-a-pe,[6]   200
Appears before them, and with solemn march
Goes slow and stately by them. Thrice he walked
By their oppressed and fear-surprisèd eyes
Within his truncheon's[7] length, whilst they, distilled
Almost to jelly with the act of fear,   205
Stand dumb and speak not to him. This to me
In dreadful secrecy impart they did,
And I with them the third night kept the watch,
Where, as they had delivered, both in time,
Form of the thing, each word made true and good,   210
The apparition comes. I knew your father.
These hands are not more like.
HAMLET   But where was this?
MARCELLUS   My lord, upon the platform where we watch.
HAMLET   Did you not speak to it?
HORATIO   My lord, I did,
But answer made it none. Yet once methought   215
It lifted up it head and did address
Itself to motion, like as it would speak;
But even then the morning cock crew loud,
And at the sound it shrunk in haste away
And vanished from our sight.

---

9. bitterest
1. moderate
2. wonder
3. attentive

4. relate
5. completely
6. from head to toe
7. baton of office

HAMLET 'Tis very strange. 220
HORATIO As I do live, my honored lord, 'tis true,
And we did think it writ down in our duty
To let you know of it.
HAMLET Indeed, sirs, but
This troubles me. Hold you the watch tonight?
ALL We do, my lord.
HAMLET Armed, say you?
ALL Armed, my lord. 225
HAMLET From top to toe?
ALL My lord, from head to foot.
HAMLET Then saw you not his face.
HORATIO O yes, my lord, he wore his beaver[8] up.
HAMLET What, looked he frowningly?
HORATIO A countenance more in sorrow than in anger. 230
HAMLET Pale or red?
HORATIO Nay, very pale.
HAMLET And fixed his eyes upon you?
HORATIO Most constantly.
HAMLET I would I had been there.
HORATIO It would have much amazed you.
HAMLET Very like.
Stayed it long? 235
HORATIO While one with moderate haste might tell a hundred.
BOTH Longer, longer.
HORATIO Not when I saw't.
HAMLET His beard was grizzled, no?
HORATIO It was as I have seen it in his life,
A sable silvered.
HAMLET I will watch tonight. 240
Perchance 'twill walk again.
HORATIO I warr'nt it will.
HAMLET If it assume my noble father's person,
I'll speak to it though hell itself should gape[9]
And bid me hold my peace. I pray you all,
If you have hitherto concealed this sight, 245
Let it be tenable[1] in your silence still,
And whatsomever else shall hap tonight,
Give it an understanding but no tongue.
I will requite your loves. So fare you well.
Upon the platform 'twixt eleven and twelve 250
I'll visit you.
ALL Our duty to your honor.
HAMLET Your loves, as mine to you. Farewell.

Exeunt all but HAMLET.

My father's spirit in arms? All is not well.
I doubt[2] some foul play. Would the night were come!

---

8. movable face protector   1. held
9. open (its mouth) wide   2. suspect

Till then sit still, my soul. Foul deeds will rise,   255
Though all the earth o'erwhelm them, to men's eyes.   *Exit.*

SCENE 3: *The dwelling of* POLONIUS. *Enter* LAERTES *and* OPHELIA.

LAERTES   My necessaries are embarked. Farewell.
And, sister, as the winds give benefit
And convoy[3] is assistant,[4] do not sleep,
But let me hear from you.
OPHELIA   Do you doubt that?
LAERTES   For Hamlet, and the trifling of his favor,   5
Hold it a fashion and a toy in blood,
A violet in the youth of primy[5] nature,
Forward, not permanent, sweet, not lasting,
The perfume and suppliance of a minute,
No more.
OPHELIA   No more but so?
LAERTES   Think it no more.   10
For nature crescent[6] does not grow alone
In thews and bulk, but as this temple[7] waxes
The inward service of the mind and soul
Grows wide withal. Perhaps he loves you now,
And now no soil nor cautel[8] doth besmirch   15
The virtue of his will, but you must fear,
His greatness weighed,[9] his will is not his own,
For he himself is subject to his birth.
He may not, as unvalued persons do,
Carve for himself, for on his choice depends   20
The safety and health of this whole state,
And therefore must his choice be circumscribed
Unto the voice[1] and yielding of that body
Whereof he is the head. Then if he says he loves you,
It fits your wisdom so far to believe it   25
As he in his particular act and place
May give his saying deed, which is no further
Than the main voice of Denmark goes withal.
Then weigh what loss your honor may sustain
If with too credent[2] ear you list[3] his songs,   30
Or lose your heart, or your chaste treasure open
To his unmastered importunity.
Fear it, Ophelia, fear it, my dear sister,
And keep you in the rear of your affection,
Out of the shot and danger of desire.   35
The chariest[4] maid is prodigal enough
If she unmask her beauty to the moon.
Virtue itself scapes not calumnious strokes.

3. means of transport
4. available
5. of the spring
6. growing
7. body
8. deceit
9. rank considered
1. assent
2. credulous
3. listen to
4. most circumspect

The canker[5] galls the infants of the spring
Too oft before their buttons[6] be disclosed,　　40
And in the morn and liquid dew of youth
Contagious blastments[7] are most imminent.
Be wary then; best safety lies in fear.
Youth to itself rebels, though none else near.

OPHELIA　　I shall the effect of this good lesson keep　　45
As watchman to my heart. But, good my brother,
Do not as some ungracious pastors do,
Show me the steep and thorny way to heaven,
Whiles like a puffed and reckless libertine
Himself the primrose path of dalliance treads　　50
And recks[8] not his own rede.[9]

LAERTES　　　　　　　　　　O, fear me not.

　　Enter POLONIUS.

I stay too long. But here my father comes.
A double blessing is a double grace;
Occasion smiles upon a second leave.

POLONIUS　　Yet here, Laertes? Aboard, aboard, for shame!　　55
The wind sits in the shoulder of your sail,
And you are stayed for. There—my blessing with thee,
And these few precepts in thy memory
Look thou character.[1] Give thy thoughts no tongue,
Nor any unproportioned thought his act.　　60
Be thou familiar, but by no means vulgar.
Those friends thou hast, and their adoption tried,
Grapple them unto thy soul with hoops of steel;
But do not dull[2] thy palm with entertainment
Of each new-hatched, unfledged comrade. Beware　　65
Of entrance to a quarrel, but being in,
Bear't[3] that th' opposéd[4] may beware of thee.
Give every man thy ear, but few thy voice;[5]
Take each man's censure, but reserve thy judgment.
Costly thy habit as thy purse can buy,　　70
But not expressed in fancy; rich not gaudy,
For the apparel oft proclaims the man,
And they in France of the best rank and station
Are of a most select and generous chief[6] in that.
Neither a borrower nor a lender be,　　75
For loan oft loses both itself and friend,
And borrowing dulls th' edge of husbandry.
This above all, to thine own self be true,
And it must follow as the night the day
Thou canst not then be false to any man.　　80
Farewell. My blessing season this in thee!

5. rose caterpillar
6. buds
7. blights
8. heeds
9. advice
1. write

2. make callous
3. conduct it
4. opponent
5. approval
6. eminence

LAERTES   Most humbly do I take my leave, my lord.
POLONIUS   The time invites you. Go, your servants tend.[7]
LAERTES   Farewell, Ophelia, and remember well
    What I have said to you.
OPHELIA   'Tis in my memory locked,   85
    And you yourself shall keep the key of it.
LAERTES   Farewell.   *Exit* LAERTES.
POLONIUS   What is't, Ophelia, he hath said to you?
OPHELIA   So please you, something touching the Lord Hamlet.
POLONIUS   Marry, well bethought.   90
    'Tis told me he hath very oft of late
    Given private time to you, and you yourself
    Have of your audience been most free and bounteous.
    If it be so—as so 'tis put on me,
    And that in way of caution—I must tell you,   95
    You do not understand yourself so clearly
    As it behooves my daughter and your honor.
    What is between you? Give me up the truth.
OPHELIA   He hath, my lord, of late made many tenders
    Of his affection to me.   100
POLONIUS   Affection? Pooh! You speak like a green girl,
    Unsifted in such perilous circumstance.
    Do you believe his tenders, as you call them?
OPHELIA   I do not know, my lord, what I should think.
POLONIUS   Marry, I will teach you. Think yourself a baby   105
    That you have ta'en these tenders for true pay
    Which are not sterling. Tender yourself more dearly,
    Or (not to crack the wind of the poor phrase,
    Running it thus) you'll tender me a fool.
OPHELIA   My lord, he hath importuned me with love   110
    In honorable fashion.
POLONIUS   Ay, fashion you may call it. Go to, go to.
OPHELIA   And hath given countenance[8] to his speech, my lord,
    With almost all the holy vows of heaven.
POLONIUS   Ay, springes[9] to catch woodcocks. I do know,   115
    When the blood burns, how prodigal the soul
    Lends the tongue vows. These blazes, daughter,
    Giving more light than heat, extinct in both
    Even in their promise, as it is a-making,
    You must not take for fire. From this time   120
    Be something scanter of your maiden presence.
    Set your entreatments[1] at a higher rate
    Than a command to parle. For Lord Hamlet,
    Believe so much in him that he is young,
    And with a larger tether may he walk   125
    Than may be given you. In few, Ophelia,
    Do not believe his vows, for they are brokers,[2]
    Not of that dye which their investments[3] show,

---

7. await
8. confirmation
9. snares

1. negotiations before a surrender
2. panders
3. garments

But mere implorators[4] of unholy suits,
Breathing like sanctified and pious bawds,   130
The better to beguile. This is for all:
I would not, in plain terms, from this time forth
Have you so slander any moment leisure
As to give words or talk with the Lord Hamlet.
Look to't, I charge you. Come your ways.   135
OPHELIA   I shall obey, my lord.   *Exeunt.*

SCENE 4: *The guard station. Enter* HAMLET, HORATIO *and*
MARCELLUS.

HAMLET   The air bites shrewdly[5]; it is very cold.
HORATIO   It is a nipping and an eager[6] air.
HAMLET   What hour now?
HORATIO   I think it lacks of twelve.
MARCELLUS   No, it is struck.
HORATIO   Indeed? I heard it not. It then draws near the season   5
Wherein the spirit held his wont to walk.
      A flourish of trumpets, and two pieces go off.
What does this mean, my lord?
HAMLET   The king doth wake tonight and takes his rouse,
Keeps wassail, and the swagg'ring up-spring[7] reels,
And as he drains his draughts of Rhenish down,   10
The kettledrum and trumpet thus bray out
The triumph of his pledge.
HORATIO   Is it a custom?
HAMLET   Ay, marry, is't,
But to my mind, though I am native here
And to the manner born, it is a custom   15
More honored in the breach than the observance.
This heavy-headed revel east and west
Makes us traduced and taxed of other nations.
They clepe[8] us drunkards, and with swinish phrase
Soil our addition,[9] and indeed it takes   20
From our achievements, though performed at height,
The pith and marrow of our attribute.[1]
So oft it chances in particular men,
That for some vicious mole of nature in them,
As in their birth, wherein they are not guilty   25
(Since nature cannot choose his origin),
By the o'ergrowth of some complexion,
Oft breaking down the pales[2] and forts of reason,
Or by some habit that too much o'er-leavens
The form of plausive[3] manners—that these men,   30
Carrying, I say, the stamp of one defect,

4. solicitors
5. sharply
6. keen
7. a German dance
8. call

9. reputation
1. honor
2. barriers
3. pleasing

Being nature's livery or fortune's star,
His virtues else, be they as pure as grace,
As infinite as man may undergo,
    Shall in the general censure take corruption   35
From that particular fault. The dram of evil
Doth all the noble substance often doubt[4]
To his own scandal.

    Enter GHOST.

HORATIO   Look, my lord, it comes.
HAMLET   Angels and ministers of grace defend us!
Be thou a spirit of health or goblin damned,   40
Bring with thee airs from heaven or blasts from hell,
Be thy intents wicked or charitable,
Thou com'st in such a questionable[5] shape
That I will speak to thee. I'll call thee Hamlet,
King, father, royal Dane. O, answer me!   45
Let me not burst in ignorance, but tell
Why thy canonized[6] bones, hearséd in death,
Have burst their cerements[7]; why the sepulchre
Wherein we saw thee quietly interred
Hath oped his ponderous and marble jaws   50
To cast thee up again. What may this mean
That thou, dead corse, again in complete steel[8]
Revisits thus the glimpses of the moon,
Making night hideous, and we fools of nature
So horridly to shake our disposition   55
With thoughts beyond the reaches of our souls?
Say, why is this? wherefore? What should we do?

    GHOST *beckons.*

HORATIO   It beckons you to go away it,
As if it some impartment[9] did desire
To you alone.
MARCELLUS   Look with what courteous action   60
It waves[1] you to a more removéd[2] ground.
But do not go with it.
HORATIO   No, by no means.
HAMLET   It will not speak; then I will follow it.
HORATIO   Do not, my lord.
HAMLET   Why, what should be the fear?
I do not set my life at a pin's fee,[3]   65
And for my soul, what can it do to that,
Being a thing immortal as itself?
It waves me forth again. I'll follow it.
HORATIO   What if it tempt you toward the flood, my lord,
Or to the dreadful summit of the cliff   70

1. put out
5. prompting question
6. buried in accordance with church
canons
    7. gravecloths

8. armor
9. communication
1. beckons
2. distant
3. price

That beetles[4] o'er his base into the sea,
And there assume some other horrible form,
Which might deprive[5] your sovereignty of reason[6]
And draw you into madness? Think of it.
The very place puts toys of desperation,[7]   75
Without more motive, into every brain
That looks so many fathoms to the sea
And hears it roar beneath.

HAMLET   It waves me still.
Go on. I'll follow thee.
MARCELLUS   You shall not go, my lord.
HAMLET   Hold off your hands.   80
HORATIO   Be ruled. You shall not go.
HAMLET   My fate cries out
And makes each petty artere in this body
As hardy as the Nemean lion's nerve.[8]
Still am I called. Unhand me, gentlemen.
By heaven, I'll make a ghost of him that lets[9] me.   85
I say, away! Go on. I'll follow thee.

Exeunt GHOST *and* HAMLET.

HORATIO   He waxes desperate with imagination.
MARCELLUS   Let's follow. 'Tis not fit thus to obey him.
HORATIO   Have after. To what issue will this come?
MARCELLUS   Something is rotten in the state of Denmark.   90
HORATIO   Heaven will direct it.
MARCELLUS   Nay, let's follow him.   *Exeunt.*

SCENE 5: *Near the guard station. Enter* GHOST *and* HAMLET.

HAMLET   Whither wilt thou lead me? Speak. I'll go no further.
GHOST   Mark me.
HAMLET   I will.
GHOST   My hour is almost come,
When I to sulph'rous and tormenting flames
Must render up myself.
HAMLET   Alas, poor ghost!
GHOST   Pity me not, but lend thy serious hearing   5
To what I shall unfold.
HAMLET   Speak. I am bound to hear.
GHOST   So art thou to revenge, when thou shalt hear.
HAMLET   What?
GHOST   I am thy father's spirit,
Doomed for a certain term to walk the night,   10
And for the day confined to fast in fires,
Till the foul crimes done in my days of nature[1]
Are burnt and purged away. But that I am forbid

4. juts out
5. take away
6. rational power
7. desperate fancies
8. The Nemean lion was a mythological

monster slain by Hercules as one of his twelve labors.
9. hinders
1. i.e., while I was alive

To tell the secrets of my prison house,
I could a tale unfold whose lightest word 15
Would harrow up thy soul, freeze thy young blood,
Make thy two eyes like stars start from their spheres,
Thy knotted and combinéd[2] locks to part,
And each particular hair to stand an end,
Like quills upon the fretful porpentine.[3] 20
But this eternal blazon[4] must not be
To ears of flesh and blood. List, list, O, list!
If thou didst ever thy dear father love—

HAMLET   O God!

GHOST   Revenge his foul and most unnatural murder. 25

HAMLET   Murder!

GHOST   Murder most foul, as in the best it is,
But this most foul, strange, and unnatural.

HAMLET   Haste me to know't, that I, with wings as swift
As meditation or the thoughts of love, 30
May sweep to my revenge.

GHOST   I find thee apt,
And duller shouldst thou be than the fat weed
That rots itself in ease on Lethe[5] wharf,—
Wouldst thou not stir in this. Now, Hamlet, hear.
'Tis given out that, sleeping in my orchard, 35
A serpent stung me. So the whole ear of Denmark
Is by a forgéd process[6] of my death
Rankly abused. But know, thou noble youth,
The serpent that did sting thy father's life
Now wears his crown.

HAMLET   O my prophetic soul! 40
My uncle!

GHOST   Ay, that incestuous, that adulterate beast,
With witchcraft of his wits, with traitorous gifts—
O wicked wit and gifts that have the power
So to seduce!—won to his shameful lust 45
The will of my most seeming virtuous queen.
O Hamlet, what a falling off was there,
From me, whose love was of that dignity
That it went hand in hand even with the vow
I made to her in marriage, and to decline[7] 50
Upon a wretch whose natural gifts were poor
To those of mine!
But virtue, as it never will be moved,
Though lewdness court it in a shape of heaven,
So lust, though to a radiant angel linked, 55
Will sate itself in a celestial bed
And prey on garbage.
But soft, methinks I scent the morning air.

2. tangled
3. porcupine
4. description of eternity
5. The Lethe was one of the rivers of the classical underworld. Its specific im-
portance was that its waters when drunk induced forgetfulness. The "fat weed" is the asphodel which grew there.
6. false report
7. sink

Brief let me be. Sleeping within my orchard,
My custom always of the afternoon, 60
Upon my secure hour thy uncle stole,
With juice of cursed hebona[8] in a vial,
And in the porches of my ears did pour
The leperous distilment, whose effect
Holds such an enmity with blood of man 65
That swift as quicksilver it courses through
The natural gates and alleys of the body,
And with a sudden vigor it doth posset[9]
And curd,[1] like eager[2] droppings into milk,
The thin and wholesome blood. So did it mine, 70
And a most instant tetter[3] barked about[4]
Most lazar-like[5] with vile and loathsome crust
All my smooth body.
Thus was I sleeping by a brother's hand
Of life, of crown, of queen at once dispatched, 75
Cut off even in the blossoms of my sin,
Unhouseled, disappointed, unaneled,[6]
No reck'ning made, but sent to my account
With all my imperfections on my head.
O, horrible! O, horrible! most horrible! 80
If thou hast nature in thee, bear it not.
Let not the royal bed of Denmark be
A couch for luxury[7] and damnéd incest.
But howsomever thou pursues this act,
Taint not thy mind, nor let thy soul contrive 85
Against thy mother aught. Leave her to heaven,
And to those thorns that in her bosom lodge
To prick and sting her. Fare thee well at once.
The glowworm shows the matin[8] to be near,
And gins to pale his uneffectual fire. 90
Adieu, adieu, adieu. Remember me. *Exit.*
HAMLET　O all you host of heaven! O earth! What else?
And shall I couple hell? O, fie! Hold, hold, my heart,
And you, my sinews, grow not instant old,
But bear me stiffly up. Remember thee? 95
Ay, thou poor ghost, whiles memory holds a seat
In this distracted globe.[9] Remember thee?
Yea, from the table[1] of my memory
I'll wipe away all trivial fond[2] records,
All saws of books, all forms, all pressures past 100
That youth and observation copied there,
And thy commandment all alone shall live
Within the book and volume of my brain,

Unmixed with baser matter. Yes, by heaven!
O most pernicious woman!
O villain, villain, smiling, damnéd villain!
My tables—meet it is I set it down   105
That one may smile, and smile, and be a villain.
At least I am sure it may be so in Denmark.
So, uncle, there you are. Now to my word[3]:   110
It is "Adieu, adieu. Remember me."
I have sworn't.

Enter HORATIO *and* MARCELLUS.

HORATIO   My lord, my lord!
MARCELLUS   Lord Hamlet!
HORATIO   Heavens secure him!
HAMLET   So be it!
MARCELLUS   Illo, ho, ho, my lord!   115
HAMLET   Hillo, ho, ho, boy![4] Come, bird, come.
MARCELLUS   How is't, my noble lord?
HORATIO   What news, my lord?
HAMLET   O, wonderful!
HORATIO   Good my lord, tell it.
HAMLET   No, you will reveal it.
HORATIO   Not I, my lord, by heaven.
MARCELLUS   Nor I, my lord.   120
HAMLET   How say you then, would heart of man once think it?
But you'll be secret?
BOTH   Ay, by heaven, my lord.
HAMLET   There's never a villain dwelling in all Denmark
But he's an arrant knave.
HORATIO   There needs no ghost, my lord, come from the grave   125
To tell us this.
HAMLET   Why, right, you are in the right,
And so without more circumstance at all
I hold it fit that we shake hands and part,
You, as your business and desire shall point you,
For every man hath business and desire   130
Such as it is, and for my own poor part,
I will go pray.
HORATIO   These are but wild and whirling words, my lord.
HAMLET   I am sorry they offend you, heartily;
Yes, faith, heartily.
HORATIO   There's no offence, my lord.   135
HAMLET   Yes, by Saint Patrick, but there is, Horatio,
And much offence too. Touching this vision here,
It is an honest ghost, that let me tell you.
For your desire to know what is between us.
O'ermaster't as you may. And now, good friends,   140
As you are friends, scholars, and soldiers,
Give me one poor request.

---

3. for my motto   4. a falconer's cry

HORATIO   What is't, my lord? We will.
HAMLET   Never make known what you have seen tonight.
BOTH   My lord, we will not.
HAMLET   Nay, but swear't.
HORATIO   In faith,   145
My lord, not I.
MARCELLUS   Nor I, my lord, in faith.
HAMLET   Upon my sword.
MARCELLUS   We have sworn, my lord, already.
HAMLET   Indeed, upon my sword, indeed.

      GHOST *cries under the stage.*

GHOST   Swear.
HAMLET   Ha, ha, boy, say'st thou so? Art thou there, truepenny[5]?
Come on. You hear this fellow in the cellarage.[6]   150
Consent to swear.
HORATIO   Propose the oath, my lord.
HAMLET   Never to speak of this that you have seen,
Swear by my sword.
GHOST [*beneath*]   Swear.
HAMLET   Hic et ubique?[7] Then we'll shift our ground.   155
Come hither, gentlemen,
And lay your hands again upon my sword.
Swear by my sword
Never to speak of this that you have heard.
GHOST [*beneath*]   Swear by his sword.   160
HAMLET   Well said, old mole! Canst work i' th' earth so fast?
A worthy pioneer![8] Once more remove, good friends.
HORATIO   O day and night, but this is wondrous strange!
HAMLET   And therefore as a stranger give it welcome.
There are more things in heaven and earth, Horatio,   165
Than are dreamt of in your philosophy.
But come.
Here as before, never, so help you mercy,
How strange or odd some'er I bear myself
(As I perchance hereafter shall think meet   170
To put an antic[9] disposition on),
That you, at such times, seeing me, never shall,
With arms encumbered[1] thus, or this head-shake,
Or by pronouncing of some doubtful phrase,
As "Well, well, we know," or "We could, and if we would"   175
Or "If we list to speak," or "There be, and if they might"
Or such ambiguous giving out, to note
That you know aught of me—this do swear,
So grace and mercy at your most need help you.
GHOST [*beneath*]   Swear.   *They swear.* 180
HAMLET   Rest, rest, perturbéd spirit! So, gentlemen,
With all my love I do commend me to you,

5. old fellow   8. soldier who digs trenches
6. below   9. grotesque
7. here and everywhere   1. folded

And what so poor a man as Hamlet is
May do t'express his love and friending[2] to you,
God willing, shall not lack. Let us go in together,   185
And still your fingers on your lips, I pray.
The time is out of joint. O curséd spite
That ever I was born to set it right!
Nay, come, let's go together.   *Exeunt.*

Act 2

SCENE 1: *The dwelling of* POLONIUS. *Enter* POLONIUS
and REYNALDO.

POLONIUS Give him this money and these notes, Reynaldo.
REYNALDO I will, my lord.
POLONIUS You shall do marvellous wisely, good Reynaldo,
Before you visit him, to make inquire[3]
Of his behavior.
REYNALDO   My lord, I did intend it.   5
POLONIUS Marry, well said, very well said. Look you, sir.
Enquire me first what Danskers[4] are in Paris,
And how, and who, what means, and where they keep,[5]
What company, at what expense; and finding
By this encompassment[6] and drift of question   10
That they do know my son, come you more nearer
Than your particular demands[7] will touch it.
Take you as 'twere some distant knowledge of him,
As thus, "I know his father and his friends,
And in part him." Do you mark this, Reynaldo?   15
REYNALDO Ay, very well, my lord.
POLONIUS "And in part him, but," you may say, "not well,
But if't be he I mean, he's very wild,
Addicted so and so." And there put on him
What forgeries[8] you please; marry, none so rank[9]   20
As may dishonor him. Take heed of that.
But, sir, such wanton, wild, and usual slips
As are companions noted and most known
To youth and liberty.
REYNALDO   As gaming, my lord.
POLONIUS Ay, or drinking, fencing, swearing, quarrelling,   25
Drabbing[1]—you may go so far.
REYNALDO My lord, that would dishonor him.
POLONIUS Faith, no, as you may season it in the charge.[2]
You must not put another scandal on him,

2. friendship
3. inquiry
4. Danes
5. live
6. indirect means

7. direct questions
8. lies
9. foul
1. whoring
2. soften the accusation

That he is open to incontinency.[3]   30
That's not my meaning. But breathe his faults so quaintly[4]
That they may seem the taints of liberty,[5]
The flash and outbreak of a fiery mind,
A savageness in unreclaiméd[6] blood,
Of general assault.[7]

REYNALDO   But, my good lord—   35
POLONIUS   Wherefore should you do this?
REYNALDO   Ay, my lord,
I would know that.
POLONIUS   Marry, sir, here's my drift,
And I believe it is a fetch of warrant.[8]
You laying these slight sullies on my son,
As 'twere a thing a little soiled i' th' working,   40
Mark you,
Your party in converse,[9] him you would sound,
Having ever seen in the prenominate[1] crimes
The youth you breathe[2] of guilty, be assured
He closes with you in this consequence,   45
"Good sir," or so, or "friend," or "gentleman,"
According to the phrase or the addition
Of man and country.
REYNALDO   Very good, my lord.
POLONIUS   And then, sir, does 'a this—'a does—What was I about to
    say?   50
By the mass, I was about to say something.
Where did I leave?
REYNALDO   At "closes in the consequence."
POLONIUS   At "closes in the consequence"—ay, marry,
He closes thus: "I know the gentleman.   55
I saw him yesterday, or th' other day,
Or then, or then, with such, or such, and as you say,
There was 'a gaming, there o'ertook in's rouse,
There falling out at tennis," or perchance
"I saw him enter such a house of sale,"   60
Videlicet,[3] a brothel, or so forth.
See you, now—
Your bait of falsehood takes this carp of truth,
And thus do we of wisdom and of reach,[4]
With windlasses and with assays of bias,[5]   65
By indirections find directions out;
So by my former lecture and advice
Shall you my son. You have me, have you not?
REYNALDO   My lord, I have.
POLONIUS   God b'wi' ye; fare ye well.
REYNALDO   Good my lord.   70

---

3. sexual excess   9. conversation
4. with delicacy   1. already named
5. faults of freedom   2. speak
6. untamed   3. namely
7. touching everyone   4. ability
8. permissible trick   5. indirect tests

POLONIUS   Observe his inclination in yourself.
REYNALDO   I shall, my lord.
POLONIUS   And let him ply[6] his music.
REYNALDO   Well, my lord.
POLONIUS   Farewell.   *Exit* REYNALDO.

     Enter OPHELIA.

                How now, Ophelia, what's the matter?
OPHELIA   O my lord, my lord, I have been so affrighted!   75
POLONIUS   With what, i' th' name of God?
OPHELIA   My lord, as I was sewing in my closet,[7]
  Lord Hamlet with his doublet[8] all unbraced,[9]
  No hat upon his head, his stockings fouled,
  Ungartered and down-gyvéd[1] to his ankle,   80
  Pale as his shirt, his knees knocking each other,
  And with a look so piteous in purport
  As if he had been looséd out of hell
  To speak of horrors—he comes before me.
POLONIUS   Mad for thy love?
OPHELIA   My lord, I do not know,   85
  But truly I do fear it.
POLONIUS   What said he?
OPHELIA   He took me by the wrist, and held me hard,
  Then goes he to the length of all his arm,
  And with his other hand thus o'er his brow,
  He falls to such perusal of my face   90
  As 'a would draw it. Long stayed he so.
  At last, a little shaking of mine arm,
  And thrice his head thus waving up and down,
  He raised a sigh so piteous and profound
  As it did seem to shatter all his bulk,[2]   95
  And end his being. That done, he lets me go,
  And with his head over his shoulder turned
  He seemed to find his way without his eyes,
  For out adoors he went without their helps,
  And to the last bended[3] their light on me.   100
POLONIUS   Come, go with me. I will go seek the king.
  This is the very ecstasy of love,
  Whose violent property[4] fordoes[5] itself,
  And leads the will to desperate undertakings
  As oft as any passion under heaven   105
  That does afflict our natures. I am sorry.
  What, have you given him any hard words of late?
OPHELIA   No, my good lord, but as you did command
  I did repel[6] his letters, and denied
  His access to me.

---

6. practice
7. chamber
8. jacket
9. unlaced
1. fallen down like fetters

2. body
3. directed
4. character
5. destroys
6. refuse

POLONIUS   That hath made him mad.   110
I am sorry that with better heed and judgment
I had not quoted[7] him. I feared he did but trifle,
And meant to wrack[8] thee; but beshrew my jealousy.
By heaven, it is as proper to our age
To cast beyond ourselves in our opinions   115
As it is common for the younger sort
To lack discretion. Come, go we to the king.
This must be known, which being kept close, might move
More grief to hide than hate to utter love.
Come.   *Exeunt.* 120

SCENE 2: *A public room. Enter* KING, QUEEN, ROSENCRANTZ
and GUILDENSTERN.

KING   Welcome, dear Rosencrantz and Guildenstern.
Moreover that[9] we much did long to see you,
The need we have to use you did provoke
Our hasty sending. Something have you heard
Of Hamlet's transformation—so call it,   5
Sith[1] nor th' exterior nor the inward man
Resembles that it was. What it should be,
More than his father's death, that thus hath put him
So much from th' understanding of himself,
I cannot deem of. I entreat you both   10
That, being of so young days[2] brought up with him,
And sith so neighbored[3] to his youth and havior,
That you vouchsafe your rest here in our court
Some little time, so by your companies
To draw him on to pleasures, and to gather   15
So much as from occasion you may glean,
Whether aught to us unknown afflicts him thus,
That opened lies within our remedy.
QUEEN   Good gentlemen, he hath much talked of you,
And sure I am two men there are not living   20
To whom he more adheres. If it will please you
To show us so much gentry[4] and good will
As to expend your time with us awhile
For the supply and profit of our hope,
Your visitation shall receive such thanks   25
As fits a king's remembrance.
ROSENCRANTZ   Both your majesties
Might, by the sovereign power you have of us,
Put your dread pleasures more into command
Than to entreaty.
GUILDENSTERN   But we both obey,
And here give up ourselves in the full bent[5]   30

7. observed
8. harm
9. in addition to the fact that
1. since

2. from childhood
3. closely allied
4. courtesy
5. completely

To lay our service freely at your feet,
To be commanded.
KING   Thanks, Rosencrantz and gentle Guildenstern.
QUEEN   Thanks, Guildenstern and gentle Rosencrantz.
And I beseech you instantly to visit   35
My too much changed son. Go, some of you,
And bring these gentlemen where Hamlet is.
GUILDENSTERN   Heavens make our presence and our practices
Pleasant and helpful to him!
QUEEN   Ay, amen!

                    Exeunt ROSENCRANTZ *and* GUILDENSTERN.

        Enter POLONIUS.

POLONIUS   Th' ambassadors from Norway, my good lord,   40
Are joyfully returned.
KING   Thou still[6] hast been the father of good news.
POLONIUS   Have I, my lord? I assure you, my good liege,
I hold my duty as I hold my soul,
Both to my God and to my gracious king;   45
And I do think—or else this brain of mine
Hunts not the trail of policy[7] so sure
As it hath used to do—that I have found
The very cause of Hamlet's lunacy.
KING   O, speak of that, that do I long to hear.   50
POLONIUS   Give first admittance to th' ambassadors.
My news shall be the fruit[8] to that great feast.
KING   Thyself do grace to them, and bring them in.

                                              Exit POLONIUS.

He tells me, my dear Gertrude, he hath found
The head and source of all your son's distemper.   55
QUEEN   I doubt it is no other but the main,
His father's death and our o'erhasty marriage.
KING   Well, we shall sift[9] him.

        Enter Ambassadors (VOLTEMAND *and* CORNELIUS) *with*
        POLONIUS.
                              Welcome, my good friends,
Say, Voltemand, what from our brother Norway?
VOLTEMAND   Most fair return of greetings and desires.   60
Upon our first,[1] he sent out to suppress
His nephew's levies, which to him appeared
To be a preparation 'gainst the Polack,
But better looked into, he truly found
It was against your highness, whereat grieved,   65
That so his sickness, age, and impotence
Was falsely borne in hand,[2] sends out arrests[3]

---

6. ever
7. statecraft
8. dessert
9. examine

1. i.e., first appearance
2. deceived
3. orders to stop

On Fortinbras, which he in brief obeys,
Receives rebuke from Norway, and in fine,
Makes vow before his uncle never more   70
To give th' assay[4] of arms against your majesty.
Whereon old Norway, overcome with joy,
Gives him threescore thousand crowns in annual fee,
And his commission to employ those soldiers,
So levied as before, against the Polack,   75
With an entreaty, herein further shown,   *Gives* CLAUDIUS *a paper.*
That it might please you to give quiet pass[5]
Through your dominions for this enterprise,
On such regards of safety and allowance
As therein are set down.

KING   It likes[6] us well,   80
And at our more considered time[7] we'll read,
Answer, and think upon this business.
Meantime we thank you for your well-took[8] labor.
Go to your rest; at night we'll feast together.
Most welcome home!   *Exeunt* AMBASSADORS.

POLONIUS   This business is well ended.   85
My liege and madam, to expostulate[9]
What majesty should be, what duty is,
Why day is day, night night, and time is time,
Were nothing but to waste night, day, and time.
Therefore, since brevity is the soul of wit,   90
And tediousness the limbs and outward flourishes,[1]
I will be brief. Your noble son is mad.
Mad call I it, for to define true madness,
What is't but to be nothing else but mad?
But let that go.

QUEEN   More matter with less art.   95

POLONIUS   Madam, I swear I use no art at all.
That he is mad, 'tis true: 'tis true 'tis pity,
And pity 'tis 'tis true. A foolish figure,
But farewell it, for I will use no art.
Mad let us grant him, then, and now remains   100
That we find out the cause of this effect,
Or rather say the cause of this defect,
For this effect defective comes by cause.
Thus it remains, and the remainder thus.
Perpend.[2]   105
I have a daughter—have while she is mine—
Who in her duty and obedience, mark,
Hath given me this. Now gather, and surmise.
    "To the celestial, and my soul's idol, the most beautified
Ophelia."—That's an ill phrase, a vile phrase, "beautified" is a   110

---

4. trial
5. safe conduct
6. pleases
7. time for more consideration

8. successful
9. discuss
1. adornments
2. consider

vile phrase. But you shall hear. Thus:
> "In her excellent white bosom, these, etc."

QUEEN   Came this from Hamlet to her?
POLONIUS   Good madam, stay awhile. I will be faithful.

> "Doubt thou the stars are fire,   115
>   Doubt that the sun doth move;
>   Doubt truth to be a liar;
>   But never doubt I love.
>
> O dear Ophelia, I am ill at these numbers.[3]
> I have not art to reckon my groans, but that I love thee best, O   120
> most best, believe it. Adieu.
>   Thine evermore, most dear lady, whilst
>   this machine[4] is to him, HAMLET."

This in obedience hath my daughter shown me,
And more above, hath his solicitings,   125
As they fell out by time, by means, and place,
All given to mine ear.
KING   But how hath she
Received his love?
POLONIUS   What do you think of me?
KING   As of a man faithful and honorable.
POLONIUS   I would fain prove so. But what might you think,   130
When I had seen this hot love on the wing,
(As I perceived it, I must tell you that,
Before my daughter told me), what might you,
Or my dear majesty your queen here, think,
If I had played the desk or table-book,   135
Or given my heart a winking, mute and dumb,
Or looked upon this love with idle sight,[5]
What might you think? No, I went round[6] to work,
And my young mistress thus I did bespeak:
"Lord Hamlet is a prince out of thy star.[7]   140
This must not be." And then I prescripts[8] gave her,
That she should lock herself from his resort,
Admit no messengers, receive no tokens.
Which done, she took[9] the fruits of my advice;
And he repelled, a short tale to make,   145
Fell into a sadness, then into a fast,
Thence to a watch, thence into a weakness,
Thence to a lightness, and by this declension,
Into the madness wherein now he raves,
And all we mourn for.
KING   Do you think 'tis this?   150
QUEEN   It may be, very like.

---

3. verses
4. body
5. Polonius means that he would have
been at fault if, having seen Hamlet's attention to Ophelia, he had winked at it or
not paid attention, an "idle sight," and if
he had remained silent and kept the information to himself, as if it were written in a
"desk" or "table-book."
6. directly
7. beyond your sphere
8. orders
9. followed

POLONIUS   Hath there been such a time—I would fain know that—
That I have positively said "'Tis so,"
When it proved otherwise?
KING   Not that I know.
POLONIUS [*pointing to his head and shoulder*]   Take this from this, if
this be otherwise.   155
If circumstances lead me, I will find
Where truth is hid, though it were hid indeed
Within the centre.[1]
KING   How may we try it further?
POLONIUS   You know sometimes he walks four hours together
Here in the lobby.
QUEEN   So he does, indeed.   160
POLONIUS   At such a time I'll loose[2] my daughter to him.
Be you and I behind an arras[3] then.
Mark the encounter. If he love her not,
And be not from his reason fall'n thereon,
Let me be no assistant for a state,   165
But keep a farm and carters.
KING   We will try it.

Enter HAMLET *reading a book.*

QUEEN   But look where sadly the poor wretch comes reading.
POLONIUS   Away, I do beseech you both away,
I'll board[4] him presently.

Exeunt KING *and* QUEEN.

O, give me leave.
How does my good Lord Hamlet?   170
HAMLET   Well, God-a-mercy.
POLONIUS   Do you know me, my lord?
HAMLET   Excellent well, you are a fishmonger.
POLONIUS   Not I, my lord.
HAMLET   Then I would you were so honest a man.   175
POLONIUS   Honest, my lord?
HAMLET   Ay, sir, to be honest as this world goes, is to be one man
picked out of ten thousand.
POLONIUS   That's very true, my lord.
HAMLET   For if the sun breed maggots in a dead dog, being a god 180
kissing carrion[5]—Have you a daughter?
POLONIUS   I have, my lord.
HAMLET   Let her not walk i' th' sun. Conception is a blessing, but as
your daughter may conceive—friend, look to't.
POLONIUS   How say you by that? [*Aside.*] Still harping on my daughter. 185
Yet he knew me not at first. 'A said I was a fishmonger. 'A is far
gone. And truly in my youth I suffered much extremity for love.
Very near this. I'll speak to him again.—What do you read, my lord?

1. of the earth
2. let loose
3. tapestry
4. accost

5. A reference to the belief of the period
that maggots were produced spontaneously
by the action of sunshine on carrion.

HAMLET   Words, words, words.

POLONIUS   What is the matter, my lord?   190

HAMLET   Between who?

POLONIUS   I mean the matter that you read, my lord.

HAMLET   Slanders, sir; for the satirical rogue says here that old men
have grey beards, that their faces are wrinkled, their eyes purging
thick amber and plum-tree gum, and that they have a plentiful lack 195
of wit, together with most weak hams[6]—all which, sir, though I
most powerfully and potently believe, yet I hold it not honesty to
have it thus set down, for yourself, sir, shall grow old as I am, if like
a crab you could go backward.

POLONIUS [*aside*]   Though this be madness, yet there is method in't. 200
—Will you walk out of the air, my lord?

HAMLET   Into my grave?

POLONIUS [*aside*]   Indeed, that's out of the air. How pregnant sometime his replies are! a happiness that often madness hits on, which
reason and sanity could not so prosperously be delivered of. I will 205
leave him, and suddenly contrive the means of meeting between
him and my daughter.—My lord, I will take my leave of you.

HAMLET   You cannot take from me anything that I will more willingly
part withal—except my life, except my life, except my life.

Enter GUILDENSTERN *and* ROSENCRANTZ.

POLONIUS   Fare you well, my lord.   210

HAMLET   These tedious old fools!

POLONIUS   You go to seek the Lord Hamlet. There he is.

ROSENCRANTZ [*to* POLONIUS]   God save you, sir!   *Exit* POLONIUS.

GUILDENSTERN   My honored lord!

ROSENCRANTZ   My most dear lord!   215

HAMLET   My excellent good friends! How dost thou, Guildenstern?
Ah, Rosencrantz! Good lads, how do you both?

ROSENCRANTZ   As the indifferent[7] children of the earth.

GUILDENSTERN   Happy in that we are not over-happy;
On Fortune's cap we are not the very button.[8]   220

HAMLET   Nor the soles of her shoe?

ROSENCRANTZ   Neither, my lord.

HAMLET   Then you live about her waist, or in the middle of her favors.

GUILDENSTERN   Faith, her privates we.

HAMLET   In the secret parts of Fortune? O, most true, she is a   225
strumpet.[9] What news?

ROSENCRANTZ   None, my lord, but that the world's grown honest.

HAMLET   Then is doomsday near. But your news is not true. Let me
question more in particular. What have you, my good friends, deserved at the hands of Fortune, that she sends you to prison hither? 230

GUILDENSTERN   Prison, my lord?

HAMLET   Denmark's a prison.

6. limbs
7. ordinary
8. i.e., on top
9. Hamlet is indulging in characteristic
ribaldry. Guildenstern means that they are

"privates" — ordinary citizens, but Hamlet
takes him to mean "privates" — sexual organs and "middle of her favors" = waist =
sexual organs.

ROSENCRANTZ　Then is the world one.

HAMLET　A goodly one, in which there are many confines, wards,[1] and dungeons, Denmark being one o' th' worst. 235

ROSENCRANTZ　We think not so, my lord.

HAMLET　Why then 'tis none to you; for there is nothing either good or bad, but thinking makes it so. To me it is a prison.

ROSENCRANTZ　Why then your ambition makes it one. 'Tis too narrow for your mind. 240

HAMLET　O God, I could be bounded in a nutshell and count myself a king of infinite space, were it not that I have bad dreams.

GUILDENSTERN　Which dreams indeed are ambition; for the very substance of the ambitious is merely the shadow of a dream.

HAMLET　A dream itself is but a shadow. 245

ROSENCRANTZ　Truly, and I hold ambition of so airy and light a quality that it is but a shadow's shadow.

HAMLET　Then are our beggars bodies, and our monarchs and outstretched heroes the beggars' shadows. Shall we to th' court? for, by my fay,[2] I cannot reason. 250

BOTH　We'll wait upon you.

HAMLET　No such matter. I will not sort[3] you with the rest of my servants; for to speak to you like an honest man, I am most dreadfully attended. But in the beaten way of friendship, what make you at Elsinore? 255

ROSENCRANTZ　To visit you, my lord; no other occasion.

HAMLET　Beggar that I am, I am even poor in thanks, but I thank you; and sure, dear friends, my thanks are too dear a halfpenny.[4] Were you not sent for? Is it your own inclining? Is it a free visitation? Come, come, deal justly with me. Come, come, nay speak. 260

GUILDENSTERN　What should we say, my lord?

HAMLET　Why anything but to th' purpose. You were sent for, and there is a kind of confession in your looks, which your modesties have not craft enough to color. I know the good king and queen have sent for you. 265

ROSENCRANTZ　To what end, my lord?

HAMLET　That you must teach me. But let me conjure you by the rights of our fellowship, by the consonancy of our youth, by the obligation of our ever-preserved love, and by what more dear a better proposer can charge you withal, be even and direct[5] with me 270 whether you were sent for or no.

ROSENCRANTZ [*aside to* GUILDENSTERN]　What say you?

HAMLET [*aside*]　Nay, then, I have an eye of you.—If you love me, hold not off.

GUILDENSTERN　My lord, we were sent for. 275

HAMLET　I will tell you why; so shall my anticipation prevent your discovery,[6] and your secrecy to the king and queen moult no feather. I have of late—but wherefore I know not—lost all my mirth, forgone all custom of exercises; and indeed it goes so heavily with my disposition, that this goodly frame the earth seems to me 280

---

1. cells
2. faith
3. include

4. not worth a halfpenny
5. straightforward
6. disclosure

a sterile promontory, this most excellent canopy the air, look you, this brave o'er-hanging firmament, this majestical roof fretted[7] with golden fire, why it appeareth nothing to me but a foul and pestilent congregation of vapors. What a piece of work is a man, how noble in reason, how infinite in faculties, in form and moving, how express[8] and admirable in action, how like an angel in apprehension, how like a god: the beauty of the world, the paragon of animals. And yet to me, what is this quintessence of dust? Man delights not me, nor woman neither, though by your smiling you seem to say so.

ROSENCRANTZ   My lord, there was no such stuff in my thoughts.

HAMLET   Why did ye laugh, then, when I said "Man delights not me"?

ROSENCRANTZ   To think, my lord, if you delight not in man, what lenten[9] entertainment the players shall receive from you. We coted[1] them on the way, and hither are they coming to offer you service.

HAMLET   He that plays the king shall be welcome—his majesty shall have tribute on me; the adventurous knight shall use his foil and target[2]; the lover shall not sigh gratis; the humorous[3] man shall end his part in peace; the clown shall make those laugh whose lungs are tickle o' th' sere[4]; and the lady shall say her mind freely, or the blank verse shall halt for't. What players are they?

ROSENCRANTZ   Even those you were wont to take such delight in, the tragedians of the city.

HAMLET   How chances it they travel? Their residence, both in reputation and profit, was better both ways.

ROSENCRANTZ   I think their inhibition comes by the means of the late innovation.

HAMLET   Do they hold the same estimation they did when I was in the city? Are they so followed?

ROSENCRANTZ   No, indeed, are they not.

HAMLET   How comes it? Do they grow rusty?

ROSENCRANTZ   Nay, their endeavor keeps in the wonted pace; but there is, sir, an eyrie of children, little eyases,[5] that cry out on the top of question,[6] and are most tyrannically clapped for't. These are now the fashion, and so berattle the common stages (so they call them) that many wearing rapiers are afraid of goose quills[7] and dare scarce come thither.[8]

HAMLET   What, are they children? Who maintains 'em? How are they escoted[9]? Will they pursue the quality no longer than they can sing? Will they not say afterwards, if they should grow themselves to common players (as it is most like, if their means are no better), their writers do them wrong to make them exclaim against their own succession[1]?

7. ornamented with fretwork
8. well built
9. scanty
1. passed
2. sword and shield
3. eccentric
4. easily set off
5. little hawks
6. with a loud, high delivery
7. pens of satirical writers
8. The passage refers to the emergence at the time of the play of theatrical companies made up of children from London choir schools. Their performances became fashionable and hurt the business of the established companies. Hamlet says that if they continue to act, "pursue the quality," when they are grown, they will find that they have been damaging their own future careers.
9. supported
1. future careers

ROSENCRANTZ   Faith, there has been much to do on both sides; and the nation holds it no sin to tarre[2] them to controversy. There was for a while no money bid for argument,[3] unless the poet and the player went to cuffs[4] in the question.   325

HAMLET   Is't possible?

GUILDENSTERN   O, there has been much throwing about of brains.

HAMLET   Do the boys carry it away?

ROSENCRANTZ   Ay, that they do, my lord, Hercules and his load too.[5]   330

HAMLET   It is not very strange, for my uncle is King of Denmark, and those that would make mouths[6] at him while my father lived give twenty, forty, fifty, a hundred ducats apiece for his picture in little.[7] 'Sblood, there is something in this more than natural, if philosophy could find it out.   *A flourish.*   335

GUILDENSTERN   There are the players.

HAMLET   Gentlemen, you are welcome to Elsinore. Your hands. Come then. th' appurtenance of welcome is fashion and ceremony. Let me comply with[8] you in this garb, lest my extent[9] to the players, which I tell you must show fairly outwards, should more appear like entertainment[1] than yours. You are welcome. But my uncle-father and aunt-mother are deceived.   340

GUILDENSTERN   In what, my dear lord?

HAMLET   I am but mad north-north-west; when the wind is southerly I know a hawk from a handsaw.[2]   345

Enter POLONIUS.

POLONIUS   Well be with you, gentlemen.

HAMLET   Hark you, Guildenstern—and you too—at each ear a hearer. That great baby you see there is not yet out of his swaddling clouts.[3]

ROSENCRANTZ   Happily he is the second time come to them, for they say an old man is twice a child.   350

HAMLET   I will prophesy he comes to tell me of the players. Mark it. —You say right, sir, a Monday morning, 'twas then indeed.

POLONIUS   My lord, I have news to tell you.

HAMLET   My lord, I have news to tell you. When Roscius was an actor in Rome—[4]   355

POLONIUS   The actors are come hither, my lord.

HAMLET   Buzz, buzz.

POLONIUS   Upon my honor—

HAMLET   Then came each actor on his ass—

POLONIUS   The best actors in the world, either for tragedy, comedy, history, pastoral, pastoral-comical, historical-pastoral, tragical-historical, tragical-comical-historical-pastoral, scene individable, or   360

2. urge
3. paid for a play plot
4. blows
5. During one of his labors Hercules assumed for a time the burden of the Titan Atlas, who supported the heavens on his shoulder. Also a reference to the effect on business at Shakespeare's theater, the Globe.
6. sneer

7. miniature
8. welcome
9. fashion
1. cordiality
2. A "hawk" is a plasterer's tool; Hamlet may also be using "handsaw" = hernshaw = heron.
3. wrappings for an infant
4. Roscius was the most famous actor of classical Rome.

poem unlimited. Seneca cannot be too heavy nor Plautus too light. For the law of writ and the liberty, these are the only men.[5]

HAMLET O Jephtha, judge of Israel, what a treasure hadst thou![6] 365
POLONIUS What a treasure had he, my lord?
HAMLET Why—

> "One fair daughter, and no more,
> The which he loved passing well."

POLONIUS [*aside*] Still on my daughter. 370
HAMLET Am I not i' th' right, old Jephtha?
POLONIUS If you call me Jephtha, my lord, I have a daughter that I love passing well.
HAMLET Nay, that follows not.
POLONIUS What follows then, my lord? 375
HAMLET Why—

> "As by lot, God wot"

and then, you know,

> "It came to pass, as most like it was."

The first row[7] of the pious chanson[8] will show you more, for look 380 where my abridgement[9] comes.

Enter the PLAYERS.

You are welcome, masters; welcome, all.—I am glad to see thee well.—Welcome, good friends.—O, old friend! Why thy face is valanced[1] since I saw thee last. Com'st thou to beard me in Denmark?—What, my young lady and mistress? By'r lady, your ladyship 385 is nearer to heaven than when I saw you last by the altitude of a chopine.[2] Pray God your voice, like a piece of uncurrent gold, be not cracked within the ring.—Masters, you are all welcome. We'll e'en to't like French falconers, fly at anything we see. We'll have a speech straight. Come give us a taste of your quality,[3] come a passionate 390 speech.

FIRST PLAYER What speech, my good lord?
HAMLET I heard thee speak me a speech once, but it was never acted, or if it was, not above once, for the play, I remember, pleased not the million; 'twas caviary[4] to the general.[5] But it was—as I received 395

---

5. Seneca and Plautus were Roman writers of tragedy and comedy, respectively. The "law of writ" refers to plays written according to such rules as the three unities; the "liberty" to those written otherwise.
6. To insure victory, Jephtha promised to sacrifice the first creature to meet him on his return. Unfortunately, his only daughter outstripped his dog and was the victim of his vow. The Biblical story is told in *Judges* 11.
7. stanza
8. song
9. that which cuts short by interrupting

1. fringed (with a beard)
2. A reference to the contemporary theatrical practice of using boys to play women's parts. The company's "lady" has grown in height by the size of a woman's thick-soled shoe, "chopine," since Hamlet saw him last. The next sentence refers to the possibility, suggested by his growth, that the young actor's voice may soon begin to change.
3. trade
4. caviar
5. masses

it, and others whose judgments in such matters cried in the top of[6] mine—an excellent play, well digested[7] in the scenes, set down with as much modesty as cunning. I remember one said there were no sallets[8] in the lines to make the matter savory, nor no matter in the phrase that might indict the author of affectation, but called it an honest method, as wholesome as sweet, and by very much more handsome than fine. One speech in't I chiefly loved. 'Twas Æneas' tale to Dido, and thereabout of it especially where he speaks of Priam's slaughter.[9] If it live in your memory, begin at this line—let me see, let me see:

400

405

"The rugged Pyrrhus, like th' Hyrcanian beast"[1]—

'tis not so; it begins with Pyrrhus—

"The rugged Pyrrhus, he whose sable arms,
Black as his purpose, did the night resemble
When he lay couchéd in th' ominous horse,[2]
Hath now this dread and black complexion smeared
With heraldry more dismal; head to foot
Now is he total gules,[3] horridly tricked[4]
With blood of fathers, mothers, daughters, sons,
Baked and impasted[5] with the parching[6] streets,
That lend a tyrannous and a damnéd light
To their lord's murder. Roasted in wrath and fire,
And thus o'er-sizéd[7] with coagulate[8] gore,
With eyes like carbuncles, the hellish Pyrrhus
Old grandsire Priam seeks."

410

415

420

So proceed you.

POLONIUS   Fore God, my lord, well spoken, with good accent and good discretion.

FIRST PLAYER   "Anon he[9] finds him[1]
Striking too short at Greeks. His antique[2] sword,
Rebellious[3] to his arm, lies where it falls,
Repugnant to command. Unequal matched,
Pyrrhus at Priam drives, in rage strikes wide.
But with the whiff and wind of his fell sword
Th' unnervéd father falls. Then senseless[4] Ilium,
Seeming to feel this blow, with flaming top
Stoops[5] to his base, and with a hideous crash

425

430

---

6. were weightier than
7. arranged
8. spicy passages
9. Aeneas, fleeing with his band from fallen Troy (Ilium), arrives in Carthage, where he tells Dido, the Queen of Carthage, of the fall of Troy. Here he is describing the death of Priam, the aged king of Troy, at the hands of Pyrrhus. the son of the slain Achilles.
1. tiger
2. i.e., the Trojan horse

3. completely red
4. adorned
5. crusted
6. burning
7. glued over
8. clotted
9. Pyrrhus
1. Priam
2. which he used when young
3. refractory
4. without feeling
5. falls

Takes prisoner Pyrrhus' ear. For, lo! his sword,
Which was declining[6] on the milky head
Of reverend Priam, seemed i' th' air to stick.   435
So as a painted tyrant Pyrrhus stood,
And like a neutral to his will and matter,[7]
Did nothing.
But as we often see, against some storm,
A silence in the heavens, the rack[8] stand still,   440
The bold winds speechless, and the orb below
As hush as death, anon the dreadful thunder
Doth rend the region; so, after Pyrrhus' pause,
A rouséd vengeance sets him new awork,[9]
And never did the Cyclops' hammers fall   445
On Mars's armor, forged for proof eterne,[1]
With less remorse than Pyrrhus' bleeding sword
Now falls on Priam.
Out, out, thou strumpet, Fortune! All you gods,
In general synod take away her power,   450
Break all the spokes and fellies[2] from her wheel,
And bowl[3] the round nave[4] down the hill of heaven
As low as to the fiends."

POLONIUS   This is too long.

HAMLET   It shall to the barber's with your beard.—Prithee say on. 455
He's for a jig,[5] or a tale of bawdry, or he sleeps. Say on; come to
Hecuba.[6]

FIRST PLAYER   "But who, ah woe! had seen the mobled[7] queen—"

HAMLET   "The mobled queen"?

POLONIUS   That's good. "Mobled queen" is good.   460

FIRST PLAYER   "Run barefoot up and down, threat'ning the flames
With bisson rheum,[8] a clout[9] upon that head
Where late the diadem stood, and for a robe,
About her lank and all o'er-teeméd loins,
A blanket, in the alarm of fear caught up—   465
Who this had seen, with tongue in venom steeped,
'Gainst Fortune's state[1] would treason have pronounced.
But if the gods themselves did see her then,
When she saw Pyrrhus make malicious sport
In mincing[2] with his sword her husband's limbs,   470
The instant burst of clamor that she made,
Unless things mortal move them not at all,
Would have made milch[3] the burning eyes of heaven,
And passion in the gods."

---

6. about to fall
7. between his will and the fulfillment of it
8. clouds
9. to work
1. Mars, as befits a Roman war god, had armor made for him by the blacksmith god Vulcan and his assistants, the Cyclops. It was suitably impenetrable, of "proof eterne."
2. parts of the rim
3. roll
4. hub

5. a comic act
6. Hecuba was the wife of Priam and Queen of Troy. Her "loins" are described below as "o'erteeméd" because of her unusual fertility. The number of her children varies in different accounts, but twenty is a safe minimum.
7. muffled (in a hood)
8. blinding tears
9. cloth
1. government
2. cutting up
3. tearful (*lit.* milk-giving)

POLONIUS   Look whe'r[4] he has not turned his color, and has tears in's 475
eyes. Prithee no more.

HAMLET   'Tis well. I'll have thee speak out the rest of this soon.—
Good my lord, will you see the players well bestowed?[5] Do you
hear, let them be well used, for they are the abstract[6] and brief
chronicles of the time; after your death you were better have a bad 480
epitaph than their ill report while you live.

POLONIUS   My lord, I will use them according to their desert.

HAMLET   God's bodkin, man, much better. Use every man after his
desert, and who shall 'scape whipping? Use them after your own
honor and dignity. The less they deserve, the more merit is in your 485
bounty. Take them in.

POLONIUS   Come, sirs.

HAMLET   Follow him, friends. We'll hear a play tomorrow. [*Aside to*
FIRST PLAYER.] Dost thou hear me, old friend, can you play "The
Murder of Gonzago"?   490

FIRST PLAYER   Ay, my lord.

HAMLET   We'll ha't tomorrow night. You could for a need study a
speech of some dozen or sixteen lines which I would set down and
insert in't, could you not?

FIRST PLAYER   Ay, my lord.   495

HAMLET   Very well. Follow that lord, and look you mock him not.

Exeunt POLONIUS *and* PLAYERS.

My good friends, I'll leave you till night. You are welcome to
Elsinore.

ROSENCRANTZ   Good my lord.

Exeunt ROSENCRANTZ *and* GUILDENSTERN.

HAMLET   Ay, so God b'wi'ye. Now I am alone.   500
O, what a rogue and peasant slave am I!
Is it not monstrous that this player here,
But in a fiction, in a dream of passion,
Could force his soul so to his own conceit[7]
That from her working all his visage wanned;[8]   505
Tears in his eyes, distraction in his aspect,[9]
A broken voice, and his whole function suiting
With forms to his conceit? And all for nothing,
For Hecuba!
What's Hecuba to him or he to Hecuba,   510
That he should weep for her? What would he do
Had he the motive and the cue for passion
That I have? He would drown the stage with tears,
And cleave the general ear with horrid speech,
Make mad the guilty, and appal the free,   515
Confound the ignorant, and amaze indeed
The very faculties of eyes and ears.
Yet I,

4. whether   7. imagination
5. provided for   8. grew pale
6. summary   9. face

A dull and muddy-mettled[1] rascal, peak[2]
Like John-a-dreams,[3] unpregnant[4] of my cause,   520
And can say nothing; no, not for a king
Upon whose property and most dear life
A damned defeat was made. Am I a coward?
Who calls me villain, breaks my pate across,
Plucks off my beard and blows it in my face,   525
Tweaks me by the nose, gives me the lie i' th' throat
As deep as to the lungs? Who does me this?
Ha, 'swounds, I should take it; for it cannot be
But I am pigeon-livered and lack gall[5]
To make oppression bitter, or ere this   530
I should 'a fatted all the region kites[6]
With this slave's offal. Bloody, bawdy villain!
Remorseless, treacherous, lecherous, kindless[7] villain!
Why, what an ass am I! This is most brave,
That I, the son of a dear father murdered,   535
Prompted to my revenge by heaven and hell,
Must like a whore unpack[8] my heart with words,
And fall a-cursing like a very drab,
A scullion![9] Fie upon't! foh!
About, my brains. Hum—I have heard   540
That guilty creatures sitting at a play,
Have by the very cunning of the scene
Been struck so to the soul that presently
They have proclaimed[1] their malefactions;
For murder, though it have no tongue, will speak   545
With most miraculous organ. I'll have these players
Play something like the murder of my father
Before mine uncle. I'll observe his looks.
I'll tent[2] him to the quick. If 'a do blench,[3]
I know my course. The spirit that I have seen   550
May be a devil, and the devil hath power
T' assume a pleasing shape, yea, and perhaps
Out of my weakness and my melancholy,
As he is very potent with such spirits,
Abuses me to damn me. I'll have grounds   555
More relative[4] than this. The play's the thing
Wherein I'll catch the conscience of the king.   *Exit.*

1. dull-spirited
2. mope
3. a man dreaming
4. not quickened by
5. bitterness
6. birds of prey of the area
7. unnatural
8. relieve

9. In some versions of the play, the word "stallion," a slang term for a prostitute, appears in place of "scullion."
1. admitted
2. try
3. turn pale
4. conclusive

Act 3

SCENE 1: *A room in the castle. Enter* KING, QUEEN, POLONIUS, OPHELIA, ROSENCRANTZ *and* GUILDENSTERN.

KING   And can you by no drift of conference[5]
Get from him why he puts on this confusion,
Grating so harshly all his days of quiet
With turbulent[6] and dangerous lunacy?

ROSENCRANTZ   He does confess he feels himself distracted,   5
But from what cause 'a will by no means speak.

GUILDENSTERN   Nor do we find him forward[7] to be sounded,[8]
But with a crafty madness keeps aloof
When we would bring him on to some confession
Of his true state.

QUEEN   Did he receive you well?   10

ROSENCRANTZ   Most like a gentleman.

GUILDENSTERN   But with much forcing of his disposition.[9]

ROSENCRANTZ   Niggard of question, but of our demands[1]
Most free in his reply.

QUEEN   Did you assay[2] him
To any pastime?   15

ROSENCRANTZ   Madam, it so fell out that certain players
We o'er-raught[3] on the way. Of these we told him,
And there did seem in him a kind of joy
To hear of it. They are here about the court,
And as I think, they have already order   20
This night to play before him.

POLONIUS   'Tis most true,
And he beseeched me to entreat your majesties
To hear and see the matter.[4]

KING   With all my heart, and it doth much content me
To hear him so inclined.   25
Good gentlemen, give him a further edge,
And drive his purpose[5] into these delights.

ROSENCRANTZ   We shall, my lord.

Exeunt ROSENCRANTZ *and* GUILDENSTERN.

KING   Sweet Gertrude, leave us too,
For we have closely sent for Hamlet hither,
That he, as 'twere by accident, may here   30
Affront[6] Ophelia.
Her father and myself (lawful espials[7])
Will so bestow ourselves that, seeing unseen,
We may of their encounter frankly judge,

And gather by him, as he is behaved,   35
If't be th' affliction of his love or no
That thus he suffers for.
QUEEN   I shall obey you.—
And for your part, Ophelia, I do wish
That your good beauties be the happy cause
Of Hamlet's wildness. So shall I hope your virtues   40
Will bring him to his wonted[8] way again,
To both your honors.
OPHELIA   Madam, I wish it may.   *Exit* QUEEN.
POLONIUS   Ophelia, walk you here.—Gracious,[9] so please you,
We will bestow ourselves.—[*To* OPHELIA.] Read on this book,
That show of such an exercise[1] may color[2]   45
Your loneliness.—We are oft to blame in this,
'Tis too much proved, that with devotion's visage
And pious action we do sugar o'er
The devil himself.
KING [*aside*]   O, 'tis too true.
How smart a lash that speech doth give my conscience!   50
The harlot's cheek, beautied with plast'ring[3] art,
Is not more ugly to the thing that helps it
Than is my deed to my most painted word.
O heavy burden!
POLONIUS   I hear him coming. Let's withdraw, my lord.   55

                         Exeunt KING *and* POLONIUS.

     Enter HAMLET.

HAMLET   To be, or not to be, that is the question:
Whether 'tis nobler in the mind to suffer
The slings and arrows of outrageous fortune,
Or to take arms against a sea of troubles,
And by opposing end them. To die, to sleep—   60
No more; and by a sleep to say we end
The heartache, and the thousand natural shocks
That flesh is heir to. 'Tis a consummation
Devoutly to be wished—to die, to sleep—
To sleep, perchance to dream, ay there's the rub;   65
For in that sleep of death what dreams may come
When we have shuffled off this mortal coil[4]
Must give us pause—there's the respect[5]
That makes calamity of so long life.
For who would bear the whips and scorns of time,   70
Th' oppressor's wrong, the proud man's contumely,[6]
The pangs of despised love, the law's delay,
The insolence of office, and the spurns[7]
That patient merit of th' unworthy takes,

8. usual
9. Majesty
1. act of devotion
2. explain

3. thickly painted
4. turmoil
5. consideration
6. insulting behavior
7. rejections

When he himself might his quietus[8] make   75
With a bare bodkin?[9] Who would fardels[1] bear,
To grunt and sweat under a weary life,
But that the dread of something after death,
The undiscovered country, from whose bourn[2]
No traveller returns, puzzles the will,   80
And makes us rather bear those ills we have
Than fly to others that we know not of?
Thus conscience does make cowards of us all;
And thus the native[3] hue of resolution
Is sicklied o'er with the pale cast of thought,   85
And enterprises of great pitch[4] and moment[5]
With this regard their currents turn awry
And lose the name of action.—Soft you now,
The fair Ophelia.—Nymph, in thy orisons[6]
Be all my sins remembered.

OPHELIA   Good my lord,   90
How does your honor for this many a day?
HAMLET   I humbly thank you, well, well, well.
OPHELIA   My lord, I have remembrances of yours
That I have longed long to re-deliver.
I pray you now receive them.
HAMLET   No, not I,   95
I never gave you aught.
OPHELIA   My honored lord, you know right well you did,
And with them words of so sweet breath composed
As made the things more rich. Their perfume lost,
Take these again, for to the noble mind   100
Rich gifts wax[7] poor when givers prove unkind.
There, my lord.
HAMLET   Ha, ha! are you honest?[8]
OPHELIA   My lord?
HAMLET   Are you fair?   105
OPHELIA   What means your lordship?
HAMLET   That if you be honest and fair, your honesty should admit
no discourse to your beauty.
OPHELIA   Could beauty, my lord, have better commerce[9] than with
honesty?   110
HAMLET   Ay, truly, for the power of beauty will sooner transform
honesty from what it is to a bawd than the force of honesty can
translate beauty into his likeness. This was sometime a paradox, but
now the time gives it proof. I did love you once.
OPHELIA   Indeed, my lord, you made me believe so.   115
HAMLET   You should not have believed me, for virtue cannot so in-
oculate[1] our old stock but we shall relish of it. I loved you not.
OPHELIA   I was the more deceived.

8. settlement   5. importance
9. dagger   6. prayers
1. burdens   7. become
2. boundary   8. chaste
3. natural   9. intercourse
4. height   1. change by grafting

HAMLET   Get thee to a nunnery.[2] Why wouldst thou be a breeder of
sinners? I am myself indifferent[3] honest, but yet I could accuse me   120
of such things that it were better my mother had not borne me: I
am very proud, revengeful, ambitious, with more offences at my
beck[4] than I have thoughts to put them in, imagination to give them
shape, or time to act them in. What should such fellows as I do
crawling between earth and heaven? We are arrant[5] knaves all; be-   125
lieve none of us. Go thy ways to a nunnery. Where's your father?

OPHELIA   At home, my lord.

HAMLET   Let the doors be shut upon him, that he may play the fool
nowhere but in's own house. Farewell.

OPHELIA   O, help him, you sweet heavens!   130

HAMLET   If thou dost marry, I'll give thee this plague for thy dowry:
be thou as chaste as ice, as pure as snow, thou shalt not escape
calumny. Get thee to a nunnery, farewell. Or if thou wilt needs
marry, marry a fool, for wise men know well enough what monsters[6]
you make of them. To a nunnery, go, and quickly too. Farewell.   135

OPHELIA   Heavenly powers, restore him!

HAMLET   I have heard of your paintings well enough. God hath given
you one face, and you make yourselves another. You jig, you amble,
and you lisp;[7] you nickname God's creatures, and make your wantonness your ignorance.[8] Go to, I'll no more on't, it hath made me mad.   140
I say we will have no more marriage. Those that are married already,
all but one, shall live. The rest shall keep as they are. To a nunnery,
go.   *Exit.*

OPHELIA   O, what a noble mind is here o'erthrown!
The courtier's, soldier's, scholar's, eye, tongue, sword,   145
Th' expectancy[9] and rose[1] of the fair state,
The glass[2] of fashion and the mould[3] of form,
Th' observed of all observers, quite quite down!
And I of ladies most deject and wretched,
That sucked the honey of his music[4] vows,   150
Now see that noble and most sovereign reason
Like sweet bells jangled, out of time and harsh;
That unmatched form and feature of blown[5] youth
Blasted with ecstasy. O, woe is me
T' have seen what I have seen, see what I see!   155

Enter KING *and* POLONIUS.

KING   Love! His affections do not that way tend,
Nor what he spake, though it lacked form a little,
Was not like madness. There's something in his soul
O'er which his melancholy sits on brood,[6]

---

2. With typical ribaldry Hamlet uses
"nunnery" in two senses, the second as a
slang term for brothel.
  3. moderately
  4. command
  5. thorough
  6. horned because cuckolded
  7. walk and talk affectedly
  8. Hamlet means that women call things

by pet names and then blame the affectation on ignorance.
  9. hope
  1. ornament
  2. mirror
  3. model
  4. musical
  5. full-blown
  6. i.e., like a hen

And I do doubt[7] the hatch and the disclose[8]   160
Will be some danger; which to prevent,
I have in quick determination
Thus set it down: he shall with speed to England
For the demand of our neglected tribute.
Haply the seas and countries different,   165
With variable objects, shall expel
This something-settled matter in his heart
Whereon his brains still beating puts him thus
From fashion of himself. What think you on't?

POLONIUS   It shall do well. But yet do I believe   170
The origin and commencement of his grief
Sprung from neglected love.——How now, Ophelia?
You need not tell us what Lord Hamlet said,
We heard it all.——My lord, do as you please,
But if you hold it fit, after the play   175
Let his queen-mother all alone entreat him
To show his grief. Let her be round[9] with him,
And I'll be placed, so please you, in the ear[1]
Of all their conference. If she find him not,[2]
To England send him; or confine him where   180
Your wisdom best shall think.

KING   It shall be so.
Madness in great ones must not unwatched go.   *Exeunt.*

SCENE 2: *A public room in the castle. Enter* HAMLET *and three of the* PLAYERS.

HAMLET   Speak the speech, I pray you, as I pronounced it to you, trippingly on the tongue; but if you mouth it as many of our players do, I had as lief the town-crier spoke my lines. Nor do not saw the air too much with your hand thus, but use all gently, for in the very torrent, tempest, and as I may say, whirlwind of your passion, you must 5
acquire and beget a temperance that may give it smoothness. O, it offends me to the soul to hear a robustious[3] periwig-pated[4] fellow tear a passion to tatters, to very rags, to split the ears of the groundlings,[5] who for the most part are capable of[6] nothing but inexplicable dumb shows and noise. I would have such a fellow whipped for 10
o'erdoing Termagant. It out-herods Herod.[7] Pray you avoid it.

FIRST PLAYER   I warrant your honor.

HAMLET   Be not too tame neither, but let your own discretion be your tutor. Suit the action to the word, the word to the action, with this special observance, that you o'erstep not the modesty of nature; 15
for anything so o'erdone is from[8] the purpose of playing, whose end both at the first, and now, was and is, to hold as 'twere the mirror up

---

7. fear
8. result
9. direct
1. hearing
2. discover his problem
3. noisy
4. bewigged

5. the spectators who paid least
6. i.e., capable of understanding
7. Termagant, a "Saracen" deity, and the Biblical Herod were stock characters in popular drama noted for the excesses of sound and fury used by their interpreters.
8. contrary to

to nature, to show virtue her own feature, scorn her own image, and the very age and body of the time his form and pressure.[9] Now this overdone, or come tardy off, though it makes the unskilful[1] laugh, 20 cannot but make the judicious grieve, the censure[2] of the which one must in your allowance o'erweigh a whole theatre of others. O, there be players that I have seen play—and heard others praise, and that highly—not to speak it profanely, that neither having th' accent of Christians, nor the gait of Christian, pagan, nor man, have so strut- 25 ted and bellowed that I have thought some of nature's journeymen[3] had made men, and not made them well, they imitated humanity so abominably.

FIRST PLAYER   I hope we have reformed that indifferently[4] with us.

HAMLET   O, reform it altogether. And let those that play your clowns 30 speak no more than is set down for them, for there be of them that will themselves laugh, to set on some quantity of barren[5] spectators to laugh too, though in the meantime some necessary question of the play be then to be considered. That's villainous, and shows a most pitiful ambition in the fool that uses it. Go, make you ready. 35

Exeunt PLAYERS.

Enter POLONIUS, GUILDENSTERN, *and* ROSENCRANTZ.

How now, my lord? Will the king hear this piece of work?

POLONIUS   And the queen too, and that presently.

HAMLET   Bid the players make haste.   *Exit* POLONIUS.
Will you two help to hasten them?

ROSENCRANTZ   Ay, my lord.   *Exeunt they two.* 40

HAMLET   What, ho, Horatio!
       Enter HORATIO.

HORATIO   Here, sweet lord, at your service.

HAMLET   Horatio, thou art e'en as just a man
As e'er my conversation coped[6] withal.

HORATIO   O my dear lord!

HAMLET   Nay, do not think I flatter, 45
For what advancement may I hope from thee,
That no revenue hast but thy good spirits
To feed and clothe thee? Why should the poor be flattered?
No, let the candied tongue lick absurd pomp,
And crook the pregnant[7] hinges of the knee 50
Where thrift[8] may follow fawning. Dost thou hear?
Since my dear soul was mistress of her choice
And could of men distinguish her election,
S'hath sealed thee for herself, for thou hast been
As one in suff'ring all that suffers nothing, 55
A man that Fortune's buffets and rewards

9. shape
1. ignorant
2. judgment
3. inferior craftsmen
4. somewhat

5. dull-witted
6. encountered
7. quick to bend
8. profit

Hast ta'en with equal thanks; and blest are those
Whose blood and judgment are so well commingled
That they are not a pipe[9] for Fortune's finger
To sound[1] what stop[2] she please. Give me that man   60
That is not passion's slave, and I will wear him
In my heart's core, ay, in my heart of heart,
As I do thee. Something too much of this.
There is a play tonight before the king.
One scene of it comes near the circumstance   65
Which I have told thee of my father's death.
I prithee, when thou seest that act afoot,
Even with the very comment[3] of thy soul
Observe my uncle. If his occulted[4] guilt
Do not itself unkennel[5] in one speech,   70
It is a damnéd ghost that we have seen,
And my imaginations are as foul
As Vulcan's stithy.[6] Give him heedful note,[7]
For I mine eyes will rivet to his face,
And after we will both our judgments join   75
In censure of his seeming.[8]
HORATIO   Well, my lord.
If 'a steal aught the whilst this play is playing,
And 'scape detecting, I will pay[9] the theft.

Enter Trumpets and Kettledrums, KING, QUEEN, POLONIUS,
OPHELIA, ROSENCRANTZ, GUILDENSTERN, *and other* LORDS *attendant.*

HAMLET   They are coming to the play. I must be idle.
Get you a place.   80
KING   How fares our cousin Hamlet?
HAMLET   Excellent, i' faith, of the chameleon's dish.[1] I eat the air,
promise-crammed. You cannot feed capons so.
KING   I have nothing with this answer, Hamlet. These words are not
mine.   85
HAMLET   No, nor mine now. [*To* POLONIUS.] My lord, you played once
i' th' university, you say?
POLONIUS   That did I, my lord, and was accounted a good actor.
HAMLET   What did you enact?
POLONIUS   I did enact Julius Cæsar. I was killed i' th' Capitol; Brutus   90
killed me.[2]
HAMLET   It was a brute part of him to kill so capital a calf there. Be
the players ready?

---

9. musical instrument
1. play
2. note
3. keenest observation
4. hidden
5. break loose
6. smithy
7. careful attention
8. manner

9. repay
1. A reference to a popular belief that
the chameleon subsisted on a diet of air.
Hamlet has deliberately misunderstood the
King's question.
2. The assassination of Julius Caesar by
Brutus and others is the subject of another
play by Shakespeare.

ROSENCRANTZ   Ay, my lord, they stay[3] upon your patience.[4]

QUEEN   Come hither, my dear Hamlet, sit by me.   95

HAMLET   No, good mother, here's metal more attractive.

POLONIUS [*to the* KING]   O, ho! do you mark that?

HAMLET   Lady, shall I lie in your lap?

Lying down at OPHELIA's *feet.*

OPHELIA   No, my lord.

HAMLET   I mean, my head upon your lap?   100

OPHELIA   Ay, my lord.

HAMLET   Do you think I meant country matters?[5]

OPHELIA   I think nothing, my lord.

HAMLET   That's a fair thought to lie between maids' legs.

OPHELIA   What is, my lord?   105

HAMLET   Nothing.

OPHELIA   You are merry, my lord.

HAMLET   Who, I?

OPHELIA   Ay, my lord.

HAMLET   O God, your only jig-maker![6] What should a man do but be   110
merry? For look you how cheerfully my mother looks, and my father
died within's two hours.

OPHELIA   Nay, 'tis twice two months, my lord.

HAMLET   So long? Nay then, let the devil wear black, for I'll have a
suit of sables. O heavens! die two months ago, and not forgotten   115
yet? Then there's hope a great man's memory may outlive his life
half a year, but by'r lady 'a must build churches then, or else shall
'a suffer not thinking on, with the hobby-horse, whose epitaph is
"For O, for O, the hobby-horse is forgot!"[7]

The trumpets sound. Dumb Show follows. Enter a KING *and a*
QUEEN *very lovingly; the* QUEEN *embracing him and he her.*
She kneels, and makes show of protestation unto him. He takes
her up, and declines[8] *his head upon her neck. He lies him down*
upon a bank of flowers; she, seeing him asleep, leaves him.
Anon come in another man, takes off his crown, kisses it, pours
poison in the sleeper's ears, and leaves him. The QUEEN *returns,*
finds the KING *dead, makes passionate action. The* POISONER
with some three or four come in again, seem to condole with
her. The dead body is carried away. The POISONER *woos the*
QUEEN *with gifts; she seems harsh awhile, but in the end accepts*
love.   *Exeunt.*

OPHELIA   What means this, my lord?   120

HAMLET   Marry, this is miching mallecho;[9] it means mischief.

OPHELIA   Belike this show imports[1] the argument[2] of the play.

---

3. wait
4. leisure
5. Presumably, rustic misbehavior, but here and elsewhere in this exchange Hamlet treats Ophelia to some ribald double meanings.
6. writer of comic scenes
7. In traditional games and dances one of the characters was a man represented as riding a horse. The horse was made of something like cardboard and was worn about the "rider's" waist.
8. lays
9. sneaking crime
1. explains
2. plot

Enter PROLOGUE.

HAMLET We shall know by this fellow. The players cannot keep counsel; they'll tell all.

OPHELIA Will 'a tell us what this show meant?   125

HAMLET Ay, or any show that you will show him. Be not you ashamed to show, he'll not shame to tell you what it means.

OPHELIA You are naught,[3] you are naught. I'll mark[4] the play.

PROLOGUE   *For us, and for our tragedy,*
           Here stooping to your clemency,   130
           We beg your hearing pa^{t}ently.   *Exit.*

HAMLET Is this a prologue, or the posy[5] of a ring?

OPHELIA 'Tis brief, my lord.

HAMLET As woman's love.

Enter the PLAYER KING *and* QUEEN.

PLAYER KING   *Full thirty times hath Phœbus' cart gone round*   135
    Neptune's salt wash and Tellus' orbéd ground,
    And thirty dozen moons with borrowed sheen[6]
    About the world have times twelve thirties been,
    Since love our hearts and Hymen did our hands
    Unite comutual[7] in most sacred bands.[8]   140

PLAYER QUEEN   *So many journeys may the sun and moon*
    Make us again count o'er ere love be done!
    But woe is me, you are so sick of late,
    So far from cheer and from your former state,
    That I distrust[9] you. Yet though I distrust,   145
    Discomfort you, my lord, it nothing must.
    For women's fear and love hold quantity,[1]
    In neither aught, or in extremity.[2]
    Now what my love is proof hath made you know,
    And as my love is sized,[3] my fear is so.   150
    Where love is great, the littlest doubts are fear;
    Where little fears grow great, great love grows there.

PLAYER KING   *Faith, I must leave thee, love, and shortly too;*
    My operant powers[4] their functions leave[5] to do.
    And thou shalt live in this fair world behind,   155
    Honored, beloved, and haply one as kind
    For husband shalt thou—

PLAYER QUEEN   *O, confound the rest!*
    Such love must needs be treason in my breast.

---

3. obscene
4. attend to
5. motto engraved inside
6. light
7. mutually
8. The speech contains several mythological references. "Phoebus" was a sun god, and his chariot or "cart" the sun. The "salt wash" of Neptune is the ocean; "Tellus" was an earth goddess, and her

"orbed ground" is the earth, or globe. Hymen was the god of marriage.
9. fear for
1. agree in weight
2. The lady means without regard to too much or too little.
3. in size
4. active forces
5. cease

In second husband let me be accurst!
None wed the second but who killed the first.[6]   160
HAMLET   That's wormwood.
PLAYER QUEEN   The instances[7] that second marriage move
Are base respects[8] of thrift, but none of love.
A second time I kill my husband dead,
When second husband kisses me in bed.   165
PLAYER KING   I do believe you think what now you speak,
But what we do determine oft we break.
Purpose is but the slave to memory,
Of violent birth, but poor validity;
Which now, like fruit unripe, sticks on the tree,   170
But fall unshaken when they mellow be.
Most necessary 'tis that we forget
To pay ourselves what to ourselves is debt.
What to ourselves in passion we propose,
The passion ending, doth the purpose lose.   175
The violence of either grief or joy
Their own enactures[9] with themselves destroy.
Where joy most revels, grief doth most lament;
Grief joys, joy grieves, on slender accident.
This world is not for aye,[1] nor 'tis not strange   180
That even our loves should with our fortunes change;
For 'tis a question left us yet to prove,
Whether love lead fortune, or else fortune love.
The great man down, you mark his favorite flies;
The poor advanced makes friends of enemies;   185
And hitherto doth love on fortune tend,
For who not needs shall never lack a friend,
And who in want a hollow[2] friend doth try,
Directly seasons him[3] his enemy.
But orderly to end where I begun,   190
Our wills and fates do so contrary run
That our devices[4] still are overthrown;
Our thoughts are ours, their ends none of our own.
So think thou wilt no second husband wed,
But die thy thoughts when thy first lord is dead.   195
PLAYER QUEEN   Nor earth to me give food, nor heaven light,
Sport and repose lock from me day and night,
To desperation turn my trust and hope,
An anchor's cheer[5] in prison be my scope,
Each opposite that blanks[6] the face of joy   200
Meet what I would have well, and it destroy,
Both here and hence[7] pursue me lasting strife,
If once a widow, ever I be wife!

6. Though there is some ambiguity, she
seems to mean that the only kind of woman
who would remarry is one who has killed
or would kill her first husband.
7. causes
8. concerns
9. actions

1. eternal
2. false
3. ripens him into
4. plans
5. anchorite's food
6. blanches
7. in the next world

HAMLET   If she should break it now!

PLAYER KING   'Tis deeply sworn. *Sweet, leave me here awhile.*   205
My spirits grow dull, and fain I would beguile
The tedious day with sleep.   *Sleeps.*

PLAYER QUEEN   *Sleep rock thy brain,*
And never come mischance between us twain!   *Exit.*

HAMLET   Madam, how like you this play?

QUEEN   The lady doth protest too much, methinks.   210

HAMLET   O, but she'll keep her word.

KING   Have you heard the argument? Is there no offence in't?

HAMLET   No, no, they do but jest, poison in jest; no offence i' th'
world.

KING   What do you call the play?   215

HAMLET   "The Mouse-trap." Marry, how? Tropically.[8] This play is the
image of a murder done in Vienna. Gonzago is the duke's name; his
wife, Baptista. You shall see anon. 'Tis a knavish piece of work, but
what of that? Your majesty, and we that have free souls, it touches
us not. Let the galled jade wince, our withers are unwrung.[9]   220

     Enter LUCIANUS.

This is one Lucianus, nephew to the king.

OPHELIA   You are as good as a chorus, my lord.

HAMLET   I could interpret between you and your love, if I could see
the puppets dallying.

OPHELIA   You are keen, my lord, you are keen.   225

HAMLET   It would cost you a groaning to take off mine edge.

OPHELIA   Still better, and worse.

HAMLET   So you mis-take your husbands.—Begin, murderer. Leave
thy damnable faces and begin. Come, the croaking raven doth bellow for revenge.   230

LUCIANUS   *Thoughts black, hands apt, drugs fit, and time agreeing,*
Confederate season,[1] else no creature seeing,
Thou mixture rank, of midnight weeds collected,
With Hecate's ban thrice blasted, thrice infected,[2]
Thy natural magic[3] and dire property   235
On wholesome life usurps immediately.

     Pours the poison in his ears.

HAMLET   'A poisons him i' th' garden for his estate. His name's Gonzago. The story is extant, and written in very choice Italian. You
shall see anon how the murderer gets the love of Gonzago's wife.

OPHELIA   The king rises.   240

HAMLET   What, frighted with false fire?

QUEEN   How fares my lord?

POLONIUS   Give o'er the play.

KING   Give me some light. Away!

POLONIUS   Lights, lights, lights!   245

---

8. figuratively
9. A "galled jade" is a horse, particularly one of poor quality, with a sore
back. The "withers" are the ridge between
a horse's shoulders; "unwrung withers" are
not chafed by the harness.

1. a helpful time for the crime
2. Hecate was a classical goddess of
witchcraft.
3. native power

Exeunt all but HAMLET *and* HORATIO.

HAMLET   Why, let the strucken deer go weep,
    The hart ungalléd[4] play.
For some must watch while some must sleep;
    Thus runs the world away.
Would not this, sir, and a forest of feathers[5]—if the rest of my for- 250
tunes turn Turk with me—with two Provincial roses on my razed
shoes, get me a fellowship in a cry[6] of players?[7]

HORATIO   Half a share.

HAMLET   A whole one, I.

    For thou dost know, O Damon dear,[8]   255
    This realm dismantled was
Of Jove himself, and now reigns here
    A very, very—peacock.

HORATIO   You might have rhymed.

HAMLET   O good Horatio, I'll take the ghost's word for a thousand 260
pound. Didst perceive?

HORATIO   Very well, my lord.

HAMLET   Upon the talk of the poisoning.

HORATIO   I did very well note[9] him.

HAMLET   Ah, ha! Come, some music. Come, the recorders.[1]   265
For if the king like not the comedy,
Why then, belike he likes it not, perdy.[2]
Come, some music.

Enter ROSENCRANTZ *and* GUILDENSTERN.

GUILDENSTERN   Good my lord, vouchsafe me a word with you.

HAMLET   Sir, a whole history.   270

GUILDENSTERN   The king, sir—

HAMLET   Ay, sir, what of him?

GUILDENSTERN   Is in his retirement[3] marvellous distempered.[4]

HAMLET   With drink, sir?

GUILDENSTERN   No, my lord, with choler.[5]   275

HAMLET   Your wisdom should show itself more richer to signify this
to the doctor, for for me to put him to his purgation[6] would perhaps
plunge him into more choler.

GUILDENSTERN   Good my lord, put your discourse[7] into some frame,[8]
and start not so wildly from my affair.   280

HAMLET   I am tame, sir. Pronounce.

---

4. uninjured
5. plumes
6. company
7. Hamlet asks Horatio if "this" recitation, accompanied with a player's costume, including plumes and rosettes on shoes which have been slashed for decorative effect, might not entitle him to become a shareholder in a theatrical company in the event that Fortune goes against him, "turn Turk."
8. Damon was a common name for a young man or a shepherd in lyric, espe-

cially pastoral poetry. Jove was the chief god of the Romans. The Reader may supply for himself the rhyme referred to by Horatio.
9. observe
1. wooden end-blown flutes
2. *par Dieu* (by God)
3. place to which he has retired
4. vexed
5. bile
6. treatment with a laxative
7. speech
8. order

GUILDENSTERN   The queen your mother, in most great affliction of spirit, hath sent me to you.

HAMLET   You are welcome.

GUILDENSTERN   Nay, good my lord, this courtesy is not of the right ²⁸⁵ breed. If it shall please you to make me a wholesome⁹ answer, I will do your mother's commandment. If not, your pardon and my return¹ shall be the end of my business.

HAMLET   Sir, I cannot.

ROSENCRANTZ   What, my lord?   ²⁹⁰

HAMLET   Make you a wholesome answer; my wit's diseased. But, sir, such answer as I can make, you shall command, or rather, as you say, my mother. Therefore no more, but to the matter. My mother, you say—

ROSENCRANTZ   Then thus she says: your behavior hath struck her into ²⁹⁵ amazement and admiration.²

HAMLET   O wonderful son, that can so stonish a mother! But is there no sequel at the heels of this mother's admiration? Impart.³

ROSENCRANTZ   She desires to speak with you in her closet⁴ ere you go to bed.   ³⁰⁰

HAMLET   We shall obey, were she ten times our mother. Have you any further trade⁵ with us?

ROSENCRANTZ   My lord, you once did love me.

HAMLET   And do still, by these pickers and stealers.⁶

ROSENCRANTZ   Good my lord, what is your cause of distemper? You ³⁰⁵ do surely bar the door upon your own liberty, if you deny your griefs to your friend.

HAMLET   Sir, I lack advancement.

ROSENCRANTZ   How can that be, when you have the voice of the king himself for your succession in Denmark?   ³¹⁰

HAMLET   Ay, sir, but "while the grass grows"—the proverb⁷ is something musty.

Enter the PLAYERS *with recorders.*

O, the recorders! Let me see one. To withdraw with you⁸—why do you go about to recover the wind of me, as if you would drive me into a toil?⁹   ³¹⁵

GUILDENSTERN   O my lord, if my duty be too bold, my love is too unmannerly.

HAMLET   I do not well understand that. Will you play upon this pipe?¹

GUILDENSTERN   My lord, I cannot.

HAMLET   I pray you.   ³²⁰

GUILDENSTERN   Believe me, I cannot.

HAMLET   I do beseech you.

GUILDENSTERN   I know no touch of it,² my lord.

9. reasonable
1. i.e., to the Queen
2. wonder
3. tell me
4. bedroom
5. business
6. hands
7. The proverb ends "the horse starves."

8. let me step aside
9. The figure is from hunting. "You will approach me with the wind blowing from me toward you in order to drive me into the net."
1. recorder
2. have no ability

HAMLET It is as easy as lying. Govern[3] these ventages[4] with your
fingers and thumb, give it breath with your mouth, and it will ³²⁵
discourse most eloquent music. Look you, these are the stops.[5]

GUILDENSTERN But these cannot I command to any utt'rance of harmony. I have not the skill.

HAMLET Why, look you now, how unworthy a thing you make of me!
You would play upon me, you would seem to know my stops, you ³³⁰
would pluck out the heart of my mystery, you would sound[6] me
from my lowest note to the top of my compass[7]; and there is much
music, excellent voice, in this little organ, yet cannot you make it
speak. 'Sblood, do you think I am easier to be played on than a pipe?
Call me what instrument you will, though you can fret[8] me, you ³³⁵
cannot play upon me.

Enter POLONIUS.

God bless you, sir!

POLONIUS My lord, the queen would speak with you, and presently.[9]

HAMLET Do you see yonder cloud that's almost in shape of a camel?

POLONIUS By th' mass, and 'tis like a camel indeed.   ³⁴⁰

HAMLET Methinks it is like a weasel.

POLONIUS It is backed like a weasel.

HAMLET Or like a whale.

POLONIUS Very like a whale.

HAMLET Then I will come to my mother by and by. [*Aside.*] They ³⁴⁵
fool me to the top of my bent.[1]—I will come by and by.

POLONIUS I will say so.   *Exit* POLONIUS.

HAMLET "By and by" is easily said. Leave me, friends.

Exeunt all but HAMLET.

'Tis now the very witching time of night,
When churchyards yawn, and hell itself breathes out   ³⁵⁰
Contagion to this world. Now could I drink hot blood,
And do such bitter business as the day
Would quake to look on. Soft, now to my mother.
O heart, lose not thy nature; let not ever
The soul of Nero[2] enter this firm bosom.   ³⁵⁵
Let me be cruel, not unnatural;
I will speak daggers to her, but use none.
My tongue and soul in this be hypocrites—
How in my words somever she be shent,[3]
To give them seals[4] never, my soul, consent!   *Exit.* ³⁶⁰

SCENE 3: *A room in the castle. Enter* KING, ROSENCRANTZ
and GUILDENSTERN.

---

3. cover and uncover
4. holes
5. wind-holes
6. play
7. range
8. "Fret" is used in a double sense, to annoy and to play a guitar or similar instrument using the "frets" or small bars on the neck.

9. at once
1. treat me as an utter fool
2. The Emperor Nero, known for his excesses, was believed to have been responsible for the death of his mother.
3. shamed
4. fulfillment in action

KING   I like him not,[5] nor stands it safe with us
   To let his madness range.[6] Therefore prepare you.
   I your commission will forthwith dispatch,
   And he to England shall along with you.
   The terms of our estate[7] may not endure   5
   Hazard so near's as doth hourly grow
   Out of his brows.
GUILDENSTERN   We will ourselves provide.[8]
   Most holy and religious fear it is
   To keep those many many bodies safe
   That live and feed upon your majesty.   10
ROSENCRANTZ   The single and peculiar[9] life is bound
   With all the strength and armor of the mind
   To keep itelf from noyance,[1] but much more
   That spirit upon whose weal[2] depends and rests
   The lives of many. The cess[3] of majesty   15
   Dies not alone, but like a gulf[4] doth draw
   What's near it with it. It is a massy[5] wheel
   Fixed on the summit of the highest mount,
   To whose huge spokes ten thousand lesser things
   Are mortised and adjoined,[6] which when it falls,   20
   Each small annexment, petty consequence,
   Attends[7] the boist'rous ruin. Never alone
   Did the king sigh, but with a general groan.
KING   Arm you, I pray you, to this speedy voyage,
   For we will fetters put about this fear,   25
   Which now goes too free-footed.
ROSENCRANTZ   We will haste us.

                    Exeunt ROSENCRANTZ *and* GUILDENSTERN.

        Enter POLONIUS.

POLONIUS   My lord, he's going to his mother's closet.
   Behind the arras I'll convey[8] myself
   To hear the process.[9] I'll warrant she'll tax him home,[1]
   And as you said, and wisely was it said,   30
   'Tis meet that some more audience than a mother,
   Since nature makes them partial, should o'erhear
   The speech, of vantage.[2] Fare you well, my liege.
   I'll call upon you ere you go to bed,
   And tell you what I know.
KING   Thanks, dear my lord.   35

                                Exit POLONIUS.

5. distrust him
6. roam freely
7. condition of the state
8. equip (for the journey)
9. individual
1. harm
2. welfare
3. cessation

4. whirlpool
5. massive
6. attached
7. joins in
8. station
9. proceedings
1. sharply
2. from a position of vantage

O, my offence is rank, it smells to heaven;
It hath the primal eldest curse[3] upon't,
A brother's murder. Pray can I not,
Though inclination be as sharp as will.
My stronger guilt defeats my strong intent,   40
And like a man to double business[4] bound,
I stand in pause where I shall first begin,
And both neglect. What if this curséd hand
Were thicker than itself with brothers' blood,
Is there not rain enough in the sweet heavens   45
To wash it white as snow? Whereto serves mercy
But to confront the visage of offence?
And what's in prayer but this twofold force,
To be forestalléd[5] ere we come to fall,
Or pardoned being down[6]? Then I'll look up.   50
My fault is past. But, O, what form of prayer
Can serve my turn? "Forgive me my foul murder"?
That cannot be, since I am still possessed
Of those effects[7] for which I did the murder—
My crown, mine own ambition, and my queen.   55
May one be pardoned and retain th' offence[8]?
In the corrupted currents of this world
Offence's gilded[9] hand may shove by justice,
And oft 'tis seen the wicked prize itself
Buys out the law. But 'tis not so above.   60
There is no shuffling; there the action[1] lies
In his true nature, and we ourselves compelled,
Even to the teeth and forehead of[2] our faults,
To give in evidence. What then? What rests[3]?
Try what repentance can. What can it not?   65
Yet what can it when one can not repent?
O wretched state! O bosom black as death!
O liméd[4] soul, that struggling to be free
Art more engaged! Help, angels! Make assay.
Bow, stubborn knees, and heart with strings of steel,   70
Be soft as sinews of the new-born babe.
All may be well.   *He kneels.*

     Enter HAMLET.

HAMLET   Now might I do it pat,[5] now 'a is a-praying,
     And now I'll do't—and so 'a goes to heaven,
     And so am I revenged. That would be scanned.[6]   75
     A villain kills my father, and for that,
     I, his sole son, do this same villain send
     To heaven.

3. i.e., of Cain
4. two mutually opposed interests
5. prevented (from sin)
6. having sinned
7. gains
8. i.e., benefits of the offence
9. bearing gold as a bribe

1. case at law
2. face-to-face with
3. remains
4. caught as with bird-lime
5. easily
6. deserves consideration

Why, this is hire and salary, not revenge.
'A took my father grossly, full of bread,[7]   80
With all his crimes broad blown,[8] as flush[9] as May;
And how his audit stands who knows save heaven?
But in our circumstance and course of thought
'Tis heavy with him; and am I then revenged
To take him in the purging of his soul,   85
When he is fit and seasoned[1] for his passage?
No.
Up, sword, and know thou a more horrid hent.[2]
When he is drunk, asleep, or in his rage,
Or in th' incestuous pleasure of his bed,   90
At game a-swearing, or about some act
That has no relish[3] of salvation in't—
Then trip him, that his heels may kick at heaven,
And that his soul may be as damned and black
As hell, whereto it goes. My mother stays.   95
This physic[4] but prolongs thy sickly days.   *Exit.*
KING [*rising*]   My words fly up, my thoughts remain below.
Words without thoughts never to heaven go.   *Exit.*

SCENE 4: *The Queen's chamber. Enter* QUEEN *and* POLONIUS.

POLONIUS   'A will come straight. Look you lay home to[5] him.
Tell him his pranks have been too broad[6] to bear with,
And that your grace hath screen'd[7] and stood between
Much heat and him. I'll silence me even here.
Pray you be round.
QUEEN   I'll warrant you. Fear[8] me not.   5
Withdraw, I hear him coming.

                            POLONIUS *goes behind the arras.*

     Enter HAMLET.

   HAMLET   Now, mother, what's the matter?
QUEEN   Hamlet, thou hast thy father much offended.
   HAMLET   Mother, you have my father much offended.
QUEEN   Come, come, you answer with an idle tongue.   10
   HAMLET   Go, go, you question with a wicked tongue.
QUEEN   Why, how now, Hamlet?
   HAMLET   What's the matter now?
QUEEN   Have you forgot me?
   HAMLET   No, by the rood,[9] not so.
You are the queen, your husband's brother's wife,
And would it were not so, you are my mother.   15
QUEEN   Nay, then I'll set those to you that can speak.

7. in a state of sin and without fasting
8. full-blown
9. vigorous
1. ready
2. opportunity
3. flavor

4. medicine
5. be sharp with
6. outrageous
7. acted as a fire screen
8. doubt
9. cross

HAMLET   Come, come, and sit you down. You shall not budge.
You go not till I set you up a glass[1]
Where you may see the inmost part of you.

QUEEN   What wilt thou do? Thou wilt not murder me?   20
Help, ho!

POLONIUS [*behind*]   What, ho! help!

HAMLET [*draws*]   How now, a rat?
Dead for a ducat, dead!

Kills POLONIUS *with a pass through the arras.*

POLONIUS [*behind*]   O, I am slain!   25

QUEEN   O me, what hast thou done?

HAMLET   Nay, I know not.
Is it the king?

QUEEN   O, what a rash and bloody deed is this!

HAMLET   A bloody deed!—almost as bad, good mother,
As kill a king and marry with his brother.   30

QUEEN   As kill a king?

HAMLET   Ay, lady, it was my word.

Parting the arras.

Thou wretched, rash, intruding fool, farewell!
I took thee for thy better. Take thy fortune.
Thou find'st to be too busy[2] is some danger.—
Leave wringing of your hands. Peace, sit you down   35
And let me wring your heart, for so I shall
If it be made of penetrable stuff,
If damnéd custom have not brazed it[3] so
That it be proof[4] and bulwark against sense.[5]

QUEEN   What have I done that thou dar'st wag thy tongue   40
In noise so rude against me?

HAMLET   Such an act
That blurs the grace and blush of modesty,
Calls virtue hypocrite, takes off the rose
From the fair forehead of an innocent love,
And sets a blister[6] there, makes marriage-vows   45
As false as dicers' oaths. O, such a deed
As from the body of contraction[7] plucks
The very soul, and sweet religion makes
A rhapsody of words. Heaven's face does glow
And this solidity and compound mass[8]   50
With heated visage, as against the doom[9]—
Is thought-sick at the act.

QUEEN   Ay me, what act,
That roars so loud and thunders in the index[1]?

HAMLET   Look here upon this picture[2] and on this,

---

1. mirror	7. the marriage contract
2. officious	8. meaningless mass (Earth)
3. plated it with brass	9. Judgment Day
4. armor	1. table of contents
5. feeling	2. portrait
6. brand	

The counterfeit presentment of two brothers.   55
See what a grace was seated on this brow:
Hyperion's curls, the front[3] of Jove himself,
An eye like Mars, to threaten and command,
A station[4] like the herald Mercury[5]
New lighted[6] on a heaven-kissing hill—   60
A combination and a form indeed
Where every god did seem to set his seal,[7]
To give the world assurance of a man.
This was your husband. Look you now what follows.
Here is your husband, like a mildewed ear   65
Blasting his wholesome brother. Have you eyes?
Could you on this fair mountain leave to feed,
And batten[8] on this moor? Ha! have you eyes?
You cannot call it love, for at your age
The heyday in the blood is tame, it's humble,   70
And waits upon the judgment, and what judgment
Would step from this to this? Sense sure you have,
Else could you not have motion, but sure that sense
Is apoplexed[9] for madness would not err,
Nor sense to ecstasy was ne'er so thralled   75
But it reserved some quantity[1] of choice
To serve in such a difference. What devil was't
That thus hath cozened[2] you at hoodman-blind[3]?
Eyes without feeling, feeling without sight,
Ears without hands or eyes, smelling sans[4] all,   80
Or but a sickly part of one true sense
Could not so mope.[5] O shame! where is thy blush?
Rebellious hell,
If thou canst mutine[6] in a matron's bones,
To flaming youth let virtue be as wax   85
And melt in her own fire. Proclaim no shame
When the compulsive ardor gives the charge,[7]
Since frost itself as actively doth burn,
And reason panders[8] will.

QUEEN   O Hamlet, speak no more!
Thou turn'st my eyes into my very soul;   90
And there I see such black and grainéd[9] spots
As will not leave their tinct.[1]

HAMLET   Nay, but to live
In the rank sweat of an enseaméd[2] bed,
Stewed in corruption, honeying and making love
Over the nasty sty—

---

3. forehead
4. bearing
5. Mercury was a Roman god who served as the messenger of the gods.
6. newly alighted
7. mark of approval
8. feed greedily
9. paralyzed
1. power
2. cheated

3. blindman's buff
4. without
5. be stupid
6. commit mutiny
7. attacks
8. pimps for
9. ingrained
1. lose their color
2. greasy

QUEEN   O, speak to me no more!   95
These words like daggers enter in my ears;
No more, sweet Hamlet.
HAMLET   A murderer and a villain,
A slave that is not twentieth part the tithe[3]
Of your precedent lord,[4] a vice of kings,[5]
A cutpurse[6] of the empire and the rule,   100
That from a shelf the precious diadem stole
And put it in his pocket—
QUEEN   No more.

Enter GHOST.

HAMLET   A king of shreds and patches—
Save me and hover o'er me with your wings,   105
You heavenly guards! What would your gracious figure?
QUEEN   Alas, he's mad.
HAMLET   Do you not come your tardy[7] son to chide,
That lapsed in time and passion lets go by
Th' important acting of your dread command?   110
O, say!
GHOST   Do not forget. This visitation
Is but to whet thy almost blunted purpose.
But look, amazement on thy mother sits.
O, step between her and her fighting soul!   115
Conceit[8] in weakest bodies strongest works.
Speak to her, Hamlet.
HAMLET   How is it with you, lady?
QUEEN   Alas, how is't with you,
That you do bend[9] your eye on vacancy,
And with th' incorporal air do hold discourse?   120
Forth at your eyes your spirits wildly peep,
And as the sleeping soldiers in th' alarm,
Your bedded hairs like life in excrements[1]
Start up and stand an end. O gentle son,
Upon the heat and flame of thy distemper   125
Sprinkle cool patience. Whereon do you look?
HAMLET   On him, on him! Look you how pale he glares.
His form and cause conjoined,[2] preaching to stones,
Would make them capable.[3]—Do not look upon me,
Lest with piteous action you convert   130
My stern effects.[4] Then what I have to do
Will want true color—tears perchance for blood.
QUEEN   To whom do you speak this?
HAMLET   Do you see nothing there?
QUEEN   Nothing at all, yet all that is I see.   135
HAMLET   Nor did you nothing hear?

3. one-tenth
4. first husband
5. The "Vice," a common figure in the popular drama, was a clown or buffoon.
6. pickpocket
7. slow to act
8. imagination
9. turn
1. nails and hair
2. working together
3. of responding
4. deeds

QUEEN   No, nothing but ourselves.

HAMLET   Why, look you there. Look how it steals away.
My father, in his habit[5] as he lived!
Look where he goes even now out at the portal.   *Exit* GHOST.   140

QUEEN   This is the very coinage[6] of your brain.
This bodiless creation ecstasy[7]
Is very cunning[8] in.

HAMLET   My pulse as yours doth temperately keep time,
And makes as healthful music. It is not madness   145
That I have uttered. Bring me to the test,
And I the matter will re-word, which madness
Would gambol[9] from. Mother, for love of grace,
Lay not that flattering unction[1] to your soul,
That not your trespass but my madness speaks.   150
It will but skin and film the ulcerous place
Whiles rank corruption, mining[2] all within,
Infects unseen. Confess yourself to heaven,
Repent what's past, avoid what is to come,
And do not spread the compost on the weeds,   155
To make them ranker. Forgive me this my virtue,
For in the fatness of these pursy[3] times
Virtue itself of vice must pardon beg,
Yea, curb[4] and woo for leave to do him good.

QUEEN   O Hamlet, thou hast cleft my heart in twain.   160

HAMLET   O, throw away the worser part of it,
And live the purer with the other half.
Good night—but go not to my uncle's bed.
Assume a virtue, if you have it not.
That monster custom[5] who all sense doth eat   165
Of habits evil, is angel yet in this,
That to the use of actions fair and good
He likewise gives a frock or livery
That aptly[6] is put on. Refrain tonight,
And that shall lend a kind of easiness   170
To the next abstinence; the next more easy;
For use almost can change the stamp of nature,
And either curb the devil, or throw him out
With wondrous potency. Once more, good night,
And when you are desirous to be blest,   175
I'll blessing beg of you. For this same lord
I do repent; but heaven hath pleased it so,
To punish me with this, and this with me,
That I must be their scourge and minister.
I will bestow[7] him and will answer well   180
The death I gave him. So, again, good night.
I must be cruel only to be kind.

5. costume
6. invention
7. madness
8. skilled
9. shy away
1. ointment

2. undermining
3. bloated
4. bow
5. habit
6. easily
7. dispose of

Thus bad begins and worse remains behind.
One word more, good lady.

QUEEN   What shall I do?

HAMLET   Not this, by no means, that I bid you do: 185
Let the bloat⁸ king tempt you again to bed,
Pinch wanton⁹ on your cheek, call you his mouse,
And let him, for a pair of reechy¹ kisses,
Or paddling in your neck with his damned fingers,
Make you to ravel² all this matter out,   190
That I essentially am not in madness,
But mad in craft. 'Twere good you let him know,
For who that's but a queen, fair, sober, wise,
Would from a paddock,³ from a bat, a gib,⁴
Such dear concernings hide? Who would so do?   195
No, in despite of sense and secrecy,
Unpeg the basket on the house's top,
Let the birds fly, and like the famous ape,
To try conclusions, in the basket creep
And break your own neck down.⁵   200

QUEEN   Be thou assured, if words be made of breath
And breath of life, I have no life to breathe
What thou hast said to me.

HAMLET   I must to England; you know that?

QUEEN   Alack,
I had forgot. 'Tis so concluded on.   205

HAMLET   There's letters sealed, and my two school-fellows,
Whom I will trust as I will adders fanged,
They bear the mandate⁶; they must sweep⁷ my way
And marshal me to knavery. Let it work,
For 'tis the sport to have the enginer   210
Hoist with his own petar; and't shall go hard
But I will delve⁸ one yard below their mines
And blow them at the moon. O, 'tis most sweet
When in one line two crafts directly meet.⁹
This man shall set me packing.   215
I'll lug the guts into the neighbor room.
Mother, good night. Indeed, this counsellor
Is now most still, most secret, and most grave,
Who was in life a foolish prating knave.
Come sir, to draw toward an end with you.   220
Good night, mother.

Exit the QUEEN. *Then exit* HAMLET *tugging* POLONIUS.

8. bloated
9. lewdly
1. foul
2. reveal
3. toad
4. tomcat
5. Apparently a reference to a now lost fable in which an ape, finding a basket containing a cage of birds on a housetop, opens the cage. The birds fly away. The ape, thinking that if he were in the basket he too could fly, enters, jumps out, and breaks his neck.

6. command
7. prepare
8. dig
9. The "enginer" or engineer is a military man who is here described as being blown up by a bomb of his own construction, "hoist with his own petar." The military figure continues in the succeeding lines where Hamlet describes himself as digging a countermine or tunnel beneath the one Claudius is digging to defeat Hamlet. In line 214 the two tunnels unexpectedly meet.

Act 4

SCENE 1: *A room in tne castle. Enter* KING, QUEEN, ROSENCRANTZ *and* GUILDENSTERN.

KING There's matter in these sighs, these profound heaves,
You must translate[1]; 'tis fit we understand them.
Where is your son?
QUEEN Bestow this place on us a little while.

Exeunt ROSENCRANTZ *and* GUILDENSTERN.

Ah, mine own lord, what have I seen tonight!   5
KING What, Gertrude? How does Hamlet?
QUEEN Mad as the sea and wind when both contend
Which is the mightier. In his lawless fit,
Behind the arras hearing something stir,
Whips out his rapier, cries "A rat, a rat!"   10
And in this brainish apprehension[2] kills
The unseen good old man.
KING   O heavy deed!
It had been so with us had we been there.
His liberty is full of threats to all—
To you yourself, to us, to every one.   15
Alas, how shall this bloody deed be answered?
It will be laid to us, whose providence[3]
Should have kept short, restrained, and out of haunt,[4]
This mad young man. But so much was our love,
We would not understand what was most fit;   20
But, like the owner of a foul disease,
To keep it from divulging, let it feed
Even on the pith of life. Where is he gone?
QUEEN To draw apart the body he hath killed,
O'er whom his very madness, like some ore   25
Among a mineral of metals base,
Shows itself pure: 'a weeps for what is done.
KING O Gertrude, come away!
The sun no sooner shall the mountains touch
But we will ship him hence, and this vile deed   30
We must with all our majesty and skill
Both countenance and excuse. Ho, Guildenstern!

Enter ROSENCRANTZ *and* GUILDENSTERN.

Friends both, go join you with some further aid.
Hamlet in madness hath Polonius slain,
And from his mother's closet hath he dragged him.   35
Go seek him out; speak fair, and bring the body
Into the chapel. I pray you haste in this.

---

1. explain
2. insane notion
3. prudence
4. away from court

Exeunt ROSENCRANTZ *and* GUILDENSTERN.

Come, Gertrude, we'll call up our wisest friends
And let them know both what we mean to do
And what's untimely done,   40
Whose whisper o'er the world's diameter,
As level[5] as the cannon to his blank,[6]
Transports his poisoned shot—may miss our name,
And hit the woundless air. O, come away!
My soul is full of discord and dismay.   *Exeunt.* 45

SCENE 2: *A passageway. Enter* HAMLET.

HAMLET   Safely stowed.—But soft, what noise? Who calls on Hamlet?
O, here they come.

Enter ROSENCRANTZ, GUILDENSTERN, *and* OTHERS.

ROSENCRANTZ   What have you done, my lord, with the dead body?
HAMLET   Compounded it with dust, whereto 'tis kin.
ROSENCRANTZ   Tell us where 'tis, that we may take it thence   5
And bear it to the chapel.
HAMLET   Do not believe it.
ROSENCRANTZ   Believe what?
HAMLET   That I can keep your counsel and not mine own. Besides, to
be demanded of[7] a sponge—what replication[8] should be made by   10
the son of a king?
ROSENCRANTZ   Take you me for a sponge, my lord?
HAMLET   Ay, sir, that soaks up the king's countenance,[9] his rewards,
his authorities. But such officers do the king best service in the end.
He keeps them like an apple in the corner of his jaw, first mouthed 15
to be last swallowed. When he needs what you have gleaned, it is
but squeezing you and, sponge, you shall be dry again.
ROSENCRANTZ   I understand you not, my lord.
HAMLET   I am glad of it. A knavish speech sleeps in a foolish ear.
ROSENCRANTZ   My lord, you must tell us where the body is, and go   20
with us to the king.
HAMLET   The body is with the king, but the king is not with the body.
The king is a thing—
GUILDENSTERN   A thing, my lord!
HAMLET   Of nothing. Bring me to him. Hide fox, and all after.[1]   25

Exeunt.

SCENE 3: *A room in the castle. Enter* KING.

KING   I have sent to seek him, and to find the body.
How dangerous is it that this man goes loose!
Yet must not we put the strong law on him.
He's loved of the distracted[2] multitude,

5. direct
6. mark
7. questioned by
8. answer

9. favor
1. Apparently a reference to a children's
game like hide-and-seek.
2. confused

Who like not in their judgment but their eyes,   5
And where 'tis so, th' offender's scourge[3] is weighed,
But never the offence. To bear all smooth and even,
This sudden sending him away must seem
Deliberate pause.[4] Diseases desperate grown
By desperate appliance are relieved,   10
Or not at all.

Enter ROSENCRANTZ, GUILDENSTERN, *and all the rest.*

How now! what hath befall'n?
ROSENCRANTZ   Where the dead body is bestowed, my lord,
We cannot get from him.
KING   But where is he?
ROSENCRANTZ   Without,[5] my lord; guarded, to know[6] your pleasure.
KING   Bring him before us.
ROSENCRANTZ   Ho! bring in the lord.   15

They enter with HAMLET.

KING   Now, Hamlet, where's Polonius?
HAMLET   At supper.
KING   At supper? Where?
HAMLET   Not where he eats, but where 'a is eaten. A certain convoca-
tion[7] of politic[8] worms are e'en at him. Your worm is your only   20
emperor for diet. We fat all creatures else to fat us, and we fat
ourselves for maggots. Your fat king and your lean beggar is but
variable service—two dishes, but to one table. That's the end.
KING   Alas, alas!
HAMLET   A man may fish with the worm that hath eat of a king, and   25
eat of the fish that hath fed of that worm.
KING   What dost thou mean by this?
HAMLET   Nothing but to show you how a king may go a progress
through the guts of a beggar.
KING   Where is Polonius?   30
HAMLET   In heaven. Send thither to see. If your messenger find him
not there, seek him i' th' other place yourself. But if, indeed, you find
him not within this month, you shall nose[9] him as you go up the
stairs into the lobby.
KING [*to* ATTENDANTS]   Go seek him there.   35
HAMLET   'A will stay till you come.   *Exeunt* ATTENDANTS.
KING   Hamlet, this deed, for thine especial safety—
Which we do tender,[1] as we dearly[2] grieve
For that which thou hast done—must send thee hence
With fiery quickness. Therefore prepare thyself.   40
The bark is ready, and the wind at help,
Th' associates tend, and everything is bent
For England.

---

3. punishment
4. i.e., not an impulse
5. outside
6. await
7. gathering
8. statesmanlike
9. smell
1. consider
2. deeply

HAMLET	For England?
KING	Ay, Hamlet.
HAMLET	Good.
KING	So it is, if thou knew'st our purposes.

HAMLET   I see a cherub that sees them. But come, for England!   45
  Farewell, dear mother.

KING   Thy loving father, Hamlet.

HAMLET   My mother. Father and mother is man and wife, man and
  wife is one flesh. So, my mother. Come, for England.   *Exit.*

KING   Follow him at foot[3]; tempt him with speed aboard.   50
  Delay it not; I'll have him hence tonight.
  Away! for everything is sealed and done
  That else leans on th' affair. Pray you make haste.

                           Exeunt all but the KING.

  And, England, if my love thou hold'st at aught—
  As my great power thereof may give thee sense,[4]   55
  Since yet thy cicatrice[5] looks raw and red
  After the Danish sword, and thy free awe
  Pays homage to us—thou mayst not coldly set[6]
  Our sovereign process,[7] which imports at full
  By letters congruing[8] to that effect   60
  The present death of Hamlet. Do it, England,
  For like the hectic[9] in my blood he rages,
  And thou must cure me. Till I know 'tis done,
  Howe'er my haps, my joys were ne'er begun.   *Exit.*

SCENE 4: *Near Elsinore. Enter* FORTINBRAS *with his army.*

FORTINBRAS   Go, captain, from me greet the Danish king.
  Tell him that by his license Fortinbras
  Craves the conveyance[1] of a promised march
  Over his kingdom. You know the rendezvous.
  If that his majesty would aught with us,   5
  We shall express our duty in his eye,[2]
  And let him know so.

CAPTAIN   I will do't, my lord.

FORTINBRAS   Go softly on.   *Exeunt all but the* CAPTAIN.

     Enter HAMLET, ROSENCRANTZ, GUILDENSTERN, *and* OTHERS.

HAMLET   Good sir, whose powers are these?

CAPTAIN   They are of Norway, sir.   10

HAMLET   How purposed, sir, I pray you?

CAPTAIN   Against some part of Poland.

HAMLET   Who commands them, sir?

CAPTAIN   The nephew to old Norway, Fortinbras.

---

3. closely	8. agreeing
4. of its value	9. chronic fever
5. wound scar	1. escort
6. set aside	2. presence
7. mandate	

HAMLET   Goes it against the main[3] of Poland, sir,   15
Or for some frontier?
CAPTAIN   Truly to speak, and with no addition,[4]
We go to gain a little patch of ground
That hath in it no profit but the name.
To pay five ducats,[5] five, I would not farm it;   20
Nor will it yield to Norway or the Pole
A ranker[6] rate should it be sold in fee.[7]
HAMLET   Why, then the Polack never will defend it.
CAPTAIN   Yes, it is already garrisoned.
HAMLET   Two thousand souls and twenty thousand ducats   25
Will not debate the question of this straw.
This is th' imposthume[8] of much wealth and peace,
That inward breaks, and shows no cause without
Why the man dies. I humbly thank you, sir.
CAPTAIN   God b'wi'ye, sir.   *Exit.*
ROSENCRANTZ   Will't please you go, my lord?   30
HAMLET   I'll be with you straight. Go a little before.

                              Exeunt all but HAMLET.

How all occasions do inform against me,
And spur my dull revenge! What is a man,
If his chief good and market[9] of his time
Be but to sleep and feed? A beast, no more.   35
Sure he that made us with such large discourse,[1]
Looking before and after, gave us not
That capability and godlike reason
To fust[2] in us unused. Now, whether it be
Bestial oblivion, or some craven scruple   40
Of thinking too precisely on th' event[3]—
A thought which, quartered, hath but one part wisdom
And ever three parts coward—I do not know
Why yet I live to say "This thing's to do,"
Sith[4] I have cause, and will, and strength, and means,   45
To do't. Examples gross as earth exhort me.
Witness this army of such mass and charge,[5]
Led by a delicate and tender prince,
Whose spirit, with divine ambition puffed,
Makes mouths at[6] the invisible event,   50
Exposing what is mortal and unsure
To all that fortune, death, and danger dare,
Even for an eggshell. Rightly to be great
Is not to stir without great argument,
But greatly to find quarrel in a straw   55

3. central part
4. exaggeration
5. i.e., in rent
6. higher
7. outright
8. abscess
9. occupation

1. ample reasoning power
2. grow musty
3. outcome
4. since
5. expense
6. scorns

When honor's at the stake. How stand I then,
That have a father killed, a mother stained,
Excitements of my reason and my blood,
And let all sleep, while to my shame I see
The imminent death of twenty thousand men   60
That for a fantasy and trick of fame
Go to their graves like beds, fight for a plot
Whereon the numbers cannot try the cause,
Which is not tomb enough and continent
To hide the slain?[7] O, from this time forth,   65
My thoughts be bloody, or be nothing worth!   *Exit.*

SCENE 5: *A room in the castle. Enter* QUEEN, HORATIO *and a*
GENTLEMAN.

QUEEN   I will not speak with her.
GENTLEMAN   She is importunate, indeed distract.
  Her mood will needs be pitied.
QUEEN   What would she have?
GENTLEMAN   She speaks much of her father, says she hears
  There's tricks i' th' world, and hems, and beats her heart,   5
  Spurns enviously at straws,[8] speaks things in doubt
  That carry but half sense. Her speech is nothing,
  Yet the unshaped use of it doth move
  The hearers to collection[9]; they yawn at it,
  And botch the words up fit to their own thoughts,   10
  Which, as her winks and nods and gestures yield them,
  Indeed would make one think there might be thought,
  Though nothing sure, yet much unhappily.
HORATIO   'Twere good she were spoken with, for she may strew
  Dangerous conjectures in ill-breeding minds.   15
QUEEN   Let her come in.   *Exit* GENTLEMAN.
  [*Aside.*] To my sick soul, as sin's true nature is,
  Each toy[1] seems prologue to some great amiss.[2]
  So full of artless jealousy is guilt,
  It spills itself in fearing to be spilt.   20

      Enter OPHELIA *distracted.*

OPHELIA   Where is the beauteous majesty of Denmark?
QUEEN   How now, Ophelia!
OPHELIA   How should I your true love know   *She sings.*
              From another one?
              By his cockle hat and staff,[3]   25
              And his sandal shoon.[4]
QUEEN   Alas, sweet lady, what imports this song?

7. The plot of ground involved is so
small that it cannot contain the number of
men involved in fighting nor furnish burial
space for the number of those who will die.
8. takes offense at trifles
9. an attempt to order
1. trifle

2. catastrophe
3. A "cockle hat," one decorated with a
shell, indicated that the wearer had made a
pilgrimage to the shrine of St. James at
Compostela in Spain. The staff also marked
the carrier as a pilgrim.
4. shoes

OPHELIA   Say you? Nay, pray you mark.

> He is dead and gone, lady,
>   He is dead and gone;   30
> At his head a grass-green turf,
>   At his heels a stone.

  O, ho!

QUEEN   Nay, but, Ophelia—

OPHELIA   Pray you mark.

    White his shroud as the mountain snow—   35

Enter KING.

QUEEN   Alas, look here, my lord.

OPHELIA   Larded all with sweet flowers;

    Which bewept to the grave did not go

       With true-love showers.

KING   How do you, pretty lady?   40

OPHELIA   Well, God dild[5] you! They say the owl was a baker's daughter. Lord, we know what we are, but know not what we may be. God be at your table!

KING   Conceit[6] upon her father.

OPHELIA   Pray let's have no words of this, but when they ask you 45 what it means, say you this:

> Tomorrow is Saint Valentine's day,
>   All in the morning betime,
> And I a maid at your window,
>   To be your Valentine.   50
> Then up he rose, and donn'd his clo'es,
>   And dupped[7] the chamber-door,
> Let in the maid, that out a maid
>   Never departed more.

KING   Pretty Ophelia!   55

OPHELIA   Indeed, without an oath, I'll make an end on't.

> By Gis[8] and by Saint Charity,
>   Alack, and fie for shame!
> Young men will do't, if they come to't;
>   By Cock,[9] they are to blame.
> Quoth she "Before you tumbled me,   60
>   You promised me to wed."

  He answers:

> "So would I 'a done, by yonder sun,
>   An thou hadst not come to my bed."   65

KING   How long hath she been thus?

OPHELIA   I hope all will be well. We must be patient, but I cannot choose but weep to think they would lay him i' th' cold ground. My brother shall know of it, and so I thank you for your good counsel.

---

5. yield   8. Jesus
6. thought   9. God
7. opened

Come, my coach! Good night, ladies, good night. Sweet ladies, good 70
night, good night.   *Exit.*
KING   Follow her close; give her good watch, I pray you.

                              Exeunt HORATIO *and* GENTLEMAN.

O, this is the poison of deep grief; it springs
All from her father's death, and now behold!
O Gertrude, Gertrude!   75
When sorrows come, they come not single spies,
But in battalions: first, her father slain;
Next, your son gone, and he most violent author
Of his own just remove; the people muddied,[1]
Thick and unwholesome in their thoughts and whispers   80
For good Polonius' death; and we have done but greenly[2]
In hugger-mugger[3] to inter him; poor Ophelia
Divided from herself and her fair judgment,
Without the which we are pictures, or mere beasts;
Last, and as much containing as all these,   85
Her brother is in secret come from France,
Feeds on his wonder, keeps himself in clouds,
And wants not buzzers to infect his ear
With pestilent speeches of his father's death,
Wherein necessity, of matter beggared,[4]   90
Will nothing stick[5] our person to arraign[6]
In ear and ear.[7] O my dear Gertrude, this,
Like to a murd'ring piece,[8] in many places
Gives me superfluous death. Attend,   *A noise within.*

        Enter a MESSENGER.

Where are my Switzers[9]? Let them guard the door.   95
What is the matter?
MESSENGER   Save yourself, my lord.
The ocean, overpeering of his list,[1]
Eats not the flats with more impiteous[2] haste
Than young Laertes, in a riotous head,[3]
O'erbears your officers. The rabble call him lord,   100
And as the world were now but to begin,
Antiquity forgot, custom not known,
The ratifiers and props of every word,
They cry "Choose we, Laertes shall be king."
Caps, hands, and tongues, applaud it to the clouds,   105
"Laertes shall be king, Laertes king."
QUEEN   How cheerfully on the false trail they cry[4]!   *A noise within.*
O, this is counter,[5] you false Danish dogs!
KING   The doors are broke.

1. disturbed
2. without judgment
3. haste
4. short on facts
5. hesitate
6. accuse
7. from both sides

8. a weapon designed to scatter its shot
9. Swiss guards
1. towering above its limits
2. pitiless
3. with an armed band
4. as if following the scent
5. backward

Enter LAERTES, *with* OTHERS.

LAERTES   Where is this king?—Sirs, stand you all without.   110
ALL   No, let's come in.
LAERTES   I pray you give me leave.
ALL   We will, we will.   *Exeunt his followers.*
LAERTES   I thank you. Keep[6] the door.—O thou vile king,
Give me my father!
QUEEN   Calmly, good Laertes.
LAERTES   That drop of blood that's calm proclaims me bastard,   115
Cries cuckold to my father, brands the harlot
Even here between the chaste unsmirchéd brow
Of my true mother.
KING   What is the cause, Laertes,
That thy rebellion looks so giant-like?
Let him go, Gertrude. Do not fear[7] our person.   120
There's such divinity doth hedge a king
That treason can but peep to[8] what it would,
Acts little of his will. Tell me, Laertes,
Why thou art thus incensed. Let him go, Gertrude.
Speak, man.
LAERTES   Where is my father?
KING   Dead.   125
QUEEN   But not by him.
KING   Let him demand[9] his fill.
LAERTES   How came he dead? I'll not be juggled with.
To hell allegiance, vows to the blackest devil,
Conscience and grace to the profoundest pit!
I dare damnation. To this point I stand,   130
That both the worlds[1] I give to negligence,[2]
Let come what comes, only I'll be revenged
Most throughly for my father.
KING   Who shall stay you?
LAERTES   My will, not all the world's.
And for my means, I'll husband[3] them so well   135
They shall go far with little.
KING   Good Laertes,
If you desire to know the certainty
Of your dear father, is't writ in your revenge
That, swoopstake,[4] you will draw both friend and foe,
Winner and loser?
LAERTES   None but his enemies.   140
KING   Will you know them, then?
LAERTES   To his good friends thus wide I'll ope my arms,
And like the kind life-rend'ring pelican,[5]
Repast them with my blood.

---

6. guard
7. fear for
8. look at over or through a barrier
9. question
1. i.e., this and the next

2. disregard
3. manage
4. sweeping the board
5. The pelican was believed to feed her young with her own blood.

KING   Why, now you speak
Like a good child and a true gentleman.   145
That I am guiltless of your father's death,
And am most sensibly in grief for it,
It shall as level[6] to your judgment 'pear
As day does to your eye.

      A noise within: "Let her come in."

LAERTES   How now? What noise is that?   150

      Enter OPHELIA.

O, heat dry up my brains! tears seven times salt
Burn out the sense[7] and virtue[8] of mine eye!
By heaven, thy madness shall be paid with weight
Till our scale turn the beam. O rose of May,
Dear maid, kind sister, sweet Ophelia!   155
O heavens! is't possible a young maid's wits
Should be as mortal as an old man's life?
Nature is fine[9] in love, and where 'tis fine
It sends some precious instance of itself
After the thing it loves.[1]   160
OPHELIA   They bore him barefac'd on the bier;
      Hey non nonny, nonny, hey nonny;
      And in his grave rain'd many a tear—

Fare you well, my dove!
LAERTES   Hadst thou thy wits, and didst persuade revenge,   165
It could not move thus.
OPHELIA   You must sing "A-down, a-down, and you call him a-down-
a." O, how the wheel becomes it! It is the false steward, that stole his
master's daughter.[2]
LAERTES   This nothing's more than matter.   170
OPHELIA   There's rosemary, that's for remembrance. Pray you, love,
remember. And there is pansies, that's for thoughts.
LAERTES   A document[3] in madness, thoughts and remembrance fitted.
OPHELIA   There's fennel for you, and columbines. There's rue for you,
and here's some for me. We may call it herb of grace a Sundays. O,   175
you must wear your rue with a difference. There's a daisy. I would
give you some violets, but they withered all when my father died.
They say 'a made a good end.

    [*Sings.*]   For bonny sweet Robin is all my joy.

LAERTES   Thought and affliction, passion, hell itself,   180
She turns to favor[4] and to prettiness.

---

6. plain
7. feeling
8. function
9. refined
1. Laertes means that Ophelia, because
of her love for her father, gave up her
sanity as a token of grief at his death.
2. The "wheel" refers to the *burden* or
refrain of a song, in this case "A-down,
a-down, and you call him a-down-a." The

ballad to which she refers was about a false
steward. Others have suggested that the
"wheel" is the Wheel of Fortune, a spinning wheel to whose rhythm such a song
might have been sung or a kind of dance
movement performed by Ophelia as she
sings.
3. lesson
4. beauty

OPHELIA   And will 'a not come again?
                   And will 'a not come again?
                      No, no, he is dead,
                      Go to thy death-bed,   185
                   He never will come again.

                   His beard was as white as snow,
                   All flaxen was his poll[5];
                      He is gone, he is gone,
                      And we cast away moan: 190
                   God-a-mercy on his soul!

      And of all Christian souls, I pray God. God b'wi'you.   *Exit.*
LAERTES   Do you see this, O God?
KING   Laertes, I must commune with your grief,
    Or you deny me right. Go but apart,   195
    Make choice of whom your wisest friends you will,
    And they shall hear and judge 'twixt you and me.
    If by direct or by collateral[6] hand
    They find us touched,[7] we will our kingdom give,
    Our crown, our life, and all that we call ours,   200
    To you in satisfaction; but if not,
    Be you content to lend your patience to us,
    And we shall jointly labor with your soul
    To give it due content.
LAERTES   Let this be so.   205
    His means of death, his obscure funeral—
    No trophy, sword, nor hatchment,[8] o'er his bones,
    No noble rite nor formal ostentation[9]—
    Cry to be heard, as 'twere from heaven to earth,
    That I must call't in question.
KING   So you shall;
    And where th' offence is, let the great axe fall.   210
    I pray you go with me.   *Exeunt.*

      SCENE 6: *Another room in the castle. Enter* HORATIO *and*
      a GENTLEMAN.

HORATIO   What are they that would speak with me?
GENTLEMAN   Sea-faring men, sir. They say they have letters for you.
HORATIO   Let them come in.   *Exit* GENTLEMAN.
    I do not know from what part of the world
    I should be greeted, if not from Lord Hamlet.   5

          Enter SAILORS.

SAILOR   God bless you, sir.
HORATIO   Let him bless thee too.
SAILOR   'A shall, sir, an't please him. There's a letter for you, sir—it

---

5. head
6. indirect
7. by guilt

8. coat of arms
9. pomp

came from th' ambassador that was bound for England —if your name be Horatio, as I am let to know[1] it is. 10

HORATIO [*reads*] "Horatio, when thou shalt have overlooked[2] this, give these fellows some means[3] to the king. They have letters for him. Ere we were two days old at sea, a pirate of very warlike appointment[4] gave us chase. Finding ourselves too slow of sail, we put on a compelled valor, and in the grapple I boarded them. On the instant they got clear of our ship, so I alone became their prisoner. They have dealt with me like thieves of mercy, but they knew what they did; I am to do a good turn for them. Let the king have the letters I have sent, and repair thou to me with as much speed as thou wouldest fly death. I have words to speak in thine ear will make thee dumb; yet are they much too light for the bore of the matter.[5] These good fellows will bring thee where I am. Rosencrantz and Guildenstern hold their course for England. Of them I have much to tell thee. Farewell. 15 20

He that thou knowest thine, HAMLET."
Come, I will give you way[6] for these your letters, 25
And do't the speedier that you may direct me
To him from whom you brought them.   *Exeunt.*

SCENE 7: *Another room in the castle. Enter* KING *and* LAERTES.

KING Now must your conscience my acquittance seal,[7]
And you must put me in your heart for friend,
Sith you have heard, and with a knowing ear,
That he which hath your noble father slain
Pursued my life.

LAERTES   It well appears. But tell me 5
Why you proceeded not against these feats,
So criminal and so capital in nature,
As by your safety, greatness, wisdom, all things else,
You mainly were stirred up.

KING   O, for two special reasons,
Which may to you, perhaps, seem much unsinewed,[8] 10
But yet to me th' are strong. The queen his mother
Lives almost by his looks, and for myself—
My virtue or my plague, be it either which—
She is so conjunctive[9] to my life and soul
That, as the star moves not but in his sphere,[1] 15
I could not but by her. The other motive,
Why to a public count[2] I might not go,
Is the great love the general gender[3] bear him,
Who, dipping all his faults in their affection,

---

1. informed
2. read through
3. access
4. equipment
5. A figure from gunnery, referring to shot which is too small for the size of the weapon to be fired.
6. means of delivery
7. grant me innocent

8. weak
9. closely joined
1. A reference to the Ptolemaic cosmology in which planets and stars were believed to revolve about the earth in crystalline spheres concentric with the earth.
2. reckoning
3. common people

Work like the spring that turneth wood to stone,[4]   20
Convert his gyves[5] to graces; so that my arrows,
Too slightly timbered[6] for so loud a wind,
Would have reverted to my bow again,
But not where I have aimed them.

LAERTES   And so have I a noble father lost,   25
A sister driven into desp'rate terms,
Whose worth, if praises may go back again,
Stood challenger on mount of all the age
For her perfections. But my revenge will come.

KING   Break not your sleeps for that. You must not think   30
That we are made of stuff so flat and dull
That we can let our beard be shook with danger,
And think it pastime. You shortly shall hear more.
I loved your father, and we love our self,
And that, I hope, will teach you to imagine—   35

Enter a MESSENGER *with letters.*

MESSENGER   These to your majesty; this to the queen.
KING   From Hamlet! Who brought them?
MESSENGER   Sailors, my lord, they say. I saw them not.
They were given me by Claudio; he received them
Of him that brought them.
KING   Laertes, you shall hear them.—   40
Leave us.   *Exit* MESSENGER.
[*Reads.*] "High and mighty, you shall know I am set naked on
your kingdom. Tomorrow shall I beg leave to see your kingly eyes;
when I shall, first asking your pardon thereunto, recount the occasion
of my sudden and more strange return.   45
                                    HAMLET."
What should this mean? Are all the rest come back?
Or is it some abuse,[7] and no such thing?
LAERTES   Know you the hand?
KING   'Tis Hamlet's character.[8] "Naked"!   50
And in a postscript here, he says "alone."
Can you devise[9] me?
LAERTES   I am lost in it, my lord. But let him come.
It warms the very sickness in my heart
That I shall live and tell him to his teeth   55
"Thus didest thou."
KING   If it be so, Laertes—
As how should it be so, how otherwise?—
Will you be ruled by me?
LAERTES   Ay, my lord,
So you will not o'errule me to a peace.
KING   To thine own peace. If he be now returned,   60

---

4. Certain English springs contain so
much lime in the water that a lime covering will be deposited on a log placed in
one of them for a length of time.
5. fetters

6. shafted
7. trick
8. handwriting
9. explain it to

As checking at[1] his voyage, and that he means
No more to undertake it, I will work him
To an exploit now ripe in my device,
Under the which he shall not choose but fall;
And for his death no wind of blame shall breathe   65
But even his mother shall uncharge[2] the practice
And call it accident.

LAERTES   My lord, I will be ruled;
    The rather if you could devise it so
    That I might be the organ.[3]

KING   It falls right.
    You have been talked of since your travel much,   70
    And that in Hamlet's hearing, for a quality
    Wherein they say you shine. Your sum of parts
    Did not together pluck such envy from him
    As did that one, and that, in my regard,
    Of the unworthiest siege.[4]

LAERTES   What part is that, my lord?   75

KING   A very riband in the cap of youth,
    Yet needful too, for youth no less becomes
    The light and careless livery that it wears
    Than settled age his sables and his weeds,[5]
    Importing health and graveness. Two months since   80
    Here was a gentleman of Normandy.
    I have seen myself, and served against, the French,
    And they can[6] well on horseback, but this gallant
    Had witchcraft in't. He grew unto his seat,
    And to such wondrous doing brought his horse,   85
    As had he been incorpsed and demi-natured
    With the brave beast. So far he topped my thought
    That I, in forgery[7] of shapes and tricks,
    Come short of what he did.[8]

LAERTES   A Norman was't?

KING   A Norman.   90

LAERTES   Upon my life, Lamord.

KING   The very same.

LAERTES   I know him well. He is the brooch indeed
    And gem of all the nation.

KING   He made confession[9] of you,
    And gave you such a masterly report   95
    For art and exercise in your defence,[1]
    And for your rapier most especial,
    That he cried out 'twould be a sight indeed
    If one could match you. The scrimers[2] of their nation

1. turning aside from
2. not accuse
3. instrument
4. rank
5. dignified clothing
6. perform
7. imagination
8. The gentleman referred to was so skilled in horsemanship that he seemed to share one body with the horse, "incorpsed." The King further extends the compliment by saying that he appeared like the mythical centaur, a creature who was man from the waist up and horse from the waist down, therefore "demi-natured."
9. gave a report
1. skill in fencing
2. fencers

He swore had neither motion, guard, nor eye,   100
If you opposed them. Sir, this report of his
Did Hamlet so envenom with his envy
That he could nothing do but wish and beg
Your sudden coming o'er, to play with you.
Now out of this—
LAERTES   What out of this, my lord?   105
KING   Laertes, was your father dear to you?
  Or are you like the painting of a sorrow,
  A face without a heart?
LAERTES   Why ask you this?
KING   Not that I think you did not love your father,
  But that I know love is begun by time,   110
  And that I see in passages of proof,[3]
  Time qualifies the spark and fire of it.
  There lives within the very flame of love
  A kind of wick or snuff that will abate it,
  And nothing is at a like goodness still,   115
  For goodness, growing to a plurisy,[4]
  Dies in his own too much.[5] That we would do,
  We should do when we would; for this "would" changes,
  And hath abatements and delays as many
  As there are tongues, are hands, are accidents,   120
  And then this "should" is like a spendthrift's sigh
  That hurts by easing. But to the quick of th' ulcer—
  Hamlet comes back; what would you undertake
  To show yourself in deed your father's son
  More than in words?
LAERTES   To cut his throat i' th' church.   125
KING   No place indeed should murder sanctuarize[6];
  Revenge should have no bounds. But, good Laertes,
  Will you do this? Keep close within your chamber.
  Hamlet returned shall know you are come home.
  We'll put on those shall praise your excellence,   130
  And set a double varnish[7] on the fame
  The Frenchman gave you, bring you in fine[8] together,
  And wager on your heads. He, being remiss,[9]
  Most generous, and free from all contriving,
  Will not peruse[1] the foils, so that with ease,   135
  Or with a little shuffling, you may choose
  A sword unbated,[2] and in a pass of practice
  Requite him for your father.
LAERTES   I will do't,
  And for that purpose I'll anoint my sword.
  I bought an unction of a mountebank,   140
  So mortal that but dip a knife in it,

---

3. tests of experience   8. in short
4. fullness   9. careless
5. excess   1. examine
6. provide sanctuary for murder   2. not blunted
7. gloss

Where it draws blood no cataplasm[3] so rare,
Collected from all simples[4] that have virtue
Under the moon, can save the thing from death
That is but scratched withal. I'll touch my point   145
With this contagion, that if I gall[5] him slightly,
It may be death.
KING   Let's further think of this,
Weigh what convenience both of time and means
May fit us to our shape. If this should fail,
And that our drift look[6] through our bad performance,   150
'Twere better not assayed. Therefore this project
Should have a back or second that might hold
If this did blast in proof.[7] Soft, let me see.
We'll make a solemn wager on your cunnings—
I ha't.   155
When in your motion you are hot and dry—
As make your bouts more violent to that end—
And that he calls for drink, I'll have preferred him
A chalice for the nonce, whereon but sipping,
If he by chance escape your venomed stuck,[8]   160
Our purpose may hold there.—But stay, what noise?

        Enter QUEEN.

QUEEN   One woe doth tread upon another's heel,
   So fast they follow. Your sister's drowned, Laertes.
LAERTES   Drowned? O, where?
QUEEN   There is a willow grows aslant the brook   165
   That shows his hoar leaves in the glassy stream.
   Therewith fantastic garlands did she make
   Of crowflowers, nettles, daisies, and long purples
   That liberal[9] shepherds give a grosser[1] name,
   But our cold[2] maids do dead men's fingers call them. 170
   There on the pendent boughs her coronet weeds
   Clamb'ring to hang, an envious[3] sliver broke,
   When down her weedy trophies and herself
   Fell in the weeping brook. Her clothes spread wide,
   And mermaid-like awhile they bore her up,   175
   Which time she chanted snatches of old tunes,
   As one incapable[4] of her own distress,
   Or like a creature native and indued[5]
   Unto that element. But long it could not be
   Till that her garments, heavy with their drink,   180
   Pulled the poor wretch from her melodious lay
   To muddy death.
LAERTES   Alas, then she is drowned?
QUEEN   Drowned, drowned.

3. poultice   9. vulgar
4. herbs   1. coarser
5. scratch   2. chaste
6. intent become obvious 3. malicious
7. fail when tried   4. unaware
8. thrust   5. habituated

LAERTES   Too much of water hast thou, poor Ophelia,
And therefore I forbid my tears; but yet   185
It is our trick; nature her custom holds,
Let shame say what it will. When these are gone,
The woman will be out. Adieu, my lord.
I have a speech o' fire that fain would blaze
But that this folly drowns it.   *Exit.*
KING   Let's follow, Gertrude.   190
How much I had to do to calm his rage!
Now fear I this will give it start again;
Therefore let's follow.   *Exeunt.*

Act 5

SCENE 1: *A churchyard. Enter two* CLOWNS.[6]

CLOWN   Is she to be buried in Christian burial when she wilfully
seeks her own salvation?
OTHER   I tell thee she is. Therefore make her grave straight. The
crowner[7] hath sat on her,[8] and finds it Christian burial.
CLOWN   How can that be, unless she drowned herself in her own de-   5
fence?
OTHER   Why, 'tis found so.
CLOWN   It must be "se offendendo";[9] it cannot be else. For here lies
the point: if I drown myself wittingly, it argues an act, and an act
hath three branches—it is to act, to do, to perform; argal,[1] she   10
drowned herself wittingly.
OTHER   Nay, but hear you, Goodman Delver.
CLOWN   Give me leave. Here lies the water; good. Here stands the
man; good. If the man go to this water and drown himself, it is, will
he, nill he, he goes—mark you that. But if the water come to him   15
and drown him, he drowns not himself. Argal, he that is not guilty
of his own death shortens not his own life.
OTHER   But is this law?
CLOWN   Ay, marry, is't; crowner's quest[2] law.
OTHER   Will you ha' the truth on't? If this had not been a gentle-   20
woman, she should have been buried out o' Christian burial.
CLOWN   Why, there thou say'st. And the more pity that great folk
should have count'nance[3] in this world to drown or hang themselves
more than their even-Christen.[4] Come, my spade. There is no ancient
gentlemen but gard'ners, ditchers, and grave-makers. They hold up   25
Adam's profession.
OTHER   Was he a gentleman?
CLOWN   'A was the first that ever bore arms.
OTHER   Why, he had none.
CLOWN   What, art a heathen? How dost thou understand the Scrip-   30

---

6. rustics
7. coroner
8. held an inquest
9. an error for *se defendendo,* in self-
defense

1. therefore
2. inquest
3. approval
4. fellow Christians

ture? The Scripture says Adam digged. Could he dig without arms?
I'll put another question to thee. If thou answerest me not to the
purpose, confess thyself—

OTHER   Go to.

CLOWN   What is he that builds stronger than either the mason, the   35
shipwright, or the carpenter?

OTHER   The gallows-maker, for that frame outlives a thousand tenants.

CLOWN   I like thy wit well, in good faith. The gallows does well. But
how does it well? It does well to those that do ill. Now thou dost ill
to say the gallows is built stronger than the church. Argal, the gal-   40
lows may do well to thee. To't again,⁵ come.

OTHER   Who builds stronger than a mason, a shipwright, or a carpenter?

CLOWN   Ay tell me that, and unyoke.⁶

OTHER   Marry, now I can tell.   45

CLOWN   To't.

OTHER   Mass, I cannot tell.

CLOWN   Cudgel thy brains no more about it, for your dull ass will not
mend his pace with beating. And when you are asked this question
next, say "a grave-maker." The houses he makes lasts till doomsday.   50
Go, get thee in, and fetch me a stoup⁷ of liquor. *Exit* OTHER CLOWN.

        Enter HAMLET *and* HORATIO *as* CLOWN *digs and sings.*

            In youth, when I did love, did love,
                Methought it was very sweet,
            To contract⁸ the time for-a my behove,⁹
                O, methought there-a was nothing-a meet.¹   55

HAMLET   Has this fellow no feeling of his business, that 'a sings in
grave-making?

HORATIO   Custom hath made it in him a property of easiness.

HAMLET   'Tis e'en so. The hand of little employment hath the daintier
sense.   60

CLOWN   But age, with his stealing steps,
                        Hath clawed me in his clutch,
                    And hath shipped me into the land,
                        As if I had never been such.

        Throws up a skull.

HAMLET   That skull had a tongue in it, and could sing once. How the   65
knave jowls² it to the ground, as if 'twere Cain's jawbone, that did
the first murder! This might be the pate of a politician, which this
ass now o'erreaches³; one that would circumvent God, might it not?

HORATIO   It might, my lord.

HAMLET   Or of a courtier, which could say "Good morrow, sweet lord!   70
How dost thou, sweet lord?" This might be my Lord Such-a-one,
that praised my Lord Such-a-one's horse, when 'a meant to beg it,
might it not?

5. guess again
6. finish the matter
7. mug
8. shorten
9. advantage
1. The gravedigger's song is a free ver

sion of "The aged lover renounceth love"
by Thomas, Lord Vaux, published in *Tot-
tel's Miscellany*, 1557.
2. hurls
3. gets the better of

HORATIO   Ay, my lord.

HAMLET   Why, e'en so, and now my Lady Worm's, chapless,[4] and   75
knock'd abut the mazzard[5] with a sexton's spade. Here's fine revolution,[6] an we had the trick to see't. Did these bones cost no more the
breeding but to play at loggets with them?[7] Mine ache to think on't.

CLOWN   A pick-axe and a spade, a spade,
                        For and a shrouding sheet: 80
                    O, a pit of clay for to be made
                    For such a guest is meet.

    Throws up another skull.

HAMLET   There's another. Why may not that be the skull of a lawyer?
Where be his quiddities now, his quillets, his cases, his tenures, and
his tricks? Why does he suffer this mad knave now to knock him   85
about the sconce[8] with a dirty shovel, and will not tell him of his
action of battery? Hum! This fellow might be in's time a great buyer
of land, with his statutes, his recognizances, his fines, his double
vouchers, his recoveries. Is this the fine[9] of his fines, and the recovery
of his recoveries, to have his fine pate full of fine dirt? Will his vouch-   90
ers vouch him no more of his purchases, and double ones too, than
the length and breadth of a pair of indentures[1]? The very convey-
ances of his lands will scarcely lie in this box, and must th' inheritor
himself have no more, ha?[2]

HORATIO   Not a jot more, my lord.   95

HAMLET   Is not parchment made of sheepskins?

HORATIO   Ay, my lord, and of calves' skins too.

HAMLET   They are sheep and calves which seek out assurance in that.
I will speak to this fellow. Whose grave's this, sirrah?

CLOWN   Mine, sir.   100

    [*Sings.*] O, a pit of clay for to be made—

HAMLET   I think it be thine indeed, for thou liest in't.

CLOWN   You lie out on't, sir, and therefore 'tis not yours. For my part,
I do not lie in't, yet it is mine.

HAMLET   Thou dost lie in't, to be in't and say it is thine. 'Tis for the   105
dead, not for the quick[3]; therefore thou liest.

CLOWN   'Tis a quick lie, sir; 'twill away again from me to you.

HAMLET   What man dost thou dig it for?

CLOWN   For no man, sir.

HAMLET   What woman, then?   110

CLOWN   For none neither.

HAMLET   Who is to be buried in't?

CLOWN   One that was a woman, sir; but, rest her soul, she's dead.

HAMLET   How absolute[4] the knave is! We must speak by the card,[5] or
equivocation will undo us. By the Lord, Horatio, this three years I   115

---

4. lacking a lower jaw
5. head
6. skill
7. "Loggets" were small pieces of wood
thrown as part of a game.
8. head
9. end

1. contracts
2. In this speech Hamlet reels off a list
of legal terms relating to property trans-
actions.
3. living
4. precise
5. exactly

have took note of it, the age is grown so picked[6] that the toe of the peasant comes so near the heel of the courtier, he galls his kibe.[7] How long hast thou been a grave-maker?

CLOWN   Of all the days i' th' year, I came to't that day that our last King Hamlet overcame Fortinbras.   120

HAMLET   How long is that since?

CLOWN   Cannot you tell that? Every fool can tell that. It was that very day that young Hamlet was born—he that is mad, and sent into England.

HAMLET   Ay, marry, why was he sent into England?   125

CLOWN   Why, because 'a was mad. 'A shall recover his wits there; or, if 'a do not, 'tis no great matter there.

HAMLET   Why?

CLOWN   'Twill not be seen in him there. There the men are as mad as he.   130

HAMLET   How came he mad?

CLOWN   Very strangely, they say.

HAMLET   How strangely?

CLOWN   Faith, e'en with losing his wits.

HAMLET   Upon what ground?   135

CLOWN   Why, here in Denmark. I have been sexton here, man and boy, thirty years.

HAMLET   How long will a man lie i' th' earth ere he rot?

CLOWN   Faith, if 'a be not rotten before 'a die—as we have many pocky[8] corses now-a-days that will scarce hold the laying in—'a will   140 last you some eight year or nine year. A tanner will last you nine year.

HAMLET   Why he more than another?

CLOWN   Why, sir, his hide is so tanned with his trade that 'a will keep out water a great while; and your water is a sore decayer of your   145 whoreson[9] dead body. Here's a skull now hath lien[1] you i' th' earth three and twenty years.

HAMLET   Whose was it?

CLOWN   A whoreson mad fellow's it was. Whose do you think it was?

HAMLET   Nay, I know not.   150

CLOWN   A pestilence on him for a mad rogue! 'A poured a flagon of Rhenish on my head once. This same skull, sir, was, sir, Yorick's skull, the king's jester.

HAMLET [*takes the skull*]   This?

CLOWN   E'en that.   155

HAMLET   Alas, poor Yorick! I knew him, Horatio—a fellow of infinite jest, of most excellent fancy. He hath bore me on his back a thousand times, and now how abhorred in my imagination it is! My gorge[2] rises at it. Here hung those lips that I have kissed I know not how oft. Where be your gibes now, your gambols, your songs, your flashes   160 of merriment that were wont to set the table on a roar? Not one now to mock your own grinning? Quite chap-fall'n[3]? Now get you to my

6. refined
7. rubs a blister on his heel
8. corrupted by syphilis
9. bastard (not literally)

1. lain
2. throat
3. lacking a lower jaw

lady's chamber, and tell her, let her paint an inch thick, to this favor⁴
she must come. Make her laugh at that. Prithee, Horatio, tell me one
thing.   165

HORATIO   What's that, my lord?

HAMLET   Dost thou think Alexander looked o' this fashion i' th' earth?

HORATIO   E'en so.

HAMLET   And smelt so? Pah!   *Throws down the skull.*

HORATIO   E'en so, my lord.   170

HAMLET   To what base uses we may return, Horatio! Why may not
imagination trace the noble dust of Alexander till 'a find it stopping
a bung-hole?

HORATIO   'Twere to consider too curiously⁵ to consider so.

HAMLET   No, faith, not a jot, but to follow him thither with modesty⁶ 175
enough, and likelihood to lead it. Alexander died, Alexander was
buried, Alexander returneth to dust; the dust is earth; of earth we
make loam; and why of that loam whereto he was converted might
they not stop a beer-barrel?

> Imperious Cæsar, dead and turned to clay,   180
> Might stop a hole to keep the wind away.
> O, that that earth which kept the world in awe
> Should patch a wall t'expel the winter's flaw!⁷

But soft, but soft awhile! Here comes the king,
The queen, the courtiers.

> *Enter* KING, QUEEN, LAERTES, *and the Corse with a* PRIEST *and*
> LORDS *attendant.*

> Who is this they follow?   185
> And with such maiméd⁸ rites? This doth betoken
> The corse they follow did with desperate hand
> Fordo⁹ it own life. 'Twas of some estate.¹
> Couch² we awhile and mark.   *Retires with* HORATIO.

LAERTES   What ceremony else³?   190

HAMLET   That is Laertes, a very noble youth. Mark.

LAERTES   What ceremony else?

PRIEST   Her obsequies have been as far enlarged⁴
As we have warranty. Her death was doubtful,
And but that great command o'ersways the order,⁵   195
She should in ground unsanctified been lodged
Till the last trumpet. For charitable prayers,
Shards, flints, and pebbles, should be thrown on her.
Yet here she is allowed her virgin crants,⁶
Her maiden strewments,⁷ and the bringing home   200
Of bell and burial.

LAERTES   Must there no more be done?

---

4. appearance
5. precisely
6. moderation
7. gusty wind
8. cut short
9. destroy
1. rank

2. conceal ourselves
3. more
4. extended
5. usual rules
6. wreaths
7. flowers strewn on the grave

PRIEST   No more be done.
We should profane the service of the dead
To sing a requiem and such rest to her
As to peace-parted souls.

LAERTES   Lay her i' th' earth,   205
And from her fair and unpolluted flesh
May violets spring! I tell thee, churlish priest,
A minist'ring angel shall my sister be
When thou liest howling.[8]

HAMLET   What, the fair Ophelia!

QUEEN   Sweets to the sweet. Farewell!   *Scatters flowers.* 210
I hoped thou shouldst have been my Hamlet's wife.
I thought thy bride-bed to have decked, sweet maid,
And not have strewed thy grave.

LAERTES   O, treble woe
Fall ten times treble on that cursèd head
Whose wicked deed thy most ingenious sense[9]   215
Deprived thee of! Hold off the earth awhile,
Till I have caught her once more in mine arms.

                              Leaps into the grave.

Now pile your dust upon the quick and dead,
Till of this flat a mountain you have made
T' o'er-top old Pelion or the skyish head   220
Of blue Olympus.[1]

HAMLET [*coming forward*]   What is he whose grief
Bears such an emphasis, whose phrase of sorrow
Conjures[2] the wand'ring stars, and makes them stand
Like wonder-wounded hearers? This is I,
Hamlet the Dane.   225

        HAMLET *leaps into the grave and they grapple.*

LAERTES   The devil take thy soul!

HAMLET   Thou pray'st not well.
I prithee take thy fingers from my throat,
For though I am not splenitive[3] and rash,
Yet have I in me something dangerous,
Which let thy wisdom fear. Hold off thy hand.   230

KING   Pluck them asunder.

QUEEN   Hamlet! Hamlet!

ALL   Gentlemen!

HORATIO   Good my lord, be quiet.

        The ATTENDANTS *part them, and they come out of the grave.*

HAMLET   Why, I will fight with him upon this theme   235
Until my eyelids will no longer wag.[4]

8. in Hell
9. lively mind
1. The rivalry between Laertes and
Hamlet in this scene extends even to their
rhetoric. Pelion and Olympus, mentioned
here by Laertes, and Ossa, mentioned below by Hamlet, were Greek mountains
noted in mythology for their height. Olym-

pus was the reputed home of the gods, and
the other two were piled one on top of the
other by the Giants in an attempt to reach
the top of Olympus and overthrow the gods.
2. casts a spell on
3. hot-tempered
4. move

QUEEN   O my son, what theme?

HAMLET   I loved Ophelia. Forty thousand brothers
Could not with all their quantity of love
Make up my sum. What wilt thou do for her?   240

KING   O, he is mad, Laertes.

QUEEN   For love of God, forbear[5] him.

HAMLET   'Swounds, show me what th'owt do.
Woo't[6] weep, woo't fight, woo't fast, woo't tear thyself,
Woo't drink up eisel,[7] eat a crocodile?   245
I'll do't. Dost come here to whine?
To outface[8] me with leaping in her grave?
Be buried quick with her, and so will I.
And if thou prate of mountains, let them throw
Millions of acres on us, till our ground,   250
Singeing his pate against the burning zone,[9]
Make Ossa like a wart! Nay, an thou'lt mouth,
I'll rant as well as thou.

QUEEN   This is mere madness;
And thus awhile the fit will work on him.
Anon, as patient as the female dove   255
When that her golden couplets[1] are disclosed,
His silence will sit drooping.

HAMLET   Hear you, sir.
What is the reason that you use me thus?
I loved you ever. But it is no matter.
Let Hercules himself do what he may,   260
The cat will mew, and dog will have his day.

KING   I pray thee, good Horatio, wait upon[2] him.

Exeunt HAMLET *and* HORATIO.

[*To* LAERTES.] Strengthen your patience in our last night's speech.
We'll put the matter to the present push.[3]—
Good Gertrude, set some watch over your son.—   265
This grave shall have a living monument.
An hour of quiet shortly shall we see;
Till then in patience our proceeding be.   *Exeunt.*

SCENE 2: *A hall or public room. Enter* HAMLET *and* HORATIO.

HAMLET   So much for this, sir; now shall you see the other.
You do remember all the circumstance?

HORATIO   Remember it, my lord!

HAMLET   Sir, in my heart there was a kind of fighting
That would not let me sleep. Methought I lay   5
Worse than the mutines[4] in the bilboes.[5] Rashly,
And praised be rashness for it—let us know,
Our indiscretion sometime serves us well,

5. bear with   1. pair of eggs
6. will you   2. attend
7. vinegar   3. immediate trial
8. get the best of   4. mutineers
9. sky in the torrid zone   5. stocks

When our deep plots do pall; and that should learn[6] us
There's a divinity that shapes our ends,   10
Rough-hew them how we will—

HORATIO   That is most certain.

HAMLET   Up from my cabin,
My sea-gown scarfed[7] about me, in the dark
Groped I to find out them, had my desire,
Fingered[8] their packet, and in fine[9] withdrew   15
To mine own room again, making so bold,
My fears forgetting manners, to unseal
Their grand commission; where I found, Horatio—
Ah, royal knavery!—an exact[1] command,
Larded[2] with many several sorts of reasons,   20
Importing Denmark's health, and England's too,
With, ho! such bugs and goblins in my life,[3]
That on the supervise,[4] no leisure bated,
No, not to stay the grinding of the axe,
My head should be struck off.

HORATIO   Is't possible?   25

HAMLET   Here's the commission; read it at more leisure.
But wilt thou hear now how I did proceed?

HORATIO   I beseech you.

HAMLET   Being thus benetted[5] round with villainies,
Or I could make a prologue to my brains,   30
They had begun the play. I sat me down,
Devised[6] a new commission, wrote it fair.[7]
I once did hold it, as our statists[8] do,
A baseness to write fair, and labored much
How to forget that learning; but sir, now   35
It did me yeoman's service. Wilt thou know
Th' effect[9] of what I wrote?

HORATIO   Ay, good my lord.

HAMLET   An earnest conjuration from the king,
As England was his faithful tributary,[1]
As love between them like the palm might flourish,   40
As peace should still her wheaten garland wear
And stand a comma 'tween their amities,[2]
And many such like as's of great charge,[3]
That on the view and knowing of these contents,
Without debatement[4] further more or less,   45
He should those bearers put to sudden death,
Not shriving-time allowed.[5]

HORATIO   How was this sealed?

HAMLET   Why, even in that was heaven ordinant,[6]
I had my father's signet in my purse,
Which was the model of that Danish seal,   50
Folded the writ up in the form of th' other,
Subscribed it, gave't th' impression,[7] placed it safely,
The changeling[8] never known. Now, the next day
Was our sea-fight, and what to this was sequent[9]
Thou knowest already.   55
HORATIO   So Guildenstern and Rosencrantz go to't.
HAMLET   Why, man, they did make love to this employment.
They are not near[1] my conscience; their defeat[2]
Does by their own insinuation grow.
'Tis dangerous when the baser nature comes   60
Between the pass[3] and fell[4] incensèd points
Of mighty opposites.
HORATIO   Why, what a king is this!
HAMLET   Does it not, think thee, stand me now upon—
He that hath killed my king and whored my mother,
Popped in between th' election and my hopes,   65
Thrown out his angle[5] for my proper life,
And with such coz'nage[6]—is't not perfect conscience
To quit[7] him with this arm? And is't not to be damned
To let this canker of our nature come
In further evil?   70
HORATIO   It must be shortly known to him from England
What is the issue[8] of the business there.
HAMLET   It will be short[9]; the interim is mine.
And a man's life's no more than to say "one."
But I am very sorry, good Horatio,   75
That to Laertes I forgot myself;
For by the image of my cause I see
The portraiture of his. I'll court his favors.
But sure the bravery[1] of his grief did put me
Into a tow'ring passion.
HORATIO   Peace; who comes here?   80

    Enter OSRIC.

OSRIC   Your lordship is right welcome back to Denmark.
HAMLET   I humbly thank you, sir. [*Aside to* HORATIO.] Dost know
this water-fly?
HORATIO [*aside to* HAMLET]   No, my good lord.
HAMLET [*aside to* HORATIO]   Thy state is the more gracious, for 'tis a   85
vice to know him. He hath much land, and fertile. Let a beast be
lord of beasts, and his crib shall stand at the king's mess. 'Tis a
chough,[2] but as I say, spacious in the possession of dirt.

6. operative
7. of the seal
8. alteration
9. followed
1. do not touch
2. death
3. thrust
4. cruel

5. fishhook
6. trickery
7. repay
8. outcome
9. soon
1. exaggerated display
2. jackdaw

OSRIC   Sweet lord, if your lordship were at leisure, I should impart a
thing to you from his majesty.   90

HAMLET   I will receive it, sir, with all diligence of spirit. Put your
bonnet to his right use. 'Tis for the head.

OSRIC   I thank your lordship, it is very hot.

HAMLET   No, believe me, 'tis very cold; the wind is northerly.

OSRIC   It is indifferent[3] cold, my lord, indeed.   95

HAMLET   But yet methinks it is very sultry and hot for my complexion.[4]

OSRIC   Exceedingly, my lord; it is very sultry, as 'twere—I cannot tell
how. My lord, his majesty bade me signify to you that 'a has laid
a great wager on your head. Sir, this is the matter—   100

HAMLET   I beseech you, remember.

> HAMLET *moves him to put on his hat.*

OSRIC   Nay, good my lord; for my case, in good faith. Sir, here is
newly come to court Laertes; believe me, an absolute[5] gentleman,
full of most excellent differences,[6] of very soft society and great
showing.[7] Indeed, to speak feelingly of him, he is the card or cal-   105
endar[8] of gentry, for you shall find in him the continent[9] of what
part a gentleman would see.

HAMLET   Sir, his definement[1] suffers no perdition in you, though I
know to divide him inventorially[2] would dozy[3] th' arithmetic of
memory, and yet but yaw[4] neither in respect of his quick sail. But   110
in the verity of extolment, I take him to be a soul of great article,[5]
and his infusion[6] of such dearth and rareness as, to make true
diction[7] of him, his semblage[8] is his mirror, and who else would
trace[9] him, his umbrage,[1] nothing more.

OSRIC   Your lordship speaks most infallibly of him.   115

HAMLET   The concernancy,[2] sir? Why do we wrap the gentleman in
our more rawer breath?[3]

OSRIC   Sir?

HORATIO   Is't not possible to understand in another tongue? You will
to't, sir, really.   120

HAMLET   What imports the nomination[4] of this gentleman?

OSRIC   Of Laertes?

HORATIO [*aside*]   His purse is empty already. All's golden words are
spent.

HAMLET   Of him, sir.   125

OSRIC   I know you are not ignorant—

HAMLET   I would you did, sir; yet, in faith, if you did, it would not
much approve me. Well, sir.

OSRIC   You are not ignorant of what excellence Laertes is—

---

3. moderately
4. temperament
5. perfect
6. qualities
7. good manners
8. measure
9. sum total
1. description
2. examine bit by bit
3. daze

4. steer wildly
5. scope
6. nature
7. telling
8. rival
9. keep pace with
1. shadow
2. meaning
3. cruder words
4. naming

HAMLET   I dare not confess that, lest I should compare[5] with him in   130
excellence; but to know a man well were to know himself.

OSRIC   I mean, sir, for his weapon; but in the imputation[6] laid on him
by them, in his meed he's unfellowed.[7]

HAMLET   What's his weapon?

OSRIC   Rapier and dagger.   135

HAMLET   That's two of his weapons—but well.

OSRIC   The king, sir, hath wagered with him six Barbary horses,
against the which he has impawned,[8] as I take it, six French rapiers
and poniards, with their assigns,[9] as girdle, hangers, and so. Three
of the carriages, in faith, are very dear to fancy,[1] very responsive to   140
the hilts, most delicate[2] carriages, and of very liberal conceit.[3]

HAMLET   What call you the carriages?

HORATIO [*aside to* HAMLET] I knew you must be edified by the
margent[4] ere you had done.

OSRIC   The carriages, sir, are the hangers.   145

HAMLET   The phrase would be more germane to the matter if we
could carry a cannon by our sides. I would it might be hangers till
then. But on! Six Barbary horses against six French swords, their
assigns, and three liberal conceited carriages; that's the French bet
against the Danish. Why is this all impawned, as you call it?   150

OSRIC   The king, sir, hath laid, sir, that in a dozen passes between
yourself and him he shall not exceed you three hits; he hath laid on
twelve for nine, and it would come to immediate trial if your lordship would vouchsafe the answer.

HAMLET   How if I answer no?   155

OSRIC   I mean, my lord, the opposition of your person in trial.

HAMLET   Sir, I will walk here in the hall. If it please his majesty, it is
the breathing time[5] of day with me. Let the foils be brought, the
gentleman willing, and the king hold his purpose; I will win for
him an I can. If not, I will gain nothing but my shame and the   160
odd hits.

OSRIC   Shall I deliver you so?

HAMLET   To this effect, sir, after what flourish your nature will.

OSRIC   I commend my duty to your lordship.

HAMLET   Yours, yours. [*Exit* OSRIC.] He does well to commend it   165
himself; there are no tongues else for's turn.

HORATIO   This lapwing runs away with the shell on his head.[6]

HAMLET   'A did comply,[7] sir, with his dug[8] before 'a sucked it. Thus
has he, and many more of the same bevy that I know the drossy age
dotes on, only got the tune of the time; and out of an habit of en-   170
counter, a kind of yesty[9] collection which carries them through and
through the most fanned and winnowed opinions; and do but blow
them to their trial, the bubbles are out.

---

5. i.e., compare myself
6. reputation
7. unequaled in his excellence
8. staked
9. appurtenances
1. finely designed
2. well adjusted
3. elegant design
4. marginal gloss

5. time for exercise
6. The lapwing was thought to be so precocious that it could run immediately after being hatched, even as here with bits of the shell still on its head.
7. deal formally
8. mother's breast
9. yeasty

Enter a LORD.

LORD   My lord, his majesty commended him to you by young Osric, who brings back to him that you attend[1] him in the hall. He sends 175 to know if your pleasure hold to play with Laertes, or that you will take longer time.

HAMLET   I am constant to my purposes; they follow the king's pleasure. If his fitness speaks, mine is ready; now or whensoever, provided I be so able as now.   180

LORD   The king and queen and all are coming down.

HAMLET   In happy time.

LORD   The queen desires you to use some gentle entertainment[2] to Laertes before you fall to play.

HAMLET   She well instructs me.   *Exit* LORD. 185

HORATIO   You will lose this wager, my lord.

HAMLET   I do not think so. Since he went into France I have been in continual practice. I shall win at the odds. But thou wouldst not think how ill[3] all's here about my heart. But it is no matter.

HORATIO   Nay, good my lord—   190

HAMLET   It is but foolery, but it is such a kind of gaingiving[4] as would perhaps trouble a woman.

HORATIO   If your mind dislike anything, obey it. I will forestall their repair[5] hither, and say you are not fit.

HAMLET   Not a whit, we defy augury. There is special providence in 195 the fall of a sparrow. If it be now, 'tis not to come; if it be not to come, it will be now; if it be not now, yet it will come. The readiness is all. Since no man of aught he leaves knows, what is't to leave betimes? Let be.

A table prepared. Enter TRUMPETS, DRUMS, *and* OFFICERS *with cushions;* KING, QUEEN, OSRIC *and* ATTENDANTS *with foils, daggers, and* LAERTES.

KING   Come, Hamlet, come and take this hand from me.   200

The KING *puts* LAERTES' *hand into* HAMLET'S.

HAMLET   Give me your pardon, sir. I have done you wrong,
But pardon 't as you are a gentleman.
This presence[6] knows, and you must needs have heard,
How I am punished with a sore distraction.
What I have done   205
That might your nature, honor, and exception,[7]
Roughly awake, I here proclaim was madness.
Was 't Hamlet wronged Laertes? Never Hamlet.
If Hamlet from himself be ta'en away,
And when he's not himself does wrong Laertes,   210
Then Hamlet does it not, Hamlet denies it.
Who does it then? His madness. If't be so,

---

1. await
2. cordiality
3. uneasy
4. misgiving

5. coming
6. company
7. resentment

Hamlet is of the faction that is wronged;
His madness is poor Hamlet's enemy.
Sir, in this audience, 215
Let my disclaiming from[8] a purposed evil
Free[9] me so far in your most generous thoughts
That I have shot my arrow o'er the house
And hurt my brother.

LAERTES   I am satisfied in nature,
Whose motive in this case should stir me most 220
To my revenge. But in my terms of honor
I stand aloof, and will no reconcilement
Till by some elder masters of known honor
I have a voice[1] and precedent of peace
To keep my name ungored.[2] But till that time 225
I do receive your offered love like love,
And will not wrong it.

HAMLET   I embrace it freely,
And will this brother's wager frankly[3] play.
Give us the foils.

LAERTES   Come, one for me.

HAMLET   I'll be your foil, Laertes. In mine ignorance 230
Your skill shall, like a star i' th' darkest night,
Stick fiery off[4] indeed.

LAERTES   You mock me, sir.

HAMLET   No, by this hand.

KING   Give them the foils, young Osric. Cousin Hamlet,
You know the wager?

HAMLET   Very well, my lord; 235
Your Grace has laid the odds o' th' weaker side.

KING   I do not fear it, I have seen you both;
But since he is bettered,[5] we have therefore odds.

LAERTES   This is too heavy; let me see another.

HAMLET   This likes[6] me well. These foils have all a[7] length? 240

They prepare to play.

OSRIC   Ay, my good lord.

KING   Set me the stoups of wine upon that table.
If Hamlet give the first or second hit,
Or quit in answer of[8] the third exchange,
Let all the battlements their ordnance fire. 245
The king shall drink to Hamlet's better breath,
And in the cup an union[9] shall he throw,
Richer than that which four successive kings
In Denmark's crown have worn. Give me the cups,
And let the kettle[1] to the trumpet speak, 250
The trumpet to the cannoneer without,

8. denying of
9. absolve
1. authority
2. unshamed
3. without rancor
4. shine brightly

5. reported better
6. suits
7. the same
8. repay
9. pearl
1. kettledrum

The cannons to the heavens, the heaven to earth,
"Now the king drinks to Hamlet." Come, begin—

Trumpets the while.

And you, the judges, bear a wary eye.
HAMLET   Come on, sir.
LAERTES   Come, my lord.   *They play.*
HAMLET   One.
LAERTES   No.
HAMLET   Judgment?   255
OSRIC   A hit, a very palpable hit.

Drums, trumpets, and shot. Flourish; a piece goes off.

LAERTES   Well, again.
KING   Stay, give me drink. Hamlet, this pearl is thine.
Here's to thy health. Give him the cup.
HAMLET   I'll play this bout first; set it by awhile.   260
Come.   *They play.*
Another hit; what say you?
LAERTES   I do confess't.
KING   Our son shall win.
QUEEN   He's fat,[2] and scant of breath.
Here, Hamlet, take my napkin, rub thy brows.   265
The queen carouses to thy fortune, Hamlet.
HAMLET   Good madam!
KING   Gertrude, do not drink.
QUEEN   I will, my lord; I pray you pardon me.
KING [*aside*]   It is the poisoned cup; it is too late.   270
HAMLET   I dare not drink yet, madam; by and by.
QUEEN   Come, let me wipe thy face.
LAERTES   My lord, I'll hit him now.
KING   I do not think't.
LAERTES [*aside*]   And yet it is almost against my conscience.
HAMLET   Come, for the third, Laertes. You do but dally.   275
I pray you pass[3] with your best violence;
I am afeard you make a wanton of me.[4]
LAERTES   Say you so? Come on.   *They play.*
OSRIC   Nothing, neither way.
LAERTES   Have at you now!   280

LAERTES *wounds* HAMLET: *then, in scuffling, they change*
rapiers, and HAMLET *wounds* LAERTES.

KING   Part them. They are incensed.
HAMLET   Nay, come again.   *The* QUEEN *falls.*
OSRIC   Look to the queen there, ho!
HORATIO   They bleed on both sides. How is it, my lord?

2. out of shape   4. trifle with me
3. attack

OSRIC   How is't, Laertes?   285
LAERTES   Why, as a woodcock to mine own springe,[5] Osric.
    I am justly killed with mine own treachery.
HAMLET   How does the queen?
KING   She swoons to see them bleed.
QUEEN   No, no, the drink, the drink! O my dear Hamlet!
    The drink, the drink! I am poisoned.   *Dies.* 290
HAMLET   O, villainy! Ho! let the door be locked.
    Treachery! seek it out.
LAERTES   It is here, Hamlet. Hamlet, thou art slain;
    No med'cine in the world can do thee good.
    In thee there is not half an hour's life.   295
    The treacherous instrument is in thy hand,
    Unbated[6] and envenomed. The foul practice
    Hath turned itself on me. Lo, here I lie,
    Never to rise again. Thy mother's poisoned.
    I can no more. The king, the king's to blame.   300
HAMLET   The point envenomed too?
    Then, venom, to thy work.   *Hurts the* KING.
ALL   Treason! treason!
KING   O, yet defend me, friends. I am but hurt.[7]
HAMLET   Here, thou incestuous, murd'rous, damnéd Dane,   305
    Drink off this potion. Is thy union here?
    Follow my mother.   *The* KING *dies.*
LAERTES   He is justly served.
    It is a poison tempered[8] by himself.
    Exchange forgiveness with me, noble Hamlet.
    Mine and my father's death come not upon thee,   310
    Nor thine on me!   *Dies.*
HAMLET   Heaven make thee free of[9] it! I follow thee.
    I am dead, Horatio. Wretched queen, adieu!
    You that look pale and tremble at this chance,[1]
    That are but mutes or audience to this act,   315
    Had I but time, as this fell sergeant Death
    Is strict in his arrest,[2] O, I could tell you—
    But let it be. Horatio, I am dead:
    Thou livest; report me and my cause aright
    To the unsatisfied.[3]
HORATIO   Never believe it.   320
    I am more an antique Roman than a Dane.
    Here's yet some liquor left.
HAMLET   As th'art a man,
    Give me the cup. Let go. By heaven, I'll ha't.
    O God, Horatio, what a wounded name,
    Things standing thus unknown, shall live behind me!   325
    If thou didst ever hold me in thy heart,
    Absent thee from felicity awhile,

5. snare   9. forgive
6. unblunted   1. circumstance
7. wounded   2. summons to court
8. mixed   3. uninformed

And in this harsh world draw thy breath in pain,
To tell my story.   *A march afar off.*
          What warlike noise is this?

OSRIC Young Fortinbras, with conquest come from Poland,   330
To th' ambassadors of England gives
This warlike volley.[4]

HAMLET   O, I die, Horatio!
The potent poison quite o'er-crows[5] my spirit.
I cannot live to hear the news from England,
But I do prophesy th' election lights   335
On Fortinbras. He has my dying voice.[6]
So tell him, with th' occurrents,[7] more and less,
Which have solicited[8]—the rest is silence.   *Dies.*

HORATIO Now cracks a noble heart. Good night, sweet prince,
And flights of angels sing thee to thy rest!   *March within.* 340
Why does the drum come hither?

      Enter FORTINBRAS, *with the* AMBASSADORS *and with drum,
colors, and* ATTENDANTS.

FORTINBRAS Where is this sight?

HORATIO   What is it you would see?
If aught of woe or wonder, cease your search.

FORTINBRAS This quarry cries on havoc.[9] O proud death,
What feast is toward[1] in thine eternal cell   345
That thou so many princes at a shot
So bloodily hast struck?

AMBASSADORS   The sight is dismal;
And our affairs from England come too late.
The ears are senseless[2] that should give us hearing
To tell him his commandment is fulfilled,   350
That Rosencrantz and Guildenstern are dead.
Where should we have our thanks?

HORATIO   Not from his mouth,
Had it th' ability of life to thank you.
He never gave commandment for their death.
But since, so jump[3] upon this bloody question,   355
You from the Polack wars, and you from England,
Are here arrived, give orders that these bodies
High on a stage be placed to the view,
And let me speak to th' yet unknowing world
How these things came about. So shall you hear   360
Of carnal, bloody, and unnatural acts;

---

4. The staging presents some difficulties
here. If Osric is not clairvoyant, he must
have left the stage at some point and returned. One possibility is that he might
have left to carry out Hamlet's order to
lock the door (line 291) and returned
when the sound of the distant march is
heard.
5. overcomes

6. support
7. circumstances
8. brought about this scene
9. The game killed in the hunt proclaims a slaughter.
1. in preparation
2. without sense of hearing
3. exactly

Of accidental judgments, casual[4] slaughters;
Of deaths put on by cunning and forced cause;
And, in this upshot,[5] purposes mistook
Fall'n on th' inventors' heads. All this can I   365
Truly deliver.
FORTINBRAS   Let us haste to hear it,
And call the noblest to the audience.[6]
For me, with sorrow I embrace my fortune.
I have some rights of memory[7] in this kingdom,
Which now to claim my vantage[8] doth invite me.   370
HORATIO   Of that I shall have also cause to speak,
And from his mouth whose voice will draw on more.
But let this same be presently performed,
Even while men's minds are wild, lest more mischance
On plots and errors happen.
FORTINBRAS   Let four captains   375
Bear Hamlet like a soldier to the stage,
For he was likely, had he been put on,[9]
To have proved most royal; and for his passage
The soldier's music and the rite of war
Speak loudly for him.   380
Take up the bodies. Such a sight as this
Becomes the field, but here shows much amiss.
Go, bid the soldiers shoot.

Exeunt marching. A peal of ordnance shot off.

ca. 1600

4. brought about by apparent accident   7. succession
5. result   8. position
6. hearing   9. elected king

Reading and Performance

3 PAGE, STAGE, AND SCREEN

So far we have examined drama as a structure built on reversal, intended for presentation on a stage before an audience. But a play has a second life, for even a mime play can be written out in words and read. Although some plays may never be performed and some never printed, the two distinct ways of looking at a play exist. Let us examine, then, some approaches by which a play can be treated purely as a work of literature.

The selection and arrangement of the plot is an important part of any writer's task, and the perfectly paralleled ironies in *Oedipus Tyrannus* provide its readers with an important way of approaching the play. Oedipus opens the action by proclaiming that he will banish the criminal responsible for the plagues upon Thebes, only to discover at play's end that to do so means exiling himself. Oedipus further learns that by fleeing his adoptive parents in Corinth to avoid fulfilling a prophecy, he has in fact murdered his real father and married his mother as foreordained by the gods. And when Oedipus spurns the words of the blind seer Teiresias, Teiresias observes that his infirmity is but physical while Oedipus has eyes but cannot see his own destruction. When Oedipus finally does "see" the truth, he blinds himself. As in the investigation of a detective who is discovered to be the criminal he has sought, all of Oedipus's words and deeds are ironically reversed as the plot unfolds.

Such parallel structures are only one way of achieving thematic resonance through plotting. In *Death of a Salesman* Willy Loman searches, like Oedipus, for himself. But the unfolding story of Willy's life moves backward and forward through time in an interpolated structure in which Willy experiences the past as if it were the present, dividing conversations between friends inhabiting his grim present and those from an idealized past. These concurrent "plots"—the stories of Willy before and after the Depression—proceed chronologically as revealed to the reader through Willy's consciousness.

Another common literary device that functions in drama is that of a recurring pattern of images. Such images often make tangible and significant connections as in the "seeing" motif of *Oedipus Tyrannus* where the concepts of both sight and knowledge are contained in this single image. In *Hamlet,* images dealing with the body are used as a metaphor of the state as the body politic, as when the Ghost tells Hamlet that his death was falsely reported: "So the whole ear of Denmark / Is by a forged process of my death / Rankly abused." Even in *Death of a Salesman,* a play whose domestic setting may seem free of such complexity, Willy's fascination with Ben's triumph in the "jungle" and the conspiratorial malfunctions of machinery—

refrigerators, cars, and run-amok wire recorders—indicate that Miller, like Sophocles and Shakespeare, is providing us with clues to help in our understanding of the play.

Some images may also be used symbolically; that is, some images may have connotations too diverse or profound to accept a single association. "Rosebud," the missing jigsaw piece of Kane's life that is the object of the newsreel reporter's search in *Citizen Kane,* is a good example. Does it represent, as Bernstein suggests, something Kane lost? Or does it stand more specifically for lost maternal love, thus explaining in some way Kane's strange infatuation with Susan Alexander on a night he might have seen "Rosebud" in the Western Manhattan Warehouse? A careful examination of the screenplay will reveal many symbolic uses of the "Rosebud" image that may provide us with insights into Charles Foster Kane's character.

Language, too, can be used to create certain effects. Some playwrights, such as Harold Pinter, render speech quite realistically. On the other hand, no crowd ever talked like the chorus in *Oedipus Tyrannus,* and *The Sacrifice of Isaac* is versified in tight rhetorical patterns. Willy Loman uses phrases such as "well liked" and "the woods are burning" as verbal crutches, and similar characteristic speech patterns can be seen in Hamlet's habit of repeating certain words and Loevborg's intimate use of Hedda's given name. The playwright makes use of the devices of language to establish something about the nature of the play and to set apart certain characters.

A play on the stage is different from a play on the page, not only because a stage production is transient, but also because every performance is a unique expression of a collaborative effort. Actors must remember hundreds of lines and perform movements on stage at certain times; the stagehands must change sets and install props between scenes; light and sound effects must occur on certain visual and aural cues. In any of these areas a single error—a forgotten piece of dialogue or a misplaced prop—guarantees that a given performance will be unique. Nor are any two audiences the same, and the character of an audience inevitably affects the performance. A warm, responsive audience will bring out the best in the performers, as any actor will tell you, while a crowd's cold indifference often results in a tepid or stiff production. For these reasons, no staged realization of a play can ever duplicate another.

Although the actors are the most visible collaborators in a performance, key decisions also rest in the hands of the producer, director, set designer, and others. These decisions may be subtle and inconsequential—a piece of humorous stage business may be given to a minor character to brighten a role—or they may present a major interpretive problem. One such decision must be made in the third act of *Hamlet.* Hamlet has a troupe of traveling players stage "The Murder of Gonzago" before the court in hopes of ascertaining his uncle Claudius's guilt or innocence. When the usurper in this play-within-the-play pours poison into the ear of the sleeping Gonzago, Claudius suddenly rises, stopping the performance, calls out, "Give me some light. Away!" and exits with his entourage. The director must here make a crucial decision. Should Claudius rise in obvious fright, call panic-stricken for lights, and bolt from the room, followed by his confused queen and retainers? Or should Claudius maintain his composure and perform this set of actions calmly and deliberately, thus emphasizing his public identity of King of the Danes over his hidden identity of usurper and murderer? The former version must confirm Hamlet's suspicions, making his later inaction more puzzling, while the latter makes his subsequent indecision seem more natural to the audience.

In preparing any performance of a play, the director and others make many such choices that affect the audience's understanding of the play. In the opening scene of *Hedda Gabler*, for example, an apparently insignificant costume decision can affect the audience's judgment. Late in the scene Hedda intentionally misidentifies Aunt Julia's hat as one belonging to Bertha, the maid, calling it "her old hat lying on the chair." Julia, insulted, responds that the hat is hers and is brand new as well. The stage directions indicate only that Aunt Julia dresses simply in gray outdoor clothes and Bertha is rather "simple and rustic-looking." Clearly, however, the hat's appearance— whether it seems new and stylish, tastefully plain, or gaudily tacky— will in some way measure the cruel aloofness with which Hedda treats her husband's aunt. This subtle choice shapes our understanding of the play and its heroine.

In some cases the playwright will provide the information that directs the visual and gestural effects on the stage. In *Hamlet*, Act 1, Scene 2, the Queen tells Hamlet to "cast thy night'd color off." This makes it clear that Hamlet is dressed in black and that the rest of the court is not. The speech that gives the reader this information occurs late in the scene, but the audience in the theater has long been aware that, by his costume, Hamlet has set himself apart from the other members of the court, calling attention to himself, to his father's death, and to the fact that Claudius has come between him and the succession to the throne. Throughout Claudius's opening speech and remarks to Laertes, the audience has been aware of Hamlet's brooding presence, even though the words have not been able to inform the reader. The reader must tax his or her imagination to get anything of the same visual effect.

Some visual effects are clearly indicated in the stage directions but are certainly less effective when witnessed only on the page and not in performance. Ibsen's description of the set of *Hedda Gabler* calls for "the portrait of a handsome old man in general's uniform" to hang above the drawing-room sofa. From this vantage point, Hedda's late father hovers over the action of the entire play, and the Tesmans' references to General Gabler, as well as the clear influence he has had in shaping Hedda's personality and desires, take on a new resonance for the audience. For the reader, however, a keen visual memory is required if in later acts he or she is to recall this telling detail, so vivid in the theater. Similarly, Willy Loman's nighttime planting at the end of *Death of a Salesman* is colored by the set design, which demands that "we see a solid vault of apartment houses around the small, fragile-seeming house." The audience must be struck by the ominous and claustrophobic atmosphere, which may be easily forgotten by the reader until later in the scene, when Willy complains to Biff, "You can't see nothing out here! They boxed in the whole goddamn neighborhood."

At its best drama establishes a tension between language and stage effects that produces a supreme dramatic event. This can be seen particularly in *Death of a Salesman,* where Willy's flood of memories often spills over into conversations and card games. Early in Act 1, Willy has trouble juggling his fantasy past and present reality as he tries to play casino with Charley and reflect with Ben at the same time:

BEN   How are you all?
WILLY   [*taking a pot, smiling*]   Fine, fine.
CHARLEY   Pretty sharp tonight.
BEN   Is Mother living with you?
WILLY   No, she died a long time ago.
CHARLEY   Who?

Here Willy is visibly and audibly torn between his two worlds. And when later in the play Biff insists that they "lay it on the line"—confront the world of fiction with "the facts"—and literally lays the rubber hose on the table, language and gesture come together in a moment of dramatic crisis. It is on such moments that the action of a play will turn; at such moments, drama possesses a power over its audience that we as readers can only attempt to realize imaginatively.

Unlike a play on the stage, a motion picture does exist as a single "performance" that can be analyzed much as we might a poem or novel. However, a feature film also represents a collaborative realization of a screenplay, and since our understanding of many films may be founded on imperfect and fleeting memories (having a print and projector on hand to settle uncertain issues is almost impossible), the script of a film often proves to be an invaluable critical tool. It may also, as in the case with the shooting script of a film like *Citizen Kane,* be worthy of examination as a literary work in its own right. For our purposes it is important to consider those elements involved in realizing a film from its script as well as the strategies required of us to "read a film" in a script.

No matter how a scene is written, the way in which that scene is shot, or captured on film by the camera, does much to affect the way we will understand what we see. The camera functions in much the same way as the narrator of a work of fiction might. It can emphasize the slightest nuance of characterization, which an actor on stage would be hard pressed to convey to the audience in the balcony. It can also focus our attention on objects or actions in a way impossible on the stage, where speech and gesture alone can do so. In scene 94 of *Kane,* for instance, the script calls only for the camera to angle "across the bed and Susan's form towards the door, from the other side of which come loud knocking." In the film a bottle of sleeping pills and glass of water fill the extreme foreground of this shot, almost rendering Susan's silhouetted form—but not her labored breathing—unrecognizable. This detail may not be a telling one, since it is soon clear that she has attempted suicide, but it is certainly compelling. A camera's position can also hide information from a film audience. When Norman Bates (Tony Perkins) wheels his mother to the basement of their home in Alfred Hitchcock's *Psycho*, the scene is shot directly downwards from the ceiling. This odd, bird's-eye perspective allows Hitchcock to maintain the illusion that Norman's mother may indeed be Janet Leigh's murderer, when if she were shot in a close-up, as she is at the end of the film, we would see this was clearly impossible. In *Kane* such manipulation of the camera becomes a thematic component in the film's realization of the script. The audience's perspective is routinely from over the shoulder of Thompson, the inquiring newsreel reporter, whose face we in fact never see. And the camera itself is always "moving in," peering so voyeuristically into Kane's affairs that we often have doors closed in our face to end a shot.

Certain other effects can be achieved during the production of a film that can only be hinted at in the shooting script. It is a rare film that does not have a musical score, yet the score is often composed only after the final edited version of the film is complete. A score may represent varying degrees of collaboration by writer, producer, director, and composer, particularly since its effect upon the audience may be so profound: anyone who has seen *Jaws* can attest to the power of a score. Special effects using models and superimposed images can also be employed even when not demanded by the script. Scene 73 of the *Kane* screenplay calls for the camera to "[continue] on up with the curtain the full height of the proscenium arch and then on up into the gridiron," where we see two stagehands offer their critical opinion of Susan's singing. In the film, what appears to be a dazzlingly long tracking shot that moves to the very ceiling of the opera house is really three separate shots, the middle one being a "miniature" sandwiched between actual shots of the proscenium arch and the gridiron that the workers stand on.

Reading a screenplay would seem to be only the crudest approximation of actually viewing a film. However, the powerfully visceral nature of the film experience itself often makes it difficult for us to understand why a film affects us as strongly as it does. The rapid play of the images across the screen contributes to this: a single shot often appears for but a few seconds, and a shot several minutes in length may seem almost unending. "Reading" a film allows us to examine at our own pace the effects the script's author seeks to create. The marvelous breakfast sequence in *Citizen Kane* (Scenes 52–58) may entrance the film audience with its use of dissolves or with its setting and makeup effects. By the scene's end the viewer knows he has seen Kane's marriage disintegrating over a period of time, but much of the dialogue and verbal nuance may have been missed or forgotten because of the scene's strong visual appeal. Kane's observation that Emily's "only corespondent is the 'Inquirer' " is, moreover, dated for the reader (1902), and reading the *Kane* screenplay helps us to develop a clearer sense of chronology in a film that moves about in time a great deal.

To read a film requires a strong visual imagination coupled with the awareness that a camera's point of view can produce a range of effects only hinted at in a screenplay's stage directions. What the reader loses in a film's camera-work, editing, and sheer visual impact may, finally, be irrecoverable from the text of a screenplay. But the reader willing to examine a script with an eye toward how a scene can be realized, willing to invest in the screenplay his or her familiarity with other films and responses to the techniques they employ, will discover that in a sense he or she has become that script's director. It is this reader who can realize the potential in film as an art form and in the screenplay as a literary work.

ARTHUR MILLER

Death of a Salesman

C H A R A C T E R S

WILLY LOMAN
LINDA
BIFF
HAPPY
BERNARD
THE WOMAN
CHARLEY

UNCLE BEN
HOWARD WAGNER
JENNY
STANLEY
MISS FORSYTHE (GIRL)
LETTA

Act 1

*A melody is heard, played upon a flute. It is small and fine, telling
of grass and trees and the horizon. The curtain rises.*

*Before us is the Salesman's house. We are aware of towering,
angular shapes behind it, surrounding it on all sides. Only the blue
light of the sky falls upon the house and forestage; the surrounding
area shows an angry glow of orange. As more light appears, we see
a solid vault of apartment houses around the small, fragile-seeming
home. An air of the dream clings to the place, a dream rising out of
reality. The kitchen at center seems actual enough, for there is a
kitchen table with three chairs, and a refrigerator. But no other
fixtures are seen. At the back of the kitchen there is a draped entrance, which leads to the living room. To the right of the kitchen,
on a level raised two feet, is a bedroom furnished only with a brass
bedstead and a straight chair. On a shelf over the bed a silver
athletic trophy stands. A window opens onto the apartment house
at the side.*

*Behind the kitchen, on a level raised six and a half feet, is the
boys' bedroom, at present barely visible. Two beds are dimly seen,
and at the back of the room a dormer window. (This bedroom is
above the unseen living room.) At the left a stairway curves up to
it from the kitchen.*

*The entire setting is wholly or, in some places, partially trans-
parent. The roof-line of the house is one-dimensional; under and
over it we see the apartment buildings. Before the house lies an
apron, curving beyond the forestage into the orchestra. This forward
area serves as the back yard as well as the locale of all WILLY's
imaginings and of his city scenes. Whenever the action is in the
present the actors observe the imaginary wall-lines, entering the
house only through its door at the left. But in the scenes of the
past these boundaries are broken, and characters enter or leave a
room by stepping "through" a wall onto the forestage.*

From the right, WILLY LOMAN, *the Salesman, enters, carrying two large sample cases. The flute plays on. He hears but is not aware of it. He is past sixty years of age, dressed quietly. Even as he crosses the stage to the doorway of the house, his exhaustion is apparent. He unlocks the door, comes into the kitchen, and thankfully lets his burden down, feeling the soreness of his palms. A word-sigh escapes his lips—it might be "Oh, boy, oh, boy." He closes the door, then carries his cases out into the living-room, through the draped kitchen doorway.*

LINDA, *his wife, has stirred in her bed at the right. She gets out and puts on a robe, listening. Most often jovial, she has developed an iron repression of her exceptions to* WILLY's *behavior—she more than loves him, she admires him, as though his mercurial nature, his temper, his massive dreams and little cruelties, served her only as sharp reminders of the turbulent longings within him, longings which she shares but lacks the temperament to utter and follow to their end.*

LINDA [*hearing* WILLY *outside the bedroom, calls with some trepidation*] Willy!

WILLY   It's all right. I came back.

LINDA   Why? What happened? [*Slight pause*]. Did something happen, Willy?

WILLY   No, nothing happened.

LINDA   You didn't smash the car, did you?

WILLY [*with casual irritation*]   I said nothing happened. Didn't you hear me?

LINDA   Don't you feel well?

WILLY   I'm tired to the death. [*The flute has faded away. He sits on the bed beside her, a little numb.*] I couldn't make it. I just couldn't make it, Linda.

LINDA [*very carefully, delicately*]   Where were you all day? You look terrible.

WILLY   I got as far as a little above Yonkers. I stopped for a cup of coffee. Maybe it was the coffee.

LINDA   What?

WILLY [*after a pause*]   I suddenly couldn't drive any more. The car kept going off onto the shoulder, y'know?

LINDA [*helpfully*]   Oh. Maybe it was the steering again. I don't think Angelo knows the Studebaker.

WILLY   No, it's me, it's me. Suddenly I realize I'm goin' sixty miles an hour and I don't remember the last five minutes. I'm—I can't seem to—keep my mind to it.

LINDA   Maybe it's your glasses. You never went for your new glasses.

WILLY   No, I see everything. I came back ten miles an hour. It took me nearly four hours from Yonkers.

LINDA [*resigned*]   Well, you'll just have to take a rest, Willy, you can't continue this way.

WILLY   I just got back from Florida.

LINDA   But you didn't rest your mind. Your mind is overactive, and the mind is what counts, dear.

WILLY   I'll start out in the morning. Maybe I'll feel better in the morning. [*She is taking off his shoes.*] These goddam arch supports are killing me.

LINDA   Take an aspirin. Should I get you an aspirin? It'll soothe you.

WILLY [*with wonder*]   I was driving along, you understand? And I was fine. I was even observing the scenery. You can imagine, me looking at scenery, on the road every week of my life. But it's so beautiful up there, Linda, the trees are so thick, and the sun is warm. I opened the windshield and just let the warm air bathe over me. And then all of a sudden I'm goin' off the road! I'm tellin' ya, I absolutely forgot I was driving. If I'd've gone the other way over the white line I might've killed somebody. So I went on again—and five minutes later I'm dreamin' again, and I nearly—[*He presses two fingers against his eyes.*] I have such thoughts, I have such strange thoughts.

LINDA   Willy, dear. Talk to them again. There's no reason why you can't work in New York.

WILLY   They don't need me in New York. I'm the New England man. I'm vital in New England.

LINDA   But you're sixty years old. They can't expect you to keep traveling every week.

WILLY   I'll have to send a wire to Portland. I'm supposed to see Brown and Morrison tomorrow morning at ten o'clock to show the line. Goddammit, I could sell them! [*He starts putting on his jacket.*]

LINDA [*taking the jacket from him*]   Why don't you go down to the place tomorrow and tell Howard you've simply got to work in New York? You're too accommodating, dear.

WILLY   If old man Wagner was alive I'd a been in charge of New York now! That man was a prince, he was a masterful man. But that boy of his, that Howard, he don't appreciate. When I went north the first time, the Wagner Company didn't know where New England was!

LINDA   Why don't you tell those things to Howard, dear?

WILLY [*encouraged*]   I will, I definitely will. Is there any cheese?

LINDA   I'll make you a sandwich.

WILLY   No, go to sleep. I'll take some milk. I'll be up right away. The boys in?

LINDA   They're sleeping. Happy took Biff on a date tonight.

WILLY [*interested*]   That so?

LINDA   It was so nice to see them shaving together, one behind the other, in the bathroom. And going out together. You notice? The whole house smells of shaving lotion.

WILLY   Figure it out. Work a lifetime to pay off a house. You finally own it, and there's nobody to live in it.

LINDA   Well, dear, life is a casting off. It's always that way.

WILLY   No, no, some people—some people accomplish something. Did Biff say anything after I went this morning?

LINDA   You shouldn't have criticized him, Willy, especially after he just got off the train. You mustn't lose your temper with him.

WILLY   When the hell did I lose my temper? I simply asked him if he was making any money. Is that a criticism?

LINDA   But, dear, how could he make any money?

WILLY   [*worried and angered*] There's such an undercurrent in him. He became a moody man. Did he apologize when I left this morning?

LINDA   He was crestfallen, Willy. You know how he admires you. I think if he finds himself, then you'll both be happier and not fight any more.

WILLY   How can he find himself on a farm? Is that a life? A farm-hand? In the beginning, when he was young, I thought, well, a young man, it's good for him to tramp around, take a lot of different jobs. But it's more than ten years now and he has yet to make thirty-five dollars a week!

LINDA   He's finding himself, Willy.

WILLY   Not finding yourself at the age of thirty-four is a disgrace!

LINDA   Shh!

WILLY   The trouble is he's lazy, goddammit!

LINDA   Willy, please!

WILLY   Biff is a lazy bum!

LINDA   They're sleeping. Get something to eat. Go on down.

WILLY   Why did he come home? I would like to know what brought him home.

LINDA   I don't know. I think he's still lost, Willy. I think he's very lost.

WILLY   Biff Loman is lost. In the greatest country in the world a young man with such—personal attractiveness, gets lost. And such a hard worker. There's one thing about Biff—he's not lazy.

LINDA   Never.

WILLY   [*with pity and resolve*] I'll see him in the morning; I'll have a nice talk with him. I'll get him a job selling. He could be big in no time. My God! Remember how they used to follow him around in high school? When he smiled at one of them their faces lit up. When he walked down the street . . . [*He loses himself in reminiscences.*]

LINDA   [*trying to bring him out of it*] Willy, dear, I got a new kind of American-type cheese today. It's whipped.

WILLY   Why do you get American when I like Swiss?

LINDA   I just thought you'd like a change—

WILLY   I don't want a change! I want Swiss cheese. Why am I always being contradicted?

LINDA   [*with a covering laugh*] I thought it would be a surprise.

WILLY   Why don't you open a window in here, for God's sake?

LINDA   [*with infinite patience*] They're all open, dear.

WILLY   The way they boxed us in here. Bricks and windows, windows and bricks.

LINDA   We should've bought the land next door.

WILLY   The street is lined with cars. There's not a breath of fresh air in the neighborhood. The grass don't grow any more, you can't raise a carrot in the back yard. They should've had a law against apartment houses. Remember those two beautiful elm trees out there? When I and Biff hung the swing between them?

LINDA   Yeah, like being a million miles from the city.

WILLY   They should've arrested the builder for cutting those down.

They massacred the neighborhood. [*Lost*] More and more I think of those days, Linda. This time of year it was lilac and wisteria. And then the peonies would come out, and the daffodils. What fragrance in this room!

LINDA   Well, after all, people had to move somewhere.

WILLY   No, there's more people now.

LINDA   I don't think there's more people. I think—

WILLY   There's more people! That's what's ruining this country! Population is getting out of control. The competition is maddening! Smell the stink from that apartment house! And another one on the other side . . . How can they whip cheese?

On WILLY's *last line,* BIFF *and* HAPPY *raise themselves up in their beds, listening.*

LINDA   Go down, try it. And be quiet.

WILLY   [*turning to Linda, guilty*]   You're not worried about me, are you, sweetheart?

BIFF   What's the matter?

HAPPY   Listen!

LINDA   You've got too much on the ball to worry about.

WILLY   You're my foundation and my support, Linda.

LINDA   Just try to relax, dear. You make mountains out of molehills.

WILLY   I won't fight with him any more. If he wants to go back to Texas, let him go.

LINDA   He'll find his way.

WILLY   Sure. Certain men just don't get started till later in life. Like Thomas Edison, I think. Or B. F. Goodrich. One of them was deaf. [*He starts for the bedroom doorway.*] I'll put my money on Biff.

LINDA   And Willy—if it's warm Sunday we'll drive in the country. And we'll open the windshield, and take lunch.

WILLY   No, the windshields don't open on the new cars.

LINDA   But you opened it today.

WILLY   Me? I didn't. [*He stops.*] Now isn't that peculiar! Isn't that a remarkable—[*He breaks off in amazement and fright as the flute is heard distantly.*]

LINDA   What, darling?

WILLY   That is the most remarkable thing.

LINDA   What, dear?

WILLY   I was thinking of the Chevvy. [*Slight pause.*] Nineteen twenty-eight . . . when I had that red Chevvy— [*Breaks off.*] That funny? I coulda sworn I was driving that Chevvy today.

LINDA   Well, that's nothing. Something must've reminded you.

WILLY   Remarkable. Ts. Remember those days? The way Biff used to simonize that car? The dealer refused to believe there was eighty thousand miles on it. [*He shakes his head.*] Heh! [*To Linda*] Close your eyes, I'll be right up. [*He walks out of the bedroom.*]

HAPPY   [*to Biff*]   Jesus, maybe he smashed up the car again!

LINDA   [*calling after Willy*]   Be careful on the stairs, dear! The cheese is on the middle shelf! [*She turns, goes over to the bed, takes his jacket, and goes out of the bedroom.*]

Light has risen on the boys' room. Unseen, WILLY *is heard talking to himself, "Eighty thousand miles," and a little laugh.*
BIFF *gets out of bed, comes downstage a bit, and stands attentively.* BIFF *is two years older than his brother* HAPPY, *well
built, but in these days bears a worn air and seems less self-
assured. He has succeeded less, and his dreams are stronger
and less acceptable than* HAPPY'S. HAPPY *is tall, powerfully
made. Sexuality is like a visible color on him, or a scent that
many women have discovered. He, like his brother, is lost, but
in a different way, for he has never allowed himself to turn his
face toward defeat and is thus more confused and hard-
skinned, although seemingly more content.*

HAPPY [*getting out of bed*]   He's going to get his license taken away
  if he keeps that up. I'm getting nervous about him, y'know, Biff?
BIFF   His eyes are going.
HAPPY   No, I've driven with him. He sees all right. He just doesn't
  keep his mind on it. I drove into the city with him last week. He
  stops at a green light and then it turns red and he goes. [*He
  laughs.*]
BIFF   Maybe he's color-blind.
HAPPY   Pop? Why he's got the finest eye for color in the business.
  You know that.
BIFF [*sitting down on his bed*]   I'm going to sleep.
HAPPY   You're not still sour on Dad, are you, Biff?
BIFF   He's all right, I guess.
WILLY [*underneath them, in the living room*]   Yes, sir, eighty thou-
  sand miles—eighty-two thousand!
BIFF   You smoking?
HAPPY [*holding out a pack of cigarettes*]   Want one?
BIFF [*taking a cigarette*]   I can never sleep when I smell it.
WILLY   What a simonizing job, heh!
HAPPY [*with deep sentiment*]   Funny, Biff, y'know? Us sleeping in
  here again? The old beds. [*He pats his bed affectionately.*] All the
  talk that went across those two beds, huh? Our whole lives.
BIFF   Yeah. Lotta dreams and plans.
HAPPY [*with a deep and masculine laugh*]   About five hundred
  women would like to know what was said in this room.

     They share a soft laugh.

BIFF   Remember that big Betsy something—what the hell was her
  name—over on Bushwick Avenue?
HAPPY [*combing his hair*]   With the collie dog!
BIFF   That's the one. I got you in there, remember?
HAPPY   Yeah, that was my first time—I think. Boy, there was a pig!
  [*They laugh, almost crudely.*] You taught me everything I know
  about women. Don't forget that.
BIFF   I bet you forgot how bashful you used to be. Especially with
  girls.
HAPPY   Oh, I still am, Biff.

BIFF   Oh, go on.

HAPPY   I just control it, that's all. I think I got less bashful and you got more so. What happened, Biff? Where's the old humor, the old confidence? [*He shakes* BIFF's *knee.* BIFF *gets up and moves restlessly about the room.*] What's the matter?

BIFF   Why does Dad mock me all the time?

HAPPY   He's not mocking you, he—

BIFF   Everything I say there's a twist of mockery on his face. I can't get near him.

HAPPY   He just wants you to make good, that's all. I wanted to talk to you about Dad for a long time, Biff. Something's—happening to him. He—talks to himself.

BIFF   I noticed that this morning. But he always mumbled.

HAPPY   But not so noticeable. It got so embarrassing I sent him to Florida. And you know something? Most of the time he's talking to you.

BIFF   What's he say about me?

HAPPY   I can't make it out.

BIFF   What's he say about me?

HAPPY   I think the fact that you're not settled, that you're still kind of up in the air . . .

BIFF   There's one or two other things depressing him, Happy.

HAPPY   What do you mean?

BIFF   Never mind. Just don't lay it all to me.

HAPPY   But I think if you just got started—I mean—is there any future for you out there?

BIFF   I tell ya, Hap, I don't know what the future is. I don't know—what I'm supposed to want.

HAPPY   What do you mean?

BIFF   Well, I spent six or seven years after high school trying to
- work myself up. Shipping clerk, salesman, business of one kind or another. And it's a measly manner of existence. To get on that subway on the hot mornings in summer. To devote your whole life to keeping stock, or making phone calls, or selling or buying. To suffer fifty weeks of the year for the sake of a two-week vacation, when all you really desire is to be outdoors, with your shirt off. And always to have to get ahead of the next fella. And still—that's how you build a future.

HAPPY   Well, you really enjoy it on a farm? Are you content out there?

BIFF   [*with rising agitation*] Hap, I've had twenty or thirty different kinds of jobs since I left home before the war, and it always turns out the same. I just realized it lately. In Nebraska when I herded cattle, and the Dakotas, and Arizona, and now in Texas. It's why I came home now, I guess, because I realized it. This farm I work on, it's spring there now, see? And they've got about fifteen new colts. There's nothing more inspiring or—beautiful than the sight of a mare and a new colt. And it's cool there now, see? Texas is cool now, and it's spring. And whenever spring comes to where I am, I suddenly get the feeling, my God, I'm not gettin' anywhere! What the hell am I doing, playing around with horses, twenty-eight dollars a week! I'm thirty-four years old, I oughta be makin' my future. That's when I come running home. And now, I get here, and I don't know what to do with myself. [*After a pause*] I've always made a point of not wasting my life, and every time I come back here I know that all I've done is to waste my life.

HAPPY　You're a poet, you know that, Biff? You're a—you're an idealist!

BIFF　No, I'm mixed up very bad. Maybe I oughta get married. Maybe I oughta get stuck into something. Maybe that's my trouble. I'm like a boy. I'm not married, I'm not in business, I just—I'm like a boy. Are you content, Hap? You're a success, aren't you? Are you content?

HAPPY　Hell, no!

BIFF　Why? You're making money, aren't you?

HAPPY　[*moving about with energy, expressiveness*]　All I can do now is wait for the merchandise manager to die. And suppose I get to be merchandise manager? He's a good friend of mine, and he just built a terrific estate on Long Island. And he lived there about two months and sold it, and now he's building another one. He can't enjoy it once it's finished. And I know that's just what I would do. I don't know what the hell I'm workin' for. Sometimes I sit in my apartment—all alone. And I think of the rent I'm paying. And it's crazy. But then, it's what I always wanted. My own apartment, a car, and plenty of women. And still, goddammit, I'm lonely.

BIFF　[*with enthusiasm*]　Listen, why don't you come out West with me?

HAPPY　You and I, heh?

BIFF　Sure, maybe we could buy a ranch. Raise cattle, use our muscles. Men built like we are should be working out in the open.

HAPPY　[*avidly*]　The Loman Brothers, heh?

BIFF　[*with vast affection*]　Sure, we'd be known all over the counties!

HAPPY　[*enthralled*]　That's what I dream about, Biff. Sometimes I want to just rip my clothes off in the middle of the store and outbox that goddam merchandise manager. I mean I can outbox, outrun, and outlift anybody in that store, and I have to take orders from those common, petty sons-of-bitches till I can't stand it any more.

BIFF　I'm tellin' you, kid, if you were with me I'd be happy out there.

HAPPY　[*enthused*]　See, Biff, everybody around me is so false that I'm constantly lowering my ideals . . .

BIFF　Baby, together we'd stand up for one another, we'd have someone to trust.

HAPPY　If I were around you—

BIFF　Hap, the trouble is we weren't brought up to grub for money. I don't know how to do it.

HAPPY　Neither can I!

BIFF　Then let's go!

HAPPY　The only thing is—what can you make out there?

BIFF　But look at your friend. Builds an estate and then hasn't the peace of mind to live in it.

HAPPY　Yeah, but when he walks into the store the waves part in front of him. That's fifty-two thousand dollars a year coming through the revolving door, and I got more in my pinky finger than he's got in his head.

BIFF   Yeah, but you just said—

HAPPY   I gotta show some of those pompous, self-important executives over there that Hap Loman can make the grade. I want to walk into the store the way he walks in. Then I'll go with you, Biff. We'll be together yet, I swear. But take those two we had tonight. Now weren't they gorgeous creatures?

BIFF   Yeah, yeah, most gorgeous I've had in years.

HAPPY   I get that any time I want, Biff. Whenever I feel disgusted. The only trouble is, it gets like bowling or something. I just keep knockin' them over and it doesn't mean anything. You still run around a lot?

BIFF   Naa. I'd like to find a girl—steady, somebody with substance.

HAPPY   That's what I long for.

BIFF   Go on! You'd never come home.

HAPPY   I would! Somebody with character, with resistance! Like Mom, y'know? You're gonna call me a bastard when I tell you this. That girl Charlotte I was with tonight is engaged to be married in five weeks. [*He tries on his new hat.*]

BIFF   No kiddin'!

HAPPY   Sure, the guy's in line for the vice-presidency of the store. I don't know what gets into me, maybe I just have an overdeveloped sense of competition or something, but I went and ruined her, and furthermore I can't get rid of her. And he's the third executive I've done that to. Isn't that a crummy characteristic? And to top it all, I go to their weddings! [*Indignantly, but laughing*] Like I'm not supposed to take bribes. Manufacturers offer me a hundred-dollar bill now and then to throw an order their way. You know how honest I am, but it's like this girl, see. I hate myself for it. Because I don't want the girl, and, still, I take it and—I love it!

BIFF   Let's go to sleep.

HAPPY   I guess we didn't settle anything, heh?

BIFF   I just got one idea that I think I'm going to try.

HAPPY   What's that?

BIFF   Remember Bill Oliver?

HAPPY   Sure, Oliver is very big now. You want to work for him again?

BIFF   No, but when I quit he said something to me. He put his arm on my shoulder, and he said, "Biff, if you ever need anything, come to me."

HAPPY   I remember that. That sounds good.

BIFF   I think I'll go to see him. If I could get ten thousand or even seven or eight thousand dollars I could buy a beautiful ranch.

HAPPY   I bet he'd back you. 'Cause he thought highly of you, Biff. I mean, they all do. You're well liked, Biff. That's why I say to come back here, and we both have the apartment. And I'm tellin' you, Biff, any babe you want . . .

BIFF   No, with a ranch I could do the work I like and still be something. I just wonder though. I wonder if Oliver still thinks I stole that carton of basketballs.

HAPPY   Oh, he probably forgot that long ago. It's almost ten years. You're too sensitive. Anyway, he didn't really fire you.

BIFF   Well, I think he was going to. I think that's why I quit. I was never sure whether he knew or not. I know he thought the world of me, though. I was the only one he'd let lock up the place.

WILLY [*below*]   You gonna wash the engine, Biff?

HAPPY   Shh!

> BIFF *looks at* HAPPY, *who is gazing down, listening.* WILLY *is mumbling in the parlor.*

HAPPY   You hear that?

> *They listen.* WILLY *laughs warmly.*

BIFF [*growing angry*]   Doesn't he know Mom can hear that?

WILLY   Don't get your sweater dirty, Biff!

> *A look of pain crosses* BIFF's *face.*

HAPPY   Isn't that terrible? Don't leave again, will you? You'll find a job here. You gotta stick around. I don't know what to do about him, it's getting embarrassing.

WILLY   What a simonizing job!

BIFF   Mom's hearing that!

WILLY   No kiddin', Biff, you got a date? Wonderful!

HAPPY   Go on to sleep. But talk to him in the morning, will you?

BIFF [*reluctantly getting into bed*]   With her in the house. Brother!

HAPPY [*getting into bed*]   I wish you'd have a good talk with him.

> *The light on their room begins to fade.*

BIFF [*to himself in bed*]   That selfish, stupid . . .

HAPPY   Sh . . . Sleep, Biff.

> *Their light is out. Well before they have finished speaking,* WILLY's *form is dimly seen below in the darkened kitchen. He opens the refrigerator, searches in there, and takes out a bottle of milk. The apartment houses are fading out, and the entire house and surroundings become covered with leaves. Music insinuates itself as the leaves appear.*

WILLY   Just wanna be careful with those girls, Biff, that's all. Don't make any promises. No promises of any kind. Because a girl, y'know, they always believe what you tell 'em, and you're very young, Biff, you're too young to be talking seriously to girls.

> *Light rises on the kitchen.* WILLY, *talking, shuts the refrigerator door and comes downstage to the kitchen table. He pours milk into a glass. He is totally immersed in himself, smiling faintly.*

WILLY   Too young entirely, Biff. You want to watch your schooling first. Then when you're all set, there'll be plenty of girls for a boy like you. [*He smiles broadly at a kitchen chair.*] That so? The girls pay for you? [*He laughs.*] Boy, you must really be makin' a hit.

WILLY *is gradually addressing—physically—a point offstage, speaking through the wall of the kitchen, and his voice has been rising in volume to that of a normal conversation.*

WILLY I been wondering why you polish the car so careful. Ha! Don't leave the hubcaps, boys. Get the chamois to the hubcaps. Happy, use newspaper on the windows, it's the easiest thing. Show him how to do it, Biff! You see, Happy? Pad it up, use it like a pad. That's it, that's it, good work. You're doin' all right, Hap. [*He pauses, then nods in approbation for a few seconds, then looks upward.*] Biff, first thing we gotta do when we get time is clip that big branch over the house. Afraid it's gonna fall in a storm and hit the roof. Tell you what. We get a rope and sling her around, and then we climb up there with a couple of saws and take her down. Soon as you finish the car, boys, I wanna see ya. I got a surprise for you, boys.

BIFF [*offstage*] Whatta ya got, Dad?

WILLY No, you finish first. Never leave a job till you're finished—remember that. [*Looking toward the "big trees"*] Biff, up in Albany I saw a beautiful hammock. I think I'll buy it next trip, and we'll hang it right between those two elms. Wouldn't that be something? Just swingin' there under those branches. Boy, that would be . . .

YOUNG BIFF *and* YOUNG HAPPY *appear from the direction* WILLY *was addressing.* HAPPY *carries rags and a pail of water.* BIFF, *wearing a sweater with a block "S," carries a football.*

BIFF [*pointing in the direction of the car offstage*] How's that, Pop, professional?

WILLY Terrific. Terrific job, boys. Good work, Biff.

HAPPY Where's the surprise, Pop?

WILLY In the back seat of the car.

HAPPY Boy! [*He runs off.*]

BIFF What is it, Dad? Tell me, what'd you buy?

WILLY [*laughing, cuffs him*] Never mind, something I want you to have.

BIFF [*turns and starts off*] What is it, Hap?

HAPPY [*offstage*] It's a punching bag!

BIFF Oh, Pop!

WILLY It's got Gene Tunney's[1] signature on it!

HAPPY *runs onstage with a punching bag.*

BIFF Gee, how'd you know we wanted a punching bag?

WILLY Well, it's the finest thing for the timing.

HAPPY [*lies down on his back and pedals with his feet*] I'm losing weight, you notice, Pop?

WILLY [*to Happy*] Jumping rope is good too.

BIFF Did you see the new football I got?

WILLY [*examining the ball*] Where'd you get a new ball?

---

1. Tunney (b. 1897) was world heavy-weight boxing champion from 1926 to 1928.

BIFF   The coach told me to practice my passing.

WILLY   That so? And he gave you the ball, heh?

BIFF   Well, I borrowed it from the locker room. [*He laughs confidentially.*]

WILLY [*laughing with him at the theft*]   I want you to return that.

HAPPY   I told you he wouldn't like it!

BIFF [*angrily*]   Well, I'm bringing it back!

WILLY [*stopping the incipient argument, to* HAPPY]   Sure, he's gotta practice with a regulation ball, doesn't he? [*To* BIFF] Coach'll probably congratulate you on your initiative!

BIFF   Oh, he keeps congratulating my initiative all the time, Pop.

WILLY   That's because he likes you. If somebody else took that ball there'd be an uproar. So what's the report, boys, what's the report?

BIFF   Where'd you go this time, Dad? Gee we were lonesome for you.

WILLY [*pleased, puts an arm around each boy and they come down to the apron*]   Lonesome, heh?

BIFF   Missed you every minute.

WILLY   Don't say? Tell you a secret, boys. Don't breathe it to a soul. Someday I'll have my own business, and I'll never have to leave home any more.

HAPPY   Like Uncle Charley, heh?

WILLY   Bigger than Uncle Charley! Because Charley is not—liked. He's liked, but he's not—well liked.

BIFF   Where'd you go this time, Dad?

WILLY   Well, I got on the road, and I went north to Providence. Met the Mayor.

BIFF   The Mayor of Providence!

WILLY   He was sitting in the hotel lobby.

BIFF   What'd he say?

WILLY   He said, "Morning!" And I said, "You got a fine city here, Mayor." And then he had coffee with me. And then I went to Waterbury. Waterbury is a fine city. Big clock city, the famous Waterbury clock. Sold a nice bill there. And then Boston—Boston is the cradle of the Revolution. A fine city. And a couple of other towns in Mass., and on to Portland and Bangor and straight home!

BIFF   Gee, I'd love to go with you sometime, Dad.

WILLY   Soon as summer comes.

HAPPY   Promise?

WILLY   You and Hap and I, and I'll show you all the towns. America is full of beautiful towns and fine, upstanding people. And they know me, boys, they know me up and down New England. The finest people. And when I bring you fellas up, there'll be open sesame for all of us, 'cause one thing, boys: I have friends. I can park my car in any street in New England, and the cops protect it like their own. This summer, heh?

BIFF and HAPPY [*together*]   Yeah! You bet!

WILLY   We'll take our bathing suits.

HAPPY   We'll carry your bags, Pop!

WILLY   Oh, won't that be something! Me comin' into the Boston stores with you boys carryin' my bags. What a sensation!

BIFF *is prancing around, practicing passing the ball.*

WILLY   You nervous, Biff, about the game?

BIFF   Not if you're gonna be there.

WILLY   What do they say about you in school, now that they made you captain?

HAPPY   There's a crowd of girls behind him everytime the classes change.

BIFF [*taking* WILLY's *hand*]   This Saturday, Pop, this Saturday—just for you, I'm going to break through for a touchdown.

HAPPY   You're supposed to pass.

BIFF   I'm takin' one play for Pop. You watch me, Pop, and when I take off my helmet, that means I'm breakin' out. Then you watch me crash through that line!

WILLY [*kisses* BIFF]   Oh, wait'll I tell this in Boston!

> BERNARD *enters in knickers. He is younger than* BIFF, *earnest and loyal, a worried boy.*

BERNARD   Biff, where are you? You're supposed to study with me today.

WILLY   Hey, looka Bernard. What're you lookin' so anemic about, Bernard?

BERNARD   He's gotta study, Uncle Willy. He's got Regents[2] next week.

HAPPY [*tauntingly, spinning* BERNARD *around*]   Let's box, Bernard!

BERNARD   Biff! [*He gets away from* HAPPY.] Listen, Biff, I heard Mr. Birnbaum say that if you don't start studyin' math he's gonna flunk you, and you won't graduate. I heard him!

WILLY   You better study with him, Biff. Go ahead now.

BERNARD   I heard him!

BIFF   Oh, Pop, you didn't see my sneakers! [*He holds up a foot for* WILLY *to look at.*]

WILLY   Hey, that's a beautiful job of printing!

BERNARD [*wiping his glasses*]   Just because he printed University of Virginia on his sneakers doesn't mean they've got to graduate him, Uncle Willy!

WILLY [*angrily*]   What're you talking about? With scholarships to three universities they're gonna flunk him?

BERNARD   But I heard Mr. Birnbaum say—

WILLY   Don't be a pest, Bernard! [*To his boys*] What an anemic!

BERNARD   Okay, I'm waiting for you in my house, Biff.

> BERNARD *goes off. The Lomans laugh.*

WILLY   Bernard is not well liked, is he?

BIFF   He's liked, but he's not well liked.

HAPPY   That's right, Pop.

WILLY   That's just what I mean. Bernard can get the best marks in school, y'understand, but when he gets out in the business world, y'understand, you are going to be five times ahead of him. That's why I thank Almighty God you're both built like Adonises.[3] Be-

---

2. A statewide examination administered to New York high school students.

3. In Greek mythology Adonis was a beautiful youth, the favorite of Aphrodite, Goddess of Love.

cause the man who makes an appearance in the business world, the man who creates personal interest, is the man who gets ahead. Be liked and you will never want. You take me, for instance. I never have to wait in line to see a buyer. "Willy Loman is here!" That's all they have to know, and I go right through.

BIFF Did you knock them dead, Pop?

WILLY Knocked 'em cold in Providence, slaughtered 'em in Boston.

HAPPY [*on his back, pedaling again*] I'm losing weight, you notice, Pop?

> LINDA *enters, as of old, a ribbon in her hair, carrying a basket of washing.*

LINDA [*with youthful energy*] Hello, dear!

WILLY Sweetheart!

LINDA How'd the Chevvy run?

WILLY Chevrolet, Linda, is the greatest car ever built. [*To the boys*] Since when do you let your mother carry wash up the stairs?

BIFF Grab hold there, boy!

HAPPY Where to, Mom?

LINDA Hang them up on the line. And you better go down to your friends, Biff. The cellar is full of boys. They don't know what to do with themselves.

BIFF Ah, when Pop comes home they can wait!

WILLY [*laughs appreciatively*] You better go down and tell them what to do, Biff.

BIFF I think I'll have them sweep out the furnace room.

WILLY Good work, Biff.

BIFF [*goes through wall-line of kitchen to doorway at back and calls down*] Fellas! Everybody sweep out the furnace room! I'll be right down!

VOICES All right! Okay, Biff.

BIFF George and Sam and Frank, come out back! We're hangin' up the wash! Come on, Hap, on the double! [*He and* HAPPY *carry out the basket.*]

LINDA The way they obey him!

WILLY Well, that's training, the training. I'm tellin' you, I was sellin' thousands and thousands, but I had to come home.

LINDA Oh, the whole block'll be at that game. Did you sell anything?

WILLY I did five hundred gross in Providence and seven hundred gross in Boston.

LINDA No! Wait a minute, I've got a pencil. [*She pulls pencil and paper out of her apron pocket.*] That makes your commission . . . Two hundred—my God! Two hundred and twelve dollars!

WILLY Well, I didn't figure it yet, but . . .

LINDA How much did you do?

WILLY Well, I—I did—about a hundred and eighty gross in Providence. Well, no—it came to—roughly two hundred gross on the whole trip.

LINDA [*without hesitation*] Two hundred gross. That's . . . [*She figures.*]

WILLY   The trouble was that three of the stores were half closed for inventory in Boston. Otherwise I woulda broke records.

LINDA   Well, it makes seventy dollars and some pennies. That's very good.

WILLY   What do we owe?

LINDA   Well, on the first there's sixteen dollars on the refrigerator—

WILLY   Why sixteen?

LINDA   Well, the fan belt broke, so it was a dollar eighty.

WILLY   But it's brand new.

LINDA   Well, the man said that's the way it is. Till they work themselves in, y'know.

They move through the wall-line into the kitchen.

WILLY   I hope we didn't get stuck on that machine.

LINDA   They got the biggest ads of any of them!

WILLY   I know, it's a fine machine. What else?

LINDA   Well, there's nine-sixty for the washing machine. And for the vacuum cleaner there's three and a half due on the fifteenth. Then the roof, you got twenty-one dollars remaining.

WILLY   It don't leak, does it?

LINDA   No, they did a wonderful job. Then you owe Frank for the carburetor.

WILLY   I'm not going to pay that man! That goddam Chevrolet, they ought to prohibit the manufacture of that car!

LINDA   Well, you owe him three and a half. And odds and ends, comes to around a hundred and twenty dollars by the fifteenth.

WILLY   A hundred and twenty dollars! My God, if business don't pick up I don't know what I'm gonna do!

LINDA   Well, next week you'll do better.

WILLY   Oh, I'll knock 'em dead next week. I'll go to Hartford. I'm very well liked in Hartford. You know, the trouble is, Linda, people don't seem to take to me.

They move onto the forestage.

LINDA   Oh, don't be foolish.

WILLY   I know it when I walk in. They seem to laugh at me.

LINDA   Why? Why would they laugh at you? Don't talk that way, Willy.

WILLY moves to the edge of the stage. LINDA goes into the kitchen and starts to darn stockings.

WILLY   I don't know the reason for it, but they just pass me by. I'm not noticed.

LINDA   But you're doing wonderful, dear. You're making seventy to a hundred dollars a week.

WILLY   But I gotta be at it ten, twelve hours a day. Other men—I don't know—they do it easier. I don't know why—I can't stop myself—I talk too much. A man oughta come in with a few words.

One thing about Charley. He's a man of few words, and they respect him.

LINDA You don't talk too much, you're just lively.

WILLY [*smiling*] Well, I figure, what the hell, life is short, a couple of jokes. [*To himself*] I joke too much! [*The smile goes.*]

LINDA Why? You're—

WILLY I'm fat. I'm very—foolish to look at, Linda. I didn't tell you, but Christmas time I happened to be calling on F. H. Stewarts, and a salesman I know, as I was going in to see the buyer I heard him say something about—walrus. And I—I cracked him right across the face. I won't take that. I simply will not take that. But they do laugh at me. I know that.

LINDA Darling . . .

WILLY I gotta overcome it. I know I gotta overcome it. I'm not dressing to advantage, maybe.

LINDA Willy, darling, you're the handsomest man in the world—

WILLY Oh, no, Linda.

LINDA To me you are. [*Slight pause.*] The handsomest.

From the darkness is heard the laughter of a woman. WILLY *doesn't turn to it, but it continues through* LINDA's *lines.*

LINDA And the boys, Willy. Few men are idolized by their children the way you are.

Music is heard as behind a scrim, to the left of the house, THE WOMAN, *dimly seen, is dressing.*

WILLY [*with great feeling*] You're the best there is, Linda, you're a pal, you know that? On the road—on the road I want to grab you sometimes and just kiss the life outa you.

The laughter is loud now, and he moves into a brightening area at the left, where THE WOMAN *has come from behind the scrim and is standing, putting on her hat, looking into a "mirror" and laughing.*

WILLY 'Cause I get so lonely—especially when business is bad and there's nobody to talk to. I get the feeling that I'll never sell anything again, that I won't make a living for you, or a business, a business for the boys. [*He talks through* THE WOMAN's *subsiding laughter;* THE WOMAN *primps at the "mirror."*] There's so much I want to make for—

THE WOMAN Me? You didn't make me, Willy. I picked you.

WILLY [*pleased*] You picked me?

THE WOMAN [*who is quite proper-looking,* WILLY's *age*] I did. I've been sitting at that desk watching all the salesmen go by, day in, day out. But you've got such a sense of humor, and we do have a good time together, don't we?

WILLY Sure, sure. [*He takes her in his arms.*] Why do you have to go now?

THE WOMAN It's two o'clock . . .

WILLY   No, come on in! [*He pulls her.*]

THE WOMAN   . . . my sisters'll bo scandalized. When'll you be back?

WILLY   Oh, two weeks about. Will you come up again?

THE WOMAN   Sure thing. You do make me laugh. It's good for me. [*She squeezes his arm, kisses him.*] And I think you're a wonderful man.

WILLY   You picked me, heh?

THE WOMAN   Sure. Because you're so sweet. And such a kidder.

WILLY   Well, I'll see you next time I'm in Boston.

THE WOMAN   I'll put you right through to the buyers.

WILLY   [*slapping her bottom*]   Right. Well, bottoms up!

THE WOMAN   [*slaps him gently and laughs*]   You just kill me, Willy. [*He suddenly grabs her and kisses her roughly.*] You kill me. And thanks for the stockings. I love a lot of stockings. Well, good night.

WILLY   Good night. And keep your pores open!

THE WOMAN   Oh, Willy!

> THE WOMAN *bursts out laughing, and* LINDA'*s laughter blends in.* THE WOMAN *disappears into the dark. Now the area at the kitchen table brightens.* LINDA *is sitting where she was at the kitchen table, but now is mending a pair of her silk stockings.*

LINDA   You are, Willy. The handsomest man. You've got no reason to feel that—

WILLY   [*coming out of* THE WOMAN'*s dimming area and going over to* LINDA]   I'll make it all up to you, Linda, I'll—

LINDA   There's nothing to make up, dear. You're doing fine, better than—

WILLY   [*noticing her mending*]   What's that?

LINDA   Just mending my stockings. They're so expensive—

WILLY   [*angrily, taking them from her*]   I won't have you mending stockings in this house! Now thrown them out!

> LINDA *puts the stockings in her pocket.*

BERNARD   [*entering on the run*]   Where is he? If he doesn't study!

WILLY   [*moving to the forestage, with great agitation*]   You'll give him the answers!

BERNARD   I do, but I can't on a Regents! That's a state exam! They're liable to arrest me!

WILLY   Where is he? I'll whip him, I'll whip him!

LINDA   And he'd better give back that football, Willy, it's not nice.

WILLY   Biff! Where is he? Why is he taking everything?

LINDA   He's too rough with the girls, Willy. All the mothers are afraid of him!

WILLY   I'll whip him!

BERNARD   He's driving the car without a license!

> THE WOMAN'*s laugh is heard.*

WILLY   Shut up!

LINDA   All the mothers—

WILLY   Shut up!

BERNARD   [*backing quietly away and out*]   Mr. Birnbaum says he's stuck up.

WILLY   Get outa here!

BERNARD   If he doesn't buckle down he'll flunk math! [*He goes off.*]

LINDA   He's right, Willy, you've gotta—

WILLY   [*exploding at her*]   There's nothing the matter with him! You want him to be a worm like Bernard? He's got spirit, personality . . .

> As he speaks, LINDA, *almost in tears, exits into the living room.* WILLY *is alone in the kitchen, wilting and staring. The leaves are gone. It is night again, and the apartment houses look down from behind.*

WILLY   Loaded with it. Loaded! What is he stealing? He's giving it back, isn't he? Why is he stealing? What did I tell him? I never in my life told him anything but decent things.

> HAPPY *in pajamas has come down the stairs;* WILLY *suddenly becomes aware of* HAPPY's *presence.*

HAPPY   Let's go now, come on.

WILLY   [*sitting down at the kitchen table*]   Huh! Why did she have to wax the floors herself? Every time she waxes the floors she keels over. She knows that!

HAPPY   Shh! Take it easy. What brought you back tonight?

WILLY   I got an awful scare. Nearly hit a kid in Yonkers. God! Why didn't I go to Alaska with my brother Ben that time! Ben! That man was a genius, that man was success incarnate! What a mistake! He begged me to go.

HAPPY   Well, there's no use in—

WILLY   You guys! There was a man started with the clothes on his back and ended up with diamond mines!

HAPPY   Boy, someday I'd like to know how he did it.

WILLY   What's the mystery? The man knew what he wanted and went out and got it! Walked into a jungle, and comes out, the age of twenty-one, and he's rich! The world is an oyster, but you don't crack it open on a mattress!

HAPPY   Pop, I told you I'm gonna retire you for life.

WILLY   You'll retire me for life on seventy goddam dollars a week? And your women and your car and your apartment, and you'll retire me for life! Christ's sake, I couldn't get past Yonkers today! Where are you guys, where are you? The woods are burning! I can't drive a car!

> CHARLEY *has appeared in the doorway. He is a large man, slow of speech, laconic, immovable. In all he says, despite what he says, there is pity, and, now, trepidation. He has a robe over pajamas, slippers on his feet. He enters the kitchen.*

CHARLEY   Everything all right?

HAPPY   Yeah, Charley, everything's . . .

WILLY   What's the matter?

CHARLEY   I heard some noise. I thought something happened. Can't we do something about the walls? You sneeze in here, and in my house hats blow off.

HAPPY   Let's go to bed, Dad. Come on.

CHARLEY *signals to* HAPPY *to go.*

WILLY   You go ahead, I'm not tired at the moment.

HAPPY [*to* WILLY]   Take it easy, huh? [*He exits.*]

WILLY   What're you doin' up?

CHARLEY [*sitting down at the kitchen table opposite Willy*]   Couldn't sleep good. I had a heartburn.

WILLY   Well, you don't know how to eat.

CHARLEY   I cat with my mouth.

WILLY   No, you're ignorant. You gotta know about vitamins and things like that.

CHARLEY   Come on, let's shoot. Tire you out a little.

WILLY [*hesitantly*]   All right. You got cards?

CHARLEY [*taking a deck from his pocket*]   Yeah, I got them. Some-place. What is it with those vitamins?

WILLY [*dealing*]   They build up your bones. Chemistry.

CHARLEY   Yeah, but there's no bones in a heartburn.

WILLY   What are you talkin' about? Do you know the first thing about it?

CHARLEY   Don't get insulted.

WILLY   Don't talk about something you don't know anything about.

They are playing. Pause.

CHARLEY   What're you doin' home?

WILLY   A little trouble with the car.

CHARLEY   Oh. [*Pause.*] I'd like to take a trip to California.

WILLY   Don't say.

CHARLEY   You want a job?

WILLY   I got a job, I told you that. [*After a slight pause*] What the hell arc you offering me a job for?

CHARLEY   Don't get insulted.

WILLY   Don't insult me.

CHARLEY   I don't see no sense in it. You don't have to go on this way.

WILLY   I got a good job. [*Slight pause.*] What do you keep comin' in here for?

CHARLEY   You want me to go?

WILLY [*after a pause, withering*]   I can't understand it. He's going back to Texas again. What the hell is that?

CHARLEY   Let him go.

WILLY   I got nothin' to give him, Charley, I'm clean, I'm clean.

CHARLEY   He won't starve. None a them starve. Forget about him.

WILLY   Then what have I got to remember?

CHARLEY   You take it too hard. To hell with it. When a deposit bottle is broken you don't get your nickel back.

WILLY   That's easy enough for you to say.

CHARLEY   That ain't easy for me to say.

WILLY   Did you see the ceiling I put up in the living room?

CHARLEY   Yeah, that's a piece of work. To put up a ceiling is a mystery to me. How do you do it?

WILLY   What's the difference?

CHARLEY   Well, talk about it.

WILLY   You gonna put up a ceiling?

CHARLEY   How could I put up a ceiling?

WILLY   Then what the hell are you bothering me for?

CHARLEY   You're insulted again.

WILLY   A man who can't handle tools is not a man. You're disgusting.

CHARLEY   Don't call me disgusting, Willy.

> UNCLE BEN, *carrying a valise and an umbrella, enters the fore-stage from around the right corner of the house. He is a stolid man, in his sixties, with a mustache and an authoritative air. He is utterly certain of his destiny, and there is an aura of far places about him. He enters exactly as* WILLY *speaks.*

WILLY   I'm getting awfully tired, Ben.

> BEN'*s music is heard.* BEN *looks around at everything.*

CHARLEY   Good, keep playing; you'll sleep better. Did you call me Ben?

> BEN *looks at his watch.*

WILLY   That's funny. For a second there you reminded me of my brother Ben.

BEN   I only have a few minutes. [*He strolls, inspecting the place.* WILLY *and* CHARLEY *continue playing.*]

CHARLEY   You never heard from him again, heh? Since that time?

WILLY   Didn't Linda tell you? Couple of weeks ago we got a letter from his wife in Africa. He died.

CHARLEY   That so.

BEN [*chuckling*]   So this is Brooklyn, eh?

CHARLEY   Maybe you're in for some of his money.

WILLY   Naa, he had seven sons. There's just one opportunity I had with that man . . .

BEN   I must make a train, William. There are several properties I'm looking at in Alaska.

WILLY   Sure, sure! If I'd gone with him to Alaska that time, everything would've been totally different.

CHARLEY   Go on, you'd froze to death up there.

WILLY   What're you talking about?

BEN   Opportunity is tremendous in Alaska, William. Surprised you're not up there.

WILLY   Sure, tremendous.

CHARLEY Heh?

WILLY There was the only man I ever met who knew the answers.

CHARLEY Who?

BEN How are you all?

WILLY [*taking a pot, smiling*] Fine, fine.

CHARLEY Pretty sharp tonight.

BEN Is Mother living with you?

WILLY No, she died a long time ago.

CHARLEY Who?

BEN That's too bad. Fine specimen of a lady, Mother.

WILLY [*to* CHARLEY] Heh?

BEN I'd hoped to see the old girl.

CHARLEY Who died?

BEN Heard anything from Father, have you?

WILLY [*unnerved*] What do you mean, who died?

CHARLEY [*taking a pot*] What're you talkin' about?

BEN [*looking at his watch*] William, it's half-past eight!

WILLY [*as though to dispel his confusion he angrily stops* CHARLEY's hand] That's my build!

CHARLEY I put the ace—

WILLY If you don't know how to play the game I'm not gonna throw my money away on you!

CHARLEY [*rising*] It was my ace, for God's sake!

WILLY I'm through, I'm through!

BEN When did Mother die?

WILLY Long ago. Since the beginning you never knew how to play cards.

CHARLEY [*picks up the cards and goes to the door*] All right! Next time I'll bring a deck with five aces.

WILLY I don't play that kind of game!

CHARLEY [*turning to him*] You ought to be ashamed of yourself!

WILLY Yeah?

CHARLEY Yeah! [*He goes out.*]

WILLY [*slamming the door after him*] Ignoramus!

BEN [*as* WILLY *comes toward him through the wall-line of the kitchen*] So you're William.

WILLY [*shaking* BEN's hand] Ben! I've been waiting for you so long! What's the answer? How did you do it?

BEN Oh, there's a story in that.

LINDA *enters the forestage, as of old, carrying the wash basket.*

LINDA Is this Ben?

BEN [*gallantly*] How do you do, my dear.

LINDA Where've you been all these years. Willy's always wondered why you—

WILLY [*pulling* BEN *away from her impatiently*] Where is Dad? Didn't you follow him? How did you get started?

BEN Well, I don't know how much you remember.

WILLY Well, I was just a baby, of course, only three or four years old—

BEN   Three years and eleven months.

WILLY   What a memory, Ben!

BEN   I have many enterprises, William, and I have never kept books.

WILLY   I remember I was sitting under the wagon in—was it Nebraska?

BEN   It was South Dakota, and I gave you a bunch of wild flowers.

WILLY   I remember you walking away down some open road.

BEN [*laughing*]   I was going to find Father in Alaska.

WILLY   Where is he?

BEN   At that age I had a very faulty view of geography, William. I discovered after a few days that I was heading due south, so instead of Alaska, I ended up in Africa.

LINDA   Africa!

WILLY   The Gold Coast!

BEN   Principally diamond mines.

LINDA   Diamond mines!

BEN   Yes, my dear. But I've only a few minutes—

WILLY   No! Boys! Boys! [YOUNG BIFF *and* HAPPY *appear.*] Listen to this. This is your Uncle Ben, a great man! Tell my boys, Ben!

BEN   Why, boys, when I was seventeen I walked into the jungle, and when I was twenty-one I walked out. [*He laughs.*] And by God I was rich.

WILLY [*to the boys*]   You see what I been talking about? The greatest things can happen!

BEN [*glancing at his watch*]   I have an appointment in Ketchikan Tuesday week.

WILLY   No, Ben! Please tell about Dad. I want my boys to hear. I want them to know the kind of stock they spring from. All I remember is a man with a big beard, and I was in Mamma's lap, sitting around a fire, and some kind of high music.

BEN   His flute. He played the flute.

WILLY   Sure, the flute, that's right!

New music is heard, a high, rollicking tune.

BEN   Father was a very great and a very wild-hearted man. We would start in Boston, and he'd toss the whole family into the wagon, and then he'd drive the team right across the country; through Ohio, and Indiana, Michigan, Illinois, and all the Western states. And we'd stop in the towns and sell the flutes that he'd made on the way. Great inventor, Father. With one gadget he made more in a week than a man like you could make in a lifetime.

WILLY   That's just the way I'm bringing them up, Ben—rugged, well liked, all-around.

BEN   Yeah? [*To* BIFF] Hit that, boy—hard as you can. [*He pounds his stomach.*]

BIFF   Oh, no, sir!

BEN [*taking boxing stance*]   Come on, get to me! [*He laughs.*]

WILLY   Go to it, Biff! Go ahead, show him!

BIFF   Okay! [*He cocks his fists and starts in.*]

LINDA [*to* WILLY]   Why must he fight, dear?

BEN [*sparring with* BIFF] Good boy! Good boy!

WILLY How's that, Ben, heh?

HAPPY Give him a left, Biff!

LINDA Why are you fighting?

BEN Good boy! [*Suddenly comes in, trips* BIFF, *and stands over him, the point of his umbrella poised over* BIFF's *eye.*]

LINDA Look out, Biff!

BIFF Gee!

BEN [*patting* BIFF's *knee*] Never fight fair with a stranger, boy. You'll never get out of the jungle that way. [*Taking* LINDA's *hand and bowing*] It was an honor and a pleasure to meet you, Linda.

LINDA [*withdrawing her hand coldly, frightened*] Have a nice—trip.

BEN [*to* WILLY] And good luck with your—what do you do?

WILLY Selling.

BEN Yes. Well . . . [*He raises his hand in farewell to all.*]

WILLY No, Ben, I don't want you to think . . . [*He takes* BEN's *arm to show him.*] It's Brooklyn, I know, but we hunt too.

BEN Really, now.

WILLY Oh, sure, there's snakes and rabbits and—that's why I moved out here. Why, Biff can fell any one of these trees in no time! Boys! Go right over to where they're building the apartment house and get some sand. We're gonna rebuild the entire front stoop right now! Watch this, Ben!

BIFF Yes, sir! On the double, Hap!

HAPPY [*as he and* BIFF *run off*] I lost weight, Pop, you notice?

CHARLEY *enters in knickers, even before the boys are gone.*

CHARLEY Listen, if they steal any more from that building the watchman'll put the cops on them!

LINDA [*to* WILLY] Don't let Biff . . .

BEN *laughs lustily.*

WILLY You shoulda seen the lumber they brought home last week. At least a dozen six-by-tens worth all kinds of money.

CHARLEY Listen, if that watchman—

WILLY I gave them hell, understand. But I got a couple of fearless characters there.

CHARLEY Willy, the jails are full of fearless characters.

BEN [*clapping* WILLY *on the back, with a laugh at* CHARLEY] And the stock exchange, friend!

WILLY [*joining in* BEN's *laughter*] Where are the rest of your pants?

CHARLEY My wife bought them.

WILLY Now all you need is a golf club and you can go upstairs and go to sleep. [*To* BEN] Great athlete! Between him and his son Bernard they can't hammer a nail!

BERNARD [*rushing in*] The watchman's chasing Biff!

WILLY [*angrily*] Shut up! He's not stealing anything!

LINDA [*alarmed, hurrying off left*] Where is he? Biff, dear! [*She exits.*]

WILLY [*moving toward the left, away from* BEN]   There's nothing wrong. What's the matter with you?

BEN   Nervy boy. Good!

WILLY [*laughing*]   Oh, nerves of iron, that Biff!

CHARLEY   Don't know what it is. My New England man comes back and he's bleedin', they murdered him up there.

WILLY   It's contacts, Charley, I got important contacts!

CHARLEY [*sarcastically*]   Glad to hear it, Willy. Come in later, we'll shoot a little casino. I'll take some of your Portland money. [*He laughs at* WILLY *and exits.*]

WILLY [*turning to* BEN]   Business is bad, it's murderous. But not for me, of course.

BEN   I'll stop by on my way back to Africa.

WILLY [*longingly*]   Can't you stay a few days? You're just what I need, Ben, because I—I have a fine position here, but I—well, Dad left when I was such a baby and I never had a chance to talk to him and I still feel—kind of temporary about myself.

BEN   I'll be late for my train.

They are at opposite ends of the stage.

WILLY   Ben, my boys—can't we talk? They'd go into the jaws of hell for me, see, but I—

BEN   William, you're being first-rate with your boys. Outstanding, manly chaps!

WILLY [*hanging on to his words*]   Oh, Ben, that's good to hear! Because sometimes I'm afraid that I'm not teaching them the right kind of—Ben, how should I teach them?

BEN [*giving great weight to each word, and with a certain vicious audacity*]   William, when I walked into the jungle, I was seventeen. When I walked out I was twenty-one. And, by God, I was rich! [*He goes off into darkness around the right corner of the house.*]

WILLY   . . . was rich! That's just the spirit I want to imbue them with! To walk into a jungle! I was right! I was right! I was right!

BEN *is gone, but* WILLY *is still speaking to him as* LINDA, *in nightgown and robe, enters the kitchen, glances around for* WILLY, *then goes to the door of the house, looks out and sees him. Comes down to his left. He looks at her.*

LINDA   Willy, dear? Willy?

WILLY   I was right!

LINDA   Did you have some cheese? [*He can't answer.*] It's very late, darling. Come to bed, heh?

WILLY [*looking straight up*]   Gotta break your neck to see a star in this yard.

LINDA   You coming in?

WILLY   Whatever happened to that diamond watch fob? Remember? When Ben came from Africa that time? Didn't he give me a watch fob with a diamond in it?

LINDA   You pawned it, dear. Twelve, thirteen years ago. For Biff's radio correspondence course.

WILLY   Gee, that was a beautiful thing. I'll take a walk.

LINDA   But you're in your slippers.

WILLY [*starting to go around the house at the left*] I was right! I was! [*Half to* LINDA, *as he goes, shaking his head*] What a man! There was a man worth talking to. I was right!

LINDA [*calling after* WILLY]   But in your slippers, Willy!

> WILLY *is almost gone when* BIFF, *in his pajamas, comes down the stairs and enters the kitchen.*

BIFF   What is he doing out there?

LINDA   Sh!

BIFF   God Almighty, Mom, how long has he been doing this?

LINDA   Don't, he'll hear you.

BIFF   What the hell is the matter with him?

LINDA   It'll pass by morning.

BIFF   Shouldn't we do anything?

LINDA   Oh, my dear, you should do a lot of things, but there's nothing to do, so go to sleep.

> HAPPY *comes down the stair and sits on the steps.*

HAPPY   I never heard him so loud, Mom.

LINDA   Well, come around more often; you'll hear him. [*She sits down at the table and mends the lining of* WILLY's *jacket.*]

BIFF   Why didn't you ever write me about this, Mom?

LINDA   How would I write to you? For over three months you had no address.

BIFF   I was on the move. But you know I thought of you all the time. You know that, don't you, pal?

LINDA   I know, dear, I know. But he likes to have a letter. Just to know that there's still a possibility for better things.

BIFF   He's not like this all the time, is he?

LINDA   It's when you come home he's always the worst.

BIFF   When I come home?

LINDA   When you write you're coming, he's all smiles, and talks about the future, and—he's just wonderful. And then the closer you seem to come, the more shaky he gets, and then, by the time you get here, he's arguing, and he seems angry at you. I think it's just that maybe he can't bring himself to—to open up to you. Why are you so hateful to each other? Why is that?

BIFF [*evasively*]   I'm not hateful, Mom.

LINDA   But you no sooner come in the door than you're fighting!

BIFF   I don't know why. I mean to change. I'm tryin', Mom, you understand?

LINDA   Are you home to stay now?

BIFF   I don't know. I want to look around, see what's doin'.

LINDA   Biff, you can't look around all your life, can you?

BIFF   I just can't take hold, Mom. I can't take hold of some kind of a life.

LINDA   Biff, a man is not a bird, to come and go with the springtime.

BIFF   Your hair . . . [*He touches her hair*]. Your hair got so gray.

LINDA   Oh, it's been gray since you were in high school. I just stopped dyeing it, that's all.

BIFF   Dye it again, will ya? I don't want my pal looking old. [*He smiles.*]

LINDA   You're such a boy! You think you can go away for a year and . . . You've got to get it into your head now that one day you'll knock on this door and there'll be strange people here—

BIFF   What are you talking about? You're not even sixty, Mom.

LINDA   But what about your father?

BIFF   [*lamely*]   Well, I meant him too.

HAPPY   He admires Pop.

LINDA   Biff, dear, if you don't have any feeling for him, then you can't have any feeling for me.

BIFF   Sure I can, Mom.

LINDA   No. You can't just come to see me, because I love him. [*With a threat, but only a threat, of tears*] He's the dearest man in the world to me, and I won't have anyone making him feel unwanted and low and blue. You've got to make up your mind now, darling, there's no leeway any more. Either he's your father and you pay him that respect, or else you're not to come here. I know he's not easy to get along with—nobody knows that better than me—but . . .

WILLY   [*from the left, with a laugh*]   Hey, hey, Biffo!

BIFF   [*starting to go out after* WILLY]   What the hell is the matter with him? [HAPPY *stops him.*]

LINDA   Don't—don't go near him!

BIFF   Stop making excuses for him! He always, always wiped the floor with you. Never had an ounce of respect for you.

HAPPY   He's always had respect for—

BIFF   What the hell do you know about it?

HAPPY   [*surlily*]   Just don't call him crazy!

BIFF   He's got no character— Charley wouldn't do this. Not in his own house—spewing out that vomit from his mind.

HAPPY   Charley never had to cope with what he's got to.

BIFF   People are worse off than Willy Loman. Believe me, I've seen them!

LINDA   Then make Charley your father, Biff. You can't do that, can you? I don't say he's a great man. Willy Loman never made a lot of money. His name was never in the paper. He's not the finest character that ever lived. But he's a human being, and a terrible thing is happening to him. So attention must be paid. He's not to be allowed to fall into his grave like an old dog. Attention, attention must be finally paid to such a person. You called him crazy—

BIFF   I didn't mean—

LINDA   No, a lot of people think he's lost his—balance. But you don't have to be very smart to know what his trouble is. The man is exhausted.

HAPPY   Sure!

LINDA   A small man can be just as exhausted as a great man. He works for a company thirty-six years this March, opens up unheard-of territories to their trademark, and now in his old age they take his salary away.

HAPPY [*indignantly*]   I didn't know that, Mom.

LINDA   You never asked, my dear! Now that you get your spending money someplace else you don't trouble your mind with him.

HAPPY   But I gave you money last—

LINDA   Christmas time, fifty dollars! To fix the hot water it cost ninety-seven fifty! For five weeks he's been on straight commission, like a beginner, an unknown!

BIFF   Those ungrateful bastards!

LINDA   Are they any worse than his sons? When he brought them business, when he was young, they were glad to see him. But now his old friends, the old buyers that loved him so and always found some order to hand him in a pinch—they're all dead, retired. He used to be able to make six, seven calls a day in Boston. Now he takes his valises out of the car and puts them back and takes them out again and he's exhausted. Instead of walking he talks now. He drives seven hundred miles, and when he gets there no one knows him any more, no one welcomes him. And what goes through a man's mind, driving seven hundred miles home without having earned a cent? Why shouldn't he talk to himself? Why? When he has to go to Charley and borrow fifty dollars a week and pretend to me that it's his pay? How long can that go on? How long? You see what I'm sitting here and waiting for? And you tell me he has no character? The man who never worked a day but for your benefit? When does he get the medal for that? Is this his reward—to turn around at the age of sixty-three and find his sons, who he loved better than his life, one a philandering bum—

HAPPY   Mom!

LINDA   That's what you are, my baby! [*To* BIFF] And you! What happened to the love you had for him? You were such pals! How you used to talk to him on the phone every night! How lonely he was till he could come home to you!

BIFF   All right, Mom. I'll live here in my room, and I'll get a job. I'll keep away from him, that's all.

LINDA   No, Biff. You can't stay here and fight all the time.

BIFF   He threw me out of this house, remember that.

LINDA   Why did he do that? I never knew why.

BIFF   Because I know he's a fake and he doesn't like anybody around who knows!

LINDA   Why a fake? In what way? What do you mean?

BIFF   Just don't lay it all at my feet. It's between me and him—that's all I have to say. I'll chip in from now on. He'll settle for half my pay check. He'll be all right. I'm going to bed. [*He starts for the stairs.*]

LINDA   He won't be all right.

BIFF [*turning on the stairs, furiously*]   I hate this city and I'll stay here. Now what do you want?

LINDA   He's dying, Biff.

HAPPY *turns quickly to her, shocked.*

BIFF [*after a pause*]   Why is he dying?

LINDA   He's been trying to kill himself.

BIFF [*with great horror*]   How?

LINDA   I live from day to day.

BIFF   What're you talking about?

LINDA   Remember I wrote you that he smashed up the car again? In February?

BIFF   Well?

LINDA   The insurance inspector came. He said that they have evidence. That all these accidents in the last year—weren't—weren't—accidents.

HAPPY   How can they tell that? That's a lie.

LINDA   It seems there's a woman . . . [*She takes a breath as*

(BIFF, *sharply but contained*]   What woman?

(LINDA, *simultaneously*] . . . and this woman . . .

LINDA   What?

BIFF   Nothing. Go ahead.

LINDA   What did you say?

BIFF   Nothing. I just said what woman?

HAPPY   What about her?

LINDA   Well, it seems she was walking down the road and saw his car. She says that he wasn't driving fast at all, and that he didn't skid. She says he came to that little bridge, and then deliberately smashed into the railing, and it was only the shallowness of the water that saved him.

BIFF   Oh, no, he probably just fell asleep again.

LINDA   I don't think he fell asleep.

BIFF   Why not?

LINDA   Last month . . . [*With great difficulty*] Oh, boys, it's so hard to say a thing like this! He's just a big stupid man to you, but I tell you there's more good in him than in many other people. [*She chokes, wipes her eyes.*] I was looking for a fuse. The lights blew out, and I went down the cellar. And behind the fuse box—it happened to fall out—was a length of rubber pipe—just short.

HAPPY   No kidding?

LINDA   There's a little attachment on the end of it. I knew right away. And sure enough, on the bottom of the water heater there's a new little nipple on the gas pipe.

HAPPY [*angrily*]   That—jerk.

BIFF   Did you have it taken off?

LINDA   I'm—I'm ashamed to. How can I mention it to him? Every day I go down and take away that little rubber pipe. But, when he comes home, I put it back where it was. How can I insult him that way? I don't know what to do. I live from day to day, boys. I tell you, I know every thought in his mind. It sounds so old-fashioned and silly, but I tell you he put his whole life into you and you've turned your backs on him. [*She is bent over in the chair, weeping, her face in her hands.*] Biff, I swear to God! Biff, his life is in your hands!

HAPPY [*to* BIFF]   How do you like that damned fool!

BIFF [*kissing her*]   All right, pal, all right. It's all settled now. I've been remiss. I know that, Mom. But now I'll stay, and I swear to you, I'll apply myself. [*Kneeling in front of her, in a fever of self-*

reproach.] It's just—you see, Mom, I don't fit in business. Not that I won't try. I'll try, and I'll make good.

HAPPY Sure you will. The trouble with you in business was you never tried to please people.

BIFF I know, I—

HAPPY Like when you worked for Harrison's. Bob Harrison said you were tops, and then you go and do some damn fool thing like whistling whole songs in the elevator like a comedian.

BIFF [*against* HAPPY] So what? I like to whistle sometimes.

HAPPY You don't raise a guy to a responsible job who whistles in the elevator!

LINDA Well, don't argue about it now.

HAPPY Like when you'd go off and swim in the middle of the day instead of taking the line around.

BIFF [*his resentment rising*] Well, don't you run off? You take off sometimes, don't you? On a nice summer day?

HAPPY Yeah, but I cover myself!

LINDA Boys!

HAPPY If I'm going to take a fade the boss can call any number where I'm supposed to be and they'll swear to him that I just left. I'll tell you something that I hate to say, Biff, but in the business world some of them think you're crazy.

BIFF [*angered*] Screw the business world!

HAPPY All right, screw it! Great, but cover yourself!

LINDA Hap, Hap!

BIFF I don't care what they think! They've laughed at Dad for years, and you know why? Because we don't belong in this nut-house of a city! We should be mixing cement on some open plain, or—or carpenters. A carpenter is allowed to whistle!

WILLY *walks in from the entrance of the house, at left.*

WILLY Even your grandfather was better than a carpenter. [*Pause. They watch him.*] You never grew up. Bernard does not whistle in the elevator, I assure you.

BIFF [*as though to laugh* WILLY *out of it*] Yeah, but you do, Pop.

WILLY I never in my life whistled in an elevator! And who in the business world thinks I'm crazy?

BIFF I didn't mean it like that, Pop. Now don't make a whole thing out of it, will ya?

WILLY Go back to the West! Be a carpenter, a cowboy, enjoy yourself!

LINDA Willy, he was just saying—

WILLY I heard what he said!

HAPPY [*trying to quiet* WILLY] Hey, Pop, come on now . . .

WILLY [*continuing over* HAPPY'*s line*] They laugh at me, heh? Go to Filene's, go to the Hub, go to Slattery's, Boston. Call out the name Willy Loman and see what happens! Big shot!

BIFF All right, Pop.

WILLY Big!

BIFF All right!

WILLY   Why do you always insult me?

BIFF   I didn't say a word. [*To* LINDA]   Did I say a word?

LINDA   He didn't say anything, Willy.

WILLY   [*going to the doorway of the living room*]   All right, good night, good night.

LINDA   Willy, dear, he just decided . . .

WILLY   [*to* BIFF]   If you get tired hanging around tomorrow, paint the ceiling I put up in the living room.

BIFF   I'm leaving early tomorrow.

HAPPY   He's going to see Bill Oliver, Pop.

WILLY   [*interestedly*]   Oliver? For what?

BIFF   [*with reserve, but trying, trying*]   He always said he'd stake me. I'd like to go into business, so maybe I can take him up on it.

LINDA   Isn't that wonderful?

WILLY   Don't interrupt. What's wonderful about it? There's fifty men in the City of New York who'd stake him. [*To* BIFF] Sporting goods?

BIFF   I guess so. I know something about it and—

WILLY   He knows something about it! You know sporting goods better than Spalding, for God's sake! How much is he giving you?

BIFF   I don't know, I didn't even see him yet, but—

WILLY   Then what're you talkin' about?

BIFF   [*getting angry*]   Well, all I said was I'm gonna see him, that's all!

WILLY   [*turning away*]   Ah, you're counting your chickens again.

BIFF   [*starting left for the stairs*]   Oh, Jesus, I'm going to sleep!

WILLY   [*calling after him*]   Don't curse in this house!

BIFF   [*turning*]   Since when did you get so clean?

HAPPY   [*trying to stop them*]   Wait a . . .

WILLY   Don't use that language to me! I won't have it!

HAPPY   [*grabbing* BIFF, *shouts*]   Wait a minute! I got an idea. I got a feasible idea. Come here, Biff, let's talk this over now, let's talk some sense here. When I was down in Florida last time, I thought of a great idea to sell sporting goods. It just came back to me. You and I, Biff—we have a line, the Loman Line. We train a couple of weeks, and put on a couple of exhibitions, see?

WILLY   That's an idea!

HAPPY   Wait! We form two basketball teams, see? Two water polo teams. We play each other. It's a million dollars' worth of publicity. Two brothers, see? The Loman Brothers. Displays in the Royal Palms—all the hotels. And banners over the ring and the basketball court: "Loman Brothers." Baby, we could sell sporting goods!

WILLY   That is a one-million-dollar idea!

LINDA   Marvelous!

BIFF   I'm in great shape as far as that's concerned.

HAPPY   And the beauty of it is, Biff, it wouldn't be like a business. We'd be out playin' ball again . . .

BIFF   [*enthused*]   Yeah, that's . . .

WILLY   Million-dollar . . .

HAPPY   And you wouldn't get fed up with it, Biff. It'd be the family again. There'd be the old honor, and comradeship, and if you wanted to go off for a swim or somethin'—well, you'd do it! Without some smart cooky gettin' up ahead of you!

WILLY   Lick the world! You guys together could absolutely lick the civilized world.

BIFF   I'll see Oliver tomorrow. Hap, if we could work that out . . .

LINDA   Maybe things are beginning to—

WILLY   [*wildly enthused, to* LINDA]   Stop interrupting! [*To* BIFF] But don't wear sport jacket and slacks when you see Oliver.

BIFF   No, I'll—

WILLY   A business suit, and talk as little as possible, and don't crack any jokes.

BIFF   He did like me. Always liked me.

LINDA   He loved you!

WILLY   [*to* LINDA]   Will you stop! [*To* BIFF] Walk in very serious. You are not applying for a boy's job. Money is to pass. Be quiet, fine, and serious. Everybody likes a kidder, but nobody lends him money.

HAPPY   I'll try to get some myself, Biff. I'm sure I can.

WILLY   I see great things for you kids, I think your troubles are over. But remember, start big and you'll end big. Ask for fifteen. How much you gonna ask for?

BIFF   Gee, I don't know—

WILLY   And don't say "Gee." "Gee" is a boy's word. A man walking in for fifteen thousand dollars does not say "Gee!"

BIFF   Ten, I think, would be top though.

WILLY   Don't be so modest. You always started too low. Walk in with a big laugh. Don't look worried. Start off with a couple of your good stories to lighten things up. It's not what you say, it's how you say it—because personality always wins the day.

LINDA   Oliver always thought the highest of him—

WILLY   Will you let me talk?

BIFF   Don't yell at her, Pop, will ya?

WILLY   [*angrily*]   I was talking, wasn't I?

BIFF   I don't like you yelling at her all the time, and I'm tellin' you, that's all.

WILLY   What're you, takin' over this house?

LINDA   Willy—

WILLY   [*turning on her*]   Don't take his side all the time, goddammit!

BIFF   [*furiously*]   Stop yelling at her!

WILLY   [*suddenly pulling on his cheek, beaten down, guilt ridden*] Give my best to Bill Oliver—he may remember me. [*He exits through the living room doorway.*]

LINDA   [*her voice subdued*]   What'd you have to start that for? [BIFF *turns away.*] You see how sweet he was as soon as you talked hopefully? [*She goes over to* BIFF.] Come up and say good night to him. Don't let him go to bed that way.

HAPPY   Come on, Biff, let's buck him up.

LINDA   Please, dear. Just say good night. It takes so little to make him happy. Come. [*She goes through the living room doorway, calling upstairs from within the living room*] Your pajamas are hanging in the bathroom, Willy!

HAPPY   [*looking toward where* LINDA *went out*]   What a woman! They broke the mold when they made her. You know that, Biff?

BIFF   He's off salary. My God, working on commission!

HAPPY   Well, let's face it: he's no hot-shot selling man. Except that sometimes, you have to admit, he's a sweet personality.

BIFF [*deciding*]   Lend me ten bucks, will ya? I want to buy some new ties.

HAPPY   I'll take you to a place I know. Beautiful stuff. Wear one of my striped shirts tomorrow.

BIFF   She got gray. Mom got awful old. Gee, I'm gonna go in to Oliver tomorrow and knock him for a—

HAPPY   Come on up. Tell that to Dad. Let's give him a whirl. Come on.

BIFF [*steamed up*]   You know, with ten thousand bucks, boy!

HAPPY [*as they go into the living room*]   That's the talk, Biff, that's the first time I've heard the old confidence out of you! [*From within the living room, fading off*] You're gonna live with me, kid, and any babe you want just say the word . . . [*The last lines are hardly heard. They are mounting the stairs to their parents' bedroom.*]

LINDA [*entering her bedroom and addressing* WILLY, *who is in the bathroom. She is straightening the bed for him*]   Can you do anything about the shower? It drips.

WILLY [*from the bathroom*]   All of a sudden everything falls to pieces! Goddam plumbing, oughta be sued, those people. I hardly finished putting it in and the thing . . . [*His words rumble off.*]

LINDA   I'm just wondering if Oliver will remember him. You think he might?

WILLY [*coming out of the bathroom in his pajamas*]   Remember him? What's the matter with you, you crazy? If he'd've stayed with Oliver he'd be on top by now! Wait'll Oliver gets a look at him. You don't know the average caliber any more. The average young man today—[*he is getting into bed*]—is got a caliber of zero. Greatest thing in the world for him was to bum around.

   BIFF *and* HAPPY *enter the bedroom. Slight pause.*

WILLY [*stops short, looking at* BIFF]   Glad to hear it, boy.

HAPPY   He wanted to say good night to you, sport.

WILLY [*to* BIFF]   Yeah. Knock him dead, boy. What'd you want to tell me?

BIFF   Just take it easy, Pop. Good night. [*He turns to go.*]

WILLY [*unable to resist*]   And if anything falls off the desk while you're talking to him—like a package or something—don't you pick it up. They have office boys for that.

LINDA   I'll make a big breakfast—

WILLY   Will you let me finish? [*To* BIFF]   Tell him you were in the business in the West. Not farm work.

BIFF   All right, Dad.

LINDA   I think everything—

WILLY [*going right through her speech*]   And don't undersell yourself. No less than fifteen thousand dollars.

BIFF [*unable to bear him*]   Okay. Good night, Mom. [*He starts moving.*]

WILLY   Because you got a greatness in you, Biff, remember that. You got all kinds a greatness . . . [*He lies back, exhausted.* BIFF *walks out.*]

LINDA [*calling after* BIFF]   Sleep well, darling!

HAPPY   I'm gonna get married, Mom. I wanted to tell you.

LINDA   Go to sleep, dear.

HAPPY   [*going*]   I just wanted to tell you.

WILLY   Keep up the good work. [HAPPY *exits.*] God . . . remember
that Ebbets Field[4] game? The championship of the city?

LINDA   Just rest. Should I sing to you?

WILLY   Yeah. Sing to me. [LINDA *hums a soft lullaby.*] When that
team came out—he was the tallest, remember?

LINDA   Oh, yes. And in gold.

> BIFF *enters the darkened kitchen, takes a cigarette, and leaves
> the house. He comes downstage into a golden pool of light. He
> smokes, staring at the night.*

WILLY   Like a young god. Hercules—something like that. And the
sun all around him. Remember how he waved to me? Right up from
the field, with the representatives of three colleges standing by?
And the buyers I brought, and the cheers when he came out—
Loman, Loman, Loman! God Almighty, he'll be great yet. A star
like that, magnificent, can never really fade away!

> *The light on* WILLY *is fading. The gas heater begins to glow
> through the kitchen wall, near the stairs, a blue flame beneath
> red coils.*

LINDA   [*timidly*]   Willy dear, what has he got against you?

WILLY   I'm so tired. Don't talk any more.

> BIFF *slowly returns to the kitchen. He stops, stares toward the
> heater.*

LINDA   Will you ask Howard to let you work in New York?

WILLY   First thing in the morning. Everything'll be all right.

> BIFF *reaches behind the heater and draws out a length of
> rubber tubing. He is horrified and turns his head toward
> WILLY's room, still dimly lit, from which the strains of LINDA's
> desperate but monotonous humming rise.*

WILLY   [*staring through the window into the moonlight*]   Gee, look
at the moon moving between the buildings!

> BIFF *wraps the tubing around his hand and quickly goes up
> the stairs.*

CURTAIN

---

4. A Brooklyn sports stadium named after Charles H. Ebbets (1859–1925) and
torn down in 1960.

Act 2

Music is heard, gay and bright. The curtain rises as the music fades away. WILLY, *in shirt sleeves, is sitting at the kitchen table, sipping coffee, his hat in his lap.* LINDA *is filling his cup when she can.*

WILLY   Wonderful coffee. Meal in itself.

LINDA   Can I make you some eggs?

WILLY   No. Take a breath.

LINDA   You look so rested, dear.

WILLY   I slept like a dead one. First time in months. Imagine, sleeping till ten on a Tuesday morning. Boys left nice and early, heh?

LINDA   They were out of here by eight o'clock.

WILLY   Good work!

LINDA   It was so thrilling to see them leaving together. I can't get over the shaving lotion in this house!

WILLY [*smiling*]   Mmm—

LINDA   Biff was very changed this morning. His whole attitude seemed to be hopeful. He couldn't wait to get downtown to see Oliver.

WILLY   He's heading for a change. There's no question, there simply are certain men that take longer to get—solidified. How did he dress?

LINDA   His blue suit. He's so handsome in that suit. He could be a—anything in that suit!

WILLY *gets up from the table.* LINDA *holds his jacket for him.*

WILLY   There's no question, no question at all. Gee, on the way home tonight I'd like to buy some seeds.

LINDA [*laughing*]   That'd be wonderful. But not enough sun gets back there. Nothing'll grow any more.

WILLY   You wait, kid, before it's all over we're gonna get a little place out in the country, and I'll raise some vegetables, a couple of chickens . . .

LINDA   You'll do it yet, dear.

WILLY *walks out of his jacket.* LINDA *follows him.*

WILLY   And they'll get married, and come for a weekend. I'd build a little guest house. 'Cause I got so many fine tools, all I'd need would be a little lumber and some peace of mind.

LINDA [*joyfully*]   I sewed the lining . . .

WILLY   I could build two guest houses, so they'd both come. Did he decide how much he's going to ask Oliver for?

LINDA [*getting him into the jacket*]   He didn't mention it, but I imagine ten or fifteen thousand. You going to talk to Howard today?

WILLY   Yeah. I'll put it to him straight and simple. He'll just have to take me off the road.

LINDA   And Willy, don't forget to ask for a little advance, because we've got the insurance premium. It's the grace period now.

WILLY   That's a hundred . . . ?

LINDA   A hundred and eight, sixty-eight. Because we're a little short again.

WILLY   Why are we short?

LINDA   Well, you had the motor job on the car . . .

WILLY   That goddam Studebaker!

LINDA   And you got one more payment on the refrigerator . . .

WILLY   But it just broke again!

LINDA   Well, it's old, dear.

WILLY   I told you we should've bought a well-advertised machine. Charley bought a General Electric and it's twenty years old and it's still good, that son-of-a-bitch.

LINDA   But, Willy—

WILLY   Whoever heard of a Hastings refrigerator? Once in my life I would like to own something outright before it's broken! I'm always in a race with the junkyard! I just finished paying for the car and it's on its last legs. The refrigerator consumes belts like a goddam maniac. They time those things. They time them so when you finally paid for them, they're used up.

LINDA   [*buttoning up his jacket as he unbuttons it*]   All told, about two hundred dollars would carry us, dear. But that includes the last payment on the mortgage. After this payment, Willy, the house belongs to us.

WILLY   It's twenty-five years!

LINDA   Biff was nine years old when we bought it.

WILLY   Well, that's a great thing. To weather a twenty-five-year mortgage is—

LINDA   It's an accomplishment.

WILLY   All the cement, the lumber, the reconstruction I put in this house! There ain't a crack to be found in it any more.

LINDA   Well, it served its purpose.

WILLY   What purpose? Some stranger'll come along, move in, and that's that. If only Biff would take this house, and raise a family . . . [*He starts to go.*] Good-by, I'm late.

LINDA   [*suddenly remembering*]   Oh, I forgot! You're supposed to meet them for dinner.

WILLY   Me?

LINDA   At Frank's Chop House on Forty-eighth near Sixth Avenue.

WILLY   Is that so! How about you?

LINDA   No, just the three of you. They're gonna blow you to a big meal!

WILLY   Don't say! Who thought of that?

LINDA   Biff came to me this morning, Willy, and he said, "Tell Dad, we want to blow him to a big meal." Be there six o'clock. You and your two boys are going to have dinner.

WILLY   Gee whiz! That's really somethin'. I'm gonna knock Howard for a loop, kid. I'll get an advance, and I'll come home with a New York job. Goddammit, now I'm gonna do it!

LINDA   Oh, that's the spirit, Willy!

WILLY   I will never get behind a wheel the rest of my life!

LINDA   It's changing, Willy, I can feel it changing!

WILLY   Beyond a question. G'by, I'm late. [*He starts to go again.*]

LINDA   [*calling after him as she runs to the kitchen table for a hand-*

kerchief]   You got your glasses?

WILLY [*feels for them, then comes back in*]   Yeah, yeah, got my glasses.

LINDA [*giving him the handkerchief*]   And a handkerchief.

WILLY   Yeah, handkerchief.

LINDA   And your saccharin?

WILLY   Yeah, my saccharin.

LINDA   Be careful on the subway stairs.

She kisses him, and a silk stocking is seen hanging from her hand. WILLY *notices it.*

WILLY   Will you stop mending stockings? At least while I'm in the house. It gets me nervous. I can't tell you. Please.

LINDA *hides the stocking in her hand as she follows* WILLY *across the forestage in front of the house.*

LINDA   Remember, Frank's Chop House.

WILLY [*passing the apron*]   Maybe beets would grow out there.

LINDA [*laughing*]   But you tried so many times.

WILLY   Yeah. Well, don't work hard today. [*He disappears around the right corner of the house.*]

LINDA   Be careful!

As WILLY *vanishes,* LINDA *waves to him. Suddenly the phone rings. She runs across the stage and into the kitchen and lifts it.*

LINDA   Hello? Oh, Biff! I'm so glad you called, I just . . . Yes, sure, I just told him. Yes, he'll be there for dinner at six o'clock, I didn't forget. Listen, I was just dying to tell you. You know that little rubber pipe I told you about? That he connected to the gas heater? I finally decided to go down the cellar this morning and take it away and destroy it. But it's gone! Imagine? He took it away himself, it isn't there! [*She listens.*] When? Oh, then you took it. Oh—nothing, it's just that I'd hoped he'd taken it away himself. Oh, I'm not worried, darling, because this morning he left in such high spirits, it was like the old days! I'm not afraid any more. Did Mr. Oliver see you? . . . Well, you wait there then. And make a nice impression on him, darling. Just don't perspire too much before you see him. And have a nice time with Dad. He may have big news too! . . . That's right, a New York job. And be sweet to him tonight, dear. Be loving to him. Because he's only a little boat looking for a harbor. [*She is trembling with sorrow and joy.*] Oh, that's wonderful, Biff, you'll save his life. Thanks, darling. Just put your arm around him when he comes into the restaurant. Give him a smile. That's the boy . . . Good-by, dear. . . . You got your comb? . . . That's fine. Good-by, Biff dear.

In the middle of her speech, HOWARD WAGNER, *thirty-six, wheels on a small typewriter table on which is a wire-recording*

*machine and proceeds to plug it in. This is on the left fore-
stage. Light slowly fades on* LINDA *as it rises on* HOWARD.
HOWARD *is intent on threading the machine and only glances
over his shoulder as* WILLY *appears.*

WILLY   Pst! Pst!
HOWARD   Hello, Willy, come in.
WILLY   Like to have a little talk with you, Howard.
HOWARD   Sorry to keep you waiting. I'll be with you in a minute.
WILLY   What's that, Howard?
HOWARD   Didn't you ever see one of these? Wire recorder.
WILLY   Oh. Can we talk a minute?
HOWARD   Records things. Just got delivery yesterday. Been driving
me crazy, the most terrific machine I ever saw in my life. I was up
all night with it.
WILLY   What do you do with it?
HOWARD   I bought it for dictation, but you can do anything with it.
Listen to this. I had it home last night. Listen to what I picked up.
The first one is my daughter. Get this. [*He flicks the switch and
"Roll out the Barrel" is heard being whistled.*] Listen to that kid
whistle.
WILLY   That is lifelike, isn't it?
HOWARD   Seven years old. Get that tone.
WILLY   Ts, ts. Like to ask a little favor if you . . .

The whistling breaks off, and the voice of HOWARD's *daughter
is heard.*

HIS DAUGHTER   "Now you, Daddy."
HOWARD   She's crazy for me! [*Again the same song is whistled.*]
That's me! Ha! [*He winks.*]
WILLY   You're very good!

*The whistling breaks off again. The machine runs silent for a
moment.*

HOWARD   Sh! Get this now, this is my son.
HIS SON   "The capital of Alabama is Montgomery; the capital of
Arizona is Phoenix; the capital of Arkansas is Little Rock; the
capital of California is Sacramento . . ." [*and on, and on.*]
HOWARD [*holding up five fingers*]   Five years old. Willy!
WILLY   He'll make an announcer some day!
HIS SON [*continuing*]   "The capital . . ."
HOWARD   Get that—alphabetical order! [*The machine breaks off sud-
denly.*] Wait a minute. The maid kicked the plug out.
WILLY   It certainly is a—
HOWARD   Sh, for God's sake!
HIS SON   "It's nine o'clock, Bulova watch time. So I have to go to
sleep."
WILLY   That really is—
HOWARD   Wait a minute! The next is my wife.

They wait.

HOWARD'S VOICE   "Go on, say something." [*Pause.*] "Well, you gonna talk?"

HIS WIFE   "I can't think of anything."

HOWARD'S VOICE   "Well, talk—it's turning."

HIS WIFE [*shyly, beaten*]   "Hello." [*Silence.*] "Oh, Howard, I can't talk into this . . ."

HOWARD [*snapping the machine off*]   That was my wife.

WILLY   That is a wonderful machine. Can we—

HOWARD   I tell you, Willy, I'm gonna take my camera, and my band-saw, and all my hobbies, and out they go. This is the most fascinating relaxation I ever found.

WILLY   I think I'll get one myself.

HOWARD   Sure, they're only a hundred and a half. You can't do without it. Supposing you wanna hear Jack Benny,[5] see? But you can't be at home at that hour. So you tell the maid to turn the radio on when Jack Benny comes on, and this automatically goes on with the radio . . .

WILLY   And when you come home you . . .

HOWARD   You can come home twelve o'clock, one o'clock, any time you like, and you get yourself a Coke and sit yourself down, throw the switch, and there's Jack Benny's program in the middle of the night!

WILLY   I'm definitely going to get one. Because lots of time I'm on the road, and I think to myself, what I must be missing on the radio!

HOWARD   Don't you have a radio in the car?

WILLY   Well, yeah, but who ever thinks of turning it on?

HOWARD   Say, aren't you supposed to be in Boston?

WILLY   That's what I want to talk to you about, Howard. You got a minute? [*He draws a chair in from the wing.*]

HOWARD   What happened? What're you doing here?

WILLY   Well . . .

HOWARD   You didn't crack up again, did you?

WILLY   Oh, no. No . . .

HOWARD   Geez, you had me worried there for a minute. What's the trouble?

WILLY   Well, tell you the truth, Howard. I've come to the decision that I'd rather not travel any more.

HOWARD   Not travel! Well, what'll you do?

WILLY   Remember, Christmas time, when you had the party here? You said you'd try to think of some spot for me here in town.

HOWARD   With us?

WILLY   Well, sure.

HOWARD   Oh, yeah, yeah. I remember. Well, I couldn't think of anything for you, Willy.

WILLY   I tell ya, Howard. The kids are all grown up, y'know. I don't

5. Jack Benny (1894–1974), a vaude-   star, hosted America's most popular radio
ville, radio, television, and motion picture   show from 1932 to 1955.

need much any more. If I could take home—well, sixty-five dollars a week, I could swing it.

HOWARD   Yeah, but Willy, see I—

WILLY   I tell ya why, Howard. Speaking frankly and between the two of us, y'know—I'm just a little tired.

HOWARD   Oh, I could understand that, Willy. But you're a road man, Willy, and we do a road business. We've only got a half-dozen salesmen on the floor here.

WILLY   God knows, Howard, I never asked a favor of any man. But I was with the firm when your father used to carry you in here in his arms.

HOWARD   I know that, Willy, but—

WILLY   Your father came to me the day you were born and asked me what I thought of the name of Howard, may he rest in peace.

HOWARD   I appreciate that, Willy, but there just is no spot here for you. If I had a spot I'd slam you right in, but I just don't have a single solitary spot.

He looks for his lighter. WILLY *has picked it up and gives it to him. Pause.*

WILLY [*with increasing anger*]   Howard, all I need to set my table is fifty dollars a week.

HOWARD   But where am I going to put you, kid?

WILLY   Look, it isn't a question of whether I can sell merchandise, is it?

HOWARD   No, but it's a business, kid, and everybody's gotta pull his own weight.

WILLY [*desperately*]   Just let me tell you a story, Howard—

HOWARD   'Cause you gotta admit, business is business.

WILLY [*angrily*]   Business is definitely business, but just listen for a minute. You don't understand this. When I was a boy—eighteen, nineteen—I was already on the road. And there was a question in my mind as to whether selling had a future for me. Because in those days I had a yearning to go to Alaska. See, there were three gold strikes in one month in Alaska, and I felt like going out. Just for the ride, you might say.

HOWARD [*barely interested*]   Don't say.

WILLY   Oh, yeah, my father lived many years in Alaska. He was an adventurous man. We've got quite a little streak of self-reliance in our family. I thought I'd go out with my older brother and try to locate him, and maybe settle in the North with the old man. And I was almost decided to go when I met a salesman in the Parker House. His name was Dave Singleman. And he was eighty-four years old, and he'd drummed merchandise in thirty-one states. And old Dave, he'd go up to his room, y'understand, put on his green velvet slippers—I'll never forget—and pick up his phone and call the buyers, and without ever leaving his room, at the age of eighty-four, he made his living. And when I saw that, I realized that selling was the greatest career a man could want. 'Cause what could be more satisfying than to be able to go, at the age of eighty-four, into twenty or thirty different cities, and pick up a phone, and be remembered and loved and helped by so many different people? Do you know? when he died—and by the way he died the death of a salesman, in his green velvet slippers in the smoker of the New York, New Haven and Hartford, going into Boston—when he died, hundreds of salesmen and buyers were at his funeral. Things were sad on a lotta trains for months after that. [*He stands up.* HOWARD *has not looked at him.*] In those days there was personality in it, Howard. There was respect, and comradeship, and gratitude in it. Today, it's all cut and dried, and there's no chance for bringing friendship to bear—or personality. You see what I mean? They don't know me any more.

HOWARD [*moving away, to the right*]   That's just the thing, Willy.

WILLY   If I had forty dollars a week—that's all I'd need. Forty dollars, Howard.

HOWARD   Kid, I can't take blood from a stone, I—

WILLY [*desperation is on him now*]   Howard, the year Al Smith[6] was nominated, your father came to me and—

HOWARD [*starting to go off*]   I've got to see some people, kid.

WILLY [*stopping him*]   I'm talking about your father! There were promises made across this desk! You mustn't tell me you've got people to see—I put thirty-four years into this firm, Howard, and now I can't pay my insurance! You can't eat the orange and throw the peel away—a man is not a piece of fruit! [*After a pause*] Now pay attention. Your father—in 1928 I had a big year. I averaged a hundred and seventy dollars a week in commissions.

HOWARD [*impatiently*]   Now, Willy, you never averaged—

WILLY [*banging his hand on the desk*]   I averaged a hundred and seventy dollars a week in the year of 1928! And your father came to me—or rather, I was in the office here—it was right over this desk—and he put his hand on my shoulder—

HOWARD [*getting up*]   You'll have to excuse me, Willy, I gotta see some people. Pull yourself together. [*Going out*] I'll be back in a little while.

On HOWARD's *exit, the light on his chair grows very bright and strange.*

WILLY   Pull myself together! What the hell did I say to him? My God, I was yelling at him! How could I! [WILLY *breaks off, staring at the light, which occupies the chair, animating it. He approaches this chair, standing across the desk from it.*] Frank, Frank, don't you remember what you told me that time? How you put your hand on my shoulder, and Frank . . . [*He leans on the desk and as he speaks the dead man's name he accidentally switches on the recorder, and instantly:*]

HOWARD'S SON   ". . . of New York is Albany. The capital of Ohio is Cincinnati, the capital of Rhode Island is . . ." [*The recitation continues.*]

---

6. Alfred E. Smith (1873–1944) was the Democratic presidential nominee who lost to Herbert Hoover in 1928.

WILLY [*leaping away with fright, shouting*] Ha! Howard! Howard! Howard!

HOWARD [*rushing in*] What happened?

WILLY [*pointing at the machine, which continues nasally, childishly, with the capital cities*] Shut it off! Shut it off!

HOWARD [*pulling the plug out*] Look, Willy . . .

WILLY [*pressing his hands to his eyes*] I gotta get myself some coffee. I'll get some coffee . . .

WILLY *starts to walk out.* HOWARD *stops him.*

HOWARD [*rolling up the cord*] Willy, look . . .

WILLY I'll go to Boston.

HOWARD Willy, you can't go to Boston for us.

WILLY Why can't I go?

HOWARD I don't want you to represent us. I've been meaning to tell you for a long time now.

WILLY Howard, are you firing me?

HOWARD I think you need a good long rest, Willy.

WILLY Howard—

HOWARD And when you feel better, come back, and we'll see if we can work something out.

WILLY But I gotta earn money, Howard. I'm in no position to—

HOWARD Where are your sons? Why don't your sons give you a hand?

WILLY They're working on a very big deal.

HOWARD This is no time for false pride, Willy. You go to your sons and you tell them that you're tired. You've got two great boys, haven't you?

WILLY Oh, no question, no question, but in the meantime . . .

HOWARD Then that's that, heh?

WILLY All right, I'll go to Boston tomorrow.

HOWARD No, no.

WILLY I can't throw myself on my sons. I'm not a cripple!

HOWARD Look, kid, I'm busy this morning.

WILLY [*grasping* HOWARD'S *arm*] Howard, you've got to let me go to Boston!

HOWARD [*hard, keeping himself under control*] I've got a line of people to see this morning. Sit down, take five minutes, and pull yourself together, and then go home, will ya? I need the office, Willy. [*He starts to go; turns, remembering the recorder, starts to push off the table holding the recorder.*] Oh, yeah. Whenever you can this week, stop by and drop off the samples. You'll feel better, Willy, and then come back and we'll talk. Pull yourself together, kid, there's people outside.

HOWARD *exits, pushing the table off left.* WILLY *stares into space, exhausted. Now the music is heard—*BEN'S *music—first distantly, then closer, closer. As* WILLY *speaks,* BEN *enters from the right. He carries valise and umbrella.*

WILLY Oh, Ben, how did you do it? What is the answer? Did you wind up the Alaska deal already?

BEN   Doesn't take much time if you know what you're doing. Just a short business trip. Boarding ship in an hour. Wanted to say good-by.

WILLY   Ben, I've got to talk to you.

BEN [*glancing at his watch*]   Haven't the time, William.

WILLY [*crossing the apron to* BEN]   Ben, nothing's working out. I don't know what to do.

BEN   Now, look here, William. I've bought timberland in Alaska and I need a man to look after things for me.

WILLY   God, timberland! Me and my boys in those grand outdoors!

BEN   You've a new continent at your doorstep, William. Get out of these cities, they're full of talk and time payments and courts of law. Screw on your fists and you can fight for a fortune up there.

WILLY   Yes, yes! Linda, Linda!

LINDA *enters as of old, with the wash.*

LINDA   Oh, you're back?

BEN   I haven't much time.

WILLY   No, wait! Linda, he's got a proposition for me in Alaska.

LINDA   But you've got— [*To* BEN]He's got a beautiful job here.

WILLY   But in Alaska, kid, I could—

LINDA   You're doing well enough, Willy!

BEN [*to* LINDA]   Enough for what, my dear?

LINDA [*frightened of* BEN *and angry at him*]   Don't say those things to him! Enough to be happy right here, right now. [*To* WILLY, *while* BEN *laughs*] Why must everybody conquer the world? You're well liked, and the boys love you, and someday—[*to* BEN]—why, old man Wagner told him just the other day that if he keeps it up he'll be a member of the firm, didn't he, Willy?

WILLY   Sure, sure. I am building something with this firm, Ben, and if a man is building something he must be on the right track, mustn't he?

BEN   What are you building? Lay your hand on it. Where is it?

WILLY [*hesitantly*]   That's true, Linda, there's nothing.

LINDA   Why? [*To* BEN] There's a man eighty-four years old—

WILLY   That's right, Ben, that's right. When I look at that man I say, what is there to worry about?

BEN   Bah!

WILLY   It's true, Ben. All he has to do is go into any city, pick up the phone, and he's making his living and you know why?

BEN [*picking up his valise*]   I've got to go.

WILLY [*holding* BEN *back*]   Look at this boy!

Biff, *in his high school sweater, enters carrying suitcase.* HAPPY *carries* BIFF's *shoulder guards, gold helmet, and football pants.*

WILLY   Without a penny to his name, three great universities are begging for him, and from there the sky's the limit, because it's not what you do, Ben. It's who you know and the smile on your face! It's contacts, Ben, contacts! The whole wealth of Alaska passes over the lunch table at the Commodore Hotel, and that's the wonder, the wonder of this country, that a man can end with diamonds here on the basis of being liked! [*He turns to* BIFF.] And that's why when you get out on that field today it's important. Because thousands of people will be rooting for you and loving you. [*To* BEN, *who has again begun to leave*] And Ben! when he walks into a business office his name will sound out like a bell and all the doors will open to him! I've seen it, Ben, I've seen it a thousand times! You can't feel it with your hand like timber, but it's there!

BEN   Good-by, William.

WILLY   Ben, am I right? Don't you think I'm right? I value your advice.

BEN   There's a new continent at your doorstep, William. You could walk out rich. Rich! [*He is gone.*]

WILLY   We'll do it here, Ben! You hear me? We're gonna do it here!

YOUNG BERNARD *rushes in. The gay music of the Boys is heard.*

BERNARD   Oh, gee, I was afraid you left already!

WILLY   Why? What time is it?

BERNARD   It's half-past one!

WILLY   Well, come on, everybody! Ebbets Field next stop! Where's the pennants? [*He rushes through the wall-line of the kitchen and out into the living room.*]

LINDA [*to* BIFF]   Did you pack fresh underwear?

BIFF [*who has been limbering up*]   I want to go!

BERNARD   Biff, I'm carrying your helmet, ain't I?

HAPPY   No, I'm carrying the helmet.

BERNARD   Oh, Biff, you promised me.

HAPPY   I'm carrying the helmet.

BERNARD   How am I going to get in the locker room?

LINDA   Let him carry the shoulder guards. [*She puts her coat and hat on in the kitchen.*]

BERNARD   Can I, Biff? 'Cause I told everybody I'm going to be in the locker room.

HAPPY   In Ebbets Field it's the clubhouse.

BERNARD   I meant the clubhouse. Biff!

HAPPY   Biff!

BIFF [*grandly, after a slight pause*]   Let him carry the shoulder guards.

HAPPY [*as he gives* BERNARD *the shoulder guards*]   Stay close to us now.

WILLY *rushes in with the pennants.*

WILLY [*handing them out*]   Everybody wave when Biff comes out on the field. [HAPPY *and* BERNARD *run off.*] You set now, boy?

The music has died away.

BIFF   Ready to go, Pop. Every muscle is ready.

WILLY [*at the edge of the apron*]   You realize what this means?

BIFF　That's right, Pop.

WILLY　[*feeling* BIFF's *muscles*]　You're comin' home this afternoon captain of the All-Scholastic Championship Team of the City of New York.

BIFF　I got it, Pop. And remember, pal, when I take off my helmet, that touchdown is for you.

WILLY　Let's go! [*He is starting out, with his arm around* BIFF, *when* CHARLEY *enters, as of old, in knickers*]　I got no room for you, Charley.

CHARLEY　Room? For what?

WILLY　In the car.

CHARLEY　You goin' for a ride? I wanted to shoot some casino.

WILLY　[*furiously*]　Casino! [*Incredulously*]　Don't you realize what today is?

LINDA　Oh, he knows, Willy. He's just kidding you.

WILLY　That's nothing to kid about!

CHARLEY　No, Linda, what's goin' on?

LINDA　He's playing in Ebbets Field.

CHARLEY　Baseball in this weather?

WILLY　Don't talk to him. Come on, come on! [*He is pushing them out.*]

CHARLEY　Wait a minute, didn't you hear the news?

WILLY　What?

CHARLEY　Don't you listen to the radio? Ebbets Field just blew up.

WILLY　You go to hell! [CHARLEY *laughs. Pushing them out*]　Come on, come on! We're late.

CHARLEY　[*as they go*]　Knock a homer, Biff, knock a homer!

WILLY　[*the last to leave, turning to* CHARLEY]　I don't think that was funny, Charley. This is the greatest day of his life.

CHARLEY　Willy, when are you going to grow up?

WILLY　Yeah, heh? When this game is over, Charley, you'll be laughing out the other side of your face. They'll be calling him another Red Grange.[7] Twenty-five thousand a year.

CHARLEY　[*kidding*]　Is that so?

WILLY　Yeah, that's so.

CHARLEY　Well, then, I'm sorry, Willy. But tell me something.

WILLY　What?

CHARLEY　Who is Red Grange?

WILLY　Put up your hands. Goddam you, put up your hands!

CHARLEY, *chuckling, shakes his head and walks away, around the left corner of the stage.* WILLY *follows him. The music rises to a mocking frenzy.*

WILLY　Who the hell do you think you are, better than everybody else? You don't know everything, you big, ignorant, stupid . . . Put up your hands!

Light rises, on the right side of the forestage, on a small table in the reception room of CHARLEY's *office. Traffic sounds are*

---

7. Harold Edward Grange, All-American halfback at the University of Illinois (1923–1925) who played professionally with the Chicago Bears.

heard. BERNARD, *now mature, sits whistling to himself. A pair of tennis rackets and an overnight bag are on the floor beside him.*

WILLY [*offstage*]   What are you walking away for? Don't walk away! If you're going to say something say it to my face! I know you laugh at me behind my back. You'll laugh out of the other side of your goddam face after this game. Touchdown! Touchdown! Eighty thousand people! Touchdown! Right between the goal posts.

BERNARD *is a quiet, but self-assured young man.* WILLY's *voice is coming from right upstage now.* BERNARD *lowers his feet off the table and listens.* JENNY, *his father's secretary, enters.*

JENNY [*distressed*]   Say, Bernard, will you go out in the hall?
BERNARD   What is that noise? Who is it?
JENNY   Mr. Loman. He just got off the elevator.
BERNARD [*getting up*]   Who's he arguing with?
JENNY   Nobody. There's nobody with him. I can't deal with him any more, and your father gets all upset everytime he comes. I've got a lot of typing to do, and your father's waiting to sign it. Will you see him?
WILLY [*entering*]   Touchdown! Touch— [*He sees* JENNY.] Jenny, Jenny, good to see you. How're ya? Workin'? Or still honest?
JENNY   Fine. How've you been feeling?
WILLY   Not much any more, Jenny. Ha, ha! [*He is surprised to see the rackets.*]
BERNARD   Hello, Uncle Willy.
WILLY [*almost shocked*]   Bernard! Well, look who's here! [*He comes quickly, guiltily, to* BERNARD *and warmly shakes his hand.*]
BERNARD   How are you? Good to see you.
WILLY   What are you doing here?
BERNARD   Oh, just stopped by to see Pop. Get off my feet till my train leaves. I'm going to Washington in a few minutes.
WILLY   Is he in?
BERNARD   Yes, he's in his office with the accountant. Sit down.
WILLY [*sitting down*]   What're you going to do in Washington?
BERNARD   Oh, just a case I've got there, Willy.
WILLY   That so? [*Indicating the rackets*] You going to play tennis there?
BERNARD   I'm staying with a friend who's got a court.
WILLY   Don't say. His own tennis court. Must be fine people, I bet.
BERNARD   They are, very nice. Dad tells me Biff's in town.
WILLY [*with a big smile*]   Yeah, Biff's in. Working on a very big deal, Bernard.
BERNARD   What's Biff doing?
WILLY   Well, he's been doing very big things in the West. But he decided to establish himself here. Very big. We're having dinner. Did I hear your wife had a boy?
BERNARD   That's right. Our second.
WILLY   Two boys! What do you know!
BERNARD   What kind of a deal has Biff got?

WILLY   Well, Bill Oliver—very big sporting-goods man—he wants Biff very badly. Called him from the West. Long distance, carte blanche, special deliveries. Your friends have their own private tennis court?

BERNARD   You still with the old firm, Willy?

WILLY [*after a pause*]   I'm—I'm overjoyed to see how you made the grade, Bernard, overjoyed. It's an encouraging thing to see a young man really—really— Looks very good for Biff—very— [*He breaks off, then*] Bernard— [*He is so full of emotion, he breaks off again.*]

BERNARD   What is it, Willy?

WILLY [*small and alone*]   What—what's the secret?

BERNARD   What secret?

WILLY   How—how did you? Why didn't he ever catch on?

BERNARD   I wouldn't know that, Willy.

WILLY [*confidentially, desperately*]   You were his friend, his boyhood friend. There's something I don't understand about it. His life ended after that Ebbets Field game. From the age of seventeen nothing good ever happened to him.

BERNARD   He never trained himself for anything.

WILLY   But he did, he did. After high school he took so many correspondence courses. Radio mechanics; television; God knows what, and never made the slightest mark.

BERNARD [*taking off his glasses*]   Willy, do you want to talk candidly?

WILLY [*rising, faces* BERNARD]   I regard you as a very brilliant man, Bernard. I value your advice.

BERNARD   Oh, the hell with the advice, Willy. I couldn't advise you. There's just one thing I've always wanted to ask you. When he was supposed to graduate, and the math teacher flunked him—

WILLY   Oh, that son-of-a-bitch ruined his life.

BERNARD   Yeah, but, Willy, all he had to do was go to summer school and make up that subject.

WILLY   That's right, that's right.

BERNARD   Did you tell him not to go to summer school?

WILLY   Me? I begged him to go. I ordered him to go!

BERNARD   Then why wouldn't he go?

WILLY   Why? Why! Bernard, that question has been trailing me like a ghost for the last fifteen years. He flunked the subject, and laid down and died like a hammer hit him!

BERNARD   Take it easy, kid.

WILLY   Let me talk to you—I got nobody to talk to. Bernard, Bernard, was it my fault? Y'see? It keeps going around in my mind, maybe I did something to him. I got nothing to give him.

BERNARD   Don't take it so hard.

WILLY   Why did he lay down? What is the story there? You were his friend!

BERNARD   Willy, I remember, it was June, and our grades came out. And he's flunked math.

WILLY   That son-of-a-bitch!

BERNARD   No, it wasn't right then. Biff just got very angry, I remember, and he was ready to enroll in summer school.

WILLY [*surprised*]   He was?

BERNARD   He wasn't beaten by it·at all. But then, Willy, he disappeared from the block for almost a month. And I got the idea that he'd gone up to New England to see you. Did he have a talk with you then?

WILLY *stares in silence.*

BERNARD Willy?

WILLY [*with a strong edge of resentment in his voice*] Yeah, he came to Boston. What about it?

BERNARD Well, just that when he came back—I'll never forget this, it always mystifies me. Because I'd thought so well of Biff, even though he'd always taken advantage of me. I loved him, Willy, y'know? And he came back after that month and took his sneakers—remember those sneakers with "University of Virginia" printed on them? He was so proud of those, wore them every day. And he took them down in the cellar, and burned them up in the furnace. We had a fist fight. It lasted at least half an hour. Just the two of us, punching each other down the cellar, and crying right through it. I've often thought how strange it was that I knew he'd given up his life. What happened in Boston, Willy?

WILLY *looks at him as at an intruder.*

BERNARD I just bring it up because you asked me.

WILLY [*angrily*] Nothing. What do you mean, "What happened?" What's that got to do with anything?

BERNARD Well, don't get sore.

WILLY What are you trying to do, blame it on me? If a boy lays down is that my fault?

BERNARD Now, Willy, don't get—

WILLY Well, don't—don't talk to me that way! What does that mean, "What happened?"

CHARLEY *enters. He is in his vest, and he carries a bottle of bourbon.*

CHARLEY Hey, you're going to miss that train. [*He waves the bottle.*]

BERNARD Yeah, I'm going. [*He takes the bottle.*] Thanks, Pop. [*He picks up his rackets and bag.*] Good-by, Willy, and don't worry about it. You know, "If at first you don't succeed . . ."

WILLY Yes, I believe in that.

BERNARD But sometimes, Willy, it's better for a man just to walk away.

WILLY Walk away?

BERNARD That's right.

WILLY But if you can't walk away?

BERNARD [*after a slight pause*] I guess that's when it's tough. [*Extending his hand*] Good-by, Willy.

WILLY [*shaking* BERNARD'S *hand*] Good-by, boy.

CHARLEY [*an arm on* BERNARD'S *shoulder*] How do you like this kid? Gonna argue a case in front of the Supreme Court.

BERNARD [*protesting*] Pop!

WILLY [*genuinely shocked, pained, and happy*] No! The Supreme Court!
BERNARD   I gotta run. 'By, Dad!
CHARLEY   Knock 'em dead, Bernard!

BERNARD *goes off.*

WILLY [*as* CHARLEY *takes out his wallet*] The Supreme Court! And he didn't even mention it!
CHARLEY [*counting out money on the desk*] He don't have to—he's gonna do it.
WILLY   And you never told him what to do, did you? You never took any interest in him.
CHARLEY   My salvation is that I never took any interest in anything. There's some money—fifty dollars. I got an accountant inside.
WILLY   Charley, look . . . [*With difficulty*] I got my insurance to pay. If you can manage it—I need a hundred and ten dollars.

CHARLEY *doesn't reply for a moment; merely stops moving.*

WILLY   I'd draw it from my bank but Linda would know, and I . . .
CHARLEY   Sit down, Willy.
WILLY [*moving toward the chair*] I'm keeping an account of everything, remember. I'll pay every penny back. [*He sits.*]
CHARLEY   Now listen to me, Willy.
WILLY   I want you to know I appreciate . . .
CHARLEY [*sitting down on the table*] Willy, what're you doin? What the hell is goin' on in your head?
WILLY   Why? I'm simply . . .
CHARLEY   I offered you a job. You can make fifty dollars a week. And I won't send you on the road.
WILLY   I've got a job.
CHARLEY   Without pay? What kind of a job is a job without pay? [*He rises.*] Now, look, kid, enough is enough. I'm no genius but I know when I'm being insulted.
WILLY   Insulted!
CHARLEY   Why don't you want to work for me?
WILLY   What's the matter with you? I've got a job.
CHARLEY   Then what're you walkin' in here every week for?
WILLY [*getting up*] Well, if you don't want me to walk in here—
CHARLEY   I am offering you a job.
WILLY   I don't want your goddam job!
CHARLEY   When the hell are you going to grow up?
WILLY [*furiously*] You big ignoramus, if you say that to me again I'll rap you one! I don't care how big you are! [*He's ready to fight.*]

Pause.

CHARLEY [*kindly, going to him*] How much do you need, Willy?
WILLY   Charley, I'm strapped. I'm strapped. I don't know what to do. I was just fired.

CHARLEY Howard fired you?

WILLY That snotnose. Imagine that? I named him. I named him Howard.

CHARLEY Willy, when're you gonna realize that them things don't mean anything? You named him Howard, but you can't sell that. The only thing you got in this world is what you can sell. And the funny thing is that you're a salesman, and you don't know that.

WILLY I've always tried to think otherwise, I guess. I always felt that if a man was impressive, and well liked, that nothing—

CHARLEY Why must everybody like you? Who liked J. P. Morgan?[8] Was he impressive? In a Turkish bath he'd look like a butcher. But with his pockets on he was very well liked. Now listen, Willy, I know you don't like me, and nobody can say I'm in love with you, but I'll give you a job because—just for the hell of it, put it that way. Now what do you say?

WILLY I—I just can't work for you, Charley.

CHARLEY What're you, jealous of me?

WILLY I can't work for you, that's all, don't ask me why.

CHARLEY [*angered, takes out more bills*] You been jealous of me all your life, you damned fool! Here, pay your insurance. [*He puts the money in* WILLY's *hand.*]

WILLY I'm keeping strict accounts.

CHARLEY I've got some work to do. Take care of yourself. And pay your insurance.

WILLY [*moving to the right*] Funny, y'know? After all the highways, and the trains, and the appointments, and the years, you end up worth more dead than alive.

CHARLEY Willy, nobody's worth nothin' dead. [*After a slight pause*] Did you hear what I said?

WILLY *stands still, dreaming.*

CHARLEY Willy!

WILLY Apologize to Bernard for me when you see him. I didn't mean to argue with him. He's a fine boy. They're all fine boys, and they'll end up big—all of them. Someday they'll all play tennis together. Wish me luck, Charley. He saw Bill Oliver today.

CHARLEY Good luck.

WILLY [*on the verge of tears*] Charley, you're the only friend I got. Isn't that a remarkable thing? [*He goes out.*]

CHARLEY Jesus!

CHARLEY *stares after him a moment and follows. All light blacks out. Suddenly raucous music is heard, and a red glow rises behind the screen at right.* STANLEY, *a young waiter, appears, carrying a table, followed by* HAPPY, *who is carrying two chairs.*

STANLEY [*putting the table down*] That's all right, Mr. Loman, I

8. John Pierpont Morgan (1887–1943), famous New York banker and financier.

can handle it myself. [*He turns and takes the chairs from* HAPPY *and places them at the table.*]

HAPPY [*glancing around*]   Oh, this is better.

STANLEY   Sure, in the front there you're in the middle of all kinds a noise. Whenever you got a party, Mr. Loman, you just tell me and I'll put you back here. Y'know, there's a lotta people they don't like it private, because when they go out they like to see a lotta action around them because they're sick and tired to stay in the house by theirself. But I know you, you ain't from Hackensack. You know what I mean?

HAPPY [*sitting down*]   So how's it coming, Stanley?

STANLEY   Ah, it's a dog's life. I only wish during the war they'd a took me in the Army. I coulda been dead by now.

HAPPY   My brother's back, Stanley.

STANLEY   Oh, he come back, heh? From the Far West.

HAPPY   Yeah, big cattle man, my brother, so treat him right. And my father's coming too.

STANLEY   Oh, your father too!

HAPPY   You got a couple of nice lobsters?

STANLEY   Hundred per cent, big.

HAPPY   I want them with the claws.

STANLEY   Don't worry, I don't give you no mice. [HAPPY *laughs.*] How about some wine? It'll put a head on the meal.

HAPPY   No. You remember, Stanley, that recipe I brought you from overseas? With the champagne in it?

STANLEY   Oh, yeah, sure. I still got it tacked up yet in the kitchen. But that'll have to cost a buck apiece anyways.

HAPPY   That's all right.

STANLEY   What'd you, hit a number or somethin'?

HAPPY   No, it's a little celebration. My brother is—I think he pulled off a big deal today. I think we're going into business together.

STANLEY   Great! That's the best for you. Because a family business, you know what I mean?—that's the best.

HAPPY   That's what I think.

STANLEY   'Cause what's the difference? Somebody steals? It's in the family. Know what I mean? [*Sotto voce*] Like this bartender here. The boss is goin' crazy what kinda leak he's got in the cash register. You put it in but it don't come out.

HAPPY [*raising his head*]   Sh!

STANLEY   What?

HAPPY   You notice I wasn't lookin' right or left, was I?

STANLEY   No.

HAPPY   And my eyes are closed.

STANLEY   So what's the—?

HAPPY   Strudel's comin'.

STANLEY [*catching on, looks around*]   Ah, no, there's no—

He breaks off as a furred, lavishly dressed GIRL *enters and sits at the next table. Both follow her with their eyes.*

STANLEY   Geez, how'd ya know?

HAPPY   I got radar or something. [*Staring directly at her profile*] Oooooooo . . , Stanley.

STANLEY   I think that's for you, Mr. Loman.

HAPPY   Look at that mouth. Oh, God. And the binoculars.

STANLEY   Geez, you got a life, Mr. Loman.

HAPPY   Wait on her.

STANLEY [*going to the* GIRL'*s table*]   Would you like a menu, ma'am?

GIRL   I'm expecting someone, but I'd like a—

HAPPY   Why don't you bring her—excuse me, miss, do you mind? I sell champagne, and I'd like you to try my brand. Bring her a champagne, Stanley.

GIRL   That's awfully nice of you.

HAPPY   Don't mention it. It's all company money. [*He laughs.*]

GIRL   That's a charming product to be selling, isn't it?

HAPPY   Oh, gets to be like everything else. Selling is selling, y'know.

GIRL   I suppose.

HAPPY   You don't happen to sell, do you?

GIRL   No, I don't sell.

HAPPY   Would you object to a compliment from a stranger? You ought to be on a magazine cover.

GIRL [*looking at him a little archly*]   I have been.

STANLEY *comes in with a glass of champagne.*

HAPPY   What'd I say before, Stanley? You see? She's a cover girl.

STANLEY   Oh, I could see, I could see.

HAPPY [*to the* GIRL]   What magazine?

GIRL   Oh, a lot of them. [*She takes the drink.*] Thank you.

HAPPY   You know what they say in France, don't you? "Champagne is the drink of the complexion"—Hya, Biff!

BIFF *has entered and sits with* HAPPY.

BIFF   Hello, kid. Sorry I'm late.

HAPPY   I just got here. Uh, Miss—?

GIRL   Forsythe.

HAPPY   Miss Forsythe, this is my brother.

BIFF   Is Dad here?

HAPPY   His name is Biff. You might've heard of him. Great football player.

GIRL   Really? What team?

HAPPY   Are you familiar with football?

GIRL   No, I'm afraid I'm not.

HAPPY   Biff is quarterback with the New York Giants.

GIRL   Well, that is nice, isn't it? [*She drinks.*]

HAPPY   Good health.

GIRL   I'm happy to meet you.

HAPPY   That's my name. Hap. It's really Harold, but at West Point they called me Happy.

GIRL [*now really impressed*]   Oh, I see. How do you do? [*She turns her profile.*]

BIFF   Isn't Dad coming?

HAPPY   You want her?

BIFF   Oh, I could never make that.

HAPPY   I remember the time that idea would never come into your head. Where's the old confidence, Biff?

BIFF   I just saw Oliver—

HAPPY   Wait a minute. I've got to see that old confidence again. Do you want her? She's on call.

BIFF   Oh, no. [*He turns to look at the* GIRL.]

HAPPY   I'm telling you. Watch this. [*Turning to the* GIRL] Honey? [*She turns to him.*] Are you busy?

GIRL   Well, I am . . . but I could make a phone call.

HAPPY   Do that, will you, honey? And see if you can get a friend. We'll be here for a while. Biff is one of the greatest football players in the country.

GIRL   [*standing up*]   Well, I'm certainly happy to meet you.

HAPPY   Come back soon.

GIRL   I'll try.

HAPPY   Don't try, honey, try hard.

> *The* GIRL *exits.* STANLEY *follows, shaking his head in bewildered admiration.*

HAPPY   Isn't that a shame now? A beautiful girl like that? That's why I can't get married. There's not a good woman in a thousand. New York is loaded with them, kid!

BIFF   Hap, look—

HAPPY   I told you she was on call!

BIFF   [*strangely unnerved*]   Cut it out, will ya? I want to say something to you.

HAPPY   Did you see Oliver?

BIFF   I saw him all right. Now look, I want to tell Dad a couple of things and I want you to help me.

HAPPY   What? Is he going to back you?

BIFF   Are you crazy? You're out of your goddam head, you know that?

HAPPY   Why? What happened?

BIFF   [*breathlessly*]   I did a terrible thing today, Hap. It's been the strangest day I ever went through. I'm all numb, I swear.

HAPPY   You mean he wouldn't see you?

BIFF   Well, I waited six hours for him, see? All day. Kept sending my name in. Even tried to date his secretary so she'd get me to him, but no soap.

HAPPY   Because you're not showin' the old confidence, Biff. He remembered you, didn't he?

BIFF   [*stopping* HAPPY *with a gesture*]   Finally, about five o'clock, he comes out. Didn't remember who I was or anything. I felt like such an idiot, Hap.

HAPPY   Did you tell him my Florida idea?

BIFF   He walked away. I saw him for one minute. I got so mad I could've torn the walls down! How the hell did I ever get the idea

I was a salesman there? I even believed myself that I'd been a salesman for him! And then he gave me one look and—I realized what a ridiculous lie my whole life has been! We've been talking in a dream for fifteen years. I was a shipping clerk.

HAPPY What'd you do?

BIFF [*with great tension and wonder*] Well, he left, see. And the secretary went out. I was all alone in the waiting room. I don't know what came over me, Hap. The next thing I know I'm in his office—paneled walls, everything. I can't explain it. I—Hap, I took his fountain pen.

HAPPY Geez, did he catch you?

BIFF I ran out. I ran down all eleven flights. I ran and ran and ran.

HAPPY That was an awful dumb—what'd you do that for?

BIFF [*agonized*] I don't know, I just—wanted to take something, I don't know. You gotta help me, Hap, I'm gonna tell Pop.

HAPPY You crazy? What for?

BIFF Hap, he's got to understand that I'm not the man somebody lends that kind of money to. He thinks I've been spiting him all these years and it's eating him up.

HAPPY That's just it. You tell him something nice.

BIFF I can't.

HAPPY Say you got a lunch date with Oliver tomorrow.

BIFF So what do I do tomorrow?

HAPPY You leave the house tomorrow and come back at night and say Oliver is thinking it over. And he thinks it over for a couple of weeks, and gradually it fades away and nobody's the worse.

BIFF But it'll go on forever!

HAPPY Dad is never so happy as when he's looking forward to something!

WILLY *enters.*

HAPPY Hello, scout!

WILLY Gee, I haven't been here in years!

STANLEY *has followed* WILLY *in and sets a chair for him.* STANLEY *starts off but* HAPPY *stops him.*

HAPPY Stanley!

STANLEY *stands by, waiting for an order.*

BIFF [*going to* WILLY *with guilt, as to an invalid*] Sit down, Pop. You want a drink?

WILLY Sure, I don't mind.

BIFF Let's get a load on.

WILLY You look worried.

BIFF N-no. [*To* STANLEY] Scotch all around. Make it doubles.

STANLEY Doubles, right. [*He goes.*]

WILLY You had a couple already, didn't you?

BIFF Just a couple, yeah.

WILLY   Well, what happened, boy? [*Nodding affirmatively, with a smile*] Everything go all right?

BIFF   [*takes a breath, then reaches out and grasps* WILLY's *hand*] Pal . . . [*He is smiling bravely, and* WILLY *is smiling too.*] I had an experience today.

HAPPY   Terrific, Pop.

WILLY   That so? What happened?

BIFF   [*high, slightly alcoholic, above the earth*] I'm going to tell you everything from first to last. It's been a strange day. [*Silence. He looks around, composes himself as best he can, but his breath keeps breaking the rhythm of his voice.*] I had to wait quite a while for him, and—

WILLY   Oliver?

BIFF   Yeah, Oliver. All day, as a matter of cold fact. And a lot of— instances—facts, Pop, facts about my life came back to me. Who was it, Pop? Who ever said I was a salesman with Oliver?

WILLY   Well, you were.

BIFF   No, Dad, I was a shipping clerk.

WILLY   But you were practically—

BIFF   [*with determination*] Dad, I don't know who said it first, but I was never a salesman for Bill Oliver.

WILLY   What're you talking about?

BIFF   Let's hold on to the facts tonight, Pop. We're not going to get anywhere bullin' around. I was a shipping clerk.

WILLY   [*angrily*] All right, now listen to me—

BIFF   Why don't you let me finish?

WILLY   I'm not interested in stories about the past or any crap of that kind because the woods are burning, boys, you understand? There's a big blaze going on all around. I was fired today.

BIFF   [*shocked*] How could you be?

WILLY   I was fired, and I'm looking for a little good news to tell your mother, because the woman has waited and the woman has suffered. The gist of it is that I haven't got a story left in my head, Biff. So don't give me a lecture about facts and aspects. I am not interested. Now what've you got to say to me?

STANLEY *enters with three drinks. They wait until he leaves.*

WILLY   Did you see Oliver?

BIFF   Jesus, Dad!

WILLY   You mean you didn't go up there?

HAPPY   Sure he went up there.

BIFF   I did. I—saw him. How could they fire you?

WILLY   [*on the edge of his chair*] What kind of a welcome did he give you?

BIFF   He won't even let you work on commission?

WILLY   I'm out! [*Driving*] So tell me, he gave you a warm welcome?

HAPPY   Sure, Pop, sure!

BIFF   [*driven*] Well, it was kind of—

WILLY   I was wondering if he'd remember you. [*To* HAPPY] Imagine, man doesn't see him for ten, twelve years and gives him that kind of a welcome!

HAPPY   Damn right!

BIFF [*trying to return to the offensive*] Pop, look—

WILLY   You know why he remembered you, don't you? Because you impressed him in those days.

BIFF   Let's talk quietly and get this down to the facts, huh?

WILLY [*as though* BIFF *had been interrupting*] Well, what happened? It's great news, Biff. Did he take you into his office or'd you talk in the waiting room?

BIFF   Well, he came in, see, and—

WILLY [*with a big smile*] What'd he say? Betcha he threw his arm around you.

BIFF   Well, he kinda—

WILLY   He's a fine man. [*To* HAPPY] Very hard man to see, y'know.

HAPPY [*agreeing*] Oh, I know.

WILLY [*to* BIFF] Is that where you had the drinks?

BIFF   Yeah, he gave me a couple of—no, no!

HAPPY [*cutting in*] He told him my Florida idea.

WILLY   Don't interrupt. [*To* BIFF] How'd he react to the Florida idea?

BIFF   Dad, will you give me a minute to explain?

WILLY   I've been waiting for you to explain since I sat down here! What happened? He took you into his office and what?

BIFF   Well—I talked. And—and he listened, see.

WILLY   Famous for the way he listens, y'know. What was his answer?

BIFF   His answer was— [*He breaks off, suddenly angry.*] Dad, you're not letting me tell you what I want to tell you!

WILLY [*accusing, angered*] You didn't see him, did you?

BIFF   I did see him!

WILLY   What'd you insult him or something? You insulted him, didn't you?

BIFF   Listen, will you let me out of it, will you just let me out of it!

HAPPY   What the hell!

WILLY   Tell me what happened!

BIFF [*to* HAPPY] I can't talk to him!

A single trumpet note jars the ear. The light of green leaves stains the house, which holds the air of night and a dream. YOUNG BERNARD *enters and knocks on the door of the house.*

YOUNG BERNARD [*frantically*] Mrs. Loman, Mrs. Loman!

HAPPY   Tell him what happened!

BIFF [*to* HAPPY] Shut up and leave me alone!

WILLY   No, no! You had to go and flunk math!

BIFF   What math? What're you talking about?

YOUNG BERNARD   Mrs. Loman, Mrs. Loman!

LINDA *appears in the house, as of old.*

WILLY [*wildly*] Math, math, math!

BIFF   Take it easy, Pop!

YOUNG BERNARD   Mrs. Loman!

WILLY [*furiously*] If you hadn't flunked you'd've been set by now!

BIFF   Now, look, I'm gonna tell you what happened, and you're going to listen to me.

YOUNG BERNARD   Mrs. Loman!

BIFF   I waited six hours—

HAPPY   What the hell are you saying?

BIFF   I kept sending in my name but he wouldn't see me. So finally he . . . [*He continues unheard as light fades low on the restaurant.*]

YOUNG BERNARD   Biff flunked math!

LINDA   No!

YOUNG BERNARD   Birnbaum flunked him! They won't graduate him!

LINDA   But they have to. He's gotta go to the university. Where is he? Biff! Biff!

YOUNG BERNARD   No, he left. He went to Grand Central.

LINDA   Grand— You mean he went to Boston!

YOUNG BERNARD   Is Uncle Willy in Boston?

LINDA   Oh, maybe Willy can talk to the teacher. Oh, the poor, poor boy!

Light on house area snaps out.

BIFF   [*at the table, now audible, holding up a gold fountain pen*] . . . so I'm washed up with Oliver, you understand? Are you listening to me?

WILLY   [*at a loss*]   Yeah, sure. If you hadn't flunked—

BIFF   Flunked what? What're you talking about?

WILLY   Don't blame everything on me! I didn't flunk math—you did! What pen?

HAPPY   That was awful dumb, Biff, a pen like that is worth—

WILLY   [*seeing the pen for the first time*]   You took Oliver's pen?

BIFF   [*weakening*]   Dad, I just explained it to you.

WILLY   You stole Bill Oliver's fountain pen!

BIFF   I didn't exactly steal it! That's just what I've been explaining to you!

HAPPY   He had it in his hand and just then Oliver walked in, so he got nervous and stuck it in his pocket!

WILLY   My God, Biff!

BIFF   I never intended to do it, Dad!

OPERATOR'S VOICE   Standish Arms, good evening!

WILLY   [*shouting*]   I'm not in my room!

BIFF   [*frightened*]   Dad, what's the matter? [*He and* HAPPY *stand up.*]

OPERATOR   Ringing Mr. Loman for you!

WILLY   I'm not there, stop it!

BIFF   [*horrified, gets down on one knee before* WILLY]   Dad, I'll make good, I'll make good. [WILLY *tries to get to his feet.* BIFF *holds him down.*] Sit down now.

WILLY   No, you're no good, you're no good for anything.

BIFF   I am, Dad, I'll find something else, you understand? Now don't worry about anything. [*He holds up* WILLY's *face*] Talk to me, Dad.

OPERATOR   Mr. Loman does not answer. Shall I page him?

WILLY   [*attempting to stand, as though to rush and silence the Operator*]   No, no, no!

HAPPY   He'll strike something, Pop.

WILLY No, no . . .

BIFF [*desperately, standing over* WILLY] Pop listen! Listen to me! I'm telling you something good. Oliver talked to his partner about the Florida idea. You listening? He—he talked to his partner, and he came to me . . . I'm going to be all right, you hear? Dad, listen to me, he said it was just a question of the amount!

WILLY Then you . . . got it?

HAPPY He's gonna be terrific, Pop!

WILLY [*trying to stand*] Then you got it, haven't you? You got it! You got it!

BIFF [*agonized, holds* WILLY *down*] No, no. Look, Pop. I'm supposed to have lunch with them tomorrow. I'm just telling you this so you'll know that I can still make an impression, Pop. And I'll make good somewhere, but I can't go tomorrow, see?

WILLY Why not? You simply—

BIFF But the pen, Pop!

WILLY You give it to him and tell him it was an oversight!

HAPPY Sure, have lunch tomorrow!

BIFF I can't say that—

WILLY You were doing a crossword puzzle and accidentally used his pen!

BIFF Listen, kid, I took those balls years ago, now I walk in with his fountain pen? That clinches it, don't you see? I can't face him like that! I'll try elsewhere.

PAGE'S VOICE Paging Mr. Loman!

WILLY Don't you want to be anything?

BIFF Pop, how can I go back?

WILLY You don't want to be anything, is that what's behind it?

BIFF [*now angry at* WILLY *for not crediting his sympathy*] Don't take it that way! You think it was easy walking into that office after what I'd done to him? A team of horses couldn't have dragged me back to Bill Oliver!

WILLY Then why'd you go?

BIFF Why did I go? Why did I go! Look at you! Look at what's become of you!

Off left, THE WOMAN *laughs.*

WILLY Biff, you're going to go to that lunch tomorrow, or—

BIFF I can't go. I've got no appointment!

HAPPY Biff, for . . . !

WILLY Are you spiting me?

BIFF Don't take it that way! Goddammit!

WILLY [*strikes* BIFF *and falters away from the table*] You rotten little louse! Are you spiting me?

THE WOMAN Someone's at the door, Willy!

BIFF I'm no good, can't you see what I am?

HAPPY [*separating them*] Hey, you're in a restaurant! Now cut it out, both of you! [*The girls enter.*] Hello, girls, sit down.

THE WOMAN *laughs, off left.*

MISS FORSYTHE   I guess we might as well. This is Letta.

THE WOMAN   Willy, are you going to wake up?

BIFF [*ignoring* WILLY]   How're ya, miss, sit down. What do you drink?

MISS FORSYTHE   Letta might not be able to stay long.

LETTA   I gotta get up very early tomorrow. I got jury duty. I'm so excited! Were you fellows ever on a jury?

BIFF   No, but I been in front of them! [*The girls laugh.*] This is my father.

LETTA   Isn't he cute? Sit down with us, Pop.

HAPPY   Sit him down, Biff!

BIFF [*going to him*]   Come on, slugger, drink us under the table. To hell with it! Come on, sit down, pal.

> On BIFF's *last insistence*, WILLY *is about to sit.*

THE WOMAN [*now urgently*]   Willy, are you going to answer the door!

> THE WOMAN's *call pulls* WILLY *back. He starts right, befuddled.*

BIFF   Hey, where are you going?

WILLY   Open the door.

BIFF   The door?

WILLY   The washroom . . . the door . . . where's the door?

BIFF [*leading* WILLY *to the left*]   Just go straight down.

> WILLY *moves left.*

THE WOMAN   Willy, Willy, are you going to get up, get up, get up, get up?

> WILLY *exits left.*

LETTA   I think it's sweet you bring your daddy along.

MISS FORSYTHE   Oh, he isn't really your father!

BIFF [*at left, turning to her resentfully*]   Miss Forsythe, you've just seen a prince walk by. A fine, troubled prince. A hard-working, unappreciated prince. A pal, you understand? A good companion. Always for his boys.

LETTA   That's so sweet.

HAPPY   Well, girls, what's the program? We're wasting time. Come on, Biff. Gather round. Where would you like to go?

BIFF   Why don't you do something for him?

HAPPY   Me!

BIFF   Don't you give a damn for him, Hap?

HAPPY   What're you talking about? I'm the one who—

BIFF   I sense it, you don't give a good goddam about him. [*He takes the rolled-up hose from his pocket and puts it on the table in front of* HAPPY.] Look what I found in the cellar, for Christ's sake. How can you bear to let it go on?

HAPPY   Me? Who goes away? Who runs off and—

BIFF   Yeah, but he doesn't mean anything to you. You could help him—I can't! Don't you understand what I'm talking about? He's going to kill himself, don't you know that?

HAPPY   Don't I know it! Me!

BIFF   Hap, help him! Jesus . . . help him . . . Help me, help me, I can't bear to look at his face! [*Ready to weep, he hurries out, up right.*]

HAPPY   [*starting after him*]   Where are you going?

MISS FORSYTHE   What's he so mad about?

HAPPY   Come on, girls, we'll catch up with him.

MISS FORSYTHE   [*as* HAPPY *pushes her out*]   Say, I don't like that temper of his!

HAPPY   He's just a little overstrung, he'll be all right!

WILLY   [*off left, as* THE WOMAN *laughs*]   Don't answer! Don't answer!

LETTA   Don't you want to tell your father—

HAPPY   No, that's not my father. He's just a guy. Come on, we'll catch Biff, and, honey, we're going to paint this town! Stanley, where's the check! Hey, Stanley!

They exit. STANLEY *looks toward left.*

STANLEY   [*calling to* HAPPY *indignantly*]   Mr. Loman! Mr. Loman!

STANLEY *picks up a chair and follows them off. Knocking is heard off left.* THE WOMAN *enters, laughing.* WILLY *follows her. She is in a black slip; he is buttoning his shirt. Raw, sensuous music accompanies their speech.*

WILLY   Will you stop laughing? Will you stop?

THE WOMAN   Aren't you going to answer the door? He'll wake the whole hotel.

WILLY   I'm not expecting anybody.

THE WOMAN   Whyn't you have another drink, honey, and stop being so damn self-centered?

WILLY   I'm so lonely.

THE WOMAN   You know you ruined me, Willy? From now on, whenever you come to the office, I'll see that you go right through to the buyers. No waiting at my desk any more, Willy. You ruined me.

WILLY   That's nice of you to say that.

THE WOMAN   Gee, you are self-centered! Why so sad? You are the saddest, self-centeredest soul I ever did see-saw. [*She laughs. He kisses her.*] Come on inside, drummer boy. It's silly to be dressing in the middle of the night. [*As knocking is heard*] Aren't you going to answer the door?

WILLY   They're knocking on the wrong door.

THE WOMAN   But I felt the knocking. And he heard us talking in here. Maybe the hotel's on fire!

WILLY   [*his terror rising*]   It's a mistake.

THE WOMAN   Then tell him to go away!

WILLY   There's nobody there.

THE WOMAN   It's getting on my nerves, Willy. There's somebody standing out there and it's getting on my nerves!

WILLY [*pushing her away from him*]   All right, stay in the bathroom here, and don't come out. I think there's a law in Massachusetts about it, so don't come out. It may be that new room clerk. He looked very mean. So don't come out. It's a mistake, there's no fire.

> *The knocking is heard again. He takes a few steps away from her, and she vanishes into the wing. The light follows him, and now he is facing* YOUNG BIFF, *who carries a suitcase.* BIFF *steps toward him. The music is gone.*

BIFF   Why didn't you answer?

WILLY   Biff! What are you doing in Boston?

BIFF   Why didn't you answer? I've been knocking for five minutes, I called you on the phone—

WILLY   I just heard you. I was in the bathroom and had the door shut. Did anything happen home?

BIFF   Dad—I let you down.

WILLY   What do you mean?

BIFF   Dad . . .

WILLY   Biffo, what's this about? [*Putting his arm around* BIFF] Come on, let's go downstairs and get you a malted.

BIFF   Dad, I flunked math.

WILLY   Not for the term?

BIFF   The term. I haven't got enough credits to graduate.

WILLY   You mean to say Bernard wouldn't give you the answers?

BIFF   He did, he tried, but I only got a sixty-one.

WILLY   And they wouldn't give you four points?

BIFF   Birnbaum refused absolutely. I begged him, Pop, but he won't give me those points. You gotta talk to him before they close the school. Because if he saw the kind of man you are, and you just talked to him in your way, I'm sure he'd come through for me. The class came right before practice, see, and I didn't go enough. Would you talk to him? He'd like you, Pop. You know the way you could talk.

WILLY   You're on. We'll drive right back.

BIFF   Oh, Dad, good work! I'm sure he'll change it for you!

WILLY   Go downstairs and tell the clerk I'm checkin' out. Go right down.

BIFF   Yes, sir! See, the reason he hates me, Pop—one day he was late for class so I got up at the blackboard and imitated him. I crossed my eyes and talked with a lithp.

WILLY [*laughing*]   You did? The kids like it?

BIFF   They nearly died laughing!

WILLY   Yeah? What'd you do?

BIFF   The thquare root of thixthy twee is . . . [WILLY *bursts out laughing;* BIFF *joins him.*] And in the middle of it he walked in!

> WILLY *laughs and* THE WOMAN *joins in offstage.*

WILLY [*without hesitation*]   Hurry downstairs and—

BIFF   Somebody in there?

WILLY No, that was next door.

THE WOMAN *laughs offstage*.

BIFF Somebody got in your bathroom!

WILLY No, it's the next room, there's a party—

THE WOMAN [*enters, laughing. She lisps this*] Can I come in? There's something in the bathtub, Willy, and it's moving!

WILLY *looks at* BIFF, *who is staring open-mouthed and horrified at* THE WOMAN.

WILLY Ah—you better go back to your room. They must be finished painting by now. They're painting her room so I let her take a shower here. Go back, go back . . . [*He pushes her.*]

THE WOMAN [*resisting*] But I've got to get dressed, Willy, I can't—

WILLY Get out of here! Go back, go back . . . [*Suddenly striving for the ordinary*] This is Miss Francis, Biff, she's a buyer. They're painting her room. Go back, Miss Francis, go back . . .

THE WOMAN But my clothes, I can't go out naked in the hall!

WILLY [*pushing her offstage*] Get outa here! Go back, go back!

BIFF *slowly sits down on his suitcase as the argument continues offstage.*

THE WOMAN Where's my stockings? You promised me stockings, Willy!

WILLY I have no stockings here!

THE WOMAN You had two boxes of size nine sheers for me, and I want them!

WILLY Here, for God's sake, will you get outa here!

THE WOMAN [*enters holding a box of stockings*] I just hope there's nobody in the hall. That's all I hope. [*To* BIFF] Are you football or baseball?

BIFF Football.

THE WOMAN [*angry, humiliated*] That's me too. G'night. [*She snatches her clothes from* WILLY, *and walks out.*]

WILLY [*after a pause*] Well, better get going. I want to get to the school first thing in the morning. Get my suits out of the closet. I'll get my valise. [BIFF *doesn't move.*] What's the matter? [BIFF *remains motionless, tears falling.*] She's a buyer. Buys for J. H. Simmons. She lives down the hall—they're painting. You don't imagine— [*He breaks off. After a pause*] Now listen, pal, she's just a buyer. She sees merchandise in her room and they have to keep it looking just so . . . [*Pause. Assuming command*] All right, get my suits. [BIFF *doesn't move.*] Now stop crying and do as I say. I gave you an order. Biff, I gave you an order! Is that what you do when I give you an order? How dare you cry! [*Putting his arm around* BIFF] Now look, Biff, when you grow up you'll understand about these things. You mustn't—you mustn't overemphasize a thing like this. I'll see Birnbaum first thing in the morning.

BIFF Never mind.

WILLY [*getting down beside* BIFF]   Never mind! He's going to give you those points. I'll see to it.

BIFF   He wouldn't listen to you.

WILLY   He certainly will listen to me. You need those points for the U. of Virginia.

BIFF   I'm not going there.

WILLY   Heh? If I can't get him to change that mark you'll make it up in summer school. You've got all summer to—

BIFF [*his weeping breaking from him*]   Dad . . .

WILLY [*infected by it*]   Oh, my boy . . .

BIFF   Dad . . .

WILLY   She's nothing to me, Biff. I was lonely, I was terribly lonely.

BIFF   You—you gave her Mama's stockings! [*His tears break through and he rises to go.*]

WILLY [*grabbing for* BIFF]   I gave you an order!

BIFF   Don't touch me, you—liar!

WILLY   Apologize for that!

BIFF   You fake! You phony little fake! You fake! [*overcome, he turns quickly and weeping fully goes out with his suitcase,* WILLY *is left on the floor on his knees.*]

WILLY   I gave you an order! Biff, come back here or I'll beat you! Come back here! I'll whip you!

STANLEY *comes quickly in from the right and stands in front of* WILLY.

WILLY [*shouts at* STANLEY]   I gave you an order . . .

STANLEY   Hey, let's pick it up, pick it up, Mr. Loman. [*He helps* WILLY *to his feet.*] Your boys left with the chippies. They said they'll see you home.

A second waiter watches some distance away.

WILLY   But we were supposed to have dinner together.

Music is heard, WILLY's *theme.*

STANLEY   Can you make it?

WILLY   I'll—sure, I can make it. [*Suddenly concerned about his clothes*] Do I—I look all right?

STANLEY   Sure, you look all right. [*He flicks a speck off* WILLY's *lapel.*]

WILLY   Here—here's a dollar.

STANLEY   Oh, your son paid me. It's all right.

WILLY [*putting it in* STANLEY's *hand*]   No, take it. You're a good boy.

STANLEY   Oh, no, you don't have to . . .

WILLY   Here—here's some more, I don't need it any more. [*After a slight pause*] Tell me—is there a seed store in the neighborhood?

STANLEY   Seeds? You mean like to plant?

As WILLY *turns,* STANLEY *slips the money back into his jacket pocket.*

WILLY   Yes. Carrots, peas . . .

STANLEY   Well, there's hardware stores on Sixth Avenue, but it may be too late now.

WILLY [*anxiously*]   Oh, I'd better hurry. I've got to get some seeds. [*He starts off to the right.*] I've got to get some seeds, right away. Nothing's planted. I don't have a thing in the ground.

WILLY *hurries out as the light goes down.* STANLEY *moves over to the right after him, watches him off. The other waiter has been staring at* WILLY.

STANLEY [*to the waiter*]   Well, whatta you looking at?

The waiter picks up the chairs and moves off right. STANLEY *takes the table and follows him. The light fades on this area. There is a long pause, the sound of the flute coming over. The light gradually rises on the kitchen, which is empty.* HAPPY *appears at the door of the house, followed by* BIFF. HAPPY *is carrying a large bunch of long-stemmed roses. He enters the kitchen, looks around for* LINDA. *Not seeing her, he turns to* BIFF, *who is just outside the house door, and makes a gesture with his hands, indicating "Not here, I guess." He looks into the living room and freezes. Inside,* LINDA, *unseen, is seated,* WILLY's *coat on her lap. She rises ominously and quietly and moves toward* HAPPY, *who backs up into the kitchen, afraid.*

HAPPY   Hey, what're you doing up? [LINDA *says nothing but moves toward him implacably.*] Where's Pop? [*He keeps backing to the right, and now* LINDA *is in full view in the doorway to the living room.*] Is he sleeping?

LINDA   Where were you?

HAPPY [*trying to laugh it off*]   We met two girls, Mom, very fine types. Here, we brought you some flowers. [*Offering them to her*] Put them in your room, Ma.

She knocks them to the floor at BIFF's *feet. He has now come inside and closed the door behind him. She stares at* BIFF, *silent.*

HAPPY   Now what'd you do that for? Mom, I want you to have some flowers—

LINDA [*cutting* HAPPY *off, violently to* BIFF]   Don't you care whether he lives or dies?

HAPPY [*going to the stairs*]   Come upstairs, Biff.

BIFF [*with a flare of disgust, to* HAPPY]   Go away from me! [*To* LINDA] What do you mean, lives or dies? Nobody's dying around here, pal.

LINDA   Get out of my sight! Get out of here!

BIFF   I wanna see the boss.

LINDA   You're not going near him!

BIFF   Where is he? [*He moves to the living room and* LINDA *follows.*]

LINDA [*shouting at* BIFF]   You invite him for dinner. He looks forward to it all day—[BIFF *appears in his parents' bedroom, looks around, and exits*]—and then you desert him there. There's no stranger you'd do that to!

HAPPY   Why? He had a swell time with us. Listen, when I—[LINDA *comes back into the kitchen*]—desert him I hope I don't outlive the day!

LINDA   Get out of here!

HAPPY   Now look, Mom . . .

LINDA   Did you have to go to women tonight? You and your lousy rotten whores!

BIFF *re-enters the kitchen.*

HAPPY   Mom, all we did was follow Biff around trying to cheer him up! [*To* BIFF] Boy, what a night you gave me!

LINDA   Get out of here, both of you, and don't come back! I don't want you tormenting him any more. Go on now, get your things together! [*To* BIFF] You can sleep in his apartment. [*She starts to pick up the flowers and stops herself.*] Pick up this stuff, I'm not your maid any more. Pick it up, you bum, you!

HAPPY *turns his back on her in refusal.* BIFF *slowly moves over and gets down on his knees, picking up the flowers.*

LINDA   You're a pair of animals! Not one, not another living soul would have had the cruelty to walk out on that man in a restaurant!

BIFF [*not looking at her*]   Is that what he said?

LINDA   He didn't have to say anything. He was so humiliated he nearly limped when he came in.

HAPPY   But, Mom, he had a great time with us—

BIFF [*cutting him off violently*]   Shut up!

Without another word, HAPPY *goes upstairs.*

LINDA   You! You didn't even go in to see if he was all right!

BIFF [*still on the floor in front of* LINDA, *the flowers in his hand; with self-loathing*]   No. Didn't. Didn't do a damned thing. How do you like that, heh? Left him babbling in a toilet.

LINDA   You louse. You . . .

BIFF   Now you hit it on the nose! [*He gets up, throws the flowers in the wastebasket.*] The scum of the earth, and you're looking at him!

LINDA   Get out of here!

BIFF   I gotta talk to the boss, Mom. Where is he?

LINDA   You're not going near him. Get out of this house!

BIFF [*with absolute assurance, determination*]   No. We're gonna have an abrupt conversation, him and me.

LINDA   You're not talking to him!

Hammering is heard from outside the house, off right. BIFF *turns toward the noise.*

LINDA [*suddenly pleading*]   Will you please leave him alone?

BIFF   What's he doing out there?

LINDA   He's planting the garden!

BIFF [*quietly*]   Now? Oh, my God!

> BIFF *moves outside,* LINDA *following. The light dies down on them and comes up on the center of the apron as* WILLY *walks into it. He is carrying a flashlight, a hoe, and a handful of seed packets. He raps the top of the hoe sharply to fix it firmly, and then moves to the left, measuring off the distance with his foot. He holds the flashlight to look at the seed packets, reading off the instructions. He is in the blue of night.*

WILLY   Carrots . . . quarter-inch apart. Rows . . . one-foot rows. [*He measures it off.*] One foot. [*He puts down a package and measures off.*] Beets [*He puts down another package and measures again.*] Lettuce. [*He reads the package, puts it down.*] One foot— [*He breaks off as* BEN *appears at the right and moves slowly down to him.*] What a proposition, ts, ts. Terrific, terrific. 'Cause she's suffered, Ben, the woman has suffered. You understand me? A man can't go out the way he came in, Ben, a man has got to add up to something. You can't, you can't— [BEN *moves toward him as though to interrupt.*] You gotta consider, now. Don't answer so quick. Remember, it's a guaranteed twenty-thousand-dollar proposition. Now look, Ben, I want you to go through the ins and outs of this thing with me. I've got nobody to talk to, Ben, and the woman has suffered, you hear me?

BEN [*standing still, considering*]   What's the proposition?

WILLY   It's twenty thousand dollars on the barrelhead. Guaranteed, gilt-edged, you understand?

BEN   You don't want to make a fool of yourself. They might not honor the policy.

WILLY   How can they dare refuse? Didn't I work like a coolie to meet every premium on the nose? And now they don't pay off? Impossible!

BEN   It's called a cowardly thing, William.

WILLY   Why? Does it take more guts to stand here the rest of my life ringing up a zero?

BEN [*yielding*]   That's a point, William. [*He moves, thinking, turns.*] And twenty thousand—that *is* something one can feel with the hand, it is there.

WILLY [*now assured, with rising power*]   Oh, Ben, that's the whole beauty of it! I see it like a diamond, shining in the dark, hard and rough, that I can pick up and touch in my hand. Not like—like an appointment! This would not be another damn-fool appointment, Ben, and it changes all the aspects. Because he thinks I'm nothing, see, and so he spites me. But the funeral— [*Straightening up*] Ben, that funeral will be massive! They'll come from Maine, Massachusetts, Vermont, New Hampshire! All the old-timers with the strange license plates—that boy will be thunder-struck, Ben, because he never realized—I am known! Rhode Island, New York, New Jersey—I am known, Ben, and he'll see it with his eyes once and for all. He'll see what I am, Ben! He's in for a shock, that boy!

BEN [*coming down to the edge of the garden*] He'll call you a coward.

WILLY [*suddenly fearful*] No, that would be terrible.

BEN   Yes. And a damned fool.

WILLY   No, no, he mustn't, I won't have that! [*He is broken and desperate.*]

BEN   He'll hate you, William.

> *The gay music of the Boys is heard.*

WILLY   Oh, Ben, how do we get back to all the great times? Used to be so full of light, and comradeship, the sleigh-riding in winter, and the ruddiness on his cheeks. And always some kind of good news coming up, always something nice coming up ahead. And never even let me carry the valises in the house, and simonizing, simonizing that little red car! Why, why can't I give him something and not have him hate me?

BEN   Let me think about it. [*He glances at his watch.*] I still have a little time. Remarkable proposition, but you've got to be sure you're not making a fool of yourself.

> BEN *drifts off upstage and goes out of sight.* BIFF *comes down from the left.*

WILLY [*suddenly conscious of* BIFF, *turns and looks up at him, then begins picking up the packages of seeds in confusion*] Where the hell is that seed? [*Indignantly*] You can't see nothing out here! They boxed in the whole goddam neighborhood!

BIFF   There are people all around here. Don't you realize that?

WILLY   I'm busy. Don't bother me.

BIFF [*taking the hoe from* WILLY] I'm saying good-by to you, Pop. [WILLY *looks at him, silent, unable to move.*] I'm not coming back any more.

WILLY   You're not going to see Oliver tomorrow?

BIFF   I've got no appointment, Dad.

WILLY   He put his arm around you, and you've got no appointment?

BIFF   Pop, get this now, will you? Every time I've left it's been a fight that sent me out of here. Today I realized something about myself and I tried to explain it to you and I—I think I'm just not smart enough to make any sense out of it for you. To hell with whose fault it is or anything like that. [*He takes* WILLY's *arm.*] Let's just wrap it up, heh? Come on in, we'll tell Mom. [*He gently tries to pull* WILLY *to left.*]

WILLY [*frozen, immobile, with guilt in his voice*] No, I don't want to see her.

BIFF   Come on! [*He pulls again, and* WILLY *tries to pull away.*]

WILLY [*highly nervous*] No, no, I don't want to see her.

BIFF [*tries to look into* WILLY's *face, as if to find the answer there*] Why don't you want to see her?

WILLY [*more harshly now*] Don't bother me, will you?

BIFF   What do you mean, you don't want to see her? You don't want them calling you yellow, do you? This isn't your fault; it's me, I'm a bum. Now come inside! [WILLY *strains to get away.*] Did you hear what I said to you?

> WILLY *pulls away and quickly goes by himself into the house.* BIFF *follows.*

LINDA [*to* WILLY]   Did you plant, dear?
BIFF [*at the door, to* LINDA]   All right, we had it out. I'm going and I'm not writing any more.
LINDA [*going to* WILLY *in the kitchen*]   I think that's the best way, dear. 'Cause there's no use drawing it out, you'll just never get along.

> WILLY *doesn't respond.*

BIFF   People ask where I am and what I'm doing, you don't know, and you don't care. That way it'll be off your mind and you can start brightening up again. All right? That clears it, doesn't it? [WILLY *is silent, and* BIFF *goes to him.*] You gonna wish me luck, scout? [*He extends his hand.*] What do you say?
LINDA   Shake his hand, Willy.
WILLY [*turning to her, seething with hurt*]   There's no necessity to mention the pen at all, y'know.
BIFF [*gently*]   I've got no appointment, Dad.
WILLY [*erupting fiercely*]   He put his arm around . . . ?
BIFF   Dad, you're never going to see what I am, so what's the use of arguing? If I strike oil I'll send you a check. Meantime forget I'm alive.
WILLY [*to* LINDA]   Spite, see?
BIFF   Shake hands, Dad.
WILLY   Not my hand.
BIFF   I was hoping not to go this way.
WILLY   Well, this is the way you're going. Good-by.

> BIFF *looks at him a moment, then turns sharply and goes to the stairs.*

WILLY [*stops him with*]   May you rot in hell if you leave this house!
BIFF [*turning*]   Exactly what is it that you want from me?
WILLY   I want you to know, on the train, in the mountains, in the valleys, wherever you go, that you cut down your life for spite!
BIFF   No, no.
WILLY   Spite, spite, is the word of your undoing! And when you're down and out, remember what did it. When you're rotting somewhere beside the railroad tracks, remember, and don't you dare blame it on me!
BIFF   I'm not blaming it on you!
WILLY   I won't take the rap for this, you hear?

HAPPY *comes down the stairs and stands on the bottom step, watching.*

BIFF   That's just what I'm telling you!

WILLY [*sinking into a chair at the table with full accusation*]   You're trying to put a knife in me—don't think I don't know what you're doing!

BIFF   All right, phony! Then let's lay it on the line. [*He whips the rubber tube out of his pocket and puts it on the table.*]

HAPPY   You crazy—

LINDA   Biff! [*She moves to grab the hose, but* BIFF *holds it down with his hand.*]

BIFF   Leave it there! Don't move it!

WILLY [*not looking at it*]   What is that?

BIFF   You know goddam well what that is.

WILLY [*caged, wanting to escape*]   I never saw that.

BIFF   You saw it. The mice didn't bring it into the cellar! What is this supposed to do, make a hero out of you? This supposed to make me sorry for you?

WILLY   Never heard of it.

BIFF   There'll be no pity for you, you hear it? No pity!

WILLY [*to* LINDA]   You hear the spite!

BIFF   No, you're going to hear the truth—what you are and what I am!

LINDA   Stop it!

WILLY   Spite!

HAPPY [*coming down toward* BIFF]   You cut it now!

BIFF [*to* HAPPY]   The man don't know who we are! The man is gonna know! [*To* WILLY] We never told the truth for ten minutes in this house!

HAPPY   We always told the truth!

BIFF [*turning on him*]   You big blow, are you the assistant buyer? You're one of the two assistants to the assistant, aren't you?

HAPPY   Well, I'm practically—

BIFF   You're practically full of it! We all are! And I'm through with it. [*To* WILLY] Now hear this, Willy, this is me.

WILLY   I know you!

BIFF   You know why I had no address for three months? I stole a suit in Kansas City and I was in jail. [*To* LINDA, *who is sobbing*] Stop crying. I'm through with it.

LINDA *turns away from them, her hands covering her face.*

WILLY   I suppose that's my fault!

BIFF   I stole myself out of every good job since high school!

WILLY   And whose fault is that?

BIFF   And I never got anywhere because you blew me so full of hot air I could never stand taking orders from anybody! That's whose fault it is!

WILLY   I hear that!

LINDA   Don't, Biff!

BIFF   It's goddam time you heard that! I had to be boss big shot in two weeks, and I'm through with it!

WILLY   Then hang yourself! For spite, hang yourself!

BIFF   No! Nobody's hanging himself, Willy! I ran down eleven flights with a pen in my hand today. And suddenly I stopped, you hear me? And in the middle of that office building, do you hear this? I stopped in the middle of that building and I saw—the sky. I saw the things that I love in this world. The work and the food and time to sit and smoke. And I looked at the pen and said to myself, what the hell am I grabbing this for? Why am I trying to become what I don't want to be? What am I doing in an office, making a contemptuous, begging fool of myself, when all I want is out there, waiting for me the minute I say I know who I am! Why can't I say that, Willy? [*He tries to make* WILLY *face him, but* WILLY *pulls away and moves to the left.*]

WILLY [*with hatred, threateningly*]   The door to your life is wide open!

BIFF   Pop! I'm a dime a dozen, and so are you!

WILLY [*turning on him now in an uncontrolled outburst*]   I am not a dime a dozen! I am Willy Loman, and you are Biff Loman!

BIFF *starts for* WILLY, *but is blocked by* HAPPY. *In his fury,* BIFF *seems on the verge of attacking his father.*

BIFF   I am not a leader of men, Willy, and neither are you. You were never anything but a hard-working drummer who landed in the ash can like all the rest of them! I'm one dollar an hour, Willy! I tried seven states and couldn't raise it. A buck an hour! Do you gather my meaning? I'm not bringing home any prizes any more, and you're going to stop waiting for me to bring them home!

WILLY [*directly to* BIFF]   You vengeful, spiteful mut!

BIFF *breaks from* HAPPY. WILLY, *in fright, starts up the stairs.* BIFF *grabs him.*

BIFF [*at the peak of his fury*]   Pop, I'm nothing! I'm nothing, Pop. Can't you understand that? There's no spite in it any more. I'm just what I am, that's all.

BIFF's *fury has spent itself, and he breaks down, sobbing, holding on to* WILLY, *who dumbly fumbles for* BIFF's *face.*

WILLY [*astonished.*]   What're you doing? What're you doing? [*To* LINDA] Why is he crying?

BIFF [*crying, broken*]   Will you let me go, for Christ's sake? Will you take that phony dream and burn it before something happens? [*Struggling to contain himself, he pulls away and moves to the stairs.*] I'll go in the morning. Put him—put him to bed. [*Exhausted,* BIFF *moves up the stairs to his room.*]

WILLY [*after a long pause, astonished, elevated*]   Isn't that—isn't that remarkable? Biff—he likes me!

LINDA   He loves you, Willy!

HAPPY   [*deeply moved*]   Always did, Pop.

WILLY   Oh, Biff! [*Staring wildly*] He cried! Cried to me. [*He is choking with his love, and now cries out his promise*] That boy— that boy is going to be magnificent!

BEN *appears in the light just outside the kitchen.*

BEN   Yes, outstanding, with twenty thousand behind him.

LINDA   [*sensing the racing of his mind, fearfully, carefully*]   Now come to bed, Willy. It's all settled now.

WILLY   [*finding it difficult not to rush out of the house*]   Yes, we'll sleep. Come on. Go to sleep, Hap.

BEN   And it does take a great kind of a man to crack the jungle.

In accents of dread, BEN's *idyllic music starts up.*

HAPPY   [*his arm around* LINDA]   I'm getting married, Pop, don't forget it. I'm changing everything. I'm gonna run that department before the year is up. You'll see, Mom. [*He kisses her.*]

BEN   The jungle is dark but full of diamonds, Willy.

WILLY *turns, moves, listening to* BEN.

LINDA   Be good. You're both good boys, just act that way, that's all.

HAPPY   'Night, Pop. [*He goes upstairs.*]

LINDA   [*to* WILLY]   Come, dear.

BEN   [*with greater force*]   One must go in to fetch a diamond out.

WILLY   [*to* LINDA, *as he moves slowly along the edge of the kitchen, toward the door*]   I just want to get settled down, Linda. Let me sit alone for a little.

LINDA   [*almost uttering her fear*]   I want you upstairs.

WILLY   [*taking her in his arms*]   In a few minutes, Linda. I couldn't sleep right now. Go on, you look awful tired. [*He kisses her.*]

BEN   Not like an appointment at all. A diamond is rough and hard to the touch.

WILLY   Go on now. I'll be right up.

LINDA   I think this is the only way, Willy.

WILLY   Sure, it's the best thing.

BEN   Best thing!

WILLY   The only way. Everything is gonna be—go on, kid, get to bed. You look so tired.

LINDA   Come right up.

WILLY   Two minutes.

LINDA *goes into the living room, then reappears in her bedroom.* WILLY *moves just outside the kitchen door.*

WILLY   Loves me. [*Wonderingly*] Always loved me. Isn't that a remarkable thing? Ben, he'll worship me for it!

BEN   [*with promise*]   It's dark there, but full of diamonds.

WILLY   Can you imagine that magnificence with twenty thousand dollars in his pocket?

LINDA   [*calling from her room*]   Willy! Come up!

WILLY   [*calling into the kitchen*]   Yes! Coming! It's very smart, you realize that, don't you, sweetheart? Even Ben sees it. I gotta go, baby. 'By! 'By! [*Going over to* BEN, *almost dancing*] Imagine? When the mail comes he'll be ahead of Bernard again!

BEN   A perfect proposition all around.

WILLY   Did you see how he cried to me? Oh, if I could kiss him, Ben!

BEN   Time, William, time!

WILLY   Oh, Ben, I always knew one way or another we were gonna make it, Biff and I!

BEN   [*looking at his watch*]   The boat. We'll be late [*He moves slowly off into the darkness.*]

WILLY   [*elegiacally, turning to the house*]   Now when you kick off, boy, I want a seventy-yard boot, and get right down the field under the ball, and when you hit, hit low and hit hard, because it's important, boy. [*He swings around and faces the audience.*] There's all kinds of important people in the stands, and the first thing you know . . . [*Suddenly realizing he is alone*] Ben! Ben, where do I . . . [*He makes a sudden movement of search.*] Ben, how do I . . . ?

LINDA   [*calling*]   Willy, you coming up?

WILLY   [*uttering a gasp of fear, whirling about as if to quiet her*]   Sh! [*He turns around as if to find his way; sounds, faces, voices, seem to be swarming in upon him and he flicks at them, crying*] Sh! Sh! [*Suddenly music, faint and high, stops him. It rises in intensity, almost to an unbearable scream. He goes up and down on his toes, and rushes off around the house.*] Shhh!

LINDA   Willy?

There is no answer. Linda waits. BIFF *gets up off his bed. He is still in his clothes.* HAPPY *sits up.* BIFF *stands listening.*

LINDA   [*with real fear*]   Willy, answer me! Willy!

There is the sound of a car starting and moving away at full speed.

LINDA   No!

BIFF   [*rushing down the stairs*]   Pop!

As the car speeds off, the music crashes down in a frenzy of sound, which becomes the soft pulsation of a single cello string. BIFF *slowly returns to his bedroom. He and* HAPPY *gravely don their jackets.* LINDA *slowly walks out of her room. The music has developed into a dead march. The leaves of day are appearing over everything.* CHARLEY *and* BERNARD, *somberly dressed, appear and knock on the kitchen door.* BIFF *and* HAPPY *slowly descend the stairs to the kitchen as* CHARLEY *and* BER- *NARD* enter. All stop a moment when LINDA, *in clothes of mourning, bearing a little bunch of roses, comes through the draped doorway into the kitchen. She goes to* CHARLEY *and takes his arm. Now all move toward the audience, through the wall-line of the kitchen. At the limit of the apron,* LINDA *lays down the flowers, kneels, and sits back on her heels. All stare down at the grave.*

Requiem

CHARLEY   It's getting dark, Linda.

LINDA *doesn't react. She stares at the grave.*

BIFF   How about it, Mom? Better get some rest, heh? They'll be closing the gate soon.

LINDA *makes no move. Pause.*

HAPPY [*deeply angered*]   He had no right to do that. There was no necessity for it. We would've helped him.

CHARLEY [*grunting*]   Hmmm.

BIFF   Come along, Mom.

LINDA   Why didn't anybody come?

CHARLEY   It was a very nice funeral.

LINDA   But where are all the people he knew? Maybe they blame him.

CHARLEY   Naa. It's a rough world, Linda. They wouldn't blame him.

LINDA   I can't understand it. At this time especially. First time in thirty-five years we were just about free and clear. He only needed a little salary. He was even finished with the dentist.

CHARLEY   No man only needs a little salary.

LINDA   I can't understand it.

BIFF   There were a lot of nice days. When he'd come home from a trip; or on Sundays, making the stoop; finishing the cellar; putting on the new porch; when he built the extra bathroom; and put up the garage. You know something, Charley, there's more of him in that front stoop than in all the sales he ever made.

CHARLEY   Yeah. He was a happy man with a batch of cement.

LINDA   He was so wonderful with his hands.

BIFF   He had the wrong dreams. All, all, wrong.

HAPPY [*almost ready to fight* BIFF]   Don't say that!

BIFF   He never knew who he was.

CHARLEY [*stopping* HAPPY*'s movement and reply. To* BIFF]   Nobody dast blame this man. You don't understand: Willy was a salesman. And for a salesman, there is no rock bottom to the life. He don't put a bolt to a nut, he don't tell you the law or give you medicine. He's a man way out there in the blue, riding on a smile and a shoeshine. And when they start not smiling back—that's an earthquake. And then you get yourself a couple of spots on your hat, and you're finished. Nobody dast blame this man. A salesman is got to dream, boy. It comes with the territory.

BIFF   Charley, the man didn't know who he was.

HAPPY [*infuriated*]   Don't say that!

BIFF   Why don't you come with me, Happy?

HAPPY   I'm not licked that easily. I'm staying right in this city, and I'm gonna beat this racket! [*He looks at* BIFF, *his chin set.*] The Loman Brothers!

BIFF   I know who I am, kid.

HAPPY   All right, boy. I'm gonna show you and everybody else that Willy Loman did not die in vain. He had a good dream. It's the only dream you can have—to come out number-one man. He fought it out here, and this is where I'm gonna win it for him.

BIFF [*with a hopeless glance at* HAPPY, *bends toward his mother*] Let's go, Mom.

LINDA   I'll be with you in a minute. Go on, Charley. [*He hesitates.*] I want to, just for a minute. I never had a chance to say good-by.

> CHARLEY *moves away, followed by* HAPPY. BIFF *remains a slight distance up and left of* LINDA. *She sits there, summoning herself. The flute begins, not far away, playing behind her speech.*

LINDA   Forgive me, dear. I can't cry. I don't what it is, but I can't cry. I don't understand it. Why did you ever do that? Help me, Willy, I can't cry. It seems to me that you're just on another trip. I keep expecting you. Willy, dear, I can't cry. Why did you do it? I search and search and search, and I can't understand it, Willy. I made the last payment on the house today. Today, dear. And there'll be nobody home. [*A sob rises in her throat.*] We're free and clear. [*Sobbing more fully, released*] We're free. [BIFF *comes slowly toward her.*] We're free . . . We're free . . .

> BIFF *lifts her to her feet and moves out up right with her in his arms.* LINDA *sobs quietly.* BERNARD *and* CHARLEY *come together and follow them, followed by* HAPPY. *Only the music of the flute is left on the darkening stage as over the house the hard towers of the apartment buildings rise into sharp focus, and*

THE CURTAIN FALLS

1949

HERMAN J. MANKIEWICZ AND ORSON WELLES

Citizen Kane

Prologue

Fade In
1 *Ext.*[1] *Xanadu—Faint Dawn—1940 (Miniature)*
   *Window, very small in the distance, illuminated. All around this
an almost totally black screen. Now, as the camera moves slowly
towards this window, which is almost a postage stamp in the
frame, other forms appear; barbed wire, cyclone fencing, and now,
looming up against an early morning sky, enormous iron grillwork.
Camera travels up what is now shown to be a gateway of gigantic
proportions and holds on the top of it—a huge initial "K" showing
darker and darker against the dawn sky. Through this and beyond
we see the fairy-tale mountaintop of Xanadu, the great castle a
silhouette at its summit, the little window a distant accent in the
darkness.*

                                                              Dissolve

*(A series of setups, each closer to the great window, all telling
something of:)*
2 *The Literally Incredible Domain of Charles Foster Kane*
   *Its right flank resting for nearly forty miles on the Gulf Coast, it
truly extends in all directions farther than the eye can see. Designed
by nature to be almost completely bare and flat—it was, as will
develop, practically all marshland when Kane acquired and changed
its face—it is now pleasantly uneven, with its fair share of rolling
hills and one very good-sized mountain, all man-made. Almost all
the land is improved, either through cultivation for farming purposes or through careful landscaping in the shape of parks and lakes.
The castle itself—an enormous pile, compounded of several genuine
castles, of European origin, of varying architecture—dominates the
scene, from the very peak of the mountain.*

                                                              Dissolve

3 *Golf Links (Miniature)*
   *Past which we move. The greens are straggly and overgrown, the
fairways wild with tropical weeds, the links unused and not seriously tended for a long time.*

                                                          Dissolve Out

Dissolve In
4 *What Was Once a Good-Sized Zoo (Miniature)*

---

1. An exterior or outdoor shot. A glossary of film terms used in *Citizen Kane* appears
on pages 1233–1234.

Of the Hagenbeck type.[2] *All that now remains, with one excep tion, are the individual plots, surrounded by moats, on which the animals are kept, free and yet safe from each other and the land-scape at large. (Signs on several of the plots indicate that here there were once tigers, lions, giraffes.)*

Dissolve

5 *The Monkey Terrace (Miniature)*
In the f.g.[3] *a great obscene ape is outlined against the dawn murk. He is scratching himself slowly, thoughtfully, looking out across the estates of Charles Foster Kane, to the distant light glow-ing in the castle on the hill.*

Dissolve

6 *The Alligator Pit (Miniature)*
The idiot pile of sleepy dragons. Reflected in the muddy water —the lighted window.

7 *The Lagoon (Miniature)*
The boat landing sags. An old newspaper floats on the surface of the water—a copy of the New York "Inquirer." As it moves across the frame, it discloses again the reflection of the window in the castle, closer than before.

8 *The Great Swimming Pool (Miniature)*
It is empty. A newspaper blows across the cracked floor of the tank.

Dissolve

9 *The Cottages (Miniature)*
In the shadows, literally the shadows, of the castle. As we move by, we see that their doors and windows are boarded up and locked, with heavy bars as further protection and sealing.

Dissolve Out

Dissolve In
10 *A Drawbridge (Miniature)*
Over a wide moat, now stagnant and choked with weeds. We move across it and through a huge solid gateway into a formal garden, perhaps thirty yards wide and one hundred yards deep, which extends right up to the very wall of the castle. The land-scaping surrounding it has been sloppy and casual for a long time, but this particular garden has been kept up in perfect shape. As the camera makes its way through it, towards the lighted window of the castle, there are revealed rare and exotic blooms of all kinds. The dominating note is one of almost exaggerated tropical lush-

2. Carl Hagenbeck, a German animal trainer, opened in 1907 a zoological gar-den near Hamburg where for the first time animals were kept in uncovered, bar-less pits.
3. Foreground.

ness, hanging limp and despairing—Moss, moss, moss. Angkor Wat,[4] *the night the last king died.*

Dissolve

11 *The Window (Miniature)*
    Camera moves in until the frame of the window fills the frame of the screen. Suddenly the light within goes out. This stops the action of the camera and cuts the music which has been accompanying the sequence. In the glass panes of the window we see reflected the ripe dreary landscape of Mr. Kane's estate behind and the dawn sky.

Dissolve

12 *Int.*[5] *Kane's Bedroom—Faint Dawn—1940*
    A very long shot of Kane's enormous bed, silhouetted against the enormous window.

Dissolve

13 *Int. Kane's Bedroom—Faint Dawn—1940*
    A snow scene. An incredible one. Big impossible flakes of snow, a too picturesque farmhouse and a snowman. The jingling of sleigh bells in the musical score now makes an ironic reference to Indian temple bells—the music freezes—

KANE'S OLD OLD VOICE   Rosebud!

    The camera pulls back, showing the whole scene to be contained in one of those glass balls which are sold in novelty stores all over the world. A hand—Kane's hand, which has been holding the ball—relaxes. The ball falls out of his hand and bounds down two carpeted steps leading to the bed, the camera following. The ball falls off the last step onto the marble floor, where it breaks, the fragments glittering in the first ray of the morning sun. This ray cuts an angular pattern across the floor, suddenly crossed with a thousand bars of light as the blinds are pulled across the window.

14 *The Foot of Kane's Bed*
    The camera very close. Outlined against the shuttered window, we can see a form—the form of a nurse, as she pulls the sheet up over his head. The camera follows this action up the length of the bed and arrives at the face after the sheet has covered it.

Fade Out

Fade In
15 *Int. of a Motion Picture Projection Room*
    On the screen as the camera moves in are the words:

MAIN TITLE

---

4. A twelfth-century temple complex at   5. Interior.
Angkor, Cambodia.

Stirring brassy music is heard on the sound track (which, of course, sounds more like a sound track than ours).

The screen in the projection room fills our screen as the second title appears:

CREDITS

(NOTE: *Here follows a typical news digest short, one of the regular monthly or bimonthly features based on public events or personalities. These are distinguished from ordinary newsreels and short subjects in that they have a fully developed editorial or story line. Some of the more obvious characteristics of the "March of Time," for example, as well as other documentary shorts, will be combined to give an authentic impression of this now familiar type of short subject. As is the accepted procedure in these short subjects, a narrator is used as well as explanatory titles.*)

Fade Out

U.S.A.
Xanadu's Landlord
CHARLES FOSTER KANE

NARRATOR Legendary was the Xanadu where Kubla Khan decreed his stately pleasure dome [*With quotes in his voice*]:

OPENING SHOT *of great desolate expanse of Florida coastline. (Day—1940)*

Dissolve

"Where twice five miles of fertile ground
With walls and towers were girdled round."[6]

[*Dropping the quotes*] Today, almost as legendary is Florida's Xanadu—world's largest private pleasure ground. Here, on the deserts of the Gulf Coast, a private mountain was commissioned, successfully built for its landlord. . . . Here for Xanadu's landlord will be held 1940's biggest, strangest funeral; here this week is laid to rest a potent figure of our century—America's Kubla Khan—Charles Foster Kane.

TITLE:[7]

TO FORTY-FOUR MILLION U.S. NEWSBUYERS, MORE NEWSWOR-

6. Lines six and seven of Samuel Taylor Coleridge's poem "Kubla Khan" (1816). In the film the poem's opening lines, "In Xanadu did Kubla Khan / A stately plea-sure dome decree," appear on the screen.
7. Words superimposed on the images that appear on the screen.

THY THAN THE NAMES IN HIS
OWN HEADLINES WAS KANE HIM-
SELF, GREATEST NEWSPAPER TY-
COON OF THIS OR ANY OTHER
GENERATION.

SHOT *of a huge, screen-filling picture of Kane.*

PULL BACK *to show that it is a
picture on the front page of the
"Inquirer," surrounded by the
reversed rules of mourning, with
masthead and headlines.*[8] *(1940)
Dissolve*

In journalism's history other
names are honored more than
Charles Foster Kane's, more
justly revered. Among publishers, second only to James Gor-
don Bennett the First: his dashing expatriate son; England's
Northcliffe and Beaverbrook;
Chicago's Patterson and Mc-
Cormick; Denver's Bonfils and
Sommes; New York's late great
Joseph Pulitzer; America's emperor of the news syndicate,
another editorialist and landlord the still mighty and once
mightier Hearst.[9] Great names
all of them—but none of these
so loved—hated—feared, so
often spoken—as Charles Foster
Kane.

A GREAT NUMBER *of headlines,
set in different types and different
styles, obviously from different
papers, all announcing Kane's
death, all appearing over photographs of Kane himself. (Perhaps
a fifth of the headlines are in
foreign languages.) An important
item in connection with the headlines is that many of them—positively not all—reveal passionately
conflicting opinions about Kane.
Thus, they contain variously the
words, "patriot," "Democrat,"
"pacifist," "warmonger," "traitor,"
"idealist," "American," etc.*

TITLE:

1895 TO 1940
ALL OF THESE YEARS HE
COVERED, MANY OF THESE
YEARS HE WAS.

—The San Francisco earth-
quake.[1] First with the news

NEWSREEL SHOTS *of San Francisco
during and after the fire, followed*

---

8. Rules are thin metal strips used to
produce boxes around headlines, copy, and
pictures; *masthead* here means the name
of the newspaper across the first page,
more often called the *nameplate.*
9. Bennett, Northcliffe, et al. were prominent editors and publishers in England as
well as in America. Pulitzer (1847–1911)

published the *St. Louis Post-Dispatch* and
along with William Randolph Hearst (1863–
1951), publisher of the *New York Journal-
American,* promoted the Spanish-American
War and the spread of "yellow journalism."
1. Great fire and earthquake of 1906,
which leveled San Francisco's central business district.

were the Kane Papers. First with relief of the sufferers, first with the news of their relief of the sufferers.

—Kane Papers scoop the world on the Armistice—publish, eight hours before competitors, complete details of the Armistice terms granted the Germans by Marshal Foch from his railroad car in the Forest of Compiègne.[2]

For forty years appeared in Kane newsprint no public issue on which Kane Papers took no stand.

No public man whom Kane himself did not support or denounce—often support, then denounce.

by shots of special trains with large streamers: "Kane Relief Organization." Over these shots superimpose the date—1906.

ARTIST'S PAINTING *of Foch's railroad car and peace negotiators, if actual newsreel shot unavailable. Over this shot superimpose the date—1918.*

SHOTS *with the date—1898—(to be supplied).*
SHOTS *with the date—1910 (to be supplied).*
SHOTS *with the date—1922—(to be supplied).*

HEADLINES, *cartoons, contemporary newsreels or stills of the following:*
  1. Woman suffrage. (The celebrated newsreel shot of about 1914.)
  2. Prohibition. (Breaking up of a speakeasy and such.)
  3. T.V.A.[3]
  4. Labor riots.

BRIEF CLIPS *of old newsreel shots of William Jennings Bryan, Theodore Roosevelt, Stalin, Walter P. Thatcher, Al Smith, McKinley, Landon, Franklin D. Roosevelt and such. (Also recent newsreels of the elderly Kane with such Nazis as Hitler, Goering and England's Chamberlain and Churchill.)[1]*

2. Ferdinand Foch (1851–1929) was marshal of France and commander of Allied forces when the World War I armistice was signed near the Forest of Compiègne in northern France.
3. The Tennessee Valley Authority, a federal agency established in 1933 to control floods, improve navigation, and produce electric power along the Tennessee River.
4. William Jennings Bryan (1860–1925), a Democrat and Populist who ran three times unsuccessfully for the presidency;

Alfred E. Smith (1873–1944), unsuccessful presidential candidate in 1928; Alfred M. Landon (b. 1887), a 1936 Republican candidate who lost to Roosevelt; Hermann Goering (1893–1946), a leader of the Nazi party and Adolph Hitler's most loyal supporter; Neville Chamberlain (1869–1940), Britain's prime minister from 1937 to 1940 and best known for his policy of "appeasement" toward Hitler, replaced by Winston Churchill (1874–1965), who served as prime minister until 1945.

Its humble beginnings a dying daily—

SHOT *of a ramshackle building with old-fashioned presses showing through plate-glass windows and the name 'Inquirer' in old-fashioned gold letters. (1892)*

Dissolve

Kane's empire, in its glory, held dominion over thirty-seven newspapers, thirteen magazines, a radio network. An empire upon an empire. The first of grocery stores, paper mills, apartment buildings factories, forests, ocean liners—

THE MAGNIFICENT INQUIRER BUILDING of today.

A MAP OF THE U.S.A., 1891–1911, *covering the entire screen, which an animated diagram shows the Kane publications spreading from city to city. Starting from New York, miniature newsboys speed madly to Chicago, Detroit, St. Louis, Los Angeles, San Francisco, Washington, Atlanta, El Paso, etc., screaming, "Wuxtry,[5] Kane Papers, Wuxtry."*

An empire through which for fifty years flowed, in an unending stream, the wealth of the earth's third richest gold mine. . . .

SHOT *of a large mine going full blast, chimneys belching smoke, trains moving in and out, etc. A large sign reads "Colorado Lode Mining Co." (1940) Sign reading: "Little Salem, Colo., 25 Miles."*

Dissolve

AN OLD STILL SHOT *of Little Salem as it was seventy years ago. (Identified by copperplate caption beneath the still.) (1870)*

Famed in American legend is the origin of the Kane fortune. . . . How, to boarding-housekeeper Mary Kane, by a defaulting boarder, in 1868, was left the supposedly worthless deed to an abandoned mine shaft: the Colorado Lode.

SHOT *of early tintype stills of Thomas Foster Kane and his wife Mary on their wedding day. A similar picture of Mary Kane some four or five years later with her little boy, Charles Foster Kane.*

SHOT *of Capitol in Washington, D.C.*

Fifty-seven years later, before a congressional investigation, Walter P. Thatcher grand old

SHOT *of congressional investigating committee. (Reproduction of existing J. P. Morgan[6] newsreel.)*

5. Slang for "extra."
6. John Pierpont Morgan (1887–1943),

New York banker and financier.

man of Wall Street, for years chief target of Kane Papers' attacks on 'trusts," recalls a journey he made as a youth. . . .

This runs silent under narration. Walter P. Thatcher is on the stand. He is flanked by his son, Walter P. Thatcher, Jr., and other partners. He is being questioned by some Merry-Andrew congressmen. At this moment a baby alligator has just been placed in his lap, causing considerable confusion and embarrassment.

NEWSREEL CLOSEUP *of Thatcher, the sound track of which now fades in.*

THATCHER . . . because of that trivial incident . . .

INVESTIGATOR It is a fact, however, is it not, that in 1870 you did go to Colorado?

THATCHER I did.

INVESTIGATOR In connection with the Kane affairs?

THATCHER Yes. My firm had been appointed trustee by Mrs. Kane for the fortune, which she had recently acquired. It was her wish that I should take charge of this boy, Charles Foster Kane.

INVESTIGATOR Is it not a fact that on that occasion the boy personally attacked you after striking you in the stomach with a sled?

Loud laughter and confusion

THATCHER Mr. Chairman, I will read to this committee a prepared statement I have brought with me—and I will then refuse to answer any further questions. Mr. Johnson, please!

A young assistant hands him a sheet of paper from a briefcase.

THATCHER [*Reading it*] "With full awareness of the meaning of my words and the responsibility of what I am about to say, it is my considered belief that Mr. Charles Foster Kane, in every essence of his social beliefs and by the dangerous manner in which he has persistently attacked the American traditions of private property, initiative and opportunity for advancement, is—in fact—nothing more or less than a Communist."

That same month in Union Square—

NEWSREEL OF UNION SQUARE MEETING, *section of crowd carrying banners urging boycott of Kane Papers. A speaker is on the platform above the crowd.*

SPEAKER [*Fading in on sound track*] . . . till the words "Charles Foster Kane" are a menace to every workingman in this land. He is today what he has always been and always will be—*a Fascist!*

And yet another opinion— Kane's own.

SILENT NEWSREEL *on a windy platform, flag-draped, in front of the magnificent Inquirer Building. On platform, in full ceremonial dress, is Charles Foster Kane. He orates silently.*

TITLE:
"I AM, HAVE BEEN, AND WILL BE ONLY ONE THING—AN AMERICAN."
CHARLES FOSTER KANE

Same locale, Kane shaking hands out of frame.

DECK OF BOAT—*Authentic newsreel interview on arrival in New York Harbor. Kane is posing for photographers (in his early seventies).*

REPORTER This is a microphone, Mr. Kane.
KANE I know it's a microphone.

You people still able to afford microphones with all that new income tax?[7]

An embarrassed smile from the radio interviewer

REPORTER   The transatlantic broadcast says you're bringing back ten million dollars' worth of art objects. Is that correct?

KANE   Don't believe everything you hear on the radio. Read the "Inquirer"!

REPORTER   How'd you find business conditions abroad, Mr. Kane?

KANE   How did I find business conditions, Mr. Bones?[8] With great difficulty! [*Laughs heartily*]

REPORTER   Glad to be back, Mr. Kane?

KANE   I'm always glad to get back, young man. I'm an American. [*Sharply*] Anything else? Come, young man—when I was a reporter we asked them faster than that.

REPORTER   What do you think of the chances for a war in Europe?

KANE   Young man, there'll be no war. I have talked with all the responsible leaders of the Great Powers, and I can assure you that England, France, Germany and Italy are too intelligent to embark upon a project that must mean the end of civilization as we now know it. There will be no war!

Dissolve

TITLE:

FEW PRIVATE LIVES WERE MORE PUBLIC

7. The 16th Amendment establishing the personal income tax was ratified in 1916.

8. A stock name for the minstrel end man who answers the interlocutor, thus creating the show's comic repartee.

PERIOD STILL *of Emily Norton.* *(1900)*

Dissolve

Twice married—twice divorced —first to a President's niece, Emily Norton—who left him in 1916—died 1918 in a motor accident with their son.

RECONSTRUCTION *of very old silent newsreel of wedding party on the back lawn of the White House. Many notables, including Kane, Emily, Thatcher Sr., Thatcher Jr., and recognizably Bernstein, Leland, et al., among the guests. Also seen in this group are period newspaper photographers and newsreel cameramen. (1900)*

PERIOD STILL *of Susan Alexander.*

Dissolve

Two weeks after his divorce from Emily Norton, Kane married Susan Alexander, singer, at the town hall in Trenton, New Jersey.

RECONSTRUCTED SILENT NEWSREEL. *Kane, Susan and Bernstein emerging from side doorway of town hall into a ring of press photographers, reporters, etc. Kane looks startled, recoils for an instant, then charges down upon the photographers, laying about him with his stick, smashing whatever he can hit. (1917)*

For Wife Two, onetime operasinging Susan Alexander, Kane built Chicago's Municipal Opera House. Cost: Three million dollars.

STILL *of architect's sketch with typically glorified "rendering" of the Chicago Municipal Opera House. (1919)*

Dissolve

Conceived for Susan Alexander Kane, half finished before she divorced him, the still unfinished Xanadu. Cost: No man can say.

A GLAMOROUS SHOT *of the almost finished Xanadu, a magnificent fairy-tale estate built on a mountain. (1927–1929)*

SHOTS *of its preparation. (1920–1929)*

SHOTS *of truck after truck, train after train, flashing by with tremendous noise.*

SHOTS *of vast dredges, steam shovels.*

SHOT *of ship standing offshore unloading into lighters.*

In quick succession SHOTS *follow each other, some reconstructed, some in miniature, some real shots (maybe from the dam projects) of building, digging, pouring concrete, etc.*

One hundred thousand trees, twenty thousand tons of marble, are the ingredients of Xanadu's mountain.

MORE SHOTS *as before, only this time we see (in miniature) a large mountain—at different periods in its development—rising out of the sands.*

Xanadu's livestock: the fowl of the air, the fish of the sea, the beast of the field and jungle—two of each; the biggest private zoo since Noah.

SHOTS *of elephants, apes, zebras, etc., being herded, unloaded, shipped, etc. in various ways.*

Contents of Xanadu's palace: paintings, pictures, statues, and more statues, the very stones of many another pallace, shipped to Florida from every corner of the earth. Enough for ten museums—the loot of the world.

SHOTS *of packing cases being unloaded from ships, from trains, from trucks, with various kinds of lettering on them (Italian, Arabian, Chinese, etc.) but all consigned to Charles Foster Kane, Xanadu, Florida.*

A RECONSTRUCTED STILL *of Xanadu—the main terrace. A group of persons in clothes of the period of 1929. In their midst, clearly recognizable, are Kane and Susan.*

TITLE:

FROM XANADU, FOR THE PAST TWENTY-FIVE YEARS, ALL KANE ENTERPRISES HAVE BEEN DIRECTED, MANY OF THE NATION'S DESTINIES SHAPED.

SHOTS *of various authentically worded headlines of American papers since 1895.*

Kane urged his country's entry into one war—

Spanish-American War SHOTS. *(1898)*

—Opposed participation in another—

A GRAVEYARD *in France of the world war and hundreds of crosses. (1919)*

—Swung the election to one American President at least—so furiously attacked another as to be blamed for his death—called his assassin—burned in effigy.

OLD NEWSREELS *of a political campaign.*

NIGHT SHOT *of crowd burning Charles Foster Kane in effigy. The dummy bears a grotesque, comic resemblance to Kane. It is tossed into the flames, which burn up . . . and then down. . . . (1916)*

Fade Out

TITLE:

IN POLITICS—ALWAYS A
BRIDESMAID, NEVER A
BRIDE

Kane, molder of mass opinion though he was, in all his life was never granted elective office by the voters of his country. Few U.S. news publishers have been. Few, like one-time Congressman Hearst, have ever run for any office—most know better—conclude with other political observers that no man's press has power enough for himself. But Kane Papers were once strong indeed, and once the prize seemed almost his. In 1916, as independent candidate for governor, the best elements of the state behind him —the White House seemingly the next easy step in a lightning political career—

NEWSREEL SHOTS *of great crowds streaming into a building—Madison Square Garden—then*

SHOTS *inside the vast auditorium, at one end of which is a huge picture of Kane. (1916)*

SHOT OF BOX *containing the first Mrs. Kane and young Charles Foster Kane aged nine and a half. They are acknowledging the cheers of the crowd. (Silent shot) (1916)*

NEWSREEL SHOT *of dignitaries on platform, with Kane alongside of speaker's table, beaming, hand upraised to silence the crowd. (Silent shot) (1916)*

NEWSREEL SHOT—*close-up of Kane delivering speech. (1916)*

Then, suddenly—less than one week before election—defeat! Shameful ignominious—Defeat that set back for twenty years the cause of reform in the U.S.,

THE FRONT PAGE *of a contemporary paper—a screaming headline—twin photos of Kane and Susan. (1916) Headline reads:*

forever canceled political chances for Charles Foster Kane.

Then in the third year of the Great Depression . . . as to all publishers it sometimes must— to Bennett, to Munsey and Hearst it did—a paper closes! For Kane, in four short years: collapse. Eleven Kane Papers, four Kane magazines merged, more sold, scrapped—

Then four long years more— alone in his never finished, already decaying, pleasure palace, aloof, seldom visited, never photographed, Charles Foster Kane continued to direct his failing empire . . . vainly attempting to sway, as he once did, the destinies of a nation that had ceased to listen to him . . . ceased to trust him. . . .

Then, last week, as it must to all men, death came to Charles Foster Kane.

CANDIDATE KANE CAUGHT IN LOVE NEST WITH "SINGER"

PRINTED TITLE *about depression.* ONCE MORE REPEAT THE MAP OF THE U.S.A., *1932–1939. Suddenly the cartoon goes into reverse, the empire begins to shrink, illustrating the narrator's words.*

THE DOOR OF A NEWSPAPER OFFICE *with the sign: "Closed."*

SHOTS OF XANADU. *(1940)*

SERIES OF SHOTS, *entirely modern, but rather jumpy and obviously bootlegged, showing Kane in a bathchair, swathed in steamer rugs, being perambulated through his rose garden, a desolate figure in the sunshine. (1935)*

EXT. THE NEW INQUIRER BUILDING. NEW YORK—NIGHT *(1940) (Painting and Double Printing)*[9]

A moving electric sign, similar to the one on the Times Building— spells out the words:

CHARLES FOSTER KANE—DEAD

INSERT: DOOR *with the sign* PROJECTION ROOM *on it.*
16 Int. Projection Room—Day—1940
(A fairly large one, with a long throw[1] *to the screen.) It is dark. Present are the editors of a news digest short, and of the Rawlston*

---

9. A special effect by which the electric sign message would be superimposed on a painting of the Times Building.

1. Throw is the distance from the projector to the screen. The longer the throw, generally, the larger the image.

magazines. Rawlston himself is also present. During this scene, nobody's face is really seen. Sections of their bodies are picked out by a table light, a silhouette is thrown on the screen, and their faces and bodies are themselves thrown into silhouette against the brilliant slanting rays of light from the projection booth.

THOMPSON   That's it.

He rises, lighting a cigarette, and sits on corner of table. There is movement of men shifting in seats and lighting cigarettes.

FIRST MAN [*Into phone*]   Stand by. I'll tell you if we want to run it again. [*Hangs up*]

THOMPSON   Well?—How about it, Mr. Rawlston?

RAWLSTON [*Has risen*]   How do you like it boys?

A short silence.

Almost together
{ SECOND MAN   Well . . . er . . .
{ THIRD MAN   Seventy years of a man's life . . .
{ FOURTH MAN   That's a lot to try to get into a newsreel . . .

Thompson turns on the table lamp.

RAWLSTON [*As he walks to* THOMPSON]   It's a good short, Thompson, but what it needs is an angle. All that picture tells us is that Charles Foster Kane is dead. I know that—I read the papers—

Laughter greets this.

RAWLSTON [*Cont'd*]   What do you think, boys?

THIRD MAN   I agree.

FIRST MAN   You're right, Mr. Rawlston—it needs an angle.

RAWLSTON   You see, Thompson, it isn't enough to show what a man did—you've got to tell us who he was—

THOMPSON   Umhum—

SECOND MAN   It needs that angle, Thompson.

RAWLSTON   Certainly! [*Getting an idea*] Wait a minute!

All lean forward, interested.

RAWLSTON [*Cont'd*]   What were Kane's last words? Do you remember, boys?

THIRD MAN   Kane's last words—

SECOND MAN   Death speech—

RAWLSTON   What were the last words Kane said on earth? Maybe he told us all about himself on his deathbed.

THOMPSON   Yes, and maybe he didn't. Maybe—

RAWLSTON [*Riding over him*]   All we saw on that screen was a big American—[*Walks toward the screen*]

THIRD MAN   One of the biggest.

RAWLSTON   But how is he different from Ford? Or Hearst, for that matter? Or Rockefeller—or John Doe?

There is a murmur of accord.

RAWLSTON [*Cont'd*] [*Walks toward Thompson*]   I tell you, Thompson—a man's dying words—
SECOND MAN   What were they?
THOMPSON [*To Second Man*]   You don't read the papers.

Laughter

RAWLSTON   When Mr. Charles Foster Kane died he said just one word—
THOMPSON   Rosebud!

FIRST MAN   Is that what he said? Just Rosebud?
Almost SECOND MAN   Umhum—Rosebud—
together FOURTH MAN   Tough guy, huh? [*Derisively*] Dies calling for Rosebud!

Laughter

RAWLSTON [*Riding over them*]   Yes, Rosebud!—Just that one word—But who was she—
SECOND MAN   Or what was it?

Tittering.

RAWLSTON   Here's a man who might have been President. He's been loved and hated and talked about as much as any man in our time—but when he comes to die, he's got something on his mind called Rosebud. What does that mean?
THIRD MAN   A race horse he bet on once, probably—
FOURTH MAN   Yeh—that didn't come in—
RAWLSTON   All right—[*Strides toward* THIRD *and* FOURTH *men*] But what was the race?

There is a short silence.

RAWLSTON [*Cont'd*]   Thompson!
THOMPSON   Yes, Mr. Rawlston.
RAWLSTON   Hold the picture up a week—two weeks if you have to—
THOMPSON [*Feebly*]   Don't you think, right after his death, if we release it now—it might be better than—
RAWLSTON [*Decisively; cutting in on above speech*]   Find out about Rosebud!—Go after everybody that knew him—that manager of his—[*Snaps fingers*]—Bernstein—his second wife—she's still living—
THOMPSON   Susan Alexander Kane—
SECOND MAN   She's running a nightclub in Atlantic City—
RAWLSTON [*Crosses to Thompson*]   See 'em all—all the people who worked for him—who loved him—who hated his guts—[*Pause*] I

don't mean go through the city directory, of course.

The Third Man gives a hearty "yes-man" laugh. Others titter.

THOMPSON [*Rising*]   I'll get to it right away, Mr. Rawlston.
RAWLSTON [*Pats his arm*]   Good! Rosebud dead or alive! It'll probably turn out to be a very simple thing.

Fade Out

> (NOTE: *Now begins the story proper—the search by Thompson for the facts about Kane—his researches—his interviews with the people who knew Kane.*)

Fade In
17 *Ext. Cheap Cabaret—"El Rancho"—Atlantic City—Rain—Night—1940 (Miniature)*
    The first image to register is a sign:

"EL RANCHO"
Floor Show
Susan Alexander Kane
Twice Nightly

These words, spelled out in neon, glow out of the darkness. Then there is lightning which reveals a squalid rooftop on which the sign stands. Camera moves close to the skylight. We see through the skylight down into the cabaret. Directly below at a table sits the lone figure of a woman, drinking by herself.

Dissolve

18 *Int. "El Rancho" Cabaret—Night—1940*
    The lone figure at the table is Susan. She is fifty, trying to look much younger, cheaply blonded, in a cheap, enormously generous evening dress. The shadows of Thompson and the Captain are seen moving toward the table from direction of doorway. The Captain appears, across to Susan, and stands behind her. Thompson moves into the picture in close f.g., his back to camera

CAPTAIN [*To Susan*]   Miss Alexander—this is Mr. Thompson, Miss Alexander.
SUSAN [*Without looking up*]   I want another drink, John.

Low thunder from outside.

CAPTAIN   Right away. Will you have something, Mr. Thompson?
THOMPSON [*Starting to sit down*]   I'll have a highball.
SUSAN [*Looks at Thompson*]   Who told you you could sit down here?
THOMPSON   I thought maybe we could have a drink together.
SUSAN   Think again!

There is an awkward pause.

SUSAN [*Cont'd*] Why don't you people let me alone? I'm minding my own business. You mind yours.

THOMPSON If you'd just let me talk to you for a little while, Miss Alexander. All I want to ask you—

SUSAN Get out of here! [*Almost hysterical*] Get out!

THOMPSON [*Rising*] I'm sorry.

SUSAN Get out.

THOMPSON Maybe some other time—

SUSAN Get out.

> *Thompson looks up at the Captain. The Captain indicates the door with a slight jerk of his head, then walks away from the table toward a waiter who is leaning against the wall in front of the door. Thompson follows.*

CAPTAIN Gino—get her another highball. [*To Thompson as he passes them*] She's just not talking to anybody, Mr. Thompson.

THOMPSON Okay.

> *Walks to phone booth.*

WAITER Another double?

CAPTAIN Yeh—

> *During above Thompson has dropped coin into phone slot and dialed long distance operator (112) The waiter exits for the drink.*

THOMPSON [*Into phone*] Hello—I want New York City—Courtland 7-9970. . . .

> *The Captain steps closer to the phone booth.*

THOMPSON [*Cont'd*] This is Atlantic City 4-6827—All right—[*Puts coins into slot; turns to Captain*] Hey—do you think she ought to have another drink?

CAPTAIN Yeh. She'll snap out of it. Why, until he died, she'd just as soon talk about Mr. Kane as about anybody. Sooner—

THOMPSON [*Into phone*] Hello—this is Thompson. Let me talk to the Chief, will you? [*Closes booth door*] Hello, Mr. Rawlston. She won't talk—

> *During above, waiter enters and sets highball in front of Susan. She drinks thirstily.*

RAWLSTON'S VOICE Who

THOMPSON The second Mrs. Kane—about Rosebud or anything else! I'm calling from Atlantic City.

RAWLSTON'S VOICE Make her talk!

THOMPSON All right—I'm going over to Philadelphia in the morning—to the Thatcher Library, to take a look of that diary of his— they're expecting me. Then I've got an appointment in New York with Kane's general manager—what's his name—Bernstein. Then I'll come back here.

RAWLSTON'S VOICE   See everybody

THOMPSON   Yes, I'll see everybody—that's still alive. Good-bye, Mr. Rawlston. [*Hangs up; opens door*] Hey—er—

CAPTAIN   John—

THOMPSON   John—you just might be able to help me. When she used to talk about Kane—did she ever happen to say anything—about Rosebud?

CAPTAIN [*Looks over at Susan*]   Rosebud?

Thompson slips him a bill.

CAPTAIN [*Cont'd*] [*Pocketing it*]   Oh, thank you, Mr. Thompson. Thanks. As a matter of fact, just the other day, when all that stuff was in the papers—I asked her—she never heard of Rosebud.

Fade Out

Fade
19 *Int. Thatcher Memorial Library—Day—1940*
   A noble interpretation of Mr. Thatcher himself, executed in expensive marble, his stone eyes fixed on the camera.
   We move down off of this, showing the pedestal on which the words "Walter Parks Thatcher" are engraved. Immediately below the inscription we encounter, in a medium shot, Bertha Anderson, an elderly, mannish spinster, seated behind her desk. Thompson, his hat in his hand, is standing before her.

BERTHA [*Into a phone*]   Yes. I'll take him in now. [*Hangs up and looks at Thompson*] The directors of the Thatcher Memorial Library have asked me to remind you again of the condition under which you may inspect certain portions of Mr. Thatcher's unpublished memoirs. Under no circumstances are direct quotations from his manuscript to be used by you.

THOMPSON   That's all right.

BERTHA   You may come with me.

She rises and starts towards a distant door. Thompson follows.
Dissolve

20 *Int. The Vault Room—Thatcher Memorial Library—Day—1940*
   A room with all the warmth and charm of Napoleon's tomb. As we dissolve in, the door opens in and we see past Thompson's shoulders the length of the room. The floor is marble. There is a gigantic, mahogany table in the center of everything. Beyond this is a safe from which a guard, with a revolver holster at his hip, is extracting the journal of Walter P. Thatcher. He brings it to Bertha.

BERTHA [*To the guard*]   Pages eighty-three to one hundred and forty-two, Jennings.

GUARD   Yes, Miss Anderson.

BERTHA [*To Thompson*] You will confine yourself, it is our understanding, to the chapter dealing with Mr. Kane.

THOMPSON That's all I'm interested in.

BERTHA You will be required to leave this room at four-thirty
promptly.

> *She leaves. Thompson starts to light a cigarette. The guard
> shakes his head. With a sigh, Thompson bends over to read
> the manuscript. Camera moves down over his shoulder onto
> page of manuscript.*

INSERT: MANUSCRIPT, *neatly and precisely written:*

CHARLES FOSTER KANE

When these lines appear in print, fifty years after my death, I
am confident that the whole world will agree with my opinion
of Charles Foster Kane, assuming that he is not then completely
forgotten, which I regard as extremely likely. A good deal of
nonsense has appeared about my first meeting with Kane, when
he was six years old. . . . The facts are simple. In the winter of
1870 . . .

> *Dissolve*

21 Ext. Mrs. Kane's Boardinghouse—Day—1870
*The white of a great field of snow. In the same position as the
last word in above insert appears the tiny figure of Charles Foster
Kane, aged five. He throws a snowball at the camera. It sails
toward us and out of scene.*

22 Reverse Angle—on the house, featuring a large sign reading:

MRS. KANE'S BOARDINGHOUSE
HIGH CLASS MEALS AND LODGING
INQUIRE WITHIN

Charles Kane's snowball hits the sign.

23 Int. Parlor—Mrs. Kane's Boardinghouse—Day—1870
*Camera is angling through the window, but the window frame
is not cut into scene. We see only the field of snow again. Charles is
manufacturing another snowball. Now—
Camera pulls back, the frame of the window appearing, and we
are inside the parlor of the boardinghouse. Mrs. Kane, aged about
twenty-eight, is looking out towards her son.*

MRS. KANE [*Calling out*] Be careful, Charles!

THATCHER'S VOICE Mrs. Kane—

MRS. KANE [*Calling out the window*] Pull your muffler around your
neck, Charles—

> *But Charles runs away. Mrs. Kane turns into camera and we*

see her face—a strong face, worn and kind.

THATCHER'S VOICE   I think we'll have to tell him now—

Camera now pulls back further, showing Thatcher standing before a table on which is his stovepipe hat and documents. He is twenty-six and a very stuffy young man.

MRS. KANE   I'll sign those papers now, Mr. Thatcher.
KANE SR.   You people seem to forget that I'm the boy's father.

At the sound of Kane Sr's. voice, both have turned to him and camera pulls back still further, taking him in

MRS. KANE   It's going to be done exactly the way I've told Mr. Thatcher—
KANE SR.   If I want to, I can go to court. A father has the right to— A boarder that beats his bill and leaves worthless stock behind— that property is just as much my property as anybody's if it turns out to be valuable. I knew Fred Graves and if he'd had any idea this was going to happen—he'd have made out those certificates in both our names—
THATCHER   However, they were made out in Mrs. Kane's name.
KANE   He owed the money for the board to both of us. Besides, I don't hold with signing my boy away to any bank as guardeen just because—
MRS. KANE   [*Quietly*]   I want you to stop this nonsense, Jim.
THATCHER   The bank's decision in all matters concerning his education, his places of residence and similar subjects are to be final.
KANE SR.   The idea of a bank being the guardeen . . .

Mrs. Kane has met his eye. Her triumph over him finds expression in his failure to finish his sentence.

MRS. KANE   [*Even more quietly*]   I want you to stop all this nonsense, Jim.
THATCHER   We will assume full management of the Colorado Lode— of which you, Mrs. Kane, I repeat, are the sole owner.

Kane Sr. opens his mouth once or twice, as if to say something, but chokes down his opinion.

MRS. KANE   Where do I sign, Mr. Thatcher?
THATCHER   Right here, Mrs. Kane.
KANE SR.   [*Sulkily*]   Don't say I didn't warn you—Mary, I'm asking you for the last time—anyone'd think I hadn't been a good husband and a—

Mrs. Kane looks at him slowly. He stops his speech.

THATCHER   The sum of fifty thousand dollars a year is to be paid to yourself and Mr. Kane as long as you both live, and thereafter the survivor—

Mrs. Kane signs

KANE SR.   Well, let's hope it's all for the best.

MRS. KANE   It is—Go on, Mr. Thatcher—

Mrs. Kane, listening to Thatcher, of course, has had her other ear bent in the direction of the boy's voice. Kane Sr. walks over to close the window.

24 *Ext. Mrs. Kane's Boardinghouse—Day—1870*
Kane Jr., seen from the window. He is advancing on the snowman, snowballs in his hands. He drops to one knee.

KANE   If the rebels want a fight, boys, let's give it to 'em! The terms are unconditional surrender. Up and at 'em! The Union forever!

25 *Int. Parlor—Mrs. Kane's Boardinghouse—Day—1870*
Kane Sr. closes the window.

THATCHER   Everything else—the principal as well as all monies earned —is to be administered by the bank in trust for your son, Charles Foster Kane, until his twenty-fifth birthday, at which time he is to come into complete possession.

Mrs. Kane rises and goes to the window, opening it.

MRS. KANE   Go on, Mr. Thatcher.

26 *Ext. Mrs. Kane's Boardinghouse—Day—1870*
Kane Jr. seen from the window.

KANE   You can't lick Andy Jackson! Old Hickory, that's me!

He fires his snowball, well wide of the mark and falls flat on his stomach, starting to crawl carefully toward the snowman.

THATCHER'S VOICE   It's nearly five, Mrs. Kane—don't you think I'd better meet the boy—

27 *Int. Parlor—Mrs. Kane's Boardinghouse—Day—1870*
Mrs. Kane at the window. Thatcher is now standing at her side.

MRS. KANE   I've got his trunk all packed—[*She chokes a little*] I've had it packed for a couple of weeks—
She can't say any more. She starts for the hall door.

THATCHER   I've arranged for a tutor to meet us in Chicago. I'd have brought him along with me, but you were so anxious to keep everything secret—

He stops. Mrs. Kane is already well into the hall. He looks at Kane Sr., tightens his lips, and follows Mrs. Kane. Kane follows him.

28 Ext. Mrs. Kane's Boardinghouse—Day—1870
  *Kane, in the snow-covered field. He holds the sled in his hand.
The Kane house, in the b.g.,[2] is a dilapidated, shabby, two-story
frame building, with a wooden outhouse. Kane looks up as he sees
the procession, Mrs. Kane at its head, coming toward him.*

KANE   H'ya, Mom. [*Gesturing at the snowman*] See, Mom? I took the
  pipe out of his mouth. If it keeps on snowin', maybe I'll make some
  teeth and—

MRS. KANE   You better come inside, son. You and I have got to get
  you all ready for—for—

THATCHER   Charles, my name is Mr. Thatcher—

MRS. KANE   This is Mr. Thatcher, Charles.

THATCHER   How do you do, Charles.

KANE SR.   He comes from the East—

KANE   Hello. Hello, Pop.

KANE SR.   Hello, Charlie!

MRS. KANE   Mr. Thatcher is going to take you on a trip with him
  tonight, Charles. You'll be leaving on Number Ten.

KANE SR.   That's the train with all the lights.

KANE   You goin', Mom?

THATCHER   Your mother won't be going right away, Charles—

KANE   Where'm I going?

KANE SR.   You're going to see Chicago and New York—and Washington, maybe . . . isn't he, Mr. Thatcher?

THATCHER [*Heartily*]   He certainly is. I wish I were a little boy and
  going to make a trip like that for the first time.

KANE   Why aren't you comin' with us, Mom?

MRS. KANE   We have to stay here, Charles.

KANE SR.   You're going to live with Mr. Thatcher from now on,
  Charlie! You're going to be rich. Your Ma figures—that is—er—she
  and I have decided that this isn't the place for you to grow up in.
  You'll probably be the richest man in America someday and you
  ought to—

MRS. KANE   You won't be lonely, Charles . . .

THATCHER   We're going to have a lot of good times together, Charles
  . . . really we are.

  Kane stares at him.

THATCHER [*Cont'd*]   Come on, Charles. Let's shake hands. [*Kane
  continues to look at him*] Now, now! I'm not as frightening as all
  that! Let's shake, what do you say?

  *He reaches out for Charles's hand. Without a word, Charles
  hits him in the stomach with the sled. Thatcher stumbles
  back a few feet, gasping.*

THATCHER [*Cont'd*] [*With a sickly grin*]   You almost hurt me,
  Charles. Sleds aren't to hit people with. Sleds are to—to sleigh on.

---

2. Background.

When we get to New York, Charles, we'll get you a sled that will—

> *He's near enough to try to put a hand on Kane's shoulder. As he does, Kane kicks him in the ankle.*

MRS. KANE   Charles!

> *He throws himself on her, his arms around her. Slowly Mrs. Kane puts her arms around him.*

KANE [*Frightened*]   Mom! Mom!
MRS. KANE   It's all right, Charles, it's all right.
KANE SR.   Sorry, Mr. Thatcher! What that kid needs is a good thrashing!
MRS. KANE   That's what you think, is it, Jim?
KANE SR.   Yes.
MRS. KANE [*Looks at Mr. Kane; slowly*]   That's why he's going to be brought up where you can't get at him.

> *Dissolve*

INSERT: (NIGHT—1870) (STOCK OR MINIATURE) OLD-FASHIONED RAIL-ROAD WHEELS *underneath a sleeper, spinning along the track.*

> *Dissolve*

29 *Int. Train—Old-Fashioned Drawing Room—Night—1870*
Thatcher, with a look of mingled exasperation, annoyance, sympathy and inability to handle the situation, is standing alongside a berth, looking at Kane. Kane, his face in the pillow, is crying with heartbreaking sobs.

KANE   Mom! Mom!

> *Dissolve*

INSERT: THE THATCHER MANUSCRIPT, *which fills the screen. It reads:*
. . . nothing but a lucky scoundrel, spoiled, unscrupulous, irresponsible. He acquired his first newspaper through a caprice. His whole attitude as a publisher . . .

> *Dissolve Out*

Dissolve In
30 *Int. Kane's Office—"Inquirer"—Day—1898*
Close-up on printed headline, which reads:
GALLEONS OF SPAIN OFF JERSEY COAST
Camera pulls back to reveal Thatcher, holding the "Inquirer" with its headline, standing in front of Kane's desk. Kane is seated behind the desk.

THATCHER   Is this really your idea of how to run a newspaper?
KANE   I don't know how to run a newspaper, Mr. Thatcher. I just try everything I can think of.
THATCHER [*Reading the headline*]   Galleons of Spain off Jersey Coast.

You know you haven't the slightest proof that this—this armada is off the Jersey coast.

KANE   Can you prove that it isn't?

Bernstein rushes in, a cable in his hand. He stops when he sees Thatcher.

KANE [*Cont'd*] [*Genially*]   Mr. Bernstein, Mr. Thatcher.

BERNSTEIN   How are you, Mr. Thatcher?

Thatcher gives him the briefest of nods.

BERNSTEIN [*Cont'd*]   We just had a wire from Cuba, Mr. Kane.

He stops, embarrassed.

KANE   That's all right. We have no secrets from our readers. Mr. Thatcher is one of our most devoted readers, Mr. Bernstein. He knows what's wrong with every copy of the "Inquirer" since I took charge. Read the cable.

BERNSTEIN [*Reading*]   Food marvelous in Cuba—girls delightful stop could send you prose poems about scenery but don't feel right spending your money stop there's no war in Cuba signed Wheeler. Any answer?

KANE   Yes. Dear Wheeler—[*Pauses a moment*]—you provide the prose poems—I'll provide the war.

BERNSTEIN   That's fine, Mr. Kane.

Thatcher, bursting with indignation, sits down.

KANE   I kinda like it myself. Send it right away.

BERNSTEIN   Right away.

Bernstein leaves. After a moment of indecision, Thatcher decides to make one last try.

THATCHER   Charles, I came to see you about this—campaign of yours . . . er . . . the "Inquirer's" campaign—against the Metropolitan Transfer Company.

KANE   Good. You got some material we can use against them?

THATCHER   You're still a college boy, aren't you, Charles?

KANE   Oh, no, I was expelled from college—several colleges. Don't you remember?

Thatcher glares at him.

KANE [*Cont'd*]   I remember. I think that's when I first lost my belief that you were omnipotent, Mr. Thatcher—when you told me that the dean's decision at Harvard, despite all your efforts, was irrevocable—[*He thinks, and looks at Thatcher inquiringly*]— irrevocable—

Thatcher stares at him angrily, tight-lipped.

KANE [*Cont'd*] I can't tell you how often I've learned the correct pronunciation of that word, but I always forget.

THATCHER [*Not interested, coming out with it*] I think I should remind you, Charles, of a fact you seem to have forgotten. You are yourself one of the company's largest individual stockholders.

KANE   The trouble is, Mr. Thatcher, you don't realize you're talking to two people. As Charles Foster Kane, who has eighty-two thousand, six hundred and thirty-one shares of Metropolitan Transfer—you see, I do have a rough idea of my holdings—I sympathize with you. Charles Foster Kane is a dangerous scoundrel, his paper should be run out of town and a committee should be formed to boycott him. You may, if you can form such a committee, put me down for a contribution of one thousand dollars.

THATCHER [*Angrily*] Charles, my time is too valuable for me—

KANE   On the other hand—[*His manner becomes serious*] I am the publisher of the "Inquirer." As such, it is my duty—I'll let you in on a little secret, it is also my pleasure—to see to it that the decent, hardworking people of this city are not robbed blind by a group of money-mad pirates because, God help them, they have no one to look after their interests!

Thatcher has risen. He now puts on his hat and walks away.

KANE [*Cont'd*]   —I'll let you in on another little secret, Mr. Thatcher.

Thatcher stops. Kane walks up to him.

KANE [*Cont'd*]   I think I'm the man to do it. You see I have money and property. If I don't defend the interests of the underprivileged, somebody else will—maybe somebody *without* any money or any property—and that would be too bad.

THATCHER [*Puts on his hat*]   I happened to see your consolidated statement this morning, Charles. Don't you think it's rather unwise to continue this philanthropic enterprise—this "Inquirer"—that's costing you one million dollars a year?

KANE   You're right. We did lose a million dollars last year. We expect to lose a million next year, too. You know, Mr. Thatcher—at the rate of a million a year—we'll have to close this place—in sixty years.

Dissolve

31 *Int. The Vault Room—Thatcher Memorial Library—Day*
THE MANUSCRIPT:

The ordinary decencies of human life were, I repeat, unknown to him. His incredible vulgarity, his utter disregard . . .

Before the audience has had a chance to read this, Thompson, with a gesture of annoyance, has closed the manuscript. He turns to confront Miss Anderson, who has come to shoo him out.

MISS ANDERSON   You have enjoyed a very rare privilege, young man.

Did you find what you were looking for?

THOMPSON   No. Tell me something. Miss Anderson. You're not Rose-bud, are you?

MISS ANDERSON   What?

THOMPSON   I didn't think you were. Well, thanks for the use of the hall.

> *He puts his hat on his head and starts out, lighting a cigarette as he goes. Miss Anderson, scandalized, watches him.*
>
> *Dissolve*

32 Int. Bernstein's Office—Inquirer Skyscraper—Day—1940
   Close-up of a still of Kane, aged about sixty-five. Camera pulls back, showing it as a framed photograph on the wall. Under it sits Bernstein, back of his desk. Bernstein, always an undersized Jew, now seems even smaller than in his youth. He is bald as an egg, spry, with remarkably intense eyes. As camera continues to travel back, the back of Thompson's head and his shoulders come into the picture.

BERNSTEIN [*Wryly*]   Who's a busy man? Me? I'm chairman of the board. I got nothing but time. . . . What do you want to know?

THOMPSON   Well, we thought maybe—[*Slowly*] if we could find out what he meant by his last words—as he was dying—

BERNSTEIN   That Rosebud, huh? [*Thinks*] Maybe some girl? There were a lot of them back in the early days and—

THOMPSON [*Amused*]   It's hardly likely, Mr. Bernstein, that Mr. Kane could have met some girl casually and then, fifty years later, on his deathbed—

BERNSTEIN   You're pretty young, Mr.—[*Remembers the name*]—Mr. Thompson. A fellow will remember things you wouldn't think he'd remember. You take me. One day, back in 1896, I was crossing over to Jersey on a ferry and as we pulled out there was another ferry pulling in—[*Slowly*]—and on it there was a girl waiting to get off. A white dress she had on—and she was carrying a white para-sol—and I only saw her for one second and she didn't see me at all—but I'll bet a month hasn't gone by since that I haven't thought of that girl. [*Triumphantly*] See what I mean? [*Smiles*]

THOMPSON   Yes. [*A near sigh*] But about Rosebud. I wonder—

BERNSTEIN   Who else you been to see?

THOMPSON   Well, I went down to Atlantic City—

BERNSTEIN   Susie? I called her myself the day after he died. I thought maybe somebody ought to—[*Sadly*] She couldn't even come to the phone.

THOMPSON [*Ruefully*]   She wasn't exactly in a condition to talk to me either. I'm going down to see her again in a couple of days [*Pauses*] About Rosebud, Mr. Bernstein—

BERNSTEIN   If I had any idea who it was, believe me, I'd tell you.

THOMPSON   If you'd kind of just talk, Mr. Bernstein—about anything connected with Mr. Kane that you can remember—After all, you were with him from the beginning.

BERNSTEIN From *before* the beginning, young fellow—[*Not too maudlinly*] And now it's after the end. [*After a pause*] Have you tried to see anybody else except Susie?

THOMPSON I haven't seen anybody else, but I've been through that stuff of Walter Thatcher's. That journal of his—

BERNSTEIN Thatcher! That man was the biggest darned fool I ever met.

THOMPSON He made an awful lot of money.

BERNSTEIN It's no trick to make a lot of money, if all you want is to make a lot of money. You take Mr. Kane—it wasn't money he wanted. Mr. Thatcher never did figure him out. Sometimes, even, I I couldn't—[*Suddenly*] You know who you ought to talk to? Mr. Jed Leland. That is, if—he was Mr. Kane's closest friend, you know. They went to school together.

THOMPSON Harvard, wasn't it?

BERNSTEIN Harvard—Yale—Cornell—Princeton—Switzerland. Mr. Leland—he never had a nickel—one of those old families where the father is worth ten million, then one day he shoots himself and it turns out there's nothing but debts. [*Reflectively*] He was with Mr. Kane and me the first day Mr. Kane took over the "Inquirer."

Dissolve

33 *Ext. The Old Inquirer Building—Day—1890*
(*The same shot as in news digest but this is the real thing, not a still.*) *A hansom cab comes into the scene. In it are Kane and Leland. They are both dressed like New York dandies. It is a warm summer day. Kane jumps from the cab, as Leland follows more slowly.*

KANE [*Pointing with his stick*] Take a look at it, Jed. It's going to look a lot different one of these days.

He is boisterously radiant. Jed agrees with a thoughtful smile. As they start across the sidewalk toward the building, which they then enter, a delivery wagon draws up and takes the place vacated by the cab. In its open back, almost buried by a bed, bedding, trunks, framed pictures, etc., is Bernstein, who climbs out with difficulty.

BERNSTEIN [*To the driver*] Come on! I'll give you a hand with this stuff.

DRIVER There ain't no bedrooms in this joint. That's a newspaper building.

BERNSTEIN You're getting paid, mister, for opinions—or for hauling?

Dissolve

34 *Int. City Room—Inquirer Building—Day—1890*
The front half of the second floor constitutes one large city room. Despite the brilliant sunshine outside, very little of it is actually getting into the room because the windows are small and narrow. There are about a dozen tables and desks, of the old-fashioned

*type, not flat, available for reporters. Two tables, on a raised plat-
form at the end of the room, obviously serve the city room executives. To the left of the platform is an open door which leads into
the sanctum.*

*As Kane and Leland enter the room an elderly, stout gent on the
raised platform strikes a bell and the other eight occupants of the
room—all men—rise and face the new arrivals. Carter, the elderly
gent, in formal clothes, rises and starts toward them.*

CARTER   Welcome, Mr. Kane, to the "Inquirer." I am Herbert Carter.
KANE   Thank you, Mr. Carter. This is Mr. Leland.
CARTER [*Bowing*]   How do you do, Mr. Leland?
KANE   Mr. Leland is your new dramatic critic, Mr. Carter. I hope I
haven't made a mistake, Jedediah. It is dramatic critic you want to
be, isn't it? [*Pointing to the reporters*] Are they standing for me?
CARTER   I thought it would be a nice gesture—the new publisher—
KANE [*Grinning*]   Ask them to sit down.
CARTER   You may resume your work, gentlemen. [*To Kane*] I didn't
know your plans and so I was unable to make any preparations.
KANE   I don't know my plans myself. As a matter of fact, I haven't
got any. Except to get out a newspaper.

> *There is a terrific crash at the doorway. They all turn to see
> Bernstein sprawled at the entrance. A roll of bedding, a suit-
> case and two framed pictures were too much for him.*

KANE [*Cont'd*]   Oh, Mr. Bernstein! If you would come here a moment
please, Mr. Bernstein?

> *Bernstein rises and comes over.*

KANE [*Cont'd*]   Mr. Carter, this is Mr. Bernstein. Mr. Bernstein is
my general manager.
CARTER [*Frigidly*]   How do you do, Mr. Bernstein?
KANE   You've got a private office here, haven't you?

> *The delivery-wagon driver has now appeared in the entrance
> with parts of the bedstead and other furniture.*

CARTER   My little sanctum is at your disposal. But I don't think I
understand—
KANE   I'm going to live right here. [*Reflectively*] As long as I have to.
CARTER   But a morning newspaper, Mr. Kane—After all, we're prac-
tically closed for twelve hours a day—except for the business offices—
KANE   That's one of the things I think must be changed, Mr. Carter.
The news goes on for twenty-four hours a day.

Dissolve

35 *Int. Kane's Office—Late Day—1890*
*Kane, in his shirt-sleeves, at a rolltop desk, is working feverishly
on copy and eating a very sizable meal at the same time. Carter,*

still formally coated, is seated alongside him. Leland, seated in a corner, is looking on, detached, amused. On a corner of the desk, Bernstein is writing down figures.

KANE I'm not criticizing, Mr. Carter, but here's what I mean. There's a front-page story in the "Chronicle" [*Points to it*] and a picture— of a woman in Brooklyn who is missing. Probably murdered. A Mrs. Harry Silverstone. Why didn't the "Inquirer" have that this morning?
CARTER [*Stiffly*] Because we're running a newspaper, Mr. Kane, not a scandal sheet.

Kane has finished eating. He pushes away his plates.

KANE I'm still hungry, Jed.
LELAND We'll go over to Rector's later and get something decent.
KANE [*Pointing to the "Chronicle"*] The "Chronicle" has a two-column headline, Mr. Carter. Why haven't we?
CARTER The news wasn't big enough.
KANE If the headline is big enough, it *makes* the news big enough. The murder of this Mrs. Harry Silverstone—
CARTER There's no proof that the woman was murdered—or even that she's dead.
KANE [*Smiling a bit*] The "Chronicle" doesn't say she's murdered, Mr. Carter. It says she's missing; the neighbors are getting suspicious.
CARTER It's not our function to report the gossip of housewives. If we were interested in that kind of thing, Mr. Kane, we could fill the paper twice over daily—
KANE [*Gently*] That's the kind of thing we *are* going to be interested in from now on, Mr. Carter. I wish you'd send your best man up to see Mr. Silverstone. Have him tell Mr. Silverstone if he doesn't produce his wife at once, the "Inquirer" will have him arrested. [*Gets an idea*] Have him tell Mr. Silverstone he's a detective from the Central Office. If Mr. Silverstone asks to see his badge, your man is to get indignant and call Mr. Silverstone an anarchist. Loudly, so that the neighbors can hear.
CARTER Really, Mr. Kane, I can't see that the function of a respectable newspaper—
KANE Mr. Carter, you've been most understanding. Good day.

Carter leaves the room, closing the door behind him.

LELAND Poor Mr. Carter!
KANE What makes these fellows think that a newspaper is something rigid, something inflexible, that people are supposed to pay two cents for—
BERNSTEIN Three cents.
KANE [*Calmly*] Two cents.

Bernstein lifts his head and looks at Kane.

BERNSTEIN [*Tapping on the paper*]   This is all figured at three cents a copy.

KANE   Refigure it, Mr. Bernstein, at two cents. Ready for dinner, Jed?

BERNSTEIN   Mr. Leland, if Mr. Kane he should decide at dinner to cut the price to one cent, or maybe even he should make up his mind to give the paper away with a half-pound of tea—

LELAND   You people work too fast for me! Talk about new brooms!

BERNSTEIN   Who said anything about brooms?

KANE   It's a saying, Mr. Bernstein. A new broom sweeps clean.

BERNSTEIN   Oh!

Dissolve

36 *Int. Primitive Composing and Pressroom—New York "Inquirer"—Night—1890*
   The ground floor with the windows on the street. It is almost midnight. Grouped around a large table, on which are several locked forms of type,[3] *are Kane and Leland in elegant evening clothes, Bernstein, unchanged from the afternoon, Carter and Smathers, the composing room foreman, nervous and harassed.*

KANE   Mr. Carter, front pages don't look like this any more. Have you seen the "Chronicle"?

CARTER   The "Inquirer" is not in competition with a rag like the "Chronicle."

BERNSTEIN   We should be publishing such a rag. The "Inquirer"—I wouldn't wrap up the liver for the cat in the "Inquirer"—

CARTER   Mr. Kane, I must ask you to see to it that this—this person learns to control his tongue. I don't think he's ever been in a newspaper office before.

KANE   You're right. Mr. Bernstein is in the wholesale jewelry business.

BERNSTEIN   *Was* in the wholesale jewelry business.

KANE   His talents seemed to be what I was looking for.

CARTER [*Sputtering; he's really sore*]   I warn you, Mr. Kane, it would go against my grain to desert you when you need me so badly—but I would feel obliged to ask that my resignation be accepted.

KANE   It *is* accepted, Mr. Carter, with assurances of my deepest regret.

CARTER   But Mr. Kane, I meant—

KANE [*Turning to Smathers; quietly*]   Let's do these pages over again.

SMATHERS [*As though Kane were talking Greek*]   We can't remake them, Mr. Kane.

KANE   Remake? Is that the right word?

SMATHERS   We go to press in five minutes.

KANE [*Quietly*]   Well, let's remake these pages, Mr. Smathers.

SMATHERS   We go to press in five minutes, Mr. Kane.

KANE   We'll have to publish half an hour late, that's all.

SMATHERS   You don't understand, Mr. Kane. We go to press in five minutes. We can't remake them, Mr. Kane.

   Kane reaches out and shoves the forms onto the floor, where they scatter into hundreds of bits.

3. The set type and other printing elements locked in a chase for the press.

KANE   You can remake them now, can't you, Mr. Smathers? After the type's been reset and the pages remade according to the way I told you before, Mr. Smathers, kindly have proofs[4] pulled—is that right, Jed—proofs pulled?—and bring them to me. Then, if I can't find any way to improve them again—I suppose we'll have to go to press.

He starts out of the room, followed by Leland.

BERNSTEIN   In case you don't understand, Mr. Smathers, he's a new broom.

Dissolve Out

Dissolve In
37 Ext. New York Street—Very Early Dawn—1890
    The picture is mainly occupied by the Inquirer Building, identified by sign. Over this newsboys are heard selling the "Chronicle." As the dissolve completes itself, camera moves toward the one lighted window—the window of Kane's office.

Dissolve

38 Int. Kane's Office—Very Early Dawn—1890
    The newsboys are still heard from the street below. Kane, in his shirt-sleeves, stands at the open window looking out. On the bed is seated Bernstein. Leland is in a chair.

NEWSBOYS' VOICES   "Chronicle"!—Chronicle"!—H'ya—the "Chronicle"! —Get ya' "Chronicle"!

Kane closes the window and turns to the others.

LELAND   We'll be on the street soon, Charlie—another ten minutes.
BERNSTEIN   It's three hours and fifty minutes late—but we did it—

Leland rises from the chair, stretching painfully.

KANE   Tired?
LELAND   It's been a tough day.
KANE   A wasted day.
BERNSTEIN   Wasted?
LELAND   Charlie?
BERNSTEIN   You just made the paper over four times tonight, Mr. Kane—that's all—
KANE   I've changed the front page a little, Mr. Bernstein. That's not enough—There's something I've got to get into this paper besides pictures and print—I've got to make the New York "Inquirer" as important to New York as the gas in that light.
LELAND   What're you going to do, Charlie?
KANE   My Declaration of Principles—don't smile, Jed—[*Getting the idea*] Take dictation, Mr. Bernstein—

4. A preliminary impression of the set type produced by hand to be read for corrections.

BERNSTEIN   I can't write shorthand, Mr. Kane—

KANE   I'll write it myself.

> *Kane grabs a piece of rough paper and a grease crayon. Sitting down on the bed next to Bernstein, he starts to write.*

BERNSTEIN [*Looking over his shoulder*]   You don't wanta make any promises, Mr. Kane, you don't wanta keep.

KANE [*As he writes*]   These'll be kept. [*Stops and reads what he has written*] I'll provide the people of this city with a daily paper that will tell all the news honestly. [*Starts to write again; reading as he writes*] I will also provide them—

LELAND   That's the second sentence you've started with "I"—

KANE [*Looking up*]   People are going to know who's responsible. And they're going to get the news—the true news—quickly and simply and entertainingly. [*With real conviction*] And no special interests will be allowed to interfere with the truth of that news. [*Writes again; reading as he writes*] I will also provide them with a fighting and tireless champion of their rights as citizens and human beings— Signed—Charles Foster Kane.

LELAND   Charlie—

> *Kane looks up.*

LELAND [*Cont'd*]   Can I have that?

KANE   I'm going to print it—[*Calls*] Mike!

MIKE   Yes, Mr. Kane.

KANE   Here's an editorial. I want to run it in a box on the front page.

MIKE [*Very wearily*]   Today's front page, Mr. Kane?

KANE   That's right. We'll have to remake again—better go down and let them know.

MIKE   All right, Mr. Kane.

> *He starts away*

LELAND   Just a minute, Mike.

> *Mike turns*

LELAND [*Cont'd*]   When you're done with that, I'd like to have it back.

> *Mike registers that this, in his opinion, is another screwball and leaves. Kane looks at Leland*

LELAND [*Cont'd*]   —I'd just like to keep that particular piece of paper myself. I've got a hunch it might turn out to be one of the important papers—of our time. [*A little ashamed of his ardor*] A document—like the Declaration of Independence—and the Constitution— and my first report card at school.

> *Kane smiles back at him, but they are both serious. The voices of the newsboys fill the air*

VOICES OF NEWSBOYS   "Chronicle"!—H'ya, the "Chronicle"! Get ya' "Chronicle"!—the "Chronicle"!

> *Dissolve Out*

Dissolve In

39 *Ext. "Inquirer" Windows on Street Level—Day—1890*
    Close-up—front page of the "Inquirer" shows big boxed editorial with heading:

MY PRINCIPLES—A DECLARATION
By Charles Foster Kane

Camera continues pulling back and shows newspaper to be on the top of a pile of newspapers. As we draw further back, we see four piles—then six piles—until we see finally a big field of piles of "Inquirers." Hands come into the frame and start picking up the piles.
    Camera pans to glass window on the street level of the "Inquirer." Painted on the glass are the words NEW YORK DAILY IN-QUIRER—CIRCULATION 26,000—*this very prominent. Through the glass we can see Kane, Leland and Bernstein, leaning on the little velvet-draped rail at the back of the window, peering out through the glass to the street, where "Inquirer" newsboys are seen to be moving. During this, camera tightens on window until* CIRCULATION 26,000 *fills frame. Then—*

Dissolve

40 *Ext. "Chronicle" Window—On Street Level—Day—1890*
    Close-up of sign which reads: CIRCULATION 495,000
    Camera pulls back to show this is a similar window on the street level of the Chronicle Building. The words NEW YORK DAILY CHRONICLE *are prominently painted above this and through the glass we can see a framed photograph of some nine men. A sign over this reads:* EDITORIAL AND EXECUTIVE STAFF OF THE NEW YORK CHRONICLE. *A sign beneath it reads:* GREATEST NEWSPAPER STAFF IN THE WORLD. *Then camera continues pulling back to show Kane, Leland and Bernstein standing in front of the window, looking in. They look very tired and cold.*

KANE   I know you're tired, gentlemen, but I brought you here for a reason. I think this little pilgrimage will do us good.
LELAND [*Wearily*] The "Chronicle" is a good newspaper.
KANE   It's a good idea for a newspaper. Notice the circulation?
BERNSTEIN [*Sullenly*] Four hundred ninety-five thousand.
KANE   Well, as the rooster said to his hens when they looked at the ostrich eggs—I am not criticizing, ladies—I am merely trying to show you what is being done in the same line by your competitors.
BERNSTEIN Ah, Mr. Kane—with them fellows on the "Chronicle"— [*Indicates photograph*] it's no trick to get circulation.
KANE   You're right, Mr. Bernstein.
BERNSTEIN [*Sighs*] You know how long it took the "Chronicle" to get that staff together? Twenty years.
KANE   I know.

Kane smiling, lights a cigarette, looking into the window. Camera moves in to hold on the photograph of the nine men.

Dissolve

41 *Int. City Room—The "Inquirer"—Night—1898*
*The same nine men, arrayed as in the photograph but with Kane
in the center of the first row.*
*Camera pulls back, revealing that they are being photographed
in a corner of the room. It is 1:30 at night. Desks, etc., have been
pushed against the wall. Running down the center of the room is a
long banquet table.*

PHOTOGRAPHER　That's all. Thank you.

The photographic subjects rise.

KANE [*A sudden thought*]　Make up an extra copy and mail it to the
"Chronicle."

Kane makes his way to the head of the table.

KANE [*Cont'd*]　Gentlemen of the "Inquirer"! Eight years ago—eight
long, very busy years ago—I stood in front of the "Chronicle"
window and looked at a picture of the nine greatest newspapermen
in the world. I felt like a kid in front of a candy shop. Tonight I got
my candy. Welcome, gentlemen, to the "Inquirer." It will make you
happy to learn that our circulation this morning was the greatest in
New York—six hundred and eighty-four thousand.
BERNSTEIN　Six hundred eighty-four thousand one hundred and
thirty-two.

General applause.

KANE　All of you—new and old—you're all getting the best salaries
in town. Not one of you has been hired because of his loyalty. It's
your talent I'm interested in—I like talent. Talent has made the
"Inquirer" the kind of paper I want—the best newspaper in the
world.

Applause.

KANE [*Cont'd*]　Having thus welcomed you, perhaps you'll forgive
my rudeness in taking leave of you. I'm going abroad next week
for a vacation.

Murmurs.

KANE [*Cont'd*]　I have promised my doctor for some time that I would
leave when I could. I now realize that I can. This decision is in
every way the best compliment that I could pay you.

Gratified murmurs.

KANE [*Cont'd*]　I have promised Mr. Bernstein, and I herewith repeat
that promise publicly, for the next three months to forget all about

the new feature sections—the Sunday supplement—and not to try to think up any ideas for comic sections—and not to—

BERNSTEIN [*Interrupting*] Say, Mr. Kane, so long as you're promising—there's a lot of statues in Europe you ain't bought yet—

KANE [*Interrupting*] You can't blame me, Mr. Bernstein. They've been making statues for two thousand years, and I've only been buying for five.

BERNSTEIN Nine Venuses already we got, twenty-six Virgins—two whole warehouses full of stuff—promise me, Mr. Kane.

KANE I promise you, Mr. Bernstein.

BERNSTEIN Thank you.

KANE Oh, Mr. Bernstein—

BERNSTEIN Yes?

KANE You don't expect me to keep *any* of my promises, do you, Mr. Bernstein?

Terrific laughter.

KANE [*Cont'd*] Do you, Mr. Leland?

LELAND Certainly not.

Laughter and applause.

KANE And now, gentlemen, your complete attention, please!

Kane puts his two fingers in his mouth and whistles. This is a signal. A band strikes up and enters in advance of a regiment of very magnificent maidens. As some of the girls are detached from the line and made into partners for individual dancing—

BERNSTEIN Isn't it wonderful? Such a party!

LELAND Yes.

BERNSTEIN [*To Leland*] What's the matter?

LELAND —Bernstein, these men who are now with the "Inquirer"—who were with the "Chronicle" until yesterday—weren't they just as devoted to the "Chronicle" kind of paper as they are now to—our kind of paper?

BERNSTEIN Sure. They're like anybody else. They got work to do. They do it. [*Proudly*] Only they happen to be the best men in the business.

LELAND [*After a minute*] Do we stand for the same things the "Chronicle" stands for, Bernstein?

BERNSTEIN [*Indignantly*] Certainly not. What of it? Mr. Kane he'll have them changed to his kind of newspapermen in a week.

LELAND There's always a chance, of course, that they'll change Mr. Kane—without his knowing it.

KANE [*Lightly*] Well, gentlemen, are we going to declare war on Spain?

LELAND The "Inquirer" already has.

KANE You long-faced, overdressed anarchist.

LELAND I am not overdressed.

KANE   You are, too. Look at that necktie, Mr. Bernstein.

> *Bernstein embarrassed, beams from one to the other.*

LELAND   Charlie, I wish—

KANE   Are you trying to be serious?

LELAND   [*Holding the look for a minute and recognizing there isn't a chance*] No. [*Out of the corner of his mouth—almost as an after-thought*] Only I'm not going to Cuba.

KANE   [*To Bernstein*] He drives me crazy. Mr. Bernstein, we get two hundred applications a day from newspapermen all over the country who want to go to Cuba—don't we, Mr. Bernstein?

> *Bernstein is unable to answer.*

LELAND   Bernstein, don't you like my necktie?

KANE   [*Ignoring him*] I offer him his own byline—[*Pompously*] By Jed Leland—The "Inquirer's" Special Correspondent at the Front— I guarantee him—[*Turns to Leland*] Richard Harding Davis[5] is doing all right. They just named a cigar after him.

LELAND   It's hardly what you'd call a cigar.

KANE   A man of very high standards, Mr. Bernstein.

LELAND   And it's hardly what you'd call a war either.

KANE   It's the best I can do. [*Looking up*] Hello, Georgie.

> *Georgie, a very handsome madam, has walked into the picture. She leans over and speaks quietly in his ear.*

GEORGIE   Hello, Charlo.

LELAND   You're doing very well.

GEORGIE   Is everything the way you want it, dear?

KANE   [*Looking around*] If everybody's having fun, that's the way I want it.

GEORGIE   I've got some other little girls coming over—

LELAND   [*Interrupting*] If you want to know what you're doing— you're dragging your country into a war. Do you know what a war is, Charlie?

KANE   I've told you about Jed, Georgie. He needs to relax.

LELAND   There's a condition in Cuba that needs to be remedied maybe—but between that and a war.

KANE   You know Georgie, Jed, don't you?

GEORGIE   Glad to meet you, Jed.

KANE   Jed, how would the "Inquirer" look with no news about this nonexistent war with Pulitzer and Hearst devoting twenty columns a day to it.

LELAND   They only do it because you do.

KANE   And I only do it because they do it—and they only do it—it's a vicious circle, isn't it? [*Rises*] I'm going over to Georgie's, Jed— You know Georgie, don't you, Mr. Bernstein?

---

5. Davis (1864–1916) was a novelist and the best-known war correspondent of his generation.

Bernstein shakes hands with Georgie.

KANE Georgie knows a young lady whom I'm sure you'd adore, Jed—
Wouldn't he, Georgie?

LELAND The first paper that had the courage to tell the actual truth
about Cuba—

KANE Why only the other evening I said to myself, if Jedediah were
only here to adore this young lady—this—[*Snaps his fingers*] What's
her name again?

Dissolve Out

Dissolve In
42 *Int. Georgie's Place—Night—1898*
    *Georgie is introducing a young lady to Leland. On sound track
we hear piano music.*

GEORGIE [*Right on cue from preceding scene*] Ethel—this gentleman
has been very anxious to meet you—Mr. Leland, this is Ethel.

ETHEL Hello, Mr. Leland.

*Camera pans to include Kane, seated at piano, with Bernstein
and girls gathered around him.*

ONE OF THE GIRLS Charlie! Play the song about you.

ANOTHER GIRL Is there a song about Charlie?

KANE You buy a bag of peanuts in this town and you get a song
written about you.

*Kane has broken into "Oh, Mr. Kane!" and he and the girls
start to sing. Ethel leads the unhappy Leland over to the
group. Kane, seeing Leland and taking his eye, motions to the
professor who has been standing next to him to take over. The
professor does so. The singing continues. Kane rises and crosses
to Leland.*

KANE [*Cont'd*] Say, Jed—you don't have to go to Cuba if you don't
want to. You don't have to be a war correspondent if you don't want
to. I'd want to be a war correspondent. [*Silence*] I've got an idea.

LELAND Pay close attention, Bernstein. The hand is quicker than the
eye.

KANE I mean I've got a job for you.

LELAND [*Suspiciously*] What is it?

KANE The "Inquirer" is probably too one-sided about this Cuban
thing—me being a warmonger and all. How's about your writing a
piece every day—while I'm away—saying exactly what you think—
[*Ruefully*] Just the way you say it to me, unless I see you coming.

LELAND Do you mean that?

Kane nods.

LELAND [*Cont'd*] No editing of my copy?

KANE [*No one will ever be able to know what he means*] No-o.

Leland keeps looking at him with loving perplexity, knowing he will never solve the riddle of this face.

KANE [*Cont'd*] We'll talk some more about it at dinner tomorrow night. We've only got about ten more nights before I go to Europe. Richard Carle's opening in *The Spring Chicken*.[6] I'll get the girls. You get the tickets. A drama critic gets them free.

LELAND Charlie—

KANE It's the best I can do.

LELAND [*Still smiling*] It doesn't make any difference about me, but one of these days you're going to find out that all this charm of yours won't be enough—

KANE You're wrong. It does make a difference about you—Come to think of it, Mr. Bernstein, I don't blame Mr. Leland for not wanting to be a war correspondent. It isn't much of a war. Besides, they tell me there isn't a decent restaurant on the whole island.

Dissolve

43 *Int. Kane's office—Day—1898*
   The shot begins on a close-up of a label. The words "From C. F. Kane, Paris, France," fill the screen. This registers as camera pulls back to show remainder of label in larger letters, which read: "To Charles Foster Kane, New York—HOLD FOR ARRIVAL." Camera continues pulling back, showing the entire sanctum piled to the ceiling with packing boxes, crated statues and art objects. One-third of the statues have been uncrated. Leland is in his shirt-sleeves; clearly he has been opening boxes, with claw hammer in one hand. Bernstein has come to the door.

BERNSTEIN I got here a cable from Mr. Kane—Mr. Leland, why didn't you go to Europe with him? He wanted you to.

LELAND I wanted him to have fun—and with me along—

This stops Bernstein. Bernstein looks at him.

LELAND [*Cont'd*] Bernstein, I wish you'd let me ask you a few questions—and answer me truthfully.

BERNSTEIN Don't I always? Most of the time?

LELAND Bernstein, am I a stuffed shirt? Am I a horse-faced hypocrite? Am I a New England schoolmarm?

BERNSTEIN Yes.

Leland is surprised.

BERNSTEIN [*Cont'd*] If you thought I'd answer you different from what Mr. Kane tells you—well, I wouldn't.

Pause as Bernstein looks around the room.

---

6. Richard Carle's *The Spring Chicken*   years in London and opened in the U.S.
was a musical comedy that played two   in 1906.

BERNSTEIN [*Cont'd*]   Mr. Leland, it's good he promised not to send back any statues.

LELAND   I don't think you understand, Bernstein. This is one of the rarest Venuses in existence.

BERNSTEIN [*Studying the statue carefully*]   Not so rare like you think, Mr. Leland. [*Handing cable to Leland*] Here's the cable from Mr. Kane.

Leland takes it, reads it, smiles.

BERNSTEIN [*Cont'd*] [*As Leland reads cable*]   He wants to buy the world's biggest diamond.

LELAND   I didn't know Charles was collecting diamonds.

BERNSTEIN   He ain't. He's collecting somebody that's collecting diamonds. Anyway—[*Taking his eye*] he ain't only collecting statues.
                                                                      Dissolve

44 *Int. City Room—Day—1898*
  Dissolve to elaborate loving cup on which is engraved:
  WELCOME HOME, MR. KANE—From 730 employees of the New York "Inquirer."
  As camera pulls back, it reveals that this cup is on a little table at the far end of the "Inquirer" city room. Next to the table stand Bernstein, rubbing his hands, Hillman and a few other executives. Throughout the entire city room, there is a feeling of cleanliness and anticipation.
COPY BOY [*At stairway*]   Here he comes!

  Bernstein and Hillman start toward the door. All the others rise. Just as Bernstein gets to the door, it bursts open and Kane, an envelope in his hand, storms in.

KANE   Hello, Mr. Bernstein!

  Kane continues at the same rate of speed with which he entered, Bernstein following behind him, at the head of a train which includes Hillman and others. The race stops a couple of steps beyond the society editor's desk by Kane, who moves back to the desk, making something of a traffic jam. (A plaque on the desk which reads "Society Editor" is what caught Kane's eye.)

KANE [*Cont'd*]   Excuse me, I've been away so long, I don't know your routine. Miss—

BERNSTEIN [*Proudly*]   Miss Townsend, Mr. Charles Foster Kane!

KANE   Miss Townsend, I'd—[*He's pretty embarrassed by his audience*] I—have a little social announcement here. [*He puts it on the desk*] I wish you wouldn't treat this any differently than you would—you would—any other—anything else.

  He looks around at the others with some embarrassment. At that moment, Hillman hands Bernstein the cup.

BERNSTEIN [*Holding the cup*]   Mr. Kane, on behalf of all the employees of the "Inquirer"—
KANE [*Interrupting*]   Mr. Bernstein, I can't tell you how much I appreciate—[*He takes the cup and starts to take a few steps—realizes that he is being a little boorish—turns around and hands the cup back to Bernstein.*] Look, Mr. Bernstein—everybody—I'm sorry—I—I can't take it now.

Murmurs.

KANE [*Cont'd*]   I'm busy. I mean—please—give it to me tomorrow.

He starts to run out. There is surprised confusion among the rest.

BERNSTEIN   Say, he's in an awful hurry!
SAME COPY BOY [*At window*]   Hey, everybody! Lookee out here!

The whole staff rushes to the window.

45 *Ext. Street in Front of Inquirer Building—Day—1898*
Angle down from window—shot of Emily sitting in a barouche.

46 *Ext. Window of "Inquirer" City Room—Day—1898*
Up shot of faces in the window, reacting and grinning.

47 *Int. City Room—Day—1898*
Miss Townsend stands frozen at her desk. She is reading and re-reading with trembling hands the piece of flimsy which Kane gave her.

TOWNSEND   Mr. Bernstein!

Mr. Bernstein, at window, turns around.

BERNSTEIN   Yes, Miss Townsend.
TOWNSEND   This—this announcement—[*She reads shakily*] Mr. and Mrs. Thomas Monroe Norton announce the engagement of their daughter, Emily Monroe Norton, to Mr. Charles Foster Kane.

Bernstein reacts.

TOWNSEND [*Cont'd*]   Emily Monroe Norton—she's the niece of the President of the United States.

Bernstein nods his head proudly and turns back to look out the window.

48 *Ext. Street in Front of Inquirer Building—Day—1898*
Down shot of Kane, crossing the curb to the barouche. He looks up in this shot, sees the people in the window, waves gaily, steps

*into the barouche. Emily looks at him smilingly. He kisses her full
on the lips before he sits down. She acts a bit taken aback because
of the public nature of the scene, but she isn't really annoyed.*

Dissolve

49 *Int. City Room—"Inquirer"—Day—1898*

   Bernstein and group at window.

BERNSTEIN   A girl like that, believe me, she's lucky! President's niece,
huh! Say, before he's through, she'll be a President's wife!

Dissolve

INSERT: FRONT PAGE "INQUIRER" (1898–1900)
   *Large picture of the young couple—Kane and Emily—occupying
four columns—very happy.*

INSERT: NEWSPAPER—KANE'S MARRIAGE TO EMILY WITH STILL OF
GROUP ON WHITE HOUSE LAWN (1900)
   (Same setup as early newsreel in news digest.)

Dissolve

50 *Int. Bernstein's Office—"Inquirer"—Day—1940*
   *Bernstein and Thompson. As the dissolve comes, Bernstein's voice
is heard.*

BERNSTEIN   The way things turned out, I don't need to tell you—Miss
Emily Norton was no rosebud!

THOMPSON   It didn't end very well, did it?

BERNSTEIN   It ended—Then there was Susie—That ended too.
[*Shrugs, a pause*] I guess he didn't make her very happy—You know,
I was thinking—that Rosebud you're trying to find out about—

THOMPSON   Yes—

BERNSTEIN   Maybe that was something he lost. Mr. Kane was a man
that lost—almost everything he had. You ought to talk to Mr. Leland. Of course, he and Mr. Kane didn't exactly see eye to eye.
You take the Spanish-American War. I guess Mr. Leland was right.
That was Mr. Kane's war. We didn't really have anything to fight
about—[*Chuckles*] But do you think if it hadn't been for that war
of Mr. Kane's, we'd have the Panama Canal? I wish I knew where
Mr. Leland was—[*Slowly*] Maybe even he's—a lot of the time now
they don't tell me those things—maybe even he's dead.

THOMPSON   In case you'd like to know, Mr. Bernstein, he's at the
Huntington Memorial Hospital on 180th Street.

BERNSTEIN   You don't say! Why I had no idea—

THOMPSON   Nothing particular the matter with him, they tell me.
Just—

BERNSTEIN   Just old age. [*Smiles sadly*] It's the only disease, Mr.
Thompson, you don't look forward to being cured of.

Dissolve Out

Dissolve In
51 *Ext. Hospital Roof—Day—1940*
   Close shot—Thompson. He is tilted back in a chair, leaning against a chimney. Leland's voice is heard for a few moments before Leland is seen.

LELAND'S VOICE   When you get to my age, young man, you don't miss anything. Unless maybe it's a good drink of bourbon. Even that doesn't make much difference, if you remember there hasn't been any good bourbon in this country for twenty years.

> *Camera has pulled back, revealing that Leland, wrapped in a blanket, is in a wheelchair, talking to Thompson. They are on the flat roof of a hospital.*

THOMPSON   Mr. Leland, you were—
LELAND   You don't happen to have a cigar, do you? I've got a young physician who thinks I'm going to stop smoking. . . . I changed the subject, didn't I? Dear, dear! What a disagreeable old man I've become. You want to know what I think of Charlie Kane?—Well—I suppose he had some private sort of greatness. But he kept it to himself. [*Grinning*] He never . . . gave himself away . . . He never gave anything away. He just . . . left you a tip. He had a generous mind. I don't suppose anybody ever had so many opinions. That was because he had the power to express them, and Charlie lived on power and the excitement of using it—But he didn't believe in anything except Charlie Kane. He never had a conviction except Charlie Kane in his life. I guess he died without one—That must have been pretty unpleasant. Of course, a lot of us check out with no special conviction about death. But we do know what we're leaving . . . we believe in something. [*Looks sharply at Thompson*] You're absolutely sure you haven't got a cigar?
THOMPSON   Sorry, Mr. Leland.
LELAND   Never mind—Bernstein told you about the first days at the office, didn't he?—Well, Charlie was a bad newspaperman even then. He entertained his readers but he never told them the truth.
THOMPSON   Maybe you could remember something that—
LELAND   I can remember everything. That's my curse, young man. It's the greatest curse that's ever been inflicted on the human race. Memory . . . I was his oldest friend. [*Slowly*] As far as I was concerned, he behaved like a swine. Not that Charlie ever was brutal. He just did brutal things. Maybe I wasn't his friend. If *I* wasn't, he never had one. Maybe I was what nowadays you call a stooge.
THOMPSON   Mr. Leland, what do you know about Rosebud?
LELAND   Rosebud? Oh! His dying words—Rosebud—Yeh. I saw that in the "Inquirer." Well, I've never believed anything I saw in the "Inquirer." Anything else?

> *Thompson is taken aback.*

LELAND [*Cont'd*]   I'll tell you about Emily. I used to go to dancing school with her. I was very graceful. Oh!—we were talking about the first Mrs. Kane—

THOMPSON   What was she like?

LELAND   She was like all the other girls I knew in dancing school. They were nice girls. Emily was a little nicer. She did her best— Charlie did his best—well, after the first couple of months they never saw much of each other except at breakfast. It was a marriage just like any other marriage.

Dissolve

(NOTE: *The following scenes cover a period of nine years—are played in the same set with only changes in lighting, special effects outside the window, and wardrobe.*)

52 *Int. Kane's Home—Breakfast Room—Day—1901*
   Kane, in white tie and tails, and Emily formally attired. Kane is pouring a glass of milk for Emily out of a milk bottle. As he finishes, he leans over and playfully nips the back of her neck.

EMILY [*Flustered*]   Charles! [*She's loving it*] Go sit down where you belong.

KANE [*On the way to his own place*]   You're beautiful.

EMILY   I can't be. I've never been to six parties in one night before. I've never been up this late.

KANE   It's just a matter of habit.

EMILY   What do you suppose the servants will think?

KANE   They'll think we enjoyed ourselves. Didn't we?

EMILY [*She gives him a purring smile. Then—*]   Dearest—I don't see why you have to go straight off to the newspaper.

KANE   You never should have married a newspaperman. They're worse than sailors. I absolutely love you.

   They look at each other.

EMILY   Charles, even newspapermen have to sleep.

KANE [*Still looking at her*]   I'll call up Bernstein and tell him to put off my appointments till noon—What time is it?

EMILY   I don't know—it's late.

KANE   It's early.

Dissolve Out

Dissolve In
53 *Int. Kane's Home—Breakfast Room—Day—1902*
   Kane and Emily—different clothes—different food.

EMILY   Do you know how long you kept me waiting while you went to the office last night for ten minutes? Really, Charles, we were dinner guests at the Boardmans'—we weren't invited for the weekend.

KANE   You're the nicest girl I ever married.

EMILY   Charles, if I didn't trust you—What do you do on a newspaper

in the middle of the night?
KANE   My dear, your only corespondent is the "Inquirer."

Dissolve

54 Int. Kane Home—Breakfast Room—1904
  Kane and Emily—change of costume and food. Emily is dressed for the street.

EMILY [*Kidding on the level*]   Sometimes I think I'd prefer a rival of flesh and blood.
KANE   Ah, Emily—I don't spend that much time—
EMILY   It isn't just time—it's what you print—attacking the President—
KANE   You mean Uncle John.
EMILY   I mean the President of the United States.
KANE   He's still Uncle John, and he's still a well-meaning fathead—
EMILY [*Interrupting*]   Charles—
KANE [*Continuing on top of her*]   —who's letting a pack of high-pressure crooks run his administration. This whole oil scandal—
EMILY   He happens to be the President, Charles—not you.
KANE   That's a mistake that will be corrected one of these days.

Dissolve

55 Int. Kane's Home—Breakfast Room—1905
  Kane and Emily—change of costume and food.

EMILY   Charles, when people make a point of not having the "Inquirer" in their homes—Margaret English says that the reading room at the Assembly already has more than forty names that have agreed to cancel the paper—
KANE   That's wonderful. Mr. Bernstein will be delighted. You see, Emily, when your friends cancel the paper, that just takes another name off our deadbeat list. You know, don't you, it's practically a point of honor among the rich not to pay the newsdealer.

Dissolve Out

Dissolve In
56 Int. Kane's Home—Breakfast Room—1906
  Kane and Emily—change of costume and food.

EMILY   Your Mr. Bernstein sent Junior the most incredible atrocity yesterday. I simply can't have it in the nursery.
KANE   Mr. Bernstein is apt to pay a visit to the nursery now and then.
EMILY   Does he have to?
KANE [*Shortly*]   Yes.

Dissolve

57 Int. Kane's Home—Breakfast Room—1908
  Kane and Emily—change of costume and food.

EMILY   Really, Charles—people have a right to expect—
KANE   What I care to give them.

Dissolve

58 *Int. Kane's Home—Breakfast Room—1909*
    Kane and Emily—change of costume and food. They are both silent, reading newspapers. Kane is reading his "Inquirer." Emily is reading a copy of the "Chronicle."

                                                            Dissolve Out

Dissolve In
59 *Ext. Hospital Roof—Day—1940*
    Leland and Thompson.

THOMPSON   Wasn't he ever in love with her?
LELAND   He married for love—[*A little laugh*] That's why he did everything. That's why he went into politics. It seems we weren't enough. He wanted all the voters to love him, too. All he really wanted out of life was love—That's Charlie's story—how he lost it. You see, he just didn't have any to give. He loved Charlie Kane, of course, very dearly—and his mother, I guess he always loved her.
THOMPSON   How about his second wife?
LELAND   Susan Alexander? [*He chuckles*] You know what Charlie called her?—The day after he'd met her he told me about her—he said she was a cross-section of the American public—I guess he couldn't help it—she must have had something for him. [*With a smile*] That first night, according to Charlie—all she had was a toothache.

                                                            Dissolve Out

Dissolve In
60 *Ext. Corner Drugstore and Street on the West Side of New York—Night—1915*
    Susan, aged twenty-two, neatly but cheaply dressed, is leaving the drugstore. (It's about eight o'clock at night.) With a large, man-sized handkerchief pressed to her cheek, she is in considerable pain. A carriage crosses in front of the camera—passes—Susan continues down the street—Camera following her—encounters Kane—very indignant, standing near the edge of the sidewalk, covered with mud. She looks at him and smiles. He glares at her. She starts on down the street; turns, looks at him again, and starts to laugh.

KANE [*Glowering*]   It's not funny.
SUSAN   I'm sorry, mister—but you *do* look awful funny.

    Suddenly the pain returns and she claps her hand to her jaw.

SUSAN [*Cont'd*]   Ow!
KANE   What's the matter with you?
SUSAN   Toothache.
KANE   Hmmm!

    He has been rubbing his clothes with his handkerchief.

SUSAN   You've got some on your face. [*Starts to laugh again.*]
KANE   What's funny now?

SUSAN   You are. [*The pain returns.*] Oh!

KANE   Ah ha!

SUSAN   If you want to come in and wash your face—I can get you some hot water to get that dirt off your trousers—

KANE   Thanks.

Susan starts, with Kane following her.

Dissolve

61 Int. Susan's Room—Night—1915
    Susan comes into the room, carrying a basin, with towels over her arm. Kane is waiting for her. She doesn't close the door.

SUSAN   [*By way of explanation*]   My landlady prefers me to keep this door open when I have a gentleman caller. She's a very decent woman. [*Making a face*] Ow!

> *Kane rushes to take the basin from her, putting it on the chiffonier. To do this, he has to shove the photograph to one side with the basin. Susan grabs the photograph as it is about to fall over.*

SUSAN   [*Cont'd*]   Hey, you should be more careful. That's my Ma and Pa.

KANE   I'm sorry. They live here too?

SUSAN   No. They've passed on.

Again she puts her hand to her jaw.

KANE   You poor kid, you are in pain, aren't you?

> *Susan can't stand it any more and sits down in a chair, bent over, whimpering a bit.*

KANE [*Cont'd*]   Look at me.

She looks at him.

KANE [*Cont'd*]   Why don't you laugh? I'm just as funny in here as I was on the street.

SUSAN   I know, but you don't like me to laugh at you.

KANE   I don't like your tooth to hurt, either.

SUSAN   I can't help it.

KANE   Come on, laugh at me.

SUSAN   I can't—what are you doing?

KANE   I'm wiggling both my ears at the same time. [*He does so*] It took me two solid years at the finest boys' school in the world to learn that trick. The fellow who taught me is now president of Venezuela. [*He wiggles his ears again*]

Susan starts to smile.

KANE [*Cont'd*]   That's it.

> *Susan smiles very broadly—then starts to laugh.*
>
> > Dissolve

62 *Int. Susan's Room—Night—1915*
   Close-up of a duck, camera pulls back, showing it to be a shadow-graph on the wall, made by Kane, who is now in his shirt-sleeves.

SUSAN [*Hesitatingly*]   A chicken?

KANE   No. But you're close.

SUSAN   A rooster?

KANE   You're getting further away all the time. It's a duck.

SUSAN   A duck. You're not a professional magician, are you?

KANE   No. I've told you. My name is Kane—Charles Foster Kane.

SUSAN   I know. Charles Foster Kane. Gee—I'm pretty ignorant, I guess you caught on to that—

KANE   You really don't know who I am?

SUSAN   No. That is, I bet it turns out I've heard your name a million times, only you know how it is—

KANE   But you like me, don't you? Even though you don't know who I am?

SUSAN   You've been wonderful! I can't tell you how glad I am you're here, I don't know many people and—[*She stops*]

KANE   And I know too many people. Obviously, we're both lonely. [*He smiles*] Would you like to know where I was going tonight—when you ran into me and ruined my Sunday clothes?

SUSAN   I didn't run into you and I bet they're not your Sunday clothes. You've probably got a lot of clothes.

KANE   I was only joking! [*Pauses*] I was on my way to the Western Manhattan Warehouse—in search of my youth.

> *Susan is bewildered.*

KANE [*Cont'd*]   You see, my mother died too—a long time ago. Her things were put into storage out West because I had no place to put them then. I still haven't. But now I've sent for them just the same. And tonight I'd planned to make a sort of sentimental journey —and now—

> *Kane doesn't finish. He looks at Susan. Silence.*

KANE [*Cont'd*]   Who am I? Well, let's see. Charles Foster Kane was born in New Salem, Colorado, in eighteen six—[*He stops on the word "sixty"—obviously a little embarrassed*] I run a couple of newspapers. How about you?

SUSAN   Me?

KANE   How old did you say you were?

SUSAN [*Very bright*]   I didn't say.

KANE   I didn't think you did. If you had, I wouldn't have asked you again, because I'd have remembered. How old?

SUSAN   Pretty old. I'll be twenty-two in August.

KANE   That's a ripe old age—What do you do?

SUSAN   I work at Seligman's.

KANE   Is that what you want to do?

SUSAN   I wanted to be a singer. I mean, I didn't. Mother did for me.

KANE   What happened to the singing?

SUSAN   Mother always thought—she used to talk about grand opera for me. Imagine!—Anyway, my voice isn't that kind. It's just—you know what mothers are like.

KANE   Yes.

SUSAN   As a matter of fact, I do sing a little.

KANE   Would you sing for me?

SUSAN   Oh, you wouldn't want to hear me sing.

KANE   Yes, I would. That's why I asked.

SUSAN   Well, I—

KANE   Don't tell me your toothache is bothering you again?

SUSAN   Oh, no, that's all gone.

KANE   Then you haven't any alibi at all. Please sing.

> *Susan, with a tiny ladylike hesitancy, goes to the piano and sings a polite song. Sweetly, nicely, she sings with a small, untrained voice. Kane listens. He is relaxed, at ease with the world.*

Dissolve Out

Dissolve In

INSERT: "INQUIRER" HEADLINE. *(1916)*

BOSS ROGERS PICKS DEMOCRATIC NOMINEE

Dissolve

INSERT: "INQUIRER" HEADLINE. *(1916)*

BOSS ROGERS PICKS REPUBLICAN NOMINEE

Dissolve

INSERT: FOUR COLUMN CARTOON ON BACK PAGE OF "INQUIRER." *(1916)*

> *This shows Boss Rogers, labeled as such, in convict stripes, dangling little marionette figures—labeled Democratic Candidate and Republican Candidate—from each hand. As camera pans to remaining four columns it reveals box. This is headed:*

Put this man in jail, people of New York.

> *It is signed, in bold type, "Charles Foster Kane." The text between headline and signature, little of which need be read, tells of the boss-ridden situation.*

Dissolve Out

Dissolve In

63 *Int. Madison Square Garden—Night—1916*

> *The evening of the final great rally. Emily and Junior are to be*

seen in the front of a box. Emily is tired and wears a forced smile on her face. Junior, now aged nine and a half, is eager, bright-eyed and excited. Kane is just finishing his speech.

KANE It is no secret that I entered upon this campaign with no thought that I could be elected governor of this state! It is no secret that my only purpose was to bring as wide publicity as I could to the domination of this state—of its every resource—of its every income—of literally the lives and deaths of its citizens by Boss Edward G. Rogers! It is now no secret that every straw vote, every independent poll, shows that I will be elected. And I repeat to you—my first official act as governor will be to appoint a special district attorney to arrange for the indictment, prosecution and conviction of Boss Edward G. Rogers!

Terrific screaming and cheering from the audience.

Dissolve

64 Int. Madison Square Garden—Night—1916
The speaker's platform. Numerous officials and civic leaders are crowding around Kane. Cameramen take flash photographs.

FIRST CIVIC LEADER Great speech, Mr. Kane.
SECOND LEADER [*Pompous*] One of the most notable public utterances ever made by a candidate in this state—
KANE Thank you, gentlemen. Thank you.

He looks up and notices that the box in which Emily and Junior were sitting is now empty. He starts toward rear of the platform, through the press of people. Hillman approaches him.

HILLMAN A wonderful speech, Mr. Kane.

Kane pats him on the shoulder as he walks along.

HILLMAN [*Cont'd*] If the election were held *today*, you'd be elected by a hundred thousand votes—on an Independent ticket there's never been anything like it!

Kane is very pleased. He continues with Hillman slowly through the crowd—a band playing off.

KANE It does seem too good to be true.
HILLMAN Rogers isn't even pretending. He isn't just scared any more. He's sick. Frank Norris told me last night he hasn't known Rogers to be that worried in twenty-five years.
KANE I think it's beginning to dawn on Mr. Rogers that I mean what I say. With Mr. Rogers out of the way, Hillman, I think we may really begin to hope for a good government in this state. [*Stopping*]
A WELL-WISHER Great speech, Mr. Kane!
ANOTHER WELL-WISHER Wonderful, Mr. Kane!

Ad libs from other well-wishers.

Dissolve Out

Dissolve In
65 *Ext. One of the Exits—Madison Square Garden—Night—1916*
Emily and Junior are standing, waiting for Kane.

JUNIOR   Is Pop governor yet, Mom?

Kane appears with Hillman and several other men. He rushes toward Emily and Junior. The men politely greet Emily.

KANE   Hello, Butch! Did you like your old man's speech?
JUNIOR   I was in a box, Father. I could hear every word.
KANE   I saw you! Good night, gentlemen.

There are good-nights. Kane's car is at the curb and he starts to walk toward it with Junior and Emily.

EMILY   I'm sending Junior home in the car, Charles—with Oliver—
KANE   But I'd arranged to go home with you myself.
EMILY   There's a call I want you to make with me, Charles.
KANE   It can wait.
EMILY   No, it can't. [*Kisses Junior*] Good night, darling.
JUNIOR   Good night, Mom.
KANE [*As car drives off*]   What's this all about, Emily? I've had a very tiring day and—
EMILY   It may not be about anything at all. [*Starting to a cab at curb*] I intend to find out.
KANE   I insist on being told exactly what you have in mind.
EMILY   I'm going to—[*She looks at a slip of paper*] 185 West 74th Street.

Kane's reaction indicates that the address definitely means something to him.

EMILY [*Cont'd*]   If you wish, you can come with me . . .
KANE [*Nods*]   I'll come with you.

He opens the door and she enters the cab. He follows her.

Dissolve

66 *Int. Cab—Night—1916*
Kane and Emily. He looks at her in search of some kind of enlightenment. Her face is set and impassive.

Dissolve Out

Dissolve In
67 *Ext. Susan's Apartment House Door—Night—1916*
Kane and Emily, in front of an apartment door. Emily is pressing the bell.

KANE   I had no idea you had this flair for melodrama, Emily.

> *Emily does not answer. The door is opened by a maid, who recognizes Kane.*

THE MAID   Come in, Mr. Kane, come in.

> *She stands to one side for Kane and Emily to enter. This they start to do. Beyond them we see into the room.*

68 *Int. Susan's Apartment—Night—1916*
> As Kane and Emily enter, Susan rises from a chair. The other person in the room—a big, heavyset man, a little past middle age—stays where he is, leaning back in his chair, regarding Kane intently.

SUSAN   It wasn't my fault, Charlie. He made me send your wife a note. He said I'd—oh, he's been saying the most terrible things, I didn't know what to do . . . I—[*She stops*]

ROGERS   Good evening, Mr. Kane. [*He rises*] I don't suppose anybody would introduce us. Mrs. Kane, I'm Edward Rogers.

EMILY   How do you do?

ROGERS   I made Miss—Miss Alexander send you the note. She was a little unwilling at first—[*Smiles grimly*] but she did it.

SUSAN   I can't tell you the things he said, Charlie. You haven't got any idea—

KANE   [*Turning on Rogers*] Rogers, I don't think I *will* postpone doing something about you until I'm elected. [*Starts toward him*] To start with, I think I'll break your neck.

ROGERS   [*Not giving way an inch*] Maybe you can do it and maybe you can't, Mr. Kane.

EMILY   Charles! [*He stops to look at her*] Your—your breaking this man's neck—[*She is clearly disgusted*] would scarcely explain this note—[*Glancing at the note*] Serious consequences for Mr. Kane—[*Slowly*] for myself, and for my son. What does this note mean, Miss—

SUSAN   [*Stiffly*] I'm Susan Alexander. [*Pauses*] I know what you think, Mrs. Kane, but—

EMILY   [*Ignoring this*] What does this note mean, Miss Alexander?

SUSAN   It's like this, Mrs. Kane. I happened to be studying singing—I always wanted to be an opera singer—and Mr. Kane happened—I mean, he's been helping me—

EMILY   What does this note mean, Miss Alexander?

ROGERS   She doesn't know, Mrs. Kane. She just sent it—because I made her see it wouldn't be smart for her not to send it.

KANE   In case you don't know, Emily, this—this gentleman—is—

ROGERS   I'm not a gentleman, Mrs. Kane, and your husband is just trying to be funny, calling me one. I don't even know what a gentleman is. You see, my idea of a gentleman, Mrs. Kane—well, if I owned a newspaper and if I didn't like the way somebody else was doing things—some politician, say—I'd fight them with everything I had. Only I wouldn't show him in a convict suit with

stripes—so his children could see the picture in the paper. Or his
mother.

EMILY   Oh!!

KANE   You're a cheap, crooked grafter—and your concern for your
children and your mother—

ROGERS   Anything you say, Mr. Kane. Only we're talking now about
what *you* are. That's what that note is about, Mrs. Kane. I'm going
to lay all my cards on the table. I'm fighting for my life. Not just
my political life. My life. If your husband is elected governor—

KANE   I'm *going* to be elected governor. And the first thing I'm going
to do—

EMILY   Let him finish, Charles.

ROGERS   I'm protecting myself every way I know how, Mrs. Kane.
This last week, I finally found out how I can stop your husband
from being elected. If the people of this state learn what I found
out this week, he wouldn't have a chance to—he couldn't be elected
dog catcher.

KANE   You can't blackmail me, Rogers. You can't—

SUSAN [*Excitedly*]   Charlie, he said, unless you withdraw your name—

ROGERS   That's the chance I'm willing to give you, Mr. Kane. More of
a chance than you'd give me. Unless you make up your mind by
tomorrow that you're so sick that you've got to go away for a year
or two—Monday morning every paper in this state—except yours—
will carry the story I'm going to give them.

EMILY   What story, Mr. Rogers?

ROGERS   The story about him and Miss Alexander, Mrs. Kane.

> *Emily looks at Kane.*

SUSAN   There *is* no story. It's all lies. Mr. Kane is just—

ROGERS [*To Susan*]   Shut up! [*To Kane*] We've got evidence that
would stand up in any court of law. You want me to give you the
evidence, Mr. Kane?

KANE   You do anything you want to do.

ROGERS   Mrs. Kane, I'm not asking *you* to believe me. I'd like to show
you—

EMILY   I believe you, Mr. Rogers.

ROGERS   I'd rather Mr. Kane withdrew without having to get the
story published. Not that I care about him. But I'd be better off
that way—and so would you, Mrs. Kane.

SUSAN   What about me? [*To Kane*] He said my name'd be dragged
through the mud. He said everywhere I'd go from now on—

EMILY   There seems to me to be only one decision you can make,
Charles. I'd say that it has been made for you.

KANE   Have you gone completely mad, Emily? You don't think I'm
going to let this blackmailer intimidate me, do you?

EMILY   I don't see what else you can do, Charles. If he's right—and
the papers publish this story he has—

KANE   Oh, they'll publish it all right. I'm not afraid of the story. You
can't tell me that the voters of this state—

EMILY   I'm not interested in the voters of this state right now. I am interested in—well, Junior, for one thing.

SUSAN Charlie! If they publish this story—

EMILY They won't. Good night, Mr. Rogers. There's nothing more to be said. Are you coming, Charles?

KANE No.

She looks at him. He starts to work himself into a rage.

KANE [*Cont'd*] There's only one person in the world to decide what I'm going to do—and that's me. And if you think—if any of you think—

EMILY You decided what you were going to do, Charles—some time ago. Come on, Charles.

KANE Go on! Get out! I can fight this all alone! Get out!

ROGERS You're making a bigger fool of yourself than I thought you would, Mr. Kane. You're licked. Why don't you—

KANE [*Turning on him*] Get out! I've got nothing to talk to you about. If you want to see me, have the warden write me a letter.

Rogers nods, with a look that says "So you say."

SUSAN [*Starting to cry*] Charlie, you're just excited. You don't realize—

KANE I know exactly what I'm doing. [*He is screaming*] Get out!

EMILY [*Quietly*] Charles, if you don't listen to reason, it may be too late—

KANE Too late for what? Too late for you and this—this public thief to take the love of the people of this state away from me? Well, you won't do it, I tell you. You won't do it!

SUSAN Charlie, there are other things to think of. [*A sly look comes into her eyes*] Your son—you don't want him to read in the papers—

EMILY It *is* too late now, Charles.

KANE [*Rushes to the door and opens it*] Get out, both of you!

SUSAN [*Rushes to him*] Charlie, please don't—

KANE What are you waiting here for? Why don't you go?

EMILY Good night, Charles.

She walks out. Rogers stops directly in front of Kane.

ROGERS You're the greatest fool I've ever known, Kane. If it was anybody else, I'd say what's going to happen to you would be a lesson to you. Only you're going to need more than one lesson. And you're going to get more than one lesson.

KANE Don't worry about me. I'm Charles Foster Kane. I'm no cheap, crooked politician, trying to save himself from the consequences of his crimes—

69 Int. Apt. House Hallway—Night—1916
    Camera angling toward Kane from other end of the hall, Rogers and Emily are already down the hall, moving toward f.g. Kane in apartment doorway b.g.

KANE [*Screams louder*]   I'm going to send you to Sing Sing,[7] Rogers. Sing Sing!

> *Kane is trembling with rage as he shakes his fist at Rogers's back. Susan, quieter now, has snuggled into the hollow of his shoulder as they stand in the doorway*
>
> *Dissolve*

INSERT: *The "Chronicle" front page with photograph (as in the news digest) revealing Kane's relations with Susan. Headline reads:*

CANDIDATE KANE FOUND IN
LOVE NEST WITH "SINGER"

Dissolve

70 Int. Composing Room—"Inquirer"—Night—1916
   Camera angles down on enormous headline in type with proof on top. In back of this headline lies complete front page, except for headline. Headline reads:

KANE GOVERNOR
Camera tilts up showing Bernstein, actually crying, standing with composing room foreman, Jenkins.

BERNSTEIN [*To foreman*]   With a million majority already against him, and the church counties still to be heard from—I'm afraid we got no choice. This one.

> *Camera pans to where he is pointing; shows enormous headline, the proof of which in small type reads:*

KANE DEFEATED

and in large type screams:
FRAUD AT POLLS!

Dissolve Out

Dissolve In
71 Int. Kane's Office—"Inquirer"—Night—1916
   Kane looks up from his desk as there is a knock on the door.

KANE   Come in.

> *Leland enters.*

KANE [*Surprised*]   I thought I heard somebody knock.
LELAND [*A bit drunk*]   I knocked. [*He looks at him defiantly.*]
KANE [*Trying to laugh it off*]   Oh! An official visit of state, eh? [*Waves his hand*] Sit down, Jedediah.
LELAND [*Sitting down angrily*]   I'm drunk.
KANE   Good! It's high time—
LELAND   You don't have to be amusing.

7. A New York state penitentiary.

KANE   All right. Tell you what I'll do. I'll get drunk, too.

LELAND   [*Thinks this over*]   No. That wouldn't help. Besides, you never get drunk. [*Pauses*] *I want to talk to you—about—about—* [*He can't get it out*]

KANE   [*Looks at him sharply a moment*]   If you've got yourself drunk to talk to me about Susan Alexander—I'm not interested.

LELAND   She's not important. What's much more important—[*He keeps glaring at Kane*]

KANE   [*As if genuinely surprised*]   Oh! [*He gets up*] I frankly didn't think I'd have to listen to that lecture from you. [*Pauses*] I've betrayed the sacred cause of reform, is that it? I've set back the sacred cause of reform in this state twenty years. Don't tell me, Jed, *you—*

Despite his load, Leland manages to achieve a dignity about the silent contempt with which he looks at Kane.

KANE   [*An outburst*]   What makes the sacred cause of reform so sacred? Why does the sacred cause of reform have to be exempt from all the other facts of life? Why do the laws of this state have to be executed by a man on a white charger?

Leland lets the storm ride over his head.

KANE   [*Cont'd*] [*Calming down*]   But, if that's the way they want it— they've made their choice. The people of this state obviously prefer Mr. Rogers to me. [*His lips tighten*] So be it.

LELAND   You talk about the people as though they belong to you. As long as I can remember you've talked about giving the people their rights as though you could make them a present of liberty—in reward for services rendered. You remember the workingman? You used to write an awful lot about the workingman. Well, he's turning into something called organized labor, and you're not going to like that a bit when you find out it means that he thinks he's entitled to something as his right and not your gift. [*He pauses*] And listen, Charles. When your precious underprivileged really do get together—that's going to add up to something bigger—than your privilege—and then I don't know what you'll do. Sail away to a desert island, probably, and lord it over the monkeys.

KANE   Don't worry about it too much, Jed. There's sure to be a few of them there to tell me where I'm wrong.

LELAND   You may not always be that lucky. [*Pauses*] Charlie, why can't you get to look at things less personally? Everything doesn't have to be between you and—the personal note doesn't always—

KANE   [*Violently*]   The personal note is all there is to it. It's all there ever is to it. It's all there ever is to anything! Stupidity in our government—crookedness—even just complacency and self-satisfaction and an unwillingness to believe that anything done by a certain class of people can be wrong—you can't fight those things impersonally. They're not impersonal crimes against the people. They're being done by actual persons—with actual names and positions and—the right of the American people to their own country is not an academic issue, Jed, that you debate—and then the judges retire to return a verdict—and the winners give a dinner for the losers.

LELAND   You almost convince me, almost. The truth is, Charlie, you just don't care about anything except you. You just want to convince people that you love them so much that they should love you back. Only you want love on your own terms. It's something to be played your way—according to your rules. And if anything goes wrong and you're hurt—then the game stops, and you've got to be soothed and nursed, no matter what else is happening—and no matter who else is hurt!

They look at each other.

KANE [*Trying to kid him into a better humor*]   Hey, Jedediah!

Leland is not to be seduced.

LELAND   Charlie, I wish you'd let me work on the Chicago paper— you said yourself you were looking for someone to do dramatic criticism there—

KANE   You're more valuable here.

There is silence.

LELAND   Well, Charlie, then I'm afraid there's nothing I can do but to ask you to accept—

KANE [*Harshly*]   All right. You can go to Chicago.

LELAND   Thank you.

There is an awkward pause. Kane opens a drawer of his desk and takes out a bottle and two glasses.

KANE   I guess I'd better *try* to get drunk, anyway.

Kane hands Jed a glass, which he makes no move to take.

KANE [*Cont'd*]   But I warn you, Jedediah, you're not going to like it in Chicago. The wind comes howling in off the lake, and the Lord only knows if they've ever heard of lobster Newburg.

LELAND   Will a week from Saturday be all right?

KANE [*Wearily*]   Anytime you say.

LELAND   Thank you.

Kane looks at him intently and lifts the glass.

KANE   A toast, Jedediah—to love on *my* terms. Those are the only terms anybody knows—his own.

                                                                    Dissolve

72 *Ext. Town Hall in Trenton (as in News Digest)—Day*—1917
    Kane (as in news digest) is just emerging with Susan. He smashes one camera and before he begins on a second, a cop removes a

newsreel cameraman. He smashes a second camera, and is just about to start on a third.

PHOTOGRAPHER   Mr. Kane! Mr. Kane! It's the "Inquirer"!

Kane sees the "Inquirer" painted on the side of the camera and stops.

REPORTER [*Quickly*]   How about a statement, Mr. Kane?
ANOTHER REPORTER   On the level, Mr. Kane, are you through with politics?
KANE   I would say vice versa, young man. [*Smiles*] We're going to be a great opera star.
REPORTER   Are you going to sing at the Metropolitan, Mrs. Kane?
KANE   We certainly are.
SUSAN   Charlie said if I didn't, he'd build me an opera house.
KANE   That won't be necessary.

Dissolve

INSERT: FRONT PAGE CHICAGO "INQUIRER," *with photograph proclaiming that Susan Alexander opens at new Chicago Opera House in Thaïs[8] (as in news digest). (1919)*
On sound track during above we hear the big expectant murmur of an opening-night audience and the noodling of the orchestra.

Dissolve

73 *Int. Chicago Opera House—Night—Set for Thaïs—1919*
The camera is just inside the curtain, angling upstage. We see the set for Thaïs—and in the center of all this, in an elaborate costume, looking very small and very lost, is Susan. She is almost hysterical with fright. Applause is heard, and the orchestra starts thunderously. The curtain starts to rise—the camera with it. Susan squints and starts to sing. Camera continues on up with the curtain the full height of the proscenium arch and then on up into the gridiron. Susan's voice still heard but faintly. Two typical stagehands fill the frame, looking down on the stage below. They look at each other. One of them puts his hand to his nose.

Dissolve

74 *Int. City Room—Chicago "Inquirer"—Night—1919*
It is late. The room is almost empty. Nobody is at work at the desks. Bernstein is waiting anxiously with a little group of Kane's hirelings, most of them in evening dress with overcoats and hats. Everybody is tense and expectant.

CITY EDITOR [*Turns to a young hireling; quietly*]   What about Jed Leland? Has he got in his copy?
HIRELING   Not yet.
BERNSTEIN   Go in and ask him to hurry.

8. An 1894 opera written by Jules Massenet. Thaïs was an Athenian courtesan who traveled with the army of Alexander the Great during its invasion of Persia.

CITY EDITOR   Well, why don't you, Mr. Bernstein? You know Mr. Leland.

BERNSTEIN [*Slowly*] I might make him nervous. Mr. Leland, he's writing it from the dramatic angle?

CITY EDITOR   Yes, I thought it was a good idea. We've covered it from the news end, of course.

BERNSTEIN   And the social. How about the music notice? You got that in?

CITY EDITOR   Oh, yes, it's already made up. Our Mr. Mervin wrote a swell review.

BERNSTEIN   Enthusiastic?

CITY EDITOR   Yes, very! [*Quietly*] Naturally.

BERNSTEIN   Well, well—isn't that nice?

KANE'S VOICE   Mr. Bernstein—

Bernstein turns.

74A Med. *Long Shot of Kane*
   He is in white tie, wearing his overcoat and carrying a folded opera hat.

BERNSTEIN   Hello, Mr. Kane.

   The hirelings rush, with Bernstein, to Kane's side. Widespread, half-suppressed sensation.

CITY EDITOR   Mr. Kane, this *is* a surprise!

KANE   We've got a nice plant here.

   Everybody falls silent. There isn't anything to say.

CITY EDITOR   Everything has been done exactly to your instructions, Mr. Kane. We've got two spreads of pictures and—

KANE   The music notice on the first page?

CITY EDITOR   Yes, Mr. Kane. [*Hesitantly*] There's still one notice to come. The dramatic.

KANE   That's Leland, isn't it?

CITY EDITOR   Yes, Mr. Kane.

KANE   Has he said when he'll finish?

CITY EDITOR   We haven't heard from him.

KANE   He used to work fast—didn't he, Mr. Bernstein?

BERNSTEIN   He sure did, Mr. Kane.

KANE   Where is he?

ANOTHER HIRELING   Right in there, Mr. Kane.

   The hireling indicates the closed glass door of a little office at the other end of the city room. Kane takes it in.

BERNSTEIN [*Helpless but very concerned*]   Mr. Kane—

KANE   That's all right, Mr. Bernstein.

   Kane crosses the length of the long city room to the glass door

indicated before by the hireling. The city editor looks at Bern-
stein. Kane opens the door and goes into the office, closing the
door behind him.

BERNSTEIN   Mr. Leland and Mr. Kane—they haven't spoken together
for four years—
CITY EDITOR   You don't suppose—
BERNSTEIN   There's nothing to suppose. [*A long pause; finally . . .*]
Excuse me. [*Starts toward the door*]

Dissolve Out

Dissolve In
75 *Int. Leland's Office—Chicago "Inquirer"—Night—*1919
Bernstein comes in. An empty bottle is standing on Leland's desk.
He has fallen asleep over his typewriter, his face on the keys. A
sheet of paper is in the machine. A paragraph has been typed. Kane
is standing at the other side of the desk looking down at him. This
is the first time we see murder in Kane's face. Bernstein looks at
Kane, then crosses to Leland. He shakes him.

BERNSTEIN [*Straightens, looks at Kane; a pause*]   He ain't been drinking before, Mr. Kane. Never. We would have heard.
KANE [*Finally, after a pause*]   What does it say there?

Bernstein stares at him.

KANE [*Cont'd*]   What's he written?

Bernstein leans over nearsightedly, painfully reading the para-
graph written on the page.

BERNSTEIN [*Reading*]   "Miss Susan Alexander, a pretty but hopelessly
incompetent amateur—[*Waits for a minute to catch his breath;*
doesn't like it] last night opened the new Chicago Opera House in
a performance of—of—" [*Looks up miserably*] I still can't pronounce
that name, Mr. Kane.

Kane doesn't answer. Bernstein looks at Kane for a moment,
then looks back, tortured.

BERNSTEIN [*Cont'd*] [*Reading again*]   "Her singing, happily, is no
concern of this department. Of her acting, it is absolutely impossible
to—" [*Continues to stare at the page.*]
KANE [*After a short silence*]   Go on!
BERNSTEIN [*Without looking up*]   That's all there is.

Kane snatches the paper from the roller and reads it for him-
self. Slowly a queer look comes into his face. Then he speaks,
very quietly.

KANE   Of her acting, it is absolutely impossible to say anything except
that it represents in the opinion of this reviewer a new low— [*Then*

sharply] Have you got that, Mr. Bernstein? In the opinion of this reviewer—

BERNSTEIN [*Miserably*]   I didn't see that.

KANE   It isn't there, Mr. Bernstein. I'm dictating it.

BERNSTEIN   But Mr. Kane, I can't—I mean—I—

KANE   Get me a typewriter. I'll finish the notice.

Bernstein retreats from the room.

Dissolve Out

Dissolve In
    76 *Int. Leland's Office—Chicago "Inquirer"—Night—1919*
    Long shot—of Kane in his shirt-sleeves, illuminated by a desk light, typing furiously. As the camera starts to pull even further away from this . . .

Dissolve

    77 *Int. Leland's Office—Chicago "Inquirer"—Night—1919*
    Leland, sprawled across his typewriter. He stirs and looks up drunkenly, his eyes encountering Bernstein, who stands beside him.

BERNSTEIN   Hello, Mr. Leland.

LELAND   Hello, Bernstein. Where is it—where's my notice—I've got to finish it!

BERNSTEIN [*Quietly*]   Mr. Kane is finishing it.

LELAND   Kane?—Charlie?—[*Painfully rises*] Where is he?

    During all this, the sound of a busy typewriter has been heard. Leland's eyes follow the sound. Slowly he registers Kane out in the city room

    78 *Int. City Room—Chicago "Inquirer"—Night—1919*
    Kane, in white tie and shirt-sleeves, is typing away at a machine, his face, seen by the desk light before him, set in a strange half-smile. Leland stands in the door of his office, staring across at him.

LELAND   I suppose he's fixing it up—I knew I'd never get that through.

BERNSTEIN [*Moving to his side*]   Mr. Kane is finishing your piece the way you started it.

Leland turns incredulously to Bernstein.

BERNSTEIN [*Cont'd*]   He's writing a bad notice like you wanted it to be—[*Then with a kind of quiet passion, rather than triumph*] I guess that'll show you.

Leland picks his way across to Kane's side. Kane goes on typing, without looking up.

KANE [*After pause*]   Hello, Jedediah.

LELAND   Hello, Charlie—I didn't know we were speaking.

Kane stops typing, but doesn't turn.

KANE   Sure, we're speaking, Jed—You're fired.

He starts typing again; the expression on his face doesn't change.

Dissolve

79 *Ext. Hospital Roof—Day—1940*
   Thompson and Leland. It is getting late. The roof is now deserted.

THOMPSON   Everybody knows that story, Mr. Leland, but—why did he do it? How could he write a notice like that when—
LELAND   You just don't know Charlie. He thought that by finishing that piece he could show me he was an honest man. He was always trying to prove something. That whole thing about Susie being an opera singer—that was trying to prove something. Do you know what the headline was the day before the election? Candidate Kane found in love nest with quote singer unquote. He was going to take the quotes off the singer [*Pauses*] Hey, nurse! Five years ago he wrote from that place of his down South—[*As if trying to think*] you know. Shangri-La? El Dorado?[9] [*Pauses*] Sloppy Joe's? What's the name of that place? . . . All right. Xanadu. I knew what it was all the time. You caught on, didn't you?
THOMPSON   Yes.
LELAND   I guess maybe I'm not as hard to see through as I think. Anyway, I never even answered his letter. Maybe I should have. He must have been pretty lonely down there in that coliseum those last years. He hadn't finished it when she left him—he never finished it—he never finished anything, except my notice. Of course, he built the joint for her.
THOMPSON   That must have been love.
LELAND   I don't know. He was disappointed in the world. So he built one of his own—an absolute monarchy—It was something bigger than an opera house anyway—[*Calls*] Nurse! [*Lowers his voice*] Say, I'll tell you one thing you can do for me, young fellow.
THOMPSON   Sure.
LELAND   On your way out, stop at a cigar store, will you, and send me up a couple of cigars?
THOMPSON   Sure, Mr. Leland. I'll be glad to.
LELAND   Hey, nurse!

A nurse has already appeared and stands behind him.

NURSE   Yes, Mr. Leland.
LELAND   I'm ready to go in now. You know when I was a young man, there was an impression around that nurses were pretty. It was no truer then than it is now.

9. Shangri-La is a utopian retreat in the novel *Lost Horizon* (1933); El Dorado is a legendary South American city of   fabulous wealth which sixteenth-century explorers sought in vain.

NURSE   Here, let me take your arm, Mr. Leland.

LELAND [*Testily*]   All right, all right. You won't forget, will you,
about the cigars? And tell them to wrap them up to look like tooth-
paste, or something, or they'll stop them at the desk. That young
doctor I was telling you about, he's got an idea he wants to keep
me alive.

Fade Out

Fade In
80 Ext. "El Rancho" Cabaret in Atlantic City—Early Dawn—1940
     Neon sign on the roof:

"EL RANCHO"
Floor Show
Susan Alexander Kane
Twice Nightly

     *Camera, as before, moves through the lights of the sign and
down on the skylight, through which is seen Susan at her regular
table, Thompson seated across from her. Very faintly during this,
idle piano music playing.*

Dissolve

81 Int. "El Rancho" Cabaret—Early Dawn—1940
     *Susan and Thompson are facing each other. The place is almost
deserted. Susan is sober. On the other side of the room somebody
is playing a piano.*

THOMPSON   I'd rather you just talked. Anything that comes into your
mind—about yourself and Mr. Kane.

SUSAN   You wouldn't want to hear a lot of what comes into my mind
about myself and Mr. Charlie Kane. [*She tosses down a drink*] You
know—maybe I shouldn't ever have sung for Charlie that first time.
Hah!—I did a lot of singing after that. To start with, I sang for
teachers at a hundred bucks an hour. The teachers got that, I didn't.

THOMPSON   What did you get?

SUSAN   What do you mean?

     Thompson doesn't answer.

SUSAN [*Cont'd*]   I didn't get a thing. Just the music lessons. That's all
there was to it.

THOMPSON   He married you, didn't he?

SUSAN   He never said anything about marriage until it all came out
in the papers about us—and he lost the election and that Norton
woman divorced him. What are you smiling about? I tell you he
was really interested in my voice. [*Sharply*] What do you think he
built that opera house for? I didn't want it. I didn't want to sing.
It was his idea—everything was his idea—except my leaving him.

Dissolve

82 Int. Living Room—Kane's Home in New York—Day—1917–1918
     *Susan is singing. Matisti, her voice teacher, is playing the piano.
Kane is seated nearby. Matisti stops.*

MATISTI   Impossible! Impossible!

KANE   It is not your job to give Mrs. Kane your opinion of her talents. You're supposed to train her voice. Nothing more.

MATISTI   [*Sweating*]   But, it is impossible. I will be the laughingstock of the musical world! People will say—

KANE   If you're interested in what people will say, Signor Matisti, I may be able to enlighten you a bit. The newspapers, for instance. I'm an authority on what the papers will say, Signor Matisti, because I own eight of them between here and San Francisco. . . . It's all right, dear. Signor Matisti is going to listen to reason. Aren't you, maestro?

MATISTI   Mr. Kane, how can I persuade you—

KANE   You can't.

> *There is a silence. Matisti rises.*

KANE   [*Cont'd*]   I knew you'd see it my way.

Dissolve

83 *Int. Chicago Opera House—Night—1919*
> *It is the same opening night—it is the same moment as before—except that the camera is now upstage angling toward the audience. The curtain is down. We see the same tableau as before. As the dissolve commences, there is the sound of applause and now, as the dissolve completes itself, the orchestra begins—the stage is cleared—Susan is left alone. The curtain rises. Susan starts to sing. Beyond her, we see the prompter's box,[1] containing the anxious face of the prompter. Beyond that, an apprehensive conductor.*

84 *Close-up*
> *Kane's face—he is seated in the audience—listening.*
> *A sudden but perfectly correct lull in the music reveals a voice from the audience—a few words from a sentence.*

THE VOICE   —really pathetic.

> *Music crashes in and drowns out the rest of the sentence, but hundreds of people around the voice have heard it (as well as Kane) and there are titters which grow in volume.*

85 *Close-up*
> *Susan's face—singing.*

86 *Close-up*
> *Kane's face—listening.*
> *There is the ghastly sound of three thousand people applauding as little as possible. Kane still looks. Then, near the camera, there is the sound of about a dozen people applauding very, very loudly. Camera moves back, revealing Bernstein and Hillman and other Kane stooges, seated around him, beating their palms together.*

---

1. A low box projecting above the floor of a stage with its opening toward the actors.

87 The Stage from Kane's Angle

The curtain is down—Still the polite applause, dying fast. Nobody comes out for a bow.

88 Close-up

Kane—breathing heavily. Suddenly he starts to applaud furiously.

89 The Stage from the Audience Again

Susan appears for her bow. She can hardly walk. There is a little polite crescendo of applause, but it is sickly.

90 Close-up

Kane—still applauding very, very hard, his eyes on Susan.

91 The Stage Again

Susan, finishing her bow, goes out through the curtains. The light on the curtain goes out and the houselights go up.

92 Close-up

Kane—still applauding very, very hard.

Dissolve Out

Dissolve In

93 Int. Hotel Room—Chicago—Day—1919

Kane—Susan in a negligee. The floor is littered with newspapers.

SUSAN   Stop telling me he's your friend. [*She points at the paper*] A friend don't write that kind of an article. Anyway, not the kind of friends I know. Of course, I'm not high-class like you and I didn't go to any swell schools—
KANE   That's enough, Susan.

A look at him convinces Susan that he really means it's enough. There's a knock at the door.

SUSAN [*Screeching*]   Come in!

A copy boy enters.

COPY BOY   Mr. Leland said I was to come right up—He was very anxious—
KANE [*Interrupting*]   Thanks, son.

He shoves the kid out. He opens the envelope as Susan returns to the attack.

SUSAN   The idea of him trying to spoil my debut!

Kane has taken a folded piece of paper out of the envelope and is holding it—looking into the envelope.

KANE   He won't spoil anything else, Susan.

SUSAN And you—you ought to have your head examined! Sending him a letter he's fired with a twenty-five-thousand-dollar check! What kind of firing do you call that? You did send him a twenty-five-thousand-dollar check, *didn't* you?

KANE [*Slowly tipping over the envelope as pieces of torn paper fall to the floor*] Yes, I sent him a twenty-five-thousand-dollar check.

Kane now unfolds the piece of paper and looks at it.

INSERT: *Kane's original grease pencil copy of his Declaration of Principles.*

SUSAN'S VOICE What's that?

KANE'S VOICE An antique.

BACK TO SCENE:

SUSAN You're awful funny, aren't you? Well, I can tell you one thing you're not going to keep on being funny about—my singing. I'm through. I never wanted to—

KANE [*Without looking up*] You are continuing your singing, Susan. [*He starts tearing the paper*] I'm not going to have myself made ridiculous.

SUSAN You don't propose to have *yourself* made ridiculous? What about me? I'm the one that has to do the singing. I'm the one that gets the razzberries.[2] Why can't you just—

KANE [*Looking up—still tearing the paper*] My reasons satisfy me, Susan. You seem to be unable to understand them. I will not tell them to you again. [*He has started to walk menacingly toward her, tearing the paper as he walks*] You are to continue with your singing.

His eyes are relentlessly upon her. She sees something that frightens her. She nods slowly; indicating surrender.

Dissolve

INSERT: FRONT PAGE *of the San Francisco "Inquirer" (1919) containing a large portrait of Susan as Thaïs. It is announced that Susan will open an independent season in San Francisco in Thaïs. The picture remains constant but the names of the papers change from New York to St. Louis, to Los Angeles to Cleveland, to Denver to Philadelphia—all "Inquirers."*
During all this, on the sound track, Susan's voice is heard singing her aria very faintly.

Dissolve

94 *Int. Susan's Bedroom—Kane's N.Y. Home—Late Night—1920*
Camera angles across the bed and Susan's form towards the door, from the other side of which comes loud knocking and Kane's voice calling Susan's name. Then:

2. Critical jeers by the audience.

KANE'S VOICE   Joseph!
JOSEPH'S VOICE   Yes, sir.
KANE'S VOICE   Do you have the keys to Mrs. Kane's bedroom?
JOSEPH'S VOICE   No, Mr. Kane. They must be on the inside.
KANE'S VOICE   We'll have to break down the door.
JOSEPH'S VOICE   Yes, sir.

> *The door crashes open. Light floods the room, revealing Susan, fully dressed, stretched out on the bed. She is breathing, but heavily. Kane rushes to her, kneels at the bed, and feels her forehead. Joseph has followed him.*

KANE   Get Dr. Corey.

> *Joseph rushes out.*

> > > > *Dissolve*

95 *Int. Susan's Bedroom—Kane's N.Y. Home—Late Night—1920*
  A little later. All the lights are lit. At start of scene, Dr. Corey removes his doctor's bag from in front of camera lens, revealing Susan, in a nightgown, is in bed. She is breathing heavily. A nurse is bending over the bed, straightening the sheets.

DR. COREY'S VOICE   She'll be perfectly all right in a day or two, Mr. Kane.
> *The nurse walks away from the bed toward b.g. We now see Kane, who was hidden by the nurse's body, seated beyond the bed. He is holding an empty medicine bottle. Dr. Corey walks to him.*

KANE   I can't imagine how Mrs. Kane came to make such a foolish mistake. [*Susan turns her head away from Kane*] The sedative Dr. Wagner gave her is in a somewhat larger bottle—I suppose the strain of preparing for the new opera has excited and confused her. [*Looks sharply up at Dr. Corey*]
DR. COREY   Yes, yes—I'm sure that's it.

> *Dr. Corey turns and walks toward the nurse.*

KANE   There are no objections to my staying here with her, are there?
DR. COREY   No—not at all. But I'd like the nurse to be here, too. Good night, Mr. Kane.

> *Dr. Corey hurries out the door.*

> > > > *Dissolve*

96 *Int. Susan's Bedroom—Kane's N.Y. Home—Very Early Dawn—1920*
  The lights are out. Camera pans from nurse, who is seated stiffly in a chair, toward Kane, seated beside the bed staring at Susan, to Susan, who is asleep.

> > > > *Dissolve*

97 *Int. Susan's Bedroom—Kane's N.Y. Home—Day—1920*
  Sunlight is streaming into the room. A hurdy-gurdy is heard. Kane is still seated beside the bed, looking at Susan, who is asleep. After a moment Susan gasps and opens her eyes. She looks toward the window, Kane leans toward her. She looks up at him, then away.

SUSAN [*Painfully*]   Charlie—I couldn't make you see how I felt—I just couldn't go through with the singing again—You don't know what it's like to feel that people—that a whole audience doesn't want you.
KANE [*Angrily*]   That's when you've got to fight them!

  She looks up at him silently with pathetic eyes.

KANE [*Cont'd*] [*After a moment; gently*]   All right. You won't have to fight them any more—It's their loss.

  She continues to look at him, but now gratefully.

                                                    Dissolve

98 *Ext. Establishing Shot of Xanadu—Half Built—1925*
                                                    Dissolve

99 *Int. Great Hall—Xanadu—1929*
  Close-up of an enormous jigsaw puzzle. A hand is putting in the last piece. Camera moves back to reveal jigsaw puzzle spread out on the floor.
  Susan is on the floor before her jigsaw puzzle. Kane is in an easy chair. Candelabra illuminates the scene.

SUSAN   What time is it?
  There is no answer.
SUSAN [*Cont'd*]   Charlie! I said, what time is it?
KANE [*Looks up—consults his watch*]   Eleven-thirty.
SUSAN   I mean in New York. [*No answer*] I said what time is it in New York!
KANE   Eleven-thirty.
SUSAN   At night?
KANE   Umhmm. The bulldog's[3] just gone to press.
SUSAN [*Sarcastically*]   Hurray for the bulldog! [*Sighs*] Eleven-thirty! The shows're just getting out. People are going to nightclubs and restaurants. Of course, we're different because we live in a palace.
KANE   You always said you wanted to live in a palace.
SUSAN   A person could go nuts in this dump.

  Kane doesn't answer.

SUSAN [*Cont'd*]   Nobody to talk to—nobody to have any fun with.
KANE   Susan—

---

3. The early edition of a newspaper.

SUSAN   Forty-nine thousand acres of nothing but scenery and—statues. I'm lonesome.

KANE   I thought you were tired of house guests. Till yesterday morning, we've had no less than fifty of your friends at any one time. As a matter of fact, Susan, if you'll look carefully in the west wing, you'll probably find a dozen vacationists still in residence.

SUSAN   You make a joke out of everything! Charlie, I want to go back to New York. I'm tired of being a hostess. I wanta have fun. Please, Charlie, please!

KANE   Our home is here, Susan. I don't care to visit New York.

Dissolve

100 *Another Picture Puzzle*
    Susan's hands fitting in a missing piece. (1930)

Dissolve

101 *Another Picture Puzzle*
    Susan's hands fitting in a missing piece. (1931)

Dissolve

102 *Int. Great Hall—Xanadu—Day—*1932
    Close-up of another jigsaw puzzle. Camera pulls back to show Kane and Susan in much the same positions as before, except that they are older.

KANE   One thing I've never been able to understand, Susan. How do you know that you haven't done them before?

Susan shoots him an angry glance. She isn't amused.

SUSAN   It makes a whole lot more sense than collecting Venuses.

KANE   You may be right—I sometimes wonder—but you get into the habit—

SUSAN [*Snapping*]   It's not a habit. I do it because I like it.

KANE   I was referring to myself [*Pauses*] I thought we might have a picnic tomorrow—Invite everybody to go to the Everglades—

SUSAN   *Invite* everybody!—Order everybody, you mean, and make them sleep in tents! Who wants to sleep in tents when they have a nice room of their own—with their own bath, where they know where everything is?

Kane has looked at her steadily, not hostilely.

KANE   I thought we might invite everybody to go on a picnic tomorrow. Stay at Everglades overnight.

Dissolve

103 *Ext. Xanadu—Road—Day—*1932
    Tight two-shot—Kane and Susan seated in an automobile, silent, glum, staring before them. Camera pulls back revealing that there are twenty cars full of picnickers following them, on their way through the Xanadu estate.

SUSAN You never give me anything I really care about.

Dissolve Out

Dissolve In
104 Ext. The Everglades Camp—Night—1932
   Long shot—of a number of classy tents.

Dissolve

105 Int. Large Tent—Everglades Camp—Night—1932
   Two real beds have been set up on each side of the tent. A rather classy dressing table is in the rear, at which Susan is preparing for bed. Kane, in his shirt-sleeves, is in an easy chair, reading. Susan is very sullen.

SUSAN I'm not going to put up with it.

Kane turns to look at her.

SUSAN [*Cont'd*] I mean it. Oh, I know I always say I mean it, and then I don't—or *you* get me so I don't do what I say I'm going to—but—

KANE [*Interrupting*] You're in a tent, darling. You're not at home. And I can hear you very well if you just talk in a normal tone of voice.

SUSAN I'm not going to have my guests insulted, just because you—[*In a rage*] if people want to bring a drink or two along on a picnic, that's their business. You've got no right—

KANE [*Quickly*] I've got more than a right as far as you're concerned, Susan.

SUSAN I'm sick and tired of your telling me what I mustn't do! And what I—

KANE We can discuss all this some other time, Susan. Right now—

SUSAN I'll discuss what's on my mind when *I* want to. I'm sick of having you run my life the way you want it.

KANE Susan, as far as you're concerned, I've never wanted anything—I don't want anything now—except what you want.

SUSAN What *you* want me to want, you mean. What you've decided I ought to have—what you'd want if you were me. Never what I want—

KANE Susan!

SUSAN You've never given me anything that—

KANE I really think—

SUSAN Oh sure, you give me things—that don't mean anything to you—What's the difference between giving me a bracelet or giving somebody else a hundred thousand dollars for a statue you're going to keep crated up and never look at? It's only money.

KANE [*He has risen*] Susan, I want you to stop this.

SUSAN I'm not going to stop it!

KANE Right now!

SUSAN [*Screams*] You never gave me anything in your life! You just tried to—to buy me into giving *you* something. You're—it's like you were bribing me!

KANE   Susan!

SUSAN   That's all you ever done—no matter how much it cost you—your time, your money—that's all you've done with everybody. Tried to bribe them!

KANE   *Susan!*

She looks at him, with no lessening of her passion.

KANE [Cont'd] [*Quietly*]   Whatever I do—I do—because I love you.

SUSAN   You don't love me! You just want me to love you—sure—I'm Charles Foster Kane. Whatever you want—just name it and it's yours. But you gotta love me!

Without a word, Kane slaps her across the face. He continues to look at her.

SUSAN [Cont'd]   You'll never get a chance to do that again. Don't tell me you're sorry.

KANE   I'm not sorry.

Dissolve

106 Int. *Great Hall—Xanadu—Day—1932*
    Kane is at the window looking out. He turns as he hears Raymond enter.

RAYMOND   Mrs. Kane would like to see you, Mr. Kane.

KANE   All right.

Raymond waits as Kane hesitates.

KANE [Cont'd]   Is Mrs. Kane—[*He can't finish*]

RAYMOND   Marie has been packing her since morning, Mr. Kane.

Kane impetuously walks past him out of the room.

107 Int. *Susan's Room—Xanadu—Day—1932*
    Packed suitcases are on the floor. Susan is completely dressed for traveling. Kane bursts into the room.

SUSAN   Tell Arnold I'm ready, Marie. He can get the bags.

MARIE   Yes, Mrs. Kane.

She leaves. Kane closes the door behind her.

KANE   Have you gone completely crazy?

Susan looks at him.

KANE [Cont'd]   Don't you realize that everybody here is going to know about this? That you've packed your bags and ordered the car and—

SUSAN —And left? Of course they'll hear. I'm not saying good-bye—except to you—but I never imagined that people wouldn't know.

Kane is standing against the door as if physically barring her way.

KANE I won't let you go.
SUSAN [*Reaches out her hand*] Good-bye, Charlie.
KANE [*Suddenly*] Don't go, Susan.

Susan just looks at him.

KANE [*Cont'd*] Susan, don't go! Susan, please!

He has lost all pride. Susan stops. She is affected by this.

KANE [*Cont'd*] You mustn't go, Susan. Everything'll be exactly the way you want it. Not the way *I* think you want it—but your way. Please, Susan—Susan!

She is staring at him. She might weaken.

KANE [*Cont'd*] Don't go, Susan! You mustn't go! [*Almost blubbering*] You—you can't do this to me, Susan—

It's as if he had thrown ice water into her face. She freezes.

SUSAN I see—it's *you* that this is being done to! It's not me at all. Not how I feel. Not what it means to me. Not—[*She laughs*] I can't do this to *you!* [*She looks at him*] Oh yes I can.

She walks out, past Kane, who turns to watch her go, like a very tired old man.

Dissolve

108 *Int. "El Rancho" Cabaret—Night—1940*
Susan and Thompson at table. There is silence between them for a moment as she accepts a cigarette from Thompson and he lights it for her.

SUSAN In case you've never heard of how I lost all my money—and it was plenty, believe me—
THOMPSON The last ten years have been tough on a lot of people—
SUSAN Aw, they haven't been tough on me. I just lost my money—[*Takes a deep puff*] So you're going down to Xanadu.
THOMPSON Monday, with some of the boys from the office. Mr. Rawlston wants the whole place photographed carefully—all that art stuff. We run a picture magazine, you know—
SUSAN Yeah, I know. If you're smart, you'll talk to Raymond—[*Nervously douses out the cigarette*] That's the butler. You can learn a lot from him. He knows where the bodies are buried.

She grabs a glass and holds it tensely in both hands.

THOMPSON   You know, all the same I feel kind of sorry for Mr. Kane.
SUSAN [*Harshly*]   Don't you think I do?

> *She lifts the glass, and as she drains it she notices the dawn light coming through the skylight. She shivers and pulls her coat over her shoulders.*

SUSAN [*Cont'd*]   Well, what do you know? It's morning already. [*Looks at him for a moment*] You must come around and tell me the story of your life sometime.

Dissolve Out

Dissolve In
109 *Ext. Xanadu—Late Dusk—1940*
> *The distant castle on the hill, seen through the great iron "K" as in the opening shot of the picture. Several lights are on.*

Dissolve

110 *Int. Great Hall—Xanadu—Late Dusk—1940*
> *Camera is in close on Thompson and Raymond—will subsequently reveal surrounding scene.*

RAYMOND   Rosebud? I'll tell you about Rosebud—how much is it worth to you? A thousand dollars?
THOMPSON   Okay.
RAYMOND   He was a little gone in the head sometimes, you know.
THOMPSON   No, I didn't.
RAYMOND   He did crazy things sometimes—I've been working for him eleven years now—the last years of his life and I ought to know. Yes, sir, the old man was kind of queer, but I knew how to handle him.
THOMPSON   Need a lot of service?
RAYMOND   Yeah. But I knew how to handle him.

Dissolve Out

Dissolve In
111 *Int. Corridor and Telegraph Office—Xanadu—Night—1932*
> *Raymond walking rapidly along corridor. He pushes open a door. At a desk sits a wireless operator. Near him at a telephone switchboard sits a female operator.*

RAYMOND [*Reading*]   Mr. Charles Foster Kane announced today that Mrs. Charles Foster Kane has left Xanadu, his Florida home, under the terms of a peaceful and friendly agreement with the intention of filing suit for divorce at an early date. Mrs. Kane said that she does not intend to return to the operatic career which she gave up a few years after her marriage, at Mr. Kane's request. Signed, Charles Foster Kane.

Fred finishes typing and then looks up.

RAYMOND [*Cont'd*] Exclusive for immediate transmission. Urgent priority all Kane Papers.
FRED Okay.

There is the sound of the buzzer on the switchboard.

KATHERINE Yes . . . yes . . . Mrs. Tinsdall. Very well. [*Turns to Raymond*] It's the housckeeper.
RAYMOND Yes?
KATHERINE She says there's some sort of disturbance up in Miss Alexander's room. She's afraid to go in.

Dissolve Out

112 *Int. Corridor Outside Susan's Bedroom—Xanadu—Night—1932*
The housekeeper, Mrs. Tinsdall, and a couple of maids are near the door but too afraid to be in front of it. From inside can be heard a terrible banging and crashing. Raymond hurries into scene, opens the door, and goes in.

113 *Int. Susan's Bedroom—Xanadu—1932*
Kane, in a truly terrible and absolutely silent rage, is literally breaking up the room—yanking pictures, hooks and all off the wall, smashing them to bits—ugly, gaudy pictures—Susie's pictures in Susie's bad taste. Off of tabletops, off of dressing tables, occasional tables, bureaus, he sweeps Susie's whorish accumulation of bric-a-brac.
Raymond stands in the doorway watching him. Kane says nothing. He continues with tremendous speed and surprising strength still wordlessly, tearing the room to bits. The curtains (too frilly—overly pretty) are pulled off the window in a single gesture, and from the bookshelves he pulls down double armloads of cheap novels—discovers a half-empty bottle of liquor and dashes it across the room. Finally he stops. Susie's cozy little chamber is an incredible shambles all around him. He stands for a minute breathing heavily, and his eye lights on a hanging whatnot in a corner which had escaped his notice. Prominent on its center shelf is the little glass ball with the snowstorm in it. He yanks it down. Something made of china breaks, but not the glass ball. It bounces on the carpet and rolls to his feet, the snow in a flurry. His eye follows it. He stoops to pick it up—can't make it. Raymond picks it up for him; hands it to him. Kane takes it sheepishly—looks at it—moves painfully out of the room into the corridor.

114 *Int. Corridor Outside Susan's Bedroom—Xanadu—1932*
Kane comes out of the door. Mrs. Tinsdall has been joined now by a fairly sizable turnout of servants. They move back away from Kane, staring at him. Raymond is in the doorway behind Kane. Kane still looks at the glass ball.

KANE [*Without turning*] Close the door, Raymond.
RAYMOND Yes, sir. [*Closes it*]
KANE Lock it—and keep it locked.

Raymond locks the door and comes to his side. There is a long pause—servants staring in silence. Kane gives the glass ball a gentle shake and starts another snowstorm.

KANE [*Almost in a trance*]   Rosebud.
RAYMOND   What's that, sir?

One of the younger servants giggles and is hushed up. Kane shakes the ball again. Another flurry of snow. He watches the flakes settle—then looks up. Finally, taking in the pack of servants and something of the situation, he puts the glass ball in his coat pocket. He speaks very quietly to Raymond, so quietly it only seems he's talking to himself.

KANE   Keep it locked.

He slowly walks off down the corridor, the servants giving way to let him pass, and watching him as he goes. The mirrors which line the hall reflect his image as he moves. He is an old, old man!
    Kane turns into a second corridor—sees himself reflected in the mirror—stops. His image is reflected again in the mirror behind him—multiplied again and again and again in long perspectives—Kane looks. We see a thousand Kanes.

Dissolve

115 Int. Great Hall—Xanadu—Night—1940
    Thompson and Raymond.

RAYMOND [*Callously*]   That's the whole works, right up to date.
THOMPSON   Sentimental fellow, aren't you?
RAYMOND   Yes and no.
THOMPSON   And that's what you know about Rosebud?
RAYMOND   That's more than anybody knows. I tell you, he was a little gone in the head—the last couple of years anyway—but I knew how to handle him. That Rosebud—I heard him say it that other time too. He just said Rosebud, then he dropped that glass ball and it broke on the floor. He didn't say anything after that, so I knew he was dead. He said all kinds of things that didn't mean anything.
THOMPSON   That isn't worth anything.
RAYMOND   You can go on asking questions if you want to.
THOMPSON [*Coldly*]   We're leaving tonight. As soon as they're through photographing the stuff—

Thompson has risen. Raymond gets to his feet.

RAYMOND   Allow yourself plenty of time. The train stops at the junction on signal—but they don't like to wait. Not now. I can remember when they'd wait all day . . . if Mr. Kane said so.

Camera has pulled back to show long shot of the great hall, revealing the magnificent tapestries, candelabra, etc., are still there, but now several large packing cases are piled against the walls, some broken open, some shut, and a number of objects, great and small, are piled pell-mell all over the place. Furniture, statues, paintings, bric-a-brac—things of obviously enormous value are standing beside a kitchen stove, an old rocking chair and other junk, among which is also an old sled, the self-same story.

In the center of the hall a photographer and his assistant are busy photographing the sundry objects. In addition there are a girl and two newspapermen—also Thompson and Raymond.

The girl and the second man, who wears a hat, are dancing somewhere in the back of the hall to the music of a phonograph playing "Oh, Mr. Kane!"

116 *Int. Great Hall—Xanadu—Night—1940*
The photographer has just photographed a picture, obviously of great value, an Italian primitive. The assistant consults a label on the back of it.

ASSISTANT   No. 9182.

The third newspaperman jots this information down.

ASSISTANT [*Cont'd*] *Nativity*—attributed to Donatello,[4] acquired Florence, 1921, cost: 45,000 lire. Got that?
THIRD NEWSPAPERMAN Yeh.
PHOTOGRAPHER All right! Next! Better get that statue over there.
ASSISTANT Okay.
RAYMOND What do you think all this is worth, Mr. Thompson?
THOMPSON Millions—if anybody wants it.
RAYMOND The banks are out of luck, eh?
THOMPSON Oh, I don't know. They'll clear all right.
ASSISTANT *Venus*, fourth century. Acquired 1911. Cost: twenty-three thousand. Got it?
THIRD NEWSPAPERMAN Okay.
ASSISTANT [*Patting the statue on the fanny*] That's a lot of money to pay for a dame without a head.
SECOND ASSISTANT [*Reading a label*] No. 483. One desk from the estate of Mary Kane, Little Salem, Colorado. Value: $6.00. We're supposed to get everything. The junk as well as the art.
THIRD NEWSPAPERMAN Okay.

A flashlight bulb goes off. Thompson has opened a box and is idly playing with a handful of little pieces of cardboard.

THIRD NEWSPAPERMAN [*Cont'd*] What's that?
RAYMOND It's a jigsaw puzzle.
THIRD NEWSPAPERMAN We got a lot of those. There's a Burmese temple and three Spanish ceilings down the hall.

4. Donato di Niccolo di Betto Bardi (1386?–1466), an Italian sculptor.

Raymond laughs.

PHOTOGRAPHER   Yeh, all in crates.

THIRD NEWSPAPERMAN   There's a part of a Scotch castle over there, but we haven't bothered to unwrap it.

PHOTOGRAPHER   I wonder how they put all those pieces together?

ASSISTANT [*Reading a label*]   Iron stove. Estate of Mary Kane. Value: $2.00.

PHOTOGRAPHER   Put it over by that statue. It'll make a good setup.

GIRL [*Calling out*]   Who is she anyway?

SECOND NEWSPAPERMAN   Venus. She always is.

THIRD NEWSPAPERMAN   He sure liked to collect things, didn't he?

PHOTOGRAPHER   Anything and everything—he was a regular crow.

THIRD NEWSPAPERMAN   I wonder—You put all this together—the palaces and the paintings and the toys and everything—what would it spell?

Thompson has turned around. He is facing the camera for the first time.

THOMPSON   Charles Foster Kane.

PHOTOGRAPHER   Or Rosebud? How about it, Jerry?

THIRD NEWSPAPERMAN [*To the dancers*]   Turn that thing off, will you? It's driving me nuts!—What's Rosebud?

PHOTOGRAPHER   Kane's last words, aren't they, Jerry? [*To the third newspaperman*] That was Jerry's angle, wasn't it. Did you ever find out what it means?

THOMPSON   No, I didn't.

The music has stopped. The dancers have come over to Thompson.

SECOND NEWSPAPERMAN   Say, what did you find out about him anyway?

THOMPSON   Not much.

SECOND NEWSPAPERMAN   Well, what have you been doing?

THOMPSON   Playing with a jigsaw puzzle—I talked to a lot of people who knew him.

GIRL   What do they say?

THOMPSON   Well—it's become a very clear picture. He was the most honest man who ever lived, with a streak of crookedness a yard wide. He was a liberal and a reactionary. He was a loving husband —and both his wives left him. He had a gift for friendship such as few men have—and he broke his oldest friend's heart like you'd throw away a cigarette you were through with. Outside of that—

THIRD NEWSPAPERMAN   Okay, okay.

GIRL   If you could have found out what that Rosebud meant, I bet that would've explained everything.

THOMPSON   No, I don't. Not much anyway. Charles Foster Kane was a man who got everything he wanted, and then lost it. Maybe Rosebud was something he couldn't get or something he lost, but it wouldn't have explained anything. I don't think any word explains a man's life. No—I guess Rosebud is just a piece in a jigsaw puzzle— a missing piece.

> *He drops the jigsaw pieces back into the box, looking at his watch.*

THOMPSON [*Cont'd*]   We'd better get along. We'll miss the train.

> *He picks up his overcoat—it has been resting on a little sled— the little sled young Charles Foster Kane hit Thatcher with at the opening of the picture. Camera dosn't close in on this. It just registers the sled as the newspaper people, picking up their clothes and equipment, move out of the great hall.*
>
> *Dissolve Out*

Dissolve In
117 Int. Cellar—Xanadu—Night—1940
   A large furnace, with an open door, dominates the scene. Two laborers, with shovels, are shoveling things into the furnace. Raymond is about ten feet away.

RAYMOND   Throw that junk in, too.

> *Camera travels to the pile that he has indicated. It is mostly bits of broken packing cases, excelsior, etc. The sled is on top of the pile. As camera comes close, it shows the faded rosebud and, though the letters are faded, unmistakably the word "Rosebud" across it. The laborer drops his shovel, takes the sled in his hand and throws it into the furnace. The flames start to devour it.*

118 Ext. Xanadu—Night—1940
   No lights are to be seen. Smoke is coming from a chimney. Camera reverses the path it took at the beginning of the picture, perhaps omitting some of the stages. It moves finally through the gates, which close behind it. As camera pauses for a moment, the letter "K" is prominent in the moonlight.
   Just before we fade out, there comes again into the picture the pattern of barbed wire and cyclone fencing. On the fence is a sign which reads:

PRIVATE—NO TRESPASSING

> *Fade Out*
> *1940*

A GLOSSARY OF FILM TERMS
USED IN *Citizen Kane*

Angle—Angle usually refers to the vertical tilt or up-and-down movement of the camera. **Angle down (down shot)** indicates that the

camera is photographing the subject from above, and **angle up**
(**tilt up**) indicates the camera is on a plane beneath the subject. A
reverse angle shot, however, is a shot taken from a position 180°
opposed to the position of the previous shot.

Dissolve—The superimposition of a fade in onto a fade out in which
the darkening shot is gradually replaced by the brightening one.

Fade—A gradual brightening or darkening of the screen image. A **fade
in** begins in darkness and slowly lightens to full brightness; a **fade
out** reduces a shot from normal brightness to a black screen.

Frame—The "line" separating the edges of the screen image from
the darkness inside the theater.

Insert—A shot, often a close-up, taken at another time or place, which
has been edited into the film so that it seems continuous with the
scene in which it appears.

Miniature—A model photographed so as to appear life-size.

Pan—The horizontal movement of the camera either left or right.

Shot—The series of images recorded on film while the camera operates
at any one time. A **long shot** generally covers a complete setting,
while a **medium shot** reveals a fair amount of detail. A **close-up** is
a detailed shot of a person or thing. A **two-shot** is a medium shot
featuring two actors.

Stock—Footage from another source—often other films or newsreels—
included so reduplication of standard shots (crowds, airplanes, ships,
trains, etc.) is unnecessary.

Contexts

4   THE AUTHOR'S WORK

Every important author leaves an individual stamp on his or her work, the mark of a personal vision and distinctive ideas. As an example, let us examine two works of the contemporary American playwright Tennessee Williams, *The Glass Menagerie* and *The Long Goodbye*. Although both plays came early in his career, they set forth ideas and patterns that recur in later plays. *The Glass Menagerie*, Williams's first success, is better known, but the two plays share many features, especially some that are related to Williams's own life. Information about Williams's early life is available from a number of sources, including Williams's memoirs and those of his mother.

Williams's father was a man primarily interested in his work and in amusements that were, at that time, considered masculine, such as poker and heavy drinking. We suspect that the elder Williams felt confined and restricted in the company of women and small children. Mrs. Williams was the daughter of a clergyman and accustomed to a more "refined" life style than her husband cared for. The son himself was a sickly child, closely attached to his older sister Rose, and temperamentally and physically repelled by the rough games and activities in which "all-American" boys were expected to engage. When he was quite small, he spent substantial periods, either alone or with his mother and Rose, living in his grandparents' home, with his father absent. There was little empathy between father and son. The family's move to St. Louis while Williams and his sister were still very young must have been a shock to Mrs. Williams and her children, who had been living in small towns where her father was an important person. The metropolis was ill prepared to be impressed by the daughter and grandchildren of a small-town Episcopal priest. The change must have made the strange city seem even more forbidding and hostile than it was. Yet, as is clear from all the accounts, Mrs. Williams was a woman who could take care of herself, a "survivor." Williams's personal situation was further exacerbated when his sister had to be hospitalized on several occasions for nervous conditions. Finally, she underwent a lobotomy, an operation that solved some of her problems but caused her to spend almost all of her life since in an institution. During his adolescence and youth Williams sought refuge from his problems in writing. After college and a period spent working for the shoe-making company where his father was employed, the aspiring writer left his home in St. Louis.

This sketchy account contains much information useful for understanding the relation between this author's work and his life, enabling us to demonstrate how art transmutes the autobiographical. In both plays, for example, the father is the least substantial figure; indeed, in *Menagerie* he has deserted his family years before the action of the play. The older Williams did not in fact "desert" his family, but he must have been a rather shadowy figure with his frequent business trips and his evenings out with the "boys," coming home to eat and sleep. Further, the physical setting of the plays is probably more impoverished than the actual dwellings in which the family lived, but they are an artistic expression of a situation in which the father, who had absolute control of the family finances, did not share his wife and children's interest in gracious living. To Mrs. Williams, raised in rectories, where the rector's wife would have been criticized by parishioners for not maintaining a "suitable" standard of living, the circumstances of her life in St. Louis might well have seemed harsher than they were.

Mrs. Williams's ability to survive, her underlying strength of character, appears in the mother in both plays. The willingness of the mother in *The Long Goodbye* to die rather than face a long series of expensive and debilitating treatments and the expedients that Amanda Wingfield employs to provide for herself and her family are not factual, but they show the same strength that Edwina Williams possessed. When *Menagerie* opened in Chicago, Laurette Taylor, who played Amanda, asked Mrs. Williams how she had liked seeing herself on stage. Mrs. Williams expressed a proper incredulity, for, of course, Amanda is not Tennessee Williams's mother. She is a woman who has had some similar experiences and who shares certain traits of character with her, but the character has been transmuted into something different and unique by the playwright's art.

In a similar way, both Myra and Laura are and are not Rose. Rose Williams was not crippled and she did have dates, but according to Williams she was much affected by the fact that one of her suitors stopped seeing her when her father suffered business reverses, apparently having been attracted more by her father's business position than by Rose herself. Williams himself describes Rose thus: "She was a very normal—but highly sexed—girl who was tearing herself apart mentally and physically by those repressions imposed upon her by [our mother's] monolithic Puritanism." Laura's physical handicap is a transmutation of Rose's emotional one, and the sexuality implicit in Laura's relation to the glass unicorn with his single phallic horn is based on Williams's understanding of Rose's plight. Both the young man from the country club who expects ready sexual compliance from a girl of Myra's social standing and the ambitious gentleman caller of *Menagerie* are transmutations of the ambitious suitor who deserted a girl whose father could no longer assist his career advancement. The two dramatic characters based on Rose go different ways—Myra apparently into promiscuity or prostitution and Laura into withdrawal from the world, two possible outcomes for such a personality—sensitive, but desiring love and acceptance.

Even more important in understanding the relation between the artist and his creation are typical ideas and motifs that appear in work after work. Several typical Williams themes may be seen in these two plays. First, throughout Williams's work there is a strong concern with sexuality. Williams was very interested in the work of D. H. Lawrence, and he shares with Lawrence a conviction that sexuality is a powerful and intense force in the lives of human beings. For Williams, however, the physical aspects of sex, its connection with the earthy, is a more dangerous, if not malevolent, force than it is for Lawrence. Because sexuality is so intense, it is even more dangerous for a sensitive person. In the brief glimpse that we have of Myra, we see a young woman being destroyed by her sexuality. While she is young and attractive, it may seem to work to her benefit, but it will ultimately lead her nowhere. Even Amanda, the survivor, has been trapped by sexual attraction into an unsuitable and unfortunate marriage. Still, as she tells Tom, she loved his father. But Laura is perhaps the most poignant victim. Before the intrusion of Jim she lives content in the fairy-tale world where she is a princess held captive by the gentle and undemanding unicorn. Jim comes into her fantasy as a knight-errant, who by his embrace and kiss overthrows his rival, figuratively castrating him when the horn breaks off. Even so slight an introduction to the physical aspect of sexuality makes retreat to the fairy kingdom impossible, and we feel that Laura has been destroyed by the experience.

A second theme that repeats itself in Williams's plays is the plight of the outsider. Of himself, Williams says that he "existed outside of conventional society, while contriving somewhat precariously to remain in contact with it. For me this was not only precarious but a matter of dark unconscious disturbances." Many of the important figures in Williams's plays are persons who live on the outskirts of normality and respectability; some do not come that close. They are unable to participate meaningfully in the life of every day. Tom in *Menagerie* is barely able to keep a menial job in a shoe factory. Both he and Joe in *The Long Goodbye* seek to move away from the world of the average, into the Merchant Marine or to South America, someplace where they hope to find more congenial life styles, settings more hospitable to their difference from the normal.

Closely associated with this is a third theme common in Williams— that art comes out of suffering and deprivation. Williams himself has said that "there is more sensibility" among homosexuals because "they must compensate for so much [suffering]." Art, he believes, is a compensation for pain or loss, and we can see this in both Joe and Tom, though more fully in the latter. The unhappiness, the sense of lost or unexperienced adventure, the routine of life makes him into a poet. This is expressed most poignantly in his description of the young couples coming out of the dance hall across the alley and embracing among the garbage cans. The pleasure of those stolen embraces is denied him, but the deprivation provides him with the artistic impulse to describe them. He cannot take on the role of the gentleman caller, the young man who sets about making himself ready to be a good husband and father. He cannot take a girl out into the alley and embrace her because that would constitute a promise, a disposition to become something he is not: an ordinary person. He is a loner, an outsider, a sufferer, and therefore potentially an artist.

TENNESSEE WILLIAMS

The Glass Menagerie

THE CHARACTERS

AMANDA WINGFIELD (*the mother*)

A little woman of great but confused vitality clinging frantically to another time and place. Her characterization must be carefully created, not copied from type. She is not paranoiac, but her life is paranoia. There is much to admire in Amanda, and as much to love and pity as there is to laugh at. Certainly she has endurance and a kind of heroism, and though her foolishness makes her unwittingly cruel at times, there is tenderness in her slight person.

LAURA WINGFIELD (*her daughter*)

Amanda, having failed to establish contact with reality, continues to live vitally in her illusions, but Laura's situation is even graver. A childhood illness has left her crippled, one leg slightly shorter than the other, and held in a brace. This defect need not be more than suggested on the stage. Stemming from this, Laura's separation increases till she is like a piece of her own glass collection, too exquisitely fragile to move from the shelf.

TOM WINGFIELD (*her son*)

And the narrator of the play. A poet with a job in a warehouse. His nature is not remorseless, but to escape from a trap he has to act without pity.

JIM O'CONNOR (*the gentleman caller*)

A nice, ordinary, young man.

PRODUCTION NOTES

Being a "memory play," *The Glass Menagerie* can be presented with unusual freedom of convention. Because of its considerably delicate or tenuous material, atmospheric touches and subtleties of direction play a particularly important part. Expressionism and all other unconventional techniques in drama have only one valid aim, and that is a closer approach to truth. When a play employs unconventional techniques, it is not, or certainly shouldn't be, trying to escape its responsibility of dealing with reality, or interpreting experience, but is actually or should be attempting to find a closer approach, a more penetrating and vivid expression of things as they are. The straight realistic play with its genuine Frigidaire and authentic ice-cubes, its characters who speak exactly as its audience speaks, corresponds to the academic landscape and has the same virtue of a photographic likeness. Everyone should know nowadays the unimportance of the photographic in art: that truth, life, or reality is an organic thing which the poetic imagination can represent or suggest, in essence, only through transformation, through changing into other forms than those which were merely present in appearance.

These remarks are not meant as a preface only to this particular play. They have to do with a conception of a new, plastic theatre which must take the place of the exhausted theatre of realistic conventions if the theatre is to resume vitality as a part of our culture.

THE SCREEN DEVICE: There is *only one important difference between the original and the acting version of the play* and that is the *omission* in the latter of the device that I tentatively included in my *original* script. This device was the use of a screen on which were projected magic-lantern slides bearing images or titles. I do not regret the omission of this device from the original Broadway production. The extraordinary power of Miss Taylor's[1] performance made it suitable to have the utmost simplicity in the physical production. But I think it may be interesting to some readers to see how this device was conceived. So I am putting it into the published manuscript. These images and legends, projected from behind, were cast on a section of wall between the front-room and dining-room areas, which should be indistinguishable from the rest when not in use.

The purpose of this will probably be apparent. It is to give accent to certain values in each scene. Each scene contains a particular point (or several) which is structurally the most important. In an episodic play, such as this, the basic structure or narrative line may be obscured from the audience; the effect may seem fragmentary rather than architectural. This may not be the fault of the play so much as a lack of attention in the audience. The legend or image upon the screen will strengthen the effect of what is merely allusion in the writing and allow the primary point to be made more simply and lightly than if the entire responsibility were on the spoken lines. Aside from this structural value, I think the screen will have a definite emotional appeal, less definable but just as important. An imaginative producer or director may invent many other uses for this device than those indicated in the present script. In fact the possibilities of the device seem much larger to me than the instance of this play can possibly utilize.

THE MUSIC: Another extra-literary accent in this play is provided by the use of music. A single recurring tune, "The Glass Menagerie,"[2] is used to give emotional emphasis to suitable passages. This tune is like circus music, not when you are on the grounds or in the

---

1. The role of Amanda was created by Laurette Taylor (1884–1946). Her first great success had been in 1912 (*Peg o'My Heart*), and she had been in virtual retirement for a number of years until her performance in this play.

2. Music for the play, including this theme, was composed by the American composer Paul Bowles.

immediate vicinity of the parade, but when you are at some distance and very likely thinking of something else. It seems under those circumstances to continue almost interminably and it weaves in and out of your preoccupied consciousness; then it is the lightest, most delicate music in the world and perhaps the saddest. It expresses the surface vivacity of life with the underlying strain of immutable and inexpressible sorrow. When you look at a piece of delicately spun glass you think of two things: how beautiful it is and how easily it can be broken. Both of those ideas should be woven into the recurring tune, which dips in and out of the play as if it were carried on a wind that changes. It serves as a thread of connection and allusion between the narrator with his separate point in time and space and the subject of his story. Between each episode it returns as reference to the emotion, nostalgia, which is the first condition of the play. It is primarily Laura's music and therefore comes out most clearly when the play focuses upon her and the lovely fragility of glass which is her image.

THE LIGHTING: The lighting in the play is not realistic. In keeping with the atmosphere of memory, the stage is dim. Shafts of light are focused on selected areas or actors, sometimes in contradistinction to what is the apparent center. For instance, in the quarrel scene between Tom and Amanda, in which Laura has no active part, the clearest pool of light is on her figure. This is also true of the supper scene, when her silent figure on the sofa should remain the visual center. The light upon Laura should be distinct from the others, having a peculiar pristine clarity such as light used in early religious portraits of female saints or madonnas. A certain correspondence to light in religious paintings, such as El Greco's,[3] where the figures are radiant in atmosphere that is relatively dusky, could be effectively used throughout the play. (It will also permit a more effective use of the screen.) A free, imaginative use of light can be of enormous value in giving a mobile, plastic quality to plays of a more or less static nature.

Tennessee Williams

Scene 1

The Wingfield apartment is in the rear of the building, one of those vast hive-like conglomerations of cellular living-units that flower as warty growths in overcrowded urban centers of lower middle-class population and are symptomatic of the impulse of this largest and fundamentally enslaved section of American society to avoid fluidity and differentiation and to exist and function as one interfused mass of automatism.

---

3. The Spanish painter Kyriakos Theo-tokopoulos (c. 1548–c. 1614), was called El Greco (the Greek) because he had been born in Crete. His paintings are so individual in style that such features as the relation between foreground and background lighting can be identified by his name.

The apartment faces an alley and is entered by a fire escape, a structure whose name is a touch of accidental poetic truth, for all of these huge buildings are always burning with the slow and implacable fires of human desperation. The fire escape is part of what we see—that is, the landing of it and steps descending from it.

The scene is memory and is therefore nonrealistic. Memory takes a lot of poetic license. It omits some details; others are exaggerated, according to the emotional value of the articles it touches, for memory is seated predominantly in the heart. The interior is therefore rather dim and poetic.

At the rise of the curtain, the audience is faced with the dark, grim rear wall of the Wingfield tenement. This building is flanked on both sides by dark, narrow alleys which run into murky canyons of tangled clotheslines, garbage cans, and the sinister latticework of neighboring fire escapes. It is up and down these side alleys that exterior entrances and exits are made during the play. At the end of TOM's opening commentary, the dark tenement wall slowly becomes transparent and reveals the interior of the ground-floor Wingfield apartment.

Nearest the audience is the living room, which also serves as a sleeping room for LAURA, the sofa unfolding to make her bed. Just beyond, separated from the living room by a wide arch or second proscenium with transparent faded portieres (or second curtain), is the dining room. In an old-fashioned whatnot[1] in the living room are seen scores of transparent glass animals. A blown-up photograph of the father hangs on the wall of the living room, to the left of the archway. It is the face of a very handsome young man in a doughboy's[2] First World War cap. He is gallantly smiling, ineluctably smiling, as if to say "I will be smiling forever."

Also hanging on the wall, near the photograph, are a typewriter keyboard chart and a Gregg shorthand diagram. An upright typewriter on a small table stands beneath the charts.

The audience hears and sees the opening scene in the dining room through both the transparent fourth wall of the building and the transparent gauze portieres of the dining-room arch. It is during this revealing scene that the fourth wall slowly ascends, out of sight. This transparent exterior wall is not brought down again until the very end of the play, during TOM's final speech.

The narrator is an undisguised convention of the play. He takes whatever license with dramatic convention is convenient to his purposes.

TOM enters, dressed as a merchant sailor, and strolls across to the fire escape. There he stops and lights a cigarette. He addresses the audience.

---

1. A light open set of shelves for storing bric-a-brac.

2. An infantryman, especially an American infantryman in World War I.

TOM   Yes, I have tricks in my pocket, I have things up my sleeve.
But I am the opposite of a stage magician. He gives you illusion
that has the appearance of truth. I give you truth in the pleasant
disguise of illusion.

To begin with, I turn back time. I reverse it to that quaint
period, the thirties, when the huge middle class of America was
matriculating in a school for the blind. Their eyes had failed them,
or they had failed their eyes, and so they were having their fingers pressed forcibly down on the fiery Braille alphabet of a dissolving economy.

In Spain there was revolution. Here there was only shouting and
confusion. In Spain there was Guernica.[3] Here there were disturbances of labor, sometimes pretty violent, in otherwise peaceful cities such as Chicago, Cleveland, Saint Louis[4] . . . This is the
social background of the play.

> *Music begins to play.*

The play is memory. Being a memory play, it is dimly lighted,
it is sentimental, it is not realistic. In memory everything seems
to happen to music. That explains the fiddle in the wings.

I am the narrator of the play, and also a character in it. The
other characters are my mother, Amanda, my sister, Laura, and a
gentleman caller who appears in the final scenes. He is the most
realistic character in the play, being an emissary from a world of
reality that we were somehow set apart from. But since I have a
poet's weakness for symbols, I am using this character also as a
symbol; he is the long-delayed but always expected something
that we live for.

There is a fifth character in the play who doesn't appear except
in this larger-than-life-size photograph over the mantel. This is our
father who left us a long time ago. He was a telephone man who
fell in love with long distances; he gave up his job with the telephone company and skipped the light fantastic out of town . . .

The last we heard of him was a picture postcard from Mazatlan,
on the Pacific coast of Mexico, containing a message of two words:
"Hello—Goodbye!" and no address.

I think the rest of the play will explain itself. . . .

> AMANDA's *voice becomes audible through the portieres.*

> *Legend on screen:* "Ou sont les neiges."[5]

> TOM *divides the portieres and enters the dining room.* AMANDA
> *and* LAURA *are seated at a drop-leaf table. Eating is indi-*

3. A Spanish village heavily bombed
during the Spanish Civil War, and the
subject of a famous painting by Pablo
Picasso.
4. The combination of the Great Depression and the rise of labor unions in
the 1930s led to violence in varying degrees in such cities as Toledo, Minneapolis,
and San Francisco in 1934 and in Chicago, Cleveland, and other places in 1937.
5. The refrain, "Where are the snows
(of yesteryear)?" of the *Ballade des Dames
du Temps Jadis* (The Ballade of Dead
Ladies) by the French poet Francois Vil-
lon (1431–c. 1463).

cated by gestures without food or utensils. AMANDA *faces the audience.* TOM *and* LAURA *are seated profile. The interior has lit up softly and through the scrim we see* AMANDA *and* LAURA *seated at the table.*

AMANDA [*calling*] Tom?
TOM   Yes, Mother.
AMANDA   We can't say grace until you come to the table!
TOM   Coming, Mother. [*He bows slightly and withdraws, reappearing a few moments later in his place at the table.*]
AMANDA [*to her son*] Honey, don't *push* with your fingers. If you have to push with something, the thing to push with is a crust of bread. And chew—chew! Animals have secretions in their stomachs which enable them to digest food without mastication, but human beings are supposed to chew their food before they swallow it down. Eat food leisurely, son, and really enjoy it. A well-cooked meal has lots of delicate flavors that have to be held in the mouth for appreciation. So chew your food and give your salivary glands a chance to function!

TOM *deliberately lays his imaginary fork down and pushes his chair back from the table.*

TOM   I haven't enjoyed one bite of this dinner because of your constant directions on how to eat it. It's you that make me rush through meals with your hawklike attention to every bite I take. Sickening—spoils my appetite—all this discussion of—animals' secretion—salivary glands—mastication!
AMANDA [*lightly*] Temperament like a Metropolitan star![6]

TOM *rises and walks toward the living room*

You're not excused from the table.
TOM   I'm getting a cigarette.
AMANDA   You smoke too much.

LAURA *rises.*

LAURA   I'll bring in the blanc mange.[7]

TOM *remains standing with his cigarette by the portieres.*

AMANDA [*rising*] No, sister, no, sister[8]—you be the lady this time and I'll be the darky.
LAURA   I'm already up.
AMANDA   Resume your seat, little sister—I want you to stay fresh and pretty—for gentlemen callers!
LAURA [*sitting down*] I'm not expecting any gentlemen callers.

6. Star of the Metropolitan Opera.
7. A kind of pudding.
8. In many Southern families of

Amanda's time the oldest daughter was called "Sister" by her parents and siblings.

AMANDA [*crossing out to the kitchenette, airily*] Some times they come when they are least expected! Why, I remember one Sunday afternoon in Blue Mountain[9]—

She enters the kitchenette.

TOM   I know what's coming!
LAURA   Yes. But let her tell it.
TOM   Again?
LAURA   She loves to tell it.

AMANDA *returns with a bowl of dessert.*

AMANDA   One Sunday afternoon in Blue Mountain—your mother received—*seventeen!*—gentlemen callers! Why, sometimes there weren't chairs enough to accommodate them all. We had to send the nigger over to bring in folding chairs from the parish house.
TOM [*remaining at the portieres*] How did you entertain those gentlemen callers?
AMANDA   I understood the art of conversation!
TOM   I bet you could talk.
AMANDA   Girls in those days *knew* how to talk, I can tell you.
TOM   Yes?

Image on screen: AMANDA *as a girl on a porch, greeting callers.*

AMANDA   They knew how to entertain their gentlemen callers. It wasn't enough for a girl to be possessed of a pretty face and a graceful figure—although I wasn't slighted in either respect. She also needed to have a nimble wit and a tongue to meet all occasions.
TOM   What did you talk about?
AMANDA   Things of importance going on in the world! Never anything coarse or common or vulgar.

She addresses TOM *as though he were seated in the vacant chair at the table though he remains by the portieres. He plays this scene as though reading from a script.*

My callers were gentlemen—all! Among my callers were some of the most prominent young planters of the Mississippi Delta[1]— planters and sons of planters!

TOM *motions for music and a spot of light on* AMANDA. *Her eyes lift, her face glows, her voice becomes rich and elegiac.*

Screen legend: "Ou sont les neiges d'antan?"

---

9. Although there is a town in Mississippi called Blue Mountain, Williams customarily uses the name to refer to a larger town, usually Clarksdale, in which he spent some time as a child.

1. An alluvial plain in northwest Mississippi, whose fertile soil supports a number of large and productive plantations. Clarksdale (Blue Mountain in the play) is at the northern limit of the region.

There was young Champ Laughlin who later became vice-president of the Delta Planters Bank. Hadley Stevenson who was drowned in Moon Lake and left his widow one hundred and fifty thousand in Government bonds. There were the Cutrere brothers, Wesley and Bates. Bates was one of my bright particular beaux! He got in a quarrel with that wild Wainwright boy. They shot it out on the floor of Moon Lake Casino. Bates was shot through the stomach. Died in the ambulance on his way to Memphis. His widow was also well provided-for, came into eight or ten thousand acres, that's all. She married him on the rebound—never loved her—carried my picture on him the night he died! And there was that boy that every girl in the Delta had set her cap for! That beautiful, brilliant young Fitzhugh boy from Greene County!

TOM What did he leave his widow?

AMANDA He never married! Gracious, you talk as though all of my old admirers had turned up their toes to the daisies!

TOM Isn't this the first you've mentioned that still survives?

AMANDA That Fitzhugh boy went North and made a fortune—came to be known as the Wolf of Wall Street! He had the Midas touch,[2] whatever he touched turned to gold! And I could have been Mrs. Duncan J. Fitzhugh, mind you! But—I picked your *father!*

LAURA [*rising*] Mother, let me clear the table.

AMANDA No, dear, you go in front and study your typewriter chart. Or practice your shorthand a little. Stay fresh and pretty!— It's almost time for our gentlemen callers to start arriving. [*She flounces girlishly toward the kitchenette.*] How many do you suppose we're going to entertain this afternoon?

TOM *throws down the paper and jumps up with a groan.*

LAURA [*alone in the dining room*] I don't believe we're going to receive any, Mother.

AMANDA [*reappearing airily*] What? No one?—not one? You must be joking!

LAURA *nervously echoes her laugh. She slips in a fugitive manner through the half-open portieres and draws them gently behind her. A shaft of very clear light is thrown on her face against the faded tapestry of the curtains. Faintly the music of "The Glass Menagerie" is heard as she continues lightly:*

Not one gentleman caller? It can't be true! There must be a flood, there must have been a tornado!

LAURA It isn't a flood, it's not a tornado, Mother. I'm just not popular like you were in Blue Mountain. . . .

---

2. The mythological King Midas was granted the power that everything he touched would turn to gold.

TOM *utters another groan.* LAURA *glances at him with a faint, apologetic smile. Her voice catches a little:*

Mother's afraid I'm going to be an old maid.

The scene dims out with the "Glass Menagerie" music.

Scene 2

On the dark stage the screen is lighted with the image of blue roses. Gradually LAURA's *figure becomes apparent and the screen goes out. The music subsides.*

LAURA *is seated in the delicate ivory chair at the small clawfoot table. She wears a dress of soft violet material for a kimono—her hair is tied back from her forehead with a ribbon. She is washing and polishing her collection of glass.* AMANDA *appears on the fire escape steps. At the sound of her ascent,* LAURA *catches her breath, thrusts the bowl of ornaments away, and seats herself stiffly before the diagram of the typewriter keyboard as though it held her spellbound. Something has happened to* AMANDA. *It is written in her face as she climbs to the landing: a look that is grim and hopeless and a little absurd. She has on one of those cheap or imitation velvety-looking cloth coats with imitation fur collar. Her hat is five or six years old, one of those dreadful cloche hats that were worn in the late Twenties, and she is clutching an enormous black patent-leather pocketbook with nickel clasps and initials. This is her full-dress outfit, the one she usually wears to the D.A.R.[3] Before entering she looks through the door. She purses her lips, opens her eyes very wide, rolls them upward and shakes her head. Then she slowly lets herself in the door. Seeing her mother's expression,* LAURA *touches her lips with a nervous gesture.*

LAURA   Hello, Mother, I was— [*She makes a nervous gesture toward the chart on the wall.* AMANDA *leans against the shut door and stares at* LAURA *with a martyred look.*]

AMANDA   Deception? Deception? [*She slowly removes her hat and gloves, continuing the sweet suffering stare. She lets the hat and gloves fall on the floor—a bit of acting.*]

LAURA [*shakily*]   How was the D.A.R. meeting?

AMANDA *slowly opens her purse and removes a dainty white handkerchief which she shakes out delicately and delicately touches to her lips and nostrils.*

Didn't you go to the D.A.R. meeting, Mother?

AMANDA [*faintly, almost inaudibly*]   —No.—No. [*then more forcibly:*] I did not have the strength—to go to the D.A.R. In fact, I did not

---

3. The Daughters of the American Revolution, an organization of women descended from participants in the American Revolution.

have the courage! I wanted to find a hole in the ground and hide myself in it forever! [*She crosses slowly to the wall and removes the diagram of the typewriter keyboard. She holds it in front of her for a second, staring at it sweetly and sorrowfully—then bites her lips and tears it in two pieces.*]

LAURA [*faintly*]   Why did you do that, Mother?

> AMANDA *repeats the same procedure with the chart of the Gregg Alphabet.*

Why are you—

AMANDA   Why? Why? How old are you, Laura?

LAURA   Mother, you know my age.

AMANDA   I thought that you were an adult; it seems that I was mistaken. [*She crosses slowly to the sofa and sinks down and stares at* LAURA.]

LAURA   Please don't stare at me, Mother.

> AMANDA *closes her eyes and lowers her head. There is a ten-second pause.*

AMANDA   What are we going to do, what is going to become of us, what is the future?

> *There is another pause.*

LAURA   Has something happened, Mother?

> AMANDA *draws a long breath, takes out the handkerchief again, goes through the dabbing process.*

Mother, has—something happened?

AMANDA   I'll be all right in a minute, I'm just bewildered—[*She hesitates.*]—by life. . . .

LAURA   Mother, I wish that you would tell me what's happened!

AMANDA   As you know, I was supposed to be inducted into my office at the D.A.R. this afternoon.

> *Screen image: A swarm of typewriters.*

But I stopped off at Rubicam's Business College to speak to your teachers about your having a cold and ask them what progress they thought you were making down there.

LAURA   Oh. . . .

AMANDA   I went to the typing instructor and introduced myself as your mother. She didn't know who you were.

"Wingfield," she said, "We don't have any such student enrolled at the school!"

I assured her she did, that you had been going to classes since early in January.

"I wonder," she said, "If you could be talking about that terribly shy little girl who dropped out of school after only a few days' attendance?"

"No," I said, "Laura, my daughter, has been going to school every day for the past six weeks!"

"Excuse me," she said. She took the attendance book out and there was your name, unmistakably printed, and all the dates you were absent until they decided that you had dropped out of school.

I still said, "No, there must have been some mistake! There must have been some mix-up in the records!"

And she said, "No—I remember her perfectly now. Her hands shook so that she couldn't hit the right keys! The first time we gave a speed test, she broke down completely—was sick at the stomach and almost had to be carried into the wash room! After that morning she never showed up any more. We phoned the house but never got any answer"—While I was working at Famous-Barr,[4] I suppose, demonstrating those—

She indicates a brassiere with her hands.

Oh! I felt so weak I could barely keep on my feet! I had to sit down while they got me a glass of water! Fifty dollars' tuition, all of our plans—my hopes and ambitions for you—just gone up the spout, just gone up the spout like that.

LAURA *draws a long breath and gets awkwardly to her feet. She crosses to the Victrola and winds it up.*

What are you doing?

LAURA   Oh! [*She releases the handle and returns to her seat.*]

AMANDA   Laura, where have you been going when you've gone out pretending that you were going to business college?

LAURA   I've just been going out walking.

AMANDA   That's not true.

LAURA   It is. I just went walking.

AMANDA   Walking? Walking? In winter? Deliberately courting pneumonia in that light coat? Where did you walk to, Laura?

LAURA   All sorts of places—mostly in the park.

AMANDA   Even after you'd started catching that cold?

LAURA   It was the lesser of two evils, Mother.

Screen image: Winter scene in a park.

I couldn't go back there. I—threw up—on the floor!

AMANDA   From half past seven till after five every day you mean to tell me you walked around in the park, because you wanted to make me think that you were still going to Rubicam's Business College?

LAURA   It wasn't as bad as it sounds. I went inside places to get warmed up.

AMANDA   Inside where?

---

4. A department store in St. Louis.

LAURA   I went in the art museum and the bird houses at the Zoo. I visited the penguins every day! Sometimes I did without lunch and went to the movies. Lately I've been spending most of my afternoons in the Jewel Box, that big glass house where they raise the tropical flowers.

AMANDA   You did all this to deceive me, just for deception? [LAURA *looks down.*] Why?

LAURA   Mother, when you're disappointed, you get that awful suffering look on your face, like the picture of Jesus' mother in the museum!

AMANDA   Hush!

LAURA   I couldn't face it.

There is a pause. A whisper of strings is heard. Legend on screen: "The Crust of Humility."

AMANDA   [*hopelessly fingering the huge pocketbook*]   So what are we going to do the rest of our lives? Stay home and watch the parades go by? Amuse ourselves with the glass menagerie, darling? Eternally play those worn-out phonograph records your father left as a painful reminder of him? We won't have a business career— we've given that up because it gave us nervous indigestion! [*She laughs wearily.*] What is there left but dependency all our lives? I know so well what becomes of unmarried women who aren't prepared to occupy a position. I've seen such pitiful cases in the South —barely tolerated spinsters living upon the grudging patronage of sister's husband or brother's wife!—stuck away in some little mousetrap of a room—encouraged by one in-law to visit another—little birdlike women without any nest—eating the crust of humility all their life!

Is that the future that we've mapped out for ourselves? I swear it's the only alternative I can think of! [*She pauses.*] It isn't a very pleasant alternative, is it? [*She pauses again.*] Of course—some girls *do marry.*

LAURA *twists her hands nervously.*

Haven't you ever liked some boy?

LAURA   Yes. I liked one once. [*She rises.*] I came across his picture a while ago.

AMANDA   [*with some interest*]   He gave you his picture?

LAURA   No, it's in the yearbook.

AMANDA   [*disappointed*]   Oh—a high school boy.

Screen image: JIM *as the high school hero bearing a silver cup.*

LAURA   Yes. His name was Jim. [*She lifts the heavy annual from the claw-foot table.*] Here he is in *The Pirates of Penzance.*[5]

AMANDA   [*absently*]   The what?

5. An operetta (1879) by William S. Gilbert and Arthur Sullivan.

LAURA   The operetta the senior class put on. He had a wonderful voice and we sat across the aisle from each other Mondays, Wednesdays and Fridays in the Aud. Here he is with the silver cup for debating! See his grin?

AMANDA [*absently*]   He must have had a jolly disposition.

LAURA   He used to call me—Blue Roses.

Screen image: Blue roses.

AMANDA   Why did he call you such a name as that?

LAURA   When I had that attack of pleurosis—he asked me what was the matter when I came back. I said pleurosis—he thought that I said Blue Roses! So that's what he always called me after that. Whenever he saw me, he'd holler, "Hello, Blue Roses!" I didn't care for the girl that he went out with. Emily Meisenbach. Emily was the best-dressed girl at Soldan. She never struck me, though, as being sincere . . . It says in the Personal Section—they're engaged. That's—six years ago! They must be married by now.

AMANDA   Girls that aren't cut out for business careers usually wind up married to some nice man. [*She gets up with a spark of revival.*] Sister, that's what you'll do!

LAURA *utters a startled, doubtful laugh. She reaches quickly for a piece of glass.*

LAURA   But, Mother—

AMANDA   Yes? [*She goes over to the photograph.*]

LAURA [*in a tone of frightened apology*]   I'm—crippled!

AMANDA   Nonsense! Laura, I've told you never, never to use that word. Why, you're not crippled, you just have a little defect—hardly noticeable, even! When people have some slight disadvantage like that, they cultivate other things to make up for it—develop charm—and vivacity—and—*charm!* That's all you have to do! [*She turns again to the photograph.*] One thing your father had plenty of—was *charm!*

The scene fades out with music.

Scene 3

Legend on screen: "After the fiasco—"

TOM *speaks from the fire escape landing.*

TOM   After the fiasco at Rubicam's Business College, the idea of getting a gentleman caller for Laura began to play a more and more important part in Mother's calculations. It became an obsession. Like some archetype of the universal unconscious, the image of the gentleman caller haunted our small apartment. . . .

Screen image: A young man at the door of a house with flowers.

An evening at home rarely passed without some allusion to this image, this specter, this hope. . . . Even when he wasn't mentioned, his presence hung in Mother's preoccupied look and in my sister's frightened, apologetic manner—hung like a sentence passed upon the Wingfields!

Mother was a woman of action as well as words. She began to take logical steps in the planned direction. Late that winter and in the early spring—realizing that extra money would be needed to properly feather the nest and plume the bird—she conducted a vigorous campaign on the telephone, roping in subscribers to one of those magazines for matrons called *The Homemaker's Companion,* the type of journal that features the serialized sublimations of ladies of letters who think in terms of delicate cuplike breasts, slim, tapering waists, rich, creamy thighs, eyes like wood smoke in autumn, fingers that soothe and caress like strains of music, bodies as powerful as Etruscan sculpture.

Screen image: The cover of a glamor magazine.

AMANDA *enters with the telephone on a long extension cord. She is spotlighted in the dim stage.*

AMANDA   Ida Scott? This is Amanda Wingfield! We *missed* you at the D.A.R. last Monday! I said to myself: She's probably suffering with that sinus condition! How is that sinus condition?

Horrors! Heaven have mercy!—You're a Christian martyr, yes, that's what you are, a Christian martyr!

Well, I just now happened to notice that your subscription to the *Companion's* about to expire! Yes, it expires with the next issue, honey!—just when that wonderful new serial by Bessie Mae Hopper is getting off to such an exciting start. Oh, honey, it's something that you can't miss! You remember how *Gone with the Wind* [6] took everybody by storm? You simply couldn't go out if you hadn't read it. All everybody *talked* was Scarlett O'Hara. Well, this is a book that critics already compare to *Gone with the Wind.* It's the *Gone with the Wind* of the post-World-War generation!—What?— Burning?—Oh, honey, don't let them burn, go take a look in the oven and I'll hold the wire! Heavens—I think she's hung up!

The scene dims out.

Legend on screen: "You think I'm in love with Continental Shoemakers?"

Before the lights come up again, the violent voices of TOM *and*

---

6. A popular novel by Margaret Mitchell, published in 1936. Scarlett O'Hara, the heroine, is one of the most famous characters in modern fiction.

AMANDA *are heard. They are quarreling behind the portieres. In front of them stands* LAURA *with clenched hands and panicky expression. A clear pool of light is on her figure throughout this scene.*

TOM　What in Christ's name am I—
AMANDA [*shrilly*]　Don't you use that—
TOM　—supposed to do!
AMANDA　—expression! Not in my—
TOM　Ohhh!
AMANDA　—presence! Have you gone out of your senses?
TOM　I have, that's true, *driven* out!
AMANDA　What is the matter with you, you—big—big—IDIOT!
TOM　Look!—I've got *no thing*, no single thing—
AMANDA　Lower your voice!
TOM　—in my life here that I can call my OWN! Everything is—
AMANDA　Stop that shouting!
TOM　Yesterday you confiscated my books! You had the nerve to—
AMANDA　I took that horrible novel back to the library—yes! That hideous book by that insane Mr. Lawrence.[7]

> TOM *laughs wildly.*

I cannot control the output of diseased minds or people who cater to them—

> TOM *laughs still more wildly.*

BUT I WON'T ALLOW SUCH FILTH BROUGHT INTO MY HOUSE! No, no, no, no, no!
TOM　House, house! Who pays rent on it, who makes a slave of himself to—
AMANDA [*fairly screeching*]　Don't you DARE to—
TOM　No, no, *I* mustn't say things! *I've* got to just—
AMANDA　Let me tell you—
TOM　I don't want to hear any more!

> *He tears the portieres open. The dining-room area is lit with turgid smoky red glow. Now we see* AMANDA; *her hair is in metal curlers and she is wearing a very old bathrobe, much too large for her slight figure, a relic of the faithless Mr. Wingfield. The upright typewriter now stands on the drop-leaf table, along with a wild disarray of manuscripts. The quarrel was probably precipitated by* AMANDA's *interruption of* TOM's *creative labor. A chair lies overthrown on the floor. Their gesticulating shadows are cast on the ceiling by the fiery glow.*

7. D(avid) H(erbert) Lawrence (1885–1930), English writer, most popularly known as an advocate of healthy sexuality as an important part of human life.

AMANDA   You *will* hear more, you—
TOM   No, I won't hear more, I'm going out!
AMANDA   You come right back in—
TOM   Out, out, out! Because I'm—
AMANDA   Come back here, Tom Wingfield! I'm not through talking to you!
TOM   Oh, go—
LAURA [*desperately*]   —Tom!
AMANDA   You're going to listen, and no more insolence from you! I'm at the end of my patience!

He comes back toward her.

TOM   What do you think I'm at? Aren't I supposed to have any patience to reach the end of, Mother? I know, I know. It seems unimportant to you, what I'm *doing*—what I *want* to do—having a little *difference* between them! You don't think that—
AMANDA   I think you've been doing things that you're ashamed of. That's why you act like this. I don't believe that you go every night to the movies. Nobody goes to the movies night after night. Nobody in their right minds goes to the movies as often as you pretend to. People don't go to the movies at nearly midnight, and movies don't let out at two A.M. Come in stumbling. Muttering to yourself like a maniac! You get three hours' sleep and then go to work. Oh, I can picture the way you're doing down there. Moping, doping, because you're in no condition.
TOM [*wildly*]   No, I'm in no condition!
AMANDA   What right have you got to jeopardize your job? Jeopardize the security of us all? How do you think we'd manage if you were—
TOM   Listen! You think I'm crazy about the *warehouse*? [*He bends fiercely toward her slight figure.*] You think I'm in love with the Continental Shoemakers? You think I want to spend fifty-five *years* down there in that—*celotex* [8] *interior!* with—*fluorescent—tubes!* Look! I'd rather somebody picked up a crowbar and battered out my brains—than go back mornings! I *go!* Every time you come in yelling that God damn "*Rise and Shine!*" "*Rise and Shine!*" I say to myself, "How *lucky dead* people are!" But I get up. I *go!* For sixty-five dollars a month I give up all that I dream of doing and being *ever!* And you say self—*self's* all I ever think of. Why, listen, if self is what I thought of, Mother, I'd be where he is—GONE! [*He points to his father's picture.*] As far as the system of transportation reaches! [*He starts past her. She grabs his arm.*] Don't grab at me, Mother!
AMANDA   Where are you going?
TOM   I'm going to the *movies!*
AMANDA   I don't believe that lie!

TOM *crouches toward her, overtowering her tiny figure. She backs away, gasping.*

8. A composition building material used for insulation and soundproofing.

TOM   I'm going to opium dens! Yes, opium dens, dens of vice and criminals' hangouts, Mother. I've joined the Hogan Gang,[9] I'm a hired assassin, I carry a tommy gun in a violin case! I run a string of cat houses in the Valley! They call me Killer, Killer Wingfield, I'm leading a double-life, a simple, honest warehouse worker by day, by night a dynamic *czar* of the *underworld, Mother.* I go to gambling casinos, I spin away fortunes on the roulette table! I wear a patch over one eye and a false mustache, sometimes I put on green whiskers. On those occasions they call me—*El Diablo!* Oh, I could tell you many things to make you sleepless! My enemies plan to dynamite this place. They're going to blow us all sky-high some night! I'll be glad, very happy, and so will you! You'll go up, up on a broomstick, over Blue Mountain with seventeen gentlemen callers! You ugly—babbling old—*witch.* . . .

> *He goes through a series of violent, clumsy movements, seizing his overcoat, lunging to the door, pulling it fiercely open. The women watch him, aghast. His arm catches in the sleeve of the coat as he struggles to pull it on. For a moment he is pinioned by the bulky garment. With an outraged groan he tears the coat off again, splitting the shoulder of it, and hurls it across the room. It strikes against the shelf of* LAURA's *glass collection, and there is a tinkle of shattering glass.* LAURA *cries out as if wounded.*

> *Music.*

> *Screen legend: "The Glass Menagerie."*

LAURA [*shrilly*]   My glass!—menagerie. . . . [*She covers her face and turns away.*]

> *But* AMANDA *is still stunned and stupefied by the "ugly witch" so that she barely notices this occurrence. Now she recovers her speech.*

AMANDA [*in an awful voice*]   I won't speak to you—until you apologize!

> *She crosses through the portieres and draws them together behind her.* TOM *is left with* LAURA. LAURA *clings weakly to the mantel with her face averted.* TOM *stares at her stupidly for a moment. Then he crosses to the shelf. He drops awkwardly on his knees to collect the fallen glass, glancing at* LAURA *as if he would speak but couldn't.*

> *"The Glass Menagerie" music steals in as the scene dims out.*

---

9. One of five major criminal organizations in St. Louis at the time of the play.

Scene 4

The interior of the apartment is dark. There is a faint light in the alley. A deep-voiced bell in a church is tolling the hour of five.

TOM *appears at the top of the alley. After each solemn boom of the bell in the tower, he shakes a little noisemaker or rattle as if to express the tiny spasm of man in contrast to the sustained power and dignity of the Almighty. This and the unsteadiness of his advance make it evident that he has been drinking. As he climbs the few steps to the fire escape landing light steals up inside.* LAURA *appears in the front room in a nightdress. She notices that* TOM's *bed is empty.* TOM *fishes in his pockets for his door key, removing a motley assortment of articles in the search, including a shower of movie ticket stubs and an empty bottle. At last he finds the key, but just as he is about to insert it, it slips from his fingers. He strikes a match and crouches below the door.*

TOM [*bitterly*]   One crack—and it falls through!

LAURA *opens the door.*

LAURA   Tom! Tom, what are you doing?
TOM   Looking for a door key.
LAURA   Where have you been all this time?
TOM   I have been to the movies.
LAURA   All this time at the movies?
TOM   There was a very long program. There was a Garbo[1] picture and a Mickey Mouse and a travelogue and a newsreel and a preview of coming attractions. And there was an organ solo and a collection for the Milk Fund—simultaneously—which ended up in a terrible fight between a fat lady and an usher!
LAURA [*innocently*]   Did you have to stay through everything?
TOM   Of course! And, oh, I forgot! There was a big stage show! The headliner on this stage show was Malvolio the Magician. He performed wonderful tricks, many of them, such as pouring water back and forth between pitchers. First it turned to wine and then it turned to beer and then it turned to whisky. I know it was whisky it finally turned into because he needed somebody to come up out of the audience to help him, and I came up—both shows! It was Kentucky Straight Bourbon. A very generous fellow, he gave souvenirs. [*He pulls from his back pocket a shimmering rainbow-colored scarf.*] He gave me this. This is his magic scarf. You can have it, Laura. You wave it over a canary cage and you get a bowl of goldfish. You wave it over the goldfish bowl and they fly away canaries. . . . But the wonderfullest trick of all was the coffin trick. We nailed him into a coffin and he got out of the coffin

1. Greta Garbo (b. 1905), a Swedish star of both silent films and early sound films, known for her beauty and air of mystery.

without removing one nail. [*He has come inside.*] There is a trick that would come in handy for me—get me out of this two-by-four situation! [*He flops onto the bed and starts removing his shoes.*]

LAURA   Tom—shhh!

TOM   What're you shushing me for?

LAURA   You'll wake up Mother.

TOM   Goody, goody! Pay 'er back for all those "Rise an' Shines." [*He lies down, groaning.*] You know it don't take much intelligence to get yourself into a nailed-up coffin, Laura. But who in hell ever got himself out of one without removing one nail?

> *As if in answer, the father's grinning photograph lights up. The scene dims out.*

> *Immediately following, the church bell is heard striking six. At the sixth stroke the alarm clock goes off in* AMANDA's *room, and after a few moments we hear her calling: "Rise and Shine! Rise and Shine! Laura, go tell your brother to rise and shine!"*

TOM [*sitting up slowly*]   I'll rise—but I won't shine.

> *The light increases.*

AMANDA   Laura, tell your brother his coffee is ready.

> LAURA *slips into the front room.*

LAURA   Tom!—It's nearly seven. Don't make Mother nervous.

> *He stares at her stupidly.*

[*Beseechingly.*] Tom, speak to Mother this morning. Make up with her, apologize, speak to her!

TOM   She won't to me. It's her that started not speaking.

LAURA   If you just say you're sorry she'll start speaking.

TOM   Her not speaking—is that such a tragedy?

LAURA   Please—please!

AMANDA [*calling from the kitchenette*]   Laura, are you going to do what I asked you to do, or do I have to get dressed and go out myself?

LAURA   Going, going—soon as I get on my coat!

> *She pulls on a shapeless felt hat with a nervous, jerky movement, pleadingly glancing at* TOM. *She rushes awkwardly for her coat. The coat is one of* AMANDA's, *inaccurately made-over, the sleeves too short for* LAURA.

Butter and what else?

AMANDA [*entering from the kitchenette*]   Just butter. Tell them to charge it.

LAURA   Mother, they make such faces when I do that.

AMANDA   Sticks and stones can break our bones, but the expression on Mr. Garfinkel's face won't harm us! Tell your brother his coffee is getting cold.

LAURA [*at the door*]   Do what I asked you, will you, will you, Tom?

He looks sullenly away.

AMANDA   Laura, go now or just don't go at all!

LAURA [*rushing out*]   Going —going!

A second later she cries out. TOM *springs up and crosses to the door.* TOM *opens the door.*

TOM   Laura?

LAURA   I'm all right. I slipped, but I'm all right.

AMANDA [*peering anxiously after her*]   If anyone breaks a leg on those fire-escape steps, the landlord ought to be sued for every cent he possesses! [*She shuts the door. Now she remembers she isn't speaking to* TOM *and returns to the other room.*]

As TOM *comes listlessly for his coffee, she turns her back to him and stands rigidly facing the window on the gloomy gray vault of the areaway. Its light on her face with its aged but childish features is cruelly sharp, satirical as a Daumier print.*[2]

The music of "Ave Maria," is heard softly.

TOM *glances sheepishly but sullenly at her averted figure and slumps at the table. The coffee is scalding hot; he sips it and gasps and spits it back in the cup. At his gasp,* AMANDA *catches her breath and half turns. Then she catches herself and turns back to the window.* TOM *blows on his coffee, glancing sidewise at his mother. She clears her throat.* TOM *clears his. He starts to rise, sinks back down again, scratches his head, clears his throat again.* AMANDA *coughs.* TOM *raises his cup in both hands to blow on it, his eyes staring over the rim of it at his mother for several moments. Then he slowly sets the cup down and awkwardly and hesitantly rises from the chair.*

TOM [*hoarsely*]   Mother. I—I apologize, Mother.

AMANDA *draws a quick, shuddering breath. Her face works grotesquely. She breaks into childlike tears.*

---

2. Honoré Daumier (1808–1879), a French painter and caricaturist, known for the realism and satire of his work.

I'm sorry for what I said, for everything that I said, I didn't mean it.

AMANDA [*sobbingly*]   My devotion has made me a witch and so I make myself hateful to my children!

TOM   *No,* you *don't.*

AMANDA   I worry so much, don't sleep, it makes me nervous!

TOM [*gently*]   I understand that.

AMANDA   I've had to put up a solitary battle all these years. But you're my right-hand bower![3] Don't fall down, don't fail!

TOM [*gently*]   I try, Mother.

AMANDA [*with great enthusiasm*]   Try and you will *succeed!* [*The notion makes her breathless.*] Why, you—you're just *full* of natural endowments! Both of my children—they're *unusual* children! Don't you think I know it? I'm so—*proud!* Happy and—feel I've—so much to be thankful for but—promise me one thing, son!

TOM   What, Mother?

AMANDA   Promise, son, you'll—never be a drunkard!

TOM [*turns to her grinning*]   I will never be a drunkard, Mother.

AMANDA   That's what frightened me so, that you'd be drinking! Eat a bowl of Purina!

TOM   Just coffee, Mother.

AMANDA   Shredded wheat biscuit?

TOM   No. No, Mother, just coffee.

AMANDA   You can't put in a day's work on an empty stomach. You've got ten minutes—don't gulp! Drinking too-hot liquids makes cancer of the stomach. . . . Put cream in.

TOM   No, thank you.

AMANDA   To cool it.

TOM   No! No, thank you, I want it black.

AMANDA   I know, but it's not good for you. We have to do all that we can to build ourselves up. In these trying times we live in, all that we have to cling to is—each other. . . . That's why it's so important to—Tom, I—I sent out your sister so I could discuss something with you. If you hadn't spoken I would have spoken to you. [*She sits down.*]

TOM [*gently*]   What is it, Mother, that you want to discuss?

AMANDA   *Laura!*

TOM *puts his cup down slowly.*

Legend on screen: "Laura." Music: "The Glass Menagerie."

TOM   —Oh.—Laura . . .

AMANDA [*touching his sleeve*]   You know how Laura is. So quiet but—still water runs deep! She notices things and I think she—broods about them.

TOM *looks up.*

3. An anchor carried at the bow of a ship.

A few days ago I came in and she was crying.

TOM   What about?

AMANDA   You.

TOM   Me?

AMANDA   She has an idea that you're not happy here.

TOM   What gave her that idea?

AMANDA   What gives her any idea? However, you do act strangely.
  I—I'm not criticizing, understand *that!* I know your ambitions do
  not lie in the warehouse, that like everybody in the whole wide
  world—you've had to—make sacrifices, but—Tom—Tom—life's not
  easy, it calls for—Spartan endurance! There's so many things in
  my heart that I cannot describe to you! I've never told you but I—
  loved your father. . . .

TOM [*gently*]   I know that, Mother.

AMANDA   And you—when I see you taking after his ways! Staying
  out late—and—well, you *had* been drinking the night you were in
  that—terrifying condition! Laura says that you hate the apartment
  and that you go out nights to get away from it! Is that true, Tom?

TOM   No. You say there's so much in your heart that you can't describe to me. That's true of me, too. There's so much in my heart
  that I can't describe to *you!* So let's respect each other's—

AMANDA   But, why—*why,* Tom—are you always so *restless?* Where
  do you *go* to, nights?

TOM   I—go to the movies.

AMANDA   Why do you go to the movies so much, Tom?

TOM   I go to the movies because—I like adventure. Adventure is
  something I don't have much of at work, so I go to the movies.

AMANDA   But, Tom, you go to the movies *entirely* too *much!*

TOM   I like a lot of adventure.

> AMANDA *looks baffled, then hurt. As the familiar inquisition
> resumes,* TOM *becomes hard and impatient again.* AMANDA
> slips back into her querulous attitude toward him.*

> *Image on screen: A sailing vessel with Jolly Roger.*[4]

AMANDA   Most young men find adventure in their careers.

TOM   Then most young men are not employed in a warehouse.

AMANDA   The world is full of young men employed in warehouses
  and offices and factories.

TOM   Do all of them find adventure in their careers?

AMANDA   They do or they do without it! Not everybody has a craze
  for adventure.

TOM   Man is by instinct a lover, a hunter, a fighter, and none of those
  instincts are given much play at the warehouse!

AMANDA   Man is by instinct! Don't quote instinct to me! Instinct is

---

4. A black flag, bearing a white skull and crossbones, traditionally associated with
pirate ships.

something that people have got away from! It belongs to animals!
Christian adults don't want it!

TOM   What do Christian adults want, then, Mother?

AMANDA   Superior things! Things of the mind and the spirit! Only
animals have to satisfy instincts! Surely your aims are somewhat
higher than theirs! Than monkeys—pigs—

TOM   I reckon they're not.

AMANDA   You're joking. However, that isn't what I wanted to discuss.

TOM [*rising*]   I haven't much time.

AMANDA [*pushing his shoulders*]   Sit down.

TOM   You want me to punch in red[5] at the warehouse, Mother?

AMANDA   You have five minutes. I want to talk about Laura.

Screen legend: "Plans and Provisions."

TOM   All right! What about Laura?

AMANDA   We have to be making some plans and provisions for her.
She's older than you, two years, and nothing has happened. She just
drifts along doing nothing. It frightens me terribly how she just
drifts along.

TOM   I guess she's the type that people call home girls.

AMANDA   There's no such type, and if there is, it's a pity! That is
unless the home is hers, with a husband!

TOM   What?

AMANDA   Oh, I can see the handwriting on the wall as plain as I
see the nose in front of my face! It's terrifying! More and more you
remind me of your father! He was out all hours without explanation!
—Then *left! Goodbye!* And me with the bag to hold. I saw that
letter you got from the Merchant Marine. I know what you're dreaming of. I'm not standing here blindfolded. [*She pauses.*] Very well,
then. Then *do* it! But not till there's somebody to take your place.

TOM   What do you mean?

AMANDA   I mean that as soon as Laura has got somebody to take care
of her, married, a home of her own, independent—why, then you'll
be free to go wherever you please, on land, on sea, whichever
way the wind blows you! But until that time you've got to look
out for your sister. I don't say me because I'm old and don't matter!
I say for your sister because she's young and dependent.

I put her in business college—a dismal failure! Frightened her so
it made her sick at the stomach. I took her over to the Young
People's League at the church. Another fiasco. She spoke to nobody, nobody spoke to her. Now all she does is fool with those
pieces of glass and play those worn-out records. What kind of a
life is that for a girl to lead?

TOM   What can I do about it?

AMANDA   Overcome selfishness! Self, self, self is all that you ever
think of!

5. Record a late arrival on the timeclock at work.

TOM *springs up and crosses to get his coat. It is ugly and bulky. He pulls on a cap with earmuffs.*

Where is your muffler? Put your wool muffler on!

He snatches it angrily from the closet, tosses it around his neck and pulls both ends tight.

Tom! I haven't said what I had in mind to ask you.
TOM   I'm too late to—
AMANDA   [*catching his arm—very importunately; then shyly*]   Down at the warehouse, aren't there some—nice young men?
TOM   No!
AMANDA   There *must* be—*some* . . .
TOM   Mother— [*He gestures.*]
AMANDA   Find out one that's clean-living—doesn't drink and ask him out for sister!
TOM   What?
AMANDA   For *sister!* To *meet!* Get *acquainted!*
TOM   [*stamping to the door*]   Oh, my go-osh!
AMANDA   Will you? [*He opens the door. She says, imploringly:*] Will you?

He starts down the fire escape.

Will you? *Will* you, dear?
TOM   [*calling back*]   Yes!

AMANDA *closes the door hesitantly and with a troubled but faintly hopeful expression.*

Screen image: The cover of a glamor magazine.

The spotlight picks up AMANDA *at the phone.*

AMANDA   Ella Cartwright? This is Amanda Wingfield! How are you honey? How is that kidney condition?

There is a five-second pause.

Horrors!

There is another pause.

You're a Christian martyr, yes, honey, that's what you are, a Christian martyr! Well, I just now happened to notice in my little red book that your subscription to the *Companion* has just run out! I knew that you wouldn't want to miss out on the wonderful serial starting in this new issue. It's by Bessie Mae Hopper, the first thing she's written since *Honeymoon for Three.* Wasn't that a strange and interesting story? Well, this one is even lovelier, I believe. It has a sophisticated, society background. It's all about the horsey set on Long Island!

The light fades out.

Scene 5

Legend on the screen: "Annunciation."

Music is heard as the light slowly comes on.
It is early dusk of a spring evening. Supper has just been finished in the Wingfield apartment. AMANDA *and* LAURA, *in light-colored dresses, are removing dishes from the table in the dining room, which is shadowy, their movements formalized almost as a dance or ritual, their moving forms as pale and silent as moths.* TOM, *in white shirt and trousers, rises from the table and crosses toward the fire escape.*

AMANDA [*as he passes her*]   Son, will you do me a favor?
TOM   What?
AMANDA   Comb your hair! You look so pretty when your hair is combed!

> TOM *slouches on the sofa with the evening paper. Its enormous headline reads: "Franco Triumphs."*[6]

There is only one respect in which I would like you to emulate your father.
TOM   What respect is that?
AMANDA   The care he always took of his appearance. He never allowed himself to look untidy.

He throws down the paper and crosses to the fire escape.

Where are you going?
TOM   I'm going out to smoke.
AMANDA   You smoke too much. A pack a day at fifteen cents a pack. How much would that amount to in a month? Thirty times fifteen is how much, Tom? Figure it out and you will be astounded at what you could save. Enough to give you a night-school course in accounting at Washington U.! Just think what a wonderful thing that would be for you, son!

> TOM *is unmoved by the thought.*

6. Francisco Franco (1892–1975), ruler of Spain from the end of the Civil War until his death, led the victorious Falan- gist (rightist) forces in the Spanish Civil War, 1937–39. The headline refers to one of his victories in that war.

TOM   I'd rather smoke. [*He steps out on the landing, letting the screen door slam.*]

AMANDA [*sharply*]   I know! That's the tragedy of it. . . . [*Alone, she turns to look at her husband's picture.*]

Dance music: "The World Is Waiting for the Sunrise!"[7]

TOM [*to the audience*]   Across the alley from us was the Paradise Dance Hall. On evenings in spring the windows and doors were open and the music came outdoors. Sometimes the lights were turned out except for a large glass sphere that hung from the ceiling. It would turn slowly about and filter the dusk with delicate rainbow colors. Then the orchestra played a waltz or a tango, something that had a slow and sensuous rhythm. Couples would come outside, to the relative privacy of the alley. You could see them kissing behind ash pits and telephone poles. This was the compensation for lives that passed like mine, without any change or adventure. Adventure and change were imminent in this year. They were waiting around the corner for all these kids. Suspended in the mist over Berchtesgaden,[8] caught in the folds of Chamberlain's umbrella. In Spain there was Guernica! But here there was only hot swing music and liquor, dance halls, bars, and movies, and sex that hung in the gloom like a chandelier and flooded the world with brief, deceptive rainbows. . . . All the world was waiting for bombardments!

AMANDA *turns from the picture and comes outside.*

AMANDA [*sighing*]   A fire escape landing's a poor excuse for a porch. [*She spreads a newspaper on a step and sits down, gracefully and demurely as if she were settling into a swing on a Mississippi veranda.*] What are you looking at?

TOM   The moon.

AMANDA   Is there a moon this evening?

TOM   It's rising over Garfinkel's Delicatessen.

AMANDA   So it is! A little silver slipper of a moon. Have you made a wish on it yet?

TOM   Um-hum.

AMANDA   What did you wish for?

TOM   That's a secret.

AMANDA   A secret, huh? Well, I won't tell mine either. I will be just as mysterious as you.

TOM   I bet I can guess what yours is.

AMANDA   Is my head so transparent?

TOM   You're not a sphinx.

AMANDA   No, I don't have secrets. I'll tell you what I wished for on the moon. Success and happiness for my precious children! I wish

---

7. A popular song of 1919, words by Eugene Lockhart, music by Ernest Seitz.

8. Berchtesgaden is a Bavarian resort, best known as the summer retreat of Adolf Hitler. Neville Chamberlain (1869–1940) was the British prime minister 1937–40. After a famous conference with Hitler at Munich in 1938, he proclaimed there would be "peace in our time." His name became a symbol of appeasement.

for that whenever there's a moon, and when there isn't a moon, I wish for it, too.

TOM   I thought perhaps you wished for a gentleman caller.

AMANDA   Why do you say that?

TOM   Don't you remember asking me to fetch one?

AMANDA   I remember suggesting that it would be nice for your sister if you brought home some nice young man from the warehouse. I think that I've made that suggestion more than once.

TOM   Yes, you have made it repeatedly.

AMANDA   Well?

TOM   We are going to have one.

AMANDA   *What?*

TOM   A gentleman caller!

The annunciation is celebrated with music.

AMANDA *rises.*

Image on screen: A caller with a bouquet.

AMANDA   You mean you have asked some nice young man to come over?

TOM   Yep. I've asked him to dinner.

AMANDA   You really did?

TOM   I did!

AMANDA   You did, and did he—*accept?*

TOM   He did!

AMANDA   Well, well—well, well! That's—lovely!

TOM   I thought that you would be pleased.

AMANDA   It's definite then?

TOM   Very definite.

AMANDA   Soon?

TOM   Very soon.

AMANDA   For heaven's sake, stop putting on and tell me some things, will you?

TOM   What things do you want me to tell you?

AMANDA   *Naturally* I would like to know when he's *coming!*

TOM   He's coming tomorrow.

AMANDA   *Tomorrow?*

TOM   Yep. Tomorrow.

AMANDA   But, Tom!

TOM   Yes, Mother?

AMANDA   Tomorrow gives me no time!

TOM   Time for what?

AMANDA   Preparations! Why didn't you phone me at once, as soon as you asked him, the minute that he accepted? Then, don't you see, I could have been getting ready!

TOM   You don't have to make any fuss.

AMANDA   Oh, Tom, Tom, Tom, of course I have to make a fuss! I want things nice, not sloppy! Not thrown together. I'll certainly have to do some fast thinking, won't I?

TOM   I don't see why you have to think at all.

AMANDA   You just don't know. We can't have a gentleman caller in a pigsty! All my wedding silver has to be polished, the monogrammed table linen ought to be laundered! The windows have to be washed and fresh curtains put up. And how about clothes? We have to *wear* something, don't we?

TOM   Mother, this boy is no one to make a fuss over!

AMANDA   Do you realize he's the first young man we've introduced to your sister? It's terrible, dreadful, disgraceful that poor little sister has never received a single gentleman caller! Tom, come inside! [*She opens the screen door.*]

TOM   What for?

AMANDA   I want to ask you some things.

TOM   If you're going to make such a fuss, I'll call it off, I'll tell him not to come!

AMANDA   You certainly won't do anything of the kind. Nothing offends people worse than broken engagements. It simply means I'll have to work like a Turk! We won't be brilliant, but we will pass inspection. Come on inside.

  TOM *follows her inside, groaning.*

Sit down.

TOM   Any particular place you would like me to sit?

AMANDA   Thank heavens I've got that new sofa! I'm also making payments on a floor lamp I'll have sent out! And put the chintz covers on, they'll brighten things up! Of course I'd hoped to have these walls re-papered. . . . What is the young man's name?

TOM   His name is O'Connor.

AMANDA   That, of course, means fish[9]—tomorrow is Friday! I'll have that salmon loaf—with Durkee's dressing! What does he do? He works at the warehouse?

TOM   Of course! How else would I—

AMANDA   Tom, he—doesn't drink?

TOM   Why do you ask me that?

AMANDA   Your father *did!*

TOM   Don't get started on that!

AMANDA   He *does* drink, then?

TOM   Not that I know of!

AMANDA   Make sure, be certain! The last thing I want for my daughter's a boy who drinks!

TOM   Aren't you being a little bit premature? Mr. O'Connor has not yet appeared on the scene!

AMANDA   But will tomorrow. To meet your sister, and what do I know about his character? Nothing! Old maids are better off than wives of drunkards!

TOM   Oh, my God!

AMANDA   Be still!

TOM [*leaning forward to whisper*]   Lots of fellows meet girls whom they don't marry!

9. At the time of the play Roman Catholics were required to abstain from meat on Fridays. Main dishes using seafood or fish were often served on Fridays.

AMANDA   Oh, talk sensibly, Tom—and don't be sarcastic! [*She has gotten a hairbrush.*]

TOM   What are you doing?

AMANDA   I'm brushing that cowlick down! [*She attacks his hair with the brush.*] What is this young man's position at the warehouse?

TOM   [*submitting grimly to the brush and the interrogation*] This young man's position is that of a shipping clerk, Mother.

AMANDA   Sounds to me like a fairly responsible job, the sort of a job *you* would be in if you just had more *get-up*. What is his salary? Have you any idea?

TOM   I would judge it to be approximately eighty-five dollars a month.

AMANDA   Well—not princely, but—

TOM   Twenty more than I make.

AMANDA   Yes, how well I know! But for a family man, eighty-five dollars a month is not much more than you can just get by on. . . .

TOM   Yes, but Mr. O'Connor is not a family man.

AMANDA   He might be, mightn't he? Some time in the future?

TOM   I see. Plans and provisions.

AMANDA   You are the only young man that I know of who ignores the fact that the future becomes the present, the present the past, and the past turns into everlasting regret if you don't plan for it!

TOM   I will think that over and see what I can make of it.

AMANDA   Don't be supercilious with your mother! Tell me some more about this—what do you call him?

TOM   James D. O'Connor. The D. is for Delaney.

AMANDA   Irish on *both* sides! *Gracious!* And he doesn't drink?

TOM   Shall I call him up and ask him right this minute?

AMANDA   The only way to find out about those things is to make discreet inquiries at the proper moment. When I was a girl in Blue Mountain and it was suspected that a young man drank, the girl whose attentions he had been receiving, if any girl *was*, would sometimes speak to the minister of his church, or rather her father would if her father was living, and sort of feel him out on the young man's character. That is the way such things are discreetly handled to keep a young woman from making a tragic mistake!

TOM   Then how did you happen to make a tragic mistake?

AMANDA   That innocent look of your father's had everyone fooled! He *smiled*—the world was *enchanted!* No girl can do worse than put herself at the mercy of a handsome appearance! I hope that Mr. O'Connor is not too good-looking.

TOM   No, he's not too good-looking. He's covered with freckles and hasn't too much of a nose.

AMANDA   He's not right-down homely, though?

TOM   Not right-down homely. Just medium homely, I'd say.

AMANDA   Character's what to look for in a man.

TOM   That's what I've always said, Mother.

AMANDA   You've never said anything of the kind and I suspect you would never give it a thought.

TOM   Don't be so suspicious of me.

AMANDA   At least I hope he's the type that's up and coming.

TOM   I think he really goes in for self-improvement.

AMANDA   What reason have you to think so?

TOM   He goes to night school.

AMANDA [*beaming*]   Splendid! What does he do, I mean study?

TOM   Radio engineering and public speaking!

AMANDA   Then he has visions of being advanced in the world! Any young man who studies public speaking is aiming to have an executive job some day! And radio engineering? A thing for the future! Both of these facts are very illuminating. Those are the sort of things that a mother should know concerning any young man who comes to call on her daughter. Seriously or—not.

TOM   One little warning. He doesn't know about Laura. I didn't let on that we had dark ulterior motives. I just said, why don't you come and have dinner with us? He said okay and that was the whole conversation.

AMANDA   I bet it was! You're eloquent as an oyster. However, he'll know about Laura when he gets here. When he sees how lovely and sweet and pretty she is, he'll thank his lucky stars he was asked to dinner.

TOM   Mother, you mustn't expect too much of Laura.

AMANDA   What do you mean?

TOM   Laura seems all those things to you and me because she's ours and we love her. We don't even notice she's crippled any more.

AMANDA   Don't say crippled! You know that I never allow that word to be used!

TOM   But face facts, Mother. She is and—that's not all—

AMANDA   What do you mean "not all"?

TOM   Laura is very different from other girls.

AMANDA   I think the difference is all to her advantage.

TOM   Not quite all—in the eyes of others—strangers—she's terribly shy and lives in a world of her own and those things make her seem a little peculiar to people outside the house.

AMANDA   Don't say peculiar.

TOM   Face the facts. She is.

The dance hall music changes to a tango that has a minor and somewhat ominous tone.

AMANDA   In what way is she peculiar—may I ask?

TOM [*gently*]   She lives in a world of her own—a world of little glass ornaments, Mother. . . .

He gets up. AMANDA *remains holding the brush, looking at him, troubled.*

She plays old phonograph records and—that's about all—[*He glances at himself in the mirror and crosses to the door.*]

AMANDA [*sharply*]   Where are you going?

TOM   I'm going to the movies. [*He goes out the screen door.*]

AMANDA   Not to the movies, every night to the movies! [*She follows quickly to the screen door.*] I don't believe you always go to the movies!

He is gone. AMANDA *looks worriedly after him for a moment. Then vitality and optimism return and she turns from the door, crossing to the portieres.*

Laura! Laura!

LAURA *answers from the kitchenette.*

LAURA   Yes, Mother.
AMANDA   Let those dishes go and come in front!

LAURA *appears with a dish towel.* AMANDA *speaks to her gaily.*

Laura, come here and make a wish on the moon!

Screen image: The Moon.

LAURA [*entering*]   Moon—moon?
AMANDA   A little silver slipper of a moon. Look over your left shoulder, Laura, and make a wish!

LAURA *looks faintly puzzled as if called out of sleep.* AMANDA *seizes her shoulders and turns her at an angle by the door.*

Now! Now, darling, *wish!*
LAURA   What shall I wish for, Mother?
AMANDA [*her voice trembling and her eyes suddenly filling with tears*]   Happiness! Good fortune!

The sound of the violin rises and the stage dims out.

Scene 6

The light comes up on the fire escape landing. Tom is leaning against the grill, smoking.
Screen image: The high school hero.

TOM   And so the following evening I brought Jim home to dinner. I had known Jim slightly in high school. In high school Jim was a hero. He had tremendous Irish good nature and vitality with the scrubbed and polished look of white chinaware. He seemed to move in a continual spotlight. He was a star in basketball, captain of the debating club, president of the senior class and the glee club and he sang the male lead in the annual light operas. He was always running or bounding, never just walking. He seemed always at the point of defeating the law of gravity. He was shooting with such velocity through his adolescence that you would logically expect him to arrive at nothing short of the White House by the time he was thirty. But Jim apparently ran into more interference after his graduation from Soldan. His speed had definitely slowed. Six years after he left high school he was holding a job that wasn't much better than mine.

Screen image: The Clerk.

He was the only one at the warehouse with whom I was on friendly terms. I was valuable to him as someone who could remember his former glory, who had seen him win basketball games and the silver cup in debating. He knew of my secret practice of retiring to a cabinet of the washroom to work on poems when business was slack in the warehouse. He called me Shakespeare. And while the other boys in the warehouse regarded me with suspicious hostility, Jim took a humorous attitude toward me. Gradually his attitude affected the others, their hostility wore off and they also began to smile at me as people smile at an oddly fashioned dog who trots across their path at some distance.

I knew that Jim and Laura had known each other at Soldan, and I had heard Laura speak admiringly of his voice. I didn't know if Jim remembered her or not. In high school Laura had been as unobtrusive as Jim had been astonishing. If he did remember Laura, it was not as my sister, for when I asked him to dinner, he grinned and said, "You know, Shakespeare, I never thought of you as having folks!"

He was about to discover that I did. . . .

Legend on screen: "The accent of a coming foot."

The light dims out on Tom *and comes up in the Wingfield living room—a delicate lemony light. It is about five on a Friday evening of late spring which comes "scattering poems in the sky."*

AMANDA *has worked like a Turk in preparation for the gentleman caller. The results are astonishing. The new floor lamp with its rose silk shade is in place, a colored paper lantern conceals the broken light fixture in the ceiling, new billowing white curtains are at the windows, chintz covers are on the chairs and sofa, a pair of new sofa pillows make their initial appearance. Open boxes and tissue paper are scattered on the floor.*

LAURA *stands in the middle of the room with lifted arms while* AMANDA *crouches before her, adjusting the hem of a new dress, devout and ritualistic. The dress is colored and designed by memory. The arrangement of* LAURA's *hair is changed; it is softer and more becoming. A fragile, unearthly prettiness has come out in* LAURA: *she is like a piece of translucent glass touched by light, given a momentary radiance, not actual, not lasting.*

AMANDA [*impatiently*]   Why are you trembling?

LAURA   Mother, you've made me so nervous!

AMANDA   How have I made you nervous?

LAURA   By all this fuss! You make it seem so important!

AMANDA   I don't understand you, Laura. You couldn't be satisfied with just sitting home, and yet whenever I try to arrange something for you, you seem to resist it. [*She gets up.*] Now take a look at yourself. No, wait! Wait just a moment—I have an idea!

LAURA   What is it now?

> AMANDA *produces two powder puffs which she wraps in hand-kerchiefs and stuffs in* LAURA's *bosom.*

LAURA   Mother, what are you doing?

AMANDA   They call them "Gay Deceivers"!

LAURA   I won't wear them!

AMANDA   You will!

LAURA   Why should I?

AMANDA   Because, to be painfully honest, your chest is flat.

LAURA   You make it seem like we were setting a trap.

AMANDA   All pretty girls are a trap, a pretty trap, and men expect them to be.

> *Legend on screen: "A pretty trap."*

Now look at yourself, young lady. This is the prettiest you will ever be! [*She stands back to admire* LAURA.] I've got to fix myself now! You're going to be surprised by your mother's appearance!

> AMANDA *crosses through the portieres, humming gaily.* LAURA *moves slowly to the long mirror and stares solemnly at herself. A wind blows the white curtains inward in a slow, graceful motion and with a faint, sorrowful sighing.*

AMANDA [*from somewhere behind the portieres*]   It isn't dark enough yet.

> LAURA *turns slowly before the mirror with a troubled look.*

> *Legend on screen: "This is my sister: Celebrate her with strings!" Music plays.*

AMANDA [*laughing, still not visible*]   I'm going to show you something. I'm going to make a spectacular appearance!

LAURA   What is it, Mother?

AMANDA   Possess your soul in patience—you will see! Something I've resurrected from that old trunk! Styles haven't changed so terribly much after all. . . . [*She parts the portieres.*] Now just look at your mother! [*She wears a girlish frock of yellowed voile with a blue silk sash. She carries a bunch of jonquils—the legend of her youth is nearly revived. Now she speaks feverishly:*] This is the dress in which I led the cotillion. Won the cakewalk twice at Sunset Hill, wore one Spring to the Governor's Ball in Jackson! See how I sashayed around the ballroom, Laura? [*She raises her skirt and does a mincing step around the room.*] I wore it on Sundays for my gentlemen callers! I had it on the day I met your father. . . . I had malaria fever all that Spring. The change of climate from East Tennessee to the Delta—weakened resistance. I had a little temperature all the time—not enough to be serious—just enough to make me restless and giddy! Invitations poured in—parties all over the Delta! "Stay in bed," said Mother, "you have a fever!"—but I just wouldn't. I took quinine[1] but kept on going, going! Evenings, dances! Afternoons, long, long rides! Picnics—lovely! So lovely, that country in May—all lacy with dogwood, literally flooded with jonquils! That was the spring I had the craze for jonquils. Jonquils became an absolute obsession. Mother said, "Honey, there's no more room for jonquils." And still I kept on bringing in more jonquils. Whenever, wherever I saw them, I'd say, "Stop! Stop! I see jonquils!" I made the young men help me gather the jonquils! It was a joke, Amanda and her jonquils. Finally there were no more vases to hold them, every available space was filled with jonquils. No vases to hold them? All right, I'll hold them myself! And then I—[*She stops in front of the picture. Music plays.*] met your father! Malaria fever and jonquils and then—this—boy. . . . [*She switches on the rose-colored lamp.*] I hope they get here before it starts to rain. [*She crosses the room and places the jonquils in a bowl on the table.*] I gave your brother a little extra change so he and Mr. O'Connor could take the service car home.

LAURA [*with an altered look*] What did you say his name was?
AMANDA   O'Connor.
LAURA   What is his first name?
AMANDA   I don't remember. Oh, yes, I do. It was—Jim!

LAURA *sways slightly and catches hold of a chair.*

Legend on screen: "Not Jim!"

LAURA [*faintly*]   Not—Jim!
AMANDA   Yes, that was it, it was Jim! I've never known a Jim that wasn't nice!

The music becomes ominous.

LAURA   Are you sure his name is Jim O'Connor?
AMANDA   Yes. Why?
LAURA   Is he the one that Tom used to know in high school?
AMANDA   He didn't say so. I think he just got to know him at the warehouse.
LAURA   There was a Jim O'Connor we both knew in high school—

1. A medicine formerly used against malaria. Later a synthetic medicine, atabrine, was developed for the same purpose.

[*Then, with effort.*] If that is the one that Tom is bringing to dinner—you'll have to excuse me, I won't come to the table.

AMANDA What sort of nonsense is this?

LAURA You asked me once if I'd ever liked a boy. Don't you remember I showed you this boy's picture?

AMANDA You mean the boy you showed me in the yearbook?

LAURA Yes, that boy.

AMANDA Laura, Laura, were you in love with that boy?

LAURA I don't know, Mother. All I know is I couldn't sit at the table if it was him!

AMANDA It won't be him! It isn't the least bit likely. But whether it is or not, you will come to the table. You will not be excused.

LAURA I'll have to be, Mother.

AMANDA I don't intend to humor your silliness, Laura. I've had too much from you and your brother, both! So just sit down and compose yourself till they come. Tom has forgotten his key so you'll have to let them in, when they arrive.

LAURA [*panicky*] Oh, Mother—*you* answer the door!

AMANDA [*lightly*] I'll be in the kitchen—busy!

LAURA Oh, Mother, please answer the door, don't make me do it!

AMANDA [*crossing into the kitchenette*] I've got to fix the dressing for the salmon. Fuss, fuss—silliness!—over a gentleman caller!

The door swings shut. LAURA *is left alone.*

Legend on screen: "Terror!"

She utters a low moan and turns off the lamp—sits stiffly on the edge of the sofa, knotting her fingers together.

Legend on screen: "The Opening of a Door!"

TOM *and* JIM *appear on the fire escape steps and climb to the landing. Hearing their approach,* LAURA *rises with a panicky gesture. She retreats to the portieres. The doorbell rings.* LAURA *catches her breath and touches her throat. Low drums sound.*

AMANDA [*calling*] Laura, sweetheart! The door!

LAURA *stares at it without moving.*

JIM I think we just beat the rain.

TOM Uh-huh. [*He rings again, nervously.* JIM *whistles and fishes for a cigarette.*]

AMANDA [*very, very gaily*] Laura, that is your brother and Mr. O'Connor! Will you let them in, darling?

LAURA *crosses toward the kitchenette door.*

LAURA [*breathlessly*] Mother—you go to the door!

AMANDA *steps out of the kitchenette and stares furiously at* LAURA. *She points imperiously at the door.*

LAURA   Please, please!

AMANDA [*in a fierce whisper*]   What is the matter with you, you silly thing?

LAURA [*desperately*]   Please, you answer it, *please!*

AMANDA   I told you I wasn't going to humor you, Laura. Why have you chosen this moment to lose your mind?

LAURA   Please, please, please, you go!

AMANDA   You'll have to go to the door because I can't!

LAURA [*despairingly*]   I can't either!

AMANDA   *Why?*

LAURA   I'm *sick!*

AMANDA   I'm sick, too—of your nonsense! Why can't you and your brother be normal people? Fantastic whims and behavior!

TOM *gives a long ring.*

Preposterous goings on! Can you give me one reason—[*She calls out lyrically.*] *Coming! Just one second!*—why you should be afraid to open a door? Now you answer it, Laura!

LAURA   Oh, oh, oh . . . [*She returns through the portiers, darts to the Victrola, winds it frantically and turns it on.*]

AMANDA   Laura Wingfield, you march right to that door!

LAURA   Yes—yes, Mother!

A faraway, scratchy rendition of "Dardanella"[2] *softens the air and gives her strength to move through it. She slips to the door and draws it cautiously open.* TOM *enters with the caller,* JIM O'CONNOR.

TOM   Laura, this is Jim. Jim, this is my sister, Laura.

JIM [*stepping inside*]   I didn't know that Shakespeare had a sister!

LAURA [*retreating, stiff and trembling, from the door*]   How—how do you do?

JIM [*heartily, extending his hand*]   Okay!

LAURA *touches it hesitantly with hers.*

JIM   Your hand's *cold*, Laura!

LAURA   Yes, well—I've been playing the Victrola. . . .

JIM   Must have been playing classical music on it! You ought to play a little hot swing music to warm you up!

LAURA   Excuse me—I haven't finished playing the Victrola. . . . [*She turns awkwardly and hurries into the front room. She pauses a second by the Victrola. Then she catches her breath and darts through the portieres like a frightened deer.*]

2. A popular songs of 1919, words by Fred Fisher, music by Felix Bernard and Johnny S. Black.

JIM [*grinning*]   What was the matter?

TOM   Oh—with Laura? Laura is—terribly shy.

JIM   Shy, huh? It's unusual to meet a shy girl nowadays. I don't believe you ever mentioned you had a sister.

TOM   Well, now you know. I have one. Here is the *Post Dispatch*. You want a piece of it?

JIM   Uh-huh.

TOM   What piece? The comics?

JIM   Sports! [*He glances at it.*] Ole Dizzy Dean[3] is on his bad behavior.

TOM [*uninterested*]   Yeah? [*He lights a cigarette and goes over to the fire-escape door.*]

JIM   Where are *you* going?

TOM   I'm going out on the terrace.

JIM [*going after him*]   You know, Shakespeare—I'm going to sell you a bill of goods!

TOM   What goods?

JIM   A course I'm taking.

TOM   Huh?

JIM   In public speaking! You and me, we're not the warehouse type.

TOM   Thanks—that's good news. But what has public speaking got to do with it?

JIM   It fits you for—executive positions!

TOM   Awww.

JIM   I tell you it's done a helluva lot for me.

Image on screen: Executive at his desk.

TOM   In what respect?

JIM   In every! Ask yourself what is the difference between you an' me and men in the office down front? Brains?—No!—Ability?—No! Then what? Just one little thing—

TOM   What is that one little thing?

JIM   Primarily it amounts to—social poise! Being able to square up to people and hold your own on any social level!

AMANDA [*from the kitchenette*]   Tom?

TOM   Yes, Mother?

AMANDA   Is that you and Mr. O'Connor?

TOM   Yes, Mother.

AMANDA   Well, you just make yourselves comfortable in there.

TOM   Yes, Mother.

AMANDA   Ask Mr. O'Connor if he would like to wash his hands.

JIM   Aw, no—no—thank you—I took care of that at the warehouse. Tom—

TOM   Yes?

JIM   Mr. Mendoza was speaking to me about you.

TOM   Favorably?

JIM   What do you think?

TOM   Well—

---

3. Jay Hanna (or Jerome Herman) Dean (1911–74) was an outstanding   pitcher for the St. Louis Cardinals, 1932–36.

JIM   You're going to be out of a job if you don't wake up.

TOM   I am waking up—

JIM   You show no signs.

TOM   The signs are interior.

Image on screen: The sailing vessel with the Jolly Roger again.

TOM   I'm planning to change. [*He leans over the fire-escape rail, speaking with quiet exhilaration. The incandescent marquees and signs of the first-run movie houses light his face from across the alley. He looks like a voyager.*] I'm right at the point of committing myself to a future that doesn't include the warehouse and Mr. Mendoza or even a night-school course in public speaking.

JIM   What are you gassing about?

TOM   I'm tired of the movies.

JIM   Movies!

TOM   Yes, movies! Look at them— [*A wave toward the marvels of Grand Avenue.*] All of those glamorous people—having adventures— hogging it all, gobbling the whole thing up! You know what happens? People go to the *movies* instead of *moving!* Hollywood characters are supposed to have all the adventures for everybody in America, while everybody in America sits in a dark room and watches them have them! Yes, until there's a war. That's when adventure becomes available to the masses! *Everyone's* dish, not only Gable's![4] Then the people in the dark room come out of the dark room to have some adventures themselves—goody, goody! It's our turn now, to go to the South Sea Island—to make a safari—to be exotic, far-off! But I'm not patient. I don't want to wait till then. I'm tired of the *movies* and I am *about* to *move!*

JIM [*incredulously*]   Move?

TOM   Yes.

JIM   When?

TOM   Soon!

JIM   Where? Where?

The music seems to answer the question, while TOM *thinks it over. He searches in his pockets.*

TOM   I'm starting to boil inside. I know I seem dreamy, but inside— well, I'm boiling! Whenever I pick up a shoe, I shudder a little thinking how short life is and what I am doing! Whatever that means, I know it doesn't mean shoes—except as something to wear on a traveler's feet! [*He finds what he has been searching for in his pockets and holds out a paper to* JIM.] Look—

JIM   What?

TOM   I'm a member.

JIM [*reading*]   The Union of Merchant Seamen.

TOM   I paid my dues this month, instead of the light bill.

---

4. Clark Gable (1901–60) was a leading romantic star of films in the 1930s, 1940s, and 1950s.

JIM You will regret it when they turn the lights off.

TOM I won't be here.

JIM How about your mother?

TOM I'm like my father. The bastard son of a bastard! Did you notice how he's grinning in his picture in there? And he's been absent going on sixteen years!

JIM You're just talking, you drip. How does your mother feel about it?

TOM Shhh! Here comes Mother! Mother is not acquainted with my plans!

AMANDA [*coming through the portieres*] Where are you all?

TOM On the terrace, Mother.

> *They start inside. She advances to them.* TOM *is distinctly shocked at her appearance. Even* JIM *blinks a little. He is making his first contact with girlish Southern vivacity and in spite of the night-school course in public speaking is somewhat thrown off the beam by the unexpected outlay of social charm. Certain responses are attempted by* JIM *but are swept aside by* AMANDA's *gay laughter and chatter.* TOM *is embarrassed but after the first shock* JIM *reacts very warmly. He grins and chuckles, is altogether won over.*
>
> *Image on screen:* AMANDA *as a girl.*

AMANDA [*coyly smiling, shaking her girlish ringlets*] Well, well, well, so this is Mr. O'Connor. Introductions entirely unnecessary. I've heard so much about you from my boy. I finally said to him, Tom— good gracious!—why don't you bring this paragon to supper? I'd like to meet this nice young man at the warehouse!—instead of just hearing him sing your praises so much! I don't know why my son is so stand-offish—that's not Southern behavior!

Let's sit down and—I think we could stand a little more air in here! Tom, leave the door open. I felt a nice fresh breeze a moment ago. Where has it gone to? Mmm, so warm already! And not quite summer, even. We're going to burn up when summer really gets started. However, we're having—we're having a very light supper. I think light things are better fo' this time of year. The same as light clothes are. Light clothes an' light food are what warm weather calls fo'. You know our blood gets so thick during th' winter—it takes a while fo' us to *adjust* ou'selves!—when the season changes . . . It's come so quick this year. I wasn't prepared. All of a sudden—heavens! Already summer! I ran to the trunk an' pulled out this light dress—terribly old! Historical almost! But feels so good—so good an' co-ol, y' know. . . .

TOM Mother—

AMANDA Yes, honey?

TOM How about—supper?

AMANDA Honey, you go ask Sister if supper is ready! You know that Sister is in full charge of supper! Tell her you hungry boys are waiting for it. [*To* JIM.] Have you met Laura?

JIM She—

AMANDA Let you in? Oh, good, you've met already! It's rare for a girl as sweet an' pretty as Laura to be domestic! But Laura is, thank heavens, not only pretty but also very domestic. I'm not at all. I never was a bit. I never could make a thing but angel-food cake. Well, in the South we had so many servants. Gone, gone, gone. All vestige of gracious living! Gone completely! I wasn't prepared for what the future brought me. All of my gentlemen callers were sons of planters and so of course I assumed that I would be married to one and raise my family on a large piece of land with plenty of servants. But man proposes—and woman accepts the proposal! To vary that old, old saying a little bit—I married no planter! I married a man who worked for the telephone company! That gallantly smiling gentleman over there! [*She points to the picture.*] A telephone man who—fell in love with long-distance! Now he travels and I don't even know where! But what am I going on for about my—tribulations? Tell me yours—I hope you don't have any! Tom?

TOM [*returning*] Yes, Mother?

AMANDA Is supper nearly ready?

TOM It looks to me like supper is on the table.

AMANDA Let me look— [*She rises prettily and looks through the portieres.*] Oh lovely! But where is Sister?

TOM Laura is not feeling well and she says that she thinks she'd better not come to the table.

AMANDA What? Nonsense! Laura? Oh, Laura!

LAURA [*from the kitchenette, faintly*] Yes, Mother.

AMANDA You really must come to the table. We won't be seated until you come to the table! Come in, Mr. O'Connor. You sit over there and I'll. . . . Laura? Laura Wingfield! You're keeping us waiting, honey! We can't say grace until you come to the table!

> The kitchenette door is pushed weakly open and LAURA comes in. She is obviously quite faint, her lips trembling, her eyes wide and staring. She moves unsteadily toward the table.
>
> Screen legend: "Terror!"
>
> Outside a summer storm is coming on abruptly. The white curtains billow inward at the windows and there is a sorrowful murmur from the deep blue dusk.
>   LAURA suddenly stumbles; she catches at a chair with a faint moan.

TOM Laura!

AMANDA Laura!

> There is a clap of thunder.
>
> Screen legend: "Ah!"

[*Despairingly.*] Why, Laura, you *are* ill, darling! Tom, help your

sister into the living room, dear! Sit in the living room, Laura—
rest on the sofa. Well! [*To* JIM *as* TOM *helps his sister to the sofa in
the living room.*] Standing over the hot stove made her ill! I told
her that it was just too warm this evening, but—

TOM *comes back to the table.*

Is Laura all right now?
TOM   Yes.
AMANDA   What *is* that? Rain? A nice cool rain has come up! [*She
gives* JIM *a frightened look.*] I think we may—have grace—now . . .
[TOM *looks at her stupidly.*] Tom, honey—you say grace!
TOM   Oh . . . "For these and all thy mercies—"

They bow their heads, AMANDA *stealing a nervous glance at*
JIM. *In the living room* LAURA, *stretched on the sofa, clenches
her hand to her lips, to hold back a shuddering sob.*

God's Holy Name be praised—

The scene dims out.

Scene 7

*It is half an hour later. Dinner is just being finished in the din-
ing room,* LAURA *is still huddled upon the sofa, her feet drawn
under her, her head resting on a pale blue pillow, her eyes wide
and mysteriously watchful. The new floor lamp with its shade of
rose-colored silk gives a soft, becoming light to her face, bringing
out the fragile, unearthly prettiness which usually escapes attention. From outside there is a steady murmur of rain, but it is
slackening and soon stops; the air outside becomes pale and
luminous as the moon breaks through the clouds. A moment after
the curtain rises, the lights in both rooms flicker and go out.*

JIM   Hey, there, Mr. Light Bulb!

AMANDA *laughs nervously.*

Legend on screen: "*Suspension of a public service.*"

AMANDA   Where was Moses when the lights went out? Ha-ha. Do
you know the answer to that one, Mr. O'Connor?
JIM   No, Ma'am, what's the answer?
AMANDA   In the dark!

JIM *laughs appreciatively.*

Everybody sit still. I'll light the candles. Isn't it lucky we have
them on the table? Where's a match? Which of you gentlemen can
provide a match?

JIM Here.

AMANDA Thank you, Sir.

JIM Not at all, Ma'am!

AMANDA [*as she lights the candles*] I guess the fuse has burnt out. Mr. O'Connor, can you tell a burnt-out fuse? I know I can't and Tom is a total loss when it comes to mechanics. [*They rise from the table and go into the kitchenette, from where their voices are heard.*] Oh, be careful you don't bump into something. We don't want our gentleman caller to break his neck. Now wouldn't that be a fine howdy-do?

JIM Ha-ha! Where is the fuse-box?

AMANDA Right here next to the stove. Can you see anything?

JIM Just a minute.

AMANDA Isn't electricity a mysterious thing? Wasn't it Benjamin Franklin who tied a key to a kite? We live in such a mysterious universe, don't we? Some people say that science clears up all the mysteries for us. In my opinion it only creates more! Have you found it yet?

JIM No, Ma'am. All these fuses look okay to me.

AMANDA Tom!

TOM Yes, Mother?

AMANDA That light bill I gave you several days ago. The one I told you we got the notices about?

> *Legend on screen: "Ha!"*

TOM Oh—yeah.

AMANDA You didn't neglect to pay it by any chance?

TOM Why, I—

AMANDA Didn't! I might have known it!

JIM Shakespeare probably wrote a poem on that light bill, Mrs. Wingfield.

AMANDA I might have known better than to trust him with it! There's such a high price for negligence in this world!

JIM Maybe the poem will win a ten-dollar prize.

AMANDA We'll just have to spend the remainder of the evening in the nineteenth century, before Mr. Edison made the Mazda lamp!

JIM Candlelight is my favorite kind of light.

AMANDA That shows you're romantic! But that's no excuse for Tom. Well, we got through dinner. Very considerate of them to let us get through dinner before they plunged us into everlasting darkness, wasn't it, Mr. O'Connor?

JIM Ha-ha!

AMANDA Tom, as a penalty for your carelessness you can help me with the dishes.

JIM Let me give you a hand.

AMANDA Indeed you will not!

JIM I ought to be good for something.

AMANDA Good for something? [*Her tone is rhapsodic.*] You? Why, Mr. O'Connor, nobody, *nobody's* given me this much entertainment in years—as you have!

JIM Aw, now, Mrs. Wingfield!

AMANDA I'm not exaggerating, not one bit! But Sister is all by her lonesome. You go keep her company in the parlor! I'll give you this lovely old candelabrum that used to be on the altar at the Church of the Heavenly Rest. It was melted a little out of shape when the church burnt down. Lightning struck it one spring. Gypsy Jones[5] was holding a revival at the time and he intimated that the church was destroyed because the Episcopalians gave card parties.

JIM Ha-ha.

AMANDA And how about you coaxing Sister to drink a little wine? I think it would be good for her! Can you carry both at once?

JIM Sure. I'm Superman!

AMANDA Now, Thomas, get into this apron!

> JIM *comes into the dining room, carrying the candelabrum, its candles lighted, in one hand and a glass of wine in the other. The door of the kitchenette swings closed on* AMANDA's *gay laughter; the flickering light approaches the portieres.* LAURA *sits up nervously as* JIM *enters. She can hardly speak from the almost intolerable strain of being alone with a stranger.*
>
> *Screen legend: "I don't suppose you remember me at all!"*
>
> *At first, before* JIM's *warmth overcomes her paralyzing shyness,* LAURA's *voice is thin and breathless, as though she had just run up a steep flight of stairs.* JIM's *attitude is gently humorous. While the incident is apparently unimportant, it is to* LAURA *the climax of her secret life.*

JIM Hello there, Laura.

LAURA [*faintly*] Hello.

> *She clears her throat.*

JIM How are you feeling now? Better?

LAURA Yes. Yes, thank you.

JIM This is for you. A little dandelion wine. [*He extends the glass toward her with extravagant gallantry.*]

LAURA Thank you.

JIM Drink it—but don't get drunk!

> *He laughs heartily.* LAURA *takes the glass uncertainly; she laughs shyly.*

Where shall I set the candles?

LAURA Oh—oh, anywhere . . .

JIM How about here on the floor? Any objections?

---

5. The name was probably suggested by the English evangelist Rodney "Gipsy" Smith (1860–1947), who toured the United States a number of times.

LAURA   No.

JIM   I'll spread a newspaper under to catch the drippings. I like to sit on the floor. Mind if I do?

LAURA   Oh, no.

JIM   Give me a pillow?

LAURA   What?

JIM   A pillow!

LAURA   Oh . . . [*She hands him one quickly.*]

JIM   How about you? Don't you like to sit on the floor?

LAURA   Oh—yes.

JIM   Why don't you, then?

LAURA   I—will.

JIM   Take a pillow!
   [LAURA *does. She sits on the floor on the other side of the candela-brum.* JIM *crosses his legs and smiles engagingly at her.*] I can't hardly see you sitting way over there.

LAURA   I can—see you.

JIM   I know, but that's not fair, I'm in the limelight.

   LAURA *moves her pillow closer.*

   Good! Now I can see you! Comfortable?

LAURA   Yes.

JIM   So am I. Comfortable as a cow! Will you have some gum?

LAURA   No, thank you.

JIM   I think that I will indulge, with your permission. [*He musingly unwraps a stick of gum and holds it up.*] Think of the fortune made by the guy that invented the first piece of chewing gum. Amazing, huh? The Wrigley Building[6] is one of the sights of Chicago—I saw it when I went up to the Century of Progress. Did you take in the Century of Progress?[7]

LAURA   No, I didn't.

JIM   Well, it was quite a wonderful exposition. What impressed me most was the Hall of Science. Gives you an idea of what the future will be in America, even more wonderful than the present time is! [*There is a pause.* JIM *smiles at her.*] Your brother tells me you're shy. Is that right, Laura?

LAURA   I—don't know.

JIM   I judge you to be an old-fashioned type of girl. Well, I think that's a pretty good type to be. Hope you don't think I'm being too personal—do you?

LAURA   [*hastily, out of embarrassment*]   I believe I *will* take a piece of gum, if you—don't mind. [*Clearing her throat.*] Mr. O'Connor, have you—kept up with your singing?

JIM   Singing? Me?

LAURA   Yes. I remember what a beautiful voice you had.

JIM   When did you hear me sing?

6. One of the earliest skyscrapers (1921–24) in the United States.
7. A world's fair held in 1933–34 to celebrate the centennial of the founding of Chicago.

LAURA *does not answer, and in the long pause which follows a man's voice is heard singing offstage.*

VOICE:
O blow, ye winds, heigh-ho,
A-roving I will go!
I'm off to my love
With a boxing glove—
Ten thousand miles away!

JIM   You say you've heard me sing?

LAURA   Oh, yes! Yes, very often . . . I—don't suppose—you remember me—at all?

JIM [*smiling doubtfully*]   You know I have an idea I've seen you before. I had that idea soon as you opened the door. It seemed almost like I was about to remember your name. But the name that I started to call you—wasn't a name! And so I stopped myself before I said it.

LAURA   Wasn't it—Blue Roses?

JIM [*springing up, grinning*]   Blue Roses! My gosh, yes—Blue Roses! That's what I had on my tongue when you opened the door! Isn't it funny what tricks your memory plays? I didn't connect you with high school somehow or other. But that's where it was; it was high school. I didn't even know you were Shakespeare's sister! Gosh, I'm sorry.

LAURA   I didn't expect you to. You—barely knew me!

JIM   But we did have a speaking acquaintance, huh?

LAURA   Yes, we—spoke to each other.

JIM   When did you recognize me?

LAURA   Oh, right away!

JIM   Soon as I came in the door?

LAURA   When I heard your name I thought it was probably you. I knew that Tom used to know you a little in high school. So when you came in the door—well, then I was—sure.

JIM   Why didn't you *say* something, then?

LAURA [*breathlessly*]   I didn't know what to say, I was—too surprised!

JIM   For goodness' sakes! You know, this sure is funny!

LAURA   Yes! Yes, isn't it, though . . .

JIM   Didn't we have a class in something together?

LAURA   Yes, we did.

JIM   What class was that?

LAURA   It was—singing—chorus!

JIM   Aw!

LAURA   I sat across the aisle from you in the Aud.

JIM   Aw.

LAURA   Mondays, Wednesdays, and Fridays.

JIM   Now I remember—you always came in late.

LAURA   Yes, it was so hard for me, getting upstairs. I had that brace on my leg—it clumped so loud!

JIM   I never heard any clumping.

LAURA [*wincing at the recollection*]   To me it sounded like—thunder!

JIM   Well, well, well, I never even noticed.

LAURA   And everybody was seated before I came in. I had to walk in front of all those people. My seat was in the back row. I had to go clumping all the way up the aisle with everyone watching!

JIM   You shouldn't have been self-conscious.

LAURA   I know, but I was. It was always such a relief when the singing started.

JIM   Aw, Yes, I've placed you now! I used to call you Blue Roses. How was it that I got started calling you that?

LAURA   I was out of school a little while with pleurosis. When I came back you asked me what was the matter. I said I had pleurosis—you thought I said *Blue Roses*. That's what you always called me after that!

JIM   I hope you didn't mind.

LAURA   Oh, no—I liked it. You see, I wasn't acquainted with many— people. . . .

JIM   As I remember you sort of stuck by yourself.

LAURA   I—I—never have had much luck at—making friends.

JIM   I don't see why you wouldn't.

LAURA   Well, I—started out badly.

JIM   You mean being—

LAURA   Yes, it sort of—stood between me—

JIM   You shouldn't have let it!

LAURA   I know, but it did, and—

JIM   You were shy with people!

LAURA   I tried not to be but never could—

JIM   Overcome it?

LAURA   No, I—I never could!

JIM   I guess being shy is something you have to work out of kind of gradually.

LAURA   [*sorrowfully*]   Yes—I guess it—

JIM   Takes time!

LAURA   Yes—

JIM   People are not so dreadful when you know them. That's what you have to remember! And everybody has problems, not just you, but practically everybody has got some problems. You think of yourself as having the only problems, as being the only one who is disappointed. But just look around you and you will see lots of people as disappointed as you are. For instance, I hoped when I was going to high school that I would be further along at this time, six years later, than I am now. You remember that wonderful write-up I had in *The Torch?*

LAURA   Yes! [*She rises and crosses to the table.*]

JIM   It said I was bound to succeed in anything I went into!

LAURA *returns with the high school yearbook.*

Holy Jeez! *The Torch!*

He accepts it reverently. They smile across the book with mutual wonder. LAURA *crouches beside him and they begin to turn the pages.* LAURA's *shyness is dissolving in his warmth.*

LAURA   Here you are in *The Pirates of Penzance!*
JIM [*wistfully*]   I sang the baritone lead in that operetta.
LAURA [*raptly*]   So—*beautifully!*
JIM [*protesting*]   Aw—
LAURA   Yes, yes—beautifully—beautifully!
JIM   You heard me?
LAURA   All three times!
JIM   No!
LAURA   Yes!
JIM   All three performances?
LAURA [*looking down*]   Yes.
JIM   Why?
LAURA   I—wanted to ask you to—autograph my program. [*She takes the program from the back of the yearbook and shows it to him.*]
JIM   Why didn't you ask me to?
LAURA   You were always surrounded by your own friends so much that I never had a chance to.
JIM   You should have just—
LAURA   Well, I—thought you might think I was—
JIM   Thought I might think you was—what?
LAURA   Oh—
JIM [*with reflective relish*]   I was beleaguered by females in those days.
LAURA   You were terribly popular!
JIM   Yeah—
LAURA   You had such a—friendly way—
JIM   I was spoiled in high school.
LAURA   Everybody—liked you!
JIM   Including you?
LAURA   I—yes, I—did, too— [*She gently closes the book in her lap.*]
JIM   Well, well, well! Give me that program, Laura.

She hands it to him. He signs it with a flourish.

There you are—better late than never!
LAURA   Oh, I—what a—surprise!
JIM   My signature isn't worth very much right now. But some day—maybe—it will increase in value! Being disappointed is one thing and being discouraged is something else. I am disappointed but I am not discouraged. I'm twenty-three years old. How old are you?
LAURA   I'll be twenty-four in June.
JIM   That's not old age!
LAURA   No, but—
JIM   You finished high school?
LAURA [*with difficulty*]   I didn't go back.
JIM   You mean you dropped out?
LAURA   I made bad grades in my final examinations. [*She rises and replaces the book and the program on the table. Her voice is strained.*] How is—Emily Meisenbach getting along?

JIM   Oh, that kraut-head!
LAURA   Why do you call her that?
JIM   That's what she was.
LAURA   You're not still—going with her?
JIM   I never see her.
LAURA   It said in the "Personal" section that you were—engaged!
JIM   I know, but I wasn't impressed by that—propaganda!
LAURA   It wasn't—the truth?
JIM   Only in Emily's optimistic opinion!
LAURA   Oh—

> Legend: "What have you done since high school?"

> JIM *lights a cigarette and leans indolently back on his elbows smiling at* LAURA *with a warmth and charm which lights her inwardly with altar candles. She remains by the table, picks up a piece from the glass menagerie collection, and turns it in her hands to cover her tumult.*

JIM *[after several reflective puffs on his cigarette]*   What have you done since high school?

> *She seems not to hear him.*

Huh?

> LAURA *looks up.*

I said what have you done since high school, Laura?
LAURA   Nothing much.
JIM   You must have been doing something these six long years.
LAURA   Yes.
JIM   Well, then, such as what?
LAURA   I took a business course at business college—
JIM   How did that work out?
LAURA   Well, not very—well—I had to drop out, it gave me—indigestion—

> JIM *laughs gently.*

JIM   What are you doing now?
LAURA   I don't do anything—much. Oh, please don't think I sit around doing nothing! My glass collection takes up a good deal of time. Glass is something you have to take good care of.
JIM   What did you say—about glass?
LAURA   Collection I said—I have one— *[She clears her throat and turns away again, acutely shy.]*
JIM *[abruptly]*   You know what I judge to be the trouble with you? Inferiority complex! Know what that is? That's what they call it when someone low-rates himself! I understand it because I had it too. Although my case was not so aggravated as yours seems to be.

I had it until I took up public speaking, developed my voice, and learned that I had an aptitude for science. Before that time I never thought of myself as being outstanding in any way whatsoever! Now I've never made a regular study of it, but I have a friend who says I can analyze people better than doctors that make a profession of it. I don't claim that to be necessarily true, but I can sure guess a person's psychology, Laura! [*He takes out his gum.*] Excuse me, Laura. I always take it out when the flavor is gone. I'll use this scrap of paper to wrap it in. I know how it is to get it stuck on a shoe. [*He wraps the gum in paper and puts it in his pocket.*] Yep—that's what I judge to be your principal trouble. A lack of confidence in yourself as a person. You don't have the proper amount of faith in yourself. I'm basing that fact on a number of your remarks and also on certain observations I've made. For instance that clumping you thought was so awful in high school. You say that you even dreaded to walk into class. You see what you did? You dropped out of school, you gave up an education because of a clump, which as far as I know was practically non-existent! A little physical defect is what you have. Hardly noticeable even! Magnified thousands of times by imagination! You know what my strong advice to you is? Think of yourself as *superior* in some way!

LAURA   In what way would I think?

JIM   Why, man alive, Laura! Just look about you a little. What do you see? A world full of common people! All of 'em born and all of 'em going to die! Which of them has one-tenth of your good points! Or mine! Or anyone else's, as far as that goes—gosh! Everybody excels in some one thing. Some in many! [*He unconsciously glances at himself in the mirror.*] All you've got to do is discover in *what!* Take me, for instance. [*He adjusts his tie at the mirror.*] My interest happens to lie in electro-dynamics. I'm taking a course in radio engineering at night school, Laura, on top of a fairly responsible job at the warehouse. I'm taking that course and studying public speaking.

LAURA   Ohhhh.

JIM   Because I believe in the future of television! [*Turning his back to her*] I wish to be ready to go up right along with it. Therefore I'm planning to get in on the ground floor. In fact I've already made the right connections and all that remains is for the industry itself to get under way! Full steam—[*His eyes are starry.*] *Knowledge* —Zzzzzp! *Money*—Zzzzzp!—Power! That's the cycle democracy is built on!

> His attitude is convincingly dynamic. LAURA *stares at him, even her shyness eclipsed in her absolute wonder. He suddenly grins.*

I guess you think I think a lot of myself!

LAURA   No—o-o-o, I—

JIM   Now how about you? Isn't there something you take more interest in than anything else?

LAURA   Well, I do—as I said—have my—glass collection—

A peal of girlish laughter rings from the kitchenette.

JIM   I'm not right sure I know what you're talking about. What kind
of glass is it?

LAURA   Little articles of it, they're ornaments mostly! Most of them
are little animals made out of glass, the tiniest little animals in the
world. Mother calls them a glass menagerie! Here's an example of
one, if you'd like to see it! This one is one of the oldest. It's nearly
thirteen.

Music: "The Glass Menagerie."

He stretches out his hand.

Oh, be careful—if you breathe, it breaks!

JIM   I'd better not take it. I'm pretty clumsy with things.

LAURA   Go, on, I trust you with him! [*She places the piece in his
palm.*] There now—you're holding him gently! Hold him over the
light, he loves the light! You see how the light shines through
him?

JIM   It sure does shine!

LAURA   I shouldn't be partial, but he is my favorite one.

JIM   What kind of a thing is this one supposed to be?

LAURA   Haven't you noticed the single horn on his forehead?

JIM   A unicorn, huh?

LAURA   Mmmm-hmmm!

JIM   Unicorns—aren't they extinct in the modern world?

LAURA   I know!

JIM   Poor little fellow, he must feel sort of lonesome.

LAURA   [*smiling*]   Well, if he does, he doesn't complain about it. He
stays on a shelf with some horses that don't have horns and all of
them seem to get along nicely together.

JIM   How do you know?

LAURA   [*lightly*]   I haven't heard any arguments among them!

JIM   [*grinning*]   No arguments, huh? Well, that's a pretty good sign!
Where shall I set him?

LAURA   Put him on the table. They all like a change of scenery once
in a while!

JIM   Well, well, well, well—[*He places the glass piece on the table,
then raises his arms and stretches.*] Look how big my shadow is
when I stretch!

LAURA   Oh, oh, yes—it stretches across the ceiling!

JIM   [*crossing to the door*]   I think it's stopped raining. [*He opens the
fire-escape door and the background music changes to a dance
tune.*] Where does the music come from?

LAURA   From the Paradise Dance Hall across the alley.

JIM   How about cutting the rug a little, Miss Wingfield?

LAURA   Oh, I—

JIM   Or is your program filled up? Let me have a look at it. [*He *grasps an imaginary card.*] Why, every dance is taken! I'll just have to scratch some out.

    Waltz music: "La Golondrina."[8]

    Ahh, a waltz! [*He executes some sweeping turns by himself, then holds his arms toward* LAURA.]

LAURA [*breathlessly*] I—can't dance!

JIM There you go, that inferiority stuff!

LAURA I've never danced in my life!

JIM Come on, try!

LAURA Oh, but I'd step on you!

JIM I'm not made out of glass.

LAURA How—how—how do we start?

JIM Just leave it to me. You hold your arms out a little.

LAURA Like this?

JIM [*taking her in his arms*] A little bit higher. Right. Now don't tighten up, that's the main thing about it— relax.

LAURA [*laughing breathlessly*] It's hard not to.

JIM Okay.

LAURA I'm afraid you can't budge me.

JIM What do you bet I can't? [*He swings her into motion.*]

LAURA Goodness, yes, you can!

JIM Let yourself go, now, Laura, just let yourself go.

LAURA I'm—

JIM Come on!

LAURA —trying!

JIM Not so stiff—easy does it!

LAURA I know but I'm—

JIM Loosen th' backbone! There now, that's a lot better.

LAURA Am I?

JIM Lets, lots better! [*He moves her about the room in a clumsy waltz.*]

LAURA Oh, my!

JIM Ha-ha!

LAURA Oh, my goodness!

JIM Ha-ha-ha!

    They suddenly bump into the table, and the glass piece on it falls to the floor. JIM *stops the dance.*

    What did we hit on?

LAURA Table.

JIM Did something fall off it? I think—

LAURA Yes.

JIM I hope that it wasn't the little glass horse with the horn!

LAURA Yes. [*She stoops to pick it up.*]

JIM Aw, aw, aw. Is it broken?

LAURA Now it is just like all the other horses.

---

8. A Mexican song, first printed in 1883, by Narciso Seradell (1843–1910).

JIM   It's lost its—

LAURA   Horn! It doesn't matter. Maybe it's a blessing in disguise.

JIM   You'll never forgive me. I bet that that was your favorite piece of glass.

LAURA   I don't have favorites much. It's no tragedy, Freckles.[9] Glass breaks so easily. No matter how careful you are. The traffic jars the shelves and things fall off them.

JIM   Still I'm awfully sorry that I was the cause.

LAURA   [*smiling*]   I'll just imagine he had an operation. The horn was removed to make him feel less—freakish!

> *They both laugh.*

Now he will feel more at home with the other horses, the ones that don't have horns. . . .

JIM   Ha-ha, that's very funny! [*Suddenly he is serious.*] I'm glad to see that you have a sense of humor. You know—you're—well—very different! Surprisingly different from anyone else I know! [*His voice becomes soft and hesitant with a genuine feeling.*] Do you mind me telling you that?

> LAURA *is abashed beyond speech.*

I mean it in a nice way—

> LAURA *nods shyly, looking away.*

You make me feel sort of—I don't know how to put it! I'm usually pretty good at expressing things, but—this is something that I don't know how to say!

> LAURA *touches her throat and clears it—turns the broken unicorn in her hands. His voice becomes softer.*

Has anyone ever told you that you were pretty?

> *There is a pause, and the music rises slightly.* LAURA *looks up slowly, with wonder, and shakes her head.*

Well, you are! In a very different way from anyone else. And all the nicer because of the difference, too.

> *His voice becomes low and husky.* LAURA *turns away, nearly faint with the novelty of her emotions.*

I wish that you were my sister. I'd teach you to have some confidence in yourself. The different people are not like other people, but being different is nothing to be ashamed of. Because other

---

9. Apparently a nickname used by Jim's high school friends. Since Laura had not been friendly with him then, her use of the name indicates her understanding of the situation between them at this point.

people are not such wonderful people. They're one hundred times one thousand. You're one times one! They walk all over the earth. You just stay here. They're common as—weeds, but—you—well, you're—*Blue Roses!*

Image on screen: Blue Roses.

The music changes.

LAURA   But blue is wrong for—roses. . . .
JIM   It's right for you! You're—pretty!
LAURA   In what respect am I pretty?
JIM   In all respects—believe me! Your eyes—your hair—are pretty! Your hands are pretty! [*He catches hold of her hand.*] You think I'm making this up because I'm invited to dinner and have to be nice. Oh, I could do that! I could put on an act for you, Laura, and say lots of things without being very sincere. But this time I am. I'm talking to you sincerely. I happened to notice you had this inferiority complex that keeps you from feeling comfortable with people. Somebody needs to build your confidence up and make you proud instead of shy and turning away and—blushing. Somebody—ought to—*kiss* you, Laura!

His hand slips slowly up her arm to her shoulder as the music swells tumultuously. He suddenly turns her about and kisses her on the lips. When he releases her, LAURA *sinks on the sofa with a bright, dazed look.* JIM *backs away and fishes in his pocket for a cigarette.*

Legend on screen: "A souvenir."

Stumblejohn!

He lights the cigarette, avoiding her look. There is a peal of girlish laughter from AMANDA *in the kitchenette.* LAURA *slowly raises and opens her hand. It still contains the little broken glass animal. She looks at it with a tender, bewildered expression.*

Stumblejohn! I shouldn't have done that—that was way off the beam. You don't smoke, do you?

She looks up, smiling, not hearing the question. He sits beside her rather gingerly. She looks at him speechlessly—waiting. He coughs decorously and moves a little further aside as he considers the situation and senses her feelings, dimly, with perturbation. He speaks gently.

Would you—care for a mint?

She doesn't seem to hear him but her look grows brighter even.

Peppermint? Life Saver? My pocket's a regular drugstore—
wherever I go. . . . [*He pops a mint in his mouth. Then he
gulps and decides to make a clean breast of it. He speaks slowly and
gingerly.*] Laura, you know, if I had a sister like you, I'd do the same
thing as Tom. I'd bring out fellows and—introduce her to them. The
right type of boys—of a type to—appreciate her. Only—well—he
made a mistake about me. Maybe I've got no call to be saying
this. That may not have been the idea in having me over. But what
if it was? There's nothing wrong about that. The only trouble is
that in my case—I'm not in a situation to—do the right thing. I can't
take down your number and say I'll phone. I can't call up next
week and—ask for a date. I thought I had better explain the situation in case you—misunderstood it and—I hurt your feelings. . . .

> *There is a pause. Slowly, very slowly,* LAURA'*s look changes, her
> eyes returning slowly from his to the glass figure in her palm.*
> AMANDA *utters another gay laugh in the kitchenette.*

LAURA [*faintly*]   You—won't—call again?
JIM   No, Laura, I can't. [*He rises from the sofa.*] As I was just explaining, I've—got strings on me. Laura, I've—been going steady! I
go out all the time with a girl named Betty. She's a home-girl like
you, and Catholic, and Irish, and in a great many ways we—get
along fine. I met her last summer on a moonlight boat trip up the
river to Alton,[1] on the *Majestic.* Well—right away from the start it
was—love!

> *Legend: Love!*

> LAURA *sways slightly forward and grips the arm of the sofa.
> He fails to notice, now enrapt in his own comfortable being.*

Being in love has made a new man of me!

> *Leaning stiffly forward, clutching the arm of the sofa,* LAURA
> *struggles visibly with her storm. But* JIM *is oblivious; she is a
> long way off.*

The power of love is really pretty tremendous! Love is something
that—changes the whole world, Laura!

> *The storm abates a little and* LAURA *leans back. He notices
> her again.*

It happened that Betty's aunt took sick, she got a wire and had
to go to Centralia.[2] So Tom—when he asked me to dinner—I naturally just accepted the invitation, not knowing that you—that he—that
I —[*He stops awkwardly.*] Huh—I'm a stumblejohn!

---

1. A city in Illinois about 20 miles
north of St. Louis.

2. A city in Illinois about 60 miles east
of St. Louis.

He flops back on the sofa. The holy candles on the altar of
LAURA's *face have been snuffed out. There is a look of almost*
infinite desolation. JIM *glances at her uneasily.*

I wish that you would—say something.

She bites her lip which was trembling and then bravely smiles.
She opens her hand again on the broken glass figure. Then
she gently takes his hand and raises it level with her own. She
carefully places the unicorn in the palm of his hand, then
pushes his fingers closed upon it.

What are you—doing that for? You want me to have him?
Laura?

She nods.

What for?

LAURA   A—souvenir. . . .

She rises unsteadily and crouches beside the Victrola to wind
it up.

Legend on screen: "Things have a way of turning out so badly!"
Or image: "Gentleman caller waving goodbye—gaily."

At this moment AMANDA *rushes brightly back into the living*
room. She bears a pitcher of fruit punch in an old-fashioned
cut-glass pitcher, and a plate of macaroons. The plate has a
gold border and poppies painted on it.

AMANDA   Well, well, well! Isn't the air delightful after the shower?
I've made you children a little liquid refreshment. [*She turns gaily*
to JIM.] Jim, do you know that song about lemonade?
   "Lemonade, lemonade
   Made in the shade and stirred with a spade—
   Good enough for any old maid!"

JIM [*uneasily*]   Ha-ha! No—I never heard it.

AMANDA   Why, Laura! You look so serious!

JIM   We were having a serious conversation.

AMANDA   Good! Now you're better acquainted!

JIM [*uncertainly*]   Ha-ha! Yes.

AMANDA   You modern young people are much more serious-minded
that my generation. I was so gay as a girl!

JIM   You haven't changed, Mrs. Wingfield.

AMANDA   Tonight I'm rejuvenated! The gaiety of the occasion, Mr.
O'Connor! [*She tosses her head with a peal of laughter, spilling some*
lemonade.] Oooo! I'm baptizing myself!

JIM   Here—let me—

AMANDA [*setting the pitcher down*]   There now. I discovered we had
some maraschino cherries. I dumped them in, juice and all!

JIM   You shouldn't have gone to that trouble, Mrs. Wingfield.

AMANDA   Trouble, trouble? Why, it was loads of fun! Didn't you hear me cutting up in the kitchen? I bet your ears were burning! I told Tom how outdone with him I was for keeping you to himself so long a time! He should have brought you over much, much sooner! Well, now that you've found your way, I want you to be a very frequent caller! Not just occasional but all the time. Oh, we're going to have a lot of gay times together! I see them coming! Mmm, just breathe that air! So fresh, and the moon's so pretty! I'll skip back out—I know where my place is when young folks are having a —serious conversation!

JIM   Oh, don't go out, Mrs. Wingfield. The fact of the matter is I've got to be going.

AMANDA   Going, now? You're joking! Why, it's only the shank of the evening,[3] Mr. O'Connor!

JIM   Well, you know how it is.

AMANDA   You mean you're a young workingman and have to keep workingmen's hours. We'll let you off early tonight. But only on the condition that next time you stay later. What's the best night for you? Isn't Saturday night the best night for you workingmen?

JIM   I have a couple of time-clocks to punch, Mrs. Wingfield. One at morning, another one at night!

AMANDA   My, but you *are* ambitious! You work at night, too?

JIM   No; Ma'am, not work but—Betty!

He crosses deliberately to pick up his hat. The band at the Paradise Dance Hall goes into a tender waltz.

AMANDA   Betty? Betty? Who's—Betty!

There is an ominous cracking sound in the sky.

JIM   Oh, just a girl. The girl I go steady with!

He smiles charmingly. The sky falls.

Legend: "The Sky Falls."

AMANDA   [*a long-drawn exhalation*]   Ohhhh . . . Is it a serious romance, Mr. O'Connor?

JIM   We're going to be married the second Sunday in June.

AMANDA   Ohhh—how nice! Tom didn't mention that you were engaged to be married.

JIM   The cat's not out of the bag at the warehouse yet. You know how they are. They call you Romeo and stuff like that. [*He stops at the oval mirror to put on his hat. He carefully shapes the brim and the crown to give a discreetly dashing effect.*] It's been a wonderful evening, Mrs. Wingfield. I guess this is what they mean by Southern hospitality.

3. The best part of the evening.

AMANDA   It really wasn't anything at all.

JIM   I hope it don't seem like I'm rushing off. But I promised Betty I'd pick her up at the Wabash depot, an' by the time I get my jalopy down there her train'll be in. Some women are pretty upset if you keep 'em waiting.

AMANDA   Yes, I know—the tyranny of women! [*She extends her hand.*] Goodbye, Mr. O'Connor. I wish you luck—and happiness—and success! All three of them, and so does Laura! Don't you, Laura?

LAURA   Yes!

JIM   [*taking* LAURA's *hand*]   Goodbye, Laura. I'm certainly going to treasure that souvenir. And don't you forget the good advice I gave you. [*He raises his voice to a cheery shout.*] So long, Shakespeare! Thanks again, ladies. Good night!

> *He grins and ducks jauntily out. Still bravely grimacing,* AMANDA *closes the door on the gentleman caller. Then she turns back to the room with a puzzled expression. She and* LAURA *don't dare to face each other.* LAURA *crouches beside the Victrola to wind it.*

AMANDA   [*faintly*]   Things have a way of turning out so badly. I don't believe that I would play the Victrola. Well, well—well! Our gentleman caller was engaged to be married! [*She raises her voice.*] Tom!

TOM   [*from the kitchenette*]   Yes, Mother?

AMANDA   Come in here a minute. I want to tell you something awfully funny.

TOM   [*entering with a macaroon and a glass of the lemonade*]   Has the gentleman caller gotten away already?

AMANDA   The gentleman caller has made an early departure. What a wonderful joke you played on us!

TOM   How do you mean?

AMANDA   You didn't mention that he was engaged to be married.

TOM   Jim? Engaged?

AMANDA   That's what he just informed us.

TOM   I'll be jiggered! I didn't know about that.

AMANDA   That seems very peculiar.

TOM   What's peculiar about it?

AMANDA   Didn't you call your best friend down at the warehouse?

TOM   He is, but how did I know?

AMANDA   It seems extremely peculiar that you wouldn't know your best friend was going to be married!

TOM   The warehouse is where I work, not where I know things about people!

AMANDA   You don't know things anywhere! You live in a dream; you manufacture illusions!

> *He crosses to the door.*

Where are you going?

TOM   I'm going to the movies.

AMANDA   That's right, now that you've had us make such fools of ourselves. The effort, the preparations, all the expense! The new floor lamp, the rug, the clothes for Laura! All for what? To entertain some other girl's fiancé! Go to the movies, go! Don't think about us, a mother deserted, an unmarried sister who's crippled and has no job! Don't let anything interfere with your selfish pleasure! Just go, go, go—to the movies!

TOM   All right, I will! The more you shout about my selfishness to me the quicker I'll go, and I won't go to the movies!

AMANDA   Go, then! Go to the moon—you selfish dreamer!

> TOM *smashes his glass on the floor. He plunges out on the fire escape, slamming the door.* LAURA *screams in fright. The dance-hall music becomes louder.* TOM *stands on the fire escape, gripping the rail. The moon breaks through the storm clouds, illuminating his face.*
>
> *Legend on screen: "And so goodbye . . ."*
>
> TOM'S *closing speech is timed with what is happening inside the house. We see, as though through soundproof glass, that* AMANDA *appears to be making a comforting speech to* LAURA, *who is huddled upon the sofa. Now that we cannot hear the mother's speech, her silliness is gone and she has dignity and tragic beauty.* LAURA'S *hair hides her face until, at the end of the speech, she lifts her head to smile at her mother.* AMANDA'S *gestures are slow and graceful, almost dancelike, as she comforts her daughter. At the end of her speech she glances a moment at the father's picture—then withdraws through the portieres. At the close of* TOM'S *speech,* LAURA *blows out the candles, ending the play.*

TOM   I didn't go to the moon, I went much further—for time is the longest distance between two places. Not long after that I was fired for writing a poem on the lid of a shoe-box. I left Saint Louis. I descended the steps of this fire escape for a last time and followed, from then on, in my father's footsteps, attempting to find in motion what was lost in space. I traveled around a great deal. The cities swept about me like dead leaves, leaves that were brightly colored but torn away from the branches. I would have stopped, but I was pursued by something. It always came upon me unawares, taking me altogether by surprise. Perhaps it was a familiar bit of music. Perhaps it was only a piece of transparent glass. Perhaps I am walking along a street at night, in some strange city, before I have found companions. I pass the lighted window of a shop where perfume is sold. The window is filled with pieces of colored glass, tiny transparent bottles in delicate colors, like bits of a shattered rainbow. Then all at once my sister touches my shoulder. I turn around and look into her eyes. Oh, Laura, Laura, I tried to leave you behind me, but I am more faithful than I intended to be!

I reach for a cigarette, I cross the street, I run into the movies or a bar, I buy a drink, I speak to the nearest stranger—anything that can blow your candles out!

LAURA *bends over the candles.*

For nowadays the world is lit by lightning! Blow out your candles, Laura—and so goodbye. . . .

She blows the candles out.

1944–45

TENNESSEE WILLIAMS

The Long Goodbye

CHARACTERS

JOE
MYRA, *his sister*
MOTHER *of Joe and Myra*

SILVA, *a friend of Joe's*
BILL, *Myra's date*
FOUR MOVERS

SCENE: *Apartment F, third floor south, in a tenement apartment situated in the washed-out middle of a large midwestern American city.[1] Outside the trucks rumble on dull streets and children cry out at their games in the area-ways between walls of dusty-tomato-colored brick. Through the double front windows in the left wall, late afternoon sunlight streams into the shabby room. Beyond the windows is the door to the stair hall, and in the center of the back wall a large door opening on a corridor in the apartment where a telephone stand is located. A door in the right wall leads to a bedroom. The furnishings are disheveled and old as if they had witnessed the sudden withdrawal of twenty-five years of furious, desperate living among them and now awaited only the moving men to cart them away. From the apartment next door comes the sound of a radio broadcasting the baseball game from Sportsman's Park.* JOE, *a young man of twenty-three, is sitting at a table by the double windows, brooding over a manuscript. In front of him is a portable typewriter with a page of the manuscript in it, and on the floor beside the table is a shabby valise.* JOE *wears an undershirt and wash-pants. The noise of the broadcast game annoys him and he slams down the windows, but the sound is as loud as ever. He raises them and goes out the door on the right and slams other windows. The shouting of the radio subsides and* JOE *comes back in lighting a cigarette, a desperate scowl on his face.* SILVA, *an Italian youth, small, graceful and good-natured, opens the entrance door and comes in. He is about* JOE's *age. By way of greeting he grins and then takes off his shirt.*

JOE   Radios, baseball games! That's why I write nothing but crap!
SILVA   Still at it?
JOE   All night and all day.
SILVA   How come?
JOE   I had a wild hair. Couldn't sleep.
SILVA [*glancing at page in machine*]   You're burning the candle at both ends, Kid . . . [*He moves from the table across the room.*] And

---

1. St Louis, Missouri, where Williams spent much of his boyhood. The play contains many references to places, including Laclede, a street named for the founder of the city; Ladue and Huntleigh, fashionable residential neighborhoods; the Belle-rive Country Club and the Chase (Hotel) Roof.

in my humble opinion the light ain't worth it. I thought cha was moving today.

JOE   I am. [*He flops in table-chair and bangs out a line. Then he removes the sheet.*] Phone the movers. They oughta been here.

SILVA   Yeh? Which one?

JOE   Langan's Storage.

SILVA   Storin' this stuff?

JOE   Yeh.

SILVA   What for? Why don't you sell it?

JOE   For six bits to the junk man?

SILVA   Store it you gotta pay storage. Sell it you got a spot a cash to start on.

JOE   Start on what?

SILVA   Whatever you're going to start on.

JOE   I got a spot a cash. Mother's insurance. I split it with Myra, we both got a hundred and fifty. Know where I'm going?

SILVA   No. Where?

JOE   Rio. Or Buenos Aires. I took Spanish in high school.

SILVA   So what?

JOE   I know the language. I oughta get on okay.

SILVA   Working for Standard Oil?

JOE   Maybe. Why not? Call the movers.

SILVA   [*going to the phone*]   You better stay here. Take your money outa the bank and go on the Project.[2]

JOE   No. I'm not gonna stay here. All of this here is dead for me. The goldfish is dead. I forgot to feed it.

SILVA   [*into the phone*]   Lindell 0124. . . . Langan's Storage? This is the Bassett apartment. Why ain't the movers come yet? . . . Aw! [*He hangs up the receiver.*] The truck's on the way. June is a big moving month. I guess they're kept busy.

JOE   I shouldn't have left the bowl setting right here in the sun. It probably cooked the poor bastard.

SILVA   He stinks. [SILVA *picks up the bowl.*]

JOE   What uh you do with him?

SILVA   Dump 'im into the tawlut.

JOE   The tawlut's turned off.

SILVA   Oh, well. [*He goes out the bedroom door.*]

JOE   Why is it that Jesus makes a distinction between the goldfish an' the sparrow![3] [*He laughs.*] There is no respect for dead bodies.

SILVIA   [*coming back in*]   You are losing your social consciousness, Joe. You should say "unless they are rich"! I read about once where a millionaire buried his dead canary in a small golden casket studded with genuine diamonds. I think it presents a beautiful picture. The saffron feathers on the white satin and the millionaire's tears falling like diamonds in sunlight—maybe a boy's choir singing! Like death in the movies. Which is always a beautiful thing. Even for an artist

2. The W(orks) P(rogress) A(dministration, a New Deal program in operation from 1935 to 1941, was designed to provide work for unemployed people. Several of its projects were directed toward the arts, including a Writers Project.

3. A reference to *Matthew* 10:29, "Are not two sparrows sold for a farthing? and one of them shall not fall on the ground without your Father." A similar passage is found in *Luke* 12:6.

I'd say that your hair was too long. A little hip motion you'd pass for a female Imp. Cigarette?

JOE   Thanks. Christ!

SILVA   What's the matter?

JOE   How does this stuff smell to you? [*He gives him a page of the manuscript.*]

SILVA   Hmm. I detect a slight odor of frying bacon.

JOE   Lousy?

SILVA   Well, it's not you at your best. You'd better get on the Project. We're through with the city guide.

JOE   What are you going to write next?

SILVA   God Bless Harry L. Hopkins[4] 999 times. Naw . . . I got a creative assignment. I'm calling it "Ghosts in the Old Court-house." Days when the slaves were sold there! . . . This is bad. This speech of the girl's—"I want to get you inside of my body—not just for the time that it takes to make love on a bed between the rattle of ice in the last highball and the rattle the milk-wagons make—"

JOE [*tearing the page from his hands*]   I must've been nuts.

SILVA   You must've had hot britches!

JOE   I did. Summer and celibacy aren't a very good mix. Buenos Aires. . . .

1ST MOVER [*from the hall outside*]   Langan's Storage!

JOE [*going to the door*]   Right here. [*He opens the door and the four burly* MOVERS *crowd in, sweating, shuffling, looking about with quick, casual eyes.*] Take out the back stuff first, will yuh, boys?

1ST MOVER   Sure.

SILVA   Hot work, huh?

2ND MOVER   Plenty.

3RD MOVER [*walking in hastily*]   "I got a pocketful of dreams!"[5] What time's it, kid?

JOE   Four-thirty-five.

3RD MOVER   We oughta get time an' a ha'f w'en we finish this job. How'd the ball game come out?

JOE   Dunno. [*He watches them, troubled.*]

2ND MOVER   What's it to you, Short Horn? Get busy! [*They laugh and go out the rear corridor. Later they are heard knocking down a bed.*]

SILVA [*noting* JOE'*s gloom*]   Let's get out of this place. It's depressing.

JOE   I got to look out for the stuff.

SILVA   Come on get a beer. There's a twenty-six-ounce-a-dime joint open up on Laclede.

JOE   Wait a while, Silva.

SILVA   Okay. [*The* MOVERS *come through with parts of a bed.* JOE *watches them, motionless, face set.*]

JOE   That is the bed I was born on.

SILVA   Jeez! And look how they handle it—just like it was an ordinary bed!

4. Hopkins (1894–1946) was an influential adviser to President Franklin D. Roosevelt and was regarded as largely responsible for such programs as the W.P.A.

5. The Mover is singing a line from a popular song of the same title. It appeared in 1938, words by Johnny Burke and music by James V. Monaco.

JOE   Myra was born on that bed, too. [*The* MOVERS *go out the door.*] Mother died on it.

SILVA   Yeah? She went pretty quick for cancer. Most of 'em hang on longer an' suffer a hell of a lot.

JOE   She killed herself. I found the empty bottle that morning in a waste-basket. It wasn't the pain, it was the doctor an' hospital bills that she was scared of. She wanted us to have the insurance.

SILVA   I didn't know that.

JOE   Naw. We kept it a secret—she an' me an' the doctor. Myra never found out.

SILVA   Where is Myra now?

JOE   Last I heard, in Detroit. I got a card from her. Here.

SILVA   Picture of the Yacht Club. What's she doin'—yachting?

JOE [*gruffly*]   Naw, I dunno what she's doin'. How should I know?

SILVA   She don't say? [JOE *doesn't answer.*] She was a real sweet kid—till all of a sudden she—

JOE   Yeh. Ev'rything broke up—when Mom died.

SILVA [*picking up a magazine*]   Four bit magazines! No wonder you stick up your nose at the Project. Hemingway! You know he's got a smooth style. [JOE *stands as if entranced as the* MOVERS *pass through to the rear.*] He's been with the Loyalist forces in Spain. Fighting in front-line trenches, they say. And yet some a the critics say that he wears a toupee on his chest![6] Reactionaries! [SILVA *begins to read.* MYRA *comes quietly into the room—young, radiant, vibrant with the glamor that memory gives.*]

JOE   You got a date tonight, Myra?

MYRA   Uh-huh.

JOE   Who with?

MYRA   Bill.

JOE   Who's Bill?

MYRA   Fellow I met at the swimming meet out at Bellerive Country Club.

JOE   I don't think a swimming pool's the best place in the world to pick up your boyfriends, Myra.

MYRA   Sure it is. If you look good in a Jantzen. [*She slips off her kimono.*] Get my white summer formal. No, I better. You got sweaty hands. [*She goes out the bedroom door.*]

JOE   What happened to Dave and Hugh White and that—that K. City boy?

MYRA [*coming back with a white evening dress on*]   Who? Them? My God, I don't know. Here. Hook this for me.

JOE   I guess what you've got in your heart's a revolving door.

MYRA   You know it. The radio's great institution, huh, Joe? [*Rapidly brushing her hair.*] I get so tired of it. Pop's got it on all the time. He gripes my soul. Just setting there, setting there, setting there! Never says nothing no more.

JOE   You oughta watch your English. It's awful.

MYRA   Hell, I'm not a book-worm. How's it look?

JOE   Smooth. Where you going?

6. The American writer Ernest Hemingway (1899–1961) cultivated a public personality of virile masculinity.

MYRA   Chase Roof. Bill is no piker. His folks have got lotsa mazooma. They live out in Huntleigh—offa Ladue. Christ, it's— whew! Open that window! Cloudy?

JOE   No. Clear as a bell.

MYRA   That's good. Dancing under the stars! [*The doorbell rings.*] That's him. Get the door. [JOE *faces the door as* BILL *enters.*]

JOE   Why go to Switzerland, huh?

BILL   What? [*He laughs indifferently.*] Oh, yeah. She ready?

JOE   Sit down. She'll be right out.

BILL   Good.

JOE   [*sweeping papers off the sofa*] You see we read the papers. Keep up with events of the day. Sport sheet?

BILL   No, thanks.

JOE   The Cards won a double-header. Joe Medwick hit a home run with two men on in the second. Comics?

BILL   No, thanks. I've seen the papers.

JOE   Oh. I thought you might've missed 'em because it's so early.

BILL   It's eight-forty-five.

JOE   It's funny, isn't it?

BILL   What?

JOE   The chandelier. I thought you were looking at it.

BILL   I hadn't noticed—particularly.

JOE   It always reminds me a little of mushroom soup. [BILL *regards him without amusement.*] Myra says that you live in Huntleigh Village.

BILL   Yes?

JOE   It must be very nice out there. In summer.

BILL   We like it [*He stands up.*] Say, could you give your little sister a third-alarm—or whatever it takes?

JOE   She'll be out when she's ready.

BILL   That's what I'm afraid of.

JOE   Is this your first date, Bill?

BILL   How do you mean?

JOE   In my experience girls don't always pop right out of their boudoirs the minute a guy calls for 'em.

BILL   No? But you sort of expect more speed of a swimming champ. [*Calling.*] Hey! Myra!

MYRA   [*She faces the wall as though it were a mirror.*] Yeh, Bill, I'm coming right out!

JOE   Excuse me, will you?

BILL   Oh, yes. [*He faces* MYRA.]

JOE   This Bill of yours is a son-of-a-bitch. If I'd stayed in the room with him another minute I'd have busted him one.

MYRA   Then you'd better stay out. 'Cause I like him. What're you doing tonight, Joe?

JOE   Stay home and write.

MYRA   You stay home and write too much. Broke? Here's a dollar. Get you a date with that girl who writes poetry. Doris. She oughta bat out a pretty good sonnet under the proper influences. Oh, hell— I'm not gonna wear any stockings. Coming, Bill! Look! How is the back of my neck? Is it filthy? Christ! [*She sprays herself with per-*

fume.] You gotta bathe three times a day to keep fresh in this weather. Doris. Is that her name? I bet that she could be had without too much effort!

JOE   Myra. Don't talk that way.

MYRA   You kill me!

JOE   Naw, it doesn't sound right in a kid your age.

MYRA   I'm twice your age! G'bye, Joe!

JOE   G'bye, Myra.

MYRA [*faces* BILL *with a dazzling smile*]   Hello, darling!

BILL   Hi. Let's get outa this sweat-box.

MYRA   Yeah. [*They go out. The* MOVERS *come in with a dresser.*]

1ST MOVER   Easy.

2ND MOVER   Got it?

1ST MOVER   Yep. Who the fuck closed that door?

JOE   I'll get it. Careful down those stairs.

SILVA [*glancing up from the magazine*]   A broken mirror is seven years' bad luck.

JOE   Aw. Is that right? The stork must've dropped us through a whole bunch of 'em when we were born. How's the story?

SILVA   It's good strong stuff.

JOE [*glancing at the title*]   Butterfly and the Tank. I read that one.

CHILD [*from the street below*]   Fly, Sheepie, fly! Fly, Sheepie, fly!

JOE [*reflectively*]   Fly, Sheepie, fly! You ever played that game?[7]

SILVA   Naw. Kids that play games are sissies in our neighborhood.

JOE   We played it. Myra an' me. Up and down fire-escapes, in an' out basements. . . . Jeez! We had a swell time. What happens to kids when they grow up?

SILVA   They grow up. [*He turns a page.*]

JOE   Yeh, they grow up. [*The sound of roller-skates on the sidewalk rises in the silence, as the light fades. Only the door to the bedroom on the right is clear in a spotlight.*]

MOTHER [*softly from the bedroom*]   Joe? Oh, Joe!

JOE   Yes, Mother? [MOTHER *appears in the door—a worn, little woman in a dingy wrapper with an expression that is personally troubled and confused.*]

MOTHER   Joe, aren't you going to bed?

JOE   Yes. In a minute.

MOTHER   I think you've written enough tonight, Joe.

JOE   I'm nearly finished. I just wanta finish this sentence.

MOTHER   Myra's still out.

JOE   She went to the Chase Roof.

MOTHER   Couldn't you go along with her sometimes? Meet the boys that she goes out with?

JOE   No, I can't horn in on her dates. Hell, if I had a job I couldn't pay tips for that crowd!

MOTHER   I'm worried about her.

JOE   What for? She says she's older than I am, Mom, an' I guess she's right.

---

7. Probably a variant of a catching game "Sheep, Sheep, Come Home," in which one player is the Wolf, another the Shepherd, and the remainder Sheep.

MOTHER No, she's only a baby. You talk to her, Joe.

JOE Okay.

MOTHER I regret that she took that job now, Joe. She should've stayed on at high-school.

JOE She wanted things—money, clothes—you can't blame her. 'S Dad out?

MOTHER Yes. . . . She's given up her swimming.

JOE She got kicked off the Lorelei team.

MOTHER What for, Joe?

JOE She broke training rules all the time. Hell, I can't stop her.

MOTHER She listens to you.

JOE Not much.

MOTHER Joe—

JOE Yes?

MOTHER Joe, it's come back on me, Joe.

JOE [*facing her slowly*] What?

MOTHER The operation wasn't no use. And all it cost us, Joe, the bills not paid for it yet!

JOE Mother—what makes you think so?

MOTHER That same pain's started again.

JOE How long?

MOTHER Oh, some time now.

JOE Why didn't you—?

MOTHER Joe . . . what's the use?

JOE Maybe it's—not what you think! You've got to go back. For examination, Mom!

MOTHER No. This is the way I look at it, Joe. Like this. I've never liked being cramped. I've always wanted to have space around me, plenty of space, to live in the country on the top of a hill. I was born in the country, raised there, and I've hankered after it lots in the last few years.

JOE Yes. I know. [*Now he speaks to himself.*] Those Sunday after-noon rides in the country, the late yellow sun through an orchard, the twisted shadows, the crazy old wind-beaten house, vacant, lop-sided, and you pointing at it, leaning out of the car, trying to make Dad stop—

MOTHER Look! That house, it's for sale! It oughta go cheap! Twenty acres of apple, a hen-house, and look, a nice barn! It's run-down now but it wouldn't cost much to repair! Stop, Floyd, go slow along here!

JOE But he went by fast, wouldn't look, wouldn't listen! The snake-fence[8] darted away from the road and a wall of stone rose and the sun disappeared for a moment. Your face was dark, your face looked desperate, Mother, as though you were starving for some-thing you'd seen and almost caught in your hands—but not quite. And then the car stopped in front of a road-side stand. "We need eggs." A quarter, a dime—you borrowed a nickel from Dad. And the sun was low then, slanting across winter fields, and the air was cold. . . .

8. A zigzag fence composed of crossed rails supporting one another.

MOTHER Some people think about death as being laid down in a box under earth. But I don't. To me it's the opposite, Joe, it's being let out of a box. And going upwards, not down. I don't take stock in heaven, I never did. But I do feel like there's lots of room out there and you don't have to pay rent on the first of each month to any old tight-fisted Dutchman who kicks about how much water you're using. There's freedom, Joe, and freedom's the big thing in life. It's funny that some of us don't ever get it until we're dead. But that's how it is and so we've got to accept it. The hard thing to me is leaving things not straightened out. I'd like to have some assurance, some definite knowledge of what you were going to do, of how things'll work out for you. . . . Joe!

JOE Yes?

MOTHER What would you do with three hundred dollars?

JOE I'm not going to think about that.

MOTHER I want you to, Joe. The policy's in your name. It's in the right hand drawer of the chiffonier, folded up under the handkerchief box and it's got . . . [*Her voice fades out and two of the* MOVERS *come in carrying a floor-lamp.*]

JOE [*clearing his throat*] Where's the shade to that lamp? [MOTHER *slips quietly out as the sunlight brightens.*]

1ST MOVER It's comin'. [*He knocks the lamp slightly against the wall.*]

JOE God damn you! Why don't you look what you're doing?

2ND MOVER What's eating you?

1ST MOVER Lissen, buddy—

JOE You don't care about people's things! Any old way is all right!

SILVA [*looking up from the magazine*] Joe, take it easy. They're not going to damage this stuff.

JOE They're not going to damage it—no!

1ST MOVER Damage it? Shit! [*The two* MOVERS *laugh as they go out.*]

SILVA If they break a thing you collect on it.

3RD MOVER [*entering with some cardboard boxes*] What's in these here boxes?

JOE China. Glass things. So don't go tossing 'em around like—

SILVA Joe, let's get outa this place. I can't concentrate on a story with all this commotion. What uh yuh stayin' here for anyhow, screwball? It's only—makin' yuh feel—depressed, ain't it?

JOE You go on if you want. I've got to wait here.

4TH MOVER [*coming in with a handful of bottles*] Some empty powder an' perfume bottles offa that dresser—you want 'em or not?

JOE Leave 'em here on the floor. [*The* 4TH MOVER *takes up a chair from the room and goes out the door to the stair hall.* JOE *examines the articles on the floor. He removes the stopper from a perfume bottle and sniffs. The light in the room dims again and the front door is caught in a spotlight.* MYRA's *voice can be heard in the hall outside.*]

MYRA Bill, I had a swell time.

BILL Zat all? . . . It's dark. They're all in bed. [JOE *rises and straightens attentively.*]

MYRA [*appearing in the doorway*] Joe's light's still on.

BILL   I'll be quiet, honey. We don't have to make any noise. I'm a *wee* little mouthie!

MYRA [*kissing him*]   Yes, and you've got to go home.

BILL   C'mere closer. Unh!

MYRA   Bill!

BILL   Whatsamatter? Aren't you the little free-style swimming an' fancy diving champion of St. Louis?

MYRA   What if I am?

BILL   Well, I can do a swell breast-stroke, too—outa water.

MYRA   Shut up. I want to go to bed.

BILL   So do I.

MYRA   Goodnight.

BILL   Lissen!

MYRA   What?

BILL   I go out with debutantes.

MYRA   What of it?

BILL   Nothing. Except that . . .

MYRA   How should I take that remark?

BILL   Okay, I'll tell you. I'll take "Goodnight I've had a swell time" from the V.P. Queen![9] But when girls like you try to sell me that stuff—

JOE [*stepping into the spotlighted area*]   Get out!

BILL   Aw. It's big brother. I thought you'd be out on the milk-route by now.

JOE   Get out, you stinking—

MYRA   Joe!

JOE   Before I hang one on you! [BILL *laughs weakly and goes out.*]

MYRA   You were right about him. He's no good. [JOE *looks at her.*] Joe, what do they mean by—"girls like me"?

JOE [*bending slowly and removing a small object[1] from the floor*]   I guess they mean—this.

MYRA [*without looking*]   What?

JOE   Something he—dropped from his pocket.

MYRA [*dully*]   Oh. [*Raising her voice.*] Joe, I don't want you to think I—

JOE   Shut up. . . . Mother's sick.

MYRA [*excitedly*]   Oh, I know, I know, it's all a rotten dirty mess! The Chase Roof, dancing under the stars! . . . And then on the way home, puking over the side of the car—puking! And then he stops in the park and tries to—Oh, Christ, I want to have a good time! You don't think I have it sewing hooks an' eyes on corsets down at Werber & Jacobs? Nights I wanta get out, Joe, I wanta go places, have fun! But I don't want things like him crawling on me, worse than filthy cock-roaches!

JOE   Hush up!

MOTHER [*faintly from another room*]   Joe—Myra . . . [*She moans.*]

---

9. The Veiled Prophet Parade and Ball was a social highlight of the year in St. Louis, somewhat like Mardi Gras in New Orleans. A young unmarried girl from St. Louis society was chosen each year as Queen and thus titular ruler of society during the next year. Such a young lady could offer advantages of wealth and/or social position which Myra could not.

1. A condom.

MYRA [*frightened*]　What's that?

JOE　It's Mother, she's sick, she's— [MYRA *runs out the hall door and the lights come up again.*]—dead!

SILVA　What?

JOE　Nothing. You want some perfume?

SILVA　What kinda perfume?

JOE　Carnation.

SILVA　Naw. I resent the suggestion. [*The* MOVERS *crowd in again.*]

1ST MOVER [*to* 3RD MOVER]　Quit horsin' around on a job. Git them rugs.

3RD MOVER　Awright, straw boss. They should've put in a pinch-hitter. Meighan or Flowers.

2ND MOVER　Flowers? He couldn't hit an elephant's ass. Grab an end a the sofa. Hup!

4TH MOVER　Cabbage for supper nex' door.

WOMAN [*calling mournfully from the street*]　May-zeeee! Oh, May-zeeee!

3RD MOVER　In that game a' Chicago . . . [*The* MOVERS *carry the sofa and other furniture out the entrance door.* JOE *removes a picture from wall.*]

SILVA [*looking up from the magazine*]　Myra's, huh?

JOE　One she had in the rotogravure,[2] time she broke a record in the Mississippi Valley relays.

SILVA [*taking the picture*]　She had a sweet shape on her, huh?

JOE　Yes.

SILVA　What makes a girl go like that.

JOE　Like what?

SILVA　You know.

JOE　No, I *don't* know! Why don't you get out of here and leave me alone?

SILVA　Because I don't want to. Because I'm reading a story. Because I think you're nuts.

JOE　Yeah? Gimme that picture. [*He bends over his suitcase to pack the photograph with his things and as he does so the lights dim a little and* MYRA *comes in. She is appreciably cheaper and more sophisticated and wears a negligee she could not have bought with her monthly salary.*]

MYRA　I wish you'd quit having that dago around the place.

JOE [*rising*]　Silva?

MYRA　Yeah. I don't like the way he looks at me.

JOE　Looks at you?

MYRA　Yeh. I might as well be standing naked in front of him the way that he looks.[JOE *laughs harshly.*] You think it's funny—him looking at me that way?

JOE　Yes. It *is* funny.

MYRA　My sense a the comical don't quite agree with yours.

JOE [*looking at her*]　You're getting awfully skittish—objecting to guys looking at you.

MYRA　Well, that boy is repulsive.

2. A special section of the (Sunday) newspaper devoted to pictures reproduced by the rotogravure method.

JOE Because he don't live somewhere offa Ladue?

MYRA No. Because he don't take a bath.

JOE That's not true. Silva takes a shower ev'ry morning at the party headquarters.

MYRA Party headquarters! You better try to associate with people that will do you some good instead of—radical dagoes and niggers an'—

JOE Shut up! My God, you're getting common. Snobbishness, that's always the first sign. I've never known a snob yet that wasn't fundamentally as common as dirt!

MYRA Is it being a snob not to like dirty people?

JOE Dirty people are what *you* run around with! Geezers in fifty dollar suits with running sores on the back of their necks. You better have your blood tested!

MYRA You—you—you can't insult me like that! I'm going to—call Papa—tell him to—

JOE I used to have hopes for you, Myra. But not any more. You're goin' down the toboggan like a greased pig. Take a look at yourself in the mirror. Why did Silva look at you that way? Why did the newsboy whistle when you walked past him last night? Why? 'Cause you looked like a whore—like a cheap one, Myra, one he could get for six![3] [MYRA *looks at him, stunned, but does not answer for a moment.*]

MYRA [*quietly*] You never would have said a thing to me like that—when Mother was living.

JOE No. When Mother was living, you wouldn't have been like this. And stayed on here in the house.

MYRA The house? This isn't a house. It's five rooms and a bath and I'm getting out as quick as I can and I mean it! I'm not going to hang around here with a bunch of long-haired lunatics with eyes that strip the clothes off you, and then be called—dirty names!

JOE If my sister was clean . . . I'd kill any fellow that dared to look at her that way!

MYRA You got a swell right—you that just loaf around all day writing crap that nobody reads. You never do nothing, nothing, you don't make a cent! If I was Papa—I'd kick you out of this place so fast it would—Ahhhhh! [*She turns away in disgust.*]

JOE Maybe that won't be necessary.

MYRA Oh, no? You been saying that a long time. They'll move every stick a furniture out a this place before they do you! [*She laughs and goes out. The lights come up.*]

JOE [*to himself*] Yeah. . . . [*The* 1ST *and* 2ND MOVERS *come back and start rolling the carpet.* JOE *watches them and then speaks aloud.*] Every stick a furniture out—before me! [*He laughs.*]

SILVA What?

JOE I got a card from her last week.

SILVA Who?

JOE Myra.

---

3. A prostitute whose fee was $.75 or "six bits."

SILVA   Yeah. You told me that. [*He throws the magazine aside.*] I wonder where your old man is.

JOE   Christ. I don't know.

SILVA   Funny an old bloke like him just quittin' his job and lamming out to God knows where—after fifty—or fifty-five years of livin' a regular middle-class life.

JOE   I guess he got tired of living a regular middle-class life.

SILVA   I used to wonder what he was thinking about nights— sitting in that big overstuffed chair. [*The* 3RD *and* 4TH MOVERS *have come back and now they remove the big chair.* JOE *takes his shirt from the chair as they pass and slowly puts it on.*]

JOE   So did I. I'm still wondering. He never said a damn thing.

SILVA   Naw?

JOE   Just sat there, sat there, night after night after night. Well, he's gone now, they're all gone.

SILVA [*with a change of tone*]   You'd better go, too.

JOE   Why don't you go on ahead an' wait for me, Silva. I'll be along in a while.

SILVA   Because I don't like the way you're acting and for some goddam reason I feel—responsible for you. You might take a no- tion to do a Steve Brody[4] out one a them windows.

JOE [*laughing shortly*]   For Chrissakes what would I do that for?

SILVA   Because your state of mind is abnormal. I've been lookin' at you. You're starin' off into space like something's come loose in your head. I know what you're doing. You're taking a morbid pleasure in watchin' this junk hauled off like some dopes get in mooning around a bone-orchard after somebody's laid under. This place is done for, Joe. You can't help it. [*Far down at the end of the block an organ grinder has started winding out an old blues tune of ten or fifteen years ago. It approaches gradually with a melancholy gaiety throughout rest of play.*] Write about it some day. Call it "An Elegy for an Empty Flat." But right now my advice is to get out of here and get drunk! 'Cause the world goes on. And you've got to keep going on with it.

JOE   But not so fast that you can't even say goodbye.

SILVA   Goodbye? 'S not in my vocabulary! Hello's the word nowadays.

JOE   You're kidding yourself. You're saying goodbye all the time, every minute you live. Because that's what life is, just a long, long goodbye! [*With almost sobbing intensity.*] To one thing after an- other! Till you get to the last one, Silva, and that's—goodbye to yourself! [*He turns sharply to the window.*] Get out of here now, get out and leave me alone!

SILVA   Okay. But I think you're weeping like Jesus and it makes me sick. [*He begins to put on his shirt.*] I'll see you over at Weston's if I can still see. [*Grinning wryly.*] Remember, kid, what Socrates said. "Hemlock's a damn bad substitute for a twenty-six-ounce glass a beer!" [*He laughs and puts on his hat.*] So long. [SILVA *goes out the door, leaving* JOE *in the bare room. The yellow stains on the walls,*

4. A suicidal leap, named from Steve Brody or Brodie, a newsboy alleged to   have jumped from the Brooklyn Bridge in 1886.

the torn peeling paper with its monotonous design, the fantastically hideous chandelier now show up in cruel relief. The sunlight through the double windows is clear and faded as weak lemon water and a fly is heard buzzing during a pause in the organ-grinder's music. The tune begins again and is drowned in the starting roar of the moving van which ebbs rapidly away. JOE walks slowly to the windows.]

CHILD [calling in the street] Olly—olly—oxen-free! Olly—olly—oxen-free![5] [JOE looks slowly about him. His whole body contracts in a spasm of nostalgic pain. Then he grins wryly, picks up his suit-case and goes over to the door. He slips a hand to his forehead in a mocking salute to the empty room, then thrusts the hand in his pocket and goes slowly out.] Olly—olly—oxen-free! [Scattered shouting and laughter floats up to the room. The music is now fading.]

pub. 1945

---

5. In one form of hide-and-seek, a player found by "It" might outrun "It" to the home base and free himself (and any others who had been found) by saying "Olly—olly—oxen-free" as he touched the base.

5   TRAGEDY, COMEDY, AND THE MODERN DRAMA

Genre is the notion that groups of literary works have resemblances that make comparison between them meaningful. We know what a novel is because of the novels we have read. Our earliest surviving notion of tragedy comes from Aristotle's *Poetics,* but even there Aristotle was not defining what tragedy should be but what the tragedies he knew were like. Departures from genre standards may be as important as adherences to them in understanding a particular work. We do not solve the problems of *Hamlet* by saying that it is a tragedy, but saying that it has certain resemblances to *Oedipus Tyrannus* or Racine's *Phèdre* helps us to understand certain aspects better. However, the play itself is unique, and ultimately must be understood on its own terms.

With these points in mind, we will examine three features of several dramatic genres: the order of values implicit in the play, the nature of character in the play, and the nature of the conclusion. The three genres we will examine are **tragedy, comedy,** and the serious modern play, a form for which no really satisfactory critical term has yet been found.

In a tragedy like *Oedipus Tyrannus,* values are universal and beyond the control of mankind. Right and wrong are determined not by any agreement between men, but by the will of the gods, or some other preterhuman force. When the oracle tells Oedipus that his fate is to kill his father and marry his mother, he is revolted by the prospect. In human terms such a fate is unthinkable, and Oedipus refuses to accept the will of the gods. In human terms, Oedipus is certainly right in trying to avoid such a fate—but in terms of the value system that rules the play, his attempt to circumvent the will of the gods is what destroys him. On the other hand, in a comedy like *The Importance of Being Earnest,* values are social and determined by the general opinion of society. In moral terms there is no reason why Jack and Gwendolen should not marry and get about the business of establishing a family. They are healthy unmarried people of opposite sexes; the only problems about their intention to marry are social ones. Gwendolen's children cannot achieve their "proper" place in society unless her husband is a suitable choice, a man of good family, some social position, and suitable means to provide an appropriate education for them. Implicit in this consideration is the fact that comedy tends to endorse the values of the society. Lady Bracknell may be amusing, but she is also right, because she understands how her society works, what is acceptable and what is not.

Between the two sets of values found in tragedy and comedy are those found in *The Glass Menagerie*. Here there are no clear-cut rules that make decisions easy. On the one hand, Tom feels a real claim on him by his mother and his sister. On the other, he feels the claim of his talent and the development of his own individual potential. How much does he owe to himself and how much to others? He can stay at home, stifling himself and growing bitter, or he can run away, carrying with him memories and guilt feelings. Whatever he does, he will bear the sole responsibility for his act, for neither the gods nor the society will make him do either.

A second characteristic feature of a dramatic genre is its treatment of character. Tragedy, for example, centers around a single individual, a person of high rank who confronts the universe and his fate as an individual, a hero. He is ultimately doomed to defeat because, although a good and noble person, the tragic figure has a flaw of character, a mark of humanity, that offsets all his goodness. Oedipus wishes to know and to control his own destiny, but he learns too much and is destroyed. Had Oedipus been the son of a shepherd rather than of a king, perhaps the gods would not have taken such an unfortunate interest in his fate.

Comic figures are quite different. Since the plays are concerned with society and social roles, comic characters are often defined in those terms. In *The Importance of Being Earnest* both Jack and Algernon are, for plot purposes, unmarried young men who are not eminently eligible husbands-to-be, Jack because of his uncertain parentage and Algernon because of his lack of money. They have individual traits—Algernon eats too much and enjoys pretense, Jack is more straightforward, or wishes to be—but their individuality is not so important as their definition by the common social standard. Many comic characters go even further and become **stereotypes,** characters with little or no individuality, representatives of social types. Lady Bracknell, for example, is a middle-aged meddling matron, ideally placed by age and position to exert tremendous social influence. However ridiculous Lady Bracknell appears, she understands her society and its rules thoroughly. Other stereotypes in the same play are Miss Prism, the desperate spinster, and Dr. Chasuble, the slightly dim clergyman.

Between the poles of character in comedy and tragedy lies the style of characterization in a serious modern play like *The Glass Menagerie.* We may not know everything about these characters, but we do know enough to understand why they behave in the way they do. When Amanda talks about her past, for example, we can never be sure about her truthfulness. Was she, in fact, visited by seventeen beaux in one afternoon? We do not know the facts, but we can know the meaning. Amanda's stories, whether true or imaginary, provide her with an escape from all the difficulties of her present life. She has not lost touch with reality as Laura has, but she refuses to accept the present reality as the only one. She walks a line between existing in the now and living in the then. As for Laura, we can understand how her father's desertion and her physical handicap have motivated her retreat. They are both complex human beings with a real mixture of good and bad traits and motives.

A third feature of the dramatic genres can be found in their endings. In most tragedies, the hero is enlightened; he comes to understand what he has done and to accept his punishment. At the end of *Oedipus Tyrannus* the blind hero sees and understands. He accepts his ostracism and leaves Thebes, a chastened but wiser man. Many tragic heroes die, as Hamlet does, but it is not death that ends the tragedy, it is understanding. Hamlet understands what has happened and in his last moments tries to restore order to the kingdom, asking for himself only that people may know the truth about what he has done. In comedy, on the other hand, the resolution occurs when one or more characters take a proper social role. This is most frequently defined in terms of the marriage of an eligible young woman and an equally eligible young man. The society of *Earnest* believes that young men like Jack and Algernon and young women like Gwendolen and Cecily should marry and get about the business of having children and raising them to provide for the continuation of the society. Even the marriage of Miss Prism and Dr. Chasuble serves social purposes. The society of the play prefers married clergymen to celibates and has no really useful function for a middle-aged spinster. In a serious modern play like *The Glass Menagerie* there are less simple endings. Tom may leave home, as Oedipus was ostracized, but he does so without serenity or enlightenment. He carries with him his memories and guilt. Amanda must make some kind of new life for herself and Laura. Probably neither Tom nor Laura will ever marry and settle into socially acceptable roles. The image of the merchant seaman is that of the self-designated outcast, a man who has given up normal family and social life, and Laura is close to retreating so far from reality that normal people must label her insane. Some characters in similar plays find a final escape in death, but it is usually without enlightenment. The characters get out of a difficult situation either by placing themselves in a different (but still difficult) situation or by dying.

SOPHOCLES

Oedipus Tyrannus*

CHARACTERS

OEDIPUS, *Ruler of Thebes*[1]
JOCASTA, *Wife of* OEDIPUS
CREON, *Brother of* JOCASTA
TEIRESIAS, *A Blind Prophet*
A PRIEST
MESSENGER 1
MESSENGER 2

A SHEPHERD
AN ATTENDANT
ANTIGONE } *Daughters of*
ISMENE } OEDIPUS *and*
} JOCASTA
CHORUS OF THEBAN ELDERS

OEDIPUS   What is it, children, sons of the ancient house of Cadmus?
Why do you sit as suppliants crowned with laurel branches? What is
the meaning of the incense which fills the city? The pleas to end
pain? The cries of sorrow? I chose not to hear it from my messengers,
but came myself—I came, Oedipus, Oedipus, whose name is known
to all. You, old one—age gives you the right to speak for all of them
—you tell me why they sit before my altar. Has something frightened
you? What brings you here? Some need? Some want? I'll help you
all I can. I would be cruel did I not greet you with compassion when
you are gathered here before me.

PRIEST   My Lord and King, we represent the young and old; some
are priests and some the best of Theban youth. And I—I am a priest
of Zeus. There are many more who carry laurel boughs like these—
in the market-places, at the twin altars of Pallas, by the sacred ashes
of Ismenus' oracle.[2] You see yourself how torn our city is, how she
craves relief from the waves of death which now crash over her.
Death is everywhere—in the harvests of the land, in the flocks that
roam the pastures, in the unborn children of our mothers' wombs. A
fiery plague is ravaging the city, festering, spreading its pestilence,
wasting the house of Cadmus, filling the house of Hades with
screams of pain and of fear. This is the reason why we come to you,
these children and I. No, we do not think you a god. But we deem
you a mortal set apart to face life's common issues and the trials
which the gods dispense to men. It was you who once before came to
Thebes and freed us from the spell that hypnotized our lives. You
did this, and yet you knew no more than we—less even. You had no
help from us. God aided you. Yes, you restored our life. And now a
second time, great Oedipus, we turn to you for help. Find some relief
for us, whether with god or man to guide your way. You helped us
then. Yes. And we believe that you will help us now. O Lord, revive
our city, restore her life. Think of your fame, your own repute. The

* Translated by Luci Berkowitz and
Theodore F. Brunner.
1. See the note on Thebes and the
House of Cadmus, p. 1116.
2. Zeus was the king of the Greek gods.
His daughter Pallas, or Athena, was specifically a goddess of wisdom, but she had
played an important part in the founding
of Thebes. Apollo (or Phoebus), the sun
god, had a shrine near Thebes, close to
the river Ismenus.

people know you saved us from our past despair. Let no one say you raised us up to let us fall. Save us and keep us safe. You found good omens once to aid you and brought us fortune then. Find them again. If you will rule this land as king and lord, rule over men and not a wall encircling emptiness. No city wall, no ship can justify its claim to strength if it is stripped of men who give it life.

OEDIPUS   O my children, I know well the pain you suffer and understand what brings yòu here. You suffer—and yet not one among you suffers more than I. Each of you grieves for himself alone, while my heart must bear the strain of sorrow for all—myself and you and all our city's people. No, I am not blind to it. I have wept and in my weeping set my thoughts on countless paths, searching for an answer. I have sent my own wife's brother Creon, son of Menoeceus, to Apollo's Pythian shrine[3] to learn what I might say or do to ease our city's suffering. I am concerned that he is not yet here—he left many days ago. But this I promise: whenever he returns, whatever news he brings, whatever course the god reveals—*that* is the course that I shall take.

PRIEST   Well spoken. Look! They are giving signs that Creon is returning.

OEDIPUS   O God! If only he brings news as welcome as his smiling face.

PRIEST   I think he does. His head is crowned with laurel leaves.

OEDIPUS   We shall know soon enough. There. My Lord Creon, what word do you bring from the god?

Enter CREON.

CREON   Good news. I tell you this: if all goes well, our troubles will be past.

OEDIPUS   But what was the oracle? Right now I'm swaying between hope and fear.

CREON   If you want to hear it in the presence of these people, I shall tell you. If not, let's go inside.

OEDIPUS   Say it before all of us. I sorrow more for them than for myself.

CREON   Then I shall tell you exactly what the god Apollo answered. These are his words: Pollution. A hidden sore is festering in our land. We are to stop its growth before it is too late.

OEDIPUS   Pollution? How are we to save ourselves?

CREON   Blood for blood. To save ourselves we are to banish a man or pay for blood with blood. It is a murder which has led to this despair.

OEDIPUS   Murder? Whose? Did the god say whose . . . ?

CREON   My Lord, before you came to rule our city, we had a king. His name was Laius . . .

OEDIPUS   I know, although I never saw him.

CREON   He was murdered. And the god's command is clear: we must find the assassin and destroy him.

OEDIPUS   But where? Where is he to be found? How can we find the traces of a crime committed long ago?

3. The oracle at Delphi was the principal shrine of Apollo and was called "Pythian" because it celebrated his victory over the monster Python.

CREON   He lives among us. If we seek, we will find; what we do not seek cannot be found.

OEDIPUS   Where was it that Laius met his death? At home? The country? In some foreign land?

CREON   One day he left and told us he would go to Delphi. That was the last we saw of him.

OEDIPUS   And there was no one who could tell what happened? No one who traveled with him? Did no one see? Is there no evidence?

CREON   All perished. All—except one who ran in panic from the scene and could not tell us anything for certain, except . . .

OEDIPUS   Except? What? What was it? One clue might lead to many. We have to grasp the smallest shred of hope.

CREON   He said that robbers—many of them—fell upon Laius and his men and murdered them.

OEDIPUS   Robbers? Who committed *murder*? Why? Unless they were paid assassins?

CREON   We considered that. But the king was dead and we were plagued with trouble. No one came forth as an avenger.

OEDIPUS   Trouble? What could have kept you from investigating the death of your king?

CREON   The Sphinx.[4] The Sphinx was confounding us with her riddles, forcing us to abandon our search for the unknown and to tend to what was then before us.

OEDIPUS   Then I—I shall begin again. I shall not cease until I bring the truth to light. Apollo has shown, and you have shown, the duty which we owe the dead. You have my gratitude. You will find me a firm ally, and together we shall exact vengeance for our land and for the god. I shall not rest till I dispel this defilement—not just for another man's sake, but for my own as well. For whoever the assassin—he might turn his hand against me too. Yes, I shall be serving Laius and myself. Now go, my children. Leave the steps of my altar. Go. Take away your laurel branches. Go to the people of Cadmus. Summon them. Tell them that I, their king, will leave nothing untried. And with the help of God, we shall find success—or ruin.

Exit OEDIPUS.

PRIEST   Come, children. We have learned what we came to learn. Come, Apollo, come yourself, who sent these oracles!
Come as our savior! Come! Deliver us from this plague!

CHORUS
O prophecy of Zeus, sweet is the sound of your words
as they come to our glorious city of Thebes
from Apollo's glittering shrine.
Yet I quake and I dread and I tremble at those words.
Io, Delian Lord![5]

4. The Sphinx was a winged monster with the head of a woman and the body of a lion who had terrorized Thebes, demanding the answer to her riddle, "What walks on four feet in the morning, two at noon, and three in the evening?" When the young Oedipus appeared at Thebes, he saved the city by answering her riddle, "Man," thus bringing about her death.

5. "Io" was a cry of generalized meaning used by worshippers in praise or supplication. Apollo was called "Delian Lord" because he had been born on the island of Delos.

What will you bring to pass? Disaster unknown,
or familiar to us, as the ever recurring seasons?
Tell me, O oracle,
heavenly daughter of blessèd hope.

Foremost I call on you, daughter of Zeus,
Athena, goddess supreme;
and on Artemis[6] shielding the world,
shielding this land from her circular shrine
graced with renown.
And on you I call, Phoebus, Lord of the unerring bow.

Come to my aid, you averters of doom!
Come to my aid if ever you came!
Come to my aid as once you did, when you quenched
the fires of doom that fell on our soil!
Hear me, and come to my aid!

Boundless the pain, boundless the grief I bear;
sickness pervades this land,
affliction without reprieve.
Barren the soil, barren of fruit;
children are born no longer to light;
all of us flutter in agony
winging our way into darkness and death.

Countless the number of dead in the land;
corpses of children cover the plain,
children dying before they have lived,
no one to pity them,
reeking, and spreading diseases and death.

Moaning and wailing our wives,
moaning and wailing our mothers
stream to the altars this way and that,
scream to the air with helpless cries.
Hear us, golden daughter of Zeus,
hear us! Send us release!

Ares[7] now rages in our midst
brandishing in his hands
the firebrands of disease,
raving, consuming, rousing the screams of death.
Hear us, O goddess!
Help us, and still his rage!
Turn back his assault!
Help us! Banish him from our land!

---

6. Artemis (called Diana by the Romans) was the twin sister of Apollo. She was primarily a moon goddess.
7. Ares (Roman Mars) was the war god.

Drive him into the angry sea,
to the wave-swept border of Thrace![8]

We who escape him tonight
will be struck down at dawn.
Help us, O father Zeus,
Lord of the thunderbolt,
crush him! Destroy him!
Burn him with fires of lightning!

Help us, Apollo, Lycean Lord!
Stand at our side with your golden bow!
Artemis, help us!
Come from the Lycian[9] hills!
Come with your torches aflame!
Dionysus,[1] protector, come to our aid,
come with your revelers' band!
Burn with your torch the god
hated among the gods!

    Enter OEDIPUS.

OEDIPUS   I have heard your prayers and answer with relief and help,
if you will heed my words and tend the sickness with the cure it
cries for. My words are uttered as a stranger to the act, a stranger to
its tale. I cannot trace its path alone, without a sign. As a citizen
newer to Thebes than you, I make this proclamation: If one among
you knows who murdered Laius, the son of Labdacus, let him tell us
now. If he fears for his life, let him confess and know a milder penalty. He will be banished from this land. Nothing more. Or if you
know the assassin to be an alien, do not protect him with your silence. You will be rewarded. But if in fear you protect yourself or
any other man and keep your silence, then hear what I say now:
Whoever he is, this assassin must be denied entrance to your homes.
Any man where I rule is forbidden to receive him or speak to him or
share with him his prayers and sacrifice or offer him the holy rites of
purification. I command you to drive this hideous curse out of your
homes; I command you to obey the will of Pythian Apollo. I will
serve the god and the dead. On the assassin or assassins, I call down
the most vile damnation—for this vicious act, may the brand of
shame be theirs to wear forever. And if I knowingly harbor their
guilt within my own walls, I shall not exempt myself from the curse
that I have called upon them. It is for me, for God, and for this city
that staggers toward ruin that you must fulfill these injunctions. Even
if Heaven gave you no sign, you had the sacred duty to insure that
this act did not go unexamined, unavenged! It was the assassination
of a noble man—your king! Now that I hold the powers that he

---

8. Thrace was a region to the east and
north of Macedonia, a relatively uncivilized
section and a favorite haunt of Ares.
9. Apollo was called "Lycean" apparently because he was regarded as a pro-

tector against wolves. Lycia was a region
of Asia Minor associated with Apollo and
Artemis.
1. Dionysus, the god of wine, was related to the royal house of Thebes.

once held, his bed, his wife—had fate been unopposed, his children would have bound us closer yet—and now on him has this disaster fallen. I will avenge him as I would avenge my own father. I will leave nothing untried to expose the murderer of Laius, the son of Labdacus, heir to the house of Cadmus and Agenor. On those who deny me obedience, I utter this curse: May the gods visit them with barrenness in their harvests, barrenness in their women, barrenness in their fate. Worse still—may they be haunted and tormented and never know the peace that comes with death. But for you, my people, in sympathy with me—I pray that Justice and all the gods attend you forever.

CHORUS   You have made me swear an oath, my Lord, and under oath I speak. I did not kill the king and cannot name the man who did. The question was Apollo's. He could name the man you seek.

OEDIPUS   I know. And yet no mortal can compel a god to speak.

CHORUS   The next-best thing, it seems to me . . .

OEDIPUS   Tell me. Tell me all your thoughts. We must consider everything.

CHORUS   There is one man, second only to Apollo, who can see the truth, who can clearly help us in our search—Teiresias.

OEDIPUS   I thought of this. On Creon's advice, I sent for him. Twice. He should be here.

CHORUS   There were some rumors once, but no one hears them now.

OEDIPUS   What rumors? I want to look at every tale that is told.

CHORUS   They said that travelers murdered Laius.

OEDIPUS   I have heard that too. And yet there's no one to be found who saw the murderer in the act.

CHORUS   He will come forth himself, once he has heard your curse, if he knows what it means to be afraid.

OEDIPUS   Why? Why should a man now fear words if then he did not fear to kill?

CHORUS   But there is one man who can point him out—the man in whom the truth resides, the god-inspired prophet. And there—they are bringing him now.

Enter TEIRESIAS, *guided by a servant.*

OEDIPUS   Teiresias, all things are known to you—the secrets of heaven and earth, the sacred and profane. Though you are blind, you surely see the plague that rakes our city. My Lord Teiresias, we turn to you as our only hope. My messengers may have told you—we have sent to Apollo and he has answered us. We must find Laius' murderers and deal with them. Or drive them out. Then—only then will we find release from our suffering. I ask you not to spare your gifts of prophecy. Look to the voices of prophetic birds or the answers written in the flames. Spare nothing. Save all of us—yourself, your city, your king, and all that is touched by this deathly pollution. We turn to you. My Lord, it is man's most noble role to help his fellow man the best his talents will allow.

TEIRESIAS   O God! How horrible wisdom is! How horrible when it does not help the wise! How could I have forgotten? I should not have come.

OEDIPUS   Why? What's wrong?

TEIRESIAS   Let me go. It will be better if you bear your own distress and I bear mine. It will be better this way.

OEDIPUS   This city gave you life and yet you refuse her an answer! You speak as if you were her enemy.

TEIRESIAS   No! No! It is because I see the danger in your words. And mine would add still more.

OEDIPUS   For God's sake, if you know, don't turn away from us! We are pleading. We are begging you.

TEIRESIAS   Because you are blind! No! I shall not reveal my secrets. I shall not reveal yours.

OEDIPUS   What? You know, and yet you refuse to speak? Would you betray us and watch our city fall helplessly to her death?

TEIRESIAS   I will not cause you further grief. I will not grieve myself. Stop asking me to tell; I will tell you nothing.

OEDIPUS   You will not tell? You monster! You could stir the stones of earth to a burning rage! You will never tell? What will it take?

TEIRESIAS   Know yourself, Oedipus. You denounce me, but you do not yet know yourself.

OEDIPUS   Yes! You disgrace your city. And then you expect us to control our rage!

TEIRESIAS   It does not matter if I speak; the future has already been determined.

OEDIPUS   And if it has, then it is for you to tell me, *prophet!*

TEIRESIAS   I shall say no more. Rage, if you wish.

OEDIPUS   I *am* enraged. And now I will tell you what *I* think. I think this was *your* doing. *You* plotted the crime, *you* saw it carried out. It was *your* doing. All but the actual killing. And had you not been blind, you would have done *that,* too!

TEIRESIAS   Do you believe what you have said? Then accept your own decree! From this day on, deny yourself the right to speak to anyone. You, Oedipus, are the desecrator, the polluter of this land!

OEDIPUS   You traitor! Do you think that you can get away with this?

TEIRESIAS   The truth is my protection.

OEDIPUS   Who taught you this? It did not come from prophecy!

TEIRESIAS   *You* taught me. *You* drove me, *you* forced me to say it against my will.

OEDIPUS   Say it again. I want to make sure that I understand you.

TEIRESIAS   Understand me? Or are you trying to provoke me?

OEDIPUS   No, I want to be sure, I want to know. Say it again.

TEIRESIAS   I say that you, Oedipus Tyrannus, are the murderer you seek.

OEDIPUS   So! A second time! Now twice you will regret what you have said!

TEIRESIAS   Shall I tell you more? Shall I fan your flames of anger?

OEDIPUS   Yes. Tell me more. Tell me more—whatever suits you. It will be in vain.

TEIRESIAS   I say you live in shame with the woman you love, blind to your own calamity.

OEDIPUS   Do you think you can speak like this forever?

TEIRESIAS   I do, if there is any strength in truth.

OEDIPUS   There is—for everyone but you. You—you cripple! Your ears are deaf, your eyes are blind, your mind—your *mind* is crippled!

TEIRESIAS   You fool! You slander me when one day you will hear the same . . .

OEDIPUS   You live in night, Teiresias, in night that never turns to day. And so, you cannot hurt me—or any man who sees the light.

TEIRESIAS   No—it is not I who will cause your fall. That is Apollo's office—and he will discharge it.

OEDIPUS   Was this *your* trick—or Creon's?

TEIRESIAS   No, not Creon's. No, Oedipus. You are destroying yourself!

OEDIPUS   Ah, wealth and sovereignty and skill surpassing skill in life's contentions, why must envy always attend them? This city *gave* me power; I did not ask for it. And Creon, my friend, my trusted friend, would plot to overthrow me—with this charlatan, this impostor, who auctions off his magic wares! His eyes see profit clearly, but they are blind in prophecy. Tell me, Teiresias, what makes you a prophet? Where were you when the monster was here weaving her spells and taunts? What words of relief did Thebes hear from you? Her riddle would stagger the simple mind; it demanded the mind of a seer. Yet, put to the test, all your birds and god-craft proved useless; you had no answer. Then *I* came—ignorant Oedipus—*I* came and smothered her, using only my wit. There were no birds to tell me what to do. I am the man you would overthrow so you can stand near Creon's throne. You will regret—you and your conspirator—you will regret your attempt to purify this land. If you were not an old man, I would make you suffer the pain which you deserve for your audacity.

CHORUS   Both of you, my Lord, have spoken in bitter rage. No more —not when we must direct our every thought to obey the god's command.

TEIRESIAS   Though you are king, the right to speak does not belong to you alone. It is *my* right as well and I shall claim it. I am not your servant and Creon is not my patron. I serve only Loxian Apollo.[2] And I tell you this, since you mock my blindness. You have eyes, Oedipus, and do not see your own destruction. You have eyes and do not see what lives with you. Do you know whose son you are? I say that you have sinned and do not know it; you have sinned against your own—the living and the dead. A double scourge, your mother's and your father's curse, will drive you from this land. Then darkness will shroud those eyes that now can see the light. Cithaeron—the whole earth will resound with your mournful cries when you discover the meaning of the wedding-song that brought you to this place you falsely thought a haven. More sorrow still awaits you—more than you can know—to show you what you are and what our children are. Damn Creon, if you will; damn the words I say. No man on earth will ever know the doom that waits for you.

OEDIPUS   How much of this am I to bear? Leave! Now! Leave my house!

---

2. Apollo was called "Loxian" because the answer given by his oracles at Delphi and elsewhere were frequently ambiguous.

TEIRESIAS   I would not be here had you not sent for me.

OEDIPUS   I never would have sent for you had I known the madness I would hear.

TEIRESIAS   To you, I am mad; but not to your parents . . .

OEDIPUS   Wait! My parents? Who are my parents?

TEIRESIAS   This day shall bring you birth *and* death.

OEDIPUS   Why must you persist with riddles?

TEIRESIAS   Are you not the best of men when it comes to riddles?

OEDIPUS   You mock the very skill that proves me great.

TEIRESIAS   A great misfortune—which will destroy you.

OEDIPUS   I don't care. If I have saved this land, I do not care.

TEIRESIAS   Then I shall go. [*To his servant.*] Come, take me home.

OEDIPUS   Yes, go home. You won't be missed.

TEIRESIAS   I will go when I've said all that I came to say. I am not afraid of you. You cannot hurt me. And I tell you this: The man you seek—the man whose death or banishment you ordered, the man who murdered Laius—that man is here, passing as an alien, living in our midst. Soon it will be known to all of you—he is a native Theban. And he will find no joy in that discovery. His eyes now see, but soon they will be blind: rich now, but soon a beggar. Holding a scepter now, but soon a cane, he will grope for the earth beneath him—in a foreign land. Both brother and father to the children that he loves. Both son and husband to the woman who bore him. Both heir and spoiler of his father's bed and the one who took his life. Go, think on this. And if you find the words I speak are lies, *then* say that I am blind.

Exeunt OEDIPUS, TEIRESIAS.

CHORUS
Who is he? Who is the man?
Who is the man whom the voice of the Delphian shrine
denounced as the killer, the murderer,
the man who committed the terrible crime?
Where is he? Where is he now?
Let him run, let him flee!
Let him rush with the speed of the wind on his flight!
For with fire and lightning the god will attack,
and relentlessy fate will pursue him and haunt him
and drive him to doom.

Do you hear? Do you hear the command of the god?
From Parnassus[3] he orders the hunt.
In vain will the murderer hide,
in vain will he run,
in vain will he lurk in the forests and caves
like an animal roaming the desolate hills.
Let him flee to the edge of the world:
On his heels he will find
the command of the god!

3. Parnassus was a mountain near Delphi, sacred to Apollo and the Muses, minor goddesses associated with the arts.

Confusion and fear
have been spread by the prophet's words.
For I cannot affirm, yet I cannot refute
what he spoke. And I'm lost, I am lost—
What am I to believe?
Now foreboding is gripping my heart.
Was there ever a strife between Laius and Polybus' house?[4]
Can I test? Can I prove?
Can I ever believe that the name of my king
has been soiled by a murder unknown?

It is Zeus and Apollo who know,
who can see the affairs of men.
But the seer and I,
we are mortal, and blind.
Who is right? Who can judge?
We are mortal, our wisdom assigned in degrees.
Does the seer know? Do I?
No, I will not believe in the prophet's charge
till the charge has been proved to my mind.
For I saw how the king
in the test with the Sphinx
proved his wisdom and worth
when he saved this city from doom.
No! I can *never* condemn the king!

Enter CREON.

CREON   My fellow citizens, anger has impelled me to come because
I have heard the accusation which Oedipus has brought against me
—and I will not tolerate it. If he thinks that I—in the midst of this
torment—*I* have thought to harm him in any way, I will not spend
the rest of my life branded by his charge. Doesn't he see the implications of such slander? To you, to my friends, to my city—I would be
a traitor!
CHORUS   He spoke in anger—without thinking.
CREON   Yes—and who was it who said that the prophet lied on my
advice?
CHORUS   It was said, but I don't know how it was meant.
CREON   And was this a charge leveled by one whose eyes were clear?
Whose head was clear?
CHORUS   I don't know. I do not judge my master's actions. But here he
comes.

Enter OEDIPUS.

OEDIPUS   Why have you come, Creon? Do you have the audacity to
show your face in my presence? Assassin! And now you would steal
my throne! What drove you to this plot? Did you see cowardice in
me? Stupidity? Did you imagine that I would not see your treachery? Did you expect that I wouldn't act to stop you? You fool! Your

4. Polybus, the King of Corinth, and his wife Merope were the reputed parents of
Oedipus.

plot was mad! You go after a throne without money, without friends! How do you think thrones are won?

CREON   You listen to me! And when you have heard me out, when you have heard the truth, *then* judge for yourself.

OEDIPUS   Ah yes, your oratory! I can learn nothing from that. This is what I have learned—you are my enemy!

CREON   Just let me say . . .

OEDIPUS   Say one thing—say that you are not a traitor.

CREON   If you think that senseless stubbornness is a precious gift, you are a fool.

OEDIPUS   If you think that you can threaten the house of Cadmus— your own house—and not pay for it, you are mad.

CREON   I grant you that. But tell me: just what is this terrible thing you say I have done to you?

OEDIPUS   Did you or did you not tell me to send for that—that— prophet?

CREON   I did. And I would again.

OEDIPUS   Then, how long since Laius . . . ?

CREON   What? I do not follow . . .

OEDIPUS   . . . Disappeared?

CREON   A long time ago.

OEDIPUS   Your Teiresias—was he—was he a prophet then?

CREON   Yes—and just as honored and just as wise.

OEDIPUS   Did he ever mention me—then?

CREON   Not in my presence.

OEDIPUS   But didn't you investigate the murder?

CREON   Of course we did—

OEDIPUS   And why didn't the prophet say anything *then?*

CREON   I do not know. It's not for me to try to understand.

OEDIPUS   You know this much which you will try to tell me . . .

CREON   What is it? I will tell you if I can.

OEDIPUS   Just this: Had he not acted under your instructions, he would not have named *me* killer of Laius.

CREON   If this is what he said, you ought to know. You heard him. But now I claim the right to question you, as you have me.

OEDIPUS   Ask what you wish. I am not the murderer.

CREON   Then answer me. Did you marry my sister?

OEDIPUS   Of course I did.

CREON   And do you rule on equal terms with her?

OEDIPUS   She has all that she wants from me.

CREON   And am I not the third and equal partner?

OEDIPUS   You are—and that is where you have proved yourself a traitor.

CREON   Not true. Consider rationally, as I have done. First ask your- self—would any man prefer a life of fear to one in which the self- same rank, the self-same rights are guaranteed untroubled peace? I have no wish to be a king when I can act as one without a throne. And any man would feel the same, if he were wise. I share with you a king's prerogatives, yet you alone must face the danger lurking around the throne. If *I* were king, I would have to act in many ways against my pleasure. What added benefit could kingship hold when

I have rank and rule without the threat of pain? I am not deluded
—no, I would not look for honors beyond the ones which profit me.
I have the favor of every man; each greets me first when he would
hope to have *your* favor. Why should I exchange this for a throne?
Only a fool would. No, I am not a traitor nor would I aid an act of
treason. You want proof? Go to Delphi; ask if I have brought you
the truth. Then, if you find me guilty of conspiracy with the prophet,
command my death. I will face that. But do not condemn me without
proof. You are wrong to judge the guilty innocent, the innocent guilty
—without proof. Casting off a true friend is like casting off your
greatest prize—your life. You will know in time that this is true.
Time alone reveals the just; a single day condemns the guilty.

CHORUS   He is right, my Lord. Respect his words. A man who plans in
haste will gamble the result.

OEDIPUS   This is a plot conceived in rashness. It must be met with
quick response. I cannot sit and wait until the plot succeeds.

CREON   What will you do then? Do you intend to banish me?

OEDIPUS   No. No, not banish you. I want to see you *dead*—to make
you an example for all aspiring to my throne.

CREON   Then you won't do as I suggest? You won't believe me?

OEDIPUS   You have not shown that you deserve belief.

CREON   No, because I see that you are mad.

OEDIPUS   In my own eyes, I am sane.

CREON   You should be sane in mine as well.

OEDIPUS   No. You are a traitor!

CREON   And what if you are wrong?

OEDIPUS   Still—*I* will rule.

CREON   Not when you rule treacherously.

OEDIPUS   O Thebes! My city! Listen to him!

CREON   *My* city too!

CHORUS   My Lords, no more. Here comes Jocasta. Perhaps the queen
can end this bitter clash.

Enter JOCASTA.

JOCASTA   Why do you behave like senseless fools and quarrel without
reason? Are you not ashamed to add trouble of your own when your
city is sick and dying? Go, Creon. Go and leave us alone. Forget
those petty grievances which you exaggerate. How important can
they be?

CREON   This important, sister: Oedipus, your husband, in his insanity,
has threatened me with banishment or death.

OEDIPUS   Yes, for I have realized his plot—a plot against my person.

CREON   May the gods haunt me forever, if that is true—if I am guilty
of that charge.

JOCASTA   In the name of God, believe him, Oedipus! Believe him for
the sake of his oath, for my own sake, and for theirs!

CHORUS   Listen to her, my Lord. I beg you to consider and comply.

OEDIPUS   What would you have me do?

CHORUS   Respect the oath that Creon gave you. Respect his past integrity.

OEDIPUS Do you know what you are asking?

CHORUS Yes, I know.

OEDIPUS Then, tell me what you mean.

CHORUS I mean that you are wrong to charge a friend who has invoked a curse upon his head. You are wrong to slander without proof and be the cause for his dishonor.

OEDIPUS Then you must know that when you ask for this, you ask for banishment or doom—for *me*.

CHORUS

O God, no!
O Helios,[5] no!
May Heaven and Earth exact my doom
if that is what I thought!
When our city is torn by sickness
and my heart is torn with pain—
do not compound the troubles
that beset us!

OEDIPUS Then, let him go, although it surely means my death—or banishment with dishonor. *Your* words—not his—have touched my heart. But Creon—wherever he may be—I will hate him.

CREON You are hard when you should yield, cruel when you should pity. Such natures deserve the pain they bear.

OEDIPUS Just go—and leave me in peace.

CREON I will go—my guilt pronounced by you alone. Behold my judge and jury—Oedipus Tyrannus!

Exit CREON.

CHORUS My queen, persuade your husband to rest awhile.

JOCASTA I will—when I have learned the truth.

CHORUS Blind suspicion has consumed the king. And Creon's passions flared beneath the sting of unjust accusations.

JOCASTA Are *both* at fault?

CHORUS Yes, both of them.

JOCASTA But what is the reason for their rage?

CHORUS Don't ask again. Our city is weary enough from suffering. Enough. Let the matter rest where it now stands.

OEDIPUS Do you see what you have done? Do you see where you have come—with your good intentions, your noble efforts to dull the sharpness of my anger?

CHORUS

My Lord, I have said before
and now I say again:
I would be mad,
a reckless fool
to turn away my king,
who saved us from a sea of troubles
and set us on a fairer course,
and who will lead us once again
to peace, a haven from our pain.

5. Helios was the name of a sun god, hence Apollo.

JOCASTA   In the name of Heaven, my Lord, tell me the reason for your bitterness.

OEDIPUS   I will—because you mean more to me than anyone. The reason is Creon and his plot against my throne.

JOCASTA   But can you *prove* a plot?

OEDIPUS   He says that I—Oedipus—bear the guilt of Laius' death.

JOCASTA   How does he justify this charge?

OEDIPUS   He does not stain his own lips by saying it. No. He uses that false prophet to speak for him.

JOCASTA   Then, you can exonerate yourself because no mortal has the power of divination. And I can prove it. An oracle came to Laius once from the Pythian priests—I'll not say from Apollo himself— that he would die at the hands of his own child, his child and mine. Yet the story, which *we* heard was that robbers murdered Laius in a place where three roads meet. As for the child—when he was three days old, Laius drove pins into his ankles and handed him to someone to cast upon a deserted mountain path—to die. And so, Apollo's prophecy was unfulfilled—the child did not kill his father. And Laius' fears were unfulfilled—he did not die by the hand of his child. Yet, these had been the prophecies. You need not give them any credence. For the god will reveal what he wants.

OEDIPUS   Jocasta—my heart is troubled at your words. Suddenly, my thoughts are wandering, disturbed . . .

JOCASTA   What is it? What makes you so frightened?

OEDIPUS   Your statement—that Laius was murdered in a place where three roads meet. Isn't that what you said?

JOCASTA   Yes. That was the story then; that is the story now.

OEDIPUS   Where is this place where three roads meet?

JOCASTA   In the land called Phocis where the roads from Delphi and from Daulia converge.[6]

OEDIPUS   How long a time has passed since then?

JOCASTA   We heard it shortly before you came.

OEDIPUS   O God, what have you planned for me?

JOCASTA   What is it, Oedipus? What frightens you?

OEDIPUS   Do not ask me. Do not ask. Just tell me—what was Laius like? How old was he?

JOCASTA   He was tall and his hair was lightly cast with silver tones, the contour of his body much like yours.

OEDIPUS   O God! Am I cursed and cannot see it?

JOCASTA   What is it, Oedipus? You frighten me.

OEDIPUS   It cannot be—that the prophet sees! Tell me one more thing.

JOCASTA   You frighten me, my Lord, but I will try to tell you what I know.

OEDIPUS   Who traveled with the king? Was he alone? Was there a guide? An escort? A few? Many?

JOCASTA   There were five—one of them a herald—and a carriage in which Laius rode.

OEDIPUS   O God! O God! I see it all now! Jocasta, who told you this?

JOCASTA   A servant—the only one who returned alive.

6. The Oracle at Delphi was located in the region of central Greece called Phocis. Daulia was a city to the east of Delphi.

OEDIPUS   Is he here now? In our house?

JOCASTA   No. When he came back and saw you ruling where once his master was, he pleaded with me—begged me—to send him to the fields to tend the flocks, far from the city. And so I did. He was a good servant and I would have granted him more than that, if he had asked.

OEDIPUS   Could we arrange to have him here—now?

JOCASTA   Yes, but what do you want with him?

OEDIPUS   I am afraid, Jocasta. I have said too much and now I have to see him.

JOCASTA   Then he shall be brought. But I, too, must know the cause of your distress. I have the right to know.

OEDIPUS   Yes, you have that right. And I must tell you—now. You, more than anyone, will have to know what I am going through. My father was Polybus of Corinth, my mother a Dorian—Merope. I was held in high regard in Corinth until—until something strange occurred—something uncanny and strange, although I might have given it too much concern. There was a man dining with us one day who had had far too much wine and shouted at me—half-drunk and shouting that I was not rightly called my father's son. I could barely endure the rest of that day and on the next I went to my parents and questioned them. They were enraged at the remark. I felt relieved at their response. But still, this—this thing—kept gnawing at my heart. And it was spread about in vulgar whispers. And then, without my parents' knowledge, I went to Delphi, but Apollo did not say what I had gone to hear. Instead, he answered questions I had not asked and told of horror and misery beyond belief—how I would know my mother's bed and bring to the world a race of children too terrible for men to see and cause the death of my own father. I trembled at those words and fled from Corinth—as far as I could—to where no star could ever guide me back, where I could never see that infamous prophecy fulfilled. And as I traveled, I came to that place where you say the king was murdered. This is the truth, Jocasta—I was in that place where the three roads meet. There was a herald leading a carriage drawn by horses and a man riding in the carriage—just as you described. The man in front, and the old one, ordered me out of the path. I refused. The driver pushed. In anger, I struck him. The old man saw it, reached for his lash and waited till I had passed. Then he struck me on the head. But he paid—oh yes, he paid. He lost his balance and fell from the carriage and as he lay there helpless—on his back—I killed him. I killed them all. But if this stranger had any tie with Laius—O God —who could be more hated in the eyes of Heaven and Earth? *I* am the one whom strangers and citizens are forbidden to receive! *I* am the one to whom all are forbidden to speak! *I* am the one who must be driven out! *I* am the one for whom my curse was meant! I have touched his bed with the very hands that killed him! O God! The sin! The horror! *I* am to be banished, never to see my people, never to walk in my fatherland. Or else I must take my mother for a bride and kill my father Polybus, who gave me life and cared for me. What cruel god has sent this torture? Hear me, you gods, you holy gods—I will never see that day! I will die before I ever see the stain of this abominable act!

CHORUS   Your words frighten us, my Lord. But you must have hope until you hear the story from the man who saw.

OEDIPUS   Yes—hope. My only hope is waiting for this shepherd.

JOCASTA   Why? What do you hope to find with him?

OEDIPUS   This—if his story agrees with what you say, then I am safe.

JOCASTA   What did I say that makes you sure of this?

OEDIPUS   You said he told of *robbers*—that *robbers* killed the king. If he still *says robbers*, then I am not the guilty one—because no man can talk of many when he means a single one. But if he names a *single* traveler, there will be no doubt—the guilt is mine.

JOCASTA   You can be sure that this was what he said—and he cannot deny it. The whole city heard him—not I alone. But even if he alters what he said before, he cannot prove that Laius met his death as it was prophesied. For Apollo said that he would die at the hand of a child—of mine. And as it happens, the child is dead. So prophecy is worthless. I wouldn't dignify it with a moment's thought.

OEDIPUS   You are right. But still—send someone for the shepherd. Now.

JOCASTA   I shall—immediately. I shall do what you ask. But now— let us go inside.

Exeunt OEDIPUS, JOCASTA.

CHORUS
I pray, may destiny permit
that honestly I live my life
in word and deed.
That I obey the laws
the heavens have begotten
and prescribed.
Those laws created by Olympus,[7]
laws pure, immortal,
forever lasting, essence of the god
who lives in them.
On arrogance and pride
a tyrant feeds.
The goad of insolence,
of senseless overbearing, blind conceit,
of seeking things unseasonable,
unreasonable,
will prick a man to climb to heights
where he must lose his footing
and tumble to his doom.
Ambition must be used
to benefit the state;
else it is wrong, and God
must strike it from this earth.
Forever, God, I pray,
may you stand at my side!

7. The highest mountain of the Greek peninsula and the reputed home of the gods.

A man who goes through life
with insolence in word and deed,
who lacks respect for law and right,
and scorns the shrines and temples of the gods,
may he find evil fate and doom
as his reward for wantonness,
for seeking ill-begotten gains
and reaching after sacred things
with sacrilegious hands.
No! Surely no such man
escapes the wrath, the vengeance of the god!
For if he did, if he could find reward
in actions which are wrong,
why should I trouble to acclaim,
to honor you, God, in my song?

No longer shall my feet
take me to Delphi's sacred shrine;
no longer shall they Abae or Olympia's altars[8] seek
unless the oracles are shown to tell the truth
to mortals without fail!
Where are you, Zeus, all-powerful, all-ruling?
You must be told,
you must know in your all-pervading power:
Apollo's oracles now fall into dishonor,
and what the god has spoken about Laius
finds disregard.
Could God be dead?

    Enter JOCASTA.

JOCASTA My Lords, I want to lay these laurel wreaths and incense offerings at the shrines of Thebes—for Oedipus is torturing himself, tearing his heart with grief. His vision to weigh the present against the past is blurred by fear and terror. He devours every word of dread, drinks in every thought of pain, destruction, death. And I no longer have the power to ease his suffering. Now I turn to you, Apollo, since you are nearest, with prayer and suppliant offerings. Find some way to free us, end our agony! O God of Light, release us! You see the fear that grips us—like sailors who watch their captain paralyzed by some unknown terror on the seas.

    Enter MESSENGER 1.

MESSENGER 1 Strangers, would you direct me to the house of Oedipus? Or if you know where I might find the king himself, please tell me.
CHORUS This is his house, stranger. He is inside. But this is the queen —his wife, and mother of his children.
MESSENGER 1 Then, blessings on the house of Oedipus—his house, his children, and his wife.
JOCASTA Blessings on you as well, stranger. Your words are kind. But why have you come? What is it?

8. Important oracles were located at Abae and Olympia in ancient times.

MESSENGER 1   Good news, my lady—for your husband and your house.

JOCASTA   What news? Where do you come from?

MESSENGER 1   From Corinth, my lady. My news will surely bring you joy—but sorrow, too.

JOCASTA   What? How can that be?

MESSENGER 1   Your husband now is ruler of the Isthmus!

JOCASTA   Do you mean that Polybus of Corinth has been deposed?

MESSENGER 1   Deposed by death, my lady. He has passed away.

JOCASTA   What! Polybus dead?

MESSENGER 1   I swear on my life that this is true.

JOCASTA   [to a servant] Go! Quickly! Tell your master. [To the heavens.] You prophecies—you divinely-uttered prophecies! Where do you stand now? The man that Oedipus feared, the man he dared not face lest he should be his killer—that man is dead! Time claimed his life—not Oedipus!

　　　　Enter OEDIPUS.

OEDIPUS   Why, Jocasta? Why have you sent for me again?

JOCASTA   I want you to listen to this man. Listen to him and judge for yourself the worth of those holy prophecies.

OEDIPUS   Who is he? What news could he have for me?

JOCASTA   He comes from Corinth with the news that—that Polybus— is dead.

OEDIPUS   What! Tell me.

MESSENGER 1   If you must know this first, then I shall tell you— plainly. Polybus has died.

OEDIPUS   How? An act of treason? Sickness? How?

MESSENGER 1   My Lord, only a slight shift in the scales is required to bring the agèd to their rest.

OEDIPUS   Then it was sickness. Poor old man.

MESSENGER 1   Sickness—yes. And the weight of years.

OEDIPUS   Oh, Jocasta! Why? Why should we even look to oracles, the prophetic words delivered at their shrines or the birds that scream above us? They led me to believe that I would kill my father. But he is dead and in his grave, while I stand here—never having touched a weapon. Unless he died of longing for his son. If that is so, then I *was* the instrument of his death. And those oracles! Where are they now? Polybus has taken them to his grave. What worth have they now?

JOCASTA   Have I not been saying this all along?

OEDIPUS   Yes, you have. But I was misled by fear.

JOCASTA   Now you will no longer have to think of it.

OEDIPUS   But—my mother's bed. I still have *that* to fear.

JOCASTA   No. No, mortals have no need to fear when chance reigns supreme. The knowledge of the future is denied to us. It is better to live as you will, live as you can. You need not fear a union with your mother. Men often, in their dreams, approach their mothers' beds, lie with them, possess them. But the man who sees that this is meaningless can live without the threat of fear.

OEDIPUS   You would be right, Jocasta, if my mother were not alive. But she *is* alive. And no matter what you say, I have reason to fear.

JOCASTA   At least your father's death has brought some comfort.

OEDIPUS   Yes—some comfort. But my fear is of *her* as long as she lives.

MESSENGER 1   Who is *she?* The woman you fear?

OEDIPUS   Queen Merope, old man, the wife of Polybus.

MESSENGER 1   But why does *she* instill fear in you?

OEDIPUS   There was an oracle—a dreadful oracle sent by the gods.

MESSENGER 1   Can you tell me—a stranger—what it is?

OEDIPUS   Yes, it is all right to tell. Once Loxian Apollo said that I would take my mother for my bride and murder my father with my own hands. This is the reason that I left Corinth long ago. Fortunately. And yet, I have often longed to see my parents.

MESSENGER 1   Is this the fear that drove you away from Corinth?

OEDIPUS   Yes. I did not want to kill my father.

MESSENGER 1   But I can free you from this fear, my Lord. My purpose for coming was a good one.

OEDIPUS   And I shall see that you receive a fitting reward.

MESSENGER 1   Yes—that's why I came. To fare well myself by your returning home.

OEDIPUS   Home? To Corinth? To my parents? Never.

MESSENGER 1   My son, you do not realize what you are doing.

OEDIPUS   What do you mean, old man? For God's sake, tell me what you mean.

MESSENGER 1   I mean—the reasons why you dread returning home.

OEDIPUS   I dread Apollo's prophecy—and its fulfillment.

MESSENGER 1   You mean the curse—the stain they say lies with your parents?

OEDIPUS   Yes, old man. That is the fear that lives with me.

MESSENGER 1   Then you must realize that this fear is groundless.

OEDIPUS   How can that be—if I am their son?

MESSENGER 1   Because Polybus was no relative of yours.

OEDIPUS   What are you saying! Polybus was *not* my father?

MESSENGER 1   No more than I.

OEDIPUS   No more than you? But you are nothing to me.

MESSENGER 1   He was not your father any more than I.

OEDIPUS   Then why did he call me his son?

MESSENGER 1   You were a gift to him—from me.

OEDIPUS   A gift? From you? And yet he loved me as his son?

MESSENGER 1   Yes, my Lord. He had been childless.

OEDIPUS   And when you gave me to him—had you bought me? Or found me?

MESSENGER 1   I found you—in the hills of Cithaeron.

OEDIPUS   What were you doing there?

MESSENGER 1   Tending sheep along the mountain side.

OEDIPUS   Then you were a—hired shepherd?

MESSENGER 1   Yes, my son—a hired shepherd who saved you at that time.

OEDIPUS   Saved me? Was I in pain when you found me? Was I in trouble?

MESSENGER 1   Yes, your ankles are the proof of that.

OEDIPUS   Ah, you mean this old trouble. What has that to do with it?

MESSENGER 1   When I found you, your ankles were pierced with rivets. And I freed you.

OEDIPUS   Yes, I have had this horrible stigma since infancy.

MESSENGER 1   And so it was the swelling in your ankles that caused your name: Oedipus—"Clubfoot."

OEDIPUS   Oh! Who did this to me? My father? Or my mother?

MESSENGER 1   I don't know. You will have to ask the man who handed you to me.

OEDIPUS   You mean—you did not find me? It was someone else?

MESSENGER 1   Another shepherd.

OEDIPUS   Who? Do you remember who he was?

MESSENGER 1   I think—he was of the house of Laius.

OEDIPUS   The king who ruled this city?

MESSENGER 1   Yes. He was a shepherd in the service of the king.

OEDIPUS   Is he still alive? Can I see him?

MESSENGER 1 [*addressing the* CHORUS]   You—you people here—could answer that.

OEDIPUS   Do any of you know this shepherd? Have you seen him in the fields? Here in Thebes? Tell me now! Now is the time to unravel this mystery—once and for all.

CHORUS   I think it is the shepherd you asked to see before. But the queen will know.

OEDIPUS   Jocasta, is that the man he means? Is it the shepherd we have sent for? Is *he* the one?

JOCASTA   Why? What difference does it make? Don't think about it. Pay no attention to what he said. It makes no difference.

OEDIPUS   No difference? When I must have every clue to untangle the line of mystery surrounding my birth?

JOCASTA   In the name of God, if you care at all for your own life, you must not go on with this. I cannot bear it any longer.

OEDIPUS   Do not worry, Jocasta. Even if I am a slave—a third-generation slave, it is no stain on your nobility.

JOCASTA   Oedipus! I beg you—don't do this!

OEDIPUS   I can't grant you that. I cannot leave the truth unknown.

JOCASTA   It is for *your* sake that I beg you to stop. For your own good.

OEDIPUS   My own good has brought me pain too long.

JOCASTA   God help you! May you never know what you are!

OEDIPUS   Go, someone, and bring the shepherd to me. Leave the queen to exult in her noble birth.

JOCASTA   God help you! This is all that I can say to you—now or ever.

Exit JOCASTA.

CHORUS   Why has the queen left like this—grief-stricken and tortured with pain? My Lord, I fear—I fear that from her silence some horror will burst forth.

OEDIPUS   Let it explode! I will still want to uncover the secret of my birth—no matter how horrible. She—she is a woman with a woman's pride—and she feels shame for my humble birth. But I am the child of Fortune—beneficent Fortune—and I shall not be shamed! She is my mother. My sisters are the months and they have seen me rise and fall. This is my family. I will never deny my birth—and I will learn its secret!

Exit OEDIPUS.

CHORUS
Ah Cithaeron,
if in my judgment I am right,
if I interpret what I hear correctly,
then—by Olympus' boundless majesty!—
tomorrow's full moon will not pass
before, Cithaeron, you will find
that Oedipus will honor you
as mother and as nurse!
That we will praise you in our song,
benevolent and friendly to our king.
Apollo, our Lord, may you find joy in this!

Who bore you, Oedipus? A nymph?
Did Pan beget you in the hills?
Were you begotten by Apollo?
Perhaps so, for he likes the mountain glens.
Could Hermes be your father?[9]
Or Dionysus? Could it be
that he received you as a gift
high in the mountains from a nymph
with whom he lay?

> *Enter* OEDIPUS.

OEDIPUS My Lords, I have never met him, but could that be the shepherd we have been waiting for? He seems to be of the same age as the stranger from Corinth. And I can see now—those are my servants who are bringing him here. But, perhaps you know—if you have seen him before. Is he the shepherd?

> *Enter* SHEPHERD.

CHORUS Yes. I recognize him. He was a shepherd in the service of Laius—as loyal as any man could be.
OEDIPUS Corinthian, I ask you—is this the man you mean?
MESSENGER 1 Yes, my Lord. This is the man.
OEDIPUS And you, old man, look at me and answer what I ask. Were you in the service of Laius?
SHEPHERD I was. But not bought. I was reared in his house.
OEDIPUS What occupation? What way of life?
SHEPHERD Tending flocks—for most of my life.
OEDIPUS And where did you tend those flocks?
SHEPHERD Sometimes Cithaeron, sometimes the neighboring places.
OEDIPUS Have you ever seen this man before?
SHEPHERD What man do you mean? Doing what?
OEDIPUS This man. Have you ever met him before?
SHEPHERD Not that I recall, my Lord.
MESSENGER 1 No wonder, my Lord. But I shall help him to recall. I am sure that he'll remember the time we spent on Cithaeron—

---

9. Pan was a woodland god and a protector of herds. Hermes (Roman Mercury) was the messenger of the gods.

he with his two flocks and I with one. Six months—spring to autumn
—every year—for three years. In the winter I would drive my
flocks to my fold in Corinth, and he to the fold of Laius. Isn't that
right, sir?

SHEPHERD   That is what happened. But it was a long time ago.

MESSENGER 1   Then tell me this. Do you remember a child you gave
me to bring up as my own?

SHEPHERD   What are you saying? Why are you asking me this?

MESSENGER 1   This, my friend, this—is that child.

SHEPHERD   Damn you! Will you keep your mouth shut!

OEDIPUS   Save your reproaches, old man. It is you who deserve them—
your words deserve them.

SHEPHERD   But master—how have I offended?

OEDIPUS   By refusing to answer his question about the child.

SHEPHERD   He doesn't know what he's saying. He's crazy.

OEDIPUS   If you don't answer of your own accord, we'll make you talk.

SHEPHERD   No! My Lord, please! Don't hurt an old man.

OEDIPUS [*to the* CHORUS]   One of you—twist his hands behind his back!

SHEPHERD   Why? Why? What do you want to know?

OEDIPUS   Did you or did you not give him that child?

SHEPHERD   I did. I gave it to him—and I wish that I had died that day.

OEDIPUS   You tell the truth, or you'll have your wish now.

SHEPHERD   If I tell, it will be worse.

OEDIPUS   Still he puts it off!

SHEPHERD   I said that I gave him the child!

OEDIPUS   Where did you get it? Your house? Someone else's? Where?

SHEPHERD   Not mine. Someone else's.

OEDIPUS   Whose? One of the citizens'? Whose house?

SHEPHERD   O God, master! Don't ask me any more.

OEDIPUS   This is the last time that I ask you.

SHEPHERD   It was a child—of the house of Laius.

OEDIPUS   A slave? Or of his own line?

SHEPHERD   Ah master, do I *have* to speak?

OEDIPUS   You have to. And I *have* to hear.

SHEPHERD   They said—it was his child. But the queen could tell you
best.

OEDIPUS   Why? Did *she* give you the child?

SHEPHERD   Yes, my Lord.

OEDIPUS   Why?

SHEPHERD   To—kill!

OEDIPUS   Her own child!

SHEPHERD   Yes. Because she was terrified of some dreadful prophecy.

OEDIPUS   What prophecy?

SHEPHERD   The child would kill his father.

OEDIPUS   Then why did you give him to this man?

SHEPHERD   I felt sorry for him, master. And I thought that he would
take him to his own home. But he saved him from his suffering—
for worse suffering yet. My Lord, if you are the man he says you are
—O God—you were born to suffering!

OEDIPUS   O God! O no! I see it all now! All clear! O Light! I will never

look on you again! Sin! Sin in my birth! Sin in my marriage! Sin in
blood!

Exit OEDIPUS.

CHORUS

O generations of men, you are nothing!
You are nothing!
And I count you as not having lived at all!
Was there ever a man,
was there ever a man on this earth
who could say he was happy,
who knew happiness, true happiness,
not an image, a dream,
an illusion, a vision, which would disappear?
Your example, Oedipus,
your example, your fate, your disaster,
show that none of us mortals
ever knew, ever felt what happiness truly is.

Here is Oedipus,
fortune and fame and bliss
leading him by the hand,
prodding him on to heights
mortals had never attained.
Zeus, it was he who removed
the scourge of the riddling maid,
of the sharp-clawed, murderous Sphinx!
He restored me to life from the brink
of disaster, of doom and of death.
It was he who was honored and hailed,
who was crowned and acclaimed as our king.

Here is Oedipus:
Who on this earth has been
struck by a harder blow
or stung by a fate more perverse?
Wretched Oedipus!
Father and son alike,
pleasures you took from where
once you were given life.
Furrows your father ploughed
bore you in silence. How, how, oh how could it be?

Time found you out,
all-seeing, irrepressible time.
Time sits in judgment on
the union that never could be,
judges you, father and son,
begot and begetter alike.

Would that I never had
laid eyes on Laius' child!
Now I wail and I weep,
and my lips are drenched in lament.
It was you, who offered me life;
it is you, who now bring me death.

Enter MESSENGER 2.

MESSENGER 2   O you most honored citizens of Thebes, you will mourn
for the things you will hear, you will mourn for the things you will
see, and you will ache from the burden of sorrow—if you are true
sons of the house of Labdacus, if you care, if you feel. The waters
of Ister and Phasis[1] can never cleanse this house of the horrors
hidden within it and soon to be revealed—horrors willfully done!
Worst of the sorrows we know are those that are willfully done!

CHORUS   We have mourned enough for sorrows we have known. What
more is there that you can add?

MESSENGER 2   One more and only one—Jocasta, the queen, is dead.

CHORUS   O God—no! How!

MESSENGER 2   By her own hand. But the most dreadful pain you have
not seen. You have not seen the worst. I have seen it and I shall tell
you what I can of her terrible suffering. She ran in frenzied despair
through the palace halls and rushed straight to her bridal bed—her
fingers clutching and tearing at her hair. Then, inside the bedroom,
she flung the doors closed and cried out to Laius, long since dead.
She cried out to him, remembering the son that she had borne long
ago, the son who killed his father, the son who left her to bear a
dread curse—the children of her own son! She wept pitifully for that
bridal bed which she had twice defiled—husband born of husband,
child born of child. I didn't see what happened then. I didn't see her
die. At that moment the king rushed in and shrieked in horror. All
eyes turned to him as he paced in frantic passion and confusion. He
sprang at each of us and begged to have a sword. He begged to
know where he could find the wife that was no wife to him, the
woman who had been mother to him and to his children. Some
power beyond the scope of man held him in its sway and guided
him to her. It was none of us. Then—as if somebody had beckoned
to him and bade him follow—he screamed in terror and threw himself against the doors that she had locked. His body's weight and
force shattered the bolts and thrust them from their sockets and he
rushed into the room. There we saw the queen hanging from a noose
of twisted cords. And when the king saw her, he cried out and
moaned in deep, sorrowful misery. Then he untied the rope that
hung about her neck and laid her body on the ground. But what
happened then was even worse. Her gold brooches, her pins—he
tore them from her gown and plunged them into her eyes again and
again and again and screamed, "No longer shall you see the suffering

---

1. The Ister was a name for the lower Danube. The Phasis flowed from the Caucasus
to the Black Sea. They are invoked here together as examples of large rivers.

you have known and caused! You saw what was forbidden to be seen, yet failed to recognize those whom you longed to see! Now you shall see only darkness!" And as he cried out in such desperate misery, he struck his eyes over and over—until a shower of blood and tears splattered down his beard, like a torrent of crimson rain and hail. And now suffering is mingled with pain for man and wife for the sins that both have done. Not one alone. Once—long ago—this house was happy—and rightly so. But now—today—sorrow, destruction, death, shame—all torments that have a name—all, all are theirs to endure.

CHORUS   But the king—does he have any relief from his suffering now?

MESSENGER 2   He calls for someone to unlock the gates and reveal to Thebes his father's killer, his mother's—I can't say it. I cannot say this unholy word. He cries out that he will banish himself from the land to free this house of the curse that he has uttered. But he is weak, drained. There is no one to guide his way. The pain is more than he can bear. You will see for yourselves. The palace gates are opening. You will see a sight so hideous that even his most bitter enemy would pity him.

Enter OEDIPUS.

CHORUS
Ah!
Dread horror for men to see!
Most dreadful of all that I have seen!
Ah!
Wretched one,
what madness has possessed you?
What demon has descended upon you
and bound you to this dire fate?
Ah!
Wretched one,
I cannot bear to look at you.
I want to ask you more
and learn still more
and understand—
but I shudder at the sight of you!

OEDIPUS   Ah! Ah! Where has this misery brought me? Is this my own voice I hear—carried on the wings of the air? O Fate! What have you done to me?

CHORUS   Terrible! Too terrible to hear! Too terrible to see!

OEDIPUS   O cloud of darkness! Cruel! Driven by the winds of fate! Assaulting me! With no defense to hold you back! O God! The pain! The pain! My flesh aches from its wounds! My soul aches from the memory of its horrors!

CHORUS   Body and soul—each suffers and mourns.

OEDIPUS   Ah! You still remain with me—a constant friend. You still remain to care for me—a blind man now. Now there is darkness and I cannot see your face. But I can hear your voice and I know that you are near.

CHORUS   O my Lord, how could you have done this? How could you blind yourself? What demon drove you?

OEDIPUS   Apollo! It was Apollo! *He* brought this pain, this suffering to me. But it was my own hand that struck the blow. Not his. O God! Why should I have sight when all that I would see is ugliness?

CHORUS   It is as you say.

OEDIPUS   What is there for me to see and love? What sight would give me joy? What sound? Take me away! Take me out of this land! I am cursed! Doomed! I am the man most hated by the gods!

CHORUS   You have suffered equally for your fortune and for your disaster. I wish that you had never come to Thebes.

OEDIPUS   Damn the man who set me free! Who loosed the fetters from my feet and let me live! I never will forgive him. If he had let me die, I would never have become the cause—the grief . . .

CHORUS   I wish that it had been this way.

OEDIPUS   If it had been, I would not have come to this—killer of my father, bridegroom of the woman who gave me birth, despised by the gods, child of shame, father and brother to my children. Is there any horror worse than these—any horror that has not fallen upon Oedipus.

CHORUS   My Lord, I cannot condone what you have done. You would have been better dead than alive and blind.

OEDIPUS   I did what I had to. You know I did. No more advice. Could these eyes have looked upon my father in the house of Hades? Could these eyes have faced my mother in her agony? I sinned against them both—a sin no suicide could purge. Could I have joy at the sight of my children—born as they were born? With these eyes? Never! Could I look upon the city of Thebes? The turrets that grace her walls? The sacred statues of her gods? Never! Damned! I—the noblest of the sons of Thebes—I have damned myself. It was I who commanded that Thebes must cast out the one who is guilty, unholy, cursed by the heavenly gods. *I* was the curse of Thebes! Could these eyes look upon the people? Never! And if I could raise a wall to channel the fountain of my hearing, I would spare nothing to build a prison for this defiled body where sight and sound would never penetrate. Then only would I have peace—where grief could not reach my mind. O Cithaeron! Why did you receive me? Why did you not let me die then? Why did you let me live to show the world how I was born? O Polybus! O Corinth! My home that was no home! You raised me, thinking I was fair and never knowing the evil that festered beneath. Now—now see the evil from which I was born, the evil I have become. O God! The three roads! The hidden glen! The thickets! The pathway where three roads meet! The blood you drank from my hands—do you not know—it was the blood of my father! Do you remember? Do you remember what I did then and what I did for Thebes? Wedding-rites! You gave me birth and gave my children birth! Born of the same womb that bore my children! Father! Brother! Child! Incestuous sin! Bride! Wife! Mother! All of one union! All the most heinous sins that man can know! The most horrible shame—I can no longer speak of it. For the love of God, hide me somewhere. Hide me away from this land! Kill me! Cast me into the sea where you will never have to look at me again! I beg you—touch me—in my misery. Touch me. Do not be afraid. My sins are mine alone to bear and touch no other man.

> *Enter* CREON.

CHORUS   My Lord, Creon is here to act or counsel in what you ask. In your stead—he is now our sole protector.

OEDIPUS   What can I say to him? How can I ask for his trust? I have wronged him. I know that now.

CREON   I have not come to mock you, Oedipus, nor to reproach you for the past. But you—if you have no respect for men, at least respect the lord of the sun whose fires give life to men. Hide your naked guilt from his sight. No earth or sacred rain or light can endure its presence. [*To a servant.*] Take him inside. It is impious for any but his own family to see and hear his suffering.

OEDIPUS   I ask you in the name of God to grant me one favor. You have been kinder to me than I deserved. But one favor. I ask it for you—not for myself.

CREON   What do you ask of me?

OEDIPUS   Cast me out of this land. Cast me out to where no man can see me. Cast me out now.

CREON   I would have done so, you can be sure. But I must wait and do the will of the god.

OEDIPUS   He has signified his will—with clarity. Destroy the parricide! Destroy the unholy one! Destroy Oedipus!

CREON   That was the god's command, I know. But now—with what has happened—I think it better to wait and learn what we must do.

OEDIPUS   You mean that you would ask for guidance for a man so sorrowful as I?

CREON   Surely, you are ready to put your trust in the god—now.

OEDIPUS   Yes, I am ready now. But I ask this of you. Inside—she is lying inside—give her whatever funeral rites you wish. You will do the right thing for her. She is your sister. But for me—do not condemn this city—my father's city—to suffer any longer from my presence as long as I live. Let me go and live upon Cithaeron—O Cithaeron, your name is ever linked with mine! Where my parents chose a grave for me. Where they would have had me die. Where I shall die in answer to their wish. And yet, I know, neither sickness nor anything else will ever bring me death. For I would not have been saved from death that once. No—I was saved for a more dreadful fate. Let it be. Creon, do not worry about my sons. They are boys and will have all they need, no matter where they go. But my daughters—poor creatures! They never ate a single meal without their father. We shared everything together. Creon, take care of them. Creon, let me touch them one last time. And let me weep—one last time. Please, my Lord, please, allow it—you're generous, you're kind. If I could only touch them and feel that they are with me—as I used to—when I could see them. [*Enter* ANTIGONE *and* ISMENE.] What is that crying? Is it my daughters? Has Creon taken pity on me? Has he sent my daughters to me? Are they here?

CREON   Yes, Oedipus, they are here. I had them brought to you. I know how much you love them, how much you have always loved them.

OEDIPUS   Bless you for this, Creon. Heaven bless you and grant you greater kindness than it has granted me. Ah, children, where are you? Come—come, touch my hands, the hands of your father, the hands of your brother, the hands that blinded these eyes which once were bright—these eyes—your father's eyes which neither saw nor knew what he had done when he became your father. I weep for you, my children. I cannot see you now. But when I think of the bitterness that waits for you in life, what you will have to suffer—the festivals, the holidays—the sadness you will know when you should share in gaiety! And when you are old enough to marry—who will there be, who will be the man strong enough to bear the slander that will haunt you—because you are *my* children? What disgrace will you not know? Your father killed his father. And lay with the woman that bore him and his children. These are the taunts that will follow you. And what man will marry you? No man, my children. You will spend your lives unwed—without children of your own—barren and wasted. Ah, Creon, you are the only father left to them. We—their parents—are lost. We gave them life. And we are lost to them. Take care of them. See that they do not wander poor and lonely. Do not let them suffer for what I have done. Pity them. They are so young. So lost. They have no one but you. Take my hand and promise me. And oh, my children, if you were older, I could make you understand. But now, make this your prayer—to find some place where you can live and have a better life than what your father knew.

CREON   Enough, my Lord. Go inside now.

OEDIPUS   Yes. I do not want to, but I will go.

CREON   All things have their time and their place.

OEDIPUS   I shall go—on this condition.

CREON   What condition? I am listening.

OEDIPUS   That you will send me away.

CREON   That is the god's decision, not mine.

OEDIPUS   The gods will not care where I go.

CREON   Then you shall have your wish.

OEDIPUS   Then—you consent?

CREON   It has nothing to do with my consent.

OEDIPUS   Let me go away from here.

CREON   Go then—but leave the children.

OEDIPUS   No! Do not take them away from me!

CREON   Do not presume that you are still in power. Your power has not survived with you.

CHORUS

There goes Oedipus—
he was the man who was able
to answer the riddle proposed by the Sphinx.
Mighty Oedipus—
he was an object of envy
to all for his fortune and fame.

There goes Oedipus—
now he is drowning in waves of dread and despair.
Look at Oedipus—
proof that none of us mortals
can truly be thought of as happy
until he is granted deliverance from life,
until he is dead
and must suffer no more.

ca. 429 B.C.

THEBES AND THE HOUSE OF CADMUS

Many of the principal myths of the Greeks centered about royal families who seemed particularly susceptible to sensational crimes and punishments. Few families had more lurid histories than that of Cadmus, the founder of Thebes.

When Cadmus' sister Europa was stolen by Zeus, in the form of a white bull, his father, Agenor of Sidon, sent Cadmus and his brothers forth to search for her. After various adventures, Cadmus, led by Athena, set out to establish a city. Led by a cow chosen by the goddess, he came to a spring where he was to establish the city. When most of his men were killed by a serpent who lived there, Cadmus killed the serpent and, again following the instructions of the goddess, sowed its teeth. From the teeth sprang up armed men who began fighting among themselves until Cadmus stopped them by throwing a stone into their midst. These "Sown Men" and their descendants were the great families of Thebes. Among them were Echion, the father of Pentheus, and an ancestor of Menoeceus, the father of Jocasta and Creon.

The chart below shows the relations of the members of the house of Cadmus who are mentioned in *Oedipus Tyrannus* and *The Bacchae*. A number of their relatives with equally spectacular destinies are omitted to make the chart more useful to readers of these two plays.

Cadmus ── Harmonia

Polydorus Semele ── Zeus Autonoe ── Aristaeus Ino Agauë ── Echion

Labdacus   Dionysus   Actaeon   Pentheus

Menoeceus

1. Laius ── Jocasta ── ? Oedipus Creon

Oedipus Antigone Eteocles Polynices Ismene

Although *Oedipus Tyrannus* and *The Bacchae* occur in different generations, the figure of Teiresias, the blind prophet, occurs in both. The name may have designated an office rather than an individual.

Thebes was the principal city of Boeotia, a district to the northwest of Attica in which Athens was located. This may help to explain its prominence in the Athenian drama. The two plays here considered make frequent reference to some of the features of the city, including its seven gates (where *The Seven Against Thebes* fought), the great mountain Cithaeron, which was nearby, the streams Ismenus, Dirce, and Asopus, and the neighboring villages of Hysiae and Erythrae.

OSCAR WILDE

The Importance of Being Earnest

CHARACTERS

JOHN WORTHING, J.P.

ALGERNON MONCRIEFF

REV. CANON CHASUBLE D. D.

LANE, *Manservant*

MERRIMAN, *Butler*

LADY BRACKNELL

HON. GWENDOLEN FAIRFAX

CECILY CARDEW

MISS PRISM, *Governess*

A FOOTMAN

The first act takes place in ALGERNON's *flat in Half-Moon Street, London. The remaining acts take place at the Manor House, Woolton, Hertfordshire, the second in the garden and the third in the drawing-room.*

Act 1

Morning-room in ALGERNON's *flat in Half-Moon Street.[1] The room is luxuriously and artistically furnished. The sound of a piano is heard in the adjoining room.*

LANE is arranging afternoon tea on the table, and after the music has ceased, ALGERNON enters.

ALGERNON   Did you hear what I was playing, Lane?

LANE   I didn't think it polite to listen, sir.

ALGERNON   I'm sorry for that, for your sake. I don't play accurately —any one can play accurately—but I play with wonderful expression. As far as the piano is concerned, sentiment is my forte. I keep science for Life.

LANE   Yes, sir.

ALGERNON   And, speaking of the science of Life, have you got the cucumber sandwiches cut for Lady Bracknell?

LANE   Yes, sir. [*Hands them on a salver.*]

ALGERNON [*inspects them, takes two, and sits down on the sofa*] Oh! . . . by the way, Lane, I see from your book that on Thursday night, when Lord Shoreman and Mr. Worthing were dining with me, eight bottles of champagne are entered as having been consumed.

LANE   Yes, sir; eight bottles and a pint.

ALGERNON   Why is it that at a bachelor's establishment the servants invariably drink the champagne? I ask merely for information.

LANE   I attribute it to the superior quality of the wine, sir. I have often observed that in married households the champagne is rarely of a first-rate brand.

---

1. Half-Moon Street runs north from Piccadilly near Hyde Park. Like many of the addresses in the play, it is in Mayfair, a very fashionable section of London.

ALGERNON   Good heavens! Is marriage so demoralizing as that?

LANE   I believe it is a very pleasant state, sir. I have had very little experience of it myself up to the present. I have only been married once. That was in consequence of a misunderstanding between myself and a young person.

ALGERNON [*languidly*]   I don't know that I am much interested in your family life, Lane.

LANE   No, sir; it is not a very interesting subject. I never think of it myself.

ALGERNON   Very natural, I am sure. That will do, Lane, thank you.

LANE   Thank you, sir. [*Goes out.*]

ALGERNON   Lane's views on marriage seem somewhat lax. Really, if the lower orders don't set us a good example, what on earth is the use of them? They seem, as a class, to have absolutely no sense of moral responsiblity.

   Enter LANE.

LANE   Mr. Ernest Worthing.

   Enter JACK. LANE *goes out.*

ALGERNON   How are you, my dear Ernest? What brings you up to town?

JACK   Oh, pleasure, pleasure! What else should bring one anywhere? Eating as usual, I see, Algy!

ALGERNON [*stiffly*]   I believe it is customary in good society to take some slight refreshment at five o'clock. Where have you been since last Thursday?

JACK [*sitting down on the sofa*]   In the country.

ALGERNON   What on earth do you do there?

JACK [*pulling off his gloves*]   When one is in town one amuses oneself. When one is in the country one amuses other people. It is excessively boring.

ALGERNON   And who are the people you amuse?

JACK [*airily*]   Oh, neighbors, neighbors.

ALGERNON   Got nice neighbors in your part of Shropshire?

JACK   Perfectly horrid! Never speak to one of them.

ALGERNON   How immensely you must amuse them! [*Goes over and takes sandwich.*] By the way, Shropshire is your county, is it not?

JACK   Eh? Shropshire? Yes, of course.[2] Hallo! Why all these cups? Why cucumber sandwiches? Why such reckless extravagance in one so young? Who is coming to tea?

ALGERNON   Oh! merely Aunt Augusta and Gwendolen.

JACK   How perfectly delightful!

ALGERNON   Yes, that is all very well; but I am afraid Aunt Augusta won't quite approve of your being here.

JACK   May I ask why?

2. As we learn later, Jack's country place is in Hertfordshire, to the north of London. He is attempting to deceive Algernon by giving a false location to the west, on the Welsh border.

ALGERNON   My dear fellow, the way you flirt with Gwendolen is perfectly disgraceful. It is almost as bad as the way Gwendolen flirts with you.

JACK   I am in love with Gwendolen. I have come up to town expressly to propose to her.

ALGERNON   I thought you had come up for pleasure? . . . I call that business.

JACK   How utterly unromantic you are!

ALGERNON   I really don't see anything romantic in proposing. It is very romantic to be in love. But there is nothing romantic about a definite proposal. Why, one may be accepted. One usually is, I believe. Then the excitement is all over. The very essence of romance is uncertainty. If ever I get married, I'll certainly try to forget the fact.

JACK   I have no doubt about that, dear Algy. The Divorce Court was specially invented for people whose memories are so curiously constituted.

ALGERNON   Oh! there is no use speculating on that subject. Divorces are made in Heaven—

JACK *puts out his hand to take a sandwich.* ALGERNON *at once interferes.*

Please don't touch the cucumber sandwiches. They are ordered specially for Aunt Augusta. [*Takes one and eats it.*]

JACK   Well, you have been eating them all the time.

ALGERNON   That is quite a different matter. She is my aunt. [*Takes plate from below.*] Have some bread and butter. The bread and butter is for Gwendolen. Gwendolen is devoted to bread and butter.

JACK [*advancing to table and helping himself*]   And very good bread and butter it is too.

ALGERNON   Well, my dear fellow, you need not eat as if you were going to eat it all. You behave as if you were married to her already. You are not married to her already, and I don't think you ever will be.

JACK   Why on earth do you say that?

ALGERNON   Well, in the first place, girls never marry the men they flirt with. Girls don't think it right.

JACK   Oh, that is nonsense!

ALGERNON   It isn't. It is a great truth. It accounts for the extraordinary number of bachelors that one sees all over the place. In the second place, I don't give my consent.

JACK   Your consent!

ALGERNON   My dear fellow, Gwendolen is my first cousin. And before I allow you to marry her, you will have to clear up the whole question of Cecily. [*Rings bell.*]

JACK   Cecily! What on earth do you mean? What do you mean, Algy, by Cecily? I don't know any one of the name of Cecily.

Enter LANE.

ALGERNON Bring me that cigarette case Mr. Worthing left in the smoking-room the last time he dined here.

LANE Yes, sir. [*Goes out.*]

JACK Do you mean to say you have had my cigarette case all this time? I wish to goodness you had let me know. I have been writing frantic letters to Scotland Yard[3] about it. I was very nearly offering a large reward.

ALGERNON Well, I wish you would offer one. I happen to be more then usually hard up.

JACK There is no good offering a large reward now that the thing is found.

> Enter LANE *with the cigarette case on a salver.* ALGERNON *takes it at once.* LANE *goes out.*

ALGERNON I think that is rather mean of you. Ernest, I must say. [*Opens case and examines it.*] However, it makes no matter, for now that I look at the inscription inside, I find that the thing isn't yours after all.

JACK Of course it's mine. [*Moving to him.*] You have seen me with it a hundred times, and you have no right whatsoever to read what is written inside. It is a very ungentlemanly thing to read a private cigarette case.

ALGERNON Oh! it is absurd to have a hard and fast rule about what one should read and what one shouldn't. More than half of modern culture depends on what one shouldn't read.

JACK I am quite aware of the fact, and I don't propose to discuss modern culture. It isn't the sort of thing one should talk of in private. I simply want my cigarette case back.

ALGERNON Yes; but this isn't your cigarette case. This cigarette case is a present from someone of the name of Cecily, and you said you didn't know anyone of that name.

JACK Well, if you want to know, Cecily happens to be my aunt.

ALGERNON Your aunt!

JACK Yes. Charming old lady she is, too. Lives at Tunbridge Wells.[4] Just give it back to me, Algy.

ALGERNON [*retreating to back of sofa*] But why does she call herself little Cecily if she is your aunt and lives at Tunbridge Wells. [*Reading.*] "From little Cecily with her fondest love."

JACK [*moving to sofa and kneeling upon it*] My dear fellow, what on earth is there in that? Some aunts are tall, some aunts are not tall. That is a matter that surely an aunt may be allowed to decide for herself. You seem to think that every aunt should be exactly like your aunt! That is absurd. For Heaven's sake give me back my cigarette case. [*Follows* ALGERNON *round the room.*]

ALGERNON Yes. But why does your aunt call you her uncle? "From little Cecily, with her fondest love to her dear Uncle Jack." There is no objection, I admit, to an aunt being a small aunt, but why an

3. The headquarters of the London Metropolitan Police are in Scotland Yard, near the Houses of Parliament.

4. Tunbridge Wells is a resort town in Kent, to the southeast of London.

aunt, no matter what her size may be, should call her own nephew her uncle, I can't quite make out. Beside, your name isn't Jack at all; it is Ernest.

JACK   It isn't Ernest; it's Jack.

ALGERNON   You have always told me it was Ernest. I have introduced you to everyone as Ernest. You answer to the name of Ernest. You look as if your name was Ernest. You are the most earnest-looking person I ever saw in my life. It is perfectly absurd your saying that your name isn't Ernest. It's on your cards. Here is one of them. [*Taking it from case.*] "Mr. Ernest Worthing, B.4, The Albany."[5] I'll keep this as a proof that your name is Ernest if ever you attempt to deny it to me, or to Gwendolen, or to any one else. [*Puts the card in his pocket.*]

JACK   Well, my name is Ernest in town and Jack in the country, and the cigarette case was given to me in the country.

ALGERNON   Yes, but that does not account for the fact that your small Aunt Cecily, who lives at Tunbridge Wells, calls you her dear uncle. Come, old boy, you had much better have the thing out at once.

JACK   My dear Algy, you talk exactly as if you were a dentist. It is very vulgar to talk like a dentist when one isn't a dentist. It produces a false impression.

ALGERNON   Well, that is exactly what dentists always do. Now, go on! Tell me the whole thing. I may mention that I have always suspected you of being a confirmed and secret Bunburyist; and I am quite sure of it now.

JACK   Bunburyist? What on earth do you mean by a Bunburyist?

ALGERNON   I'll reveal to you the meaning of that incomparable expression as soon as you are kind enough to inform me why you are Ernest in town and Jack in the country.

JACK   Well, produce my cigarette case first.

ALGERNON   Here it is. [*Hands cigarette case.*] Now produce your explanation, and pray make it improbable. [*Sits on sofa.*]

JACK   My dear fellow, there is nothing improbable about my explanation at all. In fact it's perfectly ordinary. Old Mr. Thomas Cardew, who adopted me when I was a little boy, made me in his will guardian to his granddaughter, Miss Cecily Cardew. Cecily, who addresses me as her uncle from motives of respect that you could not possibly appreciate, lives at my place in the country under the charge of her admirable governess, Miss Prism.

ALGERNON   Where is that place in the country, by the way?

JACK   That is nothing to you, dear boy. You are not going to be invited. . . . I may tell you candidly that the place is not in Shropshire.

ALGERNON   I suspected that, my dear fellow! I have Bunburyed all over Shropshire on two separate occasions. Now, go on. Why are you Ernest in town and Jack in the country?

JACK   My dear Algy, I don't know whether you will be able to understand my real motives. You are hardly serious enough. When

5. An apartment building for single gentlemen on Piccadilly, to the east of Algernon's flat.

one is placed in the position of guardian, one has to adopt a very high moral tone on all subjects. It's one's duty to do so. And as a high moral tone can hardly be said to conduce very much to either one's health or one's happiness, in order to get up to town I have always pretended to have a younger brother of the name of Ernest, who lives in the Albany, and gets into the most dreadful scrapes. That, my dear Algy, is the whole truth pure and simple.

ALGERNON   The truth is rarely pure and never simple. Modern life would be very tedious if it were either, and modern literature a complete impossibility!

JACK   That wouldn't be at all a bad thing.

ALGERNON   Literary criticism is not your forte, my dear fellow. Don't try it. You should leave that to people who haven't been at a University. They do it so well in the daily papers. What you really are is a Bunburyist. I was quite right in saying you were a Bunburyist. You are one of the most advanced Bunburyists I know.

JACK   What on earth do you mean?

ALGERNON   You have invented a very useful young brother called Ernest, in order that you may be able to come up to town as often as you like. I have invented an invaluable permanent invalid called Bunbury, in order that I may be able to go down into the country whenever I choose. Bunbury is perfectly invaluable. If it wasn't for Bunbury's extraordinary bad health, for instance, I wouldn't be able to dine with you at Willis's[6] tonight, for I have been really engaged to Aunt Augusta for more than a week.

JACK   I haven't asked you to dine with me anywhere tonight.

ALGERNON   I know. You are absurdly careless about sending out invitations. It is very foolish of you. Nothing annoys people so much as not receiving invitations.

JACK   You had much better dine with your Aunt Augusta.

ALGERNON   I haven't the smallest intention of doing anything of the kind. To begin with, I dined there on Monday, and once a week is quite enough to dine with one's own relations. In the second place, whenever I do dine there I am always treated as a member of the family, and sent down with either no woman at all, or two. In the third place, I know perfectly well whom she will place me next to, tonight. She will place me next to Mary Farquhar, who always flirts with her own husband across the dinner table. That is not very pleasant. Indeed, it is not even decent . . . and that sort of thing is enormously on the increase. The amount of women in London who flirt with their own husbands is perfectly scandalous. It looks so bad. It is simply washing one's clean linen in public. Besides, now that I know you to be a confirmed Bunburyist I naturally want to talk to you about Bunburying. I want to tell you the rules.

JACK   I'm not a Bunburyist at all. If Gwendolen accepts me, I am going to kill my brother, indeed I think I'll kill him in any case. Cecily is a little too much interested in him. It is rather a bore. So I am going to get rid of Ernest. And I strongly advice you to

6. A well-known establishment for dining on King Street, off St. James's Street and quite near Piccadilly.

do the same with Mr. . . . with your invalid friend who has the absurd name.

ALGERNON   Nothing will induce me to part with Bunbury, and if you ever get married, which seems to me extremely problematic, you will be very glad to know Bunbury. A man who marries without knowing Bunbury has a very tedious time of it.

JACK   That is nonsense. If I marry a charming girl like Gwendolen, and she is the only girl I every saw in my life that I would marry, I certainly won't want to know Bunbury.

ALGERNON   Then your wife will. You don't seem to realize, that in married life three is company and two is none.

JACK [*sententiously*]   That, my dear young friend, is the theory that the corrupt French Drama has been propounding for the last fifty years.[7]

ALGERNON   Yes! and that the happy English home has proved in half the time.

JACK   For heaven's sake, don't try to be cynical. It's perfectly easy to be cynical.

ALGERNON   My dear fellow, it isn't easy to be anything nowadays. There's such a lot of beastly competition about.

> *The sound of an electric bell is heard.*

Ah! that must be Aunt Augusta, Only relatives, or creditors, ever ring in that Wagnerian manner.[8] Now, if I get her out of the way for ten minutes, so that you can have an opportunity for proposing to Gwendolen, may I dine with you tonight at Willis's?

JACK   I suppose so, if you want to.

ALGERNON   Yes, but you must be serious about it. I hate people who are not serious about meals. It is so shallow of them.

> *Enter* LANE.

LANE   Lady Bracknell and Miss Fairfax.

> ALGERNON *goes forward to meet them. Enter* LADY BRACKNELL *and* GWENDOLEN.

LADY BRACKNELL   Good afternoon, dear Algernon, I hope you are behaving very well.

ALGERNON   I'm feeling very well, Aunt Augusta.

LADY BRACKNELL   That's not quite the same thing. In fact the two things rarely go together. [*Sees* JACK *and bows to him with icy coldness.*]

ALGERNON [*to* GWENDOLEN]   Dear me, you are smart!

---

7. Beginning in the middle of the 19th century, such diverse forces as the theatrical sensationalism of Eugene Scribe (1791–1861) and Victorien Sardou (1832–1908) and the movement toward realism in Alexandre Dumas *fils* (1824–1895) and Emil Augier (1820–1889) produced plays dealing with subjects such as adultery, prostitution, and illegitimacy. The heavily censored English theater either avoided such subjects or dealt with them more circumspectly.

8. Many earlier hearers of the music of Richard Wagner found it extremely loud and, consequently, peremptory in demanding attention.

GWENDOLEN   I am always smart! Am I not, Mr. Worthing?

JACK   You're quite perfect, Miss Fairfax.

GWENDOLEN   Oh! I hope I am not that. I would leave no room for developments, and I intend to develop in many directions.

GWENDOLEN *and* JACK *sit down together in the corner.*

LADY BRACKNELL   I'm sorry if we are a little late, Algernon, but I was obliged to call on dear Lady Harbury. I hadn't been there since her poor husband's death. I never saw a woman so altered; she looks quite twenty years younger. And now I'll have a cup of tea and one of those nice cucumber sandwiches you promised me.

ALGERNON   Certainly, Aunt Augusta. [*Goes over to tea-table.*]

LADY BRACKNELL   Won't you come and sit here, Gwendolen?

GWENDOLEN   Thanks. mamma, I'm quite comfortable where I am.

ALGERNON [*picking up empty plate in horror*]   Good heavens! Lane! Why are there no cucumber sandwiches? I ordered them specially.

LANE [*gravely*]   There were no cucumbers in the market this morning, sir. I went down twice.

ALGERNON.   No cucumbers!

LANE   No, sir. Not even for ready money.

ALGERNON   That will do, Lane, thank you.

LANE   Thank you, sir. [*Goes out.*]

ALGERNON   I am greatly distressed, Aunt Augusta, about there being no cucumbers, not even for ready money.

LADY BRACKNELL   It really makes no matter, Algernon. I had some crumpets with Lady Harbury, who seems to me to be living entirely for pleasure now.

ALGERNON   I hear her hair has turned quite gold from grief.

LADY BRACKNELL   It certainly has changed its color. From what cause I, of course, cannot say.

ALGERNON *crosses and hands tea.*

Thank you. I've quite a treat for you tonight, Algernon. I am going to send you down with Mary Farquhar. She is such a nice woman, and so attentive to her husband. It's delightful to watch them.

ALGERNON   I am afraid, Aunt Augusta, I shall have to give up the pleasure of dining with you tonight after all.

LADY BRACKNELL [*frowning*]   I hope not, Algernon. It would put my table completely out. Your uncle would have to dine upstairs. Fortunately he is accustomed to that.

ALGERNON   It is a great bore, and, I need hardly say, a terrible disappointment to me, but the fact is I have just had a telegram to say that my poor friend Bunbury is very ill again. [*Exchanges glances with* JACK.] They seem to think I should be with him.

LADY BRACKNELL   It is very strange. This Mr. Bunbury seems to suffer from curiously bad health.

ALGERNON   Yes; poor Bunbury is a dreadful invalid.

LADY BRACKNELL   Well, I must say, Algernon, that I think it is high time that Mr. Bunbury made up his mind whether he was going to live or to die. This shilly-shallying with the question is absurd. Nor do I in any way approve of the modern sympathy with invalids. I consider it morbid. Illness of any kind is hardly a thing to be encouraged in others. Health is the primary duty of life. I am always telling that to your poor uncle, but he never seems to take much notice . . . as far as any improvement in his ailments goes. I should be much obliged if you would ask Mr. Bunbury, from me, to be kind enough not to have a relapse on Saturday, for I rely on you to arrange my music for me. It is my last reception, and one wants something that will encourage conversation, particularly at the end of the season when everyone has practically said whatever they had to say, which, in most cases, was probably not much.

ALGERNON   I'll speak to Bunbury, Aunt Augusta, if he is still conscious, and I think I can promise you he'll be all right by Saturday. Of course the music is a great difficulty. You see, if one plays good music, people don't listen, and if one plays bad music, people don't talk. But I'll run over the program I've drawn out, if you will kindly come into the next room for a moment.

LADY BRACKNELL   Thank you, Algernon. It is very thoughtful of you. [*Rising, and following* ALGERNON.] I'm sure the program will be delightful, after a few expurgations. French songs I cannot possibly allow. People always seem to think that they are improper, and either look shocked, which is vulgar, or laugh, which is worse. But German sounds a thoroughly respectable language, and, indeed I believe is so. Gwendolen, you will accompany me.

GWENDOLEN   Certainly, mamma.

>   LADY BRACKNELL *and* ALGERNON *go into the music-room;* GWENDOLEN *remains behind.*

JACK   Charming day it has been, Miss Fairfax.

GWENDOLEN   Pray don't talk to me about weather, Mr. Worthing. Whenever people talk to me about the weather, I always feel quite certain that they mean something else. And that makes me so nervous.

JACK   I do mean something else.

GWENDOLEN   I thought so. In fact, I am never wrong.

JACK   And I would like to be allowed to take advantage of Lady Bracknell's temporary absence . . .

GWENDOLEN   I would certainly advise you to do so. Mamma has a way of coming back suddenly into a room that I have often had to speak to her about.

JACK [*nervously*]   Miss Fairfax, ever since I met you I have admired you more than any girl . . . I have ever met since . . . I met you.

GWENDOLEN   Yes, I am quite aware of the fact. And I often wish that in public, at any rate, you had been more demonstrative. For me you have always had an irresistible fascination. Even before I met you I was far from indifferent to you.

>   JACK *looks at her in amazement.*

We live, as I hope you know, Mr. Worthing, in an age of ideals. The fact is constantly mentioned in the more expensive monthly magazines, and has reached the provincial pulpits, I am told; and my ideal has always been to love some one of the name of Ernest. There is something in that name that inspires absolute confidence. The moment Algernon first mentioned to me that he had a friend called Ernest, I knew I was destined to love you.

JACK   You really love me, Gwendolen?

GWENDOLEN   Passionately!

JACK   Darling! You don't know how happy you've made me.

GWENDOLEN   My own Ernest! ·

JACK   But you don't really mean to say that you couldn't love me if my name wasn't Ernest?

GWENDOLEN   But your name is Ernest.

JACK   Yes, I know it is. But supposing it was something else? Do you mean to say you couldn't love me then?

GWENDOLEN   [*glibly*]   Ah! that is clearly a metaphysical speculation, and like most metaphysical speculations has very little reference at all to the actual facts of real life, as we know them.

JACK   Personally, darling, to speak quite candidly, I don't much care about the name of Ernest. . . . I don't think the name suits me at all.

GWENDOLEN   It suits you perfectly. It is a divine name. It has a music of its own. It produces vibrations.

JACK   Well, really, Gwendolen, I must say that I think there are lots of other much nicer names. I think Jack, for instance, a charming name.

GWENDOLEN   Jack? . . . No, there is very little music in the name Jack, if any at all, indeed. It does not thrill. It produces absolutely no vibrations. . . . I have known several Jacks, and they all, without exception, were more than usually plain. Besides, Jack is a notorious domesticity for John! And I pity any woman who is married to a man called John. She would probably never be allowed to know the entrancing pleasure of a single moment's solitude. The only really safe name is Ernest.

JACK   Gwendolen, I must get christened at once—I mean we must get married at once. There is no time to be lost.

GWENDOLEN   Married, Mr. Worthing?

JACK   [*astounded*]   Well . . . surely. You know that I love you, and you led me to believe, Miss Fairfax, that you were not absolutely indifferent to me.

GWENDOLEN   I adore you. But you haven't proposed to me yet. Nothing has been said at all about marriage. The subject has not even been touched on.

JACK   Well . . . may I propose to you now?

GWENDOLEN   I think it would be an admirable opportunity. And to spare you any possible disappointment, Mr. Worthing, I think it only fair to tell you quite frankly beforehand that I am fully determined to accept you.

JACK   Gwendolen!

GWENDOLEN   Yes, Mr. Worthing, what have you got to say to me?

JACK   You know what I have got to say to you.

GWENDOLEN   Yes, but you don't say it.

JACK   Gwendolen, will you marry me? [*Goes on his knees.*]

GWENDOLEN   Of course I will, darling. How long you have been about it! I am afraid you have had very little experience in how to propose.

JACK   My own one, I have never loved any one in the world but you.

GWENDOLEN   Yes, but men often propose for practice. I know my brother Gerald does. All my girl-friends tell me so. What wonderfully blue eyes you have, Ernest! They are quite, quite blue. I hope you will always look at me just like that, especially when there are other people present.

> *Enter* LADY BRACKNELL.

LADY BRACKNELL   Mr. Worthing! Rise, sir, from this semi-recumbent posture. It is most indecorous.

GWENDOLEN   Mamma! [*He tries to rise; she restrains him.*] I must beg you to retire. This is no place for you. Besides, Mr. Worthing has not quite finished yet.

LADY BRACKNELL   Finished what, may I ask?

GWENDOLEN   I am engaged to Mr. Worthing, mamma.

> *They rise together.*

LADY BRACKNELL   Pardon me, you are not engaged to anyone. When you do become engaged to some one, I, or your father, should his health permit him, will inform you of the fact. An engagement should come on a young girl as a surprise, pleasant or unpleasant, as the case may be. It is hardly a matter that she could be allowed to arrange for herself. . . . And now I have a few questions to put to you, Mr. Worthing. While I am making these inquiries, you, Gwendolen, will wait for me below in the carriage.

GWENDOLEN [*reproachfully*]   Mamma!

LADY BRACKNELL   In the carriage, Gwendolen!

> GWENDOLEN *goes to the door. She and* JACK *blow kisses to each other behind* LADY BRACKNELL's *back.* LADY BRACKNELL *looks vaguely about as if she could not understand what the noise was. Finally turns around.*

Gwendolen, the carriage!

GWENDOLEN   Yes. mamma. [*Goes out, looking back at* JACK.]

LADY BRACKNELL [*sitting down*]   You can take a seat, Mr. Worthing. [*Looks in her pocket for notebook and pencil.*]

JACK   Thank you, Lady Bracknell, I prefer standing.

LADY BRACKNELL [*pencil and notebook in hand*]   I feel bound to tell you that you are not down on my list of eligible young men, although I have the same list as the dear Duchess of Bolton has. We work together, in fact. However, I am quite ready to enter your name, should your answers be what a really affectionate mother requires. Do you smoke?

JACK   Well, yes, I must admit I smoke.

LADY BRACKNELL   I am glad to hear it. A man should always have an occupation of some kind. There are far too many idle men in London as it is. How old are you?

JACK   Twenty-nine.

LADY BRACKNELL   A very good age to be married at. I have always been of the opinion that a man who desires to get married should know either everything or nothing. Which do you know?

JACK [*after some hestitation*]   I know nothing, Lady Bracknell.

LADY BRACKNELL   I am pleased to hear it. I do not approve of anything that tampers with natural ignorance. Ignorance is like a delicate exotic fruit; touch it and the bloom is gone. The whole theory of modern education is radically unsound. Fortunately in England, at any rate, education produces no effect whatsoever. If it did, it would prove a serious danger to the upper classes, and probably lead to acts of violence in Grosvenor Square.[9] What is your income?

JACK   Between seven and eight thousand a year.[1]

LADY BRACKNELL [*makes a note in her book*]   In land, or in investments?

JACK   In investments, chiefly.

LADY BRACKNELL   That is satisfactory. What between the duties expected of one during one's lifetime, and the duties exacted from one after one's death, land has ceased to be either a profit or a pleasure. It gives one position, and prevents one from keeping it up. That's all that can be said about land.

JACK   I have a country house with some land, of course, attached to it, about fifteen hundred acres, I believe; but I don't depend on that for my real income. In fact, as far as I can make out, the poachers are the only people who make anything out of it.

LADY BRACKNELL   A country house! How many bedrooms? Well, that point can be cleared up afterwards. You have a town house, I hope? A girl with a simple, unspoiled nature, like Gwendolen, could hardly be expected to reside in the country.

JACK   Well, I own a house in Belgrave Square,[2] but it is let by the year to Lady Bloxham. Of course, I can get it back whenever I like, at six months' notice.

LADY BRACKNELL   Lady Bloxham? I don't know her.

JACK   Oh, she goes about very little. She is a lady considerably advanced in years.

LADY BRACKNELL   Ah, nowadays that is no guarantee of respectability of character. What number in Belgrave Square?

JACK   149.

---

9. A fashionable location in Mayfair.

1. At the time of the play, the pound was worth about $4.87. Jack's income was thus about thirty thousand dollars a year, a not inconsiderable figure when the New York *Times* was three cents daily and five cents on Sundays, when a can of corn was on sale at nine cents, and when $45 would purchase first-class passage from New York to Amsterdam.

2. Belgrave Square is near the southeast corner of Hyde Park in Belgravia, another fashionable section of London.

LADY BRACKNELL [*shaking her head*]   The unfashionable side. I thought there was something. However, that could easily be altered.

JACK   Do you mean the fashion, or the side?

LADY BRACKNELL [*sternly*]   Both, if necessary, I presume. What are your politics?

JACK   Well, I am afraid I really have none. I am a Liberal Unionist.

LADY BRACKNELL   Oh, they count as Tories.[3] They dine with us. Or come in the evening, at any rate. Now to minor matters. Are your parents living?

JACK   I have lost both my parents.

LADY BRACKNELL   To lose one parent, Mr. Worthing, may be regarded as a misfortune; to lose both looks like carelessness. Who was your father? He was evidently a man of some wealth. Was he born in what the Radical papers call the purple of commerce, or did he rise from the ranks of the aristocracy?

JACK   I am afraid I really don't know. That fact is, Lady Bracknell, I said I had lost my parents. It would be nearer the truth to say that my parents seem to have lost me. . . . I don't actually know who I am by birth. I was . . . well, I was found.

LADYBRACKNELL   Found!

JACK   The late Mr. Thomas Cardew, an old gentleman of a very charitable and kindly disposition, found me, and gave me the name of Worthing, because he happened to have a first-class ticket for Worthing in his pocket at the time. Worthing is a place in Sussex. It is a seaside resort.

LADY BRACKNELL   Where did the charitable gentleman who had a first-class ticket for this seaside resort find you?

JACK [*gravely*]   In a handbag.

LADY BRACKNELL   A handbag?

JACK [*very seriously*]   Yes, Lady Bracknell. I was in a handbag—a somewhat large, black leather handbag, with handles to it—an ordinary handbag in fact.

LADY BRACKNELL   In what locality did this Mr. James, or Thomas, Cardew come across this ordinary handbag?

JACK   In the cloakroom at Victoria Station.[4] It was given to him in mistake for his own.

LADY BRACKNELL   The cloakroom at Victoria Station?

JACK   Yes. The Brighton line.

LADY BRACKNELL   The line is immaterial. Mr. Worthing, I confess I feel somewhat bewildered by what you have just told me. To be born, or at any rate bred, in a handbag, whether it had handles or not, seems to me to display a contempt for the ordinary decencies of family life that reminds one of the worst excesses of the French Revolution. And I presume you know what the unfortunate movement led to? As for the particular locality in which the handbag was found, a cloakroom at a railway station might serve to conceal a

---

3. Liberal Unionists were a late 19th-century political group which had split from the Liberal Party over home rule for Ireland. "Tories" were members of the Conservative Party—the latter was the more customary designation after the First Re- form Bill of 1832.

4. Victoria Station is a major railroad terminus in London, particularly for trains to the south of England, including those going to the popular seaside resort of Brighton.

social indiscretion—has probably, indeed, been used for that purpose before now—but it could hardly be regarded as an assured basis for a recognized position in good society.

JACK   May I ask you then what you would advise me to do? I need hardly say I would do anything in the world to ensure Gwendolen's happiness.

LADY BRACKNELL   I would strongly advise you, Mr. Worthing, to try and acquire some relations as soon as possible, and to make a definite effort to produce at any rate one parent, of either sex, before the season is quite over.

JACK   Well, I don't see how I could possibly manage to do that. I can produce the handbag at any moment. It is in my dressing-room at home. I really think that should satisfy you, Lady Bracknell.

LADY BRACKNELL   Me, sir! What has it to do with me? You can hardly imagine that I and Lord Bracknell would dream of allowing our only daughter—a girl brought up with the utmost care—to marry into a cloakroom, and form an alliance with a parcel. Good morning, Mr. Worthing!

LADY BRACKNELL *sweeps out in majestic indignation.*

JACK   Good morning!

ALGERNON, *from the other room, strikes up the Wedding March.* JACK *looks perfectly furious, and goes to the door.*

For goodness' sake don't play that ghastly tune, Algy! How idiotic you are!

The music stops and ALGERNON *enters cheerily.*

ALGERNON   Didn't it go off all right, old boy? You don't mean to say Gwendolen refused you? I know it is a way she has. She is always refusing people. I think it is most ill-natured of her.

JACK   Oh, Gwendolen is as right as a trivet.[5] As far as she is concerned, we are engaged. Her mother is perfectly unbearable. Never met such a Gorgon.[6] . . . I don't really know what a Gorgon is like, but I am quite sure that Lady Bracknell is one. In any case, she is a monster, without being a myth, which is rather unfair. . . . I beg your pardon, Algy, I suppose I shouldn't talk about your own aunt in that way before you.

ALGERNON   My dear boy, I love hearing my relations abused. It is the only thing that makes me put up with them at all. Relations are simply a tedious pack of people, who haven't got the remotest knowledge of how to live, nor the smallest instinct about when to die.

JACK   Oh, that is nonsense!

5. A proverbial expression, referring to the solidity of a tripod on its three legs.
6. A mythological creature of horrible aspect, particularly because the Gorgon had snakes in place of hair. According to myth, those who looked on a Gorgon were turned to stone by the experience.

ALGERNON   It isn't!

JACK   Well, I won't argue about the matter. You always want to argue about things.

ALGERNON   That is exactly what things were originally made for.

JACK   Upon my word, if I thought that, I'd shoot myself. . . . [*A pause.*] You don't think there is any chance of Gwendolen becoming like her mother in about a hundred and fifty years, do you, Algy?

ALGERNON   All women become like their mothers. That is their tragedy. No man does. That's his.

JACK   Is that clever?

ALGERNON   It is perfectly phrased! and quite as true as any observation in civilized life should be.

JACK   I am sick to death of cleverness. Everybody is clever nowadays. You can't go anywhere without meeting clever people. The thing has become an absolute public nuisance. I wish to goodness we had a few fools left.

ALGERNON   We have.

JACK   I should extremely like to meet them. What do they talk about?

ALGERNON   The fools? Oh! about the clever people, of course.

JACK   What fools.

ALGERNON   By the way, did you tell Gwendolen the truth about your being Ernest in town, and Jack in the country?

JACK   [*in a very patronizing manner*]   My dear fellow, the truth isn't quite the sort of thing one tells to a nice, sweet, refined girl. What extraordinary ideas you have about the way to behave to a woman!

ALGERNON   The only way to behave to a woman is to make love to her, if she is pretty, and to someone else, if she is plain.

JACK   Oh, that is nonsense.

ALGERNON   What about your brother? What about the profligate Ernest?

JACK   Oh, before the end of the week I shall have got rid of him. I'll say he died in Paris of apoplexy. Lots of people die of apoplexy, quite suddenly, don't they?

ALGERNON   Yes, but it's hereditary, my dear fellow. It's a sort of thing that runs in families. You had much better say a severe chill.

JACK   You are sure a severe chill isn't hereditary, or anything of that kind?

ALGERNON   Of course it isn't!

JACK   Very well, then. My poor brother Ernest is carried off suddenly, in Paris, by a severe chill. That gets rid of him.

ALGERNON   But I thought you said that . . . Miss Cardew was a little too much interested in your poor brother Ernest? Won't she feel his loss a good deal?

JACK   Oh, that is all right. Cecily is not a silly romantic girl, I am glad to say. She has got a capital appetite, goes on long walks, and pays no attention at all to her lessons.

ALGERNON   I would rather like to see Cecily.

JACK   I will take very good care you never do. She is excessively pretty, and she is only just eighteen.

ALGERNON Have you told Gwendolen yet that you have an excessively pretty ward who is only just eighteen?

JACK Oh! one doesn't blurt these things out to people. Cecily and
Gwendolen are perfectly certain to be extremely great friends. I'll
bet you anything you like that half an hour after they have met,
they will be calling each other sister.

ALGERNON Women only do that when they have called each other
a lot of other things first. Now, my dear boy, if we want to get a
good table at Willis's, we really must go and dress. Do you know
it is nearly seven?

JACK [*irritably*] Oh! it always is nearly seven.

ALGERNON Well, I'm hungry.

JACK I never knew you when you weren't. . . .

ALGERNON What shall we do after dinner? Go to a theatre?

JACK Oh no! I loathe listening.

ALGERNON Well, let us go to the Club?

JACK Oh, no! I hate talking.

ALGERNON Well, we might trot round to the Empire[7] at ten?

JACK Oh, no! I can't bear looking at things. It is so silly.

ALGERNON Well, what shall we do?

JACK Nothing!

ALGERNON It is awfully hard work doing nothing. However, I don't
mind hard work where there is no definite object of any kind.

Enter LANE.

LANE Miss Fairfax.

Enter GWENDOLEN. LANE *goes out*.

ALGERNON Gwendolen, upon my word!

GWENDOLEN Algy, kindly turn your back. I have something very
particular to say to Mr. Worthing.

ALGERNON Really, Gwendolen, I don't think I can allow this at all.

GWENDOLEN Algy, you always adopt a strictly immoral attitude
towards life. You are not quite old enough to do that.

ALGERNON *retires to the fireplace*.

JACK My own darling!

GWENDOLEN Ernest, we may never be married. From the expression
on mamma's face I fear we never shall. Few parents nowadays pay
any regard to what their children say to them. The old-fashioned
respect for the young is fast dying out. Whatever influence I ever
had over mamma, I lost at the age of three. But although she may
prevent us from becoming man and wife, and I may marry someone
else, and marry often, nothing that she can possibly do can alter my
eternal devotion to you.

7. The Empire Theatre of Varieties, a music hall on Leicester Square.

JACK   Dear Gwendolen!

GWENDOLEN   The story of your romantic origin, as related to me by
mamma, with unpleasing comments, has naturally stirred the
deeper fibres of my nature. Your Christian name has an irresistible
fascination. The simplicity of your character makes you exquisitely
incomprehensible to me. Your town address at the Albany I have.
What is your address in the country?

JACK   The Manor House, Woolton, Hertfordshire.

ALGERNON, *who has been carefully listening, smiles to himself,
and writes the address on his shirt-cuff. Then picks up the
Railway Guide.*

GWENDOLEN   There is a good postal service, I suppose? It may be
necessary to do something desperate. That of course will require
serious consideration. I will communicate with you daily.

JACK   My own one!

GWENDOLEN   How long do you remain in town?

JACK   Till Monday.

GWENDOLEN   Good! Algy, you may turn round now.

ALGERNON   Thanks, I've turned round already.

GWENDOLEN   You may also ring the bell.

JACK   You will let me see you to your carriage, my own darling?

GWENDOLEN   Certainly.

JACK [*to* LANE, *who now enters*]   I will see Miss Fairfax out.

LANE   Yes, sir.

JACK *and* GWENDOLEN *go off.* LANE *presents several letters on a
salver to* ALGERNON. *It is to be surmised that they are bills, as*
ALGERNON, *after looking at the envelopes, tears them up.*

ALGERNON   A glass of sherry, Lane.

LANE   Yes, sir.

ALGERNON   Tomorrow, Lane, I'm going Bunburying.

LANE   Yes, sir.

ALGERNON   I shall probably not be back till Monday. You can put up
my dress clothes, my smoking jacket, and all the Bunbury suits . . .

LANE   Yes, sir. [*Handing sherry.*]

ALGERNON   I hope tomorrow will be a fine day, Lane.

LANE   It never is, sir.

ALGERNON   Lane, you're a perfect pessimist.

LANE   I do my best to give satisfaction, sir.

Enter JACK. LANE *goes off.*

JACK   There's a sensible, intellectual girl; the only girl I ever cared
for in my life.

ALGERNON *is laughing immoderately.*

What on earth are you so amused at?

ALGERNON   Oh, I'm a little anxious about poor Bunbury, that is all.

JACK   If you don't take care, your friend Bunbury will get you into a serious scrape some day.

ALGERNON   I love scrapes. They are the only things that are never serious.

JACK   Oh, that's nonsense, Algy. You never talk anything but nonsense.

ALGERNON   Nobody ever does.

> JACK *looks indignantly at him, and leaves the room.* ALGERNON *lights a cigarette, reads his shirt-cuff, and smiles.*

Act 2

> *Garden at the Manor House. A flight of gray stone steps leads up to the house. The garden, an old-fashioned one, full of roses. Time of year, July. Basket chairs, and a table covered with books, are set under a large yew-tree.*
>
> MISS PRISM *discovered seated at the table.* CECILY *is at the back, watering flowers.*

MISS PRISM [*calling*]   Cecily, Cecily! Surely such a utilitarian occupation as the watering of flowers is rather Moulton's duty than yours? Especially at a moment when intellectual pleasures await you. Your German grammar is on the table. Pray open it at page fifteen. We will repeat yesterday's lesson.

CECILY [*coming over very slowly*]....But I don't like German. It isn't at all a becoming language. I know perfectly well that I look quite plain after my German lesson.

MISS PRISM   Child, you know how anxious your guardian is that you should improve yourself in every way. He laid particular stress on your German, as he was leaving for town yesterday. Indeed, he always lays stress on your German when he is leaving for town.

CECILY   Dear Uncle Jack is so very serious! Sometimes he is so serious that I think he cannot be quite well.

MISS PRISM [*drawing herself up*]   Your guardian enjoys the best of health, and his gravity of demeanor is especially to be commended in one so comparatively young as he is. I know no one who has a higher sense of duty and responsibility.

CECILY   I suppose that is why he often looks a little bored when we three are together.

MISS PRISM   Cecily! I am surprised at you. Mr. Worthing has many troubles in his life. Idle merriment and triviality would be out of place in his conversation. You must remember his constant anxiety about that unfortunate young man, his brother.

CECILY   I wish Uncle Jack would allow that unfortunate young man, his brother, to come down here sometimes. We might have a good influence over him, Miss Prism. I am sure you certainly would. You know German, and geology, and things of that kind influence a man very much. [CECILY *begins to write in her diary.*]

MISS PRISM [*shaking her head*]   I do not think that even I could produce any effect on a character that according to his own brother's admission is irretrievably weak and vacillating. Indeed I am not sure that I would desire to reclaim him. I am not in favor of this modern mania for turning bad people into good people at a moment's notice. As a man sows so let him reap. You must put away your diary, Cecily. I really don't see why you should keep a diary at all.

CECILY   I keep a diary in order to enter the wonderful secrets of my life. If I didn't write them down, I should probably forget all about them.

MISS PRISM   Memory, my dear Cecily, is the diary that we all carry about with us.

CECILY   Yes, but it usually chronicles the things that have never happened, and couldn't possibly have happened. I believe that Memory is responsible for nearly all the three-volume novels that Mudie sends us.[8]

MISS PRISM   Do not speak slightingly of the three-volume novel, Cecily. I wrote one myself in earlier days.

CECILY   Did you really, Miss Prism? How wonderfully clever you are! I hope it did not end happily! I don't like novels that end happily. They depress me so much.

MISS PRISM   The good ended happily, and the bad unhappily. That is what Fiction means.

CECILY   I suppose so. But it seems very unfair. And was your novel ever published?

MISS PRISM   Alas! no. The manuscript unfortunately was abandoned.

> CECILY *starts.*

I used the word in the sense of lost or mislaid. To your work, child, these speculations are profitless.

CECILY [*smiling*]   But I see dear Dr. Chasuble coming up through the garden.

MISS PRISM [*rising and advancing*]   Dr. Chasuble! This is indeed a pleasure.

> *Enter* CANON CHASUBLE.

CHASUBLE   And how are we this morning? Miss Prism, you are, I trust, well?

CECILY   Miss Prism has just been complaining of a slight headache. I think it would do her so much good to have a short stroll with you in the Park, Dr. Chasuble.

MISS PRISM   Cecily, I have not mentioned anything about a headache.

CECILY   No, dear Miss Prism, I know that, but I felt instinctively that you had a headache. Indeed I was thinking about that, and not about my German lesson, when the Rector came in.

8. From the 1860s to the 1880s most novels were published in three volumes. Because of the resultant price, most readers could not afford to buy copies and obtained them by subscription from lending libraries, of which Mudie's in London was by far the largest.

CHASUBLE   I hope, Cecily, you are not inattentive.

CECILY   Oh, I am afraid I am.

CHASUBLE   That is strange. Were I fortunate enough to be Miss Prism's pupil, I would hang upon her lips.

MISS PRISM *glares.*

I spoke metaphorically.—My metaphor was drawn from bees. Ahem! Mr. Worthing, I suppose, has not returned from town yet?

MISS PRISM   We do not expect him till Monday afternoon.

CHASUBLE   Ah yes, he usually likes to spend his Sunday in London. He is not one of those whose sole aim is enjoyment, as, by all accounts, that unfortunate young man his brother seems to be. But I must not disturb Egeria[9] and her pupil any longer.

MISS PRISM   Egeria? My name is Laetitia, Doctor.

CHASUBLE   [*bowing*]   A classical allusion merely, drawn from the Pagan authors. I shall see you both no doubt at Evensong?

MISS PRISM   I think, dear, Doctor, I will have a stroll with you. I find I have a headache after all, and a walk might do it good.

CHASUBLE   With pleasure, Miss Prism, with pleasure. We might go as far as the schools and back.

MISS PRISM   That would be delightful. Cecily, you will read your Political Economy in my absence.[1] The chapter on the Fall of the Rupee you may omit. It is somewhat too sensational. Even these metallic problems have their melodramatic side. [*Goes down the garden with* DR. CHASUBLE.]

CECILY   [*picks up books and throws them back on table*]   Horrid Political Economy! Horrid Geography! Horrid, horrid German!

Enter MERRIMAN *with a card on a salver.*

MERRIMAN   Mr. Ernest Worthing has just driven over from the station. He has brought his luggage with him.

CECILY   [*takes the card and reads it*]   "Mr. Ernest Worthing, B.4, The Albany, W." Uncle Jack's brother! Did you tell him Mr. Worthing was in town?

MERRIMAN   Yes, Miss. He seemed very much disappointed. I mentioned that you and Miss Prism were in the garden. He said he was anxious to speak to you privately for a moment.

CECILY   Ask Mr. Ernest Worthing to come here. I suppose you had better talk to the housekeeper about a room for him.

MERRIMAN   Yes, Miss. [*Goes off.*]

CECILY   I have never met any really wicked person before. I feel rather frightened. I am so afraid he will look just like every one else.

Enter ALGERNON, *very gay and debonair.*

9. A nymph in classical mythology, famous as the wise counselor of Numa Pompilius, the second of the legendary kings of Rome.

1. Political Economy was a branch of social science which dealt with the reve-nues and general financial resources of nations. The term came into use at the beginning of the 17th century. In this century it has developed into the study we call Economics. The rupee is the currency unit of India.

He does!

ALGERNON [*raising his hat*]   You are my little cousin Cecily, I'm sure.

CECILY   You are under some strange mistake. I am not little. In fact, I believe I am more than usually tall for my age.

ALGERNON *is rather taken aback.*

But I am your cousin Cecily. You, I see from your card, are Uncle Jack's brother, my cousin Ernest, my wicked cousin Ernest.

ALGERNON   Oh! I am not really wicked at all, Cousin Cecily. You mustn't think that I am wicked.

CECILY   If you are not, then you have certainly been deceiving us all in a very inexcusable manner. I hope you have not been leading a double life, pretending to be wicked and being really good all the time. That would be hypocrisy.

ALGERNON [*looks at her in amazement*]   Oh! Of course I have been rather reckless.

CECILY   I am glad to hear it.

ALGERNON   In fact, now you mention the subject, I have been very bad in my own small way.

CECILY   I don't think you should be so proud of that, though I am sure it must have been very pleasant.

ALGERNON   It is much pleasanter being here with you.

CECILY   I can't understand how you are here at all. Uncle Jack won't be back till Monday afternoon.

ALGERNON   That is a great disappointment. I am obliged to go up by the first train on Monday morning. I have a business appointment that I am anxious . . . to miss!

CECILY   Couldn't you miss it anywhere but in London?

ALGERNON   No: the appointment is in London.

CECILY   Well, I know, of course, how important it is not to keep a business engagement, if one wants to retain any sense of the beauty of life, but still I think you had better wait till Uncle Jack arrives. I know he wants to speak to you about your emigrating.

ALGERNON   About my what?

CECILY   Your emigrating. He has gone up to buy your outfit.

ALGERNON   I certainly wouldn't let Jack buy my outfit. He has no taste in neckties at all.

CECILY   I don't think you will require neckties. Uncle Jack is sending you to Australia.

ALGERNON   Australia! I'd sooner die.

CECILY   Well, he said at dinner on Wednesday night, that you would have to choose between this world, the next world, and Australia.

ALGERNON   Oh, well! The accounts I have received of Australia and the next world are not particularly encouraging. This world is good enough for me, Cousin Cecily.

CECILY   Yes, but are you good enough for it?

ALGERNON   I'm afraid I'm not that. That is why I want you to reform me. You might make that your mission, if you don't mind, Cousin Cecily.

CECILY   I'm afraid I've no time, this afternoon.

ALGERNON   Well, would you mind my reforming myself this afternoon?

CECILY   It is rather Quixotic of you. But I think you should try.

ALGERNON   I will. I feel better already.

CECILY   You are looking a little worse.

ALGERNON   That is because I am hungry.

CECILY   How thoughtless of me. I should have remembered that when one is going to lead an entirely new life, one requires regular and wholesome meals. Won't you come in?

ALGERNON   Thank you. Might I have a buttonhole first?[2] I never have any appetite unless I have a buttonhole first.

CECILY   A Maréchal Niel? [*Picks up scissors.*]

ALGERNON   No, I'd sooner have a pink rose.

CECILY   Why? [*Cuts a flower.*]

ALGERNON   Because you are like a pink rose, Cousin Cecily.

CECILY   I don't think it can be right for you to talk to me like that. Miss Prism never says such things to me.

ALGERNON   Then Miss Prism is a shortsighted old lady.

> CECILY *puts the rose in his buttonhole.*

You are the prettiest girl I ever saw.

CECILY   Miss Prism says that all good looks are a snare.

ALGERNON   They are a snare that every sensible man would like to be caught in.

CECILY   Oh, I don't think I would care to catch a sensible man. I shouldn't know what to talk to him about.

> *They pass into the house.* MISS PRISM *and* DR. CHASUBLE *return.*

MISS PRISM   You are too much alone, dear Dr. Chasuble. You should get married. A misanthrope I can understand—a womanthrope, never!

CHASUBLE [*with a scholar's shudder*]....Believe me, I do not deserve so neologistic a phrase. The precept as well as the practice of the Primitive Church was distinctly against matrimony.

MISS PRISM [*sententiously*]   That is obviously the reason why the Primitive Church has not lasted up to the present day. And you do not seem to realize, dear Doctor, that by persistently remaining single, a man converts himself into a permanent public temptation. Men should be more careful; this very celibacy leads weaker vessels astray.

CHASUBLE   But is a man not equally attractive when married?

MISS PRISM   No married man is ever attractive except to his wife.

CHASUBLE   And often, I've been told, not even to her.

MISS PRISM   That depends on the intellectual sympathies of the woman. Maturity can always be depended on. Ripeness can be trusted. Young women are green.

---

2. A "buttonhole" is a flower to be worn on the lapel of a man's coat, in this case a popular yellow rose of the period. Hardier varieties are available now, and the Maréchal Niel is seldom grown.

DR. CHASUBLE *starts.*

I spoke horticulturally. My metaphor was drawn from fruits. But where is Cecily?

CHASUBLE   Perhaps she followed us to the schools.

Enter JACK *slowly from the back of the garden. He is dressed in the deepest mourning, with crepe hatband and black gloves.*

MISS PRISM   Mr. Worthing!

CHASUBLE   Mr. Worthing?

MISS PRISM   This is indeed a surprise. We did not look for you till Monday afternoon.

JACK [*shakes* MISS PRISM's *hand in a tragic manner*]   I have returned sooner than I expected. Dr. Chasuble, I hope you are well?

CHASUBLE   Dear Mr. Worthing, I trust this garb of woe does not betoken some terrible calamity?

JACK   My brother.

MISS PRISM   More shameful debts and extravagance?

CHASUBLE   Still leading his life of pleasure?

JACK [*shaking his head*]   Dead!

CHASUBLE   Your brother Ernest dead?

JACK   Quite dead.

MISS PRISM   What a lesson for him! I trust he will profit by it.

CHASUBLE   Mr. Worthing, I offer you my sincere condolence. You have at least the consolation of knowing that you were always the most generous and forgiving of brothers.

JACK   Poor Ernest! He had many faults, but it is a sad, sad blow.

CHASUBLE   Very sad indeed. Were you with him at the end?

JACK   No. He died abroad; in Paris, in fact. I had a telegram last night from the manager of the Grand Hotel.

CHASUBLE   Was the cause of death mentioned?

JACK   A severe chill, it seems.

MISS PRISM   As a man sows, so shall he reap.

CHASUBLE [*raising his hand*]   Charity, dear Miss Prism, charity! None of us is perfect. I myself am peculiarly susceptible to drafts. Will the interment take place here?

JACK   No. He seems to have expressed a desire to be buried in Paris.

CHASUBLE   In Paris! [*Shakes his head.*] I fear that hardly points to any very serious state of mind at the last. You would no doubt wish me to make some slight allusion to this tragic domestic affliction next Sunday.

JACK *presses his hand convulsively.*

My sermon on the meaning of the manna in the wilderness can be adapted to almost any occasion, joyful, or, as in the present case, distressing.

All sigh.

1 have preached it at harvest celebrations, christenings, confirmations, on days of humiliation and festal days. The last time I delivered it was in the Cathedral, as a charity sermon on behalf of the Society for the Prevention of Discontent among the Upper Orders. The Bishop, who was present, was much struck by some of the analogies I drew.

JACK   Ah! that reminds me, you mentioned christenings, I think, Dr. Chasuble? I suppose you know how to christen all right?

DR. CHASUBLE *looks astounded.*

I mean, of course, you are continually christening, aren't you?

MISS PRISM   It is, I regret to say, one of the Rector's most constant duties in this parish. I have often spoken to the poorer classes on the subject. But they don't seem to know what thrift is.

CHASUBLE   But is there any particular infant in whom you are interested, Mr. Worthing? Your brother was, I believe, unmarried, was he not?

JACK   Oh yes.

MISS PRISM [*bitterly*]   People who live entirely for pleasure usually are.

JACK   But it is not for any child, dear Doctor. I am very fond of children. No! the fact is, I would like to be christened myself, this afternoon, if you have nothing better to do.

CHASUBLE   But surely, Mr. Worthing, you have been christened already?

JACK   I don't remember anything about it.

CHASUBLE   But have you any grave doubts on the subject?

JACK   I certainly intend to have. Of course I don't know if the thing would bother you in any way, or if you think I am a little too old now.

CHASUBLE   Not at all. The sprinkling, and, indeed, the immersion of adults is a perfectly canonical practice.

JACK   Immersion!

CHASUBLE   You need have no apprehensions. Sprinkling is all that is necessary, or indeed I think advisable. Our weather is so changeable. At what hour would you wish the ceremony performed?

JACK   Oh, I might trot round about five if that would suit you.

CHASUBLE   Perfectly, perfectly! In fact I have two similar ceremonies to perform at that time. A case of twins that occurred recently in one of the outlying cottages on your own estate. Poor Jenkins the carter, a most hard-working man.

JACK   Oh! I don't see much fun in being christened along with other babies. It would be childish. Would half-past five do?

CHASUBLE   Admirably! Admirably! [*Takes out watch.*] And now, dear Mr. Worthing, I will not intrude any longer into a house of sorrow. I would merely beg you not to be too much bowed down by grief. What seem to us bitter trials are often blessings in disguise.

MISS PRISM   This seems to me a blessing of an extremely obvious kind.

Enter CECILY *from the house.*

CECILY   Uncle Jack! Oh, I am pleased to see you back. But what horrid clothes you have got on. Do go and change them.

MISS PRISM   Cecily!

CHASUBLE   My child! My child!

> CECILY *goes towards* JACK; *he kisses her brow in a melancholy manner.*

CECILY   What is the matter, Uncle Jack? Do look happy! You look as if you had toothache, and I have got such a surprise for you. Who do you think is in the dining-room? Your brother!

JACK   Who?

CECILY   Your brother Ernest. He arrived about half an hour ago.

JACK   What nonsense! I haven't got a brother.

CECILY   Oh, don't say that. However badly he may have behaved to you in the past he is still your brother. You couldn't be so heartless as to disown him. I'll tell him to come out. And you will shake hands with him, won't you, Uncle Jack? [*Runs back into the house.*]

CHASUBLE   These are very joyful tidings.

MISS PRISM   After we had all been resigned to his loss, his sudden return seems to me peculiarly distressing.

JACK   My brother is in the dining-room? I don't know what it all means. I think it is perfectly absurd.

> *Enter* ALGERNON *and* CECILY *hand in hand. They come slowly up to* JACK.

JACK   Good heavens! [*Motions* ALGERNON *away.*]

ALGERNON   Brother John, I have come down from town to tell you that I am very sorry for all the trouble I have given you, and that I intend to lead a better life in the future.

> JACK *glares at him and does not take his hand.*

CECILY   Uncle Jack, you are not going to refuse your own brother's hand?

JACK   Nothing will induce me to take his hand. I think his coming down here disgraceful. He knows perfectly well why.

CECILY   Uncle Jack, do be nice. There is some good in everyone. Ernest has just been telling me about his poor invalid friend Mr. Bunbury whom he goes to visit so often. And surely there must be much good in one who is kind to an invalid, and leaves the pleasures of London to sit by a bed of pain.

JACK   Oh! he has been talking about Bunbury, has he?

CECILY   Yes, he has told me all about poor Mr. Bunbury, and his terrible state of health.

JACK   Bunbury! Well, I won't have him to talk to you about Bunbury or about anything else. It is enough to drive one perfectly frantic.

ALGERNON   Of course I admit that the faults were all on my side.

But I must say that I think that Brother John's coldness to me is peculiarly painful. I expected a more enthusiastic welcome, especially considering it is the first time I have come here.

CECILY   Uncle Jack, if you don't shake hands with Ernest I will never forgive you.

JACK   Never forgive me?

CECILY   Never, never, never!

JACK   Well, this is the last time I shall ever do it. [*Shakes hands with* ALGERNON *and glares.*]

CHASUBLE   It's pleasant, is it not, to see so perfect a reconciliation? I think we might leave the two brothers together.

MISS PRISM   Cecily, you will come with us.

CECILY   Certainly, Miss Prism. My little task of reconciliation is over.

CHASUBLE   You have done a beautiful action today, dear child.

MISS PRISM   We must not be premature in our judgments.

CECILY   I feel very happy.

They all go off except JACK *and* ALGERNON.

JACK   You young scoundrel, Algy, you must get out of this place as soon as possible. I don't allow any Bunburying here.

Enter MERRIMAN.

MERRIMAN   I have put Mr. Ernest's things in the room next to yours, sir. I suppose that is all right?

JACK   What?

MERRIMAN   Mr. Ernest's luggage, sir. I have unpacked it and put it in the room next to your own.

JACK   His luggage?

MERRIMAN   Yes sir. Three portmanteaus, a dressing-case, two hat-boxes, and a large luncheon-basket.

ALGERNON   I am afraid I can't stay more than a week this time.

JACK   Merriman, order the dogcart[3] at once. Mr. Ernest has been suddenly called back to town.

MERRIMAN   Yes, sir. [*Goes back into the house.*]

ALGERNON   What a fearful liar you are, Jack. I have not been called back to town at all.

JACK   Yes, you have.

ALGERNON   I haven't heard any one call me.

JACK   Your duty as a gentleman calls you back.

ALGERNON   My duty as a gentleman has never interfered with my pleasures in the smallest degree.

JACK   I can quite understand that.

ALGERNON   Well, Cecily is a darling.

JACK   You are not to talk of Miss Cardew like that. I don't like it.

ALGERNON   Well, I don't like your clothes. You look perfectly ridiculous in them. Why on earth don't you go up and change? It is

---

3. A light, two wheeled carriage, usually drawn by one horse; it has two transverse seats positioned back to back.

perfectly childish to be in deep mourning for a man who is actually staying for a whole week with you in your house as a guest. I call it grotesque.

JACK   You are certainly not staying with me for a whole week as a guest or anything else. You have got to leave . . . by the four-five train.

ALGERNON   I certainly won't leave you so long as you are in mourning. It would be most unfriendly. If I were in mourning you would stay with me, I suppose. I should think it very unkind if you didn't.

JACK   Well, will you go if I change my clothes?

ALGERNON   Yes, if you are not too long. I never saw anybody take so long to dress, and with such little result.

JACK   Well, at any rate, that is better than being always overdressed as you are.

ALGERNON   If I am occasionally a little overdressed, I make up for it by being always immensely overeducated.

JACK   Your vanity is ridiculous, your conduct an outrage, and your presence in my garden utterly absurd. However, you have got to catch the four-five, and I hope you will have a pleasant journey back to town. This Bunburying, as you call it, has not been a great success for you. [*Goes into the house.*]

ALGERNON   I think it has been a great success. I'm in love with Cecily, and that is everything.

Enter CECILY *at the back of the garden. She picks up the can and begins to water the flowers.*

But I must see her before I go, and make arrangements for another Bunbury. Ah, there she is.

CECILY   Oh, I merely came back to water the roses. I thought you were with Uncle Jack.

ALGERNON   He's gone to order the dogcart for me.

CECILY   Oh, is he going to take you for a nice drive?

ALGERNON   He's going to send me away.

CECILY   Then have we got to part?

ALGERNON   I am afraid so. It's a very painful parting.

CECILY   It is always painful to part from people whom one has known for a very brief space of time. The absence of old friends one can endure with equanimity. But even a momentary separation from anyone to whom one has just been introduced is almost unbearable.

ALGERNON   Thank you.

Enter MERRIMAN.

MERRIMAN   The dogcart is at the door, sir.

ALGERNON *looks appealingly at* CECILY.

CECILY   It can wait, Merriman . . . for . . . five minutes.

MERRIMAN   Yes, miss. [*Exit.*]

ALGERNON   I hope, Cecily, I shall not offend you if I state quite frankly and openly that you seem to me to be in every way the visible personification of absolute perfection.

CECILY   I think your frankness does you great credit, Ernest. If you will allow me, I will copy your remarks into my diary. [*Goes over to table and begins writing in diary.*]

ALGERNON   Do you really keep a diary? I'd give anything to look at it. May I?

CECILY   Oh no. [*Puts her hand over it.*] You see, it is simply a very young girl's record of her own thoughts and impressions, and consequently meant for publication. When it appears in volume form I hope you will order a copy. But pray, Ernest, don't stop. I delight in taking down from dictation. I have reached "absolute perfection." You can go on. I am quite ready for more.

ALGERNON [*somewhat taken aback*]   Ahem! Ahem!

CECILY   Oh, don't cough, Ernest. When one is dictating one should speak fluently and not cough. Besides, I don't know how to spell a cough. [*Writes as* ALGERNON *speaks.*]

ALGERNON [*speaking very rapidly*]   Cecily, ever since I first looked upon your wonderful and incomparable beauty, I have dared to love you wildly, passionately, devotedly, hopelessly.

CECILY   I don't think that you should tell me that you love me wildly, passionately, devotedly, hopelessly. Hopelessly doesn't seem to make much sense, does it?

ALGERNON   Cecily.

Enter MERRIMAN.

MERRIMAN   The dogcart is waiting, sir.

ALGERNON   Tell it to come round next week, at the same hour.

MERRIMAN [*looks at* CECILY, *who makes no sign*].   Yes, sir. [MERRIMAN *retires.*]

CECILY   Uncle Jack would be very much annoyed if he knew you were staying on till next week, at the same hour.

ALGERNON   Oh, I don't care about Jack. I don't care for anybody in the whole world but you. I love you, Cecily. You will marry me, won't you?

CECILY   You silly boy! Of course. Why, we have been engaged for the last three months.

ALGERNON   For the last three months?

CECILY   Yes, it will be exactly three months on Thursday.

ALGERNON   But how did we become engaged?

CECILY   Well, ever since dear Uncle Jack first confessed to us that he had a younger brother who was very wicked and bad, you of course have formed the chief topic of conversation between myself and Miss Prism. And of course a man who is much talked about is always very attractive. One feels there must be something in him, after all. I daresay it was foolish of me, but I fell in love with you, Ernest.

ALGERNON   Darling. And when was the engagement actually settled?

CECILY   On the 14th of February last. Worn out by your entire
ignorance of my existence, I determined to end the matter one
way or the other, and after a long struggle with myself I accepted
you under this dear old tree here. The next day I bought this little
ring in your name, and this is the little bangle with the true lovers'
knot I promised you always to wear.

ALGERNON   Did I give you this? It's very pretty, isn't it?

CECILY   Yes, you've wonderfully good taste, Ernest. It's the excuse
I've always given for your leading such a bad life. And this is the
box in which I keep all your dear letters. [*Kneels at table, opens
box, and produces letters tied up with blue ribbon.*]

ALGERNON   My letters! But, my own sweet Cecily, I have never
written you any letters.

CECILY   You need hardly remind me of that, Ernest. I remember only
too well that I was forced to write your letters for you. I wrote
always three times a week, and sometimes oftener.

ALGERNON   Oh, do let me read them, Cecily?

CECILY   Oh, I couldn't possibly. They would make you far too conceited. [*Replaces box.*] The three you wrote me after I had
broken off the engagement are so beautiful, and so badly spelled,
that even now I can hardly read them without crying a little.

ALGERNON   But was our engagement ever broken off?

CECILY   Of course it was. On the 22nd of last March. You can see the
entry if you like. [*Shows diary.*] "Today I broke off my engagement
with Ernest. I feel it is better to do so. The weather still continues
charming."

ALGERNON   But why on earth did you break it off? What had I
done? I had done nothing at all. Cecily, I am very much hurt indeed to hear you broke it off. Particularly when the weather was
so charming.

CECILY   It would hardly have been a really serious engagement if it
hadn't been broken off at least once. But I forgave you before the
week was out.

ALGERNON [*crossing to her, and kneeling*]   What a perfect angel you
are, Cecily.

CECILY   You dear romantic boy. [*He kisses her, she puts her fingers
through his hair.*]   I hope your hair curls naturally, does it?

ALGERNON   Yes darling, with a little help from others.

CECILY   I am so glad.

ALGERNON   You'll never break off our engagement again, Cecily?

CECILY   I don't think I could break it off now that I have actually
met you. Besides, of course, there is the question of your name.

ALGERNON   Yes, of course. [*Nervously.*]

CECILY   You must not laugh at me, darling, but it had always been
a girlish dream of mine to love some one whose name was Ernest.

ALGERNON *rises,* CECILY *also.*

There is something in that name that seems to inspire absolute
confidence. I pity any poor married woman whose husband is not
called Ernest.

ALGERNON   But, my dear child, do you mean to say you could not love me if I had some other name?

CECILY   But what name?

ALGERNON   Oh, any name you like—Algernon—for instance . . .

CECILY   But I don't like the name of Algernon.

ALGERNON   Well, my own dear sweet, loving little darling, I really can't see why you should object to the name of Algernon. It is not at all a bad name. In fact, it is rather an aristocratic name. Half of the chaps who get into the Bankruptcy Court are called Algernon. But seriously, Cecily . . . [*Moving to her.*] if my name was Algy, couldn't you love me?

CECILY   [*rising*]   I might respect you, Ernest, I might admire your character, but I fear that I should not be able to give you my undivided attention.

ALGERNON   Ahem! Cecily! [*Picking up hat.*] Your Rector here is, I suppose, thoroughly experienced in the practice of all the rites and ceremonials of the Church?

CECILY   Oh, yes. Dr. Chasuble is a most learned man. He has never written a single book, so you can imagine how much he knows.

ALGERNON   I must see him at once on a most important christening— I mean on most important business.

CECILY   Oh!

ALGERNON   I shan't be away more than half an hour.

CECILY   Considering that we have been engaged since February the 14th, and that I only met you today for the first time, I think it is rather hard that you should leave me for so long a period as half an hour. Couldn't you make it twenty minutes?

ALGERNON   I'll be back in no time. [*Kisses her and rushes down the garden.*]

CECILY   What an impetuous boy he is! I like his hair so much. I must enter his proposal in my diary.

    Enter MERRIMAN.

MERRIMAN   A Miss Fairfax just called to see Mr. Worthing. On very important business, Miss Fairfax states.

CECILY   Isn't Mr. Worthing in his library?

MERRIMAN   Mr. Worthing went over in the direction of the Rectory some time ago.

CECILY   Pray ask the lady to come out here; Mr. Worthing is sure to be back soon. And you can bring tea.

MERRIMAN   Yes. Miss. [*Goes out.*]

CECILY   Miss Fairfax! I suppose one of the many good elderly women who are associated with Uncle Jack in some of his philanthropic work in London. I don't quite like women who are interested in philanthropic work. I think it is so forward of them.

    Enter MERRIMAN.

MERRIMAN   Miss Fairfax.

Enter GWENDOLEN. *Exit* MERRIMAN.

CECILY [*advancing to meet her*]   Pray let me introduce myself to you. My name is Cecily Cardew.

GWENDOLEN   Cecily Cardew? [*Moving to her and shaking hands.*] What a very sweet name! Something tells me that we are going to be great friends. I like you already more than I can say. My first impressions of people are never wrong.

CECILY   How nice of you to like me so much after we have known each other such a comparatively short time. Pray sit down.

GWENDOLEN [*still standing up*]   I may call you Cecily, may I not?

CECILY   With pleasure!

GWENDOLEN   And you will always call me Gwendolen, won't you?

CECILY   If you wish.

GWENDOLEN   Then that is all quite settled, is it not?

CECILY   I hope so. [*A pause. They both sit down together.*]

GWENDOLEN   Perhaps this might be a favorable opportunity for my mentioning who I am. My father is Lord Bracknell. You have never heard of papa, I suppose?

CECILY   I don't think so.

GWENDOLEN   Outside the family circle, papa, I am glad to say, is entirely unknown. I think that is quite as it should be. The home seems to me to be the proper sphere for the man. And certainly once a man begins to neglect his domestic duties he becomes painfully effeminate, does he not? And I don't like that. It makes men so very attractive. Cecily, mamma, whose views on education are remarkably strict, has brought me up to be extremely short-sighted; it is part of her system; so do you mind my looking at you through my glasses?

CECILY   Oh! not at all, Gwendolen. I am very fond of being looked at.

GWENDOLEN [*after examining* CECILY *carefully through a lorgnette*] You are here on a short visit, I suppose.

CECILY   Oh no! I live here.

GWENDOLEN [*severely*]   Really? Your mother, no doubt, or some female relative of advanced years, resides here also?

CECILY   Oh no! I have no mother, nor, in fact, any relations.

GWENDOLEN   Indeed?

CECILY   My dear guardian, with the assistance of Miss Prism, has the arduous task of looking after me.

GWENDOLEN   Your guardian?

CECILY   Yes, I am Mr. Worthing's ward.

GWENDOLEN   Oh! It is strange he never mentioned to me that he had a ward. How secretive of him! He grows more interesting hourly. I am not sure, however, that the news inspires me with feelings of unmixed delight. [*Rising and going to her.*] I am very fond of you, Cecily; I have liked you ever since I met you! But I am bound to state that now I know that you are Mr. Worthing's ward, I cannot help expressing a wish you were—well, just a little older than you seem to be—and not quite so very alluring in appearance. In fact, if I may speak candidly—

CECILY Pray do! I think that whenever one has anything unpleasant to say, one should always be quite candid.

GWENDOLEN Well, to speak with perfect candor, Cecily, I wish that you were fully forty-two, and more than usually plain for your age. Ernest has a strong upright nature. He is the very soul of truth and honor. Disloyalty would be as impossible to him as deception. But even men of the noblest possible moral character are extremely susceptible to the influence of the physical charms of others. Modern, no less than Ancient History, supplies us with many most painful examples of what I refer to. If it were not so, indeed, History would be quite unreadable.

CECILY I beg your pardon, Gwendolen, did you say Ernest?

GWENDOLEN Yes.

CECILY Oh, but it is not Mr. Ernest Worthing who is my guardian. It is his brother—his elder brother.

GWENDOLEN [*sitting down again*] Ernest never mentioned to me that he had a brother.

CECILY I am sorry to say they have not been on good terms for a long time.

GWENDOLEN Ah! that accounts for it. And now that I think of it I have never heard any man mention his brother. The subject seems distasteful to most men. Cecily, you have lifted a load from my mind. I was growing almost anxious. It would have been terrible if any cloud had come across a friendship like ours, would it not? Of course you are quite, quite sure that it is not Mr. Worthing who is your guardian?

CECILY Quite sure. [*A pause.*] In fact, I am going to be his.

GWENDOLEN [*inquiringly*] I beg your pardon?

CECILY [*rather shy and confidingly*] Dearest Gwendolen, there is no reason why I should make a secret of it to you. Our little country newspaper is sure to chronicle the fact next week. Mr. Ernest Worthing and I are engaged to be married.

GWENDOLEN [*quite politely, rising*]....My darling Cecily, I think there must be some slight error. Mr. Ernest Worthing is engaged to me. The announcement will appear in the *Morning Post* on Saturday at the latest.

CECILY [*very politely, rising*] I am afraid you must be under some misconception. Ernest proposed to me exactly ten minutes ago. [*Shows diary.*]

GWENDOLEN [*examines diary through her lorgnette carefully*] It is very curious, for he asked me to be his wife yesterday afternoon at 5:30. If you would care to verify the incident, pray do so. [*Produces diary of her own.*] I never travel without my diary. One should always have something sensational to read in the train. I am so sorry, dear Cecily, if it is any disappointment to you, but I am afraid I have the prior claim.

CECILY It would distress me more than I can tell you, dear Gwendolen, if it caused you any mental or physical anguish, but I feel bound to point out that since Ernest proposed to you he clearly has changed his mind.

GWENDOLEN [*meditatively*]   If the poor fellow has been entrapped into any foolish promise I shall consider it my duty to rescue him at once, and with a firm hand.

CECILY [*thoughtfully and sadly*]   Whatever unfortunate entanglement my dear boy may have got into, I will never reproach him with it after we are married.

GWENDOLEN   Do you allude to me, Miss Cardew, as an entanglement? You are presumptuous. On an occasion of this kind it becomes more than a moral duty to speak one's mind. It becomes a pleasure.

CECILY   Do you suggest, Miss Fairfax, that I entrapped Ernest into an engagement? How dare you? This is no time for wearing the shallow mask of manners. When I see a spade I call it a spade.

GWENDOLEN [*satirically*]   I am glad to say that I have never seen a spade. It is obvious that our social spheres have been widely different.

> Enter MERRIMAN, *followed by the* FOOTMAN. *He carries a salver, table cloth, and plate stand.* CECILY *is about to retort. The presence of the servants exercises a restraining influence, under which both girls chafe.*

MERRIMAN   Shall I lay tea here as usual, Miss?

CECILY [*sternly, in a calm voice*]   Yes, as usual.

> MERRIMAN *begins to clear table and lay cloth. A long pause.* CECILY *and* GWENDOLEN *glare at each other.*

GWENDOLEN   Are there many interesting walks in the vicinity, Miss Cardew?

CECILY   Oh! yes! a great many. From the top of one of the hills quite close one can see five counties.

GWENDOLEN   Five counties! I don't think I should like that; I hate crowds.

CECILY [*sweetly*]   I suppose that is why you live in town?

> GWENDOLEN *bites her lip, and beats her foot nervously with her parasol.*

GWENDOLEN [*looking around*]   Quite a well-kept garden this is, Miss Cardew.

CECILY   So glad you like it, Miss Fairfax.

GWENDOLEN   I had no idea there were any flowers in the country.

CECILY   Oh, flowers are as common here, Miss Fairfax, as people are in London.

GWENDOLEN   Personally I cannot understand how anybody manages to exist in the country, if anybody who is anybody does. The country always bores me to death.

CECILY   Ah! This is what the newspapers call agricultural depression, is it not? I believe the aristocracy are suffering very much from it

just at present. It is almost an epidemic amongst them, I have been
told. May I offer you some tea, Miss Fairfax?

GWENDOLEN [*with elaborate politeness*] Thank you. [*Aside.*] Detest-
able girl! But I require tea!

CECILY [*sweetly*] Sugar?

GWENDOLEN [*superciliously*] No, thank you. Sugar is not fashionable
any more.

> CECILY *looks angrily at her, takes up the tongs and puts four
> lumps of sugar into the cup.*

CECILY [*severely*] Cake or bread and butter?

GWENDOLEN [*in a bored manner*]....Bread and butter, please. Cake is
rarely seen at the best houses nowadays.

CECILY [*cuts a very large slice of cake and puts it on the tray*] Hand
that to Miss Fairfax.

> MERRIMAN *does so, and goes out with* FOOTMAN. GWENDOLEN
> *drinks the tea and makes a grimace. Puts down cup at once,
> reaches out her hand to the bread and butter, looks at it, and
> finds it is cake. Rises in indignation.*

GWENDOLEN You have filled my tea with lumps of sugar, and though
I asked most distinctly for bread and butter, you have given me
cake. I am known for the gentleness of my disposition, and the
extraordinary sweetness of my nature, but I warn you, Miss Cardew, you may go too far.

CECILY [*rising*] To save my poor, innocent, trusting boy from the
machinations of any other girl there are no lengths to which I would
not go.

GWENDOLEN From the moment I saw you I distrusted you. I felt that
you were false and deceitful. I am never deceived in such matters.
My first impressions of people are invariably right.

CECILY It seems to me, Miss Fairfax, that I am trespassing on your
valuable time. No doubt you have many other calls of a similar
character to make in the neighbourhood.

> *Enter* JACK.

GWENDOLEN [*catching sight of him*] Ernest! My own Ernest!

JACK Gwendolen! Darling! [*Offers to kiss her.*]

GWENDOLEN [*drawing back*] A moment! May I ask if you are engaged
to be married to this young lady? [*Points to* CECILY.]

JACK [*laughing*] To dear little Cecily! Of course not! What could
have put such an idea into your pretty little head?

GWENDOLEN Thank you. You may! [*Offers her cheek.*]

CECILY [*very sweetly*] I knew there must be some misunderstanding,
Miss Fairfax. The gentleman whose arm is at present round your
waist is my dear guardian, Mr. John Worthing.

GWENDOLEN I beg your pardon?

CECILY This is Uncle Jack.

GWENDOLEN [*receding*]   Jack! Oh!

> *Enter* ALGERNON.

CECILY   Here is Ernest.

ALGERNON [*goes straight over to* CECILY *without noticing anyone else*]   My own love! [*Offers to kiss her.*]

CECILY [*drawing back*]   A moment, Ernest! May I ask you—are you engaged to be married to this young lady?

ALGERNON [*looking around*]   To what young lady? Good heavens! Gwendolen!

CECILY   Yes: to good heavens, Gwendolen, I mean to Gwendolen.

ALGERNON [*laughing*]   Of course not! What could have put such an idea into your pretty little head?

CECILY   Thank you. [*Presenting her cheek to be kissed.*] You may.

> ALGERNON *kisses her.*

GWENDOLEN   I felt there was some slight error, Miss Cardew. The gentleman who is now embracing you is my cousin, Mr. Algernon Moncrieff.

CECILY [*breaking away from* ALGERNON]   Algernon Moncrieff! Oh!

> *The two girls move towards each other and put their arms round each other's waists as if for protection.*

CECILY   Are you called Algernon?

ALGERNON   I cannot deny it.

CECILY   Oh!

GWENDOLEN   Is your name really John?

JACK [*standing rather proudly*]   I could deny it if I liked. I could deny anything if I liked. But my name certainly is John. It has been John for years.

CECILY [*to* GWENDOLEN]   A gross deception has been practiced on both of us.

GWENDOLEN   My poor wounded Cecily!

CECILY   My sweet wronged Gwendolen!

GWENDOLEN [*slowly and seriously*]   You will call me sister, will you not?

> *They embrace.* JACK *and* ALGERNON *groan and walk up and down.*

CECILY [*rather brightly*]   There is just one question I would like to be allowed to ask my guardian.

GWENDOLEN   An admirable idea! Mr. Worthing, there is just one question I would like to be permitted to put to you. Where is your brother Ernest? We are both engaged to be married to your brother Ernest, so it is a matter of some importance to us to know where your brother Ernest is at present.

JACK [*slowly and hesitatingly*]   Gwendolen—Cecily—it is very painful for me to be forced to speak the truth. It is the first time in my life that I have ever been reduced to such a painful position, and I am really quite inexperienced in doing anything of the kind. However, I will tell you quite frankly that I have no brother Ernest. I have no brother at all. I never had a brother in my life, and I certainly have not the smallest intention of ever having one in the future.

CECILY [*surprised*]　No brother at all?

JACK [*cheerily*]　None!

GWENDOLEN [*severely*]　Had you never a brother of any kind?

JACK [*pleasantly*]　Never. Not even of any kind.

GWENDOLEN　I am afraid it is quite clear, Cecily, that neither of us is engaged to be married to anyone.

CECILY....It is not a very pleasant position for a young girl suddenly to find herself in. Is it?

GWENDOLEN　Let us go into the house. They will hardly venture to come after us there.

CECILY　No, men are so cowardly, aren't they?

　They retire into the house with scornful looks.

JACK　This ghastly state of things is what you call Bunburying, I suppose?

ALGERNON　Yes, and a perfectly wonderful Bunbury it is. The most wonderful Bunbury I have ever had in my life.

JACK　Well, you've no right whatsoever to Bunbury here.

ALGERNON　That is absurd. One has a right to Bunbury anywhere one chooses. Every serious Bunburyist knows that.

JACK　Serious Bunburyist? Good heavens!

ALGERNON　Well, one must be serious about something, if one wants to have any amusement in life. I happen to be serious about Bunburying. What on earth you are serious about I haven't got the remotest idea. About everything, I should fancy. You have such an absolutely trivial nature.

JACK　Well, the only small satisfaction I have in the whole of this wretched business is that your friend Bunbury is quite exploded. You won't be able to run down to the country quite so often as you used to do, dear Algy. And a very good thing too.

ALGERNON　Your brother is a little off color, isn't he, dear Jack? You won't be able to disappear to London quite so frequently as your wicked custom was. And not a bad thing either.

JACK　As for your conduct towards Miss Cardew, I must say that you taking in a sweet, simple, innocent girl like that is quite inexcusable. To say nothing of the fact that she is my ward.

ALGERNON　I can see no possible defense at all for your deceiving a brilliant, clever, thoroughly experienced young lady like Miss Fairfax. To say nothing of the fact that she is my cousin.

JACK　I wanted to be engaged to Gwendolen, that is all. I love her.

ALGERNON　Well, I simply wanted to be engaged to Cecily. I adore her.

JACK　There is certainly no chance of your marrying Miss Cardew.

ALGERNON   I don't think there is much likelihood, Jack, of you and Miss Fairfax being united.

JACK   Well, that is no business of yours.

ALGERNON   If it was my business, I wouldn't talk about it. [*Begins to eat muffins.*] It is very vulgar to talk about one's business. Only people like stockbrokers do that, and then merely at dinner parties.

JACK   How you can sit there, calmly eating muffins, when we are in this horrible trouble, I can't make out. You seem to me to be perfectly heartless.

ALGERNON   Well, I can't eat muffins in an agitated manner. The butter would probably get on my cuffs. One should always eat muffins quite calmly. It is the only way to eat them.

JACK   I say it's perfectly heartless your eating muffins at all, under the circumstances.

ALGERNON   When I am in trouble, eating is the only thing that consoles me. Indeed, when I am in really great trouble, as any one who knows me intimately will tell you, I refuse everything except food and drink. At the present moment I am eating muffins because I am unhappy. Besides, I am particularly fond of muffins. [*Rising.*]

JACK [*rising*]....Well, there is no reason why you should eat them all in that greedy way. [*Takes muffins from* ALGERNON.]

ALGERNON [*offering tea-cake*]   I wish you would have tea-cake instead. I don't like tea-cake.

JACK   Good heavens! I suppose a man may eat his own muffins in his own garden.

ALGERNON   But you have just said it was perfectly heartless to eat muffins.

JACK   I said it was perfectly heartless of you, under the circumstances. That is a very different thing.

ALGERNON   That may be. But the muffins are the same. [*He seizes the muffin-dish from* JACK.]

JACK   Algy, I wish to goodness you would go.

ALGERNON   You can't possibly ask me to go without having some dinner. It's absurd. I never go without my dinner. No one ever does, except vegetarians and people like that. Besides I have just made arrangements with Dr. Chasuble to be christened at a quarter to six under the name of Ernest.

JACK   My dear fellow, the sooner you give up that nonsense the better. I made arrangements this morning with Dr. Chasuble to be christened myself at 5:30, and I naturally will take the name of Ernest. Gwendolen would wish it. We can't both be christened Ernest. It's absurd. Besides, I have a perfect right to be christened if I like. There is no evidence at all that I have ever been christened by anybody. I should think it extremely probable I never was, and so does Dr. Chasuble. It is entirely different in your case. You have been christened already.

ALGERNON   Yes, but I have not been christened for years.

JACK   Yes, but you have been christened. That is the important thing.

ALGERNON   Quite so. So I know my constitution can stand it. If you are not quite sure about your ever having been christened, I must say I think it rather dangerous your venturing on it now. It might make you very unwell. You can hardly have forgotten that someone very closely connected with you was very nearly carried off this week in Paris by a severe chill.

JACK Yes, but you said yourself that a severe chill was not hereditary.

ALGERNON It usen't to be, I know—but I daresay it is now. Science is always making wonderful improvements in things.

JACK [*picking up the muffin-dish*] Oh, that is nonsense; you are always talking nonsense.

ALGERNON Jack, you are at the muffins again! I wish you wouldn't. There are only two left. [*Takes them.*] I told you I was particularly fond of muffins.

JACK But I hate tea-cake.

ALGERNON Why on earth then do you allow tea-cake to be served up for your guests? What ideas you have of hospitality!

JACK Algernon! I have already told you to go. I don't want you here. Why don't you go?

ALGERNON I haven't quite finished my tea yet! and there is still one muffin left.

> JACK *groans, and sinks into a chair.* ALGERNON *still continues eating.*

Act 3

Drawing room at the Manor House. GWENDOLEN *and* CECILY *are at the window, looking out into the garden.*

GWENDOLEN The fact that they did not follow us at once into the house, as any one else would have done, seems to me to show that they have some sense of shame left.

CECILY They have been eating muffins. That looks like repentance.

GWENDOLEN [*after a pause*] They don't seem to notice us at all. Couldn't you cough?

CECILY But I haven't got a cough.

GWENDOLEN They're looking at us. What effrontery!

CECILY They're approaching. That's very forward of them.

GWENDOLEN Let us preserve a dignified silence.

CECILY Certainly. It's the only thing to do now.

> *Enter* JACK *followed by* ALGERNON. *They whistle some dreadful popular air from a British opera.*

GWENDOLEN This dignified silence seems to produce an unpleasant effect.

CECILY A most distasteful one.

GWENDOLEN But we will not be the first to speak.

CECILY Certainly not.

GWENDOLEN Mr. Worthing, I have something very particular to ask you. Much depends on your reply.

CECILY   Gwendolen, your common sense is invaluable. Mr. Moncrieff, kindly answer me the following question. Why did you pretend to be my guardian's brother?

ALGERNON   In order that I might have an opportunity of meeting you.

CECILY [*to* GWENDOLEN]   That certainly seems a satisfactory explanation, does it not?

GWENDOLEN   Yes, dear, if you can believe him.

CECILY   I don't. But that does not affect the wonderful beauty of his answer.

GWENDOLEN   True. In matters of grave importance, style, not sincerity, is the vital thing. Mr. Worthing, what explanation can you offer to me for pretending to have a brother? Was it in order that you might have an opportunity of coming up to town to see me as often as possible?

JACK   Can you doubt it, Miss Fairfax?

GWENDOLEN   I have the gravest doubts about the subject. But I intend to crush them. This is not the moment for German skepticism.[4] [*Moving to* CECILY.] Their explanations appear to be quite satisfactory, especially Mr. Worthing's. That seems to me to have the stamp of truth upon it.

CECILY   I am more than content with what Mr. Moncrieff said. His voice alone inspires one with absolute credulity.

GWENDOLEN   Then you think we should forgive them?

CECILY   Yes. I mean no.

GWENDOLEN   True! I had forgotten. There are principles at stake that one cannot surrender. Which of us should tell them? The task is not a pleasant one.

CECILY   Could we not both speak at the same time?

GWENDOLEN   An excellent idea! I nearly always speak at the same time as other people. Will you take the time from me?

CECILY   Certainly.

GWENDOLEN *beats time with uplifted finger.*

GWENDOLEN *and* CECILY [*speaking together*]   Your Christian names are still an insuperable barrier. That is all!

JACK *and* ALGERNON [*speaking together*]   Our Christian names! Is that all? But we are going to be christened this afternoon.

GWENDOLEN [*to* JACK]   For my sake you are prepared to do this terrible thing?

JACK   I am.

CECILY [*to* ALGERNON]   To please me you are ready to face this fearful ordeal?

ALGERNON   I am!

GWENDOLEN   How absurd to talk of the equality of the sexes! Where questions of self-sacrifice are concerned, men are infinitely beyond us.

---

4. A reference to such philosophical movements as the Materialism of Ludwig Feuerbach (1804–1872) and such theological movements as the "Higher Criticism," a movement which subjected the Bible to the same kind of study as that accorded other books.

JACK   We are. [*Clasps hands with* ALGERNON.]
CECILY   They have moments of physical courage of which we women
  know absolutely nothing.
GWENDOLEN [*to* JACK]   Darling!
ALGERNON [*to* CECILY]   Darling!

> *They fall into each other's arms. Enter* MERRIMAN. *When he
> enters he coughs loudly, seeing the situation.*

MERRIMAN   Ahem! Ahem! Lady Bracknell.
JACK   Good heavens!

> *Enter* LADY BRACKNELL. *The couples separate in alarm. Exit*
> MERRIMAN.

LADY BRACKNELL   Gwendolen! What does this mean?
GWENDOLEN   Merely that I am engaged to be married to Mr. Worthing, mamma.
LADY BRACKNELL   Come here. Sit down. Sit down immediately.
  Hesitation of any kind is a sign of mental decay in the young, of
  physical weakness in the old. [*Turns to* JACK.] Apprised, sir, of my
  daughter's sudden flight by her trusty maid, whose confidence I
  purchased by means of a small coin, I followed her at once by a
  luggage train. Her unhappy father is, I am glad to say, under the
  impression that she is attending a more than usually lengthy lecture
  by the University Extension Scheme on the Influence of a Permanent Income on Thought. I do not propose to undeceive him. Indeed
  I have never undeceived him on any question. I would consider it
  wrong. But, of course, you will clearly understand that all communication between yourself and my daughter must cease immediately
  from this moment. On this point, as indeed on all points, I am
  firm.
JACK   I am engaged to be married to Gwendolen, Lady Bracknell!
LADY BRACKNELL   You are nothing of the kind, sir. And now as re-
  gards Algernon! . . . Algernon!
ALGERNON   Yes, Aunt Augusta.
LADY BRACKNELL   May I ask if it is in this house that your invalid
  friend Mr. Bunbury resides?
ALGERNON [*stammering*]   Oh! no! Bunbury doesn't live here. Bunbury
  is somewhere else at present. In fact, Bunbury is dead.
LADY BRACKNELL   Dead! When did Mr. Bunbury die? His death
  must have been extremely sudden.
ALGERNON [*airily*]   Oh! I killed Bunbury this afternoon. I mean poor
  Bunbury died this afternoon.
LADY BRACKNELL   What did he die of?
ALGERNON   Bunbury? Oh, he was quite exploded.
LADY BRACKNELL   Exploded! Was he the victim of a revolutionary
  outrage? I was not aware that Mr. Bunbury was interested in social
  legislation. If so, he is well punished for his morbidity.
ALGERNON   My dear Aunt Augusta, I mean he was found out! The

doctors found out that Bunbury could not live, that is what I mean —so Bunbury died.

LADY BRACKNELL   He seems to have had great confidence in the opinion of his physicians. I am glad, however, that he made up his mind at the last to some definite course of action, and acted under proper medical advice. And now that we have finally got rid of this Mr. Bunbury, may I ask, Mr. Worthing, who is that young person whose hand my nephew Algernon is now holding in what seems to me a peculiarly unnecessary manner?

JACK   That lady is Miss Cecily Cardew, my ward.

LADY BRACKNELL *bows coldly to* CECILY.

ALGERNON   I am engaged to be married to Cecily, Aunt Augusta.

LADY BRACKNELL   I beg your pardon?

CECILY   Mr. Moncrieff and I are engaged to be married, Lady Bracknell.

LADY BRACKNELL [*with a shiver, crossing to the sofa and sitting down*] I do not know whether there is anything peculiarly exciting in the air of this particular part of Hertfordshire, but the number of engagements that go on seems to me considerably above the proper average that statistics have laid down for our guidance. I think some preliminary inquiry on my part would not be out of place. Mr. Worthing, is Miss Cardew at all connected with any of the larger railway stations in London? I merely desire information. Until yesterday I had no idea that there were any families or persons whose origin was a Terminus.

JACK *looks perfectly furious, but restrains himself.*

JACK [*in a cold, clear voice*]   Miss Cardew is the granddaughter of the late Mr. Thomas Cardew of 149 Belgrave Square, S.W.; Gervase Park, Dorking, Surrey; and the Sporran, Fifeshire, N.B.[5]

LADY BRACKNELL   That sounds not unsatisfactory. Three addresses always inspire confidence, even in tradesmen. But what proof have I of their authenticity?

JACK   I have carefully preserved the Court Guides of the period. They are open to your inspection, Lady Bracknell.

LADY BRACKNELL [*grimly*]   I have known strange errors in that publication.

JACK   Miss Cardew's family solicitors are Messrs. Markby, Markby, and Markby.

LADY BRACKNELL   Markby, Markby, and Markby? A firm of the very highest position in their profession. Indeed I am told that one of the Mr. Markbys is occasionally to be seen at dinner parties. So far I am satisfied.

JACK [*very irritably*]   How extremely kind of you, Lady Bracknell! I have also in my possession, you will be pleased to hear, certifi-

5. In addition to his London residence in Belgrave Square (already referred to in Act 1), Mr. Cardew maintained establish- ments in the south of England (Dorking, Surrey) and in Scotland (Fifeshire).

cates of Miss Cardew's birth, baptism, whooping cough, registration, vaccination, confirmation, and the measles; both the German and the English variety.

LADY BRACKNELL   Ah! A life crowded with incident, I see; though perhaps somewhat too exciting for a young girl. I am not myself in favor of premature experiences. [*Rises, looks at her watch.*] Gwendolen! the time approaches for our departure. We have not a moment to lose. As a matter of form, Mr. Worthing, I had better ask you if Miss Cardew has any little fortune?

JACK   Oh! about a hundred and thirty thousand pounds in the Funds.[6] That is all. Good-bye, Lady Bracknell. So pleased to have seen you.

LADY BRACKNELL [*sitting down again*]   A moment, Mr. Worthing. A hundred and thirty thousand pounds! And in the Funds! Miss Cardew seems to me a most attractive young lady, now that I look at her. Few girls of the present day have any really solid qualities, any of the qualities that last, and improve with time. We live, I regret to say, in an age of surfaces. [*To* CECILY.] Come over here, dear.

CECILY *goes across.*

Pretty child! your dress is sadly simple, and your hair seems almost as Nature might have left it. But we can soon alter all that. A thoroughly experienced French maid produces a really marvellous result in a very brief space of time. I remember recommending one to young Lady Lancing, and after three months her own husband did not know her.

JACK   And after six months nobody knew her.

LADY BRACKNELL [*glares at* JACK *for a few moments. Then bends, with a practiced smile, to* CECILY]   Kindly turn round, sweet child.

CECILY *turns completely round.*

No, the side view is what I want.

CECILY *presents her profile.*

Yes, quite as I expected. There are distinct social possibilities in your profile. The two weak points in our age are its want of principle and its want of profile. The chin a little higher, dear. Style largely depends on the way the chin is worn. They are worn very high, just at present. Algernon!

ALGERNON   Yes, Aunt Augusta!

LADY BRACKNELL   There are distinct social possibilities in Miss Cardew's profile.

ALGERNON   Cecily is the sweetest, dearest, prettiest girl in the whole world. And I don't care twopence about social possibilities.

LADY BRACKNELL   Never speak disrespectfully of Society, Algernon.

6. Stock of the British National Debt.

Only people who can't get into it do that. [*To* CECILY.] Dear child, of course you know that Algernon has nothing but his debts to depend upon. But I do not approve of mercenary marriages. When I married Lord Bracknell I had no fortune of any kind. But I never dreamed for a moment of allowing that to stand in my way. Well, I suppose I must give my consent.

ALGERNON   Thank you, Aunt Augusta.

LADY BRACKNELL   Cecily, you may kiss me!

CECILY [*kisses her*]   Thank you, Lady Bracknell.

LADY BRACKNELL   You may also address me as Aunt Augusta for the future.

CECILY   Thank you, Aunt Augusta.

LADY BRACKNELL   The marriage, I think, had better take place quite soon.

ALGERNON   Thank you, Aunt Augusta.

CECILY   Thank you, Aunt Augusta.

LADY BRACKNELL   To speak frankly, I am not in favor of long engagements. They give people the opportunity of finding out each other's character before marriage, which I think is never advisable.

JACK   I beg your pardon for interrupting you, Lady Bracknell, but this engagement is out of the question. I am Miss Cardew's guardian, and she cannot marry without my consent until she comes of age. That consent I absolutely decline to give.

LADY BRACKNELL   Upon what grounds, may I ask? Algernon is an extremely, I may almost say an ostentatiously, eligible young man. He has nothing, but he looks everything. What more can one desire?

JACK   It pains me very much to have to speak frankly to you, Lady Bracknell, about your nephew, but the fact is that I do not approve at all of his moral character. I suspect him of being untruthful.

ALGERNON *and* CECILY *look at him in indignant amazement.*

LADY BRACKNELL   Untruthful! My nephew Algernon? Impossible! He is an Oxonian.[7]

JACK   I fear there can be no possible doubt about the matter. This afternoon during my temporary absence in London on an important question of romance, he obtained admission to my house by means of the false pretense of being my brother. Under an assumed name he drank, I've just been informed by my butler, an entire pint bottle of my Perrier-Jouet, Brut, '89;[8] wine I was specially reserving for myself. Continuing his disgraceful deception, he succeeded in the course of the afternoon in alienating the affections of my only ward. He subsequently stayed to tea, and devoured every single muffin. And what makes his conduct all the more heartless is, that he was perfectly well aware from the first that I have no brother, that I never had a brother, and that I don't intend to have a brother, not even of any kind. I distinctly told him so myself yesterday afternoon.

---

7. A graduate of Oxford University.   8. A very dry champagne.

LADY BRACKNELL   Ahem! Mr. Worthing, after careful consideration I have decided entirely to overlook my nephew's conduct to you.

JACK   That is very generous of you, Lady Bracknell. My own decision, however, is unalterable. I decline to give my consent.

LADY BRACKNELL [*to* CECILY]   Come here, sweet child.

CECILY *goes over.*

How old are you, dear?

CECILY   Well, I am really only eighteen, but I always admit to twenty when I go to evening parties.

LADY BRACKNELL   You are perfectly right in making some slight alteration. Indeed, no woman should ever be quite accurate about her age. It looks so calculating. . . . [*In a meditative manner.*] Eighteen, but admitting to twenty at evening parties. Well, it will not be very long before you are of age and free from the restraints of tutelage. So I don't think your guardian's consent is, after all, a matter of any importance.

JACK   Pray excuse me, Lady Bracknell, for interrupting you again, but it is only fair to tell you that according to the terms of her grandfather's will Miss Cardew does not come legally of age till she is thirty-five.

LADY BRACKNELL   That does not seem to me to be a grave objection. Thirty-five is a very attractive age. London society is full of women of the very highest birth who have, of their own free choice, remained thirty-five for years. Lady Dumbleton is an instance in point. To my own knowledge she has been thirty-five ever since she arrived at the age of forty, which was many years ago now. I see no reason why our dear Cecily should not be even still more attractive at the age you mention than she is at present. There will be a large accumulation of property.

CECILY   Algy, could you wait for me till I was thirty-five?

ALGERNON   Of course I could, Cecily. You know I could.

CECILY   Yes, I felt it instinctively, but I couldn't wait all that time. I hate waiting even five minutes for anybody. It always makes me rather cross. I am not punctual myself, I know, but I do like punctuality in others, and waiting, even to be married, is quite out of the question.

ALGERNON   Then what is to be done, Cecily?

CECILY   I don't know, Mr. Moncrieff.

LADY BRACKNELL   My dear Mr. Worthing, as Miss Cardew states positively that she cannot wait till she is thirty-five—a remark which I am bound to say seems to me to show a somewhat impatient nature—I would beg of you to reconsider your decision.

JACK   But my dear Lady Bracknell, the matter is entirely in your own hands. The moment you consent to my marriage with Gwendolen, I will most gladly allow your nephew to form an alliance with my ward.

LADY BRACKNELL [*rising and drawing herself up*]   You must be quite aware that what you propose is out of the question.

JACK   Then a passionate celibacy is all that any of us can look forward to.

LADY BRACKNELL   That is not the destiny I propose for Gwendolen. Algernon, of course, can choose for himself. [*Pulls out her watch.*] Come, dear [GWENDOLEN *rises.*], we have already missed five, if not six, trains. To miss any more might expose us to comment on the platform.

Enter DR. CHASUBLE.

CHASUBLE   Everything is quite ready for the christenings.

LADY BRACKNELL   The christenings, sir! Is not that somewhat premature?

CHASUBLE   [*looking rather puzzled, and pointing to* JACK *and* ALGERNON] Both these gentlemen have expressed a desire for immediate baptism.

LADY BRACKNELL   At their age? The idea is grotesque and irreligious! Algernon, I forbid you to be baptized. I will not hear of such excesses. Lord Bracknell would be highly displeased if he learned that that was the way in which you wasted your time and money.

CHASUBLE   Am I to understand then that there are to be no christenings at all this afternoon?

JACK   I don't think that, as things are now, it would be of much practical value to either of us, Dr. Chasuble.

CHASUBLE   I am grieved to hear such sentiments from you, Mr. Worthing. They savour of the heretical views of the Anbaptists,[9] views that I have completely refuted in four of my unpublished sermons. However, as your present mood seems to be one peculiarly secular, I will return to the church at once. Indeed, I have just been informed by the pew-opener[1] that for the last hour and a half Miss Prism has been waiting for me in the vestry.

LADY BRACKNELL   [*starting*] Miss Prism! Did I hear you mention a Miss Prism?

CHASUBLE   Yes, Lady Bracknell. I am on my way to join her.

LADY BRACKNELL   Pray allow me to detain you for a moment. This matter may prove to be one of vital importance to Lord Bracknell and myself. Is this Miss Prism a female of repellent aspect, remotely connected with education?

CHASUBLE   [*somewhat indignantly*]....She is the most cultivated of ladies, and the very picture of respectability.

LADY BRACKNELL   It is obviously the same person. May I ask what position she holds in your household?

CHASUBLE   [*severely*]   I am a celibate, madam.

JACK   [*interposing*]   Miss Prism, Lady Bracknell, has been for the last three years Miss Cardew's esteemed governess and valued companion.

9. A 16th-century religious group, most nearly like contemporary Mennonites. Dr. Chasuble, however, is probably using the term loosely to apply to a group more like contemporary Baptists.

1. An usher. Since most pews were completely enclosed, his duties would have included opening the gate that provided entrance for the worshipers. In addition, since most pews were rented for the use of specific persons, he would have been responsible for seeing that worshipers were seated in the correct pews.

LADY BRACKNELL   In spite of what I hear of her, I must see her at once. Let her be sent for.

CHASUBLE [*looking off*]   She approaches; she is nigh.

Enter MISS PRISM *hurriedly.*

MISS PRISM   I was told you expected me in the vestry, dear Canon. I have been waiting for you there for an hour and three-quarters. [*Catches sight of* LADY BRACKNELL, *who has fixed her with a stony glare.* MISS PRISM *grows pale and quails. She looks anxiously round as if desirous to escape.*]

LADY BRACKNELL [*in a severe, judicial voice*]   Prism!

MISS PRISM *bows her head in shame.*

Come here, Prism!

MISS PRISM *approaches in a humble manner.*

Prism! Where is that baby?

General consternation. The CANON *starts back in horror.* ALGERNON *and* JACK *pretend to be anxious to shield* CECILY *and* GWENDOLEN *from hearing the details of terrible public scandal.*

Twenty-eight years ago, Prism, you left Lord Bracknell's house, Number 104, Upper Grosvenor Square, in charge of a perambulator that contained a baby of the male sex. You never returned. A few weeks later, through the elaborate investigations of the Metropolitan police, the perambulator was discovered at midnight standing by itself in a remote corner of Bayswater.[2] It contained the manuscript of a three-volume novel of more than usually revolting sentimentality.

MISS PRISM *starts in involuntary indignation.*

But the baby was not there.

Everyone looks at MISS PRISM.

Prism! Where is that baby?

A pause.

MISS PRISM   Lady Bracknell, I admit with shame that I do not know. I only wish I did. The plain facts of the case are these. On the morning of the day you mention, a day that is for ever branded on my memory, I prepared as usual to take the baby out in its

2. Bayswater is a residential section to the north of Hyde Park and Kensington Gardens.

perambulator. I had also with me a somewhat old, but capacious handbag in which I had intended to place the manuscript of a work of fiction that I had written during my few unoccupied hours. In a moment of mental abstraction, for which I can never forgive myself, I deposited the manuscript in the bassinette and placed the baby in the handbag.

JACK [*who has been listening attentively*] But where did you deposit the handbag?

MISS PRISM Do not ask me, Mr. Worthing.

JACK Miss Prism, this is a matter of no small importance to me. I insist on knowing where you deposited the handbag that contained that infant.

MISS PRISM I left it in the cloakroom of one of the larger railway stations in London.

JACK What railway station?

MISS PRISM [*quite crushed*] Victoria. The Brighton line. [*Sinks into a chair.*]

JACK I must retire to my room for a moment. Gwendolen, wait here for me.

GWENDOLEN If you are not too long, I will wait here for you all my life.

> Exit JACK *in great excitement.*

CHASUBLE What do you think this means, Lady Bracknell?

LADY BRACKNELL I dare not even suspect, Dr. Chasuble. I need hardly tell you that in families of high position strange coincidences are not supposed to occur. They are hardly considered the thing.

> Noises *heard overhead as if some one was throwing trunks about. Everyone looks up.*

CECILY Uncle Jack seems strangely agitated.

CHASUBLE Your guardian has a very emotional nature.

LADY BRACKNELL This noise is extremely unpleasant. It sounds as if he was having an argument. I dislike arguments of any kind. They are always vulgar, and often convincing.

CHASUBLE [*looking up*] It has stopped now.

> The noise is redoubled.

LADY BRACKNELL I wish he would arrive at some conclusion.

GWENDOLEN This suspense is terrible. I hope it will last.

> Enter JACK *with a handbag of black leather in his hand.*

JACK [*rushing over to* MISS PRISM] Is this the handbag, Miss Prism? Examine is carefully before you speak. The happiness of more than one life depends on your answer.

MISS PRISM [*calmly*] It seems to be mine. Yes, here is the injury it received through the upsetting of a Gower Street omnibus in younger and happier days. Here is the stain on the lining caused by the explosion of a temperance beverage, an incident that occurred at Leamington. And here, on the lock, are my initials. I had forgotten that in an extravagant mood I had had them placed there. The bag is undoubtedly mine. I am delighted to have it so unexpectedly restored to me. It has been a great inconvenience being without it all these years.

JACK [*in a pathetic voice*]   Miss Prism, more is restored to you than this handbag. I was the baby you placed in it.

MISS PRISM [*amazed*]   You?

JACK [*embracing her*]   Yes . . . mother!

MISS PRISM [*recoiling in indignant astonishment*]   Mr. Worthing, I am unmarried!

JACK   Unmarried! I do not deny that is a serious blow. But after all, who has the right to cast a stone against one who has suffered? Cannot repentance wipe out an act of folly? Why should there be one law for men, and another for women? Mother. I forgive you. [*Tries to embrace her again.*]

MISS PRISM [*still more indignant*]   Mr. Worthing, there is some error. [*Pointing to* LADY BRACKNELL.] There is the lady who can tell you who you really are.

JACK [*after a pause*]   Lady Bracknell, I hate to seem inquisitive, but would you kindly inform me who I am?

LADY BRACKNELL   I am afraid that the news I have to give you will not altogether please you. You are the son of my poor sister, Mrs. Moncrieff, and consequently Algernon's elder brother.

JACK   Algy's elder brother! Then I have a brother after all. I knew I had a brother! I always said I had a brother! Cecily—how could you have ever doubted that I had a brother? [*Seizes hold of* ALGERNON.] Dr. Chasuble, my unfortunate brother. Miss Prism, my unfortunate brother. Gwendolen, my unfortunate brother. Algy, you young scoundrel, you will have to treat me with more respect in the future. You have never behaved to me like a brother in all your life.

ALGERNON   Well, not till today, old boy, I admit. I did my best, however, though I was out of practice. [*Shakes hands.*]

GWENDOLEN [*to* JACK]   My own! But what own are you? What is your Christian name, now that you have become someone else?

JACK   Good heavens! . . . I had quite forgotten that point. Your decision on the subject of my name is irrevocable, I suppose?

GWENDOLEN   I never change, except in my affections.

CECILY   What a noble nature you have, Gwendolen!

JACK   Then the question had better be cleared up at once. Aunt Augusta, a moment. At the time when Miss Prism left me in the handbag, had I been christened already?

LADY BRACKNELL   Every luxury that money could buy, including christening, had been lavished on you by your fond and doting parents.

JACK   Then I was christened! That is settled. Now, what name was I given? Let me know the worst.

LADY BRACKNELL   Being the eldest son you were naturally christened after your father.

JACK [*irritably*]   Yes, but what was my father's Christian name?

LADY BRACKNELL [*meditatively*]   I cannot at the present moment recall what the General's Christian name was. But I have no doubt he had one. He was eccentric, I admit. But only in later years. And that was the result of the Indian climate, and marriage, and indigestion, and other things of that kind.

JACK   Algy! Can't you recollect what our father's Christian name was?

ALGERNON   My dear boy, we were never even on speaking terms. He died before I was a year old.

JACK   His name would appear in the Army Lists of the period, I suppose, Aunt Augusta?

LADY BRACKNELL....The General was essentially a man of peace, except in his domestic life. But I have no doubt his name would appear in any military directory.

JACK   The Army Lists of the last forty years are here. These delightful records should have been my constant study. [*Rushes to bookcase and tears the books out.*] M. Generals . . . Mallam, Maxbohm, Magley—what ghastly names they have—Markby, Migsby, Mobbs, Moncrieff! Lieutenant 1840, Captain, Lieutenant-Colonel, Colonel, General 1869, Christian names, Ernest John. [*Puts book very quietly down and speaks quite calmly.*] I always told you, Gwendolen, my name was Ernest, didn't I? Well, it is Ernest after all. I mean it naturally is Ernest.

LADY BRACKNELL   Yes, I remember now that the General was called Ernest. I knew I had some particular reason for disliking the name.

GWENDOLEN   Ernest! My own Ernest! I felt from the first that you could have no other name!

JACK   Gwendolen, it is a terrible thing for a man to find out suddenly that all his life he has been speaking nothing but the truth. Can you forgive me?

GWENDOLEN   I can. For I feel that you are sure to change.

JACK   My own one!

CHASUBLE [*to* MISS PRISM]   Laetitia! [*Embraces her.*]

MISS PRISM [*enthusiastically*]   Frederick! At last!

ALGERNON   Cecily! [*Embraces her.*] At last!

JACK   Gwendolen! [*Embraces her.*] At last!

LADY BRACKNELL   My nephew, you seem to be displaying signs of triviality.

JACK   On the contrary, Aunt Augusta, I've now realized for the first time in my life the vital Importance of Being Earnest.

1895

6   HISTORICAL SETTING

A play is written in some historical time and place, and in many cases is set in that same framework. A knowledge of the historical context is worth knowing for all plays, but for those like Chekhov's *Three Sisters*, which describe their own times, the knowledge may be particularly valuable. The particular time and place are the turn of the century in a provincial Russian town. However accurate Chekhov's reflection of that milieu may be, many aspects of the names by which characters are called are strange to us, and the unwary reader may miss subtleties. Why, for example, is the middle sister sometimes called "Masha," sometimes "Marya Sergeyevna," sometimes "Mashenka"? Why does Irina call one of her suitors "Solyony" when he is not present and "Vassily Vassilyevitch" when he is? Some suggestions about these matters can be found in the note on Russian names (p. 1441).

Another problem that can trouble the reader of the play is hindsight. When Tusenbach says, "The time is at hand, an avalanche is moving down upon us, a mighty clearing storm which is coming, is already near and will soon blow the laziness, the indifference, the distaste for work, the rotten boredom out of our society," we are tempted to see him as a prophet of the Russian Revolution of 1917. Perhaps that is what he meant, but probably his contemporaries would have regarded him as a harmless eccentric rather than a seer.

What do we need to know about the society described in order to understand the play? First, we must remember that it takes place in Russia, a country slower to industrialize and urbanize than the England of *The Importance of Being Earnest*. Wealth and position were more closely tied to the possession of land and the close association with the land and its people. Perhaps this can be illustrated by servants in the plays. Lane in *Earnest* is skilled and obedient, but he cherishes no illusions about his master. Indeed, "master" is largely metaphorical; Algernon is really his employer. If his wages are not forthcoming promptly, Lane would seek new employment and be just as skilled and obedient in his new position. Anfisa, the old nurse in *Three Sisters,* however, is more a member of an extended family than an employee or even a servant. She still calls the sisters by the names she used for them as children. They do not object, because she has earned the privilege by her service and devotion to the family. Natasha treats Anfisa completely differently because Natasha represents the new forces in society. She and her beau (later, her lover) Protopopov are bourgeoisie. She wears the wrong color belt in Act 1, and on several occasions she displays her execrable French, both signs that she is from a lower social class than the Prozorovs. From her view Anfisa is merely an employee who can no longer do the job and must therefore be shipped off somewhere to die.

The rise of the bourgeoisie is shown by the relative positions of Andrey and Protopopov. Early in the play Natasha throws Protopopov over to marry Andrey, hoping to rise in society. By the end of the play, however, Protopopov is in control; Andrey is working for him and Natasha has become his mistress. The takeover of the new is also presented graphically in the play by Natasha's usurpation of the house. In Act 1 she is a diffident guest in the public rooms. By the beginning of Act 2 she has taken possession as mistress in these same rooms, and is planning to displace Irina by asking her to share Olga's room. In Act 3 she enters that bedroom and exerts her authority by threatening to get rid of Anfisa. Olga must take the position of headmistress, though she does not want it, in order to provide for Anfisa. In Act 4, Olga is gone, Irina is about to leave, and they are in the garden. Natasha has taken complete possession of the house and is planning to replace the old trees with flowers.

The position of the Prozorovs in the society is another example of how a knowledge of the historical situation can help us to understand more fully some points of the play. For us, university professors and army officers do not possess exalted social status because of their professions, as they do in the society of *Three Sisters*. As the daughters of General Prozorov, the sisters had been the center of a glittering social circle. Her sisters felt that Masha had married beneath her because her husband was merely a secondary-school teacher. All that has changed with the death of the father. "In the old days, when father was alive, we always had thirty or forty officers here on namedays; it was noisy, but today there is only a man and a half, and it is as still as the desert." Indeed, the general's social position did not outlast his funeral. "Though he was a general in command of a brigade, yet there weren't many people there." Andrey's ambition is to become a university professor in Moscow, and his sisters see that goal as a way to reenter their former life. When he marries Natasha and loses his ambitions, they realize that they are condemned to drab lives in a provincial backwater. Although they have pensions and will not starve, they can never have the kind of life they had expected.

Another social change reflected in this play, and in *Earnest*, is the importance of the metropolitan center, generally the capital of the country. One may have income-producing property in the country and even spend a part of the year there, but the big city is the center of the action. One may live in the provinces for various reasons, the Prozorovs because they cannot afford a proper style in Moscow, or Cecily Cardew because her guardian wishes to insulate her from the vices of the city, but to any right-thinking person of the upper classes the city is the place to be.

ANTON CHEKHOV

Three Sisters[*]

CHARACTERS

ANDREY SERGEYEVITCH PROZOROV[1]

NATALYA IVANOVNA (*also called* NATASHA), *his fiancée, afterwards his wife*

OLGA ⎫
MASHA ⎬ *his sisters*
IRINA ⎭

FYODOR ILYITCH KULIGIN, *a high-school teacher, husband of Masha*

LIEUTENANT COLONEL ALEXANDR IGNATYEVITCH VERSHININ, *Battery Commander*

BARON NIKOLAY LVOVITCH TUSENBACH, *Lieutenant*

VASSILY VASSILYEVITCH SOLYONY, *Captain*

IVAN ROMANITCH TCHEBUTYKIN, *army doctor*

ALEXEY PETROVITCH FEDOTIK, *Second Lieutenant*

VLADIMIR KARLOVITCH RODDEY, *Second Lieutenant*

FERAPONT, *an old porter from the Rural Board*[2]

ANFISA, *the nurse, an old woman of eighty*

The action takes place in a provincial town.

Act 1

In the house of the PROZOROVS. *A drawing room with columns beyond which a large room is visible. Midday; it is bright and sunny. The table in the farther room is being laid for lunch.*

OLGA, *in the dark blue uniform of a high-school teacher, is correcting exercise books, at times standing still and then walking up and down;* MASHA, *in a black dress, with her hat on her knee, is reading a book;* IRINA, *in a white dress, is standing plunged in thought.*

OLGA Father died just a year ago, on this very day—the fifth of May, your name-day, Irina.[3] It was very cold, snow was falling. I felt as though I should not live through it; you lay fainting as though you were dead. But now a year has passed and we can think of it calmly; you are already in a white dress, your face is radiant. [*The clock strikes twelve.*] The clock was striking then too. [*A pause.*] I remem-

---

[*] Translated by Constance Garnett.

[1] See the note on Russian names, p. 1441.

[2] The Rural Board was the local arm of the Imperial government. It was somewhat more powerful than the locally elected *zemstvo*, which is mentioned later in the play.

[3] Like many Europeans, Irina observes not her birthday but the feast of the saint whose name she bears. Several Saint Irenes share May 5 as feast day, including a Byzantine martyr of the first century, beheaded during the reign of Domitian or Trajan and a Greek martyr burned to death in Thessalonica in 304 A.D.

ber the band playing and the firing at the cemetery as they carried the coffin. Though he was a general in command of a brigade, yet there weren't many people there. It was raining, though. Heavy rain and snow.

IRINA   Why recall it!

> BARON TUSENBACH, TCHEBUTYKIN, *and* SOLYONY *appear near the table in the dining room, beyond the columns.*

OLGA   It is warm today, we can have the windows open, but the birches are not in leaf yet. Father was given his brigade and came here with us from Moscow eleven years ago and I remember distinctly that in Moscow at this time, at the beginning of May, everything was already in flower; it was warm, and everything was bathed in sunshine. It's eleven years ago, and yet I remember it all as though we had left it yesterday. Oh, dear! I woke up this morning, I saw a blaze of sunshine. I saw the spring, and joy stirred in my heart. I had a passionate longing to be back at home again!

TCHEBUTYKIN   The devil it is!

TUSENBACH   Of course, it's nonsense.

> MASHA, *brooding over a book, softly whistles a song.*

OLGA   Don't whistle, Masha. How can you! [*A pause.*] Being all day in school and then at my lessons till the evening gives me a perpetual headache and thoughts as gloomy as though I were old. And really these four years that I have been at the high-school I have felt my strength and my youth oozing away from me every day. And only one yearning grows stronger and stronger. . . .

IRINA   To go back to Moscow. To sell the house, to make an end of everything here, and off to Moscow. . . .

OLGA   Yes! To Moscow, and quickly.

> TCHEBUTYKIN *and* TUSENBACH *laugh.*

IRINA   Andrey will probably be a professor, he will not live here anyhow. The only difficulty is poor Masha.

OLGA   Masha will come and spend the whole summer in Moscow every year.

> MASHA *softly whistles a tune.*

IRINA   Please God it will all be managed. [*Looking out of window.*] How fine it is today. I don't know why I feel so lighthearted! I remembered this morning that it was my name-day and at once I felt joyful and thought of my childhood when mother was living. And I was thrilled by such wonderful thoughts, such thoughts!

OLGA   You are radiant today and looking lovelier than usual. And Masha is lovely too. Andrey would be nice-looking, but he has grown too fat and that does not suit him. And I have grown older and ever so much thinner. I suppose it's because I get so cross with the girls at school. Today now I am free, I am at home, and my head doesn't ache, and I feel younger than yesterday. I am only twenty-eight. . . . It's all quite right, it's all from God, but it seems to me that if I were married and sitting at home all day, it would be better. [*A pause.*] I should be fond of my husband.

TUSENBACH [*to* SOLYONY]   You talk such nonsense, I am tired of listening to you. [*Coming into the drawing room.*] I forgot to tell you, you will receive a visit today from Vershinin, the new commander of our battery. [*Sits down to the piano.*]

OLGA   Well, I shall be delighted.

IRINA   Is he old?

TUSENBACH   No, nothing to speak of. Forty or forty-five at the most. [*Softly plays the piano.*] He seems to be a nice fellow. He is not stupid, that's certain. Only he talks a lot.

IRINA   Is he interesting?

TUSENBACH   Yes, he is all right, only he has a wife, a mother-in-law and two little girls. And it's his second wife too. He is paying calls and telling everyone that he has a wife and two little girls. He'll tell you so too. His wife seems a bit crazy, with her hair in a long plait like a girl's, always talks in a high-flown style, makes philosophical reflections and frequently attempts to commit suicide, evidently to annoy her husband. I should have left a woman like that years ago, but he puts up with her and merely complains.

SOLYONY [*coming into the drawing room with* TCHEBUTYKIN]   With one hand I can only lift up half a hundredweight, but with both hands I can lift up a hundredweight and a half or even a hundredweight and three-quarters.[4] From that I conclude that two men are not only twice but three times as strong as one man, or even more. . . .

TCHEBUTYKIN [*reading the newspaper as he comes in*]   For hair falling out . . . two ounces of naphthaline in half a bottle of spirit . . . to be dissolved and used daily. . . . [*Puts it down in his notebook.*] Let's make a note of it! No, I don't want it. . . . [*Scratches it out.*] It doesn't matter.

IRINA   Ivan Romanitch, dear Ivan Romanitch!

TCHEBUTYKIN   What is it, my child, my joy?

IRINA   Tell me, why is it I am so happy today? As though I were sailing with the great blue sky above me and big white birds flying over it. Why is it? Why?

TCHEBUTYKIN [*kissing both her hands, tenderly*]   My white bird. . . .

IRINA   When I woke up this morning, got up and washed, it suddenly seemed to me as though everything in the world was clear to me and that I knew how one ought to live. Dear Ivan Romanitch, I know all about it. A man ought to work, to toil in the sweat of his brow, whoever he may be, and all the purpose and meaning of his life, his happiness, his ecstasies lie in that alone. How delightful to be a workman who gets up before dawn and breaks stones on the road, or a shepherd, or a schoolmaster teaching children, or an engine-driver. . . . Oh, dear! to say nothing of human beings, it would be better to be an ox, better to be a humble horse and work, than a young woman who wakes at twelve o'clock, then has coffee in bed, then spends two hours dressing. . . . Oh, how awful that is! Just as

4. I.e., 150 to 175 pounds.

one has a craving for water in hot weather I have a craving for work. And if I don't get up early and work, give me up as a friend, Ivan Romanitch.

TCHEBUTYKIN [*tenderly*]   I'll give you up, I'll give you up. . . .

OLGA   Father trained us to get up at seven o'clock. Now Irina wakes at seven and lies in bed at least till nine thinking. And she looks so serious! [*Laughs.*]

IRINA   You are used to thinking of me as a child and are surprised when I look serious. I am twenty!

TUSENBACH   The yearning for work, oh dear, how well I understand it! I have never worked in my life. I was born in cold, idle Petersburg, in a family that had known nothing of work or cares of any kind. I remember, when I came home from the school of cadets, a footman used to pull off my boots. I used to be troublesome, but my mother looked at me with reverential awe, and was surprised when other people did not do the same. I was guarded from work. But I doubt if they have succeeded in guarding me completely, I doubt it! The time is at hand, an avalanche is moving down upon us, a mighty clearing storm which is coming, is already near and will soon blow the laziness, the indifference, the distaste for work, the rotten boredom out of our society. I shall work, and in another twenty-five or thirty years everyone will have to work. Everyone!

TCHEBUTYKIN   I am not going to work.

TUSENBACH   You don't count.

SOLYONY   In another twenty-five years you won't be here, thank God. In two or three years you will kick the bucket, or I shall lose my temper and put a bullet through your head, my angel.

> *Pulls a scent-bottle out of his pocket and sprinkles his chest and hands.*

TCHEBUTYKIN [*laughs*]   And I really have never done anything at all. I haven't done a stroke of work since I left the University, I have never read a book, I read nothing but newspapers. . . . [*Takes another newspaper out of his pocket.*] Here . . . I know, for instance, from the newspapers that there was such a person as Dobrolyubov, but what he wrote, I can't say.[5] . . . Goodness only knows. . . .

> *A knock is heard on the floor from the story below.*

There . . . they are calling me downstairs, someone has come for me. I'll be back directly. . . . Wait a minute. . . . [*Goes out hurriedly, combing his beard.*]

IRINA   He's got something up his sleeve.

TUSENBACH   Yes, he went out with a solemn face; evidently he is just going to bring you a present.

IRINA   What a nuisance!

OLGA   Yes, it's awful. He is always doing something silly.

MASHA   By the sea-strand an oak tree green . . . upon that oak a chain

5. Nicholas A. Dobrolyubov (1836–1861) was a distinguished literary critic and advanced social thinker, a forerunner of populism.

of gold . . . upon that oak a chain of gold.[6] [*Gets up, humming softly.*]

OLGA   You are not very cheerful today, Masha.

MASHA, *humming, puts on her hat.*

OLGA   Where are you going?

MASHA   Home.

IRINA   How queer! . . .

TUSENBACH   To go away from a name-day party!

MASHA   Never mind. . . . I'll come in the evening. Good-bye, my darling. . . . [*Kisses* IRINA.] Once again I wish you, be well and happy. In old days, when father was alive, we always had thirty or forty officers here on name-days; it was noisy, but today there is only a man and a half, and it is as still as the desert. . . . I'll go. . . . I am in the blues today, I am feeling glum, so don't you mind what I say. [*Laughing through her tears.*] We'll talk some other time, and so for now good-bye, darling, I am going. . . .

IRINA [*discontentedly*]   Oh, how tiresome you are. . . .

OLGA [*with tears*]   I understand you, Masha.

SOLYONY   If a man philosophizes, there will be philosophy or sophistry, anyway, but if a woman philosophizes, or two do it, then you may just snap your fingers!

MASHA   What do you mean to say by that, you terrible person?

SOLYONY   Nothing. He had not time to say "alack," before the bear was on his back.[7] [*A pause.*]

MASHA [*to* OLGA, *angrily*]   Don't blubber!

Enter ANFISA *and* FERAPONT *carrying a cake.*

ANFISA   This way, my good man. Come in, your boots are clean. [*To* IRINA.] From the Rural Board, from Mihail Ivanitch Protopopov. . . . A cake.

IRINA   Thanks. Thank him. [*Takes the cake.*]

FERAPONT   What?

IRINA [*more loudly*]   Thank him from me!

OLGA   Nurse dear, give him some pie. Ferapont, go along, they will give you some pie.

FERAPONT   Eh?

ANFISA   Come along, Ferapont Spiridonitch, my good soul, come along . . .

Goes out with FERAPONT.

MASHA   I don't like that Protopopov, that Mihail Potapitch or Ivanitch. He ought not to be invited.

IRINA   I did not invite him.

MASHA   That's a good thing.

6. Masha is quoting from the opening of *Ruslan and Ludmila,* a long narrative poem by Alexander S. Pushkin (1799–1837), the most famous Russian poet of the nineteenth century. Several of the literary quotations in the play, including this one, appear more than once.

7. A quotation from the fable "The Peasant and the Laborer" by Ivan A. Krylov (1769–1844).

Enter TCHEBUTYKIN, *followed by an orderly with a silver samovar; a hum of surprise and displeasure.*

OLGA [*putting her hands over her face*]   A samovar! How awful! [*Goes out to the table in the dining room.*]

IRINA   My dear Ivan Romanitch, what are you thinking about!

TUSENBACH [*laughs*]   I warned you!

MASHA   Ivan Romanitch, you really have no conscience!

TCHEBUTYKIN   My dear girls, my darlings, you are all that I have, you are the most precious treasures I have on earth. I shall soon be sixty, I am an old man, alone in the world, a useless old man. . . . There is nothing good in me, except my love for you, and if it were not for you, I should have been dead long ago. . . . [*To* IRINA.] My dear, my little girl, I've known you from a baby. . . . I've carried you in my arms. . . . I loved your dear mother. . . .

IRINA   But why such expensive presents?

TCHEBUTYKIN [*angry and tearful*]   Expensive presents. . . . Get along with you! [*To the orderly.*] Take the samovar in there. . . . [*Mimicking.*] Expensive presents. . . .

The orderly carries the samovar into the dinng room.

ANFISA [*crossing the room*]   My dears, a colonel is here, a stranger. . . . He has taken off his greatcoat, children, he is coming in here. Irinushka, you must be nice and polite, dear. . . . [*As she goes out.*] And it's time for lunch already . . . mercy on us. . . .

TUSENBACH   Vershinin, I suppose.

Enter VERSHININ.

TUSENBACH   Colonel Vershinin.

VERSHININ [*to* MASHA *and* IRINA]   I have the honor to introduce myself, my name is Vershinin. I am very, very glad to be in your house at last. How you have grown up! Aie-aie!

IRINA   Please sit down. We are delighted to see you.

VERSHININ [*with animation*]   How glad I am, how glad I am! But there are three of you sisters. I remember—three little girls. I don't remember your faces, but that your father, Colonel Prozorov, had three little girls I remember perfectly, and saw them with my own eyes. How time passes! Hey-ho, how it passes!

TUSENBACH   Alexandr Ignatyevitch has come from Moscow.

IRINA   From Moscow? You have come from Moscow?

VERSHININ   Yes. Your father was in command of a battery there, and I was an officer in the same brigade. [*To* MASHA.] Your face, now, I seem to remember.

MASHA   I don't remember you.

IRINA   Olya! Olya! [*Calls into the dining room.*] Olya, come!

OLGA *comes out of the dining room into the drawing room.*

IRINA   Colonel Vershinin is from Moscow, it appears.

VERSHININ   So you are Olga Sergeyevna, the eldest. . . . And you are Marya. . . . And you are Irina, the youngest. . . .

OLGA   You come from Moscow?

VERSHININ   Yes. I studied in Moscow. I began my service there, I served there for years, and at last I have been given a battery here— I have come here as you see. I don't remember you exactly, I only remember you were three sisters. I remember your father. If I shut my eyes, I can see him as though he were living. I used to visit you in Moscow. . . .

OLGA   I thought I remembered everyone, and now all at once . . .

VERSHININ   My name is Alexandr Ignatyevitch.

IRINA   Alexandr Ignatyevitch, you have come from Moscow. . . . What a surprise!

OLGA   We are going to move there, you know.

IRINA   We are hoping to be there by the autumn. It's our native town, we were born there. . . . In Old Basmanny Street.[8] . . . [*Both laugh with delight.*]

MASHA   To see someone from our own town unexpectedly! [*Eagerly.*] Now I remember! Do you remember, Olya, they used to talk of the "love-sick major"? You were a lieutenant at that time and were in love, and for some reason everyone called you "major" to tease you. . . .

VERSHININ   [*laughs*]   Yes, yes. . . . The love-sick major, that was it.

MASHA   You only had a moustache then. . . . Oh, how much older you look! [*Through tears.*] How much older!

VERSHININ   Yes, when I was called the love-sick major I was young, I was in love. Now it's very different.

OLGA   But you haven't a single grey hair. You have grown older but you are not old.

VERSHININ   I am in my forty-third year, though. Is it long since you left Moscow?

IRINA   Eleven years. But why are you crying, Masha, you queer girl? . . . [*Through her tears.*] I shall cry too. . . .

MASHA   I am all right. And in which street did you live?

VERSHININ   In Old Basmanny.

OLGA   And that's where we lived too. . . .

VERSHININ   At one time I lived in Nyemetsky Street. I used to go from there to the Red Barracks. There is a gloomy-looking bridge on the way, where the water makes a noise. It makes a lonely man feel melancholy. [*A pause.*] And here what a broad, splendid river! A marvelous river!

OLGA   Yes, but it is cold. It's cold here and there are gnats. . . .

VERSHININ   How can you! You've such a splendid healthy Russian climate here. Forest, river . . . and birches here too. Charming, modest birches, I love them better than any other trees. It's nice to live here. The only strange thing is that the railway station is fifteen miles away. . . . And no one knows why it is so.

SOLYONY   I know why it is. [*They all look at him.*] Because if the station had been near it would not have been so far, and if it is far, it's because it is not near.

8. Old Basmanny Street (now Karl Marx/ Bakunin Street) and Nyemetsky Street (now Bauman Street) were in the part of Moscow called Lefortov (now Baumanski), where many foreigners lived along with army officers and technical and professional people.

An awkward silence.

TUSENBACH   He is fond of his joke, Vassily Vassilyevitch.
OLGA   Now I recall you, too. I remember.
VERSHININ   I knew your mother.
TCHEBUTYKIN   She was a fine woman, the Kingdom of Heaven be hers.
IRINA   Mother is buried in Moscow.
OLGA   In the Novo-Dyevitchy.[9]. . .
MASHA   Would you believe it, I am already beginning to forget her face. So people will not remember us either . . . they will forget us.
VERSHININ   Yes. They will forget us. Such is our fate, there is no help for it. What seems to us serious, significant, very important, will one day be forgotten or will seem unimportant. [*A pause.*] And it's curious that we can't possibly tell what exactly will be considered great and important, and what will seem paltry and ridiculous. Did not the discoveries of Copernicus or Columbus, let us say, seem useless and ridiculous at first,[1] while the nonsensical writings of some wiseacre seemed true? And it may be that our present life, which we accept so readily, will in time seem queer, uncomfortable, not sensible, not clean enough, perhaps even sinful. . . .
TUSENBACH   Who knows? Perhaps our age will be called a great one and remembered with respect. Now we have no torture-chamber, no executions, no invasions, but at the same time how much unhappiness there is!
SOLYONY   [*in a high-pitched voice*]   Chook, chook, chook. . . . It's bread and meat to the baron to talk about ideas.
TUSENBACH   Vassily Vassilyevitch, I ask you to let me alone. . . . [*Moves to another seat.*] It gets boring, at last.
SOLYONY   [*in a high-pitched voice*]   Chook, chook, chook. . . .
TUSENBACH   [*to* VERSHININ]   The unhappiness which one observes now—there is so much of it—does indicate, however, that society has reached a certain moral level.
VERSHININ   Yes, yes, of course.
TCHEBUTYKIN   You said just now, baron, that our age will be called great; but people are small all the same. . . .[*Gets up.*] Look how small I am.

A violin is played behind the scenes.

MASHA   That's Andrey playing, our brother.
IRINA   He is the learned one of the family. We expect him to become a professor. Father was a military man, but his son has gone in for a learned career.
MASHA   It was father's wish.
OLGA   We have been teasing him today. We think he is a little in love.
IRINA   With a young lady living here. She will come in today most likely.

9. The most famous nunnery in Moscow, construction of which was begun in 1524 by Grand Duke Vassily III, father of Ivan the Terrible. Many distinguished people are buried there, including Chekhov himself.
1. The Polish astronomer Nicolaus Co-pernicus (1473–1543) and the Italian navigator Christopher Columbus (1451–1506) are popularly believed to have discovered, respectively, that the earth revolves around the sun rather than *vice versa* and that the earth is spherical rather than flat.

MASHA Oh, how she dresses! It's not that her clothes are merely ugly or out of fashion, they are simply pitiful. A queer gaudy yellowish skirt with some sort of vulgar fringe and a red blouse. And her cheeks scrubbed till they shine! Andrey is not in love with her— I won't admit that, he has some taste anyway—it's simply for fun, he is teasing us, playing the fool. I heard yesterday that she is going to be married to Protopopov, the chairman of our Rural Board. And a very good thing too. . . . [*At the side door.*] Andrey, come here, dear, for a minute!

Enter ANDREY.

OLGA This is my brother, Andrey Sergeyevitch.

VERSHININ My name is Vershinin.

ANDREY And mine is Prozorov. [*Mops his perspiring face.*] You are our new battery commander?

OLGA Only fancy, Alexandr Ignatyevitch comes from Moscow.

ANDREY Really? Well, then, I congratulate you. My sisters will let you have no peace.

VERSHININ I have had time to bore your sisters already.

IRINA See what a pretty picture-frame Andrey has given me today! [*Shows the frame.*] He made it himself.

VERSHININ [*looking at the frame and not knowing what to say*] Yes . . . it is a thing. . . .

IRINA And that frame above the piano, he made that too!

ANDREY *waves his hand in despair and moves away.*

OLGA He is learned, and he plays the violin, and he makes all sorts of things with the fretsaw. In fact he is good all round. Andrey, don't go! That's a way he has—he always tries to make off! Come here!

MASHA *and* IRINA *take him by the arms and, laughing, lead him back.*

MASHA Come, come!

ANDREY Leave me alone, please!

MASHA How absurd he is! Alexandr Ignatyevitch used to be called the love-sick major at one time, and he was not a bit offended.

VERSHININ Not in the least!

MASHA And I should like to call you the love-sick violinist!

IRINA Or the love-sick professor!

OLGA He is in love! Andryusha is in love!

IRINA [*claps her hands*] Bravo, bravo! Encore! Andryusha is in love!

TCHEBUTYKIN [*comes up behind* ANDREY *and puts both arms round his waist*] Nature our hearts for love created![2] [*Laughs, then sits down and reads the newspaper which he takes out of his pocket.*]

ANDREY Come, that's enough, that's enough. . . . [*Mops his face.*] I haven't slept all night and this morning I don't feel quite myself, as they say. I read till four o'clock and then went to bed, but it was no use. I thought of one thing and another, and then it gets light so

2. A line from a Russian popular song of the 1890s.

early; the sun simply pours into my bedroom. I want while I am here during the summer to translate a book from the English. . . .

VERSHININ   You read English then?

ANDREY   Yes. Our father, the Kingdom of Heaven be his, oppressed us with education. It's absurd and silly, but it must be confessed I began to get fatter after his death, and I have grown too fat in one year, as though a weight had been taken off my body. Thanks to our father we all know English, French, and German, and Irina knows Italian too. But what it cost us!

MASHA   In this town to know three languages is an unnecessary luxury! Not even a luxury, but an unnecessary encumbrance, like a sixth finger. We know a great deal that is unnecessary.

VERSHININ   What next! [*Laughs.*] You know a great deal that is unnecessary! I don't think there can be a town so dull and dismal that intelligent and educated people are unnecessary in it. Let us suppose that of the hundred thousand people living in this town, which is, of course, uncultured and behind the times, there are only three of your sort. It goes without saying that you cannot conquer the mass of darkness round you; little by little, as you go on living, you will be lost in the crowd. You will have to give in to it. Life will get the better of you, but still you will not disappear without a trace. After you there may appear perhaps six like you, then twelve and so on until such as you form a majority. In two or three hundred years life on earth will be unimaginably beautiful, marvelous. Man needs such a life and, though he hasn't it yet, he must have a presentiment of it, expect it, dream of it, prepare for it; for that he must see and know more than his father and grandfather. [*Laughs.*] And you complain of knowing a great deal that's unnecessary.

MASHA [*takes off her hat*]   I'll stay to lunch.

IRINA [*with a sigh*]   All that really ought to be written down. . . .

ANDREY *has slipped away unobserved.*

TUSENBACH   You say that after many years life on earth will be beautiful and marvelous. That's true. But in order to have any share, however far off, in it now one must be preparing for it, one must be working. . . .

VERSHININ [*gets up*]   Yes. What a lot of flowers you have! [*Looking round.*] And delightful rooms. I envy you! I've been knocking about all my life from one wretched lodging to another, always with two chairs and a sofa and stoves which smoke. What I have been lacking all my life is just such flowers. . . . [*Rubs his hands.*] But there, it's no use thinking about it!

TUSENBACH   Yes, we must work. I'll be bound you think the German is getting sentimental.[3] But on my honor I am Russian and I can't even speak German. My father belonged to the Orthodox Church. . . . [*A pause.*]

VERSHININ [*walks about the stage*]   I often think, what if one were to

3. Great numbers of foreigners (known generically as "Germans") immigrated to Russia, beginning early in the 17th century. At various times they were the subject of distrust and prejudice from conservative elements in Russia, particularly the Orthodox Church.

begin life over again, knowing what one is about! If one life, which has been already lived, were only a rough sketch so to say, and the second were the fair copy! Then, I fancy, every one of us would try before everything not to repeat himself, anyway he would create a different setting for his life; would have a house like this with plenty of light and masses of flowers. . . . I have a wife and two little girls, my wife is in delicate health and so on and so on, but if I were to begin life over again I would not marry. . . . No, no!

Enter KULIGIN *in the uniform of a schoolmaster.*

KULIGIN [*goes up to* IRINA] Dear sister, allow me to congratulate you on your name-day and with all my heart to wish you good health and everything else that one can desire for a girl of your age. And to offer you as a gift this little book. [*Gives her a book.*] The history of our high-school for fifty years, written by myself. An insignificant little book, written because I had nothing better to do, but still you can read it. Good morning, friends. [*To* VERSHININ.] My name is Kuligin, teacher in the high-school here. [*To* IRINA.] In that book you will find a list of all who have finished their studies in our high-school during the last fifty years. *Feci quod potui, faciant meliora potentes.*[4] [*Kisses* MASHA.]

IRINA   Why, but you gave me a copy of this book at Easter.

KULIGIN [*laughs*] Impossible! If that's so, give it back, or better still, give it to the Colonel. Please accept it, Colonel. Some day when you are bored you can read it.

VERSHININ   Thank you. [*Is about to take leave.*] I am extremely glad to have made your acquaintance. . . .

OLGA   You are going? No, no!

IRINA   You must stay to lunch with us. Please do.

OLGA   Pray do!

VERSHININ [*bows*]   I believe I have chanced on a name-day. Forgive me, I did not know and have not congratulated you. . . . [*Walks away with* OLGA *into the dining room.*]

KULIGIN   Today, gentlemen, is Sunday, a day of rest. Let us all rest and enjoy ourselves each in accordance with our age and our position. The carpets should be taken up for the summer and put away till the winter . . . Persian powder or naphthaline.[5] . . . The Romans were healthy because they knew how to work and they knew how to rest, they had *mens sana in corpore sano.*[6] Their life was molded into a certain framework. Our headmaster says that the most important thing in every life is its framework. . . . What loses its framework, comes to an end—and it's the same in our everyday life. [*Puts his arm round* MASHA's *waist, laughing.*] Masha loves me. My wife loves me. And the window curtains, too, ought to be put away together with the carpets. . . . Today I feel cheerful and in the best of spirits. Masha, at four o'clock this afternoon we have to be at the head-

---

4. Latin for "I have done what I can; let those who are more capable do better things."

5. Persian (insect) powder is a form of pyrethrum.

6. Latin for "a sound mind in a sound body."

master's. An excursion has been arranged for the teachers and their families.

MASHA   I am not going.

KULIGIN [*grieved*]   Dear Masha, why not?

MASHA   We'll talk about it afterward. . . . [*Angrily.*] Very well, I will go, only let me alone, please. . . . [*Walks away.*]

KULIGIN   And then we shall spend the evening at the headmaster's. In spite of the delicate state of his health, that man tries before all things to be sociable. He is an excellent, noble personality. A splendid man. Yesterday, after the meeting, he said to me, "I am tired, Fyodor Ilyitch, I am tired." [*Looks at the clock, then at his watch.*] Your clock is seven minutes fast. "Yes," he said, "I am tired."

   Sounds of a violin behind the scenes.

OLGA   Come to lunch, please. There's a pie!

KULIGIN   Ah, Olga, my dear Olga! Yesterday I was working from early morning till eleven o'clock at night and was tired out, and today I feel happy. [*Goes up to the table in the dining room.*] My dear. . . .

TCHEBUTYKIN [*puts the newspaper in his pocket and combs his beard*] Pie? Splendid!

MASHA [*to* TCHEBUTYKIN, *sternly*]   Only mind you don't drink today! Do you hear? It's bad for you to drink.

TCHEBUTYKIN   Oh, come, that's a thing of the past. It's two years since I got drunk. [*Impatiently.*] But there, my good girl, what does it matter!

MASHA   Anyway, don't you dare to drink. Don't dare. [*Angrily, but so as not to be heard by her husband.*] Again, damnation take it, I am to be bored a whole evening at the headmaster's!

TUSENBACH   I wouldn't go if I were you. . . . It's very simple.

TCHEBUTYKIN   Don't go, my love.

MASHA   Oh, yes, don't go! . . . It's a damnable life, insufferable. . . . [*Goes to the dining room.*]

TCHEBUTYKIN [*following her*]   Come, come. . . .

SOLYONY [*going to the dining room*]   Chook, chook, chook. . . .

TUSENBACH   Enough, Vassily Vassilyevitch! Leave off!

SOLYONY   Chook, chook, chook. . . .

KULIGIN [*gaily*]   Your health, Colonel! I am a schoolmaster and one of the family here, Masha's husband. . . . She is very kind, really, very kind. . . .

VERSHININ   I'll have some of this dark-colored vodka. . . . [*Drinks.*] To your health! [*To* OLGA.] I feel so happy with all of you!

   No one is left in the drawing room but IRINA *and* TUSENBACH.

IRINA   Masha is in low spirits today. She was married at eighteen, when she thought him the cleverest of men. But now it's not the same. He is the kindest of men, but he is not the cleverest.

OLGA [*impatiently*]   Andrey, do come!

ANDREY [*behind the scenes*]   I am coming. [*Comes in and goes to the table.*]

TUSENBACH   What are you thinking about?

IRINA   Nothing. I don't like that Solyony of yours, I am afraid of him. He keeps on saying such stupid things. . . .

TUSENBACH   He is a queer man. I am sorry for him and annoyed by him, but more sorry. I think he is shy. . . . When one is alone with him he is very intelligent and friendly, but in company he is rude, a bully. Don't go yet, let them sit down to the table. Let me be by you. What are you thinking of? [*A pause.*] You are twenty, I am not yet thirty. How many years have we got before us, a long, long chain of days full of my love for you. . . .

IRINA   Nikolay Lvovitch, don't talk to me about love.

TUSENBACH [*not listening*]   I have a passionate craving for life, for struggle, for work, and that craving is mingled in my soul with my love for you, Irina, and just because you are beautiful it seems to me that life too is beautiful! What are you thinking of?

IRINA   You say life is beautiful. . . . Yes, but what if it only seems so! Life for us three sisters has not been beautiful yet, we have been stifled by it as plants are choked by weeds. . . . I am shedding tears. . . . I mustn't do that. [*Hurriedly wipes her eyes and smiles.*] I must work, I must work. The reason we are depressed and take such a gloomy view of life is that we know nothing of work. We come of people who despised work. . . .

> *Enter* NATALYA IVANOVNA; *she is wearing a pink dress with a green sash.*

NATASHA   They are sitting down to lunch already. . . . I am late. . . . [*Steals a glance at herself in the glass and sets herself to rights.*] I think my hair is all right. [*Seeing* IRINA.] Dear Irina Sergeyevna, I congratulate you! [*Gives her a vigorous and prolonged kiss.*] You have a lot of visitors, I really feel shy. . . . Good day, Baron!

OLGA [*coming into the drawing room*]   Well, here is Natalya Ivanovna! How are you, my dear? [*Kisses her.*]

NATASHA   Congratulations on the name-day. You have such a big party and I feel awfully shy. . . .

OLGA   Nonsense, we have only our own people. [*In an undertone, in alarm.*] You've got on a green sash! My dear, that's not nice!

NATASHA   Why, is that a bad omen?

OLGA   No, it's only that it doesn't go with your dress . . . and it looks queer. . . .

NATASHA [*in a tearful voice*]   Really? But you know it's not green exactly, it's more a neutral color. [*Follows* OLGA *into the dining room.*]

> *In the dining room they are all sitting down to lunch; there is no one in the drawing room.*

KULIGIN   I wish you a good husband, Irina. It's time for you to think of getting married.

TCHEBUTYKIN   Natalya Ivanovna, I hope we may hear of your engagement, too.

KULIGIN   Natalya Ivanovna has got a suitor already.

MASHA [*strikes her plate with her fork*]   Ladies and gentlemen, I want to make a speech!

KULIGIN   You deserve three bad marks for conduct.

VERSHININ   How nice this cordial is! What is it made of?

SOLYONY   Beetles.

IRINA [*in a tearful voice*]   Ugh, ugh! How disgusting.

OLGA   We are going to have roast turkey and apple pie for supper. Thank God I am at home all day and shall be at home in the evening. . . . Friends, won't you come this evening?

VERSHININ   Allow me to come too.

IRINA   Please do.

NATASHA   They don't stand on ceremony.

TCHEBUTYKIN   Nature our hearts for love created! [*Laughs.*]

ANDREY [*angrily*]   Do leave off, I wonder you are not tired of it!

FEDOTIK *and* RODDEY *come in with a big basket of flowers.*

FEDOTIK   I say, they are at lunch already.

RODDEY [*speaking loudly, with a lisp*]   At lunch? Yes, they are at lunch already. . . .

FEDOTIK   Wait a minute. [*Takes a snapshot.*] One! Wait another minute. . . . [*Takes another snapshot.*] Two! Now it's ready.

They take the basket and walk into the dining room, where they are greeted noisily.

RODDEY [*loudly*]   My congratulations! I wish you everything, everything! The weather is delightful, perfectly magnificent. I've been out all the morning for a walk with the high-school boys. I teach them gymnastics.

FEDOTIK   You may move, Irina Sergeyevna, you may move. [*Taking a photograph.*] You look charming today. [*Taking a top out of his pocket.*] Here is a top, by the way. . . . It has a wonderful note. . . .

IRINA   How lovely!

MASHA   By the seashore an oak tree green. . . . Upon that oak a chain of gold. . . . [*Complainingly.*] Why do I keep saying that? That phrase has been haunting me all day. . . .

KULIGIN   Thirteen at table!

RODDEY [*loudly*]   Surely you do not attach importance to such superstitions? [*Laughter.*]

KULIGIN   If there are thirteen at table, it means that someone present is in love. It's not you, Ivan Romanovitch, by any chance? [*Laughter.*]

TCHEBUTYKIN   I am an old sinner, but why Natalya Ivanovna is overcome, I can't imagine . . .

Loud laughter; NATASHA *runs out from the dining room into the drawing room followed by* ANDREY.

ANDREY   Come, don't take any notice! Wait a minute . . . stop, I entreat you. . . .

NATASHA   I am ashamed. . . . I don't know what's the matter with me and they make fun of me. I know it's improper for me to leave the table like this, but I can't help it. . . . I can't . . . [*Covers her face with her hands.*]

ANDREY   My dear girl, I entreat you, I implore you, don't be upset. I assure you they are only joking, they do it in all kindness. My dear, my sweet, they are all kind, warmhearted people and they are fond of me and of you. Come here to the window, here they can't see us. . . . [*Looks round.*]

NATASHA   I am so unaccustomed to society! . . .

ANDREY   Oh youth, lovely, marvelous youth! My dear, my sweet, don't be so distressed! Believe me, believe me. . . . I feel so happy, my soul is full of love and rapture. . . . Oh, they can't see us, they can't see us! Why, why, I love you, when I first loved you—oh, I don't know. My dear, my sweet, pure one, be my wife! I love you, I love you . . . as I have never loved anyone . . . [*A kiss.*]

> *Two officers come in and, seeing the pair kissing, stop in amazement.*

Act 2

> *The same scene as in Act 1. Eight o'clock in the evening. Behind the scenes in the street there is the faintly audible sound of a concertina. There is no light.* NATALYA IVANOVNA *enters in a dressing gown, carrying a candle; she comes in and stops at the door leading to* ANDREY'S *room.*

NATASHA   What are you doing, Andryusha? Reading? Never mind, I only just asked. . . .

> *Goes and opens another door and, peeping into it, shuts it again.*

Is there a light?

ANDREY [*enters with a book in his hand*]   What is it, Natasha?

NATASHA   I was looking to see whether there was a light. . . . It's Carnival, the servants are not themselves; one has always to be on the lookout for fear something goes wrong. Last night at twelve o'clock I passed through the dining room, and there was a candle left burning. I couldn't find out who had lighted it. [*Puts down the candle.*] What's the time?

ANDREY [*looking at his watch*]   A quarter past eight.

NATASHA   And Olga and Irina aren't in yet. They haven't come in. Still at work, poor dears! Olga is at the teachers' council and Irina at the telegraph office. . . . [*Sighs.*] I was saying to your sister this morning, "Take care of yourself, Irina darling," said I. But she won't listen. A quarter past eight, you say? I am afraid our Bobik is not at all well. Why is he so cold? Yesterday he was feverish and today he is cold all over. . . . I am so anxious!

ANDREY   It's all right, Natasha. The boy is quite well.

NATASHA   We had better be careful about his food, anyway. I am anxious. And I am told that the mummers are going to be here for the Carnival at nine o'clock this evening. It would be better for them not to come, Andryusha.

ANDREY   I really don't know. They've been invited, you know.

NATASHA   Baby woke up this morning, looked at me, and all at once he gave a smile; so he knew me. "Good morning, Bobik!" said I.

"Good morning, darling!" And he laughed. Children understand; they understand very well. So I shall tell them, Andryusha, not to let the carnival party come in.

ANDREY [*irresolutely*]   That's for my sisters to say. It's for them to give orders.

NATASHA   Yes, for them too; I will speak to them. They are so kind. . . . [*Is going.*] I've ordered junket for supper. The doctor says you must eat nothing but junket, or you will never get thinner. [*Stops.*] Bobik is cold. I am afraid his room is chilly, perhaps. We ought to put him in a different room till the warm weather comes, anyway. Irina's room, for instance, is just right for a nursery: it's dry and the sun shines there all day. I must tell her; she might share Olga's room for the time. . . . She is never at home, anyway, except for the night. . . . [*A pause.*] Andryushantchik, why don't you speak?

ANDREY   Nothing. I was thinking. . . . Besides, I have nothing to say.

NATASHA   Yes . . . what was it I meant to tell you? . . . Oh, yes; Ferapont has come from the Rural Board, and is asking for you.

ANDREY [*yawns*]   Send him in.

> NATASHA *goes out;* ANDREY, *bending down to the candle which she has left behind, reads. Enter* FERAPONT; *he wears an old shabby overcoat, with the collar turned up, and has a scarf over his ears.*

ANDREY   Good evening, my good man. What is it?

FERAPONT   The chairman has sent a book and a paper of some sort here. . . . [*Gives the book and an envelope.*]

ANDREY   Thanks. Very good. But why have you come so late? It is past eight.

FERAPONT   Eh?

ANDREY [*louder*]   I say, you have come late. It is eight o'clock.

FERAPONT   Just so. I came before it was dark, but they wouldn't let me see you. The master is busy, they told me. Well, of course, if you are busy, I am in no hurry. [*Thinking that* ANDREY *has asked him a question.*] Eh?

ANDREY   Nothing. [*Examines the book.*] Tomorrow is Friday. We haven't a sitting, but I'll come all the same . . . and do my work. It's dull at home. . . . [*A pause.*] Dear old man, how strangely life changes and deceives one! Today I was so bored and had nothing to do, so I picked up this book—old university lectures—and I laughed. . . . Good heavens! I am the secretary of the Rural Board of which Protopopov is the chairman. I am the secretary, and the most I can hope for is to become a member of the Board! Me, a member of the local Rural Board, while I dream every night I am professor of the University of Moscow—a distinguished man, of whom all Russia is proud!

FERAPONT   I can't say, sir. . . . I don't hear well. . . .

ANDREY   If you did hear well, perhaps I should not talk to you. I must talk to somebody, and my wife does not understand me. My sisters I am somehow afraid of—I'm afraid they will laugh at me and make me ashamed. . . . I don't drink, I am not fond of restaurants, but how I should enjoy sitting at Tyestov's in Moscow at this moment, dear old chap!

FERAPONT   A contractor was saying at the Board the other day that there were some merchants in Moscow eating pancakes; one who ate forty, it seems, died. It was either forty or fifty, I don't remember.

ANDREY   In Moscow you sit in a huge room at a restaurant; you know no one and no one knows you, and at the same time you don't feel a stranger. . . . But here you know everyone and everyone knows you, and yet you are a stranger—a stranger. . . . A stranger, and lonely. . . .

FERAPONT   Eh? [*A pause.*] And the same contractor says—maybe it's not true—that there's a rope stretched right across Moscow.

ANDREY   What for?

FERAPONT   I can't say, sir. The contractor said so.

ANDREY   Nonsense. [*Reads.*] Have you ever been in Moscow?

FERAPONT [*after a pause*]   No, never. It was not God's will I should. [*A pause.*] Am I to go?

ANDREY   You can go. Good-bye. [FERAPONT *goes out.*] Good-bye. [*Reading.*] Come tomorrow morning and take some papers here. . . . Go. . . . [*A pause.*] He has gone. [*A ring.*] Yes, it is a business. . . . [*Stretches and goes slowly into his own room.*]

> *Behind the scenes a* NURSE *is singing, rocking a baby to sleep. Enter* MASHA *and* VERSHININ. *While they are talking a maid-servant is lighting a lamp and candles in the dining room.*

MASHA   I don't know. [*A pause.*] I don't know. Of course habit does a great deal. After father's death, for instance, it was a long time before we could get used to having no orderlies in the house. But apart from habit, I think it's a feeling of justice makes me say so. Perhaps it is not so in other places, but in our town the most decent, honorable, and well-bred people are all in the army.

VERSHININ   I am thirsty. I should like some tea.

MASHA [*glancing at the clock*]   They will soon be bringing it. I was married when I was eighteen, and I was afraid of my husband because he was a teacher, and I had only just left school. In those days I thought him an awfully learned, clever, and important person. And now it is not the same, unfortunately. . . .

VERSHININ   Yes. . . . I see. . . .

MASHA   I am not speaking of my husband—I am used to him; but among civilians generally there are so many rude, ill-mannered, badly brought-up people. Rudeness upsets and distresses me: I am unhappy when I see that a man is not refined, not gentle, not polite enough. When I have to be among the teachers, my husband's colleagues, it makes me quite miserable.

VERSHININ   Yes. . . . But, to my mind, it makes no difference whether they are civilians or military men—they are equally uninteresting, in this town anyway. It's all the same! If one listens to a man of the educated class here, civilian or military, he is worried to death by his wife, worried to death by his house, worried to death by his estate, worried to death by his horses. . . . A Russian is peculiarly given to exalted ideas, but why is it he always falls so short in life? Why?

MASHA   Why?

VERSHININ   Why is he worried to death by his children and by his wife? And why are his wife and children worried to death by him?

MASHA   You are rather depressed this evening.

VERSHININ   Perhaps. . . . I've had no dinner today, and had nothing to eat since the morning. My daughter is not quite well, and when my little girls are ill I am consumed by anxiety; my conscience reproaches me for having given them such a mother. Oh, if you had seen her today! She is a wretched creature! We began quarreling at seven o'clock in the morning, and at nine I slammed the door and went away. [*A pause.*] I never talk about it. Strange, it's only to you I complain. [*Kisses her hand.*] Don't be angry with me. . . . Except for you I have no one—no one. . . .

    A pause.

MASHA   What a noise in the stove! Before father died there was howling in the chimney. There, just like that.

VERSHININ   Are you superstitious?

MASHA   Yes.

VERSHININ   That's strange. [*Kisses her hand.*] You are a splendid, wonderful woman. Splendid! Wonderful! It's dark, but I see the light in your eyes.

MASHA [*moves to another chair*]   It's lighter here.

VERSHININ   I love you—love, love. . . . I love your eyes, your movements, I see them in my dreams. . . . Splendid, wonderful woman!

MASHA [*laughing softly*]   When you talk to me like that, for some reason I laugh, though I am frightened. . . . Please don't do it again. . . . [*In an undertone.*] You may say it, though; I don't mind. . . . [*Covers her face with her hands.*] I don't mind. . . . Someone is coming. Talk of something else.

    IRINA *and* TUSENBACH *come in through the dining room.*

TUSENBACH   I've got a three-barreled name. My name is Baron Tusenbach-Krone-Altschauer, but I belong to the Orthodox Church and am just as Russian as you. There is very little of the German left in me—nothing, perhaps, but the patience and perseverance with which I bore you. I see you home every evening.

IRINA   How tired I am!

TUSENBACH   And every day I will come to the telegraph office and see you home. I'll do it for ten years, for twenty years, till you drive me away. . . . [*Seeing* MASHA *and* VERSHININ, *delightedly.*] Oh, it's you! How are you?

IRINA   Well, I am home at last. [*To* MASHA.] A lady came just now to telegraph to her brother in Saratov that her son died today, and she could not think of the address. So she sent it without an address—simply to Saratov.[7] She was crying. And I was rude to her for no sort of reason. Told her I had no time to waste. It was so stupid. Are the Carnival people coming tonight?

MASHA   Yes.

IRINA [*sits down in an armchair*]   I must rest. I am tired.

TUSENBACH [*with a smile*]   When you come from the office you seem so young, so forlorn. . . . [*A pause.*]

7. A town of some size, located on the Volga about 450 miles southeast of Moscow.

IRINA   I am tired. No, I don't like telegraph work, I don't like it.

MASHA   You've grown thinner. . . . [*Whistles.*] And you look younger, rather like a boy in the face.

TUSENBACH   That's the way she does her hair.

IRINA   I must find some other job, this does not suit me. What I so longed for, what I dreamed of, is the very thing that it's lacking in. . . . It is work without poetry, without meaning. . . . [*A knock on the floor.*] There's the doctor knocking. . . . [*To* TUSENBACH.] Do knock, dear. . . . I can't. . . . I am tired.

TUSENBACH *knocks on the floor.*

IRINA   He will come directly. We ought to do something about it. The doctor and our Andrey were at the Club yesterday and they lost again. I am told Andrey lost two hundred roubles.[8]

MASHA [*indifferently*]   Well, it can't be helped now.

IRINA   A fortnight ago he lost money, in December he lost money. I wish he'd make haste and lose everything, then perhaps we should go away from this town. By God, every night I dream of Moscow, it's perfect madness. [*Laughs.*] We'll move there in June and there is still left February, March, April, May . . . almost half a year.

MASHA   The only thing is Natasha must not hear of his losses.

IRINA   I don't suppose she cares.

TCHEBUTYKIN, *who has only just got off his bed—he has been resting after dinner—comes into the dining room combing his beard, then sits down to the table and takes a newspaper out of his pocket.*

MASHA   Here he is . . . has he paid his rent?

IRINA [*laughs*]   No. Not a kopek[9] for eight months. Evidently he has forgotten.

MASHA [*laughs*]   How gravely he sits. [*They all laugh; a pause.*]

IRINA   Why are you so quiet, Alexandr Ignatyevitch?

VERSHININ   I don't know. I am longing for tea. I'd give half my life for a glass of tea. I have had nothing to eat since the morning.

TCHEBUTYKIN   Irina Sergeyevna!

IRINA   What is it?

TCHEBUTYKIN   Come here. *Venez ici.*[1] [IRINA *goes and sits down at the table.*] I can't do without you. [IRINA *lays out the cards for patience.*]

VERSHININ   Well, if they won't bring tea, let us discuss something.

TUSENBACH   By all means. What?

VERSHININ   What? Let us dream . . . for instance of the life that will come after us, in two or three hundred years.

TUSENBACH   Well? When we are dead, men will fly in balloons, change the fashion of their coats, will discover a sixth sense, perhaps, and develop it, but life will remain just the same, difficult, full of mysteries and happiness. In a thousand years man will sigh just the same,

8. At the time of the play, one rouble was worth approximately 50 cents in American money. In the States the New York *Times* sold for one cent daily (two cents outside the metropolitan area) and three cents on Sundays. Bedsheets cost from 28 to 45 cents apiece. Old Crow was $1.10 a fifth, and a used grand piano could be purchased for from $175 to $300.

9. There are 100 kopeks in one rouble.

1. French for "Come here." At this period all cultivated, upper-class Russians spoke French.

"Ah, how hard life is," and yet just as now he will be afraid of death and not want it.

VERSHININ [*after a moment's thought*]   Well, I don't know. . . . It seems to me that everything on earth is bound to change by degrees and is already changing before our eyes. In two or three hundred, perhaps in a thousand years—the time does not matter—a new, happy life will come. We shall have no share in that life, of course, but we are living for it, we are working, well, yes, and suffering for it, we are creating it—and that alone is the purpose of our existence, and is our happiness, if you like.

MASHA *laughs softly.*

TUSENBACH   What is it?

MASHA   I don't know. I've been laughing all day.

VERSHININ   I was at the same school as you were, I did not go to the Military Academy; I read a great deal, but I do not know how to choose my books, and very likely I read quite the wrong things, and yet the longer I live the more I want to know. My hair is turning gray, I am almost an old man, but I know so little, oh so little! But all the same I fancy that I do know and thoroughly grasp what is essential and matters most. And how I should like to make you see that there is no happiness for us, that there ought not to be and will not be. . . . We must work and work, and happiness is the portion of our remote descendants. [*A pause.*] If it is not for me, at least it is for the descendants of my descendants. . . . [FEDOTIK *and* RODDEY *appear in the dining room; they sit down and sing softly, playing the guitar.*]

TUSENBACH   You think it's no use even dreaming of happiness! But what if I am happy?

VERSHININ   No.

TUSENBACH [*flinging up his hands and laughing*]   It is clear we don't understand each other. Well, how am I to convince you? [MASHA *laughs softly.* TUSENBACH *holds up a finger to her.*] Laugh! [*To* VERSHININ.] Not only in two or three hundred years but in a million years life will be just the same; it does not change, it remains stationary, following its own laws which we have nothing to do with or which, anyway, we shall never find out. Migratory birds, cranes for instance, fly backward and forward, and whatever ideas, great or small, stray through their minds, they will still go on flying just the same without knowing where or why. They fly and will continue to fly, however philosophic they may become; and it doesn't matter how philosophical they are so long as they go on flying. . . .

MASHA   But still there is a meaning?

TUSENBACH   Meaning. . . . Here it is snowing. What meaning is there in that? [*A pause.*]

MASHA   I think man ought to have faith or ought to seek a faith, or else his life is empty, empty. . . . To live and not to understand why cranes fly; why children are born; why there are stars in the sky. . . . One must know what one is living for or else it is all nonsense and waste. [*A pause.*]

VERSHININ   And yet one is sorry that youth is over. . . .

MASHA   Gogol says: it's dull living in this world, friends![2]

TUSENBACH   And I say: it is difficult to argue with you, my friends, God bless you. . . .

TCHEBUTYKIN [*reading the newspaper*]   Balzac was married at Berdit-chev.[3] [IRINA *hums softly.*] I really must put that down in my book. [*Writes.*] Balzac was married at Berditchev. [*Reads the paper.*]

IRINA [*lays out the cards for patience, dreamily*]   Balzac was married at Berditchev.

TUSENBACH   The die is cast. You know, Marya Sergeyevna, I've resigned my commission.

MASHA   So I hear. And I see nothing good in that. I don't like civilians.

TUSENBACH   Never mind. . . . [*Gets up.*] I am not good-looking enough for a soldier. But that does not matter, though. . . . I am going to work. If only for one day in my life, to work so that I come home at night tired out and fall asleep as soon as I get into bed. . . . [*Going into the dining room.*] Workmen must sleep soundly!

FEDOTIK [*to* IRINA]   I bought these chalks for you just now as I passed the shop. . . . And this penknife. . . .

IRINA   You've got into the way of treating me as though I were little, but I am grown up, you know. . . . [*Takes the chalks and the penknife, joyfully.*] How lovely!

FEDOTIK   And I bought a knife for myself . . . look . . . one blade, and another blade, a third, and this is for the ears, and here are scissors, and that's for cleaning the nails. . . .

RODDEY [*loudly*]   Doctor, how old are you?

TCHEBUTYKIN   I? Thirty-two. [*Laughter.*]

FEDOTIK   I'll show you another patience. . . . [*Lays out the cards.*]

> *The samovar is brought in;* ANFISA *is at the samovar; a little later* NATASHA *comes in and is also busy at the table;* SOLYONY *comes in and, after greeting the others, sits down at the table.*

VERSHININ   What a wind there is!

MASHA   Yes. I am sick of the winter. I've forgotten what summer is like.

IRINA   It's coming out right, I see. We shall go to Moscow.

FEDOTIK   No, it's not coming out. You see, the eight is over the two of spades. [*Laughs.*] So that means you won't go to Moscow.

TCHEBUTYKIN [*reads from the newspaper*]   Tsi-tsi-kar.[4] Smallpox is raging there.

ANFISA [*going up to* MASHA]   Masha, come to tea, my dear. [*To* VERSHININ.] Come, your honor . . . excuse me, sir, I have forgotten your name. . . .

MASHA   Bring it here, nurse, I am not going there.

IRINA   Nurse!

ANFISA   I am coming!

2. The concluding line of the short story "How the Two Ivans Quarreled" by Nikolai V. Gogol (1809–1852), best known outside Russia for his novel *Dead Souls* and his play *The Inspector General.*

3. Honoré de Balzac (1799–1850), the famous French novelist, married Countess Eveline Hanska in the Ukrainian town of Berditchev on March 14, 1850. They had begun to correspond as early as 1832, although she was married to an older man. Her husband died in 1841, but financial and other considerations delayed their marriage.

4. A city in Manchuria, also called Tsitsihar.

NATASHA [*to* SOLYONY] Little babies understand very well. "Good morning, Bobik, good morning, darling," I said. He looked at me in quite a special way. You think I say that because I am a mother, but no, I assure you! He is an extraordinary child.

SOLYONY If that child were mine, I'd fry him in a frying-pan and eat him.

Takes his glass, comes into the drawing room and sits down in a corner.

NATASHA [*covers her face with her hands*] Rude, ill-bred man!

MASHA Happy people don't notice whether it is winter or summer. I fancy if I lived in Moscow I should not mind what the weather was like. . . .

VERSHININ The other day I was reading the diary of a French minister written in prison. The minister was condemned for the Panama affair.[5] With what enthusiasm and delight he describes the birds he sees from the prison window, which he never noticed before when he was a minister. Now that he is released, of course, he notices birds no more than he did before. In the same way, you won't notice Moscow when you live in it. We have no happiness and never do have, we only long for it.

TUSENBACH [*takes a box from the table*] What has become of the sweets?

IRINA Solyony has eaten them.

TUSENBACH All?

ANFISA [*handing tea*] There's a letter for you, sir.

VERSHININ For me? [*Takes the letter.*] From my daughter. [*Reads.*] Yes, of course. . . . Excuse me, Marya Sergeyevna, I'll slip away. I won't have tea. [*Gets up in agitation.*] Always these upsets. . . .

MASHA What is it? Not a secret?

VERSHININ [*in a low voice*] My wife has taken poison again. I must go. I'll slip off unnoticed. Horribly unpleasant it all is. [*Kisses* MASHA's *hand.*] My fine, dear, splendid woman. . . . I'll go this way without being seen. . . . [*Goes out.*]

ANFISA Where is he off to? I've just given him his tea. . . . What a man.

MASHA [*getting angry*] Leave off! Don't pester, you give one no peace. . . . [*Goes with her cup to the table.*] You bother me, old lady.

ANFISA Why are you so huffy? Darling!

ANDREY's *voice:* "Anfisa!"

ANFISA [*mimicking*] Anfisa! he sits there. . . . [*Goes out.*]

5. From 1880 to 1889 a French group headed by Ferdinand de Lesseps, the builder of the Suez Canal, attempted to dig a canal across the Isthmus of Panama. It was a disaster, both from an engineering standpoint and from a financial one. In 1892 charges of fraud and bribery were made against the principals of the company and a number of politicians; a spectacular scandal resulted. Several officers of the company and Charles Baïhaut (1843–1905), a former Minister of Public Works, were convicted in 1893. After his release from several years in prison, Baïhaut published a book about his experiences called *Impressions Cellulaires* (1898).

MASHA [*by the table in the dining room, angrily*]   Let me sit down!
[*Mixes the cards on the table.*] You take up all the table with your
cards. Drink your tea!

IRINA   How cross you are, Masha!

MASHA   If I'm cross, don't talk to me. Don't interfere with me.

TCHEBUTYKIN [*laughing*]   Don't touch her, don't touch her!

MASHA   You are sixty, but you talk rot like a schoolboy.

NATASHA [*sighs*]   Dear Masha, why make use of such expressions in
conversation? With your attractive appearance, I tell you straight
out, you would be simply fascinating in a well-bred social circle if it
were not for the things you say. *Je vous prie, pardonnez-moi, Marie,
mais vous avez des manières un peu grossières.*[6]

TUSENBACH [*suppressing a laugh*]   Give me . . . give me . . . I think
there is some brandy there.

NATASHA   *Il paraît que mon Bobik déjà ne dort pas,*[7] he is awake. He
is not well today. I must go to him, excuse me. . . . [*Goes out.*]

IRINA   Where has Alexandr Ignatyevitch gone?

MASHA   Home. Something queer with his wife again.

TUSENBACH [*goes up to* SOLYONY *with a decanter of brandy in his hand*]
You always sit alone, thinking, and there's no making out what you
think about. Come, let us make it up. Let us have a drink of brandy.
[*They drink.*] I shall have to play the piano all night, I suppose, play
all sorts of trash. . . . Here goes!

SOLYONY   Why make it up? I haven't quarreled with you.

TUSENBACH   You always make me feel as though something had gone
wrong between us. You are a queer character, there's no denying
that.

SOLYONY [*declaims*]   I am strange, who is not strange! Be not wroth,
Aleko![8]

TUSENBACH   I don't see what Aleko has got to do with it. . . .

SOLYONY   When I am *tête-à-tête*[9] with somebody, I am all right, just
like anyone else, but in company I am depressed, ill at ease and . . .
say all sorts of idiotic things, but at the same time I am more conscientious and straightforward than many. And I can prove it. . . .

TUSENBACH   I often feel angry with you, you are always attacking me
when we are in company, and yet I somehow like you. Here goes,
I am going to drink a lot today. Let's drink!

SOLYONY   Let us. [*Drinks.*] I have never had anything against you,
Baron. But I have the temperament of Lermontov.[1] [*In a low voice.*]
In fact I am rather like Lermontov to look at . . . so I am told. [*Takes
out scent-bottle and sprinkles scent on his hands.*]

TUSENBACH   I have sent in my papers. I've had enough of it! I have

---

6. French for "I beg your pardon, Marie
(i.e., Masha), but you have manners which
are a bit gross."
7. French for "It seems that my Bobik
is already no longer asleep." Natasha's
unidiomatic French identifies her as
coming from a lower social class than the
Prozorovs and their friends.
8. The first part of the speech is a
quotation from the play *Woe from Wit* or
The Trouble with Reason by Alexander S.
Griboyedov (1795–1829). The second part
refers to Aleko, the hero of "The Gypsies,"

a narrative poem by Pushkin. In the poem,
Aleko, a young Russian, joins a Gypsy
tribe and lives happily for a while with a
Gypsy girl. When she deserts him for
another, he stabs both the girl and her
new lover and is ostracized by the tribe.
9. French for face-to-face (literally,
head to head).
1. Mikhail Yurievitch Lermontov (1814–
1841) was the great Romantic poet of 19th-
century Russia, known for his melancholy
and his fondness for morbid self-examina-
tion.

been thinking of it for five years and at last I have come up to the scratch. I am going to work.

SOLYONY [*declaims*]   Be not wroth, Aleko. . . . Forget, forget thy dreams. . . .

> *While they are talking* ANDREY *comes in quietly with a book and sits down by a candle.*

TUSENBACH   I am going to work.

TCHEBUTYKIN [*coming into the drawing room with* IRINA]   And the food too was real Caucasian stuff: onion soup and for the meat course *tchehartma.* . . .

SOLYONY   *Tcheremsha* is not meat at all, it's a plant rather like our onion.

TCHEBUTYKIN   No, my dear soul, it's not onion, but mutton roasted in a special way.

SOLYONY   But I tell you that *tcheremsha* is an onion.

TCHEBUTYKIN   And I tell you that *tchehartma* is mutton.

SOLYONY   And I tell you that *tcheremsha* is an onion.

TCHEBUTYKIN   What's the use of my arguing with you? You have never been to the Caucasus or eaten *tchehartma.*

SOLYONY   I haven't eaten it because I can't bear it. *Tcheremsha* smells like garlic.

ANDREY [*imploringly*]   That's enough! Please!

TUSENBACH   When are the Carnival party coming?

IRINA   They promised to come at nine, so they will be here directly.

TUSENBACH [*embraces* ANDREY *and sings*]   "Oh my porch, oh my new porch . . ."

ANDREY [*dances and sings*]   "With posts of maple wood. . . ."

TCHEBUTYKIN [*dances*]   "And lattice work complete. . . ."[2] [*Laughter.*]

TUSENBACH [*kisses* ANDREY]   Hang it all, let us have a drink. Andryusha, let us drink to our everlasting friendship. I'll go to the University when you do, Andryusha.

SOLYONY   Which? There are two universities in Moscow.

ANDREY   There is only one university in Moscow.

SOLYONY   I tell you there are two.

ANDREY   There may be three for aught I care. So much the better.

SOLYONY   There are two universities in Moscow! [*A murmur and hisses.*] There are two universities in Moscow: the old one and the new one. And if you don't care to hear, if what I say irritates you, I can keep quiet. I can even go into another room. [*Goes out at one of the doors.*]

TUSENBACH   Bravo, bravo! [*Laughs.*] Friends, begin, I'll sit down and play! Funny fellow that Solyony. . . . [*Sits down to the piano and plays a waltz.*]

MASHA [*dances a waltz alone*]   The baron is drunk, the baron is drunk, the baron is drunk.

> *Enter* NATASHA.

NATASHA [*to* TCHEBUTYKIN]   Ivan Romanitch!

2. A traditional Russian dance-song.

Says something to TCHEBUTYKIN, *then goes out softly.* TCHEBUTY-
KIN *touches* TUSENBACH *on the shoulder and whispers something
to him.*

IRINA   What is it?

TCHEBUTYKIN   It's time we were going. Good night.

TUSENBACH   Good night. It's time to be going.

IRINA   But I say . . . what about the Carnival party?

ANDREY [*with embarrassment*]   They won't be coming. You see, dear,
Natasha says Bobik is not well, and so. . . . In fact I know nothing
about it, and don't care either.

IRINA [*shrugs her shoulders*]   Bobik is not well!

MASHA   Well, it's not the first time we've had to lump it! If we are
turned out, we must go. [*To* IRINA.] It's not Bobik that is ill, but she
is a bit . . . [*Taps her forehead with her finger.*] Petty, vulgar creature!

ANDREY *goes by door on right to his own room,* TCHEBUTYKIN
following him; they are saying good-bye in the dining room.

FEDOTIK   What a pity! I was meaning to spend the evening, but of
course if the child is ill . . . I'll bring him a toy tomorrow.

RODDEY [*loudly*]   I had a nap today after dinner on purpose, I thought
I would be dancing all night. . . . Why, it's only nine o'clock.

MASHA   Let us go into the street; there we can talk. We'll decide what
to do.

Sounds of "Good-bye! Good night!" The good-humored laugh of
TUSENBACH *is heard. All go out.* ANFISA *and the maidservant
clear the table and put out the light. There is the sound of the
nurse singing.* ANDREY, *in his hat and coat, and* TCHEBUTYKIN
come in quietly.

TCHEBUTYKIN   I never had time to get married, because life has flashed
by like lightning and because I was passionately in love with your
mother, who was married.

ANDREY   One shouldn't get married. One shouldn't, because it's boring.

TCHEBUTYKIN   That's all very well, but what about loneliness? Say
what you like, it's a dreadful thing to be lonely, my dear boy. . . .
But no matter, though!

ANDREY   Let's make haste and go.

TCHEBUTYKIN   What's the hurry? We have plenty of time.

ANDREY   I am afraid my wife may stop me.

TCHEBUTYKIN   Oh!

ANDREY   I am not going to play today, I shall just sit and look on. I
don't feel well. . . . What am I to do, Ivan Romanitch, I am so short
of breath?

TCHEBUTYKIN   It's no use asking me! I don't remember, dear boy. . . .
I don't know. . . .

ANDREY   Let us go through the kitchen. [*They go out.*]

*A ring, then another ring; there is a sound of voices and laugh-
ter.*

IRINA [*enters*]   What is it?

ANFISA [*in a whisper*]   The mummers, all dressed up. [*A ring.*]

IRINA   Nurse, dear, say there is no one at home. They must excuse us.

ANFISA *goes out.* IRINA *walks about the room in hesitation; she is excited. Enter* SOLYONY.

SOLYONY [*in perplexity*]   No one here. . . . Where are they all?

IRINA   They have gone home.

SOLYONY   How queer. Are you alone here?

IRINA   Yes. [*A pause.*] Good night.

SOLYONY   I behaved tactlessly, without sufficient restraint just now. But you are not like other people, you are pure and lofty, you see the truth. You alone can understand me. I love you, I love you deeply, infinitely.

IRINA   Good night! You must go.

SOLYONY   I can't live without you. [*Following her.*] Oh, my bliss! [*Through his tears.*] Oh, happiness! Those glorious, exquisite, marvelous eyes such as I have never seen in any other woman.

IRINA [*coldly*]   Don't, Vassily Vassilyitch!

SOLYONY   For the first time I am speaking of love to you, and I feel as though I were not on earth but on another planet. [*Rubs his forehead.*] But there, it does not matter. There is no forcing kindness, of course. . . . But there must be no happy rivals. . . . There must not. . . . I swear by all that is sacred I will kill any rival. . . . O exquisite being!

NATASHA *passes with a candle.*

NATASHA [*peeps in at one door, then at another and passes by the door that leads to her husband's room*]   Andrey is there. Let him read. Excuse me, Vassily Vassilyitch, I did not know you were here, and I am in my dressing gown. . . .

SOLYONY   'I don't care. Good-bye! [*Goes out.*]

NATASHA   You are tired, my poor, dear little girl! [*Kisses* IRINA.] You ought to go to bed earlier. . . .

IRINA   Is Bobik asleep?

NATASHA   He is asleep, but not sleeping quietly. By the way, dear, I keep meaning to speak to you, but either you are out or else I haven't the time. . . . I think Bobik's nursery is cold and damp. And your room is so nice for a baby. My sweet, my dear, you might move for a time into Olya's room!

IRINA [*not understanding*]   Where?

The sound of a three-horse sledge with bells driving up to the door.

NATASHA   You would be in the same room with Olya, and Bobik in your room. He is such a poppet. I said to him today, "Bobik, you are mine, you are mine!" and he looked at me with his funny little eyes. [*A ring.*] That must be Olya. How late she is!

The maid comes up to NATASHA *and whispers in her ear.*

NATASHA   Protopopov? What a queer fellow he is! Protopopov has come, and asks me to go out with him in his sledge. [*Laughs.*] How strange men are! . . . [*A ring.*] Somebody has come. I might go for a quarter of an hour. . . . [*To the maid.*] Tell him I'll come directly. [*A ring.*] You hear . . . it must be Olya. [*Goes out.*]

> The maid runs out; IRINA sits lost in thought; KULIGIN, OLGA and VERSHININ come in.

KULIGIN   Well, this is a surprise! They said they were going to have an evening party.

VERSHININ   Strange! And when I went away half an hour ago they were expecting the Carnival people. . . .

IRINA   They have all gone.

KULIGIN   Has Masha gone too? Where has she gone? And why is Protopopov waiting below with his sledge? Whom is he waiting for?

IRINA   Don't ask questions. . . . I am tired.

KULIGIN   Oh, you little cross-patch. . . .

OLGA   The meeting is only just over. I am tired out. Our headmistress is ill and I have to take her place. Oh, my head, my head does ache; oh, my head! [*Sits down.*] Andrey lost two hundred roubles yesterday at cards. . . . The whole town is talking about it. . . .

KULIGIN   Yes, I am tired out by the meeting too. [*Sits down.*]

VERSHININ   My wife took it into her head to give me a fright, she nearly poisoned herself. It's all right now, and I'm glad, it's a relief. . . . So we are to go away? Very well, then, I will say good night. Fyodor Ilyitch, let us go somewhere together! I can't stay at home, I absolutely can't. . . . Come along!

KULIGIN   I am tired. I am not coming. [*Gets up.*] I am tired. Has my wife gone home?

IRINA   I expect so.

KULIGIN [*kisses* IRINA's *hand*]   Good-bye! I have all day tomorrow and next day to rest. Good night! [*Going.*] I do want some tea. I was reckoning on spending the evening in pleasant company. . . . *O fallacem hominum spem!*[3] . . . Accusative of exclamation.

VERSHININ   Well, then, I must go alone. [*Goes out with* KULIGIN, *whistling.*]

OLGA   My head aches, oh, how my head aches. . . . Andrey has lost at cards. . . . The whole town is talking about it. . . . I'll go and lie down. [*Is going.*] Tomorrow I shall be free. . . . Oh, goodness, how nice that is! Tomorrow I am free, and the day after I am free. . . . My head does ache, oh, my head. . . . [*Goes out.*]

IRINA [*alone*]   They have all gone away. There is no one left.

> A concertina plays in the street, the nurse sings.

NATASHA [*in a fur cap and coat crosses the dining room, followed by the maid*]   I shall be back in half an hour. I shall only go a little way. [*Goes out.*]

IRINA [*left alone, in dejection*]   Oh, to go to Moscow, to Moscow!

---

3. Latin for "Oh, deceitful hope of mankind!"

Act 3

The bedroom of OLGA *and* IRINA. *On left and right beds with screens round them. Past two o'clock in the night. Behind the scenes a bell is ringing on account of a fire in the town, which has been going on for some time. It can be seen that no one in the house has gone to bed yet. On the sofa* MASHA *is lying, dressed as usual in black. Enter* OLGA *and* ANFISA.

ANFISA   They are sitting below, under the stairs. . . . I said to them, "Come upstairs; why, you mustn't stay there"—they only cried. "We don't know where father is," they said. "What if he is burned!" What an idea! And the poor souls in the yard . . . They are all undressed too.

OLGA [*taking clothes out of the cupboard*]   Take this gray dress . . . and this one . . . and the blouse too . . . and that skirt, nurse. . . . Oh, dear, what a dreadful thing! Kirsanov Street is burned to the ground, it seems. . . . Take this . . . take this. . . . [*Throws clothes into her arms.*] The Vershinins have had a fright, poor things. . . . Their house was very nearly burned. Let them stay the night here . . . we can't let them go home. . . . Poor Fedotik has had everything burned, he has not a thing left. . . .

ANFISA   You had better call Ferapont, Olya darling, I can't carry it all.

OLGA [*rings*]   No one will answer the bell. [*At the door.*] Come here, whoever is there!

Through the open door can be seen a window red with fire; the fire brigade is heard passing the house.

How awful it is! And how sickening!

Enter FERAPONT.

OLGA   Here take these, carry them downstairs. . . . The Kolotilin young ladies are downstairs . . . give it to them . . . and give this too.

FERAPONT   Yes, miss. In 1812 Moscow was burned too. . . . Mercy on us! The French marveled.[4]

OLGA   You can go now.

FERAPONT   Yes, miss. [*Goes out.*]

OLGA   Nurse darling, give them everything. We don't want anything, give it all to them. . . . I am tired, I can hardly stand on my feet. . . . We mustn't let the Vershinins go home. . . . The little girls can sleep in the drawing room, and Alexandr Ignatyevitch down below at the baron's. . . . Fedotik can go to the baron's, too, or sleep in our dining room. . . . As ill-luck will have it, the doctor is drunk, frightfully drunk, and no one can be put in his room. And Vershinin's wife can be in the drawing room too.

ANFISA [*wearily*]   Olya darling, don't send me away; don't send me away!

---

4. In the summer of 1812 Napoleon invaded Russia. The Russians retreated before him, burning and destroying everything in his path. He reached Moscow to find it abandoned and in flames. His disastrous retreat followed.

OLGA   That's nonsense, nurse. No one is sending you away.

ANFISA [*lays her head on* OLGA's *shoulder*] My own, my treasure, I
work, I do my best. . . . I'm getting weak, everyone will say "Be off!"
And where am I to go? Where? I am eighty. Eighty-one.

OLGA   Sit down, nurse darling. . . . You are tired, poor thing. . . .
[*Makes her sit down.*] Rest, dear good nurse. . . . How pale you are!

   Enter NATASHA.

NATASHA   They are saying we must form a committee at once for the
assistance of those whose houses have been burned. Well, that's a
good idea. Indeed, one ought always to be ready to help the poor,
it's the duty of the rich. Bobik and baby Sophie are both asleep,
sleeping as though nothing were happening. There are such a lot of
people everywhere, wherever one goes, the house is full. There is in-
fluenza in the town now; I am so afraid the children may get it.

OLGA   [*not listening*]   In this room one does not see the fire, it's quiet
here.

NATASHA   Yes . . . my hair must be untidy. [*In front of the looking
glass.*] They say I have grown fatter . . . but it's not true! Not a bit!
Masha is asleep, she is tired out, poor dear. . . . [*To* ANFISA *coldly.*]
Don't dare to sit down in my presence! Get up! Go out of the room!
[ANFISA *goes out; a pause.*] Why you keep that old woman, I can't
understand!

OLGA   [*taken aback*]   Excuse me, I don't understand either. . . .

NATASHA   She is no use here. She is a peasant; she ought to be in the
country. . . . You spoil people! I like order in the house! There ought
to be no useless servants in the house. [*Strokes her cheek.*] You are
tired, poor darling. Our headmistress is tired! When baby Sophie is
a big girl and goes to the high-school, I shall be afraid of you.

OLGA   I shan't be headmistress.

NATASHA   You will be elected, Olya. That's a settled thing.

OLGA   I shall refuse. I can't. . . . It's too much for me. . . . [*Drinks
water.*] You were so rude to nurse just now. . . . Excuse me, I can't
endure it. . . . It makes me feel faint.

NATASHA   [*perturbed*].   Forgive me, Olya; forgive me. . . . I did not
mean to hurt your feelings.

   MASHA *gets up, takes her pillow, and goes out in a rage.*

OLGA   You must understand, my dear, it may be that we have been
strangely brought up, but I can't endure it. . . . Such an attitude
oppresses me, it makes me ill. . . . I feel simply unnerved by it. . . .

NATASHA   Forgive me; forgive me. . . . [*Kisses her.*]

OLGA   The very slightest rudeness, a tactless word, upsets me. . . .

NATASHA   I often say too much, that's true, but you must admit, dear,
that she might just as well be in the country.

OLGA   She has been thirty years with us.

NATASHA   But now she can't work! Either I don't understand, or you
won't understand me. She is not fit for work. She does nothing but
sleep or sit still.

OLGA   Well, let her sit still.

NATASHA   [*surprised*]   How, sit still? Why, she is a servant. [*Through tears.*] I don't understand you, Olya. I have a nurse to look after the children as well as a wet nurse for baby, and we have a housemaid and a cook, what do we want that old woman for? What's the use of her?

The alarm bell rings behind the scenes.

OLGA This night has made me ten years older.

NATASHA We must come to an understanding, Olya. You are at the high-school, I am at home; you are teaching while I look after the house, and if I say anything about the servants, I know what I'm talking about; I do know what I'm talking about. . . . And that old thief, that old hag . . . [*stamps*] that old witch shall clear out of the house tomorrow! . . . I won't have people annoy me! I won't have it! [*Feeling that she has gone too far.*] Really, if you don't move downstairs, we shall always be quarreling. It's awful.

Enter KULIGIN.

KULIGIN Where is Masha? It's time to be going home. The fire is dying down, so they say. [*Stretches.*] Only one part of the town has been burned, and yet there was a wind; it seemed at first as though the whole town would be destroyed. [*Sits down.*] I am exhausted. Olya, my dear . . . I often think if it had not been for Masha I should have married you. You are so good. . . . I am tired out. [*Listens.*]

OLGA What is it?

KULIGIN It is unfortunate the doctor should have a drinking bout just now; he is helplessly drunk. Most unfortunate. [*Gets up.*] Here he comes, I do believe. . . . Do you hear? Yes, he is coming this way. . . . [*Laughs.*] What a man he is, really. . . . I shall hide. [*Goes to the cupboard and stands in the corner.*] Isn't he a ruffian!

OLGA He has not drunk for two years and now he has gone and done it. . . . [*Walks away with* NATASHA *to the back of the room.*]

TCHEBUTYKIN *comes in; walking as though sober without staggering, he walks across the room, stops, looks round; then goes up to the washing-stand and begins to wash his hands.*

TCHEBUTYKIN [*morosely*] The devil take them all . . . damn them all. They think I am a doctor, that I can treat all sorts of complaints, and I really know nothing about it, I have forgotten all I did know, I remember nothing, absolutely nothing.

OLGA *and* NATASHA *go out unnoticed by him.*

The devil take them. Last Wednesday I treated a woman at Zasyp— she died, and it's my fault that she died. Yes . . . I did know something twenty-five years ago, but now I remember nothing, nothing. Perhaps I am not a man at all but only pretend to have arms and legs and head; perhaps I don't exist at all and only fancy that I walk about, eat and sleep. [*Weeps.*] Oh, if only I did not exist! [*Leaves off weeping, morosely.*] I don't care! I don't care a scrap! [*A pause.*] Goodness knows. . . . The day before yesterday there was a conversation at the club: they talked about Shakespeare, Voltaire.[5] . . . I have read nothing, nothing at all, but I looked as though I had read them. And the others did the same as I did. The vulgarity! The meanness! And that woman I killed on Wednesday came back to my mind . . . and it all came back to my mind and everything seemed nasty, disgusting and all awry in my soul. . . . I went and got drunk. . . .

> *Enter* IRINA, VERSHININ, *and* TUSENBACH; TUSENBACH *is wearing a fashionable new civilian suit.*

IRINA   Let us sit here. No one will come here.

VERSHININ   If it had not been for the soldiers, the whole town would have been burned down. Splendid fellows! [*Rubs his hands with pleasure.*] They are first-rate men! Splendid fellows!

KULIGIN [*going up to them*]   What time is it?

TUSENBACH   It's past three. It's getting light already.

IRINA   They are all sitting in the dining room. No one seems to think of going. And that Solyony of yours is sitting there too. . . . [*To* TCHEBUTYKIN.] You had better go to bed, doctor.

TCHEBUTYKIN   It's all right. . . . Thank you! [*Combs his beard.*]

KULIGIN [*laughs*]   You are a bit fuddled, Ivan Romanitch! [*Slaps him on the shoulder.*] Bravo! *In vino veritas,*[6] the ancients used to say.

TUSENBACH   Everyone is asking me to get up a concert for the benefit of the families whose houses have been burned down.

IRINA   Why, who is there? . . .

TUSENBACH   We could get it up, if we wanted to. Marya Sergeyevna plays the piano splendidly, to my thinking.

KULIGIN   Yes, she plays splendidly.

IRINA   She has forgotten. She has not played for three . . . or four years.

TUSENBACH   There is absolutely no one who understands music in this town, not one soul, but I do understand and on my honor I assure you that Marya Sergeyevna plays magnificently, almost with genius.

KULIGIN   You are right, Baron. I am very fond of her; Masha, I mean. She is a good sort.

TUSENBACH   To be able to play so gloriously and to know that no one understands you!

KULIGIN [*sighs*]   Yes. . . . But would it be suitable for her to take part in a concert? [*A pause.*] I know nothing about it, my friends. Perhaps it would be all right. There is no denying that our director is a fine man, indeed a very fine man, very intelligent, but he has such views. . . . Of course it is not his business, still if you like I'll speak to him about it.

> TCHEBUTYKIN *takes up a china clock and examines it.*

VERSHININ   I got dirty all over at the fire. I am a sight. [*A pause.*]

<hr>

5. Shakespeare and François Marie Arouet, called Voltaire (1694–1778), the French philosopher and playwright, are cited as examples of the culture of Western Europe as opposed to that of Russia.

6. Latin for "In wine (there is) truth," i.e., that people who have been drinking are likely to speak the truth.

I heard a word dropped yesterday about our brigade being transferred ever so far away. Some say to Poland, and others to Tchita.[7]

TUSENBACH   I've heard something about it too. Well! The town will
be a wilderness then.

IRINA   We shall go away too.

TCHEBUTYKIN [*drops the clock, which smashes*]   To smithereens!

KULIGIN [*picking up the pieces*]   To smash such a valuable thing—oh,
Ivan Romanitch, Ivan Romanitch! I should give you minus zero for
conduct!

IRINA   That was mother's clock.

TCHEBUTYKIN   Perhaps. . . . Well, if it was hers, it was. Perhaps I did
not smash it, but it only seems as though I had. Perhaps it only seems
to us that we exist, but really we are not here at all. I don't know
anything—nobody knows anything. [*By the door.*] What are you
staring at? Natasha has got a little affair with Protopopov, and you
don't see it. . . . You sit here and see nothing, while Natasha has a
little affair with Protopopov. . . . [*Sings.*] May I offer you this date?[8]
. . . [*Goes out.*]

VERSHININ   Yes. . . . [*Laughs.*] How very queer it all is, really! [*A
pause.*] When the fire began I ran home as fast as I could. I went up
and saw our house was safe and sound and out of danger, but my
little girls were standing in the doorway in their nightgowns; their
mother was nowhere to be seen, people were bustling about, horses
and dogs were running about, and my children's faces were full of
alarm, horror, entreaty, and I don't know what; it wrung my heart
to see their faces. My God, I thought, what more have these children
to go through in the long years to come! I took their hands and ran
along with them, and could think of nothing else but what more
they would have to go through in this world! [*A pause.*] When I
came to your house I found their mother here, screaming, angry.
[MASHA *comes in with the pillow and sits down on the sofa.*] And
while my little girls were standing in the doorway in their nightgowns and the street was red with the fire, and there was a fearful
noise, I thought that something like it used to happen years ago
when the enemy would suddenly make a raid and begin plundering
and burning. . . . And yet, in reality, what a difference there is between what is now and has been in the past! And when a little more
time has passed—another two or three hundred years—people will
look at our present manner of life with horror and derision, and
everything of today will seem awkward and heavy, and very strange
and uncomfortable. Oh, what a wonderful life that will be—what a
wonderful life! [*Laughs.*] Forgive me, here I am airing my theories
again! Allow me to go on. I have such a desire to talk about the
future. I am in the mood. [*A pause.*] It's as though everyone were
asleep. And so, I say, what a wonderful life it will be! Can you only
imagine? . . . There are only three of your sort in the town now, but
in generations to come there will be more and more and more; and
the time will come when everything will be changed and be as you

---

7. A town in Siberia some 3000 miles
from Moscow; also Chita.
    8. Chekhov identified this passage as a
line from an operetta which he had heard
and of which he had forgotten the name.

would have it; they will live in your way, and later on you too will
be out of date—people will be born who will be better than you. . . .
[*Laughs.*] I am in such a strange state of mind today. I have a fiend-
ish longing for life. . . . [*Sings.*] Young and old are bound by love,
and precious are its pangs[9]. . . . [*Laughs.*]

MASHA   Tram-tam-tam!
VERSHININ   Tam-tam!
MASHA   Tra-ra-ra?
VERSHININ   Tra-ta-ta! [*Laughs.*]

    Enter FEDOTIK.

FEDOTIK [*dances*]   Burned to ashes! Burned to ashes! Everything I
had in the world. [*Laughter.*]
IRINA   A queer thing to joke about. Is everything burned?
FEDOTIK [*laughs*]   Everything I had in the world. Nothing is left. My
guitar is burned, and the camera and all my letters. . . . And the
notebook I meant to give you—that's burned too.

    Enter SOLYONY.

IRINA   No; please go, Vassily Vassilyitch. You can't stay here.
SOLYONY   How is it the baron can be here and I can't?
VERSHININ   We must be going, really. How is the fire?
SOLYONY   They say it is dying down. No, I really can't understand why
the baron may be here and not I. [*Takes out a bottle of scent and
sprinkles himself.*]
VERSHININ   Tram-tam-tam!
MASHA   Tram-tam!
VERSHININ [*laughs, to* SOLYONY]   Let us go into the dining room.
SOLYONY   Very well; we'll make a note of it. I might explain my mean-
ing further, but fear I may provoke the geese.[1] . . . [*Looking at*
TUSENBACH.] Chook, chook, chook! . . . [*Goes out with* VERSHININ
and FEDOTIK.]
IRINA   How that horrid Solyony has made the room smell of tobacco! . . . [*In surprise.*] The baron is asleep! Baron, Baron!
TUSENBACH [*waking up*]   I am tired, though. . . . The brickyard. I am
not talking in my sleep. I really am going to the brickyard directly,
to begin work. . . . It's nearly settled. [*To* IRINA, *tenderly.*] You are
so pale and lovely and fascinating. . . . It seems to me as though
your paleness sheds a light through the dark air. . . . You are melancholy; you are dissatisfied with life. . . . Ah, come with me; let
us go and work together!
MASHA   Nikolay Lvovitch, do go!
TUSENBACH [*laughing*]   Are you here? I didn't see you. . . . [*Kisses*
IRINA's *hand.*] Good-bye, I am going. . . . I look at you now, and I
remember as though it were long ago how on your name-day you
talked of the joy of work, and were so gay and confident. . . . And
what a happy life I was dreaming of then! What has become of it?

9. The song is from the opera *Eugene
Onegin* by Peter I. Tchaikovsky, based on
a novel in verse of the same name by
Pushkin. It is sung in the opera by Prince
Gremin, the husband of the heroine.
    1. A quotation from the fable "The
Geese" by Krylov.

[*Kisses her hand.*] There are tears in your eyes. Go to bed, it's getting light . . . it is nearly morning. . . . If it were granted to me to give my life for you!

MASHA   Nikolay Lvovitch, do go! Come, really. . . .

TUSENBACH   I am going. [*Goes out.*]

MASHA [*lying down*]   Are you asleep, Fyodor?

KULIGIN   Eh?

MASHA   You had better go home.

KULIGIN   My darling Masha, my precious girl! . . .

IRINA   She is tired out. Let her rest, Fedya.

KULIGIN   I'll go at once. . . . My dear, charming wife! . . . I love you, my only one! . . .

MASHA [*angrily*]   Amo, amas, amat; amamus, amatis, amant.[2]

KULIGIN [*laughs*]   Yes, really she is wonderful. You have been my wife for seven years, and it seems to me as though we were only married yesterday. Honor bright! Yes, really you are a wonderful woman! I am content, I am content, I am content!

MASHA   I am bored, I am bored, I am bored! . . . [*Gets up and speaks, sitting down.*] And there's something I can't get out of my head. . . . It's simply revolting. It sticks in my head like a nail; I must speak of it. I mean about Andrey. . . . He has mortgaged this house in the bank and his wife has grabbed all the money, and you know the house does not belong to him alone, but to us four! He ought to know that, if he is a decent man.

KULIGIN   Why do you want to bother about it, Masha? What is it to you? Andryusha is in debt all round, so there it is.

MASHA   It's revolting, anyway. [*Lies down.*]

KULIGIN   We are not poor. I work—I go to the high-school, and then I give private lessons. . . . I do my duty. . . . There's no nonsense about me. *Omnia mea mecum porto,*[3] as the saying is.

MASHA   I want nothing, but it's the injustice that revolts me. [*A pause.*] Go, Fyodor.

KULIGIN [*kisses her*]   You are tired, rest for half an hour, and I'll sit and wait for you. . . . Sleep. . . . [*Goes.*] I am content, I am content, I am content. [*Goes out.*]

IRINA   Yes, how petty our Andrey has grown, how dull and old he has become beside that woman! At one time he was working to get a professorship and yesterday he was boasting of having succeeded at last in becoming a member of the Rural Board. He is a member, and Protopopov is chairman. . . . The whole town is laughing and talking of it and he is the only one who sees and knows nothing. . . . And here everyone has been running to the fire while he sits still in his room and takes no notice. He does nothing but play his violin. . . . [*Nervously.*] Oh, it's awful, awful, awful! [*Weeps.*] I can't bear it anymore, I can't! I can't, I can't! [OLGA *comes in and begins tidying up her table.* IRINA *sobs loudly.*]   Turn me out, turn me out, I can't bear it any more!

---

2. Latin for "I love, you love, he loves, we love, you love, they love," the present tense of the verb *amo,* frequently used as a sample verb in grammar texts.
3. Latin for "I carry all my (belongings about) with me."

OLGA [*alarmed*]   What is it? What is it, darling?

IRINA [*sobbing*]   Where? Where has it all gone? Where is it? Oh, my God, my God! I have forgotten everything, everything . . . everything is in a tangle in my mind. . . . I don't remember the Italian for window or ceiling . . . I am forgetting everything; every day I forget something more and life is slipping away and will never come back, we shall never, never go to Moscow. . . . I see that we shan't go. . . .

OLGA   Darling, darling. . . .

IRINA [*restraining herself*]   Oh, I am wretched. . . . I can't work, I am not going to work. I have had enough of it, enough of it! I have been a telegraph clerk and now I have a job in the town council and I hate and despise every bit of the work they give me. . . . I am nearly twenty-four, I have been working for years, my brains are drying up, I am getting thin and old and ugly and there is nothing, nothing, not the slightest satisfaction, and time is passing and one feels that one is moving away from a real, fine life, moving farther and farther away and being drawn into the depths. I am in despair and I don't know how it is I am alive and have not killed myself yet. . . .

OLGA   Don't cry, my child, don't cry. It makes me miserable.

IRINA   I am not crying, I am not crying. . . . It's over. . . . There, I am not crying now. I won't . . . I won't.

OLGA   Darling, I am speaking to you as a sister, as a friend, if you care for my advice, marry the baron! [IRINA *weeps.* OLGA *speaks softly.*]   You know you respect him, you think highly of him. . . . It's true he is ugly, but he is such a thoroughly nice man, so good. . . . One doesn't marry for love, but to do one's duty. . . . That's what I think, anyway, and I would marry without love. Whoever proposed to me I would marry him, if only he were a good man. . . . I would even marry an old man. . . .

IRINA   I kept expecting we should move to Moscow and there I should meet my real one. I've been dreaming of him, loving him. . . . But it seems that was all nonsense, nonsense. . . .

OLGA [*puts her arms round her sister*]   My darling, lovely sister, I understand it all; when the baron left the army and came to us in a plain coat, I thought he looked so ugly that it positively made me cry. . . . He asked me, "Why are you crying?" How could I tell him! But if God brought you together I should be happy. That's a different thing, you know, quite different.

> NATASHA *with a candle in her hand walks across the stage from door on right to door on left without speaking.*

MASHA [*sits up*]   She walks about as though it were she had set fire to the town.

OLGA   Masha, you are silly. The very silliest of the family, that's you. Please forgive me. [*A pause.*]

MASHA   I want to confess my sins, dear sisters. My soul is yearning. I am going to confess to you and never again to anyone. . . . I'll tell you this minute. [*Softly.*] It's my secret, but you must know everything. . . . I can't be silent. . . . [*A pause.*] I am in love, I am in love. . . . I love that man. . . . You have just seen him. . . . Well, I may as well say it straight out. I love Vershinin.

OLGA [*going behind her screen*]   Leave off. I don't hear anyway.

MASHA   But what am I to do? [*Clutches her head.*] At first I thought
him queer . . . then I was sorry for him . . . then I came to love
him . . . to love him with his voice, his words, his misfortunes, his
two little girls. . . .

OLGA [*behind the screen*]   I don't hear you anyway. Whatever silly
things you say I shan't hear them.

MASHA   Oh, Olya, you are silly. I love him—so that's my fate. It means
that that's my lot. . . . And he loves me. . . . It's all dreadful. Yes? Is
it wrong? [*Takes* IRINA *by the hand and draws her to herself.*] Oh,
my darling. . . . How are we going to live our lives, what will become of us? . . . When one reads a novel it all seems stale and easy
to understand, but when you are in love yourself you see that no
one knows anything and we all have to settle things for ourselves. . . .
My darling, my sister. . . . I have confessed it to you, now I'll hold
my tongue. . . . I'll be like Gogol's madman[4] . . . silence . . . silence. . . .

   Enter ANDREY *and after him* FERAPONT.

ANDREY [*angrily*].   What do you want? I can't make it out.

FERAPONT [*in the doorway, impatiently*]   I've told you ten times already, Andrey Sergeyevitch.

ANDREY   In the first place I am not Andrey Sergeyevitch, but Your
Honor, to you!

FERAPONT   The firemen ask leave, Your Honor, to go through the
garden on their way to the river. Or else they have to go round and
round, an awful nuisance for them.

ANDREY   Very good. Tell them, very good. [FERAPONT *goes out.*] I
am sick of them. Where is Olga? [OLGA *comes from behind the
screen.*] I've come to ask you for the key of the cupboard, I have lost
mine. You've got one, it's a little key.

   OLGA *gives him the key in silence;* IRINA *goes behind her screen;
   a pause.*

ANDREY   What a tremendous fire! Now it's begun to die down. Hang it
all, that Ferapont made me so cross I said something silly to him.
Your Honor. . . . [*A pause.*] Why don't you speak, Olya? [*A pause.*]
It's time to drop this foolishness and sulking all about nothing. . . .
You are here, Masha, and you too, Irina—very well, then, let us have
things out thoroughly, once for all. What have you against me?
What is it?

OLGA   Leave off, Andryusha. Let us talk tomorrow. [*Nervously.*] What
an agonizing night!

ANDREY [*greatly confused*]   Don't excite yourself. I ask you quite
coolly, what have you against me? Tell me straight out.
[VERSHININ'S *voice:* "Tram-tam-tam!"]

MASHA [*standing up, loudly*]   Tra-ta-ta! [*To* OLGA.] Good night, Olya,
God bless you. . . .

4. The hero of Gogol's story "Memoirs of a Madman."

Goes behind the screen and kisses IRINA.

Sleep well. . . . Good night, Andrey. You'd better leave them now, they are tired out . . . you can go into things tomorrow. [*Goes out.*]

OLGA　Yes, really, Andryusha, let us put it off until tomorrow. . . . [*Goes behind her screen.*] It's time we were in bed.

ANDREY　I'll say what I have to say and then go. Directly. . . . First, you have something against Natasha, my wife, and I've noticed that from the very day of my marriage. Natasha is a splendid woman, conscientious, straightforward, and honorable—that's my opinion! I love and respect my wife, do you understand? I respect her, and I insist on other people respecting her too. I repeat, she is a conscientious, honorable woman, and all your disagreements are simply caprice, or rather the whims of old maids. Old maids never like and never have liked their sisters-in-law—that's the rule. [*A pause.*] Secondly, you seem to be cross with me for not being a professor, not working at something learned. But I am in the service of the Zemstvo,[5] I am a member of the Rural Board, and I consider this service just as sacred and elevated as the service of learning. I am a member of the Rural Board and I am proud of it, if you care to know. . . . [*A pause.*] Thirdly . . . there's something else I have to say. . . . I have mortgaged the house without asking your permission. . . . For that I am to blame, yes, and I ask your pardon for it. I was driven to it by my debts . . . thirty-five thousand. . . . I am not gambling now—I gave up cards long ago; but the chief thing I can say in self-defense is that you are, so to say, of the privileged sex—you get a pension . . . while I had not . . . my wages, so to speak. . . . [*A pause.*]

KULIGIN [*at the door*]　Isn't Masha here? [*Perturbed.*] Where is she? It's strange. . . . [*Goes out.*]

ANDREY　They won't listen. Natasha is an excellent, conscientious woman. [*Paces up and down the stage in silence, then stops.*] When I married her, I thought we should be happy . . . happy, all of us. . . . But, my God! [*Weeps.*] Dear sisters, darling sisters, you must not believe what I say, you mustn't believe it. . . . [*Goes out.*]

KULIGIN [*at the door, uneasily*]　Where is Masha? Isn't Masha here? How strange! [*Goes out.*]

The firebell rings in the street. The stage is empty.

IRINA [*behind the screen*]　Olya! Who is that knocking on the floor?

OLGA　It's the doctor, Ivan Romanitch. He is drunk.

IRINA　What a troubled night! [*A pause.*] Olya! [*Peeps out from behind the screen.*] Have you heard? The brigade is going to be taken away; they are being transferred to some place very far off.

OLGA　That's only a rumor.

IRINA　Then we shall be alone. . . .Olya!

OLGA　Well?

IRINA　My dear, my darling, I respect the baron, I think highly of him, he is a fine man—I will marry him, I consent, only let us go to

---

5. An elected assembly at the county or provincial level which dealt with local economic and social problems.

Moscow! I entreat you, do let us go! There's nothing in the world better than Moscow! Let us go, Olya! Let us go!

Act 4

Old garden of the PROZOROVS' *house. A long avenue of fir trees, at the end of which is a view of the river. On the farther side of the river there is a wood. On the right the veranda of the house; on the table in it are bottles and glasses; evidently they have just been drinking champagne. It is twelve o'clock noon. People pass occasionally from the street across the garden to the river; five soldiers pass rapidly.* TCHEBUTYKIN, *in an affable mood, which persists throughout the act, is sitting in an easy chair in the garden, waiting to be summoned; he is wearing a military cap and has a stick.* IRINA, KULIGIN *with a decoration on his breast and with no moustache, and* TUSENBACH, *standing on the veranda, are saying good-bye to* FEDOTIK *and* RODDEY, *who are going down the steps; both officers are in marching uniform.*

TUSENBACH [*kissing* FEDOTIK] You are a good fellow; we've got on so happily together. [*Kisses* RODDEY.] Once more. . . . Good-bye, my dear boy. . . .

IRINA Till we meet again!

FEDOTIK No, it's good-bye for good; we shall never meet again.

KULIGIN Who knows! [*Wipes his eyes, smiles.*] Here I am crying too.

IRINA We shall meet some day.

FEDOTIK In ten years, or fifteen perhaps? But then we shall scarcely recognize each other—we shall greet each other coldly. . . . [*Takes a snapshot.*] Stand still. . . . Once more, for the last time.

RODDEY [*embraces* TUSENBACH] We shall not see each other again. . . . [*Kisses* IRINA's *hand.*] Thank you for everything, everything. . . .

FEDOTIK [*with vexation*] Oh, do wait!

TUSENBACH Please God we shall meet again. Write to us. Be sure to write to us.

RODDEY [*taking a long look at the garden*] Good-bye, trees! [*Shouts.*] Halloo! [*A pause.*] Good-bye, echo!

KULIGIN I shouldn't wonder if you get married in Poland. . . . Your Polish wife will clasp you in her arms and call you *kochany!*[6] [*Laughs.*]

FEDOTIK [*looking at his watch*] We have less than an hour. Of our battery only Solyony is going on the barge; we are going with the rank and file. Three divisions of the battery are going today and three more tomorrow—and peace and quiet will descend upon the town.

TUSENBACH And dreadful boredom too.

RODDEY And where is Marya Sergeyevna?

KULIGIN Masha is in the garden.

FEDOTIK We must say good-bye to her.

6. A Polish term of endearment.

RODDEY   Good-bye. We must go, or I shall begin to cry. . . .

Hurriedly embraces TUSENBACH *and* KULIGIN *and kisses* IRINA'S *hand.*

We've had a splendid time here.

FEDOTIK [*to* KULIGIN]   This is a little souvenir for you . . . a notebook with a pencil. . . . We'll go down here to the river. . . . [*As they go away both look back.*]

RODDEY [*shouts*]   Halloo-oo!

KULIGIN [*shouts*]   Good-bye!

RODDEY *and* FEDOTIK *meet* MASHA *in the background and say good-bye to her; she walks away with them.*

IRINA   They've gone. . . . [*Sits down on the bottom step of the veranda.*]

TCHEBUTYKIN   They have forgotten to say good-bye to me.

IRINA   And what were you thinking about?

TCHEBUTYKIN   Why, I somehow forget, too. But I shall see them again soon, I am setting off tomorrow. Yes . . . I have one day more. In a year I shall be on the retired list. Then I shall come here again and shall spend the rest of my life near you. . . . There is only one year now before I get my pension. [*Puts a newspaper into his pocket and takes out another.*] I shall come here to you and arrange my life quite differently. . . . I shall become such a quiet . . . God-fearing . . . well-behaved person.

IRINA   Well, you do need to arrange your life differently, dear Ivan Romanitch. You certainly ought to somehow.

TCHEBUTYKIN   Yes, I feel it. [*Softly hums.*] "Tarara-boom-dee-ay— Tarara-boom-dee-ay."[7]

KULIGIN   Ivan Romanitch is incorrigible! Incorrigible!

TCHEBUTYKIN   You ought to take me in hand. Then I should reform.

IRINA   Fyodor has shaved off his moustache. I can't bear to look at him!

KULIGIN   Why, what's wrong?

TCHEBUTYKIN   I might tell you what your countenance looks like now, but I really can't.

KULIGIN   Well! It's the thing now, *modus vivendi.*[8] Our headmaster is clean-shaven and now I am second to him I have taken to shaving too. Nobody likes it, but I don't care. I am content. With moustache or without moustache I am equally content. [*Sits down.*]

In the background ANDREY *is wheeling a baby asleep in a perambulator.*

IRINA   Ivan Romanitch, darling, I am dreadfully uneasy. You were on the boulevard yesterday, tell me what was it that happened?

TCHEBUTYKIN   What happened? Nothing. Nothing much. [*Reads the newspaper.*] It doesn't matter!

---

7. A passage from a popular nonsense song of the 1890s, attributed to Henry J. Sayers, an American, which had its first notable success in England.

8. Latin for "manner of living."

KULIGIN   The story is that Solyony and the baron met yesterday on the boulevard near the theater. . . .

TUSENBACH   Oh, stop it! Really. . . . [*With a wave of his hand walks away into the house.*]

KULIGIN   Near the theater. . . . Solyony began pestering the baron and he couldn't keep his temper and said something offensive. . . .

TCHEBUTYKIN   I don't know. It's all nonsense.

KULIGIN   A teacher at a divinity school wrote "nonsense" at the bottom of an essay and the pupil puzzled over it thinking it was a Latin word. . . . [*Laughs.*] It was fearfully funny. . . . They say Solyony is in love with Irina and hates the baron. . . . That's natural. Irina is a very nice girl.

From the background behind the scenes, "Aa-oo! Halloo!"

IRINA   [*starts*]   Everything frightens me somehow today. [*A pause.*] All my things are ready, after dinner I shall send off my luggage. The baron and I are to be married tomorrow, tomorrow we go to the brickyard and the day after that I shall be in the school. A new life is beginning. God will help me! How will it fare with me? When I passed my exam as a teacher I felt so happy, so blissful, that I cried. . . . [*A pause.*] The cart will soon be coming for my things. . . .

KULIGIN   That's all very well, but it does not seem serious. It's all nothing but ideas and very little that is serious. However, I wish you success with all my heart.

TCHEBUTYKIN   [*moved to tenderness*]   My good, delightful darling. . . . My heart of gold. . . .

KULIGIN   Well, today the officers will be gone and everything will go on in the old way. Whatever people may say, Masha is a true, good woman. I love her dearly and am thankful for my lot! . . . People have different lots in life. . . . There is a man called Kozyrev serving in the Excise here.[9] He was at school with me, but he was expelled from the fifth form because he could never understand *ut consecutivum*.[1] Now he is frightfully poor and ill, and when I meet him I say, "How are you, *ut consecutivum?*" "Yes," he says, "just so—*consecutivum*" . . . and then he coughs. . . . Now I have always been successful, I am fortunate, I have even got the order of the Stanislav of the second degree[2] and I am teaching others that *ut consecutivum*. Of course I am clever, cleverer than very many people, but happiness does not lie in that. . . . [*A pause.*]

In the house the "Maiden's Prayer" is played on the piano.[3]

IRINA   Tomorrow evening I shall not be hearing that "Maiden's Prayer," I shan't be meeting Protopopov. . . . [*A pause.*] Protopopov

---

9. The Excise is the local tax office.
1. A reference to the practice in Latin grammar of introducing clauses of result with the conjunction *ut* and of using the subjunctive mood for the verb in the result clauses.
2. The Order of St. Stanislav was originally created in 1765 by Stanislav II, the last king of Poland. It was reestablished in 1815 by Czar Alexander I and included

four classes. In 1831 it was made an Imperial and Royal Order (three classes, plus a special class for foreigners). It was an order of merit rather than a military decoration.
3. "The Maiden's Prayer" was a popular piano piece of the period, the best known work of the Polish pianist and composer Teckla Badarzewska (1838–1864).

is sitting there in the drawing room; he has come again today. . . .

KULIGIN   The headmistress has not come yet?

IRINA   No. They have sent for her. If only you knew how hard it is for
me to live here alone, without Olya. . . . Now that she is headmistress
and lives at the high-school and is busy all day long. I am alone, I
am bored, I have nothing to do, and I hate the room I live in. . . . I
have made up my mind, since I am not fated to be in Moscow, that
so it must be. It must be destiny. There is no help for it. . . . It's all
in God's hands, that's the truth. When Nikolay Lvovitch made me an
offer again . . . I thought it over and made up my mind. . . . He is a
good man, it's wonderful really how good he is. . . . And I suddenly
felt as though my soul had grown wings, my heart felt so light and
again I longed for work, work. . . . Only something happened yesterday, there is some mystery hanging over me.

TCHEBUTYKIN   Nonsense.

NATASHA [*at the window*]   Our headmistress!

KULIGIN   The headmistress has come. Let us go in. [*Goes into the house
with* IRINA.]

TCHEBUTYKIN [*reads the newspaper, humming softly*]   "Tarara-boom-
dee-ay."

> MASHA *approaches; in the background* ANDREY *is pushing the
> perambulator.*

MASHA   Here he sits, snug and settled.

TCHEBUTYKIN   Well, what then?

MASHA [*sits down*]   Nothing. . . . [*A pause.*] Did you love my mother?

TCHEBUTYKIN   Very much.

MASHA   And did she love you?

TCHEBUTYKIN [*after a pause*]   That I don't remember.

MASHA   Is my man here? It's just like our cook Marfa used to say about
her policeman: is my man here?

TCHEBUTYKIN   Not yet.

MASHA   When you get happiness by snatches, by little bits, and then
lose it, as I am losing it, by degrees one grows coarse and spiteful.
. . . [*Points to her bosom.*] I'm boiling here inside. . . . [*Looking at*
ANDREY, *who is pushing the perambulator.*] Here is our Andrey. . . .
All our hopes are shattered. Thousands of people raised the bell, a lot
of money and of labor was spent on it, and it suddenly fell and
smashed.[4] All at once, for no reason whatever. That's just how it is
with Andrey. . . .

ANDREY   When will they be quiet in the house? There is such a noise.

TCHEBUTYKIN   Soon. [*Looks at his watch.*] My watch is an old-fashioned one with a repeater. . . . [*Winds his watch, it strikes.*] The first,
the second, and the fifth batteries are going at one o'clock. [*A pause.*]
And I am going tomorrow.

ANDREY   For good?

---

4. Masha is perhaps referring to the
gigantic bell called the Tsar Kolokol (or
"King of Bells") in the Kremlin. It was
originally cast at the behest of Boris
Godunov to hang in the Ivan Bell Tower
of the Kremlin, but it proved too heavy.
The platform on which it rested fell on
several occasions as a result of fire weakening its supports. It weighs about 200
tons and is over 20 feet high and more
than 20 feet in diameter.

TCHEBUTYKIN   I don't know. Perhaps I shall come back in a year. Though goodness knows. . . . It doesn't matter one way or another.

   There is the sound of a harp and violin being played far away in the street.

ANDREY   The town will be empty. It's as though one put an extinguisher over it. [*A pause.*] Something happened yesterday near the theater; everyone is talking of it, and I know nothing about it.

TCHEBUTYKIN   It was nothing. Foolishness. Solyony began annoying the baron and he lost his temper and insulted him, and it came in the end to Solyony's having to challenge him. [*Looks at his watch.*] It's time, I fancy. . . . It was to be at half-past twelve in the Crown forest that we can see from here beyond the river. . . . Piff-paff! [*Laughs.*] Solyony imagines he is a Lermontov and even writes verses. Joking apart, this is his third duel.

MASHA   Whose?

TCHEBUTYKIN   Solyony's.

MASHA   And the baron's?

TCHEBUTYKIN   What about the baron? [*A pause.*]

MASHA   My thoughts are in a muddle. . . . Anyway, I tell you, you ought not to let them do it. He may wound the baron or even kill him.

TCHEBUTYKIN   The baron is a very good fellow, but one baron more or less in the world, what does it matter? Let them! It doesn't matter. [*Beyond the garden a shout of* "Aa-oo! Halloo!"] You can wait. That is Skvortsov, the second, shouting. He is in a boat. [*A pause.*]

ANDREY   In my opinion to take part in a duel, or to be present at it even in the capacity of a doctor, is simply immoral.

TCHEBUTYKIN   That only seems so. . . . We are not real, nothing in the world is real, we don't exist, but only seem to exist. . . . Nothing matters!

MASHA   'How they keep on talking, talking all day long. [*Goes.*] To live in such a climate, it may snow any minute, and then all this talk on the top of it. [*Stops.*] I am not going indoors, I can't go in there. . . . When Vershinin comes, tell me. . . . [*Goes down the avenue.*] And the birds are already flying south. . . . [*Looks up.*] Swans or geese. . . . Darlings, happy things. . . . [*Goes out.*]

ANDREY   Our house will be empty. The officers are going, you are going, Irina is getting married, and I shall be left in the house alone.

TCHEBUTYKIN   What about your wife?

   Enter FERAPONT *with papers.*

ANDREY   A wife is a wife. She is a straightforward, upright woman, good-natured, perhaps, but for all that there is something in her which makes her no better than some petty, blind, hairy animal. Anyway she is not a human being. I speak to you as to a friend, the one man to whom I can open my soul. I love Natasha, that is so, but sometimes she seems to me wonderfully vulgar, and then I don't know what to think, I can't account for my loving her or, anyway, having loved her.

TCHEBUTYKIN   [*gets up*]   I am going away tomorrow, my boy, perhaps

we shall never meet again, so this is my advice to you. Put on your
cap, you know, take your stick and walk off . . . walk off and just
go, go without looking back. And the farther you go, the better. [*A
pause.*] But do as you like! It doesn't matter. . . .

> SOLYONY *crosses the stage in the background with two officers;
> seeing* TCHEBUTYKIN *he turns toward him; the officers walk on.*

SOLYONY   Doctor, it's time! It's half-past twelve. [*Greets* ANDREY.]

TCHEBUTYKIN   Directly. I am sick of you all. [*To* ANDREY.] If anyone
asks for me, Andryusha, say I'll be back directly. . . . [*Sighs.*] Oho-
ho-ho!

SOLYONY   He had not time to say alack before the bear was on his
back. [*Walks away with the doctor.*] Why are you croaking, old
chap?

TCHEBUTYKIN   Come!

SOLYONY   How do you feel?

TCHEBUTYKIN [*angrily*]   Like a pig in clover.[5]

SOLYONY   The old chap need not excite himself. I won't do anything
much, I'll only shoot him like a snipe. [*Takes out scent and sprinkles
his hands.*] I've used a whole bottle today, and still they smell. My
hands smell like a corpse. [*A pause.*] Yes. . . . Do you remember the
poem? "And, restless, seeks the stormy ocean, as though in tempest
there were peace."[6] . . .

TCHEBUTYKIN   Yes. He had not time to say alack before the bear was
on his back.

> *Goes out with* SOLYONY. *Shouts are heard:* "Halloo! Oo-oo!" AN-
> DREY *and* FERAPONT *come in.*

FERAPONT   Papers for you to sign. . . .

ANDREY [*nervously*]   Let me alone! Let me alone! I entreat you!
[*Walks away with the perambulator.*]

FERAPONT   That's what the papers are for—to be signed. [*Retires into
the background.*]

> *Enter* IRINA *and* TUSENBACH *wearing a straw hat;* KULIGIN
> *crosses the stage shouting* "Aa-oo, Masha, aa-oo!"

TUSENBACH   I believe that's the only man in the town who is glad that
the officers are going away.

IRINA   That's very natural. [*A pause.*] Our town will be empty now.

TUSENBACH   Dear, I'll be back directly.

IRINA   Where are you going?

TUSENBACH   I must go into the town, and then . . . to see my comrades
off.

IRINA   That's not true. . . . Nikolay, why are you so absentminded today? [*A pause.*] What happened yesterday near the theater?

TUSENBACH [*with a gesture of impatience*]   I'll be here in an hour and
with you again. [*Kisses her hands.*] My beautiful one . . . [*Looks into
her face.*] For five years now I have loved you and still I can't get

---

5. "To turn the pigs into the grass" is a
proverbial expression meaning to create a
diversion. Tchebutykin means that he is

distracted.
6. A quotation from "The Sail," a poem
by Lermontov.

used to it, and you seem to me more and more lovely. What wonderful, exquisite hair! What eyes! I shall carry you off tomorrow, we will work, we will be rich, my dreams will come true. You shall be happy. There is only one thing, one thing: you don't love me!

IRINA   That's not in my power! I'll be your wife and be faithful and obedient, but there is no love, I can't help it. [*Weeps.*] I've never been in love in my life! Oh, I have so dreamed of love, I've been dreaming of it for years, day and night, but my soul is like a wonderful piano of which the key has been lost. [*A pause.*] You look uneasy.

TUSENBACH   I have not slept all night. There has never been anything in my life so dreadful that it could frighten me, and only that lost key frets at my heart and won't let me sleep. . . . Say something to me. . . . [*A pause.*] Say something to me. . . .

IRINA   What? What am I to say to you? What?

TUSENBACH   Anything.

IRINA   There, there! [*A pause.*]

TUSENBACH   What trifles, what little things suddenly *à propos*[7] of nothing acquire importance in life! One laughs at them as before, thinks them nonsense, but still one goes on and feels that one has not the power to stop. Don't let us talk about it! I am happy. I feel as though I were seeing these pines, these maples, these birch trees for the first time in my life, and they all seem to be looking at me with curiosity and waiting. What beautiful trees, and, really, how beautiful life ought to be under them! [*A shout of* "Halloo! Aa-oo!"] I must be off; it's time. . . . See, that tree is dead, but it waves in the wind with the others. And so it seems to me that if I die I shall still have part in life, one way or another. Good-bye, my darling. . . . [*Kisses her hands.*] Those papers of yours you gave me are lying under the calendar on my table.

IRINA   I am coming with you.

TUSENBACH   [*in alarm*]   No, no! [*Goes off quickly, stops in the avenue.*] Irina!

IRINA   What is it?

TUSENBACH   [*not knowing what to say*]   I didn't have any coffee this morning. Ask them to make me some. [*Goes out quickly.*]

> IRINA *stands lost in thought, then walks away into the background of the scene and sits down on the swing. Enter* ANDREY *with the perambulator, and* FERAPONT *comes into sight.*

FERAPONT   Andrey Sergeyevitch, the papers aren't mine; they are Government papers. I didn't invent them.

ANDREY   Oh, where is it all gone? What has become of my past, when I was young, gay, and clever, when my dreams and thoughts were exquisite, when my present and my past were lighted up by hope? Why on the very threshold of life do we become dull, grey, uninteresting, lazy, indifferent, useless, unhappy? . . . Our town has been going on for two hundred years—there are a hundred thousand people living in it; and there is not one who is not like the rest, not one saint in the past, or the present, not one man of learning, not one

---

7. A French phrase meaning "relating to" or "having to do with."

artist, not one man in the least remarkable who could inspire envy or a passionate desire to imitate him. . . . They only eat, drink, sleep, and then die . . . others are born, and they also eat and drink and sleep, and not to be bored to stupefaction they vary their lives by nasty gossip, vodka, cards, litigation; and the wives deceive their husbands, and the husbands tell lies and pretend that they see and hear nothing, and an overwhelmingly vulgar influence weighs upon the children, and the divine spark is quenched in them and they become the same sort of pitiful, dead creatures, all exactly alike, as their fathers and mothers. . . . [*To* FERAPONT, *angrily.*] What do you want?

FERAPONT   Eh? There are papers to sign.

ANDREY   You bother me!

FERAPONT [*handing him the papers*]   The porter from the local treasury was saying just now that there was as much as two hundred degrees of frost in Petersburg this winter.[8]

ANDREY   The present is hateful, but when I think of the future, it is so nice! I feel so lighthearted, so free. A light dawns in the distance, I see freedom. I see how I and my children will become free from sloth, from kvass,[9] from goose and cabbage, from sleeping after dinner, from mean, parasitic living. . . .

FERAPONT   He says that two thousand people were frozen to death. The people were terrified. It was either in Petersburg or Moscow, I don't remember.

ANDREY [*in a rush of tender feeling*]   My dear sisters, my wonderful sisters! [*Through tears.*] Masha, my sister!

NATASHA [*in the window*]   Who is talking so loud out there? Is that you, Andryusha? You will wake baby Sophie. *Il ne faut pas faire de bruit, la Sophie est dormée déja. Vous êtes un ours.*[1] [*Getting angry.*] If you want to talk, give the perambulator with the baby to somebody else. Ferapont, take the perambulator from the master!

FERAPONT   Yes, ma'am. [*Takes the pram.*]

ANDREY [*in confusion*]   I am talking quietly.

NATASHA [*petting her child, inside the room*]   Bobik! Naughty Bobik! Little rascal!

ANDREY [*looking through the papers*]   Very well, I'll look through them and sign what wants signing, and then you can take them back to the Board. . . .

> *Goes into the house reading the papers,* FERAPONT *pushes the pram further into the garden.*

NATASHA [*speaking indoors*]   Bobik, what is mamma's name? Darling, darling! And who is this? This is Auntie Olya. Say to Auntie, "Good morning, Olya!"

> *Two wandering musicians, a man and a girl, enter and play a*

---

8. Two hundred degrees of frost normally means 200 degrees below the freezing point of water, which is very cold even for the Russian winter. Joseph Nicholas Delisle, a French astronomer, was in St. Petersburg from 1725 to 1747 at the invitation of Peter the Great. With the assistance of Josias Weithrecht, he devised a thermometer which read 0 at the boiling point of water, 150 at the freezing point of water, and was graduated farther down to 200 or 205. Ferapont's temperature reading may have been on his scale.

violin and a harp; from the house enter VERSHININ *with* OLGA *and* ANFISA, *and stand for a minute listening in silence;* IRINA *comes up.*

OLGA   Our garden is like a public passage; they walk and ride through. Nurse, give those people something.

ANFISA [*gives money to the musicians*]   Go away, and God bless you, my dear souls! [*The musicians bow and go away.*] Poor things. People don't play if they have plenty to eat. [*To* IRINA.] Good morning, Irisha! [*Kisses her.*] Aye, aye, my little girl, I am having a time of it! Living in the high-school, in a government flat, with dear Olya— that's what the Lord has vouchsafed me in my old age! I have never lived so well in my life, sinful woman that I am. . . . It's a big flat, and I have a room to myself and a bedstead. All at the government expense. I wake up in the night and, O Lord, Mother of God, there is no one in the world happier than I!

VERSHININ [*looks at his watch*]   We are just going, Olga Sergeyevna. It's time to be off. [*A pause.*] I wish you everything, everything. . . . Where is Marya Sergeyevna?

IRINA   She is somewhere in the garden. . . . I'll go and look for her.

VERSHININ   Please be so good. I am in a hurry.

ANFISA   I'll go and look for her too. [*Shouts.*] Mashenka, aa-oo! [*Goes with* IRINA *into the farther part of the garden.*] Aa-oo! Aa-oo!

VERSHININ   Everything comes to an end. Here we are parting. [*Looks at his watch.*] The town has given us something like a lunch; we have been drinking champagne, the mayor made a speech. I ate and listened, but my heart was here, with you all. . . . [*Looks round the garden.*] I've grown used to you. . . .

OLGA   Shall we ever see each other again?

VERSHININ   Most likely not. [*A pause.*] My wife and two little girls will stay here for another two months; please, if anything happens, if they need anything . . .

OLGA   Yes, yes, of course. Set your mind at rest. [*A pause.*] By to-morrow there won't be a soldier in the town—it will all turn into a memory, and of course for us it will be like beginning a new life. . . . [*A pause.*] Nothing turns out as we would have it. I did not want to be a headmistress, and yet I am. It seems we are not to live in Moscow. . . .

VERSHININ   Well. . . . Thank you for everything. . . . Forgive me if anything was amiss. . . . I have talked a great deal: forgive me for that too— don't remember evil against me.

OLGA [*wipes her eyes*]   Why doesn't Masha come?

VERSHININ   What else am I to say to you at parting? What am I to theorize about? . . . [*Laughs.*] Life is hard. It seems to many of us blank and hopeless; but yet we must admit that it goes on getting clearer and easier, and it looks as though the time were not far off when it will be full of happiness. [*Looks at his watch.*] It's time for me to go! In old days men were absorbed in wars, filling all their existence with marches, raids, victories, but now all that is a thing of the past, leaving behind it a great void which there is so far nothing to fill: humanity is searching for it passionately, and of course will find it. Ah, if only it could be quickly! [*A pause.*] If, don't you

know, industry were united with culture and culture with industry.
. . . [*Looks at his watch.*] But, I say, it's time for me to go. . . .

OLGA   Here she comes.

MASHA *comes in.*

VERSHININ   I have come to say good-bye. . . .

OLGA *moves a little away to leave them free to say good-bye.*

MASHA [*looking into his face*]   Good-bye. . . . [*A prolonged kiss.*]

OLGA   Come, come. . . .

MASHA *sobs violently.*

VERSHININ   Write to me. . . . Don't forget me! Let me go! . . . Time is
up! . . . Olga Sergeyevna, take her, I must . . . go . . . I am late. . . .
[*Much moved, kisses* OLGA'S *hands; then again embraces* MASHA
and quickly goes off.]

OLGA   Come, Masha! Leave off, darling.

Enter KULIGIN.

KULIGIN [*embarrassed*]   Never mind, let her cry—let her. . . . My good
Masha, my dear Masha! . . . You are my wife, and I am happy, anyway. . . . I don't complain; I don't say a word of blame. . . . Here
Olya is my witness. . . . We'll begin the old life again, and I won't
say one word, not a hint. . . .

MASHA [*restraining her sobs*]   By the sea-strand an oak tree green. . . .
Upon that oak a chain of gold. . . . Upon that oak a chain of gold.
. . . I am going mad. . . . By the sea-strand . . . an oak tree green. . . .

OLGA   Calm yourself, Masha. . . . Calm yourself. . . . Give her some
water.

MASHA   I am not crying now. . . .

KULIGIN   She is not crying now . . . she is good. . . .

The dim sound of a faraway shot.

MASHA   By the sea-strand an oak tree green, upon that oak a chain of
gold. . . . The cat is green . . . the oak is green. . . . I am mixing it
up. . . . [*Drinks water.*] My life is a failure. . . . I want nothing now.
. . . I shall be calm directly. . . . It doesn't matter. . . . What does
"strand" mean? Why do these words haunt me? My thoughts are in
a tangle.

Enter IRINA

OLGA   Calm yourself, Masha. Come, that's a good girl. Let us go indoors.

MASHA [*angrily*]   I am not going in. Let me alone! [*Sobs, but at once
checks herself.*] I don't go into that house now and I won't.

IRINA   Let us sit together, even if we don't say anything. I am going
away tomorrow, you know. . . . [*A pause.*]

KULIGIN   I took a false beard and moustache from a boy in the third
grade yesterday, just look. . . . [*Puts on the beard and moustache.*]
I look like the German teacher. . . . [*Laughs.*] Don't I? Funny creatures, those boys.

MASHA   You really do look like the German teacher.

OLGA [*laughs*]   Yes.

> MASHA *weeps.*

IRINA   There, Masha!

KULIGIN   Awfully like. . . .

> *Enter* NATASHA.

NATASHA [*to the maid*]   What? Mr. Protopopov will sit with Sophie, and let Andrey Sergeyitch wheel Bobik up and down. What a lot there is to do with children. . . . [*To* IRINA.] Irina, you are going away tomorrow, what a pity. Do stay just another week.

> *Seeing* KULIGIN *utters a shriek; the latter laughs and takes off the beard and moustache.*

Well, what next, you gave me such a fright! [*To* IRINA.] I am used to you and do you suppose that I don't feel parting with you? I shall put Andrey with his violin into your room—let him saw away there! —and we will put baby Sophie in his room. Adorable, delightful baby! Isn't she a child! Today she looked at me with such eyes and said "Mamma"!

KULIGIN   A fine child, that's true.

NATASHA   So tomorrow I shall be all alone here. [*Sighs.*] First of all I shall have this avenue of fir trees cut down, and then that maple. . . . It looks so ugly in the evening. . . . [*To* IRINA.] My dear, that sash does not suit you at all. . . . It's in bad taste. You want something light. And then I shall have flowers, flowers planted everywhere, and there will be such a scent. . . . [*Severely.*] Why is there a fork lying about on that seat? [*Going into the house, to the maid.*] Why is there a fork lying about on this seat, I ask you? [*Shouts.*] Hold your tongue!

KULIGIN   She is at it!

> *Behind the scenes the band plays a march; they all listen.*

OLGA   They are going.

> *Enter* TCHEBUTYKIN.

MASHA   Our people are going. Well . . . a happy journey to them! [*To her husband.*] We must go home. . . . Where are my hat and cape?

KULIGIN   I took them into the house. . . . I'll get them directly. . . .

OLGA   Yes, now we can go home, it's time.

TCHEBUTYKIN   Olga Sergeyevna!

OLGA   What is it? [*A pause.*] What?

TCHEBUTYKIN   Nothing. . . . I don't know how to tell you. [*Whispers in her ear.*]

OLGA [*in alarm*]   It can't be!

TCHEBUTYKIN   Yes . . . such a business. . . . I am so worried and worn out, I don't want to say another word. . . . [*With vexation.*] But there, it doesn't matter!

MASHA   What has happened?

OLGA [*puts her arms round* IRINA]   This is a terrible day. . . . I don't know how to tell you, my precious. . . .

IRINA   What is it? Tell me quickly, what is it? For God's sake! [*Cries.*]

TCHEBUTYKIN   The baron has just been killed in a duel.

IRINA [*weeping quietly*]   I knew, I knew. . . .

TCHEBUTYKIN [*in the background of the scene sits down on a garden seat*]   I am worn out. . . . [*Takes a newspaper out of his pocket.*] Let them cry. . . . [*Sings softly.*] "Tarara-boom-dee-ay." . . . It doesn't matter.

The three sisters stand with their arms round one another.

MASHA   Oh, listen to that band! They are going away from us; one has gone altogether, gone forever. We are left alone to begin our life over again. . . . We've got to live . . . we've got to live. . . .

IRINA [*lays her head on* OLGA's *bosom*]   A time will come when everyone will know what all this is for, why there is this misery; there will be no mysteries and, meanwhile, we have got to live . . . we have got to work, only to work! Tomorrow I shall go alone; I shall teach in the school, and I will give all my life to those to whom it may be of use. Now it's autumn; soon winter will come and cover us with snow, and I will work, I will work.

OLGA [*embraces both her sisters*]   The music is so gay, so confident, and one longs for life! O my God! Time will pass, and we shall go away for ever, and we shall be forgotten, our faces will be forgotten, our voices, and how many there were of us; but our sufferings will pass into joy for those who will live after us, happiness and peace will be established upon earth, and they will remember kindly and bless those who have lived before. Oh, dear sisters, our life is not ended yet. We shall live! The music is so gay, so joyful, and it seems as though a little more and we shall know what we are living for, why we are suffering. . . . If we only knew—if we only knew!

The music grows more and more subdued; KULIGIN, *cheerful and smiling, brings the hat and cape;* ANDREY *pushes the perambulator in which* BOBIK *is sitting.*

TCHEBUTYKIN [*humming softly*]   "Tarara-boom-dee-ay!" [*Reads his paper.*] It doesn't matter, it doesn't matter.

OLGA   If we only knew, if we only knew!

1901

RUSSIAN NAMES

The use of names in Russian literature will confuse American students unless they bear certain facts in mind. Russian names, generally, consist of three parts: the given name; the patronymic (ending in *itch* for men and *vna* for women) based on the given name of the character's father; and the family name. The name Ivan Romanitch Tchebutykin, for example, tells us that the character's given name is Ivan, that his father's given name was Roman and that the family name is Tchebutykin. In general, strangers, or relative strangers, would use the family name or an appropriate title to refer to or speak to a character.

For example, Tusenbach at first calls Vershinin either "Vershinin" or "Colonel," but later calls him Alexandr Ignatyevitch. Friends of the same rank would use the given name plus patronymic, *e.g.* Ivan Romanitch, as all of the Prozorovs do for Tchebutykin. More intimate relations are indicated by the use of the given name only or by nicknames of varying degrees of intimacy. Andrey, Irina, and Marya, for example, would be called Andryusha, Irisha, and Masha or Andryushantchik, Irinushka, and Mashenka, as dictated by circumstance. Natasha, for example, calls Irina "Irina Sergeyevna" before her marriage to Andrey and "Irina" afterward. In the same way, Irina calls Kuligin either Fyodor, his given name, or Fedya, a nickname, as the particular moment renders appropriate.

The nurse Anfisa shows that in dealing with characters of various ranks, the usual rules may be modified. She calls the three sisters "Olya," "Mashenka," and "Irisha" or "Irinushka" with impunity because she knew them as children. A different view is shown when Andrey takes umbrage at being called Andrey Sergeyevitch, instead of "Your Honor," by Ferapont.

Another point to be noted is that speakers in general use a more formal term in speaking of someone in the second person than they do in the third. Irina, for example, refers to "Solyony" in the third person but calls him "Vassily Vassilyevitch" in person.

Plays for Further Reading

HENRIK IBSEN

Hedda Gabler*

CHARACTERS

GEORGE TESMAN, *research gradu-
ate in cultural history*
HEDDA, *his wife*
MISS JULIANA TESMAN, *his aunt*

MRS. ELVSTED
JUDGE BRACK
EILERT LOEVBORG
BERTHA, *a maid*

*The action takes place in Tesman's villa, in the fashionable quarter
of town.*

Act 1

*A large drawing room, handsomely and tastefully furnished; deco-
rated in dark colors. In the rear wall is a broad open doorway, with
curtains drawn back to either side. It leads to a smaller room, decorated in the same style as the drawing room. In the right-hand
wall of the drawing room, a folding door leads out to the hall. The
opposite wall, on the left, contains french windows, also with
curtains drawn back on either side. Through the glass we can see
part of a verandah, and trees in autumn colors. Downstage stands
an oval table, covered by a cloth and surrounded by chairs. Downstage right, against the wall, is a broad stove tiled with dark porcelain; in front of it stand a high-backed armchair, a cushioned foot-
rest, and two footstools. Upstage right, in an alcove, is a corner
sofa, with a small, round table. Downstage left, a little away from
the wall, is another sofa. Upstage of the french windows, a piano.
On either side of the open doorway in the rear wall stand what-nots
holding ornaments of terra cotta and majolica. Against the rear
wall of the smaller room can be seen a sofa, a table, and a couple
of chairs. Above this sofa hangs the portrait of a handsome old man
in general's uniform. Above the table a lamp hangs from the ceiling,
with a shade of opalescent, milky glass. All round the drawing room
bunches of flowers stand in vases and glasses. More bunches lie on
the tables. The floors of both rooms are covered with thick carpets.
Morning light. The sun shines in through the french windows.*

* Translated by Michael Meyer.

MISS JULIANA TESMAN, *wearing a hat and carrying a parasol,
enters from the hall, followed by* BERTHA, *who is carrying a bunch
of flowers wrapped in paper.* MISS TESMAN *is about sixty-five, of
pleasant and kindly appearance. She is neatly but simply dressed
in gray outdoor clothes.* BERTHA, *the maid, is rather simple and
rustic-looking. She is getting on in years.*

MISS TESMAN [*stops just inside the door, listens, and says in a hushed
voice*]   No, bless my soul! They're not up yet.

BERTHA [*also in hushed tones*]   What did I tell you, miss? The boat
didn't get in till midnight. And when they did turn up—Jesus, miss,
you should have seen all the things Madam made me unpack before she'd go to bed!

MISS TESMAN   Ah, well. Let them have a good lie in. But let's have
some nice fresh air waiting for them when they do come down.

Goes to the french windows and throws them wide open.

BERTHA [*bewildered at the table, the bunch of flowers in her hand*]
I'm blessed if there's a square inch left to put anything. I'll have
to let it lie here, miss.

Puts it on the piano.

MISS TESMAN   Well, Bertha dear, so now you have a new mistress.
Heaven knows it nearly broke my heart to have to part with you.

BERTHA [*snivels*]   What about me, Miss Juju? How do you suppose
I felt? After all the happy years I've spent with you and Miss Rena?

MISS TESMAN   We must accept it bravely, Bertha. It was the only
way. George needs you to take care of him. He could never manage
without you. You've looked after him ever since he was a tiny boy.

BERTHA   Oh, but, Miss Juju, I can't help thinking about Miss Rena,
lying there all helpless, poor dear. And that new girl! She'll never
learn the proper way to handle an invalid.

MISS TESMAN   Oh, I'll manage to train her. I'll do most of the work
myself, you know. You needn't worry about my poor sister, Bertha
dear.

BERTHA   But Miss Juju, there's another thing. I'm frightened Madam
may not find me suitable.

MISS TESMAN   Oh, nonsense, Bertha. There may be one or two little
things to begin with—

BERTHA   She's a real lady. Wants everything just so.

MISS TESMAN   But of course she does! General Gabler's daughter!
Think of what she was accustomed to when the General was alive.
You remember how we used to see her out riding with her father?
In that long black skirt? With the feather in her hat?

BERTHA   Oh, yes, miss. As if I could forget! But, Lord! I never
dreamed I'd live to see a match between her and Master Georgie.

MISS TESMAN   Neither did I. By the way, Bertha, from now on you
must stop calling him Master Georgie. You must say: Dr. Tesman.

BERTHA   Yes, Madam said something about that too. Last night—the
moment they'd set foot inside the door. Is it true, then, miss?

MISS TESMAN Indeed it is. Just imagine, Bertha, some foreigners have made him a doctor.[1] It happened while they were away. I had no idea till he told me when they got off the boat.

BERTHA Well, I suppose there's no limit to what he won't become. He's that clever. I never thought he'd go in for hospital work, though.

MISS TESMAN No, he's not that kind of doctor.

Nods impressively.

In any case, you may soon have to address him by an even grander title.

BERTHA You don't say! What might that be, miss?

MISS TESMAN [*smiles*] Ah! If you only knew!

Moved.

Dear God, if only poor dear Joachim could rise out of his grave and see what his little son has grown into!

Looks round.

But, Bertha, why have you done this? Taken the chintz covers off all the furniture!

BERTHA Madam said I was to. Can't stand chintz covers on chairs, she said.

MISS TESMAN But surely they're not going to use this room as a parlor?

BERTHA So I gathered, miss. From what Madam said. He didn't say anything. The Doctor.

> GEORGE TESMAN *comes into the rear room, from the right, humming, with an open, empty traveling bag in his hand. He is about thirty-three, of medium height and youthful appearance, rather plump, with an open, round, contented face, and fair hair and beard. He wears spectacles, and is dressed in comfortable, indoor clothes.*

MISS TESMAN Good morning! Good morning, George!

TESMAN [*in open doorway*] Auntie Juju! Dear Auntie Juju!

Comes forward and shakes her hand.

You've come all the way out here! And so early! What?

MISS TESMAN Well, I had to make sure you'd settled in comfortably.

TESMAN But you can't have had a proper night's sleep.

MISS TESMAN Oh, never mind that.

TESMAN We were so sorry we couldn't give you a lift. But you saw how it was—Hedda had so much luggage—and she insisted on having it all with her.

---

1. Awarded him a doctoral degree.

MISS TESMAN   Yes, I've never seen so much luggage.

BERTHA [*to* TESMAN]   Shall I go and ask Madam if there's anything I can lend her a hand with?

TESMAN   Er—thank you, Bertha; no, you needn't bother. She says if she wants you for anything she'll ring.

BERTHA [*over to right*]   Oh. Very good.

TESMAN   Oh, Bertha—take this bag, will you?

BERTHA [*takes it*]   I'll put it in the attic.

Goes out into the hall.

TESMAN   Just fancy, Auntie Juju, I filled that whole bag with notes for my book. You know, it's really incredible what I've managed to find rooting through those archives. By Jove! Wonderful old things no one even knew existed—

MISS TESMAN   I'm sure you didn't waste a single moment of your honeymoon, George dear.

TESMAN   No, I think I can truthfully claim that. But, Auntie Juju, do take your hat off. Here. Let me untie it for you.

MISS TESMAN [*as he does so*]   Oh dear, oh dear! It's just as if you were still living at home with us.

TESMAN [*turns the hat in his hand and looks at it*]   I say! What a splendid new hat!

MISS TESMAN   I bought it for Hedda's sake.

TESMAN   For Hedda's sake? What?

MISS TESMAN   So that Hedda needn't be ashamed of me, in case we ever go for a walk together.

TESMAN [*pats her cheek*]   You still think of everything, don't you, Auntie Juju?

Puts the hat down on a chair by the table.

Come on, let's sit down here on the sofa. And have a little chat while we wait for Hedda.

They sit. She puts her parasol in the corner of the sofa.

MISS TESMAN [*clasps both his hands and looks at him*]   Oh, George, it's so wonderful to have you back, and be able to see you with my own eyes again! Poor dear Joachim's own son!

TESMAN   What about me! It's wonderful for me to see you again, Auntie Juju. You've been a mother to me. And a father, too.

MISS TESMAN   You'll always keep a soft spot in your heart for your old aunties, won't you, George dear?

TESMAN   I suppose Auntie Rena's no better? What?

MISS TESMAN   Alas, no. I'm afraid she'll never get better, poor dear. She's lying there just as she has all these years. Please God I may be allowed to keep her for a little longer. If I lose her I don't know what I'd do. Especially now I haven't you to look after.

TESMAN [*pats her on the back*]   There, there, there!

MISS TESMAN [*with a sudden change of mood*]   Oh but George, fancy

you being a married man! And to think it's you who've won Hedda
Gabler! The beautiful Hedda Gabler! Fancy! She was always so
surrounded by admirers.

TESMAN [*hums a little and smiles contentedly*]   Yes, I suppose there
are quite a few people in this town who wouldn't mind being in
my shoes. What?

MISS TESMAN   And what a honeymoon! Five months! Nearly six.

TESMAN   Well, I've done a lot of work, you know. All those archives
to go through. And I've had to read lots of books.

MISS TESMAN   Yes, dear, of course.

Lowers her voice confidentially.

But tell me, George—haven't you any—any extra little piece of
news to give me?

TESMAN   You mean, arising out of the honeymoon?

MISS TESMAN   Yes.

TESMAN   No, I don't think there's anything I didn't tell you in my
letters. My doctorate, of course—but I told you about that last
night, didn't I?

MISS TESMAN   Yes, yes, I didn't mean that kind of thing. I was just
wondering—are you—are you expecting—?

TESMAN   Expecting what?

MISS TESMAN   Oh, come on George, I'm your old aunt!

TESMAN   Well actually—yes, I am expecting something.

MISS TESMAN   I knew it!

TESMAN   You'll be happy to hear that before very long I expect to
become a professor.

MISS TESMAN   Professor?

TESMAN   I think I may say that the matter has been decided. But,
Auntie Juju, you know about this.

MISS TESMAN [*gives a little laugh*]   Yes, of course. I'd forgotten.

Changes her tone.

But we were talking about your honeymoon. It must have cost a
dreadful amount of money, George?

TESMAN   Oh well, you know, that big research grant I got helped a
good deal.

MISS TESMAN   But how on earth did you manage to make it do for
two?

TESMAN   Well, to tell the truth it was a bit tricky. What?

MISS TESMAN   Especially when one's traveling with a lady. A little
bird tells me that makes things very much more expensive.

TESMAN   Well, yes, of course it does make things a little more expensive. But Hedda has to do things in style, Auntie Juju. I mean,
she has to. Anything less grand wouldn't have suited her.

MISS TESMAN   No, no, I suppose not. A honeymoon abroad seems to
be the vogue nowadays. But tell me, have you had time to look
round the house?

TESMAN   You bet. I've been up since the crack of dawn.

MISS TESMAN   Well, what do you think of it?

TESMAN   Splendid. Absolutely splendid. I'm only wondering what we're going to do with those two empty rooms between that little one and Hedda's bedroom.

MISS TESMAN [*laughs slyly*]   Ah, George dear, I'm sure you'll manage to find some use for them—in time.

TESMAN   Yes, of course, Auntie Juju, how stupid of me. You're thinking of my books. What?

MISS TESMAN   Yes, yes, dear boy. I was thinking of your books.

TESMAN   You know, I'm so happy for Hedda's sake that we've managed to get this house. Before we became engaged she often used to say this was the only house in town she felt she could really bear to live in. It used to belong to Mrs. Falk—you know, the Prime Minister's widow.

MISS TESMAN   Fancy that! And what a stroke of luck it happened to come into the market. Just as you'd left on your honeymoon.

TESMAN   Yes, Auntie Juju, we've certainly had all the luck with us. What?

MISS TESMAN   But, George dear, the expense! It's going to make a dreadful hole in your pocket, all this.

TESMAN [*a little downcast*]   Yes, I—I suppose it will, won't it?

MISS TESMAN   Oh, George, really!

TESMAN   How much do you think it'll cost? Roughly, I mean? What?

MISS TESMAN   I can't possibly say till I see the bills.

TESMAN   Well, luckily Judge Brack's managed to get it on very favorable terms. He wrote and told Hedda so.

MISS TESMAN   Don't you worry, George dear. Anyway I've stood security for all the furniture and carpets.

TESMAN   Security? But dear, sweet Auntie Juju, how could you possibly stand security?

MISS TESMAN   I've arranged a mortgage on our annuity.

TESMAN [*jumps up*]   What? On your annuity? And—Auntie Rena's?

MISS TESMAN   Yes. Well, I couldn't think of any other way.

TESMAN [*stands in front of her*]   Auntie Juju, have you gone completely out of your mind? That annuity's all you and Auntie Rena have.

MISS TESMAN   All right, there's no need to get so excited about it. It's a pure formality, you know. Judge Brack told me so. He was so kind as to arrange it all for me. A pure formality; those were his very words.

TESMAN   I dare say. All the same—

MISS TESMAN   Anyway, you'll have a salary of your own now. And, good heavens, even if we did have to fork out a little—tighten our belts for a week or two—why, we'd be happy to do so for your sake.

TESMAN   Oh, Auntie Juju! Will you never stop sacrificing yourself for me?

MISS TESMAN [*gets up and puts her hands on his shoulders*]   What else have I to live for but to smooth your road a little, my dear boy? You've never had any mother or father to turn to. And now at last we've achieved our goal. I won't deny we've had our little difficulties now and then. But now, thank the good Lord, George dear, all your worries are past.

TESMAN   Yes, it's wonderful really how everything's gone just right for me.

MISS TESMAN   Yes! And the enemies who tried to bar your way have been struck down. They have been made to bite the dust. The man who was your most dangerous rival has had the mightiest fall. And now he's lying there in the pit he dug for himself, poor misguided creature.

TESMAN   Have you heard any news of Eilert? Since I went away?

MISS TESMAN   Only that he's said to have published a new book.

TESMAN   What! Eilert Loevborg? You mean—just recently? What?

MISS TESMAN   So they say. I don't imagine it can be of any value, do you? When your new book comes out, that'll be another story. What's it going to be about?

TESMAN   The domestic industries of Brabant[2] in the Middle Ages.

MISS TESMAN   Oh, George! The things you know about!

TESMAN   Mind you, it may be some time before I actually get down to writing it. I've made these very extensive notes, and I've got to file and index them first.

MISS TESMAN   Ah, yes! Making notes; filing and indexing; you've always been wonderful at that. Poor dear Joachim was just the same.

TESMAN   I'm looking forward so much to getting down to that. Especially now I've a home of my own to work in.

MISS TESMAN   And above all, now that you have the girl you set your heart on, George dear.

TESMAN [*embraces her*]   Oh, yes, Auntie Juju, yes! Hedda's the loveliest thing of all!

    Looks towards the doorway.

I think I hear her coming. What?

    HEDDA *enters the rear room from the left, and comes into the drawing room. She is a woman of twenty-nine. Distinguished, aristocratic face and figure. Her complexion is pale and opalescent. Her eyes are steel-gray, with an expression of cold, calm serenity. Her hair is of a handsome auburn color, but is not especially abundant. She is dressed in an elegant, somewhat loose-fitting morning gown.*

MISS TESMAN [*goes to greet her*]   Good morning, Hedda dear! Good morning!

HEDDA [*holds out her hand*]   Good morning, dear Miss Tesman. What an early hour to call. So kind of you.

MISS TESMAN [*seems somewhat embarrassed*]   And has the young bride slept well in her new home?

HEDDA   Oh—thank you, yes. Passably well

TESMAN [*laughs*]   Passably. I say, Hedda, that's good! When I jumped out of bed, you were sleeping like a top.

HEDDA   Yes. Fortunately. One has to accustom oneself to anything new, Miss Tesman. It takes time.

---

2. Prosperous duchy (1190–1477), now divided between Belgium and the Netherlands

Looks left.

Oh, that maid's left the french windows open. This room's flooded with sun.

MISS TESMAN [*goes towards the windows*]   Oh—let me close them.

HEDDA   No, no, don't do that. Tesman dear, draw the curtains. This light's blinding me.

TESMAN [*at the windows*]   Yes, yes, dear. There, Hedda, now you've got shade and fresh air.

HEDDA   This room needs fresh air. All these flowers— But my dear Miss Tesman, won't you take a seat?

MISS TESMAN   No, really not, thank you. I just wanted to make sure you have everything you need. I must see about getting back home. My poor dear sister will be waiting for me.

TESMAN   Be sure to give her my love, won't you? Tell her I'll run over and see her later today.

MISS TESMAN   Oh yes, I'll tell her that. Oh, George—

Fumbles in the pocket of her skirt.

I almost forgot. I've brought something for you.

TESMAN   What's that, Auntie Juju? What?

MISS TESMAN [*pulls out a flat package wrapped in newspaper and gives it to him*]   Open and see, dear boy.

TESMAN [*opens the package*]   Good heavens! Auntie Juju, you've kept them! Hedda, this is really very touching. What?

HEDDA [*by the what-nots, on the right*]   What is it, Tesman?

TESMAN   My old shoes! My slippers, Hedda!

HEDDA   Oh, them. I remember you kept talking about them on our honeymoon.

TESMAN   Yes, I missed them dreadfully.

Goes over to her.

Here, Hedda, take a look.

HEDDA [*goes away towards the stove*]   Thanks, I won't bother.

TESMAN [*follows her*]   Fancy, Hedda, Auntie Rena's embroidered them for me. Despite her being so ill. Oh, you can't imagine what memories they have for me.

HEDDA [*by the table*]   Not for me.

MISS TESMAN   No, Hedda's right there, George.

TESMAN   Yes, but I thought since she's one of the family now—

HEDDA [*interrupts*]   Tesman, we really can't go on keeping this maid.

MISS TESMAN   Not keep Bertha?

TESMAN   What makes you say that, dear? What?

HEDDA [*points*]   Look at that! She's left her old hat lying on the chair.

TESMAN [*appalled, drops his slippers on the floor*]   But, Hedda—!

HEDDA   Suppose someone came in and saw it?

TESMAN   But, Hedda—that's Auntie Juju's hat.

HEDDA   Oh?

MISS TESMAN [*picks up the hat*]   Indeed it's mine. And it doesn't happen to be old, Hedda dear.

HEDDA   I didn't look at it very closely, Miss Tesman.

MISS TESMAN [*tying on the hat*] As a matter of fact, it's the first time I've worn it. As the good Lord is my witness.

TESMAN   It's very pretty, too. Really smart.

MISS TESMAN   Oh, I'm afraid it's nothing much really.

Looks round.

My parasol? Ah, here it is.

Takes it.

This is mine, too.

Murmurs.

Not Bertha's.

TESMAN   A new hat and a new parasol! I say, Hedda, fancy that!

HEDDA   Very pretty and charming

TESMAN   Yes, isn't it? What? But Auntie Juju, take a good look at Hedda before you go. Isn't she pretty and charming?

MISS TESMAN   Dear boy, there's nothing new in that. Hedda's been a beauty ever since the day she was born.

Nods and goes right.

TESMAN [*follows her*] Yes, but have you noticed how strong and healthy she's looking? And how she's filled out since we went away?

MISS TESMAN [*stops and turns*] Filled out?

HEDDA [*walks across the room*] Oh, can't we forget it?

TESMAN   Yes, Auntie Juju—you can't see it so clearly with that dress on. But I've good reason to know—

HEDDA [*by the french windows, impatiently*] You haven't good reason to know anything.

TESMAN   It must have been the mountain air up there in the Tyrol—

HEDDA [*curtly, interrupts him*] I'm exactly the same as when I went away.

TESMAN   You keep on saying so. But you're not. I'm right, aren't I, Auntie Juju?

MISS TESMAN [*has folded her hands and is gazing at her*] She's beautiful—beautiful. Hedda is beautiful.

Goes over to HEDDA, *takes her head between her hands, draws it down and kisses her hair.*

God bless and keep you, Hedda Tesman. For George's sake.

HEDDA [*frees herself politely*] Oh—let me go, please.

MISS TEMAN [*quietly, emotionally*] I shall come and see you both every day.

TESMAN   Yes, Auntie Juju, please do. What?

MISS TESMAN   Good-bye! Good-bye!

> *She goes out into the hall.* TESMAN *follows her. The door remains open.* TESMAN *is heard sending his love to Aunt Rena and thanking* MISS TESMAN *for his slippers. Meanwhile* HEDDA *walks up and down the room raising her arms and clenching her fists as though in desperation. Then she throws aside the curtains from the french windows and stands there, looking out. A few moments later,* TESMAN *returns and closes the door behind him.*

TESMAN [*picks up his slippers from the floor*]   What are you looking at, Hedda?

HEDDA [*calm and controlled again*]   Only the leaves. They're so golden. And withered.

TESMAN [*wraps up the slippers and lays them on the table*]   Well, we're into September now.

HEDDA [*restless again*]   Yes. We're already into September.

TESMAN   Auntie Juju was behaving rather oddly, I thought, didn't you? Almost as though she was in church or something. I wonder what came over her. Any idea?

HEDDA   I hardly know her. Does she often act like that?

TESMAN   Not to the extent she did today.

HEDDA [*goes away from the french windows*]   Do you think she was hurt by what I said about the hat?

TESMAN   Oh, I don't think so. A little at first, perhaps—

HEDDA   But what a thing to do, throw her hat down in someone's drawing room. People don't do such things.

TESMAN   I'm sure Auntie Juju doesn't do it very often.

HEDDA   Oh well, I'll make it up with her.

TESMAN   Oh Hedda, would you?

HEDDA   When you see them this afternoon invite her to come out here this evening.

TESMAN   You bet I will! I say, there's another thing which would please her enormously.

HEDDA   Oh?

TESMAN   If you could bring yourself to call her Auntie Juju. For my sake, Hedda? What?

HEDDA   Oh no, really, Tesman, you mustn't ask me to do that. I've told you so once before. I'll try to call her Aunt Juliana. That's as far as I'll go.

TESMAN [*after a moment*]   I say, Hedda, is anything wrong? What?

HEDDA   I'm just looking at my old piano. It doesn't really go with all this.

TESMAN   As soon as I start getting my salary we'll see about changing it.

HEDDA   No, no, don't let's change it. I don't want to part with it. We can move it into that little room and get another one to put in here.

TESMAN [*a little downcast*]   Yes, we—might do that.

HEDDA [*picks up the bunch of flowers from the piano*]   These flowers weren't here when we arrived last night.

TESMAN   I expect Auntie Juju brought them.
HEDDA   Here's a card.

Takes it out and reads.

"Will come back later today." Guess who it's from?
TESMAN   No idea. Who? What?
HEDDA   It says: "Mrs. Elvsted."
TESMAN   No, really? Mrs. Elvsted! She used to be Miss Rysing, didn't she?
HEDDA   Yes. She was the one with that irritating hair she was always showing off. I hear she used to be an old flame of yours.
TESMAN   [*laughs*]   That didn't last long. Anyway, that was before I got to know you, Hedda. By Jove, fancy her being in town!
HEDDA   Strange she should call. I only knew her at school.
TESMAN   Yes, I haven't seen her for—oh, heaven knows how long. I don't know how she manages to stick it out up there in the north. What?
HEDDA   [*thinks for a moment, then says suddenly*]   Tell me, Tesman, doesn't he live somewhere up in those parts? You know—Eilert Loevborg?
TESMAN   Yes, that's right. So he does.

BERTHA *enters from the hall.*

BERTHA   She's here again, madam. The lady who came and left the flowers.

Points.

The ones you're holding.
HEDDA   Oh, is she? Well, show her in.

BERTHA *opens the door for* MRS. ELVSTED *and goes out.* MRS. ELVSTED *is a delicately built woman with gentle, attractive features. Her eyes are light blue, large, and somewhat prominent, with a frightened, questioning expression. Her hair is extremely fair, almost flaxen, and is exceptionally wavy and abundant. She is two or three years younger than* HEDDA. *She is wearing a dark visiting dress, in good taste but not quite in the latest fashion.*

HEDDA   [*goes cordially to greet her*]   Dear Mrs. Elvsted, good morning. How delightful to see you again after all this time.
MRS. ELVSTED   [*nervously, trying to control herself*]   Yes, it's many years since we met.
TESMAN   And since *we* met. What?
HEDDA   Thank you for your lovely flowers.
MRS. ELVSTED   Oh, please—I wanted to come yesterday afternoon. But they told me you were away—
TESMAN   You've only just arrived in town, then? What?
MRS. ELVSTED   I got here yesterday, around midday. Oh, I became

almost desperate when I heard you weren't here.

HEDDA   Desperate? Why?

TESMAN   My dear Mrs. Rysing—Elvsted—

HEDDA   There's nothing wrong, I hope?

MRS. ELVSTED   Yes, there is. And I don't know anyone else here whom I can turn to.

HEDDA [*puts the flowers down on the table*]   Come and sit with me on the sofa—

MRS. ELVSTED   Oh, I feel too restless to sit down.

HEDDA   You must. Come along, now.

She pulls MRS. ELVSTED *down on to the sofa and sits beside her.*

TESMAN   Well? Tell us, Mrs.—er—

HEDDA   Has something happened at home?

MRS. ELVSTED   Yes—that is, yes and no. Oh, I do hope you won't misunderstand me—

HEDDA   Then you'd better tell us the whole story, Mrs. Elvsted.

TESMAN   That's why you've come. What?

MRS. ELVSTED   Yes—yes, it is. Well, then—in case you don't already know—Eilert Loevborg is in town.

HEDDA   Loevborg here?

TESMAN   Eilert back in town? By Jove, Hedda, did you hear that?

HEDDA   Yes, of course I heard.

MRS. ELVSTED   He's been here a week. A whole week! In this city. Alone. With all those dreadful people—

HEDDA   But my dear Mrs. Elvsted, what concern is he of yours?

MRS. ELVSTED [*gives her a frightened look and says quickly*]   He's been tutoring the children.

HEDDA   Your children?

MRS. ELVSTED   My husband's. I have none.

HEDDA   Oh, you mean your stepchildren.

MRS. ELVSTED   Yes.

TESMAN [*gropingly*]   But was he sufficiently—I don't know how to put it—sufficiently regular in his habits to be suited to such a post? What?

MRS. ELVSTED   For the past two to three years he has been living irreproachably.

TESMAN   You don't say! By Jove, Hedda, hear that?

HEDDA   I hear.

MRS. ELVSTED   Quite irreproachably, I assure you. In every respect. All the same—in this big city—with money in his pockets—I'm so dreadfully frightened something may happen to him.

TESMAN   But why didn't he stay up there with you and your husband?

MRS. ELVSTED   Once his book had come out, he became restless.

TESMAN   Oh, yes—Auntie Juju said he'd brought out a new book.

MRS. ELVSTED   Yes, a big new book about the history of civilization. A kind of general survey. It came out a fortnight ago. Everyone's been buying it and reading it—it's created a tremendous stir—

TESMAN   Has it really? It must be something he's dug up, then.

MRS. ELVSTED   You mean from the old days?

TESMAN Yes.

MRS. ELVSTED No, he's written it all since he came to live with us.

TESMAN Well, that's splendid news, Hedda. Fancy that!

MRS. ELVSTED Oh, yes! If only he can go on like this!

HEDDA Have you met him since you came here?

MRS. ELVSTED No, not yet. I had such dreadful difficulty finding his address. But this morning I managed to track him down at last.

HEDDA [*looks searchingly at her*] I must say I find it a little strange that your husband—hm—

MRS. ELVSTED [*starts nervously*] My husband! What do you mean?

HEDDA That he should send you all the way here on an errand of this kind. I'm surprised he didn't come himself to keep an eye on his friend.

MRS. ELVSTED Oh, no, no—my husband hasn't the time. Besides, I— er wanted to do some shopping here.

HEDDA [*with a slight smile*] Ah. Well, that's different.

MRS. ELVSTED [*gets up quickly, restlessly*] Please, Mr. Tesman, I beg you—be kind to Eilert Loevborg if he comes here. I'm sure he will. I mean, you used to be such good friends in the old days. And you're both studying the same subject, as far as I can understand. You're in the same field, aren't you?

TESMAN Well, we used to be, anyway.

MRS. ELVSTED Yes—so I beg you earnestly, do please, please, keep an eye on him. Oh, Mr. Tesman, do promise me you will.

TESMAN I shall be only too happy to do so, Mrs. Rysing.

HEDDA Elvsted.

TESMAN I'll do everything for Eilert that lies in my power. You can rely on that.

MRS. ELVSTED Oh, how good and kind you are!

Presses his hands.

Thank you, thank you, thank you.

Frightened.

My husband's so fond of him, you see.

HEDDA [*gets up*] You'd better send him a note, Tesman. He may not come to you of his own accord.

TESMAN Yes, that'd probably be the best plan, Hedda. What?

HEDDA The sooner the better. Why not do it now?

MRS. ELVSTED [*pleadingly*] Oh yes, if only you would!

TESMAN I'll do it this very moment. Do you have his address, Mrs.— er—Elvsted?

MRS. ELVSTED Yes.

Takes a small piece of paper from her pocket and gives it to him.

TESMAN Good, good. Right, well I'll go inside and—

Looks round.

Where are my slippers? Oh yes, here.

Picks up the package and is about to go.

HEDDA   Try to sound friendly. Make it a nice long letter.
TESMAN   Right, I will.
MRS. ELVSTED   Please don't say anything about my having seen you.
TESMAN   Good heavens no, of course not. What?

Goes out through the rear room to the right.

HEDDA [*goes over to* MRS. ELVSTED, *smiles, and says softly*]   Well!
Now we've killed two birds with one stone.
MRS. ELVSTED   What do you mean?
HEDDA   Didn't you realize I wanted to get him out of the room?
MRS. ELVSTED   So that he could write the letter?
HEDDA   And so that I could talk to you alone.
MRS. ELVSTED [*confused*]   About this?
HEDDA   Yes, about this.
MRS. ELVSTED [*in alarm*]   But there's nothing more to tell, Mrs. Tes-
man. Really there isn't.
HEDDA   Oh, yes there is. There's a lot more. I can see that. Come
along, let's sit down and have a little chat.

She pushes MRS. ELVSTED *down into the armchair by the stove
and seats herself on one of the footstools.*

MRS. ELVSTED [*looks anxiously at her watch*]   Really, Mrs. Tesman,
I think I ought to be going now.
HEDDA   There's no hurry. Well? How are things at home?
MRS. ELVSTED   I'd rather not speak about that.
HEDDA   But my dear, you can tell me. Good heavens, we were at
school together.
MRS. ELVSTED   Yes, but you were a year senior to me. Oh, I used to
be terribly frightened of you in those days.
HEDDA   Frightened of me?
MRS. ELVSTED   Yes, terribly frightened. Whenever you met me on the
staircase you used to pull my hair.
HEDDA   No, did I?
MRS. ELVSTED   Yes. And once you said you'd burn it all off.
HEDDA   Oh, that was only in fun.
MRS. ELVSTED   Yes, but I was so silly in those days. And then after-
wards—I mean, we've drifted so far apart. Our backgrounds were so
different.
HEDDA   Well, now we must try to drift together again. Now listen.
When we were at school we used to call each other by our Christian
names—
MRS. ELVSTED   No, I'm sure you're mistaken.
HEDDA   I'm sure I'm not. I remember it quite clearly. Let's tell each
other our secrets, as we used to in the old days.

Moves closer on her footstool.

There, now.

Kisses her on the cheek.

You must call me Hedda.

MRS. ELVSTED [*squeezes her hands and pats them*] Oh you're so kind. I'm not used to people being so nice to me.

HEDDA Now, now, now. And I shall call you Tora, the way I used to.

MRS. ELVSTED My name is Thea.

HEDDA Yes, of course. Of course. I meant Thea.

Looks at her sympathetically.

So you're not used to kindness, Thea? In your own home?

MRS. ELVSTED Oh, if only I had a home! But I haven't. I've never had one.

HEDDA [*looks at her for a moment*] I thought that was it.

MRS. ELVSTED [*stares blankly and helplessly*] Yes—yes—yes.

HEDDA I can't remember exactly now, but didn't you first go to Mr. Elvsted as a housekeeper?

MRS. ELVSTED Governess, actually. But his wife—at the time, I mean —she was an invalid, and had to spend most of her time in bed. So I had to look after the house too.

HEDDA But in the end, you became mistress of the house.

MRS. ELVSTED [*sadly*] Yes, I did.

HEDDA Let me see. Roughly how long ago was that?

MRS. ELVSTED When I got married, you mean?

HEDDA Yes.

MRS. ELVSTED About five years.

HEDDA Yes; it must be about that.

MRS. ELVSTED Oh, those five years! Especially the last two or three. Oh, Mrs. Tesman, if you only knew—!

HEDDA [*slaps her hand gently*] Mrs. Tesman? Oh, Thea!

MRS. ELVSTED I'm sorry, I'll try to remember. Yes—if you had any idea—

HEDDA [*casually*] Eilert Loevborg's been up there too, for about three years, hasn't he?

MRS. ELVSTED [*looks at her uncertainly*] Eilert Loevborg? Yes, he has.

HEDDA Did you know him before? When you were here?

MRS. ELVSTED No, not really. That is—I knew him by name, of course.

HEDDA But up there, he used to visit you?

MRS. ELVSTED Yes, he used to come and see us every day. To give the children lessons. I found I couldn't do that as well as manage the house.

HEDDA I'm sure you couldn't. And your husband—? I suppose being a magistrate he has to be away from home a good deal?

MRS. ELVSTED Yes. You see, Mrs.—you see, Hedda, he has to cover the whole district.

HEDDA [*leans against the arm of* MRS. ELVSTED'S *chair*] Poor, pretty

little Thea! Now you must tell me the whole story. From beginning
to end.

MRS. ELVSTED   Well—what do you want to know?

HEDDA   What kind of a man is your husband, Thea? I mean, as a
person. Is he kind to you?

MRS. ELVSTED [*evasively*]   I'm sure he does his best to be.

HEDDA   I only wonder if he isn't too old for you. There's more than
twenty years between you, isn't there?

MRS. ELVSTED [*irritably*]   Yes, there's that too. Oh, there are so many
things. We're different in every way. We've nothing in common.
Nothing whatever.

HEDDA   But he loves you, surely? In his own way?

MRS. ELVSTED   Oh, I don't know. I think he just finds me useful. And
then I don't cost much to keep. I'm cheap.

HEDDA   Now you're being stupid.

MRS. ELVSTED [*shakes her head*]   It can't be any different. With him.
He doesn't love anyone except himself. And perhaps the children—
a little.

HEDDA   He must be fond of Eilert Loevborg, Thea.

MRS. ELVSTED [*looks at her*]   Eilert Loevborg? What makes you think
that?

HEDDA   Well, if he sends you all the way down here to look for him—

Smiles almost imperceptibly.

Besides, you said so yourself to Tesman.

MRS. ELVSTED [*with a nervous twitch*]   Did I? Oh yes, I suppose I
did.

Impulsively, but keeping her voice low.

Well, I might as well tell you the whole story. It's bound to come
out sooner or later.

HEDDA   But my dear Thea—?

MRS. ELVSTED   My husband had no idea I was coming here.

HEDDA   What? Your husband didn't know?

MRS. ELVSTED   No, of course not. As a matter of fact, he wasn't even
there. He was away at the assizes. Oh, I couldn't stand it any longer,
Hedda! I just couldn't. I'd be so dreadfully lonely up there now.

HEDDA   Go on.

MRS. ELVSTED   So I packed a few things. Secretly. And went.

HEDDA   Without telling anyone?

MRS. ELVSTED   Yes. I caught the train and came straight here.

HEDDA   But my dear Thea! How brave of you!

MRS. ELVSTED [*gets up and walks across the room*]   Well, what else
could I do?

HEDDA   But what do you suppose your husband will say when you
get back?

MRS. ELVSTED [*by the table, looks at her*]   Back there? To him?

HEDDA   Yes. Surely—?

MRS. ELVSTED   I shall never go back to him.

HEDDA [*gets up and goes closer*]   You mean you've left your home for good?

MRS. ELVSTED   Yes, I didn't see what else I could do.

HEDDA   But to do it so openly!

MRS. ELVSTED   Oh, it's no use trying to keep a thing like that secret.

HEDDA   But what do you suppose people will say?

MRS. ELVSTED   They can say what they like.

> *Sits sadly, wearily on the sofa.*

I had to do it.

HEDDA [*after a short silence*]   What do you intend to do now? How are you going to live?

MRS. ELVSTED   I don't know. I only know that I must live wherever Eilert Loevborg is. If I am to go on living.

HEDDA [*moves a chair from the table, sits on it near* MRS. ELVSTED *and strokes her hands*]   Tell me, Thea, how did this—friendship between you and Eilert Loevborg begin?

MRS. ELVSTED   Oh, it came about gradually. I developed a kind of—power over him.

HEDDA   Oh?

MRS. ELVSTED   He gave up his old habits. Not because I asked him to. I'd never have dared to do that. I suppose he just noticed I didn't like that kind of thing. So he gave it up.

HEDDA [*hides a smile*]   So you've made a new man of him. Clever little Thea!

MRS. ELVSTED   Yes—anyway, he says I have. And he's made a—sort of—real person of me. Taught me to think—and to understand all kinds of things.

HEDDA   Did he give you lessons too?

MRS. ELVSTED   Not exactly lessons. But he talked to me. About—oh, you've no idea—so many things! And then he let me work with him. Oh, it was wonderful. I was so happy to be allowed to help him.

HEDDA   Did he allow you to help him!

MRS. ELVSTED   Yes. Whenever he wrote anything we always—did it together.

HEDDA   Like good pals?

MRS. ELVSTED [*eagerly*]   Pals! Yes—why, Hedda, that's exactly the word he used! Oh, I ought to feel so happy. But I can't. I don't know if it will last.

HEDDA   You don't seem very sure of him.

MRS. ELVSTED [*sadly*]   Something stands between Eilert Loevborg and me. The shadow of another woman.

HEDDA   Who can that be?

MRS. ELVSTED   I don't know. Someone he used to be friendly with in—in the old days. Someone he's never been able to forget.

HEDDA   What has he told you about her?

MRS. ELVSTED   Oh, he only mentioned her once, casually.

HEDDA   Well! What did he say?

MRS. ELVSTED   He said when he left her she tried to shoot him with a pistol.

HEDDA [*cold, controlled*]   What nonsense. People don't do such things. The kind of people we know.

MRS. ELVSTED   No. I think it must have been that red-haired singer he used to—

HEDDA   Ah yes, very probably.

MRS. ELVSTED   I remember they used to say she always carried a loaded pistol.

HEDDA   Well then, it must be her.

MRS. ELVSTED   But, Hedda, I hear she's come back, and is living here. Oh, I'm so desperate—!

HEDDA [*glances towards the rear room*]   Ssh! Tesman's coming.

> *Gets up and whispers.*

Thea, we mustn't breathe a word about this to anyone.

MRS. ELVSTED [*jumps up*]   Oh, no, no! Please don't!

> GEORGE TESMAN *appears from the right in the rear room with a letter in his hand, and comes into the drawing room.*

TESMAN   Well, here's my little epistle all signed and sealed.

HEDDA   Good. I think Mrs. Elvsted wants to go now. Wait a moment —I'll see you as far as the garden gate.

TESMAN   Er—Hedda, do you think Bertha could deal with this?

HEDDA [*takes the letter*]   I'll give her instructions.

> BERTHA *enters from the hall.*

BERTHA   Judge Brack is here and asks if he may pay his respects to Madam and the Doctor.

HEDDA   Yes, ask him to be so good as to come in. And—wait a moment —drop this letter in the post box.

BERTHA [*takes the letter*] Very good, madam.

> *She opens the door for* JUDGE BRACK, *and goes out.* JUDGE BRACK *is forty-five; rather short, but well-built, and elastic in his movements. He has a roundish face with an aristocratic profile. His hair, cut short, is still almost black, and is carefully barbered. Eyes lively and humorous. Thick eyebrows. His moustache is also thick, and is trimmed square at the ends. He is wearing outdoor clothes which are elegant but a little too youthful for him. He has a monocle in one eye; now and then he lets it drop.*

BRACK [*hat in hand, bows*]   May one presume to call so early?

HEDDA   One may presume.

TESMAN [*shakes his hand*]   You're welcome here any time. Judge Brack—Mrs. Rysing.

> HEDDA *sighs.*

BRACK [*bows*]   Ah—charmed—

HEDDA [*looks at him and laughs*]   What fun to be able to see you by
daylight for once, Judge.
BRACK   Do I look—different?
HEDDA   Yes. A little younger, I think.
BRACK   Obliged.
TESMAN   Well, what do you think of Hedda? What? Doesn't she look
well? Hasn't she filled out—?
HEDDA   Oh, do stop it. You ought to be thanking Judge Brack for all
the inconvenience he's put himself to—
BRACK   Nonsense, it was a pleasure—
HEDDA   You're a loyal friend. But my other friend is pining to get
away. Au revoir, Judge. I won't be a minute.

> *Mutual salutations.* MRS. ELVSTED *and* HEDDA *go out through
> the hall.*

BRACK   Well, is your wife satisfied with everything?
TESMAN   Yes, we can't thank you enough. That is—we may have to
shift one or two things around, she tells me. And we're short of one
or two little items we'll have to purchase.
BRACK   Oh? Really?
TESMAN   But you mustn't worry your head about that. Hedda says
she'll get what's needed. I say, why don't we sit down? What?
BRACK   Thanks, just for a moment.

> *Sits at the table.*

There's something I'd like to talk to you about, my dear Tesman.
TESMAN   Oh? Ah yes, of course.

> *Sits.*

After the feast comes the reckoning. What?
BRACK   Oh, never mind about the financial side—there's no hurry
about that. Though I could wish we'd arranged things a little less
palatially.
TESMAN   Good heavens, that'd never have done. Think of Hedda, my
dear chap. You know her. I couldn't possibly ask her to live like a
suburban housewife.
BRACK   No, no—that's just the problem.
TESMAN   Anyway, it can't be long now before my nomination[3] comes
through.
BRACK   Well, you know, these things often take time.
TESMAN   Have you heard any more news? What?
BRACK   Nothing definite.

> *Changing the subject.*

Oh, by the way, I have one piece of news for you.
TESMAN   What?

---

3. To a professorship at the university.

BRACK   Your old friend Eilert Loevborg is back in town.

TESMAN   I know that already.

BRACK   Oh? How did you hear that?

TESMAN   She told me. That lady who went out with Hedda.

BRACK   I see. What was her name? I didn't catch it.

TESMAN   Mrs. Elvsted.

BRACK   Oh, the magistrate's wife. Yes, Loevborg's been living up near them, hasn't he?

TESMAN   I'm delighted to hear he's become a decent human being again.

BRACK   Yes, so they say.

TESMAN   I gather he's published a new book, too. What?

BRACK   Indeed he has.

TESMAN   I hear it's created rather a stir.

BRACK   Quite an unusual stir.

TESMAN   I say, isn't that splendid news! He's such a gifted chap— and I was afraid he'd gone to the dogs for good.

BRACK   Most people thought he had.

TESMAN   But I can't think what he'll do now. How on earth will he manage to make ends meet? What?

As he speaks his last words, HEDDA *enters from the hall.*

HEDDA   [*to* BRACK, *laughs slightly scornfully*]   Tesman is always worrying about making ends meet.

TESMAN   We were talking about poor Eilert Loevborg, Hedda dear.

HEDDA   [*gives him a quick look*]   Oh, were you?

Sits in the armchair by the stove and asks casually.

Is he in trouble?

TESMAN   Well, he must have run through his inheritance long ago by now. And he can't write a new book every year. What? So I'm wondering what's going to become of him.

BRACK   I may be able to enlighten you there.

TESMAN   Oh?

BRACK   You mustn't forget he has relatives who wield a good deal of influence.

TESMAN   Relatives? Oh, they've quite washed their hands of him, I'm afraid.

BRACK   They used to regard him as the hope of the family.

TESMAN   Used to, yes. But he's put an end to that.

HEDDA   Who knows?

With a little smile.

I hear the Elvsteds have made a new man of him.

BRACK   And then this book he's just published—

TESMAN   Well, let's hope they find something for him. I've just written him a note. Oh, by the way, Hedda, I asked him to come over and see us this evening.

BRACK   But my dear chap, you're coming to me this evening. My bachelor party. You promised me last night when I met you at the boat.

HEDDA   Had you forgotten, Tesman?

TESMAN   Good heavens, yes, I'd quite forgotten.

BRACK   Anyway, you can be quite sure he won't turn up here.

TESMAN   Why do you think that? What?

BRACK   [*a little unwillingly, gets up and rests his hands on the back of his chair*]   My dear Tesman—and you, too, Mrs. Tesman—there's something I feel you ought to know.

TESMAN   Concerning Eilert?

BRACK   Concerning him and you.

TESMAN   Well, my dear Judge, tell us, please!

BRACK   You must be prepared for your nomination not to come through quite as quickly as you hope and expect.

TESMAN   [*jumps up uneasily*]   Is anything wrong? What?

BRACK   There's a possibility that the appointment may be decided by competition—

TESMAN   Competition! By Jove, Hedda, fancy that!

HEDDA   [*leans further back in her chair*]   Ah! How interesting!

TESMAN   But who else—? I say, you don't mean—?

BRACK   Exactly. By competition with Eilert Loevborg.

TESMAN   [*clasps his hands in alarm*]   No, no, but this is inconceivable! It's absolutely impossible! What?

BRACK   Hm. We may find it'll happen, all the same.

TESMAN   No, but—Judge Brack, they couldn't be so inconsiderate towards me!

Waves his arms.

I mean, by Jove, I—I'm a married man! It was on the strength of this that Hedda and I *got* married! We ran up some pretty hefty debts. And borrowed money from Auntie Juju! I mean, good heavens, they practically promised me the appointment. What?

BRACK   Well, well, I'm sure you'll get it. But you'll have to go through a competition.

HEDDA   [*motionless in her armchair*]   How exciting, Tesman. It'll be a kind of duel, by Jove.

TESMAN   My dear Hedda, how can you take it so lightly?

HEDDA   [*as before*]   I'm not. I can't wait to see who's going to win.

BRACK   In any case, Mrs. Tesman, it's best you should know how things stand. I mean before you commit yourself to these little items I hear you're threatening to purchase.

HEDDA   I can't allow this to alter my plans.

BRACK   Indeed? Well, that's your business. Good-bye.

To TESMAN.

I'll come and collect you on the way home from my afternoon walk.

TESMAN   Oh, yes, yes. I'm sorry, I'm all upside down just now.

HEDDA   [*lying in her chair, holds out her hand*]   Good-bye, Judge. See you this afternoon.

BRACK   Thank you. Good-bye, good-bye.

TESMAN [*sees him to the door*] Good-bye, my dear Judge. You will excuse me, won't you?

JUDGE BRACK *goes out through the hall.*

TESMAN [*pacing up and down*] Oh, Hedda! One oughtn't to go plunging off on wild adventures. What?

HEDDA [*looks at him and smiles*] Like you're doing?

TESMAN Yes. I mean, there's no denying it, it was a pretty big adventure to go off and get married and set up house merely on expectation.

HEDDA Perhaps you're right.

TESMAN Well, anyway, we have our home, Hedda. By Jove, yes. The home we dreamed of. And set our hearts on. What?

HEDDA [*gets up slowly, wearily*] You agreed that we should enter society. And keep open house. That was the bargain.

TESMAN Yes. Good heavens, I was looking forward to it all so much. To seeing you play hostess to a select circle. By Jove! What? Ah, well, for the time being we shall have to make do with each other's company, Hedda. Perhaps have Auntie Juju in now and then. Oh dear, this wasn't at all what you had in mind—

HEDDA I won't be able to have a liveried footman. For a start.

TESMAN Oh no, we couldn't possibly afford a footman.

HEDDA And that thoroughbred horse you promised me—

TESMAN [*fearfully*] Thoroughbred horse!

HEDDA I mustn't even think of that now.

TESMAN Heaven forbid!

HEDDA [*walks across the room*] Ah, well. I still have one thing left to amuse myself with.

TESMAN [*joyfully*] Thank goodness for that. What's that, Hedda? What?

HEDDA [*in the open doorway, looks at him with concealed scorn*] My pistols, George darling.

TESMAN [*alarmed*] Pistols!

HEDDA [*her eyes cold*] General Gabler's pistols.

She goes into the rear room and disappears.

TESMAN [*runs to the doorway and calls after her*] For heaven's sake, Hedda dear, don't touch those things. They're dangerous. Hedda— please—for my sake! What?

Act 2

The same as in Act One, except that the piano has been removed and an elegant little writing table, with a bookcase, stands in its place. By the sofa on the left a smaller table has been placed. Most of the flowers have been removed. MRS. ELVSTED's bouquet stands on the larger table, downstage. It is afternoon.

HEDDA, *dressed to receive callers, is alone in the room. She is*

*standing by the open french windows, loading a revolver. The pair
to it is lying in an open pistol case on the writing table.*

HEDDA [*looks down into the garden and calls*] Good afternoon,
Judge.

BRACK [*in the distance, below*] Afternoon, Mrs. Tesman.

HEDDA [*raises the pistol and takes aim*] I'm going to shoot you,
Judge Brack.

BRACK [*shouts from below*] No, no, no! Don't aim that thing at me!

HEDDA This'll teach you to enter houses by the back door.

Fires.

BRACK [*below*] Have you gone completely out of your mind?

HEDDA Oh dear! Did I hit you?

BRACK [*still outside*] Stop playing these silly tricks.

HEDDA All right, Judge. Come along in.

JUDGE BRACK, *dressed for a bachelor party, enters through the
french windows. He has a light overcoat on his arm.*

BRACK For God's sake! Haven't you stopped fooling around with
those things yet? What are you trying to hit?

HEDDA Oh, I was just shooting at the sky.

BRACK [*takes the pistol gently from her hand*] By your leave, ma'am.

Looks at it.

Ah, yes—I know this old friend well.

Looks around.

Where's the case? Oh, yes.

Puts the pistol in the case and closes it.

That's enough of that little game for today.

HEDDA Well, what on earth *am* I to do?

BRACK You haven't had any visitors?

HEDDA [*closes the french windows*] Not one. I suppose the best
people are all still in the country.

BRACK Your husband isn't home yet?

HEDDA [*locks the pistol away in a drawer of the writing table*] No.
The moment he'd finished eating he ran off to his aunties. He wasn't
expecting you so early.

BRACK Ah, why didn't I think of that? How stupid of me.

HEDDA [*turns her head and looks at him*] Why stupid?

BRACK I'd have come a little sooner.

HEDDA [*walks across the room*] There'd have been no one to receive
you. I've been in my room since lunch, dressing.

BRACK You haven't a tiny crack in the door through which we might
have negotiated?

HEDDA   You forgot to arrange one.

BRACK   Another stupidity.

HEDDA   Well, we'll have to sit down here. And wait. Tesman won't be back for some time.

BRACK   Sad. Well, I'll be patient.

> HEDDA *sits on the corner of the sofa.* BRACK *puts his coat over the back of the nearest chair and seats himself, keeping his hat in his hand. Short pause. They look at each other.*

HEDDA   Well?

BRACK   [*in the same tone of voice*]   Well?

HEDDA   I asked first.

BRACK   [*leans forward slightly*]   Yes, well, now we can enjoy a nice, cozy little chat—Mrs. Hedda.

HEDDA   [*leans further back in her chair*]   It seems such ages since we had a talk. I don't count last night or this morning.

BRACK   You mean: *à deux*?

HEDDA   Mm—yes. That's roughly what I meant.

BRACK   I've been longing so much for you to come home.

HEDDA   So have I.

BRACK   You? Really, Mrs. Hedda? And I thought you were having such a wonderful honeymoon.

HEDDA   Oh, yes. Wonderful!

BRACK   But your husband wrote such ecstatic letters.

HEDDA   He! Oh, yes! He thinks life has nothing better to offer than rooting around in libraries and copying old pieces of parchment, or whatever it is he does.

BRACK   [*a little maliciously*]   Well, that *is* his life. Most of it, anyway.

HEDDA   Yes, I know. Well, it's all right for him. But for me! Oh no, my dear Judge. I've been bored to death.

BRACK   [*sympathetically*]   Do you mean that? Seriously?

HEDDA   Yes. Can you imagine? Six whole months without ever meeting a single person who was one of us, and to whom I could talk about the kind of things we talk about.

BRACK   Yes, I can understand. I'd miss that, too.

HEDDA   That wasn't the worst, though.

BRACK   What was?

HEDDA   Having to spend every minute of one's life with—with the same person.

BRACK   [*nods*]   Yes. What a thought! Morning; noon; and—

HEDDA   [*coldly*]   As I said: every minute of one's life.

BRACK   I stand corrected. But dear Tesman is such a clever fellow, I should have thought one ought to be able—

HEDDA   Tesman is only interested in one thing, my dear Judge. His special subject.

BRACK   True.

HEDDA   And people who are only interested in one thing don't make the most amusing company. Not for long, anyway.

BRACK   Not even when they happen to be the person one loves?

HEDDA   Oh, don't use that sickly, stupid word.

BRACK   [*starts*]   But, Mrs. Hedda—!

HEDDA [*half laughing, half annoyed*] You just try it, Judge. Listening to the history of civilization morning, noon and—

BRACK [*corrects her*] Every minute of one's life.

HEDDA All right. Oh, and those domestic industries of Brabant in the Middle Ages! That really is beyond the limit.

BRACK [*looks at her searchingly*] But, tell me—if you feel like this why on earth did you—? Ha—

HEDDA Why on earth did I marry George Tesman?

BRACK If you like to put it that way.

HEDDA Do you think it so very strange?

BRACK Yes—and no, Mrs. Hedda.

HEDDA I'd danced myself tired, Judge. I felt my time was up—

> *Gives a slight shudder.*

No, I mustn't say that. Or even think it.

BRACK You've no rational cause to think it.

HEDDA Oh—cause, cause—

> *Looks searchingly at him.*

After all, George Tesman—well, I mean, he's a very respectable man.

BRACK Very respectable, sound as a rock. No denying that.

HEDDA And there's nothing exactly ridiculous about him. Is there?

BRACK Ridiculous? N-no, I wouldn't say that.

HEDDA Mm. He's very clever at collecting material and all that, isn't he? I mean, he may go quite far in time.

BRACK [*looks at her a little uncertainly*] I thought you believed, like everyone else, that he would become a very prominent man.

HEDDA [*looks tired*] Yes, I did. And when he came and begged me on his bended knees to be allowed to love and to cherish me, I didn't see why I shouldn't let him.

BRACK No, well—if one looks at it like that—

HEDDA It was more than my other admirers were prepared to do, Judge dear.

BRACK [*laughs*] Well, I can't answer for the others. As far as I myself am concerned, you know I've always had a considerable respect for the institution of marriage. As an institution.

HEDDA [*lightly*] Oh, I've never entertained any hopes of you.

BRACK All I want is to have a circle of friends whom I can trust, whom I can help with advice or—or by any other means, and into whose houses I may come and go as a—trusted friend.

HEDDA Of the husband?

BRACK [*bows*] Preferably, to be frank, of the wife. And of the husband too, of course. Yes, you know, this kind of—triangle is a delightful arrangement for all parties concerned.

HEDDA Yes, I often longed for a third person while I was away. Oh, those hours we spent alone in railway compartments—

BRACK Fortunately your honeymoon is now over.

HEDDA [*shakes her head*] There's a long, long way still to go. I've only reached a stop on the line.

BRACK   Why not jump out and stretch your legs a little, Mrs. Hedda?
HEDDA   I'm not the jumping sort.
BRACK   Aren't you?
HEDDA   No. There's always someone around who—
BRACK   [*laughs*]   Who looks at one's legs?
HEDDA   Yes. Exactly.
BRACK   Well, but surely—
HEDDA   [*with a gesture of rejection*]   I don't like it. I'd rather stay where I am. Sitting in the compartment. *À deux.*
BRACK   But suppose a third person were to step into the compartment?
HEDDA   That would be different.
BRACK   A trusted friend—someone who understood—
HEDDA   And was lively and amusing—
BRACK   And interested in—more subjects than one—
HEDDA   [*sighs audibly*]   Yes, that'd be a relief.
BRACK   [*hears the front door open and shut*]   The triangle is completed.
HEDDA   [*half under breath*]   And the train goes on.

> GEORGE TESMAN, *in gray walking dress with a soft felt hat, enters from the hall. He has a number of paper-covered books under his arm and in his pockets.*

TESMAN   [*goes over to the table by the corner sofa*]   Phew! It's too hot to be lugging all this around.

> *Puts the books down.*

I'm positively sweating, Hedda. Why, hullo, hullo! You here already, Judge? What? Bertha didn't tell me.
BRACK   [*gets up*]   I came in through the garden.
HEDDA   What are all those books you've got there?
TESMAN   [*stands glancing through them*]   Oh, some new publications dealing with my special subject. I had to buy them.
HEDDA   Your special subject?
BRACK   His special subject, Mrs. Tesman.

> BRACK *and* HEDDA *exchange a smile.*

HEDDA   Haven't you collected enough material on your special subject?
TESMAN   My dear Hedda, one can never have too much. One must keep abreast of what other people are writing.
HEDDA   Yes. Of course.
TESMAN   [*rooting among the books*]   Look—I bought a copy of Eilert Loevborg's new book, too.

> *Holds it out to her.*

Perhaps you'd like to have a look at it, Hedda? What?
HEDDA   No, thank you. Er—yes, perhaps I will, later.
TESMAN   I glanced through it on my way home.

BRACK   What's your opinion—as a specialist on the subject?

TESMAN   I'm amazed how sound and balanced it is. He never used to write like that.

Gathers his books together.

Well, I must get down to these at once. I can hardly wait to cut the pages. Oh, I've got to change, too.

To BRACK.

We don't have to be off just yet, do we? What?

BRACK   Heavens, no. We've plenty of time yet.

TESMAN   Good, I needn't hurry, then.

Goes with his books, but stops and turns in the doorway.

Oh, by the way, Hedda, Auntie Juju won't be coming to see you this evening.

HEDDA   Won't she? Oh—the hat, I suppose.

TESMAN   Good heavens, no. How could you think such a thing of Auntie Juju? Fancy—! No, Auntie Rena's very ill.

HEDDA   She always is.

TESMAN   Yes, but today she's been taken really bad.

HEDDA   Oh, then it's quite understandable that the other one should want to stay with her. Well, I shall have to swallow my disappointment.

TESMAN   You can't imagine how happy Auntie Juju was in spite of everything. At your looking so well after the honeymoon!

HEDDA   [*half beneath her breath, as she rises*]   Oh, these everlasting aunts!

TESMAN   What?

HEDDA   [*goes over to the french windows*]   Nothing.

TESMAN   Oh. All right.

Goes into the rear room and out of sight.

BRACK   What was that about the hat?

HEDDA   Oh, something that happened with Miss Tesman this morning. She'd put her hat down on a chair.

Looks at him and smiles.

And I pretended to think it was the servant's.

BRACK   [*shakes his head*]   But my dear Mrs. Hedda, how could you do such a thing? To that poor old lady?

HEDDA   [*nervously, walking across the room*]   Sometimes a mood like that hits me. And I can't stop myself.

Throws herself down in the armchair by the stove.

Oh, I don't know how to explain it.

BRACK [*behind her chair*]   You're not really happy. That's the answer.

HEDDA [*stares ahead of her*]   Why on earth should I be happy? Can you give me a reason?

BRACK   Yes. For one thing you've got the home you always wanted.

HEDDA [*looks at him*]   You really believe that story?

BRACK   You mean it isn't true?

HEDDA   Oh, yes, it's partly true.

BRACK   Well?

HEDDA   It's true I got Tesman to see me home from parties last summer—

BRACK   It was a pity my home lay in another direction.

HEDDA   Yes. Your interests lay in another direction, too.

BRACK [*laughs*]   That's naughty of you, Mrs. Hedda. But to return to you and Tesman—

HEDDA   Well, we walked past this house one evening. And poor Tesman was fidgeting in his boots trying to find something to talk about. I felt sorry for the great scholar—

BRACK [*smiles incredulously*]   Did you? Hm.

HEDDA   Yes, honestly I did. Well, to help him out of his misery, I happened to say quite frivolously how much I'd love to live in this house.

BRACK   Was that all?

HEDDA   That evening, yes.

BRACK   But—afterwards?

HEDDA   Yes. My little frivolity had its consequences, my dear Judge.

BRACK   Our little frivolities do. Much too often, unfortunately.

HEDDA   Thank you. Well, it was our mutual admiration for the late Prime Minister's house that brought George Tesman and me together on common ground. So we got engaged, and we got married, and we went on our honeymoon, and— Ah well, Judge, I've —made my bed and I must lie in it, I was about to say.

BRACK   How utterly fantastic! And you didn't really care in the least about the house?

HEDDA   God knows I didn't.

BRACK   Yes, but now that we've furnished it so beautifully for you?

HEDDA   Ugh—all the rooms smell of lavender and dried roses. But perhaps Auntie Juju brought that in.

BRACK [*laughs*]   More likely the Prime Minister's widow, rest her soul.

HEDDA   Yes, it's got the odor of death about it. It reminds me of the flowers one has worn at a ball—the morning after.

> *Clasps her hands behind her neck, leans back in the chair and looks up at him.*

Oh, my dear Judge, you've no idea how hideously bored I'm going to be out here.

BRACK   Couldn't you find some kind of occupation, Mrs. Hedda? Like your husband?

HEDDA   Occupation? That'd interest me?

BRACK   Well—preferably.

HEDDA   God knows what. I've often thought—

Breaks off.

No, that wouldn't work either.

BRACK   Who knows? Tell me about it.

HEDDA   I was thinking—if I could persuade Tesman to go into politics, for example.

BRACK   [*laughs*]   Tesman! No, honestly, I don't think he's quite cut
out to be a politician.

HEDDA   Perhaps not. But if I could persuade him to have a go at it?

BRACK   What satisfaction would that give you? If he turned out to
be no good? Why do you want to make him do that?

HEDDA   Because I'm bored.

After a moment.

You feel there's absolutely no possibility of Tesman becoming
Prime Minister, then?

BRACK   Well, you know, Mrs. Hedda, for one thing he'd have to be
pretty well off before he could become that.

HEDDA   [*gets up impatiently*]   There you are!

Walks across the room.

It's this wretched poverty that makes life so hateful. And ludicrous.
Well, it is!

BRACK   I don't think that's the real cause.

HEDDA   What is, then?

BRACK   Nothing really exciting has ever happened to you.

HEDDA   Nothing serious, you mean?

BRACK   Call it that if you like. But now perhaps it may.

HEDDA   [*tosses her head*]   Oh, you're thinking of this competition for
that wretched professorship? That's Tesman's affair. I'm not going
to waste my time worrying about that.

BRACK   Very well, let's forget about that then. But suppose you were
to find yourself faced with what people call—to use the conventional phrase—the most solemn of human responsibilities?

Smiles.

A new responsibility, little Mrs. Hedda.

HEDDA   [*angrily*]   Be quiet! Nothing like that's going to happen.

BRACK   [*warily*]   We'll talk about it again in a year's time. If not
earlier.

HEDDA   [*curtly*]   I've no leanings in that direction, Judge. I don't want
any—responsibilities.

BRACK   But surely you must feel some inclination to make use of that
—natural talent which every woman—

HEDDA   [*over by the french windows*]   Oh, be quiet, I say! I often
think there's only one thing for which I have any natural talent.

BRACK   [*goes closer*]   And what is that, if I may be so bold as to ask?

HEDDA [*stands looking out*] For boring myself to death. Now you know.

> *Turns, looks toward the rear room and laughs.*

Talking of boring, here comes the Professor.

BRACK [*quietly, warningly*] Now, now, now, Mrs. Hedda!

> GEORGE TESMAN, *in evening dress, with gloves and hat in his hand, enters through the rear room from the right.*

TESMAN Hedda, hasn't any message come from Eilert? What?

HEDDA No.

TESMAN Ah, then we'll have him here presently. You wait and see.

BRACK You really think he'll come?

TESMAN Yes, I'm almost sure he will. What you were saying about him this morning is just gossip.

BRACK Oh?

TESMAN Yes. Auntie Juju said she didn't believe he'd ever dare to stand in my way again. Fancy that!

BRACK Then everything in the garden's lovely.

TESMAN [*puts his hat, with his gloves in it, on a chair, right*] Yes, but you really must let me wait for him as long as possible.

BRACK We've plenty of time. No one'll be turning up at my place before seven or half past.

TESMAN Ah, then we can keep Hedda company a little longer. And see if he turns up. What?

HEDDA [*picks up* BRACK'S *coat and hat and carries them over to the corner sofa*] And if the worst comes to the worst, Mr. Loevborg can sit here and talk to me.

BRACK [*offering to take his things from her*] No, please. What do you mean by "if worst comes to worst"?

HEDDA If he doesn't want to go with you and Tesman.

TESMAN [*looks doubtfully at her*] I say, Hedda, do you think it'll be all right for him to stay here with you? What? Remember Auntie Juju isn't coming.

HEDDA Yes, but Mrs. Elvsted is. The three of us can have a cup of tea together.

TESMAN Ah, that'll be all right then.

BRACK [*smiles*] It's probably the safest solution as far as he's concerned.

HEDDA Why?

BRACK My dear Mrs. Tesman, you always say of my little bachelor parties that they should be attended only by men of the strongest principles.

HEDDA But Mr. Loevborg is a man of principle now. You know what they say about a reformed sinner—

> BERTHA *enters from the hall.*

BERTHA Madam, there's a gentleman here who wants to see you—

HEDDA Ask him to come in.

TESMAN [*quietly*] I'm sure it's him. By Jove. Fancy that!

EILERT LOEVBORG *enters from the hall. He is slim and lean, of the same age as* TESMAN, *but looks older and somewhat haggard. His hair and beard are of a blackish-brown; his face is long and pale, but with a couple of reddish patches on his cheekbones. He is dressed in an elegant and fairly new black suit, and carries black gloves and a top hat in his hand. He stops just inside the door and bows abruptly. He seems somewhat embarrassed.*

TESMAN [*goes over and shakes his hand*] My dear Eilert! How grand to see you again after all these years!

EILERT LOEVBORG [*speaks softly*] It was good of you to write, George.

Goes nearer to HEDDA.

May I shake hands with you, too, Mrs. Tesman?

HEDDA [*accepts his hand*] Delighted to see you, Mr. Loevborg.

With a gesture.

I don't know if you two gentlemen—

LOEVBORG [*bows slightly*] Judge Brack, I believe.

BRACK [*also with a slight bow*] Correct. We—met some years ago—

TESMAN [*puts his hands on* LOEVBORG'S *shoulders*] Now you're to treat this house just as though it were your own home, Eilert. Isn't that right, Hedda? I hear you've decided to settle here again? What?

LOEVBORG Yes, I have.

TESMAN Quite understandable. Oh, by the bye—I've just bought your new book. Though to tell the truth I haven't found time to read it yet.

LOEVBORG You needn't bother.

TESMAN Oh? Why?

LOEVBORG There's nothing much in it.

TESMAN By Jove, fancy hearing that from you!

BRACK But everyone's praising it.

LOEVBORG That was exactly what I wanted to happen. So I only wrote what I knew everyone would agree with.

BRACK Very sensible.

TESMAN Yes, but my dear Eilert—

LOEVBORG I want to try to re-establish myself. To begin again—from the beginning.

TESMAN [*a little embarrassed*] Yes, I—er—suppose you do. What?

LOEVBORG [*smiles, puts down his hat and takes a package wrapped in paper from his coat pocket*] But when this gets published—George Tesman—read it. This is my real book. The one in which I have spoken with my own voice.

TESMAN Oh, really? What's it about?

LOEVBORG It's the sequel.

TESMAN Sequel? To what?

LOEVBORG To the other book.

TESMAN   The one that's just come out?

LOEVBORG   Yes.

TESMAN   But my dear Eilert, that covers the subject right up to the present day.

LOEVBORG   It does. But this is about the future.

TESMAN   The future! But, I say, we don't know anything about that.

LOEVBORG   No. But there are one or two things that need to be said about it.

Opens the package.

Here, have a look.

TESMAN   Surely that's not your handwriting?

LOEVBORG   I dictated it.

Turns the pages.

It's in two parts. The first deals with the forces that will shape our civilization.

Turns further on towards the end.

And the second indicates the direction in which that civilization may develop.

TESMAN   Amazing! I'd never think of writing about anything like that.

HEDDA   [*by the french windows, drumming on the pane*]   No. You wouldn't.

LOEVBORG   [*puts the pages back into their cover and lays the package on the table*]   I brought it because I thought I might possibly read you a few pages this evening.

TESMAN   I say, what a kind idea! Oh, but this evening—?

Glances at BRACK.

I'm not quite sure whether—

LOEVBORG   Well, some other time, then. There's no hurry.

BRACK   The truth is, Mr. Loevborg, I'm giving a little dinner this evening. In Tesman's honor, you know.

LOEVBORG   [*looks round for his hat*]   Oh—then I mustn't—

BRACK   No, wait a minute. Won't you do me the honor of joining us?

LOEVBORG   [*curtly, with decision*]   No I can't. Thank you so much.

BRACK   Oh, nonsense. Do—please. There'll only be a few of us. And I can promise you we shall have some good sport, as Mrs. Hed—as Mrs. Tesman puts it.

LOEVBORG   I've no doubt. Nevertheless—

BRACK   You could bring your manuscript along and read it to Tesman at my place. I could lend you a room.

TESMAN   By Jove, Eilert, that's an idea. What?

HEDDA   [*interposes*]   But, Tesman, Mr. Loevborg doesn't want to go.

I'm sure Mr. Loevborg would much rather sit here and have supper with me.

LOEVBORG [*looks at her*] With you, Mrs. Tesman?

HEDDA And Mrs. Elvsted.

LOEVBORG Oh.

Casually.

I ran into her this afternoon.

HEDDA Did you? Well, she's coming here this evening. So you really must stay, Mr. Loevborg. Otherwise she'll have no one to see her home.

LOEVBORG That's true. Well—thank you, Mrs. Tesman, I'll stay then.

HEDDA I'll just tell the servant.

She goes to the door which leads into the hall, and rings. BERTHA *enters.* HEDDA *talks softly to her and points towards the rear room.* BERTHA *nods and goes out.*

TESMAN [*to* LOEVBORG, *as* HEDDA *does this*] I say, Eilert. This new subject of yours—the—er—future—is that the one you're going to lecture about?

LOEVBORG Yes.

TESMAN They told me down at the bookshop that you're going to hold a series of lectures here during the autumn.

LOEVBORG Yes, I am. I—hope you don't mind, Tesman.

TESMAN Good heavens, no! But—?

LOEVBORG I can quite understand it might queer your pitch a little.

TESMAN [*dejectedly*] Oh well, I can't expect you to put them off for my sake.

LOEVBORG I'll wait till your appointment's been announced.

TESMAN You'll wait! But—but—aren't you going to compete with me for the post? What?

LOEVBORG No. I only want to defeat you in the eyes of the world.

TESMAN Good heavens! Then Auntie Juju was right after all! Oh, I knew it, I knew it! Hear that, Hedda? Fancy! Eilert *doesn't* want to stand in our way.

HEDDA [*curtly*] Our? Leave me out of it, please.

She goes towards the rear room, where BERTHA *is setting a tray with decanters and glasses on the table.* HEDDA *nods approval, and comes back into the drawing room.* BERTHA *goes out.*

TESMAN [*while this is happening*] Judge Brack, what do you think about all this? What?

BRACK Oh, I think honor and victory can be very splendid things—

TESMAN Of course they can. Still—

HEDDA [*looks at* TESMAN *with a cold smile*] You look as if you'd been hit by a thunderbolt.

TESMAN Yes, I feel rather like it.

BRACK   There was a black cloud looming up, Mrs. Tesman. But it seems to have passed over.

HEDDA [*points towards the rear room*]   Well, gentlemen, won't you go in and take a glass of cold punch?

BRACK [*glances at his watch*]   A stirrup cup? Yes, why not?

TESMAN   An admirable suggestion, Hedda. Admirable! Oh, I feel so relieved!

HEDDA   Won't you have one, too, Mr. Loevborg?

LOEVBORG   No, thank you. I'd rather not.

BRACK   Great heavens, man, cold punch isn't poison. Take my word for it.

LOEVBORG   Not for everyone, perhaps.

HEDDA   I'll keep Mr. Loevborg company while you drink.

TESMAN   Yes, Hedda dear, would you?

> He and BRACK *go into the rear room, sit down, drink punch, smoke cigarettes and talk cheerfully during the following scene.* EILERT LOEVBORG *remains standing by the stove.* HEDDA *goes to the writing table.*

HEDDA [*raising her voice slightly*]   I've some photographs I'd like to show you, if you'd care to see them. Tesman and I visited the Tyrol[4] on our way home.

> *She comes back with an album, places it on the table by the sofa and sits in the upstage corner of the sofa.* EILERT LOEV-BORG *comes towards her, stops and looks at her. Then he takes a chair and sits down on her left, with his back towards the rear room.*

HEDDA [*opens the album*]   You see these mountains, Mr. Loevborg? That's the Ortler group. Tesman has written the name underneath. You see: "The Ortler Group near Meran."

LOEVBORG [*has not taken his eyes from her; says softly, slowly*]   Hedda—Gabler!

HEDDA [*gives him a quick glance*]   Ssh!

LOEVBORG [*repeats softly*]   Hedda Gabler!

HEDDA [*looks at the album*]   Yes, that used to be my name. When we first knew each other.

LOEVBORG   And from now on—for the rest of my life—I must teach myself never to say: Hedda Gabler.

HEDDA [*still turning the pages*]   Yes, you must. You'd better start getting into practice. The sooner the better.

LOEVBORG [*bitterly*]   Hedda Gabler married? And to George Tesman?

HEDDA   Yes. Well—that's life.

LOEVBORG   Oh, Hedda, Hedda! How could you throw yourself away like that?

HEDDA [*looks sharply at him*]   Stop it.

LOEVBORG   What do you mean?

---

4. Region in the Alps, now primarily in Austria.

TESMAN *comes in and goes towards the sofa.*

HEDDA [*hears him coming and says casually*] And this, Mr Loevborg, is the view from the Ampezzo valley. Look at those mountains.

Glances affectionately up at TESMAN.

What did you say those curious mountains were called, dear?
TESMAN   Let me have a look. Oh, those are the Dolomites.
HEDDA   Of course. Those are the Dolomites, Mr. Loevborg.
TESMAN   Hedda, I just wanted to ask you, can't we bring some punch
in here? A glass for you, anyway. What?
HEDDA   Thank you, yes. And a biscuit or two, perhaps.
TESMAN   You wouldn't like a cigarette?
HEDDA   No.
TESMAN   Right.

He goes into the rear room and over to the right. BRACK *is
sitting there, glancing occasionally at* HEDDA *and* LOEVBORG.

LOEVBORG [*softly, as before*]   Answer me, Hedda. How could you do
it?
HEDDA [*apparently absorbed in the album*]   If you go on calling me
Hedda I won't talk to you any more.
LOEVBORG   Mayn't I even when we're alone?
HEDDA   No. You can think it. But you mustn't say it.
LOEVBORG   Oh, I see. Because you love George Tesman.
HEDDA [*glances at him and smiles*]   Love? Don't be funny.
LOEVBORG   You don't love him?
HEDDA   I don't intend to be unfaithful to him. That's not what I want.
LOEVBORG   Hedda—just tell me one thing—
HEDDA   Ssh!

TESMAN *enters from the rear room, carrying a tray.*

TESMAN   Here we are! Here come the goodies!

Puts the tray down on the table.

HEDDA   Why didn't you ask the servant to bring it in?
TESMAN [*fills the glasses*]   I like waiting on you, Hedda.
HEDDA   But you've filled both glasses. Mr. Loevborg doesn't want to
drink.
TESMAN   Yes, but Mrs. Elvsted'll be here soon.
HEDDA   Oh, yes, that's true. Mrs. Elvsted—
TESMAN   Had you forgotten her? What?
HEDDA   We're so absorbed with these photographs.

Shows him one.

You remember this little village?

TESMAN   Oh, that one down by the Brenner Pass. We spent a night there—

HEDDA   Yes, and met all those amusing people.

TESMAN   Oh yes, it was there, wasn't it? By Jove, if only we could have had you with us, Eilert! Ah, well.

Goes back into the other room and sits down with BRACK.

LOEVBORG   Tell me one thing, Hedda.

HEDDA   Yes?

LOEVBORG   Didn't you love me either? Not—just a little?

HEDDA   Well now, I wonder? No, I think we were just good pals— Really good pals who could tell each other anything.

Smiles.

You certainly poured your heart out to me.

LOEVBORG   You begged me to.

HEDDA   Looking back on it, there was something beautiful and fascinating—and brave—about the way we told each other everything. That secret friendship no one else knew about.

LOEVBORG   Yes, Hedda, yes! Do you remember? How I used to come up to your father's house in the afternoon—and the General sat by the window and read his newspaper—with his back towards us—

HEDDA   And we sat on the sofa in the corner—

LOEVBORG   Always reading the same illustrated magazine—

HEDDA   We hadn't any photograph album.

LOEVBORG   Yes, Hedda. I regarded you as a kind of confessor. Told you things about myself which no one else knew about—then. Those days and nights of drinking and— Oh, Hedda, what power did you have to make me confess such things?

HEDDA   Power? You think I had some power over you?

LOEVBORG   Yes—I don't know how else to explain it. And all those— oblique questions you asked me—

HEDDA   You knew what they meant.

LOEVBORG   But that you could sit there and ask me such questions! So unashamedly—

HEDDA   I thought you said they were oblique.

LOEVBORG   Yes, but you asked them so unashamedly. That you could question me about—about that kind of thing!

HEDDA   You answered willingly enough.

LOEVBORG   Yes—that's what I can't understand—looking back on it. But tell me, Hedda—what you felt for me—wasn't that—love? When you asked me those questions and made me confess my sins to you, wasn't it because you wanted to wash me clean?

HEDDA   No, not exactly.

LOEVBORG   Why did you do it, then?

HEDDA   Do you find it so incredible that a young girl, given the chance to do so without anyone knowing, should want to be allowed a glimpse into a forbidden world of whose existence she is supposed to be ignorant?

LOEVBORG So that was it?

HEDDA One reason. One reason—I think.

LOEVBORG You didn't love me, then. You just wanted—knowledge. But if that was so, why did you break it off?

HEDDA That was your fault.

LOEVBORG It was you who put an end to it.

HEDDA Yes, when I realized that our friendship was threatening to develop into something—something else. Shame on you, Eilert Loevborg! How could you abuse the trust of your dearest friend?

LOEVBORG [*clenches his fists*] Oh, why didn't you do it? Why didn't you shoot me dead? As you threatened to?

HEDDA I was afraid. Of the scandal.

LOEVBORG Yes, Hedda. You're a coward at heart.

HEDDA A dreadful coward.

> *Changes her tone.*

Luckily for you. Well, now you've found consolation with the Elvsteds.

LOEVBORG I know what Thea's been telling you.

HEDDA I dare say you told her about us.

LOEVBORG Not a word. She's too silly to understand that kind of thing.

HEDDA Silly?

LOEVBORG She's silly about that kind of thing.

HEDDA And I am a coward.

> *Leans closer to him, without looking him in the eyes, and says quietly.*

But let me tell you something. Something you don't know.

LOEVBORG [*tensely*] Yes?

HEDDA My failure to shoot you wasn't my worst act of cowardice that evening.

LOEVBORG [*looks at her for a moment, realizes her meaning and whispers passionately*] Oh, Hedda! Hedda Gabler! Now I see what was behind those questions. Yes! It wasn't knowledge you wanted! It was life!

HEDDA [*flashes a look at him and says quietly*] Take care! Don't you delude yourself!

> *It has begun to grow dark.* BERTHA, *from outside, opens the door leading into the hall.*

HEDDA [*closes the album with a snap and cries, smiling*] Ah, at last! Come in, Thea dear!

> MRS. ELVSTED *enters from the hall, in evening dress. The door is closed behind her.*

HEDDA [*on the sofa, stretches out her arms towards her*] Thea darling, I thought you were never coming!

MRS. ELVSTED *makes a slight bow to the gentlemen in the rear room as she passes the open doorway, and they to her. Then she goes to the table and holds out her hand to* HEDDA. EILERT LOEVBORG *has risen from his chair. He and* MRS. ELVSTED *nod silently to each other.*

MRS. ELVSTED   Perhaps I ought to go in and say a few words to your husband?
HEDDA   Oh, there's no need. They're happy by themselves. They'll be going soon.
MRS. ELVSTED   Going?
HEDDA   Yes, they're off on a spree this evening.
MRS. ELVSTED [*quickly, to* LOEVBORG]   You're not going with them?
LOEVBORG   No.
HEDDA   Mr. Loevborg is staying here with us.
MRS. ELVSTED [*takes a chair and is about to sit down beside him*]   Oh, how nice it is to be here!
HEDDA   No, Thea darling, not there. Come over here and sit beside me. I want to be in the middle.
MRS. ELVSTED   Yes, just as you wish.

She goes round the table and sits on the sofa, on HEDDA's *right.* LOEVBORG *sits down again in his chair.*

LOEVBORG [*after a short pause, to* HEDDA]   Isn't she lovely to look at?
HEDDA [*strokes her hair gently*]   Only to look at?
LOEVBORG   Yes. We're just good pals. We trust each other implicitly. We can talk to each other quite unashamedly.
HEDDA   No need to be oblique?
MRS. ELVSTED [*nestles close to* HEDDA *and says quietly*]   Oh, Hedda, I'm so happy. Imagine—he says I've inspired him!
HEDDA [*looks at her with a smile*]   Dear Thea! Does he really?
LOEVBORG   She has the courage of her convictions, Mrs. Tesman.
MRS. ELVSTED   I? Courage?
LOEVBORG   Absolute courage. Where friendship is concerned.
HEDDA   Yes. Courage. Yes. If only one had that—
LOEVBORG   Yes?
HEDDA   One might be able to live. In spite of everything.

Changes her tone suddenly.

Well, Thea darling, now you're going to drink a nice glass of cold punch.
MRS. ELVSTED   No, thank you. I never drink anything like that.
HEDDA   Oh. You, Mr. Loevborg?
LOEVBORG   Thank you, I don't either.
MRS. ELVSTED   No, he doesn't either.
HEDDA [*looks into his eyes*]   But if I want you to?
LOEVBORG   That doesn't make any difference.
HEDDA [*laughs*]   Have I no power over you at all? Poor me!
LOEVBORG   Not where this is concerned.
HEDDA   Seriously, I think you should. For your own sake.

MRS. ELVSTED   Hedda!

LOEVBORG   Why?

HEDDA   Or perhaps I should say for other people's sake.

LOEVBORG   What do you mean?

HEDDA   People might think you didn't feel absolutely and unashamedly sure of yourself. In your heart of hearts.

MRS. ELVSTED [*quietly*]   Oh, Hedda, no!

LOEVBORG   People can think what they like. For the present.

MRS. ELVSTED [*happily*]   Yes, that's true.

HEDDA   I saw it so clearly in Judge Brack a few minutes ago.

LOEVBORG   Oh. What did you see?

HEDDA   He smiled so scornfully when he saw you were afraid to go in there and drink with them.

LOEVBORG   Afraid! I wanted to stay here and talk to you.

MRS. ELVSTED   That was only natural, Hedda.

HEDDA   But the Judge wasn't to know that. I saw him wink at Tesman when you showed you didn't dare to join their wretched little party.

LOEVBORG   Didn't dare! Are you saying I didn't dare?

HEDDA   I'm not saying so. But that was what Judge Brack thought.

LOEVBORG   Well, let him.

HEDDA   You're not going, then?

LOEVBORG   I'm staying here with you and Thea.

MRS. ELVSTED   Yes, Hedda, of course he is.

HEDDA [*smiles, and nods approvingly to* LOEVBORG]   Firm as a rock! A man of principle! That's how a man should be!

Turns to MRS. ELVSTED *and strokes her cheek.*

Didn't I tell you so this morning when you came here in such a panic—

LOEVBORG [*starts*]   Panic?

MRS. ELVSTED [*frightened*]   Hedda! But—Hedda!

HEDDA   Well, now you can see for yourself. There's no earthly need for you to get scared to death just because—

Stops.

Well! Let's all three cheer up and enjoy ourselves.

LOEVBORG   Mrs. Tesman, would you mind explaining to me what this is all about?

MRS. ELVSTED   Oh, my God, my God, Hedda, what are you saying? What are you doing?

HEDDA   Keep calm. That horrid Judge has his eye on you.

LOEVBORG   Scared to death, were you? For my sake?

MRS. ELVSTED [*quietly, trembling*]   Oh, Hedda! You've made me so unhappy!

LOEVBORG [*looks coldly at her for a moment. His face is distorted*]   So that was how much you trusted me.

MRS. ELVSTED   Eilert dear, please listen to me—

LOEVBORG [*takes one of the glasses of punch, raises it and says quietly, hoarsely*]   Skoal, Thea!

Empties the glass, puts it down and picks up one of the others.

MRS. ELVSTED [*quietly*]   Hedda, Hedda! Why did you want this to happen?

HEDDA   *I*—want it? Are you mad?

LOEVBORG   Skoal to you too, Mrs. Tesman. Thanks for telling me the truth. Here's to the truth!

Empties his glass and refills it.

HEDDA [*puts her hand on his arm*]   Steady. That's enough for now. Don't forget the party.

MRS. ELVSTED   No, no, no!

HEDDA   Ssh! They're looking at you.

LOEVBORG [*puts down his glass*]   Thea, tell me the truth—

MRS. ELVSTED   Yes!

LOEVBORG   Did your husband know you were following me?

MRS. ELVSTED   Oh, Hedda!

LOEVBORG   Did you and he have an agreement that you should come here and keep an eye on me? Perhaps he gave you the idea? After all, he's a magistrate. I suppose he needed me back in his office. Or did he miss my companionship at the card table?

MRS. ELVSTED [*quietly, sobbing*]   Eilert, Eilert!

LOEVBORG [*seizes a glass and is about to fill it*]   Let's drink to him, too.

HEDDA   No more now. Remember you're going to read your book to Tesman.

LOEVBORG [*calm again, puts down his glass*]   That was silly of me, Thea. To take it like that, I mean. Don't be angry with me, my dear. You'll see—yes, and they'll see, too—that though I fell, I— I have raised myself up again. With your help, Thea.

MRS. ELVSTED [*happily*]   Oh, thank God!

BRACK *has meanwhile glanced at his watch. He and* TESMAN *get up and come into the drawing room.*

BRACK [*takes his hat and overcoat*]   Well, Mrs. Tesman, it's time for us to go.

HEDDA   Yes, I suppose it must be.

LOEVBORG [*gets up*]   Time for me too, Judge.

MRS. ELVSTED [*quietly, pleadingly*]   Eilert, please don't!

HEDDA [*pinches her arm*]   They can hear you.

MRS. ELVSTED [*gives a little cry*]   Oh!

LOEVBORG [*to* BRACK]   You were kind enough to ask me to join you.

BRACK   Are you coming?

LOEVBORG   If I may.

BRACK   Delighted.

LOEVBORG [*puts the paper package in his pocket and says to* TESMAN]   I'd like to show you one or two things before I send it off to the printer.

TESMAN   I say, that'll be fun. Fancy—! Oh, but, Hedda, how'll Mrs. Elvsted get home? What?

HEDDA   Oh, we'll manage somehow.

LOEVBORG [*glances over towards the ladies*]   Mrs. Elvsted? I shall come back and collect her, naturally.

Goes closer.

About ten o'clock, Mrs. Tesman? Will that suit you?

HEDDA   Yes. That'll suit me admirably.

TESMAN   Good, that's settled. But you mustn't expect me back so early, Hedda.

HEDDA   Stay as long as you c— as long as you like, dear.

MRS. ELVSTED [*trying to hide her anxiety*]   Well then, Mr. Loevborg, I'll wait here till you come.

LOEVBORG [*his hat in his hand*]   Pray do, Mrs. Elvsted.

BRACK   Well, gentlemen, now the party begins. I trust that, in the words of a certain fair lady, we shall enjoy good sport.

HEDDA   What a pity the fair lady can't be there, invisible.

BRACK   Why invisible?

HEDDA   So as to be able to hear some of your uncensored witticisms, your honor.

BRACK [*laughs*]   Oh, I shouldn't advise the fair lady to do that.

TESMAN [*laughs too*]   I say, Hedda, that's good. By Jove! Fancy that!

BRACK   Well, good night, ladies, good night!

LOEVBORG [*bows farewell*]   About ten o'clock, then.

> BRACK, LOEVBORG *and* TESMAN *go out through the hall. As they do so,* BERTHA *enters from the rear room with a lighted lamp. She puts it on the drawing-room table, then goes out the way she came.*

MRS. ELVSTED [*has got up and is walking uneasily to and fro*]   Oh, Hedda, Hedda! How is all this going to end?

HEDDA   At ten o'clock, then. He'll be here. I can see him. With a crown of vine-leaves[5] in his hair. Burning and unashamed!

MRS. ELVSTED   Oh, I do hope so!

HEDDA   Can't you see? Then he'll be himself again! He'll be a free man for the rest of his days!

MRS. ELVSTED   Please God you're right.

HEDDA   That's how he'll come!

Gets up and goes closer.

You can doubt him as much as you like. I believe in him! Now we'll see which of us—

MRS. ELVSTED   You're after something, Hedda.

HEDDA   Yes, I am. For once in my life I want to have the power to shape a man's destiny.

MRS. ELVSTED   Haven't you that power already?

HEDDA   No, I haven't. I've never had it.

---

5 Worshippers of Dionysus, Greek god of vegetation and wine, wore garlands of vine leaves as a sign of divine intoxication.

MRS. ELVSTED   What about your husband?

HEDDA   Him! Oh, if you could only understand how poor I am. And you're allowed to be so rich, so rich!

Clasps her passionately.

I think I'll burn your hair off after all!

MRS. ELVSTED   Let me go! Let me go! You frighten me, Hedda!

BERTHA [*in the open doorway*]   I've laid tea in the dining room, madam.

HEDDA   Good, we're coming.

MRS. ELVSTED   No, no, no! I'd rather go home alone! Now—at once!

HEDDA   Rubbish! First you're going to have some tea, you little idiot. And then—at ten o'clock—Eilert Loevborg will come. With a crown of vine-leaves in his hair!

She drags MRS. ELVSTED *almost forcibly towards the open doorway.*

Act 3

The same. The curtains are drawn across the open doorway, and also across the french windows. The lamp, half turned down, with a shade over it, is burning on the table. In the stove, the door of which is open, a fire has been burning, but it is now almost out.

   MRS. ELVSTED, *wrapped in a large shawl and with her feet resting on a footstool, is sitting near the stove, huddled in the armchair.* HEDDA *is lying asleep on the sofa, fully dressed, with a blanket over her.*

MRS. ELVSTED [*after a pause, suddenly sits up in her chair and listens tensely. Then she sinks wearily back again and sighs*]   Not back yet! Oh, God! Oh, God! Not back yet!

   BERTHA *tiptoes cautiously in from the hall. She has a letter in her hand.*

MRS. ELVSTED [*turns and whispers*]   What is it? Has someone come?

BERTHA [*quietly*]   Yes, a servant's just called with this letter.

MRS. ELVSTED [*quickly, holding out her hand*]   A letter! Give it to me!

BERTHA   But it's for the Doctor, madam.

MRS. ELVSTED   Oh. I see.

BERTHA   Miss Tesman's maid brought it. I'll leave it here on the table.

MRS. ELVSTED   Yes, do.

BERTHA [*puts down the letter*]   I'd better put the lamp out. It's starting to smoke.

MRS. ELVSTED   Yes, put it out. It'll soon be daylight.

BERTHA [*puts out the lamp*]   It's daylight already, madam.

MRS. ELVSTED   Yes. Broad day. And not home yet.

BERTHA   Oh dear, I was afraid this would happen.

MRS. ELVSTED   Were you?

BERTHA   Yes. When I heard that a certain gentleman had returned to town, and saw him go off with them. I've heard all about him.

MRS. ELVSTED   Don't talk so loud. You'll wake your mistress.

BERTHA [*looks at the sofa and sighs*]   Yes. Let her go on sleeping, poor dear. Shall I put some more wood on the fire?

MRS. ELVSTED   Thank you, don't bother on my account.

BERTHA   Very good.

Goes quietly out through the hall.

HEDDA [*wakes as the door closes and looks up*]   What's that?

MRS. ELVSTED   It was only the maid.

HEDDA [*looks round*]   What am I doing here? Oh, now I remember.

Sits up on the sofa, stretches herself and rubs her eyes.

What time is it, Thea?

MRS. ELVSTED   It's gone seven.

HEDDA   When did Tesman get back?

ELVSTED   He's not back yet.

HEDDA   Not home yet?

MRS. ELVSTED [*gets up*]   No one's come.

HEDDA   And we sat up waiting for them till four o'clock.

MRS. ELVSTED   God! How I waited for him!

HEDDA [*yawns and says with her hand in front of her mouth*]   Oh, dear. We might have saved ourselves the trouble.

MRS. ELVSTED   Did you manage to sleep?

HEDDA   Oh, yes. Quite well, I think. Didn't you get any?

MRS. ELVSTED   Not a wink. I couldn't, Hedda. I just couldn't.

HEDDA [*gets up and comes over to her*]   Now, now, now. There's nothing to worry about. I know what's happened.

MRS. ELVSTED   What? Please tell me.

HEDDA   Well, obviously the party went on very late—

MRS. ELVSTED   Oh dear, I suppose it must have. But—

HEDDA   And Tesman didn't want to come home and wake us all up in the middle of the night.

Laughs.

Probably wasn't too keen to show his face either, after a spree like that.

MRS. ELVSTED   But where could he have gone?

HEDDA   I should think he's probably slept at his aunts'. They keep his old room for him.

MRS. ELVSTED   No, he can't be with them. A letter came for him just now from Miss Tesman. It's over there.

HEDDA   Oh?

Looks at the envelope.

Yes, it's Auntie Juju's handwriting. Well, he must still be at Judge Brack's, then. And Eilert Loevborg is sitting there, reading to him. With a crown of vine-leaves in his hair.

MRS. ELVSTED   Hedda, you're only saying that. You don't believe it.

HEDDA   Thea, you really are a little fool.

MRS. ELVSTED   Perhaps I am.

HEDDA   You look tired to death.

MRS. ELVSTED   Yes. I am tired to death.

HEDDA   Go to my room and lie down for a little. Do as I say, now; don't argue.

MRS. ELVSTED   No, no. I couldn't possibly sleep.

HEDDA   Of course you can.

MRS. ELVSTED   But your husband'll be home soon. And I must know at once—

HEDDA   I'll tell you when he comes.

MRS. ELVSTED   Promise me, Hedda?

HEDDA   Yes, don't worry. Go and get some sleep.

MRS. ELVSTED   Thank you. All right, I'll try.

She goes out through the rear room. HEDDA *goes to the french windows and draws the curtains. Broad daylight floods into the room. She goes to the writing table, takes a small hand mirror from it and arranges her hair. Then she goes to the door leading into the hall and presses the bell. After a few moments,* BERTHA *enters.*

BERTHA   Did you want anything, madam?

HEDDA   Yes, put some more wood on the fire. I'm freezing.

BERTHA   Bless you, I'll soon have this room warmed up.

She rakes the embers together and puts a fresh piece of wood on them. Suddenly she stops and listens.

There's someone at the front door, madam.

HEDDA   Well, go and open it. I'll see to the fire.

BERTHA   It'll burn up in a moment.

She goes out through the hall. HEDDA *kneels on the footstool and puts more wood in the stove. After a few seconds,* GEORGE TESMAN *enters from the hall. He looks tired, and rather worried. He tiptoes towards the open doorway and is about to slip through the curtains.*

HEDDA [*at the stove, without looking up*]   Good morning.

TESMAN [*turns*]   Hedda!

Comes nearer.

Good heavens, are you up already? What?

HEDDA   Yes, I got up very early this morning.

TESMAN   I was sure you'd still be sleeping. Fancy that!

HEDDA   Don't talk so loud. Mrs. Elvsted's asleep in my room.

TESMAN   Mrs. Elvsted? Has she stayed the night here?

HEDDA   Yes. No one came to escort her home.

TESMAN   Oh. No, I suppose not.

HEDDA [*closes the door of the stove and gets up*]   Well. Was it fun?

TESMAN   Have you been anxious about me? What?

HEDDA   Not in the least. I asked if you'd had fun.

TESMAN   Oh yes, rather! Well, I thought, for once in a while— The first part was the best; when Eilert read his book to me. We arrived over an hour too early—what about that, eh? By Jove! Brack had a lot of things to see to, so Eilert read to me.

HEDDA [*sits at the right-hand side of the table*]   Well? Tell me about it.

TESMAN [*sits on a footstool by the stove*]   Honestly, Hedda, you've no idea what a book that's going to be. It's really one of the most remarkable things that's ever been written. By Jove!

HEDDA   Oh, never mind about the book—

TESMAN   I'm going to make a confession to you, Hedda. When he'd finished reading a sort of beastly feeling came over me.

HEDDA   Beastly feeling?

TESMAN   I found myself envying Eilert for being able to write like that. Imagine that, Hedda!

HEDDA   Yes. I can imagine.

TESMAN   What a tragedy that with all those gifts he should be so incorrigible.

HEDDA   You mean he's less afraid of life than most men?

TESMAN   Good heavens, no. He just doesn't know the meaning of the word moderation.

HEDDA   What happened afterwards?

TESMAN   Well, looking back on it I suppose you might almost call it an orgy, Hedda.

HEDDA   Had he vine-leaves in his hair?

TESMAN   Vine-leaves? No, I didn't see any of them. He made a long, rambling oration in honor of the woman who'd inspired him to write this book. Yes, those were the words he used.

HEDDA   Did he name her?

TESMAN   No. But I suppose it must be Mrs. Elvsted. You wait and see!

HEDDA   Where did you leave him?

TESMAN   On the way home. We left in a bunch—the last of us, that is—and Brack came with us to get a little fresh air. Well, then, you see, we agreed we ought to see Eilert home. He'd had a drop too much.

HEDDA   You don't say?

TESMAN   But now comes the funny part, Hedda. Or I should really say the tragic part. Oh, I'm almost ashamed to tell you. For Eilert's sake, I mean—

HEDDA   Why, what happened?

TESMAN   Well, you see, as we were walking towards town I happened to drop behind for a minute. Only for a minute—er—you understand—

HEDDA   Yes, yes—?

TESMAN   Well then, when I ran on to catch them up, what do you think I found by the roadside. What?

HEDDA   How on earth should I know?

TESMAN   You mustn't tell anyone, Hedda. What? Promise me that—for Eilert's sake.

Takes a package wrapped in paper from his coat pocket.

Just fancy! I found this.

HEDDA   Isn't this the one he brought here yesterday?

TESMAN   Yes! The whole of that precious, irreplaceable manuscript! And he went and lost it! Didn't even notice! What about that? By Jove! Tragic.

HEDDA   But why didn't you give it back to him?

TESMAN   I didn't dare to, in the state he was in.

HEDDA   Didn't you tell any of the others?

TESMAN   Good heavens, no. I didn't want to do that. For Eilert's sake, you understand.

HEDDA   Then no one else knows you have his manuscript?

TESMAN   No. And no one must be allowed to know.

HEDDA   Didn't it come up in the conversation later?

TESMAN   I didn't get a chance to talk to him any more. As soon as we got into the outskirts of town, he and one or two of the others gave us the slip. Disappeared, by Jove!

HEDDA   Oh? I suppose they took him home.

TESMAN   Yes, I imagine that was the idea. Brack left us, too.

HEDDA   And what have you been up to since then?

TESMAN   Well, I and one or two of the others—awfully jolly chaps, they were—went back to where one of them lived, and had a cup of morning coffee. Morning-after coffee—what? Ah, well. I'll just lie down for a bit and give Eilert time to sleep it off, poor chap, then I'll run over and give this back to him.

HEDDA   [*holds out her hand for the package*]   No, don't do that. Not just yet. Let me read it first.

TESMAN   Oh no, really, Hedda dear, honestly, I daren't do that.

HEDDA   Daren't?

TESMAN   No—imagine how desperate he'll be when he wakes up and finds his manuscript's missing. He hasn't any copy, you see. He told me so himself.

HEDDA   Can't a thing like that be rewritten?

TESMAN   Oh no, not possibly, I shouldn't think. I mean, the inspiration, you know—

HEDDA   Oh, yes. I'd forgotten that.

Casually.

By the way, there's a letter for you.

TESMAN   Is there? Fancy that!

HEDDA   [*holds it out to him*]   It came early this morning.

TESMAN   I say, it's from Auntie Juju! What on earth can it be?

Puts the package on the other footstool, opens the letter, reads it and jumps up.

Oh, Hedda! She says poor Auntie Rena's dying.

HEDDA   Well, we've been expecting that.

TESMAN   She says if I want to see her I must go quickly. I'll run over at once.

HEDDA [*hides a smile*]   Run?

TESMAN   Hedda dear, I suppose you wouldn't like to come with me? What about that, eh?

HEDDA [*gets up and says wearily and with repulsion*]   No, no, don't ask me to do anything like that. I can't bear illness or death. I loathe anything ugly.

TESMAN   Yes, yes. Of course.

In a dither.

My hat? My overcoat? Oh yes, in the hall. I do hope I won't get there too late, Hedda? What?

BERTHA *enters from the hall.*

HEDDA   You'll be all right if you run.

BERTHA   Judge Brack's outside and wants to know if he can come in.

TESMAN   At this hour? No, I can't possibly receive him now.

HEDDA   I can.

To BERTHA.

Ask his honor to come in.

BERTHA *goes.*

HEDDA [*whispers quickly*]   The manuscript, Tesman.

She snatches it from the footstool.

TESMAN   Yes, give it to me.

HEDDA   No, I'll look after it for now.

She goes over to the writing table and puts it in the bookcase. TESMAN *stands dithering, unable to get his gloves on.* JUDGE BRACK *enters from the hall.*

HEDDA [*nods to him*]   Well, you're an early bird.

BRACK   Yes, aren't I?

To TESMAN.

Are you up and about, too?

TESMAN   Yes, I've got to go and see my aunts. Poor Auntie Rena's dying.

BRACK   Oh dear, is she? Then you mustn't let me detain you. At so tragic a—

TESMAN   Yes, I really must run. Good-bye! Good-bye!

Runs out through the hall.

HEDDA [*goes nearer*]   You seem to have had excellent sport last night —Judge.

BRACK   Indeed yes, Mrs. Hedda. I haven't even had time to take my clothes off.

HEDDA   *You* haven't either?

BRACK   As you see. What's Tesman told you about last night's escapades?

HEDDA   Oh, only some boring story about having gone and drunk coffee somewhere.

BRACK   Yes, I've heard about that coffee party. Eilert Loevborg wasn't with them, I gather?

HEDDA   No, they took him home first.

BRACK   Did Tesman go with him?

HEDDA   No, one or two of the others, he said.

BRACK [*smiles*]   George Tesman is a credulous man, Mrs. Hedda.

HEDDA   God knows. But—has something happened?

BRACK   Well, yes, I'm afraid it has.

HEDDA   I see. Sit down and tell me.

She sits on the left of the table, BRACK *at the long side of it, near her.*

HEDDA   Well?

BRACK   I had a special reason for keeping track of my guests last night. Or perhaps I should say some of my guests.

HEDDA   Including Eilert Loevborg?

BRACK   I must confess—yes.

HEDDA   You're beginning to make me curious.

BRACK   Do you know where he and some of my other guests spent the latter half of last night, Mrs. Hedda?

HEDDA   Tell me. If it won't shock me.

BRACK   Oh, I don't think it'll shock you. They found themselves participating in an exceedingly animated *soirée.*

HEDDA   Of a sporting character?

BRACK   Of a highly sporting character.

HEDDA   Tell me more.

BRACK   Loevborg had received an invitation in advance—as had the others. I knew all about that. But he had refused. As you know, he's become a new man.

HEDDA   Up at the Elvsteds', yes. But he went?

BRACK   Well, you see, Mrs. Hedda, last night at my house, unhappily, the spirit moved him.

HEDDA   Yes, I hear he became inspired.

BRACK   Somewhat violently inspired. And as a result, I suppose, his thoughts strayed. We men, alas, don't always stick to our principles as firmly as we should.

HEDDA   I'm sure you're an exception, Judge Brack. But go on about Loevborg.

BRACK   Well, to cut a long story short, he ended up in the establishment of a certain Mademoiselle Danielle.

HEDDA   Mademoiselle Danielle?

BRACK   She was holding the *soirée*. For a selected circle of friends and admirers.

HEDDA   Has she got red hair?

BRACK   She has.

HEDDA   A singer of some kind?

BRACK   Yes—among other accomplishments. She's also a celebrated huntress—of men, Mrs. Hedda. I'm sure you've heard about her. Eilert Loevborg used to be one of her most ardent patrons. In his salad days.

HEDDA   And how did all this end?

BRACK   Not entirely amicably, from all accounts. Mademoiselle Danielle began by receiving him with the utmost tenderness and ended by resorting to her fists.

HEDDA   Against Loevborg?

BRACK   Yes. He accused her, or her friends, of having robbed him. He claimed his pocketbook had been stolen. Among other things. In short, he seems to have made a bloodthirsty scene.

HEDDA   And what did this lead to?

BRACK   It led to a general free-for-all, in which both sexes participated. Fortunately, in the end the police arrived.

HEDDA   The police too?

BRACK   Yes. I'm afraid it may turn out to be rather an expensive joke for Master Eilert. Crazy fool!

HEDDA   Oh?

BRACK   Apparently he put up a very violent resistance. Hit one of the constables on the ear and tore his uniform. He had to accompany them to the police station.

HEDDA   Where did you learn all this?

BRACK   From the police.

HEDDA   [*to herself*]   So that's what happened. He didn't have a crown of vine-leaves in his hair.

BRACK   Vine-leaves, Mrs. Hedda?

HEDDA   [*in her normal voice again*]   But, tell me, Judge, why do you take such a close interest in Eilert Loevborg?

BRACK   For one thing it'll hardly be a matter of complete indifference to me if it's revealed in court that he came there straight from my house.

HEDDA   Will it come to court?

BRACK   Of course. Well, I don't regard that as particularly serious. Still, I thought it my duty, as a friend of the family, to give you and your husband a full account of his nocturnal adventures.

HEDDA   Why?

BRACK   Because I've a shrewd suspicion that he's hoping to use you as a kind of screen.

HEDDA   What makes you think that?

BRACK   Oh, for heaven's sake, Mrs. Hedda, we're not blind. You wait and see. This Mrs. Elvsted won't be going back to her husband just yet.

HEDDA   Well, if there were anything between those two there are plenty of other places where they could meet.

BRACK   Not in anyone's home. From now on every respectable house will once again be closed to Eilert Loevborg.

HEDDA   And mine should be too, you mean?

BRACK   Yes. I confess I should find it more than irksome if this gentleman were to be granted unrestricted access to this house. If he were superfluously to intrude into—

HEDDA   The triangle?

BRACK   Precisely. For me it would be like losing a home.

HEDDA   [*looks at him and smiles*]   I see. You want to be the cock of the walk.

BRACK   [*nods slowly and lowers his voice*]   Yes, that is my aim. And I shall fight for it with—every weapon at my disposal.

HEDDA   [*as her smile fades*]   You're a dangerous man, aren't you? When you really want something.

BRACK   You think so?

HEDDA   Yes, I'm beginning to think so. I'm deeply thankful you haven't any kind of hold over me.

BRACK   [*laughs equivocally*]   Well, well, Mrs. Hedda—perhaps you're right. If I had, who knows what I might not think up?

HEDDA   Come, Judge Brack. That sounds almost like a threat.

BRACK   [*gets up*]   Heaven forbid! In the creation of a triangle—and its continuance—the question of compulsion should never arise.

HEDDA   Exactly what I was thinking.

BRACK   Well, I've said what I came to say. I must be getting back. Good-bye, Mrs. Hedda.

Goes towards the french windows.

HEDDA   [*gets up*]   Are you going out through the garden?

BRACK   Yes, it's shorter.

HEDDA   Yes. And it's the back door, isn't it?

BRACK   I've nothing against back doors. They can be quite intriguing —sometimes.

HEDDA   When people fire pistols out of them, for example?

BRACK   [*in the doorway, laughs*]   Oh, people don't shoot tame cocks.

HEDDA   [*laughs too*]   I suppose not. When they've only got one.

They nod good-bye, laughing. He goes. She closes the french windows behind him, and stands for a moment, looking out pensively. Then she walks across the room and glances through the curtains in the open doorway. Goes to the writing table, takes LOEVBORG's *package from the bookcase and is about to leaf through the pages when* BERTHA *is heard remonstrating loudly in the hall.* HEDDA *turns and listens. She hastily puts the package back in the drawer, locks it and puts the key on the inkstand.* EILERT LOEVBORG, *with his overcoat on and his hat in his hand, throws the door open. He looks somewhat confused and excited.*

LOEVBORG   [*shouts as he enters*]   I must come in, I tell you! Let me pass!

He closes the door, turns, sees HEDDA, *controls himself immediately and bows.*

HEDDA [*at the writing table*]   Well, Mr. Loevborg, this is rather a late hour to be collecting Thea.

LOEVBORG   And an early hour to call on you. Please forgive me.

HEDDA   How do you know she's still here?

LOEVBORG   They told me at her lodgings that she has been out all night.

HEDDA [*goes to the table*]   Did you notice anything about their behavior when they told you?

LOEVBORG [*looks at her, puzzled*]   Notice anything?

HEDDA   Did they sound as if they thought it—strange?

LOEVBORG [*suddenly understands*]   Oh, I see what you mean. I'm dragging her down with me. No, as a matter of fact I didn't notice anything. I suppose Tesman isn't up yet?

HEDDA   No, I don't think so.

LOEVBORG   When did he get home?

HEDDA   Very late.

LOEVBORG   Did he tell you anything?

HEDDA   Yes. I gather you had a merry party at Judge Brack's last night.

LOEVBORG   He didn't tell you anything else?

HEDDA   I don't think so. I was so terribly sleepy—

MRS. ELVSTED *comes through the curtains in the open doorway.*

MRS. ELVSTED [*runs towards him*]   Oh, Eilert! At last!

LOEVBORG   Yes—at last. And too late.

MRS. ELVSTED   What is too late?

LOEVBORG   Everything—now. I'm finished, Thea.

MRS. ELVSTED   Oh, no, no! Don't say that!

LOEVBORG   You'll say it yourself, when you've heard what I—

MRS. ELVSTED   I don't want to hear anything!

HEDDA   Perhaps you'd rather speak to her alone? I'd better go.

LOEVBORG   No, stay.

MRS. ELVSTED   But I don't want to hear anything, I tell you!

LOEVBORG   It's not about last night.

MRS. ELVSTED   Then what—?

LOEVBORG   I want to tell you that from now on we must stop seeing each other.

MRS. ELVSTED   Stop seeing each other!

HEDDA [*involuntarily*]   I knew it!

LOEVBORG   I have no further use for you, Thea.

MRS. ELVSTED   You can stand there and say that! No further use for me! Surely I can go on helping you? We'll go on working together, won't we?

LOEVBORG   I don't intend to do any more work from now on.

MRS. ELVSTED [*desperately*]   Then what use have I for my life?

LOEVBORG   You must try to live as if you had never known me.

MRS. ELVSTED   But I can't!

LOEVBORG   Try to, Thea. Go back home—

MRS. ELVSTED   Never! I want to be wherever you are! I won't let myself be driven away like this! I want to stay here—and be with you when the book comes out.

HEDDA [*whispers*]   Ah, yes! The book!

LOEVBORG [*looks at her*]   Our book; Thea's and mine. It belongs to both of us.

MRS. ELVSTED   Oh, yes! I feel that, too! And I've a right to be with you when it comes into the world. I want to see people respect and honor you again. And the joy! The joy! I want to share it with you!

LOEVBORG   Thea—our book will never come into the world.

HEDDA   Ah!

MRS. ELVSTED   Not—?

LOEVBORG   It cannot. Ever.

MRS. ELVSTED   Eilert—what have you done with the manuscript? Where is it?

LOEVBORG   Oh Thea, please don't ask me that!

MRS. ELVSTED   Yes, yes—I must know. I've a right to know. Now!

LOEVBORG   The manuscript. I've torn it up.

MRS. ELVSTED [*screams*]   No, no!

HEDDA [*involuntarily*]   But that's not—!

LOEVBORG [*looks at her*]   Not true, you think?

HEDDA [*controls herself*]   Why—yes, of course it is, if you say so. It just sounded so incredible—

LOEVBORG   It's true, nevertheless.

MRS. ELVSTED   Oh, my God, my God, Hedda—he's destroyed his own book!

LOEVBORG   I have destroyed my life. Why not my life's work, too?

MRS. ELVSTED   And you—did this last night?

LOEVBORG   Yes, Thea. I tore it into a thousand pieces. And scattered them out across the fjord. It's good, clean, salt water. Let it carry them away; let them drift in the current and the wind. And in a little while, they will sink. Deeper and deeper. As I shall, Thea.

MRS. ELVSTED   Do you know, Eilert—this book—all my life I shall feel as though you'd killed a little child!

LOEVBORG   You're right. It is like killing a child.

MRS. ELVSTED   But how could you? It was my child, too!

HEDDA [*almost inaudibly*]   Oh—the child—!

MRS. ELVSTED [*breathes heavily*]   It's all over, then. Well—I'll go now, Hedda.

HEDDA   You're not leaving town?

MRS. ELVSTED   I don't know what I'm going to do. I can't see anything except—darkness.

She goes out through the hall.

HEDDA [*waits a moment*]   Aren't you going to escort her home, Mr. Loevborg?

LOEVBORG   I? Through the streets? Do you want me to let people see her with me?

HEDDA   Of course I don't know what else may have happened last night. But is it so utterly beyond redress?

LOEVBORG   It isn't just last night. It'll go on happening. I know it.

But the curse of it is, I don't want to live that kind of life. I don't want to start all that again. She's broken my courage. I can't spit in the eyes of the world any longer.

HEDDA [*as though to herself*]   That pretty little fool's been trying to shape a man's destiny.

   Looks at him.

But how could you be so heartless towards her?

LOEVBORG   Don't call me heartless!

HEDDA   To go and destroy the one thing that's made her life worth living? You don't call that heartless?

LOEVBORG   Do you want to know the truth, Hedda?

HEDDA   The truth?

LOEVBORG   Promise me first—give me your word—that you'll never let Thea know about this.

HEDDA   I give you my word.

LOEVBORG   Good. Well; what I told her just now was a lie.

HEDDA   About the manuscript?

LOEVBORG   Yes. I didn't tear it up. Or throw it in the fjord.

HEDDA   You didn't? But where is it, then?

LOEVBORG   I destroyed it, all the same. I destroyed it, Hedda!

HEDDA   I don't understand.

LOEVBORG   Thea said that what I had done was like killing a child.

HEDDA   Yes. That's what she said.

LOEVBORG   But to kill a child isn't the worst thing a father can do to it.

HEDDA   What could be worse than that?

LOEVBORG   Hedda—suppose a man came home one morning, after a night of debauchery, and said to the mother of his child: "Look here. I've been wandering round all night. I've been to—such-and-such a place and such-and-such a place. And I had our child with me. I took him to—these places. And I've lost him. Just—lost him. God knows where he is or whose hands he's fallen into."

HEDDA   I see. But when all's said and done, this was only a book—

LOEVBORG   Thea's heart and soul were in that book. It was her whole life.

HEDDA   Yes. I understand.

LOEVBORG   Well, then you must also understand that she and I cannot possibly ever see each other again.

HEDDA   Where will you go?

LOEVBORG   Nowhere. I just want to put an end to it all. As soon as possible.

HEDDA [*takes a step towards him*]   Eilert Loevborg, listen to me. Do it—beautifully!

LOEVBORG   Beautifully?

   Smiles.

With a crown of vine-leaves in my hair? The way you used to dream of me—in the old days?

HEDDA   No, I don't believe in that crown any longer. But—do it beautifully, all the same. Just this once. Good-bye. You must go now. And don't come back.

LOEVBORG   Adieu, madam. Give my love to George Tesman.

Turns to go.

HEDDA   Wait. I want to give you a souvenir to take with you.

She goes over to the writing table, opens the drawer and the pistol-case, and comes back to LOEVBORG *with one of the pistols.*

LOEVBORG [*looks at her*]   This? Is this the souvenir?

HEDDA [*nods slowly*]   You recognize it? You looked down its barrel once.

LOEVBORG   You should have used it then.

HEDDA   Here! Use it now!

LOEVBORG [*puts the pistol in his breast pocket*]   Thank you.

HEDDA   Do it beautifully, Eilert Loevborg. Only promise me that!

LOEVBORG   Good-bye, Hedda Gabler.

He goes out through the hall. HEDDA *stands by the door for a moment, listening. Then she goes over to the writing table, takes out the package containing the manuscript, glances inside it, pulls some of the pages half out and looks at them. Then she takes it to the armchair by the stove and sits down with the package in her lap. After a moment, she opens the door of the stove; then she opens the packet.*

HEDDA [*throws one of the pages into the stove and whispers to herself*]   I'm burning your child, Thea! You with your beautiful wavy hair!

She throws a few more pages into the stove.

The child Eilert Loevborg gave you.

Throws the rest of the manuscript in.

I'm burning it! I'm burning your child!

Act 4

The same. It is evening. The drawing room is in darkness. The small room is illuminated by the hanging lamp over the table. The curtains are drawn across the french windows. HEDDA, *dressed in black, is walking up and down in the darkened room. Then she goes into the small room and crosses to the left. A few chords are heard from the piano. She comes back into the drawing room.*

BERTHA *comes through the small room from the right with a lighted lamp, which she places on the table in front of the corner sofa in the drawing room. Her eyes are red with crying, and she has black ribbons on her cap. She goes quietly out, right.* HEDDA *goes over to the french windows, draws the curtains slightly to one side and looks out into the darkness.*

A few moments later, MISS TESMAN *enters from the hall. She is dressed in mourning, with a black hat and veil.* HEDDA *goes to meet her and holds out her hand.*

MISS TESMAN   Well, Hedda, here I am in the weeds of sorrow. My poor sister has ended her struggles at last.

HEDDA   I've already heard. Tesman sent me a card.

MISS TESMAN   Yes, he promised me he would. But I thought, no, I must go and break the news of death to Hedda myself—here, in the house of life.

HEDDA   It's very kind of you.

MISS TESMAN   Ah, Rena shouldn't have chosen a time like this to pass away. This is no moment for Hedda's house to be a place of mourning.

HEDDA [*changing the subject*]   She died peacefully, Miss Tesman?

MISS TESMAN   Oh, it was quite beautiful! The end came so calmly. And she was so happy at being able to see George once again. And say good-bye to him. Hasn't he come home yet?

HEDDA   No. He wrote that I mustn't expect him too soon. But please sit down.

MISS TESMAN   No, thank you, Hedda dear—bless you. I'd like to. But I've so little time. I must dress her and lay her out as well as I can. She shall go to her grave looking really beautiful.

HEDDA   Can't I help with anything?

MISS TESMAN   Why, you mustn't think of such a thing! Hedda Tesman mustn't let her hands be soiled by contact with death. Or her thoughts. Not at this time.

HEDDA   One can't always control one's thoughts.

MISS TESMAN [*continues*]   Ah, well, that's life. Now we must start to sew poor Rena's shroud. There'll be sewing to be done in this house too before long, I shouldn't wonder. But not for a shroud, praise God.

GEORGE TESMAN *enters from the hall.*

HEDDA   You've come at last! Thank heavens!

TESMAN   Are you here, Auntie Juju? With Hedda? Fancy that!

MISS TESMAN   I was just on the point of leaving, dear boy. Well, have you done everything you promised me?

TESMAN   No, I'm afraid I forgot half of it. I'll have to run over again tomorrow. My head's in a complete whirl today. I can't collect my thoughts.

MISS TESMAN   But George dear, you mustn't take it like this.

TESMAN   Oh? Well—er—how should I?

MISS TESMAN   You must be happy in your grief. Happy for what's happened. As I am.

TESMAN   Oh, yes, yes. You're thinking of Aunt Rena.

HEDDA   It'll be lonely for you now, Miss Tesman.

MISS TESMAN For the first few days, yes. But it won't last long, I hope. Poor dear Rena's little room isn't going to stay empty.

TESMAN Oh? Whom are you going to move in there? What?

MISS TESMAN Oh, there's always some poor invalid who needs care and attention.

HEDDA Do you really want another cross like that to bear?

MISS TESMAN Cross! God forgive you, child. It's been no cross for me.

HEDDA But now—if a complete stranger comes to live with you—?

MISS TESMAN Oh, one soon makes friends with invalids. And I need so much to have someone to live for. Like you, my dear. Well, I expect there'll soon be work in this house too for an old aunt, praise God!

HEDDA Oh—please!

TESMAN By Jove, yes! What a splendid time the three of us could have together if—

HEDDA If?

TESMAN [*uneasily*] Oh, never mind. It'll all work out. Let's hope so—what?

MISS TESMAN Yes, yes. Well, I'm sure you two would like to be alone.

>   *Smiles.*

Perhaps Hedda may have something to tell you, George. Good-bye. I must go home to Rena.

>   *Turns to the door.*

Dear God, how strange! Now Rena is with me and with poor dear Joachim.

TESMAN Fancy that. Yes, Auntie Juju! What?

>   MISS TESMAN *goes out through the hall.*

HEDDA [*follows* TESMAN *coldly and searchingly with her eyes*] I really believe this death distresses you more than it does her.

TESMAN Oh, it isn't just Auntie Rena. It's Eilert I'm so worried about.

HEDDA [*quickly*] Is there any news of him?

TESMAN I ran over to see him this afternoon. I wanted to tell him his manuscript was in safe hands.

HEDDA Oh? You didn't find him?

TESMAN No. He wasn't at home. But later I met Mrs. Elvsted and she told me he'd been here early this morning.

HEDDA Yes, just after you'd left.

TESMAN It seems he said he'd torn the manuscript up. What?

HEDDA Yes, he claimed to have done so.

TESMAN You told him we had it, of course?

HEDDA No.

>   *Quickly.*

Did you tell Mrs. Elvsted?

TESMAN No, I didn't like to. But you ought to have told him. Think if he should go home and do something desperate! Give me the manuscript, Hedda. I'll run over to him with it right away. Where did you put it?

HEDDA [*cold and motionless, leaning against the armchair*]   I haven't got it any longer.

TESMAN   Haven't got it? What on earth do you mean?

HEDDA   I've burned it.

TESMAN [*starts, terrified*]   Burned it! Burned Eilert's manuscript!

HEDDA   Don't shout. The servant will hear you.

TESMAN   Burned it! But in heaven's name—! Oh, no, no, no! This is impossible!

HEDDA   Well, it's true.

TESMAN   But, Hedda, do you realize what you've done? That's appropriating lost property! It's against the law! By Jove! You ask Judge Brack and see if I'm not right.

HEDDA   You'd be well advised not to talk about it to Judge Brack or anyone else.

TESMAN   But how could you go and do such a dreadful thing? What on earth put the idea into your head? What came over you? Answer me! What?

HEDDA [*represses an almost imperceptible smile*]   I did it for your sake, George.

TESMAN   For my sake?

HEDDA   When you came home this morning and described how he'd read his book to you—

TESMAN   Yes, yes?

HEDDA   You admitted you were jealous of him.

TESMAN   But, good heavens, I didn't mean it literally!

HEDDA   No matter. I couldn't bear the thought that anyone else should push you into the background.

TESMAN [*torn between doubt and joy*]   Hedda—is this true? But—but but I never realized you loved me like that! Fancy—

HEDDA   Well, I suppose you'd better know. I'm going to have—

Breaks off and says violently.

No, no—you'd better ask your Auntie Juju. She'll tell you.

TESMAN   Hedda! I think I understand what you mean.

Clasps his hands.

Good heavens, can it really be true! What?

HEDDA   Don't shout. The servant will hear you.

TESMAN [*laughing with joy*]   The servant! I say, that's good! The servant! Why, that's Bertha! I'll run out and tell her at once!

HEDDA [*clenches her hands in despair*]   Oh, it's destroying me, all this —it's destroying me!

TESMAN   I say, Hedda, what's up? What?

HEDDA [*cold, controlled*]   Oh, it's all so—absurd—George.

TESMAN   Absurd? That I'm so happy? But surely—? Ah, well—perhaps I won't say anything to Bertha.

HEDDA   No, do. She might as well know too.

TESMAN   No, no, I won't tell her yet. But Auntie Juju—I must let her knew! And you—you called me George! For the first time! Fancy that! Oh, it'll make Auntie Juju so happy, all this! So very happy!

HEDDA   Will she be happy when she hears I've burned Eilert Loevborg's manuscript—for your sake?

TESMAN   No, I'd forgotten about that. Of course no one must be allowed to know about the manuscript. But that you're burning with love for me, Hedda, I must certainly let Auntie Juju know that. I say, I wonder if young wives often feel like that towards their husbands? What?

HEDDA   You might ask Auntie Juju about that too.

TESMAN   I will, as soon as I get the chance.

Looks uneasy and thoughtful again.

But I say, you know, that manuscript. Dreadful business. Poor Eilert!

> MRS. ELVSTED, *dressed as on her first visit, with hat and overcoat, enters from the hall.*

MRS. ELVSTED [*greets them hastily and tremulously*] Oh, Hedda dear, do please forgive me for coming here again.

HEDDA   Why, Thea, what's happened?

TESMAN   Is it anything to do with Eilert Loevborg? What?

MRS. ELVSTED   Yes—I'm so dreadfully afraid he may have met with an accident.

HEDDA [*grips her arm*] You think so?

TESMAN   But, good heavens, Mrs. Elvsted, what makes you think that?

MRS. ELVSTED   I heard them talking about him at the boarding-house, as I went in. Oh, there are the most terrible rumors being spread about him in town today.

TESMAN   Fancy. Yes, I heard about them too. But I can testify that he went straight home to bed. Fancy that!

HEDDA   Well—what did they say in the boarding-house?

MRS. ELVSTED   Oh, I couldn't find out anything. Either they didn't know, or else— They stopped talking when they saw me. And I didn't dare to ask.

TESMAN [*fidgets uneasily*] We must hope—we must hope you misheard them, Mrs. Elvsted.

MRS. ELVSTED   No, no, I'm sure it was he they were talking about. I heard them say something about a hospital—

TESMAN   Hospital!

HEDDA   Oh no, surely that's impossible!

MRS. ELVSTED   Oh, I became so afraid. So I went up to his rooms and asked to see him.

HEDDA   Do you think that was wise, Thea?

MRS. ELVSTED   Well, what else could I do? I couldn't bear the uncertainty any longer.

TESMAN   But *you* didn't manage to find him either? What?

MRS. ELVSTED   No. And they had no idea where he was. They said he hadn't been home since yesterday afternoon.

TESMAN   Since yesterday? Fancy that!

MRS. ELVSTED   I'm sure he must have met with an accident.

TESMAN   Hedda, I wonder if I ought to go into town and make one or two inquiries?

HEDDA   No, no, don't you get mixed up in this.

> JUDGE BRACK *enters from the hall, hat in hand.* BERTHA, *who has opened the door for him, closes it. He looks serious and greets them silently.*

TESMAN   Hullo, my dear Judge. Fancy seeing you!

BRACK   I had to come and talk to you.

TESMAN   I can see Auntie Juju's told you the news.

BRACK   Yes, I've heard about that too.

TESMAN   Tragic, isn't it?

BRACK   Well, my dear chap, that depends how you look at it.

TESMAN   [*looks uncertainly at him*]   Has something else happened?

BRACK   Yes.

HEDDA   Another tragedy?

BRACK   That also depends on how you look at it, Mrs. Tesman.

MRS. ELVSTED   Oh, it's something to do with Eilert Loevborg!

BRACK   [*looks at her for a moment*]   How did you guess? Perhaps you've heard already—?

MRS. ELVSTED   [*confused*]   No, no, not at all—I—

TESMAN   For heaven's sake, tell us!

BRACK   [*shrugs his shoulders*]   Well, I'm afraid they've taken him to the hospital. He's dying.

MRS. ELVSTED   [*screams*]   Oh God, God!

TESMAN   The hospital! Dying!

HEDDA   [*involuntarily*]   So quickly!

MRS. ELVSTED   [*weeping*]   Oh, Hedda! And we parted enemies!

HEDDA   [*whispers*]   Thea—Thea!

MRS. ELVSTED   [*ignoring her*]   I must see him! I must see him before he dies!

BRACK   It's no use, Mrs. Elvsted. No one's allowed to see him now.

MRS. ELVSTED   But what's happened to him? You must tell me!

TESMAN   He hasn't tried to do anything to himself? What?

HEDDA   Yes, he has. I'm sure of it.

TESMAN   Hedda, how can you—?

BRACK   [*who has not taken his eyes from her*]   I'm afraid you've guessed correctly, Mrs. Tesman.

MRS. ELVSTED   How dreadful!

TESMAN   Attempted suicide! Fancy that!

HEDDA   Shot himself!

BRACK   Right again, Mrs. Tesman.

MRS. ELVSTED   [*tries to compose herself*]   When did this happen, Judge Brack?

BRACK   This afternoon. Between three and four.

TESMAN   But, good heavens—where? What?

BRACK   [*a little hesitantly*]   Where? Why, my dear chap, in his rooms of course.

MRS. ELVSTED   No, that's impossible. I was there soon after six.

BRACK   Well, it must have been somewhere else, then. I don't know exactly. I only know that they found him. He'd shot himself— through the breast.

MRS. ELVSTED   Oh, how horrible! That he should end like that!

HEDDA [*to* BRACK]   Through the breast, you said?

BRACK   That is what I said.

HEDDA   Not through the head?

BRACK   Through the breast, Mrs. Tesman.

HEDDA   The breast. Yes; yes. That's good, too.

BRACK   Why, Mrs. Tesman?

HEDDA   Oh—no, I didn't mean anything.

TESMAN   And the wound's dangerous, you say? What?

BRACK   Mortal. He's probably already dead.

MRS. ELVSTED   Yes, yes—I feel it! It's all over. All over. Oh Hedda—!

TESMAN   But, tell me, how did you manage to learn all this?

BRACK [*curtly*]   From the police. I spoke to one of them.

HEDDA [*loudly, clearly*]   At last! Oh, thank God!

TESMAN [*appalled*]   For God's sake, Hedda, what are you saying?

HEDDA   I am saying there's beauty in what he has done.

BRACK   Hm—Mrs. Tesman—

TESMAN   Beauty! Oh, but I say!

MRS. ELVSTED   Hedda, how can you talk of beauty in connection with a thing like this?

HEDDA   Eilert Loevborg has settled his account with life. He's had the courage to do what—what he had to do.

MRS. ELVSTED   No, that's not why it happened. He did it because he was mad.

TESMAN   He did it because he was desperate.

HEDDA   You're wrong! I know!

MRS. ELVSTED   He must have been mad. The same as when he tore up the manuscript.

BRACK [*starts*]   Manuscript? Did he tear it up?

MRS. ELVSTED   Yes. Last night.

TESMAN [*whispers*]   Oh, Hedda, we shall never be able to escape from this.

BRACK   Hm. Strange.

TESMAN [*wanders round the room*]   To think of Eilert dying like that. And not leaving behind him the thing that would have made his name endure.

MRS. ELVSTED   If only it could be pieced together again!

TESMAN   Yes, fancy! If only it could! I'd give anything—

MRS. ELVSTED   Perhaps it can, Mr. Tesman.

TESMAN   What do you mean?

MRS. ELVSTED [*searches in the pocket of her dress*]   Look! I kept the notes he dictated it from.

HEDDA [*takes a step nearer*]   Ah!

TESMAN   You kept them, Mrs. Elvsted! What?

MRS. ELVSTED   Yes, here they are. I brought them with me when I left home. They've been in my pocket ever since.

TESMAN   Let me have a look.

MRS. ELVSTED [*hands him a wad of small sheets of paper*]   They're in a terrible muddle. All mixed up.

TESMAN I say, just fancy if we can sort them out! Perhaps if we work on them together—?

MRS. ELVSTED Oh, yes! Let's try, anyway!

TESMAN We'll manage it. We must! I shall dedicate my life to this.

HEDDA *You,* George? Your *life?*

TESMAN Yes—well, all the time I can spare. My book'll have to wait. Hedda, you do understand? What? I owe it to Eilert's memory.

HEDDA Perhaps.

TESMAN Well, my dear Mrs. Elvsted, you and I'll have to pool our brains. No use crying over spilt milk, what? We must try to approach this matter calmly.

MRS. ELVSTED Yes, yes, Mr. Tesman. I'll do my best.

TESMAN Well, come over here and let's start looking at these notes right away. Where shall we sit? Here? No, the other room. You'll excuse us, won't you, Judge? Come along with me Mrs. Elvsted.

MRS. ELVSTED Oh, God! If only we can manage to do it!

> TESMAN *and* MRS. ELVSTED *go into the rear room. He takes off his hat and overcoat. They sit at the table beneath the hanging lamp and absorb themselves in the notes.* HEDDA *walks across to the stove and sits in the armchair. After a moment,* BRACK *goes over to her.*

HEDDA [*half aloud*] Oh, Judge! This act of Eilert Loevborg's—doesn't it give one a sense of release!

BRACK Release, Mrs. Hedda? Well, it's a release for him, of course—

HEDDA Oh, I don't mean him—I mean me! The release of knowing that someone can do something really brave! Something beautiful!

BRACK [*smiles*] Hm—my dear Mrs. Hedda—

HEDDA Oh, I know what you're going to say. You're a bourgeois at heart too, just like—ah, well!

BRACK [*looks at her*] Eilert Loevborg has meant more to you than you're willing to admit to yourself. Or am I wrong?

HEDDA I'm not answering questions like that from you. I only know that Eilert Loevborg has had the courage to live according to his own principles. And now, at last, he's done something big! Something beautiful! To have the courage and the will to rise from the feast of life so early!

BRACK It distresses me deeply, Mrs. Hedda, but I'm afraid I must rob you of that charming illusion.

HEDDA Illusion?

BRACK You wouldn't have been allowed to keep it for long, anyway.

HEDDA What do you mean?

BRACK He didn't shoot himself on purpose.

HEDDA Not on purpose?

BRACK No. It didn't happen quite the way I told you.

HEDDA Have you been hiding something? What is it?

BRACK In order to spare poor Mrs. Elvsted's feelings, I permitted myself one or two small—equivocations.

HEDDA What?

BRACK To begin with, he is already dead.

HEDDA   He died at the hospital?

BRACK   Yes. Without regaining consciousness.

HEDDA   What else haven't you told us?

BRACK   The incident didn't take place at his lodgings.

HEDDA   Well, that's utterly unimportant.

BRACK   Not utterly. The fact is, you see, that Eilbert Loevborg was found shot in Mademoiselle Danielle's boudoir.

HEDDA   [*almost jumps up, but instead sinks back in her chair*]   That's impossible. He can't have been there today.

BRACK   He was there this afternoon. He went to ask for something he claimed they'd taken from him. Talked some crazy nonsense about a child which had got lost—

HEDDA   Oh! So that was the reason!

BRACK   I thought at first he might have been referring to his manuscript. But I hear he destroyed that himself. So he must have meant his pocketbook—I suppose.

HEDDA   Yes, I suppose so. So they found him there?

BRACK   Yes; there. With a discharged pistol in his breast pocket. The shot had wounded him mortally.

HEDDA   Yes. In the breast.

BRACK   No. In the—hm—stomach. The—lower part—

HEDDA   [*looks at him with an expression of repulsion*]   That too! Oh, why does everything I touch become mean and ludicrous? It's like a curse!

BRACK   There's something else, Mrs. Hedda. It's rather disagreeable, too.

HEDDA   What?

BRACK   The pistol he had on him—

HEDDA   Yes? What about it?

BRACK   He must have stolen it.

HEDDA   [*jumps up*]   Stolen it! That isn't true! He didn't.

BRACK   It's the only explanation. He must have stolen it. Ssh!

TESMAN *and* MRS. ELVSTED *have got up from the table in the rear room and come into the drawing room.*

TESMAN   [*his hands full of papers*]   Hedda, I can't see properly under that lamp. Think!

HEDDA   I am thinking.

TESMAN   Do you think we could possibly use your writing table for a little? What?

HEDDA   Yes, of course.

Quickly.

No, wait! Let me tidy it up first.

TESMAN   Oh, don't you trouble about that. There's plenty of room.

HEDDA   No, no, let me tidy it up first, I say. I'll take this in and put them on the piano. Here.

She pulls an object, covered with sheets of music, out from under the bookcase, puts some more sheets on top and carries it all into the rear room and away to the left. TESMAN *puts his papers on the writing table and moves the lamp over from the corner table. He and* MRS. ELVSTED *sit down and begin working again.* HEDDA *comes back.*

HEDDA [*behind* MRS. ELVSTED's *chair, ruffles her hair gently*]   Well, my pretty Thea! And how is work progressing on Eilert Loevborg's memorial?

MRS. ELVSTED [*looks up at her, dejectedly*]   Oh, it's going to be terribly difficult to get these into any order.

TESMAN   We've got to do it. We must! After all, putting other people's papers into order is rather my specialty, what?

HEDDA *goes over to the stove and sits on one of the footstools.* BRACK *stands over her, leaning against the armchair.*

HEDDA [*whispers*]   What was that you were saying about the pistol?

BRACK [*softly*]   I said he must have stolen it.

HEDDA   Why do you think that?

BRACK   Because any other explanation is unthinkable, Mrs. Hedda, or ought to be.

HEDDA   I see.

BRACK [*looks at her for a moment*]   Eilert Loevborg was here this morning. Wasn't he?

HEDDA   Yes.

BRACK   Were you alone with him?

HEDDA   For a few moments.

BRACK   You didn't leave the room while he was here?

HEDDA   No.

BRACK   Think again. Are you sure you didn't go out for a moment?

HEDDA   Oh—yes, I might have gone into the hall. Just for a few seconds.

BRACK   And where was your pistol-case during this time?

HEDDA   I'd locked it in that—

BRACK   Er—Mrs. Hedda?

HEDDA   It was lying over there on my writing table.

BRACK   Have you looked to see if both the pistols are still there?

HEDDA   No.

BRACK   You needn't bother. I saw the pistol Loevborg had when they found him. I recognized it at once. From yesterday. And other occasions.

HEDDA   Have you got it?

BRACK   No. The police have it.

HEDDA   What will the police do with this pistol?

BRACK   Try to trace the owner.

HEDDA   Do you think they'll succeed?

BRACK [*leans down and whispers*]   No, Hedda Gabler. Not as long as I hold my tongue.

HEDDA [*looks nervously at him*]   And if you don't?

BRACK [*shrugs his shoulders*]   You could always say he'd stolen it.

HEDDA   I'd rather die!

BRACK [*smiles*]   People say that. They never do it.

HEDDA [*not replying*] And suppose the pistol wasn't stolen? And they trace the owner? What then?

BRACK There'll be a scandal, Hedda.

HEDDA A scandal!

BRACK Yes, a scandal. The thing you're so frightened of. You'll have to appear in court. Together with Mademoiselle Danielle. She'll have to explain how it all happened. Was it an accident, or was it— homicide? Was he about to take the pistol from his pocket to threaten her? And did it go off? Or did she snatch the pistol from his hand, shoot him and then put it back in his pocket? She might quite easily have done it. She's a resourceful lady, is Mademoiselle Danielle.

HEDDA But I had nothing to do with this repulsive business.

BRACK No. But you'll have to answer one question. Why did you give Eilert Loevborg this pistol? And what conclusions will people draw when it is proved you did give it to him?

HEDDA [*bows her head*] That's true. I hadn't thought of that.

BRACK Well, luckily there's no danger as long as I hold my tongue.

HEDDA [*looks up at him*] In other words, I'm in your power, Judge. From now on, you've got your hold over me.

BRACK [*whispers, more slowly*] Hedda, my dearest—believe me—I will not abuse my position.

HEDDA Nevertheless, I'm in your power. Dependent on your will, and your demands. Not free. Still not free!

Rises passionately.

No. I couldn't bear that. No.

BRACK [*looks half-derisively at her*] Most people resign themselves to the inevitable, sooner or later.

HEDDA [*returns his gaze*] Possibly they do.

She goes across to the writing table.

HEDDA [*represses an involuntary smile and says in* TESMAN's *voice*] Well, George. Think you'll be able to manage? What?

TESMAN Heaven knows, dear. This is going to take months and months.

HEDDA [*in the same tone as before*] Fancy that, by Jove!

Runs her hands gently through MRS. ELVSTED's *hair.*

Doesn't it feel strange, Thea? Here you are working away with Tesman just the way you used to work with Eilert Loevborg.

MRS. ELVSTED Oh—if only I can inspire your husband too!

HEDDA Oh, it'll come. In time.

TESMAN Yes—do you know, Hedda, I really think I'm beginning to feel a bit—well—that way. But you go back and talk to Judge Brack.

HEDDA Can't I be of use to you two in any way?

TESMAN No, none at all.

Turns his head.

You'll have to keep Hedda company from now on, Judge, and see she doesn't get bored. If you don't mind.

BRACK [*glances at* HEDDA] It'll be a pleasure.

HEDDA Thank you. But I'm tired this evening. I think I'll lie down on the sofa in there for a little while.

TESMAN Yes, dear—do. What?

> HEDDA *goes into the rear room and draws the curtains behind her. Short pause. Suddenly she begins to play a frenzied dance melody on the piano.*

MRS. ELVSTED [*starts up from her chair*] Oh, what's that?

TESMAN [*runs to the doorway*] Hedda dear, please! Don't play dance music tonight! Think of Auntie Rena, And Eilert.

HEDDA [*puts her head out through the curtains*] And Auntie Juju. And all the rest of them. From now on I'll be quiet.

> *Closes the curtains behind her.*

TESMAN [*at the writing table*] It distresses her to watch us doing this. I say, Mrs. Elvsted, I've an idea. Why don't you move in with Auntie Juju? I'll run over each evening, and we can sit and work there. What?

MRS. ELVSTED Yes, that might be the best plan.

HEDDA [*from the rear room*] I can hear what you're saying, Tesman. But how shall I spend the evenings out here?

TESMAN [*looking through his papers*] Oh, I'm sure Judge Brack'll be kind enough to come over and keep you company. You won't mind my not being here, Judge?

BRACK [*in the armchair, calls gaily*] I'll be delighted, Mrs. Tesman. I'll be here every evening. We'll have great fun together, you and I.

HEDDA [*loud and clear*] Yes, that'll suit you, won't it, Judge? The only cock on the dunghill—!

> *A shot is heard from the rear room.* TESMAN, MRS. ELVSTED *and* JUDGE BRACK *start from their chairs.*

TESMAN Oh, she's playing with those pistols again.

> *He pulls the curtains aside and runs in.* MRS. ELVSTED *follows him.* HEDDA *is lying dead on the sofa. Confusion and shouting.* BERTHA *enters in alarm from the right.*

TESMAN [*screams to* BRACK] She's shot herself! Shot herself in the head! By Jove! Fancy that!

BRACK [*half paralyzed in the armchair*] But, good God! People don't do such things!

ED BULLINS

A Son, Come Home

CHARACTERS

MOTHER, *early 50s*   THE GIRL
SON, *30 years old*   THE BOY

The BOY *and the* GIRL *wear black tights and shirts. They move the
action of the play and express the* MOTHER's *and the* SON's *moods
and tensions. They become various embodiments recalled from
memory and history: they enact a number of personalities and
move from mood to mood. The players are Black.*

*At rise: Scene: Bare stage but for two chairs positioned so as not
to interfere with the actions of the* BOY *and the* GIRL. *The* MOTHER
*enters, sits in chair and begins to use imaginary iron and board.
She hums a spiritual as she works.*

MOTHER   You came three times . . . Michael? It took you three times
to find me at home?

> *The* GIRL *enters, turns and peers through the cracked, imaginary
> door.*

SON'S VOICE [*offstage*]   Is Mrs. Brown home?
GIRL [*an old woman*]   What?
MOTHER   It shouldn't have taken you three times. I told you that I
would be here by two and you should wait, Michael.

> *The* SON *enters, passes the* GIRL *and takes his seat upon the
> other chair. The* BOY *enters, stops on other side of the imaginary
> door and looks through at the* GIRL.

BOY   Is Mrs. Brown in?
GIRL   Miss Brown ain't come in yet. Come back later . . . She'll be in
before dark.
MOTHER   It shouldn't have taken you three times . . . You should lis-
ten to me, Michael. Standin' all that time in the cold.
SON   It wasn't cold, Mother.
MOTHER   I told you that I would be here by two and you should wait,
Michael.
BOY   Please tell Mrs. Brown that her son's in town to visit her.
GIRL   You little Miss Brown's son? Well, bless the Lord.

> *Calls over her shoulder.*

Hey, Mandy, do you hear that? Little Miss Brown upstairs got a son
. . . a great big boy . . . He's come to visit her.
BOY   You'll tell her, won't you?
GIRL   Sure, I'll tell her.

> *Grins and shows gums.*

1508

I'll tell her soon as she gets in.

MOTHER   Did you get cold, Michael?

SON   No, Mother. I walked around some . . . sightseeing.

BOY   I walked up Twenty-third Street toward South. I had phoned that I was coming.

MOTHER   Sightseeing? But this is your home, Michael . . . always has been.

BOY   Just before I left New York I phoned that I was taking the bus. Two hours by bus, that's all. That's all it takes. Two hours.

SON   This town seems so strange. Different than how I remember it.

MOTHER   Yes, you have been away for a good while . . . How long has it been, Michael?

BOY   Two hours down the Jersey Turnpike, the trip beginning at the New York Port Authority Terminal . . .

SON   . . . and then straight down through New Jersey to Philadelphia . . .

GIRL   . . . and home . . . Just imagine . . . little Miss Brown's got a son who's come home.

SON   Yes, home . . . an anachronism.

MOTHER   What did you say, Michael?

BOY   He said . . .

GIRL [*late teens*]   What's an anachronism, Mike?

SON   Anachronism: 1: an error in chronology; *esp:* a chronological misplacing of persons, events, objects, or customs in regard to each other; 2: a person or a thing that is chronologically out of place— anachronistic/ *also* anachronic/ *or* anachronous—anachronistically/ *also* anachronously.

MOTHER   I was so glad to hear you were going to school in California.

BOY   College.

GIRL   Yes, I understand.

MOTHER   How long have you been gone, Michael?

SON   Nine years.

BOY   Nine years it's been. I wonder if she'll know me . . .

MOTHER   You've put on so much weight, son. You know that's not healthy.

GIRL [*20 years old*]   And that silly beard . . . how . . .

SON   Oh . . . I'll take it off. I'm going on a diet tomorrow.

BOY   I wonder if I'll know her.

SON   You've put on some yourself, Mother.

MOTHER   Yes, the years pass. Thank the Lord.

BOY   I wonder if we've changed much.

GIRL   Yes, thank the Lord.

SON   The streets here seem so small.

MOTHER   Yes, it seems like that when you spend a little time in Los Angeles.

GIRL   I spent eighteen months there with your aunt when she was sick. She had nobody else to help her . . . she was so lonely. And you were in the service . . . away. You've always been away.

BOY   In Los Angeles the boulevards, the avenues, the streets . . .

SON   . . . are wide. Yes, they have some wide ones out West. Here, they're so small and narrow. I wonder how cars get through on both sides.

MOTHER   Why, you know how . . . we lived on Derby Street for over ten years, didn't we?

SON   Yeah, that was almost an alley.

MOTHER   Did you see much of your aunt before you left Los Angeles?

SON   What?

GIRL [*middle-aged woman to* BOY]   Have you found a job yet, Michael?

MOTHER   Your aunt. My sister.

BOY   Nawh, not yet . . . Today I just walked downtown . . . quite a ways . . . this place is plenty big, ain't it?

SON   I don't see too much of Aunt Sophie.

MOTHER   But you're so much alike.

GIRL   Well, your bags are packed and are sitting outside the door.

BOY   My bags?

MOTHER   You shouldn't be that way, Michael. You shouldn't get too far away from your family.

SON   Yes, Mother.

BOY   But I don't have any money. I had to walk downtown today. That's how much money I have. I've only been here a week.

GIRL   I packed your bags, Michael.

MOTHER   You never can tell when you'll need or want your family, Michael.

SON   That's right, Mother.

MOTHER   You and she are so much alike.

BOY   Well, goodbye, Aunt Sophie.

GIRL [*silence*]

MOTHER   All that time in California and you hardly saw your aunt. My baby sister.

BOY   Tsk tsk tsk.

SON   I'm sorry, Mother.

MOTHER   In the letters I'd get from both of you there'd be no mention of the other. All these years. Did you see her again?

SON   Yes.

GIRL [*on telephone*]   Michael? Michael who? . . . Ohhh . . . Bernice's boy.

MOTHER   You didn't tell me about this, did you?

SON   No, I didn't.

BOY   Hello, Aunt Sophie. How are you?

GIRL   I'm fine, Michael. How are you? You're looking well.

BOY   I'm getting on okay.

MOTHER   I prayed for you.

SON   Thank you.

MOTHER   Thank the Lord, Michael.

BOY   Got me a job working for the city.

GIRL   You did now.

BOY   Yes, I've brought you something.

GIRL   What's this, Michael . . . ohhh . . . it's money.

BOY   It's for the week I stayed with you.

GIRL   Fifty dollars. But, Michael, you didn't have to.

MOTHER   Are you still writing that radical stuff, Michael?

SON   Radical?

MOTHER   Yes . . . that stuff you write and send me all the time in those little books.

SON   My poetry, Mother?

MOTHER   Yes, that's what I'm talking about.

SON   No.

MOTHER   Praise the Lord, son. Praise the Lord. Didn't seem like anything I had read in school.

BOY   [*on telephone*]   Aunt Sophie? . . . Aunt Sophie? . . . It's me, Michael . . .

GIRL   Michael?

BOY   Yes . . . Michael . . .

GIRL   Oh . . . Michael . . . yes . . .

BOY   I'm in jail, Aunt Sophie . . . I got picked up for drunk driving.

GIRL   You did . . . how awful . . .

MOTHER   When you going to get your hair cut, Michael?

BOY   Aunt Sophie . . . will you please come down and sign my bail. I've got the money . . . I just got paid yesterday . . . They're holding more than enough for me . . . but the law says that someone has to sign for it.

MOTHER   You look almost like a hoodlum, Michael.

BOY   All you need to do is come down and sign . . . and I can get out.

MOTHER   What you tryin' to be . . . a savage or something? Are you keeping out of trouble, Michael?

GIRL   Ohhh . . . Michael . . . I'm sorry but I can't do nothin' like that . . .

BOY   But all you have to do is sign . . . I've got the money and everything.

GIRL   I'm sorry . . . I can't stick my neck out.

BOY   But, Aunt Sophie . . . if I don't get back to work I'll lose my job and everything . . . please . . .

GIRL   I'm sorry, Michael . . . I can't stick my neck out . . . I have to go now . . . Is there anyone I can call?

BOY   No.

GIRL   I could call your mother. She wouldn't mind if I reversed the charges on her, would she? I don't like to run my bills up.

BOY   No, thanks.

MOTHER   You and your aunt are so much alike.

SON   Yes, Mother. Our birthdays are in the same month.

MOTHER   Yes, that year was so hot . . . so hot and I was carrying you . . .

> As the MOTHER *speaks the* BOY *comes over and takes her by the hand and leads her from the chair, and they stroll around the stage, arm in arm. The* GIRL *accompanies them and she and the* BOY *enact scenes from the* MOTHER's *mind.*

. . . carrying you, Michael . . . and you were such a big baby . . . kicked all the time. But I was happy. Happy that I was having a baby of my own . . . I worked as long as I could and bought you everything you might need . . . diapers . . . and bottles . . . and your own spoon . . . and even toys . . . and even books . . . And it was so hot in Philadelphia that year . . . Your Aunt Sophie used to

come over and we'd go for walks . . . sometimes up on the avenue
. . . I was living in West Philly then . . . in that old terrible section
they called "The Bottom." That's where I met your father.

GIRL   You're such a fool, Bernice. No nigger . . . man or boy's . . . ever
going to do a thing to me like that.

MOTHER   Everything's going to be all right, Sophia.

GIRL   But what is he going to do? How are you going to take care of a
baby by yourself?

MOTHER   Everything's going to be all right, Sophia. I'll manage.

GIRL   You'll manage? How? Have you talked about marriage?

MOTHER   Oh, please, Sophia!

GIRL   What do you mean "please"? Have you?

MOTHER   I just can't. He might think . . .

GIRL   Think! That dirty nigger better think. He better think before he
really messes up. And you better too. You got this baby comin' on.
What are you going to do?

MOTHER   I don't know . . . I don't know what I can do.

GIRL   Is he still tellin' you those lies about . . .

MOTHER   They're not lies.

GIRL   Haaaa . . .

MOTHER   They're not.

GIRL   Some smooth-talkin' nigger comes up from Georgia and tell you
he escaped from the chain gang and had to change his name so he
can't get married 'cause they might find out . . . What kinda shit is
that, Bernice?

MOTHER   Please, Sophia. Try and understand. He loves me. I can't
hurt him.

GIRL   Loves you . . . and puts you through this?

MOTHER   Please . . . I'll talk to him . . . Give me a chance.

GIRL   It's just a good thing you got a family, Bernice. It's just a good
thing. You know that, don't cha?

MOTHER   Yes . . . yes, I do . . . but please don't say anything to him.

SON   I've only seen my father about a half dozen times that I remember, Mother. What was he like?

MOTHER   Down in The Bottom . . . that's where I met your father. I
was young and hinkty[1] then. Had big pretty brown legs and a small
waist. Everybody used to call me Bernie . . . and me and my sister
would go to Atlantic City on the weekends and work as waitresses in
the evenings and sit all afternoon on the black part of the beach at
Boardwalk and Atlantic . . . getting blacker . . . and having the times
of our lives. Your father probably still lives down in The Bottom . . .
perched over some bar down there . . . drunk to the world . . . I can
see him now . . . He had good white teeth then . . . not how they
turned later when he started in drinkin' that wine and wouldn't
stop . . . he was so nice then.

BOY   Awwww, listen, kid. I got my problems too.

GIRL   But Andy . . . I'm six months gone . . . and you ain't done
nothin'.

_____
1. A Black slang word which means that she was snobbish or aloof because of her
certainty of her own good looks and general worth.

BOY   Well, what can I do?

GIRL   Don't talk like that . . . What can you do? . . . You know what you can do.

BOY   You mean marry you? Now lissen, sweetheart . . .

GIRL   But what about our baby?

BOY   Your baby.

GIRL   Don't talk like that! It took more than me to get him.

BOY   Well . . . look . . . I'll talk to you later, kid. I got to go to work now.

GIRL   That's what I got to talk to you about too, Andy. I need some money.

BOY   Money! Is somethin' wrong with your head, woman? I ain't got no money.

GIRL   But I can't work much longer, Andy. You got to give me some money. Andy . . . you just gotta.

BOY   Woman . . . all I got to *ever* do is die and go to hell.

GIRL   Well, you gonna do that, Andy. You sho are . . . you know that, don't you? . . . You know that.

MOTHER   . . . Yes, you are, man. Praise the Lord. We all are . . . All of us . . . even though he ain't come for you yet to make you pay. Maybe he's waitin' for us to go together so I can be a witness to the retribution that's handed down. A witness to all that He'll bestow upon your sinner's head . . . A witness! . . . That's what I am, Andy! Do you hear me? . . . A witness!

SON   Mother . . . what's wrong? What's the matter?

MOTHER   Thank the Lord that I am not blinded and will see the fulfillment of divine . . .

SON   Mother!

MOTHER   Oh . . . is something wrong, Michael?

SON   You're shouting and walking around . . .

MOTHER   Oh . . . it's nothing, son. I'm just feeling the power of the Lord.

SON   Oh . . . is there anything I can get you, Mother?

MOTHER   No, nothing at all.

She sits again and irons.

SON   Where's your kitchen? . . . I'll get you some coffee . . . the way you like it. I bet I still remember how to fix it.

MOTHER   Michael . . . I don't drink anything like that no more.

SON   No?

MOTHER   Not since I joined the service of the Lord.

SON   Yeah? . . . Well, do you mind if I get myself a cup?

MOTHER   Why, I don't have a kitchen. All my meals are prepared for me.

SON   Oh . . . I thought I was having dinner with you.

MOTHER   No. There's nothing like that here.

SON   Well, could I take you out to a restaurant? . . . Remember how we used to go out all the time and eat? I've never lost my habit of liking to eat out. Remember . . . we used to come down to this part of town and go to restaurants. They used to call it home cooking then . . . now, at least where I been out West and up in Harlem . . .

we call it soul food. I bet we could find a nice little restaurant not four blocks from here, Mother. Remember that old man's place we used to go to on Nineteenth and South? I bet he's dead now . . . but . . .

MOTHER   I don't even eat out no more, Michael.

SON   No?

MOTHER   Sometimes I take a piece of holy bread to work . . . or some fruit . . . if it's been blessed by my Spiritual Mother.

SON   I see.

MOTHER   Besides . . . we have a prayer meeting tonight.

SON   On Friday?

MOTHER   Every night. You'll have to be going soon.

SON   Oh.

MOTHER   You're looking well.

SON   Thank you.

MOTHER   But you look tired.

SON   Do I?

MOTHER   Yes, those rings around your eyes might never leave. Your father had them.

SON   Did he?

MOTHER   Yes . . . and cowlicks . . . deep cowlicks on each side of his head.

SON   Yes . . . I remember.

MOTHER   Do you?

> *The* BOY *and the* GIRL *take crouching positions behind and in front of them. They are in a streetcar. The* BOY *behind the* MOTHER *and* SON, *the* GIRL *across the aisle, a passenger.*

MOTHER [*young woman to the* BOY]   Keep your damn hands off him, Andy!

BOY [*chuckles*]   Awww, c'mon . . . Bernie. I ain't seen him since he was in the crib.

MOTHER   And you wouldn't have seen neither of us . . . if I had anything to do with it . . . Ohhh . . . why did I get on this trolley?

BOY   C'mon . . . Bernie . . . don't be so stuckup.

MOTHER   Don't even talk to us . . . and stop reaching after him.

BOY   Awww . . . c'mon . . . Bernie. Let me look at him.

MOTHER   Leave us alone. Look . . . people are looking at us.

> *The* GIRL *across the aisle has been peeking at the trio but looks toward front at the mention of herself.*

BOY   Hey, big boy . . . do you know who I am?

MOTHER   Stop it, Andy! Stop it, I say . . . Mikie . . . don't pay any attention to him . . . you hear?

BOY   Hey, big boy . . . know who I am? . . . I'm your daddy. Hey, there . . .

MOTHER   Shut up . . . shut up, Andy . . . you nothin' to us.

BOY   Where you livin' at . . . Bernie? Let me come on by and see the little guy, huh?

MOTHER   No! You're not comin' near us . . . ever . . . you hear?

BOY   But I'm his father . . . look . . . Bernie . . . I've been an ass the way I've acted but . . .

MOTHER   He ain't got no father.

BOY   Oh, come off that nonsense, woman.

MOTHER   Mikie ain't got no father . . . his father's dead . . . you hear?

BOY   Dead?

MOTHER   Yes, dead. My son's father's dead.

BOY   What you talkin' about? . . . He's the spittin' image of me.

MOTHER   Go away . . . leave us alone, Andrew.

BOY   See there . . . he's got the same name as me. His first name is Michael after your father . . . and Andrew after me.

MOTHER   No, stop that, you hear?

BOY   Michael Andrew . . .

MOTHER   You never gave him no name . . . his name is Brown . . . Brown. The same as mine . . . and my sister's . . . and my daddy . . . You never gave him nothin' . . . and you're dead . . . go away and get buried.

BOY   You know that trouble I'm in . . . I got a wife down there, Bernie. I don't care about her . . . what could I do?

MOTHER   [*rises, pulling up the* SON]   We're leavin' . . . don't you try and follow us . . . you hear, Andy? C'mon . . . Mikie . . . watch your step now.

BOY   Well . . . bring him around my job . . . you know where I work. That's all . . . bring him around on payday.

MOTHER   [*leaving*]   We don't need anything from you . . . I'm work-ing . . . just leave us alone.

> The BOY *turns to the* GIRL.

BOY   [*shrugs*]   That's the way it goes . . . I guess. Ships passing on the trolley car . . . Hey . . . don't I know you from up around 40th and Market?

> The GIRL *turns away.*

SON   Yeah . . . I remember him. He always had liquor on his breath.

MOTHER   Yes . . . he did. I'm glad that stuff ain't got me no more . . . Thank the Lord.

GIRL   [*35 years old*]   You want to pour me another drink, Michael?

BOY   [*15 years old*]   You drink too much, Mother.

GIRL   Not as much as some other people I know.

BOY   Well, me and the guys just get short snorts, Mother. But you really hide some port.

GIRL   Don't forget you talkin' to your mother. You gettin' more like your father every day.

BOY   Is that why you like me so much?

GIRL   [*grins drunkenly*]   Oh, hush up now, boy . . . and pour me a drink.

BOY   There's enough here for me too.

GIRL   That's okay . . . when Will comes in he'll bring something.

SON   How is Will, Mother?

MOTHER   I don't know . . . haven't seen Will in years.

SON   Mother.

MOTHER   Yes, Michael.

SON   Why you and Will never got married? . . . You stayed together for over ten years.

MOTHER   Oh, don't ask me questions like that, Michael.

SON   But why not?

MOTHER   It's just none of your business.

SON   But you could be married now . . . not alone in this room . . .

MOTHER   Will had a wife and child in Chester[2] . . . you know that.

SON   He could have gotten a divorce, Mother . . . Why . . .

MOTHER   Because he just didn't . . . that's why.

SON   You never hear from him?

MOTHER   Last I heard . . . Will had cancer.

SON   Oh, he did.

MOTHER   Yes.

SON   Why didn't you tell me? . . . You could have written.

MOTHER   Why?

SON   So I could have known.

MOTHER   So you could have known? Why?

SON   Because Will was like a father to me . . . the only one I've really known.

MOTHER   A father? And you chased him away as soon as you got big enough.

SON   Don't say that, Mother.

MOTHER   You made me choose between you and Will.

SON   Mother.

MOTHER   The quarrels you had with him . . . the mean tricks you used to play . . . the lies you told to your friends about Will . . . He wasn't much . . . when I thought I had a sense of humor I us'ta call him just plain Will.[3] But we was his family.

SON   Mother, listen.

MOTHER   And you drove him away . . . and he didn't lift a hand to stop you.

SON   Listen, Mother.

MOTHER   As soon as you were big enough you did all that you could to get me and Will separated.

SON   Listen.

MOTHER   All right, Michael . . . I'm listening.

> *Pause.*

SON   Nothing.

> *Pause. Lifts an imaginary object.*

Is this your tambourine?

MOTHER   Yes.

SON   Do you play it?

MOTHER   Yes.

SON   Well?

---

2. A town in Delaware to the southwest of Philadelphia.
3. The central character of a popular and long-running radio serial *Just Plain Bill* was presented as a man of good heart but without other characteristics to raise him above the average.

MOTHER   Everything I do in the service of the Lord I do as well as He allows.

SON   You play it at your meetings.

MOTHER   Yes, I do. We celebrate the life He has bestowed upon us.

SON   I guess that's where I get it from.

MOTHER   Did you say something, Michael?

SON   Yes. My musical ability.

MOTHER   Oh . . . you've begun taking your piano lessons again?

SON   No . . . I was never any good at that.

MOTHER   Yes, three different teachers and you never got past the tenth lesson.

SON   You have a good memory, Mother.

MOTHER   Sometimes, son. Sometimes.

SON   I play an electric guitar in a combo.

MOTHER   You do? That's nice.

SON   That's why I'm in New York. We got a good break and came East.

MOTHER   That's nice, Michael.

SON   I was thinking that Sunday I could rent a car and come down to get you and drive you up to see our show. You'll get back in plenty of time to rest for work Monday.

MOTHER   No, I'm sorry. I can't do that.

SON   But you would like it, Mother. We could have dinner up in Harlem, then go down and . . .

MOTHER   I don't do anything like that any more, Michael.

SON   You mean you wouldn't come to see me play even if I were appearing here in Philly?

MOTHER   That's right, Michael. I wouldn't come. I'm past all that.

SON   Oh, I see.

MOTHER   Yes, thank the Lord.

SON   But it's my life, Mother.

MOTHER   Good . . . then you have something to live for.

SON   Yes.

MOTHER   Well, you're a man now, Michael . . . I can no longer live it for you. Do the best with what you have.

SON   Yes . . . Yes, I will, Mother.

GIRL'S VOICE [*offstage*]   Sister Brown . . . Sister Brown . . . hello.

MOTHER [*uneasy; peers at watch*]   Oh . . . it's Mother Ellen . . . I didn't know it was so late.

GIRL [*enters*]   Sister Brown . . . how are you this evening?

MOTHER   Oh, just fine, Mother.

GIRL   Good. It's nearly time for dinner.

MOTHER   Oh, yes, I know.

GIRL   We don't want to keep the others waiting at meeting . . . do we?

MOTHER   No, we don't.

GIRL [*self-assured*]   Hello, son.

SON   Hello.

MOTHER   Oh, Mother . . . Mother . . .

GIRL   Yes, Sister Brown, what is it?

MOTHER   Mother . . . Mother . . . this is . . . this is . . .

Pause.

. . . this is . . .

SON   Hello, I'm Michael. How are you?

MOTHER   [*relieved*]   Yes, Mother . . . This is Michael . . . my son.

GIRL   Why, hello, Michael. I've heard so much about you from your mother. She prays for you daily.

SON   [*embarrassed*]   Oh . . . good.

GIRL   [*briskly*]   Well . . . I have to be off to see about the others.

MOTHER   Yes, Mother Ellen.

GIRL   [*as she exits; chuckles*]   Have to tell everyone that you won't be keeping us waiting, Bernice.

Silence.

SON   Well, I guess I better be going, Mother.

MOTHER   Yes.

SON   I'll write.

MOTHER   Please do.

SON   I will.

MOTHER   You're looking well . . . Thank the Lord.

SON   Thank you, so are you, Mother.

He moves toward her and hesitates.

MOTHER   You're so much like your aunt. Give her my best . . . won't you?

SON   Yes, I will, Mother.

MOTHER   Take care of yourself, son.

SON   Yes, Mother. I will.

The SON *exits. The* MOTHER *stands looking after him as the lights go slowly down to* . . .

BLACKNESS

1968

ACKNOWLEDGMENTS

Woody Allen: "The Kugelmass Episode," reprinted by permission; © 1977 The New Yorker Magazine, Inc.

Sherwood Anderson: "The Egg" from *The Triumph of the Egg* by Sherwood Anderson. Copyright © 1921 by B. W. Huebsch. Renewed 1948 by Eleanor Copenhaver Anderson. Reprinted by permission of Harold Ober Associates, Inc.

James Baldwin: "Sonny's Blues" excerpted from the book *Going to Meet the Man* by James Baldwin. Copyright © 1957 by James Baldwin. Originally appeared in *Partisan Review*. Reprinted by permission of The Dial Press.

Toni Cade Bambara: "My Man Bovanne" copyright © by Toni Cade Bambara. Reprinted from *Gorilla, My Love,* by Toni Cade Bambara, by permission of Random House, Inc.

Hal Bennett: "Dotson Gerber Resurrected" by George H. Bennett; copyright © 1970 by George H. Bennett. Reprinted by permission of William Morris Agency, Inc. on behalf of the author.

Jorge Luis Borges: "Garden of Forking Paths" from *Labyrinths*, translated by Donald A. Yates. Copyright © 1962 by New Directions Publishing Corporation. Reprinted by permission of New Directions.

John Cheever: "The Country Husband" from *The Housebreaker of Shady Hill* is reprinted by permission of John Cheever.

Arthur C. Clarke: "Hide and Seek," copyright 1949 by Street and Smith Publications, Inc. Reprinted from *The Nine Billion Names of God* by Arthur C. Clarke, by permission of Harcourt Brace Jovanovich.

Richard Connell: "The Most Dangerous Game" copyright 1924 by Richard Connell, renewed © 1952 by Louis Fox Connell. Reprinted by permission of Brandt & Brandt.

Joseph Conrad: "The Secret Sharer." Copyright 1910 by Harper & Brothers from the book *Twixt Land and Sea* by Joseph Conrad. Reprinted by permission of Doubleday & Company, Inc.

William Faulkner: "The Old People" from *Go Down Moses*. Copyright 1940, 1942; renewed 1968, 1970 by Estelle Faulkner and Jill Summers. Reprinted by permission of Random House, Inc. "Spotted Horses" copyright 1931 and renewed 1959 by William Faulkner. Reprinted from Scribner's Magazine by permission of Random House, Inc. An expanded version of this story appears as part of *The Hamlet* by William Faulkner.

F. Scott Fitzgerald: "Babylon Revisited" from *Taps at Reveille* is used with the permission of Charles Scribner's Sons. Copyright 1931 The Curtis Publishing Company; renewal copyright © 1959 Frances S. F. Lanahan.

Gabriel Garcia Marquez: "A Very Old Man With Enormous Wings" from *Leaf Storm and Other Stories* by Gabriel Garcia Marquez. Copyright © 1971 by Gabriel Garcia Marquez. Reprinted by permission of Harper & Row, Publishers, Inc.

Ernest Hemingway: "The Short Happy Life of Francis Macomber" (copyright 1936 Ernest Hemingway) is reprinted by permission of Charles Scribner's Sons from *The Short Stories of Ernest Hemingway*.

Spencer Holst: "The Zebra Storyteller" reprinted by permission of E. P. Dutton from *The Language of Cats and Other Stories* by Spencer Holst. Copyright © 1971 by Spencer Holst. A Saturday Review Press edition.

Shirley Jackson: "The Lottery" from *The Lottery*, copyright 1948, 1949 by Shirley Jackson. Copyright renewed © 1976 by Laurence Hyman, Barry Hyman, Mrs. Sarah Webster, and Mrs. Joanne Schnurer. First published in *The New Yorker*. Reprinted by permission of Farrar, Straus & Giroux, Inc.

James Joyce: "Araby" from *Dubliners* by James Joyce, Copyright © 1967 by the Estate of James Joyce. Reprinted by permission of Viking Penguin, Inc.

Franz Kafka: "A Hunger Artist" from *The Penal Colony*. Copyright © 1948, renewed 1967 by Schocken Books, Inc. Reprinted by permission of Schocken Books, Inc.

D. H. Lawrence: "The Rocking Horse Winner" from *The Complete Short Stories, Vol. I*, copyright © 1962 by Angelo Ravagli and C. M. Weekley, Executors of the Estate of Frieda Lawrence Ravagli. "Odour of Chrysanthemums," copyright © 1962 by Angelo Ravagli and C. M. Weekley, Executors of the Estate of Frieda Lawrence Ravagli, and "Horse Dealer's Daughter," copyright 1922 by Thomas Seltzer, Inc., renewed 1950 by Frieda Lawrence, from *The Complete Short Stories of D. H. Lawrence, Vol. II*. Reprinted by permission of Viking Penguin Inc. Excerpts from *Selected Literary Criticism*, edited by Anthony Beal, copyright © 1956 by Frieda Lawrence. Selections from *Phoenix I*, edited by Edward O. McDonald, copyright © 1936 by Frieda Lawrence, © renewed 1964 by the Estate of the late Frieda Lawrence Ravagli. Reprinted by permission of Viking Penguin, Inc.

Ursula K. Le Guin: "The Ones Who Walk Away from Omelas," copyright 1973 by Ursula K. Le Guin. Reprinted by permission of the author and the author's agent, Virginia Kidd.

Doris Lessing: "Our Friend Judith" from *A Man and Two Women*, copyright 1958, 1962, 1963 by Doris Lessing. Reprinted by permission of Simon & Schuster, a Division of Gulf and Western, and Curtis Brown Ltd.

Katherine Mansfield: "Her First Ball," copyright 1922 by Alfred A. Knopf, Inc., and renewed 1950 by John Middleton Murry. Reprinted from *The Short Stories of Katherine Mansfield* by permission of Alfred A. Knopf, Inc.

Alice Munro: "Boys and Girls" from *The Dance of the Happy Shades* by Alice Munro. Copyright © Alice Munro, 1968. Reprinted by permission of McGraw-Hill Ryerson Limited, Toronto.

Albert Murray: "Train Whistle Guitar" is reprinted by permission of the author, Albert Murray, and his agent, James Brown Associates, Inc. Copyright © 1953 by Albert Murray.

Joyce Carol Oates: "The Lady With the Pet Dog" from *Marriages and Infidelities* by Joyce Carol Oates by permission of the publisher, Vanguard Press, Inc. Copyright © 1968, 1969, 1970, 1971, 1972 by Joyce Carol Oates.

Flannery O'Connor: "The Artificial Nigger," copyright © 1955 by Flannery O'Connor. Reprinted from her volume *A Good Man Is Hard to Find and Other Stories* by permission of Harcourt Brace Jovanovich, Inc.

C. Day Lewis: "Come Live With Me and Be My Love" from *Two Songs* in *Collected Poems*, 1954, is reprinted by permission of the Executors of the Estate of C. Day Lewis, Jonathan Cape, Ltd. and The Hogarth Press.

Walter de la Mare: "Slim Cunning Hands" from *The Complete Poems of Walter de la Mare* is reprinted by permission of the Literary Executors of Walter de la Mare and The Society of Authors as their representative.

Peter de Vries: "Bacchanal" from *The Tents of Wickedness* by Peter de Vries. Copyright 1950 by Peter de Vries. Originally appeared in *The New Yorker*. Reprinted by permission of Little, Brown and Company.

Ann Deagon: "Certified Copy" and "There is no Balm in Birmingham" from *There is No Balm in Birmingham* by Ann Deagon. Copyright © 1972, 1974, 1975, 1976, 1978 by Ann Deagon. Reprinted by permission of David R. Godine, Publisher, Inc.

James Dickey: "Cherrylog Road" and "The Leap" from *Poems 1957–1967*, by James Dickey. Copyright © 1963, 1964 by James Dickey. Reprinted by permission of Wesleyan University Press. "Cherrylog Road" first appeared in *The New Yorker*.

Emily Dickinson: #'s 341, 712, 657, 986, and 632 are reprinted by permission of the Publishers and the Trustees of Amherst College from *The Poems of Emily Dickinson*, edited by Thomas H. Johnson, Cambridge, Mass.: The Belknap Press of Harvard University Press, Copyright © 1951, 1955 by the President and Fellows of Harvard College. #'s 341 and 657 are also reprinted by permission of Little, Brown and Company from *The Complete Poems of Emily Dickinson* edited by Thomas H. Johnson. Copyright 1929 by Martha Dickinson Bianchi. Copyright © 1957 by Mary L. Hampson.

Bob Dylan: "Mister Tambourine Man" © 1964 Warner Bros., Inc. All Rights Reserved. Used by Permission.

T. S. Eliot: "The Journey of the Magi" and "The Love Song of J. Alfred Prufrock" from *Collected Poems 1909–1962* by T. S. Eliot, copyright, 1936 by Harcourt Brace Jovanovich, Inc.; copyright © 1963, 1964 by T. S. Eliot. Reprinted by permission of Harcourt Brace Jovanovich, Inc. and Faber and Faber Ltd.

James A. Emanuel: "Emmett Till" from *The Treehouse and Other Poems* © 1968 by James A. Emanuel. Reprinted by permission of Broadside/Crummel Press, Detroit, Michigan.

Kenneth Fearing: "Dirge" from *New and Selected Poems* by Kenneth Fearing. Reprinted by permission of the publisher, Indiana University Press.

Lawrence Ferlinghetti: "Christ Climbed Down" from *A Coney Island of the Mind* by Lawrence Ferlinghetti. Copyright © 1958 by Lawrence Ferlinghetti. Reprinted by permission of New Directions.

Julia Fields: "Madness One Monday Evening" is reprinted by permission of the author.

Richard Harter Fogle: "A Hawthorne Garland: The Scarlet Letter" is reprinted by permission of the author.

Robert Frost: "Range-Finding," "The Rose Family," "Stopping By Woods on a Snowy Evening" and "U.S. 1946 King's X" from *The Poetry of Robert Frost* edited by Edward Connery Lathem. Copyright 1916, 1923, 1928, 1947, © 1968 by Holt, Rinehart and Winston. Copyright 1944, 1951, © 1956 by Robert Frost. Copyright © 1975 by Leslie Frost Ballentine. Reprinted by permission of Holt, Rinehart and Winston, Publishers.

Nikki Giovanni: "Poetry" from *The Woman and the Men* by Nikki Giovanni, Copyright © 1970, 1974, 1975 by Nikki Giovanni. Reprinted by permission of William Morrow & Company.

Edgar A. Guest: "The Things That Make A Soldier Great" from *Collected Verse* by Edgar Guest. Contemporary Books, Inc., Chicago, 1934. Reprinted by permission of Contemporary Books, Inc.

Michael Harper: "Dear John, Dear Coltrane" from *Dear John, Dear Coltrane* published by the University of Pittsburgh Press. First published in the *Carolina Quarterly*, 1970. Reprined by permission.

Anthony Hecht: "The Dover Bitch" and "It Out-Herod's Herod. Pray You, Avoid It" are used by permission of Atheneum Publishers from *The Hard Hours* by Anthony Hecht. Copyright © 1960, 1967 by Anthony Hecht.

Robert G. Holland: "Eve in Old Age" is reprinted by permission of the author, Robert Holland.

John Hollander: "Adam's Task" from *The Night Mirror*, copyright © 1970, 1971 by John Hollander and "A State of Nature" from *Types of Shape*, copyright © 1967, 1969 by John Hollander are reprinted by permission of Atheneum Publishers.

Robert Hollander: "You too? Me too—Why not? Soda Pop" is reprinted from *The Massachusetts Review* © 1968 by The Massachusetts Review, Inc. by permission of the publisher.

M. Carl Holman: "Three Brown Girls Singing" is reprinted by permission of the author.

A. E. Housman: "Terence, This Is Stupid Stuff" and "To an Athlete Dying Young" from "A Shropshire Lad"—Authorized Edition from *The Collected Poems of A. E. Housman*. Copyright 1939 1940, © 1965 by Holt, Rinehart and Winston. Copyright © 1967, 1968 by Robert E. Symons. Reprinted by permission of Holt, Rinehart and Winston Publishers, The Society of Authors as the Literary representative of the Estate of A. E. Housman, and Jonathan Cape Ltd.

Langston Hughes: "The Negro Speaks of Rivers" copyright 1926 by Alfred A. Knopf, Inc. and renewed 1954 by Langston Hughes. Reprinted from *Selected Poems of Langston Hughes*, by permission of Alfred A. Knopf, Inc. "Dream Deferred" copyright 1959 by Langston Hughes. Reprinted from *The Panther and the Lash*, by Langston Hughes, by permission of Alfred A. Knopf, Inc.

Richard Hugo: "To Women" from *White Center*, published by W. W. Norton & Co., Inc., is reprinted by permission of the author, Richard Hugo. "What Thou Lovest Well Remains American" is reprinted from *What Thou Lovest Well Remains American, Poems* by Richard Hugo, by permission of W. W. Norton & Co., Inc. Copyright © 1975 by W. W. Norton & Co. Inc.

Randall Jarrell: "The Death of the Ball Turret Gunner" is reprinted by permission of Farrar, Straus & Giroux, Inc. from *The Complete Poems* by Randall Jarrell. Copyright

© 1945, 1947, 1969 by Mrs. Randall Jarrell.

Robinson Jeffers: "To the Stonecutters" copyright 1924 and renewed 1952 by Robinson Jeffers. Reprinted from *Selected Poetry of Robinson Jeffers*, by Robinson Jeffers, by permission of Random House, Inc.

Donald Justice: "Here in Katmandu," "Counting the Mad" and "Southern Gothic" from *The Summer Anniversaries*, copyright © 1956, 1957, 1958 by Donald Justice. Reprinted by permission of Wesleyan University Press. "Here in Katmandu" and "Southern Gothic" first appeared in *Poetry*.

Bob Kaufman: "Blues Note" reprinted by permission of the Broadside Press.

X. J. Kennedy: "Epitaph for a Postal Clerk," copyright © 1956 by X. J. Kennedy and "In a Prominent Bar in Secaucus One Day" are reprinted from the book *Nude Descending a Staircase* by X. J. Kennedy by permission of Doubleday & Company, Inc.

Galway Kinnell: "To Christ, Our Lord" from *What A Kingdom It Was* by Galway Kinnell, copyright © 1960 by Galway Kinnell. Reprinted by permission of Houghton Mifflin Company.

A. M. Klein: "Heirloom" from *Half Not A Jew*, by A. M. Klein, copyright by Behrman House Inc. Used with permission.

Etheridge Knight: "Hard Rock Returns to Prison From the Hospital for the Criminal Insane" and "The Idea of Ancestry" from *Poems from Prison* by Etheridge Knight, © 1968 by Etheridge Knight. Reprinted by permission of Broadside/Crummel Press, Detroit, Michigan.

Kenneth Koch: "Variations on a Theme by William Carlos Williams" from *Thank You and Other Poems*, Copyright © 1962 by Kenneth Koch. Reprinted by permission of Grove Press, Inc.

Maxine Kumin: "Woodchucks" from *Up Country: Poems of New England*, copyright © 1971 by Maxine Kumin. Reprinted by permission of Harper & Row, Publisher, Inc.

Philip Larkin: "Church Going" is reprinted from *The Less Deceived* by permission of The Marvell Press, England.

D. H. Lawrence: "Piano" and "Snake" from *The Complete Poems of D. H. Lawrence*. Copyright © 1964, 1971 by Angelo Ravagli and C. M. Weekley, Executors of the Estate of Frieda Lawrence Ravagli. Reprinted by permission of Viking Penguin, Inc.

Denise Levertov: "What Were They Like?" from *The Sorrow Dance*, Copyright © 1966 by Denise Levertov Goodman. Reprinted by permission of New Directions.

Dorothy Livesay: "Green Rain" from *Collected Poems: The Two Seasons* by Dorothy Livesay. Copyright © 1972. Reprinted by permission of McGraw Hill-Ryerson, Toronto.

Donald Lloyd: "Bridal Couch" first appeared in *Prairie Schooner* and is reprinted here by permission of the author.

Audre Lorde: "Outside," "Recreation" and "Hanging Fire" are reprinted from *The Black Unicorn, Poems* by Audre Lorde by permission of W. W. Norton & Company, Inc. Copyright © 1978 by Audre Lorde.

Robert Lowell: "Skunk Hour" from *Life Studies* by Robert Lowell. Copyright © 1956, 1959 by Robert Lowell. Reprinted by permission of Farrar, Straus & Giroux, Inc.

Eugene J. McCarthy: "Kilroy" from *Other Things and the Aardvark*, copyright © 1970 by Eugene J. McCarthy. Reprinted by permission of Doubleday & Company, Inc.

David McCord: "Waiter" from *Bay Window Ballads* by David McCord. Copyright 1935 by Charles Scribner's Sons; renewal copyright © 1963 by David McCord. Reprinted by permission of Charles Scribner's Sons. "History of Education" from *What Cheer* reprinted by permission of the author.

Claude McKay: "America" from *Selected Poems of Claude McKay*, copyright 1953 by Twayne Publishers, Inc. and reprinted with the permission of Twayne Publishers, A Division of G. K. Hall & Co.

Archibald MacLeish: "Ars Poetica" and "Not Marble, Nor the Gilded Monuments" from *New and Collected Poems 1917–1976* by Archibald MacLeish. Copyright © 1976 by Archibald MacLeish. Reprinted by permission of Houghton Mifflin Company.

Louis MacNeice: "Aubade" from *The Collected Poems of Louis MacNeice* is reprinted by permission of Faber and Faber Ltd.

Eli Mandel: "Houdini" from *An Idiot's Journey* by Eli Mandel is reprinted by permission of the author.

John Masefield: "The Lemmings" is reprinted with the permission of Macmillan Publishing Co., Inc. from *Poems* by John Masefield. Copyright 1920 by John Masefield, renewed 1948 by John Masefield.

James Merrill: "Watching the Dance" from *Nights and Days* by James Merrill is used by permission of Atheneum Publishers. Copyright © 1966 by James Merrill.

Edna St. Vincent Millay: "What Lips My Lips Have Kissed" from *Collected Poems*, Harper & Row. Copyright 1923, 1951 by Edna St. Vincent Millay and Norma Millay Ellis. Reprinted by permission of Norma Millay Ellis, Literary Executor.

Vassar Miller: "Adam's Footprint" from *Wage War on Silence*, copyright © 1960 by Vassar Miller. Reprinted by permission of Wesleyan University Press.

Czeslaw Milosz: "A Poor Christian Looks at the Ghetto," from *Postwar Polish Poetry*, translated by Czeslaw Milosz. Copyright © 1965 by Czeslaw Milosz. Reprinted by permission of Doubleday & Company, Inc.

Joni Mitchell: "Woodstock" © 1969 by Siquomb Publishing Corp. All Rights Reserved. Used by permission of Warner Bros. Music.

Susan Mitchell: "From the Journals of the Frog Prince" reprinted by permission; © 1978 The New Yorker Magazine, Inc.

Arthur W. Monks: "Twilight's Last Gleaming" by Arthur Monks from *Jiggery-Pokery* edited by Anthony Hecht and John Hollander. Copyright © 1966 by Anthony Hecht and John Hollander. Used by permission of Atheneum Publishers.

Marianne Moore: "Poetry" from *Collected Poems*, copyright 1935 by Marianne Moore, renewed 1963 by Marianne Moore and T. S. Eliot. Reprinted with permission of Macmillan Publishing Co., Inc.

Edwin Morgan: "Message Clear" and "The Computer's First Christmas Card" from *The Second Life*. Reprinted by permission of Edinburgh University Press.

Ogden Nash: "The Turtle"; copyright 1940 by Ogden Nash. Reprinted from *Verses 1929 On* by Ogden Nash by permission of Little, Brown and Co.

Howard Nemerov: "Boom!," "The Goose Fish," "Epigram: Political Reflexion," "Life Cycle of Common Man," "The Vacuum" and "A Way of Life" from *The Collected Poems of Howard Nemerov*. University of Chicago Press 1977. Reprinted by permission of the author.

Gabriel Okara: "Piano and Drums" which originally appeared in *Black Orpheus* is reprinted by permission of the author.

Sharon Olds: "Leningrad Cemetery: Winter of 1941" reprinted by permission; © 1979 The New Yorker Magazine, Inc.

Wilfred Owen: "Dulce et Decorum Est" from *The Collected Poems* by Wilfred Owen. Copyright © Chatto & Windus, Ltd., 1946, 1963. Reprinted by permission of New Directions.

Dorothy Parker: "A Certain Lady," "Comment" and "One Perfect Rose" from *The Portable Dorothy Parker*. Copyright 1926, renewed 1954 by Dorothy Parker. Reprinted by permission of Viking Penguin, Inc.

Linda Pastan: "Marks" from *The Five Stages of Grief, Poems* by Linda Pastan is reprinted by permission of W. W. Norton & Company, Inc. Copyright © 1978 by Linda Pastan. "A Symposium: Apples" from *Aspects of Eve, Poems* by Linda Pastan is reprinted by permission of Liveright Publishing Corporation. Copyright Linda Pastan.

Raymond Patterson: "You Are the Brave" from *26 Ways of Looking at a Black Man*, an *Award* book published by Universal-Award House Inc. Copyright 1969 by Raymond Patterson. Reprinted by permission of Universal Publishing and Distributing Corporation.

Marge Piercy: "Barbie Doll" from *To Be of Use* by Marge Piercy. Copyright © 1969, 1971, 1973 by Marge Piercy. Reprinted by permission of Doubleday & Company, Inc.

Sylvia Plath: "Lady Lazarus" from *Ariel* by Sylvia Plath, copyright © 1963 by Ted Hughes and "Black Rook in Rainy Weather" (first published in somewhat different form by William Heinemann Ltd.) from *Crossing the Water* by Sylvia Plath, copyright © 1971 by Ted Hughes, are reprinted by permission of Harper & Row, Publishers, Inc. and Faber and Faber Ltd. "Point Shirley" copyright © 1959 by Sylvia Plath. Reprinted from *The Colossus and Other Stories*, by Sylvia Plath, by permission of Alfred A. Knopf, Inc. and Faber and Faber Ltd.

Ezra Pound: "In a Station of the Metro," "The River Merchant's Wife: A Letter," "Hugh Selwyn Mauberly, V (There died a Myriad)," and "A Virginal" from *Personae* by Ezra Pound Copyright 1926 by Ezra Pound. Reprinted by permission of New Directions.

John Press: "Womanizers" from *Guy Fawkes Night* by John Press is reprinted by permission of A. M. Heath & Company Ltd as representative of the author.

Jarold Ramsey: "Lupine Dew" is reprinted by permission of the author. "The Tally Stick" is reprinted by permission of *Northwest Review*.

John Crowe Ransom: "Bells for John Whiteside's Daughter" Copyright 1924 by Alfred A. Knopf, Inc. and renewed by John Crowe Ransom. Reprinted from *Selected Poems* Third Edition, Revised and Enlarged, by John Crowe Ransom, by permission of Alfred A. Knopf, Inc.

Dudley Randall: "Ballad of Birmingham" from *Poem Counter Poem*, © 1969 by Margaret Danner and Dudley Randall, and "Roses and Revolutions" from *Cities Burning*, © 1968 by Dudley Randall are reprinted by permission of Broadside/Crummel Press, Detroit, Michigan.

David Ray: "A Piece of Shrapnel" from *Gathering Firewood*, copyright © 1969 by David Ray. Reprinted by permission of Wesleyan University Press.

Henry Reed: "Lessons of the War: Judging Distances" from *A Map of Verona* is reprinted by permission of the author and Jonathan Cape Ltd.

Ishmael Reed: "beware; do not read this poem" and "Sermonette," Copyright 1972 by Ishmael Reed, are reprinted by permission of the author.

Adrienne Rich: "A Clock in the Square" is reprinted by permission of the author. "Origins and History of Consciousness" is reprinted from *Dream of a Common Language, Poems 1974–1977*, by Adrienne Rich, by permission of W. W. Norton & Co., Inc. Copyright 1978 by W. W. Norton & Co., Inc. "At a Bach Concert," "Snapshots of a Daughter-in-Law," "Necessities of Life," "Orion," "Planetarium," "Trying to Talk with a Man," "Diving into the Wreck," "Storm Warnings," "Two Songs," and "Aunt Jennifer's Tigers" are reprinted from *Poems, Selected and New 1950–1974* by Adrienne Rich, by permission of W. W. Norton & Co., Inc. Copyright © 1975, 1973, 1971, 1969, 1966 by W. W. Norton & Co., Inc. Copyright 1967, 1963, 1962, 1961, 1960, 1959, 1958, 1957, 1956, 1955, 1954, 1953, 1952, 1951 by Adrienne Rich. "An Interview With Adrienne Rich" by David Kalstone, copyright © 1972 by Saturday Review, Inc. Reprinted by permission of Saturday Review, Inc. "Talking With Adrienne Rich" from *The Ohio Review*, Vol. XIII, No. 1, copyright 1971. Selections reprinted by permission of *The Ohio Review*. "When We Dead Awaken: Writing as Re-Vision" from *College English*, reprinted by permission of National Council of Teachers of English and Adrienne Rich. The chronology of the poetry of Adrienne Rich is reprinted from *Adrienne Rich's Poetry*, A Norton Critical Edition, Selected and Edited by Barbara Charlesworth Gelpi and Albert Gelpi, with the permission of W. W. Norton & Company, Inc. Copyright © 1975 by W. W. Norton & Company, Inc.

Edward Arlington Robinson: "Mr. Flood's Party" is reprinted from *Collected Poems* by Edward Arlington Robinson copyright 1921 by Edward Arlington Robinson, renewed by Ruth Nivison, with permission of Macmillan Publishing Co., Inc. "Richard Cory" from *The Children of the Night* by Edward Arlington Robinson is reprinted by permission of Charles Scribner's Sons and is fully protected by copyright. "Uncle Ananias" from *The Town Down the River* by Edward Arlington Robinson is reprinted by permission of Charles Scribner's Sons. Copyright 1910 by Charles Scribner's Sons; renewal copyright 1938 by Ruth Nivison.

Theodore Roethke: "My Papa's Waltz" copyright 1942 by Hearst Magazines Inc., "I Knew a Woman" copyright 1954 by Theodore Roethke, "The Waking" copyright 1953 by Theodore Roethke, "The Mistake" copyright © 1957 by Beatrice Roethke, Administratrix of the Estate of Theodore Roethke, "She" copyright © 1956 by

INDEX OF AUTHORS

ADAMS, FRANKLIN P. (1881–1960)
  Composed in the Composing Room, 705
ALDRICH, HENRY (1647–1710)
  Why I Drink, 734
ALLEN, WOODY (b. 1935)
  The Kugelmass Episode, 506
AMMONS, A. R. (b. 1926)
  Cascadilla Falls, 830
  Needs, 609
ANDERSON, SHERWOOD (1876–1941)
  The Egg, 88
ANGELOU, MAYA (b. 1924)
  Africa, 818
ANONYMOUS
  [Epigrams], 730
  Frankie and Johnny, 669
  The Lady Fortune, 597
  Limericks, 696
  Lord Randal, 680
  Love Knot, 708
  My Love in Her Attire, 548
  The Sacrifice of Isaac, 938
  Sir Patrick Spens, 682
  The Silver Swan, 597
  The Twenty-Third Psalm, 655
  Western Wind, 531
ARMOUR, RICHARD (b. 1906)
  Hiding Place, 635
ARNOLD, MATTHEW (1822–1888)
  Dover Beach, 628
ATWOOD, MARGARET (b. 1939)
  Five Poems for Dolls, 831
AUDEN, W. H. (1907–1973)
  In Memory of W. B. Yeats, 832
  Musée des Beaux Arts, 834
  The Unknown Citizen, 599

BALDWIN, JAMES (b. 1924)
  Sonny's Blues, 336
BAMBARA, TONI CADE
  My Man Bovanne, 95
BARAKA, AMIRI (b. 1934)
  In Memory of Radio, 783
BENNETT, HAL (b. 1930)
  Dotson Gerber Resurrected, 223
BERRYMAN, JOHN (1914–1972)
  1 September 1939, 835
BETJEMAN, JOHN (b. 1906)
  In Westminster Abbey, 612
BIERCE, AMBROSE (1842–1914?)
  An Occurrence at Owl Creek Bridge, 59
BIRNEY, EARLE (b. 1904)
  From the Hazel Bough, 835
  Irapuato, 836

BLAKE, WILLIAM (1757–1827)
  Ah Sunflower, 837
  Her Whole Life Is an Epigram, 730
  The Lamb, 837
  London, 567
  The Sick Rose, 664
  The Tiger, 838
BOGAN, LOUISE (1897–1970)
  The Dragonfly, 838
BOND, JULIAN (b. 1940)
  The Bishop of Atlanta: Ray Charles, 839
  Rotation, 839
BOOTH, PHILIP (b. 1925)
  One Man's Wife, 657
BORGES, JORGE LUIS (b. 1899)
  The Garden of Forking Paths, 215
BROOKE, RUPERT (1887–1915)
  The Soldier, 791
BROOKS, GWENDOLYN (b. 1917)
  First Fight. Then Fiddle, 723
BROWNING, ELIZABETH BARRETT (1806–1861)
  How Do I Love Thee?, 538
BROWNING, ROBERT (1812–1889)
  My Last Duchess, 629
  Soliloquy of the Spanish Cloister, 604
BULLINS, ED (b. 1935)
  A Son, Come Home, 1508
BUNYAN, JOHN (1628–1688)
  Of the Boy and the Butterfly, 573
BURNS, ROBERT (1759–1796)
  A Red, Red Rose, 653

CARROLL, LEWIS (1832–1898)
  How Doth the Little Crocodile, 576
CHASIN, HELEN
  Joy Sonnet in a Random Universe, 725
  The Word Plum, 687
CHEEVER, JOHN (b. 1912)
  The Country Husband, 466
CHEKHOV, ANTON (1860–1904)
  The Lady with the Dog, 151
  Three Sisters, 1393
CHOPIN, KATE (1851–1904)
  Beyond the Bayou, 320
CLARE, JOHN (1793–1864)
  Love's Emblem, 663
CLARKE, ARTHUR C. (b. 1917)
  Hide and Seek, 207
CLEGHORN, SARAH (1876–1959)
  Quatrain, 733
CLEMENS, SAMUEL (1835–1910)
  The Celebrated Jumping Frog of Calaveras County, 296

CLIFTON, LUCILLE (b. 1936)
  At Last We Killed the Roaches, 682
COHEN, LEONARD (b. 1934)
  Suzanne Takes You Down, 840
COLERIDGE, SAMUEL TAYLOR (1772–1834)
  Kubla Khan: or, a Vision in a Dream, 841
  Metrical Feet, 695
  What Is an Epigram?, 730
CONGREVE, WILLIAM (1670–1729)
  Song, 553
CONNELL, RICHARD (1893–1949)
  The Most Dangerous Game, 17
CONRAD, JOSEPH (1857–1924)
  The Secret Sharer, 403
CONSTABLE, HENRY (1562–1613)
  My Lady's Presence Makes the Roses Red, 718
CORNFORD, FRANCES (1886–1960)
  Parting in Wartime, 736
CULLEN, COUNTEE (1903–1946)
  For a Lady I Know, 735
CUMMINGS, E. E. (1894–1962)
  anyone lived in a pretty how town, 645
  chanson innocente, 844
  l(a, 532
  poem, or beauty hurts mr. vinal, 784
  (ponder, darling, these busted statues, 798
  portrait, 705
  the season 'tis, my lovely lambs, 842
CUNNINGHAM, J. V. (b. 1911)
  All in Due Time, 736
  Here Lies My Wife, 732

DAY LEWIS, C. (1904–1972)
  Song, 800
DEAGON, ANN (b. 1930)
  Certified Copy, 645
  There Is No Balm in Birmingham, 583
DE LA MARE, WALTER (1873–1956)
  Slim Cunning Hands, 638
DELAWARE INDIAN SONG
  Who Are They?, 597
DE VRIES, PETER (b. 1910)
  Bacchanal, 801
DICKEY, JAMES (b. 1923)
  Cherrylog Road, 619
  The Leap, 659
DICKINSON, EMILY (1830–1886)
  After Great Pain, 644
  Because I Could Not Stop for Death, 557
  The Brain Is Wider than the Sky, 844
  I Dwell in Possibility, 590
  My Life Closed Twice, 845
  A Narrow Fellow in the Grass, 573
  Wild Nights! Wild Nights!, 845
DONNE, JOHN (1572–1631)
  The Bait, 800
  Batter My Heart, 655
  The Canonization, 846
  Death Be Not Proud, 558
  The Flea, 623
  The Good-Morrow, 846
  Song ("Go, and catch a falling star"), 617
  The Sun Rising, 740
  A Valediction: Forbidding Mourning, 631
DOYLE, SIR ARTHUR CONAN (1859–1930)
  The Adventure of the Speckled Band, 432
DRYDEN, JOHN (1631–1700)
  To the Memory of Mr. Oldham, 697
DYER, LADY CATHERINE
  Epitaph On the Monument of Sir William Dyer at Colmworth, 1641, 548
DYLAN, BOB (b. 1941)
  Mister Tambourine Man, 656

ELIOT, T. S. (1888–1965)
  Journey of the Magi, 848
  The Love Song of J. Alfred Prufrock, 849
EMANUEL, JAMES A. (b. 1921)
  Emmett Till, 786

FAULKNER, WILLIAM (1897–1962)
  The Old People, 191
  Spotted Horses, 300
FEARING, KENNETH (1902–1961)
  Dirge, 690
FERLINGHETTI, LAWRENCE (b. 1919)
  Christ Climbed Down, 852
FIELDS, JULIA (b. 1938)
  Madness One Monday Evening, 854
FITZGERALD, F. SCOTT (1896–1940)
  Babylon Revisited, 320
FOGLE, RICHARD HARTER (b. 1911)
  A Hawthorne Garland: Scarlet Letter, 735
FROST, ROBERT (1874–1963)
  Range-Finding, 855
  The Rose Family, 666
  Stopping by Woods on a Snowy Evening, 686
  U.S. 1946 King's X, 624

GAY, JOHN (1685–1732)
  My Own Epitaph, 732
GARCIA MARQUEZ, GABRIEL (b. 1928)
  A Very Old Man With Enormous Wings, 234
GIOVANNI, NIKKI (b. 1943)
  Poetry, 589
GUEST, EDGAR A. (1881–1959)
  The Things that Make a Soldier Great, 789

HABINGTON, WILLIAM (1605–1654)
  To Roses in the Bosom of Castara, 665

HARDY, THOMAS (1840–1928)
Channel Firing, 857
The Darkling Thrush, 855
During Wind and Rain, 856
Hap, 857
The Ruined Maid, 601
HARINGTON, SIR JOHN (1561–1612)
Epigram: Of Treason, 734
HARPER, MICHAEL (b. 1938)
Dear John, Dear Coltrane, 702
HARRIS, GEORGE WASHINGTON (1814–1869)
Mrs. Yardley's Quilting, 359
HAWTHORNE, NATHANIEL (1804–1864)
Young Goodman Brown, 117
HECHT, ANTHONY (b. 1923)
The Dover Bitch, 803
"It Out-Herods Herod, Pray You, Avoid It," 858
HEMINGWAY, ERNEST (1899–1961)
The Short Happy Life of Francis Macomber, 32
HERBERT, GEORGE (1593–1633)
The Collar, 616
Easter Wings, 707
HERRICK, ROBERT (1591–1674)
Delight in Disorder, 640
The Pillar of Fame, 707
To the Virgins, to Make Much of Time, 794
Upon Julia's Clothes, 549
HOLLAND, ROB (b. 1946)
Eve in Old Age, 811
HOLLANDER, JOHN (b. 1929)
Adam's Task, 807
A State of Nature, 711
HOLLANDER, ROBERT (b. 1933)
You Too? Me Too—Why Not? Soda Pop, 712
HOLMAN, M. CARL (b. 1919)
Three Brown Girls Singing, 678
HOLST, SPENCER
The Zebra Storyteller, 3
HOPKINS, GERARD MANLEY (1844–1889)
Pied Beauty, 643
Spring and Fall, 700
The Windhover, 860
HOUSMAN, A. E. (1859–1936)
Terence, This Is Stupid Stuff, 586
To an Athlete Dying Young, 554
HUGHES, LANGSTON (1902–1967)
Harlem (A Dream Deferred), 600
The Negro Speaks of Rivers, 817
HUGO, RICHARD (b. 1923)
To Women, 860
What Thou Lovest Well, Remains American, 580

IBSEN, HENRIK (1828–1906)
Hedda Gabler, 1443

JACKSON, SHIRLEY (1919–1965)
The Lottery, 66

JAMES, HENRY (1843–1916)
The Tree of Knowledge, 392
JARRELL, RANDALL (1914–1965)
The Death of the Ball Turret Gunner, 655
JEFFERS, ROBINSON (1887–1962)
To the Stone-Cutters, 594
JONES, LEROI
see Baraka, Amiri
JONSON, BEN (1572?–1637)
Come, My Celia, 796
Epitaph on Elizabeth, L. H., 731
On My First Son, 545
Still to Be Neat, 639
JOYCE, JAMES (1882–1941)
Araby, 165
JUSTICE, DONALD (b. 1925)
Counting the Mad, 699
Here in Katmandu, 634
Southern Gothic, 667

KAFKA, FRANZ (1883–1924)
A Hunger Artist, 451
KAUFMAN, BOB (b. 1925)
Blues Note, 703
KEATS, JOHN (1795–1821)
Bright Star, 744
Chronology, 756
Endymion (Book I), from, 743
Endymion, Preface to, dated April 10, 1818, from, 755
The Eve of St. Agnes, 861
La Belle Dame Sans Merci (original version), 744
Letter to Benjamin Bailey, November 22, 1817, from, 751
Letter to George and Thomas Keats, December 21, 1817, from, 752
Letter to James Augustus Hessey, October 8, 1818, from, 755
Letter to John Hamilton Reynolds, February 19, 1818, 753
Letter to John Taylor, February 27, 1818, from, 754
Ode on a Grecian Urn, 748
Ode on Melancholy, 749
Ode to a Nightingale, 746
On First Looking into Chapman's Homer, 723
On the Grasshopper and the Cricket, 742
On the Sonnet, 720
To Autumn, 750
When I Have Fears, 743
KENNEDY, X. J. (b. 1929)
Epitaph for a Postal Clerk, 735
In a Prominent Bar in Secaucus One Day, 602
KINNELL, GALWAY (b. 1927)
To Christ Our Lord, 632
KLEIN, A. M. (1909–1972)
Heirloom, 585

KNIGHT, ETHERIDGE (b. 1933)
  Hard Rock Returns to Prison from the
    Hospital for the Criminal Insane, 566
  The Idea of Ancestry, 584
KOCH, KENNETH (b. 1925)
  Variations on a Theme by William
    Carlos Williams, 802
KUMIN, MAXINE (b. 1925)
  Woodchucks, 569

LANDOR, WALTER SAVAGE (1775–1864)
  Various the Roads of Life, 733
LARKIN, PHILIP (b. 1922)
  Church Going, 674
LAWRENCE, D. H. (1885–1930)
  The Horse Dealer's Daughter, 259
  Odour of Chrysanthemums, 244
  Passages from Essays and Letters, 282
  Piano, 871
  The Rocking-Horse Winner, 271
  Snake, 871
LE GUIN, URSULA K. (b. 1929)
  The Ones Who Walk Away from
    Omelas, 501
LESSING, DORIS (b. 1919)
  Our Friend Judith, 100
LEVERTOV, DENISE (b. 1923)
  What Were They Like?, 596
LIVESAY, DOROTHY (b. 1909)
  Green Rain, 583
LLOYD, DONALD J. (b. 1910)
  Bridal Couch, 796
LONGSTREET, AUGUSTUS BALDWIN (1790–
    1870)
  The Horse-Swap, 290
LORDE, AUDRE (b. 1934)
  Hanging Fire, 614
  Outside, 598
  Recreation, 550
LOVELACE, RICHARD (1618–1658)
  To Amarantha, that She Would Dishevel
    Her Hair, 795
LOWELL, ROBERT (1917–1977)
  Skunk Hour, 874

MC CARTHY, EUGENE (b. 1918)
  Kilroy, 785
MC CORD, DAVID (b. 1897)
  Epitaph on a Waiter, 735
  History of Education, 734
MC KAY, CLAUDE (1891–1948)
  America, 600
MACLEISH, ARCHIBALD (b. 1892)
  Ars Poetica, 590
  "Not Marble Nor the Gilded Monu-
    ments," 593
MACNEICE, LOUIS (1907–1964)
  Aubade, 534
MANDEL, ELI (b. 1922)
  Houdini, 875

MANKIEWICZ, HERMAN J. (1897–1953),
    AND ORSON WELLES (b. 1915)
  Citizen Kane, 1156
MANSFIELD, KATHERINE (1888–1923)
  Her First Ball, 146
MARLOWE, CHRISTOPHER (1564–1593)
  The Passionate Shepherd to His Love,
    727
MARTIAL (c.40–c.104)
  Tomorrow You Will Live, 732
  You've Told Me, Maro, 731
MARVELL, ANDREW (1621–1678)
  The Garden, 876
  To His Coy Mistress, 796
MASEFIELD, JOHN (1878–1967)
  The Lemmings, 579
MELEAGER (ca. 140–ca. 70 B.C.)
  I'll Twine White Violets, 731
MELVILLE, HERMAN (1819–1891)
  Bartleby, the Scrivener, 365
MERRILL, JAMES (b. 1926)
  Watching the Dance, 878
MILLAY, EDNA ST. VINCENT (1892–1950)
  What Lips My Lips Have Kissed, 552
MILLER, ARTHUR (b. 1915)
  Death of a Salesman, 1083
MILLER, VASSAR (b. 1924)
  Adam's Footprint, 808
MILOSZ, CZESLAW (b. 1911)
  A Poor Christian Looks at the Ghetto,
    878
MILTON, JOHN (1608–1674)
  [Before the Fall], 805
  On the Late Massacre in Piedmont, 722
  Paradise Lost, *from*, 646
MITCHELL, JONI (b. 1943)
  Woodstock, 564
MITCHELL, SUSAN
  From the Journals of the Frog Prince,
    576
MONKS, ARTHUR W.
  Twilight's Last Gleaming, 695
MOORE, MARIANNE (1887–1972)
  Poetry, 587
MORGAN, EDWIN (b. 1920)
  The Computer's First Christmas Card,
    710
  Message Clear, 709
MUNRO, ALICE (b. 1931)
  Boys and Girls, 169
MURRAY, ALBERT
  Train Whistle Guitar, 484

NASH, OGDEN (1902–1972)
  The Turtle, 575
NASHE, THOMAS (1567–1601)
  Spring, the Sweet Spring, 700
NEMEROV, HOWARD (b. 1920)
  Boom!, 615
  Epigram: Political Reflexion, 734
  The Goose Fish, 671
  Life Cycle of Common Man, 879

1530   *Index of Authors*

Nemerov, Howard (*continued*)
The Vacuum, 546
A Way of Life, 738

OATES, JOYCE CAROL (b. 1938)
The Lady with the Pet Dog, 515
O'CONNOR, FLANNERY (1925–1964)
The Artificial Nigger, 127
OKARA, GABRIEL (b. 1921)
Piano and Drums, 818
OLDS, SHARON
Leningrad Cemetery, Winter of 1941, 658
OLSEN, TILLIE (b. 1913)
O Yes, 180
OWEN, WILFRED (1893–1918)
Dulce Et Decorum Est, 787

PALEY, GRACE (b. 1922)
A Conversation with My Father, 497
PARKER, DOROTHY (1893–1967)
A Certain Lady, 607
Comment, 736
One Perfect Rose, 666
PASTAN, LINDA (b. 1932)
Marks, 652
A Symposium: Apples, 807
PATTERSON, RAYMOND R. (b. 1929)
You Are the Brave, 779
PIERCY, MARGE (b. 1936)
Barbie Doll, 561
PINTER, HAROLD (b. 1930)
The Dumb Waiter, 950
PLATH, SYLVIA (1932–1963)
Black Rook in Rainy Weather, 880
Lady Lazarus, 558
Point Shirley, 626
POE, EDGAR ALLAN (1809–1849)
The Cask of Amontillado, 12
To Helen, 831
POPE, ALEXANDER (1688–1744)
[Sound and Sense], 692
POUND, EZRA (1885–1972)
In a Station of the Metro, 882
The River-Merchant's Wife: A Letter, 540
There Died a Myriad, 788
A Virginal, 882
PRESS, JOHN (b. 1920)
Womanizers, 882
PRIOR, MATTHEW (1664–1721)
A True Maid, 733

QUARLES, FRANCIS (1592–1644)
Be Sad, My Heart, 736

RALEGH, SIR WALTER (1552?–1618)
The Nymph's Reply to the Shepherd, 799

RAMSEY, JAROLD (b. 1937)
Lupine Dew, 632
The Tally Stick, 538
RANDALL, DUDLEY (b. 1914)
Ballad of Birmingham, 595
Roses and Revolutions, 667
RANSOM, JOHN CROWE (b. 1888)
Bells for John Whiteside's Daughter, 544
RAY, DAVID (b. 1932)
A Piece of Shrapnel, 883
REED, HENRY (b. 1914)
Lessons of the War: Judging Distances, 613
REED, ISHMAEL (b. 1938)
beware : do not read this poem, 591
Sermonette, 820
RICH, ADRIENNE (b. 1929)
At a Bach Concert, 757
Aunt Jennifer's Tigers, 570
Chronology, 776
A Clock in the Square, 757
Diving into the Wreck, 767
Interview with Adrienne Rich, An, *from,* 773
Necessities of Life, 762
Origins and History of Consciousness, 770
Orion, 764
Planetarium, 765
Snapshots of a Daughter-in-Law, 758
Storm Warnings, 758
Talking with Adrienne Rich, *from,* 771
Trying to Talk with a Man, 766
Two Songs, 553
When We Dead Awaken: Writing as Re-Vision, *from,* 775
RICHLER, MORDECAI (b. 1931)
The Summer My Grandmother Was Supposed to Die, 72
ROBINSON, EDWIN ARLINGTON (1869–1935)
Mr. Flood's Party, 883
Richard Cory, 885
Uncle Ananias, 885
ROETHKE, THEODORE (1908–1963)
The Dream, 886
Epigram: The Mistake, 733
I Knew a Woman, 549
My Papa's Waltz, 642
She, 887
The Waking, 887
ROSENBERG, ISAAC (1890–1918)
Break of Day in the Trenches, 788
ROSSETTI, CHRISTINA (1830–1894)
Echo, 550
Eve, 809

SASSOON, SIEGFRIED (1886–1967)
Base Details, 790
Repression of War Experience, 789
SCHWARTZ, DELMORE (1913–1966)

The Heavy Bear Who Goes with Me, 577

SEXTON, ANNE (1928–1974)
The Kiss, 888
The Truth the Dead Know, 633

SHAKESPEARE, WILLIAM (1564–1616)
Th' Expense of Spirit, 889
Hamlet, 984
Hark, Hark! the Lark, 889
Let Me Not to the Marriage of True Minds, 552
Like as the Waves, 701
My Mistress' Eyes Are Nothing like the Sun, 725
Not Marble, Nor the Gilded Monuments, 592
Spring, 890
That Time of Year, 650
Winter, 890

SHAPIRO, KARL (b. 1913)
Auto Wreck, 681
The Fly, 574

SHELLEY, PERCY BYSSHE (1792–1822)
England in 1819, 891
Ode to the West Wind, 684
Ozymandias, 721

SIDNEY, SIR PHILIP (1554–1586)
When Nature Made Her Chief Work, Stella's Eyes, 724

SINGER, ISAAC BASHEVIS (b. 1904)
Tanhum, 457

SKIRROW, DESMOND
Ode on a Grecian Urn Summarized, 802

SNODGRASS, W. D. (b. 1926)
Leaving the Motel, 562

SOPHOCLES (496?–406 B.C.)
Oedipus Tyrannus, 1313

SPENDER, STEPHEN (b. 1909)
An Elementary School Classroom in a Slum, 891
The Express, 701
Judas Iscariot, 892

SPENSER, EDMUND (1552–1599)
Happy Ye Leaves, 683
Penelope for Her Ulysses' Sake, 817

STARBUCK, GEORGE (b. 1931)
On First Looking in on Blodgett's *Keats's "Chapman's Homer,"* 724

STEVENS, WALLACE (1879–1955)
Anecdote of the Jar, 893
The Emperor of Ice-Cream, 895
The Idea of Order at Key West, 894
Sunday Morning, 896
The World as Meditation, 816

STONE, JOHN (b. 1936)
Coming Home, 580
Explaining About the Dachsund, 578

SUCKLING, SIR JOHN (1609–1642)
Song, 697

SULLIVAN, NANCY (b. 1929)
The Death of the First Man, 812

SWIFT, JONATHAN (1667–1745)
On Stella's Birthday, 1719, 899

TENNYSON, ALFRED, LORD (1809–1892)
Break, Break, Break, 699
Ulysses, 812

THOMAS, DYLAN (1914–1953)
Do Not Go Gentle into That Good Night, 556
Fern Hill, 899
The Force that Through the Green Fuse Drives the Flower, 901
In My Craft or Sullen Art, 901

TWAIN, MARK (1835–1910)
Ode to Stephen Dowling Bots. Dec'd, 555

VAN DUYN, MONA (b. 1921)
What the Motorcycle Said, 688

VIERECK, PETER (b. 1916)
Kilroy, 814

WAKOSKI, DIANE (b. 1937)
The Photos, 581
Uneasy Rider, 542

WALLER, EDMUND (1606–1687)
Song, 794

WALSH, WILLIAM (1663–1708)
An Epigram, 730

WAYMAN, TOM (b. 1945)
Wayman in Love, 543
Picketing Superman, 594

WELLES, ORSON
see Mankiewicz, Herman J.

WHITMAN, WALT (1819–1892)
When Lilacs Last in the Dooryard Bloomed, 902

WILBUR, RICHARD (b. 1921)
The Beautiful Changes, 908
Love Calls Us to the Things of This World, 909

WILDE, OSCAR (1854–1900)
The Importance of Being Earnest, 1342

WILLIAMS, TENNESSEE (b. 1914)
The Glass Menagerie, 1238
The Long Goodbye, 1297

WILLIAMS, WILLIAM CARLOS (1883–1963)
Poem ("The rose fades"), 668
The Red Wheelbarrow, 644
This Is Just to Say, 910

WILMOT, JOHN, EARL OF ROCHESTER (1647–1680)
Love and Life, 551

WINTERS, YVOR (1900–1968)
At the San Francisco Airport, 636

WORDSWORTH, WILLIAM (1770–1850)
Lines Composed a Few Miles above Tintern Abbey, 910
London, 1802, 722
Nuns Fret Not, 717
Scorn Not the Sonnet, 720
She Dwelt Among the Untrodden Ways, 610
A Slumber Did My Spirit Seal, 555

WOTTON, SIR HENRY (1568–1639)
Upon the Death of Sir Albert Morton's
Wife, 732
WRIGHT, BRUCE MCM.
The African Affair, 819
WRIGHT, JAMES (b. 1927)
Arrangements with Earth for Three
Dead Friends, 676
WYATT, SIR THOMAS (1503–1542)
They Flee from Me, 913

YEATS, WILLIAM BUTLER (1865–1939)
Among School Children, 825
Byzantium, 827
The Circus Animals' Desertion, 828
Easter 1916, 820
Leda and the Swan, 823
On Being Asked for a War Poem, 791
Sailing to Byzantium, 824
The Second Coming, 823

INDEX OF TITLES AND FIRST LINES

About suffering they were never wrong, 834

About two thousand miles, 580

"A cold coming we had of it, 848

Adam's Footprint, 808

Adam's Task, 807

Adulterers and customers of whores, 882

Adventure of the Speckled Band, The, 432

Africa, 818

African Affair, The, 819

After Great Pain, 644

After the first powerful, plain manifesto, 701

A great land and a wide land was the east land, 597

Ah Sunflower, 837

All in Due Time, 736

All my past life is mine no more, 551

Also Ulysses once—that other war, 814

Although she feeds me bread of bitterness, 600

Amarantha sweet and fair, 795

America, 600

am   I, 709

Among School Children, 825

Among the agents used by counterfeiters, 583

And did young Stephen sicken, 555

Anecdote of the Jar, 893

An Epigram should be—if right—, 730

An old, mad, blind, despised, and dying king—, 891

anyone lived in a pretty how town, 645

A poem should be palpable and mute, 590

a poet was busted by a topless judge, 820

Araby, 165

Arrangements with Earth for Three Dead Friends, 676

Artificial Nigger, The, 127

Ars Poetica, 590

A single flow'r he sent me, since we met, 666

A snake came to my water-trough, 871

A sudden blow; the great wings beating still, 823

As virtuous men pass mildly away, 631

A sweet disorder in the dress, 640

At a Bach Concert, 757

A thing of beauty is a joy for ever, 743

At last Wayman gets the girl into bed, 543

At Last We Killed the Roaches, 682

At stated .ic times, 705

At the San Francisco Airport, 636

Aubade, 533

Aunt Jennifer's Tigers, 570

Auto Wreck, 681

Avenge, O Lord, thy slaughtered saints, whose bones, 722

A woman in the shape of a monster, 765

Babylon Revisited, 320

Bacchanal, 801

Bait, The, 800

Ballad of Birmingham, 595

Barbie Doll, 561

Bartleby, the Scrivener, 365

Base Details, 790

Batter My Heart, 655

Beautiful Changes, The, 908

Because all this food is grown in the store, 594

Because I Could Not Stop for Death, 557

Bees build around red liver, 878

[Before the Fall], 805

Behind glass in Mexico, 831

Behold, how eager this our little boy, 573

Bells for John Whiteside's Daughter, 544

Bent double, like old beggars under sacks, 787

Be Sad, My Heart, 736

beware   :   do not read this poem, 591

Beyond the Bayou, 320

Bishop of Atlanta: Ray Charles, The, 839

Black is what the prisons are, 819

Black Rook in Rainy Weather, 880

Blues Note, 703

Boom! 615

Boys and Girls, 169

Brain Is Wider than the Sky, The, 844

Break, Break, Break, 699

Break of Day in the Trenches, 788

Bridal Couch, 796

Bright Star, 744

Br-r-r-am-m-m, rackety-am-m, OM, Am, 688

Buffalo Bill's, 705

Busy old fool, unruly sun, 740

But most by numbers judge a poet's song, 692

By and by, 735

Byzantium, 827

Call the roller of big cigars, 895

Canonization, The, 846

Cascadilla Falls, 830

Cask of Amontillado, The, 12
Celebrated Jumping Frog of Calaveras County, The, 296
Certain Lady, A, 607
Certified Copy, 645
Channel Firing, 857
chanson innocente, 844
Cherrylog Road, 619
Christ Climbed Down, 852
Church Going, 674
Circus Animals' Desertion, The, 828
Citizen Kane, 1156
Clock in the Square, A, 757
Collar, The, 616
Come live with me and be my love (Marlowe), 727
Come live with me, and be my love (Donne), 800
Come, live with me and be my love (Day Lewis), 800
"Come live with me and be my love" (De Vries), 801
Come, My Celia, 796
Come to me in the silence of the night, 550
Coming by evening through the wintry city, 757
Coming Home, 580
Coming together, 550
Comment, 736
Complacencies of the peignoir, and late, 896
Composed in the Composing Room, 705
Computer's First Christmas Card, The, 710
Conversation with My Father, A, 497
Counting the Mad, 699
Country Husband, The, 466

Darkling Thrush, The, 855
Dear John, Dear Coltrane, 702
Death Be Not Proud, 558
Death of a Salesman, 1083
Death of the Ball Turret Gunner, The, 655
Death of the First Man, The, 812
Delight in Disorder, 640
Did the people of Viet Nam, 596
Dirge, 690
Diving into the Wreck, 767
Do Not Go Gentle into That Good Night, 556
Dotson Gerber Resurrected, 223
Dover Beach, 628
Dover Bitch, The, 803
Dragonfly, The, 838
Dream, The, 886
Dulce Et Decorum Est, 787
Dumb Waiter, The, 950
During Wind and Rain, 856

Easter 1916, 820
Easter Wings, 707

Echo, 550
Egg, The, 88
Elementary School Classroom in a Slum, An, 891
Emmett Till, 786
Emperor of Ice-Cream, The, 895
Endymion, from, 743
Endymion, Preface to, dated April 10, 1818, from, 755
England in 1819, 891
Epigram, An, 730
Epigram: Of Treason, 734
Epigram: Political Reflexion, 734
Epigram: The Mistake, 733
[Epigrams], 738
Epitaph for a Postal Clerk, 735
Epitaph on a Waiter, 735
Epitaph on Elizabeth, L. H., 731
Epitaph On the Monument of Sir William Dyer at Colmworth, 735
Eve, 809
Eve in Old Age, 811
Eve of St. Agnes, The, 861
Expense of Spirit, Th', 889
Explaining About the Dachsund, 578
Express, The, 701

Falling in love with a mustache, 542
Fame's pillar here, at last, we set, 707
Far back when I went zig-zagging, 764
Farewell, thou child of my right hand, and joy, 545
Farewell, too little and too lately known, 697
Far far from gusty waves these children's faces, 891
Fern Hill, 899
First Fight. Then Fiddle, 723
First having read the book of myths, 767
Five Poems for Dolls, 831
Five years have passed; five summers, with the length, 910
Flea, The, 623
Fly, The, 574
Follows this a narrower bed, 796
For a Lady I Know, 735
Force that Through the Green Fuse Drives the Flower, The, 901
For God's sake hold your tongue and let me love!, 846
For reasons any, 836
Frankie and Johnny, 669
From my mother's sleep I fell into the State, 655
From the Hazel Bough, 835
From the Journals of the Frog Prince, 576
From Water-Tower Hill to the brick prison, 626

Garden, The, 876
Garden of Forking Paths, The, 215

Gassing the woodchucks didn't turn out right, 569

Gather ye rosebuds while ye may, 794

Glass Menagerie, The, 1238

Glory be to God for dappled things, 643

Go, and catch a falling star, 617

Gods chase, 802

Go, lovely rose!, 794

Gone, I say and walk from church, 633

Good Morrow, The, 846

Goose Fish, The, 671

Go, rose, my Chloe's bosom grace, 663

Green Rain, 583

Gr-r-r—there go, my heart's abhorence!, 604

Had we but world enough, and time, 797

Hamlet, 984

Hanging Fire, 614

Hap, 857

Happy Ye Leaves, 683

Hard Rock Returns to Prison from the Hospital for the Criminal Insane, 566

Hark, Hark! the Lark, 889

Harlem, 600

Having bitten on life like a sharp apple, 533

Having invented a new Holocaust, 624

Hawthorne Garland, A, 735

Heavy Bear Who Goes with Me, The, 577

Hedda Gabler, 1443

He disappeared in the dead of winter, 832

He first deceased; she for a little tried, 732

Heirloom, 585

He left his pants upon a chair, 733

Here at the Vespasian-Carlton, it's just one, 615

Here from the start, from our first of days, look:, 538

Here in Katmandu, 634

Here Lies My Wife, 732

Here lies wrapped up tight in sod, 735

Her First Ball, 146

Her Whole Life Is an Epigram, 730

He was found by the Bureau of Statistics to be, 599

Hey, Mister Tambourine Man, play a song for me, 656

Hide and Seek, 207

Hiding Place, 635

Higgledy-piggledy, 695

History of Education, 734

His words were magic and his heart was true, 885

Horse Dealer's Daughter, The, 259

Horse-Swap, The, 290

Houdini, 875

How Do I Love Thee?, 538

How Doth the Little Crocodile, 576

How long ago Hector took off his plume, 736

How vainly men themselves amaze, 876

Hunger Artist, A, 451

I am, 712

I am fourteen, 614

I came upon a child of God, 564

I caught this morning morning's minion, king-, 860

I chopped down the house that you had been saving to live in next summer, 802

Idea of Ancestry, The, 584

Idea of Order at Key West, The, 894

I Dwell in Possibility, 590

If all the world and love were young, 799

If but some vengeful god would call to me, 857

If by dull rhymes our English must be chained, 720

If I should die, think only this of me, 791

If I were fierce, and bald, and short of breath, 790

If on my theme I rightly think, 734

I have done it again, 558

I have eaten, 610

I have met them at close of day, 820

I have xeroxed my navel, 645

I hear a whistling, 786

I Knew a Woman, 549

I leant upon a coppice gate, 855

I'll Twine White Violets, 731

I met a lady, 835

I met a traveler from an antique land, 721

I met her as a blossom on a stem, 886

Importance of Being Earnest, The, 1342

In a Prominent Bar in Secaucus One Day, 602

In a Station of the Metro, 882

in Just-, 844

In March I dreamed of Mud, 576

In Memory of Radio, 783

In Memory of W. B. Yeats, 832

In My Craft or Sullen Art, 901

Interview with Adrienne Rich, An, from, 773

In the center of a harsh and spectrumed city, 598

In the ribs of an ugly school building, 678

In Westminster Abbey, 612

In Xanadu did Kubla Khan, 841

I placed a jar in Tennessee, 893

Irapuato, 836

I remember long veils of green rain, 583

Is it Ulysses that approaches from the east, 816

I sought a theme and sought for it in vain, 828

I struck the board and cried, "No more, 616

I suspect he knew that trunks are metaphors, 875

I think it better that in times like these, 791

I think the dead are tender. Shall we kiss?, 887

It little profits that an idle king, 812

I, too, dislike it: there are things that are important beyond all this fiddle, 587

"*It Out-Herods Herod, Pray You, Avoid It,*" 858

It's been going on a long time, 738

Its quick soft silver bell beating, beating, 681

I've known rivers, 817

I wake to sleep, and take my waking slow, 887

I walk through the long schoolroom questioning, 825

I wander through each chartered street, 567

I want something suited to my special needs, 609

I went down by Cascadilla, 830

I wonder, by my troth, what thou and I, 846

jollymerry, 710

Journey of the Magi, 848

Joy Sonnet in a Random Universe, 725

Judas Iscariot, 892

Kilroy (McCarthy), 785

Kilroy (Viereck), 814

Kiss, The, 888

Kubla Khan: or, a Vision in a Dream, 841

Kugelmass Episode, The, 506

l)a, 531

La Belle Dame sans Merci, 744

Lady Fortune, The, 597

Lady Lazarus, 558

Lady with the Dog, The, 151

Lady with the Pet Dog, The, 515

Lamb, The, 837

Late that mad Monday evening, 854

Leap, The, 659

Leaving the Motel, 562

Leda and the Swan, 823

Lemmings, The, 579

Leningrad Cemetery, Winter of 1941, 658

Lessons of the War, 613

Let Me Not to the Marriage of True Minds, 552

Let me take this other glove off, 612

Letter to Benjamin Bailey, November 22, 1817, from, 751

Letter to George and Thomas Keats, December 21, 1817, from, 752

Letter to James Augustus Hessey, October 8, 1818, from, 755

Letter to John Hamilton Reynolds, February 19, 1818, 753

Letter to John Taylor, February 27, 1818, from, 754

Let us go then, you and I, 849

Life Cycle of Common Man, 879

Life is a jest; and all things show it, 732

Like as the Waves, 701

Like plump green floor plans, 839

Limericks, 696

Lines Composed a Few Miles Above Tintern Abbey, 910

Little Lamb, who made thee?, 837

London, 567

London, 1802, 722

Long Goodbye, The, 1297

Lord Randal, 680

Lord, who createdst man in wealth and store, 707

Lottery, The, 66

Love and Life, 551

Love Calls Us to the Things of This World, 909

Love Knot, 708

Love's Emblem, 663

Love Song of J. Alfred Prufrock, The, 849

Lupine Dew, 632

Madness One Monday Evening, 854

Márgarét áre you gríeving, 700

Mark but this flea, and mark in this, 623

Marks, 652

Mellifluous as bees, these brittle men, 724

Message Clear, 709

Metrical Feet, 695

Milton! thou should'st be living at this hour, 722

Mr. Flood's Party, 883

Mister Tambourine Man, 656

Most Dangerous Game, The, 17

"Mother dear, may I go downtown, 595

Move over, ham, 635

Mrs. Yardley's Quilting, 359

Much have I traveled in the realms of gold, 723

Musée des Beaux Arts, 834

Musing on roses and revolutions, 667

My dearest dust, could not thy hasty day, 548

My father bequeathed me no wide estates, 585

My heart aches, and a drowsy numbness pains, 746

My husband gives me an A, 652

My Lady's Presence Makes the Roses Red, 718

My Last Duchess, 629

My Life Closed Twice, 845

My Love in Her Attire, 548

My Man Bovanne, 95

My Mistress' Eyes Are Nothing like the Sun, 725

My mouth blooms like a cut, 888
My Own Epitaph, 732
My Papa's Waltz, 642
My sister in her well-tailored silk blouse hands me, 581

Narrow Fellow in the Grass, A, 573
Nautilus Island's hermit, 874
Necessities of Life, 762
Needs, 609
Negro Speaks of Rivers, The, 817
Night life. Letters, journals, bourbon, 770
No bars are set too close, no mesh too fine, 734
No, no; for my virginity, 733
No, no! Go from me. I have left her lately, 882
No, no, go not to Lethe, neither twist, 749
Not Marble, Nor the Gilded Monuments, 592
"*Not Marble Nor the Gilded Monuments*," 593
Not only far away, but the way that you say it, 613
Not that he promised not to windowshop, 657
Now as I was young and easy under the apple boughs, 899
Now light the candles; one; two; there's a moth, 789
Nuns Fret Not, 717
Nymph's Reply to the Shepherd, The, 799

Occurrence at Owl Creek Bridge, An, 59
Ode on a Grecian Urn, 748
Ode on a Grecian Urn Summarized, 802
Ode on Melancholy, 749
Ode to a Nightingale, 746
Ode to Stephen Dowling Bots, Dec'd, 555
Ode to the West Wind, 684
Odour of Chrysanthemums, 244
Oedipus Tyrannus, 1313
Off Highway 106, 619
Of man's first disobedience, and the fruit, 646
Of the Boy and Butterfly, 573
Oh, I can smile for you, and tilt my head, 607
O hideous little bat, the size of snot, 574
Oh, life is a glorious cycle of song, 736
Old Eben Flood, climbing alone one night, 883
Old People, The, 191
"O 'Melia, my dear, this does everything crown!, 601
O, my luve's like a red, red rose, 653
On Being Asked for a War Poem, 791
Once as a child I loved to hop, 808
Once I am sure there's nothing going on, 674

Once in a hundred years the Lemmings come, 579
One Man's Wife, 657
One Perfect Rose, 666
1 September 1939, 835
1-2-3 was the number he played but today the number came 3-2-1, 690
Ones Who Walk Away from Omelas, The, 501
One wading a Fall meadow finds on all sides, 908
On First Looking in on Blodgett's Keats's "Chapman's Homer," 724
On First Looking into Chapman's Homer, 723
On My First Son, 545
On Stella's Birthday, 1719, 899
On the Grasshopper and the Cricket, 742
On the Late Massacre in Piedmont, 722
On the long shore, lit by the moon, 671
On the Sonnet, 720
On the stiff twig up there, 880
Origins and History of Consciousness, 770
Orion, 764
O rose, thou art sick, 664
Our Friend Judith, 100
Out in this desert we are testing bombs, 766
Outside, 598
Outside, the last kids holler, 562
Over her shoulder, the window framed the stars, 811
O what can ail thee, knight-at-arms, 744
"O where hae ye been, Lord Randal, my son?, 680
O wild West Wind, thou breath of Autumn's being, 684
O Yes, 180
Ozymandias, 721

Paradise Lost, from, 646
Parting in Wartime, 736
Passages from Essays and Letters, (Lawrence), 282
Passionate Shepherd to His Love, The, 727
Penelope, for Her Ulysses' Sake, 817
Photos, The, 581
Piano, 871
Piano and Drums, 818
Picketing Supermarkets, 594
Piece by piece I seem, 762
Piece of Shrapnel, A, 883
Pied Beauty, 643
Pillar of Fame, The, 707
Pious Selinda goes to prayers, 553
Planetarium, 765
Poem (Williams), 668
poem, or beauty hurts mr. vinal, 784
Poetry (Giovanni), 589
Poetry (Moore), 587
Point Shirley, 626
(ponder, darling, these busted statues, 798

Poor Christian Looks at the Ghetto, A, 878
Poor savage, doubting that a river flows, 878
portrait, 705

Quatrain, 733

Range-Finding, 855
Ray Charles is the black wind of Kilimanjaro, 703
Recreation, 550
Red, Red Rose, A, 653
Red Wheelbarrow, The, 644
Remember a season, 807
Repression of War Experience, 789
Richard Cory, 885
River-Merchant's Wife: A Letter, The, 540
Rocking-Horse Winner, The, 271
Rose Family, The, 666
Roses and Revolutions, 667
Rotation, 839
Roughly figured, this man of moderate habits, 879
Ruined Maid, The, 601

Sacrifice of Isaac, The, 938
Sailing to Byzantium, 824
St. Agnes' Eve—Ah, bitter chill it was!, 861
Scorn Not the Sonnet, 720
Season of mists and mellow fruitfulness, 750
season 'tis my lovely lambs, the, 842
Second Coming, The, 823
Secret Sharer, The, 403
Sermonette, 820
Sex, as they harshly call it, 553
Sex fingers toes, 702
She, 887
She as a veil down to the slender waist, 805
She Dwelt Among the Untrodden Ways, 610
She even thinks that up in heaven, 735
She sang beyond the genius of the sea, 894
Short Happy Life of Francis Macomber, The, 32
Sick Rose, The, 664
Silver Swan, The, 597
Sir Patrick Spens, 682
Skunk Hour, 874
Slim Cunning Hands, 638
Slumber Did My Spirit Seal, A, 555
Snake, 871
Snapshots of a Daughter-in-law, 758
Softly, in the dusk, a woman is singing to me, 871
Soldier, The, 791
Soliloquy of the Spanish Cloister, 604

Some broken, 711
Something of how the homing bee at dusk, 667
Sometimes I'm happy: la la la la la la la, 725
so much depends, 644
Son, Come Home, A, 1508
Song ("Come, live with me"), 800
Song ("Go, and catch a falling star"), 617
Song ("Go, lovely rose!"), 794
Song ("Pious Selinda goes"), 553
Song ("Why so pale"), 697
Sonny's Blues, 336
So there stood Matthew Arnold and this girl, 803
[Sound and Sense], 692
Southern Gothic, 667
Spotted Horses, 300
Spring, 890
Spring and Fall, 700
Spring, the Sweet Spring, 700
State of Nature, A, 711
Stella this day is thirty-four, 899
Still to Be Neat, 639
Stone-cutters fighting time with marble, you foredefeated, 594
Stopping by Woods on a Snowy Evening, 686
Storm Warnings, 758
Summer My Grandmother Was Supposed to Die, The, 72
Sunday Morning, 896
Sun Rising, The, 740
Suzanne Takes You Down, 840
Sweet earth, he ran and changed his shoes to go, 676
Symposium: Apples, A, 807

take it from me kiddo, 784
Talking with Adrienne Rich, from, 771
Tally Stick, The, 538
Tanhum, 457
Taped to the wall of my cell are 47 pictures: 47 black, 584
Terence, This is Stupid Stuff, 586
That is no country for old men. The young, 824
That night your great guns, unawares, 857
That's my last duchess painted on the wall, 629
That summer, you were game for anything, 632
That Time of Year, 650
That winter, the dead could not be buried, 658
The apparition of these faces in the crowd, 882
The battle rent a cobweb diamond-strung, 855
The Brain—is wider than the Sky—, 844
The darkness crumbles away, 788

The decent docent doesn't doze, 734

Th' expense of spirit in a waste of shame, 889

The eyes of twenty centuries, 892

The eyes open to a cry of pulleys, 909

The first, scattering rain on Polish cities, 835

The force that through the green fuse drives the flower, 901

The glass has been falling all the afternoon, 758

The golf links lie so near the mill, 733

The heavy bear who goes with me, 577

The house is so quiet now, 546

The king sits in Dumferling towne, 682

The lady Fortune is bothe freend and fo, 597

The legs of the elk punctured the snow's crust, 632

The Lord is my shepherd; I shall not want, 655

The only thing I have of Jane MacNaughton, 659

The poetry of earth is never dead, 742

The praisers of women in their proud and beautiful poems, 593

There Died a Myriad, 788

There Is No Balm in Birmingham, 583

There once was a spinster of Ealing, 696

There's no badger in this sandbox, 578

There was such speed in her little body, 544

The Rock That Doesn't Break, she calls, 883

The rose fades, 668

The rose is a rose, 666

The sea is calm tonight, 628

the season 'tis my lovely lambs, 842

The silver swan, who living had no note, 597

The things that make a soldier great and send him out to die, 789

The time you won your town the race, 554

The turtle lives 'twixt plated decks, 575

The unpurged images of day recede, 827

The whiskey on your breath, 642

The word *plum* is delicious, 687

They Flee from Me, 913

They sing their dearest songs—, 856

Things that Make a Soldier Great, The, 789

This girlchild was born as usual, 561

This handless clock stares blindly from its tower, 757

This Is Just to Say, 910

This is the terminal: the light, 636

This one was put in a jacket, 699

Thou still unravished bride of quietness, 748

Thou, paw-paw-paw; thou, glurd; thou, spotted, 807

Three Brown Girls Singing, 678

Three Sisters, 1393

Three things must epigrams, like bees, have all, 730

Thus she had lain, 818

Tiger, The, 838

To Amarantha, that She Would Dishevel Her Hair, 795

To an Athlete Dying Young, 554

To Autumn, 750

To Christ Our Lord, 632

To His Coy Mistress, 797

Tomorrow You Will Live, 732

Tonight my children hunch, 858

Tonite, thriller was, 591

To Roses in the Bosom of Castara, 665

To the Memory of Mr. Oldham, 697

To the Stone-Cutters, 594

To the Virgins, to Make Much of Time, 794

To Women, 860

Train Whistle Guitar, 484

Treason doth never prosper, what's the reason?, 734

Tree of Knowledge, The, 392

Trochee trips from long to short, 695

True Maid, A, 733

Truth the Dead Know, The, 633

Trying to Talk with a Man, 766

Turning and turning in the widening gyre, 823

Turtle, The, 575

Twenty-Third Psalm, The, 655

Twilight's Last Gleaming, 695

Two Songs, 553

Ulysses, 812

Uncle Ananias, 885

Uneasy Rider, 542

Unknown Citizen, The, 599

Upon Julia's Clothes, 549

Upon the Death of Sir Albert Morton's Wife, 732

U.S. 1946 King's X, 624

Vacuum, The, 546

Valediction: Forbidding Mourning, A, 631

Variations on a Theme by William Carlos Williams, 802

Various the Roads of Life, 733

Very Old Man with Enormous Wings, A, 234

Virginal, A, 882

Waking, The, 887

Watching the Dance, 878

Wayman in Love, 543

Way of Life, A, 738

We have climbed the mountain, 634

Western Wind, 531

What happens to a dream deferred?, 600

What Is an Epigram?, 730

What Lips My Lips Have Kissed, 552
What the Motorcycle Said, 688
What Thou Lovest Well, Remains Ameri-
can, 581
What was it?, 812
What Were They Like?, 596
Whenas in silks my Julia goes, 549
When at break of day at a riverside, 818
When daisies pied and violets blue, 890
Whenever Richard Cory went down town,
885
When icicles hang by the wall, 890
When I Have Fears, 743
When Lilacs Last in the Dooryard
Bloomed, 902
When Nature Made Her Chief Work,
Stella's Eyes, 724
When We Dead Awaken: Writing as Re-
Vision, from, 775
"While I sit at the door, 809
While my hair was still cut straight across
my forehead, 540
Who Are They?, 597
Who has ever stopped to think of the di-
vinity of Lamont Cranston?, 783
Whose woods these are I think I know,
686

Why I Drink, 734
Why so pale and wan, fond Lover, 697
Wild Nights! Wild Nights!, 845
Windhover, The, 860
Winter, 890
Womanizers, 882
Woodchucks, 569
Woodstock, 564
Word Plum, The, 687
World as Meditation, The, 816
Wouldst thou hear what man can say, 731
Wrote the clergy: "Our Dear Madame
Prynne, 735

Ye blushing virgins happy are, 665
You are made of almost nothing, 838
You Are the Brave, 779
Young Goodman Brown, 117
You, once a belle in Shreveport, 758
You remember the name was Jensen. She
seemed old, 580
You start it all. You are lovely, 860
You Too? Me Too—Why Not? Soda Pop,
712
You've Told Me, Maro, 731